THE

MERCK/MERIAL

MANUAL

FOR

PET HEALTH

HOME EDITION

THE
MERCK/MERIAL
MANUAL
FOR
PET HEALTH

HOME EDITION

Cynthia M. Kahn, BA, MA
Editor

Scott Line, DVM, PhD, Dipl ACVB
Associate Editor

Published by

MERCK & CO., INC.
WHITEHOUSE STATION, NJ, USA

In educational partnership with
MERIAL LIMITED
A Merck and sanofi-aventis company

2007

Editorial and Production Staff

Editor: Cynthia M. Kahn, BA, MA
Associate Editor: Scott Line, DVM, PhD, DACVB
Consulting Editor: Susan E. Aiello, BS, DVM, ELS

Project Coordinator: Odilia Achu
Administrative Coordinators: Deborah Flot, Linda St. Clair
Technical Advisor: Michael DeFerrari

Design: Jerilyn Bockorick, Nesbitt Graphics, Inc.
Text Preparation and Illustrations: Publication Services, Champaign IL
Composition: Nesbitt Graphics, Inc., Fort Washington PA

Publisher: Gary Zelko
Advertising and Promotions Supervisor: Pamela J. Barnes-Paul
Subsidiary Rights Coordinator: Jeanne Nilsen
Systems Administrator: Leta Bracy

Library of Congress Catalog Number: 2007933381

Hardcover Edition
ISBN-10: 0-911910-22-0
ISBN-13: 978-0-911910-22-3

Trade Paperback Edition
ISBN-10: 0-911910-99-9
ISBN-13: 978-0-911910-99-5

First Printing: September 2007

Printed by Courier Westford, Inc.
Westford, Massachusetts U.S.A.

PREFACE

Humans and animals have always had a special bond. The role of a pet has developed over the years from that of a simple outdoor guardian, working animal, or mouse-catcher to one of a true companion and family member. Dogs, cats, and other pets have become integral parts of our everyday lives.

Animals have also benefited from their closer association with people. In the past few decades, veterinary drugs, procedures, and vaccines have been developed specifically for animals that have eliminated many of the diseases that once shortened their lives. With these advances has also come an increase in the volume of medical information that is available to pet owners. Books, magazines, and web sites devoted to pet health have proliferated. Some contain good information, while others perpetuate outdated practices and unproven treatments. As with human health, the critical question facing pet owners today is where to find the most trusted and accurate information on pet health care?

The Merck/Merial Manual for Pet Health has been developed to meet the needs of pet owners for detailed yet easily understood medical information on every aspect of pet health. The book is closely based on the text of *The Merck Veterinary Manual*, a reference that has served as the most comprehensive and reliable source of information on animal health care for veterinarians for over 50 years. Our goal is to provide a resource—in everyday language—for pet owners that will provide the same comprehensive, up-to-date, and trusted information on all common diseases of pets that their veterinarians have relied on for the past half century.

The Merck/Merial Manual for Pet Health covers not only dogs and cats but also horses, ferrets, birds, rabbits, rodents, reptiles, amphibians, fish, and even exotic pets such as potbellied pigs and sugar gliders. In addition to the information extracted from the most recent edition of *The Merck Veterinary Manual*, we have added chapters covering the basics of pet health care, as well as useful information on emergency care and first aid (including poisonings), diagnostic tests and imaging, common drugs and vaccines for pets, and traveling with pets. Almost 300 illustrations have been specially developed to complement the text. In no other book will the reader find the breadth of coverage contained in this single volume.

In bringing this book to fruition, the editors have relied heavily on the expertise of the many authors and expert reviewers who have contributed to *The Merck Veterinary Manual* over the years and who have shaped the content of this book. The material included here represents the collective knowledge and experience of over 200 of the top veterinary experts from around the world. In addition to providing the original content on which *The Merck/Merial Manual for Pet Health* is based, most have also graciously reviewed the revised material and corrected any inaccuracies. Their names are listed on the pages that follow. We also recognize the efforts of the Merial Publication Services editorial staff and of the Merck Publishing Group who have worked tirelessly over the last two years to make this book a reality.

Pets bring joy and companionship into our daily lives. But pets require more than just love from us. They require a nutritionally sound diet and an appropriate environment that is clean, safe, and mentally stimulating. They require basic care and, in some cases, training. Perhaps most of all, they require preventive health care to ensure a good quality of life and access to appropriate veterinary care when they are injured or ill.

Communicating with your veterinarian is a key part of ensuring good health care for your pet. Our hope in developing this book is that readers will gain a better understanding of not only the many diseases that can affect their pet or pets, but also how to prevent disease, how to tell when their pet is ill, and how to effectively communicate with their veterinarian to ensure the best possible treatment when illness or injury occurs. Of course, no book can or should replace the expertise and training of a veterinarian who is familiar with and has an ongoing relationship with you and your pet. *The Merck/Merial Manual for Pet Health* is not intended as a manual to be used by pet owners to diagnose and treat their pets but rather as a tool to increase knowledge and promote responsible pet ownership.

Before diving into the text, readers are urged to review the Guide for Readers found on page xxvii for basic information on how the book is organized and how best to locate specific topics. A Glossary, found in the back of the book, is provided to help readers understand any unfamiliar medical terminology they may encounter.

The Merck/Merial Manual for Pet Health is published in an educational partnership between Merck & Co., Inc. and Merial Limited on a not-for-profit basis. The editors hope that you find the information useful, and we warmly welcome your suggestions for improvement.

Cynthia M. Kahn
Editor

Scott Line
Associate Editor

Special Note to Readers

The authors, reviewers, editors, and publisher have made extensive efforts to ensure that the information is accurate and conforms to the standards accepted at the time of publication. However, constant changes in information resulting from continuing research and clinical experience, reasonable differences in opinions among authorities, unique aspects of individual situations, and the possibility of human error in preparing such an extensive text require that the reader exercise judgment when making decisions and consult and compare information from other sources. In particular, the reader is advised to discuss information obtained in this book with a veterinarian or other qualified animal health practitioner.

CONTENTS

Preface v

Contributors.. xiii

A Guide for Readers.. xxvii

SECTION
1

DOG BASICS

1 Description and Physical Characteristics............................2

2 Selecting and Providing a Home for a Dog 7

3 Routine Care and Breeding 11

4 Behavior...17

SECTION
2

DISORDERS AND DISEASES OF DOGS

5 Blood Disorders 33

6 Heart and Blood Vessel Disorders.....................................53

7 Digestive Disorders 77

8 Hormonal Disorders...128

9 Eye Disorders..140

10 Ear Disorders 155

11 Immune Disorders 164

12 Bone, Joint, and Muscle Disorders..................................176

13 Brain, Spinal Cord, and Nerve Disorders 194

14 Reproductive Disorders 214

15 Lung and Airway Disorders 224

16 Skin Disorders 238

17 Kidney and Urinary Tract Disorders 283

18 Metabolic Disorders 300

19 Disorders Affecting Multiple Body Systems 305

SECTION
3
CAT BASICS

20 Description and Physical Characteristics 330

21 Selecting and Providing a Home for a Cat 334

22 Routine Care and Breeding 338

23 Behavior 345

SECTION
4
DISORDERS AND DISEASES OF CATS

24 Blood Disorders 359

25 Heart and Blood Vessel Disorders 370

26 Digestive Disorders 383

27 Hormonal Disorders 415

28 Eye Disorders 423

29 Ear Disorders 433

30 Immune Disorders 439

31 Bone, Joint, and Muscle Disorders 445

32 Brain, Spinal Cord, and Nerve Disorders 455

33 Reproductive Disorders 469

34 Lung and Airway Disorders 475

35 Skin Disorders 488

36 Kidney and Urinary Tract Disorders 514

37 Metabolic Disorders 525

38 Disorders Affecting Multiple Body Systems 528

SECTION 5 — HORSE BASICS

39 Description and Physical Characteristics 550

40 Selecting and Providing a Home for a Horse 557

41 Routine Care and Breeding 560

42 Behavior 566

SECTION 6 — DISORDERS AND DISEASES OF HORSES

43 Blood Disorders 581

44 Heart and Blood Vessel Disorders 592

45 Digestive Disorders 602

46 Hormonal Disorders 641

47 Eye Disorders 646

48 Ear Disorders 655

49 Immune Disorders 659

50 Bone, Joint, and Muscle Disorders 664

51 Brain, Spinal Cord, and Nerve Disorders 708

52 Reproductive Disorders 726

53 Lung and Airway Disorders 736

54 Skin Disorders 755

55 Kidney and Urinary Tract Disorders 781

56 Metabolic Disorders..788

57 Disorders Affecting Multiple Body Systems 793

SECTION
7

BIRDS

58 Description and Physical Characteristics of Birds 816

59 Selecting and Providing a Home for a Pet Bird.................827

60 Routine Care and Breeding....................................832

61 Disorders and Diseases of Birds 839

SECTION
8

EXOTIC PETS

62 Amphibians 864

63 Chinchillas 873

64 Ferrets 886

65 Fish...899

66 Gerbils 919

67 Guinea Pigs..925

68 Hamsters...940

69 Mice 953

70 Prairie Dogs 962

71 Potbellied Pigs 970

72 Rabbits 983

73 Rats 1003

74 Reptiles 1013

75 Sugar Gliders 1039

SECTION
9

SPECIAL SUBJECTS

76 Emergencies...1050

77 Diagnostic Tests and Imaging 1070

78 Infections 1078

79 Diseases Spread from Animals to People (Zoonoses).....1088

80 Drugs and Vaccines...1118

81 Poisoning 1145

82 Pain Management 1211

83 Travel with Pets 1216

84 Health and the Human-Animal Bond.............................1228

85 Cancer and Tumors...1233

Glossary...1251
Index..1285

CONTRIBUTORS

Susan E. Aiello, DVM, ELS
WordsWorld Consulting, Dayton, OH
Cat Basics; Dog Basics; Horse Basics

Dana G. Allen, DVM, MSc, DACVIM
Professor of Internal Medicine
Department of Clinical Studies
Ontario Veterinary College
University of Guelph, Ontario, Canada
Digestive Disorders

Christine Andreoni
Senior Manager
Department of Immunology/Discovery
Merial Limited, Lyon, France
Immune Disorders

Max J. Appel, DMV, PhD
Professor Emeritus, Ithaca, NY
Disorders Affecting Multiple Body Systems

Donald Armstrong, MD
Emeritus Chief, Infectious Disease Service
Memorial Sloan Kettering Cancer Center, NY
Professor of Medicine, Cornell University
Medical College, Ithaca, NY
*Diseases Spread from Animal to People
(Zoonoses)*

David A. Ashford, DVM, MPH, DSc
Assistant Area Director
International Services, APHIS, USDA
Sao Paulo, Brazil
Disorders Affecting Multiple Body Systems

Joerg A. Auer, DMV, DACVS, DECVS
Equine Hospital, Vetsuisse Faculty
University of Zurich, Switzerland
Bone, Joint, and Muscle Disorders

David G. Baker, DVM, MS, PhD, DACLAM
Director and Professor
Division of Laboratory Animal Medicine
School of Veterinary Medicine, Louisiana
State University, Baton Rouge, LA
Eye Disorders

Gordon J. Baker, BVSc, PhD, MRCVS, DACVS
Professor, Equine Medicine and Surgery
College of Veterinary Medicine
University of Illinois, Urbana, IL
Digestive Disorders

Stephen C. Barr, BVSc, MVS, PhD, DACVIM
Professor of Medicine
Department of Clinical Sciences
College of Veterinary Medicine
Cornell University, Ithaca, NY
Disorders Affecting Multiple Body Systems

George M. Barrington, DVM, PhD, DACVIM
Assistant Professor, Department of
Veterinary Clinical Sciences
College of Veterinary Medicine
Washington State University, Pullman, WA
Metabolic Disorders

Joseph W. Bartges, DVM, PhD, DACVIM, DACVN
Professor of Medicine and Nutrition
The Acree Chair of Small Animal Research
Department of Small Animal Clinical
Sciences, College of Veterinary Medicine
University of Tennessee, Knoxville, TN
Kidney and Urinary Tract Disorders

Andrew P. Bathe, MA, VetMB, DACVS, DEO, MRCVS
Rossdale & Partners, Beaufort Cottage
Equine Hospital, Exning, Newmarket
Suffolk, UK
Bone, Joint, and Muscle Disorders

Daniela Bedenice, DMV, DACVIM
Clinical Assistant Professor
Large Animal Clinic
School of Veterinary Medicine
Tufts University, North Grafton, MA
*Brain, Spinal Cord, and Nerve Disorders;
Kidney and Urinary Tract Disorders;
Disorders Affecting Multiple Body Systems*

Michael Bernstein, DVM, DACVIM
Director, Medical Services
Angell Animal Medical Center, Boston, MA
Blood Disorders

Rob Bildfell, DVM, MSc, DACVP
Assistant Professor
Department of Biomedical Sciences
College of Veterinary Medicine
Oregon State University, Corvallis, OR
Poisoning

William D. Black, MSc, DVM, PhD
Professor
Department of Biomedical Sciences
Ontario Veterinary College
University of Guelph, Ontario, Canada
Poisoning

Barry R. Blackley, DVM, PhD
Professor
Department of Veterinary Biomedical
Sciences, Western College of Veterinary
Medicine, University of Saskatchewan
Saskatoon, Saskatchewan, Canada
Poisoning

Herman J. Boermans, DVM, MSc, PhD
Director of Toxicology Program
Associate Professor of Toxicology
Department of Biomedical Sciences
Ontario Veterinary College
University of Guelph, Ontario, Canada
Poisoning

Rosemary J. Booth, BVSc
Lecturer and Wildlife Veterinarian
School of Animal Studies
University of Queensland, Australia
Sugar Gliders

**Dawn M. Boothe, DVM, PhD, DACVIM,
  DACVCP**
Professor
Department of Veterinary Physiology
and Pharmacology
College of Veterinary Medicine
Texas A&M University, College Station, TX
Drugs and Vaccines

**Davin J. Borde, DVM, DACVIM
  (Cardiology)**
Staff Cardiologist
Veterinary Heart Institute, Gainesville, FL
Heart and Blood Vessel Disorders

Kenneth R. Boschert, DVM, DACLAM
Associate Director
Division of Comparative Medicine
Washington University, St. Louis, MO
*Mice; Gerbils; Prairie Dogs; Chinchillas;
Hamsters; Rats; Guinea Pigs*

**Kyle G. Braund, BVSc, MVSc, PhD, FRCVS,
  DACVIM (Neurology)**
Director
Veterinary Neurological Consulting
Services, Dadeville, AL
Brain, Spinal Cord, and Nerve Disorders

Scott A. Brown, VMD, PhD, DACVIM
Department of Physiology and Pharmacology
College of Veterinary Medicine
University of Georgia, Athens, GA
Kidney and Urinary Tract Disorders

**Cecil F. Brownie, DVM, PhD, DABVT,
  DABT, DABFE, DABFM, FACFE**
Professor of Pharmacology/Toxicology
Dept of Molecular and Biomedical Sciences
College of Veterinary Medicine
North Carolina State University
Raleigh, NC
Poisoning

David Bruyette, DVM, DACVIM
Medical Director
VCA West Los Angeles Animal Hospital
Los Angeles, CA
Hormonal Disorders

John A. Bukowski, DVM, MPH, PhD
WordsWorld Consulting, Dayton, OH
Dog Basics; Cat Basics; Horse Basics

Raymond Cahill-Morasco, MS, DVM
Boston, MA
Poisoning

Clay A. Calvert, DVM, DACVIM
Professor
Dept of Small Animal Medicine and Surgery
College of Veterinary Medicine
University of Georgia, Athens, GA
Heart and Blood Vessel Disorders

Karen L. Campbell, MS, DVM, DACVIM, DACVD
Professor and Section Head
Specialty Medicine
Department of Veterinary Clinical Medicine
College of Veterinary Medicine
University of Illinois, Urbana, IL
Blood Disorders

Sharon Campbell, DVM, MS, DACVIM
Manager, Pharmacovigilance
Regulatory Affairs, Veterinary Medicine
Research and Development
Pfizer Inc., Kalamazoo, MI
Digestive Disorders

Ivan W. Caple, BVSc, PhD, MACVSc, MRCVS
Dean, Faculty of Veterinary Sciences
Clinical Centre, University of Melbourne,
Werribee, Victoria, Australia
Metabolic Disorders

Cheryl L. Chrisman, DVM, MS, EDS, DACVIM (Neurology)
Professor of Veterinary Neurology
College of Veterinary Medicine
University of Florida, Gainesville, FL
Brain, Spinal Cord, and Nerve Disorders

Keith A. Clark, DVM, PhD
Retired Director
Zoonosis Control Division
Texas Department of Health, Austin, TX
Poisoning

Ben H. Colmery III, DVM, DAVDC
Dixboro Veterinary Dental & Medical
Center, Ann Arbor, MI
Digestive Disorders

Peter D. Constable, BVSc, MS, PhD, DACVIM
Associate Professor
Department of Veterinary Clinical Medicine
University of Illinois, Urbana, IL
Digestive Disorders

Susan M. Cotter, DVM, DACVIM (Internal Medicine and Oncology)
Distinguished Professor
Department of Clinical Sciences
School of Veterinary Medicine
Tufts University, North Grafton, MA
Blood Disorders

Benjamin J. Darien, DVM, MS, DACVIM
Associate Professor of Internal Medicine
School of Veterinary Medicine
University of Wisconsin, Madison, WI
Heart and Blood Vessel Disorders

Autumn P. Davidson, DVM, MS, DACVIM
Clinical Professor
Department of Medicine and Epidemiology
School of Veterinary Medicine
University of California, Davis, CA
Reproductive Disorders

Fabio Del Piero, DVM, DACVP, PhD
Associate Professor of Pathology
School of Veterinary Medicine, New Bolton
Center, University of Pennsylvania
Kennett Square, PA
Reproductive Disorders

Joseph A. DiPietro, DVM, MS
Vice President for Agriculture
Institute of Agriculture
University of Tennessee, Knoxville, TN
Digestive Disorders

Thomas J. Divers, DVM, DACVIM, DACVECC
Professor of Medicine
College of Veterinary Medicine
Cornell University, Ithaca, NY
Kidney and Urinary Tract Disorders

Michael W. Dryden, DVM, MS, PhD
Professor of Veterinary Parasitology
College of Veterinary Medicine
Kansas State University, Manhattan, KS
Skin Disorders

J. P. Dubey, MVSc, PhD
Microbiologist
Animal Parasitic Diseases Laboratory
Animal and Natural Resources Institute
U.S. Department of Agriculture
Beltsville, MD
Disorders Affecting Multiple Body Systems

Gregg A. DuPont, DVM, DAVDC, Fellow AVD
Director
Shoreline Veterinary Dental Clinic
Seattle, WA
Digestive Disorders

Neil W. Dyer, DVM, MS
Director, Veterinary Diagnostic Laboratory
North Dakota State University, Fargo, ND
Lung and Airway Disorders

Ron Erskine, DVM, PhD
Professor
Dept of Large Animal Clinical Sciences
College of Veterinary Medicine
Michigan State University, East Lansing, MI
Reproductive Disorders

Paul Ettestad, DVM, MS
State Public Health Veterinarian
Office of Epidemiology, New Mexico
Department of Health, Santa Fe, NM
Disorders Affecting Multiple Body Systems

A. K. Eugster, DVM, PhD
Director and Head, Diagnostic Services
Texas Veterinary Medical Diagnostic
Laboratory
College Station, TX
Eye Disorders

David L. Evans, BVSc, PhD
Associate Professor
Faculty of Veterinary Science
University of Sydney, NSW, Australia
Metabolic Disorders

Timothy M. Fan, DVM, DACVIM
Assistant Professor
Department of Veterinary Clinical Medicine
University of Illinois, Urbana, IL
Blood Disorders

Scott D. Fitzgerald, DVM, PhD, DACVP
Professor, Department of Pathobiology
and Diagnostic Investigation
College of Veterinary Medicine
Michigan State University, East Lansing, MI
Kidney and Urinary Tract Disorders

James A. Flanders, DVM, DACVS
Associate Professor
Department of Clinical Sciences
College of Veterinary Medicine
Cornell University, Ithaca, NY
Reproductive Disorders

Carol S. Foil, DVM, MS, DACVD
Professor
Dept of Veterinary Clinical Sciences
School of Veterinary Medicine
Louisiana State University, Baton Rouge, LA
Skin Disorders

James G. Fox, DVM, MS, DACLAM
Professor and Director
Division of Comparative Medicine
Massachusetts Institute of Technology
Cambridge, MA
Digestive Disorders

Ruth Francis-Floyd, DVM, MS, DACZM
Professor and Director
Aquatic Animal Program
Dept of Large Animal Clinical Sciences
College of Veterinary Medicine
University of Florida, Gainesville, FL
Fish

Don A. Franco, DVM, MPH, DACVPM
President
Center for Biosecurity, Food Safety and
Public Health, Lake Worth, FL
Metabolic Disorders

Kirk N. Gelatt, VMD
Distinguished Professor of Comparative
Ophthalmology
Dept of Small Animal Clinical Sciences
College of Veterinary Medicine
University of Florida, Gainesville, FL
Eye Disorders; Emergencies

Paul Gibbs, BVSc, PhD, FRCVS
Professor of Virology
Dept of Pathology and Infectious Diseases
College of Veterinary Medicine University
of Florida, Gainesville, FL
Skin Disorders

Robert O. Gilbert, BVSc, MMV, DACT, MRCVS
Professor of Theriogenology
Department of Clinical Sciences
College of Veterinary Medicine
Cornell University, Ithaca, NY
Reproductive Disorders

Gregory F. Grauer, DVM, MS, DACVIM (Internal Medicine)
Professor and Head
Department of Clinical Sciences
College of Veterinary Medicine
Kansas State University, Manhattan, KS
Poisoning

Deborah S. Greco, DVM, MS
Staff Internist
The Animal Medical Center, New York, NY
Hormonal Disorders

Craig E. Greene, DVM, MS
Professor
Department of Small Animal Medicine
College of Veterinary Medicine
University of Georgia, Athens, GA
Disorders Affecting Multiple Body Systems

Jorge Guerrero, DVM, PhD, DEVPC
Adjunct Professor of Parasitology
Department of Pathobiology
School of Veterinary Medicine
University of Pennsylvania, PA
Heart and Blood Vessel Disorders

Sharon M. Gwaltney-Brant, DVM, PhD, DABVT, DABT
Director of Veterinary Toxicology Training
ASPCA Animal Poison Control Center
Urbana, IL
Poisoning

Carlton L. Gyles, DVM, PhD
Professor
Department of Pathobiology
Ontario Veterinary College
University of Guelph, Ontario, Canada
Digestive Disorders; Disorders Affecting Multiple Body Systems

Caroline N. Hahn, DVM, MSc, PhD, MRCVS
Neuromuscular Disease Laboratory
Royal (Dick) School of Veterinary Studies
University of Edinburgh, Midlothian, UK
Brain, Spinal Cord, and Nerve Disorders

Jean A. Hall, DVM, MS, PhD, DACVIM
Associate Professor
Department of Biomedical Sciences
College of Veterinary Medicine
Oregon State University, Corvallis, OR
Metabolic Disorders

Farouk M. Hamdy, DVM, MSc, PhD, MPA (Deceased)
Animal Health Consultant, Silverspring, MD
Disorders Affecting Multiple Body Systems

Larry G. Hansen, PhD
Professor
Department of Veterinary Biosciences
University of Illinois, Urbana, IL
Poisoning

Russel Reid Hanson, DVM, DACVS, DACVECC
Professor of Surgery
Department of Clinical Sciences
College of Veterinary Medicine
Auburn University, Auburn, AL
Bone, Joint, and Muscle Disorders

Joseph Harari, MS, DVM, DACVS
Veterinary Surgeon
Veterinary Surgical Specialists, Spokane, WA
Bone, Joint, and Muscle Disorders

Kenneth R. Harkin, DVM, DACVIM
Associate Professor
College of Veterinary Medicine
Kansas State University, Manhattan, KS
Disorders Affecting Multiple Body Systems

Lynette A. Hart, PhD
Professor
Dept of Population Health and Reproduction
Director, UC Center for Animal Alternatives
School of Veterinary Medicine
University of California, Davis, CA
Health and the Human-Animal Bond

Joe Hauptman, DVM, MS, DACVS
Professor of Surgery
Dept of Small Animal Clinical Sciences
College of Veterinary Medicine
Michigan State University, East Lansing, MI
Lung and Airway Disorders

William W. Hawkins, BS, DVM
Hawkins Veterinary Service, Dillon, MT
Skin Disorders

Peter Hellyer, DVM, MS, DACVA
Professor of Anesthesiology
Department of Clinical Sciences, College of
Veterinary Medicine & Biomedical Sciences
Colorado State University
Fort Collins, CO
Pain Management

Charles M. Hendrix, DVM, PhD
Professor
Department of Pathobiology
College of Veterinary Medicine
Auburn University, Auburn, AL
*Brain, Spinal Cord, and Nerve Disorders;
Travel with Pets*

Dolores E. Hill, PhD
Parasitologist
U.S. Department of Agriculture
Beltsville, MD
Disorders Affecting Multiple Body Systems

Katrin Hinrichs, DVM, PhD, DACT
Professor, Veterinary Physiology
and Pharmacology
College of Veterinary Medicine
Texas A&M University, College Station, TX
Reproductive Disorders

Steven R. Hollingsworth, DVM, DACVO
Lecturer
Dept of Surgical and Radiological Sciences
School of Veterinary Medicine
University of California, Davis, CA
Eye Disorders

**Peter H. Holmes, BVMS, PhD, MRCVS,
FRSE**
Professor
Veterinary School
University of Glasgow, Scotland, UK
Blood Disorders

Johnny D. Hoskins, DVM, PhD
Small Animal Consultant, Choudrant, LA
Disorders Affecting Multiple Body Systems

Walter Ingwersen, DVM, DVSc, DACVIM
Specialist
Companion Animals, Boehringer Ingelheim
(Canada) Ltd, Vetmedica, Burlington
Ontario, Canada
Digestive Disorders

Charles J. Issel, DVM, PhD
Wright-Market Chair of Equine Infectious
Diseases
Gluck Equine Research Center
University of Kentucky, Lexington, KY
Disorders Affecting Multiple Body Systems

Nemi C. Jain, MVSc, PhD
Professor Emeritus of Clinical Pathology
Department of Veterinary Pathology,
Microbiology, and Immunology
School of Veterinary Medicine
University of California, Davis, CA
Blood Disorders

Eugene D. Janzen, BA, DVM, MVS
Associate Dean, Clinical Programs
Faculty of Veterinary Medicine
University of Calgary
Alberta, Canada
Disorders Affecting Multiple Body Systems

**Leo B. Jeffcott, MA, BVM, PhD, FRCVS,
DVSc, VD**
Dean
Faculty of Veterinary Science
University of Sydney, NSW, Australia
Bone, Joint, and Muscle Disorders

Cheri A. Johnson, DVM, MS, DACVIM
Professor and Chief of Staff
Dept of Small Animal Clinical Sciences
College of Veterinary Medicine
Michigan State University, East Lansing, MI
Reproductive Disorders

Wayne K. Jorgensen, PhD
Senior Principal Research Scientist
(Parasitology)
Dept of Primary Industries and Fisheries
Queensland, Australia
Blood Disorders

Robert J. Kemppainen, DVM, PhD
Professor, Dept of Anatomy, Physiology,
and Pharmacology
College of Veterinary Medicine
Auburn University, Auburn, AL
Hormonal Disorders

Morag G. Kerr, BVMS, BSc, PhD, CBiol,
FIBiol, MRCVS
Director of Science and Laboratories
VetLab Services, Southwater, Horsham
West Sussex, UK
Diagnostic Tests and Imaging

Safdar A. Khan, DVM, MS, PhD, DABVT
Director of Toxicology Research
ASPCA Animal Poison Control Center
Urbana, IL
Poisoning

Rebecca Kirby, DVM, DACVECC,
DACVIM
Chief of Medicine
Animal Emergency Center and Referral
Services, Milwaukee, WI
Emergencies

Thomas R. Klei, PhD
Boyd Professor
Department of Pathobiological Science
School of Veterinary Medicine, Louisiana
State University, Baton Rouge, LA
Skin Disorders

Roger J. Klingenberg, DVM
Greeley, CO
Reptiles

Svend E. Kold, DMV, MRCVS, RCVS
Specialist in Equine Surgery
(Orthopedics)
Willesley Equine Clinic, North Tetbury
Gloucestershire, UK
Bone, Joint, and Muscle Disorders

Ned F. Kuehn, DVM, MS, DACVIM
(Internal Medicine)
Chief of Internal Medicine Services
Michigan Veterinary Specialists
Southfield, MI
Lung and Airway Disorders

Garrick C. M. Latch, MASc, PhD
Consultant, Palmerston North
New Zealand
Poisoning

Jimmy C. Lattimer, DVM, Ms, DACVR,
DACVRO
Associate Professor
Veterinary Medicine and Surgery
University of Missouri, Columbus, MO
Diagnostic Tests and Imaging

D. Bruce Lawhorn, DVM, MS
Professor and Extension Swine Veterinarian
Dept of Large Animal Medicine and Surgery
College of Veterinary Medicine
Texas A&M University, College Station, TX
Potbellied Pigs

Teresa L. Lightfoot, DVM, DABVP (Avian)
Florida Veterinary Specialists, Tampa, FL
Birds

John E. Lloyd, BS, PhD
Professor of Entomology
University of Wyoming, Laramie, WY
Skin Disorders

Maureen T. Long, DVM, PhD, DACVIM
(Large Animals)
Assistant Professor
Large Animal Clinical Sciences
University of Florida, Gainesville, FL
Brain, Spinal Cord, and Nerve Disorders

Bertrand J. Losson, DVM, PhD
Professor
Dept of Parasitology and Parasitic Diseases
Faculty of Veterinary Medicine
University of Liege, Belgium
Skin Disorders

Jodie Low Choy, BVMS
Veterinary Quarantine Facility
Territory Wildlife Park
Palmerston, Australia
Disorders Affecting Multiple Body Systems

Katharine F. Lunn, BVMS, MS, PhD, MRCVS, DACVIM
Assistant Professor
Department of Clinical Sciences
Colorado State University, Fort Collins, CO
Metabolic Disorders

Robert J. MacKay, BVSc, PhD
Professor
Dept of Large Animal Clinical Sciences
University of Florida, Gainesville, FL
Brain, Spinal Cord, and Nerve Disorders

Dennis W. Macy DVM, MS, DACVIM
Professor of Medicine and Oncology
College of Veterinary Medicine and
Biomedical Sciences, Colorado State
University, Fort Collins, CO
Disorders Affecting Multiple Body Systems

John E. Madigan, DVM, MS
Professor
Department of Medicine and Epidemiology
School of Veterinary Medicine
University of California, Davis, CA
Digestive Disorders; Disorders Affecting Multiple Body Systems

John B. Malone, DVM, PhD
Professor
Department of Medicine and Epidemiology
School of Veterinary Medicine
University of California, Davis, CA
Diagnostic Tests and Imaging

Richard A. Mansmann, VMD, PhD
Clinical Professor
Department of Clinical Sciences
College of Veterinary Medicine
North Carolina State University
Raleigh, NC
Horse Basics

Steven L. Marks, BVSc, MS, MRCVS, DACVIM
Clinical and Associate Professor of Critical
Care and Internal Medicine
Department of Clinical Sciences
College of Veterinary Medicine
North Carolina State University, Raleigh, NC
Lung and Airway Disorders

Dudley L. McCaw, DVM
Associate Professor
Dept of Veterinary Medicine and Surgery
College of Veterinary Medicine
University of Missouri, Columbia, MO
Disorders Affecting Multiple Body Systems

Diane McClure, DVM, PhD, DACLAM
Consulting Veterinarian
Comparative Medicine - Stanford Veterinary
Service Center, Stanford School of Medicine
Stanford University, Stanford, CA
Rabbits

Brian J. McCluskey, DVM, MS, PhD, DACVPM
National Surveillance Coordinator
Centers for Epidemiology and Animal
Health, National Surveillance Unit
APHIS, USDA, Fort Collins, CO
Disorders Affecting Multiple Body Systems

C. Wayne McIlwraith, BVSc, PhD, DSc, FRCVS, DACVS
Professor of Surgery
Director of Orthopedic Research
Gail Holmes Equine Orthopedic Research
Center, Colorado State University
Fort Collins, CO
Bone, Joint, and Muscle Disorders

Gavin L. Meerdink, DVM, DABVT
Clinical Professor
Veterinary Diagnostic Laboratory
College of Veterinary Medicine
University of Illinois, Urbana, IL
Poisoning

Mushtaq A. Memon, BVSc, MS, PhD, DACT
Theriogenologist
Dept of Veterinary Clinical Sciences
Washington State University
Pullman, WA
Reproductive Disorders

Bernard Mignon, DVM, PhD
Assistant Professor
Department of Parasitology, Mycology
University of Liege, Belgium
Skin Disorders

Maureen H. Milne, BVMS, MVM, DCHP, MRCVS
Farm Animal Division, Veterinary Clinical
Studies, University of Glasgow, Scotland, UK
Lung and Airway Disorders

Dale A. Moore, MS, DVM, MPVM, PhD
Associate Professor
Veterinary Medical Teaching and Research
Center
University of California-Davis, Tulare, CA
*Bone, Joint, and Muscle Disorders;
Disorders Affecting Multiple Body Systems*

James N. Moore, DVM, PhD
Distinguished Research Professor
Department of Large Animal Medicine
College of Veterinary Medicine
University of Georgia, Athens, GA
Digestive Disorders

Lisa E. Moore, DVM, DACVIM
Affiliated Veterinary Specialists
Maitland, FL
Digestive Disorders

Karen A. Moriello, DVM, DACVD
Professor
Department of Medical Science
School of Veterinary Medicine
University of Wisconsin, Madison, WI
Skin Disorders

James K. Morrisey, DVM, DABVP (Avian Practice)
Department of Clinical Science
College of Veterinary Medicine
Cornell University, Ithaca, NY
Ferrets

Karen R. Munana, DVM, MS, DACVIM (Neurology)
Associate Professor
Department of Clinical Sciences
College of Veterinary Medicine
North Carolina State University, Raleigh, NC
Brain, Spinal Cord, and Nerve Disorders

Lisa A. Murphy, VMD
Veterinary Poison Information Specialist
ASPCA Animal Poison Control Center
Urbana, IL
Poisoning

Michael J. Murray, DVM, MS
Technical Marketing Director
Merial Limited, Duluth, GA
Digestive Disorders

Sofie Muylle, DVM, PhD
Department of Morphology
Faculty of Veterinary Medicine
University of Ghent, Merelbeke, Belgium
Digestive Disorders

T. Mark Neer, DVM, DACVIM (Internal Medicine)
Professor, Dept of Clinical Sciences
College of Veterinary Medicine
Louisiana State University, Baton Rouge, LA
*Ear Disorders; Brain, Spinal Cord, and
Nerve Disorders*

Paul Nicoletti, DVM, MS
Professor Emeritus, Pathobiology
College of Veterinary Medicine
University of Florida, Gainesville, FL
Reproductive Disorders

Jerome C. Nietfeld, DVM, PhD, DACVP
Associate Professor
Dept of Diagnostic Medicine/Pathobiology
College of Veterinary Medicine
Kansas State University, Manhattan, KS
Reproductive Disorders

Frederick W. Oehme, DVM, PhD
Professor of Toxicology, Pathobiology,
Medicine, and Physiology
Comparative Toxicology Laboratories
Kansas State University, Manhattan, KS
Poisoning

Gary D. Osweiler, DVM, MS, PhD, DABVT
Professor and Director
Veterinary Diagnostic and Production
Animal Medicine
Iowa State University, Ames, IA
Poisoning

**Karen L. Overall, MA, VMD, PhD, DACVB,
ABS Certified Applied Animal Behaviorist**
Research Associate, Psychiatry Department
Center for Neurobiology & Behavior
University of Pennsylvania
Philadelphia, PA
Behavior

Sheldon Padgett, DVM, MS, DACVS
Metropolitan Veterinary Referral Group
Akron, OH
Bone, Joint, and Muscle Disorders

Sharon Patton, MS, PhD
Professor of Parasitology
Department of Comparative Medicine
College of Veterinary Medicine
University of Tennessee, Knoxville, TN
Digestive Disorders

Sarah E. Payne, DVM, DACVIM
Upstate Veterinary Specialists
Greenville, SC
Blood Disorders

**Andrew S. Peregrine, BVMS, PhD, DVM,
DEVPC, MRCVS**
Department of Pathobiology
Ontario Veterinary College
University of Guelph, Ontario, Canada
Digestive Disorders

Donald Peter, DVM, MS, DACT
Veterinarian/Owner
Frontier Genetics, Hermiston, OR
Reproductive Disorders

Mark E. Peterson, DVM, DACVIM
Head, Division of Endocrinology
The Caspary Research Institute and
the Bobst Hospital
The Animal Medical Center, New York, NY
Hormonal Disorders

**Katherine E. Quesenberry, DVM, DABVP
(Avian Practice)**
The Animal Medical Center, New York, NY
*Chinchillas; Gerbils; Guinea Pigs;
Hamsters; Mice; Prairie Dogs; Rats*

Karen W. Post, DVM, MS, DACVM
Veterinary Bacteriologist
North Carolina Department of Agriculture
and Consumer Services
Rollins Animal Disease Diagnostic
Laboratory
Raleigh, NC
Diagnostic Tests and Imaging

**Otto M. Radostits, CM, DVM, MSc,
DACVIM *(Deceased)***
Professor Emeritus
Dept of Large Animal Clinical Sciences
Western College of Veterinary Medicine
University of Saskatchewan
Saskatoon, Saskatchewan, Canada
Disorders Affecting Multiple Body Systems

Philip T. Reeves, BVSc, PhD, FACVSc
Principal Scientist
Residues and Veterinary Medicines
Australian Pesticides and Veterinary
Medicines Authority, Canberra, Australia
Drugs and Vaccines

Ase Risberg, VMD
Large Animal Internal Medicine
School of Veterinary Medicine
University of Wisconsin, Madison, WI
Heart and Blood Vessel Disorders

**Barton W. Rohrbach, VMD, MPH,
DACVPM (Epidemiology)**
Associate Professor
Dept of Large Animal Clinical Sciences
College of Veterinary Medicine
University of Tennessee, Knoxville, TN
Disorders Affecting Multiple Body Systems

Michele R. Rosenbaum, VMD, DACVD
Veterinary Specialists of Rochester
Rochester, NY
Ear Disorders

Wayne Rosenkrantz, DVM, DACVD
Owner-Partner
Animal Dermatology Clinic, Tustin, CA
Skin Disorders

Robert C. Rosenthal, DVM, MS, PhD, DACVIM, DACVR
SouthPaws Veterinary Referral Center
Fairfax, VA
Hormonal Disorders; Reproductive Disorders

Stanley I. Rubin, DVM, MS, DACVIM
Director, Veterinary Teaching Hospital
Western College of Veterinary Medicine
University of Saskatchewan
Saskatoon, Saskatchewan, Canada
Digestive Disorders

Charles E. Rupprecht, VMD, MS, PhD
Chief, Rabies Section
Centers for Disease Control and Prevention
Atlanta, GA
Brain, Spinal Cord, and Nerve Disorders

Bonnie R. Rush, DVM, MS, DACVIM
Professor, Equine Medicine
College of Veterinary Medicine
Kansas State University, Manhattan, KS
Lung and Airway Disorders

H. Carolien Rutgers, DVM, MS, DACVIM, DECVIM-CA, DSAM, MRCVS
Senior Lecturer
The Royal Veterinary College
University of London, Hertfordshire, UK
Digestive Disorders

Sherry Sanderson, BS, DVM, PhD, DACVIM, DACVN
Associate Professor
Department of Physiology and Pharmacology
College of Veterinary Medicine
University of Georgia, Athens, GA
Kidney and Urinary Tract Disorders

Donald C. Sawyer, DVM, PhD, DACVA, Hon. DABVP
Professor Emeritus
Michigan State University
Manager, Veterinary Product Development
and Support
Minrad Inc., Buffalo, NY
Metabolic Disorders

Mary M. Schell, DVM
Veterinary Poison Information Specialist
ASPCA Animal Poison Control Center
Urbana, IL
Poisoning

David G. Schmitz, DVM, MS, DACVIM
Associate Professor of Medicine
Department of Veterinary Large Animal
Medicine & Surgery
College of Veterinary Medicine
Texas A&M University, College Station, TX
Poisoning

Norman R. Schneider, DVM, MSc, DABVT
Veterinary Toxicologist Emeritus
Dept of Veterinary and Biomedical Sciences
University of Nebraska
Lincoln, NE
Poisoning

Kevin T. Schultz, DVM, PhD
Chief Scientific Officer
Head of Global Research and Development
Merial Limited, Duluth, GA
Immune Disorders

Maya M. Scott, BS, DVM
Resident, Clinical Pharmacology
Department of Veterinary Physiology and
Pharmacology
College of Veterinary Medicine
Texas A&M University, College Station, TX
Drugs and Vaccines

Brad E. Seguin, DVM, MS, PhD DACT
Professor Emeritus
Dept of Clinical and Population Sciences
College of Veterinary Medicine
University of Minnesota, St. Paul, MN
Reproductive Disorders

Susan D. Semrad, VMD, PhD, DACVIM
Associate Professor
Department of Medical Sciences
School of Veterinary Medicine
University of Wisconsin, Madison, WI
Digestive Disorders

Patricia L. Sertich, MS, VMD, DACT
Associate Professor-Clinician Educator
School of Veterinary Medicine, New Bolton
Center, University of Pennsylvania
Kennett Square, PA
Reproductive Disorders

J. Glenn Songer, PhD
Professor
Dept of Veterinary Science and Microbiology
University of Arizona, Tucson, AZ
Disorders Affecting Multiple Body Systems

Sharon J. Spier, DVM, PhD, DACVIM
Associate Professor
Dept of Veterinary Medicine and
Epidemiology
School of Veterinary Medicine
University of California, Davis, CA
Metabolic Disorders

**Richard A. Squires, BVSc, PhD, DVR,
  DACVIM, DECVIM, MRCVS**
Associate Professor
Institute of Veterinary, Animal, and
Biomedical Sciences, Massey University
Palmerston North, New Zealand
Disorders Affecting Multiple Body Systems

James H. Steele, DVM, MPH
Professor Emeritus
Center for Infectious Diseases
School of Public Health
University of Texas, Houston, TX
*Diseases Spread from Animals to People
(Zoonoses)*

**Jörg M. Steiner, DMV, PhD, DACVIM,
  DECVIM-CA**
Associate Professor
GI Laboratory, Texas A&M University
College Station, TX
Digestive Disorders; Drugs and Vaccines

David Stiller, MS, PhD
Research Entomologist
Animal Disease Research Unit
U.S. Department of Agriculture
Agricultural Research Service
University of Idaho, Moscow, ID
Skin Disorders

Bert E. Stromberg, PhD
Professor and Associate Dean
College of Veterinary Medicine
University of Minnesota, St. Paul, MN
Disorders Affecting Multiple Body Systems

Thomas W. Swerczek, DVM, PhD
Professor of Veterinary Pathology
Department of Veterinary Science
University of Kentucky, Lexington, KY
Digestive Disorders

Joseph Taboada, DVM, DACVIM
Professor and Associate Dean
Office of Student and Academic Affairs
School of Veterinary Medicine
Louisiana State University
Baton Rouge, LA
Disorders Affecting Multiple Body Systems

**Patricia A. Talcott, MS, DVM, PhD,
  DABVT**
Associate Professor
Department of Food Science and Toxicology
Holm Research Center
University of Idaho, Moscow, ID
Skin Disorders

**Stuart M. Taylor, PhD, BVMS, MRCVS,
  DECVP**
VetPar Services
Bangor, United Kingdom
Lung and Airway Disorders

Charles O. Thoen, DVM, PhD
Professor
Veterinary Microbiology and Preventive
Medicine
College of Veterinary Medicine
Iowa State University, Ames, IA
Disorders Affecting Multiple Body Systems

William B. Thomas, DVM, MS, DACVIM (Neurology)
Associate Professor of Neurology/
Neurosurgery
Dept of Small Animal Clinical Sciences
University of Tennessee, Knoxville, TN
Brain, Spinal Cord, and Nerve Disorders

John F. Timoney, MVB, MS, PhD, DSc, MRCVS
Keeneland Chair of Infectious Diseases
Gluck Equine Research Center
University of Kentucky, Lexington, KY
Disorders Affecting Multiple Body Systems

Peter J. Timoney, MVB, MS, PhD, FRCVS
Chairman and Director
Gluck Equine Research Center
Department of Veterinary Science
University of Kentucky, Lexington, KY
Disorders Affecting Multiple Body Systems

Ian Tizard, BVMS, PhD
Richard M. Schubot Professor
Department of Pathobiology
College of Veterinary Medicine
Texas A&M University, College Station, TX
*Disorders Affecting Multiple Body Systems;
Drugs and Vaccines*

Susan Tornquist, DVM, PhD, DACVP
Associate Professor
Department of Biomedical Sciences
College of Veterinary Medicine
Oregon State University, Corvallis, OR
Diagnostic Tests and Imaging

Josie L. Traub-Dargatz, DVM, MS, DACVIM
Professor of Equine Internal Medicine
Department of Clinical Sciences
College of Veterinary Medicine and
Biomedical Sciences
Colorado State University
Fort Collins, CO
*Digestive Disorders; Brain, Spinal Cord,
and Nerve Disorders*

Tracy A. Turner, DVM, MS
Professor, Equine Surgery
College of Veterinary Medicine
University of Minnesota, St. Paul, MN
Bone, Joint, and Muscle Disorders

Wendy E. Vaala, VMD, DACVIM
Clinical Associate
B. W. Furlong and Associates, Oldwick, NJ
Lung and Airway Disorders

Stephanie J. Valberg, DVM, PhD
Professor
Dept of Clinical and Population Sciences
University of Minnesota
St. Paul, MN
Bone, Joint, and Muscle Disorders

John F. Van Vleet, DVM, PhD
Professor of Veterinary Pathology
School of Veterinary Medicine
Purdue University, West Lafayette, IN
Bone, Joint, and Muscle Disorders

Jozef Vercruysse, DVM, DEVPC
Professor
Faculty of Veterinary Medicine
University of Ghent, Merelbeke, Belgium
Drugs and Vaccines

Alice Villalobos, BS, DVM
Animal Oncology Consultation Service
Woodland Hills, Torrance
Hermosa Beach, CA
Skin Disorders

Cheryl L. Waldner, DVM, PhD
Associate Professor
Dept of Large Animal Clinical Sciences
Western College of Veterinary Medicine
University of Saskatchewan
Saskatoon, Saskatchewan, Canada
Poisoning

Michelle Wall, DVM, DACVIM
Upstate Veterinary Specialists, Greenville, SC
Heart and Blood Vessel Disorders

Melissa S. Wallace, DVM, DACVIM
Regional Medical Director
VCA Animal Hospitals, Aurora, IL
Kidney and Urinary Tract Disorders

David J. Waltisbuhl, BASc, MSc
Senior Scientist DPI&F Actest
Yeerongpilly Veterinary Laboratory
Yeerongpilly, Queensland, Australia
Blood Disorders

Stephen C. Waring, DVM, PhD
Assistant Professor
Epidemiology and Environmental Science
Associate Director of Research
Center for Biosecurity and Public Health
Preparedness, School of Public Health
University of Texas Health Science Center
Houston, TX
*Diseases Spread from Animals to People
(Zoonoses)*

Brent R. Whitaker, MS, DVM
Director of Animal Health
National Aquarium in Baltimore
Baltimore, MD
Amphibians

**Trevor J. Whitbread, BSc, BVSc, MRCVS,
    DECVP**
Histopathology and Cytology Diagnostic
Laboratories, Abbey Veterinary Services
Devon, UK
Diagnostic Tests and Imaging

Patricia D. White, DVM, MS, DACVD
Atlanta Veterinary Skin & Allergy Clinic
Atlanta, GA
Ear Disorders; Skin Disorders

Stephen D. White, DVM, DACVD
Professor
Department of Medicine and Epidemiology
School of Veterinary Medicine
University of California, Davis, CA
Skin Disorders

Susan L. White, DVM, MS, DACVIM
Professor of Large Animal Internal Medicine
Department of Large Animal Medicine
College of Veterinary Medicine
University of Georgia, Athens, GA
Brain, Spinal Cord, and Nerve Disorders

**Pamela A. Wilkins, DVM, MS, PhD,
    DACVIM, DACVECC**
Chief
Section of Emergency/Critical Care and
Anesthesia
University of Pennsylvania New Bolton
Center, Kennett Square, PA
Emergencies

Robert Wylie, BVSc, QDA
Narangba, Queensland, Australia
Brain, Spinal Cord, and Nerve Disorders

Reviewers for Selected Chapters

Dale E. Bjorling, DVM, MS
Doug Carithers, DVM, EVP
Jack Easley, DVM, MS, DABVP (Equine)
James Harp, PhD
Margaret V. Root Kustritz, DVM, PhD,
    DACT

Vernon C. Langston, DVM, PhD, DACVCP
Thomas Rosol, DVM, PhD
Mats H. T. Troedsson, DVM, PhD, DACT
J. Michael Walters, DVM, MS, DACVECC

A GUIDE FOR READERS

The Merck/Merial Manual for Pet Health is organized into sections and chapters. Understanding this organization will help the reader navigate through the book and find desired information. Topics of interest can be quickly located by reviewing the Table of Contents or Index.

■ SECTIONS

In the first portion of the book sections cover either basic information or the disorders of one species. Dogs, cats, and horses are treated in this way. The disorders within these sections are grouped by body system.

Following that is a section on birds and then one that includes fish, reptiles, amphibians, and a variety of other small or exotic animals. In this section, there is one chapter covering both basic information and disorders for each animal.

The final section covers a variety of special topics, such as travel with pets, emergencies, drugs and vaccines, poisoning, and the human-animal bond. Each section has its own detailed table of contents to assist in easily locating information.

■ CHAPTERS

Some chapters describe a single body system. Other chapters cover the diseases of an entire species. In either case, the discussion of a disorder usually begins with a definition of the disorder. The information that follows typically includes causes, signs, methods your veterinarian will use to diagnose the condition, treatment, and preventive techniques.

In the sections on dogs, cats, horses, and birds, early chapters describe the normal anatomy and physiology of the animals. These are followed by chapters on select-

ing and providing a home for the animal, routine care and feeding, and behavior.

■ CROSS-REFERENCES

Cross-references are located throughout the book. These identify other important discussions that are related to the original topic. Cross-references include the page and in some cases the subject title of the related information. Some cross-references point the reader to an illustration, sidebar, or table on a specific page.

■ GLOSSARY

In many cases the technical terms that are used by veterinarians to describe medical conditions and disorders are explained or defined in the text. In addition, such terms are also defined in the glossary at the back of the book. The definitions provided in the glossary are not necessarily complete; however, they represent the most frequent usage of the term in this book.

■ INDEX

The index is located at the back of the book and provides an easy way of locating a particular topic of interest. The index is very detailed and includes all specific diseases, disorders, and conditions discussed in the book, as well as many tests, treatments, and other pertinent topics. In many cases, the animal species affected is also identified.

■ ILLUSTRATIONS, SIDEBARS, AND TABLES

The book contains many illustrations, sidebars, and tables that have been developed specifically for this reference. They help explain or highlight material in the text or give additional, related information.

1 DOG BASICS

1 **Description and Physical Characteristics** 2
Introduction 2
Description and Physical Characteristics 2

2 **Selecting and Providing a Home for a Dog** 7
Selecting a Dog 7

3 **Routine Care and Breeding** 11
Routine Health Care 11
Breeding and Reproduction 15
Puppy Care 15

4 **Behavior** 17
Introduction 17
Diagnosing Behavior Problems 17
Behavior Modification 19
Normal Social Behavior in Dogs 24
Behavior Problems in Dogs 25

CHAPTER 1

Description and Physical Characteristics

■ INTRODUCTION

Dogs are descendents of wolves that roamed wild over much of the world in ancient times. People have associated with dogs for thousands of years, originally domesticating them as beasts of burden and guard animals. Today, there are still many working breeds, and the service roles of dogs have greatly expanded to include assisting disabled individuals (for example, those with visual or hearing impairments), working with human law enforcement by sniffing out illegal drugs and other contraband, locating survivors in search-and-rescue missions, and even using their incredible sense of smell for early detection of cancer cells in human patients. Of course, the primary role of most dogs is that of loyal companion.

There are many breeds and sizes of dogs.

■ DESCRIPTION AND PHYSICAL CHARACTERISTICS

Although dogs look very different from people, they share many of our body's characteristics. They have a heart and circulatory system to transport blood, lungs to take in oxygen and rid the body of carbon dioxide, a digestive tract to absorb nutrients from food, and so on. However, it is the differences between dogs and people that are most interesting and that give dogs their unique characteristics as family members.

Body Size

Dogs come in many shapes and sizes. The smallest breeds include the toy and miniature varieties, such as the Toy Poodle, Papillon, Chihuahua, and Shih Tzu. These dogs usually weigh only 5 to 10 pounds (2.3 to 4.5 kilograms), or even less. Medium-sized dogs include many of the terriers and spaniels, which weigh in the 10 to 50 pound (4.5 to 23 kilograms) range. Larger still are the retrievers,

shepherds, and setters, which often weigh 65 to 100 pounds (30 to 45 kilograms). Finally, the giant breeds, such as the Mastiff, Komondor, and Saint Bernard, can approach or exceed 200 pounds (91 kilograms). Of course, sizes vary within breeds, with males usually being larger than females. Mixed-breed dogs include all size ranges.

Metabolism

Dogs have a higher metabolism than people. They breathe faster, pump blood faster, mature faster, and have a higher normal body temperature (*see* TABLE 1).

Table 1. Normal Canine Physiologic Values	
Body temperature (average)	102°F (38.9°C)
Heart rate	70 to 120 beats per minute
Respiratory rate (at rest)	18 to 34 breaths per minute
Average life span	8 to 16 years (depends on breed)

Table 2. Dog Years versus People Years	
Dog Years	**People Years**
6 to 12 months	10 to 15 years
12 to 18 months	15 to 20 years
18 to 24 months	20 to 24 years
4 years	32 years
6 years	40 years
8 years	48 years
10 to 12 years	56 to 64 years
13 to 14 years	68 to 72 years
15 to 20 years	76 to 96 years

Young dogs seem to have even more energy than children. However, this high metabolism comes with a shorter life span. A common rule of thumb is that 1 dog year equals about 10 to 12 people years for the first 2 years, and then 4 people years (per dog year) after that (*see* TABLE 2). Actual life span depends on health and size, with small breeds generally living longer than larger ones.

Temperature Regulation

Dogs are generally much better at conserving heat than at cooling themselves. In sled dogs, who can survive outdoors even in bitterly cold temperatures, the fur acts as an insulating "blanket" that retains the heat generated by the dog's high metabolism. However, in hot or humid weather, most dogs have difficulty. Dogs cannot sweat, which is an effective form of evaporative cooling. Instead, dogs lose heat primarily by panting. These rapid breaths (10 times faster than normal) are an attempt to lose heat through evaporation by moving hot, moisture-filled air in and out. During the short, shallow breaths in panting, little air can be exchanged in the lungs. In fact, dogs must stop panting periodically to take a good respiratory breath. Drinking water also helps dogs cool down, and the canine hair coat helps insulate from the sun.

Because the cooling system of dogs is relatively poor, certain summer situations can be dangerous and even life threatening. Sadly, many dogs die of heat stroke every year (*see* page 1053). The most common problem is associated with being shut in a parked car. Even with the windows rolled down, the inside of a parked car can quickly reach 150°F (66°C) or more in the summer, which can cause heat stroke and death in a matter of minutes. Other dangerous situations involve being penned or tied out in the sun (without access to shade) or being locked in a poorly ventilated travel crate.

Ways to keep dogs cool during hot weather include air conditioning, spray misters, shade, dips in a wading pool, or gentle spraying with a garden hose. Keeping dogs wet during the heat of the day provides a method of evaporative cooling. Plenty of cool, fresh drinking water should be available at all times.

The Senses

Dogs have the same 5 senses that people do but to very different degrees. Some senses are less developed than in people, with others being extraordinarily more sensitive.

Sight

Dogs can see movement and light much better than people. In the retina of the eye, dogs have more of a specific type of cell called a **rod**, which is good at collecting dim light, so they have better night vision. A reflective layer in the dog's eye, called the **tapetum lucidum**, magnifies incoming light. This reflective layer lends a characteristic blue or greenish glint to dogs' eyes when light (for example, headlights of passing cars) shines into them at night. However, dogs do not have as much visual acuity as people, meaning that they cannot distinguish fine details as well. They also cannot differentiate colors as well because they have fewer of the cells in the retina called **cones**, which are responsible for color vision. Contrary to popular belief, however, dogs are not completely colorblind.

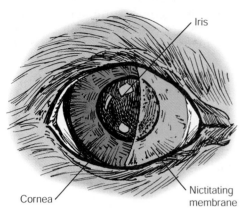

Iris

Cornea

Nictitating membrane

Dogs have a third eyelid, called the nictitating membrane.

A unique feature of the dog eye is the **nictitating membrane**, which is also called the third eyelid. This additional eyelid is a whitish pink color, and it is found under the other eyelids in the inside corner (near the nose) of the eye. The third eyelid extends up when needed to protect the eyeball from scratches (for example, while traveling through brush) or in response to inflammation. (For a more detailed discussion of EYE DISORDERS, *see* page 140.)

Hearing

The ear canal of the dog is much deeper than that of people and creates a better funnel to carry sound to the ear drum. The average dog can hear about 4 times better than the average person, including sounds at higher frequencies than can be detected by the human ear. Dogs are also better at distinguishing the direction of a sound, which is an adaptation useful for hunting. Unfortunately, this deeper ear canal predisposes dogs to ear problems. Grease, wax, and moisture can build up in the ear, leading to inflammation and infection. Floppy ears or hair within the ears further limit ventilation, making matters worse. This is why many dogs need frequent preventive ear cleaning (*see* EAR DISORDERS, page 155).

Smell and Taste

Dogs have an extraordinarily acute sense of smell; it is about a million times more sensitive than that of people. They can detect odors at extremely low levels and can distinguish odors that are subtly different. This is why dogs are able to sniff out drugs and explosives at airports, search for human victims at disaster sites (including victims deep under water), and follow the scent track of criminals.

Odor molecules dissolve in the moisture that coats the inside of the canine nose. Signals are then sent from the olfactory membranes in the nose to the olfactory center of the brain, which is 40 times bigger in dogs than in people.

Dogs also have an organ on the roof of the mouth that allows them to "taste" certain smells. As in people, taste and smell in dogs are closely linked. However, dogs gain much more information about food from smell than from taste. Dogs have only about one sixth the number of taste buds that people do, and their distinct sense of taste is actually quite poor.

Locomotion

Dogs have most of the same muscles, tendons, joints, and ligaments as people. All 4 of the dog's limbs are maximized for locomotion, from a steady walk to a rapid sprint. In many respects, dogs run like horses, and have the same 4 gaits: walk, trot, canter, and gallop. The canine bones that are comparable to the long bones of our hands and feet are located in the dog's lower legs. The angular hock in the hind legs is comparable to the ankle in people. Most dogs can swim, although some breeds specifically developed for swimming (for example, retrievers) can swim better than others (such as Bulldogs).

Pads and Nails

The canine paw contains specialized structures that help the dog move over different surfaces. The bottom of the paw is covered by thick, resilient pads that become callused after years of steady wear in direct contact with the ground. These pads protect the paw and help provide a secure grip on many types of surfaces. The toenails help provide traction while running and are also used for digging. Canine toenails are thick, brittle structures made up of a protein called keratin (just like hair). A large blood supply runs down the middle and feeds the cuticle (or "quick") of the growing nail. Avoiding these blood vessels when trimming toenails can be difficult, especially when the nails are dark. Regardless, keeping nails trimmed is important because nails that snag or break during running or jumping can cause considerable bleeding and pain. Broken nails should be examined by a veterinarian, who can trim away the fractured part of the nail, treat the wound to stop any bleeding, and prevent infection. Dogs have rudimentary equivalents of human thumbs called dew claws that are found on the middle

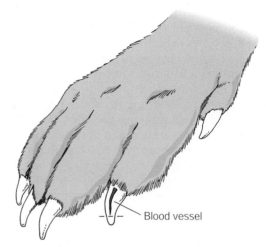

Proper trimming of the nails is important. Avoid cutting the blood vessel that runs through the nail.

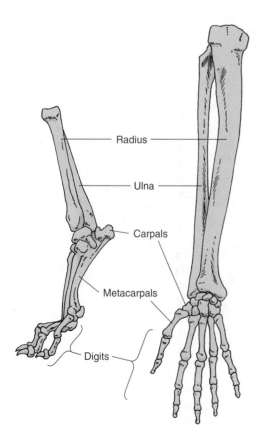

The bones in a dog's leg are similar to those in a human arm.

side of the front paws or lower front legs. Dew claws have no function, but they commonly snag and break. Dew claws should also be trimmed periodically to prevent snagging and to keep them from curling around and growing into the foot. They are commonly removed in very young puppies or as an additional surgical procedure when dogs are spayed or neutered.

Skin and Hair

Canine skin has several layers, including an outer epidermis that is constantly being replaced and an inner dermis that contains nerves and blood vessels. Canine skin is thinner and much more sensitive than human skin. Dogs should be bathed only with shampoos made specifically for pets. Shampoos and other topical products for people can be irritating to canine skin and should be avoided.

Canine fur grows from hair follicles in the skin. Dogs have compound hair follicles, with a central (guard) hair surrounded by 3 to 15 secondary hairs growing out of the same pore. Sebaceous (oil) glands within the skin lubricate the hair, keeping the coat shiny and water resistant. Hair growth is controlled by several factors, including nutrition, hormones, and time of year. In general, dogs shed at a slow steady rate all year round, with periods of increased shedding in the spring and fall. Shedding replaces hair gradually, without bald patches (which can be a sign of illness and should be investigated).

The main functions of the hair coat are to protect the skin and to help regulate temperature. Fur traps air, which provides a layer of insulation against the cold. Small muscles attached to the guard hairs allow dogs to raise these hairs, which improves air trapping. Dogs also raise their hackles as a threatening gesture in response to danger.

Different breeds of dogs have different types of hair coats. Breeds from northern climates (such as Huskies and Malamutes) have a soft, downy undercoat that provides better insulation in cold weather. Water breeds (retrievers, for example) have more long and stiff guard hairs to protect the skin and undercoat from harsh environmental conditions. Water breeds also have ample oil secretions to lubricate the hair. Breeds from warmer climates have shorter coats designed only to shade the skin. Poodles have very fine, curly hair that sheds far less than that of other breeds.

Teeth and Mouth

Like their wolf ancestors, dogs are carnivores with teeth designed for rending and tearing meat. They have 28 deciduous (baby) teeth that are replaced by 42 permanent (adult) teeth between 2 and 7 months of age (*see* TABLE 3). The different types of teeth have specialized functions, depending on their position in the mouth. The front teeth, which include the 12 incisors and 4 large canine teeth (eye teeth), are designed for

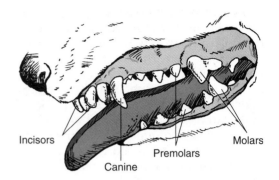

Adult dogs have incisors, canines, premolars, and molars.

grasping and tearing. The rearward premolar and molar teeth grind food into smaller pieces that can be swallowed.

The mouth also contains the salivary glands, which secrete saliva that lubricates the food and begins digestion. The tongue helps guide food to the back of the throat and is important for licking up small food pieces and lapping up water. Dogs also lick as a sign of affection or subservience, or both.

Digestive and Urinary Tracts

The gastrointestinal tract includes the stomach, the small intestine, and the large intestine (colon). This system digests food into useful nutrients, absorbs water, and eliminates waste. Digestive problems often show up as vomiting or diarrhea, which can have many causes, including viral infections; worms; stress; or ingestion of bones, sticks, or other foreign material.

The urinary system eliminates nitrogenous wastes from protein breakdown and

Table 3. Canine Adult Dentition			
Type of Tooth	Number (Upper/Lower)	Age (Months) at Eruption	Function
Incisors	6/6	2 to 5	Grasping
Canines	2/2	5 to 6	Tearing
Premolars	8/8	4 to 6	Grinding
Molars	4/6	4 to 7	Grinding

helps control fluid levels. Waste products are filtered by the kidneys and then sent through the ureters to the urinary bladder for storage. Urine is passed out of the body through the urethra. In males, the urethra doubles as a channel for sperm during copulation. Urinary infections are much more common in females and usually show up as frequent dribbles of urine that may be tinged with blood.

Both urinary and digestive problems are often associated with straining while urinating or defecating. At first glance, it may be difficult for dog owners to tell the source of the problem. Therefore, it is important to watch your dog while it eliminates and to note the character and color of the urine and feces. Your veterinarian may request a sample of the urine or feces, or both. Diarrhea usually consists of frequent, soft or runny feces that may be a different color (often yellow, gray, or black) than usual. Any sign of blood in the feces calls for veterinary attention. Repeated, unproductive attempts to pass a bowel movement can be a sign of serious constipation or bowel obstruction, which can be an emergency. Prompt veterinary attention is needed if the dog has a tense, painful abdomen or is passing only small amounts of bloody, gel-like feces. (*See also* DIGESTIVE DISORDERS, page 77, and KIDNEY AND URINARY TRACT DISORDERS, page 283.)

Anal Glands

Rump rubbing or "scooting" is usually associated with impacted anal glands, although it can be confused with a digestive problem. The anal glands are located in a layer of muscle at the 4 and 8 o'clock positions around the anus. These scent glands contain a foul-smelling secretion that is normally expressed during a bowel movement. The secretions often thicken, which can plug the duct, causing pressure and irritation that can lead to infection. Many dogs need to have their anal glands manually emptied by their veterinarian on a regular schedule.

CHAPTER 2

Selecting and Providing a Home for a Dog

▦ SELECTING A DOG

Choosing the dog that is right for you and your family is very important. The large variety of breeds means that dogs come in all sizes, shapes, and colors, and have a range of temperaments. Many dog breeds have been developed for specific purposes and behaviors. A mismatch can result in unnecessary stress and lead to behavioral problems, which can be difficult to correct.

Size, Activity, and Temperament

Size, activity level, temperament, and breed characteristics (including hair coat) should be considered in choosing a dog. Your dog will live with you for many years, so you must consider how these factors will best fit your lifestyle and situation. For example, large dogs (such as retrievers) and very active dogs (Jack Russell Terriers, for example) need room to run and play. These active dogs do better when they have access to a fenced yard for regular exercise and may not be the best choice for a city dweller who lives in a small apartment. Some dogs, such as Border Collies, appear to have a need to work (for example, herd), or they often become bored and out of sorts. Keep in mind that size is not always a good indicator of activity level. Many small dogs require significant amounts of exercise and attention, while some large breeds (Newfoundlands are a good example) can be relatively inactive when mature. Dogs with high activity levels may not be a good choice for someone whose mobility is limited. Smaller, active dogs (such as small poodles or terriers) may not be able to tolerate the rough play of young children.

One critically important consideration is whether the dog will be good with children or infants. Some breeds are generally better with children than others, but most dogs that are raised with children see them as just another family member. In these situations, the dog should be trained to respond properly to all members of the family. Adult dogs that are accustomed to a household without children may resent the attention given to a new child, resulting in behavioral problems such as aggression or soiling in the house. In any event, the early interactions when children are introduced into a household with dogs, and vice versa, should be closely monitored. Children or infants should never be left alone with a dog until you are certain that neither the dog nor the child will injure the other.

Climate

When choosing a dog, it makes sense to consider regional climate. Heavy-coated breeds will have difficulty staying cool in hot southern climates, while thin, short-haired breeds may have problems in extremely cold winter temperatures. Small dogs that stay inside most of the time can generally get along fine in any region, provided their trips outdoors in potentially dangerous weather conditions are kept short.

Age

Selecting either a puppy or an adult dog has advantages and disadvantages. Puppies raised with your family usually integrate well into your environment, and a strong bond usually forms naturally. However, the adult size and activity level of a mixed-breed puppy can be

difficult to predict. All puppies have a lot of energy and require a great deal of attention and supervision, especially during the early, housetraining period. Puppies also require a greater initial investment in veterinary care (*see* page 15). On the other hand, adult dogs may have some initial difficulty adapting to your family or lifestyle and many need additional time and attention to adjust to their new environment. If you are able to obtain a medical and behavioral history from the previous owner or a shelter, this can be invaluable in assessing whether a particular dog is right for you.

Finding the Right Dog

Dogs can be obtained from a variety of sources (*see* BOX). Again, there are advantages and disadvantages associated with each. For example, many pet shops obtain puppies from reputable kennels and shelters, while others purchase them from factory-like "puppy mills," which raise dogs of questionable quality often under extremely poor conditions. If you want a purebred dog, you should search for registered breeders in your area. Shelters are often a good source of mixed-breed puppies, and purebred dogs are also often available. Regardless of the source, your best approach to selecting a pet is to research the source, ask questions, and carefully observe both the dog and its environment.

Ask Questions

Checking out the source of your dog before you acquire it is important. If the source is a friend, neighbor, or ad in the paper, ask to see the dog's parents (if possi-

---

Potential Sources for Obtaining a Pet Dog

- Responsible breeders
- Humane shelters
- Breed rescue associations
- Pet stores
- Neighbors or relatives
- Ads in the paper

ble). Ask about the health history, including any illness, vaccinations, heartworm preventive, and whether the dog has been spayed or neutered. Ask for and check references for breeders and pet shops. Ask why an animal is up for adoption and if it has any known medical or behavioral problems. If you are getting a purebred dog, ask if the parents have been tested for, and found free of, diseases common to the breed.

Watch Closely

Keep your eyes open when visiting the kennel, pet shop, or shelter. It is worthwhile visiting before you are ready to make your selection so that you can check things over without the distraction of falling in love with a new pet. Is the facility clean and well organized? Do the dogs look happy, or scared and timid? Do the dogs look healthy, or thin and sickly? Is the temperature of the building comfortable, with fresh water available to all animals? Many problems can also be "sniffed out." Foul odors or dank, humid air suggest a building that is dirty or poorly ventilated. A clean kennel should smell slightly of disinfectant, not strongly of urine or feces. The puppies themselves should not smell of urine or feces.

Providing a Home for a Dog

Pet ownership carries responsibilities that should not be taken lightly. Pets are family members that need to be cared for throughout their entire lives, not disposable possessions that can be discarded if they become inconvenient. Pets also carry financial responsibilities for housing, a quality diet, and veterinary care. The latter includes routine veterinary examinations, preventive vaccinations, parasite control including heartworm prevention, treatment during an illness or emergency, dental cleanings, and so forth.

The money and time devoted to pet care are substantial, but the rewards are much greater. Research has shown that the bond that can develop between people and animals as a result of owning and caring for a pet has significant social and health benefits (*see also* page 1228). Dogs provide companionship, a sense of purpose, and unconditional love. These qualities can especially benefit lonely, elderly, or mentally disturbed people. Research has also shown that pet ownership can prolong both length and quality of life by reducing stress, blood pressure, anxiety, and depression. Under proper supervision, pet ownership also teaches children about responsibility, caring, and commitment.

Judging the Physical and Social Health of a New Dog

Positive Attributes

- Active, friendly, sociable, curious
- Healthy weight
- Clean, shiny coat free of mats, sores, or fleas
- Clean ears and eyes
- History of vaccination and veterinary care
- History of eating a high-quality dog food

Negative Attributes

- Timid or aggressive (snarls, backs away, snaps)
- Thin or scrawny, with ribs or hip bones sticking out (*Note:* A pot belly on a thin puppy may be a sign of worms, a very common and easily treatable condition.)
- Dirty coat stained with urine or feces
- Fleas or "flea dirt" (reddish brown granules or flecks, commonly seen over the rump)
- Red, inflamed, crusty, or painful ears
- Red spots or sores on the skin
- Signs of respiratory problems (for example, a cough or runny eyes or nose)
- History of illness (vomiting, diarrhea, or similar signs)

Provide your dog with a place to sleep.

Housing

Indoor dogs share the roof over our heads and, sometimes, our furniture as well. Puppies, and some mature dogs as well, benefit from having a crate, which can help greatly in housetraining and other training. Many dogs also feel secure in a crate because it is their own space, or "den." You may also want to provide a comfortable dog bed for your pet. In addition, your dog should have a designated, quiet place where food and water bowls are placed.

Special Needs of Outdoor Dogs

Hunting and guard dogs are often kept outdoors year round. These dogs have special needs that relate primarily to shelter, nutrition, and companionship. In addition, it is important to remember that dogs are social animals that do not like to be by themselves or kept in isolation. Outside dogs need frequent attention and human contact for health and happiness.

Diet

Proper nutrition is an important and often overlooked aspect of pet ownership. The pet food industry is large, offering many choices, and all dog foods are not of equal quality. Name-brand dog foods are backed by scientific research and quality control to provide complete, balanced nutrition for your pet. Dry food is generally preferable to canned because it promotes healthy teeth and gums (while

providing the same nutrition). Diets that are specifically formulated for the various stages of a dog's life (including puppy, adult, and senior) are widely available in grocery stores, pet shops, and other outlets such as pet "superstores." Specialty diets for specific problems (such as obesity, food allergy, or kidney disease) have also been developed; many of these diets are prescription diets that are available only through veterinarians.

Most adult dogs are fed 1 to 2 times daily, although puppies require more frequent feeding (*see* page 16). Large-breed dogs should be fed at least twice a day to

Special Needs of Outdoor Dogs

Shelter Requirements

▪ Dogs should always have access to a shelter that protects them from the elements (heat, sun, rain, cold, or other bad weather).

▪ Shelters should be large enough for the dog to turn around but not so large that they can't be warmed by body heat.

▪ Shelters should have a good roof and be high enough off the ground to keep the dog dry in heavy rain or snow.

▪ Shelters that have flexible working doors can help keep the elements out, while allowing dogs to go in and out at will.

Nutritional Requirements

▪ In cold weather, outside dogs need twice as many calories as usual to produce enough body heat to keep themselves warm. They should be fed *double* their regular amount of high-quality dog food, split into several feedings to prevent digestive problems from eating meals that are too large.

Companionship Requirements

▪ Outside dogs need companionship, which can be provided by housing outside dogs together and by frequent human contact.

▪ Dogs that are housed together require a shelter large enough to accommodate more than one dog, or multiple smaller shelters should be available.

prevent eating large amounts that can lead to bloat. Your veterinarian can help you estimate your dog's daily caloric needs, which can then be provided in multiple feedings of equal size. Meals should be provided in a quiet corner, away from the hustle and bustle of family life. This fosters proper digestion and avoids gorging and possessive aggression.

One of the biggest problems in pets is overfeeding, which can lead to obesity, other serious diseases (such as heart disease and arthritis), and a shortened life span. Only the proper amounts of a quality dog food, with few (if any) table scraps, should be fed. In any case, table food should *never* exceed 10% of your dog's daily caloric requirements. Your veterinarian can provide an estimate of the proper type and amount of food for your dog to maintain your dog's ideal weight. As a general rule, a dog is at proper weight when the ribs and spinal vertebrae (backbones) can be felt, with only a small amount of underlying fat and other body tissues.

Fresh, clean water should *always* be available to your dog. Never restrict access to water unless instructed by your veterinarian.

Exercise

Dogs need regular exercise. Sedentary dogs tend to gain weight and are prone to both medical and behavioral problems. Dogs that get enough exercise have improved muscle tone, metabolism, weight control, and temperature regulation. However, overly strenuous exercise can also cause problems, especially in dogs that are out of shape, very young, or very old. Human athletes should keep this in mind before taking their dogs on long, strenuous runs, especially in hot or humid weather.

Temperament

Dogs are pack animals that bond closely to people, making them excellent family pets. They are very social by nature and need attention from their human companions. Bored or lonely dogs often develop behavioral problems, such as destruction of property or even self-mutilation, as an outlet for loneliness and anxiety. Certainly, some breeds of dogs, such as Irish Setters, Dalmatians, and terriers in general, tend to be more energetic and high-strung than other mellower breeds, such as Newfoundlands or Bassett Hounds. These more energetic dogs tend to have a greater need for human companionship and may be more likely to develop problems, even if left for only short periods. Temperament also needs to be considered if there are small children or other dogs or pets in the household.

CHAPTER **3**

Routine Care and Breeding

◼ ROUTINE HEALTH CARE

In addition to feeding and exercising your dog, other aspects of general care are needed to keep your dog healthy throughout its life. These include routine veterinary care for vaccinations, parasite control, and dental care; grooming; and protection from household hazards.

Importance of Veterinary Care

Adult dogs should have a complete veterinary examination at least once a year.

Puppies need veterinary visits usually every 3 to 4 weeks until they are about 4 months old. Geriatric dogs (older than 7 to 8 years old) should see their veterinarian twice a year or more frequently because illness is more common in older pets and it can be identified sooner. Your veterinarian may recommend a wellness program for your pet, including routine blood work to monitor for problems such as early kidney or liver disease.

Signs of Illness

Because you are more familiar with your dog than anyone else, you should watch it carefully for subtle signs of illness that another person or even a veterinarian may miss. General signs of illness include a lack of appetite or decreased activity. Other more specific signs include vomiting and diarrhea, urinating more (or less) frequently, coughing and sneezing, or a discharge from the eyes, ears, or nose. Illness can also show up as a loss of hair or itchy areas on the skin or around the ears. Problems with the musculoskeletal system are often seen as stiffness or lameness, such as not putting weight on a leg. If your dog shows any of these signs for more than a day or two, a visit with your veterinarian is a good idea.

Giving Medication

Pills and chewable medications are usually relatively easy to administer to dogs. Most dogs will readily eat a pill that is hidden in a small treat, such as a piece of cheese or a bit of peanut butter. Sometimes, gently holding the dog's muzzle closed until you are sure that it has swallowed can be helpful. Liquid medications are sometimes prescribed, particularly for puppies. Liquids can be given via a syringe into the rear of the dog's mouth by inserting the tip of the syringe near the back teeth on either side. Holding the dog's head pointing partially upward can help prevent spills. Spot-on products or other topical medications are administered directly on the coat or skin. If your dog needs eye drops or ear medication, your veterinarian or veterinary technician will

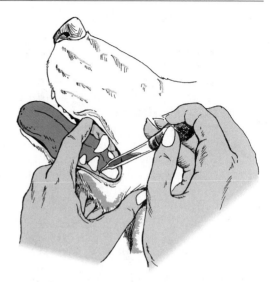

Liquid medicine is easiest given by eyedropper or syringe.

give you a demonstration. Regardless of the type of medication or how it is to be given, it is important to read and follow all label instructions.

Vaccinations

Vaccination is a key component of preventive medicine in dogs, just as in people. Vaccinations are given to stimulate the immune system against infection before exposure to a disease. Several vaccines are routinely given to dogs as the core defense against serious infectious illness. Several others (referred to as non-core) are important in certain regions and situations (see TABLE 4). Your veterinarian can advise which vaccines are necessary in your local area and circumstances.

Traditionally, booster vaccinations have been given every year throughout the dog's life to ensure ongoing protection. However, the need for yearly revaccination has been questioned in recent years. Some data indicate that after the first year of life, immunity lasts long enough so that booster vaccinations are needed only every few years. However, the debate is ongoing. Your veterinarian will be aware of the most recent findings and can advise you about the best vaccination program for your pet.

Table 4. Vaccines Required or Recommended for Dogs*

Disease	Description	Vaccination Frequency and Comments
Core vaccines		
Distemper	A viral infection that can affect several body systems, including the respiratory and nervous systems	First vaccination at 6 to 8 weeks of age, followed by additional vaccinations at 3- to 4-week intervals until 14 to 16 weeks old; booster at 1 year, then every 3 years or more
Hepatitis	A viral infection that causes liver inflammation	Same schedule as distemper (usually given as combination vaccine)
Parvovirus	A viral infection that can affect many body systems, including the respiratory, digestive, and nervous systems	Same schedule as distemper (usually given as combination vaccine)
Rabies	A viral disease of the nervous system that is both fatal and transmissible to people	Initial vaccination as early as 3 months of age; boosters at 1 year and every 1 to 3 years after that, depending on local laws
Noncore vaccines		
Bordetella	A bacterial component of kennel cough	Two doses 4 weeks apart; booster every 6 to 12 months depending on risk; vaccine usually administered into the nose
Leptospirosis	A bacterial infection of the urinary system	Two doses are given, 2 to 4 weeks apart; annual revaccination; used in areas with a known risk
Lyme disease	A bacterial infection that can affect many body systems, especially the joints	Similar schedule as distemper; revaccinate yearly just prior to start of tick season in areas with a known risk
Tracheobronchitis (kennel cough)	A viral infection that is a key component of kennel cough	Same schedule as distemper (often given as combination vaccine)
Not recommended		
Coronavirus	A viral infection of the digestive tract	Similar schedule as distemper; rarely causes disease and typically does not require treatment when it does occur
Giardiasis	A protozoal infection of the digestive tract	Vaccination can prevent shedding of infective cysts but does not prevent infection

*These recommendations were developed after referring to the 2006 American Animal Hospital Association Canine Vaccine Guidelines, Revised.

Parasite Control

The primary intestinal parasites of dogs include roundworms, hookworms, whipworms, and tapeworms. These worms damage the digestive tract or interfere with absorption of essential nutrients, or both. Intestinal parasite infections are diagnosed by finding worm eggs (or sometimes actual worms or worm segments) in fecal samples. Fecal samples should be tested periodically (yearly or on the schedule recommended by your veterinarian) in all dogs and more frequently in puppies, which are especially prone to parasite infection. These worms usually do not cause intestinal infection in people; however, hookworm infections leading to abdominal pain and inflammation have developed in people with weakened immune systems. Roundworm larvae also have the potential to infect people. When infective roundworm eggs are ingested, they can develop into larvae in the intestine and potentially migrate into sensitive organs. This migration is much more likely to occur in children and people with weakened immune systems. Sanitation is key to prevention because roundworm eggs take about 30 days to become infective; thus, promptly cleaning up feces from your yard can essentially eliminate potential exposure.

Heartworm is an especially serious parasite that is transmitted by mosquito bites. These worms live in the major blood vessels of the lung, causing inflammation of the blood vessels and potentially resulting in heart damage and early death. Because treatment of heartworm infection carries a number of serious health risks and is also potentially fatal, prevention is critical. The Companion Animal Parasite Council, an assembly of experts in veterinary medicine and parasitology, recommend year-round heartworm prevention for dogs, because it is impossible to accurately predict all times when mosquitoes will be present. Additionally, most heartworm preventives contain medications that also treat for intestinal parasites, which can be transmitted at all times of the year. Blood tests to check for heartworm disease should be done yearly. (*See also* page 73.)

Common external parasites include fleas, ticks, and mange mites. Monthly preventive treatments are available to control fleas and ticks, and are administered as body sprays or "spot-on" preparations that are placed on the skin between the shoulder blades. Mange mites can be detected by scraping the skin of infected areas for signs of mites or their eggs. Signs of mange include red, scaly areas or bald patches on the skin, or both. (*See also* page 260.)

Dental Care

Dogs need dental attention throughout their lives. You can help keep your dog's teeth and gums in good condition by feeding dry food, providing certain toys (for example, "flossie"-style bones), brushing your dog's teeth regularly, and following a program of professional dental cleanings and oral care performed by your veterinarian. Good dental care reduces the development of plaque which, if untreated, can progress to gingivitis and periodontal disease. In severe cases of dental disease, extraction is common. (*See also* page 87.)

Grooming

Your dog's hair coat should be brushed regularly to remove shed hair and prevent hair mats. Grooming is especially important for dogs with thick or shaggy hair coats that mat or tangle easily. Mats can irritate the skin, and the moist, stuffy conditions underneath them leaves the skin more susceptible to bacterial or parasite infections. Mats should be removed with electric clippers (not scissors) to avoid cutting the skin underneath. Periodic bathing with a pet shampoo is also important for maintaining healthy skin and fur. However, excessive bathing can irritate and dry the skin and hair. On average, most dogs

Dogs with long or shaggy hair require grooming to keep their hair from becoming matted.

do not need to be bathed more than once a month, depending on time of year and weather conditions.

Household Hazards

Your dog must be protected from household hazards, including chemicals, pesticides, cleaning supplies, antifreeze, electrical cords, drugs, alcohol, and poisonous plants (*see also* page 1145). Curious puppies that tend to investigate and chew everything are at greatest risk; however, these products must be kept out of reach of *all* dogs. Dangerous items (especially electrical cords) can be frequently coated with a foul-tasting spray to discourage chewing. Elements of house design, such as steep stairs, slippery floors, and open windows also pose potential hazards for pets (and people) and should be corrected as much as possible.

Spaying/Neutering

All dogs should be spayed or neutered unless they are to be used for breeding. This prevents unwanted puppies and avoids potentially serious future medical problems, such as prostate disease in males, and uterine infection or mammary cancer in females (*see* page 214). Spaying and neutering can also improve behavior. Females are usually spayed around 6 months of age, before their first

Estrous (Heat) Cycle in Female Dogs

- Proestrus—Start of heat. Lasts 7 to 10 days. Vulva swells and blood flows. Females attract males but will not allow mounting.
- Estrus—Mating period. Lasts 5 to 10 days. Blood flow lessens and then stops. Females attract and accept males. Ovulation occurs during this time, usually 2 to 3 days after mating.
- Diestrus. The period 10 to 140 days after heat, when the dog is either pregnant or in a resting phase.
- Anestrus. The resting period between diestrus and the next heat cycle.

heat cycle. Allowing a female to go through a heat or to have a litter is *not* necessary. In fact, the surgery is safest and the future medical benefits are greatest when it is done before the first heat, or estrus, has started. Males are usually neutered between 5 and 10 months of age, depending on breed and size.

▓ BREEDING AND REPRODUCTION

The reproductive cycle in female dogs has 4 phases. Female dogs that have not been spayed (bitches) typically have 2 estrus or "heat" periods per year (about 6 months apart), each lasting about 2 to 3 weeks. In some dogs, the intervals between estrus are much longer. The first heat occurs between 6 and 15 months of age, depending on the size of the dog (later in larger breeds). Females can become pregnant during their first heat or any later heat period.

Male dogs do not have a sexual "cycle." Rather, they respond to females in heat at any time of year. Males are most fertile when fully mature.

▓ PUPPY CARE

Puppies can generally be taken from their mother and littermates beginning at 7 to 8 weeks of age. Puppies, like babies, require a lot of attention, including veterinary care, feeding, socialization, and training.

Importance of Veterinary Care

Just like people, dogs receive a certain degree of immunity (known as maternal immunity) that is passed from their mothers at birth and also shortly thereafter through her milk. Vaccinations cannot effectively stimulate the puppy's immune system until this maternal immunity wears off. Because maternal immunity declines slowly over time, puppies should be vaccinated every 2 to 3 weeks until they are about 4 months old. This ensures that the puppy receives an effective dose of vaccine soon after maternal protection is gone.

Puppies need frequent vaccinations until they are 4 to 5 months old.

Table 5. Feeding Schedule for Dogs		
Age	Number of Daily Meals	Type of Food
6 to 12 weeks	4	Puppy diet
3 to 6 months	3	Puppy diet
6 to 12 months (up to 24 months in the largest breeds)	2	Puppy diet
Adult	1 or 2	Adult diet

Restricting access to unvaccinated dogs until the full series of vaccinations has been given is important to avoid disease.

Intestinal parasites are most common in puppies. Larvae are often passed through the placenta or mother's milk. Worms are so common that new puppies are often treated with a broad-spectrum wormer as a routine preventive measure. Fecal examinations, with additional treatments as necessary, are usually done every 2 to 4 weeks, until 2 successive fecal examinations are negative.

Diet

Proper nutrition is important throughout a dog's life and is especially critical during puppyhood. It is difficult for growing puppies to take in enough calories, fat, protein, vitamins, and minerals to meet their needs for rapid growth and development. Puppies need multiple daily feedings of a specially formulated puppy food. The number of daily feedings can be gradually decreased as the puppy ages, but feeding with a name-brand puppy diet should continue until adulthood, which is about 9 to 12 months in most dogs but up to 2 years in giant breeds (*see* TABLE 5).

Socialization and Training

The earliest training that your puppy must learn is housetraining. With patience, persistence, and consistency, housetraining usually takes only a few weeks. The key is to take the puppy outdoors at the times that dogs naturally eliminate and to praise them enthusiastically when they do. Establishing a designated area that the puppy can associate with elimination can be helpful. If accidents happen, take your pet outside to the designated elimination area and praise it for eliminating (if it does so). Punishment, such as rubbing a dog's nose in urine or feces, does no good and can even have a negative effect on training. Each accident indoors sets the process back a little, so the fewer accidents, the better.

All dogs should learn to pay attention and respond to everyone in the household.

Times When Puppies Naturally Eliminate

- First thing in the morning
- Last thing at night
- After each meal
- After drinking a lot of water
- After waking from a nap
- During or after rough play or other activity
- On waking during the night (generally only very young puppies)

Teaching young dogs basic obedience commands, including sit, stay, down, come, and heel, increases the control that you have over your dog, which can prevent potentially dangerous situations (such as running away or running into the street). Dogs have an early socialization period, lasting from roughly 2 to 4 months of age. During this time, they more easily learn to accept new people, places, animals, and other experiences. Giving your puppy positive experience with new events during this period can help reduce the chances of fearful behavior and other problems later in life.

Many good books are available on raising and training puppies. In addition, many local trainers, kennels, and community services offer socialization and obedience classes. Socialization classes can begin as early as 8 weeks of age, with obedience classes generally starting at 4 to 6 months of age. In general, obedience training is an activity that you and your dog learn together. The trainer teaches you, and you teach your dog. It takes only a few hours per week, is generally fun for both you and your pet, and can establish good behavior and a strong family bond for the life of your dog.

CHAPTER 4

Behavior

■ INTRODUCTION

Behavioral medicine is the scientific study of everything animals do, whether the animals are insects, birds, mammals, fish, or humans. The field of animal behavior is concerned with understanding the causes, functions, development, and evolution of behavior. Behavior refers to the actions or reactions of an organism. Behavior is usually in relation to the environment, and is controlled by the endocrine and nervous systems. The complexity of animal behavior is related to the complexity of its nervous system. Generally, animals with complex nervous systems have a greater capacity to learn new responses and thus adjust their behavior.

An animal's behavior is influenced by many factors. Some of these factors include genetic predisposition, experience and learning, environment, and physiology. Several dog studies have shown that behavior can be inherited to some degree. In addition, maternal influences can affect personality and temperament. If puppies are separated from a fearful mother, the puppies are less likely to be fearful than if they are left with their mother. The effect

of other puppies in the litter, the amount and type of human handling, and exposure to new objects and experiences all influence a dog's behavior. The brain and its associated neurotransmitters also play a fundamental role in temperament and behavior. Abnormal levels of various hormones play a role in certain forms of aggression and fear.

Understanding the nature of behavior problems is essential to developing a rational basis for their treatment. While this chapter focuses primarily on the abnormal behavior of dogs, the extent to which a dog's behavior is abnormal is defined by how much it deviates from "normal" or by the severity of the problem that this behavior poses to its owner.

■ DIAGNOSING BEHAVIOR PROBLEMS

Many "health" problems faced by pet dogs are associated with behavior problems or unmet expectations about the pet's behavior. Your veterinarian will take a behavioral history before making any diagnosis. A behavioral history generally includes the following: 1) the sex, breed, and age of the dog; 2) the age at onset of the condition; 3) the duration of the condition; 4) a description of the actual behavior; 5) the frequency of the problem behavior (hourly, daily, weekly, monthly); 6) the duration of a typical episode (seconds, minutes, hours); 7) any change in pattern, frequency, intensity, and duration of episodes; 8) any corrective measures tried and the response; 9) any activities that stopped the behavior (for example, the dog falls asleep); 10) the 24-hour schedule of the dog and owner, as well as any day-to-day changes; 11) the dog's family history (in other words, are there signs of similar problems in the dog's parents or littermates?); 12) anything else that the owner thinks is relevant.

Modern veterinary care includes routine screening questions about specific behavior complaints—such as inappropriate or undesirable chewing, growling, or odd behavior—in addition to routine questions that alert your veterinarian to potential medical problems. This routine screening helps establish what is normal for your dog.

Because behavioral diagnoses cannot be made on the basis of a one-time event, pet owners can complete a questionnaire at each visit to clarify the pattern of the dog's behavior. Your veterinarian can then identify whether the signs (barking, growling, lunging) create a pattern that meets specific diagnostic criteria such as fear aggression or protective aggression (*see* page 25). Both you and your veterinarian must use the same definitions for the same nonspecific signs. You both must also accurately recognize and describe behaviors that are of concern.

Videotapes of your dog's behavior can help ensure that your veterinarian makes an accurate diagnosis. The questionnaire relies on your description and, because of this, is more subjective. However, when combined with videotapes, your veterinarian can use questionnaires to diagnose the behavior problem. When you recognize the behaviors leading to or associated with the problematic ones, you can avoid or prevent the situation

that leads up to the problem. By viewing the problematic behavior on videotape, your veterinarian can work with you to help treat the condition.

Defining the Problem

The following is a brief glossary of terms that are commonly used when discussing behavior.

An **abnormal behavior** is one that is dysfunctional and unusual.

Aggression in animals is everything related to a threat or attack. There are various kinds of aggressive behavior in animals, such as territorial defense, predatory aggression, and inter-male aggression (*see* page 25). Examples of aggressive acts include biting, growling, and scratching.

Anxiety is the anticipation of danger accompanied by signs of tension (vigilance, increased movement, and tense muscles). The focus of anxiety can be internal or external.

A dog in **conflict** has tendencies to perform more than one type of activity at once. For example, a dog may want to approach a person to get a treat, but may also be afraid of the person and unwilling to come too close. The motivation for the conflict, except for extreme instances associated with survival functions (for example, eating), is very hard to identify in animals.

Displacement activity is the resolution of a conflict by performing a seemingly unrelated activity. When a dog is in conflict between sex and aggression or between aggression and fear, it will often perform an apparently irrelevant activity. Examples of these irrelevant activities are grooming, feeding, scratching, and sleeping.

Dominance refers to competition over a limited resource (for example, a treat, a favorite toy, or a comfortable resting place). A higher-ranking animal can displace a lower-ranking one from the resource. Rank or hierarchy is usually defined by an ability to control the resource. A dominant animal is not the one engaged in the most fighting. Most high-ranking animals can be identified by the submissive behavior exhibited toward them by others in their group.

Fear is a feeling of apprehension associated with the presence of an object, individual, or social situation and is part of normal behavior. Deciding whether a fear is abnormal depends on the context. For example, fire is a useful tool, and fear of being burned by it is normal. However, if the house were not on fire, such a fear would be irrational. If this fear was constant or recurrent, it would probably be considered an abnormal behavior. Normal

Where to Get Help

Owners seeking help for a behavior problem with their pet can turn to several sources. The American Veterinary Medical Association recognizes a variety of specialties within veterinary medicine. Similar to specialties in human medicine, these include veterinarians who are board-certified in surgery, internal medicine, ophthalmology (eye care), dentistry, behavior, and 14 other areas of expertise. As of 2007, there are 42 board-certified veterinary behaviorists. Most of these work in veterinary colleges or private referral practices.

There are also veterinarians who are not board-certified, but who have a special interest in behavior. These veterinarians have a range of experience and expertise in the field, and many offer consultations as a part of their regular veterinary practice.

In addition, nonveterinarians may call themselves behaviorists and offer counseling on behavior problems of pets. Some have a doctoral or master's degree in psychology or a related field, and some of these individuals are certified by a scientific organization called the Animal Behavior Society. Others, primarily dog trainers, have no formal education in behavior but offer advice on solving behavior problems. Owners who need help for their pet should ask about the background and training of the person offering the behavior consultation before setting up an appointment. Because many behavior problems in pets can be influenced by medical conditions, veterinarians are the professionals who can offer the most comprehensive care.

and abnormal fears usually vary in intensity. The intensity increases as the real or imagined nearness of the object that causes the fear increases.

Frustration arises when a dog is unable to complete a behavior due to physical or psychological obstacles. This term, like dominance, is overused and usually undefined, which means it often is not very helpful when diagnosing a behavior problem.

Most fearful reactions are learned and can be unlearned with gradual exposure. **Phobias**, though, are profound and quickly developed fearful reactions that do not diminish either with gradual exposure to the object or without exposure over time. A phobia involves sudden, all-or-nothing, profound, abnormal reactions resulting in panic. Phobias develop quickly, with little change between episodes. Fear may develop more gradually and, within an episode of fearful behavior, there may be more variation in intensity than would be seen in a phobic reaction. Once a phobic event has been experienced, any event associated with it or the memory of it is enough to generate the reaction. Even without re-exposure, such as the use of a shock collar on a dog, phobias can remain at or exceed their former high level for years. Phobic situations are either avoided at all costs or, if unavoidable, are endured with intense anxiety or distress. There also appears to be a genetic or hereditary basis for these responses in some canine breeds.

Stereotypic behaviors are repetitious, relatively unvaried actions that have no obvious purpose or function. They are usually derived from normal behavior, such as grooming, eating, or walking. These behaviors are abnormal because they interfere with the normal functioning of the animal.

■ BEHAVIOR MODIFICATION

The techniques used most commonly to modify dog behavior include habituation, extinction, desensitization, counterconditioning, and shaping. A behavior modification technique called flooding, described below, is not used very often because it is more likely to make animals worse. While it is claimed that punishment is frequently used with varying degrees of success, few people use punishment correctly. For punishment (such as screaming at the dog) to be successful, it must occur at the beginning of the behavior, be consistently delivered, and be strong enough to stop the unwanted behavior. Most punishments are not given at the right time or are not the appropriate type for the situation.

Behavior Modification Techniques

Most of the techniques involved in behavior modification are not hard to learn and can be successfully used as preventive techniques. They do require a regular investment of time and effort, however. The following is a short review of the basic principles involved in these techniques.

Habituation is a simple form of learning that involves no rewards. It is merely the ending of or decrease in a response to a stimulus that results from repeated or prolonged exposure to that stimulus. For example, horses placed in a pasture bordering a road may at first run away when traffic passes, but eventually learn to ignore it. A dog that habituates to one type of sound does not, as a consequence of this habituation, automatically become habituated to other sounds. Habituation is not the same as failing to respond to stimulation as a result of fatigue, sensory adaptation, or injury. The effects of habituation are generally long lasting. However, if an animal is repeatedly exposed to a potentially harmful stimulus (such as a predator) without being harmed, habituation does not generally occur. Because of this, scientists believe that responses to dangerous stimuli may have an inherited resistance to habituation.

Spontaneous recovery is associated with habituation. If there is a long period of time between when a dog has experienced an event to which it had habituated

Guidelines for Selecting a Dog Trainer

- Look for trainers who use positive reinforcement for good behavior rather than punishment for unacceptable behavior.

- Observe an obedience class without your pet. Are the dogs and people having a good time? Talk with some of the participants after the class. If someone will not let you sit in on a class, do not enroll.

- Do not allow trainers to work with your dog unless they tell you beforehand exactly what they plan to do.

- Do not be afraid to tell a trainer to stop if she or he does something (or tells you to do something) to your dog that you do not feel comfortable with.

- Avoid trainers who offer guarantees. Such trainers are either ignoring or do not understand the complexities of animal behavior.

- Avoid trainers who object to using food as a training reward. Food is one of the best ways to motivate a dog.

- Avoid trainers who insist on using a choke chain. Head collars are humane alternatives to choke chains and pinch collars.

- If you believe your dog has been subjected to cruel treatment by a trainer, get the names and phone numbers of witnesses. Take your dog to your veterinarian immediately for a complete physical examination. Tell them that the results of the examination may be used as evidence in a court case so that your veterinarian will document the procedures with that in mind.

and re-exposure to the same event, the dog may again react. For example, a puppy barks to get a reaction. The more the owner attempts to quiet it, the more the puppy barks. It will continue this pattern because it is getting the attention it wanted. Even if the attention is "negative," some puppies will find it rewarding. The best method to discourage the behavior is to ignore it. Eventually the puppy stops barking if the owner consistently ignores it. However, the bad behavior

Giving a small food treat is a good way to reward your dog for obeying a command.

comes back every now and then. This is called spontaneous recovery.

Conditioning refers to associations between stimuli and behavior. For example, a hungry dog drools (the behavior) when it sees food (the stimulus). After this, every time that the hungry dog sees the food a bell is rung (a second stimulus). Once the food and bell have been paired several times, the dog will drool even if it just hears the bell. This is called conditioning. The bell generates the same response as the sight of food. After several times, the dog has learned to associate the bell with the food.

Reinforcement is any event that increases the chances that a certain behavior will be repeated. Reinforcements can be positive or negative. When positive reinforcement (a reward) is used in training, there is a positive relationship between the behavior and its consequences. The more the pet does a behavior, the more it gets positive reinforcement. This makes that behavior increase. A negative reinforcement (which is mistakenly thought of as punishment by many people) is something unpleasant that increases a behavior when it is removed. For example, being held tightly may be unpleasant to a squirming puppy. But the hold is released only when the puppy calms

down. After several times, the release from restraint will increase the chance that the puppy will relax faster.

Second-order reinforcers are signals that can be used at a distance to let the dog know that a reward is coming. Commonly used second-order reinforcers are words, such as "good girl," hand signals, and whistles. By carefully pairing these with a primary reward (such as food or petting), second-order reinforcers can elicit the same response that the reward would. For example, a clicker can be associated with patting on the head as a reward for sitting and staying. By associating the clicker with a reward, you can train the dog to sit and stay from farther away and still reward the behavior by using the clicker. Positive training and "clicker" training have become very popular. However, it is possible to do an excellent job at positive training without using any second-order reinforcers. Clicker training requires frequent practice and excellent timing. In some situations involving problem behaviors, the incorrect use of a clicker may hinder, rather than help, a behavior modification program.

Extinction is a response that stops when a reward is removed. A classic example of extinction involves a dog that jumps up on people for attention. If people pet the dog, the behavior continues. If they stop petting the dog, the dog will eventually stop jumping up because the reward is no longer there. However, even occasional petting of the dog in response to its jumping will reinforce the pattern. The more valuable the original reward, the longer it has been present, and the more uncertainty there is about whether the reward has been truly removed, the greater the resistance to extinction. Resistance to extinction can also occur even without reinforcement if the reward was good enough and was tightly linked to the behavior.

Because there is often an association between getting the reward and the intensity of the behavior, the intensity or frequency of the behavior you are trying to eliminate usually increases at the beginning of extinction. In other words, a behavior you are trying to extinguish may get worse before it gets better. It is critical that you do not give in. Giving in will only make extinction more difficult. The dog will learn that, although your threshold has increased, the dog can override it by working harder.

Overlearning is the repeated performance of an already learned behavior. It is frequently used in training for specific events, and may also be useful for preventing fearful responses in dogs. Overlearning accomplishes 3 things: it delays forgetting, it increases the resistance to extinction, and it increases the chance that the behavior will become an automatic or "knee-jerk" response in similar situations. This aspect can be extremely useful in teaching a dog to overcome a fear or anxiety.

Shaping is a learning technique that works well for dogs that do not know what response is desired by the trainer. Shaping works through gradual approximations and allows the dog to be rewarded initially for any behavior that resembles the desired behavior. For example, when teaching a puppy to sit, giving the puppy a food treat for squatting will increase the chance that squatting will be repeated. This squatting behavior is then rewarded only when it becomes more exaggerated, and finally, when it becomes a true sit.

Avoidance of a problem behavior is essential until you can seek qualified help, particularly in a case of aggression. With treatment it may be possible to reduce the aggressive behavior, but avoidance is the key in minimizing danger. Avoidance does not mean that the pet has control, or that you are giving in to the dog. Instead, it may help extinguish the aggressive behavior. Every time a dog becomes aggressive, it learns that aggression may help it cope with the situation, thus reinforcing the problem.

Desensitization is a way to gradually teach a dog to tolerate a situation by carefully exposing it to that situation in small steps. If a puppy gets overexcited at the sound of the doorbell, a tape recording of the doorbell could help stop the undesirable behavior. If the tape is played very softly at first and then only gradually increased in volume as long as the puppy remains calm, then the puppy may stop reacting to the doorbell.

Counterconditioning is a method for reducing unwanted behavior by teaching the dog to replace it with another more favorable behavior. In the doorbell example above, the puppy will learn faster if it is first taught to sit, stay, and then relax in exchange for a treat. The puppy must be absolutely quiet and calm, and convey by its eyes, body posture, and facial expressions that it would do anything for its owner. Once this behavior is learned, the desensitization is added by playing the tape recording at a gradually increasing volume. If at any time the puppy starts to get too excited, the tape recording should be lowered in volume until the puppy relaxes. Relaxing is the key and is the first step to changing the behavior. Counterconditioning and desensitization can take a lot of time and effort. The exercises must be frequently repeated so that the unwanted behavior decreases until it is no longer a problem.

Flooding is prolonged exposure to a stimulus until the dog eventually stops reacting. This is the opposite of the approach taken in desensitization. It is far more stressful than any of the other treatment strategies and if not used correctly will make things worse. The most common problem is increased fear. This technique should be used only by a professional and only as a last resort.

Punishment is also known as aversive conditioning. It is any unpleasant event that lowers the chance that a behavior will be repeated. Punishment is not the same as negative reinforcement (*see* page 21). To be most successful, punishment must occur as early as possible (within a few seconds of the start of the behavior), and it must be consistent and appropriate. Critical factors in punishment include timing, consistency, appropriate intensity, and the presence of a reward after the undesirable behavior ends. This is the most frequently ignored part of treatment for people whose pets have behavior problems. Owners often resort to physical punishment as the first choice, but punishment does not need to be physical. Furthermore, punishment is just as hard to use correctly as counterconditioning and desensitization. Punishment is never an "easy out" and has a high chance of failure. It can also lead to other negative consequences, such as increasing the chance of fear or aggression.

Use of Medication to Treat Behavior Problems

Your veterinarian may, in some cases, prescribe medication to help treat a behavior problem of your pet. Drug treatment for almost any behavior change is most useful when combined with behavior modification.

In recent years there has been an increase in the use of medication to treat a variety of behavior problems in pets (*see* TABLE 6). There are a number of potential

Table 6. Drugs Used to Treat Behavior Problems in Dogs

Drug	Uses	Comments
Tricyclic antidepressants		
Amitriptyline	Anxiety, aggression, compulsive disorders	Cheaper than many other drugs, but may be more likely to cause adverse effects
Clomipramine	Anxiety, aggression, compulsive disorders	FDA approved for use in separation anxiety in dogs
Selective serotonin reuptake inhibitors		
Fluoxetine	Anxiety, aggression, compulsive disorders	May take 3 to 4 weeks before affecting behavior; also FDA approved for treating separation anxiety in dogs
Paroxetine	Anxiety, aggression, compulsive disorders	
Sertraline	Anxiety, aggression, compulsive disorders	
Azapirones		
Buspirone	Anxiety	
Benzodiazepines		
Alprazolam	Thunderstorm phobia, anxiety	Longer acting than other drugs of this class
Diazepam	Anxiety, noise phobia	May cause physical dependence
Monoamine oxidase inhibitors		
Selegiline	FDA approved for use in cognitive dysfunction in dogs	Must not be combined with serotonin reuptake inhibitors or tricyclic drugs due to adverse drug interactions
Hormones		
Megestrol acetate	Aggression, urine marking, roaming	Rarely used due to high risk of adverse effects
Medroxyprogesterone acetate	Aggression, urine marking, roaming	Injectable; rarely used due to high risk of adverse effects

disadvantages to the use of medication for treating these problems, however, and you should know that there is no "magic bullet" that will easily and quickly solve the problem. The limitations of medication use include the potential for adverse effects, cost, the need to treat for a considerable length of time before the medication takes effect, limited information on what medication is most effective, and the potential that the problem will reappear once the medication is withdrawn.

All medications have the potential to cause adverse effects. Fortunately, most of the modern antianxiety and antidepressant medications used in pets are well tolerated. Gastrointestinal upsets (leading to reduced appetite, vomiting, or diarrhea) are the most common adverse effects seen. In some pets, decreased activity or lethargy may occur in the first week or so of treatment as the animal adjusts to the medication. (This reaction typically disappears on its own.) More serious adverse effects, including potentially fatal inflammation of the liver, seizures, or other signs of toxicity have been reported in rare cases. Most of the medications used for behavior problems in pets were designed for use in people. Few have been directly approved by the Food and Drug Administration for use in animals, although such use is not prohibited. This means that there may be limited information available on safety, toxicity, and effectiveness in a particular animal species.

Because this is a relatively new area of veterinary medicine, demonstration of effectiveness through research has not been done in many cases. Veterinarians often must rely on case reports, their own clinical experience, and presentations at meetings to learn which medications and what dosage to recommend. Individual pets vary in their response to medication, just as people do. As a result, there will always be some element of trial and error in determining whether a particular medication will help solve a behavior problem.

If medication is used without behavior modification or environmental changes (and even when it is used with these techniques in some cases), the unwanted behavior may return once the medication is discontinued. Some problems may require treatment for a year or longer. In most cases medication is used for a period of several months.

Despite these limitations, medication has the potential to be very helpful in a wide range of pet behavior problems, including fear-related problems like separation anxiety and thunderstorm phobias, compulsive behaviors like lick granulomas, and some types of aggression. Your veterinarian can discuss whether medication might be appropriate for your dog.

■ NORMAL SOCIAL BEHAVIOR IN DOGS

Dogs are highly social animals and are well adapted to living in groups. Recent studies have also shown that they are very good at interpreting human gestures and behavior.

In nature or under free-ranging conditions, dogs live in groups that include both males and females of a variety of ages. Relative social ranking or hierarchy (also referred to as dominance) is determined by age, although sex may play a role. Females appear to be responsible for guiding most group activities. Social hierarchies are maintained primarily by lower-ranking dogs giving way to higher-ranking ones and not, as commonly believed, by fighting. Sexual maturity in domestic dogs occurs between 6 to 9 months of age (later for giant breeds), while social maturity develops at 12 to 36 months of age. In free-ranging groups, dogs that challenge the established social hierarchy may leave and form their own groups if they do not succeed in gaining a high rank. This situation may be similar to one form of inter-dog aggression that occurs in multiple-dog households (*see* below). Social maturity is also the time when problems with aggression and anxiety develop. Roaming, mounting, urine marking, and fighting are stimulated by sex hormones, particularly testosterone. These problems are often greatly reduced in males by neutering.

Between 3 to 8 weeks of age, dogs tend to focus on other dogs (if available) for social interaction, and between 5 to 12 weeks of age they shift their focus to people. Dogs are most receptive to learning how to deal with new situations until about 16 to 20 weeks of age. After this age, dogs do not stop learning from exposure; they just do so at a much slower rate and perhaps in a different way. It is not critical to change the focus of exposure at one specific period, because given adequate opportunities, puppies will learn about the social and physical environments when they are ready. Dogs that are kept exclusively kenneled or not exposed to people by 14 weeks of age may have severely undeveloped social skills. The best age to adopt a puppy is at about 8 weeks of age. Unless there is no other choice, puppies should not be adopted until at least 7½ weeks of age.

Most domestic dogs, except for Basenjis, have 2 heat (estrous) cycles per year. All members of the group may assist in puppy care. In multiple-dog groups, the highest-ranking dogs may be the only ones to breed.

■ BEHAVIOR PROBLEMS IN DOGS

The most common behavior problems in dogs are those associated with aggression, primarily dominance/impulsive control aggression and fear aggression.

Behavior Problems Associated with Aggression

Dominance aggression, which is also called **impulse control aggression** is a threat or attack shown by dogs toward people under any circumstance that involves correction of the dog's behavior by its owner. Diagnosis of this problem is difficult and cannot be based on a single event. Situations that often provoke aggression from the dog include physical restraint and control of food, toys, or resting places.

Fear aggression occurs in situations that make a dog afraid. Aggression is often accompanied by urination or defecation. In contrast to dominance aggression, in fear aggression the dog withdraws and is passive. Only when the dog can no longer avoid or withdraw does aggression occur.

Food-related aggression is shown around pet food, bones, rawhides, biscuits, or human food in dogs that are not starved or abused.

Idiopathic aggression has no known cause. It is unpredictable and unprovoked. This type of aggression is extremely rare.

Interdog aggression is aggression that is directed at other dogs. The target can be another dog in the household or dogs that are encountered away from the home.

Maternal aggression is excessive aggression directed toward puppies by the mother dog. A small amount of aggression may be normal, especially around the time of weaning. High levels of aggression may harm the puppies. This abnormal behavior may be inherited.

Pain aggression is a defensive reaction that occurs when a dog is in pain. It may happen when a dog anticipates being moved or touched.

Play aggression occurs along with play behaviors, such as play bows, chases, and charges. In contrast to previously held beliefs, energetic play by humans with dogs (for example, tug-of-war) does not necessarily produce play aggression.

Possessive aggression is constantly directed toward another individual that approaches or attempts to obtain a non-food object or toy that the dog possesses.

Predatory aggression is behavior associated with predation (for example, stalking, hunting, and catching small animals). It is usually a quiet, sudden attack, and involves a fierce bite and shake of the prey animal.

Protective aggression is an attempt by a dog to guard its owner from an approach by another person, in the absence of a real threat from the other person. The aggression intensifies as the other person gets closer.

Redirected aggression occurs when a dog is prevented from reaching its intended target. The attack is then directed at another dog or person. The aggression is not accidental and the dog will actively pursue the second dog or person, particularly if they are directly associated with the interruption of the dog's attack on its first target.

Territorial aggression is the protection of a place, such as a yard or a car, from the approach of another dog or person. It includes actions like chasing, growling, barking, or biting. The territorial dog reacts regardless of whether or not the individual approaching acts in any sort of threatening manner.

Other types of aggression can also occur in dogs. In rare cases, aggression can result from infection, toxicity, or side effects from a medication.

Treatment

Treatment of aggression in dogs is typically complex and should ideally be designed by a specialist. Avoidance of situations that provoke aggression is always a good idea and can help reduce the risk of bites. Almost without exception, physical punishment, including the use of prong collars and electric shock collars can make an already aggressive dog worse. These techniques are not recommended, especially in the absence of professional supervision.

Behavior Problems Associated with Elimination

Excitement urination is the release of a small amount of urine that occurs when a dog is active and excited, but not afraid.

Incomplete housetraining is consistent elimination in undesirable locations that is not associated with a lack of access or an illness. At 8 to 9 weeks of age dogs start to develop a habit of eliminating in certain places, so early attention to housetraining is important.

Marking behavior is urination or defecation that is used to send a social signal. For example, male dogs often lift a leg to urinate small amounts on fences, trees, or other objects. This can be an attempt to claim the area as their territory or just a way of letting other dogs know they've been there recently.

Submissive urination occurs in an otherwise housetrained dog only when the dog is showing postures associated with submission (for example, head lowered, ears back). The dog does not show any signs of fear or aggression.

Treatment

There are two main aspects of housetraining: 1) encouraging a preference for a specific surface (for example, dirt or grass) or location, and 2) encouraging inhibition of urination or defecation until the appropriate location is accessible. The first age at which a dog is able to voluntarily inhibit elimination is at 8½ weeks of age. Appropriate housetraining for dogs involves exposure to the preferred surface for elimination starting at that age, absence of physical punishment, emphasis on positive reinforcement, frequent trips to the desired area, quickly and completely cleaning up any accidents, and startling the dog to interrupt it only when the dog is caught in the act of eliminating in an inappropriate place. Punishment is not helpful and may be counterproductive. Dogs with submissive urination should never be startled. These are already anxious, uncertain dogs, and any punishment will reinforce the inappropriate behavior.

Taking dogs outside 15 to 30 minutes after eating and immediately after play, awakening, or if they slow down, can help speed housetraining. Housetraining an older dog is more a matter of fine-tuning the dog's behavior and encouraging it to select a more appropriate surface or location. For small breed young puppies, litter boxes may be a good option. The presence of an older dog may help when housetraining a puppy, because the puppy can follow the lead of the older dog. Prevention is important and owners should know that puppies obtained from pet stores are usually much more difficult to housetrain than those obtained from other sources. Puppies in a pet store are generally not taken out of their cages often and do not have to inhibit elimination. They also may have learned to play with or eat feces.

Other Canine Behavior Problems

Some common behavior problems of dogs are identified below. Many can be treated with behavior modification programs that focus on desensitization and counterconditioning (*see* page 22). This is very important in the early treatment of fears, phobias, and anxieties. Your veterinarian might also prescribe medication to help your pet.

Abnormal ingestive behavior is eating unusual amounts or types of food or non-food items. This includes pica (eating nonfood items), drinking too much water, anorexia (eating too little), and gorging.

Attention-seeking behavior occurs when the dog acts in a way that gets the attention of people who are doing something not directly involving the dog. An example of this would be a puppy that barks to get attention when it is not being actively played with. The owner then reacts to the dog's bark by giving it attention; both positive (playing with the dog) and negative (yelling at the dog) attention from the owner reinforces this behavior. This may be an undesirable behavior, but it is common and it is certainly a behavior that people unconsciously reinforce in their pets.

Senility, which is also called **cognitive dysfunction**, is similar to Alzheimer's disease in people. Signs include a decrease in social interaction, loss of housetraining, disorientation (getting lost in familiar surroundings), and changes in sleep patterns. Medication and a special diet are available for treatment. These can delay

the progression of signs, but will not reverse them.

Fear occurs with physical signs such as withdrawal, passivity, and avoidance in the absence of any aggression. Fear and anxiety have signs that overlap. Some nonspecific signs such as avoidance, shaking, and trembling, can be characteristic of both fear and anxiety.

Hyperactivity is an extremely high level of activity that does not respond to correction, redirection, or restraint. True hyperactivity is rare in dogs and is different from overactivity. Overactive dogs are highly energetic and active, but are able to calm down and respond to human control.

Neophobia is active avoidance, escape, or anxiety directed at unfamiliar objects and situations.

Noise phobia consists of a sudden and profound response to noise that leads to intense anxiety (in other words, panic) or attempts to escape confinement. The most common form is fear of thunderstorms, although fear of fireworks or other loud noises is also frequent.

Compulsive disorders are repetitive behaviors that occur out of their normal circumstances, or much more often or for much longer periods than is normal (for example, incessant licking). The dog spends so much time doing the compulsive behavior that it does not have time for normal activities.

False pregnancy is a condition during which a dog acts as though it is pregnant, but is not. The dog may make a nest and may gather small objects that it protects as if they were puppies.

Separation anxiety is a syndrome in which a dog panics when it is left alone. It causes intense anxiety and may lead the dog to bark, pace, or eliminate inside the house. Dogs that are confined commonly destroy kennels, walls, or doors in an attempt to reunite with their owners. Signs are often most severe within the first 15 to 20 minutes of the dog being left alone.

DISORDERS AND DISEASES OF DOGS

5 **Blood Disorders** 33
Introduction 33
Red Blood Cells 33
White Blood Cells 35
Platelets 36
Blood Groups and Blood Transfusions 37
Anemia 37
Blood Parasites 42
Canine Malignant Lymphoma 45
Bleeding Disorders 46
White Blood Cell Disorders 51
Polycythemia 52

6 **Heart and Blood Vessel Disorders** 53
Introduction 53
Heart Disease and Heart Failure 55
Diagnosis of Cardiovascular Disease 56
Treatment of Cardiovascular Disease 56
Congenital and Inherited Disorders of the Cardiovascular System 58
Heart Failure 65
Acquired Heart and Blood Vessel Disorders 68
Heartworm Disease 73
Blood Clots and Aneurysms 76

7 **Digestive Disorders** 77
Introduction 77
Congenital and Inherited Disorders 82
Dental Development 86
Dental Disorders 87
Disorders of the Mouth 90
Disorders of the Pharynx 97
Disorders of the Esophagus 97
Vomiting 100
Disorders of the Stomach and Intestines 100
Disorders Caused by Bacteria 109
Gastrointestinal Parasites 110
Disorders Caused by Protozoa 115
Disorders of the Pancreas 117
Disorders of the Liver and Gallbladder 120
Disorders of the Rectum and Anus 125

8 **Hormonal Disorders** 128
Introduction 128
Disorders of the Adrenal Glands 131
Disorders of the Pancreas 132
Disorders of the Parathyroid Glands and of Calcium Metabolism 134
Disorders of the Pituitary Gland 136
Disorders of the Thyroid Gland 139
Neuroendocrine Tissue Tumors 140

9   Eye Disorders.. **140**

Eye Structure and Function 140
Disorders of the Eyelids 143
Disorders of the Nasal Cavity and Tear Ducts 144
Disorders of the Conjunctiva 145
Disorders of the Cornea 146
Disorders of the Anterior Uvea 148
Glaucoma 149
Disorders of the Lens 149
Disorders of the Retina, Choroid, and Optic Disk (Ocular Fundus) 151
Disorders of the Optic Nerve 152
Disorders of the Orbit 153
Prolapse of the Eye 153
Eyeworm Disease (Thelaziasis) 154
Cancers and Tumors of the Eye 154

10   Ear Disorders.. **155**

Ear Structure and Function 155
Deafness 157
Disorders of the Outer Ear 158
Otitis Externa 160
Otitis Media and Interna 161
Tumors of the Ear Canal 163

11   Immune Disorders.. **164**

The Immune System 164
Immune System Responses 164
Disorders Involving Anaphylactic Reactions (Type I Reactions, Atopy) 167
Disorders Involving Cytotoxic Antibodies (Type II Reactions) 169
Disorders Involving Immune Complexes (Type III Reactions) 171
Disorders Involving Cell-mediated Immunity (Type IV Reactions) 172
Immune-deficiency Diseases 173
Immune System Tumors 175
Gammopathies 175

12   Bone, Joint, and Muscle Disorders **176**

Introduction 176
Components of the Musculoskeletal System 176
Overview of Musculoskeletal Disorders and Diseases 176
Lameness 178
Congenital and Inherited Disorders of Bones, Joints, and Muscles 179
Disorders Associated with Calcium, Phosphorus, and Vitamin D 180
Joint Disorders 183
Muscle Disorders 188
Bone Disorders 190
Sarcocystosis 194

13   Brain, Spinal Cord, and Nerve Disorders **194**

The Nervous System 194
Parts of the Nervous System 195
Nervous System Disorders and Effects of Injuries 196
The Neurologic Evaluation 197
Principles of Therapy 199
Congenital and Inherited Disorders 200
Disorders of the Peripheral Nerves 202
Disorders of the Spinal Column and Cord 204
Dysautonomia 207
Facial Paralysis 208

Central Nervous System Disorders Caused by Parasites 208
Leg Paralysis 209
Meningitis and Encephalitis 210
Motion Sickness 211
Rabies 211
Tick Paralysis 213

14 Reproductive Disorders... 214
Introduction 214
The Gonads and Genital Tract 214
Management of Reproduction in Dogs 215
Infertility 217
Reproductive Disorders of Male Dogs 218
Reproductive Disorders of Female Dogs 220
Mammary (Breast) Tumors 222
Brucellosis 223
Transmissible Venereal Tumor 223

15 Lung and Airway Disorders 224
Introduction 224
Accumulation of Fluid or Air in the Chest Cavity 227
Allergic Pneumonitis 227
Cancers and Tumors 228
Canine Nasal Mites 230
Diaphragmatic Hernia 230
Emphysema 231
Kennel Cough (Infectious Tracheobronchitis) 231
Laryngitis 231
Lung Flukes 232
Lungworm Infection 232
Paralysis of the Larynx 233
Pharyngitis 233
Pneumonia 233
Pulmonary Edema 235
Rhinitis and Sinusitis 235
Tonsillitis 236
Tracheal Collapse 237
Tracheobronchitis (Bronchitis) 237

16 Skin Disorders 238
Structure of the Skin 238
Dermatitis and Dermatologic Problems 240
Diagnosis of Skin Disorders 240
Treatment of Skin Disorders 241
Congenital and Inherited Skin Disorders 242
Allergies 245
Abscesses Between the Toes (Interdigital Furunculosis) 247
Contagious Ecthyma (Orf, Contagious Pustular Dermatitis, Sore Mouth) 248
Dermatophilosis 248
Eosinophilic Granuloma Complex 248
Fleas 249
Flies and Mosquitoes 251
Hair Loss (Alopecia) 255
Hives and Rashes (Urticaria) 256
Hygroma 257
Hyperpigmentation 257
Itching (Pruritus) 258
Lice 259
Mite Infestation (Mange, Acariasis, Scabies) 260

Nasal Dermatoses of Dogs 263
Parasitic Worms of the Skin 263
Photosensitization 264
Pyoderma 265
Ringworm (Dermatophytosis) 266
Seborrhea 266
Ticks 268
Tumors of the Skin 269
Whole-body Disorders that Affect the Skin 282

17 **Kidney and Urinary Tract Disorders** **283**
The Urinary System 283
Detecting Disorders of the Kidneys and Urinary Tract 283
Congenital and Inherited Disorders of the Urinary System 285
Infectious Diseases of the Urinary System 287
Noninfectious Diseases of the Urinary System 290

18 **Metabolic Disorders** **300**
Introduction 300
Disorders of Calcium Metabolism 302
Disorders of Magnesium Metabolism 303
Fatigue and Exercise 303
Fever of Unknown Origin 303
Malignant Hyperthermia 304

19 **Disorders Affecting Multiple Body Systems** **305**
Introduction 305
Congenital and Inherited Disorders 305
Actinobacillosis 306
Actinomycosis 307
Amyloidosis 307
Anthrax 308
Botulism 309
Canine Distemper (Hardpad Disease) 309
Canine Herpesvirus 310
Ehrlichiosis and Related Infections 310
Enterotoxemia 311
Fungal Infections 312
Glanders (Farcy) 317
Infectious Canine Hepatitis 318
Leishmaniasis (Visceral Leishmaniasis) 318
Leptospirosis 319
Lyme Disease (Lyme Borreliosis) 320
Melioidosis 321
Neosporosis 322
Nocardiosis 322
Peritonitis 323
Plague 323
Rocky Mountain Spotted Fever (Tick Fever) 324
Salmon Poisoning Disease and Elokomin Fluke Fever 325
Tetanus 326
Toxoplasmosis 326
Trichinellosis (Trichinosis) 327
Tuberculosis 327
Tularemia 328

CHAPTER 5

Blood Disorders

■ INTRODUCTION

Blood cells form and develop mostly in the bone marrow, that is, the tissue located in the cavities of bones. Blood performs a variety of important functions as it circulates throughout the body. It delivers oxygen and vital nutrients (such as vitamins, minerals, fats, and sugars) to the tissues. It carries carbon dioxide to the lungs to be exhaled and waste products to the kidneys and liver to be eliminated from the body. It transports hormones, which are chemical messengers, to various parts of the body, allowing those parts to communicate with each other. Blood also includes cells that fight infection and control bleeding.

There are 3 cellular elements of blood: red blood cells, white blood cells, and platelets. Basically, **red blood cells** supply the body with oxygen, **white blood cells** protect against infection, and **platelets** start the formation of blood clots.

Blood disorders are quite diverse. They can occur as normal responses to abnormal situations; for example, a significant increase in the number of white blood cells in response to an infection or disease. They may also occur as primary abnormalities of the blood; for example, a deficiency of all cellular elements of the blood due to bone marrow failure. Furthermore, abnormalities may be quantitative (too many or too few cells) or qualitative (abnormalities in the way cells function). It is helpful to understand what the names of some blood disorders mean, as they often provide a description of the disorder itself (*see* TABLE 1).

Just as there are various blood types in humans, there are multiple blood types in dogs, cats, horses, and other animals. A few blood banks for animals have been established. Like human blood banks, they depend on donated blood and can provide type-matched blood for use in emergencies or surgeries.

■ RED BLOOD CELLS

The main function of red blood cells (also called erythrocytes) is to carry oxygen to the tissues, where it is required for cellular metabolism. Oxygen molecules attach themselves to carrier molecules, called hemoglobin, which are the iron-containing proteins in red blood cells that give the cells their red color. Oxygen is carried from the lungs and delivered to all body tissues by the hemoglobin within red blood cells. Oxygen is used by cells to produce energy that the body needs. Carbon dioxide is left behind as a waste product during this process. The red blood cells then carry that carbon dioxide away from the tissues and back to the lungs, where it is exhaled. When the number of red blood cells is too low, this is called anemia. Having too few red blood cells means the blood carries less oxygen. The result is that fatigue and weakness develop. When the number of red blood cells is too high, this is called polycythemia. The result is that blood can become too thick,

Blood is a complex mixture of plasma (the liquid component), red blood cells, white blood cells, and platelets.

Suffix	Definition	Example
"philia"	Increase in blood levels of that type of cell	Neutrophilia
"osis"	An abnormal increase in blood levels of that type of cell; can also refer to a disease process	Lymphocytosis
"penia"	Decrease in blood levels of that type of cell	Neutropenia
"lysis"	Destruction of that type of cell	Hemolysis
"emia"	Denotes the presence of a substance in the blood	Polycythemia
"stasis"	To stop or stabilize	Hemostasis

Table 1. Suffixes used in Names of Blood Disorders

and impair the ability of the heart to deliver oxygen throughout the body. An animal's metabolism is geared to protect both the red blood cells and the hemoglobin from damage. Interference with the formation or release of hemoglobin, or with production or survival of red blood cells, causes disease.

The total number of red cells, and thus the oxygen-carrying capacity, remains constant over time in healthy animals. Mature red blood cells have a limited life span; their production and destruction must be carefully balanced, or disease develops.

Production of red blood cells begins with stem cells in the bone marrow and ends with the release of mature red blood cells into the body's circulation. Within the bone marrow, all blood cells begin from a single cell called a stem cell. The stem cell divides to form immature forms of red blood cells, white blood cells, or a platelet-producing cell. Those immature cells then divide again, mature even more, and ultimately become mature red blood cells, white blood cells, or platelets.

The rate of blood cell production is determined by the body's needs. Erythropoietin, a hormone produced by the kidneys, stimulates development of red blood cells in the bone marrow. Erythropoietin increases if the body lacks oxygen (a condition called hypoxia). In most species, the kidney is both the sensor organ that determines how much oxygen the body's tissues are receiving and the

major site of erythropoietin production; so chronic kidney failure leads to anemia. Erythropoietin plays a major role in determining whether to increase the number of stem cells entering red blood cell production, to shorten maturation time of the red blood cells, or to cause early release of red blood cells. Other factors that affect red blood cell production are the supply of nutrients (such as iron and vitamins) and cell-cell interactions between compounds that aid in their production. Some disorders are the direct result of abnormal red blood cell metabolism. For example, an inherited enzyme deficiency reduces the life span of red blood cells, causing a condition known as hemolytic anemia. (*See also* ANEMIA, page 37.)

It is important to remember that a decrease in the total number of red blood cells in the body (anemia) is a sign of disease, not a specific diagnosis. Anemia may be caused by blood loss, destruction of red blood cells (hemolysis), or decreased production. In severe blood loss anemia, red blood cells are lost, but death usually results from the loss of total blood volume, rather than from the lack of oxygen caused by loss of red blood cells. Hemolysis may be caused by toxins, infections, abnormalities present at birth, drugs, or antibodies that attack the red blood cells. In dogs the most common cause of serious hemolysis is an antibody directed against that dog's own red blood cells (immune-mediated hemolytic anemia).

Factors that may prevent red blood cell production include bone marrow failure or malignancy, loss of erythropoietin secondary to kidney failure, certain drugs or toxins, longterm debilitating diseases, or antibodies targeted at developing red blood cells. The outlook and treatment depend on the underlying cause of the anemia.

■ WHITE BLOOD CELLS

The function of white blood cells (also called leukocytes) is to defend the body against infection. There are 2 main types of white blood cells formed in the bone marrow: phagocytes and lymphocytes.

Phagocytes

Phagocytes (from the Greek word meaning "to eat") are cells in the bloodstream and tissues that surround and consume foreign particles, cell waste material, and bacteria. Their main function is to defend against invading microorganisms by surrounding and destroying them. There are 2 types of phagocytes: granulocytes and monocytes.

Granulocytes protect against bacteria, fungi, and parasites. Some types of granulocytes are involved in allergic reactions. Neutrophils are the most numerous of the white blood cells and are the first line of defense against bacterial invasion. Eosinophils and basophils are involved both in protection against some parasites and in the response to allergy. **Monocytes** travel from the blood to tissues where they become large cells called macrophages that consume foreign particles and cell debris.

As with red blood cells, the production and number of phagocytes are tightly regulated by chemical messengers of the blood, including interleukins (chemicals found in white blood cells that stimulate them to fight infection). Unlike the red blood cells, which remain circulating in the blood, the phagocytes use the blood's circulatory system as a pathway to the tissues. Because of this, the number of phagocytes in the blood can provide an indication of circumstances in the tissues.

For example, the number of neutrophils increases when inflammation is present anywhere in the body, An abnormal response, such as a low number of circulating white blood cells due to marrow failure, infections, drugs, or toxins, can lower resistance to bacterial infections. Finally, those elements that produce phagocytes may become cancerous, resulting in a disease called myelogenous leukemia.

Lymphocytes

Lymphocytes are white blood cells that produce antibodies to attack infectious organisms. They are also responsible for rejecting foreign tissue or cancer cells. Lymphocyte production in mammals begins in the bone marrow. Lymphocytes then become 1 of 2 types: T cells or B cells. Lymphocytes destined to protect cells from disease travel to the thymus (an organ located at the base of the neck) where they become T cells under the influence of hormones there. **T cells** are responsible for a variety of functions, especially fighting off viral infections and cancers. Most T cells remain in the circulation, but some are also present in the spleen and lymph nodes. The **B cells** are responsible for producing antibodies that coat invading organisms or foreign substances. For example, bacteria coated with antibody are more easily recognized and removed by neutrophils or macrophages. If lymphocytes are reduced or abnormal, the dog is immunodeficient and susceptible to a wide range of infections.

Antibody molecules are called **immunoglobulins**. They fall into several classes, each of which has a different function. For example, one class is commonly found in the lungs and intestines; another is the first antibody produced in response to newly recognized foreign microorganisms; a third is the main antibody in the bloodstream; and a fourth is involved in allergic reactions.

Lymphocytes usually act appropriately to rid the body of foreign "invaders" that cause disease. However, sometimes lymphocytes do not react appropriately. One

Types of Blood Cells*

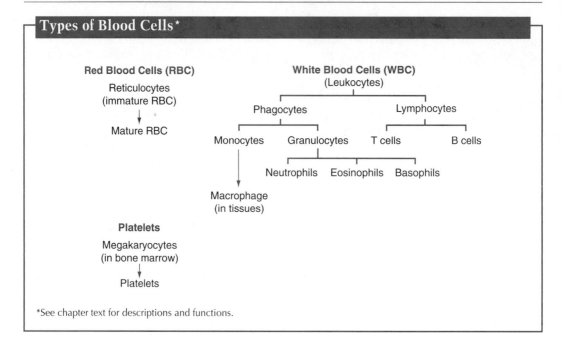

*See chapter text for descriptions and functions.

inappropriate response occurs when antibodies are produced against the body's own cells, such as red blood cells. Another inappropriate response of the immune system is allergy. When exposure to an allergen occurs, the reaction may be mild or life-threatening.

An increase in the number of lymphocytes in the bloodstream occurs in some species as a response to the secretion of epinephrine (a hormone also known as adrenaline). A reduction in the number of circulating lymphocytes may be caused by corticosteroid hormones that may also be secreted in times of stress. Unusual lymphocytes may be seen in the blood in response to antigenic stimulation, such as vaccination.

Malignant tumors originating in a lymph node (lymphoma) or lymphoid leukemia can also occur.

■ PLATELETS

Platelets are small, cell-like particles produced in the bone marrow. They function to start the formation of blood clots. Platelets gather where bleeding occurs and clump together to form the initial plug that stops or slows the flow of blood. Platelets also release substances that are needed to complete the clotting process.

Platelet disorders can result from having too few or too many platelets or from impaired platelet function. In general, when platelet counts fall very low there is an increased risk of bleeding. Decreased numbers of platelets may be caused by autoantibodies, drugs, toxins, or disorders of the bone marrow.

An abnormal increase in the number of platelets is rare and often the cause is not known. It may be associated with bone marrow disease or with longterm blood loss and iron deficiency.

There are also disorders in which platelets do not function properly. Von Willebrand disease is one example. Other hereditary disorders of platelet function have been described but are rare. Probably the most common platelet function defect in animals is a side effect of aspirin. Do not give your dog aspirin—or any other medication—unless it is prescribed by your veterinarian.

BLOOD GROUPS AND BLOOD TRANSFUSIONS

Blood groups are determined by the presence or absence of certain antigens (proteins and sugars) on the red blood cell membrane. Normally dogs do not have antibodies against any of the antigens present on their own red blood cells or against other canine blood group antigens unless they have been previously exposed to them by transfusion. In some species (such as humans and cats), however, antibodies from one individual that react with antigens of another individual of the same species may be present without any prior exposure.

Dogs have many blood groups, and their red blood cells may contain any combination of these since each blood group is inherited independently. The most important of these is called Dog Erythrocyte Antigen (DEA) 1.1. Typing of blood donors and recipients is done before transfusion. Approximately 40% of dogs are positive for DEA 1.1, meaning that they have that antigen on their red blood cells. By selecting donor animals that lack DEA 1.1 or that match the recipient, the risk of sensitizing the recipient can be minimized. If a dog is DEA 1.1-negative and is given DEA 1.1-positive blood, it may develop antibodies that rapidly destroy the red blood cells if a second DEA 1.1-positive transfusion is given. A DEA 1.1-positive dog may receive either positive or negative blood.

Blood Typing

An animal's blood group is determined by measuring the reaction of a small sample of blood to certain antibodies. Dogs are routinely typed only for the most potent antigen, DEA 1.1. In addition to DEA 1.1 at least 12 other blood group systems are present. Although the risk is less, any antigen might cause a reaction if those cells are given to a previously sensitized dog. Any dog that has had a previous transfusion may have antibodies to any of the blood group antigens not present on their own red blood cells. These antibodies can be detected by testing the red blood cells from a potential donor with plasma (the clear, yellowish liquid part of blood) taken from the recipient. This procedure is called a **major crossmatch**. If agglutination occurs, the recipient has antibodies that could destroy the donated red blood cells. That donor is incompatible and should not be used.

Blood Transfusions

Often, the need for a blood transfusion is an emergency, such as severe bleeding or sudden destruction of red blood cells due to other disease. Transfusions may also be needed to treat anemia. Animals with blood clotting disorders often require repeated transfusions of whole blood, red blood cells, plasma, or platelets. The most serious risk of transfusion is acute destruction of red blood cells, usually caused by a previously formed antibody to DEA 1.1, or to another antigen. Fortunately, this is rare. A more common problem in dogs that have received multiple transfusions is delayed destruction of the red blood cells, caused by antibodies to some of the minor blood group antigens.

Other complications of transfusions include infection from contaminated blood, a decrease in blood calcium levels, and accumulation of fluid in the lungs as a result of giving too large a volume of blood. Skin hives, fever, or vomiting are seen occasionally. Fortunately most transfusions are safe and effective.

ANEMIA

Anemia occurs when there is a decrease in the number of red blood cells, which can be measured by red blood cell count or hemoglobin concentration. It can develop from loss, destruction, or lack of production of red blood cells. Anemia is classified as regenerative or nonregenerative. In a **regenerative anemia**, the bone marrow responds appropriately to the decreased number of red blood cells by increasing production of new blood cells. In a **nonregenerative anemia**, the bone marrow responds inadequately to the increased need for red blood cells. Anemias due to bleeding or the destruction of existing red blood cells are usually regenerative. Anemias that are caused by a decrease in the hormone that stimulates red blood cell production or by an abnormality in the bone marrow are nonregenerative.

Signs and Diagnosis

The signs of anemia in animals depend on the severity, the duration (short- or longterm), and the underlying cause of the illness. Sudden anemia can result in shock and even death if more than a third of the blood volume is lost rapidly and not replaced. In severe blood loss, the animal usually has an increased heart rate, pale gums, and low blood pressure. The cause of the blood loss may be obvious, for example, a major injury. If no evidence of external bleeding is found, your veterinarian will look for a source of internal or hidden blood loss, for example, a ruptured tumor on the spleen, a stomach ulcer, or parasites. If red blood cells are being destroyed, the animal may appear jaundiced (a yellowish color of the whites of the eyes, skin, or gums). Animals with longterm anemia have had time to adjust, and their signs are usually slower to develop. These include loss of energy, weakness, and loss of appetite. Affected animals will have similar physical examination findings, such as pale gums, an increased heart rate, and possibly enlargement of the spleen or a heart murmur.

A complete medical history is an important part of diagnosing anemia. Questions a veterinarian may ask include how long signs have been present; if there is a history of exposure to toxins such as rodent poisons, heavy metals, or toxic plants; what drug treatments and vaccinations the pet has had; where the pet has traveled; and any prior illnesses.

A complete blood count is another diagnostic tool your veterinarian will use to provide information on the severity of the anemia, the degree of bone marrow response, and the condition of other types of blood cells. A test should be performed to evaluate red blood cell size and to check for red blood cell parasites (some of which are discussed later in this chapter).

Both blood and urine tests can be used to evaluate how well the internal organs are functioning. If blood loss within the stomach or intestines is suspected, an examination of the animal's feces under a microscope for trace amounts of blood and parasites can be useful. X-rays can help identify hidden disease, such as a penny in the stomach of a puppy leading to zinc poisoning and anemia. Bruising or bleeding may be signs of a disease or condition affecting the blood's ability to clot and indicate the need for a test called a coagulation profile. If hemolytic disease (a condition in which there is destruction of red blood cells) is suspected, other tests can be performed. A blood test for infectious agents may also be helpful in defining the cause of anemia.

Bone marrow evaluation is typically done for any animal with an unexplained, nonregenerative anemia. Sampling the bone marrow will require anesthetizing your pet, which may mean it will need to stay at the veterinary hospital overnight.

Blood Loss Anemia

Sudden and severe blood loss can lead to shock and even death if more than 30 to 40% of the total blood volume is lost and the condition is not treated quickly with intravenous fluids or blood transfusions, or both. Causes of severe loss include major injury or surgery. If the reason for blood loss is not obvious, your veterinarian will look for other causes, such as conditions affecting the blood's ability to clot, bleeding tumors, stomach ulcers, or parasites. Internal parasites, such as hookworms in dogs, can lead to severe blood loss, especially in puppies. Low-grade, longterm blood loss eventually results in iron-deficiency anemia. This leads to abnormally small red blood cells and a lack of hemoglobin. In young animals this

How are Blood Cell Counts Done?

A blood sample is taken and placed in a test tube containing an anticoagulant to stop it from clotting. It is then transported to a laboratory.

The process is generally done using automated equipment. The blood is well mixed and placed on a special rack on the analyzer. This instrument has many different components to analyze different elements in the blood. The cell counting component counts the numbers of red and white blood cells and platelets. The results are printed out or sent to a computer for review by a technician.

Because an automated cell counter samples and counts so many cells, the results are very precise. However, certain abnormal cells in the blood may be identified incorrectly. To be sure the results are correct, a technician reviews the blood smear on a slide and identifies any abnormal cells or blood parasites present.

In addition to counting, measuring, and analyzing red blood cells, white blood cells, and platelets, automated blood analyzers also measure the average size and the amount of hemoglobin in red blood cells. This information can be helpful when trying to identify the cause of an anemia.

is often caused by parasites (for example, fleas, lice, or intestinal worms), but in older animals, bleeding from stomach ulcers or tumors is more common.

Hemolytic Anemia

Hemolytic anemias occur when red blood cells are destroyed. They are usually regenerative. Toxins, red blood cell trauma, infections, immune system defects, and red blood cell membrane defects can all cause hemolytic anemias.

Immune-mediated Hemolytic Anemia

In dogs, the most common cause of hemolytic anemia is immune mediated. This type of anemia can occur on its own or as a result of tumors, infection, drugs, or vaccinations. The body no longer recognizes red blood cells as self and develops antibodies to circulating red blood cells, leading to their destruction.

Dogs with immune-mediated hemolytic anemia are usually jaundiced, sometimes have a fever, and may have an enlarged spleen. They can show mild, slow-developing signs and not appear to be in any pain, or they can suddenly be in severe crisis. Your veterinarian will tailor treatment to the animal's signs. Any underlying infections will be treated and unnecessary drug therapy discontinued. Fluid therapy may be started and supplemented with blood transfusions if necessary. Drugs are also given to suppress the immune system in order to stop the destruction of red blood cells.

Blocking of a blood vessel in the lungs by a piece that has broken away from a blood clot (known as pulmonary thromboembolism) is a risk for dogs with immune-mediated hemolytic anemia. The underlying cause is unknown, but the risk may be reduced by supportive care with fluids and blood transfusions. Fluids are important to keep kidneys functioning properly and to protect the kidneys from the high concentrations of circulating bilirubin (the reddish yellow pigments in blood that cause jaundice). If the risk for forming blood clots is high, anticoagulant medication may also be given.

Alloimmune Hemolysis

Alloimmune hemolysis is the production of antibodies that are directed against red blood cells of another individual of the same species. Neonatal isoerythrolysis is an example of such a disease and is seen rarely in dogs. It is caused when pups nurse from a mother whose colostrum (the yellowish fluid rich in antibodies and minerals that is produced after giving birth and before producing true milk) contains antibodies to the newborn's red blood cells. The antibodies develop in the mother during unmatched blood transfusions. Newborns with neonatal isoerythrolysis are normal at birth but develop severe hemolytic anemia within 2 to 3 days and become weak and jaundiced. A veterinarian can perform tests to confirm the diagnosis. Treatment consists of stopping any colostrum while giving supportive care with transfusions. Neonatal isoerythrolysis can be avoided by withholding colostrum from the puppy's own mother and giving colostrum free of the antibodies. A veterinarian can perform a test to check for alloimmune hemolysis before the newborn is allowed to receive maternal colostrum.

Microangiopathic Hemolysis

Microangiopathic hemolysis occurs when red blood cells are damaged due to turbulent flow through abnormal blood vessels. It can be seen in dogs after having severe heartworm infection, blood vessel tumors (for example, hemangiosarcoma), twisting of the spleen, and disseminated intravascular coagulation, a condition in which small blood clots develop throughout the bloodstream, blocking small blood vessels and depleting the platelets and clotting factors needed to control bleeding. Treatment requires correcting the underlying disease.

Metabolic Causes of Hemolysis

A deficiency of phosphorus in the blood, leading to destruction of red blood cells, is seen in dogs with diabetes, hepatic lipidosis (a disorder of fat metabolism in the liver), and refeeding syndrome (chemical and fluid abnormalities that occur during recovery from fasting or starvation). Providing additional phosphorus, either by mouth or by injection depending on the severity of the illness, is the recommended treatment.

Toxins (Drugs, Plants, Chemicals)

Many classes of drugs can cause anemia if they are ingested accidentally or if their prescribed use is not closely monitored. These include common human and animal drugs such as acetaminophen, aspirin, naproxen, penicillin, and many other antibiotic and antiparasitic agents. Other anemia-causing toxins include plants such as oak, red maple, and bracken fern; foods such as fava beans and onions; chemicals; and heavy metals such as copper, lead, and zinc. It is always important to give as

complete a history as possible to the veterinarian when anemia is suspected, in order to help pinpoint the cause.

Infections

Many infections—caused by bacteria, viruses, or other organisms—can lead to anemia, by direct damage to red blood cells (leading to their destruction) or by effects on the elements that produce red blood cells in the bone marrow. In dogs, for example, infections involving certain organisms in the genuses *Ehrlichia* and *Babesia* are known to cause anemia.

Inherited Diseases

Several inherited red blood cell disorders cause anemia. Pyruvate kinase (enzyme) deficiencies are seen in Basenjis, Beagles, West Highland White Terriers, Cairn Terriers, and other breeds. Phosphofructokinase (enzyme) deficiency occurs in English Springer Spaniels. Deficiencies in these enzymes lead to shortened red blood cell life span and a regenerative anemia. In dogs with phosphofructokinase deficiency, the sudden destruction of red blood cells is caused by a high blood pH created after excessive excitement or exercise. If such situations are minimized, these dogs may have a normal life expectancy. There is no treatment for pyruvate kinase deficiency, and affected dogs will have a shortened life span due to abnormalities of the bone marrow.

Nonregenerative Anemias

Nonregenerative anemias can be caused by nutritional deficiencies, chronic disease, kidney disease, or bone marrow diseases.

Nutritional Deficiencies

Nutritional deficiency anemias develop when the nutrients needed for red blood cell formation are not present in adequate amounts. Anemia develops gradually and may initially be regenerative, but ultimately becomes nonregenerative. Starvation causes anemia by a combination of vitamin and mineral deficiencies as well as a negative energy and protein balance. The deficiencies most likely to cause anemia are iron, copper, vitamin B_{12}, vitamin B_6, riboflavin, niacin, vitamin E, and vitamin C.

Iron deficiency is the most common deficiency seen in dogs. It is rarely nutritional in origin—it most commonly occurs after blood loss (*see* BLOOD LOSS ANEMIA, page 38). Young animals do not have much stored iron, and milk contains very little iron. Your veterinarian may recommend oral iron supplements for anemic newborns. Your veterinarian will also look for any hidden source of blood loss and treat it if needed.

B vitamin deficiencies are rare. Some drugs, such as anticonvulsants and drugs that interfere with B vitamin metabolism, may cause anemia. Poor absorption of vitamin B_{12} has been reported in Giant Schnauzers. These dogs respond to injections of vitamin B_{12}.

Anemia of Chronic Disease

Anemia caused by a longterm (chronic) disease is usually classified as mild to moderate and nonregenerative. It is the most common form of anemia seen in animals. The anemia can occur after a longterm inflammation or infection, a tumor, liver disease, or hormonal disorders such as hyper- or hypoadrenocorticism (disorders of the adrenal gland) or hypothyroidism (an underactive thyroid gland). Proteins called cytokines, which are produced by inflammatory cells, lead to decreases in iron availability, red blood cell survival, and the bone marrow's ability to regenerate, resulting in anemia. Treatment of the underlying disease leads to correction of the anemia.

Kidney Disease

Longterm kidney disease is a common cause of nonregenerative anemia in animals. Animals with kidney disease produce less of a kidney hormone that stimulates development of red blood cells in the bone marrow, leading to anemia. A synthetic form of the hormone has been used for treatment. Animals receiving the treatment require supplemental iron to support red blood cell production.

Bone Marrow Diseases

Bone marrow disease or failure from any cause can lead to nonregenerative anemia and a reduction in the number of all types of blood cells—red, white, and platelets. With widespread marrow involvement, white blood cells are affected first, followed by platelets, and finally red blood cells.

Aplastic anemia (anemia in which the ability of bone marrow to generate all blood cells is reduced) has been reported in dogs. Most cases have no known cause, but some are caused by infections, drug therapy, toxins, or total body irradiation. To treat the condition, the underlying cause must be determined and eliminated. Supportive care such as antibiotics and transfusions may also be needed. Drugs that stimulate the bone marrow can be used until the marrow recovers. If the disease has no known cause or if marrow recovery is unlikely (for example, phenylbutazone poisoning in dogs), bone marrow transplantation is helpful if a suitable donor is available.

In **pure red cell aplasia**, only the red blood cells or the elements that produce the red blood cells are affected. It is characterized by a nonregenerative anemia with severe reduction of the elements that produce the red blood cells in the bone marrow. It has been reported in dogs. Cases that are immune-related often respond to therapy that suppresses the immune system. A synthetic hormone that stimulates blood cell production has been reported to cause pure red cell aplasia in some dogs. Stopping the hormone treatment may eventually lead to recovery.

Primary leukemias are a type of cancer in which abnormal white blood cells replace normal blood cells. This leads to anemia and a lack of normal white blood cells and platelets. Primary leukemias are uncommon, but they have been reported in dogs. Leukemias can develop in bone marrow or the lymphatic system and are classified as acute (sudden and often severe) or chronic (long-lasting, with signs that are generally less severe). Acute leukemias, in which the marrow is filled with immature blood cells, generally respond poorly to chemotherapy. In animals that do respond, remission times are usually short. In dogs, the response rate to chemotherapy for the most common type of acute leukemia is about 30%, with about half the dogs surviving for at least 4 months. Other types of acute leukemia are less common and even less responsive to treatment. Chronic leukemias, in which there is greatly increased production of one blood cell line, are less likely to cause anemia and are more responsive to treatment.

Myelodysplasia (also called myelodysplastic syndrome) is a bone marrow disorder in which growth and maturation of blood-forming cells in the bone marrow is defective. This leads to nonregenerative anemia or shortages of white blood cells or platelets. It is considered a preleukemic syndrome (occurring before leukemia fully develops). Myelodysplasia occurs in dogs, cats, and humans. The disease can occur as the result of mutations in stem cells or be caused by tumors in other organs or drug therapy. Some dogs respond to treatment with synthetic hormones and steroids. Supportive care with transfusions may be helpful. Survival rates vary because myelodysplasia can progress to leukemia. Many animals with this condition are put to sleep or die of infection, bleeding, or anemia.

Myelofibrosis is a progressive disease leading to anemia and enlargement of the spleen and liver. It brings on bone marrow failure after it causes normal marrow elements to be replaced with fibrous tissue. It can be the initial disease or occur as a result of cancer, immune-mediated hemolytic anemia (*see* page 39), whole body irradiation, or hereditary anemias. Diagnosis can be made by bone marrow biopsy, a procedure requiring anesthesia and often an overnight stay at the veterinary hospital. Treatment depends on the underlying cause but usually involves suppressing the immune system. Because suppressing the immune system increases the chances that your pet will catch other diseases, carefully follow your veterinarian's recommendations for controlling exposure to disease-causing agents.

■ BLOOD PARASITES

Blood parasites are organisms that live in the blood of their animal hosts. These parasites can range from single-celled protozoa to more complex bacteria and rickettsiae. The method of transmission varies, depending on the parasite, but often they are transmitted through the bites of ticks or flies.

Babesiosis

Babesiosis is a disease transmitted by ticks. It is caused by protozoan parasites of the genus *Babesia*, which infect the red blood cells. Babesiosis affects a wide range of domestic and wild animals and, occasionally, humans. While the major economic impact of babesiosis is on the cattle industry, infections in dogs occur at various rates throughout the world.

Signs of infection vary from a mild illness that passes quickly to a severe disease that rapidly results in death. In some cases, the parasite causes a longterm disease with severe and progressive anemia as the main symptom. Babesiosis can be confused with other conditions that cause fever, anemia, destruction of red blood cells, jaundice, or red urine. Therefore, laboratory tests should be performed to confirm the diagnosis.

Your veterinarian will be able to prescribe the appropriate medication. Supportive treatment is helpful and may include the use of anti-inflammatory drugs, antioxidants, and corticosteroids. Blood transfusions may be life saving in very anemic animals.

A vaccine based on the variety of *Babesia* found in Europe is available, but does not protect against other types. Preventing exposure to ticks by using appropriate tick control products and removing any ticks promptly will help keep your dog from being exposed to this parasite.

A small number of cases of human babesiosis have been reported, but it is unclear whether the species of *Babesia* that infect dogs are the same as those that cause infection in people. Fatal cases have been reported in people whose spleen had been removed or who had a weakened immune system. Human *Babesia* infections are acquired by way of bites from infected ticks or through contaminated blood transfusions.

Hepatozoonosis

Hepatozoonosis is a disease of wild and domestic carnivores (meat-eating animals) caused by a protozoan called *Hepatozoon canis*. This organism is transmitted by the brown dog tick, but its mode of transmission is unusual. The tick picks up the organism from an infected host while biting the animal. An uninfected dog gets the disease by eating the tick, not from being bitten by the tick. In North America, the signs in infected dogs are different and more severe than in other parts of the world and the disease is caused by a different *Hepatozoon* species, which is now called *Hepatozoon americanum*. This species is transmitted by the Gulf Coast tick instead of by the brown dog tick. Because of these differences, the disease in North America is referred to as American canine hepatozoonosis (*see* below).

In much of the world (India, Africa, southeast Asia, the Middle East, southern Europe, and islands in the Pacific and Indian Oceans), infected dogs have no signs of infection or only mild signs. Having a suppressed immune system due to another disease appears to play an important role in the development of significant signs. In the United States, more severe signs may occur. Most cases in the US have been diagnosed in Texas (primarily along the Gulf Coast), Oklahoma, and Louisiana, but cases have also been reported as far east as Tennessee, Alabama, Georgia, and Florida. This is a recent disease that has primarily spread north and east from the Gulf Coast of Texas, where it was originally detected in 1978.

Dogs older than 4 to 6 months old are usually resistant to infection with *H. canis*. However, *H. americanum* causes severe signs even in adult dogs.

American Canine Hepatozoonosis

Infection by *H. americanum* creates areas of inflammation within body tissues, which can cause signs of disease such as fever, depression, weight loss, poor body condition, muscle loss and weakness, discharge from the eyes, and bloody diarrhea. These signs may come and go. Fluctuating fevers of from 102.7 to 106°F (39.3 to 41.0°C) may also be seen. Surprisingly, many dogs have a normal appetite. Severe sensitivity or pain near the spine is also common, as are stiffness and a general reluctance to move. Eventually, hepatozoonosis may lead to inflammation of the kidneys or amyloidosis of the kidneys (a condition in which there is a buildup of an abnormal protein called amyloid in kidney tissues).

There are specific laboratory tests a veterinarian can perform to confirm the presence of this disease. Muscle biopsies may also help with diagnosis. Other laboratory findings may include a significant increase in the white blood cell count and a mild to moderate anemia.

Hepatozoonosis is a life-long infection in dogs. No known treatment completely clears the body of the organism. In the past, most dogs showed only temporary improvement, with frequent relapses within 3 to 6 months and death within 2 years of diagnosis. However, remission can now usually be achieved by using new drug combinations. These new therapies have resulted in a marked improvement in the outlook for dogs with hepatozoonosis.

Prevention of access to ticks is the most effective form of control for this disease. Be sure to provide your pet with good tick control, especially if you live in an area where this disease has been reported.

There is no known risk of transferring this disease to humans.

African Tsetse-transmitted Trypanosomiasis

Tsetse are small, winged biting flies that feed on the blood of humans and other animals. They only occur in sub-Saharan Africa, where they are responsible for transmitting a group of diseases caused by protozoa of the genus *Trypanosoma,* which affect all domestic animals. Tsetse flies are restricted to Africa; however, horseflies and other biting flies can transmit the disease in other locations (such as in Central and South America). In dogs, *Trypanosoma brucei* is most likely to cause disease. Domestic animals may be a source of human infections.

Infected tsetse flies inject the protozoa into the skin of animals, where they grow for a few days and cause localized swellings called chancres. They enter the lymph nodes, then the bloodstream, where they multiply quickly. The immune response is very strong; however, not all trypanosomes are vulnerable to the immune response, which results in longterm infection.

The severity of disease varies with the species and age of the animal infected and the species of trypanosome involved. The incubation period is usually 1 to 4 weeks. In dogs, the onset of disease may be rapid. The primary signs are fever, anemia, and weight loss. The eyes are often affected. Internally, the lymph nodes and spleen are usually swollen. The diagnosis is confirmed by laboratory testing to identify trypanosomes in the blood of an infected dog.

Several drugs can be used for treatment; however, most drugs only work if the correct dose is given. It is very important to follow the prescribed dosage exactly. Some trypanosomes have become resistant to certain drugs, which may be the cause in cases that do not respond to medical treatment.

The risk of infection can be reduced in areas where the disease is common by keeping dogs indoors or by getting rid of tsetse flies and using preventive drugs, which are given to stop an infection from getting started. Flies can be partially controlled by using sprays or dips on the pets to be protected, spraying insecticides on fly-breeding areas, using screens coated with insecticide, and clearing brush to reduce the habitat for the flies. Animals can be given preventive drugs in areas of high risk for infections, but this is rarely undertaken in domestic dogs. There is no vaccine.

Surra (*Trypanosoma evansi* Infection)

Surra is separated from the tsetse-transmitted diseases because it is usually transmitted by other biting flies that are found within and outside tsetse fly areas. It occurs in North Africa, the Middle East, Asia, the Far East, and Central and South America. It is mostly a disease of horses, but all domestic animals are susceptible. The disease can be deadly, particularly in horses and dogs. The development and effects of the disease, signs, physical changes, diagnosis, and treatment are similar to those of the tsetse-transmitted trypanosomes (*see* above).

Chagas' Disease (*Trypanosoma cruzi* Infection)

Chagas' disease is caused by infection with another trypanosome. Insects transmit the disease between susceptible species of animals, including opossums, armadillos, rodents, and wild carnivores. The trypanosome also causes disease in humans and occasionally in young dogs and cats. The disease occurs in Central and South America and localized areas of the southern US. Domestic animals may become infected and introduce the trypanosome into houses where the bugs are present. People then become infected by contamination of wounds or by eating food contaminated with insect droppings that contain trypanosomes. Other domestic animals act as carriers of the disease without showing signs of illness. Affected dogs may die suddenly or have short- or long-term inflammation of the heart muscle.

■ CANINE MALIGNANT LYMPHOMA

Canine malignant lymphoma is a common cancer in dogs. It is a progressive, deadly disease caused by the harmful growth of lymphoid cells. Lymphoma most commonly arises from organized lymphoid tissues including the bone marrow, thymus, lymph nodes, and spleen. Other common sites include the skin, eye, central nervous system, testis, and bone. Although it is common, the causes and origin of the disease are not well understood. Possible causes or contributing factors include viral infection, environmental contamination with herbicides, magnetic field exposure, genetic abnormalities, and dysfunction of the immune system.

The signs of canine lymphoma will vary somewhat depending on the part of the body involved and the extent of the disease. In dogs, 4 distinct forms of lymphoma can occur: 1) multicentric, which originates in multiple places; 2) alimentary, which occurs in the digestive system, 3) mediastinal, which occurs within the chest; and 4) extranodal, which may involve the kidneys, central nervous system, or skin.

Multicentric lymphoma is by far the most common form, accounting for about 80% of cases. An early sign of multicentric lymphoma is the rapid and nonpainful enlargement of lymph nodes, which may become 3 to 10 times their normal size (*see also* page 175). In addition to this, cancerous lymphocytes may move into internal organs including the spleen, liver, bone marrow, and other sites. Late in the course of disease, when there are multiple, large tumors, dogs may show general signs of illness, including lack of energy, weakness, fever, loss of appetite, and depression.

Alimentary lymphoma is much less common and accounts for less than 10% of all canine lymphomas. Dogs with this form of the disease may have signs related to stomach upset, such as vomiting and abdominal pain. When the disease affects most of the intestinal tract, dogs may

have loss of appetite, vomiting, diarrhea, and continued weight loss because they cannot digest food properly.

Mediastinal lymphoma is also uncommon. Dogs with this form of the disease may have an enlarged thymus, lymph nodes, or both. As the disease advances, signs may include trouble breathing as fluid builds up in the chest and puts pressure on the lungs. The tumor may block the vein that routes blood from the upper part of the body into the heart. In addition to symptoms related to breathing, some dogs with mediastinal lymphoma pass large amounts of urine and drink more than normal. This can be caused by an increase in calcium in the blood, a syndrome seen in 10% to 40% of dogs with lymphoma.

The medical problems associated with **extranodal lymphoma** vary and depend on which organ is affected. Skin lymphoma may appear as single, raised, slow-healing sores or widespread, scaly regions. Signs of lymphoma at other extranodal sites include difficulty breathing (lungs), kidney failure (kidneys), blindness (eyes), and seizures (central nervous system).

Canine lymphoma is often relatively easy to diagnose by testing the affected organ system. In dogs with multicentric lymphoma, a needle biopsy of enlarged lymph nodes usually provides enough cells to test to confirm the diagnosis.

Treatment and Outlook

Treatment of multicentric canine lymphoma with chemotherapy using a combination of drugs is often successful, with more than 90% of all dogs improving to some degree. Individual treatment plans vary with respect to the drugs used, dosage, and frequency and duration of treatment. With chemotherapy, the expected survival time for dogs with B-cell lymphoma is about 9 to 12 months. For dogs with T-cell lymphoma, expected survival times are shorter (6 months). Dogs that do not respond to the usual drugs may improve when other treatment plans are used. These alternate plans may include other drugs or radiation.

Treating other forms of lymphoma is often more difficult. Alimentary lymphoma, if concentrated in one area, can be treated effectively with surgery to remove the tumor, together with combination chemotherapy. However, if lymphoma is spread throughout the intestinal tract, the response to treatment is less dramatic and survival times are shorter (often less than 3 months). The use of combination chemotherapy with or without radiation therapy can give dogs with mediastinal lymphoma considerable improvement in survival times and quality-of-life scores, but remission averages about 6 months for T-cell lymphoma. Dogs with an abnormally high level of calcium in the blood, a condition often associated with mediastinal lymphoma, are also less likely to have prolonged survival times. Lymphoma involving other extranodal sites, such as the skin, can be managed with surgery, radiation, and whole system chemotherapy as appropriate; however, the disease often does not respond to medical treatment.

■ BLEEDING DISORDERS

When bleeding occurs in an organ or body part, a process is set in motion to stop the bleeding. This is called **hemostasis**. In order to work, hemostasis requires an adequate number of platelets, the right amount of blood clotting proteins (often referred to as factors), and blood vessels that constrict properly. When an injury occurs, the wall of the blood vessel breaks. A normally responsive blood vessel will narrow so that blood flows more slowly, allowing the clotting process to begin. Platelets also rush to the broken wall where certain proteins change the platelets' shape from round to spiny so that they can stick to blood cells, the broken vessel wall, and to each other. Other proteins form long strands called fibrin. These fibrin strands form a net that traps and helps hold together the platelets and blood cells, creating a clot that plugs the break in the vessel wall. After the clot has formed and stabilized, other proteins stop the clotting process and eventually dissolve the clot.

Bleeding disorders may be present at birth (congenital) or occur later. Defects in blood clotting proteins usually show up as delayed bleeding and bruising deep in tissues, while platelet defects usually show up as superficial small bruises, nosebleeds, black stools caused by bleeding into the bowels, or prolonged bleeding at injection and surgery sites.

Abnormal clotting leading to blocked arteries may be inherited disorders of anticlotting proteins or acquired disorders. Acquired clotting diseases are more common in animals than are inherited disorders.

Blood clotting tests can help identify animals with defective clotting proteins. However, the tests are not very sensitive,

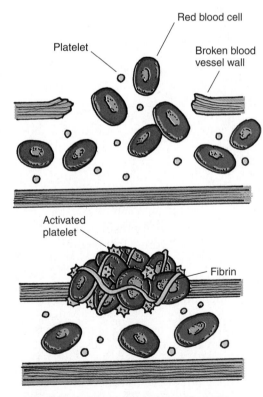

How blood clots are formed (modified with permission from *The Merck Manual of Medical Information*, Second Home Edition, 2003)

so an animal must have a severe deficiency for the tests to find the problem.

Congenital Clotting Protein Disorders

Many different proteins are involved in the clotting process. Deficiencies of any of these proteins can cause bleeding disorders. In a severe deficiency or defect of clotting proteins, signs will appear at an early age. Severe defects are usually deadly. Animals may be stillborn or die shortly after birth. Lack of clotting proteins or vitamin K (which is also part of the clotting process) in a newborn animal may make a clotting defect worse. If the amount of any particular clotting protein is 5 to 10% of normal, the newborn may survive, but will usually show signs of illness before 6 months of age. It is during this time, when numerous routine procedures (for example, vaccination, dewclaw removal, and neutering or spaying) are usually done, that a bleeding tendency may be noticed by your veterinarian. Most of the clotting protein disorders present at birth in domestic animals are defects of a single protein.

Hypofibrinogenemia (an abnormal shortage of fibrinogen in the blood), accompanied by severe bleeding, has been reported in Saint Bernards and Vizslas. **Dysfibrinogenemia** (abnormally functioning fibrinogen) has been reported in an inbred family of Russian Wolfhounds (Borzois). Dogs with the disorder had mild bleeding problems (such as nosebleeds), but injury or surgery resulted in life-threatening bleeding. Intravenous transfusion with fresh or fresh-frozen plasma (the liquid portion of blood) is the best treatment to stop the bleeding.

Factor II (prothrombin) disorders are rare. Prothrombin is one of the proteins that plays a role in clotting of blood. Boxer dogs have been reported to have prothrombin that is present in normal amounts in the body but does not function normally. A disorder of Factor II has been reported in English Cocker Spaniels. Signs in affected puppies, such as nosebleeds and bleeding

gums, decrease with age. Adults bruise easily or have inflamed skin. Treatment is by transfusion of whole blood or plasma.

Deficiency of Factor VII, another clotting protein, has been reported in Beagles, English Bulldogs, Alaskan Malamutes, Miniature Schnauzers, Boxers, and mixed-breed dogs. Usually, it is not associated with sudden, unexplained bleeding, but affected dogs may have bruising or excessive bleeding after surgery. Prolonged bleeding after giving birth has been reported. Factor VII deficiency is most often diagnosed coincidentally when clotting tests are performed.

Hemophilia A (Factor VIII deficiency) is the most common inherited bleeding disorder in dogs. Usually, females carry the gene for the disease without showing any signs, while males do show signs. In affected puppies, prolonged bleeding is seen from the umbilical cord after birth, from the gums during teething, and after surgery. Lameness due to bleeding into a joint, sudden clot formation, and oozing of blood in the body cavity also are common signs in dogs with less than 5% of normal Factor VIII activity. Animals with 5 to 10% of normal activity typically do not bleed spontaneously but bleed more than usual after an injury or surgery. Small dogs may be less likely to show signs of illness. Carrier animals have higher levels of Factor VIII (40 to 60% of normal), and the results of their clotting tests are usually normal. The diagnosis is harder to confirm in animals less than 6 months old because their livers may not yet have produced enough of the clotting proteins. Treatment requires repeated transfusions of whole blood or plasma until bleeding has been controlled.

Hemophilia B (Factor IX deficiency) is less common than hemophilia A. It has been reported in several breeds of purebred dogs and a mixed-breed dog. Females are usually carriers and rarely have signs of the disease. Signs are similar to those of hemophilia A. Animals with extremely low Factor IX activity (less than 1% of normal) usually die at birth or shortly thereafter. Animals with 5 to 10% of normal Factor IX activity may suddenly develop blood clots, bleeding in the joints, oozing of blood in the body cavity, or organ bleeding. Gums may bleed excessively during teething. Some animals have no signs until injury or surgery. Carrier animals with 40 to 60% of normal Factor IX activity usually have no signs and normal results on blood clotting tests. Treatment requires transfusion with fresh or fresh-frozen plasma. Often, internal bleeding into the abdomen, chest, central nervous system, or muscles occurs, and may not be noticed until a crisis happens.

Congenital clotting protein disorders involving deficiencies of Factor X, Factor XI, Factor XII, and prekallikrein have been reported in a few dogs but appear to be extremely rare.

Acquired Clotting Protein Disorders

Most clotting proteins are produced in the liver. Therefore, liver disease can lead to decreased levels of clotting proteins, particularly Factors VII, IX, X, and XI. Severe liver disease can also lead to a condition known as disseminated intravascular coagulation (*see* below). Fibrinogen, the protein in blood that is made in the liver and converted to fibrin in response to tissue damage, and von Willebrand's factor, which is produced outside the liver and helps platelets stick to the blood vessel wall and to each other, can be increased in liver disease.

Dogs that eat rat poison may have blood clotting problems because the poison reduces the liver's production of clotting proteins (*see* RODENTICIDE POISONING, page 1201). Affected animals may have blood clots and bruising of superficial and deep tissues. Often, the animals do not bleed within the first 24 hours after eating the poison. Vitamin K, given by injection and then by mouth, is the usual treatment, but may cause side effects, including anemia or allergic reactions. If you suspect your dog has eaten any type of rat or mouse poison, this is an emergency and an immediate trip to your veterinarian is recommended.

Disseminated intravascular coagulation (DIC) is a condition in which small blood clots develop throughout the bloodstream, blocking small blood vessels and destroying the platelets and clotting factors needed to control bleeding. It usually develops after numerous triggering events such as severe infections, heat stroke, burns, tumors, or severe injury. In many cases, the signs are uncontrolled bleeding and the inability to form a normal clot. Death is caused by extensive blood clots or collapse of circulation, leading to the failure of one or several organs. If the animal survives this crisis, a chronic form of DIC can occur. Your veterinarian will determine and attempt to correct the underlying problem causing this condition. Intravenous fluids are extremely important for maintaining normal circulation. DIC is a very serious disorder and is often fatal.

Platelet Disorders

Disorders of platelets include having too few platelets (thrombocytopenia) or having platelets that do not work properly. Each type of disorder can be either congenital (present at birth) or acquired later in life. Thrombocytosis is having too many platelets. It may occur as a response to a physiologic or disease process or, rarely, it may be a component of blood cancer.

Congenital Thrombocytopenia

A lack of platelets can occur in fetuses and newborn animals when the mother's body produces antibodies against proteins in the fetus' platelets that are related to the father and absent from the mother.

Gray Collies may develop a disorder called **cyclic hematopoiesis** (*see* GRAY COLLIE SYNDROME, page 52), which is characterized by 12-day cycles during which all types of blood cells, including platelets, decrease. All cell types are affected, but neutrophils (the most common type of white blood cells) are most affected. Mild to severe platelet shortages can be seen, and excessive bleeding is a potential complication. This disorder is deadly; most dogs with the disease die from infections before 6 months of age. Even dogs that receive frequent antibiotic treatments usually die by 3 years of age from amyloidosis, a condition in which abnormal proteins build up in the body's organs.

Acquired Thrombocytopenia

Acquired thrombocytopenias are common in dogs. Many causes have been identified, most involving the immune system destroying platelets.

Ehrlichial diseases, caused by organisms in the genus *Ehrlichia*, cause mild to severe loss of platelets in dogs. Infection may include short- and longterm changes in the number of platelets and other blood cells. Ticks are the usual carriers of the infection. Infected dogs may have nosebleeds, bleeding into the bowels (resulting in black stools), bleeding of the gums, and prolonged bleeding after vaccination or surgery.

Thrombocytopenia due to immune system dysfunction occurs when the immune system makes antibodies that destroy platelets or platelet-producing cells in the bone marrow. Signs include tiny, purplish red spots on the gums or skin, bruising, bleeding into the bowels resulting in black stools, or nosebleeds. An evaluation of the bone marrow may be necessary to help determine if circulating platelets or the platelet-forming cells are targeted by the antibodies. Corticosteroids are the usual treatment, although other drugs are sometimes used. If an animal has repeated episodes of the disease, the spleen is sometimes removed.

Thrombocytopenia caused by vaccination has been reported in dogs that have been vaccinated repeatedly with certain types of vaccines (modified live adenovirus or paramyxovirus vaccines). The platelet loss occurs 3 to 10 days after repeat vaccination, usually lasts for only a short time, and may be so mild that it is not noticed unless it happens at the same time as another clotting disorder.

Thrombocytopenia caused by drugs has been reported in dogs. Some drugs and classes of drugs (including estrogen and some antibiotics) suppress the production of platelets in the bone marrow. Other drugs (including aspirin, acetaminophen, penicillin, and others) destroy platelets circulating in the bloodstream. Drug reactions are rare and unpredictable. Platelets usually return to normal shortly after the drug is discontinued. Drug-induced bone marrow suppression may last longer, however. If your dog is taking one of these drugs, your veterinarian will likely monitor the blood count to check for any serious reductions in the number of platelets.

Congenital Platelet Function Disorders

Several types of platelet function disorders can be present at birth (congenital). Specialized tests are usually required to detect them.

Canine thrombopathia has been reported in Basset Hounds. Affected dogs have nosebleeds, tiny purplish red spots, and bleeding of the gums. This disorder should be suspected in Basset Hounds that have these signs, along with normal levels of platelets and von Willebrand's factor. Specific diagnosis of this disorder requires specialized platelet function testing. There is no specific treatment, but in cases of severe bleeding, plasma or whole blood transfusions may be needed.

Thrombasthenic thrombopathia has been diagnosed in Otterhounds. Affected dogs have prolonged bleeding times and form large bruises easily. A large number of oddly shaped, giant platelets are seen in blood tests. Platelets from dogs with this disorder do not clump together or separate as they normally should. There is no specific treatment. In cases of severe bleeding, transfusions of plasma or whole blood can be given.

Von Willebrand's disease is caused by a defective or deficient von Willebrand's factor. Von Willebrand's factor is the protein that carries an important clotting factor (Factor VIII) in the blood and that regulates the first step in clot formation. It is the most common inherited bleeding disorder in dogs and occurs in nearly all breeds and in mixed breeds. The disorder is most common in Doberman Pinschers, German Shepherds, Golden Retrievers, Miniature Schnauzers, Pembroke Welsh Corgis, Shetland Sheepdogs, Basset Hounds, Scottish Terriers, Standard Poodles, and Standard Manchester Terriers.

Two types of the disease are known. In the less common form, the condition is either deadly, or results in the dog being a carrier that has no symptoms. In the more common form, the dog can have bleeding of the gums, nosebleeds, and blood in the urine. Some puppies may bleed excessively only after injection or surgery. Signs of von Willebrand's disease are similar to those of platelet disorders. Laboratory tests are required to confirm the diagnosis. Treatment requires transfusion with whole blood or plasma.

Acquired Platelet Function Disorders

Dogs with thrombocytopenia due to immune system dysfunction (*see* page 49) also may have an acquired platelet functional defect. Dogs can have excessive bleeding tendencies without a severe drop in the number of platelets.

Several diseases have been associated with acquired platelet function disorders. A bone marrow tumor called multiple myeloma increases the amount of antibodies circulating in the blood. This can affect platelets and reduce their ability to form a blood clot. Longterm kidney disease can also decrease the ability of platelets to stick together. Liver disease may also decrease the number of platelets produced by the bone marrow. Many drugs can also impair platelet function; however, the impairment may not be noticed unless another clotting disorder is also present.

Blood Vessel Disorders

Certain defects present at birth or diseases can cause severe inflammation of the blood vessels and bleeding disorders.

Ehlers-Danlos Syndrome

This syndrome, also known as rubber puppy disease or cutaneous asthenia, is caused by a defect (present at birth) in protein connective tissue in the skin. This causes weak structural support of blood vessels and can lead to blood clots and easy bruising. The disorder has been reported in dogs and people but is rare. The most striking sign is loose skin that stretches to a greater than normal degree and tears easily. There is no treatment.

Rocky Mountain Spotted Fever

This disease is caused by an organism (*Rickettsia rickettsii*), which is transmitted by ticks (*see* ROCKY MOUNTAIN SPOTTED FEVER [TICK FEVER], page 324). The rickettsial organisms invade and kill blood cells, which leads to blood vessel swelling and bleeding. Infected dogs may have nosebleeds, bruises, blood in the urine, bleeding into the bowel, or bleeding of the retina (the membrane at the back of the eye). In severely affected dogs, disseminated intravascular coagulation may occur (*see* page 48).

Canine Herpesvirus

This virus generally affects puppies that are 7 to 21 days old. Widespread inflammation and destruction of the blood vessels is accompanied by bleeding of tissues surrounding blood vessels. The disease usually results in death within 24 hours after signs begin.

Blood Clotting Disorders

Abnormal blood clotting (known as pathologic thrombosis) is the uncontrolled clotting of blood, which causes blocked arteries. Inherited blood clotting disorders that occur in humans are not known in animals. However, there are several acquired clotting disorders that can occur. Certain diseases in animals have been associated with increased risk of blood clots. These have been seen in dogs with kidney disease, overactive adrenal glands, longterm decrease in the production of thyroid hormones, and rarely, immune-mediated hemolytic anemia (*see* page 39).

Some kidney diseases cause a decrease in the anticlotting protein called antithrombin III. Other abnormalities found in kidney disease include an increased tendency for platelets to clump together and a decrease in the enzyme that dissolves blood clots. Increased blood clotting is thought to be caused by several different factors.

Having too much cholesterol in the blood has been associated with increased risk of blood clots. Diseases that cause this include an increase in adrenal gland activity, diabetes, kidney disease, deficiency of thyroid hormones, and inflammation of the pancreas. All have been associated with increased risk of blood clot formation, often in the lungs.

The best treatment for an animal with blood clots is to diagnose and treat the underlying disease, along with providing good supportive care. Maintaining blood flow to the tissues is critical. Your veterinarian may prescribe medication to dissolve or prevent clots. In other cases, transfusions may be the most effective treatment.

■ WHITE BLOOD CELL DISORDERS

Leukocytes, or white blood cells, include neutrophils, lymphocytes, monocytes, eosinophils, and basophils (*see* page 35). These cells vary with regard to where they are produced, how long they circulate in the bloodstream, and the factors that stimulate them into going in or out of the intricate network of blood vessels that branch out through the tissues of the body. The normal numbers of each type of white blood cell also vary between species. **Leukocytosis** is an increase in the total number of circulating white blood cells; **leukopenia** is a decrease. In addition to an overall increase or decrease in white blood cells, increases or decreases in each type of white blood cell can lead to—and help diagnose—disorders.

Leukograms are blood tests that count the number of different white blood cells circulating in the bloodstream. By counting the cells and examining their form your veterinarian gains valuable information that can help diagnose a wide variety of disorders.

Disorders Related to Increased or Decreased White Blood Cells

Neutrophilia is an increase in the number of neutrophils in the bloodstream and is caused by inflammation. Structural changes in neutrophils may occur during severe inflammation and are referred to as toxic changes. **Neutropenia** is a decrease in the number of neutrophils in the bloodstream. It may occur due to the white blood cells sticking to the walls of damaged blood vessels, destruction of neutrophils, or reduced formation in the bone marrow. Neutropenia may occur in all species during overwhelming bacterial infections. Adverse reactions to drugs may result in neutropenia or even pancytopenia (a reduction in red and white blood cells and platelets).

Eosinophilia is an increase in the number of eosinophils, which are involved in allergic reactions and in controlling parasites. Increases are caused by substances that promote allergic reactions (for example, histamine) and by certain antibodies. Eosinophils increase during infections with parasites such as heartworms or fleas. Eosinophilia also may occur with inflammation of the intestines, kidneys, lungs, or skin. A decrease in eosinophils is known as **eosinopenia**. It is a common reaction to stress or treatment with corticosteroids.

Basophils are rare in domestic animals. Basophils produce histamine and, like eosinophils, are involved in allergic reactions and combating parasites. **Basophilia** (an increase in basophils) is uncommon, but does occur in some dogs with heartworm disease.

Lymphocytosis is an increase in the number of lymphocytes in the bloodstream. It can be caused by certain hormones, stimulation of the immune system by infections, chronic diseases like arthritis, and leukemia, which is a cancer of the immune system. **Lymphopenia** is a decrease in the number of lymphocytes.

It is most commonly caused by corticosteroids (either those naturally occurring in the body or given as treatment for a disease). Lymphopenia may also be caused by other conditions, such as decreased production of lymphocytes, some viral infections, and hereditary diseases.

Monocytosis is an increase in monocytes and may be associated with longterm inflammation.

Leukemia and Lymphoma

Leukemia is a malignant cancer that is characterized by an increase in abnormal white blood cells in the bloodstream. Lymphoma is a related cancer of certain white blood cells that begins in a lymph node or other lymphoid tissue (*see* page 45). Leukemia should be considered a potential cause when there is an increase in the number of white blood cells in the bloodstream.

Gray Collie Syndrome

This syndrome, also called cyclic hematopoiesis, is an inherited deficiency of the immune system that affects gray (but not merle) Collies. Signs of the disease include an extensive decrease of neutrophils that occurs in 12-day cycles, overwhelming reoccurring bacterial infections, bleeding, and a pale coat and nose color. The start of this disease is thought to be a defect in the maturation of the cells that form red and white blood cells and platelets in the bone marrow. Blood cell growth factors and other hormones also have a cyclic pattern.

Affected puppies often die at birth or during their first week. Most dogs with the disease die by 6 months of age. Surviving dogs may be stunted and weak and develop serious bacterial infections during the periods when neutrophil numbers are low. They also develop amyloidosis, an accumulation of an abnormal protein called amyloid (*see* page 307).

Your veterinarian can diagnose the disease based on the signs and results of blood tests. Treatment by bone marrow transplantation at an early age may be effective.

Pelger-Huët Anomaly

This inherited condition is caused by the failure of white blood cells to mature normally. White blood cell function is normal, and most animals do not have any signs of illness. A rare form of the disease also causes skeletal deformities and increased susceptibility to infection. This type of the disease is fatal. Pseudo-Pelger-Huët anomaly is an acquired maturation defect of white blood cells that may follow longterm infection, viral disease, drug therapy, and some tumors; it has been reported in dogs.

▨ POLYCYTHEMIA

Polycythemia is an increase in the amount of red blood cells in the bloodstream. It can be relative, transient, or absolute.

Relative polycythemia occurs when a decrease in the volume of plasma (the liquid part of blood) results in an apparent increase in red blood cell numbers. Relative polycythemia can be caused by anything that causes fluid loss from the blood, such as dehydration from vomiting or diarrhea.

Transient polycythemia is a type of relative polycythemia that occurs when excitement or fear causes the spleen to contract, resulting in the release of large numbers of red blood cells into the circulation. Treatment consists of giving fluids to the animal and addressing the underlying cause.

Absolute polycythemia is a real increase in red blood cell numbers resulting from increased production. Diagnosis requires directly measuring the total number of red blood cells, a test that is not available in most veterinary clinics. Your veterinarian will use tests of blood and urine to help diagnose polycythemia. In some cases, x-rays and other tests may also be required. Signs of the disorder include red mucous membranes, bleeding tendencies, the passing of large amounts of urine, excessive thirst, seizures or behavioral changes, lack of coordination, weakness, and blindness.

Treatment of polycythemia includes removing red blood cells by withdrawing blood through a catheter placed in a vein, then replacing the lost blood with fluids. Drugs such as hydroxyurea or clorambucil may also be added to the treatment. In some cases, the underlying disease must be treated.

CHAPTER **6**

Heart and Blood Vessel Disorders

▓ INTRODUCTION

The cardiovascular system includes the heart and the blood vessels (the veins and the arteries). The function of the heart is to pump blood. The right side of the heart pumps blood to the lungs, where oxygen is added to the blood and carbon dioxide is removed from it. The left side pumps blood to the rest of the body, where oxygen and nutrients are delivered to tissues, and waste products (including carbon dioxide) are transferred to the blood for removal by other organs (such as the lungs and kidneys). The heart is a hollow, muscular organ which, in mammals and birds, is divided into 4 chambers. The muscular tissue is called the myocardium. There are upper chambers on both the left and ride sides of the heart called the left and the right atria (the plural form of atrium). There are also 2 lower chambers called the left and right ventricles.

A series of valves keep blood flowing in one direction through the heart. The **atrioventricular valves** are valves between the atria and the ventricles. The **semilunar valves** are valves between the heart and the aorta and between the heart and the pulmonary artery. Each ventricle has an inlet and an outlet valve. In the left ventricle, the inlet valve is called the **mitral valve**, and the outlet valve is called the **aortic valve**. In the right ventricle, the inlet valve is called the **tricuspid valve**, and the outlet valve is called the **pulmonary valve**.

Blood from the body flows through the 2 largest veins, called the **venae cavae**, into the right atrium. When the right ventricle relaxes, blood in the right atrium pours through the tricuspid valve into the right ventricle. When the right ventricle is nearly full, the right atrium contracts, pushing additional blood into the right ventricle. The right ventricle then contracts, pushing blood through the pulmonary valve into the pulmonary arteries, which lead to the lungs. In the lungs, blood absorbs oxygen and gives up carbon dioxide. The blood then flows through the pulmonary veins into the left atrium. When the left ventricle relaxes, the blood in the left atrium pours through the mitral valve into the left ventricle. When the left ventricle is nearly full, the left atrium contracts, pushing additional blood into the left ventricle.

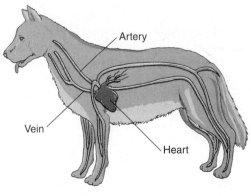

The cardiovascular system of the dog

The left ventricle then contracts, pushing blood through the aortic valve into the aorta, the largest artery in the body. This blood carries oxygen to all of the body except to the lungs.

Each heartbeat consists of 2 parts: diastole and systole. The first half of a heartbeat is the sound of the mitral and tricuspid valves closing. The second half is the sound of the aortic and pulmonary valves closing. During diastole, the ventricles relax and fill with blood. During systole, they contract and pump blood out to the body.

The rate and force of contraction of the heart and the degree of narrowing or widening of blood vessels are controlled by different hormones and by the autonomic nervous system (the part of the nervous system that controls involuntary activity).

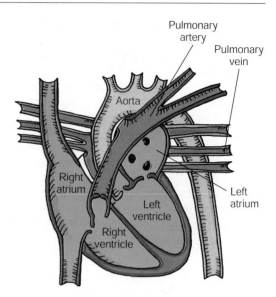

A look inside a dog's heart (modified with permission from *The Merck Manual of Medical Information*, Second Home Edition, 2003)

Heart Rate

The heart beats because of a tiny electrical current that originates in the heart's pacemaker called the **sinoatrial node**. Rhythmic electrical impulses or discharges cause the contraction of muscle fibers in the heart. While an animal is at rest, the sinoatrial node discharges many times each minute: about 15 times per minute in the horse, more than 200 times per minute in the cat, and 60 to 160 times per minute in the dog. In general, the larger the species, the slower the rate of sinoatrial node discharge and the slower the heart rate.

In quiet, healthy dogs, the heart rate is usually irregular. It increases while breathing in and decreases while breathing out. This is called respiratory sinus arrhythmia. A change in heart rate coinciding with breathing in and out is a good indicator of health. This change in heart rate usually does not occur during excitement or during heart diseases that may reduce the quality or duration of life.

Heart rate is also inversely related to blood pressure. When blood pressure increases, heart rate decreases; when blood pressure decreases, heart rate increases. In heart failure, nerve endings

that are sensitive to blood pressure changes, called baroreceptors, mistakenly report to the brain that blood pressure is too low and begin mechanisms (such as narrowing the blood vessels and increasing heart rate) that are designed to increase blood pressure. Unfortunately, these mechanisms also injure the heart.

Heart Sounds and Murmurs

Heart sounds are produced by the rapid acceleration and deceleration of blood and the resulting vibrations in the heart due to the circulation of blood. They can be heard using a stethoscope. In dogs, 2 heart sounds can normally be distinguished.

Heart murmurs are vibrations that can be heard coming from the heart or major blood vessels and generally are the result of turbulent blood flow or vibrations of heart structures such as part of a valve. Murmurs are typically described by their timing (that is, whether they occur continuously or only intermittently), their intensity (that is, whether they can be heard easily or with difficulty), and their location. Not every murmur indicates a heart disorder; for example, murmurs are commonly detected in puppies less than 6 months of age.

Arrhythmias

Arrhythmias are abnormalities of the rate, regularity, or site of heartbeat formation. An arrhythmia does not necessarily indicate heart disease. Many arrhythmias are functionally insignificant and require no specific treatment. Some arrhythmias, however, may cause severe signs such as loss of consciousness due to lack of blood flow to the brain or lead to sudden death. Many disorders are associated with abnormal heart rhythms.

Pulse

A pulse is the rhythmic expansion of an artery that can be felt with the fingertips during physical examination. In dogs, pulses are typically felt at the femoral artery (in the thigh). A jugular pulse in the neck can be noted in normal animals. A pulse may be absent, increased (strong), or decreased (weak)—each of which may indicate a specific type of heart disease or defect.

▧ HEART DISEASE AND HEART FAILURE

Slightly more than 10% of the animals examined by a veterinarian have some form of cardiovascular disease. Unlike diseases of many other organ systems, cardiovascular diseases generally do not go away but almost always become more serious and may lead to death. In addition, cardiovascular diseases may be more difficult to detect and quantify because the heart cannot be seen and is protected so well by the rib cage.

Heart disease can be defined as any abnormality of the heart. It encompasses a wide range of conditions, including congenital abnormalities (*see* page 58) and disorders of physical structure and function. It can be classified by various methods, including whether the disease was present at birth or not (that is, congenital or acquired), causes (for example, infectious or degenerative), duration (for example, long- or short-term), clinical status (for example, left heart failure, right heart failure, or biventricular failure), or by physical structure malformation (for example, ventricular septal defect).

Heart failure is any heart abnormality that results in failure of the heart to pump enough blood to meet the body's needs. It is not a specific disease; rather, it is a condition in which congestion or an abnormal accumulation of fluid, decreased blood flow to the body, and/or abnormally low blood pressure arise as the final consequence of severe heart disease. Heart disease can be present without ever leading to heart failure. Heart failure, however, can only occur if heart disease is present because it is a consequence of heart disease. (For a more detailed discussion of HEART FAILURE, *see* page 65.)

Abnormalities of the Cardiovascular System

The following abnormalities of the cardiovascular system can lead to heart disease: 1) the heart valves fail to close or open properly (valvular disease); 2) the heart muscle pumps too weakly or relaxes inadequately (myocardial disease); 3) the heart beats too slowly, too rapidly, or too irregularly (arrhythmia); 4) the blood vessels offer too great an interference to blood flow (vascular disease); 5) there may be openings between chambers of the left side and right side of the heart (cardiac shunts); 6) there is too little or too much blood compared with the ability of the blood vessels to store that blood; and 7) there is parasitism of the cardiovascular system, such as heartworm disease.

Signs associated with any of these diseases are due either to inadequate blood flow through the organs (signs include exercise intolerance, weakness, and fainting) or to blood damming up in organs, which causes fluid to leak from blood vessels into tissues (signs include abnormal accumulation of fluid in the lungs or abdomen). A dog showing signs of having too little blood in the tissues to sustain normal function is said to be in heart failure. A dog showing signs caused by blood damming up in poorly drained organs is said to be in congestive heart failure. When there is not enough oxygen in the blood, the mucous membranes develop a blue tinge, and often there is an increased concentration of red blood cells.

The diseases of greatest importance in dogs, due to the number of cases that exist, are mitral regurgitation due to mitral valve dysplasia (*see* page 63), dilated cardiomyopathy (*see* page 69), arrhythmic cardiomyopathy in Boxers (*see* page 71), and heartworm disease (*see* page 73).

DIAGNOSIS OF CARDIOVASCULAR DISEASE

A veterinarian often diagnoses cardiovascular disease by reviewing the medical history and signs, conducting a physical examination, and interpreting the results of specific tests or imaging procedures. The physical examination includes using a stethoscope to listen to the sounds made by the dog's internal organs, especially the heart, lungs, and abdominal organs, and examining parts of the body by feeling with hands and fingers to distinguish between solid and fluid-filled swellings. Imaging techniques include x-rays; electrocardiography (recording electrical activity of the heart); and echocardiography (a type of ultrasonography). Most cardiovascular diseases can be diagnosed by physical examination and x-rays. Electrocardiography is specific for diagnosis of arrhythmias. Echocardiography is excellent for confirming tentative diagnoses, for detecting heart tumors, or for detecting pericardial disease. Occasionally, more specialized tests such as cardiac catheterization (using a thin flexible tube inserted and threaded through an artery into the heart) or nuclear studies (x-ray tests that include injection of radioactive isotopes) are necessary. Heartworm disease is diagnosed best by performing a

blood test to detect the presence of female heartworms.

Many heart disorders are more common in certain breeds. For example, mitral regurgitation is more common in Cavalier King Charles Spaniels and in older, male Cocker Spaniels. Older Miniature Schnauzers may develop specific types of arrhythmias, and tetralogy of Fallot is more common in young Wirehaired Fox Terriers. Knowledge of these and other breed associations with heart disease can often help your veterinarian make a diagnosis.

General Signs of Cardiovascular Disease

Dogs showing signs of heart disease may have a history of exercise intolerance, weakness, coughing, difficulty breathing, increased breathing rate, abdominal swelling (caused by fluid pooling in the abdomen), loss of consciousness due to lack of blood flow to the brain (fainting), a bluish tinge to skin and membranes due to a lack of oxygen in the blood, or loss of appetite and weight. More rarely, swelling of the legs, jaundice (yellowing of the eyes, skin, or membranes), or coughing up blood or bloody mucous may be noted.

TREATMENT OF CARDIOVASCULAR DISEASE

Treatment of cardiovascular disease should be specific for the type of disease. Some defects can be repaired or corrected with surgery, while other conditions can be managed with medical therapy using one or a combination of drugs. In dogs with congestive heart failure, a low-sodium diet may be recommended to help eliminate excess fluid in the body.

In general, the goals of treatment are to minimize damage to the heart muscle, control the accumulation of fluids in the lungs, improve circulation, regulate the heart rate and rhythm, ensure that there is enough oxygen in the blood, and minimize the risk of blood clot formation. In heartworm disease, the mature heartworms and larvae should be killed.

Common Types of Imaging Used to Diagnose Heart Disease

X-rays

X-rays (also called radiographs) of the chest frequently help diagnose heart disease in pets. Finding generalized enlargement of the heart or enlargement of specific heart chambers makes the presence of heart disease more likely. The images may also provide clues as to the specific disease present. For example, fluid in the lungs is a common finding in congestive heart failure. Although chest x-rays are useful in evaluating patients with heart disease, they have certain limitations. The presence of fluid in the lungs does not definitively confirm a disease originating from the heart or exclude another origin such as pulmonary (lung) disease. Also, assessment of overall heart size and the size of specific heart chambers is typically far less accurate than testing by echocardiography (ultrasonography).

Electrocardiography

Electrocardiography is the recording of the heart's electrical activity from the body surface with the use of electrodes. It can be used to identify heart arrhythmias such as bradycardia (slower than expected rhythm), tachycardia (faster than expected rhythm), or other abnormalities of rhythm (such as sinus arrhythmia or sinus arrest).

Electrocardiography can also detect conduction disturbances, or failures of the electrical signals that cause the heart to contract to pass through the heart tissue. These include first-, second-, and third-degree atrioventricular block.

Finally, electrocardiography can identify chamber enlargement, which is indicated by waveform abnormalities shown on the electrocardiogram recording. Different readings suggest enlargement of the different chambers. While the electrocardiogram may suggest chamber enlargement, chest x-rays and echocardiography (ultrasonography) are more sensitive.

Echocardiography

Echocardiography is a type of ultrasonography used to evaluate the heart, the aorta, and the pulmonary artery. Echocardiography complements other diagnostic procedures by examining and displaying the working heart and moving images of its action. Heart chamber and wall dimensions can be determined; the physical structure and motion of valves can be seen; and pressure differences, blood flow volumes, and several measurements of heart function can be calculated. There are 3 main types of echocardiography: 2-dimensional, m-mode, and doppler. Two-dimensional echocardiography provides a wedge-shaped, 2-dimensional image of the heart in real-time motion. M-mode echocardiography is produced by a 1-dimensional beam of ultrasound that penetrates the heart, providing an "ice-pick view." The tissue interfaces that are encountered by the beam are then plotted on a screen. This mode of evaluation is typically used to measure chamber dimensions, wall thickness, valve motion, and the dimensions of the aorta and pulmonary artery. Doppler echocardiography employs the principle of changing frequency of the ultrasonic beam after it contacts a moving red blood cell to measure the speed of blood flow and thus identify turbulent or high-speed flow. This can locate heart murmurs.

Cardiac Catheterization

Cardiac catheterization involves the placement of specialized catheters (thin, flexible tubes) into the heart, aorta, or pulmonary artery. Cardiac catheterization may be performed when other diagnostic tests are insufficient to identify specific heart abnormalities or are unable to identify the severity of a lesion. It may also be used for presurgical evaluation, treatment, and in clinical research. Diagnostic and presurgical cardiac catheterization, however, have largely been replaced by echocardiography (*see* above).

Common Types of Drugs for Cardiovascular Disease

There are many medications that a veterinarian can prescribe for dogs with cardiovascular disease. The type of disease will determine the type of medication prescribed. Medications must be given exactly as prescribed; otherwise, they may not be effective and may even cause serious complications and harm.

One commonly used medication for heart problems is a diuretic. **Diuretics** are medicines that increase urine output. These medicines are important and effective means for removing fluids that accumulate in dogs with heart problems. The use of a diuretic can be life saving over the short run.

Some drugs, such as **digitalis glycosides** and **digoxin**, increase the force of heart muscle contraction, slow the heart rate, and allow blood pressure receptors to work better. They are often used to treat heart failure. Drugs called **ACE inhibitors** are also used in heart failure in dogs. They can reduce blood pressure, improve cardiac output, and reduce mitral regurgitation (*see* page 68).

Other types of drugs can strengthen respiratory muscles and improve breathing. Some medications are prescribed to control arrhythmias, slow or speed heart rate, and prevent blood clots. In other cases, medications are provided to kill heartworms or other parasites in the cardiovascular system.

As with any disorder, your veterinarian will evaluate your pet and provide medication appropriate for its condition. It is the responsibility of the pet owner to follow through and provide their pet with the correct dose of medicine on the schedule prescribed by the veterinarian.

■ CONGENITAL AND INHERITED DISORDERS OF THE CARDIOVASCULAR SYSTEM

Congenital abnormalities of the cardiovascular system are defects that are present at birth. They can occur as a result of genetic defects, environmental conditions, infections, poisoning, medication taken by the mother, or poor maternal nutrition. In some cases, it is a combination of these factors that causes the defect. For several defects, an inherited basis is suspected based on breed and breeding studies. However, some studies have suggested that fewer than 1% of dogs are affected by congenital heart disease.

In addition to the congenital heart defects, many other cardiovascular disorders have been shown, or are suspected, to have a genetic basis. Diseases such as hypertrophic cardiomyopathy or dilated cardiomyopathy (*see* page 69), and degenerative valve disease of small breeds of dogs (*see* page 68) may have a significant genetic component.

Among the few dogs that do have congenital heart disease, common defects (from most to least common) include patent ductus arteriosus, pulmonic stenosis, aortic stenosis, persistent right aortic arch, and ventricular septal defect. Less common congenital cardiac defects (occurring in less than 5% of cases) include tetralogy of Fallot, atrial septal defect, persistent left cranial vena cava, mitral valve dysplasia, tricuspid dysplasia, and cor triatriatum dexter. There are regional differences, however, in the occurrence of these defects. The most common congenital canine heart defects in the United States vary from those reported in the United Kingdom and may likely differ from those in other parts of Europe and other regions.

Detecting Congenital Heart Defects

It is important to detect a congenital heart defect as early as possible. Certain defects can be corrected with surgery, and treatment should be performed before the defect leads to congestive heart failure or irreversible heart damage. If the defect is discovered in a recently purchased dog, you may be able to return it for a refund. Pets with congenital heart defects are likely to die prematurely, causing emotional distress. Early detection also allows owners to avoid breeding dogs with genetic defects and prevent continuing genetic defects in breeding lines.

The evaluation of most animals with a congenital heart defect may include a physical examination, electrocardiography (recording electrical activity of the heart), x-rays, and echocardiography (ultrasonography). These steps allow diagnosis and assessment of the severity of the defect.

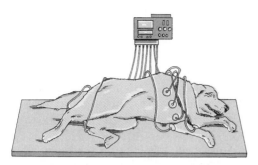

Electrocardiograms can show cardiac arrhythmias and other abnormalities in dogs.

Congenital heart defects produce signs that vary depending on the type of heart failure involved. Possible signs include shortness of breath or difficulty breathing, coughing, fainting, fatigue, or an accumulation of fluid in the lungs or abdomen.

General Treatment and Outlook

The medical importance of congenital heart disease depends on the particular defect and its severity. Mildly affected dogs may show no ill effects and live a normal life span. Defects causing significant circulatory disturbances will likely cause death in newborn (and unborn) puppies. Medical or surgical treatments are most likely to benefit animals with congenital heart defects of moderate severity. Surgical correction is indicated in most affected dogs as long as no other diseases or abnormalities are present that would pose a risk to anesthesia or surgery.

Innocent Murmurs

It is very important to understand that the presence of a heart murmur in a young puppy does not necessarily indicate a congenital heart defect. Many puppies have a low-grade systolic murmur (heard while the ventricles contract) that is not associated with a congenital heart defect. These murmurs usually disappear by 6 months of age. However, loud systolic murmurs and diastolic murmurs (heard while the ventricles relax) do indicate cardiac dis-

ease and should prompt further investigation by your veterinarian.

Common Congenital Heart Abnormalities

The defects discussed below are those that occur with the greatest frequency in dogs. However, it is important to stress that these defects are rare.

Patent Ductus Arteriosus

The ductus arteriosus is a short, broad vessel in the unborn fetus that connects the pulmonary artery with the aorta and allows most of the blood to flow directly from the right ventricle to the aorta. Before birth, oxygenated blood within the main pulmonary artery passes into the descending aorta through the ductus arteriosus, bypassing the nonfunctional lungs. At birth, inflation of the lungs upon the puppy's first breath causes the ductus to close and allows the blood to flow to the lungs.

If the ductus does not close, the blood flow is forced from chambers of the left side of the heart to those of the right side; these defects are called left-to-right shunts. They result in overcirculation of the lungs and enlargement of the heart chambers, which may result in arrhythmias. Over time, signs of left-side congestive heart failure develop.

Dogs with a small ductus may reach adulthood without signs of heart failure but are at an increased risk of an inflammation and infection of the lining of the heart (infective endocarditis). Occasionally, a large patent ductus arteriosus may cause high blood pressure in the arteries of the lungs, creating an increased workload for the heart. This can cause shunting through the ductus to slow and reverse (that is, it becomes a right-to-left shunt).

In dogs with a **patent ductus arteriosus with left-to-right shunting**, a very noticeable, continuous, machinery-like murmur can be detected. In some newborn puppies, the ductus remains open for several days after birth. Most young puppies do not exhibit any signs. Those with a large shunt and older dogs often have signs of left-sided congestive heart failure. Arrhythmias (abnormal heart rhythms) may also be heard. Large abnormalities may show up on x-rays. Echocardiography is valuable in excluding coexisting heart defects present since birth, as well as showing the presence of the patent ductus arteriosus.

Surgery to tie off the ductus in dogs with left-to-right shunting patent ductus arteriosus usually cures the problem and is almost always the best treatment option. Drugs to treat congestive heart failure may be needed before surgery can be performed. An alternative to surgically tying off the ductus is interventional closure. This can be accomplished by using a catheter to place a device in the patent ductus arteriosus that results in blood clot formation or physical obstruction of the ductus.

In animals with a **patent ductus arteriosus with right-to-left shunting**, there is usually a history of fatigue, exercise intolerance, and collapse. Careful examination may reveal a slight bluish tinge to skin and membranes. Your veterinarian may note other abnormalities such as a split heart sound, a soft murmur, or an abnormal increase in red blood cells. Electrocardiography and echocardiography may be useful in diagnosis.

Surgically tying off the ductus should not be performed in this situation because this will cause an increase in blood pressure in the arteries of the lungs and typically death. Treatment involves control of the increase in red blood cells through periodic blood-letting. The longterm outlook for affected dogs is poor.

Pulmonic Stenosis

Pulmonic stenosis causes an obstruction to the blood flow from the right ventricle. In most cases, the obstruction is due to abnormal development of the flaps on the valves between the pulmonary artery and the right ventricle. However, the stenosis can also occur in the cone-shaped opening, the subvalvular region (within the outflow tract of the right ventricle), or in the area beyond the pulmonary valve.

The right ventricle must generate increased pressure during contraction to overcome the stenosis. In moderate to severe cases, the increased pressure can lead to severe enlargement of the right ventricle with thickening of the muscle fibers. As muscle fibers of the right ventricle thicken, the ability of the ventricle to do its job diminishes, leading to increased right atrial pressure and congestion in the veins. The increased speed of blood flow results in an enlarged artery. In severe cases, right-sided congestive failure may be noted.

Dogs with pulmonic stenosis may have a history of failure to thrive and exercise intolerance. Signs of right-sided congestive heart failure, such as accumulation or fluid in the abdomen or limbs, may be present. A loud murmur can be heard, and a swollen and pulsating jugular vein may also be present. Electrocardiography, x-rays, and echocardiography may be helpful in diagnosing this condition. Doppler echocardiography is valuable in determining the severity of the stenosis.

Dogs with moderate or severe pulmonic stenosis may improve following surgery. The choice of surgical procedure depends to some degree on the presence and degree of thickening of the muscle fibers below the valve. Your veterinarian will best be able to determine the appropriate treatment for your pet. Drugs such as diuretics and vasodilators (drugs that widen blood vessels) should be started if right-sided congestive heart failure is present. The outlook is poor if atrial fibrillation or right-sided congestive heart failure is present. If atrial fibrillation is noted, your veterinarian may prescribe digitalis to control the arrhythmia.

Aortic Stenosis

Blood flow from the left ventricle may be obstructed in several ways. A ridge of fibrous tissue located within the outflow tract of the left ventricle can reduce flow. This is called **subaortic stenosis**. In other cases, the obstruction may be within the valve leading out of the left ventricle (**valvular stenosis**) or even past the aortic valve (**supravalvular stenosis**). Among dogs, supravalvular stenosis occurred most frequently in Boxers, Golden Retrievers, Rottweilers, German Shepherds, and Newfoundlands.

Aortic stenosis causes thickening of the muscle fibers of the left ventricle. A major effect of this thickening of the muscle fibers is the creation of areas of poor blood flow throughout the heart. When the supply of blood to the heart muscle is low, the heart does not get enough oxygen and is unable to rid itself of carbon dioxide and other cellular waste products. This condition is a major factor in the development of life-threatening ventricular rhythm problems.

In some cases of aortic stenosis, there may be a history of loss of consciousness (fainting) due to lack of blood flow to the brain and problems with normal levels of exercise. In other cases, animals with no history of illness may die suddenly and the defect is detected only after death. Sometimes a murmur can be detected with a stethoscope. If stenosis is suspected, the veterinarian may check the electrical activity of the heart using electrocardiography. In cases where a dog faints frequently or shows other signs of possible heart rhythm problems, the veterinarian may monitor heart activity over a full day. Other tests, such as x-rays or ultrasonography, may also be used.

Treatment options include medication to reduce problems associated with exercise intolerance or fainting. Surgery may also help, although the procedures are costly to perform and may be risky. Mildly affected dogs commonly require no treatment and the outlook can be fair to good. Your veterinarian will be able to determine the most appropriate course of treatment for your dog. Dogs with aortic stenosis should not be used for breeding.

Persistent Right Aortic Arch

When this abnormality is present at birth, the right aortic arch passes behind the the esophagus. This squeezes the esophagus and constricts it near the heart. Persistent right aortic arch has been reported in horses, cats, and dogs. German Shepherds and Irish Setters develop this abnormality more frequently than other breeds.

Ventricular Septal Defects

Ventricular septal defects (openings between the left and right ventricles) vary in size and effects on blood circulation. Ventricular septal defects may occur with other abnormalities of the heart present at birth.

Shunting of blood from the left ventricle into the right ventricle is the most common result of this defect, due to the higher pressures of the left ventricle. Blood shunted into the right ventricle is recirculated through the blood vessels in the lungs and left heart chambers, which causes enlargement of these structures. The right ventricle may enlarge as well. Significant shunting through the pulmonary arteries can induce narrowing of these vessels, leading to reduced blood flow or increased blood pressure. As resistance rises, the shunt may reverse (that is, become a right-to-left shunting of blood).

Signs depend on the severity of the defect and the shunt direction. A small defect usually causes minimal or no signs. Larger defects may result in severe left-sided congestive heart failure. The development of a right-to-left shunt is indicated by a bluish tinge, fatigue, and exercise intolerance. Most affected animals have a loud murmur; however, this murmur is absent or faint when a very large defect is present or when shunting is right to left. Chest x-rays, echocardiography (ultrasonography), and other more specialized techniques may be used to confirm the defect.

Treatment also depends on the severity of signs and direction of the shunt. Dogs with small ventricular septal defects do not typically require treatment and the outlook is good. Dogs with a moderate to severe defect more commonly develop signs, and treatment should be considered. Surgery to close the defect or decrease shunting or drugs to reduce blood pressure may be considered in the treatment of dogs with a large ventricular septal defect and left-to-right shunting. With right-to-left shunting, surgical closure of the defect is generally not advised. Bloodletting to relieve the effects of increased red blood cells or the use of certain drugs may be considered to relieve signs; however, the outlook for the dogs is poor to guarded. Dogs with a ventricular septal defect should not be bred. The defect has been shown to be inherited in English Springer Spaniels.

Tetralogy of Fallot

Tetralogy of Fallot is a defect that produces a bluish tinge to skin and membranes because there is not enough oxygen in the blood. It is caused by a combination of pulmonic stenosis (*see* page 60), a ventricular septal defect (*see* page 61), thickening of the muscle fibers of the right ventricle, and varying degrees of the aorta rotating to the right. Breeds most inclined to have tetralogy of Fallot include Keeshonds, English Bulldogs, Miniature Poodles, Miniature Schnauzers, and Wirehaired Fox Terriers. The trait is inherited in Keeshonds and presumably in other breeds. However, this defect has been recognized in other breeds of dogs.

The effect on the animal of this grouping of defects depends primarily on the severity of the pulmonic stenosis, the size of the ventricular septal defect, and the amount of resistance to blood flow provided by the blood vessels. Consequences may include reduced blood flow to the lungs (resulting in fatigue and shortness of breath) and generalized lack of oxygen in the blood causing a bluish tinge to skin and membranes. Red blood cells may be abnormally increased, leading to the development of blood clots and poor circulation of blood. Typical signs in dogs include stunted growth, exercise intolerance, collapse, and seizures. Electrocardiographs, x-rays, and echocardiography (ultrasonography) can help confirm the diagnosis.

Treatment options include surgery and medical management. Surgery to correct the defects or to relieve pain has been reported in dogs but is rarely performed. In some cases, reducing pulmonic steno-sis helps to reduce pain and signs of disease. Beta-adrenergic blocking drugs and bloodletting have been used in dogs with tetralogy of Fallot. The outlook is guarded, but dogs with mild to moderate shunting may reach adulthood.

Atrial Septal Defects

Before birth a flapped oval opening of the membrane between the atria allows shunting of blood from the right to the left side in order to bypass the nonfunctional lungs. At birth, the drop in right atrial pressure causes the flapped oval opening to close and shunting to stop. Increased right atrial pressure may reopen the flap where the membranes have not sealed and allow shunting to resume. This is not a true atrial septal defect because the membranes have formed normally. A true atrial septal defect is a consistent opening of the membranes, which allows blood to shunt from one atrium to the other.

In most cases, blood flows from the left atrium to the right atrium, causing an overload of the right-sided chambers. The volume of shunting depends on the size of the defect and the change in pressure across the defect. Excessive blood flow through the right-sided chambers results in their enlargement and thickening of their muscle fibers. Narrowing of the pulmonary blood vessels may occur as a consequence of excessive pulmonary blood flow and may quickly cause right-sided congestive heart failure. In situations in which right atrial pressure increases (for example, pulmonic stenosis) shunting from right to left across an opening that failed to close or an atrial septal defect may occur.

Signs of right-sided heart failure (for example, accumulation of fluid in the abdomen, fluid accumulation in tissues, bluish tinge to skin and mucous membranes) may be present. A murmur is usually present, and arrhythmias may be noted. Electrocardiography, x-rays, and echocardiography may be useful in visualizing the defect. The results show varying degrees of enlargement of the right atrium and right ventricle.

Surgery to correct the defect may be attempted but is associated with high cost and a high death rate. Dogs with certain types of defects can tolerate the defects well and many of these defects are only found during routine examinations of older animals. Other types of defects, however, are more likely to cause right-sided congestive heart failure. High blood pressure in the arteries of the lungs can also occur. The outlook for recovery is guarded to poor in these cases.

Mitral Valve Dysplasia

Mitral valve dysplasia refers to abnormal development or malformation of the mitral valve of the heart, allowing regurgitation of blood back into the left atrium. Breeds of dogs most likely to have mitral valve dysplasia are Bull Terriers, German Shepherds, and Great Danes.

Longterm mitral regurgitation results in enlargement of the left ventricle and atrium. When the regurgitation is severe, blood flow from the heart decreases, producing signs of heart failure. Arrhythmias may develop. In some cases, malformation of the mitral valve causes stenosis, or narrowing, of the valve (*see* MITRAL STENOSIS, below).

The signs of mitral valve dysplasia depend on the severity of the defect. Signs of left-sided congestive heart failure, such as coughing and difficulty breathing, are often seen. An electrocardiogram may show arrhythmias in severely affected dogs. Chest x-rays, echocardiography, and other specialized techniques help to confirm the defect.

The outlook for dogs with signs and severe disease is poor. Mildly affected animals may remain free of signs for several years. Signs of left-sided congestive heart failure can be treated (*see* page 65).

Mitral Stenosis

Mitral valve stenosis is a narrowing of the mitral valve opening caused by abnor-

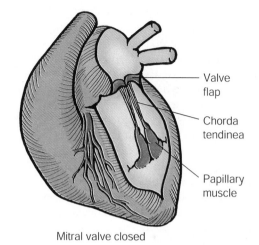

Valve flap

Chorda tendinea

Papillary muscle

Mitral valve closed

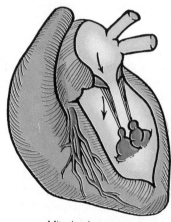

Mitral valve open

The mitral valve has flaps that open and close like swinging doors. Tethers prevent the valves from swinging backward and leaking.

malities of the mitral valve. This obstructs blood inflow to the left ventricle. The defect is rare in dogs, but it can occur together with other congenital defects such as subaortic stenosis, mitral valve dysplasia, and pulmonic stenosis (all discussed earlier in this chapter).

Mitral stenosis results in enlargement of the left atrium and an increase in blood pressure within the veins of the lungs. Fluid in the lungs can develop as a consequence. Loss of consciousness due to lack of blood flow to the brain occurs in some dogs with these defects. A low-grade heart murmur can sometimes be detected. If mitral valve dysplasia (*see* page 63) is present together with the stenosis, a louder murmur may be heard. X-rays and electrocardiography are useful in showing the effects of stenosis; echocardiography (ultrasonography) can confirm the diagnosis.

Dogs with mitral valve stenosis may be prescribed diuretics (to help eliminate fluid buildup) and put on a low-salt diet. Diuretic use should be carefully monitored because it can cause excessive urine output, which may severely reduce blood flow from the heart. Surgery and other treatments are rarely performed because they involve both considerable risk for the animal and high cost.

Tricuspid Dysplasia

Tricuspid dysplasia refers to abnormal development or malformation of the tricuspid valve of the heart, allowing regurgitation of blood back into the right atrium. This defect is seen occasionally in dogs at birth. Breeds most likely to have tricuspid dysplasia are Labrador Retrievers and German Shepherds. Rarely, stenosis (narrowing) of the tricuspid valve can be noted. Other defects of the heart may also be noted in affected dogs.

Longterm tricuspid regurgitation leads to volume overload of the right heart, enlarging the right ventricle and atrium. Blood flow to the lungs may be decreased, leading to fatigue and an increased rate of respiration. As the pressure in the right atrium increases, blood pools in the veins returning to the heart, causing an accumulation of fluid in the abdomen.

The more severe the defect, the more obvious the signs will be in affected dogs. Signs of right-sided congestive heart failure, such as accumulation of fluid in the abdomen and lungs, may be seen. A loud heart murmur is very noticeable. Arrhythmias, especially the sudden onset of a very high heart rate, are common and may cause death. Electrocardiography and x-rays may show enlargement of the right ventricle and atrium, while the malformed tricuspid valve can sometimes be seen using echocardiography (ultrasonography).

The outlook for dogs with these signs is guarded. Periodic draining of fluid from the abdomen may be needed. Medications such as diuretics, vasodilators, and digoxin may also be prescribed.

Hernias Between the Abdomen and Membrane Surrounding the Heart

An abnormal opening between the abdomen and the membrane surrounding the heart (peritoneopericardial diaphragmatic hernia) occurs as a birth defect in dogs. A diaphragmatic hernia is an abnormal opening in the membrane that separates the abdomen from the chest cavity. The result is a hole through which the abdominal organs can protrude up into the chest. The liver is most commonly herniated, followed by the small intestine, spleen, and stomach. Signs vary, with many patients showing no signs and the defect being discovered only after death. Chest x-rays or specialized contrast x-rays can show the intestine or liver crossing the membrane into the sac surrounding the heart (the pericardium). The diagnosis can also be made using echocardiography (ultrasonography). Patients with vomiting, signs of hepatic encephalopathy (a disease of the brain due to a buildup of toxic substances that are normally removed by the liver), or other adverse conditions resulting from the hernia should have surgery to repair the hernia.

Cor Triatriatum Dexter

Cor triatriatum dexter results from a fibrous membrane dividing the right atrium and has been reported in dogs. The affected atrium is divided into 2 chambers. There are commonly one or more perforations in the separating membrane, allowing communication between the 2 portions of the atrium. Surgery can be performed to correct this disease.

Normal Valve Mechanisms

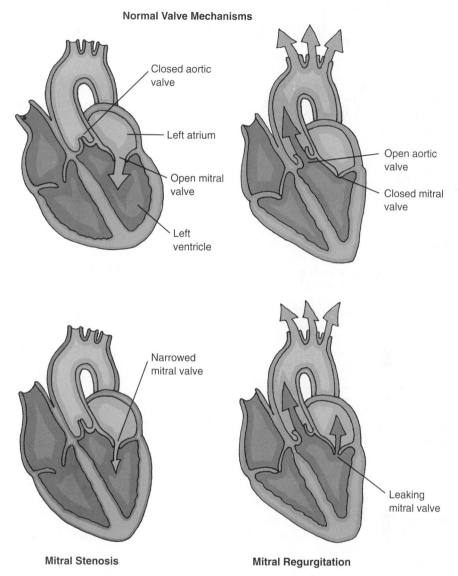

Mitral stenosis and regurgitation (modified with permission from *The Merck Manual of Medical Information*, Second Home Edition, 2003)

◼ HEART FAILURE

Heart failure is not a specific disease or diagnosis. It is a syndrome in which severe dysfunction results in failure of the cardiovascular system to maintain adequate blood circulation. There are limited and specific mechanisms by which heart disease can result in failure of the cardio-vascular system. Therefore, there are limited and specific signs that can develop as a result of heart failure.

Types of Heart Failure

Heart failure can be divided into 4 functional classifications: systolic myocardial failure, impedance to cardiac inflow, pressure overload, and volume overload.

Heart Failure, Congestive Heart Failure, and the Failing Heart

Any heart with a reduced ability to contract is considered a **failing heart**. Almost any dog with heart disease that leads to chamber enlargement or increased wall thickness has a failing heart, but the body usually is able to compensate in other ways for these physical changes. As a result, the dog has no signs and is not in heart failure or congestive heart failure.

Heart failure and congestive heart failure are medical syndromes in which a dog exhibits signs related to a complex interaction between a failing heart and the blood vessels.

In **heart failure**, the blood flow is insufficient to supply organs with enough oxygenated blood for proper function. Depending on the degree of severity, signs of heart failure may appear while the dog is at rest, during mild exertion, or during moderate or extreme exercise.

In **congestive heart failure**, blood dams up in organs—usually the lungs but occasionally in the body's other major organs—and causes the congested organs to function abnormally, become swollen with fluid, or both.

Systolic myocardial failure is a general reduction in the ability of the heart muscle to contract. This can be identified with echocardiography (ultrasonography). There is reduced wall motion during contraction of the ventricles. If the reduction is significant, normal blood flow cannot be maintained. It may be caused by trauma, infection, drugs or poisons, electric shock, heat stroke, or tumors. Some cases have no known cause.

Heart failure resulting from the **impedance (obstruction) to cardiac inflow** may result in a decrease in blood flow. This may be caused by external compression of the heart (for example, fluid in the sac surrounding the heart), diastolic dysfunction resulting in a stiff ventricle and reduced ventricular filling, or abnormalities to physical structures of the heart.

Heart failure caused by **pressure overload** occurs as a result of longterm increases in stress to the heart wall during contraction. This may result from the obstruction of blood flow from the heart or increased blood pressure throughout the body or in the arteries of the lungs.

Volume overload heart failure occurs as a result of any disease that increases volume of blood in the ventricle(s), thus increasing blood flow. Eventually, this can bring on signs of congestive heart failure. Diseases that result in volume overload myocardial failure include valve disease (for example, degenerative valve disease of the atrioventricular valves), left-to-right shunts (for example, patent ductus arteriosus, ventricular septal defect), or high-output states (such as those caused by hyperthyroidism or anemia).

Compensatory Mechanisms

The cardiovascular system maintains normal blood pressure and blood flow. In heart disease, the body uses specific mechanisms to attempt to normalize these functions and offset the negative effects the disease is having on the body. In an animal with dilated cardiomyopathy, for example, the blood flow is slowed by the heart's reduced ability to contract. This leads to a reduced blood pressure because less blood is pumped with each beat. The body compensates by using the sympathetic nervous system to increase the ability of the heart muscle to contract and to increase heart rate. These responses increase cardiac output and blood pressure. Unfortunately, longterm use of the sympathetic nervous system in this way damages the heart muscle and other organs. The damage again reduces the ability of the heart muscle to contract and leads to a cascade of actions, including the release of various hormones, that result in another increase in blood volume and blood flow. Blood volume can increase as much as 30% in pets with severe congestive heart failure. Eventually, progressive heart muscle failure and longterm activation of these hormones in an effort to normalize blood flow result in continued heart muscle failure. Blood flow becomes further compromised with progressive signs of congestive heart failure.

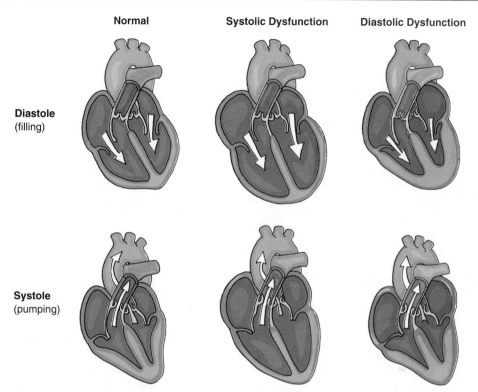

Normal   Systolic Dysfunction   Diastolic Dysfunction

Diastole
(filling)

Systole
(pumping)

Heart failure may involve systolic or diastolic dysfunction. In diastolic dysfunction, not enough blood is able to fill the heart before pumping. In systolic dysfunction, the heart is too weak to pump out enough blood. Both conditions lead to poor circulation. See the text for more details (modified with permission from *The Merck Manual of Medical Information*, Second Home Edition, 2003).

Signs of Heart Failure

Signs associated with heart failure depend on the causes of the heart failure and the heart chamber that is affected. With **left-sided congestive heart failure**, signs are associated with a backup of pressure in the vessels delivering blood to the left ventricle. Fluid in the lungs and congestion (coughing, difficulty breathing) are the most common signs. Many dogs with left-sided congestive heart failure faint due to lack of blood flow to the brain. They may also have a low heart rate and low blood pressure and may collapse.

Right-sided congestive heart failure results in increased pressure in the vessels delivering blood to the right ventricle and the body's veins and capillaries. This may cause fluid to build up in the abdomen (ascites), the chest cavity, and the limbs.

Biventricular failure can arise when both the right and left ventricles are not working properly, such as in dogs with heart muscle failure resulting from dilated cardiomyopathy or poisoning. Signs attributable to both forms of congestive heart failure can be noted, although it is common for signs of one to outweigh the other.

Treatment

It is important to treat heart failure in order to improve heart muscle performance, control arrhythmias and blood pressure, improve blood flow, and reduce the amount of blood filling the heart before contraction. All of these can further damage the heart and blood vessels if not controlled. It is also necessary to reduce the amount of fluid in the lungs, abdomen, or chest cavity.

Drugs

There are many types of drugs available for treating heart failure. The specific drugs, dosage, and frequency used will vary depending on the cause and severity of the heart failure and other factors. Your veterinarian is best able to decide on the appropriate drugs for your pet. All drugs prescribed by a veterinarian must be given to the animal as directed. Otherwise, they may not be effective and may even cause serious complications or harm.

Diuretics are usually prescribed for managing fluid overload in animals. Digitalis and digoxin, part of a group of drugs known as positive inotropes, may be used to help the heart muscle contract. ACE inhibitors (ACE stands for angiotensin-converting enzyme) and vasodilators can widen blood vessels and thus lower blood pressure. Beta-adrenergic blocking drugs (also called beta-blockers) and calcium channel blockers are helpful in some cases of congestive heart failure.

Nutrition

Some types of heart failure are caused by a deficiency of a nutrient and can be treated by supplementation with the missing nutrient. However, this type of heart failure is rare.

A **low-sodium diet** is frequently recommended for dogs with severe congestive heart failure that does not respond well to conventional treatment. In dogs with mild to moderate congestive heart failure, severe sodium restriction is not needed, but diets high in salt should be avoided. Prescription diets tailored for these differing levels of sodium restriction are readily available, as are recipes for home-made salt restricted diets. Sodium-free snacks should also be given in place of regular treats. Salt should not be restricted in dogs with heart disease that have no sign of congestive heart failure, because this can result in early activation of certain hormones.

Other Treatments

Dogs with severe left-sided congestive heart failure and fluid in the lungs (pulmo-nary edema) may not get enough oxygen. **Oxygen** can be given by way of an oxygen cage, tight-fitting mask, or nose tube.

Thoracentesis and **abdominocentesis** are surgical procedures in which a needle is inserted into the chest cavity or abdomen, respectively, to withdraw excess fluid. It may be used to treat dogs with congestive heart failure that have an accumulation of fluid in these areas. The procedure can lead to rapid improvement in signs, has no significant adverse effects, and can be performed on a regular basis, if needed.

Bronchodilator treatment is generally reserved for patients with longterm airway disease. It is not typically used to treat congestive heart failure. The exception to this is for dogs that faint as a result of a brief cardiac arrhythmia associated with heart disease such as degenerative valve disease.

Cough suppressants are generally not recommended in the treatment of congestive heart failure, because masking signs of cough can worsen the underlying fluid in the lungs. If, however, a dog diagnosed with severe heart disease is coughing, and heart enlargement on chest x-rays shows no fluid in the lungs, the coughing may be caused by the enlarged heart pressing on the airways. Cough suppressants may be helpful for these dogs.

■ ACQUIRED HEART AND BLOOD VESSEL DISORDERS

Dogs can have a variety of cardiovascular diseases. The most common ones are discussed below.

Degenerative Valve Disease

Degenerative valve disease is the most common heart disease in dogs and accounts for about 75% of cardiovascular disease in this species. This disease is characterized by thickening of the heart valves. It most commonly affects the mitral or tricuspid valve. The disease is age- and breed-related. The cause is unknown, but, in Cavalier King Charles Spaniels (which are prone to this disease), it is believed to be inherited.

It is more common in older, small-breed dogs. Male dogs are also more likely to develop it than female dogs.

Failure of the valve to close properly results in turbulent blood flow. Blood is regurgitated into the atrium, leading to an increase in pressure. If the mitral valve is affected, the result is elevated blood pressure in the capillaries of the lungs and, ultimately, fluid in the lungs. If the tricuspid valve is affected, elevated blood pressure in the body's veins occurs, and accumulation of fluid in the abdomen may develop. Further damage to the heart can occur due to the continued high-speed flow of blood back into the atrium and also to the body's attempts to compensate for the decreased blood flow. Over time, these compensatory mechanisms become harmful rather than beneficial.

In dogs, there are no signs during the early stages of the disease, although a heart murmur can be heard. As the disease progresses, affected dogs may be unwilling to move or exercise, have difficulty breathing, and develop a cough. Fainting may also occur due to decreased blood flow or arrhythmia. Sudden death is rare, but may occur.

A veterinarian can often diagnose degenerative valve disease based on physical examination findings and appropriate imaging procedures, which may include chest x-rays and echocardiography (ultrasonography). Arrhythmias may develop as the disease progresses and can be detected with electrocardiography.

Treatment in small-breed dogs should begin when signs start to appear or when fluid in the lungs is found on chest x-rays. Optimal treatment should be planned by your veterinarian for each stage of disease.

Treatment for early signs of congestive heart failure includes ACE inhibitors (*see* page 1122) to reduce adverse hormonal effects caused by activation of the certain hormones, and to reduce mitral regurgitation and signs of fluid in the lungs. Control of fluid in the lungs is also accomplished by use of diuretics. Arrhythmias can be controlled with the use of medications to improve heart function and reduce signs of congestive heart failure. Other drugs or therapy (such as administration of oxygen) may be added as needed. Affected dogs can live for years with appropriate treatment.

Disorders of the Heart Muscle (Cardiomyopathy)

Cardiomyopathy is the name for any disease that mostly affects the heart muscle. The cardiomyopathies of animals are diseases with no known cause that are not the result of any generalized or primary heart disease. Several types of cardiomyopathy occur in animals; however, dilated cardiomyopathy is the only type commonly seen in dogs. Cardiomyopathy can also occur as a result of other diseases. In these cases, they are usually called secondary myocardial diseases.

Dilated Cardiomyopathy

Dilated cardiomyopathy is an acquired disease that causes the progressive loss of the heart muscle's ability to contract. The cause is not known. It has a very long early phase in dogs, during which no signs are detectable. Signs then become evident for a relatively short period of time.

Dilated cardiomyopathy is one of the most common acquired heart diseases of dogs, only surpassed by degenerative valve disease and, in some parts of the world, heartworm disease. The disease is typically seen in middle-aged dogs. More males are affected than females. It most commonly affects large-breed dogs, with a few exceptions such as American Cocker Spaniels, Springer Spaniels, and English Cocker Spaniels. Some large-breed dogs that are particularly at risk include Doberman Pinschers, Boxers, Great Danes, German Shepherds, Irish Wolfhounds, Scottish Deerhounds, Newfoundland Retrievers, Saint Bernards, and Labrador Retrievers.

The signs of dilated cardiomyopathy may vary by breed, but include episodes of weakness or collapse, fainting, difficulty breathing, coughing, unwillingness to move, and accumulation of fluid in the chest or abdomen.

A low-grade murmur may be heard during a veterinary examination; sometimes a third heart sound or gallop heart sound is also present. Femoral pulses (in the thigh) may be weak, and an arrhythmia may be noted. Chest x-rays are helpful in showing enlargement of the heart and, if present, fluid in the lungs. Many veterinarians consider echocardiography (ultrasonography) the ideal test to diagnose dilated cardiomyopathy. Electrocardiograms may show arrhythmias or enlargement of the left atrium and ventricle.

The objectives of treatment are to control the congestion and fluid accumulation (diuretics are often prescribed), improve the ability of the heart to contract, and reduce adverse effects of hormonal changes.

Some cardiomyopathies result from a lack of a particular amino acid or enzyme and can be treated by reversing the lack. For example, myocardial failure due to the lack of an amino acid called taurine occurs in some breeds, particularly American Cocker Spaniels, Golden Retrievers, and Dalmatians, and possibly Welsh Corgis, Tibetan Terriers, and other breeds. In many of these breeds, blood tests can confirm a diagnosis of taurine deficiency. Response to taurine supplementation (which may take 2 to 4 weeks) can be dramatic, many times eliminating the need for other heart medications. Carnitine-responsive cardiomyopathy has been reported in Boxers and Doberman Pinschers; however, supplementation with L-carnitine may be cost prohibitive. Administration of fish oil may reduce the severity of weight and muscle loss in dogs with dilated cardiomyopathy. Your veterinarian will recommend a treatment program that meets your pet's needs.

Congestive heart failure, which may be severe, often occurs and should be treated appropriately (*see* HEART FAILURE, page 65). As fluid in the lungs resolves, your veterinarian is likely to prescribe medications to improve the ability of your pet's heart to function. Antiarrhythmic treatment is frequently indicated, especially for Doberman Pinschers and Boxers with severe arrhythmias.

Dogs that are taurine or carnitine responsive have a fair to good outlook once signs of congestive heart failure lessen. The outlook is poor in most Doberman Pinschers. About 65% die within 8 weeks of diagnosis of heart failure. The outlook in other breeds is better but remains guarded—75% die within 6 months of diagnosis. Dogs with severe heart failure, particularly left-sided congestive heart failure, have a worse outlook than those with milder signs or signs of right-sided congestive heart failure.

Hypertrophic Cardiomyopathy

Hypertrophic cardiomyopathy is a condition in which the walls of the left ventricle thicken and become stiff as a result of a heart muscle disorder. This can lead to decreased blood flow and volume, accumulation of fluid in the chest and lungs, and the formation of blood clots. Hypertrophic cardiomyopathy is rare in dogs. Signs may include those of heart failure (coughing, difficulty breathing), collapse, and paralysis of the back legs; sometimes no signs are noted. Treatment should include medication to relieve signs of congestive heart failure, restore heart muscle function, and prevent blood clots.

Myocarditis

Myocarditis is a local or widespread inflammation of the heart muscle with degeneration or death of the heart muscle cells. There are numerous causes, including viruses (for example, canine parvovirus), bacteria (for example, *Borrelia burgdorferi*, which causes Lyme disease), and protozoa (for example, *Trypanosoma cruzi*, which causes Chagas' disease). Deficiencies of minerals such as iron, selenium, or copper can also result in degeneration of the heart muscle. Deficiencies of vitamin E or selenium may cause death of the heart muscle. Certain antibiotics and plant toxins (poisons) can also cause myocarditis.

Signs include the typical signs of congestive heart failure, including heart murmurs and arrhythmias. Your veterinarian may request echocardiography (ultrasonography) and certain blood tests for diagnosis.

Treatment is directed at improving the ability of the heart to contract, relieving congestion, and controlling the narrowing of blood vessels (which can increase blood pressure). Your veterinarian will prescribe the most appropriate medication or drug combination for your pet.

Other Causes of Heart Muscle Failure

A form of cardiomyopathy called **atrial standstill** destroys the muscle wall of the atrium. In some dogs it affects the muscle wall of the ventricle as well. Eventually, heart muscle failure occurs. The condition has been reported in English Springer Spaniels, Old English Sheepdogs, Shih Tzus, German Shorthaired Pointers, and mixed-breed dogs.

Signs are similar to those of dilated cardiomyopathy (*see* page 69), with right or left heart failure being noted. Treatment is similar to that provided for other heart muscle failure disorders, but it may not be effective. Pacemaker implantation may improve heart rate and blood flow.

Endocardial fibroelastosis is a disease of unknown cause that leads to thickening of the thin membranous lining of the left atrium, left ventricle, and mitral valve. It is a rare cause of heart muscle failure in young dogs. Affected animals are usually less than 6 months of age and have signs of left-sided heart failure. Breeds affected by this disease include Labrador Retrievers, Great Danes, English Bulldogs, Springer Spaniels, Boxers, and Pit Bull Terriers. Signs, treatment, and outlook are similar to those for dilated cardiomyopathy.

Arrhythmogenic right ventricular cardiomyopathy is a rare cause of heart muscle failure in dogs. It is restricted primarily to the right side of the heart, but may also involve the left ventricle. It is characterized by a fibrous and fatty muscle of the right ventricle causing progressive heart muscle failure. Difficulty breathing, increased breathing rate, fainting, and nonspecific signs such as loss of appetite and lethargy may be seen.

Treatment is similar to that for dilated cardiomyopathy.

Duchenne's cardiomyopathy is an inherited disorder associated with the X chromosome. It has been reported in dogs, particularly Golden Retrievers. A similar disease called X-linked muscular dystrophy has been reported in Irish Terriers, Samoyeds, and Rottweilers. These diseases may affect heart muscle as well as nerve and muscle tissue elsewhere in the body. Tissue changes usually develop by 6 to 7 months of age and decrease in size over the next 2 years. In patients that survive, heart muscle failure may develop.

Infective Endocarditis

The endocardium is the thin membrane that lines the heart cavity. Infection of the endocardium typically involves one of the heart valves, although endocarditis of the cavity's wall may occur. Infection is caused by bacteria carried in the blood. The infection gradually destroys the valve and keeps it from working properly. In dogs, the aortic and mitral valves are most commonly affected. Middle-aged dogs and large breeds are most likely to develop endocarditis. Males are more commonly affected than females.

Bacteria released from the infected valves enter the circulation and can infect other organs. Therefore, infective endocarditis can produce a wide range of signs from various body systems, including primary cardiovascular effects or signs related to the nervous, digestive, urinary, or reproductive systems, or joints. Fever that comes and goes, lameness that shifts from one leg to another, weight loss, and lethargy are seen in many cases. If a right-sided valve is affected, fluid may accumulate in the abdomen, and a large pulse in the jugular vein may be present. Blood and pus in the urine may also be noted. A heart murmur is present in most cases; the exact type depends on the valve involved.

Bacteria most often found in affected pets include *Streptococcus*, *Staphylococcus*, and *Klebsiella* species, and *Escherichia coli*.

Other bacteria or fungi may be involved. Various blood samples may be needed for diagnosis and to monitor the effects of the infection. X-rays may show enlargement of a heart chamber; however, echocardiography (ultrasonography) is the diagnostic test of choice for most veterinarians, because blood tests are positive in only 50 to 90% of dogs. Electrocardiography (recording electrical activity of the heart) may show arrhythmias.

Treatment and Prevention

Treatment is directed at controlling signs of congestive heart failure, resolving any significant arrhythmias, killing the bacteria that started the infection, and eliminating the spread of infection. Controlling heart failure requires the use of diuretics, ACE inhibitors, and, in some cases, digoxin. The outlook is poor in most dogs. Those that respond to treatment will likely require longterm heart medications and frequent reevaluations. Your veterinarian will prescribe a drug treatment program that is appropriate for your pet.

Considering the poor outlook for this infection, prevention is vital. When animals with a heart disease that could lead to infective endocarditis (for example, subaortic stenosis, patent ductus arteriosus, ventricular septal defect, cyanotic congenital heart disease) are to undergo procedures with a potential to introduce bacteria into the blood—such as dental scaling or tooth extractions—the preventive use of a broad-spectrum antibiotic may be appropriate. Your veterinarian will evaluate both the condition of the animal's heart and the risk of bacterial infection before prescribing any antibiotic.

Pericardial Disease

The pericardium is the membrane surrounding the heart. When fluid builds up in the pericardium, the pressure is increased. The increased pressure compresses the heart, interfering with its ability to pump blood. This condition is called **cardiac tamponade**. The compression significantly affects blood circulation and causes swollen jugular veins and accumulation of fluid in the abdomen. In addition, too little oxygen reaches the body's tissues. In an attempt to increase the oxygen supply, the animal's breathing rate goes up.

This condition is uncommon compared with other acquired cardiovascular diseases; however, it does occur in dogs. Golden Retrievers, Great Danes, and Great Pyrenees are among the most commonly affected breeds. Overall, most cases involve middle-aged, mostly male, large- and giant-breed dogs. Cancer is the most common cause of fluid in the membrane surrounding the heart in dogs. Tumors in the right atrium are the most frequently seen cardiac tumor, followed by heart base tumors. Less common causes of this accumulation of fluid in dogs are infections, trauma, chamber rupture, and congestive heart failure.

Signs may include unwillingness to move or exercise, loss of appetite, listlessness, and an accumulation of fluid in the abdomen. The severity of the signs depends on the rate of fluid accumulation in the sac surrounding the heart. A veterinarian may notice a swollen jugular vein and muffled heart sounds during examination of the dog. X-rays may show an enlarged heart. In most cases, an electrocardiogram is normal or just shows an increased heart rate. Echocardiography (ultrasonography) examination is the most sensitive and specific test for the detection of cardiac tamponade.

Animals with cardiac tamponade require urgent treatment. The best way to rapidly reduce fluid in the sac surrounding the heart is pericardiocentesis. This procedure involves inserting a needle into the sac to withdraw the fluid. Pericardiocentesis is relatively easy to perform and serious complications are rare. Broad-spectrum antibiotics and intravenous fluids may be given immediately before and after pericardiocentesis. If the fluid returns, the procedure may be repeated.

Heart base tumors are usually benign in dogs, and if the fluid in the sac surrounding the heart is due to a heart base tumor, surgical removal of part of the pericardium is commonly performed. Many dogs survive with no signs up to 2 years following surgery.

High Blood Pressure (Hypertension)

Systemic hypertension is an increase in the body's blood pressure. There are 2 major types of systemic hypertension. Essential (primary) hypertension is of unknown cause. This type of hypertension is common in humans, but is rare in dogs. Secondary hypertension results from a specific underlying disease. In dogs, the most common cause of hypertension is kidney disease. An increase in adrenal gland hormones (hyperadrenocorticism), diabetes mellitus, and pheochromocytoma (a type of pituitary gland tumor) are other causes of high blood pressure in dogs.

Dogs with extremely high blood pressure may have no signs that are visible to the owner. Blood tests may help with diagnosis of the cause of high blood pressure. Treatment should be started in dogs with sustained and severe high blood pressure, or in dogs with sustained high blood pressure and a documented underlying cause such as kidney failure.

Pulmonary hypertension is elevation of blood pressure in the lungs. Possible causes include increased thickness of blood (for example, an abnormal increase in red blood cells) and increased pulmonary blood flow (caused by, for example, a ventricular septal defect, patent ductus arteriosus, or an atrial septal defect). Other causes include abnormalities of the blood vessels in the lungs, which may be caused by heartworm disease, narrowing of the arteries within the lungs, or blood clots within the lungs. Primary pulmonary hypertension is rare in dogs. Signs are similar to those seen in right-sided congestive heart failure, such as accumulation of fluid in the lungs or abdomen. A swollen and pulsating jugular vein may be noted. Doppler echocardiography (ultrasonography) is the most likely method of confirming the diagnosis. Treatment is usually not effective, and the outlook is poor. The best chance for a successful outcome is the identification and treatment of the underlying disease.

■ HEARTWORM DISEASE

Heartworm disease is a potentially fatal, but preventable, infection caused by a worm parasite, *Dirofilaria immitis*. The organism is transmitted by mosquitoes, which carry the heartworm larvae (called microfilariae) from an infected animal host to a new animal host. Once the larvae arrive in a new host, they grow into adult worms in several months and live in the blood vessels that serve the heart and lungs. In advanced infections, the heartworms enter the heart as well. The presence of parasites stresses the dog's heart and causes inflammation of the blood vessels and lungs. In addition, severe complications are possible when the number of worms present becomes high or when the heartworms die. Susceptible animals can be reinfected numerous times, so different stages of heartworm infections may be present in the same animal.

At least 70 species of mosquitoes can transmit heartworm disease. Heartworm disease has been reported in most countries with temperate, semitropical, or tropical climates around the world, including the United States, Canada, and southern Europe. The infection risk is greatest in dogs that are housed outdoors. Any dog, whether it is an indoor or an outdoor pet, is capable of being infected; all it takes is a bite from a mosquito carrying the infective heartworm larvae.

The severity of a heartworm infection and the signs depend on the number of worms present, the immune response of the infected dog, the duration of infection, and the activity level of the animal. Most dogs are highly susceptible to heartworm infection, and the majority of infective larvae develop into adult worms. The presence of heartworms in the vessels serving the heart and

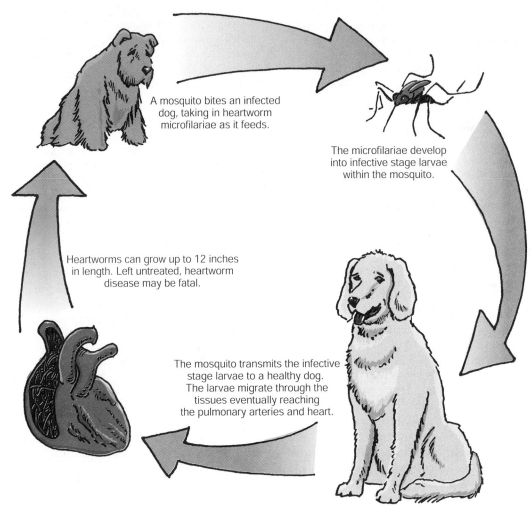

A mosquito bites an infected dog, taking in heartworm microfilariae as it feeds.

The microfilariae develop into infective stage larvae within the mosquito.

Heartworms can grow up to 12 inches in length. Left untreated, heartworm disease may be fatal.

The mosquito transmits the infective stage larvae to a healthy dog. The larvae migrate through the tissues eventually reaching the pulmonary arteries and heart.

The life cycle of the heartworm

lungs, and in the heart itself, causes irritation and inflammation of the affected vessels or heart chamber. With longterm infection (over 1 year in duration), the constant irritation will lead to scarring and reduced flexibility of the blood vessels. Heartworms can live for over 5 years.

In general, small dogs do not tolerate heartworm infections or treatments as well as large dogs do. This is mostly because small dogs have smaller blood vessels and heart chambers, so they can tolerate fewer worms without vessel damage or blockage.

Signs and Diagnosis

Common signs of heartworm infection include coughing, exercise intolerance, failure to grow, labored breathing, a blue or purplish discoloration of the skin, spitting up blood, fainting, nose bleeding, and the accumulation of fluid in the abdominal cavity. The severity of the signs is often related to the dog's activity level. Active dogs (such as hunters and performers) will typically show more dramatic signs of infection than will less active dogs. Even though they may have many worms, sedentary dogs may show few or no signs.

Your veterinarian has a number of options for diagnosing heartworm infection. The **antigen detection test** is the preferred method for diagnosis of infection or for verification of a suspected heartworm infection. This test is considered the most sensitive method available for dogs. Other diagnostic tools include echocardiography (a type of ultrasonography), blood tests, and chest x-rays. Your veterinarian will select a test based on your history of use of preventive medication and the overall health of the dog.

Treatment

Prior to treating your dog for heartworm infection, your veterinarian will want a comprehensive medical history. Selecting the most appropriate treatment regimen will depend on many factors, including whether the dog has another disease that may influence the course of treatment.

The only drug currently available to treat infection with adult heartworms is melarsomine dihydrochloride, an arsenical compound. Appropriate treatment kills both mature and some immature heartworms. There are 2 approved treatment protocols, or methods, used for treating existing infections; a 2-dose protocol or a 3-dose protocol. In both cases the medication is delivered by injection deep into the muscles of the dog's back, alternating sides of the back between treatments. About one-third of dogs will have some local pain, swelling, soreness with movement, or rarely a sterile abscess at the sites of the injections. The 2-dose protocol consists of 2 doses, 24 hours apart. The 3-dose protocol introduces a delay in the treatment schedule. Under this schedule, the dog would first receive a single injection. One month later, the second and third injections will be administered 24 hours apart. Many veterinarians choose to use the 3-injection treatment, regardless of the dog's stage of heartworm disease, because it may be safer for the dog and more efficient at killing all the parasites.

As a result of treatment, there is a risk that dead heartworms will cause severe respiratory problems, especially if dogs are not properly confined to restrict activity following treatment. These problems can occur from several days to 6 weeks after treatment of a heartworm-infected dog. The signs of post-treatment complications include coughing, spitting up blood, labored or rapid breathing, lethargy, lack of appetite, and fever. In dogs with complications of heartworm treatment, cage confinement, with several days of oxygen treatment and drugs to control inflammation and reduce blood clotting, may help alleviate the problem. If properly cared for, most dogs begin to recover from treatment complications within 24 hours.

To reduce the potential for such "dead worm reactions," all dogs should be confined (or maintained in a calm environment) throughout treatment and for at least 1 month following the final injection of melarsomine. Dogs treated for heartworm should be placed on heartworm preventive drugs and tested after 6 months to be sure that all worms were killed. For those dogs that test positive, retesting might be required and, if infection is confirmed, a new round of treatment will be needed.

Prevention

Heartworm infection is preventable. Several medications that are both safe and effective at preventing infection are available from your veterinarian. Preventive treatment in dogs is recommended beginning at 6 to 8 weeks of age. No pretesting is necessary at this age. When beginning preventive treatment in older dogs, an antigen test (to make sure the dog is not already infected) is recommended, followed by an additional negative test 6 months later (due to the 6-month development period of the worms) to ensure that the dog is not infected. Year-round preventive treatment is recommended for most dogs; however, you should check with your veterinarian about the best schedule for your pet.

The most important thing that pet owners can do to protect their companions from heartworm infection is to be absolutely sure their pet receives the prescribed dose of medication at the correct time. Because the most common preventive drugs for dogs are given only once a month, many pet owners may forget to administer the medication. Pet owners may find it helpful to post the heartworm medication dates on their refrigerator door and then check off the administration dates as the prescription is provided. Free e-mail reminder services are also available from most manufacturers of heartworm preventive drugs.

Missing an administration date may have serious consequences. If you miss a dose, you should contact your veterinarian regarding administration of the medication.

■ BLOOD CLOTS AND ANEURYSMS

A **thrombus** is a blood clot that may form when the blood flow of an artery or vein is restricted. It frequently causes obstruction to blood vessels at its site of origin. All or part of a clot may break off and be carried through the bloodstream as an **embolus** that lodges someplace else at a point of narrowing. Blockage of a blood vessel can also occur when foreign material (for example, bacteria, air, or fat) is carried into the bloodstream. Some clots are infected. Life-threatening blood clots are most commonly encountered in animals with underlying diseases that affect the blood's ability to clot. If left untreated or uncontrolled, these conditions can result in a tendency to bleed and/or a life-threatening condition in which small blood clots develop throughout the bloodstream, blocking small blood vessels and depleting the platelets and clotting factors needed to control bleeding.

Thrombus formation can occur in both large and small arteries and veins. Blood

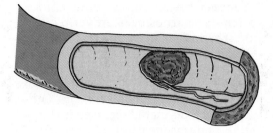
Blood clots may obstruct blood flow.

clots generally result in an inadequate supply of blood reaching nearby tissues. In addition, pus-filled clots can spread of bacteria and localized infection. Blood clots can affect the heart or the central nervous system.

An **aneurysm** is an enlargement of a blood vessel caused by weakening of the middle layer of the blood vessel. Disruption of the inner layer of a blood vessel associated with an aneurysm can cause formation of a blood clot, with subsequent blockage of the blood vessel by the clot.

Signs and Diagnosis

A sudden onset of breathing difficulty may be a sign of a blood clot in the lungs, and some dogs may cough up blood or bloody mucus. Infective clots in the heart are associated with endocarditis, an inflammation of the membranes lining the heart cavity (*see* page 71). Clots in the heart that are not infective are associated with heart muscle disease. Blood in the urine or abdominal pain can indicate blockage of certain blood vessels (within the genital or urinary systems, for example) or the loss of blood supply caused by clots. Blockage of blood vessels to abdominal organs may cause similar signs, although dogs may vomit or be unable to control their bladder and bowels.

Heartworm disease may lead to blood clots in arteries of the lungs. Blood clots in the pulmonary artery most commonly produce difficulty breathing and an increased breathing rate. Affected dogs often seem normal until they have a sudden onset of respiratory distress. Chest x-rays may show changes such as an enlarged main pulmonary artery and right heart, not enough blood getting to the affected region, an accumulation of fluid in the chest cavity, or bleeding or tissue death within the lungs. Additional tests are essential for the diagnosis of underlying diseases.

Bacterial infection of the lining of the heart cavity can lead to blood clots in the lungs and pneumonia. Other diseases associated with blood clots in the lungs include diabetes mellitus, kidney disease, increased adrenal gland hormones (hyperadrenocorticism), immune-mediated hemolytic anemia (a disorder in which the dog's immune system destroys its own red blood cells), and cancer.

Treatment

Treatment of pneumonia caused by a blood clot due to endocarditis includes longterm antibiotics, a treatment program lasting several weeks. Some cases require anti-inflammatory drugs to reduce fever. The outlook for recovery is guarded at best.

Treatment of blood clots in veins is usually limited to supportive care, including hydrotherapy of accessible veins, anti-inflammatory drugs, and antibiotics given by mouth or injection to control secondary infection. Thrombosis of the large veins that empty into the right atrium generally does not respond to treatment and the outlook is poor.

CHAPTER 7
Digestive Disorders

▨ INTRODUCTION

The digestive system includes all of the organs that are involved in taking in and processing food. It begins with the mouth and includes the esophagus, stomach, liver, pancreas, intestines, rectum, and anus.

The process of digestion begins when your pet picks up food with its mouth and starts chewing. Enzymes found in saliva begin breaking down the food chemically. The process continues with swallowing, additional breakdown of food in the stomach, absorption of nutrients in the intestines, and elimination of waste. Digestion is critical not only for providing nutrients but also for maintaining the proper balance of fluid and electrolytes (salts) in the body.

The functions of the digestive system can be divided into 4 main categories: digestion, absorption of nutrients, motility (movement through the digestive tract), and elimination of feces.

When treating a digestive system problem, the veterinarian's goal is to first identify the part of the system where the problem lies and then to determine the specific cause and appropriate treatment.

General Signs of Digestive System Disorders

Signs of digestive system disease can include excessive drooling, diarrhea, constipation, vomiting or regurgitation, loss of appetite, bleeding, abdominal pain and bloating, shock, and dehydration. The location and nature of the disease often can be determined by the signs your pet shows. For example, abnormalities of biting, chewing, and swallowing usually

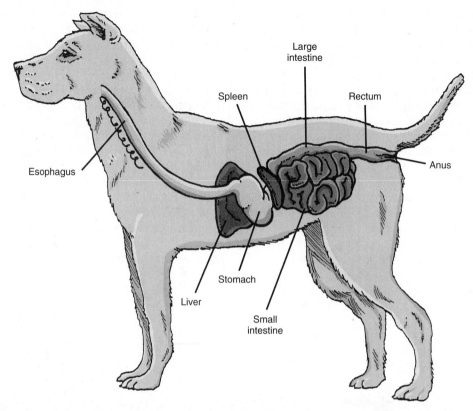

The major digestive organs of a dog

are associated with diseases of the mouth, the teeth, the jaw, or the esophagus. Vomiting is usually due to inflammation of the lining of stomach or intestines (gastroenteritis) caused by infection or irritation. However, vomiting can also be caused by a nondigestive condition such as kidney disease.

Diarrhea is often a sign of digestive system disorders, but it can have many causes. Large-volume, watery diarrhea usually is associated with hypersecretion, a condition in which excess fluid is secreted into the intestines. This can be caused by bacterial infection.

Diarrhea can also be caused by malabsorption, the failure to properly absorb nutrients. Malabsorption is due to a defect in the intestinal cells responsible for absorption. This condition can be caused by several viruses (for example, canine parvovirus, coronavirus, rotavirus). Malabsorption may also be caused by any defect that limits the ability of the intestines to absorb liquids, or by defects in the pancreatic secretions needed for effective digestion. In rare cases, newborn pups may have diarrhea while they are being fed milk because they are unable to digest lactose. Dehydration and electrolyte (salt) imbalance, which may lead to shock, are seen when large quantities of fluid are lost (for example, from diarrhea).

Changes in the color, consistency, or frequency of feces are another sign of digestive problems. Black, tarry feces may be a sign of bleeding in the stomach or small intestine. Straining during bowel movements is usually associated with inflammation of the rectum and anus. Abdominal distention (bloating) can result from accumulation of gas, fluid, or ingested food, usually due to reduced activity of the muscles that move food through the digestive system. Distention can also be caused by a physical obstruction such as a foreign object or intussusception ("telescoping" of one part of the intestines into another), or from something as simple as overeating.

Abdominal pain is due to stretching or inflammation of abdominal membranes, and it can vary in severity. A dog may react to abdominal pain by whining, pacing, and abnormal postures (for example, the forelimbs outstretched, the chest on the floor, and the back legs raised).

Examination of the Digestive System

Your complete, accurate description of your dog's history (age, signs of illness, current diet, past problems, and so on) combined with a veterinarian's clinical examination can often determine the cause of a digestive system problem. When a digestive system disorder is suspected, your veterinarian's initial examination might include a visual inspection of the mouth and abdomen for changes in size or shape; a "hands on" inspection of the abdomen (through the abdominal wall or through the rectum) to evaluate shape, size, and position of the abdominal organs; and listening through a stethoscope for any abnormal abdominal sounds. The veterinarian may also want to inspect your dog's feces. When you call to make an appointment with your veterinarian, it is a good idea to ask whether you should bring along a recent stool sample to help with diagnosis.

Depending on what the initial examination reveals, additional tests might be needed to determine the cause of the problem. These might include laboratory tests on samples containing blood or feces to determine whether bacteria or viruses are involved, as well as specialized procedures such as x-ray imaging, ultrasonography, or using an endoscope to perform an internal examination of the esophagus, stomach, duodenum, colon, and/or rectum. Sometimes it is necessary to collect fluid from

swollen abdominal organs or from the abdominal cavity for analysis; this is done with a long, hollow needle. Other tests

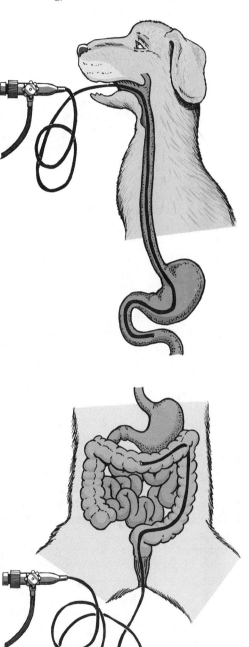

Examination of the digestive tract with an endoscope (modified with permission from *The Merck Manual of Medical Information*, Second Home Edition, 2003)

that are sometimes needed include biopsies (sampling and microscopic analysis) of liver or intestinal tissue and blood tests to detect possible malabsorption or maldigestion.

Infectious Diseases

Because it is easy for foreign organisms and other "invaders" to enter the digestive tract through the mouth, this body system is prone to infection by bacteria, viruses, parasites, and other organisms (*see* TABLE 2). These infections spread in various ways, but the most common are by direct contact or by contamination of food or water by feces.

People and animals all have small numbers of certain intestinal microorganisms that are found within the digestive tract—most commonly in the intestines—and that become established within a few hours after birth. These so-called intestinal flora are actually beneficial, in some cases aiding in digestion and in others helping to prevent infection. However, sometimes infections occur when these organisms, normally found in small numbers, suddenly multiply. This can occur after a period of stress, under unhygienic conditions, or in an animal whose immune system is weakened.

Diagnosis of a specific infectious disease depends on finding and identifying the organism suspected to cause the disease. This may require one or more fecal samples, which will be submitted to a diagnostic laboratory.

Parasites are a frequent cause of digestive tract disorders in animals. Many species of parasites can infect the digestive tract and cause disease. The life cycles of some parasites are direct, which means that there is only one host. Eggs and larvae are passed in the feces, develop into an infective stage, and are eaten by your pet. No other animals or organisms are needed to complete the life cycle. Other parasites have complex life cycles that involve an intermediate host such as an insect. In this situation, infection is acquired when the intermediate host—or parasite shed by that host—is consumed by your pet. The extent to which a parasite affects an animal depends on the parasite itself, as well as the animal's own resistance, age, nutrition, and overall health.

Parasites can cause severe disease or simply decrease your dog's overall fitness. Some of these parasites also infect humans. Because parasite infection is easily confused with other illnesses, diagnosis depends on the veterinarian's knowledge of seasonal cycles of parasite infection, as well as examination of feces for evidence of parasite eggs or larvae. In some cases, blood tests can also be used to detect the

Table 2. Infections of the Digestive System in Dogs

Organism	Examples
Viruses	Canine parvovirus, canine coronavirus, canine rotaviruses, canine astroviruses
Rickettsiae	*Neorickettsia helminthoeca* (salmon poisoning)
Bacteria	*Salmonella* species, *Yersinia enterocolitica, Campylobacter jejuni, Bacillus piliformis, Clostridium* species, *Mycobacterium* species, *Shigella* species
Protozoa	*Isospora* species, *Sarcocystis* species, *Besnoitia* species, *Hammondia* species, *Toxoplasma* species, *Giardia* species, *Trichomonas* species, *Entamoeba histolytica, Balantidium coli, Cryptosporidium* species
Fungi	*Histoplasma capsulatum, Aspergillus* species, *Candida albicans*, phycomycetes
Algae	*Prototheca* species
Parasites	Numerous (*See* page 110.)

presence of parasites. (For a more detailed discussion of GASTROINTESTINAL PARASITES, *see* page 110.)

Noninfectious Diseases

Many digestive system diseases are not caused by infective organisms. Their causes include overeating, eating poor-quality food, chemicals, obstruction caused by swallowing foreign objects, or injury to the digestive system. Digestive system disease can also be caused by enzyme deficiencies, damage to the digestive tract such as from gastric ulcers, or birth defects. Digestive system signs such as vomiting and diarrhea may also occur because of kidney, liver, or adrenal gland disease. The causes are uncertain in several diseases, including twisting of the stomach (gastric torsion) in dogs. In noninfectious diseases of the digestive tract, usually only a single animal is affected at one time; exceptions are diseases associated with excessive food intake or poisons, in which multiple animals living together can be affected.

Treatment Overview of Digestive System Disorders

Specific disorders and their treatments are described later in this chapter; however, some general principles are listed in this section. Eliminating the cause of the disease is the primary objective of veterinary treatment; however, a major part of treatment is often directed at the signs of the disease and is intended to relieve pain, correct abnormalities, and allow healing to occur.

Elimination of the cause of the disease may involve drugs that kill bacteria or parasites, antidotes for poisons, or surgery to correct defects or displacements.

Use of drugs to correct diarrhea or constipation is done depending on the specific case. Although such drugs might seem to be a logical choice, they are not beneficial in every situation. For example, diarrhea can actually be a defense mechanism for the animal, helping it to eliminate harmful organisms and their toxins.

In addition, the available drugs may not always give consistent results.

Replacement of fluids and electrolytes (salts) is necessary in cases where the animal is at risk of dehydration, such as from excessive vomiting or diarrhea.

Relief of distension (bloating) by stomach tube or surgery may be required if the digestive tract has become distended with gas, fluid, or food.

Pain relief is sometimes provided. However, a dog being given pain medicine must be watched carefully to ensure that the pain relief is not masking a condition that is becoming worse.

Treatment and Control of Infectious Disease

Bacterial and parasitic diseases of the digestive system are often treated with medications designed to kill the infectious organisms. There are currently no specific medications for treatment of viral diseases. Antibiotics (drugs effective against bacteria) are commonly given daily by mouth for several days until recovery is apparent, although their effectiveness in treating digestive system disease is still uncertain. Antibiotics may be given by injection when septicemia (blood poisoning) is apparent or likely to occur. Your veterinarian will make the decision whether to prescribe antibacterial medication based on the suspected disease, likelihood of benefits, previous results, and cost of treatment.

Advances in understanding the life cycles of parasites, coupled with the discovery of effective antiparasitic drugs, have made successful treatment and control of gastrointestinal parasites possible. Response to treatment is usually rapid, and a single treatment is often all that is needed unless reinfection occurs or the damage caused by the parasites is particularly severe.

Control of digestive diseases and parasites depends on practicing good sanitation and hygiene. This is achieved primarily by providing adequate space for your dog and by regular cleaning of its living areas. In addition, adequate nutrition and housing will minimize the stress on your dog and help it to stay healthy.

▓ CONGENITAL AND INHERITED DISORDERS

Congenital abnormalities are conditions that an animal is born with; they are often called "birth defects." Some of these conditions are inherited and tend to occur within particular families or breeds, while others are caused by chemicals or injury during pregnancy. For still others, the cause is unknown. Some of the most common congenital abnormalities of the digestive tract in dogs are described below.

Mouth

A **cleft palate** or **cleft lip** (harelip) is caused by a defect in the formation of the jaw and face during embryonic development. It leads to a gap or cleft in the center of the lip, the roof of the mouth (hard palate), or both. Often this condition leaves an open space through the roof of the mouth into the breathing passages. These conditions have a wide range in severity. Usually the upper lip and palate are affected; a cleft in the lower lip is rare.

Certain breeds are more prone to cleft palate than others. The defect is more common in Beagles, Cocker Spaniels, Dachshunds, German Shepherds, Labrador Retrievers, Schnauzers, and Shetland Sheepdogs. Dog breeds with short heads (brachycephalic breeds) can have up to a 30% risk of the disorder. Most cases are inherited, although nutritional deficiencies during pregnancy, drug or chemical exposure, injury to the fetus, and some viral infections during pregnancy have also been suggested as causes.

Cleft palate or lip will usually be noticed shortly after birth when the puppy might have problems nursing. For example, milk might be seen dripping from the nostrils or the puppy might have difficulty suckling and swallowing. The veterinarian can readily identify the problem by examining the puppy's mouth. Affected puppies require intensive nursing care, including

hand or tube feeding and possibly antibiotics to treat respiratory infections. Surgical correction is effective only in minor cases, and is usually done when puppies are 6 to 8 weeks old to minimize further complications. A variety of surgical techniques are used, and the success rate in dogs is improving. The decision to perform surgery should be made carefully, and the affected animal should be spayed or neutered to prevent passing the defect on to its offspring.

Brachygnathia occurs when the lower jaw is shorter than the upper jaw. It can be a minor problem or a serious defect depending on the degree of abnormality. Mild cases may cause no problems. More severe cases can cause damage to the hard palate (roof of the mouth) or restriction of normal jaw growth. The lower canine teeth are often removed or shortened to prevent this damage.

Prognathia occurs when the lower jaw is longer than the upper jaw. This characteristic is normal in some breeds (for example, Boxers, Bulldogs, Pugs, and other breeds with shortened heads) and does not usually require treatment.

Ankyloglossia or **microglossia** refers to incomplete or abnormal development of the tongue. The condition in dogs is often

---

What Is a Brachycephalic Dog Breed?

"Brachycephalic" comes from Greek words meaning "short" and "head." The term refers to breeds that might be described as having a short or "pushed-in" face. Because of their unique head structure, these breeds can be prone to certain respiratory, dental, and eye abnormalities.

Examples of brachycephalic dog breeds include the following:

▓ Boston Terrier

▓ Boxer

▓ Bulldog

▓ Pekingese

▓ Pug

▓ Shih Tzu

referred to as "bird tongue." Affected puppies have difficulty nursing and do not grow properly. Examination of the mouth reveals missing or underdeveloped portions of the tongue. This condition is generally fatal.

Some Chinese Shar-Peis have a condition called **tight-lip syndrome** in which the lower lip covers the lower front teeth and folds over the teeth toward the tongue. Contact between the upper front teeth and the lower lip worsens the lip position and may cause the lower front teeth to shift. This condition can be corrected by surgery.

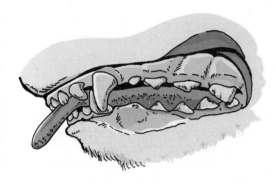

Brachygnathia

Prognathia

Common congenital defects in dogs include brachygnathia (shortened lower jaw) and prognathia (elongated lower jaw).

Teeth

In most animals, having too few teeth is rare, although in dogs, molars and premolars may fail to develop or erupt. In dogs, **extra teeth** are seen most often in the upper jaw. Although rare, sometimes a single tooth bud will split to form 2 teeth. The result may be crowding and rotation of the teeth; this condition requires tooth extraction to prevent or correct abnormalities of the bite that can lead to further dental problems.

Delayed loss of deciduous ("baby") teeth in dogs is common. The teeth that do not fall out get in the way of the permanent teeth that are starting to erupt beneath them, altering the position of the permanent teeth within as little as 2 to 3 weeks. This results in bite problems or entrapment of food, leading to tooth and gum disease. For these reasons, retained deciduous teeth should be removed by your veterinarian as soon as possible.

Abnormalities in placement or shape of teeth are reported in various breeds of dogs. The effect on an animal's health is variable and based on severity. In certain dog breeds with short, flattened heads (brachycephalic breeds), the upper third premolar and occasionally other teeth may rotate. Usually, this does not cause any problems, but it may require extraction of some teeth if crowding or bite abnormalities occur.

Abnormal development of tooth enamel (the hard outer surface of the tooth) can be caused by fever, trauma, malnutrition, poisoning, or infections such as distemper virus. The damage to the enamel depends on the severity and duration of the cause and can range from pitting to the absence of enamel with incomplete tooth development. Affected teeth are prone to plaque and tartar accumulation, which lead to tooth decay. Resin restoration is sometimes used to cover defects, although careful dental hygiene and home care is critical in reducing the incidence of complications (*see* DENTAL DISORDERS, page 87). **Discoloration of the enamel** may also occur. Giving tetracycline antibiotics to pregnant females or to puppies less than 6 months old may result in permanent brownish-yellow stains on the teeth.

Cysts of the Head and Neck

Cysts (lumps) in the head and neck can be caused by defects during fetal development. These need to be distinguished by your veterinarian from abscesses or lumps caused by infection or other disease. These cysts tend to occur in specific locations and may have a characteristic feel to them, which can help the veterinarian to diagnose their cause.

Esophagus

The muscular tube that leads from the back of the mouth to the stomach is known as the esophagus. Some congenital abnormalities of the esophagus seen in dogs include megaesophagus, vascular ring anomalies, and crichopharyngeal achalasia (*see* TABLE 3). Signs of defects in the esophagus generally include regurgitation and problems with swallowing. These signs are especially noticeable when your dog starts to eat solid food. Surgical correction of some esophageal abnormalities (for example, vascular ring anomalies, in which abnormal blood vessels surround and restrict the esophagus) is effective if done early. If not, the esophagus can become permanently damaged by the stretching caused by trapped food.

Small pouches in the lining of the esophagus, called **esophageal diverticula**, will sometimes form. Signs depend on

severity and are seen in only 10 to 15% of cases. When they do occur, they may cause accumulation of food or become inflamed. In rare cases they rupture. Treatment (if necessary) is by surgical removal of the pouch. This disorder may be more common in English Bulldogs.

Hernias

A hernia is the protrusion of a portion of an organ or tissue through an abnormal opening. One common congenital type involves an abnormal opening in the wall of the diaphragm (the sheet of muscle that separates the chest from the abdomen) or abdomen. The defect may allow abdominal organs to pass into the chest or bulge beneath the skin. Hernias may be congenital (present at birth) or result from injury. Signs of a hernia vary from none to severe and depend on the amount of herniated tissue and its effect on the organ involved. **Hiatal hernias** involve extension of part of the stomach through the diaphragm. These hernias may be "sliding" and result in signs (such as loss of appetite, drooling, or vomiting) that come and go. Hernias are diagnosed using x-rays; contrast studies (x-rays that include special dyes to outline organs) are often needed. Endoscopy may be used to diagnose sliding hiatal hernias. In many cases, correction of a hernia involving the diaphragm requires surgery. However, the use of antacid preparations and dietary modification may control signs of a hiatal hernia, if they are mild.

Table 3. Congenital Esophageal Disorders of Dogs

Type	Cause	Breeds Most Often Affected
Congenital megaesophagus	Abnormal nerve development in esophagus; sometimes part of more widespread nerve problems	Chinese Shar-Peis, Fox Terriers, German Shepherds, Great Danes, Irish Setters, Labrador Retrievers, Miniature Schnauzers, Newfoundlands; often part of laryngeal paralysis-polyneuropathy complex in Dalmatians
Vascular ring entrapment	Physical constriction of the esophagus by other tissues	Boston Terriers, German Shepherds, Irish Setters
Cricopharyngeal achalasia	Failure of the cricopharyngeal muscle (in the throat) to relax during swallowing	Toy breeds

Table 4. Types of Hernias

General Area	Specific Type	Description
Diaphragm	Peritoneopericardial	Abdominal contents extend into the sac surrounding the heart
	Pleuroperitoneal	Abdominal contents extend into the sac surrounding the lungs
	Hiatal	Stomach and/or lower esophagus protrude through the esophageal opening (hiatus) into the chest cavity
Abdomen	Umbilical	Abdominal contents protrude at the site of the navel; most often genetic but sometimes caused by strain on the umbilical cord during or after birth
	Inguinal	Abdominal contents protrude into the groin, above the scrotum of male animals
	Scrotal	Abdominal contents protrude into the scrotum (the sac surrounding the testes) of male animals

Hernias involving the abdominal wall are called umbilical, inguinal, or scrotal, depending on their location (*see* TABLE 4). Diagnosis of **umbilical hernias** is usually simple, especially if the veterinarian is able to push the hernia back through the abdominal wall (called "reducing the hernia"). These hernias are corrected by surgery. Small hernias are often corrected at the same time that the dog is spayed or neutered. The tendency to develop hernias may be inherited.

Stomach

Besides hiatal hernia (*see* above), another common abnormality involving the stomach is **pyloric stenosis**. It is likely that pyloric stenosis is inherited. This condition results from muscular thickening of the pyloric sphincter (the "exit" of the stomach). The thickening of this opening slows or blocks the flow of digested food from the stomach to the small intestine. Affected breeds include smaller breeds and those with flattened, shortened heads, especially Boxers and Boston Terriers. Because the flow of food out of the stomach is restricted, dogs with this condition will often vomit food for several hours after a meal. Treatment is through dietary modification and medication. In more severe cases, surgery may help.

Small and Large Intestine

Maldigestion is a condition in which certain foods are not properly digested. **Malabsorption** occurs when nutrients are not properly absorbed into the bloodstream. These conditions often cause persistent digestive system problems, including vomiting, weight loss, diarrhea, or a combination of these signs. There are many potential causes of maldigestion and malabsorption. Some are inherited; some are acquired. Most are associated with inflammation of the intestines (called inflammatory bowel disease). Inherited conditions may occur more often in specific breeds. For example, Irish Setters have a family tendency for sensitivity to wheat protein (gluten), with signs beginning as early as 6 months of age. The wheat sensitivity is both confirmed and treated through the use of gluten-free diets. Malabsorption and maldigestion are often treated with a combination of dietary changes and medication; the exact treatment will depend on the condition being treated. In certain conditions in which protein loss is severe (for example, in Soft-coated Wheaten Terriers with protein-losing enteropathy and nephropathy), neither dietary changes nor treatment have been proven effective, and the outlook is poor.

Various **malformations of the intestines** can occur as birth defects, including duplication of sections of the intestine or rectum, failure of the rectum to connect with the anus, and openings between the rectum and other structures such as the urethra or vagina. Surgical correction is usually needed. The success rate depends on the extent of the malformation.

Liver

The most common liver defect present at birth is **portosystemic shunt** (*see* page 122). In a healthy animal, blood coming from the intestines is processed by the liver, which removes toxins from the bloodstream before they reach the brain or other organs. In an animal with a portosystemic shunt, however, blood bypasses the liver through one or more "shortcuts" (shunts) and enters directly into the general circulatory system. Breeds with an increased risk of this defect include Yorkshire Terriers, Miniature Schnauzers, Cairn Terriers, Maltese, Scottish Terriers, Pugs, Irish Wolfhounds, Golden Retrievers, Labrador Retrievers, German Shepherds, and Poodles. Signs of a portosystemic shunt include nervous system disturbances and a failure to grow and thrive. In the late stages, protein-containing fluid may accumulate in the abdomen, a condition called **ascites**. Your veterinarian may also notice enlargement of the kidneys and kidney stones. A definite diagnosis is made by using an opaque dye to highlight the blood vessels, followed by x-rays. This procedure can identify the location of the shunt and determine whether it is single or multiple. It also allows the veterinarian to assess whether surgical correction is possible. Animals with multiple shunts tend to do poorly.

Hepatoportal microvascular dysplasia is another disorder that results in blood entering the circulatory system without being detoxified by the liver. In this disease, the shunting occurs within the liver itself. The syndrome occurs with some frequency in Cairn and Yorkshire Terriers and has also been reported in Maltese, Dachshunds, Toy and Miniature Poodles, Bichon Frise, Pekingese, Shih Tzus, and Lhasa Apsos. It generally causes no signs. Dogs that do exhibit signs may be treated with medication. Surgery is not an option because the shunting is caused by many small blood vessels, not a single prominent one that can easily be corrected.

Copper-associated hepatopathy is a defect that causes copper accumulation in the liver. This results in development of chronic hepatitis and cirrhosis of the liver. The condition is found in Bedlington Terriers. An acute form of the disease in seen in young (less than 6-year-old) dogs, and chronic liver failure is seen in older dogs. Carrier dogs, which have no signs of the disease, are also seen. Elevated copper levels have also been observed as part of the inherited liver disease of West Highland White Terriers, Skye Terriers, and Doberman Pinschers. There are apparent variations even within breeds; for example, liver copper levels are worse in Bedlington and West Highland White Terriers of North American descent than in the same breeds from Europe or other regions. Treatment involves the use of drugs that bind copper (chelators), low-copper diets, and other supportive measures directed at helping animals with liver disease. If your dog has copper-associated hepatopathy, follow your veterinarian's directions for medication, diet, and other treatment carefully and fully.

Other liver developmental anomalies include **hepatic (liver) cysts**, which generally cause no signs of illness. They are of significance mainly because they must be differentiated from abscesses in the liver. A veterinarian who finds a hepatic cyst will often want to examine the kidneys, because hepatic cysts often occur along with polycystic kidney disease. (For a more detailed discussion of POLYCYSTIC KIDNEYS, *see* page 285.)

■ DENTAL DEVELOPMENT

Each species of animal has its own unique type of teeth, depending on what type of food the animal normally eats. For example, a meat-eating animal such as a cat has quite different teeth than a grass-eating animal such as a horse. However, all domestic animals have 2 sets of teeth during their lives, as humans do: a set of deciduous ("baby") teeth that fall out, and a set of permanent teeth that develop later.

Most dogs have 28 deciduous teeth and 42 permanent teeth. The deciduous teeth begin to erupt at 3 to 5 weeks of age, while permanent teeth usually begin to appear at around 4 to 5 months. All permanent teeth are present by the time the dog reaches 7 months of age. (*See* TABLE 3, page 6.)

Estimation of Age by Examination of the Teeth

In species with relatively short incisors, such as dogs, age determination of young animals using the teeth is only somewhat accurate and is mostly based on the time at which each tooth erupts. For the majority of large adult dogs with normal teeth and jaws, veterinarians can examine wear patterns on the teeth and give an estimate of age. Determining the age of small and toy breeds by examining the teeth is more difficult.

■ DENTAL DISORDERS

Many of the dental disorders of dogs are similar to those found in people. Proper dental care, including preventive methods like tooth brushing, can help keep your dog's teeth and gums healthy.

Gum Disease

Bacterial infection of the tissue surrounding the teeth causes inflammation of the gums, the ligaments that anchor the teeth, and the surrounding bone. If gum (periodontal) disease goes untreated, teeth can be lost due to the loss of their supporting tissues. This is the major reason for tooth loss in dogs.

Gum disease is caused by accumulation of bacteria (plaque) at the gum line due in part to a lack of proper oral hygiene. Other contributing factors may include breed, genetics, age, and diet. As the number of bacteria below the gumline increases, bacterial waste products such as hydrogen sulfide, ammonia, acids, and other compounds accumulate and damage tissues. The dog's own response to this infection also causes tissue breakdown and loss of the tooth's supporting tissues. There are 2 forms of gum disease: gingivitis and periodontitis.

Dental Terms

What Most People Call It	What Your Veterinarian Might Call It
Adult tooth	Permanent tooth
Baby tooth	Deciduous tooth
Bad breath	Halitosis
Bite	Occlusion
Cavities or tooth decay	Dental caries, tooth infection
Extra teeth	Polyodontia
Eye teeth	Canines
Front teeth	Incisors and canines
Gum	Gingiva
Gum disease	Periodontal disease, periodontitis
Lower jaw	Mandible
Roof of the mouth	Palate
Root canal	Endodontic treatment
Tartar	Calculus
Teeth cleaning	Dental prophylaxis
Uneven bite	Malocclusion
Upper jaw	Maxilla

Gingivitis

In gingivitis, the gums become inflamed because of bacterial plaque, but the ligaments and bone are not yet affected. The gums change in color from coral-pink to red or purple, and the edge of the gum swells. The gums tend to bleed on contact. Bad breath is common. Gingivitis can be reversed with proper tooth cleaning but, if untreated, may lead to periodontitis (*see* below).

Gingivitis usually can be treated by thorough professional cleaning of the teeth. This should include cleaning below the gum line. If gingivitis does not improve, the dog should be examined again in case more extensive cleaning is required. When cleanings are completed, your veterinarian may apply a sealant to the teeth to prevent bacterial buildup and improve healing. Dogs that do not respond to treatment

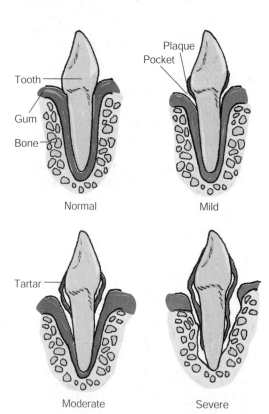

Progression of gum disease in dogs (modified with permission from *The Merck Manual of Medical Information*, Second Home Edition, 2003)

should be evaluated for other disease such as immune system problems and diabetes. Gingivitis will reoccur if the teeth are not kept clean and free of plaque. Therefore, at-home oral hygiene methods such as brushing as well as regular cleanings by your veterinarian are important.

Periodontitis

In periodontitis, the tissue damage is more severe and includes the gums, ligaments, and bone. It usually is seen after years of development of plaque, tartar, and gingivitis. It is irreversible and results in permanent loss of tooth support. Small-breed dogs usually experience more problems with periodontitis than large-breed dogs. Dogs that have a regular diet of hard kibble develop fewer problems due to the mechanical cleaning effect on the teeth as the food is chewed. Back teeth are affected more often than front teeth. The upper teeth are affected more severely than the lower teeth, and the cheek surfaces of the teeth have more disease than the surfaces near the tongue. Gingivitis is often first noticed at about 2 years of age but improves if treated. Periodontitis usually begins at 4 to 6 years of age and, if untreated, progresses to tooth loss.

Periodontitis is treated with thorough professional cleaning above and below the gum line. In some cases, surgery will be needed to gain access to the root surface for cleaning. Teeth can generally be saved until they have lost about 66% of their bone support from one or more of their roots. Your veterinarian can determine the extent of bone support loss by taking x-rays of the jaws. These are usually recommended as a normal part of periodontal disease diagnosis and treatment planning.

If your dog has been treated for periodontitis, you will need to continue oral hygiene care at home. Follow your veterinarian's instructions, which might include daily toothbrushing, dietary changes, plaque prevention gel, and oral rinses. Regular (every 6 months to 1 year) preventive cleanings will help to avoid relapse and prevent further bone loss.

Prevention

The most important thing to remember is that gum disease will not develop around clean teeth. At-home methods to keep your pet's teeth clean, such as toothbrushing and diet, along with regular dental examinations, are the best ways to help prevent gum disease. Your veterinarian might also apply a barrier sealant or recommend a plaque prevention gel. These products form a barrier to repel bacteria-laden saliva from the tooth surface and prevent plaque formation on teeth. In the future, vaccines may be available to help prevent this disease.

Endodontic Disease

Endodontic disease occurs inside the teeth. Several different conditions fall into this category. The causes include injury, tooth fracture, and tooth decay. Treatment is either tooth extraction or a root canal procedure. Signs can include painful teeth that your pet resists having touched or tapped, a tooth with a reddish-brown or gray color, or a decrease in appetite. In advanced cases dental fistulas (draining tracts) occur. However, most dogs mask their pain, making diagnosis difficult. X-rays of the mouth are used to identify affected teeth and help determine the proper treatment.

Developmental Abnormalities

There are several developmental abnormalities that affect the teeth of dogs. Many of these have a genetic component.

Improper Bite

Proper growth and development of the mouth and teeth depend on a series of events that must occur in proper sequence or longterm complications will occur. Early detection and intervention is the best way to prevent more serious problems. Dental development can be divided into 3 stages, each of which can have its own set of problems that require inspection by a veterinarian. Stage 1 is from 0 to 16 weeks of age, Stage 2 is from 16 weeks to 7 months of age, and Stage 3 is from 7 months to 1½ years of age.

Stage 1: Puppies are born with relatively long upper jaws ("overbite"), which allow them to nurse. As the dog grows and begins to eat solid food, the lower jaw goes through a growth spurt. If certain of the lower baby teeth come in before the growth spurt, they can get caught behind the upper teeth and prevent the lower jaw from developing to its proper length. If your veterinarian notices this pattern in a puppy, he or she will probably recommend removing several lower baby (deciduous) teeth. If this is done, the lower jaw will have the opportunity to reach its full length, thus averting problems with the permanent teeth. Some dogs will naturally develop a significant overbite, whether or not tooth extraction is performed.

The reverse situation can also occur. In these cases, the lower jaw grows faster than usual and becomes too long for the upper jaw, producing an "underbite." This condition can be detected as early as 8 weeks of age. Again, certain teeth from the upper jaw may become caught behind those of the lower jaw, preventing proper growth of the upper jaw. The usual treatment is to extract several upper baby teeth. Early detection and correction of such problems will produce the best longterm results.

Other congenital and developmental problems in Stage 1 that may require treatment include extra teeth (which should be extracted only if they are causing problems) or incorrect position of a baby tooth, which should be extracted if it is interfering with other teeth. If jaw growth is different between the left and right sides, teeth may be extracted from the less-developed side. This procedure provides the best opportunity for the uneven growth to correct itself.

Stage 2: The most important problem that can occur during this stage is the retention of baby teeth. Normally, shedding begins around 14 weeks of age with the loss of the upper central incisors. For the next 3 months, the baby teeth are replaced with permanent teeth. Additional permanent teeth that complete the dog's tooth pattern also erupt during this stage. If the baby teeth are not lost at the time the corresponding permanent teeth are coming in, abnormal tooth position and bite may result. If retained baby teeth are removed by a veterinarian as soon as they are noticed; complications can usually be prevented from occurring later on.

Another developmental problem noted in Stage 2 is abnormal positioning (tilting) of lower or upper canine teeth. Depending on the specific situation and age of the dog, orthodontic treatment (that is, "braces" for your pet) can be used to align teeth in their correct positions. Tilting of the upper canines typically is seen in Shetland Sheepdogs, although it has been reported in many other small breeds. Overbite is sometimes noticed during this stage and can be treated with a special plate fitted in the mouth. In more severe cases, tooth shortening or extractions might be necessary.

Stage 3: Additional types of incorrect tooth placement can occur during this stage of your pet's growth. Treatment, if necessary, may include orthodontic treatment or tooth extraction. Crowding of teeth is resolved by extracting one or more teeth. Likewise, teeth that are significantly rotated, as are often found in flat-faced (brachycephalic) breeds, are usually removed.

Enamel Defects

During the development of tooth enamel on both baby and permanent teeth, fevers and the deposition of chemicals within the tooth may cause permanent damage. The canine distemper virus is especially damaging because it both attacks the enamel-producing cells of the teeth and causes a fever. This results in tooth enamel that is thinner than normal. Other fever-causing diseases may result in enamel that does not develop properly and is weaker than normal. Severe malnutrition in young dogs may result in enamel defects. Enamel defects in

isolated teeth are most likely the result of trauma or infection. Often, the infections in fractured baby teeth affect the enamel of the permanent teeth that come in behind them. Enamel defects may also be inherited, especially in Siberian Huskies.

Treatment of these conditions can include bonding of synthetic materials to the teeth, fluoride treatment, and frequent dental preventive care.

Trauma to the Face and Jaw

Fractured teeth should be inspected by a veterinarian to determine whether there has been damage to the tooth pulp. If fractures extend into the pulp, root canal (endodontic) treatment or tooth extraction will be needed. Restorative techniques such crowns can repair defects in tooth structure if the damage is limited to the hard tissues or the pulp has already been treated with root canal treatment. Wounds to the gums or other soft tissues should be treated by the veterinarian as well.

Fractures of the bone will need to be stabilized by the veterinarian. Stabilization may require the use of wires, pins, or other materials. As long as the correct bite position can be maintained, healing is rapid and most of the supporting material can be removed by the veterinarian in about 6 to 8 weeks. A feeding tube may be needed if the dog has difficulty eating while the injury heals.

Tooth Decay (Cavities)

Tooth decay is uncommon in dogs. When it does occur, decay usually is seen as pits on the bite surfaces or on the sides of the molar teeth, near the gum line. If cavities do occur, they can be filled in a way similar to that used in human dentistry.

▓ DISORDERS OF THE MOUTH

The primary function of the mouth is to obtain and introduce food into the digestive tract. Some of its additional functions include communication and social interaction, grooming, protection, and heat regulation (particularly in dogs). Picking up food, chewing, and swallowing require a complex interaction of the muscles of the jaw, the teeth, the tongue, and the upper throat. When any of these functions becomes compromised through disease or trauma, malnutrition and dehydration may result. A complete oral examination should be a part of your animal's physical examination, because oral diseases are most effectively treated with early diagnosis. Otherwise, many will remain hidden in the mouth and progress to an advanced stage.

Oral Inflammatory and Ulcerative Diseases

Gum disease (*see* page 87), is the most common oral problem in small animals. Other causes for oral inflammatory conditions include immune system disease, chemical agents, infections, trauma, metabolic disease, developmental abnormalities, burns, radiation treatment, and cancer. Infections that have been associated with oral inflammation include canine distemper virus and leptospirosis. Traumatic mouth inflammation may be seen after an animal tries to eat sharp plant material (such as plant awns) or fiberglass insulation. The houseplant *Dieffenbachia* may cause oral inflammation and sores if chewed. Chronic kidney failure can cause inflammation and sores in the mouth.

Signs vary with the cause and extent of inflammation. Loss of appetite may be seen. Bad breath and drooling are common with mouth inflammation, tongue inflammation, and sore throat. The saliva may be tinged with blood. The animal may paw at its mouth and, due to pain, resent or resist any attempt to examine its mouth. Lymph nodes in the region may be enlarged.

Chronic Ulcerative Stomatitis

Chronic ulcerative stomatitis involves inflammation of the mucous membranes of the mouth. Signs include severe gum inflammation, receding gums in several sites, and large sores on the mouth surface near the surfaces of large teeth. The problem commonly affects Greyhounds, but it has also been seen in Maltese, Miniature Schnauzers, Labrador Retrievers, and other breeds. The characteristic feature is the contact ulcer or sore that develops where the lip contacts the tooth surface, most commonly on the inner surface of the upper lip next to the upper canine teeth. These abnormalities have also been termed "kissing ulcers" because they are found where the lips "kiss" the teeth.

The cause of this disease is an immune system dysfunction that results in an excessive inflammatory response to dental plaque. For this reason, thorough plaque control through professional cleaning and excellent home oral hygiene (including tooth brushing) may resolve the problem. Supplemental antibacterial measures, such as topical chlorhexidine rinses or gels, may be prescribed by your veterinarian. In severe cases, topical anti-inflammatory preparations may provide comfort. Discomfort caused by the ulcers can make it difficult to brush your pet's teeth and give oral medications. If discomfort is severe and you are unable to brush the teeth, extraction of the adjacent teeth may be necessary to remove the contact surfaces on which plaque accumulates. Although extraction may aid in control of the sores, it may not completely cure the problem, as plaque grows on all surfaces in the mouth and animals can continue to develop sores.

Lip Disorders

Lip fold dermatitis is a chronic skin inflammation that occurs in breeds with drooping upper lips and lower lip folds (such as spaniels, English Bulldogs, and Saint Bernards). These lips often accumulate moisture, causing inflammation to develop. The condition may be worsened when poor oral hygiene results in high salivary bacterial counts. The lower lip folds can become very bad-smelling, inflamed, uncomfortable, and swollen.

Treatment of lip fold dermatitis includes clipping the hair, cleaning the folds 1 to 2 times a day with benzoyl peroxide or a mild skin cleanser, and keeping the area dry. Your veterinarian may prescribe a daily application of a topical diaper rash cream. Surgical correction of deep lip folds is a more long-lasting remedy for severe cases.

Lip wounds, resulting from fights or chewing on sharp objects, are common and vary widely in severity. Thorns, grass awns, plant burrs, and fishhooks may embed in the lips and cause severe irritation or wounds. Irritants such as plastic or plant material may produce inflammation of the lips. Lip infections may develop. Wounds of the lips should be cleaned and sutured by your veterinarian, if necessary.

Direct extension of severe gum disease or inflammation inside the mouth can produce inflammation of the lips (**cheilitis**). Licking areas of bacterial dermatitis or infected wounds may spread the infection to the lips and lip folds. Inflammation of the lips also can be associated with parasitic infections, autoimmune skin diseases, and tumors.

Inflammation of the lips and lip folds can be short- or longterm. Animals may paw, scratch, or rub at their mouth or lip; have a foul odor on the breath; and occasionally salivate excessively or refuse to eat. With chronic infection of the lip margins or folds, the hair in these areas is discolored, moist, and matted with a thick, yellowish or brown, foul-smelling discharge overlying red skin that may have open sores. Sometimes the infection extends to another area of the body; this is easily diagnosed because of the lip inflammation that accompanies it.

Inflammation of the lips that is unrelated to lip folds usually resolves with minimal cleansing, appropriate antibiotics (if a bacterial infection is present), and specific treatment of the cause. Treatment of periodontal disease or mouth inflammation is necessary to prevent recurrence.

Infectious cheilitis that has spread from a location away from the mouth usually improves with treatment of the primary spot, but treatment of the lip area also is necessary. With severe infection, care includes clipping the hair from the infected area. The area will then be gently cleaned and dried. Antibiotics may be prescribed if the infection is severe or spreads to other locations.

Fungal Stomatitis

Fungal stomatitis is caused by overgrowth of the fungus *Candida albicans*. It is an uncommon cause of oral inflammation in dogs. The main sign is the appearance of creamy white flat areas (plaques) on the tongue or mucous membranes. It is usually thought to be associated with other oral diseases, longterm antibiotic treatment, or a suppressed immune system. In most cases, both the underlying disease and the fungal infection itself will be treated. Follow your veterinarian's recommendations about diet carefully to support your pet's recovery. Your veterinarian will also recommend a treatment program to control the fungus causing the problem. This is a critical phase of the treatment because the outlook is poor if the underlying disease cannot be adequately treated or controlled.

Trenchmouth

This relatively uncommon disease of dogs is characterized by severe inflammation of the gums (gingivitis), ulceration, and death of the tissue lining the mouth. The cause of this disease is unknown, but it has been suggested that normal mouth bacteria and other microorganisms may cause this disease after some predisposing factor either increases their levels or decreases the mouth's resistance to infection. Other potential factors are stress, excess use of corticosteroids, and poor nutrition.

The disease first appears as reddening and swelling of the gum edges, which are painful, bleed easily, and may lead to receding gums. Extension to other areas of the inner mouth is common. In severe cases, this results in sores and exposed bone. Bad breath is severe, and the animal may be unwilling to eat due to pain. Excessive drooling may be present, and the saliva may be tinged with blood. The disease is diagnosed by excluding other possible causes.

Treatment generally consists of treatment for gum disease, professional cleaning of wounds, oral hygiene, antibiotics, and oral antiseptics.

Inflammation of the Tongue

Inflammation of the tongue is called **glossitis**. It may be due to infection, irritation, wounds, disease, or other causes such as electrical burns or insect stings. A thread, string, or other foreign object may get caught under the tongue. Glossitis can also occur in long-haired dogs that use the mouth and tongue in an attempt to remove plant burrs from their coats.

Drooling and a reluctance to eat are common signs, but the cause may go undiscovered unless the mouth is carefully examined. Gum disease may result in reddening, swelling, and occasionally sores on the edge of the tongue. There may be no inflammation of the upper surface of the tongue, but the lower surface may be painful, irritated, and cut by the foreign body. Porcupine quills, plant material, and other foreign materials may become embedded so deeply that they cannot be easily detected. Insect stings can cause sudden swelling of the tongue. Some animals have a tongue with a deep central groove, which often becomes filled with hairs that act as an irritant. In chronic cases of inflammation, a thick, brown, foul-smelling discharge (occasionally with bleeding) may be present. Frequently, the animal is reluctant to allow examination of its mouth.

Glossitis is treated by the veterinarian removing any foreign objects and any broken or diseased teeth. Infection may be treated with an appropriate antibiotic. Cleaning of the wounds and use of anti-septic mouthwashes are beneficial in some cases. A soft diet and intravenous fluids may be necessary. If the animal is weak and unable to eat well for a prolonged period, tube feeding may also be required. Sudden glossitis due to insect stings may require emergency treatment. If the glossitis is caused by another condition, the primary disease will also be treated. The tongue heals rapidly after irritation and infection have been eliminated.

Soft Tissue Trauma

Injuries to the cheeks or mouth are common in dogs, but usually respond well to treatment.

Cheek Biting

A wound along the side of the cheek may be caused by self-trauma when the tissue becomes trapped between the teeth during chewing. Surgical removal of the excess tissue prevents further injury.

Mouth Burns

Thermal (heat), chemical, or electrical burns involving the mouth are common in dogs. Your veterinarian will look for any injuries to other body systems. The injuries may be mild, with only temporary discomfort, or may be very destructive with loss of tissue and scar formation, followed by deformity or tissue loss. In some cases, these other injuries can be life-threatening. Sometimes puppies will be burned by chewing on an electrical cord. These animals often have a scar across the back of the tongue, outlining the path of the electrical cord. One or both lip corners may have a scar or wound, and the adjacent teeth may be discolored and eventually require a root canal treatment.

A dog with a burn to the mouth may hesitate to eat or drink, drool, or resent handling of its mouth or face. If tissue destruction is noticeable, sores and mouth inflammation may develop. Such wounds can easily become infected. If you observed the burn yourself, provide the details to your veterinarian. If the animal is seen by a veterinarian shortly after receiving a chemical burn to the mouth, he or she may be able to neutralize the chemical and/or flush it out with water. More commonly, the dog is seen by the veterinarian too long after exposure for neutralization to be effective.

If the animal has only a reddened mouth lining without tissue damage, it may require no treatment other than a soft or liquid diet until the soreness has healed. If tissue damage is extensive, the veterinarian may rinse the tissues with a chlorhexidine solution and perform some cleansing to remove dead tissue and debris. Antibiotics may be prescribed to reduce the chance of infection.

Viral Warts and Papillomas

Viral warts are noncancerous growths caused by a virus. The mouth lining and corners of the lip are most frequently affected, but the roof and back of the mouth can also be involved. Viral warts are most common in young dogs and often appear suddenly, with rapid growth and spread. Signs are seen when the growths interfere with picking up food, chewing, or swallowing. Occasionally, if the growths are numerous, the dog may bite them when chewing, causing them to bleed and become infected. The warts may disappear spontaneously within a few weeks, and removal is generally not necessary. If necessary, a veterinarian can remove the warts surgically.

Papillomas look very much like viral warts, but they tend to grow more slowly and are less likely to be found in groups. They normally do not spread, and can be cured by surgical removal.

Oral Tumors

Tumors in the mouth and upper throat may be either benign (not cancerous) or malignant (cancerous).

Benign Tumors

The most common benign oral tumors in dogs are **epulides**. They may be seen in dogs of any age but are seen most frequently in dogs 6 years of age or older.

Epulides are firm masses involving the tissue of the gums. They arise from the ligament of the involved tooth. These masses generally occur alone, although multiple masses may be present. They can become quite extensive.

There are 2 general categories of epulides: peripheral odontogenic fibromas and canine peripheral ameloblastoma. Peripheral odontogenic fibromas may develop centers within the mass(es) that harden and turn into bone-like tissue. Canine peripheral ameloblastomas are benign but grow quickly. They routinely invade nearby tissues including bone. Because of their aggressive nature, these epulides should be surgically removed. Radiation treatment may help to minimize disfigurement if there are large tumors.

Due to the varied nature of epulides and other oral tumors, your veterinarian will want to biopsy the tumors prior to surgery. The results of the biopsy will guide the veterinarian in planning the surgery and any other required treatment.

A **gingival fibroma** is a benign growth on the gums that usually originates near the gum line. The growth is relatively insensitive and tough and is the color of the normal gum or more pale. The growth may become large enough to completely cover the surfaces of several teeth. Breeds with flat faces (brachycephalic breeds) may be more likely to develop this condition than other breeds. Gingival fibroma is most common in older dogs and usually causes no signs of illness. Hair, food, and debris may collect between the growth and the teeth and cause irritation and bad breath. Surgical removal is the most satisfactory treatment. After surgery, your pet may be prescribed a daily oral rinse to be used until the site is healed.

Malignant Tumors

In dogs, the most common types of malignant tumors are malignant melanoma, squamous cell carcinoma, and fibrosarcoma. The gums are affected most frequently. Signs vary depending on the location and extent of the tumor. Bad breath, reluctance to eat, and excessive drooling are common. If the back of the mouth and throat are involved, swallowing may be difficult. The tumors frequently ulcerate and bleed. The face may become swollen as the tumor enlarges and invades surrounding tissue. Lymph nodes near the tumor often become swollen before the tumor itself can be seen.

A tissue biopsy is usually required to confirm the diagnosis. If your veterinarian suspects that the tumor has spread, nearby lymph nodes and the lungs may be evaluated as well.

The treatment and outlook depend on the specific kind of tumor and whether it has spread. Malignant melanomas are highly invasive and spread readily; consequently, the outlook is guarded to poor. Surgical removal of the tumor can extend survival and may cure the condition; however, recurrence is common. Squamous cell carcinomas that do not involve the tonsils have a low rate of spread, and the outlook is good with aggressive surgery, radiation treatment, or both. Squamous cell carcinomas affecting the tonsils spread rapidly and have a poor outlook. Fibrosarcomas have a guarded outlook, and recurrence of tumor growth after surgery is common.

Salivary Disorders

Saliva moistens the mouth and helps begin the digestion of food. As with any other part of the body, there can be medical problems involving the glands that produce the saliva.

Excessive Salivation (Ptyalism or Sialosis)

Excessive salivation has 2 main causes: either the animal is producing too much saliva (a condition called ptyalism or sialosis), or the animal cannot effectively swallow the saliva that is produced. In either situation, the animal drools. There are a number of underlying causes for this condition (see BOX). The most serious of these is rabies, so your veterinarian will attempt to exclude that first. The underlying cause may be within or near the mouth, or it can be a sign of a more general condition. Whatever the cause, it will have to be determined and treated to control the condition. Short-term moist inflammation of the lips and face may develop if the skin is not kept as dry as possible. Cleansing with an antiseptic solution may be recommended.

Salivary Mucocele

In a salivary mucocele, saliva accumulates under the skin after damage to the salivary duct or gland. This is the most common salivary gland disorder of dogs. While any of the salivary glands may be affected, those under the tongue and in the jaw are involved most commonly. Usually, the cause is not determined.

The signs depend on the site of saliva accumulation. The first sign noticed may be a nonpainful, slowly enlarging mass, frequently in the neck. A mucocele under the tongue may not be seen until it is traumatized and bleeds. A pharyngeal (throat) mucocele may obstruct the airways and result in difficulty breathing. Pain or fever may occur if the mucocele

---

Causes of Excessive Salivation

- Drugs or poisons
- Irritation associated with inflammation of the mouth or tongue, foreign objects in the mouth, tumors, injuries, or other defects of the mouth
- Infectious diseases such as rabies, the nervous form of distemper, or other convulsive disorders
- Motion sickness, fear, nervousness, or excitement
- Reluctance to swallow from irritation of the esophagus
- Inflamed tonsils (tonsillitis)
- Administration of medicine
- Conformational defects of the mouth
- Metabolic disorders such as hepatic encephalopathy or kidney failure
- Abscess or other blockage or disorder of the salivary glands

becomes infected. A veterinarian can distinguish the mucocele from abscesses, tumors, and other types of cysts by using a needle to draw a sample of fluid from inside the mucocele.

Surgery is often recommended to remove the damaged salivary gland and duct. Mucoceles in the neck or under the tongue can be managed with periodic drainage if surgery is not an option. Complete gland and duct removal is often recommended for mucoceles in the throat to avoid the possibility of future life-threatening airway obstruction. Your veterinarian will consider your pet's specific condition when making a treatment recommendation.

Salivary Fistula

Fistulas are abnormal paths or openings between 2 organs in the body or from an organ inside the body to the body surface. Fistulas involving the salivary glands in dogs and cats are rare. When they do occur, the cause may be an injury to the salivary glands in the lower jaw, the cheeks or face, or under the tongue. Other causes include bite wounds, abscess drainage, or the opening of a closed surgical incision.

Your veterinarian will want to be sure to correctly identify the fistula before recommending treatment. Draining sinuses should be eliminated as a source of the problem. If a fistula is the problem, surgery is often required. Tying off the involved salivary duct usually resolves the problem, although the associated gland may need to be removed.

Salivary Gland Tumors

Salivary gland tumors are rare in dogs. Most are seen in dogs that are more than 10 years old. Poodles and spaniel breeds may be predisposed. Most salivary gland tumors are malignant, with carcinomas and adenocarcinomas the most common. Spread to nearby lymph nodes and the lungs is common. Tumors removed by surgery alone tend to recur, so radiation

treatment, with or without surgery, is often recommended.

Inflammation of the Salivary Glands

Inflammation of the salivary glands is rarely a problem in dogs. When it is found, it is frequently an incidental finding in addition to another disease or condition. Salivary gland infections may be caused by trauma (often from bites or other penetrating wounds) or from generalized infections such as rabies, distemper, and the virus that causes mumps in humans.

Signs of inflamed salivary glands include fever, depression, and painful, swollen salivary glands. Occasionally, an abscessed gland discharges pus into the surrounding tissue or the mouth. Rupture through the skin may cause a salivary fistula to form.

Mild inflammation may require no treatment. Recovery is often rapid and complete. If there are abscesses, these are normally drained and antibiotics given. If recovery is not complete within a few days, or if the infection recurs, your veterinarian will want to do laboratory tests on a tissue sample and a biopsy. Occasionally, surgical removal of the infected salivary gland is required.

Dry Mouth (Xerostomia)

Xerostomia is a decreased secretion of saliva that causes a dry mouth. It can cause significant discomfort and difficulty with eating. Historically, this condition is uncommon in dogs and cats, but is very common in humans who have damaged salivary glands following radiation treatment for tumors of the head and neck. As radiation treatment is used more commonly in veterinary medicine, this condition may become more frequent in pets. Decreased salivary secretion may also result from use of certain drugs, extreme dehydration, fever, anesthesia, or disease of the salivary gland. Finding and treating the underlying cause is important in controlling xerostomia. Specially formulated mouthwashes can often help relieve the discomfort that results from this condition. Fluids may be administered to correct dehydration, if present. If the condition is immune related, appropriate immunosuppressive treatment may be prescribed.

■ DISORDERS OF THE PHARYNX

The upper throat is called the pharynx. **Pharyngeal paralysis** refers to paralysis of the upper throat (pharynx) that makes swallowing difficult or impossible. It may be caused by a nervous system disorder or other disease or trauma that causes collapse, obstruction, or malfunction of the pharynx. In some instances, the condition may be partial or affect only one side of the throat and the dog may be able to swallow, although complications may occur.

Pharyngeal paralysis results in severe problems with swallowing; food and saliva come back out through the mouth and nose. In most species, collapse of throat tissues occurs. Affected dogs are at risk of pneumonia from inhaling food and liquid (aspiration pneumonia), dehydration, and circulatory and respiratory failure. Signs of pharyngeal paralysis include fever, coughing, gagging, and choking. This condition may be fatal. In many cases, emergency surgery to provide an airway (tracheostomy) must be done before any more detailed analysis of the condition can be performed.

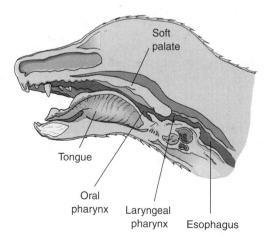

The throat and pharynx in a dog

In general, treatment for pharyngeal paralysis is directed toward alleviating the signs of the disease. Treatment may include drugs to control inflammation, antibiotics to control the complications of aspiration pneumonia, draining of abscesses (if they are present), and alternative routes of nutrition. Tubes can be inserted (intubation) to help the dog breathe, eat, and drink. In many of these cases, the outlook is poor. Your veterinarian will consider the welfare of your pet when determining what course of treatment to follow.

■ DISORDERS OF THE ESOPHAGUS

Signs of problems with the esophagus include difficulty swallowing and regurgitation (return of food or liquid before it has reached the stomach). Regurgitation is effortless and has few warning signs, in contrast to vomiting which is an active process preceded by signs of nausea.

Congenital abnormalities of the esophagus (those present at birth) are discussed earlier in this chapter (*see* page 84).

Disorders of Swallowing (Cricopharyngeal Achalasia)

The cricopharyngeal muscle opens and closes to allow food and liquids from the mouth into the esophagus. Cricopharyngeal achalasia is a condition in which this muscle does not adequately relax. This can lead to an inability to swallow foods or liquids. Though it is usually an inherited defect, adult dogs can also develop the condition. A dog will try to swallow and end up gagging and vomiting. A common complication of this disorder is aspiration pneumonia: liquids that a dog tries to swallow can end up going down the trachea and to the lungs. The cause is usually unknown, but it may be associated with neuromuscular disorders in adult dogs.

Treatment of this condition usually involves surgery to cut the abnormal muscle. Normal swallowing is usually possible immediately after the surgery. About 70% of the surgeries are successful. Dogs that have other neuromuscular disorders are less responsive to surgery, but may respond to treatment with successful management of the neuromuscular disorder. If the dog develops aspiration pneumonia, it must be treated immediately and aggressively.

Expansion of the Esophagus (Megaesophagus)

Abnormal dilation or stretching of the esophagus (also called megaesophagus) can be caused by a congenital defect (*see* page 84), or it can occur in an adult dog, either alone or together with other diseases. Congenital megaesophagus (generally diagnosed in dogs soon after weaning) is a hereditary defect that occurs in Wire-haired Fox Terriers and Miniature Schnauzers. A tendency to occur in families has been reported in German Shepherds, Newfoundlands, Great Danes, Irish Setters, Chinese Shar-Peis, Greyhounds, and cats. Some causes of megaesophagus include myasthenia gravis, systemic lupus erythematosus, polymyositis, hypoadrenocorticism, lead poisoning, dysautonomia, nervous system disorders including cancer, and possibly hypothyroidism. Megaesophagus can also occur as a result of injury of the esophagus, the presence of a foreign object in the esophagus, or compression of the esophagus.

The primary sign of megaesophagus is regurgitation. Dogs with megaesophagus will suddenly start regurgitating undigested food soon after eating and will lose weight. Respiratory signs such as coughing and difficulty breathing may occur. A chest x-ray will show air, fluid, or food in the distended esophagus. Other tests may also be performed to view the esophagus and determine the cause and extent of the enlargement.

If an associated disease is causing megaesophagus, it must be treated. Surgery is often needed to correct blood vessel abnormalities. There is no specific medical treatment for megaesophagus with no known cause, but it may be managed by feeding the dog with the upper body in an elevated position of at least 45 degrees. Allowing the dog to eat in this position—by having the dog stand on a ramp or with its front legs on a platform with the food bowl higher—has been found to help. Keeping the dog in this position for at least 15 minutes after eating allows gravity to help the food move down the esophagus.

Changing the texture of the dog's diet is usually necessary. The type of food that will best prevent vomiting varies from dog to dog. Soft gruel might work for some dogs, and others might do best with dry or canned foods. Feeding the dog in frequent small meals is usually helpful. The food should be high in calories to help the dog maintain its weight.

The overall outlook for dogs with this condition is guarded. Sixty per cent of dogs with megaesophagus tend to develop aspiration pneumonia or fibrosis of the lungs due to recurrent pneumonia, which may shorten their lifespan.

Esophageal Strictures

Esophageal stricture is a narrowing of the esophagus. It may develop after trauma (for example, ingestion of a foreign object or caustic substance), inflammation of the esophagus, gastroesophageal reflux (gastric acid flowing back into the esophagus), or tumor invasion. Signs include regurgitation, excessive drooling, difficulty swallowing, and pain. Examining the esophagus using fluoroscopy or endoscopy are the preferred methods for diagnosis. These tests enable your veterinarian to actually see the number, location, and types of strictures.

Treatment of the stricture by stretching it with a balloon catheter has been successful. The catheter is a tube that is placed in the esophagus and then advanced to where the stricture occurs. The tip of the catheter is then inflated like a balloon, which stretches the esophagus and relieves the stricture. Other methods, including surgery, have been less successful.

Inflammation of the Esophagus (Esophagitis)

Inflammation of the esophagus is usually caused by foreign objects or acid reflux from the stomach into the esophagus. Occasionally certain drugs, cancer, or caustic substances will cause this condition. In many cases, a veterinarian will use an endoscope (a flexible tube with a tiny camera at one end) to explore the esophagus, search for foreign objects, and assess the extent of tissue damage.

Mild inflammation may produce no visible signs and often requires no treatment. If signs are present, drugs may be prescribed. For example, if the problem is caused by acid reflux (a cause of heartburn in people), drugs that reduce stomach acid can provide relief for your pet. Other prescription medications increase muscle tone in the lower esophagus, reducing the amount of acid that escapes upward. Your veterinarian may recommend feeding your pet a diet of soft food, low in fat and fiber, in small, frequent meals. If inflammation is severe, a feeding tube placed through the body wall into the stomach, bypassing the esophagus, may need to be inserted to allow the esophagus to rest. Antibiotics are sometimes prescribed to prevent bacterial infection.

Foreign Objects in the Esophagus

Because of their eating habits, foreign objects in the esophagus are more common in dogs than in cats. Bones are the most common, but needles, fishhooks, wood, rawhide pieces, and other objects may also become lodged in the esophagus. Sudden and excessive drooling, gagging, regurgitation, and repeated attempts to swallow are signs of an esophageal foreign object. A partial obstruction may allow fluids but not food to pass. If an obstruction is not treated, loss of appetite, weight loss, and lethargy may occur. In addition, the foreign object can perforate the esophagus, which may require surgery. An esophageal stricture, which is a narrowing of the width of the esophagus

(*see* page 98), is the most common complication of an esophageal foreign object. Aspiration pneumonia may also be seen if regurgitated material is inhaled into the lungs.

Many foreign objects can be seen on x-rays. In some cases, a contrast esophagram (a specialized test in which a dye that shows up on x-rays is swallowed) or esophagoscopy (examination of the esophagus with an endoscope) is needed. If a foreign object is detected in the esophagus, it should be removed immediately. Removal will depend on the object and on its current location. In many cases, your veterinarian will be able to remove the foreign object through the dog's mouth, using a flexible endoscope and forceps (large tweezers) or other instrument. If the object cannot be removed by mouth, sometimes it can be pushed into the stomach where it can be digested and passed in the feces, or removed via surgery. Surgery is necessary if the esophagus has been perforated or the foreign object cannot be removed using endoscopy; in these cases, the overall recovery rate has been reported to be greater than 90%.

Esophageal Diverticula

Diverticula are pouch-like expansions (dilations) of the esophageal wall. They can be inherited or acquired. They are rare in dogs. Small diverticula may cause no signs. Large diverticula can trap food in the pouch, causing the dog to have trouble breathing after eating, vomit, or stop eating. Contrast x-rays can be used to diagnose the disorder. Endoscopy (using a tiny video camera in a flexible fiber optic tube) can allow the veterinarian to see the actual pouch and any ulceration or scarring that may be present.

Small diverticula can usually be treated with a bland, soft food diet. The animal should also eat in an upright position (having the forelegs raised higher than the hindlegs, such as on a ramp or platform, and holding this position for a short period of time after eating). Large diverticula require surgery involving removal of the pouch and rebuilding of the esophageal wall. The outlook for recovery after surgery is guarded to fair.

▓ VOMITING

Vomiting is the forceful ejection of the contents (such as food, fluids, or debris) of the stomach and upper small intestine. It is typically preceded by other signs, such as nausea, excessive drooling, retching, and forceful contractions of the abdominal muscles and the diaphragm. Vomiting can be caused by digestive system disease, kidney or liver failure, pancreatitis, nervous system disorders, and ingestion of irritating substances and poisons.

Vomiting differs from regurgitation, which is a passive motion. With regurgitation, the expelled food and fluid tends to be undigested and may have a cylindrical shape reflecting the shape of the esophagus. Coughing or difficulty breathing are more often associated with regurgitation than with vomiting.

Short-term or even occasional vomiting is generally not associated with other abnormalities. Coughing or longterm, repeated vomiting may be associated with weakness, lethargy, weight loss, dehydration, and electrolyte (salt) imbalance. Whenever possible, vomiting is controlled by identifying and eliminating the cause, while allowing the digestive system time to recover.

Short-term or Occasional Vomiting

When a dog has been vomiting for only a short time (less than 3 to 4 days) and no other signs are present, your veterinarian's examination may be limited to a detailed history (including questions about your pet's possible access to garbage or poisons), a physical examination (including the abdomen), examination of the mouth, and a rectal examination (checking for evidence of eating table scraps or other inappropriate items). If nothing of significance is found, treatment to relieve signs may be all that is needed.

Generally, the treatment for short-term vomiting requires withholding food and limiting access to water for 24 hours. Dehydrated animals and animals with kidney or heart disease may require intravenous fluids during this time. If the vomiting has stopped after 24 hours, the dog may be offered small amounts (for example, a teaspoonful) of easily digested food. If no further vomiting occurs, feeding can usually be slowly resumed. Follow the treatment directions provided by your veterinarian carefully. Providing too much or too little water or food during this time can hurt your pet.

Longterm or Severe Vomiting

Longterm vomiting, vomiting that occurs more often than once or twice daily, and vomiting accompanied by blood, abdominal pain, depression, dehydration, weakness, fever, or other signs requires a more detailed examination. This may include blood and urine tests as well as x-rays of the digestive system. In many cases, endoscopic evaluation and biopsy of the stomach and small intestine may be required to determine the nature of the disease.

Treatment for longterm vomiting is directed at elimination of the cause, if it can be identified. In addition, your veterinarian may need to treat conditions such as dehydration, electrolyte (salt) imbalances, and acid-base disorders that may have developed. Drugs to control vomiting can be prescribed for animals with persistent vomiting, dehydration, and weakness. Your veterinarian will evaluate your pet's overall condition before prescribing any medication or treatment.

▓ DISORDERS OF THE STOMACH AND INTESTINES

Diseases that affect the stomach and intestines are common in dogs. They include infectious diseases such as bacterial, viral, and parasitic diseases and noninfectious disorders such as tumors, bloat, and obstruction.

Canine Parvovirus

Canine parvovirus infection is a potentially fatal viral disease that most often affects puppies or unvaccinated adult dogs. The virus itself is resistant to a number of common disinfectants and may survive for several months in contaminated areas. Rottweilers, American Pit Bull Terriers, Doberman Pinschers, and German Shepherds are at increased risk of disease. The death rate associated with canine parvovirus infection is reported to range from 16 to 48%.

The virus is transmitted by direct contact with infected dogs. Indirect transmission, such as from objects contaminated by feces, is also an important source of infection. The virus is present in the feces for up to 3 weeks after infection. Recovered dogs may serve as carriers.

After it is ingested, the virus replicates and spreads to the bloodstream. It attacks rapidly dividing cells throughout the body, especially those in the bone marrow, blood cell-producing tissue, and the lining of the small intestine. Production of the virus in the intestinal lining causes severe damage and bloody diarrhea. Normal intestinal bacteria may enter the damaged tissue and the bloodstream, worsening the disease.

Infected dogs may not show signs of illness. Clinical disease may be triggered by stress such as boarding, and signs may be worsened by other infections of the digestive system. Prolonged contact with a dog shedding high levels of virus increases the likelihood of becoming infected. An infected dog may be contagious before the onset of signs.

Gastroenteritis (inflammation of the stomach and intestines) is most common in pups 6 to 20 weeks old. During this time, the level of antibodies provided by the mother during nursing is falling, but vaccination may not yet have adequately protected the pup against infection. More than 85% of affected dogs are less than 1 year old. Dogs with the intestinal form may show sudden lethargy, loss of appetite, fever, vomiting, and diarrhea. The feces are loose and may contain mucus or blood. The severity of signs varies. Most dogs recover within a few days with appropriate supportive care; others can die within hours of the onset of signs.

Diagnosis is based on the dog's history and signs and is confirmed by a positive fecal or blood test. The fecal test, which detects viral protein, may be negative despite infection if it is done too early in the disease course. Thus, your veterinarian may need to repeat the test if the history and signs support the likely presence of the virus.

Treatment and Control

There is no specific treatment to eliminate the virus. Most dogs recover with appropriate supportive care, which is focused on replacing lost fluids. Oral electrolyte solutions (used to replace sodium and potassium that is lost through the intestines) may be used in mildly dehydrated dogs without a history of vomiting. More severely affected dogs will need intravenous fluids. Most dogs that survive the first 2 to 3 days of disease recover. Persistent vomiting can be controlled with prescription medication. Antibiotics are generally used only in cases where secondary bacterial infection is likely to be present.

Follow your veterinarian's instructions for your pet's diet. Typically, food and water should be withheld until vomiting has subsided, followed by frequent, small amounts of a bland diet such as cottage cheese and rice or a prescription diet. If signs recur after feeding, contact your veterinarian for directions. In many cases, food will need to be withheld for an additional 12 or 24 hours. If food can be tolerated, the bland diet is usually continued for 1 or 2 weeks, after which the dog's regular diet can be gradually reintroduced.

Contaminated areas should be thoroughly cleaned. Household bleach (diluted to 1 part bleach to 30 parts water) or commercial products labeled for use against parvovirus can inactivate the virus. The same solutions may be used as footbaths to disinfect household footwear. Disinfection of hands, clothing, and the dog's food and water bowls and toys is recommended. Pups should be kept isolated from adult dogs returning from shows or field trials.

Vaccination is critical in the control of canine parvovirus. Vaccination of pups should begin at 5 to 8 weeks of age. The last vaccination should be given at 16 to 20 weeks of age, and annual vaccination thereafter is usually recommended. Follow your veterinarian's parvovirus vaccination recommendations to protect your pet.

Inflammation of the Large Intestine

The large intestine (also called colon or large bowel) helps maintain fluid and electrolyte (salt) balance and absorb nutrients; it also temporarily stores feces and provides an environment for normal intestinal bacteria. When the colon is damaged by inflammation, parasites, or other causes, diarrhea is often the result.

Inflammation of the colon may be short- or longterm. In most cases, the cause is unknown; bacterial, parasitic, and allergic causes are suspected. Inflammation may be the result of a defect in the function of the immune system in the colon. An exaggerated reaction to dietary or bacterial factors within the intestine, genetic predisposition, or results of previous infectious or parasitic disease have also been implicated.

Animals with inflammation of the colon may strain to defecate and may pass mucus-laden feces, sometimes containing blood. Feces are often of a small volume and a more liquid consistency. Weight loss and vomiting are rare and much less common than in dogs with diseases of the small intestine.

If possible, the cause of the inflammation should be identified and eliminated. Your veterinarian will conduct a physical examination, followed by appropriate tests (which may include taking blood and fecal samples, endoscopy, or biopsy, as needed). Treatment is based on the cause of inflammation.

Follow your veterinarian's recommendations for diet. You may be asked to withhold food for 1 or 2 days to "rest" the animal's digestive system. Once feeding is resumed, dissolvable fiber may be added to the diet. Over time, the fiber dose can be often be reduced or eliminated and a standard dog food substituted without causing a return of the diarrhea. When feeding is first resumed, you may be advised to provide food with a type of protein that your dog has not previously eaten, such as duck, lamb, kangaroo, or venison. This change is to reduce the chance that your pet will have an allergic reaction to the food proteins.

Supplementing the diet with fiber improves diarrhea in many animals. However, the addition of fiber alone will not usually resolve signs of large-intestinal diarrhea in dogs. To help the inflammation resolve more rapidly, your veterinarian may add anti-inflammatory medication to the change in diet. Some animals require additional short-term use of antidiarrheal medications until inflammation is brought under control.

Constipation

Constipation is a common problem in dogs. In most instances, the problem is easily corrected; however, in sicker animals, the condition can be severe. The longer feces remain in the colon, the drier, harder, and more difficult to pass they become. **Obstipation** is constipation that resists treatment, in which the animal is unable to successfully defecate.

How Can Fiber Help with Diarrhea?

Dietary fiber reduces free water in the feces, prolongs the length of time food is in the intestines (increasing the opportunity for the food to absorb water), absorbs poisons, increases fecal bulk, stretches the smooth muscle of the colon, and improves the ability of the intestines to contract.

Longterm constipation may be due to an obstruction inside the intestines, constriction from outside the intestines, or because of neuromuscular problems with the colon itself. Obstruction is most common and is due to the dog's inability to pass poorly digestible, often firm matter (such as hair or bones) that has become mixed with fecal material. A lack of water intake or the reluctance to defecate on a regular basis due to environmental stress or pain that occurs while defecating contributes to the formation of hard, dry feces. In other cases, tumors may block the passage of feces. Constriction may be caused by compression of the colon or rectum by a narrowed pelvic bone (for example, if a broken pelvis heals incorrectly) or an enlarged prostate gland. Some drugs may cause constipation as a side effect.

Signs of constipation include straining to defecate and the passage of firm, dry feces. If the passage of feces is hindered by an enlarged prostate or lymph nodes, the feces may be thin or ribbon-like in appearance. Passed feces are often foul-smelling. Some animals are quite ill and also have lethargy, depression, loss of appetite, vomiting, and abdominal discomfort. Your veterinarian can confirm the presence of retained fecal matter by feeling the abdomen and performing a rectal examination. Abdominal x-rays may help establish the cause of fecal retention and indicate whether the feces contain foreign matter such as bones. Be sure to tell your veterinarian about any tendency your pet has to eat bones, garbage, or other hard matter. Other tests may be needed in cases of longterm constipation or obstipation.

Affected dogs should receive plenty of water. Mild constipation can often be treated by switching to a high-fiber diet, keeping the dog from eating bones or other objects, providing ready access to water, and using appropriate laxatives (usually for a short time only). If laxatives are prescribed, they will be ones suitable for your pet. Laxatives formulated for humans can be very dangerous for animals. In more severe cases of constipation, a veterinar-

ian can remove retained feces using enemas or manual extraction while your pet is under general anesthesia. Complete removal of all feces may require 2 or 3 attempts over several days.

Bloat

Bloat is a life-threatening emergency. It is caused by the twisting of the stomach along its axis and the accumulation of gas with or without fluid in the stomach.

Bloat tends to primarily affect large, deep-chested dogs. Stress may trigger an acute episode of bloat. The incidence increases with age, being most common in dogs 7 to 10 years old. Doberman Pinschers, German Shepherds, Standard Poodles, Great Danes, Saint Bernards, Irish Setters, and Gordon Setters are affected most frequently.

Dogs with bloat commonly have eaten a large meal followed by exercise and repeated attempts to vomit. Signs of bloat may include restlessness, apparent discomfort, rapid breathing, abdominal pain and swelling, repeated dry retching, and excessive drooling. Your veterinarian may note a rapid and weak pulse, pale mucous membranes, and other signs of shock. An irregular heart rate can also develop. Veterinarians usually use x-rays to diagnose stomach rotation, but other imaging techniques can be helpful.

A successful outcome depends on prompt diagnosis and treatment by a veterinarian. The first goals of treatment are to stabilize the animal and decompress the stomach. The dog may require intravenous fluids to counteract shock. The pressure within the stomach will be relieved as soon as possible. This may be done by passing a tube through the mouth into the stomach. Once the tube enters the stomach, gas readily escapes. Excess fluid and food can then be removed via gravity and suction. After the stomach has been decompressed, the veterinarian may rinse it with warm water or saline to remove any remaining debris. If a tube cannot be passed into the stomach, excess gas may be relieved by inserting a large, hollow needle and catheter directly into the stomach through the skin.

Surgery may be performed to assess the condition of the stomach and spleen, to reposition the stomach to its normal location, and to attach the stomach to the abdominal wall in an attempt to decrease the likelihood that it will twist again. Food is usually withheld for 24 to 48 hours after surgery. Drugs may be prescribed to control vomiting, if necessary.

If your dog has a tendency to develop bloat, your veterinarian may recommend that it be fed smaller meals more frequently over the course of the day, rather than a few large meals. Excessive exercise should be avoided to decrease the likelihood of bloat, and consumption of large volumes of water after exercise should be avoided to limit distention of the stomach.

Inflammation of the Stomach (Gastritis)

Gastritis, or inflammation of the stomach, is usually caused by eating something that injures the stomach lining. Vomiting is the usual sign of gastritis. In cases of acute gastritis, the vomited material may contain evidence of whatever the pet ate (grass, for example). Bile, froth, fresh blood, or digested blood that looks like coffee grounds may also be present. Abdominal pain may be signaled by a dog that displays a "praying" position, with the hindquarters raised and chest and forelegs held close to the floor; this position appears to provide some relief. Excessive thirst is often followed by immediate vomiting in dogs with sudden gastritis. Diarrhea may also be noted. Short-term or occasional vomiting is generally not associated with other abnormalities; however, longterm vomiting may be associated with weakness, lethargy, weight loss, dehydration, and electrolyte (salt) imbalance and acid-base disorders.

Treatment and control are the same as for vomiting (page 100). The outlook depends on the cause of the vomiting and the ability to stop or control it. Short-term gastritis often responds well to fasting and avoiding further consumption of whatever triggered the condition. The outlook for longterm gastritis is variable. Research is ongoing in this area and trials of various diets and medications may provide new treatments in the coming years.

Cancers of the Digestive System

Cancer of the digestive system is uncommon and represents less than 1% of all cancers in small animals. Older animals are predisposed, and adenocarcinoma and lymphosarcoma are seen more frequently in male dogs. Colorectal tumors are more prevalent in Boxers, German Shepherds, Poodles, Great Danes, and spaniels. No specific cause(s) has been identified for most gastrointestinal tumor types. Intestinal tumors in dogs tend to be malignant.

Signs of a possible tumor vary depending on the location and extent of the tumor and associated consequences. Vomiting (sometimes with blood), diarrhea (also with blood), weight loss, constipation, straining to defecate, abdominal pain, the accumulation of fluid in the abdomen, and abdominal infection associated with the rupture of an affected bowel have been reported. Dogs with gastrointestinal cancer may also have signs of anemia, such as pale gums.

A tumor may be detected by a veterinarian when feeling the abdomen and confirmed by x-rays or by abdominal ultrasound. Bleeding of a tumor may also be found during a rectal examination. Biopsy samples may be taken during abdominal surgery. Microscopic examination of the biopsy by a pathologist can confirm the diagnosis.

Surgical removal is usually the preferred treatment. Your veterinarian will also attempt to determine the extent of spread of the cancer. The outlook can vary from excellent to poor, depending on the specific type of tumor, the number of tumors present, and whether all of the cancer can be removed.

Gastrointestinal Obstruction

In order for an animal to absorb the nutrients in its food, the food must move from the stomach into the intestines. The movement of food out of the stomach can be restricted or stopped due to tumors, foreign objects, polyps, ulcers, and overgrowth of the stomach lining.

Intestinal obstruction may be partial or complete and may be caused by foreign objects, "telescoping" of the intestine, bloat, incarceration (such as being constricted in a hernia), and tumors.

Signs of **small-intestinal obstruction** may include lethargy, loss of appetite, vomiting, diarrhea, abdominal pain, abdominal swelling, fever or subnormal body temperature, dehydration, and shock. The intestines become distended from built-up gas, which develops within the first 12 to 35 hours after obstruction. This is followed by the loss of fluid into the intestines. Without treatment, death from shock caused by the fluid loss may occur within 3 or 4 days.

Obstruction occurring near the beginning of the intestines (closest to the stomach) tends to cause more severe and more frequent vomiting. Lethargy, loss of appetite, weight loss, and eventual starvation in untreated dogs lead to death within 3 or 4 weeks, although some survive longer.

Intussusception (telescoping of the intestines) may cause vomiting, abdominal pain, and scant bloody diarrhea. In long-term cases of intussusception, diarrhea with or without blood is seen. Intussusception is more common in young dogs (less than 8 months old).

In **intestinal incarceration**, digested food is trapped in the intestine. The dog will typically have abdominal pain that rapidly progresses to shock. This occurs because the incarceration of the affected intestine leads to bacterial growth within the stagnant bowel loop and to tissue death, leading to shock.

Many dogs with a history of eating inappropriate objects continue that practice even after having experienced discomfort in the past. When you take your dog in for examination, be sure to tell the veterinarian about your pet's eating habits and any access to string or yarn, fabric, sewing needles, or similar objects. If there are missing objects, such as toys, in your home, this information can be important and should be reported to the veterinarian. Abdominal infection and death associated with swallowing foreign objects such as string or thread is much more common in dogs than in cats.

Examination of the abdomen can provide the veterinarian with evidence of pain, peritonitis, organ enlargement, thickened bowel loops, or gas. A rectal examination can provide evidence of eating nonfood objects or blood. Abdominal x-rays may reveal foreign objects, masses, obstruction, abdominal fluid, or bloat. Contrast x-rays or ultrasonography are useful for diagnosing intussusception. Endoscopic examination employs a tiny camera at the end of a flexible tube. This procedure is useful in identifying foreign objects, tumors, and intussusception. If an obstruction is found, the veterinarian may be able to use the endoscope to help remove the object. If the object cannot be removed in this manner, surgery may be needed.

Animals with general signs of illness, such as weakness and dehydration, benefit from intravenous fluids. The overall mortality rate for both large- and small-intestinal surgery is reported to be 12%, although

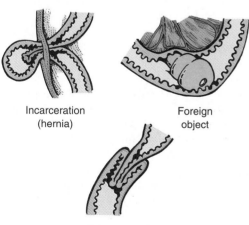

Incarceration (hernia)

Foreign object

Intussusception

Causes of gastrointestinal obstruction in dogs (modified with permission from *The Merck Manual of Medical Information*, Second Home Edition, 2003)

the recovery time may be longer with large-intestinal surgery.

Gastrointestinal Ulcers

Gastrointestinal ulcers can be caused by several factors, including drugs, tumors, infections, and generalized diseases. Stomach ulcers result from a breakdown of the normal stomach lining and are aggravated by an increase in hydrochloric acid or pepsin (a digestive enzyme). Conditions that lead to increased acid production or that damage the stomach lining speed up ulcer formation.

Animals with stomach ulcers may have no signs. In other cases, they can have a history that includes vomiting, sometimes with fresh or digested blood, and abdominal discomfort that may appear less severe after a meal. Dark stools stained with blood and pale gums suggesting anemia may be seen. Some signs may indicate the cause of the ulcer (for example, signs related to kidney failure).

In dogs that have a history of vomiting, abdominal discomfort, loss of appetite, or unexplained weight loss, there are several tests that might be performed by your veterinarian in an attempt to diagnose the cause. These may include a complete blood count, biochemical profile, urinalysis, and evaluation for parasites. Abdomi-

nal ultrasound scans or x-rays may be used to confirm the diagnosis. In cases in which the cause is unclear or in those with apparent gastrointestinal disease, endoscopy and biopsy are often recommended.

The goal of ulcer management is to determine the cause of the ulceration and then eliminate or control it. Providing supportive care is also critical. Medication directed at the ulcer itself reduces gastric acidity, prevents further destruction of the stomach lining, and promotes ulcer healing. In general, treatment is continued for 6 to 8 weeks. Dietary management includes the use of bland diets (often cottage cheese and rice or chicken and rice).

Ideally, ulcer healing should be monitored with endoscopy, although costs and the animal's tolerance for the procedure may limit its use. If ulcers do not respond to appropriate medical management, a biopsy of the stomach and small bowel becomes necessary. Several biopsies may be needed because obvious lesions may not be apparent or may be located sporadically throughout the gut.

The outlook for dogs with peptic ulcers and benign stomach tumors is good. However, the outlook is poor for those with ulcers associated with renal or liver failure and for animals with cancers such as stomach carcinoma and gastrinoma.

Common Causes of Gastrointestinal Ulcers in Dogs

- Drugs—nonsteroidal anti-inflammatory drugs (including aspirin, phenylbutazone, ibuprofen, indomethacin, carprofen, flunixin meglumine, naproxen, and piroxicam) and corticosteroids
- Cancer—lymphosarcoma, adenocarcinoma, gastrinoma, and mastocytosis
- Disease of other organs or systems— kidney or liver disease, shock, low adrenal gland function, blood poisoning, spinal injury, and pancreatitis
- Other causes—*Helicobacter* infection, stomach outlet obstruction, inflammatory bowel disease, chronic stomach inflammation

Hemorrhagic Gastroenteritis

Hemorrhagic gastroenteritis is characterized by a sudden onset of bloody diarrhea in formerly healthy dogs. The cause is unknown, but it may involve an abnormal response to bacteria, bacterial poisons, or diet. Dogs of either sex or any age may be affected. Young, toy, and miniature breeds of dogs appear to be predisposed to this condition. King Charles Spaniels, Shetland Sheepdogs, Pekingese, Yorkshire Terriers, Poodles, and Schnauzers may be more frequently affected than other breeds. Hyperactivity and stress are possible contributing factors.

The disease is often seen in dogs 2 to 4 years old and is characterized by a sudden onset of vomiting and bloody diarrhea, loss of appetite, and depression. The disease is not contagious and may occur without obvious changes in diet, environment, or daily routine.

Most dogs respond to supportive veterinary treatment, including fluid treatment and antibiotics. Dogs may develop shock unless fluid support is provided. Less severely affected dogs may be treated with antibiotics. Food and water should be withheld for 2 to 3 days while vomiting comes under control. When vomiting has stopped, food can be gradually reintroduced. Because of the possibility that food sensitivity may contribute to the disorder, your veterinarian may recommend that the protein source in the food be one not previously fed to the dog. Based on your pet's typical diet, cottage cheese, lamb, or tofu, mixed with rice may be recommended. This diet is fed for 1 to 2 weeks, after which the dog's regular diet can be gradually reintroduced. Serious complications are uncommon, and most dogs recover from hemorrhagic gastroenteritis. Fewer than 10% of treated dogs die, and 10 to 15% have repeated occurrences.

Inflammatory Bowel Disease

Inflammatory bowel disease is actually a group of digestive system diseases that are recognized by certain persistent signs and by inflammation without a known cause. The various forms of the disease are classified by their location and the type of cell that is involved.

The cause of inflammatory bowel disease is unknown. Although food allergies are an unlikely cause in most cases, they may contribute to the development of disease in certain ways (such as causing inflammation through excessive allergic reactions to food, bacteria, or parasites inside the intestine). Inflammation damages the mucosal barrier that protects the intestinal lining, making it even more sensitive to antigens. Persistent inflammation results in thickening and other changes in the lining of the intestine.

Inflammatory bowel disease appears to affect all ages, sexes, and breeds of dogs, though it may be more common in German Shepherds, Yorkshire Terriers, and Cocker Spaniels. The average age reported for the onset of disease signs is 6 years in dogs, but it may occur in dogs less than 2 years old. Signs are often present over long periods and sometimes come and go. Vomiting, diarrhea, changes in appetite, and weight loss may occur. Vomiting, dark stools, and abdominal pain are often seen with ulcers and erosion of the stomach and small intestine. Signs of large-intestinal diarrhea, including loss of appetite and watery diarrhea are common.

Inflammatory bowel disease can be difficult to diagnose because many of its signs are found in other diseases as well. Intestinal changes caused by the disease may be seen using an endoscope in most cases.

The goals of treatment are to reduce diarrhea, promote weight gain, and decrease intestinal inflammation. If a cause can be identified (such as diet or parasites), it should be eliminated. Modifying the diet, without other treatment, may be effective in some cases. In other cases, changes in diet can enhance medical treatment, allowing for the drug dosage to be reduced or discontinued once signs improve. Glucocorticoids, drugs that are anti-inflammatory and suppress the immune system, are among the drugs most often used in the management of inflammatory bowel disease.

Your veterinarian may recommend feeding your pet a hypoallergenic or elimination diet. This means providing your pet with a new source of protein and other changes. The recommended diet may be homemade—such as a diet of lamb and rice or venison and rice—or commercial. Commercial diets with these ingredients are usually available from veterinary clinics rather than commercial outlets. The new diet should be the only source of food for a minimum period (often 4 to 6 weeks), and no treats of any kind should be fed unless approved by the veterinarian. Dogs with large-intestinal diarrhea may benefit from diets high in fiber. However, supplementation of dietary fiber alone is rarely effective in severe cases. Your veterinarian will prescribe a diet that is tailored to your pet, its previous diet, and the severity of the disease.

Malabsorption

Malabsorption is poor absorption of a nutrient resulting from interference with its digestion, absorption, or both. Interference with food digestion in dogs is typically due to lack of certain enzymes from the pancreas, called exocrine pancreatic insufficiency (*see* page 118), whereas most cases of absorption failure are caused by small intestinal disease.

The signs of malabsorption are mainly due to lack of nutrient uptake and loss of nutrients in the feces. Signs typically include longterm diarrhea, weight loss, and altered appetite (loss of appetite or excessive eating). However, diarrhea may be absent even when disease is severe. Weight loss may be substantial despite a good appetite, sometimes characterized by eating of feces. Dogs with malabsorption usually appear healthy in other respects unless there is severe inflammation or cancer. Nonspecific signs may include dehydration, anemia, dark blood in the stools, or fluid retention. A veterinarian may be able to detect thickened bowel loops or enlarged abdominal lymph nodes.

Diagnosing malabsorption can be complex, because longterm diarrhea and weight loss are signs that are common in several diseases, including malabsorption. An exact diagnosis may take more than a single visit. A thorough examination is needed for dogs with signs of malabsorption to determine whether the signs are caused by an underlying generalized or metabolic disease. Certain tests can help determine whether the signs are due to a condition such as inflammatory bowel disease (*see* page 107), liver disease, or parasites. The dog's history is particularly important because it may suggest a specific food allergy, consumption of non-food items, or other sensitivity. Weight loss may indicate malabsorption or protein-losing disease but may also be due to loss of appetite, vomiting, or a non-digestive disease. There are certain features that help distinguish small-intestinal diarrhea from large-intestinal diarrhea. Suspected large intestine disease in dogs may be further evaluated by a biopsy of the intestinal lining. However, if signs are accompanied by weight loss or large volumes of feces, then the small intestine is probably also affected.

Treatment of malabsorption involves dietary change, management of complications, and treatment of the cause, if it can be identified. If malabsorption is caused by exocrine pancreatic insufficiency (*see* page 118), treatment involves feeding a special low-fiber diet that contains moderate levels of fat or highly digestible fat, very digestible carbohydrate, and high-quality protein. Supplementation with pancreatic extract to provide missing enzymes is also necessary. If the dog's response to pancreatic replacement treatment is poor, small-intestinal bacterial overgrowth may be suspected. In this case, the dog may be treated with oral antibiotics for about 1 month to reduce the bacterial overgrowth. Effective treatment of small-intestinal disease depends on the nature of the disorder, but when a specific diagnosis cannot be made, treatments may be given on a trial basis.

Dietary modification is an important aspect of the management of small intestinal disease. Your veterinarian may recommend feeding your pet an exclusion diet consisting of a single protein source (one to which your dog has not previously been exposed) as a test when dietary sensitivity is suspected. It is very important that you provide the special diet and prescribed medication(s) for your pet exactly as instructed. Often, owners are tempted to provide a "special treat" not on the diet even though they have been instructed not to do so. Failure to follow the prescribed diet can delay diagnosis and delay the treatment their pet needs. Owners can reward their pets during this time with petting, a new blanket or suitable toy, or some other reward that is not food. Often the best reward for the pet is extended periods of attention.

▓ DISORDERS CAUSED BY BACTERIA

Certain bacteria may cause gastrointestinal disease in dogs. The most common of these are discussed below.

Campylobacter Infection

Gastrointestinal campylobacteriosis is a bacterial disease. It is caused by 2 related bacteria of the *Campylobacter* genus. These organisms, along with a number of other species of *Campylobacter*, can be isolated from infected dogs that do not show signs of infection (carriers) as well as from dogs that show signs of the illness. This disease can be transmitted to humans. Animals, including dogs (especially those recently adopted from shelters), and wild animals maintained in captivity can serve as sources of human infection.

Exposure to feces of infected animals and food- or waterborne transmission appear to be the most common routes of infection. One suspected source of infection for pets is eating undercooked poultry and other raw meat products. Wild birds also may be important sources of water contamination.

The diarrhea appears to be most severe in young dogs. Typical signs include mucus-laden, watery, or bile-streaked diarrhea (with or without blood) that lasts 3 to 7 days; reduced appetite; and occasional vomiting. Fever may also be present. Intermittent diarrhea may persist for more than 2 weeks; in some, the intermittent diarrhea may continue for months. To diagnose campylobacteriosis, a veterinarian will test the animal's feces and blood for evidence of infection.

Antibiotic treatment for dogs found to carry these bacteria is usually reserved for those that are young, severely affected, or a potential source of human infection. This is because other organisms are likely to be involved and antibiotic treatment is often not effective.

Helicobacter Infection

In humans, *Helicobacter pylori* bacteria have been associated with stomach inflammation, ulcers, and gastric adenocarcinoma. Although *H. pylori* has not been found in dogs, several other species of *Helicobacter* have been isolated. So far, the evidence suggests that the bacteria cause a mild inflammation that has no signs. Whether their presence predisposes the infected animal to food allergies, inflammatory bowel disease, ulcers, or cancer is not yet known. In dogs, the bacteria have been associated with occasional vomiting.

Several tests, including biopsy of the stomach lining, may be used by your veterinarian to diagnose the presence of the bacteria. Confirming the diagnosis requires culturing the bacteria in a laboratory. Several types of antibiotics have been used to treat the infection in dogs. In many cases, however, the bacteria recur. Whether this is due to reinfection or failure of the antibiotics to completely eliminate them following treatment is not known.

Salmonella Infection

Many species of *Salmonella* bacteria can cause gastrointestinal illness. A *Salmonella* infection can cause severe blood poisoning (septicemia) or inflammation of the intestine. The disease is infrequent in dogs. Infected dogs may become carriers of *Salmonella* but often do not show any signs of disease.

When disease is seen, it is often associated with hospitalization, another infection or disease in adult dogs, or exposure to large numbers of the bacteria in puppies. Signs include sudden diarrhea and blood poisoning. Pneumonia may be evident. *Salmonella* infection is likely to cause miscarriage in pregnant dogs. Diagnosis is based on signs of disease and on the laboratory examination of feces.

Early treatment is essential for blood poisoning. In many cases, antibiotics are given intravenously. Fluids may be given intravenously as well. The intestinal form of the disease is difficult to treat effectively. Antibiotics are not always recommended, due to concerns about the development of antibiotic resistant bacteria, as well as concerns about the effects of antibiotics on normal intestinal bacteria of dogs. Although the signs of disease may disappear, eliminating the bacteria from the body is difficult, particularly in adult dogs.

Because of the above problems, it is particularly important to follow your veterinarian's directions carefully if your pet is infected with *Salmonella*. The medication selected and both the timing of the doses and the duration of treatment are important in eliminating the infection.

Salmonella can be transmitted from dogs to humans, so care should be taken to avoid contact with feces from an infected dog.

Tyzzer's Disease

Tyzzer's disease is an infection caused by the bacterium *Clostridium piliforme*. It affects a wide range of animals; however, the disease is rare in dogs. Infection most likely results from oral exposure to infective spores from the environment or contact with carrier animals. The bacteria primarily affect cells in the intestine, liver, and heart. The disease most often affects young, healthy animals that are subjected to stress. In some species, the disease occurs along with other diseases, such as distemper and mycotic pneumonia in dogs.

Signs vary, but may include decreased activity, loss of appetite, fever, jaundice, and diarrhea. Before death, there are convulsions and coma. A diagnosis of Tyzzer's disease is based on laboratory examination of tissue samples for the presence of the bacteria. Little is known about the effectiveness of antibiotics for treatment; some antibiotics are known to aggravate the disease. Dogs suspected of being infected may be treated with intravenous fluids and appropriate antibiotics.

▨ GASTROINTESTINAL PARASITES

Many parasites can infect the digestive system of dogs (*see* TABLE 5). The most common ones are described below. Some gastrointestinal parasites of dogs can also cause disease in people (*see* TABLE 6).

Roundworms

The large roundworms known as ascarids are common in dogs, especially in puppies. The most important species is *Toxocara canis*, not only because its larvae may migrate in people, but also because infections are common. Fatal infections may occasionally be seen in young pups. *Toxascaris leonina* is typically much less common and is generally seen in older dogs.

In puppies, infection with *Toxocara canis* usually occurs by transfer into the developing fetus through the placenta. The worms can be found in the intestines of the puppies as early as 1 week after birth. Pups may also be infected while nursing. If pups less than 3 months old eat the eggs that have been in the environment for at least 4 weeks, the eggs hatch, releasing larvae that penetrate the intestinal wall. The larvae migrate through the liver, reach the lungs via the bloodstream, are coughed up, swallowed, and mature to egg-producing adults in the small intestine. Many larvae will be carried by the bloodstream to other parts of the dog's body and remain in the tissues of the dog for years in an inactive form. If immune system suppression occurs, these larvae can become active.

Normally, adult dogs have some resistance to infection. However, during the period around the birth of a litter, the immunity of the female dog to infection is partially suppressed, and the inactive larvae become active, crossing the placenta to the pups and sequestering in the mammary tissue, where they are transmitted in the colostrum and milk. Due to immune system suppression at the time of whelping, active infections may occur in the pregnant dog, with substantial numbers of eggs passed in the feces.

Table 5. Gastrointestinal Parasites of Dogs

Common Name (Scientific Name)	How Contracted	Signs	Control and Prevention*
Esophageal worm (*Spirocerca lupi*)	Dogs eat intermediate host (dung beetle) or transport host (chickens, reptiles, rodents)	Most show no signs. When severe, dog has difficulty swallowing and may vomit repeatedly after trying to eat. Occasionally, death from rupture of aorta damaged by worms. Diagnosed by microscopic fecal examination.	In areas where the worm is common (southern US, tropics), dogs should be prevented from eating dung beetles, frogs, mice, lizards, or other small animals, and not fed raw chicken scraps.
Hookworms (*Ancylostoma caninum, A. braziliense, Uncinaria stenocephala*)	Eating infective larvae, transmission during nursing, or by direct skin penetration	*A. caninum*—Anemia and poor growth of puppies; in severe cases diarrhea with dark, tarry stools. Often no signs, particularly with other hookworm infections. Diagnosed by microscopic fecal examination.	Puppies should be dewormed on multiple occasions in the first 3 months of life. Some monthly heartworm preventives also control hookworms. Housing areas for pregnant dogs and puppies should be free of contamination and cleaned regularly.
Roundworms (*Toxocara canis, Toxascaris leonina*)	*T. canis*—commonly passed from mother to pups. Also acquired during nursing. Both parasites acquired by ingestion of eggs or transport hosts.	Often no signs. Diarrhea, poor growth, or a distended, swollen abdomen; worms may be passed in feces. Most often diagnosed by microscopic fecal examination.	Puppies should be dewormed on multiple occasions, during the first 3 months of life. Mothers should be treated prior to giving birth to reduce transmission to pups. Monthly heartworm preventives will also prevent roundworm infection.
Stomach worm (*Physaloptera* species)	Dogs eat hosts (beetles, cockroaches, crickets, mice, frogs)	Stomach inflammation which can result in vomiting, loss of appetite, and dark feces. In heavy infections, anemia and weight loss. Most often diagnosed when whole worms are found in vomitus, typically with no signs.	Several drugs from your veterinarian can be used to treat infection.
Tapeworms (cestodes)	Eating infected prey animals or fleas	Most infections have few signs. Poor absorption of food or diarrhea may occur. Most often diagnosed by observing proglottids in the feces or perianal area of the dog.	Control requires medication to treat the tapeworms and preventing access to prey animals so the dog is not reinfected. Flea control is also important.
Threadworm (*Strongyloides stercoralis*)	Infective stage in environment penetrates skin; also swallowed	Often no signs. Blood-streaked diarrhea, especially in hot humid weather; reduced growth rate. In severe cases, fever and shallow breathing. Diagnosed by microscopic fecal examination.	Isolation of sick animals; thorough washing of pet living areas. Disease is more severe in animals with a weakened immune system.
Whipworms (*Trichuris vulpis*)	Shed in feces; become infective in 2 to 4 weeks. Infective eggs are eaten by dogs.	No signs are seen in light infection; heavy infection produces weight loss and diarrhea. Fresh blood may be seen in feces, and anemia may be present. Diagnosed by microscopic fecal examination.	Eggs are susceptible to drying out, so maintaining cleanliness and eliminating moist areas can help reduce likelihood of infection. A limited number of drugs are available.

*A number of antiparasitic drugs (anthelmintics) are available to treat parasites in dogs.

Table 6. Gastrointestinal Parasites of Dogs and Cats that also Infect People

Species	Comments
Strongyloides stercoralis	Caution should be exercised in handling infected dogs. Disease is more likely to be severe if the person has a weakened immune system.
Roundworms (*Toxicara canis* and *T. cati*)	Most infected people show no symptoms, but fever, a persistent increase in eosinophils, and an enlarged liver (sometimes with lung involvement) may occur. These signs result from a condition known as visceral larva migrans, which occurs when roundworm larvae migrate through different organs. Rarely, a larva may settle in the retina of the eye and impair vision, resulting in a condition known as ocular larva migrans. Because the eggs adhere to many surfaces and become mixed in soil and dust, strict hygiene should be observed by people (especially children) exposed to potentially contaminated animals or areas. The risk of infection is greater if puppies or kittens are in the environment.
Hookworms (*Ancylostoma braziliense*; less of an issue with *A. caninum*, *A. tubaeforme* and *Uncinaria stenocephala*)	The infective larvae of canine hookworms, particularly those of *A. braziliense*, may penetrate and wander under the skin of people and cause cutaneous larva migrans. Intestinal inflammation (eosinophilic enteritis) may also occur.
Tapeworms (cestodes, *Echinococcus* and some *Taenia* species)	These tapeworms can be contracted by humans in association with infected dogs. Eggs are passed in dog feces. Disease in people depends on where the intermediate stage goes in the body.
Tapeworms (cestodes, (*Dipylidium caninum*)	This tapeworm of dogs and cats occasionally infects people. Infection occurs when the person accidentally ingests a dog or cat flea containing the parasite. Infection in the intestine is not generally harmful but the eggs or worm segments can be seen in the feces.
Trematodes (flukes, *Alaria* species)	This fluke of dogs and cats occasionally infects people and may invade various organs.

The first indication of infection in young animals is lack of growth and loss of condition. Infected animals have a dull coat and often appear "potbellied." Worms may be vomited and are often passed in the feces. In the early stages, migrating larvae may cause pneumonia, which can be associated with coughing. Diarrhea with mucus may be evident. Infection in dogs and cats is diagnosed by detection of the roundworm eggs in feces.

There are a number of compounds available for treating roundworm infections in dogs. Certain preventive programs for heartworm infection also control intestinal roundworm infections. Transmission of infection from mother to newborn can be greatly reduced by a program of antiparasitic drugs given during pregnancy and after the birth of a litter. Otherwise, the pups should be treated as early as pos-

sible. Ideally, treatment should be given 2 weeks after birth and repeated at 2- to 3-week intervals to 3 months of age, then monthly to 6 months of age. Nursing dogs should be treated on the same schedule as their pups. Your veterinarian will prescribe the appropriate medication for this infection.

Hookworms

Several types of hookworms can cause disease in dogs. *Ancylostoma caninum* is the principal cause of canine hookworm disease in most tropical and subtropical areas of the world. *Ancylostoma braziliense* infects dogs and is sparsely distributed from Florida to North Carolina and along the Gulf Coast in the United States. It is also found in Central and South America and Africa. *Uncinaria stenocephala* is the principal canine hookworm in cooler regions. It is the primary canine hookworm in Canada and the northern fringe of the United States, but it is found with frequency across the country.

Hookworm eggs are first passed in the feces 15 to 20 days after infection. They hatch in 2 or 3 days when deposited on warm, moist soil. Transmission may result when larvae are ingested or, in the case of *A. caninum*, from the colostrum or milk of infected dogs. Infections with *Ancylostoma* species can also result from larval invasion through the skin. Skin penetration in young pups is followed by migration of the larvae through the blood to the lungs, where they are coughed up and swallowed to mature in the small intestine. However, in animals more than 3 months old, larvae may remain in the body tissues in a state of arrested development. These larvae are activated after removal of adult worms from the intestine or during pregnancy, when they accumulate in the small intestine or mammary glands of the mother.

Anemia in young puppies is the characteristic, and often fatal, sign of *Ancylostoma caninum* hookworm infection. The anemia is the result of the bloodsucking and the bleeding internal wounds that occur when these hookworms shift their internal feeding sites in the small intestine, leaving open wounds in their wake. Surviving puppies develop some immunity and show less severe signs. Nevertheless, malnourished and weakened animals may continue to grow poorly and suffer from longterm anemia. Mature, well-nourished dogs may harbor a few worms without showing signs; these dogs are often the direct or indirect source of infection for pups. Diarrhea with dark, tarry feces accompanies severe infections. Anemia, loss of appetite, weight loss, and weakness develop in longterm disease. Pneumonia may occur in pups with overwhelming infections, making breathing difficult.

Neither of the other common species of hookworms tends to cause anemia.

However, blood fluid loss around the site of attachment in the intestine may reduce blood protein by greater than 10%. Dermatitis (particularly in the spaces between the toes) due to larval invasion of the skin may be seen with *Ancylostoma braziliense.*

A diagnosis can often be made from the identification of hookworm eggs in fresh feces from infected dogs. Even though infections may be severe, eggs will not typically be seen on fecal examinations of pups prior to 16 days (the length of time needed for a new infection to produce eggs). Thus, severe anemia and death from infections acquired from nursing may be seen in young pups before eggs are passed in their feces. This can occur as early as 1 or 2 weeks of age.

A number of drugs and drug combinations are approved for treatment of hookworm infections. In addition, many heartworm medications also control certain species of hookworms. When anemia is severe, blood transfusion or supplemental iron may be needed, followed by a high-protein diet until the blood hemoglobin level is normal.

When newborn pups die from hookworm infection, subsequent litters from the same mother should be treated twice weekly for hookworms for about 12 weeks beginning at 1 to 2 weeks of age. In addition, your veterinarian may prescribe daily medication for pregnant dogs from day 40 of pregnancy to day 14 after whelping. This greatly reduces the transmission of the disease to the pups through nursing. Your veterinarian will prescribe the most appropriate medication program for your dog.

Female dogs should be free of hookworms before breeding and kept out of contaminated areas during pregnancy. Housing and bedding for pregnant and nursing dogs must be sanitary and cleaned regularly. Consult your veterinarian about any special disinfectants to add to cleaning solutions or laundry water. For outside activities, concrete runways that can be washed at least twice a week in warm weather are best. Sunlit clay or sandy runways can be decontaminated with sodium borate.

Whipworms

Adult whipworms (*Trichuris vulpis*) in dogs are typically found in the cecum, a part of the large intestine. They attach themselves firmly to the intestinal wall. Eggs are passed in the feces and become infective in about 4 weeks. Under ideal conditions, whipworm eggs can remain dormant in the environment for several years, unless they become dried out. Once infective eggs are ingested, larvae develop in the small intestine and then move to the cecum, where the adults mature. Infections are more common in adult dogs, especially those in kennels.

No signs are seen in light infections, but as the number of worms increases the cecum can become inflamed, which can cause diarrhea and weight loss. Fresh blood might be seen in the feces in heavy infections and anemia may also result.

Because whipworm eggs take a month to become infective, whipworms can easily be controlled with good sanitation. Prompt removal and proper disposal of feces is critical. Whipworms are susceptible to drying; therefore, keeping the dog in an environment that is clean and dry reduces the risk of infection considerably. For this reason, kenneled dogs should be maintained on concrete slabs, and never on dirt. A variety of medications—including some monthly drugs that prevent infections with other parasites like heartworms—are available for treating whipworm infections. Your veterinarian will choose one that is appropriate for your dog.

Tapeworms

Several types of tapeworms—properly known as cestodes—may infect dogs. Adult tapeworms are segmented worms found in the intestines of dogs. They rarely cause serious disease.

Most urban dogs eat prepared foods and have restricted access to natural prey.

These dogs may acquire *Dipylidium caninum* (the common tapeworm of dogs and cats) from eating fleas. Suburban, rural, and hunting dogs have more access to various small mammals, in addition to raw meat and offal from large mammals. The possibility of exposure to a number of different tapeworm species can be expected in such dogs and typically are *Taenia* species or *Echinococcus granulosus*. Other species of tapeworms that may infect dogs include *Spirometra mansonoides* and *Diphyllobothrium* and *Mesocestoides* species.

Signs of infection vary from a failure to digest and absorb food normally, malaise, irritability, variable appetite, and shaggy coat to colic and mild diarrhea. There may be no signs in mild cases. In rare cases, telescoping of the intestine (intussusception), emaciation, and seizures are seen. Diagnosis is based on finding tapeworm segments or eggs in the feces or stuck to the hair around the anus.

Control of tapeworms requires both treatment and prevention. Even confined dogs can contract *Dipylidium caninum* because it can cycle through fleas. Thus, flea control is the critical preventive step even for indoor dogs. Animals that roam freely usually become reinfected by eating dead or prey animals. Preventing such feeding will limit exposure to other tapeworm species. An accurate diagnosis will enable the veterinarian to provide effective advice on treating the infection and preventing reinfection.

Flukes

Flukes (also called trematodes) are a class of parasites that can infect dogs and many other types of animals (*see* TABLE 7). They have a complex life cycle that can involve multiple intermediate hosts.

Intestinal Flukes

In general, intestinal flukes do not cause illness unless there are large numbers of flukes. Heavy infections can cause intestinal inflammation, especially of the

Table 7. Flukes that Infect Dogs

Class	Species (Common Name)	How Contracted	Signs
Intestinal flukes	*Nanophyetus salmincola* (Salmon poisoning fluke), found in northwestern US, southwestern Canada, and other countries in the northern Pacific Rim	Dogs eat intermediate host (raw or improperly prepared salmon and similar fish)	Heavy infection causes intestinal inflammation. Infection is compounded by rickettsial infection carried by flukes (salmon poisoning disease).
	Alaria species, found in North America, Europe, Australia, and Japan.	Dogs eat intermediate hosts (frogs, snakes, mice)	Heavy infection can cause bleeding in the lungs or enteritis.
	Heterobilharzia americana, found in southeastern US	Dogs are infected by a stage shed into water by snails (the intermediate host)	Heavy infection can cause intestinal inflammation and wasting. "Water dermatitis" may be seen where parasites enter the skin.
Liver flukes	*Opisthorchis* species, found in eastern Europe, parts of Asia	Dogs eat intermediate hosts including certain snails and fish	Longterm presence causes thickening and fibrosis of bile and pancreatic duct walls. Severe cases have been associated with cancer in the liver or pancreas.
	Metorchis species, found in North America, Europe, former Soviet Union	Dogs eat intermediate hosts (certain raw or undercooked fish)	Seldom causes disease.

small intestine. Several antiparasitic medications are effective against intestinal flukes. Consult your veterinarian about preventing fluke infections in your pet as the risk of infection varies greatly in different parts of the world.

Liver Flukes

Flukes in the bile ducts and gallbladder cause mild to severe liver disease (fibrosis). Various species of flukes have been reported from the liver of dogs in most parts of the world. Infections are generally uncommon. Mild infections may pass unnoticed. However, in severe infections, dogs may develop progressive weakness, ending in complete exhaustion and death in some cases.

▓ DISORDERS CAUSED BY PROTOZOA

Protozoa are single-celled organisms that can sometimes cause disease. They may be free-living or parasites. Some of the more common diseases caused by protozoa in dogs are discussed below.

Amebiasis

Amebiasis is a disease caused by the amoeba *Entamoeba histolytica*. It causes inflammation of the large intestine, which leads to persistent diarrhea. Amebiasis is common in tropical and subtropical areas worldwide. Its prevalence has declined in the US over the past several decades, but the disease is still important in many tropical areas, particularly in times of disasters. It is common in people, sometimes seen in dogs and cats, and rare in other mammals. Humans are the natural host for this species and are the usual source of infection for domestic animals. Dogs become infected by ingesting food or water contaminated with feces that contain infective cysts, which are a dormant form of the parasite.

Entamoeba histolytica lives inside the large intestine and will sometimes produce no obvious signs; on the other hand, it can invade the intestinal lining and produce inflammation, wounds, and bleeding. In short-term disease, severe diarrhea may develop. This disease may be fatal, become long-lasting, or improve spontaneously. Signs in longterm cases include weight loss, loss of appetite, straining to defecate, and diarrhea. Any of these signs may be continuous or may come and go. In addition to the large intestine, the infecting amoebae may invade skin around the anus, genitals, liver, brain, lungs, kidneys, and other organs. Signs may resemble those of other diseases of the large intestine.

The disease is diagnosed by the presence of active or dormant *E. histolytica* in feces. If infection has occurred outside of the intestine, the parasites may be difficult to detect. In some cases, your veterinarian may examine the large intestine directly using specialized instruments. This procedure is called a colonoscopy.

Medication may be prescribed to treat this illness, although the effectiveness of treatment has not been fully evaluated. Dogs may continue to shed amoebae in the feces even after drug treatment. Be sure to follow treatment and care instructions fully.

Coccidiosis

Coccidiosis is an invasion and destruction of intestinal tissues by any of several protozoa. It can cause illness in dogs but while infections are relatively common, most infected dogs show no signs.

Coccidia tend to infect dogs or puppies that have been weakened in some way. Therefore, signs of illness caused by coccidiosis are most prevalent under conditions of poor nutrition, poor sanitation, or overcrowding, or after stresses such as weaning. Infection results when a dog ingests infective eggs (oocysts). These oocysts enter the environment in the feces of an infected dog, but they are unable to cause infection until they develop further under the right environmental conditions.

The most common signs of infection in severe cases are diarrhea (sometimes bloody), weight loss, and dehydration. The veterinarian will combine the results of fecal examinations with observations of signs and intestinal abnormalities to confirm the diagnosis.

Infection usually ends on its own within a few weeks unless reinfection occurs. Medication may lessen the likelihood of reinfection and spread. Sick dogs should be isolated to prevent exposure of other animals.

Sanitation is important, especially in kennels or where large numbers of dogs are housed. Feces should be removed frequently and fecal contamination of feed and water should be prevented. Runs, cages, and utensils should be disinfected daily. Raw meat should not be fed. Insect control is also important.

Giardiasis

Giardiasis is a longterm, intestinal protozoal infection caused by species of *Giardia*. It is seen worldwide in most domestic and wild mammals, many birds, and people. Infection is common in dogs. *Giardia* has been reported to be found in up to 39% of fecal samples from pet and shelter dogs, with a higher rate of infection in younger animals.

Giardia protozoa live in the small intestine, where they attach and multiply. They produce cysts that are passed in the feces. Transmission occurs by spread from feces to the mouth. Shedding of cysts by an infected dog may be continuous over several days and weeks but is often intermittent. It is currently unclear whether the same species of *Giardia* can infect both domestic animals and people. It appears that some *Giardia* species can infect a variety of mammals, while others only infect a single species.

Giardia infection in dogs sometimes causes no signs. In other cases, it causes weight loss and longterm diarrhea, which can be continual or intermittent, particularly in puppies. Feces are usually soft, poorly formed, pale, and foul-smelling. Watery diarrhea is unusual, and blood is not present in feces. Occasionally vomiting occurs. Giardiasis causes malabsorption of nutrients and must be distinguished from other conditions that also affect the dog's ability to absorb nutrients properly (*see* MALABSORPTION, page 108). A diagnosis is usually made by identification of *Giardia* cysts or *Giardia* antigen in stool samples.

To treat giardiasis, your veterinarian will likely prescribe a drug or combination of drugs that are effective against protozoa. A vaccine is available for dogs in some countries. Some studies indicate that the vaccine may reduce signs as well as the number and length of time cysts are shed into the environment.

Giardia cysts in the feces are a source of infection and reinfection for dogs, particularly those in crowded conditions such as kennels. Prompt removal of feces from cages, runs, and yards limits environmental contamination. Cysts are inactivated by disinfectants such as quaternary ammonium compounds, household bleach (1 part bleach to 16 or 32 parts water), steam, and boiling water. To increase the effectiveness of disinfectant treatment, solutions should be left for 5 to 20 minutes before being rinsed off kennel or run surfaces. Disinfection of grass yards or runs is impossible. These areas should be considered contaminated for at least 1 month after infected dogs last had access. Cysts are susceptible to drying, so areas should be allowed to dry thoroughly after cleaning. Shampooing and rinsing the dogs well can help remove cysts from hair.

Dogs may be infected with a type of *Giardia* species that normally infects cats. They may occasionally be infected by a type that also infects people. Dog feces should be disposed of promptly. It is important to wash hands properly after handling infected animals or their feces.

▧ DISORDERS OF THE PANCREAS

The pancreas is an organ that has 2 main functions: endocrine and exocrine. The endocrine pancreas produces the hormones insulin and glucagon, which regulate blood sugar levels. The exocrine pancreas produces enzymes that are essential for the digestion of complex dietary components such as proteins, triglycerides, and complex carbohydrates. The exocrine pancreas also secretes large amounts of bicarbonate, which buffers stomach acid.

Disorders of the exocrine pancreas are discussed here, because they relate to digestion. Endocrine functions of the pancreas are discussed in the Hormonal Disorders chapter.

Inflammation of the Pancreas (Pancreatitis)

Pancreatitis is the most common exocrine pancreatic disease in both dogs and cats. It can be short- or longterm, depending on whether or not the disease has permanently damaged the pancreatic tissue. Both forms can be severe.

For most cases of pancreatitis no specific cause can be identified. However, eating trash, large amounts of table scraps, or other inappropriate food is believed to be a common risk factor in dogs. Severe trauma or surgery can lead to pancreatitis. Use of some drugs may also be linked to pancreatitis.

In the initial stages of disease, the secretion of pancreatic juice decreases. This is followed by a series of steps that lead to activation of pancreatic enzymes inside the pancreas, rather than in the intestinal tract. The enzymes begin to digest the pancreas itself, causing damage within the pancreas and triggering inflammation, which leads to damage in other parts of the body. Loss of appetite, vomiting, weakness, abdominal pain, dehydration, and diarrhea are the most common signs reported in dogs with severe pancreatitis.

A thorough history (including any dietary indiscretions) combined with vomiting and abdominal pain may suggest a diagnosis of pancreatitis. Blood tests may be used by your veterinarian to confirm the diagnosis, along with abdominal x-rays, ultrasound, or exploratory surgery, if needed.

Treatment for pancreatitis includes careful monitoring and supportive veterinary care. Hospitalization may be required. Early intervention will help prevent complications. If the cause is known, specific treatment may be started. Resting the pancreas by restricting all food or water by mouth for 3 to 4 days is recommended when the dog is vomiting. Severely ill dogs are given intravenous fluids. Pain medication is usually given because the animal is assumed to have abdominal pain.

In mild cases of pancreatitis, dogs will usually be switched to a low-fat diet and low-fat treats. Pancreatic enzyme supplementation may help in cases when abdominal pain is present or for animals with consistently poor appetites, which may be the only indicator of abdominal pain. Patients with mild, longterm pancreatitis should be monitored for potential complications, such as exocrine pancreatic insufficiency (*see* below) and diabetes mellitus.

The outlook in mild cases is good, but the outlook in severe cases of pancreatitis is poor. About half of dogs with severe pancreatitis may die.

Exocrine Pancreatic Insufficiency

Exocrine pancreatic insufficiency is a syndrome caused by insufficient production and secretion of digestive enzymes by the pancreas. Deterioration of the structures that produce pancreatic enzymes is the most common cause of this syndrome in dogs. This can either be due to the slow decline of cells that produce the enzymes in German Shepherds or due to destruction resulting from long-term pancreatic inflammation in other breeds. Less common causes are tumors that lead to obstruction of the pancreatic duct. German Shepherds with exocrine pancreatic insufficiency are usually young

adult dogs, while dogs with exocrine pancreatic insufficiency due to other causes are usually middle-aged to older and can be of any breed.

Pancreatic enzymes play a critical role in the assimilation of all major dietary components, and a lack of pancreatic digestive enzymes leads to problems with digestion and to malabsorption (*see* page 108). The lack of nutrients also causes weight loss and may lead to vitamin deficiencies. Animals with exocrine pancreatic insufficiency caused by longterm pancreatitis may develop diabetes mellitus.

Signs most commonly reported are excessive eating, weight loss, and diarrhea. Vomiting and loss of appetite are sometimes seen, but these may be a sign of a concurrent condition. The feces are most commonly pale, loose, and voluminous and may be foul-smelling. In rare cases, watery diarrhea may be seen. Diagnosis can be made using a blood test that indicates a decrease in the functional capacity of the exocrine pancreas.

Most dogs with exocrine pancreatic insufficiency can be successfully treated by supplementing each meal with pancreatic enzymes (powdered or from fresh tissue). Follow your veterinarian's directions for this dietary supplement carefully. Avoid providing too much or too little and follow the schedule prescribed. Be sure to report any bleeding from the mouth to your veterinarian. This adverse effect can often be eliminated by lowering the enzyme dose. When signs have improved, it may be possible to gradually decrease the dose.

If enzyme supplementation alone does not resolve the condition, vitamin B_{12} (cobalamin) deficiency may be a possible cause. Cobalamin deficiency is seen in about half of dogs with exocrine pancreatic insufficiency. Dogs with vitamin B_{12} deficiency can be given this vitamin by injection. Other vitamin deficiencies have also been reported.

Most dogs can continue eating their normal food, but a highly digestible, low-fiber, moderate-fat diet can be useful in those that do not respond satisfactorily to treatment. It is important to avoid radical changes in diet, however.

In most cases, exocrine pancreatic insufficiency is the result of an irreversible loss of pancreatic tissue, and a cure is rare. However, with appropriate enzyme supplementation and monitoring, dogs with this disorder usually gain weight quickly, pass normal stools, and can live a normal life.

Pancreatic Cancers

Cancers of the exocrine pancreas can be either benign or malignant. **Pancreatic adenomas** are benign (nonspreading) tumors. **Pancreatic adenocarcinomas** are the most common malignant tumor of the exocrine pancreas in dogs. A few other types of cancer have also been reported in the pancreas.

A diagnosis may be made based on a combination of blood tests, x-rays, biopsy, or exploratory surgery as appropriate.

Pancreatic Adenomas

Benign tumors of the pancreas can lead to the displacement of organs in the abdominal cavity. However, these changes cause no signs in most cases. In rare cases, the tumor can obstruct the pancreatic duct and cause deterioration of the remaining exocrine pancreas, leading to exocrine pancreatic insufficiency (*see* page 118).

Pancreatic adenomas are benign and theoretically do not require any treatment unless they cause signs. However, because the tumors are often found during surgery and the appearance of both benign and malignant tumors is similar, removal of the affected pancreatic tissue is usually recommended. The outlook in these cases is excellent.

Pancreatic Adenocarcinomas

Adenocarcinomas may lead to death of part of the cancerous tissue if the tumor outgrows its blood supply. This causes local inflammation, which can lead to signs of pancreatitis. Malignant tumors may also spread to neighboring or distant organs.

Many dogs show no signs until late in the disease. Some dogs have signs that suggest inflammation of the pancreas. Jaundice may be seen if bile duct obstruction develops. Signs related to spread—such as lameness, bone pain, or difficulty breathing—have also been reported in some cases of pancreatic adenocarcinoma.

Pancreatic adenocarcinomas are usually not detected until the disease is advanced and the cancer has already spread. In those few cases when it appears the cancer has not yet spread, your veterinarian may attempt surgical removal. However, it is difficult to completely remove such tumors and surgery is often unsuccessful. Both chemotherapy and radiation treatment have shown little success in human or veterinary patients with pancreatic adenocarcinomas. Thus, the outlook for dogs with pancreatic adenocarcinoma is grave.

Pancreatic Abscesses

A pancreatic abscess is a collection of pus, usually near the pancreas, which is considered a complication of pancreatitis (*see* page 117). Signs may include vomiting, depression, abdominal pain, loss of appetite, fever, diarrhea, and dehydration. In some animals, a mass in the abdomen can be felt. Dogs may respond favorably to surgical drainage of the abscess. However, the risks and expense of surgery may outweigh the benefit, unless there is clear evidence of an enlarging mass or bacterial infection. Your veterinarian will make a surgical recommendation based on your dog's specific condition, overall health, and related considerations.

Pancreatic Pseudocyst

A pancreatic pseudocyst is a collection of sterile pancreatic fluid enclosed by a wall of tissue. Signs are similar to those of pancreatitis. Vomiting is the most consistent sign. The cysts can be seen by using ultrasound. Use of a long needle to draw fluid from the cyst can provide fluid for analysis and diagnosis. Drawing fluid is also a method of treating such cysts. Surgery may be needed if the dog has signs that persist or if the pseudocyst does not decrease in size.

DISORDERS OF THE LIVER AND GALLBLADDER

The liver is an organ that performs numerous functions. It has a large storage capacity and functional reserve and is capable of regenerating. These properties provide some protection against permanent damage. However, the liver is also susceptible to injury because of its role in metabolizing, detoxifying, and storing various toxic compounds.

Signs that a dog has liver disease can vary and include loss of appetite, vomiting, stomach ulceration, diarrhea, seizures or other neurologic problems, fever, blood clotting problems, jaundice (a yellow tinge noticeable in the skin, mucous membranes, and eyes), fluid collection in the abdomen, excessive urination and thirst, changes in liver size, and weight loss. Gastrointestinal bleeding can be seen in animals with liver disease due to ulcers or problems with blood clotting. The veterinarian's understanding of the potential causes of each of these signs helps him or her to diagnose illness and provide appropriate treatment.

A variety of blood tests can be useful in detecting and diagnosing liver disease. X-rays and ultrasonography can help your veterinarian determine liver size and find irregularities, gallstones, and diseases of the gallbladder. Aspiration or biopsy procedures can be used to obtain samples for bacterial culture, cell and tissue analysis, and, when appropriate, toxicologic analysis. Other, less common tests, such as nuclear scintigraphy, may be used in some cases to identify portosystemic shunts (*see* page 122) and other blood vessel abnormalities.

Early treatment is critical for dogs with acute liver failure. Your veterinarian will prescribe specific treatment if an underlying cause be identified. In cases of long-term or end-stage liver disease, and in cases of acute liver disease when no underlying cause has been identified, supportive

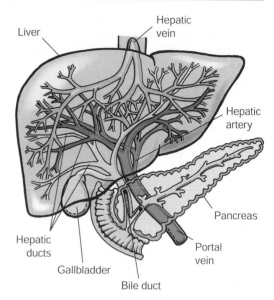

The liver, gallbladder, and pancreas of a dog (modified with permission from *The Merck Manual of Medical Information*, Second Home Edition, 2003)

treatment is directed at slowing progression of disease and minimizing complications.

The diet usually recommended for dogs with liver disease includes adequate calorie intake, with the bulk of energy supplied by carbohydrates (20 to 40% of the diet) in the form of complex carbohydrates such as rice and pasta. A diet higher in soluble fiber may be recommended

Functions of the Liver

- Metabolizes fats, carbohydrates, and proteins
- Metabolizes drugs (inactivates or makes it easier for the body to excrete them)
- Stores and metabolizes vitamins
- Stores minerals, glycogen, and triglycerides
- Manufactures proteins needed for various body functions, such as blood clotting
- Produces bile acids needed for digestion
- Detoxifies harmful products manufactured within the body (such as ammonia) or consumed by the animal (such as poisons)

because the fermentation of fiber in the large intestine decreases ammonia production and absorption and reduces the chances of hepatic encephalopathy. Protein restriction is usually required only for dogs that are at risk of developing hepatic encephalopathy. Follow the specific advice provided by your veterinarian. Dogs that refuse to eat may require tube feeding.

Prescribed vitamin and mineral supplements may include zinc, B vitamins, and vitamin C. Zinc may help to protect the liver by preventing the absorption of copper from the gut. Low potassium levels and decreased levels of B vitamins are common complications with liver disease, and supplementation is often recommended. Vitamin C deficiency has been reported in dogs with liver disease, and supplementation may be beneficial. Injections of vitamin K are sometimes given to dogs with bleeding tendencies.

Complications of Liver Disease

The liver has multiple functions, including removing many toxins from the bloodstream and producing blood clotting proteins. When it is not working properly, many other organs can be affected.

Hepatic Encephalopathy

Hepatic encephalopathy, a syndrome of neurologic problems caused by poor liver function, is seen in a number of liver diseases. While the development of this condition is not completely understood, failure of the liver to clear poisons from the bloodstream and changes in amino acid metabolism caused by the liver disease may act together to cause this disorder. Signs of hepatic encephalopathy include circling, head pressing, aimless wandering, weakness, poor coordination, blindness, excessive drooling, aggression, dementia, seizures, and coma.

Treatment of hepatic encephalopathy is aimed at providing supportive care and rapidly reducing the poisons being produced by the colon. Affected dogs are usually comatose or semicomatose and should not be fed until their status improves. Treatment is likely to include intravenous fluids to correct dehydration and electrolyte (salt) imbalances. Enemas may be used to cleanse the intestines of ammonia and other poisons, and to introduce nutrients that help decrease poison production. Once the dog has been stabilized, treatment is aimed at preventing recurrence. A protein-restricted diet may be prescribed.

Ascites

Ascites is a condition in which fluid collects in the abdomen. In patients with liver disease, ascites is caused by a combination of high blood pressure in the liver and an imbalance in sodium and water metabolism. The first step in the control of ascites is restriction of sodium in the dog's diet. However, sodium-restricted diets alone are often not sufficient, and diuretics (medications that promote loss of fluid by the kidneys) may also be needed. If ascites interferes with breathing, fluid can be removed from the abdomen using a long needle in a process called abdominocentesis. Periodic abdominocentesis can also be used if ascites does not respond to treatment with medication.

Clotting Defects

Clotting problems can be treated using transfusions of blood or plasma to provide the necessary clotting factors. Heparin and vitamin K can also be administered to aid in clotting. Your veterinarian will prescribe the treatment most appropriate for your pet, its overall condition, and blood type.

Bacterial Infections

Dogs with acute liver failure and long-standing liver disease are susceptible to bacterial infections. Your veterinarian will be alert to this possibility because signs of the liver disease itself (for example, fever or low blood sugar) can be similar to those of infection. One or more antibiotics may be necessary to adequately treat the types of bacteria associated with the infection.

Fibrosis

Fibrosis, the formation of fibrous scar tissue in the liver, can eventually lead to liver cirrhosis. Cirrhosis is a serious disease that disrupts liver function. However, fibrosis can sometimes be reversed or reduced by the use of appropriate medications. Your veterinarian can determine which, if any, of the available medications would be beneficial for your pet.

Portosystemic Shunts and Other Vessel Abnormalities

Portosystemic shunts have already been described as a congenital (inborn) defect (*see* page 86). However, in some cases they can develop as a part of illness. In these instances they are called acquired shunts. They can be caused by high blood pressure in the vessels entering the liver. The diseased liver can be thought of as resisting blood flow into the organ. In this case, new blood vessels open to bypass the liver and connect to the blood system of the rest of the body, where the blood pressure is lower. It is as if the blood system were finding a detour around a traffic jam. Acquired shunts are usually seen in older animals and are more frequent in dogs than in cats.

Signs of an acquired shunt include excessive thirst, vomiting, and diarrhea. Fluid accumulation in the abdomen (ascites) is common. Laboratory tests can identify abnormalities associated with the underlying liver disease. Medical treatment of the disease, along with placing a band around the caudal vena cava to slightly raise the blood pressure outside the liver and reduce shunting, can result in a favorable outlook for some dogs with this condition.

Poisons Affecting the Liver

Because of the liver's function in metabolizing drugs, some drugs have been associated with liver dysfunction in dogs. The specific signs and effects depend on the the drug and dosage. In many cases your veterinarian will be aware of the potential for liver disease when prescribing these drugs and will monitor your dog for any signs of decreased or altered function.

Other substances that are toxic to the liver include heavy metals, certain herbicides, fungicides, insecticides, rodent poisons, aflatoxins (produced by mold), amanita mushrooms, and blue-green algae. These can cause life-threatening liver damage.

If your dog has had an accidental overdose of a medication, has had an adverse reaction to a medication (even at the prescribed dose), or has eaten a poison, a veterinarian should be consulted immediately. If necessary, the veterinarian can take steps to minimize absorption of the drug or poison. Depending on the situation, the veterinarian may induce vomiting, administer activated charcoal, pump the animal's stomach, and/or administer an appropriate antitoxin. (For a more detailed discussion of POISONING, *see* page 1145.)

Infectious Diseases of the Liver

Several types of infections may affect the liver, including viral, bacterial, fungal, and parasitic diseases.

Viral diseases of dogs associated with liver dysfunction include infectious canine hepatitis, canine acidophil hepatitis, and canine herpesvirus. **Infectious canine hepatitis** (*see* page 318) can cause longterm inflammation and scarring of the liver in addition to causing death of liver tissue. Canine acidophil hepatitis and canine herpesvirus are uncommon.

Leptospirosis (*see* page 319) is a bacterial infection, caused by *Leptospira interrogans*, that can cause liver disease. The diagnosis is usually made with a blood test and identification of the organism in body tissue samples obtained by biopsy. Treatment includes supportive care and treatment with penicillin or other appropriate antibiotics. Special precautions are recommended when handling dogs suspected of leptospirosis, because this organism may also infect humans.

The most common fungal infections associated with liver dysfunction are coccidioidomycosis and histoplasmosis (*see* page 312). Signs of liver dysfunction include fluid accumulation in the abdomen (ascites), jaundice, and an enlarged liver. Histoplasmosis is generally treated with a prescription antifungal drug. Depending on the level of illness, the outlook for recovery may be poor. In some cases, coccidioidomycosis can be treated with the longterm (6 to 12 months) use of antifungal medications. However, relapses do sometimes occur.

Toxoplasmosis (*see* page 326) is a parasitic disease that can kill liver cells and cause sudden liver failure. Jaundice, fever, lethargy, vomiting, and diarrhea are seen in addition to signs of central nervous system or eye involvement. Liver disease associated with toxoplasmosis in dogs is most often seen in young dogs. A high percentage of dogs with toxoplasmosis are also infected with canine distemper virus. The disease is sudden in onset and rapidly fatal. Diagnosis can be difficult. Treatment usually involves appropriate antibiotics. The outlook for recovery depends on the severity of the illness.

Canine Chronic Hepatitis

Chronic hepatitis is a longterm inflammation of the liver. It is more common in dogs than in cats. Several breeds of dogs are predisposed to this condition, including Bedlington Terriers, Cocker Spaniels, Doberman Pinschers, Skye Terriers, Standard Poodles, and West Highland White Terriers. Although the cause can be determined in some cases of chronic hepatitis, in many cases the cause remains unknown. Copper accumulation is often seen in chronic hepatitis of Bedlington Terriers, West Highland White Terriers, Doberman Pinschers, Skye Terriers, and Cocker Spaniels. Other conditions that have been associated with chronic hepatitis include viral infection (such as infectious canine hepatitis), leptospirosis, and drug toxicity.

Depending on the signs, the cause (if known), and the breed and history of the dog, your veterinarian will determine the appropriate plan for treating and managing chronic hepatitis.

Endocrine Diseases Affecting the Liver

Several diseases involving the endocrine glands can cause liver problems in dogs. These diseases include diabetes mellitus (*see* page 133), Cushing's disease (*see* page 132), and hyperthyroidism (*see* page 140).

Dogs with **diabetes mellitus** have an increased risk of developing fatty degeneration of the liver because diabetes mellitus increases the metabolism and mobilization of lipids. Lipids include any of a group of water-soluble fats and fatlike chemical substances that are sources of fuel for the body. However, when too many lipids are deposited in the liver, the function of the organ is impaired. Insulin replacement may or may not correct this storage problem.

Dogs with **hyperadrenocorticism** are likely to develop changes in the liver similar to those seen in overdoses of corticosteroids. These problems are controlled when the underlying disorder is treated.

Liver Cysts and Nodular Hyperplasia

Liver cysts can be acquired (usually single cysts) or present at birth (usually multiple cysts). Congenital polycystic disease of the liver has been reported in Cairn Terriers and West Highland White Terriers. Occasionally, the cysts can become large and cause abdominal swelling and other signs such as lethargy, vomiting, and excessive thirst. Your veterinarian may be able to feel masses in the abdomen that usually are not painful. Fluid may accumulate in the abdomen. The problem can be identified using x-rays or ultrasonography, although a definitive diagnosis is made by biopsy. Surgical removal of the cysts usually cures the condition.

Nodular hyperplasia is a nonspreading, age-related condition in dogs. It does not usually cause disease or affect liver function. If it is detected, a biopsy may be needed to distinguish these changes from those caused by hepatocellular carcinoma, a form of cancer.

Cancers of the Liver

Tumors that originate in the liver (called primary tumors) are less common than those caused by spread from another part in the body. Primary tumors are most often seen in animals more than 10 years old. These tumors can be either malignant or benign and may spread (metastasize) to other locations such as the lymph nodes, abdominal wall, and lungs.

Cancers that can spread to the liver include pancreatic cancer, mammary (breast) cancer, and several others. Metastatic tumors usually occur at multiple sites.

Signs can include excessive urination and thirst, vomiting, weight loss, jaundice, bleeding problems, hepatic encephalopathy (*see* page 121), enlarged liver, and fluid accumulation in the abdomen. Seizures may develop because of hepatic encephalopathy, low blood sugar, or the spread of cancer to the brain. An abdominal tumor may be found by your veterinarian during an examination. A biopsy is often needed for a definitive diagnosis. If a single liver lobe is involved, surgical removal of the involved lobe is often recommended. Chemotherapy may be effective for some other cancer types. The outlook is poor for primary liver tumors that involve multiple lobes because an effective treatment is not yet available.

Other Liver Diseases

Several other noninfectious chronic diseases may also affect the liver.

Glycogen Storage Disease

Glycogen is a form of stored sugar found in animals. It is converted to glucose when the body needs energy. Glycogen storage diseases are caused by a deficiency of certain enzymes and result in failure of glycogen to be released from cells. When this occurs, glycogen accumulates within the liver and other organs and is unavail-

able for conversion to glucose. Signs of this disorder include an enlarged liver, retarded growth, and weakness due to low blood sugar levels. Analysis of samples of liver, muscle, or skin is needed for diagnosis. Treatment is based on signs of illness and includes frequent small meals of high-carbohydrate food. The outlook in most cases is poor, and most dogs with these diseases die at a young age.

Hepatic Amyloidosis

Amyloid is a protein that is not folded into the correct shape. The misfolded protein causes damage by displacing normal cells. Amyloidosis is an inherited disease of Chinese Shar-Peis; however, the liver is not always affected. Although some dogs may show no signs, typical signs include loss of appetite, excessive thirst and urination, vomiting, jaundice, and an enlarged liver. Affected animals may collapse and have pale mucous membranes due to rupture of the liver and subsequent internal bleeding. Diagnosis is made by identifying amyloid deposits in liver biopsy samples. Drugs are available that may slow the progression of amyloidosis, but the outlook is poor, especially if the diagnosis is made late in the disease.

Idiopathic Liver Fibrosis

Liver fibrosis in young dogs that is not associated with any underlying inflammatory conditions is referred to as idiopathic hepatic (liver) fibrosis. Fibrosis is accumulation of tough scar tissue that replaces normal liver tissue. Affected dogs are usually less than 2 years of age. Signs include fluid accumulation in the abdomen (ascites) and hepatic encephalopathy (*see* page 121). Other signs include weight loss, vomiting, and diarrhea. X-rays of the liver show a decrease in size, and abnormalities of the blood vessels between the intestines and liver can be identified by ultrasound. Treatment to manage signs of illness, particularly hepatic encephalopathy and ascites, is usual.

Diseases of the Gallbladder and Bile Duct

The liver secretes bile, a substance that assists with digestion and absorption of fats and with elimination of certain waste products from the body. Bile is stored in the gallbladder and is released into the duodenum through the bile duct.

Jaundice (a yellow tinge noticeable in the skin, mucous membranes, and eyes) is often the main sign of diseases of the gallbladder and bile duct. An exception is cancer of the gallbladder, which may not cause jaundice.

Obstruction of the Bile Duct

Obstruction of the bile duct is most often caused by pancreatic disease. Pancreatic swelling, inflammation, or fibrosis can cause compression of the bile duct. Diagnosis is based on laboratory tests, x-rays, and ultrasonographic evidence of pancreatic disease. Treatment of pancreatitis will often relieve the obstruction. If this is not successful, surgery may be necessary to connect the gallbladder directly to the intestine. If gallstones are the cause of obstruction, the gallbladder may need to be removed. Cancer of the pancreas, bile ducts, liver, intestines, and lymph nodes can also cause obstruction. A biopsy is needed to confirm the diagnosis. When cancer is present, surgery can provide some relief but is not a cure.

Inflammation of the Gallbladder (Cholecystitis)

Inflammation of the gallbladder (cholecystitis) is usually caused by bacterial infections that start in the intestines and either travel up the common bile duct or are spread through the blood. In some cases, the wall of the gallbladder is damaged, and bile leaks into the abdomen causing severe abdominal infection and inflammation, which can be fatal. Loss of appetite, abdominal pain, jaundice, fever, and vomiting are common signs. The dog may be in a state of shock due to abdominal inflammation.

The inflammation can also spread to the surrounding branches of the bile duct and the liver. Diagnosis can be confirmed by biopsy for bacterial cultures and tissue analysis. Treatment usually consists of removal of the gallbladder and appropriate antibiotic medication to treat infection. The outlook is good if appropriate antibiotics are started early but is less favorable if diagnosis and treatment are delayed.

Gallstones

Gallstones rarely cause disease. When it does occur, disease is usually seen in older, female, small-breed dogs. Signs include vomiting, jaundice, abdominal pain, and fever. Treatment consists of removal of the stones and appropriate antibiotics.

Rupture of the Gallbladder or Bile Duct

Rupture of the gallbladder or bile duct is most often due to gallstone obstruction, inflammation of the gallbladder, or blunt trauma. Rupture of the bile duct may also occur as a result of cancer or certain parasites. Rupture leads to leakage of bile into the abdomen, causing a serious condition called bile peritonitis, which may be fatal if the rupture is not repaired. Treatment includes surgery, which consists of tying off the bile duct, removing the gallbladder, or connecting the gallbladder with the small intestine.

■ DISORDERS OF THE RECTUM AND ANUS

Diseases of the rectum and anus can be congenital (inherited) or occur later in life. (For a more detailed discussion of CONGENITAL AND INHERITED DISORDERS, *see* page 82.)

Anal Sac Disease

Anal sac disease is caused by clogging or infection of glands called anal sacs located on each side of the anus. It is the most common disease of the anal region in dogs. The anal sacs are related to the scent glands in skunks and produce a small amount of dark, foul-smelling liquid. The liquid is normally squeezed out during defecation. Small breeds are predisposed to anal sac disease; large or giant breeds are rarely affected.

Anal sacs may become clogged (impacted), infected, abscessed, or cancerous. There are several common causes of clogged anal sacs, including failure of the sacs to be squeezed out during defecation, poor muscle tone in obese dogs, and excessive secretion of the gland. When the gland contents are not periodically squeezed out, this can make the glands susceptible to bacterial overgrowth, infection, and inflammation.

The signs of anal sac disease are related to pain and discomfort associated with sitting. The dog may scoot its buttocks on the ground, lick or bite at the anal area, and have painful defecation with straining. If the glands are impacted, hard masses can be felt in the area of the sacs. When the sacs are infected or abscessed, severe pain and discoloration of the area are often present. Open tracts of tissue can lead from abscessed sacs and rupture through the skin, causing a wound. Tumors involving the anal sacs are sometimes present. A rectal examination by a veterinarian will usually be done to diagnose anal sac disease. Additional tests may be needed if infection or a tumor is suspected.

Your veterinarian can often squeeze out impacted anal sacs by hand. If the material in the sacs is too hard or dry, the veterinarian may inject a softening agent into the sac. If infection is present, antibiotics might be prescribed. Your veterinarian might recommend applying hot compresses if an abscess (infection) is present. Supplemental fiber may be recommended to increase fecal bulk, which facilitates anal sac compression and emptying. If treatment is ineffective or the condition keeps coming back, the anal sac can be surgically removed. A common complication from this surgery is fecal incontinence; however, the incontinence is usually temporary.

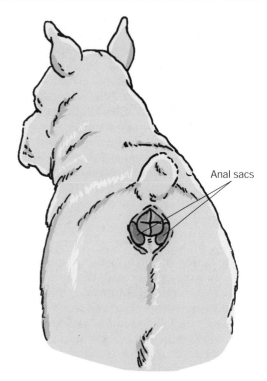

Anal sacs

The anal sacs of a dog

Perianal Fistula

Perianal fistula is characterized by chronic, foul-smelling wounds in the tissues surrounding the anus. The cause is unknown. It is most common in German Shepherds but is also seen in setters and retrievers. Dogs more than 7 years old are at higher risk.

Contamination of the hair follicles and glands of the anal area by fecal material and anal sac secretions may result in tissue damage and longterm inflammation of the skin and tissues surrounding the anus. Dogs that are susceptible to skin problems may be affected more often. Low thyroid hormone levels or an immune system defect may also contribute to susceptibility. The likelihood of contamination is greater in dogs with a broad-based tail; deep anal folds may cause feces to be retained within rectal glands and play a major role. Prompt treatment is necessary to keep infection from spreading deeper into the body.

Signs in dogs include attitude change, straining and painful defecation, loss of appetite, lethargy, diarrhea, and attempts to bite and lick the anal area.

Until recently, management of perianal fistulas usually involved surgery to remove the anal sacs and the diseased tissues. Because of complications such as incontinence and rectal narrowing, surgery is now recommended only for dogs that do not improve with medical treatment. Several medications have been shown to provide effective treatment. Your pet may also be prescribed stool softeners to reduce painful defecation. Antibiotics (if prescribed) and cleansing the anal area may reduce inflammation. For your pet's comfort, follow all treatment instructions carefully.

Perineal Hernia

Perineal hernia is a type of hernia that occurs near the anus. It occurs most often in unneutered 6- to 8-year-old male dogs. Welsh Corgis, Boston Terriers, Boxers, Collies, Kelpies and Kelpie mixes, Dachshunds and Dachshund mixes, Old English Sheepdogs, and Pekingese are at higher risk than other breeds. Many factors are involved in the development of this condition, including breed predisposition, hormonal imbalance, prostate disease, chronic constipation, and pelvic muscle weakness.

Common signs include constipation, straining, and painful defecation. Urinary obstruction may develop if the bladder and/or prostate gland become displaced into the hernia. A swelling below and to the side of the anus may be evident. Hernias may occur on both sides, but two-thirds of cases occur on one side only and more than 80% of these are on the right side. Diagnosis is done by rectal examination to determine what organs and tissues are involved.

Perineal hernia is rarely an emergency, except when the dog is unable to urinate. If this occurs, the veterinarian will attempt to insert a catheter into the bladder or remove the urine using a needle. This is followed by an attempt to correct the hernia surgically. If your pet is an unneutered male, neutering may be recommended to reduce the chance of recurrence. In up to half of affected dogs, perianal hernias will happen again. Postoperative complications such as infection, nerve damage, and other anal or rectal problems can occur.

Rectal and Anorectal Narrowing (Strictures)

Rectal and anorectal strictures are narrowings caused by scar tissue. The scarring may be the result of injury from foreign objects or trauma (such as bite wounds or accidents) or may be a complication of inflammation. In dogs, strictures usually involve both the rectum and the anus, but they are not common. Strictures are more frequent in German Shepherds, Beagles, and Poodles than in other breeds.

Rectal Tumors

Signs of rectal tumors can include straining, painful defecation, blood in the feces, or diarrhea. Surgery is the treatment of choice for rectal tumors, but it may not be effective because the disease may have spread beyond the rectum before any signs are visible.

Rectal Polyps

The growths called rectal polyps occur infrequently in dogs. The polyps are usually benign and do not spread to other tissues. The larger the polyp, the greater the probability that it is malignant (cancerous). Signs include straining to defecate, blood in the feces, and diarrhea. The polyp can be felt by a veterinarian during a rectal examination, and its surface tends to bleed easily. Periodically, the polyp may protrude from the anus. Surgical removal is usually followed by rapid recovery and lengthy survival time. New polyps may develop after surgery. Your veterinarian may submit a tissue sample from the polyp for microscopic analysis to confirm the diagnosis.

Rectal Prolapse

Rectal prolapse is a condition in which one or more layers of the rectum protrude through the anus. Prolapse may be classified as incomplete (only the innermost rectal layer is protruding) or complete (all rectal layers are protruding).

The condition commonly occurs in young dogs that have severe diarrhea or that routinely strain to defecate. Prolapse can be caused by a number of intestinal, anorectal, or urinary diseases. Perineal hernia (*see* page 127) or other conditions that affect the nerves of the anal sphincter may also produce prolapse.

An elongated, cylinder-shaped mass protruding through the anal opening is usually a sign of rectal prolapse. However, prolapses involving other parts of the intestine can have a similar appearance. No matter what type of prolapse is present, any tissue mass protruding from the anal opening should be promptly examined by a veterinarian.

Identifying and eliminating the cause of prolapse is a key part of treatment. Small or incomplete prolapses can often be manually replaced by the veterinarian while the dog is anesthetized. This is usually followed by partial closure of the anus with stitches for 5 to 7 days to prevent the prolapse from happening again. The dog may be given a topical anesthetic or epidural injection before or after the procedure to reduce straining. In some cases, surgery to repair the prolapse may be required. After treatment, a moist diet and a stool softener are likely to be recommended. Diarrhea occurring shortly after surgery may require additional treatment and should be discussed with your veterinarian.

Rectal Tears

A tear in the rectum or anus can be caused by a dog swallowing a sharp object (such as a sharp bone, needle, or other rough material) or from injury such as a bite. The tear may involve only the surface layers of the rectum (partial tear) or penetrate all layers (complete tear). Signs may include constipation, straining, rectal bleeding, and reluctance to defecate. A diagnosis is based on these signs and inspection of the rectum and anus. Swelling may be present when the injury has been present for some time.

Treatment to avoid infection and close the wound will be started immediately. The tear will be cleansed and stitched closed. Depending on the location, the wound may be accessible through the anus or may require abdominal surgery. Antibiotics and stool softeners will probably be prescribed after surgery.

CHAPTER 8

Hormonal Disorders

▓ INTRODUCTION

Hormones are chemical messengers that have many different functions. The effects of hormones in the body are wide-ranging and varied. Some familiar examples of hormones include insulin, which is important in the development of diabetes, and estrogen and progesterone, which are involved in the female reproductive cycle.

The **endocrine system** consists of a group of tissues that release hormones into the bloodstream for travel to other parts of the body (*see* TABLE 8). Most endocrine tissues are glands (such as the thyroid gland) that release hormones directly into small blood vessels within and around the tissue. Several important hormones are released from tissues other than glands, such as the heart, kidney, and

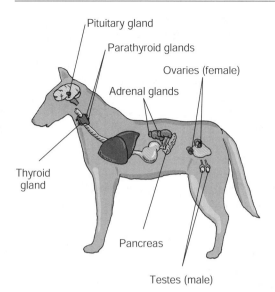

- Pituitary gland
- Parathyroid glands
- Ovaries (female)
- Adrenal glands
- Thyroid gland
- Pancreas
- Testes (male)

The major endocrine glands in the dog (modified with permission from *The Merck Manual of Medical Information*, Second Home Edition, 2003)

liver. Some hormones act only on a single tissue, while others have effects on virtually every cell in the body. Hormones are present in the blood in very small quantities, so laboratory tests done to measure hormone levels must be very sensitive.

Development of Endocrine System Disease

The body monitors and adjusts the level of each hormone by using a feedback system specifically for that hormone. Hormones function to keep factors such as temperature and blood sugar (glucose) levels within certain ranges. Sometimes, pairs of hormones with opposite functions work together to keep body functions in balance.

Endocrine system diseases can develop when too much or not enough hormone is produced, or when normal pathways for hormones to be used and removed are disrupted. Signs can develop because of a problem in the tissues that are the source of the hormone, or because of a problem in another part of the body that is affecting the secretion or action of a particular hormone.

A tumor or other abnormal tissue in an endocrine gland often causes it to produce too much hormone. When an endocrine gland is destroyed, not enough hormone is produced. Diseases caused by overproduction or excess of a hormone often begin with the prefix **hyper-**. For example, in hyperthyroidism, the thyroid gland produces too much thyroid hormone. Diseases caused by a lack or deficiency of a hormone often begin with the prefix **hypo-**. For example, in hypothyroidism, the thyroid gland does not produce enough thyroid hormone.

In many cases, the abnormal gland not only overproduces hormone, it also does not respond normally to feedback signals. This causes hormone to be released in situations in which its levels would normally be reduced. Sometimes, the overproduction is caused by stimulation from another part of the body. Occasionally, a tumor outside the endocrine system can produce a substance similar to a hormone, causing the body to respond as though that hormone were being produced.

Diseases caused by not enough hormone secretion can also have multiple causes. Endocrine tissue can be destroyed by an autoimmune process, in which the body incorrectly identifies some of its own tissue as foreign and destroys the tissue cells. In early stages of tissue loss, the body may compensate by producing additional hormone from the remaining tissue. In these cases, signs of disease may be delayed until the tissue has been destroyed completely.

Disorders resulting in signs of reduced endocrine activity may also develop because tissues distant from the hormone source are disrupted. This can occur when the function of one hormone is to stimulate the production of a second hormone. For example, the pituitary gland secretes a hormone that stimulates the thyroid gland to secrete thyroid hormones. If the levels of the thyroid-stimulating hormone from the pituitary gland are abnormally low, the levels of thyroid hormones will also be low even if the thyroid gland is healthy. Another potential cause for reduced endocrine function is tissue loss caused by tumors that do not produce hormones themselves but compress or destroy the nearby endocrine gland.

Table 8. Major Hormones

Endocrine Gland	Hormone(s) Produced	Function
Pituitary gland (anterior lobe)		
	Corticotropin (adreno-corticotropic hormone)	Stimulates the production and secretion of hormones by the adrenal cortex
	Growth hormone	Promotes growth of the body and influences the metabolism of proteins, carbohydrates, and lipids
	Follicle-stimulating hormone	Stimulates the growth of follicles in the ovaries and induces the formation of sperm in the testes
	Luteinizing hormone	Stimulates ovulation and the development of the corpus luteum in the female and the production of testosterone by the testes in the male
	Prolactin	Stimulates the mammary glands to secrete milk
	Thyroid-stimulating hormone	Stimulates the production and secretion of thyroid hormones by the thyroid gland
Pituitary gland (posterior lobe)		
	Antidiuretic hormone; also known as arginine vasopressin	Causes the kidneys to conserve water by concentrating the urine and reducing urine volume; also has lesser role in regulating blood pressure
	Oxytocin	Stimulates the contraction of smooth muscle of the uterus during labor and facilitates ejection of milk from the breast during nursing
Parathyroid glands		
	Parathyroid hormone	Raises the blood calcium concentration by promoting absorption of calcium by the intestine, mobilizing calcium salts from bones, and increasing the ability of the kidney to recover calcium from urine; also lowers phosphate by enhancing its excretion by the kidneys
Thyroid glands		
	Thyroid hormones (T_3 and T_4)	Increase the basal metabolic rate; also regulate protein, fat, and carbohydrate metabolism
	Calcitonin	Participates in calcium and phosphorus metabolism; tends to have the opposite effects of parathyroid hormone
Adrenal glands		
	Aldosterone	Helps regulate salt and water balance by retaining sodium (salt) and water and excreting potassium
	Cortisol	Has widespread effects throughout the body; involved in the response to stress; active in carbohydrate and protein metabolism; helps maintain blood sugar level, blood pressure, and muscle strength
	Epinephrine (adrenaline) and norepinephrine	Released in response to stress; stimulates heart action and increases blood pressure, metabolic rate, and blood glucose concentration; also raises blood sugar and fatty acid levels

Table 8. Major Hormones—*(Continued)*		
Endocrine Gland	**Hormone(s) Produced**	**Function**
Pancreas		
	Insulin	Lowers blood sugar level; affects the metabolism of sugar, protein, and fat
	Glucagon	Raises blood sugar level, thus opposing the action of insulin
Ovaries		
	Estrogen	Controls female reproductive system, along with other hormones; responsible for promoting estrus and the development and maintenance of female secondary sex characteristics
	Progesterone	Prepares the uterus for implantation of the fertilized egg, maintains pregnancy, and promotes development of the mammary glands
Testes		
	Testosterone	Responsible for the development of the male reproductive system and secondary male sexual characteristics

Endocrine diseases and related conditions also result from changes in the response of tissues targeted by a hormone. An important example is type 2 diabetes mellitus, in which the body produces insulin but the cells no longer respond to it. This condition is often associated with obesity.

Treatment of Endocrine System Disease

Endocrine diseases caused by the presence of too much hormone may be treated surgically (tumor removal), by radiotherapy (such as the use of radioactive iodine to destroy an overactive thyroid gland), or with medication. Syndromes of hormone deficiency are often successfully treated by replacing the missing hormone, such as insulin injections to treat diabetes mellitus. Steroid and thyroid hormone replacements can usually be given orally.

Pets taking hormone replacement treatment must be monitored for adverse effects and periodically retested to make sure the dosage is correct. In some cases, such as after surgical removal of an endocrine tumor, the diseased gland will recover and hormone replacement will no longer be needed. However, most of the time, lifelong treatment is required.

▓ DISORDERS OF THE ADRENAL GLANDS

The adrenal glands are located just in front of the kidneys. The adrenal gland has 2 parts—the cortex and the medulla.

The **adrenal cortex** is subdivided into 3 layers, and each layer produces a different set of steroid hormones. The outer layer produces the mineralocorticoids, which help to control the body's balance of sodium and potassium salts. The middle layer produces glucocorticoids, which are involved in metabolizing nutrients as well as in reducing inflammation. The inner layer produces sex hormones such as estrogen and progesterone.

The **adrenal medulla** plays an important role in response to stress or low blood sugar (glucose). It releases epinephrine (sometimes also called adrenaline) and norepinephrine, both of which increase heart output, blood pressure, and blood glucose, and slow digestion.

Cushing's Disease

Cushing's disease, also referred to as **hyperadrenocorticism**, is a common endocrine disease in adult and aged dogs. The signs result primarily from chronic excess of the hormone cortisol. Increased cortisol levels in dogs may result from one of several mechanisms. The most common cause (85% to 90% of cases) is a tumor in the pituitary gland. The pituitary tumor produces a hormone that triggers excessive development of the adrenal gland. Less common (10% to 15% of cases) is a tumor in the adrenal glands themselves. Longterm use of corticosteroid drugs (for example, to decrease inflammation or treat an immune disorder) can also cause signs of Cushing's disease. (For a more detailed discussion of CUSHING'S DISEASE, *see* page 136.)

Addison's Disease

Addison's disease, also called **hypoadrenocorticism**, is caused by a deficiency of adrenal gland hormones. It is most common in young to middle-aged dogs. The cause is usually not known, but an autoimmune condition in which the body destroys some of its own tissue is likely. The adrenal gland can also be destroyed by other conditions, including cancer in other parts of the body. Secretion of aldosterone, the main mineralocorticoid hormone, is reduced, which affects the levels of potassium, sodium, and chloride in the blood. Potassium gradually builds up in the blood and, in severe cases, may cause the heart to slow down or beat irregularly. Some dogs have such a slow heart rate (50 beats per minute or lower) that they can become weak or go into shock.

Signs of Addison's disease include repeated episodes of vomiting and diarrhea, loss of appetite, dehydration, and a gradual loss of body condition. Weight loss is often severe. Although signs can be hard to identify while Addison's disease is developing, severe consequences, such as shock and evidence of kidney failure, can develop suddenly.

A veterinarian can make a tentative diagnosis based on the history, signs, and certain laboratory abnormalities, such as very low levels of sodium and very high levels of potassium in the blood. The diagnosis is confirmed by specific evaluation of adrenal function. This is done by measuring the level of cortisol in the blood, treating the dog with adrenocorticotropin (a hormone that stimulates the adrenal gland in healthy animals), and then measuring the level of cortisol in the blood a second time. Affected dogs have low baseline cortisol levels, and there is little response to administration of adrenocorticotropin.

An adrenal crisis is a medical emergency and requires treatment with intravenous fluids to restore levels of body fluids, salt, and sugar to normal. Hormone replacement treatment can often be started while the pet is being stabilized. Laboratory values are monitored regularly to assess response to treatment and adjust doses if needed. For longterm treatment, replacement hormones can be given by mouth or injection. Additional sodium may need to be added to the diet.

Pheochromocytomas

Pheochromocytomas are tumors of the adrenal medulla that are able to secrete epinephrine (adrenaline), norepinephrine, or both. Often, there are no signs, and the tumor is found by chance during treatment for other conditions. When signs are present, they may include increased thirst and urination, increased heart rate, restlessness, and a distended abdomen. Diagnosis is often made based on signs and ultrasonography. Treatment involves surgery (if feasible) and management of high blood pressure. Other tumors in the adrenal glands, such as neuroblastomas and ganglioneuromas, can develop from nerve cells.

▓ DISORDERS OF THE PANCREAS

The pancreas is composed of several types of cells that have distinct functions involved in the production of hormones and digestive enzymes. The **exocrine pancreas** produces enzymes that are essential for the digestion of complex dietary components such as proteins, triglycerides, and complex carbohydrates. The exocrine pancreas also secretes large amounts of bicarbonate, which buffers stomach acid. Disorders of the exocrine pancreas are discussed in the section on digestive disorders, because they relate to digestion (*see* page 117). The **endocrine pancreas** produces the hormones insulin and glucagon, which regulate blood sugar levels. The functions and disorders of the endocrine pancreas are discussed in this section.

The **islets of Langerhans** in the pancreas consist of 3 types of cells, each of which produces a different hormone. Most of the cells, which are called beta cells, produce insulin. Insulin affects, either directly or indirectly, the function of every organ in the body, particularly the liver, fat cells, and muscle. In general, insulin increases the transfer of glucose (sugar) and other compounds into body cells. It also decreases the rate of fat, protein, and carbohydrate breakdown.

The other 2 cell types in the islets of Langerhans produce the hormones glucagon and somatostatin. When blood glucose levels drop, glucagon is released. Glucagon helps convert stored carbohydrates into glucose so they can be used as energy.

Insulin and glucagon work together to keep the concentration of glucose in the blood and other body fluids within a relatively narrow range. Glucagon controls glucose release from the liver, and insulin controls glucose transport into numerous body tissues.

Diabetes Mellitus

Diabetes mellitus (often called simply diabetes) is a chronic disorder of carbohydrate metabolism caused by either a deficiency of insulin or a resistance to insulin. Middle-aged dogs are affected most commonly, with females affected twice as often as males. Certain small breeds, such as Miniature Poodles, Dachshunds, Schnauzers, Cairn Terriers, and Beagles, seem to develop diabetes more often than other breeds, but any breed can be affected.

A number of mechanisms are responsible for decreased insulin production and secretion, but usually they involve destruction of islet cells. Insulin resistance and diabetes mellitus are also seen in many dogs with Cushing's disease (*see* page 136). Longterm treatment with glucocorticoids or progestins can make an animal more likely to develop diabetes mellitus. During their heat cycles, unspayed female dogs produce the hormone progesterone, which can lead to high blood sugar and insulin resistance. Obesity increases the risk of insulin resistance. Increased glucagon also appears to contribute to development of high blood sugar by releasing liver stores of glucose.

Diabetes can often develop gradually, and the signs may not be noticed at first. Common signs include increased thirst and urination, along with increased appetite and weight loss. Diabetic animals often develop chronic or recurrent infections. An enlarged liver is common. Cataracts develop often in dogs with poorly controlled diabetes mellitus. A diagnosis of diabetes mellitus is based on finding high levels of sugar in the blood and urine after a period of fasting.

Your understanding of the disease and daily care of your pet are critical to successfully managing diabetes. Treatment involves a combination of weight loss, diet, insulin injections, and possibly oral medications. Usually, animals are hospitalized for a day or two, and multiple blood samples are taken to measure the blood sugar level throughout the day. This information is used to determine the amount and timing of your pet's meals, and the dosage and timing of insulin injections. After this initial stabilization, your veterinarian will provide appropriate instructions on managing this regimen at home. Periodic reevaluation is necessary to ensure that the disease is being controlled; these checkups may lead to changes in treatment over time.

Functional Islet Cell Tumors (Insulinomas)

Tumors in the islet cells of the pancreas often produce and secrete the hormones normally secreted by the gland. The most common pancreatic islet tumor affects the insulin-secreting beta cells and is called an insulinoma. Insulinomas are most common in middle-aged to older dogs.

Signs result from excessive insulin secretion, which leads to low blood sugar (hypoglycemia). Initially, signs include weakness, fatigue after exercise, muscle twitching, lack of coordination, confusion, and possibly changes of temperament. Dogs are easily agitated, occasionally becoming excited and restless. Periodic seizures may occur. A dog might also collapse, appearing to have fainted.

Signs occur infrequently at first, but become more frequent and last longer as the disease progresses. Attacks may be brought on by exercise, or by fasting or eating (which stimulates the release of insulin and lowers blood sugar levels). Signs resolve quickly after glucose treatment. Repeated episodes of prolonged and severe low blood sugar can result in irreversible brain damage. Diagnosis is based on a history of periodic weakness, collapse, or seizures, along with tests indicating low blood sugar.

Removing the tumor surgically can correct the low blood sugar and nervous system signs unless permanent damage has already occurred. However, if the tumor has already spread, blood sugar levels may remain low after surgery. Unfortunately, insulinomas are often malignant, and dogs often live only a year or so. Quality of life can sometimes be maintained in affected dogs by modifying the diet and giving glucocorticoids.

Gastrin-secreting Islet Cell Tumors (Gastrinomas)

Gastrin is a hormone that prompts the release of gastric acid in the stomach. Gastrin is normally secreted only by the stomach and small intestine. In rare cases, it can also be secreted by tumors of the pancreatic islet cells called gastrinomas.

Signs of a gastrinoma may include loss of appetite, vomiting blood, intermittent diarrhea (usually containing dark blood), weight loss, and dehydration. Many of these signs result from stomach ulcers caused by too much gastrin. In dogs with repeated stomach or intestinal ulcers, exploratory surgery can be done to check for pancreatic tumors. However, in all known cases, the pancreatic cancer has been inoperable because of spread to other areas. Medications for the stomach and intestinal ulcers can make the dog more comfortable.

■ DISORDERS OF THE PARATHYROID GLANDS AND OF CALCIUM METABOLISM

The way in which the body processes calcium and phosphate, the function of vitamin D (which acts more like a hormone than a vitamin), and the formation of bone are all tied together into a system that involves 2 other hormones— parathyroid hormone and calcitonin— that are secreted by the parathyroid glands.

Disorders of calcium and phosphorus metabolism that affect the skeletal system are discussed in the chapter on bone, joint, and muscle disorders (*see* page 180).

Calcium-regulating Hormones

Calcium is an essential component of the skeleton, and it has important functions in muscle contraction, blood clotting, enzyme activity, the nervous system, and hormone release, among others. Precise control of calcium in the body is vital to health. Parathyroid hormone, vitamin D, and calcitonin all interact to keep the level of calcium steady, despite variations in intake and excretion. Other hormones may also contribute to maintaining the balance of calcium in the body.

Parathyroid hormone is synthesized and stored in the parathyroid glands, which are located on either side of the thyroid gland in the neck. The synthesis of this hormone is regulated by a feedback mechanism that involves the level of blood calcium. The primary function of parathyroid hormone is to control the level of calcium by affecting the movement of calcium into and out of bone, the retention of calcium by the kidneys, and absorption of calcium from the digestive tract.

Vitamin D is the second major hormone involved in the regulation of calcium metabolism. In several species, including horses and people, vitamin D is formed in the skin after exposure to ultraviolet light (such as sunshine). In contrast, dogs are not able to form enough vitamin D in the skin and depend on dietary intake. Parathyroid hormone and conditions that stimulate its secretion, as well as reduced phosphate levels, increase the formation of vitamin D.

Calcitonin is a hormone secreted by certain cells of the thyroid gland in mammals. When the level of blood calcium increases, calcitonin is released to prevent hypercalcemia (abnormally high levels of calcium).

Hypercalcemia

Hypercalcemia is an abnormally high level of calcium in the blood. The signs associated with this condition depend on how high the calcium level is, how quickly it develops, and how long it lasts. The most common signs are increased thirst and urination, followed by reduced appetite, vomiting, constipation, weakness, depression, muscle twitching, and seizures.

In dogs, hypercalcemia is often associated with tumors, an underactive adrenal gland (Addison's disease), or kidney disease. Less common causes include an overactive parathyroid gland, vitamin D overdose, and granulomatous disease (*see* TABLE 9).

Hypercalcemia is treated by identifying and treating the underlying condition that is causing it. However, the cause may not always be apparent. Supportive treatment, including fluids, diuretics ("water pills"), sodium bicarbonate, and glucocorticoids, is often needed to lower the level of calcium in the blood.

Hypocalcemia

Hypocalcemia is an abnormally low level of calcium in the blood, leading to twitching, muscle tremors, and seizures. The causes of hypocalcemia include previous surgical removal of the parathyroid glands (leading to hypoparathyroidism), kidney disease or failure, and calcium imbalance in nursing females.

Hypoparathyroidism is characterized by low calcium levels, high phosphate levels, and either temporary or permanent insufficiency of parathyroid hormone. It is uncommon in dogs, but can be caused by previous removal of the parathyroid glands as a treatment for hyperthyroidism or for a parathyroid tumor. Common signs of hypocalcemia include muscle tremors and twitches, muscle contraction, and generalized convulsions. Diagnosis is based on history, signs, low calcium and high phosphorus levels, and the blood parathyroid hormone level. Other causes of hypocalcemia must be eliminated.

The goal of treatment is to return the level of blood calcium to normal and to eliminate the underlying cause. If an animal is having muscle spasms or seizures because of low calcium levels, immediate treatment with intravenous calcium is needed. Dietary supplements of calcium, often along with vitamin D, are prescribed for longterm treatment.

Chronic kidney failure is probably the most common cause of hypocalcemia. However, the hypocalcemia that occurs with kidney failure does not tend to lead to the nervous system signs that are seen in hypoparathyroidism. Treatment usually involves dietary restriction and treatment to lower phosphate concentration in the blood.

Several other disorders can also cause hypocalcemia (*see* TABLE 10).

Table 9. Causes and Treatment of Increased Blood Calcium Levels (Hypercalcemia)

Cause	Reason	Treatment
Primary hyperparathyroidism (relatively rare in dogs)	Parathyroid glands are overactive (often due to a tumor) and secrete excessive parathyroid hormone	Removal or destruction of tumor
Hypercalcemia caused by cancer (malignant hypercalcemia)	Increased bone breakdown and resorption triggered by cancer cells causes higher levels of calcium in blood	Depends on specific type of cancer
Hypoadrenocorticism (Addison's disease)	Multiple factors involved; up to 30% of dogs with Addison's disease have increased calcium levels	Treatment of underlying disease normalizes calcium levels
Chronic kidney failure	Exact mechanism unknown	Supportive care
Vitamin toxicity	Vitamin D supplements taken in excess (for example, to treat hypoparathyroidism); accidental ingestion of calcipotriene (a human psoriasis medicine) or of rodent poisons containing calcitriol	Adjustment of vitamin D dosage (if from medication)
Granulomatous disease	Inflammation activates the type of white blood cells that can increase levels of vitamin D	Treatment of underlying disease, for example, antifungal drugs or surgery
Houseplants (*Cestrum diurnum* [the day-blooming jessamine], *Solanum malacoxylon, Triestum flavescens*)	Contain substance similar to vitamin D that may cause hypercalcemia when accidentally eaten	Supportive care; corticosteroids
Bone tumors (rare)	Breakdown of bone increases blood calcium levels	Depends on specific type of cancer

■ DISORDERS OF THE PITUITARY GLAND

The pituitary gland is located near the center and bottom of the brain. It produces a number of critical hormones that control many parts of the body, including several other endocrine glands. Because of this central role, it is sometimes called a "master gland." Because large numbers of hormones are produced by the pituitary gland, a variety of different conditions can be caused by pituitary disease or tumors. The specific illness and signs depend on the cause and the area(s) of the pituitary gland that is affected.

Cushing's Disease

Cushing's disease, also called **hyperadrenocorticism**, is caused by too much cortisol. Cushing's disease is common in dogs but not in other species. Miniature Poo-

dles, Dachshunds, Boxers, Boston Terriers, and Beagles are at increased risk. In most affected dogs (85 to 90%), the cause is a small, benign pituitary tumor. In the remaining 10 to 15% of dogs, the cause is a tumor of the adrenal gland itself.

This condition tends to occur in middle-aged to older dogs. Common signs include increased thirst and urination, increased appetite, heat intolerance, lethargy, a "potbelly," panting, obesity, weakness, thin skin, hair loss, and bruising. Rarely, calcinosis cutis develops, a condition in which minerals are deposited in the skin and can appear as small, thickened "dots" on the abdomen.

Diagnosis of Cushing's disease can be difficult because laboratory test results may be inconclusive and false-positive test results are common in dogs that have other diseases. Retesting may be needed 3 to 6 months later. Once the disease is con-

Table 10. Causes and Treatment of Low Blood Calcium Levels (Hypocalcemia)

Cause	Reason	Treatment
Hypoparathyroidism	Deficiency of parathyroid hormone leads to low blood calcium levels	(*See* HYPOCALCEMIA, page 135.)
Chronic kidney failure	Damaged kidney does not effectively regulate calcium levels	Most cases are mild; if needed, lower blood phosphate concentration through diet and medication
Eclampsia (puerperal tetany)	Occurs in lactating females; may be due to imbalance between intake and outflow of calcium	Intravenous calcium; weaning of litter if possible
Chelating agents (for example, ethylene glycol in antifreeze)	Chelating agent binds to calcium	(*See* ETHYLENE GLYCOL (ANTIFREEZE) POISONING, page 1150.)

firmed, additional laboratory tests are usually done to determine whether the cause is a tumor of the pituitary gland or of the adrenal gland. The pituitary and adrenal glands can be further evaluated using abdominal x-rays, ultrasonography, or more sophisticated methods of diagnostic imaging such as computed tomography (CT) or magnetic resonance imaging (MRI).

Hyperadrenocorticism can be treated with mitotane, a drug that acts on the adrenal glands to decrease the production of cortisol. Dogs should be monitored for signs that the cortisol level has dropped too low, such as reduced appetite, vomiting, and diarrhea. After 7 to 10 days of treatment, a test may be performed to determine if cortisol levels are low enough. Often, mitotane treatment is continued, with blood tests done periodically to monitor cortisol levels. Gradually increasing doses of mitotane are often needed to keep the disease under control. Adverse effects of mitotane can include vomiting and loss of appetite, lack of coordination, weakness, seizures, and mildly low blood sugar. These effects sometimes stop if the daily dose is divided into 2 equal parts and given 8 to 12 hours apart.

Another medication called trilostane has been shown to be effective in treating pituitary-dependent Cushing's disease in some studies, and it may have fewer adverse effects. However, it is not currently available in the United States except through special permission of the Food and Drug Administration.

If adrenal gland tumors are present, surgical removal is sometimes an option. In some cases, radiation treatment of the pituitary gland is a possibility, although it may take several months for signs of the disease to resolve.

Adult-onset Panhypopituitarism

In adult-onset panhypopituitarism, the pituitary gland and nearby tissues, including the hypothalamus, are compressed or damaged. As a result of this damage, the secretion of many of the anterior pituitary hormones becomes inadequate or absent. This disrupts a number of other hormone-producing glands, resulting in a variety of signs.

Inactive pituitary tumors develop most commonly in adult to older dogs. All breeds appear to be equally affected. Other conditions, infections, or injuries that lead to destruction of pituitary tissue can also cause panhypopituitarism.

Affected dogs are often depressed and uncoordinated, collapse with exercise, and lose weight. Occasionally, they show a change in attitude, do not respond to people, and tend to hide. In chronic cases, the animal may become blind because the growing pituitary tumor puts pressure on the optic nerves. Animals with panhypopituitarism appear dehydrated despite drinking more water. Dogs may urinate in large volumes and break housetraining.

Inactive pituitary tumors usually become quite large before they cause obvious signs or death. The entire hypothalamus may be compressed and replaced by tumor, and the thyroid and adrenal glands may be smaller than normal.

External beam radiation therapy offers the best means of treatment for dogs with large pituitary tumors through reduction in the size of the mass. In dogs with severe signs and very large tumors, however, the response is often inadequate and the outlook for these dogs is very poor.

Juvenile-onset Panhypopituitarism (Pituitary Dwarfism)

In juvenile-onset panhypopituitarism, also called pituitary dwarfism, the front portion of the pituitary gland does not fully develop or is disrupted by a tumor. This affects several other hormone-producing glands, leading to a variety of signs. In particular, the lack of growth hormone causes the young animal to be dwarfed.

Pituitary dwarfism is most common in German Shepherds and has been seen in the Spitz, Miniature Pinscher, and Karelian Bear Dog. It is inherited and occurs equally in male and female dogs.

Dwarf pups appear the same as their normal littermates up to about 2 months of age. After that, they grow slower than their littermates and keep their puppy coat. Primary guard hairs do not develop. Hair is gradually lost on both sides of the body, and hair loss often becomes complete except for the head and tufts of hair on the legs. Permanent teeth do not come in, or come in late. Closure of the growing ends of the bones can be delayed as long as 4 years. The testes and penis of male dogs are small. In female dogs, heat cycles are irregular or absent. Because the pituitary gland affects the production of other hormones in the body, the levels of thyroid hormones and cortisol are reduced, and the thyroid and adrenal glands show signs of deterioration. Affected dogs have a shortened life span.

Unfortunately, effective treatment of pituitary dwarfism is not possible in dogs. Daily thyroid hormone replacement should be started as soon as there is evidence of secondary hypothyroidism. Canine growth hormone is not yet available for use as a therapy, and only porcine or human growth hormone has been tried. Because of the differences between canine and human growth hormone, the formation of antibodies against the human growth hormone is common in dogs, making this treatment ineffective. Porcine growth hormone appears to work better, but it is expensive and is not widely available. Recently, the use of progestogens to treat congenital growth hormone deficiency in dogs has been reported. This treatment was reported to slightly increase body size and hair regrowth in a few young dogs, but it has many potential adverse effects.

The outlook for dogs with pituitary dwarfism is poor if treatment is not attempted. By 3 to 5 years of age, affected dogs are usually bald, thin, mentally dull, and lethargic. These changes are due to the progressive loss of pituitary function, as well as the continuing expansion of pituitary cysts.

Diabetes Insipidus

Despite its name, diabetes insipidus is not related to the more commonly known diabetes mellitus, and it does not involve insulin or sugar metabolism.

Diabetes insipidus is caused by problems with antidiuretic hormone or vasopressin, a pituitary gland hormone responsible for maintaining the correct level of fluid in the body. Either the pituitary gland does not secrete enough of this hormone (called **central diabetes insipidus**), or the kidneys do not respond normally to the hormone (called **nephrogenic diabetes insipidus**).

Affected dogs urinate in large volumes and drink equally large amounts of water. The urine is very dilute even if the animal is deprived of water. (Normally, urine becomes more concentrated when an animal is dehydrated.)

If the animal is not dehydrated and does not have kidney disease, a water deprivation test can be done to assist in diagnosing diabetes insipidus. A second test that measures the animal's response to treatment with antidiuretic hormone is then performed to distinguish between central and nephrogenic diabetes insipidus.

Increased urination may be controlled using desmopressin acetate, a drug that acts in a way similar to antidiuretic hormone. Water should not be restricted. Treatment is usually lifelong.

■ DISORDERS OF THE THYROID GLAND

The thyroid gland is a 2-lobed gland in the neck. It produces 2 iodine-containing hormones, T_3 and T_4, which affect many processes in the body. In general, the thyroid hormones regulate metabolic rate, or the speed at which body processes "run." Too little hormone causes body processes to be sluggish. Too much causes them to run too fast.

The secretion of thyroid hormone is regulated by a chain of events starting in the hypothalamus. The hypothalamus secretes thyrotropin-releasing hormone, which acts on the pituitary gland by stimulating it to secrete thyroid-stimulating hormone, which in turn, acts on the thyroid gland by stimulating it to secrete T_3 and T_4.

Thyroid hormones act on many different cellular processes. Some of their actions occur within minutes to hours, while others take several hours or longer. Thyroid hormones in normal quantities work along with other hormones, such as growth hormone and insulin, to build tissues. However, when they are secreted in excess, they can contribute to breakdown of proteins and tissues.

Hypothyroidism

In hypothyroidism, decreased levels of thyroid hormones result in a slower metabolic rate. More than 95% of cases of hypothyroidism in dogs are caused by destruction of the thyroid gland itself.

Another cause is a tumor of the pituitary gland, which usually causes deficiencies of other pituitary hormones as well.

Hypothyroidism is most common in dogs 4 to 10 years old. It usually affects mid- to large-size breeds and is rare in toy and miniature breeds. Breeds most commonly affected include the Golden Retriever, Doberman Pinscher, Irish Setter, Miniature Schnauzer, Dachshund, Cocker Spaniel, and Airedale Terrier. Hypothyroidism occurs equally in both males and females.

Because a deficiency of thyroid hormone affects the function of all organ systems, signs vary. Most signs are directly related to slowing of metabolism, which results in lethargy, unwillingness or inability to exercise, and weight gain without an increase in appetite. Some dogs have trouble keeping warm and seek sources of heat. Changes in the skin and coat are common, including dryness, excessive shedding, delayed regrowth of hair, and hair thinning or hair loss (usually the same pattern on both sides), sometimes associated with increased pigmentation over points of wear. In more severe cases, the skin can thicken, especially on the forehead and face, resulting in a puffy appearance and thickened skin folds above the eyes. This puffiness, together with slight drooping of the upper eyelid, gives some dogs a "tragic" facial expression.

In non-neutered dogs, hypothyroidism may cause various reproductive disturbances. Females may have irregular or no heat cycles and become infertile, or litter survival may be poor. Males may have lack of libido, small testicles, low sperm count, or infertility.

During the fetal period and in the first few months of life, thyroid hormones are crucial for growth and development of the skeleton and central nervous system. Animals that are born with thyroid deficiency or that develop it early in life often show dwarfism and impaired mental development. An enlarged thyroid gland also may be detected, depending on the cause of the hypothyroidism.

Accurately diagnosing hypothyroidism requires close evaluation of signs and various laboratory tests, including demonstration of low serum concentrations of thyroid hormones (especially T_4) that do not respond to administration of thyroid-stimulating hormone.

Treatment involves increasing or replacing the missing thyroid hormone. Thyroxine (T_4) is the thyroid hormone replacement most often used in dogs. The success of treatment can be measured by the amount of improvement in signs. Usually, treatment must be tried for 4 to 8 weeks before any changes in coat and body weight can be evaluated. Serum thyroid hormone concentrations are also monitored to determine whether the dosage of thyroid hormone needs adjustment. Once the dose has been stabilized, thyroid hormone levels are usually checked once or twice a year. Treatment is generally lifelong.

Hyperthyroidism

Hyperthyroidism is caused by excess of the thyroid hormones, T_3 and T_4. Signs include weight loss, increased appetite, and increased heart rate, all of which reflect an increased metabolic rate. Hyperthyroidism is much more common in cats than in dogs. (For a more detailed discussion of HYPERTHYROIDISM, *see* page 422.)

■ NEUROENDOCRINE TISSUE TUMORS

Neuroendocrine tissues are tissues that have both nervous system and hormone-producing functions. They are found in a number of locations throughout the body. Tumors develop occasionally from neuroendocrine cells in the adrenal or thyroid glands. These can be benign or malignant. Even if benign, a growing tumor can disrupt nearby normal tissues and, in some cases, secrete excess hormone.

Chemoreceptor organs are derived from neuroendocrine tissue. They can detect very small changes in the carbon dioxide and oxygen content and pH of the blood, and they help regulate breathing and circulation. Tumors in chemoreceptor tissue usually develop principally in either the aortic body (found in the chest) or in the carotid bodies (found in the neck). Tumors of the aortic and carotid bodies are seen most often in brachycephalic breeds of dogs, such as Boxers and Boston Terriers. The tumors do not secrete excess hormone but may cause problems by placing pressure on the heart, blood vessels, and nerves.

CHAPTER **9**

Eye Disorders

■ EYE STRUCTURE AND FUNCTION

The eyes of animals, including dogs, function much like your eyes. (For a more complete discussion of SIGHT, *see* page 3.) Animals also develop many of the same eye problems that people can have, including cataracts, glaucoma, and other problems. It is important for your dog to receive good eye care to protect its sight and allow it to interact comfortably with its environment.

The eye is an active organ that constantly adjusts the amount of light it lets in and focuses on objects near and far. It produces continuous images that are quickly relayed to the brain.

The bony cavity or socket that contains the eyeball is called the **orbit**. The orbit is

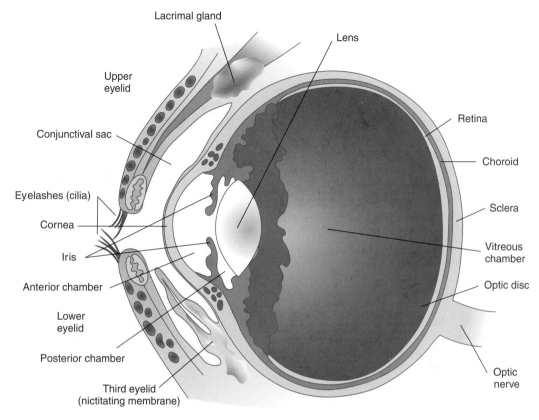

Anatomy of the eye

a structure that is formed by several bones. The orbit also contains muscles, nerves, blood vessels, and the structures that produce and drain tears.

The white of the eye is called the **sclera**. This is the relatively tough outer layer of the eye. It is covered by a thin membrane, called the **conjunctiva**, located near the front of the eye. The conjunctiva runs to the edge of the cornea and covers the inside of the eyelid. The **cornea** is a clear dome on the front surface of the eye that lets light in. The cornea not only protects the front of the eye, but also helps focus light on the retina at the back of the eye. The **iris** is the circular, colored area of the eye. It controls the amount of light that enters the eye by making the pupil larger or smaller. The **pupil** is the black area in the middle of the eye. The pupil is controlled by the

circular sphincter muscle. When the environment is dark, the pupil enlarges to let in more light; when the environment is bright, the pupil becomes smaller to let in less light.

The **lens**, which sits behind the iris, changes its shape to focus light onto the retina. Small muscles (ciliary muscles) contract to cause the lens to become thicker, which allows the lens to focus on nearby objects. The ciliary muscles relax to cause the lens to become thinner when it focuses on distant objects. The **retina** contains the cells that sense light (photoreceptors). These lens changes are limited in dogs. The most sensitive area of the retina is called the area centralis in dogs; this area contains thousands of tightly packed photoreceptors that make visual images sharp. Each photoreceptor is attached to a nerve fiber. All the nerve fibers are bundled together to form the **optic nerve**. The photoreceptors in the retina convert the image into electrical impulses, which are carried to the brain by the optic nerve.

The upper and lower eyelids are thin folds of skin that can cover the eye and reflexively blink to protect the eye. Blinking also helps spread tears over the surface of the eye, keeping it moist and clearing away small particles. The eyes of a dog are protected not only by the same types of eyelids that people have, but also by the **nictitating membrane**, which is sometimes called the third eyelid. This additional eyelid is a whitish pink color, and it is found under the other eyelids in the inside corner of the eye (near the nose). The third eyelid extends across the eye when needed to protect the eyeball from scratches (for example, while traveling through brush) or in response to inflammation.

To function properly, eyes must be kept moist. Tears are the source of this needed moisture. Tears are produced by 2 types of glands. **Lacrimal glands** produce the watery portion of tears. They are located at the top outer edge of each eye. Mucus glands in the conjunctiva produce mucus that mixes with the watery portion. This creates a more protective tear that is slower to evaporate. Nasolacrimal ducts allow tears to drain from each eye into the nose. Each of these ducts has openings at the edge of the upper and lower eyelids near the nose.

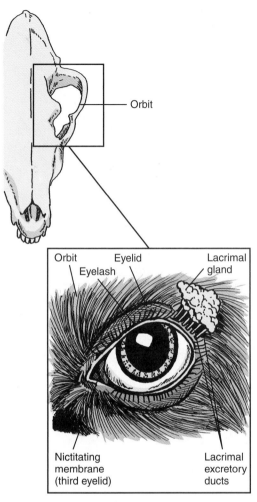

Structures that protect the eye (modified with permission from *The Merck Manual of Medical Information*, Second Home Edition, 2003)

Physical Examination of the Eye

Because of the importance of sight to your dog, one of the critical aspects of any examination or checkup will be an examination of your pet's eyes. Be prepared to provide any background or medical history (such as any previous injury to the eye, history of treatments or medications used, any signs of visual problems, and vaccination history) that might help with the diagnosis of any eye problem.

The first step of the examination involves checking to be sure that the shape and outline of the eyes are normal and that there are no obvious abnormalities. Then, using light and magnification in a darkened room, the reflexes of the pupils and the front part of the eye are examined. Depending on these findings and the reasons for the checkup, additional tests may be needed. Some parts of the examination may require sedation or anesthesia.

A test, called the Schirmer tear test, may be performed to ensure that the eyes are producing enough tears to keep them moist. This is a relatively simple test in which a small paper strip is inserted under the eyelid to measure the amount of moisture produced. A small drop of fluorescein staining may be put into each eye, allowing defects—such as scratches in the cornea of the eye—to be detected.

Pressure within the eye is measured painlessly using an instrument called a tonometer. (If eye pressure is too high, optic nerve damage can occur, leading to irreversible blindness.) A swab may also be done to culture for bacteria or fungi. The eyelids may be turned inside out to examine the underside. The nasolacrimal tear duct may be flushed to evaluate the external parts of the eye. Drops may be added to the eyes to allow the pupils to become dilated so that the veterinarian may examine the internal part of the eye using an ophthalmoscope.

▓ DISORDERS OF THE EYELIDS

Problems affecting the eyelids may be congenital (present at birth) or may occur as a result of injury, infection, or exposure to various types of irritants.

Entropion

Entropion is the turning in of the edges of the eyelid so that the eyelashes rub against the eye surface. It is the most frequent inherited eyelid defect in many dog breeds. It may also follow scar formation and severe involuntary winking due to pain in the eye or the surrounding area. The turning in of eyelashes or facial hairs causes discomfort and irritation of the conjunctiva and cornea. Extremely long lashes can cause scarring, abnormal coloring, and possibly the formation of slow-healing sores on the cornea.

Early spasms of entropion may be reversed if the cause is removed or if pain is lessened. Turning the lid hairs back away from the eye with stitches in the lid, injections of medication into the lid close to the area where the lid is turning in, or using anesthetics to block the nerves in the eyelids are some of the methods that have been used to lessen the pain. Established entropion may require surgery to correct the defect.

Ectropion

Ectropion is a slack eyelid edge that is turned out, usually with a large notch or "crack" in the eyelid. It is a common abnormality affecting both eyelids in a number of dog breeds, including the Bloodhound, Bull Mastiff, Great Dane, Newfoundland, St. Bernard, and several Spaniel breeds. Developing scars in the eyelid or facial nerve paralysis may produce ectropion in one eyelid in any species. Exposure of the conjunctiva to environmental irritants and secondary bacterial infection can result in longterm or recurrent conjunctivitis (inflammation of the conjunctiva). Topical antibiotics may temporarily control infections, but surgical lid-shortening procedures are often necessary to resolve the condition. Repeated, periodic cleansing of the affected eyelid with mild decongestant solutions can control mild cases. To protect your pet's eyesight, follow your veterinarian's treatment program carefully.

Lagophthalmos

Lagophthalmos is an inability to fully close the eyelids and protect the cornea from drying and trauma. It may result

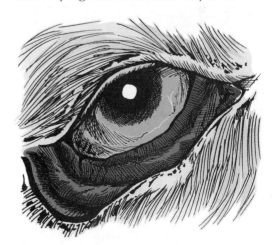

Ectropion is a common abnormality in some dog breeds.

from extremely shallow orbits, a common condition in breeds with short, broad, flattened heads (brachycephalic breeds such as Bulldogs and Pugs, for example). It may also be caused by an abnormal protrusion of the eyeball due to a mass in the eye socket, or facial nerve paralysis. Scarring, abnormal coloring, and the formation of slow-healing sores of the cornea are common problems with this condition. Unless the cause can be corrected, treatment involves frequent use of lubricating ointments and surgical shortening or closure of the corners of the eye either temporarily or permanently. Excessive nasal skin folds and facial hair may aggravate the damage caused by lagophthalmos.

Abnormalities of the Eyelashes

Abnormalities of the eyelashes include extra eyelashes or misdirected eyelashes on the edge of the eyelid. These conditions may cause watering eyes, development of blood vessels in the cornea, and slow-healing sores and scarring in the cornea. In many instances, irregular eyelashes are very fine and do not cause signs of irritation or damage the eye. However, eyelashes in an unusual position sticking out through the back of the eyelid can cause profound pain. If the extra lashes cause damage to the cornea or conjunctiva, it may be necessary to surgically cut out or freeze and remove the eyelash follicles. Irregularities of the eyelashes are common in some dog breeds and are probably inherited.

Inflammation of the Eyelids (Blepharitis)

Inflammation of the eyelids can result from the spreading of a generalized inflammation of the skin, inflammation of the conjunctiva, local glandular infections, or irritants such as plant oils or sunlight. Fungi, mites, or bacteria can infect the eyelids, which can then lead to a generalized inflammation.

Lesions of immune-mediated diseases can occur where the skin and conjunctiva join. Pemphigus (*see* page 170) is an example of a disease in which large blisters occur on the skin and mucous membranes. Pemphigus is often accompanied by itching or burning sensations. Skin scrapings, cultures, and biopsies may be required for an accurate diagnosis. Localized glandular infections may be short-term (for example, a stye) or longterm (for example, a meibomian abscess).

When inflammation of the eyelids is caused by a generalized condition, whole-body therapy often is necessary in addition to treatment of the eye itself. Supportive therapy of hot packing and frequent cleansing is often used in severe cases. Your veterinarian will recommend a treatment program designed to control the generalized condition, make your pet more comfortable, and treat the eye condition. Be sure you thoroughly understand the treatment program your veterinarian recommends. Do not hesitate to ask for detailed instructions regarding any eye drops or other medication you will need to give to your pet. It is often helpful to have the veterinarian demonstrate the administration of these medications.

■ DISORDERS OF THE NASAL CAVITY AND TEAR DUCTS

The lacrimal or tear gland, located at the top outer edge of the eye, produces the watery portion of tears. Nasolacrimal ducts allow tears to drain from each eye into the nose. Disorders of these structures can lead to either eyes that water excessively or dry eyes. They may be congenital (present at birth) or caused by infection, foreign objects in the eye, or trauma.

Cherry Eye (Prolapsed Nictitans Gland)

Cherry eye is a common disorder in young dogs and certain breeds (for example, American Cocker Spaniel, Lhasa Apso, Beagle, and English Bulldog). In this disorder, the gland of the nictitating membrane thickens and slips out of its proper place. In the severe stage of cherry eye, the red glandular mass swells and sticks out over the edge of the membrane, leading to the name "cherry eye." A pus-filled discharge may also be seen. Although the swelling may go down for short periods, the nictitating membrane gland often remains dislocated.

Because this gland appears to be important in the production of tears, your veterinarian will want to preserve it, if possible. The gland is often put back in place and stitched to the connective tissue around the edge of the eye or covered with nearby mucous membrane using an envelope or pocket technique. Partial removal of the gland is usually avoided. Dogs that have cherry eye appear to be more likely to develop dry eye (*see* below) later in life.

Inflammation of the Tear Sac (Dacryocystitis)

Inflammation of the tear sac is usually caused by obstruction of the tear sac and the attached nasal tear duct by inflammatory debris, foreign objects, or masses pressing on the duct. It results in watering eyes, conjunctivitis that is resistant to treatment, and occasionally a draining opening in the middle of the lower eyelid. If your veterinarian suspects an obstruction of the duct, he or she may attempt to unblock it by flushing it with sterile water or a saline solution. X-rays of the skull after injection of a dye into the duct may be necessary to determine the site, cause, and

outlook of longterm obstructions. The usual therapy consists of keeping the duct unblocked and using eyedrops containing antibiotics. When the tear duct has been irreversibly damaged, surgery may be necessary to create a new drainage pathway to empty tears into the nasal cavity, sinus, or mouth.

Absence of Nasal Tear Duct Openings

Absence of the nasal tear duct openings at birth is known as imperforate lacrimal puncta. This is an infrequent cause of watering eyes in young dogs. Therapy consists of surgically opening the blocked duct and keeping it open by inserting a tube or suture during healing.

Dry Eye (Keratoconjunctivitis Sicca)

The condition known as dry eye results from inadequate tear production. It often causes persistent mucus and pus-filled conjunctivitis and slow-healing sores and scarring on the cornea. In dogs, it is often associated with an autoimmune inflammation of both the tear and nictitans glands. Less frequent causes of dry eye in dogs are distemper (a viral disease), therapy with sulfonamide antibiotics, heredity, and injury. To treat this condition, your veterinarian may prescribe cyclosporine, artificial tear solutions, ointments, and, if there are no sores on the cornea, an antibiotic-corticosteroid combination. In longterm dry eye resistant to medical therapy, surgery may be required to correct the condition.

▨ DISORDERS OF THE CONJUNCTIVA

The conjunctiva is a thin membrane that lines the inside of the eyelids and extends over the globe of the eye. It plays a role in creating tears, providing protection for the eye from foreign invaders, and healing of the cornea after injury. It is important to identify and treat problems of the conjunctiva, because some can indicate generalized disease, while others can lead to blindness if not treated.

Cherry eye generally requires surgery.

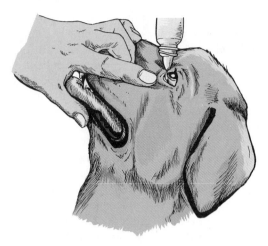

Your veterinarian can demonstrate the proper way to administer eye drops (modified with permission from *The Merck Manual of Medical Information*, Second Home Edition, 2003).

Ruptured Blood Vessels (Subconjunctival Hemorrhage)

Ruptured blood vessels beneath the conjunctiva may be the result of trauma, a blood disorder, or certain infectious diseases. This condition, by itself, does not require therapy, but close inspection is necessary to determine if more serious changes within the eye have occurred. If definite evidence or history of trauma is not present, then your veterinarian will perform a complete examination to determine the cause of the spontaneous bleeding.

Swelling of Conjunctival Tissue (Chemosis)

Swelling of the conjunctival tissue around the cornea occurs to some degree with all cases of conjunctivitis, but the most dramatic examples are seen with trauma, a deficiency of proteins in the blood (hypoproteinemia), allergic reactions, and insect bites. Insect bites are treated with topical corticosteroids and usually heal rapidly. In other cases, specific therapy to treat the original cause is required.

Conjunctivitis (Pink Eye)

Conjunctivitis, also known as pink eye, is common in dogs. The causes vary from infections to environmental irritants. The signs are excess blood flow to the eye, swelling of the tissue around the cornea, discharge from the eye, and mild eye discomfort. The appearance of the conjunctiva usually is not enough, by itself, to allow your veterinarian to diagnose the cause with only a physical examination. A specific diagnosis often requires a medical history, tests on conjunctival scrapings, Schirmer tear test, and occasionally biopsy.

Conjunctivitis in only one eye may result from a foreign object, inflammation of the tear sac, or dry eye (*see* page 145). Conjunctivitis occurring in both eyes is commonly caused by infection with a virus or bacteria. Environmental irritants and allergens are other common causes of conjunctivitis. If a mucus and pus-filled discharge is present, your veterinarian may prescribe a topical antibiotic. However, the antibiotic alone may not bring about healing if other factors are involved. Your veterinarian will also check for foreign objects in the eye, environmental irritants, parasites, and defects of eyelid shape, outline, or form, as these factors also contribute to pink eye. Because conjunctivitis can have multiple causes, your veterinarian may prescribe a combination of treatments.

▓ DISORDERS OF THE CORNEA

The cornea helps to protect the front of the eye and is also important in focusing light on the retina at the back of the eye. Because the cornea is critical for proper vision, it is important to address any disorders or injuries promptly.

Inflammation of the Outer Cornea

Inflammation and swelling of the outer cornea is common in all species. The most common sign is the development of blood vessels in the cornea. In addition, the cornea often becomes cloudy due to fluid build-up, cellular infiltrates, pigmentation, or the formation of fibrous tissue. If slow-healing sores or ulcers are present, pain—shown by watering eyes and spasmodic winking—is common. If inflammation and swelling of the cornea is in one eye only, injury or trauma is often the cause. Your veterinarian will also check for other factors, such as abnormalities in the shape, outline, or form of the eye and foreign objects. This check is important because your dog's condition will not improve until any such conditions are under control.

Inflammation and swelling of the outer cornea in both eyes may be caused by a response from the immune system or may be associated with a lack of tears, abnormalities in the shape, outline, or form of the eye, or infectious agents.

Pannus, or **Uberreiter's disease**, is a rapidly spreading, longterm inflammation and swelling of the outside of the cornea in both eyes. The disease begins on the edge of the cornea where the cornea and the white of the eye meet. It eventually spreads from all edges to cover the cornea. It is common in German Shepherds, Belgian Tervurens, Border Collies, Greyhounds, Siberian Huskies, and Australian Shepherds. Treatment for pannus consists of topical corticosteroids and/or cyclosporine (usually given as eye drops). Because this disease is caused by the immune system, treatment needs to be continued indefinitely. In these cases, routine veterinary examinations are needed to monitor your pet's response to the treatment and make adjustments as required.

Inflammation within the Cornea

Inflammation and swelling within the cornea is a deep involvement of the connective tissue that provides the structure of the cornea. Interstitial keratitis is present in all longterm and in many short-term, severe cases of inflammation of the lining of the front of the eye (*see also* INFLAMMATION OF THE ANTERIOR UVEA, page 148). Swelling of the cornea is often very noticeable. Some generalized diseases can cause this type of inflammation in one or both eyes. These diseases include infectious canine hepatitis, whole system diseases caused by fungi, and diseases caused by toxic microorganisms in the bloodstream.

In these cases, therapy is directed at the inflammation of the eye, the generalized infection, or both. Your veterinarian will prescribe the most effective treatment for your pet.

Corneal Ulcers (Ulcerative Keratitis)

Inflammation and swelling of the cornea with slow-healing sores may occur on the surface of the cornea (superficial) or they may be deeper. When deep ulcers occur, the membrane that covers the inner surface of the cornea may protrude through the cornea, or the ulcer can create a full-thickness hole in the cornea. In dogs, most ulcers are caused by injury such as nail scratches, foreign objects in the eye, or chemicals that enter the eye. Pain, irregularity of the cornea, swelling, and eventually development of blood vessels are signs of ulceration. Infection is another cause of ulcers; however, bacterial infection often occurs after the ulcer is already present. A dense, white material at the edge of the ulcer indicates the presence of white blood cells and bacterial involvement.

To detect small ulcers, a veterinarian may put drops of a specialized dye into the eye. Therapy for shallow ulcers usually consists of topical antibiotic(s) and correction of any causes such as removal of a small splinter from the eye. The ulcers usually heal within a week. Another topical medication called atropine may be used to treat the loss of movement of the iris and reduce eye pain. However, atropine may reduce tear production. Your veterinarian will prescribe the most appropriate combination of medication and other treatments to control the condition.

Syndromes of very slow-healing and recurrent shallow ulcers occur in dogs, especially in older animals. They may be due to a membrane disease causing faulty attachment of the thin layer of cells lining the cornea. Initial therapy often includes removal of the dead, damaged, or infected tissue of the ulcer by a veterinarian, followed by prescription topical medication. For resistant cases, surgery may be required to stimulate new membrane growth. Nictitating membrane flaps (or soft contact lenses or collagen shields) may be used as a pressure bandage.

Medical treatment of deep ulcers is similar to that of shallow ulcers, but many deep ulcers also require grafts of conjunctival tissue to strengthen the cornea.

Corneal Deterioration

Deterioration in the structure and function of the cornea occurs in dogs. Corneal degenerations often occur in only one eye and are usually the result of other eye or generalized diseases. Corneal dystrophies that occur in both eyes are likely inherited or breed-predisposed in dogs, and often consist of triglyceride, cholesterol, and calcium deposits within the connective tissue of the cornea. Treatment is not usually necessary.

▓ DISORDERS OF THE ANTERIOR UVEA

The uvea (or the uveal tract) is the colored inside lining of the eye consisting of the iris, the ciliary body, and the choroid. The iris is the colored ring around the black pupil. The ciliary body is the set of muscles that contract and relax to allow the lens to focus on objects; it is also the major source of aqueous humor, the clear fluid within the eye. The choroid is the inner lining of the eyeball and extends from the ciliary muscles to the optic nerve at the back of the eye. The choroid also contains layers of blood vessels that nourish the inside parts of the eye, especially the retina.

Persistent Membranes across the Pupil

Persistent membranes across the pupil are the remains of the normal prenatal vascular network that fills the region of the pupil. The persistence of colored strands across the pupil from one area of the iris to another, or to the lens or cornea, is common in dogs and occurs occasionally in other species. In Basenjis, the condition is inherited.

Atrophy of the Iris

A weakening and shrinking (atrophy) of the iris is common in older dogs and may involve the edge of the pupil or the connective tissue. Shrinkage of the edge of the pupil creates a scalloped border and a weakening of the sphincter muscle, which results in a dilated pupil or slowed reflexes of the pupil in response to light. Shrinkage of the connective tissue results in dramatic holes in the iris, and often, displacement of the pupil. Neither of these types of atrophy appears to affect vision. Animals lacking a functional sphincter muscle (which controls the opening and closing of the iris) may show increased sensitivity to bright light.

Cysts of the Iris

Cysts of the iris are usually free-floating, colored spheres in the liquid part within the eye. Although harmless in most breeds of dogs, cysts of the anterior uvea (the iris and the tissue and muscle surrounding the lens) in Golden Retrievers and Great Danes are associated with longterm inflammation of the uvea, abnormally high pressure within the eyeball (glaucoma), and the formation of cataracts. Therapy is rarely necessary in most breeds, but removal or rupture of a cyst may occasionally be required. Your veterinarian can assess your pet's condition and recommend the best treatment.

Inflammation of the Anterior Uvea

Inflammation of the iris and ciliary body (anterior uveitis or iridocyclitis), when severe, results in a contraction of the pupil of the eye, increased protein and cells in the anterior chamber, low pressure within the eye, an abnormally high level of blood in the conjunctiva, swelling of the iris, low tolerance to light, and spasmodic winking. As a result, complications may occur, such as glaucoma (*see* below), the formation of a cataract covering the lens of the eye, and cloudiness of the cornea. Inflammation of the membrane (the choroid) between the retina and the white of the eye (the sclera) frequently occurs at the same time.

Trauma and, rarely, tumors or worms within the eye are causes of inflammation of the uvea in only one eye. Common causes of inflammation of the uvea in both eyes include infectious diseases such as infectious canine hepatitis (a viral infection), toxoplasmosis (a parasitic disease), fungal infections, and bacterial infections such as canine brucellosis, leptospirosis, and canine ehrlichiosis. Immune system problems may also cause this condition in dogs. Your veterinarian will want a thorough medical history of your pet to help in diagnosing this condition. Other diagnostic steps may include examination of the cornea for injuries, a physical examination, blood tests, and tests on fluid from your pet's eye.

Treatment of the inflammation consists of topical medications to maintain eye movement capabilities, a darkened environment, and other prescription medications, such as antibacterial drugs to treat bacterial infections. Your veterinarian will select the most appropriate treatment program for your pet's specific condition.

▩ GLAUCOMA

Dogs, like people, can develop glaucoma. Glaucoma occurs when an imbalance in production and drainage of fluid in the eye (aqueous humor) causes a buildup of fluid that increases eye pressure to unhealthy levels. The increased pressure can cause the destruction of the retina and optic disk (the spot where the optic nerve enters the eye). **Open-angle glaucoma** is a painless and gradual development of blind spots or loss of vision over a long period of time. **Closed-angle glaucoma** is a sudden increase in eye pressure with severe pain, redness, and loss of vision. Glaucoma occurs in about 1.7% of the dogs in North America. The frequency of breed-predisposed glaucoma in both eyes in purebred dogs is the highest of any animal species, except humans.

Most dogs with early to moderate long-term glaucoma are not taken to the veterinarian because the early signs—sluggish to slightly dilated pupils, mild congestion of the veins in the conjunctiva, and early enlargement of the eye—are so subtle that owners are not aware of the changes. To detect early glaucoma, a veterinarian uses a tonometer to measure the pressure within the eye. This is often done for high-risk breeds of dogs as part of the general physical examination.

Prolonged increases of pressure within the eye can result in enlargement of the eyeball, displacement of the lens, and breaks in a membrane of the cornea. Pain usually shows itself as behavioral changes and occasional pain around the eye rather than by spasmodic winking.

There are various instruments a veterinarian can use to evaluate and manage glaucoma. The choice of medical or surgical treatment or, most frequently, a combination of both, depends on the type of glaucoma present. It is important to decrease the pressure within the eye as quickly as possible in order to minimize damage. Drugs that can draw fluid out of the eye and others that decrease production of fluid are often prescribed. After the pressure is lowered, it must be stabilized to prevent future problems. Your veterinarian will be able to suggest the appropriate medical and/or surgical treatment for your pet. Most glaucomas require long-term management.

▩ DISORDERS OF THE LENS

The lens is a soft, transparent tissue that sits behind the iris. It helps focus incoming light onto the retina. Common disorders of the lens include those that affect its transparency (such as cataracts), and those that affect the position of the lens.

Cataracts

A cataract occurs when the lens becomes cloudy or opaque, which effectively blocks light from reaching the retina. This causes a loss of eyesight that can range from mild vision problems to partial blindness. Cataracts should not be confused with the minor lens imperfections in young dogs or with the normal increase in the thickening and hardening of central lens tissue that occurs in older animals. Cataracts are often inherited in dogs (*see* TABLE 11). Other causes include diabetes, malnutrition, radiation, inflammation, and trauma. In some cases, sight may be regained in young dogs, cats, or horses when cataracts disappear on their own.

Cataracts that are present at birth in young animals may reduce in size as the lens grows, allowing for some restoration of vision as the animal matures. Animals with immature and incomplete cataracts

Table 11. Inherited Cataracts in Dogs

Breed	Age of Onset
Afghan Hound	6 to 12 months
American Cocker Spaniel	6 months or older
Bichon Frise	Older than 2 years
Boston Terrier	Present at birth, late onset
Chesapeake Bay Retriever	1 year or older
German Shepherd	8 weeks or older
Golden Retriever	6 months or older
Labrador Retriever	6 months or older
Miniature Schnauzer	Present at birth, 6 months, or older
Norwegian Buhund	1 year or older
Old English Sheepdog	Present at birth
Rottweiler	10 months or older
Siberian Husky	6 months or older
Staffordshire Bull Terrier	6 months or older
Standard Poodle	1 year or older
Welsh Springer Spaniel	Present at birth
West Highland White Terrier	Present at birth

may benefit from topical medication (eye drops) 2 to 3 times per week.

Because dogs can often use their keen senses of hearing and smell to compensate for loss of vision, it can be difficult for a pet owner to detect cataracts at an early stage. Some owners report that their dogs have more difficulty in bright light, while others report the opposite. Dogs with vision loss may appear more cautious in their movements and tend to stay closer than usual to their owner.

In general, treatment for cataracts involves surgery to remove the affected lens or lenses. In dogs, removal of the cataract is most likely to be successful when performed before cataract maturation is complete and before inflammation in the front chamber of the eye occurs due to leakage of lens material. Advances have been made in this procedure, but complications are possible. In animals in which cataract surgery is not performed, continued monitoring is very important. Follow your veterinarian's recommendations for treatment of cataracts.

Lens Displacement

Lens displacement can occur in any dog but is common as a primary inherited defect in several Terrier breeds. Lens displacements also can be produced by trauma, enlargement of the eyeball due to glaucoma, and degenerative changes that occur as a result of long-standing cataracts.

Complete displacement of the lens into the front chamber of the eye produces severe signs and frequently is accompanied by glaucoma and swelling of the cornea. The only effective treatment is surgical removal of the lens.

Displacement backward into the main eye chamber (called the vitreous cavity) may cause no signs or be associated with inflammation of the eye or glaucoma. Partially dislocated lenses are recognized by a trembling of the iris and lens. The decision to remove partially dislocated lenses is based on the severity of the signs.

Procedures to remove the lens because of lens displacement are associated with

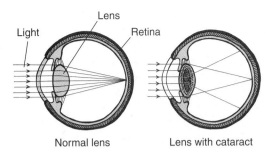

Normal lens   Lens with cataract

Normally, the lens receives light and focuses it on the retina. A cataract keeps some light from reaching the lens and distorts the light being focused on the retina (modified with permission from *The Merck Manual of Medical Information, Second Home Edition*, 2003).

higher levels of postoperative complications of glaucoma and detachment of the retina. Your veterinarian will carefully evaluate your pet's condition and recommend a program to provide your pet with the best possible outcome.

■ DISORDERS OF THE RETINA, CHOROID, AND OPTIC DISK (OCULAR FUNDUS)

The **ocular fundus** is the back of the eye opposite the pupil and includes the retina, the membrane (the choroid) between the retina and the white of the eye, and the optic disk. Diseases of the ocular fundus may occur on their own or as a part of generalized diseases. Inherited abnormalities, trauma, metabolic disturbances, generalized infections, tumors, blood disorders, high blood pressure, and nutritional deficiencies are possible underlying causes for diseases of the retina in all species.

Inherited Diseases of the Retina

Inherited abnormalities may be present at birth or appear later, and are important in the development of diseases of the retina in dogs.

Collie Eye Anomaly

Collie eye anomaly is an inherited eye defect present at birth in varying degrees in rough- and smooth-coated Collies. It also occurs in Shetland Sheepdogs, Border Collies, Australian Shepherds, Lancashire Heelers, and the Nova Scotia Duck Tolling Retriever. The main abnormality is an area of the choroid or the retina and choroid that fails to develop fully. More severely affected dogs may also have abnormalities close to where the optic nerve enters the eye, and some will have detachment of the retina. Blood vessel ruptures within the eye may occur. Vision is not noticeably affected unless detachment of the retina is present.

Abnormal Development of the Retina (Retinal Dysplasia)

An abnormal development of the retina called retinal dysplasia is present at birth and may arise from trauma, genetic defect, or damage occurring while in the womb from conditions such as viral infections. Most forms of retinal dysplasia in dogs are inherited. Viral infections of the mother (for example, herpesvirus in dogs), especially during early fetal development, can result in many eye abnormalities with retinal dysplasia in puppies. Retinal dysplasia is thought to be inherited in American Cocker Spaniels, Beagles, Labrador Retrievers, Rottweilers, and Yorkshire Terriers. Small areas of retinal dysplasia may not cause any signs or interfere with vision. Generalized retinal dysplasia with detachment of the retina, visual impairment, or blindness is inherited in English Springer Spaniels, Bedlington Terriers, Sealyham Terriers, Labrador Retrievers, Doberman Pinschers, and Australian Shepherds. Other eye abnormalities, including abnormally small eyes and cataracts that are present at birth, often occur together with the generalized forms of retinal dysplasia.

Progressive Retinal Atrophy

Progressive retinal atrophy is the name for a group of diseases that cause degeneration of the retina. This includes inherited abnormalities of the light-sensitive cells (photoreceptor dysplasia) and degenerations that have similar signs. The inherited photoreceptor dysplasias in which signs develop in the first year occur in Irish Setters, Collies, Norwegian Elkhounds, Miniature Schnauzers, and Belgian Sheepdogs. The inherited photoreceptor degenerations in which signs develop at 3 to 5 years occur in Miniature and Toy Poodles, English and American Cocker Spaniels, Labrador Retrievers, Tibetan Terriers, Miniature Longhaired Dachshunds, Akitas, and Samoyeds. Progressive retinal atrophy is also inherited in Siberian Huskies and Bull Mastiffs. Many other breeds of dogs are also suspected of having inherited progressive retinal atrophy.

The first sign of progressive retinal atrophy is usually night blindness. This progresses to total blindness over a period ranging from months to years. Cataracts are common late in the course of progressive retinal atrophy in many breeds and may mask the underlying disease of the retina. No effective treatment is available, although DNA tests have been developed to detect carrier and affected dogs before signs develop in many breeds.

Retinal Pigment Epithelial Dystrophy

This type of retinal degeneration occurs in Labrador Retrievers, smooth and rough Collies, Border Collies, Shetland Sheepdogs, and Briards. The condition is inherited in Labrador Retrievers. In many cases, early eye examinations can detect this disease before signs are apparent. Progressive vision loss occurs gradually over several years. Cataract formation occurs late in the disease. There is no treatment. Recent studies suggest systemic vitamin E disorders may also be important in the development of this disease complex.

Inflammation of the Retina and Choroid (Chorioretinitis)

Inflammation of the retina and choroid is frequently a result of a generalized infection that affects many areas of the body. Unless the abnormalities are widespread or involve the optic nerve, they often go undetected. Inflammation of the retina and choroid may be present with canine distemper (a viral disease), fungal infec-

tions, prototheosis (an algal disease), toxoplasmosis (a disease caused by a parasitic microorganism), tuberculosis, and bacterial septicemias (infections of the blood by toxic microorganisms). Therapy is directed at the systemic disease causing the inflammation.

It is important to make sure that your pet receives regular, routine eye examinations. These examinations are important because they can often help diagnose many generalized diseases quickly and accurately.

Retinal Detachments

When the retina becomes detached, it is separated from the back of the eye and from part of its blood supply, preventing it from functioning properly. In dogs, detachments of the retina are associated with retinal disorders present at birth (retinal dysplasia and Collie eye anomaly), inflammation of the retina and choroid (chorioretinitis), injury and other trauma, eye surgery, and certain tumors.

Signs that the retina has become detached include excessive or prolonged dilation of the pupil, pupils of different sizes, vision impairment, and bleeding within the eye. Eye examinations must be performed to confirm the diagnosis.

Detachments of the retina are treated medically with therapy directed at the primary disease or surgically to correct the detachment. Your veterinarian will select the treatment approach most appropriate for your pet's condition.

▓ DISORDERS OF THE OPTIC NERVE

The optic nerve carries the electrical impulses from the eye to the area in the back of the brain where vision is sensed and interpreted. Injury to the optic nerve usually leads to partial or complete loss of sight.

Optic Nerve Hypoplasia

Optic nerve hypoplasia is a failure of the optic nerve to develop fully. It may be inherited in Miniature Poodles. The condition may occur in only one eye or both, and it can occur with or without other eye abnormalities. If the optic nerves of both eyes fail to develop, the newborn will be blind. Involvement of only one of the optic nerves often goes undetected or may be discovered later in life if the other eye acquires a blinding disease.

Papilledema

Papilledema is swelling and protrusion of the optic disk caused by fluid buildup. It is uncommon in most animals. The condition is often associated with tumors of the orbit. The optic disk appears raised above the surface of the nearby retina, and veins appear swollen. Vision and the light reflexes of the pupil are not usually affected unless the optic disk degenerates.

Optic Atrophy

Optic degeneration or atrophy may occur after glaucoma, trauma, advanced degeneration of the retina, prolonged low pressure within the eye, or inflammation. The optic disk appears flattened and smaller than normal; it is darkly colored, with very noticeable reduction in the optic nerve and blood vessels of the retina. Both direct reflex of the pupil and vision are absent. There is no treatment.

■ DISORDERS OF THE ORBIT

The orbit is the bony cavity that contains the eyeball and all of its associated muscles, vessels, and nerves. Inflammation of the orbital area, called **orbital cellulitis**, is common in large and hunting breeds of dogs and much less common in other breeds. This condition may be caused by foreign objects in the eye (such as a porcupine quill, thorn, or grass awn) or by an infection that spreads from another part of the body. The most common signs are severe pain on opening the mouth, swelling of the eyelid and conjunctiva, extension of the nictitating membrane (the third eyelid, a thin membrane beneath the eyelid that can extend across the eyeball), and "bulging" of the eyeball. Inflammation

and swelling of the cornea may develop due to the dog's inability to close the eyelid fully.

In severe cases, antibiotics given by mouth or injection are usually effective, but if swelling behind the last molar is present, drainage of this area may be required. Warm compresses and topical lubricants such as eyedrops to protect the cornea are often used to treat these conditions. Relapses may occur, and x-rays and ultrasonography of the adjacent teeth, sinuses, and nasal cavity are often used to check for other factors that might be contributing to the condition.

■ PROLAPSE OF THE EYE

Severe prolapse (slipping out of place) and/or bulging of the eye can be caused by trauma. It is common in dogs. The chances of a good outcome depend on the severity of the injury, the breed of dog, depth of the eye socket, the condition of the eye and how long it was displaced, and other damage near the eye. The eyeball should be put back in place surgically as soon as possible if the animal is in good enough health to have general anesthesia. Treatment

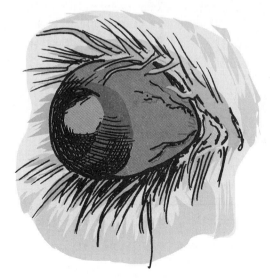

A dog's eyeball might bulge or come out of the eye socket entirely after an injury. Prompt surgery can save the eyeball and sometimes prevent blindness.

includes antibiotics (given by mouth or injection, as well as topical ointments or creams) to prevent infection. Occasionally other medications are needed as well.

Although recovery of sight cannot be guaranteed, the eyeball can usually be saved. Return of vision occurs in about half of dogs. If such an accident happens to your dog, immediately take your pet to the veterinarian and, following surgery, carefully follow the recommended treatment program.

▨ EYEWORM DISEASE (THELAZIASIS)

Eyeworms (*Thelazia californiensis* and *T. callipaeda*) are parasites found in dogs, cats, and other animals, including humans, in the western United States and Asia. They are whitish, 0.5 to 0.75 inches (7 to 19 millimeters) long, and move in a rapid snake-like motion across the eye. Up to 100 eyeworms may be seen in the conjunctival sac, tear ducts, and on the conjunctiva under the nictitating membrane (third eyelid) and eyelids. Filth flies (including the common house fly) serve as intermediate hosts and deposit the infective eyeworm larvae on the eye while feeding on secretions from the eyes.

Signs include excessive watering of the eyes, inflammation of the conjunctiva, opaque corneas with slow-healing sores,

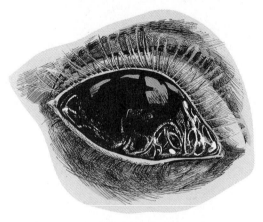

To diagnose, examine, and remove eyeworms, a veterinarian might numb the affected areas.

and rarely, blindness. After a local anesthetic is applied, diagnosis and treatment are accomplished by observing and carefully removing the parasites with forceps. Some veterinarians have reported the successful elimination of *Thelazia* infections from dogs with injected medication. Certain eye solutions or ointments also may be effective. Your veterinarian will evaluate your pet's situation and take the most appropriate treatment approach.

▨ CANCERS AND TUMORS OF THE EYE

The different tissues of the eye and associated structures can develop primary tumors or can be the site of spreading tumor cells.

Eyelid tumors are the most frequent group of eye tumors in dogs. Adenoma (a benign tumor) and adenocarcinoma (a malignant tumor) of the meibomian glands in the eyelid are the most common lid tumors. Because these tumors tend to be disfiguring as well as irritating to the dog, they are usually surgically removed—a process that is usually successful. Adenocarcinomas of the eyelid glands are locally invasive and harmful but are not known to spread elsewhere throughout the body. Lid melanomas, seen as spreading colored masses on the eyelid edges, are usually surgically removed. Other frequent eyelid tumors include histiocytoma, mastocytoma, and papilloma.

Orbital tumors in dogs cause the eyeball to protrude forward and produce swelling of the conjunctiva, cornea, and eyelid. They also cause the affected eye to be unable to move in tandem with the other eye. The eyeball cannot be pushed back. Usually, there is no pain. The longterm survival in affected dogs is often poor, because about 90% of these tumors are malignant and about 75% arise within the orbit. A veterinarian will determine the type of tumor and the extent of the mass through physical examination, skull x-rays, and ultrasonography before surgical removal or radiation of the tumor. Surgically removing the orbital mass with the eyeball and all orbital tissues (including nearby bone) may decrease the possibility of recurrence.

Tumors of the cornea and those at the edge of the cornea are uncommon in dogs and can be confused with nodular fasciitis (benign cells that grow rapidly into a bumpy mass) and proliferative keratoconjunctivitis (inflammation of the cornea and conjunctiva) in Collies. Malignant melanomas at the edge of the cornea are usually superficial, in which case surgical removal is usually successful. If the melanoma has penetrated into the eyeball, the eyeball must be removed.

Malignant melanomas are the most common **tumors of the uvea**. They are usually black and most frequently involve the iris and the tissue and muscle that surround the lens. Signs of tumors of the uvea may include an obvious mass, persistent inflammation of the iris and the tissue and muscle that surround the lens, blood vessel ruptures within the anterior chamber of the eye, glaucoma (high pressure within the eye), and pain. Adenoma

and adenocarcinoma of the tissue and muscle that surround the lens are the most frequent tumors of the outer layer of the uvea. Signs may include blood vessel ruptures within the anterior chamber of the eye, glaucoma, and usually a white to pink mass behind the iris and in the pupil. Treatment is usually removal of the eyeball. Recent studies in melanomas of the iris, especially in Labrador Retrievers, suggest noninvasive laser surgery may be effective and can be repeated if necessary. Adenocarcinomas from other sites in the body do not commonly spread to the uvea.

Other tumors such as a venereal tumor and hemangiosarcoma may spread to the anterior uvea. Lymphosarcoma frequently involves the anterior uvea and other eye structures, and may occur in both eyes. Therapy with topical and/or whole-body anti-inflammatory treatment for lymphoma within the eye may be attempted using one of several standard treatment plans, but dogs with lymphoma within the eye often have short survival times.

CHAPTER **10**

Ear Disorders

▉ EAR STRUCTURE AND FUNCTION

The ear is an organ of hearing and an organ of balance. It consists of the outer, middle, and inner ear.

The **outer ear** includes the pinna (the part you see that is made of cartilage and covered by skin, fur, or hair) and the ear canal. The pinna is shaped to capture sound waves and funnel them through the ear canal to the eardrum. In dogs, the pinnae are mobile and can move independently of each other. The size and shape of the pinnae vary by breed. The ear canal of the dog is much deeper than that of people

and creates a better funnel to carry sound to the eardrum. The average dog can hear about 4 times better than the average person, including sounds at higher frequencies than can be detected by the human ear.

The **middle ear** includes the eardrum and a small, air-filled chamber that contains 3 tiny bones: the hammer, anvil, and stirrup. It also includes 2 muscles, the oval window, and the eustachian tube (a small tube that connects the middle ear with the back of the nose, allowing air to enter the middle ear).

The **inner ear** is a complex structure that includes the cochlea (the organ of

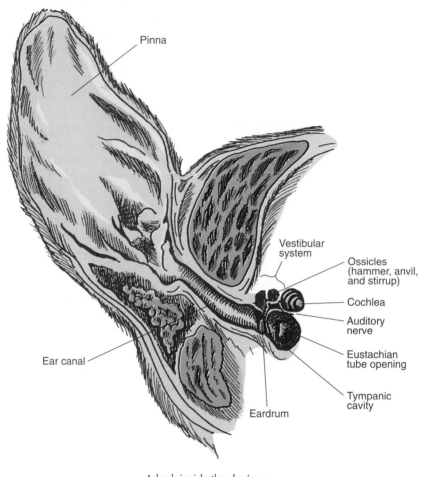

A look inside the dog's ear

hearing) and the vestibular system (the organ of balance).

Physical Examination of the Ear

Infections of the ear and other ear disorders are common in dogs. Your veterinarian will examine your dog's ears at every routine checkup. If the dog has a history of previous ear infections or other problems with the ear, you should provide that information to the veterinarian.

To start, your veterinarian will visually inspect the outer ears, noting any signs of inflammation, injury from trauma, swelling, secretions, or excessive ear wax. He or she will then use an instrument called an otoscope to view the ear canal and eardrum. In some cases, hair may need to be removed from the ear canals to allow the veterinarian a clear view of the ear drum.

If an infection is suspected, tests will be performed on samples of fluid or secretions from the ear to determine the organisms involved and the proper treatment. Infections in dogs are most commonly caused by bacteria or yeasts. Sometimes excessive overgrowth of tissue or the development of a tumor is seen.

To diagnose a tumor of the ear, it may be necessary to do a pinch biopsy for evaluation. This can usually be done using forceps and an otoscope. Further tests, including x-rays, neurologic tests, and electronic tests may be needed to confirm certain conditions such as deafness.

DEAFNESS

Deafness may be congenital (present at birth) or acquired as a result of infection, trauma, or degeneration of the cochlea (the organ of hearing).

Deafness present at birth can be inherited or result from toxic or viral damage to the developing unborn puppy. Merle and white coat colors are associated with deafness at birth in dogs and other animals. Dog breeds commonly affected include the Dalmatian, Australian Heeler, Catahoula, English Setter, Australian Shepherd, Boston Terrier, Old English Sheepdog, Great Dane, West Highland White Terrier, and Boxer. The list of affected breeds (now more than 48) continues to expand and may change due to breed popularity and elimination of the defect through selective breeding. For example, Cocker Spaniels were known to have hereditary deafness, but the trait is no longer common in the breed.

Acquired deafness may result from blockage of the external ear canal due to longterm inflammation (**otitis externa**). It may also occur after destruction of the middle or inner ear. Other causes include trauma to the hard portion of the temporal bone that surrounds the inner ear, loud noises (for example, gunfire), conditions in which there is a loss or destruction of myelin (the fatty material that surrounds some nerve cells), drugs toxic to the ear (for example, aminoglycoside antibiotics or aspirin), tumors involving the ear or brainstem, and degeneration of the cochlea in aged dogs. Deafness in one ear or partial hearing loss, or both, is possible in some of these instances. Degeneration of the cochlea in aged dogs is the most common cause of acquired deafness.

Diagnosis of deafness requires careful observation of the animal's response to sound. The response to touch, smell, and objects that can be seen must be differentiated from the response to sound. In young animals or in animals kept in groups, deafness may be difficult to detect, because the individual being evaluated will follow the response of others in the group. If the animal is observed on its own, after an age when responses to sound are predictable (about 3 to 4 weeks for dogs), then the deafness may be detected.

The primary sign of deafness is failure to respond to a sound, for example, failure of noise to awaken a sleeping dog, or failure to alert to the source of a sound. Other signs include unusual behavior such as excessive barking, unusual voice, hyperactivity, confusion when given vocal commands, and lack of ear movement. An animal that has gradually become deaf, as in old age, may become unresponsive to the surroundings and refuse to answer the owner's call.

Deafness in one ear is difficult to detect, except by careful observation or by electronic diagnostic tests that a veterinarian can perform. Examination of the external ear using an otoscope (an instrument that allows a veterinarian to see into the ear canal), x-rays, computed tomography (CT scan), magnetic resonance imaging (MRI), and neurologic examination may reveal the cause, especially in cases of acquired deafness. Electronic testing is useful in assessing hearing in puppies of breeds prone to deafness at birth.

Deafness due to blockage of the external ear canal usually responds to appropriate surgical or medical treatment. This deafness is usually not complete. Deafness due to bacterial infections of the middle and inner ear may respond to antibiotic treatment. If deafness is due to persistent intense noise, trauma, or viral infection, after treatment the animal may experience complete recovery, partial recovery, or no recovery of hearing at all. Recovery from deafness caused by drugs that are toxic to the ear is rare.

Hereditary deafness may be eliminated from a breed by removal of identifiable carriers from the breeding program.

▓ DISORDERS OF THE OUTER EAR

A variety of skin conditions affect the outside part of the ear, called the pinna. Most conditions cause tissue changes elsewhere as well. Rarely, a disease affects the outer ear alone or affects it first. As with all skin conditions, a diagnosis is best made when combined with the results of a thorough history, a complete physical and skin examination, and carefully selected diagnostic tests.

Insects and parasites commonly cause inflammation of the pinna—resulting in redness, swelling, itching or blistering—either through direct damage from the bite of the parasite or as a result of hypersensitivity. Tiny skin mites burrow under a dog's skin, often on the edges of the ears. Because they are so hard to see and find, a veterinarian might take several skin scrapings before making a diagnosis.

Canine Juvenile Cellulitis

Canine juvenile cellulitis is an infection and inflammation of the tissues beneath the skin of young dogs. It is an uncommon disorder of puppies and is characterized

Tiny mites burrow under the skin, often on the edges of the ears.

by masses of small, round raised areas of inflamed skin filled with pus on the face and ears. The lymph nodes below the lower jaw are usually noticeably enlarged. It occurs in puppies 3 weeks to 4 months of age and rarely in older animals. Golden Retrievers, Gordon Setters, and Dachshunds appear to be at greater risk than other breeds. An inflamed, pus-filled, raised area of the skin of the ear canal is common, along with swollen, thickened pinnae. Early treatment is recommended to avoid scarring. Careful observation of the condition of your puppies will help you detect any masses or lumps on their faces or ears. Any lumps or masses, even small ones, are a good reason to take your puppy in for a checkup as soon as possible.

Ear Hematomas

Ear hematomas are fluid-filled swellings that develop on the inward curving surface of the outer ears in dogs. The cause for their development is unknown. Signs include head shaking or ear scratching due to itchiness. In dogs, the condition is seen with hereditary environmental allergies and food allergies in which the ear canals are the primary sites of allergic inflammation and itching. Treatment usually involves surgery to drain and flush the swellings. Frequently, the veterinarian will place a drain made out of a soft tube in the area to help prevent fluid from building up again.

Flies

Fly strike (irritation of the ears caused by biting flies) is a worldwide problem caused by the stable fly and typically affects dogs and horses. The fly bite causes small, hard, round bumps and raised, reddened areas with central bloody crusts that itch. Tissue changes are found on the tips or on the folded surface of the outer ears of dogs with flopped ears. Treatment includes fly repellents, controlling the fly population with environmental clean up (such as removing manure), and insecticides.

Frostbite

Frostbite may occur in dogs poorly adapted to cold climates and is more likely in wet or windy conditions. It typically affects body regions that are poorly insulated, including the tips of the ears. The skin may be pale or red, swollen, and painful. In severe cases, tissue death and shedding of the tips of the outer ears may follow. Treatment consists of rapid, gentle warming and supportive care. Amputation of affected regions may be required but should be delayed until the extent of living tissue is determined.

Hair Loss

Several ear edge skin disorders characterized by hair loss occur in dogs. Periodic loss of hair on the outer ear in Miniature Poodles involves the loss of hair on the outward curving surfaces of the ear. The hair loss starts suddenly and progresses over several months, but hair may spontaneously regrow. There are no other signs. Treatment is unnecessary.

Hair loss on the outer ear has been reported in Dachshunds, Chihuahuas, Italian Greyhounds, and Whippets and is thought to have a tendency to be hereditary. The age of onset is 1 year or more, when the hair coat begins to thin. Complete hair loss on the outer ear may occur by 8 to 9 years of age. Other commonly affected areas are the lower neck and chest and the back to the middle of the thighs. There are no other signs. No effective treatment has been reported, but certain drugs have been described as helpful.

Immune-mediated Diseases

Several immune-mediated diseases may affect the outer ear and the ear canal. (*See also* AUTOIMMUNE SKIN DISORDERS, page 170.) Other areas of the body are typically affected and may include footpads, mucous membranes, skin and mucous membrane junctions, nails and nail beds, and the tip of the tail. Immune-mediated diseases are confirmed using biopsies of primary lesions.

Mange

Sarcoptic mange is an infectious skin disease caused by a parasitic mite that burrows into the top layers of the skin. It is common in dogs throughout the world. The condition begins with small, red, round bumps on the skin. These bumps progress to scaling, crusting, and raw, irritated open sores on the ear edges and other parts of the body as a result of scratching; however, in some cases only the red bumps and itching are seen. Itching is severe. Transmission of the mite is by direct contact with infected animals.

Diagnosis is based on signs, history of exposure, and discovery of mites on multiple skin scrapings. Treatment options include dips and injections. Your veterinarian will be able to prescribe the best therapy for your pet. Because mites can survive off the host for a variable amount of time, all bedding, brushes, and objects in your pet's environment should be thoroughly cleaned.

Seborrhea and Dermatosis

Overly oily skin at the edge of the ear (seborrhea) or ear edge skin disease (dermatosis) is common in Dachshunds, although other breeds with ears that hang loose may be affected. The tips of the ears on both sides are usually affected, but the condition can progress to involve the whole ear edge. The cause is unknown. Signs include waxy gray to yellow scale sticking to the base of hair shafts. Plugs of hair can be easily pulled out, leaving behind skin with a shiny surface. In severe cases the ear edges are swollen and cracked. Treatments are available and can be prescribed by your veterinarian.

Ticks

Ticks can cause irritation at the site of attachment and may be found on the pinna or in the ear canal. The ear tick, found in the southwestern United States, South and Central America, southern Africa, and India, is a soft-shelled tick whose younger, immature forms infest and live on the external ear canal of dogs and other animals. Signs of infestation include head shaking, head rubbing, or drooped ears. Both the animal and the environment should be treated. Your veterinarian can recommend the most appropriate treatment for your pet and your local area.

▓ OTITIS EXTERNA

The tubular portion of the outer ear that carries sound to the eardrum is called the ear canal. The most common disorder of the ear canal in dogs is called otitis externa. This condition occurs when the layer of cells that line the external ear canal becomes inflamed. Signs include redness of the skin, swelling, itchiness, increased discharge, and scaly skin. The ear canal may be painful or itchy depending on the cause or duration of the condition. Otitis externa can be caused by many different factors. Some of these factors (such as parasites, foreign objects, and allergies) appear to directly cause the inflammation, while others (such as certain bacteria and yeasts) perpetuate the condition. To complicate things further, the shape or form of the pinnae or ear canals can predispose dogs to developing otitis externa. Identifying these factors is key to successful control of the inflammation. Unless all the causes are identified and treated, the condition may return.

A detailed history and thorough physical and skin examination can provide

Otitis externa, the most common ear disease in dogs, can be caused by many factors.

clues as to the cause of otitis externa. The pinnae and regions near the ear may show evidence of self-trauma (from scratching, for example), redness of skin, and primary and secondary skin abnormalities. Deformities of the pinnae, an abnormal growth of tissue in the canal, and head-shaking suggest chronic ear discomfort.

Your dog may require sedation or anesthesia to allow a thorough examination using an otoscope. This is especially true if the ear is painful, if the canal is obstructed with discharge or widespread inflammatory tissue, or if the animal is uncooperative. An examination using an otoscope will allow identification of foreign objects deep in the ear, impacted debris, low-grade infections with ear mites, and ruptured or abnormal eardrums. Tissues for culture (to identify any infection-causing microbes) are usually taken at the same time that the examination of the ear canal using an otoscope is being conducted.

Sometimes a smear taken using a cotton-tipped applicator can provide immediate diagnostic information. The external ear canals of most dogs and cats harbor small numbers of harmless microorganisms. These organisms may cause disease if the environment of the ear changes in a way that allows them to multiply. Microscopic examination of a smear can quickly determine if this type of overgrowth is present.

A dark discharge in the canal usually signals the presence of either a yeast infection or a parasite such as ear mites, but may also be seen with a bacterial or mixed infection. Your veterinarian will examine the discharge for eggs, larvae, or adults of ear mites.

Additional tests are sometimes needed to identify the factors causing the inflammation. Allergy testing may be recommended. Biopsies from animals with longterm, obstructive, inflammation of the external ear canal in only one ear may reveal whether tumors are present. X-rays may be taken when better visualization of the eardrum is needed, when inflammation of the middle ear is suspected, or when neurologic signs (such as loss of balance) are present.

Treatment

To treat these conditions, your veterinarian will need to identify and correct any underlying causes. Usually, the area around the ear is clipped of fur, and hair is removed from the ear canal. This improves the movement of air and eases cleaning and drying of the canals.

Because topical medications can be inactivated by discharge from the ears or excessive earwax, your veterinarian will probably clean the ears gently and then dry them before treatment is started. In animals with painful ears, proper cleaning requires general anesthesia.

When properly applied, the ideal medication will coat the layer of cells lining the external ear canal as a thin film. Medication given by mouth or injection will probably be included in the treatment regimen in most cases of longterm inflammation of the ear canal and in any case in which inflammation of the middle ear is suspected.

When severe bacterial infection of the external ear canal is the cause of inflammation, antibacterial drugs in combination with corticosteroids may be used to reduce discharges, pain, and swelling, and to decrease glandular secretions. Dogs that have recurring bacterial inflammation of the external ear and a history of infection with ear mites should be treated with a topical product that contains antibacterial and antiparasitic drugs to ensure that any parasitic infections are eliminated.

The treatment should continue until the infection is completely gone. For dogs with bacterial and yeast infections, you should expect weekly or bi-weekly physical examinations and tests until there is no evidence of infection. For most cases, this takes 2 to 4 weeks. Longterm cases may take months to resolve, and in some instances, treatment must be continued indefinitely. Follow your veterinarian's recommended treatment program carefully and fully for the best result for your pet.

Preventive Care

The best treatment of inflammation of the outer ear is prevention. Be sure to inspect your dog's ears regularly and note any unusual temperature changes, changes in skin color or condition, sudden increases in moisture, or other changes. When you notice changes in your pet's ears, it is time for a prompt checkup.

Your veterinarian can show you how to properly clean your dog's ears, if necessary. The frequency of cleaning usually decreases over time from daily to once or twice weekly as a preventive maintenance procedure. The ear canals should be kept dry and well ventilated. Using drying agents in the ears of dogs that swim frequently and preventing water from entering the ear canals during bathing should minimize softening of the ear canal and decrease the frequency of bacterial or fungal infections in moist ear canals. (Softening impairs the barrier function of the skin, which makes it easier for infection to start.) In some cases, clipping or plucking hair from the inside of the pinna and around the ear canal improves ventilation and decreases humidity in the ears. However, you should check with your veterinarian before removing any hair. If such a step is warranted, be sure to get a demonstration of how to do this correctly.

▓ OTITIS MEDIA AND INTERNA

Inflammation of the middle ear structures (**otitis media**) is usually caused by an extension of infection from the external ear canal or by penetration of the eardrum by a foreign object. The spread of infection through the bloodstream to these areas is also possible, but it is rare. Inflammation of the middle ear may lead to inflammation of the inner ear structures (**otitis interna**). This can in turn lead to loss of balance and deafness.

The signs of otitis media may be similar to those of otitis externa (*see* page 160). Head shaking, rubbing the affected ear on the floor, and rotating the head toward the

---

How to Clean your Dog's Ears

- When cleaning a dog's ear, it is critical not to use anything that would tend to push any debris further into the ear canal. Cotton-tipped applicators (such as Q-tips) should not be used.

- Assemble real (not synthetic) cotton balls and the ear cleaning solution. It is best to use saline eye solution to clean the ear. Do not use wax removal liquid or other over-the-counter ear cleaners.

- Squirt enough cleaner into the ear to fill the canal. Massage the base of the ear until you hear the solution "squish."

- Gently grasp the base of the ear and pull the pinna up and away from the head in order to straighten out the "L" shape of the canal.

- Wad the cotton into a tubular shape and gently insert it into the canal as far as it will go.

- Again, gently massage the base of the ear to help work debris and cleaning solution toward the cotton and dry the canal.

- Wait a few minutes before using any medication in the affected ear(s) as instructed by your veterinarian.

---

affected side are often noted. The ear is usually painful, with a discharge and inflammatory changes in the ear canal. Inflammation of the outer ear that recurs may be another sign.

Because the facial and sympathetic nerves travel through the middle ear, facial nerve paralysis, constriction of the pupil of the eye, drooping of the eyelid, sinking of the eyeball into the orbital cavity, and protrusion of the third eyelid may occur on the same side as the affected ear. If otitis interna occurs at the same time, head tilt toward the affected side will be more obvious. Additionally, an animal with inflammation of the inner ear may have an overall lack of coordination severe enough to cause difficulty in rising and walking. An involuntary rhythmic movement of the eyes from side to side (called nystagmus) may also be seen with inflammation of the inner ear.

Your veterinarian may diagnose otitis media when an examination reveals severe pus-filled inflammation of the external ear; longterm, recurrent inflammation of the external ear; or whenever the eardrum has been penetrated by a foreign object or has ruptured after longterm inflammation of the ear. Fluid in the middle ear or hardening and fibrous overgrowth of the round bone behind the ear may be detected through x-rays or computerized tomography (CT scan).

Otitis interna may be diagnosed based on similar signs with the addition of loss of balance. Examination using an otoscope and x-rays of the round bone behind the ear may confirm the presence of simultaneous middle and inner ear inflammation.

Treatment

Because of the possibility of hearing loss and damage to the organ of balance (vestibular apparatus), longterm antibiotics given by mouth or injection may be prescribed by your veterinarian to treat otitis media or interna. Treatment may last 3 to 6 weeks. If the eardrum is ruptured, your veterinarian will carefully clean the middle ear. Small perforations of the eardrum usually heal in 2 to 3 weeks. Any inflammation of the external ear canal will be treated at the same time. Additionally, anti-inflammatory medications may be prescribed during the first week of treatment to decrease inflammatory changes in nearby nerves.

If your dog's external ear is clean and normal, but the eardrum is bulging or discolored, your veterinarian may perforate the eardrum to relieve the pressure (and thus the pain) within the middle ear, to permit removal of the inflammatory discharge, and to allow for culture of the fluid for diagnosis and treatment. However, perforation of the eardrum could result in hearing loss, so alternatives may be used. Antibiotics given by mouth or injection may be prescribed for 3 to 4 weeks and possibly up to 6 weeks if inflammation of the inner ear exists. In longterm otitis media, surgery may be necessary to allow for drainage and adequate resolution of the infection.

Otitis media with an intact eardrum usually responds well to antibiotic therapy. However, if longterm inflammation of the inner ear exists and the eardrum is ruptured, the chances of successful treatment are reduced. If local nerve problems develop, they may continue even after the infection has been cleared. Inflammation of the inner ear usually responds well to longterm antibiotic therapy, but some neurologic problems (for example, lack of coordination, head tilt, deafness, drooping lips, or inability to blink) may persist for life. Animals recovering from inflammation of the inner ear should be given adequate time to adapt to any persistent nerve-related signs.

The sooner animals can be treated, the better the prospect is for a good outcome. If you notice any of the signs indicating a possible infection or inflammation in your pet's ears or if you notice any changes in your dog's normal head position or movement, a checkup should be scheduled promptly.

TUMORS OF THE EAR CANAL

Tumors may develop from any of the structures lining or supporting the ear canal, including the outer layer of skin, the glands that produce earwax and oil, or any of the bones, connective tissues, muscles, or middle layers of the skin. Tumors of the external ear canal and pinna are more common than tumors of the middle or inner ear. Cocker Spaniels are more likely to have ear canal tumors than other breeds of dogs. Middle-aged to older dogs are more likely to have ear canal tumors than younger animals.

Although the exact cause of ear canal tumors is unknown, it is thought that longterm inflammation of the ear canal may lead to an abnormal growth and development of tissue, and finally to the formation of a tumor. Thickening secretions from earwax glands during inflammation of the external ear canal may stimulate the production of cancerous cells. Ear canal tumors are more likely to be malignant than benign.

Signs of ear canal tumors include ear discharge (waxy, pus-filled, or bloody) in one ear, a foul odor, head shaking, ear scratching, swelling or draining abscesses near the ear, and deafness. If the middle or inner ear is involved, the dog may have loss of balance and coordination, head tilt, and other neurologic signs. In any case of inflammation in one ear that does not respond to treatment, a tumor of the ear canal should be suspected by your veterinarian.

Earwax Gland Tumors

Benign or malignant tumors that develop from the earwax glands in the external ear canal occur occasionally in middle-aged or older dogs. Malignant earwax tumors are more common than benign ones. Animals with a history of longterm inflammation of the ear are more likely to develop earwax gland tumors, and Cocker Spaniels are particularly susceptible. These tumors appear as firm, dome-shaped, pinkish white shapes, often with stalk-shaped lumps or flattened patches that may have slow-healing sores. Because many tumors completely obstruct the ear canal, they are often associated with inflammation of

Earwax gland tumors may be malignant or benign.

the external or middle ear accompanied by a pus-filled to bloody discharge. Loss of balance may be present if there is middle ear involvement. Malignant earwax tumors can spread to regional lymph nodes and to salivary glands, so your veterinarian may recommend that they be removed.

Surgical removal of benign ear canal tumors is possible in many cases. Laser surgery has also been used. More extensive surgery is required for malignant ear canal tumors. Average survival time of animals with malignant ear canal tumors has been reported to be almost 5 years in dogs; however, dogs with extensive tumor involvement had a less favorable outlook. Radiation therapy can be used to treat incompletely removed malignant earwax gland tumors, with a 56% 1-year survival rate reported.

Your veterinarian can discuss your pet's individual health status and provide you with a more complete outlook for the possible result of any surgery or other treatment.

CHAPTER **11**

Immune Disorders

▓ THE IMMUNE SYSTEM

The immune system consists of a network of white blood cells, antibodies, and other substances that fight off infections and reject foreign proteins (*see* TABLE 12). In addition, the immune system includes several organs. Some, such as the thymus gland and the bone marrow, are the sites where white blood cells are produced. Others, including the spleen, lymph nodes, and liver, trap microorganisms and foreign substances and provide a place for immune system cells to collect, interact with each other and with foreign substances, and generate an immune response.

▓ IMMUNE SYSTEM RESPONSES

The primary role of the immune system is to defend the body against foreign invaders or abnormal cells that invade or attack it. In order to do this, the immune system must distinguish between "self" and "non-self." By recognizing invading microorganisms (such as viruses), chemical agents, or other foreign substances that are "non-self," a body can protect itself from attack. Substances that stimulate an immune response in the body are called antigens. Antigens may be contained within or on bacteria, viruses, other microorganisms, or cancer cells. Antigens may also exist on their own—for example, as pollen or food molecules. A normal immune response consists of recognizing a foreign antigen, mobilizing forces to defend against it, and attacking it.

There are 3 lines of defense against invaders: physical barriers, nonspecific (or innate) immunity, and specific (or adaptive) immunity. Nonspecific and specific immunity involve various white blood cells.

Physical Barriers

The first lines of defense against invaders are mechanical or physical barriers. These include the skin, the cornea of the eye, and the membranes lining the respiratory, digestive, urinary, and reproductive tracts. As long as these barriers remain unbroken, many invaders cannot penetrate them. However, if a barrier is broken (for example, if the skin is broken by a wound), the risk of infection is increased.

In addition, the physical barriers are defended by secretions containing enzymes that can destroy bacteria. Examples are

Table 12. Specialized Cells and Molecules of the Immune System

Lymphocytes	Small white blood cells found in all organs and tissues. There are 2 principal types: B lymphocytes (B cells), which mature in the bone marrow, and T lymphocytes (T cells), which mature in the thymus.
B cells	These lymphocytes are responsible for the production of antibodies, an important part of the immune response.
T cells	These lymphocytes include **killer (cytotoxic) T cells**, which detect and kill cells that are abnormal (such as cancer cells), and **helper T cells**, which help other lymphocytes mount an immune response.
Antigens	Any substances that can induce an immune response.
Antigen-presenting cells	Specialized cells that engulf antigens and process them so that they can be recognized by lymphocytes.
Neutrophils	All-purpose scavenger cells that ingest and destroy antigens and cell debris.
Eosinophils	White blood cells that ingest bacteria and other foreign cells, participate in allergic reactions, and help destroy cancer cells.
Mast cells	Cells that release histamine and other substances involved in allergic reactions.
Cytokines	The immune system's messengers, which help regulate an immune response by delivering signals from one cell to another.
Antibodies	Also called **immunoglobulins**, antibodies are proteins produced by B cells that interact with specific antigens. They can form immune complexes, label antigens for removal by other cells, or block the ability of a virus to enter its target cell.

tears in the eyes and secretions in the digestive tract.

Nonspecific Immunity

Nonspecific (innate) immunity is present at birth. It is so named because its components treat all foreign substances in much the same way. The white blood cells involved in nonspecific immunity are monocytes (which develop into macrophages), neutrophils, eosinophils, basophils, and natural killer cells. (For a more detailed discussion of WHITE BLOOD CELLS, *see* page 35.) These types of white blood cells usually act on their own to destroy invaders. The complement system and cytokines are molecules produced by the immune system that also participate in nonspecific immunity.

Specific Immunity

Specific (adaptive) immunity is not present at birth; it is acquired. As the immune system encounters different antigens, it learns the best way to attack each antigen, and it begins to develop a

memory for that antigen. Specific immunity is so named because it tailors its attack to a specific antigen previously encountered. It takes time to develop specific immunity after initial exposure to a new antigen; however, when the antigen is encountered in the future, the response is more rapid and more effective than that generated by nonspecific immunity.

Most vaccines work by stimulating the development of specific immunity. Vaccinations have been developed for many diseases in animals and are an effective way of enhancing the immune response.

Mounting an Immune Response

In order to destroy invaders, the immune system must first recognize them. It can make this distinction because all cells have unique markers on their surface that identify them. A cell with markers on its surface that are not identical to those on the body's own cells is identified as being foreign. The immune system then attacks that cell.

Some white blood cells (B cells) recognize invaders, or antigens, directly. When a B cell recognizes and attaches to the antigen, it produces antibodies, which coat the surface of the virus or bacteria to stop it from multiplying or infecting other cells. This process is called neutralization. Antibodies also label the foreign invaders so that other immune defenses can find and attack them.

Other white blood cells (T cells) need help from cells that first ingest the invader and break it into fragments. The fragments are then presented to the T cells so that they can recognize and destroy them. These helper cells are called antigen presenting cells.

After an infectious organism has been eliminated, most of the immune cells and antibodies that fought the infection disappear. However, a small group of "memory" immune cells remain in the body. If the memory cells are later exposed to an antigen that they remember, they help the body respond much faster and with a stronger response. This is the reason why vaccinations are successful in preventing many diseases. Vaccinations prime the immune system to respond quickly by exposing the T and B cells to antigens present on the infectious organism.

Types of Immune System Disorders

The immune system does not always function properly. Sometimes it identifies

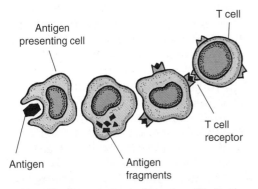

Antigen presenting cell

T cell

T cell receptor

Antigen

Antigen fragments

How T cells recognize antigens (modified with permission from *The Merck Manual of Medical Information*, Second Home Edition, 2003)

parts of its own body as foreign and attacks them, causing what is known as an autoimmune disorder. At other times, the immune system overreacts to foreign invaders by producing too many antibodies or other chemicals (known as hypersensitivity or allergic reactions). Sometimes the immune system does not react at all (immunosuppression) or cannot generate an appropriate immune response. The malfunctions are called immune-mediated disorders. There are 4 general classifications or types of these disorders.

Type I Reactions (Anaphylaxis)

Anaphylaxis is a rare, life-threatening, immediate allergic reaction to something that has entered the body (for example, eaten or injected). In a normal immune system, the binding of an antigen to an antibody activates various cells, which produce chemicals such as histamines. In anaphylaxis, the body activates an excessive number of cells, resulting in the production of very large numbers of histamines and other chemicals. These chemicals can affect various organs such as the blood vessels and muscles. The severity of the reaction depends on the type of antigen, the amount of antibodies produced, the amount of antigen, and the route of exposure. Agents that can cause anaphylactic and allergic reactions include biting insects, vaccines, drugs, food, and blood products. The most common signs include restlessness, excitement, drooling, vomiting, abdominal pain, diarrhea, shock, collapse, convulsions, and death.

Type II Reactions (Antibody-mediated Cytotoxic Reactions)

Type II reactions occur when an antibody binds to an antigen present at the surface of its own cells. This antibody–antigen complex then activates a cell-killing series of proteins called complement, resulting in cell death and tissue damage. It is unclear what triggers this antibody-mediated cell killing but, as with all immune-mediated diseases, the combination of both external factors and an infection can lead to the development of this type of reaction. It has been suggested that some viral infections can lead to changes in regulation of the immune system. This can either trigger an overreaction of the immune system or convert protective immunity into a disease.

Signs of Type II hypersensitivity vary, and they depend on the organ in which the reaction is occurring. Signs can include fever, kidney failure, vomiting, diarrhea, abdominal pain, or joint swelling. The disease is diagnosed by physical examination and by biopsies of the damaged organ. Supportive treatment consists of elimination of the infectious agent (if determined) and anti-inflammatory or immunosuppressive drug treatment.

Type III Reactions (Immune Complex Disease)

Type III reactions occur when a large number of antigen–antibody complexes lodge in certain organs, causing damage to blood vessels. There are many possible reasons for the continuous presence of antigens, including persistent infections caused by viruses, bacteria, fungi, or parasites. In addition, antibody responses to certain drugs can occur, particularly in the case of long-acting drugs or drugs that are given continually over a long period of time. Some animals can react and produce antibodies against self antigens. However, in many cases, the cause of the disease is unidentifiable.

The most commonly affected sites include the joints, skin, kidneys, lungs, and brain. Signs vary and may include fever, lameness that shifts from leg to leg, painful or swollen joints, behavioral changes, vomiting, diarrhea, and abdominal pain. An immune complex disease is usually diagnosed with blood tests. Treatment generally includes supportive treatment for the affected organ, removal of the causative agent, or treatment of the infection (such as appropriate antibiotic treatment for bacterial infection). Anti-inflammatory drugs may be needed to stop the continued formation of immune complexes and to decrease the inflammation associated with these reactions.

Type IV Reactions (Cell-mediated Reactions)

Type IV or delayed hypersensitivity occurs more than 24 hours after the body was exposed to an antigen. The antigens usually responsible for the development of Type IV reactions include bacteria, parasites, viruses, chemicals, and certain cell antigens. This type of reaction can occur in any organ. For this reason the signs will vary. The reaction is diagnosed based on excluding other causes for organ-specific diseases and by laboratory tests on the tissue. The goals of treatment are to provide supportive treatment based on the organ-specific disease process, to identify (if possible) and eliminate the source of the antigen causing the reaction, and to control inflammation and immune suppression.

■ DISORDERS INVOLVING ANAPHYLACTIC REACTIONS (TYPE I REACTIONS, ATOPY)

In a Type I reaction, the animal has been previously exposed to an antigen and produces an excess of antibodies. If this antigen appears in the blood, the result can be either anaphylactic shock or more localized reactions (such as itchy patches on the skin). If the antigen enters through the skin, the more localized reaction is typical.

Anaphylactic Shock

Anaphylactic shock is a rare, life-threatening, immediate allergic reaction to food, an injection, or an insect sting. The most common signs occur within seconds to minutes after exposure to the antigen. Dogs differ from other domestic animals in that the major organ affected by anaphylactic shock is the liver, rather than the lungs. Therefore, gastrointestinal signs are the major signs of anaphylactic shock rather than respiratory signs. These signs include sudden onset of diarrhea, excessive drooling, vomiting, shock, seizures, coma, and death. The dog's gums may be pale, and the limbs may feel cold. The heart rate is generally very fast, but the pulse is weak. There is no facial swelling.

Anaphylaxis is an extreme emergency. If you think that your dog is having an anaphylactic reaction, seek emergency veterinary assistance immediately. A veterinarian can give intravenous injections of epinephrine (adrenalin) to counteract the reaction. Treatment for other associated problems, such as difficulty breathing, may also be needed.

Hives and Swelling

Hives (**urticaria**) and areas of swelling are caused by allergic reactions to drugs, chemicals, something eaten, insect bites, or even sunlight. They generally develop within 20 minutes of exposure to the allergen (antigen). Hives are the least severe type of anaphylactic reaction. Small bumps occur on the skin. Often, the hair stands up over these swellings and sometimes they itch. Swelling is most often noticed on the face, especially on the lips, the muzzle, and around the eyes. The swelling can be so severe that the dog cannot open its eyes.

Hives and swelling are usually not life threatening and typically go away by themselves if the source of the allergic reaction is removed or passes through the body. Veterinarians treat these reactions by giving appropriate antihistamines.

Hives are a reaction to an allergen such as a drug, type of food, or insect bite.

Allergic Rhinitis (Nasal Allergies)

Like humans, dogs can suffer from seasonal allergies (usually caused by pollen exposure) that can cause a watery nasal discharge and sneezing called allergic rhinitis. Nonseasonal rhinitis may be due to exposure to such allergens as molds, dander, bedding, or feeds. The condition is diagnosed by a favorable response after treatment with antihistamines and the disappearance of signs when the offending antigen is removed. Although skin tests can diagnose the allergic reaction in people, skin testing is not presently an accurate means to diagnose nasal allergies in animals.

Chronic Allergic Bronchitis

Chronic allergic bronchitis is characterized by a dry, harsh, hacking cough that is easily brought on by physical activity. The disease may be seasonal or may occur year-round. The condition is treated with expectorants, which aid in the removal of thick, sticky mucus. Your veterinarian may prescribe additional medication to help control this type of immune-mediated bronchitis. It is usually not possible to determine the antigen causing the reaction.

PIE Syndrome (Pulmonary Infiltration with Eosinophilia)

Infiltration of the lungs with a thick fluid and white blood cells, called PIE syndrome, is caused by allergens, viruses, and parasites in dogs. Pets with PIE syndrome generally become lethargic and have difficulty breathing with normal exercise. It is usually not possible to determine the antigen causing the reaction. Medications can help control the signs of the disorder.

Food Allergies

Food allergies occur in pets as well as people. They can lead to inflammation of the lining of the stomach and intestines. In dogs, the first sign is vomiting that occurs within 1 to 2 hours of eating. The dog is usually healthy except for vomiting, although there can be weight loss, diarrhea or soft feces, and poor coat condition in severe cases. Food allergies often develop following an intestinal infection.

Both the diagnosis and treatment of food allergies are done by strictly controlling the diet at the direction of a veterinarian. Dogs should be fed low-protein diets that contain as few ingredients as possible. A basic diet of rice, cottage cheese (or tofu), and mutton, supplemented with vitamins and minerals, is a good way to begin. When the signs have disappeared, additional foods can be introduced one at a time. Commercial prescription diets are also available. In case the signs do not disappear after the dietary changes, prescription medications can provide excellent relief for dogs.

Skin Allergies (Atopy)

Skin allergy, also called atopy, occurs when a dog's skin overreacts to certain allergens in the environment. It has been estimated that 10% of all dogs suffer from these allergies, which are commonly due to inhaled substances such as dust mites, pollen, mold, or dander. Certain breeds of dogs, including terriers, Dalmatians, and retrievers, are predisposed to developing skin allergies. The most common signs of skin allergy occur in the area of the skin that is sparsely haired and directly exposed to the allergens, such as the back of the paws, abdomen, muzzle, and lips. The affected areas are very red, have small bumps, and itch.

The condition is diagnosed by history and physical examination. To determine the source of the allergy, tests may be performed. In one such test, the dog is injected with small amounts of the possible allergen into the shin. If the dog is allergic to the injected substance, a swelling will occur immediately at the injection site.

The key to managing this condition is removing or restricting exposure to the allergen or irritant in the dog's environment. Treatment consists of an extended series of injections of the offending allergen under the skin until improvement is noted. This type of treatment is effective in 60% of dogs. If the treatment fails, or is not used, treatment with prescription corticosteroids or antihistamines is often helpful. If your veterinarian prescribes a medication to control your pet's allergic reactions, be sure to follow the directions carefully and fully, including any restrictions regarding exposure to carpets, chemicals, or other potential hazards.

■ DISORDERS INVOLVING CYTOTOXIC ANTIBODIES (TYPE II REACTIONS)

Type II reactions can lead to several types of diseases in dogs, including anemia, blood clotting problems, and skin and muscle disorders. They may be associated with other immune system disturbances, such as systemic lupus erythematosus, or triggered by a drug, vaccine, or infection. Most often, the triggering cause cannot be pinpointed. Immune-mediated hemolytic anemia and thrombocytopenia are the most common Type II reactions.

Immune-mediated Hemolytic Anemia

This type of anemia is a severe and life-threatening disease in which the dog's immune system sees its own red blood cells as foreign invaders, and therefore produces antibodies to destroy them. Red blood cells are manufactured as usual in the bone marrow, but once released into the bloodstream, they are attacked and destroyed by antibodies. Signs of anemia may include fatigue, paleness of the lips and gums, and depression, along with jaundice in some cases. Other signs your veterinarian may find include an enlarged liver or spleen.

Immune-mediated hemolytic anemia has 4 basic forms, peracute, acute or subacute, chronic, and pure red cell aplasia. Most forms are treatable with medications, including corticosteroids and cytotoxic drugs (such as those often used in chemotherapy). Relapses are uncommon.

Immune-mediated Thrombocytopenia

Immune-mediated thrombocytopenia is common in dogs and occurs more often in females than males. This condition is caused by the destruction of platelets (thrombocytes) by the immune system in much the same manner as red blood cells are destroyed in immune-mediated hemolytic anemia (*see* above). When an animal has thrombocytopenia, clotting does not occur correctly. Even minor injuries can cause uncontrollable bleeding, further decreasing the number of red blood cells. The most frequent signs are bleeding of the skin and mucous membranes.

Before immune-mediated thrombocytopenia can be diagnosed, many more common diseases must be excluded, including various clotting disorders, bladder or prostate infections or cancer, and intestinal parasites. The diagnosis is usually made based on signs and response to treatment, rather than on blood tests. However, certain blood tests such as platelet counts and clotting profiles are helpful. Medication will likely be prescribed to treat this disease. Signs usually disappear after 5 to 7 days of treatment when platelet counts begin to rise. If the platelet count has not increased significantly after 7 to 10 days, additional or different medications may be prescribed. If the blood loss is life threatening, transfusions of whole blood or plasma may be necessary.

Treatment is often continued for 1 to 3 months after the platelet counts return to normal. Some dogs have persistent decreases in platelets even with drug treatment. If this is the case with your pet, you and your veterinarian will want to discuss longterm treatment and maintenance options.

Autoimmune Skin Disorders

Pemphigus foliaceus is an uncommon autoimmune disease that affects the skin. The cause of this malfunction of the immune system is usually not known. One theory is that the skin is somehow altered, making it appear "foreign" to the immune system. In the case of pemphigus foliaceus, the immune system produces antibodies against the "glue" that normally keeps skin cells (keratinocytes) attached to one another. White blood cells move in causing further damage, and the keratinocytes break apart from each other, forming pimples or crusted areas. Veterinarians frequently prescribe corticosteroids for initial treatment of pemphigus foliaceus, but other immunosuppressive drugs may be added if there is no response.

Pemphigus vulgaris is a very rare disease in dogs. It produces mouth abnormalities, but other areas of the skin are only mildly affected. The disease is often controlled with high doses of corticosteroids in combination with other drugs that suppress the immune system.

Bullous pemphigoid has been seen in Collies and Doberman Pinschers. Abnormalities are often widespread but tend to be concentrated in the groin. The involved skin resembles a severe scald and may include blisters. The disease is usually treated with corticosteroids, but continuous treatment is often needed and the longterm outlook is poor.

Myasthenia Gravis

Myasthenia gravis is an autoimmune neuromuscular disease seen in both people and animals, including dogs. It can be congenital (present at birth) or immune-mediated, developing later in life. Weakness is the primary sign. Affected animals produce antibodies to certain nerve receptors and destroy them. This leads to the inability to contract muscles and extreme muscle weakness. In older dogs, the first sign of problems may be an enlargement of the esophagus (megaesophagus) due to the muscular weakness. The enlargement of the esophagus leads to problems with swallowing. This can cause regurgitation which may, in turn, cause inhalation pneumonia. Myasthenia gravis is diagnosed using blood tests to search for the antibody to the nerve receptor and other tests for nerve activity. Your veterinarian will prescribe drugs to control this disease. Remissions can occur, and many dogs that develop this condition do well with continued treatment.

◼ DISORDERS INVOLVING IMMUNE COMPLEXES (TYPE III REACTIONS)

Immune complex disorders are among the most common immune-mediated diseases. The location in the body where the immune complexes (combinations of antibodies and antigens) are deposited determines the signs and the course of the disease.

Glomerulonephritis

Glomerulonephritis (*see* GLOMERULAR DISEASE, page 293) is inflammation of the microscopic filtering units of the kidneys known as glomeruli. The inflammation develops when immune complexes become trapped in the glomeruli. This leads to activation of the body's inflammatory defense system, which, in turn, damages the glomeruli. The immune complexes often form as a consequence of some other disease such as an infection or cancer. However, in many dogs with glomerulonephritis, the triggering cause cannot be determined. Glomerulonephritis results in an excessive loss of protein in the urine (proteinuria). The finding of protein in the urine during a urine test may be the first indication that your dog has glomerulonephritis. Treatment includes giving immunosuppressive drugs to reduce the formation of the immune complexes. If it goes untreated, the disease can lead to chronic kidney failure.

Systemic Lupus Erythematosus (Lupus)

Systemic lupus erythematosus (often simply called lupus) is a rare autoimmune disease that is seen in both people and dogs. Dogs with lupus have antibodies in their blood that are targeted against their own body tissues. Lupus causes widespread abnormalities of the skin, heart, lungs, kidneys, joints, nervous system, and blood (decreased red blood cell or platelet numbers). Multiple organs are usually affected.

Lupus causes such a wide variety of signs that it can be confused with many different diseases. The signs of lupus may be acute (sudden onset and short duration) or chronic (of long duration and recurring), and they often come and go. The signs may include a fluctuating fever; lameness that shifts from one leg to another; arthritis affecting multiple joints; painful muscles; anemia; a low white blood cell count; mouth ulcers; skin changes including hair loss, skin crusting, ulceration, and scar formation; and involvement of internal organs such as the thyroid gland, spleen, or kidneys.

A blood test is the usual method of diagnosing lupus. Blood tests are also used to check for the presence of liver or kidney damage and to look for anemia, low platelet counts, and other changes associated with the disease. Drugs are usually prescribed to treat the disorder. Your veterinarian will be able to determine the most appropriate treatment for your pet.

Vasculitis

Vasculitis (inflammation of blood vessels) caused by immune complexes occurs in dogs. At first, abnormalities are seen as purplish red dots appearing on the skin. Depending on which blood vessels are involved, signs appear on the paws, tail, ears, mouth, or tongue. Drugs are a frequent cause of vasculitis in dogs. The disorder is diagnosed by performing tests on samples removed from the affected areas. Vasculitis is treated by stopping the offending drug (if implicated as the cause) or by giving drugs that suppress the immune system.

Anterior Uveitis

One cause of anterior uveitis (*see* page 148) is the action of antibody-antigen complexes on the iris, which causes inflammation of the eye. Anterior uveitis often occurs during the recovery phase of canine hepatitis. Treatment of immune-mediated anterior uveitis may include whole-body corticosteroids and other drugs that suppress the immune system.

Immune-mediated Arthritis

Canine rheumatoid arthritis is an autoimmune disease that produces inflammation and swelling of the joints. The condition is believed to occur as a result of immune complexes that are deposited in the tissue surrounding the joints. Animals with rheumatoid arthritis often have painful joints. This can be seen as a lameness that shifts from leg to leg and difficulty rising, walking, or climbing. The carpal (wrist), tarsal (ankle), and toe joints are the most commonly affected and may have signs of inflammation such as excessive warmth or swelling. The dog may also have a persistent fever. In addition to signs, x-rays of the joints, blood testing, and laboratory analysis of fluid removed from the joints may assist in diagnosis. Your veterinarian can prescribe several drugs that can help a pet with rheumatoid arthritis. Follow the directions carefully for administration of medication.

Plasmacytic-lymphocytic synovitis may be a variant of rheumatoid arthritis. This disease occurs in medium and large breeds of dogs. The most common sign is hind limb lameness, with the knee being the joint most commonly affected. A combination of drugs that control inflammation is often needed to treat this disorder.

Idiopathic polyarthritis is an arthritis of unknown cause that affects multiple

Several types of arthritis that occur in dogs are mediated by the immune system.

joints. It is most common in large dogs, particularly German Shepherds, Doberman Pinschers, retrievers, spaniels, and pointers. In toy breeds, it is most frequent in Toy Poodles, Yorkshire Terriers, and Chihuahuas, or mixes. The most common signs are joint disease and inflammation. Diagnosis is based on the history of recurring fever that does not improve after antibiotic treatment, lethargy, poor appetite, and stiffness or lameness. The disease may be controlled with longterm corticosteroid treatment lasting about 3 to 5 months. In many cases, additional drugs are required.

Immune-mediated Meningitis

Immune-mediated meningitis causes an inflammation of the layers of tissue covering the brain and spinal cord. These coverings, called the meninges, become inflamed and thickened due to an invasion of inflammatory cells. In juvenile or young adult Beagles, Boxers, and German Shorthaired Pointers, the signs consist of recurring bouts of fever, severe neck pain and rigidity, reluctance to move, and depression. Attacks last for 5 to 10 days, with periods of a week or more between attacks in which the dog is mostly or completely normal. The disease is diagnosed through a complete medical history, physical examination, and blood test. The disease often improves on its own over several months. However, in some dogs it becomes chronic and does not respond well to treatment. Corticosteroids are used in some cases to reduce the severity of the signs. More severe forms of the disease, which are not as responsive to treatment, have been reported in Bernese Mountain Dogs and Akitas.

■ DISORDERS INVOLVING CELL-MEDIATED IMMUNITY (TYPE IV REACTIONS)

This type of reaction occurs when specific types of white blood cells (called T helper cells) respond to antigens and release toxic and inflammatory substances that can damage tissues. Cell-mediated immune reactions can occur in any organ. Treatment usually involves the use of anti-inflammatory drugs and drugs that suppress the immune system, either alone or in combination.

Granulomatous Reactions

Granulomatous reactions are masses of fibrous connective tissue infiltrated by the white blood cells that form a cell-mediated immune response. They occur in some animals following infection with certain types of bacteria or fungi. Although cell-mediated immune responses effectively fight off these infections in most individuals, in a few animals the immune response is only partially effective and results in a mass at the site of infection.

Old Dog Encephalitis

Old dog encephalitis refers to a chronic brain inflammation that can occur in a dog that had distemper many years earlier (*see also* page 309). In dogs that have an undetectable infection with the virus, cell-mediated immune reactions may target cells that have been infected by the virus for years.

Contact Hypersensitivity

Contact hypersensitivity results from chemicals reacting with skin proteins. These reactions modify skin proteins in such a way that they are perceived as foreign invaders. The body then produces a cell-mediated immune response against them and causes skin damage. This hypersensitivity usually occurs as a result of contact with sensitizing chemicals incorporated into plastic food dishes, plastic collars, and drugs placed on the skin.

Autoimmune Thyroiditis

Autoimmune thyroiditis is an immune-mediated disease that destroys the thyroid gland. The disease is particularly prevalent in Doberman Pinschers, Beagles, Golden Retrievers, and Akitas. The production of thyroid hormones may be the only detectable sign; however, this condition may occur as part of a broader immune disorder such as lupus, rheumatoid arthritis, or idiopathic polyarthritis (*see* page 171).

Autoimmune Adrenalitis

Autoimmune adrenalitis is caused by infiltration of immune cells into the adrenal glands (located next to each kidney). This causes the destruction of the glands and may lead to the signs of Addison's disease (*see* page 132), such as weakness, loss of weight and appetite, diarrhea, and vomiting. It is most common in young, adult female dogs.

Dry Eye (Keratoconjunctivitis Sicca)

Dry eye, or keratoconjunctivitis sicca (*see* page 145) is caused by an immune reaction that destroys the tear gland. It occurs in dogs, with a genetic predisposition in Cocker Spaniels. Keratoconjunctivitis sicca can follow a viral infection or continuous use of sulfonamides (a type of antibiotic). The disease is treated by giving prescription eye drops that contain cyclosporine, which inhibits the immune response that causes the disorder.

■ IMMUNE-DEFICIENCY DISEASES

Immune-deficiency diseases have serious consequences and often lower the body's defenses against infection. Some are inherited, and others are caused by viral infections or cancer.

Deficiencies in Phagocytosis

Phagocytosis is an essential mechanism of the immune system. Phagocytes are cells that engulf (phagocytize), digest, and kill foreign invaders. They can also serve as part of the adaptive immune system by presenting antigens to other cells in the adaptive system, thereby alerting them to the presence of the foreign invaders. Phagocytes are produced in the bone marrow, spread throughout the body via the bloodstream, and then gather in either tissue or the blood. They are found in the skin, spleen, lymph nodes, the coverings

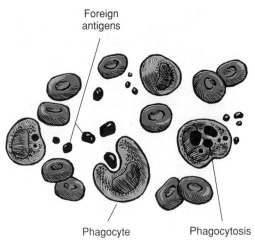

Foreign antigens

Phagocyte   Phagocytosis

Phagocytes are white blood cells that engulf and then kill invaders such as bacteria in a process called phagocytosis.

of the brain and spinal cord, bone marrow, and blood vessels throughout the body.

A deficiency in phagocytosis can be caused by a low number of phagocytes in the blood or by a viral infection or congenital defect (birth defect). The deficiency causes an increased susceptibility to bacterial infection of the skin, respiratory system, and gastrointestinal tract. These infections respond poorly to antibiotics.

Immunoglobulin Deficiency

This condition is due to a failure of the body to produce antibodies (immunoglobulins). This deficiency can be acquired (caused by other diseases) or congenital (present at birth). Congenital deficiencies of one type of immunoglobulin (immunoglobulin A, or IgA) have occurred in Beagles, German Shepherds, and Chinese Shar-Peis, leading to respiratory infections, digestive system disorders, skin disease, or allergies.

Acquired deficiencies occur in puppies that do not receive adequate maternal antibodies when nursing during the first several days of life. For older animals the cause is often a decrease in antibody production.

Immunoglobulin deficiency can occur as part of any disease that disrupts the production of antibodies in the body. For example, certain tumors (such as lymphosarcoma and plasma cell myeloma) cause the production of abnormal antibodies, which decreases production of normal antibodies. Some viral infections, including canine distemper and parvovirus, can damage the tissues that produce antibody-forming cells.

Combined Immunodeficiency Disease

Combined immunodeficiency disease involves a defect in both cell-mediated immunity and antibody production. Affected animals lack both T and B cells, which makes it impossible for the body to fight foreign invaders. Cases have been seen in Bassett Hounds, Toy Poodles, Rottweilers, and mixed-breed puppies. Affected dogs are healthy during the first several months of life but become progressively more susceptible to bacterial infections as the antibodies they received during nursing disappear. No treatment is available and the longterm outlook is poor.

Selective Immunodeficiencies

Rottweiler puppies have a predisposition for severe and often fatal canine parvovirus infections. Their resistance to other diseases is essentially normal, and the basis of this selective immunodeficiency is unknown.

Localized and whole-body fungal infections affect certain types of dogs. Long-nosed breeds, in particular German Shepherds and shepherd mixes, are more likely to develop fungal infections in their nasal passages. Whole-body aspergillosis (a type of fungal infection) is seen almost exclusively in German Shepherds and occurs more commonly in western Australia than in other areas. Signs of this disease include infection of the kidneys, bones, and the discs between the vertebrae of the spinal cord.

Immunodeficiencies Caused by Viruses

These types of diseases can be caused by a number of viruses in animals. In dogs, distemper virus causes a profound immunodeficiency in infected puppies. The infection is associated with a progressive decline in levels of antibodies and an increased susceptibility to bacterial infections that are normally controlled by the immune system. Parvovirus infection in dogs causes a huge decrease in the number of white blood cells and a weakened immune response to bacterial and fungal infections.

IMMUNE SYSTEM TUMORS

Cancer occurs when cells grow out of control. This can happen with the cells of the immune system. The normal immune system requires a rapid increase in the growth of lymphocytes to fight foreign invaders. On occasion however, this increase in the growth of lymphocytes may be uncontrolled, which causes a tumor called **lymphoma**. Lymphoma is one of the most common tumors in dogs. Boxers, Basset Hounds, and Rottweilers are predisposed to developing lymphomas, which primarily affect middle-aged and older dogs. Lymphomas can occur in the lymph nodes, spleen, liver, and other organs.

The signs of lymphoma are related to the location of the tumor(s). The only signs of tumors that develop in the lymph nodes are swelling of the nodes. The gastrointestinal form is often accompanied by vomiting, diarrhea, weight loss, and lack of appetite. Signs of the chest form of lymphoma include shortness of breath and muffled heart sounds. The skin form has several different signs including single or multiple lumps in the skin or mouth. These bumps can itch or be reddened. Lymphoma can be diagnosed with a combination of blood tests, biopsies, and ultrasonography. The treatment for canine lymphoma often includes chemotherapy, usually with a combination of drugs. Adverse effects of the chemotherapy include vomiting, diarrhea, lack of appetite, and fever. Hair loss as an adverse effect of chemotherapy does not occur in dogs. Your veterinarian can advise you about the

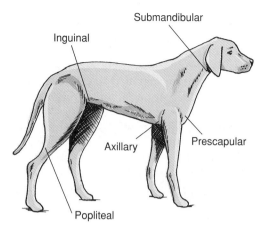

Location of lymph nodes in the dog

most appropriate treatment for your dog. Dogs with lymphomas are rarely cured, but remissions of up to 1 year are common with chemotherapy.

GAMMOPATHIES

The body sometimes produces too many antibodies (immunoglobulins). Gammopathies are conditions in which there is a dramatic rise in the production of the antibodies. There are 2 general types. In polyclonal gammopathies, levels of all the major immunoglobulins are increased. In monoclonal gammopathies, the levels of only a single type of immunoglobulin are increased.

Polyclonal gammopathies may occur when a dog has longterm skin disease or longterm viral, bacterial, or fungal infections. Some longterm parasitic infections, rickettsial diseases, and immunologic diseases (for example, rheumatoid arthritis) may also cause polyclonal gammopathies.

Monoclonal gammopathies may be either benign and associated with no known cause or potentially associated with immunoglobulin-secreting cancers. Doberman Pinschers are predisposed to monoclonal gammopathies. The signs of monoclonal gammopathies vary depending on the location and severity of the source tumor(s). For example, tumors frequently develop in the cavities of flat bones in the skull, ribs, and pelvis and in the spinal cord. Fractures of diseased bones can lead to central nervous system problems, spinal disorders, pain, and lameness. Signs can also be caused by the presence of the monoclonal antibodies themselves. In about 20% of dogs with monoclonal gammopathies, blood changes occur that can cause blood clots, bleeding problems, depression, blindness, and other nervous system signs. In some conditions, the animals develop gangrene and lose portions of the ear tips, eyelids, toes, or tail tip.

The tumors that produce immunoglobulins can be treated with several medications. Remission may occur after treatment, but the overall outlook is poor and relapse is common after 6 to 12 months.

CHAPTER 12

Bone, Joint, and Muscle Disorders

■ INTRODUCTION

The musculoskeletal system includes the bones, cartilage, muscles, ligaments, joints, tendons, and other connective tissue. It supports the body, permits movement, and protects the vital organs. Because many other body systems (including the nervous system, blood vessels, and skin) are interrelated, disorders of one of these systems may also affect the musculoskeletal system.

■ COMPONENTS OF THE MUSCULOSKELETAL SYSTEM

Bones provide rigid structure to the body and shield internal organs from damage. They also house bone marrow, where blood cells are formed, and they maintain the body's reservoir of calcium. Old bone tissue is constantly replaced with new bone tissue in a process called remodeling. This helps keep the bones healthy.

Bones come together to form **joints**. The type of joint formed determines the degree and direction of motion. For example, joints with a ball-and-socket formation allow for rotation, while hinge joints only allow bending and straightening. Some joints do not move at all. In a joint, the ends of the bones are covered with **cartilage**, which is a smooth protective tissue that helps reduce friction as joints move.

There are several different types of **muscles** in the body. Two of these kinds, skeletal muscle and smooth muscle, are part of the musculoskeletal system. Skeletal muscles are responsible for posture and movement. They are attached to bones and arranged around the joints. Smooth muscle helps facilitate many processes in the body such as the flow of blood (by surrounding arteries) and the movement of food along the digestive tract.

Tendons are tough bands of connective tissue made up mostly of a protein called collagen. They do not stretch. Tendons attach each end of a muscle to a bone. They are located within sheaths that allow them to move easily. **Ligaments** are also tough cords formed of connective tissue, but unlike tendons they can stretch to some extent. Ligaments surround joints and help to support and stabilize them. They also connect one bone to another.

■ OVERVIEW OF MUSCULOSKELETAL DISORDERS AND DISEASES

Diseases of the musculoskeletal system most often affect the dog's ability to move.

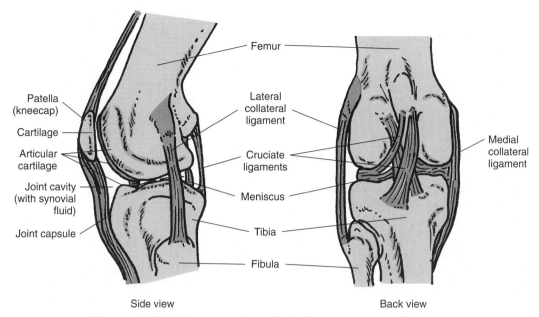

Components of the musculoskeletal system are shown for the knee of a dog (modified with permission from *The Merck Manual of Medical Information*, Second Home Edition, 2003).

How severely movement is impaired depends on the type and severity of the problem. Skeletal and joint disorders are the most common, but problems in the musculoskeletal system can also indicate diseases of the muscles, neurologic problems, toxins in the body, hormonal abnormalities, metabolic disorders, infectious diseases, blood and vascular disorders, poor nutrition, and birth defects.

Many different systems in the body rely on the muscles. A dog's ability to see, breathe, urinate, breed, and even chew and swallow may be affected a muscular condition. With many disorders, however, the musculoskeletal system is simply where signs of other underlying conditions show themselves. Veterinarians often trace the real cause of musculoskeletal trouble back to the nervous system, as in cases of tetanus or canine distemper.

Disorders that primarily affect the muscle membrane or muscle fibers are called **myopathies.** Muscle membrane disorders may be hereditary or acquired. Myopathies involving the actual muscle fiber compo-

nents include polymyositis (*see* page 188), and exertional myopathy (*see* page 189). Diagnosing a myopathy usually requires laboratory tests.

Tendons do not stretch, so they are prone to injury and may become torn if a large amount of force is applied to them. Such injuries lead to **tendinitis**, which is inflammation of the tendons. Because tendons and ligaments are relatively poorly supplied with blood, they heal slowly and sometimes imperfectly. Injuries to ligaments and tendons require patience and careful longterm rehabilitation.

Bone diseases are generally present at birth or the result of nutritional deficiencies or injuries. Inherited disorders include some cases of canine hip dysplasia or having extra toes (polydactyly). An imbalanced level of minerals in the diet, particularly of trace minerals such as copper, zinc, and magnesium, is a common dietary cause of **bone defects.** Growing animals that are fed too much protein can also develop nutritional disorders affecting bones. Getting either too much or too little of certain vitamins, particularly vitamins A and D, can influence bone growth and development.

Most **bone disorders** stem from some sort of trauma, such as fractures or cracks. Infections that cause bone tissue to break down and die can lead to bone disorders. In other situations, diseases of the ligaments or tendons may cause secondary bone troubles.

Movable joints are vulnerable to **joint diseases or disorders** affecting their membranes, as well as related ligaments, cartilage, and bone. Joint disorders may be caused by trauma to the joint, longterm inflammation, developmental problems, or infections. Traumatic injuries may produce short-term consequences such as dislocation, fracture, or the distortion of a joint. More longterm effects may include arthritis or the rupture of nearby ligaments or membranes.

Chronic or longterm inflammation is most commonly seen in joints associated with movement. The effects of longterm inflammation can be complicated. Any joint injury changes the composition and amount of fluid inside the joint, which affects the amount of pressure on the connecting bones. Injuries also raise the white blood cell count in a joint, which, over time, can break down cartilage.

Recent years have seen great advances in techniques for diagnosing and healing musculoskeletal disorders. When detected early, the disorders often can be corrected, allowing the animal a full return to healthy life.

▓ LAMENESS

Lameness is a sign of illness, not a specific disease. It may indicate a disorder in the musculoskeletal system. Signs of musculoskeletal disorders include weakness, lameness, limb swelling, and joint dysfunction. Nerve and muscle function may be impaired as a result of changes to neuromuscular tissues. Problems with the muscles and skeleton may also affect other organ systems, including the urinary, digestive, and circulatory systems.

The Lameness Examination

In order to diagnose the problem, your veterinarian will examine your dog and review any previous injuries and current overall health. A veterinarian performs a lameness examination in order to identify changes to musculoskeletal tissues. The veterinarian observes the animal resting, getting up, and walking. He or she watches to see if the injury affects one limb or several limbs and how the degree of reaction varies with each type of activity. If a forelimb is lame, the animal generally raises its head when putting weight on that limb. The stride is also shortened on the affected side. If a hindlimb is lame, the animal generally drops its head when putting weight on that limb. The veterinarian will feel the animal's bones, joints, and soft tissue for abnormalities such as swelling, pain, instability, a grating or crackling sound, reduced range of motion, and wasting away of muscle. More than one examination, sometimes with exercise in between, may be necessary. For irritable animals or certain tests, sedation may be required.

Imaging Techniques

Veterinarians may use imaging procedures to diagnose lameness. These include x-rays and ultrasonography, as well as less common techniques such as nuclear scintigraphy, computed tomography (CT), and magnetic resonance imaging (MRI). During these procedures, the veterinarian will probably use a heavy sedative or anesthesia to reduce your pet's pain and stress. (*See also* DIAGNOSTIC TESTS AND IMAGING, page 1070.)

Arthroscopy

Arthroscopy is a type of minor surgery in which a flexible tube called an endoscope is inserted into the joint through a small incision. It is relatively noninvasive and is used for diagnosis as well as treatment of lame animals. For diagnosis, the endoscope has a small camera attached to the end that allows the veterinarian to see the inside of the joint. The veterinarian is also able to remove dead or damaged cartilage or ligaments using the endoscope. This type of surgery allows for a shorter healing time than conventional surgery. Common conditions that can be diagnosed or treated by arthroscopy include osteochondrosis, tenosynovitis, joint fractures, and injuries to ligaments and cartilage.

Pain Management

Relieving pain is an important component of treatment for lame animals, and may allow faster recovery. As well, it is helpful for dogs with chronic conditions such as osteoarthritis. Nonsteroidal anti-inflammatory drugs and other pain-relieving drugs are used to control pain in lame animals. Other methods of pain relief that may be suggested in addition to (or instead of) drugs include acupuncture, massage, and changes in diet. Your veterinarian is best able to prescribe the appropriate treatment for your pet. It is very important that you follow all directions exactly as prescribed.

■ CONGENITAL AND INHERITED DISORDERS OF BONES, JOINTS, AND MUSCLES

Animals that contract viral infections in the womb may be born with diseased or deformed musculoskeletal systems. Abnormalities may also be congenital (present at birth) if a mother eats toxic plants at certain stages of the pregnancy. Some inherited (genetic) conditions affecting the musculoskeletal system may be neurologic in origin.

Dyschondroplasia

Dyschondroplasia in dogs is a hereditary skeletal disorder in which the bones of the limbs or trunk and head may be underdeveloped or deformed. Dyschondroplasia of the limbs is reported in Poodles and Scottish Terriers. The disorder may be seen in the trunk and head of Alaskan Malamutes, Basset Hounds, Dachshunds, Poodles, and Scottish Terriers. Malamutes with dyschondroplasia also have a deficiency of red blood cells (anemia). Among Basset Hounds, Dachshunds, and Pekingese, body characteristics produced by the disorder are an important feature of the breed type.

Dystrophy-like Myopathies

Numerous examples of progressive muscle diseases (myopathies) have been described in animals. They may be inherited, and many resemble various types of muscular dystrophy in humans.

Several types of muscular dystrophy are seen in dogs. One type (similar to Duchenne muscular dystrophy in humans) has been seen in Golden Retrievers in the United States and Irish Terriers in Europe. Male dogs are more likely to be affected. Signs include muscular weakening, difficulty swallowing, a stiff gait, and a loss of muscle mass. The disease is caused by the lack of a key protein required for normal functioning of muscle membranes. Some affected dogs have an accompanying heart muscle disease.

A second type of dystrophy affects Labrador Retrievers in North America, Europe, and Australia. Dogs with this type of dystrophy will show a stiff gait; they will resist exercise and begin to lose muscle mass as early as 6 months of age. Bouviers in Europe may develop another type of dystrophy that affects their ability to swallow.

Glycogen Storage Disease (Glycogenosis)

Glycogen is a complex carbohydrate that is normally stored in the liver and muscles. The body converts it to glucose (sugar) as a source of energy. Some animals with glycogen storage diseases progressively weaken until they are unable to rise from a lying position. To date, 5 of 8 types of glycogen storage diseases found in humans have also been found in animals. Affected species include dogs, cats, and horses. In particular, Type II glycogenosis has been reported in Lapland dogs.

Hip Dysplasia

Hip dysplasia is a common developmental disorder of the hip joints. The femur (the large bone of the upper leg) does not fit properly into the hip socket, which eventually leads to arthritis. An increased risk of the disorder can be inherited in many large breeds of dogs. (For a more detailed discussion of HIP DYSPLASIA, *see* page 184.)

Osteochondrosis

Osteochondrosis is most commonly seen in large and giant breeds of dogs. The condition affects bone formation in early stages of life, when the animal is growing at its fastest and the stress to the immature skeleton is greatest. In osteochondrosis, the immature joint cartilage may separate from the bone. This detached cartilage is left to float loosely in the joint cavity, where it can cause inflammation, cartilage debris, and further interference with proper bone formation. It most often affects the shoulder, elbow, and tarsal (ankle) joints, in decreasing order of frequency.

Osteogenesis Imperfecta

Dogs with osteogenesis imperfecta inherit very fragile bones and loose joints. The long bones (such as the major bones of the front and hind legs) tend to be slender with thin outer layers. A veterinarian diagnosing the condition looks for calluses on the bones that indicate recent breaks and fractures. The whites of the eyes of animals with osteogenesis imperfecta may also have a bluish tinge.

Osteopetrosis

A rare disease that appears to be inherited, osteopetrosis has been seen in dogs. Animals with osteopetrosis are stillborn 10 to 30 days before term. The condition produces a shortening of the lower jaw, impacted molar teeth, and easily broken long bones. Bone marrow cavities in the skull as well as the long bones fill with a spongy type of bone instead of marrow. The resultant thickening of the skull compresses the brain.

■ DISORDERS ASSOCIATED WITH CALCIUM, PHOSPHORUS, AND VITAMIN D

Defective bone formation is called osteodystrophy. It is caused in most cases by deficiencies or imbalances of calcium, phosphorus, and vitamin D, all of which are important in creating and maintaining strong, healthy bones.

The primary source of calcium and phosphorus is the diet, but a number of factors affect how the body absorbs calcium and phosphorus. These include the source of the minerals as well as the levels of vitamin D in the body. Vitamin D is obtained either through the diet or by exposure to sunlight. Because of the role it plays in the body, if the vitamin or its activity is decreased, calcium and phosphorus absorption are reduced. Abnormalities of the bones can result, as well as other nutritional and metabolic complications.

In general, supplementing a dog's diet with too much calcium or phosphorus can increase its susceptibility to diseases to which it is genetically prone. Specifically, giant-breed dogs fed excess calcium are more likely to develop osteochondrosis (page 184) and hypertrophic osteodystrophy (page 191).

Rickets

Rickets is a rare disease of young, growing animals that causes soft and deformed bones. It is commonly caused by insufficient phosphorus or vitamin D in the diet. More rarely, calcium deficiency is to blame. An excess of calcium has caused rickets-like signs in some dogs. As in most diets causing defective bone formation (osteodystrophies), the cause is typically an imbalance in the ratio of calcium to phosphorus in the diet. Animals fed all-meat diets commonly develop rickets.

Signs may include bone pain and swelling, a stiff gait or limp, difficulty in rising, bowed limbs, and fractures. Affected puppies may become quiet and reluctant to play. Touching the bones will cause pain, and folding fractures of long bones and vertebrae are common. In folding fractures, pressure on the bones causes them to slowly "fold" over and deform instead of fracturing. X-rays will show distortions in the bone. In advanced cases, limbs can be deformed due to the bones growing at unequal rates.

The outlook for treating rickets is good if there are no broken bones or irreversible damage to the bone. The primary treatment is to correct the diet. Exposure to sunlight (ultraviolet radiation) will also increase the production of vitamin D.

Recent studies show that many homemade diets for dogs are deficient in minerals and fail to achieve a proper calcium-to-phosphorus ratio. Therefore a high-quality commercial food, or one designed by a credentialed veterinary nutritionist, is recommended.

Adult Rickets (Osteomalacia)

Osteomalacia develops similarly to rickets but in mature bones. Because bones mature at different rates, both rickets and osteomalacia can be seen in the same animal.

Affected animals may fail to thrive or go into heat and may crave and eat substances such as paint chips, clay, plaster, or dirt. Fractures are most commonly found in the ribs, pelvis, and long bones (such as the main bones of the front and hind legs). Deformities may also be seen in the spine, including an abnormal inward curving of the spine in the lower area of the back (**lordosis**) or an abnormal outward curving of the spine (**kyphosis**).

To establish a firm diagnosis, veterinarians will evaluate a dog's diet to make sure it provides enough calcium, phosphorus, and vitamin D for healthy bones. X-rays will reveal the effects of severe osteomalacia on the skeleton.

Affected animals should be confined for the first few weeks while the diet is corrected. The response to proper nutrition is rapid. Within 1 week the animals become more active and show an improved attitude. Jumping or climbing must be prevented because the skeleton is still

susceptible to fractures. Restrictions can usually be relaxed after 3 weeks, but confinement with limited movement is recommended until the skeleton returns to normal. Response to treatment can be monitored using x-rays.

Rubber Jaw Syndrome (Fibrous Osteodystrophy)

Two metabolic disorders in dogs produce rubber jaw syndrome: primary hyperparathyroidism and hyperparathyroidism due to kidney disease.

Primary Hyperparathyroidism

In primary hyperparathyroidism, the parathyroid gland produces too much parathyroid hormone. This hormone controls the metabolism of calcium and phosphorus in the body (*see also* page 134). The disease occurs infrequently in older dogs.

When too much parathyroid hormone is released over a long period of time, minerals are leached from the skeleton and replaced by immature fibrous connective tissue. This condition, called **fibrous osteodystrophy**, affects the entire skeleton but tends to concentrate in the bones of the skull.

Dogs with primary hyperparathyroidism may become lame and develop fractures of the long bones after minor physical trauma. Compression fractures in the spine place pressure on the spinal cord, which may disable motor and sensory functions. In some cases the condition causes a thickening of facial bones. Nasal cavities may be damaged and teeth loosened. Some dogs lose the ability to close the mouth properly and develop slow-healing sores in the gums. Often the jawbones become coarsely thickened, while bones in the skull grow thin and appear "moth-eaten" in x-rays. The name "rubber jaw" syndrome refers to advanced cases in which the jaw can be twisted gently due to the degeneration of the bone.

Tests on animals with primary hyperparathyroidism will show an abnormally high level of calcium in the blood. Other tests can be performed to determine phosphorus and parathyroid hormone levels. Because abnormally high levels of calcium in the blood may be associated with many other diseases, an animal must be thoroughly examined before confirming a diagnosis of primary hyperparathyroidism.

The goal of treatment is to eliminate the source of excessive parathyroid hormone production. If a tumor is causing the increased parathyroid hormone levels, it must be removed. However, removing the source of the increased hormone production results in a rapid decrease in circulating hormone levels. Calcium levels can drop below normal within 12 to 24 hours after surgery, so the veterinarian must monitor levels closely and correct them if needed. If high levels of calcium persist a week or longer after surgery or recur after initial improvement, a second tumor or the spread of cancer from a malignant tumor may be causing the problem.

Hyperparathyroidism due to Kidney Disease

Hyperparathyroidism can be a complication of longterm kidney disease or kidney failure characterized by increased levels of parathyroid hormone. This type is more common than primary hyperparathyroidism (*see* page 181). With progressive kidney disease, excess phosphate in the blood lowers calcium levels. The lowered calcium level in turn triggers an increase in

parathyroid hormone levels. In addition, the kidneys are necessary to produce the active form of vitamin D (calcitriol). Too little calcitriol leads to further increases in parathyroid hormone levels.

Signs of hyperparathyroidism caused by kidney disease include the most common signs of kidney malfunction (vomiting, dehydration, excessive thirst and urination, and depression). Physical changes to the skeleton vary with the level of kidney malfunction from minor to severe. Severely defective fibrous bone formation may accompany advanced kidney failure. Excessive growth or thickening of bone tissue, such as facial swelling, may be seen in younger dogs.

While the entire skeleton may be affected, more dramatic changes are visible in the bones of the skull, particularly in the jaw. Jawbones become softened and pliable (known as "rubber jaw" syndrome). During early stages, the teeth may loosen and fall out, or interfere with chewing. The condition may prevent the proper closure of the jaw, resulting in drooling and causing the dog's tongue to stick out. Long bones are less dramatically affected, but lameness, stiff gait, and fractures after minor trauma may occur.

This type of hyperparathyroidism is diagnosed when laboratory test results show abnormalities consistent with kidney malfunction. Lab work will also reveal increased levels of parathyroid hormone in the blood.

Treatment options include modifying the diet, supplementing it with active vitamin D (calcitriol), and giving medication that binds phosphate. Any underlying kidney disease must be managed as well. Prescription diets with restricted dietary phosphorus are available. Your veterinarian can give you specific recommendations for proper treatment options for your pet. Be sure to follow those recommendations and any prescriptions precisely as directed.

Signs of Hyperparathyroidism Due to Kidney Disease

▓ Signs of kidney disease may be seen, including vomiting, dehydration, and increased thirst or urination.

▓ The jawbone may become soft and pliable.

▓ Teeth loosen and fall out.

▓ Growth or thickening of bones in the head may lead to facial swelling.

▓ Stiffness or lameness of the legs may occur.

▓ Fractures occur after minor trauma.

Hypoparathyroidism

In hypoparathyroidism (*see* page 135), either lower than normal amounts of parathyroid hormone are secreted or the hormone secreted is unable to function normally. This, in turn, affects the levels of calcium and phosphorus. Smaller breeds such as Miniature Schnauzers are particularly susceptible, but other breeds may be affected.

Various disorders can disable the secretion of parathyroid hormone. The parathyroid glands may be damaged or inadvertently removed during thyroid surgery. If adequate tissue remains, however, glands will often regenerate following damage, eliminating the signs.

Affected dogs are restless, nervous, and unable to control muscle movements. They may appear weak and have intermittent tremors that become convulsions. Longterm hypoparathyroidism can also cause abnormal hardening of certain parts of the body (such as ligaments), decreased mental function, cataracts, and reduction in bone volume.

To diagnose this disorder, a veterinarian will look for signs and the results of laboratory tests. Blood tests may show lowered calcium levels and higher than normal phosphorus levels. How well an animal responds to treatment may affect the diagnosis.

The prolonged contraction of muscles should be treated initially by restoring blood calcium levels to near normal. A veterinarian can accomplish this by giving calcium gluconate through the vein. Longterm maintenance of blood calcium levels is necessary if parathyroid hormone secretion is impaired. This can be attempted with a diet high in calcium, low in phosphorus, and supplemented with calcium and vitamin D_3. Your veterinarian will be able to advise you as to the appropriate treatment options.

■ JOINT DISORDERS

Some joint diseases, such as arthritis, affect the joint membranes themselves. Other types of joint conditions affect the tendons, cartilage, bursae, and fluid within the joint. Joint disorders may be congenital (present at birth) or may be the result of injury to the joint, abnormal development, immune-related conditions, or infections.

Legg-Calvé-Perthes Disease

This deterioration of the top of the femur (femoral head) seen in young miniature and small breeds of dogs is characterized by a lack of blood supply and destruction of blood vessels of the bone. The cause is unknown, although the condition may be hereditary in Manchester Terriers. The sudden loss of blood supply to the femur leads to collapse of the top of the bone.

Signs include hindlimb lameness, wasting away of the thigh muscles, and pain during movement of the hip joint. Longterm cases have evidence of degenerative joint disease. X-rays can help identify characteristic changes of this condition and may be used to confirm the diagnosis. Treatment involves surgical removal of the affected femoral head and neck and physical therapy to stimulate limb usage. If these procedures are followed, most animals with this condition recover.

Displacement of the Kneecap

This hereditary disorder is caused by abnormal development of the kneecap (patella). Displacement of the kneecap is often associated with multiple deformities of the hindlimb, involving the hip joint, femur, and tibia. Affected animals are lame or walk with a skipping gait. Dogs of any age may be affected.

Signs vary widely based on the severity of the displacement. In mild cases, the kneecap can be manually displaced but easily returned to normal position. As displacement becomes more severe, the dislocated kneecap is more often out of place, the limb is consistently lame, and bone deformities may be seen. X-rays can help your veterinarian see how severely the kneecap is displaced and what effects this has had on the limb.

There are several surgical options for treatment. The type of surgery performed is based on the severity of the displacement and can range from minor procedures to limb amputation. Mild or moderately affected dogs generally recover fully.

Osteochondrosis

Osteochondrosis is a disturbance in cartilage and bone formation of medium and large dogs that grow quickly. In this condition, the immature joint cartilage separates from the underlying bone. Fluid enters the space, and cysts may form under the cartilage. Fragments of cartilage may separate from the end of a bone and float loose in the joint cavity. This results in inflammation of the affected joint, and it can lead to arthritis and continued cartilage breakdown, severely affecting joint motion. The cause is unknown, but possible factors include high-growth diets, as well as rapid growth, trauma, and heredity.

Signs of osteochondrosis include lameness, fluid buildup within the joint, and joint stiffness. Affected areas include the head of the shoulder joint, the inside of the elbow joint, the stifle (knee) joints, and the ridges of the hock joints. Your veterinarian may use x-rays to determine the extent of the damage. Surgery using an endoscope can also be performed to identify cartilage or joint lesions.

Treatment involves surgical removal of cartilage flaps or the free-floating fragments of cartilage known as joint mice. Dogs with degenerative joint disease may benefit from nonsteroidal anti-inflammatory drugs and joint fluid modifiers. Your veterinarian is best able to advise you on the appropriate use of any relevant medication. The outlook for recovery is excellent for the shoulders, good for the stifle joint, and fair for the elbow and hock (tarsal) joints. If the affected dog also has signs of degenerative joint disease, other joint conditions, or instability of the hock joint, the chances of recovery are reduced.

Elbow Dysplasia

Elbow dysplasia is an abnormal development of the elbow joint in young, large, rapidly growing dogs. It involves abnormal bone growth, cartilage development, or joint stresses. It is considered to be one of the most common causes of osteoarthritis of the canine elbow.

Lameness can develop slowly between 4 and 8 months of age; however, some cases may not be diagnosed until the dogs are more than 1 year old. The joint may appear stiff or unable to move freely. Advanced cases develop osteoarthritis, fluid buildup within the joint, and a grating or crackling sound. Physical examination and the presence of the characteristic signs suggest the diagnosis, and x-rays can confirm it. Both elbows should be examined because the condition can develop in both at the same time.

Surgery should be performed before the degenerative changes of osteoarthritis occur. The outlook for recovery after surgery is good if degenerative joint disease has not developed in the joint. Aspirin or nonsteroidal anti-inflammatory drugs (as prescribed by your veterinarian) can reduce pain and inflammation. Joint fluid modifiers may also be helpful.

Hip Dysplasia

Hip dysplasia is an abnormal development of the hip joint in large dogs. It is characterized by a loose joint and subsequent degenerative joint disease (osteoarthritis). Excessive growth, exercise, nutrition, and hereditary factors affect the occurrence of hip dysplasia.

The signs associated with hip dysplasia vary. Lameness may be mild, moderate, or severe, and is worse after exercise. The dog may walk with a "bunny-hopping" gait. A loose joint, reduced range of motion or stiffness of the joint, and a grating sound and pain during full extension and bending of the joint may be present. X-rays are useful in determining the degree of arthritis and planning treatments.

Both medical and surgical treatments are available. Dogs that have a mild case of hip dysplasia or that cannot undergo surgery due to health or owner constraints may benefit from other treatments. These include weight reduction, restriction of exercise on hard surfaces, physical therapy, anti-inflammatory drugs, and possibly joint fluid modifiers. Surgical treatments can include a range of procedures from reducing pain and arthritis to total hip replacement.

The outlook for recovery varies greatly and depends on the overall health, degree of dysplasia and joint damage, and environment of the animal. Surgery is generally beneficial if recommended and performed correctly. Dogs that do not undergo surgery may require lifestyle changes in order to be comfortable.

Osteoarthritis (Degenerative Joint Disease)

The joint cartilage in freely moving joints may degenerate over time, leading to loss of joint movement and, in many cases, pain. This condition is characterized by thinning of cartilage, buildup of fluid within the joint, and the formation of bony outgrowths around the joint. Joint degeneration can be caused by trauma, infection, the body's own immune system, or malformation during development. This leads to inflammation of the joint membrane, continued cartilage destruction and inflammation, and abnormal joint function.

Signs of osteoarthritis include lameness, joint swelling, wasting away of muscle, and thickening and scarring of the joint membrane. Eventually enough damage can occur that a grating sound might be heard during joint movement. X-rays show increased fluid within the joint, soft-tissue swelling around the joint, the formation of bony outgrowths, hardening and thickening of bone beneath the cartilage, and sometimes a narrowed joint space.

Treatments can be either medical or surgical. Medical treatment may include the use of nonsteroidal anti-inflammatory drugs to reduce pain and inflammation. However, longterm use of these drugs in dogs can sometimes cause gastrointestinal problems such as lack of appetite, vomiting, and inflammation of the stomach and intestines. Corticosteroids also suppress

inflammation, but they are usually given only for a short period in order to avoid adverse effects of continued use. Your veterinarian will prescribe appropriate medication based on your dog's signs, age, and overall health.

Surgical options include joint fusion, joint replacement, cutting of the joint, and amputation. The outlook for recovery depends on the location and severity of the joint disease.

Other treatments that might be considered include weight reduction, carefully monitored exercise on soft surfaces, and application of warm compresses to affected joints. Joint-fluid modifiers may help prevent further cartilage degradation.

Septic Arthritis

Infectious, or septic, arthritis is usually caused by bacteria that spread through the blood or enter the body as a result of trauma (with penetrating wounds) or surgery. Other causes of septic arthritis include rickettsia (Rocky Mountain spotted fever, ehrlichiosis) and spirochetes (Lyme disease). (*See also* INFECTIONS, page 1078.)

Signs of septic arthritis include lameness, swelling, pain of affected joint(s), fever, listlessness, loss of appetite, and stiffness. X-rays may reveal increased fluid within the joint in early cases and degenerative joint disease in longterm conditions. Laboratory tests on fluid removed from the joint may be useful in confirming the diagnosis.

Treatment consists of antibiotics administered orally or intravenously, flushing of the joint cavity, and surgical removal of dead, damaged or infected tissue in severe cases.

Immune-mediated Arthritis

Arthritis caused by the body's own immune system can cause inflammation of joints. It generally affects several joints. In some types of immune-mediated arthritis, joint cartilage and bone beneath the cartilage is destroyed. **Rheumatoid arthritis** (page 172) and **Greyhound polyarthritis** are examples of arthritis that destroys joint cartilage and bone beneath the cartilage. **Systemic lupus erythematosus** (page 171) is the most common form of arthritis that causes inflammation of the joint.

Signs include lameness, pain, and swelling in multiple joints, fever, a generalized illness, and persistent loss of appetite. These signs commonly come and go. In addition to signs, the diagnosis is aided by x-rays, biopsy of joint tissue, and examination of joint fluid (commonly called a joint tap).

Treatment involves anti-inflammatory medications and chemotherapeutic agents. The outlook for recovery is uncertain. Relapses are relatively common and the cause of the reactions is often unknown.

Cancerous Arthritis

This type of arthritis is most commonly caused by a tumor known as a **synovial cell sarcoma**. It is the most common cancerous (malignant) tumor involving the joints. Signs include lameness and joint swelling. X-rays show soft-tissue swelling and a reaction around the bone. A biopsy reveals evidence of a soft-tissue tumor. Spread of the cancer to the lungs occurs in about 25% of animals; thus, amputation of the limb is usually recommended to prevent spreading.

Joint Trauma

There are many types of joint trauma that can contribute to the development of joint disorders. Some of the more common types of trauma that can affect the joints are discussed below.

Cranial Cruciate Ligament Tear

Tearing of the cranial cruciate ligament of the stifle (knee) joint is usually caused by serious injury. However injuries are more likely to occur when the joint structure is already weakened by degeneration, the animal's own immune system, or defects in conformation (such as those seen in straight-legged dogs). Most injuries involve a tear in the middle of the ligament, although some result from bone separation at the origin of the ligament. A tear of this

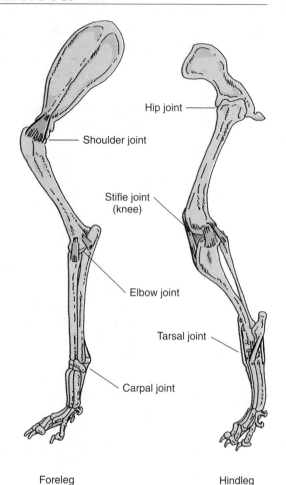

Key joints in a dog's leg

Hip joint

Shoulder joint

Stifle joint (knee)

Elbow joint

Tarsal joint

Carpal joint

Foreleg   Hindleg

type can make the stifle joint unstable and can lead to cartilage injury, buildup of joint fluid, bony outgrowths, and hardening and thickening of the joint membrane.

Signs include those generally seen in joint disorders, such as lameness, pain, joint swelling, fluid buildup, and a grating sound when the joint is moved. In addition, the joint may appear to be abnormally loose. Partial cranial crucial ligament tears are characterized by a reduced ability to move the joint, especially bending it. Cartilage injury may be identified by a clicking sound during movement or when the joint is bent and extended. X-rays may show the injury and/or damage to the joint; testing of fluid removed from the joint may also be used to help diagnose the condition.

Both medical and surgical treatment options are available. Physical therapy, weight reduction, and nonsteroidal anti-inflammatory drugs ease discomfort from inflammation and degenerative joint disease. For active dogs, surgery to stabilize the knee joint is recommended. Physical therapy following surgery is critical for recovery. The outlook after surgery is good as long as degenerative joint disease has not progressed too far.

Dislocation and Fracture of the Ankle

Injury to the ankle (tarsus) is often seen in dogs that have been hit by a car. The ankle in dogs includes several bones that connect the lower leg to the foot. Injuries may include fracture or dislocation of these bones or tearing of the ligaments that hold them together. Affected dogs will hold the injured leg up and refuse to put any weight on it. The foot may swing in unusual directions because of its loose attachment following the injury. The extent of the injury is confirmed by physical examination and x-rays. Treatment is surgery to repair the bones and ligaments. The outlook for recovery is good.

Dislocation of the Elbow

Elbow dislocation is usually the result of trauma and is a common injury in dogs. Pain is variable, and the dog will usually hold the injured leg up and refuse to put any weight on it. Physical examination and x-rays are used to diagnose the condition. Treatment generally requires surgery, but the outlook for recovery is excellent.

Dislocation of the Hip

Hip dislocation is usually the result of injury or trauma that displaces the head of the femur from the socket of the hip joint. Signs of hip dislocation include lameness, pain during movement of the hip joint, and a shortened limb. X-rays are useful in confirming the dislocation and revealing the presence of fractures. Nonsurgical treat-

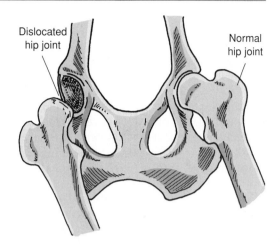

A normal and a dislocated hip joint of a dog

ment involves forcefully moving the joint back into place (closed manipulation) and using slings to keep the hip in its normal position. Surgical treatment involves stabilization using sutures or pins. Surgical resection of the bones involved or total hip replacement may be performed if more conservative treatment has not succeeded. The outlook for recovery is usually excellent.

Joint Fractures

The shoulder, elbow, carpal, hip, stifle, and tarsal joints are those most commonly involved in fractures due to injury. In young animals, the portion of the bone where growth occurs—called the growth plate and usually located at the ends of the bones—is weak compared with adjacent bones, ligaments, and joint membranes, making this area more prone to injury.

Signs of joint fractures include lameness, pain, and joint swelling. If the injury affects an active growth plate, limb deformities can result. X-rays are used to confirm and locate the fracture.

The goal of treatment is to allow the fracture to heal in proper alignment while maintaining joint and limb functions. This is usually done by holding the fracture in place internally with pins, wires, or screws in order to stabilize it. The outlook for recovery is good as long as damage to the joint is not severe.

Palmar Carpal Ligament Breakdown

Injuries sustained when falling or jumping can cause hyperextension, in which the limb extends beyond its normal range of motion. This produces excessive force on the wrist (carpus), which can cause tearing of the palmar carpal ligaments and fibrocartilage, leading to collapse of the joints. Signs include lameness, swelling of the carpal joint, and a characteristic stance in which the heel is touching the ground. For mild cases a splint or cast may be sufficient, but surgery is usually required. Surgery involves fusing the affected joints using a bone plate and screws, pins and wires, or an external system. The outlook for recovery is good.

MUSCLE DISORDERS

Myopathies are diseases that primarily cause damage to muscles or muscle tissues. They may be present at birth or occur due to nutritional imbalances, injury, or ingestion of a poisonous substance. **Myositides** are diseases that produce a mainly inflammatory reaction in muscle. Common causes include infections, parasitic diseases, and immune-mediated conditions.

Type II Muscle Fiber Deficiency

Type II muscle fiber deficiency is a muscle disease of unknown cause that is present at birth in some Labrador Retrievers. The condition appears to be inherited and has been known to occur in both yellow and black Labradors. Signs become noticeable at less than 5 months of age and include wasting away of muscle, stunted growth, and weakness. These signs progressively worsen until the animal reaches maturity (between 6 and 12 months), when they stabilize. Animals may have a normal life span. A definite diagnosis usually requires a urine test, muscle biopsy, and electromyography. There is no effective treatment.

Fibrotic Myopathy

Fibrotic myopathy is an uncommon progressive disorder that leads to degeneration of the thigh muscles. The cause is not known, but German Shepherds appear to be predisposed to developing the condition. Affected muscles are characterized by a permanent, abnormal tightening. Normal tissues are replaced by thick connective tissue. Other signs include lameness without pain. Surgery is only sometimes helpful. The outlook for recovery is guarded because signs can recur.

Myositis Ossificans

Myositis ossificans is a muscle disorder in which noncancerous bony deposits appear in the muscles and connective tissue. The cause is unknown. The disorder frequently affects tissues near the hip joint in Doberman Pinschers. It may be related to a bleeding disorder (von Willebrand's disease) in these dogs. Surgical removal of the bony mass is usually helpful.

Polymyositis

Polymyositis is an inflammatory muscle disorder in adult dogs that affects the entire body. It may be associated with immune-mediated disorders such as lupus erythematosus or myasthenia gravis. The condition can have a sudden onset, or it may be recurring and progressive. Signs include depression, lack of energy, weakness, weight loss, lameness, muscle tenderness or pain, and wasting away of muscle. Corticosteroids are generally recommended for treatment; however, other drugs that suppress the immune system may also be used. The outlook for recovery is favorable, although signs sometimes reappear.

Masticatory Myositis

Masticatory myositis is an inflammatory condition that affects the muscles used to chew. The exact cause is unknown, although the body's own immune response plays a role. In acute cases, muscles are swollen and the dog has difficulty opening the jaw. In chronic cases, signs include persistent loss of appetite, weight loss, difficulty opening the jaw, and wasting away of muscle. Blood tests, electromyography, and a muscle biopsy may help to confirm the diagnosis. Although the condition sometimes improves on its own, treatment with corticosteroids given by mouth is recommended in most cases. Relapses are common, and longterm medication may be required.

Malignant Hyperthermia

Malignant hyperthermia is a disorder of skeletal muscle usually brought on by certain types of inhaled anesthesia and stress. It is characterized by an abnormal increase in metabolic rate. Although the condition is most common in pigs, it is also known to occur in some heavily muscled dogs (particularly Greyhounds).

Signs include rapid heartbeat, increased breathing rate, fever, muscle tightness and rigidity, and heart and lung failure. Signs develop between 5 and 30 minutes after exposure to the anesthetic agent. Treatment requires immediately stopping the anesthesia and administering oxygen. Fluid injections, corticosteroids, ice packs, and muscle relaxants are also used. The outlook is poor in severe cases.

Exertional Myopathy (Rhabdomyolysis)

This muscle disorder of racing Greyhounds and working dogs is caused by overuse. It appears to be triggered by an inadequate supply of blood to the muscle after exercise or excitement. This can cause kidney disease and destruction of muscle cells. Signs include muscle pain and swelling that becomes noticeable 24 to 72 hours after racing or overuse. In severe cases, stiffness, deep or fast breathing, collapse, and kidney failure may occur. Urine tests are used to confirm the diagnosis. Treatment includes supportive care such as fluid injection, bicarbonate, body cooling, rest, and muscle relaxants. The outlook for recovery depends on the severity of the case.

Muscular or Tendon Trauma

Injury (trauma) of the muscles and the associated tendons can cause many forms of myopathy in dogs.

Abnormal Contracture of the Shoulder Muscle

Abnormal tightening or contracture of the shoulder muscle (infraspinatus) is a muscle disease that affects one or both shoulders. It usually occurs after trauma in hunting or working dogs. Signs include noticeable lameness, pain, and swelling in the shoulder region. The lameness is temporary, but an abnormal gait develops 2 to 4 weeks after injury as the muscles thicken and tighten. Other signs include the pulling in of the elbow towards the body, pulling away of the foreleg from the body, and external rotation of the carpus and paw. The limb is moved in a circular motion with each stride of the leg. Treatment consists of the surgical removal of a portion of the muscle, including cutting of a tendon. Limb and joint functions usually improve immediately following surgery, and the outlook for full recovery is excellent.

Inflammation of the Biceps Brachii Tendon and Its Covering

Inflammation of the biceps brachii tendon and its covering (sheath) due to injury can occur in one or both forelimbs. It usually affects mature, large dogs. The injury may be direct, indirect, or due to overuse or migration of bone and cartilage fragments called **joint mice** (*see* OSTEOCHONDROSIS, page 184).

Persistent lameness that may worsen over time is one sign of this condition. The lameness also worsens after exercise and improves with rest. The shoulder joint's range of motion is reduced, and the shoulder muscles may waste away. Applying pressure to the biceps tendon while bending and extending the shoulder joint causes severe pain. X-rays and ultrasonography are often used to help confirm the diagnosis. Surgical inspection using an endoscope can help your veterinarian determine the extent of the injury.

In mild cases, the recommended treatments are rest and nonsteroidal anti-inflammatory drugs given by mouth. Severe cases can be treated with injections of an anti-inflammatory agent and rest. Chronic cases that are resistant to treatment of multiple corticosteroid injections or cases involving joint mice are treated through surgery. The outlook for recovery is good, although severe degeneration in longterm cases may cause lameness to persist after treatment.

Quadriceps Contracture (Stiff Stifle Disease)

This serious thickening and tightening of the quadriceps muscles develops after improperly performed surgical operations on young dogs to repair fractures of the femur. The bone, the connective tissue surrounding the bone, and the quadriceps muscles bond together. This leads to extension and disuse of the limb, porous and easily broken bones (osteoporosis), osteoarthritis, and bone and joint deformations. The affected limb is overextended and often displaced. Surgery is usually required to remove the fibrous tissues that connect the bone and muscles and to restore motion in the stifle joint. Reconstruction of bone and soft tissues should be followed by application of bandages that restrict mobility of the joint. Physical therapy is usually required after surgery. The outlook for recovery is guarded. Careful surgical repair of bone fractures can help prevent this condition.

Achilles Tendon Disruption (Dropped Hock)

This injury to the common Achilles tendon most often afflicts fully grown working and athletic dogs. It is usually the result of trauma. The tendon can be partially or completely ruptured or torn away from the bone. Signs include a severe lameness that keeps the animal from putting weight on the leg, overextension of the tarsus, and a stance in which the heel touches the ground. Swelling, pain, and torn or thickened tendon ends may also be seen. X-rays are useful for diagnosis and may reveal fragments torn from the bone.

Surgical treatment can repair the torn ends and reattach the tendon to the bone. External splints are generally used after surgery to immobilize the joint for several weeks. The outlook for recovery varies, based on the duration of the injury, the success of the surgery, and the dog's expected performance when healthy.

Muscle Tumors

Tumors that originate in the skeletal muscle can be benign or cancerous (malignant). Malignant tumors can spread and invade nearby muscle. They can also spread to other parts of the body.

Signs include localized swelling and lameness. The diagnosis is confirmed by taking a small tissue sample called a biopsy. The tumor generally must be surgically removed or the limb amputated. Chemotherapy and radiation may be used depending on the type of tumor. (*See also* CANCER AND TUMORS, page 1233.)

▪ BONE DISORDERS

Bone disorders can be developmental, infectious, nutritional, or due to bone tumors, trauma, or unknown causes.

Developmental Bone Disorders

Developmental bone disorders appear in young animals when the bones do not grow correctly. They may be congenital (present at birth) or occur as the animal grows. Some of the more common causes include hereditary breed characteristics and dietary imbalances.

Angular Limb Deformities

Abnormal development of the bones of the foreleg (the radius and ulna) can occur after injury to growth plates. It may also be hereditary in some breeds (such as Bulldogs, Pugs, Boston Terriers, Basset Hounds, and Dachshunds). Irregular growth of the 2 bones leads to shortened limbs, bowing of the bones, partial displacement of the elbow joint, and bending or twisting of the carpus.

This condition results in lameness. Movement of the elbow or carpal joints is pain-

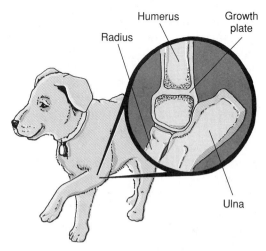

Humerus

Growth plate

Radius

Ulna

Growth plates are found near the ends of bones in young animals.

ful, and range of motion is reduced. X-rays may reveal the extent of bone deformity.

Treatment is based on correcting the position, shape, and length of the limb, and reestablishing normal joint movement. Surgical procedures include corrective surgery and stabilization with internal or external braces. The outlook for recovery is good as long as the limb deformities are not severe.

Craniomandibular Osteopathy

Craniomandibular osteopathy is a bone disorder of growing dogs that affects the lower jaw (mandible) and the round bones behind the ears (tympanic bullae) of Terrier breeds. Certain portions of the normal bone are resorbed and replaced by immature bone. The cause is unknown, but it is probably genetic.

Signs may vary widely. They include mouth discomfort, weight loss, fever, and painful enlargement of the lower jaw. X-rays are used to confirm the diagnosis. Treatment may involve the prescription of appropriate pain relievers or corticosteroids to reduce inflammation and discomfort. A soft-food diet is usually recommended. The outlook for recovery is good, because the bone growth stops when the animal matures.

Hypertrophic Osteodystrophy

This disorder affects the areas where growth occurs in the long bones of young, growing dogs, usually of large or giant breeds. The exact cause is unknown, although feeding puppies a diet that is very high in protein and/or calories may play a role.

Signs include pain and swelling in the radius and ulna, fever, loss of appetite, and depression. Affected dogs may be lame and reluctant to move. These signs may come and go. Deformities may develop in severely affected dogs.

Treatment is aimed at relieving pain; for example, nonsteroidal anti-inflammatory drugs may be prescribed. Supportive fluid care and dietary changes (as recommended by a veterinarian) may also be helpful.

Osteochondromatosis (Multiple Exostoses)

Osteochondromatosis is an uncommon disorder of young dogs characterized by multiple bony growths (known as osteochondromas) that arise from the surface of the long bones, vertebrae, and ribs. Animals may have no signs, and diagnosis is confirmed by x-rays and physical examination of the growths. If lameness or pain develops, the masses can be surgically removed.

Panosteitis

Panosteitis causes bone inflammation, primarily of the long bones, in young, rapidly growing dogs of large and giant breeds. The inflammation may involve single or multiple bones. It appears spontaneously and lasts only as long as the dog is growing, whether or not it is treated. The exact cause is unknown, although some factors thought to play a role include genetics (in German Shepherds), stress, infection, or the body's own metabolic and immune responses.

The condition generally affects dogs 6 to 16 months old. Animals are lame and feverish, have no appetite, and show signs of pain when the affected bones are handled. These signs may come and go. X-rays are used to confirm the diagnosis. Treatment is aimed at relieving pain and discomfort.

Nonsteroidal anti-inflammatory drugs or corticosteroids as prescribed by a veterinarian can be used when signs are present. Although it is uncertain whether diets high in protein and calories or dietary supplementation play a role in the development of this condition, it is suggested that such diets be avoided in young, growing dogs.

Retained Ulnar Cartilage Cores

Retained ulnar cartilage cores is a disorder of the growth plate of the ulna in young large and giant dogs. Abnormal bone formation, in which bone does not harden appropriately, occurs. As a result, bone growth is restrained in the affected forelimb. The exact cause is uncertain, although diet may play a role.

Signs include lameness and angular limb deformities (*see* page 190). X-rays are useful to confirm the diagnosis. Dietary supplementation should be stopped, and appropriate nutrition discussed with your veterinarian. Surgical division or removal of the bone may also be necessary to reduce limb deformation. The outlook for recovery is based on the severity of the condition.

Osteomyelitis

Osteomyelitis is inflammation of the bone. The condition is most often associated with bacterial infection, although fungal diseases may also cause osteomyelitis. Factors contributing to infection include an inadequate blood supply to the bone, trauma, inflammation, bone damage, and the spread of an infectious agent through the bloodstream.

General signs of osteomyelitis include lameness and pain. Dogs may have pus-filled sores at the wound site, fever, persistent lack of appetite, and depression. X-rays, laboratory tests, and cultures to identify the source of infection can all help to confirm the diagnosis.

Longterm treatment with antibiotics, either injected or given by mouth, is the usual treatment. Additionally, flushing of the wound; removal of dead, damaged, or infected tissue; and removal of loose implants are recommended. Open or closed wound drainage and bone grafting can also be performed. In persistent cases, limb amputation may be necessary. The outlook for recovery varies based on the severity of the infection and on how long it has remained untreated.

Hypertrophic Osteopathy

Hypertrophic osteopathy is excessive thickening or growth of bone tissues of long bones in dogs occurring after tumors or infectious masses develop in the chest or abdominal cavity. The exact cause is unknown, but may be related to a reduced flow to blood to the bones.

Signs include lameness, long-bone pain, and signs of body cavity tumors. X-rays are used to reveal the primary tumors and bone reactions. Treatment includes chest or abdominal surgery to remove tumors and the surgical cutting of the nerve to block the associated bone changes.

Nutritional Osteopathies

(*See also* DISORDERS ASSOCIATED WITH CALCIUM, PHOSPHORUS, AND VITAMIN D, page 180.)

Reduced bone mass, bone deformities, bony growths, fractures, and loose teeth (rubber jaw) are all conditions that can result from nutritional disturbances. These disturbances affect parathyroid hormone function and the metabolism of calcium and vitamins in the body. Specific causes may include an unbalanced diet resulting in an abnormally high level of parathyroid hormone (secondary nutritional hyperparathyroidism) or an abnormally high level of parathyroid hormone causing kidney damage (renal hyperparathyroidism), a deficiency of vitamin D, and excessive intake of vitamin A. Diagnosis is by blood tests, x-rays, and identification of any underlying nutritional cause. Treatment is aimed at reversing the specific cause. Surgery is rarely needed.

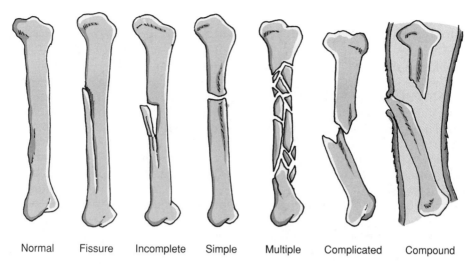

| Normal | Fissure | Incomplete | Simple | Multiple | Complicated | Compound |

Fracture types can range from incomplete to compound.

Bone Tumors

Skeletal tumors can be benign or malignant (cancerous). They can either begin in the bone or spread from other areas of the body. The most common primary bone tumor is osteosarcoma of the radius, humerus, femur, or tibia.

Signs include lameness, bone swelling, and fractures of the bone that are not caused by injury. X-rays of the affected limb can help confirm the diagnosis. Chest x-rays should be performed to look for any original tumors that may be spreading to the bones. A bone biopsy is required to confirm the diagnosis.

The outlook for recovery is guarded. Untreated animals rarely live more than several months. The recommended treatments are limb amputation and chemotherapy, which in many cases can double survival times. On average, dogs live for 5 months after amputation.

Bone Fractures

Bone fractures are often caused by car accidents, firearms, fights, or falls. Fractures can involve single or multiple breaks in the bone and may be open (also called compound) or closed. Open fractures have a wound or break in the skin that is

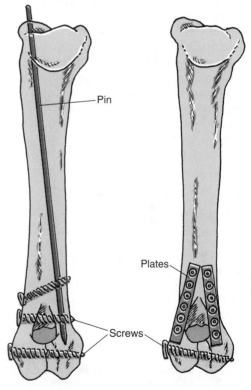

Common treatments for bone fractures involve the use of bone plates, screws, orthopedic wires, and pins (This figure was published in *Saunders Manual of Small Animal Practice*, 2nd edition, Birchard SJ, Sherding RG, page 1108, Copyright Saunders, 2000).

associated with the fracture; closed fractures are those that do not produce an open wound. The shape and severity of the fracture depends on the force and type of the trauma. (*See also* EMERGENCIES, page 1050.)

Signs of fracture are general and include lameness, pain, and swelling. X-rays are useful in determining the type and extent of the fracture. Treatment is based on the type of fracture, the dog's age and health, the owner's finances, and the surgeon's technical expertise.

Incomplete fractures in young, healthy dogs can be treated with external splints or casts. Other injuries are treated with bone plates, screws, orthopedic wires, or pins. Bone grafts are frequently used to help healing. Antibiotics are given to keep open fractures from becoming infected. Appropriate pain-relieving medication is used to reduce discomfort.

The outlook for recovery is usually good, depending on the injury and the success of the surgery. Followup care includes x-rays and veterinary checkups to assess how the fracture is healing. Removal of internal implants like bone plates or screws is not necessary unless complications such as stress protection, infection, and soft-tissue irritation develop.

◾ SARCOCYSTOSIS

In sarcocystosis, the muscles and other soft tissues are invaded by single-celled organisms, called protozoans, of the genus *Sarcocystis*. Although their final hosts are predators such as dogs and cats, these organisms form cysts in various intermediate hosts, including cattle, pigs, humans, rodents, and reptiles. Some cysts are visible to the naked eye, but others are too small to see. Their size depends on the species of the host and the species of *Sarcocystis*. A dog can develop sarcocystosis after eating undercooked beef or pork containing sporocysts or after eating food infected with sporocysts from another animal's feces. Infected dogs often have no signs, although a mild diarrhea may be seen.

As noted above, humans may serve as intermediate hosts and can develop inflammation and soreness of muscles and blood vessels. This condition is rare, and the source of human infection has never been determined. Signs include nausea, abdominal pain, and diarrhea lasting up to 48 hours. The extent of human illness caused by infected meat has not been documented.

Because most adult cattle and sheep and many pigs harbor cysts in their muscles, dogs should not be allowed to eat raw meat, edible organs (such as heart, liver, tongue, and brains), or dead animals. Supplies of grain and feed should be kept covered. Dogs should not be allowed in buildings used to store feed or house animals. There are no available vaccines. Experiments have shown that infected pork can be made safe for consumption by cooking at 158°F (70°C) for 15 minutes or by freezing at 25°F (-4°C) for 2 days or -4°F (-20°C) for 1 day.

CHAPTER **13**

Brain, Spinal Cord, and Nerve Disorders

◾ THE NERVOUS SYSTEM

The nervous system is made up of the brain, spinal cord, and several different kinds of nerves that are found throughout the body. These create complex circuits through which animals experience and respond to sensations.

A familiar type of nervous system circuit is a reflex. Reflexes are simple networks found in the nervous system of all animals. For example, when the eyelid is

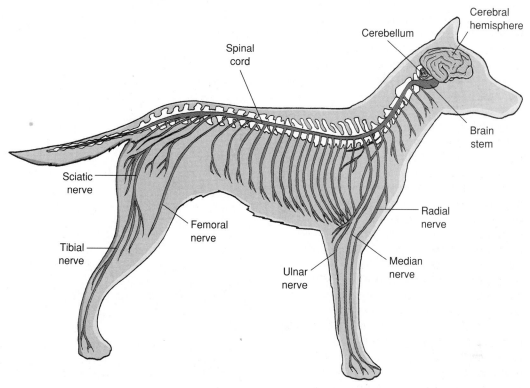

The nervous system of the dog

touched, it closes; when the toe is pinched, the foot pulls away "automatically."

Many different types of diseases can affect the nervous system, including birth defects, infections, inflammatory conditions, poisoning, metabolic disorders, nutritional disorders, injuries, degenerative diseases, or cancer. Neurologic diseases are often more common in a particular breed or sex, or tend to occur at a certain age.

■ PARTS OF THE NERVOUS SYSTEM

The **central nervous system** includes the spinal cord and the brain. The brain is divided into 3 main sections—the **brain stem**, which controls many basic life functions, the **cerebrum**, which is the center of conscious decision-making, and the **cerebellum**, which is involved in movement and motor control. The spinal cord of dogs is divided into regions that correspond to the vertebral bodies (the bones that make up the spine) in the following order from neck to tail: cervical, thoracic, lumbar, sacral, and caudal segments. Specialized tissues called the **meninges** cover the brain and spinal cord, and cerebrospinal fluid surrounds and protects the brain and spinal cord.

The **peripheral nervous system** consists of the nerves that are found throughout the rest of the body.

Neurons

Both the central and peripheral nervous systems contain billions of cells known as neurons. Neurons connect with each other to form neurological circuits. Information travels along these circuits via electrical signals.

All neurons have a center portion called a **cell body** and 2 extensions called **dendrites** and **axons**. Dendrites receive signals from other neurons and transmit electrical charges *to* the cell body. Axons transmit the electrical charges *away* from the cell body. When the current reaches the end of the axon, the axon releases chemicals called **neurotransmitters**. Neurotransmitters pass the signal to the dendrites of other neurons, or to muscles or glands.

Neurons in the peripheral nervous system combine to form pairs of **spinal nerves** and pairs of **cranial nerves**. The spinal nerves arise from the spinal cord and extend axons outward into the front and hind legs and to the bladder, anus, and tail. These nerves subdivide into smaller nerves that cover the entire surface and interior of the body. The cranial nerves include sensory and motor neurons that connect the head and face to the brain.

Types of Neurons

Sensory neurons carry information from the body to the spinal cord or brain stem, and then on to the cerebellum and cerebrum for interpretation. Sensory information includes sensations of pain, position, touch, temperature, taste, hearing, balance, vision, and smell.

Motor neurons carry responses to the sensory information from the spinal cord and brain to the rest of the body. Inside the spinal cord, the axons of motor neurons form bundles known as **tracts**, which transmit this information to motor peripheral nerves going to muscles in the limbs. Motor neurons are important for voluntary movements and muscle control.

A specialized set of neurons controls and regulates basic, unconscious bodily functions that support life, such as the pumping of the heart and digestion. These neurons make up what is called the **autonomic nervous system**, which sends axons from the brain stem and spinal cord to various areas of the body such as the heart muscle, the digestive system, and the pupils of the eyes.

■ NERVOUS SYSTEM DISORDERS AND EFFECTS OF INJURIES

A change in an animal's ability to sense its environment can be caused by disease in either the central nervous system or the peripheral nervous system. The primary signs of nervous system disorders include behavioral changes, seizures, tremors, pain, numbness, lack of coordination, and weakness or paralysis of one or more legs. The effects of an injury on sensory and motor functions depend on its location and severity.

A spinal cord injury can cause loss of feeling and paralysis below the level of the injury. Mild spinal cord injuries can result in clumsy movement and mild weakness of the limbs. Moderate spinal cord injuries can cause a greater weakness of the limbs. In severe spinal cord injuries, a complete loss of movement (paralysis) and feeling can occur. However, not all spinal cord injuries cause paralysis. For example, injury to the spinal cord in the lower back can result not in limb paralysis but in loss of bladder control.

Brain injuries result in different effects, again depending on which part of the brain is affected. Injuries to the brain stem can cause a loss of balance, weakness of the limbs, hyperactive reflexes, stupor, or coma. Injuries to the cerebellum can result in a lack of coordination of the head and legs, tremors, and a loss of balance. Injuries to the cerebrum can cause complete or partial blindness, loss of the sense of smell, seizures, coma, stupor, pacing or circling behavior, and inability to recognize an owner.

Some injuries to the nervous system can cause damage that is not evident until 24 to 48 hours after the injury occurs. Long-term damage is usually caused by swelling or internal bleeding of the vessels in the brain. Strokes caused by clogged arteries or high blood pressure are rare in pets.

Mechanisms of Disease

In addition to the effects of injuries, nervous system disorders can include birth defects, infections and inflammations, poisoning, metabolic disorders, nutritional deficiencies, degenerative diseases, or cancer.

Most birth defects, often called **congenital disorders**, are obvious at birth or shortly after. Some genetic diseases cause the neurons to degenerate slowly and irreversibly in the first year of life. In other inherited diseases, such as epilepsy, the animal may not show any signs for 2 to 3 years.

Infections of the nervous system are caused by specific viruses or microorganisms. Other inflammations such as certain types of meningitis can be caused by the body's own overactive immune system. These are known as **autoimmune disorders**. Various chemicals can cause a toxic reaction in the nervous system. These include certain pesticides and herbicides, rat poisons, antifreeze, chocolate, and sedatives. Botulism, tetanus, and tick bites, as well as coral and tiger snake venom, can also affect the nervous system and cause paralysis.

Some metabolic disorders affect the function of the nervous system, including low blood sugar, shortness or loss of breath, liver disease, and kidney failure. Thyroid gland abnormalities can also cause neurologic signs. A lack of thiamine (a vitamin) in the diet can cause a loss of motor control, stupor, seizures, and coma in dogs.

Tumors of the Nervous System

Tumors of the nervous system are classified by the cell type affected, the behavior of the tumor, the pattern of growth, and any secondary changes seen in and around the tumor.

Brain tumors are occasionally found in young animals, but most are found in mature and older animals. In dogs, the brain is the more common site of primary tumors of the nervous system than the spinal cord (see page 207) or peripheral nerves (see page 203). Adult dogs of several brachycephalic breeds—Boxers, English Bulldogs, and Boston Terriers—are often reported as having the highest incidence of brain tumors among domestic animals. (Brachycephalic dog breeds are those that have characteristically flattened faces and short noses.)

A variety of tests are used to confirm the presence of a brain tumor. Plain x-rays, myelography, computed tomography scans, and magnetic resonance imaging are all used to diagnose nervous system tumors. Cerebrospinal fluid analysis may also be useful.

The outlook for animals with nervous system tumors is guarded to poor, and depends on the location, extent of tissue damage, access by surgery, and rate of tumor growth. Recent improvements in treatment have centered on surgical removal, radiation therapy, and chemotherapy. (See also CANCER TREATMENT, page 1240.)

■ THE NEUROLOGIC EVALUATION

Evaluation of the nervous system begins with an accurate history and general physical examination, followed by a neurologic examination. There are a number of specific physical tests that can be carried out to evaluate the functioning of the various components of the nervous system. These include tests of various reflexes, muscle function and control, and posture and gait.

Laboratory tests are often needed to diagnose the specific problem. Common laboratory tests include blood tests, urinalysis, analysis of the cerebrospinal fluid, x-rays, computed tomography (CT) scans, magnetic resonance imaging (MRI), and evaluation of the electrical activity of the brain, peripheral nerves, and muscles.

The Neurologic Examination

A neurologic examination evaluates 1) the cranial nerves, 2) the gait, or walk, 3) the neck and front legs, and 4) the torso, hind legs, anus, and tail. Your pet's reflexes will also be tested to determine, if possible, the location of the injury in the brain, spinal cord, or nerves in the peripheral nervous system.

Evaluation of the Cranial Nerves

The 12 pairs of cranial nerves extend from specific segments of the brain stem to the left and right sides of the head (*see* TABLE 13). They include the nerves that transmit smell, those responsible for vision and the movement of the eyes, those that control facial movements, those responsible for hearing and balance, and those responsible for chewing, swallowing, barking, and movement of the tongue. Testing the reflexes of these nerves can help identify the location of the damage. Your veterinarian will perform specific tests designed to pinpoint any signs of dysfunction in these nerves.

An evaluation of the cranial nerves tests mental activity, head posture and coordination, and reflexes on the head. Signs identified during this evaluation indicate an injury or disease of the brain. Signs of damage to the cerebrum and brain stem can include mental deterioration, constant pacing, seizures, depression or coma, or a head turn or circling in one direction.

A head tilt, bobbing, tremors, or other unusual head movements may indicate damage to the cerebellum.

Evaluation of Gait (Walking)

Your veterinarian will evaluate the gait by watching your pet as it walks, runs, turns, steps to the side, and backs up. Signs of dysfunction include circling, weakness or complete paralysis of any limbs, falling, stumbling, rolling, or loss of coordination.

Evaluation of the Neck and Front Legs

Evaluation of the neck and front legs will include searching for evidence of pain and loss of muscle size or tone, which may indicate an injury to the upper spinal cord. Various types of tests are done to help detect minor spinal cord injuries.

Some examples of tests that are commonly used to evaluate the neck and front legs include the wheelbarrow test (in which the back legs are lifted slightly and the animal is evaluated while walk-

Table 13. The Cranial Nerves

Nerve	Function
Olfactory nerves	Transmit smell
Optic nerves	Necessary for vision; carry the sensory nerves for certain eye reflexes
Oculomotor nerves	Carry motor neurons that control most of the muscles of the eye
Trochlear nerves	Carry motor neurons that control other muscles of the eye
Trigeminal nerves	Include 3 main branches: the motor nerve to the muscles of the jaw, sensory nerves to the mouth and nasal cavity, and sensory nerves that carry pain sensations from the cornea (the sensitive outermost part of the eyeball)
Abducent nerves	Carry motor neurons that control other muscles of the eye
Facial nerves	Control the muscles responsible for facial expression (ears, eyelids, nose, and mouth)
Vestibulocochlear nerves	These nerves are divided into 2 parts: the cochlear nerve, which responds to sound; and the vestibular nerve, which functions to maintain posture and balance
Glossopharyngeal nerves	Provide sensory and motor control of the throat and vocal chords
Vagus nerves	Provide sensory and motor control for the major internal organs, including the heart and the digestive tract
Spinal accessory nerves	Carry sensory and motor information for the muscles of the head and upper neck
Hypoglossal nerves	The motor nerves to the tongue

ing on its front legs), the righting test (in which the dog is placed on its side or upside down to see how well it can right itself), and the positioning test (in which a foot or limb is moved from its normal position in order to evaluate how quickly and accurately the dog resumes its normal stance). Spinal reflexes and muscle condition are also evaluated.

Evaluation of the Torso, Hind Legs, Anus, and Tail

The trunk, or torso, is evaluated for abnormal posture or position of the vertebrae, pain, loss of feeling or hypersensitivity to light touch or pinpricking, and loss of muscle mass. Some tests used to evaluate the nerves of the neck and front legs (*see* above) are also used to evaluate the torso and hind legs. Various reflexes can also be evaluated. Loss of muscle around the torso or hind legs can indicate damage to a nerve associated with that muscle.

Laboratory Tests and Imaging

Blood tests are often used to detect metabolic disorders, some of which can affect nervous system activity. Blood tests can also identify other conditions, including lead poisoning, certain infections, and myasthenia gravis, an autoimmune disease in which the connections between nerve and muscle are blocked and weakness results.

Analysis of cerebrospinal fluid (the fluid that surrounds the brain and spinal cord) is often useful for diagnosing a central nervous system disorder. Cerebrospinal fluid is collected from the base of the skull or from the lower back in a procedure called a **spinal tap**. An unusually high amount of protein in the cerebrospinal fluid may indicate encephalitis (inflammation of the brain), meningitis (inflammation of the covering of the brain), cancer, or a compressive injury of the spinal cord. Increased numbers of white blood cells in the cerebrospinal fluid indicate an inflammation or infection. Other disorders that can be identified by cerebrospinal fluid analysis include bacterial or fungal infec-

tions, internal bleeding, brain abscesses, and some types of tumors. Cerebrospinal fluid can also be tested for the presence of canine distemper virus, Rocky Mountain spotted fever, and some other infectious diseases.

Several different types of radiographic tests can be used to detect disorders of the nervous system. **Plain x-rays** of the skull and spine can detect fractures, infections, or bone cancer. However, in most infections or cancers of the brain and spinal cord, plain x-rays appear normal. In a procedure known as **myelography**, a special dye that is visible on x-rays is injected into the cerebrospinal canal. This dye can highlight specific types of spinal problems, such as herniated ("slipped") disks and spinal cord tumors. **Computed tomography (CT)** and **magnetic resonance imaging (MRI) scans** can also help evaluate changes in bone structure, internal bleeding, abscesses, inflammation, and certain nervous system cancers.

Other tests may be used in some cases. An **electroencephalogram** records electrical activity in the brain. Results are abnormal in meningitis or encephalitis, head injuries, and brain tumors. An electroencephalogram can sometimes help determine the cause and severity of a seizure. An **electromyogram** records electrical activity in muscles and nerves. In this test, a nerve is stimulated electrically, and the speed of conduction along the neurons is calculated. This technique can detect nerve injury and myasthenia gravis. A **brain stem auditory evoked response (BAER)** records electrical activity in the pathway from the sound receptors in the ear to the brain stem and cerebrum. In cases of deafness caused by nerve damage, the BAER generates no response. Brain-stem disorders may also change the BAER.

■ PRINCIPLES OF THERAPY

Once a diagnosis is made, appropriate therapy can be considered. There are several groups of drugs that are used to treat disorders of the nervous system. Drugs used to treat epileptic seizures are known as anticonvulsants. Anti-inflammatory medications, including corticosteroids, are used to reduce swelling and inflammation in many types of injuries. These medications may be given intravenously in some cases (such as spinal cord injury) and by mouth in others. Other medications may be needed to relieve muscle spasms caused by neurologic disorders or to treat infections of the nervous system.

After cranial surgery, and in animals with brain tumors or head injuries, there is a risk of swelling caused by an accumulation of fluid in the brain. Mannitol or corticosteroid medications can be given intravenously to reduce the swelling. (For a more detailed discussion, *see* DRUGS USED TO TREAT BRAIN, SPINAL CORD, AND NERVE DISORDERS, page 1130.)

Nursing Care

Paraplegic or quadriplegic animals need intensive nursing care. The dog should be kept on padding and turned every 4 to 6 hours to help prevent sores from developing on the skin. The skin must be kept clean and free of urine and feces. Urinalyses must be done every 2 to 4 weeks to monitor for bladder infection. Quadriplegic animals need to be hand fed and given plenty of water. Manually flexing and massaging the dog's joints and muscles can delay muscle wasting in paralyzed limbs.

■ CONGENITAL AND INHERITED DISORDERS

Some congenital defects (defects present at birth), are inherited from the parents, while others are caused by environmental factors in the womb, such as nutritional deficiencies or some viral infections. For many, the cause is unknown.

Puppies are born with a nervous system that is not fully developed, and birth defects may not become apparent until they begin to walk. In some cases, evidence of an inherited disorder may not be seen until the dog has reached adulthood, even though the defect has been present since birth.

Birth defects of the nervous system are categorized according to the primary region of the nervous system affected: forebrain, cerebellum, spinal cord, peripheral nerve and muscle disorders, or multifocal disorders that include signs of more than one area. Many of these inherited disorders are rare or breed-specific, or both. A few of the more common disorders of each area are described below.

Forebrain Disorders

Forebrain disorders (defects in the cerebrum) often result in vision problems, changes in awareness or behavior, abnormal movements or postures, and seizures.

Hydrocephalus, commonly known as "water on the brain," is an excess of fluid that puts pressure on the brain and may damage the cerebrum. This condition is not uncommon in puppies, especially in toy and brachycephalic breeds, such as Pugs, Bulldogs, and Bull Mastiffs. Hydrocephalus usually results in signs similar to those of a cerebral injury, and may worsen over time. However, some animals may not show any obvious signs. Blindness or impaired vision can also develop. Ultrasonography or magnetic resonance imaging (MRI) can confirm the diagnosis. This condition may be treated with corticosteroids, but surgery may be necessary in severe cases.

Idiopathic epilepsy refers to epileptic seizures of unknown cause. It may be inherited in certain breeds, including Beagles, Keeshonden, Irish Setters, Belgian Tervurens, Siberian Huskies, Springer Spaniels, Labrador Retrievers, Golden Retrievers, and German Shepherds. A diagnosis of idiopathic epilepsy depends on eliminating other causes of seizures, particularly structural brain abnormalities (such as hydrocephalus), encephalitis, or metabolic disorders such as hepatic encephalopathy.

Hepatic encephalopathy is usually caused by a birth defect that leads to blood vessel abnormalities within the liver, or in rare cases it may result from an enzyme deficiency in the liver. Breeds often affected include Miniature Schnauzers, Yorkshire Terriers, Cairn Terriers, Australian Cattle Dogs, Old English Sheepdogs, and Maltese Terriers. Nervous system signs are usually evident before the pup is 6 months old. Signs include "staring into space," inappropriate barking or whining, aggression, and agitation. In advanced disease, depression, blindness, sudden jerking motions, stupor, coma, or seizures can be seen. Hepatic encephalopathy is diagnosed by using radiographic imaging techniques, such as computed tomography or ultrasonography.

Puppy hypoglycemia, or low blood sugar, is seen in toy breeds in the first 6 months of life. It seems to relate to a relative immaturity of the liver. This condition can usually be managed by feeding frequent meals of a commercial puppy food. The problem usually disappears as the animal matures.

Cerebellar Disorders

Cerebellar disorders (defects in the cerebellum) usually result in a tremor and a lack of coordination in both the head and legs.

Cerebellar hypoplasia is a condition in which the cerebellum does not develop completely. The animal typically has a tremor that does not worsen as the animal matures, and affected animals can be good pets. Hydrocephalus can also be found in animals with a cerebellar disorder.

Cerebellar abiotrophies develop when cells in the cerebellum age prematurely and degenerate. Signs are similar to those seen in severe cerebellar injury, including tremor and poor motor control. The signs get progressively worse over time.

Spinal Cord Disorders

Spinal cord disorders do not affect coordination of head movement but cause a loss of motor function and coordination in the legs or sense of position.

Congenital vertebral malformations involve the bones of the spinal column, called vertebrae. These malformations can cause damage to the spinal cord. They include **hemivertebrae** (shortened or misshapen vertebrae), **block vertebrae** (fused together), and **butterfly vertebrae** (cleft vertebrae). Hemivertebrae are most common in screw-tailed dog breeds, such as Pugs, Bulldogs, and Boston Terriers. Specialized imaging techniques such as computed tomography (CT) scanning may be necessary to determine whether a spinal defect can be corrected by surgery.

In **caudal cervical spondylomyelopathy**, also called wobbler syndrome, the spine in the neck area is deformed. The most commonly affected breeds include Borzois, Basset Hounds, Doberman Pinschers, and Great Danes. The condition may be inherited, and signs begin to show at a variety of different ages. Signs range from mild difficulty in walking to paralysis of all 4 legs. Affected dogs often keep their neck flexed awkwardly, and the neck may be painful. Surgery can relieve pressure on the spinal cord.

Atlantoaxial subluxation is most common in young toy or miniature breeds of dogs and is seen occasionally in large breed dogs as well. Signs usually develop within the first few years of life and consist of sudden or progressively worsening neck pain or difficulty moving. Signs can be mild or progress to paralysis of all 4 legs. Surgery is necessary to stabilize the dog's condition, and the outlook for recovery is uncertain.

Peripheral Nerve and Muscle Disorders

Peripheral nerve and muscle disorders can result in muscle weakness and awkward or uncoordinated movement similar to that seen in spinal cord disorders. In addition, they often cause a loss of reflexes and pain sensation, or wasting or withering of the muscles. Although there are a number of these disorders that may affect particular breeds, they are quite rare in most dogs.

Miscellaneous Birth Defects

Congenital deafness occurs most often in Dalmatians but has also been recorded in a number of other breeds, including Australian Shepherds, English Setters, Boston Terriers, and Old English Sheepdogs. The brain stem auditory evoked response test (*see* page 199) can identify deaf puppies at an early age.

■ DISORDERS OF THE PERIPHERAL NERVES

Diseases of the peripheral nerves include degenerative diseases, inflammatory diseases, metabolic disorders, cancers, nutritional disorders, toxic disorders, disorders caused by injury, and vascular diseases.

Degenerative Diseases

Acquired laryngeal paralysis is common in middle-aged and older dogs, especially in large breeds, such as Labrador Retrievers, Golden Retrievers, and Saint Bernards. In most cases, the cause is unknown, but it can be caused by an injury or tumor affecting the neck or by thyroid disorders. Signs include voice change, noisy breathing, and a dry cough. In severe cases, the dog may have difficulty breathing, be unwilling or unable to exercise, and the tongue and gums may turn bluish. Some dogs have more general signs of a neurologic disorder, such as weakness and reduced sense of position. Although surgery cannot completely resolve the signs, it can usually relieve the breathing difficulties.

Dancing Doberman disease is a neuromuscular disorder that affects Doberman Pinschers older than 6 months. Initially, dogs repeatedly flex the hip and extend one hind leg while standing. Within several months, most dogs alternately flex and extend both hind legs in a dance-like motion. They often prefer to sit rather than stand. The condition slowly progresses to mild partial paralysis. The front legs are not affected. The cause is unknown. There is no treatment, and signs do not improve. However, this disease usually does not result in severe disability and does not appear to be painful.

Inflammatory Disorders

Acquired myasthenia gravis is a disease of the connections between the muscles and nerves. It is most common in adult German Shepherds, Golden Retrievers, and Labrador Retrievers. Common signs are stiffness (brought on by exercise), tremors, and weakness that improve with rest. Weakness of the face and throat muscles is common, and often there is difficulty swallowing or regurgitation of food after eating. Pneumonia is a frequent complication. Diagnosis requires a blood test. Medications are available for long-term treatment. The outlook for recovery is generally good, but less so for animals that suffer complications.

Acute idiopathic polyradiculoneuritis causes inflammation of peripheral nerves. Signs often develop 7 to 14 days after a raccoon bite or scratch (leading to the name of Coonhound paralysis); however, not all affected animals have been exposed to raccoons. A similar syndrome can develop in dogs within 1 to 2 weeks of a vaccination. Typically, the hind legs become weak and within 24 to 48 hours the signs progress to partial paralysis in all legs and, in some cases, weakness in the face and throat. Occasionally, the front legs are affected first. Typically, muscle wasting is severe within 2 weeks. The dog does not lose its pain perception or bladder and bowel function. There is no effective treatment other than nursing care. Most affected animals begin to improve within 3 weeks, with complete recovery by 2 to 6 months. However, animals with severe signs may not recover completely, and death can occur from respiratory paralysis. Relapses are also seen, especially in hunting dogs that frequently encounter raccoons.

Trigeminal neuritis results in inflammation of and damage to the trigeminal nerve, causing a sudden onset of jaw paralysis. Affected animals cannot close the mouth and have difficulty eating and drinking. Partial paralysis and a loss of sensation in the rest of the face are also possible. The cause is unknown. Signs usually resolve within 3 to 4 weeks. Fluid and nutritional support may be necessary.

Metabolic Disorders

Hypothyroid neuropathy can be seen in dogs with a thyroid condition. Adult dogs, especially of large breeds, are at the most risk. Signs vary widely, and may include partial paralysis, weakened reflexes, loss of paw position sense in all 4 legs, loss of balance, inability to swallow, and vomiting. In most dogs, more typical signs of a thyroid condition are present, such as obesity and hair loss (*see also* DISORDERS OF THE THYROID GLAND, page 139), but in some cases the neurologic signs are the only signs of illness. Usually, signs resolve within several months of starting thyroid replacement therapy.

Tumors

Nerve sheath tumors in dogs often arise in the peripheral nerves that extend to the front legs, initially causing weakness and pain in a leg that may be mistaken for a bone or muscle injury. A large tumor may appear as a visible lump. Partial paralysis and muscle wasting eventually develop in the affected leg. If the tumor spreads, it may eventually put pressure against the spinal cord, causing neurologic signs in other legs. Nerve sheath tumors can also form in the cranial nerves, most frequently in the trigeminal nerve. This results in muscle wasting and pain on one side of the jaw. Eventually, the brain stem can become compressed, leading to death. Surgery can be very beneficial at an early stage, but recurrence is common.

In **paraneoplastic neuropathy**, a cancer outside the nervous system causes damage to nerves. It is most common in dogs with insulinoma but has been associated with a variety of other tumors. This condition is not well understood, but it may be caused by an immune system response to a tumor that indirectly harms the nervous system. Signs typically involve partial paralysis in either 2 or 4 legs that progressively wors-

ens over several weeks. Diagnosis requires identification of the underlying tumor. Signs may improve with successful treatment of the tumor.

Toxic Disorders

Organophosphate poisoning can result from exposure to pesticides, herbicides, or other industrial chemicals. The signs depend on the severity of exposure. The **acute form** prevents the body's acetylcholinesterase from working properly. Acetylcholinesterase is an enzyme that is essential for the proper function of connections between neurons, and between nerve and muscle. Signs of severe poisoning can include vomiting, diarrhea, salivation, shortness of breath, muscle tremors and twitching, seizure, or coma.

The **intermediate form** can cause generalized muscle weakness. Affected animals may not show obvious signs at first, but partial paralysis of the legs and stiffness of the neck can develop several days after exposure. The pupils may be dilated. Treatment of acute or intermediate toxicity includes the drug atropine, which blocks the effects of the organophosphate. Other medications are used to relieve the tremors and muscle weakness. Treatment for several weeks may be necessary.

In the **delayed form** of toxicity, the nerves slowly degenerate. This form is unrelated to the effects on acetylcholinesterase. Signs develop several weeks after exposure and typically involve weakness and loss of motor control in the hind legs. There is no specific treatment. (*See also* ORGANOPHOSPHATES, page 1169.)

Tick paralysis (page 213) is caused by the bite of several species of ticks that results in rapidly progressing paralysis. In Australia, the tick *Ixodes holocyclus* causes an especially severe form of tick paralysis. Signs begin with partial paralysis in the hind legs that worsens within 24 to 72 hours to total paralysis in all 4 legs. Sensory perception and consciousness remain normal. Difficulty swallowing, facial paralysis, jaw muscle weakness, and respiratory paralysis may develop in severe cases. Treatment consists of removing the tick and applying a skin ointment to kill any hidden ticks. For all except *Ixodes holocyclus* cases in Australia, recovery usually occurs in 1 to 2 days. A serum is available for treatment of *Ixodes holocyclus* paralysis, but death from respiratory paralysis can occur despite treatment.

Injury and Trauma

Brachial plexus avulsion occurs in dogs due to injury to the spinal nerve roots in the neck and shoulder area that extend nerves into the front legs. In a severe injury, the nerve roots may stretch or tear from their attachment to the spinal cord. Signs vary depending on the severity. If the nerves are completely torn, paralysis of the leg and a loss of sensation and reflexes below the elbow result. The animal puts little or no weight on the leg and drags the paw on the ground. The leg may need to be amputated because of damage from dragging or self-mutilation. Recovery is possible in mild cases in which the nerve roots are bruised but not completely torn.

Peripheral nerve injuries are common in traumatic injuries. The **sciatic nerve**, which runs from the lower back to the hind legs, may be injured by hip fractures or during surgery to correct a broken leg. Irritants injected in or near the nerve can also cause nerve damage. The leg may be partially paralyzed, or the animal may not be able to flex the knee. The paw and digits cannot flex or extend. There may be loss of sensation below the knee. Injury to the branches of the sciatic nerve in the lower leg, such as the **tibial nerve** or the **peroneal nerve**, can result in an inability to extend the paw or flex the digits and reduced sensation over the surface of the foot.

For function to return after nerve connections are lost, the nerve must regenerate from the point of injury all the way to where it ends in the muscle. Nerve tissue regenerates or heals very slowly. Recovery is unlikely if the severed ends of the nerve are widely separated or if scar tissue interferes with healing. Anti-inflammatory drugs have been used to treat traumatic nerve injuries, although there is little evidence of any benefit. Surgery should be performed promptly in cases in which the nerve has been cut. In cases of injury from a fall or a blunt object, surgical exploration and removal of scar tissue may help. Longterm care consists of physical therapy to minimize muscle wasting and to keep the joints moving. Bandages or splints may be necessary to help protect a damaged limb.

■ DISORDERS OF THE SPINAL COLUMN AND CORD

Disorders of the spinal column and cord include congenital defects (discussed above), degenerative diseases, inflammatory and infectious diseases, tumors, nutritional diseases, injury and trauma, toxic disorders, and vascular diseases.

Degenerative Diseases

Degenerative lumbosacral stenosis is a disorder of the vertebrae in the lower back that causes compression of the nerve roots. It is most common in large breeds of dogs, especially German Shepherds. The cause is unknown. Signs typically begin at 3 to 7 years of age and may include difficulty using the hind legs, tail weakness, and incontinence. Dogs often experience pain when the lower back is touched or moved. Other signs include a loss of paw position sense, muscle wasting, or weakened reflexes in the hind legs. X-rays may show signs of degeneration, but diagnosis requires magnetic resonance imaging (MRI) or computed tomography (CT). Dogs in which mild pain is the only sign may improve with 4 to 6 weeks of rest. Specific treatment requires surgery. The outlook for recovery after surgery is good, although urinary incontinence may continue.

Intervertebral disk disease is a degenerative disease of the spinal column that results in compression of the spinal cord and spinal nerves. It is a common cause of spinal cord disorders in dogs, especially of small breeds, particularly the Dachshund, Beagle, Shih Tzu, Lhasa Apso, and Pekingese. In these breeds, spinal disks can begin degenerating in the first few months of life. A **herniated or "slipped" disk** causing severe signs can occur suddenly, as early as 1 to 2 years of age. In contrast, disk degeneration in large breeds of dogs typically occurs after the age of 5 years, and signs continue to worsen. Herniated disks are most common in the neck and the middle of the back. A herniated disk in the neck leads to neck pain, stiffness, and muscle spasms. There may be muscle weakness or other signs, ranging from mild partial paralysis in the legs to total paralysis of all legs. A herniated disk in the middle of the back leads to back pain, and possibly curvature in the spine and a reluctance to move. Neurologic signs range from a loss of motor control in the hind legs to paralysis and incontinence. In paralyzed animals, it is important to determine whether pain sensation is present by pinching the toe or tail and watching whether the dog makes a behavioral response, such as a bark or turn of the head.

Diagnosis of herniated disks requires x-rays, myelography, computed tomography (CT), or magnetic resonance imaging (MRI). Dogs with minimal to moderate signs that can still feel pain often recover with a few weeks of rest. Anti-inflammatory or pain medication can be used, but generally only if the dog can be cage-rested. If the dog increases its activity, the disk(s) may extrude further and worsen the spinal cord compression. Unfortunately, signs recur in 30 to 40% of cases. In dogs with severe neurologic signs, surgery must be performed promptly to relieve the pressure on the spinal cord. Surgery is also needed if drug therapy is unsuccessful and signs return. The outlook for recovery after surgery is good if the dog can still feel pain. If surgery is delayed for more than 48 hours after pain

perception is lost, the chances of recovery decrease.

Inflammatory and Infectious Diseases

Infectious and inflammatory diseases of the spinal column and spinal cord include bacterial, rickettsial, viral, fungal, protozoal, and parasitic infections. Many of these diseases, such as meningitis and encephalitis, can also affect the brain. Some of the more common infectious and inflammatory diseases that affect the spinal column or cord are discussed below.

Bacterial Diseases

Diskospondylitis is inflammation of the disk between 2 vertebrae (bones in the spinal column). The vertebrae can also be inflamed without infection of the disk. Causes include a bacterial or fungal infection in the bloodstream or a weakened immune system that allows infections to develop. Diskospondylitis occurs more often in larger breeds. The most common sign is spinal pain, with some dogs also having fever, depression, and weight loss. Neurologic signs can develop due to pressure on the spinal cord or, rarely, spread of infection to the spinal cord. Blood and urine samples can identify the underlying infection. Signs usually disappear within 5 days of treatment with an appropriate antibiotic, but treatment should be continued for at least 8 weeks.

Rickettsial Diseases

Dogs that develop an infection of rickettsia or related bacteria sometimes show signs of spinal cord dysfunction. These bacteria cause disorders such as **Rocky Mountain spotted fever** and **ehrlichiosis**, which can lead to swelling in the spinal cord. Blood and cerebrospinal fluid samples can help identify the infection. Antibiotic treatment is given for 2 to 3 weeks. The outlook for a full recovery is good with early treatment, although the neurologic signs occasionally worsen despite treatment. (*See also* EHRLICHIOSIS AND RELATED INFECTIONS, page 310.)

Viral Diseases

Canine distemper encephalomyelitis, a viral infection that causes swelling of the brain and spinal cord, remains one of the most common central nervous system disorders in dogs worldwide. Neurologic signs may appear suddenly or may worsen slowly and progressively, depending on the location of the swelling. Adult dogs can have fever and pain, and animals sometimes lose motor control or develop paralysis. Definitive diagnosis is difficult without a necropsy. There is no specific treatment, and the outlook for recovery is poor for dogs with severe signs. Vaccination is usually successful in preventing distemper.

Rabies (page 211) is caused by a viral infection that spreads to the central nervous system from the peripheral nerves. Rabies is common throughout the world except in Japan and some other islands, including New Zealand, Iceland, and Hawaii. Initial signs are extremely variable, and rabies should be considered a possibility in any unvaccinated animal with severe neurologic dysfunction. Signs that the infection has reached the spinal cord include a loss of motor control and progressive paralysis, usually with a loss of reflexes. Affected animals typically, but not invariably, die within 2 to 7 days of when signs begin. There is no treatment. Vaccination is essential for prevention.

Fungal Diseases

Cryptococcus neoformans is the most common fungus to cause a central nervous system infection in dogs. Other fungal organisms may also invade the central nervous system. Infections often affect other organs, such as the lungs, eyes, skin, or bones. Signs of spinal cord infection include partial or total paralysis and spinal pain. Blood or cerebrospinal fluid tests are necessary to diagnose an infection and identify the organism.

Treatment and the outlook for recovery depend on the specific fungus involved. The drug fluconazole is often effective for *Cryptococcus* infections. Infections with *Blastomyces* or *Histoplasma* fungi are difficult to treat, and the outlook for recovery in dogs infected with these fungi is uncertain.

Protozoal Diseases

Neosporosis is caused by *Neospora caninum*, a microorganism that can cause inflammation of the brain and spinal cord. Infection in young puppies typically causes paralysis with muscle rigidity in one or both hind legs. Other organs, including muscle, liver, and lungs, can also be affected. A blood test or tissue sample can be used to diagnose the infection. Early drug treatment may be effective, but the chances of recovery are poor.

Toxoplasmosis is caused by a protozoan called *Toxoplasma gondii*, which can occasionally cause inflammation of the brain and spinal cord. Dogs with toxoplasmosis often also have other diseases, such as canine distemper. A blood test or tissue sample can be used to diagnose the infection. Various drugs are recommended for treatment.

Parasitic Diseases

Verminous myelitis is inflammation of the spinal cord caused by a parasite. The most common such parasite in dogs is a roundworm called *Baylisascaris procyonis*. Signs of spinal cord inflammation strike suddenly and severely, often affecting one side of the body more than the other, and may progressively worsen over time. This condition is difficult to diagnose except by examination of tissues after death. Drug treatment can be beneficial, but a full recovery is uncertain.

Inflammatory Diseases of Unknown Cause

Granulomatous meningoencephalomyelitis is an inflammatory disease of the central nervous system that occurs in dogs worldwide. The cause is unknown, but it may be a viral infection. There are 2 different forms of the disease that have different effects within the body, but the signs are similar, and often include neck pain and partial paralysis in all 4 legs. Adult dogs of any breed can be affected, but female small-breed dogs, especially Poodles, are at highest risk. Signs can occur suddenly or slowly worsen over several months. An accurate diagnosis requires cerebrospinal fluid analysis. Dogs often improve temporarily with drug treatment, but the longterm outlook is guarded.

Tumors

Tumors that affect the spinal column and cord in dogs include cancers of the bone, connective tissue, meninges, and nerve sheath, in addition to metastatic cancers, which are cancers that have spread from other parts of the body. A specific tumor called a **nephroblastoma** can affect young dogs (from 5 to 36 months of age), with German Shepherds affected most commonly. This tumor is frequently in the middle or lower back, causing progressively worsening partial paralysis in the hind legs. Imaging (including x-rays, myelography, computed tomography, magnetic resonance imaging) and surgical biopsy are used to identify and confirm a diagnosis of spinal cancer. Surgery is possible in some cases.

Injury and Trauma

Spinal cord injuries usually occur as a result of a spinal fracture or dislocation. Common causes in dogs include automobile accidents, bite wounds, and gunshot wounds. The injury not only causes initial damage to the spinal cord, but also causes secondary damage from swelling, bleeding, destruction of the nerve sheath, and tissue decay. Signs of spinal trauma typically have a sudden and severe onset, and may progressively worsen. Severe spinal cord injury to the middle or lower back may cause a rigid paralysis, or a limp paralysis that spreads to the entire body over several days and leads to death from respiratory paralysis. Fractured or dislocated vertebrae can often be seen on x-rays. Drug treatment can be helpful if started

within the first few hours of injury. Animals with mild neurologic signs from injury often recover after 4 to 6 weeks of cage rest. Surgery is necessary for some types of injuries that cause severe neurologic signs. In dogs that have lost the ability to feel pain at locations below the spinal injury, the outlook for recovery is poor.

Poisoning and Toxic Disorders

Delayed organophosphate intoxication can be seen after ingestion or skin contact with insecticides or pesticides that contain organophosphates. In addition to the signs of severe exposure (*see* page 1169), delayed paralysis can develop 1 to 4 weeks after exposure. Partial paralysis of the hind legs worsens progressively, and occasionally all 4 legs become paralyzed. A veterinarian will need a history of the dog's possible chemical exposure to make the correct diagnosis. The outlook for recovery is poor for animals with severe signs.

Tetanus is caused by toxins produced by *Clostridium tetani* bacteria that usually enter the body at the site of a wound. Dogs are fairly resistant to tetanus, but cases do sometimes occur. Signs usually develop within 5 to 10 days of infection and include muscle stiffness and rigid leg extension, inability to swallow, protruding eyelids, and locking of the jowl and facial muscles. In severe cases, the animal may be unable to stand as a result of muscle spasms. Treatment consists of wound care, antibiotics to kill any remaining organisms, and tetanus antitoxin. In mild cases, a dog may recover completely with early treatment. In severe cases, death may occur due to respiratory paralysis.

■ DYSAUTONOMIA

Canine dysautonomia is a disorder of the autonomic nervous system, which controls many reflexes and other neurologic functions that the animal does not consciously control. Cases have been reported from both Europe and the United States, where canine dysautonomia has been seen primarily in the Midwest. Signs often include a loss of the pupillary light reflexes, with otherwise normal vision. The eyelid may droop or protrude abnormally, and the position of the eyeball may be abnormal. The dog may experience painful or difficult urination and lose anal sphincter control. Secondary signs such as pneumonia and lethargic behavior may develop. Weight loss may be dramatic. There is no treatment and the condition is ultimately fatal.

■ FACIAL PARALYSIS

Facial paralysis in dogs may result from injuries caused by rough handling or other trauma, such as automobile accidents. Paralysis on one side of the face is common when the facial nerve is damaged. Facial paralysis on both sides of the face can be more difficult to recognize, but affected animals often drool and have a dull facial expression. In total facial paralysis, the animal cannot move its eyelids, ears, lips, or nostrils. In partial paralysis, the muscles of facial expression move less than normal.

The signs of facial paralysis vary with the location and severity of the injury. One or both sides of the face can be affected. Usually, the signs include loss of motor function, including the inability to blink, a drooping ear, a drooping upper lip, and drooling from the corner of the mouth. When the animal eats or drinks, food and water may fall out of the mouth. The nose may seem to turn away from the side of the injury because muscle tone on the injured side is reduced.

Infection of the inner ear is a common cause of facial paralysis, especially in dogs with chronic skin conditions. This can be diagnosed with magnetic resonance imaging (MRI) and computed tomography (CT) scans. The prognosis for recovery can be good if the diagnosis is made early and the animal receives appropriate antibiotic treatment. However, the facial nerve paralysis can be permanent, and longterm administration of eye drops may be necessary.

A low-functioning thyroid gland (hypothyroidism) can also cause facial nerve paralysis. In such cases, thyroid replacement therapy can resolve facial paralysis completely.

Idiopathic facial paralysis (like Bell's palsy in humans) is diagnosed in the absence of infection, reduced thyroid function, injury, or trauma. There is no treatment, and regular administration of lubricating eye drops may be necessary. One or both sides of the face can be affected, and the condition can be either temporary or permanent. It can occur on one side, disappear, and then occur on the other side at a later time. Permanent paralysis may give the face an unusual appearance but does not usually affect the quality of life in dogs.

Electromyography, including electrical stimulation of the facial nerve, may be helpful to determine the severity of the injury. There is no specific therapy for injury except electroacupuncture, massage, and heat applied to the affected muscles. Some animals may also need special water containers and soft food. The facial nerve can slowly regenerate, so repeated neurologic examinations can help determine if an animal is recovering. If there has been no improvement after 6 months, the chance of recovery is poor.

■ CENTRAL NERVOUS SYSTEM DISORDERS CAUSED BY PARASITES

A number of parasites (including worms and insects) are associated with central nervous system disease. Diagnosis requires eliminating other possible causes of illness, such as rabies, and identifying the specific parasite responsible.

Tapeworms

Coenurosis (also called gid, sturdy, or staggers) is caused by *Taenia multiceps*, an intestinal tapeworm of dogs and people. Other animals, such as sheep, goats, deer, rabbits, horses, and cattle can carry and spread this parasite to dogs. The larval stage of the parasite can invade the nervous system and lead to swelling of the brain and spinal cord. The adult worm may grow to more than 2 inches in diameter and cause increased pressure on the brain, which results in loss of muscle control, blindness, head tilting, stumbling, and paralysis. Dogs that are around sheep and other livestock should not be fed body parts of infected animals and should be dewormed regularly.

Echinococcosis is caused by *Echinococcus granulosus*, a tapeworm found in the small intestine of dogs. Its eggs are ingested by intermediate hosts, including sheep, cattle, and moose. People can also serve as intermediate hosts. The larvae can form large, thick-walled cysts that spread to the nervous system and produce signs similar to those of a brain tumor. Surgery can sometimes remove the cysts, and the infection can be treated with appropriate medication.

Flukes

Two species of *Paragonimus* lung flukes can migrate to the nervous system and produce cysts in the brain and spinal cord of dogs, cats, and people.

Schistosomes, or blood flukes, normally deposit their eggs in the blood vessels of the gut and urinary bladder, from which they pass into the external environment via the feces or urine. Some eggs, however, may get into the bloodstream and reach the central nervous system, where they form capsules. This condition has been seen in people and domestic animals.

Roundworms

Several types of roundworms are found in domestic animals.

The larvae of some ascarid roundworms, including *Toxocara* species, can invade the central nervous system and cause localized damage in dogs. *Toxocara* larvae may also invade the eye and cause vision loss in people.

Baylisascaris procyonis is a roundworm found in the small intestine of raccoons.

Its larvae can infect people and domesticated animals and migrate to the central nervous system. This parasite can also cause central nervous system and eye damage in people, particularly children.

Dirofilaria immitis is the canine heartworm. In addition to the heart, other parts of the body, including the central nervous system and the eye, can be infected.

Disease Caused by Insects

Myiasis is the development of larval dipteran flies (bots and warbles) within the body's tissues or organs. The larvae of *Cuterebra*, which are deposited under the skin in dogs or cats, have been known to wander into the central nervous system and affect the cerebrum or cerebellum. Organophosphate drugs can eliminate certain dipteran larvae from the nervous system, but they can also cause nervous system damage. Corticosteroid drugs are often recommended to prevent additional inflammatory damage and pressure on the brain during treatment. (*See also* FLIES AND MOSQUITOES, page 251.)

■ LEG PARALYSIS

Paralysis of a leg often results from damage to the peripheral spinal nerves. Paralysis of a front leg is usually associated with injury to the nerve roots in the neck or shoulder, or injury to the radial, median, or ulnar nerve in the leg. Paralysis of a hind leg is usually associated with injury to the nerve roots in the lower back or tailbone, or the femoral, sciatic, peroneal, or tibial nerve in the leg.

Paralysis of a leg may be temporary or permanent.

The animal's posture and gait, spinal reflexes, pain sensation, and the condition of the muscles in the affected limb are evaluated to identify the location of the injury. The closer a nerve injury is to the muscle, the better the outlook for recovery, so it is important to determine the exact location of the injury. The ability or inability of the animal to flex the joint and bear weight on the leg, and the presence or absence of pain sensation and reflexes at various places in the leg, depend on the site of the nerve damage. Within a few days, muscles wither and lose mass because of the lost nerve connection. Electrical stimulation of the nerve can be used to determine whether the nerve is partially intact. Nerves regenerate slowly (about 1 inch per month), and full functional recovery depends on the condition of the nerve sheath and on the distance between the injury and the muscle where the nerve ends. Some nerve injuries can resolve after several weeks or months; however, when total nerve rupture occurs, surgical reattachment is required for regeneration.

If an abnormal eye condition known as Horner's syndrome (pupils small, eyelid partially closed, and third eyelid elevated) is present on the same side of the body as a paralyzed front leg, then the nerve roots have been torn and the chances for recovery are minimal. If Horner's syndrome is not present with front leg paralysis, the outlook for recovery may be better.

Applying heat, performing massage, and stretching tendons should be done as directed by your veterinarian to keep muscles, tendons, and joints of a paralyzed leg healthy while the nerve is regenerating. A light, but not tight, bandage may prevent damage to the foot from dragging. If the leg drags on the ground, it can be held up with a sling or amputated to prevent damage to the paw. Three-legged dogs generally have a good quality of life.

No specific therapy is available to help nerve regeneration. Acupuncture may help recovery. If voluntary movement, pain sensation, and spinal reflexes improve over 1 to 2 months, the outlook for recovery is good. An Elizabethan collar may be needed to prevent the dog from chewing on its leg. If the nerve injury is suspected to be permanent and the animal is chewing the leg, amputation may be the best option.

Paralysis from Tumors

Tumors affecting nerves can cause a chronic, often painful lameness or weakness of a front or hind leg that worsens over time. Tumors can be identified using computed tomography (CT) or magnetic resonance imaging (MRI) scans. Surgical removal or biopsy of the tumor is necessary to determine the diagnosis and the chance for recovery.

Nerve sheath tumors are common in dogs, and they often affect multiple nerves. These tumors are difficult to completely remove. The outlook for recovery is usually poor.

▓ MENINGITIS AND ENCEPHALITIS

Inflammation of the meninges, the membranous covering of the brain and spinal cord (**meningitis**), and inflammation of the brain (**encephalitis**) often are seen simultaneously (**meningoencephalitis**), although either can develop separately. Causes of meningitis, encephalitis, and meningoencephalitis include infection by bacteria, viruses, fungi, protozoa, rickettsia, or parasites. In some cases, the immune system is involved or the cause is unknown. In dogs, especially adult animals, viruses, protozoa, rickettsia, and fungi are more frequent causes of meningitis and encephalitis than are bacteria.

Meningitis and encephalitis are less common than infections of other organs, because the nervous system has protective barriers. However, infections may occur when these protective barriers are injured or weakened. Infections can also spread to the central nervous system from the sinuses, the inner ear, vertebrae, or spinal disks; these infections may result from bite wounds or other traumatic injuries near the head or spine. Brain abscesses also can arise from direct infections or from blood poisoning. Bacterial meningitis or meningoencephalitis is not common in dogs and is not generally contagious.

The usual signs of meningitis are fever, neck pain and rigidity, and painful muscle spasms. Dogs may have these signs without any sign of brain or spinal cord dysfunction. However, in meningoencephalitis, depression, blindness, partial paralysis of the face or the limbs, loss of balance or motor control, seizures, behavioral changes, agitation, head tilt and circling behavior, difficulty eating, and loss of consciousness (including coma) can develop, depending on the severity and location of the inflammation. The analysis of cerebrospinal fluid from a spinal tap is the most reliable and accurate means of identifying meningitis or encephalitis.

Cases resulting from an immune system disorder can be treated with corticosteroids or other medications that alter the immune system. Infections caused by rickettsia, protozoa, and certain bacteria can be treated with appropriate antibiotics, and fungal infections can be treated with specific antifungal drugs. The outlook for recovery depends on the cause, the severity of the infection, and whether or not the infection has resulted in irreversible damage to the nervous tissue. Supportive care may include pain relievers, anticonvulsant drugs, fluids, nutritional supplements, and physical therapy.

■ MOTION SICKNESS

Motion sickness results in nausea, excessive drooling, vomiting, and occasionally other signs such as poor appetite for several hours after the motion sickness event. Animals may yawn, whine, show signs of uneasiness or apprehension, or have diarrhea. Motion sickness is usually seen during travel by land, sea, or air, and signs usually disappear when the motion of the vehicle ceases.

Motion sickness can be minimized with conditioning or medication in many dogs.

The principal cause of motion sickness is due to stimulation of the sensory organ in the inner ear, which has connections to the vomiting center in the brain stem. Fear of the vehicle may be a contributing factor in dogs and cats, and signs may occur even in a vehicle that is not moving. This occurs if a dog has become preconditioned to illness associated with travel in a vehicle.

In some cases, motion sickness can be overcome by conditioning the animal to travel. (*See also* TRAVEL WITH PETS, page 1216.) In others, drug treatment can help prevent motion sickness, provide sedation, and decrease drooling. These medications can be obtained from your veterinarian and include tranquilizers, sedatives, and products to decrease nausea and/or vomiting.

■ RABIES

Rabies is an acute viral infection of the nervous system that mainly affects carnivores and bats, although it can affect any mammal. It is caused by the rabies virus. Once clinical signs appear, it is fatal. Rabies is found throughout the world, although a few countries are declared rabies-free due to successful elimination standards. Islands that have a strict quarantine program in effect are often rabies-free. In North America and Europe, rabies has been mostly eliminated in domestic dogs, although it affects wildlife.

Transmission is almost always by the bite of an infected animal, when the saliva containing the rabies virus is introduced into the body. The virus can be in the body for weeks before signs develop. Most cases in dogs develop within 21 to 80 days after exposure, but the incubation period may be considerably shorter or longer.

Signs and Diagnosis

Most rabid animals show signs of central nervous system disturbance. The most reliable indicators are sudden and severe behavioral changes and unexplained paralysis that worsens over time. Behavioral changes can include sudden loss of appetite, signs of apprehension or nervousness, irritability, and hyperexcitability. The animal may seek solitude, or an otherwise unfriendly animal may become friendly. Uncharacteristic aggressiveness can develop, and wild animals may lose their fear of people. Animals that are normally nocturnal may be seen wandering around during the daytime.

The furious form of rabies is the classic "mad-dog" syndrome, although it is seen in all species. The animal becomes irritable and may viciously and aggressively use its teeth and claws with the slightest provocation. The posture is alert and anxious, with pupils dilated. Noise can invite attack. Such animals lose fear and caution of other animals. Young pups seek out human companionship and are overly playful, but will bite even when petted and become vicious within a few hours. As the disease progresses, seizures and lack of muscle coordination are common. Death is caused by progressive paralysis.

The paralytic form of rabies usually involves paralysis of the throat and jaw muscles, often with excess salivation and inability to swallow. Drooping of the lower jaw is common. These animals may not be vicious and rarely attempt to bite.

People can be infected by this form when examining the dog's mouth or giving it medication with bare hands. Paralysis progresses throughout the body and death occurs within a few hours.

Diagnosis is difficult, especially in areas where rabies is not common. Early stages of rabies can be easily confused with other diseases or with normal aggressive tendencies. A rabies diagnosis must be verified with laboratory tests. The animal must be euthanized and the remains sent for laboratory analysis.

Control of Rabies

The World Health Organization (WHO) has strict guidelines to control rabies in the dog population. These guidelines include: 1) notification of suspected cases, with euthanasia of dogs with clinical signs and those bitten by suspected rabid animals; 2) leash laws and quarantine to reduce contact between susceptible dogs; 3) a mass immunization program with continued boosters; 4) stray dog control and euthanasia of unvaccinated dogs that roam freely; and 5) dog registration programs.

Rabies vaccination programs are strictly enforced. The Compendium of Animal Rabies Control recommends vaccination every 3 years, after an initial series of 2 vaccines, 1 year apart.

Management of Suspected Rabies Cases

In areas where rabies is known to exist in the wildlife population (including bats), an animal bitten or otherwise exposed by a wild, carnivorous mammal or a bat that is not available for testing should be regarded as having been exposed to rabies. The National Association for State Public Health Veterinarians recommends that any unvaccinated dog exposed to rabies be euthanized immediately. If the owner is unwilling to do this, the animal must be placed in strict isolation, with no human or animal contact, for 6 months and be vaccinated against rabies 1 month before release. If an exposed animal is currently vaccinated, it should be revaccinated immediately and closely observed for 45 days.

Risk of Passing Rabies to People

When a person is exposed to an animal suspected of rabies, the risk of rabies transmission should be evaluated carefully. Wild carnivores and bats present a considerable risk where the disease is found, regardless of whether or not abnormal behavior has been seen.

Any healthy domestic dog, cat, or ferret, whether vaccinated or not, that bites a person or otherwise deposits saliva into a fresh wound, should be confined for 10 days for observation. If the animal develops signs within those 10 days, it should be promptly euthanized and submitted for testing. If the animal responsible for the exposure is stray or unwanted, it should be euthanized and submitted for testing immediately.

Pre-exposure vaccination is strongly recommended for all people in high-risk groups, such as veterinary staff, animal control officers, rabies and diagnostic laboratory workers, and travelers working in countries where canine rabies is prevalent.

■ TICK PARALYSIS

Tick paralysis is a rapidly progressive motor paralysis caused by a salivary toxin that attacks the nervous system. Certain species of ticks are known to cause tick paralysis. People (especially children) and many other animals may be affected. Human cases of tick paralysis caused by the genera *Ixodes, Dermacentor*, and *Amblyomma* have been reported in Australia, North America, Europe, and South Africa. These 3 genera plus *Rhipicephalus, Haemaphysalis, Otobius*, and *Argas* have been associated with paralysis in animals.

Early signs in affected dogs include change or loss of voice, lack of coordination of the hind legs, change in breathing rate and effort, gagging or coughing, vomiting, and dilated pupils.

The presence of a tick along with the sudden (within 12 to 24 hours) appearance of leg weakness and/or difficulty breathing is diagnostic. If the tick is not still attached, the presence of a tick "crater" (a small hole surrounded by a slightly raised and red area) can help confirm diagnosis. Other diseases and disorders have the same signs as tick paralysis, but in areas where ticks are prevalent, tick paralysis is a strong possibility.

Removal of the tick(s) is necessary (*see* TICKS, page 268). In North America, the animal usually improves greatly within 24 hours of the tick being removed. If the animal does not recover, more ticks may still be attached, or the signs may be due to another condition. In Australia, the disease tends to progress even after removal of the tick and treatment of the motor and respiratory signs.

Canine tick hyperimmune serum, also called tick antiserum (TAS) is the specific treatment for tick paralysis caused by *Ixodes holocyclus*.

Stress should be kept at a minimum. Affected animals may worsen for the first 24 hours after tick removal, and then recover. During this time, animals should be kept quiet under observation at a veterinary hospital. Animals, especially if long-haired, should be examined carefully for the presence of more ticks. About 5% of animals are likely to die, despite treatment, especially if the stages of paralysis are advanced or if the animal is already weak or old. For animals that do recover, the owner should continue searching for ticks and avoid stressing or strenuously exercising the animal for the next 2 months.

Tick control products are available. However, owners should not rely only on chemical control to prevent ticks. Additional measures include keeping the hair short and routinely checking for ticks when dogs have been outdoors in an area where ticks are prevalent. There is no vaccine against the *Ixodes holocyclus* toxin.

CHAPTER 14

Reproductive Disorders

■ INTRODUCTION

The reproductive system is the group of organs that produce offspring. In both males and females, the reproductive system is composed of primary sex organs and primary regulatory centers. The primary sex organs are the testes in males and the ovaries and uterus in females. The primary regulatory centers are in the brain. They control the production of hormones that in turn influence the function of the primary sex organs.

■ THE GONADS AND GENITAL TRACT

Both sexes have a pair of sexual organs or gonads (ovaries or testes), the main function of which is to produce eggs or sperm, respectively.

The Ovaries

Ovaries are female gonads that produce eggs and female sex hormones, including estrogen and progesterone. Estrogen is necessary for the development of eggs, and progesterone prepares the uterus for

pregnancy. Once puberty is reached and the dog starts its heat or estrous cycle, the size and form of the ovaries change. Within the ovary, a group of special cells called a follicle surround each egg. The estrous cycle begins when follicle stimulating hormone stimulates follicles to grow, leading to maturation of eggs and production of the hormone estrogen. Estrogen causes the brain to release luteinizing hormone, which stimulates the release of eggs from the ovary (a process called ovulation). After ovulation, progesterone, produced by the ovary, prepares the uterus for pregnancy and the mammary glands for milk production.

The Testes

Testes are male gonads that produce sperm and male sex hormones. Sperm maturation is stimulated by the production and release of follicle stimulating hormone and testosterone. Testosterone is required for proper function of the accessory sexual glands, male sex characteristics (for example, larger size), and sexual behavior. For sperm production, the testes must descend into the scrotum (a pouch of skin outside the abdomen), because regular body temperature is too high for sperm to develop normally. The function of the testicles can be assessed by an evaluation of semen samples and hormonal tests. In addition, testicle examination and measurement can help evaluate fertility and may reveal reproductive diseases.

The Female Genital Tract

The female genital tract includes the vulva, vagina, cervix, uterus, oviducts, and ovaries, as well as the mammary glands found on the chest and abdomen. The oviducts are small tubes that connect the ovaries to the uterus. The end of the uterus is called the cervix. It separates the uterus from the vagina and provides a bar-

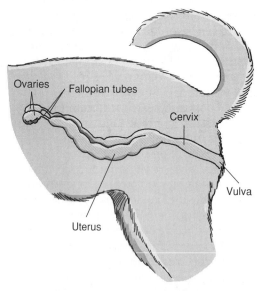

Ovaries Fallopian tubes

Cervix

Vulva

Uterus

The reproductive system of the female dog

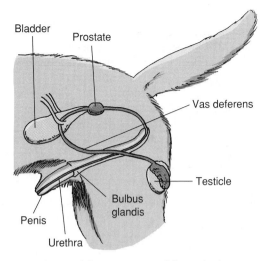

Bladder

Prostate

Vas deferens

Testicle

Bulbus glandis

Penis

Urethra

The reproductive system of the male dog

rier against infection. The vagina (a muscular tube that extends from the cervix to the outside) is connected to the vulva (skin surrounding the opening of the vagina). The vulva is the external opening of the female genitals. An oviduct is connected to each ovary. After ovulation, eggs are transported to the uterus via the oviducts. Secretion of fluid in the oviducts provides a proper environment for survival of the mature egg, fertilization, and the first few critical days of embryonic life. Proper functioning of the uterus and cervix are also required for the establishment and maintenance of pregnancy.

Infections contracted at mating can be a cause of female infertility because they interfere with the proper function of the uterus. Infertility in females can be diagnosed through various means, including x-rays, ultrasonography, physical examination, and blood tests. The vagina and vulva serve as the copulatory organs and as the last part of the birth canal. They also provide a route for infections, particularly when the vulva cannot function properly due to trauma or relaxation.

The Male Genital Tract

In males, the genital tract provides a pathway for sperm cells and semen. The epididymis connects the testicle to the ductus deferens, which carries ejaculated sperm to the urethra. Sperm mature and are stored in the epididymis. The accessory sex glands, such as the prostate, create the fluid portion of semen. Cancer and inflammation of the genital tract can be diagnosed by physical examination or ultrasonography. Other diseases or abnormal functioning can be diagnosed by testing semen samples.

■ MANAGEMENT OF REPRODUCTION IN DOGS

A complete discussion of breeding and reproduction in dogs is beyond the scope of this book. And considering the surplus of pet dogs in the US and other countries, casual rearing of litters by pet owners is not recommended. However, the following section includes a basic discussion of reproduction in dogs.

Dogs can be bred naturally or artificially. Artificial reproduction techniques include insemination with fresh, chilled, or frozen-thawed semen. Because male dogs are more likely to breed successfully in their home environment, females are generally taken to the male rather than the reverse.

Female dogs usually have estrous cycles twice a year, but the interval between cycles can range from 4 to 13 months. The **anestrus** phase is the nonbreeding portion of the cycle and is marked by inactive ovaries and a small uterus. A female dog in this phase is not attractive to male dogs and will not allow them to mount. The end of anestrus is marked by an increase in luteinizing hormone and follicle stimulating hormone.

During the **proestrus** stage, female dogs become attractive to males but still do not allow them to mate. A discharge from the vagina can be seen and the vulva starts to enlarge. Blood levels of the hormone estrogen rise during proestrus. In most dogs, proestrus lasts about 9 days.

During **estrus** female dogs are receptive to breeding by males. At this point estrogen levels are declining and progesterone levels increase. Estrus can be as short as 3 days or as long as 3 weeks, but is about 9 days long on average.

During the last phase, **diestrus**, female dogs again become resistant to breeding by males. Vaginal discharges diminish. The uterus enlarges due to stimulation by progesterone. Progesterone levels increase during the first half of diestrus, then slowly decline. Diestrus usually lasts for 2 to 3 months. If the dog becomes pregnant, progesterone levels stay high and the pregnancy lasts for about 65 days.

Unlike in other domestic species, manipulation of the estrous cycle is not easy in dogs. Prevention of estrus is typically accomplished by spaying, although short-term suppression of estrus can also be achieved by medication. Side effects of medical suppression can include inflammation of the vagina and changes in the skin and liver. It is also possible to use medications to speed up the onset of estrus in dogs that are in the late anestrus phase of the cycle.

Unplanned and unwanted mating of dogs is a common concern. Pregnancy can be completely prevented by spaying or neutering. Pregnancy can also be ended by having your veterinarian give the hormone prostaglandin F_{2alpha} or the corticosteroid dexamethasone.

Pregnancy and Delivery

Pregnancy in dogs can be detected by physical examination (palpation of the uterus) at about day 30 of gestation. A blood test is also available that measures the hormone relaxin and can detect pregnancy by day 30 to 35 of gestation. The developing fetuses can be seen on x-rays after about day 45. This is also the best way to determine the litter size. Ultrasonography can reliably detect pregnancy by 25 to 35 days and also allows your veterinarian to confirm that the fetuses are alive.

Pregnancy lasts about 65 days in dogs, but predicting the timing of delivery can be difficult. A drop in rectal temperature usually precedes delivery by about 8 to 24 hours. Labor and delivery in dogs is divided into 3 stages. Stage I lasts 12 to 24 hours. During this stage uterine contractions begin, but are not visible externally. The cervix also begins to dilate. During Stage II, abdominal contractions can be seen and the puppies are delivered. The puppies are usually delivered at intervals of 1 to 2 hours, but that can vary considerably. Stage II can last up to 24 hours. Stage III is defined as the delivery of the placenta. Dogs typically alternate between stages II and III until delivery is complete.

Abnormal labor and delivery (dystocia) can be diagnosed if the uterine contractions are too infrequent or too weak to deliver the fetuses. This can lead to prolonged labor (more than 24 hours for stage I or II or more than 4 hours between delivery of puppies during stage II). Other signs of difficult birth include puppies that are born dead or near death or excessive maternal distress. Uterine and fetal monitors can be used to assess the condition of the uterus and fetuses. Dystocia can be treated either medically or surgically. Medical treatment includes injection of calcium or the hormone oxytocin to increase the strength and frequency of uterine contractions. Neither should be given without the specific advice of a veterinarian. If these measures are not successful, cesarean section is performed to remove the fetuses.

Physical examination, and in some cases x-rays, are used to ensure that all puppies have been delivered. Post-delivery injections of oxytocin are not routinely given unless the dog has not delivered all of the placentas. Disinfection of the umbilicus (belly button) with tincture of iodine helps prevent bacterial infection in the newborn puppies. Puppies should be weighed as soon as they are dry and then twice daily for the first week. Any weight loss after the first 24 hours indicates a potential problem and should be given immediate attention, such as extra feeding, assisted nursing, or examination by a veterinarian. (For a more detailed discussion of PUPPY CARE, *see* page 15.)

Problems Associated with Delivery

Dogs should be allowed to deliver their puppies in a familiar area where they will not be disturbed. Unfamiliar surroundings or strangers may hinder delivery, interfere with milk letdown, or adversely affect maternal instincts and cause the dog to neglect her newborn puppies. This is especially true for a dog delivering her first litter. A nervous dog may either ignore the newborn puppies or give them excess attention. This can lead to nearly continuous licking and biting at the umbilical stump, which can potentially cause serious injury to the puppy. If the dog's maternal instincts fail, she may lie down in an upright position that does not allow the puppies to nurse, or she may leave the puppies unattended.

Following delivery and because of the demands of nursing, calcium levels in the bloodstream of the dog may fall to abnormally low levels (*see* page 302). This problem is most common in dogs weighing less than 45 pounds (20 kilograms) and may be worsened by an improper diet or a very large litter.

Common inflammatory diseases in the period after delivery include inflammation of the uterus (metritis) and breasts (mastitis). Retention of a placenta usually leads to metritis (page 221). Signs include continued straining as if in labor, vaginal discharge, fever, and depression. Drugs that help stimulate uterine contractions, such as oxytocin or prostaglandin F_{2alpha} may help expel the placenta. Mastitis (page 221) is usually caused by a bacterial infection and can be treated with appropriate antibiotics.

Lack of milk production (agalactia) is uncommon in dogs, but can be associated with premature delivery of the litter. Dogs that do not produce enough milk should be examined by a veterinarian to check for other underlying diseases. The normal presence of colostrum (a clear, watery fluid produced before milk and containing important antibodies) should not be confused with agalactia. Contented puppies that gain weight daily after the first 24 hours are a good indication that milk production is adequate. If necessary, milk production can be stimulated by injections of oxytocin. If milk production is inadequate, puppies may need supplemental feeding.

■ INFERTILITY

Proper ovulation in females and ejaculation of fertile and normal sperm by males are regulated through a sequence of events in the brain, nervous system, and sexual organs. For best results, ovulation and deposition of semen into the female genital tract must be closely synchronized. Failure of any step in either sex leads to infertility or sterility. The ultimate result of infertility is the failure to produce offspring. In females, infertility may be due to improper timing of breeding (the most common cause), the absence of the estrous cycle, abnormal ovulation, failure to conceive, or prenatal death. Major infertility problems in males are caused by disturbances in the production, transport, or storage of sperm; loss of libido (sexual desire); and partial or complete inability to mate. Most major infertility problems are complex. Often, several factors, singly or in combination, can cause failure to produce offspring.

Regardless of whether reproduction is attempted through natural mating or by artificial insemination, your veterinarian will determine whether it is the female or male that is infertile. Infertility can be diagnosed through laboratory tests, semen evaluation, or ultrasonography. Infertility is seldom accompanied by obvious signs of illness or infection. Lower fertility may be hereditary and your veterinarian will consider this issue when treating fertility problems.

In dogs, the focus of treatment is the individual animal. Diagnostic techniques and treatments are becoming more advanced every year. Infertility can be treated by administration of hormones that act directly on the ovaries or regulate their functions, or act to help maintain pregnancy. Hormonal treatment can also work on male dogs with low sperm counts or poor libido. On the other hand, hormonal treatment can also be used for prevention of pregnancy after undesired mating.

Antibiotics are used for treatment of infection of the reproductive tracts. The selection of the antibiotic is based on tests that determine the nature of the bacteria or infectious agent.

In some circumstances, unsatisfactory results with antibiotics and increased concerns about bacteria that develop resistance to a particular antibiotic have led veterinarians to use treatments other than antibiotics for infections of the reproductive tract. These drugs boost local immune defenses and can be used alone or in combination with antibiotics.

◼ REPRODUCTIVE DISORDERS OF MALE DOGS

Several reproductive diseases can affect male dogs. This section discusses the most common of these disorders.

Cryptorchidism

Cryptorchidism is a failure of one or both testicles to descend into the scrotum. It is the most common disorder of sexual development in dogs. The condition has a genetic basis and can be inherited from either parent. If both testicles are affected, the dog is sterile. Because the retained testicles still produce male hormones, these animals have normal mating behavior. If only one testicle is retained (unilateral cryptorchidism), the dog can still mate normally, as the one normal testicle will produce normal sperm. Because the condition is inherited, cryptorchid dogs should not be used for breeding. This condition occurs in all breeds but is commonly seen in the Toy and Miniature Poodle, Pomeranian, Dachshund, Chihuahua, Maltese, Boxer, Pekingese, English Bulldog, Miniature Schnauzer, and Shetland Sheepdog. Affected animals should be neutered due

to an increased risk of developing testicular cancer.

Inflammation of the Testes and Epididymis

Short-term inflammation of the testis or epididymis may be caused by injury or infection. Signs are pain and swelling of the testes, epididymides, or scrotum. There may be wounds or other abnormalities in the scrotal skin. The disease is diagnosed by physical examination, ultrasonography, and laboratory tests. Treatment is difficult unless the cause of the inflammation can be identified. Application of cool water packs may decrease testicular damage caused by inflammation. If there is a bacterial infection, antibiotics will be administered. If the cause is an immune disorder, medications that suppress the immune system may be administered. When maintaining fertility is not important, castration is a reasonable treatment choice for inflammation of the testes or epididymes due to any cause.

Longterm inflammation of the testis or epididymis may follow short-term inflammation, although in some cases there is no history of testicular inflammation. Many dogs do not have any signs of the disease except for infertility; however, decrease in size or softening of the testes may be present. Non-inflammatory causes of this disease include previous exposure to excessive pressure, heat, cold, or toxic agents. Hormonal causes are also possible. The diagnosis and treatment is as described above for the short-term condition.

Inflammation of the Penis and Prepuce (Balanoposthitis)

Balanoposthitis is inflammation of the penis or preputial cavity (the skin on the dog's belly that covers the penis). Mild balanoposthitis is present in many sexually mature dogs and it resolves spontaneously without any treatment. There are several causes of more severe balanoposthitis, including allergies, trauma, foreign objects, bacterial infection, and phimosis (a condition in which the prepuce cannot be drawn back to expose the penis). The most common sign is yellow-green discharge at the tip of the penis or prepuce. Swelling of the prepuce and pain are rarely present except in cases of trauma or foreign objects. The disease is diagnosed by physical examination and laboratory tests. Treatment includes correcting any predisposing factors, clipping long hair away from the opening of the prepuce, and thorough flushing of the preputial cavity with a mild antiseptic or sterile saline solution. In the case of a bacterial infection, your veterinarian may prescribe an antibiotic. Neutering will diminish preputial secretions.

Paraphimosis

Paraphimosis, or the inability to completely retract the penis into the preputial cavity usually occurs after erection. It is seen most often after semen collection or breeding. The skin at the preputial opening traps the extruded penis, impairing blood circulation. Other causes of paraphimosis include a constricting band of hair at the preputial opening or other trauma to the penis. Paraphimosis is a medical emergency because the exposed penis quickly becomes swollen (due to accumulation of fluid), dry, and painful. If recognized early, before severe swelling and pain develop, paraphimosis is easily treated. The treatment consists of gentle cleansing and lubrication of the exposed penis. The penis is replaced inside the prepuce and the swelling resolves once circulation is restored.

Phimosis

Phimosis is the inability to expose the penis and may be due to an abnormally small preputial opening. It may be hereditary or acquired as a result of trauma, inflammation, or bacterial infection. The signs are variable. Usually, the problem is unnoticed until the dog attempts to mate and is unable to copulate. Diagnosis is established by physical examination of the prepuce and penis. Treatment depends on the severity of the phimosis and the intended use of the dog. If the dog is not used for breeding, treatment probably is not needed, although neutering could be considered to prevent arousal.

Disorders of the Prostate

The prostate gland is located within the pelvis behind the bladder. The size of the prostate is determined by the hormone dihydrotestosterone in mature dogs. The prostate gland is not required for sperm production but it is important for successful breeding. The prostate gland provides the major part of the fluid in the ejaculate and is important in nourishing the sperm cells and increasing their movement.

Diseases of the prostate gland are common in dogs that have not been neutered and include enlargement of the prostate (benign prostatic hyperplasia), bacterial infection, abscesses, cysts, and tumors. These disorders cause enlargement of the prostate gland. Additional signs, such as fever, malaise, poor appetite, stiffness, and pain in the belly, are often due to bacterial infections or presence of tumors. Prostatic diseases are diagnosed by physical examination, x-rays, ultrasonography, and blood and semen tests.

Enlargement of the Prostate (Benign Prostatic Hyperplasia)

Enlargement of the prostate is the most common prostatic disorder. It is caused by male hormones. It is found in almost all unneutered dogs over the age of 6 years. There may be no signs, or straining to defecate and blood in the urine may occur. Neutering is the preferred treatment. Reduction in the size of the prostate usually follows within a few weeks of the surgery. In dogs used for breeding, medication to decrease the size of the prostate may be helpful.

Prostatitis

Inflammation of the prostate gland may be due to bacterial infections and can result in abscesses. The signs are similar to those of prostate enlargement (*see* page 219). In addition, malaise, pain, and fever are common. Dehydration and shock may occur in severe cases of prostatic abscesses. The disease is diagnosed by physical examination, x-rays, and blood tests. Longterm bacterial prostatitis may cause no signs except for recurrent urinary tract infection. Prostatitis is treated by administration of antibiotics and may require prolonged treatment. Neutering will speed recovery.

Prostatic and Paraprostatic Cysts

Large cysts are occasionally found within or near the prostate gland. The signs are similar to those seen with other types of prostatic enlargement and usually become apparent only when the cyst reaches a size sufficient to cause pressure on other organs. Large cysts may result in abdominal distention. Drug treatment may be ineffective. Your veterinarian may attempt to drain the cyst by using ultrasonography as a guide. The treatment of choice for large cysts is surgical removal. Neutering alone is unlikely to provide sufficient benefit but may be recommended after the cyst has been removed.

Prostate Cancer

Prostate cancer is a serious, yet uncommon, disorder in dogs. Neutering does not protect against future development of prostate cancer in dogs. The signs are similar to those of other prostatic diseases. Pain and fever may be present. Furthermore, the cancer may spread to other tissue and organs. There is no effective curative treatment. Consultation with a veterinary oncologist (cancer specialist) is recommended.

■ REPRODUCTIVE DISORDERS OF FEMALE DOGS

There are many reproductive diseases that can affect female dogs. The most common diseases are discussed in this section.

Abnormal or Difficult Birth (Dystocia)

Many factors can cause a difficult birth, including uterine problems, a too-small birth canal, an oversized fetus, or abnormal position of the fetus during birth. Dystocia should be considered in any of the following situations: 1) dogs that have a history of dystocia; 2) birth that does not occur within 24 hours of a drop in rectal temperature (a sign of impending birth); 3) continuous strong contraction for more than 20 to 30 minutes with no birth; 4) active labor for more than 1 to 2 hours without a birth; 5) a resting period during labor that lasts more than 2 to 4 hours; 6) obvious illness in the mother; and 7) abnormal discharge from the vulvar area. Once the cause is identified, the appropriate treatment can be determined. X-rays or ultrasonography can show how many fetuses are present. Medication may help the labor progress if the mother and fetuses are still in stable condition and there is no obstruction. Surgery (cesarean section) is performed if the mother or the fetuses are not stable or there is an obstruction.

False Pregnancy (Pseudopregnancy)

False pregnancy is common in female dogs. It occurs at the end of the heat cycle and is characterized by swelling of the mammary glands, milk production, and behavioral changes. Some dogs behave as if delivery has occurred and "mother" by nesting inanimate objects and refusing to eat. Your veterinarian will eliminate the possibility of true pregnancy by the medical history, physical examination, and x-rays or ultrasonography. Treatment is often not recommended because the condition usually ends on its own in 1 to 3 weeks. You should not milk out the mammary glands, because this will only stimulate production of more milk. Treatment can be given to animals that are uncomfortable because of milk production or to those with behavior that is troublesome.

Follicular Cysts

These fluid-filled structures develop within the ovary and lead to prolonged secretion of estrogen and continuous signs of estrus (heat) and attractiveness to males.

Ovulation may not occur during these abnormal estrous cycles. Follicular cysts should be suspected in any dog showing signs of heat for more than 40 days. The condition is diagnosed through ultrasonography and laboratory tests. The treatment of choice is removal of the ovaries and uterus, which is curative. If the dog is to be bred, administration of drugs that cause ovulation might resolve the condition; however, these dogs must be monitored closely for uterine disease.

Mastitis

Mastitis is inflammation of the mammary gland(s) that occurs in dogs after giving birth. It is caused by a bacterial infection. Risk factors for developing mastitis include poor sanitary conditions, trauma inflicted by offspring, and whole-body infection. Mastitis may involve a single gland or multiple glands. Milk is usually abnormal in color or consistency. The affected glands are hot and painful. If mastitis progresses to a generalized infection, signs of illness such as fever, depression, poor appetite, and lethargy may be seen. The disease is diagnosed based on the physical examination and the dog's medical history. Your veterinarian may test for bacteria to determine which antibiotic to use in cases of infective mastitis. Warm compresses should be applied to the affected glands 4 to 6 times daily, and the puppies should be encouraged to nurse from these glands. An abscessed mammary gland should be lanced, drained, and treated as an open wound.

At the time of weaning, there may be an abundance of milk and glands that are warm, swollen, and painful to touch, but the dog should remain alert and healthy. Lactation can be diminished by reducing food and water intake.

Metritis

Metritis is inflammation of the uterus that occurs after pregnancy. It is usually caused by bacterial infection. Factors such as prolonged delivery and retained fetuses or placentas may cause metritis. *Escheri-chia coli* bacteria are a common cause of infection of the uterus. The primary sign of infection is a pus-like discharge from the vulva. Female dogs with metritis are usually depressed, feverish, and may neglect their offspring. Pups may become restless and cry incessantly. The infection is diagnosed through physical examination, ultrasonography, and laboratory tests. Treatment includes administering fluids, supportive care, and antibiotics.

Ovarian Remnant Syndrome

Ovarian remnant syndrome is caused by ovarian tissue that was left behind when a dog was spayed. This is a complication of the surgery. The most common signs are those of heat (swelling of the vulva, flagging, and standing to be mounted). The ovarian tissue is removed by surgery.

Pyometra

Pyometra is a bacterial infection of the uterus due to hormonal changes in unspayed dogs. It is reported primarily in dogs more than 5 years old, and tends to occur 4 to 6 weeks after estrus. After estrus, the level of progesterone stays high to prepare the uterus for pregnancy by thickening its surface. If pregnancy does not occur for several cycles, the lining inside the uterus continues to thicken and cysts will form within the uterus. These cysts secrete fluids providing an ideal environment for bacterial infection. Pyometra can occur due to administration of progesterone-based medication.

The signs are variable and include lethargy, poor appetite, and vomiting. When the cervix is open, a discharge of pus, often containing blood, is present. When the cervix is closed there is no discharge and the large uterus may cause abdominal enlargement. Signs can progress rapidly to shock and death. The infection is diagnosed by physical examination, determination of the nature of the discharge, ultrasonography, x-rays, and laboratory and blood tests.

Removal of the ovaries and uterus are the recommended treatment in most cases. For animals that will be bred in the future, antibiotics and prostaglandin can be administered. Animals should be re-examined 2 weeks after completion of medical treatment to ensure complete emptying of the discharge from the uterus. Dogs with a history of pyometra should be bred on the next heat cycle after treatment, as pyometra will eventually recur. Affected dogs should be spayed as soon as their breeding life is over.

Subinvolution of Placental Sites

This disorder occurs after pregnancy as a result of abnormal repair of the lining of the uterus (where the placenta was attached). After giving birth, the uterus slowly returns to its normal size in a process called involution. Normally, a bloody discharge accompanies this process for up to 16 weeks after birth. In some dogs, the discharge lasts much longer. The condition is most common in dogs less than 3 years old after their first litter. There are no signs except for discharge from the uterus that contains blood. Blood loss is not severe with this condition. It resolves on its own and usually does not recur. Spaying is curative but it is not necessary if there is a desire to breed the dog again.

Vaginal Overgrowth (Vaginal Prolapse, Vaginal Hypertrophy)

In vaginal overgrowth, the vaginal tissue becomes swollen during estrus (heat). The swollen vaginal tissue may be seen through the vulva. This condition is caused by estrogen and is most common in young dogs. The disease is diagnosed through the medical history and physical examination. Vaginal overgrowth resolves on its own as soon as the estrogen-producing phase of the cycle is over. However, it usually recurs with every heat. Treatment may include daily cleansing of the affected area, prevention of trauma, and antibiotic ointment. An Elizabethan collar (a large funnel-shaped collar that prevents the dog from licking itself) may be necessary to prevent

self-trauma. These dogs may be bred by artificial insemination, but the female puppies may also be prone to develop this condition.

Vaginitis

Inflammation of the vagina may occur before puberty or in mature dogs. It is especially common in puppies. Vaginitis is primarily due to bacterial infection. Viral infections, vaginal foreign bodies, or cancer may also cause vaginitis. The most common sign is discharge from the vulva. Animals may also lick the vulva. The disease is diagnosed through physical examination and laboratory tests. Vaginitis in puppies usually resolves on its own when the pup has reached physical maturity. In the case of a persistent infection, antibiotics are administered. Estrogen treatment may be beneficial in the treatment of spayed dogs.

■ MAMMARY (BREAST) TUMORS

The frequency of mammary tumors in different species varies tremendously. The dog is by far the most frequently affected domestic species, with a rate that is about 3 times that found in women. About half of all tumors in female dogs are mammary tumors. Approximately 40% of canine mammary tumors are malignant (cancerous).

The cause of mammary tumors is unknown, but hormones play an important role in their development. Mammary tumors in dogs occur most often in non-spayed female dogs or females spayed late in life; they are extremely rare in male dogs. Female dogs that are spayed before their first heat cycle are no more likely to develop mammary tumors than male dogs. Breast tumors are usually diagnosed by physical examination, but confirmation and identification of the type of tumor requires a biopsy.

There are several treatment choices, including surgery to remove the tumor or the entire breast and anticancer drug

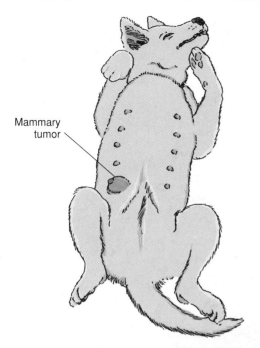

Mammary tumor

There are 10 sets of mammary glands in dogs, any of which may be the site of a tumor. Most tumors occur in the glands closest to the hind legs.

treatment. The outlook for recovery depends on multiple factors. Most canine mammary tumors that are going to cause death do so within 1 year. The risk of this disease can be greatly reduced by spaying the dog before it first comes into heat.

▣ BRUCELLOSIS

Infection with *Brucella canis* in dogs leads to abortion, infection of the sexual organs in males, and infertility. The disease occurs throughout the world and primarily affects dogs. It spreads rapidly among closely confined dogs. Infection is transmitted through ingestion of contaminated materials or via sexual transmission. Both sexes appear to be equally susceptible. The primary sign of the infection in females is abortion during the last trimester of pregnancy without previous signs of abnormality. Abortion may occur

during subsequent pregnancies. In males, the primary signs of infection are inflammation of the epididymides or testicles and reluctance to mate because of this inflammation. Transmission of brucellosis from dogs to humans occurs, but is quite rare. In humans, the disease can be very serious.

Brucellosis caused by *Brucella abortus*, *B. suis*, or *B. melitensis* is relatively rare in dogs. In cases that do occur, the dogs are usually around livestock, as they are the primary source of those strains of the bacteria.

The disease is diagnosed through laboratory tests. Spread of infection is controlled through isolation of infected dogs. Brucellosis is very difficult to treat successfully, and euthanasia of infected dogs is often recommended. In some states, cases of brucellosis must be reported to the health department. Dogs with a history of brucellosis cannot be bred.

▣ TRANSMISSIBLE VENEREAL TUMOR

Transmissible venereal tumors are cancerous tumors of the genitalia in dogs. The tumor cells are passed from dog to dog during breeding. They form cauliflower-like masses that range in size from small (less than 5 millimeters wide) to large (more than 10 centimeters wide). The surface is often ulcerated and inflamed and bleeds easily. The tumors may be single or multiple. Although they are almost always located directly on the genitalia, they may be passed on to the adjacent skin or the mucous membranes of the mouth, nose, or eyes. Diagnosis is made by examining tumor cells under a microscope. Transmissible venereal tumors are usually progressive and are treated with a combination of surgical removal, chemotherapy, and radiation treatment. The outlook for successful treatment is good, unless the tumors have already spread within the body before treatment begins.

CHAPTER 15

Lung and Airway Disorders

■ INTRODUCTION

The respiratory system consists of the large and small airways and the lungs. When a dog breathes air in through its nose or mouth, the air travels down the trachea, which divides into the tubes known as the right and left bronchi, then into the smaller airways called bronchioles in the lungs. The bronchioles end in the small sacs called alveoli, where the barrier between the air and the blood is a thin membrane.

The most important function of the respiratory system is to deliver oxygen into the blood, which distributes it throughout the body, and to remove carbon dioxide from the blood. The exchange of oxygen and carbon dioxide occurs in the alveoli. When this exchange fails or becomes inefficient because of disease, the animal can become seriously ill. The respiratory system protects its own delicate airways by warming and humidifying inhaled air and by filtering out particles. Large airborne particles usually land on the mucous lining of the nasal passages, after which they are carried to the throat to be either swallowed or coughed up. Small particles and microorganisms are destroyed by the

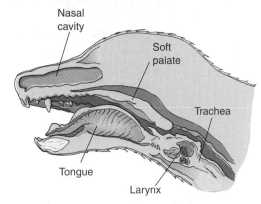

The nose and throat of a dog.

body's immune system. The upper airways also provide for the sense of smell and play a role in temperature regulation in animals such as dogs that use panting as a way to help keep cool.

Although the basic functions are the same, the anatomy of the respiratory tract varies among species. For example, the respiratory systems of dogs and cats are somewhat similar to each other, but differ from the respiratory systems of horses and humans. These differences explain in part why some diseases affect only certain species of animals.

When the level of oxygen in the blood is too low (called hypoxia or anoxia), the animal will show signs of respiratory distress. Low oxygen levels can be caused by reduced oxygen-carrying capacity of the blood cells, insufficient movement of gases in and out of the lungs, or inability of tissues to use available oxygen (a condition caused by some poisons). The animal's body attempts to compensate for low oxygen in the blood by increasing the depth and rate of breathing, increasing contraction of the spleen (to force more red blood cells into circulation), and increasing blood flow and heart rate. If the brain suffers from lack of oxygen, respi-

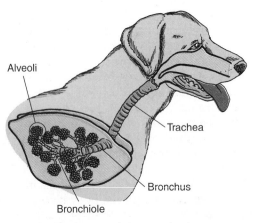

The lungs and airways of a dog

Table 14. Terms Used to Describe the Respiratory System

Medical Term	Description or Common Term
Alveoli	The sacs in the lungs where oxygen is transferred into the blood and carbon dioxide is transferred out of the blood
Bronchi	The largest branches from the trachea into the lungs
Bronchioli	The fine branches coming off of the bronchi
Epiglottis	Serves as a "trap door" on top of the larynx; keeps food out of the larynx and trachea while the animal is swallowing
Larynx	Voice box; located at the top of the windpipe (trachea)
Nasal	Pertaining to the nose
Nasopharynx	The upper part of the pharynx, at the far back of the nasal passages
Oral	Pertaining to the mouth
Oropharynx	The middle part of the pharynx, at the far back of the mouth
Paranasal sinuses	Often just called "sinuses"; the tissue-lined cavities in the skull just behind and above the eyes and along the sides of the nose
Pharynx	The passage between the back of the nose and the throat; it is separated (top to bottom) into the nasopharynx, oropharynx, and hypopharynx (throat)
Pleura	The sac that encloses the lung
Pulmonary	Pertaining to the lung
Rhino-	Pertaining to the nose
Trachea	Windpipe

ratory function may be reduced even further due to depression of nervous system activity. In addition, heart, kidney, and liver functions may be reduced, as may the normal movement and secretions of the intestine. If the body is not able to compensate for the reduced oxygen level, a "vicious cycle" may begin in which all body tissues function less efficiently.

Respiratory diseases are common in dogs. Although signs such as coughing and labored breathing are most commonly caused by problems of the respiratory tract, they may also occur because of disorders of other organ systems, such as congestive heart failure.

Both very young and older animals are at increased risk of developing respiratory disease compared to healthy adult animals. At birth, the respiratory and immune systems are not fully developed; this makes it easier for disease organisms to enter and spread within the lungs. In aged animals, a decrease in the animal's ability to filter out particles and fight off infection may render the lungs more vulnerable to airborne disease organisms and toxic particles.

Causes of Lung and Airway Disorders

Lung and airway disorders are often caused by direct infection with viruses, bacteria, fungi, or parasites, as well as by immune-mediated reactions or inhalation of irritants or toxic substances. Trauma (such as being hit by a car) may lead to the collapse of a lung or airway.

A variety of bacteria normally live in the canine nasal passages, throat, and sometimes lungs, without causing signs of illness. Infections by these usually harmless bacteria may occur when the respiratory defense mechanisms are weakened by another infection (such as distemper or parainfluenza virus), irritant (such as smoke or noxious gases), or disease (such as congestive heart failure or lung tumors). Disease organisms may continue to live in the respiratory tract of recovering animals. When stressed, these animals may relapse; they can also act as a source of infection for other animals. Poor management practices such as overcrowding are often associated with poor sanitation and environmental conditions, which can lead to more frequent and more severe infections. Conditions that favor the spread of infections often occur in kennels, pet shops, boarding facilities, and humane shelters.

Abnormalities that are present at birth, such as narrowed nostrils, elongation of the soft palate, cleft palate, and narrowing of the trachea, can cause respiratory dysfunction. Tumors, damage to the airways, and collapse of the trachea can result in difficult breathing and other signs of respiratory disease.

Diagnosing Lung and Airway Disorders

Your pet's history and the veterinarian's physical examination will help to determine the possible cause and site of respiratory disease. Chest and neck x-rays may be helpful when obstructive upper airway disease or an airway obstruction is suspected. Chest x-rays are typically done for dogs with lower respiratory signs such as cough, rapid shallow breathing, or labored breathing. Blood gas analysis or pulse oximetry may help assess the need for oxygen therapy in an animal with severe labored breathing.

When obstructive upper airway disease is suspected, your veterinarian may use various scopes to view the nose, throat, and airways. When lung disease is suspected, the veterinarian will want to examine the contents of the lung and its airways. This can be done by bathing the trachea or air sacs with a sterile fluid and examining the contents of the retrieved fluid; procedures such as transtracheal wash and bronchoalveolar lavage work in this way. When bacterial pneumonia is suspected, bacterial culture of transtracheal

Signs of Respiratory Disorders

- Discharge from the nose (mucus, pus, or blood, depending on the cause)
- Coughing that may be dry or may include mucus or blood
- Rapid breathing (not always a sign of disease, such as in healthy animals after exercise)
- Labored or difficult breathing; shortness of breath
- Shallow breathing
- Signs of pain associated with breathing in or out
- Noise (such as grunting) associated with breathing

wash or bronchoalveolar lavage fluid can reveal which type(s) of bacteria are present.

Another way the veterinarian can collect material is to use a fine needle inserted through the wall of the chest to withdraw a small amount of tissue; this procedure is called fine needle aspiration. Microscopic analysis of fluid from the lungs can also aid in the diagnosis of fungal, parasitic, or allergic lung diseases. Fine needle aspirates of lung often are useful in the diagnosis of fungal pneumonia. In dogs with fluid buildup in the chest cavity, a sample of the accumulated fluid is often removed using a needle (thoracocentesis) to allow microscopic evaluation of the fluid.

A sudden onset of a runny nose, sneezing, or both may suggest the presence of viral or bacterial infection (both very rare in adult dogs) or a tumor or foreign object in the nose. Persistent cases may require additional examination using x-rays, computed tomography (CT), examination with an endoscope, or a sample of nasal tissue. Microscopic evaluation of nasal tissue may help diagnose fungal infections. Blood tests for fungal respiratory infections are sometimes used in addition to other tests and examinations.

Control of Respiratory Conditions

Sudden dietary changes, weaning, cold, drafts, dampness, dust, poor ventilation, and the mixing of different age groups all play a role in respiratory disease in groups of animals. Stress and mixing of animals from several sources should be avoided or minimized if possible. Immunization can help control some types of respiratory infection; however, it is not a substitute for proper environmental conditions and animal care.

General Treatment of Lung and Airway Disorders

Respiratory disorders often involve the production of excess secretions in the respiratory system (for example, in the nose and lungs) that the affected animal may not be able to remove without assistance. One goal of veterinary treatment is to reduce the volume and thickness of the secretions and to make their removal easier. This can be accomplished by controlling infection, thinning the secretions, and when possible, improving drainage and mechanically removing the material.

Animals with respiratory disorders should normally receive plenty of water unless otherwise directed by the veterinarian. Adding humidity to the air may make removal of airway secretions easier. Cough medicines (expectorants) are sometimes used to thin secretions and make them easier for the animal to cough up; however, they are rarely helpful. If airway obstruction is severe, large amounts of secretions may need to be gently suctioned away by the veterinarian.

When an animal has coughing that is not helping to remove mucus (a nonproductive cough), medicines are sometimes used to suppress the coughing. Increased airway resistance caused by contraction of the bronchial airway muscles is sometimes treated with bronchodilators, which expand the airways and may be prescribed for animals with asthma-like conditions and chronic respiratory disease. Antihistamines can be used to alleviate constriction triggered by allergies. Constriction of the bronchial tubes in the lungs can also be reduced significantly by removing irritating factors, using mild sedatives, or reduc-

ing periods of excitement. If a bacterial infection is present, antibiotics are often given. Diuretics (medicines that help the body get rid of excess fluid) are sometimes used when an animal has fluid buildup in the lungs.

When a respiratory illness results in a lack of oxygen in the blood, this can usually be corrected by the administration of oxygen. However, this must be done carefully, because too much oxygen can lead to other problems.

■ ACCUMULATION OF FLUID OR AIR IN THE CHEST CAVITY

Hemothorax, the accumulation of blood in the pleural (chest) cavity, is usually caused by trauma to the chest, blood clotting disorders, or tumors in the chest. **Hydrothorax**, the accumulation of clear fluid in the pleural cavity, is usually due to interference with blood flow or lymph drainage. **Chylothorax**, the accumulation of a high-triglyceride lymphatic fluid in the pleural cavity, is relatively rare in dogs. It may be caused by rupture of the chest duct but often the cause is unknown. The signs of all 3 conditions include respiratory difficulty, such as rapid shallow breathing with labored inhalation, and weakness. Drainage of the fluid may be necessary to relieve these signs and can be helpful in diagnosing the underlying problem. However, the outlook for many disorders that cause accumulation of fluid in the chest is guarded to poor.

Air in the pleural cavity, called **pneumothorax**, may be caused by trauma or occur spontaneously. The lung collapses if a large volume of air enters the pleural cavity, causing difficulty inhaling or rapid, shallow breathing. This condition should be considered an emergency that requires immediate veterinary attention.

■ ALLERGIC PNEUMONITIS

Allergic pneumonitis is an acute or chronic allergic reaction of the lungs and small airways. The lungs "overreact" to the presence of a parasite or other irritant, causing inflammation and a chronic cough. There is often a higher than normal number of white cells called eosinophils in the blood. The underlying cause is rarely determined in these reactions in dogs.

Pulmonary infiltration with eosinophilia, known as **PIE syndrome** (*see* page 168), is associated with allergic pneumonitis. Causes of PIE syndrome include parasites, chronic bacterial or fungal infections, viruses, external antigens, and unknown factors.

Canine heartworm pneumonitis occurs when dogs become sensitized to the prelarval stage (microfilariae) of heartworms. Migrating intestinal parasites and primary lung parasites may cause mild signs of allergic pneumonitis. **Pulmonary nodular eosinophilic granulomatous syndrome** is a rare, severe allergic reaction occurring in dogs and is most often associated with heartworm infection (*see also* HEARTWORM DISEASE, page 73).

A chronic cough is the most common sign of allergic pneumonitis. The cough may be mild or severe, and it may be dry (nonproductive) or contain secretions (productive). Weight loss, rapid or difficult breathing, wheezing, intolerance to exercise, and occasionally coughing up of blood may be seen. Severely affected animals may have bluish mucous membranes at rest. The degree of labored breathing and coughing is related to the severity of inflammation within the airways and alveoli.

The diagnosis is based largely on the animal's history and signs, chest x-rays, and laboratory tests. Evidence of heartworm disease or parasitic lung disease on x-rays may suggest these as an underlying cause of the allergic reaction. Blood tests show an increase in several types of white blood cells, indicating inflammation or infection. Fecal analysis and a heartworm test are performed when lung parasites or heartworms are suspected.

When an underlying cause is identified, elimination of the offending agent and a short-term course of a corticosteroid usually resolves the problem. When heart-

worm disease or lung parasites appear to be the cause, corticosteroid treatment before or during treatment for the parasite controls the lung signs. If an underlying cause cannot be determined, prolonged corticosteroid therapy is often required. When severe airway constriction is suspected, bronchodilators or beta$_2$-agonist medications may be helpful. Animals with severe shortness of breath may require oxygen therapy.

■ BRONCHITIS

Bronchitis is an inflammation of the bronchial airways that may extend into the lungs. It is discussed later in this chapter as part of tracheobronchitis (page 237).

■ CANCERS AND TUMORS

The respiratory system can be a host to many different tumors. The following are the more common tumors found in the lungs and airways of dogs.

Tumors of the Nose and Sinuses

Tumors of the nose and sinuses account for about 1 to 2% of all canine tumors. The incidence is slightly higher in males and in older dogs. The average age at time of diagnosis is 10.5 years of age. In dogs, virtually all of these tumors are cancerous (malignant). Long-nosed and medium-nosed breeds appear to be at higher risk than short-nosed (brachycephalic) breeds. In general, if untreated, survival is 3 to 5 months after diagnosis.

Chronic nasal discharge containing mucus, pus, or blood is the most common sign. Initially, the discharge involves one side of the nose, but it often becomes 2-sided. Periodic sneezing, bleeding from the nose, and snoring may occur. Deformities of the face and mouth result from the destruction of bony or soft-tissue nasal and sinus structures. Extension of these tumors behind the eyeballs can result in protruding eyeballs, excessive tear production, and inflammation of the cornea. Late in the disease, central nervous system signs such as disorientation, blindness, seizures, stupor, and coma may develop if the tumor extends into the upper skull.

Diagnosis is based on the history and clinical signs. Nasal x-rays or computed tomography (CT) scans typically show increased density of the nasal cavity and sinuses as well as evidence of bone destruction. Nasal CT scans are preferred because they provide better detail than x-rays when attempting to distinguish tumors of the nose from other causes of chronic nasal discharge. A biopsy of tumor tissue can provide a definite diagnosis.

The recommended treatment largely depends on the tumor type and the extent of disease. Treatments such as aggressive surgical removal of the tumor, drug therapies, radiation therapy, or combinations of these provide a more favorable outlook when diagnosis is made early.

Tumors of the Larynx and Trachea

Tumors of the larynx and trachea are rare in dogs. The most common signs of tumors of the larynx include labored breathing when inhaling or after exercise; high-pitched noisy breathing; voice change (hoarse bark or loss of voice); and coughing. Similar signs, including coughing, labored breathing, and high-pitched, noisy breathing, are associated with tumors of the trachea. The animal may cough up blood, but this is rare. The degree of labored breathing often relates to the degree of obstruction of the windpipe.

A diagnosis can often be made from the history and clinical findings and by eliminating other causes of upper airway obstruction or coughing. The tumor mass may be seen by the veterinarian during examination of the larynx or trachea with an endoscope. Definitive diagnosis can be made after a biopsy. Treatment involves surgically removing the tumor. Some types of tumors respond to radiation therapy.

Primary Lung Tumors

Tumors that originate in the lung (primary lung tumors) are rare in dogs and represent approximately 1% of canine tumors. Metastatic lung cancers (cancers that spread to the lungs from other locations) are much more common in dogs than primary lung cancers. However, primary lung cancers are being seen more frequently over the last 20 years. This is likely attributable to an increased average life span, better detection and awareness, or, possibly, increasing exposure to cancer-causing agents in the environment. Most primary lung tumors are diagnosed at an average age of 10 to 12 years in dogs. All breeds and both genders appear to be equally affected. Of the primary lung tumors in dogs, virtually all are malignant (cancerous).

Primary lung tumors have variable signs, which depend on the location of the tumor, rate of tumor growth, and the presence of previous or current lung disease. Common signs include cough, poor appetite, weight loss, reduced exercise tolerance, lethargy, rapid breathing, labored breathing, wheezing, vomiting or regurgitation, fever, and lameness. The most common sign in dogs is a chronic, nonproductive cough.

Chest x-rays are the first step in making a diagnosis in animals that have signs suggesting lung cancer. A definitive diagnosis of lung cancer requires a sample of tissue (biopsy).

Surgery to remove the portion of the lung containing the tumor is the recommended treatment in most cases. Tumors that cannot be operated on or those that have spread may be treated with chemotherapy. A dog with a single primary lung tumor that has not spread to the lymph nodes has the longest average survival time (15 to 26 months); if the lymph nodes are involved or multiple tumors are found at the time of diagnosis, survival time is shortened. Recurrence or spread of the tumor is a common cause of death.

Metastatic Lung Tumors

A metastatic lung tumor is one that originates in another part of the body and then spreads to the lungs. A tumor may spread to the lungs through the blood or lymph systems or by direct extension of tumor cells from a nearby location in the body. The signs of metastatic lung disease are similar to those of primary lung tumors except that coughing is less common. The severity of signs depends on the location of the tumor and whether the lesions are single or multiple. The diagnosis and treatment is similar to that for primary lung tumors. Chemotherapy or radiation therapy may be useful with certain tumor types that are not well-suited for surgery. Because spread to the lung occurs late in the clinical course of a malignant tumor, the outlook is poor.

▓ CANINE NASAL MITES

The canine nasal mite, *Pneumonyssoides caninum*, has been reported worldwide. All breeds, ages, and sexes of dogs appear to be affected, although one report suggested that dogs older than 3 years of age were affected more often and that large breed dogs had a higher incidence than small breed dogs. The mites live in the nasal passages and sinuses. Transmission of the mite is thought to be by both direct and indirect contact between dogs. There is no evidence to suggest that this organism presents a risk to humans.

The most common signs associated with nasal mite infestation include bleeding from the nose, sneezing, "reverse sneezing" (sniffing air rapidly inward), impaired ability to pick up scents, facial itching, nasal discharge, labored breathing, head shaking, and high-pitched, noisy breathing. Other, less specific signs include coughing, restlessness, and other indications of upper respiratory disease.

Examination of the dog's nose with an endoscope and nasal flushing are useful tools for diagnosing nasal mites. Flexible scopes allow the veterinarian to observe the nasal passages, and the fluid obtained from nasal flushing can be examined for the presence of mites. Other procedures that are sometimes helpful include blood and urine tests, nasal or dental x-rays, or

nasal biopsy. It is important to locate and identify the nasal mites, as many other respiratory diseases can cause similar signs.

There is no single universally recommended treatment for canine nasal mites; however, several antiparasitic medications appear to be effective. Treatment may not completely eliminate clinical signs, particularly if infection is suspected but mites have not been found. In these cases, it is probable that the signs are the result of another upper airway disease present at the same time.

▓ DIAPHRAGMATIC HERNIA

A diaphragmatic hernia is a condition in which a break in the diaphragm allows protrusion of abdominal organs into the chest. In dogs, automobile-related trauma is a common cause of diaphragmatic hernia, although defects of the diaphragm that are present at birth (congenital) may also be a cause.

The signs of a hernia can vary. In the case of sudden trauma or injury, the dog has difficulty breathing. The degree of labored breathing may vary from barely detectable to fatal, depending on the severity of the hernia. If the stomach is trapped in the hernia, it may bloat and the animal's condition may worsen rapidly. In more mild, longterm cases, general signs such as weight loss may be more noticeable than respiratory signs. During an examination, the veterinarian may note the absence of normal lung sounds and/or the presence of digestive system sounds in the chest.

A definitive diagnosis is most frequently made from x-rays, which can reveal changes in the shape of the diaphragm and the displacement of abdominal organs. Specialized x-rays that use dyes to highlight the digestive organs are sometimes necessary to make the diagnosis. Samples of abdominal or chest fluids, electrocardiographs (EKGs), and blood work may be obtained, and surgical exploration of the abdominal cavity may be necessary in some cases.

Surgical repair of the hernia is the only treatment. If other trauma is present, the animal's condition is usually stabilized before surgical correction of the hernia is performed.

EMPHYSEMA

Emphysema is an important disease in humans; however, in other animals it typically occurs as a result of another lung disease. The condition leads to difficulty in expelling air from the lungs, making breathing more difficult. Two major forms of emphysema are generally recognized. **Alveolar emphysema** is abnormal permanent enlargement of the alveoli, which are small air sacs deep in the lungs. **Interstitial emphysema** is the presence of air within the supporting connective tissue of the lung. Chronic obstructive pulmonary (lung) disease (COPD) can cause enlargement and destruction of air spaces. The association of high numbers of white blood cells with COPD suggests that there may be allergic, infectious, and/or toxicologic causes for the condition. **Congenital lobar emphysema** of dogs (a condition seen in the Pekingese breed) occurs because of incomplete development of the bronchiolar cartilage.

KENNEL COUGH (INFECTIOUS TRACHEOBRONCHITIS)

Kennel cough results from an inflammation of the upper airways. It is fully discussed in this chapter under Tracheobronchitis (page 237).

LARYNGITIS

The larynx is the part of the throat often called the "voice box" in humans. Laryngitis is an inflammation of the larynx. It may result from upper respiratory tract infection or by direct irritation from inhalation of dust, smoke or irritating gas, or foreign objects. It can also be caused by the trauma of a breathing tube placed during surgery or excessive vocalization (barking). Laryngitis may accompany infectious tracheobronchitis and distemper in dogs.

Fluid buildup and swelling of the mucous membranes is often a key part of laryngitis; if severe, the upper airway may be obstructed. Brachycephalic dogs (dogs that have a flattened face with short nasal passages and larynx, such as a Pug) obese dogs, and dogs with paralysis of the larynx (*see* page 233), may develop laryngitis through severe panting or respiratory effort during excitement or from being overheated.

A cough is often the first noticeable sign of laryngitis. The cough is harsh, dry, and short at first, but becomes soft and moist later and may be very painful. It can be induced by pressure on the larynx, exposure to cold or dusty air, swallowing coarse food or cold water, or attempts to administer medicines. Vocal changes may be evident. Bad breath and difficult, noisy breathing may also be noted, and the animal may stand with its head lowered and mouth open. Swallowing is difficult and painful. Death due to suffocation may occur, especially if the animal is exerted; however, this is rare. When it does occur, it is not the result of laryngitis alone, but rather is due to underlying causes such as paralysis.

Fluid buildup and swelling of the larynx may develop within hours, causing an increased effort to inhale and high-pitched breathing arising from the larynx. The respiratory rate may slow as the animal's effort to breathe increases. Visible mucous membranes, such as the gums in the mouth, become bluish from lack of oxygen, the pulse rate increases, and body temperature rises. If the swelling obstructs the airways, affected dogs may be unable to cool themselves down in hot weather; a significant rise in temperature is not uncommon. Untreated animals with significant obstruction eventually collapse.

The veterinarian can make a tentative diagnosis based on the clinical signs and physical examination of the dog. A definitive diagnosis requires examination of the larynx with an endoscope; in dogs, anesthesia is usually required during this procedure.

If the larynx is obstructed, an opening will be made in the neck to allow a tracheotomy tube to be placed; this tube enables the animal to breathe while the problem is being corrected. Corticosteroids may be prescribed to reduce swelling and obstruction; these are often given along with nonsteroidal anti-inflammatory drugs (NSAIDs) and systemic antibiotics. Diuretic drugs may be used to relieve fluid buildup in the larynx and lungs. Identification and treatment of the primary cause of the laryngitis is essential. Procedures that may be recommended to speed the animal's recovery and provide comfort include inhalation of humidified air; confinement in a warm, clean environment; feeding of soft or liquid foods; and avoidance of dust. Cough-suppressing medications and antibiotics may also be needed to treat this condition.

■ LUNG FLUKES

The adult flukes *Paragonimus kellicotti* and *Paragonimus westermani* usually live in cysts or bulla, primarily in the lungs of dogs. They also have been found rarely in other organs or the brain. Infection is most common in China, Southeast Asia, and North America. The eggs from the adult flukes pass through the cyst wall, are coughed up, swallowed, and passed in the feces. The life cycle includes several snails as the first intermediate host and crayfish or crabs as the second. Dogs become infected by eating raw crayfish or crabs that contain the encysted parasite. The young flukes eventually migrate to the lungs where they become established.

Infected animals may have a chronic, deep, intermittent cough and eventually become weak and lethargic, although many infections pass unnoticed. A diagnosis is based on finding the characteristic eggs in feces or coughed-up material. The location of the flukes in the lungs is determined by x-rays. Several drugs provide effective treatment for lung fluke infections.

■ LUNGWORM INFECTION

Lungworm infections in dogs are usually caused by the parasitic nematode *Oslerus osleri*. They have been found in the United States, South Africa, New Zealand, India, Great Britain, France, and Australia. Adult lungworms live in nodules in the trachea of dogs, and larvated eggs laid by adults hatch there. Pups become infected from the feces or saliva of an infected dog (for example, when an infected mother licks her pups). Infection is infrequent in dogs.

Signs of lungworm infection range from moderate, dry coughing with slightly increased respiratory rates to severe, persistent coughing and respiratory distress or even failure. Infections with no visible signs can also occur. Death is relatively uncommon in dogs infected with these lungworms. However, some nematodes that inhabit the right ventricle of the heart, such as *Angiostrongylus vasorum* and *Dirofilaria immitis* (*see* HEARTWORM DISEASE, page 73), both found in dogs in certain areas of the world, may be associated with lung disease. Signs relating to a heart or a lung syndrome, or to a combination of both, may occur.

Diagnosis of lungworm infection is based on signs, known transmission patterns, and presence of larvae in feces. Examination of the airways with an endoscope (bronchoscopy) and x-rays can be helpful tools. It can be a challenge for the veterinarian to diagnose lungworm because infected animals do not always pass the larvae in their feces, and when they do, they may be few in number. Bronchoscopy can be used to collect washings from the trachea to examine for eggs, larvae, and white blood cells.

Lungworm infection in dogs can be difficult to treat, but there is evidence that appropriate antiparasitic drugs are effective, particularly when combined with surgical removal of the nodules in the trachea. It may be necessary to continue antiparasitic treatment for up to 2 months.

Other Lungworms

Capillaria aerophila are parasites that are usually found in the frontal sinuses, trachea, bronchi, and nasal cavities of foxes, but they can also be found in dogs and other carnivores. Female worms produce eggs in the lungs that are coughed up and swallowed, and then passed in the feces. Dogs become infected by eating food or drinking water that is contaminated with larvated eggs. After being eaten, the eggs hatch in the intestine and then travel to the lungs through the circulatory system. Larvae mature about 40 days after infection. Clinical signs include coughing, persistent sneezing, and nasal discharge. Treatment with appropriate antiparasitic drugs is usually effective.

■ PARALYSIS OF THE LARYNX

Laryngeal paralysis, a disease of the upper airway, is common in dogs. The condition occurs when the cartilages of the larynx do not open and close normally during respiration. It is an acquired problem in middle-aged to older, large and giant breeds of dogs such as Labrador Retrievers, Irish Setters, and Great Danes. It is seen less often as a hereditary, congenital disease in Bouvier des Flandres, Leonbergers, Siberian Huskies, Bulldogs, and racing sled dogs.

Signs include a dry cough, voice changes, and noisy breathing that slowly progresses to obvious difficulty in breathing during stress and exertion, and eventually to collapse. Regurgitation and vomiting may occur. The progression of signs usually takes months or even years before respiratory distress is evident. The veterinarian will generally need to examine the upper airway with an endoscope (laryngoscopy) to confirm the diagnosis. This procedure is done using light anesthesia.

Initially, treatment is directed at relieving the signs of airway obstruction. Tranquilizers and corticosteroids are temporarily effective in mild cases. Severe obstruction may require the placement of a tube into the trachea (tracheotomy).

Surgery to correct the problem is often successful.

■ PHARYNGITIS

Pharyngitis is inflammation of the walls of the throat (pharynx). It accompanies most upper airway viral and bacterial respiratory infections, such as distemper in dogs. Other causes include damage of the pharynx by a foreign object or cancer of the mouth or tonsils. In dogs, foreign objects stuck in the mouth and throat are quite common; typical objects include pins, needles, porcupine quills, and pieces of stick or bone fragments.

In general, animals with pharyngitis have a normal desire to eat and drink but may have difficulty swallowing. As a result of inflammation and abscesses, an emergency situation can develop if the airway becomes obstructed. The diagnosis is based on a complete physical examination, which may include x-rays and endoscopic examination of the throat along with cultures of fluids and sites that are draining.

The primary treatment is to identify and control or eliminate the factors leading to the disease. If pharyngitis has been caused by a foreign object, surgery to remove the object and any dead tissue is done under general anesthesia.

■ PNEUMONIA

Pneumonia is an inflammation of the lungs and airways that causes breathing difficulties and deficiency of oxygen in the blood. There are many possible causes. The most common cause of pneumonia is a viral infection of the lower respiratory tract. Canine distemper virus, adenovirus types 1 and 2, canine influenza virus, and parainfluenza virus cause damage to the airways and make the animal susceptible to the development of pneumonia.

Parasitic invasion of the bronchi can also result in pneumonia. Tuberculous pneumonia, although uncommon, is sometimes seen in dogs. Fungal pneumonia (*see* page 234) is also seen in dogs. Injury to the mucous membranes of the bronchial tubes and inhalation of irritants may cause pneumonia directly, as well as making the animal susceptible to bacterial infection. Aspiration pneumonia (*see* below) may result from persistent vomiting, abnormal movement of the esophagus, or improperly administered medications (for example, oil or barium) or food (forced feeding).

Signs of pneumonia include lethargy, loss of appetite, and a deep cough. Labored breathing, "blowing" of the lips, and bluish mucous membranes may be evident, especially after exercise. Body temperature is moderately increased. Complications such as pleurisy or infection by additional organisms may occur.

Diagnosis usually involves a combination of history, physical examination (including listening to the lungs with a stethoscope), and appropriate tests. Your veterinarian may be able to hear wheezing sounds within the lungs. In the later stages of pneumonia, the increased lung density caused by inflammation can be seen on x-rays. Analysis of fluid used to "wash" the airways is valuable for the diagnosis of bacterial infections. Bacterial culture and drug sensitivity testing help the veterinarian to determine the best course of antibiotic treatment, if needed. A viral infection generally results in an increased body temperature.

Animals with pneumonia benefit from a warm, dry environment. If the mucous membranes are very bluish (indicating poor oxygen in the blood), the veterinarian may administer oxygen. Antibiotics are usually given, although the treatment may be modified based on the results of laboratory cultures, so that the drugs given best match the type of infection found. The dog may need to be reexamined frequently, including periodic chest x-rays, to watch for improvement or recurrence, to follow an underlying disease (if one is present), or to detect any possible complications.

Aspiration Pneumonia

Aspiration pneumonia is a lung infection caused by inhalation of foreign material.

The severity of the inflammation depends on the material inhaled, the type of bacteria inhaled, and the distribution of foreign material in the lungs. A common cause of aspiration pneumonia is the improper administration of liquid medicines. Animals that breathe in vomit or attempt to eat or drink while partially choked are at risk for aspiration pneumonia as well. Disturbances in the normal swallowing mechanism, such as in anesthetized or comatose animals, or in animals with deformities such as cleft palate, may also lead to aspiration pneumonia.

A history suggesting that a foreign substance might have been inhaled is the most important clue to diagnosing this disease. Signs include labored or rapid breathing, rapid heart rate, and fever. Other signs include bluish mucous membranes and airway spasms. A sweetish, off-smelling breath may be detected, which becomes more intense as the disease progresses. This is often associated with a nasal discharge that sometimes is tinged reddish brown or green. Occasionally, evidence of the breathed-in material (for example, oil droplets) can be seen in the nasal discharge or coughed-up material.

As with nearly all disease conditions, prevention is better than treatment. This is especially the case for aspiration pneumonia, since the outlook is poor even with treatment. The rate of death is high, and recovered animals often develop lung abscesses. Veterinarians normally use drugs and other precautions to minimize the risk of an animal inhaling fluid (such as saliva) during surgery. If an animal is known to have inhaled a foreign substance, broad-spectrum antibiotics are usually prescribed without waiting for signs of pneumonia to appear. Care and supportive treatment are the same as for other types of pneumonia.

Fungal Pneumonia

Fungal pneumonia (also called mycotic pneumonia) is a fungal infection of the lung that leads to the development of pneumonia. A number of fungi have been shown to cause fungal pneumonia in domestic animals.

Often these fungi are found in animals with compromised immune systems, but they can cause disease in healthy animals as well. Infection is typically caused by inhalation of spores, which can spread through the blood and lymph systems. The source of most fungal infections is believed to be soil-related rather than spread from one animal to another.

Although fungal pneumonia cases with sudden, severe onset occur rarely, the most common course of disease is development over a long period of time. A short, moist cough is characteristic of the disease, and a thick discharge of mucous from the nose may be seen. As the disease progresses, labored breathing, weight loss, and generalized weakness develop. During examination, the veterinarian may detect harsh respiratory sounds. In advanced cases, breath sounds are decreased or almost impossible to hear. Inflammation of the lymph nodes can cause compression of the airway, making it difficult for the animal to breathe. Periodic fever can occur.

A tentative diagnosis of fungal pneumonia can be made if an animal with long-term respiratory disease exhibits typical signs and does not respond to antibiotic therapy. (Antibiotics are effective against bacteria but not against fungi or other organisms.) However, a definite diagnosis requires identification of the fungus using appropriate laboratory tests. X-rays and blood tests may be useful.

Antifungal drugs are used to treat fungal pneumonia. Extended drug therapy, which may be needed for several months after signs have disappeared, is usually necessary to effectively treat the infection.

■ PULMONARY EDEMA

Pulmonary edema, the abnormal accumulation of fluid in the tissue, airways, or air sacs (alveoli) of the lungs, may occur along with circulatory disorders or in some allergic reactions or infectious diseases. Head trauma can cause pulmonary edema in dogs. Labored breathing and open-mouth breathing may occur. Animals stand rather than lying down, lie only on their chest, or assume a sitting position. The veterinarian may be able to hear wheezing or crackling sounds in the chest.

■ RHINITIS AND SINUSITIS

The most common upper respiratory tract malfunction is rhinitis (inflammation of the mucous membranes of the nose) or other damage to the nasal mucous membranes. It is often associated with sinusitis, or inflammation of the lining of the sinuses. If the nasal passages deteriorate and fail to function properly, a major filtration function is removed. This exposes the lungs to much heavier loads of dust and microorganisms.

Viral infection is the most common cause of acute rhinitis or sinusitis in dogs. Canine distemper, canine adenovirus types 1 and 2, and canine parainfluenza are most frequently involved. Infection with bacteria frequently occurs after the initial viral infection; bacterial rhinitis without an initial viral infection is extremely rare in dogs. (One exception is infection with *Bordetella bronchiseptica*, an organism that causes infectious tracheobronchitis.) Allergic rhinitis or sinusitis occurs seasonally in association with pollen production, and year-round, probably in association with house dusts and molds. Inhalation of smoke or irritant gases, or foreign objects lodged in the nasal passages, also may cause rhinitis.

Major Causes of Fungal Pneumonia

- *Aspergillus* species
- *Blastomyces dermatitidis*
- *Candida* species
- *Coccidioides immitis*
- *Cryptococcus neoformans*
- *Histoplasma capsulatum*

Underlying causes of chronic rhinitis include chronic inflammatory disease (such as lymphoplasmacytic rhinitis), trauma, parasites, foreign bodies, tumors, or fungal infection. Rhinitis or sinusitis may result when a root abscess on an upper tooth extends further upward.

Signs of rhinitis include nasal discharge, sneezing, snoring, open-mouth breathing, and/or labored breathing. Pawing at the face is occasionally seen and often suggests the presence of a foreign object. Tears and inflammation of the membrane surrounding the eyes (conjunctivitis) often accompany inflammation of the upper respiratory passages. The nasal discharge is clear but may become mucus-like or contain pus as a result of secondary infection. Sneezing, in an attempt to clear the upper airways of discharge, is seen most frequently in acute rhinitis and tends to come and go in cases of chronic rhinitis. Affected dogs may also experience an aspiration reflex ("reverse sneeze"), a short rapid inhalation in an attempt to clear the nose. Tumors, fungal disease, or chronic inflammatory rhinitis can cause a chronic nasal discharge that starts out as 1-sided but becomes 2-sided; another sign is discharge that starts out as mucus or pus but later contains blood.

Diagnosis is based on the dog's history, physical examination, x-ray findings (especially computed tomography), endoscopic examination, nasal biopsy, and elimination of other causes of nasal discharge and sneezing.

In mild cases or those that are recent in onset, treatment to relieve signs may be effective. The veterinarian may prescribe antibiotics if bacterial infection is present or suspected (antibiotics are not effective against viruses). Fungal rhinositis and sinusitis can be treated with antifungal therapy once the particular fungus has been identified. Chronic inflammatory rhinitis is a frustrating disease that often does not respond to various therapies. Animals that evade definitive diagnosis may require surgery. Radiation therapy is usually the most successful treatment for

tumors in the nose (*see also* CANCERS AND TUMORS, page 228).

■ TONSILLITIS

Tonsillitis, an inflammation of the tonsils, usually occurs in dogs with another disorder of the lungs or airways, such as disorders of the nose, mouth, or upper throat (for example, cleft palate); chronic vomiting or regurgitation (for example, from an enlarged esophagus); or chronic coughing (for example, with bronchitis). When present, it is most frequently seen in small breeds. Chronic tonsillitis may occur in brachycephalic dogs (those bred to have flattened faced and short noses) along with inflammation of the upper throat. Bacteria are a frequent cause of disease. Plant fibers or other foreign bodies that lodge in a tonsil may produce a localized 1-sided inflammation or abscess. Other physical and chemical agents may cause irritation of the mouth and upper throat and one or both tonsils. Tonsillitis may also accompany tumors in the tonsil because of physical trauma or bacterial infection that enters the diseased tonsil.

Tonsillitis is not always accompanied by obvious signs. Gagging, followed by retching or a short, soft cough, may result in expulsion of small amounts of mucus. Poor appetite, listlessness, salivation, and difficulty swallowing are seen in severe tonsillitis. Enlargement of the tonsils may range from slight to large enough to cause difficulty swallowing or to cause high-pitched, noisy breathing.

Prompt administration of appropriate antibiotics is the usual treatment for bacterial tonsillitis. In dogs that do not respond to initial treatment, bacterial culture and drug sensitivity testing may be needed to identify the best course of treatment. Mild pain relievers are sometimes given for severe pharyngeal irritation, and a soft palatable diet is recommended for a few days until the difficulty swallowing resolves. Most cases of tonsillitis do not require removal of the tonsils (tonsillectomy). The veterinarian will probably recommend tonsillectomy when tumors of the tonsil are present or when there is chronic tonsil enlargement that interferes with airflow.

■ TRACHEAL COLLAPSE

Tracheal collapse is most common in toy and miniature breeds of dogs, although it may occasionally occur in large-breed dogs. The cause is unknown. Affected dogs have a dry, honking, chronic cough, and labored breathing. The condition occurs more frequently in dogs that are obese and in those with heart disease or another lung disease (especially chronic bronchitis). Weight loss for obese or overweight dogs is critical in the management of tracheal collapse. Other measures include exercise restriction, reduction of excitement and stress, and appropriate medications such as cough suppressants, antibiotics, and corticosteroids.

■ TRACHEOBRONCHITIS (BRONCHITIS)

Tracheobronchitis is an acute or chronic inflammation of the trachea and bronchial airways; it may also extend into the lungs. It often occurs in dogs already affected by respiratory disease or a disorder of the lungs or airways. For example, infectious tracheobronchitis (kennel cough; *see* page 238) often follows a viral infection of the respiratory system. Other causes of tracheobronchitis in dogs include parasites,

| Normal | Inflamed |
| bronchial wall | bronchial wall |

In tracheobronchitis, areas of the tracheal or bronchial wall become inflamed and swollen, causing the air passageway to narrow (modified with permission from *The Merck Manual of Medical Information*, Second Home Edition, 2003).

diseases of the mouth and pharynx, chronic coughing related to heart or lung disease, smoke inhalation, and exposure to chemical fumes.

Chronic bronchitis in middle-aged and older dogs may become worse following sudden changes in the weather or other environmental stresses. Animals with foreign bodies in the airway or developmental abnormalities such as deformities of the larynx may tend to develop bronchitis. Chronic bronchitis most often affects small breeds of dogs, although it is also seen in large breeds.

Spasms of coughing are the most prominent sign. The act of coughing is an attempt to remove accumulations of mucus and secretions from the respiratory passages; it is most severe after rest or a change of environment or at the beginning of exercise. The dog's temperature may be slightly increased. The acute stage of bronchitis passes in 2 to 3 days; the cough, however, may persist for several weeks. Severe bronchitis and pneumonia are difficult to tell apart; in fact, bronchitis often extends from the bronchial tubes into the lung cells and results in pneumonia.

The veterinarian's diagnosis is made from the history, physical examination, clinical signs and by ruling out other causes of coughing. Diagnostic tools include chest x-rays, use of an endoscope to view the bronchial tubes (bronchoscopy), and collection of biopsy and swab samples for laboratory analysis. Bronchial washing is an additional diagnostic aid that may demonstrate the agent causing the illness (for example, a parasite) or the animal's response to disease (for example, the production of certain types of red blood cells). These diagnostic tests may be needed in cases where the veterinarian's initial treatment is not effective in providing relief.

In mild cases or those with a recent onset of signs, supportive therapy may be effective, but treatment of the underlying disease (if present) is also needed. Rest, warmth, and proper hygiene are important. If bacterial infection is present, antibiotics may be prescribed. A persistent, dry (nonproductive) cough may be controlled by a prescribed cough suppressant that contains codeine. The veterinarian may perform or prescribe therapy such as use of a mist (nebulization) or steam from a hot shower to help loosen secretions and stimulate coughing up of secretions.

Infectious Tracheobronchitis of Dogs (Kennel Cough)

Infectious tracheobronchitis results from inflammation of the upper airways. It is a mild disease that normally improves on its own. However, it can progress to fatal bronchopneumonia in puppies or to chronic bronchitis in weakened, ill, or aged dogs. The disease spreads rapidly among susceptible dogs housed in close confinement such as veterinary hospitals or kennels.

A number of viral and bacterial organisms can cause kennel cough. It is common to have infections with more than one of these organisms at the same time. Stress and environmental changes such as extremes of ventilation, temperature, and humidity appear to increase the dog's susceptibility to disease as well as its severity.

The most common sign is spasms of harsh, dry coughing, which may be followed by retching and gagging. The severity of the cough usually diminishes during the first 5 days, but the disease persists for 10 to 20 days. Affected dogs have few if any additional signs except for some loss of appetite. Body temperature and white blood cell counts usually remain normal.

Development of more severe signs, including fever, pus-containing nasal discharge, depression, loss of appetite, and a productive cough, especially in puppies, usually indicates the presence of an additional infection such as distemper or bronchopneumonia. Stress, particularly from adverse environmental conditions and improper nutrition, may contribute to a relapse during recovery.

Tracheobronchitis is usually suspected whenever a dog demonstrates the distinctive harsh cough and has a history of exposure to other susceptible or affected dogs. Laboratory tests are usually normal.

In most cases, affected dogs should not be hospitalized because the disease is highly contagious and because it generally improves on its own. The dog's recovery may be hastened by good nutrition and hygiene, and (if needed) improvement of the animal's living environment as recommended by the veterinarian. Cough suppressants are sometimes prescribed to control persistent nonproductive coughing. Antibiotics are usually not needed except in severe chronic cases. Corticosteroids may be prescribed to help alleviate signs.

Vaccines are available to protect against distemper, parainfluenza, canine adenovirus-2, and *Bordetella bronchiseptica*, some of the main organisms responsible for kennel cough. Your veterinarian will recommend the types of vaccination, and vaccination schedule, most appropriate for your dog.

CHAPTER **16**

Skin Disorders

■ STRUCTURE OF THE SKIN

The skin is the largest organ of your dog's body. It provides a protective barrier against the environment, regulates temperature, and gives your dog its sense of touch. Depending on the species and age, the skin may be 12 to 24% of a dog's body weight. The skin has 3 major layers: the epidermis or outermost layer, the dermis or middle layer, and subcutis or innermost

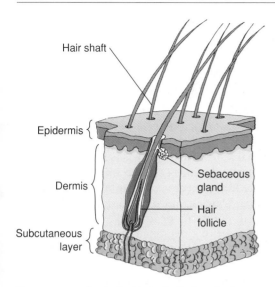

Hair shaft

Epidermis {

Dermis {

Subcutaneous layer {

Sebaceous gland

Hair follicle

The anatomy of a dog's skin includes 3 major layers, as well as hair follicles and sebaceous glands.

and the ducts of the sebaceous and sweat glands. The melanocytes produce the skin and hair coloring (pigment) called melanin. Production of melanin is controlled by both hormones and the genes received from parents. Melanin helps protect the cells from the damaging rays of the sun.

Langerhans cells are part of the immune system. These cells are damaged when exposed to excessive ultraviolet light and glucocorticoids (anti-inflammatory drugs). Langerhans cells play an important role in the skin's response to foreign substances and contribute to such things as the development of rashes when an animal is exposed to irritating materials.

Merkel cells are specialized cells associated with the sensory organs in the skin. In particular, Merkel cells help provide animals with sensory information from whiskers and the deep skin areas called tylotrich pads.

Basement Membrane Zone

This layer of the skin is located beneath the epidermis and connects the epidermis to the dermis layer below. It also serves as a protective barrier between the epidermis and the dermis. Several skin diseases, including a number of autoimmune conditions, can damage the basement membrane zone.

Dermis

The dermis supports and nourishes the epidermis and skin appendages. The blood vessels that supply the epidermis with nutrients are located in the dermis. Blood vessels also regulate skin and body temperature. Sensory nerves are located in the dermis and hair follicles. The skin responds to the sensations of touch, pain, itch, heat, and cold. The dermis secretes the proteins collagen and elastin, which give support and elasticity to the skin. There are also immune cells in the dermis that defend against infectious agents that pass through the epidermis.

Skin Appendages

Hair follicles, oil and sweat glands, and claws, are skin appendages that grow out

layer. Other important parts of the skin include skin appendages (such as hair and claws) and subcutaneous muscles and fat.

Epidermis

The epidermis is the outer layer of skin. It provides protection from foreign substances. The epidermis is composed of multiple types of cells, including keratinocytes, melanocytes, Langerhans cells, and Merkel cells. Each of these cells has special functions.

Keratinocytes provide a protective layer that is constantly being renewed in a process called keratinization. In this process, new skin cells are created near the base of the epidermis and migrate upwards. This produces a compact layer of dead cells on the skin surface. This layer keeps in fluids, salts, and nutrients, while keeping out infectious or noxious agents. The top layer of dead skin cells are continuously shed and replaced by cells from lower layers. The rate of cell replacement is affected by nutrition, hormones, tissue factors, immune cells in the skin, and genetics. Disease and inflammation also alter normal cell growth and keratinization.

Melanocytes are located at the base of the epidermis, the outer root sheath of hairs, of the epidermis and dermis. The hair follicles of dogs are compound. The follicles have a central hair surrounded by 3 to 15 smaller secondary hairs all exiting from one pore. Dogs are born with simple hair follicles that develop into compound hair follicles.

The growth of hair is affected by nutrition, hormones, and change of season. Dogs normally shed hair in the early spring and early fall. They may also shed in response to changes in temperature or amount of sunlight. The size, shape, and length of hair are controlled by genetics and hormones. Disease, drugs, nutrition, and environment also affect the health of hair.

The hair coat protects the skin from physical and ultraviolet light damage, and helps regulate body temperature. Trapping dead air space between secondary hairs conserves heat. This requires that the hairs be dry and waterproof. The cold-weather coat of many dogs is longer and finer to facilitate heat conservation. The hair coat can also help cool the skin. The warm-weather coat has shorter, thicker hairs and fewer secondary hairs. This anatomic change allows air to move easily through the coat, which facilitates cooling.

Oil glands (also called sebaceous glands) secrete an oily substance called sebum into the hair follicles and onto the skin. They are present in large numbers near the paws, back of the neck, rump, chin, and tail area. Sebum is a mixture of fatty acids. Sebum is important for keeping the skin soft, moist, and pliable. Sebum gives the hair coat sheen and has antibiotic properties.

Dogs have sweat glands on the feet that may have a minor role in cooling of the body. However, dogs primarily release excess body heat by panting and drooling.

Subcutis

The subcutis is the innermost layer of the skin. It contains the subcutaneous fat and muscles. (The word subcutaneous means "beneath the skin.") The twitch muscle is the major muscle immediately beneath the skin. The subcutaneous fat provides insulation; a reservoir for fluids, electrolytes, and energy; and a shock absorber.

▇ DERMATITIS AND DERMATOLOGIC PROBLEMS

Dermatitis is a general word for any type of inflammation of the skin. It is the word usually used to describe a skin condition until a specific diagnosis is reached. There are many causes of skin inflammation, including external irritants, burns, allergens, trauma, and infection (bacterial, viral, parasitic, or fungal).

The skin's response to insult is generically called dermatitis and manifests as any combination of itching, scaling, abnormal redness, thickening of the skin, and hair loss. The usual progression of a skin disease involves an underlying trigger that causes boils, scabs, scales, or blisters.

Abnormal itching, called **pruritus**, occurs in many skin diseases and is often present because of secondary infections. As the inflammation progresses, crusting and scaling develop. If the problem reaches from the upper layer of skin (the epidermis) to the deeper layer (the dermis), fluid discharge, pain, and sloughing or shedding of the skin may occur. Secondary bacterial and yeast infections commonly develop as a result of skin inflammation. As dermatitis persists, short-term signs of inflammation (such as redness) become obscured by signs of longterm inflammation (thickening of the skin, color changes, scaling, fluid discharge). Often the skin becomes drier and, if itching is not already a sign, it frequently develops at this stage.

Resolving dermatitis requires that your veterinarian identify the underlying cause and treat secondary infections or other complications. A review of your pet's history and a physical examination can more precisely define the problem.

▇ DIAGNOSIS OF SKIN DISORDERS

A precise diagnosis of the causes of a skin disease requires a detailed history,

Skin Disease History Checklist

When you take your dog to the veterinarian for a skin problem, you can help your veterinarian diagnose the problem by having information about the following:

- The primary complaint—what is bothering your dog?
- The length of time the problem has been present.
- The age at which the skin disease started. Some diseases are more common to particular ages of dogs.
- The breed. Some breeds are prone to specific diseases. (Also note whether related animals such as littermates have had a similar problem.)
- Behavior of the dog such as licking, rubbing, scratching, or chewing of the skin.
- How the problem started and how it has progressed. For example, problems that began with itching may lead to self-trauma that develops secondary skin wounds or infections.
- The type of skin problems you saw develop and when.
- The season when the problem first started. Some skin diseases are related to the season of the year.
- The area on the body where the problem was first noticed.
- Any previous treatments and how your dog responded to treatment. For example, if your dog did not improve when given antibiotics, this helps your veterinarian exclude certain diseases.
- How often you bathe the animal and when you last bathed it. Recent bathing may obscure or change skin problems. Excessive bathing and wetting of the skin can worsen some skin diseases.
- The presence of fleas, ticks, or mites and what you use for routine control of these problems.
- The health of other animals with which your dog has been in contact.
- The environment of your dog. Changes in your dog's environment can influence the development of certain skin diseases.

physical examination, and appropriate diagnostic tests. Many skin diseases have similar signs and an immediate diagnosis may not be possible. Based on your dog's history and the physical examination, your veterinarian may order any of a number of laboratory procedures. These may include microscopic analysis of skin scrapings and hair, cultures of skin swabs, blood and urine tests, and even biopsies. It may take several days before laboratory results are available. Your veterinarian may also evaluate how your dog responds to treatment in order to diagnose a specific skin problem. More than one visit is often required for an accurate diagnosis.

▨ TREATMENT OF SKIN DISORDERS

Successful treatment of skin disorders requires identification of the underlying cause. Not surprisingly, many treatments for skin diseases are applied directly to the skin surface (topically). It may be the preferred method of treatment for some diseases or beneficial in addition to systemic treatment (medications taken by mouth or injected and distributed throughout the body). Examples of products applied directly to the skin include antibiotic ointments, corticosteroid preparations, medicated shampoos, and topical insecticides.

Systemic drugs may be needed to treat some disorders. These include whole-body antibiotics, corticosteroids, and other anti-inflammatory drugs.

As with any treatment program, make sure that you read and understand all directions for using the prescribed product, including how to apply or give it, how much to use, and how often it should be administered.

Shampoo Therapy

Medicated shampoos are commonly used as topical treatments for specific skin conditions. Before applying a medicated shampoo, wash your dog with a cleansing shampoo and rinse well. Medicated shampoos often are not good cleansing agents, do not lather well, or do not work except on a clean hair coat.

The medicated shampoo should be applied evenly to the hair coat after being diluted in water. Diluting the shampoo will help rinse it from the coat and minimize the potential for irritating your dog. Depending on the shampoo, dilute 1 part shampoo to 3 or 4 parts water.

If possible, keep the medicated shampoo on the skin for 10 minutes, then rinse thoroughly. (The prolonged contact time is often necessary for medicated ingredients to have their full effects.) Shampoo residue is a common cause of irritation, so it is very important to rinse your dog carefully and fully follow all shampoo usage instructions.

Medicated shampoos usually need to be used regularly for the most successful results. Ask for and follow your veterinarian's instructions on shampoo frequency.

■ CONGENITAL AND INHERITED SKIN DISORDERS

Dogs can be born with or may inherit any of several different kinds of skin abnormalities. Most of these conditions are uncommon to rare. Some occur with greater frequency in particular breeds of dogs, as noted below.

Congenital Skin Disorders

Epitheliogenesis imperfecta, also called **aplasia cutis**, might be conventionally described as missing or absent skin. It is a congenital condition of unknown cause that is most frequently seen in cattle, pigs, sheep, and horses. It is a rare condition in cats and dogs. Animals with epitheliogenesis imperfecta have failed to develop part or all of the layers of the skin. As a result, the animal is born with ulcers or with areas that lack any skin covering. The condition can be fatal if it involves large portions of the skin. Small defects can be surgically corrected.

A **nevus** in humans is a congenital pigmented area on the skin that is often called a birthmark. In animals, the term is used for any area where skin is malformed, including abnormally pigmented spots. Some forms of nevi displace the normal structures of the skin, including hair follicles; thus, these patches are hairless. When not extensive, nevi can be surgically removed or treated with laser treatment or cryotherapy (freezing); otherwise no effective treatment is available.

Dermoid cysts are birth defects that may occur in Rhodesian Ridgebacks (in which they are inherited) and occasionally other breeds of dogs. These are skin pockets into which dander, hair, oil, and other debris accumulate. They are found on skin above the backbone but are rarely associated with spinal cord neural deficits. They can be surgically removed.

Hereditary Hair Loss (Alopecia)

Dogs can be born either totally or partially without hair. Hairlessness can also develop later in life. These defects can be associated with abnormal teeth, claws, and eyes, or with skeletal and other developmental defects. Hairless breeds of dogs (Mexican Hairless, Chinese Crested, American Hairless Terrier) have been bred for these defects. Many sporadic cases occur in other breeds of dogs, most often in males. Many affected dogs, including most of the hairless breeds, have patchy or pattern hairlessness as well as associated dental anomalies. All animals with abnormal follicular development are prone to hair follicle infections, and hair foreign-body inflammations.

In dogs, there are several types of abnormalities in hair follicles. A syndrome known as **color dilution alopecia** is associated with the gene that turns normally black hair blue, beige, or fawn. This syndrome is best known in Doberman Pinschers but is also commonly seen in color dilute Dachshunds, Italian Greyhounds, Greyhounds, Whippets, Yorkshire Terriers, and tricolor hounds. Affected dogs are born with normal hair coats but before

1 year of age begin to develop hair follicle inflammation and progressive hair loss in the blue or fawn-colored areas. **Black hair follicle dysplasia** develops earlier with more complete hair loss in black and white dogs. It develops shortly after birth and affects only the black-colored areas. This syndrome is most common in Papillons and Bearded Collies. Seasonal flank alopecia can appear in Boxers and Airedale Terriers. Various woolly syndromes and post-clipping alopecia can occur in Spitz-type breeds.

Abnormal Skin Growth Syndromes (Hyperplastic and Seborrheic Syndromes)

There are syndromes in which skin cells grow abnormally, resulting in scaling and thickening of the top layer of skin. Some of these syndromes are associated with various other inherited conditions and may be sex linked. Some involve only localized portions of the skin while others produce generalized signs.

Canine ichthyosiform dermatoses occur sporadically in a number of breeds, including Doberman Pinschers, Rottweilers, Irish Setters, Collies, English Springer Spaniels, Cavalier King Charles Spaniels, Golden Retrievers, Labrador Retrievers, American Bulldogs, and terriers (including Jack Russell Terriers). There is good evidence of a familial inheritance pattern for this condition in Jack Russell Terriers and Golden Retrievers. In dogs with ichthyosiform dermatosis, the body is covered with large scales that may flake off in large sheets. The nose and paws may be noticeably thickened with apparent discomfort. Treatment is difficult, but signs may be lessened with special shampoos or solutions. Some experimental treatments have been useful. Control of secondary infection is frequently required. Your veterinarian will prescribe the most appropriate treatment for your pet.

Familial footpad hyperkeratosis is a syndrome reported in Irish Terriers and Dogues de Bordeaux. Hyperkeratosis is increased thickness of the hard, outer layer of the skin. All footpads are involved starting at an early age. The disease is not usually congenital. When the hyperkeratosis is severe, horns, cracks (fissures) and secondary infections cause pain and lameness. No other skin abnormalities are present. Treatment concentrates on relief of signs and often includes soaking footpads, applying softening lotions, and treatment of any bacterial infections.

Granulomatous sebaceous adenitis destroys the oil glands and, in some breeds of dogs, is associated with a severe oil discharge and hair loss. It is hereditary in Standard Poodles and possibly in Akitas. It first appears when the dog is a young adult. Noticeable skin thickening precedes the loss of normal hair kinkiness and progresses to patchy hair loss. Akitas tend to have more oiliness and less hair loss than Poodles. Response to treatment is inconsistent and incomplete. Mildly affected dogs are treated with medicated shampoos. Secondary infections are treated as needed.

Hereditary Congenital Follicular Parakeratosis

This is a newly recognized syndrome affecting female Rottweilers and female Siberian Huskies. This is a severe defect of the process that forms the keratins that are a major component of skin. This syndrome is associated with various abnormalities in other areas of the body. Little is presently known about this syndrome.

Psoriasiform-lichenoid dermatosis affects young English Springer Spaniels. It is presumed that this syndrome is inherited (genetic in origin). The most obvious signs are red symmetric abnormalities consisting of small lumps on the skin and solid elevated areas near the ears or groin. The abnormalities are covered with scale and become increasingly thick and hard (hyperkeratotic) if left untreated. In some dogs, the abnormalities may eventually spread. Spontaneous improvement occurs in some dogs while in others, the signs come and go. In some dogs, antibiotic treatment or other medications provide relief. In most cases, however, psoriasiform-lichenoid dermatosis does not respond to treatment.

Pigmentary Abnormalities

Some skin color abnormalities may be acquired while others may be hereditary. Abnormalities in skin and coat color are sometimes related. Some of the associations are mentioned in hereditary hair loss (*see* page 242).

Albinism is rare in dogs. True albinism is always associated with pink or pale irises and with visual defects. Albinism is different from extreme white spotting. In either case, affected animals are at increased risk of skin cancer from solar radiation, especially in areas with short or thin hair. Some animals with extreme pie-baldism (spotted or blotched with black and white) or dominant white have associated neurologic anomalies or deafness in one or both ears.

Vitiligo is hereditary but not noticeable at birth. The onset is usually in young adulthood. Affected dogs develop bleached splotches of skin that occasionally also affects the hair coat and claws. Most splotches are on the face, especially the bridge of the muzzle or around the eyes. Color loss may come and go with varying amounts of severity. Vitiligo runs in some dog families, especially Belgian Tervurens and Rottweilers. Complete remission may occur but is rare. Vitiligo causes no other health problems. No treatment is available. Treatments used in people with vitiligo are unlikely to help animals.

Acquired aurotrichia is a syndrome seen in some lines of Miniature Schnauzers and occasionally in other breeds of dogs. In affected dogs, the hair along the middle of the back above the spinal cord changes from the normal black or gray to golden. This usually starts in young adulthood. The change may be associated with a thinning of the hair coat. In many cases, there are no other changes to the skin and no other whole-body signs. In most dogs, the coat color returns to normal within 1 to 2 years.

Defects of Structural Integrity

Some skin diseases are genetic defects that affect the integrity or continuity of the skin.

Cutaneous asthenia (also called **dermatosparaxis** or **Ehlers–Danlos syndrome**) is a condition in which the skin does not produce enough collagen. This causes loose, stretchy, fragile skin, and joint problems. The fragile skin is evident from birth. Wounds heal slowly or not completely. Skin hangs from the body. Cysts and bruising may develop. The disease may be fatal. Older animals develop hanging folds of skin and exhibit extensive scarring. Some have joint and eye problems. Diagnosis is based on visible signs and testing of the collagen structure. For cats and dogs, a skin extensibility index has been developed to help your veterinarian diagnose this syndrome. There have been some reports of improvement for affected dogs following vitamin C supplements and your veterinarian will be able to determine whether such supplements might help your pet.

Epidermolysis bullosa syndromes are a group of hereditary congenital defects that affect the attachments between the outer and inner layers of the skin, resulting in blistering of the skin. The several forms of epidermolysis bullosa have been reported in Collies, Shetland Sheepdogs, Toy Poodles, German Shorthaired Pointers, Golden Retrievers, Akitas, and mixed breed dogs. Minor skin trauma results in separation of the skin layers. Blisters form and soon rupture, leaving glistening, flat ulcers. Blisters may be present at birth or develop within the first weeks of life. The most severe blisters are on the feet, mouth, face, and genitals. In many cases the disease is fatal.

Cutaneous mucinosis is thought to be a familial problem in some lines of Chinese Shar-Peis. Normal Shar-Peis have more of a protein called mucin than other dogs. In some young dogs, mucin is so excessive that the skin exhibits pronounced folding and blisters. Diagnosis is by skin prick of the blisters or by skin biopsy. As these dogs mature, the syndrome may become less severe. However, this condition can be exaggerated by the development of allergic skin disease, which is common in the breed.

Multisystem Disorders that Affect the Skin

Familial **dermatomyositis** is an inflammatory disease of the skin and muscles of young Collies and Shetland Sheepdogs. Problems with blood vessels of the skin and muscles occur in the early inflammatory stages of the disease, leading to decreases in size or wasting (atrophy). The onset is typically at younger than 6 months of age. The disease is variable, and individual pups within a litter may be affected differently. Ulcers, crusting, and hair loss appear on the face, ear tips, tail tip, and legs. Heat, sun exposure, and wounds worsen the condition. The muscles most affected are on the head and legs. Diagnosis is established by evaluation of littermates and family history, skin biopsy, electromyography, and muscle biopsy, which must be performed early in the course of the disease. Steroids, vitamin E, and omega-3 fatty acids may help. Severely affected dogs rarely respond well to treatment.

Familial **vasculopathy** has been described in German Shepherds and Jack Russell Terriers. In these dogs, skin ulcers develop shortly after the first set of puppy vaccinations and worsen after subsequent vaccinations. The main signs are footpad swelling and loss of color that may progress to ulcers. All footpads are typically affected. Crusting and ulcers on ear and tail tips and loss of color of the bridge of the muzzle may also occur. A severe form of neutrophilic vasculitis has recently been described in young Chinese Shar-Peis; this may be familial. As the dogs mature, the disease may go away, but pad ulcers may be so severe that euthanasia is warranted. No known treatment is uniformly effective, although some dogs appear to respond to high dosages of steroids.

Hereditary **lupoid dermatosis** is a condition reported in German Shorthaired Pointers. The condition is usually first noted when the dog is about 6 months old. The first signs are scaling and crusting on the head and upper parts of the body and legs. This quickly progresses to a generalized scaling of the skin accompanied by redness (erythema) caused by congestion of the tiny blood vessels (capillaries) in the skin. This skin condition is either painful or itchy for the affected animal. These dogs develop fevers and enlarged lymph nodes. When examined in a laboratory, skin biopsy samples show signs of a lupus-like skin condition. This disease is progressive and ultimately fatal. No successful treatment has been reported.

Hereditary **zinc deficiency syndromes** occur in some breeds. In white Bull Terriers, lethal acrodermatitis has signs of retarded growth, thickened skin on the legs, and pustules around mucous membranes. These signs are apparent by 10 weeks of age and are later accompanied by diarrhea, pneumonia, and death before 2 years of age. The lives of affected dogs can be prolonged by treating secondary infections. These dogs do not respond to zinc treatment given by mouth. In Alaskan Malamutes, Huskies, and German Shorthaired Pointers, zinc deficiency syndrome is responsive to supplemental zinc. Signs develop at weaning or later and include crusted, thickened skin on the legs and pustules around mucous membranes. Often, females develop signs associated with estrus or whelping and lactation. Secondary infections are common. Diagnosis is by skin biopsy and response to zinc supplementation by mouth.

■ ALLERGIES

Like people, dogs can be allergic to various substances, including plant particles and other substances in the air or substances in food. These substances are called allergens. Allergens are substances that, when inhaled or absorbed through the skin, respiratory tract, or gastrointestinal tract, stimulate histamine production, which results in inflammation.

Airborne Allergies (Atopy)

Fewer than 10% of dogs are thought to be genetically predisposed to become sensitized to allergens in the environment. Both male and female dogs can be allergic to materials in the air. Breeds predisposed to developing allergies include Chinese Shar-Peis, Wirehaired Fox Terriers, Golden Retrievers, Dalmatians, Boxers, Boston Terriers, Labrador Retrievers, Lhasa Apsos, Scottish Terriers, Shih Tzus, and West Highland White Terriers. However, any dog of any breed (or mixed breeds) can be allergic. The age of onset is generally between 6 months and 3 years. Signs are usually seasonal but may be seen all year. Itching is the most typical sign (*see also* page 258). The feet, face, ears, front legs, and abdomen are the most frequently affected areas, but scratching all over the body is common. Scratching can lead to secondary signs of wounds, scabbing, infection, hair loss, and scaling. Other signs of atopy include licking or chewing the paws and rubbing the face and eyes.

Allergies are identified by signs when other causes have been excluded. Allergy testing can be used to identify the offending allergens and to formulate a specific immunotherapy treatment program.

There are 3 therapeutic options: avoidance of the offending allergen(s), controlling the signs of itching, and immunotherapy (for example, an allergy vaccine). A good management plan requires the use of several different treatments, the understanding and reasonable expectations for response from the pet owner, and frequent progress evaluations so that the plan can be adjusted as needed.

Immunotherapy attempts to increase a dog's tolerance to environmental allergens. Vaccine preparation involves selection of individual allergens for a particular dog. The allergen selection is determined by matching the test results with the prominent allergens during the time of year when the dog has signs. Immunotherapy is best considered for dogs with problematic signs that occur for several months during the year. The dog must be cooperative enough to receive allergy injections. You may have to administer some injections yourself. Your veterinarian can provide training and most owners learn to administer the allergy injections very well, while others may need assistance from a capable friend or veterinary staff member. Your veterinarian will determine the frequency of the injections and the dosage given.

Treatment takes a longterm commitment. You must be willing to follow instructions accurately, be patient, and be able to communicate effectively with your veterinarian. Injections may initially increase signs. If this occurs, contact your veterinarian immediately. Improvement may not be visible for 6 months and a year of treatment may be required before you can tell if the immunotherapy is working. The best way to evaluate the treatment is to compare the degree of disease or discomfort between similar seasons. Anti-itch medication and antibiotics are often required during the initial phase of treatment.

Allergy shots improve the condition but do not cure the disease. Many animals may still require anti-itch medications during seasonal flare-ups.

Food Allergies

Among pets, food allergies are less common than airborne allergies. Signs of food allergy are similar to airborne allergies except there is little variation in the intensity of itching from one season to another. The age of onset is variable. The distribution and intensity of itching varies between animals.

There is no reliable diagnostic test other than feeding a limited foodstuff (hypoallergenic or elimination) diet and seeing if the itching resolves. Your veterinarian should be consulted to develop a specific test plan for your dog. The ideal food elimination diet should be balanced and nutritionally complete and not contain any ingredients that have been fed previously to your dog. Owners often do not understand that if *any* previously fed ingredient is present in the elimination diet, the dog may be allergic to that one ingredient and the diet trial will be a failure. The key point in any food elimination diet trial is that only novel food ingredients can be fed. This also includes treats and anything the dog eats besides its regular food.

The trial diet should be fed for up to 3 months. If marked or complete resolution in signs occurs during the elimination diet trial, food allergy can be suspected. To confirm that a food allergy exists and improvement was not just coincidental, the dog must be given the previously fed food ingredients and a relapse of signs must occur. The return of signs is usually between 1 hour and 14 days. Once a food allergy is confirmed, the elimination diet should be continued until signs disappear, which usually takes less than 14 days. At this point, previously fed individual ingredients should be added to the elimination diet for a period of up to 14 days. If signs reappear, the individual ingredient is considered a cause of the food allergy.

The foods dogs are most often allergic to include beef, chicken, eggs, corn, wheat, soy, and milk. Once the offending allergens are identified, control of the food allergy is by strict avoidance. Concurrent diseases may complicate the identification of underlying food allergies. Infrequently, a dog will react to new food allergens as it ages.

■ ABSCESSES BETWEEN THE TOES (INTERDIGITAL FURUNCULOSIS)

An abscess, or localized infection of the skin between the toes, is also called a furuncle. It is similar to a severely infected pimple on the face. These painful, pus-filled blisters often occur in the webbing between a dog's toes.

The most common cause of furuncles between the toes is a deep bacterial infection. Many dog breeds (for example, Chinese Shar-Peis, Labrador Retrievers, and English Bulldogs) are predisposed to

the condition because they have short, bristly hairs on the webbing between the toes. The short hair shafts are easily forced backward into the hair follicles while the dog is walking. Ingrown hairs are very inflammatory in the skin, and secondary bacterial infections are common. Less commonly, a hair shaft can become infected if foreign material, such as a splinter or burr, becomes embedded in the skin.

Early signs of infected hair follicles that could become furuncles are rash-like redness and small bumps in one spot or over the entire webbing between the toes. If left untreated, the bumps will rapidly develop into shiny, reddish purple boils 0.4 to 0.8 inches (1 to 2 centimeters) in diameter. The boils may rupture when pressed and leak bloody fluid. Furuncles are usually painful, and the dog may be obviously lame on the affected foot (or feet) and lick and bite at them. Furuncles caused by a foreign object are usually solitary and often occur on a front foot. Recurrence is not common. If a bacterial infection is causing the problem, there may be several furuncles with new ones developing as others heal.

Diagnosis is often based on signs alone. The furuncles can be lanced to find and remove any foreign objects. Furuncles between the toes respond best to a combination of treatment at the site and system-wide drugs. Antibiotics are frequently prescribed for an initial course lasting 4 to 6 weeks. However, because it may be difficult for antibiotics to penetrate these furuncles, more than 8 weeks of antibiotic treatment may be needed. Additional treatment for secondary fungal infections may be required. Other commonly recommended treatments include soaking the foot in warm water (with or without an antibiotic solution added to the bath) and applying antibiotic ointment. Some dogs may benefit from antibiotic wraps and bandaging. Antihistamines given for the first several weeks of treatment may help alleviate itching, if present. Pain medication may be needed in some dogs.

Using antibiotics improperly, such as not finishing the entire prescription, can lead to longterm, recurring furuncles between the toes. Furuncles can also recur if the bacteria are not susceptible to the antibiotic prescribed. If furuncles recur in spite of proper treatment, it may be a sign of an underlying disease. Furuncles in confined dogs are likely to recur unless the dog is removed from wire or concrete surfaces. In some longterm cases, surgical excision or surgical correction of the webbing may be needed. The most common causes of recurrent furuncles in dogs are atopy (page 246) and demodicosis (page 262).

■ CONTAGIOUS ECTHYMA (ORF, CONTAGIOUS PUSTULAR DERMATITIS, SORE MOUTH)

Contagious ecthyma is an infectious skin disease that most frequently affects sheep and goats. This disease has been reported in dogs that have eaten carcasses of infected sheep or goats; otherwise the disease is rare among pets.

Contagious ecthyma is caused by a parapoxvirus. Infection occurs by contact. The disease is found worldwide and is most common in late summer, fall, and winter on pasture. It also occurs during winter in feedlots.

The disease is characterized by sores that develop on the skin of the lips and frequently extend to the inside of the mouth. Occasionally, they are also found on the feet. The disease usually lasts 1 to 4 weeks. Scabs drop off and the tissues heal without scarring.

Veterinarians may prescribe antibacterial medications, not for the parapoxvirus infection, but to control secondary bacterial infections.

Humans can also catch the disease from sheep. Sheep handlers and veterinarians are most at risk. In humans, the sores are usually confined to the hands and face and can be both numerous and distressing to the infected person.

■ DERMATOPHILOSIS

This disease is seen worldwide but is more common in the tropics. It is known by a number of names, including "strawberry footrot." Among companion animals, it is seen most frequently in horses. Dogs and cats rarely have this disease. The few reported human cases have usually been associated with handling diseased animals.

The disease is caused by *Dermatophilus congolensis* bacteria. It is possible that the bacteria can live in the skin causing no signs in the animal until conditions encourage active infection. Epidemics of dermatophilosis often occur during rainy seasons. In most short-term infections, the invasion of the skin stops in 2 to 3 weeks and the animal heals spontaneously. In longterm infections, the bacteria periodically spread from infected hair follicles and scabs to uninfected patches of skin. Increased wetness enhances the growth of the infective bacteria, leading to release of infective spores.

Uncomplicated infections usually heal without scar formation. Animals with severe generalized infections often lose condition; movement and the ability to eat may be reduced, especially if the feet, lips, and mouth are involved.

Dermatophilosis is diagnosed using laboratory tests on samples taken from the skin. Because dermatophilosis usually heals rapidly and without complications, treatment is often not required. The disease is controlled by isolating infected animals and controlling skin parasites that injure the skin and increase susceptibility to the bacteria.

■ EOSINOPHILIC GRANULOMA COMPLEX

Eosinophilic granuloma complex is rare in dogs. It is recognized more commonly in cats and horses. When seen in the dog, this disorder is associated with unusual reactions to insect bites or other hypersensitivity reactions. They will often appear

Most flea-infested dogs actually have cat fleas rather than dog fleas.

as bumps or nodules anywhere on the body. Over time, these may become ulcerated or crusted. There is also a condition of unknown cause that most commonly is seen in the oral cavity of Siberian Huskies, where single or multiple nodules can appear on the tongue or in the mouth.

Some cases can be treated with antibiotics initially, although many dogs require corticosteroids. Insect control may be of some value. If the disorder returns, low-dose, corticosteroid treatment may be prescribed.

FLEAS

Fleas are small wingless insects that feed on animal blood. In addition to being a nuisance, they can also transmit diseases and cause allergies or anemia. There are more than 2,200 species of fleas recognized worldwide. In North America, only a few species commonly infest house pets. Two common species of flea are the cat flea (*Ctenocephalides felis*) and the dog flea (*Ctenocephalides canis*). However, most of the fleas found on both dogs and cats are cat fleas. Fleas cause severe irritation in other animals and humans. They also transmit a wide variety of diseases, including tapeworm infections (*see* TAPEWORMS, page 114) and the typhus-like rickettsiae (*see* RICKETTSIAL DISEASES, page 205).

Transmission and Life Cycle

Cat fleas begin reproduction about 1 or 2 days after a blood meal from a host. Female fleas lay eggs as they feed and move about on the surface of the skin. A single female flea can produce up to 50 eggs per day and about 2,000 in her lifetime. The eggs are pearly white, oval, and tiny. They readily fall from the fur and drop onto bedding, carpet, or soil, where they hatch in 1 to 6 days. Newly hatched flea larvae are mobile and free-living, feeding on organic debris found in their environment and on adult flea droppings. Flea larvae avoid direct light and actively move deep into carpet fibers or under organic debris (grass, branches, leaves, or soil).

Larvae can easily dry out, and exposure to relative humidity under 50% will kill them. However, they are capable of moving as far as 3 feet (1 meter) to find locations suitable for their survival. Indoors, flea larvae best survive in the protected environment deep within carpet fibers, in cracks between hardwood floor boards, and on unfinished concrete floors in damp basements. Flea development occurs outdoors only where the ground is shaded and moist. The larval stage usually lasts 5 to 11 days but may be prolonged for 2 to 3 weeks, depending on the availability of food and the environmental conditions.

After completing its development, the mature larva produces a silk-like cocoon in which it pupates. The pupa is fully developed in 1 to 2 weeks, but the adult flea may remain in the cocoon for several weeks until a suitable host arrives. When it emerges from the cocoon, it can survive 1 to 2 weeks before finding a host on which to feed. It is the newly emerged, unfed fleas that infest pets and bite people. Fleas generally do not leave their host unless forced off by grooming or insecticides. Cat fleas in any stage of the life cycle cannot survive cold temperatures. They will die if the environmental temperature falls below 37°F (3°C) for several days.

Depending on temperature and humidity, the entire life cycle of the flea can be completed in as little as 12 to 14 days or last up to 350 days. However, under most conditions, fleas complete their life cycle in 3 to 6 weeks. Fleas mate after feeding, and females lay eggs within 1 to 2 days of their first blood meal.

A flea-infested dog or cat can easily introduce fleas into a home where they deposit eggs that then develop into newly emerging fleas. These then infest other pets and bite people.

Flea Allergy Dermatitis

When feeding, fleas inject saliva into the host on which they are living. Many dogs and cats are allergic to flea saliva. Even nonallergic animals will scratch due to the annoyance of flea bites. Allergic dogs itch intensely in some or all areas of the body. They are likely to be restless and uncomfortable, spending much time scratching, licking, rubbing, chewing, and even nibbling at their skin. This often leads to hair loss, scabbing, and secondary infections. In heavy infestations (or in young puppies), anemia may develop due to the loss of blood.

Most cases of flea allergy dermatitis occur in the late summer, corresponding to the peak of flea populations. Animals younger than 1 year old do not usually have flea allergy dermatitis. Usually, diagnosis is made by visual observation. Slowly parting the hair often reveals flea excrement or rapidly moving fleas. Flea excrement is reddish black, cylindrical, and pellet- or comma-shaped. Placed in water or on a damp paper towel, the excrement dissolves, producing a reddish brown color. Examination of the pet's bedding for eggs, larvae, and excrement is also useful. The presence of fleas does not exclude another disease being at least partially responsible for the dog's itching and skin

condition. Your veterinarian may do skin testing to eliminate other causes for the itching and confirm a diagnosis of flea allergy dermatitis. Other conditions that can look like flea allergy dermatitis include respiratory allergies, food allergies, mange and other skin parasite infestations, and hair follicle infections.

Flea control measures have changed dramatically in recent years. Flea control previously required repeated application of insecticides on the animal and the premises. Recently, new insecticides and insect growth regulators have been developed that provide residual control and require fewer applications. The most effective of these products are sold by veterinarians. Insect growth regulators prevent fleas from reproducing. Flea treatments include topically applied liquids, oral and injected medications, and "fogger" sprays. You should discuss flea control products with your veterinarian and select one that works well for your individual pet and the environment in which it lives.

The overall goal of treatment is to kill all fleas in all life stages on the affected animal and everywhere in the pet's environment. The first step is eliminating fleas currently on your dog. Topical spot-on treatments can take 12 to 36 hours until the medication has spread sufficiently to eliminate all existing fleas. The second step is eliminating fleas in the pet's environment. In-home studies have shown that in many cases the newer topical and oral flea control products can effectively control flea populations without the need to treat the environment itself. By using these products, it is possible to eliminate a flea infestation in a household; however, the amount of time necessary to achieve flea control will vary because of the flea's life cycle and conditions in the environment. Typically, control of an infestation can take 6 weeks to 3 months. In cases of massive flea infestation or severe pet or human flea allergy, treatment of the household environment may still be necessary. Control may be achieved using insecticides with residual activity or by repeated application of short-acting products. Areas where flea eggs and larvae gather, such as bedding, furniture, carpets, the tiny spaces in hardwood flooring, behind baseboards, and within closets, should be treated.

If your dog spends time outside regularly, also treat the outside areas it frequents. Spraying flea control products over the whole yard is not worthwhile. Instead, concentrate outdoor treatments on shaded areas, including dog houses, garages, under porches, and in animal lounging areas beneath shrubs or other shaded areas. Other outdoor spaces where fleas can be found include cracks in shaded or moist brick walks and patios and areas under decks and steps.

Despite your best efforts, it may not be possible to totally eliminate fleas rapidly enough to prevent signs of flea allergy dermatitis in your dog. Treatment may also be required to control itching and secondary skin disease in hypersensitive animals (*see* ITCHING (PRURITUS), page 258). Your veterinarian can prescribe medications to control your dog's skin condition and make your pet more comfortable.

◼ FLIES AND MOSQUITOES

Flies are winged insects that are usually just an annoyance, but they can transmit disease and cause problems in animals. They belong to a large, complex order of insects called Diptera. Flies vary greatly in size, food preference, development, and habits. As adults, flies may feed on blood, saliva, tears, or mucus. They also spread bacteria, viruses, and parasites. The order Diptera includes not only the common house fly and many other insects we commonly call flies, but also mosquitoes.

The life cycles of all of the thousands of different flies are divided into 4 stages: egg, larva (flies at this stage look like worms and are commonly known as maggots), pupa (the stage in which the fly is developing inside a cocoon), and adult. Fly eggs are laid in decaying flesh, animal

Sand fly

Black fly

Mosquito

Biting flies, including mosquitoes, black flies, and sand flies, feed on animal blood.

waste, or pools of standing water. The common characteristic of these egg locations is the presence of ample food for the maggots. Flies reproduce and grow rapidly. Depending on the season and weather conditions, a fly may take only 12 to 14 days to go from egg to adult.

Biting flies feed on animal blood. This group includes mosquitoes, black flies, sand flies, biting midges, horse flies, and deer flies. Though the bites can be painful and may bring on allergic reactions, biting flies are usually not dangerous to dogs unless they are extremely numerous or transmit a disease. Many of these flies, including black flies and mosquitoes, will bite both animals and humans.

Nonbiting flies include those that do not feed on blood and do not actually bite the host animal while feeding. Instead, these flies feed on bodily secretions. They can transmit diseases to dogs and other domestic animals.

Biting Midges

These tiny (0.04 to 0.16 inches [1 to 3 millimeters]) insects are often called gnats and are sometimes known as "no-see-ums," or "punkies." There are several species. All are associated with aquatic or semiaquatic habitats, such as mud or moist soil around streams, ponds, and marshes. They can inflict painful bites and suck the blood of both humans and animals, including horses and dogs. (For a more detailed discussion of midges, *see* page 761.)

Black Flies

There are more than 1,000 species of black flies. They feed on humans and many kinds of animals. Most black flies are small—tiny enough to slip through the mesh of many screens. They are most numerous in north temperate and subarctic zones, although there are tropical and subtropical species as well. In some cases, swarms of these flies will attack, inflicting large numbers of painful bites and even killing livestock.

Diagnosis is by appearance of bite wounds on the animal and, in some instances, the presence of the flies. Black flies are small and can hide in the fur coat. Adult female flies prefer to feed outdoors during daylight hours. Because black flies breed in streams, pets should be kept away from streams, especially during the day, to limit fly exposure. Over-the-counter insect repellents can help keep flies away from pets.

Individual pet owners usually have little control over the presence of black flies.

Because it is difficult, expensive, and can harm the environment, area-wide control of black flies is usually best done by city, county, or other governmental agencies.

Bot Fly Larvae Infestation (Grubs, Cuterebriasis)

This parasitic infestation of dogs and cats is caused by rodent or rabbit bot flies, which are different *Cuterebra* species. Most species of flies only live on one species of animal. However, the rabbit *Cuterebra* fly is a common pest on dogs and cats. Rarely, dogs and cats might also be infested with warble flies, which are types of *Hypoderma* species.

Adult *Cuterebra* flies are large and bee-like and do not feed or bite. Females deposit eggs on stones or vegetation. Dogs become infested as they pass through contaminated areas. Infestations are most common in the summer and fall when the larvae enlarge and produce a swelling about 0.4 inches (1 centimeter) in diameter. Boils are seen around the head, neck, and trunk. The hair is often matted and the skin is swollen. The boils may be painful and discharge pus.

Definitive diagnosis is made when your veterinarian finds the larvae. Suspect boils should be explored carefully by a veterinarian. The boil should not be squeezed because this may rupture the larva and lead to secondary infection or an anaphylactic (severe allergic) reaction. Healing may be slow after the larvae are removed by your veterinarian.

Eye Gnats

Eye gnats or eye flies are very small, only 0.06 to 0.1 inches (1.5 to 2.5 millimeters) long. These tiny flies usually congregate around the eyes, though some species are attracted to the genital organs. They feed by sponging up mucus, pus, and blood. In the desert and foothill regions of southern California, adult flies are present throughout the year; they are most numerous from April through November. During the peak months, they are noticeable in the early morning and late afternoon.

Often they are found in deep shade, among densely planted shrubs, or in the shade of a building.

Diagnosis is by appearance of signs on the animal and, in many cases, the presence of the offending insect. Eye gnats look much like miniature house flies. Insect repellents, such as those recommended for mosquitoes, can provide temporary relief from eye gnats. Be sure to follow your veterinarian's recommendations when using repellents. Community-wide mosquito control programs also reduce the number of eye gnats in the area. However, more adult gnats invade the area after the insecticide disperses.

Horse Flies, Deer Flies, and Other Flies of Large Animals

Horse flies (*Tabanus* species) and deer flies (*Chrysops* species) are large (up to 1.4 inches [3.5 centimeters] long), heavy bodied, and robust. They are swift fliers with powerful wings and very large eyes. The females may feed on the blood of any vertebrate animal, including dogs, though these flies usually prefer horses, deer, and cattle. Male flies are never blood feeders; instead they feed on plant nectar and pollen. Compared to other flies, they consume larger amounts of blood at a single feeding. Like other flies, they can transmit bacteria or viruses. Control of these flies is difficult. Some insecticides may be effective but may have to be used in larger than normal doses. Your veterinarian can advise you about the most effective products and dosages for your pet.

Maggots (Myiasis, Fly Strike)

Maggot infestation is also known as myiasis, fly strike, or simply strike. House flies, blow flies, bottle flies, and flesh flies will lay eggs in skin wounds of any animal (including a dog) that has an infected skin wound. In newborn puppies, the healing stub of the umbilical cord is an attractive egg-laying site for flies. Bite wounds are often sites of initial infection in older dogs. Matted hair coats contaminated with feces also attract these flies. Eggs laid in contaminated hair coats produce maggots that move rapidly to any infected wound. Once inside a wound, the larvae quickly invade the surrounding tissue.

Affected dogs often have raised, red sores at or near the strike site. Maggots may be visible in a sore or wound. You should not try to remove the maggots yourself; wound cleaning and maggot removal by your veterinarian is required. In most cases, your pet will have to be sedated or anesthetized for removal of the larvae.

Finding maggots in a sore or wound is the normal method of diagnosis. If precise identification of the fly is needed or desired, maggots can be sent to a laboratory for identification. Because the first maggots in a wound often create favorable conditions for other flies, the strike site may contain maggots from more than one type of fly.

Treating all open wounds and controlling the presence of flies are 2 steps that you can take to protect your pet from strike. To treat open wounds, gently wash the wound with mild soap, rinse well, and then apply a veterinarian-recommended medicated salve. You should carefully trim the fur around the wound to reduce the chance of infection. Check the wound several times a day to be sure it does not become inflamed or infected. Equally important is routine bathing and grooming for your pet. Keep your dog clean and do not allow urine or feces to collect on the animal.

Finally, if possible, keep your pet in a fly-free area protected by screens. To control flies in the area, be sure all garbage and decaying animal matter are removed. All garbage and trash containers should be securely covered. Remove standing water, especially places that accumulate any organic matter (including yard waste). In kennels and yards, feces should be removed and urination areas washed down daily, especially during warm months.

Pseudomyiasis (false strike) occurs when fly maggots have been consumed and are found within a dog's digestive tract.

Dogs, cats, and other animals consume the maggots while grooming or when eating flesh infested with the maggots. In most cases, these maggots pass through the animal undigested.

Screwworms

Certain species of filth-breeding flies are known for their larvae, which are called **screwworms** (so named because their shape resembles a wood screw). There are several types of screwworms, but they rarely affect dogs. The screwworms include the primary or New World screwworm (found in Central and South America and the Caribbean), and Old World screwworms (found in Africa, India, and Southeast Asia). None are currently found in the United States.

Treatment of fly strike involves removal of the maggots, cleansing of the wound, and medication to control infection and reduce the dog's discomfort. If your pet develops a screwworm infestation, it must be reported by your veterinarian to appropriate state and federal authorities.

Mosquitoes

Mosquitoes belong to the family Culicidae. They are tiny and fragile but possibly the most voracious of the blood-feeding flies. About 300 species have been described worldwide, but only about 150 species of mosquitoes are found in the temperate regions of North America.

Mosquitoes often lay their eggs on the surface of standing water. Even small amounts of standing water can attract mosquitoes. You can reduce the number of mosquitoes near your home by being sure that there is no standing water. Eliminate or turn over any container that can hold water and check your gutters to be sure that they run freely; standing water in gutters is an ideal location for mosquito eggs.

Only female mosquitoes feed on blood. They annoy animals and humans, cause blood loss, and transmit diseases. Although they are known for spreading such diseases as malaria, yellow fever, dengue, and ele-

phantiasis in people, in veterinary medicine they are also known for spreading heartworm to dogs and cats. (*See also* HEARTWORM DISEASE, page 73.)

It is difficult to protect your dog from mosquitoes, especially if the dog spends much time outside. You can reduce outdoor exposure to mosquitoes by not walking your dog in the early morning or early evening hours. Those are the hours when mosquitoes are most active. Sensitive animals, including puppies, should be housed in closed or screened buildings, and the mosquitoes inside killed with safe insecticide. Imidacloprid is a topical drug that can be used on dogs to repel adult female mosquitoes for up to 4 weeks. Mosquitoes are not attracted to light, so "bug zappers" do not help control mosquitoes; they may actually be harmful because they destroy insects that prey on mosquitoes.

Sand Flies

Sand flies are most numerous in tropical and subtropical regions. They are tiny (0.06 to 0.16 inches [1.5 to 4 millimeters] long) and have moth-like, hairy wings. Female sand flies have piercing mouthparts and feed on the blood of a variety of warm-blooded animals, including dogs and humans. They tend to be active only at night and, in contrast to black flies, are only weak fliers. During daylight hours, sand flies seek protection in crevices and caves, in vegetation, and within dark locations, including buildings. They breed in dark, humid environments that have a supply of organic matter that serves as food for the maggots.

Evidence of small bite wounds is the usual sign. The flies are rarely found on animals. Sand flies are an intermediate host for visceral leishmaniasis, a disease caused by a parasite that infects the cells of capillaries and the spleen and other organs of humans, dogs, cats, and horses. (*See* LEISHMANIASIS (VISCERAL LEISHMANIASIS), page 318.)

Successful sand fly control is not usually possible with ordinary insecticide spraying because the breeding locations are hard to reach. Removal of dense vegetation helps control sand flies in outdoor environments. Often sand flies are controlled as a side effect of mosquito control programs.

Stable Flies

Stable flies (*Stomoxys calcitrans*) are often called biting house flies. These flies are about the same size as house flies and look much like them, but are avid blood feeders. Both male and female stable flies feed on blood. They are found throughout the world. In the US, they are most commonly found in midwestern and southeastern states. Horses are the preferred host for stable flies, though they are known to feed on the tips of the ears of dogs with pointed ears, especially German Shepherds. Stable flies are known to transmit anthrax, surra, and equine infectious anemia. Good sanitation practices can reduce the stable fly population by up to 90%. Areas along fence rows, under feed bunks, or wherever manure and straw or decaying matter can accumulate should be kept clean.

Tsetse Flies

The tsetse flies (*Glossina* species) are important blood-feeding flies found in portions of Africa. Tsetse flies are the intermediate hosts for trypanosomes that cause the fatal diseases African sleeping sickness in humans and nagana in domestic animals. Both horses and dogs can die from trypanosome infection. The disease brings on a profound lethargy that ends in death. Dogs show progressive nervous system signs. Infected dogs often lose their sight, howl involuntarily, and die in what appears to be great pain.

Control of tsetse flies is critical to the control of nagana and African sleeping sickness. Tsetse fly traps, bush clearing, fly screens, insect repellents, and insecticides are the traditional control techniques. Recently, programs involving the release of sterile male tsetse flies have offered hope for an environmentally friendly and effective control procedure for these dangerous flies.

■ HAIR LOSS (ALOPECIA)

Alopecia is the partial or complete lack of hairs in areas where they are normally present. Hair loss is a sign and its underlying cause must be determined for the condition to be successfully treated. If a dog has hair loss and is also scratching the area excessively, the itching should be investigated first (*see* page 258).

There are many causes of hair loss, which can be congenital (the animal is born with the condition) or acquired. Congenital hair loss may or may not be hereditary. It is caused by a lack of normal development of hair follicles. It may be apparent at or shortly after birth. Or, the dog may be born with a normal coat and patchy or widespread hair loss occurs when the dog becomes a young adult.

In acquired hair loss, the dog is born with a normal hair coat. It has or had normal hair follicles at one time, and is or was capable of producing structurally normal hairs. Any disease that can affect hair follicles can cause hair loss. Certain diseases may destroy the hair follicle or shaft or interfere with the growth of hair. Some diseases can cause discomfort, leading to self-trauma and loss of hair. Acquired hair loss can be inflammatory or noninflammatory.

Diseases that can directly cause destruction or damage to the hair shaft or follicle include bacterial, fungal, or parasitic infections; skin trauma such as burns; and (rarely) poisonings caused by mercury, thallium, or iodine. These diseases tend to be inflammatory.

Diseases that can directly inhibit or slow hair follicle growth include nutritional deficiencies (particularly protein deficiencies), or hormonal imbalances such as hypothyroidism. Temporary hair loss can occur during pregnancy, lactation, or several weeks after a severe illness or fever. These types of hair loss tend to be noninflammatory unless a secondary infection of the skin develops.

Itching or pain is a common cause of acquired inflammatory hair loss. Diseases that commonly cause itching or pain

Shedding

Many dog owners seek veterinary assistance because their pet sheds excessively. You should remember that the natural development and growth of new hair is accompanied by the shedding of old hair. Shedding may be abnormal (excessive) if it results in obvious loss of the hair coat and bald spots. Abnormal shedding may be caused by bacterial infection. However, if the shedding is not accompanied by bald patches or symmetric hair loss, it is likely the shedding is just a stage in the natural replacement of the hair coat.

include infections, parasites, and allergies. Friction may cause local hair loss, for example, poorly fitted halters or collars. Rarely, excessive grooming may be the cause of hair loss in some dogs.

Signs of hair loss may be obvious or subtle, depending on the disease. Congenital or hereditary hair loss is commonly either symmetric (appearing similar on both sides of the body) or located in one area only. It is not usually accompanied by inflammation.

Signs of acquired hair loss are varied and often influenced by the underlying cause(s). Inflammation, color change, scaling, excessive shedding, and itching are common. Some causes may lead to the development of secondary skin diseases, such as infection or fluid discharge. Itching is variable, depending on the primary cause.

An accurate diagnosis of the cause of hair loss requires a detailed history and physical examination. Key points in the history include the breed's tendency for congenital or hereditary hair loss; the presence, duration, and progression of problems; the presence or absence of itching; evidence of infection; and general health problems.

The physical examination will cover both the dog's skin and its general health. In the physical examination, your veterinarian will note the pattern and distribution of hair loss. The hairs will be examined to determine if they are being shed from the hair follicle or broken off. Your veterinarian will also look for signs

of secondary skin infections or parasites and may perform skin scrapings and comb the hair coat for fleas, mites, and lice. The skin scrapings and the materials obtained during combing will be carefully saved and sent to a laboratory for testing.

Your veterinarian may order diagnostic laboratory tests. These usually include smears and culture of the skin to check for evidence of bacterial, fungal, or yeast infections. If these tests do not identify or suggest an underlying cause, a skin biopsy may be performed. Skin biopsies are often needed to confirm bacterial and parasitic causes of hair loss or to identify cancerous causes of hair loss. If your veterinarian suspects a hormonal problem, he or she may order testing of blood and urine samples.

Successful treatment depends on the underlying cause and specific diagnosis. Because identifying the underlying cause of a skin condition may take some time, many veterinarians will provide or prescribe medication to relieve any discomfort or itching your pet has in connection with the hair loss.

▩ HIVES AND RASHES (URTICARIA)

Hives or skin rashes (urticaria) are localized patches of red, usually itchy, skin. They often develop and disappear suddenly. Hives are relatively uncommon in dogs. The most frequent causes are insect bites or stings, shampoos, and medications. Other causes include contact with toxic plants or chemicals. Friction, sunlight, heat, exercise, stress, and genetic abnormalities may cause or intensify the rash. Hives may develop after inhaling or consuming allergens.

The wheals (eruptions) appear within a few minutes or hours of exposure to the causative agent. In severe cases, the skin eruptions are preceded by fever, poor appetite, or dullness. They can develop on any part of the body but occur mainly on the back, flanks, neck, eyelids, and legs. In advanced cases, they may be found on the mucous membranes of the mouth, nose, lining of the eyes, rectum, and vagina.

Often, hives disappear as rapidly as they arise, usually within a few hours. Treatment may not be required. They may return rapidly if exposure to the cause is not eliminated, however. Treatment may include rapid-acting corticosteroids. If hives are chronic, environmental or food allergens should be considered as potential causes.

■ HYGROMA

A **hygroma** is a fluid-filled sac that develops over bony prominences and pressure points, especially in large breeds of dogs. Repeated trauma from lying on hard surfaces leads to inflammation. This results in a dense-walled, fluid-filled cavity. A soft, flexible, fluid-filled, painless swelling develops over pressure points, especially the leg joints. If long lasting, severe inflammation may develop, with ulcers, infection, abscesses, masses of inflamed tissue with sand-like deposits, and tissue erosion. The sac contains a clear fluid yellow to red in color. If diagnosed early while they are still small, hygromas can be lanced and then bandaged. Soft bedding and padding over pressure points is important to prevent further trauma. In cases of chronic hygromas, surgical drainage and flushing are critical for relief. Areas with severe skin ulcers may require extensive drainage, surgical removal, or skin grafting.

■ HYPERPIGMENTATION

Hyperpigmentation is a darkening and thickening of the skin seen in dogs. It is not a specific disease but a reaction of a dog's body to certain conditions.

Hyperpigmentation appears as light-brown-to-black, velvety, rough areas of thickened, often hairless skin. The usual sites are in the legs and groin area. Signs are invariably a result of inflammation due to constant friction. It can be primary or secondary. Primary diseases that cause hyperpigmentation are rare and occur almost exclusively in Dachshunds. Signs

are usually evident by 1 year of age. Secondary hyperpigmentation is relatively common and can occur in any breed of dog, most commonly those breeds prone to obesity, hormonal abnormalities, allergies, contact dermatitis, and skin infections.

The edges of these abnormal areas are often red, a sign of secondary bacterial or yeast infection. With time, it may spread to the lower neck, groin, abdomen, hocks, eyes, ears, and the area between the anus and the external genital organs. Itching is variable. When it occurs, it may be caused by the underlying disease or by a secondary infection. As the condition progresses, secondary hair loss, fluid discharge, and infections develop.

Diagnosis is by appearance of signs on the animal. In a young Dachshund, your veterinarian will want to eliminate other causes of the signs. A careful history and physical examination will be performed to identify an underlying cause. Skin scrapings are taken to exclude other causes (parasites, for example), especially in young dogs. Impression smears are used to identify bacterial infections. Depending on other signs, endocrine function tests for thyroid and adrenal disease may be used to check for underlying hormonal abnormalities. Skin testing, a food trial, or both may be necessary to test for allergies. Skin biopsies may be made to check for secondary bacterial infections not previously recognized. In most cases, your veterinarian will want to treat any secondary bacterial infections before proceeding with other diagnostic tests.

Primary hyperpigmentation in Dachshunds is not curable. Early cases may respond to shampoo treatment and steroid ointments. As signs progress, other treatment, such as medication given by mouth or injection, may be useful. The concurrent treatment of secondary infections is helpful and is required before steroids are administered. Medicated shampoos are often beneficial for removing excess oil and odor.

In secondary hyperpigmentation, the affected areas will go away on their own after identification and treatment of the underlying cause. However, this will not occur if secondary bacterial and yeast infections are not treated and controlled. Many affected dogs benefit greatly from appropriate antibiotics and medicated shampoos (2 to 3 times per week). Thus, many veterinarians will prescribe such treatments. Owners need to be patient with these treatment programs. The signs of hyperpigmentation resolve slowly; it may take months for the dog's skin to return to normal.

■ ITCHING (PRURITUS)

Pruritus is defined as an unpleasant sensation within the skin that provokes the desire to scratch. Itching is a sign, not a diagnosis or specific disease. The most common causes of itching are parasites, infections, and allergies. There are many skin diseases that do not initially cause itching. Itching may develop because of secondary bacterial or yeast infections. It is possible that by the time itching develops the initial cause is long gone.

A dog with pruritus will excessively scratch, bite, or lick its skin. Itching may be general or confined to one area. Your veterinarian will perform a thorough skin history and physical examination. Parasites, including mites and fleas, are the first possible cause your veterinarian will seek to exclude.

Next, your veterinarian will look for infectious causes of skin disease. Concurrent bacterial and yeast infections are common causes of itching. Infections are often accompanied by hair loss, scaling, odor, and fluid discharge. Excessive scratching of feet and face are common in animals with concurrent yeast and bacterial infections. If such an infection is suspected, your veterinarian will often prescribe a 21- to 30-day course of antibiotics.

If the itching goes away, then the cause was a microbial infection. However, if the dog's itching is unchanged or only somewhat better, the most likely underlying cause may be an allergy. The most common causes of allergic itching are insect

bites, food allergy, and a reaction to allergens in the environment, such as pollens, molds, or dust (*see* page 246). Sensitivity to insect bites is readily identified. Dogs that have seasonal itching are likely reacting to seasonal allergens. Dogs with year-round allergic itching may have a food allergy. Food allergy is confirmed or excluded based on response to a diet trial (*see also* page 246). During a diet trial your dog is fed a diet that does not include the foods it has normally consumed. Your veterinarian will specify a diet, often one containing fish or other meats not previously fed. To help your veterinarian isolate the food allergy, you will need to follow the prescribed diet fully and carefully and avoid providing treats that do not comply with the diet. Allergy testing and intradermal skin testing show only antigen exposure patterns. These tests are used to determine the contents of an immunotherapy vaccine, but are ineffective in identifying food allergy.

Successful treatment depends on identification of the underlying cause. Dogs whose cause of itching cannot be identified, or those in which treatment of the underlying disease does not eliminate the itching, will require medical management. Commonly prescribed anti-itching medications include antihistamines, glucocorticoids, and essential fatty acids.

Treating itchiness with **antihistamines** is common, but their success in treating itching is highly variable. The most commonly used antihistamines include hydroxyzine hydrochloride, diphenhydramine, amitriptyline hydrochloride, cetirizine, and fexofenadine. A 7- to 10-day therapeutic trial of any one antihistamine is required to see maximal benefit. Your veterinarian will assess your dog's condition and prescribe antihistamines if appropriate.

Glucocorticoids are anti-inflammatory steroids. They are often considered the most effective drugs in the management of itching. However, these drugs can cause adverse side effects, including excessive hunger, thirst, and urination. These drugs also suppress the function of the adrenal glands and increase the risk of diabetes and secondary urinary tract infections. Thus, these medications are prescribed only in limited circumstances. The use of glucocorticoids to control itching caused by infections is inappropriate.

Essential fatty acids are rarely effective as sole anti-itch agents; however, they often can be successful when used in combination with antihistamines or steroids because they may enhance the effectiveness of antihistamines or allow a smaller than usual dose of steroids.

▌ LICE

Lice are small, flightless insects that live in the hair or feathers of animals and people. There are 2 basic types of lice. Biting or chewing lice (order Mallophaga) infest both birds and mammals. They feed mostly on skin debris and the secretions of their hosts. Blood-sucking lice (order Anoplura) are skin parasites of mammals only. Typically, lice are species specific; that is, they do not readily transfer from one animal species to another.

Female lice glue their eggs, called nits, to the hairs of the host near the skin. Ordinary shampooing and washing will not dislodge the nits. Nits are pale, translucent, and almost oval in shape. Once the nits hatch, the lice undergo a nymphal stage before reaching adulthood. The immature nymphs look very much like adult lice, only smaller. It takes about 3 to 4 weeks for most lice to go from nit to reproductively capable adult, although this period varies with the species.

Dogs can be infested with 2 species of lice, *Linognathus setosus* (the dog sucking louse) and *Heterodoxus spiniger* (the biting louse). Dogs in poor health can become heavily infested. The biting louse is rare in North America. It can serve as an intermediate host for intestinal tapeworms (*see* page 114).

The first signs that your dog may have lice include scratching, biting, and rubbing of infested areas. A dog with lice will

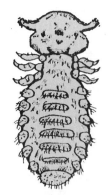

Biting louse

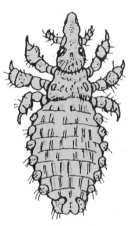

Blood-sucking louse

Biting or chewing louse (order Mallophaga) and blood-sucking louse (order Anoplura).

have a rough, dry coat. If the lice are abundant, the hair might also be matted. Sucking lice cause small wounds that can become infected. Usually, the diagnosis is made by seeing lice on the infested pet. Parting the hair often reveals the lice. Chewing lice are active and can be seen moving through the hair. Sucking lice usually move more slowly. They are often found with their mouth-parts embedded in the skin.

Using a fine-toothed comb to dislodge nits is a tedious process that will not kill lice that have hatched. Dogs, cats, and other pets are usually treated with dips, washes, sprays, or dusts that kill lice. Your veterinarian can recommend an appropriate control product for your pet and provide directions for its use.

Lice dropped or pulled from the host die in a few days, but eggs may continue to hatch over 2 to 3 weeks. Thus, lice control treatments should be repeated 7 to 10 days after the first treatment. (*See also* ANTIPARASITIC DRUGS, page 1134.) Careful inspection of your pet's coat should be continued daily for at least 2 weeks after you see the last louse. Be sure to carefully collect any lice (dead or alive) removed from your pet and dispose of them promptly in a sealed container (such as a zip-closure plastic bag).

In severe louse infestations, the dog may damage its skin by scratching. Bacterial infections and scratch wounds are common. If these conditions are present, your veterinarian may prescribe an antibiotic or other medication.

In addition to killing the lice on your pet, you will want to be sure that lice are not infesting your dog's bedding, collar, grooming tools (including bushes or combs), and other similar objects in your dog's environment. Careful cleaning and inspection of these objects can help provide your pet with continued relief from the irritation caused by lice.

The lice that infest dogs, cats, and other pets are not normally attracted to humans. Therefore, while care in dealing with the lice infecting your pet is recommended, owners should understand that people rarely get lice from their pets.

▓ MITE INFESTATION (MANGE, ACARIASIS, SCABIES)

Mange is caused by microscopic mites that invade the skin of otherwise healthy animals. The mites cause irritation of the skin, resulting in itching, hair loss, and inflammation. All forms of mange are highly contagious. Both dogs and cats are very susceptible. Horses and other domestic animals can also be infected. There are several types of mange that affect dogs, including canine scabies (sarcoptic mange), ear mites (otodectic mange), walking dandruff (cheyletiellosis), and trombiculosis.

Demodicosis is not considered mange, but it is also caused by mites.

Canine Scabies (Sarcoptic Mange)

This form of mange is caused by the mite *Sarcoptes scabiei canis*. This highly contagious parasite is found on dogs worldwide. It is often called canine scabies. Although the mites that cause mange are fairly picky in selecting their host, humans and other animals that come in contact with an infected dog may also become infected. The entire life cycle (17 to 21 days) of these mites is spent on the infested dog. Females burrow tunnels in the skin to lay eggs. Mange is easily spread between animals by contact. Indirect transmission, such as through infested bedding, is less common, but it can occur. The incubation period varies from 10 days to 8 weeks, depending on how severely the dog is infested, part of the body affected, number of mites transmitted, and the individual dog's health and hygiene.

Not all dogs have signs when they are infested with sarcoptic mange mites. Usually, though, the animal will have intense itching that comes on suddenly. The itching is probably caused by sensitivity to the mites' droppings. Initially, infested skin will erupt with small, solid bumps. Because the dog scratches or bites itself to

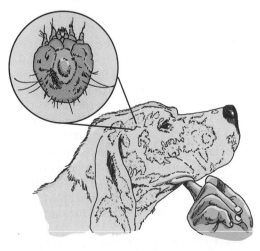

Canine scabies is caused by the *Sarcoptes scabiei canis* mite.

relieve the itch, these bumps and the surrounding skin are often damaged, causing thick, crusted sores. Secondary yeast or bacterial infections can develop in the damaged skin. Usually, the sores appear first on the abdomen, chest, ears, elbows, and legs. If the mange is not diagnosed and treated, the sores can spread over the entire body. Dogs with longterm, recurring mange develop oily dandruff (seborrhea), severe thickening of the skin with wrinkling and crust build-up, and oozing, weeping sores. Dogs affected this severely can become emaciated and may even die.

"Scabies incognito" is a term used to describe hard-to-diagnose mange. If a dog is regularly bathed and has a well-groomed coat, the mites might be hard to find, even if the dog shows signs of infestation such as itching. The other typical signs of mange—crusts and scales on the skin— are removed by regular bathing.

If mange is suspected, your veterinarian will do a physical examination, including collecting skin scrapings and possibly a stool sample. Some clinics might also use a blood test to diagnose mange. If mites are not found, but the signs are highly suggestive of mange, trial treatment is warranted. Mange is very highly contagious and can spread easily between animals of different species and even to humans. Thus, you should ask your veterinarian for advice on how to avoid contracting mange from your pet.

Treatment should include all dogs and other animals that have been in contact with one another. It may be necessary to clip the hair. The crusts and dirt should be removed by soaking with a medicated (antiseborrheic) shampoo, and an antimite dip applied. Lime-sulfur is highly effective and safe for use in young animals. This is frequently prescribed by veterinarians. Several dips may be required. Internal medicines may also be prescribed. Some internal mange medications are also used for heartworm prevention, so your veterinarian may want to test your dog for heartworms before treatment. Treatment for secondary infections may also be necessary.

Ear Mites (Otodectic Mange)

This form of mange is caused by *Otodectes cynotis* mites. These mites often infest the external ear, causing inflammation of the ear canal (*see* OTITIS EXTERNA, page 160) in dogs and especially in cats. Ear mites are usually found deep in the external ear canal, but they are sometimes seen on the body. The infested animal will shake its head and scratch its ear(s). In dogs with normally upright ears, the external ear may droop. The intensity of the itching varies. In severe cases, the external ear may be inflamed and produce pus; a torn eardrum is also possible. Dogs with ear mites should be treated with a parasiticide in the ears and whole body for 2 to 4 weeks.

Walking Dandruff (Cheyletiellosis)

Cheyletiella yasguri mites cause walking dandruff in dogs. (The dandruff that is seen "walking" is actually the mites moving about on the skin of the dog.) Although these mites often stay on their preferred hosts, infections across species are possible. Walking dandruff is very contagious, especially in kennels, catteries, or multipet households. Regular use of certain insecticides to control flea infestations has a side benefit of often controlling the mites that cause walking dandruff. Humans can also be infested with these species of mites. Mites that cause walking dandruff spend their entire 3-week life cycle on their host.

Scaling of the skin and infestation along the back are common signs of walking dandruff. Intense itching is frequent, though some animals do not itch at all. Pets that show no signs can carry the mites and transmit them to other pets and humans.

Although a definitive diagnosis is usually made by examining the mites with a microscope, a tentative diagnosis is often made based on the presence of mites and an examination of the animal's skin. The mites and eggs are hard to find, especially on animals that are bathed often.

In many cases, veterinarians will prescribe weekly dipping in an insecticide to eliminate the mites. In addition, treating the pet's environment is necessary to kill mites in bedding, carpets, and other areas. Insecticidal treatment of kennels and other multipet communities is required to halt mite infestations.

Owners of pets infested with these mites may want to check with their physicians regarding medication and other steps to control mite infestations in themselves, their family members, and the home environment. It is very easy these mites to spread from pets to owners.

Canine Demodicosis

The mites that cause canine demodicosis live in small numbers in the hair follicles and sebaceous glands of all dogs. This is normal and causes no signs of disease. However, for reasons not clearly understood, some dogs have large numbers of *Demodex canis* mites, resulting in inflammation and hair loss. There is evidence of hereditary predisposition for this condition in some dogs. It is strongly suspected that suppression of the immune response to these mites may play a role.

There are 2 clinical forms of canine demodicosis: localized (limited to a small area) and generalized (found on the entire body). Localized demodicosis is seen in dogs less than 2 years old. Affected areas are usually hairless, red or densely pigmented, raised lumps that look like acne. Itching is mild or absent. A few cases of localized demodicosis progress to the generalized form, though most cases resolve without treatment.

The generalized form of demodicosis is a severe disease with widespread inflammation of the skin. Secondary bacterial infections (pyodemodicosis) are common. Many dogs with generalized demodicosis also have inflamed foot pads. Other signs can include enlarged lymph nodes, lethargy, fever, and pus-filled inflammation of the deeper layers of skin.

Laboratory analysis of deep skin scrapings is usually used to confirm a diagnosis of demodicosis. In addition, your veterinarian will also want to test your dog for other infections or diseases that may have suppressed the immune system.

Cases of localized demodicosis often resolve without treatment. Generalized demodicosis is a serious disease that requires medical treatment. The outlook for these cases is guarded. Medicated shampoos and dips are often used to treat demodicosis. Prescription medications to kill the mites may be required. In cases where secondary bacterial infections are present, antibiotics may also be prescribed. Skin scrapings are taken at monthly intervals to monitor the number of mites in the dog.

Owners of dogs with demodicosis should understand that treatment of generalized demodicosis can take several months. The prescribed antiparasitic treatment must be continued until at least 2 consecutive negative skin scrapings have been obtained at monthly intervals.

Because it may be inherited, dogs with demodicosis should not be bred.

Trombiculosis

Trombiculosis is a type of mange caused by the parasitic larval stage of mites of the family Trombiculidae. Adults and nymphs look like tiny spiders and live on rotting material. Dogs acquire the larvae by lying on the ground or walking in suitable habitat.

The larvae attach to the host, feed for a few days, and leave when engorged. They are easily identified as tiny, orange-red, oval dots that do not move. These are usually found clustering on the head, ears, feet, or belly. Signs include redness, bumps, hair loss, and crusts. Intense itching can persist even after the larvae have left the animal. Diagnosis is based on history and signs. Your veterinarian will want to exclude other skin disorders that cause itching, such as respiratory allergies (*see* page 227). Diagnosis is confirmed by careful examination of the affected areas. Skin scrapings might also be examined under the microscope for evidence of 6-legged mite larvae.

Treatment for dogs and other pets with trombiculosis follows the pattern for the general treatment of mange (*see* page 261).

Medications to kill these mites on your pet may be different from those prescribed for other types of mites. Follow your veterinarian's treatment program. If the itching has been either severe or extended, antibiotics or other medications may be prescribed to control secondary infections in scratch and bite wounds.

Preventing reinfestation is often difficult. The most useful approach, if feasible, consists of keeping pets away from areas known to harbor mites.

NASAL DERMATOSES OF DOGS

Nasal dermatoses are diseases of the skin on or near the nose. The nose itself is often referred to as the nasal planum. These conditions are sometimes known as **Collie nose** or **nasal solar dermatitis**, depending on the cause.

Many diseases may cause these conditions in dogs. These may affect the bridge of the nose (the muzzle), the nose itself, or both. In cases of pyoderma, dermatophytosis, and demodicosis, the haired portions of the nose are affected. In systemic lupus erythematosus or pemphigus, the whole muzzle is often crusted (with occasional oozing of serum) or covered with ulcers. In systemic and discoid lupus, and occasionally in pemphigus and skin lymphoma, the nose loses color and reddens; eventually the area near the nose may develop ulcers.

Nasal dermatosis due to solar radiation is probably a rare disease and may be a misdiagnosis of the lupus variants. In true nasal solar dermatitis, the nonpigmented areas around the nostrils are affected first, and occasionally the bridge of the nose may become inflamed or ulcerated. These changes are worse in the summer, although lupus and pemphigus may also show this seasonal variation. Any of the above diseases may affect the areas around the eyes. The sudden onset of nasal swelling, redness, and fluid discharge is thought to be caused by an insect sting or bite. The parasitic disease leishmaniasis may cause color loss or ulceration on the nose.

Treatment depends on the cause. Diagnostic tests performed by your veterinarian will likely include skin scrapings, bacterial and fungal cultures, and biopsies. The prescribed treatment will depend on the results of the diagnostic tests.

If the diagnosis is nasal solar dermatitis, a topical steroid lotion may help relieve inflammation. Exposure to sunlight must be severely curtailed. Topical sunscreens may be effective but need to be applied at least twice daily. You should be aware that not all sunscreen lotions prepared for human use are safe for use on dogs. Your veterinarian can recommend a sunscreen that will be tolerated by your dog.

PARASITIC WORMS OF THE SKIN

A parasite is any living thing that lives in, on, or with another living thing (known as a host) and that depends on the host for its food and shelter. Some parasites depend on a host for their entire life while other parasites depend on a host only during a part of their life. Many worms are parasites that infect dogs, cats, horses, and other animals. Some of these worms may also infect people. The following section describes parasitic worms that affect the skin of pets.

Dracunculus Infection

Dracunculus insignis is a species of roundworm found mainly in the connective tissue beneath the skin of the legs. They are known to infect raccoons, minks, and other animals, including dogs, in North America. Female worms can reach 10 feet (3 meters) in length. Male worms are tiny in comparison, around 0.6 inches (20 millimeters) long. These worms can produce skin ulcers on their hosts. When the ulcers touch water, the worms stick their heads out of the wounds in order to lay their long, thin-tailed larvae. The larvae then develop inside of another host, the water flea. Dogs can also become infected when they drink contaminated water or eat another host, such as a frog.

Signs of *D. insignis* worm infestation include snake-like, swollen tracks under the skin and crater-like red ulcers on the skin's surface. These infections are rare, but have occasionally been found in dogs that have been around small lakes and shallow, stagnant water.

Veterinarians treat the infection by carefully and slowly extracting the parasites. Antiparasitic drugs of the miridazole or benzimidazole classes can also be useful (see also ANTHELMINTICS, page 1127).

In parts of Africa, Asia, and the Middle East, a guinea worm (*Dracunculus medinensis*) is a well-known parasite of humans that may also infest dogs and other animals.

Pelodera Dermatitis

Pelodera dermatitis is a rare skin worm infestation that causes a short-term skin infection. The condition is caused when larvae of roundworms known as *Pelodera strongyloides* invade the skin. These larvae are widespread in decaying organic matter (such as damp hay) and on or near the surface of moist soil. They are only occasionally parasitic. In most cases, animals are exposed to the larvae through direct contact with infested materials, such as damp, filthy bedding. Animals with healthy skin are not usually at risk of infection.

The sores usually only appear on parts of the body that contact the infested material, such as the legs, groin, abdomen, and chest. The affected skin is red and partially or completely hairless. In addition, there may be bumps in the skin, lumps filled with pus, crusts, or ulcers. Often—though not always—there is severe itching, causing the animal to scratch, bite, or rub the infected area. Veterinarians can usually make a definitive diagnosis by examining a skin scraping under a microscope to check for worm larvae. Animals with *Pelodera* dermatitis can be treated in the same manner as other skin worm infestations. In many cases, simply moving the animal to a dry area with clean bedding will lead to recovery.

▪ PHOTOSENSITIZATION

Photosensitization is a clinical condition in which skin is oversensitive to sunlight; this condition is not sunburn. Certain molecules present in the skin are energized by light. When the molecules return to the less energized state, the released energy causes chemical reactions in the skin. Photosensitization can be difficult to distinguish from actual sunburn.

Photosensitization is often classified according to the source of the photodynamic pigment. The types known to occur in dogs include primary (type I) photosensitivity and secondary (or type III) photosensitivity. A wide range of chemicals in plants, fungi, and bacteria may act as photosensitization agents. Photosensitization can also occur in dogs that have liver damage caused by any of several types of poisonings.

The signs associated with photosensitivity are similar regardless of the cause. Photosensitive dogs squirm in apparent discomfort when exposed to light. They scratch or rub lightly pigmented, exposed areas of skin (for example, the ears, eyelids, or muzzle). Bright sunlight can cause typical skin changes, even in black-coated animals. Redness develops rapidly and is soon followed by swelling. If exposure to light stops at this stage, the abnormalities soon resolve. When exposure is prolonged, fluid discharge, scab formation, and skin death result.

Signs are easily recognized in cases of marked photosensitivity but are similar to the effects of sunburn in early or mild cases. When examining your pet for photosensitivity, your veterinarian will not only examine the skin but also look for signs of any of the diseases that may trigger this condition. Evaluation of liver enzymes and liver biopsies may be necessary to determine if your dog has liver disease. Laboratory tests may also be performed. Your veterinarian will also ask about your dog's access to poisons and whether or not your dog may have been exposed to rat poison or other poisonous chemicals.

Treatment involves mostly soothing the signs. While photosensitivity continues, dogs should be shaded fully or, preferably, kept indoors and allowed out only during darkness. The severe stress of photosensitization and extensive death of skin tissue can cause serious illness and even death. Depending on the individual case, injectable steroids may be helpful. Secondary skin infections and fluid discharge are treated with standard wound management techniques. Exposure to flies must be prevented because the skin damage caused by photosensitivity attracts flies and may lead to maggot infestations and secondary diseases. Skin abnormalities caused by photosensitivity heal remarkably well, even after extensive damage. The outcome for a dog is related to the site and severity of the primary lesion and/or liver disease, and to the degree of healing.

PYODERMA

Pyoderma literally means "pus in the skin." It can be caused by infection, inflammation, or cancer and is common in dogs.

Most cases of pyoderma are caused by bacterial infections. Most of these are superficial and secondary to a variety of other conditions, such as allergies or parasites. Pyoderma occurs in otherwise healthy animals and resolves completely with appropriate antibiotics. Warm, moist areas on the skin, such as lip folds, facial folds, and neck folds, often have higher bacterial counts than other areas and are at an increased risk for infection. Pressure points, such as elbows, are prone to infections due to repeated pressure. Any skin disease that changes the normally dry, desert-like environment to a more humid environment can cause overcolonization of the skin with bacteria.

The most common sign of bacterial pyoderma is excessive scaling. Scales are often pierced by hairs. Itching is variable. In dogs, superficial pyoderma commonly appears as bald patches, welts around hairs, and scabbing. Shorthaired breeds often have multiple welts that look similar to hives because the inflammation in and around the follicles causes the hairs to stand more erect. These hairs are often easily removed, which distinguishes pyo-

derma from hives. Hair loss leads to small bald patches in affected areas. At the margins of the hair loss, there may be redness and welts but these signs are often absent in shorthaired breeds. The signs of deep pyoderma in dogs include pain, crusting, odor, and secretions of blood and pus. Redness, swelling, ulceration, scabs, and blisters may also be seen. The bridge of the muzzle, chin, elbows, hocks, and spaces between the toes are more prone to deep infections, but any area may be involved.

Diagnosis is based on signs. Diagnosis of pyoderma must also include steps to identify any underlying causes. These include fleas, allergies, hypothyroidism, and poor grooming. Multiple deep skin scrapings are needed to exclude parasitic infections. Bacterial cultures may also be taken.

The most common causes of recurrent bacterial pyoderma include undertreatment with prescribed antibiotic medications. You may contribute to a recurrence of pyoderma in your dog if you don't carefully follow your veterinarian's treatment directions. Even though your dog may seem better after only a few days or a week, it is still very important for you to continue the prescribed treatment program for the full length of time. The bacteria causing pyoderma can still be present and ready to multiply again if the complete course of medication is not given.

Antibiotic treatment should last for at least 3 weeks and preferably for 4 weeks. All signs (except for hair regrowth and resolution of increased pigmentation) should be gone for at least 7 days before antibiotics are discontinued. Longterm, recurrent, or deep pyodermas typically require 8 to 12 weeks or longer to heal completely.

Attention to grooming is crucial. The hair coat should be clipped in dogs with deep pyoderma and a professional grooming is recommended in medium- to long-haired dogs with superficial pyoderma. This will remove excessive hair that can trap debris and bacteria and will help grooming.

Dogs with superficial pyoderma should be bathed 2 to 3 times per week during the first 2 weeks of treatment and then 1 to

2 times per week until the infection clears. Dogs with deep pyoderma may require daily baths with medicated shampoos diluted to one-half or one-quarter strength. Shampooing will remove bacteria, crusts, and scales, and reduce itching, odor, and oiliness. Improvement may not be evident for at least 14 to 21 days, and recovery may not be as rapid as expected. Your veterinarian can recommend the appropriate bathing program for your pet's condition.

RINGWORM (DERMATOPHYTOSIS)

Ringworm is an infection of skin, hair, or claws caused by a type of fungus. In dogs, about 70% of ringworm cases are caused by the fungus *Microsporum canis*, 20% by *Microsporum gypseum*, and 10% by *Trichophyton mentagrophytes*. The infecting fungus is spread easily in the environment. People can easily be infected with these fungi. (*See also* FUNGAL INFECTIONS, page 312.)

Most cases of ringworm are spread by contact with infected animals or contaminated objects such as furniture or grooming tools. Broken hairs with associated spores are important sources for spread of the disease. Contact does not always result in infection. Whether infection is established depends on the fungal species and on host factors, including age, health, condition of exposed skin surfaces, grooming behavior, and nutrition. Infection leads to short-lived resistance to reinfection. Under most circumstances, dermatophytes grow only in the dead cells of skin and hair, and infection stops on reaching living cells or inflamed tissue. As inflammation and host immunity develop, further spread of infection stops, but this process may take several weeks.

Infected dogs develop bald, scaly patches with broken hairs in ring-like whirls. The most common sites affected by ringworm are the face, ear tips, tail, and feet. Ringworm is diagnosed by fungal culture, examination with an ultraviolet lamp, and direct microscopic examination

Ringworm, shown here on the shoulder of a dog, is caused by a type of fungus.

of hair or skin scale. Fungal culture of hairs and scrapings from the affected areas is the most accurate method. Direct microscopic examination of hairs or skin scrapings may allow early diagnosis.

Ringworm infections usually clear up without treatment, but medicated shampoos might speed recovery in some cases. Such treatments are not always effective, however. Your veterinarian can provide you with information about any treatment that may be appropriate for your pet and advise you regarding precautions you should take to avoid ringworm infection in yourself and members of your family.

SEBORRHEA

In dogs, seborrhea is a skin disease that is characterized by a defect in keratinization or cornification of the outer layer of the skin, hair follicles, or claws. Seborrhea results in increased scale formation, occasionally excessive greasiness of the skin and hair coat, and often secondary inflammation and infection.

Seborrhea is often a sign of other skin diseases, such as food or airborne allergies, ringworm, or mite infestation.

Primary seborrhea is an inherited skin disorder. It is seen most frequently in American Cocker Spaniels, English Springer Spaniels, Basset Hounds, West Highland White Terriers, Dachshunds, Labrador and Golden Retrievers, and German Shepherd dogs. Among dogs with seborrhea, there is usually a family history of the disorder, suggesting genetic factors are involved. The disease begins at a young age (usually less than 18 to 24 months) and progresses throughout the dog's life.

Secondary seborrhea is a sign of an underlying disease that causes excessive scaling, crusting, or oiliness, often accompanied by pus-filled inflammation, infection, and hair loss.

Signs and Diagnosis

A diagnosis of primary seborrhea is reserved for dogs in which all possible underlying causes of seborrhea have been excluded. Most dogs with seborrhea have the secondary form of the disease. The most common underlying causes are hormonal disorders and allergies. The goal is to identify and treat these underlying causes. Allergies are more likely to be the underlying cause if the age of onset is less than 5 years. Endocrine disorders are more likely if the seborrhea begins in middle aged or older dogs. A lack of itching helps to exclude allergies, scabies, and other itching diseases. If itching is minimal, your veterinarian will seek to exclude hormonal disorders, other internal diseases, or other primary skin diseases. If itching is significant, allergies, scabies, and fleas will be considered by your veterinarian.

Other important considerations in making a diagnosis include the presence of excessive urination, excessive drinking, heat-seeking behavior, abnormal estrous cycles, pyoderma, the season, diet, response to previous medications, fungi or bacteria present, and the environment.

Your veterinarian will give your pet a thorough physical examination, including internal organ systems and a comprehensive skin examination. This is the first step in identifying the underlying cause. The skin examination documents the type and distribution of the abnormalities; the presence of hair loss; and the degree of odor, scale, oiliness, and texture of the skin and hair coat. The presence of follicular boils, papules (pimples), crusts, and other bumps usually indicates the existence of a superficial pyoderma (bacterial infection). Darkening indicates a chronic skin irritation (such as infection or inflammation), and skin thickening indicates chronic itching. Yeast infection will always be considered during this process.

Secondary infection is a problem for dogs with seborrhea. The keratinization abnormalities in seborrheic dogs usually provide ideal conditions for bacterial and yeast infections. The self-trauma that occurs in itchy animals increases the likelihood of a secondary infection. The infections add to the itchiness and are usually responsible for a significant amount of the inflammation, papules, crusts, hair loss, and scales. Samples of the affected areas are taken to identify the quantity and type of bacteria or yeast present. In a seborrheic dog with itching, the infection may cause all or most of the signs. Other diseases may be uncovered by clearing the infections. Thus, you should be sure to comply with any follow up examination requests made by your veterinarian.

Treatment

Treatment is needed to keep your dog comfortable while the underlying cause is identified and secondary skin diseases are corrected. In addition to treating any secondary infections with antibiotics, medicated shampoos are often used to help control the seborrhea and speed the return of the skin to a normal state. Medicated shampoos can decrease the number of bacteria and yeast on the skin surface, the amount of scale and sebum present, and the level of itching. They may also help normalize skin cell replacement.

Most products contained in medicated shampoos can be classified based on their effects. **Keratolytic products** include sulfur, salicylic acid, tar, selenium sulfide, propylene glycol, fatty acids, and benzoyl peroxide. They remove excess dead skin cells. This reduces the scale and makes the skin feel softer. Shampoos containing keratolytic products frequently increase scaling during the first 14 days of treatment, due to the loosened scales getting caught in the hair coat. The scales will be removed by continued bathing. **Keratoplastic products** help normalize keratinization and reduce scale formation. Tar, sulfur, salicylic acid, and selenium sulfide are examples of keratoplastic agents. **Emollients** (lactic acid, sodium lactate, lanolin, and numerous oils, such as corn, coconut, peanut, and cottonseed) reduce water loss from the skin. They work best after the skin has been rehydrated and are excellent products after shampooing. **Antibacterial agents** include benzoyl peroxide, chlorhexidine, iodine, ethyl lactate, and triclosan. **Antifungal ingredients** include chlorhexidine, sulfur, iodine, ketoconazole, and miconazole. Boric and acetic acids are also used as topical antibiotics. Most medicated shampoos are a combination of these ingredients.

Follow the advice of your veterinarian regarding the most appropriate medicated shampoo for your pet with seborrhea. The selection of a medicated shampoo is based on hair coat and skin scaling and oiliness. Never use a shampoo formulated for people without the consent of your veterinarian.

◼ TICKS

Ticks are blood-sucking parasites that attach themselves to animals and people. Once attached to a host, ticks feed voraciously. As they feed, ticks can transmit a large number of diseases, including Rocky Mountain spotted fever, Q fever, and Lyme disease. Ticks also release toxins that can harm their hosts (*see* TICK PARALYSIS, page 213). Skin wounds caused by ticks can lead to secondary bacterial infections and screwworm infestations. Severe tick infestations can lead to anemia and death.

Technically, ticks are not insects. They are arachnids and are related to spiders. There are about 825 species of ticks belonging to 7 biological families. The Ixodidae family (commonly known as "hard" ticks) contains more than 650 species while the next largest family, the Argasidae ("soft" ticks), contains about 150 species. The remaining tick families (the Nutelliellidae, Amblyomma, Aponomma, Argas, and Boophilus) are much smaller and far less important in terms of diseases. Ticks have 4 life stages—egg, larva, nymph, and adult.

Ticks can be found worldwide. Some ticks prey on specific animals, though other species can prey on many species of animals, including humans. Blood-sucking behavior is different depending on the species. Adult feeding activity is chiefly in late summer and early fall but may begin later after a dry summer. Larvae and nymphs are active from spring through fall. Ticks can survive from several months to several years without food if environmental conditions permit.

Most species of ticks have a favored feeding area on a host, although in dense infestations, ticks may attach themselves wherever they can find a feeding location. Some ticks feed chiefly on the head, neck, shoulders, and pubic area. In other species, the favored sites may be ears, near the anus and under the tail, or in nasal passages.

The definitive sign of tick infestation is the presence of a tick on the animal. Direct contact with ticks frequently results in tick infestation. Animals that spend time outdoors, especially in wild areas, are more often affected. Thus, among dogs, hunting breeds or dogs that roam are mostly likely to be infested, though any dog spending time outside can acquire ticks.

Otobius megnini is a tick species that can hide unusually well. These ticks prefer to attach themselves in the ears of their hosts and are often overlooked by pet owners. These ticks are found in low rainfall areas of the western US and in Mexico and western Canada. Dogs and humans can suffer severe irritation from ear canal infestations. The infestations may cause paralysis. Secondary infections by larval screwworms are reported. *Otobius megnini* ticks can transmit Q fever, tularemia, Colorado tick fever, and Rocky Mountain spotted fever.

Diagnosis is by appearance of tick bite marks on the dog and the presence of the parasite. Ticks that have been on an animal only a short time (an hour to a few days) appear flat. Ticks that have been on an animal for days appear much more rounded due to the blood they have consumed.

Ticks should be removed as soon as possible to minimize disease and damage. To do this, use tweezers to carefully grasp the tick close to the skin and pull gently. Never try to remove a tick with your bare hands, as some tick-borne diseases (for example, Rocky Mountain spotted fever) can be immediately transmitted through breaks in your skin or contact with mucous membranes. The use of hot matches should also be avoided. Infested dogs should also be treated with anti-tick insecticides that kill attached larvae, nymphs, and adults. These can be given by spot-on solutions (which are applied on the back and spread rapidly over the entire body surface) dips, sprays, and dusts. Care needs to be taken in selecting the correct anti-tick product. Contact your veterinarian for a recommendation for the best tick control prod-

uct for your pet. Some of the products that are given monthly for flea control also effectively control ticks. Be sure to tell the veterinarian about any other pets you have in your household because this will make a difference in the veterinarian's recommendation.

If your dog is severely infested with ticks, you should promptly take it to a veterinarian for tick removal. Heavy infestations will not only severely damage the skin, but the chances of anemia, paralysis, and other complications are high. Your veterinarian is in the best position to provide a heavily infested pet with the care it needs. A clinic stay for such pets is likely.

Even if your pet has acquired only a few ticks, you should have your pet checked for any of the many diseases spread by these parasites. Monitor any site(s) from which you have removed ticks. If a tick bite site turns red or swells a prompt trip to the veterinarian is warranted.

Keeping animals away from tick-prone areas is the most effective step you can take to control exposure. Most ticks live in particular microhabitats, such as tall grass or the border between wooded areas and lawns. Destruction of these microhabitats reduces the number of ticks. Removing tall grass and weeds and trimming vegetation can help protect your animal. Insecticide treatment of vegetation can slightly reduce the risk of ticks. However, it is not recommended for wide use because of environmental pollution and the cost of treatment of large areas.

◼ TUMORS OF THE SKIN

Tumors are abnormal growths of cells. Tumors affecting the skin or the tissue just under the skin are the most commonly seen tumors in dogs. Skin tumors are diagnosed more frequently than other tumors in animals in part because they are the most easily seen tumors and in part because the skin is constantly exposed to many tumor-causing factors in the environment. Chemicals, solar radiation, and viruses are just some of the things that can cause skin tumors. Hormonal abnormalities and genetic factors may also play a role in the development of skin tumors.

All of the various layers and components of skin have the potential for developing distinctive tumors. Distinguishing a tumor from an inflammatory disease can sometimes be difficult. Tumors are usually small lumps or bumps, but they also can occur as hairless, discolored patches, rashes, or nonhealing ulcers. Because skin tumors are so diverse, identifying them should be left to a veterinarian.

Tumors may be benign or malignant (cancerous). Malignant tumors can spread and cause harm to the animal. Distinguishing a benign tumor from a cancerous tumor requires specialized knowledge and laboratory equipment. A veterinarian can perform a fine needle aspiration of cells or a biopsy (which removes a small amount of tissue from a tumor) for evaluation.

Treatment for a particular tumor depends largely on the type of tumor, its location and size, and the overall physical condition of the dog. For benign tumors that are not ulcerated and do not impair the dog's normal routine, treatment may not be necessary. This may be the most prudent option, especially in aged dogs.

There are several treatment options for cancerous tumors and benign tumors that inhibit normal activities or are cosmetically unpleasant. For most tumors, surgical removal is the most effective option. It is also probably the least costly option and the one with the fewest side effects. If malignancy is suspected, tissue surrounding the tumor will also be removed to increase the chance that none of the tumor cells are left behind. For tumors that cannot be completely removed, partial removal may prolong the life of the dog. Radiation treatment or chemotherapy may also be used to provide your pet with a better outcome.

In addition to skin and hair follicle tumors, there are also tumors that affect the ceruminous glands. These are discussed in the section on ear diseases (*see* page 163).

Apocrine Gland Tumors of the Anal Sac

These tumors most commonly appear as deep, firm, masses near the anal sacs. Older English Cocker Spaniels, Springer Spaniels, Dachshunds, Alaskan Malamutes, German Shepherds, and mixed-breed dogs are most at risk. As the tumors grow, they may compress the rectum and induce constipation. Some of these tumors are associated with a syndrome that is characterized by abnormally high calcium in the blood. Elevated calcium causes poor appetite, weight loss, and increased water intake and urine output. The tumors often spread to local lymph nodes and other organs. In most cases, surgery requires removal of the mass and tissues surrounding it, including involved lymph nodes. Chemotherapy and radiation treatment may also be provided. Few dogs live more than a year after this type of tumor has been diagnosed.

Basal Cell Tumors and Carcinomas

Basal cells lie at the base of the top layer of the skin (the epidermis). A benign growth of these cells is a basal cell tumor. A malignant growth is a basal cell carcinoma.

Basal cell tumors are common in dogs and most are benign. Canine basal cell tumors most commonly develop in middle-aged to older dogs. Many breeds are predisposed, especially Wirehaired Pointing Griffons and Kerry Blue and Wheaten Terriers. These tumors are found most commonly on the head (especially the ears), the neck, and forelimbs. These tumors generally appear as firm, solitary, dome-shaped elevated masses, which are often hairless or ulcerated. The lumps may stick out like stalks from the skin surface. They vary in size from less than 0.4 inches (1 centimeter) to more than 4 inches (10 centimeters) in diameter. These tumors are sometimes dark in color. Cysts may also form. Although basal cell tumors are benign, they can be large and may cause extensive ulceration and secondary inflammation. These tumors can break the skin, cause the death of skin tissue, and drain fluid or pus. The dog is often uncomfortable. Surgical removal is effective treatment and reduces the chance of secondary infection and inflammation.

Basal cell carcinomas are less common in dogs than in cats. They often appear as ulcers on the head, legs, or neck. Unlike benign basal cell tumors, these carcinomas generally are not raised above the skin surface. However, they spread, forming new ulcers. Consequently, surgical removal is the treatment of choice. These tumors generally occur in older dogs. Saint Bernards, Scottish Terriers, and Norwegian Elkhounds are most at risk. Unlike basal cell tumors, basal cell carcinomas can be found almost anywhere on the body. These tumors spread to neighboring skin but seldom spread to other organs. Surgical removal is the treatment usually recommended. When performing this surgery, the veterinarian will remove a sufficient amount of normal skin around the tumor to make certain that the entire tumor has been removed.

Benign Fibroblastic Tumors

Collagenous nevi are benign collections of fibrous proteins known as collagen. They are common in dogs. Generally collagenous nevi are found in middle-aged or older animals, most frequently on the legs, head, neck, and areas prone to trauma. They are flat to raised lumps that develop in the skin or fat beneath the skin. Surgical removal of both forms is generally effective. Infrequently, some may grow too large to be surgically removed.

Skin tags are distinctive, benign, skin lumps on older dogs. These are common, may be single or multiple, and can develop in any breed, although large breeds may be at increased risk. Most commonly, skin tags look like extended stalk-like growths, often covered by a wart-like surface. Surgical removal is optional, but a biopsy is recommended to confirm the diagnosis. Dogs that develop one are likely to develop others.

Fibromas resemble collagenous nevi or skin tags. Fibromas occur in all breeds but are primarily a tumor of aged dogs.

Doberman Pinschers, Boxers, and Golden Retrievers are most at risk. The head and legs are the most likely sites. Fibromas appear as isolated, generally raised, often hairless lumps originating under the skin surface. They feel firm and rubbery (**fibroma durum**) or soft and mushy (**fibroma molle**) These tumors are benign and treatment is optional. However, complete surgical removal is recommended because they may grow quite large.

Benign, Nonviral, Wart-like Tumors

These tumors are not, in the strictest sense, warts though they may look a lot like warts. These tumors are often easy to remove and there is little threat to the overall health of the dog. (For a more detailed discussion of WARTS (PAPILLOMAS), *see* page 282.)

Epidermal hamartomas (nevi) are dark, pointy bumps on the skin. Occasionally they are arranged in a line. They are rare and found most often in puppies. The disease may be inherited in Cocker Spaniels. Some form pimples or dark, thick skin folds. They are benign, but their appearance is unpleasant, and they are prone to secondary bacterial infection. For these reasons, epidermal hamartomas are usually removed or treated. Smaller hamartomas can be surgically removed. Dogs with large or multiple hamartomas may respond to drug treatment.

Canine warty dyskeratomas are rare, benign tumors that grow near hair follicles or sweat glands. They are bumps with a dark dot in the center. How they are formed is not known. They are usually treated by surgical removal.

Blood Vessel Tumors

Blood vessel (vascular) tumors of the skin and soft tissues are growths that closely resemble blood vessels. Some forms are benign while others are highly malignant.

Hemangiomas are benign tumors of adult dogs. Many breeds (including Gordon Setters; Boxers; and Airedale, Scottish, and Kerry Blue Terriers) are considered to be at risk. These tumors are most common on the head, legs, and abdomen. Hemangiomas are single to multiple, circular, often compressible, red to black lumps and can look like a "blood blister." Although they are benign, they tend to develop ulcers and some grow quite large. Because of this, and because it is important to identify whether the tumor is cancerous, they should be removed.

Hemangiopericytomas develop most frequently on the lower legs and chest of older dogs. They occur more often in females than in males. Siberian Huskies, Irish Setters, German Shepherds, and mixed-breed dogs are most at risk. These sarcomas are typically firm, solitary tumors with irregular looping borders. They occur most commonly in the fat under the skin. They can be malignant but rarely spread to other sites. Complete surgical removal is the treatment of choice. Regrowth is common within 1 year. If the first surgical removal of any sarcoma is not adequate, followup surgery to completely remove the tumor is normally prescribed. Followup radiation treatment may also be necessary if surgical removal is incomplete.

Cutaneous (skin) angiosarcomas start out as benign skin tumors. They occur most often in dogs with short, often white coats, with high amounts of sun exposure. The breeds prone to sun-caused angiosarcomas are Whippets, Italian Greyhounds, white Boxers, and Pit Bull Terriers. Irish Wolfhounds, Vizslas, Golden Retrievers, and German Shepherds are also prone to develop these tumors, but not in response to sun exposure. In dogs, they most frequently develop on the underside of the trunk, hip, thigh, and lower legs. Surface tumors are easily controlled with freezing as needed. Avoidance of further sun exposure may reduce the development of new tumors; however, more tumors can appear over several years.

Angiosarcomas are highly malignant and can vary greatly in appearance. Most commonly, they appear as one or more red lumps in the skin or underlying soft tissues. Less frequently, they appear as a poorly defined bruise. All grow rapidly and often cause death of nearby normal tissue. These tumors spread, especially to the lungs and liver. A biopsy is needed to confirm the diagnosis. Wide surgical removal is the treatment of choice for angiosarcomas below the skin surface.

Cornifying Epitheliomas

Other names for these benign tumors of dogs include keratoacanthoma and infundibular keratinizing acanthoma. These growths are nests of tough, layered lumps that stick up from the skin surface. They can look a little like a horn, which is why they are described as cornifying. In other cases, the epitheliomas may appear solely as cornified cysts. They most likely arise from a hair follicle. These tumors can develop anywhere on the body, but they occur most frequently on the back, tail, and legs. Middle-aged dogs are most at risk. Norwegian Elkhounds, Belgian Sheepdogs, Lhasa Apsos, and Bearded Collies are most likely to develop these tumors. Norwegian Elkhounds and Lhasa Apsos are at risk for developing widespread tumors. The condition is diagnosed by finding the tumors on the animal. Treatment is optional, provided there is no self-trauma, ulceration, or secondary infection. Some dogs find the tumors annoying and attempt to scratch, rub, or bite them off. This leads to skin trauma that can easily become infected. Surgical removal is the treatment of choice. However, dogs are prone to develop additional tumors. For animals with a generalized form of the disease, oral retinoid medications may help.

Hair Follicle Tumors

Tricholemmomas are rare, benign, hair follicle tumors of dogs, most commonly found on the head. Poodles may be predisposed. They appear as firm, oval masses, 0.4 to 2.75 inches (1 to 7 centimeters) in diameter that are compact but gradually grow. Extremely rarely, they can form funnel-shaped cysts known as **trichofolliculomas**.

Trichoepitheliomas are multiple small lumps in which an entire hair follicle is filled with condensed, yellow, granular, "cheesy" material. They occur mostly on the skin of the face. They can be either benign or malignant.

In dogs, they can occur at any age but are found most commonly during late middle age. Many breeds are predisposed, including Basset Hounds, Bull Mastiffs, Irish Setters, Standard Poodles, English Springer Spaniels, and Golden Retrievers. Tumors can develop anywhere on the body but most commonly on the trunk in dogs. Benign forms appear as cysts in or under the skin. Growth of the cysts or self-trauma may cause skin ulcers. Treatment is by surgical removal. However, dogs that develop one such tumor are prone to develop more at other sites. This is especially true for Basset Hounds and English Springer Spaniels.

Malignant trichoepitheliomas are much less common than benign trichoepitheliomas. They spread to the skin surface and cause extensive inflammation, tissue death, and fibrosis. It is uncommon for these tumors to spread to other organs. Surgery is the usual treatment. During the surgery, your veterinarian will remove tissue around the tumor to reduce the chances of it recurring.

Histiocytic Cell Tumors

These tumors form a group of poorly defined skin diseases all characterized by a proliferation of cells called histiocytes (tissue macrophages). The cause for these diseases is unknown.

Histiocytomas are common skin tumors typically seen in younger dogs (less than 3½ years old). They can occur in dogs of any age, however. English Bulldogs, Scottish Terriers, Greyhounds, Boxers, Boston Terriers, and Chinese Shar-Peis are most at risk. The head, ears, and limbs are the most common sites. The tumors appear as solitary, raised, generally ulcerated lumps that are freely movable. Diagnosis is through microscopic examination of samples of the tumor cells from fine needle aspiration or biopsy. Canine histiocytomas are normally considered benign tumors; most resolve spontaneously and without treatment within 2 to 3 months. Surgical removal is optional and normally performed only if the tumors cause severe problems for the dog.

Systemic histiocytosis affects mostly Bernese Mountain dogs as an aggressive skin disease that causes multiple skin lesions that wax and wane. The disease eventually becomes progressive.

Malignant histiocytosis affects mostly Bernese Mountain dogs. This variant first appears in the internal organs and lungs, causing illness, pain, and eventually death.

Keratinized Skin Cysts

Some dogs develop cysts that are filled with keratin, a skin protein. Such cysts have a hard or solid core. Most are malformations of hair follicles and may be the same color as the hair. There are several kinds of keratinized skin cysts. The ones found in dogs include isthmus catagen cysts, matrix cysts, hybrid cysts (panfollicular cysts), and dermoid cysts. Dermoid cysts are congenital (the animal is born with them). Among dogs, they are most commonly found in Boxers, Kerry Blue Terriers, and Rhodesian Ridgebacks. Most dermoid cysts are multiple and contain fully formed hair shafts. Diagnosis is by finding the cysts on the dog. They can be solitary or multiple and are benign. Surgical removal is the best treatment. You should not to attempt to remove the cysts by squeezing them because this can spread the cyst contents into the surrounding tissues. Your dog's body will react to the cyst contents as a foreign substance, which can cause severe inflammation.

Lipomas and Liposarcomas

Lipomas are benign tumors of fat (adipose tissue) and are common in dogs. Lipomas generally occur in older, obese females, most commonly on the trunk and near the tops of the legs. The breeds most at risk are Doberman Pinschers, Labrador Retrievers, Miniature Schnauzers, and mixed-breed dogs. In older, neutered male dogs, lipomas typically appear as soft, occasionally thin, discrete lumpy masses; most move freely when touched. A rare variant of this tumor, **diffuse lipomatosis**, has been identified in Dachshunds, in which virtually the entire skin is affected, resulting in prominent folds in the skin on the neck and trunk.

Many lipomas merge with healthy fat tissue next to them, making it difficult to determine the edges of the tumors. A fine needle aspiration is necessary in order to exclude other types of tumors that can mimic lipomas, such as mast cell tumors (*see* page 275).

Despite their benign nature, lipomas should not be ignored. Some tend to grow, and they may be indistinguishable from infiltrative lipomas or liposarcomas. Surgical removal is the cure. In dogs, dietary restriction (weight loss diet) starting several weeks before surgery may make it easier for the surgeon to identify the edges of the tumor and remove all of it.

Infiltrative lipomas are rare in dogs. They are most common in middle-aged females, usually on the chest and legs. The breeds most at risk are Doberman Pinschers, Labrador Retrievers, Miniature Schnauzers, and mixed-breed dogs. These tumors are soft, lumpy swellings in the fat layer under the skin. They can spread to underlying muscle and connective tissue.

Lipomas are one of the most common benign tumors of the skin in dogs.

Invasive lipomas are considered sarcomas of partial malignancy. They rarely spread to other sites. The treatment of choice for infiltrative lipomas is surgery to remove the tumor and a margin of normal tissue surrounding it. In some cases, this may mean amputation of a limb.

Liposarcomas are rare tumors in all domestic animals. Most are recognized in older male dogs in which they usually develop on the chest and legs. Shetland Sheepdogs and Beagles are most at risk for liposarcomas. Liposarcomas are lumpy and can be soft or firm. They are malignant tumors with a low potential to spread to other sites. Wide surgical removal (removing both tumor and some surrounding tissue) is most often recommended. Recurrence is common, so follow up radiation treatment may be required.

Lymphoid Tumors of the Skin

Canine extramedullary plasmacytomas are relatively common skin tumors in dogs. They are most frequently identified on the ears, lips, mouth, and legs of mature to aged animals. Cocker Spaniels, Airedales, Scottish Terriers, and Standard Poodles are most at risk. The tumors are generally small (less than 2 inches [5 centimeters]) in diameter and sometimes narrow. Diagnosis is by finding the tumors on the animal and confirming the type of tumor with a fine needle aspiration or a biopsy. Most of these tumors do not spread and surgical removal is the usual treatment. When these tumors develop in the mouth, they may multiply. Treatment for the multiple form is more difficult, because the tumors are more likely to return following surgery. In such cases, tissue around the tumors may have to be removed. When tumors are multiple, or surgical removal is not feasible, radiation treatment is considered. Chemotherapy is commonly recommended for patients if radiation treatment is declined or if the tumor is resistant to radiation treatment.

Cutaneous (skin) lymphosarcoma is a rare form of skin cancer that may occur in a form in which the skin is the first and primary site of lymphoid tumor involvement. However, this disease may also be secondary to whole-body, internal diseases such as canine malignant lymphoma (*see* page 45). This uncommon tumor occurs in 2 distinct forms—epitheliotropic cutaneous lymphosarcoma and nonepitheliotropic cutaneous lymphosarcoma.

Epitheliotropic lymphosarcoma is the most frequently recognized form of skin lymphosarcoma in dogs. It is primarily a disease of middle-aged and older dogs, most often found in Poodles and Cocker Spaniels. The disease progresses slowly or moderately. Signs vary widely and may include flaky skin, red patches on the skin surface, raised and ulcerated areas, or lumps deep within the skin. These changes may also appear in the mouth or on the lips, eyelids, or footpads. Because of the variable appearance, diagnosis can be very difficult. The early stages can be confused with allergies or infections. Thus, your veterinarian may suggest a tissue biopsy of any tumor or tumor-like growth found on your pet. The presence of tumors with simultaneous leukemia is known as Sézary syndrome.

Many treatments for skin lymphosarcoma have been tried, though no treatment has been shown to be completely successful. Thus far, all the tested treatment procedures improved the signs of the disease but did not lengthen an affected dog's life. Your veterinarian will have access to the latest treatment information for skin lymphosarcoma and will recommend the treatment program that is best suited for your pet and its overall health.

Nonepitheliotropic cutaneous (skin) lymphosarcoma is most common in middle-aged or older animals. The tumors are lumps or plaques that often develop on the trunk. Generally, these are multiple tumors. In many cases, nonepitheliotropic skin lymphosarcoma is, by appearance, indistinguishable from epitheliotropic skin lymphosarcoma. A definitive diagnosis is important because the nonepitheliotropic form in dogs is generally more serious than the epitheliotropic form. These tumors frequently spread to other organs and do so early in the course of the disease. Thus, an early, accurate diagnosis is extremely important in treating this disease.

Various treatments, including surgical removal, chemotherapy, and, less frequently, radiation treatment have been used both singly and in combination. Surgical removal is usually the first choice when the disease is limited to a single tumor. Removing the tumor can potentially completely cure the dog. For diffuse or multiple forms, surgical removal or freezing have been less successful. Chemotherapy can relieve signs but this form of cancer often recurs. The average remission time is 8 months.

Mast Cell Tumors

Mast cell tumors are named for the type of cell from which they grow. Mast cells are involved in allergic reactions. They release histamine, which causes irritation and itching, and other chemicals that may cause shock. Mast cell tumors may be

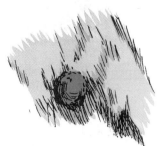

The appearance of mast cell tumors can vary widely.

seen in dogs of any age but occur most commonly in dogs 8 to 10 years old. They may develop anywhere on the body surface as well as in internal organs, but the limbs (especially the back of the upper thigh), lower abdomen, and chest are the most common sites. Tumors located near mucous membranes or on the lower surface of the body are more likely to spread than mast cell tumors in other areas. Many breeds appear to be prone to the disease, especially Boxers and Pugs (in which tumors are often multiple), Rhodesian Ridgebacks, and Boston Terriers.

These tumors vary greatly in size and rate of growth. They can mimic lipomas; therefore, visual signs alone cannot establish a diagnosis. Most commonly, a mast cell tumor appears as a raised lump or mass that may be soft to solid to the touch. Mast cell tumors are tricky and difficult to deal with because they appear as a large central tumor surrounded by a halo of smaller nests of mast cells that infiltrate normal skin. Dogs can also develop signs associated with the release of toxins from the malignant mast cells. For example, up to a quarter of dogs with mast cell tumors also have stomach ulcers due to histamine release. Diagnosis is by microscopic examination of fine needle aspirations, impression smears, or biopsy samples.

Small mast cell tumors may remain quiet and seem inactive for long periods before spreading. Thus, all mast cell tumors are normally treated as at least potential malignancies. Treatment depends on the clinical stage of the disease and the predicted spread of an individual tumor. For a small solitary tumor confined to the skin (Stage I), the preferred treatment is complete surgical removal. Most veterinarians will remove at least 1¼ inches (3 centimeters) of healthy tissue surrounding all borders of these tumors to remove both the lump and any surrounding nests of tumor cells. If, during surgery, biopsy of a sample of the removed tissue suggests that the tumor extends beyond the initial edge of the

surgery, additional surrounding tissue will be removed. Alternatively, because mast cells are sensitive to radiation, radiation treatment may be effective if there is remaining tumor. In some cases, a combination of radiation treatment and hyperthermia (carefully increasing the dog's body temperature while under anesthesia) may be more effective than radiation alone. If the margins are not clean and radiation treatment is not elected, chemotherapy is also an effective followup treatment. Some dogs grow new tumors periodically. When surgery is not performed for residual disease or for small recurrent tumors, injections of steroids and antihistamines into the tumor, which may be followed by freezing (cryotherapy), can be considered as an option.

At present, there is no agreed upon treatment for Stage II to IV mast cell tumors. Options include surgical removal of the mass and affected regional lymph nodes (if feasible), radiation, and chemotherapy. Your veterinarian may consult with a veterinary oncologist for assistance in the treatment of these tumors.

Melanomas

A melanoma is a dark-pigmented skin tumor that may be either benign (not cancerous) or malignant (cancerous). Benign melanomas are diagnosed much more frequently in dogs than malignant melanomas. They most commonly develop on the head and forelimbs in middle-aged or older dogs. Miniature and Standard Schnauzers, Doberman Pinschers, Golden Retrievers, Irish Setters, and Vizslas are the breeds in which these tumors are most commonly found. They can appear as spots or patches, or raised or flat masses. Most have a dark surface. Although generally solitary, melanomas may be multiple, especially in the breeds at risk. When these tumors are benign, surgical removal cures the condition.

Malignant melanomas most commonly develop in older animals. Among dogs, Miniature and Standard Schnauzers and Scottish Terriers are most at risk. The lips, mouth, and nail beds are the most common sites of development. Malignant melanomas on haired skin are rare, and most arise on the lower abdomen and the scrotum. Males are affected more often than females.

Most malignant melanomas appear as raised, generally ulcerated lumps that are variably darkened. When present on the lips or in the mouth, the tumors appear as dark to light gray or pink raised lumps. When present in the nail bed, they appear as swellings of the toe, often with loss of the nail and destruction of underlying bone.

For this reason, a veterinarian who finds a festering toe in an older dog will often order x-rays and remove a tissue sample from deep in the toe (including bone) for a biopsy. These steps will help the veterinarian treat this form of cancer as early as possible. Malignant melanomas grow quickly and have great potential to spread to other organs. Early treatment is critical for a positive outcome for a dog with a malignant melanoma.

Treatment consists of complete surgical removal. However, the spreading nature of the tumor may make this difficult. When present on a toe, amputation of the involved toe is the standard treatment. When present on the mouth, surgical removal of part of the jaw may allow for complete tumor removal and an acceptable postsurgical cosmetic appearance and survival. Melanomas are generally considered resistant to radiation treatment, and there is no established chemotherapy known to be highly effective. Typical survival times for dogs with malignant melanomas range from 1 to 36 months. A vaccine that helps shrink the size of malignant melanomas in dogs and prolong survival was conditionally licensed by the US Department of Agriculture in 2007.

Perianal (Hepatoid) Gland Tumors

Perianal gland tumors are a type of tumor found near the anus in dogs. They occur mostly in a specialized gland found in the anal sac. They may also occur in similar glands along the abdomen from the anus to the base of the skull, the tail, and in the skin of the back and areas near the tail. The tumors occur in male dogs much more often than in females. They are most common in aged dogs. Siberian Huskies, Samoyeds, Pekingese, and Cocker Spaniels are the breeds most commonly affected.

The tumors appear as one or (more commonly) multiple lumps 0.2 to 4 inches (0.5 to 10 centimeters) in diameter. Larger tumors commonly form ulcers and bleed. In addition, large tumors can compress the anal canal and make defecation difficult.

Up to 95% of male dogs with these tumors are cured by castration. Surgical removal of the tumors may be used to remove extremely large or ulcerated tumors that have become secondarily infected. Surgery is the treatment of choice for females but may need to be repeated because recurrence is common in females. Radiation treatment is also an option and may be prescribed either alone or in combination with surgery. Laser surgery and cryosurgery (freezing) are other options, but because fecal incontinence is very common following extensive surgery involving the sphincter, this option is used only when tumors cannot be removed using regular surgical techniques.

Perianal gland adenocarcinomas are uncommon in dogs. These tumors are found in male dogs 10 times more commonly than in females. Siberian Huskies, Alaskan Malamutes, and Bulldogs are most likely to develop this tumor. Biopsy evaluation (laboratory study of a tissue sample taken from the tumor) is the best means of diagnosis. These tumors often spread to draining lymph nodes that are located along the lower back. Therefore, during surgery the tumor itself and a wide margin of tissue around it will be removed. If any of the lymph nodes are involved, they may also be surgically removed. Radiation treatment is often added following the surgery. These tumors are generally not responsive to castration or to estrogen treatment. The outlook is guarded.

Peripheral Nerve Sheath Tumors

There are several tumors that arise from the connective tissue that provides a covering for nerves. These include amputation neuromas, neurofibromas, and neurofibrosarcomas.

Amputation neuromas are disorganized growths that form after amputation or traumatic injury. They most commonly happen after tail docking in dogs. They are most commonly found in young dogs that continuously bother a docked tail. Surgical removal is the cure.

Neurofibromas and **neurofibrosarcomas** are other tumors that grow in the connective tissue around a nerve. In dogs, they are found in older animals. These tumors appear as white, firm, lumps. There are both benign and malignant forms. In dogs, most are locally invasive but do not spread to other sites. Complete surgical removal is the treatment of choice. Followup radiation treatment may slow regrowth.

Sebaceous Gland Tumors

The sebaceous glands secrete the oil known as sebum into the hair follicles and onto the skin. Tumors of sebaceous glands are common in dogs.

Sebaceous gland hamartomas are solitary tumors of dogs. These are elongated or circular, roughly 2 inches (5 centimeters) in length or diameter. They are usually identified shortly after birth.

Sebaceous gland overgrowth (hyperplasia) occurs in old dogs and cats. It appears as lumps seldom more than 0.4 inches (1 centimeter) in diameter, often with a shiny, horn-like surface. Among dogs, Manchester, Wheaten, and Welsh Terriers are at greatest risk. The head and abdomen are affected most often.

Sebaceous gland adenomas are common in older dogs. Coonhounds, English Cocker Spaniels, Cocker Spaniels, Huskies, Samoyeds, and Alaskan Malamutes are the breeds most likely to develop these tumors. They are often indistinguishable from sebaceous gland overgrowth, but they tend to be larger (typically over 0.4 inches [1 centimeter] wide). They are

often multiple and may occur anywhere on the body but are commonly found on the head. Sebaceous adenomas may be covered with a crust and filled with pus.

Sebaceous gland adenocarcinomas are a rare malignant form of sebaceous gland tumor. They occur in middle-aged or older dogs. Cavalier King Charles Spaniels, Cocker Spaniels, and Scottish, Cairn, and West Highland White Terriers are the breeds most at risk. Male dogs may be predisposed. These may be indistinguishable from sebaceous epitheliomas or other skin carcinomas. They spread within the skin and may spread to regional lymph nodes late in the disease.

Once a diagnosis is established, surgery is optional for benign sebaceous gland tumors unless they are inflamed and infected. For malignant adenocarcinomas, surgery is the treatment of choice. Your veterinarian will remove not only the tumor but also tissue around the tumor, including involved lymph nodes. In addition, chemotherapy and radiation treatment may also be prescribed. Dogs that develop a sebaceous gland overgrowth or adenoma often develop new tumors at other sites. Your veterinarian may consult with a veterinary oncologist or veterinary dermatologist for assistance in the treatment of these tumors.

Smooth Muscle Tumors of the Skin

These tumors occur rarely and little is known about them. Those that have been reported have been malignant and found in dogs and cats. In most cases, these are firm masses that can be felt through the skin. Treatment is surgery to remove the tumor.

Soft Tissue Giant Cell Tumors (Fibrous Histiocytomas)

These tumors are not well understood. They appear more like an inflammatory reaction than a tumor and are generally treated with steroids. An abnormality called canine fibrous histiocytoma has been found in the eye of some dogs, most commonly Collies 2 to 4 years old.

Some soft tissue giant cell tumors are malignant (cancerous). **Malignant fibrous**

histiocytomas are rare in dogs. Malignant fibrous histiocytomas are firm, lumpy to diffuse swellings that may bleed. Soft tissue giant cell tumors are sarcomas that may be malignant. They seldom spread to other sites but tend to return after surgical removal. Surgery to remove these tumors is the treatment of choice. Because these tumors tend to return after surgical removal, most veterinarians will also remove a wide margin of tissue surrounding the tumor to be as sure as possible that the entire tumor has been taken out.

Soft Tissue Sarcomas

Sarcomas are a group of connective tissue tumors generally considered to be malignant. Sarcomas on the surface of the skin tend to be benign. Deep sarcomas tend to be malignant. The larger the tumor, the more likely it is to be malignant. A rapidly growing tumor is more likely to be malignant than one that develops slowly. Benign tumors have few blood vessels, whereas most malignant tumors have many blood vessels.

Diagnosis is made by biopsy of the sarcoma. Many sarcomas are shaped like an octopus, with tentacles that extend deeply into the tumor bed. They are often called "spindle-cell" sarcomas.

Wide surgical removal is the treatment of choice for soft-tissue sarcomas. The veterinarian will remove a 2- to 3-centimeter margin of tissue surrounding the sarcoma. This is necessary because there is a strong possibility that the sarcoma has spread beyond the mass that is easily identifiable as the head of the octopus. Occasionally, depending on location, amputation may be required to remove the entire tumor. It is important to remove all of the tumor during the first surgery, because sarcomas that recur have a greater potential to invade local tissue, and they may also spread to other parts of the body. Each future attempt at surgical removal can increase the rate of spread. Freezing (cryosurgery) is usually not used for sarcomas because some tumor types are resistant to freezing. Spindle-cell sarcomas generally do not respond well to conventional doses of radiation. Higher doses have been somewhat successful. Surgical removal followed by radiation is an option, as well as radiation prior to surgical removal. Chemotherapy for sarcomas has become a more common method of treatment. Although chemotherapy may improve the quality and prolong the life of an affected dog, it is seldom a complete cure. There is only a guarded outlook for dogs with soft-tissue sarcomas.

Fibromatosis is a thickening and invasive growth in tendon sheaths. They are generally seen on the heads of dogs, especially Doberman Pinschers and Golden Retrievers, where they are commonly called lumpy fasciitis. Fibromatoses are generally indistinguishable from infiltrative fibrosarcomas (*see* below) except by microscopic examination. Small lymphoid lumps are scattered throughout the tissues. Fibromatosis can spread to nearby tissue but does not spread through the bloodstream to distant organs. If feasible, surgical removal is the treatment of choice. Recurrence is common, and radiation treatment may be helpful in reducing regrowth.

Fibrosarcomas are fast-growing malignant tumors. They are common in dogs, with most located on the trunk and legs. Gordon Setters, Irish Wolfhounds, Brittany Spaniels, Golden Retrievers, and Doberman Pinschers are most likely to develop these tumors. Fibrosarcomas vary greatly in appearance and size. Tumors arising under the skin surface may look lumpy. Those arising in the fat or nearby soft tissues may require hands-on examination to detect. They are firm and fleshy and appear deep in the skin and the fat underneath. They often invade underlying muscles. When multiple tumors are present, they usually occur within the same area of the body. In dogs, about 10% of these tumors spread to other parts of the body (metastasize). Wide surgical removal is the best treatment, although complete removal is difficult. Because it is hard to determine the tumor's edges during surgery, recurrence is common (more than 70% return within 1 year of the initial surgery). Even when surgical removal is complete, recurrence is still the rule. Followup radiation treatment and chemotherapy has been recommended for tumors that are inoperable and for tumors that cannot be removed completely.

Squamous Cell Carcinomas

Squamous cell carcinomas are malignant tumors. They can be found in all domestic animals. In dogs, these are the most frequently diagnosed carcinomas of the skin. Two forms occur in dogs—skin and subungual. **Skin squamous cell carcinomas** are tumors of older dogs. Bloodhounds, Basset Hounds, and Standard Poodles are at greatest risk. They appear on the head, lower legs, abdomen, and rear. Most appear as firm, raised, frequently ulcerated patches and lumps. Sometimes they can grow outward with a surface like a wart. Some are caused by prolonged sun exposure. These usually develop on the lower abdomen, especially on or near the pubic area in white-skinned, shorthaired breeds such as Dalmatians, Bull Terriers, and Beagles. They develop on the underside of dogs because the poorly haired skin offers minimal shielding from ultraviolet radiation. Many animals sun themselves lying on their backs. They also get some solar radiation that reflects from the ground. Before a malignant tumor develops, dogs develop **solar keratosis.** Solar keratosis is thickened and discolored skin. Thus, finding areas on your dog where the skin is thick and discolored is cause for a veterinary checkup. Early diagnosis is important for successful treatment.

Subungual squamous cell carcinomas are tumors that originate under a nail (claw). They are most commonly found in Giant and Standard Schnauzers, Gordon Setters, Briards, Kerry Blue Terriers, and Standard Poodles. Generally, these are dark-haired breeds, and a dark coat color has been associated with the development of subungual squamous cell carcinomas

arising on multiple toes, often on different legs. Females are slightly more likely to develop these tumors than males and both fore- and hindlegs are equally likely to have tumors.

Most squamous cell carcinomas are solitary tumors. However, multiple tumors may develop. They appear as raised, irregular masses with either ulcers or pimples. Dogs with subungual squamous cell carcinomas first show lameness or malformation, infection, or loss of a claw. Solitary tumors grow slowly. Tumors close to each other are more likely to spread or return within 20 weeks of surgical removal. In general, when treatment fails it is due to late diagnosis and lack of control of the original tumor rather than spread of new tumors. For this reason, you need to be alert to any problems your dog may be having with toes or claws and have these problems checked by your veterinarian promptly after discovery.

For dogs, surgical removal, such as the amputation of the involved toe or ear, is the proper treatment. A margin of skin at least ¾ of an inch (2 centimeters) around the tumor needs to be removed. Surgical removal may be combined with radiation treatment or chemotherapy. Survival rates depend on the malignancy of the tumor and its size before treatment. Treatment of these carcinomas often includes medications to control infections that can develop in the area near the tumor(s).

Limiting exposure to excessive sunlight may help prevent squamous cell carcinomas. This may be accomplished by using ultraviolet window screens, sunscreen, and keeping the animals indoors during hours of peak sunlight.

Sweat Gland Tumors

There are 2 types of sweat glands in dogs, called apocrine and eccrine. **Apocrine gland cysts** are found in middle-aged or older dogs. They can occur either in or outside of hair follicles. They appear most commonly on the head and neck. One or more cysts develop in the middle to upper skin layer with a loose association with hair follicles. Another form is more diffuse and involves cysts within the glands associated with multiple hair follicles in uninjured skin. Both forms of apocrine gland cysts are benign (not cancerous). Treatment is by surgical removal, though this may be difficult if the cysts are diffused.

Apocrine gland adenomas appear as firm to soft cysts, seldom larger than 1.6 inches (4 centimeters) in diameter. They contain varying amounts of clear to brownish fluid. They are found in older dogs, cats, and, in rare cases, horses. Among dogs, Great Pyrenees, Chow Chows, and Alaskan Malamutes are the most commonly affected breeds. The head, neck, and legs are the most frequent sites.

Apocrine ductular adenomas are less common than apocrine gland adenomas. They are found in older dogs and cats and appear closer to the surface of the skin. In dogs, these tumors are most commonly recognized in Peekapoos, Old English Sheepdogs, and English Springer Spaniels. They are often smaller, firmer, and less cystic than apocrine adenomas.

Apocrine adenomas and apocrine ductular adenomas are benign, and complete surgical removal cures the condition.

Apocrine gland adenocarcinomas are malignant tumors of sweat glands. They are rare in all domestic animals but occur most often in dogs and cats. In dogs, Treeing Walker Coonhounds, Norwegian Elkhounds, German Shepherds, and mixed-breed dogs are most at risk. This tumor most commonly occurs where the legs meet the trunk and near the groin. The appearance varies from thick lumps to ulcers. They are likely to spread across the skin, but do not often spread to other organs. Complete surgical removal is the treatment of choice. Little is known about the effectiveness of chemotherapy in treatment of these tumors.

Eccrine sweat glands are found in the footpads of dogs. **Eccrine gland tumors** are extremely rare. When they do occur, most are severely malignant and have a high potential to spread to the lymph nodes. The treatment of choice involves removal of not only the malignant gland but also surrounding tissue and any involved lymph nodes. In addition, chemotherapy and radiation treatment may also be provided.

Tumors Originating Outside the Skin (Metastatic Tumors)

All malignant tumors, wherever they originate, are capable of spreading to the skin. However, the spread of a primary tumor from inside the body to the skin is unusual. Although the appearance is variable, the tumors that spread to the skin are usually multiple, ulcerated lumps. As these tumors grow, they extend deeper into the skin and surrounding tissue. Generally, it is difficult to identify the primary tumor based on the signs in the skin. This is because only a small population of cells in the primary tumor will spread to the skin, and these cells may have different microscopic features than the primary tumor. When tumors have spread from other areas of the body to the skin, the primary tumor usually grows and spreads quickly and the outlook for a positive outcome is guarded. Treatment for these tumors involves a whole-body approach that deal with both the skin tumors and the primary tumor(s).

Undifferentiated and Anaplastic Sarcomas

These are cancers of **mesenchymal** cells. Mesenchymal cells are the cells that develop into connective tissues, blood, lymph nodes, and other organs. Cancers of mesenchymal cells are difficult to identify because, like the mesenchymal cells themselves, malignant forms of these cells are loosely organized and often undeveloped or undifferentiated. Once identified, surgery is the usual treatment. When removing these cancerous cells, the veterinarian will usually remove not only the visible tumor but also a wide margin of tissue surrounding it. This reduces the chance that the malignancy will recur.

Warts (Papillomas)

Warts are caused by papillomaviruses. The virus is transmitted by direct contact or by contact with contaminated items such as bedding, clothing, dishes, and other items in the dog's environment. It is also possible that insects may spread papillomaviruses. There are several distinct papillomaviruses. Warts have been reported in all domestic animals and are most common in dogs and horses.

Multiple warts of skin or mucus membranes generally are seen in younger dogs. Single warts are more frequent in older animals, but they may not always be caused by viral infection. The period between the initial infection and the development of visible warts varies but normally takes several months.

Most warts appear as bumps with a hardened surface resembling a cauliflower. When multiple warts are present they may be sufficiently characteristic to make a working diagnosis. However, there are many things that look like warts and a definitive diagnosis may require identification of the virus or its effects on individual cells (a change known as koilocytic atypia or koilocytosis).

In dogs, there are 3 kinds of warts. The first is **canine mucous membrane papillomatosis**, which primarily affects young dogs. Multiple warts appear on mucous membranes in the mouth from the lips to (occasionally) the esophagus and on the eyelid and adjacent haired skin. When the mouth is severely affected, chewing and swallowing is difficult. The second kind of wart in dogs is **skin warts**, which are indistinguishable from the warts that develop on or around mucous membranes. However, they are more frequently solitary and develop on older dogs. Skin warts are common in Cocker Spaniels and Kerry Blue Terriers. The third type found in dogs is called a **skin inverted papilloma**. In this disease of young adult dogs, warts most commonly develop on the lower abdomen. Infrequently, viral warts in dogs may progress to invasive squamous cell carcinomas.

Warts will eventually go away on their own, although how long this takes varies considerably. A variety of treatments have been suggested, but results vary. Surgical removal is recommended if the warts are sufficiently objectionable. However, because surgery in the early growing stage of warts may lead to recurrence and stimulation of growth, the warts should be removed when near their maximal size or when regressing. Affected dogs may be isolated from susceptible ones, but with the long incubation period (months), many are likely to have been exposed before the problem is recognized.

■ WHOLE-BODY DISORDERS THAT AFFECT THE SKIN

Several whole-body disorders produce changes in the skin. In some instances, the skin changes are characteristic of the particular disease. Often, however, the signs are not obviously associated with the underlying condition and must be carefully differentiated from primary skin disorders. Some of these secondary disorders are mentioned briefly below and are also described in the chapters on the specific disorders.

Skin disorders can be associated with nutritional deficiencies, especially of proteins, fats, minerals, some vitamins, and trace elements. However, this is uncommon in dogs fed modern, balanced diets.

Multiple papillomas, or warts, are common on younger dogs.

Siberian Huskies, and occasionally other breeds, may require additional zinc in their diet. Consult your veterinarian regarding your pet's dietary needs to avoid health problems related to nutritional deficiencies.

Dermatitis (inflammation of the skin) is sometimes seen in association with disorders of internal organs, such as the liver, kidneys, or pancreas. Liver disease and diabetes can cause superficial skin tissue death (necrolytic dermatitis) in old dogs. The signs of these skin abnormalities include redness, crusting, oozing, and hair loss of the footpads, face, genitals, and lower legs. The skin disease may precede the onset of signs of the internal disease. Any ongoing or growing abnormality of the skin of your dog should be examined by your veterinarian. Early diagnosis of disease offers the best chance for effective treatment for your pet.

A generalized **lumpy skin syndrome** in German Shepherds, and occasionally other breeds, is associated with kidney cysts. Poisoning by rat poison, ergot (a fungus found in rye and other grains), mercury, and iodides may cause various skin changes. In male dogs with testicular tumors, widespread hair loss and occasional itching with a skin rash may be seen. Nonspayed female dogs with hormonal imbalances are usually itchy and have skin rashes, mammary tissue enlargement, and frequent estrous cycles. The skin tumors of both disorders may begin in the groin or flank region and progress toward the head.

Hypothyroidism (*see* page 139) can cause skin changes with diminished hair growth and hair loss. The skin is dry, scaly, thickened, and folded. Secondary bacterial infection may occur. The edges of the ears may develop excess scale. **Hypopituitarism** is a congenital disease characterized by short stature and hair loss. **Hyperadrenocorticism** (an increase in the activity of the adrenal glands; also called Cushing's disease) also causes skin changes such as darkening of skin color, hair loss, seborrhea (oily dandruff), calcium deposits in the skin, and secondary bacterial infection.

Treatment of all these conditions depends on finding the specific cause. Once this is established and managed, the skin usually needs only symptomatic care, such as control of scratching, until it returns to normal with resolution of the primary disease.

CHAPTER **17**

Kidney and Urinary Tract Disorders

■ THE URINARY SYSTEM

The urinary system or tract includes the kidneys, the ureters (tubes that connect the kidneys to the bladder), the bladder, and the urethra (the tube through which urine exits the body). The urinary system has several important functions. It gets rid of the waste products that are created when food is transformed into energy. It also maintains the correct balance of water and electrolytes (salts) within the body's cells. Another key function is the production of hormones called erythropoietin and renin, which are important in maintaining healthy blood pressure, producing blood cells, and absorbing salt correctly. Finally, the urinary system processes vitamin D.

■ DETECTING DISORDERS OF THE KIDNEYS AND URINARY TRACT

Your veterinarian can diagnose many common problems with the urinary system by taking a history of how your dog

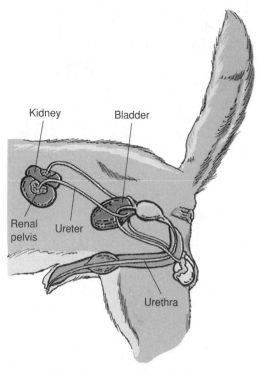

Kidney   Bladder

Renal   Ureter
pelvis

Urethra

The urinary system in male dogs

form a neurologic (nerve and brain) examination. There are many other tests a veterinarian might perform in the case of a urinary disorder. These include blood tests, blood pressure tests, urinalysis, x-rays, contrast x-rays (tests in which a special dye is given to outline the urinary tract on the x-ray), ultrasonography, biopsies, and cystoscopic tests. Cystoscopic tests involve inserting a small tube with a camera on the tip into the urethra. This allows the veterinarian to view the inside of the urethra and the bladder. Your dog will be anesthetized or given a tranquilizer for such a test.

Urinalysis is a laboratory test that evaluates urine. It is one of the most important tools a veterinarian can use to diagnose urinary tract problems. Many tests are performed as part of a urinalysis. These include urine specific gravity, which is an indication of how concentrated the urine sample is; color; turbidity or cloudiness of the urine; and pH (how acidic or alkaline the urine sample is). Urinalysis

has acted in the days prior to its becoming sick, performing a physical examination, and performing tests on the dog's blood and urine. The history that your veterinarian takes might include information regarding changes in how much water your pet drinks, how often it urinates, how much urine it produces, how the urine looks, and how your pet behaves. Your veterinarian will also need information about what medications your pet has taken or is currently taking, your pet's appetite and diet, changes in body weight, and previous illnesses or injuries.

When performing the physical examination, your veterinarian will feel your dog's kidneys and bladder, examine its genitalia and, sometimes, its rectum. In both male and female dogs, examining the rectum allows your veterinarian to feel the urethra. In male dogs, it also allows your veterinarian to examine the prostate. If your pet has trouble urinating, your veterinarian may also want to per-

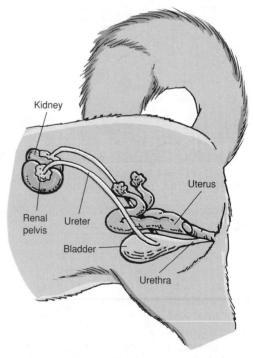

Kidney

Uterus

Renal   Ureter
pelvis

Bladder

Urethra

The urinary system in female dogs

also tests for the presence of certain chemicals or substances in the urine, such as sugar, ketones (a byproduct of the body's processing of fat), bilirubin (a pigment produced when the liver processes waste), blood, and protein. The urine sediment is also examined under a microscope to look for things such as red blood cells, white blood cells, other cells, bacteria, and crystals.

If your veterinarian suspects your dog may have a urinary tract infection, a **bacterial culture** may be performed instead of, or in addition to, urinalysis. Cystocentesis (removing urine directly from the bladder by use of a needle inserted through the abdomen) is the preferred way to collect urine for a bacterial culture.

■ CONGENITAL AND INHERITED DISORDERS OF THE URINARY SYSTEM

Certain urinary tract abnormalities are inherited or congenital (present at birth). These abnormalities are caused by abnormal genes or produced by injury, disease, or exposure to toxic substances in the womb. They may or may not cause health problems later in your pet's life. They are rare, but important to consider, if your dog has urinary tract problems.

Disorders of the Kidneys

There are many congenital and inherited problems that can affect the kidneys. Among these are kidney malformations, failure of the kidney(s) to develop, polycystic kidneys, and kidney cysts.

Kidney Malformations

Kidney malformations, called **dysplasias**, occur when a dog's kidneys do not develop properly before birth. When the kidneys are unusually small, the condition is called **hypoplasia**. These conditions have been reported in many breeds, including Alaskan Malamutes, Bedlington Terriers, Chow Chows, Cocker Spaniels, Doberman Pinschers, Keeshonden, Lhasa Apsos, Miniature Schnauzers, Norwe-

gian Elkhounds, Samoyeds, Shih Tzus, Soft-coated Wheaten Terriers, and Standard Poodles. Dysplasia can occur in either one or both kidneys. When these conditions occur, the kidneys are usually small, firm, and pale. The outer portion of the kidney that contains glomeruli (microscopic structures which are critical for filtering blood) may be smaller than normal in size.

Dogs with these conditions typically have a buildup in the blood of the toxic waste products that are normally excreted in the urine, which becomes evident between 6 months and 2 years of age. Before this occurs, however, an affected dog usually has ongoing, excessive thirst (called polydipsia) and corresponding excessive urination (polyuria). A dog whose kidneys start to fail in the first few months of life will also show signs of stunted growth. Your veterinarian can usually diagnose dysplasia or hypoplasia based on your dog's breed and the age it begins to show signs of disease. The diagnosis can be confirmed with a biopsy of the kidneys.

There is no treatment for renal dysplasia or hypoplasia. Care for affected dogs consists of managing the problems associated with the kidney failure that results from these conditions.

Failure to Develop

Rarely, one or both kidneys fail to develop. This condition is always accompanied by a lack of the tube connecting the kidney to the bladder (ureter). The reproductive organs may also be underdeveloped. A dog in which both kidneys have failed to develop will die shortly after birth. However, an animal with one functioning kidney can live a full and healthy life. In this case, the failure of one kidney to develop is usually discovered by accident.

Polycystic Kidneys

Polycystic kidneys have multiple cysts inside the functional part of the organ. The kidneys are greatly enlarged, which a veterinarian may be able to feel during a physical examination. Problems caused by this condition can range from none at all to progressive kidney failure. In dogs, this condition is inherited in Beagles and Cairn Terriers. Your veterinarian can diagnose polycystic kidneys by examining your pet, taking x-rays, using ultrasonography, or performing exploratory abdominal surgery.

Kidney Cysts

These usually occur as a single cyst. They generally do not interfere with kidney function, and the rest of the kidney is normal. It is unclear what causes these cysts. They are usually identified by accident.

Other Kidney Disorders

About 5% of dogs have 2 or more renal arteries. A normal kidney has 1 renal artery, which delivers blood to the kidneys. Other congenital problems include kidneys that are not positioned correctly, kidneys that are fused together, and **nephroblastoma**, a cancer that develops in the kidneys as a result of abnormal kidney tissue growth in the womb (*see* page 296).

Disorders of the Ureters

Several disorders can affect the ureter, the tube that connects the kidney to the bladder. Normal animals have 2 ureters, 1 for each kidney.

Ectopic Ureter

An ectopic ureter is one that opens somewhere other than into the bladder. Ectopic ureters could empty urine into the urethra (the tube used for urination), or in females, the uterus or vagina. This defect is most commonly identified in 3- to 6-month-old dogs, with females affected 8 times more frequently than males.

Other problems can occur along with an ectopic ureter. An enlarged ureter caused by blockage of urine flow may be seen. This condition eventually leads to enlargement of the kidney due to the backup of urine. Abnormally small kidneys or bladder, and urine leakage caused by problems with the urethral sphincter may also be found along with an ectopic ureter.

A common sign of ectopic ureter is continuous dripping of urine. Because urine is acidic, this dripping can cause female dogs to develop inflammation of the vagina or vulva. Animals that have one ectopic ureter and one normally-functioning ureter may be able to urinate normally. Not being able to urinate normally is a sign that both ureters are abnormally placed.

West Highland White Terriers, Fox Terriers, and Miniature and Toy Poodles are at high risk for this condition. Siberian Huskies and Labrador Retrievers are also at a somewhat higher than normal risk. Your veterinarian can diagnose this condition using x-rays taken after a special dye is given intravenously.

Ectopic ureters can be treated by surgically moving the ureter to the correct place, or, in severe cases, removing the affected ureter and the accompanying kidney.

Other Disorders of the Ureter

Other abnormalities of the ureter include failure to develop, the presence of more than the usual 2 ureters, and enlargement of the end of the ureter that connects to the bladder, a condition that can usually be successfully treated by surgery.

Disorders of the Bladder

The bladder is a muscular sac that stores urine produced by the kidneys. Several congenital and inherited problems can affect the bladder.

Urachal Remnants

The urachus is a cord of fibrous tissue that normally extends from the bladder to the navel. Before birth, the urachus is a tube that connects the bladder to the umbilical cord so that wastes can be removed. After birth, it normally closes and becomes a solid cord. In some animals, however, the urachus does not close properly after birth. Depending on which portion of the urachus remains open, these abnormalities are called a patent urachus or an umbilical urachal sinus. Other problems include urachal diverticula (small sac-like structures attached to the urachus) and urachal cysts. Signs include an inability to control urination, urine scalding (due to the fact that urine is acidic) of the skin near the navel, and urinary tract infections. Your veterinarian can diagnose these problems using x-rays taken after a special dye is given intravenously. Treatment usually includes surgery and, sometimes, antibiotics.

Other Disorders of the Bladder

Other congenital bladder conditions in dogs include the presence of more than one bladder, an abnormally developed or underdeveloped bladder, failure of the bladder to develop, and a bladder that is turned inside-out. Usually these problems occur along with other abnormalities in the urinary tract. Your veterinarian can diagnose these problems based on a physical examination, observation of your dog while it urinates, and contrast x-rays. Treatment varies depending on the type of problem. Your veterinarian will advise you about the most appropriate treatment for your pet.

Disorders of the Urethra

The urethra connects the bladder to the exterior of the body. It is the tube through which urine passes when a dog urinates. Congenital urethral problems in dogs are uncommon. Some of the conditions that occur include a urethra that does not open all the way or does not open at all, hypospadias (see below), multiple urethras, urethral diverticula (small pouches that form in the urethra), urethrorectal fistula (see below), and narrowing of the urethra.

Hypospadias

In this condition of male dogs, the opening of the urethra is on the underside of the penis rather than at the tip. In addition, the penis or testicles may not be fully developed. Hypospadias is caused by abnormal development of the fetus in the womb. The signs vary depending on where the urethral opening is located. They can include urine scalding (due to the acidity

of urine) and urinary tract infections. This condition can be treated with surgery.

Urethrorectal Fistula

In this condition, there is an abnormal opening between the urethra and the rectum. It is more common in English Bulldogs than any other breed. Dogs with a urethrorectal fistula are prone to urinary tract infections. Signs of this condition are the same signs found in urinary tract infections and include blood in the urine and painful or difficult urination. Animals with this condition may also pass urine from the rectum while urinating. This condition can be corrected by surgery.

■ INFECTIOUS DISEASES OF THE URINARY SYSTEM

Most infections of the urinary system are caused by bacteria. The infection usually develops when bacteria enter the body through the urethra. The bacteria then travel to the bladder, and in some cases they set up an infection there. Sometimes bacteria continue to move up the urinary tract to the kidneys, which can result in kidney infection (pyelonephritis). There are several factors that increase the risk of urinary system infection. These include problems with urine flow (especially not being able to empty the bladder completely during urination), overly dilute urine, sugar in the urine (often a sign of diabetes mellitus), and a weakened immune system. Female dogs are more prone to urinary tract infections than male dogs. Older, uncastrated male dogs, however, are prone to bacterial infections of the prostate. Most bacterial infections of dogs cannot be passed to humans.

Treatment of bacterial infections is important for several reasons. The bacteria that cause infections of the urinary tract can become resistant to antibiotics if the infections are not treated properly. Antibiotic resistance can lead to an infection that will not go away. In some cases, an untreated or inadequately treated bladder or prostate infection can be the cause of an infection in the kidneys, which is a more serious condition. Finally, untreated urinary tract infections in dogs are a common cause of a certain type of stone (struvite) that can form in the urinary tract.

Bladder Infection

Infection and inflammation of the bladder caused by bacteria is called **bacterial cystitis**. Signs of bladder infection include frequent urination, painful or difficult urination, and urinating in inappropriate places. There may also be blood in the urine. This may be more noticeable at the end of the urine stream. Occasionally, dogs with a bladder infection may show no signs at all. In these cases, the infection is usually diagnosed during a routine urinalysis. Dogs that are given longterm steroids or that have hyperadrenocorticism (an excess of adrenal gland hormones) are more prone to get urinary tract infections with no signs.

A urine sample is needed to diagnose bacterial cystitis. The laboratory tests your veterinarian will likely perform on the sample are a urinalysis and a bacterial culture. Treatment consists of antibiotics given by mouth for 2 weeks (simple infections) or longer, if needed. Your veterinarian may take more urine samples during and after treatment to make sure the medications have cured the infection. In dogs that have repeated infections, your veterinarian may take a urine sample at regular intervals (about every 1 to 3 months) to make sure the infection has not come back.

Longterm or recurring infections may be a sign of an underlying problem that needs to be addressed. Because certain medications can increase the risk of urinary tract infections, be sure your veterinarian knows about all the medications that your dog is being given. Additional tests such as contrast x-rays, ultrasonography, and/or cystoscopy may be needed in order to exclude problems such as cysts, growths, stones, tumors, and birth defects. Blood tests may be needed to diagnose other diseases that may contribute to the risk of infection.

Sometimes, even when nothing else appears to be wrong with your pet, bacterial cystitis simply continues to come back. In these cases, your veterinarian may prescribe low-dose antibiotics for your dog to take on a longterm basis. These medications will help prevent the recurrence of bladder infections, as well as preventing the infection from spreading upwards into the kidneys. If your dog is on longterm, low-dose antibiotics, frequent monitoring (urinalysis and bacterial culture) is usually necessary. Encouraging your dog to urinate frequently during the day may help prevent the infection from coming back.

Kidney Infection (Pyelonephritis)

Pyelonephritis is inflammation of the kidneys. This is usually caused by bacteria in the urinary tract that have climbed upwards into the bladder and then continued into the kidneys. The risk factors for pyelonephritis and those for bacterial cystitis are very similar. Anything that interferes with normal urine flow through the urinary system, such as stones in the kidneys or ureters, can increase the risk for pyelonephritis. In young dogs, birth defects such as ectopic ureters (*see* DISORDERS OF THE URETERS, page 286) can cause pyelonephritis. Dogs at risk for this condition are the very young, the very old, those that have weak immune systems, and those with kidneys that cannot properly balance the amount of water in the urine. In many cases, your veterinarian may not be able to identify what caused the pyelonephritis.

Signs of pyelonephritis include pain in the sides, especially in the area around the kidneys, fever, and a general sense of not feeling well. Other signs include vomiting, a reduced appetite, excessive thirst, or excessive urination. The kidneys might suddenly begin to fail. Dogs with longterm pyelonephritis may have few or no signs (other than excessive thirst and urination), and they are often not diagnosed until their kidneys begin to fail.

Your veterinarian may be able to diagnose pyelonephritis through urine and blood samples. In many cases, ultrasonography or contrast x-rays may be necessary for diagnosis.

Treatment includes longterm antibiotics (4 to 6 weeks), sometimes at high dosages. If your dog is very ill, your veterinarian may give intravenous fluids and injectable antibiotics. In extreme cases, the infected kidney must be removed in order to prevent the infection from spreading to the remaining, healthy kidney. Your veterinarian may take urine samples at regular intervals (about once a month) during and after treatment to make sure the infection does not come back. Dogs with pyelonephritis are at high risk for repeated infections. Because pyelonephritis can be a life-threatening disease, following your veterinarian's recommendations is important.

Animals with short-term pyelonephritis may be able to recover full kidney function, depending on the amount of damage that occurred before treatment. If both of the kidneys have already failed, your veterinarian may be able to do little more than keep your dog stable and comfortable.

Interstitial Nephritis

Interstitial nephritis is another type of inflammation of the kidney. In dogs, sudden onset (acute) interstitial nephritis is often triggered by infectious diseases. The most common cause is leptospirosis (infection by *Leptospira interrogans*). Leptospirosis is usually spread by wildlife, such as raccoons, opossums, rats, and other small mammals. It can occur in dogs living in rural, suburban, and even in urban areas. Antibiotics are needed to treat the infection. Kidney failure, if it has occurred, may be treated with supportive treatment, including fluids. Humans can also become infected with leptospirosis. Although transmission from dogs to humans is uncommon, if a dog is diagnosed with the infection, the dog owner should consult a physician.

Capillaria plica Infection

Capillaria plica is a small worm that can infect the bladder, and, less often, the ureters and kidneys of dogs. This is an uncommon parasite in pet dogs. The worms are threadlike, yellowish, and 0.5 to 2.5 inches (13 to 60 millimeters) long. This infection is most common in wild animals. Dogs catch the infection by eating earthworms that carry the larvae of the parasite. Most dogs have no signs. Some show signs of excessive urination, inability to control urination, and urinating in abnormal places. The worms' eggs come out in the urine; your veterinarian may be able to identify them when examining a urine sample. The best treatment has not been determined, but several different antiparasitic drugs are available.

Giant Kidney Worm Infection

Giant kidney worms, known as *Dioctophyma renale*, are a type of parasite that can infect the kidney and the abdomen of dogs. However, they are uncommon parasites in pet dogs. This is one of the largest parasitic worms known and can reach 40 inches (103 centimeters) in length. Female worms are bigger than males. Both sexes are blood red in color. They lay eggs that are barrel-shaped and yellow-brown in color. The urine of infected dogs contains these eggs.

Dogs catch the worm by eating infected raw fish, frogs, or certain common backyard worms (such as earthworms). Once a dog begins digesting the infected fish, frog, or worm, the giant kidney worm makes its way out of the bowels of the dog, into the liver, and finally into the kidneys. Often the worms do not make it all the way to the kidney and end up instead in the abdomen.

Once in the kidneys, the worms cause blockage and destruction of kidney tissues. The right kidney is the one most commonly infected. If both kidneys become infected, kidney failure may result. Other problems that can result from this infection include inflammation of the abdominal cavity, bands of scar tissue in the abdomen or intestines, and liver disease. Signs of the infection include blood in the urine, excessive urination, weight loss, and pain in the abdomen or in the area around the kidneys.

Your veterinarian may be able to diagnose a giant kidney worm infection by identifying eggs in a urine sample. Other tests, such as x-rays, ultrasonography, or abdominal surgery may be needed in order to make the diagnosis. The best treatment is removal of the affected kidney, as long as the other kidney is healthy. To prevent this infection, make sure your dog does not eat raw fish or other animals likely to be infected.

■ NONINFECTIOUS DISEASES OF THE URINARY SYSTEM

There are a variety of noninfectious disorders that can impair the urinary system. All of these diseases and conditions can be serious threats to the health of your dog.

Kidney Dysfunction

The kidneys' most important function is to filter waste from the blood. When this does not happen, waste products can build to dangerous levels in the blood. This is called azotemia. Azotemia can be caused by many factors, including dehydration, shock, and congestive heart failure (*see* page 67). Azotemia can also occur as a result of urine not being able to flow properly through the urinary tract.

Chronic Kidney Disease and Kidney Failure

Longterm, or chronic, disease can damage the kidney so severely that it is not able to function properly. This happens slowly. Chronic kidney disease often continues for months or years before a dog has any signs. There is rarely anything that a veterinarian can do to treat existing damage or prevent further damage once the process has started. Occasionally, chronic kidney disease results from a problem that is inherited or an abnormality present at birth (*see* CONGENITAL AND INHERITED DISORDERS OF THE URINARY SYS-

TEM, page 285). Most of the time, however, it is a problem in older animals. Starting at age 5 to 6, kidney disease becomes more common, affecting up to 10% of elderly dogs. Chronic kidney disease that is not inherited does not seem to be more common among certain dog breeds or among males or females.

Veterinarians classify chronic kidney disease into 4 stages based on laboratory tests and the results of physical examinations (*see* TABLE 15). In Stage I, the kidneys are damaged but azotemia (*see* above) has not yet developed and the dog has no signs. This is the stage at which treatment has the greatest chance of success, but because the dog has no signs, the disease is rarely diagnosed at this stage. In Stage II, the kidneys filter waste much more slowly than normal, and there is a buildup of waste chemicals in the blood, but many dogs still have no signs. Signs that may be present at this stage include an increase in the amount of water in the urine and an increased volume of urine. In Stage III, filtering slows even more, the waste chemicals are more concentrated in the blood, and the dog develops signs of disease. Stage IV, the final stage, reflects continued kidney damage and accumulation of waste products in the bloodstream. By this time the dog feels and acts very sick.

Determining the cause of chronic kidney disease, especially in the early stages, will help determine the appropriate treatment and provide an outlook for your dog. Some of the common causes include diseases of the circulatory system (such as high blood pressure, problems with blood clotting, and not having enough oxygen in the blood) or other diseases of the kidneys such as pyelonephritis (*see* page 288) or tumors. Whatever the cause, chronic kidney disease usually results in scarring of the kidneys, which gets gradually worse.

Animals usually have no signs of kidney disease until they are at Stages III or IV, when their kidneys are working at less than 25% of their usual capacity. Exceptions to this include other illnesses that

Table 15. Chronic Kidney Disease Stages

Disease Stage	Physical Conditions	Signs	Treatment
Stage I	Waste filtering slows. Waste chemicals start to appear in blood.	No easily visible signs. Laboratory or other tests required.	Identify and treat cause of kidney disease.
Stage II	Further slowing of waste filtering. Buildup of waste chemicals and imbalance of water in urine.	Dog may be urinating more than previously. Tests show increased amount of waste chemicals in blood.	Treat underlying cause of the condition. A change of diet may be required (such as a low salt or other special diet).
Stage III	Kidneys often working at less than 60% of normal capacity.	Excessive thirst and urination.	Support dog with kidney disease diet, monitor for infections, and treat underlying cause of kidney disease.
Stage IV	Kidneys working at less than 25% of normal capacity. Toxic chemicals build up in blood and affect other organs in the body.	Vomiting, depression, loss of appetite, weight loss, dehydration, mouth sores, diarrhea. Young dogs may lose teeth. Bones can become soft and easily breakable.	Provide special diet. Treat underlying conditions. Provide comfort care. In severe cases, kidney dialysis or a kidney transplant might be possible.

affect the entire body along with the kidneys, or kidneys that become unusually inflamed or sore and cause vomiting or pain. Veterinarians may be able to detect a problem in a blood test or on physical examination even before the dog starts to display signs of kidney failure. Usually, the earliest signs are excessive thirst and urination. However, these signs may signal other diseases as well, and they do not begin to appear until Stage II or III. After this, there are usually no new signs until Stage IV, when affected dogs vomit and are sluggish. As the disease progresses over months, other problems begin. These include loss of appetite, weight loss, dehydration, sores in the mouth, vomiting, and diarrhea.

To diagnose chronic kidney disease, veterinarians generally use a combination of x-rays, ultrasonography, urine and blood tests, and physical examination. These tests are also used to check the response to treatment and monitor complications related to the kidney disease.

With proper treatment, even dogs with as little as 5% of normal kidney function can survive for a long time. The recom-

mended treatment depends on the stage of disease. Identifying and treating complications, such as high blood pressure or urinary tract infections, needs to be done as well. All dogs with kidney disease should see their veterinarian every 3 to 6 months, or more frequently if there are problems. During these visits, the veterinarian will do tests on the dog's blood and urine.

Although there is no way to prevent chronic kidney disease from getting progressively worse, there are some things you can do to slow the process. These include making sure the dog's diet does not contain too much phosphorus, supplementing your dog's food with fish oil, and giving all medications as directed. Your veterinarian may suggest special food which has been designed for animals with kidney disease. If there are problems with the acidity of your pet's blood, or if the levels of phosphorus in your pet's blood are unhealthy, your veterinarian may prescribe a supplement or vitamin.

In the later stages of kidney disease (III and IV), the dog should be taken to the veterinarian every 1 to 2 months. At this stage, treatments will focus on easing some of the signs of the disease. Some approaches include limiting the amount or type of protein in your dog's diet (your veterinarian can suggest special food formulated for pets with kidney disease) and medications. Sometimes veterinarians will recommend intravenous fluids or feeding tubes. At this point, there are very few options. Dialysis machines, which do the job of the kidneys by filtering the blood, can prolong life, but dialysis is not feasible for most dogs. A kidney transplant can be done, but requires immune-suppressing drugs to prevent the body from rejecting the new kidney, which can cause other problems.

Acute Kidney Disease

Acute kidney disease is the result of sudden, major damage to the kidneys. This damage is usually caused by toxic chemi-

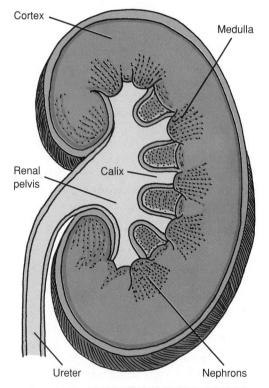

The kidneys consist of an outer part (cortex) and an inner part (medulla). The nephrons filter the blood and produce urine (modified with permission from *The Merck Manual of Medical Information*, Second Home Edition, 2003).

cals either consumed by your pet or built up by an abnormal condition in your pet's body. Kidney function can also be affected when the kidneys do not receive sufficient oxygen, such as when a blood clot blocks the flow of blood to the kidneys.

Some dogs consume toxic chemicals, such as antifreeze, or poisonous plants that can damage the kidneys. There are many substances in the average home that may be safe for humans but dangerous for dogs and other pets (*see* POISONING, page 1145). Some toxic chemicals come from inside the dog's own body. For example, there could be a buildup of calcium or other substances due to a disease in another part of the body. In these cases, the effects on kidney function can last from 1 to 8 weeks, depending on the chemical(s) that caused the injury.

Mild kidney disease often goes unnoticed. However, repeated occurrences can lead to chronic kidney disease. The stages of acute and chronic kidney disease are the same (*see* page 290). Usually, acute kidney disease becomes obvious only in Stage IV, when the signs include loss of appetite, depression, dehydration, sores in the mouth, vomiting, diarrhea, and a smaller than normal volume of urine.

It is important to determine whether the kidney disease is acute or chronic, as well as the cause of the disease. This information will help your veterinarian determine the most appropriate treatment. Usually, veterinarians can identify acute kidney disease by taking a urine sample and asking thorough questions about exactly what your pet has eaten, what medications your pet may have taken, and how your pet has been acting in the months and weeks prior to becoming ill.

An injured kidney can often regain some or most of its function. The uninjured part of the kidney (or remaining uninjured kidney) helps compensate for the injured organ. To determine how much potential your dog's kidneys have to regenerate, your veterinarian may need to do a kidney biopsy.

If the cause of the kidney injury can be determined, treatment will be aimed at this cause. Dogs that are dehydrated or not eating may require intravenous fluids or a feeding tube. Your veterinarian may suggest treatment to promote urination in dogs that are not urinating enough or not urinating at all. This treatment involves intravenous fluids, inserting a catheter into your dog's bladder, and, occasionally, medication. If none of the available treatments work, and your dog is simply not producing urine, the only remaining options are kidney dialysis, a kidney transplant, or euthanasia.

Glomerular Disease

The glomerulus is one of the structures that are essential to kidney function. It is made up of special blood vessels that help filter blood. Each kidney contains thousands of these structures. Glomerular disease is a common cause of chronic (but not acute) kidney disease in dogs. Damage to parts of the glomerulus can cause protein in the urine and low levels of a protein called albumin in the blood. This can

lead to other problems, such as swelling of the legs, high cholesterol, and blood clots.

Glomerular disease can occur due to the longterm effects of high blood pressure. However, glomerular disease can also occur along with other kidney disorders. Some glomerular disease is immune-mediated, that is, caused by the dog's immune system attacking parts of its own body. Tumors, rickettsial infections, lupus, and heartworm infection have been identified in connection with immune-mediated glomerulonephropathy.

Glomerular disease may also be caused by hyperadrenocorticism, which is an excess of a hormone called cortisol. Cortisol is produced by the adrenal gland, and is one of the hormones that helps convert food into energy and regulate blood sugar. Animals with glomerular disease caused by hyperadrenocorticism frequently also have diabetes.

Some types of glomerular disease are inherited. Dog breeds that are more prone to inherit this illness include Bernese

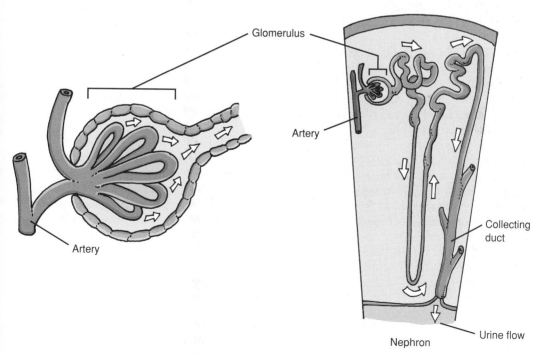

The glomeruli help filter blood (modified with permission from *The Merck Manual of Medical Information, Second Home Edition*, 2003).

Mountain Dogs, English Cocker Spaniels, Doberman Pinschers, Greyhounds, Lhasa Apsos, Poodles, Rottweilers, Samoyeds, Shih Tzus, and Soft-coated Wheaten Terriers.

Some glomerular disease is caused by **amyloidosis**, or deposits in the kidneys of a misfolded protein called amyloid. Glomerular amyloidosis usually causes protein in the urine. Amyloidosis is sometimes inherited in Chinese Shar-Peis. The non-inherited form of amyloidosis usually affects dogs that are middle-aged or older. Certain breeds, such as Beagles, Collies, and Walker Hounds, are at increased risk. Dogs with the inherited form of the disease are usually diagnosed at a young age.

Signs and Diagnosis

Disease in the glomerulus often leads to protein in the urine, low levels of protein in the blood, a buildup of fluid in the abdomen (which can cause visible swelling), shortness of breath, and swelling of the legs. Taken together, these signs are called the nephrotic syndrome. (Nephrotic means relating to the kidneys.) The loss of protein through the urine can cause loss of muscle tissues.

Protein in the urine can lead to a loss of an important protein that helps the blood to clot properly. This can cause strokes, heart attacks, and other problems that occur when the blood clots too easily. For example, if blood clots form in the lungs, dogs may have severe difficulty breathing.

Your veterinarian will look for increased levels of protein and other chemicals in your dog's urine and blood. Physical examination usually reveals that something is wrong; however the signs are often non-specific and could point to any of a wide variety of problems. A biopsy of the kidneys is often required to determine the cause of glomerular disease. In dogs, about half the cases of glomerular disease are caused by amyloidosis. Additional tests may be required in some cases, including x-rays, ultrasonography, and special blood tests.

Treatment and Outlook

Treatment for glomerular disease varies according to the cause. If the glomerular disease is immune-mediated, then the immune system problem should be treated, and drugs that suppress the immune system may be required to limit damage. If the dog has signs of nephrotic syndrome (*see* above), your veterinarian will probably recommend limiting sodium in the diet, using a diuretic, or both. For a dog whose blood clots too easily as a result of kidney disease, your veterinarian might recommend a medication that thins the blood. Because protein in the urine can cause scar tissue to build up in the kidneys, your veterinarian will probably attempt to limit how much protein is shed from the body into the urine. Options for this include limiting the amount of protein in the dog's diet and prescribing certain medications.

Dogs with glomerular disease live an average of about 3 months once the illness is diagnosed. However, if the problem can be diagnosed and treated early, dogs can live much longer. Survival times for animals with amyloidosis vary widely, with reported times ranging from 49 days to 20 months.

Renal Tubular Problems

Renal tubules are structures in the kidneys that help filter blood.

Renal Tubular Acidosis

Healthy kidneys help rid the body of acid by producing urine that is acidic. Diseased kidneys cannot get rid of acid properly, and instead of being eliminated in the urine, this acid builds up in the blood, leading to a condition called uremic acidosis. This condition can also occur when there are defects in the renal tubules, in which case it is called renal tubular acidosis. These defects are rare in dogs.

Renal tubular acidosis can cause kidney stones and can cause the bones to become soft and easily breakable. To treat this condition, your veterinarian will probably prescribe medication to help rebalance the amount of acid in the blood. However, this treatment is not effective for all cases.

Fanconi Syndrome

Fanconi syndrome is a condition in which the kidneys cannot properly absorb certain chemicals. The chemicals are glucose, sodium, potassium, phosphorus, uric acid, bicarbonate, and amino acids. All of these are required to meet the body's needs, but animals with Fanconi syndrome cannot reabsorb them through the kidneys. Instead, they are lost in the urine. Dogs can develop Fanconi syndrome in one of several ways. They can have a bad reaction to gentamicin (a type of antibiotic), the syndrome can appear suddenly and for no apparent reason, or it can be inherited. Basenjis are most likely to inherit the condition; in this case, the condition develops gradually in adults.

Signs of Fanconi syndrome include excessive thirst, excessive urination, and weight loss. There may be a buildup of toxic chemicals in the blood, called uremia. Your veterinarian can diagnose Fanconi syndrome by doing tests on your dog's blood and urine.

There is no way to correct the tubular defect that causes Fanconi syndrome. Veterinarians can try to balance the amount of acid in the blood by prescribing supplements. Treating the signs of disease can make your dog more comfortable. However, ultimately there is little a veterinarian can do beyond keeping the dog as comfortable as possible. Most dogs with the inherited form of Fanconi syndrome die from uremia.

Obstructions of the Urinary Tract

Even when the kidneys are functioning normally, a blockage in the urinary system at any point below the kidneys can lead to a backup of toxic wastes that can damage the kidneys and cause illness. In dogs, the most common cause is a kidney stone that blocks the urethra. Other possible causes include tumors or blood clots in the ureters or urethra.

If the flow of urine is blocked, the kidney becomes abnormally enlarged. When this happens suddenly to both kidneys, especially when the urine is completely blocked, the dog does not live long. When the blockage is only partial, or only occurs on one side, the dog often survives, but the kidneys often sustain permanent damage. The affected kidneys eventually become giant, useless sacs filled with urine and may become infected. The ureter may also become enlarged due to a backup of urine. This often occurs when the blockage is located far down the urinary tract and away from the kidneys.

Signs and Diagnosis

Dogs with a blockage in their urethra urinate quite frequently, urinate slowly and painfully (some dogs may whine or cry), and typically have blood in their urine. They may also have a painful abdomen. Uremia, the buildup of toxic waste in the blood, happens quickly. The signs of uremia include vomiting, dehydration, a drop in body temperature, and severe depression. The bladder is bloated and painful. The heart can be affected by the buildup of potassium in the blood and start to beat abnormally. In dogs with only one blocked kidney, the other kidney can compensate for the blockage. The blockage in these dogs often goes unnoticed unless there is another kidney disease or your veterinarian notices it during a physical examination or on an x-ray or ultrasound examination.

Your veterinarian may be able to diagnose obstructions based on the signs and physical examination. Sometimes, however, ultrasonography or other special tests are required. In cases where the heart is affected, a heart test called an electrocardiogram (EKG) may be required.

Treatment

To restore normal urine flow, the blockage must be removed. In most cases, intravenous fluids will be used to restore the balance of various chemicals in the blood. Because of increased production of urine after the blockage is removed, it is normal for a dog to urinate more than usual for 1 to 5 days after treatment. During this period, it is important that your pet not get dehydrated. Your veterinarian may want to monitor your dog daily during this time, and adjust the amount and type of fluids your pet is receiving.

Surgery is often required to remove the blockage. If the blockage is caused by stones, the stones may naturally pass and eliminate the need for surgery. However, the damage caused by the stone may require part of the ureter or urethra to be removed. In some cases, a kidney is so damaged that it needs to be removed. This is possible only if the other kidney is healthy.

If a dog has signs of a blocked urethra, it is critical to seek veterinary care immediately. Dogs with a complete blockage may die within 2 to 3 days without treatment.

Tumors

Tumors of the kidneys and urinary tract are not common in dogs. Tumors can be benign (harmless) or malignant (cancerous).

Kidney Tumors

Kidney tumors are uncommon; only about 1% of all tumors in dogs involve the kidneys. It is unusual to find benign kidney growths because they rarely affect the health of an animal. They are usually discovered only by accident and do not require treatment.

Malignant tumors that begin in the kidneys (as opposed to those that begin in other organs and spread to the kidneys) are most common in middle-aged to older dogs. In general, no breed is more prone to kidney tumors than others; however, German Shepherds can inherit a tendency to develop a very specific kind of cancer known as a **cystoadenocarcinoma**. This cancer involves many small tumors on both kidneys and usually appears when the dog is between 5 and 11 years old.

The most common malignant kidney tumor is a **carcinoma** that starts in the lining of the renal tubules. Usually, the

tumor appears on only one kidney. Cancerous tumors that begin in the kidneys spread quickly to other organs, especially the opposite kidney, the lungs, and the liver.

Blastomas are tumors composed of previously healthy young cells that never mature normally. Instead, these cells mutate into cancer. Those that originate in the kidney are known as **nephroblastomas**. (Other names for this type of tumor are embryonal nephroma and Wilms' tumor). Dogs with this type of cancer are usually diagnosed when they are less than 1 year old. Males are affected twice as often as females. Nephroblastomas usually occur in only one kidney, but occasionally they affect both kidneys. They can become quite large; it is not uncommon for a single nephroblastoma to take up all of the space inside the affected dog's abdomen. Nephroblastomas typically spread to nearby lymph nodes, the liver, and the lungs.

Transitional cell carcinomas are cancers that appear in the lining of certain parts of the urinary tract including the ureter, bladder, urethra, or the center of the kidney (referred to as the renal pelvis). The lining in these parts of the urinary tract is called transitional epithelium and is different from the lining of other organs because it is very stretchy.

Other malignant tumors rarely originate in the kidneys, but can include hemangiosarcomas (tumors from the lining of the blood vessels), fibrosarcomas (tumors of connective tissue), leiomyosarcomas (tumors of the smooth muscle), and squamous cell carcinomas (tumors of the outer layer of the kidney surface).

When cancer spreads from one organ to another, it is said to metastasize and the cancer itself is described as metastatic. The kidneys are a common second site for metastasis of cancers that begin in other organs, such as the lymph nodes. Up to half of dogs with cancer of the lymph nodes also develop cancer in their kidneys. In some cases, the cancer remains only in the lymph nodes and the kidneys. In others it also affects the brain. When cancer spreads to the kidneys, it usually takes the form of many small tumors. It can affect both kidneys and may result in the kidneys being unusually large and irregularly shaped.

Signs of kidney tumors are usually general and can point to many different illnesses. Common signs include weight loss, loss of appetite, depression, and fever. Your veterinarian will need to eliminate other causes of these signs before confirming cancer. Occasionally, tumors that appear in both kidneys can cause enough damage that the dog will develop signs of late-stage chronic kidney disease and failure (*see* page 290). Pet owners who pay close attention may notice "lumps" in the dog's belly or an enlarged belly. There may be blood in the urine, but it is usually too tiny an amount to see with the naked eye.

Your veterinarian may suspect a tumor in the kidneys based on physical examination and careful consideration of your dog's signs in the weeks and months prior to becoming ill. This suspicion can be confirmed with ultrasonography, x-rays, or contrast x-ray tests of the urinary tract. Cancer cells can also occasionally be found in the urine. A biopsy of the tumor is usually necessary to determine its type.

All kidney tumors must be surgically removed. Usually it is necessary to remove the entire affected kidney. Tumors in the lymph nodes around the kidney are usually treated with chemotherapy instead of surgery. If your dog develops a urinary cancer, the veterinarian will assess the severity of your pet's condition, the outlook for your pet, and other factors when recommending a treatment program.

Lower Urinary Tract Tumors

Tumors in the ureters, bladder, and urethra are not common in dogs. The average age of affected dogs is 9 years old. Tumors that begin in (as opposed to those that spread to) the lower urinary tract are more likely to be malignant than benign. Benign tumors that can be found in the lower urinary tract include papillomas (warts; tumors of the lining of organs), leiomyomas (smooth muscle tumors, also called fibroids), neurofibromas (tumors of the protective sheath that surrounds nerves), hemangiomas (blood vessel tumors), rhabdomyomas (another type of smooth muscle tumor), and myxomas (tumors of primitive connective tissue).

The most common type of malignant tumor that begins in the lower urinary tract is **transitional cell carcinoma**. Transitional cell carcinomas are cancers that appear in the lining of certain parts of the urinary tract including the ureter, bladder, urethra, and renal pelvis. Transitional cell carcinomas may appear as a single tumor, or as multiple wart-like growths that are visible on the membranes lining the urinary tract. Alternatively, these carcinomas may develop all over the ureter, bladder, prostate gland, or urethra. Once they appear, they have the tendency to grow and spread quickly, most often to the nearby lymph nodes and lungs.

Tumors in the ureter and bladder can cause blockage of urine, which can back up into the kidneys and cause damage (*see* page 295). Tumors in the urethra are more likely than tumors in the ureter and bladder to suddenly cut off the passage of urine. Tumors in the bladder and urethra are usually accompanied by urinary tract infections that will not go away despite treatment with antibiotics.

Other types of malignant tumors that can originate in the urinary tract include squamous cell carcinomas (cancer of the outer layer of an organ), adenocarcinomas (cancer of the lining of the walls of an organ), fibrosarcomas (cancer of the connective tissue), leiomysarcomas (cancer of the smooth muscles), rhabdomysarcomas (cancer of smooth muscle), hemangiosarcomas (cancer of the blood vessels), and osteosarcomas (bone cancer).

The most common signs of cancer of the lower urinary tract include blood in the urine; painful, slow, or difficult urination; and excessive urination. Dogs with one blocked ureter may have a painful abdomen, and a veterinarian may be able to feel an enlarged kidney. Dogs with blocked ureters on both sides or a single blocked urethra may show signs of uremia (a buildup of the toxic chemicals usually eliminated in the urine). While doing an examination, a veterinarian may be able to detect a thickened bladder wall, an irregular urethra, or masses on the urethra.

Laboratory tests on the dog's urine usually reveal blood in the urine, and sometimes reveal a bacterial or other infection that has developed in addition to the tumor. It is occasionally possible to mistake tumors in the lower urinary tract with simple urinary tract infections, especially those that do not go away or keep coming back. Thus, your veterinarian may order additional tests to confirm the diagnosis of cancer. Sometimes cancer cells can be found in the urine, especially when the cancer is in the transitional cells. Your veterinarian may use ultrasonography or specialized x-rays to locate and assess the severity of the tumor. A biopsy of the tumor is required to identify its type.

Surgical removal of the tumor, if possible, is the best treatment. Transitional cell carcinomas are frequently located in critical parts of the bladder or urethra, and removing them requires reconstruction of the lower urinary tract. Survival time tends to be short for these dogs, even with surgery, because the tumors spread quickly and often reappear. Chemotherapy may give the dog more time but can have serious side effects. You and your veterinarian will want to discuss the treatment options and the quality of life for your pet both during and after treatment.

Problems with Urination

Urination problems can be grouped into problems with storing urine and problems with eliminating urine. Urinary incontinence is the inability to prevent or control urination. Incontinent animals leak urine constantly or on and off without realizing it. An incontinent dog may leave a pool of urine where it has been lying or dribble urine while walking. The fur around the vulva or penis may be wet, and the con-

stant dribbling of urine can cause inflammation and urine scalding of the skin in these areas.

Problems with Urine Storage

Problems with urine storage are identified by inappropriate leakage of urine, and can be caused by several different disorders. These include failure of the muscles in the bladder to relax appropriately, injury or damage to the urethra or other parts of the urinary system, and overflowing of the bladder.

Urge incontinence occurs when urine leaks during the times when an animal feels the urge to urinate as opposed to urine which leaks when an animal is unaware of it. Urge incontinence is usually caused by irritation of the bladder muscle that forcibly expels the urine. This is usually due to inflammation of the bladder. Unusually low levels of sex hormones in neutered dogs are a common cause. This type of incontinence, called hormonal-responsive urethral incompetence, is particularly common in female dogs. Problems with the urethral sphincter (the muscle that allows urine to pass through the urethra) can also cause this type of incontinence.

Incontinence that results from birth defects or malformation of the urinary system usually becomes obvious while the dog is still young. For example, a dog that was born with an ectopic ureter (*see* page 286) on one side might urinate normally but dribble urine on and off, whereas dogs with ectopic ureters on both sides are less likely to be able to urinate normally at all. Although it seems contradictory, a dog can also become incontinent if its urethra is partially blocked; the blocked urethra can cause urine to back up and the bladder to overflow.

Problems with Urine Elimination

Problems with urine elimination can have many causes, including a physical blockage of the urethra by stones, growths, or scar tissue; problems related to the nervous system; or a lack of muscle tone in the muscle that closes off the bladder.

Dogs that cannot urinate normally will usually try to urinate often, but the urination will be slow and painful, and only small amounts of urine will come out. Dogs with urine elimination problems may also develop incontinence over time, if the bladder does not empty properly. The bladder can become stretched out and begin to overflow and leak.

Neurologic Problems

Neurologic problems with urination can be caused by damage to the lower half of the spine, damage to the major nerve in the pelvis, or a lack of muscle tone in the muscle that closes off the bladder. Dogs with one of these injuries may have an enlarged bladder that empties easily. Other neurologic problems with urination are caused by damage to the upper half of the spine or disease in the brain. Dogs with these disorders have an enlarged bladder that does not empty easily.

Another neurologic cause of urination problems is poor muscle coordination. The various muscles involved in the different steps of urination do not work together normally. Dogs with this condition usually urinate extraordinarily often, with the stream of urine being cut short. Some dogs with neurologic problems may leak urine. Animals with any neurologic urination problem may develop incontinence, especially if the bladder becomes too full and begins to overflow and leak.

Diagnosis and Treatment of Urination Problems

A thorough physical examination and a history of your dog's behavior can help your veterinarian determine whether your dog has problems related to urination. Your veterinarian will probably also want to watch your pet urinate. Specialized tests, such as ultrasonography, x-rays, or neurologic tests, may be helpful in some cases.

Dogs with incontinence that is caused by imbalances in sex hormones may be prescribed hormones in order to re-establish the proper balance. Urethral incontinence can be treated with medication that tar-

gets the membrane inside the urethra (called alpha-adrenergic agonist drugs). Urge incontinence can be treated with medication that targets certain nerves (called anticholinergic drugs). Weakened bladder muscles can be treated with medications that target slack muscles (called cholinergic drugs). Muscle relaxants may be useful in cases where muscle coordination issues are identified.

Complete physical blockage of the urethra is a medical emergency. The treatment varies, depending on the circumstances. A catheter may be used to push the blockage backwards out of the urethra and into the bladder. The blockage may have to be removed during surgery. Dogs with bladder muscles that have been weakened by overfill and stretching may require a special catheter that remains in place, or is placed at regular intervals every few hours for 3 to 5 days. This allows the bladder to empty properly and regain some muscle tone.

In dogs in which the bladder has lost its muscle tone due to neurologic problems, there are few medical options to restore muscle tone. For these dogs, it is usually necessary to empty the bladder with a catheter several times a day for the rest of its life. In these cases, you will need to be trained to properly insert and remove the catheter.

Urinary Stones (Uroliths, Calculi)

Uroliths are stones (also known as calculi) formed when minerals that naturally occur in urine clump together to form tiny crystals. These stones can develop anywhere in the urinary system, including in the kidneys, ureters, bladder, or urethra.

Veterinary researchers do not completely understand what causes stones to form. There are many different types of stones, each formed from a complex mixture of various minerals. Each type of stone develops only under certain conditions. They can be caused by a problem with the minerals themselves, by a problem with other chemicals that exist in urine and which, under normal circumstances, prevent stones from form-ing, or by the environment of the urinary tract. All of these conditions can be affected by urinary tract infections, diet, digestion, the amount of urine that a dog produces, how frequently a dog urinates, medications, and genetics.

Dogs with very small stones in the urinary system do not usually have any signs. However, larger stones in the lower urinary tract may interfere with urination or irritate the lining of the urethra. In turn, these problems can cause an inabil-ity to urinate, blood in the urine, and slow or painful urination. Kidney stones usu-ally cause no signs unless the kidney becomes inflamed or the stones pass into the ureter. If a ureter becomes blocked by a stone, it can cause vomiting, slowness or tiredness, and pain in the abdomen in the area around the kidneys. This sign is particularly common when both ureters are suddenly and completely blocked and a backup of fluids causes the kidneys to become enlarged. Pain is the only sign of stones in the ureter on only one side; however, pain can be difficult to detect in dogs. If the blocked ureter is not diag-nosed right away, kidney damage occurs.

Ultimately, the blocked kidney is destroyed. Veterinarians can sometimes detect stones in the bladder by pressing on the dog's abdomen. Stones in the ure-thra may also be detected during a rectal examination or when attempting to insert a catheter. There may be many stones present at once, so if one stone is located, it is important to examine the entire urinary tract to look for others. X-rays can reveal stones as small as 3 millime-ters in size. A veterinarian will also need to do tests on the dog's urine and may need to do ultrasonography or other spe-cialized tests.

The treatment of stones, and preventing their return, depends on their type and location. Treatment and prevention may include surgery, a special diet, and medi-cation. When stones are removed, the vet-erinarian will probably send them to a laboratory to be analyzed. Knowing what types of minerals are in the stone can pro-vide the information needed to prescribe medication to help prevent the formation of more stones. Dogs undergoing treat-ment will need to be monitored closely and return at regular intervals for addi-tional testing.

CHAPTER **18**

Metabolic Disorders

▦ INTRODUCTION

Metabolism refers to all processes in the body that break down and convert ingested substances to provide the energy and nutrients needed to sustain life. Foods, liquids, and drugs all generally undergo metabolic processes within the body. Many foods are complex materials that need to be broken down into simpler substances, which in turn become "building blocks" for the body to use as needed. For example, protein is broken down into amino acids, which are used in several metabolic reac-

tions. **Enzymes** made by the body are needed for many metabolic processes to occur. Whenever the function of an enzyme is affected, a metabolic disorder can de-velop. Metabolic disorders are important because they affect energy production or damage tissues. They may be genetic (inherited) or acquired. Acquired metabolic disorders are more common and significant.

Metabolic Storage Disorders

Metabolic storage disorders usually result from the body's inability to break

Table 16. Breeds of Dogs Prone to Genetic Storage Diseases

Disease	Breeds
Ceroid lipofuscinosis	Border Collies, Chihuahuas, Cocker Spaniels, Dachshunds, English Setters, Salukis
Gangliosidoses	Beagle crosses, German Shorthaired Pointers, Japanese Spaniels
Globoid cell leukodystrophy (Krabbe's disease)	Beagles, Bluetick Hounds, Cairn Terriers, Poodles, West Highland White Terriers
Glucocerebrosidosis	Australian Silky Terriers, Dalmatians
Glycogenosis	Silky Terriers
Mucopolysaccharidosis (associated with lameness)	Miniature Pinschers, Mixed-breed dogs, Plott Hounds
Phosphofructokinase deficiency	American Cocker Spaniels, English Springer Spaniels
Pyruvate kinase deficiency (associated with anemia)	Basenjis, Beagles, Cairn Terriers, West Highland White Terriers
Sphingomyelinosis	German Shepherds, Poodles

down some substance because of partial or complete lack of a certain enzyme. The substance can build up to a toxic level, or the body is unable to produce a substance that it needs. Although storage diseases are often widespread throughout the body, most clinical signs are due to the effects on the central nervous system. Metabolic storage disorders can be either genetic or acquired.

Genetic (inherited) storage diseases are named according to the specific metabolic byproduct that builds up in the body. Certain breeds are more prone to certain storage diseases than others (*see* TABLE 16). Puppies typically appear normal at birth, and clinical signs begin within a few weeks to months. These diseases are progressive and usually fatal. Specific treatments do not exist.

Acquired storage diseases can be caused by eating plants that contain inhibitors of specific enzymes. (For a more detailed discussion of PLANTS POISONOUS TO ANIMALS, *see* page 1175.)

Production-related Metabolic Disorders

Some metabolic disorders are caused by an increased demand for a specific element or nutrient that has become deficient under certain conditions. For example, in **hypoglycemia**, the animal's metabolic reserves are unable to sustain sugar (or glucose) in the blood at a level needed for normal function. Likewise, in **hypocalcemia**, the level of calcium in the blood is too low. In some cases, dietary intake of a nutrient, such as calcium, is rapidly used up for an ongoing, high metabolic need, such as lactation (or nursing puppies).

The difference between production-related metabolic diseases and nutritional deficiencies is often subtle. Typically, nutritional deficiencies are longterm conditions that develop gradually and can be corrected through dietary supplementation. Metabolic diseases usually begin suddenly and respond dramatically to administration of the deficient nutrient (although affected animals may need dietary supplements to avoid recurrence). Because production-related metabolic disorders are serious and develop suddenly, accurate and rapid diagnosis is essential. Ideally, diagnostic tests can be used to predict the chance of disease occurring so that either it can be prevented or preparations can be made for rapid treatment.

■ DISORDERS OF CALCIUM METABOLISM

Calcium is an essential component of the skeleton, and it has important functions in muscle contraction, blood clotting, enzyme activity, the nervous system, and hormone release, among others. Many different metabolic disorders affect calcium metabolism and can lead to abnormally high or low levels of calcium in the blood. (*See also* DISORDERS OF THE PARATHYROID GLANDS AND OF CALCIUM METABOLISM, page 134.)

In dogs, the most common disorder of calcium metabolism is **puerperal hypocalcemia**. Other names for this condition include postpartum hypocalcemia, periparturient hypocalcemia, puerperal tetany, and eclampsia. This life-threatening condition is usually seen 2 to 3 weeks after whelping, when the mammary glands are producing the greatest amount of milk. Small-breed dogs with large litters are affected most often, although puerperal hypocalcemia can occur in any breed of dog, with any litter size, and at any time during lactation. Hypocalcemia most likely results from loss of calcium into the milk and too little calcium in the diet.

Panting and restlessness are early clinical signs. Tremors, twitching, muscle spasms, stiffness, and incoordination may

Puerperal hypocalcemia is most common in small-breed female dogs with large litters.

also occur. The dog may become disoriented, hypersensitive, and aggressive, and whine, drool, and pace. Severe tremors, repeated and prolonged contraction of muscles, rapid heartbeat, fever, seizures, and coma may develop. Usually, the dog has been otherwise healthy, and the newborns have been thriving. Although hypocalcemia usually occurs after giving birth, clinical signs can appear before or during the act of giving birth. Hypocalcemia can contribute to ineffective contractions and a slow labor without causing other clinical signs.

A tentative diagnosis is based on the history, physical examination, clinical signs, and response to treatment. A blood test to determine the level of calcium confirms the diagnosis.

Immediate veterinary treatment is needed for dogs with puerperal hypocalcemia. Calcium solutions given intravenously usually result in rapid improvement within 15 minutes. Puppies should not be allowed to nurse for 12 to 24 hours. During this period, they should be fed a milk substitute or other appropriate diet; if mature enough, they should be weaned. If signs recur in the same lactation, the litter should be hand raised (if younger than 4 weeks) or weaned (if older than 4 weeks). After the acute crisis, calcium supplements are given for the rest of the lactation. Vitamin D supplements also may be used to increase calcium absorption from the intestines. Blood calcium levels are usually monitored weekly.

Puerperal hypocalcemia is likely to recur with future pregnancies. Preventive measures in dogs include feeding a high-quality, nutritionally balanced, and appropriate diet during pregnancy and lactation, providing food and water ad lib during lactation, and feeding puppies with supplemental milk replacer early in lactation and with solid food after 3 to 4 weeks of age. Oral calcium supplements should not be given during pregnancy because they may actually cause rather than prevent hypocalcemia after the dog gives birth.

■ DISORDERS OF MAGNESIUM METABOLISM

Most disorders of magnesium metabolism are due to problems associated with absorption of the mineral from the digestive tract. The anatomical differences between species are associated with the importance of disorders of magnesium occurring in a particular species. Disorders of magnesium metabolism are less common in dogs than in cattle and sheep. Too much magnesium in the blood (**hypermagnesemia**) is rare but has been reported in dogs after ingestion of ice melts and in animals with kidney failure that were receiving intravenous fluids. Cardiac arrest can occur with very high blood magnesium levels.

■ FATIGUE AND EXERCISE

Owners commonly report **muscular fatigue** of dogs and horses. Muscular fatigue can be caused by numerous disorders of several body systems, which are discussed in other chapters. Fatigue is an issue for working dogs, racing greyhounds, and dogs that compete in agility and other high-intensity events.

Fatigue is a normal consequence of exercise that is continued at high intensity or for prolonged periods of time. The decreased ability of the muscle to produce force is actually a safety mechanism for the body. If fatigue did not occur and force the animal to stop, the intense exercise could cause structural damage to muscle cells and supportive tissues.

During prolonged exercise (usually several hours or more), panting and/or sweating occur to remove excess heat generated by the body's metabolic processes. This leads to dehydration and acid-base and electrolyte imbalances. These factors cause fatigue, exhaustion, and may even lead to death.

Appropriate physical training is the most effective way to reduce fatigue and increase the capacity for exercise. Training leads to more effective use of oxygen in body tissues, increased blood volume, and muscle adaptations. Working animals should be acclimated to hot environments before competition.

If you have a working dog or one that competes in high-intensity events, you should consult with your veterinarian about appropriate feeding and hydration strategies to help minimize fatigue.

■ FEVER OF UNKNOWN ORIGIN

In both animals and people, fever may indicate infection, inflammation, an immune-mediated disease, or cancer. Determining the cause of a fever requires a history, physical examination, and sometimes laboratory or other diagnostic tests. Often, a fever resolves on its own or in response to antibiotic therapy. However, in a small percentage of animals, the fever continues or keeps coming back and the cause cannot be determined. This is called fever of unknown origin. In dogs, the most common causes of fever of unknown origin are infections, immune-mediated diseases, and cancer.

Body Temperature Regulation

Body temperature is regulated by an area of the brain called the **hypothalamus**. The hypothalamus acts as a thermostat to maintain temperature as close to normal as possible, and it sets off activities in the body that influence heat production, heat loss, and heat gain. In true fever, the thermostat is reset to a higher temperature.

In certain conditions, such as heat stroke, seizures, or malignant hyperthermia, the body temperature is increased above the normal range, but it is not considered a true fever, as the thermostat is not reset. Depending on their severity, these conditions can potentially result in dangerously high body temperatures of 106°F (41.1°C) or higher. In comparison, most patients with true fever have body temperatures in the range of 103 to 106°F (39.5 to 41.1°C).

Diagnosis

The diagnosis of fever of unknown origin can require considerable time and patience and demand numerous diagnostic tests.

Initial diagnostic efforts include getting a history and performing a detailed physical examination as well as eye and neurologic examinations. Vaccination status, parasite control, travel history, response to previous medications, and the presence of illness in other animals (including people) will be reviewed. Initial laboratory tests include complete blood tests, urinalysis, and usually chest and abdomen x-rays.

For further diagnostic efforts, some initial tests may need to be repeated (particularly the physical examination), and more specialized tests may be needed, depending on results of the initial tests or to more specifically investigate the most common known causes of fever of unknown origin. These tests might include additional blood tests; specialized tests for infectious diseases; withdrawal and testing of joint fluid; an ultrasound of the abdomen, chest, or heart; aspiration or biopsies of the bone marrow, lymph nodes, or other tissues to examine the cells of these tissues; analysis and bacterial cultures of various body fluids; x-rays of the bones, joints, or spinal cord; computed tomography (CT) or magnetic resonance imaging (MRI); or exploratory surgery.

Treatment

In some fever of unknown origin cases a specific diagnosis cannot be found, or diagnostic testing is discontinued, and different treatments are tried without a diagnosis. Options include antibiotics, antifungal agents, and anti-inflammatory or immunosuppressive therapy. Although trial therapy can resolve the clinical signs or may confirm a tentative diagnosis, it can also carry significant risk, and careful monitoring is needed.

In true fever, the high body temperature is being regulated by the body, so cooling methods such as water baths work against the body's own regulatory mechanisms. It is also likely that fever itself has some beneficial effects, particularly in infectious diseases. However, fever can lead to loss of appetite, loss of energy, and dehydration. Because of this, animals with fever of unknown origin may benefit from intravenous fluid therapy or from the use of fever-reducing medications.

■ MALIGNANT HYPERTHERMIA

Malignant hyperthermia is seen mostly in swine, but it has also been reported in dogs (especially Greyhounds), cats, and horses. This syndrome is characterized by abnormally high body temperature, muscle rigidity, a very rapid and irregular heartbeat, increased breathing rate, bluish tinge to skin and mucous membranes, unstable blood pressure, fluid buildup in the lungs, impaired blood coagulation, kidney failure, and death.

Malignant hyperthermia is consistently triggered in susceptible animals by excitement, apprehension, exercise, or environmental stress. Giving certain anesthetics or specific drugs that affect the neurologic and muscular systems also consistently triggers malignant hyperthermia in susceptible animals.

Diagnosis is based on development of clinical signs in an animal that has been given an anesthetic agent or is participating in a stressful event. Signs can develop slowly or rapidly and include muscle stiffness, twitching, a rapid heartbeat, and an increased breathing rate. Animals that are not under anesthesia may show open-mouthed breathing and an increased breathing rate, followed by a temporary break in breathing. Blanching and redness of the skin followed by blotchy blue tinges can be seen in light-colored animals. Body temperature increases rapidly and can reach 113°F (45°C).

Many laboratory tests have been developed to help identify animals susceptible to malignant hyperthermia, but they are not useful for diagnosis of malignant hyperthermia in a sudden crisis.

Treatment and Prevention

Usually, malignant hyperthermia episodes come on suddenly and are very severe. If the condition is recognized early in an animal under anesthesia, supportive measures may be able to save the animal. Unfortunately, regardless of treatment, malignant hyperthermia is usually fatal.

Stress must be minimized to prevent malignant hyperthermia episodes in individual animals. If an animal that is suspected to be susceptible to malignant hyperthermia (or that has survived a previous episode) needs anesthesia and surgery, certain precautions should be taken. These include administering a drug called dantrolene 1 to 2 days before anesthesia and avoiding certain anesthetic agents. Certain local anesthetics are also safe to use. All procedures must be kept as short as possible because malignant hyperthermia happens most often when the animal has been under anesthesia for longer than 1 hour. Although these precautions cannot prevent malignant hyperthermia, they can reduce the chances of a crisis developing.

Whenever a case of malignant hyperthermia is suspected, owners of siblings and breeders should be notified if possible. However, malignant hyperthermia is not always linked to a pedigree line.

CHAPTER **19**

Disorders Affecting Multiple Body Systems

▓ INTRODUCTION

There are many disorders that can affect multiple parts of the body. These may be caused by bacteria, viruses, poisonous or toxic substances in the environment, and other health hazards. Disorders affecting multiple body systems can also be inherited or develop while the animal is still in the womb. Diseases or conditions that involve multiple organ systems may also be described as systemic or generalized.

Many disorders are discussed in this chapter. A listing of congenital and inherited conditions is followed by a discussion of the most significant disorders, which have been arranged alphabetically by medical name to help you locate a particular disease or condition easily.

▓ CONGENITAL AND INHERITED DISORDERS

A variety of structural and functional defects have been described in animals. These birth defects are usually classified by the body system primarily affected, and many are discussed in this book under the appropriate body system section. Defective newborns have survived a disruptive event during embryonic or fetal development. Defective development may also cause embryonic loss, fetal death, mummification, abortion, stillbirth, or a newborn not capable of living.

Susceptibility to environmental agents or genetic abnormalities varies with the stage of development and species, and decreases with fetal age. The fertilized egg is resistant to agents or factors that cause or increase the chances of a congenital defect (teratogens), but it is susceptible to genetic mutations and changes in the chromosomes. The embryo is highly susceptible to teratogens, but this susceptibility decreases with age as the critical developmental periods of various organs or organ systems are passed. The fetus becomes increasingly resistant to teratogens except for structures that develop late such as the cerebellum, palate, urinary system, and genitals.

The frequency of individual defects varies with the species, breed, geographic location, season, and other environmental factors. It is estimated to occur at a rate of 0.2 to 3.5% of all canine births. Commonly reported congenital and inherited defects in dogs include neurologic defects, eye defects, heart defects, skeletal muscle defects, failure of one or both testicles to descend into the scrotum (known as cryptorchidism), and hip and elbow abnormalities. Most congenital defects have no clearly established cause; others are caused by genetic or environmental factors or interaction between these factors.

Genetic Factors

Inherited defects resulting from mutant genes or chromosome abnormalities tend to occur in patterns of inheritance. Such patterns include dominant (in which the defect will occur if either parent supplies an abnormal gene to its offspring), recessive (in which both parents must supply an abnormal gene) or others, such as sex-linked (in which the gene is associated with the X chromosome and not the Y chromosome).

Some common diseases or disorders caused by genetic defects include deficiencies of particular enzymes that lead to the body's inability to perform normal metabolic functions, and chromosome abnormalities that can result in sterility, abnormal growth, increased embryonic mortality, or reduced litter size. Viruses,

certain drugs, and radiation are common causes of chromosomal damage.

The complex interaction between genetic and environmental factors is being studied and is slowly becoming better understood.

Environmental Factors

Factors tending to produce abnormalities of formation include toxic plants, viral infections that occur during pregnancy, drugs, trace elements, nutritional deficiencies, and physical agents such as radiation, abnormally high body temperature, uterine positioning, and pressure during rectal examination. These factors may be difficult to identify, often follow seasonal patterns and stress, and may be linked to maternal disease. They do not follow the pattern of family inheritance that is shown by genetic changes.

◾ ACTINOBACILLOSIS

Actinobacillosis is caused by bacteria in the genus *Actinobacillus*. Several different forms of disease occur, depending on the particular species of *Actinobacillus* involved and the type of animal infected. Soft tissue infections are common, and lymph node involvement is frequently a step in the spread of the disease throughout the animal's entire body. Bony tissue close to infected muscles or other tissue may also be infected.

One type of *Actinobacillus* occasionally causes tumorous abscesses of the tongue in dogs, a condition often called "wooden tongue." The organism may also cause abnormalities in soft tissues of the head, neck, limbs, and occasionally the lungs, pleura (membranes lining the chest cavity), and tissue under the skin. The organism is normally found in the mucus of the upper gastrointestinal tract. It causes disease when it gains access to adjacent soft tissue through penetrating wounds. The organism causes localized infections and can spread through the lymphatic (immune) system to other tissues.

This form of actinobacillosis is found worldwide, but is sporadic and thus diffi-

---

Commonly Reported Congenital and Inherited Defects in Dogs

- Neurologic defects (*see also* page 200)
- Digestive tract defects (*see also* page 82)
- Heart defects (*see also* page 58)
- Skeletal muscle defects (*see also* page 179)
- Cryptorchidism (apparent absence of one or both testicles; *see also* page 218)
- Hip or elbow dysplasia (*see also* page 184)

Many other congenital and inherited conditions are also reported in dogs, though they are less common. Please see individual body system chapters for more information.

cult to prevent. Treatment may include surgical removal of the infected tissue, potassium iodide given by mouth, or antibiotics.

▓ ACTINOMYCOSIS

Actinomyces bacteria normally live in the mouth and in the nasal passages near the throat. Several species are associated with diseases in dogs.

Actinomyces bovis has been identified infrequently in infections in dogs and other mammals. Disease occurs when this bacterium is introduced to underlying soft tissue through penetrating wounds of the mouth (such as those that occur from carrying sharp objects in the mouth or running through underbrush). Involvement of the nearby bone frequently results in facial distortion, loose teeth (making chewing difficult), and difficulty breathing due to swelling of the nasal cavity. Treatment is rarely successful in longterm cases in which bone is extensively involved, due to poor penetration of antibacterial drugs into the infected area. In less advanced cases, your veterinarian may prescribe an antibiotic.

Actinomyces hordeovulneris causes abscesses on the liver and spleen and generalized infections, such as inflammation of the cavity surrounding the lungs, inflammation of the lining of the stomach, and bacterial arthritis in dogs. One factor that appears to be related to infection with this organism is the presence of foxtail grass (*Hordeum* species) particles that have migrated into the body tissues, allowing penetration of the bacteria. Treatment includes surgical removal of the contaminated tissue and drainage, followed by longterm treatment with an antibiotic.

Actinomyces viscosus causes chronic pneumonia, inflammation of the cavity surrounding the lungs, and abscesses under the skin in dogs. Lesions generally develop after a traumatic injury such as a bite wound. Treatment of inflammation of the chest cavity with an antibiotic may be successful if begun early in the disease course. Treatment is more likely to be successful with a localized infection under the skin, which your veterinarian will also treat with an antibiotic.

▓ AMYLOIDOSIS

Amyloidosis is a condition that occurs when **amyloid**, a substance composed of abnormally folded protein, is deposited in various organs of the body. Some types of amyloidosis are hereditary in dogs. (Chinese Shar-Peis are known to be at risk for hereditary amyloidosis.) Others occur as a result of diseases such as heartworm infection, various cancers, or other inflammatory or immune-related conditions. However, the cause is often unknown.

Amyloid can be deposited throughout the body, or in just one specific area. This causes damage by displacing normal cells. The disease can become fatal if amyloid is deposited into the tissue of critical organs, such as the kidneys, liver, or heart. All domestic mammals may develop amyloidosis, and aged animals commonly have minor deposits of amyloid without signs or problems.

There are several types of amyloid, and the classification of amyloidosis is based on which amyloid protein is involved. Deposits of **AA amyloid** can result from chronic inflammatory diseases, chronic bacterial infections, and cancer. The amyloid is usually deposited in organs such as the spleen or kidneys. The animal may not show any signs of disease. If AA amyloid is deposited in the kidneys, it can lead to a buildup of protein and result in kidney failure. **AL amyloid** is another common form of amyloid. AL amyloid tends to be deposited in nerve tissue and joints.

Because of its wide distribution and stealthy onset, amyloidosis is difficult to diagnose. However, your veterinarian might suspect amyloidosis if your dog has a chronic infection or inflammation and develops kidney or liver failure. No specific treatment can prevent the development of amyloidosis or promote the reabsorption of the protein deposits.

ANTHRAX

Anthrax is an often fatal infectious disease that can infect all warm-blooded animals, including dogs and humans. Underdiagnosis and unreliable reporting make it difficult to estimate the true rate of occurrence of anthrax worldwide; however, anthrax has been reported from nearly every continent. Under normal circumstances, anthrax outbreaks in the United States are extremely rare. Anthrax received much attention in 2001 in relation to the terrorist attacks on the United States because of its potential use as a biological weapon.

Anthrax is caused by infection with bacteria known as *Bacillus anthracis*. This bacterium forms spores, which make it extremely resistant to environmental conditions, such as heating, freezing, chemical disinfection, or dehydration that typically destroy other types of bacteria. Thus, it can persist for a long time within or on a contaminated environment or object. Livestock may consume the spores while grazing; however, the most common source of infection in dogs is from raw or poorly cooked contaminated meat or contact with the blood, tissues, or body fluids of infected animals that harbor spores. Although the inhalation of anthrax spores is a concern in humans, the dog appears to be quite resistant to infection by this route of exposure. A skin form of anthrax exists in humans, but this route is also thought to be of minimal significance in dogs.

After exposure to the bacteria, the typical incubation period is 3 to 7 days. Once the bacteria infect an animal or human, the organisms multiply and spread throughout the body. They produce a potent and lethal toxin that causes cell death and breakdown of the tissues infected with the bacteria. This results in inflammation and organ damage, eventually leading to organ failure. The bacteria spread throughout the body through the blood and lymphatic (immune) system.

Dogs may develop sudden, severe (acute) blood poisoning after ingesting *Bacillus anthracis* bacteria. This may lead to a rapid swelling of the throat, and sudden death. More often, a mild, chronic form is seen, in which dogs show generalized signs of illness and gradually recover with treatment. Intestinal involvement is seldom recognized because the signs (such as loss of appetite, vomiting, diarrhea or constipation) are so nonspecific.

A diagnosis based on signs is difficult because many infections and other conditions (such as poisoning), may have signs similar to anthrax. Diagnosis thus requires laboratory analysis of blood samples from the potentially infected individual to confirm the presence of the bacteria.

Anthrax is controlled through vaccination programs in large animals (such as cattle), rapid detection and reporting, quarantine, treatment of any animals exposed to the bacteria, and the burning or burial of suspected and confirmed fatal cases. In most countries, all cases of anthrax must be reported to the appropriate regulatory officials. Cleaning and disinfection of any bedding, cages, or other possibly contaminated materials is necessary to prevent further spread of the disease. Because anthrax spores are resistant to many disinfectants, check with a health official as to proper procedures for decontaminating inanimate objects. If a pet is exposed to anthrax, the fur should be decontaminated to avoid transmission to humans. Currently, no chemicals that kill spores are considered safe for use on animals; therefore, repeated bathing is necessary to mechanically remove the organism.

Human cases of anthrax may follow contact with contaminated animals or animal products. Anthrax is not directly communicable by usual social contact from one infected animal to another animal, between animal and human, or between human and human, even in the case of anthrax pneumonia. For infection to occur, spores must gain access to the new victim by ingestion, inhalation, or through open wounds. When transmission occurs between individuals it is usually through exposure to infected tissue or body fluids. Therefore, humans should use strict precautions (wearing gloves, protective clothing, goggles, and masks) when handling potentially infected animals or their remains.

BOTULISM

Botulism is a motor paralysis caused by eating food containing the toxin (a poisonous substance) produced by *Clostridium botulinum*. This bacterium grows rapidly in decomposing animal tissue and sometimes in plant material. It results in rapid death due to the paralysis of vital organs. Botulism is not an infection. The paralysis is caused by the consumption of the toxin in food.

There are 7 types of *Clostridium botulinum*; the C_1 type is most common in animals. The usual source of the toxin is decaying carcasses or spoiled vegetation. Botulism occurs only sporadically in dogs.

The signs of botulism are caused by muscle paralysis and include progressive motor paralysis, disturbed vision, difficulty chewing and swallowing, and progressive weakness. Death is usually due to paralysis of the lungs or heart. Treatment is usually not possible, although a few experimental therapies have had limited success.

CANINE DISTEMPER (HARDPAD DISEASE)

Canine distemper is a highly contagious, whole body, viral disease of dogs. It is characterized by fever, loss of white blood cells, and inflammation of the lungs and brain. The disease is seen worldwide in *Canidae* (dogs, foxes, wolves), *Mustelidae* (including ferrets, mink, and skunks), and several other species of wild animals.

Most cases of canine distemper develop after an animal breathes in the virus from droplets of moisture exhaled by an infected animal (aerosol route). Some infected dogs may spread the infectious virus for several months after outward signs of the disease have passed.

A short fever usually occurs 3 to 6 days after infection. During this stage of the disease, blood tests might show low white blood cell counts. These signs may go unnoticed or be accompanied by loss of appetite. The fever subsides for several days before a second fever occurs. The second fever lasts less than 1 week and may be accompanied by a discharge from the nose and eyes and loss of appetite. Gastrointestinal and respiratory signs may follow and are usually complicated by bacterial infections. Overgrowth of the skin of the footpads ("hardpad" disease) and the nose may be seen. Signs of central nervous system involvement are frequently seen in dogs with this overgrowth. These signs often include: 1) localized involuntary twitching of a muscle or group of muscles, such as in the leg or face, 2) slight or complete paralysis, often most noticeable in the hind limbs as failure of muscle coordination, followed by weakness and paralysis in all 4 legs, and 3) convulsions with drooling and chewing movements of the jaw ("chewing-gum fits").

The seizures become more frequent and severe as the disease progresses. The dog may fall on its side and paddle its legs. Involuntary urination and defecation often occur. Infection may be mild with few or no signs, or it may lead to severe disease showing most of the above signs. The course of the disease may be as short as 10 days, but the onset of neurologic signs may be delayed for several weeks or months.

Inflammation of the brain in longterm distemper is often marked by lack of coordination and compulsive movements such as head pressing or continual pacing. These signs may be seen in adult dogs without a history of signs related to canine distemper. The development of neurologic signs is often progressive. Dogs with this form of the disease do not spread it to other dogs.

Your veterinarian will consider distemper infection any time a puppy is feverish and has signs of widespread infection. While the typical case is not difficult to diagnose, the characteristic signs sometimes fail to appear until late in the disease. The infected dog may have other viral and bacterial infections that can complicate the picture Thus, blood work and other tests may be required to confirm the diagnosis.

Treatment is designed to limit bacterial invasion, support fluid balance, and control nervous system problems. Antibiotics, fluids, dietary supplements, medication to reduce fever, analgesics, and anticonvulsants are used as appropriate for the individual dog. No single treatment is specific or uniformly successful. Dogs may recover completely from the infection, but good nursing care is essential. Even with intensive care, some dogs do not make a satisfactory recovery. Unfortunately, treatment for the neurologic problems of distemper is usually not successful. If the neurologic signs are severe or continue to worsen, it may be appropriate to have the dog euthanized. Dogs with some of the longterm, progressive forms of neurologic distemper have responded to immune system treatment with antiinflammatory drugs or steroids.

Vaccination is the most widely used and best available prevention for canine distemper. Puppies should be vaccinated when they are 6 weeks old and then at 2- to 4-week intervals until they are 14 to 16 weeks old. Annual revaccination has been suggested because of the breaks in neurologic distemper that can occur in stressed or diseased dogs or those with weakened immune systems. Your veterinarian will recommend an appropriate vaccination schedule for your pet taking into consideration the health of your pet, the frequency of the disease in your area, and other risk factors.

CANINE HERPESVIRUS

Canine herpesviral infection is a severe, often fatal, disease of puppies. (It is sometimes referred to as fading or sudden death syndrome in puppies.) In adult dogs, it may be associated with upper respiratory infection or an inflammation of the vagina marked by pain and a pus-filled discharge (in females) or inflammation of the foreskin of the penis (in males).

The disease is caused by a canine herpesvirus that occurs worldwide. Transmission usually occurs by contact between susceptible puppies and the infected oral, nasal, or vaginal secretions of their dam or oral or nasal secretions of dogs allowed to come in contact with puppies during the first 3 weeks of life. Transmission may also occur prior to birth.

Death due to the infection usually occurs in puppies 1 to 3 weeks old, occasionally in puppies up to 1 month old, and rarely in puppies as old as 6 months. Typically, the onset of illness is sudden, and death occurs after an illness of less than 24 hours. Infections in the womb may be associated with abortions, stillbirths, and infertility.

No vaccine is available. Infected female dogs develop antibodies, and litters born after the first infected litter receive antibodies from the mother in the colostrum. Puppies that receive these maternal antibodies may be infected with the virus, but show no signs of disease. The outlook for puppies that survive early infection with canine herpesvirus is guarded because the disease can cause irreparable damage to the lymph nodes, brain, kidneys, and liver.

EHRLICHIOSIS AND RELATED INFECTIONS

Canine monocytic ehrlichiosis is usually caused by the rickettsia *Ehrlichia canis*, although other types of *Ehrlichia* are sometimes involved. (Rickettsiae are a specialized type of bacteria that live only inside other cells.) Carried by ticks, the organism infects a certain type of white blood cell and causes fever and other signs. A related organism, *Ehrlichia ewingi*, targets other types of white blood cells called granulocytes and has been isolated from dogs and people in the southern, western, and midwestern United States. *Anaplasma platys*, another rickettsia, causes infectious cyclic thrombocytopenia in dogs. This infection leads to periodic losses of platelets, which causes problems with blood clotting.

The *Ehrlichia* and *Anaplasma* rickettsiae are present in many parts of the world, including the United States. They are transmitted by ticks (including the brown dog tick, lone star tick, and black-legged tick) that become infected after feeding on infected animals. People, dogs, cats, and other domestic animals are accidental hosts of these disease-causing organisms.

In infections caused by *Ehrlichia canis*, signs commonly progress from short- to longterm, depending on the strain of the organism and the immune status of the host. In short-term cases, there is fever, widespread inflammation of the lymph nodes, enlargement of the spleen, and a decrease in the number of platelets in the bloodstream. In addition, there may be loss of appetite, depression, loss of stamina, stiffness and reluctance to walk, swelling of the limbs or scrotum, and coughing or difficulty in breathing. Most short-term cases are seen in the warmer months, when ticks are active. During this phase of infection, death is rare and the infected animal may recover spontaneously. The recovered dog may remain free of signs thereafter, or longterm disease may develop.

Longterm ehrlichiosis caused by *Ehrlichia canis* may develop in any breed of dog, but certain breeds (such as German Shepherds) may be predisposed. Longterm infection does not vary with the seasons. Signs depend on which organs are affected and may include enlargement of the spleen, kidney failure, and inflammation of the lungs, eye, brain and spinal cord. If the brain and spinal cord are involved, there may be problems with the nervous system, such as lack of coordination, depression, partial paralysis, and increased sensitivity to a normally painless touch. Severe weight loss is common.

Dogs infected with *Anaplasma platys* generally show minimal to no signs of infection, although the organism is present in the platelets. Infection with other rickettsiae causes signs similar to short-term *Ehrlichia canis* infection, but the disease is usually more self-limiting. Fever and a lameness that shifts from one leg to another may be present. Longterm disease (such as that seen with *Ehrlichia canis* infection) is not typically seen in other ehrlichial infections.

For treatment of all forms of infection caused by these organisms, your veterinarian will prescribe an antibiotic. The medication is usually given for a period of 10 to 21 days. Fever usually ends within 1 to 2 days after treatment begins. In longterm cases, the blood abnormalities may persist for 3 to 6 months, although relief from signs often occurs much sooner. Some dogs may also need supportive care. If the dog has widespread or severe bleeding, then transfusion with blood platelets or whole blood may be prescribed.

The most important preventive steps are those that control ticks, the most common source of the disease. Keeping your dog away from areas known to harbor ticks is a step you can take. Preventive medications that will keep your dog from being infested with ticks are also available from your veterinarian. Any ticks found on your dog should be promptly and properly removed to prevent the spread of disease. Remove any ticks by using fine-pointed tweezers to grasp the head of the tick (right where it enters the skin). Pull the tick straight off, making sure not to grasp or squeeze its body. If there are multiple ticks, it may be best to have your veterinarian remove them and examine your dog.

■ ENTEROTOXEMIA

Clostridium perfringens is a bacterium that is widely distributed in the soil and the gastrointestinal tract of animals. It has the ability to produce poisonous substances (toxins) outside of the bacterial cell. Inflammation of the intestines (enteritis) and absorption of toxins (known as enterotox-emia) occur when these poisonous substances are released. Five types of *Clostridium perfringens* have been identified, but only one, Type A, causes enterotoxemia in dogs. Type A is also associated with a rarely occurring bloody diarrhea in dogs. These organisms are also associated with chronic intermittent diarrhea in dogs but have not been confirmed as the cause.

Clostridium perfringens of an undetermined type have also been shown to multiply in the intestines of dogs with inflammation of the intestines caused by a parvovirus, but its contribution to the disease is not clear.

■ FUNGAL INFECTIONS

Funguses (also called fungi) are parasitic, spore-producing organisms. They obtain their nourishment by absorbing food from the hosts on which they grow. Many species of fungus exist in the environment, but only a very few cause infections. The primary source of most infections is soil. Fungal infections can be acquired by inhalation, ingestion, or through the skin (for example, through a cut or wound).

Some fungal infections can cause disease in otherwise healthy animals, while others require a host that is incapacitated or immunocompromised (by, for example, such stresses as captivity, poor nutrition, viral infections, cancer, or drugs like steroids) to establish infection. Prolonged use of antimicrobial drugs or immunosuppressive agents appears to increase the likelihood of some fungal infections. The infection itself may be localized or may affect the entire body (systemic or generalized).

Aspergillosis

Aspergillosis is a fungal infection caused by several *Aspergillus* species. It is found worldwide and in almost all domestic animals as well as in many wild species. It is primarily a respiratory infection that may become generalized; however, the susceptibility to fungal infections varies among species.

Nasal Aspergillosis

In dogs, aspergillosis is typically localized to the nasal cavity or paranasal sinuses and is usually caused by infection with *Aspergillus fumigatus*. Nasal aspergillosis is a relatively common disease in dogs. The disease usually remains confined to the nasal cavity or the sinuses, but it causes destruction of the delicate nasal bony structures known as turbinates. Occasionally, a very invasive infection may affect the orbit of the eye and the skull. Most cases of nasal aspergillosis occur in dogs with normal immune systems that are in otherwise good health.

Nasal aspergillosis is mainly seen in breeds of dogs with long, narrow heads and noses (such as Collies and Greyhounds). Signs of infection include a bloody nasal discharge, nasal pain, sneezing, ulceration surrounding the nostrils, and nosebleed. Your veterinarian will perform a number of tests before providing a diagnosis. Most cases of nasal aspergillosis can be successfully treated with antifungal drugs, which may be given orally or infused into the nasal cavity. Relapses are possible, but are uncommon.

Disseminated Aspergillosis

Disseminated aspergillosis, a more generalized form of infection, is more common in German Shepherds than in other breeds. *Aspergillus tereus* is the most common species of organism responsible, although other species of *Aspergillus* have been isolated occasionally. The fungus likely enters through the respiratory tract and goes to the lungs, then travels through the bloodstream where it spreads throughout the body, including the intervertebral

---

Signs of Nasal Aspergillosis in Dogs

- Profuse nasal discharge consisting of blood mixed with pus
- Nasal pain
- Ulceration surrounding the nostrils
- Nosebleed

discs of the spine, the eyes, or the kidneys. Other organs, muscles, or bones may also be affected.

Disseminated aspergillosis usually takes several months to develop. Signs of this disease include back pain progressing to partial or complete paralysis or lameness of a limb with pronounced swelling. Other, less specific, findings include poor appetite, weight loss, muscle wasting, fever, weakness, lethargy, vomiting, inflammation of the eye, and lymph node enlargement. Severely ill dogs have a poor prognosis. Most dogs die from the disseminated aspergillosis although a few have been treated successfully.

Candidiasis

Candidiasis is a localized fungal disease affecting the mucous membranes, the skin, and the gastrointestinal tract. It is distributed worldwide in a variety of animals and is most commonly caused by species of the yeast-like fungus, *Candida albicans*. Candidiasis is rare in dogs. Factors that may predispose an animal to infection include injury to any of the mucous membranes, the use of catheters, administration of antibiotics, and immunosuppressive drugs or diseases.

Signs of infection are variable and nonspecific (for example, diarrhea, weakness, skin lesions) and may be associated more with the primary or predisposing conditions than with the candidiasis infection itself. An ointment or topical application may be useful in the treatment of oral or skin candidiasis. Your veterinarian may also recommend different drugs given by mouth or through the vein for treatment of infected dogs.

Coccidioidomycosis (Valley Fever)

Coccidioidomycosis is a dustborne, noncontagious infection caused by the fungus *Coccidioides immitis*. Infections are limited to dry, desertlike regions of the southwestern United States and the valleys of southern California. Similar geographic areas of Mexico and Central and South America are also affected.

Signs of Coccidioidomycosis (Valley Fever) in Dogs

Coccidioidomycosis is primarily a chronic respiratory disease, but canine infections can spread to many tissues, especially eyes and bone. Dogs with generalized disease may have the following signs:

- Chronic cough
- Loss of appetite
- General ill health and malnutrition
- Lameness
- Enlarged joints
- Fever
- Intermittent diarrhea
- Spread to the skin with draining ulceration may occur (primary infection through the skin is rare)

While many species of animals, including humans, are susceptible, only dogs are affected significantly. Inhalation of fungal spores (often carried on dust particles) is the only established mode of infection. Epidemics may occur when rainy periods are followed by drought, resulting in dust storms. Coccidioidomycosis is primarily a chronic respiratory disease, but canine infections can spread throughout the dog's body infecting many tissues, especially eyes and bone. Signs can vary greatly, depending on which organs are involved and the severity of infection. Dogs with disseminated disease may have a persistant cough, poor appetite, general ill health and malnutrition, lameness, enlarged joints, fever, and intermittent diarrhea. The skin may become ulcerated.

Many dogs exposed to the fungal spores will fight off the infection without showing any signs at all. In some dogs that develop signs, the disease will resolve without treatment. However, if chronic respiratory signs occur or the infection involves many body organs and tissues, longterm antifungal treatment is needed. In cases where the infection has spread, treatment of at least 6 to 12 months is typical. With treatment, the likelihood of recovery from the primary (respiratory) form is quite good. Recovery in the disseminated case varies with the location and severity, and must be considered guarded. There is no known prevention other than decreasing your pet's exposure to desert soil and dust in areas where the fungus occurs.

Cryptococcosis

Cryptococcosis is a fungal disease that may affect the respiratory tract (especially the nasal cavity), central nervous system, eyes, and skin. The causal fungus, *Cryptococcus neoformans*, is found worldwide in soil and bird manure, especially in pigeon droppings. Transmission is by inhalation of spores or contamination of wounds. Immunosuppressed humans and animals are at increased risk for developing cryptococcosis.

In dogs, the disease often spreads throughout the body, with central nervous system or eye involvement. Nonspecific signs of illness are most common and often include weight loss and lethargy. Central nervous system problems may also occur, such as head tilt, the back-and-forth eye movements called nystagmus, paralysis of the facial nerve leading to inability to blink, poor coordination, circling, and seizures. Eye problems, such as bleeding in the retina and inflammation of the eye also are common. Other tissues that may be affected include the kidneys, lymph nodes, spleen, liver, thyroid, adrenal glands, pancreas, bone, gastrointestinal tract, and muscles.

Various antifungal drugs may be prescribed for the treatment of cryptococcosis; but most affected pets require prolonged treatment (up to several months), depending on the severity and extent of the disease. Treatment for cryptococcosis may include surgery to remove lesions in the nasal cavity or on the bridge of the nose. The outlook for recovery is poor when infected dogs have widespread nervous system involvement.

Geotrichosis

Geotrichosis is a rare fungal infection caused by *Geotrichum candidum*, a fungus of soil, decaying organic matter, and contaminated food. This fungus is part of the normal flora of the mouth and intestinal tract in humans. The organism can cause generalized disease in dogs. Signs of infection vary based on the organs involved and may include coughing, fever, poor appetite, excessive intake of water, progressive difficulty in breathing, vomiting, and jaundice (yellow appearance of the skin and mucous membranes). The disease may progress rapidly.

Treatment for disseminated geotrichosis has not been standardized. Your veterinarian will be aware of the most recent medical information and prescribe a treatment program tailored to your pet and the extent and severity of infection.

Histoplasmosis

Histoplasmosis is a noncontagious infection caused by the fungus *Histoplasma capsulatum*, which is found worldwide. The organism responsible for the disorder is a soil fungus that is widely distributed (particularly by bird and bat populations) in the midwestern and southern United States, especially in river valleys and plains. Infection occurs when spores in the air are inhaled. The lungs and the lymph nodes in the chest are the sites of primary infection, although the gastrointestinal tract may be affected in dogs. The organisms enter the bloodstream from the primary site of infection and become dispersed throughout the body; they may localize in bone marrow or the eyes.

The signs vary and are nonspecific, reflecting the various organ involvements. Occasionally, dogs with lung involvement show signs of fever, labored breathing, and coughing. The lung infection usually resolves on its own. However, if the respiratory infection extends to other tissues, a more serious, disseminated form of the disease may develop, involving a large number of organs and body systems. The organs most often involved are the lungs, intestine, lymph nodes, liver, spleen and bone marrow. Signs of illness such as depression, fever, and poor appetite are common, as well as chronic diarrhea, intestinal blood loss, anemia, and weight loss. In a few dogs, infection of the bones, eyes, skin, and central nervous system may occur. Diagnosis requires identification of the fungus in body fluids or tissues.

Treatment of disseminated histoplasmosis is difficult. It requires the use of antifungal drugs and supportive treatment such as adequate nutrition, additional liquids (hydration), and control of secondary bacterial infections. Antifungal treatment must be continued for prolonged periods of time and may be expensive.

Mycetomas

Mycetomas are infections of the skin and underlying tissues that have the appearance of nodules or tumors. When such lesions are caused by funguses, they are known as **eumycotic mycetomas**. The fungus proliferates in the lesions and organizes into aggregates known as granules or grains. Granules may be of various colors and sizes, depending on the species of fungus involved.

Most eumycotic mycetomas are confined to the tissue beneath the skin, but some may be extensions of fungal infections in the abdomen. Inflammation of the membrane lining the abdominal walls or abdominal masses is typically seen with cases of white-grain mycetomas. Black-grain mycetomas are usually characterized by skin nodules on the legs and feet or on the face. When the feet or limbs are involved, the infection may extend to the underlying bone.

The outlook for abdominal mycetomas is guarded because tissue involvement is usually extensive. Skin mycetomas, while not life-threatening, are often difficult to resolve. Surgical removal, including limb amputation, may be the only effective treatment for some cases of skin mycetomas. Antifungal medication has been reported as effective in only a few cases.

North American Blastomycosis

North American blastomycosis, caused by the fungus *Blastomyces dermatitidis*, is generally limited to geographically re-

stricted areas in the Mississippi, Missouri, Tennessee, and Ohio River basins and along the Great Lakes and the St. Lawrence Seaway. Beaver dams and other habitats where soil is moist, acidic, and rich in decaying vegetation may serve as the ecologic niche for the organism, which has also been found in pigeon and bat feces.

This fungus exists in 2 different forms: a **mycelial form** (this form is present in the environment and is contagious) and **yeast** (this form is found in the tissues and is not contagious). The mycelial form of blastomycosis can easily infect both animals and humans. When respiratory defenses are overwhelmed or immunosuppressed, the infection spreads from the lungs through the bloodstream. Infection can occur through the skin but spread from a lung infection is much more common.

Young male dogs, especially hunting dogs, are at increased risk presumably because of increased contact with contaminated soil. The prognosis depends on the extent and severity of lung involvement. In dogs, blastomycosis most commonly affects the lungs (up to 85% of cases), eyes, skin, and bones.

Most affected animals have signs such as coughing, fever, lethargy, loss of appetite, and weight loss. In addition to the cough, lung involvement leads to exercise intolerance and difficulty breathing. The animal's peripheral lymph nodes often are enlarged. These are found under the neck, in the shoulder region, and behind the knee. Bone involvement may cause pain that results in lameness. Infection of the urogenital tract (for example the prostate gland in male dogs) occasionally may occur and cause signs like blood in the urine or difficulty urinating. Eye involvement can lead to pain, light sensitivity, and glaucoma. Involvement of the retina may lead to blindness. Draining nodules may be found in the skin.

Treatment of blastomycosis is based on the severity of the condition and other factors that must be evaluated by a veterinarian. Treatment is aimed at relief of specific signs (such as difficulty breathing, coughing, or eye problems) and elimination of the fungus from the body. Treatment may include one or more anti-fungal drugs, which are given for an extended period (often 2 months or more) until active disease is not apparent. The infection can recur in about 20% of treated dogs. The recurrence can occur months to years after treatment. Most dogs will again respond to treatment. The outlook is best for dogs without severe lung disease. The outcome is more guarded for dogs with moderate to severe lung disease, and is poorest for dogs with central nervous system involvement.

Phaeohyphomycosis

Phaeohyphomycosis is a general term for an infection by any of a number of funguses of the family Dematiaceae. This type of fungal infection is uncommon in dogs. The funguses known to cause phaeo-hyphomycosis have been recovered from decaying vegetative matter and soil all over the world.

Infection may result from fungal implantation into tissue at the site of an injury. Signs of infection are uncommon and almost invariably occur in animals that are sick or that have weakened immune systems. The most common signs include ulcerated skin nodules, upper respiratory problems (coughing and difficulty breathing), and nasal or paranasal masses. Slowly enlarging masses or nodules beneath the skin are found on the head, linings of the nasal passages, limbs, and chest. In most cases, the infection is confined to the skin and tissues beneath the skin. Surgical removal of the lesion can be a cure. Treatment with antifungal drugs may be considered in cases when surgery is not possible.

Pythiosis and Lagenidiosis

Pythiosis is a disease caused by *Pythium insidiosum*, which is not a true fungus but a water mold. It occurs in some tropical and subtropical areas of the world and is seen in warmer to temperate sections of the US. In dogs, pythiosis is most often encountered in Southeast Asia, eastern coastal Australia, South America, and the United States, especially along the Gulf coast and parts of California. In the US, the disease most often is seen in fall and winter months.

These organisms cause disease when animals come into contact with the infecting zoospores in water, usually by ingestion. Pythiosis most often affects the gastrointestinal tract in young adult dogs, especially Labrador Retrievers. The usual site of infection is the stomach and the adjacent intestinal tissues, but any part of the gastrointestinal tract may be infected. Affected dogs often will have a history of upper gastrointestinal tract obstruction and may have an abdominal mass the veterinarian can feel during examination. Common signs include vomiting, weight loss, and loss of appetite. The weight loss can be severe, but affected dogs usually do not appear generally ill until the infection is well advanced.

Less frequently, dogs will have a pythiosis infection concentrated in the skin and adjacent tissues. A wound has usually allowed the entry of the infective zoospores into the skin tissues. Many of these animals have a history of swimming or being in "swampy" areas. Non-healing, tumor-like nodules may be present. They often grow rapidly. Some lesions may have a focused area of dead cells and a spongy appearance. Such lesions are usually on the legs, the wall of the chest, near the place where the tail connects to the body, or on the space between the anus and scrotum (male) or vulva (female). They can, however, be seen anywhere on the body.

Lagenidiosis is a disease involving the skin, the area beneath the skin, and multiple parts of the body. It has been recently reported in dogs from the southern United States. Lagenidiosis also is caused by a water mold (*Lagenidium* species). Lagenidiosis is very similar to the skin form of pythiosis. However, multi-organ involvement occurs more frequently in lagenidiosis.

Dogs exposed to warm, standing fresh water are more likely to be in contact with the infectious zoospores and may have increased risk for both pythiosis and lagenidiosis. Reports of animals being infected with no known history of being near water suggests that animals may be infected by contact with resistant spores that form in wet soil and on grass.

The treatment of choice for pythiosis and lagenidiosis has been aggressive surgery to remove infected tissue, but the disease is often too extensive at the time of diagnosis to allow complete removal. Whenever possible, complete amputation of affected limbs may be curative. Your veterinarian may recommend surgery followed by treatment with antifungal drugs. Approximately 20% of dogs will respond to longterm antifungal treatment. For most infections the prognosis is guarded to poor even though there have been advances in treatment.

Recently, a newly formulated vaccine has been reported to successfully treat cutaneous pythiosis in dogs. The effectiveness of the vaccine is not well established, and the vaccine is not entirely without risk; there is a possibility of complications caused by abscesses at the site of vaccine injection.

Rhinosporidiosis

Rhinosporidiosis is a chronic, nonfatal, infection, primarily of the lining of the nasal passages and, occasionally, of the skin. It is caused by the fungus *Rhinosporidium seeberi*. Uncommon in North America, it is seen most often in India, Africa, and South America.

Infection is characterized by polyp-like growths that may be soft, pink, crumbly, lobular with roughened surfaces, and large enough to obstruct or close off the nasal passages. The skin lesions may be single or multiple, attached at a base, or have a stem-like connection.

Surgical removal of the lesions is considered to be the standard treatment, but recurrence is common.

Sporotrichosis

Sporotrichosis is a sporadic chronic disease caused by *Sporothrix schenckii*. The organism is found around the world in soil, vegetation, and timber. In the United States *S. schenckii* is most commonly found in coastal regions and river valleys. Infection usually results when the organism enters the body through skin wounds via contact with plants or soil or penetrating foreign objects such as a sharp branch. Transmission of the disease from animals to humans can occur.

The infection may remain localized to the site of entry (involving only the skin) or may spread to nearby lymph nodes. Although generalized illness is not seen initially, chronic illness may result in fever, listlessness, and depression. Rarely, infection will spread through the bloodstream or tissue from the initial site of inoculation to the bone, lungs, liver, spleen, testes, gastrointestinal tract, or central nervous system.

Longterm treatment with antifungal drugs (continued 3 to 4 weeks beyond apparent cure) is usually recommended. Because sporotrichosis can be passed from your pet to you, strict hygiene must be observed when handling animals with suspected or diagnosed sporotrichosis. If your pet is diagnosed with sporotrichosis, be sure to ask your veterinarian about the precautions you and every member of your family should take while your pet is ill.

■ GLANDERS (FARCY)

Glanders is a contagious, short- or longterm, usually fatal disease of horses caused by the bacterium *Burkholderia mallei*. The disease is characterized by the development of a series of ulcerating nodules. The nodules are most commonly found in the upper respiratory tract, lungs, and skin. Humans, dogs, cats, and other species are susceptible, but infections in dogs are uncommon. Infections in humans are often fatal.

Prevention and control depend on early detection and elimination of affected animals. Complete quarantine and rigorous disinfection is required for all housing and objects that have been in contact with the infected animal. Euthanasia is usually recommended for infected animals. (For a more detailed discussion of GLANDERS, *see* page 805.)

▓ INFECTIOUS CANINE HEPATITIS

Infectious canine hepatitis is a worldwide, contagious disease of dogs with signs that vary from a slight fever and congestion of the mucous membranes to severe depression, severe reduction in white blood cells, and deficiency of blood clotting. In recent years, the disease has become uncommon in areas where routine vaccination is used.

Infectious canine hepatitis is caused by a virus, canine adenovirus 1. Consumption of urine, feces, or saliva from infected dogs is the most common route of infection. Recovered dogs shed virus in their urine for at least 6 months. The virus targets the liver, kidneys, spleen, and lungs, though other organs are occasionally involved. Longterm kidney damage and clouding of the cornea of the eye ("blue eye") result from immune-complex reactions after recovery from the disease.

Signs vary from a slight fever to death. The mortality rate is highest in very young dogs. The first sign is a fever higher than 104°F (40°C), which lasts 1 to 6 days and usually occurs in 2 stages. If the fever is of short duration, a low white blood cell count may be the only other sign. If the fever lasts for more than 1 day, other signs of illness, such as an increased heart rate, develop. On the day after the initial temperature rise, the white blood cell count drops and stays low throughout the feverish period. The severity of the fever seems to relate to the severity of the infection. Other signs of infection include apathy, loss of appetite, thirst, inflammation of the eyes, and a watery discharge from the eyes and nose. Occasionally there may be abdominal pain and vomiting. The nose and mouth may be reddened or covered with small bruises. Enlarged tonsils and swelling of the head, neck, and trunk may occur.

It may be difficult to get an infected dog's blood to clot. Respiratory signs may be seen in a few dogs with infectious canine hepatitis. Although central nervous system involvement is unusual, severely infected dogs may develop convulsions from brain damage. Slight paralysis, caused by bleeding in the brain, may also occur. After recovery, dogs eat well but regain weight slowly.

Usually, the abrupt onset and bleeding suggest a diagnosis of infectious canine hepatitis, but laboratory tests are needed for confirmation.

Because of blood loss, blood transfusions may be necessary to treat severely ill dogs. In addition, intravenous fluids are often provided. Your veterinarian will likely recommend treatment with a broad-spectrum antibiotic. Although the clouding of the cornea of the eye usually requires no treatment, the veterinarian may prescribe an eye ointment to alleviate the painful spasm that is sometimes associated with it. Dogs with corneal clouding should be protected against bright light.

Vaccination is the mostly widely used preventive step and is usually given along with canine distemper vaccinations. Annual revaccination against infectious canine hepatitis is often recommended.

▓ LEISHMANIASIS (VISCERAL LEISHMANIASIS)

Leishmaniasis is a chronic, severe disease of humans, dogs, and certain rodents caused by single-celled protozoa of the genus *Leishmania*. Visceral leishmaniasis is characterized by skin lesions, disease of the lymph nodes, weight loss, anemia, lameness, and kidney failure. Occasionally, there may be bleeding from the nose or eye lesions.

Infection in dogs is prevalent in Central and South America, the Middle East, Asia, and the Mediterranean region. The disease is found in Foxhounds in North America. Isolated cases are diagnosed around the world in animals that have visited areas where the disease is well established.

Leishmaniasis can be transmitted from dogs to people. Humans most frequently catch this disease when they are bitten by a sand fly or other insect that has previously bitten an infected animal or human. While there are only a very few human or animal cases in the US each

A dog with leishmaniasis will often have bald patches and shedding with dry skin.

year, worldwide there are about 1.5 million cases of cutaneous leishmaniasis and 500,000 cases of visceral leishmaniasis a year. Most human cases of visceral leishmaniasis are reported in India, Bangladesh, Nepal, Sudan, and Brazil.

The incubation period is quite variable, ranging from 3 months to several years. The signs vary but may include skin lesions, weight loss, poor appetite, local or generalized disease of the lymph nodes, eye lesions, kidney failure, nosebleed, lameness, and anemia. Occasionally, some dogs have chronic diarrhea or liver failure. The most common skin lesions are areas of baldness with severe dry skin shedding, usually beginning on the head and extending to the rest of the body. Other animals develop chronic ulceration, located particularly on the head and limbs. The signs invariably progress slowly.

The most reliable diagnostic test for canine leishmaniasis is direct observation of the parasite in bone marrow or lymph node smears. If your veterinarian suspects leishmaniasis, samples of bone marrow or fluid from the lymph nodes will be taken to confirm the diagnosis.

Drug treatment is available for dogs with visceral leishmaniasis and may last up to 6 months. Relapses after treatment are common. In areas where the disease is common, rapid treatment of infected dogs, control of stray and homeless dogs, and control of sand flies are recommended. At present, there is no effective vaccine.

■ LEPTOSPIROSIS

Leptospirosis is a disease caused by bacteria in the genus *Leptospira*; there are roughly 17 species. Because the organisms survive in surface waters (such as swamps, streams, and rivers) for extended periods, the disease is often waterborne.

Dogs contract leptospirosis by direct contact with infected urine or contaminated water sources, through bite wounds, by eating infected tissue, or exposure during birth. Once in the body, leptospires spread rapidly via the lymph system to the bloodstream and then to all tissues. If the animal mounts an immune response and survives, leptospires will be cleared from most organs and the bloodstream. However, the infection persists in sites hidden from the immune system; the most common hidden site is the kidneys. Persistence in the kidneys results in a carrier state; the infected animal may shed leptospires in the urine for at least a year.

Infections may be without signs or cause various early signs, including fever, jaundice, joint or muscle pain, loss of

Signs of Leptospirosis in Dogs

Early findings are nonspecific and include:
- Fever
- Depression
- Lethargy
- Loss of appetite
- Joint or muscle pain
- Eye and nasal discharge

The disease may progress within a few days to a kidney crisis characterized by:
- Vomiting
- Dehydration
- Lumbar pain from inflammation of the kidney
- Kidney failure

appetite, weakness, and discharge from the nose or eyes. This may progress within a few days to a kidney crisis characterized by loss of appetite, vomiting, dehydration, and lumbar pain from inflammation of the kidneys. Sudden kidney failure occurs in 80 to 90% of dogs that are severely affected. In dogs that develop milder forms of kidney failure, excessive intake of water followed by excessive urination may be the primary sign.

Kidney failure and liver disease are treated with fluid treatment and other supportive measures to maintain normal fluid, electrolyte, and acid-base balance. Your veterinarian will likely recommend antibiotics to treat the cause of disease.

Commercial vaccines for dogs are available for 4 of the subtypes of leptospirosis. Vaccinated dogs may still be susceptible to infections with other subtypes. Vaccination is recommended at yearly intervals. Dogs that have recently been exposed to leptospirosis may be treated with antibiotics given by mouth for 7 to 10 days to prevent infection.

▓ LYME DISEASE (LYME BORRELIOSIS)

Lyme disease, which is caused by *Borrelia burgdorferi* bacteria and transmitted through the bite of a tick, affects domestic animals and humans. At least 3 known species of ticks can transmit Lyme disease. However, the great majority of Lyme disease transmissions are due to the bite of a very tiny tick commonly called the deer tick, or black-legged tick. The scientific name of the tick involved on the west coast is *Ixodes pacificus* and *Ixodes scapularis* elsewhere. It is important to note that ticks do not cause Lyme disease; they merely harbor and transmit the bacteria that cause it.

Although the tick, during various stages of its life cycle, prefers certain creatures—such as voles, white-footed mice, or deer—upon which to feed, it is quite willing to feed on humans or dogs. Regardless of its stage of development (larva, nymph, or adult *Ixodes* tick), if the tick carries the

bacteria in its body, people and dogs can become infected if bitten. Risk of transmission is highest during periods when the nymphs (spring) and adults (spring and fall) are actively seeking hosts.

Lyme disease in dogs has been reported in every state in the United States, but certain geographical areas are much more likely to harbor bacteria-carrying ticks than others. Areas in the United States where it occurs most often include the Atlantic seaboard, upper Midwest, and Pacific coast. The disease is actually named after the town Lyme, Connecticut where an early outbreak was first described. Lyme disease is also seen in Europe, Asia, Australia, and elsewhere. The importance of Lyme disease as a zoonotic disease is increasing. Although the rate of occurrence of the disease in a geographic area is similar in both animals and humans, animals, especially dogs, are at significantly higher risk because of their greater exposure to ticks.

The signs of Lyme disease vary. Many animals can have Lyme disease and show no signs. In dogs, the most common signs

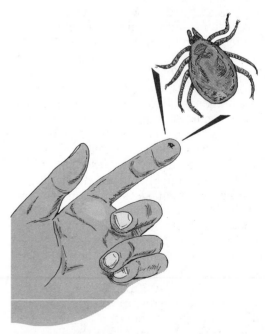

Tiny deer ticks transmit Lyme disease.

include fever, loss of appetite, painful or swollen joints, lameness that progresses from mild to severe, swollen lymph nodes, and lethargy. If Lyme disease is left untreated it can lead to damage in the kidneys, nervous system, and heart. Lyme disease affecting the kidneys is the second most common syndrome in dogs and is generally fatal. Facial paralysis and seizure disorders have been reported in the disease form affecting the nervous system. The form of the disease that affects the heart is rare.

The diagnosis of Lyme disease is often based on the signs and history. For example, a veterinarian might suspect Lyme disease in a dog with recent lameness, a mild fever, and a history that includes possible exposure to ticks. Standard blood studies are not very helpful in diagnosis because the results tend to fall within normal ranges despite signs of infection. Antibodies against the disease-causing bacteria can often be detected 4 to 6 weeks after the initial infection and help confirm the diagnosis.

Antibiotics (usually for 2 to 4 weeks) are required in all cases of Lyme disease. Rapid response is seen in limb and joint disease in most cases, although incomplete resolution of signs is seen in a significant number of affected animals. Infection in animals may persist in spite of treatment with antibiotics. Treatment directed toward the affected organ system and signs is also important, especially when the disease affects the kidneys, heart, or nerves. Some affected dogs will experience chronic, lifelong joint pain from the damage caused by the bacteria.

Tick avoidance plays a role in disease control. While highly effective products (such as sprays and monthly "spot-on" products) are available for use on dogs, they must be used consistently in order to provide effective longterm tick control. Vaccines that prevent infection in dogs are available; these appear to work best when given to dogs before they are exposed to Lyme-causing bacteria. Vaccination and annual boosters may be recommended by your veterinarian if you live in an area

Prevention of Lyme Disease

- Dogs should be routinely checked for ticks after they have been outside, especially if they have been in tall grass and brush during the spring, summer, or fall.

- Remove any ticks by using fine-pointed tweezers to grasp the head of the tick (right where it enters the skin). Pull the tick straight off, making sure not to grasp or squeeze its body.

- Dogs should be brushed regularly. Watch carefully for any ticks that are removed and capture and dispose of them before they can either reattach to the dog or migrate to other pets or people in the household.

- Dogs should be treated regularly with a readily available, effective, tick-control product. Ask your veterinarian to recommend the best product for your pet.

- In areas where Lyme disease is common, ask your veterinarian about whether vaccination is recommended.

where Lyme disease is common. Any ticks found on your dog should be promptly removed in order to help prevent transmission of Lyme disease and other diseases spread by ticks.

■ MELIOIDOSIS

Melioidosis is a bacterial infection of humans and animals. The disease-causing agent is *Burkholderia pseudomallei*, which occurs in the soil throughout southeast Asia, northern Australia, and the South Pacific. The true boundaries of this organism are unclear, as it may cause sporadic disease and outbreaks in other temperate regions. Melioidosis outbreaks have coincided with heavy rainfall, flooding, and disturbances in plumbing resulting in contamination of water supplies.

Melioidosis has been diagnosed in many animals, including dogs and humans. Species such as dogs and cats may succumb to infection due to a weakened immune system. Infection is normally transmitted from the environment to an animal rather than from animal to animal. The most common routes of infection are via skin inoculation, contamination of wounds, ingestion of soil or contaminated carcasses, or inhalation.

Signs can vary widely, and infection without signs is common. Infection may be associated with single or multiple curd-like nodules or abscesses, which can be located in any organ. When the infection enters through the skin, it often develops at distant sites without evidence of active infection at the site of entry. Pneumonia is the most common form of the disease in both animals and humans. Lameness can occur. It is possible for an infection to lie dormant before becoming apparent. Death may result in animals with sudden and intense infections or when vital organs are affected.

Treatment can be expensive and prolonged. Treatment protocols adopted for human infections are expected to have more success than the usual approach using conventional veterinary antibiotics. There is a risk that signs will return after treatment is discontinued. It is possible that this disease involves suppression of the immune system, especially in species that are less susceptible to infection. In areas where the disease-causing bacteria exist, prevention involves providing your pet with housing and sleeping areas that are not exposed to soil and providing clean drinking water that has been chlorinated and filtered (most municipal water supplies meet these requirements). Other preventive steps include restricting your pet's access to the fecal material of other animals and dead animals in the environment.

▉ NEOSPOROSIS

Neosporosis is caused by the protozoan parasite *Neospora caninum*. Neosporosis has been recognized in dogs, cattle, horses, and other animals, but the dog is the definitive host. Infection is uncommon but can be acquired by ingesting contaminated food and water, or ingesting infected tissues. It may also be transferred from

Severe neosporosis infections tend to occur in puppies.

a mother to a fetus still in the womb (transplacentally).

Both puppies and older dogs may be affected. Most severe infections occur in young puppies, which typically develop paralysis of the legs, particularly the hind legs. The paralysis is often progressive and results in rigid contracture of the muscles. In some dogs, only neurologic signs (such as inflammation of the brain and spinal cord) are seen. Disease of the peripheral nerves and spinal nerve roots appears typical of neosporosis. Skin inflammation with sores, inflammation of the liver, pneumonia, and inflammation of the brain may also occur. If not treated promptly, death is likely.

Your veterinarian will recommend proper antibiotic treatment. There is currently no vaccine.

▉ NOCARDIOSIS

Nocardiosis is a chronic, noncontagious disease caused by the bacteria of the genus *Nocardia*. These bacteria are found commonly in soil, decaying vegetation, compost, and other environmental sources. They enter the body through contamination of wounds or by inhalation. Species in this genus are found in temperate regions, as well as in tropical and subtropical areas.

Poor appetite, fever, lethargy, and weight loss are common nonspecific signs associated with all infection sites. Infections in dogs are often localized, with lesions beneath the skin, mycetomas, and inflammation of one or more lymph nodes. There may be swelling and inflammation of the gums around the teeth and ulcers in the mouth accompanied by severe bad breath. Nocardiosis affecting the chest often involves pus-producing inflammation of the chest cavity or abdominal cavity. The heart, liver, kidneys, and brain may also be affected. Occasionally, young dogs have a form of disease that begins in the lower respiratory tract after inhalation of the organism and spreads throughout the body.

Your veterinarian will prescribe antibiotics based on identification of the bacteria. Nocardial infections are resistant to some types of antibiotics. Treatment must often be continued for more than 3 months. It is important to continue treatment as directed to allow your pet the best possibility for recovery. The prognosis is guarded due to the long treatment time and the likelihood of relapse.

PERITONITIS

Peritonitis is inflammation of the membrane that lines the abdominal cavity (peritoneum). It is a serious and often fatal condition in dogs, with mortality as high as 68%. Peritonitis may be short- or long-term, localized or widespread. Most commonly it occurs due to contamination of the peritoneal cavity (for example by perforation of the abdominal cavity by a foreign object, splitting open of an abdominal wound closure, or rupture of the intestine due to the presence of a foreign object), but it also may be caused by infectious agents such as viruses or bacteria.

Fever, blood poisoning, shock, reduced blood pressure, bleeding, abdominal pain, paralytic obstruction of the intestines with reduced fecal output, and fluid accumulation may all be signs of peritonitis. Rupture of the gastrointestinal tract, with spillage of large volumes of intestinal contents, leads to short-term peritonitis. Death due to shock from the large amounts of bacterial toxins may occur suddenly.

The first priority of treatment is to stabilize the consequences of peritonitis (for example, changes in electrolytes, acid-base imbalance, fluid loss, and blood clotting abnormalities). In addition, your veterinarian will want to identify the point of origin of inflammation and correct or remove it. Antibiotics are a standard part of the treatment. Replacement fluids, electrolytes, plasma, or whole blood may be necessary to maintain heart output.

Once your pet is stabilized, surgery is done to explore the abdomen and to repair any defects. Your veterinarian will follow this with a thorough rinsing of the abdominal cavity with a saline solution, antiseptic, or antibiotics. Antibiotics are continued after surgery. Nutritional support with intravenous feeding may be needed, as many animals with peritonitis will not eat after surgery. In animals with blood poisoning and shock, fluids, electrolytes, and antibiotics are crucial elements of treatment.

PLAGUE

Plague is a sudden and sometimes fatal bacterial disease caused by *Yersinia pestis*. It is transmitted primarily by the fleas of rats and other rodents. This is the disease, often called the Black Death, that swept through Asia and then Europe in the 14th century. Over 25 million people (one third of the population) died of this disease in Europe between 1347 and 1352. Devastating outbreaks of this disease recurred with regularity throughout the next 200 years.

Today, this disease can be controlled with antibiotics and other medications; however, it has not been eradicated. Small numbers of cases occur in wild animals in the western United States and throughout the world, including Eurasia, Africa, and North and South America. On average, 10 human plague cases are reported each year in the United States; the majority are from New Mexico, California, Colorado, and Arizona. Infection in dogs is extremely rare.

Yersinia pestis is maintained in the environment in a natural cycle between susceptible rodent species and their associated fleas. Commonly affected rodent species include ground squirrels and wood rats. Dogs are usually exposed to the bacteria by oral contact with secretions or tissues of an infected rodent or rabbit or by the bite of an infected flea. Potentially, the infected fleas can be transported into homes.

Dogs are inherently resistant to the plague-causing bacteria. Dogs that do become infected with plague are less likely to show signs illness than cats. Signs of infection include fever, lethargy, inflammation of the lymph nodes below the lower jaw, a pus-like lesion along the jaw, lesions in the mouth, and cough.

Due to the rapid progression of this disease, treatment for suspected plague (and infection control practices) should be started before a definitive diagnosis is obtained. Your veterinarian will recommend an antibiotic as standard treatment.

Along with treatment and diagnostic considerations, protection of people and other animals and initiation of public health interventions are critical when an animal is suspected to have plague. Even before a diagnosis is complete, animals with signs suggestive of plague should be placed in isolation and infection control measures implemented to protect you and your family, other household pets, and any other animals or individuals that have had contact with the infected pet.

To decrease the risk of pets and humans being exposed to plague, pet owners in areas where the disease may be found should keep their pets from roaming and hunting, limit their contact with rodent or rabbit carcasses, and use appropriate flea control. Your veterinarian can suggest the most appropriate flea control product for your pet.

■ ROCKY MOUNTAIN SPOTTED FEVER (TICK FEVER)

Rocky Mountain spotted fever is a disease of humans and dogs that is caused by *Rickettsia rickettsii*. (Rickettsiae are a specialized type of bacteria that live only

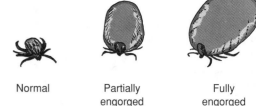

| Normal | Partially engorged | Fully engorged |

Ticks gradually enlarge as they feed. When fully engorged, they drop off.

inside other cells.) The spotted-fever group of organisms is found worldwide, but the closely related organisms within this group that cause Rocky Mountain spotted fever are only found in certain geographic areas of North, South, and Central America. They are often transmitted through the bites of infected ticks. In the United States, the American dog tick and the Rocky Mountain wood tick are considered the most important transmission agents for *Rickettsia rickettsii*.

Direct transmission from dogs to humans has not been reported. Humans can become infected following contact with tick blood and lymph fluids or excretions during the removal of engorged ticks from their pets or themselves. Human infections usually involve the transfer of tick fluids through broken skin or through the eyes.

Dogs are highly susceptible to infection. Early signs may include fever (up to 105°F [40.5°C]), loss of appetite, enlargement of the lymph nodes, inflammation of several joints together, coughing or difficulty in breathing, abdominal pain, vomiting and diarrhea, and swelling of the face or extremities. In severe cases, unraised, perfectly round, purplish red spots may be seen on the linings of the eyelids and mouth. These spots are caused by bleeding below the surfaces of these tissues. Signs of nervous system involvement, such as altered mental states and increased painful spinal sensitivity from a normally painless touch, may be seen. Between 1% and 5% of dogs with Rocky Mountain spotted fever die from the disease.

If a veterinarian suspects Rocky Mountain spotted fever, the usual response will be immediate antibiotic treatment without waiting for blood test results. Any delay in treatment may increase the chances of a severe or fatal infection. Depending on the severity of infection, supportive care for dehydration and hemorrhaging may be necessary.

The most important preventive steps are those that control ticks, the most common source of the disease. Keeping your dog away from areas known to harbor ticks is a step you can take. Preventive medications that will keep your dog from being infested with ticks are also available from your veterinarian. Any ticks found on your dog should be promptly and properly removed to prevent the spread of disease. Remove any ticks by using fine-pointed tweezers to grasp the head of the tick (right where it enters the skin). Pull the tick straight off, making sure not to grasp or squeeze its body. If there are multiple ticks, it may be best to have your veterinarian remove them and examine your dog.

■ SALMON POISONING DISEASE AND ELOKOMIN FLUKE FEVER

Salmon poisoning disease is an short-term, infectious disease of the dog family, in which the infective agent is transmitted through the various life cycle stages of a flatworm known as a fluke. The name of the disease is misleading because no poison is involved. Elokomin fluke fever resembles salmon poisoning disease but infects a wider range of animals, including members of the dog family (dogs, foxes, wolves), ferrets, bears, and raccoons. These 2 disorders occur only in the Pacific Northwest region of the United States, from San Francisco to the coast of Alaska.

Salmon poisoning disease is caused by the bacterium *Neorickettsia helminthoeca*. Sometimes the disease is complicated by a second agent, *Neorickettsia elokominica*, which causes Elokomin fluke fever. Animals become infected by eating trout, salmon, or Pacific giant salamanders that are infected with cysts that contain the larval stage of the rickettsia-infected flukes. It is the rickettsiae bacteria that cause the disease; the fluke infection itself produces few or no signs of disease. Transmission by dog to dog contact is rare.

In salmon poisoning disease, signs appear suddenly, usually 5 to 7 days after eating infected fish. In some cases, however, the onset of signs may take as long as 33 days. Signs usually continue for 7 to 10 days before culminating in death in up to 90% of untreated animals. A high fever may be seen initially, which peaks in 1 to 2 days and then gradually returns to normal. Frequently, animals have abnormally low body temperature before death. Fever is accompanied by depression and complete loss of appetite in virtually all cases. Persistent vomiting usually occurs by day 4 or 5, followed by diarrhea that may be severe or contain blood. Dehydration and extreme weight loss occur. The lymph nodes may be enlarged. Nasal or eye discharges may be present.

Elokomin fluke fever is generally a milder infection than salmon poisoning disease. The severe gastrointestinal signs seen with salmon poisoning disease are less common in Elokomin fluke fever infections. However, disease of the lymph nodes may occur more often. Death occurs in only about 10% of untreated cases. Flukes embedded in the duodenum account for little tissue damage.

In both infections, fluke eggs can usually be seen on fecal examination, which helps with the diagnosis. The eggs are oval, yellowish brown, and rough-surfaced. If your veterinarian cannot find fluke eggs in your dog's feces, then lymph fluid may be examined for evidence of the bacteria.

Currently, the only means of stopping this disease is to prevent the consumption of uncooked salmon, trout, steelhead, and similar freshwater fish. In dogs that recover, there is a strong, long-lasting immunity to future infections. However, dogs that have been infected with

Neorickettsia helminthoeca are still vulnerable to *Neorickettsia elokominica* and vice versa.

Various drugs may be given to treat these infections. Early treatment greatly increases the chances for survival. Animals that die from these infections have usually received delayed treatment. Death is often because of dehydration, electrolyte and acid-base imbalances, and anemia. Therefore, your veterinarian will prescribe general supportive treatment to maintain fluid levels and acid-base balance, while meeting nutritional requirements and controlling diarrhea. In some cases, blood transfusions may be helpful.

Dogs with tetanus usually stand with stiff legs.

■ TETANUS

Tetanus toxemia is caused by a specific poison, or toxin, that blocks inhibitory nerve signals, leading to severe muscle contractions and exaggerated muscle responses to stimuli. The toxin is produced by *Clostridium tetani* bacteria in dead tissue. Almost all mammals are susceptible to this disease, although dogs are relatively resistant.

Clostridium tetani is found in soil and intestinal tracts. In most cases, it is introduced into the body through wounds, particularly deep puncture wounds. Sometimes, the point of entry cannot be found because the wound itself may be minor or healed. The bacteria remain in the dead tissue at the original site of infection and multiply. As bacterial cells die and disintegrate, the potent nerve toxin is released. The toxin causes convulsions of the voluntary muscles.

The incubation period varies from 1 to several weeks but usually averages 10 to 14 days. Localized stiffness, often involving the jaw muscles and muscles of the neck, the hind limbs, and the region of the infected wound, is seen first. General stiffness becomes pronounced about 1 day later, and then spasms and painful sensitivity to touch become evident. Spasms are often triggered by sudden movement or noise. Because of their high resistance to tetanus toxin, dogs often have a long incubation period and frequently develop tetanus that is localized to the area of the wound. However, generalized tetanus does develop, in which the ears are erect, the tail is stiff and extended, and the mouth is partially open with the lips drawn back.

In the early stages of the disease, your veterinarian may recommend muscle relaxants, tranquilizers, or sedatives along with tetanus antitoxin. This treatment is supported by draining and cleaning the wounds and administering antibiotics.

Good nursing is invaluable during the early period of spasms. If your pet has tetanus and will be returning home with you rather than staying in a clinic, be sure to follow the nursing care instructions fully and carefully.

■ TOXOPLASMOSIS

Toxoplasmosis is caused by *Toxoplasma gondii*, a protozoan parasite that infects humans and other warmblooded animals. It is found worldwide.

Felines (members of the cat family) are the only definitive hosts of the parasite. Both wild and domestic cats serve as the main reservoir of infection. (For a more detailed discussion of TOXOPLASMOSIS, *see* page 545.) In dogs, a generalized infection may occur as the parasites travel through the body and invade the tissues.

Adult animals with vigorous immune systems control the spread of the parasite efficiently; therefore, toxoplasmosis usually causes no signs in healthy dogs. However, in puppies, the parasites may spread throughout the body. Signs of infection include fever, diarrhea, cough, difficulty breathing, jaundice, seizures, and death. Adult animals with weakened immune systems are extremely susceptible to developing sudden, generalized toxoplasmosis.

In many cases, treatment is not necessary. If warranted, your veterinarian will prescribe antibiotics to treat toxoplasmosis. Anticonvulsant medications may be used to control seizures. Fluids or other medication given by intravenous injection may be necessary for animals that are dehydrated or severely debilitated due to the infection.

◼ TRICHINELLOSIS (TRICHINOSIS)

Trichinellosis is a parasitic disease that can be transmitted to people. It is caused by a type of worm known as a nematode. The name of the disease comes from the scientific name for the worm, *Trichinella spiralis.* Humans become infected when they eat undercooked infected meat, usually pork or bear, although other animals can also be infected with this nematode. Natural infections occur in wild meat-eating animals; most mammals are susceptible.

Infection occurs when an animal eats meat with cysts containing the *Trichinella* larvae. The life cycle continues inside the animal, with larvae eventually migrating throughout the body, where they form cysts in muscles. Larvae may remain viable in the cysts for years, and their development continues only if ingested by another suitable host. If larvae pass through the intestine and are eliminated in the feces before maturation, they may be infective to other animals.

Generally, there are no signs of the disease, and most infections in domestic and wild animals go undiagnosed. In humans,

---

Preventing Trichinellosis (Trichinosis)

Trichinosis is a parasitic disease caused by the growth of infective cysts in muscle tissue. Human infections are usually caused by eating undercooked infected meat, usually pork. To protect yourself and your pets, be sure to cook meat to an internal temperature of at least 145°F (63°C). Freezing pork at an appropriate temperature for an appropriate time is also effective:

- ▨ 5°F (-15°C) for 20 days,
- ▨ -9.4°F (-23°C) for 10 days, or
- ▨ -22°F (-30°C) for 6 days.

Freezing cannot be relied on to kill cysts in meat other than pork.

---

heavy infections may produce serious illness and occasionally death. Although diagnosis before death in animals other than humans is rare, trichinellosis may be suspected if there is a history of eating either rodents or raw, infected meat.

Treatment is generally impractical in animals. Making sure that ingestion of viable *Trichinella* cysts in muscle does not occur is the best way to prevent disease in both animals and humans.

◼ TUBERCULOSIS

Tuberculosis is an infectious disease caused by bacteria of the genus *Mycobacterium.* The disease affects practically all species of vertebrates, and, before control measures were adopted, was a major disease of humans and domestic animals. Signs and lesions are generally similar in the various species.

Three main types of tubercle bacilli are recognized: human (*Mycobacterium tuberculosis*), bovine (*Mycobacterium bovis*), and avian (*Mycobacterium avium*). The 2 mammalian types are more closely related to each other than to the avian type. Each of the types may produce infection in other host species.

The breathing in of infected droplets expelled from the lungs of an infected person or animal is the usual—though not the only—route of infection. Ingestion, particularly via contaminated food or milk, may also be a common source of infection.

Most infected dogs do not have any signs, as the canine immune system actively suppresses the bacteria. When disease does occur, signs generally include chronic coughing with difficulty breathing or quick, shallow breaths. Other generalized signs include progressive emaciation, lethargy, weakness, poor appetite, and a low-grade, fluctuating fever.

The disease is easily transmitted to humans and other animals and represents a public health risk. Therefore, treatment of tuberculosis in dogs should be discussed with your veterinarian. If a dog is suspected of having advanced tuberculous lesions, it must be reported to the appropriate public health authorities, and the dog should be euthanized.

■ TULAREMIA

Tularemia is a bacterial disease that affects people and many species of wild and domestic animals. It is caused by toxins in the blood produced by the bacterium *Francisella tularensis*. The bacteria can survive for weeks or months in a moist environment. There are 2 types of organisms that differ based on the severity of the disease they produce. Type A is more likely to cause rapid and severe disease. It is found most commonly in North America. Disease resulting from Type B infection is generally mild and occurs most commonly as a result of contact with aquatic animals or ingestion of contaminated water in North America and Eurasia.

In domestic animals, sheep are infected most frequently, but infection has been reported in dogs, pigs, and horses. It is possible that many mild cases go untreated

and unreported among pets and livestock. Infection occurs most commonly in cottontail and jackrabbits, beaver, muskrat, meadow voles, and sheep in North America, and other voles, field mice, and lemmings in Europe and Asia. Although found in every state except Hawaii, tularemia is most often reported in the south central and western US (Missouri, Oklahoma, South Dakota, and Montana).

The disease can be transmitted from animals to humans by several routes. The most common mode of transmission to humans is from the bite of an infected tick. Direct transmission can occur from contact with moist tissue when skinning and preparing wild game. Other sources of infection include eating infected, undercooked game and drinking contaminated water. Rarely, the bite of a cat that has recently fed on an infected animal has been found to be a source of human infection.

In most mammals, signs of illness may include tick infestation, swollen glands, the sudden onset of high fever, lethargy, and poor appetite. Other signs may include stiffness and reduced mobility and are associated with a generalized infection. Pulse and respiratory rates may also be increased, and the infected animal may have a cough, diarrhea, and frequent urination. Prostration and death may occur in a few hours or days. Signs in dogs may include skin ulcer, swollen glands, throat infection, vomiting and diarrhea, and pneumonia. Very mild cases without signs may be common.

Veterinarians treat cases of tularemia with an antibiotic. Early treatment should prevent death; however, prolonged treatment may be necessary. Control is difficult and is limited to reducing tick infestation and to rapid diagnosis and treatment. Animals that recover develop a long-lasting immunity.

CAT BASICS

20 **Description and Physical Characteristics** 330
Introduction 330
Description and Physical Characteristics 330

21 **Selecting and Providing a Home for a Cat** 334
Selecting a Cat 334
Providing a Home for a Cat 336

22 **Routine Care and Breeding** 338
Routine Health Care 338
Breeding and Reproduction 343
Kitten Care 343

23 **Behavior** 345
Introduction 345
Diagnosing Behavior Problems 345
Behavior Modification 347
Normal Social Behavior in Cats 351
Behavior Problems in Cats 352

20

Description and Physical Characteristics

■ INTRODUCTION

People have associated with cats for thousands of years. Cats were first domesticated in Egypt between 1600 and 1500 BC. Even earlier, they were worshiped as gods: the Egyptian gods of fertility and war were given feline personalities. Feline images can also be found on early Greek and Roman vases, statues, and coins.

Wild cats (such as tigers, leopards, civets, and bobcats, for example) are among the best hunters in the animal kingdom. Domestic cats share these characteristics and are still valued "mousers" around barns, granaries, and warehouses. However, most cats in the United States are primarily pets that provide companionship, typically with fewer demands than are associated with dog ownership. The population of pet cats in the United States has steadily increased since the early 1970s, rivaling and now exceeding the number of pet dogs.

■ DESCRIPTION AND PHYSICAL CHARACTERISTICS

Like dogs, cats look very different from people but share many of our body's characteristics, such as a circulatory system, lungs, a digestive tract, a nervous system, and so on.

Breeds and Body Size

There are many different breeds of cats, including Abyssinian, Himalayan, Maine Coon, Manx, Persian, Scottish Fold, and Siamese, to name a few. The Cat Fanciers' Association, which is the world's largest registry of pedigreed cats, recognizes about 40 distinct breeds. The most familiar cats are the domestic shorthair and the domestic longhair, which are really mixtures of different breeds. Cat breeds differ in looks, coat length, and other characteristics but vary relatively little in size. On average, only 5 to 10 pounds separate the smallest and largest domestic breeds of cats.

Metabolism

Cats also share the rapid metabolism that dogs have, which results in a higher heart rate, respiratory rate, and temperature than those of people (*see* TABLE 1). Cats generally live longer than dogs, and many live to be 20 years old or older.

Temperature Regulation

Cats are better at conserving heat than at cooling themselves, although their small size relative to their large surface area makes for more effective cooling than in dogs. Cats lose heat through exter-

There are many distinct breeds of cats.

Table 1. Normal Feline Physiologic Values	
Body temperature (average)	101.5°F (38.6°C)
Heart rate	120 to 140 beats per minute
Respiratory rate (at rest)	16 to 40 breaths per minute
Average life span	12 to 20 years (depends on health care, behavior, diet, genetics, and other factors)

nal radiation. They have some sweat glands that aid in evaporative cooling, and licking their fur further improves this process. Heat is also lost through panting, although this is not as effective a method of cooling as it is in dogs. Cats typically also seek dark, cool places to shelter themselves from the heat of the day. As with all animals, cats should never be shut in cars or other hot, confined spaces. This can lead to heat stroke and death.

The Senses

Cats have the same 5 senses as people do but to very different degrees. Some senses are much better developed than in people.

Cats have an excellent sense of balance.

Sight

Cats have keen vision; they can see much more detail than dogs. Concentrated in the center of the retina of the eye, a specific type of cell called a **cone** gives cats excellent visual acuity and binocular vision. This allows them to judge speed and distance very well, an ability that helped them survive as hunters. However, although the cone cells are also responsible for color vision, it is uncertain whether cats can see colors. Like dogs, cats also have a lot of the retinal cells called **rods**, which are good at collecting dim light. In fact, cats can see 6 times better in dim light than people, giving rise to the myth that cats can see in the dark. Cats also have a reflective layer called the **tapetum lucidum**, which magnifies incoming light and lends a characteristic blue or greenish glint to their eyes at night.

A unique feature of both canine and feline eyes is the **nictitating membrane**, which is also called the third eyelid. This additional eyelid is a whitish pink color and is found under the other eyelids in the inside corner (near the nose) of the eye. The third eyelid extends up when needed to protect the eyeball from scratches (such as while traveling through brush) or in response to inflammation.

Hearing

Cats are very sensitive to sound, with a range of hearing both above and below the range of frequencies that can be detected by people. They can hear better than people and even better than most dogs. Feline hearing also acts as a direction finder, which is useful for hunting purposes. Cats generally turn their heads toward the direction of the sound while listening to pinpoint the location. The ear canal of cats is deeper and more tapered than in people. This deeper canal is subject to buildup of dirt and wax that can lead to inflammation and secondary infection, although to a lesser degree than in dogs.

The semicircular canals, which are found within the inner ear, are filled with fluid and are important for maintaining balance. These are highly developed in cats, accounting for their agility and excellent sense of balance. Cats can usually determine their body position at all times and can rapidly right themselves when falling, which explains the origin of the phrase, "Cats always land on their feet."

Smell and Taste

Cats do not rely as much on the sense of smell as some other animals. The sense of smell is less developed in cats than in dogs. Like people, cats are finicky about odors and try to cover disagreeable smells. Also like people, odor is an extremely important part of taste and enjoyment of food for cats. Cats that have lost their sense of smell due to illness (such as nasal or severe respiratory infection, nerve damage, or certain cancers) often stop eating completely.

Most cats are excited by the smell of catnip, a plant that is a member of the mint family. However, not all cats react in the same way. Some become manic, others roll and purr, others are minimally affected. This herb is harmless and can be given to your cat either directly or as part of a catnip toy or ball.

Locomotion

The muscles, tendons, joints, ligaments, and spine of cats are extremely flexible, making them agile hunters. Cats can walk, run, leap, twist, and even roll into a ball. They can leap long distances and twist in mid-air to obtain a better angle of attack. The feline bones that are comparable to the long bones of our hands and feet are located in the cat's lower legs. The angular hock in the hind legs is comparable to the ankle in people. Their normal gait is a "pace," in which both legs on one side move together.

Pads and Nails

As in dogs, the bottom of the paw in cats is covered by thick, resilient pads that cushion the foot and help provide a secure grip

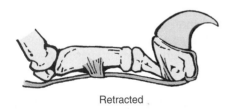

Retracted

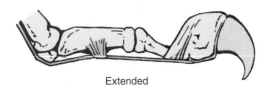

Extended

Cats' claws are highly adapted for hunting.

on many types of surfaces. Cats have claws that are much more highly adapted and complex than in the dog. Feline claws are very sharp and curved, which makes it easier to grasp prey while hunting or to slash during fights over territory. The claws are retractable, so that they do not get in the way or make noise when walking or running.

Many cats frequently scratch or knead furniture, bedding, drapes, and other types of material as a way of removing the outer layers of the front claws and keeping them sharp. Obviously, this habit can be very destructive. Solutions include providing a scratching post as an alternative and periodically clipping the nails. Nail clipping is usually easier in cats than in dogs, although caution must be used to avoid cutting the central "quick," which is the blood supply to the growing nail. A more permanent solution is a "declaw" surgery, in which the front claws are completely removed, including the dew claw, which has no function but can potentially snag and break. Although the surgery is controversial and prohibited in some countries, there is no evidence that it increases behavioral problems such as biting or failure to use a litter box. If you choose to declaw your cat, this procedure should be done before the cat is around 6 months of age. It is not recommended for adult or older cats. Declawed cats can have trouble climbing and defending themselves and should not be let outdoors.

Skin and Hair

Feline skin, like that of people and dogs, has an outer layer called the epidermis that is constantly being replaced, and an inner layer called the dermis that contains nerves and blood vessels, oil glands, and hair follicles. The oil glands secrete sebum that coats and protects the fur, giving it a glossy sheen. Feline skin is more sensitive than human skin, which is why it is important to use topical preparations that are specifically formulated for pets. Shampoos and other topical products for people can irritate your cat's skin and should be avoided.

Feline Hairs

- **Guard hairs:** coarse, long, thick hairs that come to a fine tip; insulate the body and aid the sense of touch
- **Awn hairs:** thinner hairs within the primary coat; also help insulate and protect the body
- **Secondary hairs:** the thinnest and most numerous hairs; make up the downy undercoat that is important for temperature control
- **Whiskers:** long, wiry, sensory hairs attached to the face

Cat fur protects the skin from sun, cold, scratches, and insect bites; helps regulate body temperature; and supports the sense of touch. Cat fur consists of several types of hairs. Cats also have whiskers that are attached to nerve cells in the face. These sensitive hairs can be used to judge the size of an opening, such as a rodent hole. As in dogs, cats have small muscles attached to hair follicles, which can make hair stand erect for temperature control or as a warning sign (that is, "raised hackles") in response to danger.

Different breeds of cats have different types of hair coats. Some have long hair (for example, the Persian, the domestic longhair), some have short hair (the Abyssinian, domestic shorthair), and some have "mutant" hair. The mutant hair types on Rex or wire-haired breeds are shorter and curlier than the hair of most other cats. Some breeds even lack hair on certain areas of the body, usually the chest and belly.

Cats shed hair naturally year round, although the rate of shedding depends on climate, nutrition, and general overall health. Outdoor cats shed more in fall and spring. Shedding may increase in all cats due to stress, such as a trip to the veterinarian. Excessive shedding and bald patches can be a sign of illness that should be investigated.

Teeth and Mouth

Cats are carnivores with teeth designed for piercing and tearing meat. They have 26 deciduous (baby) teeth that are replaced by 30 permanent (adult) teeth that erupt between 5 and 7 months of age (*see* TABLE 2). The different types of teeth have specialized functions, depending on their position in the mouth. The front teeth, which include the 12 incisors and 4 large canine teeth (also known as eye teeth), are designed for grasping and tearing. The rearward premolar and molar teeth grind food into smaller pieces so that it can be swallowed.

The mouth contains the salivary glands, which lubricate food and begin digestion. The tongue helps guide food to the back of the throat and is important for licking up small food pieces and lapping up water. The feline tongue is covered with tiny, thornlike structures that give it a rough, sandpapery texture. The rough tongue aids in grooming and can be used to scrape meat away from bones.

Digestive and Urinary Tracts

The gastrointestinal tract includes the stomach, the small intestine, and the large intestine (colon). This system digests food into useful nutrients, absorbs water, and eliminates waste. Digestive problems often show up as vomiting or diarrhea, which can have many causes, including viral

Table 2. Feline Adult Dentition

Type of Tooth	Number (Upper/Lower)	Age (Months) at Eruption	Function
Incisors	6/6	3.5 to 4.5	Grasping
Canines	2/2	5	Tearing
Premolars	6/4	4.5 to 6	Grinding
Molars	2/2	4 to 5	Grinding

infections; worms; stress; or ingestion of bones, string, hair, or other foreign material.

The urinary system eliminates wastes from protein breakdown and helps control fluid levels. Waste products are filtered by the kidneys and then sent through the ureters to the urinary bladder for storage. Urine is passed out of the body through the urethra. In males, the urethra doubles as a channel for sperm during copulation. The feline penis is small and "hidden" within the scrotal pouch that holds the testicles. This can sometimes make it difficult for pet owners to determine whether their cat is male or female.

Urinary infections are more common in females and usually show up as frequent dribbles of urine that may be tinged with blood. Cats commonly develop a condition called feline lower urinary tract disease, which is also called feline urologic syndrome. Signs can be similar to signs of infection. Feline lower urinary tract disease is caused by a buildup of crystals in the urine, which develop into a sludge that irritates the urinary tract. This is particularly dangerous in male cats, because their urethra, which carries urine from the bladder out of the body, is narrow and

bends and turns. If the tract becomes blocked and the cat is unable to pass urine, kidney failure and death can ultimately result without prompt treatment.

Both urinary and digestive problems are often associated with straining while urinating or defecating. At first glance, it may be difficult for cat owners to tell the source of the problem. Therefore, it is important to watch your cat while it eliminates and to check the litter for the character and color of the urine and feces. Diarrhea usually consists of frequent, soft or runny feces that may be a different color (often yellow, gray, or black) than usual. Any sign of blood in the feces calls for veterinary attention. Repeated, unproductive attempts to pass a bowel movement can be a sign of serious constipation or obstruction. Male cats that strain, dribble blood, howl, or have a painful abdomen are likely to have feline lower urinary tract disease. Blockage of either the urinary or gastrointestinal tract is an emergency, and your pet should be seen by a veterinarian immediately. (*See also* DIGESTIVE DISORDERS, page 383, and KIDNEY AND URINARY TRACT DISORDERS, page 514.)

CHAPTER *21*

Selecting and Providing a Home for a Cat

▨ SELECTING A CAT

Cats do not require the same level of attention or activity often demanded by dogs. This makes them excellent pets for people who have decreased mobility, a busy lifestyle, or limited living space (such as apartment dwellers). However, as with dogs, you should consider temperament, breed characteristics, age, and other factors when deciding whether cat ownership is right for you.

Temperament and Communication

Cats are very different than dogs in temperament and character. While dogs are pack animals that crave and need social contact, cats are mostly solitary hunters with a very different type of social structure. Some cats spend most of their time alone, while others live in groups and spend most of their time together. Because cats often tend to seek attention on their terms, some people perceive

Cats show affection by purring and rubbing against a favored individual.

them as aloof. Of course, many cats are highly affectionate and frequently solicit attention from people.

Cats show affection by purring and rubbing against a favored individual with their face and tail. Aggression and fear are associated with an arched back, raised hackles, spitting, and hissing. In addition to the purring that is associated with affection, cats communicate by making other types of vocalizations. Low-volume calls are associated with greeting or requests for attention. Loud calls include cries of complaint or bewilderment, urgent demands for attention, and the well known mating cry of a queen in heat.

Breeds

There are many breeds and types of cats. Mixed-breed cats are typically categorized by the length and color of their hair coat. For example, there are domestic short-, medium-, and long-haired cats, with colors including gray, black, brown, white, calico, and tortoise shell. Coat length is an important consideration when choosing a cat, because longer-haired cats require more grooming to prevent and eliminate mats. Long-haired cats are also more prone to hairballs.

Many breeds of purebred cats have distinctive characteristics. For example, the Abyssinian is an active, high-energy breed, while Persian and Scottish Fold cats are generally calmer. Siamese cats are very intelligent but often require more attention and tend to meow loudly when ignored. You may want to refer to one of the many cat books available that describe the characteristics of various breeds or check with your veterinarian before making your selection.

Sex

You should also consider whether you want a male or a female cat. Male cats that have not been neutered are more aggressive and usually fight for territory or dominance. They may spray urine along surfaces outside and inside the home, as a means of "marking" territory. Intact cats, both male and female, try to roam during the mating season, which can lead not only to unwanted kittens but also to bite wounds, car accidents, ingestion of poison, and other problems. Many of these undesirable behaviors can be decreased by spaying or neutering when the cat is young, although some cats may still spray when they sense their home environment is being invaded by, for example, new cats or cat odors.

Age

Kittens raised with your family usually integrate well into the environment. However, kittens have a lot of energy and require a lot of care and attention. Adult cats are usually calmer, less demanding, and less destructive.

Finding the Right Cat

Cats can be obtained from a variety of sources, each of which has advantages and disadvantages. For example, adopting a kitten from a friend or a breeder may give you a good opportunity to obtain information on the home environment, state of health, and behavior. You will probably need to locate a breeder if you have an exact type of purebred cat in mind. However, young

Table 3. Judging the Physical and Social Health of a New Cat

Positive Attributes	Negative Attributes
Active, friendly, sociable, curious	Timid or aggressive (hisses, spits, arches back)
Healthy weight	Thin or scrawny, with ribs or hip bones sticking out (**Note:** A pot belly on a thin kitten may be a sign of worms, a very common and easily treatable condition.)
Clean, shiny coat free of mats, sores, or fleas	Dirty coat stained with urine or feces; red spots or sores on the skin
Clean ears and eyes	Discharge from the eyes, excessive wax or debris in the ears
History of vaccination and veterinary care	Signs of respiratory problems (for example, a cough or runny eyes or nose)
History of eating a high-quality cat food	History of illness (such as vomiting or diarrhea) or behavior problems (such as not using the litter box)

and older adult cats at animal shelters are usually already spayed or neutered and vaccinated, and adopting from a shelter saves lives of cats that might not otherwise find a good home. Some owners choose to buy a cat at a pet store. While a pet store may provide health records or registration papers, conditions in which the cat was kept or raised before arriving at the store will likely not be known. Many people also adopt cats as strays from their neighborhood.

When choosing a cat, look for a healthy individual with a good temperament (*see* TABLE 3). Ask questions, and use your eyes and nose to look for problems. Sick kittens or cats are often listless and scrawny and have a dull hair coat. They may have urine or diarrhea stains (or associated odors) on the fur. Adult cats should be sociable and friendly. Kittens should be curious and adventurous, neither timid nor aggressive. Feral (wild) kittens or cats generally do not make good pets unless they have had considerable human contact during their first few months of life (*see* KITTEN CARE, page 343).

■ PROVIDING A HOME FOR A CAT

Pet ownership carries responsibilities that should not be taken lightly. Just like dog ownership, cat ownership carries both ethical and financial responsibilities. However, the rewards of pet ownership far outweigh the responsibilities. Research has also shown that the bond that can develop between people and animals as a result of owning and caring for a pet has significant social and health benefits (*see* page 1228).

Keeping Indoor Cats versus Outdoor Cats

People often wonder if they should keep their cat indoors, or also allow their cat to go outdoors. It is far safer for cats to be kept indoors. Cats that roam outside can get into fights, ingest poisonous substances (for example, antifreeze), get hit by cars, or find myriad other sources of trouble. Outdoor cats frequently pick up both external parasites (including fleas and ticks) and intestinal parasites (for example, from eating infected rodents). Outdoor cats also tend to kill wild birds and other small animals. In addition, outdoor cats that are not spayed or neutered add to the population of stray and unwanted kittens. Outdoor cats can spread diseases (including feline distemper) to other cats and can be exposed to rabies through encounters with infected wildlife. Unfortunately, once cats are accustomed to going outdoors, it can be difficult to break them of the habit.

Diet

Proper nutrition is an important and often overlooked aspect of pet ownership. The pet food industry is large, offering many choices, and all cat foods are not of equal quality. Dry food is generally preferable to canned because it promotes healthy teeth and gums (while providing the same nutrition). Name-brand cat foods are backed by scientific research and quality control to provide complete, balanced nutrition for your pet. This is especially important with cats, which require high-quality fat and protein in their diets, as well as certain amino acids (including taurine) that are not found in dog or people food. *Cats should never be fed dog food as a regular diet.* Diets that are specifically formulated for the various stages of a cat's life (including kitten, adult, and senior) are widely available in grocery stores, pet shops, and other outlets such as pet "superstores." Specialty diets for specific problems (such as obesity, feline lower urinary tract disorder, or kidney disease) have also been developed; many of these diets are prescription diets that are available only through veterinarians.

Most adult cats can be fed 1 to 2 times daily, although kittens require more frequent feeding (*see* page 344). Meals should be provided in a quiet corner, away from the hustle and bustle of family life. Some cats are notoriously finicky eaters, and you may need to experiment with different canned and dry foods to find those that your cat likes. For adult cats that do not overeat and gain weight, dry food can be left out all the time so that they eat whenever they want.

One of the biggest problems in pets is overfeeding, which can lead to obesity, other serious diseases such as heart disease and arthritis, and a shortened lifespan. Only the proper amounts of a quality cat food, with few (if any) table scraps, should be fed. Your veterinarian can provide an estimate of the proper type and amount of food for your cat to maintain your cat's ideal weight.

Dry food promotes healthy teeth and gums.

At the other end of the spectrum, you should also take notice if your cat is not eating enough. Lack of appetite can be a sign of serious illness. If your cat refuses to eat for more than a day, a prompt visit to your veterinarian is recommended.

Fresh, clean water should *always* be available to your cat. Although cats need less water than dogs and some cats get all the water they need from moist, canned food, access to water should never be restricted unless specifically instructed by your veterinarian.

Exercise

Sedentary cats tend to gain weight and are prone to certain medical conditions such as liver disease. Although it is much more difficult to exercise a cat than a dog, exercise can be encouraged by selecting certain toys that promote greater physical activity. For example, one popular type of toy is a short, flexible pole with a feather or other small object attached at the top. You hold the bottom of the pole and "bounce" the object for the cat to jump after and chase. You may need to try a variety of toys until you find ones that appeal to your cat.

Litter Boxes

Litter training is generally easy, because cats are naturally clean animals that seek a place to bury their waste. However, the litter box must be kept clean, or cats may refuse to use it and will soil outside the box. Solid waste should be removed every day, and the entire box cleaned at least once a week. In households with more than one cat, there should be at least one litter box per cat. In houses with multiple floors, it is also a good idea to provide a litter box on each floor.

The litter box should be placed in a secluded, low-traffic area that is readily accessible to cats. There are many dif-ferent types of litter to choose from, but most cats prefer small, clumping parti-cles (such as clay-based products). The preferred location and type of box will vary from cat to cat, which may necessi-tate a little trial and error. Sudden changes in the type of litter or the loca-tion of the litter box can lead to soiling outside the box. However, soiling out-side the box can also be a sign of illness or behavioral problems and may require veterinary attention.

CHAPTER 22

Routine Care and Breeding

▧ ROUTINE HEALTH CARE

Routine health care refers to the non-emergency, general care that is needed to keep your cat healthy throughout its life. This includes routine veterinary care for vaccinations, parasite control, and dental care; proper nutrition; grooming; and protection from household hazards.

Importance of Veterinary Care

Adult cats should have a complete vet-erinary examination at least once a year. Kittens need veterinary visits usually every 3 to 4 weeks until they are about 4 months old. Geriatric cats (older than 8 to 9 years old) should see their veterinar-ian twice a year or more frequently because illness is more common in older pets and should be identified sooner to provide proper treatment. Your veteri-narian may recommend a wellness pro-gram for your pet, such as routine blood tests to monitor for early kidney or liver disease.

Signs of Illness

Because you are more familiar with your cat than anyone else, you should watch it carefully for subtle signs of ill-ness that another person or even a vet-erinarian may miss. General signs of illness include a lack of appetite or decreased activity. Other more specific signs include vomiting and diarrhea, uri-nating more (or less) frequently, coughing and sneezing, or a discharge from the eyes, ears, or nose. Illness can also show up as a loss of hair or itchy areas on the skin or around the ears. Problems with the mus-culoskeletal system are often seen as stiff-ness or lameness, such as not putting weight on a leg. If your cat shows any of these signs for more than a day or two, a visit with your veterinarian is a good idea.

Giving Medication

Administering pills to a cat can be a challenge. Some cats will take a pill that

Getting a cat to take a pill can be a challenge.

is hidden in a small treat, such as a piece of tuna or chicken. However, many cats will eat the treat and spit out the medication. In these cases, you will need to learn how to administer a pill by tipping your cat's head so that he or she is looking up (that is, at the ceiling), opening the mouth, and placing the pill directly in the back of the mouth for swallowing. Your veterinarian or veterinary technician can give you a demonstration and additional guidance. Liquid medications are sometimes prescribed, particularly for kittens. Liquids can be given via a syringe into the rear of the cat's mouth by inserting the tip of the syringe near the back teeth on either side. Holding the cat's head pointing partially upward can help prevent spills. Spot-on products or other topical medications are administered directly on the coat or skin. If your cat needs eye drops or ear medication, your veterinarian or veterinary technician will give you a demonstration. Regardless of the type of medication or how it is to be given, it is important to read and follow all label instructions.

Vaccinations

Vaccination is a key component of preventive medicine in cats, just as in dogs and people. Vaccinations are given to stimulate the immune system against infection before exposure to disease. Several vaccines are routinely given to cats as the core defense against serious infectious illness. Several others (referred to as noncore) are important in certain regions and situations. Your veterinarian can advise which vaccines are recommended in your local area and circumstances (*see* TABLE 4).

Disease	Description	Vaccination Frequency and Comments
Table 4. Vaccines Required or Recommended for Cats*		
Core vaccines		
Panleukopenia (feline distemper)	A viral infection that can affect several body systems, especially the blood cells produced in the bone marrow	First vaccination at 8 to 10 weeks of age, followed by additional vaccinations at 12 to 14 weeks and 1 year; periodic (for example, yearly) booster vaccinations
Feline herpesvirus type 1 (feline viral rhinotracheitis)	A viral respiratory infection	Same schedule as panleukopenia (usually given as combination vaccine)
Feline calicivirus	A viral respiratory infection	Same schedule as panleukopenia (usually given as combination vaccine)
Rabies	A viral disease of the nervous system that is both fatal and transmissible to people	Initial vaccination at 3 to 4 months of age; boosters at 1 year and every 1 to 3 years after that, depending on location
Noncore vaccines		
Feline chlamydiosis	A respiratory infection caused by intracellular organisms similar to bacteria	Similar schedule as panleukopenia
Feline immunodeficiency virus (feline AIDS)	A viral infection of the immune system	Three doses are given, 2 to 3 weeks apart, followed by annual boosters

(Continued on the following page)

*These recommendations are based on the 2006 American Association of Feline Practitioners Feline Vaccine Advisory Panel Report.

Table 4. Vaccines Required or Recommended for Cats*—(Continued)

Disease	Description	Vaccination Frequency and Comments
Feline leukemia virus	A viral form of blood cancer that suppresses the immune system	Vaccination at 9 and 12 weeks of age, followed by periodic (for example, yearly) boosters
Not recommended		
Feline infectious peritonitis	A viral infection that can affect many body systems, including the liver, kidneys, and brain; inflammation of the abdominal cavity is common in some forms of this disease	Most cats are exposed to the virus early in life and will not be able to develop an immune response to the vaccine
Giardiasis	A protozoal infection of the digestive tract	Not enough information is available to determine whether the vaccine can prevent disease in cats

*These recommendations are based on the 2006 American Association of Feline Practitioners Feline Vaccine Advisory Panel Report.

Traditionally, booster vaccinations have been given every year throughout the cat's life to ensure ongoing protection. However, the need for yearly revaccination has been questioned in recent years. Some data indicate that, after the first year of life, immunity lasts long enough so that booster vaccinations are needed only every few years. In addition, some research has suggested that local inflammation, even that associated with certain types of vaccines, can lead to fibrosarcoma in cats, which is the most common soft-tissue cancer of this species. Vaccines using killed feline leukemia virus and rabies vaccines are most commonly associated with this form of cancer. Debate over the best approach to vaccination is ongoing. Your veterinarian can advise you about the best vaccination program for your cat.

Parasite Control

Several internal and external parasites can infect cats (*see* TABLE 5). Common intestinal parasites of cats include roundworms, hookworms, and tapeworms. Worm infections are often passed through eggs in feces or directly from mother to offspring through the placenta or milk. Sometimes, a secondary host is involved with infection. For example, tapeworm infections are passed through ingestion of larvae either in fleas or in tissue of infected prey (such as mice).

Intestinal worms cause damage to the digestive tract and blood loss. They also interfere with absorption of essential nutrients. Infection is diagnosed by finding worm eggs (or sometimes actual worms or worm segments) in fecal samples. Fecal samples should be tested several times in kittens, periodically (usually yearly) in all indoor cats, and at least twice a year in outdoor cats, which are especially likely to become infected with parasites.

Intestinal worms of cats usually do not cause intestinal infection in people; however, hookworm infections leading to abdominal pain and enteritis have developed in people with a weakened immune system. Roundworm larvae also have the potential to infect people; ingested larvae can wander into sensitive organs, such as the eye or into a developing fetus. Cat owners should clean all litter boxes frequently (it takes at least a week for these intestinal parasite eggs to become infective) and wash their hands thoroughly after any exposure to cat litter, feces,

Table 5. Common Parasites of Cats

Parasite	Transmission	Effect on Health
Roundworms and hookworms	Directly through ingestion of eggs in feces, or larvae pass through placenta or milk	Damage to digestive tract and loss of nutrients; migrating roundworm larvae in people can affect young children and people with a weakened immune system; hookworms can cause skin lesions or infections in people with a weakened immune system
Tapeworms	Ingestion of secondary hosts, such as fleas or prey animals (for example, mice)	Loss of nutrients
Flukes or lungworms	Ingestion of secondary hosts found near water (for example, snails or tadpoles)	Damage to lungs, liver, or intestines
Intestinal protozoa (for example, coccidia or *Toxoplasma*)	Ingestion of eggs in feces or infective cysts in prey animals	Gastrointestinal damage in cats; infection of pregnant women (toxoplasmosis) can potentially result in serious injury to fetus, young children, or immunocompromised individuals
Heartworm	Passed by infected mosquitoes, especially in southeastern US	Damage to blood vessels of the lungs, the lungs themselves, and the heart
Fleas, ticks, and mites	Passed directly outdoors or from other infected cats in household (for example, mother to kitten)	Skin damage, itching, secondary skin infection, ear infection (ear mites), flea allergy, tapeworms (fleas), and secondary bloodborne diseases (for example, infectious anemia transmitted by fleas or ticks)
Cuterebra (fly larvae)	Contact with fly larvae near rodent or rabbit burrows	Unsightly lumps on head or neck; secondary infections under the skin

vomit, and other body fluids. (*See also* GASTROINTESTINAL PARASITES OF CATS, page 403.)

Cats can also become infected with protozoa, such as coccidia or *Toxoplasma*. These are microscopic parasites that live inside the cells of the digestive tract. Of greatest concern to cat owners is toxoplasmosis, which is transmitted directly through eggs or indirectly through infective cysts in raw meat (usually from prey animals). Toxoplasmosis usually causes only mild digestive upset in cats, but it can cause more serious illness if transmitted to people. People particularly at risk include pregnant women, young children, and those who have a weakened immune system, such as people with AIDS or those receiving chemotherapy

for cancer. Ingested organisms can migrate throughout the body, causing damage to important organs (including the brain) or to a developing fetus. People at risk can prevent infection by not handling cat feces and by not eating rare or underdone meat. Cleaning cat litter should be done by someone else. All meat for consumption should be well cooked.

Other internal parasites of cats include flukes (flatworms that can infect the intestine or liver) and lungworms. Outdoor cats that hunt are prone to these infections, especially if they live or hunt near water. Aquatic animals such as snails and frogs are common hosts for the developing fluke or lungworm larvae. These infections are diagnosed by testing fecal samples.

Frequent scratching can be a sign of infestation by fleas or other parasites.

Cats can also become infected with heartworms, which are parasites transmitted by mosquitoes (*see* page 380). Heartworm disease is common in most of the United States. It is most commonly diagnosed with a blood test and can be prevented by administering monthly medication. There is no effective treatment for heartworm infection in cats, so prevention is critical.

External parasites of cats include fleas, ticks, mange mites, and ear mites. Monthly preventive treatments are available to control fleas and ticks and are administered as body sprays or "spot on" preparations that are placed on the skin between the shoulder blades. Mange mites can be detected by scraping the skin of infected areas for signs of mites or their eggs. Signs of mange include red, scaly areas or bald patches on the skin, or both (*see also* page 500). One type of mange called *Cheyletiella* is termed "walking dandruff." This large mite causes itching along the surface of the skin, while other mange mites reside deeper inside skin layers or hair follicles. People can also become infested with the burrowing mange mites (*Sarcoptes*) and *Cheyletiella*.

Outdoor cats can also become infested with a *Cuterebra* larva, which is a developmental stage of a particular fly. The larvae are commonly found around rodent and rabbit holes, and they burrow under the skin of cats. This results in a large swelling under the skin, usually around the head or neck area, with a small, round breathing hole on the skin surface. Treatment consists of removing the larva and treating the resulting wound.

Dental Care

Cats need dental attention throughout their lives. You can help keep your cat's teeth and gums in good condition by feeding dry food and following a program of professional dental cleanings performed by your veterinarian. Good dental care reduces the development of plaque which, if untreated, can progress to gingivitis and gum disease. In severe cases of dental disease, extraction is common. (*See also* page 390.)

Grooming

Cats frequently groom themselves. Short-haired breeds usually require little brushing or bathing by their owners. Routine brushing of long-haired cats, or of cats that stop grooming because of illness, is important to remove shed hair and prevent hair mats. Brushing also limits the amount of hair that cats ingest, which helps decrease the development of hairballs. Many cats like being brushed, and grooming can be used as a reward and time of bonding. Mats should be removed with electric clippers (not scissors) to avoid cutting the skin underneath.

Your cat's ears should be checked routinely for cleanliness. If dirt and wax build up in the ears, they can harbor organisms that may lead to infection. Your veterinarian can clean your cat's ears safely. If cleaning is needed on a regular basis, ask your veterinarian to demonstrate how this should be done.

Healthy cats rarely need bathing. However, if bathing is required, only pet shampoos approved for use on cats should be used.

Household Hazards

Your cat must be protected from household hazards, including chemicals, pesticides, cleaning supplies, antifreeze, electrical cords, drugs, alcohol, and common house plants that may be poisonous. Curious kittens that tend to chew on almost anything are at greatest risk, and these products must be kept out of reach of all cats. Cats are especially sensitive to many medications commonly found in the average household, including aspirin, acetaminophen, ibuprofen, and cold remedies. *Never give your cat any human medication unless specifically instructed by your veterinarian.* (*See also* POISONING, page 1145.)

Cats and kittens should be kept away from open windows or balconies in apartments or condominiums that are multiple floors above the ground. Although agile and often able to right themselves in mid air, cats can still sustain serious injuries if they fall from a great height.

Spaying/Neutering

All cats should be spayed (females) or neutered (males) unless they are to be used for breeding. This prevents unwanted kittens and avoids potentially serious future medical problems, such as uterine cancer or infection. Spaying or neutering also decreases the urge to wander outside, which can result in car accidents, fights, and other injuries. Neutered male cats are also much less likely to spray urine to mark their territory. The spay or neuter procedure is usually done when cats are about 6 to 7 months old.

▉ BREEDING AND REPRODUCTION

Like dogs, cats also have an estrous, or heat, cycle. However, female cats, which are called queens, are **induced ovulators**. This means that they do not ovulate (pass an egg) unless they are bred. This greatly increases the chances of conception when bred, which is why stray queens often have many kittens per

Kittens from the same litter can have different sires.

year. The queen can enter her first heat as young as 4 months of age, and she generally has 2 or 3 heat cycles during the breeding season (typically February to October in the northern hemisphere). During heat, the queen is receptive to males and shows characteristic mating behavior. She will roll, rub against objects, knead her back feet, and yowl repeatedly and loudly. This behavior can last 3 to 20 days and can repeat in 10 to 40 days if the queen is not bred. If the queen is bred, the cycle ends as her body prepares for pregnancy.

Gestation, or pregnancy, lasts about 2 months (60 to 63 days), with an average litter size of about 4 kittens. Queens can be bred by more than one male during a heat period, resulting in kittens from the same litter with different sires. Signs of pregnancy include a large abdomen, increased appetite, and swollen mammary glands that may release milk when squeezed. During the later stages of pregnancy, the queen seeks a nesting area and places bedding in a quiet, secluded spot. Cats that are not pregnant sometimes show these signs of pregnancy during a pseudopregnancy, or false pregnancy. This usually begins at the end of estrus and can last for several months. Your veterinarian can tell you if the pregnancy is real or false.

▉ KITTEN CARE

Kittens can generally be taken from their mother and littermates once they are weaned, beginning at 6 to 7 weeks of age. Kittens, like babies, require a lot of attention, including veterinary care, feeding, and socialization.

Importance of Veterinary Care

Like puppies and human babies, kittens receive a certain degree of immunity (known as maternal immunity) that is passed from their mothers at birth and also shortly thereafter through the milk. Vaccinations cannot effectively stimulate the kitten's immune system until this maternal immunity wears off. Because maternal immunity declines slowly over time, kittens should be vaccinated according to a regular schedule, beginning at 2 to 3 months of age (*see* TABLE 4, page 339). This ensures that the kitten receives an effective dose of vaccine soon after maternal protection is gone. Restricting access to unvaccinated cats until the full series of vaccinations has been given is important to avoid disease.

Intestinal parasites are most common in kittens. Larvae may be passed through the placenta or mother's milk. Worms are so common that new kittens are often treated with a broad-spectrum wormer as a routine preventive measure. Fecal examinations, with additional treatments as necessary, are usually repeated after worming until 2 successive fecal examinations are negative. External parasites

Kittens require frequent vaccinations.

(including fleas) should also be treated but only with products approved for use on kittens. Cats that are allowed outdoors or that live in mixed-pet households should be treated with appropriate antiparasitic products to prevent infestation of all pets and the house.

Diet

Proper nutrition is important throughout a cat's life and is especially critical during kittenhood. Growing kittens need more calories, fat, protein, vitamins, and minerals to meet their needs for rapid growth and development. Kittens need multiple daily feedings of a specially formulated kitten food. The number of daily feedings can be gradually decreased as the kitten ages, but feeding with a name-brand kitten diet should continue until adulthood (about 9 to 12 months of age).

Socialization

Cats learn how to socialize with other cats from their mother and littermates. Human contact before kittens reach 10 to 12 weeks of age is usually required for cats to become good pets. Cats that have not had this initial socialization will likely always fear and avoid human contact. This makes it difficult to turn older feral (wild) cats into household pets. Playing with your cat and providing interactive toys can help develop a close bond, as well as decrease destructive behaviors.

Introducing cats to other pets, including—and sometimes especially— other cats, can take additional socialization regardless of age. Some cats can be territorial and view a new cat as an intruder. This can lead to undesirable behaviors such as urine marking, soiling outside the litter box, or fighting with the newcomer. Cats should be introduced to any new animal gradually. For example, the cat and the new animal should be allowed to first smell each other through a gate separating rooms, then each animal should be held while allowed to investigate each other more thoroughly. After a day or two, if both animals appear calm in each other's presence, they can be allowed together while supervised for short periods, gradually leading to longer times. Patience is often necessary while animals are adjusting to one another in multi-pet households. It can take 6 months or more to completely integrate a new cat into a household with other cats.

CHAPTER 23
Behavior

▨ INTRODUCTION

Behavioral medicine is the scientific study of everything animals do, whether the animals are insects, birds, mammals, fish, or humans. The field of animal behavior is concerned with understanding the causes, functions, development, and evolution of behavior. Behavior refers to the actions or reactions of an organism. Behavior is usually in relation to the environment, and is controlled by the endocrine and nervous systems. The complexity of animal behavior is related to the complexity of the animal's nervous system. Generally, animals with complex nervous systems have a greater capacity to learn and thus adjust their behavior.

An animal's behavior is influenced by many factors. Some of these factors include genetics, experience and learning, environment, and physiology. Several studies have shown that behavior can be inherited to some degree. The effect of other kittens in the litter, the amount and type of human handling (especially true for kittens), and exposure to new objects and experiences can influence a cat's behavior and character. The brain and its neurotransmitters also play a fundamental role in temperament and behavior. Abnormal levels of various hormones play a role in certain forms of aggression and fear. Regulatory functions of the brain decrease with age, which results in an increase in fears and anxieties.

Understanding the nature of behavior problems is essential to developing a rational basis for their treatment. While this section focuses primarily on the abnormal behavior of cats, the extent to which a cat's behavior is abnormal is defined by its deviation from "normal" or by the problem that this behavior poses to its owner.

▨ DIAGNOSING BEHAVIOR PROBLEMS

Many "heath" problems faced by pet cats are associated with behavior problems or unmet expectations about behavior. Your veterinarian will take a behavioral history before making any diagnosis. A behavioral history generally includes the following items: 1) the sex, breed, and age of the cat; 2) the age at onset of the condition; 3) the duration of the condition; 4) a description of the actual behavior; 5) the frequency of the problem behavior (hourly, daily, weekly, monthly); 6) the duration of a typical episode (seconds, minutes, hours); 7) any change in pattern, frequency, intensity, and duration of episodes; 8) any corrective measures tried and the response; 9) any activities that stopped the behavior (for example, the cat falls asleep); 10) the 24-hour schedule of the cat and owner, as well as any day-to-day changes; 11) the cat's family history (in other words, are there signs of similar problems in the cat's parents or littermates?); 12) anything else that the owner thinks is relevant.

Modern veterinary care includes routine screening questions about specific behavior complaints (for example, failure to use the litter box, any fighting with other pets, any odd behavior) in addition to routine questions that alert your veterinarian to potential medical problems. This routine screening will identify what is "normal" for your cat.

Because behavioral diagnoses cannot be made on the basis of a one-time event, you can complete a questionnaire at each visit to clarify the pattern of your cat's behavior. The veterinarian can then identify whether the signs (growling, hissing) create a pattern that meets specific diagnostic criteria such as fear aggression. Both you and your veterinarian must use the same definitions for the same nonspecific signs.

Videotapes of your cat's behavior can help ensure that an accurate diagnosis is made. The questionnaire relies on your description and, because of this, is more subjective. However, when combined with a videotape, your veterinarian can use the information to diagnose the problem. Your understanding and compliance are critical if your cat's behavior disorder is to improve. Only when you recognize the behaviors leading to or associated with the problematic ones, can you avoid or prevent the problem situation from arising.

Defining the Problem

The following is a brief glossary of terms that are commonly used when discussing behavior.

An **abnormal behavior** is one that is dysfunctional and unusual.

Aggression is everything related to a threat or attack. There are various kinds of aggressive behavior in cats, such as territorial defense, predatory aggression, and inter-male aggression. Examples of aggressive acts in cats include hissing, biting, chasing, and growling.

Anxiety is the anticipation of danger accompanied by signs of tension (vigilance, increased movement, and tense muscles). The focus of anxiety can be internal or external.

A cat in **conflict** has tendencies to perform more than one type of activity at once. For example, a cat may want to approach a person to get a treat, but may also be afraid of the person and unwilling to come too close. The motivation for the conflict, except for extreme instances associated with survival functions (for example, eating), is very hard to identify in animals.

Displacement activity is the resolution of a conflict by performing a seemingly unrelated activity. When a cat is obviously in conflict between sex and aggression or between aggression and fear, it will often perform an apparently irrelevant activity. Examples of irrelevant activities are grooming, feeding, and sleeping.

Fear is a feeling of apprehension associated with the presence of an object, individual, or social situation and is part of normal behavior. Deciding whether a fear is abnormal depends on the context. For example, fire is a useful tool, and fear of being consumed by it is a normal behavior. However, if the house were not on fire, such a fear would be irrational. If this fear was constant or recurrent, it would probably be considered an abnormal behavior. Normal and abnormal fears usually vary in intensity. The intensity increases as the real or imagined closeness of the object that causes the fear increases.

Frustration arises when a cat is unable to complete a behavior due to physical or psychological obstacles. This term is overused and usually undefined, which means it often is not very helpful when diagnosing a behavior problem.

Most fearful reactions are learned and can be unlearned with gradual exposure. **Phobias**, however, are profound and quickly developed fearful reactions that do not diminish either with gradual exposure to the object or without exposure over time. A phobia involves sudden, all-or-nothing, profound, abnormal reactions resulting in panic. Phobias develop quickly, with little change between episodes. Fear may develop more gradually and, within an episode of fearful behavior, there may be more variation in intensity than would be seen in a phobic reaction. Once a phobic event has been experienced, any event associated with it or the memory of it is enough to generate the reaction. Even without re-exposure, phobias can remain at or exceed their former high level for years. Phobic situations are either avoided at all costs or, if unavoidable, are endured with intense anxiety or distress.

Stereotypic behaviors are repetitious, relatively unvaried actions that have no obvious purpose or function. They are usually derived from normal maintenance behavior such as grooming, eating, or walking. These behaviors are abnormal because they interfere with the normal functioning of the animal.

▨ BEHAVIOR MODIFICATION

The techniques used most commonly to modify cat behavior include habituation, extinction, desensitization, counterconditioning, and shaping. A behavior modification technique called flooding (*see* page 349) is not used very often because it is more likely to make animals worse. While it is claimed that punishment is frequently used with varying degrees of success, few people use punishment correctly. For punishment (such as yelling at the cat) to be successful, it must occur just as the behavior starts, be consistently delivered, and be strong enough to stop the unwanted behavior. Most punishments are not given at the right time or are not the appropriate type for the situation.

Behavior Modification Techniques

Most of the techniques involved in behavior modification are not hard to learn and can be successfully employed as preventive techniques. They do, however, require an investment of time and effort. The following is a short review of the basic principles involved in these techniques.

Habituation is a simple form of learning that involves no rewards. It is merely the ending of or decrease in a response to a stimulus that results from repeated or prolonged exposure to that stimulus. For example, horses placed in a pasture bordering a road may at first run away when traffic passes, but eventually learn to ignore it. A cat that habituates to one type of sound does not, as a consequence of this habituation, become habituated to other sounds. Habituation is not the same as failing to respond to stimulation as a result of fatigue, sensory adaptation, or injury. The effects of habituation are generally long lasting. However, if an animal is repeatedly exposed to a potentially harmful stimulus (such as a predator) without being harmed, habituation does not generally occur. Because of this, scientists believe that responses to dangerous stimuli may have an inherited resistance to habituation.

Spontaneous recovery is associated with habituation. If there is a long period of time between when a cat has experienced an event to which it had habituated and re-exposure to the same event, the animal may again react. For example, some cats will howl at night to get a reaction. The more the owner attempts to quiet it, the more the cat howls. It will continue this pattern because it is getting the attention it wanted. Even if the attention is "negative," some cats will find it rewarding. The best method to discourage the behavior is to ignore it. Eventually the cat stops howling if the owner consistently ignores it. However, the unwanted behavior comes back every now and then. This is called spontaneous recovery.

Conditioning refers to associations between stimuli and behavior. For example, a hungry cat may drool when it sees food (the stimulus). If every time that the hungry cat sees the food it also hears a can opener, after several times, the sound of the can opener alone will cause the cat to start drooling. This is called conditioning. The can opener elicits the same response as the sight of food. After several times, the cat has learned to associate the sound of the can opener with the food.

Reinforcement is any event that increases the chances that a certain behavior will be repeated. Reinforcements can be positive or negative. When positive reinforcement (a reward) is used in training, there is a positive relationship between the behavior and its consequences. The more the pet does a behavior, the more it gets positive reinforcement. This makes that behavior increase. A negative reinforcement (which is mistakenly thought of as punishment by many people) is something unpleasant that increases a behavior when it is removed. For example, some cats find being held in a lap unpleasant. When a cat squirms and escapes from your lap, it is rewarded with being freed from your hold. After several times, the release from restraint will increase the chance that your cat will try to escape again the next time.

Second-order reinforcers are signals that can be used at a distance to let the cat know that a reward is coming. Commonly used second-order reinforcers are words, such as "good kitty," clickers, and whistles. By carefully pairing these with a primary reward (such as food or petting), second-order reinforcers can generate the same response as the reward itself. For example, a clicker can be associated with a food treat as a reward for coming. By associating the clicker with the food, you can train the cat to come from farther away, and still reward the behavior by using the clicker. Positive training and "clicker" training have recently become very popular and work well with cats as well as dogs. However, it is possible to do an excellent job at positive training without using any second-order reinforcers. Clicker training requires frequent practice and excellent timing. In some situations involving problem behaviors, the incorrect use of a clicker may hinder, rather than help, a behavior modification program.

Extinction is a response that stops when the reward is removed. An example of extinction is ignoring a cat that howls at night for attention. If the owners get up to feed the cat (or even in many cases to yell at it), the behavior continues. If they stop feeding the cat or giving it attention, the cat will eventually stop howling during the night because the reward is no longer there. However, occasional feeding in response to the howling will only reinforce the pattern. The more valuable the original reward, the longer the reward has been given, and the more uncertain the cat is that the reward has been truly removed, the greater the resistance to extinction.

Because there is often an association between getting the reward and the intensity of the behavior, the intensity or frequency of the behavior you are trying to eliminate usually increases at the beginning of extinction. In other words, a behavior you are trying to extinguish often gets worse before it gets better. It is critical that you do not give in. Giving in will only make extinction more difficult. The cat has learned that, although your threshold has increased, the cat can override it by working harder.

Overlearning is the repeated performance of an already learned behavior. It is frequently used in training for specific events. Overlearning accomplishes 3 things: it delays forgetting, it increases the resistance to extinction, and it increases the chances that the response will become a "knee-jerk", or automatic response, when the circumstances are similar. This aspect can be useful in teaching a cat to overcome a fear or anxiety.

Shaping is a learning technique that works well for cats that do not know what response is desired by the trainer. Shaping works through gradual approximations and allows the cat to be rewarded at first for any behavior that resembles the desired end result. For example, when teaching a cat to come, tossing a food treat in front of the cat when it first takes a step or two in your direction will increase the chance that the cat will come closer. Then the cat can be given a treat for taking several steps toward you, and finally, only when it comes all the way to you.

Avoidance of a problem behavior is essential until you can seek qualified help, particularly in the case of cats that are biting or scratching. With treatment it may be possible to desensitize the cat to circumstances in which aggressive behavior occurs, but avoidance is the key to minimizing danger. Avoidance does not mean that the cat has control, or that you are giving in to the cat. Rather, it means that the cat is not being given the chance to reinforce the pattern by acting aggressively. Every time a cat becomes aggressive, it learns that this reaction may help it cope with the situation, thus reinforcing the problem.

Desensitization is a way to gradually teach a cat to tolerate a situation by carefully exposing it to the situation in small steps. If a cat is afraid of another cat in the household, gradual, controlled exposure to the other pet can be arranged to desensitize the fearful cat. The second cat could be placed in a carrier and kept at the far side of the room for a minute or two. The cat in the carrier could gradually be moved closer and kept in the room longer, but only if the fearful cat remains calm and relaxed,

Counterconditioning is a method for reducing unwanted behavior by teaching the cat to replace it with another more favorable behavior. In the example of the fearful cat, the cat will learn faster if it is first taught to sit and relax in exchange for a treat. The cat must be calm, and convey by its eyes, body posture, and facial expressions that it is not upset or agitated in any way. Once this routine is learned, the desensitization is added by placing the other cat (in a carrier at first) on the other side of the room for a few minutes. If at any time the cat starts to become anxious or act like it wants to leave, the other cat should be moved farther away until the nervous cat relaxes. Relaxing is the key and is the first step in changing the fearful cat's behavior. There is no point in having the cat stay if it is clearly distressed. Counterconditioning and desensitization can take a lot of time and effort. The exercises must be frequently repeated so that the unwanted behavior decreases to an acceptable level. Moving too quickly provokes anxiety and works against any progress with the behavior modification program.

Flooding is prolonged exposure to a stimulus until the cat eventually stops reacting. This is the opposite of the approach taken in desensitization. It is far more stressful than any of the other treatment strategies and if not used correctly will make things worse. This technique should be used only by a professional and only as a last resort.

Punishment is also known as aversive conditioning. It is any unpleasant event that lowers the chance that a behavior will be repeated. Punishment is not the same as negative reinforcement (*see* above). To be most successful, punishment must occur as early as possible (within a few seconds of the start of the behavior), and it must be consistent and appropriate. Critical factors in punishment include timing, consistency, appropriate intensity, and the presence of a reward after the undesirable behavior ends. This is the most frequently ignored part of treatment for people whose pets have behavior problems. Owners often resort to physical punishment as the first choice, but punishment does not need to be physical. Furthermore, punishment is just as hard to use correctly as counterconditioning and desensitization. Punishment is never an "easy out" and has a high chance of failure. It can also lead to other negative consequences, such as increasing the chance of fear or aggression.

Use of Medication to Treat Behavior Problems

Your veterinarian may, in some cases, prescribe medication to help treat a behavior problem of your cat. Drug treatment for almost any behavior change is most useful when combined with behavior modification.

In recent years there has been an increase in the use of medication to treat

Table 6. Drugs Used to Treat Behavior Problems in Cats

Drug	Uses	Comments
Tricyclic antidepressants		
Amitriptyline	Anxiety, aggression, compulsive disorders	Cheaper than many other drugs, but may be more likely to cause adverse effects
Clomipramine	Anxiety, aggression, compulsive disorders, urine marking	
Selective serotonin reuptake inhibitors		
Fluoxetine	Anxiety, aggression, compulsive disorders, urine marking	May take 3 to 4 weeks before affecting behavior; liquid form may be easier to give to some cats
Paroxetine	Anxiety, aggression, compulsive disorders, urine marking	
Sertraline	Anxiety, aggression, compulsive disorders	
Azapirones		
Buspirone	Anxiety, urine marking	
Benzodiazepines		
Alprazolam	Anxiety	Longer acting than other drugs of this class
Diazepam	Anxiety, urine marking	May cause physical dependence
Hormones		
Megestrol acetate	Aggression, urine marking, roaming	Rarely used due to high risk of adverse effects
Medroxyprogesterone acetate	Aggression, urine marking, roaming	Injectable; rarely used due to high risk of adverse effects

a variety of behavior problems in cats (*see* Table 6). There are a number of potential disadvantages to the use of medication for treating behavior problems, however, and you should know that there is no "magic bullet" that will easily and quickly solve the problem. The limitations of medication use include the potential for adverse effects, cost, the need to treat for a considerable length of time before the medication takes effect, limited information on what medication is most effective, and the potential that the problem will reappear once the medication is withdrawn.

All medications have the potential to cause adverse effects. Fortunately, most of the modern antianxiety and antidepressant medications used in cats are well tolerated. Gastrointestinal upsets (leading to reduced appetite, vomiting, or diarrhea) are the most common adverse effects seen. In some cats, decreased activity or lethargy may occur in the first week or so of treatment as the animal adjusts to the medication. (This reaction typically disappears on its own.) More serious adverse effects, including potentially fatal inflammation of the liver, seizures, or other signs of toxicity, have been reported in rare cases. Most of the medications used for behavior problems in cats were designed for use in people. None have been directly approved by the Food and Drug Administration for use in cats, although such use is not prohibited. This means that there may be limited information available on the safety, toxicity, and effectiveness in cats.

Because this is a relatively new area of veterinary medicine, demonstration of effectiveness through research has not been done in many cases. Veterinarians often must rely on case reports, their own clinical experience, and presentations at meetings to learn which medications and what dosage to recommend. Individual cats vary in their response to medication, just as people do. As a result, there will always be some element of trial and error in determining whether a particular medication will help solve a behavior problem.

If medication is used without behavior modification or environmental changes (and even when it is used with these techniques in some cases), the unwanted behavior may return once the medication is discontinued. Some problems may require treatment for a year or longer. In most cases medication is used for a period of several months.

Despite these limitations, medication has the potential to be very helpful in a wide range of cat behavior problems, including marking, fear-related problems, compulsive behaviors like overgrooming, and some types of aggression. Your veterinarian can discuss whether medication might be appropriate for your cat.

■ NORMAL SOCIAL BEHAVIOR IN CATS

Although many people think of cats as solitary animals, they are very sociable in the right circumstances. Some indoor cats may prefer living alone, but many get along well in groups. Outdoor cats will form stable groups as long as they can find enough food.

Unlike dogs, cats have not been artificially bred to perform specific tasks. Instead of selecting them based on behavior, different breeds have been created based on factors like hair color or length.

The basic feline social unit is the queen, or mother cat, and her kittens. Weaning occurs between 5 and 8 weeks, although given the chance, some kittens will occasionally suckle much later. This is probably related more to social behavior than to nutrition. In stable groups of outdoor cats, kittens will remain either with their mother or as part of her extended social group for the first 12 to 13 months of life. Male kittens more commonly leave the group before social maturity (2 to 4 years) than do females. Multiple generations of related females can be found in such groups and they may all provide care for the young.

The size of cat groups, also known as colonies, often depends on the amount of food available. Most domestic cats hunt alone. Prey species include those considered by humans to be vermin, like rats and mice, which may explain why cats are found worldwide. Kittens learn to prefer and to hunt the same type of prey that their mother hunted. Pet cats learn to prefer a certain texture of food. If you want your cat to accept a wide range of food as an adult, then it should be given a variety of foods as a kitten.

While sexual maturity is early (6 months of age), breeding may be inhibited in larger social groups, either directly (by male cats interrupting other males that are trying to breed) or indirectly by the group as a whole.

Factors such as being unfriendly, timid, or shy are hereditary and are often inherited from the father. However, kittens between 2 to 7 weeks of age that are handled by people are friendlier towards people, are more outgoing, and may be less aggressive. The effect of early human handling can add to the paternal effect on the willingness to explore. At about 12 to 14 weeks of age, kittens switch from social play to social fighting and a more predatory type of play. Early weaning will hasten this change.

The wild ancestors of cats used open, well-drained, ground (sand, for example) for elimination. This may reflect their North African origins. Cats may scratch before, after, or not at all when eliminating, and they may or may not dig to cover their urine or feces. All of these elimination behaviors are normal. Spraying (directing a thin stream of urine on a vertical surface like a wall, curtains, or a piece of furniture) can be a part of normal elimination, but is usually a way of marking or claiming territory.

Behaviors such as urine marking, roaming, and fighting with other cats are all affected by hormones. Neutering male cats will reduce or prevent their occurrence in most cases. Cats are markedly influenced by the role of scent in their environment, and they mark with urine, feces, and special scent glands under the chin and on the paws.

■ BEHAVIOR PROBLEMS IN CATS

The most common feline behavior problems are associated with elimination. Some of these are related to the litter box, while others reflect social conflicts and involve anxiety or aggression. Much feline aggression is subtle and passive, so its real frequency may be greatly underestimated.

Many behavior problems in cats are similar to those in dogs, including some types of aggression and elimination problems (*see* page 25). Additional behavior problems in cats are discussed below.

The process of diagnosing and treating behavior problems in cats is complex and requires a face-to-face meeting with a qualified behaviorist (*see* BOX). The descriptions in this chapter are intended to help you understand the types of behavior problems in cats, but are not a replacement for seeking professional help in solving a problem.

Behavior Problems Associated with Aggression

Aggression due to lack of early handling is an abnormal, out-of-context threat or attack demonstrated by cats toward peo-

ple when people approach or attempt to handle the cat. As mentioned above, early exposure to people is essential for kittens to develop into friendly adults. However, sometimes these problems are hereditary. In such cases the cat may learn to be friendly with its owner, but not other people.

Status-related aggression is scratching or biting by cats towards people that try to control the cat's behavior. This is another name for what has been called

Where to Get Help

Owners seeking help for a behavior problem with their cat can turn to several sources. The American Veterinary Medical Association recognizes a variety of specialties within veterinary medicine. Similar to specialties in human medicine, these include veterinarians who are board-certified in surgery, internal medicine, ophthalmology (eye care), dentistry, behavior, and 14 other areas of expertise. As of 2007, there are 42 board-certified veterinary behaviorists. Most of these work in veterinary colleges or private referral practices.

There are also veterinarians who are not board-certified, but who have a special interest in behavior. These veterinarians have a range of experience and expertise in the field, and many offer behavioral consultations as a part of their regular veterinary practice.

In addition, nonveterinarians may call themselves behaviorists and offer counseling on behavior problems of pets. Some have a doctoral or master's degree in psychology or a related field, and some of these individuals are certified by a scientific organization called the Animal Behavior Society. Others have no formal education in behavior but offer advice on solving behavior problems of cats. Owners who need help for their pet should ask about the background and training of the person offering the behavior consultation before setting up an appointment. Because many behavior problems in cats can be influenced by medical conditions, veterinarians are the professionals who can offer the most comprehensive care.

the "leave-me-alone bite." Unlike similar situations in dogs, this behavior in cats is not associated with resources such as food, toys, or space.

Other types of aggression in cats, including fear, inter-cat, maternal, pain, play, predatory, and redirected aggression, are similar to the same conditions in dogs (*see* page 25).

Treatment

Treatment of feline aggression is similar in principle and practice to that of canine aggression. Cats, like dogs, will work for food rewards in counterconditioning programs. It is best to seek the help of your veterinarian for a successful treatment program. The earlier a treatment program is started, the better the chances that it will be successful.

Behavior Problems Associated with Elimination

Aversion to type of litter or location involves consistent avoidance of a litter box location or litter type formerly used for elimination.

Location preference involves consistent elimination in an area outside of the litter box.

Spraying is the elimination of urine through a small stream of urine. It is done standing up, with the tail raised and quivering. The urine is directed onto a vertical surface, such as a wall, curtain, or door. Cats may spray as a form of marking or as a sign of anxiety.

Substrate preference is consistent elimination on a particular surface or substrate (for example, carpet or tile).

Treatment

Treatment of feline elimination disorders includes addressing the underlying anxieties and any associated aggressive behaviors, keeping the litter box as clean as possible, and determining what combi-

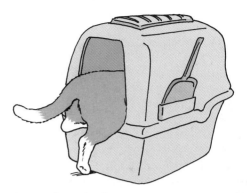

Cats can be picky about the type and location of the litter box.

nation of litter, box, and location is preferred by your cat. If anxiety or marking is part of the problem, medication may also make a big difference in managing the problem. Your veterinarian can help you to identify the best treatment program.

Other Feline Behavior Problems

Other kinds of behavior problems also occur in cats. **Hyperesthesia** is a syndrome that is not completely understood. Cats with this problem are overly sensitive to being touched, especially along the back. They may howl or become agitated when handled. **Compulsive behavior** also occurs in cats. These are otherwise normal behaviors that occur out of context or so often that they interfere with normal activity. The most common types are excessive grooming, and chewing of wool or other fabrics. In many cats compulsive behavior results from stress or anxiety. Chewing wool or other fabrics tends to occur in Siamese and similar breeds and is likely inherited. Your veterinarian can help you with a behavior modification program and medication in order to manage these types of behavior problems.

DISORDERS AND DISEASES OF CATS

24 Blood Disorders 359
Introduction 359
Red Blood Cells 359
White Blood Cells 360
Platelets 361
Blood Groups and Blood Transfusions 361
Anemia 362
Blood Parasites 364
Bleeding Disorders 366
White Blood Cell Disorders 369
Polycythemia 370

25 Heart and Blood Vessel Disorders 370
Introduction 370
Heart Disease and Heart Failure 372
Diagnosis of Cardiovascular Disease 373
Treatment of Cardiovascular Disease 373
Congenital and Inherited Disorders of the Cardiovascular System 373
Heart Failure 376
Acquired Heart and Blood Vessel Disorders 378
Heartworm Disease 380
Blood Clots and Aneurysms 382

26 Digestive Disorders 383
Introduction 383
Congenital and Inherited Disorders 387
Dental Development 390
Dental Disorders 390
Disorders of the Mouth 393
Disorders of the Pharynx 396
Disorders of the Esophagus 397
Vomiting 397
Disorders of the Stomach and Intestines 398
Disorders Caused by Bacteria 402
Gastrointestinal Parasites of Cats 403
Disorders Caused by Protozoa 405
Disorders of the Pancreas 407
Disorders of the Liver and Gallbladder 409
Disorders of the Rectum and Anus 414

27 Hormonal Disorders 415
Introduction 415
Disorders of the Adrenal Glands 417
Disorders of the Pancreas 417
Disorders of the Parathyroid Glands and of Calcium Metabolism 419
Disorders of the Pituitary Gland 420
Disorders of the Thyroid Gland 422

28 Eye Disorders **423**
Eye Structure and Function 423
Disorders of the Eyelids 425
Disorders of the Nasal Cavity and Tear Ducts 426
Disorders of the Conjunctiva 427
Disorders of the Cornea 428
Disorders of the Anterior Uvea 428
Glaucoma 429
Disorders of the Lens 429
Disorders of the Retina, Choroid, and Optic Disk (Ocular Fundus) 430
Disorders of the Optic Nerve 431
Prolapse of the Eye 431
Chlamydial Conjunctivitis (Feline Pneumonitis) 432
Eyeworm Disease (Thelaziasis) 432
Cancers and Tumors of the Eye 432

29 Ear Disorders **433**
Ear Structure and Function 433
Deafness 435
Disorders of the Outer Ear 435
Otitis Externa 437
Otitis Media and Interna 437
Tumors of the Ear Canal 437

30 Immune Disorders **439**
The Immune System 439
Disorders Involving Anaphylactic Reactions (Type I Reactions, Atopy) 439
Disorders Involving Cytotoxic Antibodies (Type II Reactions) 441
Disorders Involving Immune Complexes (Type III Reactions) 442
Disorders Involving Cell-mediated Immunity (Type IV Reactions) 443
Immune-deficiency Diseases 443
Immune System Tumors 444
Gammopathies 445

31 Bone, Joint, and Muscle Disorders **445**
Introduction 445
Components of the Musculoskeletal System 445
Lameness 446
Congenital and Inherited Disorders of Bones, Joints, and Muscles 447
Disorders Associated with Calcium, Phosphorus, and Vitamin D 447
Joint Disorders 449
Muscle Disorders 451
Bone Disorders 452
Sarcocystosis 454

32 Brain, Spinal Cord, and Nerve Disorders **455**
The Nervous System 455
Parts of the Nervous System 455
Nervous System Disorders and Effects of Injuries 456
The Neurologic Evaluation 457
Principles of Therapy 459
Congenital and Inherited Disorders 459
Disorders of the Peripheral Nerves 460
Disorders of the Spinal Column and Cord 462
Dysautonomia 464
Facial Paralysis 464

Central Nervous System Disorders Caused by Parasites 465
Leg Paralysis 466
Meningitis and Encephalitis 466
Motion Sickness 467
Rabies 467
Tick Paralysis 469

33 **Reproductive Disorders**... **469**
Introduction 469
The Gonads and Genital Tract 469
Management of Reproduction in Cats 471
Infertility 472
Reproductive Disorders of Male Cats 473
Reproductive Disorders of Female Cats 473
Mammary (Breast) Tumors 475

34 **Lung and Airway Disorders** **475**
Introduction 475
Accumulation of Fluid or Air in the Chest Cavity 478
Allergic Pneumonitis 479
Cancers and Tumors 479
Diaphragmatic Hernia 480
Emphysema 481
Feline Respiratory Disease Complex (Feline Herpesviral Rhinotracheitis, Feline
    Calicivirus) 481
Laryngitis 483
Lung Flukes 483
Lungworm Infection 484
Nasopharyngeal Polyps 484
Paralysis of the Larynx 484
Pharyngitis 484
Pneumonia 485
Pulmonary Edema 486
Rhinitis and Sinusitis 486
Tonsillitis 487
Tracheobronchitis (Bronchitis, Bronchial Asthma) 487

35 **Skin Disorders** **488**
Structure of the Skin 488
Dermatitis and Dermatologic Problems 489
Diagnosis of Skin Disorders 490
Treatment of Skin Disorders 490
Congenital and Inherited Skin Disorders 491
Allergies 492
Eosinophilic Granuloma Complex 493
Fleas 494
Flies and Mosquitoes 496
Hair Loss (Alopecia) 498
Hives and Rashes (Urticaria) 499
Itching (Pruritus) 499
Lice 500
Mite Infestation (Mange, Acariasis, Scabies) 500
Parasitic Worms of the Skin 502
Photosensitization 502
Pox Infection 503
Pyoderma 504
Ringworm (Dermatophytosis) 504

Ticks 505
Tumors of the Skin 505
Whole-body Disorders that Affect the Skin 513

36 **Kidney and Urinary Tract Disorders** **514**
The Urinary System 514
Detecting Disorders of the Kidneys and Urinary Tract 514
Congenital and Inherited Disorders of the Urinary System 515
Infectious Diseases of the Urinary System 516
Noninfectious Diseases of the Urinary System 518

37 **Metabolic Disorders** **525**
Introduction 525
Congenital Erythropoietic Porphyria 526
Disorders of Calcium Metabolism 527
Disorders of Magnesium Metabolism 527
Fever of Unknown Origin 527
Malignant Hyperthermia 528

38 **Disorders Affecting Multiple Body Systems** **528**
Introduction 528
Congenital and Inherited Disorders 529
Amyloidosis 530
Anthrax 531
Ehrlichiosis and Related Infections 532
Feline Infectious Peritonitis 532
Feline Leukemia Virus and Related Diseases 533
Feline Panleukopenia 536
Fungal Infections 537
Glanders (Farcy) 540
Leishmaniasis 541
Lyme Disease (Lyme Borreliosis) 541
Melioidosis 541
Nocardiosis 542
Peritonitis 542
Plague 543
Q Fever 544
Tetanus 544
Toxoplasmosis 545
Trichinellosis (Trichinosis) 546
Tuberculosis 546
Tularemia 547

CHAPTER 24

Blood Disorders

▨ INTRODUCTION

Blood cells form and develop mostly in the bone marrow, that is, the tissue located in the cavities of bones. Blood performs a variety of important functions as it circulates throughout the body. It delivers oxygen and vital nutrients (such as vitamins, minerals, fats, and sugars) to the tissues. It carries carbon dioxide to the lungs to be exhaled and waste products to the kidneys to be eliminated from the body. It transports hormones, which are chemical messengers, to various parts of the body, allowing those parts to communicate with each other. Blood also includes cells that fight infection and platelets that control bleeding.

There are 3 cellular elements of blood: red blood cells, white blood cells, and platelets. Basically, red blood cells supply the body with oxygen, white blood cells protect against infection, and platelets start the formation of blood clots.

▨ RED BLOOD CELLS

The main function of red blood cells (also called erythrocytes) is to carry oxygen to the tissues. When the number of red blood cells is too low, this is called anemia. Having too few red blood cells means the blood carries less oxygen. (For a more detailed discussion of RED BLOOD CELLS, see page 33.)

Red blood cells are formed in the bone marrow. Within the bone marrow, all blood cells begin from a single cell type called a stem cell. The stem cell divides to produce an immature form of a red blood cell white blood cell, or platelet-producing cell. That immature cell then divides again, matures even more, and ultimately becomes a mature red or white blood cell or platelet. The total number of red cells remains constant over time in healthy animals. Mature red blood cells have a

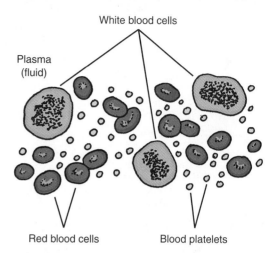

White blood cells

Plasma (fluid)

Red blood cells   Blood platelets

Blood is a complex mixture of plasma (the liquid component), red blood cells, white blood cells, and platelets.

limited life span; their production and destruction must be carefully balanced, or disease develops.

A decrease in the number of total red blood cells (anemia) may be caused by blood loss, destruction of red blood cells (hemolysis), or decreased production. In severe blood loss anemia, red blood cells are lost, but death usually results from the loss of total blood volume. Hemolysis may be caused by toxins, infections, abnormalities present at birth, or antibodies that attack the red blood cells. Certain drugs, such as acetaminophen may also cause hemolytic anemia in cats. Decreased red blood cell production may result from bone marrow diseases or from other causes such as infection with feline leukemia virus, kidney failure, drugs, toxins, or antibodies targeted at developing red blood cells. It is important to remember that anemia is a sign of disease, not a specific diagnosis. The outlook and treatment depend on the underlying cause. (*See also* ANEMIA, page 362.)

Types of Blood Cells*

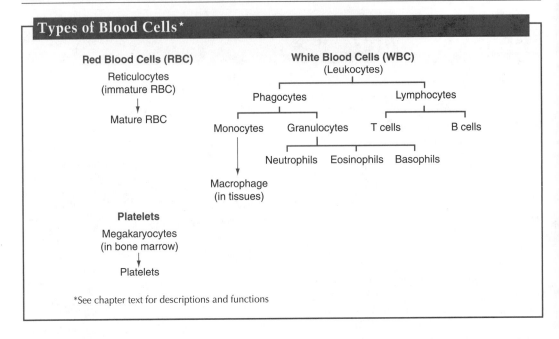

Red Blood Cells (RBC)

Reticulocytes
(immature RBC)
↓
Mature RBC

White Blood Cells (WBC)
(Leukocytes)

Phagocytes — Lymphocytes

Monocytes   Granulocytes   T cells   B cells

Neutrophils   Eosinophils   Basophils

Macrophage
(in tissues)

Platelets

Megakaryocytes
(in bone marrow)
↓
Platelets

*See chapter text for descriptions and functions

▤ WHITE BLOOD CELLS

The function of white blood cells (also called leukocytes) is to defend the body against infection. There are 2 main types of white blood cells: phagocytes and lymphocytes. (For a more complete discussion of WHITE BLOOD CELLS, see page 35.)

Phagocytes

Phagocytes are cells in the bloodstream and tissues that surround and consume foreign particles, cell waste material, and bacteria. Their main function is to defend against invading microorganisms.

There are 2 types of phagocytes: granulocytes and monocytes. **Granulocytes**, primarily neutrophils, protect against bacteria and fungi. Others, known as eosinophils and basophils, are involved in allergic reactions. **Monocytes** become macrophages in the tissues, and consume large foreign particles and cellular debris.

Unlike red blood cells, which remain circulating in the blood, phagocytes use blood vessels as a pathway to the tissues. Because of this, the number of phagocytes in the blood can provide an indication of circumstances in the tissues. For example, the neutrophil number increases in the presence of inflammation. In cats, neutrophils are normally the most numerous type of white blood cell. An abnormally low number of circulating neutrophils due to marrow failure can lower resistance to bacterial infections. Finally, those elements that produce phagocytes may become cancerous, resulting in a disease called myelogenous leukemia.

Lymphocytes

Lymphocytes are white blood cells that produce antibodies against infectious organisms. They also reject foreign tissue and cancer cells. There are 2 types of lymphocytes: T cells and B cells. **T cells** are responsible for fighting off viral infections and cancer cells. **B cells** produce antibodies that help destroy foreign invaders, such as viruses, or cells infected by them. Antibodies also can coat bacteria making it easier for phagocytes to consume them. If lymphocytes are reduced or abnormal, the cat is immunodeficient and susceptible to a wide variety of infections.

Antibody molecules are called **immunoglobulins**. They include several classes, each of which has a different function. For example, one class is commonly found in the lungs and intestines; another is the first antibody produced in response to newly recognized foreign microorganisms; a third is the main antibody in the bloodstream; and a fourth is involved in allergic reactions.

Lymphocytes usually act appropriately to rid the body of foreign "invaders" that cause disease. An inappropriate response occurs when antibodies are produced against the body's own cells. This can result in what are called autoimmune diseases (literally, immune diseases directed against the self), such as immune-mediated hemolytic anemia.

Lymphocytosis, an increase in the number of circulating lymphocytes, may occur as a response to the secretion of epinephrine (a hormone also known as adrenaline). A reduction in the number of lymphocytes circulating in the blood may be caused by corticosteroids.

▓ PLATELETS

Platelets, produced in the bone marrow, are small, cell-like particles that start the formation of blood clots. Platelets gather where bleeding occurs and clump together to form the initial plug that stops or slows down the flow of blood. Platelets also release other substances needed to complete the clotting process.

Platelet disorders can result from having too few or too many platelets or from impaired function. When the platelet count falls very low, the risk of bleeding is increased. Decreased production of platelets may be caused by drugs, toxins, or disorders of the bone marrow.

An abnormal increase in the number of platelets is rare and often the cause is not known. It may be associated with bone marrow disease or with longterm blood loss and iron deficiency.

There are also disorders in which platelets do not function properly. Von Willebrand disease is one example. Other hereditary disorders of platelet function have been described but are rare. Probably the most common platelet function defect in animals is a side effect of aspirin. Do

not give your cat aspirin—or any other medication—unless it is prescribed by your veterinarian.

▓ BLOOD GROUPS AND BLOOD TRANSFUSIONS

Blood groups are determined by the presence or absence of certain antigens (proteins or sugars) found on the red blood cell membrane. The number of blood group systems varies among domestic species. Cats have 4 known blood types, A, B, AB, and a newly described "MIC." Type A is most common (about 90% of cats are Type A). Certain breeds have a higher prevalence of Type B. Type AB is rare. There are no universal donors among cats, because they naturally have antibodies against the blood group antigen that they lack. Patients are typed to aid in the matching of donors and recipients and to identify breeding pairs potentially at risk of causing hemolytic anemia in their offspring. Type B queens have especially strong anti-A antibodies. If they have kittens that inherit Type A from the tom, the antibody goes to the kittens in the colostrum (first milk) and destroys red blood cells in the kitten (*see* Neonatal Iso-Erythrolysis, page 362).

Blood Typing

An animal's blood group is determined by measuring the reaction of a small sample of blood to certain antibodies. The blood group must be determined before a blood transfusion can be safely provided. Even the first incompatible transfusion results in the rapid destruction of the transfused cells.

Blood Transfusions

Often, the need for a blood transfusion is an emergency, such as severe bleeding or sudden destruction of red blood cells due to other disease. Transfusions may also be needed to treat anemia of any cause. Animals with blood clotting disorders often require repeated transfusions. All transfusions must be given with care because of the potential for adverse effects. The most serious risk is destruction of the red blood cells shortly after they are given. Other complications include transmission of feline leukemia or immunodeficiency viruses from an infected donor. Donors should be tested before blood is taken. If too much blood is given, edema (fluid) in the lungs could occur. Other less common or minor reactions include decreased calcium, fever, or vomiting.

ANEMIA

Anemia occurs when there is a decrease in the number of red blood cells. It can develop from loss, destruction, or lack of production of red blood cells. Anemia is classified as regenerative or nonregenerative. In a **regenerative anemia**, the bone marrow responds appropriately to the decreased number of red blood cells by increasing red blood cell production. In a **nonregenerative anemia**, the bone marrow responds inadequately to the increased need for red blood cells. Anemias due to bleeding or the destruction of existing red blood cells are usually regenerative. Anemias that are caused by a decrease in the hormone that stimulates red blood cell production or an abnormality in the bone marrow are nonregenerative. (For a more detailed discussion of ANEMIA, *see* page 37.)

Regenerative Anemias

Regenerative anemias include blood loss anemia (*see* page 38) and hemolytic anemia (*see* page 39). Hemolytic anemias may be due to immune system dysfunction, diseases of the small blood vessels, metabolic disorders, toxins, infections, and genetic diseases.

Many classes of drugs can cause anemia if they are ingested accidentally or if their prescribed use is not closely monitored. These include common human and animal drugs such as acetaminophen, aspirin, naproxen, penicillin, and many other antibiotic and antiparasitic agents. Other anemia-causing toxins include plants such as oak, red maple, and bracken fern; foods such as fava beans and onions; chemicals; and heavy metals such as copper, lead, and zinc. It is always important to give as complete a history as possible to your veterinarian when anemia is suspected, in order to help pinpoint the cause.

Many infections—caused by bacteria, viruses, or other organisms—can lead to anemia, by direct damage to red blood cells (leading to their destruction) or by effects on the elements that produce red blood cells in the bone marrow. Some infections that can cause anemia in cats include feline leukemia virus and feline immunodeficiency virus.

Inherited red blood cell disorders can also cause anemia in cats. Deficiencies of an enzyme called pyruvate kinase are seen in Abyssinian and Somali cats. Affected cats have hemolytic anemia that waxes and wanes over a long time. Signs may improve if the spleen is removed or if corticosteroids are given. A hereditary blood disorder, porphyria (*see* page 526), which leads to a build-up of porphyrins in the body occurs in cats, people, and other species. Porphyrins are proteins that become part of the hemoglobin molecule in red blood cells. Your veterinarian can check your cat for these conditions.

Neonatal Isoerythrolysis

Neonatal isoerythrolysis is an immunologic disease seen in newborn cats. It occurs when kittens nurse from a mother whose colostrum (the yellowish fluid rich in antibodies and minerals that is produced after giving birth and before producing true milk) contains antibodies to the newborns' red blood cells. This can be caused by exposure of the mother to another blood type during a previous pregnancy or an unmatched blood transfusion. Cats with blood type B also have naturally occurring antibodies to blood type A.

The kittens get the antibodies when they first begin nursing. Once absorbed, the antibodies enter the bloodstream where they attach to red blood cells and cause them to rupture. Newborns with neonatal isoerythrolysis are normal at birth but develop severe hemolytic anemia within 2 to 3 days. A veterinarian can perform tests to confirm the diagnosis. Treatment consists of stopping any colostrum while giving supportive care with transfusions. Neonatal isoerythrolysis can be avoided by withholding colostrum from the kittens' own mother and giving colostrum free of the antibodies. A veterinarian can perform a test to check for alloimmune hemolysis before the newborn is allowed to receive maternal colostrum.

Hypophosphatemia

Anemia may be noted in cats with **hypophosphatemia**, a deficiency of phosphates in the blood. Hypophosphatemia occurs in cats with diabetes or fatty degeneration of the liver. It may also occur as a complication of refeeding syndrome, which is a shift in the concentration of several minerals in the blood that happens during recovery from a period of fasting.

Nonregenerative Anemias

Nonregenerative anemias include anemias caused by poor diet, chronic diseases, kidney disease, and disorders of the bone marrow. (For a more detailed discussion of NONREGENERATIVE ANEMIAS, *see* page 40.)

Nutritional deficiencies may lead to anemia if the nutrients needed for red blood cell formation are not present in adequate amounts in the diet. Iron deficiency, for example, occurs in some cats.

Anemia of chronic disease is usually classified as mild to moderate and nonregenerative. It is the most common form of anemia seen in animals. The anemia can occur after a long-term inflammation or infection, a tumor, liver disease, or hormonal disorders such as hyper- or hypoadrenocorticism (disorders of the adrenal gland) or hypothyroidism (an underactive thyroid gland). Proteins called cytokines, which are produced by inflammatory cells, decrease iron availability, red blood cell survival, and the bone marrow's ability to regenerate, resulting in anemia. Treatment of the underlying disease leads to correction of the anemia.

Aplastic anemia is a disorder of the bone marrow, in which the ability of bone marrow to grow new blood cells is reduced. It has been reported in cats with a condition in which too few red blood cells, white blood cells, and blood platelets are found in the blood and with bone marrow that is underdeveloped and replaced by fat. Most cases have no known cause, but some are caused by infections (including feline leukemia virus and *Ehrlichia* bacteria), drug treatment, toxins, and radiation therapy. To treat the condition, the underlying cause must be determined and eliminated. Supportive care such as antibiotics and transfusions may also be needed. Drugs that stimulate the bone marrow can be used until the marrow recovers. If the disease has no known cause or if marrow recovery is unlikely, bone marrow transplantation is helpful if a suitable donor is available.

In **pure red cell aplasia**, only the red blood cells are affected. In this nonregenerative anemia, there is a severe reduction of the elements that produce red blood cells in the bone marrow. It has been reported in cats, including some with feline leukemia.

Primary leukemias are a type of cancer in which abnormal white blood cells displace normal blood cells. This leads to anemia and a lack of normal white blood cells and platelets. Primary leukemias are uncommon, but they have been reported in cats. Retroviruses are a cause in some cats. Leukemias are classified as acute (sudden and often severe) or chronic (long-term). Acute leukemias, in which the marrow is filled with immature blood cells, generally respond poorly to chemotherapy. In animals that do respond, remission times are usually short. Chronic leukemias, in which there is greatly increased production of one blood cell line, are less likely to cause anemia and are more responsive to treatment.

Myelodysplasia (also called myelodysplastic syndrome) is a bone marrow disorder in which growth and maturation of blood-forming cells in the bone marrow is defective. This leads to nonregenerative anemia or shortages of white blood cells or platelets. It is considered a preleukemic syndrome (occurring before leukemia fully develops). Myelodysplasia occurs in cats, dogs, and humans. The disease can occur as the result of mutations in stem cells or be caused by tumors in other organs or drug therapy. Some cats respond to treatment with synthetic hormones and steroids. Supportive care with blood transfusions may be helpful. Survival rates vary because myelodysplasia can progress to leukemia. Many animals with this condition are put to sleep or die of infection, bleeding, or anemia.

Myelofibrosis is a progressive disease leading to anemia and enlargement of the spleen and liver. It brings on bone marrow failure after it causes normal marrow elements to be replaced with fibrous tissue. It occurs in cats and several other species. Myelofibrosis may arise on its own or as the result of cancer, immune-mediated hemolytic anemia (*see* page 39), radiation therapy, or hereditary causes. A diagnosis can be made by bone marrow biopsy, a procedure requiring anesthesia and often an overnight stay at the veterinary hospital. Treatment depends on the underlying causes but usually involves suppressing the immune system. Because immune system suppression increases the chances that your pet will catch other diseases, carefully follow your veterinarian's recommendations for controlling exposure to disease-causing agents.

▨ BLOOD PARASITES

Blood parasites are organisms that live in the blood of their animal hosts. These parasites can range from single-celled protozoa to more complex bacteria and rickettsiae. The method of transmission varies depending on the parasite, but often they are transmitted through the bites of ticks or flies.

Babesiosis

Babesiosis is a disease that is transmitted by ticks. It is caused by protozoan parasites of the genus *Babesia*, which infect red blood cells. Babesiosis affects a wide range of domestic and wild animals and occasionally humans. While the major economic impact of babesiosis is on the cattle industry, infections in other domestic animals, including cats, occur at various rates throughout the world.

Illness of varying severity due to *Babesia felis* has been reported in domestic cats in Africa and India. An unusual feature is its lack of response to the normal medicines used to destroy *Babesia* parasites. However, your veterinarian can provide alternative medications for this disease. (For a more detailed discussion of Babesiosis, *see* page 42.)

Cytauxzoonosis

Cytauxzoonosis is caused by parasites of the genus *Cytauxzoon*. These are natural parasites of wild cats of North America, including the bobcat and the Florida panther. The parasites are transmitted to domestic cats by ticks. Most cases occur in the southern and southeastern states of the US and are usually associated with access to wooded areas. The disease progresses quickly and is usually deadly, although a strain found in northwestern Arkansas and northeastern Oklahoma may be less dangerous. The disease can also be transmitted by blood infection, which appears to have less deadly results.

Signs of infection usually begin about 10 days after a tick bite and come to a peak about 6 days later. Cats may be feverish, weak, depressed, and dehydrated, have difficulty breathing, and refuse to eat. Temperatures may be as high as 105°F (40.5°C) but usually fall below normal at the point of death. Gums and other mucous membranes are often yellow (jaundiced). Your veterinarian will perform blood tests to identify this infection. Treatment is often unsuccessful when the infection is caused by a severe strain, but new treatments have shown promise in some cases. Keeping cats out of areas where ticks are found is the best way to prevent this disease.

Feline Infectious Anemia (Hemobartonellosis)

Feline infectious anemia is an acute or chronic disease of domestic cats. It is seen in many parts of the world and is caused by a rickettsial agent (a specialized type of bacteria) that multiplies within the bloodstream. Feline infectious anemia is thought to be transmitted by bloodsucking insects such as fleas. Transmission via bite wounds is another possibility, and transmission from mother to kitten can also occur during pregnancy.

Feline infectious anemia is more common among 1- to 3-year-old cats, particularly males. The first signs of illness usually appear 1 to 5 weeks after transmission of the parasite, and recovery does not make the animal immune to reinfection. Cats that have recovered from infection may still carry the parasite and relapse when stressed. Some cats may not appear to be sick, but are carrying the infection in a suppressed (or latent) form. Signs of illness may only appear when the cat has another disease or is stressed.

Any anemic cat should be evaluated by a veterinarian for feline infectious anemia. In severe cases, fever usually reaches 103 to 106°F (39 to 41°C). The more quickly the anemia develops, the more severe the signs observed. Pale mucous membranes or jaundice, loss of appetite and energy, depression, weakness, and an enlarged spleen are common signs of this disease. In chronic cases, weight loss or emaciation may be seen, but there is less likely to be jaundice or an enlarged spleen. The degree of breathing difficulty varies with the degree of anemia.

The number of red blood cells affected depends on the severity of the infection and the stage in the life cycle of the parasite. A series of daily blood tests are normally used to confirm the diagnosis, because these red blood cell parasites are not always present in every blood sample.

To help prevent this disease in your cat, reduce the animal's exposure to bloodsucking insects and stay alert to your cat's overall condition. If unusual symptoms such as loss of energy, depression, or other signs of declining health appear, take your cat to your veterinarian for an examination.

Treatment involves both supportive care and specific drugs. Without treatment, up to one-third of cats may die in the early stages of infection. Cats that have difficulty breathing may require oxygen, and whole blood or red blood cell transfusions may be needed. Antibiotics are effective in many cases and may be prescribed by your veterinarian. If antibiotics are recommended, be sure to provide your pet with the prescribed dosages on the schedule given to you by your veterinarian.

Hepatozoonosis

Hepatozoonosis is a tick-borne disease of wild and domestic carnivores (meat-eating animals) caused by protozoa of the genus *Hepatozoon*. This organism is transmitted by the brown dog tick, but its method of transmission is unusual. The tick picks up the organism from an infected host while biting the animal. An uninfected cat then gets the disease by eating the tick, not from being bitten by the tick.

(For a more detailed description of hepatozoonosis including causes, spread, transmission, signs, diagnosis, and treatment, *see* page 43.)

African Tsetse-transmitted Trypanosomiasis

Tsetse are small, winged biting flies that feed on the blood of humans and other animals. They only occur in sub-Saharan Africa, where they are responsible for transmitting a group of diseases caused by protozoa of the genus *Trypanosoma*, which affect all domestic animals. In cats, *Trypanosoma brucei* is probably the most important disease-causing species. This disease is not common in North America. (For a more detailed discussion of TSETSE-TRANSMITTED TRYPANOSOMIASIS, *see* page 44.)

Surra (*Trypanosoma evansi* Infection)

Surra is separated from the tsetse-transmitted diseases because it is usually transmitted by other biting flies that are found within and outside tsetse fly areas. It occurs in North Africa, the Middle East, Asia, the Far East, and Central and South America. It is mostly a disease of horses, but cats and other domestic animals are susceptible. The disease can be deadly. The development and effects of the disease, signs, diagnosis, and treatment are similar to those of Tsetse-transmitted trypanosomiasis (*see* page 365).

Chagas' Disease (*Trypanosoma cruzi* Infection)

Chagas' disease is caused by infection with another trypanosome, *Trypanosoma cruzi*. Insects transmit the disease between susceptible species of animals, including opossums, armadillos, rodents, and wild meat-eating animals. The trypanosome causes disease in humans and occasionally in young cats (and dogs). The disease occurs in Central and South America and localized areas of the southern US. Domestic animals may become infected and introduce the trypanosome into houses where the bugs are present. People then become infected by contamination of eye wounds or by eating food contaminated with insect droppings that contain trypanosomes. Other domestic animals act as source hosts. Your veterinarian can tell you if you live in an area where infections are likely.

▓ BLEEDING DISORDERS

When bleeding occurs in an organ or body part, a process is set in motion to stop the bleeding. This is called **hemostasis**. In order to work, hemostasis requires an adequate number of platelets, the right amount of blood clotting proteins (often referred to as factors), and blood vessels

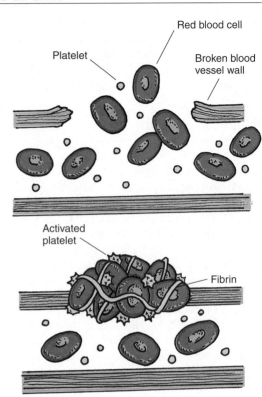

How blood clots are formed (modified with permission from *The Merck Manual of Medical Information*, Second Home Edition, 2003)

that constrict properly. When an injury occurs, the wall of the blood vessel breaks. A normally responsive blood vessel will narrow so that blood flows more slowly, allowing the clotting process to begin. Platelets also rush to the broken wall where certain proteins change the platelets' shape from round to spiny so that they can stick to blood cells, the broken vessel wall, and to each other. Other proteins form long strands called fibrin. These fibrin strands form a net that traps and helps hold together the platelets and blood cells, creating a clot that plugs the break in the vessel wall. After the clot has formed and stabilized, other proteins stop the clotting process and eventually dissolve the clot.

Bleeding disorders may be present at birth (congenital) or occur later. Defects in blood clotting proteins usually show up as delayed bleeding and bruising deep in tissues, while platelet defects usually show up as superficial small bruises, nosebleeds, black stools caused by bleeding into the bowels, or prolonged bleeding at injection and surgery sites.

Bleeding disorders include coagulation protein disorders, platelet disorders, and vascular disorders. The ones that are most common in cats are described below. (For a more detailed discussion of BLEEDING DISORDERS, *see* page 46.)

Congenital Clotting Protein Disorders

If clotting protein levels are too low, or if they do not work properly, signs appear at an early age. Severe defects are usually deadly. Animals may be stillborn or die shortly after birth. Insufficient production of clotting proteins may worsen a clotting defect. If activity of any particular clotting protein is 5 to 10% of normal, the newborn may survive, but signs usually appear before 6 months of age. It is during this time, when numerous routine procedures (for example, vaccination, castration, or spaying) are usually done, that a bleeding tendency may be noticed by your veterinarian.

Hemophilia A (Factor VIII deficiency) is the most common inherited bleeding disorder in cats. Affected cats may show prolonged bleeding after surgery or injury but rarely bleed spontaneously, probably because of their agility and light weight. The diagnosis is harder to confirm in animals less than 6 months old because their livers may not yet have produced enough of the clotting proteins. Treatment requires repeated transfusions of whole blood or plasma until bleeding has been controlled.

Hemophilia B (Factor IX deficiency) is diagnosed less often in cats than hemophilia A. It has been reported in Himalayan cats, a family of Siamese-cross cats, and a family of British Shorthaired cats. Signs are similar to those of animals with Factor VIII deficiency. Animals with extremely low Factor IX activity (less than 1%) usually die at birth or shortly thereafter. Animals with 5 to 10% of normal Factor IX activity may suddenly develop blood clots, bleeding in the joints, oozing of blood into the body cavity, or organ bleeding. Gum bleeding during teething or prolonged bleeding after surgery can occur. Some animals have no symptoms until injury or surgery. Treatment requires transfusion with fresh or fresh-frozen plasma. Often, internal bleeding into the abdomen, chest, central nervous system, or muscles occurs, and may not be noticed until a crisis happens.

Acquired Clotting Protein Disorders

Most clotting proteins are produced in the liver. Therefore, liver disease can lead to decreased production of clotting proteins, particularly Factors VII, IX, X, and XI. Small to large decreases in clotting proteins can result after severe liver disease.

Cats that eat rat poison may have blood clotting problems because the poison reduces the liver's production of clotting proteins (*see* RODENTICIDE POISONING, page 1201). Affected animals may have blood clots and bruises in multiple tissues. If you suspect your cat has eaten any type of rat or mouse poison, this is an emergency and an immediate trip to your veterinarian is recommended.

Disseminated intravascular coagulation (DIC) is a condition in which small blood clots develop throughout the bloodstream, blocking small blood vessels and destroying the platelets and clotting factors needed to control bleeding. It usually develops after numerous triggering events such as severe infections, heat stroke, burns, tumors, or severe injury. In many cases, the signs are uncontrolled bleeding and the inability to form a normal clot. Death is caused by extensive blood clots or collapse of circulation, leading to the failure of one or several organs. If the animal survives this crisis, a chronic form of DIC can occur. Your veterinarian will determine and attempt to correct the underlying problem. Intravenous fluids are extremely important for maintaining normal circulation. DIC is a very serious disorder and is often fatal.

Platelet Disorders

Disorders of platelets include having too few platelets (thrombocytopenia) or having platelets that do not work properly. Each type of disorder can be either congenital (present at birth) or acquired later in life. Thrombocytosis is having too many platelets in response to a physiologic or disease process or, rarely, as a component of cancer.

Acquired Thrombocytopenia

Acquired thrombocytopenias are reported frequently in cats and dogs and rarely in other species. Numerous causes have been identified; in most cases the immune system destroys platelets.

Thrombocytopenia caused by drugs occurs in cats. Some drugs and classes of drugs (including estrogen and some antibiotics) suppress platelet production in the bone marrow. Other drugs (including aspirin, acetaminophen, penicillin, and others) destroy platelets circulating in the bloodstream. Drug reactions are rare and unpredictable. Platelets usually return to normal shortly after the drug is discontinued. Drug-induced bone marrow suppression may last longer, however. If your cat is taking one of these drugs, your veterinarian will likely monitor the blood count to check for any serious reductions in the number of platelets.

Cats are inquisitive and investigate the world with their tongues. They may lick or eat birth control pills, aspirin, pain pills, or other medications. This is another example of why medications should be carefully stored. This simple precaution can save your pet's life.

Congenital Platelet Function Disorders

Cats with **Chédiak-Higashi syndrome** (*see* page 369) have abnormal white blood cells, melanocytes (pigment-producing skin cells), and platelets. The defect in melanocytes causes a pale coat color. White blood cells do not work properly, and platelets do not clump together or separate as they normally should when blood clots are formed or broken down.

Prolonged bleeding in blue smoke Persian cats occurs after surgery or when a blood sample is taken.

Von Willebrand's disease is caused by a defective or deficient von Willebrand's factor (also called Factor VIII-related antigen). It is more common in dogs; however, it has also been reported in cats.

Acquired Platelet Function Disorders

Several diseases have been associated with acquired platelet function disorders. In 2 studies of cats with lowered numbers of platelets circulating in their blood, up to half had infectious diseases, including feline leukemia, feline infectious peritonitis, feline distemper (panleukopenia), or toxoplasmosis (a disease caused by the protozoan parasite *Toxoplasma gondii*). Acquired defects of the immune system, longterm kidney disease, liver disease, and certain drugs can also cause disorders in platelet function. Your veterinarian can diagnose these disorders with blood tests and other tools.

Blood Vessel Disorders

Ehlers-Danlos syndrome, also known as cutaneous asthenia, is caused by a defect (present at birth) in the development of connective tissue proteins found in skin. This causes weak structural support of blood vessels and can result in blood clot formation and easy bruising. The disorder has been reported in cats but is rare. The most striking sign is loose skin that stretches to a greater than normal degree and tears easily. There is no treatment.

Blood Clotting Disorders

Certain diseases in animals have been associated with increased risk of blood clots. Cats with **cardiomyopathy** (a disease of the heart muscle) can form blood clots in large arteries. Injury to the wall of the heart and turbulent blood flow through the heart chambers and valves caused by poor functioning of the heart are thought to start blood clot formation. Cats with heart disease caused by high levels of thyroid hormone are often given drugs that lessen the signs of heart problems. These drugs appear to protect against increased risk of blood clots by changing how likely the platelets are to form a clot. Your veterinarian can prescribe the most appropriate medication for your cat.

WHITE BLOOD CELL DISORDERS

Leukocytes, or white blood cells, in the blood of mammals include neutrophils, lymphocytes, monocytes, eosinophils, and basophils. These cells vary with regard to where they are produced, how long they circulate in the bloodstream, and the factors that stimulate them into going in or out of the intricate network of tiny blood vessels that branch out through the tissues of the body. The normal numbers of each type of white blood cell also vary among species. **Leukocytosis** is an increase in the total number of circulating white blood cells; **leukopenia** is a decrease.

Leukograms are blood tests that count the number of different white blood cells circulating in the bloodstream. By counting the cells and examining their form your veterinarian gains valuable information that can help diagnose a wide variety of disorders.

Disorders Related to Increased or Decreased White Blood Cells

Neutrophilia is an increase in the number of neutrophils in the bloodstream and is caused by inflammation. Structural changes in neutrophils may occur during severe inflammation and are referred to as toxic changes. **Neutropenia** is a decrease in the number of neutrophils in the bloodstream. It may occur due to the white blood cells sticking to the walls of damaged blood vessels, destruction of neutrophils, or reduced formation in the bone marrow. Neutropenia may occur in all species during overwhelming bacterial infections. Adverse reactions to drugs may result in neutropenia or even pancytopenia (a reduction in red and white blood cells and platelets) in cats. Feline leukemia virus has also been associated with neutropenia.

Eosinophilia is an increase in the number of eosinophils, which are involved in allergic reactions and in controlling parasites. Increases are caused by substances that promote allergic reactions (for example, histamine) and by certain antibodies. Eosinophils increase during infections with parasites such as heartworms or fleas. Eosinophilia also may occur with inflammation of the intestines, kidneys, lungs, or skin. **Hypereosinophilic syndrome**—with persistent and excessive levels of eosinophils, which accumulate in various organs—has been reported in cats. The cause is unknown. Diagnosis may require several blood tests. Less commonly, eosinophilia may be associated with cancer. In some cats, eosinophils collect in skin or mouth sores. A decrease in eosinophils is known as **eosinopenia**. It is a common reaction to stress or treatment with corticosteroids.

Leukemia and Lymphoma

Leukemia is a malignant cancer that is characterized by an increase in abnormal white blood cells in the bloodstream. Lymphoma is a related cancer of certain white blood cells that begins in a lymph node or other lymphoid tissue. Leukemia should be considered a potential cause when there is an increase in the number of white blood cells in the bloodstream. (*See also* FELINE LEUKEMIA VIRUS AND RELATED DISEASES, page 533.)

Chédiak-Higashi Syndrome

This inherited syndrome occurs in Persian cats (and in humans). There is an increased susceptibility to bacterial infections due to impaired white blood cell function, an increased tendency to bleed due to platelet defects, and partial lack of color in the eyes and skin due to abnormal melanin (pigment) distribution. Diagnosis is based on abnormal skin color, presence of abnormal white blood cells, and increased susceptibility to infections.

Pelger-Huët Anomaly

This condition is characterized by the failure of certain white blood cells (granulocytes) to mature normally. White blood cell function is normal, and many cats do not have any signs of illness. In some animals, it is deadly and associated with skeletal deformities and increased susceptibility to infection.

POLYCYTHEMIA

Polycythemia is an increase in the number of red blood cells in the bloodstream. **Polycythemia rubra vera** is a disease in which the blood-producing cells in the bone marrow develop and reproduce abnormally. It has been reported in cats. Red blood cell production is dramatically increased, and levels of the hormone that stimulates development of red blood cells (erythropoietin) are low or normal. In **secondary polycythemia**, red blood cell production increases in response to increased erythropoietin levels. This may be seen in severe lung disease, congestive heart failure, or abnormalities of blood circulation.

Your veterinarian will use tests of blood and urine to help diagnose polycythemia. In some cases, X-rays and other tests may also be required. Signs of the disorder include red mucous membranes, bleeding tendencies, the passing of large amounts of urine, excessive thirst, seizures or behavioral changes, lack of coordination, weakness, and blindness. Treatment of polycythemia includes removing red blood cells by withdrawing blood through a catheter placed in a vein, then replacing the lost blood with fluids. Drugs such as hydroxyurea or clorambucil may also be added to the treatment. In some cases, the underlying disease must be treated. (For a more detailed discussion of POLYCYTHEMIA, *see* page 52.)

CHAPTER **25**

Heart and Blood Vessel Disorders

INTRODUCTION

The cardiovascular system includes the heart and the blood vessels (the veins and the arteries). The function of the heart is to pump blood. The right side of the heart pumps blood to the lungs, where oxygen is added to the blood. The left side pumps blood to the rest of the body, where oxygen and nutrients are delivered to tissues, and waste products (such as carbon dioxide) are removed. The heart is a hollow, muscular organ which, in mammals and birds, is divided into 4 chambers. The muscular tissue is called the myocardium. There are upper chambers on both the left and ride sides of the heart called the left and right **atria** (the plural form of atrium). There are also 2 lower chambers called the left and right **ventricles**.

A series of valves keep blood flowing in one direction through the heart. The **atrioventricular valves** are valves between the atria and the ventricles. The **semilunar valves** are valves between the heart and the aorta and between the heart and the pulmonary artery. Each ventricle has an inlet and an outlet valve. In the left ventricle, the inlet valve is called the **mitral valve**, and the outlet valve is called the **aortic valve**. In the right ventricle, the inlet valve is called the **tricuspid valve**, and the outlet valve is called the **pulmonary valve**.

Blood from the body flows through the 2 largest veins, called the **venae cavae**, into the right atrium. When the right ventricle relaxes, blood in the right atrium pours through the tricuspid valve into the right ventricle. When the right ventricle is nearly

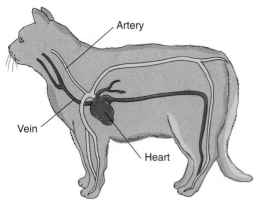

Cardiovascular system in a cat

full, the right atrium contracts, pushing additional blood into the right ventricle. The right ventricle then contracts, pushing blood through the pulmonary valve into the pulmonary arteries, which lead to the lungs. In the lungs, blood absorbs oxygen and gives up carbon dioxide. The blood then flows through the pulmonary veins into the left atrium. When the left ventricle relaxes, the blood in the left atrium pours through the mitral valve into the left ventricle.

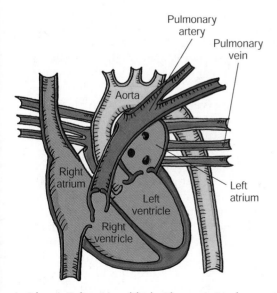

Inside a cat's heart (modified with permission from *The Merck Manual of Medical Information*, Second Home Edition, 2003)

When the left ventricle is nearly full, the left atrium contracts, pushing additional blood into the left ventricle. The left ventricle then contracts, pushing blood through the aortic valve into the aorta, the largest artery in the body. This blood carried in the aorta distributes oxygen to all of the body except the lungs.

Each heartbeat consists of 2 parts: **diastole** and **systole**. The first half of a heartbeat (diastole) is the sound of the mitral and tricuspid valves closing. The second half (systole) is the sound of the aortic and pulmonary valves closing. During diastole, the ventricles relax and fill with blood. During systole, they contract and pump blood out to the body.

The rate and force of contraction of the heart and the degree of narrowing or widening of blood vessels are controlled by several hormones and by the autonomic nervous system (the part of the nervous system that controls involuntary activity).

Heart Rate

The heart beats because of a tiny electrical current that begins in the **sinoatrial node.** The sinoatrial node is the heart's natural pacemaker. Rhythmic electrical impulses or discharges from the sinoatrial node cause the contraction of muscle fibers in the heart. While an animal is at rest, the sinoatrial node discharges many times each minute; in a resting cat, it will discharge more than 200 times per minute.

Heart rate is also inversely related to blood pressure. When blood pressure increases, heart rate decreases; when blood pressure decreases, heart rate increases. (For a more detailed discussion of HEART RATE, *see* page 54.)

Heart Sounds and Murmurs

Heart sounds are produced by the rapid acceleration and deceleration of blood and the resulting vibrations in the heart due to the circulation of blood. They can be heard using a stethoscope. In cats, 2 heart sounds can normally be distinguished.

Heart murmurs are vibrations that can be heard coming from the heart or major blood vessels and generally are the result of turbulent blood flow or vibrations of heart structures such as part of a valve. Murmurs are typically described by their timing (that is, whether they occur continuously or only intermittently), their intensity (that is, whether they can be heard easily or with difficulty), and their location. Not every murmur indicates a heart disorder; for example, murmurs are commonly detected in kittens less than 6 months of age.

Arrhythmias

Arrhythmias are abnormalities of the rate, regularity, or site of heartbeat formation. An arrhythmia does not necessarily indicate heart disease. Many arrhythmias are functionally insignificant and require no specific treatment. Some arrhythmias, however, may cause severe signs such as loss of consciousness due to lack of blood flow to the brain or lead to sudden death. Many disorders are associated with abnormal heart rhythms.

Pulse

A pulse is the rhythmic expansion of an artery that can be felt with the fingertips during physical examination. In cats, pulses are typically felt at the femoral artery (in the thigh). A jugular pulse in the neck can be noted in normal animals. A pulse may be absent, increased (strong), or decreased (weak)—each of which may indicate a specific type of heart disease or defect.

▓ HEART DISEASE AND HEART FAILURE

Slightly more than 10% of the animals examined by a veterinarian have some form of cardiovascular disease. Unlike diseases of many other organ systems, cardiovascular diseases generally do not go away but almost always become more serious and may lead to death. In addition, cardiovascular diseases may be more difficult to detect and quantify because the heart cannot be seen and is protected so well by the rib cage.

Heart disease can be defined as any abnormality of the heart. It encompasses a wide range of conditions, including congenital abnormalities (*see* page 373) and disorders of physical structure and function. It can be classified by various methods, including whether the disease was present at birth or not (that is, congenital or acquired), causes (for example, infectious or degenerative), duration (for example, long- or short-term), clinical status (for example, left heart failure, right heart failure, or biventricular failure), or by physical structure malformation (for example, ventricular septal defect).

Heart failure is any heart abnormality that results in failure of the heart to pump enough blood to meet the body's needs. It is not a specific disease; rather, it is a condition in which congestion or an abnormal accumulation of fluid, decreased blood flow to the body, and/or abnormally low blood pressure arise as the final consequence of severe heart disease. Heart disease can be present without ever leading to heart failure. Heart failure, however, can only occur if heart disease is present because it is a consequence of heart disease. (For a more detailed discussion of HEART FAILURE, *see* page 376.)

Abnormalities of the Cardiovascular System

The following abnormalities of the cardiovascular system can lead to heart disease: 1) the heart valves fail to close or open properly (valve disease); 2) the heart muscle pumps too weakly or relaxes inadequately (myocardial disease); 3) the heart beats too slowly, too rapidly, or too irregularly (arrhythmia); 4) the blood vessels offer too great an interference to blood flow (vascular disease); 5) there may be openings between chambers of the left side and right side of the heart (cardiac shunts); 6) there is too little or too much blood compared with the ability of the blood vessels to store that blood; and 7) there is parasitism of the cardiovascular system, such as heartworm disease.

Signs associated with any of these diseases are due either to inadequate blood flow through the organs (signs include exercise intolerance, weakness, and fainting) or to blood damming up in organs, which causes fluid to leak from blood vessels into tissues (signs include abnormal accumulation of fluid in the lungs or abdomen). A cat showing signs of having too little blood in the tissues to sustain normal function is said to be in heart failure. A cat showing signs caused by blood damming up in poorly drained organs is said to be in congestive heart failure. When there is not enough oxygen in the blood, the mucous membranes develop a blue tinge, and often there is an increased concentration of red blood cells.

■ DIAGNOSIS OF CARDIOVASCULAR DISEASE

A veterinarian often diagnoses cardiovascular disease by reviewing the medical history and signs, conducting a physical examination, and interpreting the results of specific tests or imaging procedures. The physical examination includes using a stethoscope to listen to the heart and lungs. Imaging techniques include x-rays, electrocardiography (recording electrical activity of the heart), and echocardiography (a type of ultrasonography). Most cardiovascular diseases can be diagnosed by physical examination and x-rays. Electrocardiography specifically tracks heart rhythm disturbances (arrhythmias). Echocardiography is excellent for confirming tentative diagnoses or detecting heart tumors or disease of the membrane that surrounds the heart (the pericardium). Occasionally, more specialized tests such as cardiac catheterization (using a thin flexible tube inserted and threaded through an artery into the heart) or nuclear studies (x-ray tests that include injection of radioactive isotopes) are necessary. (For a more detailed discussion of diagnosis of CAR-DIOVASCULAR DISEASE, *see* page 56.)

■ TREATMENT OF CARDIOVASCULAR DISEASE

Treatment of cardiovascular disease should be specific for the type of disease. Some defects can be repaired or corrected with surgery, while other conditions can be managed with medical therapy using one or a combination of drugs. In general, the goals of treatment are to minimize damage to the heart muscle, control the accumulation of fluids in the lungs, improve circulation, regulate the heart rate and rhythm, ensure that there is enough oxygen in the blood, and minimize the risk of blood clot formation. In heartworm disease, the mature heartworms and larvae should be killed.

Common Types of Drugs for Cardiovascular Disease

There are many medications that a veterinarian can prescribe for cats with cardiovascular disease. The type of disease will determine the type of medication prescribed. Medications must be given exactly as prescribed; otherwise, they may not be effective and may even cause serious complications and harm. (For a more detailed discussion of common medications for heart disease, *see* page 56.)

■ CONGENITAL AND INHERITED DISORDERS OF THE CARDIOVASCULAR SYSTEM

Congenital abnormalities of the cardiovascular system are defects that are present at birth. They can occur as a result of genetic defects, environmental conditions, infections, poisoning, medication taken by the mother, or poor maternal nutrition. In some cases, it is a combination of these factors that causes the defect. For several defects, an inherited basis is suspected.

In cats, the frequency of congenital heart disease has been estimated to be less than 1% of the population. Among the few cats that do have congenital heart disease, common defects include atrioventricular septal defects, atrioventricular valve dysplasia, endocardial fibroelastosis, patent ductus arteriosus, aortic stenosis, and tetralogy of Fallot.

Detecting Congenital Heart Defects

It is important to detect a congenital heart defect as early as possible. Certain defects can be corrected with surgery, and treatment should be performed before the defect leads to congestive heart failure or irreversible heart damage. If the defect is discovered in a recently purchased cat, you may be able to return it. Pets with congenital heart defects are likely to die prematurely, causing emotional distress. Early detection also prevents continuing genetic defects into breeding lines.

The evaluation of most cats with a congenital heart defect may include a physical examination, electrocardiography (recording electrical activity of the heart), x-rays, and echocardiography (ultrasonography). These steps allow diagnosis and assessment of the severity of the defect.

General Treatment and Outlook

The medical importance of congenital heart disease depends on the particular defect and its severity. Mildly affected cats may show no ill effects and live a normal life span. Defects causing significant circulatory disturbances will likely cause death in newborn (and unborn) kittens. Medical or surgical treatments are most likely to benefit cats with congenital heart defects of moderate severity. Left-to-right shunting patent ductus arteriosus is one notable exception. Surgical correction is recommended for most affected animals as long as no other diseases or abnormalities are present that would pose a risk for anesthesia or surgery.

Congenital heart defects produce signs that vary depending on the type of heart failure involved. Possible signs include shortness of breath, difficulty breathing, weakness or unwillingness to move, coughing, fainting, or an accumulation of fluid in the chest or abdomen.

Innocent Murmurs

It is very important to understand that the presence of a heart murmur in a young kitten does not necessarily indicate a congenital heart defect. Many young animals have a low-grade systolic murmur (heard while the ventricles contract) that is not associated with a congenital heart defect. These murmurs usually disappear by 6 months of age. Loud systolic murmurs and diastolic murmurs (heard while the ventricles relax) do indicate cardiac disease, however, and should prompt further investigation by your veterinarian.

Common Congenital Heart Abnormalities

The defects discussed below are those that occur with some frequency in cats. However, it is important to stress that these defects are rare. (For a more detailed discussion of these abnormalities, *see* page 58.)

Patent Ductus Arteriosus

The ductus arteriosus is a short, broad vessel in the unborn kitten that connects the pulmonary artery with the aorta and allows most of the blood to flow directly from the right ventricle to the aorta. Before birth, oxygenated blood within the main pulmonary artery passes into the descending aorta through the ductus arteriosus, bypassing the nonfunctional lungs. At birth, inflation of the lungs with the kitten's first breath causes the ductus to close and allows the blood to flow to the lungs.

If the ductus does not close, the blood flow is forced from chambers of the left side of the heart to those of the right side (left-to-right shunting), resulting in many problems with circulation of blood and development of abnormal heart rhythms (arrhythmias) and enlarged chambers of the heart. Over time, heart failure develops in untreated animals. Surgery is successful when left-to-right shunting is present, but the outcome is poor when right-to-left shunting occurs.

Aortic Stenosis

The aorta is the large artery that carries blood away from the heart. Obstruction (stenosis) of the aorta is an abnormality that can affect the flow of blood. Emptying of the left ventricle may be obstructed at 3 locations: subvalvular, also called subaortic, consisting of a fibrous ridge of tissue within the outflow tract of the left ventricle; valvular (the valve itself); and supravalvular (obstruction past the aortic valve). Treatment options include medication to reduce signs of heart failure; surgery may also help but is costly and may be risky for some pets.

Pulmonic Stenosis

Pulmonic stenosis causes an obstruction to the blood flow from the right ventricle. In most cases, the obstruction is due to abnormal development of the flaps on the valves between the pulmonary artery and the right ventricle. The stenosis can also occur in the opening, the subvalvular region (within the outflow tract of the right ventricle), or in the area beyond the pulmonary valve. Signs include heart failure (including fluid accumulation in the abdomen or limbs), weakness, and a failure to thrive. Surgery may help in some cases; medications to improve signs of heart failure can help lessen signs.

Atrial and Ventricular Septal Defects

The septa (plural of septum) are the membranes that divide the chambers of the heart. In an unborn kitten, there is an opening in this membrane between the atria that allows shunting of blood from the right to the left side in order to bypass the nonfunctional lungs. At birth, the opening closes and shunting stops. However, increased right atrial pressure may reopen the flap where the membranes have not sealed and allow shunting to resume. This is not a true atrial septal defect because the membranes have formed normally. A true **atrial septal defect** is a consistent opening of the membranes, which allows blood to shunt from the atrium with the greater pressure. Some of these defects cause few problems for the affected animal, while others lead to heart failure and other associated problems.

Ventricular septal defects (openings in the membrane separating the ventricles) vary in size and effects on blood circulation. These defects may occur with other abnormalities of the heart present at

birth. Treatment depends on the severity of the signs and the direction of the shunting of blood.

Tetralogy of Fallot

Tetralogy of Fallot is a defect that produces a bluish tinge to skin and membranes because there is not enough oxygen in the blood. It is caused by a combination of defects: pulmonic stenosis (*see* above), a typically high and large ventricular septal defect (*see* above), thickening of the muscle fibers of the right ventricle, and varying degrees of the aorta rotating to the right. The effect of these abnormalities depends on their severity and size. In addition to the bluish tinge of the skin and mucous membranes, signs may include fatigue, shortness of breath, stunted growth, and seizures. Certain medications may be prescribed to help alleviate signs.

Mitral and Triscuspid Valve Dysplasia

Defects of the mitral and tricuspid valves occur more commonly in cats than in many other species. **Mitral valve dysplasia** refers to abnormal development or malformation of the mitral valve of the heart, allowing blood to flow back into the left atrium (regurgitation). Any component of the mitral valve (valve flaps, the structures that anchor the flaps, or the small muscular columns that attach the flaps to the ventricle) may be malformed, and often more than one component is defective. If the defect is severe, signs of heart failure (such as coughing and difficulty breathing) and arrhythmias may develop. Although these signs can be treated, the outlook is poor in most cases.

Tricuspid valve dysplasia (abnormal development) is seen occasionally in newborn kittens. This prevents the tricuspid valve from performing adequately and leads to blood being regurgitated back into the right atrium. Other defects of the heart may also be noted in affected cats.

Signs of right-sided congestive heart failure, such as accumulation of fluid in the abdomen and lungs, may be seen. A loud heart murmur is very noticeable.

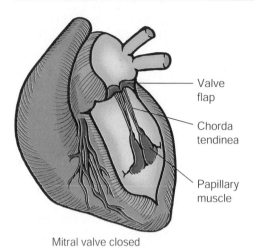

Valve flap

Chorda tendinea

Papillary muscle

Mitral valve closed

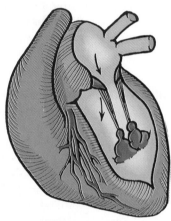

Mitral valve open

The mitral valve has flaps that open and close like swinging doors. Tethers prevent the valves from swinging backward and leaking.

Arrhythmias, especially the sudden onset of a very high heart rate, are common and may cause death. Electrocardiography and x-rays may show enlargement of the right ventricle and atrium, while the malformed tricuspid valve can sometimes be seen using echocardiography (ultrasonography).

The outlook for cats with these signs is guarded. Periodic draining of fluid from the abdomen may be needed. Medications such as diuretics, vasodilators, and digoxin may also be prescribed.

Endocardial Fibroelastosis

Endocardial fibroelastosis is a congenital defect that is seen most commonly in Siamese and Burmese cats. The wall of the left ventricle is enlarged, and the membrane that surrounds and lines the heart becomes thickened and fibrous. Signs, such as difficulty breathing, usually appear when affected kittens are from 1 to 4 months old. The aortic valve may also be affected. Treatment is rarely successful and the outlook is poor.

Cor Triatriatum Sinister

Cor triatriatum sinister results from a fibrous membrane dividing the left atrium and has been reported in cats. ("Sinister" means left.) The affected atrium is divided into 2 chambers. There are commonly one or more perforations in the separating membrane, allowing communication between the 2 portions of the atrium. Surgery can be performed to correct this disease.

■ HEART FAILURE

Heart failure is not a specific disease or diagnosis. It is a syndrome in which severe dysfunction results in failure of the cardiovascular system to maintain adequate blood circulation. There are limited and specific mechanisms by which heart disease can bring on failure of the cardiovascular system. Therefore, there are limited and specific signs that can develop as a result of heart failure.

Types of Heart Failure

Heart failure can be divided into 4 functional classifications: systolic myocardial failure, impedance to cardiac inflow, pressure overload, and volume overload (*see* FIGURE, page 65.)

Systolic myocardial failure is a general reduction in the ability of the heart muscle to contract. This can be identified with echocardiography (ultrasonography). There is reduced wall motion during contraction of the ventricles. If the reduction is significant, normal blood flow cannot be maintained. It may be caused by trauma, infection, drugs or poisons, electric shock, heat stroke, or tumors. Some cases have no known cause.

Heart failure resulting from the **impedance (obstruction) to cardiac inflow** may result in a decrease in blood flow. This may be caused by external compression of the heart (for example, fluid in the sac surrounding the heart), diastolic dysfunction resulting in a stiff ventricle and reduced ventricular filling, or abnormalities of physical structures of the heart.

Heart failure caused by **pressure overload** occurs as a result of longterm increases in stress to the heart wall during contraction. This may result from the obstruction of blood flow from the heart or increased blood pressure throughout the body or in the arteries of the lungs.

Volume overload heart failure occurs as a result of any disease that increases volume of blood in the ventricle(s), thus increasing blood flow. Eventually, this can bring on signs of congestive heart failure. Diseases that result in volume overload myocardial failure include valve disease (for example, degenerative valve disease of the atrioventricular valves), left-to-right shunts (for example, patent ductus arteriosus, ventricular septal defect), or high-output states (such as those caused by hyperthyroidism or anemia).

Compensatory Mechanisms

The cardiovascular system maintains normal blood pressure and blood flow. In heart disease, the body uses specific mechanisms to attempt to normalize these functions and offset negative effects the disease is having on the body. Unfortunately, longterm activation of these compensatory mechanisms can damage the heart muscle and other organs, leading to further heart failure. (For a more detailed discussion of COMPENSATORY MECHANISMS, *see* page 66.)

Signs of Heart Failure

Signs associated with heart failure depend on the causes of the heart failure and the heart chamber that is affected. With **left-sided congestive heart failure**, signs are associated with a backup of pressure in the vessels delivering blood to the left ventricle. Fluid in the lungs and congestion (coughing and difficulty breathing) are the most common signs, although cats with heart failure are far less likely to cough than dogs with the disease. Increased breathing rate, loss of appetite, or exercise intolerance may also be noted.

Right-sided congestive heart failure results in increased pressure in the body's veins and capillaries. This can result in an accumulation of fluid in the abdomen, chest cavity, or limbs.

Biventricular failure can arise when both the right and left ventricles are not working, such as in cats with heart failure resulting from dilated cardiomyopathy or toxin (poison) exposure. Signs attributable to both forms of congestive heart failure can be noted, although commonly signs of one type of congestive heart failure will outweigh the other.

Treatment

It is important to treat heart failure in order to improve heart muscle performance, control arrhythmias and blood pressure, improve blood flow, and reduce the amount of blood filling the heart before contraction. All of these can further damage the heart and blood vessels if not controlled. It is also necessary to reduce the amount of fluid in the lungs, abdomen, or chest cavity.

There are many types of drugs available for treating heart failure. The specific drugs, dosage, and frequency used will vary depending on the causes and severity of the heart failure and other factors. Your veterinarian is best able to decide on the appropriate medications for your cat. All drugs prescribed by your veterinarian must be given as directed. Otherwise, they may not be effective and may even cause serious complications and harm.

Diuretics are usually prescribed to reduce fluid overload. Digitalis and digoxin, part of a group of drugs known as positive inotropes, may be used to help the heart muscle contract. ACE inhibitors (ACE stands for angiotensin-converting enzyme) and vasodilators can widen blood vessels and thus lower blood pressure. Beta-adrenergic blocking drugs (also called beta-blockers) and calcium channel blockers are also helpful in some cases of congestive heart failure.

In addition to drugs, other types of treatment are sometimes recommended. These may include a low-sodium diet (prescription or commercial diets are available), oxygen therapy to raise the level of oxygen in the blood, or surgical procedures to remove excess fluid buildup from the chest cavity or abdomen.

■ ACQUIRED HEART AND BLOOD VESSEL DISORDERS

Cats can develop many different cardiovascular diseases. The ones discussed below are the most common.

Degenerative Valve Disease

This acquired disease is characterized by a thickening of the heart valves. Degenerative valve disease is uncommon in cats. A veterinarian can often diagnose degenerative valve disease based on physical examination findings and appropriate imaging procedures, which may include chest x-rays and echocardiography (ultrasonography). Affected cats can live for years with appropriate treatment. (For a more detailed discussion of degenerative valve disease, *see* page 68.)

Disorders of the Heart Muscle (Cardiomyopathy)

Cardiomyopathy is the name for any disease that mostly affects the heart muscle. The cardiomyopathies of animals are diseases with no known cause that are not the result of any generalized or primary heart disease. In cats and other animals, they have been classified as dilated cardiomyopathy, hypertrophic cardiomyopathy, and restrictive or unclassified cardiomyopathy. Cardiomyopathy can also occur as a result of other diseases. In these cases, they are usually called secondary myocardial diseases.

Dilated Cardiomyopathy

Dilated cardiomyopathy is a disease that causes the progressive loss of the heart

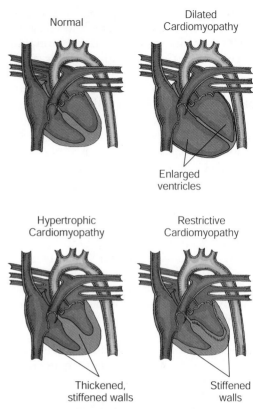

Types of cardiomyopathy in cats (modified with permission from *The Merck Manual of Medical Information*, Second Home Edition, 2003).

muscle's ability to contract. The cause is unknown. Several forms of secondary dilated cardiomyopathy exist; for example, one form in cats is caused by a deficiency of taurine, an amino acid. The incidence in cats has decreased dramatically since the discovery in 1985 that taurine deficiency was responsible for most cases. Since then, taurine levels have been increased to acceptable levels in all commercial cat foods. Today, most cases are not taurine responsive and reflect primary disease of unknown cause.

The outlook is grave for cats with dilated cardiomyopathy that is not taurine responsive. Most cats only survive 2 weeks after diagnosis. Cats that have taurine responsive cardiomyopathy also have a high risk of death. However, cats that can be kept alive long enough for taurine supplementation to become effective (2 to 3 weeks) have an excellent outlook.

Hypertrophic Cardiomyopathy

Hypertrophic cardiomyopathy is a condition in which the walls of the left ventricle thicken and become stiff as a result of a heart muscle disorder. It is the most common primary heart disease diagnosed in cats. It occurs in families in certain breeds of cats such as Maine Coon cats and American Shorthairs. The disease may be seen in cats from 3 months to 17 years of age, although most patients are middle aged. It is more common in males than females. The cause is believed to be an inherited genetic defect. Although this has not been proved in cats, the genetic factor has been documented in humans with this disease.

Affected cats may not have any signs or may have sudden onset of difficulty breathing, collapse, and weakness or paralysis of the hind limbs. A veterinarian may note abnormal heart sounds, including murmurs and gallop heart sounds. Fluid may accumulate in the lungs and in the space between the lungs and the chest wall. Blood clots may form and lodge at the point where the aorta divides near the hips (called saddle thrombi), leading to muscular weakness or paralysis of the hind limbs. X-rays and echocardiography (ultrasonography) may be helpful to diagnose the condition as well as to determine the best treatment.

Treatment is directed at controlling signs of heart failure, improving cardiac function, and reducing the incidence of blood clots. Diuretics (to reduce fluid buildup), oxygen, nitroglycerin, calcium-channel blockers, beta-blockers, or ACE inhibitors may all be considered. Many mildly affected cats have a good longterm outlook; however cats with congestive heart failure have a poorer outlook.

Restrictive Cardiomyopathy

Restrictive cardiomyopathy develops when either one or both ventricles become stiff without significant thickening of the muscle fibers. The cause is not known. The stiff heart muscle fibers cause the ventricles to resist filling with blood between heartbeats. To confirm a diagnosis, cardiac catheterization or echocardiography (ultrasonography) is usually required. Signs and treatment are similar to those for hypertrophic cardiomyopathy (*see* above); however, the outlook seems to be worse, especially in cats with congestive heart failure.

Unclassified Cardiomyopathy

Unclassified cardiomyopathy is a disease of cats with obvious abnormalities of the heart muscle on echocardiography (ultrasonography) that do not clearly fit into any other category. The cause is not known.

Other Causes of Heart Muscle Failure

A form of cardiomyopathy called **atrial standstill** destroys the muscle wall of the atrium and occasionally affects the muscle wall of the ventricle. This disease has been reported in some cats with coexisting dilated cardiomyopathy. Treatment is rarely effective.

Endocardial fibroelastosis is a disease of unknown cause that leads to thickening of the lining of the left atrium, left ventricle, and mitral valve. It is a rare cause of heart muscle failure in young cats. Signs, treatment, and outlook are similar to dilated cardiomyopathy (*see* page 378).

Arrhythmogenic right ventricular cardiomyopathy is a rare cause of heart muscle failure in cats. It is restricted primarily to the right side of the heart, but may also involve the left ventricle. It is characterized by a fibrous and fatty muscle of the right ventricle causing progressive heart muscle failure. Signs include difficulty breathing, increased breathing rate, fainting, and nonspecific signs such as loss of appetite and lethargy. Treatment is similar to that for dilated cardiomyopathy (*see* page 378).

Infective Endocarditis

The endocardium is the thin membrane that lines the heart cavity. Infection of the endocardium typically involves one of the heart valves, although endocarditis of the cavity's wall may occur. Infection is caused by bacteria carried in the blood. The infection gradually destroys the valve and keeps it from working properly. The disease is rare in cats, with the aortic and mitral valves being most commonly affected.

Treatment is directed at controlling signs of congestive heart failure, resolving any significant arrhythmias, killing the bacteria that started the infection, and eliminating the spread of infection. (For a more detailed discussion of INFECTIVE ENDOCARDITIS, *see* page 71.)

Pericardial Disease

The pericardium is the membrane surrounding the heart. When fluid builds up in the pericardium, pressure on the heart increases. The increased pressure gradually compresses the heart, interfering with its ability to pump blood. This condition is called **cardiac tamponade**. This compression of the chambers significantly affects blood circulation and causes swollen jugular veins and accumulation of fluid in the abdomen. In addition, too little oxygen reaches the body's tissues. This condition is uncommon in cats, but may be caused by cancer (usually lymphoma in cats), infections (for example, feline infectious peritonitis), injury, chamber rupture, and congestive heart failure.

Cats with cardiac tamponade require urgent treatment. Medical treatment may not be able to rapidly reduce fluid buildup within the membrane surrounding the heart. Pericardiocentesis (inserting a needle through the membrane to withdraw the fluid) is commonly used to remove fluid quickly.

High Blood Pressure (Hypertension)

Systemic hypertension is an increase in the body's blood pressure. There are 2 major types of systemic hypertension. Essential (primary) hypertension, which is of unknown cause, is common in humans but rare in cats. Secondary hypertension results from a specific underlying disease. In cats, the most common causes are kidney disease and hyperthyroidism (overproduction of thyroid hormones).

Cats with extremely high blood pressure may have no signs that are visible to the owner. Blood tests may help with diagnosis of the cause of high blood pressure. Treatment should be started in cats with sustained and severe high blood pressure, or in pets with sustained high blood pressure and an underlying cause such as kidney failure.

Pulmonary hypertension is elevation of blood pressure in the lungs. Possible causes include increased thickness of blood (for example, an abnormal increase in red blood cells) and increased pulmonary blood flow (caused by, for example, a ventricular septal defect, patent ductus arteriosus, or an atrial septal defect). Other causes include abnormalities of the blood vessels in the lungs, which may be caused by heartworm disease, narrowing of the arteries within the lungs, or blood clots within the lungs. Signs are similar to those seen in right-sided congestive heart failure, such as accumulation of fluid in the lungs or abdomen. A swollen and pulsating jugular vein may be noted. Doppler echocardiography (ultrasonography) is the most likely method of confirming the diagnosis. Treatment is usually not effective, and the outlook is poor. The best chance for a successful outcome is the identification and treatment of the underlying disease.

■ HEARTWORM DISEASE

Heartworm disease is a potentially fatal, but preventable, infection caused by a worm parasite, *Dirofilaria immitis*. The organism is transmitted by mosquitoes, which carry the heartworm larvae (called microfilariae) from an infected animal host to a new animal host. Once the larvae arrive in a new host, they grow into adult worms in several months and live in the blood vessels leading from the heart to the lungs. In advanced infections, the heartworms may enter the heart as well.

Both indoor and outdoor cats can be infected. Other infections in cats, such as those caused by the feline leukemia virus or feline immunodeficiency virus, do not appear to increase the risk of heartworm infection. The critical factor in heartworm disease is being bitten by a mosquito carrying the infectious heartworm larvae.

The development of a heartworm infection in cats follows a pattern similar to that in dogs. However, because cats have smaller blood vessels and hearts, the severity of the damage is greater. In addition, cats react more to heartworms than dogs, and the lung inflammation associated with heartworm infection leads to poor oxygenation of the blood. Cats are more likely to die of heartworm infection than are dogs.

Signs and Diagnosis

Infected cats may show no signs or exhibit only mild signs. Weight loss is common in cats with heartworm infection. The signs often resemble those of feline asthma. Cats harboring mature worms may have intermittent vomiting, lethargy, coughing, or occasional shortness of breath. The death of heartworms in a cat can lead to sudden respiratory distress and shock. This situation may be fatal.

Diagnosis of heartworm infection in cats is based on history and physical findings, chest x-rays, echocardiography, and appropriate testing. Often, multiple blood tests may be needed, as low numbers of worms and new infections are missed by antigen tests.

Treatment

There is no current satisfactory treatment for heartworm infections in cats. The death of the heartworms leads to a reaction in cats that is often fatal. Restricted activity and corticosteroids might help ease signs in some cats. Even with medication, however, timing becomes an issue as heartworms live for approximately 2 years in cats. It is estimated that 25% to 50% of infected cats survive heartworm infection.

Heartworm infection in a cat

The presence of parasites stresses the heart, blood vessels, and lungs. In addition, severe complications are possible when the heartworms die.

Cats are somewhat more resistant to heartworm infection than dogs. Therefore, a lower percentage of exposed cats develop infections of adult heartworms, and there are often only 1 to 3 worms present. Heartworms have been known to migrate to areas outside the heart, and they can even invade the central nervous system.

Prevention

Heartworm infection is preventable. Heartworm preventive medication is recommended for all cats, whether they live indoors or outdoors, in areas where the disease is common. Because heartworm infection can be fatal or severely debilitating for cats, your veterinarian will likely prescribe a preventive medication for all cats, including kittens. This program should be continued for the cat's entire life.

The most important thing that pet owners can do to protect their companions from heartworm infection is to be absolutely sure their pet receives the prescribed dose of medication at the correct time. Because the most common preventive drugs for both dogs and cats are given only once a month, pet owners might forget to administer the medication. Take advantage of e-mail or other reminder systems offered by your veterinarian or other sources to ensure proper dosing. Neglecting to give the medication can have serious consequences. If you miss a dose, you should contact your veterinarian regarding administration of the medication and the need for retesting the cat to determine if an infection has occurred.

■ BLOOD CLOTS AND ANEURYSMS

A **thrombus** is a blood clot that may form when the blood flow of an artery or vein is restricted. It frequently causes obstruction to blood vessels at its site of origin. All or part of a clot may break off and be carried through the bloodstream as an **embolus** that lodges someplace else at a point of narrowing. Blockage of a blood vessel can also occur when foreign material (for example, bacteria, air, or fat) is carried into the bloodstream. Blood clots generally result in not enough blood reaching tissues supplied by the blocked blood vessel. Some clots are infected and can spread bacteria and cause localized infection.

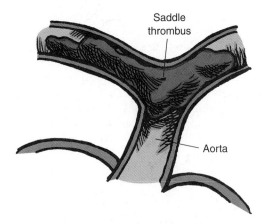

A thrombus (blood clot) may form when the blood flow of an artery or vein is restricted.

An **aneurysm** is an enlargement of a blood vessel caused by weakening of the middle layer of the blood vessel. Disruption of the inner lining of a blood vessel associated with an aneurysm can cause formation of a blood clot with subsequent blockage of the blood vessel by the clot.

Signs and Diagnosis

A sudden onset of breathing difficulty may be a sign of a blood clot in the lungs, and some cats may cough up blood or bloody mucus. Infective clots in the heart are associated with endocarditis, an inflammation of the membranes lining the heart cavity (*see* page 379). Clots in the heart that are not infective are associated with heart muscle disease. Blood in the urine or abdominal pain can indicate blockage of certain blood vessels.

Heartworm disease may lead to blood clots in arteries of the lungs. Blood clots in the pulmonary artery most commonly produce difficulty breathing and an increased breathing rate. Affected cats often seem normal until they have a sudden onset of respiratory distress. Chest x-rays may show changes such as an enlarged main pulmonary artery and right heart, not enough blood getting to the affected region, an accumulation of fluid in the chest cavity, or bleeding or tissue death within the lungs. Additional tests are essential for the diagnosis of underlying diseases.

Blood clots associated with the aorta are a frequent complication of cardiomyopathy (*see* page 378). Clots may be located in the left atrium, ventricle, or both. Clots that dislodge form emboli, which may obstruct the aorta where it branches. This happens most commonly where the aorta splits into 3 branches near the hips. Signs include paralysis and pain of the back legs, cold limbs, and signs related to congestive heart failure. Incomplete blockage of the aortic branches may cause mild neurologic signs in both hind limbs or muscle weakness in only one.

Aneurysms cause no signs unless bleeding occurs or an associated clot develops. Spontaneous bleeding from aneurysms is rare, and signs usually relate to blood clots. Ultrasonography and angiography may be helpful in confirming a diagnosis.

Treatment

Treatment of pneumonia caused by a blood clot due to endocarditis includes longterm antibiotics, a treatment program lasting several weeks. Some cases require anti-inflammatory drugs to reduce fever. The outlook for recovery is guarded at best.

Treatment of blood clots in veins is usually limited to supportive care, including hydrotherapy of accessible veins, anti-inflammatory drugs, and antibiotics to control secondary infection. Thrombosis of the large veins that empty into the right atrium generally does not respond to treatment and the outlook is poor.

Surgical removal of clots in the aorta may be attempted, but most authorities recommend medical treatment only, including analgesics, anticoagulants, careful use of intravenous fluids (to maintain hydration and blood pressure but not worsen congestive heart failure), and specific treatment for underlying heart disease.

Many cats with aortic thromboembolism die despite treatment or fail to regain hind limb function. Some cats that survive the initial cardiovascular crisis recover the ability to walk after several weeks, but may have some permanent damage (such as abnormal tightening or shortening of muscle and a degenerative disorder affecting the nervous system). The longterm outlook often depends on the severity of underlying heart disease.

CHAPTER 26

Digestive Disorders

▧ INTRODUCTION

The digestive system includes all the organs that are involved in taking in and processing food. It begins with the mouth and includes the esophagus, stomach, liver, pancreas, intestines, rectum, and anus.

The process of digestion begins when your pet picks up food with its mouth and starts chewing. Enzymes found in saliva begin breaking down the food chemically.

The process continues with swallowing, additional breakdown of food in the stomach, absorption of nutrients in the intestines, and elimination of waste. Digestion is critical not only for providing nutrients but also for maintaining the proper balance of fluid and electrolytes (salts) in the body.

The functions of the digestive system can be divided into 4 main categories: digestion, absorption of nutrients, motility (movement through the digestive tract), and elimination of feces.

When treating a digestive system problem, the veterinarian's goal is to first identify the part of the system where the problem lies and then to determine the specific cause and appropriate treatment.

General Signs of Digestive System Disorders

Signs of digestive system disease can include excessive drooling, diarrhea, constipation, vomiting or regurgitation, loss of appetite, bleeding, abdominal pain and bloating, shock, and dehydration. Your cat may indicate abdominal pain by whining, meowing, and abnormal postures (for example, crouching while arching the back).

The location and nature of the disease often can be determined by the signs your pet shows. For example, abnormalities of biting, chewing, and swallowing usually are associated with diseases of the mouth, the teeth, the jaw, or the esophagus. Vom-

iting is usually due to inflammation of the lining of stomach or intestines (gastroenteritis) caused by infection or irritation. However, vomiting can also be caused by a nondigestive condition such as kidney disease.

Diarrhea is often a sign of digestive system disorders, but it can have many causes. It is important to treat animals with continuing diarrhea, because dehydration and electrolyte (salt) imbalance, which may lead to shock, are seen when large quantities of fluid are lost.

Changes in the color, consistency, or frequency of feces are another sign of digestive problems. Black, tarry feces may be a sign of bleeding in the stomach or small intestine. Straining during bowel movements is usually associated with inflammation of the rectum and anus. Abdominal distention (bloating) can result from accumulation of gas, fluid, or ingested food, usually due to reduced activity of the muscles that move food through the digestive system. Dis-

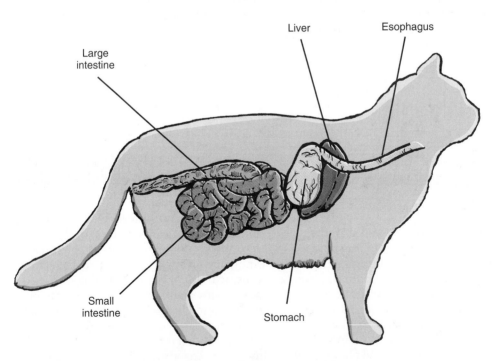

The major digestive organs of the cat

tention can also be caused by a physical obstruction such as a foreign object or intussusception ("telescoping" of one part of the intestines into another), or from something as simple as overeating.

Examination of the Digestive System

Your complete, accurate description of your cat's history (age, signs of illness, current diet, past problems, and so on) combined with a veterinarian's clinical examination can often determine the cause of a digestive system problem.

When a digestive system disorder is suspected, your veterinarian's initial examination might include a visual inspection of the mouth and abdomen for changes in size or shape; a "hands on" inspection of the abdomen (through the abdominal wall or through the rectum) to evaluate the shape, size, and position of the abdominal organs; and listening through a stethoscope for any abnormal abdominal sounds. The veterinarian may also want to inspect your cat's feces. When you make an appointment with your veterinarian, it is a good idea to ask whether you should bring along a recent stool sample to help with diagnosis.

Depending on what the initial examination reveals, additional tests might be needed to determine the cause of the problem. These might include laboratory tests on samples containing blood or feces to determine whether bacteria or viruses are involved, as well as specialized procedures such as x-ray imaging, ultrasonography, or using an endoscope to perform an internal examination of the esophagus, stomach, duodenum, colon, and/or rectum. Sometimes it is necessary to collect fluid from swollen abdominal organs or from the abdominal cavity for analysis; this is done with a long, hollow needle. Other tests that are sometimes needed include biopsies (sampling and microscopic analysis) of liver or intestinal tissue and blood tests to detect possible malabsorption or maldigestion.

Infectious Diseases

Because it is easy for foreign organisms and other "invaders" to enter the digestive tract through the mouth, this body system is prone to infection by bacteria, viruses, parasites, and other organisms (*see* TABLE 1). These infections spread in various ways, but the most common are by direct contact or by contamination of food or water by feces.

People and animals all have small numbers of certain intestinal microorganisms that are found within the digestive tract—most commonly in the intestines—and that become established within a few hours after birth. These so-called intestinal flora are actually beneficial, in some cases aiding in digestion and in others helping to prevent infection. However, sometimes infections occur when these

Table 1. Infections of the Digestive System in Cats

Organism	Examples
Viruses	Feline panleukopenia virus, feline enteric coronavirus, feline rotaviruses, feline astroviruses
Bacteria	*Salmonella* species, *Yersinia enterocolitica*, *Campylobacter jejuni*, *Bacillus piliformis*, *Clostridium* species, *Mycobacterium* species, *Shigella* species
Protozoa	*Isospora* species, *Sarcocystis* species, *Besnoitia* species, *Hammondia* species, *Toxoplasma* species, *Giardia* species, *Trichomonas* species, *Entamoeba histolytica*, *Balantidium coli*, *Cryptosporidium* species
Fungi	*Histoplasma capsulatum*, *Aspergillus* species, *Candida albicans*, phycomycetes
Algae	*Prototheca* species
Parasites	Numerous (*see* page 403)

organisms, normally found in small numbers, suddenly multiply. This can occur after a period of stress, under unhygienic conditions, or in an animal whose immune system is weakened.

Diagnosis of a specific infectious disease depends on finding and identifying the organism suspected to cause the disease. This may require one or more fecal samples, which will be submitted to a diagnostic laboratory.

Parasites are a frequent cause of digestive tract disorders in animals. Many species of parasites can infect the digestive tract and cause disease. The extent to which a parasite affects an animal depends on the parasite itself, as well as the animal's own resistance, age, nutrition, and overall health.

Parasites can cause severe disease or simply decrease your cat's overall fitness. Some of these parasites also infect humans. Because parasite infection is easily confused with other illnesses, diagnosis depends on your veterinarian's knowledge of seasonal cycles of parasite infection, as well as examination of feces for evidence of parasite eggs or larvae. In some cases, blood tests can also be used to detect the presence of parasites. (For a more detailed discussion of GASTROINTESTINAL PARASITES OF CATS, *see* page 403.)

Noninfectious Diseases

Many digestive system diseases are not caused by infective organisms. Their causes include overeating, eating poor-quality food, chemicals, obstruction caused by swallowing foreign objects, or injury to the digestive system. Digestive system disease can also be caused by enzyme deficiencies, damage to the digestive tract such as from gastric ulcers, or birth defects. Digestive system signs such as vomiting and diarrhea may also occur because of kidney, liver, or adrenal gland disease. In noninfectious diseases of the digestive tract, usually only a single animal is affected at one time; exceptions are diseases associated with excessive food intake or poisons, in which multiple animals living together can be affected.

Treatment Overview of Digestive System Disorders

Specific disorders and their treatments are described later in this chapter; however, some general principles are listed in this section. Eliminating the cause of the disease is the primary objective of veterinary treatment; however, a major part of treatment is often directed at the signs of the disease and is aimed at relieving pain, correcting abnormalities, and allowing healing to occur.

Elimination of the cause of the disease may involve drugs that kill bacteria or parasites, antidotes for poisons, or surgery to correct defects or displacements.

Use of drugs to correct diarrhea or constipation is done depending on the specific case. Although such drugs might seem to be a logical choice, they are not beneficial in every situation. For example, diarrhea can actually be a defense mechanism for the animal, helping it to eliminate harmful organisms and their toxins. In addition, the available drugs may not always give consistent results.

Replacement of fluids and electrolytes (salts) is necessary in cases where the animal is at risk of dehydration, such as from excessive vomiting or diarrhea.

Relief of distension (bloating) by stomach tube or surgery may be required if the digestive tract has become distended with gas, fluid, or food.

Pain relief is sometimes provided. However, a cat being given pain medicine must be watched carefully to ensure that the pain relief is not masking a condition that is becoming worse.

Treatment and Control of Infectious Disease

Bacterial and parasitic diseases of the digestive system are often treated with medications designed to kill the infectious organisms. There are currently no specific medications for treatment of viral diseases. Antibiotics (drugs effective against bacteria) are commonly given daily by mouth for several days until recovery is apparent, although their effectiveness in treating digestive system disease is still uncertain. Antibiotics may be given by injection when septicemia (an infection of the blood) is apparent or likely to occur. Your veterinarian will make the decision to prescribe antibacterial medication based on the suspected disease, likelihood of benefits, previous results, and cost of treatment.

Advances in understanding the life cycles of parasites, coupled with the discovery of effective antiparasitic drugs, have made successful treatment and control of gastrointestinal parasites possible. Response to treatment is usually rapid, and a single treatment is often all that is needed unless reinfection occurs or the damage caused by the parasites is particularly severe.

Control of digestive diseases and parasites depends on practicing good sanitation and hygiene. This is achieved primarily by providing adequate space for your cat and by regular cleaning of its living areas and litter box. In addition, adequate nutrition and housing will minimize the stress on your cat and help it to stay healthy.

■ CONGENITAL AND INHERITED DISORDERS

Congenital abnormalities are conditions that an animal is born with; they are often referred to as "birth defects." Some of these conditions are inherited and tend to occur within particular families or breeds, while others are caused by chemicals or injury during pregnancy. For still others, the cause is unknown. Some of the most common congenital abnormalities of the digestive system in cats are described below.

Mouth

A cleft palate or cleft lip (harelip) is caused by a defect in the formation of the jaw and face during embryonic development. It leads to a gap or cleft in the center of the lip, roof of the mouth (hard palate), or both. Often these gaps leave an opening between the roof of the mouth and the nasal cavity allowing food and liquids to pass into the breathing passages. These conditions have a wide range in severity. Usually the upper lip and palate are affected. Clefts in the lower lip are rare. The incidence of cleft lip is higher in Siamese cats than in other breeds.

Cleft palate or lip will usually be noticed shortly after birth when the kitten might have problems nursing. For example, milk might be seen dripping from the nostrils or the kitten might have difficulty suckling and swallowing. The veterinarian can readily identify the problem by examining the kitten's mouth. Affected kittens require intensive nursing care, including hand or tube feeding and possibly antibiotics to treat respiratory infections. Surgical correction is effective only in minor cases, and is usually done when kittens are 6 to 8 weeks old to minimize further complications. A variety of surgical techniques are used, and the success rate in cats is improving. The decision to perform surgery should be made carefully, and the affected animal should be spayed or neutered to prevent passing the defect on to its offspring.

Brachygnathia occurs when the lower jaw is shorter than the upper jaw. It can be a minor problem or a serious defect depending on the degree of abnormality. Mild cases may cause no problems. More severe cases can cause damage to the hard palate (roof of the mouth) or restriction of normal jaw growth. The lower canine teeth are often removed or shortened to prevent this damage.

Prognathia occurs when the lower jaw is longer than the upper jaw. This characteristic is normal in some breeds (for example, Persian cats) and does not usually require treatment.

Teeth

In most animals, having too few teeth is rare. In cats, **extra teeth** sometimes occur and may lead to crowding and poor alignment of the teeth. Extra teeth that cause crowding should be extracted by a veterinarian as soon as they are discovered to prevent further dental problems.

Delayed loss of deciduous (baby) teeth is uncommon in cats. However, because teeth that do not fall out get in the way of the permanent teeth, any retained deciduous teeth should be removed by your veterinarian as soon as possible.

Abnormal development of tooth enamel (the hard outer surface of the tooth) can be caused by fever, trauma, malnutrition, poisoning, or infections. The damage to the enamel depends on the severity and duration of the cause and can range from pitting to the absence of enamel with incomplete tooth development. Affected teeth are prone to plaque and tartar accumulation, which lead to tooth decay. Resin restoration is sometimes used to cover defects, although careful dental hygiene and home care is critical in reducing the incidence of complications (*see* DENTAL DISORDERS, page 390). **Discoloration of the enamel** may also occur. Giving tetracycline antibiotics to pregnant females or to kittens less than 6 months old may result in permanent brownish-yellow stains on the teeth.

Esophagus

The muscular tube that leads from the back of the mouth to the stomach is known as the esophagus. Some congenital abnormalities of the esophagus seen in cats include megaesophagus, vascular ring anomalies, and crichopharyngeal achalasia (*see* TABLE 2). Signs of defects in the esophagus generally include regurgitation and problems with swallowing. These signs are especially noticeable when your cat starts to eat solid food. Surgical correction of some esophageal abnormalities (for example, vascular ring anomalies, in which abnormal blood vessels surround and restrict the esophagus) is effective if done early. If not, the esophagus can become permanently damaged by the stretching caused by trapped food.

Small pouches in the lining of the esophagus, called **esophageal diverticula**, will sometimes form. Clinical signs depend on severity and are seen in only 10 to 15% of cases. When they do occur, they may cause accumulation of food or become inflamed. In rare cases they rupture. Treatment (if necessary) is by surgical removal of the pouch.

Hernias

A hernia is the protrusion of a portion of an organ or tissue through an abnormal opening. One common congenital type involves an abnormal opening in the wall of the diaphragm (the sheet of muscle that separates the chest from the abdomen) or abdomen. The defect may allow abdominal organs to pass into the chest or bulge beneath the skin. Hernias may be congenital (present at birth) or result from injury. Signs of a hernia vary from none to severe and depend on the amount of herniated tissue and its effect on the organ involved. **Hiatal hernias** involve extension of part of the stomach through the diaphragm.

Table 2. Congenital Esophageal Disorders of Cats

Type	Cause	Breeds Most Often Affected
Congenital megaesophagus	Abnormal nerve development in esophagus; sometimes part of more widespread nerve problems	Siamese
Vascular ring entrapment	Physical constriction of the esophagus by blood vessels	No breed tendencies reported
Cricopharyngeal achalasia	Failure of the cricopharyngeal muscle (in the throat) to relax during swallowing	Rare; no breed tendencies reported

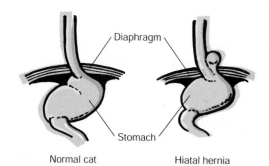

Diaphragm

Stomach

Normal cat   Hiatal hernia

A hiatal hernia involves the extension of part of the stomach through the diaphragm (modified with permission from *The Merck Manual of Medical Information*, Second Home Edition, 2003).

These hernias may be "sliding" and result in signs (such as loss of appetite, drooling, or vomiting) that come and go. Hernias are diagnosed using x-rays; contrast studies (x-rays that include special dyes to outline organs) are often needed. Endoscopy may be used to diagnose sliding hiatal hernias. In many cases, correction of a hernia involving the diaphragm requires surgery. However, the use of antacid preparations and dietary modification may control signs of a hiatal hernia, if they are mild.

Hernias involving the abdominal wall include umbilical, inguinal, or scrotal, depending on their location (*see* TABLE 4, page 85). Diagnosis of **umbilical hernias** is usually simple, especially if the veterinarian is able to push the hernia back through the abdominal wall (called "reducing the hernia"). These hernias are corrected by surgery. Small hernias are often corrected at the same time that the cat is spayed or neutered. The tendency to develop hernias may be inherited.

Stomach

Besides hiatal hernia (*see* above), another abnormality involving the stomach is **pyloric stenosis**. It is likely that pyloric stenosis is inherited. This condition results from muscular thickening of the pyloric sphincter (the "exit" of the stomach). The thickening of this opening slows or blocks the flow of digested food from the stomach to the small intestine. Siamese cats are at higher risk of this condition. Because the flow of food out of the stomach is restricted, cats with this condition will often vomit food for several hours after a meal. Treatment is through dietary modification and medication. In more severe cases, surgery may help.

Small and Large Intestine

Malabsorption occurs when nutrients are not properly absorbed into the bloodstream. These conditions often cause persistent digestive system problems, including vomiting, weight loss, diarrhea, or a combination of these signs. There are many potential causes of malabsorption. Some are inherited; some are acquired (for example, as a result of a viral infection). Most are associated with inflammation of the intestines called inflammatory bowel disease. Malabsorption is often treated with a combination of dietary changes and medication; the exact treatment will depend on the condition being treated. To provide the best life for a cat with these conditions, follow your veterinarian's medication, diet recommendations, and other guidelines carefully.

Various **malformations of the intestines** can occur as birth defects, including duplication of sections of the intestine or rectum, failure of the rectum to connect with the anus, and openings between the rectum and other structures such as the urethra or vagina. Surgical correction is usually needed. The success rate depends on the extent of the malformation.

The inability to control urination and defecation (incontinence) is often seen in Manx cats as a consequence of **spina bifida**, a birth defect in which the spine does not properly close before birth (*see also* page 460).

Liver

The most common liver defect present at birth is a **portosystemic shunt** (*see* page 411). In a healthy animal, blood coming from the intestines is processed by the liver, which removes toxins from the bloodstream before they reach the brain or other organs. In an animal with a portosystemic shunt, however, blood bypasses the liver through one or more "shortcuts" (shunts) and enters directly into the general circulatory system. Himalayan and Persian cats have an increased incidence of this condition. Signs of a portosystemic shunt include nervous system disturbances and a failure to grow and thrive. Affected cats may also salivate more than normal, have a poor appetite, and be depressed. In the late stages, protein-containing fluid may accumulate in the abdomen, a condition called **ascites**. Your veterinarian may also notice enlargement of the kidneys and kidney stones. A definite diagnosis is made by using an opaque dye to highlight the blood vessels, followed by x-rays. This procedure can identify the location of the shunt and determine whether it is single or multiple. It also allows the veterinarian to assess whether surgical correction is possible. Animals with multiple shunts tend to do poorly.

Copper-associated hepatopathy is a defect that causes levels of copper to build up in the liver. This results in development of chronic hepatitis and cirrhosis of the liver. Treatment involves the use of drugs that bind copper (chelators), low copper diets, and other supportive measures directed at helping animals with liver disease.

Other developmental liver disorders include **hepatic (liver) cysts**, which generally cause no signs. They are important mainly because they must be differentiated from abscesses in the liver. A veterinarian who finds a hepatic cyst will often want to examine the kidneys, because hepatic cysts often occur along with polycystic kidney disease, especially in cats. (For more information on POLYCYSTIC KIDNEYS, *see* page 515.)

▦ DENTAL DEVELOPMENT

Each type of companion animal has its own unique type of teeth, depending on what type of food the animal normally eats. For example, a meat-eating animal such as a cat has quite different teeth compared to a grass-eating animal such as a horse. However, all domestic animals have 2 sets of teeth during their lives, as humans do: a set of deciduous ("baby") teeth that fall out, and a set of permanent teeth that come in later.

Most cats have 26 deciduous teeth and 30 permanent teeth. The deciduous incisors begin to erupt at 2 to 4 weeks of age, and the deciduous premolars at 5 to 6 weeks of age. Permanent teeth usually begin to appear at around 4 to 7 months. (*See* TABLE 2, page 333.)

▦ DENTAL DISORDERS

Many of the dental disorders of cats are similar to those found in people. Treatment methods are also similar. Proper dental care can help keep your cat's teeth and gums healthy. Learning the terms your veterinarian uses to describe dental disorders will help you understand and discuss any dental problems your cat may develop. (*See* BOX, page 87.)

Gum Disease

Gum (periodontal) disease is inflammation of the tissue surrounding the teeth. It is caused by the accumulation of many different bacteria (plaque) at the gum line due—in part—to a lack of proper oral hygiene. This infection causes inflammation of the gums, the ligaments that anchor the teeth, and the surrounding bone. If periodontal disease goes untreated, teeth can be lost due to the loss of their supporting tissues. There are 2 forms of periodontal disease: gingivitis and periodontitis.

Gingivitis

In gingivitis, the gums become inflamed because of bacterial plaque, but the ligaments and bone are not yet affected. The gums change in color from coral-pink to red or purple, and the edge of the gum swells. The gums tend to bleed on contact. Bad breath is common. Gingivitis can be reversed with proper tooth clean-

What is Plaque?

Plaque is a thin film of food debris, bacteria, saliva, and dead cells that is continually deposited on your animal's teeth. Plaque that is present for more than 72 hours begins to harden into a substance called tartar (calculus) that accumulates at the base of the teeth. This buildup irritates the gums and contributes to the development of gum disease.

ing but, if untreated, may lead to periodontitis (*see* below).

A form of juvenile-onset gingivitis is seen in some cats at 6 to 8 months of age. Cats with this condition often have swollen gums and bad breath.

Gingivitis can usually be treated by thorough professional cleaning of the teeth. This includes cleaning below the gum line. If gingivitis does not improve, your cat should be examined again to determine if more extensive cleaning is required. When cleanings are completed, your veterinarian may apply a sealant to the teeth to prevent bacterial buildup and improve healing. Cats that do not respond to treatment should be evaluated for other diseases such as immune system problems, diabetes, and especially feline *Bartonella* infection (cat scratch fever). Gingivitis will reoccur if the teeth are not kept clean and free of plaque.

Periodontitis

In periodontitis, the tissue damage is more severe and includes the gums, the ligaments, and bone. It usually is seen after the development of plaque, tartar, and gingivitis. It is irreversible and results in permanent loss of tooth support. Gingivitis is often first noticed at about 2 years of age but improves if treated. Periodontitis usually begins at 4 to 6 years of age and, if untreated, results in tooth loss. In some cats this disease can be seen as early as 1 year of age.

Periodontitis is treated with thorough professional cleaning above and below the gum line. If your cat has been treated for periodontitis, you will need to continue oral hygiene care at home. Follow your veterinarian's instructions, which might include daily toothbrushing, dietary changes, plaque prevention gel, and oral rinses. Frequent (every 3 months to 1 year) preventive cleanings will help to avoid relapse and prevent further bone loss.

Prevention

The most important point to remember is that gum disease rarely develops around clean teeth. At-home methods to keep your pet's teeth clean, such as toothbrushing and diet, along with regular dental examinations, are the best ways to help prevent gum disease. Your veterinarian might also apply a barrier sealant or recommend a plaque prevention gel.

Endodontic Disease

Endodontic disease occurs inside the teeth. The causes include injury and tooth decay. This problem requires tooth extraction or a root canal procedure. Signs can include poor appetite, painful teeth that your cat resists having touched or tapped, or a tooth with a reddish-brown or gray color. However, most cats mask their signs, and waiting until signs occur is not in the cat's best interest. X-rays of the mouth will reveal the presence of disease before signs occur.

Feline Gingivitis/Stomatitis Syndrome

A cat's mouth may react intensely to disease and become severely inflamed. Signs include mouth pain, drooling, bad breath, and loss of appetite. A veterinarian's examination may reveal inflammation of the gums, the inside of the mouth, and the upper throat. The underlying disease must be diagnosed accurately in order for treatment to be successful. Many viral and bacterial diseases contribute to this problem. Some cats are also infected by the bacteria that cause cat scratch fever (a disease that can be passed to people), which must be considered as a possible cause.

Treatment includes controlling or eliminating the cause of the condition and aggressive dental care, including home care if possible. In cases where the pain is severe, home care might not be possible. Many cats have been successfully treated by having all of their teeth extracted; sometimes the canine teeth ("fangs") can be left in. This solution is not as bad as it sounds, because most cats can eat moist food (and eventually even solid food) even after the teeth have been extracted.

Cervical Line Lesions (Feline Odontoclastic Resorptive Lesions)

Cats do not develop cavities like those seen in humans. However, they may develop cervical line lesions, also called feline odontoclastic resorptive lesions. In fact, these are the most frequently seen dental abnormality in cats. The cause is unknown, but the condition results in the breakdown and loss of tooth material and is often associated with bright red gum inflammation. The crown of the tooth may be completely lost, with the root that is left covered over by the gum. Signs associated with cervical line lesions include pain on contact, loss of appetite, drooling, and generally not feeling well.

The condition is not thought to be contagious. Mouth infections may develop because of tooth loss, however. Damage to the roots of the teeth can be detected with x-rays of the jaws. In most cases,

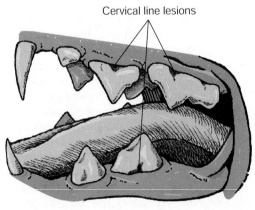

Cervical line lesions

Cervical line lesions are common in cats and lead to destruction of affected teeth.

affected teeth will need to be extracted. Techniques to restore the teeth yield only fair success rates, except for very early cases.

Developmental Abnormalities

Developmental problems with the teeth include a misaligned bite and defects in the tooth enamel. These abnormalities often have a genetic component.

Improper Bite

Proper growth and development of the mouth and teeth depends on a series of events that must occur in proper sequence or longterm complications will occur. Early detection and intervention is the best way to prevent more serious problems later in the cat's life. Dental development can be divided into 3 stages: Stage 1 is from 0 to 16 weeks of age, Stage 2 is from 16 weeks to 7 months of age, and Stage 3 is from 7 months to 1½ years of age.

Stage 1: Kittens are born with relatively long upper jaws ("overbite"), which allow them to nurse. As the kitten grows and begins to eat solid food, the lower jaw goes through a growth spurt. If certain of the lower baby teeth come in before the growth spurt, they can get caught behind the upper teeth and prevent the lower jaw from developing to its proper length. The usual treatment is to remove several of the baby lower teeth. This will allow the lower jaw to reach its full length and avert problems with the permanent teeth.

The reverse situation can also occur. In these cases, the lower jaw grows faster than usual and becomes too long for the upper jaw, producing an "underbite." This condition can be detected as early as 8 weeks of age. Again, certain teeth from the upper jaw may become caught behind those of the lower jaw, preventing proper growth of the upper jaw. As in the previous situation, the treatment is usually to extract several teeth; in this case, upper teeth are removed.

Stage 2: The most important problem that can occur during this stage is the retention of baby teeth. Abnormal tooth position and bite may result if the baby teeth are not lost at the time the corresponding permanent teeth are coming in. If retained baby teeth are removed by a veterinarian as soon as they are noticed, complications can usually be prevented.

Another developmental defect noted in this stage is abnormal positioning (tilting) of the upper canine teeth. Depending on the specific situation and age of the cat, orthodontic treatment (that is, "braces" for your pet) can be used to align teeth in their correct positions. This treatment is only effective in some cats. In most cases, tooth shortening or extractions might be necessary.

Stage 3: Additional types of incorrect tooth placement and crowding of teeth can occur during this stage of your pet's growth. Treatment, if necessary, may include orthodontic treatment and possibly tooth extraction.

Enamel Defects

During the development of tooth enamel, fevers and the deposition of certain chemicals within the tooth may cause permanent damage. Severe malnutrition in young cats or trauma to a tooth may also cause enamel defects. Treatment of these conditions can include the bonding of synthetic materials to the teeth, fluoride treatment, and frequent dental preventive care.

Trauma to the Face and Jaw

Fractured teeth should be inspected by a veterinarian to determine whether there has been damage to the tooth pulp. If fractures extend into the pulp, root canal treatment or tooth extraction will be needed. Wounds to the gums or other soft tissues should be treated by the veterinarian as well.

Bone fractures will need to be stabilized by the veterinarian using wires, pins, or other materials. As long as the correct bite position can be maintained, healing is rapid and most of the supporting material can be removed by the veterinarian in about 6 to 8 weeks. A feeding tube may be needed if the cat has difficulty eating while the injury heals.

■ DISORDERS OF THE MOUTH

Diseases of the mouth in cats can be caused by infections, injuries, tumors, or inflammatory disorders. A complete oral examination should be a part of your animal's routine physical examination, because oral diseases are most effectively treated with early diagnosis. Otherwise, many will remain hidden in the mouth and progress to an advanced stage.

Oral Inflammatory and Ulcerative Diseases

Gum disease, which was discussed earlier in this chapter, is the most common oral problem in cats. Several viruses can cause inflammation of the mouth in cats, including feline herpesvirus, feline calicivirus, feline leukemia virus, and feline immunodeficiency virus. Signs vary widely with the cause and extent of inflammation. Loss of appetite may be seen. Bad breath and drooling are common with inflammation of the mouth or tongue and saliva may be blood tinged. Pain may cause a cat to paw at its mouth and resist any attempt to examine the affected area. Lymph nodes in the region may be enlarged.

Feline Stomatitis

Cats with feline stomatitis have progressively worsening inflammation of the mouth, gums, and upper throat. The cause is unproved, but may be related to an inappropriate inflammatory response to a substance on the tooth surface. The most immediate sign is severe pain on opening the mouth. The cat may vocalize and jump when it yawns or opens its mouth to pick up food. An affected cat may have bad breath, excessive drooling, and difficulty swallowing. Cats often show an "approach-avoidance" reaction as they approach their food in hunger, then hiss and run off in anticipation of discomfort. If the condition is severe and of long duration, the animal may be noticeably thinner. If soft, palatable foods are being fed, the condition may be fairly severe before the signs are recognized.

Frequently, because of the cat's pain, a veterinarian will need to sedate it in order to perform an examination of the mouth. A complete history, assessment of the mouth, and evaluation for generalized diseases (such as renal failure) and/or viral infections will be included in the examination. A sample of tissue (biopsy) may be taken to help to exclude oral cancers or other specific mouth disorders.

Surgical removal of all the premolars and molars and removal of the connective tissue that attaches the teeth to the bone of the jaw is the only treatment that has provided some improvement and aided in overall longterm control. If the teeth are extracted early in the disease process, the procedure generally results in significant improvement or complete resolution of the inflammation. Antibiotics should be given if bacterial infections are present. Dietary changes, antibiotics, and antiseptic mouthwashes may help lessen signs. Animals that are unable or unwilling to eat and drink may require intravenous fluids or a feeding tube to prevent dehydration. Frequent feedings of tasty liquids and, later, semi-solid foods encourage eating.

Fungal Stomatitis

Fungal stomatitis is caused by overgrowth of the fungus *Candida albicans*. It is an uncommon cause of mouth inflammation in cats. The main sign is the appearance of creamy white flat areas (plaques) on the tongue or mucous membranes. It is usually thought to be associated with other oral diseases, longterm antibiotics, or a suppressed immune system. When possible, both the underlying disease and the fungal infection itself will be treated. A balanced diet should be maintained. The outlook is guarded if the underlying disease cannot be adequately treated or controlled.

Inflammation of the Tongue

Inflammation of the tongue is called **glossitis**. It may be due to infection, irrita-

tion, wounds, disease, or other causes such as electrical burns or insect stings. A thread, string, or other foreign object may get caught under the tongue. Drooling and a reluctance to eat are common signs, but the cause may go undiscovered unless the mouth is carefully examined.

Glossitis is treated by the veterinarian removing any foreign objects and any broken or diseased teeth. Infection may be treated with an appropriate antibiotic. Cleaning of the wounds and use of antiseptic mouthwashes are beneficial in some cases. A soft diet and intravenous fluids may be necessary. If the animal is unable to eat well for a prolonged period, tube feeding may also be required. Short-term glossitis due to insect stings may require emergency treatment. If the glossitis is caused by another condition, the primary disease should also be treated. The tongue tissues heal rapidly after irritation and infection have been eliminated.

Soft Tissue Trauma

Injuries to the mouth can cause significant inflammation in cats, but usually respond well to treatment.

Cheek Biting

A wound along the side of the cheek may be caused by self-trauma when the tissue becomes trapped between the teeth during chewing. Surgical removal of the excess tissue prevents further injury.

Mouth Burns

Thermal (heat), chemical, or electrical burns involving the mouth may occur. The cat should be evaluated and treated for injury to other body systems, which may be life-threatening in some cases. A cat with a burn to the mouth hesitates to eat or drink, drools, and resents handling of its mouth or face. Sores and mouth inflammation may develop. These wounds can easily become infected. If you observed the burn yourself, provide the details to your veterinarian. If the cat has only a reddened mouth lining without tissue damage, it may require no treatment other than a soft or liquid diet until the soreness has disappeared. If tissue damage is extensive, your veterinarian may rinse the tissues with an antiseptic and remove any dead tissue and debris. Antibiotics may be prescribed to reduce the chance of infection.

Oral Tumors

Benign oral tumors of the mouth and throat are less common in cats than in dogs. Instead, tumors that arise are likely to be malignant.

Benign Tumors

A **gingival fibroma** is a benign (non-spreading) growth on the gums that usually originates near the gum line. The growth is relatively insensitive and tough and is either the color of the normal gum or more pale. The growth may become large enough to completely cover the surfaces of several teeth. Surgical removal is the most satisfactory treatment. After surgery, your cat may be prescribed a daily oral rinse to be used until the site is healed.

Epulides are another type of gum tumor. They are rare in cats. This type of tumor usually involves only a single tooth. Your veterinarian can analyze a tissue sample (biopsy) to determine the proper diagnosis and treatment.

Malignant Tumors

Squamous cell carcinomas are by far the most common malignant oral tumors in cats. They commonly involve the gums and tongue and spread rapidly throughout the mouth.

Signs vary depending on the location and extent of the tumor. Bad breath, reluctance to eat, and excessive drooling are common. If the back of the mouth and throat are involved, swallowing may be difficult. The tumors frequently ulcerate and bleed. The animal's face may become swollen as the tumor enlarges and invades surrounding tissue. Lymph nodes near the tumor often become swollen before the tumor itself can be seen. A tissue biopsy is usually required for diagnosis.

The treatment and outlook depend on the specific kind of tumor and whether it has spread. Malignant melanomas are highly invasive and spread readily; consequently, the outlook is guarded to poor. Surgical removal of the tumor can extend survival and may cure the condition, but recurrence is common. In cats, squamous cell carcinoma has a poor outlook, and longterm survival is seen only if it is diagnosed and treated early. Tumor removal often requires removal of the lower jaw.

Salivary Disorders

Saliva moistens the mouth and helps begin the digestion of food. As with any other part of the body, there can be medical problems involving the glands that produce the saliva. Salivary disorders in cats include excessive drooling, salivary mucocele, and tumors.

Excessive Salivation (Ptyalism or Sialosis)

Excessive salivation has 2 main causes: either the cat is producing too much saliva (a condition called ptyalism or sialosis), or it cannot effectively swallow the saliva that is produced. In either situation, the animal drools. The most serious cause of excessive drooling is rabies, so your veterinarian will want to exclude that possibility first. The underlying cause should be determined and treated. Short-term irritation of the lips and face may develop if the skin is not kept as dry as possible. Cleansing with an appropriate antiseptic solution may be recommended.

Salivary Mucocele

In a salivary mucocele, saliva accumulates under the skin after damage to the salivary duct or gland. Although any of the salivary glands may be affected, those under the tongue and in the jaw are most commonly involved. Usually, the cause is not determined. The signs depend on the site of saliva accumulation.

The first sign may be a nonpainful, slowly enlarging mass, frequently in the neck. A mucocele under the tongue may not be seen until it is traumatized and bleeds. A pharyngeal (throat) mucocele may obstruct the airways and result in difficulty breathing. Pain or fever may occur if the mucocele becomes infected. A veterinarian can distinguish a mucocele from abscesses, tumors, and other types of cysts by using a needle to draw a sample of fluid from inside the mucocele.

Surgery is often recommended to remove the damaged salivary gland and duct. Mucoceles in the neck or under the tongue can be managed with periodic drainage if surgery is not an option. Complete gland and duct removal is often recommended for mucoceles in the throat to avoid the possibility of future life-threatening airway obstruction.

Salivary Gland Tumors

Salivary gland tumors are rare in cats, although cats are affected twice as frequently as dogs. They usually occur in cats more than 10 years old. Most salivary gland tumors are malignant, with carcinomas and adenocarcinomas the most common types. Spread to nearby lymph nodes and the lungs is common. Tumors removed by surgery alone tend to recur, so radiation treatment, with or without surgery, offers the best outlook in most cases.

Dry Mouth (Xerostomia)

This condition occurs when saliva production is decreased. Signs include interest in eating but turning away as if the food does not taste good. Lip smacking and excessive tongue thrusting when trying to eat is another sign. The gums and mucous membranes of the mouth are dry and the teeth usually have a heavy film of plaque. Older cats with kidney failure are more at risk for this disease. Treatment is supportive care—artificial saliva substitutes and wetting the food. The condition rarely reverses itself.

▮ DISORDERS OF THE PHARYNX

The upper throat is called the pharynx. **Pharyngeal paralysis** refers to paralysis of the upper throat (pharynx) that makes swallowing difficult or impossible. It may be caused by a nervous system disor-

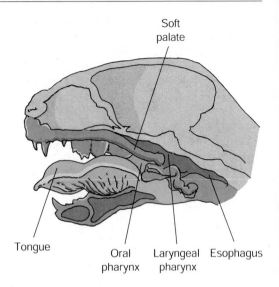

The throat and pharynx of the cat

der or other disease or trauma that causes collapse, obstruction, or malfunction of the pharynx.

Pharyngeal paralysis results in severe problems with swallowing; food and saliva come back out through the mouth and nose. In most species, collapse of throat tissues occurs. Affected cats are at risk of pneumonia from inhaling food and liquid (aspiration pneumonia), dehydration, and circulatory and respiratory failure. Signs of pharyngeal paralysis include fever, coughing, gagging, and choking. This condition may be fatal. In many cases, emergency surgery to provide an airway (tracheostomy) must be done before any more detailed analysis of the condition can be performed.

In general, treatment for pharyngeal paralysis is directed toward alleviating the signs of the disease. Treatment may include drugs to control inflammation, antibiotics to control the complications of aspiration pneumonia, draining of abscesses (if they are present), and providing alternative routes of nutrition. A feeding tube (a soft plastic tube inserted through the mouth or nose into the stomach) may be required to provide nutrition and water. In many cases, the outlook is poor. The welfare of the cat should be considered when determining what course of treatment to follow.

■ DISORDERS OF THE ESOPHAGUS

Signs of problems with the esophagus include difficulty swallowing and regurgitation (return of food or fluid before it has reached the stomach). Congenital abnormalities of the esophagus are discussed earlier in this chapter (*see* page 388).

Inflammation of the Esophagus (Esophagitis)

Inflammation of the esophagus (esophagitis) is usually caused by foreign objects or acid reflux. Other causes include certain drugs, eating an irritating or caustic substance, or cancer. Calicivirus in cats may also cause esophagitis. Mild inflammation may produce no visible signs and often requires no treatment. If the problem is caused by acid reflux (a cause of heartburn in people), drugs that reduce stomach acid can provide relief. Your veterinarian may recommend feeding your pet a diet of soft food, low in fat and fiber, in small, frequent meals. If esophagitis is severe, a feeding tube may need to be surgically placed into the stomach, bypassing the esophagus to allow it to rest. Antibiotics are sometimes prescribed to prevent bacterial infection.

Foreign Objects in the Esophagus

Cats are generally pickier eaters than dogs, but occasionally they will get foreign objects lodged in the esophagus. Bones are the most common, but other objects such as needles, string, thread, fishhooks, and wood may also become stuck. Signs include excessive drooling, gagging, regurgitation, and repeated attempts to swallow. Many foreign objects can be seen on x-rays. If a foreign object is found in the esophagus, a veterinarian will need to remove it as soon as possible. Surgery is necessary if the esophagus has been perforated or the foreign object cannot be removed using endoscopy. In these cases, the outlook for recovery is usually poor.

Esophageal Strictures

Esophageal stricture is a narrowing of the esophagus. It may develop after trauma (for example, ingestion of a foreign object, caustic substance, or certain drugs), inflammation of the esophagus, gastroesophageal reflux (gastric acid flowing back into the esophagus), or tumor invasion. Signs include vomiting, excessive drooling, difficulty swallowing, and pain. Examining the esophagus using fluoroscopy and endoscopy are the preferred methods for diagnosis. This enables the veterinarian to actually see the number, location, and types of strictures. Endoscopy may also allow the veterinarian to correct the stricture at the time of examination.

Treatment with a balloon catheter has been successful. The catheter is a tube that is placed in the esophagus and then advanced to where the stricture occurs. The tip of the catheter is then inflated like a balloon, which stretches the esophagus and relieves the stricture. Other methods, including surgery, have been less successful.

Esophageal Diverticula

Diverticula are pouch-like expansions (dilations) of the esophageal wall. They can be inherited or acquired; however, they are rare in cats. There are 2 types of acquired diverticula: pulsion and traction. **Pulsion diverticula** are caused by an increase in pressure inside the esophagus or deep esophageal inflammation, which leads to a rupture (hernia) of the inner lining. **Traction diverticula** are caused by inflammation in the chest cavity close to the esophagus. Fibrous tissue is formed and then contracts, pulling the esophageal wall outward. (For a more detailed discussion of ESOPHAGEAL DIVERTICULA, *see* page 99.)

■ VOMITING

Vomiting is the forceful ejection of the contents (such as food or fluids) of the stomach and upper small intestine. It is

Managing Hairballs in Cats

As cats groom themselves they swallow some of the loose hair from their coat. Hair cannot be digested and tends to stick together in the stomach, where it forms into a lump or hairball (also called a **trichobezoar**). Often, cats will vomit up the hairball. In some cases, however, it remains in the stomach for a long time and hardens into a dense mass. This can irritate the stomach or even block the digestive tract. Longhaired breeds are at greater risk.

You can limit the amount of hair your cat swallows and help prevent hairballs from forming by frequently brushing your cat to remove loose fur. If necessary, medications such as mineral oil can be given to help cats pass hair through the digestive tract. Some commercial cat diets and treats are also formulated to help prevent formation of hairballs. In severe cases, surgery may be required to remove the hairball.

normally preceded by excessive drooling, retching, and forceful contractions of the abdominal muscles and the diaphragm. Vomiting can be caused by digestive system disease, kidney or liver failure, pancreatitis, or nervous system disorders (including ingestion of poisons).

Vomiting differs from **regurgitation**, which is a passive motion. With regurgitation, the expelled food and fluid tends to be undigested and may have a cylindrical shape reflecting the shape of the esophagus. Coughing or difficulty breathing are more often associated with regurgitation than with vomiting.

Short-term or occasional vomiting is generally not associated with other abnormalities. Longterm vomiting may be associated with weakness, lethargy, weight loss, dehydration, and electrolyte (salt) imbalance. Whenever possible, control of vomiting is achieved by identifying and eliminating the cause while allowing the digestive system time to recover.

Short-term or Occasional Vomiting

When a cat has been vomiting for only a short time (less than 3 to 4 days) and no other signs of disease are present, treatment to relieve signs may be all that is needed. Generally, the treatment for short-term vomiting requires withholding food and limiting access to water for 24 hours. Cats with kidney or heart disease may require a hospital stay with intravenous fluid treatment during this time. If the vomiting has stopped after 24 hours, the cat may be offered small amounts of water. If no further vomiting occurs, feeding can usually be resumed slowly.

Longterm or Severe Vomiting

Longterm vomiting, vomiting that occurs more often than once or twice daily, and vomiting accompanied by blood, abdominal pain, depression, dehydration, weakness, fever, or other adverse signs requires a detailed examination by your veterinarian. This may include blood and urine tests as well as abdominal x-rays. In many cases, endoscopic evaluation and biopsy of the stomach and small intestine are the only tests that can determine the cause of the vomiting.

A cat with longterm vomiting may need to be treated for conditions such as dehydration, salt imbalances, and acid-base disorders that have developed. Drugs to control vomiting can be prescribed for animals with persistent vomiting, dehydration, and weakness.

■ DISORDERS OF THE STOMACH AND INTESTINES

Diseases that affect the stomach and intestines include infectious diseases such as bacterial, viral, and parasitic diseases and noninfectious disorders such as tumors and obstruction.

Inflammation of the Large Intestine

When the large intestine (also called colon or large bowel) is damaged by illness, parasites, or other causes, diarrhea is often the result. Cats with inflammation of the colon have a history of straining to defecate and frequent passage of mucus-laden feces, sometimes containing bright red blood. Feces are often of a small volume and a more liquid consistency. Weight loss is uncommon, and vomiting is seen in about 30% of cases.

If possible, the cause of the inflammation should be identified and eliminated. Follow your veterinarian's recommendations for diet. You may be asked to withhold food for 24 hours to rest the cat's digestive system. Once feeding is resumed, soluble fiber is often added to the diet. Over time, the fiber dose can be often be reduced or eliminated. When feeding is first resumed, you may be advised to provide food with a protein source that your cat has not previously eaten, such as mutton, lamb, venison, or rabbit. This is to identify any food allergies your cat may have. Cats with some types of inflammation may respond to dietary management alone (such as changing to lamb and rice, or a commercially available diet). To help the signs improve more rapidly, your veterinarian may add anti-inflammatory medication to the change in diet. Some animals require additional short-term use of medication to thicken the feces until inflammation is brought under control.

Constipation

Constipation is a common problem in cats. In most instances, the problem is easily corrected. However, in cats with more serious illness, accompanying signs can be severe. The longer feces remain in the colon, the drier, harder, and more difficult to pass they become. **Obstipation** is constipation that resists treatment.

Longterm constipation may be due to an obstruction inside the intestines, constriction from outside the intestines, or neuromuscular problems with the colon itself. Obstruction is most common and is due to the cat's inability to pass poorly digestible, often firm matter (such as hair, bones, or litter) that has become mixed with fecal material. Some cats with longterm constipation or obstipation may have **megacolon**, an enlarged intestine caused by a defect in the muscle strength of the colon. The cause of megacolon often remains undiagnosed. Some drugs cause constipation as a side effect.

Signs of constipation include straining to defecate and the passage of firm, dry feces. Some animals are quite ill and also have lethargy, depression, loss of appetite, vomiting, and abdominal discomfort. A visit to the veterinarian is advised. During the visit, be sure to tell your veterinarian if your cat has any tendency to eat bones, litter, or other hard matter.

Affected cats should receive plenty of water. Mild constipation can often be treated by switching to a high-fiber diet, keeping your cat from eating bones or other objects, providing ready access to water, and using appropriate laxatives (usually for a short time only). Be sure to provide your cat with the laxative prescribed by your veterinarian. Laxatives formulated for human use can be very dangerous for pets. In more severe cases of constipation, a veterinarian will need to remove retained feces using enemas or manual extraction while your pet is under general anesthesia. Cats with chronic constipation or megacolon that have been unresponsive to medical treatment may respond to removal of the affected section of the large intestine.

Feline Enteric Coronavirus

Feline enteric coronavirus is highly contagious among cats in close contact. It is very closely related to the virus that causes a more serious disease, feline infectious peritonitis. Infection with feline enteric coronavirus causes inflammation of the small intestine, but is not usually fatal.

The virus is shed in the feces of infected cats. Close contact between cats is required for transmission, although the possibility of transmission by contaminated objects also exists. In catteries, the virus may be a cause of mild to severe intestinal inflammation in kittens 6 to 12 weeks old. Recently weaned kittens may have fever, vomiting, and diarrhea lasting 2 to 5 days. More severely affected kittens may be unwilling to eat for 1 to 3 days. Adult cats often show no signs when infected.

The virus is extremely widespread in cats, and many cats that recover from the infection remain carriers. Enteric coronavirus infection can be prevented only by minimizing exposure to infected cats and their feces. Most cats develop an effective immune response after exposure and will recover from infection. Cats with the intestinal form of the disease do not develop signs of feline infectious peritonitis. However, if signs of disease develop in cats with feline infectious peritonitis, the disease is fatal. There is no specific treatment; however, affected cats should receive supportive treatment and fluids, if needed.

Inflammation of the Stomach (Gastritis)

Gastritis, or inflammation of the stomach, is often caused by eating something that injures the stomach lining. Vomiting is the usual sign of gastritis. In cases of short-term gastritis, the vomited material may contain evidence of whatever the cat has eaten (such as grass). Bile, froth, fresh blood, or digested blood that looks like coffee grounds may be seen. Diarrhea may also be present. Short-term or occasional vomiting is generally not associated with other abnormalities. Longterm vomiting, however, may be associated with weakness, lethargy, weight loss, dehydration, and electrolyte (salt) imbalance. The outlook depends on the cause of the vomiting and the likelihood of correcting the underlying disorder. (*See also* VOMITING, page 397.)

Cancers of the Digestive System

Cancer of the digestive system is uncommon and represents less than 1% of all cancers in cats. When it does occur, it most commonly develops in the small intestine. Older animals are predisposed. No specific cause has been identified for most intestinal tumors, although alimentary lymphoma in cats is believed to be caused by the feline leukemia virus, even in cats that test negative for the virus. Intestinal tumors in cats tend to spread rapidly and are usually malignant (cancerous).

Signs of a possible tumor vary depending on the location and extent of the tumor and associated consequences. Vomiting (sometimes with blood), diarrhea (also with blood), weight loss, constipation, straining to defecate, abdominal pain, abdominal swelling, and abdominal infection associated with the rupture of the affected bowel have been reported. Cats with intestinal tumors may also have signs of anemia, such as pale gums.

Diagnosis is based on a complete history and physical examination and confirmed by tissue biopsy. Surgical removal is the preferred treatment. Your veterinarian will also attempt to determine the extent of spread of the cancer. The outlook can vary from excellent to poor, depending on the specific type of tumor and whether all of it can be removed.

Gastrointestinal Obstruction

Obstruction of food movement out of the stomach can result from tumors, foreign objects, polyps, and overgrowth of stomach tissue.

Intestinal obstruction may be partial or complete and may be caused by foreign objects, intussusception (a condition in which the intestine telescopes on itself), incarceration (such as being constricted in a hernia), and tumors. Long, thin foreign objects (such as string, yarn, or fabric) may become attached at the base of the tongue. If the object is long enough to trail into the intestines, normal intestinal movement tends to cause a sawing or cutting motion on the gut, leading to intestinal perforation and abdominal infection.

Signs of **small-intestinal obstruction** may include lethargy, poor appetite, vomiting, diarrhea, abdominal pain or swelling, fever or subnormal body temperature, dehydration, and shock. To make a diagnosis, your veterinarian will need to know as much as possible about your cat's eating habits. Access to string or sewing needles or missing objects (such as toys) may be important facts and should be reported. Abdominal palpation (gently using the hands to feel the internal organs) can allow your veterinarian to detect organ enlargement, thickened bowel loops, and gas. X-rays, ultrasonography, or examination using an endoscope may be used to identify the problem.

Cats that have generalized signs of illness, such as depression or fever, benefit from intravenous fluid treatment. If an obstruction is found and cannot be removed using the endoscope, then surgery will be needed. Cats with sudden abdominal signs of unknown cause, and those that continue to worsen, may also require surgery. Many of these animals recover well.

Gastrointestinal Ulcers

Gastrointestinal ulcers are wounds in the stomach or intestinal lining caused by stomach acid or digestive enzymes. Factors that may lead to formation of ulcers include certain drugs, tumors, infections, or generalized diseases.

Cats with stomach ulceration may have no signs. In other cases, they can have a history that includes vomiting, sometimes with blood, and abdominal discomfort that may appear less severe after a meal. Dark, tarry stools, which indicate the presence of blood, and pale gums suggesting anemia may be present. Signs may also be related to the cause of the ulcer (for example, signs related to kidney failure).

In cats that have a history of vomiting, abdominal discomfort, loss of appetite, or unexplained weight loss, there are several tests that might be performed by your veterinarian in an attempt to diagnose the cause. Abdominal ultrasound scans or x-rays may be used to confirm the diagnosis. In cases in which the cause is unclear or in those with apparent gastrointestinal disease, endoscopy and biopsy of the stomach and intestines are often recommended.

The goal of ulcer management is to determine the cause of the ulceration and then eliminate or control it. Providing supportive care is also critical. Medication directed at the ulcer itself reduces stomach acidity, prevents further destruction of the stomach lining, and promotes ulcer healing. In general, treatment should be continued for 6 to 8 weeks. Dietary management should include the use of bland diets (for example, cottage cheese and rice or chicken and rice).

Ideally, ulcer healing should be monitored with endoscopy. If the ulcers do not respond to basic medical management, a biopsy of the stomach and small intestine are the next steps. The outlook for cats with peptic ulcers and benign stomach tumors is good. Outlook is poor for those with ulcers associated with kidney or liver failure and for cats with gastric carcinoma or gastrinoma.

Inflammatory Bowel Disease

Idiopathic inflammatory bowel disease is actually a group of digestive system diseases that are recognized by certain persistent signs and by inflammation without a known cause. The various forms of inflammatory bowel disease are classified by their location in the body and the type of cell that is involved.

Inflammatory bowel disease appears to affect all ages, sexes, and breeds, although it may be more common in purebred cats. The average age reported for the development of disease in cats is 7 years. Signs are often longterm and sometimes come and go. Vomiting, diarrhea, changes in appetite, and weight loss may be seen. Inflammatory bowel disease can be difficult to diagnose, because many of its signs can be seen in other diseases as well.

The goals of treatment are to reduce diarrhea, promote weight gain, and decrease intestinal inflammation. If a cause can be identified (such as diet, parasites, bacterial overgrowth, or drug reaction), it should be eliminated. Modifying the diet, without other treatment, may be effective in some cases. In other cases, changes in diet can enhance medical treatment, allowing for the drug dosage to be reduced or for the drug to be discontinued once signs improve. Glucocorticoids, which suppress the immune system, are among the drugs most often used in the management of inflammatory bowel disease.

Your veterinarian may recommend feeding your cat a hypoallergenic or elimination diet. This means feeding a source of protein that the cat has not previously eaten. Diets with these ingredients are usually available from veterinary clinics rather than commercial outlets, or they can be home-made. This diet should be the sole source of food for a minimum of 4 to 6 weeks, and no treats of any kind should be fed unless approved by your veterinarian. These types of diets are effective in controlling signs in some cats with inflammatory bowel disease, but not in cats with food sensitivity or food allergy. Supplementation of dietary fiber alone is rarely effective in severe cases.

Although feline inflammatory bowel disease can often be controlled with an appropriate combination of diet and medication, the condition is rarely cured. Relapses may occur.

Malabsorption

Malabsorption is poor absorption of a nutrient resulting from interference with its digestion, absorption, or both. Interference with digestion in cats is typically due to lack of certain enzymes from the pancreas, called pancreatic insufficiency (*see* page 408), whereas most cases of absorption failure are caused by diseases in the small intestine.

The signs of malabsorption are mainly due to lack of nutrient uptake and loss of nutrients in the feces. Signs typically include longterm diarrhea, weight loss, and altered appetite (loss of appetite or excessive eating). However, diarrhea may be absent even when disease is severe. Weight loss may be substantial despite a good appetite. Cats with malabsorption usually appear healthy in other respects unless there is severe inflammation or cancer. Nonspecific signs may include dehydration, anemia, and accumulation of fluid in the abdomen or other tissues. Your veterinarian may be able to detect thickened bowel loops or enlarged abdominal lymph nodes.

Diagnosing malabsorption can be complex, because longterm diarrhea and weight loss are signs that are common in several diseases. A thorough examination with appropriate laboratory tests can help determine whether the signs are caused

by an underlying multisystem or metabolic disease (such as hyperthyroidism).

Treatment of malabsorption involves dietary treatment, management of complications, and treatment of the cause (if it can be identified). Dietary modification is an important aspect of the management of malabsorption. Diets generally contain moderate levels of limited protein sources, highly digestible carbohydrates, and moderate levels of fat (to reduce fatty diarrhea). Cats with inflammatory bowel disease have a higher incidence of dietary sensitivity than dogs. Your veterinarian may recommend feeding your cat an exclusion diet consisting of a single novel protein source (lamb or venison, for example) as a test when dietary sensitivity is suspected. Oral anti-inflammatory medication may be prescribed if the initial response to the exclusion diet is disappointing.

■ DISORDERS CAUSED BY BACTERIA

Certain bacteria may cause gastrointestinal disease in cats. The most common of these are discussed below.

Campylobacter Infection

Gastrointestinal campylobacteriosis is a bacterial disease. It is caused by 2 related bacteria of the *Campylobacter* genus. These 2 organisms, along with a number of other species of *Campylobacter*, can be isolated from carrier cats (those that do not show signs) as well as ill cats. Cats, especially those recently obtained from shelters, can serve as sources of human infection.

Exposure to feces of infected animals and food- or waterborne transmission appears to be the most common routes of infection. One suspected source of infection for pets is eating undercooked poultry and other raw meat products. Wild birds also may be important sources of water contamination.

The diarrhea appears to be most severe in young cats. Typical signs include mucus-laden, watery, or bile-streaked diarrhea (with or without blood) that lasts 3 to 7 days; reduced appetite; and occasional vomiting. Fever may also be present. Intermittent diarrhea may persist for more than 2 weeks; in some, it may last for months. To diagnose campylobacteriosis, a veterinarian will test the animal's feces and blood for evidence of infection.

Antibiotic treatment for cats found to carry these bacteria is usually reserved for those that are young, severely affected, or a potential source of human infection. This is because other organisms are likely to be involved and antibiotic treatment is often not effective.

Salmonella Infection

Many species of *Salmonella* bacteria can cause gastrointestinal illness. A *Salmonella* infection can cause severe blood poisoning (septicemia) or inflammation of the intestine. The disease occurs in all domestic animals, as well as humans, but it is infrequent in cats. Infected cats may become carriers of *Salmonella* but often do not show any signs of disease.

Signs of disease are more likely to occur during hospitalization, in cats with another infection or debilitating condition, or in kittens exposed to large numbers of the bacteria. Signs include sudden diarrhea with blood poisoning. Pneumonia and conjunctivitis (inflammation of eye membranes) are sometimes present. Diagnosis is based on signs of disease and on the laboratory examination of feces.

Early treatment is essential for blood poisoning. In many cases, antibiotics are given intravenously. Fluids may be given intravenously as well. The intestinal form of the disease is difficult to treat effectively. Antibiotics are not always recommended, due to concerns about the development of antibiotic-resistant bacteria. Although the signs of disease may disappear, eliminating the bacteria from the body is difficult, particularly in adult cats.

Tyzzer's Disease

Tyzzer's disease is an infection caused by the bacterium *Clostridium piliforme*. It affects a wide range of animals but is rare in cats. It most often affects young, healthy animals that have been subjected to stress or other diseases (such as feline infectious peritonitis). The bacteria primarily affect cells in the intestine, liver, and heart.

Signs vary, but may include decreased activity, loss of appetite, fever, jaundice, and diarrhea. Before death, there are convulsions and coma. A diagnosis of Tyzzer's disease is based on laboratory examination of tissue sections for the presence of the bacteria.

Little is known about the effectiveness of antibiotics for treatment. Some antibiotics may aggravate the disease. Cats suspected of being infected may be treated with intravenous fluids and appropriate antibiotics.

■ GASTROINTESTINAL PARASITES OF CATS

Many parasites can infect the digestive system of cats (*see* TABLE 3). The most common ones are described below.

Roundworms

The large roundworms known as ascarids are common in cats, especially in kittens. The most important species is *Toxocara cati*, as it is both very common and will infect people. *Toxascaris leonina* also infects cats, but is typically much less common and does not infect people. In kittens, infections with *Toxocara cati* are most likely to be acquired by ingestion of parasites in the mother's milk. Adult parasites can then be found in the small intestine of kittens as early as 3 to 4 weeks of age. Cats of all ages may also be infected with *Toxocara cati* by ingesting eggs that have been in the environment for at least 2 weeks, and by eating prey such as mice that carry the parasites. Maturation of parasites typically only occurs in the gastrointestinal tract. However, in kittens that have eaten infective eggs, hatched larvae penetrate the intestinal wall, travel to the lungs via the bloodstream, are coughed up, swallowed, and mature to egg-producing adults in the small intestine. Adult cats generally have some resistance to infection.

Table 3. Gastrointestinal Parasites of Cats

Common Name (Scientific Name)	How Contracted	Signs	Control and Prevention*
Hookworms (*Ancylostoma tubaeforme, A. braziliense, A. ceylanicum, Uncinaria stenocephala*)	Ingestion of larvae in environment or by eating infected rodents; penetration of skin by larvae	Often no signs; weight loss and anemia can occur.	Several drugs are available for treating hookworm infection. Some heartworm preventives also control hookworms.
Roundworms (*Toxascaris leonina, Toxocara cati*)	*T. cati*—commonly passed from mother to kittens during nursing Both species—ingestion of eggs or eating infected rodents	Often no signs; diarrhea, poor growth, or a distended, swollen abdomen; worms may be vomited or passed in feces	Kittens should be dewormed on multiple occasions in the first 3 months of life; some monthly heartworm preventives will also prevent roundworm infection.
Stomach worms (*Physaloptera* species)	Cats eat hosts (beetles, cockroaches, crickets, mice, frogs)	Stomach inflammation which can result in vomiting, loss of appetite, and dark feces. In heavy infections, anemia and weight loss.	Several drugs from your veterinarian can be used to treat infection.
Ollulanus tricuspis	Cats pick up infection through contaminated vomit	Gastritis; causes vomiting minutes to a few hours after a meal	Drugs are available from your veterinarian to treat infection.
Tapeworms (cestodes), (*Dipylidium caninum, Taenia taeniaformis*)	Eating infected fleas or prey animals; the biting mite *Trichodectes canis*, is also an intermediate host	Most infections have few signs. Poor absorption of food or diarrhea may occur; unthrifty, potbellied.	Control requires medication to treat the tapeworms and preventing access to prey animals so the cat isn't reinfected. Flea control is also important for *D. caninum*.
Threadworms (*Strongyloides* species)	Infective stage in environment penetrates skin; also swallowed	Often no signs; sometimes watery diarrhea.	Isolation of sick animals; thorough washing of pet living areas. Disease is more severe in cats with a weakened immune system.

*A number of antiparasitic drugs (anthelmintics) are available to treat parasites in cats.

However, around the time when they give birth, immunity to infection may be suppressed and significant numbers of eggs may be present in feces. Infections are often not associated with any signs. The first indication of infection in young animals can be lack of growth and loss of condition. Infected cats can have a dull coat and often are "potbellied." Worms may be vomited or passed in the feces. In the early stages, migrating larvae occasionally cause pneumonia, which can be associated with coughing. Diarrhea with mucus may be evident. Infection is diagnosed by microscopic detection of eggs in feces.

Several drugs are effective for treatment of roundworm infections in cats. Certain preventive programs for heartworm infection also control intestinal roundworm infections. Ideally, treatment for kittens should be started at 3 to 4 weeks of age, repeated at 2-week intervals until 3 months of age, and then continued monthly until 6 months of age. Your veterinarian will prescribe the most appropriate medication for your cat.

Hookworms

Several types of hookworms can cause gastrointestinal disease in cats. *Ancylostoma tubaeforme* is the most likely to cause illness and is found globally. *Ancylostoma braziliense* is found in central and South America, southeast US, and Africa. *Ancylostoma ceylanicum* is found in southern Africa, India, and southeast Asia. *Uncinaria stenocephala* is found globally in temperate and subarctic climates, but infections with this species are rare. Cats can become infected by ingesting the larvae in the environment (passed in the feces of an infected animal or in the milk from a nursing queen), by eating infected rodents, or by larval penetration of the skin. Infection is more common in kittens. When larvae mature to adults, they live in the small intestine.

Most infected cats show no signs. Anemia occasionally occurs and is the result of bloodsucking by the worms in the small intestine. Feces may become loose and have a tarry consistency. Loss of appetite, weight loss, and weakness occasionally develop in longterm disease. A diagnosis can often be made from the microscopic identification of hookworm eggs in fresh feces from infected cats.

A number of drugs and drug combinations are approved for treatment of hookworm infections. In addition, some heartworm medications also control certain species of hookworms. Deworming programs for roundworms in cats will usually also control hookworm infections.

Tapeworms

Several types of tapeworms—properly known as cestodes—may infect cats. Adult tapeworms are segmented worms found in the intestines. They rarely cause serious disease. The common tapeworm of cats, *Dipylidium*, is acquired from eating fleas. Much less frequently, cats with access to infected house (or outdoor) mice and rats can acquire other types of tapeworm infections from these sources. The biting mite, *Trichodectes canis*, is also an intermediate host. In parts of the Middle East, southern Europe, and northern Africa, tapeworms can also be acquired by eating reptiles. Signs of tapeworm infection vary and can include a failure to digest and absorb food normally (unthriftiness), malaise, variable appetite, mild diarrhea, and a pot-bellied appearance. Often, there are no signs. Very rarely, seizures are seen. Diagnosis is based on finding tapeworm segments or eggs in the feces.

Control of tapeworms requires both treatment and prevention. Flea control is critical for tapeworm control, even for indoor cats. In addition to being exposed to fleas, cats that roam freely may also become reinfected by eating dead or prey animals. Confined animals can be reinfected by fleas. An accurate diagnosis will enable your veterinarian to provide effective advice on treating the infection and preventing reinfection.

Flukes

Flukes (also called trematodes) are a class of parasites that can infect cats. They have a complex life cycle that can involve multiple intermediate hosts. There are several types of intestinal, liver, and pancreatic flukes that can infect cats (*see* TABLE 4); however, infection of cats is uncommon in the US.

■ DISORDERS CAUSED BY PROTOZOA

Protozoa are single-celled organisms that can sometimes cause disease. They may be free-living or parasites. Some of the more common diseases caused by protozoa in cats are discussed below.

Amebiasis

Amebiasis is a disease caused by the amoeba *Entamoeba histolytica*. It causes inflammation of the large intestine, which produces persistent diarrhea. Amebiasis

Table 4. Types of Flukes that Infect Cats

Class	Species (Common Name)	How Contracted	Signs
Intestinal flukes	*Nanophyetus salmincola* (Salmon poisoning fluke); found in northwestern US, southwestern Canada, and other countries of the northern Pacific rim	Cats eat intermediate host (raw or improperly prepared salmon and similar fish)	Heavy infection causes enteritis. Infection is compounded by rickettsial infection carried by flukes ("salmon poisoning disease").
	Alaria species; found in North America, Europe, Russia, Australia, and Japan	Cats eat hosts (frogs, reptiles, rodents)	Heavy infection can cause bleeding in the lungs (larval migration damage) or enteritis (adult flukes).
Liver flukes	*Opisthorchis* species; found in eastern Europe, former Soviet Union, parts of Asia	Cats eat certain fish	Longterm presence causes thickening and fibrosis of bile and/or pancreatic duct walls. Fluid may build up in the abdomen.
	Amphimerus pseudofelineus; reported in southern and midwestern US	Rare; cats acquire by eating infected fish	Vomiting, poor appetite, lethargy, weight loss.
	Platynosomum concinnum; found in southeastern US, Puerto Rico and other Caribbean Islands, South America, Malaysia, Hawaii and other Pacific islands, and parts of Africa	Cats acquire parasite by feeding on infected lizards and toads	Mild cases seen as general unthriftiness. Severe cases ("lizard poisoning") characterized by loss of appetite, vomiting, diarrhea and jaundice, leading to death.
Pancreatic fluke	*Eurytrema procyonis*; found in North America	Rare; cats acquire by feeding on infected snails or possibly insects	Weight loss, but may cause no signs.

is common in people, sometimes seen in dogs and cats, and rare in other mammals. Humans are the natural host for this species and the usual source of infection for domestic animals. Cats become infected by eating food or water contaminated with feces containing infective cysts, which are a dormant form of the parasite.

Entamoeba histolytica lives inside the large intestine and will sometimes produce no obvious signs. On the other hand, it can invade the intestinal lining and produce inflammation, wounds, and bleeding. In short-term disease, severe diarrhea may develop. This disease may be fatal, become long-lasting, or improve spontaneously. Cats with longterm infection may show weight loss, poor appetite, straining to defecate, and diarrhea. Any of these signs may be continuous or may come and go.

The disease is diagnosed by the presence of active or dormant *E. histolytica* in feces. If infection has occurred outside of the intestine, the parasites may be difficult to detect. Antibiotics may be prescribed to treat this illness.

Coccidiosis

Coccidiosis is an invasion and destruction of intestinal tissues by any of several protozoa. Coccidiosis can cause illness in cats but while infections are very common, signs associated with infection are much less common.

Coccidia more commonly infect kittens and tend to infect animals that have been weakened in some way. Therefore, signs of illness caused by coccidiosis are most prevalent under conditions of poor nutrition, poor sanitation, or overcrowding, or after stresses such as weaning or other intestinal infections. Infection results when an animal eats infective egg cysts (oocysts). These oocysts enter the environment in the feces of an infected animal, but they are unable to cause infection until they develop further under the right environmental conditions.

The most common signs in severe cases are diarrhea (sometimes bloody), weight loss, and dehydration. Your veterinarian will combine the results of fecal examinations with observations of signs and intestinal abnormalities to confirm the diagnosis.

Treatment may be unnecessary in cats because they usually eliminate the infection spontaneously, although sick animals can be treated with medication if needed.

Sanitation is important, especially in catteries or other places where large numbers of animals are housed. Feces should be removed frequently, and fecal contamination of food and water should be prevented. Cages and utensils should be disinfected daily. Raw meat should not be fed. Insect control is also important.

Giardiasis

Giardiasis is a longterm, intestinal protozoal infection caused by species of *Giardia*. It is seen worldwide in most domestic and wild mammals, many birds, and people. Infection is common in cats. *Giardia* has been reported to be found in up to 35% of fecal samples from pet and shelter cats, with a higher rate of infection in younger animals.

Giardia protozoa live in the small intestine, where they attach and multiply. They produce cysts that are passed in the feces. Transmission occurs by spread from feces to mouth.

Giardia infection in cats sometimes causes no signs. In other cases, it causes weight loss and longterm diarrhea, which can be continual or intermittent, particu-

larly in kittens. Feces usually are soft, poorly formed, pale, foul-smelling, contain mucus, and appear fatty. Occasionally vomiting occurs. A diagnosis is usually made by identifying *Giardia* cysts or *Giardia* antigen in stool samples.

To treat giardiasis, your veterinarian will likely prescribe a drug or combination of drugs that are effective against protozoa. A vaccine is available for cats in some countries. Some studies indicate that the vaccine may reduce signs as well as the number and length of time cysts are shed into the environment. Your veterinarian can tell you whether or not this vaccine is appropriate for your cat.

Giardia cysts in the feces are a source of infection and reinfection for cats, particularly those in crowded conditions such as catteries. Prompt removal of feces limits environmental contamination. Cysts contaminating the hair of cats may be a source of reinfection. Shampooing and rinsing the animals well can help remove cysts from hair. Vaccination can aid in disease prevention by decreasing or preventing cyst shedding. Cats may be infected with a type of *Giardia* species that only infects cats, but they may occasionally have a type that also infects people. Cat feces should be disposed of promptly. It is important to wash your hands properly after handling infected animals or their feces.

◾ DISORDERS OF THE PANCREAS

The pancreas is an organ that has 2 main functions: endocrine and exocrine. The endocrine pancreas produces the hormones insulin and glucagon, which regulate blood sugar levels. The exocrine pancreas produces enzymes that are essential for the digestion of complex dietary components such as proteins, triglycerides, and complex carbohydrates. The exocrine pancreas also secretes large amounts of bicarbonate, which buffers stomach acid.

Disorders of the exocrine pancreas are discussed here, because they relate to digestion. Endocrine functions of the pancreas are discussed in the Hormonal Disorders chapter.

Inflammation of the Pancreas (Pancreatitis)

Pancreatitis, or inflammation of the pancreas, is the most common exocrine pancreatic disease in cats. It can be short-term (acute) or longterm (chronic), depending on whether or not the disease has led to permanent damage to pancreatic cells. Both forms of pancreatitis can be severe. In most cases of pancreatitis, the cause cannot be determined.

Signs of severe pancreatitis are the same as with many other digestive disorders. They can include lethargy, loss of appetite, dehydration, low body temperature, vomiting, and abdominal pain. Blood tests may be used by your veterinarian to confirm the diagnosis, along with ultrasonography or exploratory surgery, if needed.

Treatment for pancreatitis includes careful monitoring and supportive veterinary care. Hospitalization may be required. Early intervention will help prevent complications. If the cause is known, specific treatment may be started. Resting the pancreas by giving the cat nothing by mouth for 3 to 4 days is recommended only when the cat is vomiting. Treatment with intravenous fluids may be required. Pain medication is given in most cases because the cat is assumed to have abdominal pain.

In mild cases of pancreatitis, cats may be switched to a low-fat diet and low-fat treats. Pancreatic enzyme supplementation may help in cases in which abdominal pain is present or for cats with poor appetites (often the only indicator of abdominal pain). Cats with mild, long-term pancreatitis should be monitored for potential complications, such as exocrine pancreatic insufficiency (*see* below).

The outlook in mild cases is good, but outlook in severe cases of pancreatitis is poor. About half of cats with severe pancreatitis may die.

Exocrine Pancreatic Insufficiency

Exocrine pancreatic insufficiency is a syndrome caused by insufficient production and secretion of digestive enzymes by the pancreas. Longterm inflammation of the pancreas (pancreatitis) is the most common cause in cats; less commonly, tumors that lead to obstruction of the pancreatic duct cause this disorder.

Cats with exocrine pancreatic insufficiency are usually middle-aged to older and can be of any breed. The most common signs are excessive eating, weight loss, and loose stools or diarrhea. Vomiting and loss of appetite are seen in some cats and may be a sign of other disorders. Diabetes mellitus is often seen with exocrine pancreatic insufficiency, due to the destruction of pancreatic hormone-producing cells. The feces are most commonly pale, loose, and voluminous and may be foul-smelling. In rare cases watery diarrhea may be seen. The high fat content of the feces can lead to a greasy appearance of the hair coat, especially in the region around the anus and tail. Diagnosis can be made using a blood test that indicates the decreased function of the exocrine pancreas.

Most cats with exocrine pancreatic insufficiency can be successfully treated by dietary supplementation with pancreatic enzymes (powdered or from fresh tissue). Follow your veterinarian's directions for this dietary supplement carefully, and be sure to report any bleeding of the mouth, which can often be eliminated with a lower dose of the enzyme. When signs have improved, it may be possible to gradually decrease the dose.

If enzyme supplementation alone does not resolve the condition, vitamin B_{12} (cobalamin) deficiency may be a possible cause. This can be treated by injection of this vitamin. Other vitamin deficiencies have also been reported.

In most cases, exocrine pancreatic insufficiency is the result of an irreversible loss of pancreatic tissue and a cure is rare. However, with appropriate diet supplementation and monitoring, cats with exocrine pancreatic insufficiency usually gain weight quickly, pass normal stools, and can live a normal life.

Pancreatic Cancers

Cancers of the pancreas can be either benign or malignant (cancerous). **Pancreatic adenomas** are benign tumors. **Pancreatic adenocarcinomas** are malignant; however, they are uncommon in cats. The signs in cats with pancreatic tumors are very general, and many animals show no signs until late in the disease. If signs are present, they often include not eating, vomiting, or abdominal pain. If the tumor has spread to other organs, signs such as lameness, bone pain, difficulty breathing, jaundice, lack of appetite, or hair loss can occur.

Pancreatic adenomas do not usually require any treatment unless they cause signs. However, because they look similar to pancreatic adenocarcinoma, the affected pancreatic tissue is often removed. The outlook in these cases is excellent.

Pancreatic adenocarcinomas are usually not detected until the disease is advanced and the cancer has already spread. In those few cases when it appears the cancer has not yet spread, the veterinarian may remove the tumor by surgery. However, it is difficult to completely remove such tumors and surgery is often unsuccessful. The outlook for cats with pancreatic adenocarcinoma is grave.

Pancreatic Abscesses

A pancreatic abscess is a collection of pus, usually near the pancreas, which may contain dead pancreatic tissue. Signs may include vomiting, depression, abdominal pain, loss of appetite, fever, diarrhea, and dehydration. In some animals, a lump in the abdomen can be felt. Cats may respond favorably to surgical drainage of the abscess. However, the risks and expense of surgery may outweigh the benefit to the cat unless there is clear evidence of an enlarging mass or bacterial infection. Your veterinarian

will make a surgical recommendation based on your cat's specific condition, overall health, and related considerations.

Pancreatic Pseudocyst

A pancreatic pseudocyst is a collection of sterile pancreatic fluid enclosed by a wall of tissue. Signs are similar to those of pancreatitis and include poor appetite, lethargy, vomiting, or abdominal pain. Vomiting is the most consistent sign reported in cats. Pancreatic pseudocysts can be treated with or without surgery. Surgery may be needed if the cat has persistent signs or if the pseudocyst does not decrease in size.

▪ DISORDERS OF THE LIVER AND GALLBLADDER

The liver performs numerous functions. It has a large storage capacity and functional reserve and is capable of regenerating. These properties provide some protection against permanent damage. However, the liver is also susceptible to injury because of its role in metabolizing, detoxifying, and storing various toxic compounds.

Signs that a cat has liver disease can vary and include loss of appetite, vomiting, stomach ulceration, diarrhea, fever, blood clotting problems, jaundice, abdominal swelling, excessive urination and thirst, changes in liver size, weight loss, and occasionally gastrointestinal bleeding.

Hepatic encephalopathy is a neurologic syndrome seen in a number of liver diseases. Signs suggestive of hepatic encephalopathy include circling, head pressing, aimless wandering, weakness, poor coordination, blindness, excessive drooling, aggression, dementia, seizures, and coma.

Ascites is a condition in which fluid collects in the abdomen. In patients with liver disease, ascites is caused by a combination of high blood pressure in the liver and an imbalance in salt and water metabolism. The swelling may be controlled by prescribing a diuretic (a medication to increase the amount of water excreted into the urine), by extracting the excess fluid with a needle, or a combination of steps.

Hepatic Lipidosis

Hepatic lipidosis is the most common cause of liver disease in cats. Excessive accumulation of fat (triglycerides) within the liver leads to liver failure. The cause is unknown but the disease is associated with a period of poor appetite (a few days to several weeks), especially in obese cats. Factors that may trigger loss of appetite include a change of diet to initiate weight loss or other stressful events such as moving, boarding, or death of other pets or owners. Hepatic lipidosis can also be associated with a metabolic disease (such as diabetes mellitus) or digestive system disease that causes loss of appetite.

Signs of hepatic lipidosis vary but can include dramatic weight loss (up to 30 to 40% of body weight) due to loss of appetite, vomiting, lethargy, and diarrhea. Signs of hepatic encephalopathy and bleeding are unusual, but can be seen in advanced disease. Jaundice or pale mucous membranes, excessive drooling, enlarged liver, and decreased body condition with retention of abdominal fat are commonly seen.

Treatment is primarily supportive unless the underlying cause can be found. Fluid treatment is used to correct dehydration. Feeding as soon as possible is essential. Occasionally, the veterinarian will prescribe an appetite stimulant. However,

Cats with hepatic lipidosis may stop eating and lose weight but still have belly fat.

placement of a feeding tube is usually necessary. Once the cat is able to eat, a high-protein, calorie-dense, balanced diet is usually recommended unless the cat shows signs of hepatic encephalopathy, in which case a low-protein diet should be used. Initially, feedings are small and given frequently. The outlook is good if the diagnosis is made early, treatment is started promptly, and the underlying disease, if any, can be treated.

Inflammatory Liver Disease

Inflammatory liver disease is the second most common liver disease reported in cats. The 2 types of inflammatory liver disease in cats are cholangiohepatitis (both short- and longterm) and lymphocytic portal hepatitis.

Cholangiohepatitis

Cholangiohepatitis is an inflammation of the biliary tract (ducts that connect to the gallbladder) that extends into the liver. Cats with cholangiohepatitis may have other digestive disorders as well, such as inflammatory bowel disease and pancreatitis.

Short-term (acute) cholangiohepatitis is often associated with bacterial, fungal, or protozoal infections, or less frequently, liver fluke infection. Signs are usually of short duration and include fever, enlarged liver, abdominal pain, jaundice, lethargy, vomiting, poor appetite, and weight loss. Treatment consists of fluids to correct dehydration and longterm (3 to 6 months) antibiotics to treat the infection. If there is an obstruction between the liver and the gallbladder, surgery is required to restore normal function.

Longterm (chronic) cholangiohepatitis may be a variant of short-term cholangiohepatitis, an immune-mediated disease, or a condition caused by any of several infections including feline infectious peritonitis, feline leukemia, toxoplasmosis, or liver flukes. It may occur more often in Persian cats than other breeds. Abdominal swelling and jaundice are the most frequently reported signs, and the lymph nodes may be inflamed. Other signs are similar to those seen with short-term cholangiohepatitis. Progression to cirrhosis (end-stage liver disease) is possible. Supportive fluid treatment, antibiotics, and other appropriate drugs may be prescribed. Treatment with a corticosteroid is often recommended because of the suspected immune-mediated aspect of this disease. Some cats respond well to initial treatment, others relapse repeatedly, and some do not recover and die from the disease.

Lymphocytic Portal Hepatitis

Lymphocytic portal hepatitis is an inflammatory disease of the liver that does not appear to be related to cholangiohepatitis. The cause is uncertain, but it may be related to immune function. It is more common in hyperthyroid cats. Signs include loss of appetite, weight loss, and less frequently vomiting, diarrhea, lethargy, and fever. An enlarged liver is noted in about half of cats with lymphocytic portal hepatitis. A combination of antibiotics and immunosuppressive drugs has been tried with variable results. Your veterinarian will be able to provide a treatment program based on the most current information.

Poisons Affecting the Liver

Because of the liver's function in metabolizing drugs, some drugs have been associated with liver dysfunction in cats. The specific signs and effects depend on the the drug and dosage. In many cases your veterinarian will be aware of the potential for liver disease when prescribing these drugs and will monitor your cat for any signs of decreased or altered function. Other substances that are toxic to the liver include heavy metals, certain herbicides, fungicides, insecticides, rodent poisons, aflatoxins (produced by mold), amanita mushrooms, and blue-green algae.

If your pet has had an accidental overdose of a medication, has had an adverse reaction to a medication (even at the prescribed dosage), or has eaten a poison, a veterinarian should be consulted immediately. If necessary, the veterinarian can take steps to minimize absorption of the drug or poison. Depending on the situation, the veterinarian may induce vomiting, administer activated charcoal, pump the animal's stomach, or administer an appropriate antitoxin. Any information you can provide regarding the toxin can help your veterinarian provide more rapid treatment. (For a more detailed discussion of POISONING, *see* page 1145.)

Portosystemic Shunts

Portosystemic shunts have already been described as a congenital (inborn) defect (*see* page 389). However, in some cases they can develop as a part of illness. In these instances they are called acquired shunts. Signs include excessive thirst, vomiting, and diarrhea. Fluid accumulation in the abdomen (ascites) is common. Medical treatment of the underlying disease, along with placing a band around the caudal vena cava (to slightly raise the blood pressure outside the liver and reduce shunting), can lead to a favorable response in some cats.

Infectious Diseases of the Liver

Several types of infections may cause liver disease, including viral, bacterial, fungal, and parasitic disease.

Feline infectious peritonitis is caused by a virus. Infection leads to widespread inflammation in the abdomen, including the liver, and inflammation of the blood vessels (vasculitis). Jaundice, abdominal effusion, vomiting, diarrhea, and fever are common signs. (For a more detailed discussion of FELINE INFECTIOUS PERITONITIS, *see* page 532.)

The most common fungal infections associated with liver dysfunction are **coccidioidomycosis** and **histoplasmosis**. (For a more detailed discussion of FUNGAL INFECTIONS, *see* page 537.) If the liver is involved, signs may include abdominal swelling, jaundice, and liver enlargement. Coccidioidomycosis can be treated with longterm (6 to 12 months) use of antifungal medications. However, relapses sometimes occur. Histoplasmosis is often treated using prescription antifungal medications. Depending on the level of illness, the outlook for recovery may be poor.

Toxoplasmosis is a parasitic disease that can cause acute liver failure due to liver cell death. The parasite is a protozoan, *Toxoplasma gondii*, that is found worldwide. Infection is more common in cats positive for feline immunodeficiency virus. Jaundice, fever, lethargy, vomiting, and diarrhea are seen, in addition to signs of central nervous system or eye involvement. The outlook depends on the severity of the illness. (For a more detailed discussion of TOXOPLASMOSIS, *see* page 545.)

Endocrine Diseases Affecting the Liver

Several diseases involving endocrine glands can cause liver problems in cats. These diseases include diabetes mellitus (*see* page 418) and hyperthyroidism (*see* page 422).

Cats with **diabetes mellitus** have an increased risk of developing hepatic lipidosis because diabetes mellitus increases the metabolism and mobilization of lipids. Lipids include any of a group of water-soluble fats and fatlike chemical substances that are sources of fuel for the body. However, when too many lipids are deposited in the liver, the function of the organ is impaired. Insulin replacement may or may not correct this storage problem.

Cats with **hyperthyroidism** have increased levels of certain chemicals (enzymes) in the liver and, in some cases, an excessive amount of bilirubin (a yellow bile pigment). Cats with excess bilirubin may have jaundice. The liver enzyme levels almost always return to normal when the underlying causes are treated.

Hepatocutaneous Syndrome

Hepatocutaneous syndrome is rare, longterm, progressive, and usually fatal. Diabetes mellitus is often present at the same time. Crusting and abnormalities on the footpads, ears, skin around the eyes, and pressure points are typical skin changes. Poor appetite, weight loss, and lethargy are also reported. Treatment may include antifungal and antibiotics for skin infections, zinc and vitamin supplementation, high-protein diets, control of diabetes mellitus with insulin, and topical cleansing of affected skin. Unfortunately, treatment has little effect on the course of the disease, and the outlook is guarded to poor.

Liver Cysts

Liver cysts can be acquired (usually single nodules) or present at birth (usually multiple nodes). Congenital polycystic disease of the liver has been reported in Persian cats. The cysts often go undiagnosed but occasionally they enlarge and cause abdominal swelling and other signs such as lethargy, vomiting, and excessive thirst. Your veterinarian may be able to feel nonpainful masses in the abdomen. Cysts may be identified with x-rays or ultrasonography, but a biopsy is needed for a definite diagnosis. Surgical removal of the cysts usually cures the condition.

Cancers of the Liver

Tumors that originate in the liver (called primary tumors) are less common than those caused by spread from another part in the body. Primary tumors are most often seen in cats more than 10 years old, and can be either malignant or benign. Metastatic (spreading) tumors of the liver are less common in cats than in dogs. Cancers that can spread to the liver include pancreatic, intestinal, and renal cell carcinomas. Metastatic tumors usually occur at multiple sites.

Cats with liver tumors are usually uninterested in food and lethargic. Seizures may develop because of hepatic encephalopathy, low blood sugar, or spread of cancer to the brain. An enlarged liver or an abdominal mass may be found during a physical examination. Animals may be pale (due to bleeding or anemia caused by longterm liver disease) or jaundiced. A biopsy is needed for a definitive diagnosis. If a single liver lobe is involved, surgical removal of the lobe is recommended. Chemotherapy may be effective for some other cancer types. The outlook is poor for primary liver tumors that involve multiple lobes because an effective treatment is not yet available.

Hepatic Amyloidosis

Amyloid is a protein that is not folded into the correct shape. The misfolded protein causes damage by displacing normal cells. Amyloidosis is an inherited disease of Abyssinian, Siamese, and oriental cats. Although some cats may show no signs, others may have loss of appetite, excessive thirst and urination, vomiting, jaundice, and an enlarged liver. Affected cats may collapse and have pale mucous membranes due to rupture of the liver and subsequent bleeding. Diagnosis is made by identifying amyloid deposits in liver biopsy samples. Amyloidosis is progressive and the outlook for recovery is poor, especially if the diagnosis is made late in the disease.

Diseases of the Gallbladder and Bile Duct

The liver secretes bile, a substance that assists with digestion and absorption of fats and with elimination of certain waste products from the body. Bile is stored in the gallbladder and is released into the duodenum through the bile duct.

Jaundice (a yellow tinge noticeable in the skin, mucous membranes, and eyes) is often the main sign of diseases of the gallbladder and bile duct. An exception is cancer of the gallbladder, which may not cause jaundice.

Obstruction of the Bile Duct

Obstruction of the bile duct is most often caused by pancreatic disease. Pancreatic swelling, inflammation, or fibrosis can cause compression of the bile duct. Diagnosis is based on laboratory tests, x-rays, and ultrasonographic evidence of pancreatic disease. Treatment of pancreatitis will often

relieve the obstruction. If this is not successful, surgery may be necessary to rejoin the gallbladder and intestine. Gallstones rarely cause obstruction, but when this does occur, removal of the gallbladder is the preferred treatment in most cases. Cancer of the pancreas, bile ducts, liver, intestines, and lymph nodes can also cause obstruction. A biopsy is needed to confirm the diagnosis. When cancer is present, surgery can provide temporary relief but is not a cure.

Inflammation of the Gallbladder (Cholecystitis)

Inflammation of the gallbladder (cholecystitis) is usually caused by bacterial infections that start in the intestines and either travel up the bile duct or are spread through the blood. Loss of appetite, abdominal pain, jaundice, fever, and vomiting are common signs. The cat may be in a state of shock due to abdominal inflammation.

The inflammation can also spread to the surrounding branches of the bile duct and the liver. Diagnosis can be confirmed by biopsy for bacterial cultures and tissue analysis. Treatment usually consists of removal of the gallbladder and appropriate antibiotic medication to treat infection. The outlook is good if appropriate antibiotics are started early but is less favorable if diagnosis and treatment are delayed.

Gallstones

Gallstones rarely cause disease. In cats, gallstones are generally associated with bile duct inflammation. Signs include vomiting, jaundice, abdominal pain, and fever. Treatment consists of removal of the stones and appropriate antibiotics.

Liver Flukes

The liver fluke *Platynosomum concinnum* is an uncommon cause of bile duct disease in cats. It occurs in Malaysia, Hawaii, southeastern US, the Caribbean, South America, and western Africa. The fluke's life cycle includes lizards and toads as intermediate hosts. Cats are infected when they catch and eat these animals.

The flukes may not cause any signs in some cats, but in others they obstruct the bile duct, which causes severe liver dysfunction. Signs vary depending on the number of flukes involved, but may include vomiting, diarrhea, jaundice, depression, poor appetite, and an enlarged liver. The flukes can also damage the pancreas. Antiparasitic drugs can be used to treat the infection. The outlook is favorable for mild forms of the disease.

Rupture of the Gallbladder or Bile Duct

Rupture of the gallbladder or bile duct is most often due to gallstones, inflammation of the gallbladder, or blunt trauma. Rupture of the bile duct may also occur as a result of cancer or certain parasites. Rupture leads to leakage of bile into the abdomen, causing a serious condition called bile peritonitis, which may be fatal if the rupture is not repaired. Treatment includes surgery, which consists of tying off the bile duct, removing the gallbladder, or connecting the gallbladder with the small intestine.

■ DISORDERS OF THE RECTUM AND ANUS

Rectal diseases in cats can result from injuries, tumors, or infections.

Anal Sac Disease

The anal sacs are glands located on each side of the anus. They are related to the scent glands in skunks and produce small amount of dark, foul-smelling liquid which is normally squeezed out during defecation. Anal sac disease is caused by clogging or infection of the glands. Anal sacs may become clogged (impacted), infected, abscessed, or cancerous. Anal sac disease is much less common in cats than in dogs. In cats, the most common form of anal sac disease is impaction.

Signs are related to pain and discomfort associated with sitting. The cat may scoot its buttocks on the ground, lick or bite at the anal area, and have painful defecation with straining. If the glands are impacted, hard masses can be felt in the area of the sacs. A rectal examination by a veterinarian will usually be done to diagnose anal sac disease. Additional tests may be needed if infection or a tumor is suspected.

Your veterinarian can often squeeze out impacted anal sacs by hand. If the material in the sacs is too hard or dry, your veterinarian may inject a softening agent into the sac. If infection is present, antibiotics might be prescribed. Supplemental fiber may be recommended to increase fecal bulk, which facilitates anal sac compression and emptying. If treatment is ineffective or the condition keeps coming back, surgical removal of the sac(s) may be required. A common complication from this surgery is fecal incontinence; however, the incontinence is usually temporary.

Rectal and Anorectal Narrowing (Strictures)

A rectal or anorectal stricture is a narrowing of the rectum or anus caused by scar tissue. Injuries that lead to strictures may result from foreign objects or trauma (such as bite wounds or accidents), or they may be a complication of inflammation. In cats, anorectal strictures are more common than rectal strictures, but neither condition is frequent.

Rectal Tumors

Malignant rectal tumors in cats are usually cancers involving lymph tissue (lymphosarcoma). Cats with rectal lymphosarcoma are treated with chemotherapy.

Rectal Polyps

The growths called rectal polyps occur infrequently in cats. The polyps are usually benign (noncancerous) and do not spread. Signs include straining to defecate, blood in the feces, and diarrhea. The polyp can be felt by a veterinarian during a rectal examination, and its surface tends to bleed easily. An endoscopic examination may be required to see the polyp. Periodically, the polyp may protrude from the anus. Surgical removal is usually followed by rapid recovery and lengthy survival time. Your veterinarian may send a tissue sample from the polyp to a laboratory for microscopic analysis to confirm the diagnosis.

Rectal Prolapse

Rectal prolapse is a condition in which one or more layers of the rectum protrude through the anus. Prolapse may be classified as incomplete (only the innermost rectal layer is protruding) or complete (all rectal layers are protruding).

Cats of any age, breed, or sex may be affected, although the condition commonly occurs in young cats that have severe diarrhea or that routinely strain to defecate. Prolapse can be caused by a number of intestinal, anorectal, or urinary diseases.

An elongated, cylinder-shaped mass protruding through the anal opening is usually a sign of rectal prolapse. However, prolapses involving other parts of the intestine can have a similar appearance. No matter what type of prolapse is present, any tissue mass protruding from the anal opening should be promptly examined by a veterinarian.

Identifying and eliminating the cause of prolapse is a key part of treatment. Small or incomplete prolapses can often be manually replaced by the veterinarian while the cat is anesthetized. This is usually followed by partial closure of the anus with stitches for 5 to 7 days to prevent the prolapse from happening again. In cases where tissue death is evident or where the living tissue cannot easily be repositioned through the rectum, surgery may be required. After treatment, a moist diet and a stool softener are likely to be recommended. Diarrhea occurring shortly after surgery may require additional treatment and should be discussed with your veterinarian.

Rectal Tears

A tear in the rectum or anus can be caused by a sharp object (such as a bone, needle, or other rough material) making its way through the digestive tract or from injury such as a bite. The tear may involve only the surface layers of the rectum (partial tear) or penetrate all layers (complete tear). Signs may include constipation, straining, rectal bleeding, and reluctance to defecate. A diagnosis is based on these signs and inspection of the rectum and anus. Swelling may be present when the injury has been present for some time.

Treatment to avoid infection and close the wound should be started immediately. The tear will be cleaned and stitched closed. Depending on the location, abdominal surgery may be required. Antibiotics and stool softeners will probably be prescribed after surgery.

CHAPTER **27**

Hormonal Disorders

■ INTRODUCTION

Hormones are chemical messengers that have many different functions. The effects of hormones in the body are wide-ranging and varied. Some familiar examples of hormones include insulin, which is important in the development of diabetes, and estrogen and progesterone, which are involved in the female reproductive cycle. (*See* TABLE 8, page 130.)

The endocrine system consists of a group of tissues that release hormones into the bloodstream for travel to other parts of the body. Most endocrine tissues are glands (such as the thyroid gland) that release hormones directly into small blood vessels within and around the tissue. Several important hormones are released from tissues other than glands, such as the heart, kidney, and liver.

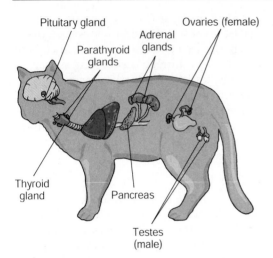

Pituitary gland

Adrenal glands

Parathyroid glands

Ovaries (female)

Thyroid gland

Pancreas

Testes (male)

The major endocrine glands in the cat (modified with permission from *The Merck Manual of Medical Information*, Second Home Edition, 2003)

Some hormones act only on a single tissue, while others have effects on virtually every cell in the body. Hormones are present in the blood in very small quantities, so laboratory tests done to measure hormone levels must be very sensitive.

Development of Endocrine System Disease

The body monitors and adjusts the level of each hormone by using a feedback system specifically for that hormone. Hormones function to keep factors such as temperature and blood sugar (glucose) levels within certain ranges. Sometimes, pairs of hormones with opposite functions work together to keep body functions in balance.

Endocrine system diseases can develop when too much or not enough hormone is produced, or when normal pathways for hormones to be used and removed are disrupted. Signs can develop because of a problem in the tissues that are the source of the hormone, or because of a problem in another part of the body that is affecting the secretion or action of a particular hormone.

A tumor or other abnormal tissue in an endocrine gland often causes it to produce too much hormone. When an endocrine gland is destroyed, not enough hormone is produced. Diseases caused by overproduction or excess of a hormone often begin with the prefix **hyper-**. For example, in hyperthyroidism, the thyroid gland produces too much thyroid hormone. Diseases caused by a lack or deficiency of a hormone often begin with the prefix **hypo-**. For example, in hypothyroidism, the thyroid gland does not produce enough thyroid hormone.

In many cases, the abnormal gland not only overproduces hormone, it also does not respond normally to feedback signals. This causes hormone to be released in situations in which its levels would normally be reduced. Sometimes, the overproduction is caused by stimulation from another part of the body. Occasionally, a tumor outside the endocrine system can produce a substance similar to a hormone, causing the body to respond as though that hormone were being produced.

Diseases caused by not enough hormone secretion can also have multiple causes. Endocrine tissue can be destroyed by an autoimmune process, in which the body incorrectly identifies some of its own tissue as foreign and destroys the tissue cells. In early stages of tissue loss, the body may compensate by producing additional hormone from the remaining tissue. In these cases, signs of disease may be delayed until the tissue has been destroyed completely.

Disorders resulting in signs of reduced endocrine activity may also develop because tissues distant from the hormone source are disrupted. This can occur when the function of one hormone is to stimulate the production of a second hormone. For example, the pituitary gland secretes a hormone that stimulates the thyroid gland to secrete thyroid hormones. If the levels of the thyroid-stimulating hormone from the pituitary gland are abnormally low, the levels of thyroid hormones will also be low even if the thyroid gland is healthy. Another potential cause for reduced endocrine function is tissue loss caused by tumors that do not produce hormones themselves but compress or destroy the nearby endocrine gland.

Endocrine diseases and related conditions also result from changes in the response of tissues targeted by a hormone. An important example is type 2 diabetes mellitus, in which the body produces insulin but the cells no longer respond to it. This condition is often associated with obesity.

Treatment of Endocrine System Disease

Endocrine diseases caused by the presence of too much hormone may be treated surgically (such as tumor removal), by radiotherapy (such as the use of radioactive iodine to destroy an overactive thyroid gland), or with medication. Syndromes of hormone deficiency are often successfully treated by replacing the missing hormone, such as insulin injections to treat diabetes mellitus. Steroid and thyroid hormone replacements can usually be given by mouth.

Pets taking hormone replacement treatment must be monitored for adverse effects and periodically retested to make sure the dosage is correct. In some cases, such as after surgical removal of an endocrine tumor, the diseased gland will recover and hormone replacement will no longer be needed. However, most of the time, lifelong treatment is required.

▨ DISORDERS OF THE ADRENAL GLANDS

The adrenal glands are located just in front of the kidneys. The adrenal gland has 2 parts—the cortex and the medulla.

The **adrenal cortex** is subdivided into 3 layers, and each layer produces a different set of steroid hormones. The outer layer produces the mineralocorticoids, which help to control the body's balance of sodium and potassium salts. The middle layer produces glucocorticoids, which are involved in metabolizing nutrients as well as in reducing inflammation. The inner layer produces sex hormones such as estrogen and progesterone.

The **adrenal medulla** plays an important role in response to stress or low blood sugar (glucose). It releases epinephrine (sometimes also called adrenaline) and norepi-

nephrine, both of which increase heart output, blood pressure, and blood glucose, and slow digestion.

Addison's Disease

Addison's disease, also referred to as **hypoadrenocorticism**, is caused by a deficiency of adrenal gland hormones. It is rare in cats. The cause is usually not known, but an autoimmune condition in which the body destroys some of its own tissue is likely. The adrenal gland can also be destroyed by other conditions, including cancer in other parts of the body. Secretion of aldosterone, the main mineralocorticoid hormone, is reduced, which affects the levels of potassium, sodium, and chloride in the blood. Potassium gradually builds up in the blood and, in severe cases, may cause the heart to slow down or beat irregularly.

Signs of Addison's disease include loss of appetite, lethargy, dehydration, and a gradual loss of body condition. Vomiting and diarrhea may be noted. Although signs can be hard to identify while Addison's disease is developing, severe consequences, such as shock and evidence of kidney failure, can develop suddenly.

A veterinarian can make a tentative diagnosis based on the history, signs, and certain laboratory abnormalities, such as very low levels of sodium and very high levels of potassium in the blood. The diagnosis is confirmed by specific evaluation of adrenal function.

An adrenal crisis is a medical emergency and requires treatment with intravenous fluids to restore levels of body fluids, salt, and sugar to normal. Hormone replacement treatment can often be started while the animal is being stabilized. The cat should be monitored regularly to assess response to treatment and adjust dosages if needed. For longterm treatment, replacement hormones can be given by mouth or injection.

▨ DISORDERS OF THE PANCREAS

The pancreas is composed of several types of cells that have distinct functions involved in the production of hormones and digestive enzymes. The **exocrine pancreas** produces enzymes that are essential for the digestion of complex dietary components such as proteins, triglycerides, and complex carbohydrates. The exocrine pancreas also secretes large amounts of bicarbonate, which buffers stomach acid. Disorders of the exocrine pancreas are discussed in the chapter on digestive disorders (*see* page 407), because they relate to digestion. The **endocrine pancreas** produces the hormones insulin and glucagon, which regulate blood sugar levels. The functions and disorders of the endocrine pancreas are discussed in this section.

The **islets of Langerhans** in the pancreas consist of 3 different types of cells, each of which produces a different hormone. Most of the cells, which are called beta cells, produce insulin. Insulin affects, either directly or indirectly, the function of every organ in the body, particularly the liver, fat cells, and muscle. In general, insulin increases the transfer of glucose and other compounds into body cells. It also decreases the rate of fat, protein, and carbohydrate breakdown.

The other 2 cell types in the islets of Langerhans produce the hormones glucagon and somatostatin. When blood glucose levels drop, glucagon is released. Glucagon helps convert stored carbohydrates into glucose so they can be used as energy.

Insulin and glucagon work together to keep the concentration of glucose in the blood and other body fluids within a relatively narrow range. Glucagon controls glucose release from the liver, and insulin controls glucose transport into numerous body tissues.

Diabetes Mellitus

Diabetes mellitus (often called simply diabetes) is a chronic disorder of carbohydrate metabolism caused by either a deficiency of insulin or a resistance to insulin. Middle-aged cats are affected most commonly. Diabetes mellitus occurs in all feline breeds equally and in both males and females.

A number of mechanisms are responsible for decreased insulin production and secretion, but usually they involve destruction of islet cells. In many cats with diabetes, a protein called amyloid collects in and damages the islet cells. Obesity increases the risk of insulin resistance in both cats and dogs.

Diabetes can often develop gradually, and the signs may not be noticed at first. Common signs include increased thirst and urination, along with increased appetite and weight loss. Diabetic animals often develop chronic or recurrent infections. An enlarged liver is common.

A diagnosis of diabetes mellitus is based on finding high levels of sugar in the blood and urine after a period of fasting. In cats, the blood sugar level commonly increases under stress, such as drawing a blood sample, and multiple evaluations may be needed to confirm the diagnosis.

Your understanding of the disease and daily care of your pet are critical to successfully managing diabetes. Treatment involves a combination of weight loss, diet, insulin injections, and possibly oral medications. Usually, animals are hospitalized for 1 or 2 days, and multiple blood samples are taken to measure the blood sugar level throughout the day. This information is used to determine the amount and timing of your pet's meals, and the dosage and timing of insulin injections. After this initial stabilization, your veterinarian will provide appropriate instructions on managing this regimen at home. Periodic reevaluation is necessary to ensure that the disease is being controlled; these evaluations may lead to changes in treatment over time.

Functional Islet Cell Tumors (Insulinomas)

Tumors in the islet cells of the pancreas often produce and secrete the hormones normally secreted by the gland. The most common pancreatic islet tumor affects the insulin-secreting beta cells and is called an insulinoma. Insulinomas are not common in cats. (For a more detailed discussion of FUNCTIONAL ISLET CELL TUMORS, *see* page 134.)

■ DISORDERS OF THE PARATHYROID GLANDS AND OF CALCIUM METABOLISM

The way in which the body processes calcium and phosphate, the function of vitamin D (which acts more like a hormone than a vitamin), and the formation of bone are all tied together into a system that involves 2 other hormones—parathyroid hormone and calcitonin—that are secreted by the parathyroid glands.

Disorders of calcium and phosphorus metabolism that affect the skeletal system are discussed in the chapter on bone, joint, and muscle disorders (*see* page 447).

Calcium-regulating Hormones

Calcium is an essential component of the skeleton, and it has important functions in muscle contraction, blood clotting, enzyme activity, the nervous system, and hormone release, among others. Precise control of calcium in the body is vital to health. Parathyroid hormone, vitamin D, and calcitonin all interact to keep the level of calcium steady, despite variations in intake and excretion. Other hormones may also contribute to maintaining the balance of calcium in the body.

Parathyroid hormone is created and stored in the parathyroid glands, which are located on either side of the thyroid gland in the neck. The creation of this hormone is regulated by a feedback mechanism that involves the level of blood calcium. The primary function of parathyroid hormone is to control the level of calcium by affecting the movement of calcium into and out of bone, the retention of calcium by the kidneys, and absorption of calcium from the digestive tract.

Vitamin D is the second major hormone involved in the regulation of calcium metabolism. In several species, including horses and people, vitamin D is formed in the skin after exposure to ultraviolet light (such as sunshine). In contrast, cats are not able to form enough vitamin D in the skin and depend on dietary intake. Parathyroid hormone and conditions that stimulate its secretion, as well as reduced phosphate levels, increase the formation of vitamin D.

Calcitonin is a hormone secreted by certain cells of the thyroid gland in mammals. When the level of blood calcium increases, calcitonin is released to prevent hypercalcemia (abnormally high levels of calcium).

Hypocalcemia

Hypocalcemia is an abnormally low level of calcium in the blood, leading to twitching, muscle tremors, and seizures. The causes of hypocalcemia include previous surgical removal of the parathyroid glands (leading to hypoparathyroidism), kidney disease or failure, and calcium imbalance in nursing females.

Hypoparathyroidism is characterized by low calcium levels, high phosphate levels, and either temporary or permanent insufficiency of parathyroid hormone. It is uncommon in cats, but can be caused by previous removal of the parathyroid glands as a treatment for hyperthyroidism or for a parathyroid tumor. Common signs of hypocalcemia include muscle tremors and twitches, muscle contraction, and generalized convulsions. Diagnosis is based on history, signs, low calcium and high phosphorus levels, and the serum parathyroid hormone level. Other causes of hypocalcemia must be eliminated.

The goal of treatment is to return the level of blood calcium to normal and to eliminate the underlying cause. If a cat is having muscle spasms or seizures because of low calcium levels, immediate treatment with intravenous calcium is needed. Dietary supplements of calcium, often along with vitamin D, are prescribed for longterm treatment.

Chronic kidney failure is probably the most common cause of hypocalcemia. However, the hypocalcemia that occurs with kidney failure does not tend to lead to the nervous system signs that are seen in hypoparathyroidism. Treatment usually

Table 5. Causes and Treatment for Hypercalcemia (Increased Blood Calcium Levels) in Cats

Cause	Mechanism	Treatment
Primary hyperparathyroidism (relatively rare in cats)	Parathyroid glands are overactive (often due to a tumor) and secrete excessive parathyroid hormone	Removal or destruction of tumor
Hypercalcemia caused by cancer (malignant hypercalcemia)	Increased bone breakdown and resorption triggered by cancer cells causes higher levels of calcium in blood	Depends on specific type of cancer
Chronic kidney failure	Exact mechanism is unknown; most common cause of hypercalcemia in cats	Supportive care
Vitamin D toxicity (hypervitaminosis D)	Vitamin D supplements taken in excess (for example, to treat hypoparathyroidism); accidental ingestion of human psoriasis medicine calcipotriene (tacalcitol) or rodent poisons containing calcitriol	Adjustment of vitamin D dosage (if from medication)
Granulomatous disease	Inflammation activates the type of white blood cells that can increase levels of active vitamin D	Treatment of underlying disease, for example, antifungal drugs or surgery
Idiopathic hypercalcemia of cats	Unknown cause; affects cats 2 to 13 years old (either sex)	High-fiber diet and/or medication (prednisone)

involves dietary restriction and treatment to lower phosphate concentration in the blood.

Several other diseases can also cause hypocalcemia (*see* TABLE 10, page 137).

Hypercalcemia

Hypercalcemia is an abnormally high level of calcium in the blood. The signs associated with this condition depend on how high the calcium level is, how quickly it develops, and how long it lasts. The most common signs are increased thirst and urination, followed by reduced appetite, vomiting, constipation, weakness, depression, muscle twitching, and seizures.

In cats, kidney failure, tumors, and a newly recognized syndrome called **idiopathic hypercalcemia** are the most common causes of hypercalcemia (*see* TABLE 5).

Hypercalcemia is treated by identifying and treating the condition causing it. However, the cause may not always be apparent. Supportive treatment, including fluids, diuretics ("water pills"), sodium bicarbon-

ate, and glucocorticoids, is often needed to lower the level of calcium in the blood.

▓ DISORDERS OF THE PITUITARY GLAND

The pituitary gland is located near the center and bottom of the brain. It produces a number of critical hormones that control many parts of the body, including several other endocrine glands. Because of this central role, it is sometimes called a "master gland." A variety of different conditions can be caused by pituitary disease or tumors. The specific illness and signs depend on the cause and the area(s) of the pituitary gland that is affected.

Cushing's Disease

Cushing's disease, also called **hyperadrenocorticism**, is caused by too much cortisol. Cushing's disease is rare in cats. In most affected cats, the cause is a pituitary tumor, although an overactive pituitary gland or a tumor of the adrenal gland itself are also possible causes.

Cats with Cushing's disease are generally middle-aged or older. The most common signs include excessive thirst, increased urination, and increased appetite. These signs are frequently seen because cats with Cushing's disease also tend to have diabetes mellitus that is resistant to insulin. (Thus, the signs develop as a result of the diabetes mellitus, not necessarily as a result of the cortisol excess seen in Cushing's disease.)

The skin of affected cats may be extremely fragile, thin, and easily infected or bruised; this is called feline fragile skin syndrome. Cats may also have an unkempt hair coat, patchy hair loss, muscle wasting, a "potbelly," and pigmented skin. Some cats may appear listless or depressed due to muscle weakness or to the effects of a large pituitary tumor.

Cushing's disease causes substantial weakness and loss of vitality in affected cats. Although therapy is difficult and the outlook is guarded, an attempt is usually made to control the disease because of the overall deteriorating effect on cats with this disorder. Surgical removal of one or both adrenal glands has provided the best results.

Adult-onset Panhypopituitarism

In adult-onset panhypopituitarism, the pituitary gland and nearby tissues, including the hypothalamus, are compressed or damaged. This disrupts a number of other hormone-producing glands, resulting in a variety of signs.

Inactive pituitary tumors are one cause of adult-onset panhypopituitarism. They are extremely rare in cats, usually developing in older animals. The tumor may become quite large before it causes obvious signs or death. All breeds appear to be equally affected. Other conditions, infections, or injuries that lead to destruction of pituitary tissue can also cause panhypopituitarism.

Affected cats are often depressed and uncoordinated, and may lose weight. Occasionally, they show a change in attitude, do not respond to people, and tend to hide. In chronic cases, the cat may become blind because the growing pituitary tumor puts pressure on the optic nerves. Animals with panhypopituitarism appear dehydrated despite drinking more water. Cats may urinate in large volumes and use areas other than the litter box.

External beam radiation therapy may reduce the pituitary tumor size and improve the signs in some cats, but the experience using this kind of treatment is limited for cats with large pituitary tumors. The outlook is poor.

Diabetes Insipidus

Despite its name, diabetes insipidus is not related to the more commonly known diabetes mellitus, and it does not involve insulin or sugar metabolism. Diabetes insipidus is caused by problems with antidiuretic hormone, a pituitary gland hormone responsible for maintaining the correct level of fluid in the body. It occurs rarely in cats; when seen, it tends to affect kittens or young adults. (For a more detailed discussion of DIABETES INSIPIDUS, see page 138.)

Feline Acromegaly

Feline acromegaly is caused by a tumor of the pituitary gland that secretes growth hormone. It occurs in cats 8 to 14 years old and appears to be more common in males. These tumors grow slowly and may be present for a long time before signs appear.

Because this disease causes diabetes mellitus, signs of diabetes such as increased thirst, urination, and appetite are present. In addition, signs of excess growth in the legs, paws, chin, skull, and other parts of the body may be seen. In particular, weight gain in cats with uncontrolled diabetes mellitus is a key sign of acromegaly. The heart, kidneys, liver, and endocrine organs are also larger than normal. Insulin levels in the blood are dramatically increased. Feline acromegaly should be suspected in any diabetic cat that has severe insulin resistance.

Signs and laboratory abnormalities can help determine a diagnosis of acromegaly, but the most definitive diagnostic test is computed tomography (CT) or magnetic resonance imaging (MRI) of the pituitary region.

Radiation treatment probably offers the greatest chance of successful treatment, but disadvantages include the slow rate of tumor shrinkage (more than 3 years), the possible development of hypopituitarism, cranial and optic nerve damage, and radiation injury to the hypothalamus.

The short-term outlook in cats with untreated acromegaly is fair to good, using various medications to treat signs. However, because this does not address the cause of the condition, the longterm outlook is relatively poor. Most cats die of congestive heart failure, chronic kidney failure, or signs related to the growing pituitary tumor.

■ DISORDERS OF THE THYROID GLAND

The thyroid gland is a 2-lobed gland in the neck. It produces 2 iodine-containing hormones, T_3 and T_4, which affect many processes in the body. In general, the thyroid hormones regulate metabolic rate, or the speed at which body processes run. Too little hormone causes body processes to be sluggish. Too much causes them to run too fast.

Thyroid hormones act on many different cellular processes. Some of their actions occur within minutes to hours, while others take several hours or longer. Thyroid hormones in normal quantities work along with other hormones, such as growth hormone and insulin, to build tissues. However, when they are secreted in excess, they can contribute to the breakdown of proteins and tissues.

Hypothyroidism

In hypothyroidism, decreased levels of thyroid hormones result in a slower metabolic rate. In cats, the most common reason for hypothyroidism is surgical removal or destruction (for example, by radioiodine or antithyroid drugs) of the thyroid gland as a treatment for hyperthyroidism. Although naturally occurring hypothyroidism is extremely rare in cats, when it does occur, it appears to be due to a disorder in the thyroid

gland itself (rather than in the pituitary gland, as is seen in some other animals).

Because a deficiency of thyroid hormone affects the function of all organ systems, signs vary. In cats, signs include lethargy, hair loss, low body temperature, and occasionally decreased heart rate. Obesity may develop, especially in cats with hypothyroidism caused by surgical removal of the thyroid gland. In cats that are born with hypothyroidism (or that develop it at a young age), signs include dwarfing, severe lethargy, mental dullness, constipation, and decreased heart rate.

Accurately diagnosing hypothyroidism requires close evaluation of signs and various laboratory tests, including demonstration of low blood concentrations of thyroid hormones (especially T_4) that do not respond to the administration of thyroid-stimulating hormone.

Hypothyroidism is treated using replacement with synthetic thyroid hormone. The success of treatment can be measured by the amount of improvement in signs. Thyroid hormone concentrations are also monitored to determine whether the dosage of thyroid hormone needs adjustment. Once the dose has been stabilized, thyroid hormone levels are usually checked once or twice a year. Treatment is generally lifelong.

Hyperthyroidism

Hyperthyroidism is caused by excess of the thyroid hormones, T_3 and T_4. It is most likely to be seen in middle-aged to old cats. A hormone-producing, benign thyroid tumor is the most common cause of feline hyperthyroidism.

Signs of hyperthyroidism reflect an increased metabolic rate. The most common signs include weight loss, excessive appetite, hyperexcitability, increased thirst and urination, vomiting, diarrhea, and increased fecal volume. Cardiovascular signs include increased heart rate, murmurs, shortness of breath, an enlarged heart, and congestive heart failure. Rarely, hyperthyroid cats have signs such as reduced appetite, lethargy, and depression.

Diagnosis is based on the history, signs, and physical examination, and confirmed by a blood test to measure the thyroid hormone level.

Cats with hyperthyroidism can be treated by radioactive iodine treatment, surgical removal of the thyroid gland, or longterm administration of an antithyroid drug. Radioactive iodine is usually recommended; it is simple, effective, and safe. The radioactive iodine concentrates within the thyroid tumor, where it irradiates and destroys the overactive thyroid tissue without affecting other tissues.

Surgically removing the thyroid gland is also effective. If the tumor affects only one side of the gland, only that half is removed and treatment with synthetic thyroid hormone usually is not needed. If the tumor affects both sides of the gland, the entire gland must be removed and treatment with synthetic thyroid hormone will be needed after surgery. The main complication is that the parathyroid glands, which sit on either side of the thyroid gland, can be injured or also removed during surgery. In this case, treatment with calcium and vitamin D will also be needed.

Daily treatment with methimazole, an antithyroid drug, blocks the production of thyroid hormone. Because most adverse effects associated with methimazole treatment develop during the first 3 months, complete blood counts and serum thyroid hormone measurements are checked frequently (every 2 to 4 weeks) during that time. The dosage of methimazole is adjusted to maintain circulating thyroid hormone levels within the normal range. After this initial period, levels of serum thyroid hormone are usually measured every 3 to 6 months to monitor response to treatment and the need for further dosage adjustments.

CHAPTER **28**

Eye Disorders

■ EYE STRUCTURE AND FUNCTION

The eyes of animals, including cats, function much like your eyes. (For a more detailed discussion of SIGHT, *see* page 331.) Animals also develop many of the same eye problems that people can have, including cataracts, glaucoma, and other disorders. It is important for your cat to receive good eye care to protect its sight and allow it to interact comfortably with its environment.

The eye is an organ that constantly adjusts the amount of light it lets in and focuses on objects near and far. It produces continuous images that are quickly relayed to the brain (*see* FIGURE, page 141).

The bony cavity or socket that contains the eyeball is called the **orbit**. The orbit is a structure that is formed by several bones. The orbit also contains muscles, nerves, blood vessels, and the structures that produce and drain tears.

The white of the eye is called the **sclera**. This is the relatively tough outer layer of the eye. It is covered by a thin membrane, called the **conjunctiva**, located near the front of the eye. The conjunctiva runs to the edge of the cornea and covers the inside of the eyelid. The **cornea** is a clear dome on the front surface of the eye that lets light in. The cornea not only protects the front of the eye, but also helps focus light on the retina at the back of the eye. The **iris** is the circular, colored area of the eye. It controls the amount of light that enters the eye by making the pupil larger or smaller.

The **pupil** is the black area in the middle of the eye. The pupil is controlled by the circular sphincter muscle. When the environment is dark, the pupil enlarges to let in more light; when the environment is bright, the pupil becomes smaller to let in less light.

The **lens**, which sits behind the iris, changes its shape to focus light onto the retina. Small muscles (ciliary muscles) contract to cause the lens to become thicker, which allows the lens to focus on nearby objects. In cats, these lens changes appear limited. The ciliary muscles relax to cause the lens to become thinner when it focuses on distant objects. The **retina** contains the cells that sense light (photoreceptors). The 2 main types of photoreceptors are cones and rods. **Cone cells** give cats excellent visual acuity and binocular vision, allowing them to judge speed and distance very well, an ability that helped them survive as hunters. However, although the cone cells are also responsible for color vision, it is uncertain whether cats can see colors. Cats also have many **rod cells**, which are good at collecting dim light. In fact, cats can see 6 times better in dim light than people, giving rise to the myth that cats can see in the dark. Cats also have a reflective layer called the tapetum lucidum, which magnifies incoming light and lends a characteristic blue or greenish glint to their eyes at night.

In cats, the most sensitive area of the retina is called the **area centralis**. This area contains thousands of tightly packed photoreceptors that make visual images sharp. Each photoreceptor is attached to a nerve fiber. All the nerve fibers are bundled together to form the **optic nerve**. The photoreceptors in the retina convert the image into electrical impulses, which are carried to the brain by the optic nerve.

The upper and lower eyelids are thin folds of skin that can cover the eye and reflexively blink to protect the eye. Blinking also helps spread tears over the surface of the eye, keeping it moist and clearing away small particles. The eyes of a cat are protected not only by the same types of eyelids that people have, but also by the **nictitating membrane**, which is sometimes called the third eyelid. This additional eyelid is a whitish pink color, and it is found under the other eyelids in the inside corner of the eye (near the nose). The third eyelid extends up when needed to protect the eyeball from scratches (for example, while traveling through brush) or in response to inflammation.

To function properly, eyes must be kept moist. Tears are the source of this needed moisture. Tears are produced by 2 types of glands. **Lacrimal glands** produce the watery portion of tears. They are located at the top outer edge of each eye. Mucus glands in the conjunctiva produce mucus that mixes with the watery portion. This creates a more protective tear that is slower

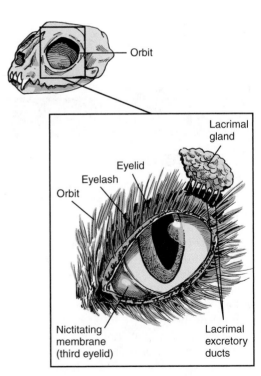

Structures that protect the eye (modified with permission from *The Merck Manual of Medical Information*, Second Home Edition, 2003)

to evaporate. Nasolacrimal ducts allow tears to drain from each eye into the nose. Each of these ducts has openings at the edge of the upper and lower eyelids near the nose.

Physical Examination of the Eye

Because of the importance of sight to your cat, one of the critical aspects of any examination or checkup will be an examination of your pet's eyes. Be prepared to provide any background or medical history (such as any previous injury to the eye, history of treatments or medications used, any signs of vision problems, and vaccination history) that might help with the diagnosis of any eye problem.

The first step of the examination involves checking to be sure that the shape and outline of the eyes are normal and that there are no obvious abnormalities. Then, using light and magnification in a darkened room, the reflexes of the pupils and the front part of the eye are examined. Depending on these findings and the reasons for the checkup, additional tests may be needed. Some parts of the examination may require sedation or anesthesia.

A test, called the Schirmer tear test, may be performed to ensure that the eyes are producing enough tears to keep them moist. This is a relatively simple test in which a small paper strip is inserted under the eyelid to measure the amount of moisture produced. A small drop of fluorescein staining may be put into each eye, allowing defects—such as scratches in the cornea of the eye—to be detected.

Pressure within the eye is measured painlessly using an instrument called a tonometer. If eye pressure is too high, optic nerve damage can occur, leading to irreversible blindness. A swab may also be done to culture for bacteria or fungi. The eyelids may be turned inside out to examine the underside. The nasolacrimal tear duct may be flushed to evaluate the external parts of the eye. Drops may be added to the eyes to allow the pupils to stay dilated so that the veterinarian may examine the internal part of the eye using an ophthalmoscope.

■ DISORDERS OF THE EYELIDS

Problems affecting the eyelids may be congenital (present at birth) or may occur as a result of injury, infection, or exposure to various types of irritants.

Abnormalities in the Shape, Outline, or Form of the Eye

Abnormalities in the shape, outline, or form of the eye include **entropion** (the turning in of the edges of the eyelid so that the eyelashes rub against the eye surface), which occurs more often in Persian cats and other breeds with shortened, flattened heads. Other defects include **ectropion** (a slack eyelid edge that is turned out, usually with a large notch in the eyelid), **lagophthalmos** (an inability to fully close the lids and protect the cornea from drying and trauma), and abnormalities of the eyelashes (including extra eyelashes or misdirected eyelashes on the lid edge). Treatment varies with the type and severity of the disorder and may include antibiotics, supportive care, or surgery. (For a more detailed discussion of entropion and ectropion, *see* page 143.)

Occasionally kittens are born with a developmental deformity of the upper eyelid called a **coloboma**, which appears as a cleft in the eyelid. The defective eyelid is often unable to function properly, leaving the eye is exposed and at risk for inflammation and the development of ulcers unless it is surgically repaired.

Inflammation of the Eyelids (Blepharitis)

Inflammation of the eyelids can result from the spreading of a generalized inflammation of the skin, inflammation of the conjunctiva, local glandular infections, or irritants such as plant oils or sunlight. Fungi, mites, or bacteria can infect the eyelids, which can then lead to a generalized inflammation.

Lesions of immune-mediated diseases can occur where the skin and conjunctiva join. Pemphigus (*see* page 442) is an example of a disease in which large blisters occur on the skin and mucous membranes. Pemphigus is often accompanied by itching or burning sensations. Skin scrapings, cultures, and biopsies may be required for an accurate diagnosis. Localized glandular infections may be short-term (for example, a stye) or longterm (for example, a meibomian abscess).

When inflammation of the eyelids is caused by a generalized condition, whole-body therapy often is necessary in addition to treatment of the eye itself. Supportive therapy of hot packing and frequent cleansing is often used in severe cases. Your veterinarian will recommend a treatment program designed to control the generalized condition, make your pet more comfortable, and treat the eye condition. Be sure you thoroughly understand the treatment program your veterinarian recommends. Do not hesitate to ask for detailed instructions regarding any eye drops or other medication you will need to provide for your pet. It is often helpful to have the veterinarian demonstrate the administration of these medications.

▥ DISORDERS OF THE NASAL CAVITY AND TEAR DUCTS

The lacrimal or tear gland, located at the top outer edge of the eye, produces the watery portion of tears. The nasolacrimal duct system allows tears to drain from each eye into the nose. Disorders of these structures can lead to either eyes that water excessively or dry eyes. They may be congenital (present at birth) or caused by infection, foreign objects in the eye, or trauma.

Disorders of the nasal cavity and tear ducts are not as common in cats as they are in dogs. However, a few disorders occasionally are seen in this species.

Blockage of the Nasal Duct (Epiphora)

Occasionally cats will experience a chronic overflow of tears due to an obstruction of the nasal duct called epiphora. This is more common in Persian and Himalayan breeds. In most cases, there is no reason for concern when this occurs, as it does not lead to any medical problems. However, if appearance is an issue, the condition can be corrected surgically.

Inflammation of the Tear Sac (Dacryocystitis)

Inflammation of the tear sac is rare in cats. It is usually caused by obstruction of the tear sac and the attached nasolacrimal tear duct by inflammatory debris, foreign objects, or masses pressing on the duct. It results in watering eyes, conjunctivitis that is resistant to treatment, and occasionally a draining opening in the middle of the lower eyelid. If your veterinarian suspects an obstruction of the duct, he or she may attempt to unblock it by flushing it with sterile water or a saline solution. X-rays of the skull after injection of a dye into the duct may be necessary to determine the site, cause, and outlook of long-term obstructions. The usual therapy

It is important to use eye drops and ointments properly so that medication is effective. Your veterinarian can demonstrate the proper technique.

consists of keeping the duct unblocked and using eyedrops containing antibiotics. When the tear duct has been irreversibly damaged, surgery may be necessary to create a new drainage pathway to empty tears into the nasal cavity, sinus, or mouth.

Dry Eye (Keratoconjunctivitis Sicca)

The condition known as dry eye results from inadequate tear production. It often causes persistent mucus and pus-filled conjunctivitis and slow-healing sores (ulcers) and scarring on the cornea. Dry eye is not common in cats but has been associated with longterm feline herpesvirus-1 infections. Topical therapy consists of artificial tear solutions, ointments, and, if there are no scars on the cornea, medications that contain steroids. In longterm dry eye resistant to medical therapy, surgery may be required to correct the condition.

■ DISORDERS OF THE CONJUNCTIVA

The conjunctiva is a thin membrane that lines the inside of the eyelids and extends over to the cornea of the globe. It plays a role in creating tears, providing protection for the eye from foreign invaders, and healing of the cornea after injury. It is important to identify and treat problems of the conjunctiva, because some can indicate generalized disease, while others can lead to blindness if not treated.

Ruptured Blood Vessels (Subconjunctival Hemorrhage)

Ruptured blood vessels beneath the conjunctiva may be the result of trauma, a blood disorder, or certain infectious diseases. This condition, by itself, does not require treatment, but close inspection is necessary to determine if more serious changes within the eye have occurred. If definite evidence or history of trauma is not present, then your veterinarian will perform a complete examination to determine the cause of the spontaneous bleeding.

Swelling of Conjunctival Tissue (Chemosis)

Swelling of the conjunctival tissue around the cornea occurs to some degree with all cases of conjunctivitis, but the most dramatic examples are seen with trauma, a deficiency of proteins in the blood (hypoproteinemia), allergic reactions, and insect bites. Insect bites are treated with topical corticosteroids and usually heal rapidly. In other cases, specific therapy to treat the original cause is required.

Pink Eye (Conjunctivitis)

Conjunctivitis, also known as pink eye, is common in cats. It often occurs as the result of an infection with feline herpesvirus-1, which is extremely widespread among cats. Other causes include various bacterial infections, foreign objects, and environmental irritants. The signs are excess blood flow to the eye, swelling of the tissue around the cornea, discharge from the eye, and mild eye discomfort. The appearance of the conjunctiva usually is not enough, by itself, to allow your veterinarian to diagnose the cause with only a physical examination. A specific diagnosis often requires a medical history, tests on scrapings taken from the conjunctiva, Schirmer tear test, and occasionally biopsy.

Conjunctivitis in only one eye may result from a foreign object, inflammation of the tear sac, or dry eye (*see* above). Conjunctivitis occurring in both eyes is commonly caused by infection with a virus or bacteria. Environmental irritants and allergens are other common causes of conjunctivitis. If a mucus and pus-filled discharge is present, your veterinarian may prescribe a topical antibiotic. However, the antibiotic alone may not bring about healing if other factors are involved. Your veterinarian will also check for foreign objects, environmental irritants, parasites, and defects of eyelid shape, outline, or form, as these factors also contribute to pink eye. Because conjunctivitis can have multiple causes, your veterinarian may prescribe a combination of treatments, including antibiotic or antiviral therapy.

Conjunctivitis is common in cats and is most often the result of an infection.

Conjunctivitis with large amounts of a thick discharge from the eye can occur in newborn kittens. It is usually the result of the same bacteria and viruses that cause infections in adult cats and is treated with topical antibiotics, such as an antibiotic eye ointment.

■ DISORDERS OF THE CORNEA

The cornea helps to protect the front of the eye and is also important in focusing light on the retina at the back of the eye. Because the cornea is critical for proper vision, it is important to address any disorders or injuries promptly.

Inflammation of the Cornea (Keratitis)

Superficial inflammation and swelling of the cornea (superficial keratitis), inflammation and swelling within the cornea (interstitial keratitis), and inflammation and swelling of the cornea with slow-healing sores (ulcerative keratitis), can all occur in cats.

Ulcerative keratitis is frequently caused by an infection with feline herpesvirus-1. This inflammation and swelling of the cornea with slow-healing sores may occur on the surface of the cornea (superficial) or it may affect deeper layers. Initial therapy is

removal of the dead, damaged, or infected tissue of the ulcer by your veterinarian, followed by topical antibiotics and other prescription medication. For resistant cases, there are surgical procedures to stimulate the replacement or development of new corneal tissue, although there are a few risks with these procedures. Your veterinarian can advise you regarding the best treatment for your cat.

Corneal Sequestration (Corneal Black Spot)

A disorder that includes darkening, inflammation, and swelling of the cornea, called corneal sequestration, appears to be unique to the cat. The condition is painful and may also involve inflammation of the cornea. There is a brown to black clouded area in or near the center of the cornea; this is composed of dead connective tissue, blood vessels, and surrounding inflammation. Corneal sequestration occurs in all breeds of cats, but Persians, Himalayans, and Burmese cats are more likely to develop the disorder. Treatment consists of removing the affected surface of the cornea and, in some cases, covering the defect with grafts of conjunctival tissue.

Corneal Deterioration

Deterioration or degeneration in the structure and function of the cornea occurs in cats. Degeneration often occurs in only one eye and is usually the result of other generalized or eye diseases. Treatment, if necessary, usually targets the underlying cause.

(For a more detailed discussion of DISORDERS OF THE CORNEA, *see* page 146.)

■ DISORDERS OF THE ANTERIOR UVEA

The uvea (or the uveal tract) is the colored inside lining of the eye consisting of the iris, the ciliary body, and the choroid. The iris is the colored ring around the black pupil. The ciliary body is the set of muscles that contract and relax to allow the lens to focus on objects; it is also the source of aqueous humor, the clear fluid in the eye.

The choroid is the inner lining of the eyeball. It extends from the ciliary muscles to the optic nerve at the back of the eye. The choroid also contains layers of blood vessels that nourish the inside parts of the eye, especially the retina.

Persistent membranes across the pupil, a weakening and shrinking in size (atrophy) of the iris, cysts of the iris, and inflammation of the iris and ciliary body (anterior uveitis or iridocyclitis) are all conditions that can affect the anterior uvea. In cats, cysts of the iris are frequently attached at the edge of the pupil. Therapy is rarely necessary, but removal or rupture of a cyst may occasionally be required.

Inflammation of the Anterior Uvea

Anterior uveitis, or inflammation of the front portion of the uvea, occurs frequently in cats. It may be seen in one eye (as a result of trauma or various types of cancers) or in both eyes (as a result of a whole-body infection or parasites). The effects of anterior uveitis may be destructive to the eye and can affect vision.

Common causes of inflammation of the uvea in both eyes of cats include immune-mediated diseases and infectious diseases such as feline infectious peritonitis and feline leukemia (both viral infections), feline immunodeficiency virus infection, toxoplasmosis (a disease caused by microscopic parasites), generalized fungal infection, and leptospirosis (a bacterial infection). Often, anterior uveitis is the only sign of these disorders, so it is very important to have your cat examined by a veterinarian if it shows signs such as a protruding third eyelid (nictitating membrane), abnormally red or bloodshot eyes, or pus or nodules in the eye.

Your veterinarian will want a thorough medical history of your pet to help in diagnosing this condition. Other diagnostic steps may include examination of the cornea for injuries, a physical examination, blood tests, and tests on fluid from your pet's eye. Reducing the eye inflammation requires treating the underlying primary disease with appropriate drugs. Cortico-

steroids are sometimes prescribed to treat cloudiness, reduce the inflammation, and reduce the chance of developing glaucoma.

(For a more detailed discussion of DISORDERS OF THE ANTERIOR UVEA, see page 148.)

■ GLAUCOMA

Cats, like people, can develop glaucoma. Glaucoma occurs when an imbalance in production and drainage of fluid in the eye (aqueous humor) causes a buildup of fluid that increases eye pressure to unhealthy levels. The increased pressure can cause the destruction of the retina and optic disk (the spot where the optic nerve enters the eye).

Glaucoma occurs less often in cats than in dogs. It usually develops following inflammation of the anterior uvea (see above) or tumors, although primary (open-angle) glaucoma does occur on its own, particularly in the Siamese breed. Prolonged increases of pressure within the eye can result in enlargement of the eyeball, displacement of the lens, and breaks in a membrane of the cornea. Pain usually shows itself as behavioral changes and occasional pain around the eye rather than by spasmodic winking.

Treatment may require a combination of surgery and medication. (For a more detailed discussion of GLAUCOMA, see page 149.)

■ DISORDERS OF THE LENS

The lens is a soft, transparent tissue that sits behind the iris. It helps focus incoming light onto the retina. Common disorders of the lens include those that affect its transparency (such as cataracts), and those that affect the placement of the lens.

Cataracts

A cataract occurs when the lens becomes cloudy or opaque, which effectively blocks light from reaching the retina. This causes a loss of eyesight that can range from mild vision problems to partial blindness. In contrast to dogs, most of the cataracts that develop in cats do not occur on their own or because of an inherited predisposition.

Instead, they often occur as the result of trauma or inflammation of the anterior uvea (*see* page 429).

In general, treatment for cataracts involves surgery to remove the affected lens or lenses. Advances have been made in this procedure, but complications are possible. In animals in which cataract surgery is not performed, continued monitoring is very important. Follow your veterinarian's recommendations for treatment of cataracts.

Lens Displacement

Lens displacement can occur in cats. The displacement may be due to trauma, long-term inflammation of the uvea, or glaucoma. Lens displacement also occurs in elderly cats. The only effective treatment is surgical removal of the lens. (For a more detailed discussion of DISORDERS OF THE LENS, *see* page 149.)

■ DISORDERS OF THE RETINA, CHOROID, AND OPTIC DISK (OCULAR FUNDUS)

The **ocular fundus** is the back of the eye opposite the pupil and includes the retina, the membrane between the retina and the white of the eye (the choroid), and the optic disk. Diseases of the ocular fundus may occur on their own or as a part of generalized diseases. Inherited abnormalities may be present at birth or appear later, and are important in the cause, development, and effect of diseases of the retina in cats. Trauma, metabolic disturbances, whole-body infections, tumors, blood abnormalities, high blood pressure, and nutritional deficiencies are possible underlying causes for diseases of the retina in cats.

Cats require a certain quantity of an amino acid, **taurine**, in their diet to prevent retinal disease and degeneration. All commercially prepared cat foods are now required to contain sufficient levels of taurine to prevent this condition, and it is rarely seen in cats kept as pets and fed a good-quality commercial diet formulated for cats.

Inherited Diseases of the Retina

Inherited abnormalities may be present at birth or appear later, and are important in the development of diseases of the retina in cats.

Abnormal Development of the Retina (Retinal Dysplasia)

An abnormal development of the retina called retinal dysplasia is present at birth and may arise from trauma, genetic defect, or damage occurring while in the womb, such as viral infections. Viral infections of the mother (for example, panleukopenia), especially during early fetal development, can result in many eye abnormalities with retinal dysplasia in kittens.

Progressive Retinal Atrophy

Progressive retinal atrophy is the name for a group of diseases that cause degeneration of the retina. This includes inherited abnormalities of the light-sensitive layer of the retina. In Abyssinian cats, progressive retinal atrophy occurs as both abnormal development and degeneration. Night blindness is noted early and progresses to total blindness over periods of months to years. Cataracts are common late in the course of progressive retinal atrophy in many breeds and may make it difficult to detect the underlying disease of the retina. No effective therapy is available.

Inflammation of the Retina and Choroid (Chorioretinitis)

Inflammation of the retina and choroid (chorioretinitis) may result from a generalized infection. In cats, infection may be associated with certain viruses (such as feline infectious peritonitis, feline leukemia virus, and feline immunodeficiency virus), fungal diseases, parasites, bacterial infections, and tuberculosis. Unless the abnormalities are widespread or involve the optic nerve, there are often no signs. Signs of inflammation include swelling, bloodshot eyes, discharge from the eyes, and nodules or masses in the eye itself. Therapy is directed at the underlying cause of disease.

It is important to make sure that your pet receives regular, routine eye examinations. These examinations are important because they can often help diagnose many generalized diseases quickly and accurately, thus permitting early therapy.

Retinal Detachments

When the retina is detached, it is separated from the back of the eye and from part of its blood supply, preventing it from functioning properly. In cats, detachment of the retina occurs with chorioretinitis associated with feline infectious peritonitis, feline leukemia, and high blood pressure.

Signs that the retina has become detached include excessive or prolonged dilation of the pupil, pupils of different sizes, loss of vision, and bleeding within the eye. Eye examinations need to be performed to confirm the diagnosis.

Detachments of the retina are treated medically with therapy directed at the primary disease or surgically to correct the detachment. Your veterinarian will select the treatment approach most appropriate for your cat's condition.

▧ DISORDERS OF THE OPTIC NERVE

The optic nerve carries the electrical impulses from the eye to the area in the back of the brain where vision is sensed and interpreted. Injury to the optic nerve usually leads to partial or complete loss of sight.

Optic Nerve Hypoplasia

Failure of the optic nerve to develop fully (optic nerve hypoplasia) in kittens may result from infections with panleukopenia (feline distemper, a viral infection) while in the mother's womb. The condition may occur in only one eye or both, and it can occur with or without other eye abnormalities. If the optic nerves of both eyes fail to develop, the newborn will be blind. Involvement of only one of the optic nerves often goes undetected or may be discovered later in life if the other eye acquires a blinding disease.

The retina may become detached as a result of infection or inflammation. As a result, one pupil may be larger than the other.

Optic Atrophy

Optic degeneration or atrophy may occur after glaucoma, trauma, advanced degeneration of the retina, prolonged low blood pressure within the eye, or inflammation. The optic disk appears flattened and smaller than normal; it is often colored, with very noticeable reduction in the optic nerve and blood vessels of the retina. The pupil of the eye will not react to light and vision is absent. There is no treatment.

▧ PROLAPSE OF THE EYE

Severe prolapse (slipping out of place) and/or bulging of the eye can be caused by trauma. It is uncommon in cats. The outcome depends on the extent of the trauma, depth of the eye socket, duration of the displacement, resting pupil size, condition of the eye, and other damage near the eye. In cats, forward displacement is usually caused by severe trauma to the head; often, facial bones are broken. The eyeball should be put back in place surgically as soon as possible if the cat is in good enough health to have general anesthesia. The upper and lower eyelids are temporarily stitched closed to protect the damaged eye and prevent recurrence. Treatment includes antibiotics (both given by mouth or injection and topical ointments or creams) to prevent infection. Occasionally other medications are needed as well. Although vision does not usually return in the injured eye, the eyeball can usually be saved.

CHLAMYDIAL CONJUNCTIVITIS (FELINE PNEUMONITIS)

Chlamydial conjunctivitis is an infection of the membranes around the eye. Different strains of *Chlamydophila psittaci* and *Chlamydia pecorum* bacteria cause significant eye infections in cats. The disease in cats is also known as feline pneumonitis, which can be misleading because these bacteria rarely cause pneumonia in cats. The infection usually involves the eye and the upper respiratory tract (the nose, sinuses, and throat).

Signs in cats range from watery to mucus- and pus-filled inflammation of the conjunctiva and inflammation of the mucous membranes of the nose. Early signs are reddened, slightly swollen conjunctivae in one eye. Conjunctivitis in both eyes develops after a few days, and the conjunctivae become full of blood and swollen around the cornea. The signs are most severe 9 to 13 days after onset and then subside over 2 to 3 weeks. In some cats, however, signs can last for weeks despite treatment, and recurrence is not uncommon.

Your veterinarian can confirm the diagnosis by taking a smear from the conjunctiva and finding the chlamydial organism under a microscope. It is important to identify the organism causing conjunctivitis in order to provide effective treatment.

There are various medications and ointments your veterinarian can prescribe after infection occurs. Be sure to follow directions carefully and for the full period prescribed by your veterinarian. To reduce recurrence, treatment in cats is usually continued for 7 to 10 days after signs disappear. So, even though your cat looks better, be sure to follow the treatment program for the full length of time prescribed.

Vaccines are available for chlamydiosis in cats. The vaccine does not completely protect the cat from infection, but it can significantly reduce the severity and likelihood of infection. You may want to discuss with your veterinarian whether vaccination is appropriate for your cat.

EYEWORM DISEASE (THELAZIASIS)

Eyeworms (*Thelazia californiensis* and *T. callipaeda*) are parasites found in cats, dogs, and other animals, including humans, in the western United States and Asia. They are whitish, 0.5 to 0.75 inches (7 to 19 millimeters) long, and move in a rapid snake-like motion across the eye. Your veterinarian may find up to 100 eyeworms in the conjunctival sac, tear ducts, and the conjunctiva under the eyelids. Filth flies (including the common house fly) serve as intermediate hosts and deposit the infective eyeworm larvae on the eye while feeding on secretions from the eyes.

Signs include excessive watering of the eyes, inflammation of the conjunctiva, cloudy corneas with slow-healing sores, and rarely, blindness. After a local anesthetic is applied, diagnosis can be confirmed by observing the worms. The veterinarian can remove the parasites with forceps. Injectable or topical treatments may be effective, but physical removal is often the first choice for treatment.

CANCERS AND TUMORS OF THE EYE

The different tissues of the eye and associated structures can develop primary tumors or can be the site of spreading tumor cells. Tumors of the eye are less frequent in cats than in dogs.

Tumors of the Eyelid and Conjunctiva

Eyelid and conjunctival tumors are the most frequent primary eye tumors. These tumors are usually malignant and more difficult to treat in cats than in dogs. Squamous cell carcinomas, which are more common in white cats with noncolored eyelid edges, can involve the eyelids, conjunctivae, and the third eyelid. These tumors are pink, roughened, irregular masses or thickened slow-healing sores. Other less frequent tumors include adenocarcinomas, fibrosarcomas, neurofibrosarcomas, and basal cell carcinomas. Treatment varies with the tumor type, location, and size and includes surgical removal, radiation therapy, and freezing (cryotherapy).

Melanoma of the Iris

The most common primary tumor within the eyes of cats is widespread melanoma of the iris. In these cases, the iris becomes progressively pigmented (dark brown or black) and develops an expanding irregular surface. Abnormalities in the pupil, glaucoma (high pressure within the eye), and enlarged eye occur late in the disease. Removal of the eyeball is recommended when these masses are fast-growing, as they may spread to other parts of the body.

Post-traumatic Sarcoma

Post-traumatic sarcoma within the eye occurs in older cats with a history of long-term inflammation of the uvea and previous damage within the eye. Signs include glaucoma (high pressure within the eye), wasting and shrinkage of the eyeball, or longterm inflammation of the uvea. Early removal of the eyeball is usually recommended in these cases.

Feline Lymphosarcoma-Leukemia Complex

Feline lymphosarcoma-leukemia complex is a common tumor of the eye associated with feline leukemia virus infection. Cats with feline lymphosarcoma-leukemia complex of the eye may have signs affecting one or both eyes, such as inflammation and swelling of the cornea or uvea, excessive formation or rupture of blood vessels in the eye, retinal detachment, abnormal size or shape of the pupil, and lack of pupil dilation. Slow healing sores may also occur. Tumors can be found in the orbit, eyeball, conjunctivae, and eyelids. Treatment for cats with eye lymphoma has not been well studied, but cats with lymphoma and feline leukemia virus infection have lower overall survival times.

CHAPTER **29**

Ear Disorders

▣ EAR STRUCTURE AND FUNCTION

Cats are very sensitive to sound, with a range of hearing both above and below the range of frequencies that can be detected by humans. They can hear better than people and even better than most dogs.

The ear is an organ of hearing and an organ of balance. It consists of the outer, middle, and inner ear.

The **outer ear** includes the pinna (the part you see that is made of cartilage and covered by skin, fur, or hair) and the ear canal. The pinna is shaped to capture sound waves and funnel them through the ear canal to the eardrum. In cats, the pinnae are mobile and can move independently of each other. The ear canal of cats is deeper and more tapered than in people, creating a better funnel to carry sound to the eardrum. This deeper canal is subject to buildup of dirt and wax that can lead to inflammation and secondary infection, although to a lesser degree than in dogs.

The **middle ear** includes the eardrum and a small, air-filled chamber that contains 3 tiny bones: the hammer, anvil, and stirrup. It also includes 2 muscles, the oval window, and the eustachian tube (a small tube that connects the middle ear with the back of the nose, allowing air to enter the middle ear).

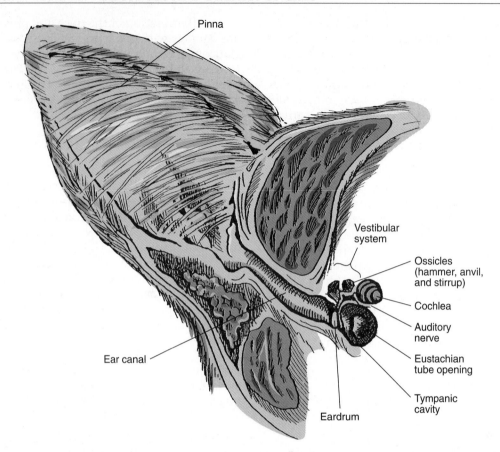

Pinna

Vestibular system

Ossicles (hammer, anvil, and stirrup)

Cochlea

Auditory nerve

Eustachian tube opening

Ear canal

Tympanic cavity

Eardrum

A look inside the cat's ear

The **inner ear** is a complex structure that includes the cochlea (the organ of hearing) and the vestibular system (the organ of balance). The semicircular canals, which are found within the inner ear, are filled with fluid and are important for maintaining balance. These are highly developed in the cat, accounting for its agility and excellent sense of balance.

Physical Examination of the Ear

Your veterinarian will examine your cat's ears at every routine checkup. If the cat has a history of previous ear infections or other problems with the ear, you should provide that information to the veterinarian. Information on how to clean your pet's ears at home can be found in the chapter on dog ear disorders (*see* BOX, page 162).

To start, your veterinarian will visually inspect the outer ears, noting any signs of inflammation, injury from trauma, swelling, secretions, or excessive ear wax. He or she will then use an instrument called an otoscope to view the ear canal and eardrum. A video-otoscope (an otoscope with a camera that can display images of the inside of the ear) is often very helpful when inspecting the ear canals. It may be necessary to use sedation or general anesthesia to examine some cats if the ear is painful and the cat is difficult to restrain. If an infection is suspected, tests will be performed on samples of fluid or secretions from the ear to determine the organisms involved and the proper treatment. Infections in cats' ears are most commonly caused by bacteria or yeasts.

To diagnose a tumor of the ear, it may be necessary to do a pinch biopsy to obtain tissue for evaluation. This can usually be done using forceps and an otoscope while the cat is under general anesthesia. Further tests, including x-rays, neurologic tests, and electronic tests may be needed to confirm certain conditions such as deafness.

DEAFNESS

Deafness in cats may be congenital (present at birth) or acquired as a result of infection, trauma, or degeneration of the ear.

Deafness present at birth can be inherited or result from toxic or viral damage to the developing unborn kitten. A certain gene in cats causes white fur, blue eyes, and deafness; however, not all blue-eyed white cats are deaf. Deafness in this instance is due to degenerative changes that occur in the first week of life.

Diagnosis of congenital deafness requires careful observation of the cat's response to sound. In young kittens or in cats kept in groups, deafness may be difficult to detect, because the suspect individual will follow the response of others in the group. If the cat is observed as an individual after an age when responses to sound are predictable (about 3 to 4 weeks), then the deafness may be detected.

Acquired deafness may result from blockage of the external ear canal which occurs in longterm inflammation of the external ear canal (**otitis externa**), or it may occur after destruction of the middle or inner ear. Other causes include trauma to the hard portion of the temporal bone that surrounds the inner ear, loud noises, conditions in which there is a loss or destruction of myelin (the fatty material that surrounds some nerve cells), drugs toxic to the ear (for example, certain antibiotics or aspirin), and tumors involving the ear or brain stem. Inflammatory polyps (*see* page 438) can sometimes cause deafness in cats. Deafness in one ear or partial hearing loss, or both, is possible in some of these instances.

Cats with deafness due to bacterial infection may recover hearing after antibiotic treatment. Recovery from other causes varies with the particular disease. There is no effective treatment for congenital deafness. Many cats with partial or complete deafness adapt very well to their condition. However, deaf cats should not be let outdoors except on a leash.

(For a more detailed discussion of DEAFNESS, *see* page 157.)

DISORDERS OF THE OUTER EAR

A variety of skin conditions affect the outside part of the ear, called the pinna. Most conditions cause tissue changes elsewhere as well. Rarely, a disease affects the outer ear alone or affects it first. As with all skin conditions, a diagnosis is best made when combined with the results of a thorough history, a complete physical and skin examination, and carefully selected diagnostic tests.

Insects and parasites commonly cause inflammation of the pinna—resulting in redness, swelling, itching or blistering—either through direct damage from the bite of the parasite or as a result of hypersensitivity.

Ear Hematomas

Ear hematomas are fluid-filled swellings that develop on the inward curving surface of the pinna (outer ear). The cause for their development is unknown. Signs include head shaking or ear scratching due to itchiness. Treatment usually involves surgery to drain and flush the swellings. Frequently, the veterinarian will place a drain made out of a soft tube in the area to help prevent fluid from building up again.

Immune-mediated Diseases

Several immune-mediated diseases may affect the outer ear and the ear canal (*see also* PEMPHIGUS, page 442). Other areas of the body are typically affected at the same time and may include footpads, mucous membranes, skin and mucous membrane junctions, nails and nail beds, and the tip of the tail. Immune-mediated diseases are confirmed using a biopsy of primary lesions.

Mange

Mange is caused by microscopic mites. There are several types of mites that cause mange. One of the most common types of inflammation of the external ear canal (otitis externa) in cats is **otodectic mange**, caused by *Otodectes cynotis* mites. The mites affect the skin as well as the ears, and signs include redness, partial loss of hair, itching, and general inflammation of the skin. It may occur on the head, neck, rump, or paws.

Sarcoptic mange, caused by the parasitic mite *Sarcoptes scabiei* is rare in cats. The condition begins with small, hard round bumps on the skin. These bumps progress to scaling, crusting, and raw, irritated areas on the ear edges and other parts of the body. Itching is severe. Transmission is by direct contact with infected animals.

Notoedric mange is also rare in cats, but can cause intense, constant itching around the ears, head, and neck. Signs include head-shaking, redness, hair loss, and crusted, grayish-yellow scabs.

The diagnosis of mange is based on signs, history of exposure, examination, and discovery of mites on multiple skin scrapings. The actual mites are small and hard to see, even with magnification. Treatment options include dips, medications effective against mites (applied to the skin or given by mouth or by injection). Corticosteroids may be given to help control severe itching. Your veterinarian will be able to prescribe the best treatment for your pet. Because mites can survive off the host for a variable amount of time, all bedding, brushes, and objects in your cat's environment should be thoroughly cleaned. Any other cats or dogs in the household should be considered infested and should also be treated.

Mosquitoes

An allergic reaction to mosquito bites can cause an inflammation of the skin with crusted, slow-healing sores on the outer ears, nose, and rarely the footpads and eyelids of cats. Often referred to as **miliary dermatitis**, these tiny "millet seed" eruptions will crust over, ooze, then dry, leaving a small patch of hair loss. In severely affected cats, the affected areas progress from small, hard round bumps to raised, white to pink tumors to crusted, slow-healing sores that merge together to affect extensive areas. The amount of itching varies and lymph nodes may enlarge. Treatment includes keeping the cat inside and using a prescribed insect repellent when exposure to mosquitoes is anticipated. Be sure to use only repellents prescribed by your veterinarian.

Solar Dermatitis (Radiation Dermatitis)

Feline solar dermatitis, also called radiation or ultraviolet dermatitis is seen most commonly in white cats or cats with white outer ears that have had longterm exposure to the sun. The first signs are a reddening of the skin and scaling on the sparsely-haired tips of the ears. Crusting, discharge, and slow-healing sores may develop as the hornlike growth on the skin undergoes transformation into a form of cancer called squamous cell carcinoma. During early stages of the disease, treatment consists of limiting exposure to sunlight through confinement indoors between the hours of 10 A.M. and 4 P.M., and the use of special topical sunscreens that your veterinarian

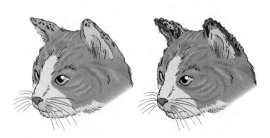

Solar dermatitis   Squamous cell
                                carcinoma

Solar dermatitis occurs in cats after prolonged periods of sun exposure. It can progress to squamous cell carcinoma, a form of cancer.

will prescribe. Squamous cell carcinoma of the outer ears is treated with surgical removal followed by radiation treatment.

Ticks

Ticks can cause irritation at the site of attachment and may be found on the pinna or in the ear canal. The **ear tick**, found in the southwestern United States, South and Central Americas, southern Africa, and India, is a soft-shelled tick whose younger, immature forms infest and live on the external ear canal of cats and other animals. Signs include head shaking, head rubbing, or attempts to scratch the ear. Both the animal and the environment (including all bedding) should be treated using the compounds prescribed or recommended by your veterinarian.

▓ OTITIS EXTERNA

The tubular portion of the outer ear that carries sound to the eardrum is called the ear canal. The most common disorder of the ear canal in cats is called otitis externa. This condition occurs when the layer of cells that line the external ear canal becomes inflamed. Signs include redness of the skin, swelling, itchiness, increased discharge, and scaly skin. The ear canal may be painful or itchy depending on the cause or duration of the condition.

Otitis externa can be caused by many different factors. Some of these factors (such as parasites, foreign objects, and allergies) appear to directly cause the inflammation, while others (such as certain bacteria and yeasts) worsen and perpetuate the condition. Identifying these factors is key to successful control of the inflammation. Unless all the causes are identified and treated, the condition may return. Thus, in addition to a physical examination, your veterinarian will ask about your pet's environment and exposure to chemicals and irritants.

The diagnosis, treatment, and preventive care for otitis externa in cats is very similar to this condition in dogs (*see* page 160).

▓ OTITIS MEDIA AND INTERNA

Inflammation of the middle ear structures (**otitis media**) is usually caused by an extension of infection from the external ear canal or by penetration of the eardrum by a foreign object. Inflammatory polyps (*see* page 438) are also a common cause of otitis media in cats. The spread of infection through the bloodstream to these areas is also possible, but it is rare. Inflammation of the middle ear may lead to inflammation of the inner ear structures (**otitis interna**). This can in turn lead to loss of balance and deafness. In general, otitis media and interna are more serious than otitis externa, and their effects on the ear may not be reversible.

If your cat is having problems with balance, walking, or jumping, you should suspect a middle ear problem and take your pet in to the veterinarian promptly. A pus-filled inflammation of the outer ear may also signal inflammation of the middle or inner ear.

The diagnosis, treatment, and preventive care for otitis media and interna in cats is very similar to this condition in dogs (*see* page 161).

▓ TUMORS OF THE EAR CANAL

Ear canal tumors may develop from any of the structures lining or supporting the ear canal, including the outer layer of skin, the glands that produce earwax and oil, or any of the bones, connective tissues, muscles, or middle layers of skin. Tumors of the external ear canal and outer ear are more common than tumors of the middle or inner ear. Ear canal tumors are more common in cats than in dogs but, overall, these tumors are relatively uncommon compared with skin tumors elsewhere on the body.

Although the exact cause of ear canal tumors is unknown, it is thought that longterm inflammation of the ear canal may lead to abnormal growth and development of tissue, and finally to the formation of a tumor. Thickening secretions from earwax glands during episodes of inflammation of the external ear canal may stimulate the production of cancerous cells. Ear canal tumors are more likely to be malignant than benign in cats.

Middle-aged to older cats are more likely to develop benign and malignant ear canal tumors, while young cats (3 months to 5 years old) are more likely to develop inflammatory polyps (*see* below). Signs of ear canal tumors include a continuing waxy, pus-filled, or bloody ear discharge in one ear, foul odor, head shaking, ear scratching, swelling, draining abscesses in the region below the affected ear, or deafness. If the middle or inner ear is involved, the cat may have loss of balance or coordination, head tilt, and other neurologic signs. In any case of inflammation in one ear that does not respond to treatment, a tumor of the ear canal is possible.

Referral to a board-certified surgical specialist is often recommended when dealing with ear canal tumors, especially when the middle ear is involved. (*See also* TUMORS OF THE SKIN, page 505.)

Inflammatory Polyps

Nasopharyngeal polyps are small, pinkish inflammatory growths of connective tissue that are found in the external ear canals of young cats (usually between the ages of 3 months and 5 years). They also occur in the mucous membranes lining the throat mucosa and auditory tube (the channel connecting the nasopharynx to the middle ear). These polyps may be present at birth or caused by viral or bacterial infection. Bacterial infection of the external or middle ear canal due to obstruction of the ear canal or round bone behind the ear may also be present. Signs of inflammatory polyps will be similar to those seen in other middle ear problems, including problems with balance, coordination, or an inflammation of the outer (visible) portion of the ear.

Diagnosis involves examination of the vertical and horizontal ear canals using an otoscope (an instrument that allows a veterinarian to see deep into the ear canal) while the cat is sedated. Pus-filled discharge may need to be gently suctioned from the ear canal to see the polyp. Additional tests such as computed tomography or magnetic resonance imaging may be used if a mass is suspected in the round bone behind the ear.

Surgery is often used to remove the polyp. Your veterinarian will take care to completely remove the entire polyp and stalk; incomplete removal usually leads to rapid regrowth of the polyp.

Earwax Gland Tumors

Benign or malignant tumors that develop from the modified earwax glands in the external ear canal occur occasionally in middle-aged or older cats. These tumors are more likely to be malignant than benign. Cats with a history of longterm inflammation of the ear are more likely to develop earwax gland tumors.

Malignant earwax tumors are firm, dome-shaped, and pink-white. They often have stalk-shaped lumps or flattened patches with slow-healing sores. Because many tumors completely obstruct the ear canal, they are often associated with inflammation of the external or middle ear and pus-filled or bloody discharge. Loss of balance is common if there is middle ear involvement. Malignant earwax tumors can spread to nearby lymph nodes and salivary glands, so your veterinarian may recommend that they be removed.

Surgical removal of benign ear canal tumors may be accomplished by removing part of the ear canal. This is helpful in most cases unless there is involvement of the round bone behind the ear. Laser surgery has also been used. Completely opening the ear canal and surgically dividing the bone in the middle ear is the only recommended surgery for removal of malignant ear canal tumors.

The best treatment program for your cat will depend on many factors, including your pet's age and the size and location of the tumor. Your veterinarian will recommend a treatment program that has the best chances for a positive result.

CHAPTER 30

Immune Disorders

▓ THE IMMUNE SYSTEM

The immune system consists of a network of white blood cells, antibodies, and other substances that fight off infections and reject foreign proteins. In addition, the immune system includes several organs. Some, such as the thymus gland and the bone marrow, are the sites where white blood cells are produced. Others, including the spleen, lymph nodes, and liver, trap microorganisms and foreign substances and provide a place for immune system cells to collect, interact with each other and with foreign substances, and generate an immune response.

The primary role of the immune system is to defend the body against foreign invaders or abnormal cells that invade or attack it. The immune system functions in the same way in cats as it does in dogs—and, indeed, in humans. For that reason, the various immune system responses to foreign substances and the types of immune system disorders are discussed in detail in the chapter on immune disorders in dogs (*see* page 164).

▓ DISORDERS INVOLVING ANAPHYLACTIC REACTIONS (TYPE I REACTIONS, ATOPY)

In a Type I reaction, the animal has been previously exposed to an antigen and produces an excess of antibodies. If this antigen appears in the blood, the result can be either anaphylactic shock or more localized reactions (such as itchy patches on the skin). If the antigen enters through the skin, the more localized reaction is typical.

Anaphylactic Shock

Anaphylactic shock is a rare, life-threatening, immediate allergic reaction to food, an injection, or an insect sting. The most common signs occur within seconds to minutes after exposure to the antigen. These signs include severe respiratory distress and the sudden onset of diarrhea, vomiting, excessive drooling, shock, seizures, coma, and death. The cat's gums are very pale, and the limbs feel cold. The heart rate is generally very fast, but the pulse is weak. Facial swelling does not usually occur, but there may be itchiness around the face and head.

Anaphylaxis is an extreme emergency. If you think that your cat is having an anaphylactic reaction, seek emergency veterinary assistance immediately. A veterinarian can give intravenous injections of epinephrine to counteract the reaction. Treatment for other problems, such as difficulty breathing, may also be needed.

Hives and Swelling

Hives (**urticaria**) and areas of swelling are caused by allergic reactions to drugs, chemicals, something eaten, insect bites, or even sunlight. They generally develop within 20 minutes of being exposed to the allergen (antigen). Hives are the least severe type of anaphylactic reaction. Small bumps occur on the skin. Often, the hair stands up over these swellings and sometimes they itch. Swelling is most often noticed on the face, especially on the lips,

A cat can develop hives in reaction to either environmental or ingested allergens.

the nose, and around the eyes. The swelling can be so severe that the cat cannot open its eyes.

Hives and swelling are usually not life threatening and typically go away by themselves once the cause of the allergic reaction is removed or passes through the body. Veterinarians often treat these reactions by providing antihistamines. Your veterinarian will make treatment decisions based on your pet's circumstances.

Allergic Bronchiolitis

Coughing and wheezing are the most common signs of allergic bronchiolitis, which is an inflammation of the lower portion (bronchioles) of the airway. This disease may be mistaken for other conditions such as asthma or lungworm disease. The early signs of the disease can easily disappear with common medications. If the disease increases in severity, more powerful medication may be required. Your veterinarian can adjust the prescribed medication based on your cat's reaction. It is usually not possible to identify the antigen causing the allergic reaction.

Allergic Asthma

Allergic asthma is more often found in cats than in other animals; however, it is still less common than in humans. It occurs more frequently in summer and after going outdoors. Asthma attacks can be moderate or lengthy and severe. The signs are shortness of breath and frantic attempts to inhale. The condition occurs as a result of constriction of the breathing passages triggered by the release of compounds, such as histamines, that combat allergens. Corticosteroids may be recom-

Signs of allergic asthma include open-mouth breathing, congestion, and shortness of breath.

mended to alleviate severe signs, but they do not treat the underlying cause of the asthma. Determining the allergic trigger can be difficult.

PIE Syndrome (Pulmonary Infiltration with Eosinophilia)

Infiltration of the lungs with a thick fluid and white blood cells, called PIE syndrome, is caused by allergens, viruses, and parasites. It is uncommon in cats. Animals with PIE syndrome generally become lethargic and have difficulty breathing with normal exercise. It is usually not possible to determine the antigen causing the reaction. Medications can help control the signs of the disorder.

Food Allergies

Food allergies occur in cats as well as people. They often develop following an intestinal infection with a virus, bacteria, or protozoan and can lead to inflammation of the lining of the stomach and intestines. In cats, the first (and sometimes only) sign is vomiting that occurs within 1 to 2 hours of eating. Weight loss, diarrhea or soft feces, and poor coat condition may also occur. Feces usually are normal in amount and frequency, but consistency varies from semi-solid to watery. They may be extremely odorous. Severe cases of food allergies are characterized by diarrhea and sometimes by bloody feces.

Both the diagnosis and treatment of food allergies are done by strictly controlling the diet at the direction of a veterinarian. Your veterinarian is likely to recommend a basic diet that includes a protein source the cat has not eaten before, such as ground, cooked turkey or lamb. Follow the recommended diet carefully to help identify the food that causes your pet's allergic reaction. Once signs have disappeared (usually after 1 to 2 weeks), additional foods can be introduced 1 at a time until the problem food is identified. Commercial prescription diets are also available. Kittens with food allergies often grow out of them. Older animals may need special and restricted diets for the rest of their lives.

Food allergies can cause weight loss and poor coat condition in cats, in addition to vomiting and diarrhea.

Skin Allergies (Atopy)

Skin allergy, also called atopy, occurs when a cat's skin overreacts to certain allergens in the environment. In cats, food allergies are probably a more common cause of skin allergies than inhaled allergens (such as pollen). Veterinarians diagnose skin allergies by a medical history, physical examination, and various tests including exclusion trials (where potential allergens are removed from the environment and then reintroduced) and skin tests.

The key to managing this condition is removing or restricting exposure to the allergen or contact irritant in the cat's environment. Treatment consists of an extended series of injections of the possible allergen under the skin until improvement is noted. Several medications are available to help control the skin allergy. Your veterinarian will select a treatment program that is appropriate for your cat and its specific allergy. (For a more detailed discussion of ALLERGIES, *see* page 492.)

■ DISORDERS INVOLVING CYTOTOXIC ANTIBODIES (TYPE II REACTIONS)

Type II reactions can lead to several types of diseases in cats, including anemia, blood clotting problems, and skin and muscle disorders. They may be associated with other immune system disturbances, such as cancers of the lymphoreticular system, or triggered by a drug, vaccine, or infection. Most often, the triggering cause cannot be pinpointed. Immune-mediated hemolytic anemia and thrombocytopenia are the most common Type II reactions.

Immune-mediated Hemolytic Anemia

This type of anemia is a severe and life-threatening disease in which the cat's immune system sees its own red blood cells as foreign invaders, and therefore produces antibodies to destroy them. Red blood cells are manufactured as usual in the bone marrow, but once released into the bloodstream, they are attacked and destroyed by antibodies. Signs of anemia may include fatigue, paleness of the lips and gums, and depression, along with jaundice in some cases. Other signs your veterinarian may find include an enlarged liver or spleen.

Immune-mediated hemolytic anemia has 4 basic forms, peracute, acute or subacute, chronic, and pure red cell aplasia. The chronic (longterm) form is most common in cats. Most forms are treatable with drugs, including corticosteroids and cytotoxic drugs, such as those often used in chemotherapy. Relapses are uncommon.

Immune-mediated Thrombocytopenia

Immune-mediated thrombocytopenia is caused by the destruction of platelets (thrombocytes) by the immune system in much the same manner as red blood cells are destroyed in immune-mediated hemolytic anemia (*see* above). When an animal has thrombocytopenia, clotting does not occur correctly. Even minor injuries can cause uncontrollable bleeding, further decreasing the number of red blood cells. The most frequent signs are bleeding of the skin and mucous membranes.

Before immune-mediated thrombocytopenia can be diagnosed, many more common diseases must be excluded, including various clotting disorders, bladder or prostate infections or cancer, and intestinal parasites. The diagnosis is usually made based on signs and response to treatment, rather than on blood tests. However, certain blood tests such as platelet counts and clotting profiles are helpful. Medication will likely be prescribed to treat this disease. Signs usually disappear after 5 to 7 days of treatment when platelet counts begin to rise. If the platelet count has not increased significantly after 7 to 10 days, additional or different medications, such as drugs that suppress the immune system, may be prescribed. If the blood loss is life threatening, transfusions of whole blood or plasma may be necessary.

Treatment is often continued for 1 to 3 months after the platelet counts return to normal. Some cats have persistent decreases in platelets even with drug treatment. If this is the case with your pet, you and your veterinarian will want to discuss longterm treatment and maintenance options.

Pemphigus

Pemphigus foliaceus is an uncommon autoimmune disease that affects the skin. It is rare in cats. The cause of this malfunction of the immune system is usually not known. One theory is that the skin is somehow altered, making it appear "foreign" to the immune system. In the case of pemphigus, the immune system produces antibodies against the "glue" that normally keeps skin cells (keratinocytes) attached to one another. White blood cells move in causing further damage, and the keratinocytes break apart from each other, forming pimples or crusted areas. Veterinarians frequently prescribe corticosteroids for initial treatment of pemphigus, but other immunosuppressive drugs may be added if there is no response.

Myasthenia Gravis

Myasthenia gravis is an autoimmune neuromuscular disease; it is rarely seen in cats. Weakness and lack of muscle control are the primary signs. Affected animals produce antibodies to certain nerve receptors and destroy them. Your veterinarian will prescribe drugs to control this disease. (For a more detailed discussion of MYASTHENIA GRAVIS, see page 170.)

■ DISORDERS INVOLVING IMMUNE COMPLEXES (TYPE III REACTIONS)

Immune complex disorders are among the most common immune-mediated diseases. The location in the body where the immune complexes (combinations of antibodies and antigens) are deposited determines the signs and the course of the disease.

Glomerulonephritis

Glomerulonephritis (see GLOMERULAR DISEASE, page 520) is inflammation of the microscopic filtering units of the kidneys known as glomeruli. The inflammation develops when immune complexes become trapped in the glomeruli. This leads to activation of the body's inflammatory defense system, which, in turn, damages the glomeruli. The immune complexes often form as a consequence of some other disease such as an infection or cancer. However, in many cats with glomerulonephritis, the triggering cause cannot be determined. Glomerulonephritis results in an excessive loss of protein in the urine (proteinuria). The finding of protein in the urine during a urine test (urinalysis) may be the first indication that your cat has glomerulonephritis. Treatment includes giving immunosuppressive drugs to reduce the formation of the immune complexes. If it goes untreated, the disease can lead to chronic kidney failure.

Systemic Lupus Erythematosus (Lupus)

Systemic lupus erythematosus (often simply called lupus) is an autoimmune disease that is rare in cats. Pets with lupus have antibodies in their blood that are targeted against their own body tissues. Lupus causes widespread abnormalities of the skin, heart, lungs, kidneys, joints, nervous system, and blood (anemia and/or decreased platelet numbers). Multiple organs are usually affected. A blood test is the usual method of diagnosing lupus. Longterm treatment with corticosteroids and other drugs that suppress the immune system are prescribed to treat the disorder.

Your veterinarian will determine the most appropriate treatment for your pet. (For a more detailed discussion of SYSTEMIC LUPUS ERYTHEMATOSUS, *see* page 171.)

Anterior Uveitis

One cause of anterior uveitis (*see* page 429) is the action of antibody-antigen complexes on the iris, which causes inflammation of the eye. Uveitis caused by *Toxoplasma* parasites or by the feline infectious peritonitis virus also has an immunologic basis. Treatment of immune-mediated anterior uveitis may include whole-body corticosteroids and other drugs that suppress the immune system.

▨ DISORDERS INVOLVING CELL-MEDIATED IMMUNITY (TYPE IV REACTIONS)

This type of reaction occurs when specific types of white blood cells (called T helper cells) respond to antigens and release toxic and inflammatory substances that can damage tissues. Cell-mediated immune reactions can occur in any organ. Treatment usually involves the use of anti-inflammatory drugs and drugs that suppress the immune system, either alone or in combination.

Granulomatous Reactions

Granulomatous reactions are masses of fibrous connective tissue infiltrated by the white blood cells that form a cell-mediated immune response. The feline infectious peritonitis virus and some bacteria and fungi may trigger these reactions in cats. These reactions may be due to long-lasting cell-mediated immune reactions. Although cell-mediated immune responses effectively fight off these infections in most cats, in a few animals the immune response is only partially effective and results in the mass at the site of infection.

▨ IMMUNE-DEFICIENCY DISEASES

Like humans, cats can develop diseases and conditions that impair the function of their immune systems. Immune defi-

ciency diseases have serious consequences and often lower the body's defenses against infection. Some are inherited, and others are caused by viral infections (for example, feline immunodeficiency virus infection) or cancer.

Deficiencies in Phagocytosis

Phagocytosis is an essential mechanism of the immune system. Phagocytes are cells that engulf (phagocytize), digest, and kill foreign invaders. They can also serve as part of the adaptive immune system by presenting antigens to other cells in the adaptive system, thereby alerting them to the presence of the foreign invaders. Phagocytes are produced in the bone marrow, spread throughout the body via the bloodstream, and then gather in either tissue or the blood. They are found in the skin, spleen, lymph nodes, the coverings of the brain and spinal cord, bone marrow, and blood vessels throughout the body.

A deficiency in phagocytosis can be caused by a low number of phagocytes in the blood or by a viral infection or a congenital (birth) defect. The deficiency increases susceptibility to bacterial infections of the skin, respiratory system, and gastrointestinal tract.

Because a cat with reduced numbers of phagocytes has trouble fighting diseases,

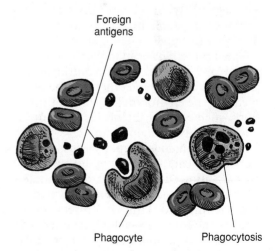

Foreign antigens

Phagocyte　　Phagocytosis

Phagocytes are white blood cells that engulf and then kill foreign antigens such as bacteria in a process called phagocytosis.

infections can easily develop into life-threatening complications. These infections respond poorly to antibiotics. Some conditions in cats that are known to affect phagocytosis include viruses such as feline leukemia, feline panleukopenia, and feline immunodeficiency; various disorders of white blood cell production; and bone marrow disorders.

Selective Immunodeficiencies

Persian cats have a tendency to develop severe and sometimes protracted infections of the skin, fur, and claws. Many are caused by fungal infections. In some Persian cats, the fungal infections invade the skin and cause the formation of small fleshy or grainy masses called **mycetomas**. Your veterinarian can recommend a treatment program for these infections.

Immunodeficiencies Caused by Viruses

Parvovirus occurs in both dogs and cats. This viral disease causes a severe and short-term reduction in the number of neutrophils and in the lymphocyte responsiveness. These failures of the immune system increase the risk of fungal infections such as aspergillosis, mucormycosis, and candidiasis.

Feline leukemia virus infection in cats (*see* page 533) causes a response similar to that seen in people infected with the human immunodeficiency virus. An infected cat will have an impaired immune system and a higher risk of acquiring infections from bacteria and other infectious agents in the environment. Dormant infections, such as feline infectious peritonitis, may suddenly flare up again.

Feline immunodeficiency virus is spread from cat to cat, primarily by biting. Cats that are allowed to roam outdoors, male cats, and older cats are more likely to become infected. This viral infection attacks the immune system, leading to signs such as anemia and low white blood cell counts, infections of the gums and mouth, cancer, or neurologic disease. Shortly after becoming infected, cats may

have a fever and enlargement of the lymph nodes (glands). However, these signs go away and the cat may appear healthy with no further signs of infection for months or years. However, once infected, cats remain infected for life and most eventually have a deterioration of immune function and increased risk of infections.

Infection with feline immunodeficiency virus is diagnosed by a complete medical history and physical examination combined with a blood test that measures antibodies against the virus. There is no effective treatment, but supportive care and treatment of signs is important. This includes giving antibiotics for bacterial infections, providing a balanced diet, controlling parasites, keeping the cat indoors and isolated from other cats, and removing tumors.

A vaccine for feline immunodeficiency virus is available, but not all vaccinated cats will be protected, so preventing exposure is important, even for vaccinated pets. Vaccination may also have an impact on future feline immunodeficiency test results. You should discuss whether or not your cat needs this vaccine with your veterinarian.

■ IMMUNE SYSTEM TUMORS

Cancer occurs when cells grow out of control. This can happen with the cells of the immune system. The normal immune system requires a rapid increase in the growth of lymphocytes to fight foreign invaders. On occasion, this increase in the growth of lymphocytes may be uncontrolled, which causes a tumor called **lymphoma**. Lymphoma occurs in middle-aged to older cats. No breed of cat is known to have a higher risk for lymphoma than other breeds. Infections with both feline leukemia virus and feline immunodeficiency virus have been shown to increase the risk for developing lymphoma.

Lymphomas can occur in lymph nodes, the spleen, the liver, and other organs. Signs in cats with lymphoma depend primarily on the location of the tumor cells, but can include enlargement of lymph nodes, vomiting, diarrhea, loss of appetite, weight loss, lethargy, difficulty breathing, and increased thirst or urination. The skin form can cause redness or flakiness of the skin, ulceration (especially near the lips and on the footpads), itching, or lumps in the skin. The disease is diagnosed by blood tests and biopsy of a lump or enlarged lymph node. It is often treated with chemotherapy involving several drugs. Adverse effects of the chemotherapy include vomiting, diarrhea, lack of appetite, and fever. Hair loss as an effect of chemotherapy does not occur in cats.

▓ GAMMOPATHIES

The body sometimes produces too many antibodies (immunoglobulins). Gammopathies are conditions in which there is a dramatic rise in the production of antibodies. There are 2 general types. In polyclonal gammopathies, levels of all the major immunoglobulins are increased. In monoclonal gammopathies, the levels of only a single type of immunoglobulin are increased.

Polyclonal gammopathies may occur when a cat has longterm skin disease or longterm viral, bacterial, or fungal infections. Some longterm parasitic infections, rickettsial diseases, and immunologic diseases (for example, systemic lupus erythematosus) may also cause polyclonal gammopathies.

Monoclonal gammopathies may be either benign and associated with no known cause or associated with immunoglobulin-secreting cancers. The signs of monoclonal gammopathies vary depending on the location and severity of the source tumor(s). For example, tumors frequently develop in the cavities of flat bones in the skull, ribs, and pelvis and in the spinal cord. Fractures of diseased bones can lead to central nervous system problems, spinal disorders, or to pain and lameness. Signs can also be caused by the presence of the monoclonal antibodies themselves.

The tumors that produce antibody secretions can be treated with several medications. Remission may occur after treatment, but the overall outlook is poor and relapse is common after 6 to 12 months.

CHAPTER **31**

Bone, Joint, and Muscle Disorders

▓ INTRODUCTION

The musculoskeletal system includes the bones, cartilage, muscles, ligaments, joints, tendons, and other connective tissue. It supports the body, permits movement, and protects the vital organs. Because many other body systems (including the nervous system, blood vessels, and skin) are interrelated, disorders of one of these systems may also affect the musculoskeletal system.

Diseases of the musculoskeletal system most often affect the body's ability to move. How severely movement is impaired depends on the type and severity of the problem. Skeletal and joint disorders are

the most common, but problems in the musculoskeletal system can also indicate diseases of the muscles, neurologic problems, toxins in the body, hormonal abnormalities, metabolic disorders, infectious diseases, blood and vascular disorders, poor nutrition, and birth defects. (For a more detailed discussion of the musculoskeletal system, *see* page 176.)

▓ COMPONENTS OF THE MUSCULOSKELETAL SYSTEM

Bones provide rigid structure to the body and shield internal organs from

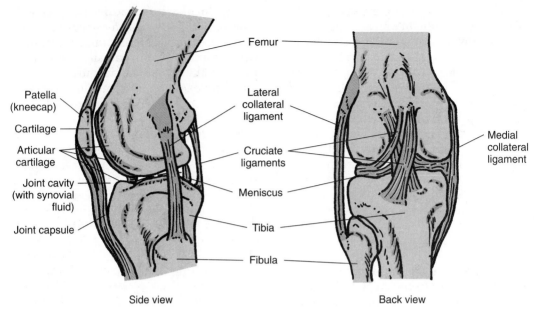

Components of the musculoskeletal system are shown for the knee of a cat (modified with permission from *The Merck Manual of Medical Information*, Second Home Edition, 2003).

damage. They also house bone marrow, where blood cells are formed, and they maintain the body's reservoir of calcium. Old bone tissue is constantly replaced with new bone tissue in a process called remodeling. This helps keep the bones healthy.

Bones come together to form **joints**. The type of joint formed determines the degree and direction of motion. For example, joints with a ball-and-socket formation allow for rotation, while hinge joints only allow bending and straightening. Some joints, such as those between bones of the skull, do not move at all. In a joint, the ends of the bones are covered with **cartilage**, which is a smooth protective tissue that helps reduce friction as joints move.

There are several different types of **muscles** in the body. Two of these kinds, skeletal muscle and smooth muscle, are part of the musculoskeletal system. Skeletal muscles are responsible for posture and movement. They are attached to bones and arranged around the joints. Smooth muscle helps facilitate many processes in the body such as the flow of blood (by surrounding arteries) and the movement of food along the digestive tract.

Tendons are tough bands of connective tissue made up mostly of a protein called collagen. They do not stretch. Tendons attach each end of a muscle to a bone. They are located within sheaths that allow them to move easily. **Ligaments** are also tough cords formed of connective tissue, but unlike tendons they can stretch to some extent. Ligaments surround joints and help to support and stabilize them. They can also connect one bone to another.

LAMENESS

Lameness is not a disease, but it may indicate a disorder in the musculoskeletal system. Signs of musculoskeletal disorders include weakness, lameness, limb swelling, and joint dysfunction. Nerve reaction and muscle function may be impaired as a result of changes to neuromuscular tissues. Problems with the muscles and skeleton may also affect other organ systems, including the urinary, digestive, and circulatory systems.

In order to diagnose the problem, a veterinarian will need to examine the cat and hear a careful recounting of any previous injuries and its overall health and history. A veterinarian may also use x-rays, ultrasonography, and other less common imaging techniques to visualize the cause of the lameness. Other techniques that might be used to aid in the diagnosis include withdrawal and examination of joint fluids, surgical inspection of the inside of a joint using an endoscope, electromyography, and tissue biopsy and examination.

Relieving pain is an important component of treatment for lame animals, and may allow faster recovery. Nonsteroidal anti-inflammatory drugs and other pain-relieving drugs are commonly used to control pain in lame animals. Other methods of pain relief, such as acupuncture, massage, and even changes to the diet may also be recommended. (For a more detailed discussion of LAMENESS, *see* page 178.)

▓ CONGENITAL AND INHERITED DISORDERS OF BONES, JOINTS, AND MUSCLES

Animals that contract viral infections in the womb may be born with diseased or deformed musculoskeletal systems. Abnormalities may also be congenital (present at birth) if a mother eats toxic plants at certain stages of the pregnancy. Some inherited (genetic) conditions affecting the musculoskeletal system may be neurologic in origin.

Dystrophy-like Myopathies

Numerous examples of progressive muscle diseases (also called myopathies) have been described in animals. Myopathies can be inherited, and many resemble various types of muscular dystrophy in humans. A Duchenne-like muscular dystrophy, similar to the one that affects dogs and humans, has been described in cats. It is a form of muscular dystrophy that

attacks the leg and pelvic muscles and can lead to disease of the heart muscle. Signs can include progressive muscular weakness, difficulty swallowing, stiffness of gait, and the wasting away of muscle. Such myopathies can lead to heart muscle disease and death. Male cats are more likely to be affected.

Glycogen Storage Disease (Glycogenosis)

Glycogen is a complex carbohydrate that is normally stored in the liver and muscles. The body converts it to glucose as a source of energy. Animals with glycogen storage diseases may weaken progressively until they are unable to rise from a lying position. To date, 5 of the 8 types of glycogen storage diseases characterized in humans have been identified in animals, including cats.

Osteogenesis Imperfecta

Cats with osteogenesis imperfecta inherit very fragile bones and loose joints. The long bones (such as the major bones of the front and hind legs) tend to be slender with thin outer layers. A veterinarian diagnosing the condition looks for evidence of recent breaks and fractures. The whites of the eyes of animals with osteogenesis imperfecta may also have a bluish tinge.

▓ DISORDERS ASSOCIATED WITH CALCIUM, PHOSPHORUS, AND VITAMIN D

Defective bone formation is called osteodystrophy. It is caused in most cases by deficiencies or imbalances of calcium, phosphorus, and vitamin D, all of which are important in creating and maintaining strong, healthy bones.

Rickets

Rickets is a disease of young, growing animals that causes soft and deformed bones. It is commonly caused by insufficient phosphorus or vitamin D in the diet. More rarely, calcium deficiencies are to blame. As in most diets causing defective

bone formation, the cause is typically
an imbalance in the ratio of calcium to
phosphorus. Animals fed all-meat diets
are commonly affected.

In affected kittens, the most common
signs are a reluctance to move, lameness
in the hind legs, bowing of the legs, and
the inability to control muscle movements. The skeletal disease becomes progressively more severe after 5 to 14 weeks.
The kittens become quiet and reluctant to
play; they assume a sitting position or lie
down with the hind legs stretched out
away from the body. Normal activities
may result in the sudden onset of severe
lameness due to incomplete or folding
fractures of one or more bones. In folding
fractures, pressure on the bones causes
them to slowly "fold" over and deform
instead of fracturing. Joints may also
appear swollen.

The outlook for treating rickets is good
if there are no broken bones or irreversible
damage to the bone. The primary treatment is to correct the diet. Exposure to
sunlight (ultraviolet radiation) will also
increase the production of vitamin D.

Recent studies show that many home-
made diets for cats are deficient in minerals
and fail to achieve a proper calcium-to-
phosphorus ratio. Therefore a high-quality
commercial food, or one designed by a
credentialed veterinary nutritionist, is
recommended.

Adult Rickets (Osteomalacia)

Osteomalacia develops similarly to rickets but in mature bones. It may be seen in
cats that remain indoors and that consume
an all-meat diet. The signs are similar to
those seen in kittens but may be less severe.
Over time, the bones become brittle and
fracture easily. Because bones mature at
different rates, both rickets and osteomalacia can be seen in the same animal.

Affected animals should be confined for
the first few weeks while the diet is corrected. The response to proper nutrition is
rapid. Within 1 week the animals become
more active and show an improved attitude.

Jumping or climbing must be prevented
because the skeleton is still susceptible to
fractures. Restrictions can usually be
relaxed after 3 weeks, but confinement
with limited movement is recommended
until the skeleton returns to normal.
Response to treatment can be monitored
using x-rays.

Metabolic Osteodystrophies (Defective Bone Formation due to Metabolic Abnormalities)

In both primary hyperparathyroidism
(see page 181) and renal secondary hyperparathyroidism (see below), defective
bone formation results from metabolic
abnormalities.

Rubber Jaw Syndrome (Renal Secondary Hyperparathyroidism)

A disorder seen occasionally in cats,
rubber jaw syndrome is caused by an
excess of parathyroid hormone (hyperparathyroidism) due to longterm kidney
disease or failure. With progressive kidney
disease, excess phosphate in the blood
leads to lower calcium levels. Decreased
calcium levels in turn trigger an increase
in parathyroid hormone levels. In addition, the kidneys are necessary to produce
the active form of vitamin D (calcitriol).
Too little calcitriol leads to further
increases in parathyroid hormone levels.

The most obvious signs include those
related to kidney malfunction (vomiting,
dehydration, excessive thirst and urination, depression), loose teeth that may fall
out while chewing, and jawbones that
become softened and pliable (rubber jaw
syndrome) and fail to close properly.

This type of hyperparathyroidism is
diagnosed when laboratory test results
show abnormalities consistent with kidney malfunction. Tests will also reveal
increased levels of parathyroid hormone
in the blood.

Treatment options include modifying the
diet, supplementing it with active vitamin
D (calcitriol), and giving medication that
binds phosphate. Any underlying kidney
disease must be managed as well. Prescrip-

tion diets with restricted dietary phosphorus are available. Your veterinarian can give you specific recommendations for proper treatment options for your cat. Be sure to follow those recommendations and any prescriptions precisely as directed.

■ JOINT DISORDERS

Some joint diseases, such as arthritis, affect the joint membranes themselves. Other types of joint conditions affect the tendons, cartilage, bursae, and fluid within the joint. Joint disorders may be congenital (present at birth) or may be the result of injury to the joint, abnormal development, immune-related conditions, or infections.

Displacement of the Kneecap

This hereditary disorder is caused by abnormal development of the kneecap (patella). Displacement of the kneecap is often associated with multiple deformities of the hindlimb, involving the hip joint, femur, and tibia.

Signs vary widely based on the severity of the displacement. In mild cases, the kneecap can be manually displaced but easily returned to normal position. As displacement becomes more severe, the dislocated kneecap is more often out of place, the limb is consistently lame, and bone deformities may be seen. X-rays can help your veterinarian see how severely the kneecap is displaced and what effects this has had on the limb.

There are several surgical options for treatment, depending on the severity of the displacement. Cats are less severely affected than dogs and have an excellent outlook for recovery.

Hip Dysplasia

Hip dysplasia is an abnormal development of the hip joints. It is rare in domestic cats but occurs more commonly in purebred cats. It is characterized by a loose hip joint that eventually leads to degenerative joint disease (osteoarthritis). Signs of hip dysplasia vary, and lameness may be mild to severe. Most cats require no surgical treatment; however, lifestyle changes such as weight reduction may help reduce discomfort.

Osteoarthritis (Degenerative Joint Disease)

The joint cartilage in freely moving joints may degenerate over time, leading to loss of joint movement and, in many cases, pain. Joint degeneration can be caused by trauma, infection, the body's own immune system, or malformation during development. This leads to inflammation of the joint membrane, continued cartilage destruction and inflammation, and abnormal joint function. Although more commonly diagnosed in dogs, this condition does occur in cats. It may not be noticed because of differences in the lifestyles of cats and dogs.

Signs of osteoarthritis include lameness, joint swelling, wasting away of muscle, thickening and scarring of the joint membrane, and a grating sound during joint movement. X-rays show increased fluid within the joint, soft-tissue swelling around the joint, the formation of bony outgrowths, hardening and thickening of bone beneath the cartilage, and sometimes a narrowed joint space.

Treatments can be either medical or surgical. Medical therapy may include the use of appropriate drugs to reduce pain and inflammation. Surgical options include joint fusion, joint replacement, cutting of the joint, and amputation. The outlook for recovery depends on the location and severity of the joint disease. Other treatments, including weight reduction, carefully monitored exercise on soft surfaces, and the use of joint-fluid modifiers, may help prevent further cartilage degeneration.

Septic Arthritis

Infectious, or septic, arthritis is usually caused by bacteria that spread through the blood or enter the body as a result of trauma (with penetrating wounds) or surgery. Other causes of septic arthritis include rickettsia and spirochetes. (*See also* INFECTIONS, page 1078.)

Signs of septic arthritis include lameness, swelling, pain of affected joint(s), fever, listlessness, loss of appetite, and stiffness. X-rays may reveal increased fluid within the joint in early cases and degenerative joint disease in longterm conditions. Laboratory tests on fluid removed from the joint may be useful in confirming the diagnosis.

Treatment consists of antibiotics administered by mouth or intravenously, flushing of the joint cavity, and surgical removal of dead, damaged, or infected tissue in severe cases.

Immune-mediated Arthritis

Arthritis caused by the body's own immune system can cause inflammation of joints. It generally affects several joints. In some types of immune-mediated arthritis, joint cartilage and bone beneath the cartilage is destroyed. **Feline progressive polyarthritis**, which resembles rheumatoid arthritis in people, is an example of the type of arthritis that destroys joint cartilage and bone beneath the cartilage. **Systemic lupus erythematosus** (*see* page 442) is the most common form of arthritis that causes inflammation of the joint without destruction of cartilage and bone. This condition may affect other organ systems, including the skin.

Signs of immune-mediated arthritis include lameness, pain and swelling in multiple joints, fever, a general feeling of illness, and persistent loss of appetite. These signs commonly come and go. In addition to signs, the diagnosis is aided by x-rays, biopsy of joint tissue, and examination of joint fluid (commonly called a joint tap).

Treatment involves anti-inflammatory medications and chemotherapeutic drugs. The outlook for recovery is uncertain. Relapses are relatively common and the cause of the reactions is often unknown.

Cancerous Arthritis

This type of arthritis is most commonly caused by a tumor known as a **synovial cell sarcoma**. It is the most common cancerous (malignant) tumor involving the joints. Signs include lameness and joint swelling. X-rays show soft-tissue swelling and a reaction around the bone. A biopsy reveals evidence of a soft-tissue tumor. Spread of the cancer to the lungs occurs in about 25% of animals; thus, amputation of the limb is usually recommended to prevent spreading.

Joint Trauma

Several types of joint trauma that can affect the joints in cats, including cranial cruciate ligament tears and palmar carpal ligament breakdown.

Cranial Cruciate Ligament Tear

Tearing of the cranial cruciate ligament of the knee joint (stifle) is usually caused by serious injury. However, injuries are more likely to occur when the joint structure is already weakened by degeneration, the animal's own immune system, or defects in conformation of the joint. Most injuries involve a tear in the middle of the ligament, although some result from bone separation at the origin of the ligament. A tear of this type can make the knee unstable and can lead to cartilage injury, buildup of joint fluid, bony outgrowths, and hardening and thickening of the joint membrane.

Signs include lameness, pain, joint swelling, fluid buildup, and a grating sound when the joint is moved. In addition, the joint may appear to be abnormally loose. Partial tears are characterized by a reduced ability to move the joint, especially bending it. X-rays may show the injury and/or damage to the joint; testing of fluid removed from the joint may also be used to help diagnose the condition.

Both medical and surgical treatment options are available. Physical therapy, weight reduction, and nonsteroidal anti-inflammatory drugs ease discomfort from inflammation and degenerative joint disease. The outlook after surgery is good as long as degenerative joint disease has not progressed too far.

Palmar Carpal Ligament Breakdown

Injuries sustained when falling or jumping can cause hyperextension, in which the limb extends beyond its normal range of motion. This produces excessive force on the wrist (carpus), which can cause tearing of the palmar carpal ligaments and fibrocartilage, leading to collapse of the joints. This is a rare problem in cats. Signs include lameness, swelling of the carpal joint, and a characteristic stance in which the heel is touching the ground. For mild cases a splint or cast may be sufficient, but surgery is usually required. Surgery involves fusing the affected joints using a bone plate and screws, pins and wires, or an external system. The outlook for recovery is good.

Dislocation of the Hip

Hip dislocation is usually the result of injury or trauma that displaces the head of the femur from the "socket" of the hip joint. Signs of hip dislocation include lameness, pain during movement of the hip joint, and a shortened limb. X-rays are useful in confirming the dislocation and

A sling may be used to help the dislocated hip remain in a normal position after treatment.

revealing the presence of fractures. Non-surgical treatment involves forcefully moving the joint back into place (closed manipulation) and using slings to keep the hip in its normal position. Surgical treatment involves stabilization using sutures or pins. Surgical resection of the bones involved or total hip replacement may be performed if more conservative treatment has not succeeded. The outlook for recovery is usually excellent.

■ MUSCLE DISORDERS

Myopathies are diseases that primarily cause damage to muscles or muscle tissues. They may be present at birth (congenital) or occur due to nutritional imbalances, muscle injury, or ingestion of a poisonous substance. **Myositides** are diseases that produce a mainly inflammatory reaction in muscle. Common causes include infections, parasitic diseases, and immune-mediated conditions.

Yellow Fat Disease (Steatitis)

Yellow fat disease is a condition in which inflammation of the fatty tissue (which develops a yellow tinge) occurs. It is thought that an excess of unsaturated fatty acids in the food, combined with a deficiency of vitamin E or other antioxidants, causes this condition. Most known cases have involved animals whose diet consists partially or completely of fish or fish byproducts. Fish are rich in fatty acids.

Affected cats are usually young and may be male or female. They are frequently obese. Early signs may include a dull hair coat or dry skin. Cats often become lethargic and lose agility. The back or abdomen becomes very tender. In advanced cases, even a light touch can cause pain. Lumpy deposits of fat under the skin may be seen. Fever is always present, and loss of appetite is common.

The cat's diet must be changed to exclude the source of excess fat. In addition, supplementing the diet with vitamin E in an appropriate form is usually recommended. Antibiotics are not helpful, as the condition is not bacterial. Because the condition is quite painful, affected cats should be handled as little as possible.

Hypokalemic Polymyopathy

Hypokalemic polymyopathy of cats is a muscle weakness disorder. It affects the whole body and is caused by potassium deficiency. Signs include generalized weakness, bending forward of the neck, stiffened posture, abnormal gait, persistent loss of appetite, and muscle pain. Blood and urine tests are used to confirm the diagnosis. The condition is treatable with dietary potassium supplements, given as recommended by a veterinarian. The outlook for recovery is excellent if the condition is diagnosed and treated quickly.

Muscle Tumors

Skeletal muscle tumors can be benign or cancerous (malignant). Malignant tumors can spread and invade nearby muscle. They can also spread to other parts of the body. Signs include localized swelling and lameness. The diagnosis is confirmed by taking a small tissue sample called a biopsy. The tumor generally must be surgically removed or the limb amputated. Chemotherapy and radiation may be used depending on the type of tumor. (*See also* CANCER, page 1233.)

▩ BONE DISORDERS

Bone diseases can be developmental, infectious, nutritional, or due to bone tumors, trauma, or unknown causes.

Developmental Bone Disorders

Developmental bone disorders appear in young animals when the bones do not grow correctly. They may be congenital (present at birth) or occur as the animal grows. Some of the more common causes include hereditary breed characteristics and dietary imbalances.

Osteochondromatosis (Multiple Exostoses)

Osteochondromatosis in young cats is an uncommon disorder characterized by multiple bony growths (known as osteochondromas) that arise from the surface of the long bones, vertebrae, and ribs. Animals may have no signs, and the diagnosis is confirmed by x-rays and physical examination of the growths. If lameness or pain develops, the masses can be surgically removed.

When osteochondromatosis occurs in older cats, it is believed to be caused by infection with the feline leukemia virus. The outlook in these cats is guarded.

Scottish Fold Osteodystrophy

This genetic condition of Scottish Fold cats is characterized by deformities of the bones of the spine (vertebrae), the metacarpal and metatarsal bones, and the toes due to the development of bony growths. Affected cats are lame, and the bones in question are deformed and swollen. Treatment involves surgery to remove the bony growths. The outlook for recovery is guarded.

Osteomyelitis

Osteomyelitis is inflammation of the bone. The condition is most often associated with bacterial infection, although fungal diseases may also cause osteomyelitis. Factors contributing to infection include an inadequate blood supply to the bone, trauma, inflammation, bone damage, and the spread of an infectious agent through the bloodstream.

General signs of osteomyelitis include lameness and pain. Cats may have pus-filled sores at the wound site, fever, persistent lack of appetite, and depression. X-rays, laboratory tests, and cultures to identify the source of infection can all help to confirm the diagnosis.

Longterm treatment with antibiotics, either injected or given by mouth, is the usual treatment. Additionally, flushing of the wound; removal of dead, damaged, or infected tissue; and removal of loose implants are recommended. Open or closed wound drainage and bone grafting can also be performed. In cases that persist or recur, limb amputation may be necessary. The outlook for recovery varies based on the severity of the infection and on how long it has remained untreated.

Nutritional Osteopathies

(*See also* DISORDERS ASSOCIATED WITH CALCIUM, PHOSPHORUS, AND VITAMIN D, page 447.)

Reduced bone mass, bone deformities, bony growths, fractures, and loose teeth (rubber jaw) are all conditions that can result from nutritional disturbances. These disturbances affect parathyroid hormone function and the metabolism of calcium and vitamins in the body. Specific causes may include an unbalanced diet resulting in an abnormally high level of parathyroid hormone (nutritional secondary hyperparathyroidism) or an abnormally high level of parathyroid hormone causing kidney damage (renal hyperparathyroidism), a deficiency of vitamin D, and excessive intake of vitamin A. Diagnosis is by blood tests, x-rays, and identification of any underlying nutritional cause. Treatment is aimed at reversing the specific cause. Surgery is rarely needed.

Nutritional secondary hyperparathyroidism refers to a calcium deficiency in cats that are fed an all-meat diet, which is high in phosphates and low in calcium. Over time, this diet causes the parathyroid glands to secrete parathyroid hormone in an effort to restore the normal balance of minerals in the body. Unfortunately, calcium is extracted from the skeleton, leading to thinning and weakening of bones. The condition is seen most often in kittens but may also occur in older indoor cats on an all-meat diet. If treated early with calcium supplementation and a balanced diet, most cats have a good outlook. However, if severe bone deformities have occurred, the outlook is poor.

Hypervitaminosis A is a condition that develops in cats whose diets contain excessive amounts of vitamin A (for example, diets that include a large quantity of liver). Although it is primarily considered a dis-

order of the nervous system, problems usually start when bony outgrowths form on the vertebrae. These cause deformities, interfere with normal movement, and can lead to nerve damage. The bony outgrowths may also occur in the elbows and other joints of the legs. If treated early (with a balanced diet), some signs may be reversed; however, skeletal changes are generally irreversible and the outlook is guarded.

Bone Tumors

Skeletal tumors can be benign or malignant (cancerous). They can either begin in the bone or spread from other areas of the body. The most common primary bone tumor is osteosarcoma of the radius, humerus, femur, or tibia.

Signs include lameness, bone swelling, and fractures of the bone that are not caused by injury. X-rays of the affected limb can help confirm the diagnosis. Chest x-rays should be performed to look for any original tumors that may be spreading to the bones. A bone biopsy is required to confirm the diagnosis.

The outlook for recovery is guarded. Untreated animals rarely live more than several months. The recommended treatments are limb amputation and chemotherapy. On average, cats live for 4 years after amputation.

Bone Fractures

Bone fractures are often caused by car accidents, firearms, fights, or falls. Fractures can involve single or multiple breaks in the bone and may be open (also called compound) or closed (*see* FIGURE, page 193). Open fractures have a wound or break in the skin that is associated with the fracture; closed fractures are those that do not produce an open wound. The shape and severity of the fracture depends on the force and type of the trauma. (*See also* EMERGENCIES, page 1050.)

Some common sites of fractures in cats include the thigh bone (femur), pelvis, jaws, and tail vertebrae. Signs of fracture are general and include lameness, pain, and swelling. X-rays are useful in determining the type and extent of the fracture. Treatment is based on the type of fracture, the cat's age and health, the owner's finances, and the surgeon's technical expertise.

Incomplete fractures in young, healthy cats can be treated with external splints or casts. Other injuries are treated with bone plates, screws, orthopedic wires, or pins. Bone grafts are frequently used to help healing. Antibiotics are given to keep open fractures from becoming infected. Appropriate pain-relieving medication is used to reduce discomfort.

The outlook for recovery is usually good, depending on the injury and the success of the surgery. Followup care includes x-rays and veterinary checkups to assess how the fracture is healing. Removal of internal implants like bone plates or screws is not necessary unless complica-tions such as stress protection, infection, and soft-tissue irritation develop. Fractures of the vertebrae that lead to damage of the spinal cord have a guarded to poor outlook, although surgical repair is sometimes possible when the damage is not extensive.

■ SARCOCYSTOSIS

In sarcocystosis, the muscles and other soft tissues are invaded by single-celled organisms called protozoans of the genus *Sarcocystis*. Although their final hosts are predators such as dogs and cats, these organisms form cysts in various intermediate hosts, including cattle, pigs, humans, rodents, and reptiles. Some cysts are visible to the naked eye, but others are too small to see. Their size depends on the species of the host and the species of *Sarcocystis*. A cat can develop sarcocystosis after eating undercooked beef or pork containing sporocysts or after eating food infected with sporocysts from another animal's feces. Infected cats often have no signs, although a mild diarrhea may be seen.

As noted above, humans may serve as intermediate hosts and may develop inflammation and soreness of muscles and blood vessels. This condition is rare, and the source of human infection has never been determined. Signs include nausea, abdominal pain, and diarrhea lasting up to 48 hours. The extent of human illness caused by infected meat has not been documented.

Because most adult cattle and sheep and many pigs harbor cysts in their muscles, cats should not be allowed to eat raw meat, edible organs (such as heart, liver, tongue, and brains), or dead animals. Supplies of grain and feed should be kept covered. Cats should not be allowed in buildings used to store feed or house animals. No vaccine is available. Experiments have shown that infected pork can be made safe for consumption by cooking at 158°F (70°C) for 15 minutes or by freezing at 25°F (-4°C) for 2 days or -4°F (-20°C) for 1 day.

An incomplete fracture may be treated by a splint or cast.

32
Brain, Spinal Cord, and Nerve Disorders

■ THE NERVOUS SYSTEM

The nervous system is made up of the **brain, spinal cord,** and several different kinds of **nerves** that are found throughout the body. These create complex circuits through which animals experience and respond to sensations.

A familiar type of nervous system circuit is a **reflex.** Reflexes are simple networks found in the nervous system of all animals. For example, when the eyelid is touched, it closes; when the toe is pinched, the foot pulls away automatically.

Many different types of diseases can affect the nervous system, including birth defects, infections, inflammatory conditions, poisoning, metabolic disorders, nutritional disorders, injuries, degenerative diseases, or cancer. Neurologic diseases are often more common in a particular breed or sex, or tend to occur at a certain age.

■ PARTS OF THE NERVOUS SYSTEM

The **central nervous system** includes the spinal cord and the brain. The brain is divided into 3 main sections—the **brain stem**, which controls many basic life functions, the **cerebrum**, which is the center of conscious decision-making, and the

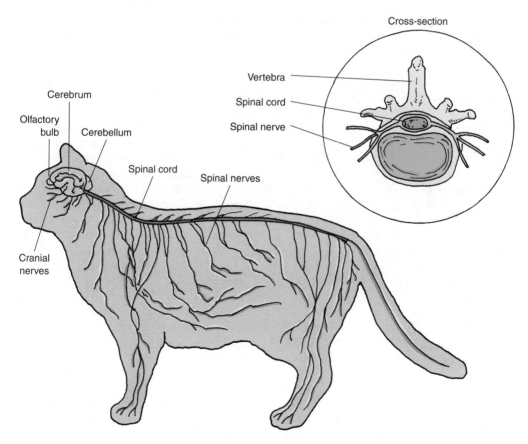

The nervous system of the cat

cerebellum, which is involved in movement and motor control. The spinal cord of cats is divided into regions that correspond to the vertebral bodies (the bones that make up the spine) in the following order from neck to tail: cervical, thoracic, lumbar, sacral, and caudal segments. Specialized tissues called **meninges** cover the brain and spinal cord, and cerebrospinal fluid surrounds and protects the brain and spinal cord.

The **peripheral nervous system** consists of the nerves that are found throughout the rest of the body.

Neurons

Both the central and peripheral nervous systems contain billions of cells known as **neurons.** Neurons connect with each other to form neurological circuits. Information travels along these circuits via electrical signals.

All neurons have a center portion called a **cell body** and 2 extensions called **dendrites** and **axons**. Dendrites receive signals from other neurons and transmit electrical charges *to* the cell body. Axons transmit the electrical charges *away* from the cell body. When the current reaches the end of the axon, the axon releases chemicals called **neurotransmitters**. Neurotransmitters pass the signal to the dendrites of other neurons, or to muscles or glands.

Neurons in the peripheral nervous system combine to form pairs of **spinal nerves** and pairs of **cranial nerves**. The spinal nerves arise from the spinal cord and extend axons outward into the front and hind legs and to the bladder, anus, and tail. These nerves subdivide into smaller nerves that cover the entire surface and interior of the body. The cranial nerves include sensory and motor neurons that connect the head and face to the brain.

Types of Neurons

Sensory neurons carry information from the body to the spinal cord or brain stem, and then on to the cerebellum and cerebrum for interpretation. Sensory information includes sensations of pain, position, touch, temperature, taste, hearing, balance, vision, and smell.

Motor neurons carry responses to the sensory information from the spinal cord and brain to the rest of the body. Inside the spinal cord, the axons of motor neurons form bundles known as **tracts**, which transmit this information to motor peripheral nerves going to muscles in the limbs. Motor neurons are important for voluntary movements and muscle control.

A specialized set of neurons controls and regulates basic, unconscious bodily functions that support life such as the pumping of the heart and digestion. These neurons make up what is called the **autonomic nervous system**, which sends axons from the brain stem and spinal cord to various areas of the body such as the heart muscle, the digestive system, and the pupils of the eyes.

■ NERVOUS SYSTEM DISORDERS AND EFFECTS OF INJURIES

A change in an animal's ability to sense its environment can be caused by disease in either the central nervous system or the peripheral nervous system. The primary signs of nervous system disorders include behavioral changes, seizures, tremors, pain, numbness, lack of coordination, and weakness or paralysis of one or more legs. The effects of an injury on sensory and motor functions depend on its location and severity.

A spinal cord injury can cause loss of feeling and paralysis below the level of the injury. Mild spinal cord injuries can result in clumsy movement and mild weakness of the limbs. Moderate spinal cord injuries can cause a greater weakness of the limbs. In severe spinal cord injuries, a complete loss of movement (paralysis) and feeling can occur. However, not all spinal cord injuries cause paralysis. For example, injury to the spinal cord in the lower back can result not in limb paralysis but in loss of bladder control.

Brain injuries result in different effects, again depending on which part of the brain is affected. Injuries to the brain stem can cause a loss of balance, weakness of the limbs, hyperactive reflexes, stupor, or coma. Injuries to the cerebellum can result in a lack of coordination of the head and legs, tremors, and a loss of balance. Injuries to the cerebrum can cause complete or partial blindness, loss of the sense of smell, seizures, coma, stupor, pacing or circling behavior, and inability to recognize an owner.

Some injuries to the nervous system can cause damage that is not evident until 24 to 48 hours after the injury occurs. Longterm damage is usually caused by swelling or internal bleeding of the vessels in the brain. Strokes caused by clogged arteries or high blood pressure are rare in pets.

Mechanisms of Disease

In addition to the effects of injuries, nervous system disorders can include birth defects, infections and inflammations, poisoning, metabolic disorders, nutritional deficiencies, degenerative diseases, or cancer.

Most birth defects, often called **congenital disorders**, are obvious at birth or shortly after. Some genetic diseases cause the neurons to degenerate slowly and irreversibly in the first year of life. In other inherited diseases, such as epilepsy, the animal may not show any signs for 2 to 3 years.

Infections of the nervous system are caused by specific viruses or microorganisms. Other inflammations such as certain types of meningitis can be caused by the body's own overactive immune system. These are known as **autoimmune disorders**. Various chemicals can cause a toxic reaction in the nervous system. These include certain pesticides and herbicides, rat poisons, antifreeze, and sedatives. Botulism, tetanus, and tick bites, as well as coral and tiger snake venom, can also affect the nervous system and cause paralysis.

Some metabolic disorders affect the function of the nervous system, including low blood sugar, shortness or loss of breath, liver disease, and kidney failure. Thyroid gland abnormalities can also cause neurologic signs.

Tumors of the Nervous System

Tumors of the nervous system are classified by the cell type affected, the behavior of the tumor, the pattern of growth, and any secondary changes seen in and around the tumor. Tumors affecting the nervous system are less common in cats than in dogs. (For a more detailed discussion, *see* page 197.)

■ THE NEUROLOGIC EVALUATION

Evaluation of the nervous system begins with an accurate history and general physical examination, followed by a neurologic examination. There are a number of specific physical tests that can be carried out to evaluate the functioning of the various components of the nervous system. These include tests of various reflexes, muscle function and control, and posture and gait.

Laboratory tests are often needed to diagnose the specific problem. Common laboratory tests include blood tests, urinalysis, analysis of the cerebrospinal fluid, x-rays, computed tomography (CT) scans, magnetic resonance imaging (MRI), and evaluation of the electrical activity of the brain, peripheral nerves, and muscles.

The Neurologic Examination

A neurologic examination evaluates 1) the cranial nerves, 2) the gait, or walk, 3) the neck and front legs, and 4) the torso, hind legs, anus, and tail. Your cat's reflexes will also be tested to determine, if possible, the location of the injury in the brain, spinal cord, or nerves in the peripheral nervous system.

Evaluation of the Cranial Nerves

The 12 pairs of cranial nerves extend from specific segments of the brain stem to the left and right sides of the head. They include the nerves that transmit smell, those responsible for vision and the movement of the eyes, those that control facial movements, those responsible for hearing and balance, and those responsible for chewing, swallowing, vocalizing, and movement of the tongue (*see* TABLE 13, page 198). Testing the reflexes of these nerves can help identify the location of the damage. Your veterinarian will perform specific tests designed to pinpoint any signs of dysfunction in these nerves.

An evaluation of the cranial nerves tests mental activity, head posture and coordination, and reflexes on the head. Signs identified during this evaluation indicate an injury or disease of the brain. Signs of damage to the cerebrum and brain stem can include mental deterioration, constant pacing, seizures, depression, coma, or a head turn or circling in one direction. A head tilt, bobbing, tremors, or other unusual head movements may indicate damage to the cerebellum.

Evaluation of Gait (Walking)

Your veterinarian will evaluate the gait by watching your cat as it walks, runs, turns, steps to the side, and backs up. Signs of dysfunction include circling, weakness or complete paralysis of any limbs, falling, stumbling, rolling, or loss of coordination.

Evaluation of the Neck and Front Legs

Evaluation of the neck and front legs will include searching for evidence of pain and loss of muscle size or tone, which may indicate an injury to the upper spinal cord. Various types of tests are done to help detect minor spinal cord injuries.

Some examples of tests that are commonly used to evaluate the neck and front legs include the wheelbarrow test (in which the back legs are lifted slightly and the cat is evaluated while walking on its front legs), the righting test (in which the cat is placed on its side or upside down to see how well it can right itself), and the positioning test (in which a foot or limb is moved from its normal position in order to evaluate how quickly and accurately

the cat resumes its normal stance). Spinal reflexes and muscle condition are also evaluated.

Evaluation of the Torso, Hind Limbs, Anus, and Tail

The trunk, or torso, is evaluated for abnormal posture or position of the vertebrae, pain, loss of feeling or hypersensitivity to light touch or pinpricking, and loss of muscle mass. Some tests used to evaluate the nerves of the neck and front legs (*see* above) are also used to evaluate the torso and hind legs. Various reflexes can also be evaluated. Loss of muscle around the torso or hind legs can indicate damage to a nerve associated with that muscle.

Laboratory Tests and Imaging

Blood tests are often used to detect metabolic disorders, some of which can affect nervous system activity. Blood tests can also identify other conditions, including lead poisoning, certain infections, and myasthenia gravis, an autoimmune disease in which the connections between nerve and muscle are blocked and weakness results.

Analysis of cerebrospinal fluid (the fluid that surrounds the brain and spinal cord) is often useful for diagnosing a central nervous system disorder. Cerebrospinal fluid is collected from the base of the skull or from the lower back in a procedure called a **spinal tap**. An unusually high amount of protein in the cerebrospinal fluid may indicate encephalitis (inflammation of the brain), meningitis (inflammation of the covering of the brain), cancer, or a compressive injury of the spinal cord. Increased numbers of white blood cells in the cerebrospinal fluid indicate an inflammation or infection. Other disorders that can be identified by cerebrospinal fluid analysis include bacterial or fungal infections, internal bleeding, brain abscesses, and some types of tumors. Cerebrospinal fluid can also be tested for the presence of infectious diseases.

Several different types of radiographic tests can be used to detect disorders of the nervous system. **Plain x-rays** of the skull and spine can detect fractures, infections, or bone cancer. However, in most infections or cancers of the brain and spinal cord, plain x-rays appear normal. In a procedure known as **myelography,** a special liquid dye is injected into the cerebrospinal canal. This dye can highlight specific types of spinal problems, such as herniated ("slipped") disks and spinal cord tumors. **Computed tomography (CT)** and **magnetic resonance imaging (MRI) scans** can also help evaluate changes in bone structure, internal bleeding, abscesses, inflammation, and certain nervous system cancers.

Other tests may be used in some cases. An **electroencephalogram** records electrical activity in the brain. Results are abnormal in meningitis or encephalitis, head injuries, and brain tumors. An electroencephalogram can sometimes help determine the cause and severity of a seizure. An **electromyogram** records electrical activity in muscles and nerves. In this test, a nerve is stimulated electrically, and the speed of conduction along the neurons is calculated. This technique can detect nerve injury and myasthenia gravis. A **brain stem auditory evoked response (BAER)** records electrical activity in the pathway from the sound receptors in the ear to the brain stem and cerebrum. In cases of deafness caused by nerve damage, the BAER generates no response. Brain-stem disorders may also change the BAER.

▨ PRINCIPLES OF THERAPY

Once a diagnosis is made, appropriate therapy can be considered. There are several groups of drugs that are used to treat disorders of the nervous system. Drugs used to treat epileptic seizures are known as anticonvulsants. Anti-inflammatory medications, including corticosteroids, are used to reduce swelling and inflammation in many types of injuries. These medications may be given intravenously in some cases (such as spinal cord injury) and by mouth in others. Other medications

may be needed to relieve muscle spasms caused by neurologic disorders or to treat infections of the nervous system.

After cranial surgery, and in animals with brain tumors or head injuries, there is a risk of swelling caused by an accumulation of fluid in the brain. Mannitol or corticosteroid medications can be given intravenously to reduce the swelling. (For a more detailed discussion of DRUGS USED TO TREAT BRAIN, SPINAL CORD, AND NERVE DISORDERS, *see* page 1130.)

Nursing Care

Paraplegic or quadriplegic animals need intensive nursing care. The cat should be kept on padding and turned every 4 to 6 hours to help prevent sores from developing on the skin. The skin must be kept clean and free of urine and feces. Urinalyses must be done every 2 to 4 weeks to monitor for bladder infection. Quadriplegic animals need to be hand fed and given plenty of water. Manually flexing and massaging the cat's joints and muscles can delay muscle wasting in paralyzed limbs.

▨ CONGENITAL AND INHERITED DISORDERS

Some congenital defects (defects present at birth), are inherited from the parents, while others are caused by environmental factors in the womb, such as nutritional deficiencies or some viral infections. For many, the cause is unknown.

Kittens are born with a nervous system that is not fully developed, and birth defects may not become apparent until they begin to walk. In some cases, evidence of an inherited disorder may not be seen until the cat has reached adulthood, even though the defect has been present since birth.

Birth defects of the nervous system are categorized according to the primary region of the nervous system affected: forebrain, cerebellum, spinal cord, peripheral nerve and muscle disorders, or multifocal disorders that include signs of more than one area. Many of these inherited disorders are rare or breed-specific, or both. A few of the more common disorders of each area are described below.

Forebrain Disorders

Hydranencephaly has been described mainly in kittens who were exposed to feline panleukopenia virus/parvovirus (*see* page 536) while in the womb. This can also cause brain stem malformations and cerebellar hypoplasia.

Cerebellar Disorders

In **cerebellar hypoplasia,** the cerebellum does not develop completely. This is caused by exposure of the kitten to feline panleukopenia virus/parvovirus (*see* page 536) while in the womb. The kitten typically has a tremor that does not worsen as the cat matures, and affected animals can be good pets. Hydrocephalus can also be found in animals with cerebellar disorders.

Spinal Cord Disorders

Spina bifida occulta is a condition seen in Manx cats as a result of the spinal changes resulting in the tailless body type.

Peripheral Nerve and Muscle Disorders

Neuropathy of hereditary hyperchylomicronemia (hyperlipidemia) is an inherited disorder that causes peripheral nerve damage in cats. Signs do not develop until the kitten is at least 8 months of age. This condition causes granules of fat to be deposited within nerves, and some studies show that the signs can be controlled by a low-fat diet. **Congenital megaesophagus** is an enlarged esophagus that is inherited in Siamese cats. Signs include frequent vomiting and pneumonia.

▦ DISORDERS OF THE PERIPHERAL NERVES

Disorders of the peripheral nerves include degenerative diseases, inflammatory diseases, metabolic disorders, cancers, nutritional disorders, toxic disorders, disorders caused by injury, and vascular diseases.

Inflammatory Disorders

Acquired myasthenia gravis is a disease of the connections between the muscles and nerves. It is uncommon in cats. (For a more detailed discussion, *see* page 202.)

Acute idiopathic polyradiculoneuritis causes inflammation of peripheral nerves. It is uncommon in cats. (For a more detailed discussion, *see* page 202.)

Chronic inflammatory demyelinating polyneuropathy is seen in adult cats. The cause is unknown. Partial paralysis slowly spreads to all 4 legs with weakened reflexes. Sometimes, the cranial nerves are also affected. Signs usually improve after treatment with corticosteroids, but relapse may occur when therapy is stopped.

Trigeminal neuritis is common in dogs, but uncommon in cats. (For a more detailed discussion, *see* page 202.)

Metabolic Disorders

Diabetic neuropathy is an uncommon complication of diabetes seen more often in cats than in dogs. Signs include weakness, loss of motor control, and muscle wasting. Affected animals often have nerve dysfunction in their lower legs, which results in a flat-footed stance. High blood sugar is the likely underlying cause. Diagnosis requires evidence of diabetes and a nerve biopsy. In some cases, insulin therapy can lead to partial or complete recovery.

Tumors

Several different types of **nerve sheath tumors** can be found in animals, but are most common in dogs and cattle. (For a more detailed discussion, *see* page 203.)

Toxic Disorders

Intermediate organophosphate poisoning is especially common in cats, due to exposure to pesticides that contain chlorpyrifos. Often, signs are not obvious initially, but instead cats develop weakness in all 4 legs and abnormal neck position several days after exposure. Cats usually recover after several weeks of drug treatment. (*See also* ORGANOPHOSPHATES, page 1169.)

Tick paralysis (*see* page 469) is caused by the bite of several species of ticks that results in rapidly progressing paralysis. In Australia, the tick *Ixodes holocyclus* causes an especially severe form of tick paralysis. Signs begin with partial paralysis in the hind legs that worsens within 24 to 72 hours to total paralysis in all 4 legs. Sensory perception and consciousness remain normal. Difficulty swallowing, facial paralysis, jaw muscle weakness, and respiratory paralysis may develop in severe cases. Treatment consists of removing the tick and applying a skin ointment to kill any hidden ticks. For all except *Ixodes holocyclus* cases in Australia, recovery usually occurs in 1 to 2 days. A serum is available for treatment of *Ixodes holocyclus* paralysis, but death from respiratory paralysis can occur despite treatment.

Injury and Trauma

Brachial plexus avulsion occurs in cats due to injury to the spinal nerve roots in the neck and shoulder area that extend nerves into the front legs. In a severe injury, the nerve roots may stretch or tear from their attachment to the spinal cord. Signs vary depending on the severity. If the nerves are completely torn, paralysis of the leg and a loss of sensation and reflexes below the elbow result. The animal puts little or no weight on the leg and drags the paw on the ground. The leg may need to be amputated because of damage from dragging or self-mutilation. Recovery is possible in mild cases in which the nerve roots are bruised but not completely torn.

Peripheral nerve injuries are common in traumatic injuries. The **sciatic nerve**, which runs from the lower back to the hind legs, may be injured by hip fractures or during surgery to correct a broken leg. Irritants injected in or near the nerve can also cause nerve damage. The leg may be partially paralyzed, or the animal may not be able to bend the knee. The paw and toes cannot flex or extend. There may be loss of sensation below the knee. Injury to the branches of the sciatic nerve in the lower leg, such as the **tibial nerve** or the **peroneal nerve**, can result in an inability to extend the paw or flex the toes and reduced sensation over the surface of the foot.

For function to return after nerve connections are lost, the nerve must regenerate from the point of injury all the way to where it ends in the muscle. Nerve tissue regenerates or heals very slowly. Recovery is unlikely if the severed ends of the nerve are widely separated or if scar tissue interferes with healing. Anti-inflammatory drugs have been used to treat traumatic nerve injuries, but there is little evidence of any benefit. Surgery should be performed promptly in cases in which the nerve has been cut. In cases of injury from a fall or a blunt object, surgical exploration and removal of scar tissue may help. Longterm care consists of physical therapy to minimize muscle wasting and to keep the joints moving. Bandages or splints may be necessary to help protect a damaged limb.

Blood Vessel (Vascular) Diseases

Ischemic neuromyopathy is most common in cats with arterial thromboembolism, a condition that develops secondary to disease of the heart muscle (*see* page 382). Emboli lodge in the arteries, blocking blood flow to the area. Blockage occurs most commonly at the aorta, resulting in damage to the muscles and nerves in the hind legs. Partial paralysis develops, and the cat may be unable to flex or extend the leg, lose the knee reflexes, and lose sensation in the lower leg. Diagnosis is based on the history and signs, as well as ultrasound scanning to analyze blood flow to the legs. Underlying heart disease must be treated. Neurologic signs can improve within 2 to 3 weeks, but 6 months may be needed for complete recovery. Permanent damage is possible. Health risks persist for many animals because of the underlying disease and high possibility of recurrence.

■ DISORDERS OF THE SPINAL COLUMN AND CORD

Diseases of the spinal column and cord include congenital defects (discussed earlier in this chapter), degenerative diseases, inflammatory and infectious diseases, tumors, nutritional diseases, injury and trauma, toxic disorders, and vascular diseases.

Degenerative Diseases

Degenerative lumbosacral stenosis is a disorder of the vertebrae in the lower back that causes compression of the nerve roots. It is uncommon in cats. (For a more detailed discussion, *see* page 204.)

Intervertebral disk disease is a degenerative disease of the spinal column that results in compression of the spinal cord and spinal nerves. It is a common cause of spinal cord disorders in dogs, but rare in cats. (For a more detailed discussion, *see* page 204.)

Inflammatory and Infectious Diseases

Infectious and inflammatory diseases of the spinal column and spinal cord include bacterial, rickettsial, viral, fungal, protozoal, and parasitic infections. Many of these diseases, such as meningitis and encephalitis, can also affect the brain. Some of the more common infectious and inflammatory diseases that affect the spinal column or cord are discussed below.

Bacterial Diseases

Diskospondylitis is inflammation of the disk between 2 vertebrae (bones in the spinal column). The vertebrae can also be inflamed without infection of the disk. It is rare in cats and is usually due to direct spread of infection from a nearby wound. (For a more detailed discussion, *see* page 205.)

Viral Diseases

Feline infectious peritonitis is a disease of domestic cats caused by an abnormal immune response to a coronavirus. This condition causes damage to the meninges and to the cells that produce cerebrospinal fluid. Signs of spinal cord inflammation include spinal pain and partial paralysis in 2 or 4 legs. Signs affecting the blood and other organs, especially the eyes, are also common. Available blood tests are unreliable. Analysis of cerebrospinal fluid can be helpful in diagnosis. There is no effective treatment, and the prognosis for recovery is poor.

Myelopathy associated with feline leukemia virus causes nerve damage and affects some cats that have been infected with the feline leukemia virus (*see* page 533) for more than 2 years. The main signs are loss of motor control and weakness in the hind legs, which can progress to paraplegic paralysis within a year. Other signs include spinal pain and abnormal behavior. Diagnosis is based on the signs, blood tests, and eliminating other possible causes. There is no treatment.

Rabies (*see* page 467) is caused by a viral infection that spreads to the central nervous system from the peripheral nerves. Rabies is common throughout the world except in Japan, and some other islands, including New Zealand, Iceland, and Hawaii. Initial signs are extremely variable, and rabies should be considered a possibility in any unvaccinated animal with severe neurologic dysfunction. Signs that the infection has reached the spinal cord include a loss of motor control and progressive paralysis, usually with a loss of reflexes. Affected animals typically, but not invariably, die within 2 to 7 days of when signs begin. There is no treatment. Vaccination is essential for prevention.

Fungal Diseases

Cryptococcus neoformans is the most common fungus to cause a central nervous system infection in cats. Other fungal organisms may also invade the central nervous system. Infections often affect other organs, such as the lungs, eyes, skin, or bones. Signs of spinal cord infection include partial or total paralysis and spinal pain. Blood or cerebrospinal fluid tests are necessary to diagnose an infection and identify the organism.

Treatment and the outlook for recovery depend on the specific fungus involved. The drug fluconazole is often effective for *Cryptococcus* infections. Infections with *Blastomyces* or *Histoplasma* fungi are difficult to treat, and the outlook for recovery in cats infected with these fungi is uncertain.

Protozoal Diseases

Toxoplasmosis (*see* page 545) is caused by a protozoan called *Toxoplasma gondii*, which can occasionally cause inflammation of the brain and spinal cord. Infected cats usually have signs of disease in other organs. A blood test or tissue sample can diagnose the infection. Various drugs are recommended for treatment.

Parasitic Diseases

Verminous myelitis is inflammation of the spinal cord caused by a parasite. The most common cause in cats is larvae of *Cuterebra* flies. Signs of spinal cord inflammation strike suddenly and severely, often affecting one side of the body more than the other, and may progressively worsen over time. This condition is difficult to diagnose except by examination of tissue after death. Drug treatment can be beneficial, but a full recovery is uncertain.

Inflammatory Diseases of Unknown Cause

Feline nonsuppurative meningoencephalomyelitis, also called feline polioencephalomyelitis or staggering disease, is a slowly progressive, inflammatory disease of the central nervous system in domestic cats. It has been reported in North America, Europe, and Australia. The cause is unknown, but a virus or some other infectious agent is probably involved. The disease causes the neurons to degenerate and is most severe in the thoracic segments of the spinal cord. The disease is difficult to diagnosis in a living animal, and there is no treatment, so the outlook is poor. Signs begin with weakness in the legs for 1 to 2 months, followed by sensitivity to touch, head tremors, and changes in behavior.

Tumors

In cats, **lymphoma** is the most common tumor to affect the spinal cord. Adult cats of any age can be affected. There is a sudden and severe or slowly progressive onset of signs that center around a specific, often painful, tumor on the spinal cord. About 85% of affected cats have positive tests for feline leukemia virus (*see* page 533). Treatment consists of combination chemotherapy. Remission is possible, but the longterm outlook is poor.

Nutritional Disorders

Hypervitaminosis A can develop in cats that are fed diets that contain excess vitamin A, such as diets that contain a large amount of liver. Signs include neck pain and rigidity with foreleg lameness. Reducing the amount of vitamin A will prevent further damage but does not reverse the damage that has already occurred.

Injury and Trauma

Spinal cord injuries usually occur as a result of a spinal fracture or dislocation. Common causes in cats include automobile accidents, bite wounds, and gunshot wounds. The injury not only causes initial damage to the spinal cord, but also causes secondary damage from swelling, bleeding, destruction of the nerve sheath, and tissue decay. Signs of spinal trauma typically have a sudden onset, and may progressively worsen. Severe spinal cord injury to the middle or lower back may cause a rigid paralysis, or a limp paralysis that spreads to the entire body over several days and leads to death from respiratory paralysis. Fractured or dislocated vertebrae can often be seen on x-rays. Drug treatment can be helpful if started within the first few hours of injury. Animals with mild neurologic signs from injury often recover after 4 to 6 weeks of cage rest. Surgery is necessary for some types of injuries that cause severe neurologic signs. In cats that have lost the ability to feel pain at locations below the spinal injury, the outlook for recovery is poor.

Poisoning and Toxic Disorders

Delayed organophosphate intoxication can be seen after ingestion or skin contact with insecticides or pesticides that contain organophosphates. In addition to the signs of severe exposure (*see* page 1169), delayed paralysis can develop 1 to 4 weeks after exposure. Partial paralysis of the hind legs worsens progressively and occasionally all 4 legs become paralyzed. A veterinarian will need a history of the cat's possible chemical exposure to make the correct diagnosis. The outlook for recovery is poor for animals with severe signs.

Tetanus is caused by toxins produced by *Clostridium tetani* bacteria that usually enter the body at the site of a wound. Cats are fairly resistant to tetanus, but cases do sometimes occur. Signs usually develop within 5 to 10 days of infection and include muscle stiffness and rigid leg extension, inability to swallow, protruding eyelids, and locking of the jowl and facial muscles. In severe cases, the animal may be unable to stand as a result of muscle spasms. Treatment consists of wound care, antibiotics to kill any remaining organisms, and tetanus antitoxin. In mild cases, a cat may recover completely with early treatment. In severe cases, death may occur due to respiratory paralysis.

▓ DYSAUTONOMIA

Feline dysautonomia is a disorder of the autonomic nervous system, which controls many reflexes and other neurologic functions. All breeds and age groups are susceptible. Feline dysautonomia was first reported in 1982 and initially became widespread in the UK; the incidence declined considerably but recently seems to have risen again. Cases have been reported throughout Europe, a few have been documented in North America, and sporadic cases have been seen in Dubai, New Zealand, and Venezuela. The cause is unknown.

Signs range widely in severity and can develop rapidly or be slowly progressive.

Initial signs include mental dullness, loss of appetite, upper respiratory signs, or diarrhea. Additional signs include dilated and unresponsive pupils, drooping or protruding eyelids, difficulty swallowing, vomiting, constipation, and dehydration. The heart rate may slow down, and the cat may develop urinary or fecal incontinence.

Definitive diagnosis requires a tissue sample. Feline leukemia virus infection (*see* page 533) can also cause some of the signs seen in dysautonomia.

The main aim of therapy is first to rehydrate the cat and then to maintain adequate fluid balance. Supportive care includes keeping the cat warm, supporting respiratory function, administering eye drops, and assisting with grooming. A laxative may be needed for constipation. A small number of cats have recovered, and others are able to survive with lingering signs. However, such improvements often take up to a year. In general, the outlook is poor for severely affected cats.

▓ FACIAL PARALYSIS

Facial paralysis in cats may result from injuries caused by rough handling or other trauma, such as automobile accidents or ear infection. Paralysis on one side of the face is common when the facial nerve is damaged. Facial paralysis on both sides of the face can be more difficult to recognize, but affected animals often drool and have a dull facial expression. In total facial paralysis, the animal cannot move its eyelids, ears, lips, or nostrils. In partial paralysis, the muscles of facial expression move less than normal.

The signs of facial paralysis vary with the location and severity of the injury. One or both sides of the face can be affected. Usually, the signs include loss of motor function, including the inability to blink, a drooping ear, a drooping upper lip, and drooling from the corner of the mouth. When the animal eats or drinks, food and water may fall out of the mouth.

Infection of the inner ear is another common cause of facial paralysis; this can be diagnosed with magnetic resonance imaging (MRI) or computed tomography (CT) scans. The prognosis for recovery can be good if the diagnosis is made early and the animal receives appropriate antibiotic treatment. However, the facial nerve paralysis can be permanent, and longterm administration of eye drops may be necessary.

Idiopathic facial paralysis (like Bell's palsy in humans) is diagnosed in the absence of infection, injury, or trauma. Domestic long-haired cats are at increased risk. There is no treatment, and regular administration of lubricating eye drops may be necessary. One or both sides of the face can be affected, and the condition can be either temporary or permanent. It can occur on one side, disappear, and then occur on the other side at a later time.

Electromyography, including electrical stimulation of the facial nerve, can be used to determine the location and severity of the injury. There is no specific therapy for injury except electroacupuncture, massage, and heat applied to the affected muscles. Some animals may also need special water containers and soft food. The facial nerve can slowly regenerate, so repeated neurologic examinations can help determine if an animal is recovering. If there has been no improvement after 6 months, the chance of recovery is poor.

Paralysis on one side of the face is common when the facial nerve is damaged.

■ CENTRAL NERVOUS SYSTEM DISORDERS CAUSED BY PARASITES

A number of parasites (including worms and insects) are associated with central nervous system disease. Diagnosis requires eliminating other possible causes of illness, such as rabies, and identifying the specific parasite responsible.

Flukes

Two species of *Paragonimus* lung flukes can migrate to the nervous system and produce cysts in the brain and spinal cord of cats, dogs, and people.

Schistosomes, or blood flukes, normally deposit their eggs in the blood vessels of the gut and urinary bladder, from which they pass into the external environment via the feces or urine. Some eggs, however, may get into the bloodstream and reach the central nervous system where they form capsules. This condition has been seen in people and domestic animals.

Roundworms

Several types of nematodes are found in domestic animals.

The larvae of some ascarid roundworms, including *Toxocara* species, can invade the central nervous system and cause localized damage in cats. *Toxocara* larvae may also invade the eye and cause vision loss in people.

Baylisascaris procyonis is a roundworm found in the small intestine of raccoons. Its larvae can infect people and domesticated animals and migrate to the central nervous system. This parasite can also cause central nervous system and eye damage in people, particularly children.

Dirofilaria immitis is more commonly known as the canine heartworm, but it can also affect cats. In addition to the heart and lungs, other parts of the body, including the central nervous system and the eye, can be infected.

Gurlita paralysans is found in the spinal veins of cats and has reportedly produced a high incidence of paralysis.

Disease from Insects

Myiasis is the development of certain types of larval flies (bots and warbles) within the body's tissues or organs. The larvae of *Cuterebra*, which are deposited under the skin in dogs or cats, have been known to wander into the central nervous system and affect the cerebrum or cerebellum. Organophosphate drugs can eliminate certain insect larvae from the nervous system, but they can also cause nervous system damage. Corticosteroid drugs are often recommended to prevent additional inflammatory damage and pressure on the brain during treatment (*see also* FLIES AND MOSQUITOES, page 496).

■ LEG PARALYSIS

Paralysis of a leg often results from damage to the peripheral spinal nerves. Paralysis of a front leg is usually associated with injury to the nerve roots in the neck or shoulder, or injury to the radial, median, or ulnar nerve in the leg. Paralysis of a hind leg is usually associated with injury to the nerve roots in the lower back or tailbone, or the femoral, sciatic, peroneal, or tibial nerve in the leg.

The animal's posture and gait, spinal reflexes, pain sensation, and the condition of the muscles in the affected limb are evaluated to identify the location of the injury. The closer a nerve injury is to the muscle, the better the outlook for recovery, so it is important to determine the exact location of the injury. The ability or inability of the animal to flex the joint and bear weight on the leg, and the presence or absence of pain sensation and reflexes at various places in the leg, depend on the site of the nerve damage. Within a few days, muscles wither and lose mass because of the lost nerve connection. Nerves regenerate slowly (at the rate of about 1 inch per month), and full functional recovery

depends on the condition of the nerve sheath and on the distance between the injury and the muscle where the nerve ends. Some nerve injuries can resolve after several weeks or months; however, when total nerve rupture occurs, surgical reattachment is required for regeneration.

If an abnormal eye condition known as Horner's syndrome (pupil small, eyelid partially closed, and third eyelid elevated) is present on the same side of the body as a paralyzed front leg, then the nerve roots have been torn and the chances for recovery are minimal. If Horner's syndrome is not present with front leg paralysis, the outlook for recovery may be better.

Applying heat, performing massage, and stretching tendons should be done as directed to keep muscles, tendons, and joints of a paralyzed leg healthy while the nerve is regenerating. A light, but not tight, bandage may prevent damage to the foot from dragging. If the leg drags on the ground, it can be held up with a sling or amputated to prevent damage to the paw. Three-legged cats generally have a good quality of life.

No specific therapy is available to help nerve regeneration. Acupuncture may help recovery. If voluntary movement, pain sensation, and spinal reflexes improve over 1 to 2 months, the outlook for recovery is good. An Elizabethan collar may be needed to prevent the cat from chewing on its leg. If the nerve injury is suspected to be permanent and the animal is chewing the leg, amputation may be the best option.

■ MENINGITIS AND ENCEPHALITIS

Inflammation of the meninges, the membranous covering of the brain and spinal cord (**meningitis**), and inflammation of the brain (**encephalitis**) often are seen simultaneously (**meningoencephalitis**), although either can develop separately. Causes of meningitis, encephalitis, and meningoencephalitis include infection by bacteria, viruses, fungi, protozoa, rickettsia or parasites. In some cases, the immune system is involved or the cause is unknown. In cats, especially adult animals, viruses, protozoa, and fungi are more frequent causes of meningitis and encephalitis than are bacteria.

The usual signs of meningitis are fever, neck pain and rigidity, and painful muscle spasms. Cats may have these signs without any sign of brain or spinal cord dysfunction. However, in meningoencephalitis, depression, blindness, partial paralysis of the face or limbs, loss of balance or motor control, seizures, behavioral changes, agitation, head tilt and circling behavior, and loss of consciousness (including coma) can develop, depending on the severity and location of the inflammation. The analysis of cerebrospinal fluid from a spinal tap is the most reliable and accurate means of identifying meningitis or encephalitis.

Cases resulting from an immune system disorder can be treated with corticosteroids or other medications that alter the immune system. Infections caused by protozoa and certain bacteria can be treated with appropriate antibiotics, and fungal infections can be treated with specific antifungal drugs. The outlook for recovery depends on the cause, the severity of the infection, and whether or not the infection has resulted in irreversible damage to the nervous tissue. Supportive care may include pain relievers, anticonvulsant drugs, fluids, nutritional supplements, and physical therapy.

▨ MOTION SICKNESS

Motion sickness results in nausea, excessive salivation, vomiting, and occasionally other signs. Animals may yawn, whine, show signs of uneasiness or apprehension, or have diarrhea. Motion sickness is usually seen during travel by land, sea, or air, and signs usually disappear when the motion of the vehicle ceases.

The principal cause of motion sickness is a problem in the inner ear, which has connections to the brain stem. Fear of the vehicle may be a contributing factor in cats, and signs may occur even in a vehicle that is not moving.

In some cases, motion sickness can be overcome by conditioning the animal to travel. (*See also* TRAVEL WITH PETS, page 1216.) In others, drug treatment can help prevent motion sickness, provide sedation, and decrease drooling.

▨ RABIES

Rabies is an acute viral infection of the nervous system that affects mainly carnivores and bats, although it can affect any mammal. It is caused by the rabies virus. Once signs appear, it is fatal. Rabies is found throughout the world, although a few countries are declared rabies-free due to successful elimination standards. Islands that have a strict quarantine program in effect are often rabies-free. In North America and Europe, rabies has been mostly eliminated in domestic animals, although it still affects wildlife.

No cat-to-cat rabies transmission has been recorded and no feline strain of rabies virus is known. However, cats are the most commonly reported rabid domestic animal in the United States. The virus is present in the saliva of rabid cats, and people have developed rabies after being bitten by a rabid cat. Reported cases in domestic cats have outnumbered those in dogs in the United States in every year since 1988.

Transmission is almost always by the bite of an infected animal, when the saliva containing the rabies virus is introduced into the body. The virus can be in the body for weeks or months before signs develop.

Signs and Diagnosis

Most rabid animals show signs of central nervous system disturbance. The most reliable indicators are sudden and severe behavioral changes and unexplained paralysis that worsens over time. Behavioral changes can include sudden loss of appetite, signs of apprehension or nervousness, irritability, and hyperexcitability. The animal may seek solitude, or an otherwise unfriendly animal may become friendly. Uncharacteristic aggressiveness can develop, and wild animals may lose their fear of people. Animals that are normally nocturnal may be seen wandering around during the daytime.

Cats are the most commonly reported rabid domestic animal in the United States.

The furious form of rabies is the classic "mad-dog" syndrome, although it is seen in all species. The animal becomes irritable and may viciously and aggressively use its teeth and claws with the slightest provocation. The posture is alert and anxious, with pupils dilated. Noise can invite attack. Such animals lose fear and caution of other animals. As the disease progresses, seizures and lack of muscle coordination are common. Death is caused by progressive paralysis.

The paralytic form of rabies is usually seen with paralysis of the throat and jaw muscles, often with excess salivation and inability to swallow. These animals may not be vicious and rarely attempt to bite. People can be infected by this form when examining the cat's mouth or giving it medication with bare hands. Again, paralysis progresses throughout the body and death occurs within a few hours.

Diagnosis is difficult, especially in areas where rabies is not common. Early stages of rabies can be easily confused with other diseases or with normal aggressive tendencies. A rabies diagnosis must be verified with laboratory tests. The animal must be euthanized and the remains sent for laboratory analysis.

Control of Rabies

The World Health Organization (WHO) has strict guidelines to control rabies in the dog population. These guidelines (which also apply to cats) include notification of suspected cases, euthanasia of animals with signs of the disease and those bitten by suspected rabid animals, leash laws and quarantine to reduce contact between susceptible animals, immunization programs with continued boosters, stray animal control, and pet registration programs.

Management of Suspected Rabies Cases

In areas where rabies is known to exist in the wildlife population (including bats), an animal bitten or otherwise exposed by a wild, carnivorous mammal or a bat that is not available for testing should be regarded as having been exposed to rabies. The National Association for State Public Health Veterinarians recommends that any unvaccinated cat exposed to rabies be euthanized immediately. If the owner is unwilling to do this, the animal must be placed in strict isolation, with no human or animal contact, for 6 months and be vaccinated against rabies 1 month before release. If an exposed animal is currently vaccinated, it should be revaccinated immediately and closely observed for 45 days.

Risk of Passing Rabies to People

When a person is exposed to an animal suspected of rabies, the risk of rabies transmission should be evaluated carefully. Wild carnivores and bats present a considerable risk where the disease is found, regardless of whether or not abnormal behavior has been seen.

Any healthy domestic dog, cat, or ferret, whether vaccinated or not, that bites a person or otherwise deposits saliva into a fresh wound, should be confined for 10 days for observation. If the animal develops signs within those 10 days, it should be promptly euthanized and submitted for testing. If the animal responsible for the exposure is stray or unwanted, it should be euthanized and submitted for testing immediately.

Pre-exposure vaccination is strongly recommended for all people in high-risk groups, such as veterinary staff, animal control officers, rabies and diagnostic laboratory workers, and travelers working in countries where canine rabies is prevalent.

TICK PARALYSIS

Tick paralysis is a sudden, progressive motor paralysis caused by a salivary toxin that attacks the nervous system. Certain species of ticks are known to cause tick paralysis. People (especially children) and many other animals may be affected. Human cases of tick paralysis caused by the genera *Ixodes, Dermacentor,* and *Amblyomma* have been reported in Australia, North America, Europe, and South Africa.

These 3 genera plus *Rhipicephalus, Haemaphysalis, Otobius,* and *Argas* have been associated with paralysis in animals. Cats seem to be resistant to the disease caused by these ticks, except in Australia where *Ixodes holocyclus* causes a severe and often fatal paralysis in cats.

Topical treatment with any product to kill attached ticks must only be done with chemicals that are safe for use in cats. In Australia, treatment for *Ixodes holocyclus* paralysis involves a specific antiserum (tick hyperimmune serum), in addition to treatment to minimize stress and support respiration. (For a more detailed discussion of TICK PARALYSIS, *see* page 213.)

CHAPTER **33**

Reproductive Disorders

INTRODUCTION

The reproductive system is the group of organs that produce offspring. In both males and females, the reproductive system is composed of primary sex organs and primary regulatory centers. The primary sex organs are testes in the male and the ovaries and uterus in the female. The primary regulatory centers are in the brain. They control the production of hormones that in turn influence the functioning of the primary sex organs.

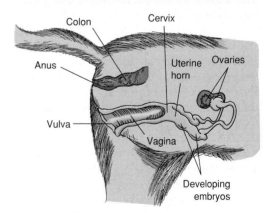

The reproductive system of the female cat

THE GONADS AND GENITAL TRACT

Both sexes have a pair of sexual organs or gonads (ovaries or testes), the main function of which is to produce eggs or sperm, respectively.

The Ovaries

Ovaries are female gonads that produce eggs and female sexual hormones, includ-

ing estrogen and progesterone. Estrogen is necessary for the development of eggs, and progesterone prepares the uterus for pregnancy. Once puberty is reached and the cat starts having estrous (heat) cycles, the size and form of the ovaries change. Within the ovary, a special group of cells called a follicle surrounds each egg.

The estrous cycle begins when follicle stimulating hormone causes follicles to grow, leading to maturation of eggs. Follicle stimulating hormone also stimulates the production and release of estrogen. Cats are induced ovulators, which means that the mechanical stimulation of the vagina and cervix during mating causes the release of luteinizing hormone from the brain, which stimulates the ovary to release the eggs (a process called ovulation). Progesterone, which is released from the ovaries, prepares the uterus for pregnancy and the mammary glands for milk production. Estrogen and progesterone are required for the development of female characteristics and sexual behavior.

Estrual cycling is seasonal in cats and is controlled by light. Cats require at least 12 hours of light in order to have estrous cycles. In the Northern Hemisphere, under natural lighting, cats reproduce in the spring and summer, with reduced or absent cycling during the shorter days of winter. Cats that are kept indoors under artificial light will tend to have heat periods more often than cats housed under natural lighting conditions.

The Testes

The testes are male gonads that produce sperm and male sexual hormones. Sperm maturation is stimulated by the production and release of follicle stimulating hormone and testosterone. During ejaculation, sperm are transported from the testes through the ductus deferens (narrow tubes connecting the testicles to the urethra). Testosterone is required for development and function of accessory glands, sexual organs, male sex characteristics, and sexual behavior. For normal sperm production, testes must descend into the scrotum (a pouch of skin outside the abdomen), because normal body temperature is too high for sperm to develop normally. The function of the testicles can be assessed by an evaluation of semen samples and hormonal tests. In addition, testicle examination and measurement can help evaluate fertility and may reveal reproductive diseases.

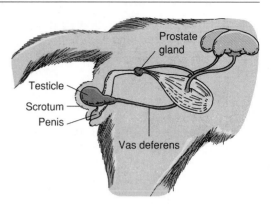

The reproductive system of the male cat

The Female Genital Tract

The female genital tract consists of the vulva, vagina, cervix, uterus, oviducts, and ovaries, as well as the mammary glands found on the chest and abdomen. The oviducts are small tubes that connect the ovaries to the uterus. The end of the uterus is called the cervix. It separates the uterus from the vagina and provides a barrier against infection. The vagina, a muscular tube that extends from the cervix to the outside, is connected to the vulva, which is the external opening of the female genitals. Oviducts are associated with each ovary. After ovulation, mature eggs are transported to the uterus via the oviducts. Secretion of fluid in the tubes provides a proper environment for survival of the mature egg, fertilization, and the first few critical days of embryonic life. The proper functioning of the uterus and cervix are also required for the establishment and maintenance of pregnancy. Infections may cause female infertility because they interfere with the proper function of the uterus. Infertility in female cats can be diagnosed through various tests, including x-rays, ultrasonography, abdominal examination, and blood tests. The vagina and vulva serve as the copulatory organ and as the last part of the birth canal.

The Male Genital Tract

In male cats, the genital tract provides a pathway for semen, which contains the sperm cells. The epididymis connects the testicle to the ductus deferens, which carries ejaculated sperm to the urethra. Sperm mature and are stored in the epididymis. The accessory sex glands, such as the prostate, create the fluid portion of semen. Cancer and inflammation of the genital tract can be diagnosed by several means, including physical examination, laboratory tests, and ultrasonography. Other diseases or abnormal functioning can be diagnosed by testing semen samples. Reproductive tract disease in male cats is very uncommon.

■ MANAGEMENT OF REPRODUCTION IN CATS

A complete discussion of breeding and reproduction in cats is beyond the scope of this book. And considering the surplus of pet cats in the US and other countries, casual rearing of litters by pet owners is not recommended. However, the following section includes a basic discussion of reproduction in cats.

Female cats (queens) are usually taken to the home of the male cat (tom) for breeding when they show signs of estrus. The breeding area should be quiet, familiar to the tom, and allow for observation with minimal interference from people. The courtship should not be interrupted unless there is a concern for the safety of either cat. Toms have been known to mate to the point of exhaustion, but queens usually go through a period of rolling and grooming after mating and may not let the tom remount for some time. Because cats are what is known as induced ovulators (see page 470), multiple breedings over several days are recommended. Periods of separation between breedings may prevent exhaustion and fighting. Evaluation for pregnancy can be done by your veterinarian by physically examining (palpating) the abdomen or by ultrasonography. Pregnancy lasts 60 to 63 days and can be detected by day 25 to 30.

Unlike in other domestic species, manipulation of the estrous cycle is not easy in cats. Prevention of estrus is typically accomplished by spaying, although short-term suppression of estrus can also be achieved by medication. The side effects of medical suppression can include inflammation and infection of the uterus, diabetes, and mammary cancer. Ovulation can be induced in cats by physical stimulation (for example, mating with a vasectomized tom) or sometimes by injections of hormones.

Unplanned and unwanted mating of cats is a common concern. Pregnancy can be completely prevented or ended by spaying or neutering. Pregnancy can also be ended by a veterinarian giving the hormone prostaglandin F_{2alpha}.

Pregnancy and Delivery

Predicting the timing of delivery can be difficult. Labor and delivery in cats is divided into 3 stages. Stage I lasts 12 to 24 hours. During this stage uterine contractions begin, but are not visible externally. The cervix also begins to dilate. During Stage II, abdominal contractions can be seen and the kittens are delivered. The kittens are usually delivered at intervals of 1 to 2 hours, but that can vary considerably. Stage II can last up to 24 hours. Stage III is defined as the delivery of the placenta. Cats typically alternate between stages II and III until delivery is complete.

Abnormal labor and delivery (dystocia) can be diagnosed if the uterine contractions are too infrequent or too weak to deliver the fetuses. This can lead to prolonged labor (more than 24 hours for stage I or II or more than 4 hours between delivery of kittens during stage II). Other signs of difficult birth include kittens that are born dead or near death or excessive maternal distress. Uterine and fetal monitors can be used to assess the condition of the uterus and fetuses. Dystocia can be treated either medically or surgically. Medical treatment includes injection of calcium or the hormone oxytocin to increase the strength and frequency of uterine contractions. Neither should be given without specific directions from your veterinarian. If these measures are not successful, cesarean section is performed to remove the fetuses.

Physical examination, and in some cases x-rays, are used to ensure that all kittens have been delivered. Injections of oxytocin are not routinely given unless the cat has not delivered all of the placentas. Disinfection of the umbilicus (belly button) with tincture of iodine helps prevent bacterial infection in the newborn kittens. Kittens should be weighed as soon as they are dry and then twice daily for the first week. Any weight loss after the first 24 hours indicates a potential problem and should be given immediate attention, such as extra feeding, assisted nursing, or examination by a veterinarian. (For a more detailed discussion of KITTEN CARE, see page 343.)

Problems Associated with Delivery

Cats should be allowed to deliver their kittens in a familiar area where they will not be disturbed. Unfamiliar surroundings or strangers may hinder delivery, interfere with milk letdown, or adversely affect maternal instincts and cause the cat to neglect her newborn kittens. This is especially true for a cat delivering her first litter. A nervous cat may either ignore the newborn kittens or give them excess attention. This can lead to nearly continuous licking and biting at the umbilical stump, which can potentially cause serious injury to the kitten. If the cat's maternal instincts fail, she may ignore the kittens, leave them unattended, or not allow them to nurse.

Common inflammatory diseases in the period after delivery include inflammation of the uterus (metritis) and breasts (mastitis). Retention of a placenta usually leads to metritis (see page 474). Signs include continued straining as if in labor, vaginal discharge, fever, and depression. Drugs that help stimulate uterine contractions such as oxytocin or prostaglandin F_{2alpha} may help expel the placenta. Mastitis (see page 474) is uncommon in cats and is usually caused by a bacterial infection. It can be treated with appropriate antibiotics.

Lack of milk production (agalactia) is uncommon in cats, but can be associated with premature delivery of the litter. Cats that do not produce enough milk should be examined by a veterinarian to check for other underlying diseases. The normal presence of colostrum (a clear, watery fluid produced before milk and containing important antibodies) should not be confused with agalactia. Contented kittens that gain weight daily after the first 24 hours are a good indication that milk production is adequate. If necessary, milk production can be stimulated by injections of oxytocin. If milk production is inadequate, kittens may need supplemental feeding.

■ INFERTILITY

Proper ovulation in females and ejaculation of fertile and normal sperm by males are regulated through a sequence of events in the brain, nervous system, and sexual organs. For optimal results, ovulation and deposition of semen into the female genital tract must be closely synchronized. Failure of any step in either sex leads to infertility or sterility. The ultimate result of infertility is the failure to produce offspring. In females, infertility may be due to the absence of the estrous cycle, abnormal ovulation, failure to conceive, or prenatal death. Major infertility problems in males are caused by disturbances in the production, transport, or storage of sperm; loss of libido; and partial or complete inability to mate or to stimulate ovulation in the female. Most major infertility problems are complex; several factors, singly or in combination, can cause failure to produce offspring.

Your veterinarian will establish whether it is the female or male that is infertile based on diagnostic tests such as semen evaluation, ultrasonography, or laboratory tests. In some cases both animals may contribute to infertility. Infertility is seldom accompanied by obvious signs of illness or infection. Lower fertility may be hereditary and your veterinarian will consider this issue when dealing with fertility problems.

Infertility can be treated by administration of hormones that act directly on the ovaries or regulate their functions, or act to help maintain pregnancy. Hormonal treatment can also work on male cats with low sperm counts or poor libido. On the other hand, hormonal treatment can also be used to prevent pregnancy after an undesired mating.

Antibiotics are used for treatment of infection of the reproductive tracts. The selection of the antibiotic is based on tests that determine the nature of the bacteria or infectious agent.

In some circumstances, unsatisfactory results with antibiotics and increased concerns about bacteria that develop resistance to a particular antibiotic have led veterinarians to use treatments other than antibiotics for infections of the reproductive tract. These drugs boost local immune defenses and can be used alone or in combination with antibiotics.

■ REPRODUCTIVE DISORDERS OF MALE CATS

Several reproductive diseases can affect male cats. Although most of these disorders (other than cryptorchidism) are rare, the most commonly encountered conditions are discussed below.

Cryptorchidism

Cryptorchidism is a failure of one or both testicles to descend into the scrotum. It is the most common reproductive disorder in male cats. The condition has a genetic basis and can be inherited from either parent. If only one testicle is affected, the cat will still be fertile. Because this is often an inherited condition, cryptorchid cats should not be used for breeding. The undescended testicle is also more likely to develop cancer, so neutering is recommended.

Inflammation of the Testes and Epididymis

Short-term inflammation of the testes or epididymis may be caused by trauma or infection. Chronic inflammation of the testes and epididymis may follow short-term inflammation of the organs. These conditions are rare in cats, however. (For additional information, *see* page 218.)

Paraphimosis

The inability to completely retract the penis into the preputial cavity usually occurs after erection. It is seen most often after semen collection or breeding. The most common cause of paraphimosis in cats is a band of hair that entangles the penis. Paraphimosis is a medical emergency because the exposed penis quickly becomes swollen (due to accumulation of fluid), dry, and painful. If recognized early, before severe swelling and pain develop, paraphimosis is easily treated. Treatment consists of trimming the hair, gentle cleansing, and lubrication of the exposed penis. The penis is replaced inside the prepuce and the swelling resolves once circulation is restored.

Phimosis

Phimosis can be due to an abnormally small preputial opening, resulting in the inability to extrude the penis. It may be hereditary or acquired as a result of trauma, inflammation, or a bacterial infection. The signs are variable. Usually, the problem is unnoticed until the cat attempts to mate and is unable to copulate. Diagnosis is established by physical examination of the prepuce and penis. Treatment depends upon the severity of the phimosis and the intended use of the cat. If the cat is not to be used for breeding, treatment probably is not needed, although neutering should be considered to prevent arousal.

Disorders of the Prostate

Prostatic diseases, including enlarged prostate, prostatitis, and prostate cancer, are not common in cats. (For a more detailed discussion of DISORDERS OF THE PROSTATE, *see* page 219.)

■ REPRODUCTIVE DISORDERS OF FEMALE CATS

There are many reproductive diseases that can affect the female cat. The most common of these diseases are discussed below.

Abnormal or Difficult Birth (Dystocia)

Many factors can cause a difficult birth, including uterine problems, a too small birth canal, an oversized fetus, or abnormal position of the fetus during birth. One of the more common situations in cats is a partially delivered kitten. Unless the head of the kitten is sticking out (so that the kitten can breathe), it must be delivered within 10 to 20 minutes or the kitten will die.

Dystocia should be considered in any of the following situations: 1) cats that have a history of dystocia; 2) strong contractions for more than 1 to 2 hours with no birth; 3) a resting period during labor that lasts more than 2 to 4 hours; 4) obvious illness in the mother; or 5) abnormal discharge from the vulvar area. Once the cause is determined, the appropriate treatment can be selected. X-rays or ultrasonography can show how many fetuses are present. Medication can sometimes help the labor progress if the mother is still in stable condition. Surgery (cesarean section) is performed if the mother or kittens are not stable or the fetuses are not able to be delivered naturally.

False Pregnancy (Pseudopregnancy)

False pregnancy occurs in cats when they have been induced to ovulate but did not conceive. The ovary will produce progesterone for about 40 days. There may be mammary development. When it does occur, treatment is often not recommended because the condition usually ends on its own in 1 to 3 weeks. (For additional information, see page 220.)

Follicular Cysts

These fluid-filled structures develop within the ovary and result in prolonged secretion of estrogen and continuous signs of estrus (heat) and attractiveness to males. Ovulation may not occur during this abnormal estrous cycle. Follicular cysts should be suspected in any female cat continuously showing signs of estrus (heat) for more than 21 days. This can sometimes be difficult to differentiate from normal, frequent cycles. The condition is diagnosed through laboratory tests or ultrasonography. The most commonly recommended treatment is removal of the ovaries and uterus. If the cat is to be bred, administration of drugs that affect ovulation might resolve the condition.

Overgrowth of Mammary Tissue (Mammary Hypertrophy)

This benign condition is characterized by rapid abnormal growth of the breasts. There are 2 types of breast swelling in cats. It occurs most often in young, cycling, or pregnant cats, but it can be seen in older, non-neutered females and in neutered males after treatment with progesterone. This condition is due to the effects of progesterone and is not cancerous. The most commonly recommended treatment is surgical removal of ovaries and uterus, although spontaneous remission can occur.

Mastitis

Mastitis is inflammation of the mammary gland(s) after giving birth. It is usually caused by a bacterial infection and can be treated with appropriate antibiotics; however, mastitis is uncommon in female cats. (For a more detailed discussion of MASTITIS, see page 221.)

Metritis

Metritis is inflammation of the uterus that may occur after pregnancy. Factors such as prolonged delivery and retained fetuses or placentas might lead to metritis. Bacteria such as Escherichia coli can also cause an infection of the uterus. The primary sign of the bacterial infection is pus-like discharge from the vulva. Female cats with metritis are usually depressed, have a fever, and may neglect their offspring. Kittens may become restless and cry incessantly. The infection is diagnosed through abdominal physical examination, ultrasonography, and laboratory tests. Treatment includes administering fluids, supportive care, and appropriate antibiotics.

Ovarian Remnant Syndrome

Ovarian remnant syndrome is caused by ovarian tissue that was left behind in a cat that has been spayed. Affected cats resume estrous cycles at variable lengths of time after surgery. This is a complication of the surgery. To diagnose this disorder, the veterinarian should see the cat when it is showing signs of heat. The remaining ovarian tissue must be surgically removed.

Pyometra

Pyometra is a bacterial infection of the uterus due to hormonal changes in unspayed cats. The signs are variable and include lethargy, poor appetite, and vomiting. When the cervix is open, a discharge of pus, often containing blood, is present. When the cervix is closed there is no discharge and the enlarged uterus may cause abdominal enlargement. Signs can progress rapidly to shock and death. The infection is diagnosed by physical examination, determination of the nature of the discharge, ultrasonography, and laboratory and blood tests. Removal of the ovaries and uterus is the recommended treatment in most cases. Medical treatment may be considered for valuable breeding females that have an open cervix. (For a more detailed discussion of PYOMETRA, *see* page 221.)

■ MAMMARY (BREAST) TUMORS

The frequency of mammary tumors in different species varies tremendously. They are relatively common in cats. Approximately 90% of mammary tumors in cats are malignant (cancerous). The cause of mammary tumors is unknown, however hormones play an important role in their development. Mammary tumors in cats are most often seen in older (average age 11 years) nonspayed females. Spaying at a young age reduces the risk, but the degree of protection is less precisely documented than that for dogs. Breast tumors are diagnosed by physical examination, x-rays, and tissue samples (biopsy). They often spread to the lungs, so chest x-rays are also taken to check for that possibility. Treatment includes removal of the tumor or the entire breast and anticancer drug treatment. The outlook is worse in cats with larger tumors and those with a high grade of malignancy, as determined by the biopsy.

CHAPTER **34**

Lung and Airway Disorders

■ INTRODUCTION

The respiratory system consists of the large and small airways and the lungs. When a cat breathes air in through its nose or mouth, the air travels down the trachea, which divides into the tubes known as the right and left bronchi, then into the smaller airways called bronchioles in the lungs. The bronchioles end in the small sacs called alveoli, where the barrier between the air and the blood is a thin membrane.

The most important function of the respiratory system is to deliver oxygen into the blood, which distributes it throughout the body, and to remove carbon dioxide from the blood. The exchange of oxygen and carbon dioxide occurs in the alveoli. When this exchange fails or becomes inefficient because of disease, the animal can become seriously ill. The respiratory system protects its own delicate airways by warming and humidifying inhaled air and by filtering out particles. Large airborne

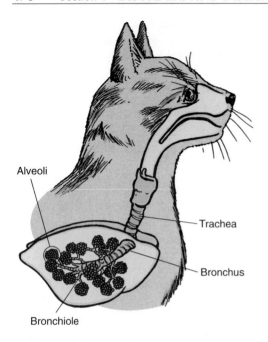

Alveoli

Trachea

Bronchus

Bronchiole

The lungs and airways in a cat

particles usually land on the mucous lining of the nasal passages, after which they are carried to the throat to be either swallowed or coughed up. Small particles and microorganisms are destroyed by the body's immune system.

Although the basic functions are the same, the anatomy of the respiratory tract varies among species. For example, the respiratory systems of dogs and cats are somewhat similar to each other, but differ from the respiratory systems of horses and humans. These differences explain in part why some diseases affect only certain species of animals.

When the level of oxygen in the blood is too low (called hypoxia or anoxia), the animal will show signs of respiratory distress. Low oxygen levels can be caused by reduced oxygen-carrying capacity of the blood cells, insufficient movement of gases in and out of the lungs, or inability of tissues to use available oxygen (a condition caused by some poisons). The animal's body attempts to compensate for low oxygen in the blood by increasing the

depth and rate of breathing, increasing contraction of the spleen (to force more red blood cells into circulation), and increasing blood flow and heart rate. If the brain suffers from lack of oxygen, respiratory function may be reduced even further due to depression of nervous system activity. In addition, heart, kidney, and liver functions may be reduced, as may the normal movement and secretions of the intestine. If the body is not able to compensate for the reduced oxygen level, a "vicious cycle" may begin in which all body tissues function less efficiently.

Respiratory diseases are common in cats. Although signs such as coughing and

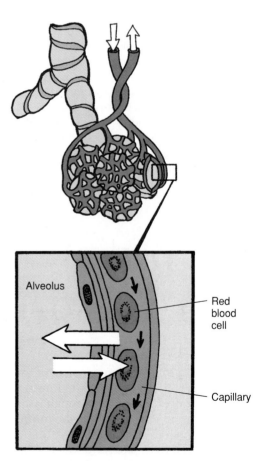

Alveolus

Red blood cell

Capillary

The alveoli and capillaries in the lung. Red blood cells take on oxygen and release carbon dioxide at the alveolus (modified with permission from *The Merck Manual of Medical Information*, Second Home Edition, 2003).

labored breathing are most commonly caused by problems of the respiratory tract, they may also occur because of disorders of other organ systems, such as congestive heart failure.

Both very young and older animals are at increased risk of developing respiratory disease compared to healthy adult animals. At birth, the respiratory and immune systems are not fully developed; this makes it easier for disease organisms to enter and spread within the lungs. In aged animals, a decrease in the animal's ability to filter out particles and fight off infection may render the lungs more vulnerable to airborne disease organisms and toxic particles.

Causes of Lung and Airway Disorders

Lung and airway disorders are often caused by direct infection with viruses, bacteria, fungi, or parasites, as well as by immune-mediated reactions or inhalation of irritants or toxic substances. Trauma (such as being hit by a car) may lead to the collapse of a lung or airway.

A variety of bacteria normally live in the feline nasal passages, throat, and sometimes lungs, without causing signs of illness. Infections by these usually harmless bacteria may occur when respiratory defense mechanisms are weakened by another infection (such as rhinotracheitis virus or calicivirus), irritant (such as smoke or noxious gases), or disease (such as congestive heart failure or lung tumors). Disease organisms may continue to live in the respiratory tract of recovering animals. When stressed, these animals may relapse; they can also act as a source of infection for other animals. Poor management practices such as overcrowding are often associated with poor sanitation and environmental conditions, which can lead to both more frequent and more severe infections. Conditions that favor the spread of infections often occur in catteries, pet shops, boarding facilities, and humane shelters.

Abnormalities that are present at birth, such as narrowed nostrils, elongation of the soft palate, cleft palate, and narrowing of the trachea, can cause respiratory dysfunction. Tumors, nasopharyngeal polyps, chronic nasal disease, damage to the airways, and collapse of the trachea can result in difficult breathing and other signs of respiratory disease.

Diagnosing Lung and Airway Disorders

Your pet's history and the veterinarian's physical examination will help to determine the possible cause and site of respiratory disease. Chest and neck x-rays may be helpful when obstructive upper airway disease or an airway obstruction is suspected (for example, by a foreign object). Chest x-rays are typically done for cats exhibiting lower respiratory signs such as cough, rapid shallow breathing, or labored breathing. Blood gas analysis or pulse oximetry may help assess the need for oxygen therapy in an animal with severe labored breathing.

When obstructive upper airway disease is suspected, your veterinarian may use various scopes to view the nose, throat, and airways. When lung disease is suspected, the veterinarian will want to examine the contents of the lung and its airways. This can be done by bathing the trachea or air sacs with a sterile fluid and examining the contents of the retrieved fluid; these procedures are called transtracheal wash and bronchoalveolar lavage, respectively.

In cats with a buildup of fluid in the pleural cavity, a sample of the accumulated fluid is often removed using a needle (thoracocentesis) then evaluated under a microscope. Fluid buildup in the pleural cavity can be a sign of heart disease in cats, so an echocardiograph may also be performed.

A runny nose, sneezing, or both may suggest the presence of viral or bacterial infection or a tumor or foreign object in the nose. Persistent cases may require additional examination using x-rays, computed tomography (CT), examination with an endoscope, or a sample of nasal tissue. Microscopic evaluation of nasal tissue may help diagnose fungal infections. Blood tests for fungal respiratory infections are sometimes used in addition to other tests and examinations.

Signs of Respiratory Disorders

- Discharge from the nose (mucus, pus, or blood, depending on the cause)
- Coughing that may be dry or may include mucus or blood
- Rapid breathing (not always a sign of disease, such as in healthy animals after exercise)
- Labored or difficult breathing; shortness of breath
- Shallow breathing
- Signs of pain associated with breathing in or out
- Noise (such as grunting) associated with breathing

Control of Respiratory Conditions

Sudden dietary changes, weaning, cold, drafts, dampness, dust, poor ventilation, and the mixing of different age groups all play a role in respiratory disease in groups of animals. Stress and mixing of animals from several sources should be avoided or minimized if possible. Immunization can help control some types of respiratory infection; however, it is not a substitute for proper environmental conditions and animal care.

General Treatment of Lung and Airway Disorders

Respiratory disorders often involve the production of excess secretions in the respiratory system (for example, in the nose and lungs) that the affected animal may not be able to remove without assistance. One goal of veterinary treatment is to reduce the volume and thickness of the secretions and to make their removal easier. This can be accomplished by controlling infection, thinning the secretions, and when possible, improving drainage and removing the material.

Animals with respiratory disorders should normally receive plenty of water unless otherwise directed by the veterinarian. Adding humidity to the air may make removal of airway secretions easier. Cough medicines (expectorants) are some-

times used to thin secretions and make them easier for the animal to cough up; however, they are rarely helpful. If airway obstruction is severe, large amounts of secretions may need to be gently suctioned away by the veterinarian.

When coughing is not helping to remove mucus (a nonproductive cough), medicines can be used to suppress the coughing. Increased airway resistance caused by contraction of the bronchial airway muscles is sometimes treated with bronchodilators, which expand the airways and may be prescribed for animals with asthma-like conditions and chronic respiratory disease. Antihistamines can be used to alleviate constriction triggered by allergies. Constriction of the bronchial tubes in the lungs can also be reduced significantly by removing irritating factors, using mild sedatives, or reducing periods of excitement. If a bacterial infection is present, antibiotics are often given. Diuretics (medicines that help the body get rid of excess fluid) are sometimes used when an animal has fluid buildup in the lungs.

When a respiratory illness results in a lack of oxygen in the blood, the condition can usually be corrected by the veterinarian administering oxygen. However, treatment must be done carefully, because too much oxygen can lead to other problems.

■ ACCUMULATION OF FLUID OR AIR IN THE CHEST CAVITY

Hemothorax, the accumulation of blood in the pleural cavity, is usually caused by trauma to the chest, blood clotting disorders, or tumors in the chest. **Hydrothorax**, the accumulation of clear fluid in the pleural cavity, is usually due to interference with blood flow or lymph drainage. **Chylothorax**, the accumulation of a high-triglyceride lymphatic fluid in the pleural cavity, is relatively rare. It may be caused by rupture of the chest duct but often the cause is unknown. The signs of all 3 conditions include respiratory difficulty, such as rapid shallow breathing with labored inhalation, and weakness. Drainage of the fluid may be necessary to relieve these signs and can be helpful in diagnosing the underlying problem. However, the outlook for many disorders that cause accumulation of fluid in the chest is guarded to poor.

Air in the pleural cavity, called **pneumothorax**, may be caused by trauma or occur spontaneously. The lung collapses if a large volume of air enters the pleural cavity, causing difficulty inhaling or rapid, shallow breathing. This condition should be considered an emergency that requires immediate veterinary attention.

ALLERGIC PNEUMONITIS

Allergic pneumonitis is an acute or chronic allergic reaction of the lungs and small airways. The lungs "overreact" to the presence of a parasite or other irritant, causing inflammation and a chronic cough. There is often a higher than normal number of white blood cells called eosinophils in the blood. The underlying cause is rarely determined.

Pulmonary infiltration with eosinophilia, known as **PIE syndrome** (*see* page 440), is associated with allergic pneumonitis. Causes of PIE syndrome include parasites, chronic bacterial or fungal infections, viruses, external antigens, and unknown factors.

Heartworm pneumonitis can occur when cats with heartworm infections become sensitized to the adult heartworms. Migrating intestinal parasites and primary lung parasites may cause mild signs of allergic pneumonitis.

A chronic cough is the most common sign of allergic pneumonitis. The cough may be mild or severe, and it may be dry (nonproductive) or contain secretions (productive). Weight loss, rapid or labored breathing, wheezing, intolerance to exercise, and occasionally coughing up of blood may be seen. Severely affected animals may have bluish mucous membranes at rest. The degree of labored breathing and coughing is related to the severity of inflammation within the airways and alveoli.

The diagnosis is based on the animal's history and signs, chest x-rays, and laboratory tests. Evidence of heartworm disease or parasitic lung disease on x-rays may suggest these as an underlying cause of the allergic reaction. Blood tests show an increase in several types of white blood cells, indicating inflammation or infection. Fecal analysis and a heartworm test are performed when lung parasites or heartworms are suspected.

When an underlying cause can be found, elimination of the offending agent and a short-term course of a corticosteroid usually resolve the problem. When heartworm disease or lung parasites appear to be the cause, corticosteroid treatment before or during treatment for the parasite controls the respiratory signs. If an underlying cause cannot be determined, prolonged corticosteroid therapy is often required. If the affected cat has severe airway constriction, bronchodilators or beta$_2$-agonist medications may be helpful. Animals with severe shortness of breath may require oxygen therapy.

BRONCHITIS

Bronchitis is an inflammation of the bronchial airways that may extend into the lungs. It is discussed later in this chapter as part of tracheobronchitis (*see* page 487).

CANCERS AND TUMORS

The respiratory system can be a host to many different types of tumors and cancers. The following are the more common tumors found in the lungs and airways of cats.

Tumors of the Nose and Sinuses

Tumors of the nose and sinuses are relatively uncommon in cats as compared to dogs. The incidence is higher in older cats. The average age at time of diagnosis is 10 years. In cats, essentially all nasal tumors are cancerous (malignant). The most common tumor types are carcinomas and lymphomas. In general, if untreated, survival is 3 to 5 months after diagnosis.

Chronic nasal discharge containing mucus, pus, or blood is the most common sign. Initially, the discharge may involve one side of the nose, but it often becomes 2-sided. Periodic sneezing, bleeding from the nose, and snoring may occur. Deformities of the face and mouth and/or protruding eyeballs may be seen depending on the tissues affected by the tumor. Excessive tearing and inflammation of the cornea may occur.

Diagnosis is based on the history and clinical signs. Nasal x-rays or computed tomography (CT) scans may show evidence of tumor presence. Nasal CT scans are preferred because they provide better detail than x-rays when attempting to distinguish tumors of the nose from other causes of chronic nasal discharge. A biopsy of tumor tissue can provide a definite diagnosis.

The recommended treatment largely depends on the tumor type and the extent of disease. Treatments such as aggressive surgical removal of the tumor, chemotherapy, radiation therapy, or combinations of these provide a more favorable outlook when the diagnosis is made early.

Tumors of the Larynx and Trachea

Tumors of the larynx and trachea are rare in cats. The most common signs of tumors of the larynx include labored breathing when inhaling or after exercise; high-pitched, noisy breathing; voice change (hoarseness or loss of voice); and coughing. Similar signs are associated with tumors of the trachea. A diagnosis can often be made from the history and clinical findings and by eliminating other causes of upper airway obstruction or coughing. The tumor mass may be seen by the veterinarian during examination of the larynx or trachea with an endoscope. Definitive diagnosis can be made after a biopsy. Treatment involves surgically removing the tumor. Some types of tumors respond to radiation therapy.

Primary Lung Tumors

Tumors that originate in the lung (primary lung tumors) are very rare in cats. Metastatic lung disease is more common than primary lung tumors in cats. Although cats are less prone to developing primary lung cancer than dogs, the reported incidence has increased during the last 20 years. This may be due to an increased average life span, better detection and awareness, or, possibly, increasing exposure to cancer-causing agents in the environment. Most primary lung tumors are diagnosed at an average age of 12 years in cats. All breeds and both genders appear to be equally affected. Of the primary lung tumors in cats, virtually all are malignant (cancerous).

The signs indicating a primary lung tumor can vary, depending on the location of the tumor, speed of tumor growth, and presence of previous or current lung disease. Coughing is uncommon in cats; general signs of illness such as poor appetite, weight loss, and rapid, labored breathing, are more common signs. Chest x-rays are the first step in making a diagnosis; however, a definitive diagnosis of lung cancer requires a sample of tissue (biopsy).

Surgery to remove the portion of the lung containing the tumor is the recommended treatment in most cases. Tumors that cannot be operated on or those that have spread may be treated with chemotherapy. Recurrence or spread of the tumor is a common cause of death.

Metastatic Lung Tumors

A metastatic lung tumor is one that originates in another part of the body and then spreads to the lungs. The signs of metastatic lung disease are similar to those of primary lung tumors (*see* above). The severity of signs depends on the location of the tumor and whether the lesions are single or multiple. The diagnosis and treatment is similar to that for primary lung tumors. Chemotherapy or radiation therapy may be useful with certain tumor types that are not well suited for surgery. Because spread to the lung occurs late in the clinical course of a malignant tumor, the outlook is poor.

▨ DIAPHRAGMATIC HERNIA

A diaphragmatic hernia is a condition in which a break in the diaphragm allows protrusion of abdominal organs into the chest. In cats, automobile-related trauma is a common cause of diaphragmatic hernia, although defects of the diaphragm that are present at birth (congenital) may also be a cause.

The signs of a hernia can vary. In the case of sudden trauma or injury, the cat has difficulty breathing. The degree of labored breathing may vary from barely detectable to fatal, depending on the severity of the hernia. If the stomach is trapped in the hernia, it may bloat and the animal's condition may worsen rapidly. In milder, longterm cases, general signs such as weight loss may be more noticeable than respiratory signs. During an examination, the veterinarian may note the absence of normal lung sounds and/or the presence of digestive system sounds in the chest.

Careful physical examination by the veterinarian, including listening to and tapping the chest and abdomen, usually suggests the presence of chest disease. A definitive diagnosis is most frequently made from x-rays, which can reveal changes in the shape of the diaphragm and the displacement of abdominal organs. Specialized x-rays that use dyes to highlight the digestive organs are sometimes necessary to make the diagnosis. Samples of abdominal or chest fluids, electrocardiographs (EKGs), and blood work may be obtained, and surgical exploration of the abdominal cavity may be necessary in some cases.

Surgical repair of the hernia is the only treatment. If other trauma is present, the animal's condition is usually stabilized before surgical correction of the hernia is performed.

EMPHYSEMA

Emphysema is an important disease in humans; however, in other animals it typically occurs as a result of another lung disease. The condition leads to difficulty in expelling air from the lungs, making breathing more difficult. Two major forms of emphysema are generally recognized. **Alveolar emphysema** is abnormal permanent enlargement of the alveoli, which are small air sacs deep in the lungs. **Interstitial**

emphysema is the presence of air within the supporting connective tissue of the lung. Chronic obstructive pulmonary (lung) disease (COPD) can cause enlargement and destruction of air spaces. The association of high numbers of white blood cells with COPD suggests that there may be allergic, infectious, and/or toxicologic causes for the condition.

FELINE RESPIRATORY DISEASE COMPLEX (FELINE HERPESVIRAL RHINOTRACHEITIS, FELINE CALICIVIRUS)

Feline respiratory disease complex is a set of respiratory illnesses caused by a group of organisms that can cause infection alone or together. It includes those illnesses with signs including inflammation of the nasal and sinus linings, inflammation of the eye lining (conjunctivitis), tears, salivation, and mouth sores. The principal diseases are feline herpesviral rhinotracheitis and feline calicivirus, although other diseases may also be involved (*see* TABLE 6).

The majority of feline upper respiratory infections are caused by feline herpesviral rhinotracheitis, although the incidence of feline calicivirus may be higher in some populations of cats. Infection with both these viruses at once may occur. Natural transmission of these agents occurs through small droplets in the air (such as from a sneeze) and contaminated objects, which can be carried to a susceptible cat by a handler. Recovering cats may harbor the virus for many months. Stress may trigger a relapse.

The onset of **feline herpesviral rhinotracheitis** is marked by fever, frequent sneezing, inflamed eyes (conjunctivitis), rhinitis, and often salivation. Excitement or movement may cause sneezing. The fever may reach 105°F (40.5°C) but subsides and then may come and go. Initially, the disease causes a clear discharge from the nose and eyes; it soon increases in amount and contains mucus and pus. At this point, depression and loss of appetite become evident. Severely affected cats may develop mouth

Table 6. Organisms Found as Part of Feline Respiratory Disease Complex

Disease Organism	Signs/Comments
Feline herpesviral rhinotracheitis (FHV-1)	Accounts for the majority of acute upper respiratory infections in cats; see text for signs
Feline calicivirus (FCV)	Often hard to distinguish from feline herpesviral rhinotracheitis; see text for signs
Feline pneumonitis (*Chlamydophila psittaci*)	Conjunctivitis, sneezing, eye discharge, fever may develop; of lesser importance than FHV-1 and FCV
Mycoplasma infections	Conjunctivitis and inflammation of the nasal lining (rhinitis); of lesser importance than FHV-1 and FCV
Feline infectious peritonitis virus	May cause signs of mild upper respiratory tract infection
Reoviruses	Virus replicates in respiratory tract; may not always cause respiratory signs

inflammation with sores, and inflammation of the cornea occurs in some cats.

Signs may persist for 5 to 10 days in milder cases and up to 6 weeks in severe cases. The outlook is generally good except for young kittens and older cats. When the illness is prolonged, weight loss may be marked. Bacteria often infect cats that are already ill with feline herpesviral rhinotracheitis.

There are many related strains of **feline caliciviruses**. Some caliciviruses cause few or no signs, while others produce fluid buildup in the lungs (pulmonary edema) and pneumonia. It is often impossible to distinguish feline herpesviral rhinotracheitis from feline calicivirus infection. Two feline calicivirus strains may produce a transient "limping syndrome" without mouth sores or pneumonia. These strains produce a short fever, leg lameness, and pain on handling of affected joints. Signs occur most often in 8- to 12-week-old kittens and usually improve without treatment. The syndrome may occur even in kittens that have been vaccinated against feline calicivirus, because no vaccine protects against both of the particular strains that produce the "limping syndrome."

Calicivirus has also been found in cats with inflammation of the gums and mouth. The lesions heal rapidly, and the infected cat regains appetite 2 to 3 days after onset, although the course of disease may last 7 to 10 days. Fever, poor appetite, and depression are common signs. Nasal inflammation (rhinitis) and conjunctivitis also can occur.

The veterinarian's initial diagnosis is based on the typical signs as described above. These characteristics may be difficult to sort out when more than one infection is present. A definite diagnosis is based on isolation and identification of the organism through appropriate tests and microscopic examination of samples from the oral and nasal mucous membranes, nostrils, or conjunctival sacs. However, diagnosis of feline herpesviral rhinotracheitis may be difficult because the virus is shed only periodically, and because even cats without symptoms can show presence of the virus.

Treatment and Prevention

Treatment is largely directed toward the signs of illness, but broad-spectrum antibiotics are useful if secondary bacterial infections are involved. Antihistamines may be prescribed early in the course of the disease. Nose and eye discharges should be removed frequently for the comfort of the cat. Treatment with a mist (nebulization) or saline nose drops may be recommended to help remove hard secretions. Nose drops containing a blood vessel constrictor and antibiotics are sometimes prescribed to reduce the amount of nasal secretion. Eye ointment containing antibiotics may also be prescribed to prevent corneal irritation produced by dried secretions from the eye. If corneal ulcers occur in feline herpesviral rhinotracheitis infections, eye preparations containing antiviral medication may be prescribed, in addition to other antibiotic eye preparations. If the cat has great difficulty breathing, it may be placed in an oxygen tent.

Vaccines that protect against feline herpesviral rhinotracheitis and feline calicivirus are available. One type is injected; the other is given as drops in the eyes and nose. Cats that have received the eye/nose vaccine may sneeze frequently for a few days after vaccination; ask your veterinarian if you should expect this or any other side effect from the vaccines. Vaccines against *Chlamydia* are also available; these vaccines are generally used in catteries or on premises where infection has been confirmed. A combination of recommended vaccinations and control of environmental factors (such as exposure to sick cats, overcrowding, and stress) provide good protection against upper respiratory disease.

LARYNGITIS

The larynx is the part of the throat often called the "voice box" in humans. Laryngitis is an inflammation of the larynx. It may result from upper respiratory tract infection or by direct irritation from inhalation of dust, smoke, irritating gas, or foreign objects. It can also be caused by a tumor of the larynx. Laryngitis may accompany infectious rhinotracheitis and calicivirus infection in cats. Fluid buildup and swelling of the mucous membranes is often a key part of laryngitis; if severe, the upper airway may be obstructed.

A cough is often the first noticeable sign of laryngitis. The cough is harsh, dry, and short at first, but becomes soft and moist later and may be very painful. Fluid buildup and swelling of the larynx may develop within hours, causing an increased effort to inhale and high-pitched breathing arising from the larynx. Vocal changes may be evident. Bad breath and difficult, noisy breathing may be evident, and the cat may stand with its head lowered and mouth open. Swallowing is difficult and painful. While death due to suffocation may occur, this is extremely unlikely unless a mass, lesion, or swelling is severely obstructing the larynx.

The veterinarian can make a tentative diagnosis based on the clinical signs and physical examination of the cat. A definitive diagnosis requires examination of the larynx with an endoscope; in cats, anesthesia is usually required during this procedure. If the larynx is obstructed, an opening will be made in the neck to allow a tracheotomy tube to be placed; this tube enables the animal to breathe while the problem is being corrected. Corticosteroids may be prescribed to reduce obstruction caused by swelling. Diuretics may be used to relieve fluid buildup in the larynx and lungs. Control of pain with medication, especially in cats, allows the animal to eat and thus speeds recovery.

LUNG FLUKES

The adult flukes *Paragonimus kellicotti* and *Paragonimus westermani* usually live in cysts or bulla, primarily in the lungs of cats. They also have been found rarely in other organs or the brain. Infection is most common in China, southeast Asia, and North America. The eggs from the adult flukes, are coughed up, swallowed, and passed in the feces. The life cycle includes several snails as the first intermediate host and crayfish or crabs as the second. Cats become infected by eating raw crayfish or crabs that contain the encysted parasite. The young flukes eventually migrate to the lungs where they become established.

Infected animals may have a chronic, deep, intermittent cough and eventually become weak and lethargic, although many infections pass unnoticed. A diagnosis is based on finding the characteristic eggs in feces or coughed-up material. The location of the flukes in the lungs is determined by x-ray. Several drugs provide effective treatment for lung fluke infections.

■ LUNGWORM INFECTION

Lungworm infection of the lower respiratory tract, usually resulting in bronchitis or pneumonia, can be caused by any of several parasitic nematodes (roundworms), including *Aelurostrongylus abstrusus* and *Capillaria aerophila* in cats. *A. abstrusus* is normally transferred to cats after eating a bird or rodent that has previously eaten a slug or snail containing the nematode. *C. aerophila* in cats has a direct cycle, with infective eggs being consumed along with food or water.

Signs of lungworm infection range from moderate coughing with slightly increased breathing rates to severe, persistent coughing, labored breathing, and respiratory distress or failure. Infections with no visible signs can also occur. Deaths are relatively uncommon with these infections, although they do occur in kittens.

Diagnosis of lungworm infection is based on signs, known transmission patterns, and presence of larvae in feces. Examination of the airways with an endoscope (bronchoscopy) and x-rays can be helpful tools. It can be a challenge for the veterinarian to diagnose lungworm because infected animals do not always pass the larvae in their feces, and when they do, they may be few in number. In cats, because of the relative infrequency of infection, diagnosis may be made only after failure of antibiotic therapy to improve the condition.

Lungworm infections can be difficult to treat, but there is evidence that appropriate antiparasitic drugs are effective. It may be necessary to continue antiparasitic treatment for up to 2 months.

■ NASOPHARYNGEAL POLYPS

Nasopharyngeal polyps can cause signs of upper respiratory disease, such as increased sounds associated with breathing, sneezing, and nasal discharge. These polyps typically arise from the middle ear and extend through the Eustachian tube into the nasopharynx. Occasionally they may arise from the Eustachian tube lining. The cause is unclear but may be related to chronic (longterm) inflammation.

Nasopharyngeal polyps are benign, but they can grow to a size that causes obstruction of the nasopharynx. Removal by surgery is recommended if this occurs.

■ PARALYSIS OF THE LARYNX

Laryngeal paralysis, a disorder of the upper airway, is rare in cats. The condition occurs when the cartilages of the larynx do not open and close normally during respiration. (For a more detailed discussion of PARALYSIS OF THE LARYNX, *see* page 233.)

■ PHARYNGITIS

Pharyngitis is inflammation of the walls of the throat (pharynx). It accompanies most upper airway viral and bacterial respiratory infections. Calicivirus infections in cats may cause lesions of the mucous membranes in the mouth and throat. Mouth pain and resistance to having the mouth opened may indicate abscesses at the back of the throat or the presence of a penetrating foreign object or growth in the mouth or tonsils.

In general, cats with pharyngitis have a normal desire to eat and drink but may have difficulty swallowing. As a result of inflammation and abscesses, an emergency situation can develop because of airway obstruction. The diagnosis is based on complete physical examination; this may include oral examination, x-rays, and endoscopic examination of the throat along with cultures of fluids and sites that are draining.

The primary treatment is to identify and control or eliminate the factors leading to the disease. If pharyngitis has been caused by a foreign object (a relatively uncommon situation in cats), surgery to remove the object and any dead tissue is done under general anesthesia.

PNEUMONIA

Pneumonia is an inflammation of the lungs and airways that causes breathing difficulties and deficiency of oxygen in the blood. There are many possible causes. The most common cause of pneumonia is a viral infection of the lower respiratory tract; *Mycoplasma* bacteria are another common cause. Feline calicivirus causes damage to the airways and makes the animal susceptible to development of pneumonia.

Parasitic invasion of the bronchi can also result in pneumonia. Fungal pneumonia (*see* page 486) also occurs in cats. Injury to the mucous membranes of the bronchial tubes and inhalation of irritants may cause pneumonia directly, as well as predispose the animal to bacterial infection. Aspiration pneumonia (*see* below) may result from persistent vomiting, force feeding, or improperly administered medications. It may also occur after suckling in a newborn with a cleft palate.

Signs of pneumonia include lethargy, loss of appetite, and a deep cough. Labored breathing, "blowing" of the lips, and bluish mucous membranes may be evident. Body temperature is moderately increased. Diagnosis usually involves a combination of history, physical examination, and appropriate tests. In the later stages of pneumonia, the increased lung density can be seen on chest x-rays. Analysis of fluid used to "wash" the airways is valuable for the diagnosis of bacterial infections.

Animals with pneumonia benefit from a warm, dry environment. If the mucous membranes are very bluish (indicating poor oxygen in the blood) the veterinarian may administer oxygen. Antibiotics are usually given, although the treatment may be modified based on the results of laboratory cultures, so that the drugs given best match the type of infection found. The cat may need to be reexamined frequently, including periodic chest x-rays, to watch for improvement or recurrence, to follow an underlying disease (if one is present), or to detect any possible complications.

Aspiration Pneumonia

Aspiration pneumonia is a lung infection caused by inhalation of foreign material. The severity of the inflammation depends on the material inhaled and the distribution of foreign material in the lungs. A common cause of aspiration pneumonia is the improper administration of liquid medicines. Animals that breathe in vomit or attempt to eat or drink while partially choked are at risk for aspiration pneumonia as well. Disturbances in the normal swallowing mechanism, such as in anesthetized or comatose animals, or in animals with deformities such as cleft palate, may also lead to aspiration pneumonia. Cats are particularly susceptible to aspiration pneumonia caused by aspiration of tasteless products such as mineral oil.

A history suggesting that a foreign substance might have been inhaled is the most important clue to diagnosing this disease. Signs include labored or rapid breathing, rapid heart rate, and fever. Other signs include bluish mucous membranes and airway spasms. A sweetish, off-smelling breath may be detected, which becomes more intense as the disease progresses. This is often associated with a nasal discharge that sometimes is tinged reddish brown or green. Occasionally, evidence of the breathed-in material (for example, oil droplets) can be seen in the nasal discharge or coughed-up material.

As with nearly all disease conditions, prevention is better than treatment. This is especially the case for aspiration pneumonia, because the outlook is poor even with treatment. The rate of death is high, and recovered animals often develop lung abscesses. Veterinarians normally use drugs and other precautions to minimize the risk of an animal inhaling fluid (such as saliva) during surgery. If a cat is known to have inhaled a foreign substance, broad-spectrum antibiotics are usually prescribed without waiting for signs of pneumonia to appear. Care and supportive treatment are the same as for other types of pneumonia.

Chlamydial Pneumonia (Feline Chlamydiosis, Pneumonitis)

Chlamydiae bacteria have been identified as a cause of pneumonia in cats. This type of pneumonia in cats usually develops in association with the more common chlaymdial conjunctivitis and rhinitis. Chlamydial pneumonia is caused by *Chlamydophila psittaci*. Treatment is with appropriate antibiotics.

Fungal Pneumonia

Fungal pneumonia (also called mycotic pneumonia) is a fungal infection of the lung that leads to the development of pneumonia. A number of fungi have been shown to cause fungal pneumonia in domestic animals (*see* BOX, page 235). Often these fungi are found in animals with compromised immune systems, but they can cause disease in healthy animals as well. The source of most fungal infections is believed to be inhalation of spores from the soil.

In cats, the fungus *Cryptococcus* tends to colonize in the nasal cavity where it causes inflammation of the nasal and sinus lining. A short, moist cough is characteristic of the disease, and a thick discharge of mucus from the nose may be seen. As the disease progresses, labored breathing, weight loss, and generalized weakness develop. Inflammation of lymph nodes can cause airway compression, making it more difficult for the cat to breathe. Periodic fever can occur, possibly caused by bacterial infections.

A tentative diagnosis of fungal pneumonia can be made if an animal with long-term respiratory disease shows the typical signs and does not respond to antibiotic therapy. (Antibiotics are effective against bacteria but not against fungi or other organisms.) However, a definite diagnosis requires identification of the fungus using appropriate laboratory tests. X-rays and blood tests may be useful.

Antifungal drugs are used to treat fungal pneumonia. Extended drug therapy, which may be needed for several months after symptoms have disappeared, is usually necessary to effectively treat the infection.

■ PULMONARY EDEMA

Pulmonary edema, the abnormal accumulation of fluid in the tissue, airways, or air sacs (alveoli) of the lungs, may occur along with circulatory disorders or in some allergic reactions or infectious diseases. Head trauma can cause pulmonary edema in cats. Labored breathing and open-mouth breathing may occur. Animals stand rather than lying down, lie only on their chest, or assume a sitting position. The veterinarian may be able to hear wheezing and crackling sounds in the chest.

■ RHINITIS AND SINUSITIS

A common upper respiratory tract disorder is rhinitis (inflammation of the mucous membranes of the nose) or other damage to the nasal mucous membranes. It is often associated with sinusitis, or inflammation of the lining of the sinuses. If the nasal passages deteriorate and fail to function properly, a major filtration function is removed. This exposes the lungs to much heavier loads of dust and microorganisms.

Viral infection is the most common cause of acute rhinitis or sinusitis in cats. Feline herpesviral rhinotracheitis and feline calicivirus are most frequently involved (*see also* FELINE RESPIRATORY DISEASE COMPLEX [FELINE HERPESVIRAL RHINOTRACHEITIS, FELINE CALICIVIRUS], page 481). Infection with bacteria frequently occurs after the initial viral infection. Allergic rhinitis or sinusitis can occur seasonally (if due to pollen production) or year-round (if due to indoor allergens such as house dusts and molds). In cats, chronic nasal and sinus inflammation frequently occurs following severe acute viral infections of the nasal and sinus mucous membranes. Fungal nasal and sinus inflammation may be caused by the fungi *Cryptococcus neoformans* (relatively common in cats) or *Aspergillus* subspecies and *Penicillium* subspecies (both relatively rare in cats).

Signs of rhinitis include nasal discharge, sneezing, pawing at the face, snoring, open-mouth breathing, and labored inhalation. Tears and inflammation of the membrane surrounding the eyes (conjunctivitis) often accompany inflammation of the upper respiratory passages. The nasal discharge is clear but may become mucuslike as a result of secondary bacterial infection. Sneezing may be frequent, or it may come and go in cases of chronic rhinitis. Affected cats may also experience an aspiration reflex ("reverse sneeze"), a short rapid inhalation in an attempt to clear the nose.

Diagnosis is based on the cat's history, physical examination, radiographic findings (especially computed tomography), rhinoscopy, nasal biopsy, and elimination of other causes of nasal discharge and sneezing.

In mild or acute cases, treatment to relieve signs may be effective. Severe cases of rhinosinusitis in kittens or adult cats may require intravenous fluids to prevent dehydration, and nutritional support via a feeding tube to maintain weight. The veterinarian may prescribe antibiotics if secondary bacterial rhinosinusitis is present or suspected. (Antibiotics are not effective against viruses.) Feline herpesvirus vaccine (administered in the nose) occasionally may help shorten and minimize recurrence of signs of viral infection. In general, chronic rhinosinusitis is a frustrating disease to manage, and cures are rare. Fungal rhinosinusitis can be treated with antifungal therapy once the particular fungal cause has been identified. Surgery may be recommended for animals that do not respond to medical therapy, although the results are often disappointing.

TONSILLITIS

Tonsillitis is inflammation of the tonsils, usually caused by another underlying condition. It sometimes does not cause any signs, but when severe, can cause poor appetite, listlessness, salivation, and difficulty swallowing. Tonsillitis is rare in cats. If a bacterial infection is the cause, appropriate antibiotics provide effective treatment. Most cases of tonsillitis do not require removal of the tonsils. (For a more detailed discussion of TONSILLITIS, *see* page 236.)

TRACHEOBRONCHITIS (BRONCHITIS, BRONCHIAL ASTHMA)

Tracheobronchitis is an acute or chronic inflammation of the trachea and bronchial airways; it may also extend into the lungs. It is more likely to occur in cats already affected by respiratory disease or a disorder of the lungs or airways. Tracheobronchitis in cats can be caused by parasites, by diseases of the mouth and pharynx, or by chronic coughing related to heart or lung disease. Other causes include smoke inhalation and exposure to chemical fumes.

Spasms of coughing are the most prominent sign; it is most severe after rest or at the beginning of exercise. A slight fever may also be noted. The acute stage of bronchitis passes in 2 to 3 days, although the cough may persist for several weeks.

Bronchial asthma (allergic bronchitis) is a syndrome in cats with similarities to asthma in humans. Young cats and Siamese and Himalayan breeds are most often affected. The sudden development of asthma in older cats is extremely uncommon. The signs of bronchial asthma include shortness of breath, coughing, or wheezing that may come and go. However, a chronic cough in older cats is often due to pneumonia (*see* page 485). If shortness of breath is severe, bluish mucous membranes (signaling a lack of oxygen in the blood) may be seen.

The veterinarian's diagnosis is made from the history, physical examination, and clinical signs and by ruling out other causes of coughing. Diagnostic tools include chest x-rays, use of an endoscope to view the bronchial tubes (bronchoscopy), and collection of biopsy and swab samples for laboratory analysis. These diagnostic tests may be needed in cases where the veterinarian's initial treatment is not effective in providing relief.

In mild cases or those with a recent onset of signs, supportive therapy may be effective, but treatment of the underlying disease (if present) is also needed. Rest, warmth, and proper hygiene are important. If bacterial infection is present, broad-spectrum antibiotics may be prescribed. The veterinarian may perform or prescribe therapy such as use of a mist (nebulization) or steam from a hot shower to help loosen secretions, making them easier to cough up.

CHAPTER **35**

Skin Disorders

▥ STRUCTURE OF THE SKIN

The skin is the largest organ of your cat's body. It provides a protective barrier against the environment, regulates temperature, and gives your cat its sense of touch. Depending on the species and age, the skin may be 12 to 24% of a cat's body weight. The skin has 3 main layers: the epidermis or outer layer, the dermis or middle layer, and the subcutis or innermost layer. Other important parts of the skin include skin appendages (such as hair and claws) and subcutaneous muscles and fat.

Epidermis

The epidermis is the top skin layer. It provides protection from foreign substances. The epidermis is constantly regenerating. New skin cells are created near the base of the epidermis and migrate upwards in a process called keratinization. This produces a compact layer of dead cells on the skin surface. This layer keeps in fluids, salts, nutrients, and water, while keeping out infectious or noxious agents. The top layer of dead skin cells are continuously shed and replaced by lower cells. The rate of cell replacement is affected by nutrition, hormones, tissue factors, immune cells in the skin, and genetics. Disease and inflammation also alter normal cell growth and keratinization.

Cells in the epidermis can be damaged by excessive ultraviolet light exposure. Healthy skin cells contain a skin and hair pigment called melanin. The presence of melanin helps protect the cells from the damaging rays of the sun.

Basement Membrane Zone

This area of the skin is located at the base of the epidermis and connects the epi-

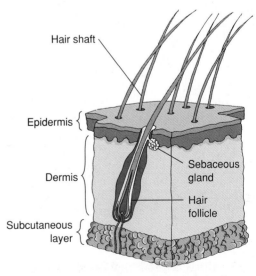

The anatomy of a cat's skin includes 3 major layers, as well as hair follicles and sebaceous glands.

dermis to the dermis layer below. It also serves as a protective barrier between the epidermis and the dermis. Several skin diseases, including a number of autoimmune conditions, can damage the basement membrane zone.

Dermis

The dermis supports and nourishes the epidermis and skin appendages. The network of blood vessels that supply the epidermis with nutrients is in the dermis. Blood vessels are also responsible for regulating skin and body temperature. Sensory nerves are located in the dermis and hair follicles. The skin responds to the sensations of touch, pain, itch, heat, and cold. The dermis produces collagen and elastin proteins that give support and elasticity to the skin. There are also immune cells in the dermis that defend against infectious agents that pass through the epidermis.

Skin Appendages

Hair follicles, oil and sweat glands, and claws are skin appendages that grow out of the epidermis and dermis. The hair follicles of cats are compound. The follicles have a central hair surrounded by 3 to 15 smaller hairs all exiting from a common pore. Cats are born with simple hair follicles that develop into compound hair follicles.

The growth of hair is affected by nutrition, hormones, and change of season. Cats normally shed hair in the early spring and early fall. They may also shed in response to changes in temperature or the amount of sunlight. The size, shape, and length of hair are controlled by genetics and hormones. Disease, drugs, nutrition, and environment also affect the health of hair.

The hair coat protects the skin from physical and ultraviolet light damage, and it also helps regulate body temperature. Trapping dead air space between secondary hairs conserves heat. This requires that the hairs be dry and waterproof. The cold-weather coat of many animals is often longer and finer to facilitate heat conservation. The hair coat can also help cool the skin. The warm-weather coat has shorter, thicker hairs and fewer secondary hairs. This anatomic change allows air to move easily through the coat, which facilitates cooling.

Oil glands (also called sebaceous glands) secrete an oily substance called sebum into the hair follicles and onto the skin. They are present in large numbers near the paws, back of the neck, rump, chin, and tail area. They are part of the cat's scent-marking system. Cats mark territories by rubbing their face on objects and depositing a layer of sebum laced with feline facial pheromones. Sebum is a mixture of fatty acids. It is important for keeping the skin soft and pliable and for maintaining proper hydration. Sebum gives the hair coat sheen and has antimicrobial properties.

Cats have sweat glands on the feet that may have a minor role in cooling the body. Cats also will sweat through their paws when excited; this is most commonly seen as wet paw prints on surfaces, such as shiny countertops or floors.

Subcutis

The subcutis is the innermost layer of the skin. It contains the subcutaneous fat and muscles. (The word subcutaneous means "beneath the skin.") The twitch muscle is the major muscle immediately beneath the skin. The subcutaneous fat provides insulation; a reservoir for fluids, electrolytes, and energy; and a shock absorber.

■ DERMATITIS AND DERMATOLOGIC PROBLEMS

Dermatitis is a general word for any type of inflammation of the skin. It is usually used until a specific diagnosis is reached. There are many causes of skin inflammation, including external irritants, burns, allergens, trauma, and infection (bacterial, viral, parasitic, or fungal).

The signs of dermatitis can include itching, scaling, abnormal redness, thickening of the skin, and hair loss. The usual progression of a skin disease involves an underlying trigger that causes boils, scabs, scales, or blisters.

Abnormal itching, called **pruritus**, occurs in many diseases and is often present because of secondary infections. As the inflammation progresses, crusting and scaling develop. If the problem reaches the deeper dermis, fluid discharge, pain, and sloughing of the skin may occur. Secondary bacterial and yeast infections commonly develop as a result of skin inflammation. If the dermatitis does not improve, early signs of inflammation (such as redness) become obscured by signs of chronic inflammation (thickening of the skin, color changes, scaling, fluid discharge). Often the skin becomes drier. If itching is not already a sign, it will often develop at this stage.

Resolving dermatitis requires that your veterinarian identify the underlying cause and treat secondary infections or other complications. A review of your cat's history and a physical examination can more precisely define the problem.

DIAGNOSIS OF SKIN DISORDERS

A precise diagnosis of the causes of a skin disease requires a detailed history, physical examination, and appropriate diagnostic tests. Many skin diseases have similar signs and an immediate diagnosis may not be possible. Based on your cat's history and the physical examination, your veterinarian may order any of a number of laboratory procedures. These may include microscopic analysis of skin scrapings and hair, cultures of skin swabs, blood and urine tests, and even biopsies. It may take several days before laboratory results are available. Your veterinarian may also evaluate how your cat responds to treatment in order to diagnose a specific skin problem. More than one visit is often required for an accurate diagnosis.

TREATMENT OF SKIN DISORDERS

Successful treatment of a skin disorder requires identification of the underlying cause. Not surprisingly, many treatments for skin diseases are applied directly to the skin surface. This may be the preferred method of treatment for some diseases or beneficial in addition to systemic drugs (medications taken by mouth or injected, then distributed throughout the body). Examples of products applied directly to the skin include antibiotic ointments, corticosteroid preparations, medicated shampoos, and topical insecticides. Most cats do not like to be bathed, so shampoo treatment is less often recommended for

---

Skin Disease History Checklist

When you bring your cat to your veterinarian for a skin problem, you can help your veterinarian diagnose the problem by having information about the following:

- The primary complaint—what is bothering your cat?

- The length of time the problem has been present.

- The age at which the skin disease started. Some diseases are more common to particular ages of animals.

- The breed. Some breeds are prone to specific diseases.

- Behavior of the cat such as licking, rubbing, scratching, or chewing of the skin.

- How the problem started and how it has progressed. For example, problems that began with itching may lead to self-trauma that develops secondary skin wounds or infections.

- The type of skin problems you saw develop and when.

- The season when the problem first started. Some skin diseases are related to the season of the year.

- The area on the body where the problem was first noticed.

- Any previous treatments and how your cat responded to treatment. For example, if your cat did not improve if given antibiotics, this helps your veterinarian exclude certain diseases.

- The presence of fleas, ticks, or mites.

- The health of other animals with which your cat has been in contact.

- The environment of your cat. Changes in the animal's environment can influence the development of certain skin diseases.

cats than it is for dogs. Instead, your veterinarian may recommend local warm packs or washing of the particular area involved (such as the chin).

Systemic drugs may be needed to treat some disorders. These include whole-body antibiotics, corticosteroids, and other anti-inflammatory drugs.

As with any treatment program, make sure that you read and understand all directions for using the prescribed product, including how to apply or give it, how much to use, and how often it should be administered.

■ CONGENITAL AND INHERITED SKIN DISORDERS

Cats can be born with or may inherit several different kinds of skin abnormalities. Most of these conditions are uncommon to rare. Some occur with greater frequency in particular breeds of cats.

Congenital Skin Disorders

Epitheliogenesis imperfecta, also called **aplasia cutis**, might be described as missing or absent skin. It is a congenital condition of unknown cause and is rare in cats. Animals with epitheliogenesis imperfecta have failed to develop part or all of the layers of the skin. As a result, the animal is born with ulcers, or areas lacking any skin covering. The condition can be fatal if it involves large portions of the skin. Small defects can be surgically corrected.

Hereditary Hair Loss (Alopecia)

Animals can be born either totally or partially without hair. Hairlessness can also develop later in life. These defects can be associated with abnormal teeth, claws, and eyes, or with skeletal and other developmental defects. Hairless breeds of cats, such as the Sphinx, have been bred for these defects. All animals with abnormal hair development are prone to hair follicle infections, and inflammation caused by foreign objects in the hair follicles.

In cats, hair growth abnormalities known as follicular dysplasia have been

reported in the Devon Rex. Hair shaft structural abnormalities called pili torti are known to occur in the American Wirehaired Cat.

Pigmentary Abnormalities

Some skin color abnormalities may be acquired, while others are hereditary. Abnormalities in skin and coat color are sometimes related. Some of the associations are mentioned in hereditary hair loss (*see* above).

Albinism is rare in cats. True albinism is always associated with pink or pale irises and with visual defects and increased risk of skin damage from sunlight. Albinism is different from extreme white spotting. Some animals with extreme piebaldism (spotted or blotched with black and white) or dominant white have associated nervous system abnormalities or deafness in one or both ears. About 75% of white cats with 2 blue eyes are deaf. Albino and white skin on piebald cats is subject to solar damage and sun-induced skin cancer, especially where the hair is short or thin (such as on the ears).

Lentigo occurs in orange and orange-faced male cats. It is marked by the development of pigmented spots. Marks are first seen on the lips and eyelids at 1 year of age. Marks later develop on the nose

Lentigo occurs in orange or orange-faced male cats.

and lips. Lentigo spots are not precancerous and have no medical consequence.

Vitiligo is hereditary but not noticeable at birth. The onset is usually in young adulthood. Affected cats develop bleached areas of skin that occasionally also involve the hair coat and claws. Most patches are on the face, especially the bridge of the nose or around the eyes. Color loss may wax and wane. Complete remission may occur but is rare. Vitiligo causes no other health problems. No treatment is available. Treatments used in people with vitiligo are unlikely to help animals.

Defects of Structural Integrity

Some skin diseases are genetic defects that affect the structural integrity of the skin. **Cutaneous asthenia** (also known as **dermatosparaxis** or **Ehlers–Danlos syndrome**) is a group of syndromes characterized by defects in collagen production. Affected animals develop loose, unusually elastic, fragile skin along with loose joints and other connective tissue dysfunctions. These syndromes have been seen in Himalayan and domestic shorthair cats. For Himalayan cats, the disease is a recessive characteristic. In some families of domestic shorthair cats, the disease is a dominant characteristic.

The signs of these syndromes include fragile skin (present from birth), wounds that heal with thin scars, delayed wound healing, hanging skin, and the formation of blood clots (hematomas) and sacs or cysts filled with fluid (hygromas).

Diagnosis in cats includes assessment of signs, measurement of skin elasticity, and laboratory tests on the collagen structure of skin samples. Prior to diagnosing cutaneous asthenia, your veterinarian will want to eliminate other disorders of acquired rather than hereditary skin fragility as a cause of the skin problems. Cutaneous asthenia is not usually fatal in cats, although older animals develop hanging folds of skin and often have extensive scarring.

Epidermolysis bullosa syndromes are a group of hereditary congenital defects in the zone between the dermis and epidermis. Minor skin trauma results in separation of the dermal and epidermal skin layers and blisters that soon rupture, leaving glistening, flat ulcers. Skin damage may be present at birth or develop within the first weeks of life. The most severe damage occurs on the feet, mouth, face, and genitals. Most occurrences of this disease are fatal.

This disease has been seen in Siamese, domestic shorthair, and Persian cats. (For more information about EPIDERMOLYSIS BULLOSA SYNDROMES, *see* page 244.)

Multisystem Disorders that Affect the Skin

Porphyria is an inherited defect in the metabolism of hemoglobin (a blood component) and its byproducts. Signs in cats include photodermatitis (inflammation of the skin brought on by exposure to light); a reddish brown discoloration of the teeth, bones, and urine; anemia; and stunted growth. The abnormal fear and avoidance of light that is a sign of this disease in other animals does not occur in cats. Laboratory tests on urine samples are commonly used to confirm the presence of porphyria, although skin biopsies are also used.

Congenital and Inherited Tumors

Abnormal growth and spread of mast cells in the skin (benign familial cutaneous mastocytosis) has been reported in young Siamese cats. This rare, inherited condition causes skin to thicken and have a leathery, bark-like appearance. Intense itching is evident. Treatment includes medication to control itching and prevent self-inflicted skin damage.

■ ALLERGIES

Like people, cats can be allergic to various substances, including plant particles and other substances in the air or in food. These substances are called allergens. Allergens are substances that, when inhaled or absorbed through the skin, respiratory tract, or gastrointestinal tract, stimulate histamine production, which results in inflammation.

Airborne Allergies (Atopy)

Airborne allergens can adversely affect the skin. **Feline atopy** (*see also* page 441) is a condition characterized by severe itching. Affected cats have an abnormal sensitivity to inhaled or contacted environmental allergens. Excessive scratching and licking produce sores and other skin conditions including hair loss, scaling, crusts, and inflammation. The age of onset varies, but is often less than 5 years. Feline atopy may be seasonal or nonseasonal. Your veterinarian will want to eliminate other possible causes of the itching before diagnosing feline atopy. (*See also* AIRBORNE ALLERGIES, page 246.)

Food Allergies

Food allergies (*see also* page 440) are known to occur in cats. Signs of food allergy are similar to airborne allergies except there is little variation in the intensity of itching from one season to another. The age of onset is variable. The distribution and intensity of itching varies between cats; however, itching that is directed at the head and face is fairly common.

There is no reliable diagnostic test other than feeding a limited foodstuff (a hypoallergenic or elimination diet) and seeing if the itching resolves. A veterinarian should be consulted to develop a specific test plan for your cat. The ideal food elimination diet should be balanced and nutritionally complete and not contain any ingredients that have been fed previously to the cat. Owners often do not understand that if *any* previously fed ingredient is present in the elimination diet, the animal may be allergic to the new food and the diet trial will be a failure. The key point in any food elimination diet trial is that only new food ingredients can be fed. This includes treats and anything else the cat eats besides its regular food.

Food elimination diets can be difficult in cats because many cats are reluctant to change diets. Cats should not be starved or forced into eating a new diet, because prolonged poor appetite can lead to serious liver damage. The trial diet should be fed for up to 3 months. If obvious or complete resolution in signs occurs during the elimination diet trial, food allergy can be suspected. Response time to the elimination diets varies from 1 to 9 weeks.

To confirm that a food allergy exists and improvement was not just coincidental, the cat must be given the previously fed food ingredients and a relapse of signs must occur. The return of signs may occur in as little as 15 minutes but usually takes place within 10 days. Once a food allergy is confirmed, the elimination diet should be continued until signs disappear, which usually takes less than 14 days. At this point, previously fed individual ingredients should be added to the elimination diet for a period of up to 14 days. If signs reappear, the individual ingredient is considered a cause in the food allergy.

The foods cats are most often allergic to include fish, beef, and milk products. Avoidance of the offending allergens will control the signs associated with the food allergy.

■ EOSINOPHILIC GRANULOMA COMPLEX

This group of skin conditions affects cats, dogs, and horses. Eosinophilic granuloma complexes have varying signs but seem to be caused most commonly by an allergic hypersensitivity.

In cats, 3 diseases have been grouped in this complex. **Eosinophilic ulcers** are well-defined, red, skin ulcers, usually not painful or itchy. They are most commonly found on the upper lip. Progression to squamous cell carcinoma is extremely rare, although it can occur. **Eosinophilic plaque,** a well-defined, red, raised wound, is most commonly found on the belly and thighs. It is extremely itchy, and cats will scratch and rub the affected sites. These lesions are often infected with bacteria, which usually make this condition worse. **Eosinophilic granulomas** are raised, circular, yellowish to pink nodules. They may be found anywhere on the body but are most common on the head, face, bridge of the nose, ears, paw pads, lips, chin, mouth, and thighs. Linear lesions are found most often on the thighs but have been seen on other body locations.

This complex can be due to insects, dietary and environmental allergies, infectious agents, and genetic or hereditary factors. Allergies should be investigated by allergy testing and dietary elimination trials. Some cases will be better defined by having additional laboratory testing performed, including skin cytology, cultures, and skin biopsies. All forms of this complex can often benefit from antibiotic treatment. Many treatment options exist depending on the underlying cause. In cases where the underlying problem cannot be identified or controlled, treatment with corticosteroids or cyclosporine many be required.

The common cat flea, *Ctenocephalides felis*

▒ FLEAS

Fleas are small, wingless insects that feed on animal blood. Besides being a nuisance, they can also transmit diseases and cause allergies or anemia. There are more than 2,200 species of fleas recognized worldwide. In North America, only a few species commonly infest house pets. Two common species of flea are the cat flea (*Ctenocephalides felis*) and the dog flea (*Ctenocephalides canis*). However, most of the fleas found on both dogs and cats are cat fleas. Fleas cause severe irritation in other animals and humans. They also transmit a wide variety of diseases, including tapeworm infections (*see* TAPEWORMS, page 405) and the typhus-like rickettsiae (*see* EHRLICHIOSIS AND RELATED INFECTIONS, page 310).

Transmission and Life Cycle

Cat fleas begin reproduction about 1 or 2 days after a blood meal from a host. Female fleas lay eggs as they feed and move about on the surface of the skin. A single female flea can produce up to 50 eggs per day and about 2,000 in her lifetime. The eggs are pearly white, oval, and tiny. They readily fall from the fur and drop onto bedding, carpet, or soil, where they hatch in 1

to 6 days. Newly hatched flea larvae are mobile and free-living, feeding on organic debris found in their environment and on adult flea droppings. Flea larvae avoid direct light and actively move deep into carpet fibers or under organic debris (grass, branches, leaves, or soil).

Larvae can easily dry out, and exposure to relative humidity under 50% will kill them. However, they are capable of moving as far as 3 feet (1 meter) to find locations suitable for their survival. Indoors, flea larvae best survive in the protected environment deep within carpet fibers, in cracks between hardwood floor boards, and on unfinished concrete floors in damp basements. Flea development occurs outdoors only where the ground is shaded and moist. The larval stage usually lasts 5 to 11 days but may be prolonged for 2 to 3 weeks, depending on the availability of food and the environmental conditions.

After completing its development, the mature larva produces a silk-like cocoon in which it pupates. The pupa is fully developed in 1 to 2 weeks, but the adult flea may remain in the cocoon for several weeks until a suitable host arrives. When it emerges from the cocoon, it can survive 1 to 2 weeks before finding a host on which to feed. It is the newly emerged, unfed fleas that infest pets and bite people. Fleas generally do not leave their host unless forced off by grooming or insecticides. Cat fleas in any stage of the life cycle cannot survive cold temperatures. They will die if the environmental temperature falls below 37°F (3°C) for several days.

Depending on temperature and humidity, the entire life cycle of the flea can be completed in as little as 12 to 14 days or last up to 350 days. However, under most conditions, fleas complete their life cycle in 3 to 6 weeks. Fleas mate after feeding, and females lay eggs within 1 to 2 days of their first blood meal.

A flea-infested cat or dog can easily introduce fleas into a home where they deposit eggs that develop into newly emerging fleas. These then infest other pets and bite people.

Flea Allergy Dermatitis

When feeding, fleas inject saliva into the host on which they are living. Many cats are allergic to flea saliva. Even non-allergic animals will occasionally scratch due to the annoyance of flea bites. Cats with flea allergy dermatitis will have itching that can range from minimal to severe, depending on how sensitive the cat is to the flea saliva. When fur is parted to inspect for skin irritation, small, solid bumps will be visible. This pattern of irritation is known as **feline miliary dermatitis** because it resembles tiny, round millet seeds. Bumps are typically spread over the back, neck, and face. They can become crusted over after the cat damages its skin by scratching. These bumps are not flea bites, but a system-wide allergic reaction to having been bitten by fleas. The allergic reaction causes the bumpy rash to develop and the cat's entire body to itch. Itching can be severe, prompting the cat to repeatedly lick, scratch, and chew its skin. Cats with flea allergy dermatitis can also have widespread hair loss.

Most cases of flea allergy dermatitis occur in the late summer, corresponding to the peak of flea populations. Animals younger than 1 year old do not usually have flea allergy dermatitis. Usually, diagnosis is made by visual observation. Slowly parting the hair often reveals flea excrement or rapidly moving fleas. Flea excrement is reddish black, cylindrical, and pellet- or comma-shaped. Placed in water or on a damp paper towel, the excrement dissolves, producing a reddish brown color. Examination of the pet's bedding for eggs, larvae, and excrement is also useful. The presence of fleas does not exclude another disease being at least partially responsible for the cat's itching and skin condition.

Your veterinarian may do skin testing to eliminate other causes for the itching and confirm a diagnosis of flea allergy dermatitis. However, skin testing does not always reliably identify flea allergy dermatitis in cats. Other diseases and conditions that can cause similar signs include infestation with other skin parasites, ringworm infection, sensitivity to medication, food allergy, respiratory allergy, and hair follicle infections.

Flea control measures have changed dramatically in recent years. Flea control previously required repeated application of insecticides on the cat and the premises. Recently, new insecticides and insect growth regulators have been developed that provide residual control and require fewer applications. The most effective of these products are sold by veterinarians. Many are given once a month and effectively control fleas and other parasites. By using these products, it is possible to eliminate a flea infestation in a household; however, the amount of time necessary to achieve flea control will vary because of the flea's life cycle and conditions in the environment. Typically, control of an infestation can take 6 weeks to 3 months.

You should discuss flea control products with your veterinarian and select one that works well for your cat and the environment in which it lives. (For a more detailed discussion of FLEA ALLERGY DERMATITIS, *see* page 250.)

FLIES AND MOSQUITOES

Flies are winged insects that are usually just an annoyance, but they can transmit disease. They belong to a large, complex order of insects called Diptera. Flies vary greatly in size, food preference, development, and habits. As adults, flies may feed on blood, saliva, tears, or mucus. They also spread bacteria, viruses, and parasites. (For a more detailed discussion of FLIES AND MOSQUITOES, *see* page 251.)

Biting flies feed on animal blood. This group includes mosquitoes, black flies, sand flies, biting midges, mosquitoes, horse flies, and deer flies. Though the bites can be painful and may bring on allergic reactions, biting flies are usually just a nuisance unless they are extremely numerous or transmit a disease. Many of these flies, including black flies and mosquitoes, will bite both animals and humans.

Nonbiting flies include those that do not feed on blood and do not actually bite the host animal while feeding. Instead, these flies feed on bodily secretions. They can transmit diseases to cats and other domestic animals.

Bot Fly Larvae Infestation (Grubs, Cuterebriasis)

This parasitic infestation of cats is caused by rodent or rabbit bot flies, which are different *Cuterebra* species. Most species of flies only live on one species of host animal. However, the rabbit *Cuterebra* fly is a common pest on cats. Rarely, cats might also be infested with warble flies, which are members of *Hypoderma* species.

Adult *Cuterebra* flies are large and bee-like and do not feed or bite. Females deposit eggs on stones or vegetation. Cats become infested as they pass through contaminated areas. Infestations are most common in the summer and fall when the larvae enlarge and produce a swelling about 0.4 inches (1 centimeter) in diameter. Swellings with

breathing pores are seen around the head, neck, and trunk. The hair is often matted and the skin is swollen. The swellings may be painful and discharge pus.

Definitive diagnosis is made when your veterinarian finds the larvae. Any suspected swellings should be explored carefully by a veterinarian. The affected area should not be squeezed because this may rupture the larva and lead to infection. Healing may be slow after the larvae are removed by your veterinarian.

Horse Flies, Deer Flies, and Other Flies of Large Animals

Horse flies (*Tabanus* species) and deer flies (*Chrysops* species) are large (up to 1.4 inches [3.5 centimeters] long), heavy bodied, and robust. They are swift fliers with powerful wings and very large eyes. The females usually prefer horses, deer, and cattle but may feed on any animal, including cats. (For additional information, *see* page 253.)

Maggots (Myiasis, Fly Strike)

House flies, blow flies, bottle flies, and flesh flies lay eggs in skin wounds of any animal (including a cat) that has an infected skin wound. In newborn kittens, the healing stub of the umbilical cord is an attractive egg-laying site for flies. Bite wounds are often sites of initial infection in older cats. Matted hair coats contaminated with feces also attract these flies. Eggs laid in contaminated hair coats produce maggots that move rapidly to any infected wound.

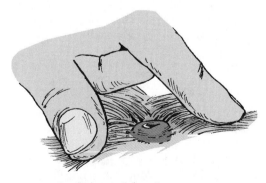

Bot fly larvae infestation on a cat

Once inside a wound, the larvae quickly invade the surrounding tissue.

Affected cats often have raised, red sores at or near the strike site. Sores may resemble swollen pockets of pus. Maggots may be visible in a sore or wound. You should not try to remove the maggots yourself; wound cleaning and maggot removal by your veterinarian is required. In most cases, your pet will have to be sedated or anesthetized for removal of the larvae.

Finding maggots in a sore or wound is the normal method of diagnosis. Maggots from more than one type of fly can be present.

Promptly treating all open wounds and reducing the number of flies are 2 steps that you can take to protect your cat from strike. To treat open wounds, gently wash the wound with mild soap, rinse well, and then apply a veterinarian-recommended medicated salve. You should carefully trim the fur around the wound to reduce the chance of infection. Check the wound several times a day to be sure it does not become inflamed or infected. Equally important is routine grooming for your cat. Keep your cat's fur clean and do not allow urine or feces to collect on the skin.

Finally, if possible, keep your cat in a fly-free area protected by screens. To control flies in the area, be sure all garbage and decaying animal matter are removed. All garbage and trash containers should be securely covered. Remove standing water, especially places that accumulate any organic matter (including yard waste).

Mosquitoes

Mosquitoes belong to the family Culicidae. They are tiny and fragile but possibly the most voracious of the blood-feeding flies. About 300 species have been described worldwide, but only about 150 species of mosquitoes are found in the temperate regions of North America.

Mosquitoes often lay their eggs on the surface of standing water. Even small amounts of standing water can attract mosquitoes. You can reduce the number of mosquitoes near your home by ensuring that there is no standing water. Eliminate or turn over any container that can hold water and check your gutters to be sure that they run freely; standing water in gutters is an ideal location for mosquito eggs.

Only female mosquitoes feed on blood. They annoy animals and humans, cause blood loss, and transmit diseases. Although they are known for spreading diseases such as malaria and yellow fever in people, in veterinary medicine they are also known for spreading heartworm to dogs and cats. (*See also* HEARTWORM DISEASE, page 380.)

It is difficult to protect your cat from mosquitoes, especially if the cat spends much time outside. You can reduce outdoor exposure to mosquitoes by not letting your cat outdoors in the early morning or early evening hours when mosquitoes are most active. Sensitive animals, including kittens, should be housed in closed or screened buildings. Mosquitoes are not attracted to light, so "bug zappers" do not help control mosquitoes; they may actually be harmful because they destroy insects that prey on mosquitoes.

Sand Flies

Sand flies are most numerous in tropical and subtropical regions. They are tiny (0.06 to 0.16 inches [1.5 to 4 millimeters] long) and have moth-like, hairy wings. Female sand flies have piercing mouthparts and feed on the blood of a variety of warm-blooded animals, including cats and people. They tend to be active only at night. They breed in dark, humid environments that have a supply of organic matter that serves as food for the maggots.

Evidence of small bite wounds is the usual sign. The flies are rarely found on animals. Sand flies are an intermediate host for leishmaniasis, a disease caused by a parasite that infects the cells of capillaries and the spleen (*see* LEISHMANIASIS, page 541).

Successful sand fly control is not usually possible with ordinary insecticide spraying because the breeding locations are hard to reach. Removal of dense vegetation helps control sand flies. Often sand flies are controlled as a side effect of mosquito control programs.

Stable Flies

Stable flies (*Stomoxys calcitrans*) are often called biting house flies. They are about the same size as house flies and look much like them, but they are avid blood feeders. Horses are the preferred host for stable flies; however, they sometimes feed on cats. (For additional information, *see* page 765.)

■ HAIR LOSS (ALOPECIA)

Alopecia is the partial or complete lack of hair in areas where it is normally present. Hair loss is a sign, and its underlying cause must be determined in order to be treated. If a cat has hair loss and is scratching the area excessively, the itching problem should be investigated first.

Hair loss can be congenital (present at birth) or acquired. Congenital hair loss may or may not be hereditary. It is caused by a lack of development of hair follicles. It may be apparent at or shortly after birth. Or, the cat may be born with a normal coat and then local or generalized hair loss occurs when the cat becomes a young adult.

In acquired hair loss, the cat is born with a normal hair coat. It has or had normal hair follicles at one time, and is or was capable of producing structurally normal hairs. Any disease that can affect hair follicles can cause hair loss. Disease may destroy the hair follicle or shaft or interfere with the growth of hair. Disease can cause the cat discomfort leading to self-trauma and loss of hair. Acquired hair loss can be inflammatory or noninflammatory.

Diseases that can directly cause destruction or damage to the hair shaft or follicle include bacterial, fungal, or parasitic infections; skin trauma such as burns; and (rarely) poisonings caused by mercury, thallium, or iodine. These diseases tend to be inflammatory.

Diseases that can inhibit or slow hair follicle growth include nutritional deficiencies (particularly protein deficiencies) or hormonal imbalances. Temporary hair loss can occur during pregnancy, while nursing, or several weeks after a severe illness or fever. These types of hair loss do not generally cause inflammation unless a secondary infection of the skin develops.

Itching or pain is a common cause of inflammatory hair loss. Diseases that commonly cause itching or pain include skin infections, parasites, and allergies. Friction may cause areas of hair loss, for example, poorly fitted halters or collars. Excessive grooming (usually caused by stress) can cause hair loss in some cats. Unlike dogs, many cats can hide their itching, and it may be hard to determine whether your cat is itchy.

Signs of hair loss may be obvious or subtle, depending on the disease. Congenital or hereditary hair loss is commonly either symmetric (appearing similar on both sides of the body) or localized to one region. It is usually not accompanied by inflammation. Signs of acquired hair loss are varied and often influenced by the underlying cause(s). Inflammation, color change, scaling, excessive shedding, and itching are common. Some causes may lead to the development of secondary skin diseases, such as infection or fluid discharge. Itching is variable, depending on the primary cause.

An accurate diagnosis of the cause of hair loss requires a detailed history and physical examination. The physical examination will cover both the cat's skin and its general health. The veterinarian will also look for signs of skin infections or parasites.

Your veterinarian may order laboratory tests in order to diagnose the cause of hair loss. These often include smears and culture of the skin to check for bacterial, fungal, or yeast infections. If these tests do not identify or suggest an underlying cause, a skin biopsy may be performed. If your veterinarian suspects a hormonal problem, he or she may order blood and urine tests.

Successful treatment depends on the underlying cause and specific diagnosis. Because identifying the underlying cause of the skin condition may take some time,

Shedding

Many cat owners seek veterinary assistance because their pet sheds excessively. You should remember that the natural development and growth of new hair is accompanied by the shedding of old hair. Shedding may be abnormal (excessive) if it results in obvious loss of the hair coat and bald spots. Abnormal shedding may be caused by bacterial infection. However, if the shedding is not accompanied by bald patches or symmetric hair loss, it is likely the shedding is just a stage in the natural replacement of the hair coat.

many veterinarians will provide or prescribe medication to relieve any discomfort or itching your pet has in connection with the hair loss.

HIVES AND RASHES (URTICARIA)

Hives or skin rashes (urticaria) are small patches of red, usually itchy, skin. They are very rare in cats and are most often associated with insect bites or stings or with medications. Hives may develop after inhaling or consuming allergens.

The wheals (eruptions) appear within a few minutes or hours of exposure to the causative agent. In severe cases, the skin eruptions are preceded by fever, poor appetite, or dullness. They can develop on any part of the body but occur mainly on the back, flanks, neck, eyelids, and legs. In advanced cases, they may be found on the mucous membranes of the mouth, nose, lining of the eyes, rectum, and vagina.

Often, hives disappear as rapidly as they arise, usually within a few hours. Treatment may not be required. They may return rapidly if exposure to the cause is not eliminated, however. Treatment may include rapid-acting corticosteroids. If hives are chronic, food or environmental allergens should be considered as potential causes.

ITCHING (PRURITUS)

The medical term for itching is pruritus. Itching is defined as an unpleasant sensation within the skin that provokes the desire to scratch.

Itching is a sign, not a diagnosis or a specific disease. The most common causes of itching are parasites, infections, and allergies. There are many skin diseases that do not initially cause itching. However, itching may develop with these diseases due to secondary bacterial or yeast infections. It is possible that by the time itching develops the initial cause is long gone.

Itching may be general or confined to one area. The cat will excessively scratch, bite, or lick its skin. Your veterinarian will perform a thorough skin history and physical examination. Parasites, including mites and fleas, are often the first possible cause your veterinarian will seek to exclude. Next, the veterinarian will look for infectious causes of skin disease. Bacterial and yeast infections are also common causes of itching. If such an infection is suspected, your veterinarian may prescribe a course of antibiotics that lasts 3 to 4 weeks.

If the itching goes away, then the cause was a microbial infection. However, if the cat's itching is unchanged or only somewhat better, then the underlying cause may be an allergy. The most common causes of allergic itching are insect bites, food allergy, and an inherited skin allergy called atopy (*see* page 493). Sensitivity to insect bites is readily identified. Cats that have seasonal itching are likely reacting to seasonal allergens. Cats with year-round allergic itching may have a food allergy or allergies to house dust mites in addition to seasonal allergens. Food allergy is identified based on response to a diet trial (*see also* page 493). During a diet trial the cat is provided with a diet that does not include the foods it has normally consumed. Your veterinarian will specify a diet, often one containing lamb or other meats not previously fed. To help your veterinarian isolate the food allergy, you will need to follow the prescribed diet fully and carefully and avoid providing treats that do not comply with the diet. Food allergies cannot be diagnosed by a blood test or skin testing.

Successful treatment depends on identification of the underlying cause. Cats with itching of unknown cause, or those in which treatment of the underlying disease does not eliminate the itching, require medical management. Usually, this means giving the cat prescription medication. In addition, essential fatty acids may be added to the anti-itching treatment program.

Lice and nits may be seen when the fur is parted.

LICE

Lice are small, flightless insects that live in the hair or feathers of animals and people. Most lice are of the biting or chewing type (order Mallophaga), including the cat louse (*Felicola subrostrata*). Lice are most often seen on older, longhaired cats that are no longer able to groom themselves.

Lice live within the environment provided by the skin and hair. They move from host to host by direct contact. In temperate regions, lice are most common during the colder months and hard to find in the summer. Most Mallophaga lice have definite preferences as to their hosts: they will often live on only one species or several closely related species.

Lice have claws on their legs that are adapted for clinging to hair. Females glue their eggs, known as nits, to the hairs of the host near the skin. The nits are tightly attached and ordinary shampooing will not dislodge them. It takes about 3 to 4 weeks for most lice to go from nit to adult.

The first signs that your cat may have lice are scratching, biting, and rubbing of infested areas. If the lice are abundant, the hair might also be matted. Usually, diagnosis is made by seeing lice on the infested cat. Parting the hair often reveals the lice. Lice are active and can be seen moving through the hair.

Using a fine-toothed comb to dislodge nits is a tedious process that will not kill lice that have hatched. Cats and other pets are more frequently treated with dips, washes, sprays, or dusts that kill lice. Your veterinarian can recommend an appropriate control product for your pet and pro-

vide directions for its use. (For a more detailed discussion of LICE, see page 259.)

The lice that infest cats and other pets are not normally attracted to humans. Therefore, while care in dealing with the lice infesting your pet is recommended, owners should understand that people rarely get lice from their pets.

MITE INFESTATION (MANGE, ACARIASIS, SCABIES)

Mange is caused by microscopic mites that invade the skin of otherwise healthy animals. The mites cause irritation of the skin, resulting in itching, hair loss, and inflammation. All forms of mange are highly contagious. Cats are very susceptible to several types of mange, including canine scabies (see page 260), feline scabies (notoedric mange), ear mites (otodectic mange), walking dandruff (cheyletiellosis), and trombiculosis. Demodicosis is not considered mange, but it is also caused by mites.

Feline Scabies (Notoedric Mange)

Infestation with *Notoedres cati* mites is a rare and a highly contagious skin disease of otherwise healthy cats. The mite's appearance and life cycle are very similar to that of the sarcoptic mange mite (see page 260). Mange is readily transmitted between cats by contact. Notoedric mange causes severe itching. Skin crusts and hair loss first appear on the ears, head, and neck, but can spread over the entire body. Veterinarians diagnose notoedric mange by using a microscope to inspect skin scrapings for mites. Treatment involves lime-sulfur dips given 10 days apart. Your veterinarian might also try treatment with other medications.

Ear Mites (Otodectic Mange)

This form of mange is caused by *Otodectes cynotis* mites. These mites often infest the external ear, causing inflammation of the ear canal (*see* page 436). Although ear mange occurs in dogs, it is especially common in cats. Ear mites are usually found deep in the external ear canal, but they are sometimes seen on the body. The infested animal will shake its head and scratch its ear(s). The external ear may droop. The intensity of the itching varies. In severe cases, the external ear may be

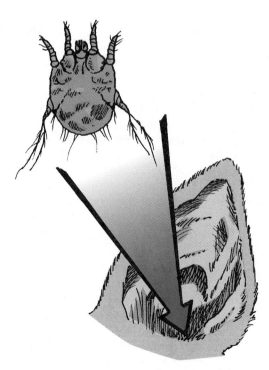

Ear mange mites cause inflammation of the ear canal and skin disease in cats.

inflamed and produce pus; a torn eardrum is also possible. Cats with ear mites should be treated with a suitable medication in the ears, as well as with whole body drugs, for 2 to 4 weeks.

Walking Dandruff (Cheyletiellosis)

Cheyletiella blakei mites are the most common cause of walking dandruff in cats. (The dandruff that is seen "walking" is actually the mites moving about on the skin of the cat.) *Cheyletiella* mites are very contagious, especially in catteries or multipet households. Regular use of certain insecticides to control flea infestations has a side benefit of often controlling the mites that cause walking dandruff. Humans are frequently infested with this mite. Mites that cause walking dandruff have 4 pairs of legs and large hook-like mouthparts. They live on the skin's surface, and they spend their entire 3-week life cycle on their host.

Scaling of the skin and infestation along the back are common signs of walking dandruff. Intense itching is frequent among infested cats, though there may be no itching at all. Cats may develop skin crusts and many small bumps along their back (*see also* FLEA ALLERGY DERMATITIS, page 495). Some cats may show no signs of infestation but carry the mites and transmit them to other pets and humans.

For treatment, your veterinarian may prescribe weekly dipping in an insecticide to eliminate the mites. In addition, treating the household is necessary to kill mites that can survive in bedding, carpets, and other areas.

Feline Demodicosis

Demodicosis is caused by *Demodex* mites. *Demodex* mites are thought to be a normal resident of feline skin. Two species of *Demodex* mites can cause demodicosis. *Demodex gatoi* is smaller and rounder than *Demodex cati*. It is commonly found in younger cats and is contagious.

These mites do not usually bother their host, but they can cause demodicosis in cats sickened by another disease. Demodicosis can be limited to one or several areas on the head and neck, where it causes hair loss, or it can spread over the entire body. When demodicosis is severe enough to affect the entire body, it causes crusting and fluid-filled sores in addition to hair loss. Whole-body demodicosis can be associated with other system-wide diseases, such as diabetes mellitus.

In some cases of demodicosis, the only sign is overproduction of earwax (*see* OTITIS EXTERNA, page 437). The severity of itching can vary; *D. gatoi* is more likely to cause severe itching than *D. cati*. Your veterinarian will diagnose demodicosis by collecting and examining deep skin scrapings for mites. However, the mites can be very difficult to find, and a response to treatment may be the only way to diagnose the infestation. Cats with generalized disease, such as diabetes, should be evaluated by a veterinarian if demodicosis is suspected. The outlook for recovery from whole-body demodicosis depends on the cat's overall health. Some cases resolve without treatment. Treatment with lime sulfur dips 1 to 2 times weekly for 4 to 5 weeks is usually safe and effective. Infested cats often have a fast response to treatment.

Trombiculosis

Trombiculosis is a type of mange caused by the parasitic larval stage of mites of the family Trombiculidae. Adults and nymphs look like very tiny spiders and live on rotting material. Cats acquire the larval lifestage as parasites when lying on the ground or walking in a suitable habitat.

The larvae attach to the host, feed for a few days, and leave when engorged. They are easily identified as tiny, orange-red, oval dots that do not move. These are usually found clustering on the head, ears, feet, or belly. Signs include redness, bumps, hair loss, and skin crusts. Intense itching can persist even after the parasites have left the animal.

Diagnosis is based on history and signs. Your veterinarian will want to exclude other skin disorders that cause itching, such as allergies (*see* page 493). Diagnosis is confirmed by careful examination of the affected areas. Skin scrapings might also be examined under the microscope for evidence of mite larvae.

Treatment for cats with trombiculosis follows the pattern for the general treatment of mange. Medications to kill these mites may be different than those prescribed for other types of mites. Follow your veterinarian's treatment program carefully. If the itching has been either severe or extended, antibiotics or other medications may be prescribed to control secondary infections in scratch and bite wounds.

Preventing reinfestation is often difficult. The most useful approach, if feasible, consists of keeping pets away from areas known to harbor mites. You should also avoid bringing your cat into contact with other animals known to have the mites.

▩ PARASITIC WORMS OF THE SKIN

Helminths are parasitic worms. *Dracunculus insignis* is a species of roundworm found mainly in the connective tissue beneath the skin of the legs. They are known to infest raccoons, minks, and other animals in North America. These worms are rare in cats, but they are occasionally found in cats that have been around small lakes and bodies of shallow, stagnant water. Cats can also become infected by drinking contaminated water or eating an infected animal such as a frog. Treatment requires careful extraction of the worm by a veterinarian. In some cases, medications are also given. (For a more detailed discussion of DRACUNCULUS INFECTION, *see* page 263.)

▩ PHOTOSENSITIZATION

Photosensitization is a condition in which skin is overly sensitive to sunlight; it is not the same as sunburn. Certain molecules present in the skin are energized by light. When the molecules return to the less energized state, the released energy causes chemical reactions in the skin. Photosensitization can be difficult to distinguish from actual sunburn.

Photosensitization is often classified according to the source of the photodynamic pigment. These categories are primary or type I photosensitivity, abnormal pigment creation or type II photosensitivity, and type III or secondary photosensitivity. A wide range of chemicals in plants, fungi, and bacteria may act as photosensitization agents. Photosensitization can also occur in cats that have liver damage caused by any of several types of poisonings.

The signs associated with photosensitivity are similar regardless of the cause. Photosensitive cats squirm in apparent discomfort when exposed to sunlight. They scratch or rub lightly pigmented, exposed areas of skin (for example, the ears, eyelids, or nose). Bright sunlight can cause typical skin changes, even in black-coated animals. Redness develops rapidly and is soon followed by swelling. If exposure to light stops at this stage, the abnormalities soon resolve. When exposure is prolonged, fluid discharge, scab formation, and skin death result.

Signs are easily recognized in cases of severe photosensitivity but are similar to the effects of sunburn in early or mild cases. When examining your cat for photosensitivity, your veterinarian will not only examine the skin but also look for signs of any of the diseases that may trigger this condition. Evaluation of liver enzymes and liver biopsies may be necessary to determine if your cat has liver disease. Laboratory tests may also be performed. Your veterinarian will also ask about your pet's access to poisons and whether or not your cat may have been exposed to rat poison or other poisonous chemicals.

Treatment involves mostly soothing the signs. While photosensitivity continues, cats should be shaded fully or, preferably, kept indoors and allowed out only during darkness. The severe stress of photosensitization and extensive death of skin tissue can cause serious illness and even death. Depending on the individual case, injectable steroids may be helpful. Sec-ondary skin infections and fluid discharge are treated with standard wound management techniques. Exposure to flies must be prevented because the skin damage caused by photosensitivity attracts flies and may lead to maggot infestations and serious diseases. Skin abnormalities caused by photosensitivity heal remarkably well, even after extensive damage. The outlook for recovery is related to the site and severity of the primary lesion and/or liver disease, and to the degree of healing.

■ POX INFECTION

One pox virus is known to infect cats. It has been reported occasionally in the United Kingdom (Great Britain) and Western Europe, but not in the United States. The virus is indistinguishable from cowpox virus. Cats are believed to contract this virus while hunting. Most infected cats are from rural environments and are known to hunt rodents, which are believed to be the reservoir host. Infection in cats is seasonal with most cases occurring between September and November.

Most cats with pox virus infections have a history of a single affected area, usually on the head, neck, or forelimb. The primary abnormality can vary from a small scabbed wound to a large abscess. Widespread secondary areas start appearing about 7 to 10 days after the primary one. These develop into well-defined, circular ulcers about 0.125 to 0.25 inches (0.5 to 1 centimeters) in diameter. The sores become covered with scabs. Healing is complete in about 6 weeks. Many cats show no signs other than the affected areas of skin, but about 25% develop mild nose or eye infections. In rare cases, cats may develop a severe generalized form of the disease that affects the liver, lungs, trachea, bronchial tissues, the mouth lining, and the small intestine.

Laboratory tests can confirm a diagnosis of pox infection. Veterinarians will usually suspect a pox infection if the cat is from an area where the disease is known and the cat has a habit of hunting.

Prompt diagnosis is important because steroid treatment (which is often used for other skin conditions) is not appropriate for pox infections. The virus can also cause localized skin disease in people, so appropriate precautions to minimize contact with infected cats should be taken. For pet cats, supportive treatment—usually including broad-spectrum antibiotics and fluid treatment—is generally successful and most cats recover from the infection.

▓ PYODERMA

Pyoderma literally means "pus in the skin" and can be caused by infection, inflammation, or cancer. It is not common in cats.

The most common sign of bacterial pyoderma is excessive scaling, particularly on the back near the tail. Scales are often pierced by hairs. Intact pustules are almost never found. Hair loss leads to small bald patches in affected areas or just excessive scaling. Deep pyoderma in a cat is most commonly seen as either a cat bite abscess or chin acne. Recurrent, nonhealing deep pyoderma in cats can be associated with multisystem disease, such as infection with feline immunodeficiency virus or feline leukemia virus, or atypical mycobacteria.

Diagnosis is based on signs. It is also important to identify any underlying causes. The most common causes include fleas, allergies, and poor grooming. However, any disease that causes itching and self-trauma can trigger a pyoderma. Multiple deep skin scrapings are needed to exclude parasitic infections. Bacterial and fungal cultures may also be done.

The most common causes of a bacterial pyoderma that recurs after treatment include failure to identify an underlying trigger or stopping antibiotics too soon. Thus, it is important to fully follow your veterinarian's instructions for any medication. Cats often have concurrent bacterial and yeast infections of the skin, and it is not uncommon for your veterinarian to treat both diseases.

Antibiotic treatment is usually prescribed for at least 3 weeks. Longterm, recurrent, or deep pyodermas typically require 8 to 12 weeks or longer to heal completely.

Attention to grooming is also crucial. The hair coat should be clipped in cats with deep pyoderma and a professional grooming is recommended in medium- to long-haired cats. This will remove excessive hair that can trap debris and bacteria and will help grooming. Carefully follow your veterinarian's instructions regarding grooming.

▓ RINGWORM (DERMATOPHYTOSIS)

Ringworm is an infection of skin, hair, or claws caused by a type of fungus known as a dermatophyte. In cats, about 98% of ringworm cases are caused by the fungus *Microsporum canis*. The fungus is spread easily in the environment and often infects people. (*See also* FUNGAL INFECTIONS, page 537.)

The fungi spread to people primarily by contact with infected cats and contaminated objects such as furniture or grooming tools. Broken hairs with associated spores are important sources for spread of the disease. Contact does not always result in infection. Whether infection is established depends on the fungal species and on host factors, including age, health, condition of exposed skin surfaces, grooming habits, and nutrition. Infection leads to temporary resistance to reinfection. Under most circumstances, dermatophytes grow only in the dead cells of skin and hair, and infection stops on reaching living cells or inflamed tissue. As inflammation and host immunity develop, further spread of infection stops, but this process may take several weeks.

Infected cats can develop circular, bald, scaly patches with broken hairs in ring-like whirls. The center of the rings can regrow darker than normal hair. The most common areas for ringworm to occur are the face, ear tips, tail, and feet.

Veterinarians diagnose ringworm by fungal culture, examination with an ultraviolet lamp, and direct microscopic examination of hair or skin scale. Fungal culture of hairs and scrapings from the affected areas is the most accurate method. Direct microscopic examination of hairs or skin scrapings may allow early diagnosis.

Ringworm infections clear up without treatment, but cats with widespread ringworm are most often treated with antifungal medications prescribed by a veterinarian. Treatment with medicated shampoos can speed healing in some cases. Such treatments are not always effective, however. Your veterinarian can provide you with information about any treatment that may be appropriate for your pet and advise you regarding precautions you should take to avoid ringworm infection in yourself and members of your family.

■ TICKS

Ticks are blood-sucking parasites that attach themselves to animals and people. As they feed, ticks can transmit diseases, including Rocky Mountain spotted fever, Q fever, and Lyme disease. Skin wounds caused by ticks can lead to bacterial infections. Severe tick infestations can lead to anemia and death.

Ticks are much less commonly found on cats than on dogs. However, cats that spend time outdoors, especially in wild areas, are often affected. Diagnosis is by appearance of tick bite marks on the animal or the presence of the parasite. Ticks that have been on an animal only a short time (an hour to a few days) appear flat. Ticks that have been on an animal for days appear much more rounded due to the blood they have consumed.

Ticks should be removed as soon as possible to minimize disease and damage. To do this, use tweezers to carefully grasp the tick close to the skin and pull gently. Never try to remove a tick with your bare hands, as some tickborne diseases (for example, Rocky Mountain spotted fever) can be immediately transmitted through breaks in the skin or contact with mucous membranes. The use of hot matches to remove ticks should also be avoided.

Infested cats can be treated with anti-tick insecticides that kill all stages from nymph to adult. These can be given as spot-on solutions (which are applied on the back and spread rapidly over the entire body surface), dips, sprays, and dusts. Care should be taken in selecting the correct anti-tick product. Some products work well on dogs but are dangerous for cats. Contact your veterinarian for a prescription or a recommendation for the best tick control product for your pet.

If your cat is severely infested with ticks, you should take it to a veterinarian for tick removal. Heavy infestations will not only severely damage the skin, but can also cause anemia, paralysis, or other complications. Your veterinarian is in the best position to provide a heavily infested cat with the care it needs. A clinic stay for such pets may be likely. Even if your pet has acquired only a few ticks, you should have your pet checked for the many diseases spread by these parasites. Monitor the site(s) from which you have removed ticks. If a tick bite turns red or swollen, a prompt trip to the veterinarian is warranted.

Keeping animals away from tick prone areas is the most effective step you can take to control exposure. Most ticks live in particular microhabitats, such as tall grass or the border between wooded areas and lawns. Cleaning and clearing of these microhabitats reduces the number of ticks. Removing tall grass and weeds and trimming vegetation from your property can help protect your animal. Insecticide treatment of vegetation can slightly reduce the risk of ticks. However, it is not recommended for wide use because of environmental pollution and the cost of treating large areas.

■ TUMORS OF THE SKIN

Tumors are abnormal growths of cells. Tumors affecting the skin or the tissue just under the skin are the most commonly seen tumors in cats. This is partly because they are the most easily seen tumors and partly because the skin is constantly exposed to many tumor-causing factors in the environment. Chemical carcinogens, solar radiation, and viruses all can cause skin tumors. Hormonal and genetic factors may also play a role.

Distinguishing a tumor from an inflammatory disease is difficult. Skin tumors can appear in many forms. They are usually small lumps or bumps, but they also can occur as hairless, discolored patches, rashes, or nonhealing sores. Because skin tumors are so diverse, identifying them should be left to a veterinarian.

Tumors can be benign or malignant (cancerous). Malignant tumors can spread and cause harm to the animal. Distinguishing a benign tumor from a cancerous tumor requires specialized knowledge and laboratory equipment. A veterinarian can perform a fine needle aspiration of cells or a biopsy (which removes a small amount of tissue from a tumor) for evaluation.

Treatment depends largely on the type of tumor, its location and size, and overall physical condition of the animal. For benign tumors that are not ulcerated and do not impair the animal's normal routine, treatment may not be necessary. This could be the most prudent option, especially in aged cats.

For malignant tumors or benign tumors that inhibit normal activities or are cosmetically unpleasant, there are several options. For most, surgical removal is the most effective, the least costly, and the option with the fewest adverse effects. Laser and cryotherapy (freezing) are also options for treating small superficial tumors. If malignancy is suspected, surrounding tissue may also be surgically removed. For tumors that cannot be completely removed, partial removal may prolong the life of the animal. Radiation treatment or chemotherapy may also be used to provide your cat with the best possible outcome.

In addition to skin and hair follicle tumors, there are tumors that affect the ceruminous gland. These are discussed in the section on ear diseases (*see* page 437).

Basal Cell Tumors and Carcinomas

Basal cells lie at the base of the top layer of the skin (the epidermis). A benign growth of these cells is a basal cell tumor. A malignant growth is a basal cell carcinoma.

Basal cell tumors are common in older cats. Domestic longhair, Himalayan, and Persian are the breeds most at risk. Tumors may develop almost anywhere on the body. These tumors generally appear as firm, solitary, often hairless or ulcerated lumps. The lumps may stick out like stalks from the skin surface. They vary in size from less than 0.4 inches (1 centimeter) to more than 4 inches (10 centimeters) in diameter. In cats, these tumors are often dark in color. Cysts may form. Although basal cell tumors are benign, some grow rapidly and may cause extensive ulceration and secondary inflammation. Surgical removal is an effective treatment.

Basal cell carcinomas are malignant tumors that occur most frequently in aged cats. Persians are more prone to them. They often appear as ulcers on the head, legs, or neck. Unlike benign basal cell tumors, these carcinomas are not usually raised up from the skin. They spread, forming new ulcers. Surgical removal is the treatment of choice. These tumors spread to neighboring skin but seldom spread to other organs.

Benign Fibroblastic Tumors

Benign fibroblastic tumors include the tumors known as collagenous nevi.

Collagenous nevi are benign buildups of collagen that are uncommon in cats. They generally are found in middle-aged or older cats, most frequently on the legs, head, neck, and areas prone to trauma. They are flat to raised lumps that develop in the dermal layer of the skin or in the fat beneath the skin. Surgical removal of both forms is generally effective. Infrequently, some may grow too large to be surgically removed.

Fibromas usually begin in the dermal layer of the skin and have well defined edges. They resemble collagenous nevi.

While they are most common in dogs, all domestic animals can develop fibromas. These are usually benign. They appear as raised, often hairless, lumps that may feel firm or rubbery. Unless fibromas are malignant or interfere with the cat's activities or appearance, treatment is optional. In some cases, fibromas may grow to be quite large. In these cases, surgical removal is recommended to make the cat more comfortable.

Benign, Nonviral, Wart-like Tumors

These tumors are not, in the strictest sense, warts, although they may resemble warts. They are often easy to remove and do not threaten the cat's overall health. (*See also* WARTS [PAPILLOMAS], page 513.)

Blood Vessel Tumors

Blood vessel tumors of the skin are benign growths that resemble normal blood vessels. These are uncommon tumors of adult cats and most often develop on the head, legs, and abdomen.

Hemangiomas are single to multiple, circular, often compressible, red to black lumps. They can look like "blood blisters." Hemangiomas are benign, but they tend to develop ulcers and grow quite large. It is important to identify the type of tumor to be sure it is not a malignant growth, so surgical removal is the treatment of choice. However, the tumors may be large and involve the lower legs, making surgical removal difficult. In these cases, freezing (cryotherapy) or radiation may be necessary. These tumors do not usually spread to new sites after complete surgical removal.

Angiosarcomas are the most likely of all soft-tissue tumors to grow quickly and spread to other locations. These tumors can arise at any time, but seem to occur most often in older, neutered male cats. When present, they are usually found on the legs and trunk of the cat. Some forms of angiosarcomas have been associated with prolonged exposure to the sun, especially in cats with white coats.

Angiosarcomas can vary greatly in appearance. Most commonly, they appear as one or more red lumps in the skin or underlying soft tissues. Less frequently, they appear as a poorly defined bruise. These tumors spread, especially to the lungs and liver. In most cases, surgical removal is the treatment of choice. Because these tumors often spread throughout the body, your veterinarian will remove both the tumor and a wide margin of tissue surrounding it. For surface tumors, cryosurgery (freezing) can be used as needed. Avoidance of further sun exposure may reduce the development of new tumors.

Keratinized Skin Cysts

Some cats develop cysts that are filled with keratin, a skin protein. These are described as keratinized skin cysts. The cysts are benign and have a hard or solid core. Most such cysts are malformations of hair follicles and may be the same color as the hair. They are only occasionally found in cats. The cysts can be solitary or multiple. Surgical removal is the usual treatment.

Dilated pores of Winer are rare, hair-follicle growths recognized only in aged cats. Males may be predisposed. Growths most often develop on the head. They are solitary and dome-shaped. They may stick out from the surface, giving them the appearance of a skin horn. As with other keratinized skin cysts, these often closely resemble a large blackhead.

Lipomas and Liposarcomas

Lipomas are benign tumors of fatty (adipose) tissue. Older, neutered, male Siamese cats are most at risk for these tumors. They are most commonly found on the abdomen. Obesity does not appear to be a factor in the development of lipomas in cats. Lipomas typically appear as soft, occasionally thin, discrete lumpy masses. Most move freely when touched. Many lipomas merge with the healthy fat tissue next to them, making it difficult for a veterinarian to identify the edge of the tumor.

Despite their benign nature, lipomas should not be ignored because they tend to grow, and they may be indistinguishable from infiltrative lipomas or liposarcomas (*see* below). Surgical removal is the treatment. In most cases, the surgeon will remove not only the visible lipoma but also tissue around it. This provides the cat with the best possibility for a positive outcome.

Infiltrative lipomas are very rare in cats. When they are found, they are usually treated as malignant tumors even though they rarely spread to other organs. These tumors are soft, lumpy swellings in the fat layer under the skin. They can spread to underlying muscle and connective tissue. Invasive lipomas are considered sarcomas of partial malignancy. They rarely spread to other locations. Failure to remove the entire tumor can result in spread to nearby tissue. Surgery to remove the tumor and a wide margin of surrounding tissue is usually the treatment of choice. Amputation may be necessary.

Liposarcomas are rare tumors that are lumpy and soft to firm. Liposarcomas are malignant tumors that have a low potential to spread to other organs. In cats, feline leukemia virus infection has been infrequently associated with these tumors. Wide surgical removal of the tumor plus surrounding tissue is recommended. Recurrence is common, so followup radiation treatment may be required.

Lymphoid Tumors of the Skin

Lymphoma or **lymphosarcoma** is a cancer of the blood and lymphatic system. A rare form of lymphoma may first occur as lymphoid infiltrations of the skin, causing distinctive tumors. Lymphosarcoma in cats generally begins in other parts of the body, such as the intestinal tract or the lymphatic system. Lymphoma is associated with infection by feline leukemia virus. (For a more detailed discussion of FELINE LEUKEMIA VIRUS, *see* page 533.)

Epitheliotropic skin lymphosarcoma is the most frequently recognized form of lymphoid skin tumors in cats. Among cats, the disease tends to develop in older animals. Signs are often extremely subtle. Tumors often appear initially as a crusty plaque that may itch. Accurate diagnosis in the early stages is difficult. Thus, skin scrapings, biopsies, and other diagnostic tools will be used to identify suspicious tissues. The tumors evolve into unmistakable skin lymphosarcoma. Unfortunately, effective treatment in cats is limited.

Nonepitheliotropic skin lymphosarcoma may occur as either single or multiple tumors in cats. The tumors are lumps or plaques that most commonly develop on the trunk. The disease occurs in middle-aged or older cats. The tumors are thick patches or lumps that can have hair loss or skin ulcers. The disease spreads quickly. Even when a solitary lump is completely surgically removed, recurrence is likely. Surgical removal is the most common treatment; the effectiveness of chemotherapy is limited.

Mast Cell Tumors

Mast cell tumors are a kind of tumor named for the type of skin cell from which they grow. Skin mast cell tumors are common. There are also generalized, blood cell, splenic, and digestive tract forms of mast cell sarcoma.

Two distinct variants occur: a mast cell type and a histiocytic type. The mast cell type is most common. They are found primarily in cats younger than 4 years old. They may develop anywhere on the body but are most commonly found on the head and neck. The tumors are benign, single, hairless lumps, generally 0.8 to 1.6 inches (2 to 3 centimeters) in diameter. Occasionally these tumors may extend into the fat beneath the skin. Surgical removal is the treatment of choice; few tumors of this kind return after surgery and, of those that do, considerably fewer spread. Freezing (cryosurgery) is an option used by veterinarians to treat multiple recurrent small tumors in cats that may have problems with anesthesia.

The histiocytic type of skin mast cell tumor in cats is seen primarily in Siamese cats younger than 4 years old. Tumors may develop anywhere on the body and appear as multiple, small (less than 0.4 inches [1 centimeter] in diameter), firm, lumps under the skin surface. Older cats generally have fewer tumors. This variant may be difficult to distinguish from simple inflammation. Because these tumors usually go away on their own, treatment may not be necessary.

Melanomas

A melanoma is a dark-pigmented skin tumor. They are rare in cats and may be either malignant or benign. Unlike in people, sun damage is seldom associated with melanomas in cats.

Melanomas in cats are found most often on the head (especially the ears and eyes), neck, and lower legs in middle-aged or older cats. They can appear as spots, patches, or raised or flat masses. Most have a dark surface. Although generally solitary, these tumors may be multiple. Surgical removal is the treatment of choice and offers a good outcome for benign tumors.

Neurofibromas and Neurofibrosarcomas

Neurofibromas and neurofibrosarcomas are tumors that grow in the connective tissue around a nerve. They are found in older cats. These tumors appear as white, firm, lumps. There are benign and mildly malignant types. Most are locally invasive but do not spread to distant organs. Complete surgical removal is the treatment of choice. Followup radiation treatment may slow regrowth of the tumor.

Sebaceous Gland Tumors

The sebaceous glands secrete oil (sebum) into the hair follicles and onto the skin. Tumors and tumor-like conditions of sebaceous glands are infrequent in cats. Older cats are more likely to develop these tumors than young or middle-aged cats. Persians are the breed most predisposed. When tumors occur, they are typically found in multiple places. They may occur anywhere on the body but are most often found on the head. Sebaceous adenomas may be covered with a crust and inflamed with pus.

Sebaceous gland adenocarcinomas are the rare malignant form of these tumors. They occur in middle-aged or older cats. Female cats may be predisposed. These are hard to distinguish from sebaceous epitheliomas or other skin carcinomas. A biopsy (laboratory study of a tissue sample from the tumor) is usually required to make a definitive diagnosis. These tumors spread within the skin and may spread to regional lymph nodes late in the disease.

Once a diagnosis is established, treatment is optional for benign sebaceous gland tumors unless they are inflamed and infected. For malignant adenocarcinomas, surgical removal (both the tumor and adjacent tissue including any involved lymph nodes) is the treatment of choice. Chemotherapy and radiation treatment may also be prescribed. Even benign sebaceous gland growths recur following surgery if the tumor is not completely removed. In addition, cats that develop one sebaceous gland tumor often develop new tumors at other sites. Your veterinarian may recommend consultation with a specialist in the treatment of cancer (oncologist) or skin disorders (dermatologist) to provide the best treatment for your cat.

Soft Tissue Giant Cell Tumors (Fibrous Histiocytomas)

Malignant fibrous histiocytomas are most frequently found in the skin and soft tissues of aged cats. They are most common on the lower legs or lower neck but may also occur at vaccination sites. They seldom spread to other locations in the body but tend to return after surgical removal. Because these tumors often recur, your veterinarian will remove the tumor and some surrounding tissue. This is necessary to provide your cat with the best possible outcome.

Soft Tissue Sarcomas

Sarcomas on the surface of the skin tend to have a more benign behavior, whereas deep sarcomas are considered malignant. Also, the larger the tumor, the more likely it is to be malignant. A rapidly growing tumor is more likely to be malignant than one that develops slowly. Some sarcomas are found at vaccine sites in cats.

Many sarcomas are shaped like an octopus, with tentacles that extend deeply into surrounding tissue. Diagnosis consists of finding a mass on the cat and confirming that the cells in the tumor are spindle cells. Cells are best obtained through a biopsy.

Surgical removal is the treatment of choice. Because groups of tumor cells that are too small to see grow out as tentacles from the main tumor, your veterinarian will remove not only the easily visible tumor (the head of the octopus) but also a wide margin of tissue surrounding it. In some cases, amputation may be required because the tumor cannot be completely removed from a leg. The best, if not only, opportunity to completely remove a sarcoma is during the initial surgery. Sarcomas that recur have a greater potential for invasion into deeper tissues and spread to other parts of the body. Later surgeries for recurrent tumors may not increase the longterm survival of the cat. Spindle-cell sarcomas generally do not respond well to conventional doses of radiation. Higher doses have been somewhat successful. Surgical removal followed by radiation treatment, or radiation treatment given prior to surgery may provide a longer tumor-free interval. Chemotherapy for sarcomas has become a more common means of treatment. Although chemotherapy may improve the quality and prolong the life of an affected cat, it seldom provides a complete cure.

Fibromatosis is a thickening and invasive growth in tendon sheaths. Fibromatoses are infrequently diagnosed in cats. They are locally invasive but do not spread to distant organs. If feasible, surgical removal is the treatment of choice. Recurrence is common, and radiation treatment may be helpful.

Fibrosarcomas grow rapidly and may spread to other locations. These are the most common soft tissue tumors in cats. Fibrosarcomas vary greatly in appearance and size. Tumors arising under the skin surface may appear lumpy. Those arising in the fat or other tissues under the skin surface may not be noticed unless a thorough, hands-on physical examination is performed. They are firm and fleshy and appear deep in the skin and the fat underneath. They often invade muscles. When tumors are multiple, they usually occur within the same area of the body.

Three forms of fibrosarcoma are recognized in cats: a multiple form generally found in cats younger than 4 years old and caused by the feline sarcoma virus; a solitary form in the young or old cat, not caused by feline sarcoma virus; and a tumor that develops in the soft tissues where cats are commonly vaccinated. Some rabies and feline leukemia virus vaccines may increase the risk of this type of tumor. These tumors appear as lumps or hard patches between the shoulder blades or in the soft tissues of the hind legs or flanks (*see* VACCINE-ASSOCIATED TUMORS, page 511).

Surgical removal by a board-certified surgeon is considered the best treatment; however, complete removal is very difficult to achieve. When removing a fibrosarcoma, the veterinary surgeon will remove not only the tumor but also a wide and deep tissue margin around the tumor as well. Because it is difficult to determine the tumor's edges, recurrence is common. More than 70% recur within

Some vaccines have been linked with an increased risk of fibrosarcoma in cats.

1 year of the initial surgery. The rate of recurrence is higher than 90% for vaccine-associated sarcomas. Even when surgical removal is complete, recurrence is still the rule. Radiation treatment is recommended prior to or following surgery to increase the tumor-free interval. Chemotherapy has been recommended for tumors that cannot be removed.

Vaccine-associated Tumors

In the 1990s an increase in the frequency of fibrosarcomas under the skin of cats was noticed by veterinarians. The tumors were often located in places where vaccines were commonly given, such as between the shoulder blades. Some vaccines, such as certain rabies and feline leukemia vaccines, have been linked with an increased risk of this tumor. Adjuvants, which are compounds added to a vaccine to boost the animal's immune response, may be a factor in causing the tumors. Because the tumors often spread locally and can be difficult to remove, vaccine recommendations have been changed. Changes may include vaccinating cats less frequently, matching which vaccines are given to the risk of infections that the cat may be exposed to, and giving the vaccine in the leg rather than between the shoulder blades. Vaccine manufacturers are also researching more effective vaccines and new ways of giving them that eliminate the need to add adjuvants.

Cat owners should be aware, however, that the overall risk of this tumor is low. Estimates run from 1 in 1,000 to as low as 1 in 10,000 cats affected. The disease protection that the vaccines provide will far outweigh the risk in most cases. Your veterinarian can recommend the vaccines and vaccination schedule best suited for your cat, taking into account factors such as your cat's age, health, and exposure to other animals.

Squamous Cell Carcinomas

In cats that are all or partially white, prolonged exposure to sunlight is a major cause of **skin squamous cell carcinomas**. Abnormalities usually develop on the ears, eye ridges, eyelids, nose, or lips of cats that have white skin in these regions. Before a malignant tumor develops, cats develop **solar keratosis**. The signs of solar keratosis include thickening and discoloration of skin. Surgery to remove the tumor is the usual treatment, but cryotherapy (freezing), topical chemotherapy, or radiation treatment may be used as needed. Limiting exposure to ultraviolet radiation may help prevent skin squamous cell carcinomas. This may be accomplished by using ultraviolet window screens, sunscreen, and keeping your cat indoors during hours of peak sunlight. Before using a sunscreen on your cat, please consult your veterinarian for recommendations. Sunscreen products prepared for human use are not always safe for cats and should never be used around the eyes.

Oral squamous cell carcinomas may appear in the mouth and on the tongue of cats and are not solar induced. The grooming habits of cats expose them to carcinogens such as cigarette smoke and flea collars, which increase their risk of developing these squamous cell carcinomas. Most oral squamous cell

Squamous cell carcinoma occurs on lightly pigmented areas that are exposed to ultraviolet light, such as the tips of the ears.

carcinomas are single, ulcerated lesions. They often mimic dental disease because they involve the teeth and the bone of the jaw or maxilla. The ulcerative lesions invade other local tissues. Specialized oral surgery to remove the involved bone is the recommended treatment, but it is difficult for cats because they will require feeding tubes. Surgery is followed by radiation treatment. Chemotherapy may be of limited help in some cases. The outcome is guarded to poor in most cases. Most cats have advanced disease at diagnosis.

Feline Bowen's disease (also known as feline multicentric squamous cell carcinoma in situ) is a disease of aged (over 10 years old) cats that may be associated with reduced immunity. Tumors appear as multiple discrete red, black, or brown patches and bumps. Their development is associated with the presence of a papillomavirus. Lesions grow on the skin surface, but eventually these tumors may change into a form that spreads into underlying tissues. No treatment has yet proven to be completely successful; however, cryotherapy (freezing), localized radiation treatment, and topical treatment may control the lesions initially.

Sweat Gland Tumors

There are 2 types of sweat glands: apocrine and eccrine. **Apocrine gland cysts** are found in middle-aged or older cats. They can occur either in or outside of hair follicles. They appear most commonly on the head and neck. Treatment is by surgical removal.

Cystic apocrine gland dilations have 2 forms. In the cystic form, one or more cysts develop in the middle to upper dermis but have little association with hair follicles. There is also a more dispersed form in which apocrine glands associated with multiple hair follicles are dilated.

Apocrine gland adenomas occur in older cats as firm to variable cysts, seldom larger than 1.5 inches (4 centimeters) in diameter, at the base of the sweat gland. They contain varying amounts of clear to brownish fluid. In cats, the fluid may be darkly pigmented. Apocrine adenomas are more likely to occur in male than in female cats. The vast majority of these adenomas occur on the head, especially the ears.

Apocrine ductular adenomas are less common. They are found in older cats and appear closer to the surface of the skin. They are often smaller, firmer, and less cystic than apocrine adenomas.

Apocrine adenomas and apocrine ductular adenomas are benign, and complete surgical removal cures the condition.

Apocrine gland adenocarcinomas are malignant tumors of sweat glands. Siamese cats may be predisposed. This tumor most commonly occurs where the legs meet the trunk and in the groin. Apocrine gland adenocarcinomas generally are larger than adenomas. Their appearance varies from thick lumps to ulcers. These tumors often spread to lymph nodes or, less commonly, to internal organs or skin. Complete surgical removal is the treatment of choice for apocrine gland adenocarcinomas. Little is known about response of these tumors to chemotherapy either alone or in combination with surgery.

Tumors of the Hair Follicle

Trichoepitheliomas are uncommon tumors involving hair follicles in cats. Both benign and malignant forms of these tumors appear. Tumors of the hair follicle can develop anywhere on the body but are most common on the head, tail, and legs. Benign forms appear as cysts 0.4 to 2 inches (1 to 5 centimeters) in diameter in the middle and lower layers of the skin. Expansion of the cysts or self-trauma may cause skin ulcers. Treatment is by surgical removal. However, cats that develop one such tumor are prone to develop more at other sites.

Malignant trichoepitheliomas are much less common than the benign form. They spread to the skin surface and cause extensive inflammation, tissue death, and fibrosis. Spread to other organs is uncommon. Surgery is required to remove malignant trichoepitheliomas. Because they spread, your veterinarian will likely remove tissue around the tumor as well.

Tumors Originating Outside the Skin (Metastatic Tumors)

Tumors that spread from a place of origin in the body to other locations in the body are described as metastatic tumors. It is unusual for tumors originating in another part of the body to spread (metastasize) to the skin. When it does happen in cats, the metastatic tumors usually appear on the paws or legs. If a metastatic tumor is found on one or more paws of a cat, veterinarians will usually check for the presence of lung cancer. Metastatic tumors that affect the skin are associated with very poor prospects for recovery.

Undifferentiated and Anaplastic Sarcomas

These are cancers of **mesenchymal cells** and are not common in cats. Mesenchymal cells are the cells that develop into connective tissues, blood, lymph nodes, and other organs. Cancers of mesenchymal cells are difficult to identify because, like the mesenchymal cells themselves, malignant forms of these cells are loosely organized and often undeveloped or undifferentiated. Once identified, surgery is the usual treatment. When removing these sarcomas, the veterinarian will usually remove not only the visible tumor but also a 2 to 3 centimeter margin of tissue surrounding it. This reduces the chance that the malignancy will recur. Radiation treatment is indicated following surgical removal to increase the tumor-free interval.

Warts (Papillomas)

Papillomaviruses cause warts in most animal species. They are transmitted by direct contact, and possibly by insects. Infection can also be transmitted when a cat comes into contact with an infected object in its environment such as bedding, dishes, collars, leashes, or toys.

In cats, papillomavirus does not cause the hard, rounded warts seen in most other species. Instead, it leads to formation of a squamous cell carcinoma (*see* page 511).

■ WHOLE-BODY DISORDERS THAT AFFECT THE SKIN

A number of whole-body diseases also affect the skin. In some instances, the skin changes are characteristic of the particular disease. Often, however, the signs are not obviously associated with the underlying condition and must be carefully distinguished from primary skin disorders. Some of these secondary disorders are mentioned briefly below and are also described in the chapters on the specific disorders. Some skin disorders may be associated with a poor diet. However, this is uncommon in cats fed modern, balanced diets.

Dermatitis (skin inflammation) is sometimes seen in association with disorders of internal organs, such as the liver, kidneys, or pancreas. Liver disease and diabetes can cause death of skin tissue in old cats. The skin changes include redness, crusting, oozing, and hair loss on the face, genitals, and lower legs, as well as thickened skin and ulcers of the footpads. The skin disease may be noted before the onset of signs of the internal disease.

Fragile skin syndrome (the skin becomes very fragile and is easily broken) in cats has been associated with pancreatic, liver, or adrenal disorders. Pancreatic cancer may cause crusting of the footpads and hair loss in cats.

Hypothyroidism (low levels of thyroid hormone, *see* page 422) is very rare in cats. The disease can cause skin changes with diminished hair growth and hair loss. The skin is dry, scaly, thickened, and folded. Secondary skin infection and seborrhea may occur.

Hyperadrenocorticism (high levels of adrenal gland hormones) also causes skin changes such as darkening, hair loss, seborrhea, and secondary infection. In cats, the skin becomes extremely fragile.

Treatment of all these conditions depends on identifying and treating the underlying disease. The earlier in the disease process your veterinarian can examine your cat, the more rapidly a diagnosis may be obtained and an outcome predicted for the animal.

CHAPTER 36

Kidney and Urinary Tract Disorders

▓ THE URINARY SYSTEM

The urinary system or tract includes the kidneys, the ureters (tubes that connect the kidneys to the bladder), the bladder, and the urethra (the tube through which urine exits the body). The urinary system has several important functions. It gets rid of the waste products that are created when food is transformed into energy. It also maintains the correct balance of water and electrolytes (salts) within the body's cells. Another key function is the production of hormones called erythropoietin and renin, which are important in maintaining healthy blood pressure, producing blood cells, and absorbing salt correctly. Finally, the urinary system processes vitamin D.

▓ DETECTING DISORDERS OF THE KIDNEYS AND URINARY TRACT

Your veterinarian can diagnose many common problems involving the urinary system by taking a medical history, performing a physical examination, and performing tests on the cat's blood and urine. The history might include information regarding changes in how much water your pet drinks, how often it urinates, how much urine it produces, how the urine looks, and how your pet behaves. Your veterinarian will also need information about what medications your pet has taken or is currently taking, your pet's appetite and diet, changes in body weight, and previous illnesses or injuries.

There are many additional tests a veterinarian might sometimes perform in the case of a urinary disorder. These include blood tests, blood pressure tests, urinalysis (laboratory tests on your pet's urine), x-rays, contrast x-rays (tests in which a special dye is given to outline the urinary tract on the x-ray), ultrasonography, biopsies, and cystoscopy. Cystoscopy involves inserting a tube with a small camera at the tip into the urethra. This allows the veterinarian to see problems or changes in the urinary tract more clearly.

Urinalysis is a laboratory test that evaluates urine. It is one of the most important tools a veterinarian can use to diagnose urinary tract problems. Many tests are performed as part of a urinalysis. These include the specific gravity, concentration, appearance, and pH of the urine. Urinalysis also tests for the presence of certain chemicals or substances in the urine, such as sugar, ketones (a byproduct of the body's processing of fat), bilirubin (a pigment produced when the liver processes waste), blood, and protein. The urine sediment is also examined under a microscope to look for things such as red blood cells, white blood cells, other cells, bacteria, and crystals.

If your veterinarian suspects your cat may have a urinary tract infection, a **bacterial culture** may be performed instead of, or in addition to, urinalysis. Cystocentesis, a procedure in which urine is removed directly from the bladder by use of a needle inserted through the abdomen, is the preferred way to collect urine for a bacterial culture.

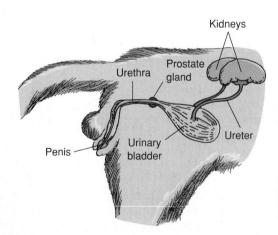

The urinary system in male cats

CONGENITAL AND INHERITED DISORDERS OF THE URINARY SYSTEM

Certain urinary tract abnormalities are inherited or congenital (present at birth). These abnormalities are caused by abnormal genes or produced by injury, disease, or exposure to toxic substances in the womb. They may or may not cause health problems later in your pet's life. These types of abnormalities are rare, but important to consider, if your cat has urinary tract problems.

Disorders of the Kidneys

There are many congenital and inherited problems that affect the kidneys. Among these are kidney dysplasia and hypoplasia, failure of the kidney(s) to develop, polycystic kidneys, and kidney cysts.

Kidney Malformations

Kidney malformations, called **dysplasias**, occur when a cat's kidneys do not develop properly before birth. When the kidneys are unusually small, the condition is called **hypoplasia**. These abnormalities occur only occasionally in cats. Signs typically develop when cats are between 6 months and 2 years of age, and may include vomiting, decreased appetite, and increased thirst or urination. There is no effective treatment. Care for affected cats consists of managing the problems associated with the kidney failure that results from these conditions.

Failure to Develop

Rarely, one or both kidneys fail to develop. This condition is always accompanied by a lack of the tube that connects the kidney to the bladder (the ureter). The reproductive organs may also be underdeveloped. A cat in which both kidneys have failed to develop will die shortly after birth. However, a cat with one functioning kidney can live a full and healthy life. In this case, the condition is usually discovered by accident.

Polycystic Kidneys

Polycystic kidneys have multiple cysts (enclosed, fluid-filled sacs) inside the func-

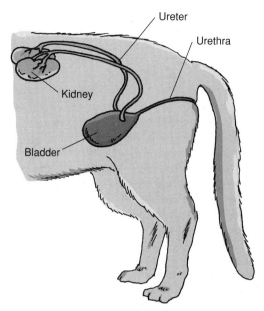

The urinary system in female cats

tional part of the organ. The kidneys may be greatly enlarged, which a veterinarian may be able to feel during a physical examination. Problems caused by this condition can range from none at all to progressive kidney failure. This condition may be inherited in Persian cats and domestic longhaired cats. Your veterinarian can diagnose polycystic kidneys by examining your pet, taking x-rays, performing ultrasonography, or performing exploratory abdominal surgery.

Kidney Cysts

These usually occur as a single cyst. They generally do not interfere with normal kidney function. It is unclear what causes them, and they are usually identified by accident.

Other Kidney Disorders

Other congenital problems include kidneys that are not positioned correctly, kidneys that are fused together, and **nephroblastoma**, a cancer that develops in the kidneys of young animals as a result of abnormal kidney tissue growth in the womb (*see* page 522).

Disorders of the Ureters

Several abnormalities can affect the ureter, the tube that connects the kidneys to the bladder. Normal, healthy cats have 2 ureters, 1 for each kidney.

Ectopic Ureter

An ectopic ureter is one that opens somewhere other than into the bladder. Ectopic ureters could empty urine into the urethra (the tube used for urination), or in females, the uterus or vagina. This defect can occur in cats, but it is much more common in dogs. (For a more detailed discussion, *see* page 286.)

Other Disorders of the Ureter

Other abnormalities of the ureter include failure to develop, the presence of more than the usual 2 ureters, and enlargement of the end of the ureter that connects to the bladder, a condition that can usually be successfully treated by surgery.

Disorders of the Bladder

The bladder is a muscular sac that stores the urine produced by the kidneys. Several congenital and inherited problems can affect the bladder.

Urachal Remnants

The **urachus** is a cord of fibrous tissue that normally extends from the bladder to the navel. Before birth, the urachus is a tube that connects the bladder to the umbilical cord so that wastes can be removed. After birth, it normally closes and becomes a solid cord. In some animals, however, the urachus does not close properly after birth. Depending on which portion of the urachus remains open, these abnormalities are called a patent urachus or an umbilical urachal sinus. Other problems include urachal diverticula (small sac-like structures attached to the urachus) and urachal cysts. Signs include an inability to control urination, urine scalding (due to the fact that urine is acidic) of the skin near the navel, and urinary tract infections. Your veterinarian can diagnose these problems using x-rays taken after a special dye is given

intravenously. Treatment usually includes surgery and, sometimes, antibiotics.

Other Disorders of the Bladder

Other inherited or congenital bladder conditions in cats include the presence of more than one bladder, an abnormally developed or underdeveloped bladder, failure of the bladder to develop, and a bladder that is turned inside-out. Usually these problems occur along with other abnormalities of the urinary tract. Your veterinarian can diagnose these problems based on physical examination, observation of your pet while it urinates, and contrast x-rays. Treatment varies depending on the type of problem.

Disorders of the Urethra

The urethra connects the bladder to the outside of the body. It is the tube through which urine passes when your cat urinates. Congenital urethral problems in cats are uncommon. Some of the conditions that do occur include failure of the urethra to develop, a urethra that does not open all the way or does not open at all, openings of the urethra that are on the underside or on top of the penis rather than on the tip in males, multiple urethras, urethral diverticula (small pouches that form in the urethra that become inflamed and painful), an abnormal opening between the urethra and the rectum, and an unusually narrow urethra.

▓ INFECTIOUS DISEASES OF THE URINARY SYSTEM

Most infections of the urinary system are caused by bacteria. The infection usually develops when bacteria enter the body through of the urethra. The bacteria then travel to the bladder, and in some cases they set up an infection there. Sometimes bacteria continue to move up the urinary tract to the kidneys and can result in kidney infection (pyelonephritis). There are several factors that increase the risk of urinary system infection. These include problems with urine flow (especially not being able to empty the bladder completely during urination), overly dilute urine, sugar in the urine (often a sign of diabetes mellitus), older age, a weakened immune system, and the presence of other diseases. Healthy adult cats are relatively resistant to urinary tract infections.

Treatment of bacterial infections is important for several reasons. The bacteria that cause infections of the urinary tract can become resistant to antibiotics if the infections are not treated properly. Antibiotic resistance can lead to an infection that will not go away. In some cases, an untreated or inadequately treated bladder infection can be the cause of an infection in the kidneys, which is a more serious condition.

Bladder Infection

Infection and inflammation of the bladder caused by bacteria is called **bacterial cystitis**. Healthy adult cats do not generally get bacterial cystitis. However, cats that are elderly, have compromised immune systems (including those with feline leukemia virus or feline immunodeficiency virus), or those with diseases that affect the whole body (such as diabetes mellitus or thyroid disease) are more prone to bacterial cystitis.

Signs of bladder infection include frequent urination, painful or difficult urination, and urinating in inappropriate places. There may also be blood in the urine. This may be more noticeable at the end of the urine stream. Rarely, cats with a bladder infection may show no signs at all. In these cases, the infection is usually diagnosed during a routine urinalysis.

A urine sample is needed to diagnose bacterial cystitis. The laboratory tests your veterinarian will likely perform on the sample are a urinalysis and a bacterial culture. Treatment consists of antibiotics. Your veterinarian may want to take more urine samples during and after treatment to make sure that the medications have controlled the infection. Longterm or recurring infections may be a sign of an underlying problem that should be addressed.

Feline Lower Urinary Tract Disease

Feline lower urinary tract disease (previously called feline urologic syndrome) does not refer to a specific disease, but rather to a grouping of problems that are associated with the lower urinary tract in cats. Both males and females are affected. Some of the problems that may be included in feline lower urinary tract disease include idiopathic cystitis (see page 521), interstitial cystitis, formation of urinary stones (see page 524), obstruction of the urethra (see page 522), and bacterial infections (see page 516). Because these disorders may occur separately, their causes, signs, and treatment are discussed separately in this chapter, rather than grouped under feline lower urinary tract disease.

Kidney Infection (Pyelonephritis)

Pyelonephritis is a bacterial infection of the kidneys. This is usually caused by bacteria in the urinary tract that climbed upwards into the bladder and then into the kidneys. The risk factors for pyelonephritis and those for bacterial cystitis are similar. Stones in the kidney or ureter, which prevent urine from flowing normally, are a common cause. In young cats, birth defects such as ectopic ureters (see page 516) can cause pyelonephritis. Cats at risk for this condition are the very young, the very old, those that have weak immune systems, or those with kidneys that cannot properly balance the amount of water in the urine. In many cases, your veterinarian may not be able to identify what caused the pyelonephritis.

Signs of pyelonephritis include pain in the sides (especially in the area around the kidneys), fever, and a general sense of not feeling well. Other signs include vomiting, decreased appetite, excessive thirst, or excessive urination. Sometimes there are no signs until kidney failure has occurred from the infection. Diagnosis of this condition requires blood and urine tests (urinalysis and bacterial culture). Longterm cases may not show abnormalities on these tests. If this is the case, contrast x-rays or ultrasonography may be needed. Treatment for pyelonephritis includes longterm antibiotics (4 to 6 weeks), sometimes using high dosages. In some cases, intravenous fluids are given. Rarely, surgery to remove the affected kidney may be required. Because pyelonephritis can be a life-threatening disease, following your veterinarian's recommendations is important.

Cats with pyelonephritis may be able to recover full kidney function, depending on the amount of damage that occurred before treatment. If both of the kidneys have already failed, your veterinarian may be able to do little more than keep your cat stable and comfortable.

Interstitial Nephritis

Interstitial nephritis is a type of inflammation of the kidney. Sudden-onset (acute) interstitial nephritis is uncommon in cats. Chronic (longstanding) progressive interstitial nephritis is common in cats and is more commonly referred to as chronic kidney disease (*see* below). Infectious diseases that affect the blood vessels (for example, feline infectious peritonitis) or diseases that activate the immune system can cause interstitial nephritis. It is usually not possible to identify the exact cause in an individual cat. Antibiotics or other drugs may be needed to treat an infectious disease, if one is diagnosed. Kidney failure, if it has occurred, may be treated with supportive treatment, including fluids, dietary changes, and other medications.

Capillaria Infection

Capillaria plica is a small worm that can infect the bladder, and, less often, the ureters and kidneys of cats. This is an uncommon condition in pet cats. The worms are threadlike, yellowish, and about 0.5 to 2.5 inches (13 to 60 millimeters) long. This infection is most common in wild animals. House pets catch the infection by eating earthworms that carry the larvae of the parasite. A similar but less common worm called *Capillaria felis cati* can also infect cats.

Most cats have no signs. Some cats will urinate frequently, become unable to control urination, or urinate in abnormal places. The worms' eggs come out in the urine; your veterinarian may be able to identify them by taking a urine sample. The best treatment has not been determined, but several different antiparasitic drugs are available.

▇ NONINFECTIOUS DISEASES OF THE URINARY SYSTEM

Not every disease is caused by infection with bacteria, viruses, or other outside agents. There are a variety of noninfectious disorders that can impair the urinary system. All of these diseases and conditions can be serious threats to the health of your cat.

Kidney Dysfunction

The kidneys' most important function is to filter waste from the blood. When this does not happen properly, waste products can build to dangerous levels in the blood. This is called azotemia. Azotemia can be caused by many factors, including dehydration, congestive heart failure (*see* page 372), and shock. Azotemia can also occur as a result of urine not being able to flow properly through the urinary tract.

Chronic Kidney Disease and Kidney Failure

Longterm, or chronic, disease can damage the kidney so severely that it is not able to function properly. This happens slowly. Chronic kidney disease often continues for many months or years before a cat has any signs. There is rarely anything that a veterinarian can do to treat existing damage. Occasionally, chronic kidney disease results from a problem that is inherited or an abnormality present at birth. Some breeds of cats are more likely to have this problem (*see* CONGENITAL AND INHERITED DISORDERS OF THE URINARY SYSTEM, page 515); however, most of the time it is a problem related to old age. Starting at age 5 to 6, chronic kidney disease becomes more common, affecting up to 35% of elderly cats. Chronic kidney disease that is not inherited does not seem to be more common among certain breeds or among males or females.

Veterinarians classify chronic kidney disease into 4 stages based on laboratory tests and the results of physical examinations (*see* TABLE 7). In **Stage I**, the kidneys are damaged but azotemia (a buildup of toxins caused by poor filtering of the blood by the kidneys) has not yet developed and the cat has no signs. This is the stage at which treatment has the greatest chance of success. However, because the cat has no signs, the disease is rarely diagnosed at this stage. In **Stage II**, the kidneys filter waste much more slowly than normal, and there is a buildup of waste chemicals in the blood, but most cats still have no signs. Signs that may be present at this stage include an increase in the amount of water in the urine and an increased volume of urine. In **Stage III**, filtering slows even more, the waste chemicals are more concentrated in the blood, and the cat develops signs of disease. **Stage IV**, the final stage, reflects continued kidney damage and accumulation of waste products in the blood. By this time, the cat feels and acts very sick.

Determining the cause of chronic kidney disease, especially in the early stages, will help determine the appropriate treatment and outlook for your cat. Some of the common causes include diseases of the circulatory system (such as high blood pressure, problems with blood clotting, and not having enough oxygen in the blood) or other diseases of the kidneys such as pyelonephritis (*see* page 517) or tumors. Whatever the cause, chronic kidney disease usually results in scarring of the kidneys, which gets gradually worse.

Cats usually have no signs of kidney disease until they are at Stages III or IV, when their kidneys are working at less than 25% of their usual capacity. Exceptions to this are cats with other illnesses that affect the entire body or kidneys that become unusually inflamed or sore and cause vomiting or pain. Veterinarians may be able to detect a problem in a blood test or on physical examination even before the cat develops signs of kidney failure. Usually, the earliest signs are excessive thirst and urination. However, these signs may signal other diseases as well, and they do not begin to appear until Stage II or III. After this, there are usually no new signs until Stage IV, when affected cats

Table 7. Chronic Kidney Disease Stages

Disease Stage	Physical Conditions	Signs	Treatment
Stage I	Waste filtering slows. Waste chemicals start to appear in blood.	No easily visible signs. Laboratory or other tests required.	Identify and treat cause of kidney disease.
Stage II	Further slowing of waste filtering. Buildup of waste chemicals and imbalance of water in urine	Cat may be urinating more than previously. Tests show increased amount of waste chemicals in blood.	Treat underlying cause of the condition. A change of diet may be required (such as a low salt or other special diet).
Stage III	Kidneys often working at less than 60% of normal capacity.	Excessive thirst and urination	Support cat with kidney disease diet, monitor for infections, and treat underlying cause of kidney disease.
Stage IV	Kidneys working at less than 25% of normal capacity. Toxic chemicals build up in blood and affect other organs in the body.	Vomiting, depression, loss of appetite, weight loss, dehydration, mouth sores, diarrhea. Young cats may lose teeth. Bones can become soft and easily breakable.	Provide special diet. Treat underlying conditions. Provide comfort care. In severe cases, kidney dialysis or a kidney transplant might be possible.

vomit and are sluggish. As the disease progresses over months, other problems begin. These include loss of appetite, weight loss, dehydration, sores in the mouth, vomiting, and diarrhea.

To diagnose chronic kidney disease, veterinarians generally use a combination of x-rays, ultrasonography, urine and blood tests, and physical examination. These tests are also used to check the response to treatment and monitor complications related to the kidney disease.

With proper treatment, even cats with as little as 5% of normal kidney function can survive for a long time. The recommended treatment depends on the stage of disease. Identifying and treating complications, such as high blood pressure or urinary tract infections, needs to be done as well. All cats with kidney disease should see their veterinarian every 3 to 6 months, or more frequently if there are problems. During these visits, the veterinarian will do tests on the cat's blood and urine.

In the later stages of kidney disease (III and IV), the cat should be taken to the veterinarian every 1 to 2 months. At this stage, treatments will focus on easing some of the signs of the disease. A commercial diet developed for cats with chronic kidney disease may be recommended, along with appropriate medications. Sometimes veterinarians will recommend intravenous fluids or feeding tubes. At this point, there are very few options. Dialysis machines, which do the job of the kidneys by filtering the blood, can prolong life, but dialysis is not feasible for most pets. A kidney transplant can be done, but requires immune-suppressing drugs to prevent the body from rejecting the new kidney, which can cause other problems.

Acute Kidney Disease

Acute kidney disease is the result of sudden, major damage to the kidneys. This damage is usually caused by toxic chemicals either consumed by your pet or built up by an abnormal condition in your pet's body. Kidney function can also be affected when the kidneys do not receive sufficient oxygen, such as when a blood clot blocks the flow of blood to the kidneys.

Some cats may consume toxic chemicals, such as antifreeze, or poisonous plants that can damage the kidneys. There are many substances in the average home that may be safe for humans but dangerous for cats and other pets (*see* POISONING, page 1145). Some toxic chemicals come from inside the cat's body. For example, a buildup of calcium or other substances can occur due to disease in another part of the body. The effects on kidney function can last from 1 to 8 weeks, depending on the chemical(s) that caused the injury.

Mild kidney disease often goes unnoticed. However, repeated occurrences can lead to chronic kidney disease. The 4 (I through IV) stages of acute and chronic kidney disease are the same (*see* page 518). Usually, acute kidney disease is not detected until Stage IV, when signs can include loss of appetite, depression, dehydration, sores in the mouth, vomiting, diarrhea, and urinating a smaller than normal volume of urine.

It is important to determine whether the kidney disease is acute or chronic, as well as the cause of the disease. This information will help your veterinarian determine the most appropriate treatment. If your veterinarian can determine what caused the kidney injury, treatment will be aimed at this cause. Cats that are dehydrated or not eating may require intravenous fluids or a feeding tube. If none of the available treatments work, and your cat is simply not producing urine, the only remaining options are kidney dialysis, a kidney transplant, or euthanasia.

Glomerular Disease

The glomerulus is one of the structures that are essential for kidney function. It is made up of special blood vessels that help filter blood. Each kidney contains thousands of these structures. Glomerular disease sometimes causes kidney disease in cats. Damage to parts of the glomerulus can cause protein in the urine and low levels of a protein called albumin in the blood.

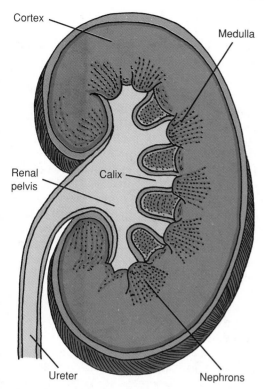

Cortex

Medulla

Renal pelvis

Calix

Ureter

Nephrons

The kidneys consist of an outer part (cortex) and an inner part (medulla). The nephrons filter the blood and produce urine (modified with permission from *The Merck Manual of Medical Information*, Second Home Edition, 2003).

This can lead to other problems, such as swelling of the legs, high cholesterol, and blood clots.

Glomerular disease can occur due to the longterm effects of high blood pressure. However, glomerular disease can also occur as a result of other disorders such as hyperadrenocorticism (an excess of cortisol) or amyloidosis. Some glomerular disease is immune-mediated, that is, caused by the cat's immune system attacking parts of its own body.

Disease in the glomerulus often leads to protein in the urine, low levels of protein in the blood, a buildup of fluid in the abdomen (which can cause visible swelling), shortness of breath, and swelling in the legs. Taken together, these signs are called the nephrotic syndrome. ("Nephrotic"

means relating to the kidneys.) The loss of protein through the urine can cause loss of muscle tissue. Most cats with glomerular disease eventually develop Stage III or IV kidney disease. Kidney disease that is accompanied by protein in the urine often leads to high blood pressure.

Your veterinarian will look for increased levels of protein and other chemicals in your cat's urine and blood. Physical examination usually reveals that something is wrong; however, the signs are often nonspecific and could point to any of a wide variety of problems.

A biopsy of the kidneys is often required to determine the cause of the glomerular disease. Additional tests may be required in some cases, including x-rays, ultrasonography, and special blood tests.

Treatment for glomerular disease varies according to the underlying cause. In addition, kidney failure should be treated with appropriate medications. (For a more detailed discussion of GLOMERULAR DISEASE, *see* page 293.)

Feline Idiopathic Cystitis and Feline Interstitial Cystitis

Feline idiopathic cystitis is an inflammation of the urinary bladder of unknown origin. This condition has also been called idiopathic feline lower urinary tract disease (idiopathic FLUTD) and feline urologic syndrome. The cause is unknown, but certain factors such as viral infections, stress, diet, and genetic factors may play a role. Both male and female cats are affected.

Signs of feline idiopathic cystitis include frequent urination, blood in the urine, straining or distress while urinating, and urination in inappropriate locations. A urinary tract obstruction may occur in male cats due to their longer and narrower urethras; this should be considered a medical emergency and requires immediate veterinary attention. Signs of this condition include frequent unsuccessful attempts to urinate, lethargy, loss of appetite, and reluctance to move.

Diagnosis depends on a complete history and physical examination, as well as appropriate laboratory tests to identify feline idiopathic cystitis and exclude other conditions. These may include urinalysis and bacterial culture of urine, blood tests, x-rays, ultrasonography, and cystoscopy.

Treatment of this condition has many approaches. If bacteria are identified, antibiotics will be prescribed. Drugs that reduce pain and inflammation may be useful in some cases. Cats should have access to plenty of fresh, clean water to encourage water intake (so the cat will have less concentrated urine). Changing from a dry to a canned food may also help add water.

Another condition that may be related to—or the same as—feline idiopathic cystitis is called **feline interstitial cystitis**. Currently, it is unclear whether these are 2 separate conditions or whether they represent the same overall disorder. Signs of both conditions are similar and both involve inflammation of the bladder with bladder pain, straining, and bloody urine.

Renal Tubular Problems

Renal tubules are structures in the kidneys that help filter blood. Healthy kidneys help the body to get rid of acid by producing urine that is very acidic. Diseased kidneys cannot get rid of acid properly, and instead of being eliminated in the urine, this acid builds up in the blood, leading to a condition called uremic acidosis. This condition can also occur when there are defects in the renal tubules, in which case it is called **renal tubular acidosis**. These defects are rare in cats. Treatment may involve medications to rebalance the amount of acid in the blood.

Obstructions of the Urinary Tract

Even when the kidneys are functioning normally, a blockage in the urinary system at any point below the kidneys can lead to a backup of toxic wastes that can damage the kidneys and cause illness. In cats, the most common cause is a "plug" composed of protein, cellular waste, and/or crystallized minerals that blocks the urethra. Other possible causes include urinary tract stones (*see* page 524), tumors, or blood clots in the ureters or urethra.

If the flow of urine is blocked, the kidney becomes abnormally enlarged. When this happens suddenly to both kidneys, especially when the urine is completely blocked, the cat does not live long. When the blockage is only partial, or only occurs on one side, the cat often survives but the kidneys may sustain permanent damage. The affected kidneys eventually become giant, useless urine-filled sacs and may become infected. The ureter may also become enlarged due to a backup of urine. This often occurs when the blockage is located further down the urinary tract and away from the kidneys.

Cats with a urinary blockage will attempt to urinate frequently. These attempts, however, may be painful and will result in only small amounts of urine being produced. Often, blood will be present in the urine. An affected cat may have a painful abdomen, lose interest in food, and become more and more depressed. As the condition progresses, the cat may vomit and become dehydrated. Your veterinarian will be able to readily diagnose urinary tract obstructions based on the signs and a physical examination.

To restore normal urine flow, the blockage must be removed. In most cases, intravenous fluids will be used to restore the balance of various chemicals in the blood. Surgery is often required to resolve the blockage of the urinary tract.

If a cat has signs of a blocked urethra, it is critical to seek veterinary care immediately. Cats with a complete blockage may die within 2 to 3 days without treatment.

Tumors

Tumors that originate in the kidneys and urinary tract are not common in cats. Tumors can be benign (harmless) or malignant (cancerous). Benign tumors, such as fatty tumors or tumors made of fibrous tissue, are usually discovered only by accident and do not require treatment.

Cancers that begin in other parts of the body may spread to the kidneys. (When cancer spreads from one organ to another, it is said to metastasize and the cancer itself is described as metastatic.) Metastatic tumors can appear on one or both kidneys. Lymphosarcoma is the type of tumor that most commonly spreads to the kidneys. Up to half of cats with cancer of the lymphatic system also develop cancer in their kidneys. In some cases, the cancer remains only in the lymph tissues and the kidneys; in others it also spreads to the brain. When cancer spreads to the kidneys, it usually takes the form of many small tumors. It can affect both kidneys and may cause the kidneys to become unusually large and irregularly shaped. Lymphosarcoma in cats frequently occurs along with infection with the feline leukemia virus (*see* page 533).

Signs of kidney tumors are usually general and can point to many different illnesses. Common signs include weight loss, poor appetite, depression, and fever. Your veterinarian will need to eliminate other causes of these signs before confirming cancer. Occasionally, tumors that appear in both kidneys can cause enough damage that the cat will develop signs of late-stage kidney disease (*see* page 518).

Your veterinarian may suspect a tumor of the kidneys based on physical examination and careful consideration of your cat's signs in the weeks and months prior to becoming ill. This suspicion can be confirmed with ultrasonography, x-rays, or contrast x-rays of the urinary tract. Cancer cells can also occasionally be found in the urine. A biopsy of the tumor is usually necessary to determine its type.

Normally, kidney tumors must be surgically removed. Usually it is necessary to remove the entire affected kidney. Tumors in the lymph nodes around the kidney are usually treated with chemotherapy instead of surgery. If your cat develops a urinary cancer, your veterinarian will assess the severity of your pet's condition, the outlook for your pet, and other factors when recommending a treatment program. (For a more detailed discussion of tumors of the kidney and urinary tract, *see* page 296.)

Problems with Urination

Urination problems can be grouped into problems with storing urine and problems with eliminating urine. Urinary incontinence is the inability to prevent or control urination. Incontinent animals leak urine constantly or occasionally without realizing it. An incontinent cat may leave a pool of urine where it has been lying or dribble urine while walking. The fur around the vulva or penis may be wet, and the constant dribbling of urine can cause inflammation and urine scalding of the skin in these areas.

Problems with Urine Storage

Problems with urine storage are identified by inappropriate leakage of urine. They can be caused by several different conditions, including failure of the muscles in the bladder to relax appropriately, injury or damage to the urethra or other parts of the urinary system, and overflowing of the bladder.

Urge incontinence occurs when urine leaks during the times when an animal feels the urge to urinate as opposed to urine that leaks when an animal is unaware of it. Urge incontinence is usually caused by irritation of the bladder muscle that forcibly expels the urine. This is usually due to inflammation of the bladder. Problems with the urethral sphincter (the muscle that opens and closes to allow urine to pass through the urethra), can also cause this type of incontinence.

Incontinence that results from birth defects or malformation of the urinary system usually becomes obvious while the cat is young. For example, a cat that was born with an ectopic ureter (*see* page 516) on one side might urinate normally but dribble urine on and off, whereas cats with ectopic ureters on both sides are less likely to be able to urinate normally at all.

Problems with Urine Elimination

Problems with urine elimination can have many causes, including physical blockage of the urethra by stones, growths, or scar tissue; a lack of muscle tone in the muscle that expels urine; or problems related to the nervous system. Cats that cannot urinate normally will usually try to urinate often, but the urination will be slow and painful and only a small amount of urine will come out. Cats with urine elimination problems may also develop incontinence over time; if the bladder does not empty properly, it can become stretched out and begin to overflow and leak.

Neurologic Problems

Problems with urination can sometimes be caused by damage or disease that affects the brain or spine, damage to the major nerve in the pelvis that connects to the bladder, or a lack of muscle tone in the muscle that controls urination. **Dysautonomia** is a condition in cats in which the nervous system does not work properly. It can also lead to urinary incontinence. Cats with any neurologic urination problem may develop incontinence over time if the bladder becomes too full and begins to overflow and then leak.

Diagnosis and Treatment of Urination Problems

A thorough physical examination and a history of the cat's behavior can help your veterinarian determine whether your cat has problems related to urination. Your veterinarian will probably also want to watch your pet urinate. Specialized tests, such as ultrasonography, x-rays, or neurologic tests, may be helpful in some cases.

Treatment of urination problems will vary depending on the cause. Urethral incontinence can be treated with medication that targets the membrane inside the urethra (called alpha-adrenergic agonist drugs). Urge incontinence can be treated with medication that targets certain nerves (called anticholinergic drugs). Weakened bladder muscles can be treated with medications that target slack muscles (called cholinergic drugs). Muscle relaxants may be useful in cases where muscle coordination issues are identified.

In cats in which the bladder has lost its muscle tone due to neurologic problems,

there are few medical options to restore muscle tone. It is usually necessary to empty the bladder with a catheter several times a day for the rest of the animal's life. In these cases, you will need to be trained to properly insert and remove the catheter.

Urinary Stones (Uroliths, Calculi)

Uroliths are stones (also known as calculi) formed when minerals that naturally occur in urine clump together to form tiny crystals. These stones can develop anywhere in the urinary system, including the kidney, ureter, bladder, or urethra. Certain types of stones appear to have increased in cats in recent years. The cause is not clear, but researchers are looking at the effects of diet to determine if there is any link.

Veterinary researchers do not completely understand what causes stones to form (*see* Box). There are many different types of stones, each formed from a complex mixture of various minerals, and each of which develops only under certain conditions. They can be caused by a problem with the minerals themselves or by a problem with other chemicals that exist in urine and which, under normal circumstances, prevent stones from forming. The environment of the urinary tract may also contribute to stone formation. All of these conditions can be affected by urinary tract infections, diet, digestion, the amount of urine that a cat produces, how frequently a cat urinates, medications, and genetics.

Cats with very tiny stones in the urinary system do not usually have any signs. However, larger stones in the lower urinary tract may interfere with urination or irritate the lining of the urethra. In turn, these problems can cause an inability to urinate, blood in the urine, and slow or painful urination. Kidney stones (which are rare in cats) usually cause no signs unless the kidney becomes inflamed or the stones pass into the ureter. If a ureter becomes blocked by a stone, it can cause vomiting, depression, or pain in the abdomen in the area around the kidneys. Such pain is particularly common when both ureters are suddenly and completely blocked; the fluids back up causing the kidneys to become enlarged. Pain is the only sign of stones in the ureter on only one side; however, pain can be difficult to detect in cats. If the blocked ureter is not diagnosed right away, kidney damage occurs. Ultimately, the blocked kidney is destroyed.

Veterinarians can sometimes detect stones in the bladder by pressing on the cat's abdomen. Stones in the urethra may also be detected during a rectal examination or when attempting to insert a catheter. There may be many stones present at once. If one stone is located, it is important to examine the entire urinary tract to look for others. X-rays can detect stones as small as 3 millimeters in size. Your veterinarian will also perform tests on the cat's urine and may need to do ultrasonography or other specialized tests.

Treating stones, and preventing their return, depends on their type and location. Treatment and prevention may include surgery, a special diet, and medication. When stones are removed, your veterinarian may send them to a laboratory to be analyzed. Knowing what types of minerals are in the stone can provide the information needed to prescribe medication

Why Cats Develop Uroliths (Stones)

Cats have highly concentrated (acidic) urine that predisposes them to form stones of the urinary tract, especially when certain minerals or other substances are abundant. This may be a result of diet, inflammation or infection, or possibly the pH level of the individual cat's urine.

The urolith itself is made up of a hardened center, with various layers that have formed around it. It is unclear what starts the process of formation, but it is likely that an excess of urolith-forming minerals in the urine form small crystals that stick together to form a stone. Once the stone is formed, it gradually increases in size—a process that can take weeks or months.

Veterinarians identify stones based on their makeup. In cats, the most common stones are generally composed of either magnesium ammonium phosphate (known as struvite) or calcium oxalate. Struvite stones tend to occur more often in the bladder, while calcium oxalate stones are more common in the kidney.

that can prevent the formation of more stones. Cats undergoing treatment for uroliths will need to be monitored closely, returning at regular intervals for additional testing.

CHAPTER **37**

Metabolic Disorders

▓ INTRODUCTION

Metabolism refers to all processes in the body that break down and convert ingested substances to provide the energy and nutrients needed to sustain life. Foods, liquids, and drugs all generally undergo metabolic processes within the body. Many foods are complex materials that must be broken down into simpler substances, which in turn become "building blocks" for the body to use as needed. For example, protein is broken down into amino acids, which are used in several metabolic reactions. Enzymes made by the body are necessary for many metabolic processes. Whenever the function of an enzyme is affected, a metabolic disorder can develop. Metabolic disorders are important because they affect energy production or damage tissues. They may be genetic (inherited) or acquired. Acquired metabolic disorders are more common and significant.

Metabolic Storage Disorders

Metabolic storage disorders usually result from the body's inability to break down some substance because of the partial or complete lack of a certain enzyme. The substance can build up to a toxic level, or the body is unable to produce a substance that it needs. Although storage diseases are often widespread throughout the body, most clinical signs are due to the effects on the central nervous system. Metabolic storage disorders can be either genetic or acquired.

Genetic (inherited) storage diseases are named according to the specific metabolic byproduct that builds up in the body. Certain breeds of cats are more prone to certain storage diseases than others (*see* TABLE 8). Kittens typically appear normal

Table 8. Breeds of Cats Prone to Genetic Storage Diseases

Disease	Breeds
Ceroid lipofuscinosis	Domestic shorthair
Gangliosidoses	Domestic shorthair Korat Siamese
Globoid cell leuko-dystrophy (Krabbe's disease)	Domestic shorthair
Glycogenosis	Domestic shorthair Norwegian forest cats
Mannosidosis	Domestic shorthair Persian
Mucopolysacchari-dosis type I	Domestic shorthair Korat Siamese
Mucopolysacchari-dosis type IV	Siamese
Porphyria (associated with anemia)	Domestic shorthair Siamese
Sphingomyelinosis	Domestic shorthair Siamese

at birth, and clinical signs begin within a few weeks to months. These diseases are progressive and usually fatal because specific treatments do not exist.

Acquired storage diseases can be caused by eating plants that contain inhibitors of specific enzymes. (*See also* PLANTS POISONOUS TO ANIMALS, page 1175.)

Production-related Metabolic Disorders

Some metabolic disorders are caused by an increased demand for a specific element or nutrient that has become deficient under certain conditions. For example, in **hypoglycemia,** the animal's metabolic reserves are unable to sustain sugar (or glucose) in the blood at a level needed for normal function. Likewise, in **hypocalcemia,** the level of calcium in the blood is too low. In some cases, dietary intake of a nutrient, such as calcium, is rapidly used up for an ongoing, high metabolic need, such as producing milk for kittens.

The difference between production-related metabolic diseases and nutritional deficiencies is often subtle. Typically, nutritional deficiencies are longterm conditions that develop gradually and can be corrected through dietary supplementation. Metabolic diseases usually begin suddenly and respond dramatically to administration of the deficient nutrient (although affected animals may need dietary supplements to avoid recurrence). Because production-related metabolic disorders are serious and develop suddenly, accurate and rapid diagnosis is essential. Ideally, diagnostic tests can be used to predict the chance of disease occurring so that either it can be prevented or preparations can be made for rapid treatment.

■ CONGENITAL ERYTHROPOIETIC PORPHYRIA

Congenital erythropoietic porphyria is a rare hereditary disease of cats, cattle, pigs, sheep, and people. It results from low levels of an enzyme involved in the production of heme. Heme is a part of hemoglobin, which is the molecule that carries oxygen in the blood. Affected animals have reddish brown discoloration of the teeth, bones, and urine at birth that continues for life. In addition, affected animals develop hemolytic anemia, a condition in which there are not enough circulating red blood cells because the body destroys them too quickly.

Cats with congenital erythropoietic porphyria have a reddish brown discoloration of the teeth.

DISORDERS OF CALCIUM METABOLISM

Calcium is an essential component of the skeleton, and it has important functions in muscle contraction, blood clotting, enzyme activity, the nervous system, and hormone release, among others. Many different metabolic disorders affect calcium metabolism and can lead to abnormally high or low levels of calcium in the blood. (*See also* DISORDERS OF THE PARATHYROID GLANDS AND OF CALCIUM METABOLISM, page 419.)

In cats, a disorder of calcium metabolism known as **puerperal hypocalcemia** may occur 2 to 3 weeks after giving birth, when the mammary glands are producing the greatest amount of milk. Other names for this condition include postpartum hypocalcemia, periparturient hypocalcemia, puerperal tetany, and eclampsia. This life-threatening condition is less common in cats than in dogs. Low levels of calcium in the blood can cause seizures. Early signs include listlessness, restlessness, and lack of appetite. The queen may be unwilling to let kittens nurse.

A tentative diagnosis is based on the history, physical examination, clinical signs, and response to treatment. A blood test to determine the level of calcium confirms the diagnosis.

Immediate veterinary medical treatment is needed for cats with puerperal hypocalcemia. Calcium solutions given intravenously usually result in improvement within 15 minutes. Kittens should not be allowed to nurse for 12 to 24 hours.

During this period, they should be fed a milk substitute or other appropriate diet. After the acute crisis, calcium supplements are given for the rest of the lactation. Vitamin D supplements also may be used to increase calcium absorption from the intestines.

DISORDERS OF MAGNESIUM METABOLISM

Most disorders of magnesium metabolism are due to problems associated with absorption of the mineral from the digestive tract. The anatomical differences between species are associated with the importance of disorders of magnesium occurring in a particular species. Disorders of magnesium metabolism are less common in cats than in cattle and sheep. Too much magnesium in the blood (**hypermagnesemia**) is rare but has been reported in cats with kidney failure that were receiving intravenous fluids. Cardiac arrest can occur with very high blood magnesium levels.

FEVER OF UNKNOWN ORIGIN

In both animals and people, fever may indicate infection, inflammation, an immune-mediated disease, or cancer. Determining the cause of a fever requires a history, physical examination, and sometimes laboratory or other diagnostic tests. Often, a fever resolves on its own or in response to antibiotic therapy. However, in a small percentage of animals, the fever continues or keeps coming back and the cause cannot be determined. This is called fever of unknown origin.

In some fever of unknown origin cases, a specific diagnosis cannot be found, or diagnostic testing is discontinued, and different treatments are tried without a diagnosis. Drugs that may be tried include antibiotics, antifungal agents, and anti-inflammatory or immunosuppressive therapy. Although trial therapy may improve the signs or confirm a tentative diagnosis, it can also carry significant risk, and careful monitoring is needed. (For a more detailed discussion of FEVER OF UNKNOWN ORIGIN, *see* page 303.)

■ MALIGNANT HYPERTHERMIA

Malignant hyperthermia is seen mostly in swine, but it has also been reported in dogs, cats, and horses. This syndrome is characterized by abnormally high body temperature, muscle rigidity, a very rapid and irregular heartbeat, increased breathing rate, bluish tinge to skin and mucous membranes, unstable blood pressure, fluid buildup in the lungs, impaired blood coagulation, kidney failure, and death.

Malignant hyperthermia is consistently triggered in susceptible animals by excitement, apprehension, exercise, or environmental stress. Giving certain anesthetics or specific drugs that affect the neurologic and muscular systems also consistently triggers malignant hyperthermia in these animals.

Diagnosis is based on the development of signs in an animal that has been given an anesthetic agent or is participating in a stressful event. Signs can develop slowly or rapidly. Signs include muscle stiffness, twitching, a rapid heartbeat, and an increased breathing rate. Animals that are not under anesthesia may show open-mouthed breathing and an increased breathing rate, followed by a temporary break in breathing. Blanching and redness of the skin followed by blotchy blue tinges can be seen in light-colored animals. Body temperature increases rapidly and can reach 113°F (45°C).

Usually, malignant hyperthermia episodes occur suddenly and are severe. If the condition is recognized early in an animal under anesthesia, supportive measures may be able to save the animal. Unfortunately, regardless of treatment, malignant hyperthermia is usually fatal.

Stress must be minimized to prevent malignant hyperthermia episodes in individual animals. If a cat that is suspected to be susceptible to malignant hyperthermia (or that has survived a previous episode) needs anesthesia and surgery, certain precautions should be taken. These include administering a drug called dantrolene 1 to 2 days before anesthesia and avoiding certain anesthetic agents.

CHAPTER **38**

Disorders Affecting Multiple Body Systems

■ INTRODUCTION

There are many disorders that can affect multiple parts of the body. These may be caused by bacteria, viruses, poisonous or toxic substances in the environment, and other health hazards. Disorders affecting multiple body systems can also be inherited or develop while the animal is still in the womb. Diseases or conditions that involve multiple organ systems may also be described as systemic or generalized.

Many disorders are discussed in this chapter. A listing of congenital and inherited conditions is followed by a discussion of the most significant disorders, which have been arranged alphabetically by medical name to help you locate a particular disease or condition easily.

■ CONGENITAL AND INHERITED DISORDERS

A variety of structural and functional defects have been described in animals. These defects are usually classified by the body system primarily affected, and many are discussed in this book under the appropriate body system section. Defective newborns have survived a disruptive event during embryonic or fetal development. Defective development may also cause embryonic loss, fetal death, mummification, abortion, stillbirth, or a newborn not capable of living.

Susceptibility to environmental agents or genetic abnormalities varies with the stage of development and species, and decreases with fetal age. The fertilized egg is resistant to agents or factors that cause or increase the rate of occurrence of a congenital defect (teratogens), but it is susceptible to genetic mutations and changes in the chromosomes. The embryo is highly susceptible to teratogens, but this susceptibility decreases with age as the critical developmental periods of various organs or organ systems are passed. The fetus becomes increasingly resistant to teratogens except for structures that develop late such as the cerebellum, palate, urinary system, and genitals.

The frequency of individual defects varies with the species, breed, geographic location, season, and other environmental factors. Among domestic animals, cats have the lowest frequency of congenital defects. Some reported congenital and inherited defects in cats include lack of development of the cerebellum (which controls the balance function), eye and eyelid defects, heart defects, cleft palate, failure of one or both testicles to descend

Commonly Reported Congenital and Inherited Defects in Cats

- Cerebellar hypoplasia, a lack of development of the cerebellum, which controls balance (*see also* page 460)
- Eye and eyelid defects (*see also* page 425)
- Heart defects (*see also* page 373)
- Cleft palate (uncommon in cats but occurs more often in Siamese; *see also* page 387)
- Cryptorchidism (apparent absence of one or both testicles; *see also* page 473)
- Polydactyly (more toes than normal; usually occurs on the front paws and rarely causes any problems for the cat)
- Deafness associated with white fur and blue eyes (*see also* page 435)

into the scrotum (known as cryptorchidism), more toes than normal (polydactyly), and diaphragmatic and umbilical hernias. Most congenital defects have no clearly established cause; others are caused by genetic or environmental factors or interaction between these factors.

Genetic Factors

Inherited defects resulting from mutant genes or chromosome abnormalities tend to occur in patterns of inheritance. Such patterns include dominant (in which the defect will occur if either parent supplies an abnormal gene to its offspring), recessive (in which both parents must supply an abnormal gene) or others, such as sex-linked (in which the gene is associated with the X chromosome and not the Y chromosome). In cats, for example, the appearance of excess toes follows a dominant pattern of inheritance, while diaphragmatic hernia follows a recessive pattern.

Some common diseases or disorders caused by genetic defects include deficiencies of particular enzymes that lead to the body's inability to perform normal metabolic functions, and chromosome abnormalities that can result in sterility, abnormal growth, increased embryonic mortality, or reduced litter size. Viruses, certain drugs, and

Polydactyly (the presence of extra toes) is fairly common in cats.

radiation are common causes of chromosomal damage.

The complex interaction between genetic and environmental factors is being studied and is slowly becoming better understood.

Environmental Factors

Factors tending to produce abnormalities of formation include toxic plants, viral infections that occur during pregnancy (such as feline panleukemia), drugs, trace elements, nutritional deficiencies, and physical agents such as radiation, abnormally high body temperature, and uterine positioning. These factors may be difficult to identify, often follow seasonal patterns and stress, and may be linked to maternal disease. They do not follow the pattern of family inheritance that is shown by genetic changes.

■ AMYLOIDOSIS

Amyloidosis is a condition that occurs when **amyloid**, a substance composed of abnormally folded protein, is deposited in various organs of the body. Some types of amyloidosis are hereditary in cats. Abys-

sinian cats are known to be at risk for hereditary amyloidosis. Other types occur as a result of infections, various cancers, or other inflammatory or immune-related conditions. However, the cause is often unknown.

Amyloid can be deposited throughout the body, or in just one specific area. The misfolded protein causes damage by displacing normal cells. The disease can become fatal if amyloid is deposited into the tissue of critical organs, such as the kidneys, liver, or heart. All domestic mammals may develop amyloidosis. Senile systemic amyloidosis is the form of amyloidosis commonly seen in older animals. Aged animals commonly have minor deposits of amyloid without signs.

There are several types of amyloid, and the classification of amyloidosis is based on which amyloid protein is involved. Deposits of **AA amyloid** can result from chronic

Calico and Black and Orange Tortoiseshell Cats

Calico and tortoiseshell cats are usually female. The reason has to do with genetics. Normal cats have 38 pairs of chromosomes. Half of these pairs of chromosomes are from the father; half are from the mother. Female cats receive an X chromosome from both the mother and father. (Male cats get a Y chromosome from the father and an X chromosome from the mother.)

The gene that determines the color of a cat's coat is on the X chromosome(s). Calico and tortoiseshell cats receive one X chromosome with the black coat color gene and one X chromosome with the orange coat color gene. The white coat color seen in calicos and tortoiseshells comes from a different gene. Because 2 X chromosomes are required for the calico and tortoiseshell coats, almost all cats showing these coat colorings are female. Thus, calico and tortoiseshell coat colors are considered to be sex-linked traits.

A few male cats are born with 2 X chromosomes (only one of which becomes active) and one Y chromosome. The XXY gene defect in male cats is very rare and also causes sterility.

inflammatory diseases, chronic bacterial infections, and cancer. The amyloid is usually deposited in organs such as the spleen or kidneys. The animal may not show any signs of illness. If AA amyloid is deposited in the kidneys, it can lead to a buildup of protein and result in kidney failure. However, kidney amyloidosis is uncommon in cats, except for Abyssinian cats, in which it is inherited. **AL amyloid** is another common form of amyloid protein. AL amyloid tends to be deposited in nerve tissue and joints.

Because of its wide distribution and stealthy onset, amyloidosis is difficult to diagnose. However, your veterinarian might suspect amyloidosis if your cat has a chronic infection or inflammation and develops kidney or liver failure. No specific treatment can prevent the development of amyloidosis or promote the reabsorption of the protein deposits.

■ ANTHRAX

Anthrax is an often fatal infectious disease that may infect all warm-blooded animals, including cats and humans. Underdiagnosis and unreliable reporting make it difficult to estimate the true frequency of anthrax worldwide; however, anthrax has been reported from nearly every continent. Under normal circumstances, anthrax outbreaks in the United States are extremely rare. Anthrax received much attention in 2001 in relation to the terrorist attacks on the United States because of its potential use as a biological weapon.

Anthrax is caused by infection with bacteria known as *Bacillus anthracis*. This bacterium forms spores, which make it extremely resistant to environmental conditions such as heating, freezing, chemical disinfection, or dehydration that typically destroy other types of bacteria. Thus, it can persist for a long time within or on a contaminated environment or object. Livestock may consume the spores while grazing; however, the most common source of infection in cats is from raw or poorly cooked contaminated meat or contact with the

blood, tissues, or body fluids of infected animals that harbor spores.

After exposure to the bacteria, the typical incubation period is 3 to 7 days. Once the bacteria infect an animal or human, the organisms multiply and spread throughout the body. They produce a potent and lethal toxin that causes cell death and breakdown of the infected tissues. This results in inflammation and organ damage, eventually leading to organ failure.

Cats may develop sudden, severe (acute) blood poisoning after ingesting *Bacillus anthracis* bacteria. This may lead to a rapid swelling of the throat and sudden death. More often, a mild, chronic form is seen, in which cats show generalized signs of illness and gradually recover with treatment. Intestinal involvement is seldom recognized because the signs (such as loss of appetite, vomiting, diarrhea or constipation) are so nonspecific.

A diagnosis based on signs is difficult because many infections and other conditions (such as poisoning) may have signs similar to anthrax. Diagnosis thus requires laboratory analysis of blood samples from the potentially infected cat to confirm the presence of the bacteria.

Anthrax is controlled through vaccination programs in large animals (such as cattle), rapid detection and reporting, quarantine, treatment of any animals exposed to the bacteria, and the burning or burial of suspected or confirmed fatal cases. In most countries, all cases of anthrax must be reported to the appropriate regulatory officials. Cleaning and disinfection of any bedding, cages, or other possibly contaminated materials is necessary to prevent further spread of the disease. Because anthrax spores are resistant to many disinfectants, check with a health official as to proper procedures for decontaminating inanimate objects. If a pet is exposed to anthrax, the fur should be decontaminated to avoid transmission to humans. Currently, no chemicals that kill spores are considered safe for use on animals; therefore, repeated bathing is necessary to mechanically remove the organism.

Human cases of anthrax may follow contact with contaminated animals or animal products. For infection to occur, spores must gain access to the new victim by ingestion, inhalation, or through open wounds. When transmission occurs between individuals, it is usually through exposure to infected tissue or body fluids. Therefore, humans should use strict precautions (wearing gloves, protective clothing, goggles, and masks) when handling potentially infected animals or their remains.

■ EHRLICHIOSIS AND RELATED INFECTIONS

Monocytic ehrlichiosis in dogs is caused by *Ehrlichia canis*. A similar disease has been identified in cats in Africa, France, and the United States; however, the exact species causing the infection has not been determined. (For a more detailed discussion of EHRLICHIOSIS, *see* page 310.)

■ FELINE INFECTIOUS PERITONITIS

Feline infectious peritonitis is caused by a feline coronavirus. Coronaviruses are a family of viruses that chiefly cause respiratory infections. The disease is seen worldwide. Although a large number of cats may be infected with the feline coronavirus, only a few show signs of disease. Cats of all ages and either sex can develop feline infectious peritonitis, but the disease is most frequent in cats 6 months to 2 years old. Kittens raised in infected colonies may contract the virus from their mothers or from carriers (infected cats with no obvious signs of disease) when their maternal immunity decreases at 5 to 10 weeks of age.

Most infections probably result from ingestion of the feline infectious peritonitis virus. Transmission by inhalation is also possible. Because cats shed particles of the virus in feces, litter box exposure and mutual grooming are important sources of infection. Cats living in multiple-cat households are at greater risk of the disease. It has been suggested that this disease can move across the placenta from mother to developing kitten; however, the frequency with which this occurs is unknown.

There are 2 forms of this disease: a wet form (effusive) and a dry (noneffusive) form. In the wet form, fluids build up in the abdomen and may restrict the lungs to the point that breathing is difficult. In the dry form, organs such as the liver and kidneys may be involved. The dry form may also involve the eyes, the brain, or both. The disease may start as the wet form and develop gradually into the dry form. If the eyes or the brain are involved, mortality, even with treatment, approaches 100%.

Signs and Diagnosis

The initial infection is often without signs. In some cases, fever, inflammation of the eyes, respiratory signs, and diarrhea may occur. This stage may last several days or weeks before signs of the wet or dry forms develop. Many cats show signs of both forms of feline infectious peritonitis.

Cats with the **wet (effusive) form** of the disease usually have noticeable fluid buildup in the abdomen. About one-third of cats with effusive disease have lung involvement and difficulty breathing. These signs are often accompanied by fever, poor appetite, weight loss, and depression.

Cats with the **dry (noneffusive) form** of the disease may have a history of vague illness. This includes repeated fever, malaise, weight loss, and occasionally organ failure (most often the kidneys or liver). Involvement of the eyes and central nervous system may occur either simultaneously or independently of other signs. When the eyes are affected, there may be bleeding or accumulation of pus in one or both eyes. The dry form of feline infectious peritonitis may also attack the ner-

Signs of Feline Infectious Peritonitis

Short-term or primary infection

Often without signs, but in some cases:

▓ Fever

▓ Inflammation of eyes

▓ Upper respiratory signs

▓ Diarrhea

This stage may last several days or weeks

Effusive disease (wet form)*

▓ Progressive distention of the abdomen due to fluid buildup

▓ Lung involvement and difficulty breathing

▓ Fever lasting 2 to 5 weeks

▓ Loss of appetite

▓ Weight loss

▓ Depression

Noneffusive disease (dry form)*

▓ History of vague illness, including long-term fever, malaise, weight loss, and occasionally major organ system failure (kidneys, liver)

▓ Eye and central nervous system signs may occur simultaneously or independently

▓ About 50% of all cats have signs related to involvement of abdominal organs (kidney, liver, spleen, pancreas, lymph nodes)

*Many cats have elements of both the effusive and noneffusive forms of feline infectious peritonitis.

vous system. The most common neurologic sign is poor coordination of muscles with slight paralysis progressing to generalized failure of muscle coordination. Convulsions, personality changes, and increased sensitivity to touch may also be seen.

Your veterinarian can diagnose feline infectious peritonitis based on the cat's medical history, signs found during a physical examination, and results of laboratory tests.

Treatment, Prevention, and Control

There is no specific treatment for feline infectious peritonitis. Although recovery from signs has been reported, it is uncommon. Up to 95% of cats with feline infectious peritonitis will die from the disease.

In cats with the wet (effusive) form of the disease, the progress is rapid and death usually comes within 2 months. The dry (noneffusive) form of the disease has a more prolonged course. Many cats live several months to a year. Treatment with drugs that reduce inflammation and suppress immune reactions, along with supportive care, can make the cat more comfortable. In some cats (probably less than 10%), treatment may extend survival time by several months. Treatment offers the most hope for cats that are still in good physical condition, still eating, have not yet developed nervous system problems, and that do not have additional disease (such as feline leukemia virus infection).

A vaccine is available to help prevent feline infectious peritonitis. It protects 60% to 90% of noninfected cats that are vaccinated. The duration of protection is unknown but is thought to be short. Because feline infectious peritonitis in the general cat population is relatively rare, vaccination of individual pet cats that live mostly or entirely indoors is probably not necessary.

Vaccination alone cannot be relied on to control the disease within a cat facility. Other measures to reduce exposure include frequent removal of feces (the primary source of coronavirus), early weaning, and isolation of cats that test positive for coronavirus antibodies. Additionally, isolation and testing of cats after shows, proper sanitation and cleaning using viral disinfectants, and vaccination against other feline viruses can reduce exposure. These control measures should be combined with an overall preventive health program.

▓ FELINE LEUKEMIA VIRUS AND RELATED DISEASES

Despite the widespread use of vaccines, feline leukemia virus remains one of the most important causes of illness and death in cats. It causes a variety of cancers. Persistent infection can also lead to severe suppression of the immune system and severe anemia. The virus is present worldwide. Young kittens are much more susceptible than adults.

The rate of feline leukemia virus infection is directly related to the population density of cats. Infection rates are highest in catteries and multiple cat households, especially when cats have access to the outdoors. In the United States, 1 to 2% of healthy stray urban cats persistently have the virus; this figure is higher for sick, "at risk" cats.

Persistently infected healthy cats are carriers of the virus. These carriers excrete large quantities of virus in their saliva. Lesser amounts of virus are excreted in tears, urine, and feces. Mouth and nose contact with infectious saliva or urine is the most likely method of transmission. Nose-to-nose contact, mutual grooming, and shared litter boxes and food dishes make it easy for the disease to spread to uninfected cats. Bite wounds from infected cats are also an efficient method of transmission. This virus may also be transmitted from mother to kitten either in the womb or in the milk.

Disorders Caused by Feline Leukemia Virus

Feline leukemia virus-related disorders are numerous. They include suppression of the immune system, cancer, anemia, immune-mediated diseases, reproductive problems, and inflammation of the intestines.

Immunosuppression

The damage to the immune system caused by feline leukemia virus is similar to that caused by feline immunodeficiency virus (*see* page 444). With a damaged immune system, a cat has an increased susceptibility to bacterial, fungal, protozoal, and other viral infections.

Tumors

Tumors, including lymphoma, lymphoid leukemia, and erythremic myelosis, develop in up to 30% of cats infected

Direct contact, mutual grooming, and shared litter boxes and food dishes can help spread feline leukemia virus.

with feline leukemia virus. Cats that test negative for the feline leukemia virus (called nonviremic cats) also develop these tumors. However, they may still be caused by feline leukemia virus that is no longer detectable in the bloodstream.

Lymphoma is the most frequently diagnosed cancer of cats. Most American cats with lymphoma of the spine, chest, or multiple locations are feline leukemia virus-positive. However, in some parts of the world, these forms of lymphoma are becoming much less common. The proportion occurring in feline leukemia virus-positive cats is decreasing. This may be related to effective control of feline leukemia virus.

Feline lymphoma can be treated with anticancer drugs, often called chemotherapy. The use of chemotherapy has improved in recent years. Most cats do not experience significant adverse effects and enjoy a good quality of life.

About 50% of cats with lymphoma that are treated will have a complete remission (no clinical evidence of disease). Feline leukemia virus-negative cats that attain a complete remission live an average of 9 months. Feline leukemia virus-positive cats have an average survival period of

6 months. Cats not treated or those not responding to treatment survive only about 6 weeks.

Leukemia is a cancerous proliferation of blood cells originating in the bone marrow. In cats, leukemia is strongly associated with feline leukemia virus infection. Leukemia is sometimes (but not always) associated with cancerous cells circulating in the blood.

Reproductive Problems

Reproductive problems, including infertility and abortion, are common in cats with the feline leukemia virus. Fetal death and reabsorption of the placenta may occur between 21 and 42 days into the pregnancy. The normal gestation period in cats is 63 to 67 days. It is likely that, in these cases, the virus was transported across the placenta and fatally infected the developing kittens. Occasionally, infected queens give birth to live kittens that were infected with the virus while in the womb. Queens that are infected but have not tested positive for the virus may pass the virus on to their kittens in their milk.

Inflammation of the Intestines

Inflammation of the intestines may develop in feline leukemia virus infections. This inflammation often resembles feline panleukopenia (*see* page 536). Signs include loss of appetite, depression, vomiting, and diarrhea (which may be bloody). Because immune system damage is associated with feline leukemia virus infection, blood poisoning may develop. Evidence suggests that the feline leukemia virus and the feline panleukopenia virus may act together to produce this syndrome.

Other Disorders

Other disorders may also develop as a result of infection with feline leukemia virus. It occasionally causes problems in the nervous system, leading to inequality in the size of the pupils, loss of bladder control, or hind limb paralysis. Certain lymphomas induced by the feline leukemia virus can produce identical signs. Thus, your veterinarian will be careful to confirm whether the cat has a form of cancer or problems with the nervous system. The treatment required for these conditions is different and, for the health of your cat, it is important that the correct treatment be provided.

Treatment

Ideally, a feline leukemia virus-infected cat would be identified early and treated to totally eliminate the infection before virus-related diseases had time to develop. Unfortunately, most infected cats have a longterm infection by the time the disease is diagnosed.

Many treatments have been administered in an attempt to reverse the presence of the virus in the blood or control the signs associated with feline leukemia virus infection. However, most of these treatments have not been found to be effective.

Cats with feline leukemia virus infection can live without major disease for several years if they have good supportive care. Stress and sources of secondary infection should be avoided. To avoid infection from bacteria and other agents, water should be changed at least daily, uneaten food should be removed at least daily, and all dishes should be thoroughly cleaned daily. The cat should remain indoors 100% of the time. This will reduce the risk of exposure to infectious agents and prevent transmission of the virus to other cats. Routine preventive care for feline leukemia virus-infected cats is more important than for uninfected cats. Infected cats should receive health checkups every 6 months or whenever you notice any health changes. Your veterinarian will provide routine vaccinations based on the risk to the cat. Rabies vaccinations will also be given to comply with local laws. Feline leukemia virus vaccinations are not administered to infected cats as there is no evidence that these vaccines provide a benefit. If the infected cat is not already neutered, this should be done.

If you have a cat with feline leukemia virus, you should ask your veterinarian to provide you with a list of signs of developing disease. This will allow you to watch for signs of virus-related disease, particularly secondary infections. Treatment for any infections or other illnesses will be started earlier and may last longer due to the cat's weakened immune system.

Prevention and Control

Testing for feline leukemia virus infection is recommended for all kittens at their first veterinary visit. If the kitten(s) test positive, your veterinarian will talk with you about the steps you should consider. Testing is also recommended for all cats prior to entering a household with existing uninfected cats, for cats in an existing household prior to admission of a new, uninfected cat, and for all cats prior to their first feline leukemia virus vaccination.

Feline leukemia virus vaccines are intended to protect cats against infection and/or to prevent persistent presence of virus in the blood. Vaccines are recommended only for uninfected cats; there is no benefit in vaccinating a feline leukemia virus-positive cat.

Your veterinarian will assess each cat's risk of exposure to feline leukemia virus and prescribe vaccines only for those cats at risk. Uninfected cats in a household with infected cats should be vaccinated. In addition, other means of protecting uninfected cats (for example, by physical separation) should also be used. Constant exposure to feline leukemia virus-infected cats is likely to result in viral transmission to a previously uninfected cat whether it has been vaccinated or not.

Some strains of feline leukemia virus can be grown in human tissue cultures. This has led to concerns about possible transmission to people. Several studies have addressed this concern; none have shown any evidence that people can be infected with this virus by exposure to infected cats.

▓ FELINE PANLEUKOPENIA

Feline panleukopenia (also called feline infectious enteritis or feline distemper) is a highly contagious, sometimes fatal,

---

Prevention and Control of Feline Leukemia Virus

Testing should be done in the following situations:

- All kittens at their first veterinary visit
- All cats prior to entering a household with existing uninfected cats
- All cats in an existing household prior to admission of a new, uninfected cat
- All cats prior to their first feline leukemia virus vaccination

Vaccines are recommended only for uninfected cats at risk.

---

viral disease of cats. Kittens are affected most severely. Feline panleukopenia virus, the parvovirus that causes this disease, occurs worldwide and can persist for more than a year in the environment unless potent disinfectants are used to inactivate it. The term "panleukopenia" refers to an abnormally low level of white blood cells. This disorder is now seen only infrequently by veterinarians, presumably as a consequence of the widespread use of vaccines. However, infection rates remain high in unvaccinated cat populations, and the disease is occasionally seen in vaccinated, pedigreed kittens that have been exposed to high amounts of the virus.

During the initial phase of the illness, virus is abundant in all secretions and excretions of infected cats including saliva, tears, urine, and feces. The virus can be shed in the feces of survivors for up to 6 weeks after recovery. Cats are infected through the mouth and nose by exposure to infected animals, their secretions, or inanimate objects harboring the virus. Most free-roaming cats are exposed to the virus during their first year of life. Those that develop low grade infection or survive short-term illness mount a long-lasting, protective immune response.

In pregnant queens, the virus may spread across the placenta to cause fetal mummification, abortion, or stillbirth. Rarely, infection of kittens in the period just after birth may destroy the lining of the cerebellum, leading to incomplete development of the brain, problems with physical coordination, and tremors.

Most cats infected with the panleukopenia virus show no signs of infection. Those that become ill are usually less than 1 year old. Severe infection may cause death with little or no warning. Short-term infection causes fever, depression, and loss of appetite after an incubation period of 2 to 7 days. Vomiting usually develops 1 to 2 days after the onset of fever. Diarrhea may occur but is not always present. Extreme dehydration develops rapidly in severe cases. Affected cats may sit for hours at their water bowl, although they may not drink much. The duration of illness is seldom more than 5 to 7 days. Kittens under 5 months of age are most likely to die from panleukopenia virus infection.

Your veterinarian will diagnose this disease based on the signs and laboratory tests. Successful treatment of severe cases requires intravenous fluids and supportive care. Electrolyte (salt) imbalances, low blood sugar, low levels of protein in the blood, anemia, and secondary infections often develop in severely affected cats.

Vaccines that provide solid, long-lasting immunity are available. The first vaccination for kittens is usually given at 6 to 9 weeks of age. Your veterinarian will make a recommendation for additional vaccinations based on the health of your cat and your cat's risk of exposure to the virus.

▨ FUNGAL INFECTIONS

Funguses (also called fungi) are parasitic, spore-producing organisms. They obtain their nourishment by absorbing food from the hosts on which they grow. Many species of fungus exist in the environment, but only some cause infections. The primary source of most infections is soil. Fungal infections can be acquired by inhalation, ingestion, or through the skin (for example, through a cut or wound).

Some fungal infections can cause disease in otherwise healthy animals, while others require a host that is sick, weakened, or immunocompromised to establish infection. Prolonged use of antibiotic drugs or immunosuppressive agents appears to increase the likelihood of some fungal infections. The infection itself may be localized, or it may affect the entire body. In general, fungal infections affecting the skin (such as ringworm) are common in cats, while generalized fungal infections are very rare.

Aspergillosis

Aspergillosis is a fungal infection caused by several *Aspergillus* species. It is primarily a respiratory infection that may become generalized. Aspergillosis is found worldwide and in almost all domestic animals as well as in many wild animals; however, the susceptibility to fungal infections varies among species. Nasal cavity, lung, and intestinal forms have been described in domestic cats. Cats that are already stressed by disease (such as viral infection) or immunosuppressed may be more likely to become infected. Signs are nonspecific and include inflammation of the sinuses or the esophagus (or both) and pneumonia. Establishing an accurate diagnosis can be difficult. Surgery and antifungal drugs are usually recommended to treat aspergillosis; however, the outlook depends on the overall condition of the cat and the extent of infection.

Candidiasis

Candidiasis is a localized fungal disease affecting the mucous membranes and the skin. It is distributed worldwide in a variety of animals and is most commonly caused by species of the yeast-like fungus, *Candida albicans*. Candidiasis is rare in cats, but has been associated with oral and upper respiratory disease, lesions of the eye, infection of the space between the lungs and chest wall, intestinal disease, and bladder infection.

Factors that may predispose an animal to infection include injury to any of the mucous membranes, the use of catheters, administration of antibiotics, and immunosuppressive drugs or diseases.

Signs of infection are variable and nonspecific (for example, diarrhea, weakness, skin lesions) and may be associated more with the primary or predisposing conditions than with the *Candida* infection itself. An ointment or topical application may be useful in the treatment of oral or skin candidiasis. Your veterinarian may also recommend different drugs given by mouth or by injection for treatment of infected cats.

Coccidioidomycosis (Valley Fever)

Coccidioidomycosis is a dustborne, noncontagious infection caused by the fungus *Coccidioides immitis*. Infections are limited to dry, desertlike regions of the southwestern United States and similar geographic areas of Mexico and Central and South America. Inhalation of fungal spores (often carried on dust particles) is the only established mode of infection. Epidemics may occur when rainy periods are followed by drought, resulting in dust storms. Infections are uncommon in cats.

Coccidioidomycosis is primarily a chronic respiratory disease. Infected cats most often have skin problems (draining skin lesions, lumps under the skin, abscesses), fever, lack of appetite, and weight loss. Less common signs in cats include difficulty breathing, lameness, neurologic signs, and eye abnormalities. A diagnosis is based on identification of the fungus in tissue samples from the animal.

Treatment involves longterm antifungal medications. The prognosis is guarded, but cats with skin infections may respond to treatment. There is no known prevention other than decreasing your pet's exposure to desert soil and dust as much as possible.

Cryptococcosis

Cryptococcosis is a fungal disease that may affect the respiratory tract (especially the nasal cavity), central nervous system, eyes, and skin (particularly of the face and neck of cats). It is caused by the fungus *Cryptococcus neoformans*, which is found worldwide in soil and bird manure, especially in pigeon droppings. Transmission is by inhalation of spores or contamination of wounds.

Cryptococcosis is most common in cats, although it also occurs in other domestic and wild animals. In cats, upper respiratory signs following infection of the nasal cavity are most common. The signs often include sneezing, bloody nasal discharge, polyp-like mass(es) in the nostril, and a firm swelling under the skin and over the bridge of the nose. Areas of small raised bumps and nodules may affect the skin; these may feel soft (liquid filled) or firm. These areas may ulcerate, leaving a raw surface. Neurologic signs associated with cryptococcosis of the central nervous system include depression, changes in temperament, seizures, circling, slight paralysis, and blindness. Eye abnormalities may also develop.

Various antifungal drugs may be prescribed for the treatment of cryptococcosis. Most affected pets require prolonged treatment (up to several months), depending on the severity and extent of the disease. Treatment for cryptococcosis may include surgery to remove lesions in the nasal cavity or on the bridge of the nose. The outlook for cats that are also infected with feline leukemia virus or feline immunodeficiency virus is guarded, because these cats have a higher likelihood of treatment failure.

Histoplasmosis

Histoplasmosis is a noncontagious infection caused by the fungus *Histoplasma capsulatum*, which is found worldwide. This soil fungus is widely distributed (particularly by bird and bat populations) in the midwestern and southern United States, especially in river valleys and plains. Infection occurs when spores in the air are inhaled. The lungs and the lymph nodes in the chest are the sites of primary infection. The organisms enter the bloodstream from

Signs of Cryptococcosis in Cats

Upper respiratory signs (most common)

- Sneezing
- Bloody chronic nasal discharge containing both mucus and pus
- Firm swelling under the skin and over the bridge of the nose
- Skin lesions
- Raised bumps or nodules that may be firm or soft
- Larger lesions that tend to ulcerate, leaving a raw surface

Neurologic signs

- Depression
- Changes in temperament
- Seizures
- Circling
- Slight paralysis
- Blindness

Eye abnormalities

- Dilated unresponsive pupils
- Blindness due to retinal detachment
- Inflammation of the tissues of the eye

these sites and become dispersed throughout the body; they may localize in bone marrow or the eyes.

The signs vary and are nonspecific, reflecting the various organ involvements. Occasionally, cats with lung involvement show signs of fever, labored breathing, and coughing. The lung infection usually resolves on its own. However, if the respiratory infection extends to other tissues, a more serious form of the disease may develop, involving a large number of organs and body systems. The organs most often involved are the lungs, intestine, lymph nodes, liver, spleen and bone marrow. Signs of illness such as depression, fever, and poor appetite are common, as well as chronic diarrhea, intestinal blood loss, anemia, and weight loss. Infection of the bones, eyes, skin, and central nervous system may occur. Diagnosis requires identification of the fungus in body fluids or tissues.

Treatment of widespread histoplasmosis is difficult. It requires the use of antifungal drugs and supportive treatment such as adequate nutrition, additional fluids (hydration), and control of secondary bacterial infections. Antifungal treatment must be continued for prolonged periods of time and may be expensive.

Mycetomas

Mycetomas are infections of the skin and underlying tissues that have the appearance of nodules or tumors. When such lesions are caused by funguses, they are known as **eumycotic mycetomas**. The fungus multiplies in the lesions and organizes into aggregates known as granules or grains. Granules may be of various colors and sizes, depending on the species of fungus involved. Mycetomas are rare in cats.

Most eumycotic mycetomas are confined to the tissue beneath the skin. In cats, mycetomas are usually characterized by skin nodules on the legs and feet or on the face. When the feet or limbs are involved, the infection may extend to the underlying bone. Skin mycetomas, while not life-threatening, are often difficult to resolve. Your veterinarian will recommend the best treatment options, which may include surgical removal or antifungal medication.

North American Blastomycosis

North American blastomycosis, caused by the fungus *Blastomyces dermatitidis*, is generally limited to geographically restricted areas in the Mississippi, Missouri, Tennessee, and Ohio River basins and along the Great Lakes and the St. Lawrence Seaway. Beaver dams and other habitats where soil is moist, acidic, and rich in decaying vegetation may serve as the ecologic niche for the organism, which has also been found in pigeon and bat feces. Blastomycosis is rare in cats.

Affected animals have signs such as fever, lethargy, poor appetite, and weight loss. Lung involvement leads to exercise intolerance, cough, and difficulty breathing. The peripheral lymph nodes may be enlarged. Bone involvement may occur and result in lameness. Central nervous system infection may lead to behavior changes, seizures, coma, or sudden death. Infection of the urogenital tract occasionally may occur and cause signs such as blood in the urine or difficulty urinating. Eye involvement can lead to pain, light sensitivity, and glaucoma. Involvement of the retina may lead to blindness. Draining nodules may be found in the skin.

Treatment of blastomycosis is based on the severity of the condition and other factors that must be evaluated by a veterinarian. Treatment is aimed at relief of specific signs (such as difficulty breathing, coughing, or eye problems) and elimination of the fungus from the body. Treatment may include one or more antifungal drugs, which are given for an extended period (often 2 months or more) until active disease is not apparent. Relapses may occur. (For a more detailed discussion of NORTH AMERICAN BLASTOMYCOSIS, *see* page 315.)

Phaeohyphomycosis

Phaeohyphomycosis is a general term for an infection by any of a number of pigmented funguses of the family Dematiaceae. Infection may result from fungal contamination of tissue at the site of an injury. Phaeohyphomycosis is uncommon in cats. In most cases, the infection is confined to the skin and tissues beneath the skin. Slowly enlarging masses beneath the skin are found on the head, the lining of the nasal passages, limbs, and chest. The nodules may ulcerate and have draining tracts. Surgical removal of the lesion can be a cure. Treatment with antifungal drugs may be considered in cases when surgery is not possible.

Rhinosporidiosis

Rhinosporidiosis is a chronic, nonfatal infection, primarily of the lining of the nasal passages and, occasionally, of the skin. It is caused by the fungus *Rhinosporidium seeberi*. Uncommon in North America, it is seen most often in India, Africa, and South America.

Infection is characterized by polyp-like growths that may be soft, pink, crumbly, lobular with roughened surfaces, and large enough to obstruct or close off the nasal passages. The skin lesions may be single or multiple, attached at a base, or have a stem-like connection.

Surgical removal of the lesions is considered to be the standard treatment, but recurrence is common.

Sporotrichosis

Sporotrichosis is a sporadic chronic disease caused by *Sporothrix schenckii*. The organism is found around the world in soil, vegetation, and timber. In the US, this fungus is most commonly found in coastal regions and river valleys. Infection usually results when the organism enters the body through skin wounds via contact with plants or soil or penetrating foreign objects such as a sharp branch. Transmission of the disease from animals to humans can occur.

Sporotrichosis is more common in cats than other species. The infection may remain localized to the site of entry (involving only the skin) or it may spread to nearby lymph nodes. Although generalized illness is not seen initially, longterm infection may result in fever, listlessness, and depression. Rarely, infection will spread through the bloodstream from the initial site of inoculation to the bone, lungs, liver, spleen, testes, gastrointestinal tract, or central nervous system.

Longterm treatment with antifungal drugs (continued 3 to 4 weeks beyond apparent cure) is usually recommended. Because sporotrichosis can be passed from your pet to you, strict hygiene must be observed when handling animals with suspected or diagnosed sporotrichosis. If your cat is diagnosed with sporotrichosis, ask your veterinarian about the precautions you and every member of your family should take while your pet is ill.

■ GLANDERS (FARCY)

Glanders is a contagious, short- or longterm, usually fatal disease of horses caused by the bacterium *Burkholderia mallei*. The disease is characterized by the development of a series of ulcerating nodules.

The nodules are most commonly found in the upper respiratory tract, lungs, and skin. Humans, cats, dogs, and other species are susceptible, but infections in cats are uncommon. Infections in humans are often fatal.

There is no vaccine for glanders. Prevention and control depend on early detection and elimination of affected animals. Complete quarantine and rigorous disinfection is required for all housing and objects that have been in contact with the infected animal. Euthanasia is usually recommended for infected animals. (For a more detailed discussion of GLANDERS, *see* page 805.)

■ LEISHMANIASIS

Leishmaniasis is a longterm, severe, protozoal disease of humans, dogs, and certain rodents. It is characterized by skin sores, disease of the lymph nodes, weight loss, anemia, lameness, kidney failure, and occasionally nosebleed or eye inflammation. Infection in dogs occurs in Central and South America, the Middle East, Asia, and in the Mediterranean region. Cats and other domestic animals are rarely infected and usually only develop skin ulcers, without showing other signs of disease. (For a more detailed discussion of LEISHMANIASIS, *see* page 318.)

■ LYME DISEASE (LYME BORRELIOSIS)

Lyme disease, which is caused by the bacteria *Borrelia burgdorferi* and transmitted through the bite of a tick, affects domestic animals and humans. At least 3 known species of ticks can transmit Lyme disease. However, the great majority of Lyme disease transmissions are due to the bite of a very tiny tick commonly called the deer tick, or black-legged tick. The scientific name of the tick species involved on the west coast of the US is *Ixodes pacificus*; *Ixodes scapularis* is the species involved elsewhere. It is important to note that ticks do not cause Lyme disease, they merely transmit the bacteria that cause it.

Lyme disease occurs much more frequently in dogs than in cats. When infected, cats may show lameness, fever, loss of appetite, fatigue, or difficulty breathing. Many cats do not show noticeable signs, despite being infected. Antibiotics are required for treatment in all cases of Lyme disease. Rapid response is seen in limb and joint disease in most cases, although the signs do not completely resolve in a significant number of affected animals. The infection may persist in spite of antibiotic treatment. (For a more detailed discussion of LYME DISEASE, *see* page 320.)

Tick avoidance plays a role in disease control. While highly effective products (such as sprays and monthly "spot-on" products) are available for use, they must be used consistently in order to provide effective longterm tick control. Your veterinarian can recommend a product that is appropriate for your cat.

■ MELIOIDOSIS

Melioidosis is an uncommon bacterial infection of humans and animals. The disease-causing agent is *Burkholderia pseudomallei*, which occurs in the soil throughout southeast Asia, northern Australia, and the South Pacific. Melioidosis has been diagnosed in many animals, including cats and humans. Cats may succumb to infection due to a weakened immune system. The most common routes of infection are via skin inoculation, contamination of wounds, ingestion of soil or contaminated carcasses, or inhalation.

Infection may be associated with single or multiple curd-like nodules or abscesses, which can be located in any organ. Pneumonia is the most common form of the disease in both animals and humans. Lameness can occur. It is possible for an infection to lie dormant before becoming apparent. Death may result in animals with sudden and intense infections or when vital organs are affected. Treatment with antibiotics can be expensive and prolonged. Treatment protocols adopted for human infections are expected to have more success than the usual approach using conventional veterinary antibiotics. There is a risk that signs will return after treatment is discontinued, however. (For a more detailed discussion of MELIOIDOSIS, *see* page 321.)

■ NOCARDIOSIS

Nocardiosis is a chronic, noncontagious disease caused by the bacteria of the genus *Nocardia*. These bacteria are found commonly in soil, decaying vegetation, compost, and other environmental sources. They enter the body through contamination of wounds or by inhalation. Species in this genus are found in temperate regions, as well as in tropical and subtropical areas.

Poor appetite, fever, lethargy, and weight loss are common nonspecific signs associated with all infection sites. Infections in cats are often localized, with lesions beneath the skin, mycetomas, and inflammation of one or more lymph nodes. There may be swelling and inflammation of the gums around the teeth and ulcers in the mouth accompanied by severe bad breath. Nocardiosis affecting the chest often involves pus-producing inflammation of the chest cavity or abdominal cavity. The heart, liver, kidneys, and brain may also be affected.

Your veterinarian will prescribe antibiotics based on identification of the bacteria. Nocardial infections are resistant to some types of antibiotics. Treatment must

Nocardia bacteria can often be found in soil, compost, or decaying vegetation.

often be continued for more than 3 months. It is important to continue treatment as directed to allow your pet the best possibility for recovery. The prognosis is guarded due to the long treatment time and the likelihood of relapse.

■ PERITONITIS

Peritonitis is inflammation of the peritoneum, the membrane that lines the abdominal cavity. It is a serious and often fatal condition. Peritonitis may be short- or longterm, localized or widespread. Most commonly it occurs due to contamination of the peritoneal cavity (for example by perforation of the abdominal cavity by a foreign object, the splitting open of an abdominal wound closure, or rupture of the intestine due to the presence of a swallowed foreign object), but it also may be caused by infectious agents such as viruses or bacteria.

Fever, blood poisoning, shock, reduced blood pressure, hemorrhage, abdominal pain, paralytic obstruction of the intestines with reduced fecal output, and fluid accumulation within the abdominal cavity may all be signs of peritonitis. Rupture of the gastrointestinal tract, with spillage of large volumes of intestinal contents, leads to short-term peritonitis. Death due to shock from the large amounts of bacterial toxins may occur suddenly.

The first priority of treatment is to stabilize the consequences of peritonitis, such as changes in electrolytes, acid-base imbalance, fluid loss, and blood clotting abnormalities. In addition, your veterinarian will want to identify the point of origin of inflammation and correct or remove it. Antibiotics are a standard part of the treatment. Replacement fluids, electrolytes, plasma, or whole blood may be necessary to maintain heart output.

Once the cat is stabilized, surgery is done to explore the abdomen and to repair any defects. Your veterinarian will follow this with a thorough rinsing of the abdominal cavity with a saline solution, antiseptics, or antibiotics. Antibiotics are continued after surgery. Nutritional support with intravenous feeding may be needed, as many cats with peritonitis will not eat after surgery. In cats with blood poisoning and shock, fluids, electrolytes, and antibiotics are crucial elements of treatment.

PLAGUE

Plague is a sudden and sometimes fatal bacterial disease caused by *Yersinia pestis*. It is transmitted primarily by the fleas of rats and other rodents. This is the disease, often called the Black Death, that swept through Asia and then Europe in the 14th century. Over 25 million people (one third of the population) died of this disease in Europe between 1347 and 1352. Devastating outbreaks of this disease recurred with regularity throughout the next 200 years.

Today, this disease can be controlled with antibiotics and other medications; however, it has not been eradicated. Small numbers of cases occur in wild animals in the western United States and throughout the world, including Eurasia, Africa, and North and South America. On average, 10 human plague cases are reported each year in the United States; the majority are from New Mexico, California, Colorado, and Arizona.

Yersinia pestis is maintained in the environment in a natural cycle between susceptible rodent species and their associated fleas. Commonly affected species include ground squirrels, prairie dogs, rabbits, and wood rats. Cats are usually exposed to the bacteria by eating an infected animal or by the bite an infected flea. Potentially, the infected fleas can be transported into homes.

In mammalian hosts, plague occurs in one of 3 forms: bubonic, septicemic, or pneumonic. In **bubonic plague**, the bacteria enter the body via the skin (by a flea bite) or the mucous membranes (by ingestion of infected animal tissue). The bacteria then travel via the lymphatic vessels to regional lymph nodes. These infected lymph nodes are called buboes, the typical lesion of bubonic plague. **Septicemic plague** can develop when the organism spreads from the affected lymph nodes via the bloodstream, but it can also occur without prior disease of the lymph nodes. Numerous organs can be affected, including the spleen, liver, heart, and lungs. **Pneumonic plague** can develop from inadequately treated septicemic plague or from infectious respiratory droplets, such as those from a coughing pneumonic plague patient.

Signs and Diagnosis

The most common presentation of plague in cats is bubonic plague. Cats with bubonic plague usually have fever, lethargy, and an enlarged lymph node that may be abscessed and draining. Ulcers in the mouth, skin abscesses, discharge from the eyes, diarrhea, vomiting, and diffuse spreading inflammation of tissues beneath the skin have also been documented. High fever may be present. Cats with primary septicemic plague have no obvious disease of the lymph nodes but have fever, lethargy, and poor appetite. Septic signs may also include diarrhea, vomiting, excessively rapid heart rate, weak pulse, and breathing distress. Primary pneumonic plague has not been documented in cats. Cats with secondary pneumonic plague may have all the signs of septicemic plague along with a cough and other abnormal lung sounds.

To diagnose plague, your veterinarian will take samples (such as blood, fluid from the lymph nodes, or a swab from the mouth or throat) for testing and confirmation of the presence of plague-causing bacteria.

Treatment and Prevention

Due to the rapid progression of this disease, treatment for suspected plague (and infection control practices) should be started before a definitive diagnosis is obtained. Your veterinarian will recommend an antibiotic as standard treatment.

The duration of infectivity in treated cats is not known with certainty, but cats are thought to be noninfectious after 72 hours of appropriate antibiotic treatment if there

---

Prevention of Plague in Cats

To decrease the risk of pets and humans being exposed to plague, pet owners in areas where the disease may be found should:

- Keep their pets from roaming and hunting
- Limit their contact with rodent or rabbit carcasses
- Use appropriate flea control

---

are indications of improvement. During the infectious period, cats should remain hospitalized, especially if there are signs of pneumonia. Human cases have occurred in cat owners trying to give medications by mouth at home, exposing them to contact with the mouth and associated infectious secretions.

Along with treatment and diagnostic considerations, protection of people and other animals and initiation of public health interventions are critical when an animal is suspected to have plague. Even before a diagnosis is complete, animals with signs that suggest plague should be placed in isolation, and infection control measures should be implemented for the protection of you and your family, other household pets, and any other animals or individuals that have had contact with the infected animal.

To decrease the risk of pets and humans being exposed to plague, pet owners in areas where the disease may be found should keep their pets from roaming and hunting, limit their contact with rodent or rabbit carcasses, and use appropriate flea control. Your veterinarian can suggest the most appropriate flea control product for your cat.

▓ Q FEVER

Q fever is a bacterial infection that rarely causes noticeable illness in animals; it can be passed from animals to people. Transmission to people usually occurs by direct or indirect contact with the bacteria that are shed in large numbers in the placenta and birth fluids of ruminants such

as cattle, sheep, and goats. Other domestic animals, including cats, can also play a role in the spread of infection to humans.

There are 2 major patterns of transmission. In one, the organism circulates between wild animals and their skin parasites, mainly ticks. The other transmission pattern occurs in domestic animals (mainly ruminants). People can become infected by direct contact with the bacteria in birth fluids or materials such as soil or bedding that were contaminated during the delivery. The organism is also found in milk, urine, and feces of infected animals. Transmission may occur by aerosolization of the bacteria attached to dust particles that are inhaled into the lungs or by ingestion of contaminated milk.

The Q fever bacteria usually do not cause signs of illness in infected animals. They have occasionally been implicated in abortion. Infected animals that contract the illness may show vague signs, such as fever, lethargy, and lack of appetite lasting several days.

Infected animals can be treated with antibiotics, but complete elimination of the organism has not been reported. Vaccines for people and animals have been developed but are not commercially available in the United States. Q fever in humans must be reported to public health officials; cases of Q fever in animals need not be reported unless humans are involved.

▓ TETANUS

Tetanus toxemia is caused by a specific toxin, or poison, that blocks the transmission of inhibitory nerve signals, resulting in severe contractions of muscles and exaggerated muscle responses to stimuli. The toxin is produced by *Clostridium tetani* bacteria in dead tissue. Almost all mammals are susceptible to this disease, although cats seem much more resistant than any other domestic animal.

Clostridium tetani is found in soil and intestinal tracts. In most cases, it is introduced into the body through wounds, particularly deep puncture wounds. The bacteria remain in the dead tissue at the original site of infection and multiply. As bacterial cells die and disintegrate, the potent nerve toxin is released. The toxin causes convulsions of the voluntary muscles.

The incubation period averages 10 to 14 days. Localized stiffness, often involving the jaw muscles and muscles of the neck, the hind limbs, and the region of the infected wound, is seen first. General stiffness becomes pronounced approximately 1 day later, and then spasms and painful sensitivity from a normally painless touch become evident. Spasms are often triggered by sudden movement or noise. Because of their high resistance to tetanus toxin, cats often have a long incubation period and frequently develop tetanus that is localized to the area of the wound. However, generalized tetanus does develop, in which the ears are erect, the tail is stiff and extended, and the mouth is partially open with the lips drawn back.

In the early stages of the disease, your veterinarian may recommend muscle relaxants, tranquilizers, or sedatives along with tetanus antitoxin. This treatment is supported by draining and cleaning the wounds and administering antibiotics.

Good nursing is critical during the early period of spasms. If your pet has tetanus and will be returning home with you rather than staying in a clinic, be sure to follow the nursing care instructions fully and carefully.

■ TOXOPLASMOSIS

Toxoplasmosis is caused by *Toxoplasma gondii*, a protozoan parasite that infects humans and other warm-blooded animals. It has been found worldwide. Wild and domestic felines (members of the cat family) are the only definitive hosts of the parasite. Infected cats can transmit the disease to humans and other animals.

There are 3 infectious stages of *Toxoplasma gondii*: tachyzoites (rapidly multiplying form), bradyzoites (tissue cyst form), and sporozoites (in oocysts). The parasite is transmitted by consumption of infectious oocysts in cat feces, consump-

---

Transmission of Toxoplasmosis to People

Exposure to feces from infected cats can cause toxoplasmosis in people, although more likely sources of infection are eating undercooked meat and handling raw meat. Still, it is recommended that pregnant women and immunocompromised individuals avoid exposure to cat feces—for example, they should not clean litter boxes or pans and should wear gloves when gardening. Any areas known to be contaminated with cat feces should be avoided.

---

tion of tissue cysts in infected meat, and by transfer of tachyzoites from mother to fetus through the placenta. Cats generally develop immunity after the initial infection; therefore, they shed oocysts only once in their lifetime (from approximately 3 days after infection and for about 20 days thereafter).

The tachyzoite is the stage responsible for tissue damage. Therefore, signs depend on the number of tachyzoites released, the ability of the infected cat's immune system to limit tachyzoite spread, and the organs damaged by the tachyzoites. Because adult animals with normally functioning immune systems control tachyzoite spread efficiently, cats with toxoplasmosis usually have no signs of illness. However, in kittens tachyzoites spread throughout the body. The signs include fever, diarrhea, cough, difficulty breathing, jaundice, seizures, and death.

In many cases, treatment is not necessary in infected cats. If warranted, your veterinarian will prescribe antibiotics to treat toxoplasmosis. Anticonvulsant medications may be used to control seizures. Fluids or intravenous feeding may be necessary for animals that are dehydrated or severely weakened due to the infection.

Toxoplasmosis is a major concern for people with immune system dysfunction (such as people infected with the human immunodeficiency virus). In these individuals, toxoplasmosis usually leads to inflammation of the brain. Toxoplasmosis is also a major concern for pregnant women because tachyzoites can migrate across the placenta and cause birth defects in human fetuses.

▓ TRICHINELLOSIS (TRICHINOSIS)

Trichinellosis is a parasitic disease that can be transmitted to people. It is caused by a type of worm known as a nematode. The name of the disease comes from the scientific name for the worm, *Trichinella spiralis*. Humans become infected when they eat undercooked infected meat, usually pork or bear, although other animals can also be infected with this nematode. Natural infections occur in wild meat-eating animals; most mammals are susceptible.

Infection occurs when an animal eats meat with cysts containing the *Trichinella* larvae. The life cycle continues inside the animal, with larvae eventually migrating throughout the body, where they form cysts in muscles. Larvae may remain viable in the cysts for years, and their development continues only if they are ingested by another suitable host. If larvae pass through the intestine and are eliminated in the feces before maturation, they may be infective to other animals.

Generally, there are no signs of the disease, and most infections in domestic and wild animals go undiagnosed. In humans, heavy infections may produce serious illness and occasionally death. Although diagnosis before death in animals other than humans is rare, trichinellosis may be suspected if there is a history of eating either rodents or raw, infected meat.

Treatment is generally impractical in animals. Making sure that ingestion of viable *Trichinella* cysts in muscle does not occur is the best way to prevent disease in both animals and humans. Raw or improperly cooked meat should not be fed to cats. Cooking meat to an internal temperature of at least 145°F (63°C) will kill the cysts. Freezing cannot be relied on to kill cysts in meat other than pork.

Diseases such as trichinellosis or tularemia can occur in cats that eat prey or raw, uncooked meat.

▓ TUBERCULOSIS

Tuberculosis is an infectious disease caused by bacteria of the genus *Mycobacterium*. The disease affects practically all species of vertebrates, and, before control measures were adopted, was a major disease of humans and domestic animals. Signs and lesions are generally similar in the various species. Tuberculosis is uncommon in cats in North America.

Three main types of tubercle bacilli are recognized: human (*Mycobacterium tuberculosis*), bovine (*Mycobacterium bovis*), and avian (*Mycobacterium avium*). Cats are quite resistant to the human form.

Ingestion, particularly via contaminated food or milk, is the most common source of infection. The bacteria may spread rapidly through the bloodstream and lymphatic channels and cause death. Alternatively, a prolonged course of disease may ensue. The signs reflect the extent and location of infection plus the underlying condition caused by the spread through the bloodstream. Generalized signs include lethargy, weakness, loss of appetite and weight, and fever. The pneumonia of the respiratory form of the disease causes a chronic, intermittent, moist cough with later signs of difficulty breathing and quick, shallow breathing.

The tuberculin skin test for diagnosis is considered unreliable in cats. Treatment of tuberculosis in cats is often not successful. If a cat is suspected of having advanced tuberculosis, it must be reported to the appropriate public health authorities. It is generally recommended that affected cats be euthanized.

TULAREMIA

Tularemia is a bacterial disease that affects people and many species of wild and domestic animals. It is caused by toxins in the blood produced by the bacterium *Francisella tularensis*. The bacteria can survive for weeks or months in a moist environment. There are 2 types of organisms that differ based on the severity of the disease they produce. Type A is more likely to cause severe disease and is found most commonly in North America. Disease resulting from Type B infection is less severe and occurs most commonly as a result of contact with aquatic animals or ingestion of contaminated water in North America and Eurasia. Cats and other carnivores may also acquire infection from eating an infected carcass.

In domestic animals, sheep are most often infected, but clinical infection has been reported in dogs, pigs, horses, and cats. Cats are at higher risk than many other domestic animals due to their predatory behavior. Cats also appear to have a greater susceptibility than other domesticated animals.

The disease can be transmitted from animals to humans by several routes. These include direct contact with bacteria in the tissue of infected animals, eating infected undercooked meat, being bitten by ticks or deer flies, and contact with contaminated water. Rarely, the bite of a cat that has recently fed on an infected animal has been found to be a source of human infection.

In most mammals, signs of illness may include heavy tick infestation, the sudden onset of high fever, swollen glands, lethargy, and poor appetite. Other signs such as stiffness, reduced mobility, increased pulse and respiratory rates, coughing, diarrhea, and frequent urination are occasionally seen. Prostration and death may occur in a few hours or days. In most cases, infection of domestic animals does not result in obvious signs of illness.

Animals with signs of disease are treated with an antibiotic. Early treatment should prevent death; however, prolonged treatment may be necessary. Control is difficult and is limited to reducing tick infestation, keeping pets confined to reduce predatory behavior, and rapid diagnosis and treatment. Animals that recover develop a long-lasting immunity.

HORSE BASICS

39 **Description and Physical Characteristics** 550
Introduction 550
Description and Physical Characteristics 550

40 **Selecting and Providing a Home for a Horse** 557
Selecting a Horse 557
Providing a Home for a Horse 558

41 **Routine Care and Breeding** 560
Routine Health Care 560
Breeding and Reproduction 565

42 **Behavior** 566
Introduction 566
Diagnosing Behavior Problems 566
Behavior Modification 568
Normal Social Behavior in Horses 570
Behavior Problems in Horses 572

CHAPTER 39

Description and Physical Characteristics

■ INTRODUCTION

Horses have evolved over millions of years from animals about the size of dogs to the much larger size they are today. The origins of their association with people are unknown, but evidence suggests that they were first domesticated by nomadic Middle Eastern tribesmen around 2000 BC, or even earlier by the Chinese (3500 BC). Unlike dogs and cats, which are predators, horses are prey animals. They feed on grains and grasses and, like all prey animals of open grasslands, they tend to herd together for protection and take flight in response to danger or any unsettling circumstance.

Horses in the United States are not generally raised for meat, hides, or milk. Rather, horses are used primarily for pleasure riding, showing, racing, and pulling carts or carriages. Horses are still used for agricultural purposes (for example, pulling plows) in some areas and by some cultures such as the Amish in Pennsylvania or central Illinois. A wide range of horse varieties and breeds have been created to perform these various functions.

■ DESCRIPTION AND PHYSICAL CHARACTERISTICS

Horses share many of the same physiologic characteristics of people and domestic pets, in that they have a circulatory system, a respiratory system, a nervous system, and so on. However, they also have many unique characteristics that differ from those of people and other companion animals. For example, horses have developed a large strong band of connective tissue, called the **nuchal ligament**, to provide support for their relatively long and heavily muscled neck.

Metabolism

Horses have a slower metabolism than other companion animals, with resting heart and respiratory rates that are slower than those of people. This slower metabolism is associated with a longer life span than that of many other companion animals. Actual life span depends on overall health, level of care, and size. For example, horses of miniature breeds routinely live 40 years or longer (*see* TABLE 1).

Temperature Regulation

Horses generate considerable heat during exercise. They lose heat primarily by evaporative cooling (usually sweating), just like people do. However, because sweat does not readily evaporate during hot, humid weather, evaporative cooling becomes ineffective under these conditions. During hot, sticky summer days, exercise should be limited to avoid heat stress. Heat stress and continued exercise can lead to dehydration and eventually shock. Adequate water, proper diet (including vitamins and minerals), and limits on exercise are all needed to avoid heat stress.

Horses are large, bulky animals that are good at conserving heat during periods of colder weather. Regardless, they still need adequate shelter, diet, water, and routine veterinary health care to prevent wintertime problems (*see* PROVIDING A HOME FOR A HORSE, page 558).

Table 1. Normal Equine Physiologic Values	
Body temperature (average)	Mare: 100°F (37.8°C) Stallion: 99.7°F (37.6°C)
Resting heart rate	28 to 40 beats per minute
Respiratory rate (at rest)	10 to 14 breaths per minute
Average life span	25 to 30 years (depends on breed, level of care, and other factors)

The Senses

Horses have the same 5 senses as people do but to very different degrees. Some senses are less developed than in people, while others are more powerful.

Sight

The primary sensory input in horses is sight. The importance of vision is reflected in the size of the equine eye, which is the largest of any land mammal, and by the fact that the visual cortex of the equine brain handles one-third of all sensory input.

Horses' eyes are set on the side of the head, rather than facing front as in people, dogs, and cats. This gives them extraordinary peripheral vision, which is useful for animals that must constantly watch for predators (for example, rabbits and most birds). Horses can generally see over a 340° arc without moving their heads, with only small blind spots directly behind and in front of them. These blind spots are caused by the body of the horse (behind)

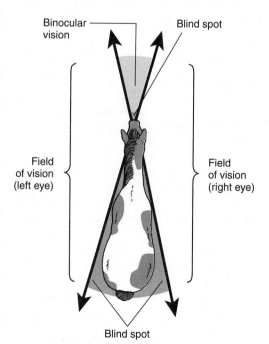

Horses can see well to either side, but have only a limited range of binocular vision.

and the large forehead and muzzle (in front) obstructing the horse's vision. Horses step slightly to the side to see things behind them, and back up and lower their head to see directly in front.

Horses see a panoramic view as a form of monocular vision, which means that each eye is viewing images independently. These images are transferred to a band of retinal cells called **cones** within a "retinal streak." A second group of cones provides binocular vision in an arc of 55 to 65° in front of the horse. The relatively large number of cones enables horses to see distinct images better than dogs do but not quite as well as people can. These cones also mean that horses have some color vision. Horses also have a large number of **rods**, which are the specific type of cells in the retina responsible for night vision, as well as the reflective **tapetum lucidum**, which is also found in both dogs and cats. For this reason, horses see considerably better in the dark than people, and even cats. Horses also share the protective third eyelid that is found in both dogs and cats (*see* Dog Basics, page 3).

Because horses rely on monocular vision, they have poor depth perception. They can misjudge the depth of a small puddle or the distance to a fence. Horses compensate for this by comparing the size of an object to their memory of what they have seen in the past. For example, if a person or fence appears smaller, then it must be farther away. A horse will lower its head to judge closer distances and raise it to judge objects farther away.

In general, horse vision is a little blurrier and a little less colorful than human vision. However, horses see movement very well throughout the 340° arc of their peripheral vision. This is why horses may "spook" when confronted with even minor changes around them—another useful survival skill for herd animals.

As horses age, their vision may worsen. Unfortunately, there are few medical treatments for poor sight in horses. However, watching for signs of poor vision can

Signs of Poor Vision in Horses

- "Spooking" more frequently or to a greater degree
- Frequent sideways head movements (possible decreased vision in one eye)
- Delayed reaction to objects, as if seeing them only when very close
- Bobbing the head while going over uneven ground

help prevent injury to both you and your horse.

Hearing

Horses have large ears that are good at magnifying sound and noting its direction. Each ear can swivel independently up to 180°, allowing horses to locate multiple sounds at the same time. The ears also provide clues to a horse's emotional state. For example, a horse with ears that are laid back may be indicating aggression, pain, or fear (such as in response to a loud or unfamiliar noise).

In general, horses hear slightly better than people do and are able to hear sounds at both higher and lower frequencies. Horses are good at hearing the high-pitched squeaks or crackles associated with the stealthy approach of a predator. Horses experience age-related hearing loss, which means that older animals may not hear your approach as well as they did when younger. Spooking can be avoided by making sure that your horse can see you or knows you are approaching. Hearing loss can also be caused by ear infection or by a mite or tick infestation, so you should ask your veterinarian to periodically check your horse's ears.

Smell and Taste

In addition to providing information about the world in general, the sense of smell is the primary way that horses recognize each other as well as people. For example, horses exchange breath on meeting, and stallions assess the sexual status of a mare through scent. The equine nose has a large internal surface area that contains many chemical receptors within the mucous membrane. The surface area devoted to scent detection is many hundred times greater than in people, again highlighting the importance of the equine sense of smell.

Horses enjoy their food through the sense of taste, which also helps them avoid unpalatable or poisonous food or water. Taste buds are located on the tongue, the soft palate, and the back of the throat. It is not known whether horses have the 4 basic types of taste (sweet, sour, bitter, and salty). However, it is known that they can at least distinguish salty and sweet. In fact, like people, horses are known to have a sweet tooth, appreciating such things as apples, carrots, and honey. Horses are also known to tolerate substances (including medications) that people generally find very bitter.

Locomotion

One of the unique features of horses is their way of movement, which is designed for maximum speed. This natural ability has been enhanced by selective breeding. For example, Thoroughbreds are designed for high-speed sprints, Arabians for endurance racing, Quarter Horses for agility and bursts of speed, and Standardbreds for trotting and pacing. Horses have 4 natural gaits of progressively increasing speed: walk, trot, canter, and gallop. All 4 hooves leave the ground simultaneously during the canter and gallop, a fact that was discovered only through early stop-action photography. Some horses are also taught to pace, which is like the trot, except that both feet on the same side move together.

The Equine Leg

The equine leg is designed for rapid movement over a variety of surfaces. The upper part of the leg is heavily muscled, while the lower part acts as a springboard to enhance the stride. The leg is supported by a suspensory apparatus of tendons and ligaments. The tendons, which can be felt along the back of the lower leg, run the length of the limb, while the many joints are held together and protected by ligaments and joint capsules. Horses also have a unique anatomical feature called the **stay apparatus**, which allows them to "rest" a rear leg while standing on the other 3 for prolonged periods. This is why horses can sleep standing up.

Horses walk and run on their hooves. The cannon and splint bones are in the lower leg, while the pastern bones are between the fetlock and the hoof.

The long, lean, flexible equine leg is excellent for its purpose, but it is also delicate and easily injured. The tremendous amount of weight that is balanced on the hooves and lower limbs make these areas particularly subject to injury.

The Hoof

The hoof consists of a wall of horny keratin (a protein) that grows down from a band called the coronet at the top of the hoof. This process is similar to the way our fingernails grow out from the cuticle. The sole of the equine foot is concave, with a resilient wedge of tissue called the frog that juts forward from the heel. Inside the hoof is the coffin bone (which is shaped like the hoof) and additional resilient tissue. The sole and the frog protect

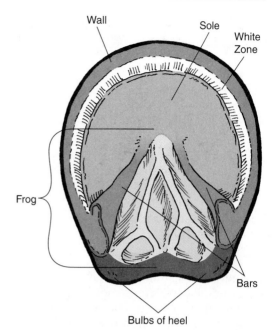

Parts of the hoof

the underside of the foot, while the resilient tissues cushion each step like a spring (*see* FIGURE).

Because the hoof is subjected to tremendous, repetitive impact, it can develop numerous problems that lead to lameness, including bruises, infections, hoof rot, and a serious inflammation in the area of the coffin bone and coronet called laminitis (*see* page 682). Therefore, hoof care is an important part of equine husbandry and preventive medicine.

Skin and Hair

Equine skin is similar to canine and feline skin, although it is not quite as sensitive. The main functions of the hair coat are to protect the skin and to help regulate temperature. The hair coat changes with the seasons, with hair being longer and coarser in the winter than in the summer. Like dogs and cats, horses are able to fluff up their hair (using small muscles attached in the hair follicles) to increase the amount of trapped air for insulation. Additional oil (sebum) is also produced by the skin

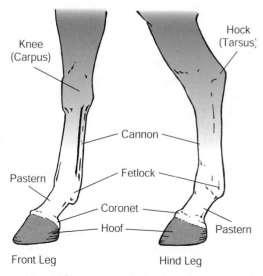

Horses' legs are complex and easily injured.

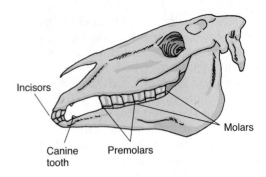

Signs of Skin Problems in Horses

- Hair loss
- Broken hairs, which can be a sign of rubbing or scratching
- Welts, scabs, scratches, bumps, or blisters
- Itching
- Sores that "weep" clear or yellowish serum (a sign of blisters) or pus (a sign of infection)
- Discoloration of the skin
- Dried, crusty material (such as dried blood or serum)

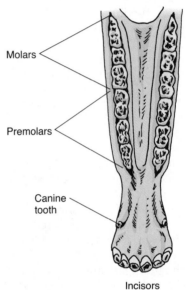

Adult horses have 40 to 42 permanent teeth.

during winter, adding insulation. Proper nutrition, daily cleaning and brushing with a curry comb, and occasional baths are generally all that is needed to keep the skin and hair clean and healthy.

All horse owners should watch for skin problems, which can be caused by infections, scratches, insect bites, parasites, allergies, or irritating chemicals. Signs vary depending on the problem and the individual horse. The location of the problem is often a clue to the cause. For example, fly bites often appear on the neck and ears, while irritation or contact allergy from the saddle or blanket is located on the back.

Teeth and Mouth

Unlike dogs and cats, horses are herbivores designed to eat grains and grasses. Incisor teeth in the front of the mouth grasp and cut grasses, while the rearward molars and premolars are designed for grinding. Equine teeth grow continuously throughout life—as the crowns are ground down, new replacement material arises from the jaw.

Horses have 24 deciduous (baby or milk) teeth; these are replaced by 40 to 42 permanent (adult) teeth that erupt between the ages of 6 months and 5 years (*see* TABLE 2). All male and some female horses have small canine teeth between the incisors and premolars. Horses may

also have up to 4 wolf teeth, which are vestigial and nonfunctional premolars. The wolf teeth are typically extracted when yearlings are being broken in the late fall or early in their 2-year-old year.

Because equine incisor teeth typically grow and wear predictably, dental wear can be used to estimate age. In adult horses, age is typically estimated by the shape and wear pattern of the incisor teeth (*see* TABLE 3).

The mouth also contains the salivary glands, which lubricate food and begin digestion. The tongue helps guide food to the back of the throat and is important for grasping grasses, drinking water, and taste.

Table 2. Equine Dentition

Type of Tooth	Number (Upper/Lower)	Age (Years) at Eruption	Function
Incisors	6/6	2.5 to 4.5	Grasping and cutting
Canines	2/2	4 to 5	—
Premolars	6 to 8/6	2.5 to 4 (wolf teeth at 6 months)	Grinding (wolf teeth nonfunctional)
Molars	6/6	1 to 4	Grinding

Digestive System

People, dogs, and cats have simple stomachs that are good at breaking down meat, fruits, and vegetables. Most animals that eat grass (including cows and sheep) have a more complex system consisting of several stomachs, including a large fermentation vat called a rumen. Grasses (such as hay) in the rumen are digested by billions of bacteria that break down roughage into volatile fatty acids. These fatty acids are absorbed for energy further down in the digestive tract. The equine digestive system combines features of both the simple stomach and the multiple-stomach digestive systems.

At the beginning of the digestive tract, horses have a simple stomach that leads to a small intestine. At the end of the digestive tract, they also have a fermentation vat called the cecum that leads to the great colon. The cecum and great colon make it possible for horses to eat grasses for energy, but because these organs are located at the end of the digestive tract, problems tend to develop. Before they can be fully digested, grasses must pass through almost the full length of the digestive tract, with its many bends and narrowings. This increases the risk of dense, fibrous material becoming impacted and blocking the digestive tract, leading

Table 3. Estimation of Age of Adult Horses by Examination of Teeth

Age (Years)	Distinguishing Dental Wear Pattern
5	Middle incisors worn flat; outer incisors beginning to wear
6	"Cup" (black cavity) gone from middle of central incisor
7	All lower incisors level; cup gone from next to last incisor on each side; telltale "hook" on edge of upper outermost incisors (wears off in 2 years then reappears at age 11); color changes from yellow to bluish white
8	Dental "stars" appear on central incisors; cup gone from outermost incisors; the "star" is the darker dentin that fills the pulp cavity as the tooth wears
9	Center incisors are rounded
10	Next to last incisor on each side is rounded; Galvayne's groove emerges on outermost upper incisors
15	Dental stars round, dark, and distinct; Galvayne's groove halfway down outermost upper incisor
16	Innermost incisor is triangular in cross section
17	Second from last incisor on each side is triangular

Common Signs of Colic

- Abdominal pain
- Pawing with the front foot
- Looking back at the flank
- Kicking at the abdomen
- Curling the upper lip
- Stretching the neck
- Laying down and rolling
- Playing in or with the water bucket
- Intense sweating at rest
- Distended abdomen
- Straining to defecate
- Decreased bowel movements
- Loss of appetite
- Increased heart rate (often a sign that surgery may be needed)

to a condition called colic (*see* page 616). Colic can be a medical emergency, so all horse owners should be familiar with the signs of this very serious, potentially life-threatening condition.

Digestive problems can also show up as changes in the number or character of bowel movements. Normal horse feces are apple-sized lumps that are well formed but somewhat moist. Digestive problems can result in feces that are too soft or too hard. Hard, dry feces can predispose horses to colic. The number of bowel movements per day, the color of the feces, and any tell-tale signs of blood should be reported to your veterinarian.

Urinary System

Equine kidneys are very efficient, constantly filtering waste from the 10 gallons of blood within the horse's body. Very few horses ever develop kidney problems. Most cases go undetected until the later stages, when signs appear as waste products build up in the blood. These signs are caused by the body's attempt to maximize the amount of remaining kidney function.

The kidneys can be injured by a variety of problems, including dehydration; heat stroke; ingestion of poisonous plants;

treatment with certain antibiotics, vitamin supplements, or pain medications; massive blood loss; shock; colic; bacterial infection; or obstruction of urine flow (for example, from stones). Your veterinarian may need to perform urine and blood tests to confirm kidney disease and decide on appropriate treatment (*see* page 781).

Respiratory System

The respiratory system of horses is very similar to that of dogs, cats, and people, although it is much larger. Horses are tremendous athletes, and they need a great deal of oxygen to perform their functions. Performance suffers noticeably when a horse's respiratory system is compromised, which is why respiratory problems in horses are usually noticed more rapidly than in dogs and cats.

The equine respiratory system can be affected by bacterial infections (such as strangles), viral infections, allergies, asthma, mechanical obstruction (for example, "roaring"), and general irritation and inflammation associated with a dirty, dusty environment (*see* page 736). Keeping your horse up to date on vaccinations and keeping his or her environment dry and clean are both important for respiratory health.

Signs of Kidney Disease in Horses

- Increased water intake ("average" intake is 5 to 7 gallons of water/day)
- Increased urination ("average" urine output is 1 to 3 gallons of urine/day)
- Changes in urine smell or color. Depending on the disease process, urine may become foul smelling and dark colored, or very pale and watery.
- Decreased appetite and weight loss. When waste products build up in the blood (a condition called uremia), the horse feels ill and stops eating. Chronic weight loss may be the only noticeable sign.
- Inflammation of the gums, which can be a sign of excess ammonia in the blood

CHAPTER 40

Selecting and Providing a Home for a Horse

■ SELECTING A HORSE

Choosing the right horse takes time and can be difficult. Horses come in many different sizes, breeds, colors, temperaments, and states of health. All these things should be considered, while keeping in mind how the horse will be used (pleasure riding, barrel racing, showing, jumping, and other sports) and the rider's skill and comfort level around horses.

Breed, Temperament, and Use

More than 150 breeds of horses and ponies are commonly found in the United States. Size ranges from large draft breeds, such as Percherons and Clydesdales, to mid-sized Saddlebred and Quarter Horses and smaller Morgans and Arabians. The size of the rider relative to the size of the horse should also be considered. In addition to size considerations, each breed has different physical characteristics to consider during horse selection. For example, breeds that have "feathering" around the hooves are not a good choice for someone who lives in a muddy area and does not have time to groom the horse every day.

Different varieties of horses have different temperaments and have been bred to excel at different activities, so it is important to

There are more than 150 recognized breeds of horses and ponies.

match the horse to both the rider and its proposed use (*see* TABLE 4). Draft breeds are usually calm and steady, while Arabians and Thoroughbreds are often more skittish. Placing an inexperienced or beginning rider on a fiery Thoroughbred would be a mistake, as would purchasing a slow draft breed for flat racing. Many good books on horse breeds are available to help you decide on the breed that is right for you. It is also wise to seek out opinions from experienced horse people (breeders, trainers, veterinarians) before you make a decision.

Table 4. Desirable Characteristics of Horses for Selected Uses		
Use	**Main Qualities**	**Temperament**
Draft horses	Strength	Calm and willing
Polo	Quick and agile	Well balanced
Show jumping	Agile	Well balanced
Steeple chasing or flat racing	Speed and stamina	Well balanced and competitive
Classic horsemanship or dressage	Elegance	Calm and well balanced
Distance riding	Stamina and endurance	Calm and dependable
Pleasure riding	Easy and sure-footed gait	Calm and dependable

Sex and Age

The sex and reproductive status of a horse are other factors to consider. Mares are generally smaller and calmer than stallions within the same breed. Males that have been gelded (castrated) are generally calmer and more easily handled than stallions (intact males). Obviously, horses kept for breeding purposes must remain intact.

Older horses are usually more docile than young ones. However, older horses may have medical conditions that affect their disposition (for example, arthritis), or they may have developed bad habits, such as cribbing, biting, stubbornness, or rolling. Breeding horses should be sexually mature and experienced enough to mate successfully but not so old as to be infertile or afflicted with conditions that inhibit mounting, such as arthritis.

State of Health

Before deciding to buy a particular horse, you should have a veterinarian perform a prepurchase examination. A prepurchase examination involves a complete evaluation of the horse, including observation during movement. The prepurchase examination is a good investment of time and money, because it not only provides you with some assurance that the horse is healthy but also makes you aware of possible problems. You should discuss your intended use of the horse with your veterinarian so that he or she can give an opinion of the horse's suitability for that purpose. However, although your veterinarian can identify problems and render an opinion, the decision to purchase is yours.

Finding the Right Horse

Take some time when looking for the horse that is right for you. You can watch competition horses perform at shows and races. Trainers, instructors, and farriers (horse shoers) may know of horses for sale that fit your needs. Asking around at your barn or riding stable can also be helpful. 4-H clubs are often good sources of avail-

Typical Veterinary Prepurchase Examination

- Detailed history, including examination of medical and reproductive records.
- Thorough physical examination in the stable, including hands-on palpation, listening to the heart and lungs with a stethoscope, and eye examination.
- Observation at the walk and trot on lead.
- Observation at the canter and gallop, then rest and re-examination.
- A Coggins test, which is a blood test for equine infectious anemia, should always be performed. A Coggins test is also almost always required by state regulation if a horse is to be transported across state lines. Your veterinarian can advise you of the current regulations in your area.
- Other special diagnostic tests, such as soundness x-rays, blood tests, or examination with an endoscope, may be recommended based on findings of the physical examination. Regional requirements and conditions may also dictate certain tests.
- State or country regulations may require vaccination for specific diseases before purchase. These are performed after the decision to buy has been made.

able horses. For specific breeds, the breed association may be able to provide a list of breeders or owners in your area. Horses are often advertised in newspapers and equine publications, which may also have information on horse auctions in your area. Be prepared to make a lot of phone calls and shopping trips before you find the horse that is right for you. You can also hire a horse broker for a fee to do most of the leg work for you.

■ PROVIDING A HOME FOR A HORSE

Horses are large animals that require large amounts of space. Some horse owners choose to board their horses because they do not have the proper facilities to keep and exercise them at home.

A clean, well-ventilated stable helps reduce disease.

Housing

The basics of winter management include shelter, adequate nutrition and water, and routine health care. Horses generally do well in cold weather, as long as they are kept dry and clean. Wet animals get chilled easily, and damp conditions promote hoof and respiratory problems. If kept indoors, horses should be stabled in quarters that provide optimal ventilation and light, temperature regulation, and minimal exposure to dust and molds. In addition, the barn or stable should be easy to clean and disinfect and should provide an ample amount of space for each horse. Stalls should have nonslip flooring and walls or partitions that prevent direct contact between horses in adjacent stalls. Keeping your horse's quarters clean and well ventilated helps cut down on ammonia, dust, and stale air that can irritate the respiratory tract during prolonged periods indoors.

Make sure that you have identified a reliable source of quality hay to maintain wintertime nutrition. Horses have greater energy needs in winter because they must burn more calories to stay warm. Therefore, during winter, additional forage, fat, or grain should be added to the normal ration. Horses must always have access to fresh water in the winter, because even mild dehydration can increase the risk of colic. Water may need to be heated to keep it from freezing in winter weather.

Daily grooming and hoof care are also important during winter. Watch for signs of respiratory disease during your daily inspection, because this is more common during long periods of indoor confinement. Wintertime veterinary check ups can help identify respiratory or hoof problems early before they develop into serious conditions.

Whenever possible, horses should have access to good quality pasture. This provides optimal ventilation, a source of good forage, and the opportunity for your horse to graze and exercise. Safe, durable fencing should be used for pastures and paddocks to reduce the risk of self-trauma. Double fencing between paddocks minimizes the transmission of contagious disease between horses. Overcrowding should be avoided as it can lead to overgrazing, which in turn can lead to dusty or muddy pasture that may contribute to disease.

In summer, the biggest danger is heat stress. Horses should have shady places to rest during the heat of the day and plenty of fresh water at all times. Horses that are sweating profusely may also need increased supplementation with salt and minerals. In the stable, ceiling or wall-mounted fans can be used to increase air circulation on hot, humid days. Stall doors that are open at the top or made of heavy mesh screening provide better ventilation.

Exercise must be limited during periods of high temperature and/or humidity. A simple guide to dangerous conditions is the comfort index, which is the sum of temperature in degrees Fahrenheit and percent relative humidity (*see* TABLE 5). For example, a temperature of 80°F (26°C) and a relative humidity of 70% results in a comfort index of 150.

Diet

Proper nutrition is an important part of equine management. Most of the energy in your horse's diet should come from forage (pasture or good quality hay). In fact, horses

Table 5. Using the Comfort Index to Avoid Summertime Heat Stress

Comfort Index	Situation	Protective Action Needed
Less than 130	Heat stress is not an issue.	None.
130 to 150	Horses will sweat but can stay safe if water intake is adequate.	None, as long as water intake is adequate.
More than 150 (and relative humidity above 75%)	Heat dissipation through sweating may be a problem.	Limit exercise and check horses frequently for signs of stress.
More than 180	Heat dissipation through sweating fails.	Stop all workouts.

doing only light work or exercise often do fine on a diet of total forage supplemented with vitamins and minerals. As energy requirements increase, such as during training or cold weather, grain can be added to provide additional calories. However, grain should be limited, because it contains starch that can upset digestion in the hindgut (cecum and great colon), leading to colic.

All grains are not created equal. Oats are among the best grains to feed, because they contain highly digestible starches that spare the hindgut. Sweet feeds can cause horses to eat too quickly and upset the digestion in the hind gut, both of which can lead to colic. Horses can also get energy from fats, which are often preferable to grains.

Pelleted rations can be an excellent source of energy, protein, fat, fiber, vitamins, and minerals. High-quality rations from a name-brand manufacturer have appropriate ingredients and quality control.

Your veterinarian can advise you on setting up a proper feeding program for your horse.

Fresh, clean water should always be available to all horses, year round. Never restrict access to water unless instructed by your veterinarian.

Exercise

Horses are natural athletes and need a level of exercise that is appropriate for their age and health. However, exercise must be limited during hot, humid weather (*see* page 559) or after periods of inactivity. Problems often develop when a horse is exercised too strenuously, especially after a long period of rest. In this situation, muscles that are out of condition become damaged, leading to lameness and the buildup of protein breakdown products in the blood. This is commonly known as "Monday morning" sickness, in which horses that have had not been exercised all week are ridden hard by their owners on the weekend.

CHAPTER 41

Routine Care and Breeding

■ ROUTINE HEALTH CARE

In addition to properly feeding and exercising your horse, other aspects of general care are needed to keep your horse healthy throughout his or her life. These include routine veterinary care for vaccinations, parasite control, and dental care; grooming and hoof care; and protection from the elements.

Importance of Veterinary Care

Adult horses should have a complete veterinary examination at least once a year. Geriatric horses (older than 20 years old) should see their veterinarian twice a year or more frequently because illness is more common in older animals and it can be identified sooner. Your veterinarian may recommend a wellness program for your horse, including routine blood tests.

Signs of Illness

You should monitor your horse regularly for signs of illness, such as during daily feeding and grooming times. General signs of illness include a lack of appetite, diarrhea, coughing and sneezing, or a discharge from the eyes or nose. Illness can also show up as a loss of hair or itchy areas on the skin. Problems with the musculoskeletal system are often seen as lameness (such as not putting weight on a particular leg), reluctance to move, or head bobbing. If your horse shows any of these signs for more than a day or two, a visit with your veterinarian is a good idea.

Giving Medication

Generally, administering medication to a horse is not difficult if you use common sense and follow good handling principles for keeping both you and your horse safe. Maintain physical contact with the horse by keeping your shoulder pressed against the horse's shoulder or flank (depending on where and what you are treating) and make sure to use a sturdy halter and lead rope (hooked to the left halter ring). *Never* let a loop of any rope that is attached to your horse get wrapped around any part of your body.

If you need to apply medication to the horse's feet or lower front legs, lift the hoof to be treated and cradle it between your knees. If you need to treat the rear legs, in addition to lifting the hoof, you will also need to bend the hock. If your horse "dances" around, have another person lift the other leg *on the same side* as the leg that you need to treat.

Oral medication is usually in the form of "horse pills" (called boluses), pastes, or drenches. When administering oral medication, identify the toothless gap directly behind your horse's incisors and in front of

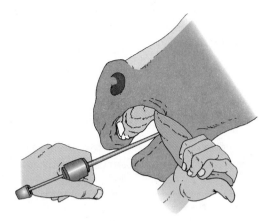

Correct administration of a bolus or "horse pill"

the molars. Insert your thumb into this gap while holding the horse's head down with your hand. Firmly pull the horse's tongue out through the gap and, and gently hold it outside the mouth. You can now administer a bolus by placing it behind the "top" of the tongue with a balling gun. Always lubricate the bolus with something like petroleum jelly or vegetable oil to keep it from getting caught in your horse's throat. Drenching guns and paste syringes can be placed far back in the mouth for administration of the fluid or paste. Hold your horse's head level or tilting slightly upward until he or she swallows the medicine.

Some medications can be administered only by injection, which is usually given in the neck area or thigh. Ask your veterinarian for a demonstration and guidance to make sure you know how to give the injection properly.

Regardless of type of medication or how it is to be given, it is important to read and follow all label instructions regarding use and storage.

Vaccinations

Vaccination is a key component of preventive medicine in horses. Vaccinations are given to stimulate the immune system against infection before exposure to disease. Several vaccines are routinely given to horses as the core defense against serious infectious illness. Several others are important in certain regions and situations. Your veterinarian can advise which vaccines are necessary in your local area and circumstances (*see* TABLE 6).

Foals born to a vaccinated mare will be protected against most infectious diseases for up to 6 months, so long as the foal consumed the antibody-rich mother's milk known as colostrum within 6 hours of birth. In this case, vaccinations should be delayed until maternal immunity has waned. Otherwise, the vaccination will be ineffective.

Vaccinations should be administered by your veterinarian or other properly trained individual. If you administer vaccines your-

Table 6. Vaccines Required or Recommended for Horses

Disease	Description	Vaccination Frequency
Core vaccines		
Tetanus	A bacterial infection that attacks the nervous system and causes the muscles to tighten (lockjaw)	First vaccine at 6 months of age, followed by 2 additional vaccinations at 3-to 6-week intervals; yearly boosters
Encephalomyelitis (sleeping sickness, Eastern equine encephalomyelitis, Western equine encephalomyelitis)	A family of viral infections carried by mosquitoes that result in inflammation of the nervous system, including the brain	Similar schedule as tetanus (usually given as combination vaccine)
Equine viral rhinopneumonitis	A highly infectious herpesvirus that can cause respiratory disease	Similar schedule as tetanus (usually given as combination vaccine) but semiannual boosters
Influenza	A highly infectious viral respiratory infection; vaccine usually sprayed into the nose	Initial vaccination at 6 to 9 months, followed by revaccination at 11 months; earlier and more frequent vaccination for foals of unvaccinated mares; periodic boosters (for example, every 6 to 12 months)
Other vaccines		
Potomac horse fever	A bacterial disease that affects many systems, causing fever, lethargy, diarrhea, and occasionally colic or laminitis (founder); vaccination recommended in areas where disease is common	Initial vaccination at 5 to 6 months followed by revaccination in 4 weeks; booster vaccinations at 1 year and annually after that
Rabies	A viral disease of the nervous system that is both fatal and transmissible to people	Initial vaccination at 6 months of age; boosters at 7 months, 1 year, and yearly after that
Rotavirus	A viral diarrheal disease; vaccination usually restricted to farms with a recurring problem	Pregnant mares are given a 3-dose series of vaccinations before foaling; foals protected through colostrum
Strangles	A bacterial infection of the throat; vaccination usually restricted to farms with a recurring problem	Initial vaccine at 4 to 6 months, followed by 2 revaccinations at 4-week intervals; boosters at 12 months and annually after that
West Nile virus	A viral infection carried by mosquitoes that results in inflammation of the nervous system, including the brain; vaccination currently recommended for horses in continental United States	Initial vaccine at 3 to 4 months, followed by revaccination 1 month later; boosters every 4 to 6 months depending on risk

Table 7. Signs Caused by Common Parasites of Horses*

Parasite	Signs
Strongyles	Anemia, dry coat, diarrhea, general loss of condition
Roundworms	Loss of condition, bowel problems, or colic when present in large numbers; migrating roundworm larvae can also injure the lungs in young horses
Pinworms	Horse rubs its tail; itching and irritation around anus; discharge and worms visible around anus
Bots	Loss of condition and colic from large numbers in the gut; occasional diarrhea or constipation
Tapeworms	Mild diarrhea, colic, failure to grow or put on weight as expected

*For a more detailed discussion, see GASTROINTESTINAL PARASITES OF HORSES, page 629.

self, learn how to do it properly. Use only vaccines from a reliable source who can verify that they have been kept clean and refrigerated. Poor-quality vaccines increase the risk of adverse reactions, which can range from inflammation at the site of the injection, fever, and malaise, to serious allergic reactions that affect the entire body (for example, anaphylaxis).

Parasite Control

Animals that graze on grasses, including horses, ingest parasite eggs that are found throughout the environment. The actual parasite burden for any individual horse depends on its age, the number of horses on the same pasture, and the pasture's size and quality. Internal parasites of horses can cause many intestinal problems, including gastrointestinal upset, diarrhea, and potentially colic.

The primary intestinal parasites of horses include roundworms (both large and small strongyles), tapeworms, pinworms, and stomach bots (see TABLE 7). These worms can cause damage to the digestive tract and blood loss, and interfere with absorption of essential nutrients. The greatest damage is caused by strongyles (also called redworms or bloodworms), and most parasite control programs are designed around strongyle control. Young horses typically are infested with more parasites and have more signs than older horses.

Most intestinal parasites are ingested while horses are grazing, from eggs and larvae deposited on the grass and upper layers of the soil. The tapeworm lifecycle involves small mites (specifically, orbatid mites) that feed on tapeworm eggs and thus contain tapeworm larvae. These mites live on grasses and are ingested while grazing. Stomach bots are larvae of flies. The adult fly deposits eggs on the muzzle, legs, and chest of horses during the spring. When the eggs are licked by the horse, they hatch and are ingested by the horse. The larvae attach to the wall of the stomach and remain for a period of time (usually until the following spring). The bot pupae then pass into the feces, where they hatch as adult flies.

All horses should be on a deworming program that consists of either a periodic deworming treatment (usually by administering a paste) every 4 to 8 weeks or a daily dewormer in the feed (see page 629). Pasture management and good grooming practices are also very important aspects of parasite control. You may want to periodically submit samples of your horse's feces to your veterinarian to check for the type and number of intestinal parasites.

External Parasites

As outdoor animals, horses are also bothered by flies and ticks. These can cause sores and subsequent infection on the head, neck, ears, face, abdomen, and

---

Suggested Practices for Controlling Intestinal Parasites in Horses

▓ Mow and harrow pastures frequently. This breaks up manure piles and exposes parasite eggs to the damaging effects of air and sun.

▓ Periodically rotate pastures to other livestock (such as cattle or sheep) if possible.

▓ In multiple-horse settings, group horses by age to maximize the efficiency of your deworming program and to reduce exposure to certain parasites.

▓ Keep the number of horses per acre to a minimum.

▓ Place hay and grain off the ground by using a feeder.

▓ Remove yellowish bot eggs from horses' coats quickly. A daily wipe-down with a warm, wet towel will stimulate the eggs to hatch, and the emerging larvae will dry out and die. Good grooming practices are necessary to remove the bot eggs, because they are firmly glued onto the hair.

▓ Rotate among different classes of deworming drugs (not just different brand names) to decrease resistance.

▓ Consult your veterinarian about an effective deworming program.

---

legs. Irritation from external parasites can also cause general upset, failure to grow and thrive, and decreased appetite (for example, fly "worry"). Horses should be checked regularly for ticks or signs of fly damage. Fly control includes proper manure management and stall cleanliness. Many different insecticidal salves, lotions, sprays, and rubs are available that can be used to remove ticks and decrease insect irritation and annoyance. Consult your veterinarian or extension service about an appropriate control program for your area and circumstances.

Dental Care

Equine teeth grow and wear down continuously throughout life. Unfortunately, they often wear unevenly, leading to sharp points, edges, and even hooks that need to be trimmed down, or "floated."

Horses require a dental checkup with their veterinarian at least once per year (older horses need more frequent check-ups). Your veterinarian will check inside the mouth for teeth with sharp points or edges, trimming them down with a file or nippers. As with hoof trimming, this procedure is best left to an experienced professional.

Grooming

Grooming is an important part of daily maintenance for horses. Daily brushing and currying helps remove dirt and debris that can allow bacteria a place to multiply. During grooming, you can also check the overall condition of your horse's skin and find sores, infections, bumps, or welts when they first arise. Vigorous currying is required to remove dirt, and horses generally enjoy it. Hair that is bound up (tail bags and mane braids) should be taken down every 10 to 14 days for brushing and cleaning. Horses can be bathed with equine shampoo, but baths should be kept to a minimum to avoid drying out the skin and coat. Horses should not be bathed when winter temperatures are below freezing, because horses need to be dry to resist the cold.

Hoof Care

Hoof care is an important part of the daily grooming routine. The hooves should be "picked" daily to remove manure, dirt, and stones, and checked for signs of bruising, odor, discoloration, or discharge. The shoes should also be

---

Signs of Dental Problems in Horses

▓ Reluctance to eat or chew

▓ Dropping food during eating (also called "quidding")

▓ Hesitating to take a bit or other signs of a sore mouth

▓ Bad breath from tooth decay or gum disease

checked for wear and tightness of the nails (*see* below). Hoof dressings may be needed, but care should be taken to apply them appropriately. For example, water-repellent dressings can be important to keep hooves dry and healthy during wet weather. However, excessive use of emollient dressings can soften the hooves and lead to problems. Antifungal solutions should be applied every 1 to 2 weeks during winter and wet weather to prevent thrush (*see* page 687). Your veterinarian and farrier can provide information on when and how frequently to treat your horse's feet.

Horses' hooves grow constantly and require trimming about every 6 weeks. Horses need to be trained to stand properly so that their hooves can be trimmed correctly and damage to the foot can be avoided. Foot trimming is best left to your farrier or veterinarian if you do not have experience with this procedure.

Shoes

Horse shoes provide traction on some surfaces and help prevent wear and tear of the hooves. The need for horse shoes depends on several factors, including foot conformation and health as well as the types of surfaces the horse will travel on. Horses with tender or bruised feet require shoes for protection, as do horses working on hard or rough surfaces. Various kinds of corrective shoes are available for particular hoof or lameness problems. For example, horses with cracked hooves or splayed feet may need a barred shoe for support, while horses with other specific lameness problems may need a shoe that slows down or stabilizes the gait. Veterinarians, farriers, and trainers can provide more information on the shoes needed for any particular problem.

▨ BREEDING AND REPRODUCTION

Mares reach puberty at about 18 months of age and undergo an estrous, or heat, cycle. Mares go into heat repeatedly during the breeding season, which usually continues while day length is long and ends when

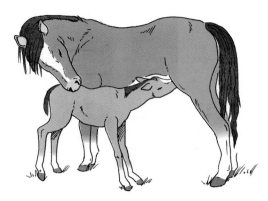

Early nursing helps protect against disease.

winter approaches. Exposing mares to increasing periods of artificial light can get the breeding season started earlier. During the breeding season, mares ovulate regularly every 3 weeks, but they are in heat and receptive to a stallion for only 2 to 8 days. Heat is generally longer early in the season (spring) and only 2 to 3 days in late June. Gestation (pregnancy) lasts 330 to 342 days, with lighter breeds generally having a longer pregnancy (340 to 342 days) than heavier breeds (330 to 340 days). Pregnant mares generally have a single foal; twins are rare. Foals can see and stand to suckle soon after birth.

Foal Care

As soon as a foal is born, you should remove any mucus or other material around its nostrils to assist the foal in breathing, and coat the umbilical stump with iodine to prevent bacteria from entering the body and causing a serious blood infection. The foal should begin to nurse within the first 1 to 2 hours. This is critical because the initial mare's milk, called colostrum, contains antibodies that provide the young foal with immunity against disease. If the mare rejects the foal, a milk replacer can be used as a substitute. Foals should also have a bowel movement within their first 2 hours or so; if they do not, you will need to give the foal an enema. Contact your veterinarian immediately if the foal does not begin to nurse, or if you observe any other problems during the first few hours after foaling.

As much as possible, the mare and the foal should not be disturbed. Many mares are very protective of their foals, and someone will likely have to hold the mare while another person attends to the foal's needs, such as removing mucus, coating the umbilical stump, and so forth.

You should spend at least 15 minutes every day with a new foal, touching its hooves, ears, nose, and other body parts, as well as tapping on its feet and generally rubbing it all over. Handling a foal early on will make it much easier to handle as an adult.

Vaccinations usually begin around the age of 3 months, with appropriate booster vaccinations 1 month later. Vaccination for equine influenza generally begins when the foal is 8 to 10 months old. Your veterinarian can advise you on the best vaccination program for your foal.

CHAPTER 42
Behavior

■ INTRODUCTION

Behavioral medicine is the scientific study of everything animals do, whether the animals are insects, birds, mammals, fish, or humans. The field of animal behavior is concerned with understanding the causes, functions, development, and evolution of behavior. Behavior refers to the actions or reactions of an animal. Behavior is controlled by the endocrine and nervous systems. The complexity of an animal's behavior is related to the complexity of its nervous system. Generally, animals with complex nervous systems have a greater capacity to learn new responses and thus adjust their behavior.

An animal's behavior is influenced by many factors. Some of these factors include genetic predisposition, experience and learning, environment, and physiology. The amount and type of human handling (especially during the first days and months of life) and exposure to novel stimuli can influence a horse's behavior and character. The brain and its associated neurotransmitters also play a fundamental role in temperament and behavior. Abnormal levels of various hormones may play a role in aggression and fear. Regulatory functions of the brain decrease with age, which results in an increase in fears and anxieties.

Understanding the nature of behavior problems is essential to developing a rational basis for their treatment. While this section focuses primarily on the abnormal behavior of horses, the extent to which a horse's behavior is abnormal is defined by its deviation from "normal" or by the problem that this behavior poses to its owner.

■ DIAGNOSING BEHAVIOR PROBLEMS

Some "health" problems faced by horses are associated with behavior problems or unmet expectations about the animal's behavior. Your veterinarian will take a behavioral history before making any diagnosis. A behavioral history includes the following: 1) sex, breed, and age of horse, 2) age at onset of the problem, 3) duration of the problem, 4) description of the actual behavior, 5) the frequency of the behavior (hourly, daily, weekly, monthly), 6) the duration of an average episode (seconds, minutes, hours), 7) the range of duration of episodes, 8) any change in the pattern, frequency, intensity, or duration of episodes, 9) any corrective measures tried and the response, 10) any activities that stopped the behavior, 11) a typical 24-hour schedule for the horse and owner, as well as any day-to-day variability, 12) the horse's breeding (to see if there are any signs of similar problems in the dam or sire), and 13) anything else that the owner thinks is relevant.

Defining the Problem

In order to properly diagnose a behavior problem, both you and your veterinarian must use the same definitions for the same behaviors. You both must also accurately recognize and describe the behaviors that are of concern. Videotapes of the horse can ensure that such communication occurs. Your understanding and compliance are critical if horses with behavior disorders are to improve. Only when you recognize the behaviors leading to the problematic ones, can you avoid or prevent the provocative situation. Therefore, by viewing a recording of the problematic behavior, your veterinarian will be able to work with you to achieve more desirable responses and help treat the condition.

The following is a brief glossary of terms that are commonly used when discussing behavior.

An **abnormal behavior** is one that is dysfunctional and unusual.

Aggression in horses may occur as a threat or as an attack. There are various kinds of aggressive behavior in horses, such as fear aggression and inter-male aggression.

Anxiety is the anticipation of future danger accompanied by signs of tension (vigilance, increased motor activity, and tense muscles). The focus of anxiety can be internal or external.

A horse in **conflict** has tendencies to perform more than one behavior at once. For example, a horse may want to approach a person to take a treat such as an apple, but be reluctant to get too close because it is nervous. The motivation for the conflict, except for extreme instances associated with survival functions (for example, eating), is often hard to identify in animals.

Displacement activity is the resolution of a conflict by performing a seemingly unrelated behavior. When a horse is in conflict between sex and aggression or between aggression and fear, it will often perform an

Where to Get Help

Owners seeking help for a behavior problem with their horse can turn to several sources. The American Veterinary Medical Association recognizes a variety of specialties within veterinary medicine. Similar to specialties in human medicine, these include veterinarians who are board-certified in surgery, internal medicine, ophthalmology (eye care), dentistry, behavior, and 14 other areas of expertise. As of 2007, there are 42 board-certified veterinary behaviorists. Most of these veterinarians work in veterinary colleges or private referral practices.

There are also veterinarians who are not board-certified, but who have a special interest in behavior. These veterinarians have a range of experience and expertise in the field, and many offer behavior consultations as a part of their regular veterinary practice.

There are also nonveterinarians who call themselves behaviorists and offer counseling on behavior problems of horses. Some have a doctoral or master's degree in psychology or a related field, and some of these individuals are certified by a scientific organization called the Animal Behavior Society. Others, primarily horse trainers, have no formal education in behavior but offer advice on solving behavior problems. Owners who need help for their horse should ask about the background and training of the person offering the behavior consultation before setting up an appointment. Because many behavior problems in horses can be influenced by medical conditions, veterinarians are the professionals who can offer the most comprehensive care.

apparently irrelevant activity. Examples of these activities include grooming, feeding, scratching, and sleeping.

Dominance refers to competition over a limited resource (for example, access to a feed bucket or water trough). A higher-ranking animal can displace a lower-ranking one from the resource. Rank or hierarchy is usually defined by an ability to control the resource. A dominant animal is not the one engaged in the most fighting. Most high-ranking animals can be identified by the submissive behavior exhibited toward them by others in their group.

Fear is a feeling of apprehension associated with the presence of an object, individual, or social situation and is part of normal behavior. Deciding whether the fear is abnormal depends on the context. For example, fire is a useful tool, and fear of being consumed by it is a normal behavior. However, if the barn were not on fire, such a fear would be irrational. If this fear was constant or recurrent, it would probably be considered an abnormal behavior. Normal and abnormal fears usually vary in intensity. The intensity of the fear increases as the real or imagined nearness of the object that causes the fear increases.

Frustration arises when a horse is unable to perform a behavior due to physical or psychological obstacles in the environment. This term, like dominance, is overused and usually undefined, which means it often is not very helpful when diagnosing a behavior problem.

Most fearful reactions are learned and can be unlearned with gradual exposure. **Phobias**, though, are profound and quickly developed fearful reactions that do not diminish either with gradual exposure to the object or without exposure over time. A phobia involves sudden, all-or-nothing, profound, abnormal reactions resulting in panic. Phobias develop quickly, with little change between episodes. Fear may develop more gradually and, within an episode of fearful behavior, there may be more variation in intensity than would be seen in a phobic reaction. Once a phobic event has been experienced, any event associated with it or the memory of it is sufficient to generate the reaction. Even without re-exposure phobias can remain at or exceed their former high level for years. Phobic situations are either avoided at all costs or, if unavoidable, are endured with intense anxiety or distress.

Stereotypic behaviors are repetitious, relatively unvaried behaviors that have no obvious purpose. They are usually derived from normal behavior, such as grooming, eating, or walking. These behaviors are abnormal because they interfere with the normal functioning of the animal.

■ BEHAVIOR MODIFICATION

The most commonly used techniques to modify animal behavior include habituation, extinction, desensitization, counterconditioning, and shaping. A behavior modification technique called flooding (*see* page 570) is not used very often because it has the potential to make most animals worse. While it is claimed that punishment is frequently used with varying degrees of success, few people correctly employ punishment. For punishment (for example, screaming at the horse) to be successful, it must occur sufficiently close to the onset of the behavior. Most punishments are inappropriate in context, duration, or time of application.

Most of the passive, or positive techniques involved in behavior modification are not hard to learn and are successfully employed as preventive techniques. They do require a regular investment of time and effort, however. The following is a short review of the basic principles involved in the techniques, and their associated strategies.

Habituation is an elementary form of learning that involves no rewards. It is merely the ending of or decrease in a response to a stimulus that results from repeated or prolonged exposure to that stimulus. For example, horses placed in a pasture bordering a road may at first run away when traffic passes, but eventually learn to ignore it. A horse that habituates to one type of sound does not, as a consequence of this habituation, become habituated to other sounds. Habituation is distinct from failing to respond to stimulation as a result of fatigue or injury. The effects of habituation are generally long lasting. If a horse is repeatedly exposed to a potentially harmful stimulus (such as to a predator) without being harmed, habituation does not generally occur. Responses to dangerous stimuli seem to have an inherited resistance to habituation.

Spontaneous recovery is associated with habituation. If there is a long time between when a horse has experienced an event to which it had habituated and re-exposure to the same event, the horse may again react.

Conditioning refers to associations between stimuli and behavior. For example, a horse that touches an electric fence will receive a painful shock. It will quickly learn to avoid touching the fence. The sight of the fence itself will then become associated with the shock.

Reinforcement is any event that increases the chance that a certain behavior will be repeated. When positive reinforcement (such as a reward) is used in training, there is a positive relationship between the behavior and its consequences. The more the horse does a behavior, the more it gets positive reinforcement and what it gets is good. This makes that behavior increase. A negative reinforcement (which is mistakenly thought of as punishment by many people) is something unpleasant that increases a behavior when it is removed. For example, most horses find the application of spurs to be painful. When the horse starts moving, the spurring stops. This reinforces the behavior the rider wanted. Over time, the horse will start moving as soon as the spurs are applied.

Second-order reinforcers are signals that can be used at a distance to let the horse know that the reward is coming. Commonly used second-order reinforcers are words, such as "good girl," hand signals, and whistles. By carefully pairing these with a primary reward (such as food), second-order reinforcers can elicit the same response that the reward would.

Extinction is a response that stops when the reward is removed. For example, if a horse was used to getting a carrot as a treat for coming up to the fence of a paddock, but then the owner stopped giving it a carrot, the horse would eventually stop coming over to the fence. The more valuable the original reinforcer, the longer the reinforcement has been continuing, and the more uncertainty there is about whether the reward has been truly removed, the greater the resistance to extinction.

Resistance to extinction can also occur even without reinforcement if the reward was good enough and was tightly linked to the behavior. Because there is often an association between getting the reward and the intensity of the behavior, the intensity or frequency of the behavior you are trying to eliminate usually increases at the beginning of extinction. In other words, a behavior you are trying to extinguish may get worse before it gets better. It is critical that you do not give in. Giving in will only make extinction more difficult. The horse will learn that, although your threshold has increased, the horse can override it by working harder.

Overlearning is the repeated performance of an already learned behavior. It is frequently used in training for specific events. Overlearning accomplishes 3 things: it delays forgetting, it increases the resistance to extinction, and it increases the chance that the response will become an automatic or "knee-jerk" response in similar situations. This aspect can be useful in teaching a horse to overcome fear or anxiety.

Shaping is a training technique that works well for horses that do not know what response is desired by the trainer. Shaping works through gradual approximations and allows the horse to be rewarded initially for any behavior that resembles the desired behavior. For example, when teaching a horse to load on a trailer, at first you might praise and stroke the horse for just taking 1 or 2 steps toward the trailer's ramp. Next, you would reward it for walking calmly up to the ramp. Finally, the horse would be rewarded only for completely entering the trailer.

Avoidance is essential until you can seek qualified help, particularly in the case of an aggressive horse. With treatment it may be possible to desensitize the horse to circumstances in which aggressive behavior occurs, but avoidance is the key in minimizing danger. Avoidance does not mean that the horse has control, or that the owner is giving in. Rather, it means that the horse is not being given the chance to exert control in its usual manner. Every time a horse becomes aggressive, it learns that aggression may help it cope with the situation, thus reinforcing the problem.

Desensitization is a way to teach a horse to tolerate a situation by exposing it to the problem in a series of small steps. For example, a horse that is fearful of having its hooves picked may need to be desensitized to having its feet handled. This could be started by first rubbing and massaging the upper leg, then gradually working down to the hoof. The leg could also be picked up and held for a few seconds, gradually increasing that to several minutes over a series of training sessions.

Counterconditioning is a method for reducing undesirable behavior by teaching the horse to replace it with another more favorable behavior. In the hoof-picking example, the horse will learn faster if it is first taught to stand calmly and relax in exchange for a treat. The horse must be absolutely quiet and calm, and convey by its eyes, body posture, and ear position that it is not alarmed. Once this behavior is learned, the desensitization is added by handling the leg closer and closer to the hoof. If at any time the horse starts to become anxious or agitated, the trainer should handle a higher part of the leg until the horse relaxes again. There is no point in forcing the horse to submit to handling if it is clearly distressed. Relaxation is the first step to changing the behavior. Counterconditioning coupled with desensitization is a time-consuming technique. The exercises must be repeated often so that the fearful response decreases until it disappears.

Flooding is prolonged exposure to a stimulus until the horse eventually stops reacting. This is the opposite of the approach taken in desensitization. It is far more stressful than any of the other treatment strategies and if not used correctly could make things worse. This technique should be used only by a professional and only as a last resort.

Punishment is also known as aversive conditioning. It is any unpleasant event that lowers the chance that a behavior will be repeated. Punishment is not the same as negative reinforcement (*see* page 569). To be most successful, punishment must occur as early as possible (within a few seconds of the start of the behavior), and it must be consistent and appropriate. Critical factors in punishment include timing, consistency, appropriate intensity, and the presence of a reward after the undesirable behavior ends. This is the most frequently ignored part of treatment for people whose horses have behavior problems. Owners often resort to physical punishment as the first choice, but punishment does not need to be physical. Furthermore, punishment is just as hard to use correctly as counterconditioning and desensitization. Punishment is never an "easy out" and has a high chance of failure. It can also lead to other negative consequences, such as increased fear or aggression.

Use of Medication to Treat Behavior Problems

Your veterinarian may, in some cases, prescribe medication to help treat a behavior problem in your horse. Drug treatment for almost any behavior change is most useful when combined with behavior modification. (For a more detailed discussion of the use of medication for behavior problems in animals, *see* page 23).

■ NORMAL SOCIAL BEHAVIOR IN HORSES

Domestic horses are social animals. In the wild, they live in a harem group or band with one to several stallions, multiple mares, and the mares' offspring. One stallion (the highest ranking or dominant animal) does most of the breeding. In many horses, rank is associated with age or the ability to survive and thrive in challenging environments. High-ranking stallions are the first to gain access to mares in heat and the first to displace a mare from another band. Unless they become pregnant, mares cycle over 21 days during the spring and summer months. Within a harem group, the highest-ranking individual is usually, but not always, a stallion. This high-ranking stallion will force colts to leave the group once they are 2 years old, as they begin to become sexually and socially mature. Snapping (tooth clapping or champing) is a facial expression given by young horses to adults, particularly stallions. It peaks in frequency at 2 months of age, after which it decreases. It may function to decrease aggression from adults, but is also compatible with displaced nursing behavior. This is not the same behavior as smacking, which is an aggressive threat in which the ears are laid back and the mouth is open with smacking lips, but the lips are not retracted. Social maturity is not attained until 5 years of age.

Most fillies and all colts leave the herd they were born in by about 5 years of age. Fillies that remain in their original group may have fewer offspring. Young stallions form bachelor herds, and the highest-ranking stallion within this group is usually the next one to acquire a mate. Fillies can join a bachelor herd but are often incorporated into other bands. Stallions are rarely solitary; when this occurs, they are usually old and infirm. While rank in males is based primarily on access to females, rank in females is determined by which mares lead group activities (for example, seeking out resources such as water holes). Horse groups are largely structured by females, and females make the decision about whether to leave or to stay within a harem. Such decisions are usually based not on specific stallions or their characteristics, but on a female's assessment of food resources. High-ranking females can successfully interfere with the nursing of foals by lower-ranking females. Mares form friendships and are more likely to groom each other. This pattern is typical of many animals—rank is

determined mainly by the way that lower-ranking animals defer to higher-ranking ones, not by the results of outright combat.

Rank within groups also depends on the ages and sexes of the group members. The more members of the herd, and the more within each age and sex group, the less likely it is for a dominance hierarchy to exist. Relationships within most horse bands are complex and depend on multiple factors and their interactions (age or length of residence in the group, sex, size, and rank of the mother). These factors are important to consider when addressing problems that may arise in stabled horses.

Rank effects also exist between herds. Multi-stallion herds are dominant over single-stallion bands, possibly because lower-ranking stallions within a herd conduct most of the fighting that occurs between groups. Herds that are currently occupying an area or using a resource (for example, a water hole) tend to retain it. Groups, as well as individuals within them, follow specific patterns of fecal marking.

Many behavior problems in horses are associated with confinement. Under free-ranging circumstances, horses will wander and spend 60% of their day foraging. The reminder of their time is spent standing, lying down, or engaging in another activity. This same pattern is the preferred one under barn conditions—even with free choice of grain, horses will choose to eat many small meals a day.

Free-ranging movement is also part of play development in horses. Until 3 months of age, most play is solitary. Interactive play peaks at 3 to 4 months of age. There are also sex differences in play. Colts play more than fillies and play different games than fillies do. Colt games focus more on fighting and mounting, while filly games focus more on running and mutual grooming. Fillies will groom both colts and fillies while colts tend to groom only fillies, which has been interpreted as practice for later courtship behavior. The social experience of play is important for normal social interaction in adult life.

■ BEHAVIOR PROBLEMS IN HORSES

A variety of behavior problems occur in horses. Some of the most common are those associated with aggression (including aggression towards people), abnormal eating habits, and undesirable stall behaviors. (*See* TABLE 8.)

The most common types of **aggression towards people** in horses are similar to dominance aggression and fear aggression in dogs. Fear can be caused by physical abuse, harsh treatment, and night blindness associated with confinement in a dark stall. Horses that are aggressive to people are sometimes too dangerous to keep. There have been cases of horses killing people in such circumstances.

Aggressive behavior can be modified using counterconditioning and desensitization (using rewards for nonaggressive reactions). Rewards could be frequent feedings of highly desirable foods (for example, molasses or apples), attention, grooming, or exercise. The purpose of the frequent feeding is to mimic the natural pattern of frequent grazing and to associate that with the person's presence. All aggressive animals should probably be neutered because aggression appears to be hereditary, and removal of sex hormones reduces some types of aggression.

Aggression towards other horses is usually associated with sex or may be secondary to fear. Horses have preferred grooming and grazing partners. The extent to which these preferences may be a factor in aggression to other horses is unknown. Treatment may include castration, desensitization, and counterconditioning (*see* page 570). This can be done gradually by introducing horses across 1 or 2 fences so that they do not injure each other. Two fences are best because they reduce the possibility that the horses could strike each other with their feet.

Wood chewing may be associated with the normal equine pattern of browsing. Under free-ranging circumstances, horses graze 12 to 14 hours per day. Most wood chewing occurs in the winter, and it appears to take place more often in horses that are fed pelleted diets. If a horse receives less than 1 kilogram of hay per 100 kilograms of body weight, wood chewing can become extreme. It is important to address the primary problem (that is, learn why the horse is doing it), rather than merely trying to prevent it. To treat this condition the owner should increase both roughage (hay, for example) and exercise through work or increased pasture time, because wood chewing is sometimes caused by boredom.

Coprophagia is the eating of feces and is a normal behavior in foals. It is most common in the first month of life, after which it usually declines. When it is seen in adults, it is usually associated with low roughage or protein in the diet or a dietary deficiency. Treatment includes increasing the amount of roughage and protein in the diet.

Pica is the consumption of soil or sand or other nonfood items. This can lead to serious and even fatal digestive complications, and therefore should not be taken lightly. By nature, horses spend much of their time grazing and if this activity is curtailed, such as when stabled, they are likely to seek other materials to consume. Lengthy periods of confinement, often combined with concentrated feeds that are quickly consumed, can cause boredom and lead to abnormal eating behaviors. Texture may be important, and the addition of roughage and salt blocks may have a role in treatment.

Horses form friendships with other horses, and **anorexia** (loss of appetite) can be associated with changes in these relationships. For example, if a horse is separated from a companion it may stop eating. Addressing the social aspects of the problem is important. Your veterinarian may also prescribe drugs that stimulate appetite. In foals, poor appetite may

Table 8. Behavior Problems in Horses*

Behavior	Description	Causes
Aggression		
Biting	Nipping during handling or when in close proximity	Boredom; bad temperament
Charging	Attacks handlers or those in close proximity	Bad temperament; meal time; overly protective of foals; hormone problems in mares
Crowding	Invades handler's personal space	Nervousness; learned avoidance mechanism
Kicking	Lifting hind foot forward and then kicking back in a sideward motion towards an object (not to be confused by just kicking to get rid of flies on legs)	Fear; bad temperament; aggressiveness (usually towards other horses)
Rearing	Striking with front legs while standing on hind legs	Fear or objection to restraint, medication, or other stimuli; harsh bit; learned avoidance mechanism
Striking	Reaches for handler with either or both front feet	Reflex to pain; fear; confinement; bad temperament
Fear		
Halter pulling	Pulls back when tied; panics when cross-tied; doesn't follow handler	Poor training; learned avoidance mechanism; pain
Evading haltering	Runs away when approached; avoids being caught	Fear or mistrust of people; anticipation of bad experience
Performance problems		
Balking	Resists moving forward	Fear; failure to establish clear cues; asking horse to perform beyond its abilities
Bucking	Kicks up hind legs forcefully	Playfulness; desire to unseat rider; frustration from unclear training cues; ill-fitting equipment
Head tossing	Throws up head when grooming exercising, or riding	Tooth infection or medical problem; painful bit pressure; learned avoidance mechanism
Eating problems		
Coprophagia	Eats manure	Normal in foals 2 to 5 weeks old; lack of roughage, minerals or proteins
Cribbing	Bites an object, pulls back flexing neck	Boredom; lack of exercise
Food bolting	Swallows food rapidly without chewing	Excessive hunger; competition for food; learned behavior
Mane and tail chewing	Chewing on manes and tails of herdmates	Boredom; playfulness; lack of roughage or minerals

(Continued on the following page)

Table 8. Behavior Problems in Horses*—*(Continued)*

Behavior	Description	Causes
Wood chewing	Chews on wood	Lack of roughage, protein, or minerals; boredom
Stall problems		
Digging or pawing	Paws floor	Anticipation of feed; nervousness; lack of exercise
Tail rubbing	Rubs tail against fences or walls	Parasites; habit
Stall walking; stall weaving; stall kicking	Continuous circling, moving, kicking	Boredom; excess energy; aggression

*Adapted with permission from EB1657—Identifying Abnormal Equine Behavior and Vices, Washington State University Extension.

be due to an aggressive mare attacking a foal that tries to share the mother's food. Barriers should be erected that safely permit normal development and feeding patterns. Foals may not eat the same plant or same plant part as the mare, and the part they choose may be based on the height of the plant. This problem should be addressed and creep feeders should be placed near the mare so that the foal does not have to choose between food and contact with its dam. Foals on pasture that are nursing do not drink water, but the mares need access to good, clean water.

Obesity can be the result of decreased exercise, increased palatable food, and understimulation (horses that eat in the absence of other activities). Food should not be abruptly removed from an obese horse. The amounts of food should be decreased gradually while increasing exercise. The diet should also be evaluated for nutritional content and adjusted to make a more balanced ration. This will help the horse lose weight.

Stall walking or circling is usually in response to separation from another horse. It is usually rapid and accompanied by vocalization. Horse owners should watch for signs of anxiety (pacing or changes in vocalization when stable mates or housing conditions change). Treatment should include increasing exercise, providing social company, allowing the horse to see other horses, and providing clean bedding. Feeding fre-

quently, providing more open stalls, and providing better access to outside views can also help. Adding toys to the stall may help if the horse is young and active.

Weaving occurs when a horse that normally stall walks is tied or prohibited from walking due to restricted space. Because they cannot circle as usual, they will still move constantly, but in a weaving motion. Treatment includes untying the horse, providing a larger stall, or best of all, turning the horse out onto pasture. The other treatments recommended for stall walking (*see* above) can also help.

Pawing can cause injury to the horse, damage the floor, and cause wear to the horse's hooves. It is a normal behavior and can occur when horses on winter pasture are forced to dig for feed. When horses are confined and fed highly palatable foods, pawing can occur more frequently and more intensely than it would otherwise. The underlying cause of the pawing needs to be determined in order to successfully treat it. Specific treatments are similar to those for stall walking (*see* above). Pawing should not be rewarded, which is what inadvertently happens when horses paw in anticipation of feeding. The food should be presented to the horse only when the horse is not pawing, or the horse should be brought to the food.

Kicking damages horses' legs and stalls. It is often an aggressive behavior that appears when another horse is nearby or when the horse perceives that another horse is nearby. Kicking can also occur in anticipation of food. It may also occur when the horse cannot achieve its goals (for example, exercise or a chance to breed). For successful treatment, the underlying causes of kicking should be determined. Treatment is as for stall walking (see above). It may also require rearranging the social grouping in the barn.

Cribbing (windsucking, crib biting) is a distinct behavior, different from wood chewing, that involves grasping a horizontal surface with the front teeth (incisors) and flexing the neck without swallowing air. The activity produces strange, non-flatulant sounds. Cribbing is most easily diagnosed by noticing the missing U-shaped pieces from the available fencing. Horses that crib have worn teeth and develop thick neck muscles. Treatment options include increasing roughage in the diet, changing companions, and providing greater access to pasture.

Self-mutilation may be due to a medical problem such as a digestive disorder or colic. The progression of the problem should help to differentiate a medical problem from one that is primarily behavioral. In horses, most self-mutilation involves biting of the limbs, chest, or flanks. Self-mutilation can appear in sexually frustrated (usually male) or socially incompatible horses. Treatment should include correction of the underlying problem. Self-mutilation associated with sexual frustration can be addressed by castration, pasturing with a mare, removing all mares, increasing exercise, increasing roughage, and decreasing grain.

Foal rejection is seen in 3 main forms: mares that will accept the foal but will not let it suckle, mares that are fearful of the foal and run away, and mares that exhibit stallion-like behavior and attempt to kick or bite the foal. Mares may paw at foals to stimulate them to rise from recumbency, which is different from rejection. Mares can kill their foals if they are underweight and not getting enough to eat, and this can be a normal, although uncommon behavior. The first step in treatment is to protect the foal. If the mare will accept the foal but not let it suckle, the mare should be helped through several nursings until she learns that suckling is pleasurable. Holding her in such a way that she cannot injure the foal may involve either cross-ties or partial barriers through which she can see and smell the foal but that prohibit her from reaching for it. The mare should be checked to make sure there is nothing wrong with her udder, such as mastitis or sores that could be causing her pain, which can explain an aversion to nursing. Pressure in the udder resulting from infrequent nursing can be treated using warm water baths and soaks, light massage using a hose, and milking the mare.

Mares that are afraid of their foals should be treated in the same manner, but the addition of relaxation cues such as darker, quieter stalls and food treats may help. Dogs have been used to evoke maternal "herding" behavior by stimulating the mare to protect the foal from a potential threat. Mares that attempt to injure their foals must be restrained using stocks or bars. At the same time, the mare can be counterconditioned using positive rewards. If the mare cannot be retrained or trusted, a replacement ("nurse") mare should be sought or other arrangements made (hand nursing) so that the foal can be adequately nourished.

Stallions have **poor libido** if they are overused for breeding, are inhibited because of the use of antimasturbation devices, are used out of season, or are injured while breeding. Masturbation is a normal equine behavior. There is no truth to the myth that masturbation depletes semen value because horses that masturbate rarely ejaculate. Stallions that have poor libido should be rested if they have been overused. Another cause of poor libido can be a poor breeding environment. Many stallions are "picky" about the environment in which they are collected and may exhibit signs of poor libido if the environment is not right. Distractions such as yelling, rapid and unexpected movement, and rough handling can lead to a stallion that has no interest in the situation at all.

Letting a stallion that exhibits poor libido watch other stallions mate may have a beneficial effect on their libido. Providing them with a variety of mares can also stimulate their interest. Pasturing with a mare may also help.

Stallions that are **aggressive during breeding** are often overused or used out of season. These stallions may benefit from the use of an artificial vagina out of season so that they learn that the experience is pleasurable. Stallions may develop mating preferences and may not be compatible with the chosen mare, so changing the mare may help. If stallions were stabled with mares when they were colts, they may have some social inhibition with mating, and forced mating can result in aggression. Successful treatment involves identifying the underlying problem.

Nymphomaniac mares "wink" (show the clitoris), squat, and urinate frequently, often when they are not in heat. Mating behaviors and those involved in solicitation are not considered abnormal if they occur every 21 days when the mare cycles. Nymphomaniac mares should be checked for underlying medical problems.

Geldings that act like stallions will mount mares, attack foals, fight with other males, and self-mutilate. These geldings may also disturb other social relationships. Laboratory tests may be helpful to exclude underlying medical problems, although about 10% of normally castrated stallions will retain stallion-like behavior.

Problems with trailering include refusing to enter or leave the trailer and scrambling. All of these can be potentially injurious to the horse and are best addressed early. Often, treatment can be as simple as backing the horse into the trailer (using a platform rather than a ramp), walking the horse slowly around and then into the trailer, using another horse that trailers well as a "buddy," and counterconditioning and desensitizing by using treats. Trailers can be designed to allow bidirectional entry and exit and a walk-through option. Walking through the trailer may help demonstrate that the horse is not walking into a dark, uncertain area. Once the horse is calm, the gate can be raised.

43 Blood Disorders **581**
Introduction 581
Red Blood Cells 581
White Blood Cells 582
Platelets 583
Blood Groups and Blood Transfusions 584
Anemia 584
Blood Parasites 586
Bleeding Disorders 587
White Blood Cell Disorders 589
Lymphangitis 591

44 Heart and Blood Vessel Disorders **592**
Introduction 592
Heart Disease and Heart Failure 594
Diagnosis of Cardiovascular Disease 595
Treatment of Cardiovascular Disease 595
Congenital and Inherited Disorders of the Cardiovascular System 596
Heart Failure 598
Acquired Heart and Blood Vessel Disorders 599
Blood Clots and Aneurysms 600

45 Digestive Disorders **602**
Introduction 602
Congenital and Inherited Disorders 606
Dental Development 609
Dental Disorders 610
Disorders of the Mouth 612
Pharyngeal Paralysis 613
Disorders of the Esophagus 613
Stomach (Gastric) Ulcers in Horses 614
Gastrointestinal Obstruction (Blockages) 615
Colic 616
Intestinal Disorders Other than Colic 621
Gastrointestinal Parasites of Horses 629
Disorders of the Liver 633
Disorders of the Rectum and Anus 640

46 Hormonal Disorders **641**
Introduction 641
Common Hormonal Disorders in Horses 643

47 Eye Disorders **646**
Eye Structure and Function 646
Disorders of the Eyelids 648
Disorders of the Nasal Cavity and Tear Ducts 648
Disorders of the Conjunctiva 649
Disorders of the Cornea 650

Disorders of the Anterior Uvea 650
Glaucoma 652
Disorders of the Lens 652
Disorders of the Retina, Choroid, and Optic Disk (Ocular Fundus) 652
Disorders of the Optic Nerve 653
Prolapse of the Eye 653
Eyeworm Disease (Thelaziasis) 654
Cancers and Tumors of the Eye 654

48 Ear Disorders.. **655**
Ear Structure and Function 655
Deafness 657
Disorders of the Outer Ear 657
Otitis Externa 659
Otitis Media and Interna 659

49 Immune Disorders.. **659**
The Immune System 659
Disorders Involving Anaphylactic Reactions (Type I Reactions, Atopy) 660
Disorders Involving Cytotoxic Antibodies (Type II Reactions) 661
Disorders Involving Immune Complexes (Type III Reactions) 662
Disorders Involving Cell-mediated Immunity (Type IV Reactions) 663
Immune-deficiency Diseases 663

50 Bone, Joint, and Muscle Disorders **664**
Introduction 664
Components of the Musculoskeletal System 664
Overview of Musculoskeletal Disorders 665
Lameness 666
Congenital and Inherited Disorders of Bones, Joints, and Muscles 669
Developmental Orthopedic Disease 671
Disorders Associated with Calcium, Phosphorus, and Vitamin D 673
Joint Disorders 675
Disorders of the Foot 678
Disorders of the Fetlock and Pastern 687
Disorders of the Carpus and Metacarpus 689
Disorders of the Shoulder and Elbow 694
Disorders of the Tarsus 696
Disorders of the Stifle 699
Disorders of the Hip 700
Disorders of the Back 701
Muscle Disorders 704
Sarcocystosis 708

51 Brain, Spinal Cord, and Nerve Disorders **708**
The Nervous System 708
Parts of the Nervous System 708
Nervous System Disorders and Effects of Injuries 710
The Neurologic Evaluation 711
Principles of Therapy 712
Congenital and Inherited Disorders 712
Disorders of the Peripheral Nerves 714
Disorders of the Spinal Column and Cord 716
Equine Dysautonomia (Grass Sickness) 718
Equine Viral Encephalomyelitis (Encephalitis) 718
Equine Protozoal Myeloencephalitis 719
Facial Paralysis 720
Central Nervous System Disorders Caused by Parasites 720

Neonatal Encephalopathy in Foals (Neonatal Maladjustment Syndrome) 721
Leg Paralysis 721
Meningitis and Encephalitis 722
Rabies 723
West Nile Encephalomyelitis 724

52   Reproductive Disorders 726

Introduction 726
The Gonads and Genital Tract 726
Management of Reproduction in Horses 727
Infertility 731
Congenital and Inherited Disorders of the Reproductive System 731
Abortion 732
Brucellosis 733
Contagious Equine Metritis 733
Equine Coital Exanthema (Genital Horsepox, Equine Venereal Balanitis) 734
Mastitis 734
Metritis 735
Pyometra 735
Retained Placenta 735
Uterine Prolapse 735
Vulvitis and Vaginitis 736

53   Lung and Airway Disorders 736

Introduction 736
Accumulation of Fluid or Air in the Chest Cavity 739
Aspiration Pneumonia 740
Choanal Atresia 740
Diaphragmatic Hernia 740
Disorders of the Larynx 741
Disorders of the Nasal Septum 742
Disorders of the Paranasal Sinuses 742
Dorsal Displacement of the Soft Palate 743
Epiglottic Entrapment 744
Equine Herpesvirus Infection (Equine Viral Rhinopneumonitis) 744
Equine Influenza 745
Equine Morbillivirus Pneumonia (Hendra Virus Infection) 746
Equine Viral Arteritis 746
Exercise-induced Pulmonary Hemorrhage ("Bleeder") 747
Foal Pneumonia 747
Guttural Pouch Empyema 749
Guttural Pouch Mycosis 749
Guttural Pouch Tympany 750
Inflammatory Airway Disease 750
Lungworm Infection 750
Nasal Polyps 751
Pharyngeal Lymphoid Hyperplasia (Pharyngitis) 751
Pleuropneumonia 752
Recurrent Airway Obstruction (Heaves) 752
Strangles (Distemper) 753
Subepiglottic Cyst 754

54   Skin Disorders 755

Structure of the Skin 755
Dermatitis and Dermatologic Problems 756
Diagnosis of Skin Disorders 757
Treatment of Skin Disorders 757
Congenital and Inherited Skin Disorders 758
Allergies 759

Dermatophilosis 760
Eosinophilic Granuloma Complex 760
Flies and Mosquitoes 761
Hair Loss (Alopecia) 766
Hives (Urticaria) 767
Itching (Pruritus) 768
Lice 768
Mange (Acariasis, Mange Mites) 769
Parasitic Worms of the Skin 770
Photosensitization 772
Ringworm (Dermatophytosis) 773
Saddle Sores (Collar Galls) 773
Ticks 774
Tumors of the Skin 775

55 **Kidney and Urinary Tract Disorders** **781**
The Urinary System 781
Detecting Disorders of the Kidneys and Urinary Tract 782
Congenital and Inherited Disorders of the Urinary System 783
Infectious Diseases of the Urinary System 784
Noninfectious Diseases of the Urinary System 785

56 **Metabolic Disorders** **788**
Introduction 788
Disorders of Calcium Metabolism 790
Disorders of Magnesium Metabolism 790
Fatigue and Exercise 790
Fever of Unknown Origin 792
Malignant Hyperthermia 793

57 **Disorders Affecting Multiple Body Systems** **793**
Introduction 793
Congenital and Inherited Disorders 794
Actinobacillosis 794
Actinomycosis 795
African Horse Sickness 795
Amyloidosis 796
Anaplasmosis (Equine Granulocytic Ehrlichiosis) 796
Anthrax 797
Besnoitiosis 798
Botulism 798
Equine Infectious Anemia 799
Equine Morbillivirus Pneumonia (Hendra Virus Infection) 799
Equine Viral Arteritis 800
Fungal Infections (Mycoses) 801
Glanders (Farcy) 805
Infectious Necrotic Hepatitis (Black Disease) 805
Intestinal Clostridiosis (Clostridia-associated Enterocolitis) 806
Leptospirosis 807
Lyme Disease (Lyme Borreliosis) 808
Malignant Edema 808
Melioidosis 808
Nocardiosis 809
Peritonitis 809
Septicemia in Foals 810
Tetanus 811
Trichinellosis (Trichinosis) 813
Tuberculosis 813
Tularemia 813
Vesicular Stomatitis 813

CHAPTER 43

Blood Disorders

■ INTRODUCTION

Blood cells form and develop mostly in the bone marrow, that is, the tissue located in the cavities of bones. Blood performs a variety of important functions as it circulates throughout the body. It delivers oxygen and vital nutrients (such as vitamins, minerals, fats, and sugars) to the body's tissues. It carries carbon dioxide to the lungs to be exhaled and waste products to the kidneys and liver to be eliminated from the body. It transports hormones, which are chemical messengers, to various parts of the body, allowing those parts to communicate with each other. Blood also includes cells that fight infection and platelets that control bleeding.

There are 3 cellular elements of blood: **red blood cells, white blood cells**, and **platelets**. Basically, red blood cells supply the body with oxygen; white blood cells protect against infection; and, platelets start the formation of blood clots.

Blood disorders are quite diverse. They can occur as normal responses to abnormal situations; for example, a significant increase in the number of white blood cells in response to an infection or disease. They may also occur as primary abnormalities of the blood; for example, a deficiency of all cellular elements of the blood due to bone marrow failure. Furthermore, abnormalities may be quantitative (too many or too few cells) or qualitative (abnormalities in the way cells function). Like people, horses have different blood groups or types. Researchers have identified 8 blood types in horses: A, C, D, K, P, Q, U, and T. Horse owners and breeders will often have a record of their horse's blood type. This should be included in the medical records for your horse.

■ RED BLOOD CELLS

The main function of red blood cells (also called erythrocytes) is to carry oxygen to the tissues, where it is required for cellular metabolism. Oxygen molecules attach themselves to carrier molecules, called hemoglobin, which are the iron-containing proteins in red blood cells that give the cells their red color. Oxygen is carried from the lungs and delivered to all body tissues by the hemoglobin within red blood cells. Oxygen is used by cells to produce energy that the body needs. Carbon dioxide is left behind as a waste product during this process. The red blood cells then carry that carbon dioxide away from the tissues and back to the lungs, where it is exhaled. When the number of red blood cells is too low, this is called anemia. Having too few red blood cells means the blood carries less oxygen. The result is that fatigue and weakness develop. When the number of red blood cells is too high, this is called polycythemia. The result is that blood can become too thick, and impair the ability of the heart to deliver oxygen throughout the body. An animal's metabolism is geared to protect both the red blood cells and the

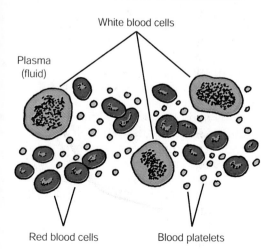

Plasma (fluid)

White blood cells

Red blood cells   Blood platelets

Blood is a complex mix of plasma (the liquid component), red blood cells, white blood cells, and platelets.

hemoglobin from damage. Interference with the formation or release of hemoglobin, or with production or survival of red blood cells, causes disease.

The total number of red cells remains constant over time in healthy animals. Mature red blood cells have a limited life span; their production and destruction must be carefully balanced, or disease develops.

Production of red blood cells begins with stem cells in the bone marrow and ends with the release of mature red blood cells into the body's circulation. Within the bone marrow, all blood cells begin from a single type of cell called a stem cell. The stem cell produces an immature form of a red blood cell, a white blood cell, or a platelet-producing cell. That immature cell then divides again, develops further, and ultimately becomes a mature red blood cell, white blood cell, or platelet.

The rate of blood cell production is determined by the body's needs. Erythropoietin, a hormone produced by the kidneys, stimulates development of red blood cells in the bone marrow. Erythropoietin increases if the body lacks oxygen (a condition called hypoxia). In most species, the kidney is both the sensor organ that determines how much oxygen the body's tissues are receiving and the major site of erythropoietin production; so chronic kidney failure leads to anemia. Erythropoietin plays a major role in determining whether to increase the number of stem cells entering red blood cell production, to shorten maturation time of the red blood cells, or to cause early release of red blood cells. Other factors that affect red blood cell production are the supply of nutrients (such as iron and vitamins) and cell-cell interactions between compounds that aid in their production.

Anemia may be caused by blood loss, the destruction of red blood cells (hemolysis), or decreased production. In severe blood loss anemia, red blood cells are lost, but death usually results from the loss of total blood volume, rather than from the lack of oxygen caused by loss of red blood cells. Red blood cells may be destroyed by toxins such as red maple leaves, infections such as equine infectious anemia, and drugs such as phenothiazine tranquilizers. Hemolytic disease of newborn foals is caused by maternal antibodies against foals' red blood cells. (*See also* ANEMIA, page 584.)

Decreased red blood cell production may be caused by primary bone marrow diseases (such as aplastic anemia or hematopoietic malignancy), kidney failure, or drugs such as phenylbutazone. Longterm debilitating diseases may also be associated with mild anemia. It is important to remember that anemia is a clinical finding, not a specific diagnosis. The prognosis and treatment depend on the underlying cause.

■ WHITE BLOOD CELLS

The function of white blood cells (also called leukocytes) is to defend the body against infection. There are 2 main types of white blood cells: phagocytes and lymphocytes.

Phagocytes

Phagocytes are cells in the bloodstream and tissues that surround and consume foreign particles, cell waste material, and bacteria. Their main function is to defend against invading microorganisms by surrounding and destroying them.

There are 2 types of phagocytes: granulocytes and monocytes. **Granulocytes**, primarily neutrophils, protect against bacteria and fungi. Others known as eosinophils and basophils are involved in allergic reactions. **Monocytes** become macrophages in the tissues and consume large foreign particles and cellular debris.

As with red blood cells, the production and number of phagocytes are tightly regulated by chemical messengers in the blood, including interleukins (chemicals found in white blood cells that stimulate them to fight infection). Unlike the red blood cells, which remain circulating in the blood, the phagocytes use the blood's circulatory system as a pathway to the tissues. Because of this, the number of phagocytes in the blood can provide an indication of disorders in the body. For example, the number of neutrophils increases when inflammation is present anywhere in the body. The number of phagocytes produced as a result of these conditions varies from species to species. An abnormal response, such as an unusually low number of circulating white blood cells due to marrow failure, drugs, or toxins, can lower resistance to bacterial infections. Finally, those elements that produce phagocytes may become cancerous, resulting in a disease called myelogenous leukemia.

Lymphocytes

Lymphocytes are white blood cells that produce antibodies to attack infectious organisms. They are also responsible for rejecting foreign tissue or cancer cells. Lymphocyte production in mammals begins in the bone marrow. Lymphocytes then become 1 of 2 types: T cells or B cells. **T cells** are responsible for a variety of functions, especially fighting off viral infections and cancers. Most T cells remain in the bloodstream, but some are also present in the spleen and lymph nodes. **B cells** are responsible for producing antibodies that coat invading organisms or foreign substances. For example, bacteria coated by antibody are more easily recognized and removed by phagocytes. If lymphocytes are decreased or abnormal, the patient is immunodeficient and is at risk for a wide variety of infections.

Antibody molecules are called **immunoglobulins**. They fall into several classes, each of which has a different function. For example, one class is commonly found in the lungs and intestines; another is the first antibody produced in response to newly recognized foreign microorganisms; a third is the main antibody in the bloodstream; and a fourth is involved in allergic reactions.

Lymphocytes usually act appropriately to rid the body of foreign "invaders" that cause disease. However, sometimes lymphocytes do not react appropriately. One inappropriate response occurs when antibodies are produced against the body's own cells. Another inappropriate response of the immune system is allergy. When exposure to the allergen occurs, the reaction can be mild or life-threatening.

An increase in the number of lymphocytes in the bloodstream occurs in some animals as a response to the secretion of epinephrine (a hormone also known as adrenaline). A reduction in the number of circulating lymphocytes may be caused by corticosteroid hormones that are secreted in times of stress. Unusual lymphocytes may be seen in the blood in response to antigenic stimulation, such as vaccination. Malignant tumors starting in a lymph node (lymphoma) or lymphoid leukemia can occur.

■ PLATELETS

Platelets are small, cell-like particles produced in the bone marrow. Their main function is to start the formation of blood clots. Platelets gather where bleeding occurs and clump together to form the initial plug that stops or slows down the flow of blood. Platelets also release other substances needed to complete the clotting process.

Platelet disorders can result from having too few or too many platelets or from impaired platelet function. In general, when platelet counts fall very low there is an increased risk of bleeding. Decreased numbers of platelets may be caused by drugs, toxins, or disorders of the bone marrow.

An abnormal increase in the number of platelets is rare and often the cause is not known. It may be associated with bone marrow disease or with longterm blood loss and iron deficiency. There are also disorders in which platelets do not function properly.

▓ BLOOD GROUPS AND BLOOD TRANSFUSIONS

Blood groups are determined by the presence or absence of certain proteins or sugars found on the red blood cell membrane. The number of blood groups varies among domestic species. Normally, individuals do not have antibodies against antigens on their own red blood cells or against other blood group antigens of that species unless they have been exposed to them by a blood transfusion or pregnancy. In some species however, antibodies from one individual that react with antigens of another individual may exist without any prior exposure. In horses, antibodies are produced in the mare against a foreign fetal red blood cell antigen when fetal blood passes through the placenta. This can be a problem in subsequent pregnancies if foals have this same foreign antigen inherited from the sire. The maternal antibodies can be transmitted to the foals in colostrum (first milk) and can destroy the foal's red blood cells.

In horses there are 8 major blood groups: A, C, D, K, P, Q, U, and T. Of these, A, C, and Q seem to be the most likely to stimulate an antibody response when given to a horse that is negative for them. These groups are identified to aid in matching of donors and recipients and to identify breeding pairs potentially at risk of causing an immune disorder, neonatal isoerythrolysis, in their offspring (*see* page 585). Because the expression of blood group antigens is genetically controlled and the ways in which they are inherited are understood, these systems also have been used to confirm pedigrees in horses. However in most cases, DNA testing has now replaced blood typing for paternity testing.

Blood Typing

Bloody typing is a procedure for testing an animal's blood by measuring the reaction of a small sample of blood to certain antibodies. In horses, it is most practical to type potential donors in advance, as it is seldom possible to type recipients on an emergency basis. By selecting donors that lack the blood group antigens (A, C, and Q), most likely to be problematic, or that match the recipient, the risk of causing a transfusion reaction can be minimized.

Blood Transfusions

Often, the need for a blood transfusion is an emergency, such as severe bleeding or sudden destruction of red blood cells due to other disease. Transfusions may also be needed to treat anemia. Animals with blood clotting disorders often require repeated transfusions.

Blood transfusions must be given with care because they have the potential to cause adverse reactions in rare cases. The most serious risk of transfusion is immediate destruction of red blood cells. In horses, a complete match is rarely possible, and even when donor and recipient are compatible, red blood cells survive only 2 to 4 days. Other rare potential complications include fever and the spread of infections.

▓ ANEMIA

Anemia occurs when there is a decrease in the number of red blood cells. It can develop from loss, destruction, or lack of production of red blood cells. Anemia is classified as regenerative or nonregenerative. In a **regenerative anemia**, the bone marrow responds appropriately to the decreased number of red blood cells by increasing red blood cell production. Anemias due to bleeding or the destruction of red blood cells are usually regenerative. In a **nonregenerative anemia**, the bone marrow responds inadequately to the increased need for red blood cells. Anemias that are caused by a decrease in the hormone that stimulates red blood cell production or by an abnormality in the bone marrow are nonregenerative.

Some infections, including equine infectious anemia, babesiosis, and trypanosomiasis, can cause anemia in horses. (For a more detailed discussion of ANEMIA, *see* page 37.)

Regenerative Anemias

Regenerative anemias include blood loss anemia (page 38) and hemolytic anemia (page 39). Hemolytic anemias may be due to immune system dysfunction, diseases of the small blood vessels, metabolic disorders, toxins, infections, and genetic diseases.

Neonatal isoerythrolysis is an immune disorder in which red blood cells are destroyed in newborn foals. It occurs when foals nurse from a mother whose colostrum (the yellowish fluid rich in antibodies and minerals that is produced after giving birth and before producing true milk) contains antibodies to the newborns' red blood cells. This can be caused by exposure of the mother to another blood type during a previous pregnancy or an unmatched blood transfusion. In horses, the antigens usually involved are A, C, and Q. Neonatal isoerythrolysis is most commonly seen in Thoroughbreds. The foals get the antibodies when they first begin nursing. Once absorbed, the antibodies enter the bloodstream where they attach to red blood cells and cause them to rupture. Newborns with neonatal isoerythrolysis are normal at birth but develop severe hemolytic anemia within 2 to 3 days. A veterinarian can perform tests to confirm the diagnosis. Treatment consists of stopping any colostrum while giving supportive care with transfusions. Neonatal isoerythrolysis can be avoided by withholding colostrum from the foal's own mother and giving colostrum free of the antibodies. A veterinarian can perform a test to check for this potential disorder before the newborn is allowed to receive maternal colostrum.

Nonregenerative Anemias

Nonregenerative anemias include anemias caused by deficiencies in vitamins or minerals (such as iron) needed for the formation of red blood cells, as well as by chronic disease, kidney disease, and primary bone marrow diseases. (For a more detailed discussion of NONREGENERATIVE ANEMIAS, *see* page 40.)

Aplastic anemia is a severe disorder of the bone marrow, in which the ability of bone marrow to generate blood cells is reduced. It has been reported in horses with pancytopenia (a condition in which there is an abnormal reduction in the number of red blood cells, white blood cells, and platelets in the blood) and with marrow that is underdeveloped and replaced by fat. Most cases have no known cause, but known causes include infections, drugs, toxins, and radiation therapy. To treat the condition, the underlying cause must be determined and eliminated. Supportive care such as antibiotics and transfusions may also be needed. Drugs that stimulate the bone marrow can be used until the marrow recovers. If the disease has no known cause or if marrow recovery is unlikely, bone marrow transplantation is helpful if a suitable donor is available.

In **pure red cell aplasia**, the number of both mature and immature red blood cells is decreased. In this nonregenerative anemia, there is a severe reduction of the elements that produce the red blood cells in the bone marrow. The use of recombinant human erythropoietin, used to treat anemia caused by kidney failure, may cause this condition in horses. Discontinuing the drug may lead to recovery in some animals.

Primary leukemias are a type of cancer in which abnormal white blood cells displace normal blood cells. This leads to anemia and a lack of normal white blood cells and platelets. Primary leukemias are uncommon to rare in most domestic species but have been reported in horses. Leukemias are classified as acute (sudden and often severe) or chronic (long-lasting, with signs that are generally less severe). Acute leukemias, in which the marrow is filled with immature blood cells, generally respond poorly to chemotherapy. In animals that do respond, remission times are usually short. Chronic leukemias, in which there is greatly increased production of one blood cell line, are less likely to cause anemia and are more responsive to treatment.

◼ BLOOD PARASITES

Blood parasites are organisms that live in the blood of their animal hosts. These parasites can range from single-celled protozoa to more complex bacteria and rickettsiae. The method of transmission varies, depending on the parasite, but often they are transmitted through the bites of ticks or flies.

Babesiosis

Babesiosis is a disease transmitted by ticks. It affects a wide range of domestic and wild animals and occasionally humans. In horses, babesiosis is caused by protozoan parasites of the genuses *Babesia* and *Theileria*, which infect red blood cells. Equine babesiosis occurs in Africa, Europe, Asia, South and Central America, and the southern US. Infection of unborn foals, particularly with *Theileria* protozoa, is relatively common.

The incubation period is approximately 8 to 10 days. Signs of infection in adult horses may include reluctance to move, lack of appetite, and fever. Swelling of the fetlocks may occur, and episodes of colic are common. In young horses, signs may be more severe and can include jaundice, weakness, and pale mucous membranes. The disease lasts for about 10 days, but death may occur in the first 24 to 48 hours. Some horses develop chronic, or longterm, infections and can become carriers for several years after the initial infection.

Babesiosis can be confused with other conditions that cause fever, anemia, destruction of red blood cells, or jaundice. Therefore, laboratory tests should be performed to confirm the diagnosis. Treatment generally involves using one or a combination of effective antiprotozoal drugs. There is no vaccine for use in horses. Controlling ticks by periodic spraying and inspection of the horse can help reduce the chance of transmission.

African Trypanosomiasis (Tsetse Fly Disease)

Tsetse flies are small, winged biting flies that feed on the blood of humans and other animals. They only occur in sub-Saharan Africa, where they are responsible for transmitting a group of diseases caused by protozoa of the genus *Trypanosoma*, which affect all domestic animals. Tsetse flies are restricted to Africa; however, horseflies and other biting flies can transmit the disease in other locations such as Central and South America. In horses, *Trypanosoma congolense*, *T. vivax*, and *T. brucei brucei* are the trypanosomes most likely to cause disease. Domestic animals may be a source of human infections.

The severity of disease varies with the species and age of the animal infected and the species of trypanosome involved. The incubation period is usually 1 to 4 weeks. The primary signs are fever that may come and go, anemia, and weight loss. Internally, the lymph nodes and spleen are usually swollen. The diagnosis is confirmed by finding trypanosomes in laboratory tests.

Several drugs can be used for treatment; however, most drugs only work if the correct dose is given. It is very important to follow the prescribed dosage exactly. Some trypanosomes have become resistant to certain drugs, which may be the cause in cases that do not respond to medical treatment.

The risk of infection can be reduced in areas where the disease is common by getting rid of tsetse flies and using preventive drugs, which are given to stop an infection from getting started. Flies can be partially controlled by using sprays approved for use on horses, spraying insecticides on fly-breeding areas, using screens coated with insecticide, and clearing brush to reduce the habitat for the flies. Animals can be given preventive drugs in areas with a high population of trypanosome-infected tsetse flies (portions of Africa and Central and South America). There is no vaccine.

Surra (*Trypanosoma evansi* Infection)

Surra is separated from the tsetse-transmitted diseases because it is usually transmitted by other biting flies that are found within and outside tsetse fly areas.

It occurs in North Africa, the Middle East, Asia, the Far East, and Central and South America. It can be a deadly disease in horses. *Trypanosoma evansi* in other animals appears not to cause disease, and these animals serve as a source of the infection.

The development and effects of the disease, signs, physical changes, diagnosis, and treatment are similar to those of the tsetse-transmitted trypanosomes (*see* above).

Dourine

Dourine is a venereal disease of horses that is transmitted during sexual intercourse. It is caused by a species of trypanosome named *Trypanosoma equiperdum*. The disease occurs on the Mediterranean coast of Africa and in the Middle East, southern Africa, and South America; however, the distribution is probably wider.

Signs may develop over weeks or months, and infection may become chronic. Early signs include mucous and pus-filled discharge from the urethra in stallions and from the vagina in mares, followed by swelling of the genitals. Later, characteristic scaly patches ¾ to 4 inches (2 to 10 centimeters) in diameter appear on the skin, and the horse becomes dangerously thin. If untreated, 50 to 70% of infected horses will die.

Getting definitive proof of this disease can be difficult. However, your veterinarian can perform certain tests to find and identify the trypanosomes in the discharges, the skin patches, or the blood.

In areas prone to this disease, horses may be treated with several different medications. When completely eliminating the disease from a stable or group of horses is desired, strict control of breeding, euthanasia of positively identified infected horses, and elimination of stray horses has been successful.

■ BLEEDING DISORDERS

When bleeding occurs in an organ or body part, a process is set in motion to stop the bleeding. This is called **hemostasis**. In order to work, hemostasis requires an adequate number of platelets, the right amount of blood clotting proteins (often referred to as factors), and blood vessels that constrict properly. When an injury occurs, the wall of the blood vessel breaks. The affected blood vessel will narrow so that blood flows more slowly, allowing the clotting process to begin. Platelets also rush to the broken wall where certain proteins change the platelets' shape from round to spiny so that they can stick to blood cells, the broken vessel wall, and to each other. Other proteins form long strands called fibrin. These fibrin strands form a net that traps and helps hold together the platelets and blood cells, creating a clot that plugs the break in the vessel wall. After the clot has formed and stabilized, other proteins stop the clotting process and eventually dissolve the clot.

Bleeding disorders may be present at birth (congenital) or occur later. Defects in blood clotting proteins usually show up as delayed bleeding and bruising deep in tissues, while platelet defects usually show up as superficial small bruises, nosebleeds, black stools caused by bleeding into the bowels, or prolonged bleeding at injection and surgery sites.

Abnormal clotting leading to blocked arteries may be inherited disorders of anticlotting proteins or acquired disorders. Acquired clotting diseases are more common in animals than are inherited disorders.

Blood clotting tests can help identify animals with defective clotting proteins. However, the tests are not very sensitive, so an animal must have a severe deficiency for the tests to find the problem. (For a more detailed discussion of BLEEDING DISORDERS, *see* page 46.)

Congenital Clotting Protein Disorders

Many different proteins are involved in the clotting process. Deficiencies of any of these proteins can cause bleeding disorders. In a severe deficiency or defect of

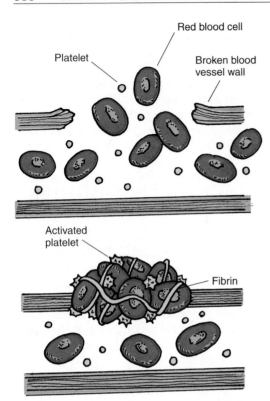

How blood clots are formed (modified with permission from *The Merck Manual of Medical Information*, Second Home Edition, 2003)

clotting proteins, signs will appear at an early age. Severe defects are usually deadly. Animals may be stillborn or die shortly after birth. Lack of clotting proteins or vitamin K (which is also part of the clotting process) in a newborn animal may make a clotting defect worse. If the amount of any particular clotting protein is 5 to 10% of normal, the newborn may survive, but will usually show signs of illness before 6 months of age. It is during this time, when numerous routine procedures (for example, vaccination or gelding) are usually done, that a bleeding tendency may be noticed.

Hemophilia A (Factor VIII deficiency) has been reported in several breeds of horses, including Arabians, Standardbreds, Quarter Horses, and Thoroughbreds. (For a more detailed discussion of hemophilia A, *see* page 47.)

Acquired Clotting Protein Disorders

Most clotting proteins are produced in the liver. Therefore, liver disease can lead to decreased levels of clotting proteins, particularly Factors VII, IX, X, and XI. The decrease in clotting proteins can range from small to large.

Disseminated intravascular coagulation (DIC) is a condition in which small blood clots develop throughout the bloodstream, blocking small blood vessels and destroying the platelets and clotting factors needed to control bleeding. It usually develops after numerous triggering events such as severe infections, heat stroke, burns, tumors, or severe injury. In many cases, the signs are uncontrolled bleeding and the inability to form a normal clot. Death is caused by extensive blood clots or collapse of circulation, leading to the failure of one or several organs. If the animal survives this crisis, a longterm form of DIC can occur. Your veterinarian will determine and attempt to correct the underlying problem causing this condition. Intravenous fluids are extremely important for maintaining normal circulation. DIC is a very serious disorder and is often fatal.

Platelet Disorders

Disorders of platelets include having too few platelets (thrombocytopenia) or having platelets that do not work properly. Each type of disorder can be either congenital (present at birth) or acquired later in life. Several acquired thrombocytopenias causing decreases in platelets in the bloodstream are reported in horses. Numerous causes have been identified, most involving the immune system. Thrombocytosis (having too many platelets in the blood) is rare.

Thrombocytopenia due to immune system dysfunction (also called idiopathic thrombocytopenia or idiopathic thrombocytopenic purpura) occurs when the immune system makes antibodies that destroy platelets or platelet-producing cells in the bone marrow. It has been seen in horses. Signs include tiny, purplish red spots on the gums or skin, bruising, bleeding into the bowels resulting in black stools, or nosebleeds. An evaluation of the bone marrow may be necessary to help determine if circulating platelets or the platelet-forming cells are targeted by the antibodies. Corticosteroids are the usual treatment, although other drugs are sometimes used. If an animal has repeated episodes of the disease, the spleen is sometimes removed.

Thrombocytopenia caused by drugs has been reported in horses. Some drugs and classes of drugs (including estrogen and some antibiotics) suppress the production of platelets in the bone marrow. Other drugs (including aspirin, acetaminophen, penicillin, and others) destroy platelets circulating in the bloodstream. Drug reactions are rare and unpredictable. Platelets usually return to normal shortly after the drug is discontinued. Drug-induced bone marrow suppression may last longer, however. If your horse is taking one of these drugs, your veterinarian will likely monitor the blood count to check for any serious reductions in the number of platelets.

Blood Vessel Disorders

Certain defects present at birth or diseases can cause severe inflammation of the blood vessels and bleeding disorders.

Ehlers-Danlos syndrome, also known as cutaneous asthenia, is caused by a defect in protein connective tissue in the skin. This causes weak structural support of blood vessels and can lead to blood clots and easy bruising. The disorder has been reported in horses but is rare. The most striking clinical abnormality is loose skin that stretches to a greater than normal degree and tears easily. No treatment is available.

Blood Clotting Disorders

Abnormal blood clotting (known as pathologic thrombosis) is the uncontrolled clotting of blood, which causes blocked arteries. It may occur because of inherited disorders of anticlotting proteins or because of acquired disorders, which are more common. Coagulation

screening tests performed by a veterinarian can identify which clotting protein is affected. Disorders most relevant to horses are described below. (For a more detailed discussion of BLOOD CLOTTING DISORDERS, see page 50.)

Blood clots have been seen in horses with generalized inflammatory diseases such as colic (a digestive disease), laminitis (inflammation of the hoof), or equine ehrlichial colitis (an infection of the colon). Catheters inserted in the jugular vein in the neck for long periods and treatment with drugs that irritate the blood vessels may also cause blood clots to form.

Horses with **colic associated with endotoxemia** (the presence of bacterial toxins in the bloodstream) have decreased activity of enzymes that break down blood-clotting agents, such as fibrin. These horses have increased death rates and a higher risk for blood clot formation. **Laminitis** is thought to be the result of several diverse whole system disorders. Tiny blood clots form in the blood vessels of the hoof in the early stages of laminitis. One theory is that bacterial toxins in the bloodstream directly affect the blood vessels and activate the clotting system. Swelling, blood vessel compression, and possibly the shifting of blood flow to the upper part of the horse's hoof increase the damage to the blood vessels. When blood flow is restored, it releases toxins into the bloodstream, which causes blood clot formation.

The best treatment for an animal with blood clots is diagnosing and treating the underlying disease, along with providing good supportive care. Maintaining blood flow to the tissues is critical. Your veterinarian may prescribe medication to dissolve or prevent clots. In other cases, transfusions may be the most effective treatment.

■ WHITE BLOOD CELL DISORDERS

Several different types of white blood cells, or leukocytes, are found in the blood of mammals, including neutrophils, lymphocytes, monocytes, eosinophils, and basophils. These cells vary with regard to where they are produced and where and how long they circulate in the bloodstream. The normal numbers of each type of white blood cell also vary among species. **Leukocytosis** is an increase in the total number of circulating white blood cells; **leukopenia** is a decrease. Leukopenia in horses occurs in equine herpesvirus infections, equine ehrlichiosis, influenza, and sometimes during the early stages of equine infectious anemia.

In addition to an overall increase or decrease in white blood cells, increases or decreases in each type of white blood cell can lead to—and help diagnose—disorders. **Leukograms** are blood tests that count the number of different white blood cells circulating in the bloodstream. By counting the cells and examining their form your veterinarian gains valuable information that can help diagnose a wide variety of disorders.

Disorders Related to Increased or Decreased White Blood Cells

An increase in white blood cells may occur as a result of exercise or excitement. This response, which is known as **physiologic leukocytosis**, is caused by increased epinephrine (the hormone adrenaline). Excitement may double the total white blood cell count within minutes. In addition, contraction of the spleen releases white blood cells and red blood cells into the bloodstream. An increase in lymphocytes (**lymphocytosis**) may also be present, especially in young horses.

Neutrophilia is an increase in the number of neutrophils in the bloodstream and is usually caused by inflammation. Structural changes in neutrophils may occur during severe inflammation and are referred to as toxic changes. Neutrophilia can occur in horses with equine viral arteritis and in those being treated with corticosteroids.

Neutropenia is a decrease in the number of neutrophils in the bloodstream. It may occur due to the white blood cells sticking to the walls of damaged blood vessels, destruction of neutrophils, or reduced formation in the bone marrow. Neutropenia may occur in all species during overwhelming bacterial infections. Destruction of neutrophils due to an immune response occurs in animals, and tests have been developed to detect antineutrophil antibodies in horses. Adverse reactions to drugs may result in neutropenia or even pancytopenia (a reduction in red and white blood cells and platelets).

Eosinophilia is an increase in the number of eosinophils, which are involved in allergic reactions and in controlling parasites. Increases are caused by substances that promote allergic reactions (for example, histamine) and by certain antibodies. Eosinophils increase during infections with parasites and sometimes during inflammation of the intestines, kidneys, lungs, or skin. A decrease in eosinophils is known as **eosinopenia**. It is a common reaction to stress or treatment with corticosteroids in horses.

Lymphocytosis is an increase in the number of lymphocytes in the bloodstream. It can be caused by certain hormones, stimulation of the immune system by infections, chronic diseases like arthritis, and leukemia, which is a cancer of the immune system. **Lymphopenia** is a decrease in the number of lymphocytes. It is most commonly caused by corticosteroids (either those naturally occurring in the body or given as treatment for a disease). Lymphopenia may also be caused by other conditions, such as decreased production of lymphocytes, some viral infections (such as equine viral arteritis), and hereditary diseases.

Monocytosis is an increase in monocytes and may be associated with longterm inflammation and the use of corticosteroids.

Leukemia and Lymphoma

Leukemia is a malignant cancer that is characterized by an increase in abnormal white blood cells in the bloodstream. It is rarely seen in horses. Lymphoma is a related cancer of certain white blood cells that begins in a lymph node or other lymphoid tissue. It is most likely to occur in horses that are 5 to 10 years old.

▧ LYMPHANGITIS

Lymphangitis is inflammation of the lymphatic vessels. These are low-pressure vessels similar to veins that collect the fluid that surrounds cells and return it to the bloodstream. Lymphangitis is usually caused by a bacterial infection that spreads to the lymphatic vessels.

Pigeon Fever (False Strangles)

Infection causing lymphangitis in horses can occur following infection with *Corynebacterium pseudotuberculosis* bacteria. The bacteria probably enter by way of skin wounds including injections, insect bites, or by contact with contaminated tack or grooming equipment. The condition is commonly known as pigeon fever, but is also called false strangles, pigeon breast, and dry land distemper. Pigeon fever in horses causes an infection of the lower limbs (ulcerative lymphangitis), inflamed and pus-filled sores in the chest region, and contagious acne. It is a common infectious diseases of horses in California and is increasingly seen in other dry, western states of the US. In these areas, infections are seasonal, with a peak in late summer and fall. Healing often occurs without treatment or with limited topical treatment. Abortion and infection of the mammary glands may also occur. In rare cases the internal organs may be affected.

Signs of the ulcerative lymphangitis caused by pigeon fever develop slowly and may include painful inflammation, small lumps or swellings, and slow-healing sores, especially on the fetlock. Occasionally, the swelling extends up the entire limb. The discharge is odorless, thick, greenish white, and blood-tinged. Usually, only one leg is involved. The sores and swelling progress slowly, and the condition can become longterm with relapses.

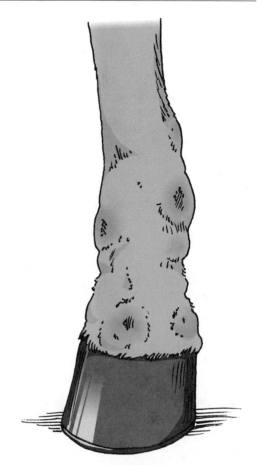

Pigeon fever is a bacterial infection that may cause nodules and sores on the lower legs, particularly in the fetlock area.

Other signs of pigeon fever include widespread or localized swellings, swelling and inflammation of the skin on the lower abdomen, lameness, sores that drain pus, fever, weight loss, and depression. An increase in white blood cells may be present. A high or prolonged fever may indicate complications such as multiple or internal pus-filled sores, or whole-body infection and abortion. Pus-filled sores can be large, up to 8 inches (20 centimeters) in diameter before rupturing, and take months to heal. Weight loss, colic, or lack of coordination may be signs of internal sores. Inflamed skin sores are painful and mildly itchy with a loss of hair, discharge, and crusting. They are also slow to heal.

To confirm the diagnosis of this disease, your veterinarian will take samples of material from the sores. Tests will then be done in a laboratory to identify the organism involved. Because the signs of this disease can easily be confused with infection by other bacteria, fungi, or worms, it is important to identify the bacteria so that proper treatment can be started.

Lymphangitis and early pus-filled swellings are often treated with hot packs, poultices, or flushing with water (hydrotherapy). In many cases, small sores are pierced to let the pus out and then flushed with iodine solution. Your veterinarian can recommend the most effective treatment for your horse. Large sores usually require surgery. For skin lesions and grossly contaminated limbs, veterinarians usually prescribe a daily scrubbing with a shampoo that contains iodine. Medications to relieve pain and promote healing may be needed. General supportive and nursing care is also important. If treatment is successful, the swelling gradually goes down over days or weeks. Severe or untreated cases often become longterm, and scarring and hardening of the tissue of the leg occurs.

Unhygienic and wet conditions increase the risk of infection, particularly of the lower legs and abdomen. Maintaining good hygiene and avoiding prolonged exposure of horses to damp or wet conditions may help limit infections. However, the disease occurs even under excellent management conditions.

CHAPTER 44

Heart and Blood Vessel Disorders

▓ INTRODUCTION

The cardiovascular system includes the heart and the blood vessels—the veins and the arteries. The function of the heart is to pump blood. The right side of the heart pumps blood to the lungs, where oxygen is added to the blood and carbon dioxide is removed from it. The left side pumps blood to the rest of the body, where oxygen and nutrients are delivered to tissues, and waste products (such as carbon dioxide) are removed. In horses, the cardiovascular system must not only efficiently supply blood to all parts of a large animal, but must also function well during strenuous racing or training, in many cases.

The heart is a hollow, muscular organ which, in mammals, is divided into 4 chambers. The muscular tissue is called the myocardium. There are upper chambers on both the left and right sides of the heart called the left and right **atria** (the plural form of atrium). There are also 2 lower chambers called the left and right **ventricles**.

A series of valves keep blood flowing in one direction through the heart. The **atrioventricular valves** are valves between the atria and the ventricles. The **semilunar valves** are valves between the heart and the aorta and between the heart and the pulmonary artery. Each ventricle has an inlet and an outlet valve. In the left ventricle, the inlet valve is called the **mitral valve,** and the outlet valve is called the **aortic valve**. In the right ventricle, the inlet valve is called the **tricuspid valve,** and the outlet valve is called the **pulmonary valve**.

Blood from the body flows through the 2 largest veins, called the **venae cavae,** into the right atrium. When the right ventricle relaxes, blood in the right atrium pours through the tricuspid valve into the

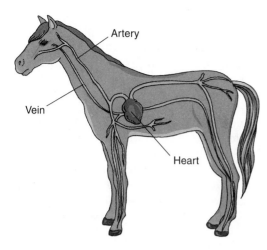

The cardiovascular system in horses

right ventricle. When the right ventricle is nearly full, the right atrium contracts, pushing additional blood into the right ventricle. The right ventricle then contracts, pushing blood through the pulmonary valve into the pulmonary arteries, which lead to the lungs. In the lungs, blood absorbs oxygen and gives up carbon dioxide. The blood then flows through the pulmonary veins into the left atrium. When the left ventricle relaxes, the blood in the left atrium pours through the mitral valve into the left ventricle. When the left ventricle is nearly full, the left atrium contracts, pushing additional blood into the left ventricle. The left ventricle then contracts, pushing blood through the aortic valve into the aorta, the largest artery in the body. This blood carries oxygen to all of the body except to the lungs.

Each heartbeat consists of 2 parts: **diastole** and **systole**. The first half of a heartbeat is the sound of the mitral and tricuspid valves closing. The second half is the sound of the aortic and pulmonary valves closing. During diastole, the ventricles relax and fill with blood. During systole they contract and pump blood out to the body.

The rate and force of contraction of the heart and the degree of narrowing or widening of blood vessels are controlled by

different hormones and the autonomic nervous system, the part of the nervous system that controls involuntary activity.

Heart Rate

The heart beats because of a tiny electrical current that originates in the heart's pacemaker, called the **sinoatrial node**. Rhythmic electrical impulses or discharges cause the contraction of muscle fibers in the heart. While a horse is at rest, its sinoatrial node discharges about 15 times per minute.

Heart Sounds and Murmurs

Heart sounds are produced by the rapid acceleration and deceleration of blood and the resulting vibrations in the heart due to the circulation of blood. They can be heard using a stethoscope. In horses, 4 heart sounds can possibly be heard. An absence or abnormality of one of these sounds may indicate a heart abnormality.

Heart murmurs are vibrations that can be heard coming from the heart or major blood vessels and generally are the result of turbulent blood flow or vibrations of heart structures such as part of a valve. Murmurs are typically described by their

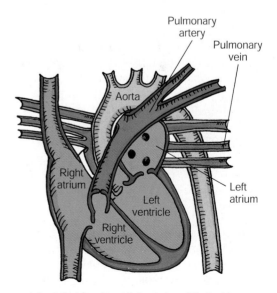

A look inside a horse's heart (modified with permission from *The Merck Manual of Medical Information*, Second Home Edition, 2003)

timing (that is, whether they occur continuously or only intermittently), intensity (that is, whether they can be heard easily or with difficulty), and location. In horses, early systolic and diastolic murmurs can be noted in the absence of heart disease or anemia (having too few red blood cells). A short, high-pitched, squeaking, early diastolic cardiac murmur is sometimes seen in healthy young horses.

Arrhythmias

Arrhythmias are abnormalities of the rate, regularity, or site of heartbeat formation. An arrhythmia does not necessarily indicate heart disease. Many arrhythmias have no functional significance and require no specific treatment. Some arrhythmias, however, may cause severe signs such as loss of consciousness due to lack of blood flow to the brain or lead to sudden death. Many disorders are associated with abnormal heart rhythms.

Atrial fibrillation is a type of arrhythmia that commonly occurs in horses. In atrial fibrillation, the electric current running through the atria is not coordinated, stimulation of the atrioventricular node is frequent but random, and the heart rate is rapid and irregular.

Pulse

A pulse is the rhythmic expansion of an artery that can be felt with the fingertips during physical examination. A jugular pulse in the neck can be noted in normal animals. A pulse may be absent, increased (strong), or decreased (weak)—each of which may indicate a specific type of heart disease or defect.

■ HEART DISEASE AND HEART FAILURE

Unlike diseases of many other organ systems, cardiovascular diseases generally do not go away but almost always become more serious. In addition, cardiovascular diseases may be more difficult to detect and quantify because the heart cannot be seen and is protected so well by the rib cage. In horses, cardiovascular disease is less common than in people, dogs, or cats. However, because horses are often expected to perform work or athletic feats, the cardiovascular condition of the animal may be relatively more important.

Heart disease can be defined as any abnormality of the heart. It encompasses a wide range of conditions, including congenital abnormalities and disorders of physical structure and function. It can be classified by various methods, including whether the disease was present at birth or not (that is, congenital or acquired), causes (for example, infectious or degenerative), duration (for example, long- or short-term), clinical status (for example, left heart failure, right heart failure, or biventricular failure), or by physical structure malformation (for example, ventricular septal defect).

Heart failure is any heart abnormality that results in failure of the heart to pump enough blood to meet the body's needs. It is not a specific disease; rather, it is a condition in which congestion or an abnormal accumulation of fluid, decreased blood flow to the body, and/or abnormally low blood pressure arise as the final consequence of severe heart disease. Heart disease can be present without ever leading to heart failure. Heart failure, however, can only occur if heart disease is present because it is a consequence of heart disease. (For a more detailed discussion of HEART FAILURE, *see* page 598.)

Abnormalities of the Cardiovascular System

The following abnormalities of the cardiovascular system can lead to heart disease: 1) the heart valves fail to close or open properly (valvular disease); 2) the heart muscle pumps too weakly or relaxes inadequately (myocardial disease); 3) the heart beats too slowly, too rapidly, or too irregularly (arrhythmia); 4) the blood vessels offer too great an interference to blood flow (vascular disease); 5) there may be openings between chambers of the left side and right side of the heart (cardiac shunts); 6) there is too little or too much blood compared with the ability of the blood vessels to store that blood; and 7) there is parasitism of the cardiovascular system.

Signs associated with any of these diseases are due either to inadequate blood flow through the organs (signs include exercise intolerance, weakness, and fainting) or to blood damming up in organs, which causes fluid to leak from blood vessels into tissues (signs include abnormal accumulation of fluid in the lungs or abdomen). A horse showing signs of having too little blood in the tissues to sustain normal function is said to be in heart failure. An animal showing signs caused by blood damming up in poorly drained organs is said to be in congestive heart failure. When there is not enough oxygen in the blood, the mucous membranes develop a blue tinge, and often there is an increased concentration of red blood cells.

Horses with heart disease may deteriorate gradually, most often due to pulmonary failure, or they may die suddenly, due to a nearly instant stoppage of blood circulation. Pulmonary failure occurs because the lungs become too stiff to bring in adequate oxygen.

■ DIAGNOSIS OF CARDIOVASCULAR DISEASE

A veterinarian often diagnoses cardiovascular disease by reviewing the medical history and signs, conducting a physical examination, and interpreting the results of specific tests or imaging procedures. The physical examination includes using a stethoscope to listen to the sounds made by the horse's internal organs, especially the heart, lungs, and abdominal organs, x-rays, electrocardiography (recording electrical activity of the heart), and echocardiography (a type of ultrasonography).

Most cardiovascular diseases can be diagnosed by physical examination and x-rays. Electrocardiography is a specific test for diagnosis of arrhythmias. Echocardiography is excellent for confirming tentative diagnoses, for detecting heart

tumors, or for detecting pericardial disease. Occasionally, more specialized tests such as cardiac catheterization (using a thin flexible tube inserted and threaded through an artery into the heart) or nuclear studies (x-ray tests that include injection of radioactive isotopes) are necessary. (For a more detailed discussion of DIAGNOSIS OF CARDIOVASCULAR DISEASE, *see* page 56.)

General Signs of Cardiovascular Disease

Horses with heart disorders or defects may have a general loss of condition, become fatigued easily (particularly after exercise), have difficulty breathing or shortness of breath, and show signs of weakness (including fainting or collapse). In addition, excess fluid that has accumulated in the chest or abdominal area may indicate heart failure. Signs may show up only after exercise, but over time they may occur even when the horse is at rest.

■ TREATMENT OF CARDIOVASCULAR DISEASE

Treatment of cardiovascular disease should be specific for the type of disease. Some defects can be repaired or corrected with surgery, while other conditions can be managed with medical therapy using one or a combination of drugs. In general, the goals of treatment are to minimize damage to the heart muscle, control the accumulation of fluids in the lungs, improve circulation, regulate the heart rate and rhythm, ensure that there is enough oxygen in the blood, and minimize the risk of blood clot formation.

Common Types of Drugs for Cardiovascular Disease

There are many medications that a veterinarian can prescribe to treat cardiovascular disease and heart failure. The type of disorder will determine the type of medication prescribed. Medications must be given directly as prescribed; otherwise, they may not be effective and may even cause serious complications and harm. (For a more detailed discussion of common medications for heart disease, *see* page 57.)

■ CONGENITAL AND INHERITED DISORDERS OF THE CARDIOVASCULAR SYSTEM

Congenital abnormalities of the cardiovascular system are defects that are present at birth. They can occur as a result of genetic defects, environmental conditions, infections, poisoning, medication taken by the dam, poor maternal nutrition, or a combination of factors. For several defects, an inherited basis is suspected based on breed and breeding studies. Congenital heart defects are significant not only for the effects they produce but also for their potential to be transmitted to offspring through breeding.

The most common congenital defects in horses are ventricular septal defect, patent ductus arteriosus, tetralogy of Fallot, and tricuspid dysplasia. Arabian horses have a relatively higher rate of congenital defects than other breeds; a variety of defects have been reported for this breed. However, it is important to understand that the overall number of horses with congenital defects is very low.

Detecting Congenital Heart Defects

It is important to detect a congenital heart defect as early as possible. Certain defects can be corrected with surgery, and treatment should be performed before the defect leads to congestive heart failure or irreversible heart damage. If the defect is discovered in a recently purchased horse, you may be able to return it for a refund. Horses with congenital heart defects are likely to die prematurely, causing emotional distress. Animals purchased for performance have limited potential and will likely be unsatisfactory. Early detection also prevents continuing genetic defects into breeding lines.

The evaluation of most animals with a congenital heart defect may include a physical examination, electrocardio-graphy (recording electrical activity of the heart), x-rays, and echocardiography (ultrasonography). These steps allow diagnosis and an assessment of the severity of the defect. Once the diagnosis has been made and the severity determined, treatment options can be developed and a medical opinion given as to the likely outcome of the disease.

Congenital heart defects produce signs that vary depending on the type of heart failure involved and the severity of the defect. Left- or right-sided heart failure may develop. Possible signs include shortness of breath or difficulty breathing, coughing, fatigue, or an accumulation of fluid in the lungs or abdomen.

General Treatment and Outlook

The medical importance of congenital heart disease depends on the particular defect and its severity. Mildly affected horses may show no ill effects and live a normal life span. Defects causing significant circulatory disturbances will likely cause death in newborn (or unborn) foals. Medical or surgical treatments are most likely to benefit horses with congenital heart defects of moderate severity. However, it is very important to understand what level of work or competition the horse will be physically able to carry out following treatment, in order to make the best decision.

Common Congenital Heart Defects

Although a wide variety of congenital defects may occur in horses, few of these occur often enough to warrant concern. The defects discussed below are those that occur with the greatest frequency in horses. However, these defects are still rare.

Ventricular Septal Defects

Ventricular septal defects (openings between the left and right ventricles) vary in both size and effects on blood circulation. Ventricular septal defects may occur with other abnormalities of the heart present at birth. They are the most common congenital defects in horses.

Shunting of blood from the left ventricle into the right ventricle is the most common result of this defect, due to the higher pressures of the left ventricle. Blood shunted into the right ventricle is recirculated through the blood vessels in the lungs and left heart chambers, which causes enlargement of these structures. The right ventricle may enlarge as well. Significant shunting through the pulmonary arteries can induce narrowing of these vessels, leading to reduced blood flow or increased blood pressure. As resistance rises, the shunt may reverse (that is, become a right-to-left shunting of blood).

Signs depend on the severity of the defect and the shunt direction. A small defect usually causes minimal or no signs, and affected horses may be able to engage in moderate levels of physical activity. Larger defects may result in severe left-sided congestive heart failure. The development of a right-to-left shunt is indicated by a bluish tinge, fatigue, and exercise intolerance. Most affected animals have a loud murmur; however, this murmur is absent or faint when a very large defect is present or when shunting is right to left. Chest x-rays, echocardiography (ultrasonography), and other more specialized techniques may be used to confirm the defect.

Treatment also depends on the severity of signs and direction of the shunt. Horses with small ventricular septal defects do not typically require treatment and the outlook is good. Animals with a moderate to severe defect more commonly develop signs, and treatment should be considered. Horses with a ventricular septal defect should not be bred.

Patent Ductus Arteriosus

The ductus arteriosus is a short, broad vessel in the unborn foal that connects the pulmonary artery with the aorta. It allows most of the blood to flow directly from the right ventricle to the aorta. In an unborn foal, oxygenated blood within the main pulmonary artery is forced into the descending aorta through the ductus arteriosus, bypassing the nonfunctional lungs. In most species, the ductus closes at birth when the animal begins to breathe, allowing blood to flow to the lungs. In foals, however, the complete closure of the ductus may be delayed for up to a week after birth, causing a heart murmur.

If the ductus does not close within the first week, the blood flow is forced from chambers of the left side of the heart to those of the right side; these defects are called left-to-right shunts. They result in overcirculation of the lungs and enlargement of the heart chambers, which may result in arrhythmias. Over time, signs of left-sided congestive heart failure develop.

Tetralogy Of Fallot

Tetralogy of Fallot is a defect that produces a bluish tinge to skin and membranes because there is not enough oxygen in the blood. It is caused by a combination of pulmonic stenosis (an obstruction of blood flow from the right ventricle), a ventricular septal defect (*see* above), thickening of the muscle fibers of the right ventricle, and varying degrees of the aorta rotating to the right.

The effect of this grouping of defects depends primarily on the severity of the pulmonic stenosis, the size of the ventricular septal defect, and the amount of resistance to blood flow provided by the blood vessels. Consequences may include reduced blood flow to the lungs (resulting in fatigue and shortness of breath) and generalized lack of oxygen in the blood causing a bluish tinge to skin and membranes. Red blood cells may be abnormally increased, leading to the development of blood clots and poor circulation of blood.

Electrocardiographs, x-rays, and echocardiography (ultrasonography) can help confirm the diagnosis. Treatment options include surgery and medical management, but the outlook is guarded to poor.

Tricuspid Dysplasia (Atresia)

Tricuspid dysplasia refers to abnormal development or malformation of the tricuspid valve of the heart, allowing regurgitation of blood back into the right atrium. This defect is seen occasionally in horses at birth. Arabian horses are more likely to have tricuspid dysplasia, suggesting that there may be a genetic basis for the defect in some cases.

Longterm tricuspid regurgitation leads to volume overload of the right heart, enlarging the right ventricle and atrium. Blood flow to the lungs may be decreased, leading to fatigue and an increased rate of respiration. As the pressure in the right atrium increases, blood pools in the veins returning to the heart, causing an accumulation of fluid in the abdomen.

The more severe the defect, the more obvious the signs will be in affected horses. Signs of right-sided congestive heart failure, such as accumulation of fluid in the abdomen and lungs, may be seen. A loud heart murmur is very noticeable. Arrhythmias, especially the sudden onset of a very high heart rate, are common and may cause death. In a severe form, called **tricuspid atresia**, the entire valve may be undeveloped or absent.

Electrocardiography and x-rays may show enlargement of the right ventricle and atrium, while the malformed tricuspid valve can sometimes be seen using echocardiography (ultrasonography). The outlook for horses with these signs is guarded, although mild defects may pose few problems.

■ HEART FAILURE

Heart failure is not a specific disease or diagnosis. It is a syndrome in which severe dysfunction results in failure of the cardiovascular system to maintain adequate blood circulation. There are limited and specific mechanisms by which heart disease can result in failure of the cardiovascular system. Therefore, there are limited and specific signs that can develop as a result of heart failure. Heart failure can be divided into 4 functional classifications: systolic myocardial failure, impedance to cardiac inflow, pressure overload, and volume overload.

Systolic myocardial failure is a general reduction in the ability of the heart muscle to contract. There is reduced wall motion during contraction of the ventricles. If the reduction is significant, normal blood flow cannot be maintained. It may be caused by trauma, infection, drugs or poisons, electric shock, heat stroke, or tumors. Some cases have no known cause.

Heart failure caused by **impedance (obstruction) to cardiac inflow** can result in a decrease in blood flow. This may be caused by external compression of the heart (for example, fluid in the sac surrounding the heart), diastolic dysfunction resulting in a stiff ventricle and reduced ventricular filling, or abnormalities to physical structures of the heart.

Heart failure caused by **pressure overload** occurs as a result of longterm increases in stress to the heart wall during contraction. This may result from the obstruction of blood flow from the heart or increased blood pressure throughout the body or in the arteries of the lungs.

Volume overload heart failure occurs as a result of any disease that increases volume of blood in the ventricle(s), thus increasing blood flow. Eventually, this can bring on signs of congestive heart failure. Diseases that result in volume overload myocardial failure include valve disease (for example, degenerative valve disease of the atrioventricular valves) and left-to-right shunts (for example, patent ductus arteriosus, ventricular septal defect).

Compensatory Mechanisms

The cardiovascular system maintains normal blood pressure and blood flow. In heart disease, the body uses compensatory mechanisms to attempt to normalize these functions and offset the negative effects of the disease on the body. Unfortunately, the longterm activation of these compensatory mechanisms can damage the heart muscle and other organs, leading to further heart failure. (For a more detailed discussion of compensatory mechanisms, *see* page 66.)

Treatment

It is important to treat heart failure in order to improve heart muscle performance, control arrhythmias and blood pressure, improve blood flow, and reduce the amount of blood filling the heart before contraction. All of these can further damage the heart and blood vessels if not controlled. It is also necessary to reduce the amount of fluid in the lungs, abdomen, or chest cavity.

There are many types of drugs available for treating heart failure. The specific drugs, dosage, and frequency used will vary depending on the causes and severity of the heart failure and other factors. Your veterinarian is best able to determine the appropriate medications for your horse. All drugs prescribed by your veterinarian must be given as directed. Otherwise, they may not be effective and may even cause serious complications and harm.

Diuretics are usually prescribed to reduce fluid overload. Digitalis and digoxin, part of a group of drugs known as positive inotropes, may be used to help the heart muscle contract. ACE inhibitors (ACE stands for angiotensin-converting enzyme) and vasodilators can widen blood vessels and thus lower blood pressure. Beta-adrenergic blocking drugs (also called beta-blockers) and calcium channel blockers are helpful in some cases of congestive heart failure. In addition to drugs, other types of treatment are sometimes recommended, such as surgical procedures to remove excess fluid buildup from the chest cavity or abdomen.

ACQUIRED HEART AND BLOOD VESSEL DISORDERS

There are many specific acquired heart diseases that have been identified in horses. The ones discussed below are the most common.

Degenerative Valve Disease

This acquired disease is characterized by thickening of the heart valves. In horses, degenerative valve disease most often affects the aortic, mitral, and tricuspid valves. The condition generally occurs slowly over time and is most common in middle-aged and older horses. In many horses, signs are uncommon because significant left ventricular volume overload and enlargement do not occur.

A veterinarian can often diagnose degenerative valve disease based on physical examination findings and appropriate imaging procedures, which may include chest x-rays and echocardiography (ultrasonography). A heart murmur may be heard.

Horses with mild or moderate valve disease and no signs have a good outlook and can usually still be used for physical activity that is not overly strenuous. Horses with more severe disease should not be ridden or exercised and have a poor outlook.

Myocarditis

Myocarditis is a local or widespread inflammation of the heart muscle, with degeneration or death of the heart muscle cells. There are numerous causes, including several viruses and bacteria, particularly *Streptococcus* species. Equine infectious anemia virus (*see* page 799) tends to cause myocarditis. Less common causes include severe deficiencies of vitamin E or selenium and ingestion of monensin (a feed additive found in some cattle feeds).

Signs of right-sided heart failure are common and include accumulation of fluid in the abdomen, congestion in veins, and large pulsations in the jugular vein. A murmur or arrhythmia may be noted on examination.

Treatment is directed at improving the ability of the heart to contract, relieving fluid buildup, and controlling the narrowing of blood vessels (which can increase blood pressure) through the use of appropriate medication.

Infective Endocarditis

The endocardium is the thin membrane that lines the heart cavity. Infection of the endocardium typically involves one of the cardiac valves, although endocarditis of the cavity's wall may occur. Infection is caused by bacteria carried in the blood. The infection gradually destroys the valve and keeps it from working properly. In horses, the aortic and mitral valves are most commonly affected. The tricuspid valve is rarely affected, and pulmonic valve infective endocarditis is exceedingly rare.

Treatment is directed at controlling signs of congestive heart failure, resolving any significant arrhythmias, killing the bacteria that started the infection, and eliminating the spread of infection. (For a more detailed discussion of INFECTIVE ENDOCARDITIS, *see* page 71.)

Pericardial Disease

The pericardium is the membrane that surrounds the heart. When fluid builds up within this membrane, the heart is compressed. The pressure on the heart reduces its ability to pump blood. This condition is called **cardiac tamponade.** The compression significantly affects blood circulation and causes swollen jugular veins and accumulation of fluid in the abdomen. In addition, too little oxygen reaches the body's tissues.

In horses, septic pericarditis (resulting from infection) and pericarditis of an unknown cause are the most commonly reported types of pericardial disease. Signs vary based on the amount of fluid that has accumulated; these may include unwillingness or inability to exercise, lack of appetite, listlessness, and abdominal swelling due to fluid accumulation. Blood tests show signs of an infection in horses with suspected septic pericarditis.

Horses with cardiac tamponade require urgent treatment. Pericardiocentesis (inserting a needle into the sac to withdraw the fluid), is the most common initial treatment. Pericardiocentesis is

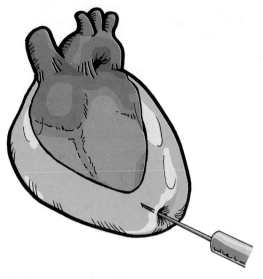

Fluid can be removed from the pericardial sac to relieve pressure on the heart muscle.

relatively easy to perform and serious complications are rare. Broad-spectrum antibiotics, intravenous fluids, and corticosteroids may also be given.

High Blood Pressure (Hypertension)

Systemic hypertension is an increase in the body's blood pressure. There are 2 major types of systemic hypertension. Essential (primary) hypertension, which is of unknown cause, is rare in most animals, but common in humans. Secondary hypertension results from a specific underlying disease. Pulmonary hypertension is elevation of blood pressure in the blood vessels of the lungs. In horses, pulmonary hypertension may occur as a result of left-sided congestive heart failure. (For more information on high blood pressure, *see* page 73.)

▉ BLOOD CLOTS AND ANEURYSMS

A **thrombus** is a blood clot that may form when the blood flow of an artery or vein is restricted. It frequently causes obstruction to blood vessels at its site of origin. The clot can be classified based on

A clot in the jugular vein usually resolves with appropriate therapy.

its location and the syndrome it produces. Examples of this condition in horses include venous thrombosis (a blood clot in a vein often associated with having a catheter inserted into it for a long period of time) and pulmonary arterial thrombosis (a blood clot in the pulmonary artery). All or part of a clot may break off and be carried through the bloodstream as an **embolus** that lodges someplace else at a point of narrowing. Blockage of a blood vessel can also occur when foreign material (for example, bacteria, air, or fat) is carried into the bloodstream. Some clots are infected. Blood clots generally result in an inadequate supply of blood reaching nearby tissues.

An **aneurysm** is an enlargement of a blood vessel caused by weakening of the middle layer of the blood vessel. Disruption of the tissue layer lining the inside of the blood vessels associated with an aneurysm can cause formation of a blood clot with subsequent blockage of a blood vessel by the clot.

Signs and Diagnosis

A sudden onset of difficulty breathing is often associated with a clot in the lungs. Infective clots in the heart are associated with endocarditis (*see* page 600). Clots in the heart that are not infective are associated with myocardial (heart muscle)

disease. Tissue death due to loss of blood supply in the kidneys or reproductive system can produce blood in the urine or abdominal pain. Blockage of blood vessels to other organs of the abdomen may cause similar signs.

In horses, cranial vena cava thrombosis may result from blockage of blood vessels due to a clot in a jugular vein or extension of an inflamed lining of the right atrium. Jugular vein thrombosis in horses often follows catheterization or an injection and will cause swelling, heat, and pain of the affected area with thickening of the jugular vein. Blockage of both jugular veins by clots can cause fluid accumulation and swelling of the head and neck due to the difficulty of blood returning to the heart. Ultrasonographic examination of the affected vein can determine the extent of the clot and degree of obstruction. Horses with colitis (inflammation of the colon) and other gastrointestinal disorders are at increased risk for developing jugular thrombosis.

The larvae of the worm *Strongylus vulgaris* migrate through the horse's arteries and can cause inflammation of the walls of an artery. This can develop into blood clots and aneurysms in horses infested by these parasites. Blockage or death of intestinal tissue can occur. Signs are those of colic, constipation, or diarrhea. The colic usually keeps returning, and attacks may be severe and prolonged. With the recent introduction of newer drugs that destroy or flush out parasitic worms and improved treatment plans, this is becoming an uncommon disorder.

Blood clots of the aorta and the iliac arteries (with or without aneurysm) produce a characteristic syndrome in horses. Affected horses appear normal at rest; however, exercise results in weakness of the hind limbs with lameness on one or both sides, muscle tremors, and sweating. Severely affected horses may show signs of exercise intolerance, weakness, and an unusual lameness that resolves after a short rest. In severe cases, the hindquarter muscles weaken and waste away, and lameness may occur after only mild exercise. Severe paralysis of both hind limbs and an inability to rise may also occur. Affected horses are anxious, appear painful, and rapidly go into shock. The hind limbs are cold, and no pulse is felt in either iliac artery. Ultrasonographic examinations can be helpful in evaluating blood flow in the aorta and iliac arteries.

Treatment

Embolic pneumonia caused by endocarditis is treated with longterm antibiotics (given for several weeks) and, in some cases, anti-inflammatory drugs and drugs to reduce fever. The outlook for recovery is guarded at best, and the performance of recovered horses is often decreased.

Treatment of blood clots in veins is usually limited to supportive care, including hydrotherapy of accessible veins, anti-inflammatory drugs, and injectable antibiotics to control infection. Surgical removal of jugular veins that have been blocked by blood clots has been performed successfully in horses, but unless both veins are severely affected, the inflammation will resolve with appropriate medication. Thrombosis of the cranial or caudal vena cava generally does not respond to treatment and the outlook is poor.

In horses, aneurysms due to *Strongylus vulgaris* rarely rupture; the chief concern is blood clots within the intestines that can cause colic. Generally, removal of the clot is impractical, as another would likely form. Antibiotics and drugs used to kill the migrating larvae are of considerable value. The best approach to cranial mesenteric and aortic-iliac thrombosis in horses is prevention and control of strongyles (*see* page 631).

CHAPTER 45

Digestive Disorders

■ INTRODUCTION

The digestive system includes all of the organs that are involved in taking in and processing food. It begins with the mouth and includes the esophagus, stomach, liver, pancreas, intestines, rectum, and anus.

The process of digestion begins when your pet picks up food with its mouth and starts chewing. Enzymes found in saliva begin breaking down the food chemically. The process continues with swallowing, additional breakdown of food in the stomach, absorption of nutrients in the intestines, and elimination of waste. Digestion is critical not only for providing nutrients but also for maintaining the proper balance of fluid and electrolytes (salts) in the body.

The functions of the digestive system can be divided into 4 main categories: digestion, absorption of nutrients, motility (movement through the digestive tract), and elimination of feces.

When treating a digestive system problem, the veterinarian's goal is to first identify the part of the system where the problem lies and then to determine the specific cause and appropriate treatment.

General Signs of Digestive System Disorders

Signs of digestive system disease can include excessive drooling, diarrhea, constipation, loss of appetite, bleeding, abdominal pain and bloating, shock, and dehydration. Horses cannot vomit or regurgitate.

Diarrhea is often a sign of digestive system disorders, but it can have many causes. Large-volume, watery diarrhea usually is associated with hypersecretion, a condi-

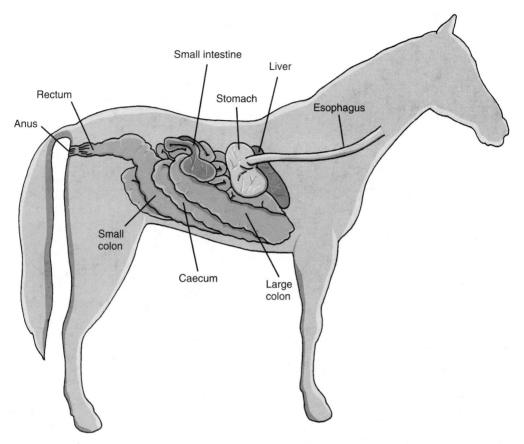

Major digestive organs of the horse

tion in which excess fluid is secreted into the intestines. This can be caused by bacterial infection.

Diarrhea can also be caused by malabsorption, the failure to properly absorb nutrients. Malabsorption is due to a defect in the intestinal cells responsible for absorption. This condition can be caused by viral infection, by a defect that limits the ability of the intestines to absorb liquids, or by defects in the pancreatic secretions needed for effective digestion. Dehydration and electrolyte (salt) imbalance, which may lead to shock, are seen when large quantities of fluid are lost (for example, from diarrhea).

Digestive problems can also show up as changes in the number or character of bowel movements. Normal horse feces

are apple-sized lumps that are well formed but somewhat moist. Digestive problems can result in feces that are too soft or too hard. Hard, dry feces can predispose horses to colic. The number of bowel movements per day, the color of the feces, and any tell-tale signs of blood should be reported to your veterinarian.

Colic (*see* page 616) is one of the most common digestive problems in horses. It usually involves intense abdominal pain, which your horse may show by pawing repeatedly at the ground, kicking at the abdomen, laying down and rolling, and looking at the flank. Other signs of colic include intense sweating, a distended or swollen abdomen, and straining to defecate. Colic is a serious condition that can have several causes; if you suspect that your horse has colic, prompt veterinary attention is necessary.

Examination of the Digestive System

A diagnosis can only be made after the horse is thoroughly examined. Your complete, accurate description of your horse's history (age, signs of illness, current diet, deworming schedule, when teeth were last floated, past problems, and so on) combined with a veterinarian's physical examination can often determine the cause of a digestive system problem. When a digestive system disorder is suspected, your veterinarian's initial examination might include the following: a visual inspection of the mouth for changes in the color and moistness of the mucous membranes; a determination of heart rate; a "hands on" examination of the abdomen and chest area to evaluate the shape, size, and position of the abdominal organs; tapping the abdomen or using a stethoscope to listen for sounds that indicate gas or for other abnormal sounds such as splashing; a rectal examination; and a visual examination of feces.

Depending on what the initial examination reveals, additional tests might include performing bacterial culture and virus isolation from feces; passing a stomach tube; using a long needle to collect fluid from distended abdominal organs or from the abdominal cavity for analysis; creating

x-ray images, which may include use of special dyes, to detect blockages and other problems; performing abdominal ultrasonography; obtaining a biopsy (sampling and microscopic analysis) of liver or intestinal tissue; or conducting additional blood tests to detect possible malabsorption or maldigestion.

Infectious Diseases

Because it is easy for foreign organisms and other "invaders" to enter the digestive tract through the mouth, this body system is prone to infection by bacteria, viruses, parasites, and other organisms (*see* TABLE 1). These infections spread in various ways, but the most common are by direct contact or by contamination of food or water by feces.

People and animals all have small numbers of certain intestinal microorganisms found within the digestive tract—most commonly in the intestines—that become established within a few hours after birth. These so-called intestinal flora are actually beneficial, in some cases aiding in digestion and in others helping to prevent infection. However, sometimes infections occur when these organisms, normally found in small numbers, suddenly multiply. This can occur after a period of stress, under unhygienic conditions, or in an animal whose immune system is weakened. For example, salmo-

Table 1. Infections of the Digestive System in Horses	
Organism	**Examples**
Viruses	Rotavirus, vesicular stomatitis
Rickettsiae	*Ehrlichia risticii* (Potomac horse fever)
Bacteria	Enterotoxigenic *Escherichia coli*, *Salmonella* species, *Rhodococcus equi*, *Actinobacillus equuli*, *Clostridium perfringens* types B and C
Protozoa	*Eimeria* species
Fungi	*Aspergillus fumigatus*
Algae	*Prototheca* species
Parasites	Numerous (*See* page 629.)

nellosis in horses can develop after transportation, extended anesthesia, or surgery.

Diagnosis of a specific infectious disease depends on finding and identifying the organism suspected to cause the disease. This may require one or more fecal samples, which will be submitted to a diagnostic laboratory.

Parasites are a frequent cause of digestive tract disorders in horses. Many species of parasites can infect the digestive tract and cause disease. The life cycles of some parasites are direct, which means that there is only one host. Eggs and larvae are passed in the feces, develop into an infective stage, and are eaten by the horse. No other animals or organisms are needed to complete the life cycle. Other parasites have complex life cycles that involve an intermediate host such as an insect. In this situation, infection is acquired when the intermediate host—or parasite shed by that host—is consumed by the horse. The extent to which a parasite affects an animal depends on the parasite itself, as well as the animal's own resistance, age, nutrition, and overall health.

Parasites can cause severe disease or simply decrease your horse's overall fitness. Some of these parasites also infect humans. Because parasite infection is easily confused with other illnesses, diagnosis depends on the veterinarian's knowledge of seasonal cycles of parasite infection, as well as examination of feces for evidence of parasite eggs or larvae. In some cases, blood tests can also be used to detect the presence of parasites. (For a more detailed discussion of GASTROINTESTINAL PARASITES OF HORSES, *see* page 629.)

Noninfectious Diseases

Many digestive system diseases are not caused by infective organisms. Their causes include overeating, eating poor-quality food, chemicals, obstruction caused by swallowing foreign objects, or injury to the digestive system. Digestive system disease can also be caused by enzyme deficiencies, damage to the digestive tract such as from stomach (gastric) ulcers, or birth defects. Digestive system signs such as diarrhea may also occur because of kidney, liver, or adrenal gland disease. The causes are uncertain in several diseases, including stomach ulcers in foals. Some conditions, such as colic, may have both infectious (such as damage from internal parasites) and noninfectious (such as excessive gas or simple obstruction) causes.

In noninfectious diseases of the digestive tract, usually only a single animal is affected at one time; exceptions are diseases associated with excessive food intake or poisons, in which multiple animals living together can be affected.

Treatment Overview of Digestive System Disorders

Specific disorders and their treatments are described later in this chapter; however, some general principles are listed in this section. Eliminating the cause of the disease is the primary objective of veterinary treatment; however, a major part of treatment is often directed at the signs of the disease and is intended to relieve pain, correct abnormalities, and allow healing to occur.

Elimination of the cause of the disease may involve drugs that kill bacteria or parasites, antidotes for poisons, or surgery to correct defects or displacements.

Use of drugs to correct diarrhea or constipation is done depending on the specific case. Although such drugs might seem to be a logical choice, they are not beneficial in every situation. For example, diarrhea can actually be a defense mechanism for the animal, helping it to eliminate harmful organisms and their toxins. In addition, the available drugs may not always give consistent results.

Replacement of fluids and electrolytes (salts) is necessary in cases where the animal is at risk of dehydration, such as from excessive diarrhea.

Relief of distension (bloating) by stomach tube or surgery may be required if the digestive tract has become distended with gas, fluid, or food.

Pain relief is sometimes provided. However, a horse being given pain medicine must be watched carefully to ensure that the pain relief is not masking a condition that is becoming worse.

Treatment and Control of Infectious Disease

Bacterial and parasitic diseases of the digestive system are often treated with medications designed to kill the infectious organisms. There are currently no specific medications for treatment of viral diseases. Antibiotics (drugs effective against bacteria) are commonly given for several days until recovery is apparent, although their effectiveness in treating digestive system disease is still uncertain. Antibiotics may be given by injection when septicemia (infection of the blood) is apparent or likely to occur. Your veterinarian will make the decision whether to prescribe antibacterial medication based on the suspected disease, likelihood of benefits, previous results, and cost of treatment.

Advances in understanding the life cycles of parasites, coupled with the discovery of effective antiparasitic drugs, have made successful treatment and control of digestive system parasites possible. Response to treatment is usually rapid, and a single treatment is often all that is needed unless reinfection occurs or the damage caused by the parasites is particularly severe.

Control of digestive diseases and parasites depends on practicing good sanitation and hygiene. This is achieved primarily by providing adequate space for your horse and by regular cleaning of its living areas. In addition, adequate nutrition and preventive medical care will minimize the stress on your horse and help it to stay healthy.

■ CONGENITAL AND INHERITED DISORDERS

Congenital abnormalities are conditions that an animal is born with; they are often called birth defects. Some of these conditions are inherited and tend to occur within particular families or breeds, while others are caused by chemicals or injury during pregnancy. For still others, the cause is unknown. The most common congenital abnormalities of the digestive tract in horses are described below.

Mouth

A **cleft palate** or **cleft lip** (harelip) is caused by a defect in the formation of the jaw and face during embryonic development. It leads to a gap or cleft in the center of the lip, the roof of the mouth (hard palate), or both. Often this condition leaves an open space through the roof of the mouth into the breathing passages. These conditions have a wide range in severity. Usually the upper lip and palate are affected; a cleft in the lower lip is rare. Most cases are inherited, although nutritional deficiencies during pregnancy, drug or chemical exposure, injury to the fetus, and some viral infections during pregnancy have also been suggested as causes.

Cleft palate or lip will usually be noticed shortly after birth when the foal might have problems with nursing. For example, milk might be seen dripping from the nostrils or the foal might have difficulty suckling and swallowing. The veterinarian can usually identify the problem by examining the foal's mouth, although a cleft involving only the soft palate may be difficult to see. Affected foals require intensive nursing care, including hand or tube feeding and possibly antibiotics to treat secondary respiratory infections. Surgical correction is effective only in minor cases. The decision to perform surgery should be made carefully, and the affected animal should be neutered to prevent passing the defect on to future offspring.

Brachygnathia occurs when the lower jaw is shorter than the upper jaw. This condition is called "parrot mouth" in horses. It can be a minor problem or a serious defect depending on the degree of abnormality. Mild cases may cause no problems. More severe cases can cause damage to the hard palate (roof of the mouth) or restriction of normal jaw growth.

Prognathia occurs when the lower jaw is longer than the upper jaw. If a foal is badly affected, nursing may be impossible. Treatment consists of rasping or shearing the points and projections on the teeth that are causing difficulty.

Teeth

In most animals, having too few teeth is rare. **Extra teeth** occur in some horses; these extra teeth are commonly found in the incisor and molar regions of the mouth. The result may be crowding and rotation of the teeth. Extra teeth are either removed or periodically rasped, especially if they interfere with chewing or are irritated by a bit.

Abnormalities in placement or shape of teeth sometimes occur. This may affect the incisors and result in rotation or over-lapping of adjacent teeth. Usually, this does not cause any problems, but it may require extraction of some teeth if crowding or bite abnormalities occur.

Enamel defects such as disruption of tooth enamel formation may be caused by fever, trauma, malnutrition, poisoning, or infection. The damage can vary, depending on the severity and duration of the cause, from pitted enamel to the absence of enamel with incomplete tooth development. Affected teeth are prone to plaque and tartar accumulation and subsequent tooth decay.

Cysts of the Head and Neck

Cysts (lumps) in the head and neck can be caused by imperfections during fetal development. These need to be distinguished by your veterinarian from abscesses or lumps caused by infection or other disease. **Dentigerous cysts** arise from abnormal tooth development and often contain tooth fragments. These cysts can be found in horses less than 3 years of age, and they may be difficult to distinguish from **cystic sinuses**, another condition which can result in face or jaw distortion. Surgical removal of the cysts is required. The veterinarian can then make a final diagnosis based on examination of the removed tissue.

Hernias

A hernia is the protrusion of a portion of an organ or tissue through an abnormal opening. One common congenital type, called a **hiatal hernia**, involves an abnormal opening in the wall of the diaphragm (the sheet of muscle that separates the chest from the abdomen) or the abdomen. The defect may allow abdominal organs to pass into the chest or bulge beneath the skin. Hernias may be congenital (present at birth) or result from injury. Signs of a hernia vary from none to severe and depend on the amount of herniated tissue and its effect on the organ involved.

Hernias involving the abdominal wall are called umbilical, inguinal, or scrotal, depending on their location (*see* TABLE 4, page 85). Diagnosis of **umbilical hernias** is usually simple, especially if the veterinarian is able to push the hernia back through the abdominal wall (called reducing the hernia). If not, the hernia must be differentiated from an umbilical abscess, which is common in horses. The veterinarian may need to use a fine needle to collect tissue or fluid for confirmation of the diagnosis. These hernias are corrected by surgery. The tendency to develop hernias may be inherited.

Inguinal hernias are sections of the intestine that break into the inguinal

Cysts

Some cysts arise from abnormal tooth development.

canal located in the groin. Inguinal hernias in colts often resolve spontaneously during the first year of life, so early corrective surgery is not recommended unless the hernia is strangulated or so large that it interferes with walking.

Stomach

Besides hiatal hernias (*see* page 607), another abnormality involving the stomach is **pyloric stenosis**. It can be acquired or inherited, but the inherited form is rare in horses. Pyloric stenosis results from muscular thickening of the "exit" of the stomach (pyloric sphincter). This obstructs the flow of digested food from the stomach to the small intestine. Signs may include loss of appetite and other signs, such as abdominal pain, that are usually associated with colic. Treatment is through dietary modification and medication. In more severely affected cases, surgery may be beneficial.

Small and Large Intestine

Maldigestion is a condition in which certain foods are not properly digested. **Malabsorption** occurs when nutrients are not properly absorbed into the bloodstream. Both of these conditions often cause chronic, persistent digestive system problems including weight loss and diarrhea. Malabsorption and maldigestion are often treated with a combination of dietary changes and medication; the exact treatment will depend on the condition being treated.

A defect in the colonic nerves called **ileocolonic agangliosis** is seen in white foals produced by matings of Overo horses. Although the foals appear normal at birth, they soon develop colic and die on the second day. The affected horses are white and have blue irises. Diagnosis can be confirmed by the lack of specific nerves in the colon.

Congenital defects of the rectum and anus generally result from arrested embryonic development. Inherited closures (atresias) of the small- and large-intestinal tracts are relatively common in large animals and are always fatal. Atresia of the colon has been reported in Percheron horses. **Segmental aplasia** (also called rectal agenesis) is a condition in which the rectum is closed off before reaching the anus. Surgical correction is difficult because the location of the closure varies, and damage to nerves in the area may occur during surgery.

Liver

The most common congenital liver defect present at birth is a portosystemic shunt (*see* page 640). In a healthy animal, blood coming from the intestines is processed by the liver, which removes toxins from the bloodstream before they reach the brain or other organs. In an animal with a portosystemic shunt, however, blood bypasses the liver through one or more "shortcuts" (shunts) and enters directly into the general circulatory system. Signs of a portosystemic shunt include nervous system disturbances and a failure to grow and thrive. In the late stages, protein-containing fluid may accumulate in the abdomen, a condition called **ascites**. Your veterinarian may also notice enlargement of the kidneys and kidney stones. A definite diagnosis is made by using an opaque dye to highlight the blood vessels, followed by x-rays. This procedure can identify the location of the shunt and determine whether it is single or multiple. It also allows the veterinarian to assess whether surgical correction is possible. Animals with multiple shunts tend to do poorly.

Other liver developmental anomalies include **hepatic (liver) cysts**, which generally cause no signs. They are significant mainly because they must be differentiated from abscesses in the liver. A veterinarian who finds a hepatic cyst will often want to examine the kidneys because hepatic cysts often occur along with polycystic kidney disease. (For a more detailed discussion of POLYCYSTIC KIDNEYS, *see* page 783.)

■ DENTAL DEVELOPMENT

Each species of animal has its own unique type of teeth, depending on what food the animal normally eats. For example, a meat-eating animal such as a cat has quite different teeth than a horse, which eats grasses and grains. However, all domestic animals have 2 sets of teeth during their lives, as humans do: a set of deciduous ("baby") teeth that fall out, and a set of permanent teeth that develop later.

Most horses have 28 deciduous teeth. Mature stallions have 40 to 42 teeth, while mature mares have 36 to 38 teeth. The difference is due to the fact that the canine teeth, which appear at around 4 to 5 years of age, are often not seen in mares. Deciduous teeth appear early—usually within 2 weeks of birth. The first permanent teeth to appear are the first premolars sometimes called "wolf teeth." They are usually found in the upper jaw; however, they are sometimes found in the lower jaw as well. The permanent molars erupt at about 1, 2, and 3.5 years of age. The replacement of deciduous incisors and premolars by the permanent successors starts at about 2.5 years of age. All permanent teeth are usually present by the time the horse reaches 5 years of age (*see* TABLE 2, page 555).

Estimation of Age by Examination of the Teeth

In horses, the structure of the teeth allows the age of the animal to be estimated by the eruption times and general appearance of the teeth, particularly the lower front teeth (lower incisors). However, tooth appearance is affected by individual and breed variations and differences in environmental conditions, so it does not provide an exact measure (*see* TABLE 3, page 555).

Equine incisor teeth develop certain wear-related visible features that are traditionally used for estimating age. For example, the "dental star" is a yellowish-brown mark that appears at the bite surface as the tooth wears. Its shape and position, as well as the appearance of the white spot in its center, are related to age. The shape, size, and time of disappearance of indentations on the bite surface are additional indicators of age. Progressive dental wear also causes an alteration of tooth shape, and the angle of the teeth changes with age. In young

Dental Terms

What Most People Call It	What Your Veterinarian Might Call It
Adult tooth	Permanent tooth
Baby tooth	Deciduous tooth
Bad breath	Halitosis
Bite	Occlusion
Cavities or tooth decay	Dental caries, tooth infection
Extra teeth	Polyodontia
Eye teeth	Canines
Front teeth	Incisors and canines
Gum	Gingiva
Gum disease	Periodontal disease, periodontitis
Lower jaw	Mandible
Roof of the mouth	Palate
Root canal	Endodontic treatment
Tartar	Calculus
Teeth cleaning	Dental prophylaxis
Uneven bite	Malocclusion
Upper jaw	Maxilla
Wolf teeth	First premolars

horses, the upper and lower incisors are positioned in a straight line. With increasing age, the angle between upper and lower front teeth becomes sharper as the teeth wear away.

■ DENTAL DISORDERS

Horses, like most other large animals, are herbivores (plant eaters). If a horse's teeth do not function well, it will be unable to eat properly and its overall health may be at risk. Unlike human teeth, a horse's teeth continue to erupt throughout its life. The continual eruption helps to compensate for the wear caused by frequent grazing. When the teeth are not worn down evenly, problems can arise. Horses require regular dental care and preventive treatment throughout their lives.

Signs of Dental Problems

Dental conditions such as broken or irregular teeth are common causes of loss of appetite or weight or a general loss of condition. The classic signs of dental disease in horses include difficulty or slowness in feeding and a reluctance to drink cold water. While chewing, the horse may stop for a few moments and then start again. Sometimes, the horse will hold its head to one side as if it were in pain. The horse may form its food into a ball in the mouth, then drop the food after it has been partially chewed. Occasionally, the semi-chewed mass of feed may become packed between the teeth and the cheek. To avoid using a painful tooth or a sore mouth, the horse may swallow its food before chewing it, leading to indigestion, colic, or choke. Uncrushed, unchewed grain may be noticed in the manure.

Other signs of dental disease in horses include excessive drooling and blood-tinged mucus in the mouth, accompanied by bad breath from tooth decay. There may be a lack of desire to eat hard grain accompanied by loss of body condition or poor coat condition. Extensive dental decay and accompanying infection around the teeth may lead to a sinus infection and occasional discharge from one nostril. Infection may cause swelling of the face or jaw. A horse with a dental problem may be reluctant to take the bit, shake its head when being ridden, or resist training due to discomfort and cuts inside the mouth.

Dental Examination and Preventive Care

If you or your veterinarian suspects a dental problem, a thorough physical examination, followed by a detailed and thorough examination of the mouth and teeth, is necessary. To do this effectively, the veterinarian may give the horse a sedative. Some cases may require general anesthesia.

Regular dental prophylaxis (preventive care) is important to maintain your horse's health. Enamel edges should be filed down twice yearly while the permanent teeth are coming in (from about 2½ to 5 years of age) and as frequently as needed after that, depending on the diet of the horse. This procedure is sometimes referred to as **floating.** Horses that graze on free range or grass usually require yearly preventive care. Horses that are kept in a stall and fed hay and grain usually require at least twice yearly oral examinations and preventive care. The objective of dental prophylaxis is to remove any sharp edges of teeth and maintain the normal biting surface. Dental prophylaxis can often be done with simple restraint or the use of sedatives and pain medication.

Normal dentition   Enamel points

Sharp enamel points can form in a horse's mouth. They can be treated by regular filing (floating).

Birth Defects and Developmental Abnormalities

In horses, the most common oral birth defect (congenital deformity) is **parrot mouth**, in which the upper jaw is relatively longer than the lower jaw. In horses, many cases of abnormal dental development result from exposure to poisons during pregnancy, although some are inherited. **Extra teeth** (polyodontia), such as double rows of incisor teeth or extra cheek teeth, are seen occasionally. Treatment is determined on a case-by-case basis and may require extraction of the extra teeth.

Abnormal Tooth Eruption

Abnormal eruption of permanent teeth is usually caused by trauma to the face or jaw, in which the bud of the permanent tooth is damaged by a fracture or by the repair process. In horses, delayed eruption or impaction of cheek teeth (such as from overcrowding) is a common cause of bone inflammation and subsequent tooth decay.

Irregular Tooth Wear (Enamel Points)

Most large animals have a lower jaw that is narrower than the upper jaw. In horses, this can eventually cause the development of enamel points on the cheek side of the upper teeth and on the tongue side of the lower teeth. Extreme forms of this condition may be seen in older horses. In such cases, treatment is often not completely effective. A special diet will probably be prescribed for affected horses. As described earlier, enamel points are best treated by regular filing.

Wave Mouth and Step Mouth

Wave mouth and step mouth refer to a bite surface that is irregular. These conditions are caused by uneven wear of the teeth and are the result of local pain. In time, gum disease usually develops. Such conditions are best prevented by regular, routine dental care. Once dental irregularities are severe, dental procedures cannot completely correct the problem. However, some improvement is usually possible, even in severe cases where dental care needs to be supplemented by a special diet.

Gum Disease

In all animals, some inflammation of the gums (periodontitis) typically occurs when teeth come in. However, if bite problems occur, severe gum disease is inevitable. In horses, this is a common result of trauma to the mouth, fractured teeth, impacted teeth, and most importantly, irregular wear.

Tooth Decay

Infection may enter the soft center (pulp) of the teeth in various ways. Some horses may be prone to tooth infection because of incomplete development of tooth enamel. Depending on the site of the decayed tooth, there may be other signs of disease such as inflammation in the mouth or sinuses. If a horse is not examined until a dental infection is advanced, it may be difficult to determine the initial cause of the problem. Abnormal eruption of teeth appears to be the primary cause of many dental problems in horses.

When tooth decay is advanced, extraction of the tooth is typically required. This procedure may require surgery with general anesthesia, although in some cases sedation and local anesthetics can be used. After tooth extraction, the surrounding teeth gradually move to close the gap where the missing tooth was located. However, this process is never complete, and the tooth opposite the gap will tend to be longer than normal because it has nothing to wear it down. These irregularities can be corrected by grinding and realigning the teeth every 6 months.

Because of the problems that a missing tooth can cause in horses, techniques to preserve the teeth are often considered. In some cases, it is possible to preserve an infected tooth by performing a root canal. This procedure involves removing the diseased tooth pulp and replacing it with synthetic material. The age of the horse and the extent of damage will guide your veterinarian's recommendation as to the best course of treatment.

■ DISORDERS OF THE MOUTH

Problems of the mouth can involve the lips, teeth, tongue, or gums. These disorders can be caused by injury, infection, or internal diseases (for example, kidney failure).

Lip Lacerations

Wounds of the lips and cheeks are common in horses. They may be caused by a fall, a kick, the use of inappropriate bits or restraint devices or, more commonly, from the horse having its lips and sometimes jaw caught as it "plays" in its stall. Lip lacerations may be accompanied by a broken jaw or teeth and additional skin tearing (especially if the horse panics). Because of the large number of blood vessels in the lip region, healing is usually rapid. However, once a wound has penetrated into the mouth, more extensive treatment is needed to avoid complications.

Paralysis of the Tongue

This condition may be seen in newborns because of the placement of obstetric snares used to aid in delivery. Such newborns need to be managed carefully to ensure that they are able to nurse. Intravenous fluids and anti-inflammatory treatments are often needed. If the condition persists for more than 10 days after birth, the likelihood of regaining normal function of the tongue is slight. Inflammatory diseases and trauma can also cause temporary paralysis of the tongue, as can conditions such as upper respiratory infections, meningitis, botulism, encephalomyelitis, or brain abscesses.

Oral Tumors

Tumors of the mouth and lips other than viral papillomas (see PAPILLAR STOMATITIS, page 613) are uncommon in young horses. In gray horses, malignant skin cancers (melanomas) may develop near the corners of the mouth and cause hard, thickened, tumorous areas that may not be detected until they are well advanced. Treatment of oral and lip melanomas in the horse is often unsuccessful, although treatment with prescription medication may provide relief.

Slaframine Poisoning

Slaframine poisoning (see page 1158) can occur when horses eat forages, particularly clovers, that are infected with the fungus *Rhizoctonia leguminicola*. The fungus produces the toxic alkaloid slaframine. There are no abnormalities inside the mouth, and the only sign that may help in diagnosis is profuse drooling. Removal of infected forage from the diet brings on rapid recovery. Most horses recover fully.

Inflammation of the Mouth (Stomatitis)

Inflammation of the mouth (stomatitis) has many possible causes. Trauma to the mouth or contact with chemical irritants (for example, horses that lick at their legs after having been blistered) may result in inflammation. Traumatic injury from the ingestion of the sharp awns of barley, foxtail, porcupine grass, and spear grass, as well as feeding on plants infested with hairy caterpillars, will result in severe stomatitis in horses. Some infectious diseases also cause inflammation of the mouth.

Frothy drooling, reluctance to eat, and resistance to examination of the mouth are the common signs of stomatitis. The veterinarian will examine the horse's mouth (usually with the animal under sedation) to allow removal of any embedded foreign matter such as grass awns. If the cause is ingestion of foreign material, changing the quality and quantity of the hay may allow recovery.

It is important to diagnose the cause of the inflammation, if possible, because a number of serious diseases can cause stomatitis. Other illnesses with similar signs include actinobacillosis, vesicular stomatitis, and malignant catarrhal fever.

Papillar Stomatitis

Viral papillomas (warts) are found around the lips and mouths of young animals. These lesions usually improve on their own. However, in some cases, they may grow together to form masses around the muzzles of young horses. If this is undesirable for cosmetic reasons, the papillomas can be treated by a veterinarian using liquid nitrogen to burn them off, vaccines, or a combination of treatments.

▥ PHARYNGEAL PARALYSIS

Pharyngeal paralysis refers to paralysis of the upper throat (pharynx). The paralysis makes swallowing difficult or impossible. It may be caused by a nervous system disorder (for example rabies or botulism) or other disease that causes collapse, obstruction, or malfunction of the pharynx. Conditions such as poisoning, head trauma, and tumor formation may dramatically affect function of the pharynx in many species. In some instances, the condition may be partial or one-sided (for example, guttural pouch disease) and the horse may be able to swallow, although complications may occur.

In general, pharyngeal paralysis results in severe problems with swallowing; food and saliva come back out through the mouth and nose. Collapse of throat tissues may cause breathing difficulties. Affected animals are at risk of pneumonia from inhaling food and liquid (aspiration pneumonia), dehydration, and circulatory and respiratory failure. Signs of pharyngeal paralysis include fever, coughing, and choking. This condition may be fatal. In many cases, emergency surgery to provide an airway (tracheostomy) must be done before any more detailed analysis of the condition can be performed.

In general, treatment for pharyngeal paralysis is directed toward relieving signs. If the paralysis is caused by another disorder, treatment of that disorder may help correct the problem. Treatment may include drugs to control inflammation, antibiotics to control the complications of aspiration pneumonia, the draining of pharyngeal abscesses (if they are present), and alternative routes of nutrition, such as a feeding tube. In many cases, the outlook is poor. Your veterinarian will consider the welfare of the animal when recommending a course of treatment.

▥ DISORDERS OF THE ESOPHAGUS

Esophageal disorders in horses include choking and esophageal narrowing (strictures).

Obstruction of the Esophagus (Choke)

Esophageal obstruction (choke) is a condition in which the esophagus is obstructed by food masses or foreign objects. It is by far the most common esophageal disease in horses. Obstruction is most common when a horse quickly eats dried grains or hay. Diseased teeth can also limit the ability of a horse to chew forage.

The classic sign associated with choke is regurgitation of food through the nostrils. When saliva and food is discharged through the nasal openings, the materials often spill into the airway. This brings on coughing. The horse is anxious and may stretch and arch its neck but may still attempt to continue to either eat or drink. The horse should be moved away from any food or water, or food and water removed from its stall. Objects lodged in the upper esophagus may be felt by the veterinarian during examination. An endoscope may be used to confirm the diagnosis.

Many cases of obstruction caused by greedily eaten grain or hay improve on their own. The horse should be kept off feed and water as directed by a veterinarian. Mild sedatives, muscle relaxants, or smooth muscle stimulants may be prescribed. Horses should be monitored, because recovery may take from a few hours to several days. The longer the obstruction is present, the greater the danger of damage from pressure on the tissues of the esophagus and complications such as aspiration pneumonia (inflammation caused by inhalation of food particles into the lungs).

If the obstruction does not dislodge spontaneously and the horse resists the veterinarian's attempts to insert a feeding tube through the nose, general anesthesia may be necessary. Repeated pumping and siphoning of warm water by the veterinarian usually loosens the impacted food. After the mass has been removed, food should be introduced gradually, as directed. The horse will probably receive injected antibiotics and pain medications, and the esophagus may need to be examined again to monitor healing.

The main complication of choke is aspiration pneumonia caused by inhalation of food. Longterm obstruction can cause tissue death in the esophagus due to prolonged contact with the mass of food. Constrictions of the esophagus from scar tissue can also result.

Some cases of obstruction are not due to food blockage of the esophagus itself. In these other cases, the cause may be injury to the neck or surrounding tissues, leading to constriction of the esophagus. Such cases may be diagnosed from a history of recurrent choke or obstruction. The veterinarian may use x-rays (possibly including contrast material) to locate the site of the obstruction within the esophagus. If the problem is outside of the esophagus, surgery may be necessary to determine and correct it.

Esophageal Strictures (Narrowing)

Esophageal strictures of unknown cause are sometimes seen in foals. Diagnosis can be difficult because the signs are similar to those seen in foals with cleft palates or cysts in the throat. The diagnosis is confirmed by inserting an endoscope (a flexible tube with a tiny camera at the end) to examine the esophagus. If the esophagus is narrowed, the condition is treated either with dilation (stretching of the narrowed region) or with surgery.

▓ STOMACH (GASTRIC) ULCERS IN HORSES

A gastric ulcer is a sore in the stomach lining that occurs when the lining has

been damaged by stomach acid and digestive enzymes. Mild stomach ulcers are seen in more than half of foals. In most cases, these ulcers cause no signs and heal without treatment. Ulcers can be found in approximately 30% of adult horses, but the percentage is much higher (up to 90%) in race horses. They are least common among horses turned out onto pasture and most common among Thoroughbred race horses at racetracks. Ulcers are found in 40 to 60% of show horses, event horses, western performance horses, and endurance horses. The prevalence and severity of ulcers increase as the intensity of exertion increases. Stomach ulcers develop in as little as 5 days.

Causes of stomach ulcers vary. Horses' stomachs secrete hydrochloric acid continuously, and the stomach acidity of a horse or foal is very high between periods of eating or nursing, as well as during intensive exercise. The upper part of the equine stomach is lined by tissue that is very similar to the esophagus and is highly sensitive to acid. The lower part of the stomach is more resistant to acid. Continuous grazing leads to low stomach acidity, while intermittent feeding or having food withheld leads to greater acid secretion and ulceration. Exercise may be linked to ulcer formation, possibly due to increased abdominal pressure during exercise pushing acidic stomach contents into the acid-sensitive upper portion of the stomach. The effects of different feeds on stomach acidity and ulcer formation have not been thoroughly studied. Excessive doses of nonsteroidal anti-inflammatory drugs (NSAIDs) are known to induce ulcers, but are not the cause in most cases. Recent research suggests that horses may be infected with a species of *Helicobacter*, bacteria associated with ulcers in humans. However, a role for this organism in stomach ulcers of horses has not been confirmed.

Most foals with stomach ulcers do not show signs unless the ulcers are widespread or severe. The classic signs for stomach ulcers in foals include diarrhea, grinding of teeth, poor nursing, lying down, and excessive drooling. None of these signs is specific for stomach ulcers, so your veterinarian will also consider other possible causes. When a foal does show signs of ulcers, the ulcers are usually severe and should be diagnosed and treated immediately. Sudden stomach perforation without prior signs sometimes occurs in foals.

Adult horses with ulcers also show nonspecific signs that can include abdominal discomfort (colic), poor appetite, mild weight loss, poor body condition, and attitude changes. In most cases, the signs of ulcers are subtle and may not be associated with the disorder until the horse receives treatment that lowers stomach acidity.

Neither signs nor laboratory tests are specific for stomach ulcers. Endoscopy is the only reliable method of diagnosis for this disorder.

Complications related to stomach ulcers are most frequent and severe in foals and include perforation of the stomach and gastroesophageal reflux (a condition similar to acid reflux in humans). Some ulcers in the region where the stomach joins the intestine can cause constriction; this complication is seen in both foals and adult horses. In rare cases, severe stomach ulceration causes thickening and contracture of the stomach.

Suppressing or reducing the level of acidity in the stomach to protect the stomach wall is the primary treatment objective. This can be accomplished with several types of medication including antacids, histamine type-2 receptor antagonists, and proton pump inhibitors. Proton pump inhibitors are the most effective way to treat and prevent ulcers. One medication, omeprazole, is licensed to treat and prevent ulcers in horses. To treat ulcers in your horse, the veterinarian will consider the animal's overall health and condition, the severity of the ulcer(s), and other factors before recommending a treatment program. Prevention of ulcers is preferable to treatment once they are present. This can be accomplished by a combination of managing the risk factors (feeding schedule, stall confinement, travel, and training) and using medication designed for ulcer prevention.

■ GASTROINTESTINAL OBSTRUCTION (BLOCKAGES)

Intestinal obstructions (blockages) are common in horses. Blockages can occur in any part of the digestive tract and can cause sharp and severe pain. These obstructions can stop the flow of food through the digestive tract and, in some instances, impair blood flow or cause damage to intestinal tissues.

It is not always possible to determine the cause of an individual blockage. Feed impactions, parasite infections or migrations, abnormal dental conditions, and changes in diet, daily activities, medications, or sudden stress may play a role in functional obstructions. Coarse feeds, reduced water consumption, and eating foreign objects are other common factors. Blockage may occur in a variety of locations within the intestines.

Twists, muscle tension changes, and changes in the position of various parts of the intestines can also bring on impaction or blockage. Altered intestinal movement and, possibly, strenuous exercise and rolling may cause or contribute to obstructions. Broodmares may be predisposed to obstructions, especially during pregnancy and shortly after giving birth. Standardbred stallions and colts develop inguinal and scrotal hernias more commonly than other breeds.

Pain is the most common sign of intestinal obstruction in horses. The horse may pace, stretch, kick at its abdomen, and, upon occasion, roll or vocalize. Otherwise, the signs are the same as for colic (*see* page 616).

For functional obstructions in horses, the treatment is the same as for colic (*see* page 616), and may include medicine to relieve pain, fluid treatment, and intestinal lubricants and possibly laxatives.

Mechanical obstructions such as a twisted intestine frequently require surgery to make a definitive diagnosis. If the obstruction is a foreign (nonfood) object that has penetrated the digestive system, care needs to be taken to locate and repair the injuries (there is often more than one injured site). This normally requires surgery. Antibiotics are usually prescribed before surgery to reduce infection. Additional supportive treatment may include fluids, electrolytes (salts), and calcium. Horses that require exploratory abdominal surgery to locate and correct an obstruction have an overall longterm survival rate of 50%, but early surgical intervention can improve that outlook.

Prevention of all—or even most—cases of intestinal obstruction is not possible. However, the likelihood is reduced if changes in diet and daily routines are gradual, adequate water is available at all times, dental care is regular and appropriate, and parasites are controlled. Access to coarse feeds and foreign materials should be avoided or corrected.

■ COLIC

Over the years, colic has become a broad term for a variety of conditions that cause horses to experience abdominal pain. Because it is such a broad term, it is used to refer to conditions that vary widely in cause and severity. Your veterinarian's understanding of your horse's digestive system structure and function is key to making a diagnosis and providing appropriate treatment for cases of colic (*see* TABLE 2).

The most common signs of colic are pawing repeatedly with a front foot, looking back at the flank region, curling the upper lip and arching the neck, repeatedly raising a rear leg or kicking at the abdomen, lying down, rolling from side to side, sweating, stretching out as if to urinate, straining to defecate, distention of the abdomen, loss of appetite, depression, and a decreased number of bowel movements. It is uncommon for a horse with colic to exhibit all of these

A horse with colic may kick at the abdomen, stretch out, or lie down and roll.

signs. Although these signs are reliable indicators of abdominal pain, they do not indicate which portion of the digestive system is affected.

Diagnosis and treatment occur only after a thorough examination of the horse, including a review of its history of any previous problems or treatments. Both the location and the cause of the colic should be determined. The list of possible conditions that cause colic is long (*see* BOX). For that reason, your veterinarian may begin treatment based on the most likely diagnosis and then make a more specific diagnosis later, if necessary or possible. Information that you can provide includes the length and severity of the colic episode, as well as the horse's deworming history (schedule, treatment dates, drugs used), when the teeth were floated last, if any changes in the type or amount of feed or water supply have occurred, and whether the horse was at rest or exercising when the colic episode started.

Treatment

Horses with colic may or may not need surgery. Almost all horses will require some form of medical treatment, but only those with certain mechanical obstructions of the intestine need surgery. The type of treatment is determined by the cause of colic and the severity of the disease. If the horse appears to have only mild pain and the

Table 2. The Veterinarian's Examination of a Horse with Colic

Type of Procedure	Why It is Done
Assessment of breathing and heart rate	Increased heart rate or breathing rate can indicate pain.
Examination of mucous membranes (inside of mouth)	Paleness indicates poor oxygen level in blood; dryness indicates dehydration; discoloration indicates poor blood flow in the tissues.
Insertion of tube through nose into stomach	Because horses cannot vomit, the tube can allow release of gas or fluid that would otherwise result in stomach rupture. For this reason, passing a stomach tube may save the horse's life in addition to helping the veterinarian diagnose the condition causing the colic.
Listening to various parts of the abdomen with a stethoscope	Sounds (or lack of sound) may indicate the presence of fluid, gas, and/or obstruction.
Sample of abdominal (peritoneal) fluid via needle	Composition (protein and white blood cells) can reveal extent of intestinal damage.
Rectal examination	Allows the veterinarian to feel the intestines, their position, and their content.
Ultrasonography	Provides a view of certain abdominal organs, including the intestines. Some conditions (such as an inguinal hernia or an intussuception) can be seen.

heart and circulatory system are functioning normally, the horse may be treated using medication or other non-surgical methods and the response evaluated. Ultrasonography can be used to evaluate the effectiveness of nonsurgical treatment in some cases. If necessary, surgery can be used for diagnosis as well as treatment.

If the horse has severe pain and has signs indicating loss of fluid from the bloodstream (high heart rate and discoloration of the mucous membranes), the initial aims of treatment are to relieve pain, restore tissue blood supply, and correct any abnormalities in the composition of the blood and body fluids.

If damage to the intestinal wall is suspected, specific antibodies or medications may be administered to prevent or counteract the ill effects of bacterial toxins that leave the intestine and enter the bloodstream. If there is evidence that the colic episode is caused by parasites, one of the first goals of treatment would be to eliminate the parasites.

Common Causes of Colic (Abdominal Pain) in Horses

- The wall of the intestine is stretched excessively by gas, fluid, or partially digested food.
- There is tension on the tissue that supports the intestines (mesentery) due to the intestine moving out of its normal position.
- There is inflammation or ulceration in the stomach or intestine.
- Part of the intestine has reduced blood flow, most often as a result of passing through a hernia or severe twisting of the intestine.
- Inflammation develops which involves either the entire intestinal wall or the covering of the intestine.
- The intestine and/or its blood supply have become obstructed by feed, sand (if horses are fed on the ground where soil is sandy), parasites, or other foreign material.
- Enteroliths (rock-like concretions of material) have developed in the large intestine.

Pain Relief

Pain is mild in most cases of colic, and pain medication is all that is needed. This is the usual treatment if the cause of colic is believed to be a spasm of intestinal muscle or excessive gas in a portion of the intestine. If the pain is due to a more serious condition, such as an intestinal twist or displacement, some of the stronger pain medications may mask the signs that would be useful in making a diagnosis. For these reasons, whenever possible a thorough physical examination is performed before any medications are given. However, because horses with severe colic or pain may hurt themselves and become dangerous to people nearby, pain medication often must be given first. In addition, many horses with less severe problems may need pain relief until the other treatments have time to be effective.

Although pain relief usually is provided by medications, pain can be reduced in other ways. For example, the veterinarian's use of a stomach tube during diagnosis will also remove any fluid that has accumulated in the stomach because of an obstruction of the small intestine. The removal of this fluid not only relieves pain caused by distention of the stomach but also prevents rupture of the stomach.

Fluid Treatment

Many horses with colic benefit from fluid treatment to prevent dehydration and maintain blood supply to the kidneys and other vital organs. The fluids may be given either through a stomach tube or intravenous catheter, depending on the particular intestinal problem. Intravenous fluids may be needed for several days until intestinal function has returned, blood electrolyte (salt) concentrations are balanced, and the horse can maintain its fluid needs by drinking.

Protection against Bacterial Endotoxins

Endotoxins are a part of the outer coating of certain bacteria. Endotoxins are released when the bacteria die or multiply rapidly. Normally, endotoxins are contained within the intestines, but if the intestinal lining is damaged, they can escape into the abdominal cavity or bloodstream. Endotoxins then trigger an inflammatory response that can include fever, depression, reduced blood pressure, blood clotting abnormalities, and eventually death. One treatment is administration of antibodies or medications designed to neutralize the endotoxin. The effectiveness of this treatment is still being studied, however. In cases of colic, your veterinarian will be on the alert for damage to the intestinal lining and the possibility of complications due to endotoxins.

Intestinal Lubricants and Laxatives

A common cause of colic in horses is obstruction of the large intestine by dried digested food, sometimes mixed with sand. In most instances, lubricants or fecal-softening agents given through a stomach tube soften the impacted material, allowing it to be passed. Sometimes intravenous fluids are given during this procedure. The horse will normally need to be muzzled to prevent further impaction of feed while the obstruction is softening. Medications include mineral oil, dioctyl sodium sulfosuccinate (a soap-like compound), and psyllium hydrophilic mucilloid (an ingredient also found in some fiber products used by humans). When mixed with water, psyllium forms a gelatin-like mass that carries ingested food along the digestive tract. Horses that live in a sandy environment or that persistently develop impactions may be given psyllium powder in their feed, as directed by a veterinarian, to help prevent impaction.

Strong laxatives that stimulate intestinal contractions are not commonly used to treat impactions and, in fact, may worsen the problem. If an impaction does not start to break down within 3 to 5 days, surgery may be necessary to remove the impacted material.

Surgery

Usually, surgery is necessary only if there is a mechanical obstruction that cannot be corrected medically or if the obstruction also interferes with the intestinal blood supply. The latter condition causes death of the horse unless surgery is performed quickly. Occasionally, surgery is needed to diagnose the problem in horses with longterm colic that have not responded to routine medical treatment.

Specific Causes of Colic and their Treatment

Colic can be caused by several disorders of the stomach and intestines. The most common ones are discussed here.

Distention and Rupture of the Stomach

Excessive gas or intestinal obstruction can lead to distention of the stomach. This may be caused by overeating fermentable feeds such as grains, lush grass, or beet pulp. If untreated, this can rapidly progress to a rupture of the stomach. Signs include severe abdominal pain, increased heart rate, and retching. Once the stomach ruptures, the horse may act relieved or depressed. The outlook for survival is excellent if the condition is recognized and treated soon enough, but stomach rupture is fatal.

Obstruction of the Small or Large Intestine

Signs of colic may occur if the small or large intestine is obstructed or inflamed. The outlook for these conditions is guarded, so rapid diagnosis and treatment are critical.

The most common condition that causes obstruction of the small intestine is impaction (blockage of the intestine by food or other materials that have been eaten). It has been linked to eating high-fiber hay and infection by the tapeworm, *Anoplocephala perfoliata*. Young horses may be affected by impaction of the small intestine with ascarid parasites following deworming. In the large intestine, obstruction has also been linked to coarse feed, insufficient water intake, and diseased teeth. In some areas sand may be the cause of intestinal obstruction and colic. This is especially true if there is not enough pasture and the horse is fed on the ground. The sand may accumulate in the large intestine and eventually cause a blockage.

Signs in horses with impaction of the small intestine include mild to severe abdominal pain, reduced intestinal sounds, stomach reflux, and increased heart rate. Because the horse's condition may remain stable and the pain may be mild at first, many horses with this condition are not immediately referred for surgery. The condition often requires surgery, although it may respond to treatment with fluids, pain-relieving drugs, and mineral oil if identified early. A lack of normal intestinal contractions may occur after surgery. Adhesions within the abdomen (*see* below) are another potential complication.

In contrast, horses with impaction of the large intestine rarely require surgery. Almost all respond well to administration of laxatives, fluids, and mild analgesics.

Adhesions

Adhesions are fibrous connections between organs within the abdomen. They generally affect the small intestine and usually constrict the inner opening of the intestine. Adhesions develop in response to abdominal injury such as surgery, longterm distention of the intestine, inflammation, or migration of larval parasites. Signs range from mild, recurrent colic to severe, continual pain. Treatment involves surgery to remove the fibrous tissue and the affected portion of the intestine. Medications are also given to try to reduce the formation of new adhesions. However, adhesions often recur and the longterm outlook for horses with extensive adhesions is poor.

Inflammation of the Small Intestine

Inflammation of the first part of the small intestine is a poorly understood condition of horses. It has been reported in the southeastern and northeastern US, as well as in England and continental Europe. There may be fluid or bleeding within the intestinal wall, or tissue death in more severe cases.

Varying degrees of abdominal pain are the most common sign of the disorder. Treatment may be either medical (such as fluids and pain medication) or surgical. About half of the cases are fatal. Laminitis, or inflammation of the hoof (*see* page 682), is a common complication.

Lipomas

Colic caused by lipomas (benign fatty tumors) is sometimes seen in horses more than 10 years old. If the tumor is attached by a stalk to connective tissue in the abdomen, then it may wrap around a part of the intestine, shutting off its blood supply. Signs may include depression and severe abdominal pain, with rapid worsening of condition. Treatment requires removal of the tumor by surgery, along with any damaged sections of the intestine. If the problem is detected early, the outlook is good, but if surgery is not done before signs are advanced, the chances for recovery are fair to poor.

Twisting or Displacement of the Small or Large Intestine

Twisting of the intestines (volvulus) occurs when the intestine rotates around its attachment to the abdominal wall. This reduces the blood supply to the intestine, leading to colic. Horses with this condition are painful and have an increased heart rate. Dehydration is caused by movement of fluid into the stomach and intestine. The horse's condition may worsen rapidly. Displacement, without twisting, of the large intestine may occur and also leads to obstruction.

Treatment requires surgery to correct the positioning of the intestine. Removal of part of the intestine may also be required if it has been compromised by a lack of blood supply for too long. The outlook for recovery is good if the condition is detected and treated soon after it occurs. Adhesions (*see* page 619) may be a complication, especially if the illness is prolonged.

Inguinal Hernia

Inguinal hernias (commonly referred to as scrotal hernias) occur when the intestine passes from the abdomen into the inguinal canal that connects the testes to the abdomen. They occur in male horses, generally after breeding, trauma, or a hard workout. If the inguinal opening is large enough, part of the intestine may become trapped, causing colic. Hernias appear to be most common in Tennessee Walking Horses, American Saddlebreds, and Standardbreds. If the condition has been present for more than a few hours, the horse's condition worsens rapidly. Surgery is the usual treatment and may require removal of the testicle on the affected side, along with a portion of the intestine if it has become too damaged. The chances for survival appear to be breed-dependent, with Standardbred horses having a good outlook and Tennessee Walking Horses a fair to poor outlook. Presumably, this is because Tennessee Walking Horse stallions with inguinal hernias show few signs of pain, which may delay recognition of the problem and treatment.

Enteroliths (Intestinal Stones)

Enteroliths are hard masses composed of magnesium ammonium phosphate crystals that form around a foreign object (such as a piece of wire, stone, or nail) in the large intestine of horses. Enteroliths may be seen singly or in groups and are commonly found in horses in certain parts of the United States, including California, the southwest, Indiana, and Florida. Most horses with enteroliths are about 10 years old; horses younger than 4 years old are rarely affected. A common factor associated with formation of enteroliths may be the consumption of alfalfa hay, which results in a higher pH and increased concentrations of calcium, magnesium, and sulfur in the large colon.

Many horses with this condition have a history of recurring colic, which may indicate that the enterolith(s) had caused partial or temporary blockage of the large intestine. Depending on the location of the enterolith, the horse may be in severe pain. Heart and respiratory rates increase, and the mucous membranes may be pale or pink. Generally, intestinal distention is evident to the veterinarian on rectal examination, but the mass cannot usually be felt. In areas where the problem is common, x-rays may be used to identify the enteroliths.

Treatment involves surgery to decompress the intestine and remove the stone(s). The outlook is excellent. Veterinary practices in areas where this condition commonly occurs report survival rates of 95%.

■ INTESTINAL DISORDERS OTHER THAN COLIC

Diarrhea, weight loss, and protein loss are common signs of intestinal disorders in horses. These signs can be caused by many different disorders, including infectious diseases, parasites, reactions to poisons or drugs, stress, changes in diet, and certain types of colic (*see* page 619). Because the signs are similar for many intestinal disorders, determining the cause can sometimes be challenging and is often best left to a veterinarian. A correct diagnosis will lead to better treatment and, in many cases, a faster recovery.

Diarrhea in adult horses can be acute (sudden and often severe) or chronic (persisting a month or more). It is often difficult to diagnose the cause of chronic diarrhea. It can occur due to inflammatory or cancerous conditions involving the intestine or disruption of normal digestion. Possible causes include sand colic and abnormalities such as those associated with inflammatory bowel disease. The body's response to certain components of feed may play a role in chronic diarrhea of horses due to bowel inflammation, but has not frequently been established as a cause. Diarrhea in adult horses should be considered a serious event.

The causes of **weight loss** in horses are numerous and can involve many body systems. This discussion will cover only diseases of the digestive tract. **Protein loss** (called hypoproteinemia) may or may not be associated with weight loss. The disorders commonly associated with either of these signs are tumors, inflammatory bowel disease, and adverse reactions to treatment with nonsteroidal anti-inflammatory medication.

Salmonellosis

Salmonellosis is one of the most common infectious causes of diarrhea in adult horses. It is caused by many species of *Salmonella* bacteria and can cause severe disease if the bacteria or toxins it produces enter the bloodstream (septicemia). It can also cause inflammation of the small or large intestine (enteritis or colitis). Signs range from none to sudden, severe diarrhea, and even death.

The usual route of entry by the bacteria is by mouth. After entry, the organism multiplies in the intestines and causes intestinal inflammation. Young horses are the most susceptible. Penetration of bacteria into the intestinal surface contributes to tissue damage and diarrhea. Entry into the bloodstream may follow. The bacteria can also live in the lymph nodes and can cause infection in other parts of the body, such as the liver, lungs, joints, or bones, especially in foals.

Some horses that show no signs of disease may be carriers of *Salmonella*. Although most horses clear the infection in a few weeks, some can carry the bacteria for prolonged periods and shed it in the manure when stressed. In adults, most cases of disease develop after the stress of surgery or anesthesia, alteration in diet,

---

Diarrhea in Horses

Because of the large volume of the intestines of horses, massive fluid losses can occur in a short time. Thus, diarrhea in adult horses can be a serious event, and rates of illness and death may exceed those in other animals and humans. Any case of diarrhea in your horse that lasts more than a day or two, or that occurs repeatedly, is a cause for concern. Your veterinarian should be contacted for evaluation of the horse. Although a definitive cause can be determined in less than 50% of cases of diarrhea, treatment of most horses and foals with diarrhea is similar and can be started despite the lack of a precise diagnosis.

treatment with antibiotics, or transport. Mares may shed the bacteria while giving birth and infect the newborn foal. Salmonellosis in horses hospitalized for other causes is a major problem for equine clinics because horses that are hospitalized experience one or more of the stressors listed above. In these circumstances, a large number of vulnerable horses are present and carriers may shed the bacteria.

In newborn foals, the bacteria or its toxins are more likely to spread beyond the intestine into the bloodstream. Illness can develop suddenly and be severe; signs generally include lethargy, reduced suckling, and a high fever. Death occurs in 24 to 48 hours. In some foals these sudden signs of illness are not noticed. If the bacteria spread to joints or bones, the foal can become lame and have a fever.

In adult horses, intestinal inflammation is the most common form of the disease. Initially, there is fever, followed by severe, watery diarrhea. Straining during defecation can occur. The feces may have a foul odor and contain mucus, shreds of mucous membrane, and in some cases, blood. Abdominal pain and colic can also occur. Affected horses are severely dehydrated and many die within 24 hours of the onset of diarrhea if not treated promptly. A milder illness may develop in some adult horses. The signs include mild fever, soft feces, poor appetite, and dehydration.

A diagnosis of salmonellosis is based on signs and identification of the organism after laboratory examination of feces and tissues from affected animals.

Early treatment is essential for cases of salmonellosis in which the horse or foal has signs of dehydration, pain, or bacteria in the bloodstream (septicemia). Broad-spectrum antibiotics are given intravenously to treat septicemia. Oral medication may be provided in drinking water because affected horses are thirsty due to dehydration, and their appetite is generally poor. Some horses with severe or ongoing fluid and electrolyte (salt) loss will require treatment with intravenous fluids.

There is controversy regarding the use of antibiotics for intestinal salmonellosis (the type seen more commonly in adults). Oral antibiotics may damage the normal population of intestinal bacteria, which aid in digestion and help protect the animal from other, disease-causing bacteria. There is also concern that antibiotic use may increase the number of bacteria that can resist antibiotics and make the infection more difficult to treat. Horses with acute intestinal salmonellosis will probably be given fluids containing electrolytes (salts) intravenously to correct deficiencies of sodium and potassium. Plasma with a high concentration of antibodies against *Salmonella* may also be given. Some horses may require treatment with medications given via a tube that is passed into the stomach. These medications are designed to help heal the intes-

Controlling Salmonellosis

Owners can take several steps to control salmonellosis:

- Buy horses only from sources that are free of the disease.
- Isolate new horses when they arrive.
- Have a veterinarian check all new horses when they arrive to determine if they appear healthy.
- Protect feed and water supplies from fecal contamination.
- Be sure housing areas are thoroughly cleaned and disinfected between uses.

If you have an ill or known infected horse:

- Isolate the ill horse.
- Have your horse examined and tested by your veterinarian to determine the cause of illness.
- Start hygiene and cleaning routines for personnel working with infected horses.
- Remove all feces promptly and dispose of them away from horse housing or grazing areas.
- Thoroughly clean and sanitize all contaminated living areas.
- Follow your veterinarian's instructions for medication and care.

tine and absorb toxins produced by the bacteria.

Although the signs of disease may disappear, eliminating the bacteria from the body is difficult, particularly in adult horses.

Control and prevention are focused on reducing the likelihood of exposure to the bacteria and promoting the overall health of the horse. A horse could be exposed to the bacteria by contacting the feces of an animal (for example, another horse or a bird or rodent) that is shedding the bacteria. It is advisable to make every effort to avoid introduction of a carrier animal that is shedding the bacteria into the environment. Horses should be purchased from farms known to be free of the disease and should be housed away from the resident horses for about 2 to 3 weeks while their health status is monitored. Feed and water supplies should be high quality and must be protected from fecal contamination by rodents, birds, or any other animal that may be shedding the bacteria in its feces. Should the bacteria be detected in the environment, any contaminated living areas should be thoroughly cleaned and disinfected. It is critical that a well-thought-out plan for cleaning be made and all label instructions on disinfecting products be followed. Because *Salmonella* can also infect humans, anyone working with infected horses or wastes from infected horses should be aware of the risks and the need for good personal hygiene.

Potomac Horse Fever

Potomac horse fever is a syndrome producing mild colic, fever, and diarrhea in horses of all ages, as well as loss of foals in pregnant mares. It is caused by *Neorickettsia risticii* bacteria. The bacteria are found in parasites called flukes, which have been isolated from freshwater snails and appear to be present in a number of insects. One route of exposure is believed to be the horse's accidental ingestion of aquatic insects containing infected flukes. The disease is seen in spring, summer,

and early fall and is associated with pastures bordering creeks or rivers. It has recently been noticed that having lights on in barns at night attracts insects, which may fall in feed or water buckets.

Infection of the small and large intestine results in inflammation of the large intestine (colitis), which is one of the principal signs of the disorder. Early signs of Potomac horse fever include mild depression and loss of appetite, followed by a mild to high fever. At this stage, a veterinarian may be able to detect decreased intestinal sounds. A definitive diagnosis is based on identifying the *Neorickettsia risticii* bacteria in the blood or feces of infected horses using a DNA test.

Within 24 to 48 hours, a moderate to severe diarrhea and abdominal discomfort develops in about 60% of affected horses. Some horses develop severe blood poisoning and dehydration. Founder or laminitis (*see* page 682) can occur as a severe complication of the disorder in up to 40% of affected horses.

Several months following disease in pregnant mares, miscarriage of the foal due to fetal infection with *Neorickettsia risticii* may occur. The miscarriage is accompanied by an enlarged and retained placenta.

Sick horses are not contagious and can be housed with other horses. Potomac horse fever can be treated successfully with an appropriate antibiotic, if it is given soon after the disease begins. A response to treatment is usually seen within 12 hours. This is associated with relief from fever, followed by an improvement in attitude, appetite, and bowel sounds. If treatment is started early, signs frequently resolve by the third day of treatment. Generally, antibiotics are given for no more than 5 days. In horses with signs of enterocolitis, fluids and a nonsteroidal anti-inflammatory drug will likely be prescribed. Founder, if it develops, is usually severe and often resistant to treatment.

Several vaccines are commercially available; however, they do not appear to be very effective. Reducing the number of snails in rivers and ditches may be attempted to lessen sources of infection. No risk to humans from this disease is known.

Clostridia-associated Intestinal Inflammation

Clostridium bacteria have been diagnosed as a cause of intestinal inflammation in horses and foals. The exact role of the bacteria is still unclear, and it may be that multiple factors—such as stress, antibiotic use, and altered diet—are involved in the development of this disorder. Disease due to this infection is more common in foals but appears to occur in adult horses as well.

Signs of this condition include diarrhea with or without blood, colic, poor appetite, lethargy, and sudden death. These signs are similar to those seen in other causes of intestinal inflammation. Affected foals (usually less than 3 days old) often have bloody diarrhea and colic. Several foals on the same farm may be affected, but usually only one case occurs on a farm at a time. Diagnosis is based on signs and identification of the bacteria or the toxins produced by the bacteria in feces or tissue samples from the infected horse or foal. If you are asked to bring in a fecal sample for testing, follow your veterinarian's instructions in regard to the handling of these samples to preserve the bacteria.

In humans, *Clostridium* bacteria have been identified as an infection common in hospitals. This may also be seen in horses receiving hospital care. Veterinary hospital personnel are aware of this possibility and take special precautions to prevent the spread of the disease.

Treatment is similar to that for other causes of intestinal inflammation but is not always effective if the newborn foal has severe disease due to the infection. Treatment includes intravenous fluids and prescription drugs. Newborn foals may be given medication to help prevent stomach ulcers. Broad-spectrum antibiotics may also be prescribed. Foals with colic associated with ingestion of milk often require intravenous fluids and nutritional support. Drugs that are given via a tube into the stomach may help absorb the toxins produced by the bacteria and help the intestine heal. Intensive treatment may be required for several days until the condition improves.

Colitis-X

Colitis-X is an extremely rapid, usually fatal disease of horses, with a sudden onset of profuse, watery diarrhea and development of shock. Many affected horses have a history of stress. The cause of colitis-X is unknown, although multiple factors have been proposed, including severe salmonellosis, infection with clostridia, and endotoxemia (absorption of bacterial toxins into the bloodstream from the gut). Disease onset is often closely associated with stress such as surgery, anesthesia, strenuous athletic events, or transport.

The disease may begin with a short period of fever, but the horse's temperature soon returns to normal or below normal. Rapid breathing, rapid heart rate, and lethargy are present. Severe diarrhea develops, followed by extreme dehydration and shock. Death may occur within 3 hours of onset of signs. In some horses the progression of the disease is so rapid that the only sign is sudden death. In less sudden cases, death occurs within 24 to 48 hours. Colitis-X is almost always fatal.

Treatment for colitis-X usually is not effective but is similar to that for salmonellosis (*see* page 621). Large volumes of intravenous fluids are needed to treat the severe dehydration, and electrolyte (salt) replacement is often necessary.

Parasites

A number of parasites are known to cause diarrhea in horses. Both large and small worms called strongyles (*see* page 631) have been linked to chronic diarrhea in horses and foals. Infections with *Giardia* (*see* page 632) and *Cryptosporidium* (*see* page 632) protozoa can cause diarrhea in horses and foals.

Intestinal Disease Caused by Eating Sand or Dirt

Consumption of large amounts of sand, which then accumulates in the large intestine, can produce diarrhea, weight loss, or colic. Sand may be eaten accidentally along with food when the horse or foal is kept on sandy pasture or is fed hay or grain in a sandy area (paddock, stall, or pasture). Some horses or foals develop a habit of eating dirt and sand if it is in their environment.

A veterinarian can diagnose this condition based on history of exposure to a sandy environment, the presence of sand in the feces, "sand sounds" in the abdomen, and abdominal x-rays or ultrasonography. Treatment involves administering a fiber product (usually psyllium seed hull) by a tube inserted up through the nostril and into the stomach or added to the concentrate feed daily. Diarrhea generally resolves within 2 to 3 days after the start of treatment; however, 3 to 4 weeks of treatment is often necessary to remove all of the sand. The treatment may need to be repeated if the horse or foal is not removed from the source of sand. Preventive treatment with a fiber product may be recommended in areas where this condition is common.

Other Causes of Diarrhea in Horses

Some horses develop soft feces when first introduced to lush pastures, alfalfa hay, or a temporarily stressful situation such as a trailer ride, racing, showing, or visit to a veterinary hospital. This change in fecal consistency is not of medical significance as long as the horse is healthy in all other regards. It is important that horses with diarrhea have a physical examination and appropriate laboratory tests to exclude infectious causes and to determine whether treatment is required. Usually, the fecal consistency returns to normal when the horse adapts to its new diet or the stressful situation resolves.

Other causes of diarrhea or semiformed to watery feces in horses include grain overload, partial failure of the heart resulting in thickening of the intestinal wall with retained fluid, peritonitis, antibiotic treatment, kidney or liver failure, and numerous poisons (such as certain chemicals, plants, and insects). Diarrhea can also be seen while an impaction of the large intestine is resolving or being treated.

Diarrhea in Foals

Diarrhea in foals may be caused by bacterial or viral infection, parasites, and nutritional or environmental changes.

Foal Heat Diarrhea

At about 4 to 14 days after birth, foals often develop a mild diarrhea that resolves on its own. Although the cause is unknown, it may be associated with changes in the normal bacteria in the foal's intestines or alteration in diet as the foal begins to eat small amounts of hay and grain. The condition is often referred to as foal heat diarrhea because it appears at about the same time as the dam is undergoing her first estrous cycle after the foal's birth.

The foal remains active and alert and has a normal appetite. Vital signs remain normal. Feces are semiformed to watery and not foul-smelling or passed more frequently than is normal. Monitoring is important to ensure the foal's condition does not worsen. Specific treatment is usually not necessary, but application of a protectant to the skin around the buttocks helps prevent irritation from the diarrhea.

Bacterial Diarrhea

Several bacterial infections can cause intestinal inflammation and blood infection in newborn and young foals. Organisms that can be involved in diarrhea include *Salmonella* and *Clostridium* species and others. Intensive antibiotic treatment, correction of fluid loss and electrolyte (salt) abnormalities, and nursing care are usually needed. If a veterinarian determines that transfer of antibodies from the mother during suckling was not sufficient, a blood plasma transfer into the foal's blood may be performed. Your veterinarian will prescribe medication based on the diagnosis, the condition of the foal, and other factors.

Intestinal infection with the bacteria *Lawsonia intracellularis* has been associated with outbreaks of diarrhea, rapid weight loss, colic, accumulation of fluid under the skin (edema), and lowered levels of protein (due to loss from the intestines) in weanling foals on breeding farms in Canada and the United States. Because it is difficult to diagnose this condition, some veterinarians will initiate treatment for this bacterium in foals when other causes of diarrhea have been excluded and there is evidence of exposure. Treatment with appropriate antibiotics has been successful, and a response to this treatment is considered confirmation of the diagnosis.

Viral Diarrhea in Foals

Rotavirus is the main cause of viral diarrhea in foals, but other viruses such as coronavirus may also be responsible. Signs of rotaviral infection can include lethargy, colic, loss of appetite, and profuse, watery, foul-smelling diarrhea. It is usually seen in foals less than 2 months old. Younger foals typically have more severe signs. The diarrhea usually lasts 4 to 7 days, although it can persist for weeks. Rotavirus destroys cells in the lining of the small intestine, causing poor absorption of nutrients. Lactase, an enzyme required for digestion of milk, becomes deficient. When this occurs, undigested lactose passing into the large intestine causes diarrhea. Treatment is generally supportive.

This type of diarrhea is highly contagious. In situations where multiple foals are housed on the same farm, sick foals should be isolated in the stall or barn in which the foal originally became ill or moved to a special isolation facility. Strict hygiene and disinfection practices should be followed, including use of disposable gloves and foot covers, handwashing, and disinfection of stalls and equipment with compounds that meet Environmental Protection Agency standards. Because stalls with dirt floors are difficult to adequately clean and disinfect, removal of the top layers of dirt may be required. Fecal material of sick foals removed from stalls should not be spread on pastures that are used for horses and foals. Care should be taken with all equipment that may contact the manure of ill foals so that it is either thoroughly cleaned and disinfected prior to use with healthy foals or is used only for care of ill foals. For example, a wheelbarrow and pitchfork used for cleaning stalls of ill foals should never be used to feed foals and should never be used to clean the stalls of healthy foals unless it is thoroughly cleaned and disinfected.

A vaccine is available for pregnant mares to help protect their foals. The vaccine causes the mares to produce antibodies to rotavirus. These protective antibodies are passed to their foals during suckling of the first milk (colostrum) from the mare.

Miscellaneous Causes of Diarrhea in Foals

Nutritional diarrhea can result from overfeeding (for example, when a foal is reunited with the mare after a period of separation) and improper nutrition (as when orphan foals are being fed calf milk, a replacer formula, or sucrose). Lactose intolerance in foals is rare and can be determined by a lactose tolerance challenge test. Diarrhea can also develop when foals consume indigestible substances such as roughage, sand, dirt, or rocks.

Diarrhea in foals has been reported to be associated with infection by the parasites *Strongyloides westeri, Parascaris equorum,* and *Cryptosporidium* species (*see* page 632).

Gastrointestinal Tumors

Several types of tumors can affect the digestive tract, with the primary sign being chronic weight loss. However, gastrointestinal tumors are rare, so veterinarians often investigate other more common causes of weight loss first. Diagnosis is usually made by excluding other possible causes of weight loss and by examining tissue collected during exploratory surgery or initial treatment. Some cancerous conditions can be diagnosed using endoscopy, ultrasound, rectal examination, or microscopic examination of abdominal fluid. Treatment of cancerous gastrointestinal tumors in horses is generally not attempted because the outlook for longterm recovery is poor. However, a few cases of gastrointestinal cancer have been treated, which improved the well being of the horses at least temporarily.

Inflammatory Bowel Disease

This disease occurs when inflammatory cells accumulate in the small and large intestine and regional lymph nodes. The inflammation may be limited to only a short segment of the bowel or it may be more widespread. This condition interferes with absorption of nutrients and causes a loss of protein from the blood. Diarrhea may or may not be present. Diagnosis is based on signs, physical examination, tests for low blood protein or malabsorption, and intestinal or rectal biopsy. Your veterinarian may detect thickened intestines or enlarged abdominal lymph nodes based on rectal examination. The cause of this disease is not well understood. An altered immune response to a common intestinal exposure (such as feed, parasites, or bacteria) has been suggested.

Medical treatments that may reduce the inflammatory response in the intestine have been tried with limited success. Supportive nutritional care is often prescribed. The usual program involves the frequent feeding of good-quality, high-energy feeds. The longterm outlook is frequently poor. If only a limited and accessible section of the bowel is affected, your veterinarian may recommend surgery to remove the affected portion of the intestine.

Nonsteroidal Anti-inflammatory Drug Toxicity

If the drugs phenylbutazone, flunixin meglumine, or other nonsteroidal antiinflammatory agents are administered at high doses or for prolonged periods, they can cause protein to be lost from the blood into the intestines. Signs include mouth sores, loss of appetite, lethargy, weight loss, diarrhea, and colic. Stomach and intestinal ulcers can also result from this condition. Your veterinarian can make a tentative diagnosis based on the history of drug administration, signs consistent with this condition, and the presence of reduced blood protein. Stomach ulcers can be confirmed using an endoscope inserted through the mouth or nasal passages and then into the stomach. Treatment includes discontinuing the use of phenylbutazone or any other nonsteroidal anti-inflammatory drug. Reducing the production of stomach acid with medications may be beneficial. Changes in diet can help some horses. Surgery may be required if scarring of the intestines has resulted in partial obstruction.

Malabsorption and Maldigestion

Sometimes horses have a defect in the ability of the digestive tract to incorporate nutrients into the body. There are 2 main causes: malabsorption and maldigestion.

Malabsorption is the failure of nutrients to pass from the inside of the intestines to the bloodstream. Many diseases can cause a malabsorption syndrome by altering the normal function of the small intestine. Protein loss may coexist with this condition and prove more harmful than the malabsorption itself. **Maldigestion** is usually caused by a missing or insufficient enzyme; it is the inability to digest certain foods within the intestines. In horses, diseases of malabsorption are much more common than are diseases of maldigestion. Some diseases involve both maldigestion and malabsorption, such as is seen in foals with

lactase deficiency, an inability to digest the sugar in milk (*see* below).

Signs of malabsorption and maldigestion vary, depending on the underlying disease condition. Insufficient energy, weight loss, and possibly low blood protein concentrations are characteristics of these syndromes. Longterm weight loss, muscle wasting, or a reduced growth rate are common. Excessive eating may be seen, because the nutrients that are taken in do not effectively stimulate the brain areas that normally indicate fullness. More commonly with small-intestinal malabsorption, loss of appetite is present. Diarrhea may occur; however, small-intestinal disease may be extensive before diarrhea develops because the large intestine can compensate and absorb the increased fluid. In adult horses, diarrhea usually indicates large-intestinal disease.

Abnormal pain may result from bowel inflammation, abscesses, adhesions, or partial obstruction. Abdominal fluid buildup (ascites) and weakness may develop later in the disease, especially if protein loss is present. Skin and eye abnormalities, arthritis, hepatitis, and kidney disease may indicate immune system reactions, particularly with inflammatory bowel disease. Skin abnormalities seen with malabsorption-related skin disease include a thin hair coat, patchy hair loss, and areas of scaling and crusting that are often symmetrical.

Small-intestinal malabsorption cannot be determined by clinical examination or by routine laboratory data. The veterinarian must exclude more common causes of weight loss before a diagnosis can be made. Determination of the primary underlying disease process is also necessary to establish an appropriate treatment regimen and outlook.

Treatment

The causes of the disease leading to malabsorption must be determined before treatment can be started. Specific treatment for most causes is not avail-able; however, if the cause is parasite damage, it can sometimes be corrected with antiparasitic medications. Anti-inflammatory agents (such as nonsteroidal anti-inflammatory drugs or corticosteroids) may help decrease inflammation within the intestine, although care must be taken in their use. Follow your veterinarian's instructions about dosages and administration times carefully.

Horses that will not eat may have to be force-fed through a stomach tube. Intravenous feeding may be necessary for horses that refuse to eat or for those that cannot tolerate force-feeding. However, intravenous nutrition is difficult to continue on a longterm basis. For most adult horses with conditions causing malabsorption or maldigestion, the treatment is often unsuccessful and the outlook for recovery is poor.

Malabsorption and weight loss sometimes occur after **viral enteritis**, because the infection destroys the villi in the intestine. The villi are hair-like projections of the inner surface of the intestine that increase the area for uptake of nutrients. The loss of the villi means a reduction in the nutrients absorbed from food. Replacement of the villi may take weeks to months in severe cases.

Foals with Lactase Deficiency (Lactose Intolerance)

Lactose deficiency may be congenital but is more commonly acquired and temporary in foals. Foals with lactase deficiency commonly have diarrhea, poor growth rate, and an unthrifty appearance. Signs include flatulence, mild abdominal discomfort, or bloating after intake of milk.

Foals with temporary lactase deficiency caused by diarrhea often respond well to feeding of lactase-treated milk until the small-intestinal lining has regenerated. Foals that can tolerate it should be fed small amounts of high-quality roughage or grain to help meet their energy needs. Young foals may benefit from intestinal rest (withdrawal of milk feeding) while the intestinal lining heals. Dietary change to a soy-based, non-lactose-containing milk replacer and early weaning may be necessary for foals with lactose deficiency that does not respond to other treatments.

■ GASTROINTESTINAL PARASITES OF HORSES

Numerous parasites can infect the digestive system of horses (*see* TABLE 3). The most common ones are described in the following text.

Ascarids

Horse ascarids (*Parascaris equorum*) are stout, whitish worms up to 12 inches (30 centimeters) long that primarily affect foals. Foals get the worms by ingesting eggs, which can remain viable for years in contaminated soil. The main sources of infection are pastures, paddocks, or stalls contaminated with eggs from foals of the previous year.

In heavy infections, migrating larvae may produce respiratory signs ("summer colds"). Infected foals can show poor condition, lack of energy, or colic. Intestinal obstruction and perforation have also been reported.

Diagnosis is based on finding eggs in feces. If infection is suspected, but the worms have not matured enough to begin producing eggs, deworming medication can be given. This will cause large numbers of immature worms to be passed in the feces.

On farms where the worms are common, most foals become infected soon after birth. Treatment with a deworming medication should be started when foals are about 8 weeks old and repeated at 6- to 8-week intervals until they are yearlings. Some medications can also prevent ascarid infection if given daily once foals begin eating grain regularly.

Horse Bots

Horse bots are found in the stomach. They are the larvae of bot flies, *Gastero-philus* species. Three common species are distributed worldwide, and a number of others are found in parts of Europe, Africa, and Asia. The adult flies lay eggs that stick to the hairs of the horse's body. When the horse grooms itself, wetting the mature eggs, the larvae then hatch and are carried by the tongue into the mouth. The larvae stay embedded in the tongue or the lining of the mouth for about 1 month, after which they pass to the stomach, where they attach themselves. The main disease effects are caused by the larvae, which attach by oral hooks to the lining of the stomach, causing wounds and ulceration.

Bots cause a mild stomach inflammation and potentially ulcers, but large numbers may be present without any signs. The larvae migrating in the mouth can cause inflammation and may produce pain during eating. The adult flies may annoy horses when they lay their eggs. Sometimes the yellow to cream-white bot eggs (1 to 2 millimeters long) on the horse's hairs can be seen. Specific diagnosis of infection is difficult; gastroscopy (viewing the inside of the stomach with an endoscope) is the most effective means of diagnosis.

Treatment usually involves appropriate antiparasitic drugs. The drug ivermectin is very effective against oral and stomach stages of bots and, when used as part of a routine parasite control program, provides effective bot control throughout the season. Moxidectin is effective against stages living in the stomach. Although there is no satisfactory method for protecting exposed horses from attack by the adult flies, bot control programs can greatly reduce fly numbers and larval infections. To control bots, your veterinarian will recommend a treatment program based on your local environment and bot fly season, the degree of infection, and the medical history of your horse. If you recognize bot eggs on your horse, you can clean the area with warm water. This causes the bots to hatch but reduces the likelihood of the horse ingesting the larvae.

Table 3. Common Gastrointestinal Parasites of Horses

Common and Scientific Names	How Contracted	Signs	Treatment and Prevention
Habronema species	Horses ingest larvae of house or stable flies that contain larvae of the stomach worms.	Worms produce tumor-like enlargements in stomach; signs usually absent unless enlargements lead to obstruction or rupture.	Some medications may be effective.
Horse bots (*Gasterophilus* species)	Ingestion of bot larvae (*see* text for details).	Stomach and sometimes mouth irritation.	Treatment includes medication. Bot control programs can be effective if done on a regional basis.
Large strongyles (*Strongylus vulgaris, S. edentatus, S. equinus*)	Infection is passed by eating larvae on grass or bedding, which migrate through the body.	Signs include weakness, emaciation, colic, diarrhea, and anemia; diagnosis is by finding eggs in feces.	Control programs limit pasture contamination by preventing fecal excretion of eggs. Regular deworming.
Ascarids (*Parascaris equorum*)	Affects mostly foals; infection sources are pastures, paddocks, and stalls contaminated with eggs from foals of previous year.	Migrating larvae can produce respiratory signs ("summer colds"). Heavily infected foals show unthriftiness, loss of energy, occasionally colic with obstruction of the intestine by the worms. Diagnosed by presence of worms or their eggs in feces.	Regular treatment of foals with antiparasitic medications beginning at 1 month of age recommended on farms where infection is common. Prevention includes daily administration of pyrantel tartrate in grain.
Pinworms (*Oxuris* species)	Most common in horses less than 18 months old.	Egg masses around anus appear as white crusty mass. Signs include horse rubbing anal and tail regions, causing bare patches.	Medications provide effective treatment.
Small stomach worm (hairworm, *Trichostrongylus axei*)	Normally a problem only in horses on pastures also used by ruminants (cows, sheep, or goats).	Stomach inflammation resulting in weight loss. Detected after culture of feces.	Some antiparasitic drugs are effective.
Small strongyles (*Cyathostomes,* multiple species)	Infection passed by eating larvae on contaminated pasture.	Often few signs; heavy infections may lead to poor absorption of nutrients and weight loss.	Several medications available, although some worms may be resistant to particular drugs.
Strongyloides westeri	Transmitted from mares to foals in milk.	Possible cause of early diarrhea in foals.	Infection of foals can be prevented by treatment of mares with ivermectin 24 hours after foaling.
Tapeworms (*Anoplocephala magna, A. perfoliata, Paranoplocephala mamillana*)	Transmitted by eating soil mites that are the intermediate host.	Diagnosed by finding eggs in feces, which may require multiple tests.	Several medications provide effective treatment (*see* text for details).

Large Strongyles

The large strongyles of horses belong to a group of parasites known as round-worms. They are also known as blood worms or red worms. Horses become infected when they ingest larvae in forage contaminated by feces. Once inside the horse, the larvae become active in the intestine and migrate extensively (in blood vessels and other organs) before developing to maturity in the large intestine. In the intestine, they cause anemia due to blood loss, weakness, weight loss, and sometimes diarrhea. One strongyle, *Strongylus vulgaris* can damage the anterior mesenteric artery and its branches, which interferes with the flow of blood to the intestines. This can cause colic, tissue death, twisting of the intestine, intussusception (telescoping on itself) of intestinal tissues, bleeding, or possibly intestinal rupture. The central nervous system can also be affected by these parasites.

Typically horses become infected with both large strongyles and small strongyles (*see* below). Diagnosis is based on the detection of eggs in the feces. When treating this infection, your veterinarian will often recommend both antiparasitic medication and measures to control the presence of the parasites in the horse's environment. Parasite control programs are designed to minimize the level of pasture contamination and thus reduce the risks associated with migrating larvae. Routine antiparasitic treatments do this by preventing excretion of strongyle eggs in the feces.

Small Strongyles

Over 40 species of small strongyles can infect domestic horses. The adult worms live within the large intestine. Unlike the large strongyles, small strongyles do not migrate outside of the intestinal wall, and they are generally less damaging. Healthy horses may have large numbers of small strongyles without signs of infection. In heavier infections, however, disruption may be extensive enough to disturb diges-tion and absorption of nutrients, resulting in loss of condition, inflammation of the mucous membranes of the large intestine, and diarrhea.

Larval cyathostomiasis is a syndrome of sudden weight loss, often with severe diarrhea, associated with the mass emergence of previously inactive strongyle larvae from the intestinal wall. It is seen in temperate areas in late winter and spring, particularly in young ponies and horses (those less than 5 years old). This condition is not common in the United States, but it occurs more frequently in Europe. The bright red larvae can sometimes be seen in the feces and are helpful in making a diagnosis. Biopsy of the large intestine also may assist in diagnosis.

Adult strongyles are easily removed from the intestines by a variety of antiparasitic drugs. Small-strongyle larvae in the intestinal tissues are much more difficult to effectively remove with medication. Horses already infected with these parasites may not respond to treatment if inflammation is too severe. In these cases, the prescribed treatment often includes supplementing antiparasitic drugs with corticosteroids and other appropriate supportive treatment.

Routine or interval antiparasitic treatments can minimize the level of pasture contamination, thereby reducing the risks associated with the accumulation of larvae and adult worms. Alternatively, infection may be prevented by daily administration of prescription medication. The interval between routine treatments depends on several factors including the drug; the horse's age, health, and value; and the level of risk of disease. Removal of feces from paddocks and pastures aids in control and may also reduce the number of antiparasitic treatments required. As is the case with other infective worms, your veterinarian may recommend a treatment program that involves medication, supportive care for the horse, and steps to reduce the presence of the worms in the horse's environment.

Tapeworms

Tapeworms (cestodes) may be found in the small or large intestine but may also be in the stomach. Infection usually occurs when horses eat pasture mites that become infected by ingesting the tapeworm eggs. Larvae develop and mature in the horse's gastrointestinal tract.

In light infections, no signs of disease are present. In heavy infections, digestive disturbances can be seen. Horses may lose weight and condition and become anemic. Ulceration may occur where the tapeworm attaches to the intestinal lining. Intestinal perforation, abdominal infection, and colic may be seen in some infections. Colic is more likely in horses with tapeworm infections, and it often recurs.

Diagnosis is made by identifying tapeworm eggs in the feces. Because the eggs are not always present, multiple fecal samples and multiple tests may be required to make a definite diagnosis.

Your veterinarian will recommend medical treatment based on the species of tapeworm. *Anoplocephala* species can be effectively treated with pyrantel salts and praziquantel. The drug praziquantel appears to be effective in removing *Paranoplocephala mamillana*, while pyrantel salts are not. In facilities where tapeworms are common, signs of tapeworm infections can be prevented by pyrantel salts routinely administered daily during the grazing season, or praziquantel administered within an interval deworming program. Follow your veterinarian's recommendations as to an appropriate treatment program for your horse.

Protozoa

Protozoa are single-celled, microscopic parasites. Several types can infect the horse's digestive tract.

Cryptosporidiosis

Cryptosporidiosis is an uncommon infection in foals caused by the parasite *Cryptosporidium parvum*. The source of infection is egg cysts (oocysts) containing the parasite. The oocysts are excreted in the feces of infected horses or other infected species (such as rodents or farm cats). Simultaneous infections, especially with rotavirus and coronavirus, are common; studies suggest that diarrhea is more severe in these mixed infections. Cryptosporidiosis is usually not fatal unless complicated by other factors such as other infections, energy deficits from inadequate intake of colostrum and milk, a weakened immune system, or chilling.

Signs include mild to moderate diarrhea that persists for several days regardless of treatment. Feces are yellow or pale, watery, and contain mucus. The diarrhea may result in weight loss and emaciation. In most cases, the diarrhea improves on its own after several days. Varying degrees of apathy, poor appetite, and mild dehydration are present. More severe dehydration, weakness, and collapse are rare. A diagnosis is based on laboratory detection of oocysts in feces.

A number of drugs have been tested for their effectiveness against *Cryptosporidium*, but at this point, few if any medications are available. As with other intestinal illnesses, cleanliness and isolation of sick animals are the best routes of control.

Infections in domestic animals may be a source of infection for susceptible people, particularly those with weakened immune systems, in whom disease can be severe. The infection is transmitted predominantly from person to person, but direct infection from animals and waterborne infection from contamination of surface water and drinking water by domestic or wild animal feces can also be important.

Giardiasis

Giardiasis is a chronic, intestinal protozoal infection that is seen worldwide in most domestic and wild mammals, many birds, and people. Though infection is common in dogs and cats, it is rare in horses. (For a more detailed discussion of GIARDIASIS, *see* page 116.)

■ DISORDERS OF THE LIVER

The liver is an organ that performs numerous functions, including metabolizing carbohydrates, proteins, and fats. It also breaks down and excretes many potentially toxic compounds. The liver has a large storage capacity and functional reserve and is capable of regenerating, which provides some protection against permanent damage. However, the liver is also susceptible to injury and disease.

When liver cells die, they are removed by inflammatory cells and replaced with either new liver cells or fibrous tissue. Unless the problem is short-term and regeneration of new liver cells is evident, the outlook for horses with liver failure is usually unfavorable. Early liver fibrosis may be reversible if recognized and treated promptly. Longterm disease with extensive loss of functioning liver tissue and the development of fibrosis is a grave sign and the outlook for recovery is poor.

Signs of Liver Insufficiency

Signs of liver insufficiency may not be evident until more than 60 to 80% of the liver is nonfunctional or when liver dysfunction is caused by disease in another organ system. Early vague signs of depression and decreased appetite may be overlooked. Jaundice (yellowing of the skin, gums, and whites of the eyes), weight loss, abdominal pain or colic, and abnormal behavior due to hepatic encephalopathy (*see* below) are common in horses with liver disease and liver failure. Skin changes due to a reaction to ultraviolet sunlight (photosensitization) may occur. Less often, harsh, high-pitched breathing sounds, diarrhea, or constipation, may be present. Anemia may be seen in horses with liver dysfunction due to parasitic diseases, chronic copper toxicity, some plant poisonings, or longterm inflammatory diseases or destruction of red blood cells. Weight loss is a common sign in longterm liver disease and may be the only sign associated with liver abscesses.

How Does Liver Disease Affect the Skin (Light Sensitivity)?

One of the main functions of the liver is the removal of toxic substances from the blood. When the liver is diseased, a toxin called phylloerythrin increases in the bloodstream. Phylloerythrin is produced by the breakdown of chlorophyll (green pigment) present in plants eaten by the horse, and it is sensitive to light. When phylloerythrin reaches the skin and is exposed to ultraviolet sunlight, it releases energy and damages the skin. Unpigmented or light-skinned areas absorb the most ultraviolet light, so they are most likely to be affected by light sensitivity.

Hepatic encephalopathy, a syndrome of neurologic problems caused by poor liver function, is seen in a number of liver diseases. The liver normally removes poisons from the bloodstream; when the liver is not working properly, poisons build up and can affect the nervous system. Signs of hepatic encephalopathy range from depression and lethargy to head pressing, circling, aimless walking, lack of coordination, difficulty swallowing, persistent yawning, sleepiness, aggressiveness, vicious behavior, stupor, seizures, or coma. Loud sounds while breathing and difficulty breathing occur in some cases of liver failure, especially in ponies. Although the signs can be dramatic, hepatic encephalopathy can often be reversed if the underlying liver disease is successfully treated. Horses with hepatic encephalopathy often show aggressive and unpredictable behavior that can result in injury to the horse or to its handlers. The animal may require sedation.

Liver disease can cause **photosensitization**, a condition in which the skin is unusually sensitive to ultraviolet sunlight. This disorder is caused by increased levels of a light-reactive chemical called phylloerythrin circulating in the bloodstream. Signs can include itching, mild to severe skin disease with reddened skin, extensive fluid accumulation (edema) beneath the skin, skin ulceration and peeling, eye inflammation and tearing, aversion to light, and cloudiness of the cornea. Skin inflammation and edema are particularly evident on nonpigmented, light-colored or hairless areas of the body (such as the lips and white markings on the face or legs) that are exposed to sun. Uncommonly, the underside of the tongue may be affected. Blindness, skin abnormalities, loss of condition, and occasionally death can result.

Either diarrhea or constipation can occur in horses with liver disease. Ponies and horses with hyperlipemia (high levels of fat in the blood) and liver failure may develop diarrhea, founder, and edema. Some horses with liver disease have alternating diarrhea and constipation. Horses with liver failure and hepatic encephalopathy frequently develop intestinal impaction or obstruction (*see* page 615) due to decreased water intake.

Initially, your veterinarian will treat your horse to reduce the signs of severe hepatic encephalopathy, stabilize its condition, and perform laboratory tests. Your veterinarian will want to perform a liver biopsy to determine the type of tissue changes, degree of liver fibrosis present, and the regenerative capabilities of the liver cells before developing a more long-term treatment plan or providing you with an outlook for the horse's recovery.

Diagnosis

Laboratory tests can often detect liver disease before liver failure occurs. Routine biochemical tests such as blood concentrations of liver-specific enzymes are sensitive indicators that liver disease is present, but they do not measure liver function. Additional biochemical tests are available that assess liver function more accurately. These provide the veterinarian with a useful tool for diagnosis.

Liver biopsy is the definitive means of diagnosis. Evaluation of the tissue provides valuable information regarding causes and severity of liver disease. Ultrasonography may also be useful to evaluate the size and appearance of the liver or bile

duct; gallstones, tumors, abscesses, or other abnormalities. Abdominal x-rays using dyes (called contrast studies) can help diagnose intestinal obstructions and secondary liver disease in foals. Additional specialized tests, such as scintigraphy (a technique in which a radioactive substance is injected into the body and its distribution studied) may be helpful in some cases.

Treatment and Management

The goals for treatment of horses with liver disease or failure are to control hepatic encephalopathy, treat the underlying disease, provide supportive care to allow time for liver regeneration, and prevent injury to the animal and persons working with the animal. Initial treatment of horses with signs of liver disease may be started before the underlying cause and extent of liver damage is known. However, specific therapies for liver disease depend on the causes, the presence of liver failure, whether or not the disease is chronic, and the degree of liver fibrosis (scarring) or bile duct obstruction.

Treatment is most successful when intervention is early, liver fibrosis is minimal, and there is evidence of regeneration in the liver. Horses with severe fibrosis respond poorly because the potential for regeneration of healthy liver cells is decreased.

If conditions such as dehydration, acid-base and electrolyte (salt) imbalances, or low blood sugar are present, they can be corrected with appropriate intravenous fluids. Adequate fresh water should be available if the horse can swallow normally. Until the nature of the underlying liver disease is known, broad-spectrum antibiotics may be prescribed if a liver infection is suspected. Pain may be controlled with low to moderate doses of nonsteroidal anti-inflammatory drugs.

Dietary management is essential for animals with hepatic encephalopathy or liver disease. Affected horses should be fed carefully because difficulty swallowing may be a problem. Follow your veterinarian's directions as to proper feeding. Normally, a horse with liver disease will need to be fed frequently in relatively small amounts. The recommended diet typically contains easily digestible carbohydrates, provides adequate but not excessive protein, has a high ratio of branched-chain amino acids to aromatic amino acids, and is high in starch. If the horse will not eat voluntarily, feeding by stomach tube or intravenous fluids will be required.

Acute Hepatitis (Short-term Liver Inflammation)

Acute hepatitis can be caused by infections, poisons, or undefined causes. Signs, which include lethargy, jaundice, and poor appetite, may appear suddenly. Sensitivity to light, diarrhea, and blood clotting abnormalities also may be seen. Neurologic signs resulting from low blood sugar and hepatic encephalopathy can be most severe in horses with sudden and severe liver disease. Signs of bacterial blood infection may be present. Loss of appetite can lead to potassium deficiency.

Idiopathic Acute Liver Disease (Serum Sickness, Theiler's Disease)

Idiopathic acute liver disease, a sudden-onset liver disease with no apparent cause, is the most common cause of acute hepatitis in horses. About 20% of horses with this disorder show signs of liver failure 4 to 10 weeks after receiving a medical product derived from horses, such as tetanus antitoxin. In these cases, the condition is sometimes called serum-associated hepatitis or serum sickness. However, horses can develop this disorder with no prior history of exposure to such a product. The cause of the disorder is unknown. Possibilities include a viral disease or an "overreaction" of the horse's immune system to tetanus antitoxin. Lactating mares that receive tetanus antitoxin at foaling seem to be more susceptible.

The onset of signs is usually sudden and may progress rapidly over 2 to 7 days. Death may occur suddenly in 50 to 60%

of affected horses. Horses with idiopathic acute liver disease typically show loss of appetite, hepatic encephalopathy (page 633), and jaundice. Nervous system signs range from lethargy to aggression or maniacal behavior, blindness, and poor coordination. Light sensitivity, colic, fever, discolored urine, and bleeding may be seen. Most cases are single, but outbreaks with several horses involved have been reported. If one horse in a group appears ill, the other horses on the same premises should be carefully observed. Most veterinarians will recommend that all the horses receive blood tests for liver disease.

Supportive treatment for the hepatic encephalopathy is often successful. Stressful situations, such as moving the horse or weaning a mare's foal, may worsen the signs of hepatic encephalopathy and should be avoided, if possible. Recovery depends on the degree of damage in the liver. Affected horses that remain stable for 3 to 5 days and that continue to eat often recover.

Tyzzer's Disease

Tyzzer's disease is caused by the bacterium *Clostridium piliforme*. The infection causes a liver infection that destroys liver tissue, inflammation of the heart muscle, and inflammation of the large intestine with diarrhea in foals 1 to 6 weeks old. It is very rare but is usually fatal. Signs of infection, including depression, fever, jaundice, loss of appetite, and diarrhea, develop quickly and may last a few hours or up to 2 days. Foals often are found dead without any preceding signs. There is no effective treatment.

Cholangiohepatitis

Cholangiohepatitis is inflammation of the bile ducts and adjacent liver, which occasionally causes liver failure in horses. It is sometimes associated with stones in the bile duct. Several causes, including bacterial infection in the bile duct, ulcers in the small intestine, and parasite migration, may cause cholangiohepatitis to develop.

Typically, cholangiohepatitis is a medium- to longterm disease. Affected horses show signs of weight loss, poor appetite, fever, or colic. Jaundice, light sensitivity, and signs of hepatic encephalopathy (page 633) may be present. Short-term cholangiohepatitis may occasionally result in severe blood poisoning and death. Diagnosis is confirmed by liver biopsy.

If test results indicate a particular type of infection, appropriate antibiotics often produce favorable results. Treatment should be continued for 4 to 6 weeks or longer. Liver enzyme tests and biopsies may need to be repeated to determine whether the treatment is successful. If test results are unclear or unavailable, broad-spectrum antibiotics can be prescribed. The outlook is good if fibrosis (scarring) is not severe.

Poisons Affecting the Liver

Hepatotoxins are poisons that damage the liver (*see* TABLE 4). Fatal liver failure may result if the initial poisoning is severe. More commonly, the liver damage from toxins occurs over a long period of time. The result may be cirrhosis, a condition in which the functional liver tissue is replaced by extensive fibrous tissue. Many hepatotoxins, especially those in plants, have toxic effects on multiple organs, particularly the kidneys, lungs, and digestive tract.

Obtaining a definite diagnosis may be difficult. Careful history, inspection of the environment, laboratory tests, and/or a liver biopsy may be needed to determine the toxic agent. With short-term plant toxicities, remains of toxic plants may be found in the stomach contents.

Specific antidotes for hepatotoxins are limited. Removal of the horses from the source is essential to decrease additional exposure. You may have to change your horse's pasture or hay or remove toxic plants from the pasture. If the poisoning is recent, your veterinarian may administer laxatives (such as mineral oil or magnesium sulfate) or absorbants (usually activated charcoal or mineral oil) to decrease the

absorption of toxic substances. These may not be helpful for longterm toxicity, such as pyrrolizidine alkaloid toxicity (*see also* page 1200) caused by plants, in which the toxic agent has been eaten over weeks to months before signs of illness are evident. Care often includes correction of electrolyte (salt), metabolic, and blood sugar disorders through fluid treatment and dietary management. Hepatic encephalopathy (page 633) must be controlled. Sunlight should be avoided if light sensitization is present. Antibiotics may be prescribed to prevent skin infection. The outlook for recovery is guarded and depends on the particular toxin.

Gallstones (Biliary Calculi, Choleliths)

Although horses do not have a gallbladder, they can get stones in their bile ducts (biliary stones or calculi). These stones in horses may block bile ducts and cause liver disease, but sometimes they do not cause any signs. Gallstones most commonly affect middle-aged (6- to 15-year-old) horses regardless of sex or breed. One or more stones may be present in the bile ducts or gallbladder. The cause of gallstone formation in horses is not known.

Signs commonly seen in horses with gallstones or bile duct inflammation include weight loss, abdominal pain, jaundice, depression, and fever. Signs of liver failure, including encephalopathy and light sensitivity, occur less frequently. These signs often come and go. Complete obstruction of the common bile duct may be accompanied by persistent abdominal pain. Blood tests provide additional evidence for the presence of this disease. Ultrasonography may reveal liver enlargement or the presence of the stones themselves.

Although bile duct obstruction in horses is often fatal, the stones can sometimes be crushed or removed surgically. When stones are small, intravenous fluids may be used to wash out or dissolve the stones. Anti-inflammatory drugs are administered to reduce inflammation and provide pain relief, and antibiotics may be

Table 4. Substances that can Cause Liver Injury in Horses

Substance	Possible Sources	Signs	Treatment and Prevention
Iron	Inappropriate iron supplementation, forages high in iron, injectable iron, and leaching of iron into water or feed.	Foals: hepatic encephalopathy, death. Adults: weight loss, jaundice, depression.	Treatment includes fluids and nutritional supplements.
Fungal toxins (mycotoxins), especially *Fusarium*	Feed or bedding contaminated with mold toxins, especially corn.	Drowsiness, neurologic signs, blindness, collapse, death.	No treatment available; screen grain to remove broken or small grains.
Blue-green algae	Contamination of drinking water by blue-green algae.	Death may occur within a few hours and may be preceded by coma, muscle tremors, and difficulty breathing; horses that survive may have light sensitivity.	Replacement of contaminated water with large amounts of fresh water; affected horses should be kept out of direct sunlight.
Pyrrolizidine alkaloid toxicity (compound found in many plant species, for example, ragwort, groundsel, fiddleneck)	Plants are normally avoided during grazing but may be eaten during drought or may be found in contaminated hay.	Exposure is usually long-term; causes loss of condition and appetite, jaundice; exercise intolerance, light sensitivity, and hepatic encephalopathy; can be fatal.	Rations high in carbohydrates and low in protein; protein should be high in branch-chain amino acids. Prevention via herbicide control of offending plants.
Kleingrass (*Panicum coloratum*)— toxin is sapogenin	Found in southwestern United States from late spring to early fall; young growing plants contain highest toxin concentration.	Jaundice, light sensitivity, intermittent colic and fever, weight loss, and hepatic encephalopathy. Light sensitivity may develop around the coronary band and cause lameness.	Affected horses should be removed from the kleingrass source, fed good-quality hay, and protected from sunlight. Antibiotic or softening creams may be needed in severe cases.
Alsike clover (*Trifolium hybridium*)	Ingestion of clover pasture, especially during wet seasons (dewy pastures); diet with high content of clover (especially blossoms) in pasture or hay.	"Dew poisoning." Light sensitivity—reddened skin after exposure to sun, followed by death of the skin or swelling and discharge. The muzzle, tongue, and feet are frequently affected.	Care of skin lesions; removal of the horse from Alsike-containing pasture or hay.
	Feeding on clover, especially blossoms at pasture or high percentage of clover in the hay. Usually seen in horses eating larger amount or grazing longer on clover than those with "dew poisoning."	"Big liver disease": loss of condition, liver failure, neurologic disturbances, colic, diarrhea, death.	Removal from Alsike-containing pasture.
Cocklebur (*Xanthium* species)	Uncommon; feeding on ground seeds or young seedlings; burs are toxic but rarely eaten.	Within hours of toxin ingestion, horses develop signs of depression, weakness, poor coordination, breathing difficulty, convulsions, and death. Signs are due to sudden liver failure.	Treatment requires intensive supportive care. Mineral oil or activated charcoal may be given by mouth to delay absorption of the toxin.

prescribed if infection is likely. Supportive care is provided to manage any liver insufficiency.

Chronic Active Hepatitis

Chronic active hepatitis describes any progressive inflammation within the liver producing sustained, progressive, longterm liver disease. Cholangiohepatitis (*see* page 635) can be a part of chronic active hepatitis. The exact cause of this inflammation is not known but may be related to infection, the immune system, or toxins. Many causes acute hepatitis can progress to chronic active hepatitis.

The main signs are weight loss, poor appetite, depression, and lethargy. Jaundice, behavioral changes, diarrhea, light sensitivity, and bleeding are occasionally present. Fever may be persistent or intermittent. Microscopic examination of a liver biopsy is needed for a definite diagnosis. Your veterinarian may also order a tissue culture to check for the presence of bacteria.

Treatment usually includes providing fluids with added potassium chloride, glucose, and vitamin supplementation; dietary management (a low-protein, high branched-chain amino acid, high-carbohydrate diet); and prevention of exposure to the sun if sensitivity is present. Medications may include corticosteroids to reduce inflammation and fibrosis and broad-spectrum antibiotics to treat infection. The outlook is fair to good in horses with less severe tissue abnormalities, especially those with a condition that responds well to corticosteroids. The outlook is poor in horses with liver failure, widespread fibrosis (scarring) in the liver, and loss of normal liver cells.

Hyperlipemia and Hepatic Lipidosis

Hyperlipemia is a syndrome in which blood levels of fats (triglycerides, lipids) are increased. Fatty changes in the liver, known as hepatic lipidosis, are another part of the syndrome. Poor feed quality or a decrease in feed intake, particularly dur-

ing a period of stress or when energy is needed (such as during pregnancy or illness), may result in hyperlipemia syndrome. Hyperlipemia is most commonly seen in the winter and spring.

In this disease, the need for energy triggers excessive movement of fatty acids out of fat tissue, leading to high blood triglyceride levels and eventually to fat accumulation in the liver. Hyperlipemia is seen most commonly in ponies, donkeys, and miniature horses, and less frequently in standard-size adult horses. Affected ponies are commonly obese with a history of recent weight loss due to stress, illness, pregnancy, or early lactation. Hyperlipemia in miniature horses and donkeys frequently develops along with some other illness.

The signs of hyperlipemia include lethargy, weakness, poor appetite, decreased water intake, jaundice, and diarrhea. Often, there is a history of prolonged loss of appetite, rapid weight loss, and previous obesity. Weight loss, colic, lack of coordination, and trembling may be seen. Impairment of liver function is common; functioning of the kidneys, heart, and skeletal muscles may also be impaired. A diagnosis is often based on the history, signs, and examination of tissues. High blood triglyceride levels confirm the diagnosis. Cholesterol may also be increased. Laboratory evidence of poor liver function provides additional evidence for this disease.

Correction of the underlying disease, intravenous fluids, and nutritional support are the most essential factors in treatment. Voluntary feeding is preferred if the horse will eat adequate quantities of food; however, supplemental tube feeding may be necessary until feed intake is adequate. For horses that will not eat, intravenous nutrition may be needed. Some horses will also require injection of insulin or heparin.

Death from hyperlipemia is rare in miniature breeds. In most instances, survival depends on the ability to successfully treat the underlying disease. The outlook is often poor in ponies and standard-size horses with hyperlipemia.

Hemochromatosis

Hemochromatosis is a disease in which excess iron is deposited in the liver cells, causing damage and dysfunction of the liver and other tissues. In horses, this disease appears to be caused by a damaged liver that cannot properly metabolize iron. There is no evidence that this disease runs in families or is caused by consumption of excess iron in the normal diet of horses.

The most common signs are weight loss, lethargy, and occasional loss of appetite. The levels of certain liver enzymes in the blood are increased. An enlarged liver and iron accumulation in the liver, lymph nodes, pancreas, spleen, thyroid, kidneys, brain, and glandular tissue are typically present. Diagnosis is based on history, signs, and laboratory findings. A high iron level in liver tissue in horses with no history of excess iron intake helps confirm the diagnosis.

Although several drugs and treatment regimens have been tried, there is currently no effective treatment for this condition.

Right Liver Lobe Atrophy

The right lobe of the liver is the largest lobe in young horses but frequently decreases in size (atrophies) in older animals and becomes fibrous. While the cause of this condition is not known, some researchers have suggested that it might be caused by longterm compression of the right lobe of the liver by expanded intestines. Feeding horses high-concentrate, low-fiber diets may contribute to this condition. Colic may be seen in some cases of right liver lobe atrophy and some horses may have signs unrelated to the digestive system.

Liver Lobe Torsion

When the liver twists, the condition causes colic in horses. Occasionally, portions of the liver tissue die. Tests of the liver may show increased enzymes or fibrinogen. Bacteria may be found in the dead portion of the liver. Exploratory surgery may be required for diagnosis.

Hepatic Amyloidosis

Amyloid is misfolded protein. It can be deposited in various organs of the body, distorting tissues and affecting their function. In horses, the liver and spleen are the most common organs affected by amyloidosis. The condition may be associated with severe parasite infection or longterm infection or inflammation. The condition progresses slowly, and there is no effective treatment. (For a more detailed discussion of AMYLOIDOSIS, *see* page 796.)

Primary Hyperammonemia

In this condition affecting adult horses, apparent blindness and severe neurologic signs are seen. The cause is unknown, but it is thought to be due to overgrowth of certain bacteria in the intestines. Although the signs are similar to some types of liver disease, this condition does not appear to be directly related to the liver. The syndrome is nearly always associated with intestinal disease, diarrhea, or colic. In most cases, diarrhea or colic are seen 24 to 48 hours before the neurologic signs. A diagnosis is often based on the signs and results of blood tests that show increased ammonia and glucose levels and low blood bicarbonate levels.

In most horses, neurologic signs resolve within 2 to 3 days with supportive treatment (intravenous fluids, potassium chloride, glucose, sodium bicarbonate) and drugs to reduce the absorption of ammonia.

Hyperammonemia of Morgan Weanlings

A syndrome of ill thrift, increased ammonia levels in the bloodstream, and potential injury to the liver is seen in Morgan foals. Affected foals have been related, but the cause of the syndrome is unknown. Signs are usually first seen around the time of weaning. Liver enzymes (which indicate inflammation of the liver) and blood ammonia levels are increased.

Portosystemic Shunts

Portosystemic shunts are conditions in which blood vessels bypass all or part of the liver, causing toxins normally removed by the liver to remain in the blood. This lack of processing causes increased ammonia levels in the blood and nervous system signs.

Although the condition is often present at birth, signs are first seen when affected foals are about 2 months old and start to eat larger amounts of grain and forage. Neurologic signs include staggering, depression, wandering, blindness, circling, and seizures. Signs may be most pronounced and associated with feedings. The shunt can often be seen using imaging techniques such as contrast x-rays, ultrasonography, or nuclear scintigraphy.

Surgical repair may be attempted in foals in which the site of the shunt can be identified, but the outlook is guarded. Restricting protein intake, carefully managing the diet, and giving products to decrease ammonia production within the intestines may control signs in some foals. Supportive care with fluids, potassium, and dextrose may be needed to help decrease neurologic signs. A high level of care on the part of the owner is required to control this disease over time.

▧ DISORDERS OF THE RECTUM AND ANUS

The rectum is the final portion of the large intestine and marks the end of the digestive tract. Feces pass through the rectum and are then excreted through the anus.

Rectal and Anorectal Narrowing (Strictures)

Rectal and anorectal strictures are narrowings of the rectum and anus due to the presence of scar tissue. The scar tissue may be caused by an injury from foreign objects or trauma (such as bite wounds or accidents) or it may be a complication of inflammatory disease.

Rectal Prolapse

Rectal prolapse is a condition in which one or more layers of the rectum protrude through the anus. A prolapse may be classified as incomplete, in which only the innermost rectal layer protrudes, or complete, in which all rectal layers protrude. The condition is common in foals in association with severe diarrhea and straining to defecate or urinate. It can be caused by intestinal, anorectal, or urinary diseases or exposure to certain fungal toxins in feed. A perineal hernia or other condition that affects the nerves of the muscle that controls the anus may also cause a prolapse.

An elongated, cylindrical mass protruding through the anus usually indicates a rectal prolapse. However, prolapses involving other parts of the intestine can look very similar. No matter what type of prolapse is present, any tissue mass protruding from the anal opening should be promptly examined by a veterinarian.

Identifying and eliminating the cause of a prolapse is a key part of treatment. For horses with rectal prolapse, epidural anesthesia (injecting anesthetic near the spinal cord) may be used to keep the horse from straining and allow the veterinarian to reposition the prolapsed tissue. Stitches will often be needed to keep the repositioned tissue in place. If neglected, rectal prolapse in mares can lead to prolapse of the small colon, a more serious condition. In some cases, surgery may be necessary to remove dead or damaged tissue or to repair the prolapse. Because of the potential complication of rectal stricture formation (*see* above), complete amputation of the rectum is generally done only in severe cases. After surgery, antibiotics and stool softeners may be prescribed.

Rectal Tears

A tear in the rectum or anus can be caused by a sharp object that is accidentally eaten, a wound such as a bite wound, or an accidental tear during a rectal examination. The tear may involve only the surface layers of the rectum (partial tear) or penetrate all layers (complete tear).

Signs may include constipation, straining or reluctance to defecate, bleeding, and discoloration of the rectum and anus. Swelling may be present when the injury has been present for more than a short time.

Treatment to avoid infection and close the wound should be started immediately.

Rectal tears in horses have been classified according to the tissue layers penetrated. Grade I tears (the least serious) can sometimes be treated without surgery, using antibiotics, intravenous fluids, and stool softeners. More serious tears require immediate surgery.

CHAPTER **46**
Hormonal Disorders

■ INTRODUCTION

Hormones are chemical messengers that have many different functions. The effects of hormones in the body are wide-ranging and varied. Some familiar examples of hormones include insulin, which is important in the development of diabetes, and estrogen and progesterone, which are involved in the female reproductive cycle.

The Endocrine System

The endocrine system consists of a group of tissues that release hormones into the bloodstream for travel to other parts of the body. Most endocrine tissues are glands (such as the thyroid gland) that release hormones directly into small blood vessels within and around the tissue. Several important hormones are released from tissues other than glands, such as the heart, kidney, and liver. Some hormones act only on a single tissue, while others have effects on virtually every cell in the body. Hormones are present in the blood in very small quantities, so laboratory tests done to measure hormone levels must be very sensitive. (*See* TABLE 8, page 130.)

The **pituitary gland** is located near the center and bottom of the brain. It produces a number of critical hormones that control many parts of the body, including several other endocrine glands. For this reason, it is sometimes called a "master gland." Because large numbers of hormones are produced by the pituitary, a variety of different conditions can be caused by pituitary disease or tumors. The specific illness and signs depend on the cause and the area of the pituitary gland that is affected.

The **adrenal glands** are located just in front of the kidneys. The adrenal gland has 2 parts—the cortex and the medulla. The adrenal cortex consists of 3 layers, each of which produces a different set of steroid hormones. The outer layer produces the mineralocorticoids, which help to control the body's balance of sodium and potassium salts. The middle layer produces glucocorticoids, which are involved in metabolizing nutrients as well as in reducing inflammation. The inner layer produces sex hormones such as estrogen and progesterone. The adrenal medulla plays an important role in response to stress or low blood sugar (glucose). It releases epinephrine (sometimes called adrenaline) and norepinephrine, both of which increase heart output, blood pressure, and blood glucose, and slow digestion.

The **pancreas** is composed of several types of cells that have distinct functions involved in the production of hormones and digestive enzymes. The islets of Langerhans in the pancreas consist of 3 types of cells, each of which produces a different hormone. Most of the cells,

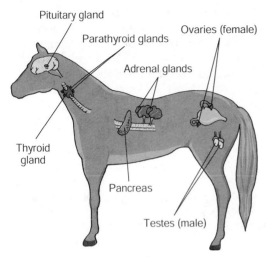

Pituitary gland

Parathyroid glands

Ovaries (female)

Adrenal glands

Thyroid gland

Pancreas

Testes (male)

The major endocrine glands in the horse (modified with permission from *The Merck Manual of Medical Information*, Second Home Edition, 2003)

which are called beta cells, produce insulin. Insulin affects, either directly or indirectly, the function of every organ in the body, particularly the liver, fat cells, and muscle. In general, insulin increases the transfer of glucose and other compounds into body cells. It also decreases the rate of fat, protein, and carbohydrate breakdown.

The other 2 cell types in the islets of Langerhans produce the hormones glucagon and somatostatin. Insulin and glucagon work together to keep the concentration of glucose in the blood and other body fluids within a relatively narrow range. Glucagon controls glucose release from the liver, and insulin controls glucose transport into numerous body tissues.

The **thyroid gland** is a 2-lobed gland in the neck. It produces the iodine-containing hormones, T_3 and T_4, which affect many processes in the body. In general, the thyroid hormones regulate metabolic rate, or the speed at which body processes "run." Thyroid hormones act on many different cellular processes. Some of their actions occur within minutes to hours, while others take several hours or longer. Thyroid hormones in normal quantities work

along with other hormones, such as growth hormone and insulin, to build tissues. However, when they are secreted in excess, they can contribute to breakdown of proteins and tissues.

The **parathyroid glands**, which extend down the sides of the neck, help to regulate the body's levels of calcium and phosphorus in the blood. The way the body processes calcium and phosphate, the function of vitamin D (which acts more like a hormone than a vitamin), and the formation of bone are all tied together into a system that involves 2 other hormones—parathyroid hormone and calcitonin—that are secreted by the parathyroid glands.

Development of Endocrine System Disease

The body monitors and adjusts the level of each hormone by using a feedback system specifically for that hormone. Hormones function to keep factors such as temperature and blood sugar (glucose) levels within certain ranges. Sometimes, pairs of hormones with opposite functions work together to keep body functions in balance.

Endocrine system diseases can develop when too much or not enough hormone is produced, or when normal pathways for hormones to be used and removed are disrupted. Signs can develop because of a problem in the tissues that are the source of the hormone, or because of a problem in another part of the body that is affecting the secretion or action of a particular hormone.

A tumor or other abnormal tissue in an endocrine gland often causes it to produce too much hormone. When an endocrine gland is destroyed, not enough hormone is produced. Diseases caused by overproduction or excess of a hormone often begin with the prefix **hyper-**. For example, in hyperthyroidism, the thyroid gland produces too much thyroid hormone. Diseases caused by a lack or deficiency of a hormone often begin with the prefix **hypo-**. For example, in hypothyroidism, the thyroid gland does not produce enough thyroid hormone.

In many cases, the abnormal gland not only overproduces hormone, it also does not respond normally to feedback signals. This causes hormone to be released in situations in which its levels would normally be reduced. Sometimes, the overproduction is caused by stimulation from another part of the body. Occasionally, a tumor outside the endocrine system can produce a substance similar to a hormone, causing the body to respond as though that hormone were being produced.

Diseases caused by not enough hormone secretion can also have multiple causes. Endocrine tissue can be destroyed by an autoimmune process, in which the body incorrectly identifies some of its own tissue as foreign and destroys the tissue cells. In early stages of tissue loss, the body may compensate by producing additional hormone from the remaining tissue. In these cases, signs of disease may be delayed until the tissue has been destroyed completely.

Disorders resulting in signs of reduced endocrine activity may also develop because tissues distant from the hormone source are disrupted. This can occur when the function of one hormone is to stimulate the production of a second hormone. For example, the pituitary gland secretes a hormone that stimulates the thyroid gland to secrete thyroid hormones. If the levels of the thyroid-stimulating hormone from the pituitary gland are abnormally low, the levels of thyroid hormones will also be low even if the thyroid gland is healthy. Another potential cause for reduced endocrine function is tissue loss caused by tumors that do not produce hormones themselves but compress or destroy the nearby endocrine gland.

Endocrine diseases and related conditions also result from changes in the response of tissues targeted by a hormone. An important example is type 2 diabetes mellitus, in which the body produces insulin but the cells no longer respond to it. This condition is often associated with obesity.

Treatment of Endocrine System Disease

Endocrine diseases caused by the presence of too much hormone may be treated surgically (tumor removal), by radiotherapy (such as the use of radioactive iodine to destroy an overactive thyroid gland), or with medication. Syndromes of hormone deficiency are often successfully treated by replacing the missing hormone, such as insulin injections to treat diabetes mellitus. Steroid and thyroid hormone replacements can usually be given by mouth.

Animals taking hormone replacement treatment must be monitored for adverse effects and periodically retested to make sure the dosage is correct. In some cases, such as after surgical removal of an endocrine tumor, the diseased gland will recover and hormone replacement will no longer be needed. However, most of the time, lifelong treatment is required.

■ COMMON HORMONAL DISORDERS IN HORSES

The most common hormonal disorders in horses affect the adrenal glands (Addison's disease and Cushing's disease), thyroid gland (hypothyroidism and goiter), and the pancreas (diabetes mellitus).

Cushing's Disease (Hypertrichosis)

Cushing's disease, also called **hyperadrenocorticism**, is the most common endocrine disease in horses. The signs are due primarily to chronic excess of the hormone cortisol. Increased cortisol levels may result from one of several mechanisms, such as destruction of a portion of the pituitary gland and overproduction of certain other hormones. Unlike Cushing's disease in dogs or people, the cause is not usually related to a pituitary tumor. However, pituitary tumors do occur, particularly later in the disease.

The disorder is seen in older horses (over 15 years of age) of any breed. Mares and geldings are most often affected. The most striking sign is development of an abnormally long or heavy hair coat (called **hypertrichosis**), which can grow up to 4 to 5 inches (10 to 12 centimeters) long, and is thick, wavy, and often matted. Other signs include excessive thirst and urination, increased appetite and weight, an enlarged abdomen, and bulging eyes. Horses with Cushing's disease tend to have a weakened immune system and may be prone to infections (such as dental disease or respiratory infections) or parasites. A diagnosis is based on a history and signs, physical examination, and appropriate blood tests.

Once a horse has been diagnosed with Cushing's disease, there are treatments available that may improve its condition and, in some cases, even return it to normal health. Pergolide and cyproheptadine are the 2 most commonly used drugs for treatment of this disorder in horses. However, treatment requires that the owner administer the drug daily and schedule regular veterinary checkups, including blood tests to monitor the horse's response. If treatment is stopped, the signs can reappear within a few weeks.

Even without medical treatment, many horses respond to careful management. This includes regular dental care, dewormings, hoof care, and an appropriate diet.

Addison's Disease

Addison's disease (**hypoadrenocorticism**) is caused by a deficiency of adrenal gland hormones. It is seen occasionally in horses. The cause is usually not known, but an autoimmune condition in which the body destroys some of its own tissue is likely. The adrenal gland can also be destroyed by other conditions, including cancer in other parts of the body. Secretion of aldosterone, the main mineralocorticoid hormone, is reduced, which affects the levels of potassium, sodium, and chloride in the blood. Potassium gradually builds up in the blood and, in severe cases, may cause the heart to slow down or beat irregularly. (*See also* DISORDERS OF THE ADRENAL GLANDS, page 131.)

Signs of Addison's disease include repeated episodes of vomiting and diarrhea, loss of appetite, dehydration, and a gradual loss of body condition. Weight loss is often severe. Although signs can be hard to identify while Addison's disease is developing, severe consequences, such as shock and evidence of kidney failure, can develop suddenly.

A tentative diagnosis is based on the history, signs, and certain laboratory abnormalities, such as very low levels of sodium and very high levels of potassium in the blood. The diagnosis is confirmed by specific evaluation of adrenal function. This is done by measuring the level of cortisol in the blood, treating the animal with adrenocorticotropin (a hormone that stimulates the adrenal gland in healthy animals), and then measuring the level of cortisol in the blood a second time. Affected horses have low baseline cortisol levels, and there is little response to administration of adrenocorticotropin.

An adrenal crisis is a medical emergency and requires treatment with intravenous fluids to restore levels of body fluids, salt, and sugar to normal. Hormone replacement therapy can often be started while the animal is being stabilized. Laboratory values are monitored regularly to assess the response to treatment and adjust doses if needed. For longterm treatment, replacement hormones can be given by mouth or injection. Supportive treatment and rest are indicated for horses with Addison's disease.

Diabetes Mellitus

Diabetes mellitus (often called simply diabetes) is a chronic disorder of carbohydrate metabolism caused by either a deficiency of insulin or a resistance to insulin. Diabetes caused by a deficiency of insulin (also called primary diabetes mellitus) is rare in horses; however, resistance to insulin (also called secondary diabetes mellitus) is more common and tends to develop in horses with Cushing's disease (*see* page 643). A diagnosis of diabetes mellitus is based on finding high levels of sugar in the blood and urine after a period of fasting. Treatment with insulin cannot reverse the insulin resistance seen in secondary diabetes mellitus.

Hypothyroidism

In hypothyroidism, decreased levels of thyroid hormones result in a slower metabolic rate. Adult horses rarely develop hypothyroidism. However, foals may be born with hypothyroidism if the pregnant mare grazed plants that contained goiter-producing substances (*see* below), or if she was fed a diet with either not enough or too much iodine. Most commonly, these foals are affected by a specific syndrome in which they have both thyroid abnormalities and multiple congenital musculoskeletal abnormalities. This syndrome has been reported most commonly in western Canada, and it may be related to feeding a high nitrate diet (for example, greenfeed) to pregnant mares.

Because a deficiency of thyroid hormone affects the function of all organ systems, signs vary. Many signs could also be caused by other diseases. Most signs are directly related to slowing of metabolism, which results in lethargy, unwillingness or inability to exercise, and weight gain without an increase in appetite.

Diagnosis requires evaluation of signs and various laboratory tests, including demonstration of low serum concentrations of thyroid hormones that do not respond to administration of thyroid-stimulating hormone. Identifying hypothyroidism can be difficult at times because other conditions in the adult horse can make it appear that thyroid hormone levels are low when they are actually normal.

Hypothyroidism is treated using replacement with synthetic thyroid hormone. The success of treatment can be measured by the amount of improvement in signs. Serum thyroid hormone concentrations are also monitored to determine whether the dosage of thyroid hormone needs adjustment. Once the dose has been stabilized, thyroid hormone levels are usually checked once or twice a year. Treatment is generally lifelong.

Goiter

A goiter is a noncancerous enlargement of the thyroid gland that develops most often when the diet does not contain enough iodine. Goiters develop in people, all domestic mammals, and birds. In addition to iodine deficiency, other major causes of goiter include goiter-causing substances, too much iodine in the diet, and inherited defects in the body's production of thyroid hormones. Many animals with goiter appear to have normal thyroid hormone levels, but signs of hypothyroidism may develop in some, especially in newborns (*see* above).

Iodine Deficiency

Goiter due to iodine deficiency was common in many areas of the world before iodized salt was routinely added to animal diets. Outbreaks of goiter caused by iodine deficiency are now sporadic and affect fewer animals, but iodine deficiency is still responsible for most goiters seen in horses.

A lack of iodine reduces the ability of the thyroid to make thyroid hormone. Because thyroid hormone levels drop, the pituitary gland secretes more thyroid-stimulating hormone, which results in the thyroid gland enlarging in an effort to make more thyroid hormone. Often, the enlarged thyroid gland can make enough thyroid hormone to bring the levels into the normal range. However, foals born of mares on iodine-deficient diets are more likely to develop severe thyroid enlargement and have signs of hypothyroidism. The neck is usually enlarged, and the skin and other tissue may be thickened, flabby, and swollen. Many foals die before or soon after birth, but treatment with iodized salt may resolve the goiter and associated signs in mildly affected foals. Prevention is much more effective than treatment, and adding stabilized, iodized salt to the diet is recommended in areas known or suspected to be deficient in iodine.

Iodine Toxicity

Foals born of mares fed too much iodine may develop extreme thyroid enlargement and die before birth or soon after. Signs include general weakness, long hair, and limb abnormalities.

Goiter-causing Substances

Certain plants can produce goiter if eaten in sufficient amounts, especially when the diet does not contain enough iodine. Soybeans, cabbage, rape, kale, and turnips all contain goitrogens. Cooking or heating (and the usual processing of soy- bean meal) destroys the goiter-causing substance in these plants. Goiter-causing substances act by interfering with production of thyroid hormone. As in iodine deficiency, the pituitary gland responds to the lower levels of thyroid hormone by increasing its secretion of thyroid-stimulating hormone. In turn, the thyroid responds by enlarging in an attempt to produce more thyroid hormone. In adult animals the disease is usually not significant, but newborn foals can develop severe thyroid enlargement and signs of hypothyroidism.

CHAPTER 47

Eye Disorders

▓ EYE STRUCTURE AND FUNCTION

The eyes of animals, including horses, function much like your eyes. (For a more complete discussion of SIGHT, *see* page 551.) Animals also develop many of the same eye problems that people can have, including cataracts, glaucoma, and other problems. Because sight is the way in which horses get the majority of their information about their surroundings, it is important for your horse to receive good eye care to protect its sight and allow the horse to interact comfortably with its environment. In general, horse vision is a little blurrier and a little less colorful than human vision. However, horses see movement very well throughout the 340° arc of their peripheral vision.

The eye is an active organ that constantly adjusts the amount of light it lets in and focuses on objects near and far. It produces continuous images that are quickly relayed to the brain.

The bony cavity or socket that contains and protects the eyeball is called the **orbit**. The orbit is a structure that is formed by several bones. The orbit also contains muscles, nerves, blood vessels, and the structures that produce and drain tears.

The white of the eye is called the **sclera**. This is the relatively tough outer layer of the eye. It is covered by a thin membrane, called the **conjunctiva**, located near the front of the eye. The conjunctiva runs to the edge of the cornea and covers the inside of the eyelid. The **cornea** is a clear dome on the front surface of the eye that lets light in. The cornea not only protects the front of the eye, but also helps focus light on the retina at the back of the eye. The **iris** is the circular, colored area of the eye. It controls the amount of light that enters the eye by making the pupil larger or smaller. The **pupil** is the black area in the middle of the eye. It is controlled by the circular sphincter muscle. When the environment is dark, the pupil enlarges to let in more light; when the environment is bright, the pupil becomes smaller to let in less light.

The **lens**, which sits behind the iris, changes its shape to focus light onto the retina. Small muscles called ciliary muscles contract to cause the lens to become thicker, which allows the lens to focus on nearby objects. The ciliary muscles relax to cause the lens to become thinner when it focuses on distant objects. In horses, the very large lens appears to have limited changes. The **retina** contains the cells that sense light (photoreceptors). The most sensitive area of the retina is called the **visual streak** in horses. This area contains thousands of tightly packed photoreceptors that make visual images sharp. Each photoreceptor is attached to a nerve fiber. All the nerve fibers are bundled together to form the **optic nerve**. The photoreceptors in the retina convert the image into electrical impulses, which are carried to the brain by the optic nerve.

The upper and lower eyelids are thin folds of skin that can cover the eye and reflexively blink to protect it. Blinking also helps spread tears over the surface of the eye, keeping it moist and clearing away small particles. The eyes of a horse are protected not only by the same types of eyelids that people have, but also by the **nictitating membrane**, which is sometimes called the third eyelid. This additional eyelid is a whitish pink color, and it is found under the other eyelids in the inside corner of the eye (near the nose). The third eyelid extends up when needed to protect the eyeball from scratches or in response to inflammation.

To function properly, eyes must be kept moist. Tears are the source of this needed moisture. Tears are produced by 2 types of glands. **Lacrimal glands** produce the watery portion of tears. They are located at the top outer edge of each eye. Mucus glands in the conjunctiva produce mucus that mixes with the watery portion. This creates a more protective tear that is slower to evaporate. Nasolacrimal ducts allow tears to drain from each eye into the nose. Each of these ducts has openings at the edge of the upper and lower eyelids near the nose.

Physical Examination of the Eye

When examining your horse's eyes, a veterinarian will begin by checking to

see that the shape and outline of the eyes are normal and that there are no obvious abnormalities. Using light and magnification in a darkened room, the reflexes of the pupils and the front part of the eye will be examined. A test, called the Schirmer tear test, may be performed to ensure that the eyes are producing enough tears to keep them moist. This is a relatively simple test in which small paper strips are inserted under the eyelid to measure the amount of moisture produced. A small drop of fluorescein staining may be put into each eye allowing defects in the cornea of the eye to be detected.

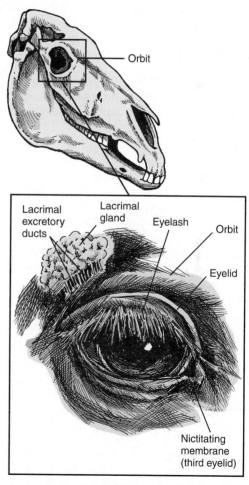

Structures that protect the eye (modified with permission from *The Merck Manual of Medical Information*, Second Home Edition, 2003)

Pressure within the eye is painlessly measured using an instrument called a tonometer. If eye pressure is too high, optic nerve damage can occur, leading to irreversible blindness. A swab may also be done to culture for bacteria or fungi. The eyelids may be turned inside out to examine the underside of the eyelids. The nasal tear duct may be flushed to evaluate the external parts of the eye. Drops may be added to the eyes to dilate the pupils so that the veterinarian may examine the internal part of the eye using an ophthalmoscope.

To ensure the safety of both horse and veterinarian, appropriate restraint during the eye examination—such as topical anesthesia, use of a nose or ear twitch, or sedation—are often necessary.

▓ DISORDERS OF THE EYELIDS

Problems affecting the eyelids may be congenital (present at birth) or may occur as a result of injury, infection, or exposure to various types of irritants.

Entropion

Entropion is the turning in of the edges of the eyelid so that the eyelashes rub against the eye surface. It occurs in foals as a congenital defect. It may also be acquired in older horses as a result of chronic eye irritation or spasms. The turning in of eyelashes or facial hairs causes discomfort and irritation of the conjunctiva and cornea. Extremely long lashes can cause scarring, abnormal coloring, and possibly the formation of slow-healing sores or ulcers on the cornea.

Early spasms of entropion may be reversed if the cause is removed or if pain is lessened. Turning the lid hairs back away from the eye with stitches in the lid, injections of medication into the lid close to the area where the lid is turning in, or using anesthetics to block the nerves in the eyelids are some of the methods that have been used to lessen the pain. Established entropion may require surgery to correct the defect.

Lacerations of the Eyelid

Eyelid lacerations (rips or tears in the eyelid) are common in horses. They must be repaired quickly to avoid infection, reduce swelling, and prevent further damage to the eye. In many cases, your veterinarian will clean the wound and use stitches to repair it so that minimal scarring occurs.

Inflammation of the Eyelids (Blepharitis)

Inflammation of the eyelids can result from the spreading of a generalized inflammation of the skin (dermatitis), conjunctivitis (inflammation of the conjunctiva), local glandular infections, or irritants such as plant oils or sunlight. Infection with certain fungi or bacteria can also lead to inflammation of the eyelids; however, this is uncommon in horses.

Parasites, such as eyeworms (*see* page 654) and the larvae of stomach worms (*Habronema* species), are a common cause of blepharitis in horses, particularly during warm-weather months. Treatment is targeted toward removing the parasites by the use of appropriate antiparasitic drugs, although eyeworms can sometimes be removed directly from the surface of the conjunctiva using forceps. If needed, topical ointments to reduce swelling may be prescribed.

▓ DISORDERS OF THE NASAL CAVITY AND TEAR DUCTS

The lacrimal or tear gland, located at the top outer edge of the eye, produces the watery portion of tears. Nasolacrimal ducts allow tears to drain from each eye into the nose. Disorders of these structures can lead to eyes that water excessively or to dry eyes. They may be congenital (present at birth) or caused by infection, foreign objects in the eye, or trauma.

Absence of Nasal Tear Duct Openings

A congenital absence of the opening of the nasal tear duct at the lower end in the

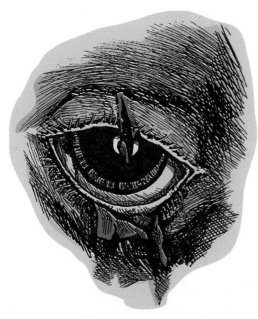

Rips or tears in the eyelid require prompt attention.

nose is a common cause of watering eyes and longterm conjunctivitis in foals. Therapy consists of surgically opening the blocked passage and keeping it open by inserting a tube during healing.

Inflammation of the Tear Sac (Dacryocystitis)

Inflammation of the tear sac is usually caused by obstruction of the tear sac and the attached nasal tear duct by inflammatory debris, foreign objects, or masses pressing on the duct. It results in watering eyes, conjunctivitis that is resistant to treatment, and occasionally a draining opening in the middle of the lower eyelid. If your veterinarian suspects an obstruction of the duct, he or she may attempt to unblock it by flushing it with sterile water or a saline solution. X-rays of the skull after injection of a dye into the duct may be necessary to determine the site, cause, and outlook of longterm obstructions. The usual therapy consists of keeping the duct unblocked and using eyedrops containing antibiotics.

Dry Eye (Keratoconjunctivitis Sicca)

The condition known as dry eye is caused by inadequate tear production. It frequently results in persistent, mucus and pus-filled conjunctivitis and slow-healing sores and scarring on the cornea. In horses, dry eye may follow head trauma. Topical therapy consists of artificial tear solutions, ointments, and, if there are no sores on the cornea, combination antibiotic/steroid medication. In longterm dry eye resistant to medical therapy, parotid duct transplantation surgery may be recommended.

▄ DISORDERS OF THE CONJUNCTIVA

The conjunctiva is a thin membrane that lines the inside of the eyelids and extends to the cornea of the eye. It plays a role in creating tears, providing protection for the eye from foreign invaders, and healing of the cornea after injury. It is important to identify and treat problems of the conjunctiva, because some can indicate generalized disease, while others can lead to blindness if not treated.

Conjunctivitis (Pink Eye)

Conjunctivitis, also known as pink eye, can occur as a result of many different diseases that affect the eye or even the whole body. The causes vary from infections to environmental irritants. The signs are excess blood flow to the eye, swelling of the tissue around the cornea, discharge from the eye, and mild eye discomfort. The appearance of the conjunctiva usually is not enough, by itself, to allow your veterinarian to diagnose the cause with only a physical examination. A specific diagnosis often requires a medical history, tests on conjunctival scrapings, Schirmer tear test, and occasionally biopsy.

Conjunctivitis in only one eye may result from a foreign object, inflammation of the tear sac, or dry eye (*see* above). Conjunctivitis occurring in both eyes is commonly caused by infection with a virus or bacteria. Environmental irritants and allergens are other common causes of conjunctivitis. If a mucus and pus-filled discharge is present, your veterinarian may prescribe a topical antibiotic. However, the antibiotic alone may not bring about healing if other factors are involved. Your veterinarian will also check for foreign objects in the eye, environmental irritants, parasites, and defects of eyelid shape, outline, or form, as these factors also contribute to pink eye. Because conjunctivitis can have multiple causes, your veterinarian may prescribe a combination of treatments.

■ DISORDERS OF THE CORNEA

The cornea protects the front of the eye and is also important in focusing light on the retina at the back of the eye. Because the cornea is critical for proper vision, it is important to address any disorders or injuries promptly.

Corneal Ulcers

Corneal ulcers are common in horses. This disorder has the potential to affect vision unless the cause is promptly diagnosed and treated. Many equine corneal ulcers occur as a result of injury to the eye, with inflammation of the cornea (called keratitis) that ranges from superficial to deep. Superficial ulcers are usually controlled with topical antibiotics and correction of any mechanical factors. In addition, veterinarians often prescribe medications to reduce eye pain.

Corneal ulcers may be complicated by a fungal invasion; this is termed **equine ulcerative keratomycosis**. The fungus, which is normally present in the conjunctiva, multiplies rapidly after injury to the cornea and causes inflammation and ulcers. The diagnosis is confirmed by identifying the fungus in cells from the cornea. Treatment must begin promptly to avoid vision loss and includes both therapy with antifungal drugs and sur-

gery. Even with aggressive treatment, vision after keratomycosis is lost in about 25% of affected eyes.

Syndromes of very slow-healing and recurrent superficial ulcers also occur in horses. In such cases, a herpesvirus is often the cause. Initial treatment involves removal of the dead, damaged, or infected tissue of the ulcer, followed by prescription topical medication.

Corneal Abscesses

Pus-filled sores in the connective tissue of the cornea (corneal stromal abscesses) in horses may be caused by healing ulcers or defects of the cornea and the trapping of bacteria or fungi (or both) within the connective tissue after healing tissue is formed. A white to yellow material in the connective tissue is surrounded by an intense inflammation and swelling of the cornea and formation of blood vessels. In addition, there may be a variable but sometimes intense inflammation of the anterior uvea. Treatments include topical and, in some cases, whole-body antibiotics, antifungal drugs, drugs to reduce pain, and nonsteroidal anti-inflammatory drugs. In addition, surgery may be required.

Corneal Lacerations

Minor lacerations of the cornea are common in horses and can usually be treated with topical antibiotics and other drugs as recommended by your veterinarian. Severe lacerations or perforations of the cornea often require surgery and more aggressive therapy. Signs of laceration include swelling or prolapse of the iris, swelling of the ciliary bodies, and blood in the eye.

■ DISORDERS OF THE ANTERIOR UVEA

The uvea (or the uveal tract) is the colored inside lining of the eye consisting of the iris, the ciliary body, and the choroid. The iris is the colored ring around the black pupil. The ciliary body consists of muscles that contract and relax to allow the lens to focus on objects; it is also the source of the aqueous humor, the clear fluid within the eye. The choroid is the inner lining of the eyeball. It extends from the ciliary muscles to the optic nerve at the back of the eye. The choroid also contains layers of blood vessels that nourish the inside parts of the eye, especially the retina.

Persistent membranes across the pupil, cysts of the iris, and inflammation of the iris and ciliary body (**anterior uveitis or iridocyclitis**) are all conditions that can affect the front of the uvea. In horses, cysts of the iris may be present in the connective tissue. Many such cysts involve blue irises. (For a more detailed discussion of DISORDERS OF THE ANTERIOR UVEA, *see* page 148.)

Common causes of inflammation of the uvea in both eyes of horses include immune-mediated diseases and infectious diseases such as toxoplasmosis (a disease caused by a parasite), systemic mycosis (a fungal infection), leptospirosis (a bacterial disease), equine viral arteritis (a viral disease), and bacterial infections of the joints, navel, and gut of newborn foals.

Equine Recurrent Uveitis (Periodic Ophthalmia, Moon Blindness)

Equine recurrent uveitis is one of the most common eye diseases in adult horses. Typically, there are periods of active inflammation of the uvea, followed by varying periods with no signs at all. During the so-called inactive periods, mild inflammation continues in most horses. If untreated, the inflammation eventually leads to harmful complications that make this syndrome the most common cause of blindness in horses throughout the world.

Equine recurrent uveitis has many potential causes, but the end result is damage to the uveal tract. Specific conditions or agents that may cause this disorder include certain bacteria, parasitic worms, equine influenza (a viral illness), tooth root

abscesses, and hoof abscesses. Inflammation can be stimulated by dead or dying larvae of parasites that have unexpectedly migrated to the eye. Therefore, active episodes of uveitis are sometimes seen after normal deworming treatments.

Signs of active uveitis include frequent squinting, watering eyes, cloudiness of the cornea, and contraction of the pupil. An active episode may include inflamed cells infiltrating the retina or choroid, partial separation of the retina, retinal bleeding, and a hazy appearance to the vitreous (the clear "jelly" that fills the eye). One or both eyes may be affected. When both eyes are affected, it is common for one eye to be more severely inflamed.

Longterm equine recurrent uveitis leads to scarring of the cornea, formation of fibrous tissue in the iris, glaucoma, cataracts, and degeneration of the retina. The importance of careful eye examinations cannot be overstated. Horses with longterm uveitis can have few or no obvious signs of eye disease but may develop degeneration of the retina. To protect your horse's vision, eye examinations should be included in its routine care.

Your veterinarian will want to identify the underlying cause of the uveitis. Because an episode of uveitis (inflammation of the uvea) can be the first sign of generalized disease, a thorough physical examination is usually performed in

Equine recurrent uveitis is the most common cause of blindness in horses.

addition to the eye examination. Blood tests are often included as part of the examination. Other tests may also be needed to identify the cause.

Therapy should begin as soon as possible. If a specific cause can be identified, your veterinarian will address it as part of the treatment plan. In addition, or in cases where no cause is identified, aggressive therapy with both topical and whole-body anti-inflammatory medications is usually started to minimize the damage to the eye. Your veterinarian will prescribe the therapy best suited for your horse. Be sure to follow the prescription instructions exactly to help your horse recover.

Good husbandry practices such as effective fly control, frequent bedding changes, routine worming and vaccinations, minimizing contact with cattle or wildlife, draining stagnant ponds or restricting access to swampy pastures, and maximizing nutrition have all been advocated as means to reduce the effects of equine recurrent uveitis. These steps should be taken in addition to providing the prescribed medications.

■ GLAUCOMA

The glaucomas represent a group of diseases characterized by increased pressure within the eye. The high pressure eventually destroys the retina and optic disk (the spot where the optic nerve enters the eye). In horses, glaucomas are probably underdiagnosed because testing of the pressure within the eye has only recently become a part of ordinary equine examinations. Among horses, glaucoma appears most frequently in older animals, in the Appaloosa breed, or together with equine recurrent uveitis (*see* page 651).

There are various instruments a veterinarian can use to evaluate and manage glaucoma. The choice of medical or surgical (including laser) treatment or, most frequently, a combination of both, depends on the type of glaucoma present. Most glaucomas require longterm management. (For a more detailed discussion of GLAUCOMA, *see* page 149.)

■ DISORDERS OF THE LENS

The lens is a soft, transparent tissue that sits behind the iris. It helps refract incoming light onto the retina. Common disorders of the lens include those that affect its transparency (such as cataracts), and those that affect the placement of the lens.

Cataracts

Cataracts are a condition in which the lens becomes covered in a cloudy film that affects sight, eventually causing total blindness.

In foals, cataracts are the most common congenital defect of the eye. They are inherited in Belgian, Morgan, and Thoroughbred horses. Cataracts usually occur in both eyes. When these cataracts interfere with vision in healthy foals, surgery followed by topical therapy is successful in a majority of cases.

In adult horses, most cataracts occur as a result of the inflammation of the anterior uvea associated with equine recurrent uveitis (*see* page 651). Horses older than 20 years of age may develop so-called senile cataracts that interfere with vision. Surgical removal of the lens is the only definitive treatment available.

Lens Displacement

Lens displacement can also occur in horses. The displacement may be due to trauma, longterm inflammation of the uvea (as occurs in equine recurrent uveitis), or glaucoma. The only effective treatment is surgical removal of the lens.

■ DISORDERS OF THE RETINA, CHOROID, AND OPTIC DISK (OCULAR FUNDUS)

The ocular fundus is the back of the eye opposite the pupil and includes the retina, the membrane between the retina and the white of the eye (the choroid), and the optic disk. Diseases of the ocular fundus may occur on their own or as a part of generalized diseases. Inherited abnormalities, trauma, metabolic disturbances, generalized infections, tumors, blood disorders, and nutritional deficiencies are possible underlying causes for diseases of the retina in all species.

Inflammation of the Retina and Choroid (Chorioretinitis)

Inflammation of the retina and choroid is frequently a result of a generalized infection. It is important as both a convenient diagnostic clue and a predictor of visual function. Unless the abnormalities are widespread or involve the optic nerve, they often are "silent." Signs of inflammation include swelling, bloodshot eyes, discharge from the eyes, and nodules or masses in the eye itself.

Your veterinarian will look for certain characteristic lesions in the eye. These include "bullet-hole" lesions (which suggest infection with equine herpesvirus), diffuse lesions (which may be caused by inflammation or severe head trauma), and "horizontal band" lesions (which may be caused by blockage of the blood vessels).

Inflammation of the retina and choroid may be present with bacterial, algal, and fungal infections, or caused by trauma or parasites. Therapy is directed at the underlying generalized disease.

Retinal Detachments

When the retina become detached, it is separated from the back of the eye and from part of its blood supply, preventing it from functioning properly. In horses, detachment of the retina occurs with chorioretinitis, trauma, surgery, and low pressure within the eye.

Signs that the retina has become detached include excessive or prolonged dilation of the pupil, pupils of different sizes, vision impairment, and bleeding within the eye. Eye examinations need to be performed to confirm the diagnosis.

Detachments of the retina are treated medically with therapy directed at the primary disease or surgically to correct the detachment. Your veterinarian will select the treatment approach most appropriate for your horse's condition.

DISORDERS OF THE OPTIC NERVE

The optic nerve carries the electrical impulses from the eye to the area in the back of the brain where vision is sensed and interpreted. Injury to the optic nerve usually leads to partial or complete loss of sight.

Optic Nerve Hypoplasia

Optic nerve hypoplasia is a failure of the optic nerve to develop fully. It is a congenital disorder in horses. The condition may occur in only one eye or both, and it can occur with or without other eye abnormalities. If the optic nerves of both eyes fail to develop, the foal will be blind. Involvement of only one of the optic nerves often goes undetected or may be discovered later in life if the other eye acquires a blinding disease.

Optic Nerve Atrophy

Optic nerve degeneration or atrophy may occur as a result of equine recurrent uveitis (*see* page 651), glaucoma, trauma, advanced degeneration of the retina, prolonged low pressure within the eye, or inflammation. The optic disk appears flattened and smaller than normal; it is often pale or white, with very noticeable reduction in the optic nerve and blood vessels of the retina. Both the direct reflex of the pupil and vision are absent. There is no treatment.

Proliferative Optic Neuropathy

This condition occurs primarily in older horses. It usually involves only one eye and has a minimal effect on vision. Signs include a yellow-white mass that protrudes from the optic disk into the vitreous (the clear "jelly" that fills the eye). There is no treatment.

PROLAPSE OF THE EYE

Severe prolapse (slipping out of place) and/or bulging of the eye can be caused by trauma. The chances of a good outcome depend on the severity of the injury, depth of the eye socket, the condition of the eye and how long it was displaced, and other damage near the eye. Without its blood supply, the equine eye quickly becomes damaged. The eyeball should be put back in place surgically as soon as possible if the animal is in good enough health to have general anesthesia; the eyelids are then sutured together to protect the globe as swelling decreases. Treatment includes antibiotics (given by mouth or injection, as well as topical ointments or creams) to prevent infection. Occasionally other medications are needed as well.

◼ EYEWORM DISEASE (THELAZIASIS)

Eyeworms (*Thelazia* species) are common parasites of horses in many countries, including several areas of North America. Horses are infected primarily by *Thelazia lacrymalis*.

The face fly, which feeds on secretions from the eye, transmits eyeworms in North America. Eyeworm larvae are ingested by the fly and become infective in 2 to 4 weeks. The infective larvae are then re-deposited in the horse's eye by the fly during feeding. Infections may occur year-round, but disease outbreaks usually are associated with the warm season activities of the flies.

Eyeworms can be found in the tear gland and its ducts, less commonly in the third eyelid and the nasal tear ducts, and

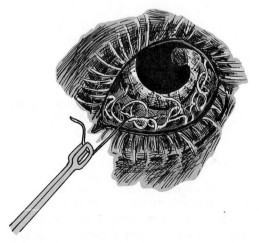

Your veterinarian may be able to remove eyeworms using forceps.

also on the cornea, in the conjunctival sac, and under the eyelids. Infections with no obvious signs in horses appear to be typical of eyeworm disease in North America. However, irritation and inflammation of the eye is likely due to the rough outer layer of the worms. Inflammation of the tear ducts and sac has also been reported in horses. Mild to severe inflammation of the conjunctiva and inflammation of affected eyelids are common. Inflammation and swelling of the cornea, including the development of an opaque film, slow-healing sores, holes, and permanent fibrous tissue, may develop in severe cases.

Currently, there is no reliable technique for detecting adult eyeworms in horses. Inspection of the eyes may reveal the worms; however, *Thelazia lacrymalis* in horses tends to be more invasive and less apt to be seen. Topical anesthetics may be administered to allow the veterinarian to detect and remove worms from the eye. Microscopic examination of tears for eggs or larvae may be attempted. Certain other parasites (such as *Onchocerca* microfilariae, *see* page 771) that affect the eyes of horses must also be excluded as causes of the inflammation.

Your veterinarian may be able to remove eyeworms with forceps after using a local anesthetic. Flushing the eyes with an iodine solution or applying an iodine ointment may also be effective. An antibiotic-steroid ointment to treat the inflammation and any bacterial infection is often recommended. Certain whole-body drugs that destroy or flush out parasitic worms have been shown to work against eyeworms.

To reduce the chance of eyeworm infections, good fly control measures—directed especially against the face fly—are critical.

◼ CANCERS AND TUMORS OF THE EYE

The different tissues of the eye and associated structures can develop primary tumors or can be the site of spreading tumor cells. In horses, tumors of the skin, eye, and genital system are the most frequent, and about 80% of eye tumors are malignant (cancerous).

Tumors of the eyelids and conjunctivae are the most frequent eye tumors in horses. Most are either squamous cell carcinoma (a common type of cancer that usually develops in the outer layer of the skin and sometimes in mucous membranes) or sarcoid (a small, lumpy collection of fibrous tissue). Eye socket tumors are rare and are usually local extensions of eyelid, conjunctiva, or sinus tumors or generalized tumors (including lymphosarcoma). Tumors within the eyes are rare. Those that do occur are usually malignant melanomas.

Squamous Cell Carcinoma

Squamous cell carcinoma is a form of skin cancer that occurs most frequently in horses 8 to 10 years old. It may be more frequent in those with lightly-pigmented or nonpigmented eyelids. Appaloosas and draft breeds are affected most frequently. Ultraviolet radiation from excessive sun exposure may be important, because the incidence in North America is higher in southern and western areas and in areas of increased altitude or higher mean solar radiation. The eyelids, conjunctivae, third eyelid, and edges of the cornea can be affected with masses of slow-healing sores or multiplying cells forming a tumor. In most cases, only one eye is involved. Squamous cell carcinomas of the third

eyelid are more likely to invade the eye socket than are those from other sites.

Anticancer drugs, surgery, and cryotherapy—alone or in various combinations—are available to control these tumors. Your veterinarian will recommend a medication program that is best for your horse.

Equine Sarcoids

Equine sarcoids are skin tumors that generally affect young horses (average 3.8 years old). They represent about 40% of all tumors in horses (*see also* page 775). When the eyes are affected, sarcoids appear as masses just below the skin in the eyelids or at the corners of the eyelids. They usually grow rapidly and may invade the skin, appearing as red, fleshy masses. Treatment can be difficult because sarcoids are destructive and have a high recurrence rate after surgery. Treatment can include laser surgery or cryotherapy (freezing the tumor) to remove the sarcoid; chemotherapy; radiation; or a combination of these therapies. After attempts to surgically remove the sarcoid, recurrence may be rapid and occur before the wound completely heals. Following surgery, veterinarians will often strengthen the body's immune system by giving a series of BCG (bacille Calmette-Guérin) preparation injections. This has about a 70% success rate. Other medications and radiation therapy may also be included in the treatment program.

CHAPTER 48

Ear Disorders

▓ EAR STRUCTURE AND FUNCTION

The ear is an organ of hearing and an organ of balance. It consists of the outer, middle, and inner ear.

The **outer ear** includes the pinna (the part you see that is made of cartilage and

covered by skin, fur, or hair) and the ear canal. The pinna is shaped to capture sound waves and funnel them through the ear canal to the eardrum. The pinnae are mobile and can move independently of each other, allowing horses to locate multiple sounds at the same time. In general,

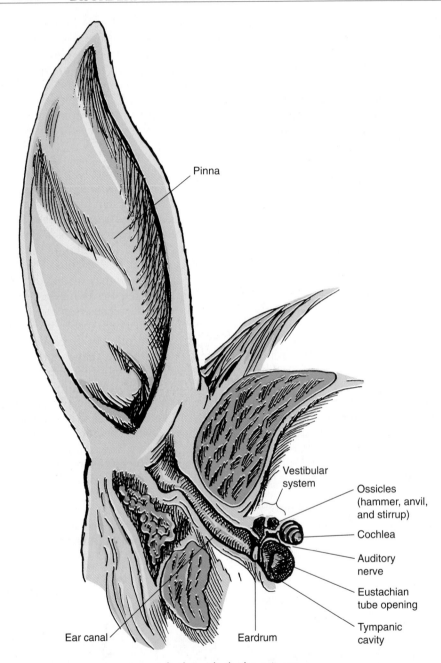

Pinna

Vestibular
system

Ossicles
(hammer, anvil,
and stirrup)

Cochlea

Auditory
nerve

Eustachian
tube opening

Tympanic
cavity

Ear canal

Eardrum

A look inside the horse's ear

horses hear slightly better than people and are able to hear sounds at both higher and lower frequencies. Horses are good at hearing the high-pitched squeaks or cracks associated with the stealthy approach of a predator.

The **middle ear** includes the eardrum and a small, air-filled chamber that contains 3 tiny bones: the hammer, anvil, and stirrup. It also includes 2 muscles, the oval window, and the eustachian tube (a small tube that connects the middle ear with the back of the nose, allowing air to enter the middle ear).

The **inner ear** is a complex structure that includes the cochlea (the organ of hearing) and the vestibular system (the organ of balance).

Physical Examination of the Ear

Infections of the ear and other ear disorders are less common in horses than in dogs or cats. Your veterinarian will examine your horse's ears at every routine checkup. If the horse has a history of previous ear infections or other problems with the ear, you should provide that information to the veterinarian.

To start, your veterinarian will visually inspect the outer ears, noting any signs of inflammation, injury from trauma, swelling, secretions, or excessive ear wax. He or she will then use an instrument called an otoscope to view the ear canal and eardrum. In some cases, hair may need to be removed from the ear canals to allow the veterinarian a clear view of the ear drum.

If an infection is suspected, tests will be performed on samples of fluid or secretions from the ear to determine the organisms involved and the proper treatment. Infections are most commonly caused by bacteria or yeasts.

To diagnose a tumor of the ear, it may be necessary to do a pinch biopsy for evaluation. This can usually be done using forceps and an otoscope. Further tests, including x-rays, neurologic tests, and electronic tests, may be needed to confirm certain conditions such as deafness.

▓ DEAFNESS

Deafness may be congenital (present at birth) or acquired as a result of infection, trauma, or degeneration of the ear.

Deafness present at birth can be inherited (as is known to occur in certain American Paint horses) or result from toxic or viral damage to the developing unborn foal.

Acquired deafness may result from blockage of the external ear canal as occurs in longterm otitis externa (inflammation of the external ear canal), or it may occur after destruction or damage of the middle or inner ear. Other causes include trauma to the hard portion of the temporal bone that surrounds the inner ear, loud noises (for example, gunfire), conditions in which there is a loss or destruction of myelin (the fatty material that surrounds some nerve cells), drugs toxic to the ear (for example, aminoglycoside antibiotics or aspirin), and tumors involving the ear or brain stem. Deafness in one ear or partial hearing loss is possible in some of these instances. (For a more detailed discussion of DEAFNESS, *see* page 157.)

▓ DISORDERS OF THE OUTER EAR

A variety of skin conditions affect the outside part of the ear, called the pinna. Most conditions cause tissue changes elsewhere as well. Rarely, a disease affects the outer ear alone, or it is the first site affected. As with all skin conditions, a diagnosis is based on a thorough history, a complete physical and skin examination, and carefully selected diagnostic tests.

Insects and parasites commonly cause inflammation of the pinna in horses—resulting in redness, swelling, itching, or blistering—either through direct damage from the bite of the parasite or as a result of hypersensitivity.

Treating Painful Bites on Your Horse's Ears

Bites from certain types of flies, such as black flies, deer flies, or stable flies, can be painful and sometimes become infected if not treated.

▓ Clip ear hairs only when absolutely necessary to see the bite or bites. The hairs in a horse's ears protect the ear against parasites and agents that spread infection.

▓ Gently clean the area around the bite, using warm, soapy water and a clean cloth. Do not let water drip into the ear.

▓ Apply a general antibiotic ointment or other medication as directed by your veterinarian.

▓ To prevent further bites, use appropriate fly repellent.

Aural Plaques

Equine aural plaques are benign, raised, pinkish tumors on the inner surface of the ear. They are caused by a papillomavirus that is likely transmitted by black flies. These flies are active at dawn and dusk, when they attack the head, ears, and lower abdomen of horses. The thickened, hard, round bumps and patches eventually grow together. Often both ears are affected. Similar lesions may be present around the anus and external genitalia. The plaques do not usually cause signs, but in some cases the direct effect of the fly bite causes skin inflammation and discomfort. Treatment includes frequent applications of fly repellent and stabling the horse during the hours when black flies are active. The plaques typically do not go away.

Flies

Fly strike (irritation of the ears caused by biting flies) is a worldwide problem in horses caused by the stable fly. The fly bite causes small, hard, round bumps and raised, reddened areas with central bloody crusts that itch. Tissue changes are found

Hard, round bumps and flaky skin are signs of fly strike.

on the tips of the ears. In horses, the stable fly can cause a hypersensitivity reaction or severe inflammation of the skin resulting in tissue changes on the hind and/or lower part of the body and face in addition to the outer ear. Treatment includes fly repellents, controlling the fly population with environmental cleanup (for example, removing manure), and insecticides.

Frostbite

Frostbite may occur in animals poorly adapted to cold climates and is more likely in wet or windy conditions. It typically affects body regions that are not well insulated, including the tips of the ears. The skin may be pale or red, swollen, and painful. In severe cases, death to tissue and shedding of the pinnae tips may follow. Treatment consists of rapid, gentle warming and supportive care. Amputation of affected regions may be required but is usually delayed until the extent of living tissue is determined.

Immune-mediated Diseases

Several immune-mediated diseases may affect the outer ear and ear canal. (*See also*

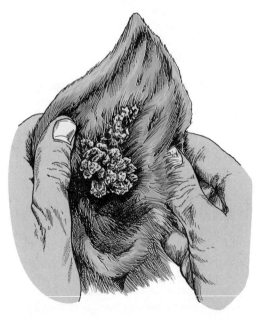

Equine aural plaques are caused by a virus spread by black flies.

AUTOIMMUNE SKIN DISORDERS, page 170.) Other areas of the body are typically affected and may include mucous membranes or skin. Immune-mediated diseases are confirmed with a biopsy of primary abnormalities.

Mites

Nonburrowing **psoroptic mites** cause an itchy, inflamed ear canal in horses. Horses may shake their heads and have a drooping ear. Diagnosis is confirmed by finding the mites on skin scrapings or in ear discharges, but mites may be difficult to find in the ear canal. Psoroptic mange is a reportable disease in some regions. Medications are available for controlling these conditions. Your veterinarian will prescribe the one that is most appropriate for your horse.

Ticks

Ticks can cause irritation at the site of attachment and may be found on the pinna or in the ear canal. The **ear tick**, found in the southwestern United States, South and Central America, southern Africa, and India, is a soft-shelled tick whose younger, immature forms infest and live on the external ear canal of horses. Signs of infestation include head shaking, head rubbing, or drooped ears. Both the animal and the environment (pasture and stable) should be treated. Your veterinarian can recommend the most appropriate treatment for your horse.

▓ OTITIS EXTERNA

The tubular portion of the outer ear that carries sound to the eardrum is called the ear canal. Inflammation of the layer of cells that line the external ear canal, called otitis externa, can be short- or longterm and may develop anywhere from the eardrum to the outer ear. Signs of inflammation include redness of the skin, swelling, itchiness, head shaking, increased discharge, and scaly skin. The ear canal may be painful or itchy depending on the cause or duration of the condition. While it is the most common disease of the ear canal in dogs and cats, it is uncommon in horses. (For a more detailed discussion of OTITIS EXTERNA, *see* page 160.)

▓ OTITIS MEDIA AND INTERNA

Inflammation of the middle ear structures (**otitis media**) is usually due to extension of infection from the external ear canal or to penetration of the eardrum by a foreign object. Spread of infection by means of blood to these areas is possible but rare. The signs of otitis media are similar to those of otitis externa (*see* above).

Inflammation of the middle ear may lead to inflammation of the inner ear structures (**otitis interna**). This can in turn lead to loss of balance and deafness. (For a more detailed discussion of OTITIS MEDIA AND INTERNA, *see* page 161.)

CHAPTER **49**
Immune Disorders

▓ THE IMMUNE SYSTEM

The immune system consists of a network of white blood cells, antibodies, and other substances that fight off infections and reject foreign proteins. In addition, the immune system includes several organs.

Some, such as the thymus gland and the bone marrow, are the sites where white blood cells are produced. Others, including the spleen, lymph nodes, and liver, trap microorganisms and foreign substances and provide a place for immune system cells to collect, interact with each other and with foreign substances, and generate an immune response.

The primary role of the immune system is to defend the body against foreign invaders or abnormal cells that invade or attack it. The immune system functions in the same way in horses as it does in dogs—and, indeed, in humans. For that reason, the various immune system responses to foreign substances and the types of immune system disorders are discussed in detail in the chapter on immune disorders in dogs (*see* page 164).

■ DISORDERS INVOLVING ANAPHYLACTIC REACTIONS (TYPE I REACTIONS, ATOPY)

In a Type I reaction, the animal has been previously exposed to an antigen and produces an excess of antibodies. If this antigen appears in the blood, the result can be either anaphylactic shock or more localized reactions, such as itchy patches or hives on the skin. If the antigen enters through the skin, a more localized reaction is typical.

Anaphylactic Shock

Anaphylactic shock is a rare, life-threatening, immediate allergic reaction to food, an injection, or an insect sting. The most common signs occur within seconds to minutes after exposure to the antigen. These signs include severe respiratory distress and the sudden onset of diarrhea, vomiting, excessive drooling, shock, seizures, coma, and death. The horse's gums are very pale, and the limbs feel cold. The heart rate is generally very fast, but the pulse is weak. Facial swelling does not usually occur, but there may be itchiness around the face and head.

Anaphylaxis is an extreme emergency. If you think that your horse is having an anaphylactic reaction, seek emergency veterinary assistance immediately. A veterinarian can give intravenous injections of epinephrine to counteract the reaction.

Treatment for related problems, such as respiratory distress, may also be needed.

Hives and Swelling

Hives (**urticaria**) and areas of swelling are caused by allergic reactions to drugs, chemicals, something eaten, insect bites, or even sunlight. They generally develop within 20 minutes of being exposed to the allergen (antigen). Hives are the least severe type of anaphylactic reaction. Small bumps occur on the skin. Often, the hair stands up over these swellings and sometimes they itch. Swelling is most often noticed on the face, especially on the lips, the muzzle, and around the eyes, but may also occur on the body or legs.

Hives and swelling are usually not life threatening and typically go away by themselves once the cause of the allergic reaction is removed or passes through the body. Veterinarians often treat these reactions by providing corticosteroids or antihistamines. Your veterinarian will make treatment decisions based on your horse's individual situation.

Milk Allergy

In some mares, a milk allergy develops when the pressure inside the mammary glands increases enough that some stored milk components (usually the protein casein) are forced into the mare's circulatory system. The mare's immune system reacts to these "foreign" proteins in her blood. This results in a hypersensitivity reaction that may be localized (hives and/or swelling involving only a small part of the mare's body) or generalized and severe (anaphylactic shock). Recovery is usually prompt once the mare's mammary gland is emptied.

Sweet Itch

Sweet itch is a skin allergy in horses that is usually seen in the warm summer months. It is associated with some insect bites, especially night-feeding *Culicoides*. These insects include midges ("no-see-ums") and a member of the black fly

Sweet itch is a seasonal skin allergy in horses caused by biting midges ("no-see-ums").

family. Sweet itch is characterized by intensely itchy patches that appear along the back of the horse from the ears to the tail and near the anus. Sweet itch is identified by skin tests. Treatment includes keeping the horse away from the biting insects and providing medication to control the itching and allergic reaction. Preventive measures include destroying the flies' breeding grounds, spraying stable areas with an approved pesticide, and using a fan to move the air around the horses.

▓ DISORDERS INVOLVING CYTOTOXIC ANTIBODIES (TYPE II REACTIONS)

Type II reactions can lead to several types of diseases in horses, including anemia, blood clotting problems, and skin and muscle disorders. They may be associated with other immune system disturbances, such as cancers of the lymphoreticular system, or triggered by a drug, vaccine, or infection. Most often, the triggering cause cannot be pinpointed.

Immune-mediated Hemolytic Anemia

This type of anemia is a severe and life-threatening disease in which the immune system sees its own red blood cells as foreign invaders, and produces antibodies to destroy them. Red blood cells are manufactured as usual in the bone marrow, but once released into the bloodstream, they are attacked and destroyed by antibodies. Signs of anemia may include fatigue, paleness of the lips and gums, and depression, along with jaundice in some cases. Other signs your veterinarian may find include an enlarged liver or spleen.

Cold Agglutinin (Hemolytic) Disease

Cold agglutinin (hemolytic) disease is also called cold antibody disease. It is a type of immune-mediated hemolytic anemia in which the body develops antibodies that attack red blood cells at temperatures lower than normal body temperature. It is more common in colder climates and seasons. The cause is usually not known, but it may follow a longterm infection, another autoimmune disorder, or cancer. The red blood cells are destroyed prematurely and bone marrow production of new cells cannot compensate for their loss. The severity of the anemia is determined by the length of time that the red blood cells survive and by the capacity of the bone marrow to produce new red blood cells. The condition is more likely to attack cooler parts of the body such as the nose, tips of the ears, legs, scrotum, and the skin over the penis. Diagnosis is based on a blood test. Medications are available to control this disease. Your veterinarian can prescribe the most appropriate for your horse.

Immune-mediated Thrombocytopenia

Immune-mediated thrombocytopenia is caused by the destruction of platelets (thrombocytes) by the immune system in much the same manner as red blood cells are destroyed in immune-mediated hemolytic anemia (*see* above). When an animal has thrombocytopenia, clotting does not occur correctly. Even minor injuries can cause uncontrollable bleeding, further decreasing the number of red blood cells. The most frequent signs are bleeding of the skin and mucous membranes.

The diagnosis is usually made based on the signs and response to treatment, rather than on blood tests. However, certain blood tests such as platelet counts and clotting profiles are helpful. Medication will likely be prescribed to treat this disease. Signs usually disappear after 5 to 7 days of treatment when platelet counts begin to rise. If the platelet count has not increased significantly after 7 to 10 days, additional or different medications, such as drugs that suppress the immune system, may be prescribed. If the blood loss is life threatening, transfusions of whole blood or plasma may be necessary.

Treatment is often continued for 1 to 3 months after the platelet counts return to normal. Some animals have persistent decreases in platelets even with drug treatment. If this is the case with your horse, you will want to discuss longterm treatment and maintenance options with your veterinarian.

■ DISORDERS INVOLVING IMMUNE COMPLEXES (TYPE III REACTIONS)

Immune complex disorders are among the most common immune-mediated diseases. The location in the body where the immune complexes (combinations of antibodies and antigens) are deposited determines the signs and the course of the disease.

Hypersensitivity Pneumonitis

This condition occurs when horses are exposed to large amounts of inhaled antigens, such as those found in dusty feeds or moldy hay. The lung tissues become inflamed, and signs of respiratory distress, such as difficulty breathing or rapid breathing, may be noticed about 4 to 6 hours after exposure to the antigen. The most effective treatment involves detecting and removing the source of the antigen. Your veterinarian may also recommend certain drugs, such as corticosteroids, to help control the allergic reaction.

Vasculitis

Vasculitis (inflammation of blood vessels) caused by immune complexes occurs in horses. At first, abnormalities are seen as purplish red dots appearing on the skin. Depending on which blood vessels are involved, signs may appear on the legs, mouth, or lips. Drugs are a frequent cause of vasculitis. The disorder is diagnosed by performing tests on samples removed from the affected areas. Vasculitis is treated by stopping the offending drug (if implicated as the cause) or by giving drugs that suppress the immune system.

Purpura Hemorrhagica

Purpura hemorrhagica is an immune reaction characterized by swelling and abscesses. It is a serious complication of infection with *Streptococcus equi* bacteria. The bacteria can spread from one horse to another by inhalation or ingestion of infected fluids or cells. It can also spread through contamination of the horse's environment. The disease ruptures lymph nodes and damages the horse's blood vessels. It can be fatal. Infected horses may lack energy, be in pain when swallowing and lose their appetite, and develop a fever or cough. Bacteria cultured from the material in the abscesses can be identified for a definitive diagnosis.

Horses suspected of having the infection should be isolated from other horses, kept warm and dry, and encouraged to eat soft, palatable feed. Complete drainage of the abscesses is necessary along with regular flushes of the ruptured lymph nodes until healing occurs. The material from the abscesses is infectious, and contaminated objects—including boots, hands, tack, hay, stall, and soil—should be cleaned and disinfected or discarded. The treatment consists of a strict quarantine of any new animals on the premises for up to 6 weeks. Recovered horses should not be considered free of infection until bacterial cultures are negative.

Anterior Uveitis

Anterior uveitis in horses is also known as moon blindness or periodic ophthalmia (*see* page 651). One cause of anterior uveitis is the action of antibody–antigen complexes on the iris, which causes inflammation of the eye. Once started, the inflammation may cause blindness if not halted. Fortunately, its progression can, in many cases, be slowed or stopped by fast, aggressive, and consistent care. Treatment of immune-mediated anterior uveitis may include whole-body corticosteroids and other drugs that suppress the immune system.

■ DISORDERS INVOLVING CELL-MEDIATED IMMUNITY (TYPE IV REACTIONS)

This type of reaction occurs when specific types of white blood cells (called T helper cells) respond to antigens and release toxic and inflammatory substances that can damage tissues. Cell-mediated immune reactions can occur in any organ. Treatment usually involves the use of anti-inflammatory drugs and drugs that suppress the immune system, either alone or in combination.

Granulomatous Reactions

Granulomatous reactions are masses of fibrous connective tissue infiltrated by the white blood cells that form a cell-mediated immune response. They occur in some animals following infection with certain types of bacteria or fungi. Although cell-mediated immune responses effectively fight off these infections in most individuals, in a few animals the immune response is only partially effective and results in a mass at the site of infection.

Contact Hypersensitivity

Contact hypersensitivity results from chemicals reacting with skin proteins. These reactions modify skin proteins in such a way that they are perceived as foreign invaders. The body then produces a cell-mediated immune response against them and causes skin damage. This hypersensitivity usually occurs as a result of contact with sensitizing chemicals, including some medications and insect repellents.

■ IMMUNE-DEFICIENCY DISEASES

Immune-deficiency diseases have serious consequences and often lower the body's defenses against infection. Some are inherited, and others are caused by viral infections or cancer.

Immunoglobulin Deficiency

This condition is due to a failure of the body to produce antibodies (immunoglobulins). The deficiency can be acquired (caused by other diseases) or congenital (present at birth). Acquired deficiencies occur in foals that do not receive adequate maternal antibodies from the colostrum produced by the dam during the first several hours of nursing. This is also called failure of passive transfer. Newborn animals that do not obtain adequate levels of these antibodies often develop fatal bacterial or viral infections of the gastrointestinal or respiratory tract.

It is important to ensure that newborn foals receive appropriate amounts of colostrum, preferably within the first 30 to 90 minutes after birth. Your veterinarian can measure the level and, if it is low, may recommend providing colostrum from another mare or from a frozen supply.

Immunoglobulin deficiency can occur as part of any disease that disrupts the production of antibodies in the body. For example, certain tumors (such as lymphosarcoma and plasma cell myeloma) cause the production of abnormal antibodies,

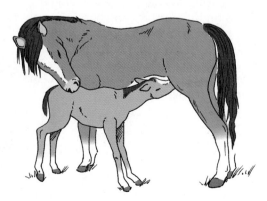

Newborn foals receive antibodies from their dams within the first few hours after birth.

which decreases production of normal antibodies. Depending on whether the deficiency is short- or longterm, treatment with antibiotics and intravenous immunoglobulins may be needed.

Combined Immunodeficiency Disease

Combined immunodeficiency disease involves a defect in both cell-mediated immunity and antibody production. This disease has been seen in Arabian foals in which the thymus (the organ that produces certain immune cells) is abnormal. Affected foals lack both T and B cells, which makes it impossible for the body to fight foreign invaders. The foals are healthy during the first several months of life but become progressively more susceptible to bacterial infections as the antibodies they received during nursing disappear. They tend to die from pneumonia or other infections, frequently by 2 months of age. No treatment is available.

CHAPTER **50**
Bone, Joint, and Muscle Disorders

▓ INTRODUCTION

The musculoskeletal system includes the bones, cartilage, muscles, ligaments, joints, tendons, and other connective tissue. It supports the body, permits movement, and protects the vital organs. Because many other body systems (including the nervous system, blood vessels, and skin) are interrelated, disorders of one of these systems may also affect the musculoskeletal system.

Musculoskeletal disorders are common in horses, in part due to the fact that they are often expected to work, perform, or carry a rider, which places additional stress on the muscles and bones. Horses also have a complex anatomy of the front and hind limbs with a number of bones, tendons, and joints. Disorders of any of these musculoskeletal components can lead to lameness and other problems.

▓ COMPONENTS OF THE MUSCULOSKELETAL SYSTEM

Bones provide rigid structure to the body and shield internal organs from damage. They also house bone marrow, where blood cells are formed, and they maintain the body's reservoir of calcium. Old bone tissue is constantly replaced with new bone tissue in a process called remodeling. This helps keep the bones healthy.

Bones come together to form **joints**. The type of joint formed determines the degree and direction of motion. For example, joints with a ball-and-socket formation allow for rotation, while hinge joints only allow bending and straightening. Some joints do not move at all. In a joint, the ends of the bones are covered with **cartilage**, which is a smooth protective tissue that helps reduce friction as joints move.

There are several different types of **muscles** in the body. Two of these, skeletal muscle and smooth muscle, are part of the musculoskeletal system. Skeletal muscles are responsible for posture and movement. They are attached to bones and arranged around the joints. Smooth muscle helps facilitate many processes in the body such as the flow of blood (by surrounding arteries) and the movement of food along the digestive tract.

Tendons are tough bands of connective tissue made up mostly of a protein called collagen. They stretch very little. Tendons attach each end of a muscle to a bone. At selected points, they are located within

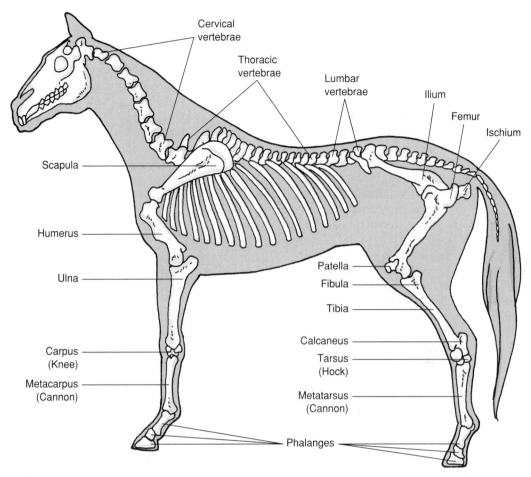

The skeleton of the horse

sheaths that allow them to move easily. **Ligaments** are also tough cords formed of connective tissue. Unlike tendons, they can stretch to some extent. Ligaments surround joints and help to support and stabilize them. They can also connect one bone to another.

▧ OVERVIEW OF MUSCULOSKELETAL DISORDERS

Disorders of the musculoskeletal system most often affect the horse's ability to move. How severely movement is impaired depends on the type and severity of the problem. Skeletal and joint disorders are the most common, but problems in the

musculoskeletal system can also indicate diseases of the muscles, neurologic problems, toxins in the body, hormonal abnormalities, metabolic disorders, infectious diseases, blood and vascular disorders, poor nutrition, and birth defects.

Many different systems in the body rely on the muscles. A horse's ability to see, breathe, urinate, breed, and even chew and swallow may be affected by a muscular condition. With many disorders, however, the musculoskeletal system is simply the location where signs of other underlying conditions show themselves. Veterinarians often trace the real cause of musculoskeletal trouble back to the nervous system.

Disorders that primarily affect the muscle membrane or muscle fibers are called **myopathies.** Muscle membrane disorders may be hereditary or acquired. Myopathies involving the actual muscle fiber components include exertional myopathy (*see* page 704). Diagnosing a myopathy usually requires laboratory tests.

Tendons stretch very little, so they are prone to injury and may become torn if a large amount of force is applied to them. Such injuries lead to **tendinitis**, which is inflammation of the tendons. Because tendons and ligaments are relatively poorly supplied with blood, they heal slowly and sometimes imperfectly. Injuries to ligaments and tendons require patience and careful longterm rehabilitation.

Bone diseases are generally present at birth or the result of nutritional deficiencies or injuries. An imbalanced level of minerals in the diet, particularly of trace minerals such as copper, zinc, and magnesium, is a common dietary cause of bone defects. Growing animals that are fed too much protein can also develop nutritional disorders affecting bones. Getting either too much or too little of certain vitamins, particularly vitamins A and D, can influence bone growth and development.

Most **bone disorders** stem from some sort of trauma, such as fractures or cracks. Bone fractures are classified as simple (the bone is broken into 2 pieces) or compound (there are 3 or more pieces). They are also divided into closed (the skin is not broken) or open (the skin is broken). Infections that cause bone tissue to break down and die can lead to bone disorders. In other situations, diseases of the ligaments or tendons may cause secondary bone troubles.

Movable joints are vulnerable to **joint diseases or disorders** affecting their membranes, as well as related ligaments, cartilage, and bone. Joint disorders may be caused by trauma to the joint, longterm inflammation, developmental problems, or infections. Traumatic injuries may produce short-term consequences such as dislocation, fracture, or the distortion of a joint. More longterm effects may include arthritis or the rupture of nearby ligaments or membranes.

Chronic or longterm inflammation is most commonly seen in joints associated with movement. The effects of longterm inflammation can be complicated. Any joint injury changes the composition and amount of fluid inside the joint, which affects the amount of pressure on the connecting bones. Injuries also raise the white blood cell count in a joint, which can break down cartilage over time.

Recent years have seen great advances in techniques for diagnosing and healing musculoskeletal disorders. When detected early, the disorders often can be corrected, allowing the horse a full return to healthy life.

▓ LAMENESS

A horse is said to be lame when its normal stance or gait is changed by a problem in one or more of the limbs, the neck, the trunk, or the quarters. Lameness is not a specific disease but may indicate a disorder in the musculoskeletal system. When unaccompanied by pain, the lameness may be mechanical. A horse with **mechanical lameness** may develop an abnormal gait as a result of scarred and thickened connective tissues or of an abnormality of movement produced by a syndrome such as stringhalt. It is important that a veterinarian properly distinguish the cause of mechanical lameness.

Physically immature horses that are subjected to repetitive stress on bones are prone to lameness. Immature bones may be anatomically normal but weak due to the age of the horse. Such bone weakness may also be caused by developmental orthopedic disease. An example of repetitive stress on bones is the continuous training of racehorses around left-handed bends. This can produce shin soreness, stress fractures, or imbalances of the feet that abnormally distribute body weight among the limbs. Other factors that cause lameness include direct or indirect trauma to a limb, fatigue in racehorses racing over long distances, or inflammation—more often than not without infection—of joints, tendons, and ligaments.

Lameness in one part of a limb will often produce soreness in another area of the limb as well. It can also lead to a secondary lameness in the fore- or hindlimb on the opposite side of the body.

The Lameness Examination

A thorough investigation of a lame horse is necessary in order to ensure a correct diagnosis and appropriate treatment. The examination begins with a full medical history. The horse's type, age, and training regimen may give important clues to the lameness. Your veterinarian will ask how much time has passed since the onset of lameness and how it has been managed. The length of time since the last shoeing will be noted, as well as any indication that the lameness improves with either rest or exercise. The horse's response to anti-inflammatory or pain-relieving medications may provide useful information. Results of laboratory tests may reveal other problems that influence overall performance.

A detailed visual inspection is followed by a hands-on examination of the limbs in weight-bearing and non-weight-bearing positions to identify any heat, pain, swelling of joints, or abnormal tissue tension. Your veterinarian will also study your horse's reactions, look for any muscle loss, and measure the range of movement in the joints. Your veterinarian will observe whether lameness seems to increase or decrease after flexing or extending the joint.

The feet are thoroughly examined, inspecting any compression of the walls or soles with hoof testers. Wear patterns of shoes and feet are noted. In addition to the legs and feet, the back and neck should be thoroughly examined with the horse restrained and standing on a level surface.

Examination during exercise is done only if the degree of lameness is minor and longterm. If lameness is major and severe (for example, a suspected fracture), additional exercise could catastrophically injure the horse. It is important to tell your veterinarian if your horse was given pain-relieving medication before a lameness examination. In some cases, a ridden assessment of the horse may be necessary, particularly with a subtle lameness or a horse that is unwilling to perform certain movements (for example, a dressage horse).

Because lameness may indicate a nerve dysfunction, a neurologic examination should always be part of the lameness examination. This might include observing the horse execute "complicated" movements such as turning short, backing, "hopping" on one forelimb (with the other forelimb held up), and negotiating a small step. These tests help identify reduced response to stimuli, weakness, or spasms, as well as abnormalities in the motor function of the major muscle groups that flex and extend the limbs.

Imaging Techniques

Imaging techniques provide important information necessary to diagnose and treat specific conditions (*see* BOX, page 668). Imaging can be divided into anatomic and physiologic methods. Anatomic methods are used to view physical structures, and physiologic methods assess how the anatomy functions. Anatomic imaging methods include x-rays and ultrasonography. Physiologic imaging methods, including scintigraphy and thermography, evaluate metabolism or circulation, completing the picture of the disorder. Imaging techniques may help narrow the problem to a specific region when other diagnostic methods fail. Imaging may also be necessary if the lameness is very subtle, or if the horse resists handling or an injection. Imaging may also help prevent injury by allowing early detection of the physiologic changes associated with injuries.

Imaging Techniques for Evaluation of Lameness

- **X-rays:** Plain x-rays allow evaluation of bony tissues and reveal longterm changes. Contrast x-rays (x-rays taken after a dye has been administered to the horse either intravenously or by mouth) provide information about joint cartilage and surfaces and are of particular value in determining whether cysts below the cartilage interfere with the joint.

- **Ultrasonography:** Ultrasonographic examination can be used to evaluate most soft tissues. It is most useful in the evaluation of tendons and ligaments but can also be used to evaluate muscle and cartilage. Used together, x-rays and ultrasonography provide a complete picture of bony tissues and the soft tissues that connect and support them.

- **Thermography:** This noninvasive technique creates a picture of the surface temperature of an object. It measures emitted heat and is useful for detecting inflammation that may contribute to lameness. Disease and injury nearly always affect blood circulation, which in turn affects the temperature of an injured area. Due to the increased blood flow to an affected area, thermography can identify "hot spots" of local inflammation. If a disease reduces blood supply to a particular area, that area of decreased heat is usually surrounded by a warmer rim, which thermography can also identify.

- **Scintigraphy:** During scintigraphy, a small amount of a radioactive substance is injected intravenously. Because inflammation causes a local increase in blood flow, the radioactive substance will accumulate in the inflamed area. A special camera that is sensitive to the injected radioactive substance is then used to locate the affected area.

Arthroscopy

Arthroscopy can be used to both evaluate and treat musculoskeletal disorders, particularly those involving the soft tissues of the joint. It is a minor surgical technique in which an endoscope (a long, flexible tube with a tiny camera in the tip) is inserted through a small surgical incision. Most arthroscopies take place with the horse under general anesthesia. Because it is a minimally invasive surgery, arthroscopy allows for rapid healing of soft tissues.

With diagnostic arthroscopies, an attached camera transmits images to a monitor allowing the veterinarian to see inside the joint. Corrective surgeries (such as removal of bone fragments or cartilage, or repair of fractures) can often be performed at the same time. Arthroscopy also enables biopsies within the joint.

Endoscopes may also be used to explore and correct problems involving the tendons or bursae, particularly in cases of infection. For a number of disorders, these techniques have revolutionized treatment and dramatically improved recovery rates.

Regional Analgesia

The use of regional, or local, painkillers (analgesics) to help diagnose lameness is an important part of the examination. This procedure is done before x-rays are taken. It is used when physical examination fails to identify the affected area (for example, in cases such as superficial foot pain, inflammation of the navicular bone and forefoot of the horse, traumatic joint disease, or inflammation of a ligament). A horse given diagnostic analgesia should be lame enough that any improvement can be detected. In conditions of severe lameness, the analgesia should be used with great care. Suddenly removing the protective effect of pain can cause a horse to further damage an injured area.

In most cases, interpreting the results of diagnostic analgesia is fairly straightforward. Pain reduction lessens the lameness, helping your veterinarian isolate the location of the injury. But various factors may complicate the procedure. Severe pain can be difficult to block fully. Also, mechanical and neurologic lameness, which are not necessarily painful to the horse, may be undetectable with analgesia. Sometimes a local anesthetic diffuses more widely than planned, reducing diagnostic accuracy. The arrangement of nerves in a given area may vary from horse to horse, and visible lameness may lessen as a horse "warms up." Overall, however, regional analgesia remains very useful for diagnosing lameness.

■ CONGENITAL AND INHERITED DISORDERS OF BONES, JOINTS, AND MUSCLES

Inherited problems of the musculoskeletal system are less common in horses than in many other species. Underlying viral infections and toxic causes may lead to congenital (birth) defects in foals but are rare. Most of the problems that arise are related to specific genetic conditions.

Contracted Flexor Tendons

Contracted flexor tendons are probably the most common abnormality of the musculoskeletal system of newborn foals. The condition, which is associated with the positioning of the foal while in the uterus, may not have a specific inherited cause.

At birth, the pastern and fetlocks of the forelegs and sometimes the carpal joints are flexed to varying degrees due to shortening of the associated muscles. A cleft palate may accompany this condition in some breeds of horses. Slightly affected animals bear weight on the soles of the feet and walk on their toes. More severely affected animals walk on the back of the pastern and fetlock joint. If not treated, the rear surfaces of these joints become damaged, and arthritis develops. This may lead to a rupture of the common digital extensor tendon.

Mildly affected animals recover without treatment. In moderate cases, your veterinarian may apply a splint to force your horse to bear weight on its toes. Care must be taken that the splint does not limit blood circulation, or tissues in the foot could be damaged. For a horse with a moderate case, your veterinarian might demonstrate how to help your horse stretch. By manually moving a horse's legs to extend these joints, you can assist in stretching the ligaments, tendons, and muscles. Severe cases require the surgical cutting of one or both flexor tendons. A cast may also be needed in some cases. Extreme cases may not respond to any treatment. (*See also* CONTRACTED FLEXOR TENDONS, page 672.)

Glycogen Storage Disease (Glycogenosis)

Glycogen is a complex carbohydrate normally stored in the liver and muscles. The body converts it to glucose (sugar) as a source of energy. Animals with glycogen storage diseases may become progressively weaker until they are unable to rise from a lying position. To date, 5 of 8 types of glycogen storage diseases found in humans have also been found in animals, including horses.

Arthrogryposis (Congenital Joint Rigidity)

This syndrome, more commonly associated with calves, has also occasionally been seen in foals. It is characterized by the "locking" of limbs in abnormal positions, and it can make foaling abnormally difficult for the mare. Affected foals may have other abnormalities, including hydrocephalus (water on the brain), resulting in an enlarged head, cleft palate, and abnormalities of the spine. The condition may be lethal, but some mildly affected animals recover completely. In some types of the syndrome, the muscle fiber dysfunctions might be the primary disorder. Most often, the syndrome has its roots in a nervous system disorder. The muscular and joint problems begin when muscles are no longer served by healthy nerves.

Osteochondritis Dissecans

Osteochondritis dissecans most commonly occurs in young horses during periods of rapid growth. It is caused by a number of factors and can have a genetic component. Damage to the joints occurs when the animal is growing at its fastest, and the stress on the immature skeleton is greatest. The damaged cartilage may become detached and float loosely in the joint cavity, where it can cause inflammation and further interference with proper bone formation. (For a more detailed discussion of OSTEOCHONDRITIS DISSECANS, *see* page 671.)

Polydactyly

Polydactyly is a congenital defect occasionally found in horses. In its most common form, the second or fourth splint bone develops into a complete lower limb and toe. One or all 4 limbs can have the condition.

Angular Limb Deformities

Angular limb deformities may be present at birth (congenital) or acquired. In these skeletal defects, a portion of a limb is bent or twisted crossways or towards the midline of the body early in the newborn's life. Angular limb deformities may be caused by the positioning of the limb while in the womb, a thyroid hormone deficiency (hypothyroidism), trauma, a poorly formed or loosely jointed limb, or underdevelopment of the carpal or tarsal and long bones. One or all 4 limbs may be affected.

The carpus is the bone affected most often, but the tarsus and fetlocks are occasionally involved. Most foals have no signs, but lameness and soft-tissue swelling can accompany severe deformities. A limb with very slight deviation may be regarded as normal. Foals with poorly conformed carpal and outermost tarsal bones or excessively loose joints often become lame as the deformity worsens. Your veterinarian may diagnose the condition by a thorough examination of the limb and x-rays.

Treatment will be determined by the severity of the condition and the tissues affected. Foals that are only mildly affected may improve on their own without treatment. In cases where joints are excessively loose, a cast or a splint may be required. Such limb support may be required for up to 6 weeks, and restricted exercise will be necessary to maintain tendon and ligament tone.

Surgery may be necessary if the growth plates have been disturbed. These surger-

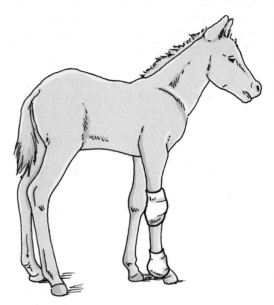

Limbs may be immobilized with casts or splints to treat angular limb deformity.

ies must be performed before the growth plates close (as early as 2 to 4 months of age). Success depends on the continued growth and development of the bones. Examinations and x-rays should be used to determine if the condition is improving or further surgery is required.

Without treatment, the outlook for recovery from severe deformity of the carpus is poor, as it can lead to degenerative joint disease. However, with early detection, careful evaluation, and proper surgery, most foals respond favorably.

Defects of the Spine

Although defects of the spine are uncommon in foals, 4 types are possible. Congenital **scoliosis**, an S-bend of the spine, is encountered occasionally. It is often difficult to assess the severity of the deformity with just a physical examination. X-rays provide a better view of the condition. Even in more severe cases, there is rarely any obvious abnormality in gait or the ability to move. Mild cases sometimes completely correct themselves.

Synostosis is fusion of a vertebra with a vertebra next to it. An x-ray is necessary for confirmation of synostosis, which is often associated with secondary scoliosis.

Swayback, known as **lordosis**, is a downward curving of the spine in the lower back. Congenital lordosis affects the spine of a horse whose vertebral joints fail to develop properly. In adult horses, degrees of acquired lordosis occur as the horse gets older. **Kyphosis** (an upward curving of the spine, also known as roach-back) is also occasionally seen. Both of these conditions contribute to back weakness. A veterinarian diagnoses the condition by thorough examination, often confirmed by x-rays that reveal an abnormal curvature of the vertebral column.

Hyperkalemic Periodic Paralysis

Hyperkalemic periodic paralysis (*see* page 706) is a hereditary condition of Quarter Horses, in which abnormally high levels of potassium in the blood produce intermittent episodes of muscle weakness or paralysis.

Glycogen Branching Enzyme Deficiency

Glycogen branching enzyme deficiency may be a common cause of newborn death in Quarter Horses. Diagnosis can be complicated by the variety of signs that resemble other diseases of newborn horses. Signs of glycogen branching enzyme deficiency may include curving or bending limb deformities lasting for only a short time, stillbirth, seizures, respiratory or heart failure, and the inability to rise from a recumbent position. Your veterinarian may notice other abnormalities on blood tests of affected foals.

■ DEVELOPMENTAL ORTHOPEDIC DISEASE

Developmental orthopedic diseases of horses are an important group of conditions that includes osteochondritis dissecans, physeal dysplasia, acquired angular limb deformities, flexor tendon deformities, and cuboidal bone malformations.

Osteochondritis Dissecans

Osteochondritis dissecans is one of the more common developmental orthopedic diseases of horses. The condition mainly affects joint growth cartilage; however, bone shape and length can be disturbed. It can lead to cysts (*see* page 676), an abnormal narrowing of the vertebral canal and, ultimately, an inability to coordinate muscle movements.

There are many causes of osteochondritis dissecans, such as rapid growth, overnutrition, mineral imbalance, and biomechanical problems (for example, trauma to cartilage). Inherited conditions have been noticed in some breeds, such as Standardbreds and Swedish Warmbloods.

The signs of osteochondritis dissecans are varied due to the wide range of causes and sites involved. The most common sign is a nonpainful joint swelling (for example, gonitis and bog spavin). Horses affected by osteochondritis dissecans do not typically become lame, except in cases of damage to particular sites. In severe cases, signs typical of other developmental orthopedic diseases also may be present. In cases involving trauma, joint damage may alter the performance of the horse and cause pain and lameness.

In foals younger than 6 months of age, the first sign noted is often a tendency to spend more time lying down. This is accompanied frequently by joint swelling, stiffness, and difficulty keeping up with other animals in the paddock. An additional sign may be the development of upright conformation of the limbs, presumably as a result of rapid growth. Osteochondritis dissecans of the fetlock is particularly seen in younger foals (less than 6 months old).

The main signs in yearlings or older horses are stiffness of joints, pain when the joint is bent, and varying degrees of lameness. These signs are usually associated with the onset of training, suggesting a preexisting biomechanical problem that the training aggravates.

A diagnosis can often be made on the basis of a detailed physical examination.

More definitive diagnosis may require the use of x-rays, ultrasonography, or exploratory surgery using an endoscope.

Treatment and Outlook

Management of osteochondritis dissecans depends on the location and severity of signs. Mild cases recover spontaneously, and a conservative approach may be appropriate. In young animals (less than 12 months old) this involves several weeks of restricted exercise and a reduced diet to slow the growth rate. Particular care should be taken to ensure appropriate mineral supplementation. (Copper deficiency can be a problem.) Veterinarians debate whether correcting the diet, once signs have developed, actually assists in resolving the condition, but it may limit further cases on stud farms. Medicating the joint with hyaluronic acid may help, and injections of long-acting corticosteroids may reduce swelling and inflammation of the joint membrane.

When surgery is necessary, it is usually performed using an endoscope. This technique has been successful in most affected sites, particularly the hock, stifle, and fetlock. Damaged cartilage and loose pieces of bone below the cartilage (known as joint mice) are removed, and the joint is flushed extensively. The outlook for recovery should be good except in cases of severe joint disruption or degenerative joint disease.

Shoulders are often more problematic to treat surgically because endoscopic access is more difficult, and there is usually more extensive bone damage below the cartilage, often with formation of many cysts. Therefore, the outlook for recovery is guarded.

Physitis

Physitis involves swelling around the growth plates of certain long bones in young horses. It can occur along with osteochondritis dissecans. Suggested causes include nutritional imbalances, defects in conformation, faulty hoof growth, toxicosis, and compression of the growth plate. Physitis is frequently seen in fast-growing foals (often 4 to 8 months of age) or in young horses (18 to 24 months of age) that have begun training. Foals affected are often those fed high-grain or high-protein diets.

The condition is characterized by swelling at the level of the growth plate, giving a "boxy" appearance to the affected joints when seen on x-rays. The bones most often affected include the radius, tibia, third metacarpal or metatarsal bone, and the first phalanx. The amount of lameness varies.

Treatment consists of reducing food intake to reduce body weight or at least growth rate; confining exercise to a yard or a large, well-ventilated loose box with a soft surface (for example, peat moss, deep straw, shavings, or sand); ensuring that the feet are carefully and frequently trimmed; and correcting any imbalances in the diet. Your veterinarian can make appropriate recommendations for dietary changes and supplements.

As a preventive measure, the older foal or yearling that is fat or heavy-topped should be watched carefully for signs of physitis, especially when the ground is hard and dry. When these conditions exist, feed rations and exercise should be restricted.

Contracted Flexor Tendons

Flexor tendon disorders may be congenital (present at birth) or acquired. They are associated with postural and foot changes, lameness, and a lack of strength and energy. A foal that is malpositioned within the uterus, genetic defects, and toxic substances that the mare was exposed to may be causes of contracted limbs in newborn foals. In horses with acquired deformities, contracted tendons are most often a response to longterm pain. The pain may arise from physitis (*see* above), osteochondritis dissecans (page 671), osteoarthritis (page 676), or soft-tissue wounds and infection. Pain may cause the horse to withdraw the limb, walking on its toes or knuckles in the fetlocks. This withdrawn position causes the tendon to contract.

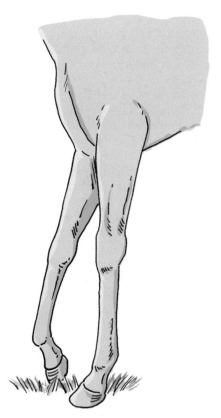

Foal with contracted flexor tendons

Nutritional imbalances that are known to cause problems with bone growth (as seen in osteochondritis dissecans and physitis) are also associated with the syndrome.

Signs vary widely in newborn foals. Some cannot stand, some attempt to walk on the upper part of their fetlocks, and others can stand but knuckle in the fetlocks or carpi. One foal may improve spontaneously, while another, seemingly healthy at birth, may become progressively worse. The onset of signs may be rapid in foals 3 to 12 months old; such animals may walk on their toes with their heels off the ground. A slower onset may produce a "boxy" hoof with an elongated heel and toe that curves inward. Physitis may also occur in these horses. Usually both forelimbs are involved, although one or the other tends to be worse. Sores on the toes are a frequent complication that adds to the pain and deformity.

Slightly older horses (1 to 2 years old) commonly knuckle in the fetlock joints, which swell and enlarge. These horses are upright and straight-legged in both fore- and hindlimbs. Yearlings usually are more severely affected and more difficult to treat than younger animals. A complete examination by a veterinarian is necessary to determine the specific tendons involved. Any underlying bone or joint diseases or nutrition problems must be identified and corrected.

Various types of splints and casts are used for foals with contracted tendons. Cases in foals less than 1 year old can be managed conservatively with nutritional correction, proper hoof trimming, and treatment to control pain. Surgically cutting the accessory ligament of the deep digital flexor tendon is the most successful and commonly used procedure and does not interfere with future performance. Other types of surgery, including surgical cutting of the tendon and tendon lengthening, tend to be less successful. In long-term cases, complications such as abnormal tightening of the joint membrane, malformation of accompanying ligaments, and bone involvement may prevent full recovery. Nutritional correction, proper foot trimming, and treatment to relieve pain are essential to proper healing, even when surgery is recommended. The outlook for recovery is fair to good for horses diagnosed early and managed properly.

■ DISORDERS ASSOCIATED WITH CALCIUM, PHOSPHORUS, AND VITAMIN D

Defective bone formation is called osteodystrophy. It is caused in most cases by deficiencies or imbalances of calcium, phosphorus, and vitamin D, all of which are important in creating and maintaining strong, healthy bones.

The primary source of calcium and phosphorus is the diet, but a number of factors affect how the body absorbs calcium and phosphorus. These include the source of the minerals as well as the levels of vitamin D in the body. Vitamin D is obtained either through the diet or by exposure to sunlight. Because of the role it plays in the body, if the vitamin or its activity is decreased, calcium and phosphorus absorption are reduced. Bone deformities can result, as well as other nutritional and metabolic complications.

Osteomalacia (Adult Rickets, Bran Disease)

Osteomalacia causes soft and deformed bones, commonly due to insufficient phosphorus or vitamin D in the diet. It develops similarly to rickets but in mature bones.

In horses, osteomalacia is sometimes known as **bran disease, miller's disease**, and "**big head**." The diet of pampered horses often contains too much grain and too little forage, making it high in phosphorus and low in calcium. In cases where a horse becomes lame for no apparent reason, the cause is frequently attributed to osteomalacia. In severe cases the disease may cause structural changes and swelling of the bones of the head. Signs may include breaks in bone beneath cartilage (followed by degeneration of the joint cartilage and tearing of ligaments).

To establish a firm diagnosis, your veterinarian will evaluate your horse's diet to make sure it provides enough calcium, phosphorus, and vitamin D for healthy bones. X-rays will reveal the effects of osteomalacia on the skeleton.

Affected horses should be confined for the first few weeks after the diet is corrected. The response to proper nutrition is rapid. Within 1 week the horses become more active and show an improved attitude. Restrictions on activity can usually be relaxed after several weeks, but confinement with limited movement is recommended until the skeleton returns to normal. Response to treatment can be monitored using x-rays.

Enzootic Calcinosis

In enzootic calcinosis large deposits of calcium in the body contribute to the hardening of soft body tissues. The condition can be caused by plant poisoning or less commonly mineral imbalances in the soil.

Wild jasmine, day-blooming jessamine, king-of-the-day (*Cestrum diurnum*), golden oats, or yellow oat grass (*Trisetum flavescens*), as well as some other plants (*Nierembergia veitchii*, *Solanum* species) contain a substance in their leaves that bypasses the body's feedback mechanism for regulating levels of the active form of vitamin D (calcitriol). An excess of vitamin D in turn may trigger the deposit of excessive calcium in the soft tissues called calcinosis. Dietary mineral imbalances such as excessive phosphate or calcium, as well as deficiencies of magnesium, potassium, and nitrogen, may worsen the tissue hardening that is caused by plant poisoning. Certain soils in Hawaii, India, Austria, and elsewhere contain these mineral imbalances.

Calcinosis progressively worsens over weeks or months. The earliest signs are a stiffened and painful gait, which is most obvious when the horse rises after prolonged rest. Severely affected horses stand with their forelimbs somewhat pulled away from the central line of the limb and displaced at the shoulder joints. The flexor tendons, particularly the suspensory ligaments, are painfully sensitive. The fetlock joints are overextended to varying degrees. When affected horses are forced to walk, they take short steps, and their gait is awkward, stiff, and slow. Examination by a veterinarian often reveals a heart murmur as well.

As the disease progresses, the horse loses weight and becomes weak and listless. The coat becomes shaggy, dull, and faded. As the animal loses muscle mass, the skeleton may become pronounced and the abdomen tucked up. The spine may curve upward (causing the animal to appear hunched over), and the tailhead may rise. Appetite is usually unaffected, although it may become poor.

Diagnosis may be difficult at early stages but is usually based on a medical history and examination of physical changes to the horse. X-rays and electro-cardiography help confirm the diagnosis.

If poisonous plants are to blame, they must be removed from the pastures. When the disease is associated with the mineral content of the soil, however, control may be more difficult. A change of pasture, forage, and environment may reduce the signs and even diminish the soft-tissue mineral deposits.

▨ JOINT DISORDERS

Some joint disorders, such as arthritis, affect the joint membranes themselves. Other types of joint conditions affect the tendons, cartilage, bursae, and fluid within the joint (synovial fluid).

Arthritis

Arthritis refers to inflammation in a joint. All joint diseases that affect large animals produce some degree of inflammation, often with accompanying swelling, pain, redness or heat.

Important arthritic conditions include traumatic arthritis, osteochondritis dissecans, subchondral cystic lesions, septic (infectious) arthritis, and osteoarthritis.

Traumatic Arthritis

Traumatic arthritis includes inflammation of the synovial membrane and joint capsule, chip fractures within the joint, tears (sprains) of ligaments or cartilage near or within a joint, and the gradual loss of cartilage of the joints known as osteoarthritis. It may be seen in any horse but typically occurs in horses that are athletes. A similar condition occurs in human athletes that undergo traumatic or repeated injury of a particular joint, such as the knee.

In its early stage, excess fluid enters injured joints, which can make the surrounding tissues swollen and warm. In more severe cases, manipulation of the joint causes pain. The chronic stage includes a general thickening and scarring of connective tissue, which reduces the range of joint motion. The horse's gait may change mildly, or it may become severely lame.

Veterinarians take x-rays to exclude other traumatic conditions, such as bone disease or fractures in bone or cartilage. Examination with an endoscope may be necessary to exclude tearing of ligaments or cartilage in the leg joints.

Treatment of traumatic joint inflammation includes rest and physical therapy regimens such as cold water treatment, ice, passive bending of the joint, and swimming. Nonsteroidal anti-inflammatory drugs are routinely prescribed to relieve pain and inflammation; corticosteroids may be recommended in some cases. In more severe cases, a veterinarian will flush the joint with water to remove any inflammatory or cartilage debris. This is more effective than joint drainage alone.

Arthroscopic surgery may be recommended to remove fragments of bone and cartilage (most commonly seen in the carpus and fetlock) to minimize the ongoing development of osteoarthritis. After such surgery, 2 to 6 months of rest follows, with physical therapy during the recovery period. The success rate in returning horses to previous performance levels is high if the degeneration is minimal at the time of surgery.

Osteochondritis Dissecans

In osteochondritis dissecans, the immature joint cartilage separates from the underlying bone. Fluid enters the space, and cysts may form under the cartilage. The cartilage may break away completely or, if the joint is rested or protected, reattach itself to bone. Osteochondritis dissecans usually is seen in young animals (less than 1 year old), most commonly at the femoropatellar (knee) joint, tarsal joint, fetlock joints, and the shoulder. The exact cause is unknown but contributing factors likely include a genetic predisposition in the animal, rapid growth, high caloric intake, disproportionate levels of copper and zinc in the diet, and hormonal factors. (For a more detailed discussion of OSTEOCHONDRITIS DISSECANS, *see* page 671.)

Cysts beneath the Cartilage (Subchondral Cysts)

Cysts beneath the cartilage, called sub-chondral cysts, occur in the femorotibial joint and in the fetlock, pastern, elbow, shoulder, and distal phalanx of horses. Lameness is the usual sign. Levels of excessive joint fluid vary, so the diagnosis is usually made on the basis of the location of lameness and the responsiveness to pain within the joint. X-rays are necessary to confirm the diagnosis.

Surgery using an arthroscope is currently recommended in the femorotibial joint whenever a complete cyst is present. Smaller cysts are treated conservatively at first. Athletic soundness is achieved in 65 to 70% of these horses. More recently, some horses have been treated with an injection of corticosteroids.

Surgery is usually recommended for cysts beneath the cartilage in the fetlock. Single cysts associated with the pastern and elbow joints are treated conservatively and have a fair outlook for recovery. If possible, surgery is recommended for cysts of the distal phalanx because results with conservative treatment are very poor.

Septic Arthritis

Infectious, or septic, arthritis is usually caused by bacterial infection in a joint. Infection may occur after a traumatic injury, surgery, or injections, or it may enter the joint through the bloodstream. A common example of bloodborne infection is called **navel ill**, in which the infection reaches the foal through the umbilical cord. Infections in a horse's digestive tract or lungs can also travel to a joint through the blood.

Septic arthritis usually produces severe lameness and swelling of the joint. When fluid from the joint is obtained and examined, it is cloudy and contaminated. In foals, the infection often inflames the bone and bone marrow.

Septic arthritis must be treated promptly to avoid permanent damage. Infections are treated with injectable broad-spectrum antibiotics, as well as antibiotics injected directly in the joint. Nonsteroidal anti-inflammatory drugs may be prescribed as well. Other useful therapies include flushing the joint with saline solution and cleaning and draining the joint with an endoscope. The effectiveness of treatment is monitored carefully by watching for signs and repeating the examination and analysis of the joint fluid.

Osteoarthritis

Osteoarthritis, which is sometimes called degenerative joint disease, is a progressive deterioration of the joint cartilage. It represents the end stage of most of the other diseases discussed above, such as traumatic arthritis involving the synovial membrane and joint capsule, joint fractures, traumatic damage to cartilage, osteochondritis dissecans, cysts beneath cartilage, and infective arthritis.

Osteoarthritis produces lameness. There may be varying degrees of excess fluid in the joint, an abnormal thickening and scarring of the membranes, and restricted motion of the involved joints. X-rays show decreased joint space, bony outgrowths, inflammation of the muscles or tendons, and a hardening and thickening of the tissue below the cartilage. In less severe cases, an endoscope is used to observe the degree of joint damage.

Treatment of osteoarthritis is generally limited to reducing joint pain and stiffness. Nonsteroidal anti-inflammatory drugs (for example, firocoxib, ketoprofen, and phenylbutazone) or corticosteroids may provide relief. Physical therapy may prove helpful. In advanced cases, surgical fusion may be performed on selected joints. Some horses return to athletic soundness following surgical fusion of the pastern or tarsal joints. For very valuable animals, the fetlocks may be surgically fused, making the horse comfortable and capable of breeding.

Bursitis

A bursa is a small fluid-filled sac between a tendon and a bone (or other tissues that rub against one another) that reduces friction around the joint. Common in horses, bursitis is an inflammatory reaction within a bursa that can range from mild inflammation to infection. **True bursitis** involves inflammation of a natural bursa, for example, fistulous withers. In contrast, **acquired bursitis** is the development or inflammation of a bursa where none previously existed, as with capped elbow or hock.

Bursitis may develop suddenly with swelling, warmth, and pain, or it may persist over a long time with excess fluid and generalized thickening. Chronic bursitis often develops as a result of repeated trauma, abnormal thickening and scarring of connective tissue, and other longterm changes. The cold, painless swellings associated with chronic bursitis do not severely interfere with joint function unless they are greatly enlarged.

Infective bursitis is more serious and may produce pain and lameness in the joint. Infections may begin locally following an injection or travel from elsewhere to the bursa through the bloodstream.

Bursitis pain may be relieved with cold packs, by draining the bursal sac, or by directly medicating the bursa. (Repeated injections, however, pose a risk of infection.) Chronic bursitis is treated with surgery. Treating infective bursitis requires injectable antibiotics as well as drainage of the infected area.

Fistulous Withers and Poll Evil

Fistulous withers is the name of a condition in which the bursa in a horse's withers region (the ridge between the shoulder bones) becomes infected and inflamed. Poll evil is a virtually identical condition, except that the location of infection is the bursa behind the horse's ears in the area known as the poll. In each instance, a ruptured bursal sac creates an opening that makes the bursa susceptible to infection. Both conditions are rare.

Both fistulous withers and poll evil may be caused by trauma or an infection. Infections frequently are caused by *Brucella abortus* bacteria. If tests reveal the presence of *Brucella*, owners should be aware that this bacterium can be transmitted to people. Outbreaks of brucellosis in cattle have occured after contact with horses with open bursitis.

The inflammation caused by fistulous withers and poll evil thickens the bursa wall. The bursal sacs swell and may rupture if unprotected. In more advanced cases, nearby ligaments and the tips of the vertebral spines are affected, sometimes causing the death of these tissues.

The earlier treatment is started, the better the outlook for recovery. The most successful treatment is complete surgical removal of the infected bursa. However, the cost of treatment required in longterm cases often exceeds the value of the animal, and the risk of human infection (in cases in which *Brucella* is involved) should be carefully considered. It is prudent to keep horses separated from *Brucella*-infected cattle, and to keep cattle separated from horses with discharging fistulous withers.

Capped Elbow and Hock

Capped elbow and hock are acquired forms of bursitis. Bursas beneath the hock and elbow can become inflamed if a horse suffers trauma from falling in or kicking its stall, from lying on poorly bedded hard floors, riding a trailer tailgate, wearing iron shoes that project beyond the heels, or from leaning or reclining for long periods of time.

Capped elbow and hock rarely cause lameness, but fluid-filled swellings may develop on and around the affected bursa. The bursa may be soft at first but is soon surrounded by a fibrous capsule, especially in the case of a recurrent, older injury. The amount of initial swelling may vary. Infection may occur in chronic cases.

If detected early, the condition may respond well to applications of cold water, followed in a few days by fluid drainage and a corticosteroid injection. The bursa may also be reduced in size by ultrasonic radiation therapy. Another method involves the application of a substance called a counterirritant that irritates the skin and thereby reduces the inflammation of the bursa. Older bursas are more resistant to treatment. Surgery is recommended for advanced longterm cases or when infection is present. If a capped elbow has been caused by the heel or the shoe, a shoe-boil roll should be used to prevent reinjury. For a capped hock, modifying the horse's behavior so it does not kick the stall may offer the only hope of a permanent solution.

Tendinitis

Tendinitis is the inflammation of a tendon. Tendon inflammation may be short-term (acute tendinitis), or build up over a period of time (chronic tendinitis). The condition is most common among horses that do fast work, such as racehorses. The flexor tendons are generally involved, and the forelegs are more likely to be affected than the hind legs. The condition ruptures the tendon fibers to varying degrees. Blood vessels are also ruptured, and fluid may accumulate in the affected area.

Tendinitis usually appears after a horse is exercised improperly. Contributing factors may include fatigue or overextension, poor conditioning, and poor racetrack conditions. Tendinitis also develops when horses are trained despite prior inflammation of the tendon. Improper shoeing increases a horse's vulnerability to tendinitis, as do any malformations of the joints.

Horses with acute tendinitis are severely lame, with affected joints that are hot, painful, and swollen. In chronic tendinitis, fibrous tissues around the tendon join together, thicken, and scar. The horse may appear sound while walking or trotting but becomes lame again when put to a gallop. Your veterinarian may use ultrasonography to locate defects or injuries that are otherwise undetectable.

Horses with acute tendinitis should be stall-rested. Swelling and inflammation should be treated aggressively with cold packs and anti-inflammatory drugs; however, corticosteroid injections directly into the tendon are not recommended. Depending on the amount of damage, inflamed tendons may need to be supported and immobilized. In some cases, tendon splitting is recommended to decrease pressure within the tendon due to fluid or blood buildup. Recently, bone marrow injections that introduce stem cells and growth factors have produced encouraging results.

Rehabilitation following tendinitis should include a regimen of increasing exercise. Regardless of treatment, the outlook for full recovery in a racehorse is guarded.

Tenosynovitis

Tenosynovitis is an inflammation of the synovial membrane and usually the outer fibrous covering of the tendon. Possible causes include a response to traumatic injury or infection. When seen in young animals where the cause is uncertain, the condition is called **idiopathic synovitis**.

Lameness and swelling of the tendon sheath varies depending on severity of the condition. Where infection is involved, the horse will be very noticeably lame. Long-term tenosynovitis is common in the tendon coverings near the hock and fetlock.

In cases where the cause is unknown, no treatment is recommended initially. When inflammation is severe, cold packs, nonsteroidal anti-inflammatory drugs, and rest may relieve the signs. In more chronic cases, counterirritants and bandaging may be tried. Radiation therapy may be helpful. Infective tenosynovitis requires whole-body antibiotics and drainage of the affected site.

■ DISORDERS OF THE FOOT

Among the many disorders that can affect the foot of a horse are bone cysts, bruises, corns, cankers, and fractures.

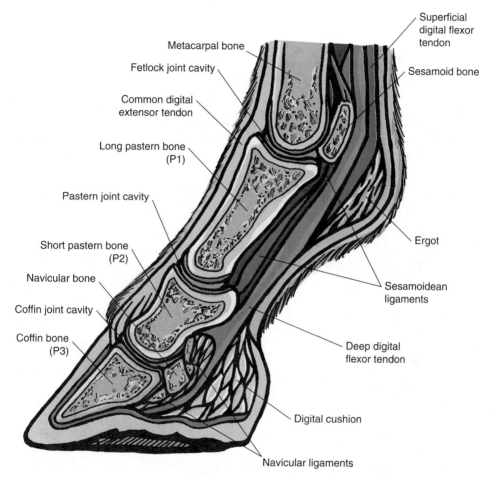

Anatomy of the horse's foot

Labels (clockwise from top): Superficial digital flexor tendon · Sesamoid bone · Metacarpal bone · Fetlock joint cavity · Common digital extensor tendon · Long pastern bone (P1) · Pastern joint cavity · Short pastern bone (P2) · Navicular bone · Coffin joint cavity · Coffin bone (P3) · Ergot · Sesamoidean ligaments · Deep digital flexor tendon · Digital cushion · Navicular ligaments

Bone Cyst in the Pedal Bone

A large cyst in the pedal bone (the distal phalanx) can cause longterm lameness that may be severe and unresponsive to anti-inflammatory medication. This uncommon condition, caused by trauma, may be seen in any foot but more often affects a hindfoot. The diagnosis may be confirmed by your veterinarian through the use of regional analgesia and x-rays. Progressive weakening of the pedal bone can lead to a secondary fracture. Because of the cyst's location and size, surgery is not always successful. However, some horses do return to performance status, while others may be used for less strenuous activity such as breeding.

Bruised Sole and Corns

Bruising on the sole of the foot usually is caused by direct injury from stones, irregular ground, or other trauma. Poor shoeing, especially in horses with flat feet or dropped soles, can increase the risk of bruising, usually around the outside edge of the sole. Bruising may or may not be associated with lameness, but if it becomes longterm, the affected area can become infected.

A **corn** is a type of bruise that appears in the sole at the buttress (that is, the angle between the wall and the bar). It is most common in the forefeet on the inner buttress. Corns may arise from pressure applied to the sole by the heel of a shoe

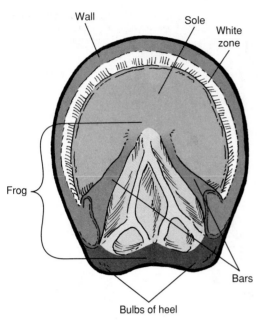

Anatomy of the hoof

improperly placed or left on too long. Shoes that have been fitted too closely at the quarters can also cause corns. Malformations of the feet, such as straight walls that tend to turn in at the quarters, increase a horse's vulnerability. Other causes include excess trimming of the sole (which exposes the sensitive tissue to injury) or neglect of the feet to the extent that they become long and irregular.

Corns may be dry, with only mild inflammation, or moist, with extensive inflammation. If infection sets in, they may discharge pus. The sole of the foot looks discolored, either red or reddish yellow, and lameness sometimes occurs in the supporting leg. Applying pressure may cause discomfort or pain. If not promptly treated, a corn may lead to the formation of a pus-filled tract that runs to where the horn of the hoof meets the skin (the coronet).

The outlook for recovery is favorable. In uncomplicated dry corns, the first step is to relieve pressure on the affected area. Shortening a too-long toe or using an appropriate type of bar shoe (such as a three-quarter-bar shoe) can relieve pressure. A corn that produces pus must be surgically drained, then bandaged to allow continued drainage. Hot foot baths and poultices may help, and the horse should be kept in a dry, clean box stall. After the infection is controlled, the cavity can be packed with sterile gauze and topical antibiotic ointment. A metal, rubber, or leather sole may be placed between the shoe and the foot.

Canker

Canker is an enlargement of the horn-producing tissues of the foot, involving the tough flexible pad in the middle of the sole (the frog) and the sole, with obvious production of pus. The cause is unknown. Primarily a disease of heavy draft horses, canker is seldom seen today, although it has been seen in certain stables of light horses in the southern United States.

Canker is most often found in the hind-feet and is frequently well advanced before detection. The frog may appear to be intact but has a ragged, oiled appearance. The horn tissue of the frog loosens easily and reveals a swollen, foul-smelling layer covered with dry, diseased, dead tissue. The disease may extend to the sole and even to the wall of the hoof and show no tendency to heal.

The outlook for recovery for canker is guarded. Treatment must be intensive. All loose horn and affected tissue should be removed, and an antiseptic or antibiotic dressing applied daily. A clean, dry wound environment must be maintained to allow healing, which may take weeks or months. If the horse is not lame, it may be able to return to work during the healing period by use of a special shoe to maintain the dressing.

Contracted Heels

Contracted heels are seen primarily in the forefeet of light horses. The condition may be caused by improper shoeing that draws in the quarters. This prevents hoof expansion and adequate frog pressure. Dry hooves, excess scraping of the wall, and trimming of the bars make a horse more prone to contracted heels. However, this condition may also occur after the use of a hoof-immobilizing shoe, such as that used for fracture of the third phalanx (pedal bone).

When the heel is contracted, the frog is narrow and shrunken, and the bars may be curved or almost parallel to each other. The quarters and heels are noticeably contracted and drawn in. The hoof horn is dry and hard, and heat may be noticed around the heels and quarters. If the horse is worked at speed, it may become lame, and its stride length will be shortened.

The outlook for recovery is guarded. In advanced cases, recovery can take 6 to 12 months. The most important factors in treatment are to moisturize the hooves and to promote expansion. This can be achieved by soaking the feet in water daily for 10 to 14 days followed by corrective shoeing. Hoof-moisturizing products that contain oils or waxy substances should be used with caution because they can keep water out of the hoof. Slipper shoes with no more than 3 nails in each branch promote hoof expansion. Quarter clips and the fourth shoe nail must be avoided.

A veterinarian can thin the wall of the quarters or groove the walls parallel to the coronet to aid in expanding the heels. As the quarters grow out, the procedure may need to be repeated until the heels and quarters are expanded normally.

Fracture of the Navicular Bone

The navicular bone may fracture as a result of trauma or a jarring injury to the foot. It may also break as a consequence of navicular disease (page 683). Fracture of the navicular bone is much less common than that of the pedal bone, but it may be seen in either the fore- or hindfeet. Pain may vary, but a hoof tester usually can locate the general area of the fracture. Lameness is persistent. X-rays and regional analgesia can confirm the diagnosis.

Treatment is prolonged rest and corrective trimming, although the fracture seldom heals entirely. Surgical repair using lag screws is an option, but the outlook for recovery remains guarded to poor.

Fracture of the Pedal Bone

Pedal bone fractures (fracture of the third phalanx, os pedis, or distal phalanx) generally follow a jarring injury, producing a sudden onset of lameness during exercise or racing. Most fractures are through the wing (flat side) of the pedal bone and often extend up into the adjacent joint.

A horse that fractures its pedal bone immediately becomes lame. Compressing the foot with hoof testers causes pain. Lightly tapping the hoof with a hammer also may cause pain, and turning the horse or making it pivot on the affected leg worsens the lameness. Lameness may improve considerably after 48 hours of stall rest, unless the fracture extends into the joint.

Diagnosis is confirmed by regional analgesia and x-rays. X-ray confirmation may be difficult immediately after the injury because the fracture may be only a hairline at this stage. Repeating the x-ray 2 or 3 days later may be necessary for confirmation and to determine the extent of the fracture.

Conservative treatment of 6 to 9 months' rest is usually all that is required for fractures that do not involve the joint. The horse should return to soundness, although the fracture will remain visible on x-rays. It is usual to fit a plain bar shoe with a clip well back on each quarter to limit expansion and contraction of the heels. In young horses (less than 3 years old), fractures into the joint usually heal satisfactorily, provided a 12-month rest period is given. Horses older than 3 years have a much less favorable outlook for recovery, and insertion of a bone screw is recommended. However, infection is a frequent complication. Many fractures heal in the presence of infection, but the screw must be removed at a second surgery to restore the horse to complete working soundness.

Keratoma

A keratoma is a hard, thickened area of the horn, usually at the toe. It is believed to follow longterm inflammation caused by nail bind, which occurs when a horseshoe nail is driven close to, but not into, the soft tissue. A keratoma may also be caused by mechanical injury to the wall or coronet, or by hoof-grooving. The condition may be difficult to detect until the growth is well advanced. Examining the surface of the underside of the horse's forefoot shows that the growth has pushed the white line in toward the center of the sole. In severe cases, the pressure shrinks the pedal bone. Surgical removal of the mass is recommended. In mild cases, corrective shoeing may give some temporary relief. The outlook for recovery is guarded.

Laminitis (Founder)

A horse's foot has 2 types of laminae (tissue layers). The **sensitive laminae** are attached to the pedal bone. The **insensitive laminae** are the layers of tissue just inside the hard exterior of the hoof. The word laminitis means "inflammation of the laminae," and it can refer to either a short-term (acute) inflammation or the disease caused by longterm or repeated (chronic) attacks of inflammation. Laminitis can develop in the forefeet, in all 4 feet, or in the hindfeet only. Biomechanical laminitis can be seen in a single foot, usually as a complication of a severe lameness or bone injury in the limb on the opposite side of the body.

Acute laminitis occurs when an inadequate supply of blood reaches the laminae. The reduced blood flow causes tissue to break down where the sensitive and insensitive laminae come together, eventually leading to a degeneration of the union between the layers of tissue. When treatment is unsuccessful, the pedal bone often rotates. If rotation progresses, a hole may form through the sole of the foot.

The most common causes of laminitis are ingestion of too much grain, grazing of lush pastures (especially in ponies), and excessive exercise or repetitive trauma. Other causes include generalized infections, colic, and treatment with corticosteroids and certain other medications. The risk is higher in ponies and in horses that are overweight and unfit. The number of cases of acute laminitis tends to increase whenever there is a flush of new grass.

Initially, the disturbances in the circulation to the foot are reversible. However, if the condition is severe or lasts for a long time, the outlook for recovery is poor. The pedal bone may rotate, or the hoof may alter its shape or separate from the underlying tissues. These changes may be irreversible, and secondary infection is common.

Signs and Diagnosis

In acute laminitis, the horse is depressed, has no appetite, and stands reluctantly. The horse resists exercise and attempts to shift weight off of the affected feet. If forced to walk, it has a slow, crouching, short-striding gait. Each foot, once lifted, is set down as quickly as possible.

Usually, heat is apparent in the whole hoof, especially near the coronary band. Pain can cause muscle trembling, and pressure reveals tenderness in the feet. If an effective treatment is not given quickly, the pedal bone may rotate. X-ray evidence of rotation can be present as early as the third day. Horses with laminitis typically have elevated vital signs, such as increased body temperature, heart rate, and respiration. In exceptionally severe cases, for which the outlook for recovery is unfavorable, a blood-stained discharge may seep from the coronary bands.

In less severe cases, the horse may exhibit any or all of the above signs but to a lesser degree. Often, there is only a mild change in stance, with reluctance to walk and some increased sensitivity in the soles of the affected feet. Episodes of acute laminitis tend to come back at varying intervals and may develop into a chronic condition.

Chronic laminitis is characterized by changes in the shape of the hoof and usually follows one or more acute attacks. Bands of irregular horn growth may appear in the hoof, and the hoof itself may narrow and become elongated, with the wall almost vertical at the heel and horizontal at the toe. As the condition progresses, the sole thickens and either flattens or begins to curve outward. When standing, the horse continually shifts its body weight from one foot to the other. X-rays reveal rotation of the pedal bone, as well as a diseased state in which the bone has become very porous. The top of the bone is forced downward and presses on the sole. In severe cases, it may poke through the sole just in front of the point of the frog.

To diagnose laminitis, a medical history is taken, noting possible contributing factors such as a grain overload in the diet. The physical examination will pay close attention to the posture of the horse, any abnormalities of the hooves, and a reluctance to move. Mild cases with no visible hoof deformity can be identified by x-rays of the affected feet.

Treatment and Outlook

Acute laminitis is considered a medical emergency because pedal rotation can occur quickly. If laminitis is suspected, your veterinarian should be contacted immediately.

In cases of grain overload, it is critical to prevent the absorption of toxic material from the gastrointestinal tract. Mineral oil is usually recommended— 1 gallon (4 liters), by mouth. Purgation should not be performed on horses in the acute phase as they tend to be dehydrated.

Traditionally, cold packs or ice packs applied to the affected feet have been encouraged, but recent evidence suggests that hot packs used early in the course of the disease may be more beneficial.

Your veterinarian may prescribe certain nonsteroidal anti-inflammatory medications to lessen inflammation. Administration of corticosteroids is not recommended. Follow prescriptions exactly as described.

Heart-bar shoes have been used in acute cases of laminitis in an attempt to distrib-ute sole pressure and avoid pedal rotation. Because an improperly fitted heart-bar shoe aggravates the pain, correct fitting is essential.

Treatments of chronic laminitis have attempted to restore the normal alignment of the rotated coffin bone and encourage frog pressure by lowering the heels, removing excess toe, and protecting the dropped sole. This requires corrective hoof trimming and the use of full leather pads or a heart-bar shoe. The hoof should be trimmed and the shoe reset at 4- to 6-week intervals. This approach can be successful in selected cases but is expensive, labor intensive, and prolonged.

Surgical removal of the separated hoof wall may also be recommended and has been used in cases of both acute and chronic laminitis. This procedure carries risk and should follow consultation between the veterinarian and the person who makes and fits the horseshoes (farrier).

Despite prompt treatment, the outlook for recovery is guarded until recovery is complete and it is evident that the hoof structure is not altered.

Navicular Disease

Navicular disease is essentially a long-term, degenerative condition of the navicular bursa and navicular bone that involves damage to the surface of the bone and the flexor tendon with abnormal outgrowth of bone on the borders of the bone. Thus, it is a syndrome with a complex disease development. It is one of the most common causes of longterm forelimb lameness in horses. Navicular disease is essentially unknown in ponies and donkeys.

The exact cause is unknown, but many factors involving the navicular bone and its blood supply, as well as the nearby ligament, joint, bursa, and tendon, may contribute. It is most often a disease of the more mature riding horse, although it has been seen in 3-year-olds. Navicular disease may be partially hereditary. Defective shoeing that stops the action of the frog and the quarters may also be a contributing factor, as well as trauma or a jarring injury.

Usually, navicular disease is slowly and subtly harmful in onset. An early sign may be the way in which the horse relieves pressure on the painful area by pointing or advancing the affected foot with the heel off the ground. If both fore-feet are affected, the horse points them alternately. Lameness tends to come and go early in the course of the disease. The stride is shortened, and the horse may tend to stumble. Turning the horse in a tight circle usually produces a short-term worsening of lameness. There may be soreness in the shoulder muscles after the changes in posture and gait, resulting in a common complaint of "shoulder lameness."

Diagnosis is based on a complete history and careful physical examination. The lameness can be eliminated by the use of regional analgesia (*see* page 668). X-rays show degenerative changes involving the navicular bone, including some abnormal outgrowths of bone and bone reshaping.

Because the condition is both longterm and degenerative, it can be managed in some horses but not cured. With severe lameness, rest is recommended. Foot care includes trimming and shoeing that restores normal bone alignment and balance. Nonsteroidal anti-inflammatory drugs, along with proper foot management, extend serviceable soundness in some horses. The injection of corticosteroids into the bursa may relieve pain but is not curative.

Surgical removal of part of the palmar digital nerve ("denerving") may provide relief from pain and prolong the usefulness of the horse, but this should not be considered curative. The surgical removal of nerves can be accompanied by severe complications such as a painful tumor formation.

The outlook for recovery is guarded to poor, but a carefully designed treatment plan can prolong the usefulness of most horses. Athletes may even temporarily return to competitive status. However, over months or years, all affected horses eventually stop responding to treatment.

Pedal Osteitis

Pedal osteitis is an inflammation of the sensitive structures of the soles of the forefeet, associated with inflammation of bony tissue and mineral loss from the coffin bone. Repeated jarring injuries, laminitis (*see* page 682), persistent corns, and chronic bruised soles have been implicated as causes. Pedal osteitis is common in performance horses and usually is associated with work on hard tracks.

Lameness may not be obvious because usually both forelimbs are affected. There may be a stilted or shuffling action in front, with signs of discomfort in the hoof region. Tapping and pressure from hoof testers usually reveal tenderness over the entire sole. X-rays are helpful in diagnosis and can be used to help differentiate this condition from others with similar signs.

Treatment involves prolonged rest, anti-inflammatory medication, and careful shoeing to relieve sole pressure. The outlook for recovery is guarded, but the serviceable soundness of many horses can be extended by proper management.

Puncture Wounds of the Foot

Puncture wounds are usually the result of poor horse-shoeing technique but can occur when a horse steps on a penetrating foreign object. **Nail bind** implies that a nail has been driven close to the sensitive structures of the foot, causing severe pain and lameness. **Nail prick** means that the thick, sensitive layer of connective tissue beneath the outer layer of skin has been pierced.

When a foreign object penetrates the sole of the foot, it can introduce microorganisms that can cause infection. Lameness is usually severe following a puncture wound, especially when the foot bears weight; the degree of lameness may be similar to that produced by a fracture. The horse may stand and point the affected foot. The foot will show increased pain and may be warm to the touch. Infection may progress to the coronary band, and abscesses may form. Subsequently, the pastern and fetlock areas accumulate fluid and swell. Diagnosis requires confirming the site of pain by pulling the shoe, applying hoof testers, and paring down the suspect area to locate the foreign object or its path of entry.

Prompt treatment with disinfectants and poultices is important for nail bind and nail prick. Ensuring adequate wound drainage helps prevent the formation of abscesses. In pricked foot, the outlook for recovery is good, provided diagnosis is made and treatment begun early. If an abscess has developed below the sole of the foot, treatment may be prolonged, and the outlook for recovery is guarded. If infection spreads to the joints, the outlook for recovery is unfavorable.

Any foreign object must always be found and removed, and the infected area pared with a hoof knife to allow adequate drainage. The foot should then be kept in a rubber or plastic boot for 3 to 5 days with a cotton pad soaked in saturated magnesium sulfate solution or other suitable poultice. All horses with puncture wounds should be immunized against tetanus. If the pain is severe, regional analgesia provides temporary relief. Antibiotic treatment is not necessary, provided the infection is localized and good drainage has been achieved. Deep punctures of the foot that involve the deep digital flexor tendon, navicular bursa, navicular bone, or third phalanx require emergency surgery.

Pyramidal Disease (Buttress Foot)

Pyramidal disease, also called buttress foot, involves inflammation of the covering of connective tissue that surrounds the coffin bone. The disease may arise after trauma or from a separating fracture caused by excess tension on the tendon. Secondary arthritis is a likely complication. In early stages, the area will be hot and painful. The toe region above the coronet usually enlarges, creating the "buttress foot" appearance.

There is no specific treatment for pyramidal disease. Anti-inflammatory medication given by mouth or injection may be beneficial. Corrective shoeing can help minimize lameness. Surgery has been successful for the separating fractures. The outlook is guarded to poor for a return to soundness.

Quittor

Quittor is a chronic inflammation of the cartilage of the pedal bone characterized by death of the cartilage and one or more sinus tracts extending from the diseased cartilage through the skin. It is seldom encountered today but once was common in working draft horses.

In most cases, injury to the coronet or pastern introduces infection into the deep tissues, forming a pus-filled sore called an abscess. Quittor may also occur after a penetrating wound through the sole. The first sign is an inflammatory swelling over the cartilage, followed by the formation of abscesses. During the inflammatory stage, lameness occurs.

Surgery to remove the diseased tissue and cartilage is usually successful. Drug treatment without surgery is likely to fail. Without treatment and drainage the cartilage will die, and abscesses will recur and extend to deep structures, leading to longterm lameness. If damage is extensive and the distal phalangeal joint has been invaded, the outlook for recovery is unfavorable.

Sandcrack (Toe Crack, Quarter Crack, Heel Crack)

In sandcrack, cracks in the wall of the hoof begin at the coronet and run down the hoof. They are most common in racehorses. Excess drying of the hoof makes the hoof more prone to cracking, but trauma or structural factors are usually to blame. Extensive injury to the coronet may leave a crack in the wall characterized by an overlapping buildup in the wall at the site of injury. This latter condition is referred to as **false quarter**.

A crack in the horn coming from the coronet is the most obvious sign of sandcrack. Lameness varies depending on the site and extent of the injury; if infection is involved, lameness may be accompanied by a bloody or pus-filled discharge and signs of inflammation.

Treatment involves surgery and corrective shoeing to change the distribution of weight on the hoof. The use of bar shoes is often recommended. If the crack has become infected, an antiseptic pack may be used. The hoof is then bandaged until new horn formation is evident.

Scratches (Greasy Heel)

Scratches, sometimes referred to as greasy heel, is a longterm inflammation of the skin in which the rear surface of the pastern and fetlock enlarge and ooze discharge. It often is associated with poor stable hygiene, but no specific cause is known. Heavy horses are particularly susceptible, and the hindlimbs more commonly are affected. Standardbreds often are affected in the spring when tracks are wet. The common use of limestone on racetracks has been associated with scratches.

Scratches may go unnoticed if hidden by the "feather" at the back of the pastern. The skin is itchy, sensitive, and swollen during the early stages; later, it thickens and loses all but its shorter hairs, which stand in an upright position. The surface of the skin is soft, and the grayish discharge has a rotten odor. If the condition becomes chronic, small masses of tissue may appear. Lameness may or may not be present, but it can be severe if inflamed tissues beneath the skin of the limb become infected. As the condition progresses, the skin of the affected regions thickens and hardens.

Persistent and aggressive treatment is usually successful. This consists of removing the hair, regular washing and cleansing with warm water and soap to remove all soft discharge, drying, and applying an astringent dressing. If small masses appear, a veterinarian should remove them. Infec-

tion requires whole-body antibiotics and preventive treatment for tetanus.

Seedy Toe (Hollow Wall)

Seedy toe is a condition of the hoof wall in the toe region, characterized by changes in or loss of the tissue that makes up the horn. It is most often a consequence of mild, longterm laminitis (page 682). The outer surface of the wall appears sound, but the inner surface of the wall is mealy, and there may be a cavity due to loss of horn substance. Tapping on the outside of the wall at the toe produces a hollow sound over the affected portion. The disease may affect only a small area or nearly the entire width of the wall at the toe. Lameness is infrequent but may occur if infection or an abscess is also present.

The outlook for recovery is usually good. The diseased portion of the hoof wall should be cleaned and packed with juniper tar and oakum. In the absence of lameness, shoeing and work can continue. If the condition is extensive, the outer wall may need to be removed over the affected area.

Sheared Heels

In sheared heels, unevenness of the heels produces a severe imbalance of the foot. This results in one side of the heel contacting the ground before the other, creating a shearing force at the rounded parts of the heel, uneven growth of the toe, and severe overriding contraction of the heels. The heel develops longterm soreness similar to that of navicular disease (page 683). Hoof cracks, deep cracks between the rounded parts of the heel, and an infection of the frog frequently accompany the problem. Navicular disease may occur at the same time.

Heel alignment and foot balance may be restored with corrective trimming and shoeing. A full bar shoe with a reinforcing diagonal bar to support the affected quarter and heel is used. Improvement will likely require several shoe resettings. The outlook for recovery is good in uncomplicated cases, if corrective measures are consistently applied until new hoof growth occurs.

Sidebone

Sidebone is the hardening (calcification) of the cartilage of the coffin or pedal bone. It is most common in the forefeet of heavy horses working on hard surfaces. It also is frequent in hunters and jumpers but is rare in racing Thoroughbreds. Repeated jarring injuries to the quarters of the feet are probably the most basic cause. Improper shoeing that stops normal movement of the quarters may also lead to sidebone. Other cases arise from direct trauma.

The hardened cartilage may stick out above the coronet. The presence of lameness depends on the stage of the hardening process, the amount of jarring injury sustained by the feet, and the type of terrain underfoot. Often, no lameness is noted. A narrow or contracted foot makes lameness more likely. Lameness also may occur if sidebone is accompanied by another condition such as navicular disease. The stride may be shortened, and walking the horse across a slope may exaggerate the soreness.

Sidebone may be diagnosed using examination and palpation (hands-on evaluation of the leg); however, x-rays are necessary for confirmation. When lameness is present, corrective shoeing to promote expansion of the quarters and to protect the foot from jarring injury often helps. Grooving the hooves also may promote expansion of the wall.

Thrush

Thrush is a degeneration of the frog with secondary bacterial infection. It results from poor management and hygiene, such as allowing the horse to stand too long in wet conditions and failing to clean the hooves regularly. The condition is more common in the hindfeet. The affected area is moist and contains a black, thick discharge with a characteristic foul odor. These signs alone are sufficient to make the diagnosis.

Treatment should begin by providing dry, clean material underfoot and cleaning out the hoof, including the removal of all softened horn. An astringent lotion, used with daily hoof cleaning, aids recovery after removal of the diseased tissue. Use of a bar shoe after the disease has been stopped may help the frog regenerate. The outlook for recovery is usually favorable, but if the connective tissue of the frog has been damaged, all diseased tissue must be removed.

■ DISORDERS OF THE FETLOCK AND PASTERN

Fetlock is a term used for the joint where the cannon bone, the proximal sesamoid bones, and the distal phalanx (pedal bone) meet. In some ways it is comparable to the ankle joint in humans. The pastern is the area between the hoof and the fetlock joint. Disorders of the fetlock and pastern include conditions such as fractures, osselets, ringbone, sesamoiditis, synovitis, and windgalls.

Fractures of Phalanges and Proximal Sesamoids

Fractures of the long pastern bone (first phalanx) are not uncommon in racehorses. They may be small "chip" fractures, fractures along the length of the bone (split pastern), or fractures in which the bone is broken into fragments. Another category, seen only in Standardbreds, involves chips or loose fragments on the back of the long pastern bone called Birkeland fractures.

Signs of longitudinal fractures involve sudden, severe weightbearing lameness after work or a race. There may be little or no swelling initially, but there is intense pain on feeling or bending the fetlock joint. Lameness may be less obvious with chip or fragmented fractures, but bending the joint worsens the problem. X-rays confirm the diagnosis, although it can be difficult to see the fine line of the fracture.

Chip and fragmented fractures can be surgically removed using an endoscope. Long, split fractures can be repaired using

2 or more bone screws. Conservative treatment of severely fragmented fractures involves using a plaster or fiberglass cast for up to 12 weeks. However, complications include poor alignment at the fracture site and secondary arthritis.

Fractures of the short pastern bone (second phalanx) are similar to those of the long pastern bone, but they are less common. The treatment and outlook for recovery are similar.

Fractures of the fetlock (proximal sesamoid) bones are relatively common. They are caused by overextension and often are associated with damage to the ligament, as in the forelimb of Thoroughbreds. Shoeing with a trailer-type shoe may cause fractures of the fetlock in the hindlimb of Standardbreds. Signs of fracture include heat, pain, and sudden onset of lameness; these tend to worsen when the fetlock joint is bent. There is bleeding and fluid buildup in the fetlock joint. X-rays confirm the diagnosis.

The outlook for recovery is fairly good if small fragments are surgically removed as soon as possible. Standardbreds respond more favorably than Thoroughbreds. The outlook for recovery in large fractures at the base of the fetlock bone is poor, regardless of the treatment. Very severe damage to the suspensory ligaments, including fracture of both sesamoid bones, is a catastrophic injury and can cause a compromise of blood flow to the foot. Some horses can still be used for breeding by surgical immobilization of the fetlock joint so that the bones grow solidly together.

Osselets

Osselets refers to inflammation of the connective tissue that surrounds the cannon bone (between the fetlock joint and the carpus) and the fetlock joint. The inflammation may involve arthritis and can progress to degenerative joint disease. The condition is an occupational hazard for young Thoroughbreds and is caused by the strain and repeated trauma of hard training in young horses.

The gait of a horse with osselets becomes short and choppy. Applying firm pressure and bending the fetlock joint will cause pain. Swelling, which may be warm and sensitive, is seen over the front and sometimes the side of the joint. In the initial stages, x-rays may show no evidence of new bone formation, in which case the condition is called "green osselets." Later, a disorder may be seen in the attachments of bones to the fetlock joint. Bone spurs or newly formed bone in the affected area may break off and float loosely in the joint. Such loose fragments are called **joint mice**.

Early cases may be cured by rest, which is very important to treatment. The application of cold packs over several days may relieve inflammation. Anti-inflammatory drugs given by mouth or injection may also be used. Corticosteroids may be injected into the joint as well. However, this and other forms of anti-inflammatory medication, if used along with continued training or racing, will inevitably lead to the destruction of the joint surfaces.

Ringbone

Ringbone is inflammation of the connective tissue surrounding the pastern bone or osteoarthritis in the digits. It leads to the development of spurs or outgrowths of bone. Causes include poor conformation, improper shoeing, or repeated jarring injury from working on hard ground. Trauma and infection, especially wire-cut wounds, are other causes. In light horses, the condition may result from strains on ligaments and tendons in the pastern region.

The pastern may become bell-shaped when affected by ringbone. Inflammation of the connective tissue will initially cause lameness. The lameness may subside once the bony outgrowths appear, particularly if the surfaces of the joint are unaffected. If joint surfaces are involved, lameness tends to persist, sometimes leading to the fusion of the bones to the joint. Your veterinarian will diagnose the condition by physical examination of your horse, use of regional analgesia to identify the location of pain, and x-rays to confirm the findings.

Complete rest is the most important requirement for treatment. Cold and astringent applications as well as radiation therapy in the early stages may be beneficial. Anti-inflammatory medication may relieve the signs of lameness. Surgically immobilizing the pastern joint so that the bones grow solidly together will cure the condition.

Sesamoiditis

The sesamoid bones in the fetlock are kept in position by ligaments. Due to the great stress placed on the fetlock during racing, the attachment of some of these ligaments can tear, resulting in sesamoiditis.

The signs of sesamoiditis are similar to—but less severe than—those resulting from sesamoid fracture (page 687). The amount of lameness or swelling will depend on the extent of the damage. Reduced speed may be the only sign of lameness. A veterinarian will look for pain and heat while bending the fetlock joint, but x-rays are necessary for accurate diagnosis and evaluation.

The recommended treatment is a 2- to 3-week course of an anti-inflammatory drug. Mild cases of sesamoiditis require 6 or more months of rest; severe cases require 9 to 12 months. Despite various treatments, the outlook for recovery is guarded or poor. Even after 9 to 12 months of rest, many horses become lame within weeks after resuming training.

Villonodular Synovitis

The cause of this inflammation of the membrane surrounding the forelimb fetlock joints is unknown. Affected horses may be 2 to 18 years old, with a slightly higher incidence in males. Signs include nodules that form around the fetlock joint. Swelling and lameness may or may not be present. Changes to the surrounding bone and cartilage may occur.

To diagnose villonodular synovitis, your veterinarian will examine your horse for the presence of nodules or small lumps around the joint. X-rays confirm the diagnosis. The nodules are surgically removed; smaller masses can be surgically removed by using an endoscope. Radiation therapy appears to help prevent recurrence after surgery.

Windgalls (Windpuffs)

These puffy, fluid-filled swellings around the fetlock joints may affect the forelimbs, hindlimbs, or both. They generally are not accompanied by heat, pain, or lameness. Trauma and hard exercise are believed to contribute to the condition, but the exact cause is uncertain. Some horses, particularly heavy ones, seem to be more susceptible than others. In the absence of lameness, treatment is not warranted. Windgalls may disappear spontaneously or respond to periods of rest, bandaging, and exercise. Recurrence is common, however.

■ DISORDERS OF THE CARPUS AND METACARPUS

The carpus actually involves 3 joints, any of which could be a cause of a carpal or metacarpal disorder. Veterinarians use a number of diagnostic techniques to pinpoint disorders in the area, including examination of any lameness, swelling, fluid buildup, or pain in the joint. Sometimes the only observable evidence of carpal problems is fluid buildup (swelling) and minor gait problems. Regional analgesia may be used, injecting directly into the joint and observing a spread of the anesthetic throughout the connected joints.

X-rays of the carpus are critical for specific diagnosis of fractures within the joint, osteochondritis dissecans, cysts beneath the cartilage, osteoarthritis, septic (infectious) arthritis, and benign tumors containing both bone and cartilage.

Bucked Shins (Sore Shins, Saucer Fractures)

Bucked shins is a painful inflammation of the connective tissues on the shinbones. The condition most often affects the forelimbs of young Thoroughbreds in training and racing, and less commonly Standardbreds and Quarter Horses.

Strains sustained during high-speed exercise usually cause this condition in young horses whose bones are not fully conditioned. The condition may begin with microfractures (such as stress fractures) that can develop into major fractures. Affected bones will show a warm, painful swelling. The horse usually becomes lame, with a shortened stride. Exercise may worsen the lameness.

Rest from training is important until the soreness and inflammation go away. Severe inflammation may be relieved by anti-inflammatory, pain-relieving drugs and application of cold packs. Older horses not responding to rest and medication may require surgical screws to treat the fractures.

Degeneration of the Carpal Bones beneath the Cartilage

Most fractures that occur within the joint are likely preceded by the death of cells in the carpal bone. This degeneration of cells is believed to be caused by recurring trauma. Bone disease beneath the cartilage elsewhere in the carpus may also cause degeneration of carpal bones. Depending on the location, degeneration can be diagnosed either by using x-rays or by surgically inspecting the inside of the joint with an endoscope. Treatment involves surgically removing any dead, damaged, or infected tissue. The outlook for recovery is relatively good.

Desmitis or Sprain of the Inferior Check Ligament

Desmitis (inflammation) of the inferior check ligament is a common diagnosis, but it can be easily confused with inflammation of nearby ligaments. Ultrasonography can help confirm the diagnosis. The primary sign is lameness, which is lessened by the use of injected anesthetic. This condition has been treated conservatively in the past, but more recently veterinarians have surgically cut the ligament (called sectioning) with good results.

Fracture of the Carpal Bones

Fractures of the carpal bones may include chip fragments, slab fractures, and fractures of the accessory bones.

Chip Fragments

Chip fragments of bone and cartilage are the most common fractures in the carpal joints of racehorses. They occur less commonly in working Quarter Horses and sport horses. The primary cause is trauma, usually associated with fast exercise. Diagnosis generally involves examination of the inflamed joint membranes together with x-rays that reveal the chip fragments. Surgery using an endoscope is the treatment of choice. The overall outlook for recovery is excellent. However, in conditions persisting over a long time, the loss of joint cartilage and bone will be greater, lowering the horse's chances of returning to previous performance levels.

Carpal Slab Fractures

Slab fractures extend from one joint surface to another joint surface. The most common slab fracture is repaired with lag screws (placed surgically with an endoscope). Such a fracture is considered routine if the joint does not collapse, and the treatment returns many horses to full athletic activity.

However, slab fractures can also lead to a collapse of a row of carpal bones. If untreated, the affected leg gradually turns inward, causing laminitis (founder) in the hoof of the opposite forelimb. Collapsing slab fractures require surgery. Immobilization in a cast for up to 6 weeks helps minimize the chance of another collapse of the joint.

Accessory Carpal Fractures

These are less common than other fractures in the carpus. Accessory carpal fractures may lead to an increase in fluid in the joint and will usually make the horse lame. Diagnosis requires x-rays for confirmation. With rest and conservative treatment, the fracture may heal. The formation of a fibrous union at the site of the fracture may allow a horse to return to athletic activity.

Fractures of the Splint Bones

Fractures of the splint bones (the second and fourth metacarpal and metatarsal bones) may occur as a result of direct trauma or, more often, after inflammation of the suspensory ligament (*see* INFLAMMATION OF THE SUSPENSORY LIGAMENT [SUSPENSORY DESMITIS], page 692) and the resulting buildup of fibrous tissue at the end of the bone. Immediately following fracture, severe inflammation (usually involving the suspensory ligament) may occur. Lameness may affect a supporting leg. It may go away after several days' rest but return after work.

Longstanding fractures lead to lameness in the supporting leg, which is apparent when the horse is worked at speed. The suspensory ligament thickens at and above the fracture site, where a considerable amount of callus may build up without the fracture actually healing.

X-rays confirm the diagnosis. Surgical removal of the fractured tip and callus is the treatment of choice. The outlook for recovery depends on the severity of the suspensory desmitis (inflammation), which has a greater bearing on future performance than the splint fracture itself.

Fracture of the Cannon Bone

The most common reason for fractures of the third metacarpal bone (cannon bone) is the cyclic trauma of racing. Fractures occur into the fetlock joint (condylar fractures); stress fractures are also possible in the body of the cannon bone. X-rays are used to confirm diagnosis of cannon bone fractures.

These fractures are treated with surgery using compression plates and bone screws. More conservative treatments risk delayed healing and the development of osteoarthritis. (*See also* BUCKED SHINS, page 689.)

Hygroma

A hygroma is inflammation of an acquired bursa. Acquired bursas are fluid-filled sacs that develop as a result of trauma. Excessive fluid accumulates in the bursa, and the bursal wall thickens with fibrous tissue. The condition rarely produces lameness. Diagnosis is made by feeling the swollen bursa together with x-ray confirmation. Hygromas can be treated in the early stage with drainage, steroid injections, and bandaging. At later stages, drains must be implanted.

Osteoarthritis (Degenerative Joint Disease)

In the carpus, osteoarthritis typically occurs together with a longterm thickening of the joint. The range of motion of affected joints is decreased, and x-rays reveal a gradual loss of joint cartilage that may become severe. Treatment of severe osteoarthritis is limited mostly to pain relief, but removal of dead or damaged tissue from the joint, followed by joint and whole system treatment may help. (*See also* OSTEOARTHRITIS, page 676.)

Osteochondroma of the Distal Radius

The formation of an osteochondroma (a benign tumor containing both bone and cartilage) at the lower end of the radius usually occurs in young animals. In affected horses, the carpus will typically swell after exercise, with the swelling subsiding after a few hours. Moderate lameness during exercise is also seen. Deep inside, the carpal joint may be tender, and the area is sensitive to pressure. Rapid bending of the carpus causes pain. Diagnosis is usually made with x-rays, but ultrasonography may be necessary to define the extent of the osteochondroma. Treatment is generally successful when the osteochondroma, along with any resulting damage to the deep flexor tendon, is removed with an endoscope.

Rupture of the Common Digital Extensor Tendon

This developmental problem is present at birth or is seen shortly after. Foals usually show a carpal or fetlock deformity, forcing the joint to remain in a flexed position. If not noticed immediately, the condition may cause an abnormal tightening of the flexor muscle-tendon unit. A veterinarian confirms the condition by feeling the swollen, disrupted ends of the extensor tendon. When appropriate, splints are used to prevent the secondary tightening of the tendons that can lead to knuckling. The outlook is good for a full recovery.

Splints

Splints is a condition in which painful, bony outgrowths occur on the upper part of the cannon bones, usually on the inner sides of the legs. Trauma from a jarring injury, strain from excess training (especially in young horses), poor conformation, imbalanced diet or excessive food intake, or improper shoeing may be factors that contribute to the condition.

Lameness is seen only when the bony outgrowths are forming. It is seen most often in young horses and is more obvious after the horse has been worked. In the early stages, there is no visible enlargement of the affected area, but your veterinarian may be able to feel some local, painful swelling. In the later stages, a calcified growth appears. Lameness disappears, except in rare cases in which the growth interferes with the suspensory ligament or the carpal joint. X-rays are necessary to differentiate splints from fractured splint bones.

Complete rest and treatment with appropriate anti-inflammatory drugs is recommended. Injected corticosteroids, together with counterpressure bandaging, may reduce inflammation and prevent excessive bone growth. If the growth affects the suspensory ligament, however, it may be necessary to remove the growth surgically.

Cysts beneath the Cartilage and Septic Arthritis

Cysts beneath the cartilage (page 676) may be seen in the lower part of the radius or the carpus. Many of these cysts cause no problems; however, in certain areas of

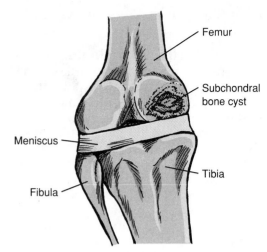

Cysts may form beneath cartilage at various joints in the limbs.

the carpus they can cause signs. They are diagnosed using x-rays, and if conservative treatment does not solve the problem, surgically removing them using an endoscope is recommended.

Infectious or septic arthritis (page 676) of the carpal joints is relatively rare. It most commonly follows injections given to the joint. Horses show severe lameness as well as fluid buildup and swelling in the joint. The veterinarian will detect heat, pain, and fluid in the joint. Treatment with appropriate antibiotics is required.

Inflammation of the Suspensory Ligament (Suspensory Desmitis)

Injuries of the suspensory ligament, which supports and protects the fetlock, are common in both forelimbs and hindlimbs. Signs often are restricted to the top one-third of the ligament, to the body of the ligament, or to one or both ligament branches.

Inflammation of the Top Third of the Suspensory Ligament

Inflammation of the top one-third of the suspensory ligament is relatively common and can affect the forelimbs or hindlimbs of horses of all ages. Unlike inflammation of other portions of the ligament, inflammation of the upper third causes lameness, poor performance, or poor action. It is often seen in horses with poor foot balance. Straight hock conformation or hyperextension of the fetlock joints may make a horse more prone to this type of injury.

Lameness can vary from mild to severe and, in early cases, is generally worsened by work and improved by rest. Forelimb lameness may be more noticeable by bending the fetlock and interphalangeal joints but is generally unaffected by bending the carpus, whereas hindlimb lameness may be increased by bending the fetlock and interphalangeal joints or by bending the hock and stifle joints.

In severe cases, localized heat may be felt just below the back of the carpus (or tarsus). Swelling may or may not be present. In more chronic cases, often no obvious abnormality can be detected.

Local anesthesia and ultrasonography may help in the diagnosis of this condition. Treatment is stall rest, followed by a graduated program of exercise combined with correction of foot imbalance.

Inflammation of the Body of the Suspensory Ligament

This is an injury seen mostly in racehorses, affecting usually the forelimbs of Thoroughbreds and both the forelimbs and hindlimbs of Standardbreds. Signs vary and may include enlargement of the ligament, local heat, swelling, lameness, and pain. The diagnosis can be confirmed using ultrasonography. Treatment is aimed at reducing inflammation by using nonsteroidal anti-inflammatory drugs, hydrotherapy, and controlled exercise.

Inflammation of the Branches of the Suspensory Ligament

This relatively common injury can affect the forelimbs and hindlimbs in all types of horses. Usually only a single branch in a single limb is affected, although both branches may be affected, especially in hindlimbs. Horses that develop this condition often have imbalanced feet.

Signs depend on the degree of damage and how long the condition has existed. The affected area may be hot, and fluid buildup in the affected branch can cause swelling. Direct pressure applied to the injured branch may cause pain, as may bending the fetlock. Lameness varies and is sometimes absent altogether.

Diagnosis is based on observation of the signs and ultrasonography. Management of the condition depends on the severity of signs as well as on the breed and use of the horse. The outlook for recovery is guarded. Injuries are slow to heal; some signs take 6 months or more to improve, after which the condition may return.

Hernias, Lumps, and Splints in the Synovial Joint Membrane

These conditions are relatively uncommon but must be considered when fluid-filled swellings occur across the back of the carpus. A synovial hernia is a swelling arising from the rupture of the synovial membrane by a defect in the joint capsule or the tendon sheath. Diagnosis is confirmed using contrast x-rays. When it is accessible, the hernia or splint is surgically repaired.

Torn Medial Palmar Intercarpal Ligament

This injury, first described in 1990, is usually diagnosed when there is an inflammation of the membranes of the carpal joint that does not respond to treatment. Bone chips may be present in the carpus, and the horse may be exceedingly lame. Diagnosis is made by surgical inspection of the joint using an endoscope. An endoscope is also used for treatment to remove the torn fibers. If the ligament is torn less than 50%, the outlook for recovery is excellent.

Inflammation of the Tendon Sheaths Associated with the Carpus

There are several forms of inflammation that can affect the tendon sheaths, including those caused by trauma, infection, and others whose cause is unknown (in which there is no evident lameness).

The only sign may be joint fluid buildup around the tendon sheath. Inflammation caused by trauma is usually seen in older animals. In the acute form, a fluid-filled swelling appears; in the chronic form, the connective tissues may show abnormal thickening and scarring.

Treatment consists of generalized and local anti-inflammatory treatment. Surgical removal of any dead or damaged tissue may be helpful in treating the chronic form seen in jumpers. The infectious (septic) form of inflammation is rare. When it is seen, the signs include lameness, heat, and swelling as seen in septic arthritis.

Inflammation of the Synovial Membrane and Fibrous Joint Capsule

Inflammation of the membrane and capsule surrounding the carpal joint is a common condition and is usually the result of training or racing in athletic horses. In addition to affecting the joint membrane and capsule, the inflammation can also affect the ligaments and cause bone and cartilage damage.

Signs include varying degrees of lameness with heat and swelling around the joint. In longterm inflammation of the synovial membrane, x-rays may show bony growths, but in many instances no significant changes show up on x-rays. Treatment is as described under osteoarthritis (*see* page 676). The most common treatments are corticosteroids injected into the joint, either alone or in combination with hyaluronic acid, as well as appropriate nonsteroidal anti-inflammatory drugs. If the inflammation does not respond to joint treatment, diagnostic surgery using an endoscope to inspect the inside of the joint may be necessary to exclude other causes of inflammation.

▨ DISORDERS OF THE SHOULDER AND ELBOW

Disorders of the shoulder and elbow include arthritis of the shoulder joint, bicipital bursitis, fractures, and sweeney.

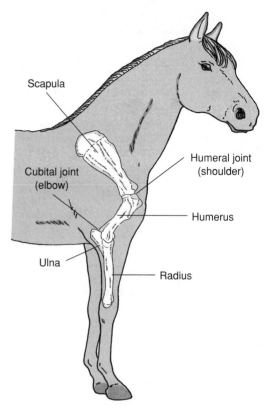

Anatomy of the horse's shoulder and elbow

Arthritis of the Shoulder Joint

Inflammation of the structures of the shoulder joint is uncommon. Causes include changes in the joint membrane or, more often, in the joint surfaces of the humerus or scapula, such as might be caused by osteochondritis dissecans (*see* page 671). Fractures affecting the joint surfaces or trauma to the shoulder may also produce inflammation. Septic (infectious) arthritis (for example, from a puncture wound to the joint) may also occur.

In severe cases, lameness may be present in both the swinging (non-weight-bearing) and supporting (weight-bearing) legs. Milder cases may produce lameness only in the swinging leg. Typically, the forward movement is shortened, with the horse moving the leg in a circular motion to avoid bending the joint. The toe shows signs of wear. Forcing the leg to extend, which pulls the shoulder forward, often causes pain. X-rays of the shoulder joint, preferably taken with the horse lying down under general anesthesia, may show changes that are typical of arthritis.

When arthritis is severe, treatment often is ineffective. Injections of a corticosteroid into the joint may be of some benefit. Whole-body steroids or other anti-inflammatory drugs may relieve signs of pain. Hyaluronic acid, which lubricates joints and seems to benefit cases of degenerative disease in other joints, may also provide some relief.

Bicipital Bursitis

In bicipital bursitis, the bursa between the tendon of the biceps and the bicipital groove of the humerus becomes inflamed. Direct trauma to the point of the shoulder usually causes the inflammation.

Bicipital bursitis tends to produce lameness that shortens the forward phase of movement in the swinging leg. The horse may fail to lift the toe sufficiently to clear the ground, causing it to stumble. In severe cases, the horse rests the supporting leg in a semi-flexed position. Forced extension of the leg usually causes pain, as can firm pressure over the bursa and the tendon of the biceps. Ultrasonography can show the excess fluid and associated physical changes of the biceps tendon. In longterm cases, x-rays may show calcification of the bursa, a common consequence.

Horses afflicted with bicipital bursitis require prolonged rest, often for more than 6 months. Injection of hyaluronic acid or corticosteroids within the bursa may help. Anti-inflammatory drugs and oral steroids may also be helpful. The outlook for recovery is guarded.

Elbow Fractures

Fractures of the bones of the elbow occur most often as a result of a kick or fall. The most frequent is fracture of the ulna. The onset of lameness is sudden, with pain and swelling of the elbow. The fractures typically affect the joint, causing the elbow to drop and be incapable of extension. The carpus and fetlock are bent, with the toe resting on the ground. The diagnosis is confirmed using x-rays.

Treatment may be nonsurgical or surgical. In fractures that are not displaced or that do not involve the joint, full-leg splinting and stall rest are sufficient. Otherwise, surgery is recommended. With proper treatment, the outlook for recovery is favorable.

Shoulder Fractures

Fractures of the scapula and humerus are the most common shoulder fractures. They usually result from falls or kicks. Lameness is severe and sudden in onset. The local soft tissues swell, often with the formation of a large blood clot. Diagnosis of the fracture is confirmed using x-rays. Conservative treatment, including prolonged stall rest, often produces improvement. Surgery may be advised in certain cases. The outlook for recovery is poor if joint surfaces are involved.

Sweeney (Shoulder Atrophy)

Sweeney is wasting of the muscles of the shoulder caused by damage to the muscles' nerve supply. Muscles may also waste away due to disuse following damage to the limb or foot that leads to prolonged, reduced use of the limb. The condition occasionally affects polo ponies following collisions during competition.

If the horse has not been obviously injured, it may feel no pain, and lameness may be difficult to detect until the muscles have weakened. Injury usually makes extension of the shoulder difficult. As weakness progresses, there is loss of muscle from each side of the spine of the scapula, resulting in prominence of the spine. Weakness of the muscles leads to a looseness in the shoulder joint. The shoulder pulls away from the body and, in severe cases, is sometimes incorrectly diagnosed as a dislocation. When the horse is at rest, the lower part of the limb (in addition to the shoulder) also pulls away from the body.

When disuse of the muscles is to blame, wasted muscles can be restored by correcting the original problem. When nerve tissue is damaged, massaging with stimulating liniments or an electrical vibrator can be of major benefit. Passive exercise techniques, such as the application of an alternating electric current to stimulate nerve and muscle function, may help maintain muscle bulk until the nerve regenerates. Surgery to free the nerve from scar tissue has also been recommended. For best results, the surgery should be performed before looseness and slipping of the shoulder joint are advanced.

When muscles atrophy due to disuse, the outlook for recovery depends on removing the cause of the disuse and allowing the muscle to rebuild. When nerve damage is involved, the outlook for recovery is guarded. Mild cases should recover in 6 to 8 weeks. In cases of severe nerve damage, spontaneous recovery may take many months, if it occurs at all. Such cases are candidates for surgery. If the nerve has been severed, recovery is unlikely.

■ DISORDERS OF THE TARSUS

Disorders of the tarsus include the conditions known as bog spavin, bone spavin, and curb. The tarsus can also be affected by displacement of the tendon from the hock, fracture of the tarsus, hindlimb tendon and muscle ruptures, stringhalt, and thoroughpin.

(*See also* FRACTURES OF THE SPLINT BONES, page 691.)

Bog Spavin (Inflammation of the Hock Joint)

Bog spavin is a longterm, low-grade inflammation of the synovial membrane that surrounds the tarsal, or hock, joint. Poor conformation may lead to weakness of the hock joint and increased production of joint fluid. In such cases, both limbs are affected. Inflammation of just one hock is more likely to be a consequence of a sprain or some underlying problem within the joint (for example, osteochondritis dissecans).

The horse usually is not lame. The joint swells mainly on the middle back surface of the hock, with smaller swellings on each side of the joint near the back. Uncomplicated bog spavin rarely interferes with the usefulness of the horse but is an unsightly blemish. It should be evaluated by a veterinarian, including x-rays. The swelling may spontaneously appear and disappear in weanlings and yearlings.

Excess fluid within the joint membrane may be removed by a veterinarian using a needle and syringe. Corticosteroid injections to the joint provide variable and short-term relief. Surgery using an endoscope may be necessary when bone and cartilage involvement is suspected. Bog spavin tends to recur, especially in cases where poor conformation is involved.

Bone Spavin

Bone spavin is a degenerative condition with a gradual loss of cartilage of the joint (osteoarthritis) or inflammation of the bone or bony tissue (osteitis) of the hock joint. Portions of the joint may degenerate, particularly the upper middle part of the hock, and the formation of new bone near the joint may eventually cause the bones to fuse. Although bone spavin usually causes lameness, this may not always be obvious. The cause is not always clear, but may be related to improper conformation of the hock, excessive jarring injury, or mineral imbalance. All breeds can be affected, but it is most common in Standardbreds and Quarter Horses.

In cases of lameness, the horse tends to drag the toe. The forward movement of the hoof is shortened, and hock action is decreased. If the surfaces of the joint have been affected, lameness can be continuous. The heel may become elongated. Standardbreds develop soreness in the gluteal muscles—known as trochanteric bursitis (page 701)—as a result of the spavin. When standing, the horse may rest the toe on the ground with the heel slightly raised. The lameness often disappears with exercise and returns after rest. The bones of the affected joints may fuse spontaneously, leading to a return to soundness.

Diagnosis of bone spavin is based on the horse's history, a physical examination, and x-rays to look for joint degeneration and bony growth. Local anesthesia of the individual tarsal joints may be necessary to isolate the exact site of the pain responsible for the lameness.

In the early stages, injection of corticosteroids to the joint may help. Nonsteroidal anti-inflammatory drugs (for example, phenylbutazone) may minimize or eliminate signs. After treatment the horse may be worked to increase the fusion rate of the bones. Fusion may also be done surgically. Corrective shoeing by raising the heels and rolling the toe may help in milder cases but is unlikely to get rid of lameness on its own.

Curb

Curb is a thickening or bowing of the plantar tarsal ligament that runs down the back of the hock. The cause is typically strain. This ligament may become inflamed and thickened after falling, slipping, jumping, or pulling. The condition is most common in Standardbreds, in which poor conformation of the hock makes the horse more inclined to develop the condition. An enlargement over the bone about 4 inches (10 centimeters) below the point of the hock may be seen when observing the horse from the side. A recently formed curb typically produces noticeable inflammation and lameness. The horse stands and favors the limb with the heel elevated. In cases of chronic curb, there is rarely any lameness or pain.

Cold packs and rest are recommended for acute cases. Little can be done to overcome curb that results from poor conformation of the hock. Fortunately, the problem seems to be self-limiting, without lasting effects on performance.

Displacement of the Superficial Flexor Tendon from the Point of the Hock

The superficial flexor tendon can be dislocated by damage to its attachment to the point of the hock. A sudden bending of the hock typically causes the injury, after which the tendon may slip to the inside of the hock. The limb may initially become lame with heat and swelling at the point of injury. Treatment involves rest for up to 3 months, possibly with a cast. The horse may be left with a permanently displaced flexor tendon and a rather jerky hock action. This usually causes no difficulty during fast exercise or jumping, but dressage movements may be affected. Surgery has been reported in a limited number of cases, but the results have not been very successful, particularly in larger horses.

Fracture of the Tarsus

Fractures of the tarsus or hock are usually caused by trauma or the complications of degenerative joint disease. Because the hock is a complex joint made up of 8 bones, a wide range of fractures can occur. Specific diagnosis depends on careful x-ray examination.

Chip fractures are among the more common fractures of the tarsus. Slab fractures are also seen, particularly in Standardbreds.

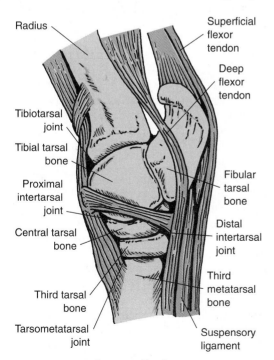

Radius

Superficial flexor tendon

Deep flexor tendon

Tibiotarsal joint

Tibial tarsal bone

Proximal intertarsal joint

Central tarsal bone

Fibular tarsal bone

Distal intertarsal joint

Third metatarsal bone

Third tarsal bone

Tarsometatarsal joint

Suspensory ligament

Side view of hock joint

Because these often are quite small and may not cause lameness, your veterinarian may need to use local anesthesia to positively identify the site of lameness. In many instances, a rest period of 3 to 6 months is all that is required for full recovery, although with large chip fragments surgical removal may be better. The condition responds well to surgery with an endoscope. Slab fractures may require the placement of bone screws.

Hindlimb Tendon and Muscle Ruptures

Horses rarely tear an entire **Achilles tendon** (involving both the calf muscle and superficial flexor), but in such cases the outlook for recovery is grave. The hock drops towards the ground and is unable to bear weight.

Gastrocnemius (calf muscle) rupture is more common and can result from excess stress applied to the hock, such as when the horse has to stop suddenly. It can occur in both hindlimbs and weight can be borne, but the excess bending of the hock makes walking difficult. No satisfactory treatment exists. Splinting the limb and slinging the horse have been attempted but are usually unsuccessful.

Hindlimb tears often injure the **extensor tendons and digital extensors** as well. When only one tendon is involved, the outlook for recovery is usually good. If both extensor tendons are severed, the horse's performance gait may be lost, although the horse may remain useful for slower work or for breeding. Conservative treatment will heal the wound, but surgical repair and casting should be considered if both tendons are completely severed or if a return to performance status is desired.

Racing injuries sometimes rupture the **superficial and deep flexor tendons**. The tendons may also rupture when other tendons are torn. These are serious injuries with obvious lameness and varying degrees of overextension of the fetlock and pastern. Treatment involves surgical repair with splinting and casting the limb, but

the outlook for recovery is poor for future performance.

Injury to the **peroneus tertius muscle** affects the hindlimb and disrupts the action of the stifle and hock joints. The most characteristic identifying feature of this condition is the ability to extend the hock and flex the stifle at the same time. The horse is lame but usually is able to bear weight on the limb. The affected hindlimb exhibits a jerking motion as it is brought forward. Treatment consisting of prolonged rest (usually 4 months) is recommended, and the outlook for recovery is favorable.

Stringhalt (Springhalt)

Stringhalt is the involuntary contraction (spasm) of the muscles of one or both hindlimbs and is seen as overflexing of the joints. Its cause is unknown, but it is possible that an abnormality in the nervous system may be involved in some cases. Severe forms have been attributed to sweet pea poisoning in the United States and possibly to flat weed or dandelion intoxication in Australia. Horses of any breed may be affected, although it is rare in foals.

Any degree of overflexion in the joint may be seen; in mild cases the horse may spasmodically lift and lower the foot, while in extreme cases the foot is drawn sharply up until it touches the belly and then is struck violently on the ground. In severe cases, the side thigh muscles waste away. In Australian stringhalt and sweet pea poisoning, the condition may be progressive, and the gait abnormality may become so severe that euthanasia must be considered.

Mild stringhalt may come and go. Signs may diminish or even disappear during warmer weather. The signs are most obvious when the horse is sharply turned or backed. In some cases, the condition is seen only during the first few steps the horse takes out of its stall. Stringhalt may not materially hinder the horse's ability to work, except in severe cases when the constant jarring injuries give rise to secondary complications. The condition may also make the horse unsuitable for equestrian sports (for example, dressage).

Diagnosis is based on a veterinarian's examination but can be confirmed by electromyography, which measures the electrical activity of the muscles and associated nerves. False stringhalt sometimes appears as a result of some temporary irritation to the lower pastern area or even a painful sore in the foot. A stringhalt-like gait may occasionally be seen in a horse with momentary "locking" of the patella (kneecap) in an extended position.

When sweet pea (US) or flat weed (Australia) ingestion is suspected, moving the horse to another paddock may correct the problem. Many such cases recover spontaneously. In longterm cases, surgical cutting of a digital extensor, including removal of a portion of the muscle, may yield good results. Improvement may not be evident until 2 to 3 weeks after surgery, however. The outlook for recovery after surgery is considered guarded; not all cases respond.

Thoroughpin

Thoroughpin is a swelling of the covering of the deep digital flexor tendon just above the hock. It is characterized by fluid-filled swellings on both sides above the tarsal joint (distinguishing it from bog spavin). It usually affects only one limb and varies in size. It may produce no detectable inflammation, pain, or lameness. Essentially a blemish, thoroughpin is chiefly important in show horses. It is treated by withdrawing the fluid and injecting hyaluronic acid or a long-acting corticosteroid. This procedure may need to be repeated until the swelling does not come back. Radiation therapy also helps reduce the fluid buildup from the tendon sheath.

■ DISORDERS OF THE STIFLE

The stifle is made up of the femorotibial and femoropatellar joints. It corresponds to the knee joint in humans. Disorders of the stifle include fractures, gonitis, dislocation, and bone cysts.

Fracture of the Stifle

Severe fractures of the stifle involving either the femur or the tibia are uncommon. Treatment is difficult or impossible, owing to the damage to the joint, ligaments, and cartilage, and the soft-tissue swelling that occurs. Fractures of the kneecap usually cause much less severe lameness and swelling. X-rays are necessary to confirm the diagnosis. The condition may respond to conservative treatment or, if a large bone fragment is involved, require surgical repair.

Gonitis

Gonitis is inflammation of the stifle. Because of the joint's complexity, there are many possible causes, including osteochondritis dissecans (page 671), "locking" of the kneecap in an extended position, injuries to the ligaments or cartilage, erosions of the joint cartilage, or infection, whether as a result of a puncture wound or a bloodborne bacteria (for example, pyosepticemia).

Signs may vary, depending on the condition's cause and how advanced it is. The joint membrane may swell just below the kneecap. Lameness may be visible in the swinging leg as a shortening of the forward phase. At rest, the horse will keep the fetlock bent with only the toe touching the ground. In moderately severe cases, lameness may be seen in both the supporting and the swinging legs. In severe cases, the horse may carry the leg in a bent position. If the cartilage or ligaments of the joint have ruptured, a grating or crackling sound may be audible. X-rays help confirm bone or cartilage involvement, whereas ultrasonography allows your veterinarian to view ligaments, cartilage, and soft tissue.

Treatment requires prolonged rest. Repeated injections of steroids or hyaluronic acid into the joint may be useful. Anti-inflammatory drugs and whole-body steroids may relieve the lameness in less severe cases. Cases of gonitis that are due to rupture of ligaments or damage to the joint cartilage rarely respond satisfactorily and rapidly progress to secondary arthritis. The outlook for recovery is poor if the condition is longterm or if severe injuries to the joint surface, ligaments, or the joint cartilage have occurred.

Dislocation of the Kneecap (Patella)

True dislocation of the kneecap is uncommon in horses. When it does occur, it is usually a serious injury and the dislocation is very obvious. Some breeds are prone to a congenital form of dislocation.

The most frequent problem involving the kneecap is upward fixation or locking of the patellar ligament. Some pony breeds inherit a tendency to develop this condition. Dislocation may also be seen in immature animals with poorly developed thigh muscles. It may occur in one or both hindlimbs. Signs include an intermittent locking of the limb in extension followed by a sudden jerk or overbending of the joint when the patellar ligament unlocks. These signs are more common after the horse has been standing still for any period (for example, overnight in the stable, or after traveling in a trailer). However, the signs are often much less dramatic, which makes diagnosis difficult. There may simply be a lack of hindlimb forward motion associated with a rather jerky patellar action.

In many cases, a general improvement in fitness and muscle tone of the hindquarters can eliminate the problem. In the more severe and persistent cases, surgery to realign the kneecap may be recommended. Following surgery, rest must be sufficient to permit complete healing (4 to 6 weeks) before resuming any training.

Bone Cyst beneath Cartilage

Large, cyst-like structures may occur in various sites in a horse's body, particularly in the stifle. Their cause and development are not completely understood, but they may arise after trauma to the joint cartilage or as a result of a bone or

cartilage disorder (for example, osteochondritis dissecans).

In the stifle, cysts are most common in young Thoroughbreds (aged 1 to 2 years). Lameness is first noticed when training begins or while the horse is being broken in. The condition commonly produces swelling of the knee joint, although the cysts can cause severe lameness with no swelling or pain. X-rays can confirm the diagnosis. Some horses respond well to rest for 4 to 6 months and treatment with anti-inflammatory drugs. If this conservative treatment fails, particularly in more mature animals, surgery is recommended. A variety of surgical techniques are in use, and because of the favorable results surgery tends to produce, it may be considered before more conservative treatment.

■ DISORDERS OF THE HIP

Disorders of the hip include coxitis, dislocations, fractures, and bursitis.

Coxitis

Coxitis is inflammation of the hip and may lead to osteoarthritis of the hip joint. Most cases are caused by trauma, such as following a fall or after a cast has been applied while the horse is lying down. Hip bone (pelvic) fractures and infections, particularly pyosepticemia in young animals, may also be causes.

Lameness may be seen in both the supporting and the swinging leg. In severe cases, the horse may carry the leg. In less severe cases, the horse develops a rolling gait, elevating the affected quarter during weight-bearing and advancing the limb in a semicircular manner with a shortened forward stride. The toe may be worn from dragging. The horse often stands with the limb partially bent, the stifle turned out, and the point of the hock turned inward. The muscles of the quarter waste away in longterm cases. X-rays of the joint confirm the diagnosis.

The outlook for recovery is poor. Treatment involves rest, and steroids injected into the joint may relieve the lameness temporarily in milder cases. Anti-inflammatory drugs are useful, but many horses are in too much pain for the drug to have a beneficial effect.

Dislocation of the Hip

The hip can dislocate when ligaments or joint membranes are ruptured due to trauma; however dislocation of the hip is uncommon in horses. When dislocation does occur, fracture of the hip bone or "locking" of the kneecap in an extended position often accompanies it.

When the round ligament of the hip joint ruptures, the stifle and toe of the hindlimb visibly rotate outward, while the hock rotates inward. The hip joint does not always completely dislocate, but when it does the gait is obviously affected. The thighbone rotates outward, and the horse resists bearing weight on that leg.

Relocation of the hip joint may be attempted under general anesthesia, but the longterm outlook for recovery is usually poor.

Pelvic Fracture

A horse may fracture its pelvis at any age, but the injury is most common in horses 6 months to 2 years old. Almost any part of the pelvic girdle may be involved. The outlook for recovery depends on the specific location of the injury and the extent of soft-tissue damage. A pelvic fracture can usually be confirmed by a veterinarian after a rectal examination, especially if the fragments are displaced. Considerable pain and lameness in the hindlimbs immediately follow the injury. If the lameness is not too severe, but a fracture is suspected, it is better to rest the horse for 4 to 6 weeks before giving a general anesthetic to do x-rays.

In more longterm cases, the lameness produces a wasting away of the gluteal muscles. X-rays can aid the diagnosis. Depending on the site of the fracture, there may be a hopeful outlook for recovery, particularly in young horses. Rest (for as long as 9 to 12 months) is usually the only treatment necessary. However, some pelvic fractures have a much more guarded outlook for recovery.

Trochanteric Bursitis ("Whirlbone" Lameness)

In trochanteric bursitis, inflammation is seen in the tendon of the middle quarters muscle, in the bursa between this tendon and the top part of the thighbone, or in the attached cartilage. It is most common in Standardbreds, in which bursitis and inflammation and soreness of the quarters muscle occur after hock problems.

The condition shifts weight to the middle wall of the foot, wearing it down more than the side wall. The stride of the affected leg is shorter, and the leg rotates inward. The horse tends to carry its hindquarters toward the sound side. In longterm cases, the muscles of the hindquarters waste away, giving them a flat appearance. Pressure applied to the trochanter (the joint of the hip and thigh) will cause pain.

If the inflammation is severe, the horse should be rested and hot packs applied to the affected area. Injection of corticosteroids into the bursa temporarily relieves the inflammation. In longterm cases, a veterinarian may inject a counter-irritant around the bursa.

■ DISORDERS OF THE BACK

Disorders of the back include fractures, muscle and ligament strain, degenerative diseases, kissing spines syndrome, and injuries to the sacroiliac junction (the joint between the back and pelvis).

Fractures

Multiple fractures in the upper portions of the vertebrae of the withers are sometimes seen in young horses that have reared up and fallen over backward. After the initial pain and local reaction have subsided, the horse usually recovers with no permanent effect on performance. A persistent swelling over the withers, however, may require use of a special saddle. Occasionally, other spinal fractures occur, and their presence can be confirmed with x-rays. The signs in these cases are variable.

Fractures of the main body of the vertebrae are more serious. Such fractures usually result from a bad fall entailing a somersault. Damage to the spinal cord may cause complete or partial paralysis of the limbs. The outlook for recovery is grave.

Muscle and Ligament Strain

(*See also* MUSCLE DISORDERS, page 704.)

Damage to the soft tissues is the most common cause of back soreness in the horse. This mostly involves the group of muscles along the back. Usually, all or parts of these muscles are strained while the horse is being ridden. The principal sites of damage are located just in front of and behind the saddle area. Signs include alteration of the horse's performance and acute back pain. Most of these injuries respond to rest and physiotherapy, although several weeks may be needed for full recovery.

Another fairly common site of soft-tissue damage is the ligament that runs down the middle of the back. Signs of damage to this ligament typically persist longer, and the chances of complete recovery are not as good as for the uncomplicated muscle strains.

There is considerable controversy over the diagnosis and treatment of back problems in horses. Much credit is given to the value of physiotherapy, particularly chiropractic and osteopathic manipulation, but there is often little to substantiate their effectiveness.

Degenerative Diseases of the Spine

Degenerative diseases of the spine in the thoracic region (chest area of the back) are uncommon in working horses. However, when they are seen, they have serious effects, and little can be done to keep the horse working.

Arthritis with the degenerative loss of cartilage of the joints of the lumbar vertebrae (rear area of the back) is much more common, especially in older horses. Lumbar arthritis, however, appears to cause little inconvenience to the horse because this part of the spine is kept particularly rigid even when the horse is jumping.

Kissing Spine Syndrome

The spinous processes are the bony structures that protrude upwards from the vertebrae. You can feel their upper points in the midline of the back between the large back muscles. They do not normally touch each other; however, with kissing spines syndrome, 2 or more do. This may be partially due to the effects of bearing a rider. When this occurs beneath the saddle area, some horses develop back pain. The condition may also cause a local bone reaction, small bone cysts, and false joint

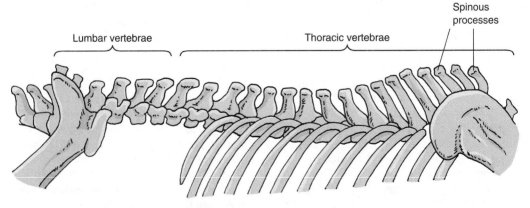

Lumbar vertebrae   Thoracic vertebrae   Spinous processes

The vertebrae of the horse's spine

formation. Diagnosis can be aided by injection of local anesthetic into the affected spaces between the spinous processes. Many cases respond to rest and physiotherapy, but persistent cases may require surgically removing one or more of the tops of the spinous processes to relieve the crowding of the spines.

Sacroiliac Injury (Dislocation, Strain, Arthrosis, Hunter's Bumps)

Acute and severe strain of the sacroiliac ligaments typically results from an injury. It can produce severe pain in the pelvic or sacroiliac region and lameness in the hindlimbs. Longterm sacroiliac strain is a cause of back soreness. It may indicate incomplete healing or reinjury of an ear-

lier strain. Sacroiliac injury may affect a horse's performance, producing intermittent, often shifting, hindlimb lameness. The action of the hindlimbs may be reduced, and the horse may drag the toe of one or both hooves.

Sacroiliac injury is common in Standardbreds and hunter-jumper horses. It is sometimes confused with longterm stifle problems. Usually, the quarters muscles will be poorly developed and, when viewed from behind, the hindquarters may be asymmetrical. This may be due to some tilting or rotation of the pelvis or muscle wastage of one quarter, or both. In the early stages of injury, pressure applied to the area may cause pain. The horse may hold its tail slightly to the side and be

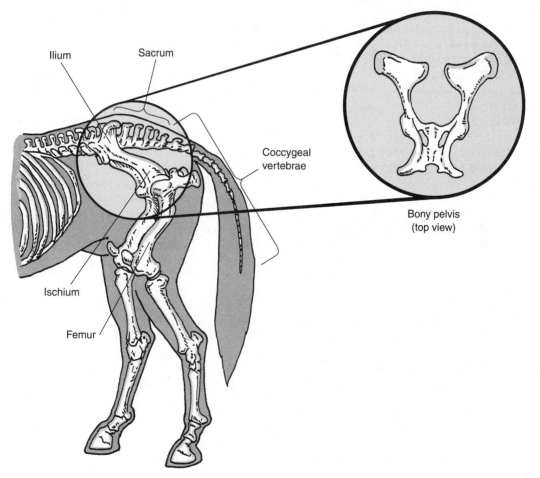

The sacroiliac region of the horse

reluctant to bend its back. If a diagnosis is made early and the horse is rested long enough to allow complete healing of the damaged ligaments (6 to 9 months), recovery can occur. However, Standardbreds usually do not compete well following a sacroiliac injury. Horses with lasting injuries continue to perform poorly despite rest and anti-inflammatory medication.

■ MUSCLE DISORDERS

Myopathies are diseases that primarily cause damage to muscles. They may be present at birth (congenital) or occur due to nutritional imbalances, injury, or ingestion of a poisonous substance. **Myositides** are diseases that produce a mainly inflammatory reaction in muscle. Common causes include infections, parasitic diseases, and immune-mediated conditions.

Muscle weakness or damage can also occur as a sign of many different disorders (such as nerve trauma or influenza). Only conditions in which myopathy or myositis are primarily involved are discussed in this section.

Nutritional Myopathies of Horses

Disorders related to vitamin E, selenium (an element required in small amounts for normal nutrition), and fat metabolism can all affect the muscles, leading to inflammation and degeneration.

Selenium or Vitamin E Deficiency

Degeneration of muscle is sometimes associated with a deficiency of selenium or vitamin E. The condition may cause rapid, unexpected death in adult horses. Other affected horses may show a staggering gait, difficulty swallowing, swelling of the cheek and tongue muscles, difficulty breathing, and a rapid heartbeat. Physical changes involve the skeletal muscles and the heart muscle. Blood tests are used to confirm a selenium or vitamin E deficiency.

In foals, this nutritional myopathy may be seen at birth or shortly thereafter and may be accompanied by inflammation

of fatty tissue or "yellow fat disease" (*see* below). Stiffness and pain are noticeable when feeling for the firm, fat masses below the skin, and severely affected foals may be unable to suckle. Treatment involves addressing the underlying dietary deficiency. Vitamin E supplementation appears to be effective.

Yellow Fat Disease (Steatitis)

Yellow fat disease is characterized by a noticeable inflammation of the fatty tissue, which develops a yellow tinge. This condition may occur in foals together with muscle degeneration due to vitamin E deficiency (*see* above).

It is thought that an excess of unsaturated fatty acids in the food, combined with a deficiency of vitamin E or other antioxidants, causes yellow fat disease. Most known cases have involved animals whose diet consists partially or completely of fish or fish byproducts. The most effective treatment involves removing fish from the diet and restoring any dietary imbalances.

Exertional Myopathies in Horses

Exertional myopathies in horses involve muscle fatigue, pain, or cramping associated with exercise. Most exercise-associated myopathies result in death of skeletal muscle, which is called **exertional rhabdomyolysis**.

Signs are usually seen shortly after the horse begins to exercise. Excessive sweating, increased breathing rate, rapid heartbeat, reluctance or refusal to move, and firm, painful hindquarters are common. The severity varies between horses and even between episodes in the same horse. Severe episodes may involve muscle damage with kidney failure and reluctance to stand. A diagnosis of exertional rhabdomyolysis is confirmed using blood tests.

Exertional rhabdomyolysis can be sporadic, with single or very infrequent episodes occurring with exercise. It can also be chronic, with repeated episodes, often occurring after mild exertion. Horses of any breed may develop sporadic exertional rhabdomyolysis.

Sporadic Exertional Rhabdomyolysis (Tying Up)

The most common cause of sporadic exertional rhabdomyolysis is exercise that exceeds the horse's training. Respiratory disease and deficiencies of sodium, calcium, vitamin E, or selenium in the diet may also play a role. Affected horses generally have no previous history of the condition.

Signs include muscle cramping and stiffness following exercise. Blood tests will reveal elevated levels of certain enzymes. As soon as the condition is diagnosed, exercise should stop and the horse should be moved to a stall with comfortable bedding and access to fresh water. Treatment should aim to relieve anxiety and muscle pain and to correct dehydration and metabolic imbalances. Appropriate tranquilizers or pain relievers may be prescribed to relieve pain and inflammation. Most horses are relatively free of pain within 18 to 24 hours.

Severe rhabdomyolysis can lead to kidney problems. In severely affected animals, regular blood and urine tests are advised to assess the kidney damage. Treatments that induce urination (diuretics) are not recommended except in certain cases (such as in horses receiving intravenous fluid treatment). Your veterinarian will monitor your horse's kidney function and develop an appropriate treatment plan.

Horses should be kept on a hay diet and stall rest for a few days. The horse should continue to rest with regular access to a paddock until the blood muscle enzyme levels are normal. Because the cause is generally temporary, most horses recover with rest, a gradual return to normal training levels, and dietary changes. Horses ridden for endurance should be encouraged to drink electrolyte-supplemented water during an endurance ride. They should be watched especially closely in hot, humid weather for signs of dehydration or muscle cramping.

Chronic Exertional Rhabdomyolysis

Some horses have multiple episodes of rhabdomyolysis that occur after even light exercise. Two forms of chronic exertional rhabdomyolysis have been identified from samples of muscle tissue (biopsies)—polysaccharide storage myopathy and recurrent exertional rhabdomyolysis.

Polysaccharide storage myopathy is most often seen in Warmbloods, draft horses, and breeds related to the Quarter Horse. It is an inherited disorder in Quarter Horse-related breeds. Light-breed horses with this condition often have episodes of rhabdomyolysis at a young age with little exercise. Resting for several days prior to exercise increases the risk of an episode. Signs include a tucked-up abdomen, a camped-out stance (in which the cannon and fetlock are further back rather than in line with the point of the buttock), muscle twitching, sweating, irregular gait, hindlimb stiffness, and reluctance to move. Some horses paw or roll in a way that resembles colic. Certain blood enzyme levels are increased during an episode. Signs in draft horses may include loss of muscle mass, difficulty standing with a hindleg raised, difficulty backing up without hindlimb shaking, progressive weakness, and reluctance to stand. Blood tests, urinalysis, exercise testing, muscle biopsy, and an analysis of the diet may all be useful in diagnosing this condition.

When fed a high-starch meal, Quarter Horses with polysaccharide storage myopathy store a higher proportion of absorbed glucose in their muscles than do healthy horses. Your veterinarian can recommend a diet for a horse with polysaccharide storage myopathy, adjusting the amount of forage and grain or replacing it with a fat supplement. Caloric needs should be assessed first to prevent horses becoming obese on a high-fat diet. Improvement in horses with this condition requires both dietary changes and gradual increases in the amount of daily exercise and turn-out.

Recurrent exertional rhabdomyolysis is most often seen in Thoroughbreds (in which it may be an inherited condition), Standardbreds, and Arabian horses. It is likely due to problems with regulation of calcium within muscle cells. Muscle contraction is intermittently disrupted in otherwise healthy horses.

Your veterinarian can perform tests to determine the cause of the condition, including blood and urine tests, dietary analysis, exercise testing, and muscle biopsy. An exercise challenge test is useful to detect less severe cases. Determining the severity of the condition during mild exercise is helpful in deciding how quickly to resume training.

Management of this condition is best done by minimizing the factors that lead to an episode and regulating calcium within muscle cells through the use of medication. Techniques include decreasing stall confinement by using turn-out or a hot walker, exercising and feeding horses with this condition before other horses, providing the company of compatible horses, and careful use of low-dose tranquilizers during training. A high-fat, low-starch diet is helpful.

Unlike horses with polysaccharide storage myopathy, horses that have recurrent exertional rhabdomyolysis often require higher-calorie diets. At these high caloric intakes, specialized feeds designed for horses with this condition are necessary. Simply adding vegetable oil or rice bran cannot supply enough calories for athletes in intense training. Your veterinarian can recommend a diet for a horse with recurrent exertional rhabdomyolysis.

Hyperkalemic Periodic Paralysis

Hyperkalemic periodic paralysis is a hereditary condition that affects American Paint horses, Appaloosas, Quarter Horses, and Quarter Horse crossbreeds. About 4% of Quarter Horses are affected by this condition, which results from an abnormally high level of potassium in the blood.

Signs are not always obvious but may include intermittent muscle spasms and weakness. They are usually first identified in foals and young horses up to 3 years of age. A brief period in which muscles stay contracted for much longer than normal and have difficulty in relaxing is often the first sign. In some horses, the third eyelid also slips out of place. Muscle spasms begin on the flanks, neck, and shoulders and may spread to other parts of the body. Most horses remain standing during mild attacks, but weakness with swaying, staggering, dogsitting, or lying down may be seen. Severe attacks last anywhere from 15 minutes to an hour or longer. Breathing and heart rate may increase, but horses remain alert and attentive. Some horses have difficulty breathing due to upper respiratory muscle paralysis. Once an episode is over, the horse can walk or stand normally.

Episodes can be triggered by sudden dietary changes or foods with high potassium content, such as those containing alfalfa hay, molasses, electrolyte supplements, and kelp-based supplements. Lack of food, anesthesia or heavy sedation, trailer rides, and stress may also cause an episode. However, the condition is often unpredictable. Exercise does not appear to trigger episodes.

Many horses recover from episodes of hyperkalemic periodic paralysis without treatment. Owners may treat early mild episodes with light exercise or feeding of grain or corn syrup. In severe cases, emergency treatment from a veterinarian is necessary. If breathing is severely obstructed due to upper respiratory muscle paralysis, a veterinarian may need to perform a tracheostomy (create a hole in the trachea) to allow the horse to breathe. Sudden death is common in severe cases.

To prevent episodes in affected horses, the level of potassium in the body should be reduced. High-potassium feeds, such as alfalfa hay, brome hay, canola oil, soybean meal or oil, sugar molasses, and beet molasses, should be avoided. Grains such as oats, corn, wheat, and barley; beet pulp; and late cuts of timothy and bermuda grass should be fed in small meals several times a day. Horses should also have regular exercise and frequent access to a large paddock or yard. Pasture is ideal for horses with this condition, because the high water content of live grass reduces potassium intake. Special feeds for horses with this condition are available without a prescription. For horses with recurrent episodes even with dietary changes, there are some drugs that may be helpful. However, use of these drugs during competition is restricted.

Toxic Myopathies

Some myopathies in horses are caused by ingestion of certain plants, drugs, or other toxins.

Ionophore Toxicity

Certain feed additives (of a type called **ionophores**) that are often added to feeds for poultry or livestock other than horses may cause muscle disease. Usually this is the result of exposure to feeding or mixing errors of these drugs. The toxic effects may be compounded due to various other drugs incorporated into feeds. Signs include persistent loss of appetite, heart failure with rapid heartbeat, difficulty breathing, diarrhea, stiffness, muscle weakness, and reluctance to stand. Diagnosis requires history of exposure to these drugs and physical signs, along with appropriate laboratory tests.

Plant Intoxication

Degeneration of skeletal and heart muscles results when some animals consume the toxic portions (often the leaves, fruit, or beans) of certain plants. Coyotillo (*Karwinskia humboldtiana*), sennas (*Cassia* species), and white snakeroot (*Eupatorium rugosum*) have been suggested, but other species also may cause similar damage. Sennas (such as coffee senna and sickle-

pod) are common in fields and pastures. Affected animals show weakness and trouble walking, and severely affected animals have unhealthy-looking, degenerated muscles and a strong reluctance to stand. Treatment consists of supplemental feeding and removal of animals from the area in which they ingested the toxic plants.

Circulatory Disturbances

Some myopathies in horses are caused by problems in the animal's circulatory system. In **ischemic myopathy**, the formation of blood clots that block the iliac artery results in extensive damage and death of muscle tissue of the hindlimb due to a lack of blood supply. In **postanesthetic myopathy**, complications of general anesthesia may cause changes to muscle tissue due to abnormally low arterial blood pressure induced by gas anesthesia.

Fibrotic and Ossifying Myopathy in Quarter Horses

This condition is seen primarily in working Quarter Horses as a result of injury to the inner thigh muscles. Usually, it affects one leg at a time and involves thickening and scarring of connective tissue that progressively worsens. The muscles bond together and eventually harden. The gait is distinctive in affected horses; the forward stride is jerky, and the foot is pulled back a short distance before being placed back on the ground. The hardening of the muscles can be felt in some cases. X-rays and ultrasonography help to establish the degree of bonding and hardening. Treatment involves surgery to cut out the thickened and scarred tissue or to cut the ligament attached at the stifle. Most horses improve after surgery but only about half make a full recovery.

Immune-mediated Myositis

Ruptured blood vessels and death of skeletal muscle accompanied by injury to blood vessels may be an immune-mediated consequence of equine respiratory diseases associated with *Streptococcus equi* (the bacteria that cause strangles in horses).

▓ SARCOCYSTOSIS

In sarcocystosis, the muscles and other soft tissues are invaded by single-celled organisms called protozoans of the genus *Sarcocystis*. Although their final hosts are predators such as dogs and cats, these organisms form cysts in various intermediate hosts, including horses and humans (*see also* page 194).

Researchers believe that one *Sarcocystis* species (*Sarcocystis neurona*) causes equine protozoal myeloencephalitis

(page 719). The source of infection is unknown, but the condition occurs primarily in the United States. One sign of infection is an abnormal gait; the horse might lose coordination, knuckle over, or cross over. Muscle wasting, usually on one side only, is also possible. The muscle tissue changes caused by equine protozoal myeloencephalitis are usually focused in a particular area, often involving the brain stem. Other possible signs of equine protozoal myeloencephalitis include depression, weakness, head tilt, and difficulty swallowing. Treatment involves long-term (1 to 4 months) treatment with antiparasitic drugs, along with other anti-inflammatory or immune-boosting drugs as appropriate. Even when treated, many horses do not make a full recovery.

CHAPTER **51**

Brain, Spinal Cord, and Nerve Disorders

▓ THE NERVOUS SYSTEM

The nervous system is made up of the brain, spinal cord, and several different kinds of nerves that are found throughout the body. These create complex circuits through which animals experience and respond to sensations.

A familiar type of nervous system circuit is a reflex. Reflexes are simple networks found in the nervous system of all animals. For example, when the eyelid is touched, it closes; when the toe is pinched, the foot pulls away "automatically."

Many different types of diseases can affect the nervous system, including birth defects, infections, inflammatory conditions, poisoning, metabolic disorders, nutritional disorders, injuries, degenerative diseases, or cancer. Neurologic diseases are often more common in a particular breed or sex, or tend to occur at a certain age.

▓ PARTS OF THE NERVOUS SYSTEM

The **central nervous system** includes the spinal cord and the brain. The brain is divided into 3 main sections—the **brain stem**, which controls many basic life functions; the **cerebrum**, which is the center of conscious decision-making; and the **cerebellum**, which is involved in movement and motor control. The spinal cord of horses is divided into regions that correspond to the vertebral bodies (the bones that make up the spine) in the following order from neck to tail: cervical, thoracic, lumbar, sacral, and caudal segments. Specialized tissue called the **meninges** cover the brain and spinal cord, and cerebrospinal fluid surrounds and protects the brain and spinal cord.

The **peripheral nervous system** consists of the nerves that are found throughout the rest of the body.

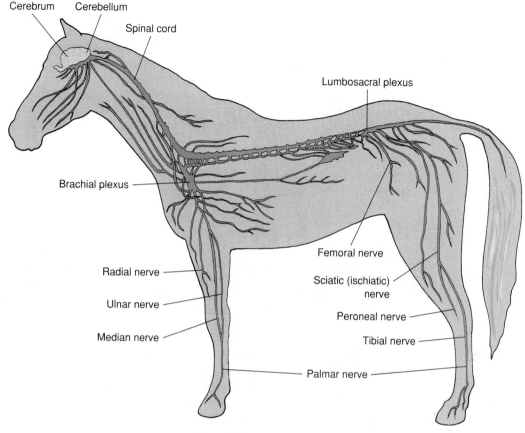

The nervous system of the horse

Neurons

Both the central and peripheral nervous systems contain billions of cells known as **neurons**. Neurons connect with each other to form neurological circuits. Information travels along these circuits via electrical signals.

All neurons have a center portion called a **cell body** and 2 extensions called **dendrites** and **axons**. Dendrites receive signals from other neurons and transmit electrical charges *to* the cell body. Axons transmit the electrical charges *away* from the cell body. When the current reaches the end of the axon, the axon releases chemicals called **neurotransmitters**. Neurotransmitters pass the signal to the dendrites of other neurons, or to muscles or glands.

Neurons in the peripheral nervous system combine to form pairs of **spinal nerves** and pairs of **cranial nerves**. The spinal nerves arise from the spinal cord and extend axons outward into the front and hind legs and to the chest, abdomen, and tail. These nerves subdivide into smaller nerves that cover the entire surface and interior of the body. The cranial nerves include sensory and motor neurons that connect the head and face to the brain.

Types of Neurons

Sensory neurons carry information from the body to the spinal cord or brain stem, and then on to the cerebellum and cerebrum for interpretation. Sensory information includes sensations of pain, position, touch, temperature, taste, hearing, balance, vision, and smell.

Motor neurons carry responses to the sensory information from the spinal cord and brain to the rest of the body. Inside the spinal cord, the axons of motor neurons form bundles known as **tracts**, which transmit this information to motor peripheral nerves going to muscles in the limbs. Motor neurons are important for voluntary movements and muscle control.

A specialized set of neurons controls and regulates basic, unconscious bodily functions that support life, such as the pumping of the heart and digestion. These neurons make up what is called the **autonomic nervous system**, which sends axons from the brain stem and spinal cord to various areas of the body such as the heart muscle, the digestive system, and the pupils of the eyes.

▨ NERVOUS SYSTEM DISORDERS AND EFFECTS OF INJURIES

A change in an animal's ability to sense its environment can be caused by disease in either the central nervous system or the peripheral nervous system. The primary signs of nervous system disorders include behavioral changes, seizures, tremors, pain, numbness, lack of coordination, and weakness or paralysis of one or more legs. The effects of an injury on sensory and motor functions depend on its location and severity.

A spinal cord injury can cause loss of feeling and paralysis below the level of the injury. Mild spinal cord injuries can result in clumsy movement and mild weakness of the limbs. Moderate spinal cord injuries can cause a greater weakness of the limbs. In severe spinal cord injuries, a complete loss of movement (paralysis) and feeling can occur. However, not all spinal cord injuries cause paralysis. For example, injury to the spinal cord in the lower back can result not in limb paralysis but in loss of bladder control.

Brain injuries result in different effects, again depending on which part of the brain is affected. Injuries to the brain stem can cause a loss of balance, weakness of the limbs, hyperactive reflexes, stupor, or coma. Injuries to the cerebellum can result in a lack of coordination of the head and legs, tremors, and a loss of balance. Injuries to the cerebrum can cause complete or partial blindness, loss of the sense of smell, seizures, coma, stupor, pacing or circling behavior, and inability to recognize an owner.

Some injuries to the nervous system can cause damage that is not evident until 24 to 48 hours after the injury occurs. Long-term damage is usually caused by swelling or internal bleeding of the vessels in the brain. Strokes caused by clogged arteries or high blood pressure are rare in animals.

Mechanisms of Disease

In addition to the effects of injuries, nervous system disorders can include birth defects, infections and inflammations, poisoning, metabolic disorders, nutritional deficiencies, degenerative diseases, or cancer.

Most birth defects, often called **congenital disorders**, are obvious at birth or shortly after. Some genetic diseases cause the neurons to degenerate slowly and irreversibly in the first year of life. In other inherited diseases, such as epilepsy, the animal may not show any signs for 2 to 3 years.

Infections of the nervous system are caused by specific viruses or microorganisms. Other inflammations such as certain types of meningitis can be caused by the body's own overactive immune system. These are known as **autoimmune disorders**. Various chemicals can cause a toxic reaction in the nervous system. These include certain pesticides and herbicides, rat poisons, antifreeze, and sedatives. Botulism, tetanus, and tick bites, as well as coral and tiger snake venom, can also affect the nervous system and cause paralysis.

Some metabolic disorders affect the function of the nervous system, including low blood sugar, shortness or loss of breath, liver disease, and kidney failure. Thyroid gland abnormalities can also cause neurologic signs.

■ THE NEUROLOGIC EVALUATION

Evaluation of the nervous system begins with an accurate history and general physical examination, followed by a neurologic examination. Laboratory tests are often needed to diagnose the specific problem. Common tests include blood tests, urinalysis, analysis of the cerebrospinal fluid, x-rays, computed tomography (CT) scans, magnetic resonance imaging (MRI), and evaluation of the electrical activity of the brain, peripheral nerves, and muscles.

The Neurologic Examination

A neurologic examination evaluates 1) the cranial nerves, 2) the gait, or walk, 3) the neck and front legs, and 4) the torso, hind legs, anus, and tail. Your pet's reflexes will also be tested to determine, if possible, the location of the injury in the brain, spinal cord, or nerves in the peripheral nervous system.

Evaluation of the Cranial Nerves

The 12 pairs of cranial nerves extend from specific segments of the brain stem to the left and right sides of the head. They include the nerves that transmit smell, those responsible for vision and the movement of the eye, those that control facial movements, those responsible for hearing and balance, and those responsible for chewing, swallowing, vocalizing, and movement of the tongue (*see* TABLE 13 on page 198). Testing the reflexes of these nerves can help identify the location of the damage. Your veterinarian will perform specific tests designed to pinpoint any signs of dysfunction in these nerves.

An evaluation of the cranial nerves tests mental activity, head posture and coordination, and reflexes on the head. Signs identified during this evaluation indicate an injury or disease of the brain. Signs of damage to the cerebrum and brain stem can include mental deterioration, constant pacing, seizures, depression, coma, or a head turn or circling in one direction. A head tilt, bobbing, tremors, or other unusual head movements may indicate damage to the cerebellum.

Evaluation of Gait (Walking)

Your veterinarian will watch your horse as it walks, trots, runs, turns, steps to the side, and backs up. Signs of dysfunction include circling, weakness or complete paralysis of any limbs, falling, stumbling, rolling, or loss of coordination. Walking horses up and down a hill or on and off a curb may make subtle problems easier to notice. Evaluation of gait is especially important in horses because spinal reflexes usually are not tested unless the horse is lying down.

Evaluation of the Neck and Front Legs

Evaluation of the neck and front legs will include searching for evidence of pain, loss of muscle tone, or numbness in the neck, which may indicate an injury to the upper spinal cord. Various types of tests are done to help detect minor spinal cord injuries.

Evaluation of the Torso, Hind Legs, Anus, and Tail

The trunk, or torso, is evaluated for abnormal posture or position of the vertebrae, pain, loss of feeling or hypersensitivity to light touch or pinpricking, and loss of muscle mass. Some tests used to evaluate the nerves of the neck and front legs are also used to evaluate the torso and hind legs. Loss of muscle around the torso or hind legs can indicate damage to a nerve associated with that muscle.

Laboratory Tests and Imaging

Blood tests are often used to detect metabolic disorders, some of which can affect nervous system activity. Blood tests can also identify other conditions, including lead poisoning, certain infections, and myasthenia gravis, an autoimmune disease in which the connections between nerve and muscle are blocked and weakness results.

Analysis of cerebrospinal fluid (the fluid that surrounds the brain and spinal cord) is often useful for diagnosing a central nervous system disorder. Cerebrospinal fluid is collected from the base of the skull or from the lower back in a procedure called a **spinal tap**. An unusually high amount of protein in the cerebrospinal fluid may indicate encephalitis (inflammation of the brain), meningitis (inflammation of the covering of the brain), cancer, or a compressive injury of the spinal cord. Increased numbers of white blood cells in the cerebrospinal fluid indicate an inflammation or infection. Other disorders that can be identified by cerebrospinal fluid analysis include bacterial or fungal infections, internal bleeding, brain abscesses, and some types of tumors.

Several different types of radiographic tests can be used to detect disorders of the nervous system. **Plain x-rays** of the skull and spine can detect fractures, infections, or bone cancer. However, in most infections or cancers of the brain and spinal cord, plain x-rays appear normal. In a procedure known as **myelography,** a special dye that is visible on x-rays is injected into the cerebrospinal canal. This dye can highlight specific types of spinal problems, such as herniated ("slipped") disks and spinal cord tumors. **Computed tomography (CT)** and **magnetic resonance imaging (MRI) scans** can also help evaluate changes in bone structure, internal bleeding, abscesses, inflammation, and certain nervous system cancers.

Other tests may be used in some cases. An **electroencephalogram** records electrical activity in the brain. Results are abnormal in meningitis or encephalitis, head injuries, and brain tumors. An electroencephalogram can sometimes help determine the cause and severity of a seizure. An **electromyogram** records electrical activity in muscles and nerves. In this test, a nerve is stimulated electrically, and the speed of conduction along the neurons is calculated. This technique can detect nerve injury and myasthenia gravis. A **brain stem auditory evoked response (BAER)** records electrical activity in the pathway from the sound receptors in the ear to the brain stem and cerebrum. In cases of deafness caused by nerve damage, the BAER generates no response. Brainstem disorders may also change the BAER.

■ PRINCIPLES OF THERAPY

Once a diagnosis is made, appropriate therapy can be considered. There are several groups of drugs that are used to treat disorders of the nervous system. Drugs used to treat epileptic seizures are known as anticonvulsants. Anti-inflammatory medications, including corticosteroids, are used to reduce swelling and inflammation in many types of injuries. These medications may be given intravenously in some cases (such as spinal cord injury) and by mouth in others. Other medications may be needed to relieve muscle spasms caused by neurologic disorders or to treat infections of the nervous system.

After head surgery, and in animals with brain tumors or head injuries, there is a risk of swelling caused by an accumulation of fluid in the brain. Mannitol or corticosteroid medications can be given intravenously to reduce the swelling. (For a more detailed discussion, *see* Drugs Used to Treat Brain, Spinal Cord and Nerve Disorders, page 1130.)

■ CONGENITAL AND INHERITED DISORDERS

Some congenital defects (defects present at birth), are inherited from the parents, while others are caused by environmental factors in the womb (such as nutritional deficiencies or some viral infections). For many, the cause is unknown. Foals are born with a well-developed nervous system, and disorders may be recognizable soon after birth.

Birth defects of the nervous system are categorized according to the primary region of the nervous system affected: forebrain, cerebellum, spinal cord, peripheral nerve and muscle disorders, or multifocal disorders that include signs of more than one area. Many of these inherited disorders are rare or breed-specific, or both. A few of the more common disorders of each area are described below.

Forebrain Disorders

Juvenile epilepsy (also called **idiopathic or familial epilepsy**) occurs in young foals, particularly Arabians, up to 12 months of age. The foal can have seizures that result in head injuries or blindness. Foals may recover without treatment, but anticonvulsant medication is usually recommended for the first 1 to 3 months.

Narcolepsy occurs in several equine breeds, particularly Shetland ponies. Signs include excessive sleepiness or sudden attacks of paralysis during which the animal is limp and paralyzed but conscious. The animal is otherwise healthy. During narcoleptic episodes, rapid eye movements occur, and at the same time, the animal may also have muscle weakness or collapse.

Cerebellar Disorders

Cerebellar disorders (defects in the cerebellum) usually result in a tremor and a lack of coordination in both the head and legs.

Cerebellar hypoplasia is a condition in which the cerebellum does not develop completely. The horse typically has a tremor that does not worsen as the animal matures. Hydrocephalus can also be found in animals with cerebellar disorder.

Cerebellar abiotrophies develop when cells in the cerebellum age prematurely and degenerate. In Arabian foals and Swedish Gotland ponies, the onset of signs is from birth to 9 months. Signs are similar to those seen in severe cerebellar

injury, including tremor and poor motor control. The signs get progressively worse over time.

Spinal Cord Disorders

Neuraxonal dystrophy is inherited in Morgan horses, and signs usually develop around 6 to 12 months of age. It occurs occasionally in the German horse breed Hafflinger. The legs become weak and movement can appear stiff, awkward, or uncoordinated. It is now thought that neuraxonal dystrophy in horses is the same as equine degenerative myeloencephalopathy (*see* below).

Equine degenerative myeloencephalopathy (*see also* page 716) has been mainly associated with vitamin E deficiency, but it may be inherited in the Appaloosa and other breeds. The connections between the spine and the cerebellum degenerate, and results in a slowly progressive loss of coordination or paralysis of all 4 legs that starts as early as 1 week to 1 month after birth.

Cervical stenotic myelopathy (wobbler syndrome) may have some genetic basis in young, rapidly growing horses, particularly Thoroughbreds. Males are affected more commonly than females. Excessive weight is an important contributory factor, and the signs may be reversed in animals less than 9 months of age if the diagnosis is made early. Signs are caused by injuries to the vertebrae in the neck and usually appear between 6 months and 3 years of age. Diagnosis involves x-rays or other spinal examinations to look for deformity of the neck vertebrae. Treatment usually involves surgery to decompress these areas. The outlook for recovery is uncertain.

Occipitoatlantoaxial malformation is inherited in Arabian foals and may also be seen in foals of miniature horses. Signs include a progressive loss of coordination, partial paralysis of all 4 legs, and standing with an extended neck. Affected foals usually are partially paralyzed at birth, although other neurologic signs may not develop for several years. Diagnosis requires x-rays.

Spina bifida is seen in most species and usually results in dysfunction of the tail and anus, incontinence, and sometimes hind leg weakness.

Peripheral Nerve and Muscle Disorders

Hyperkalemic periodic paralysis (page 706) is an inherited disorder of Quarter Horses or Quarter Horse-derived breeds. Signs usually appear between the ages of 2 to 3 years and include episodes of muscle tremor and sometimes recumbency, both of which may be brought on by exercise. Blood potassium levels are increased during these episodes. Diagnosis involves testing for the causative gene and is supported by results of needle electromyography. Exercise, nutritional management, and drug treatment can lessen the severity and frequency of episodes, but it does not cure the disease.

Myotonia congenita is an inherited disorder that causes muscle rigidity, marked dimpling when tapping the muscle belly, and a stiff, stilted gait. Diagnosis is via an electromyogram.

■ DISORDERS OF THE PERIPHERAL NERVES

Diseases of the peripheral nerves include degenerative diseases, inflammatory diseases, metabolic disorders, cancers, nutritional disorders, toxic disorders, disorders caused by injury, and vascular diseases.

Degenerative Diseases

Stringhalt in horses is characterized by brisk, involuntary flexing of one or both hind legs during the lengthening phase of the gait. Severity ranges from a mild jerk in the leg to contractions so severe that the horse can hardly walk. Muscle wasting may occur in the lowest parts of the affected leg(s).

Stringhalt is seen in 2 forms. **Ordinary or classic stringhalt** is seen sporadically throughout the world and usually affects individual horses. The cause is unknown. Some cases resolve spontaneously, while removal of the affected portion of lateral digital extensor tendon is done in others. **Australian stringhalt** occurs in outbreaks, affecting multiple horses in a region and often affecting both hind legs. Horses in Australia, New Zealand, and the United States have contracted the disorder, usually in late summer or autumn. Australian stringhalt may be caused by eating Australian dandelion, European dandelion, or mallow, and it is possibly caused by toxic molds in these plants. Horses with Australian stringhalt usually recover spontaneously when removed from pastures with these plant varieties.

Inflammatory Disorders

Polyneuritis equi (neuritis of the cauda equina) causes inflammation of the nerves around the sacral vertebrae at the rear of the spine, near the pelvis. It can occasionally affect other nerves, including cranial nerves. The cause is unknown, although it may be an immune response to a viral infection. The disorder is seen in adult horses of all breeds in Europe and North America. Signs include urinary and fecal incontinence, tail paralysis, loss of sensation in the perineum, and mild loss of coordination in the hind legs. Affected horses may rub the tail. A rectal examination and x-rays are done to check for a fracture of the vertebrae in the tail, which can cause similar signs. If a diagnosis of polyneuritis equi is determined, there is no treatment, and the outlook is poor.

Toxic Disorders

Botulism (*see* page 798) is an intoxication with a neurotoxin that is produced by a microorganism called *Clostridium botulinum*. The toxin is often found in rotting carcasses or vegetation. Multiple animals can be affected from a single source. Less commonly, botulism can develop from wound infection in which the spores germinate in the wound. Partial paralysis develops rapidly, and reflexes are lost in all 4 legs. Cranial nerves can also be affected, leading to a loss of motor control in the head and face. Definitive diagnosis requires identifying the toxin in the food, blood, or feces. Treatment is generally limited to supportive therapy while the body clears out the toxin. The outlook is poor for large animals that are recumbent. To help prevent botulism, feed should be kept dry and free from contamination by rodent carcasses. A vaccine is available for horses in areas where botulism is common.

Occasionally *Clostridium botulinum* has been found to grow in the gastrointestinal tract and produce toxins there. When the toxins are released, they cause typical botulism. This occurs in foals up to about 8 months of age and results in the **shaker foal syndrome**. Most often, foals show signs of paralysis that slowly progresses. Stilted gait, muscle tremors, and the inability to stand for more than 4 to 5 minutes are common signs. Other signs include difficulty swallowing, constipation, dilated pupils, and frequent urination. As the disease progresses, labored breathing with extension of the head and neck, rapid heart rate, and respiratory arrest occur. Death occurs most often 1 to 3 days after signs are first noted.

Ionophores are antiprotozoal drugs used in the poultry industry but also included in some animal feeds as growth promotants. The ionophores include monensin and lasalocid. **Ionophore toxicity** occurs when horses accidentally ingest these feeds. It is often fatal in horses. Signs include lethargy, depression, degeneration of heart muscle, and death. There is no antidote. It is critical to provide only feeds and mineral supplements that are formulated for horses to avoid this toxicity.

Organophosphate poisoning can result from exposure to pesticides, herbicides, or other industrial chemicals. The signs depend on the severity of exposure. The **acute form**, or suddenly form, prevents the body's acetylcholinesterase from working properly. Acetylcholinesterase is an enzyme that is essential for the proper function of connections between neurons, and between nerve and muscle. Signs of severe

poisoning can include vomiting, diarrhea, salivation, shortness of breath, muscle tremors and twitching, seizure, or coma.

The **intermediate form** can cause generalized muscle weakness. Affected animals may not show obvious signs at first, but partial paralysis of the legs and stiffness of the neck can develop several days after exposure. The pupils may appear to be dilated. Treatment of acute or intermediate toxicity includes the drug atropine, which blocks the effects of the organophosphate. Other medications are used to relieve the tremors and muscle weakness. Treatment for several weeks may be necessary.

In the **delayed form** of toxicity, the nerves slowly degenerate. This form is unrelated to the effects on acetylcholinesterase. Signs develop several weeks after exposure and typically involve weakness and loss of motor control in the hind legs. There is no specific treatment. (*See also* ORGANOPHOSPHATES, page 1169.)

Injury and Trauma

Peripheral nerve injuries are common in traumatic injuries. The **sciatic nerve**, which runs from the lower back to the hind legs, may be injured by hip fractures or during surgery to correct a broken leg. Irritants injected in or near the nerve can also cause nerve damage. The leg may be partially paralyzed, or the animal may not be able to bend the knee. There may be loss of sensation below the knee. The **femoral nerve** may be injured in foals during a difficult birth. The foal is unable to bear weight on the leg because of an inability to extend the stifle. The patellar reflex is weak or lost. The **suprascapular nerve** is most commonly damaged in large animals in an injury to the shoulder region. Damage to the suprascapular nerve causes muscle wasting and difficulty moving the shoulder joint. In horses, the nerve may be damaged by the growth of connective tissue in the shoulder after an injury.

Facial nerve injuries are most common in large animals that lie down for long periods of time with pressure on the side of the face. It can be caused by pressure from a halter in horses after general anesthesia. Signs include lip paralysis on the same side of the face as the injury, the muzzle twisted away from the injury, and weak or lost facial reflexes. A drooping ear can also result from injuries to the nerve.

For function to return after nerve connections are lost, the nerve must regenerate from the point of injury all the way to where it ends in the muscle. Nerve tissue regenerates or heals very slowly. Recovery is unlikely if the severed ends of the nerve are widely separated or if scar tissue interferes with healing. Although anti-inflammatory drugs have been used to treat traumatic nerve injuries, there is little evidence of any benefit. Surgery should be performed promptly in cases in which the nerve has been cut. In cases of injury from a fall or a blunt object, surgical exploration and removal of scar tissue may help. Longterm care consists of physical therapy to minimize muscle wasting and to keep the joints moving. Bandages or splints may be necessary to help protect a damaged leg.

▉ DISORDERS OF THE SPINAL COLUMN AND CORD

Disorders of the spinal column and cord include birth defects (discussed earlier in this chapter), degenerative diseases, inflammatory and infectious diseases, tumors, nutritional diseases, injury and trauma, toxic disorders, and vascular diseases.

Degenerative Diseases

Equine degenerative myeloencephalopathy is a neurologic disorder of horses and zebras. It has been seen in many equine breeds in North America, Australia, and England, and is believed to be related to a vitamin E deficiency and to involve genetic factors. Various parts of the central nervous system degenerate, and signs, which appear during the first year of life, may stabilize or slowly continue to worsen. All 4 legs become weak and uncoordinated, with the hind legs being affected more severely. There is

no definitive way to diagnose equine degenerative myeloencephalopathy, although finding low blood levels of vitamin E is supportive. Vitamin E supplements may help horses improve and can be preventive in some cases.

Equine motor neuron disease is a progressive, noninflammatory degeneration of motor neurons in the spinal cord and brain stem of horses. Adult horses of any age and breed can be affected, although Quarter Horses are affected most commonly. This disease is most common in the northeastern United States, but it has been reported in several areas of North and South America, Europe, and Japan. The disease has been reproduced by longterm feeding of diets low in vitamin E.

Signs include weakness, trembling, and muscle wasting all over the body. Horses often stand with their head held low and their feet camped under their body, frequently shifting their weight from one leg to another. Loss of coordination is not seen in this disease. Many horses develop a distinct pigment pattern on their retinas or other abnormalities in their eyes. There is no specific treatment, but some horses improve partially after 2 to 3 months.

Inflammatory and Infectious Diseases

Infectious and inflammatory diseases of the spinal column and spinal cord include bacterial, rickettsial, viral, fungal, protozoal, and parasitic infections. Many of these diseases, such as meningitis and encephalitis, can also affect the brain. Some of the more common infectious and inflammatory diseases that affect the spinal column or cord are discussed below.

Viral Diseases

Equine infectious anemia (page 799) occasionally infects the brain in horses. Neurologic signs include lack of coordination and weakness in the hind legs. Analysis of the cerebrospinal fluid is required for diagnosis. There is no treatment, and affected horses are usually euthanized to prevent spread of the disease.

Equine herpesvirus-1 (EHV-1) myeloencephalopathy can affect horses of any age; however, horses older than 4 years are most susceptible. Although there is a vaccine for the virus, it does not protect from this particular disorder. The equine herpesvirus-1 infects blood vessels within the central nervous system and causes cell death and bleeding throughout the brain and spinal cord. The neurologic signs may be the first sign of the disease, or they may occur after a nasal infection or an abortion. Signs begin abruptly but usually do not progress after 48 hours. They include urine dribbling, retention of feces, sensory deficits in the perineum and tail, mild lack of coordination in the hind legs, and possibly paralysis and an inability to rise after lying down. There is no specific treatment, but mildly affected horses often recover with supportive care. Some horses that cannot rise also eventually recover. The antiviral drug acyclovir has been advocated for treatment and prevention of EHV-1 myeloencephalopathy; however, the efficacy is unknown.

Fungal Diseases

Cryptococcus neoformans is the most common fungus to cause a central nervous system infection in dogs and cats, and is seen occasionally in horses. Other fungal organisms may also invade the central nervous system. Infections often affect other organs, such as the lungs, eyes, skin, or bones. Signs of spinal cord infection include partial or total paralysis and spinal pain. Blood or cerebrospinal fluid tests are necessary to diagnose an infection and identify the organism.

Treatment and the outlook for recovery depend on the specific fungus involved. The drug fluconazole is often effective for *Cryptococcus* infections. Infections with *Blastomyces* or *Histoplasma* fungi are difficult to treat, and the outlook for recovery in horses infected with these fungi is uncertain.

Protozoal Diseases

Equine protozoal myeloencephalitis (page 719) causes signs of spinal cord disease and encephalitis in horses. It results from an infection with *Sarcocystis neurona*, which is carried by opossums, or with *Neospora hughesi*. Any age horse can be affected, although signs are very rare in horses less than 12 months old. Signs vary depending on the location of the infection. A loss of motor control and partial paralysis of the legs are common. Other potential signs include weakness and wasting of leg muscles and cranial nerve dysfunction. Diagnosis is based on signs, analysis of cerebrospinal fluid, and response to drug treatment. Many horses recover with treatment, but permanent neurologic damage is possible. Prevention is difficult but involves keeping opossums away from the horse and its feed and water.

Parasitic Diseases

Verminous myelitis and encephalitis are inflammatory conditions of the spinal cord and brain, respectively, caused by a parasite. The most common such parasites in horses in Asia are *Setaria* species. *Halicephalobus gingivalis* is a sporadic cause of verminous encephalitis worldwide. Signs of central nervous system inflammation strike suddenly, often affecting one side of the body more than the other, and may worsen over time. This condition is difficult to diagnosis, but may be suspected on the basis of cerebrospinal fluid analysis. Drug treatment can be beneficial, but a full recovery is uncertain.

Poisoning and Toxic Disorders

Delayed organophosphate intoxication can be seen after ingestion or skin contact with insecticides or pesticides that contain organophosphates. In addition to the signs of severe exposure (*see* page 1169), delayed paralysis can develop 1 to 4 weeks after exposure. Partial paralysis of the hind legs worsens progressively and occasionally all 4 legs become paralyzed. A veterinarian will need a history of the horse's possible chemical exposure to make the correct diagnosis. The outlook for recovery is poor for animals with severe signs.

Sorghum subspecies, such as **Sorghum, Sudan**, and **Johnson grass**, can cause degeneration of the spinal cord in horses. This may be caused by the high levels of hydrocyanide in these grasses. Signs include lack of coordination, weakness of the hind legs, and incontinence or urine retention. Diagnosis is based on signs and a history of exposure. Signs may improve once the feed is removed.

Tetanus is caused by toxins produced by *Clostridium tetani* bacteria that usually are produced at the site of a wound. Signs usually develop within 5 to 10 days of infection and include muscle stiffness and rigid leg extension, inability to swallow, protruding eyelids, and locking of the jowl and facial muscles. In severe cases, the animal may be unable to stand as a result of muscle spasms. Treatment consists of wound care, antibiotics to kill any remaining organisms, and tetanus antitoxin. In mild cases, a horse may recover completely with early treatment. In severe cases, death may occur due to respiratory paralysis.

EQUINE DYSAUTONOMIA (GRASS SICKNESS)

The exact causes of grass sickness are still controversial, although there is strong evidence implicating *Clostridium botulinum* type C toxin. Grass sickness can occur at any age after weaning and at any time of year, but it is most common in the spring and in horses between 2 and 7 years of age. It is rarely seen in housed stock and is most common in Great Britain. Horses with grass sickness develop paralysis of their gut. Visible signs include patchy sweating, twitching of the muscles of the shoulders and flanks, a dropping of the penis, "droopy" eyelashes, drooling, hard feces, and the regurgitation of food out through the nose. Some horses assume a "tucked-up" stance with the legs held close together. Less visible signs include an increase in the size of the intestines and stomach, displacement of the large intestine, rupture of the gastric system due to fluid, and degeneration of

neurons. There is no reliable laboratory test for diagnosis.

The severity of the toxicity varies: some horses survive for weeks or months and, in some instances, the horse can recover. In more severe cases, death occurs within 24 hours to 1 week. Mildly affected horses can survive with nursing care and a wide variety of feeds. For severe cases, veterinarians often recommend euthanasia on humane grounds, because the disorder is very painful.

EQUINE VIRAL ENCEPHALOMYELITIS (ENCEPHALITIS)

These viral disorders, usually transmitted by mosquitoes or other blood-feeding insects, involve central nervous system dysfunction and moderate to high mortality. **West Nile encephalomyelitis**, caused by infection with the West Nile virus, is currently the best-known encephalitis of this type (*see also* page 724). Other viruses that cause encephalomyelitis are Eastern equine encephalitis (found primarily in eastern Canada, US states east of the Mississippi river, and the Caribbean islands), Western equine encephalitis (found in western Canada, US states west of the Mississippi river, Mexico, and South America), and Venezuelan equine encephalitis (found in Mexico, and Central and South America).

The severity of the disease depends on the individual virus. Infections with Eastern equine encephalitis are generally severe and can progress to death over a short period of time. West Nile virus and Western equine encephalomyelitis are less severe. Not all infected animals develop signs of disease; a horse may be infected with the virus, develop antibodies to it, and eliminate the virus without showing any obvious signs of illness.

Nervous system signs may vary, depending on the type of virus involved. Observable signs can include impaired vision, aimless wandering, head pressing, circling, inability to swallow, irregular gait, weakness and paralysis, convulsions, and death. Many horses have a fever. Horses with West Nile encephalomyelitis may have spinal cord incoordination, muscle contractions, and an abnormal sensitivity to touch. Nearly half of affected horses have a distinctive twitching of the muzzle early in the course of the disease.

A tentative diagnosis is made based on signs and by comparing the location of the affected horse(s) and the season of the year with known data on the insects that carry the disease. Detection of certain blood antibodies (IgM) against the causative virus provides additional support for the diagnosis.

There is no specific treatment for viral encephalitis. Supportive care includes intravenous fluids if the horse is unable to drink, use of appropriate anti-inflammatory agents, and anticonvulsants if necessary. Good nursing care is essential.

Vaccines are currently available for Eastern equine encephalitis, Western equine encephalitis, Venezuelan encephalitis, and West Nile encephalomyelitis. Your veterinarian can recommend the appropriate vaccine and booster schedule for your horse depending on the geographic location and current guidelines.

The outlook depends greatly on the specific viral cause. Horses that recover may or may not have permanent neurologic damage. The disorder can be fatal. Deaths occur within 2 to 3 days after signs appear with Eastern equine encephalitis. Signs of West Nile virus infection may wax and wane over several days to weeks.

Risk to People

People can be infected by all of the viruses that commonly cause viral encephalitis in horses. Signs in people vary from mild flu-like symptoms to death. Children, the elderly, and people whose immune systems are suppressed are the most susceptible. People usually develop permanent neurologic impairment. Human disease is reported infrequently and generally follows equine infections by about 2 weeks.

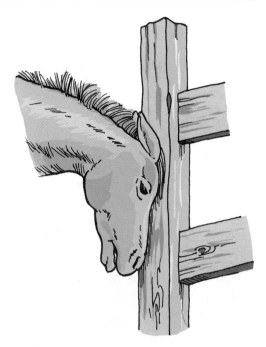

A horse with encephalomyelitis may exhibit behaviors such as head pressing and circling.

■ EQUINE PROTOZOAL MYELOENCEPHALITIS

Equine protozoal myeloencephalitis is a neurologic disease of horses that occurs in endemic form in the Americas and sporadically in other countries. The endemic form is caused by ingesting sporocysts of the protozoan *Sarcocystis neurona* in contaminated feed or water. Sporadic disease occurs worldwide and is caused by *Neospora hughesi*.

The protozoa can infect any part of the central nervous system, so almost any neurologic sign can develop. Infection of the spinal cord is particularly common and causes weakness, loss of coordination, and muscle wasting in the legs and torso. When the disease infects other parts of the central nervous system, signs can include spontaneous sweating, loss of reflexes, diminished sensitivity to touch, dullness, abnormal head tilt, facial paralysis, vision problems, behavioral abnormalities, and seizures.

The disease is difficult to diagnose, but it can be treated effectively with antiprotozoal drugs. These are applied as a paste, and the treatment lasts from 28 days to 6 months, depending on the particular treatment used. Without treatment, equine protozoal myeloencephalitis is often fatal, but the severe signs, particularly recumbency, may not occur for years after infection. The disease can progress steadily or in a stop-start fashion.

Antiprotozoal drugs may also be useful for prevention, although there is no scientific consensus.

The likeliest source of the protozoa that causes endemic equine protozoal myeloencephalitis is opossum feces, so horse owners should attempt to keep opossums away from horse feeding areas. Horse feed or pet food should not be left out, and open feed bags should be kept in closed containers. Bird feeders, garbage, and fallen fruit should be removed from the area.

■ FACIAL PARALYSIS

Facial paralysis in horses may result from injuries caused by rough handling, halter injuries, facial surgery or skull fracture. Paralysis on one side of the face is common when the facial nerve is damaged. Facial paralysis on both sides of the face can be more difficult to recognize, but affected animals often drool and have a dull facial expression and a collapsed nostril. In total facial paralysis, the animal cannot move its eyelids, ears, lips, or nostrils. In partial paralysis, the muscles of facial expression move less than normal.

The signs of facial paralysis vary with the location and severity of the injury. One or both sides of the face can be affected. Usually, the signs include loss of motor function, including the inability to blink, a drooping ear, a drooping upper lip, drooling from the corner of the mouth, and absence of nostril flaring. When the animal eats or drinks, food and water may fall out of the mouth. The muzzle may seem to turn away from the side of the injury because muscle tone on the injured side is reduced.

Electromyography, including electrical stimulation of the facial nerve, can be used to determine the location and severity of the injury. There is no specific therapy for injury except electroacupuncture, massage, and heat applied to the affected muscles. Some animals may also need special water containers and soft food. The facial nerve can regenerate over time, so repeated neurologic examinations can help determine if an animal is recovering. If there has been no improvement after 6 months, the chance of recovery is poor.

Infection of the inner ear and arthritis of the joint between the hyoid bones and the skull are additional causes of facial paralysis. The outlook for recovery can be good if the diagnosis is made early and the animal receives appropriate antibiotic and anti-inflammatory treatment. Surgery to remove part of the hyoid apparatus may be helpful. However, the facial nerve paralysis can be permanent, and longterm administration of eye drops may be necessary.

■ CENTRAL NERVOUS SYSTEM DISORDERS CAUSED BY PARASITES

A number of parasites (including worms and insects) are associated with central nervous system disease. Diagnosis requires eliminating other possible causes of illness and identifying the specific parasite responsible.

Tapeworms

Coenurosis (also called gid, sturdy, or staggers) is caused by *Taenia multiceps*, an intestinal tapeworm of dogs and people. Other animals, such as sheep, goats, deer, rabbits, horses, and cattle can carry and spread this parasite to dogs. The larval stage of the parasite can invade the nervous system and lead to swelling of the brain and spinal cord. The adult worm may grow to more than 2 inches in diameter and cause increased pressure on the brain, which results in loss of motor control, blindness, head tilting, stumbling, and paralysis.

Roundworms

Several types of roundworms are found in domestic animals.

Setaria digitata is found in Asia and is a common parasite of cattle. Mosquitoes are intermediate hosts. In horses, the developing worms invade the central nervous system and cause weakness, lack of coordination, lameness, drooping eyelids or ears, and paralysis.

Migrating larvae of strongyles (*Strongylus vulgaris* and *Draschia megastoma*) and rhabditids (*Halicephalobus gingivales*) have been reported in the central nervous system of horses.

Disease Caused by Insects

Myiasis is the development of larval dipteran flies (bots and warbles) within the body's tissues or organs. *Hypoderma* subspecies have been found in horses. Organophosphate drugs can eliminate certain dipteran larvae from the nervous system, but they can also cause nervous system damage. Corticosteroid drugs are often recommended to prevent additional inflammatory damage and pressure on the brain during treatment. (*See also* FLIES AND MOSQUITOES, page 761.)

◼ NEONATAL ENCEPHALOPATHY IN FOALS (NEONATAL MALADJUSTMENT SYNDROME)

The term neonatal encephalopathy is used to describe a variety of behavioral disturbances in a newborn foal. It may also be called neonatal maladjustment syndrome, hypoxic ischemic encephalopathy, or "dummy foal" syndrome. It is believed to result from decreased oxygen reaching the foal's tissues during birth. This causes varying degrees of damage to the central nervous system, depending on the age of the fetus, the length of oxygen deprivation, and on how low the oxygen level was.

Signs vary, ranging from a slow suckle response at birth to hyperexcitability, aimless wandering, depression, lying prone, loss of muscle tone, and seizures. In a common scenario, the foal appears normal at birth and progressively loses interest in its dam, loses its suckle reflex, can no longer stand, and begins to have seizures. The foal may start vocalizing, which has been described as sounding like a barking dog; thus, the term "barker foal" is also sometimes used to describe this condition.

If the foal does not also have an infection or limb paralysis, the outlook for neonatal encephalopathy is fair to good: about 80% of these foals recover and grow to be normal adults. With good supportive care, improvement can be seen every day. Mildly affected foals can recover in 2 days, but more severely affected foals may take more than a week before they are able to recognize their dam and suckle.

Providing warmth and nutrition is essential. If the foal does not have a suckle response, it should be tube-fed mare's milk or an appropriate mare milk substitute to keep it hydrated and maintain glucose levels. Foals should be fed 20 to 30% of their body weight over each 24-hour period. Antibiotics are often given to prevent secondary infections. Treatment may be needed to control seizures, and a protected or padded environment and a human holder to cradle the foal when recumbent can prevent the foal from injury during seizures. These foals are especially susceptible to eye trauma during seizures. A plasma transfusion may be needed if the foal did not receive enough colostrum (initial milk from the dam that contains antibodies).

◼ LEG PARALYSIS

Paralysis of a leg often results from damage to the peripheral spinal nerves. Paralysis of a front leg is usually associated with injury to the nerve roots in the neck or shoulder, or injury to the radial, median, or ulnar nerve in the leg. Paralysis of a hind leg is usually associated with injury to the nerve roots in the lower back or tailbone, or the femoral, sciatic, peroneal, or tibial nerve in the leg.

The horse's posture and gait, spinal reflexes, pain sensation, and the condition of the muscles in the affected limb are evaluated to identify the location of the injury. The closer a nerve injury is to the muscle, the better the outlook for recovery, so it is important to determine the exact location of the injury. The ability or inability of the animal to flex the joint and bear weight on the leg, and the presence or absence of pain sensation and reflexes at various places in the leg, depend on the site of the nerve damage. Within a few days, muscles wither and lose mass because of the lost nerve connection. Electrical stimulation of the nerve can be used to determine whether the nerve is partially intact. Nerves regenerate slowly (at a rate of about 1 inch per month), and full functional recovery depends on the condition of the nerve sheath and on the distance between the injury and the muscle where the nerve ends. Some nerve injuries can resolve after several weeks or months, but in total nerve rupture, surgical reattachment is required for regeneration.

Applying heat, performing massage, and stretching tendons should be done as directed by the veterinarian to keep muscles, tendons, and joints of a paralyzed leg healthy while the nerve is regenerating. Acupuncture may help recovery. A light, but not tight, bandage may prevent damage to the foot from dragging. No specific treatment is available to help nerve regeneration, but nonsteroidal anti-inflammatory drugs can help control swelling. If voluntary movement, pain sensation, and spinal reflexes improve over 1 to 2 months, the outlook for recovery is good.

■ MENINGITIS AND ENCEPHALITIS

Inflammation of the meninges, the membranous covering of the brain and spinal cord (**meningitis**), and inflammation of the brain (**encephalitis**) often are seen simultaneously (**meningoencephali-tis**), although either can develop separately. Causes of meningitis, encephalitis, and meningoencephalitis include infection by bacteria, viruses, fungi, protozoa, or parasites. Viruses and protozoa are more frequent causes of meningitis and encephalitis than are bacteria.

Meningitis and encephalitis are less common than infections of other organs, because the nervous system has protective barriers. However, infections may occur when these protective barriers are injured or weakened. Infections can also spread to the central nervous system from the sinuses, guttural pouches, the inner ear, vertebrae, or spinal disks; these infections may result from bite wounds or other traumatic injuries near the head or spine. Brain abscesses also can arise from direct infections or from blood poisoning.

Bacterial meningoencephalitis often affects very young farm animals because of blood poisoning caused by *Escherichia coli* or a streptococcal infection. *Actinobacillus equuli* is an important cause of meningoencephalitis in foals. Meningoencephalitis caused by *Mannheimia haemolytica* has been reported in horses, donkeys, and mules. *Actinomyces*, *Klebsiella*, and *Streptococcus* species are sporadic causes of meningitis in horses.

The usual signs of meningitis are fever, neck pain and rigidity, and painful muscle spasms. Horses may have these signs without any sign of brain or spinal cord dysfunction. However, in meningoencephalitis, signs such as depression, blindness, partial paralysis of the face or the limbs, loss of balance or motor control, seizures, behavior changes, agitation, head tilt and circling behavior, difficulty eating, and loss of consciousness can develop, depending on the severity and location of the inflammation. The analysis of cerebrospinal fluid from a spinal tap is the most reliable and accurate means of identifying meningitis or encephalitis.

Cases resulting from rickettsial and bacterial infections can be treated with appropriate antibiotics, while fungal infections can be treated with specific antifungal drugs. The outlook for recovery depends on the cause, the severity of the infection, and whether or not the infection has resulted in irreversible damage to the nervous tissue. Supportive care may include pain relievers, anticonvulsant drugs, fluids, nutritional supplements, and physical therapy.

▨ RABIES

Rabies is an acute viral infection of the nervous system that mainly affects carnivores and bats, although it can affect any mammal. It is caused by the rabies virus. Once signs appear, it is fatal. Rabies is found throughout the world, although a few countries are declared rabies-free due to successful elimination or prevention standards. Islands that have a strict quarantine program in effect are also often rabies-free. In North America and Europe, rabies has been mostly eliminated in domestic animals, although it still affects wildlife.

Transmission is almost always by the bite of an infected animal, when the saliva containing the rabies virus is introduced into the body. In horses, the virus can be in the body for 2 to 9 weeks before signs develop.

The signs of rabies can vary. There are 2 major forms of the disease. The furious form of rabies is the classic "mad-dog" syndrome; it is not common in horses. The animal becomes irritable and may become vicious or aggressive without provocation. The posture is alert and anxious, with pupils dilated. As the disease progresses, seizures and lack of muscle coordination are common. Death is caused by paralysis that worsens over time.

The paralytic form of rabies usually involves paralysis of the throat and jaw muscles, often with excess salivation and inability to swallow. Drooping of the lower jaw is common. People can be infected by this form when examining the horse's mouth or giving it medication with bare hands. Paralysis progresses throughout the body and death occurs within a few hours.

Diagnosis is difficult, especially in areas where rabies is not common. Early stages of rabies can be easily confused with other diseases or with normal aggressive tendencies. A rabies diagnosis must be verified with laboratory tests. The animal must be euthanized and the remains sent for laboratory analysis. There is no effective treatment.

Guidelines for the control of rabies are updated yearly. In general, any animal that has bitten a person and has signs of rabies should be euthanized. An unvaccinated horse that has been bitten by or exposed to a rabid animal must be either euthanized or quarantined for 6 months and vaccinated for rabies 1 month before release. A vaccinated horse that is bitten by or exposed to a rabid animal should be given a rabies booster and observed for 45 days for any signs of rabies.

Several rabies vaccines are available for horses; these appear to be both safe and effective in preventing rabies. Your veterinarian can recommend an appropriate vaccine and booster schedule based on current guidelines.

Risk of Passing Rabies to People

When a person is exposed to an animal suspected of rabies, the risk of rabies transmission should be evaluated carefully. Wild carnivores and bats present a considerable risk where the disease is found, regardless of whether or not abnormal behavior has been seen.

Any healthy domestic animal, whether vaccinated or not, that bites a person or otherwise deposits saliva into a fresh wound, should be confined for 10 days for observation. If the animal develops signs within those 10 days, it should be promptly euthanized and submitted for testing.

Pre-exposure vaccination is strongly recommended for all people in high-risk groups, such as veterinary staff, animal control officers, rabies and diagnostic laboratory workers, and travelers working in countries where rabies is prevalent.

◼ WEST NILE ENCEPHALOMYELITIS

Encephalomyelitis is inflammation in the brain and/or spinal cord. West Nile virus, the cause of West Nile encephalomyelitis, was first found in North America in 1999. This viral disease, transmitted primarily by mosquitoes, is characterized by central nervous system dysfunction and can be fatal or (if the horse survives) can result in prolonged signs of disease.

Encephalomyelitis in horses caused by infection with the West Nile virus has been called Near Eastern equine encephalitis or lordige in France. In the United States, 10 to 39% of infected horses show signs. Once signs appear, the death rate is approximately 30%. The number of equine cases of West Nile virus infection in the US has been declining since it hit a high of more than 15,000 cases in 2002. This decline is thought to be because of availability and increased use of vaccines, increased awareness of the need to control mosquito populations, and increased immunity to the virus within wild bird populations (the reservoir hosts).

All horses are susceptible to West Nile virus encephalomyelitis if not vaccinated against the disease. Any age horse can be affected, but adults are affected most commonly, and older horses develop more severe disease.

The signs and course of the disease are highly variable. Not all horses infected with the virus develop the disease, and some horses can die without showing signs of illness prior to death. The first signs of the disease may be general and include signs of discomfort or anxiety, lameness, low-grade fever, or malaise. Neurologic signs can include muzzle twitching, impaired vision, aimless wan-

dering, head pressing, circling, inability to swallow, irregular gait, trembling, lack of coordination, weakness, muscle contractions, paralysis, convulsions, and death. Horses may become abnormally sensitive to sights, sounds, or touch. Once complete paralysis has developed in one or more legs, the death rate can reach 60 to 80%. A presumptive diagnosis is made by blood test.

Serum or plasma products containing antibodies to the virus can be given as part of the treatment; however, treatment of signs and supportive care to keep the horse comfortable and safe are the most commonly administered treatments. Anti-inflammatory drugs, including nonsteroidal drugs and/or corticosteroids, are often prescribed, but do not always result in improvement. Several different therapies may need to be tried to find one that helps. Good supportive care is important. In horses that recover, most return to normal functioning within 1 to 6 months, but at least 10% of owners of horses with West Nile virus infection have reported some longterm effects.

Vaccination helps protect against West Nile virus encephalomyelitis. Most horses given one of the available vaccines according to the manufacturer's recommendations will be fully protected from disease. In the unlikely event that a horse vaccinated against West Nile virus contracts the disease, the signs tend to be less severe and recovery better. Your veterinarian can recommend an appropriate vaccination schedule for your horse based on current guidelines.

Good environmental management can also help prevent West Nile virus infection. Because mosquitoes breed in standing, stagnant water, all water tanks and buckets should be cleaned at least once a week, and areas where stagnant water can collect, such as empty flower pots and used tires, should be eliminated. Fans that blow over horses in the barn area can reduce mosquitoes and other flying insects. (Be sure that all electrical cords for fans

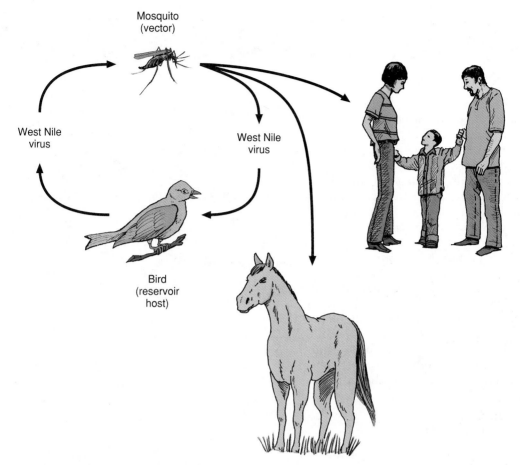

The transmission cycle of West Nile virus. Mosquitoes are the disease vector, and birds are the reservoir hosts. Horses and people are incidentally infected.

are out of the horses' reach to avoid electrical shock.) Appropriate insecticides should be used according to label directions in the summer and other times when mosquitoes are common.

Transmission to People

Mosquitoes can also transmit the West Nile virus to people. Most people who contract the virus never develop symptoms. However, about 1 in 150 people exposed to the virus develop the severe form of the disease. Infection is more common in the elderly. West Nile fever in people is a syndrome characterized by fever, headache, and weakness.

Horses do not act as a source of West Nile virus for mosquitoes, and horses do not pose a risk to humans who perform routine care for infected horses. Special precautions should be taken if people will be involved in assisting with a necropsy (animal autopsy) or when handling blood products from infected horses.

CHAPTER 52

Reproductive Disorders

▨ INTRODUCTION

The reproductive system is the group of organs that produce offspring. In both males and females, the reproductive system is composed of primary sex organs and primary regulatory centers. The primary sex organs are the testes in males and the ovaries and uterus in females. The primary regulatory centers are in the brain. They control the production of hormones that in turn influence the function of the primary sex organs.

A full discussion of breeding issues in horses is beyond the scope of this chapter. If you intend to purchase a horse for the purpose of breeding, you should seek the advice of a veterinarian (who will likely conduct a breeding soundness examination) and of other responsible horse breeders prior to purchasing the animal.

▨ THE GONADS AND GENITAL TRACT

Both sexes have a pair of sexual organs or gonads (ovaries or testes), the main function of which is to produce eggs or sperm, respectively.

The Ovaries

Ovaries are female gonads that produce eggs and female sex hormones, including estrogen and progesterone. These hormones are necessary for the development of eggs and preparation of the uterus for pregnancy. Once puberty is reached and the horse starts its heat or estrous cycle, the size and form of the ovaries change. Within the ovary, a group of special cells form a follicle, which surrounds each egg. The estrous cycle begins when follicle stimulating hormone causes follicles to grow, leading to maturation of eggs and production of the hormone estrogen. Estrogen causes the brain to release luteinizing hormone, which stimulates the release

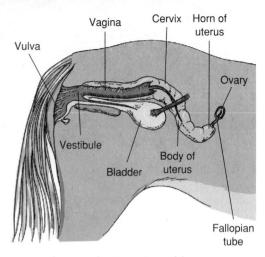

The reproductive system of the mare

of eggs from the ovary (a process called ovulation). After ovulation, the follicle becomes a corpus luteum, which produces progesterone. Progesterone causes the mare to go out of heat and prepares the uterus for pregnancy. If the mare does not become pregnant, the corpus luteum is destroyed and the mare returns to heat.

The Testes

Testes are male gonads that produce sperm and male sex hormones. Sperm maturation is stimulated by the production and release of follicle stimulating hormone and testosterone. Testosterone is required for proper function of the accessory sexual glands, male sex characteristics, and sexual behavior. For sperm production, the testes must descend into the scrotum (a pouch of skin outside the abdomen), because regular body temperature is too high for sperm to develop normally. The function of the testicles can be assessed by an evaluation of semen samples and hormonal tests. In addition, testicle examination and measurement may reveal reproductive diseases.

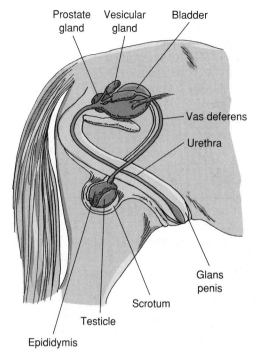

The reproductive system of the stallion

The Female Genital Tract

The female genital tract includes the vulva, vagina, cervix, uterus, oviducts, and ovaries. The oviducts are small tubes that connect the ovaries to the uterus. The end of the uterus is called the cervix. It separates the uterus from the vagina and provides a barrier against infection. The vagina (a muscular tube that extends from the cervix to the outside) is connected to the vulva (skin surrounding the opening of the vagina). The vulva is the external opening of the female genitals. After ovulation, eggs are transported to the uterus via the oviducts. Secretion of protein-rich fluid in the oviducts provides a proper environment for survival of the mature egg, fertilization, and the first few critical days of embryonic life. Proper functioning of the uterus and cervix are also required for the establishment and maintenance of pregnancy. Infections contracted at mating are common causes of female infertility because they interfere

with the proper function of the uterus. Infertility in females can be diagnosed through various means, including physical examination, ultrasonography, hormonal tests, uterine culture, and biopsy of the uterine lining. The vagina and vulva serve as the copulatory organs and as the last part of the birth canal. Mares that have poor function of the vulva and vagina may be prone to recurrent contamination of the reproductive tract, leading to the development of chronic uterine infections and infertility.

The Male Genital Tract

In males, the genital tract provides a pathway for sperm cells and semen. The testicles produce sperm and testosterone (the main male hormone). Sperm pass from the testicles into the epididymis, where they mature and are stored. The epididymis is connected to the ductus deferens, which carries sperm to the urethra. The accessory sex glands, such as the prostate and seminal vesicles, create the fluid portion of semen. Abnormalities of the genital tract can be diagnosed by physical examination or ultrasonography. A semen evaluation can provide information regarding the quality and quantity of sperm and can give some estimate of fertility.

▧ MANAGEMENT OF REPRODUCTION IN HORSES

A fully detailed discussion of the reproductive biology and management of reproduction in horses is beyond the scope of this book. However, an overview of key aspects of the horse's reproductive cycle, pregnancy, and foaling are provided in this section.

Reproductive Cycle and Breeding Management

Most mares only have estrous cycles during the seasons of the year when day length is long. During winter, the ovaries are inactive, and the reproductive hormones are at baseline levels in the bloodstream. As the days get longer in the spring, mares go through a transitional stage as the reproductive tract starts to prepare for the breeding season. During this transition, mares will have 3 to 4 episodes of sexual receptivity due to the development of waves of large follicles on the ovaries. Mares are not fertile at this time of year because the ovaries do not release eggs. After 8 to 10 weeks, the level of luteinizing hormone will be high enough to cause one of the follicles to ovulate. Once this occurs, the mare will then establish a normal estrous cycle with regular ovulation. Mares ovulate every 21 days throughout the breeding season, with periods of estrus (receptivity to breeding with a stallion) lasting 2 to 8 days. During estrus, follicles on the ovary enlarge. One of these will become dominant and release a mature egg. The follicle becomes a corpus luteum and produces the hormone progesterone, which prepares the uterus for implantation of the egg. If the mare breeds and the egg is fertilized, the egg passes into the uterus and begins a pregnancy. Otherwise, the corpus luteum is destroyed and another estrous cycle begins.

After the period of winter inactivity and transition, mares naturally begin estrous cycles in April in the northern hemisphere. Because the changes in cycling are stimulated by increasing amounts of daylight, it is possible to hasten the onset of cycles by exposing the mare to increased amounts of artificial light during the winter. The timing of ovarian cycles can also be manipulated by giving injections of various reproductive hormones. This is typically done to facilitate breeding appointments and to allow mares and stallions to remain in competition during much of the breeding season. Your veterinarian can advise you on how this is done.

Detecting Estrus

A successful breeding program revolves around good estrus detection. The mare should be presented to a stallion (teaser) daily or every other day during the breeding season, and an accurate interpretation and record of her response should be made. A mare in estrus (the receptive phase of the cycle) raises her tail, squats, urinates, and presents her rear to the stallion. She will also allow the stallion to mount and copulate. A mare in diestrus (the nonreceptive phase of the cycle) usually squeals, kicks, bites, and rejects the stallion's attempts to sniff the mare or mount. Adequate exposure to the teaser stallion is necessary to determine the mare's receptivity. Prolonged and irregular periods of estrus are common at the beginning and end of the breeding season.

A mare in estrus may not appear receptive at first due to nervousness or inexperience. Some mares with a foal at their side will appear less receptive because they are protective of the foal. The mare's behavior should be consistent with the condition of her reproductive tract as determined by a physical examination. The response to teasing can determine if estrus has begun and indicate when a mare should be bred. Failure to return to estrus 2 to 3 weeks after breeding may suggest that the mare is pregnant. Pregnancy can be confirmed by several methods. Ultrasonography of the uterus (through the rectum) allows the earliest detection. Examination by rectal palpation (feeling a bulge in the uterus) can detect pregnancy from as early as day 28 in some mares. Hormonal tests are most accurate after about day 60 of pregnancy.

Health Programs During Pregnancy

Proper health care of pregnant mares is important to help ensure delivery of a healthy foal. Consult your veterinarian to make sure that your horse's vaccination and deworming programs are up to date.

Parasite Control

Most horse dewormers are safe for use throughout pregnancy, but your veterinarian's recommendations should be followed. In general, mares should not be given antiworming medications during the first 2 months of pregnancy, or during the last few weeks before foaling. Otherwise, mares should be dewormed every 6 to 8 weeks. It is recommended that the specific medication used be switched periodically to prevent development of resistance in the parasites. Mares can also be dewormed 1 or 2 days after foaling to reduce the number of small strongyle worms passed to the foal. (For additional information, *see* page 631.) Foals should be dewormed at 6 to 8 weeks of age on the same day as the mare and again at weaning.

Vaccinations

Immunizations should follow an annual schedule based on local health problems. Vaccination against rhinopneumonitis should be given at 3, 5, 7, and 9 months of pregnancy. Vaccinations that require annual boosters should be given 30 days before the estimated foaling date of the mare (*see* TABLE 5). This will allow the mare to produce protective antibodies that are passed to the foal in the colostrum. (For a more detailed discussion of VACCINATIONS, *see* page 561.)

Foaling

General preparations for managing delivery and caring for the newborn foal are described below (*see also* page 565).

Preparation

The mare should be taken to a foaling location 3 to 4 weeks before the expected foaling date so she can produce antibodies to any disease-causing organisms present in that environment. These antibodies will be passed to the foal via the colostrum (the first milk produced by the mare after foaling).

Foaling box stalls should be large (at least 12 by 16 feet [4 by 5 meters]). The foaling area should have good ventilation and be well bedded with clean, dry straw. The walls should be solidly constructed and free of sharp edges. Observation of the mare should be possible without disturbance.

Although certain signs occur before delivery, they do not allow any accurate prediction of the time delivery will occur. The mammary glands (udder) start develop-

Table 5. Sample Vaccination Schedule for Broodmares

Vaccine	Timing
Equine rhinopneumonitis	3, 5, 7, and 9 months of pregnancy and after foaling
Tetanus	4 to 6 weeks before foaling
Equine influenza	4 to 6 weeks before foaling; every 2 to 3 months during pregnancy for mares exposed to new horses
Eastern and Western equine encephalomyelitis	Usually given to mares in late spring or early summer before the onset of insect season; depends on location; if foaling late in the season, should be given again 4 to 6 weeks before foaling
Rabies	4 to 6 weeks before foaling; annual if rabies occurs regularly in the region
Botulism	Initially 3 injections at 1-month intervals, then annual booster 4 to 6 weeks before foaling
Equine viral arteritis	Viral titer should be checked before vaccination; pregnant mares should not be vaccinated; mares should be vaccinated before breeding to a positive stallion that is shedding the virus; mares must be isolated from other horses for 3 weeks after vaccination; positive titers may cause problems if the mare is to be shipped internationally; stallions should also be vaccinated 3 months before breeding
Strangles	Not routinely given; used only if warranted for a specific mare and situation; occasionally causes problems with abscesses and sore muscles; questionable effectiveness
West Nile virus	Initially 2 injections at a 3- to 6-week interval, then annual booster 4 to 6 weeks before foaling

ing 2 to 4 weeks before foaling and distend with colostrum in most mares 1 to 3 days before delivery. Colostrum drips from the teats and dries to form a waxy material at each teat opening. This "waxing" develops in almost all mares 6 to 48 hours before foaling, but in some cases it occurs much earlier or not at all.

Stages of Delivery

It is critical to understand the normal progression of events during delivery of a foal. This allows you to know if something is going wrong and whether intervention is needed. Delivery is divided into 3 stages.

Stage I is characterized by signs of abdominal pain and restlessness due to contractions of the uterus. Patches of sweat usually appear on the neck and flank and behind the elbows a few hours before foaling. The uterine contractions increase in frequency and intensity, causing the fetus to move into the pelvic canal. This causes the cervix to open. The fetus changes from a pelvis-up to a pelvis-down position prior to delivery. Mares may roll during this stage, which is thought to assist with the rotation of the fetus. Increasing pressure in the uterus causes the fetal membranes to bulge out of the opening cervix. Rupture of the fetal membranes and release of the fetal fluids (sometimes referred to as "water breaking") marks the end of the first stage of delivery.

Stage II starts when the fetal membranes rupture and ends when the foal is delivered. An uncomplicated labor usually takes 10 to 30 minutes. The pressure of the fetus on the cervix stimulates abdominal contractions in the mare. The fetal membrane that normally appears between the lips of the vulva is a white, fluid-filled structure. The straining efforts of the mare consist of 3 or 4 strong contractions, followed by a short period of rest. The mare usually lies on her side with her legs extended during labor. The foal is normally delivered head-first, with

the head, neck, and forelegs extended. One front hoof usually precedes the other, allowing the elbows and shoulders to pass through the pelvic canal more easily. The foal is usually born with the umbilical cord intact. The white amnion is usually intact, but is easily torn open by the movements of the mare or foal. If the membranes remain covering the nose, they should be removed by an attendant to prevent suffocation. If left undisturbed, the mare may lie for a few minutes with the foal's hindlegs in her vagina. If the foal has not been delivered within 30 minutes of the rupture of the fetal membranes and release of the tea-colored amniotic fluid, veterinary assistance is warranted.

Stage III involves the expulsion of the afterbirth (fetal membranes). Normally, the afterbirth is passed within 3 hours of birth of the foal. The weight of the membranes helps them separate from the inner surface of the uterus. Powerful contractions of the uterus complete the separation of the membranes from the uterus. The mare will stand with the fetal membranes hanging from the vulva. The membranes may extend past the level of the hock. If the mare kicks, which can endanger the foal, the membranes should be tied above the hocks. You should never manually pull on the membranes, as this can tear the membranes or cause damage to the uterus. If the fetal membranes have not been passed by 3 hours after delivery of the foal, your veterinarian may decide to give injections of the hormone oxytocin at 15- to 30-minute intervals until they have been completely expelled. (For a more detailed discussion of RETAINED PLACENTA, see page 735.)

If the fetal membranes separate from the uterus too early, then the fetal membranes that are first seen at the vulva in Stage II of labor will appear bright red and velvety instead of pale and white. This means the separation has occurred before the foal is able to breathe air on its own. The fetal membranes must immediately be ruptured and the foal delivered manu-

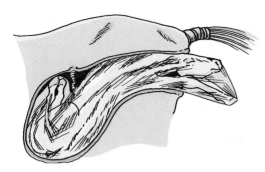

Foals are normally delivered head-first, with the head, neck, and forelegs extended.

ally, or it will not receive enough oxygen. Depending on the degree of oxygen deprivation, the foal may not survive or may have permanent brain damage.

The Early Postdelivery Period

The uterus contracts and returns to its nonpregnant size soon after delivery of the foal and fetal membranes. Horses have an average pregnancy length of about 340 days (about 11 months). It is possible to breed a mare during the "foal heat" that occurs 5 to 11 days after delivery. However, mares that have had a difficult birth, retained fetal membranes, or metritis should not be bred on the foal heat. Foal heat pregnancy rates are higher for mares bred at least 10 days after delivery.

▓ INFERTILITY

Proper ovulation in females and ejaculation of fertile and normal sperm by males are regulated through a sequence of events in the brain, nervous system, and sexual organs. For optimal results, ovulation and deposition of semen into the female genital tract must be closely synchronized. Failure of any single functional event in either sex leads to infertility or sterility. The ultimate result of infertility is the failure to produce offspring. In females, infertility may be due to the absence of the estrous cycle, abnormal ovulation, failure to conceive, failure of normal fetal development, or prenatal death. Major infertility problems in males are caused by disturbances

in the production, transport, or storage of sperm; loss of libido; and partial or complete inability to mate. Most major infertility problems are complex; several factors, singly or in combination, can cause failure to produce offspring.

Your veterinarian will first attempt to determine whether it is the mare or the stallion that is infertile. Infertility can be diagnosed through laboratory tests, semen evaluation, and ultrasonography. Infertility is seldom accompanied by obvious signs of illness or infection. Often, infertility is caused by the mare not being bred with sufficient amounts of good quality semen at the correct time during her estrous cycle.

Infertility may be helped by the administration of hormones that act directly on the ovaries or regulate their functions, or act to help maintain pregnancy. Antibiotics are used for treatment of infection of the reproductive tract. The selection of the antibiotic is based on tests that determine the nature of the bacteria or infectious agent. Unfortunately, there are few medications that can cause a stallion to make better quality semen. However, good intensive management of both the stallion and the mare can help in producing offspring.

▓ CONGENITAL AND INHERITED DISORDERS OF THE REPRODUCTIVE SYSTEM

Cryptorchidism is a failure of one or both testicles to descend into the scrotum and is seen in all domestic animals. It is the most common disorder of sexual development in horses. It is thought to be a genetic disorder inherited from either parent. If both testicles are retained in the abdomen, the horse will be sterile. Because a retained testicle still produces male hormones, cryptorchid animals have normal mating behavior. If only 1 testicle is retained (unilateral cryptorchidism), the horse may still be fertile because the normal testicle produces normal sperm. However, it is highly recommended that you not breed a cryptorchid horse because the condition is hereditary and will likely be passed on to any offspring.

Mares that are missing one of the sex chromosomes (designated as XO) have hereditary **underdevelopment of the ovaries** and are sterile. Affected mares may be smaller than average and may not have an estrous cycle because the ovaries do not have any eggs. The ovaries are smooth and firm and have no follicles. There is no treatment for this condition.

■ ABORTION

Abortion is the premature termination of pregnancy. There can be many causes of abortion, from infection to noninfectious causes such as exposure to toxins in the environment or genetics. It may be difficult to pinpoint the cause, as the abortion often occurs weeks or months after an infection or exposure to toxin, so the cause is no longer apparent. In order to diagnose the cause of an abortion, it may be necessary for your veterinarian to collect samples from the placenta or fetus for testing in a diagnostic laboratory.

Noninfectious Causes

The most common noninfectious cause of abortion in horses is a twin pregnancy. Most abortions related to twinning occur at 8 to 9 months of pregnancy (normal pregnancy length is about 11 months in horses) and may be preceded by premature lactation. Abnormalities of the umbilical cord, which connects the developing fetus to the placenta, (such as twisting) are another cause of abortion in horses.

Mare reproductive loss syndrome was first identified in 2001. There was a large increase in abortions affecting all breeds of horses in central Kentucky. Foals aborted in late gestation were dead or, if alive, were weak and dehydrated. Foals in the first trimester of gestation usually died in the uterus before being aborted. An infectious cause (such as a bacteria or virus) is not thought to be responsible. The outbreak occurred after a colder than normal March, followed by above-normal temperatures in

April. During the third week of April, there was a frost followed by warm weather. Abortions increased after a similar weather pattern in 1980 and 1981, but not to the extent seen in 2001. The warm weather in early April resulted in rapid plant growth and unusually high numbers of eastern tent caterpillars. An absence of eastern tent caterpillars and feeding hay to the mares when they were on the pasture were associated with few or no abortions. In experiments to test whether the caterpillars were the cause, pregnant mares fed crushed caterpillars mixed in water aborted. Current recommendations for control of mare reproductive loss syndrome consist of controlling tent caterpillars, removing wild cherry trees (the principle food source for the caterpillars), frequently mowing pastures used by pregnant mares, and feeding hay to the mares when on pasture. Secondary measures include increasing the ratio of grass to clover in pastures and reducing the time mares spend on pasture when a hard freeze following a warm spell is expected.

Fescue grass poisoning occurs when horses graze on fescue grass that is infected with a fungus called *Acremonium*. The fungus lives in plant cells and produces a toxic chemical that causes prolonged pregnancy in mares and stillborn or weak foals. The placenta is thickened and does not separate normally during birth. The foal becomes trapped in fetal membranes during birth and dies because it cannot breathe. The source of infected fescue can be pasture, hay, or bedding. The best practice to prevent abortion of this type is the removal of mares from the fescue pasture or removal of infected fescue and replanting another grass.

Infectious Causes

Infectious causes of abortion include viral, bacterial, and fungal infections.

Equine rhinopneumonitis is caused by equine herpesvirus 1 and is the most important viral cause of abortion in horses. Abortion usually occurs after 7 months of pregnancy and there is no corresponding maternal illness. The disease is diagnosed by a blood test or isolation of the virus from fetal tissues. Prevention is based on vaccinating at 5, 7, and 9 months of pregnancy as well as preventing exposure of pregnant mares to horses that attend shows or other equine events where they may have been exposed to the disease.

Equine viral arteritis (*see* page 800) may also cause abortion in horses 6 to 29 days after signs of infection appear. Signs of the disease include fever, swelling of the limbs, poor appetite, nasal discharge, and swelling of mammary glands. Stallions can be infected with the virus and carry the disease. Equine viral arteritis can be spread sexually or through the air. Infected horses usually recover without treatment. Prevention is based on vaccinating both the mare and the stallion.

Potomac horse fever, caused by *Ehrlichia risticii* bacteria, can be followed by abortion in mid to late pregnancy. Inflammation of the placenta and retained placentas can occur. Aborted fetuses have been found to have the bacteria in them. It is not known how effective the vaccine for Potomac horse fever is in preventing abortions. (For a more detailed discussion of POTOMAC HORSE FEVER, *see* page 623.)

Leptospirosis has recently been identified as an occasional cause of abortion in horses in Kentucky, England, and Northern Ireland. Most fetuses were aborted at 6 months of pregnancy. The mares were otherwise healthy. Usually only a single horse on a farm will abort in this manner—it does not seem to spread from horse to horse.

Abortion can also be caused by other bacteria, such as *Streptococcus zooepidemicus*, other *Streptococcus* species, *Salmonella*, *Escherichia coli*, *Pseudomonas*, and *Klebsiella*. These abortions are usually caused by the bacteria entering through the cervix and causing inflammation of the placenta (placentitis).

Infection by several types of fungi can also lead to abortion in horses. These include *Aspergillus*, *Mucor*, and *Candida* species. Fetuses aborted late in pregnancy may show signs of delayed growth. Fungi

may be found in the placenta, or the lungs, liver, or stomach of the fetus.

▓ BRUCELLOSIS

Brucellosis in horses is caused by *Brucella abortus* or *Brucella suis* bacteria. The infection is rare, especially in countries that have control programs for the infection in food animals. It can cause abortion, infection of the sexual organs in stallions, and infertility. The disease is present in most countries of the world. The most common abnormality associated with brucellosis in horses is suppurative bursitis, a pus-filled inflammation of connective tissue over the shoulders or poll. It is commonly called fistulous withers or poll evil (*see* page 677). Infection is diagnosed through laboratory tests that isolate the bacteria in the blood, semen, or milk of the infected horse or blood tests that detect antibodies to the bacteria. Antibiotics are the usual treatment, although elimination of the infection is difficult to accomplish. It is unlikely that infected horses are a source of the disease for other horses, other animals, or people.

▓ CONTAGIOUS EQUINE METRITIS

Contagious equine metritis is a highly contagious, but uncommon, sexually transmitted disease of horses. The disease occurs primarily in Europe and is uncommon in the United States. The disease is caused by infection with *Taylorella equigenitalis* bacteria, also known as the contagious equine metritis organism. It is primarily transmitted at mating, but contaminated instruments and equipment also play a role. Stallions show no signs of infection and carry the bacteria in the prepuce and on the surface of the penis, especially in the opening of the urethra. The transmission rate is very high; virtually every mare mated by an infected stallion becomes infected.

The signs of infection include a large volume of vaginal discharge seen 10 to 14 days after mating. Mares may return to estrus after a shortened estrous cycle. Although the discharge subsides after a few days, mares may remain infected for several months. Chronically infected mares show no signs of the disease. Most mares do not become pregnant after an infected mating. If they do, they may infect the foal at or shortly after birth. Infected foals can become carriers of the disease when they reach sexual maturity. Diagnosis is based on identification of the causative bacteria. Although other bacteria may infect the mare's genital tract, most do not produce the same large volume of vaginal discharge seen with contagious equine metritis, and no other sexually transmitted disease of horses is as contagious.

Stallions and mares can be treated by thoroughly cleaning the penis or vagina with antiseptics and applying antibiotic ointment. Strict import regulations are in place in many countries to prevent spread of the disease.

EQUINE COITAL EXANTHEMA (GENITAL HORSEPOX, EQUINE VENEREAL BALANITIS)

Equine coital exanthema is a benign (noncancerous) sexually transmitted disease of horses that probably occurs worldwide. It affects both sexes and is caused by equine herpesvirus type 3. Although the primary route of transmission is through sexual activity, outbreaks have been documented in which transmission occurred through contaminated supplies and instruments or by the use of a single glove for rectal examination of numerous mares. The infection is probably transmitted only in the early phase of the disease; after the sores have healed, horses do not appear to transmit the virus. Immunity against a second infection is very short, but there is little evidence of recurrence within a single breeding season.

Signs in mares develop 4 to 8 days after sexual contact or veterinary examination. Signs include the appearance of multiple, circular, red spots on the vulva and vagina. These may become infected by

bacteria and develop into abscesses. The abscesses eventually rupture, leaving shallow, painful sores. Occasionally these spots may be found on the teats, lips, and nasal tissue (mucosa). Unless another bacterial infection occurs, the skin heals within 3 weeks, but spots in the vagina heal more slowly. Affected areas in stallions are similar to those in mares and are found on both the penis and prepuce. As a result, the stallion may be reluctant to copulate. Diagnosis is based on physical examination and blood tests.

Sexual rest is essential to allow affected spots to heal and prevent the spread of the disease. The use of antibiotic ointments to prevent secondary bacterial infections is also recommended. Affected horses should be isolated until healed, and disposable equipment should be used for examinations. During the early phase of the disease, mares should be bred only by artificial insemination. No vaccine is available. All horses should be examined carefully before they are allowed to breed, keeping in mind that the signs of the infection may not appear for up to 10 days.

MASTITIS

Mastitis is inflammation of the mammary gland (breast) and is almost always due to a bacterial infection. It occurs occasionally in mares nursing foals, most commonly in the drying-off period (the end of milk production, when the glands are reducing and stopping the production of milk). Mastitis can occur in one or both breasts. Milk from inflamed mammary glands may appear normal or may be abnormal in color or consistency. In the early stage of mastitis, the affected glands are hot and painful. Other signs of illness such as fever and depression may occur. The mare may walk stiffly or stand with hindlegs apart due to the discomfort. The disease is diagnosed by physical examination and blood tests. Mastitis is treated by the administration of appropriate antibiotics.

■ METRITIS

Metritis is inflammation of the uterus that occurs just after giving birth. It results from the placenta being retained or severe contamination of the reproductive tract during delivery. Factors such as prolonged or complicated delivery and a retained fetus or placenta may cause metritis. The most common cause of metritis in mares is infection by *Streptococcus zooepidemicus* bacteria. Other bacteria, such as *Escherichia coli*, *Pseudomonas aeruginosa*, and *Klebsiella pneumoniae* can also cause metritis. The infection is diagnosed through physical examination, monitoring body temperature, ultrasonography, and laboratory tests. The primary treatment includes the use of anti-inflammatory drugs and antibiotics, as well as management of the retained placenta (*see* below).

■ PYOMETRA

Pyometra is an infection of the uterus characterized by the accumulation of large amounts of pus. This condition is often caused by an abnormal cervix or poor uterine clearance mechanisms. Infected mares may continue to cycle normally, or the cycle may be interrupted. Discharge from the genital tract (vagina) may be absent or intermittent and correspond to the periods of estrus.

Although pyometra causes the mare to be infertile, it rarely affects the general health and well-being of the mare. Your veterinarian will perform tests to distinguish between pregnancy and pyometra before prescribing any treatment. The condition may be managed by uterine lavage and the administration of drugs that will cause the uterus to contract and empty. However, in severe cases, treatment may require surgical removal of the uterus.

■ RETAINED PLACENTA

In mares, the fetal portion of the placenta, or fetal membranes, are normally expelled within 3 hours after birth. Although some mares may retain the fetal membranes longer without suffering ill effects, many mares with retained membranes become toxic and may even die. The cause of placental retention is not known. If none of the fetal membranes have been expelled, the condition will be obvious by the membranes hanging from the mare's vulva. However, retention of only a small portion of the placenta within the uterus may not be noticed and will result in serious complications.

Once passed, the fetal membranes should always be carefully examined to ensure that they have been completely expelled. The fetal membranes from the side (horn) of the uterus that contained the foal will be thicker, and the other, nonfetal side (horn) will be thin and puckered. It is important that both tips be present. The puckered tip, or nonfetal horn, is most commonly retained.

If the entire fetal membranes have not been passed by 3 hours after the foal is born, you should contact your veterinarian so that oxytocin can be administered. The oxytocin will cause uterine contraction and expulsion of the fetal membranes. If the membranes have still not passed by 8 hours after the foal's birth, your veterinarian will administer antibiotics and anti-inflammatory drugs. The placenta should never be manually pulled out, as this may cause parts of the placenta to be retained or cause damage to the lining of the uterus.

A retained placenta should always be treated promptly. Failure to treat this condition can lead to serious consequences for the mare, including endotoxemia, founder (laminitis), and death.

■ UTERINE PROLAPSE

Uterine prolapse is a disorder in which the uterus turns inside out and protrudes out of the vagina. It is rare in horses, but may occur immediately after or within a few hours of delivery of a foal. When it does occur, uterine prolapse is a serious problem that requires immediate veterinary attention because a major blood vessel can be damaged, causing the mare to bleed to death.

After careful cleansing and repair of any injuries to the uterus, your veterinarian will manually return the uterus to its normal position within the abdomen. Once the uterus is back in place, the hormone oxytocin is given to help contract the uterus and keep it in position. Complications, such as infection, bleeding, and shock, may occur if treatment is delayed. The outlook for recovery depends on the amount of contamination and injury of the uterus. The sooner treatment is given, the better the ouotlook. There is no tendency for the disorder to recur during subsequent deliveries.

▓ VULVITIS AND VAGINITIS

Vulvitis (inflammation of the vulva) and vaginitis (inflammation of the vagina) can develop due to difficult labor, chronic contamination of the reproductive tract due to poor conformation, sexually trans-

mitted diseases, or mating. Bruises and hematomas (a pool of blood under the surface of the skin) of the vagina may be found in mares following delivery of a foal. Severe inflammation of the vulva and vagina, including local tissue death, may also occur. The signs of severe inflammation can include an arched back, elevated tail, poor appetite, straining, swelling of the vulva, and a foul-smelling, watery discharge. Signs begin 1 to 4 days after birth and last for 2 to 4 weeks. In most cases, supportive care and treatment with antibiotics is sufficient.

Equine coital exanthema (page 734) is caused by a viral infection and may lead to vaginitis and vulvitis. The disease causes discomfort, but does not decrease fertility.

Dourine is a sexually transmitted disease of horses caused by the protozoan parasite, *Trypanosoma equiperdum*. Early signs of the disease include swelling of the vagina and vulva. Dourine occurs primarily in the Mediterranean coast of Africa, the Middle East, southern Africa, and South America (*see also* page 587).

CHAPTER **53**

Lung and Airway Disorders

▓ INTRODUCTION

The respiratory system consists of the large and small airways and the lungs. When a horse inhales, the air travels down the trachea, which divides into the tubes known as the right and left bronchi, then into the smaller airways called bronchioles in the lungs. The bronchioles end in the small sacs called alveoli, where the barrier between the air and the blood is a thin membrane.

The most important function of the respiratory system is to deliver oxygen into the blood, which distributes it throughout the body, and to remove carbon dioxide from the blood. The exchange of oxygen

and carbon dioxide occurs in the alveoli. When this exchange fails or becomes inefficient because of disease, the animal can become seriously ill. The respiratory system protects its own delicate airways by warming and humidifying inhaled air and by filtering out particles. Large airborne particles usually land on the mucous lining of the nasal passages, after which they are carried to the throat to be either swallowed or coughed up. Small particles and microorganisms are destroyed by the body's immune system.

Although the basic functions are the same, the anatomy of the respiratory tract varies among species. For example, the

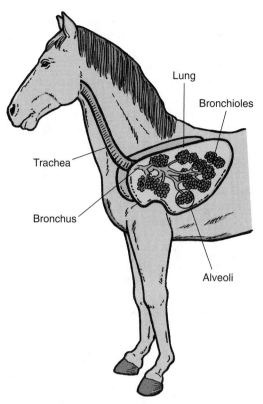

The lungs and airways in a horse

respiratory systems of dogs and cats are somewhat similar to each other, but differ from the respiratory systems of horses and humans. These differences explain in part why some diseases affect only certain species of animals. Horses are nasal breathers, and are not able to breathe through their mouths. Because of this, the horse's nasal passages are large and can expand somewhat during strenuous exercise in order to increase the intake of air.

When the level of oxygen in the blood is too low (called hypoxia or anoxia), the animal will show signs of respiratory distress. Low oxygen levels can be caused by reduced oxygen-carrying capacity of the red blood cells, insufficient movement of gases in and out of the lungs, or inability of tissues to use available oxygen (a condition caused by some poisons). The animal's body attempts to compensate for low oxygen in the blood by increasing the depth and rate of breathing, increasing contraction of the spleen (to force more red blood cells into circulation), and increasing blood flow and heart rate. If the brain suffers from lack of oxygen, respiratory function may be reduced even further due to depression of nervous system activity. In addition, heart, kidney, and liver functions may be reduced, as may the normal movement and secretions of the intestine. If the body is not able to compensate for the reduced oxygen level, a "vicious cycle" may begin in which all body tissues function less efficiently.

Causes of Lung and Airway Disorders

Lung and airway disorders are often caused by direct infection with viruses, bacteria, fungi, or parasites, as well as by immune-mediated reactions or inhalation of irritants or toxic substances. Trauma (such as crashing into a fence) may lead to the collapse of a lung or airway.

Viral respiratory infections are common in horses. Most bacterial respiratory infections (with the exception of strangles) occur after an attack of a viral disease. This is because viral respiratory infections impair and/or destroy respiratory defense mechanisms, making the horse more susceptible to additional infections.

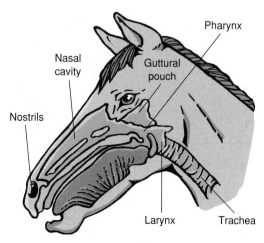

The upper portion of the horse's respiratory system

Signs of Respiratory Disorders

- Discharge from the nose (mucus, pus, or blood, depending on the cause)
- Coughing that may be dry or may include mucus or blood
- Rapid breathing (not always a sign of disease, such as in healthy animals after exercise; however, rapid breathing at rest is never normal)
- Labored or difficult breathing; shortness of breath
- Shallow breathing
- Signs of pain associated with breathing in or out
- Noise (such as grunting) associated with breathing
- Head shaking or abnormal carriage of head (low or extended)

The most common organisms associated with pneumonia in horses are bacteria normally present in the upper respiratory tract that take advantage of the horse's weakened state (called opportunistic bacteria). Secondary bacterial disease may result in bacterial infections of the mucous membranes (rhinitis and tracheitis), or may produce more serious invasive disease such as pneumonia and pleuropneumonia. *Streptococcus equi equi*, the organism that causes strangles, is a primary bacterial disease organism of the upper respiratory tract and is capable of causing infection without predisposing factors such as a previous viral disease. *Rhodococcus equi* is a disease organism of the lower respiratory tract of foals less than 5 months of age, which produces lung hardening and formation of abscesses.

Noninfectious respiratory disease (disease not caused by a bacterium or other microorganism) may occur in adult horses of various ages and can limit their performance. Inflammatory airway disease is characterized by excessive mucus in the airways and poor exercise performance in young horses. The cause is unclear, but viral respiratory infection, allergy, and environmental factors may play a role. Reactive airway disease (heaves) is triggered by exposure to organic dusts in older horses with a genetic susceptibility to allergic airway disease. The small airways in the

Table 6. Diagnosing Lung and Airway Disorders in Horses

Type of Test	How Used
Endoscopic examination	Allows the veterinarian to directly view the upper respiratory tract, guttural pouches, trachea, and upper airways of the lungs. Reasons for endoscopic examination include upper airway noise, difficulty inhaling, poor exercise performance, and 1- or 2-sided nasal discharge.
X-rays of the skull	Used to investigate facial deformity, abnormalities of the sinuses, guttural pouch, and tissues at the back of the mouth and throat.
X-rays of the neck	Used to investigate possible airway obstruction.
Transtracheal wash	Used to obtain secretions for bacterial and fungal culture.
Bronchoalveolar lavage	Used to obtain respiratory secretions for microscopic examination.
Nasal swab culture	Used to obtain samples for bacterial culture.
X-rays of the chest	Detects abnormalities of the lungs, heart, and diaphragm.
Chest ultrasonography	Used to identify the volume, location, and character of fluid or air within the chest cavity.
Pleurocentesis	Sampling of fluid from the chest cavity; guided by ultrasonography.
Lung biopsy and fine needle aspirate	Used to obtain tissue samples for final diagnosis of lung tumors, lung fibrosis, and other disease.

lungs are obstructed by constriction and excessive mucus production. The severity of signs ranges from exercise intolerance to labored breathing at rest.

Diagnosing Lung and Airway Disorders

Your horse's history and the veterinarian's physical examination will help to determine the possible cause and site of respiratory disease. Other techniques commonly used for diagnosis include x-rays of the chest or neck; the use of various types of endoscopes to view the nose, throat, and airways; and examination of the contents of the lung and airways, which can be obtained through aspiration or retrieval of fluid used to "bathe" the airways (*see* TABLE 6).

Control of Respiratory Conditions

Sudden dietary changes, weaning, cold, drafts, dampness, dust, poor ventilation, and the mixing of different age groups all play a role in respiratory disease in groups of animals. Stress and mixing of animals from several sources should be avoided or minimized if possible. Immunization can help control respiratory infection; however, it is not a substitute for proper environmental conditions and animal care.

Immunization does not always prevent respiratory infections in horses, but the duration and severity of illness is usually lessened in horses with regular vaccination depending on factors such as the disease and specific vaccine. The veterinarian will help weigh the cost and hazards of each vaccination against the probability of the horse's exposure and potential disease and the effectiveness of the vaccines. Vaccination recommendations and schedules will vary according to the use of the horse and its potential for exposure to contagious animals.

General Treatment of Lung and Airway Disorders

Respiratory disorders often involve the production of excess secretions in the respiratory system (for example, in the nose and lungs) that the affected animal may not be able to remove without assistance. One goal of veterinary treatment is to reduce the volume and thickness of the secretions and to make their removal easier. This can be accomplished by controlling infection, thinning the secretions, and when possible, improving drainage and mechanically removing the material.

Therapies can include altering the inhaled air as well as the use of expectorants (which help an animal to cough up the secretions), cough suppressants, bronchodilators (to help open airways), antibiotics, diuretics (to reduce fluid buildup), and other drugs.

Regardless of the type of respiratory disease, environmental factors and supportive care are important to aid recovery. A dust- and ammonia-free stable environment prevents further damage to the respiratory system. Highly palatable feeds help to prevent weight loss and weakness during the treatment and recovery period. Adequate water intake will decrease the thickness of respiratory secretions, making their removal from the lower respiratory tract easier. A comfortable, dry, temperature-appropriate environment will allow the horse to rest and will lessen the need for the respiratory tract to work at regulating the horse's body temperature.

ACCUMULATION OF FLUID OR AIR IN THE CHEST CAVITY

Hemothorax, the accumulation of blood in the pleural (chest) cavity, is usually caused by trauma to the chest, blood clotting disorders, or tumors in the chest. **Hydrothorax,** the accumulation of clear fluid in the pleural cavity, is usually due to interference with blood flow or lymph drainage. **Chylothorax,** the accumulation of a high-triglyceride lymphatic fluid in the pleural cavity, is relatively rare. It may be caused by rupture of the chest duct but often the cause is unknown. The signs of all 3 conditions include respiratory difficulty, such as rapid shallow breathing with labored inhalation, and weakness. Drainage of the fluid may be necessary to relieve these signs and can be helpful in diagnosing the underlying problem. However, the outlook for many disorders that cause accumulation of fluid in the chest is guarded to poor.

Air in the pleural cavity, called **pneumothorax**, may be caused by trauma or occur spontaneously. The lung collapses if a large volume of air enters the pleural cavity, causing difficulty inhaling or rapid, shallow breathing. This condition should be considered an emergency that requires immediate veterinary attention.

■ ASPIRATION PNEUMONIA

Aspiration pneumonia is a lung infection caused by inhalation of foreign material. The severity of the inflammation depends on the material inhaled, the type of bacteria inhaled, and the distribution of foreign material in the lungs. A common cause of aspiration pneumonia is the improper administration of liquid medicines. If an animal needs to be given liquids through a drench or dose syringe, they should not be administered any faster than the animal can swallow. Animals that attempt to eat or drink while partially choked are at risk for aspiration pneumonia as well. Disturbances in the normal swallowing mechanism, such as in anesthetized or comatose animals, or in animals with deformities such as cleft palate, are frequent causes.

A history suggesting that a foreign substance might have been inhaled is the most important clue to diagnosing this disease. Signs include labored or rapid breathing, rapid heart rate, and fever. Other signs include bluish mucous membranes and airway spasms. A sweetish, off-smelling breath may be detected, which becomes more intense as the disease progresses. This is often associated with a nasal discharge that sometimes is tinged reddish brown or green. Occasionally, evidence of the breathed-in material can be seen in the nasal discharge or coughed-up material.

As with nearly all disease conditions, prevention is better than treatment. This is especially the case for aspiration pneumonia, since the outlook is poor even with treatment. The rate of death is high, and recovered animals often develop lung abscesses. If an animal is known to have inhaled a foreign substance, broad-spectrum antibiotics are usually prescribed without waiting for signs of pneumonia to appear.

■ CHOANAL ATRESIA

Choanal atresia is caused by the bucconasal membrane, a membrane that separates portions of the mouth and nose during fetal development but is normally gone by birth. In choanal atresia, the membrane is still present at birth and one or both nostrils are partially or completely shut off from the rest of the respiratory system. Clinical signs are evident immediately after birth in foals in which both nostrils are affected, because labored breathing is severe and air cannot be detected passing through the nostrils. This is a life-threatening condition. Immediately after birth, a tube must be inserted through the neck into the trachea (tracheotomy) to allow the foal to breathe until the condition can be corrected. The situation is less severe if only one nostril is affected.

■ DIAPHRAGMATIC HERNIA

A diaphragmatic hernia is a condition in which a break in the diaphragm allows protrusion of abdominal organs into the chest. It may be caused by trauma, a difficult birth, or recent strenuous activity. The condition is not very common in horses.

The signs of hernia can vary, depending on the duration of the disease and the species affected. In horses, the most frequent sign is acute, severe colic caused by the displaced intestines; respiratory signs occur less frequently.

Careful physical examination by the veterinarian, including listening to and tapping the chest and abdomen, usually suggests the presence of the hernia. The definitive diagnosis is most frequently made from x-rays, which can reveal changes in the shape of the diaphragm and the displacement of abdominal organs. Ultrasonography can be useful in cases where obtaining an x-ray is difficult. Surgical repair of the hernia is the only treatment.

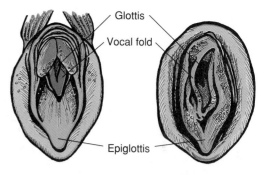

Normal larynx   Laryngeal hemiplegia

Laryngeal hemiplegia is a condition in which paralysis of the larynx occurs.

■ DISORDERS OF THE LARYNX

The larynx is the part of the throat often called the "voice box" in humans. It is located near the top of the trachea. The larynx is composed of muscles and cartilage, and it includes the vocal cords. Several disorders of the larynx are seen in horses.

Arytenoid Chondritis (Laryngeal Chondropathy)

In horses, fluid buildup and swelling of the larynx can lead to arytenoid chondritis, a condition that causes swelling in the cartilage in the larynx. It is believed to result from microbial infection, often following the inhalation of irritants. Initially, there is often severe inflammation. Later, there is progressive enlargement of the cartilages that results in a fixed upper airway obstruction; this causes high-pitched breathing sounds and reduced exercise tolerance. Arytenoid chondritis occurs most often in young male horses. Thoroughbred horses in race training are more likely than other breeds to develop this condition. Removal of some of the cartilage is an effective remedy, although a competitive horse may not be able to return to full athletic capacity.

Laryngeal Hemiplegia (Roaring)

Laryngeal hemiplegia is a condition in which paralysis of the larynx occurs. For reasons that are not completely understood, this occurs more commonly on the left side than on the right side or on both sides. The nerve that controls the left side of the larynx is the longest nerve in the body. Paralysis is caused by a gradual deteriora-

tion of nerve fibers in the larynx, leading to deterioration of the associated muscles. Because muscle control is lost, the cartilage in the larynx can collapse, reducing the size of the "tube" through which the horse breathes. The resistance to airflow makes breathing more difficult. When the horse inhales during strenuous exercise, the airway can be essentially blocked.

The condition develops in young horses and is familial in most cases. Less common causes include injury to the nerve, accidental injection of irritating substances, and plant (for example, *Cicer arietinum* [chick peas] and *Lathyrus* subspecies) or chemical poisoning. If a horse has laryngeal paralysis on both sides, lead poisoning may be the cause. Although all breeds are affected, there is a higher prevalence in males and long-necked and larger breeds.

The most common signs of laryngeal hemiplegia are noise when inhaling during exercise and intolerance to exercise. Affected horses show no signs when at rest except for an unusual whinny in many cases. Using an endoscope, the veterinarian can observe reduced movement (or no movement) of specific tissues in the larynx.

Surgery can be done to reconstruct the larynx, which will stabilize the affected side during inhalation and prevent collapse of the airway during exercise. This is commonly done in racing horses and is the only technique that reduces the blockage of inhalation. Potential complications after surgery include chronic cough, chronic inhalation of feed, implant failure, and implant infection. Athletic performance will improve after surgery; however, horses may not reach (or return to) their full performance potential.

Fourth Branchial Arch Defect

Fourth branchial arch defect is a condition in which one or more structures of the larynx have not fully developed. Incomplete development may occur on one or both sides. Right-sided defects are more common than left-sided defects or defects of both sides. The severity of clinical signs is based on the extent of the defect. The most common sign is respiratory noise, although coughing and mild difficulty swallowing have been reported. Your veterinarian may be able to feel the defect when examining your horse's neck, or detect it using radiography or endoscopic examination. Affected horses are unlikely to become effective athletes.

■ DISORDERS OF THE NASAL SEPTUM

Diseases of the nasal septum (the "wall" between the nostrils) are uncommon. A traumatic injury to the bridge of the nose of a young horse can produce nasal septal deviation and thickening. Other less common diseases of the nasal septum include fungal infection and squamous cell carcinoma (a type of cancer). Thickening or deviation of the nasal septum causes low-pitched noisy breathing during exercise. Facial deformity may be observed. Your veterinarian may be able to detect septal abnormalities by physical examination or endoscopic examination. X-rays of the skull can provide evidence of septal deformity, deviation, and thickening. Microscopic examination of any nodules or lesions on the septum will identify tumors, amyloidosis, or fungal infections.

Surgical repair of the nasal septum is the only treatment option in most cases. The incisions heal in a few weeks, but horses should be rested for about 2 months before returning to normal activity. After surgery, most horses make breathing noise during work, although less than before surgery, and exercise tolerance is improved. Shortening of the upper jaw, poor alignment of the incisors, or nostril collapse can develop if the procedure is performed in immature horses, so the surgery should be delayed until the horse has reached maturity, if possible.

■ DISORDERS OF THE PARANASAL SINUSES

The paranasal sinuses are tissue-lined cavities in the skull, located behind the nose and eyes. They are divided into a number of different compartments that are interconnected to the nasal passages and to each other in various ways. Diseases that originate in one sinus cavity may extend to and involve others.

Most diseases of the paranasal sinuses cause pus-containing or bloody discharge from one nostril. Swelling on one side of

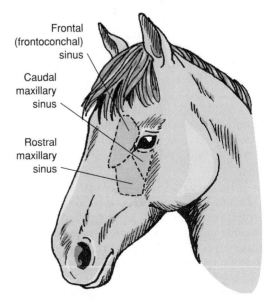

Frontal (frontoconchal) sinus

Caudal maxillary sinus

Rostral maxillary sinus

The paranasal sinuses in the horse

the face, excessive tears from one eye, and noise when the horse inhales are common signs of disorders of the sinuses.

Using an endoscope, the veterinarian can observe pus-containing material, a mass, or blood in the nasal passage originating from higher up in the head. X-rays of the skull and computed tomography (CT) can also be useful. With sedation and local anesthesia, the veterinarian can obtain a sample from the sinus of a standing horse. Fluid can be sampled from the maxillary or frontal sinuses for bacterial culture, drug sensitivity testing, and microscopic examination.

Sinusitis

Primary sinusitis, or inflammation of the sinuses, occurs after an upper respiratory tract infection that has involved the paranasal sinuses. It usually involves all sinus cavities but can be confined to just one. This cavity is difficult to detect on x-rays and is also difficult to access surgically. Secondary sinusitis can result from tooth root infection, fracture, or sinus cyst. The first molar, fourth premolar, and third premolar (from more to less likely) are the most likely to develop tooth root abscesses. Signs of secondary sinusitis closely resemble those of primary sinusitis, including 1-sided nasal discharge and facial deformity. Tooth root abscesses typically produce a foul-smelling nasal discharge. Treatment of primary sinusitis involves rinsing (lavage) of the sinus cavity and antibiotic therapy based the results of bacterial culture and drug sensitivity testing. Secondary sinusitis requires removal of affected cheek teeth or cysts.

Ethmoid Hematoma

Progressive ethmoid hematoma is a destructive mass in the nasal passages and sinuses. The cause is unknown. Masses originating in the sinus extend into the nasal passage. An expanding hematoma can cause damage to the surrounding bone but rarely causes facial distortion. It is primarily observed in horses older than 6 years. Periodic bleeding from one nostril is the most common sign. Horses with extensive masses may have reduced airflow through the affected nasal passage and bad breath. In longterm cases, the mass may protrude from the nostril. In most instances, the veterinarian can see the lesion extending into the nasal passages on endoscopic examination, and the extent of the mass can be determined with x-rays. Your veterinarian can shrink the mass by injecting it with a chemical. This works rapidly, but recurrence is common. Surgical removal can be performed if needed.

Sinus Cysts

Sinus cysts are fluid-filled cavities. They are typically found in horses less than 1 year old, but can also be seen in those greater than 9 years old. The primary signs are facial deformity, nasal discharge, and partial airway obstruction. X-rays are more likely to identify a sinus cyst than endoscopic examination. Treatment involves surgical removal of the cyst and associated lining of the sinus. The outlook for complete recovery is good, and the recurrence is low. Some horses may have a permanent, mild discharge of mucus after surgery.

■ DORSAL DISPLACEMENT OF THE SOFT PALATE

Dorsal displacement of the soft palate is a condition of the upper respiratory tract that can limit performance in horses. It is a relatively common cause of upper respiratory noise during maximal exercise. During dorsal displacement of the soft palate, the free edge of the soft palate moves from its normal position below the epiglottis and creates a functional obstruction within the airway. The cross-sectional area of the throat is reduced, and airflow resistance and turbulence are increased.

The condition may result from several disease mechanisms. Inflammation of the upper respiratory tract due to infection may cause dysfunction of the nerves that control the soft palate. Similarly, inflamed lymph nodes can cause compression and irritation of the nerves. Inborn defects in the epiglottis may also contribute to dorsal displacement of the soft palate, due to insufficient tissue to maintain the soft palate in its normal location.

Dorsal displacement of the soft palate creates a characteristic gurgling breathing noise, primarily during exhaling, due to vibration of the soft palate. Horses may make no noise at the onset of exercise but displace their palate during high-speed exercise, causing them to "choke down." Head position (flexed) may contribute to displacement.

The most effective treatment for dorsal displacement of the soft palate in young horses (2-year-olds) and horses with evidence of upper respiratory tract infection is rest and anti-inflammatory medication. Placing a tongue tie during exercise helps keep the palate in a better position and can improve signs. Various types of surgery can also be performed and a procedure called soft palate resection (staphylectomy) is frequently performed in horses with dorsal displacement of the soft palate. This procedure has a success rate of about 50%.

▓ EPIGLOTTIC ENTRAPMENT

Epiglottic entrapment is an uncommon cause of respiratory noise and exercise intolerance. The epiglottis is a flap of tissue that, in normal situations, functions something like a "trap door" to keep food from entering the trachea and airways while the animal is swallowing. In this disease, the epiglottis is partially trapped by other tissues and cannot move normally. Signs of epiglottic entrapment include respiratory noise during exercise and poor exercise performance. Less common signs include cough, nasal discharge, and headshaking. Diagnosis is determined by endoscopic examination. The condition can be corrected by surgery to free the epiglottis and allow it to move normally. This procedure generally cures the condition and has a relapse rate of only 5%.

▓ EQUINE HERPESVIRUS INFECTION (EQUINE VIRAL RHINOPNEUMONITIS)

Equine herpesvirus 1 (EHV-1) and equine herpesvirus-4 (EHV-4) make up 2 distinct groups of viruses. Both are widespread in horse populations worldwide and are a major cause of respiratory disease. Transmission occurs by direct or indirect contact with infectious nasal secretions, miscarried fetuses, placentas, or fluids from the placenta. A horse's susceptibility to infection depends on the strain of virus, the immune status of the animal, pregnancy status, and possibly age. The infection is mild or unseen in horses immunologically sensitized to the virus by a previous infection. Most horses carry the EHV-1 and EHV-4 viruses in an inactive state. The infection remains dormant for most of the horse's life, although stress or immune system problems may result in "reawakening" of disease and shedding of infectious virus.

Outbreaks of respiratory disease occur annually among foals in areas with concentrated horse populations. Most of these outbreaks are caused by strains of EHV-4. Infection of pregnant mares with EHV-1 may result in abortion 2 to 12 weeks after infection. Nervous system disease is another possible outcome of a specific strain of EHV-1 infection.

Signs of infection include fever, nasal discharge, depression, throat inflammation (pharyngitis), cough, poor appetite, and enlarged lymph nodes. Horses infected with EHV-1 strains often develop a fever that rises, falls, and then rises again. Infected horses may also develop bacterial infections that cause nasal discharge and lung disease. If nervous system disease develops, signs may vary from mild incoordination to paralysis of the hind end (forcing the horse to be unable to rise or stand), loss of bladder and tail function, and loss of sensation to the skin around the rectal, genital, and groin areas. In rare cases, the paralysis can progress to all 4 legs (quadriplegia) and death.

Equine herpesvirus infection cannot be differentiated from other causes of equine respiratory disease, such as equine influenza (*see* below), solely on the basis of signs. The definitive diagnosis is determined by identifying the virus in samples obtained from the nose and throat and from blood testing early in the course of the infection.

There is no specific treatment for this infection. Rest and good nursing care may minimize the chance of secondary bacterial infection. Fever-reducing medications may be recommended in some cases, such as for horses with a fever greater than 104°F (40°C). Antibiotic therapy is usually initiated when there is suspicion of secondary bacterial infection, such as pus-containing nasal discharge or lung disease. If horses with EHV-1-associated nervous system disease remain able to walk, or are down for only 2 to 3 days, the outlook is usually favorable. Intensive nursing care is necessary to avoid lung congestion, pneumonia, ruptured bladder, or intestinal problems. Recovery may be complete, but a small percentage of cases have nervous system damage.

For prevention and control of EHV-4- and EHV-1-related diseases, management practices that reduce viral spread are recommended. New horses (or those returning from other premises) should be isolated for 3 to 4 weeks before mixing with resident horses, especially pregnant mares. Pregnant mares should be maintained in a group away from the weanlings, yearlings, and horses out of training. In an outbreak of respiratory disease or miscarriage, affected horses should be isolated and appropriate measures taken for disinfection of contaminated premises.

Several types of vaccines have been developed but are not available in all countries. Your veterinarian can provide appropriate information about types of vaccines and the need for vaccination in your area. The immunity induced by vaccination against EHV-1 and EHV-4 generally lasts for only 2 to 4 months, and available vaccines do not cover all strains to which horses can be exposed. Vaccination usually begins when foals are 3 to 4 months old and, depending on the vaccine used, a second dose may be given 4 to 8 weeks later. Periodic booster vaccinations may be given until the horse reaches maturity. Vaccination programs against EHV-1 should include all horses on the premises.

▮ EQUINE INFLUENZA

Equine influenza is highly contagious and spreads rapidly among susceptible horses. Two distinct influenza viruses have been found in horse populations worldwide, although only one of these strains has been seen since 1980. Disease varies from a mild, undetected infection to severe disease in susceptible animals. Influenza is rarely fatal except in sick, weakened, or stressed horses. Transmission occurs by inhalation of respiratory secretions. Epidemics can arise when one or more infected horses are introduced into a susceptible group.

The incubation period of influenza is about 1 to 3 days after exposure to an infected horse. Signs develop rapidly and include a high fever (up to 106°F [41°C]), clear nasal discharge, swollen lymph nodes, and coughing that is dry, harsh, and nonproductive. Depression, loss of appetite, and weakness are frequently seen. These signs usually last less than 3 days in uncomplicated cases, although the cough can persist for several weeks. Nasal discharge may become filled with mucous and pus due to bacterial infection. Disease is rare in foals less than 9 months of age. Mildly affected horses recover in 2 to 3 weeks, but severely affected horses may take up to 6 months to fully recover. Complications are minimized by restricting exercise, controlling dust, providing superior ventilation, and practicing good stable hygiene.

The presence of a rapidly spreading respiratory infection with high fever, depression, and cough in a group of horses suggests the possibility of equine influenza. However, equine influenza cannot be differentiated from other causes of equine respiratory disease, such as equine herpesvirus infection (*see* page 744), solely on the basis of signs. A definite diagnosis can be made by identifying the virus in samples obtained from the nose and throat early in the course of the infection.

Horses that do not develop complications generally require no treatment aside from rest and supportive care. Horses should be rested 1 week for every day of fever with a minimum of 3 weeks rest, to allow healing of damaged respiratory tissues. Nonsteroidal anti-inflammatory drugs (NSAIDs) are usually given to horses with a fever higher than 104°F (40°C). Antibiotics may be prescribed when fever persists beyond 3 to 4 days or when pus-containing nasal discharge or pneumonia are present.

Prevention of influenza requires hygienic management practices and vaccination. Exposure can be reduced by isolation of newly introduced horses for 2 weeks. A number of vaccines are commercially available for the prevention of equine influenza; however booster vaccines are recommended every 6 months to maintain immunity. Vaccination should not begin in foals until 9 months of age. As is done with human influenza vaccines (flu shots), vaccine manufacturers monitor continuously to ensure that the content of the currently available vaccine reflects, as closely as possible, the strains of virus causing infection at that time.

EQUINE MORBILLIVIRUS PNEUMONIA (HENDRA VIRUS INFECTION)

Hendra virus is a newly identified virus seen so far only in Australia and Papua New Guinea. The viral agent is commonly found in specific species of fruit bats (also called flying foxes), and close contact among horses and these bats is suspected to have caused transfer of the virus to horses. The disease, called equine morbillivirus pneumonia, develops in horses that are infected by direct contact with the virus particles in urine, saliva, and respiratory secretions. Humans in very close contact with infected horses can become infected as well and develop flu-like symptoms.

Infected horses develop severe and often fatal respiratory disease, characterized by labored breathing and fluid and swelling in the lungs. Damage to the heart and blood vessels may occur. Depression, loss of appetite, fever, respiratory difficulty, poor coordination, increased heart rate, and frothy nasal discharge are other common signs. (For a more detailed discussion of EQUINE MORBILLIVIRUS PNEUMONIA [HENDRA VIRUS INFECTION], *see* page 799.)

EQUINE VIRAL ARTERITIS

Equine viral arteritis is another viral infection that causes significant respiratory disease and blood vessel inflammation. It is caused by the equine arteritis virus. The most important consequences of this virus are the carrier state in the stallion and abortion in the mare.

Infected horses show fever, loss of appetite, and depression. The signs of respiratory infection with the equine arteritis virus are clear nasal discharge, cough, eye reddening (conjunctivitis), tears, and swelling of the eyelids and tissue around the eyes. Signs of disease persist for 2 to 9 days. As with equine influenza and equine herpesvirus infection, a diagnosis is determined by identifying the virus in appropriate samples.

Treatment consists of supportive care and nonsteroidal anti-inflammatory drugs to reduce fever and inflammation. Antibiotics are usually unnecessary. A carrier state occurs in most stallions after natural infection and is primarily responsible for the persistence of the virus in the horse population. Semen from carrier stallions has a tremendous viral content that is unaffected by freezing or semen extenders. Stallions and mares can be protected from equine arteritis virus infection by vaccination prior to the breeding season. The carrier state does not affect semen quality. Persistently infected stallions can be used for breeding by using specific vaccination strategies for the mares.

▓ EXERCISE-INDUCED PULMONARY HEMORRHAGE ("BLEEDER")

Exercise-induced pulmonary (lung) bleeding occurs in the majority of racehorses and is observed in many other equine sports (such as polo, barrel racing, and 3-day events) that require strenuous exercise for short periods of time. Bleeding from the nose is actually observed in only about 5% of horses with exercised-induced lung hemorrhage; however, examination of racehorses has shown that bleeding in the airways is present in a majority of horses.

Possible causes include high lung blood pressures during intense exercise, new blood vessel formation caused by lung inflammation, and shear forces within the chest generated during exercise. Some research suggests that exercise-induced lung hemorrhage results from failure of the horse's lungs to accommodate the massive increase in heart output to meet the demands of high-intensity exercise.

Diagnosis of exercise-induced lung hemorrhage involves observation of blood in the airways 30 to 90 minutes after exercise. This can be detected using an endoscope. Other sources of bleeding in the upper airway must be exluded during the examination. Examination of fluid from the lungs is sometimes used if the horse cannot be examined after exercise.

The use of a specific diuretic drug, furosemide, can reduce the severity of exercise-induced lung hemorrhage by 70% and improve race performance, although it does not prevent bleeding entirely. Nasal dilator bands also appear to reduce bleeding by approximately 30%.

▓ FOAL PNEUMONIA

Pneumonia is an infection of the lungs and airways that causes disturbance in respiration and deficiency of oxygen in the blood. It is common in foals up to 6 months of age. The causes of foal pneumonia include viral infections (such as equine herpesvirus infection, discussed earlier in this chapter), bacterial infections (such as *Rhodococcus equi* infection), parasitic migration, and environmental stresses (such as weather fluctuations, dusty conditions, or overcrowding). Often, a combination of factors appears to be involved in the development of foal pneumonia. Some of the more significant types of foal pneumonia are discussed below.

Rhodococcus equi Pneumonia

Although it is not the most common cause of pneumonia, *Rhodococcus equi* is the most serious cause of pneumonia in foals 1 to 5 months old. It has significant economic consequences due to death, prolonged treatment, surveillance programs for early detection, and relatively expensive prevention strategies. This type of pneumonia is rare in horses older than 6 months of age.

Rhodococcus equi bacteria are widespread in soil and are likely present on all premises to some degree. However, the incidence of disease varies from farm to farm. High summer temperatures, sandy soil, and dusty conditions favor the multiplication and spread of the organism in the environment. Inhalation of dust particles containing disease-causing strains of the bacteria is the major route of lung infection. Manure from infected foals is a major source of bacteria contaminating the environment. Foals are exposed or infected during the first week of life.

Infection progresses slowly, and signs of disease are difficult to detect until lung lesions reach a critical mass. These lung lesions include pneumonia, abscesses in the lungs, and swelling of lymph nodes. When signs begin, most foals are lethargic, run a fever, and have rapid breathing. Cough is an occasional sign, while pus-containing nasal discharge is less common. The veterinarian can hear crackles and wheezes in the chest.

In addition to lung abscesses, intestinal and abdominal abscesses may occur in *Rhodococcus equi* infection. Foals with abdominal involvement often show fever, depression, loss of appetite, weight loss, colic, and diarrhea. The outlook for foals with the abdominal form of *R. equi* is less favorable than for those with the lung form. The bone is another, less common site of infection. If the vertebrae are affected, vertebral fracture and spinal cord compression can result. Other sites of abscesses such as the liver and kidneys have been reported.

Routine blood testing reveals abnormalities consistent with infection and inflammation. Particular lesions seen on chest x-rays can suggest the presence of *R. equi*; however, identification of the bacteria in fluid from the airways is needed for a definitive diagnosis.

Treatment and Prevention

For treatment, a combination of antibiotics is more effective in fighting the infection than any antibiotic given alone. The use of combination antibiotic therapy has greatly improved the survival of foals. The length of antibiotic therapy typically ranges from 4 to 9 weeks. Supportive therapy includes a clean, comfortable environment and highly palatable, dust-free feeds. Your veterinarian may use intravenous fluid therapy and saline mist (nebulization) to help your horse cough up lung secretions. Nonsteroidal anti-inflammatory drugs (NSAIDs) may be prescribed when fever is present. Treatment with oxygen is necessary in foals with severe respiratory difficulty.

Prompt veterinary attention and appropriate treatment is critical. The survival rate of foals with *R. equi* pneumonia is approximately 70 to 90% with appropriate

therapy. Without therapy (or with inappropriate therapy), the death rate is about 80%.

To help prevent *R. equi* pneumonia on farms where the disease is present, foals should be maintained in well-ventilated, dust-free areas, avoiding dirt paddocks and overcrowding. Commercially available plasma with antibodies against *R. equi* should be administered to foals on the first day of life on at-risk premises. Foals with pneumonia should be isolated and their manure composted. Herd surveillance programs (including periodic physical examinations and blood testing) can be put in place for early detection of sick foals on farms where the disease is present.

Acute Bronchointerstitial Pneumonia in Foals

Acute bronchointerstitial pneumonia is a sporadic, rapidly developing disease of foals characterized by severe respiratory distress and high mortality. This sporadic disease has been reported in North America, Australia, and parts of Europe. The cause is not clear. It is likely that a number of different factors can start a chain of events resulting in severe lung damage and acute respiratory distress. Warm weather (temperatures higher than 85°F [29°C]) is a common factor. Many foals have a history of receiving antibiotics (particularly erythromycin) at the time signs developed. No virus is consistently isolated, and no bacterial agent has been consistently identified in infected foals.

The age of affected foals ranges from 1 week to 8 months. Acute bronchointerstitial pneumonia has a sudden onset and is accompanied by high fever. The disease progresses rapidly and may result in sudden death from respiratory failure. Foals are unable or reluctant to move and usually have bluish mucous membranes from lack of oxygen. Severe respiratory distress is the most striking clinical sign. Veterinary evaluation of foals with respiratory distress typically includes arterial blood gas, blood tests, chest x-rays, and culture of samples for identification of bacteria or viruses. The arterial blood gas findings measure the severity of respiratory impairment and are used to monitor the foal's response to therapy.

Because the cause of bronchointerstitial pneumonia is unknown, treatment is directed toward relieving the signs. Treatment includes anti-inflammatory drugs to control fever and inflammation, antibiotics, drugs to dilate constricted airways, supplemental oxygen, and supportive care. Anti-inflammatory therapy with corticosteroids appears to improve survival. When directed by your veterinarian, measures such as an alcohol bath, an air-conditioned stall, and/or a fan are used in conjunction with nonsteroidal anti-inflammatory drugs to help control fever. Additional supportive therapy includes provision of a clean, comfortable environment, highly palatable, dust-free feeds, and medications to prevent ulcer.

Although the death rate is high, affected foals that receive aggressive medical care have a reasonably favorable outlook for survival (70%). However, some foals will have longterm lung damage that may affect performance.

■ GUTTURAL POUCH EMPYEMA

The guttural pouch is a structure that is only found in equine species. It is an outpouching of the Eustachian tube, the tube that connects the ears to the nose and mouth and helps to regulate air pressure. Guttural pouch empyema is a condition in which pus- and bacteria-containing secretions accumulate in the guttural pouch.

The condition usually develops after a bacterial infection of the upper respiratory tract. Signs include intermittent nasal discharge that contains pus, painful swelling, and in severe cases, stiff head carriage and noisy breathing. Fever, depression, and loss of appetite may or may not be seen. A diagnosis can often be made after endoscopic examination of the guttural pouch. Guttural pouch empyema should be considered a *Streptococcus equi equi* infec-

tion until proven otherwise, and isolation or quarantine procedures should be instituted in affected horses until the bacterial culture results are obtained.

Antibiotic therapy alone will not resolve the infection; the guttural pouch must be rinsed out by lavage. Guttural pouch empyema may compress the throat and produce upper airway obstruction. If this occurs, a tube through the trachea (tracheotomy) may be necessary to provide a temporary alternative airway. If guttural pouch empyema is not treated, the material in the pouch continues to provide a source of bacteria for infection.

■ GUTTURAL POUCH MYCOSIS

Guttural pouch mycosis is a fungal infection of the guttural pouch, an outpouching of the Eustachian tube that connects the ears to the nose and mouth and helps to regulate air pressure. *Aspergillus* species of fungus are common causes of these infections, although other species are sometimes identified. The infection is usually seen in mature horses that are stabled. Guttural pouch mycosis causes damage to the cranial nerves and to the arteries found in the lining of the guttural pouch.

The most common sign of infection is bleeding from the nose due to arterial damage. The bleeding occurs without any obvious cause and is often severe. Difficulty swallowing is another common sign. Horses that have difficulty swallowing often have a poor outlook. Other signs include respiratory distress, extended or low carriage of the head, and fluid buildup and swelling of the head. The diagnosis is based on the history, signs, and examination of the guttural pouch with an endoscope.

Treatment can be difficult, and it is not always effective. Antifungal drugs that are infused directly into the guttural pouch are the usual treatment for guttural pouch mycosis. If damage to the arteries has occurred, it may be necessary to perform surgery to close the affected blood vessel. This can help prevent a fatal hemorrhage. Nerve function may or may not return after the infection resolves.

▊ GUTTURAL POUCH TYMPANY

Guttural pouch tympany occurs when the guttural pouch (a pouch in the Eustachian tube that connects the ears to the nose and mouth and helps to regulate air pressure) becomes abnormally filled with air, causing nonpainful swelling just behind the jaw. The condition occurs in young horses (from birth to 1 year of age) and is more common in fillies than in colts. It may be caused by inflammation or by a congenital (present at birth) defect that allows air to enter the pouch but prevents it from returning to the pharynx.

Often, the swelling is the only noticeable sign; it may occur on one or both sides of the head. Other signs may include difficulty breathing, nasal discharge, and carrying the head in an extended position. The diagnosis is based on the signs and x-rays of the skull.

Treatment with nonsteroidal antiinflammatory drugs (NSAIDs) and appropriate antibiotics is successful in most horses in which inflammation is the cause. If tympany is due to a congenital defect, surgery is required to provide a route for the air to be expelled from the affected guttural pouch. The outlook for recovery is good in most cases.

▊ INFLAMMATORY AIRWAY DISEASE

Inflammatory airway disease is a group of inflammatory conditions of the lower respiratory tract that do not appear to be caused by disease organisms. Inflammatory airway disease occurs in up to 50% of athletic horses, and it is a common cause of impaired performance and interruption of training.

Factors that may be involved in the development of inflammatory airway disease include allergic airway disease, recurrent lung stress, deep inhalation of dust, pollutants in the atmosphere, and persistent respiratory viral infections. Inflammatory airway disease often develops following a viral respiratory infection, and may result from an inability of the immune system to fully eliminate viruses or bacteria from small airways. The bacterium *Streptococcus pneumoniae* has been isolated from young horses (less than 2 years of age) with inflammatory airway disease. Its role in the disease is unclear because inflammatory airway disease does not respond to antibiotic therapy.

The most common signs are a chronic cough and poor tolerance for strenuous exercise. Affected horses appear normal at rest; fever and abnormal lung sounds are rare. Endoscopic examination reveals mucous and pus in the upper throat, windpipe, and lungs. A diagnosis of inflammatory airway disease is often based on poor race performance and signs. Microscopic examination of fluid from the lungs can help determine whether infection or inflammation are involved and can help determine appropriate therapy.

Horses with inflammatory airway disease (regardless of the specific type) typically are prescribed aerosolized bronchodilator medication for use prior to exercise in order to prevent exercise- or irritant-induced airway constriction. In addition, drugs such as antiviral medication or corticosteroids (for relief of inflammation) may be prescribed.

▊ LUNGWORM INFECTION

Lungworm is an infection of the lower respiratory tract in horses, usually resulting in bronchitis or pneumonia, caused by the parasitic roundworm *Dictyocaulus arnfieldi*. The infection can cause severe coughing in horses and can be difficult to distinguish from other respiratory diseases.

Donkeys, which usually show few signs of the infection, are the prime source of pasture contamination for horses. Horses that share pasture with donkeys or follow them into grazing used by donkeys within a few months are most likely to become infected. Adult female worms in the lungs of infected donkeys (and less commonly horses) lay eggs that hatch in host feces after being coughed up and swallowed. After a short period, the larvae become infective in feces on pasture; they may remain infective unless killed by drought or very cold conditions. The severity of disease is related to the number of larvae ingested. Once infected, adults generally become immune to further disease, but some will contract very mild infections. Such animals can act as a source of further larval contamination, although infected horses do not produce many infective larvae. Previously infected adults can become reinfected if they have not been exposed to the lungworm larvae for over a year (and therefore have lost some of their natural resistance).

Signs of lungworm infection range from moderate coughing with slightly increased respiratory rates to severe, persistent coughing and respiratory distress or failure. Infections with no visible signs can occur. Diagnosis is based on these signs, known transmission patterns, and the presence of first-stage larvae in feces. Examination of the airways with an endoscope and x-rays can be helpful tools. Bronchoscopy can be used to collect washings from the trachea to examine for eggs, larvae, and white blood cells. It can be a challenge for a veterinarian to diagnose lungworm because infected animals do not always pass the larvae in their feces, and when they do, they may be few in number. Because of the relative infrequency of infection in horses, diagnosis may be made only after failure of antibiotic therapy to improve the condition.

Several antiparasitic drugs, especially moxidectin and ivermectin, are very effective for treatment of lungworms. Horses at pasture should be moved inside for treatment, and supportive care may be needed for complications that can arise in all species. Sporadic infections can be controlled more easily by management, such as avoidance of grazing horses with donkeys.

NASAL POLYPS

Nasal polyps are noncancerous growths that arise from the mucous membranes of the nasal cavity, nasal septum, or tooth socket. Polyps are usually single but can be multiple. They form in response to chronic inflammation by excess growth of the mucous membrane or fibrous connective tissue. They occur in all ages and breeds of horses.

Signs include poor airflow through the affected nasal passage, labored inhalation, a bad-smelling nasal discharge containing mucus and pus, and low-volume bleeding from the nose. The polyp may extend until it protrudes beyond the nostrils. Polyps are detected via endoscopic and radiographic examination, and microscopic evaluation of tissue samples provide a definitive diagnosis. They can be removed surgically.

PHARYNGEAL LYMPHOID HYPERPLASIA (PHARYNGITIS)

Pharyngeal lymphoid hyperplasia is a condition that occurs in young horses (1 to 3 years old). Unlike humans, horses do not have masses of lymphoid tissue that make up tonsils. Instead, there are follicles of this tissue spread over the pharynx. The follicles blend with normal mucosal tissue as the horse ages, but they are prominent in younger horses. Overgrowth (hyperplasia) may occur. While it was previously thought that the overgrowth was a cause of poor performance in younger horses, it is now thought to be of little significance in most cases. Occasionally these follicles may appear inflamed and produce a discharge that contains mucus or pus; this is likely the result of a mild viral infection, and treatment is usually not needed. Rest and nonsteroidal anti-inflammatory drugs can be used for horses showing signs of pain.

■ PLEUROPNEUMONIA

Pleuropneumonia is an infection of the lungs and the sac surrounding them (the pleural space). In most instances, it develops as a result of bacterial infection or penetrating chest wounds. Pleuropneumonia is more likely to occur in horses already weakened by previous viral respiratory infection, long-distance transportation (more than 500 miles), general anesthesia, or strenuous exercise. These factors can impair lung defense mechanisms, allowing bacteria to invade. Race and sport horses are particularly at risk. The majority of horses with pleuropneumonia are athletic horses younger than 5 years old.

Signs of pleuropneumonia in horses include fever, depression, lethargy, and poor appetite. Pleural pain is specific to this condition and causes short strides, guarding, flinching on tapping of the chest, and shallow breathing. Horses with pleural pain may have an anxious facial expression and are reluctant to move, cough, or lie down. Their gait may be stiff or stilted, and some horses will grunt in response to chest pressure or examination. Bad breath or foul-smelling nasal discharge indicates bacterial infection. Rapid, shallow breathing is due to pleural pain and restricted ability of the lungs to expand because of secretions accumulated in the pleural cavity.

In horses with a recent onset of pleuropneumonia, laboratory findings reflect the presence of infection in the blood. Horses with more longstanding disease often have anemia. During physical examination, the veterinarian can hear a lack of breath sounds in parts of the chest and abnormal lung sounds (often crackles) in others. Heart sounds may be muffled or absent. Chest ultrasonography is an effective tool for examining secretions in the pleural cavity and should be used to assist with removal of fluid from the

pleural cavity, so the veterinarian can determine the best site for maximal drainage. The fluid removal serves 2 purposes: it provides a sample for use in diagnosis, and it relieves the pressure caused by the fluid. Chest x-rays are used after pleurocentesis to evaluate lesions in the lungs as well as to detect air in the pleural cavity (pneumothorax). Bacterial culture is performed to identify the bacteria involved.

Monitoring of affected horses is important to check for fluid in the pleural cavity, determine whether drainage is effective, identify isolated fluid pockets, and assess lung disease. The amount and characteristics of the pleural fluid determine whether continual drainage is needed. Medical therapy includes appropriate broad-spectrum antibiotics, nonsteroidal anti-inflammatory drugs (NSAIDs), pain relievers, and supportive care. Some horses do not eliminate the pleural infection even after weeks to months of antibiotics and drainage. If needed, an opening in the chest can be created to allow the veterinarian to remove materials and dead lung tissue; however, this technique is used only when the condition has become chronic.

The outlook for horses with pleuropneumonia has greatly improved over the past 20 years due to early recognition, advancements in diagnostic testing, and aggressive therapy. The survival rate is reported to be as high as 90% by some investigators with a 60% chance to return to athletic performance. Even in cases where a chest tube has been necessary, it is still possible for the horse to return to athletic condition. Prompt treatment is important, because if appropriate therapy is delayed by more than 48 hours, infection can worsen and lead to a poor outcome.

■ RECURRENT AIRWAY OBSTRUCTION (HEAVES)

Recurrent airway obstruction is a common, allergic respiratory disease of horses that is similar to asthma in people. Exposure to the allergen causes inflammation and constriction of the small airways, leading to chronic cough, nasal discharge, and breathing difficulty. Episodes of airway obstruction tend to occur when susceptible horses are stabled, bedded on straw, or fed hay, whereas elimination of these factors results in remission or lessening of signs. The average age at onset is 9 years. Approximately 12% of mature horses have some degree of lower airway inflammation induced by allergens. The disease affects horses of all breeds. There does appear to be an inherited component to susceptibility.

Horses with recurrent airway obstruction typically have signs such as flared nostrils, rapid breathing with labored exhalation, and cough. The cough may be productive and often occurs during feeding or exercise. The abdominal muscles must work hard to assist with exhaling, and overdevelopment of these muscles produces a line along both sides of the abdomen known as a "heave line." Wheezing may be caused by airflow through narrowed airways, and is most obvious when the horse is exhaling. Mild to moderately affected horses may have few signs at rest, but coughing and exercise intolerance are seen during athletic performance.

The diagnosis of recurrent airway obstruction is made on the basis of the horse's history and physical examination. Chest x-rays may not be necessary in horses with typical signs, unless there is no response to standard treatment after several weeks of therapy. However, x-rays are sometimes used to distinguish between recurrent airway obstruction and other diseases with similar signs, such as interstitial pneumonia, pulmonary fibrosis, or bacterial pneumonia.

The single most important treatment is environmental management to reduce the horse's exposure to allergens. Medication will improve the signs of disease, but respiratory disease will return after medication is discontinued if the horse remains in an environment where allergens are present. The most common culprits are organic dusts present in hay.

Horses should be maintained at pasture with fresh grass as the source of roughage, supplemented with pelleted feed. Round bale hay is particularly allergenic and is a common cause of treatment failure for horses on pasture. Horses that remain stalled should be maintained in a clean, controlled environment. Complete commercial feeds eliminate the need for roughage. Hay cubes and hay silage are acceptable low-allergen alternative sources of roughage and may be preferred by horses over the complete feeds. Soaking hay with water prior to feeding may control signs in mildly affected horses but is not effective for highly sensitive horses. Horses maintained in a stall should not be housed in the same building as an indoor arena, hay should not be stored overhead, and straw bedding should be avoided.

Medical treatment typically consists of a combination of bronchodilating agents to open up the air passages and provide rapid relief of airway obstruction and corticosteroids to reduce lung inflammation. Some of these medications are given in an aerosol form.

Summer Pasture-associated Obstructive Lung Disease

Horses on late-summer pasture in the southeastern United States may have signs similar to those of horses with heaves. This likely reflects sensitivity to molds or grass pollens and is referred to as summer pasture-associated obstructive lung disease. The management is similar to that of a horse with heaves, with the addition of pasture avoidance. These horses should be maintained in a dust-free stable.

▧ STRANGLES (DISTEMPER)

Strangles is an infectious, contagious disease of horses caused by *Streptococcus equi equi* bacteria. It is characterized by abscesses in the lymph tissue of the upper respiratory tract. Strangles is a highly contagious disease, but it has a low death rate in otherwise healthy horses. Transmission occurs through infected objects and direct contact with infectious secretions. Infected horses may become carriers that show no signs but harbor and spread the disease. Paddocks and barn facilities used by infected horses should be regarded as contaminated for about 2 months after resolution of an outbreak.

The incubation period of strangles is 3 to 14 days after exposure. The first sign of infection is usually fever. Within 24 to 48 hours of the initial fever spike, the horse will exhibit signs typical of strangles, including nasal discharge containing mucus and pus, depression, and swollen lymph nodes under the jaw. Horses with swollen lymph nodes at the back of the throat will have difficulty swallowing, noisy inhalation, and will extend the head and neck. Older animals with some immunity from a previous infection may develop a less typical form of the disease with nasal mucous discharge, cough, and mild fever. Metastatic strangles (sometimes called "bastard strangles") is a condition in which lymph nodes in other parts of the body, such as the abdomen and chest, are affected.

The diagnosis of strangles is confirmed by bacterial culture of secretions from abscesses or nasal swab samples. Complicated cases may require endoscopic examination of the upper respiratory tract, ultrasonography of the throat, or x-ray examination of the skull to identify the location and extent of abscesses.

Treatment and Control

Although strangles is a bacterial infection, there are pros and cons to using antibiotics to treat it. Most researchers agree that antibiotic therapy will provide temporary improvement in fever and depression; however, it may also prolong the course of the disease by delaying maturation and drainage of the abscesses. Antibiotic therapy can also reduce the horse's natural buildup of immunity,

making it more susceptible to reinfection. Despite the disadvantages, antibiotic therapy is often necessary when the horse has labored breathing, difficulty swallowing, prolonged high fever, and severe lethargy or loss of appetite. Your veterinarian will weigh the pros and cons of antibiotic therapy based on your horse's specific condition.

The veterinarian may recommend applying warm compresses to the sites of swollen lymph nodes to help abscesses drain more quickly. Ruptured abscesses may need to be flushed with dilute iodine or a similar treatment until drainage stops. Nonsteroidal anti-inflammatory drugs (NSAIDs) may be prescribed to reduce pain and fever and improve appetite in horses with rapidly developing disease.

The horse should be kept in an environment that is warm, dry, and dust-free. It should be isolated from any other horses as soon as strangles is suspected, and appropriate procedures to prevent spread of infection should be followed. Flies can transmit infection mechanically; therefore, efforts should be made to control the fly population during an outbreak. Individuals, such as trainers, who visit multiple horse facilities should wear protective clothing or change clothes prior to traveling to the next facility. Horses being newly introduced to a group should be carefully scrutinized for evidence of disease. Consult your veterinarian for advice on testing, vaccination, and quarantine procedures.

Most horses continue to shed the infectious bacteria for about 1 month following recovery from disease. Analysis of swabs from the nose and throat can be used by the veterinarian to assess whether it is safe to introduce (or reintroduce) a previously infected horse into a group.

■ SUBEPIGLOTTIC CYST

Subepiglottic cysts are sometimes seen at the back of the pharynx and soft palate. They are an uncommon cause of respiratory noise in young horses. Although they are usually present from birth, they often remain undetected until the horse begins exercise training. Signs include respiratory noise and exercise intolerance. Large cysts may produce coughing, difficulty swallowing, and inhalation of foreign materials in foals. The condition is diagnosed by endoscopic examination of the upper respiratory tract. Treatment involves complete removal of the lining of the cyst. Rupture of the cyst will temporarily "deflate" it, but recurrence is common.

CHAPTER **54**

Skin Disorders

▨ STRUCTURE OF THE SKIN

The skin is the largest organ of your horse's body. It provides a protective barrier against the environment, regulates temperature, and gives your horse its sense of touch. Depending on the species and age, the skin may be 12 to 24% of an animal's body weight. The skin has 3 major layers: the epidermis or outermost layer, the dermis or middle layer, and the subcutis or innermost layer. Other important components include skin appendages (such as hair and hooves), and subcutaneous muscles and fat.

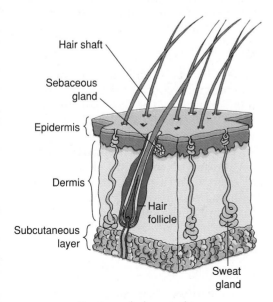

Hair shaft

Sebaceous gland

Epidermis {

Dermis {

Hair follicle

Subcutaneous layer {

Sweat gland

Structure of a horse's skin

Epidermis

The epidermis is the outer layer of skin, which is composed of several layers of cells. It provides a barrier of protection from foreign substances. The epidermis is thickest in large animals like horses. It includes multiple types of cells, including keratinocytes, melanocytes, Langerhans cells, and Merkel cells. Each of these cells has special functions.

Keratinocytes provide a protective layer that is constantly being renewed in a process called keratinization. In this process, new skin cells are created near the base of the epidermis and migrate upwards. This produces a compact layer of dead cells on the skin surface. This layer keeps in fluids, electrolytes, and nutrients, while keeping out infectious or noxious agents. The top layer of dead skin cells are continuously shed and replaced by cells from lower layers. The rate of cell replacement is affected by nutrition, hormones, tissue factors, immune cells in the skin, and genetics. Disease and inflammation can also change normal cell growth and keratinization.

Melanocytes are located at the base of the epidermis, the outer root sheath of hairs, and the ducts of the sebaceous and sweat glands. The melanocytes produce the skin and hair coloring (pigment) called melanin. Production of melanin is controlled by both hormones and the genes received from parents. Melanin helps protect the cells from the damaging rays of the sun.

Langerhans cells are part of the immune system. These cells are damaged when exposed to excessive ultraviolet light and glucocorticoids (anti-inflammatory drugs). Langerhans cells play an important role in the skin's response to foreign substances and contribute to such things as the development of rashes when an animal is exposed to irritating materials.

Merkel cells are specialized cells associated with the sensory organs in the skin. In particular, Merkel cells help provide animals with sensory information from whiskers and the deep skin areas called tylotrich pads.

Basement Membrane Zone

This layer of skin is located at the base of the epidermis and connects the epidermis to the dermis layer below. It also serves as a protective barrier between the epidermis and the dermis. Several skin diseases, including a number of autoimmune conditions, can damage the basement membrane zone.

Dermis

The dermis supports and nourishes the epidermis and skin appendages. The blood vessels that supply the epidermis with nutrients are located in the dermis. Blood vessels also regulate skin and body temperature. Sensory nerves are located in the dermis and hair follicles. The skin responds to the sensations of touch, pain, itch, heat, and cold. The dermis secretes the proteins collagen and elastin that give support and elasticity to the skin. Also present are immune cells that defend against infectious agents that pass through the epidermis.

Skin Appendages

Hair follicles, oil and sweat glands, and hooves are all skin appendages that grow out of the epidermis and dermis. The hair follicles of horses are simple—the follicles have 1 hair emerging from each pore.

The growth of hair is affected by nutrition, hormones, and change of season.

The size, shape, and length of hair are controlled by genetics and hormones. Disease, drugs, nutrition, and environment also affect the health of hair.

The hair coat protects the skin from physical and ultraviolet light damage, and helps regulate body temperature. Trapping air between secondary hairs conserves heat. This requires that the hairs be dry and waterproof. The cold-weather coat of many animals is often longer and finer to facilitate heat conservation. The hair coat can also help cool the skin. The warm-weather coat has shorter thicker hairs and fewer secondary hairs. This anatomic change allows air to move easily through the coat, which facilitates cooling.

Oil glands (also called sebaceous glands) secrete an oily substance called sebum into the hair follicles and onto the skin. They are present in large numbers near the hooves, back of the neck, rump, mouth, and tail area. Sebum is important for keeping the skin soft, moist, and pliable. It gives the hair coat sheen and has antimicrobial properties.

Sweat glands are part of the horse's system to regulate body temperature. They are found over most of the body except the legs. The evaporation of sweat from the skin is the primary cooling mechanism of the body for horses.

Subcutis

The subcutis is the innermost major layer of skin. It contains the subcutaneous fat and muscles. (The word subcutaneous means "beneath the skin.") The twitch muscle is the major subcutaneous muscle. The subcutaneous fat provides insulation; a reservoir for fluids, electrolytes, and energy; and a shock absorber. Nerves and blood vessels that supply the skin are also found in the subcutis.

▓ DERMATITIS AND DERMATOLOGIC PROBLEMS

Dermatitis is a general word for any type of inflammation of the skin. It is the word usually used to describe a skin condition before a specific diagnosis is reached. There are many causes of skin inflammation, including external irritants, burns, allergens, trauma, and infection (bacterial, viral, parasitic, or fungal).

Dermatitis may have many signs including any combination of itching, scaling, abnormal redness, thickening of the skin, and hair loss. The usual progression of a skin disease involves an underlying trigger that causes boils, scabs, scales, or blisters.

Abnormal itching, called **pruritus**, occurs in many skin diseases. As the inflammation progresses, crusting and scaling develop. If the problem reaches the deeper layer (the dermis), fluid discharge, pain, and sloughing or shedding of the skin may occur. Secondary bacterial and yeast infections commonly develop as a result of skin inflammation. If the dermatitis does not improve, the early signs of inflammation (such as redness) become obscured by signs of chronic inflammation (thickening of the skin, color changes, scaling, fluid discharge). Often the skin becomes drier and, if itching is not already a sign, it will often develop at this stage.

Resolving dermatitis requires that a veterinarian identify the underlying cause and treat secondary infections or other complications. A review of your horse's history and a physical examination can more precisely define the problem.

▓ DIAGNOSIS OF SKIN DISORDERS

A precise diagnosis of the causes of a skin disease requires a detailed history, physical examination, and appropriate diagnostic tests. Many skin diseases have similar signs, and an immediate diagnosis may not be possible. Based on your horse's history and the physical examination, your veterinarian may order any of a number of laboratory procedures. These may include microscopic analysis of skin scrapings and hair, cultures of skin swabs, blood and urine tests, and even biopsies.

It may take several days before laboratory results are available. Your veterinarian may also evaluate how your horse responds to treatment in order to diagnose a specific skin problem. More than one visit is often required for an accurate diagnosis.

▓ TREATMENT OF SKIN DISORDERS

Successful treatment of skin disorders requires identification of the underlying cause. Not surprisingly, many treatments for skin diseases are applied directly to the skin surface. Even though topical treatments may not cure the condition, they are often beneficial in improving the cosmetic appearance or odor of the animal, pending the final diagnosis. Topical skin medications may be the preferred method of treatment for some diseases or beneficial in addition to systemic drugs (medications

Shampoo Therapy

▪ Shampoos are commonly used topical treatments. Before applying a medicated shampoo, wash the horse with a cleansing shampoo and rinse well. Medicated shampoos often are not good cleansing agents, do not lather well, or do not work except on a clean hair coat.

▪ The medicated shampoo should be applied evenly to the hair coat after being diluted in water. (The shampoo should never be applied directly to the skin.) Diluting the shampoo will help rinse it from the coat and minimize the potential for irritating the skin. Depending on the shampoo, dilute 1 part shampoo to 3 or 4 parts water. The water used should be lukewarm, never hot.

▪ If possible, keep the medicated shampoo on the skin for 10 minutes (or as directed) then rinse thoroughly. Shampoo residue is a common cause of skin irritation or allergic reactions in horses, so it is very important to rinse your horse carefully and fully follow all instructions.

▪ Medicated shampoos usually need to be used frequently for the most successful results. Ask for and follow your veterinarian's instructions on shampoo frequency.

usually given by mouth or injection and distributed throughout the body). Examples of products applied directly to the skin include antibiotic ointments, corticosteroid preparations, medicated shampoos, and topical insecticides.

Systemic drugs may be needed to treat some disorders. These include whole-body antibiotics and corticosteroids and other anti-inflammatory drugs.

As with any treatment program, make sure that you read and understand all directions for using the prescribed product, including how to apply or give it, how much to use, and how often it should be administered.

■ CONGENITAL AND INHERITED SKIN DISORDERS

Horses may be born with any of several different kinds of skin abnormalities. The disorder may be present at birth or may develop weeks to months later.

Congenital Skin Disorders

Epitheliogenesis imperfecta (aplasia cutis) is a congenital skin deformity. Foals are born with small to extensive areas where skin is missing. Secondary infection is common. One or more hooves may be deformed or absent; in some affected animals, there are other associated congenital anomalies. The condition is fatal when extensive, but small defects can be surgically corrected.

A **nevus** in humans is a congenital pigmented area on the skin that is often called a birthmark. In animals, the term is used for any area where skin is malformed, including abnormally pigmented spots. Some forms of nevi displace the normal structures of the skin, including hair follicles; thus, these patches are hairless. When not extensive, nevi can be surgically removed; otherwise there is no effective treatment.

Dermoid sinuses or cysts occur in Thoroughbred horses. These cysts are lined with skin. Exfoliated skin, hair, and glandular debris accumulate in the cysts,

which can lead to infection. The cysts are found on the midline of the back and in rare cases are associated with spinal cord deficits. They can be removed by surgical excision.

Follicular cysts develop by abnormal hair follicle growth and by retention of follicular or glandular products. They may be congenital when the hair follicle does not develop normally. **Periauricular (dentigerous) cysts** are seen in horses. Although they are present at birth, they may not be recognized until adulthood.

Pigmentary Abnormalities

Skin color abnormalities may be either acquired or hereditary. Abnormalities in skin and coat color are sometimes related.

True **albinism** is always associated with pink or pale irises and with visual defects and increased risk of skin damage from solar radiation. Albinism is different from extreme white spotting. Lethal white foal syndrome is one that results from breeding 2 Overo Paints. Some animals with extreme piebaldism (spotted or blotched with black and white) or dominant white have associated neurologic anomalies or deafness in one or both ears.

Vitiligo is hereditary but not noticeable at birth. It is mostly seen in Arabian horses (Arabian fading syndrome, pinky syndrome). The onset is usually in young adulthood. Affected animals develop bleached splotches of skin that occasionally also affect the hair coat and hooves. Most splotches are on the face, especially the bridge of the muzzle or around the eyes. Color loss may wax and wane. Complete remission may occur but is rare. Vitiligo causes no other health problems. No treatment is available. Treatments used in people with vitiligo are unlikely to help animals.

Defects of Structural Integrity

Some genetic defects affect the integrity of the skin. **Hereditary equine regional dermal asthenia (HERD)** is a condition in which the skin produces abnormal collagen and/or elastin. This causes patches or large areas of loose, stretchy, fragile skin and joint problems. Wounds heal slowly or not completely. This condition has been reported in Quarter horses and Arabian cross horses. The condition is often first noticed during training, at the time saddles and tack are first placed on a young horse. Diagnosis is based on visible signs and testing of the collagen structure.

Epidermolysis bullosa syndromes are a group of hereditary congenital defects that affect the attachments between the outer and inner layers of the skin. There are 3 types of epidermolysis bullosa syndromes. In all 3 forms, minor skin trauma results in dermal-epidermal separation and blisters that soon rupture, leaving glistening, flat ulcers. Blisters may be present at birth or develop within the first weeks of life. The most severe blisters are on the lower legs (with sloughing of hooves), mouth, face, and genitals. Except for the simplex form, most occurrences of the disease are fatal. All 3 forms of epidermolysis bullosa have been reported in Belgian foals.

▨ ALLERGIES

Like people, horses can be allergic to various substances, including plant particles and other substances in the air (called allergic inhalant dermatitis or atopy) or in food. These substances are called allergens. Allergens are substances that, when inhaled or absorbed through the skin, respiratory tract, or gastrointestinal tract, stimulate histamine production, leading to inflammation. Allergic reactions can also be triggered by medications or vaccination.

Airborne Allergies (Atopy)

Horses often live in environments that have a high level of dust, mold, or other common allergens in the air. While the horse's immune system normally provides protection for the animal, the immune system of some horses overreacts to the presence of one or more airborne allergens. Airborne allergens can adversely affect the skin. The most common skin problems associated with the inhalation of allergens include hives and rashes (page 767). However, itching (page 768) is also a common allergic reaction to such things as hay dust, mold, mildew, pollen, and dust mites.

Once an allergy is diagnosed, treatment usually involves avoiding the allergen, if possible, and use of corticosteroids to control the inflammatory reaction. If a horse is allergic to dust in the environment, you may consider keeping it outside rather than stabling it. Feeding the horse haylage or some other feed with little dust may also help. Conversely, if the horse has seasonal pollen allergies, it can be kept inside during the months when pollen is normally present.

Allergy testing is also available in some areas. Allergy testing allows your veterinarian or veterinary dermatologist to identify the specific allergens that are a problem for your horse and to formulate an allergy vaccine, if appropriate.

Food Allergies

Horses can also develop food allergies, although documented cases are rare. For example, there are reports that certain types of grains or hay have caused hives in horses. In some cases, the food allergies were associated with high-protein food concentrates.

One common approach to identifying a food allergy starts with a trial or elimination diet. The horse receives a diet that does not include any of the foods previously fed, including supplements. For horses that have been on pasture, the diet may include a change of pasture or isolation from pasture. The trial diet is normally provided for up to 3 months. If signs of the allergy improve or resolve during this period, then a food allergy is likely. To confirm the food allergy, the previously fed foods must be returned to the diet 1 at a time. If signs return in response to a particular food given, then that food is likely the cause. The suspect food is again eliminated from the diet. If the signs resolve (often in less than 14 days), the food allergy is usually confirmed.

Once the offending allergens are identified, control of the food allergy involves strict avoidance of the food. Concurrent diseases may complicate the identification of underlying food allergies. Infrequently, a horse will react to new food allergens as it ages.

DERMATOPHILOSIS

This infection of the epidermis (top layer of the skin) is seen worldwide but is more prevalent in tropical environments where rain is frequent and humidity is high. Lameness and loss of performance may occur in horses that are severely affected around the pasterns.

The infection is caused by a species of actinomycete, a microorganism that resembles bacteria and funguses. Factors such as prolonged wetting by rain, high humidity, and high temperature, increase the occurrence of dermatophilosis. The organism can live in the skin quietly until infection is stimulated by climatic conditions. High humidity and moisture increases the release of spores and spreads the infection. Epidemics usually occur during the rainy season.

Dermatophilosis is most common in the young, animals continually exposed to moisture, and animals with weakened immune systems. Most infections subside in 2 to 3 weeks and the wounds heal without scarring. In general, the onset of dry weather speeds healing. In chronic infections, scabs and crusts can spread over a large portion of the body, particularly along the back. Itching is variable. Some wounds may be painful. Wounds on horses with long winter coats develop with matted hair and paintbrush wounds leading to crust or scab formation with yellow-green pus. With short summer hair, matting and scab formation is uncommon. However, loss of hair with a fine paintbrush effect can be extensive.

Animals with severe generalized infections often lose condition, and movement is difficult if the hooves, lips, and muzzle are severely affected. The condition is painful. Severely infected animals may have to be euthanized.

Diagnosis depends on the appearance of wounds in diseased animals and the finding of the actinomycete in skin smears or culture. The most practical diagnostic test is microscopic examination of scabs or impression smears of the underside of fresh wounds. Thus, your veterinarian will likely take sample scabs or smears for laboratory examination.

Treatment involves appropriate antibiotics. The lesions should be gently soaked and removed. Your veterinarian can provide instructions for this. Topical antibacterial shampoo treatment is often effective and may be prescribed along with other medications. Clipping of the hair coat may be required. Successful treatment requires removing the horse from the damp or wet environment that triggered the infection.

Infected horses should be isolated from other animals to reduce spread of the disease. Careful attention to the cleanliness of living areas, tack, blankets, grooming tools, and other accessories is required and can help control spread of the disease. Insect controls are often recommended for the same reason because insects can carry the disease from an infected horse to a healthy one.

EOSINOPHILIC GRANULOMA COMPLEX

Equine eosinophilic granuloma (also called nodular necrobiosis or collagenolytic granuloma with collagen degeneration) is the most common nodular skin disease in horses. There are many proposed causes; however, insect bite reactions are the most likely. Trauma and other environmental allergies may also be involved. Many collagenolytic granulomas occur during the warmer months of the year and may recur seasonally. Some may persist year round or distinctively occur under tack and saddle areas where pressure and trauma occur.

Lesions vary in size and number from less than ¼ inch (0.5 centimeter) to larger than 2 inches (5 centimeters) and usually occur over the neck, trunk and back. Some horses can develop a generalized form with hundreds of pea-sized nodules over most of the body. The overlying skin is usually normal but on occasion may open and ulcerate. More chronic lesions may calcify and become "rock hard;" such lesions are often the most difficult to treat effectively.

Treatment most often involves relatively high doses of corticosteroids given by mouth or injection. Persistent lesions can be injected with more potent forms of corticosteroids. Antibiotics can also be helpful in controlling secondary infection related to foreign body reactions. Occasionally surgical removal is needed for more calcified lesions. Fly control, along with allergy testing and desensitization in recurrent cases, are often indicated.

▓ FLIES AND MOSQUITOES

Flies are winged insects that are usually just an annoyance. However, they can transmit disease and cause problems in animals. They belong to a large, complex order of insects called Diptera. Flies vary greatly in size, food preference, development, and habits. As adults, flies may feed on blood, saliva, tears, or mucus. They also spread bacteria, viruses, and parasites.

Biting flies feed on animal blood. This group includes mosquitoes, black flies, sand flies, biting midges, horse flies, and deer flies. Though the bites can be painful and may bring on allergic reactions, biting flies are usually not dangerous and are just a nuisance unless they are extremely numerous in the horse's environment or transmit a disease. Many of these flies, including black flies and mosquitoes, will bite both animals and humans.

Nonbiting flies include those that do not feed on blood and do not actually bite the host animal while feeding. Instead, these flies feed on bodily secretions. Both biting and nonbiting flies can transmit diseases to horses and other domestic animals.

Stable fly

Horse fly

Biting midge

Some common flying pests of horses

Finally, some flies have larvae that may develop in the subcutaneous tissues of the skin or organs of animals, producing a condition known as **myiasis (fly strike)**. The larvae, or maggots, may be free-living or may be parasites of the host animal.

The flies and mosquitoes that are most commonly involved in transmitting or causing disorders that affect the skin are discussed below.

Biting Midges (Gnats, No-see-ums)

These tiny insects are often called gnats and are sometimes known as "no-see-ums," or "punkies." There are several species. All are associated with habitats in and around bodies of water, such as the mud or moist soil around streams, ponds, and marshes. They can inflict painful bites and suck the blood of both humans and animals, including horses. Midges can transmit the parasite that causes onchocerciasis (page 771) in horses.

Midges fly only during the warm months of the year and are most active before and during dusk. They can cause intense irritation of the skin. The preferred feeding site for biting midges is usually on the back and belly; however, this varies by species of midge. Horses often become allergic to the bites. Allergic horses scratch and rub the affected areas, causing hair loss, abrasions, and thickening of the skin. This condition is known by various names around the world: culicoid hypersensitivity (in Canada), Queensland itch (in Australia), Kasen (in Japan), sweat itch, sweet itch, summer dermatitis, and seasonal dermatitis.

Your veterinarian can provide treatment as needed for the midge bite wounds and sores caused by scratching and rubbing. Veterinarians and extension insect specialists can recommend approved midge control methods and products. Keeping your horse inside a stable during dusk will also help reduce the animal's exposure to midges. Because they are weak fliers, air movement also reduces exposure to midges. Some owners have had success using fans in stables, fine screens on windows and doors, stable blankets, and topical applications. Although they are not approved for use in the United States, fly repellent ear tags attached to manes and tails can also be effective.

Black Flies

There are more than 1,000 species of black flies. They feed on humans and all groups of animals. Most black flies are small, tiny enough to slip through the mesh of many screens. They are most numerous in north temperate and subarctic zones, although there are tropical and subtropical

species as well. In some cases, swarms of these flies will attack, inflicting large numbers of painful bites and causing whole-body reactions.

Because the female black flies have tiny, serrated mouthparts, the bites are often more painful or itchy than the bites of other flies and are more likely to become infected. There are occasional animal deaths from black fly bites, usually involving attacks by swarms of black flies. These rare deaths occur either because the animal is unusually sensitive to black fly bites or because the animal was attacked by a very large number of the flies. If the animal survives a mass black fly attack, it usually recovers quickly. Diagnosis is by appearance of bite wounds on the animal and, in some instances, the presence of the offending insect.

Control of black flies is difficult due to the distances the adult flies can travel. Some control is possible by using insecticides on the horse as directed. Stabling horses during daylight hours when the flies are active can provide some protection. Area-wide control for black flies is usually best done by city, county, or other government agencies.

Buffalo Flies

Buffalo flies are primarily a pest of cattle and water buffalo, but they occasionally infest horses as well. They are dark in color and about half the size of an ordinary house fly or stable fly. Thus far, they have not been found in the US. They are native to north Australia and New Guinea and can be found in parts of southern, southeastern, and eastern Asia as well as Oceania. Buffalo flies are not found in New Zealand. Animals infested with buffalo flies have blood loss and irritation from the bites. Because these flies stay on the infested animal, diagnosis is usually through finding the flies on the animal. The bite wounds are visible and may be infected.

Insecticides should be avoided in controlling buffalo flies. Many of these flies have developed resistance to the commonly used insecticides. To date, the most effective controls are the walk-through buffalo fly traps developed in Australia.

Eye Gnats

The eye gnats or eye flies are very small flies that congregate around the eyes. Some species are attracted to the genitals. They feed by sponging up mucous, pus, and blood. Although adult flies are present throughout the year in some regions, they only bother horses from spring through fall. During the peak months, they are noticeable in the early morning and late afternoon. They enjoy the deep shade, such as among densely planted shrubs or in the shade of a building.

These gnats do not bite. However, their mouth parts have spines that can cause small scars that open the skin to disease-causing organisms. They are persistent and, if brushed away, quickly return to continue engorging themselves. Large quantities of eye gnats can stress an animal. Diagnosis is by appearance of characteristic wounds or scars on the skin and the presence of eye gnats on the animal.

Insect repellents, such as those recommended for mosquitoes, can provide temporary relief from eye gnats. Be sure to follow veterinary instructions when using repellents. Community-wide mosquito control programs also reduce the number of eye gnats in the area. However, more adult gnats invade the area after the insecticide disperses.

Face Flies

Face flies are so named because they gather around the eyes and muzzle. Adult face flies are similar to house flies. They usually affect cattle but can also affect horses. In general, if a medium-sized fly is found feeding around the eyes and nostrils of a horse, it is most probably a face fly. They may also be found on the withers, neck, chest, and flanks. Face flies do not bite. Their mouthparts are adapted for sponging up saliva, tears, and mucus. However, they follow blood-feeding flies. After a biting fly has fed, the face flies move in and lap up the blood and body fluids on the host's skin. Face flies are found on animals that are outdoors. They usually do not follow animals into barns.

Feeding around the host's eyes causes irritation that stimulates the flow of tears, attracting even more flies. Because face flies have small, rough spines on their sponging mouthparts, even a few flies can cause irritation and damage to the eyes of the host. Face flies can also transmit diseases and parasites. Diagnosis is by finding the flies on the animal and finding the characteristic bite wounds especially near eyes, ears, and noses.

Control of face flies is difficult. Much research has gone into developing products and application techniques that are safe for horses but fatal to face flies; however, progress has been slow. Face flies do not like to be inside, so stabling horses can provide some protection.

Filth-breeding Flies

This group includes the common house fly (*Musca domestica*) and many other species, including blow flies, bottle flies, and flesh flies. Animal feces attract large numbers of filth-breeding flies because animal wastes offer an ideal location for the eggs and larvae of these flies. While these flies do not suck blood, they use their sponging mouthparts to suck semiliquid food. Thus, any liquid or semiliquid body secretions will attract these flies. They are "vomit drop" feeders and fly from feces to food, spreading bacteria on their feet and within the stomach contents they leave behind.

Good sanitation programs can go a long way toward reducing the number of filth-breeding flies. Make sure all manure is removed quickly; it should not be allowed to accumulate. If manure handling is done on site, it should be handled in a manner to reduce fly breeding. If large numbers of flies are seen, consult your veterinarian regarding the use of insecticides, fly baits, and other control measures appropriate for your situation.

Fly Strike (Myiasis)

In addition to spreading disease, filth-breeding flies may lay eggs in skin wounds that have become contaminated with bacteria or in a matted hair coat contaminated with feces. The larvae (maggots) develop in and around the wound and can tear the skin to obtain more food. This type of infestation is known as myiasis or fly strike. Finding maggots in a sore or wound is the normal method of diagnosis. If precise identification of the fly is needed or desired, removed maggots can be sent to a laboratory for identification. Because the first maggots in a wound often create favorable conditions for other flies, the strike site may contain maggots from more than one type of fly.

Certain species of filth-breeding flies are known for their larvae, which are called **screwworms** (so named because their shape resembles a wood screw). There are several types of screwworms that can affect horses, including primary or New World screwworms (found in Central and South America and the Caribbean), and Old World screwworms (found in Africa, India, and Southeast Asia). None are currently found in the United States.

Treatment of fly strike involves removal of the maggots, cleansing and removal of dead tissue from the strike site, and medication to control infection and reduce the horse's discomfort. If your horse develops a screwworm infestation, it must be reported to appropriate state and federal authorities.

Horn Flies

Horn flies (*Haematobia irritans*) are a common pest of cattle in Europe, North Africa, Asia Minor, and the Americas. However, they will also feed on horses. The flies themselves are about half the size of a stable fly and dark in color. They have a bayonet-like mouthpart that juts out from the head.

The common name for these flies comes from the fact that they often cluster around the base of the horns of cattle. They also cluster around the shoulders, back, and sides of an animal, all areas where tail switching is usually ineffective. Horn flies spend their entire lives on their host except for the period when females leave to deposit their eggs in fresh feces. In some warmer climates (such as Florida or far southern Texas), these flies reproduce actively throughout the year.

Horn flies feed frequently, up to 20 times a day. They suck blood and other body fluids. Horn fly bites and wounds are painful and cause blood loss and irritation in afflicted horses. Infested horses may lose weight and show painful lesions wherever the flies cluster. Diagnosis is by finding the bite wounds and the flies on the horse.

Treatment of the bite wounds may require antibiotics to control bacterial or other infections. Relief from horn fly infestation will encourage normal food consumption and allow the animal to recover from any blood loss.

Controlling horn flies often involves the use of chemical liquids and sprays. Because horn flies generally prefer to feed on cattle, keeping horses separated from cattle and cow manure may help reduce their exposure.

Horse Flies

Horse flies are large, heavy bodied, robust insects with powerful wings and very large eyes. They may exceed 1 inch (3 centimeters) in length. Many are highly colored. The females feed on animal blood. These flies can transmit such diseases as anthrax, anaplasmosis, tularemia, and the virus of equine infectious anemia.

Adult horse flies lay eggs in the vicinity of open water. Larval stages develop in aquatic to semiaquatic environments, often buried deep in mud at the bottom of lakes and ponds. Adults are seen near water in summer, particularly in sunlight.

Adult females have scissor-like mouthparts that they use to slice into the skin and lap up the oozing blood. Mass horse fly attacks can cause significant blood loss in a horse. Bites are painful and irritating. Horses become restless when the flies are present. Flies usually attack the underside of the abdomen around the navel, the legs, or the neck and withers. When disturbed by the animal's swatting tail or by the muscle twitch reflex, the flies leave the host, yet blood continues to ooze from the open wound. Secondary infection from bacteria or other parasites is possible. Horse fly bites are diagnosed by the presence of the flies near the horse and the characteristic bite wounds.

Horse flies are the most difficult to control of all of the blood-sucking flies. A number of insecticides will kill horse flies. However, because these flies are occasional feeders that land on the horse for only a short time, the flies may not be exposed to ordinary doses of fly control products for long enough to kill them. Larger doses of the insecticide may be required. To protect your horse, follow the advice of your veterinarian for the use of fly control insecticides. Horse fly traps are effective when used around horses confined to manageable areas. Insect repellants are only slightly effective in discouraging horse flies around individual animals.

Mosquitoes

Mosquitoes belong to the family Culicidae. They are tiny and fragile but possibly the most voracious of the blood-feeding flies. About 300 species have been described worldwide; only about 150 species of mosquitoes are found in the temperate regions of North America. Only adult female mosquitoes are blood feeders.

Although they are known for spreading such diseases as malaria, yellow fever, dengue, and elephantiasis, mosquitoes pose a concern for horse owners because they spread viral encephalitides, including Western and Eastern equine encephalomyelitis and the West Nile virus. (*See also* BRAIN, SPINAL CORD, AND NERVE DISORDERS, page 708.)

The toxins injected at the time of biting may cause allergic reactions to mosquito bites. Hives (wheals of raised flesh) and itching can accompany the bites. In addition to the skin irritation, there is the possibility that a serious disease may have been transmitted by the biting mosquito. Adult mosquitoes are rarely found on bitten animals. However, the bite locations are usually raised and itchy. Horses may scratch, lick, or rub the location. The bite location can then be further injured and infected with bacteria or other disease-causing organisms. Your veterinarian can guide you in the selection of the most appropriate medication(s) for mosquito bite wounds.

It is difficult to protect your horse from mosquitoes. Insect repellents and insecticides are not widely effective. You can reduce outdoor exposure to mosquitoes by keeping your horse stabled in the early morning or early evening hours, when mosquitoes are most active.

Mosquitoes often lay their eggs on the surface of standing water. Even small amounts of standing water can attract mosquitoes. Eliminating sources of standing water or applying appropriate insecticides may help limit the mosquito population.

Stable Flies

The stable fly (*Stomoxys calcitrans*) is often called the biting house fly. It is about the same in size and general appearance as the common house fly. It has a bayonet-like, needle-sharp mouth. In the US, stable flies are found in the midwestern and southeastern states. Adults may live 3 to 4 weeks.

The larvae develop in decaying organic matter, including grass clippings, the edges of hay stacks, and seaweed along beaches. Breeding can occur where hay has become mixed with urine and feces.

Both male and female stable flies are blood feeders, and horses are the preferred hosts. The fly usually lands on the legs, abdomen, or ears, with its head pointed upward and inflicts painful bites that puncture the skin and bleed freely. Secondary infection from bacteria or other parasites is possible. The painful bite, blood loss, and irritation results in stress to the animal. Stable flies stay on the host for only short periods of time. This is an outdoor fly; however, in the late fall and during rainy weather, it may enter barns. Diagnosis is by the presence of stable flies and the appearance of the characteristic bite wounds on the animal.

The best way to control stable flies is by good sanitation practices. Areas along fence rows, under feed bunks, or wherever manure and straw or decaying matter can build up should be kept clean. These provide the conditions in which the larval flies develop. If good sanitation is maintained, chemical control is less likely to be needed. Various insecticides can be sprayed where flies may rest in barns or on fence rows. However, insecticides on animals are not usually effective. Stable flies usually feed only once or twice daily for short periods, thus minimizing exposure to any insecticides.

In cases where stable fly bites have become infected or inflamed, your veterinarian can recommend appropriate medications to make your horse more comfortable and speed healing. Blood tests may be recommended to check for diseases that can be transmitted by stable flies.

Tsetse Flies

Tsetse flies (*Glossina* species) are important blood-feeding flies found in portions of Africa. Tsetse flies are the intermediate hosts for trypanosomes that cause fatal diseases in both humans and domestic animals. In humans, the disease is often called African sleeping sickness; it is known as nagana in animals. Horses can die from trypanosome infection. The disease brings on a profound lethargy that ends in death.

Control of tsetse flies is critical to the control of nagana and African sleeping sickness. Tsetse fly traps, bush clearing, fly screens, insect repellents, and insecticides are the traditional control techniques. Recently, programs involving the release of sterile male tsetse flies have offered hope for an environmentally friendly and effective control procedure for these flies.

■ HAIR LOSS (ALOPECIA)

Alopecia is the partial or complete lack of hairs in areas where they are normally present. Hair loss is a sign, not a disease. Its underlying cause must be determined for the condition to be successfully treated. If an animal has hair loss and is also scratching the area excessively, the itching problem should be investigated first (*see* ITCHING [PRURITUS], page 768).

There are many causes of hair loss, which can be congenital (the animal is born with the condition) or acquired. Any disease that can affect hair follicles can cause hair loss. Certain diseases may destroy the hair follicle or shaft or interfere with the growth of hair. Some diseases can cause the animal discomfort leading to self-trauma and loss of hair. Acquired hair loss can be inflammatory or noninflammatory.

Diseases that can directly cause destruction or damage to the hair shaft or follicle include bacterial, fungal, or parasitic infections; skin trauma such as burns; and (rarely) poisonings. Diseases that can directly inhibit or slow hair follicle growth include nutritional deficiencies (particularly protein deficiencies), or hormonal imbalances such as hypothyroidism. Temporary hair loss can occur during pregnancy, lactation, or several weeks after a severe illness or fever. Bald patches can occur during the normal shedding process. These types of hair loss tend to be noninflammatory unless a secondary infection of the skin develops.

Itching or pain is a common cause of acquired inflammatory hair loss. Diseases that commonly cause itching or pain include infections, parasite infestations, and allergies. Friction may cause local hair loss, for example, poorly fitted halters or saddles.

An accurate diagnosis of the cause of hair loss requires a detailed history and physical examination. In the physical examination, your veterinarian will note the pattern and distribution of hair loss. He or she will examine the hairs to determine if they are being shed from the hair follicle or broken off and will also look for signs of secondary skin infections or parasites. Often, this involves taking skin scrapings and combing of the hair coat to collect samples for microscopic examination. Fungal cultures are commonly performed on horses with hair loss, as ringworm (which is caused by a fungus) is one of the most common causes of this condition.

Your veterinarian may order diagnostic laboratory tests. These usually include smears and culture of the skin to check for evidence of bacterial, fungal, or yeast infections. If these tests do not identify or suggest an underlying cause, a skin biopsy may be performed. Skin biopsies are often needed to confirm bacterial and parasitic causes of hair loss or to identify cancerous causes of hair loss. In the rare event your veterinarian suspects an endocrine problem, blood and urine samples may be tested.

Successful treatment depends on the underlying cause and specific diagnosis. Because identifying the cause of a skin condition may take some time, many veterinarians will provide or prescribe medication to relieve any discomfort or itching your horse may be experiencing in connection with the hair loss.

▒ HIVES (URTICARIA)

Hives (urticaria) are groups of itchy eruptions of localized swelling in the dermis. They often develop and disappear suddenly. The most common causes of hives in horses are insect bites or stings, medications, and exposure to allergens. Other potential causes include vasculitis (inflammation of the blood vessels of the skin), food allergy, ringworm (page 773), and pemphigus foliaceus.

Common causes of hives in horses are insect bites or stings, medications, and exposure to allergens.

Hives appear within a few minutes or hours of exposure to the causative agent. They are elevated, round, flat-topped, and 0.5 to 8 inches (1 to 20 centimeters) in diameter; they may be slightly depressed in the center. Hives can develop on any part of the body but occur mainly on the back, flanks, neck, eyelids, and legs. In advanced cases, they may be found on the mucous membranes of the mouth, nose, eyes, rectum, and vagina. In severe cases, the skin eruptions are preceded by fever, poor appetite, or dullness. Horses often become excited and restless.

The usual treatment for hives is antihistamines; however, antihistamines are often ineffective and unnecessary. In most cases, the hives disappear as rapidly as they arise, often within a few hours. Hives are very seldom harmful to the horse. Fatalities are even rarer. If hives are chronic, allergens in an environment should be considered potential causes, and steps taken to prevent exposure to the allergen, if possible. The hives promptly disappear but return rapidly if the allergen is not eliminated. Topical medication may be prescribed to control itching and reduce the chance of further skin damage.

Sensitive animals, particularly purebred horses, also may exhibit **dermographism**, a phenomenon in which rubbing or whipping produces hive-like inflammations. These are of no medical significance.

ITCHING (PRURITUS)

Itching is a sign, not a diagnosis or specific disease. The most common causes of itching are parasites, infections, and allergies. There are many skin diseases that do not initially cause itching; however, itching may develop because of secondary bacterial or yeast infections. It is possible that by the time itching develops the initial cause is long gone.

Itching may be general or confined to one area. A horse with itchy skin will rub up against fences, stalls, trees, or other objects in an attempt to scratch the itch. The animal may excessively bite or lick its skin to the point of drawing blood or causing damage to the skin.

Your veterinarian will perform a thorough skin history and physical examination. Parasites are a common cause of itchy skin disorders in horses and are the first possible causes the veterinarian will seek to exclude. Infections are common causes of itching and may be accompanied by hair loss, scaling, odor, and fluid discharge. Many infections can be effectively treated with appropriate antibiotics.

The underlying cause of itching may be allergic. The most common causes of allergic itching are insect bites, food allergy, and skin allergies. Sensitivity to insect bites is readily identified. Animals that have seasonal itching are likely reacting to seasonal allergens. Allergens in the feed are another possibility.

Successful treatment depends on identifying the underlying cause. For example, if parasites are identified as the cause of itching, appropriate antiparasitic drugs are prescribed. Horses with itching of unknown cause, or those in which treatment of the underlying disease does not eliminate the itching, will require medical management. Commonly prescribed anti-itching medications include antihistamines, corticosteroids, and essential fatty acids.

A program that stresses preventive control of parasites in the horse's environment—including insect control and regular deworming programs—can help eliminate or reduce some causes of itching.

LICE

Lice are small flightless insects that live in the feathers or hair of animals and people. All lice live within the environment provided by the skin and its hair or feathers. They move from host to host, primarily by direct contact. In temperate regions, lice are most common during the colder months.

There are 2 basic types of lice. The largest group is the biting or chewing lice (order Mallophaga). The smaller group is the blood-sucking lice (order Anoplura). Two species of lice can infest horses, *Haematopinus asini*, the horse sucking louse, and *Damalinia equi*, the horse biting louse. Normally, the horse sucking louse is found at the roots of the forelock and mane, around the base of the tail, and on the hairs just above the hoof. The horse biting louse prefers to lay its eggs on the finer hairs of the body. It is found on the sides of the neck, the flank, and the base of the tail.

Females glue their eggs, known as nits, to the hairs of the host near the skin. Ordinary shampooing and washing will not dislodge the nits. Nits are pale, translucent, and almost oval in shape. Once the nits hatch, the lice go through 3 nymph stages before reaching adulthood. The nymphs look very much like adult lice, only smaller. It takes about 3 to 4 weeks for most lice to go from nit to adult, although this period varies with the species.

Lice can be found anywhere on the body, but they are more commonly seen on the head, neck, mane, and the base of the tail. The first signs that your horse may be infested with lice are biting at and rubbing infested areas. Hair loss and even skin loss may occur. If the lice are abundant, the hair might also be matted. Sucking lice cause small wounds that can become infected. Usually, diagnosis is made by visual observation of lice on the infested animal. Parting the hair often reveals the lice. Chewing lice are active and can be seen moving through the hair.

Horses can be treated with sprays of permethrin, coumaphos, or malathion to kill lice. A wipe-on formula is also available and is especially useful for treating horses that react to sprayer noises. Your veterinarian can recommend an appropriate control product and provide directions for its use. Reapplication may be necessary to kill all lice.

The lice that infest horses are not normally attracted to humans. Therefore, while care in dealing with the lice infecting your horse is recommended, owners should understand that people rarely get lice from their horses.

■ MANGE (ACARIASIS, MANGE MITES)

Mange is caused by microscopic mites that invade the skin of otherwise healthy animals. The mites cause irritation of the skin and a hypersensitivity reaction, resulting in itching, hair loss, and inflammation. Mange is rare in horses. There are several types of mange that affect horses, including sarcoptic mange (equine scabies), psoroptic mange (mane mange), chorioptic mange (leg mange), demodectic mange, harvest mites (chiggers, trombiculids), and straw itch mites (forage mites).

Sarcoptic Mange (Scabies, Body Mange)

Although rare, sarcoptic mange is the most severe type of mange in horses. The first sign of mange is intense itching, which is caused by hypersensitivity to mite saliva and feces. Anti-itch medications do not help. The animal will rub and chew on its skin, causing sores and bald patches to appear on the head, neck, flanks, and abdomen. The sores start as small bumps and blisters that later develop into crusts. Hair loss and crusting spreads, and the skin becomes thickened. If untreated, the sores may spread over the entire body, leading to emaciation, weakness, and loss of appetite.

Diagnosing mange is sometimes difficult. If mange is suspected, your veterinarian will do a physical examination, including skin scrapings. However, the mites that cause mange are not always found in skin scrapings. If mites are not found, but the signs are highly suggestive of mange, a skin biopsy might be performed.

Sarcoptic mange is highly contagious. Treatment must be thorough and should include all horses and other animals that have been in contact with one another. Your veterinarian will prescribe an organophosphate insecticide or a lime-sulfur solution, to be applied by dip, spray, or sponge. Three or 4 treatments, applied 12 to 14 days apart, are often recommended. A group of drugs called macrocyclic lactones are highly effective against sarcoptic mange. These drugs are usually given by mouth in horses. Treatment for secondary infections may also be necessary.

Psoroptic Mange (Mane Mange)

Psoroptic mange is rare in horses and, in fact, has been eradicated from horses in the United States. It produces lesions on thickly haired regions of the body, such as under the forelock and mane, at the base of the tail, under the chin, between the hindlegs, and in the armpits. The mites can sometimes infect ears and may cause head shaking. Signs start as bumps and hair loss. Eventually, thick scabs develop. Itching is characteristic. The lesions start as small raised areas that soon lose hair and develop into thick crusts that bleed easily. Treatment is the same as for sarcoptic mange (*see* above).

Chorioptic Mange (Leg Mange)

Leg mange tends to occur in heavy breeds of horses. Signs start as itching affecting the legs (most often the hind legs) around the foot and fetlock. Raised bumps are seen first, followed by hair loss, crusting, and thickening of the skin. The signs lessen in summer but return with cold weather. The disease persists without treatment, but usually clears when treated. Topical treatments recommended for other types of mange are usually effective.

Demodectic Mange

Demodectic mange is rare in horses. The mites live in the hair follicles and oil glands or in the eyelids and muzzle. The signs of demodectic mange in horses can include patchy hair loss and scaling or skin lumps. Signs appear on the face, neck, shoulders, and forelimbs. There is no itching. No effective treatments have been developed.

Harvest Mites (Chiggers, Trombiculids)

Harvest mites usually live on other animals but can infest the skin of horses, especially during the late summer and fall. Signs consist of severely itchy bumps and hives. Specific treatment is not required. The itching can be controlled with medication. Repellents may help prevent infestation.

Straw Itch Mites (Forage Mites)

Straw itch mites usually feed on organic material in straw and grain but can infest the skin of horses. Raised bumps and hives appear on the face and neck if horses are fed from a hay rack, and on the muzzle and legs if fed from the ground. Itching is variable and can be controlled with medication.

PARASITIC WORMS OF THE SKIN

Some parasitic worms, particularly nematodes (roundworms), can cause diseases of the skin in horses and other animals. The most common are discussed below.

Cutaneous Habronemiasis (Summer Sores)

Cutaneous habronemiasis is a skin disease of horses caused by the larvae of spirurid stomach worms (*see also*

Habronemiasis of the skin is caused by a gastrointestinal parasite.

GASTROINTESTINAL PARASITES OF HORSES, page 629). The larvae move from flies feeding on preexisting wounds or on moisture of the genitalia or eyes, into the skin of a horse. When in the skin, they cause irritation and wounds. These wounds generally occur during the summer and are commonly called summer sores. The wounds are reddish brown, greasy areas of skin that contain yellow, calcified material the size of rice grains. Healing is slow. Diagnosis is by skin biopsy. Larvae, recognized by spiny knobs on their tails, can sometimes be found in scrapings of the boils.

Many different treatments have been used, most with poor results. Use of insect repellents may help, and organophosphates rubbed onto the area of the wound may kill the larvae. Some products (such as those containing ivermectin or moxidectin) with broad-spectrum activity against parasites have been shown to be effective. Surgical removal or cauterization of the excessive granulation tissue may be necessary. Control of the fly hosts and regular collection and stacking of manure may reduce the incidence of the disease. As with many other diseases, good sanitation practices significantly reduce the number of cases of cutaneous habronemiasis and can go a long way toward protecting your horse.

Onchocerciasis

Equine onchocerciasis is a disease caused by a parasitic worm and transmitted by biting midges (*see* page 761). It causes skin lumps and crusty dry patches that are irritating. The life cycle of the worm begins when a midge takes a blood meal containing the larvae of the worm. Larvae develop to the infective stage in the fly and then pass into the horse host when the flies feed on other horses. The larvae migrate to the connective tissues of the neck, where they mature into adult worms over a period of 1 to 3 months. After the worms have matured they mate. Female worms produce eggs, which hatch to produce new larvae. The larvae are then sucked up by a biting midge and the life cycle continues. Adult worms are very thin and 1.2 to 23.5 inches (3 to 60 centimeters) long. The larvae are tiny, only 0.008 inches (0.2 millimeters) long.

Adult worms live in the nuchal ligament (the large, powerful ligament in the neck that helps support the head). They cause inflammation which can lead to hardened lumps. These lumps are more common in older horses. Large numbers of larvae can cause skin inflammation of the face, neck, chest, withers, forelegs, and abdomen. Signs often include areas of scaling, crusts, ulcers, hair loss, and color loss. There may also be itching. Larvae can also accumulate in the eyes of horses.

The most effective method of diagnosis is by skin biopsy. Allergic reactions to the bites of flies can cause similar signs. Therefore, diagnosis of onchocerciasis may be based on laboratory tests and a positive response to antiworm treatment.

No treatment is effective against the adult worms. Drugs with a broad spectrum of activity against worms and other parasites (such as those containing ivermectin or moxidectin) are very effective against larvae. A small portion of horses infected react to the treatment with a noticeable swelling of affected areas 1 to 3 days after treatment. These conditions may resolve on their own; however, treatment of the signs may be necessary for the comfort of your horse.

Parafilaria multipapillosa Infestation (Summer Bleeding)

Parasitic worms known as *Parafilaria multipapillosa* infest the tissue just beneath the skin of horses in various parts of the world. They are especially common in the Russian steppes and Eastern Europe. In the spring and summer, the worms cause skin nodules primarily on the head and upper forequarters. Bleeding from the nodules is seen periodically and may be heavy. This condition is sometimes called summer bleeding. As the parasite moves under the skin, new nodules develop. Occasionally, the nodules will accumulate or discharge pus. The nodules are unique in formation and their presence is a clear sign of this disease. Both the nodules and the bleeding are unsightly and may interfere with the harnessing of working horses. Otherwise, they do not seem to bother the animal. No satisfactory treatment is available, but fly control may reduce the incidence.

Pelodera Dermatitis

Pelodera dermatitis is a rare skin worm infestation that causes a sudden, serious skin infection. The condition is caused when larvae of the roundworm *Pelodera strongyloides* invade the skin. These larvae are widespread in decaying organic matter (such as damp hay) and on or near the surface of moist soil. They are only occasionally parasitic. In most cases, animals are exposed to the larvae through direct contact with infested materials, such as damp, filthy bedding. Animals with healthy skin are not usually at risk of infection.

The sores usually only appear on parts of the body that contact the infested material, such as the legs, groin, abdomen, and chest. The affected skin is red and partially or completely hairless. In addition, there may be bumps in the skin, or lumps filled with pus, crusts, or ulcers. Often—though not always—there is severe itching, causing the animal to scratch, bite, or rub the infected area.

Veterinarians can usually make a definitive diagnosis by examining a skin scraping under a microscope to check for worm larvae. Animals with *Pelodera* dermatitis can be treated in the same manner as those with other skin worm infestations. In many cases, simply moving the animal to a dry area with clean bedding will lead to recovery.

■ PHOTOSENSITIZATION

Photosensitization is a condition in which skin becomes overly sensitive to ultraviolet light (sunlight). This condition is not sunburn, although the difference can be difficult to distinguish. Photosensitization occurs when certain compounds that are activated by light are present in the skin, and the skin is then exposed to ultraviolet light. The molecules present in the skin are energized by the light. When the molecules return to a less energized state, the energy released causes chemical reactions in the skin. Many chemicals, including some that are fungal and bacterial in origin, may act as photosensitizing agents. Affected areas are usually those that are lightly pigmented or that have little hair, such as the lips, eyelids, and tips of the ears.

Photosensitization is often classified according to the source of the photodynamic pigment. The categories seen most often in horses include **systemic photosensitivity** (also known as primary or type I photosensitivity) and **contact photosensitivity** (also known as secondary photosensitivity). Contact photosensitivity is more common in horses and often involves impaired liver function. A common cause of contact photosensitivity is poisoning by grazing certain plants (such as red and alsike clover) or

ingesting substances such as phosphorus or cyanobacteria.

The signs associated with photosensitivity are similar regardless of the cause. Photosensitive animals are hypersensitive when exposed to sunlight and squirm in apparent discomfort. They scratch or rub lightly pigmented, exposed areas of skin such as the ears, eyelids, or muzzle. Bright sunlight can cause typical skin lesions (ranging from hives to redness and scaling of skin), even in black-coated animals. Redness develops rapidly and is soon followed by swelling. If exposure to light stops at this stage, the abnormalities soon resolve. When exposure is prolonged, fluid discharge, scab formation, and death of skin tissue can result.

Signs are easily recognized in advanced cases of photosensitivity but are similar to the effects of sunburn in early or mild cases. Reference to the specific diseases in which photosensitization is a sign may assist your veterinarian in diagnosing the underlying disease. Evaluation of liver enzymes and liver biopsies may be necessary to confirm the presence of liver disease. Examination of blood, feces, and urine for porphyrins may also be performed.

Treatment involves mostly soothing the signs. While photosensitivity continues, animals should be shaded fully or, preferably, housed and allowed out only at night. The severe stress of photosensitization and extensive death of skin tissue can be highly harmful, even deadly. Corticosteroid injections may be helpful in the early stages. Wounds to the skin should be kept clean to minimize secondary skin infections. Exposure to flies must be prevented because skin damaged during photosensitivity attracts flies and other insects. The skin lesions heal remarkably well, even after extensive damage. The outcome for an individual horse is related to the site and severity of the primary lesion and/or liver disease, and to the degree of healing.

RINGWORM (DERMATOPHYTOSIS)

Ringworm is an infection of the skin or hair caused by a type of fungus. In horses, *Trichophyton equinum* and *Trichophyton mentagrophytes* are the primary causes of ringworm, although other fungi have also been found in ringworm infections. All of these spread easily in the environment, and some can be transmitted from horses to people.

These fungi live in the soil and cause disease in animals that are exposed while digging, rolling, and lying down. They can also spread by contact with infected individuals and contaminated objects such as stalls or grooming tools. Broken hairs with associated spores are important sources for spread of the disease. Contact does not always result in infection. Whether infection is established depends on the fungal species and on such factors as the age, health, condition of exposed skin surfaces, grooming behavior, and nutrition of the animal.

Under most circumstances, dermatophytes grow only in the dead cells of skin and hair, and infection stops on reaching living cells or inflamed tissue. As inflammation and host immunity develop, further spread of infection stops, but this process may take several weeks.

Infected animals will develop circular, bald, scaly patches with broken hairs. Common areas for ringworm to occur are the withers and saddle area, but the infection may spread to the neck, flanks, chest, or head. Occasionally 1 or more legs may also be involved.

Ringworm is diagnosed by fungal culture and direct microscopic examination of hair or skin scale. Fungal culture of hairs and scrapings from the affected areas is the most accurate method. Direct microscopic examination of hairs or skin scrapings may allow early diagnosis.

Ringworm infections usually clear up without treatment. Treatment with medicated shampoos can speed recovery in some cases. Such treatments are not always effective, however. Your veterinarian can provide you with information about any treatment that may be appropriate for your horse and advise you regarding precautions you should take to avoid ringworm infection in yourself and members of your family.

SADDLE SORES (COLLAR GALLS)

This skin condition of horses is caused by the constant rubbing of poorly fitted saddles and harness. The area of riding horses that is under the saddle, or the shoulder area of those driven in harness, is frequently the site of injuries to the skin and deeper soft and bony tissues.

Signs vary according to the depth of injury and the presence of any secondary infections. Sores affecting only the skin are characterized by inflammation; redness; the presence of bumps, cysts, or blisters; and finally skin tissue death. Frequently, the condition starts as an inflammation of the hair follicles; the follicles may become filled with pus. Affected areas show hair loss and are swollen, warm, and painful. The pus dries and forms crusts. Advanced sores are called galls. When the skin and underlying tissues are damaged more seriously, abscesses may develop. Severe damage to the skin and deeper tissues results in skin death. If the sores are not treated (and the cause corrected), deep abscesses, scarring, and localized loss of feeling may occur.

Identification and elimination of the offending portion of tack is more important

Typical saddle sores on a horse

than any other treatment. Wounds and inflammation of the skin of the saddle and harness regions are treated as any other skin wounds. Absolute rest of the affected parts is necessary. During the early or acute stages, astringent packs are often prescribed. Chronic sores and those superficially infected may be treated by warm applications and appropriate antibiotics. Hematomas (pockets of bloody fluid) should be drained. Dead tissue should be removed surgically. If infections are present, antibiotics will be prescribed.

▨ TICKS

Ticks are blood-sucking parasites that attach themselves to animals and people. As they feed, ticks can transmit a number of diseases. Skin wounds caused by ticks can lead to secondary bacterial infections and screwworm infestations. Severe tick infestations can lead to anemia and death. The international movement of horses infected with the tick-transmitted blood parasites *Theileria*, *Babesia*, *Anaplasma*, and *Cowdria* species is widely restricted.

Each species of tick has a favored feeding site on a host, although in dense infestations, ticks may attach themselves wherever they can find a feeding location. Some ticks feed chiefly on the head, neck, shoulders, and pubic area. In other species, the favored sites may be ears, near the anus and under the tail, or in nasal passages.

Direct contact with ticks frequently results in tick infestation. Animals that spend time outdoors, especially in wild areas, are more often affected. Thus, among horses, animals roaming in the wild or being ridden in wilderness areas are mostly likely to be infested, although any horse spending time outside can acquire ticks.

There is one tick that can hide unusually well. This is the *Otobius megnini*, also called the **spinous ear tick**. These ticks prefer to attach themselves in the ears of their hosts and are often overlooked by horse owners and other animal

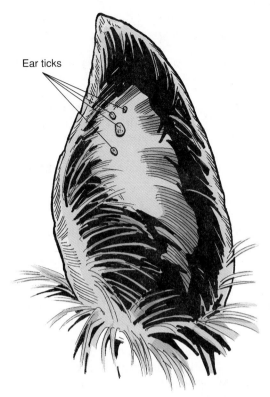

Spinous ear tick (*Otobius megnini*)

care givers. These ticks are found in dry areas of the western US and in Mexico and western Canada. Horses can suffer severe irritation from ear canal infestations. The infestations may cause paralysis. Secondary infections by larval screwworms are also reported.

The definitive sign of tick infestation is the presence of a tick on the animal. Ticks that have been on an animal only a short time (an hour to a few days) appear flat. Ticks that have been on an animal for several hours or days appear much more rounded due to the blood they have consumed. Diagnosis is by appearance of tick bite marks on the animal and the presence of the offending pest.

Treatment and Control

Ticks should be removed as soon as possible to minimize disease and damage. To remove a tick correctly, use tweezers to carefully grasp the tick close to the skin and pull gently. Never try to remove a tick with your bare hands, as some tick-borne diseases can be immediately transmitted through breaks in your skin or contact with mucous membranes. The use of hot matches to remove ticks should also be avoided. Infested horses should also be treated with insecticides that kill attached larvae, nymphs, and adults. Contact your veterinarian for a prescription or a recommendation for the best tick control product for your horse. Be sure to tell the veterinarian what other animals you have because this may make a difference in the veterinarian's recommendation. Monitor the site(s) from which you have removed ticks. If a tick bite site turns red or swells, a call to the veterinarian is warranted.

If a horse is severely infested with ticks, it is recommended that you immediately contact your veterinarian regarding tick removal. Heavy infestations will not only severely damage the skin, but the chances of anemia and other complications are high.

Keeping animals away from tick-prone areas is the most effective step you can take to control exposure. Most ticks live in particular microhabitats, such as tall grass or the borders between pastures and woodlands. Destruction of these microhabitats reduces the number of ticks. Removing tall grass and weeds from your property and keeping pastures mowed can help protect your horse. Insecticide treatment of vegetation can slightly reduce the risk of ticks. However, it is not recommended for wide use because of environmental pollution and the cost of treating large areas.

■ TUMORS OF THE SKIN

Tumors are abnormal growths of cells. Tumors affecting the skin or the tissue just under the skin are the most commonly seen tumors in horses. Skin tumors are diagnosed more frequently in part because they are the most easily seen tumors and in part because the skin is constantly exposed to the external environment and the many tumor-causing factors in the environment. Chemicals, solar radiation, and viruses are just some of the things that can cause skin tumors. Hormonal abnormalities and genetic factors may also play a role in the development of tumors in and close to the skin.

All of the various layers and components of skin have the potential of developing distinctive tumors. Skin tumors can appear in many forms. Distinguishing a tumor from an inflammatory disease can sometimes be difficult. Tumors are usually small lumps or bumps, but they also can occur as hairless or discolored patches, wheals, or nonhealing ulcers. Because skin tumors are so diverse, identifying them should be left to a veterinarian.

Tumors may be benign or malignant (cancerous). Benign tumors do not spread to other parts of the body. Malignant tumors can spread and cause harm to the horse. Several types of malignant tumors of the skin are relatively common in horses, including melanoma, squamous cell carcinoma, and sarcoids. Distinguishing a benign tumor from a malignant tumor requires specialized knowledge and laboratory equipment. A veterinarian can perform a fine needle aspiration of cells or a biopsy (a procedure that removes a small amount of tissue from a tumor) for further examination.

Treatment depends largely on the type of tumor, its location and size, and the overall physical condition of the horse. For benign tumors that are not ulcerated and do not impair the horse's normal routine, no treatment may be necessary. This may be the most prudent option, especially in aged horses. For malignant tumors or benign tumors that inhibit normal activities or are cosmetically unpleasant, there are several treatment options. For most tumors, surgical removal is the most effective. It is also probably the least costly option and the one with the fewest adverse effects. If malignancy is suspected, a margin of tissue surrounding the tumor will also be removed. For tumors that cannot be completely removed, partial removal may prolong the life of the horse. Radiation treatment or chemotherapy may also be used to provide your horse with a better outcome.

Basal Cell Tumors and Carcinomas

Basal cell tumors and basal cell carcinomas include tumors of the hair roots, cysts on the base of hairs, sweat gland tumors, connective tissue tumors, and more. Even though tumors commonly occur in or near the skin, many of these are either benign (not cancerous) or treatable if found early. Thus, as with human tumors, early treatment offers the best possibility for a successful outcome.

Basal cell tumors are uncommon in horses. Most basal cell tumors in horses are benign. These tumors generally appear as firm, solitary, often hairless or ulcerated lumps. The lumps may stick out like stalks from the skin surface. They vary in size from less than 0.4 inches to more than 4 inches (less than 1 to more than 10 centimeters) in diameter. These tumors are sometimes dark in color. Cysts may also form. Although basal cell tumors are benign, their growth may cause extensive ulceration and secondary inflammation. Surgical removal is effective and the treatment most often used for these tumors.

Basal cell carcinomas are the malignant (cancerous) form of these tumors. They are not common in horses. These often appear as ulcers on the head, extremities, or neck. Unlike benign basal cell tumors, these carcinomas generally are not raised up from the skin. Also, they spread, forming new ulcers. Consequently, surgical removal is the treatment of choice. These tumors spread to neighboring skin but seldom spread to other organs. Surgical removal is the best treatment.

Collagenous Nevi

Collagenous nevi are a benign buildup of collagen. They are rare in horses. They generally are found in middle-aged or older animals, most frequently on the legs, head, neck, and areas prone to trauma. They are flat to raised lumps that develop in the dermis skin layer or fat beneath the skin. Surgical removal is generally effective. Infrequently, some may grow too large to be surgically removed. Surgical removal is optional, but a biopsy is recommended to confirm the diagnosis.

Equine Sarcoids

Equine sarcoids are the most frequently recognized tumor in horses. A viral cause is suspected, and both papillomavirus and retrovirus particles have been identified in these tumors. Sarcoids are probably transmitted by direct contact or contaminated brushes and needles. Sarcoids tend to develop in families and occur most commonly in horses less than 4 years of age. They may be found anywhere on the body, and most affected horses have multiple tumors. The limbs are affected most frequently.

Sarcoids vary greatly in appearance, and 4 manifestations are recognized: 1) warty, which may be confused with papillomas

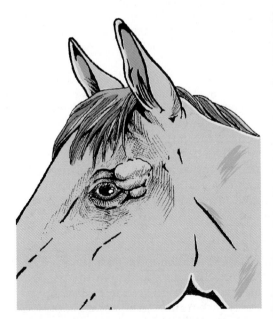

The appearance of sarcoids can resemble a fleshy or wart-like growth (shown), a slightly raised nodule, or a patch of ringworm (uncommon).

or squamous cell carcinomas; 2) fibroblastic, which may be confused with granulation tissue or fibromas; 3) flat, which may be confused with flat warts; and 4) mixed verrucous and fibroblastic, which may be confused with fibropapillomas. They should be considered tumors of partial malignancy; they may not spread to distant locations but are locally invasive.

Treatment generally involves surgery to remove the greater part of larger tumors, followed by freezing (cryosurgery). Nontreated tumors may regress spontaneously, although more than 50% of equine sarcoids recur after surgery. Radiation treatment may be used when sarcoids develop in locations not suitable for cryosurgery or surgical removal.

Fibromatosis

Fibromatosis is a thickening and invasive growth in tendon sheaths. Fibromatosis appears only infrequently in horses. The growths appear as locally invasive, well-defined nodules or lumps scattered throughout the tissues. They do not spread to other areas of the body, although they can be locally invasive. Surgical removal is the recommended treatment in most cases; however, the nodules are likely to recur. Radiation treatment may be used for local control.

Keratinized Skin Cysts

A cyst is a thin-walled sac that fills with fluid or semifluid material. In some cases, cysts develop that are filled with keratins (fiber-like proteins that form nails, hooves, and horns). These are described as keratinized skin cysts. Such cysts have a hard or solid core. They are rare in horses.

There are several kinds of keratinized skin cysts. The ones found in horses are usually limited to dermoid cysts and keratomas.

Dermoid cysts are congenital malformations found on the back of the head or along the spine. Thoroughbred horses are the breed most likely to develop dermoid cysts. These cysts are different from other cysts in that they contain fully formed hair shafts.

Keratomas are cystic lesions in the hoof wall of the toe or, less frequently, the quarter or heel in horses. They often occur following a traumatic injury. Although the horse with a keratoma in its early stages may show no signs of the cyst, keratomas often cause lameness and deformity of the hoof wall or sole and may be associated with degradation in bones associated with the hoof.

Diagnosis is by finding the cysts on the animal. These skin cysts can be solitary or multiple. They are benign and do not spread to other parts of the body. In many cases, surgical removal is the best treatment for keratinized cysts. Because these cysts usually look like large pimples, some owners are tempted to squeeze the cyst. This should be avoided, as squeezing the cyst often releases the contents of the cyst into the body where they can cause a severe inflammatory response. Your veterinarian will have the tools and knowledge to safely deal with the cysts on your horse.

Lipomas and Liposarcomas

Lipomas are benign tumors of fat (adipose) tissue. These are occasionally found in horses. Affected horses are generally younger than 2 years of age. Lipomas typically appear as soft, occasionally thin, discrete lumpy masses, and most move freely when touched.

Surgical removal is the recommended treatment. Many lipomas merge with healthy fat tissue next to them, making it difficult for the surgeon to identify the edges of the tumor. Despite their benign nature, lipomas should not be ignored because they tend to grow.

Liposarcomas are rare tumors of fat tissue. They are malignant tumors that have a low growth potential. Liposarcomas are lumpy and soft to firm. Surgical removal of both the tumor and surrounding tissue is recommended. Recurrence is common, so followup radiation treatment may be required.

Lymphoid Skin Tumors

Nonepitheliotropic cutaneous lympho-sarcoma is the most frequently recognized form of skin lymphosarcoma in horses. The disease may be recognized at any age but is most common in young and middle-aged animals. Firm lumps are noted in the fat under the skin surface of the lower body surface. There are 2 types of nonepitheliotropic cutaneous lymphosarcoma in horses. Differentiation between these forms is important because the monomorphic form of the disease progresses rapidly. In contrast, the lymphohistiocytic form seldom spreads and affected horses may live for years. As the lympho-histiocytic form progresses, the lumps tend to become more frequent on the lower neck regions. In many cases, eutha-nasia may be necessary when tumors cause difficulty in breathing.

Because of the expense of antitumor drugs, treatment is generally limited to corticosteroids administered by mouth or by injection. Remission, if it happens at all, is usually short term.

Mast Cell Tumors

Skin mast cell tumors are a unique tumor form named for the type of skin cell from which they grow. Other names for these tumors are mastocytomas and mast cell sarcomas. In horses, mast cell tumors are uncommon, benign tumors.

These tumors may develop anywhere on the body but are most common on the head and legs. Typically, there is a single, solitary mass in the dermis skin layer or in fat under the skin that may expand to involve the underlying muscles. The tumor begins as a lump. As the tumor evolves, the central lump becomes sur-rounded by dead tissue and pus. In the late stages, the dead tissue hardens and mast cells may be very difficult to identify. Hair loss and ulcers can occur. A variant of skin mast cell tumor is seen in new-born foals, in which the tumors may become widespread but disappear over time. Surgical removal is the treatment of choice. These tumors do not spread to other organs and surgical removal usually cures the disease.

Melanomas

A melanoma is a dark-pigmented skin tumor. In human medical terminology, all melanomas are malignant. Among ani-mals, however, melanomas may be either benign (not cancerous) or malignant (can-cerous). Most melanomas found in horses occur in those with gray coats, in which the coat turns gray (or white) with age. They are especially common in Lipizzan-ers, Arabians, and Percherons. It has been found that up to 80% of gray or white horses of these breeds may be affected.

Tumors can appear as spots or patches, or raised or flat masses. Most have a dark surface. Although often solitary, tumors may be multiple, especially in the breeds at risk. They generally occur in older horses but usually begin their develop-ment when the animals are 3 to 4 years old. The perineum and the base of the tail are the most common sites of develop-ment, but these tumors may develop in any location, including the ears. They increase in size and number over time. Although most are benign, there are malignant variants that spread to other organs.

Melanomas of nongray horses are rare tumors usually found on the trunk and legs of young horses less than 2 years old. Masses appear as solitary lumps. Most are benign. However, congenital malignant melanomas may infrequently develop. Such tumors are invasive, but with little potential to spread to other organs.

Treatment consists of surgical removal or freezing. However, affected animals tend to develop additional tumors. Little is known about the use of radiation or chemotherapy for treatment. If the tumors are benign, the outcome is excellent. For malignant tumors, the outlook is guarded.

Neurofibromas and Neurofibrosarcomas

Neurofibromas and neurofibrosarcomas are tumors that grow in the connective tissue around a nerve. These tumors appear as white, firm lumps. There are benign and somewhat malignant types. In horses, most are locally invasive but do not spread to other locations. Complete surgical removal is the treatment of choice. Followup radiation treatment is often prescribed to slow regrowth of the tumor.

Sebaceous Gland Tumors

The sebaceous glands secrete the oil known as sebum into the hair follicles and onto the skin. Tumors and tumor-like conditions of sebaceous glands are rare in horses. **Sebaceous gland adenomas** are typically over 0.4 inches (1 centimeter) in size. They are often multiple and may occur anywhere on the body but are commonly found on the head. Sebaceous adenomas may be covered with a crust and inflamed. Treatment is optional for benign sebaceous gland tumors unless they are inflamed and infected, in which case surgical removal is necessary. Animals that develop one sebaceous gland tumor often develop new tumors at other sites. Your veterinarian may consult with a veterinary oncologist or veterinary dermatologist for assistance in the treatment of these tumors.

Soft Tissue Giant Cell Tumors (Malignant Fibrous Histiocytomas)

Soft tissue giant cell tumors are occasionally found in horses. Occurring in young adult to middle-aged horses, they are firm, lumpy to diffuse swellings, with variable bleeding. Soft tissue giant cell tumors are sarcomas of possible malignancy. They seldom spread but tend to return after surgical removal. Surgical removal is the normal recommended treatment for these tumors. Both the tumor and some of the surrounding tissue will be removed to reduce the chance of recurrence.

Squamous Cell Carcinomas

Squamous cell carcinomas are thought to arise from regions in the outer root

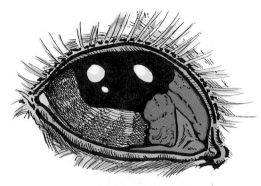

Squamous cell carcinoma is relatively common in horses.

sheath of the hair follicle. Although most arise without known cause, prolonged exposure to sunlight is believed to be a major predisposing factor. Squamous cell carcinomas are the most common malignant skin tumor in horses. They are most frequently seen in adult or aged horses with white or part-white coats. The breeds most at risk are Appaloosa, Belgian, American Paint, and Pinto.

Although squamous cell carcinomas can arise on any part of the body, in horses they are seen most frequently in nonpigmented, poorly haired areas near mucous membranes. Thus, the tumors can be seen most frequently around the eyes, lips, nose, anus, and external genitalia (especially the sheath around the penis). Most squamous cell carcinomas are solitary tumors. They appear as raised, irregular masses with either ulcers or pimples. Solitary tumors grow slowly. Thus, these tumors are often overlooked until defects appear on the ear tips, openings of the nose, or eyelids.

For horses, radiotherapy using surface or interstitial brachytherapy is the treatment of choice for squamous cell carcinomas. Other options include chemotherapy implants, freezing (cryosurgery), and surgical removal. If surgery is used to remove these tumors, the skin needs to be removed at least 0.8 inches (2 centimeters) around the tumor. Surgical removal may be combined with radiation or chemotherapy. Survival rates depend on the malignancy of the tumor and its size before treatment. Tumors close to each other are more likely to spread or return within 20 weeks of surgical removal. In general, when surgery fails to eliminate the tumors, the problem can be traced to late diagnosis and uncontrolled local disease rather than to spread of the cancer to distant tissues.

Limiting exposure to ultraviolet radiation may help prevent squamous cell carcinomas, especially in horses with white or partially white coats. This may be accomplished by providing face shades, providing shade in pastures and other open areas where the horse spends time, or keeping the horse stabled during hours of peak sunlight.

Sweat Gland Tumors

There are 2 types of sweat glands: eccrine and apocrine. Horses do not have eccrine sweat glands. Apocrine glands are present in all hair follicles across the body. **Apocrine gland adenomas** are rare in horses. They appear as firm to variable cysts, seldom larger than 1.6 inches (4 centimeters) in diameter. They occur at the base of the sweat gland and contain varying amounts of clear to brownish fluid. The ears and vulva are the most likely regions to develop these tumors. Apocrine adenomas are benign, and complete surgical removal cures the condition.

Apocrine gland adenocarcinomas are malignant tumors of sweat glands. They are also rare in horses. Apocrine gland adenocarcinomas generally are larger than adenomas. Appearance varies from thick lumps to ulcers. They spread frequently across the skin and, less commonly, to other organs. Complete surgical removal, including removal of surrounding tissue, is the recommended treatment.

Tumors Originating Outside the Skin (Metastatic Tumors)

The spread of a primary tumor to the skin is unusual. All malignant tumors are capable of spreading to the skin. Although appearance is variable, the tumors most commonly are multiple, ulcerated lumps. As these tumors evolve, they extend deeper into the skin and surrounding tissue. Generally, it is difficult to identify the primary tumor based on the signs in the skin. This is because only a small population of cells in the primary tumor will spread to the skin, and these cells may have different microscopic features.

Vascular Tumors

Vascular tumors of the skin and soft tissues are benign growths that closely resemble blood vessels. These tumors are usually found on the head, legs, and abdomen. In horses, they are most common on the lower legs of animals less than 1 year old. **Hemangiomas** are single to multiple, circular, often compressible, red to black lumps that may resemble a "blood blister." Hemangiomas are benign, but they tend to develop ulcers and grow quite large. Surgical removal is the recommended treatment. However, the tumors may be large and involve the lower legs, making removal difficult. In these cases, freezing or radiation treatment may be needed. More tumors do not usually develop at new sites after complete surgical removal.

Angiosarcomas can vary greatly in appearance. Most commonly, they appear as 1 or more red lumps in the skin or underlying soft tissues. Less frequently, they appear as a poorly defined bruise. Tumors that appear in the underlying soft tissues tend to be more aggressive. Surgical removal of both the tumor and a margin of surrounding tissue is the recommended treatment. The tumors in the skin do not seem to spread or invade local tissues, and recurrence rather than spread to distant locations is more common after surgical removal. These tumors seem to arise spontaneously, but chronic injury due to sun exposure may play a role in their development, especially in white-coated animals. Surface tumors are easily controlled with freezing (cryosurgery) as needed. Avoidance of further sun exposure may reduce the development of new tumors.

Warts (Papillomas)

Warts are caused by papillomaviruses. The virus is transmitted by direct contact or by contact with infected items such as bedding, blankets, saddles and other tack, and hard surfaces in the horse's environment. It is also possible that insects may spread papillomaviruses. There are several distinct papillomaviruses. Among companion animals, papillomas are most common in horses and dogs.

Multiple warts of skin or mucus membranes generally are seen in younger animals. Single warts are more frequent in older animals, but they may not always be caused by viral infection. The period between the initial infection and the development of visible warts varies but normally takes several months.

Most warts appear as bumps with a hardened surface resembling a cauliflower. When multiple warts are present they may be sufficiently characteristic to make a diagnosis. However, there are many things that look like warts and a definitive diagnosis may require identification of the virus or its effects on individual cells.

In horses, small, scattered papillomas develop on the nose, lips, eyelids, bottoms of legs, penis, vulva, mammary glands, and inner surfaces of the ears. Warts are often seen following mild skin abrasions. They can be a problem in a herd, especially when young horses are kept together. Warts on foals may shrink or disappear in a few months as the foal's immune system matures. When warts develop in mature horses, they often persist for over a year. Equine warts are disfiguring but benign. They should, however, be distinguished from verrucose equine sarcoids (*see* page 776). Warts will usually go away on their own, although the duration of warts varies considerably. A variety of treatments have been advocated with uncertain results. Surgical removal is recommended if the warts are sufficiently objectionable. However, because surgery in the early growing stage of warts may lead to recurrence and stimulation of growth, the warts should be removed when near their maximum size or when regressing. Affected animals may be isolated from susceptible ones, but with the long incubation period (months), many are likely to have been exposed before the problem is recognized.

Congenital papillomas of foals are rare and are probably a developmental defect rather than a result of papilloma virus infection. They are found anywhere on the body but most commonly on the head. Thoroughbreds may be predisposed. Present at birth, the lesions are often several centimeters in diameter, hairless, highly raised, with an uneven surface reminiscent of a cauliflower. They are benign, and surgical removal cures the condition.

CHAPTER **55**

Kidney and Urinary Tract Disorders

▓ THE URINARY SYSTEM

The urinary system or tract includes the kidneys, the ureters (tubes that connect the kidneys to the bladder), the bladder, and the urethra (the tube through which urine exits the body). The urinary system has several important functions. It gets rid of the waste products that are created when food is transformed into energy. It also maintains the correct balance of

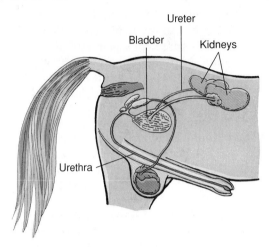

The urinary system in male horses

water and electrolytes (salts) within the body's cells. Another key function is the production of hormones called erythropoietin and renin, which are important in maintaining healthy blood pressure, producing blood cells, and absorbing salt correctly. Finally, the urinary system processes vitamin D.

■ DETECTING DISORDERS OF THE KIDNEYS AND URINARY TRACT

Your veterinarian can diagnose most urinary system problems by taking a history of how your horse has acted in the days prior to becoming sick, performing a physical examination, and performing tests on the horse's blood and urine. The history that your veterinarian takes might include information regarding changes in how much water your horse drinks, how often it urinates, how much urine it produces, how the urine looks, and how your horse behaves. Your veterinarian will also need information about what medications your horse has taken or is currently taking, your horse's appetite, diet, changes in body weight, and previous illnesses or injuries.

There are many tests a veterinarian might perform in the case of a urinary disorder. These include blood tests, blood pressure measurement, urinalysis, x-rays, contrast x-rays (tests in which a special dye is given to outline the urinary tract on the x-ray), ultrasonography, biopsies, and endoscopic evaluation of the urethra and bladder.

Urinalysis is a laboratory test that evaluates urine. It is one of the most important tools a veterinarian can use to diagnose urinary tract problems. Many tests are performed as part of a urinalysis. These include urine specific gravity, which is an indication of how concentrated the urine sample is; color; turbidity or cloudiness of the urine; and pH (how acidic or alkaline the urine sample is). Urinalysis also tests for the presence of certain chemicals or substances in the urine, such as sugar, ketones (a byproduct of the body's processing of fat), bilirubin (a pigment produced when the liver processes waste), blood, and protein. The urine sediment is examined under a microscope to look for things such as red blood cells, white blood cells, other cells, bacteria, and crystals.

Endoscopic evaluation is another valuable source of diagnostic information for a veterinarian. A small flexible tube with a camera located at its tip is inserted through the horse's urethra and can be used to visualize the urethra and sometimes the bladder. This provides a good way to identify problems such as obstructions of the urethra, tumors, or malformations.

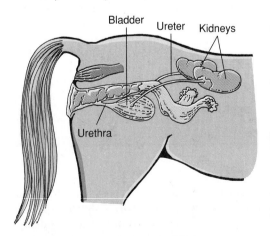

The urinary system in female horses

CONGENITAL AND INHERITED DISORDERS OF THE URINARY SYSTEM

Certain urinary tract abnormalities are inherited or congenital (present at birth). These abnormalities are caused by abnormal genes or produced by injury, disease, or exposure to toxic substances in the womb. They may or may not cause health problems for your horse later in life. These types of abnormalities are very rare in horses, but they are important to consider if your horse has urinary tract problems.

Kidney Malformations

Kidney malformations, called **dysplasias**, occur when a horse's kidneys do not develop properly before birth. When the kidneys are unusually small, the condition is called **hypoplasia**. Dysplasia can occur in either one or both kidneys. When these conditions occur, the kidneys are usually small, firm, and pale. The outer portion of the kidney that contains glomeruli (microscopic structures that are critical for filtering blood) may be smaller than normal in size.

Horses with these conditions typically have a buildup in the blood of the toxic waste products that are normally excreted in the urine. An affected horse usually has ongoing, excessive thirst (called polydipsia) and corresponding excessive urination (polyuria), as well as other signs of kidney disease such as weakness, lack of appetite, abdominal pain, fever, or swelling of the legs.

Your veterinarian can usually diagnose dysplasia or hypoplasia based on these signs and appropriate tests. The diagnosis can be confirmed with a biopsy of the kidneys.

Failure to Develop

Rarely, one or both kidneys fail to develop. This condition is always accompanied by a lack of the tube connecting the kidney to the bladder (ureter). The reproductive organs may also be underdeveloped. A foal in which both kidneys have failed to develop will die shortly after birth. However, a horse with one functioning kidney can usually live a full and healthy life. In this case, the failure of one kidney to develop is usually discovered by accident.

Polycystic Kidneys

Polycystic kidneys have multiple cysts inside the functional part of the organ. The kidneys are greatly enlarged, which a veterinarian may be able to feel during a physical examination. Horses with this condition sometimes also have cysts in the bile ducts of the liver. Problems caused by this condition can range from none at all to progressive kidney failure. Your veterinarian can diagnose polycystic kidneys based on examining your horse, using x-rays or ultrasonography, or performing exploratory abdominal surgery.

Other Kidney Disorders

Other congenital problems include kidneys that are not positioned correctly, kidneys that are fused together, and **nephroblastoma**, a cancer that develops in the kidneys during embryonic development (before birth).

Disorders of the Ureters

Several abnormalities can affect the ureter, the tube that connects the kidneys to the bladder. Normal, healthy horses have 2 ureters, 1 for each kidney.

An **ectopic ureter** is one that opens somewhere other than into the bladder. Ectopic ureters can connect to the urethra (the tube used for urination), or in females, the uterus or vagina. This defect is rare in horses.

Other abnormalities of the ureter include failure to develop or abnormal development, the presence of more than the usual 2 ureters, and ureterocele (enlargement of the portion of the ureter that connects to the bladder). Ureterocele can usually be successfully treated with surgery.

Urachal Remnants

The urachus is a cord of fibrous tissue that normally extends from the bladder to the navel. Before birth, the urachus is a tube that connects the bladder to the umbilical cord so that wastes can be removed. After birth, it normally closes and becomes a solid cord. In some animals, however, the urachus does not close properly after birth. Depending on which portion of the urachus remains open, these abnormalities are called a **patent urachus** or an **umbilical urachal sinus**. Other problems include urachal diverticula (small sac-like structures attached to the urachus) and urachal cysts. Signs include an inability to control urination, urine scalding (due to the fact that urine is acidic) of the skin near the navel, and urinary tract infections. Your veterinarian can diagnose these problems using x-rays taken after a special dye is given intravenously. Treatment usually includes surgery and, sometimes, antibiotics.

Disorders of the Bladder

The bladder is a muscular sac that stores urine produced by the kidneys. Several congenital and inherited problems can affect the bladder. These include the presence of more than one bladder, an abnormally developed or underdeveloped bladder, failure of the bladder to develop, and a bladder that is turned inside-out. Usually these problems occur along with other abnormalities in the urinary tract. Your veterinarian can diagnose these problems based on physical examination, observation of your horse while it urinates, and contrast x-rays. Treatment varies depending on the type of problem.

Disorders of the Urethra

The urethra connects the bladder to the exterior of the body. It is the tube through which urine passes when a horse urinates. Congenital urethral problems are rare in horses. Some of the conditions that do occur include failure of the urethra to develop, a urethra that does not open all the way or does not open at all, openings of the urethra that are on the underside or on top of the penis rather than on the tip in males, multiple urethras, urethral diverticula (small pouches that form in the urethra that

become inflamed and painful), an abnormal opening between the urethra and the rectum, and an unusually narrow urethra.

■ INFECTIOUS DISEASES OF THE URINARY SYSTEM

Infections of the urinary system are often caused by bacteria. The infection may develop on its own (for example, when bacteria enter the body through the urethra) or as the result of a problem in the urinary tract (for example, obstruction of the lower urinary tract by stones).

Several factors increase the risk of urinary system infection. These include problems with urine flow (especially not being able to empty the bladder completely during urination), overly dilute urine, sugar in the urine (often a sign of diabetes), older age, a weakened immune system, and the presence of other diseases. Healthy horses seem to be relatively resistant to urinary tract infections.

Bladder Infection

Infection and inflammation of the bladder caused by bacteria is called **bacterial cystitis**. In horses, cystitis is likely to be the result of an obstruction in the urinary tract or paralysis of the bladder (which may be the result of nerve damage). Cystitis can also occur in mares with chronic inflammation of the vagina.

Signs of cystitis include loss of control over urination, frequent urination, urine dribbling, urine scalding, and straining to urinate. There may also be blood in the urine. If nerve damage is the cause, other signs such as paralysis of the anus or tail may also occur.

A urine sample is needed to diagnose bacterial cystitis. Treatment includes antibiotics targeted to be effective against the bacteria causing infection, as well as identifying and treating any underlying causes for the cystitis.

Kidney Infection (Pyelonephritis)

Pyelonephritis is inflammation of the kidneys. This is usually caused by a bacterial infection in the urinary tract that climbed upwards into the bladder and then continued into the kidneys. The risk factors for pyelonephritis and those for bacterial cystitis are similar. Stones in the kidney or ureter, which prevent urine from flowing normally, are a common cause.

Signs of pyelonephritis include pain in the sides, especially in the area around the kidneys; fever; weight loss; and a general sense of not feeling well. Other signs include excessive thirst or excessive urination. Diagnosis of this condition requires blood and urine tests. Longterm cases may not show abnormalities on these tests. If this is the case, x-rays or ultrasonography may be needed. Treatment for pyelonephritis includes high dosages of antibiotics. In some cases, intravenous fluids or even surgery to remove the affected kidney may be required.

Interstitial Nephritis

Interstitial nephritis is another type of inflammation of the kidney and is usually the result of bacterial infection. Infectious diseases that affect the blood vessels can spread to become interstitial nephritis. As part of the immune response to these infections, collections of antibodies damage the kidneys and cause kidney failure. Antibiotics may be needed to treat the infection. Kidney failure, if it has occurred, may be treated with supportive treatment, including fluids.

Leptospirosis

Infection with *Leptospira* bacteria is most commonly associated with eye infections (uveitis) and abortions in adult horses. However, in foals it can also lead to kidney failure (for additional information, *see* page 807). Infection can be effectively treated with appropriate antibiotics.

▓ NONINFECTIOUS DISEASES OF THE URINARY SYSTEM

Not every disease is caused by infection with bacteria, viruses, or other outside agents. There are a variety of noninfectious disorders that can impair the urinary system. All of these diseases and condi-

tions can be serious threats to the health of your horse.

Kidney Dysfunction

The kidneys' most important function is to filter waste from the blood. When this does not happen properly, waste products can build to dangerous levels in the blood. This is called azotemia. Azotemia can also occur as a result of urine not being able to flow properly through the urinary tract. This process damages the kidneys and, over time, leads to kidney failure.

Chronic Kidney Disease and Kidney Failure

Longterm, or chronic, disease can damage the kidney so severely that it is not able to function properly. This happens slowly. Chronic kidney disease often continues for many months or years before any signs appear. There is rarely anything

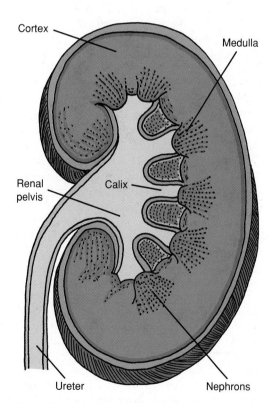

The kidneys consist of an outer part (cortex) and an inner part (medulla). The nephrons filter the blood and produce urine (modified with permission from *The Merck Manual of Medical Information*, Second Home Edition, 2003).

that a veterinarian can do to treat existing damage or prevent further damage once the process has started. Occasionally, chronic kidney disease results from a problem that is inherited or an abnormality present at birth; however, most of the time it is a problem related to old age.

Determining the cause of chronic kidney disease, especially in the early stages, will help determine the appropriate treatment and allow your veterinarian to determine the outlook for your horse. Some of the common causes include diseases of the circulatory system (such as high blood pressure, problems with blood clotting, and not having enough oxygen in the blood) or other diseases of the kidneys such as pyelonephritis (see page 784) or tumors. Whatever the cause, chronic kidney disease usually results in scarring of the kidneys, which worsens over time.

Veterinarians may be able to detect a problem in a blood test or on physical examination even before the horse develops signs of kidney failure. Usually, the earliest signs are unexplained weight loss, excessive thirst, and excessive urination. However, these signs may signal other diseases as well. To diagnose chronic kidney disease, veterinarians generally use a combination of x-rays, ultrasonography, urine and blood tests, and physical examination. These tests are also used to check the response to treatment and monitor complications related to the kidney disease.

Treatment involves identifying the underlying cause of kidney disease and treating it, if possible, along with any complications. The recommended treatment depends on the stage of disease. If kidney failure has occurred, supportive treatment such as intravenous fluids and feeding tubes may be recommended. In most cases, the outlook for longterm survival in horses with kidney failure is poor.

Acute Kidney Disease

Acute kidney disease is the result of sudden, major damage to the kidneys. This damage is usually caused by toxic chemicals either consumed by your horse or built up by an abnormal condition in your horse's body. Kidney function can also be affected when the kidneys do not receive sufficient oxygen, such as when a blood clot blocks the flow of blood to the kidneys. Other causes of acute kidney disease include severe dehydration, bleeding, infections involving the entire body, and general anesthesia.

Mild kidney disease often goes unnoticed. However, repeated occurrences can lead to chronic kidney disease (see page 785). It is important to determine whether the kidney disease is acute or chronic, as well as the cause of the disease. This information will help your veterinarian determine the most appropriate treatment.

Glomerular Disease

The glomerulus is one of the structures that are essential for kidney function (see FIGURE, page 293). It is made up of special blood vessels that help filter blood. Each kidney contains hundreds of thousands of these structures, or glomeruli. Glomerular disease sometimes causes kidney disease.

Glomerular disease can occur due to the effects of high blood pressure, hyperadrenocorticism (an excess of cortisol), or amyloidosis (a disorder in which abnormally folded protein is deposited in the glomeruli). Some glomerular disease is immune-mediated, that is, caused by the horse's immune system attacking parts of its own body.

Disease in the glomerulus often leads to protein in the urine, low levels of protein in the blood, a buildup of fluid in the abdomen (which can cause visible swelling), shortness of breath, and swelling in the legs. The loss of protein through the urine can cause loss of muscle tissue. Most horses with glomerular disease eventually develop chronic kidney disease and kidney failure.

A biopsy of the kidneys is often required to determine the cause of the glomerular disease. Additional tests may be necessary in some cases, including x-rays, ultrasonography, and special blood tests.

Treatment for glomerular disease varies according to the underlying cause. In addition, kidney failure should be treated with appropriate medications.

Renal Tubular Problems

Renal tubules are structures in the kidneys that help filter blood. Healthy kidneys help the body to get rid of acid by producing urine that is very acidic. Diseased kidneys cannot get rid of acid properly, and instead of being eliminated in the urine, this acid builds up in the blood, leading to a condition called **uremic acidosis**. This condition can also occur when there are defects in the renal tubules, in which case it is called **renal tubular acidosis**. These defects are rare in horses. Treatment may involve medications to rebalance the amount of acid in the blood. Some horses may recover with treatment, but the outlook is guarded.

Tumors

Tumors that originate in the urinary tract are rare in horses. In the kidney, **renal cell carcinoma** occurs in older horses. Usually only one kidney is involved. If the tumor spreads to the lungs or lymph nodes, the outlook is poor. Tumors that may develop in the bladder include **squamous cell carcinoma** and **transitional cell carcinoma**. Bladder tumors are usually malignant, and there is no effective treatment. Signs of tumors in the urinary tract include blood in the urine, abdominal pain, and, for tumors of the kidney, signs of kidney disease or failure.

Urinary Stones (Uroliths, Calculi)

Uroliths are stones (also known as calculi) formed when minerals that naturally occur in urine clump together to form tiny crystals. These stones can develop anywhere in the urinary tract, including the kidney, ureter, bladder, or urethra. The formation of uroliths is not common in horses. It can affect young horses but is seen most frequently to adults. There is no one breed that is more prone to urolithiasis than another; however, it is seen more frequently in males than females.

Uroliths in horses can be anywhere from 0.2 to 8 inches (0.5 to 20 centimeters) in size, weigh as much as 14 pounds (6.5 kilograms), and are found most often in the bladder. There are many different types of stones, each formed from a complex mixture of various minerals. Veterinarians are not sure how or why stones form in horses, although they suspect that feeding your horse food or water that is high in mineral content may play a role. Kidney stones may develop in horses with renal papillary necrosis, a disorder of the kidney in which areas of the kidney die off.

Signs and Diagnosis

Signs vary depending on where the stone is located. Most stones are located in the bladder and cause blood in the urine and increased thirst and urination. Occasionally, stones are found in other parts of the urinary system, including the kidneys.

Blood in the urine is most obvious after exercise and toward the end of a urine stream. Horses with this condition usually stretch out in order to urinate and may maintain this pose for some time before and after urinating. Additional signs include scalding of the area around the urethra (the area between the vulva and the anus in females, and the inside of the hind legs in males). The scalding occurs because urine is acidic and constant contact with urine can burn the skin over time. Geldings and stallions may protrude the penis for prolonged periods of time while dribbling urine on and off. Horses with this condition may occasionally have recurring bouts of colic or an altered gait. The urethra may become blocked as a result of a trapped stone; this usually causes restlessness, sweating, colic, and frequent attempts to urinate. On doing a rectal examination, your veterinarian will be able to tell that the bladder is overly full.

Kidney stones in both kidneys are common in adult horses that have been used for performance. Over time, these stones may repeatedly block the ureter and cause kidney failure (*see* page 785).

Your veterinarian can usually detect the stones by the signs listed above in addition to performing a thorough physical examination. Sometimes x-rays or ultrasonography are used to confirm the diagnosis. Your veterinarian may want to insert a catheter (a narrow, flexible tube) through the urethra and into the bladder in order to empty the bladder and make sure there is no stone or other growth blocking the urethra. An analysis of the urine may also be done to provide more information.

Treatment

Urinary stones in horses are best removed by surgery. There are several different types of surgery; the most appropriate type for your horse depends on the size, location, and number of stones and the sex and health of the horse.

Uroperitoneum in Foals

Uroperitoneum is the leakage of urine into the abdominal cavity. In foals, this most commonly results from tearing of the bladder during birth or rupture of the urachus (*see* page 783) following an infection. Bladder rupture may be more common in male foals.

Foals with this condition usually appear normal at birth, but gradually become ill over 1 to 2 days. They are weak, lack energy and interest in their surroundings, and have an increased heart rate. Gradually, the abdomen will enlarge. Most of these foals attempt to urinate often, but only produce a small amount of urine.

Tests of blood and fluid from the abdomen can help your veterinarian make the diagnosis. Other diseases with signs that could be confused with uroperitoneum include blood infection (septicemia), nervous system disorders, and colic.

Surgery is generally required to correct the defect and is successful in most uncomplicated cases. The foal should be stabilized before surgery to prevent complications due to poor lung function (a consequence of distension of the abdomen) or electrolyte imbalances (especially high potassium, which can affect the heart). If the problem is recognized early, the outlook for correction is excellent. If the foal becomes infected or is born prematurely, other complications may decrease the chances of recovery.

CHAPTER 56
Metabolic Disorders

■ INTRODUCTION

Metabolism refers to all processes in the body that break down and convert ingested substances to provide the energy and nutrients needed to sustain life. Foods, liquids, and drugs all generally undergo metabolic processes within the body. Many foods are complex materials that need to be broken down into simpler substances, which in turn become "building blocks" for the body to use as needed. For example, protein is broken down into amino acids, which are used in several metabolic reactions. **Enzymes** made by the body are needed for many metabolic processes to occur. Whenever the function of an enzyme is affected, a metabolic disorder can develop. Metabolic disorders are important because they affect energy production or damage tissues. They may be inherited or acquired. Acquired metabolic disorders are more common and significant.

Metabolic Storage Disorders

Metabolic storage disorders usually result from the body's inability to break

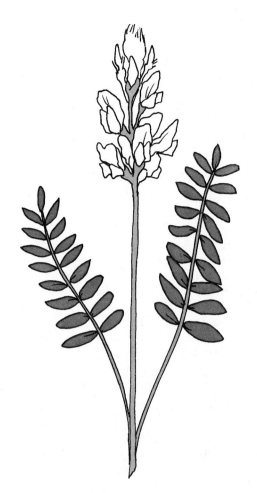

Longterm ingestion of locoweed plants (*Astragalus* or *Oxytropis* species) causes a metabolic storage disease that affects the central nervous system of horses.

down some substance because of partial or complete lack of a certain enzyme. The substance can build up to a toxic level, or the body is unable to produce a substance that it needs. Although storage diseases are often widespread throughout the body, most signs are due to the effects on the central nervous system. Metabolic storage disorders can be either genetic or acquired.

Genetic (inherited) storage diseases are named according to the specific metabolic byproduct that builds up in the body. These diseases are progressive and usually fatal because specific treatments do not exist. Genetic storage diseases have not been reported in horses.

Acquired storage diseases can be caused by eating plants that contain inhibitors of specific enzymes. Eating locoweed plants (*Astragalus* or *Oxytropis* species) for a long time can result in an acquired neurologic storage disease. Several toxic components of these plants interfere with the activity of a specific enzyme. Horses are highly susceptible to intoxication. (*See also* PLANTS POISONOUS TO ANIMALS, page 1175.)

Production-related Metabolic Disorders

Some metabolic disorders are caused by an increased demand for a specific element or nutrient that has become deficient under certain conditions. For example, in **hypoglycemia**, the animal's metabolic reserves are unable to sustain sugar (glucose) in the blood at a level needed for normal function. Likewise, in **hypocalcemia**, the level of calcium in the blood is too low. In some cases, dietary intake of a nutrient, such as calcium, is rapidly used up for an ongoing, high metabolic need, such as lactation or nursing a foal. Another production-related disorder of horses is **exertional rhabdomyolysis** (page 704), which is also called "tying-up" or "cording-up." In this condition, draft or race horses are forced to work or exercise after a period of rest during which feed has not been restricted. When the horses go back to work, certain compounds (such as glycogen and lactate) can build up in and damage the muscle tissue.

The difference between production-related metabolic diseases and nutritional deficiencies is often subtle. Typically, nutritional deficiencies are longterm conditions that develop gradually and can be corrected through dietary supplementation. Metabolic diseases usually begin suddenly and respond dramatically to administration of the deficient nutrient (although affected animals may need dietary supplements to avoid recurrence). Because production-related metabolic disorders are serious and develop suddenly, accurate and rapid diagnosis is essential. Ideally, diagnostic tests can be used to predict the chance of disease occurring so that it can be prevented or preparations can be made for rapid treatment.

DISORDERS OF CALCIUM METABOLISM

Hypocalcemic tetany in horses is uncommon but can develop after prolonged physical exercise, such as endurance rides, or transport (**transport tetany**) and in lactating or nursing mares (**lactation tetany**). A low level of calcium in the blood (hypocalcemia) can be caused by decreased absorption from the intestines, by increased loss through the milk, urine, or sweat, or by changes in bone metabolism. Producing large amounts of milk and grazing lush pastures make lactating mares more inclined to develop the condition.

Signs correspond to the level of calcium in the blood, and most relate to muscular spasms, tremors, and stiffness. Other signs include inability to chew, spasm of the jaw muscles, drooling, lying down, seizures, and irregular heart rhythms. In severe cases, synchronous diaphragmatic flutter may develop. In this condition, the diaphragm contracts at the same time as the heart to produce loud thumping noises (heard with a stethoscope) and usually visible contractions in the flank area.

Calcium solutions given intravenously usually result in full recovery. Some horses need repeated treatments over several days. Throughout pregnancy, mares should be fed a balanced ration that contains adequate amounts of calcium and phosphorus in the correct ratio. When calcium demands are increased, for example when nursing a foal, mares should be fed high-quality forage such as alfalfa or calcium-containing mineral mixes. Stress and fasting during transport should be minimized.

DISORDERS OF MAGNESIUM METABOLISM

Most disorders of magnesium metabolism are due to problems associated with absorption of the mineral from the digestive tract. The differences in anatomy between species are associated with the importance of disorders of magnesium occurring in a particular species. In horses, disorders of magnesium metabolism are much less common than in cattle and sheep, in which magnesium is mainly absorbed from the rumen in adult animals. Horses are able to absorb magnesium from the small intestine. Too much magnesium in the blood (**hypermagnesemia**) is rare, but horses receiving excessive doses of magnesium sulfate for constipation may show signs of sweating, muscle weakness, and rapid heartbeat and breathing rate. Cardiac arrest can occur with very high blood magnesium levels.

FATIGUE AND EXERCISE

Owners commonly report **muscular fatigue** of horses. Muscular fatigue can be caused by numerous disorders of several body systems, which are discussed in other chapters.

Fatigue is a normal consequence of exercise that is continued at high intensity or for prolonged periods of time. The decreased ability of the muscle to produce force is actually a safety mechanism for the body. If fatigue did not occur and force the animal to stop, the intense exercise could cause structural damage to muscle cells and supportive tissues.

Most knowledge concerning fatigue in animals has been described in horses because horses can easily be trained to exercise on high-speed treadmills that allow investigation of respiratory, cardiovascular, and metabolic responses. When the horse becomes fatigued, it is generally unable or unwilling to maintain the same speed as the treadmill when the treadmill speed is increased. Changes in the gait and joint movements are seen, and these changes may be an important factor contributing to musculoskeletal injuries of racehorses. Because of these changes, training of racehorses should avoid fatiguing the animal.

Fatigue during High-intensity Exercise

In general, the cause of fatigue during exercise depends greatly on the duration and energy demands of the event. Endurance events can last many hours or days, while many Quarter Horse, Standardbred, and Thoroughbred races require intense exercise at maximal speeds lasting 3 minutes or less. Generally, exercise at an individual animal's highest attainable speed cannot be maintained for more than about 30 to 40 seconds. After that, fatigue sets in and the animal slows down.

Synchronous diaphragmatic flutter, a condition in which the diaphragm contracts at the same time as the heart to produce loud thumping noises (heard with a stethoscope) and usually visible contractions in the flank area, is sometimes seen after races in Thoroughbreds and Standardbreds. It is more often associated with fatigue during prolonged exercise. The condition occurs primarily when there is a significant electrolyte or acid-base imbalance. It often resolves within 30 to 60 minutes without treatment, but close monitoring is needed.

Very intense training over many weeks can result in a form of longterm fatigue referred to as **overtraining**. This condition causes weight loss and decreased performance during intense exercise that is not reversed by 1 to 2 weeks of rest. Horses must be given many weeks of rest from training and racing to recover from this condition.

Fatigue during Prolonged Exercise

During exercise lasting many hours, heat is generated within the body. The body tries to cool off by sweating, which can result in dehydration and metabolic disturbances. These factors are usually implicated in the fatigue, exhaustion, and even death that can occur after prolonged exercise in horses.

Washing the horse repeatedly with water that is very cold (near ice temperature) is the most effective way of cooling a horse.

Environmental temperature and humidity also have a major impact on the degree of disturbance to body fluids during prolonged exercise.

Horses competing in 3-day events or endurance rides may show signs of exhaustion, despite current practices of evaluation of recovery at rest stops. Horses can lose large amounts of fluid by sweating, and show signs of depression, fatigue, dehydration, increased heart and breathing rates, and high body temperature. These horses need urgent treatment. Horses with a high body temperature should be continuously hosed with very cold water, stood in the shade (in a cooling breeze if possible), and given fluid therapy (both oral and intravenous).

Prevention of Fatigue

Physical training is the most effective way of reducing fatigue and increasing the capacity for exercise. Physical training not only builds up muscle size and strength, it also transports more oxygen to and produces more energy within the muscle. Skeletal muscle responds to training depending on the training intensity, which can be guided by heart rate meters. In horses, maximal heart rates range from about 210 to 240 beats per minute. Heart rates that are about 60 to 90% of the horse's maximal heart rate are ideal during training of Standardbred and Thoroughbred horses. If the maximal heart rate is not known, training should be kept at heart rates of 120 to 190 beats per minute, with the addition of occasional high speed exercise later in the training program.

Warmup before competition at high speeds is likely to reduce fatigue in Quarter Horse, Thoroughbred, and Standardbred races. A 10-minute warmup with trot and canter should be used whenever possible.

Horses should be well hydrated before any intense or prolonged exercise and given access to fluids during and after events. Horses that are dehydrated or that have not been acclimated to a hot environment before exercise have higher body temperatures and earlier fatigue. Horses should not be given large meals 1 to 2 hours before competition. Feeding small portions every 4 hours is best. Reduced fiber intake before racing can also decrease fatigue during intense exercise. Horses that are overweight also fatigue earlier.

During high-intensity exercise, energy comes from the metabolic conversion of various compounds, including glycogen, a compound stored in the liver and muscles and converted to glucose (sugar) as a source of energy. Glycogen concentration in skeletal muscle before performance has an effect on fatigue during both short-term/intense and prolonged exercise. Horses should not be depleted of glycogen before short-term or endurance events. Intense or prolonged exercise depletes the muscle glycogen stores, and it is sensible to allow at least 48 hours for glycogen levels in horses to return to normal after exercise. No method of glycogen loading using adjustments to normal feeding has been described in horses. Use of glucose or other carbohydrate solutions before racing to improve performance in Standardbred and Thoroughbred racehorses has no scientific basis.

Feeding fat can increase performance during prolonged exercise. Adding fat to the diet affects various metabolic responses to exercise, including body temperature. Feeding vegetable oil at a rate of 100 to 120 grams per kilogram of weight has been suggested as ample.

Recovery

Recovery of horses after endurance rides is influenced by the rehydration strategy used. Horses offered a saline solution as initial rehydration recover more rapidly than horses offered water. However, horses may need to be trained to drink a saline solution. Use of saline solutions should be encouraged, especially for horses that compete in endurance events or other events over multiple days. Owners should consult with their veterinarian concerning the most suitable saline solution to use.

Blood lactate concentrations do decrease more quickly after racing and intense training if the horse is trotted for 30 minutes, but there is no obvious benefit for the horse of this so-called "warm-down."

■ FEVER OF UNKNOWN ORIGIN

In both animals and people, fever may indicate infection, inflammation, immune-mediated disease, or cancer. Determining the cause of a fever requires a history, physical examination, and sometimes laboratory or other diagnostic tests. Withdrawal and analysis of joint fluid is an important diagnostic test in horses and other large animals because infectious polyarthritis (arthritis involving 2 or more joints) is a common cause of fever.

Often, a fever resolves on its own or in response to antibiotic therapy. However, in a small percentage of animals, the fever continues or keeps coming back and the cause cannot be determined. This is called fever of unknown origin. In a case series of horses with fever of unknown origin, 43% had infectious disease, 22% had tumors, 6.5% had immune-mediated disease, 19% had miscellaneous causes, and in 9.5% the cause was not determined.

In some fever of unknown origin cases, a specific diagnosis cannot be found, or diagnostic testing is discontinued, and different treatments are tried without a diagnosis. Options include antibiotics, antifungal agents, and anti-inflammatory or immunosuppressive therapy. Although trial therapy can resolve the clinical signs or may confirm a tentative diagnosis, it can also carry significant risk, and careful monitoring is needed. (For a more detailed discussion of FEVER OF UNKNOWN ORIGIN, *see* page 303.)

▧ MALIGNANT HYPERTHERMIA

Malignant hyperthermia is seen mostly in swine, but it has also been reported in horses, dogs, and cats. This syndrome is characterized by abnormally high body temperature, muscle rigidity, a very rapid and irregular heartbeat, increased breathing rate, bluish tinge to skin and mucous membranes, unstable blood pressure, fluid buildup in the lungs, impaired blood coagulation, kidney failure, and death.

Malignant hyperthermia is consistently triggered in susceptible animals by excitement, apprehension, exercise, or environmental stress. Giving certain anesthetics or specific drugs that affect the neurologic and muscular systems also consistently triggers malignant hyperthermia in susceptible animals.

Diagnosis is based on development of signs in an animal that has been given an anesthetic agent or is participating in a stressful event. Signs can develop slowly or rapidly. They include muscle stiffness, twitching, a rapid heartbeat, and an increased breathing rate. Body temperature increases rapidly and can reach 113°F (45°C).

Usually, malignant hyperthermia episodes occur suddenly and are severe. If the condition is recognized early in an animal under anesthesia, supportive measures may be able to save the animal. Unfortunately, regardless of treatment, malignant hyperthermia is usually fatal.

Stress must be minimized to prevent malignant hyperthermia episodes in individual animals. If an animal that is suspected to be susceptible to malignant hyperthermia (or that has survived a previous episode) needs anesthesia and surgery, certain precautions should be taken. These include administering a drug called dantrolene 1 to 2 days before anesthesia and avoiding certain anesthetic agents.

CHAPTER **57**

Disorders Affecting Multiple Body Systems

▧ INTRODUCTION

There are many disorders or conditions that can affect multiple parts of the body. These disorders and conditions may be caused by bacteria, viruses, poisonous or toxic substances in the environment, and other health hazards. Disorders affecting multiple body systems can also be inherited or can develop while the animal is still in the womb. When these disorders or conditions involve multiple organ systems they are often described as systemic or generalized.

Many disorders are discussed in this chapter. A listing of congenital and inherited conditions is followed by a discussion of the most significant disorders, which have been arranged alphabetically by medical name to help you locate a particular disease or condition easily.

CONGENITAL AND INHERITED DISORDERS

A variety of structural and functional defects have been described in animals. These birth defects are usually classified by the body system primarily affected, and many are discussed in this book under the appropriate body system section. Defective newborns have survived a disruptive event during embryonic or fetal development.

The frequency of individual defects varies with the species, breed, geographic location, season, and other environmental factors. It occurs at an estimated rate of 0.2 to 3.5% of all foal births.

Commonly reported congenital and inherited defects in horses include the following: contracted tendons, hydrocephalus ("water on the brain"), failure of one or both testicles to descend into the scrotum (known as cryptorchidism), displacement of the kneecap, cataracts, and failure of the umbilical opening to close ("leaky navel"). Other congenital defects are known, but they are reported less often. Most congenital defects have no clearly established cause; others are caused by genetic or environmental factors or interaction between these factors.

Genetic Factors

Inherited defects resulting from mutant genes or chromosome abnormalities tend to occur in patterns of inheritance. Such patterns include dominant (in which the defect will occur if either parent supplies an abnormal gene to its offspring), recessive (in which both parents must supply an abnormal gene) or others, such as sex-linked (in which the gene is nearly always associated with the X chromosome and not the Y chromosome).

Some common diseases or disorders caused by genetic defects include deficiencies of particular enzymes that lead to the body's inability to perform normal metabolic functions, and chromosome abnormalities that can result in sterility, abnormal growth or development, or fetal death. Viruses, certain drugs, and radiation are common causes of chromosomal damage.

The complex interaction between genetic and environmental factors is being studied and is slowly becoming better understood.

Environmental Factors

Factors that tend to produce abnormalities in body formation include toxic plants (such as poison hemlock, which may contribute to contracted tendons in foals), viral infections that occur during pregnancy, drugs, trace elements, nutritional deficiencies, and physical agents such as radiation, abnormally high body temperature, uterine positioning, and twisting of the umbilical cord. These factors may be difficult to identify. They often follow seasonal patterns and stress and may be linked to maternal disease. They do not follow the pattern of family inheritance that is shown by genetic changes.

ACTINOBACILLOSIS

Actinobacillosis is caused by bacteria in the genus *Actinobacillus*. Several different forms of disease occur, depending on the particular species of *Actinobacillus* involved and the type of animal infected. Soft tissue infections are common, and lymph node involvement is frequently a step in the spread of the disease throughout the animal's entire body. Bony tissue close to muscles or other infected tissue may also be infected.

Actinobacillus equuli infects both foals and adult horses. Foals may become infected through a contaminated umbilical cord or by inhaling or ingesting the

---

Some Congenital and Inherited Defects in Horses

- Contracted flexor tendons (*see* page 669)
- Cryptorchidism (apparent absence of one or both testicles; *see* page 731)
- Angular limb deformities (*see* page 670)
- Cataracts (for more information, see section starting on page 652)

bacteria. Signs of infection include diarrhea, followed by inflammation of the brain and spinal cord, pneumonia, inflammation of the kidneys, or bacterial arthritis. The chance of infection in foals can be reduced with careful attention to sanitation in the birthing environment and to ensuring that the foal receives milk containing antibodies from the nursing mother shortly after birth. An infection in an adult can result in abortion, blood poisoning, and inflammation of the kidneys or heart. Infection may be treated with antibacterial drugs.

Actinobacillus lignieresii causes tumorous abscesses of the tongue, a condition often called **wooden tongue**. This infection occurs most frequently in cattle, but is also seen in horses. Treatment may include surgical removal of the contaminated tissue, potassium iodide given by mouth, or antibacterial drugs.

▪ ACTINOMYCOSIS

Actinomyces bacteria normally live in the mouth and in the nasal passages near the throat. One species, *Actinomyces bovis*, has been identified infrequently in infections in horses, including chronic fistulous withers and chronic poll evil (*see* page 677). Disease occurs when this bacterium is introduced to underlying soft tissue through penetrating wounds of the mouth (such as those that occur from chewing wire or coarse hay). Involvement of the nearby bone frequently results in facial distortion, loose teeth (making chewing difficult), and difficulty breathing due to swelling of the nasal cavity. Treatment is rarely successful in long-term cases in which bone is involved, due to the poor penetration of antibacterial drugs into the affected area. In less advanced cases, your veterinarian may prescribe an antibiotic.

▪ AFRICAN HORSE SICKNESS

African horse sickness is a short-term insect-borne viral disease of horses that is widespread in Africa. It is characterized by signs of lung and blood system impairment. African horse sickness is caused by a virus of the family Reoviridae. The appearance of African horse sickness follows seasons of heavy rain that alternate with hot and dry climatic conditions. Outbreaks in central and east Africa have extended to Egypt, the Middle East, and southern Arabia. Epidemics have also occurred in Spain. During epidemics, the fatality rate can reach 90%.

African horse sickness virus is most frequently transmitted by midges, although other insects, including mosquitoes, may also transmit the disease. Stray dogs, dog ticks, and camel ticks have also been shown to carry the disease and may also play a role in disease transmission, especially in areas where the disease is widespread.

In the respiratory form of the disease, signs develop in 3 to 5 days, with death occurring in about a week. Signs include fever, coughing, difficulty breathing, and dilated nostrils. The heart form of the disease is slower to develop. The incubation period is 1 to 2 weeks. Fever lasts about 1 week, followed by swelling near the eyes. The swelling usually extends to the neck, shoulders, and chest. Death usually follows within a week and may be preceded by colic. The mortality rate of this form is about 50%.

In areas where the disease is common, the signs and tissue changes may allow a veterinarian to make a provisional diagnosis. However, laboratory testing is needed to confirm the diagnosis and identify the strain of virus involved. Knowing the strain can be important for control measures.

The outlook for recovery in infected horses depends on the viral strain involved and the susceptibility of the infected horse. Infected horses that survive develop immunity to the viral type with which they were infected. However, they remain susceptible to other types of the virus. There are vaccines for all 9 types that provide long-lasting protection. When the disease first appears in an area, affected horses should be eliminated immediately, and uninfected animals should be vaccinated and rested for 2 weeks. At the same time, attention should be paid to control of the insects that most frequently transmit this disease. Your veterinarian can recommend the most appropriate pest control program for your horses. Note that vaccinated horses should be kept in insect-proof housing because vaccine failure may occur. In the US, horses, donkeys, mules and other equids from African countries are quarantined for 2 months and then tested for the virus. The presence of antibodies does not interfere with importation of horses into countries free of the disease.

■ AMYLOIDOSIS

Amyloidosis is a condition that occurs when **amyloid**, a substance composed of abnormally folded protein, is deposited in various organs of the body. Some types of amyloidosis are hereditary. Others occur as a result of various infections, cancers, or other inflammatory or immune-related conditions. However, the cause is often unknown.

Amyloid can be deposited throughout the body, or in just one specific area. This causes damage by displacing normal cells. The disease can become fatal if amyloid is deposited into the tissue of critical organs, such as the kidneys, liver, or heart. All domestic mammals may develop amyloidosis, and aged animals commonly have minor deposits of amyloid without signs or problems. Tumor-like amyloid nodules and amyloid deposits under the skin have been reported in horses.

There are several types of amyloid, and the classification of amyloidosis is based on which amyloid protein is involved. Deposits of **AA amyloid** can result from chronic inflammatory diseases, chronic bacterial infections, and cancer. The amyloid is usually deposited in organs such as the spleen or kidneys. The animal may not show any signs. If AA amyloid is deposited in the kidneys, it can lead to

a buildup of protein and result in kidney failure. **AL amyloid** is another common form of amyloid protein. AL amyloid tends to be deposited in nerve tissue and joints.

Because of its wide distribution and stealthy onset, amyloidosis is difficult to diagnose. However, your veterinarian might suspect amyloidosis if your horse has a chronic infection or inflammation and develops kidney or liver failure. No specific treatment can prevent the development of amyloidosis or promote the reabsorption of the protein deposits.

■ ANAPLASMOSIS (EQUINE GRANULOCYTIC EHRLICHIOSIS)

Anaplasmosis (formerly called equine granulocytic ehrlichiosis) is an infectious, seasonal disease, seen chiefly in the United States. Most cases occur in northern California but cases have been seen in several other states, including Connecticut, Illinois, Arkansas, Washington, Pennsylvania, Colorado, Minnesota, and Florida. Cases have also been confirmed in British Columbia, Sweden, Great Britain, and South America. The disease is seasonal in California, occurring in the late fall, winter, and spring.

This disease is caused by the bacterium *Anaplasma phagocytophilum*, which is found in the bloodstream. The disease is transmitted by ticks. The risk of transmission to people is unclear at this time. Although horses and people appear to be infected with strains of the same bacteria, it is believed that people also acquire the infection from tick bites, and not directly from infected horses.

The severity of signs varies with the age of the animal and duration of the illness. Signs may be mild. Horses less than 1 year old may have a fever only; horses 1 to 3 years old develop fever, depression, mild limb swelling, and lack of coordination. Adults exhibit the characteristic signs of fever, poor appetite, depression, reluctance to move, limb swelling, and jaundice. Fever is highest during the first 1 to 3 days of infection, but may last for 6 to 12 days. Signs become more severe over several days. Any existing infection (such as a leg wound or respiratory infection) can be made worse.

The disease is easily treated in the early stages using appropriate antibiotics. The severity of the disease is variable; many horses recover after 14 days without treatment. However, rare fatalities have occurred that are believed to be associated with secondary infections. Horses with severe signs and neurologic signs may benefit from injectable corticosteroids. Recovered horses develop immunity for at least 2 years and are not carriers. Tick control measures are mandatory for control of the disease. There is no vaccine.

ANTHRAX

Anthrax is an often fatal infectious disease that can infect all warm-blooded animals, including horses and humans. Underdiagnosis and unreliable reporting make it difficult to estimate the true frequency of anthrax worldwide; however, anthrax has been reported from nearly every continent. Under normal circumstances, anthrax outbreaks in the United States are extremely rare. Anthrax received much attention in 2001 in relation to the terrorist attacks on the United States because of its potential use as a biological weapon.

Anthrax is caused by infection with a bacterium known as *Bacillus anthracis*. This bacterium forms spores, which make it extremely resistant to environmental conditions such as heating, freezing, chemical disinfection, or dehydration that typically destroy other types of bacteria. Thus, it can persist for a long time within or on a contaminated environment or object. Horses may consume the spores while grazing in areas where anthrax has been a problem. Optimal growth conditions for the bacteria often occur in neutral or alkaline, calcium- or lime-rich soils. Flies and other insects may also spread the disease from infected animals to other animals.

After exposure, the typical incubation period is from 3 to 7 days. Once the bacteria infect an animal or human, the organisms multiply and spread throughout the body. They produce a potent and lethal poison (toxin) that causes cell death and breakdown of the infected tissues. This results in inflammation and organ damage eventually leading to organ failure. The bacteria spread throughout the body through the blood and lymphatic (immune) system.

Signs occur rapidly in a previously healthy animal. High fever and agitation are quickly followed by chills, severe colic, loss of appetite, depression, disorientation, difficulty breathing or exercise intolerance, muscle weakness, and seizures. Bloody diarrhea may be observed. Swelling often occurs around the neck and may be so severe that suffocation is possible. Swelling of the chest, lower abdomen, and external genitals may also occur. If spores infect open cuts or abrasions, a localized skin infection occurs. Without rapid treatment, death usually occurs within 2 to 3 days of onset.

A diagnosis based on signs is difficult because many infections and other conditions (such as colic, sunstroke, or acute infectious anemia in horses) may have signs similar to anthrax. Diagnosis thus requires laboratory analysis of blood samples from the potentially infected animal or human to confirm the presence of the bacteria.

Human cases of anthrax may follow contact with contaminated animals or animal products. You should use strict precautions (wearing gloves, protective clothing, goggles, and masks) when handling potentially infected animals or their remains.

Anthrax is controlled through vaccination programs, rapid detection and reporting, quarantine, antibiotic treatment of any animals exposed to the bacteria, and the burning or burial of dead animals that had suspected or confirmed anthrax infection. Early treatment and vigorous implementation of a preventive program are essential. Vaccination of horses is done only when horses are pastured in an area that is known to be contaminated. In most countries, all cases of anthrax must be reported to the appropriate regulatory officials. Uninfected horses should be moved to another pasture away from where infected animals had pastured and from any possible site of soil contamination. Stables and equipment must be cleaned and disinfected.

■ BESNOITIOSIS

Although mainly a disease of cattle, besnoitiosis can cause infection in horses and other herbivores. This disease is caused by a tiny single-celled organism called a protozoan; in this case, the protozoan is known as *Besnoitia bennetti*. It has been reported in horses in Africa, southern France, and Mexico. Although it has not been reported in horses in the United States, it has been reported in donkeys.

The disease is transmitted by certain biting flies (including the tsetse) and ticks or by ingesting the feces of an infected cat. (Cats are the primary host of the protozoa.) The organisms form cysts in and under the skin and in blood vessels, mucous membranes of the upper respiratory tract, and other tissues. Other signs include fever, fluid buildup in the tissues, loss of appetite, intolerance to light, inflammation of the mucous membranes of the nose, chronic hardening and thickening of the skin, and hair loss. The skin becomes hard, thick, and wrinkled and develops cracks that allow bacterial infections to develop. Severely affected animals become emaciated. The signs in horses tend to be less severe than in other animals.

Affected animals should be isolated and treated for specific signs. Recovery is slow in severe cases, and affected animals remain carriers of the disease for life. Reducing the number of biting insects and ticks may reduce transmission.

■ BOTULISM

Botulism is a motor paralysis caused most commonly by eating food contaminated with the toxin (a type of poison) produced by *Clostridium botulinum* bacteria. This organism grows rapidly in decomposing animal tissue and sometimes in plant material. It results in rapid death due to the paralysis of vital organs. Botulism is not usually an infection. The paralysis is usually caused by the consumption of the toxin in food. The frequency of botulism in animals is not known with accuracy, but it is low in horses.

There are 7 types of *Clostridium botulinum*; the C_1 toxin is seen in most animal species, although types A and B may also be implicated in horses. The usual source of the toxin is decaying carcasses or vegetable materials such as decaying grass, hay, grain, or spoiled silage.

The signs of botulism are caused by muscle paralysis. They include paralysis that becomes progressively more severe, disturbed vision, difficulty in chewing and swallowing, and overall weakness. Death is usually due to paralysis of the lungs or heart. Diagnosis of this condition is difficult, and it is often made by excluding any other possible causes of paralysis and by association with a likely source of the toxin.

Botulism may also originate in 2 other ways. *Clostridium botulinum* has occasionally been found to grow in the gastrointestinal tract and produce toxins there. When the toxins are released, they cause typical botulism. This occurs in foals up to about 8 months of age and results in the **shaker foal syndrome**. Most often, foals show signs of paralysis that slowly progresses. Stilted gait, muscle tremors, and the inability to stand for more than 4 to 5 minutes are common signs. Other signs include difficulty swallowing, constipation, dilated pupils, and frequent urination. As the disease progresses, labored breathing with extension of the head and neck, rapid heart rate, and respiratory arrest occur. Death occurs most often 1 to 3 days after signs are first noted.

A third form of botulism occurs in humans—and sometimes in adult horses—when the bacterium grows and produces toxin in a wound. This is referred to as **wound botulism**.

EQUINE INFECTIOUS ANEMIA

Equine infectious anemia is a blood-borne infection that affects horses and other equids. It is caused by a virus. In many infected animals, the signs of illness are minimal; however, equine infectious anemia may also infect many animals in a region simultaneously with severe infections and a high death rate. Infection appears to persist for life.

Blood-feeding insects transfer the virus from an infected animal to nearby uninfected animals while feeding. The most efficient transfer of the infection seems to involve horseflies and deer flies. The reason is simple; when these insects bite, the pain causes the horse to switch its tail and take other defensive behavior that interrupts the insect's feeding and the insect flies off to bite yet another animal and transfer the virus.

There are 2 forms of the disease. One form exists without noticeable signs or with subtle signs (such as fever or lack of appetite) that go unrecognized. Often, infection is noted only after routine surveillance testing for the disease or when the horse develops recurring bouts of fever accompanied by anemia, depression, weight loss, general ill health, malnutrition, and swelling (hallmarks of the long-term form of the disease). This most often occurs in horses on pasture. Thus, the virus frequently enters a herd without the knowledge of the owner and spreads until a high percentage of the herd is infected.

No specific treatment or vaccine is available. If a horse tests positive for equine infectious anemia, euthanasia is often recommended as the most prudent option, albeit a difficult one. Lifelong quarantine in a screened stall is another, less acceptable, alternative. Infected horses will always pose a health risk to other horses, whether or not they show signs of illness. Even in the best management situations, blood-feeding insects cannot be totally controlled or eliminated.

Horses testing positive for equine infectious anemia are often required by law to be permanently identified via branding or tattooing and to be quarantined. Transportation and housing are severely restricted. Owners who choose quarantine must post signs clearly stating the housing of a quarantined animal. As equine infectious anemia-positive horses present the only known source of infection, horses should be quarantined at least 200 meters (220 yards) away from all other animals. A screened enclosure is best.

EQUINE MORBILLIVIRUS PNEUMONIA (HENDRA VIRUS INFECTION)

Equine morbillivirus pneumonia is a frequently fatal viral respiratory infection of horses caused by Hendra virus. Disease due to Hendra virus infection has only been reported in horses and people. The virus appears to be limited to Australia and Papua New Guinea.

Hendra virus does not appear to be highly contagious. Transmission between infected and uninfected horses occurs infrequently. Based on available field and laboratory data, infection of humans or animals appears to require direct contact with virus-infective secretions (lung discharges), urine, or tissues.

In infected horses, signs include fever (up to 106°F [41°C]), poor appetite, lethargy, elevated respiratory and heart rates, difficulty breathing, pneumonia, and frothy clear to blood-tinged nasal discharge. Additional signs seen in some affected horses include bluish-colored or jaundiced mucous membranes, tissue swelling, and neurologic signs. As many as 60 to 70% of infected horses die of the disease. The course of the disease is short; death may occur within 1 to 3 days.

There is no specific antiviral treatment and, as yet, no vaccine for this disease. Hendra virus is transmissible to humans. The infection has been fatal in a high percentage of the handful of cases recorded so far, either from severe pneumonia or from inflammation of the brain. Direct contact with infectious respiratory secretions, urine, or tissues appears to be necessary for viral transmission.

■ EQUINE VIRAL ARTERITIS

Equine viral arteritis is a contagious, viral disease that affects members of the horse family. The disease is caused by the equine arteritis virus and is of short duration. Signs can include fever; depression; swelling of the limbs, scrotum, and the covering fold of skin on the penis in stallions; inflammation of the conjunctival lining of the eye; nasal discharge; and abortion. Occasionally, it will cause death in young foals.

The virus is present in horse populations in many countries throughout the world; Japan and Iceland are notable exceptions. However, outbreaks of the virus are uncommon and are usually associated with the movement of horses or shipment of semen. While the virus is known to infect many breeds of horses, the rate of infection varies widely, usually being highest in Standardbreds and Warmbloods. To date, there is no evidence of infection in populations of wild horses.

The virus may be spread by the respiratory route (such as breathing in particles of virus exhaled by an infected animal) or may be transmitted by sexual contact, from mare to foal, or by indirect contact. Infected stallions can become carriers and readily spread the infection due to the fact that the virus is continually shed in the semen. Mares can be infected by either natural breeding or artificial insemination with infective semen. Viral transmission may be widespread at racetracks or on breeding farms. Transmission of the virus is not always associated with the appearance of the signs characteristic of equine viral arteritis. In fact, most infected horses show no signs of disease. The virus may persist in some otherwise healthy stallions for years.

Most cases of infection are without signs. When signs are observed, they may include any combination of the following: fever of 2 to 9 days duration, low blood white cell counts, depression, poor appetite, leg swelling (especially of the hind legs), and swelling of the covering fold of skin on the penis and the scrotum in stallions. Less consistent signs include inflammation of the conjunctival lining of the eye, tearing, abnormal sensitivity to light, swelling around the eyes, inflammation of the lining of the nose and nasal discharge, swelling of the ventral body wall (including the mammary glands of mares), a skin reaction visible on the sides of the neck or head (although it can sometimes occur elsewhere on the body), a stiff gait, difficulty breathing, diarrhea, jaundice, and lack of coordination. Signs are more severe in young, old, and weakened horses. Death is rare but has been reported in foals up to several months old.

The reason equine arteritis virus causes abortion is unclear. Abortion may occur while the horse is displaying signs of disease or while it is recovering from the infection. It may also occur in infected mares that do not develop any signs of illness. Mares may abort any time from 3 months to over 10 months of gestation. Abortion rates in a herd can vary from less than 10% to as high as 70%. Abortion is not the result of a mare being bred to a carrier stallion or inseminated with infective semen. Mares that abort are already pregnant at the time of exposure. Mares infected late in gestation may not abort, but give birth to a congenitally infected foal.

Stallions affected with equine viral arteritis may undergo a period of short-term reduced fertility. This is believed to be the result of increased temperature in the testicles caused by prolonged high fever and severe scrotal swelling that can occur during infection.

Treatment and Control

There is no specific antiviral treatment for equine viral arteritis. Because virtually all horses recover completely, supportive treatment (including fever reducing, anti-inflammatory drugs, and diuretic agents) is appropriate only in severe cases, especially in stallions in which prolonged fever and extensive scrotal swelling can result in short-term reduced fertility. Good nursing care and rest, with a gradual return to normal activity are usually sufficient. As yet, there is no proven treatment that will successfully eliminate the carrier state in stallions.

Equine viral arteritis is a preventable disease that can be controlled by good management practices and selective use of vaccination. All national, state, and local guidelines should be followed regarding testing of horses or semen for the equine arteritis virus and appropriate vaccination. Pregnant mares should not be vaccinated.

Prevention and Control of Equine Viral Arteritis

Equine viral arteritis is a preventable disease that can be controlled by sound management practices and selective use of a commercial, modified live virus vaccine. Management practices that help control this disease include:

- Follow any national, state, or local guidelines regarding testing of horses for the equine arteritis virus and vaccination

- Separately manage carrier stallions to avoid the risk of inadvertent spread of the virus to previously uninfected or unvaccinated horses on the premises

- Breed carrier stallions only to naturally positive mares or mares adequately immunized against equine viral arteritis

- If recommended, vaccinate breeding stallions and colts against the disease between 6 and 12 months of age (before puberty and before significant risk of infection)

- Test fresh-cooled or frozen semen used for artificial insemination, especially if imported, for virus

---

■ FUNGAL INFECTIONS (MYCOSES)

Funguses (also called fungi) are parasitic, spore-producing organisms. They obtain their nourishment by absorbing food from the hosts on which they grow. Many species of fungus exist in the environment, but only some cause infections. The primary source of most infections is soil. Fungal infections can be acquired by inhalation, ingestion, or through the skin (for example, through a cut or wound).

Some fungal infections can cause disease in otherwise healthy animals, while others require a host that is incapacitated or immunocompromised (by, for example, such stresses as poor nutrition, viral infections, or cancer) to establish infection. Prolonged use of antimicrobial drugs or immunosuppressive agents appears to increase the likelihood of some fungal infections. The infection itself may be localized or may affect the entire body (systemic or generalized).

Aspergillosis (Guttural Pouch Mycosis)

Aspergillosis is a fungal infection caused by several *Aspergillus* species. It is primarily a respiratory infection that may become generalized. Aspergillosis is found worldwide and in almost all domestic animals as well as in many wild animals; however, the susceptibility to fungal infections varies among species.

The most common form in horses is fungal disease affecting the guttural pouch. The 2 guttural pouches are sacs formed by the auditory tube, which connects the middle ear with the back of the throat. Infection usually occurs only in 1 guttural pouch. The infected guttural pouch becomes thickened, and bleeding into the tissue may occur. Nosebleed and difficulty in breathing or swallowing are common signs. Other signs include holding the head extended or low, head-shaking, swelling of the head, neurologic signs, and nasal discharge.

Aspergillosis in horses can be rapidly fatal when the infection invades the lungs. In these cases, inflammation of the intestine is often a predisposing factor thought to weaken the immune system of the horse. This is followed by the invasion of *Aspergillus* from a disrupted lining of the intestines. Physical coordination is impaired and visual disturbances, including blindness, may occur when the infection spreads to the brain and optic nerve.

In horses, surgery to expose and remove fungal material has been used to treat guttural pouch mycosis. Topical and oral antifungal agents have been reported to be effective in cases of *Aspergillus* infection. The outlook is guarded; horses may survive but not recover completely, particularly if the nerves are damaged.

Candidiasis

Candidiasis is a localized fungal disease affecting the mucous membranes and the skin. It is distributed worldwide in a variety of animals and is most commonly caused by species of the yeast-like fungus, *Candida albicans*. Superficial infections limited to the mucous membranes of the intestinal tract have been described in foals. Widespread candidiasis has also been described in foals undergoing prolonged antibiotic or corticosteroid treatment. Infections are rare in horses. However, *Candida* species have been considered a cause of arthritis in horses.

Signs are variable and nonspecific and may be associated more with the primary or predisposing conditions than with the candidiasis itself. An ointment or topical application may be useful in the treatment of oral or skin candidiasis. Your veterinarian may also recommend different drugs given by mouth or through the vein to successfully resolve arthritis induced by *Candida fumata* infection in a horse or to treat generalized candidiasis in foals.

Coccidioidomycosis (Valley Fever)

Coccidioidomycosis is a dustborne, noncontagious infection caused by the fungus *Coccidioides immitis*. Infections are limited to dry, desertlike regions of the southwestern United States and to similar areas of Mexico and Central and South America. Inhalation of fungal spores (often carried on dust particles) is the only established mode of infection. Epidemics may occur when rainy periods are followed by drought, resulting in dust storms.

The disease varies from infections with few or no signs to progressive, disseminated, and fatal forms. In horses, the most common signs include loss of weight, coughing, fever, musculoskeletal pain, and abscesses of the skin. Placental infections leading to abortion and inflammation of bone have been described in horses. A diagnosis is confirmed by identifying the fungus in body tissues.

Coccidioidomycosis may resolve without treatment, but if chronic respiratory signs or multisystemic disease are present, longterm antifungal treatment is needed. At the present time there is no known prevention other than decreasing your horse's exposure to the desert soil and dust as much as possible in areas where the fungus is known to exist.

Cryptococcosis

Cryptococcosis is a systemic fungal disease. The causal fungus, *Cryptococcus neoformans*, exists in the environment and in tissues in a yeast form. The fungus is found worldwide in soil and bird manure, especially in pigeon droppings. Transmission is by inhalation of spores or contamination of wounds. Cryptococcosis is uncommon in horses.

The disease in horses is, almost invariably, a respiratory ailment with obstructive growths in the nasal cavities. Treatment for cryptococcosis may include surgery to remove lesions in the nasal cavity. Various antifungal drugs can be used for the treatment of cryptococcosis.

Epizootic Lymphangitis

Epizootic lymphangitis is a disease that affects the skin, lymph vessels, and lymph nodes of the limbs and neck of horses. It is caused by the fungus *Histoplasma farciminosum*. Infection seems to be limited to horses, donkeys, and occasionally mules. Epizootic lymphangitis occurs in Asian and Mediterranean areas but is unknown in the United States. Infection probably is acquired by wound infection or transmission by bloodsucking insects such as mosquitoes.

The disease most typically involves the skin and associated lymph vessels and nodes. Occasionally there is involvement of the respiratory tract. Some horses develop small, inconspicuous lesions that heal spontaneously. More typically, nodules develop under the skin. These increase in size and undergo cycles of granulation and partial healing followed by renewed eruption. The surrounding tissues become hard, painful, and swollen. Lesions may be seen on the skin of the face, around and in the eyes and nose, and on the forelegs, thorax, neck, and occasionally the inside of the rear legs. Other internal organs may be involved.

No completely satisfactory treatment is known. Surgical removal of lesions combined with antifungal drugs may be tried. In most areas of the world, however, this is a reportable disease; treatment of animals is not permitted, and destruction of affected horses is usually mandatory.

Strict hygienic precautions are essential to prevent spread of epizootic lymphangitis. Great care should be taken to prevent spread on grooming or harness equipment. Contaminated bedding should be burned. The organism may persist in the environment for many months.

Pythiosis

Pythiosis is a disease caused by *Pythium insidiosum*, which is not a true fungus but a water mold. It occurs in some tropical and subtropical areas of the world and is seen in warmer sections of the US. In the US, the disease most often is seen in fall and winter months. Horses are the most commonly affected animals, followed by dogs and, rarely, cats and people.

Infections in horses are most commonly restricted to the skin and the tissues just inside the skin. There may be large, circu-lar nodules or areas of swelling that can become open, draining sores. These lesions are usually on the lower legs, abdomen, and chest but may occur anywhere on the body. The lesions are usually intensely itchy, and horses may mutilate the wounds if not closely monitored. Skin lesions often contain firm, yellowish masses of dead tissue known as "kunkers."

Following the initial infection, the organism may spread to distant areas through the lymph system. The lymph nodes, bones, or lungs may be involved.

Horses rarely develop gastrointestinal disease similar to that occurring in dogs (*see* page 316). Horses with gastrointestinal pythiosis may have signs of gastrointestinal obstruction, weight loss, poor appetite, diarrhea, and acute abdominal pain. In other horses, gastrointestinal disease may be unaccompanied by signs of generalized illness.

Pythiosis nodules are usually found on the lower legs, abdomen, and chest.

A diagnosis may be based on the appearance of the distinctive lesions and confirmed by identification of the organism in infected tissues. Surgical removal of lesions, antifungal treatment, treatment directed at the immune system, or a combination of these may be recommended to treat affected horses. The outlook is guarded, but timely recognition and treatment may lead to a more successful outcome. Other factors that influence the outlook include the size and location of lesions and the length of infection.

Phaeohyphomycosis

Phaeohyphomycosis is a general term for an infection by any of a number of funguses of the family Dematiaceae. This type of fungal infection is uncommon in horses. The funguses known to cause phaeohyphomycosis have been recovered from decaying vegetative matter and soil all over the world. Infection may result when the fungus enters the body at the site of an injury.

In most cases, the infection is confined to the skin and tissues beneath the skin. The most common signs include nodules in the skin, upper respiratory signs, and masses that form in the lining of the nasal passages and on the legs and chest. The nodules may ulcerate and have draining tracts.

Surgical removal of the lesion can be a cure. Treatment with antifungal drugs may be considered in cases when surgery is not possible.

Rhinosporidiosis

Rhinosporidiosis is a chronic infection, primarily of the lining of the nasal passages and occasionally of the skin. It is caused by the fungus *Rhinosporidium seeberi*. Uncommon in North America, it is seen most often in India, Africa, and South America. This disease is not considered transmissible.

Infection of the nasal mucosa is characterized by polyp-like growths that may be soft, pink, crumbly, and lobular with roughened surfaces. The growths may become large enough to obstruct or close off the nasal passages. The skin lesions may be single or multiple, attached at a base or have a stem-like connection. Signs of infection include nasal discharge and sneezing.

Surgical removal of the lesions is considered to be the standard treatment, but recurrence is common.

Sporotrichosis

Sporotrichosis is a sporadic chronic disease caused by *Sporothrix schenckii*. The organism is found around the world in soil, vegetation, and timber. In the United States, *Sporothrix schenckii* is most commonly found in coastal regions and river valleys. Infection usually results when the organism enters the body through skin wounds via contact with plants or soil or penetrating foreign objects such as a sharp branch. Transmission of the disease from animals to humans can occur.

The infection may remain localized to the site of entry (involving only the skin) or it may spread to nearby lymph nodes. Both of these forms occur in horses. Small, firm nodules develop at the site where infection enters the body. Although generalized illness is not seen initially, chronic illness may result in fever, listlessness, and depression. Rarely, infection will spread through the bloodstream or tissue from the initial site of inoculation to the bone, lungs, liver, spleen, testes, gastrointestinal tract, or central nervous system.

In order to diagnose sporotrichosis in horses, it may be necessary to take samples of infected tissues, culture them, and then examine them for evidence of the fungus.

Longterm treatment with antifungal drugs (continued 3 to 4 weeks beyond apparent cure) is usually recommended. Alternatively, a solution of potassium iodide, administered by mouth, has been used with some success; treatment is continued 30 days beyond apparent cure. During treatment, the horse should be monitored for signs of iodide toxicity.

Because sporotrichosis can be passed from your horse to you, strict hygiene must be observed when handling animals with suspected or diagnosed sporotrichosis.

Zygomycosis (Basidiobolomycosis, Conidiobolomycosis)

Zygomycosis is the term used to describe infection with funguses in the class Zygomycetes and 2 genera in the order Entomophthorales (*Basidiobolus* and *Conidiobolus*). These funguses are found throughout the natural environment and are present in soil and decaying vegetation. True zygomycete infections are rare, but conidiobolomycosis and basidiobolomycosis are more common and cause lesions that are similar to those caused by pythiosis (*see* page 803).

This is primarily an infection of the lining of the mouth, nasal passages, and tissue beneath the skin of horses (*Conidiobolus* and *Basidiobolus* species) or the sides of the head, neck, and body (*Basidiobolus* species).

When infection causes ulcers or nodular growths in the mucous membrane of the nostril or mouth, the lesions may grow so large that they block the passages. Such mechanical blockages cause difficulty in breathing and nasal discharge. When *Basidiobolus* affects the skin of the upper body, nodules that are large, usually single, circular, ulcerative, and itchy may form. Infection may extend to nearby lymph nodes, causing swelling of the nodes and development of focused yellow areas of dead cells.

Your veterinarian may recommend surgical removal of the lesion, antifungal drugs, medication to improve immune system response, or a combination of these.

GLANDERS (FARCY)

Glanders is a contagious, short- or long-term, usually fatal disease of the horse family caused by the bacterium *Burkholderia mallei*. The disease is characterized by the development of ulcerating growths that are most commonly found in the upper respiratory tract, lungs, and skin. Humans and other animals are also susceptible, and infections are usually fatal. Glanders once was prevalent worldwide. It has now been eradicated or effectively controlled in many countries, including the United States. In recent years, the disease has been reported in Iraq, Turkey, Pakistan, India, Mongolia, China, Brazil, and the United Arab Emirates.

The disease is commonly contracted by consuming food or water contaminated by the nasal discharge of carrier animals. The organism can survive in a contaminated area for more than 1 year, particularly under humid, wet conditions.

After an incubation period of about 2 weeks, affected animals usually have blood infection and a high fever (up to 106°F [41°C]). Later, a thick nasal discharge is seen and the animal has trouble breathing and other respiratory signs. Death can occur within a few days. The longterm form of the disease is common in horses. It is a debilitating condition with ulcers and growths on the skin and in the nose. Infected animals may live for years and spread the bacteria widely. The outlook is unfavorable. Recovered animals may not develop immunity.

In the skin form (also called **farcy**), growths appear along the course of the lymph vessels, particularly on the legs. These growths degenerate and form ulcers that discharge highly infectious, sticky pus.

There is no vaccine. Prevention and control depend on early detection and elimination of affected animals, as well as complete quarantine and rigorous disinfection of the area involved. Euthanasia is usually recommended for affected horses.

INFECTIOUS NECROTIC HEPATITIS (BLACK DISEASE)

Infectious necrotic hepatitis is an infectious disease of sheep and cattle that is rarely seen in horses. The bacteria that cause the disease, *Clostridium novyi* type B, are found in the soil and are frequently present in the intestines of plant-eating animals (herbivores). They may be present on skin surfaces and are a potential source of wound infections. Contamination of pasture by the feces of carrier animals is the most important source of infection for horses. The organism multiplies in areas of dead cells in the liver caused by migration of liver flukes and produces a powerful cell-killing toxin. The disease is worldwide in distribution. Affected animals tend to become lethargic, lie down, and die within a few hours. Abdominal pain and inflammation may occur. Most cases occur in the summer and early fall when liver fluke infection is at its peak. Usually, there is extensive rupture of the blood capillaries in the tissue under the skin, which causes the adjacent skin to turn black (hence the common name, black disease). There is no effective treatment.

Reducing the numbers of snails (usually *Lymnaea* species) that act as intermediate hosts for liver flukes or otherwise reducing the number of liver flukes may reduce the occurrence of infectious necrotic hepatitis. However, these procedures are not always practical. There is currently no vaccine available for use in horses.

▓ INTESTINAL CLOSTRIDIOSIS (CLOSTRIDIA-ASSOCIATED ENTEROCOLITIS)

This intestinal disease of horses and foals is characterized by diarrhea and sudden stomach pain. It has been associated with various species of *Clostridium* bacteria, which are likely responsible for the disease. The bacteria are normally present in the soil or the environment and may be ingested by horses. They are commonly found in the intestine of healthy horses. The factors that trigger disease are not well understood, but it may be that some alteration in the organisms normally found in the digestive tract—such as a change of diet or antibiotic treatment—permits excessive multiplication of the bacteria and the production of toxins

Intestinal Clostridiosis

Clostridium difficile and *Clostridium perfringens* have been implicated in this intestinal disease of horses characterized by diarrhea and stomach pain. Both organisms may be present in soil or the environment and be ingested by horses. The factors that trigger disease are not well known, but there are established predisposing factors.

Predisposing factors:

▓ Change in diet

▓ Antibiotic treatment

▓ Age

▓ Immunity

▓ Presence of receptors for the clostridial toxins in the intestines

▓ Elimination of roughage from the diet prior to surgery

(poisonous substances) capable of causing intestinal damage and disease.

Certain antibiotics (notably, erythromycin, beta-lactam antibiotics, and trimethoprim/sulfonamide), are more likely than others to be associated with intestinal clostridiosis. Mares with foals that are being treated with erythromycin appear to be at high risk. Cutting down on the amount of roughage in the diet prior to surgery may also be a factor.

Typically, the signs include abdominal pain and diarrhea with or without blood. The abdomen may be distended. Dehydration, spread of bacterial toxins through the bloodstream, and shock may develop. One or several horses in a stable or on a farm may be affected. The identification of *Clostridium* species as the cause of diarrhea depends on finding the specific toxin in the intestines or the gene for the toxin in the feces or intestinal fluid. Your veterinarian is more likely to suspect this condition if your horse has a history of recent treatment with antibiotics.

Your veterinarian will recommend an antibiotic given by mouth for treatment of this condition. In addition, steps may be taken to reduce the opportunity for intestinal clostridiosis in horses. Careful selection of certain antibiotics for high-risk horses is recommended. The sources of the bacterial spores may be attacked by the regular use of disinfectants that kill spores. Good hygiene, including hand washing and isolation of infected horses and foals, should always be practiced.

Enterotoxemia Caused by *Clostridium* in Foals

One type of *Clostridium* associated with intestinal clostridiosis (*Clostridium perfringens*) also causes severe inflammation of the intestines, abdominal pain, and release of toxins that are responsible for severe intestinal damage and high mortality in foals. This condition, called enterotoxemia, usually occurs in foals in the first week of life.

Treatment involves administration of antibiotics by mouth to destroy the *C. perfringens* in the intestine, giving fluids to compensate for losses due to diarrhea, and appropriate use of drugs to relieve pain. Serum from horses that have been immunized with toxins of *C. perfringens* is sometimes administered as well. Despite these interventions, some affected foals will die.

LEPTOSPIROSIS

Leptospirosis is a disease caused by a *Leptospira* bacteria; there are approximately 17 species. Because the organisms survive in surface waters (such as swamps, streams, and rivers) for extended periods, the disease is often waterborne.

Horses may contract leptospirosis by direct contact with infected urine or urine-contaminated feed or water. Less commonly, transmission of the bacteria may occur via bite wounds, eating infected tissue, or during birth. Once in the body, leptospires spread rapidly via the lymph system to the bloodstream and then to all tissues. If the animal mounts an immune response and survives, leptospires will be cleared from most organs and the bloodstream. However, the infection persists in sites hidden from the immune system; the most common hidden site is the kidneys. Persistence in the kidneys results in a carrier state. An infected animal may shed leptospires in the urine for at least a year.

Leptospirosis in horses is most commonly associated with inflammation of the inner part of the eye (also called uveitis or periodic ophthalmia) or abortions. The disease is typically seen as a mild fever with loss of appetite, although severe forms can cause the presence of free hemoglobin in the urine, low blood counts, jaundice, depression, and weakness. Kidney failure has been seen in affected foals.

Recurrent uveitis, or moon blindness, (*see* page 651) develops any time from 2 to 8 months after the initial infection. Leptospirosis appears to be a significant cause of recurrent uveitis in horses, accounting for up to 67% of the cases. Leptospirosis is responsible for 3 to 4% of all equine abortions annually, although flooding and other environmental catastrophes may result in abortion outbreaks.

Your veterinarian will likely recommend antibiotics for leptospirosis. Uveitis is treated as needed to reduce the inflammation and prevent adhesion of the iris to the cornea or the lens of the eye. No vaccine is currently available for horses.

Leptospirosis is a common cause of equine uveitis.

■ LYME DISEASE (LYME BORRELIOSIS)

Lyme disease, which is caused by the bacteria *Borrelia burgdorferi* and transmitted through the bite of a tick, affects domestic animals and humans. At least 3 known species of ticks can transmit Lyme disease. However, the great majority of Lyme disease transmissions are due to the bite of a very tiny tick commonly called the deer tick, or black-legged tick. The scientific name of the tick species involved is *Ixodes pacificus* on the west coast of the US; *Ixodes scapularis* is the species involved elsewhere. It is important to note that ticks do not cause Lyme disease; they merely harbor and transmit the bacteria that cause it.

Lyme disease occurs much more frequently in dogs than in other animals. Although horses have tested positive for exposure to the disease-causing bacteria, it is unclear whether there is a relationship between the exposure and any signs of infection such as lameness, fever, loss of appetite, fatigue, or difficulty breathing. It is best to consult with your veterinarian regarding the cause if any of these signs appear, particularly in areas where Lyme disease is common (including the northeastern and mid-Atlantic states in the United States). Antibiotics are required for treatment. (For a more detailed description of LYME DISEASE, *see* page 320.)

The best protection against Lyme disease is to avoid exposing your horses to the ticks that transmit the *Borrelia burgdorferi* bacteria. Keep pastures mowed and remove areas where rodents nest. Ask your veterinarian to recommend an appropriate tick repellent for your horse. Daily grooming away from stalls or exercise areas can remove ticks resting on your horse's coat. If possible, capture and properly dispose of any ticks you find; otherwise they may reattach themselves to another horse or other animal. Remove any ticks by using fine-pointed tweezers to grasp the head of the tick (right where it enters the skin). Pull the tick straight off, making sure not to grasp or squeeze its body.

■ MALIGNANT EDEMA

Malignant edema is a disease in which there is a severe, usually fatal spread of bacterial toxins through the bloodstream of horses and other large mammals. It is usually caused by *Clostridium septicum* bacteria, often accompanied by other clostridial species. The bacteria are found in soil and intestinal contents of animals (including humans) throughout the world. Infection ordinarily occurs through the contamination and infection of wounds such as those caused by accident, castration, tail docking, unsanitary injections, or during birth.

Signs, such as loss of appetite, intoxication, and high fever, as well as swelling around the site of the infection, develop within a few hours to a few days after a predisposing injury. The swellings extend rapidly because of the formation of large quantities of material under the skin and within the connective tissue. The muscle in such areas is dark brown to black. Malignant edema associated with lacerations of the vulva during labor is characterized by swelling of the vulva, spread of bacterial toxins through the bloodstream, and death in 24 to 48 hours. Treatment with high doses of penicillin or broad-spectrum antibiotics early in the disease may be attempted, but death usually occurs rapidly after infection.

■ MELIOIDOSIS

Melioidosis is an uncommon bacterial infection of humans and animals. The disease-causing agent is *Burkholderia pseudomallei*, which occurs in the soil throughout southeast Asia, northern Australia, and the South Pacific. The disease is not known to occur in the US. Outbreaks have coincided with heavy rainfall and flooding and are associated with high humidity or temperature. Major excavations and disturbances in plumbing resulting in contamination of water supplies have also led to outbreaks. Animals become infected through inhalation, contamination of wounds, or ingestion.

Melioidosis has been diagnosed in many animals, including horses. In horses, signs may be similar to those of glanders (*see* page 805), although infection without signs is common. The disease may be associated with single or multiple curd-like nodules or abscesses, which can be located in any organ. When the infection enters through the skin, it often develops at distant sites without evidence of active infection at the site of entry. Central nervous system disease has been seen in horses. Pneumonia is the most common form of disease caused by the bacteria in animals and humans. Lameness can occur. It is possible for an infection to lie dormant before becoming apparent. Death may occur in sudden and intense infections or when vital organs are affected.

Treatment can be expensive and prolonged. It is often unsuccessful and there is a risk that signs will return after treatment is discontinued. There is a possibility that this disease involves suppression of the immune system, especially in species that are less susceptible to infection. Treatment regimens using guidelines for human melioidosis include antibiotics. In areas where the bacteria are common, preventive measures such as minimizing environmental contamination by diseased animals and providing clean (chlorinated and filtered) drinking water may be helpful.

■ NOCARDIOSIS

Nocardiosis is a chronic, noncontagious disease caused by the bacteria of the genus *Nocardia*. These bacteria are found commonly in soil, decaying vegetation, compost, and other environmental sources. They enter the body through contamination of wounds or by inhalation. Species in this genus are found in temperate regions, as well as in tropical and subtropical areas.

Poor appetite, fever, lethargy, and weight loss are common nonspecific signs associated with all infection sites. Skin infection and lymph node abscesses (localized collections of pus) are common signs in horses, with respiratory or disseminated disease occurring in animals with weakened immune systems. The first sign of infection is the appearance of a hardened nodule or pustule, which ruptures and produces pus. Individual lesions may be connected by channels, with frequent development of chronic, progressive disease. Nocardial inflammation of the mouth produces swelling and inflammation of the gums around the teeth and ulceration of the oral cavity, with severe bad breath. Abortion may occur in infected mares.

Your veterinarian will prescribe an antibiotic based on identification of the bacteria. Nocardial infections are resistant to some types of antibiotics. Treatment must often be continued for more than 3 months. It is important to continue treatment as directed to allow the best possibility for recovery. The outlook is guarded due to the long treatment time and the likelihood of relapse.

■ PERITONITIS

Peritonitis is inflammation of the peritoneum, the membrane that lines the abdominal cavity. Peritonitis may be short- or longterm, local or diffuse. Most commonly it occurs due to contamination (for example by perforation of the abdominal cavity by a foreign object, the splitting open of an abdominal wound closure, or the rupture of the intestine due to a foreign object or compromised intestinal wall), but it also may be caused by infectious agents such as viruses or bacteria.

Signs vary depending on the type and cause of peritonitis. Abdominal pain (colic) may be generalized and severe. The affected horse may guard the abdomen, walk with a stiff gait, or lie down and roll. Diarrhea or constipation may be noted, along with fever and loss of appetite. Abdominal distention, which may not be easily seen, is usually due to an accumulation of fluids and other material in the abdomen. Distention may be accompanied by bleeding, blood poisoning, paralytic obstruction of the intestines, shock, and adhesions. Jaundice may be present in generalized gallbladder peritonitis.

Diagnosis of peritonitis can be difficult due to the nonspecific signs. Your veterinarian will likely use a combination of signs, x-rays or ultrasonography, rectal examination, and examination of peritoneal fluid (obtained from the abdomen) to make a diagnosis.

The first priority of treatment is to stabilize the consequences of peritonitis (for example, changes in electrolytes, acid-base imbalance, fluid loss, and blood clotting abnormalities), In addition, your veterinarian will want to identify the source of inflammation or infection and correct or remove it. Antibiotics are usually needed. Replacement fluids, electrolytes, plasma, or whole blood may be necessary to maintain heart output.

Once the horse is stabilized, surgery is done to explore the abdomen and to repair any defects. Your veterinarian will follow this with a thorough rinsing of the abdominal cavity with a saline solution, antiseptic, or antibiotics. Antibiotics are continued after surgery. Nutritional support with intravenous feeding may be needed, as many horses with peritonitis will not eat after surgery. In animals with blood poisoning and shock, fluids and electrolytes are crucial elements of treat-

ment, especially for horses during the first 24 to 72 hours after surgery. Peritonitis caused by infection is frequently fatal, despite intensive treatment.

■ SEPTICEMIA IN FOALS

Septicemia or sepsis (blood infection) is a whole-body disease in which bacteria circulate in the bloodstream. It is most commonly found in very young foals less than 4 weeks of age. Bacteria can spread through the blood to various organs, such as the lungs, intestines, eyes, central nervous system, bones, and joints causing lameness and joint swelling. The condition implies an extensive, whole body infection from single or multiple sources. The most common bacteria identified in septic foals is *Escherichia coli* (*E. coli*). Others that may be involved include *Klebsiella, Enterobacter, Actinobacillus, Salmonella*, and *Streptococcus* species. Some of these bacteria contain a toxin in their cell walls called **endotoxin**. When endotoxin is released into the bloodstream, or when whole bacteria are present in the blood, it causes the release of other chemicals in the body called cytokines. These cytokines cause the signs of depression, poor appetite, and fever.

The major risk factor for septicemia in foals is the failure to receive an adequate quantity of good quality colostrum (the first milk produced by mares, which contains high levels of antibodies) during the first few hours after birth. Other factors that increase the risk of disease include a dirty environment, prematurity at birth (a weak foal), poor health and condition of the dam, a difficult birth, and the presence of new disease-causing agents in the environment against which the mare has no antibodies.

A foal with septicemia may show evidence of single or multiple organ dysfunction. The earliest sign may be that the foal is slightly depressed or does not act as lively as other foals. This progresses to a foal that will not eat and lies down fre-

---

Common Causes of Peritonitis in Horses

■ Traumatic perforation or injury to the abdomen

■ Leakage of material from damaged intestines

■ Leakage from damaged spleen, liver, or umbilical organs

■ Injury caused by infections, chemical toxins, or parasites

■ Rupture of the intestines, stomach, or rectum

Risk Factors for Septicemia in Foals

- Failure to receive an adequate quality and quantity of colostral antibodies
- Unsanitary environmental conditions
- Gestational age of the foal (prematurity)
- Poor health and condition of the dam
- A difficult birth
- Presence of new disease-causing agents in the environment against which the mare has no antibodies

quently. The mare's udder is often distended with milk, indicating that the foal is not nursing with normal frequency.

In the advanced stage of illness (septic shock), the body becomes overwhelmed. Such foals are often severely depressed and dehydrated, can only rise with assistance, and have a rapid heart rate. Low blood pressure, shown by such signs as cold extremities and a weak pulse, is evident. Foals may have elevated or reduced body temperature. Gums become either bright red or pale. In the final stages, foals become unconscious and go into cardiac and respiratory arrest.

Diagnosis is based in part on a thorough physical examination and medical history. Laboratory tests are required to assess organ function and identify the type of bacteria responsible for the infection.

Treatment and Outlook

Foals suspected of being septic are usually given broad-spectrum antibiotics (antibiotics that are effective against a wide range of bacteria) to kill the bacteria causing the infection. In cases of neonatal sepsis, veterinarians often recommend plasma transfusions to help the foal's immune system by supplying antibodies that were not received in colostrum. In addition, intravenous fluids may be given to help counter the effects of bacterial toxins and infection. Many septic foals have low blood sugar, so a sugar solution is often added to the fluid treatment.

Nutritional support is also important. If the foal is not nursing adequately, it should be fed mare's milk or a milk substitute at 15 to 25% of its body weight over each 24-hour period. Sometimes, the foal does not tolerate a large volume of milk and must be fed small amounts very frequently. It may be necessary to insert a feeding tube through the nose in foals with a decreased suckle reflex. Foals should never be fed milk by a syringe, because there is a risk of inhaling the milk into the lungs (aspiration).

Other treatments that may be required include flushing out infected joints with sterile fluids and providing nasal oxygen or ventilation for foals with septic pneumonia. Surgical removal of infected umbilical cord remnants may be needed. Eye infections and ulcers on the cornea of the eye are treated with antibiotic and anti-inflammatory eye ointments.

Recovery from neonatal sepsis depends on the severity and form of the infection. Current survival rates are 55 to 75% in equine intensive care units of large veterinary hospitals. An average of 1 to 3 weeks of intensive care should be expected. Early recognition and intensive treatment of foal sepsis improves the outcome. If the foal survives the initial problems, it has the potential of becoming a healthy adult.

■ TETANUS

Tetanus toxemia is caused by a specific poison, or toxin, that blocks transmission of inhibitory nerve signals. This leads to severe muscle contraction and an exaggerated response to stimuli. The toxin is produced by the bacterium *Clostridium tetani* in dead tissue. Most mammals are susceptible, but horses and humans appear to be the most sensitive of all species. Although tetanus occurs worldwide, there are some areas, such as the northern Rocky Mountain section of the United States, where the organism is rarely found in the soil and where tetanus is almost unknown. In general, the occurrence of the bacteria in the soil and the frequency of tetanus in humans and horses are higher in the warmer parts of the various continents.

Clostridium tetani is found in soil and intestinal tracts. In most cases, it is introduced into the body through wounds, particularly deep puncture wounds. Sometimes, the point of entry cannot be found because the wound itself may be minor or healed. The bacteria remain in the dead tissue at the original site of infection and multiply. As bacterial cells die and disintegrate, the potent nerve toxin is released. The toxin spreads and causes spasms of the voluntary muscles.

The incubation period varies from 1 to several weeks but usually averages 10 to 14 days. Localized stiffness, often involving the jaw muscles and muscles of the neck, the hind limbs, and the region of the infected wound, is seen first. General stiffness becomes pronounced about 1 day later, and then spasms and painful sensitivity to touch become evident.

As the disease progresses, the reflexes increase in intensity and the animal is easily excited into more violent, general spasms by sudden movement or noise. The spasms may be so severe that they cause bone fractures. Spasms of head muscles cause difficulty in grasping and chewing of food, hence the common name, lockjaw.

In horses, the ears are erect, the tail stiff and extended, the nostrils dilated, and the third eyelid sunken. Walking, turning, and backing are difficult. Spasms of the neck and back muscles cause extension of the head and neck, while stiffness of the

A horse with tetanus often has a typical "sawhorse" stance.

leg muscles causes the animal to assume a "sawhorse" stance. Sweating is common. General spasms disturb blood circulation and breathing, which results in increased heart rate, rapid breathing, congestion of mucous membranes, and possible respiratory failure. About 80% of affected animals die. In horses that recover, there is a recovery period of 2 to 6 weeks.

The diagnosis of tetanus is usually based on the distinctive signs and history of recent trauma. Your veterinarian may be able to confirm the diagnosis by finding the tetanus toxin in a blood sample taken from the affected animal. Treatment involves thorough cleaning and disinfection of the wound, the use of antibiotics, and tetanus antitoxin (which helps protect against the effects of additional toxin being released). Whether or not the horse has been immunized, another injection of toxoid is usually given to increase the production of antibodies to the toxin. In the early stages of the disease, your veterinarian may recommend muscle relaxants, tranquilizers, or sedatives, in conjunction with tetanus antitoxin. Good results with tetanus antitoxin injections have been obtained in horses.

Recovering horses require supportive nursing care and should be kept in a dark, quiet stall. Feeding and watering devices should be high enough to allow the horse to use them without lowering the head. Slings may be useful for horses having difficulty standing or rising. Ask for and follow your veterinarian's advice regarding any other steps you should take.

Immunization can be accomplished with tetanus toxoid and is usually recommended for all horses. Yearly booster injections of toxoid are advisable. Mares should be vaccinated during the last 6 weeks of pregnancy and the foals vaccinated at 5 to 8 weeks of age. In high-risk areas, foals may be given tetanus antitoxin immediately after birth and every 2 to 3 weeks until they are 3 months old, at which time they can be given toxoid.

TRICHINELLOSIS (TRICHINOSIS)

Trichinellosis is a parasitic disease that can be transmitted to people. It is caused by the nematode *Trichinella spiralis*. People become infected when they eat insufficiently cooked infected meat, usually pork or bear, although meat from other animals has also been implicated. Natural infections occur in wild carnivores, and most mammals are susceptible. Trichinellosis has occasionally been found in horses.

Generally, there are no signs of the disease in horses. Making sure that ingestion of viable *Trichinella* cysts in muscle does not occur is the best way to prevent disease in both animals and humans. (For a more detailed discussion of TRICHINELLOSIS, *see* page 327.)

TUBERCULOSIS

Tuberculosis, an infectious disease caused by bacteria of the genus *Mycobacterium*, is rare in the United States. Most infections in horses are caused by *Mycobacterium bovis* and are likely acquired by close contact with infected cattle. The disease affects practically all species of vertebrates, and, before control measures were adopted, was an important disease of humans and domestic animals. Signs and lesions are generally similar in the various species.

Three main types of tubercle bacilli are recognized: human (*Mycobacterium tuberculosis*), bovine (*M. bovis*), and avian (*M. avium*). The 2 mammalian types are more closely related to each other than to the avian type. All the types may produce infection in host species other than their own. Ingestion (particularly via contaminated feed) occurs, especially with *M. avium*. The breathing in of infected droplets expelled from the lungs of an infected person or animal may also occur.

The signs reflect the extent and location of lesions. Generalized signs include progressive emaciation, lethargy, weakness, loss of appetite, and fever. Horses infected with *M. bovis* often have signs related to the respiratory form of the disease, including coughing and difficulty breathing.

M. bovis may be transmitted to humans and other animals and represents a public health risk. If a horse is suspected of having advanced tuberculous lesions, it must be reported to the appropriate public health authorities. Treatment of a horse with tuberculosis should be discussed with your veterinarian.

TULAREMIA

Tularemia is a bacterial disease that affects people and many species of wild and domestic animals. It is caused by toxins in the blood produced by the bacterium *Francisella tularensis*. The bacteria can survive for weeks or months in a moist environment. Tularemia can infect people and can be transmitted by aerosol, direct contact, ingestion, or ticks and deer flies.

Among domestic animals, sheep are the most likely to show signs of the disease, but disease has also been reported in horses. The most common source of infection for people and horses is the bite of an infected tick. Signs of infection in the horse include the sudden onset of high fever, swollen lymph nodes, and lethargy. Prostration and death may occur in a few hours or days. Sporadic cases are best recognized based on signs of illness and observation of heavy tick infestation. Very mild cases without signs may be common.

Animals with signs of illness are treated with an antibiotic. Early treatment should prevent death; however, prolonged treatment may be necessary. Control is difficult and is limited to reducing tick infestation and to rapid diagnosis and treatment. Animals that recover develop a long-lasting immunity.

VESICULAR STOMATITIS

Vesicular stomatitis is caused by a virus and affects horses and other livestock. The virus can be transmitted to humans and may cause flu-like disease. Vesicular stomatitis is seen only sporadically in the US. Outbreaks have historically occurred in all regions of the country, but since the 1980s have been limited to the southwestern states. Vesicular stomatitis viruses are prevalent in South America, Central America, and parts of Mexico but have not been seen naturally outside the Western hemisphere.

The virus can be transmitted through direct contact with infected animals that have signs of disease (those with sores) or by blood-feeding insects. In the southwestern US, black flies are the most likely carrier. In areas where this disease is common, sand flies are also known to transmit it.

Excessive drooling is often the first sign of disease. Blisters in the mouth are rarely seen in naturally occurring cases because they rupture soon after formation. Ulcers and erosions of the mouth linings, shedding of the surface of the tongue, and ulcers at the junctions of the lips are commonly seen. Inflammation and erosions at the cushion of the hoof are sometimes observed; lameness soon follows. Crusting lesions of the muzzle, lower abdomen, the covering of the penis, and udder of horses are typical during outbreaks in the southwestern US. Loss of appetite due to mouth ulcers and lameness due to foot ulcers are normally of short duration, as the disease generally resolves within 2 weeks. However, reinfection can occur following a second exposure.

No specific treatment is needed. When infected animals are identified, they should be isolated until the disease has run its course. Other animals on the property should be restricted to the property to reduce the chance of the disease spreading. General ill health and malnutrition can be avoided by providing softened

Crusts and blisters around the lips and sores inside the mouth may be seen in horses with vesicular stomatitis.

feeds. Cleaning ulcers with mild antiseptics may help avoid bacterial infections.

To reduce the risk of exposure to the virus, owners may limit pasture time, provide shelters or barns during insect feeding times, and take other steps to reduce animal contact with insects. Your veterinarian can provide advice about insecticides that may be appropriate for use with horses. Vesicular stomatitis is a reportable disease in most areas, including the US. Veterinarians are required to notify animal health officials when it is suspected. Vaccines are not available in the US but are available in some Latin American countries.

SECTION

7

BIRDS

58 **Description and Physical Characteristics of Birds** **816**
Introduction 816
Description and Physical Characteristics 816
Special Considerations 826

59 **Selecting and Providing a Home for a Pet Bird** **827**
Introduction 827
Selecting a Pet Bird 828
Providing a Home for a Pet Bird 829

60 **Routine Care and Breeding** **832**
Introduction 832
Importance of Veterinary Care 832
Signs of Illness 832
Giving Medication 833
Grooming and Routine Care 834
Household Hazards 835
Breeding and Reproduction 836

61 **Disorders and Diseases of Birds** **839**
Introduction 839
Heart and Blood Vessel Disorders 839
Digestive Disorders 840
Hormonal Disorders 843
Eye Disorders 843
Bone and Muscle Disorders 843
Nutritional Disorders 844
Lung and Airway Disorders 846
Reproductive Disorders 848
Skin and Feather Disorders 850
Kidney and Urinary Tract Disorders 852
Disorders Affecting Multiple Body Systems 854
Cancers and Tumors 858
Injuries and Accidents 859

58

CHAPTER

Description and Physical Characteristics of Birds

■ INTRODUCTION

There are some 35 to 45 million pet birds in the United States. Modern bird owners are continuing a pet bird tradition that goes back at least 4,000 years to the ancient Egyptians, who are often credited with keeping the first pet birds. The ancient Chinese are known to have kept pheasants. From writings dating back almost 3,000 years, we know that both Persians and Indians kept parrots and other birds as pets, as did the ancient Greeks. Aristotle studied and wrote about his pet bird, Psittace. The name of Aristotle's bird is the root of the scientific name for all parrots, *Psittacine*. The Alexandrine parakeet is named for Alexander the Great; tradition has it that one of Alexander's generals granted him one of these birds as a gift following the invasion of northern India in 327 A.D.

Birds have often performed important tasks for their human owners. For example, the breeding and use of pigeons for rapid message delivery was widely practiced in the Middle East and northern Africa from ancient times, spread to Europe and the New World, and continued well into the 1900s. Most individuals are familiar with the use of canaries in mines to detect dangerous coal gases and carbon monoxide. If the canary fainted or died, the miners knew that the air was dangerous and they should get out quickly. The use of canaries in mines started as early as the 15th century and continued into the 20th century. Canaries were also used to detect poison gas following the terrorist attacks in Japanese subways in 1995.

During the Medieval period, interest in bird keeping of all kinds was keen. Parrots in particular were highly prized and often kept by royalty and high ranking clergymen. Marco Polo saw many types of parrots during his journey to China, and Christopher Columbus brought Cuban Amazon parrots back to Spain as gifts for Queen Isabella and King Ferdinand.

Canaries were brought to Europe by Portuguese sailors about 1478. These birds originated on the Canary Islands, the location for which they were named. In some countries, such as Germany, the birds were bred for singing capabilities. In other areas, the interest was in body shape, body type, or feather color. Today, there are 3 general types of domestic canaries. There are those bred for color (such as the well-known yellow canary), those that are bred for their song (the Roller Canary), and those bred for characteristics of shape, plumage, and size (the Frilled Canary).

Interest in owning birds has been strong for hundreds of years. In Europe, bird shows were first organized in the 1600s. Both canaries and parrots were popular in these early events. Today, bird fanciers hold over 200 shows each year in the United States alone.

■ DESCRIPTION AND PHYSICAL CHARACTERISTICS

There are between 8,700 and 9,600 living species of birds today. These range in size from tiny (such as hummingbirds) to huge (such as ostriches and condors). Bird species are divided into 2 superfamilies, the Paleognathae or "old jaws," and the Neognathae or "new jaws."

The Paleognathae family includes 5 orders, the Tinamiformes, the Rheiformes, the Casuariiformes, the Apterygiformes, and the Struthioniformes. The Tinamiformes order is comprised of some 45 species, most in South and Central America. Members of the other orders are flightless and very large. Collectively, they are often known as ratites and include the ostriches, the emus and cassowaries, the kiwis, and the rheas.

The superfamily Neognathae is huge and includes most of the bird species that are alive today. While over the millennia, individuals from a large number of these species have been kept as pets at one time or another and some have been domesticated, only a relatively small number of species have been widely kept as companion animals. With some exceptions (such as swans and peacocks) these pet species have been birds that have adapted to caged life and have some specific appeal such as very colorful feathers, a pleasing range of calls, the ability to mimic human speech, or engaging behaviors.

Up until the mid-twentieth century, canaries were one of the most popular pet birds, prized for their beautiful songs and often colorful feathers. Parrots have long been another popular companion bird. For many bird owners, the attraction of these birds has been the often colorful feathers and the ability to thrive under human control. Today, members of the order Psittaciformes (the parrot order) include the cockatoo family (Cacatuidae) and parrots (Psittacidae). Other popular companion birds in this same order include budgerigars, lovebirds, and lorikeets (*see* Table 1).

Table 1. Popular Companion Birds

Popular Name of Bird	Origin	Varieties	Average Lifespan	Ownership Considerations
Amazon Parrots	Mexico, Central and South America	Most are green with various bright colors on the head.	40 to 50 years	Most are great talkers and singers and do so loudly. Medium to large birds. Can be temperamental and often bond closely to one person.
Brotogeris Parakeets	South America (feral colonies in Puerto Rico, Los Angeles)	Bee Bee, gray-cheeked, orange-winged, and other color varieties	15 to 20 years	Small and lively. Sometimes called "dwarf" parrots. Only some talk.
Budgerigars (Budgies)	Australia	Usually green in wild; many colors available in the pet trade.	5 to 10 years	Suitable for apartment living as not usually loud. Can learn to talk.
Caiques	South America	Black-headed, white-bellied (yellow-thighed)	20 to 30 years	Personalities vary. Active birds that actually "hop." Some talk a little; most males whistle well.
Canaries	Canary Islands and Madeira	There are 3 main groups: colorbred (bred for their colors, including yellow), type (bred for their shape and feathering), and song (bred for the song patterns).	Up to 15 years	Males often have a lovely song, which is how they are distinguished from females. Territorial in temperament, canaries prefer to be housed singly or in mated pairs. Suitable for most apartments.
Cockatiels	Australia and South Pacific Islands	Have muted feather colors.	Up to 20 years	The rarer color mutations may be more fragile. Often have lively personalities. Relatively quiet compared with macaws or cockatoos, but are still vocal.

(Continued on the following page)

Table 1. Popular Companion Birds—*(Continued)*

Popular Name of Bird	Origin	Varieties	Average Lifespan	Ownership Considerations
Cockatoos	Australia and South Pacific Islands	Most are predominantly white; the rose-breasted is gray and pink. Several rare species are available.	25 to 50 years	Some talk, and their speaking voices are quiet. Enjoy and may demand a lot of handling, cuddling and attention, which can add to hormonal behavioral problems. Very loud when they decide to scream. Not for inexperienced owners. The most prone to extensive chewing of wood, plastic, et cetera.
Small conures (*Pyrrura* species)	Mexico, Central and South America	Small in size, peach-fronted, maroon bellied, green cheeked	Up to 25 years	Often described as charming. Relatively quiet. Most are smaller than cockatiels.
Larger conures (*Aratinga* species)		Sun, Jenday, Nanday, gold-capped	Up to 30 years	Active, beautifully colored, small to medium in size. Temperaments vary. Voice is piercing when they scream. Not known for their talking ability.
Doves	America, Mexico, Europe	Relatives of the common pigeon. Many species available.	Up to 20 years	Considered beautiful and elegant. Less demonstrative than parrots, and quiet except for their cooing.
Eclectus Parrots	Indonesia, Pacific islands	Males are emerald green with patches of reds and yellows. Females are shades of deep red, often with a blue bib.	40 to 50 years	Ability to talk varies. Not as prone to screaming as cockatoos and macaws.
Finches (Fringillidae)	Africa, primarily	Many colors available	5 to 10 years	Usually kept as aviary birds; do not generally interact with humans. Not loud but "peep" over extended periods.
Grass parakeets	Australia	Bourkes, turquosines, scarlet-chested. Many species and colors available.	8 to 13 years	Small, quiet, usually not aggressive; tendency to be nervous. Generally do not talk.
African Grey Parrots	Africa	A medium-large bird. Gray feathers and red tail.	40 to 50 years	The most intelligent of the parrot species, and therefore have the most potential problems with behavior. Require a great deal of time and attention. Do not scream, but they do growl. Excellent mimics with the largest potential vocabularies, but do not like to talk in front of strangers.

Table 1. Popular Companion Birds—*(Continued)*

Popular Name of Bird	Origin	Varieties	Average Lifespan	Ownership Considerations
Lories and Lorikeets	Australia and Pacific islands	Many species including Moluccan (red), multicolor, red and blue, and others	15 years	Intelligent, curious, fairly nervous temperament. Striking coloration. Require special diet, which creates increased mess.
Lovebirds	Africa	4 or 5 species commonly available. Peach-face, black-mask, blue-mask, and Fischer's are popular.	Up to 20 years	Sweet voices, not usually loud. Can be temperamental during breeding season.
Macaws	Central and South America	Blue and gold (blue and yellow), scarlet, green-winged, military, and hyacinth are available.	50 to 60 years	Largest of the parrots. Can talk, but usually more limited vocabularies than Amazons or African Greys. Screaming voice is very loud, with potential to irritate neighbors! Require a lot of exercise and a lot of time and attention.
Mynas (Mynahs)	Southeast Asia and Indonesia	Feathers are usually dark though some species have yellow head feathers. The Bali Mynah is light in color.	12 or more years	Excellent talkers. Not demonstrably affectionate. Very messy stools.
Parrotlets	Mexico, Central and South America	Green and blue in color. Common species include Mexican and Pacific (Celestial).	Up to 20 years	Also known as "pocket parrots." Relatively easily tamed when young. Small in size. Quiet for parrots.
Pionus parrots	South America	Blue-headed Maximilian's, white-capped, Dusky, and bronze-winged.	25 to 30 years	Quieter than Amazons, to which they are closely related. Known for gentle dispositions. A medium-sized parrot.
Poicephalus parrots	Africa	Small to medium size. Senegal is most common. Others include Meyer's, Jardine's, and red-bellied.	2 to 25 years	Engaging birds with distinctive colors, comparatively quiet voices. Very playful when young.
Pigeons	Europe and other areas	Relatives of the common pigeon living in cities.	Up to 20 years	Relatively quiet. Often kept in colonies. Some are raised and trained for racing.

(Continued on the following page)

Table 1. Popular Companion Birds—*(Continued)*

Popular Name of Bird	Origin	Varieties	Average Lifespan	Ownership Considerations
Psitticula parakeets	India, Southeast Asia, Africa	Indian ring-necked (rose ringed-necked), moustached, plum-headed, Derbyan, Alexandrine	Up to 20 years	Very colorful. Medium in size. Can be very affectionate if given sufficient attention and care. Many are good, quiet talkers. Their screaming voice is piercing but they are less prone to excessive screaming than many other psittacines.
Quaker (monk) parakeets	South America (feral in many locations, including Florida and New York)	Usually green with gray face and chest, blue and yellow mutations available.	20 to 30 years	Banned in several states (California, Massachusetts, Pennsylvania, New Jersey, Maryland, and Georgia) and considered a pest by farmers in many countries. Hand-reared birds can be very affectionate and decent talkers. Sometimes loud. Known for chewing.
Rosellas	Australia	Brilliantly colored parrots of the family Platycercus. Crimson, eastern, and western most common.	10 to 15 years	Tend to be nervous; require constant handling to remain tame. Often found in larger aviary settings.
Toucans and Toucanets	Central and South America	Toucanets are smaller versions of toucans.	10 to 25 years	Toucanets are more nervous. Must be acquired young to make good pets. Require soft food diet and can be extremely messy.

Although birds are very different from human beings, they also share certain characteristics with people. For example, birds have all of the same senses (sight, hearing, touch, taste, and smell) that we have. While their front limbs are wings and their feet, beaks, and tongues have taken on many tasks for which we use our hands, birds are still creatures with appendages that they use to interact with their environment. A bird uses its beak as an additional appendage to assist with communication, mobility, and social interaction, such as grooming.

Some birds, such as canaries, have melodious voices while others may vocalize in screeches at volumes loud enough to cause ear pain in their owners. Individuals desiring a pet bird may select from hundreds of possible birds and should match their interests and lives to a suitable bird.

Body Size

Birds kept as pets come in sizes from tiny (many finches are only 4 inches [10 centimeters] from the beak to the end of their tail feathers) to large (wing spans of parrots can easily reach 40 inches [1 meter]) and in colors from dull grays and browns to brilliant reds, yellows, greens, and blues. Because they are specially adapted for flight, most birds weigh very little. Even the largest captive parrots (some types of Macaws) rarely exceed about 2.5 pounds (1,200 grams), and medium to large parrots may weigh from a half pound to 2 pounds (250 to 900 grams). Their bones are particularly light, and some are filled with air.

Metabolism

Birds have a much more rapid metabolism than people. Pet birds' normal body temperatures usually range from 101 to 107°F (38.3 to 41.7°C), depending on the species. The more active a bird is, the more food it must consume relative to its body weight. Highly active birds, such as hummingbirds, may consume their body weight in food each day. Birds have very efficient digestive systems that allow them to eat enough to provide their bodies with needed energy while minimizing their body weight to allow flight.

While there are wide differences between types of birds, most birds' heart rates will be faster than that of a healthy human. For example, a normal human heart beats about 70 times per minute, while a small songbird's heart may beat 500 times in a minute and a hummingbird's heart will beat about 1,000 times in a minute. Birds' heart rates vary much more than people's do, increasing dramatically following stress or exercise. An Umbrella Cockatoo, for example, may have a resting heart rate of 120 beats per minute, but that will increase to over 300 if it is nervous or startled.

There are differences in the lungs as well. Human lungs operate rather like bellows; we breathe in and out. Birds, however, have lungs that are filled continuously and possess air sacs to take in fresh air and expel used air including carbon dioxide. The air sacs also divert warm air into bones to help water birds and other species remain buoyant in water, maintain warmth in cold weather, and dissipate some of the heat generated during flight.

Temperature Regulation

Birds do not sweat, but they have developed other strategies to stay cool in very warm conditions. Most birds will hold their wings out to cool off. If water is available, they will bathe and cool as the water evaporates. Another cooling technique in birds is panting. In many cases involving pet birds, panting is a sign that the bird is seriously overheated. Panting involves a more rapid breathing rate (more breaths per minute) and, in many species, a rapid fluttering of the throat. Fluttering causes heat loss from the mucus membranes of the throat and from heavily filled blood vessels.

Overheated birds will often have hot feet, red nares (nasal openings), and hot beaks. The bird's breath will feel obviously hot against your skin. This is an emergency, and you should contact your veterinarian immediately for advice on cooling the bird. While holding the wings out, panting, and hot feet and beaks may be signs of overheating, they can also signal other problems such as fever or respiratory distress. You should quickly evaluate your bird's environment to determine whether overheating is the likely cause of distress.

If it is clear that the bird has been overheated, your veterinarian may recommend that you place the bird in a shallow pool of tepid water (not cold water, as this could bring on shock in the bird). Be careful that the bird's beak and face are not covered with water. The bird must not inhale any water. Allow the bird to stay in the water until the nares return to a normal color and the bird's breath is a normal temperature. Then, return the bird to a cage placed in an area that is not too warm.

Feathers provide good insulation for any bird and, within limits for each species, provide protection from low temperatures. Birds will often sit with their feathers covering their feet to reduce heat loss when it is cold. Fluffing their feathers also helps protect against the cold. Sitting with their darkest colored feathers toward the sun is a technique used by some birds to absorb additional heat. While tropical birds, especially canaries, are less susceptible to chilling due to drafts than has often been reported, abnormally cool temperatures are not good for your bird's health.

If your bird is fluffing its feathers for extended periods or sitting on its feet, it may be chilled. Check the air temperature close to the cage and along its sides. Your bird may be exposed to cold drafts or air that is colder than appropriate. Cages placed close to windows are often colder than other areas of the room. Relocating the cage to a warmer spot can help your bird feel more comfortable and stay healthy. *Fluffed feathers may also be a sign that your bird is seriously ill.* If your bird is fluffing its feathers for an extended period, the bird should be checked for health problems.

The Senses

Like humans, birds have the senses of sight, hearing, smell, taste, and touch. They use these senses much as we do.

Sight

Birds depend heavily on the ability to see. Not only is good eyesight needed for flight, it is also critical to finding food and water, finding a mate, and avoiding predators. The degree to which a bird depends on sight is evident in the size of a bird's eye in relationship to its body. In humans, the eyes take up only about 1% of the weight of the head. In birds, the eye makes up a much larger portion. For example, European Starlings have eyes that make up about 15% of the head. In many birds, the weight of the 2 eyes is greater than the weight of the brain. And, in comparison with human brains, the optic lobe in a bird's brain is larger and better developed.

The keen eyesight of birds is also due to the position of the eyes in the head, the shape of the eyeball, the ability to focus rapidly, light regulation, and special variations in the retina of the eye. A bird's eye adjusts to the level of light about twice as fast as a 20-year-old human. The lens in the eyes of many birds is very flexible, allowing them to rapidly change their focus from near to far. This is an advan-

tage for birds that must spot their dinner from above and then accurately swoop down to catch it. Color vision is not universal in birds, but it does occur in many. Some birds can even see colors outside the range of humans. For example, several species of birds are known to be able to see ultraviolet light. It is believed that birds with ultraviolet light perception use this ability to help them choose mates.

These abilities, critical as they are, would be of little help to birds if they did not have a way to protect their eyes from drying out during flight. This task is accomplished by a third eyelid, known as the nictitating membrane. The nictitating membrane is clear, allowing birds to see while using the membrane to cover and protect the eye during flight. It also helps them "blink" and keeps their eyes moist and clear of debris. The easily visible eyelids in birds are normally closed only when the bird sleeps.

Hearing

Most birds have ears located somewhat behind and just below the level of the eye. The opening of the ear is concealed by specialized feathers known as ear coverts. These feathers have a texture that differs from other feathers on the head. If you very gently move these feathers aside, you can see the opening of your bird's outer ear. The exact shape and size of the ear opening varies between species. Sound captured by the outer ear is passed to the middle ear and then on to the inner ear. The inner ear passes these signals to the brain, which interprets the sounds.

Some birds may suffer an injury to, or infection of, the outer ear that can affect hearing. For example, macaws that started life as stunted chicks may have outer ear problems due to early infection or scarring. Lovebirds appear to be more prone to external ear infections than other species of birds, but all species of birds can experience outer ear infections. A regular check of your bird's outer ears for signs of inflammation or accumulations of debris can help you catch such infections early when they are more easily treated. If you find reddened outer ear tissue or debris in an outer ear of your bird, you should take your bird to the veterinarian for a physical examination.

In birds, as in humans, the middle ear not only processes sounds, it also provides the sensory information the animal needs for balance and equilibrium.

Many birds have excellent hearing, although the frequency range over which they hear is somewhat narrower than the human hearing range. What is lost due to narrower frequency range is often more than compensated for by the ability to distinguish small changes in pitch and beat. Owls, for example, can sense rapid fluctuations in pitch and intensity 10 times more accurately than humans. Some owls use this ability to find their prey, even in complete darkness.

In their natural environments, birds use their voices and their hearing to help them find mates, avoid danger, stake out their territory, and communicate with other members of their flock. These same abilities are used when the birds are companions. For example, many parrots will listen carefully to the sounds they hear and can accurately imitate the words their owners use frequently. Many will exchange vocalizations with their owners, and it is quite common for birds to react to the sounds that are a part of their daily life. For example, many pet birds have learned that opening a refrigerator or cabinet door precedes the arrival of food. When they hear the sound of the refrigerator or cabinet being opened, they will often vocalize or start their own particular prefeeding behavior.

Smell and Taste

It was long believed that smell is a poorly developed sense in most birds. However, research over the past 20 years has shown that, while birds' sense of smell may be more limited than some animals, birds do rely on this sense for feeding and navigation. Many birds, including vultures and sea birds, depend on their sense of smell to find food. The sense of smell also helps pet birds pick out their favorite foods. Many bird owners know that, even when they hide a preferred food, their pets will use smell to locate their favorites. In other cases, smell may be a critical sense in navigation. For example, homing pigeons were tested for the use of smell in finding their home nests; birds with experimentally plugged nostrils took longer to find their way home.

Taste is another sense which is believed to be similar to that of humans. In birds, the taste buds are located on the back part of the tongue and the bottom of the throat. Birds have fewer taste buds than humans, but as any bird owner will agree, birds do have taste preferences and have favorite foods based, at least partly, on taste. Parrots, hummingbirds, and other fruit and nectar feeders are known to have a fine sense for the differences in sweet and sour foods, while seed eaters seem to have no preferences for sweet or sour foods. Most birds can sense salt levels in foods. Bitter tastes are also sensed by birds and many will reject highly bitter foods. Research published in 2004 reported that caged cockatiels were able to detect and reject water with very small amounts of quinine, gamine, hydrolysable tannin, and condensed tannin. This research suggests that cockatiels—and probably other birds—use taste to detect and possibly avoid consumption of potentially toxic chemicals. This same sense of taste, along with texture, temperature, and color can be used to select preferred or favorite foods.

Touch

A bird's skin possesses nerve endings that relay information to the brain about its environment and its condition. Birds are aware of any injury and sense pain, just as people do. Some birds have sensory bristle feathers located around the eyes, nostrils, and mouth. There are also concentrated nerve endings called Herbst corpuscles located in the bills or beaks and the tongues of some birds. Similar sensory cells are also found at the base of flight feathers and it is likely that these special sensory areas play an important role in flight.

Locomotion

Over many thousands of years, birds' front limbs have become specially adapted for flight. The wings, together with the feathers, are what allow a bird to fly. They provide the lift that is needed to get off the ground and move in the air. The bones of the wing are particularly strong and light, and they serve as an anchor for the feathers and for the powerful muscles and tendons needed for flight.

Each bird has a wing shape that is appropriate for its life pattern. For example, long narrow soaring wings are typical of birds (such as the albatross) that spend much of their life soaring along thermal winds. High-speed wings are useful for birds that travel at fast speeds, such as swallows. Eagles, falcons, and other raptors have high-lift wings that allow them to get off the ground even with a heavy weight in their talons. Elliptical wings are shaped like a half of an oval. This shape increases maneuverability in the air and allows birds to rapidly change direction in flight—a useful skill for songbirds, sparrows, and others that must avoid becoming another bird's dinner.

The speed at which a bird can fly varies greatly based on species and breed. As a general rule, the flight speed of birds varies from about 15 miles (24 kilometers) per hour to about 50 miles (81 kilometers) per hour. Most birds will have 2 flight speeds, one for ordinary flight and a second accelerated speed they use for escaping predators and chasing other birds. The accelerated speed may be up to twice their normal flight speed. Small songbirds and perching birds will, in the wild, have a normal flight speed close to 15 miles (24 kilometers) per hour. Larger birds in their original habitat will often reach 25 miles (40 kilometers) per hour. These flight speeds are for birds that have developed their flying skills over almost their entire lives and have strong flight muscles. In general, pet bird flight speeds are somewhat lower than those of the same species that have lived and flown in the wild. One exception to this general guideline is racing pigeons. Racing pigeons are raised and trained for speedy flight. These birds, also known as homing pigeons, can often cover 30 miles (48 kilometers) per hour over extended distances.

Beaks and Feet

Over time, both the beaks and feet of birds have adapted to the many different environments in which birds live. As Charles Darwin first noted during his famous visit to the Galapagos Islands, beaks have developed to help a particular bird eat its preferred diet. For example, hummingbirds have long, narrow beaks suited for eating nectar from flowers; hawks have sharp beaks useful for tearing apart their prey; and birds on islands where cacti are plentiful have beaks that allow them to efficiently find and eat cactus fruit.

Parrots have beaks that are strong and shaped rather like hooks. With their flexible necks, parrots can use their beaks not only to crack tough outer shells on nuts and fruit, but also to preen and groom and to defend themselves. In addition, their strong beaks can be used to help them climb and swing and to help build nests and feed their chicks.

By way of comparison, canaries have straight, short beaks. These beaks are ideally shaped for finding and consuming the seeds and grubs that comprise their diet in their native environment on the Canary Islands and Madeira. However, the short beaks are not as useful for climbing or defending themselves.

Birds do not have teeth; their jaws, therefore, are light in weight. This is just one of many adaptations in birds to reduce body weight and make flight easier. Birds use a special body organ, known as the crop, to store their food before it is passed on to the stomach. Many, though not all, birds will eat and store sand and small stones in their ventriculus (gizzard) to assist in grinding food.

Birds' feet have also adapted to their particular habitat. Waterbirds, including ducks

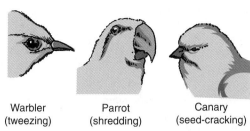

Warbler	Parrot	Canary
(tweezing)	(shredding)	(seed-cracking)

Birds have developed different types of beaks.

and geese, have webbed feet. As any scuba diver can confirm, webbed feet are very helpful in moving in the water. Owls, hawks, falcons, eagles, and other raptors have feet with sharp talons that help catch their prey. Perching birds (passerines and psittacines) have feet with specialized tendons for grasping tree branches. And smaller birds, such as sparrows, have feet that adapt to flat surfaces as well as branches.

Parrots, many of which are native to jungles, have feet that have evolved to function very efficiently. Parrots use their feet not only to help them perch securely on branches, but also to hold and move objects and foods in their environment. Unlike most other birds, parrots frequently use their feet in ways that people would use their hands.

Skin and Feathers

Birds have a sensitive skin that allows them to feel and sense pressure, heat, and cold. The feathers of a bird grow from the inner layer of skin (the dermis). Feathers provide assistance in flight, insulation from cold, waterproofing, and—in some cases—camouflage. In some species, the feathers can also indicate sex and mating status.

There are 8 main types of feathers, including 3 types of contour feathers, semiplumes, down feathers, natal down, bristles, and filoplumes. Contour feathers cover most of a bird's body and are used for flight. Each contour feather has a central hollow quill that starts at the base of the feather and connects to a central shaft known as the rachis. Branching out from the rachis are vanes which, in turn, support

the barbs. Each barb has many smaller, hooked segments known as barbules. The barbules hook together, making the feather strong and uniform. There are 3 types of contour feathers: body feathers, flight feathers (wing feathers called remiges and tail feathers called retices), and ear coverts.

Down feathers are small and soft. They grow between the contour feathers and keep the bird warm. Adult down feathers are structurally different than the down feathers found on chicks (natal down feathers). Some newly hatched chicks have only natal down feathers. Anyone who has ever slept under a down comforter knows how soft and warm these feathers are.

Sensory bristles are located around a bird's eyes, nostrils, and mouth. They play a role in the sense of touch.

Filoplume feathers are long and shaped like hairs. Their function is not fully understood, although it is probable that some birds (for example, psittacines) use these feathers to sense vibrations and changes in pressure—abilities that would be very helpful during flight. Not all species of birds have filoplume feathers.

Preening is how birds maintain their feathers. They use their beaks or bills to clean their feathers and keep them aligned correctly. At the same time, some birds waterproof their feathers using an oil produced by a gland (called the uropygial or preen gland) located near the tail. Other birds use a powder formed by powder down feathers to waterproof their feathers.

Flight and normal rubbing against objects in their environment can damage and wear feathers. Molting is the process by which birds renew their feathers. During the molt, an old feather is pushed out of the skin by the growth of new feather cells at the base of the old feather. The weight of a feather has nothing to do with its loss; it is the growth of a new feather that dislodges the old one. In most birds, feathers are discarded on both sides of the bird simultaneously to avoid problems with flying. Most birds replace all their feathers at least once a year, most often after the breeding season. Some birds molt

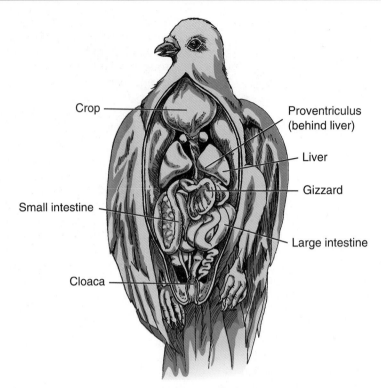

Crop

Proventriculus
(behind liver)

Liver

Gizzard

Small intestine

Large intestine

Cloaca

Digestive system of a bird

more frequently. No matter how frequently a bird molts, their bodies naturally time the loss of feathers in such a
way that the bird always has sufficient
feathers for warmth and flight.

Mouth and Digestive System

Birds do not have teeth. They use their
beaks to break up the food they eat. Also,
birds lack a soft palate at the back of their
mouths. The food is pushed along by the
muscles in the esophagus (the tube that
connects the mouth to the stomach) until
it reaches the crop, where it is stored and
is sometimes partially digested before
passing on to the stomach.

Unlike humans, birds have a 2-part
stomach consisting of the proventriculus
and the ventriculus or gizzard. The
proventriculus produces digestive fluids
that help break down the food. Once the
digestive fluids have soaked into the food,
it moves on to the gizzard where it is

ground up. In some birds, the work of the
gizzard is enhanced by sand and small
stones that the bird has swallowed for this
purpose. This grinding material is called
grit. Not all birds need it, but some do.
Your veterinarian can advise you on the
amount and type of grit that is most
appropriate for your particular bird.

From the gizzard, the bird's food passes
into the intestines, where intestinal
enzymes as well as secretions from the
liver and pancreas help finish digestion.
Food then passes into the large intestine,
colon, and finally into the cloaca. Here
both liquid and solid waste (urine and
feces) are stored prior to exiting the body
through the vent. The vent is located near
the base of the tail feathers.

■ SPECIAL CONSIDERATIONS

Becoming the owner of a pet bird can be
a lifelong commitment. Many parrots live
20 to 50 years—with larger birds generally

living longer. Parrots can form very strong bonds with their owners. When this occurs, they may have difficulty adjusting to a new owner. While smaller birds such as budgies, canaries, and finches tend to live between 10 and 20 years in captivity, and not every type of bird becomes so tied to an owner, bird ownership should never be considered a short-term commitment. Your home and your life will be changed for years—possibly decades—to come.

Many birds, including most parrots, are naturally vocal. In the wild environment, they will scream, screech, call, trill, and routinely make a great deal of noise. Such birds may not make suitable pets for individuals living in apartment complexes or in close proximity to other people. Many highly vocal pet birds have been abandoned when their owners were faced with choosing between keeping their apartment and keeping their bird. Before adding a pet bird to your household, it is best to research the vocal habits of the bird you are considering. Apartment dwellers and those living in condominiums may want to select a bird that is quieter. For example, canaries or finches are quiet when compared to the highly vocal macaws. Modifying a bird's vocalizations may be possible, but it requires time and a great deal of consistent training. Consult your veterinarian, local bird club, library, or Internet sources for this information.

Small birds may not be suitable for households that have small children because children can easily injure a bird unintentionally. Larger birds can injure children who place their hands or faces in or near the cage.

Birds do not sweat and therefore regulating their body temperature can cause problems for caged birds. They can rapidly overheat if forced to endure periods of exposure to direct sunlight. Be sure you can provide a cage location out of direct sun exposure. Related cage location considerations include a spot out of the direct path of chilling air conditioning ducts and drying hot air ducts.

Kitchens make poor locations for birds because of the high risk of exposure to toxic fumes, aerosols, and smoke from cooking. All of these fumes can be dangerous—or even lethal—for birds. Also, birds should not be exposed to secondhand cigarette or other tobacco smoke. (*See also* HOUSEHOLD HAZARDS, page 835.)

Birds are rarely neat. Some birds throw food all over their cages and any area surrounding it. Thus, before you select a bird, decide how much messiness you are willing to tolerate. Even with pelleted diets presented in deep food cups, some birds will scatter food throughout their cages. If you cannot stand the sight of food littering a cage floor and surroundings, a bird may not be for you. If neatness is important to you, be sure to check out the feeding habits of any bird that interests you before you bring it into your home.

CHAPTER **59**

Selecting and Providing a Home for a Pet Bird

▉ INTRODUCTION

As with any pet, it is important to do some research before you buy a bird. You want a bird that meets your expectations and can live comfortably and happily in your home. To make a good decision about a bird, you need to learn more about individual types of birds, their natural behaviors, and their requirements in terms of housing, diet, and care. This information will help you select the best bird for you and your family. It will also allow you to plan more carefully for the arrival of a new family member.

■ SELECTING A PET BIRD

Individuals seeking information about selecting a bird can turn to their local library for information about breeds, cage and diet requirements, typical temperament, and other important information. Once you have developed more specific questions, your local bird club or avian veterinarian can be great sources of practical information. Bookstores offer many current books with information on companion birds. In addition, there are hundreds of web sites that have information on birds and offer guidance on selecting the bird most appropriate for your family.

The temperament and behavior of a bird is important (*see also* page 831). Canaries and finches, for example, rarely like to be handled and are quite happy "doing their own thing" in their cages. In contrast, large parrots and some cockatoos often demand attention and require daily interaction with their owners. You need to consider how much time and attention you will provide for the bird and select a bird that will be happy with that level of attention from you.

Other factors to consider include cost of the bird and its upkeep, size, and noise level. Rare birds and many larger birds can be quite expensive, and larger birds require a larger cage (thus taking up more space). The cost of cages, diets, and veterinary care should also be considered. Some birds are quite noisy and may not be the best choice for people concerned with neighbors and noise.

Sources for Pet Birds

Once you have decided what breed of bird you want to acquire, you will have to locate a source. It is best to buy directly from a breeder or a high quality pet store that specializes in birds. Whatever the

source, you should ensure that the bird you purchase was bred and raised in captivity. Not only are wild-caught birds less tame, they can also carry diseases that may shorten their lifespan or even diseases that can be transmitted to humans. Many birds are smuggled illegally into countries such as the United States. Although this practice is less common than it once was, beware of anyone selling birds for a much cheaper price than other sources, and always ask for documentation regarding the source of the bird you are considering.

Choosing a Healthy Bird

If you are considering bringing home a companion bird, take the time to ensure that it is healthy before purchasing it. No matter where you buy the bird, look carefully at how the birds are housed. Your bird should come from a clean environment in which the handlers show care and consideration for the animals. Birds should be housed in roomy cages with fresh, appropriate food and clean water.

Look carefully for any signs of illness or other physical problems. Birds should be clean and alert with bright, clear eyes. A healthy bird should move easily in its environment and interact with other birds in the cage. Huddled birds or those with bunched or drooping feathers should be avoided. There should be no obvious injuries or feather loss. Check for any unusual discharge or staining around the eyes, beak, or tail that could indicate illness. The feet should be clean and free of injury. Wings should be carried normally, not dragged or held awkwardly.

Any new bird should have a wellness check before it permanently joins your home. Preferably, this should be done by a veterinarian specially trained in bird care. The seller should be willing to accept back (and refund the purchase cost for) any bird that is not found to be healthy. It may be wise to get this agreement in writing from the seller, particularly if the bird you are purchasing is expensive.

■ PROVIDING A HOME FOR A PET BIRD

Understanding your bird and providing an appropriate habitat can go a long way toward building a good relationship with your pet. Learn everything you can about your bird, its normal habits, and how to keep it healthy and happy. This knowledge will help you provide a home that supports your pet's needs. Libraries, books you purchase, and the Internet offer many helpful sources of such information.

Housing

The cage you provide must be large enough to allow the bird room for movement. Overly small cages can cause stress, which often leads to behavior problems. An absolute minimum cage size for larger birds is one and a half times the bird's wingspan in width, depth, and height. These dimensions give the bird room to stretch and move without damaging the wing or tail feathers on the cage bars. Of course, if you plan on housing more than

The cage should be large enough to allow plenty of room for movement.

one bird in the cage, the amount of space should be increased appropriately. Birds of the same species will not necessarily be compatible when placed in the same cage. Cagemate trauma is fairly common, and the individual birds' personalities will dictate whether they can live together peacefully. Larger birds can potentially inflict serious or even fatal injuries on other birds, even those of their own species. Conversely, some birds of different species may be successfully housed together. Check with your avian veterinarian or an experienced bird owner for methods of introducing birds prior to attempting to place them in the same enclosure.

Cage location can also be critical. Some birds are very social and need to be in the middle of the family as much of the day as possible. Some nervous birds need to be in a quieter room, but one that is still occupied by the family for social interaction. Placing the cage so that one side is against a wall or providing a hiding place in the cage may relieve stress as the bird is able to relax and stop looking for predators. It is not advisable to place the cage in front of a window as a permanent location because the bird cannot relax its search for enemies.

Covering the cage each night may not be necessary. Except for eliminating drafts, covering a cage will not significantly increase the ambient temperature. If a bird's cage is suitably large, a bird will not generate sufficient body heat to warm the air in a cage that is simply covered, so other means of generating heat must be provided if needed. The advantage of covering the cage at night is that it can give your bird a daily period of privacy and, for some birds, a sense of security. However, some birds find the presence of a cage cover frightening, possibly because it prevents them from sensing the presence of a dangerous animal. In general, whether or not to cover the cage should be based on your pet's reaction. If your bird quiets down and goes to sleep when the cover is on the cage, then go ahead and use it. If your bird becomes agitated when the cage is covered, you should leave it off.

Diet

By providing a pet bird with a healthy, nutritious diet, and by practicing good sanitation and hygiene, combined with preventative veterinary care, owners can increase the likelihood that their bird will live a long, disease-free life. An unbalanced diet is the main cause of disease and early death in pet birds. The understanding of the nutritional needs of birds has improved greatly over the past decade, but the precise nutritional requirements for individual species are still mostly unknown.

Diets for Pet Birds

Formulated diets for pet birds are available from many reputable manufacturers, pet stores, and veterinarians. The food is a blend of grains, seeds, vegetables, fruits, and various types of proteins, as well as additional vitamins and minerals. The ingredients are mixed and then baked. The food may be in the form of pellets, crumbles, or nuggets. Unlike a seed mixture, the bird cannot select particular components out of a formulated diet, so nutritional imbalances are much less likely to occur. There are commercial foods for different species, so be sure to select one appropriate for your particular bird.

Specialized Diets

Diets for lories and lorikeets, which consume nectar naturally as a large part of their diet, are available in commercially prepared formulas. Some of these may be fed dry or moistened; others must be made into a solution and fed as nectar. The nectar needs to be replaced several times daily and at least every 4 hours in hot weather. The diet should also include some fruits, such as apples, pomegranates, papaya, grapes, cantaloupe, pineapple, figs, or kiwi. Some lory diets contain excessive vitamin A and this may contrib-

ute to iron storage disease in the liver in these species. Check with your veterinarian or other reputable source for current information as more research is completed on the dietary needs of lories.

Other Nutritional Needs

Fruits and vegetables can be added to a formulated diet in moderation to provide psychological stimulation and variety. Caged bird owners can add appeal to fruit and vegetables by hanging food from the cage top or sides, weaving food into the bars of the cage, or stuffing food in the spaces of toys. This creativity helps entertain the bird and provides physical and mental stimulation.

For most adult birds, supplements are not necessary and should only be provided if recommended by a veterinarian. Using vitamin supplements could result in overdoses of certain vitamins and even poisoning.

Grit is necessary for proper digestion in some passerine birds. Not all birds need grit. If grit is overeaten, blockages can occur in the digestive system. Finches and canaries may benefit from having periodic access to a very small amount of grit, but most budgies, cockatiels, and other parrots do not need it.

Providing Food and Water

Natural feeding times for many wild birds occur at about half an hour after sunrise and again just before sunset. Following these feeding times will be the most natural routine for your pet. Some birds may enjoy having fruits and vegetables left in the cage throughout the day for snacking and entertainment. Smaller birds may need to eat more frequently throughout the day due to a higher metabolic rate.

Birds should be offered only what they can eat in a day in order to easily monitor daily intake. A decreased appetite may be the first sign that a bird is ill. Feeding dishes should be washed daily in hot, soapy water. No food should remain in the cage for longer than 24 hours as the risk of contamination or spoiling is high.

Fresh, clean water should always be available. If a water bottle is used, you must first determine that your bird knows how to get water from the bottle. The water should be changed daily and the tip should be checked daily to make sure it is working. Dehydration is a serious problem that can occur within 1 to 2 days if water is unavailable.

Exercise

Like people, birds need exercise to stay healthy and fit. Be sure your bird has sufficient room in its cage to exercise its wings and has perches and toys to encourage activity within the cage. However, just providing toys is not enough stimulation. Interaction, especially in the form of training, will use the bird's mental and physical energies and decrease the likelihood of abnormal behaviors.

Most parrots must be allowed time outside of their cages in order to provide sufficient exercise and psychological stimulation; many other birds also enjoy the opportunity to venture outside their cages. However, ensuring a safe environment and close supervision of the bird when it is out of its cage is necessary to avoid potential dangers (*see* HOUSEHOLD HAZARDS, page 835).

Temperament

Many birds are sociable and can develop close bonds with people. However, they require a certain amount of training and attention to help prevent the development of behavior problems. Although such behavioral problems can usually be treated over time, treatment is much more difficult than prevention. Behavior problems such as biting, screaming, feather plucking, and phobias are common reasons that owners give up their pet birds.

Parrots should not be allowed to perch on shoulders. Although this is a favorite position for many birds, it gives them an equal height advantage with the owner, and it is difficult if not impossible to control a bird in this location. Birds perched on a human shoulder are within easy range of the owner's eyes, ears, nose, and lips and can cause severe injury. The bird may cause damage intentionally (biting or pecking) or unintentionally (grabbing onto something to keep from falling). Either way, the damage to the owner and to the owner-pet bond has occurred.

Boredom is a major factor in behavior problems. Birds are intelligent and need an outlet for their curiosity and energy. In the wild, a bird divides its time between interacting with its flock and mate, finding and eating food, and preening. If family members are gone most of the day, they must provide toys and other items so the bird can entertain itself. Food can be hidden in toys, hung in the cage, or provided in large pieces that must be broken up before eating. Having routine times for training and interaction with household members can give a bird a sense of purpose and position within its surrogate "flock", serving to prevent or minimize behavioral problems.

Many companion birds are native to the tropics, which have 10 to 12 hours of darkness year round. Adult parrots should receive 10 to 12 hours of sleep each night. This sleep requirement is best satisfied by moving the parrot from the center of family activity to a quiet, darkened room for sleeping. In the morning, the bird is then moved back to a room where it can interact with the family. A small "sleep cage" can be set up and left in a quiet place and the regular cage left in the family's activity room.

Birds are not necessarily compatible when placed in the same cage, even those of the same species. Cage mate trauma is fairly common, and the individual birds' personalities will dictate whether they can live together peacefully. Larger birds can potentially inflict serious or even fatal injuries on other birds, even those of their own species.

CHAPTER 60

Routine Care and Breeding

▨ INTRODUCTION

Recent advances in medicine for pet birds—and the change from wild-caught birds to those raised in captivity—have changed the emphasis from infectious diseases and emergency medicine to wellness care. The importance of nutrition and behavior in the health of caged birds has been acknowledged and plays a major role in pet bird wellness programs. Understanding the natural behavior of birds will help make the relationship between owner and bird more enjoyable for both.

▨ IMPORTANCE OF VETERINARY CARE

Your veterinarian plays an important role in your bird's health because birds tend to mask illness until it is far advanced. Owners who recognize a slight difference in behavior, attitude, or physical condition of their pet bird should seek the immediate attention of a veterinarian. Other important services your veterinarian provides include grooming and identification.

New bird owners should try to locate an ABVP (American Board of Veterinary Practitioners) Avian board-certified Diplomate in their area. These veterinarians have undertaken further training in relation to birds and are dedicated to and knowledgeable about pet birds. Pet owners may want to start with a recommendation from a friend, neighbor, pet store, or animal shelter. The local animal shelter can often provide advice on locating an avian practice. You can also check the yellow pages of the phone book under "veterinarians" and "animal hospitals," specifically looking for a practice with veterinarians that have this certification. Other sources of informa-tion include the Internet; a check of the web site for your state's Veterinary Medical Association can help you locate a veterinary practice with special knowledge of birds.

A newly purchased bird should be examined by a veterinarian, preferably before it is taken to its new home. Newly acquired birds, or those exposed to other birds outside the household at bird shows or during pet store visits, are most likely to be affected by contagious diseases. It is also important for companion birds to have a regular annual physical examination. The bird should be brought to the veterinarian in its own cage if practical. Some disorders (for example, zinc toxicity from galvanized wire or dishes, loose perches, territorial or sexual behavior, and nutritional disorders) can be diagnosed in part by an examination of the cage. The veterinarian will likely ask you a number of questions about the history of your bird, particularly regarding its general health, diet, and environment, including exposure to other birds or animals.

Blood work taken during a wellness examination may detect disease before it has progressed sufficiently that the bird can no longer "mask" its illness. Treatment of disease is almost always more successful when it is diagnosed early.

▨ SIGNS OF ILLNESS

Owners should use special times with their pets to observe their habits and look for subtle changes in behavior, food consumption, water consumption, and feather condition (*see* BOX). In the wild, most birds are instinctively aware that they are the prey of many other animals. Under these conditions, birds will often attempt to hide any weakness or illness. Pet bird owners should be aware of this

General Signs of Disease in Birds

- Fluffed feathers
- Increased sleeping or eyes closed
- Inactivity or lack of interest in surroundings
- Decreases or changes in vocalization or singing
- Sitting low on the perch
- Sitting on the bottom of the cage
- Hanging onto the side of the cage by the beak rather than perching
- Weakness
- Losing balance, teetering, or falling off of perch
- Walking in circles
- Trembling or seizures
- Changes in breathing, such as breathing with open beak, wheezing or clicking sounds when breathing, sneezing, tail bobbing when taking a breath

- Discharge or crusts around the nostrils
- Exercise intolerance (heavy breathing after exercise, or inability to exercise)
- Eyes dull, sunken, or abnormal color
- Drooped or elevated wing(s)
- Lumps or swelling of any portion of the body
- Picking at the feathers or body
- Not preening
- Changes in color, consistency, quantity or frequency of droppings or urine
- Increased or decreased appetite or thirst
- Vomiting or regurgitation
- Weight loss (use a scale) and/or prominent keel (breast bone)

built-in defense mechanism and be alert to subtle changes in their bird. Any changes in activity, appetite, behavior, or feather condition are a signal that your bird should be examined for possible illness or injury. One of the first signs of illness noted by astute parrot owners may be a decrease in talking or other vocalizing. Owners often overlook these early changes and medical care is delayed until the condition is too far advanced for optimal care. With alertness on your part, care can be provided more promptly and your pet can live a longer and healthier life.

When a bird is ill, the veterinarian will often collect and analyze a sample of the bird's blood. Blood tests, x-rays, and other diagnostic tests can help in the diagnosis of disease, just as they do in humans and other animals.

▦ GIVING MEDICATION

If your bird is ill, your veterinarian may prescribe medication. Occasionally, medications can be provided in food or water. However, unless you can provide the medication inside something that can be swallowed in one gulp (for example, inside a small piece or fruit or vegetable), or your bird will accept hand feeding, controlling dosages and administration times in food or water is not very precise. Your bird may not consume enough of the medication because it does not like the taste or it simply is not hungry.

In many cases, your veterinarian will instruct you to provide medication using an eye dropper or needle-less syringe. It is important to follow your veterinarian's instructions as closely as possible regarding the amount of medication and how often it must be given. Your bird may not be very cooperative, but it is important to administer the medication with as little fuss as possible to avoid stressing the sick bird further. If you are uncertain how to give the medication, ask your veterinarian or veterinary technician to demonstrate the technique before you leave the office.

Be sure that you understand all of the instructions given by your veterinarian, including the correct dosage, the number of times you need to give the medication each day, and how long the treatment should continue. You should also find out if there are any special storage requirements

Administering Medication to Your Pet Bird

Almost all birds will require holding and restraint when medication must be given. It is best to have this demonstrated by your avian veterinarian or technician prior to attempting it yourself at home. Here is a procedure that works for many birds:

- Prepare the dosage in the eyedropper or needle-less syringe, following the instructions from your veterinarian.

- Have 2 people available if possible.

- Be sure that there are no other pets or unfamiliar people in the vicinity and that the lights are soft and any sounds (such as music) are soothing and soft. Have a comfortable place to sit or stand as it will take a few moments to get the medication into your bird.

- Lay out any towel or other restraint you will use. You may also want to wear gloves.

- Quietly talk with your bird as you open the cage and gently pick it up.

- Remove your bird from the cage and, following the instructions provided by your veterinarian, gently restrain your bird. Be very careful not to hold your bird too tightly. You do not want to restrict your bird's breathing.

- Throughout the process of delivering medication, monitor your bird's stress level. If your bird goes from struggling to panic, or panting, be prepared to release your bird and wait while your bird recovers. Your bird is less likely to panic if you remain calm and supportive throughout the process.

- Place the tip of the eye dropper or syringe in one side of your bird's mouth and aim the tip toward the opposite side of the mouth. For example, if the dropper is on the bird's left side you need to aim the end toward the right side of the mouth. Be careful not to put more than the tip of the dropper or syringe into the mouth. You do not want to restrict your bird's ability to swallow and breathe.

- Gently and very slowly deliver the medication. Going too quickly can force medication into the lungs or allow medication to run out of the bird's mouth. Watch your bird as it swallows the medication. Do not provide more than your bird can swallow at one time.

- Many birds respond better if you talk with them gently during this process.

- If possible, leave the tip of the dropper or syringe just inside the mouth until all of the medication is delivered.

- Check to see if any medication ended up outside the mouth. Using a small amount of clear water, gently clean any soiled feathers or other areas.

- Once all of the medication has been provided, praise your bird and, if the bird seems receptive, offer a treat or other reward.

- Return the bird to its cage.

- Make sure all medications are stored correctly.

- Disassemble the dropper or syringe and thoroughly clean all parts of the device in soap and warm water. Rinse all parts thoroughly and allow the pieces to air dry on a clean towel.

Possible indirect methods of administration:

- If your bird is still eating well, has a favorite soft food that it receives as a treat (for example, oatmeal, yogurt, or mashed potatoes) and does not object to the taste of the medicine, it may be administered by mixing it directly into a small amount of this food.

- If your bird was hand (syringe) fed, and will still take syringe-feeding, the medication may be mixed in hand-feeding formula and delivered.

(such as keeping the medicine in the refrigerator) or preparations needed.

A very few birds will take some medications without restraint. In these rare cases, you can simply provide the medication while the bird is sitting on a perch or grabbing the bars of its cage. However, most birds will require holding and restraint (*see* Box).

GROOMING AND ROUTINE CARE

Birds, like all pets, require routine care and grooming. The next section covers the specifics of routine care for pet birds.

Wing Clipping or Trimming

Wing trims help protect against loss or escape of pet birds. Trimming should be done by a trained veterinarian or other individual who is familiar with the type of trim needed. It is important to understand that trimming the wings is not a guarantee against escape. A bird that can only glide to the floor indoors may be able to fly outside on a windy day.

Nail Trimming

Nail trimming is usually done to prevent scratching of the owner's skin rather than due to overgrowth of the nails. However, over-trimming a bird's nails decreases its stability and increases the chance that it will fall from its perch. Generally, a good compromise can be reached by trimming the needle-like tip of the nail just enough to blunt it, while still leaving enough nail to allow a stable grip. Trimming the nails of birds is not difficult if the bird becomes accustomed to it at a young age. All birds, regardless of age, should be trained to allow trimming, especially large birds. Having to use a restraint for trimming can be an unnecessarily traumatic experience for your bird.

The use of cement perches (available in various sizes and textures) may eliminate the need for nail trimming in some birds if the perch is selected and placed appropriately. If used, it is best to place a cement perch where the bird stands for brief periods (such as in front of a food bowl or treat cup). To avoid irritation to the bottom of the feet, the cement perch should not be the main perch used by the bird to preen or sleep.

Beak Trimming

Sometimes excess keratin accumulates on a bird's beak and needs to be removed. Your veterinarian can do this with specialized sanding tools. Normal, healthy birds that are provided with abrasive surfaces (such as rough wood, or the commercially available concrete perches) rarely require beak trims.

Means of Identification

There are 2 common methods for identifying caged birds. Many birds are leg banded, either for individual identification or to indicate a proper quarantine history. Bands represent certain hazards to the bird (for example, they can become caught on a loose wire) and their removal entails some risk if the proper equipment is not available.

Leg banding is being replaced or augmented by microchipping as a means of permanent identification. In pet birds, microchips are normally placed deep in the left pectoral (chest) muscle. This procedure is normally done under local or general anesthesia as the needle used to place the chip in the muscle is large, and the process can be painful for the bird. Adverse reactions or microchip failures in birds are uncommon.

Vaccinations

A few vaccines are available for pet birds (notably polyomavirus vaccine), but most caged birds are not routinely vaccinated. If you have questions about the need to vaccinate your bird, you should discuss your concerns with your veterinarian.

■ HOUSEHOLD HAZARDS

While time outside a cage can be a positive experience your bird, it can also be dangerous, especially for small birds that

A cement perch can help keep nails blunted without trimming.

Common Household Poisons

This list is not inclusive because there may be other substances toxic to birds that have not been widely documented. The bird's environment should be limited to those items known to be safe.

Acetone (nail polish remover)	Garden sprays	Paint
Ammonia	Gasoline	Paint remover
Antifreeze	Gun cleaner	Paint thinner
Ant syrup or paste	Gunpowder	Perfume
Avocado	Hair dyes	Permanent wave solutions
Bathroom bowl cleaner	Hexachlorophene (in some	Pesticides
Bleach	soaps)	Photographic solutions
Boric acid	House plants (including calla	Pine oil
Camphophenique	lilies, mistletoe, poinsettia,	Prescription and nonprescrip-
Carbon tetrachloride	and others)	tion drugs
Charcoal lighter	Indelible markers	Red squill
Clinitest tablets	Insecticides	Rodenticides
Copper and brass cleaners	Iodine	Rubbing alcohol
Corn and wart remover	Kerosene	Shaving lotion
Crayons	Lighter fluid	Silver polish
Deodorants	Linoleum (contains lead)	Snail bait
Detergents	Matches	Spot remover
Disinfectants	Model glue	Spray starch
Drain cleaners	Mothballs	Sulphuric acid
Epoxy or super glue	Muriatic acid	Suntan lotion
Fabric softeners	Mushrooms (some varieties)	Turpentine
Fluoropolymer fumes	Nail polish	Weed killers
Galvanized materials	Oven cleaner	Window cleaners

can be easily stepped on or injured in falls. Birds also do not understand the nature of glass windows or mirrors. Like wild birds that fly into windows from the outside, pet birds can be injured flying into these barriers. Birds outside their cages should be carefully monitored to ensure they cannot escape and to avoid accidents and injury. All windows and doors in the area should be fully closed before you release your bird from its cage.

Other hazards for birds outside their cages include access to toxic materials (including certain house plants and dangerous foods and medicines), electrical cords, stove tops, open toilets, and other seemingly innocent household objects (*see* Box). Birds have been caught in blankets, trapped in clothes dryers, drowned in sinks and toilets and even sucked into vacuum cleaners. Be sure to monitor your bird any time it is outside its cage.

■ BREEDING AND REPRODUCTION

All birds reproduce by laying eggs. Eggs are produced inside the female and then deposited in a nest. In captive female birds, egg laying, which is actually the equivalent of ovulation in mammals, can happen without fertilization or even the presence of a male. In some species, both female and male birds sit on the nest, while other species either leave this chore to the female only or leave it to nature to provide the warmth needed by the developing chick. In most species of pet birds, both parents are actively involved in incubation, feeding, and caring for the chicks.

Breeding birds and rearing chicks is best undertaken by an experienced bird owner. Most individual pet birds will not breed successfully in captivity. Requirements for breeding are complex and vary by species. Giving the full range of information is beyond the scope of this book.

If you are planning to breed your bird, you should have a thorough understanding of what is involved. By contacting and talking with an experienced breeder, you can learn about incubating, hatching, feeding, and judging whether or not your bird can or will take care of the chicks. Many inexperienced birds have trouble learning to care for their offspring, leaving the owner no choice but hand rearing the chicks. This can be quite challenging and time consuming, as the chicks must be fed on a regular schedule throughout the day. Hand raising also decreases a bird's immune system strength, increases the chance of infection, and decreases necessary parental bonds. This can lead to behavioral problems later in life, similar to the relative attachment disorder seen in human babies deprived of physical contact.

Males

Most male birds do not have a penis, which can be confusing for pet owners when trying to identify the sex of their birds. Identification of a male bird may be possible based on feather coloration or other physical features. However, most parrots are not sexually dimorphic—that is, males and females look the same. Sperm is produced in reproductive organs located well inside the body and then expelled into the female during copulation, in what is termed cloacal kissing.

Females

In most female birds, only the left ovary is present. The ovary produces an unshelled egg which may then be fertilized by the deposited sperm. The newly fertilized egg then travels through the female, passing through several glands that add the egg white fluid (albumin) and deposit layers of shell material over the egg. The shelled egg is then expelled through the cloaca and deposited in the nest.

Female birds are receptive to male attention only at certain times of the year and under certain conditions (such as the presence of adequate nest boxes).

Ask your veterinarian about breeding cycles for your species of bird. Also, female birds can be quite choosy about their mates; you may find that it will take several tries and exposure to different males, for your female to mate successfully. Factors such as age, environment, light cycle, presence of a suitable nest box, available food types, socialization, presence of other birds, and the presence or absence of potential predators (for example, dogs) will all influence whether birds will mate.

The time between mating to laying a fertilized egg and the length of egg incubation also varies between species. Your avian veterinarian can provide accurate estimates for your bird.

Care of Newborns and Young Birds

Successfully breeding and rearing birds is difficult and not something that most bird owners will do. This section is meant to provide general information, but not to provide a comprehensive guide to rearing young birds.

Chicks of most pet bird species are born blind and without feathers. Depending on the type of bird, the eyes open within 1 to 2 weeks. Feathering is complete in about 1 month for smaller birds but can take up to 5 months in larger birds, such as macaws.

Proper care during breeding, good sanitation and nutrition, nursery management, and egg incubation (if needed) can help reduce diseases in newborn chicks. Be sure to keep the cage in a warm spot away from any drafts. In general, chicks should not be disturbed but should be closely monitored to ensure that they are receiving proper care from the parents. If the newborns do not appear to be thriving, contact your avian veterinarian immediately for instructions on hand rearing.

Swallowing Foreign Objects

As chicks get older, it is common for them to eat nonfood items that may be found in the cage. Loose bedding is a favorite for the curious chick. This habit may be related to normal curiosity, boredom, or a seemingly insatiable appetite. The result is that young birds often end up with foreign objects in the crop. A veterinarian may be able to manipulate the item back up the esophagus where it can be retrieved manually. In many cases, as with foreign objects such as jewelry screws, glass and other potentially abrasive items, surgery may be required.

Crop Burns

Crop burns occur when birds eat food that is too hot. This is seen most commonly in baby birds being hand-fed. It usually occurs when the powdered formula is mixed with water that has been heated in a bowl in the microwave. Even when the temperature appears to be acceptable (103 to 105°F, 39.4 to 40.6°C), the formula will continue to warm as it absorbs heat from the bowl. The severity of the burn and the bird's reaction vary greatly. Some birds become ill from the tissue damage and may die despite intensive care. Other birds have no signs and the burn is only detected when either food or a hole is noticed in the area of the crop.

If the burn is mild, swelling and redness will appear on the surface of the skin within several days. If the burn is severe, the chick may be very ill, refuse subsequent feedings, and need immediate veterinary care. The type of treatment depends on the degree of tissue damage. Mild burns may be treated with antibiotics and topical ointments, while severe burns may require life-saving supportive care, and later surgery to repair the damage.

Fatty Liver Disease

This disease is caused by a high fat diet and may be seen in chicks (particularly cockatoo chicks) that are being hand reared. Often owners are unaware of the dangers of adding peanut butter, oil, or other high fat foods to the regular commercial formula, or they feed high-fat formulas (designed for macaws) to inappropriate species. Fat accumulates in the liver, interfering with normal liver func-

tion. Parrot chicks with fatty liver disease typically are heavy for their age and have severe trouble breathing.

Treatment includes removing sources of excess fat, reducing the amount of food provided in a single feeding, and adding digestive aids such as lactulose to the formula. Birds should be handled gently and as little as possible. If this disease is not detected early, and breathing difficulty has occurred, it is often necessary for the veterinarian to give oxygen, injectable fluids, antibiotics, and other supportive care to attempt to save the chick.

Birth Defects and Developmental Problems

Young, recently purchased cockatiels may have **low body weights** for their age and a stunted appearance. These birds may have underlying congenital or developmental problems, including decreased liver function and decreased immune system competence. With supportive care, some of these birds will survive, but many will not. Birds that survive may have a fairly normal life or may require repeated veterinary care.

Another problem seen in young cockatiels is nicknamed the **"one week post-purchase syndrome."** Cockatiels with this syndrome are often only partially weaned and are purchased soon after arriving at the pet store. In nature, they would be eating partially on their own but still receiving supplementation from their parents. When such a bird is sold as "weaned" to an uninformed owner, it generally takes about a week for the bird's decreased food intake to create noticeable weakness. At this point, the infant bird is emaciated and dehydrated and may or may not respond to medical treatment.

Splay leg occurs when one or both legs are bent so that the chick is unable to stand properly. The cause of this abnormality is unknown. It can occur in most pet bird species but is most common in cockatiels. Parental "over-sitting," nest box flooring that is too slick, birth defects, and nutritional deficiencies in the parents or young bird may all contribute. For young birds with splay leg, it may be helpful to keep each baby in a small container that does not allow the legs to slide out from under them sideways and to provide flooring that provides some traction. In cases where the legs are already splayed, a veterinarian can often correct the problem with splints, hobbles, or traction. The younger the bird is at the time of the attempted correction, the faster the recovery and the greater the success rate.

An **underbite** is a genetic abnormality in which the lower jaw outgrows the upper jaw. It commonly occurs in clutches (that is, several chicks from a single clutch of eggs). If the underbite is not too severe and is detected early, the jaw of the bird can be manually manipulated to avoid surgery. However, surgery can be successfully performed by veterinarians experienced in this technique and may be necessary in advanced cases.

Constricted toe syndrome is fairly common in infant birds, often affecting more than 1 toe. A band of fibrous tissue forms at the joint of the toe and interferes with normal blood circulation. This results in swelling, loss of blood supply, and finally death of the end of the toe. If circulation loss is severe and the tissue has died, amputation of the toe may be necessary. If this condition is recognized early, the fibrous band may be surgically removed to restore circulation. The cause of constricted toe syndrome is unknown.

Some birds are born with a condition called **eyelid atresia**, in which the eyelids are missing and the skin surrounding the eyes is fused together. The condition is most common in cockatiels and usually occurs in several members of the same clutch. If a sufficient opening for vision remains, the bird may lead a close to normal life. Attempts to slit the skin in this area and maintain the opening are rarely successful because the skin tend to seal together again as it heals.

"Lockjaw" is a bacterial infection of the sinuses and jaw joint of the chick. This syndrome can appear in clutches, most commonly in cockatiels. When the jaw joints are affected, the young bird may not be able to open its beak and may therefore starve to death, as it will be unable to eat.

CHAPTER **61**

Disorders and Diseases of Birds

▨ INTRODUCTION

Many of the most common causes of illness or death in birds are due to nutritional deficiencies, trauma or poisoning due to household hazards, and unsanitary housing conditions. All of these can be prevented or minimized by providing proper care. Other causes of illness include parasites and bacterial, viral, or fungal infections that can be spread by exposure to sick birds or lack of good sanitation.

It is important to recognize signs of illness promptly in sick birds so that appropriate care can be given. Due to their relatively small size and rapid metabolism, birds can become ill very quickly, and delays in treatment can lessen the chance of recovery.

▨ HEART AND BLOOD VESSEL DISORDERS

Some older birds develop signs of chronic heart disease, such as an inability to move or fly without discomfort and shortness of breath or other breathing difficulties. The ability to diagnose some forms of avian heart disease, using the same techniques as in people (x-rays, electrocardiograms, and

Care of Sick Birds

There are 5 important elements to consider in supportive care of a sick (or injured) bird. (Note that these are supportive measures, and do not address the cause of and treatment for your bird's illness. Your veterinarian must diagnose and prescribe specific treatment for your bird.)

1. **Heat:** Keeping your sick bird in a slightly warmer environment than usual may help it conserve the energy it usually uses to keep its body temperature normal. However, be careful not to overheat the bird. (Panting and spreading the wings are signs of overheating.)

2. **Humidity:** Raising the level of humidity can be helpful for birds with respiratory disease or signs of illness. Higher humidity eases the breathing and helps the bird keep the air passages clear and moist. A vaporizer or humidifier can be used to provide extra humidity.

3. **Fluids:** A sick bird can become dehydrated easily, especially because it may not drink as much on its own. In many cases a veterinarian may administer fluids under the skin, and follow-up oral fluids are also very helpful. Favorite foods high in moisture content (leafy greens, fruit) will add to water intake, but check with your veterinarian first to make sure they will not worsen your bird's illness. Adding a bit of juice (of your bird's favorite fruit, like apple or grape) to the water will often encourage drinking.

4. **Nutrition:** Inadequate nutrition will severely impact the bird's ability to recover from the illness. The best foods to give a sick bird are high in simple carbohydrates and easy to digest. Ask your veterinarian for appropriate suggestions.

5. **Quiet/Level of Activity:** Keep an ill or injured bird quiet and inactive. Remove toys from the cage and limit noisy activities or move the bird to a quiet part of the house. Make sure that your bird gets adequate (10 to 12 hours) uninterrupted sleep.

echocardiograms) has progressed rapidly over the past decade. Once the type of heart disease has been diagnosed, your avian veterinarian may be able to prescribe medications to limit the effects of the condition.

Parasites such as protozoa or the larvae of certain worms are occasionally found in the blood of various pet bird species. This problem has become less common since importation of exotic pet birds was halted in the 1980s. Most of these blood-borne parasites do not cause any disease or signs of illness unless a bird is already ill or stressed. If signs do occur, they may include general listlessness, diarrhea, and loss of appetite. A veterinarian can diagnose most types of blood parasites by microscopic examination of a blood sample.

■ DIGESTIVE DISORDERS

Birds have various digestive disorders, including infections and parasites, that can cause problems. The next section discusses some of the more commonly seen disorders in detail.

Avian Gastric Yeast (*Macrorhabdus*)

Avian gastric yeast colonizes the digestive tract of birds. Birds that have weakened immune systems are most often infected. The most common sign of infection is chronic weight loss, regurgitation, and/or excessive eating followed by decreased food intake. Droppings may contain undigested seeds or pellets. The percentage of deaths varies from 10 to 80% of affected birds, depending on the species and strain of the yeast. In birds that recover, both relapses and potential shedding of the organism in the droppings are likely.

The goals of treatment are to reduce the number of organisms and improve the general health and immune status of the bird. Your veterinarian may prescribe various medications to achieve this goal. This disease can be transmitted between birds.

Candidiasis (Thrush)

Candidiasis is caused by infection with the yeast *Candida albicans*. It is the same organism that causes "thrush" in the mouths of human babies. This yeast is common in the environment and may be present in small numbers in a normal bird's digestive tract. It may, however, cause illness under certain conditions. Very young, unweaned birds, especially those on antibiotics, may develop candidiasis due to their immature immune systems. Adult birds on longterm antibiotics or suffering from malnutrition or other illnesses may also develop candidiasis. This occurs because some antibiotics can disturb digestion by killing off beneficial bacteria that normally live in the digestive tract, allowing other organisms, such as the *Candida* yeast, to overgrow.

Candidiasis most often affects the crop, although the stomach and intestines may be affected as well. It can also affect the skin, respiratory tract, and rarely, the central nervous system and other organs. The severity of infection often depends on the age of the bird and the state of its immune system. A very young or very ill bird may develop an infection that spreads to the blood, bone marrow, and other organs.

Regurgitation of food, lack of appetite, and general signs of illness may be caused by delayed crop emptying caused by candidiasis. Some birds develop a swollen, mucus-filled crop. Adult birds can harbor low-grade candidiasis with few signs of illness. White spots may be present in the mouth if oral *Candida* is present. A veterinarian can determine whether these white spots are due to candidiasis or another disease.

Good hygiene, including proper cleaning and disinfection of the cage, nest box, and any feeding utensils, is critical to minimize the amount of *Candida* in the environment. In baby chicks affected with candidiasis, the crop must be emptied more often and smaller amounts fed until the crop begins to function normally again. Your veterinarian may prescribe medications to aid in effectively clearing the infection.

Proventricular Dilatation Disease (Macaw Wasting Disease)

Proventricular dilatation disease, also known as macaw wasting disease, affects not only macaws, but many other species of pet birds. Cockatoos, conures, *Eclectus* parrots, and many African and Asian species have been infected. The condition appears to be caused by a virus.

Proventricular dilatation disease affects the nerves of the digestive tract and results in stretching of the stomach and lack of normal muscular contractions. Signs include chronic weight loss (often following an initial increase in appetite), the passage of undigested food (most easily recognized when whole seeds are found in the droppings), and regurgitation. Widespread outbreaks are uncommon, but the infection is often fatal.

The transmission of proventricular dilatation disease appears to be by exposure to feces of infected birds, but other routes may exist. Isolation of affected birds is the only way to prevent transmission of the disease to other birds. Disinfection and improved ventilation is recommended and may help reduce transmission.

Isolation or euthanasia of affected birds is necessary in order to prevent transmission to other birds. Treatment with antiviral drugs has not been effective to date, but preliminary trials of drugs that modulate the immune system, the use of anti-inflammatory medication, and feeding a liquid diet show some promise at improving an infected pet bird's quality and length of life.

Papillomatosis

Pink, cauliflower-like growths or tissue thickening called papillomas may occur anywhere from the oral cavity, through the digestive tract, to the cloaca of a bird. The most common, or at least the most readily detected locations, are the mouth and cloaca. Papillomatosis is most likely caused by a herpesvirus that is spread through close contact between birds.

The highest incidence of these growths occurs in green wing macaws, but it is also common in other macaws, Amazon parrots, and hawk-headed parrots. Papillomatosis tends to occur as a flock problem, particularly in breeding colonies of macaws and Amazon parrots.

The signs exhibited depend on where the papillomas occur. Growths in the mouth may cause wheezing, difficulty swallowing, and open-mouth breathing. Papillomas in the gastrointestinal tract may cause vomiting, loss of appetite, and wasting. Cloacal papillomas may look like and be mistaken for a cloacal prolapse (page 849). Papillomas may be seen protruding from the vent when the bird becomes stressed or during elimination. Straining to produce stool, blood in the droppings, passing gas, and an abnormal odor to the droppings may occur.

Surgical removal of the papillomas may be attempted by your avian veterinarian, but the growths often recur. There is no permanent cure, but control for many years is possible.

In Amazon parrots, there is a high incidence of liver or bile duct cancer in birds affected with papillomatosis.

Gastrointestinal Parasites

Giardiasis occurs when protozoa (microscopic, single-celled parasites) of the genus *Giardia* invade the intestines. It most often affects cockatiels, lovebirds, and budgerigars (budgies), although parrots, macaws, cockatoos, and other pet birds may also become infected. Transmission occurs when infected material is eaten, and adult birds may be carriers. *Giardia* may cause diarrhea, malnutrition, and problems with absorption of nutrients. In some birds, especially cockatiels, *Giardia* may lead to itching; causing a bird to scream and pull its feathers or dig at the skin with the beak. (Note: many other causes of feather plucking exist that will cause the same symptoms.) With giardiasis, droppings may be more numerous than normal, and have a "popcorn" appearance. If baby birds are infected, they may be thin, with poor feathering, cry excessively to be fed and may die prior to fledging. The veterinarian will most often prescribe a medication taken by mouth (*see* Giving Medication, page 833).

Trichomoniasis (known as **frounce** or **canker** in non-pet bird species) is also the result of infection with a protozoan parasite, *Trichomonas gallinae*. It is occasionally seen in pet birds, notably budgies. Whitish-yellow lesions resembling cheese or curds stick to the lining of the mouth and throat, crop, and esophagus. Infected budgies may have signs such as increased salivation and regurgitation. Transmission may occur by direct contact (such as infected parents feeding young) or indirect contact (eating contaminated food or water). Treatment requires a medication taken by mouth.

Various types of **roundworms** occur in the digestive tract of pet birds, and wild birds may transmit certain roundworms to parrots housed outdoors. Transmission occurs when birds eat the roundworm eggs. Signs of infection include loss of condition, weakness, emaciation, and death. In heavy infections, the intestines can become obstructed. The veterinarian will most often prescribe a medication to kill the worms. In warm climates where exposure in outdoor aviaries is likely, a routine deworming with one of these oral medications is often performed.

Tapeworms have become uncommon in pet birds now that most are bred in captivity. These parasites are most common in cockatoos, African Grey parrots, and finches. The tapeworms are transferred from infected animals by an intermediate host that bites the animal or picks up the tapeworm organism from droppings or other discharges and then transfers the infecting parasite to a previously healthy animal. Intermediate hosts for tapeworms are most likely insects and spiders of various types, earthworms, and slugs. Signs of illness are rarely present, but segments of the tapeworm can sometimes be recognized in the droppings of affected birds. Your veterinarian will most often prescribe medication to kill the tapeworms; medicine may be given by mouth or injected into a muscle. Recurrence is rare unless the bird continues to be exposed to the intermediate host.

HORMONAL DISORDERS

Diabetes mellitus is seen in pet birds and causes signs similar to those seen in people with diabetes, including passing a large volume of urine, excessive thirst, and high sugar (glucose) levels in the blood and urine. Diabetes is often seen in birds that are overweight or that have pancreatic or reproductive problems. A veterinarian can diagnose diabetes by laboratory blood testing. Depending on the species of bird, a deficiency of insulin or relative increase in glucagon (another hormone secreted by the pancreas) may be noted.

Treatment with insulin often results in extremely short-term correction of blood sugar elevations. The veterinarian may prescribe drugs to lower the sugar levels; some of these can be put in the bird's water to allow the bird to self-regulate its sugar levels (in other words, as the blood sugar levels drop back toward normal, the bird will not want to drink as much water, and the amount of medicated water consumed decreases). Other medications that are given by mouth may also be used.

Diabetes in some birds may be temporary, being caused by another illness or condition. In other birds, as in most people, it is a life-long disease requiring constant medication to control.

EYE DISORDERS

Swelling and inflammation of the eyes is called **conjunctivitis**. It may be an infection of just the eye, often caused by bacteria, or it may be a sign of a more widespread respiratory infection.

Inflammation of the internal structures of the eye is called **uveitis,** which may be a sign of a generalized disease. If the inflammation goes untreated, it may lead to the formation of a **cataract** in the affected eye.

If you notice any swelling, redness, discharge from the eye, excessive blinking, or holding the eye(s) closed, you should consult your veterinarian immediately for treatment. Most eye infections can be treated successfully with antibiotic eye drops or salves.

BONE AND MUSCLE DISORDERS

Like people, birds can break bones and develop diseases that cause problems with their musculoskeletal system. In this section, some of the most common problems involving bones and muscles in birds are covered.

Fractures

Birds do break bones and suffer joint dislocations. These problems can be challenging to treat, because some of the bones are pneumatic (air filled) structures that are part of the bird's respiratory system. Also, bird bones contain more calcium than human bones. The high calcium content tends to make bird bones brittle and more prone to developing multiple fractures in the break area.

Despite these challenges, treatment for fractures in birds has advanced greatly in the past 20 years. Fracture stabilization techniques have been developed to help many birds with broken bones. Because bird bones often heal more quickly than bones in people, dogs, cats, and other mammals, rigid stabilization during the natural healing process may be all that is required. In other cases, surgery or implanted supports might be required to return the bird's bones to normal functioning.

The repair of fractured bones in birds can be complicated by bone diseases. For example, **osteomyelitis** is a painful inflammatory disease of bones often caused by bacterial infection. This disease can cause repeated infection of other locations in the body. Antibiotics are critical to prevent this infection from spreading through your bird's bloodstream and becoming life-threatening. If osteomyelitis is present in a bird with bone fractures, repair and healing of fractures can be complicated. Blood tests and x-rays can be used to determine the presence of this disease.

During recovery from fractures, physical therapy may be prescribed for your bird. This prevents joints from becoming frozen or stiff and preserves as much range of motion as possible. Your avian veterinarian or the orthopedic specialist will provide you with instructions for any physical therapy your bird may need. To ensure a complete recovery for your bird, you will need to carefully and completely follow these instructions.

In addition to therapy, pain medication may be prescribed for your bird. These medications may be given in food or water or by mouth (*see* GIVING MEDICATION, page 833).

Gout

Gout (*see* page 852) is not actually a primary bone or muscle disorder, but it is a disease that can cause severe pain in the joints and muscles of birds. The cause of gout is the abnormal deposition and accumulation of uric acid crystals in the body, often in the joints or feet. Walking and perching will often be so painful that the bird will rest on the bottom of the cage or on any available flat surface in its environment. The bird will move only when it must and may vocalize if it must walk or move.

Sarcocystosis

Sarcocystosis (*see* page 848) is a disease caused by microscopic parasites. It is the cause of death in many parrots housed in outdoor cages in the southern United States. The parasites invade soft tissues, including the lungs, kidneys and muscles.

■ NUTRITIONAL DISORDERS

Avian nutrition has greatly improved in the past decade. Pellets and even organic formulated diets are now available, and domestically raised birds generally accept these readily. However, the nutritional requirements for individual species are still largely unknown. Many of the illnesses seen in pet birds have their basis in malnutrition. These include liver disease, kidney insufficiency, respiratory impairment, musculoskeletal disease, and reproductive problems.

Some special nutritional concerns in pet birds should be noted. Individual birds may be sensitive to the dyes and preservatives that are added to some seed and pelleted foods. Mold that contaminates improperly stored seed and pet-grade peanuts can cause liver disease, so be sure that any feed is fresh and is properly stored.

Be aware of what your bird actually eats and drinks. Many owners provide a varied diet for their birds to eat (such as table foods, formulated pelleted diet, vegetables, and other foods), but fail to realize that what the birds actually consume is mostly seeds, which can lead to nutritional deficiencies and imbalances. Also, birds do not like the taste of most vitamin and mineral supplements added to water. This not only makes them ineffective, it can also lead to decreased water consumption and dehydration.

Vitamin A Deficiency

A deficiency of vitamin A frequently goes unrecognized in pet birds. Birds that eat only seeds and nuts (especially sunflower seeds and peanuts) are most prone to this problem because an all-seed diet is deficient in many ways, including being low in vitamin A. Conversely, excessive vitamin A supplementation can cause serious side effects, including reproductive failure, bone abnormalities, and liver disease in some species.

The diets of all pet birds should be evaluated for vitamin A and vitamin A precursor content. Signs of vitamin A deficiency depend on which organ system is affected (for instance the reproductive, digestive, or respiratory tracts). Initially, small white spots may be seen in and around the mouth, eyes, and sinuses of the bird. The spots ultimately become infected, forming large, obvious abscesses. The abscesses can distort the glottis (opening of the windpipe), causing labored breathing and eventually suffocation. The abscesses can even grow so large that they block the choana (the slit in the roof of the mouth). When this happens, the bird will exhibit profuse nasal discharge and obvious swelling around the eyes. Other signs of vitamin A deficiency may include any of the following: sneezing, wheezing, crusted or plugged nostrils, lethargy, depression, diarrhea, tail-bobbing, thinness, poor feather color, swollen eyes, discharge from the eyes, lack of appetite, gagging, foul-smelling breath, and "slimy mouth."

The best preventive against vitamin A deficiency is to provide a formulated diet with sufficient, but not excessive, vitamin A precursors. A precursor is a substance that can be converted into vitamin A in the body. These precursors, such as beta-carotene, are much less likely to cause the toxicity that can occur with excessive vitamin A consumption.

Some birds, particularly lories and lorikeets, may need a decreased amount of vitamin A in their diet to avoid conditions such as iron storage disease of the liver (*see* page 846).

If your bird is not on a formulated diet, foods containing vitamin A or its precursors include cantaloupe, papaya, chili peppers, broccoli leaves and flowers, sweet potatoes, turnip leaves, collards, endive, butter, liver, egg yolks, beets, dandelion greens, and spinach.

Iodine Deficiency

Goiters caused by iodine deficiency used to be a common problem of pet budgies and still occur in certain areas. The thyroid gland in budgies is normally about 3 millimeters long, but can enlarge to more than 1 centimeter. Classic signs include loud or harsh breathing, wheezing, or clicking. Regurgitation is seen in some severe cases. Affected birds tolerate stress poorly. Lugol's iodine (1 drop per 1 cup [250 milliliters] of drinking water) can be used to treat the deficiency. The bird should be switched to a pelleted diet that includes sufficient iodine to prevent the formation of goiters.

Calcium, Phosphorus, and Vitamin D₃ Imbalance

Seed diets are known to lead to an imbalance in the calcium to phosphorus ratio in birds, as well as creating amino acid deficiencies. This ratio is important because calcium, phosphorus, and vitamin D_3 work together to perform vital functions, and a lack or excess of any of these nutrients can affect the body's ability to use all of them. Sunflower seeds, which tend to be preferred by many pet birds of the parrot family, are low in calcium, deficient in amino acids, and high in fat. Safflower seeds are actually higher in fat content than sunflower seeds, contrary to popular belief, and also contain inadequate amino acids and calcium. Providing a nutritionally sound diet that includes only a limited amount of seeds and nuts (*see* DIET, page 830) will help prevent these imbalances.

Acute Hypocalcemia in African Grey Parrots

This syndrome, caused by deficient levels of calcium in the blood, is characterized by weakness, tremors, and seizures. The exact cause is unknown, although parathyroid hormone abnormalities and vitamin D_3 requirements in this species of parrot are being studied. Treatment with calcium may lead to immediate improvement. In cases involving calcium deficiencies, your veterinarian may prescribe calcium supplements and exposure of the affected bird to outdoor-quality light for several hours each day. This light would include light in the UV (ultraviolet) spectrum. Exposure to UV rays is important because UV light can help your bird use calcium more efficiently. Bulbs and tubes emitting UV light are often available. (Note: these are not the same as plant lights.) Your avian veterinarian or a bird expert can recommend bulbs or tubes that provide the essential UV rays.

Vitamin D Toxicosis

Although excess calcium intake is not thought to cause problems in most cases, excess vitamin D_3 can cause harmful calcium accumulation in tissues such as the kidneys. Supplements should be used carefully, and excess vitamin D_3 should not be given to susceptible species, such as macaws.

Iron Storage Disease

Iron storage disease occurs when too much iron accumulates in the liver and other major organs of the body. The body needs a certain amount of iron to produce hemoglobin, which is the means of transporting oxygen molecules from the lungs to all the other cells in the body. However, when too much iron builds up, the body begins to store it in the liver, then the heart, lungs, and other organs, where it can do significant damage, eventually leading to death.

In most cases, there are no signs of iron storage disease until shortly before death. When signs do occur, they include difficulty breathing, fluid in the air sacs, paralysis, and distended abdomen.

The condition is common in pet mynahs and toucans, as well as certain zoo birds such as the bird of paradise. It has also been reported in pet birds of the parrot family, particularly lories. Although iron storage disease seems to be associated with excessive intake of dietary iron, not all birds become affected when kept on similar diets. Stress or genetic factors may also play a role. Certain foods rich in vitamin C, such as citrus fruits, increase dietary iron uptake. Excessive vitamin A consumption may also be involved.

It is recommended that low-iron diets be given routinely for pet mynahs and toucans, and commercial formulas are available. Certain foods such as peaches, plums, honeydew melon, and apples without skin are low in iron. Bananas, mangoes, papaya, summer squashes, and boiled potatoes without skin are a bit higher in iron content but can still be within the acceptable range. Foods to avoid include baby foods and juices and nectars that contain iron, foods that are enriched with iron or ferrous sulfate (including table scraps), animal products, such items as primate biscuits, and large quantities of citrus fruit.

▓ LUNG AND AIRWAY DISORDERS

In pet birds, diseases of the respiratory tract are very common. They can be caused by bacteria, viruses, fungi, or parasites. It is critical to recognize and treat these diseases in the early stages, when it is much more likely that treatment will be effective.

Aspergillosis

Aspergillosis is the most common fungal infection in birds. It occurs in 2 forms. The first form primarily occurs in young birds and newly imported birds and is the result of exposure to a large number of spores of the *Aspergillus* fungus. The second, more chronic form is more likely to occur in older birds that have been in captivity. Contaminated food, water, and nesting material with poor ventilation are sources of concentrated spores. *Aspergillus* spores are also widespread in the environment. Birds that inhale the spores may carry them into their lungs and air sacs. When the bird becomes weakened or stressed, the disease is triggered. Aspergillosis has been diagnosed in many species of birds. Long-term malnutrition, especially vitamin A deficiency, is the most common cause of a weakened respiratory system defense that predisposes birds to the chronic form of aspergillosis.

Aspergillosis usually affects the lower respiratory tract. Although the lungs and air sacs are usually involved, the trachea, syrinx (voice organ), and bronchi may be affected as well. Infection can spread from the respiratory tract to other organs.

Signs of infection in the severe, short-term form that affects young and newly imported birds include loss of appetite and labored breathing. Sudden death may occur. White mucous congestion of the lungs and air sacs, and nodules in the lungs may be noted during examination of the bird. The air sacs may become inflamed, leading to a condition sometimes called **airsacculitis**.

In the chronic form, labored breathing, voice change, lack of energy, depression, and emaciation may occur. Infection of the respiratory tract can be severe before signs are noted. Extensive or chronic fungal infection may lead to bone changes and permanent malformation of the upper respiratory architecture. If the central nervous system is affected, the bird may have a lack of coordination and paralysis.

The symptoms caused by aspergillosis are similar to those seen with other respiratory infections. Treatment with antifungal drugs is often successful if the infection is caught in its early stages. It is important to check with your veterinarian whenever your bird has signs of a respiratory illness.

To help prevent aspergillosis, good hygiene, including proper ventilation of the cage or aviary area and proper nutrition, should be maintained at all times.

Avian Influenza (Bird Flu)

Avian influenza is caused by a virus that originated in wild birds but has recently become a significant concern both because of its ability to infect domestic poultry and other birds and because of its potential to infect people. With the recent discovery of new mutations, this virus may become a more significant health threat in birds and in humans.

Because of the risk of infection, the Centers for Disease Control and Prevention (CDC) in the United States has banned the importation of pet birds from certain countries in Africa, Europe, and Asia where avian influenza has been reported. Before purchasing a new bird, you should always find out where it has come from, as well as getting it checked by a veterinarian to determine whether it has any infectious diseases.

The avian influenza virus is transmitted by direct contact with respiratory secretions and feces from an infected wild, domesticated, or pet bird. Signs of infection may include depression, loss of appetite, difficulty breathing, swelling of the head, discharge from the eyes, and diarrhea. Some infected birds may have no signs and recover, while others may die suddenly, without any signs of illness. Birds showing signs of respiratory illness should be promptly separated from other birds and examined by a veterinarian, who can diagnose avian influenza by submitting samples for isolation and identification of the virus.

Although vaccines have been developed for some types of avian influenza in domestic poultry, it is not known whether they would protect other species of birds from infection. An important way of preventing exposure to the virus is preventing contact between domestic birds and wild birds that may carry the virus.

Macaw Respiratory Hypersensitivity (Macaw Asthma)

An asthma-like disorder affecting macaws (primarily blue and gold macaws) has been recognized for several decades. The source of the irritant causing the hypersensitivity may vary, and may be difficult to determine. One common cause of respiratory irritation in macaws is the powder-down produced from "dusty" bird species (such as cockatoos and African Grey parrots). This does not mean that all macaws must be kept in separate areas from cockatoos or African Greys. As with people, only some macaws are sensitive to allergies.

Your veterinarian may need to do several procedures to determine if your macaw's respiratory condition is due to this hypersensitivity or to other causes such as bacterial or fungal infection. A blood cell count and x-rays are often performed. A tracheal wash may be necessary to determine if a combination of these diseases is present, and to select the appropriate treatment. A lung biopsy is the only way to confirm the diagnosis.

Initially, the best treatment for a bird that is in respiratory distress from this condition is oxygen. Your veterinarian may also consider the use of glucocorticoids or other anti-inflammatory drugs. Longterm management requires optimal air quality and ventilation. A good air filter (such as a HEPA filter) located near the cage is invaluable. Repeat crises may occur and necessitate rehospitalization and treatment, but a change of environment and increased ventilation will reduce the likelihood of severe relapse. Some permanent lung damage is usually present, and exercise intolerance often persists due to interstitial fibrosis (scarring) of the lungs.

Polycythemia, an increase in the percentage of red blood cells, is a very common finding on the blood work and may be the best method to screen for this disease before it becomes a noticeable problem.

Newcastle Disease

Newcastle disease, caused by a virus, is a significant threat to the poultry industry but can also infect pet birds. Transmission is by respiratory aerosols, fecal contamination of food or water, direct contact with infected birds, and contact with inanimate objects that harbor the virus. It is rarely seen in pet birds in the United States.

Signs of infection include depression, loss of appetite and weight, sneezing, discharge from the eyes or nostrils, difficulty breathing, bright yellow-green diarrhea, lack of coordination, head bobbing, and spasms. In later stages, paralysis of the wings or legs, involuntary or jerky movements, twisting of the neck and unnatural position of the head, and dilated pupils may also be seen. Birds may die suddenly without any signs.

There is no cure, and treatment is not recommended. If suspected, Newcastle disease must be reported to the appropriate authorities due to its potentially devastating effects on domestic poultry. Vaccination is prohibited in birds entering the United States because it does not eliminate the carrier state and makes it difficult to detect the virus during quarantine.

Respiratory Parasites

Air sac mites are parasites that can be found in the entire respiratory tract of affected birds, most frequently in canaries and Gouldian finches. All stages of the mite are found within the respiratory tissues. In mild infections, birds do not usually have any signs; in heavy infections, difficult breathing with high-pitched noises and clicking, sneezing, tail bobbing, and open-mouthed breathing are noted. Excessive salivation may also be present. Signs are made worse by handling, exercise, and other stresses. Mortality can be high in heavy infections. The veterinarian will most likely prescribe an antiparasitic medication that is given by mouth or by injection.

Gapeworms are parasites that live in the wall of the trachea, usually in finches and canaries. Infected birds often have difficulty breathing and will "gape" for air—hence the name. Gapeworms are rare in caged birds, but when present, they can cause death due to lack of oxygen or pneumonia. Effective treatment is possible when it is begun early.

Sarcocystosis is caused by a protozoan parasite that invades the body's soft tissues and forms cysts in the respiratory tract, kidneys, nervous tissues, and eventually in the muscles. It is a major cause of death in parrots housed outdoors in the southern United States. In severely affected areas, even indoor birds can be infected by contaminated food. The infection occurs when birds are exposed to infected opossum feces, usually carried by insects such as cockroaches, or by rats that get into the bird's feed. The feces of these transport hosts are then consumed by birds, and a rapidly fatal disease can develop. A high death rate is observed in untreated birds such as cockatoos, African Grey parrots, *Eclectus* parrots, and other Old World species that have not been exposed to this parasite. Signs of infection may include a lack of energy, passive regurgitation of water, and anemia. Treatment includes supportive care with injectable fluids, supplemental feeding if needed, treatment for anemia, and longterm antiprotozoal medications.

■ REPRODUCTIVE DISORDERS

There are a number of reproductive disorders that can occur in pet birds. The following are some of the more common disorders.

Cloacal Prolapse (Vent Prolapse)

The cloaca is the area where the urine, feces, and urates are stored prior to being passed. The vent is the outermost part of the cloaca; these cloacal lips control the frequency with which your bird will eliminate its droppings. A prolapse of the cloaca occurs when the inner tissue protrudes through the vent opening, resulting in exposed intestines, cloaca, or uterus. It can be caused by a physical or psychological problem or both. The condition requires immediate emergency care by a veterinarian.

This syndrome is extremely common in adult Umbrella and Moluccan cockatoos. The exact cause has not been determined, but birds that develop cloacal prolapses are frequently hand-raised, had delayed weaning and/or continued begging for food, have a close attachment to at least one person (with signs of either a child/parent or mate/mate relationship with the person), and have a tendency to hold the stool in the vent for prolonged periods (for example, overnight), rather than defecating in the cage. Cockatoos that are independent of humans do not have this medical problem. It is possible that the condition is caused by prolonged begging for food, causing straining and dilation of the vent; misplaced sexual attraction to a person, causing vent straining and movement; retention of stool in the vent for prolonged periods, stretching and dilating the vent; or a combination of these factors.

If detected and treated early, surgery and behavior modification can correct the problem. However, behavior modification is often difficult for owners because in many ways it involves breaking the close bond that they have with their bird. If the bird still perceives its owner as either parent or mate, it will continue to strain and the problem will likely recur. Behaviors that should be avoided include stroking the bird, especially on the back; feeding the bird warm foods or food by hand or mouth; and cuddling the bird close to the body. If an owner is serious about trying to change their bird's behavior, the aid of a behavioral consultant will likely be necessary (*see* WHERE TO GET HELP, page 19).

Egg Binding

Egg binding occurs when a bird is unable to expel an egg from the reproductive tract. It is most commonly seen in overweight, female birds that get little exercise. Calcium deficiency is another factor often seen in birds with this condition. Cockatiels, budgies, and lovebirds are commonly affected, but larger parrots may also experience egg binding.

Signs of egg binding include tail wagging, swelling of the abdomen, and a swaying or unsteady posture on the perch. If the egg is putting pressure on a nerve, signs of leg paralysis may also occur. It is not recommended that bird owners attempt to remove the bound egg, because a bird may become paralyzed or die if this is done incorrectly.

A veterinarian will attempt to extract the egg by providing calcium, humidity, lubrication, hydration (fluids), and warmth. X-rays may be needed to determine if the egg is abnormal and to pinpoint its location. Following this, injections such as oxytocin or prostaglandins may be given to help induce movement of the egg. If the egg does not pass with medical management, the veterinarian may need to use manual extraction or even surgery to remove the egg.

Cockatoos that are hand fed and have an extremely close bond with their owner are at risk for cloacal prolapse.

SKIN AND FEATHER DISORDERS

Skin and feather disorders are among the most common health problems seen in pet birds. Loss of feathers and skin disorders can be signs of a local disorder (that is, one that only involves the skin or feathers), or they can be signs of general, system-wide disease.

Feather Cysts

Feather cysts occur when a growing feather is unable to protrude through the skin and curls within the follicle. The ingrown feather results in a lump or mass that continues to grow as the feather enlarges. Feather cysts appear as oval or elongated swellings involving a single or several feather follicles. Although they may occur anywhere, in parrots they most commonly involve the primary feathers of the wings.

Feather cysts may be seen in all species; however, they are most common in blue and gold macaws and certain breeds of canaries. The cysts may be the result of an inherited predisposition, as in certain species of canaries, or acquired as a result of infection or trauma involving the feather follicle. The condition can be treated by surgically removing the involved feather follicles. If the follicle is not removed, the condition will usually recur. In canaries with multiple cysts, surgery is not usually practical.

Feather Plucking

Feather plucking refers to behaviors in birds that can range from mild overpreening to self-mutilation. There are many different possible causes of feather plucking, both physical (such as disease, parasites, or allergies) and psychological (such as stress or boredom). Good communication with your veterinarian concerning the problem is necessary in order to improve the health of the bird and to reduce or eliminate the plucking behavior if possible.

Feather plucking seldom has a single factor as the cause, and all possible reasons should be explored, including underlying medical problems. Possible medical causes for feather plucking include skin or internal parasites, liver disease, cancer, allergies and other inflammatory skin conditions, infectious diseases, metabolic or nutritional disorders, or heavy metal poisoning (notably zinc).

Malnutrition is a common contributing factor to feather plucking. Basic seed and table food diets often create nutritional deficiencies that cause abnormal skin and feather development. This can result in plucking behavior, as well as many other medical problems. The dyes and preservatives added to seeds and many pelleted diets may be detrimental to birds or can cause allergies. The relatively low humidity in most households also has a drying effect on the skin. Being deprived of natural sunlight, fresh air, humidity, and the normal light/dark cycle has negative physiologic and psychological effects on birds.

Addressing the medical and environmental factors may reduce the severity of feather plucking, but a strong behavioral component is often involved as well. Treatment of some of the above-mentioned problems may lead to initial improvement, followed by a relapse. Psychological stressors can lead to feather plucking. Psychological conditions that may cause feather plucking in birds vary. Excessive stimulation may cause plucking in one bird, while another bird might pluck out of boredom. Unfortunately, once the stress has been relieved, the habit may still remain.

Feather plucking does not occur in the wild, where birds are occupied with finding food, maintaining their social status in the flock, seeking a mate, avoiding predators, and breeding and raising young. Therefore, often the best-kept birds, which have all their apparent needs met, will pluck feathers for behavioral reasons. Owners of these birds often report that their birds are more territorial, more aggressive, and may be showing sexual behavior toward a perceived human mate or inanimate objects.

A thorough understanding of the bird's environment and the associated behavioral changes that have accompanied the

Reducing Feather Plucking

Once feather plucking is diagnosed and medical reasons for plucking have been excluded or treated, a few changes in the bird's environment may aid in reducing the plucking behavior.

- Make sure the bird receives at least 12 hours of light and 12 hours of dark and quiet each day. Covering the cage with a dark blue or black blanket for at least 12 hours will help.

- Spend time with your bird. Setting a schedule that allows you to interact with your bird at the same time daily may help to reduce anxiety and concurrent feather plucking.

- It is important that your bird has toys to help occupy free time and distract from plucking. Changing the toys daily or rearranging them within the cage may maintain its interest.

- Observe your bird when it is plucking. There may be something in its environment that stimulates it to pick. Identifying "triggers" is the first step in decreasing the behavior.

- Mist or bathe your bird on a regular basis. The amount of bathing needed will vary with the species and its natural habitat. Daily bathing is enjoyed by many rainforest species (such as Amazons and macaws) while weekly may be enough for birds from more arid climates that have powder down (for example, cockatoos and African Grey parrots). Spray or mist with water to lightly coat the plumage or take the bird into the shower with you and allow it to perch on the shower bar or door. Many birds love to preen in the sun and groom their plumage after a bath. Bathing induces normal preening behaviors and deters plucking.

- New foods may interest your bird and occupy its time. Feed fun things such as rotelle pasta, spray millet, breads, unsweetened cereals, or bean mixes.

- If your bird picks from a stressful situation, then avoid that situation. For example, some birds do not like to have their plumage stroked but enjoy merely perching on your hand. Let them perch and keep hands away.

- Additionally, "stroking" birds on the back simulates mating behavior, and although enjoyed by many birds, particularly cockatoos, it can increase hormone levels and therefore can increase behavioral feather plucking.

- Frequent trips to or consults with your avian veterinarian or avian behaviorist may be necessary for follow-up care. Many treatments are available for reducing feather destructive behaviors and several may need to be tried to find which ones work best for a particular bird.

- Finally, realize that if you have excluded or treated all medical problems and done your best to correct any environmental, nutritional or social inadequacies in your bird's environment, that your bird may still pluck some feathers. Take comfort in the fact this usually reflects that the bird lives in an environment where all its needs have been met. As many avian veterinarians state, "Generally the best kept birds are the ones that can afford to pluck."

---

onset of plucking is required in order to treat the problem. In some cases, simple changes in the environment, such as moving the bird's cage to an area where the family often gathers, will help. In other birds, environmental changes are combined with medical treatments such as hormones or drugs to reduce anxiety or aggression. However, available drugs do not tend to produce longterm positive results, and side effects may be seen. In addition to traditional medical therapies, acupuncture and dietary supplementation with omega fatty acids have been reported to be helpful in some cases. Referral to a behavioral consultant may be useful.

Skin Infections

Inflammation of the skin may result from infection with various organisms. Bacteria, including staphylococci, streptococci, and *Bacillus* species, are thought to be responsible for most skin infections in parrots. Staphylococci are often isolated from areas of pododermatitis (bumblefoot) in many avian species. Your veterinarian can identify and prescribe appropriate antibiotics for these bacterial infections, if necessary.

Ringworm, a fungal infection, is occasionally reported in pet birds. *Cryptococcus* fungi have been rarely reported to cause facial dermatitis in birds, but because this organism may also cause infections in people, it should be considered in cases of true skin infection. Skin inflammation caused by the yeast *Malassezia* has been reported in caged birds. Your veterinarian may prescribe a medication given by mouth or a topical spray to treat these infections.

Parasites

Scaly face or leg mites are common in budgies but rare in other parrots. They cause a mange-like condition on the face or legs of affected birds. Signs of infestation include white crusts around the corners of the mouth, nostrils, beak, and occasionally the area around the eyes or the legs that may cause deformities if not treated. Even after successful treatment, beak deformity may still persist. Other species of birds such as canaries and finches can also become infested with this parasite, but have different signs, such as crusts that form on the legs and surfaces of the toes (commonly called **tassel foot**). Itching is not usually seen. The mites can be diagnosed from skin scrapings taken from affected areas. The veterinarian will most likely prescribe an antiparasitic drug that is given by mouth or by injection.

Feather mites rarely affect pet birds, despite popular belief. Occasionally, infestation with red mites may be found in outdoor aviaries. Signs of feather mite infestation include restlessness (especially at night), anemia, and death, particularly in young chicks confined to the nest box. Covering the cage at night with a white sheet and examining the underside of the cover the following morning aids in collecting and identifying mites. The veterinarian may prescribe a spray, powder, or other medication that is given by mouth or by injection for treatment. Nest box treatment includes mixing a medicated powder into the nest box bedding. Cages should be cleaned thoroughly, and wooden nest boxes may need to be discarded and replaced.

Psittacine Beak and Feather Disease (Circovirus)

Psittacine beak and feather disease is caused by a virus. The name "beak and feather disease" is somewhat misleading, because the typical signs do not include beak abnormalities and are less likely to have the severe feather abnormalities that were seen in cockatoos when the disease was first documented. This serious infection has been reported in wild and domestic birds. Screening for the virus has greatly decreased its presence in cockatoos; however, the disease is still noted in African Grey parrots, *Eclectus* parrots, lovebirds, lorikeets, and other species from Old World locations such as Asia, Africa, and Australia.

Infection occurs primarily in young birds, with few instances of infection seen in birds over 3 years of age. Typical signs include feather loss, (including areas where the bird could not reach to pluck itself), abnormal pin feathers (constricted, clubbed, or stunted), abnormal mature feathers (blood in shaft), and lack of powder down in some species. Pigment loss may occur in colored feathers. More rapid infections can also occur, with several days of depression and sudden death.

Psittacine beak and feather disease is spread by direct contact with affected birds and by spread of feather dust, dander, and fecal material. It may be spread from adults to offspring and may even be contracted from a nest box which has been unused for many months or years. The virus is very stable in the environment and is resistant to disinfectants.

Affected birds should be isolated; often it is recommended that they be euthanized. There is no effective treatment, but supportive measures may increase the length and quality of life. Strict hygiene with attention to dust control, diagnostic screening methods, and lengthy quarantines are highly recommended in cockatoo breeding colonies to prevent the establishment and spread of this disease.

■ KIDNEY AND URINARY TRACT DISORDERS

Gout is the abnormal deposit of uric acid crystals in the body. Uric acid is

Feather Loss

Molting

Birds lose and replace most of their feathers at least once yearly; some species will normally have a partial molt 6 months later. In North America, most species start their major molt around mid-February and end it about a month later. South American parrots usually skip the fall molt but Old World parrots (especially cockatiels) will sometimes drop feathers in early September.

It is important to know if your bird is undergoing normal feather replacement or has feather loss for other reasons.

Types of Feather Damage

Feathers can be chewed off at the level of skin, chewed off with the downy aftershaft left behind, or chewed at just the tips; leaving a moth-eaten appearance. Some birds will extract the feathers completely, oftentimes vocalizing painfully during this process. Other birds simply chew, abnormally preen, or fray their plumage.

Feather damage can also occur from wear and tear, infectious causes, parasites, barbering by cagemates, and cage trauma. Parasites cause feather breakage or rubbing of the plumage and skin, which also breaks the plumage.

Causes of Feather Damage

- **Parasites**—Contrary to public opinion, parasites are rarely a cause for feather loss. Red mites, feather mites, and lice are occasionally found.

- **Bacteria and Fungi**—Both types of organisms can cause follicle infection and usually respond well to medication.

- **Nutrition**—Malnutrition can cause feather abnormalities directly and by affecting a bird's organ function and immune system.

- **Barbering**—Cage mates frequently pick feathers of birds housed with them.

- **Behavior**—Besides the lack of natural stressors that act to prevent any wild bird from plucking, other factors that can contribute to behavioral feather damage in captive parrots include sexual frustration, boredom, territoriality, compulsive behavior, predator stress from household pets, and lack of parental training for preening.

- **Medical**—Organ disease such as liver damage, kidney failure, tumors, respiratory infection and other infections can contribute to stress-induced feather loss or self-trauma.

- **Other Causes**—Irritants such as insect bites, tonics applied to the plumage, ointments, hand creams or oils from the owner that are inadvertently transferred to the bird's feathers, or improperly trimmed flight feathers can lead to chewing.

produced by the liver and excreted through the kidneys. The uric acid, when not properly removed from the bloodstream, will begin to crystallize and collect in various places in the bird's body. It is not toxic or harmful in itself, but the buildup of crystals can severely damage tissues.

Gout is rare in canaries and finches, but birds in the parrot family are more frequently affected. The disease is most often seen in older budgies, cockatiels, and parrots that have been fed an unbalanced diet (protein levels above 20 to 25%). Also contributing to this condition are diets that are too high in calcium or vitamin D_3 or too low in vitamin A. Gout that affects the joints of birds tends to be severely painful. If pain control cannot be accomplished,

euthanasia may be considered to prevent suffering. Surgical removal of the crystal deposits is not practical in most cases because they are often located close to blood vessels and the chance of fatal bleeding is high. Additionally, unless the underlying condition can be corrected or controlled, new crystal deposits will appear very rapidly. Your veterinarian may prescribe medications given by mouth that are helpful in the control of gout and the associated pain in some cases.

Gout crystals may also affect internal organs; this type of gout is rarely diagnosed before death of the bird. The membranes on the surface of various organs and the tubules of the kidney are the location of uric acid crystal deposits. Death is often the only sign noted.

The genetic, nutritional, and environmental factors that predispose a bird to gout are not fully understood. However, uric acid levels should be determined in birds with gout, and birds with elevated levels should be placed on a low-protein diet.

■ DISORDERS AFFECTING MULTIPLE BODY SYSTEMS

A number of diseases may involve multiple parts or organ systems of a bird's body. Signs can be general (such as weakness or lack of interest in food or activities) or more specific. Sometimes no signs are noted. The more common of these disorders are discussed here.

Polyomavirus

Polyomavirus was first identified in budgerigars (budgies), then in other parrots and parakeets, and most recently has been shown to cause disease in finches. Polyomavirus can infect birds of all ages, but nestlings and juveniles are the most susceptible. Affected birds may have a lack of appetite, diarrhea, and generalized weakness, and the onset of these signs is usually rapid. Bruising of the skin and muscles may also occur, and the infection may target the heart, liver, and kidneys. Infection is usually fatal, and death may occur in 24 to 48 hours. If a bird survives, it may have abnormal feather growth, heart disease, and liver damage as an adult. Adult birds may be carriers of the virus and can spread infection. The prevalence of this virus in adult parrots and budgies is thought to be high.

Polyomavirus can be passed from the female to the egg, but most infections are spread by direct contact, feather dander, and exposure to feces. Exposed females may develop protective antibodies that are passed on to nestlings and may provide temporary immunity. Offspring from unexposed females are at higher risk of infection because they lack protective antibodies.

There is no treatment available for infected birds. Spread of the virus can be controlled through testing and isolation of all infected birds and by vaccination. Because infected adults shed the virus only under certain conditions, identifying infected adults can be difficult. Control during an outbreak can be maintained by disinfecting handfeeding utensils, incubators, and brooders and by vaccination. The chances of exposure to polyomavirus can be reduced by following standard hygiene procedures closely, preventing access to baby birds by visitors or any returned bird or outside bird, and using appropriate quarantine procedures for all new birds. Screening by a veterinarian should first be done to make sure that avian polyomavirus is not already present.

A vaccine to prevent polyomavirus infection is available and is given in 2 doses. The first dose may be given by the veterinarian as early as 4 weeks of age to properly complete the vaccination series and allow full immunity to develop. Older birds receive 2 vaccines 2 to 4 weeks apart, then 1 booster annually. Both negative and positive adult and juvenile parrots can be vaccinated.

Pacheco's Disease (Pacheco's Herpesvirus)

Pacheco's disease is a highly contagious, fast-developing disease of parrots (psittacines) caused by a herpesvirus. This disease is associated with stress, which can cause healthy-looking birds that carry the virus to pass the infection to susceptible birds. It is spread by direct contact between birds, airborne secretions, or contamination of food or water with feces. Macaws, Amazon parrots, Monk parakeets, and conures are often involved in outbreaks of the disease. Old World species are less likely to be either carriers or susceptible to infection.

Infected birds may not show any signs of disease until just before dying. The birds are usually in good condition and have a good appetite. Fluffing, loss of energy, and watery feces are signs that sometimes can be seen in infected birds. Most birds do not recover from the infection. Diagnosis of Pacheco's disease must be made quickly in order to prevent further spread of the infection.

Other Herpesvirus Infections

Other important herpesviruses of pet birds include the strain responsible for wart-like foot growths (called papillomas) in *Cacatua* species and an abnormal loss of color noted on the feet of macaws. The internal papillomatous disease of macaws (most notably green-wing macaws, *Ara chloroptera*) and Amazon parrots is thought to be caused by a herpesvirus related to the one causing Pacheco's disease. Amazon tracheitis (inflammation of the trachea), which is an uncommon infection, is also caused by a herpesvirus.

Poxvirus Infections

Because of import restrictions, the poxvirus that was historically common in imported blue-fronted Amazon parrots is rarely seen in pet birds. However, poxvirus infections may still occur in canaries and pigeons and in several species of wild birds. These viruses are not contagious to psittacines (parrots).

Pet birds may show one of 3 different types of clinical signs. The first type, skin infection, is the most common. These birds have individual growths, small abscesses, or crusty scabs on the skin of unfeathered areas, such as the face (especially around the eyes and the mouth) and the legs and feet. The diphtheritic or "wet" form is the second type, which may follow the skin form or occur on its own. Swelling and discharges from the eyes are followed by injuries on the mucous membranes of the throat, upper airways, and esophagus. The third and most severe form occurs with a rapid onset of generalized signs of illness, including depression, bluish discoloration of the skin, loss of appetite, and rapid death.

Veterinarians often recommend treatment with vitamin A and antibiotics, ointments for the eyes, heat, humidity, daily cleansing of the affected areas, and attention to diet. Poxvirus infections are trans-mitted by insect (usually mosquito) bites or through breaks in the skin. Therefore, mosquito control and indoor housing are vital to prevent outbreaks. Vaccines for canarypox and pigeonpox are available, but are protective only for their host species.

Mycobacteriosis (Avian Tuberculosis)

Mycobacteriosis is a bacterial infection that is sometimes called avian tuberculosis, although it differs from tuberculosis in mammals. Three species of *Mycobacterium* bacteria are most frequently linked with mycobacteriosis in pet birds.

Mycobacteriosis is seen most frequently in pet birds of the parrot family, in which it usually affects the intestinal tract. This bacterial infection can also occur in toucans, finches, and pigeons. Most birds that are infected are adults. For many birds, infection is fatal.

Signs of infection may include weight loss (in spite of having a good appetite), diarrhea, increased thirst, difficulty breathing, and masses in the skin, eyes, and internal organs such as the liver, spleen, and lungs.

Treatment can be difficult and may take up to a year. In addition, the disease can potentially be transmitted from birds to humans, so great care must be taken to avoid infection by thoroughly washing hands with soap and water after contact with a sick bird, wearing gloves, and practicing other good hygiene. Although some evidence suggests that the risk of transmission from pet birds to people is low, people who are elderly, very young, or have weakened immune systems (such as individuals infected with the HIV virus) should avoid any contact with infected birds.

Psittacosis (Chlamydiosis, Parrot Fever)

Psittacosis or chlamydiosis is a serious infection that is caused by the bacteria *Chlamydophila psittaci*. The bacteria are found in the nasal secretions and in the stool from infected birds, recovering birds, and carriers. Because the disease can be transmitted from birds to people, there are certain regulations in the United States regarding the reporting and quarantine of birds that are suspected of having psittacosis. Although still a disease of concern, chlamydial infection has decreased dramatically since the importation of South American birds has been curtailed.

Some birds, because of their genetic resistance, are less likely to become ill when infected and, consequently, are more likely to develop into carriers. These include pigeons, doves, budgies, cockatiels, cockatoos, and about 100 additional species. Other species, such as rosellas, lorikeets, mynahs, canaries, and some parrots have low natural resistance.

Depending on the species of bird affected, the signs of psittacosis will vary. Typical signs of infection include a bird that is ruffled, depressed, has labored breathing, discharge from the eyes and nose, and is neither eating nor vocalizing. The appearance of lime-green or yellow droppings, especially when the urine is also discolored, is often present with psittacosis. One form of psittacosis that occurs infrequently involves the central nervous system and includes signs such as tremors, shaking, head twisting, and convulsions. This form has most often been recognized in African Grey parrots and cockatoos. Additionally, cockatiels and *Neophema* species (turquoisines, scarlet-chested parakeets) may seem to have an eye disease resembling conjunctivitis or a stye. Various internal organs may be affected by psittacosis, including the liver and heart.

Once psittacosis is diagnosed, treatment usually involves giving antibiotics (often added to the food or water) for an extended period of time. Birds in chlamydial crisis need intense, supportive care (injectable antibiotics, fluids, heat, isolation, extremely clean conditions, absence of stress), as well as treatment for any other signs of illness.

The best way to control psittacosis is to keep susceptible birds away from the infectious agent. Because the bacteria can

remain infective for many months in dried excrement, cleanliness and disinfection are essential. Eliminating drafts and spraying the area with appropriate disinfectants will help keep infectious feathers and dust to a minimum. Birds that have had the disease or are under treatment can be reinfected.

Because the bacteria can cause illness in people as well as birds, care should be taken to always practice good hygiene when caring for a sick bird. This includes wearing gloves when handling the bird, thorough hand washing with soap and water, and disinfecting cages, feeders, and other utensils daily. All new birds should be tested for psittacosis before being introduced into your household.

In most areas, physicians must report cases of psittacosis to local health authorities, and treatment may need to be coordinated with and approved by the governing agency.

Clostridial Diseases

Clostridial bacteria cause several disorders in birds depending on the species of the bacteria involved and the location of infection. Birds become infected by eating contaminated food or water, inhaling spores or bacteria from the air or other contaminated surfaces, or by infection of wounds. One common method of entry in birds occurs

Table 2. Diseases that can be Spread from Birds to People	
Disease	**Causative Organism**
Avian tuberculosis	*Mycobacterium avium*
Psittacosis (chlamydiosis)	*Chlamydophila psittaci*
Avian influenza	Influenza virus A H5N1
Giardiasis	*Giardia lamblia*
Cryptococcosis	*Cryptococcus neoformans*
Ringworm (dermatophytosis)	*Trichophyton* and *Microsporum* species
Histoplasmosis	*Histoplasma capsulatum*

when the bacteria invade damaged cloacal tissue (the area where the urine, feces, and urates wait to be passed) in birds with cloacal prolapse or papillomatosis.

Signs vary depending on the type of clostridial infection. Disease-causing strains of the bacteria produce a toxin in the small intestines of birds, resulting in rapid loss of condition and weight loss, lethargic behavior, decreased appetite, and bloodstained or undigested food. The toxin and its effects may remain in the system for a long time even after the original bacterial infection has been treated.

For prevention, minimize stress and overcrowding, ensure proper ventilation, and provide a nutritionally sound diet. Make sure feed is properly stored and is free of bacterial growth. Spores may be present in corn and grain products as well as manufactured pellets or extruded food and may develop bacterial growth if they are not properly stored. The stool of household pets (dogs and cats) may also harbor these bacteria.

Other Bacterial Diseases

Several types of bacteria can cause disease in birds. Some are normally present in the bird's body or environment, but do not cause disease except under certain circumstances, such as in birds that are very young, old, weak, stressed, or that have an impaired immune system. *Escherichia coli, Pseudomonas, Aeromonas, Serratia marcescens, Salmonella, Klebsiella, Enterobacter, Proteus,* and *Citrobacter* species are bacteria that are frequently isolated in birds. *Pasteurella* species have been reported as possible agents causing infection in birds bitten by other animals, such as pet cats or rats.

Heavy Metal Poisoning

Heavy metals such as lead and zinc are common throughout the environment, so limiting your bird's exposure to them is important. Birds should not be allowed to play outside their cages without supervision. The environment should be inspected for the presence of heavy metals, and the sources should be removed from the area if possible. Because cage and fencing materials are common sources of heavy metals, proper selection of nontoxic materials is important. Stainless steel and welded wire should be used. Cage clips should be made from alloys that do not contain lead or zinc.

Lead and zinc poisoning are the 2 most common poisonings in caged birds. Zinc poisoning is now more common than lead poisoning, due to the heightened awareness of the dangers of lead, and the increased use of galvanized materials. Galvanization is a process of coating other metals such as iron with a zinc-based surface to prevent rust. This galvanization is found on much of the manufactured wire and other hardware used in home-made cage construction.

Potential sources of lead include old paint, stained glass, lead curtain weights, lead fishing weights, and lead solder. Signs of heavy metal poisoning include regurgitation of water, excessive thirst, depression, lack of energy, and weakness. Trembling, lack of coordination, excitability, or seizures may occur in lead poisoning.

Your veterinarian will suspect heavy metal poisoning when signs of this toxicity are accompanied by the presence of metal in the gizzard on an x-ray. This diagnosis can be confirmed by determining levels of lead or zinc in the blood. The initial treatment, besides supportive care, is usually one of a class of drugs called chelating agents that is injected into the muscle until the bird no longer has signs. Once your bird is stable, you can give a chelating agent by mouth at home. If the toxicity is not severe, the bird's response to treatment is usually rapid. As with all poisonings, prevention is the key.

Poisoning from Fumes and Aerosols

Many bird owners are aware of the hazard that occurs when surfaces coated with Teflon®, Silverstone®, Tefzel®, or other fluoropolymers are overheated. Nonstick cookware and bakeware, some heat lamp bulbs (those manufactured for use in the food industry), self-cleaning ovens, and irons are often coated with fluoropolymers. Fluoropolymers start releasing particles at temperatures as low as 396°F (202°C) and release vaporized fluoropolymer particles starting at 464°F (240°C). These temperatures are commonly reached during normal cooking. For example, when cooking meat, the normal frying temperature is between 400 to 450°F (204 to 232°C). When heated to 680°F (360°C) or higher, fluoropolymers give off acidic fumes that can be lethal for birds. This temperature may be reached when cooking meat in broilers or when using the cleaning feature on some self-cleaning ovens.

Fluoropolymer fumes are not the only potential home chemical hazard for birds. A number of aerosol products (including some carpet fresheners), plastics melted or burned in a microwave oven, or new heating duct systems may also be irritating or toxic to caged birds. (*See also* HOUSEHOLD HAZARDS, page 835.)

Signs of poisoning include labored breathing, neurologic signs, and sudden death. Most exposures are deadly before action can be taken, but if you have time, get the bird into fresh air and then to the veterinarian as soon as possible. It is best to locate your bird's cage in an area well away from any fumes that might be created as a result of cooking. Cages should always be well ventilated.

■ CANCERS AND TUMORS

As the average age of the pet bird has increased, so has the incidence of cancers and tumors. Avian cancers include most of the common locations and categories seen in other companion animals.

Internally, cancer may occur in the ovaries, kidneys, liver, stomach (often not identified until the bird has died), pituitary and thyroid glands, and the muscles and bones. Both surgery and chemotherapy have been used successfully in treating these internal cancers.

Skin cancers (**squamous cell carcinomas**) are most likely to occur around the eyes and beak, on the tips of the wings, and on the toes. Radiation therapy has been used to

Lipomas most often occur on the breastbone or chest area of budgerigars (budgies).

treat these cancers with some success. Tumors called fibrosarcomas may also be noticed as reddened patches on the skin.

Lipomas are fatty tumors that occur most frequently in budgerigars. They are most often located on the keel (breast bone) or in the chest area and are benign. It is not necessary to remove the lipoma unless it is large enough to cause discomfort to the bird.

Xanthomas are yellow, fatty masses that occur under the skin. The wing tips, keel, and the chest area are common locations, although xanthomas may be found anywhere. Xanthomas are seen in many bird species, and the incidence is very high in cockatiels and budgies. The cause is unknown, but dietary improvement, including diets with sufficient vitamin A precursors (such as beta carotene) may be helpful in treatment. Surgical removal is an option in advanced cases. Like lipomas, xanthomas are benign, but tend to become ulcerated and bleed as they enlarge.

Lymphoma occurs in pet birds, as it does in other companion animals (*see* page 45). Both radiation therapy and chemotherapy have been used successfully in the treatment of lymphoma in birds.

Pituitary adenomas are most common in budgerigars and cockatiels. They may be seen as acute conditions of the nervous system, with signs such as seizures and muscle spasms. Affected birds may also show signs related to the pituitary hormone(s) that are involved, for example causing excessive thirst and increased urination.

■ INJURIES AND ACCIDENTS

Pet birds have an innate desire to try to hide any illness or injury. In the wild, showing signs of illness increases the chance they will be attacked by other animals. Thus, any behavior that is out of the ordinary is a sign that your bird may be ill. In particular, if you notice limping, the inability to move the wings properly, any unusual discharge, any changes in droppings, or a general lack of physical activity, you should seek veterinary advice or care promptly. If your bird is huddled, lethargic, unresponsive, or lying on the bottom of the cage, you have an emergency. Alert your veterinarian and transport the bird immediately.

When a bird has a "bleeding" emergency, it is important to distinguish between obvious active bleeding (such as from the wing, beak, or foot) and blood on the cage or on the bird with no active bleeding. Continued bleeding requires immediate veterinary intervention, whereas bleeding that has stopped is best left undisturbed. However, even if bleeding has ceased, it is wise to take your bird in for an examination.

If your bird is in respiratory distress, your veterinarian will place the bird in an incubator with oxygen. Shock and infection are of concern in birds that have penetrating or extensive wounds.

Injuries should be treated with the goal of the bird's survival first and treatment of the traumatized area second. For example, a bird that has been struggling for hours with its leg band caught—and that may possibly have a fractured bone—is in more danger of dying from stress related to the prolonged struggling than from the fracture.

First Aid Kit for Pet Birds

Phone Numbers

Phone numbers are by far the most important thing any emergency kit can contain. Have an alternative number recorded in case your regular avian veterinarian is not available. Find the closest emergency clinic to you that will treat birds and keep their number handy as well.

Flour

Flour can be placed in the bottom of a shoe box or comparable container. A bird with a bleeding toenail can be placed in the box to walk around. This will not require restraint and therefore will not elevate the bird's blood pressure and cause more bleeding.

File

Birds can be acclimated to the use of a nail file to take just the very sharp points off of their nails. Unless they are diseased or malnourished, birds' nails do not overgrow in length, but the needle sharp tips can get caught in clothing or carpeting, and can be uncomfortable for the owner.

Hemostat

A hemostat is a medical clamp referred to as "forceps." A substitute is tweezers or thumb forceps with "teeth" to catch hold of what you are trying to grasp. Forceps are good for unknotting string wound around small feet.

Scissors

Scissors are great for trimming broken, mature feathers. It is not recommended that inexperienced bird owners trim broken, bleeding quills as the quill may bleed more profusely.

(Continued on the following page)

First Aid Kit for Pet Birds—*(Continued)*

Cotton swabs

Cotton swabs can help control bleeding. They are also best for cleaning stains off of feathers and skin (such as lipstick or oils) and for swabbing out lower beaks (such as food debris in baby birds).

Gauze pads

Gauze pads can also help control bleeding. Use only sterile pads on open wounds. Small size pads are easier to use but may be difficult to find.

Bandage material

Bleeding emergencies often warrant the use of pressure wraps to aid in the application of direct pressure to open cuts, abrasions, and fractures. Do not apply a wrap if you are uncertain of the proper method. Most bleeding skin wounds will clot on their own or be "protected" by the bird from further injury. Good materials that won't adhere to the plumage are vet wrap (which clings to itself like cling wrap), roll gauze, cellophane tape, and some masking tapes.

Toothpick

A rounded-end toothpick can be used by experienced bird owners to remove debris from the nostrils. (This type of emergency can wait until the next day when you can consult your avian veterinarian).

Disinfectant

Many disinfectants are available. Only use topical disinfectants on open wounds and skin. Hydrogen peroxide and dilute chlorhexidine are safe and effective if used away from the mouth, ear canals, and eyes. **Do not** use salves, ointments, petroleum jelly, or other thick or oily substances on birds without veterinary recommendation. These products may matt the plumage and prevent the bird from insulating itself.

Syringe

A 3-milliliter syringe without a needle can be used to flush small wounds with water or dilute disinfectant and also to "syringe feed" a bird that will not eat. It is strongly recommended not to force feed a bird unless specifically instructed to do so by your avian veterinarian. Many birds will inhale food into the lungs if fed in this manner and this may cause respiratory infections.

Restraining towel

A washcloth is good for most cockatiels, small conures, and small parakeets. Big, fluffy bath towels are good for large Amazons, macaws, and cockatoos.

Hospital area

The carrying cage used to take the bird to the veterinarian often makes a perfect "bed" for the ill bird. It can be covered with a towel or blanket on all but one side to keep out drafts.

A spare bathroom is a good area in which to place the cage of a sick bird. The heating vents can be adjusted to more quickly elevate the temperature, providing additional warmth. This area also has less foot traffic and fewer disturbances.

Heat source

A heating pad (set only on low, producing a temperature safe for skin contact) and insulated with 2 towels above and 1 towel between the pad and cage can be used to keep most small cages between 75 to 85°F (24 to 29°C). Alternatively, a shaded light bulb (60 to 100 watts) can be placed outside the cage (far enough away that the bird cannot reach the shade or bulb). Cover both the cage and the shaded light bulb with a towel or sheet being sure that the towel or sheet does not come in direct contact with the hot bulb. The heat from the lighted bulb will gently warm the cage area.

Thermometer

Remote probe digital thermometers sold in electronics stores and photographic thermometers measure from 60 to 120°F (16 to 49°C) and can be safely used to monitor the room temperature. An ill bird should be kept at 80 to 90°F (27 to 32°C) until it is taken to your avian veterinarian.

EXOTIC PETS

62 Amphibians **864**
Introduction 864
Description and Physical Characteristics 864
Special Considerations 864
Housing 865
Diet 867
Disorders and Diseases 868

63 Chinchillas **873**
Introduction 873
Description and Physical Characteristics 873
Special Considerations 873
Selecting a Chinchilla 874
Providing a Home for a Chinchilla 874
Routine Health Care 876
Breeding and Reproduction 878
Disorders and Diseases 878

64 Ferrets **886**
Introduction 886
Description and Physical Characteristics 886
Special Considerations 887
Providing a Home for a Ferret 889
Routine Health Care 891
Emergencies 892
Breeding and Reproduction 893
Infectious Diseases 894
Cancers and Tumors 896
Hormonal Disorders 897
Other Noninfectious Diseases 898

65 Fish **899**
Introduction 899
Description and Physical Characteristics 899
Special Considerations 900
Selection 901
Providing a Home for Fish 901
Routine Health Care 906
Emergencies 908
Breeding and Reproduction 908
Disorders and Diseases 910

66 Gerbils **919**
Introduction 919
Description and Physical Characteristics 919
Special Considerations 920
Selecting a Gerbil 920
Providing a Home for a Gerbil 920
Routine Health Care 921
Breeding and Reproduction 922
Disorders and Diseases 922

67 Guinea Pigs **925**
Introduction 925
Description and Physical Characteristics 926
Special Considerations 926
Selecting a Guinea Pig 927
Providing a Home for a Guinea Pig 927
Routine Health Care 929
Breeding and Reproduction 930
Disorders and Diseases 931

68 Hamsters **940**
Introduction 940
Description and Physical Characteristics 940
Special Considerations 940
Selecting a Hamster 941
Providing a Home for a Hamster 941
Routine Health Care 943
Breeding and Reproduction 945
Disorders and Diseases 946

69 Mice **953**
Introduction 953
Description and Physical Characteristics 953
Special Considerations 953
Selecting a Mouse 954
Providing a Home for Mice 954
Routine Health Care 955
Breeding and Reproduction 956
Diseases and Disorders 956

70 Prairie Dogs **962**
Introduction 962
Description and Physical Characteristics 963
Special Considerations 963
Providing a Home for a Prairie Dog 964
Routine Health Care 965
Disorders and Diseases 966

71 Potbellied Pigs **970**
Introduction 970
Description and Physical Characteristics 970
Special Considerations 970
Selecting a Potbellied Pig 970
Providing a Home for a Potbellied Pig 971
Routine Health Care 973
Breeding and Reproduction 974
Disorders and Diseases 976

72 Rabbits **983**
Introduction 983
Description and Physical Characteristics 983
Special Considerations 984
Selecting a Rabbit 985
Providing a Home for a Rabbit 985
Routine Health Care 989
Breeding and Reproduction 992
Disorders and Diseases 992

73 Rats **1003**
Introduction 1003
Description and Physical Characteristics 1004
Special Considerations 1004
Selecting a Rat 1004
Providing a Home for a Rat 1005
Routine Health Care 1006
Breeding and Reproduction 1007
Disorders and Diseases 1008

74 Reptiles **1013**
Introduction 1013
Description and Physical Characteristics 1013
Special Considerations 1015
Selecting a Reptile 1016
Providing a Home for a Reptile 1018
Routine Health Care 1025
Emergencies 1026
Disorders and Diseases 1027

75 Sugar Gliders **1039**
Introduction 1039
Description and Physical Characteristics 1039
Special Considerations 1039
Providing a Home for a Sugar Glider 1040
Routine Health Care 1042
Breeding and Reproduction 1043
Disorders and Diseases 1044

CHAPTER 62

Amphibians

■ INTRODUCTION

The word amphibian comes from the Greek word for "double-life," referring to the fact that amphibians start life in water breathing through gills before maturing into lung-breathing land animals, although most never stray too far from water. The class Amphibia is composed of only 3 orders. Anura, which refers to tailless amphibians, includes frogs and toads (*see* TABLE 1). This is the largest order with more than 3,500 species. Caudata refers to amphibians with tails—salamanders, newts, and sirens—and has about 375 species (*see* TABLE 2). The Gymnophiona order is made up of caecilians, legless, tailless amphibians that spend most of their time burrowing. It has about 160 species.

■ DESCRIPTION AND PHYSICAL CHARACTERISTICS

Amphibians come in a wide range of sizes and colorings. The largest amphibian, the Japanese giant salamander, can grow to 6 feet long (1.8 meters) and weigh up to 140 pounds (63 kilograms). The smallest include some species of poison dart frogs measuring less than 0.5 inches long (1.3 centimeters) and weighing only grams (less than an ounce). One thing that most amphibians do have in common is a moist

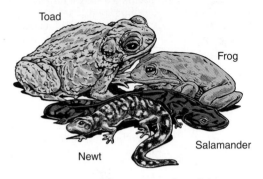

There are many different types of amphibians, including frogs, toads, salamanders, and newts.

skin, often coated with a slimy mucus. Adult amphibians breathe not only through their lungs but also through their skin, and the moisture is necessary for proper oxygen exchange. The life span of amphibians varies widely, from a few months to many years.

■ SPECIAL CONSIDERATIONS

Amphibians can make excellent pets; however, they should not be handled any more than is absolutely necessary due to their delicate skin. In addition, some amphibians release irritating toxins from their skin or special glands. Wearing disposable gloves that have been rinsed free

Table 1. Similarities and Differences Between Frogs and Toads

Similarities	Differences	
	Frogs	**Toads**
Both hatch from eggs	Lay eggs in clusters	Lay eggs in chains
Young have gills	Teeth in upper jaw	Have no teeth
Adults have lungs	Moist, smooth skin	Dry, lumpy skin
Young live in water	Jump	Walk
	Bulging eyes	Eyes do not protrude

Table 2. Some Common Salamanders and Newts

Type	Location	Size
Tiger salamander (*Ambystoma tigrinum*)	Western-central Canada south to Mexico and east and north to Long Island New York; sandy soils; common as pets	Varies according to type; can be up to 12 inches (31 centimeters)
Axolotl salamander (*Ambystoma mexicanum*)	Native to Xochimilco and Chalco lakes, Mexico City; strictly aquatic; common as pets	8 to 11 inches (20 to 28 centimeters)
Marbled salamander (*Ambystoma opacum*)	From southern New England, west to parts of Texas, Illinois, Oklahoma, and south to north Florida; variety of habitats	Up to 4.25 inches (11 centimeters) in length
Redback salamander (*Plethodon cynereus*)	Canada, northern United States to Midwest; woodland	Small: 2.6 to 4.9 inches (6.5 to 12.5 centimeters)
Seal salamander (*Desmognathus monticola*)	Southwestern Pennsylvania, to Georgia and Alabama; streams, ravines, and similar habitat	Size varies
Blackbelly and shovelnose salamanders (*Desmognathus quadramaculatus, D. marmoratus*)	Appalachia; springs and streams	Medium to large
Two-lined and Junaluska salamanders (*Eurycea bislineata, E. junaluska*)	Eastern half of North America	Small: up to 4.7 inches (12 centimeters)
Eastern or red-spotted newt (*Notophthalmus viridescens*)	Eastern half of North America, southern Canada, Texas, Oklahoma, Florida; watery areas	Varies
California newt (*Taricha torosa*)	California, west coast of United States	Up to 8 inches (20 centimeters)
Rough-skinned Oregon newt (*Taricha granulosa*)	Coastal Pacific northwest from southeast Alaska to San Francisco, California; aquatic or woodlands	5 to 8.5 inches (13 to 22 centimeters)
Fire-bellied newt (*Cynops pyrrhogastea*)	China and Japan; however, they are commonly bred and kept as pets	Varies; generally from 3 to 5 inches (8 to 13 centimeters)

of powder protects both you and your pet and is recommended when handling amphibians or cleaning their enclosure.

▪ HOUSING

Amphibians that are kept as pets require proper environmental conditions in order to remain healthy. The most important conditions are water and air temperature. Amphibians do not regulate their body temperature as mammals do, making them very sensitive to climate and temperature. As cold-blooded animals, amphibians regulate their body temperature by shuttling back and forth between different temperatures in their environment. The range of temperatures necessary to maintain health varies between species. Infections and malnutrition are common problems in tropical amphibians kept at less than ideal temperatures. A thermometer and a humidity gauge should be placed in the enclosure so that you can easily monitor the environment. Most amphibians do best at temperatures between 60 to 70°F (16 to 21°C), with humidity at 75 to 80%. However, tropical amphibians

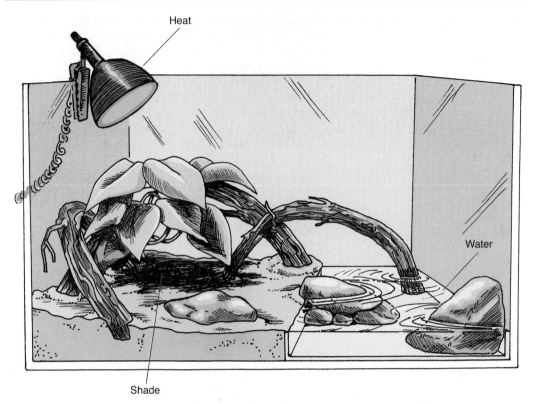

Heat

Water

Shade

Providing proper amounts of heat, shade, and water is vital to the health of your amphibian.

may require slightly higher temperatures (75 to 80°F [24 to 27°C]) and humidity (85 to 90%). Your veterinarian or the store where you purchased your amphibian should be able to tell you the appropriate range for your pet.

For most terrestrial amphibians, humidity is also very important. Amphibians require moisture to prevent their bodies from drying out. Aquatic amphibians may be kept in aquariums with appropriate areas for swimming. Even land-dwelling amphibians need a shallow container of water in the enclosure. Moisture may also be provided by incorporating small streams, waterfalls, or ultrasonic humidifiers into enclosures, or by misting frequently with a spray bottle.

An amphibian's skin is semipermeable, meaning the animal can readily absorb water in the environment through the skin. However, this means it can also readily absorb potentially harmful substances. Therefore water must be clean and free of toxins such as chlorine, ammonia, nitrite, pesticides, and heavy metals.

Chlorine can be removed from tap water by placing the water in a barrel and circulating it through a carbon filter for at least 24 hours prior to use. Some municipal water supplies may use chemicals called chloramines for disinfection. Such water must be treated with specific dechlorinating agents, after which the water can be filtered to remove the chlorine and ammonia. Bottled water may or may not be safe for use. Carefully read the label on bottled water. If in doubt, have the water tested for problem chemicals before using it for your amphibian. Basic water quality testing should be done once a week for aquatic amphibians. This includes monitoring the temperature, pH level, hardness, and testing for levels of ammonia, nitrite, and nitrate. Aquarium water test kits can be purchased in pet stores and may be used to periodically check basic water quality. Biological filtration provided by external canister filters or undergravel filters helps maintain water quality in aquatic habitats.

Substances that can be used to cover the floor of an enclosure include gravel, soil, sphagnum moss, and mulch. Gravel should be either too large for your pet to swallow or small enough to easily pass in the feces. Soils with chemical additives such as fungicides must not be used. Substances such as untreated hardwood mulches and leaf litter can be used, but cedar and pine mulches contain toxic oils and should be avoided. Some amphibians cannot tolerate low pH and may develop skin irritation if they come into contact with peat moss and sphagnum moss. Heating soils to 200°F (93°C) for 30 minutes is recommended to kill any mites or parasites. Freezing substances below 32°F (0°C) is also effective for removing many infectious organisms.

Amphibians need adequate ventilation (1 to 2 fresh air changes per hour) in order to prevent disease. Aquarium-type enclosures should be fitted with a secure top that contains multiple holes for ventilation. Live plants are recommended for terrestrial amphibians because they purify the air, remove organic wastes in the soil, filter light, generate humidity, and provide hiding and perching places. Aquatic plants replenish oxygen in the water, remove waste, provide hiding places, and are often a source of nutrition for larval amphibians.

Full-spectrum lighting (available at most pet stores) using bulbs that emit biologically active ultraviolet-B light is recommended in order to prevent metabolic bone disease. Bulbs must be changed every 6 to 8 months or according to the manufacturer's specification.

Keeping your amphibian's home clean is important to prevent disease. Food and water should be replaced daily. Uneaten food and waste material should be removed daily. In an established aquatic environment, at least 10% of the water should be changed weekly. Mosses and hardwood mulches provide an excellent home for microorganisms that help clean the environment. For this reason, changing small portions of the bedding or moss material every few weeks as needed is recommended. Bleach (30 milliliters per liter of water) can be used to disinfect tools and housing materials. A minimum of 30 minutes of contact time is recommended. Humidifiers and spray bottles must be disinfected weekly to remove potentially disease-causing bacteria. Disposable gloves should be worn when cleaning an amphibian enclosure to prevent the possible spread of disease.

■ DIET

Longterm maintenance of most amphibians requires live food. Most adult terrestrial and aquatic amphibians feed on invertebrates (animals that do not have backbones) including earthworms, bloodworms, black worms, white worms, tubifex worms, springtails, fruit flies, fly larvae, mealworms, and crickets. However, some amphibians feed on vertebrates (animals with backbones) and require live minnows, guppies, goldfish, or newborn mice or rats. Most invertebrates raised as food sources lack the proper ratio of calcium to phosphorus needed for the maintenance of healthy bones. (Earthworms are the exception.) They also lack vitamins that help prevent other diseases. For these reasons, owners of amphibians must include vitamin and mineral supplements in the diet to prevent nutritional disease. This is commonly done by **gut loading**, or feeding commercially available diets high in calcium to insects 48 hours prior to feeding them to your pet. It can also be done by coating insects with powdered multiple-vitamin preparations that include vitamin D_3 and calcium (also known as **dusting**). Your veterinarian can provide appropriate guidelines for supplementation.

■ DISORDERS AND DISEASES

Disease in amphibians can best be minimized through prevention or early treatment. Proper care and housing are important, in part because ideal environments for amphibians are often moist and warm—the same ideal conditions that lead to the growth of many bacteria and molds. Amphibians are sensitive to their environments and easily become ill due to poor environmental conditions, such as poor water quality, poor diet, improper tank set up, overcrowding, and improper or too frequent handling. Owners of amphibians must pay close attention to sanitation and hygiene in order to prevent illness.

Diseases Caused by Bacteria

Bacterial infection is usually caused by bacteria that are normally found in the environment. Such bacteria can become a problem when the balance in the enclosure is disrupted by changes in the various elements such as temperature, diet, crowding, or cleanliness.

Chlamydiosis

Chlamydiosis is a serious infection that can lead to death in amphibians. Infected frogs may die suddenly or show signs of lethargy, loss of balance, loss of skin color, tiny red spots on the skin, and swelling due to excess fluid in body tissues. An examination of the animal's tissue by your veterinarian may show enlargement of the liver and inflammation within the liver, spleen, kidney, and other organs. Chlamydiosis may be accompanied by other bacterial infections, which must also be treated appropriately. Antibiotics are often prescribed to treat chlamydial infection.

Mycobacteriosis

Mycobacteriosis is caused by several bacteria known as *Mycobacterium* species. It occurs most commonly in injured amphibians with weakened immune systems. While mycobacteriosis is often an infection of the skin, ingesting organisms in food or water may also lead to gastrointestinal disease and infection throughout the body. Affected amphibians may have small gray lumps in the skin or in body organs such as the liver, kidneys, spleen, and lungs. Toes, webs, and the mouth are common areas of infection. Skin ulcers may also be present. Infected amphibians may eat well but still lose weight. Your veterinarian can look for the bacteria on the amphibian's skin or test for it in feces and in the mucus of the throat.

Treatment is not recommended for this disease. If you have more than one animal, immediately isolate the suspect amphibian from any companions by removing it from the tank. The best defense is prevention. Mycobacteria typically live in the slime layer that builds up in aquatic habitats over time. For this reason, weekly cleaning and removal of this film is recommended.

Mycobacteriosis can pass from animals to humans and can result in skin infection. Always wear protective eyewear and gloves when handling infected animals or cleaning their environment.

Red-leg Syndrome

Red-leg syndrome refers to a common condition in which there is a reddening of the lower body—usually the legs and sometimes the abdomen—due to a dilation of capillaries under the skin. It accompanies widespread infection in frogs, toads, and salamanders. Red-leg syndrome is most often associated with *Aeromonas* bacteria, although other bacteria can cause this syndrome. Viruses and fungi may also cause similar reddening.

Underfed, newly acquired amphibians that are kept in poor-quality water or other less-than-ideal environmental conditions are particularly susceptible. Signs include lethargy; extreme thinness; open sores on the skin, nose, and toes that do not heal; and the characteristic reddening of the legs and abdomen. Bleeding may also occur in the skeletal muscles, tongue, and "third eyelid," or protective fold of skin in the eyes of amphibians. When the onset of disease is sudden, however, these signs may be absent. Your veterinarian will look for signs of widespread infection—which could include inflammation or dead cells localized in the liver, spleen, and other abdominal organs—and will likely test the blood or body fluids for bacteria before beginning therapy. Treatment can be started immediately with any of several prescription medications before the test results are available. If the disease is due to fungi, the treatment will be different than if it is caused by bacteria. Follow your veterinarian's instructions for the most favorable results.

Maintaining a high-quality environment, including thorough sanitation, will go a long way toward preventing red-leg syndrome. If an animal does become affected, be sure to isolate it from other amphibians in the home and seek immediate veterinary care.

Diseases Caused by Fungi

Fungal infections are common in amphibians. Many of the fungi that infect amphibians are difficult to tell apart because they produce similar signs, including lethargy and open sores on the skin. Sometimes white or yellow furry growths on the skin may be seen. Your veterinarian can identify some fungi by examining a skin scraping under a microscope. Others require that tissue samples be prepared using special stains and then examined under a microscope. Samples may also be taken so that the veterinarian can try to grow, or culture, the fungus. This is done so that the fungus can be identified and the best possible treatment selected. Treatment includes proper hygiene and the use of antifungal agents, often given in a dip or bath. Carefully follow your veterinarian's prescribed dosage and treatment schedule.

Chromomycosis

Chromomycosis is caused by several types of pigmented fungi that may be found in organic substances such as topsoil and decaying plant matter. These fungi are capable of growing on tank walls. Amphibians with cuts or sores are at risk, because the fungus typically infects the body through broken skin.

Infection is common and often fatal. Signs may include loss of appetite, weight loss, wounds on the skin or open sores that do not heal and become inflamed, swelling of the abdominal area, and evidence of neurologic impairment such as head tilt or the inability to move correctly.

Confirmation of this disease usually requires examination of the animal's internal organs and tissues after it has died. Amphibians that are suspected of having chromomycosis may be treated with antifungal drugs, but the chance of survival is poor once the infection has spread to the central nervous system.

Red-leg syndrome is caused by a widespread bacterial infection.

The best defense is to improve sanitation. Chromomycosis can cause skin lesions in humans, so be sure to wear powderless gloves and follow careful sanitary procedures when cleaning your pet's cage, handling any items in the cage, and when handling your pet.

Chytridiomycosis

Chytridiomycosis is the most serious fungal infection in amphibians and is thought to play a role in the decline of frog populations in many parts of the world. It is caused by *Batrachochytrium dendrobatidis*, a fungus related to water molds. The fungus feeds on keratin, a protein found in the outermost layers of the skin. It can survive in most environments even without a host. Death is common in infected animals. Signs include a persistent loss of appetite, lethargy, excessive shedding of skin, constriction of the pupil of the eye, and an inability to coordinate the muscles. Placing an infected animal in a shallow dish of water will often confirm the sloughing of skin associated with this disease.

If you suspect this disease, seek medical attention immediately. Entire collections have been lost in a matter of days. Veterinarians diagnose the disease by examining skin scrapings that are stained and put under a light microscope. Treatment includes applying a prescription antifungal medicine (usually as a bath) to the surface of the skin and making sure that animals are kept well within their preferred temperature range.

Saprolegniasis

Saprolegniasis is a disease caused by several kinds of fungi or "water molds" that infect the gills and/or skin of aquatic and immature amphibians. It commonly affects newts, mudpuppies, aquatic frogs, and tadpoles. When in water, newly affected animals appear to have a whitish cotton-like growth on their skin. As time goes on, the growth may become greenish due to the presence of algae. This growth, sometimes called a fungal mat, can be difficult to see when the amphibian is not in the water. Other signs of saprolegniasis include lethargy, difficulty breathing, lack of appetite, and weight loss. Sores on the skin that do not heal may occur as the infection progresses.

Veterinarians diagnose the disease by identifying the fungus in a scraping taken from the animal's skin. Treatment with a medicated dip, used as directed by your veterinarian, may be effective. Poor water quality is often the root cause of saprolegniasis. Changing water frequently and providing a correct and constant temperature for the species being kept are necessary for successful treatment. All water containers should be cleaned and sanitized daily.

Additional bacterial and parasitic infections may occur in amphibians with open sores on the skin. Be sure you understand the correct procedures for applying the medication prescribed by your veterinarian. Ask for a demonstration if you are new to the procedures.

Diseases Caused by Parasites

Many of the single-celled organisms and other microorganisms found in and on amphibians are not associated with disease unless the amphibian becomes stressed or its immune system is weakened. Recently caught or transported amphibians are particularly susceptible to parasites, as are those kept in unhealthy conditions or in environments outside their preferred temperature range.

Whether or not a parasite becomes a threat to the health of an amphibian in an enclosed environment often depends on whether it needs another animal host to properly develop. Amphibians may act as a temporary or intermediate host for some parasites; in other words, they help the parasite mature before it moves on to its final host. Or amphibians may act as the final destination after the parasite reached maturity on another host. Parasites that require more than 1 host are said to have an indirect life cycle. They tend to die out when wild-caught amphibians are brought into captivity, as long as the other host is not present. The opposite is also true. Parasites that do not need a third party to fully develop—those with a direct life cycle—may thrive in a closed environment.

Good hygiene is essential for parasite control and includes the prompt removal of sloughed skin, droppings, uneaten food, and carcasses from animal enclosures. Parasites of the skin can sometimes be seen by close examination of amphibians using magnification and a bright, cool light. Your veterinarian may need to do a skin scraping or biopsy to identify parasites causing lumps or other skin abnormalities. Fresh fecal samples may be needed to identify internal parasites. (It is a good practice to bring fresh droppings, if available, any time your pet visits the veterinarian.) Some small frogs are translucent enough to allow your veterinarian to see parasites inside the body by shining a bright light through the body of the frog, a procedure called transillumination. In some cases, parasites are found only on examination after death.

It is common for your veterinarian to find various microorganisms in the droppings. These do not require treatment in healthy amphibians. While many immature roundworms found in the feces do not cause disease, treatment is recommended because disease-causing and non-disease-causing worms cannot be readily distinguished from one another.

Pseudocapillaroides xenopi Infection

The roundworm *Pseudocapillaroides xenopi* burrows into the skin and is known to affect colonies of the aquatic African clawed frog. Signs include blotchy, rough, and pitted skin, and the formation of sores on the skin. As the infection progresses, lethargy, loss of appetite, and sloughing of the skin occur. The disease may also make amphibians more susceptible to bacterial infections that can lead to death.

Diagnosis is made by finding small, white roundworms beneath the mucus on the skin. A veterinarian can confirm the presence of these parasites by performing a skin scraping that is examined immediately under a microscope. Treatment with drugs used to destroy parasitic worms, called anthelmintics, may be effective. Follow the dosage and treatment schedule prescribed by your pet's veterinarian. Frequent water changes with removal of shed skin containing the parasite are required to prevent the infection from getting worse and spreading to other amphibians in the enclosure.

Rhabdiasis

Rhabdiasis is caused by the lungworm *Rhabdias*, which damages the lungs of captive amphibians. Associated infections may occur as a result of this damage. The lungworm has a direct life cycle with free-living phases. Adult worms live in the lungs where they deposit eggs that are coughed up, swallowed, and then excreted into the environment. Larvae then burrow through the skin of a new host where they mature and migrate to the lungs, repeating the cycle. Affected animals may appear thin, are generally weak, and lose appetite.

Your veterinarian may diagnose this disease by examining fresh feces or secretions from the mouth and nose for lungworms or their eggs. When rhabdiasis is suspected, treatment usually involves 1 of 2 commonly prescribed drugs (fenbendazole or ivermectin) that are used to remove worms or other parasites. Following the second day of each 2-day fenbendazole treatment or each dose of ivermectin, the animals should be moved into a newly established environment to prevent re-infection from free-living life stages that have become established in the material (such as moss or mulch) in their enclosure. The relocation to a clean environment is critical to the recovery of your pet and any instructions from your veterinarian should be followed precisely.

Diseases Caused by Viruses

Like other species, amphibians are susceptible to a variety of viral infections. Some viruses that affect amphibians can also cause cancer. No specific treatments are available for viral infections in amphibians, so general supportive care is provided.

Iridoviruses

Iridoviruses have been identified in many wild populations of amphibians across the world. Some of these cause signs very similar to those seen with bacterial skin infections. The original viral infection may lead to secondary infections—many outbreaks of red-leg syndrome (*see* page 868) may have had an underlying and undiagnosed iridovirus infection. There is no treatment for iridoviral disease other than supportive care and appropriate treatment for the secondary infections of bacteria or fungi.

Renal Adenocarcinomas (Lucké Tumors)

Renal adenocarcinomas (Lucké tumors), caused by a herpesvirus, may occur in leopard frogs (*Rana pipiens*) that are wild-caught in the northeastern and north central United States. Few frogs with tumors are seen in the summer because the virus needs cold temperatures to grow. The virus is thought to be transmitted through breeding ponds, and then matures while infected frogs are hibernating at 41° to 50°F (5° to 10°C). Tumors are most common in the early spring when frogs emerge from hibernation.

The spread of the tumor to the liver, lungs, and other organs is common; both the original tumor and its offshoots can become very large. Signs are lethargy and bloating. There is no known treatment.

Metabolic Bone Disease

Metabolic bone disease often results from an imbalance of calcium, phosphorus, and vitamin D_3 in the diet. It is frequently seen in amphibians that are fed a diet of invertebrates without supplementation (*see* DIET, page 867). With the exception of earthworms, most invertebrates used as food are deficient in calcium. Crickets are often a culprit; amphibians fed a cricket-only diet are at high risk for developing metabolic bone disease.

The disease results in deformity of the lower jaw, fractures, and scoliosis (curvature of the spine). In severe cases, muscle spasms and bloating occur. Your veterinarian will diagnose the condition by examining x-rays for the thinning of the outer layers of leg bones, deformities of the lower jaw and the bone at the base of the tongue, fractures caused by disease, and in severe cases, gastrointestinal gas.

Treatment includes correcting the diet and administering a calcium supplement as directed by your veterinarian. Full spectrum lighting with biologically active ultraviolet-B light should be provided. Vitamin D_3 can also be administered in severe cases. Follow your veterinarian's treatment program carefully for the best results.

Thiamine Deficiency

Thiamine deficiency is typically seen in amphibians that are fed frozen fish. Many frozen fish contain the enzyme thiaminase, which destroys thiamine (vitamin B_1). Thiamine is required by many tissues in the body, especially those of the central nervous system. Signs of thiamine deficiency include tremors, seizures, and severe arching of the back and neck. Initial treatment is the injection of thiamine by your veterinarian, followed by thiamine supplements with each meal for a prescribed period of time. Thiamine deficiency can be prevented by routinely supplementing diets with 250 milligrams of thiamine per kilogram of fish fed.

Obesity

Obesity is also considered a disease. Overfeeding is the primary cause of obesity. Owners often fail to realize that many amphibians will continue to consume prey as long as it is available and without regard for their energy needs. As in mammals, it is assumed that obesity in amphibians can cause stress on certain organs. Your veterinarian can examine the body using gentle finger pressure to feel for fat deposits; however, in females, ultrasonography may be necessary to differentiate fat deposits from egg masses.

Treatment for active species includes increasing the size of the enclosure to allow increased activity. Maintaining the amphibian at the upper end of its preferred temperature range will accelerate metabolic rate and increase caloric use. However, you should never exceed the maximum recommended temperature. Lastly, reducing the amount of food given to an animal will help control weight. Ask your veterinarian for guidance in determining the appropriate amount of food for your pet.

CHAPTER **63**

Chinchillas

▥ INTRODUCTION

Chinchillas are members of the rodent family. Their scientific name is *Chinchilla lanigera*. They originated in the Andes mountains of South America. During the eighteenth century, chinchillas were hunted for their fur and faced extinction until laws banned hunting them. Today there are about 3,000 ranches throughout the United States and Canada that breed chinchillas, and chinchillas are increasingly popular as pets.

▥ DESCRIPTION AND PHYSICAL CHARACTERISTICS

Chinchillas have a very thick coat of fur (as many as 60 hairs per follicle) that was originally a blue-gray in color; however, today chinchillas have been bred with coats that are black, gray, white, beige, and combinations of each. Their thick fur not only keeps them warm, it also protects them from fleas, lice, and predators.

Chinchillas have thick, soft fur.

Chinchillas have a rounded body, large mouse-like ears, short legs, and a long tail. A healthy baby weighs 2 to 2.5 ounces (60 to 70 grams) at birth. A mature chinchilla's weight ranges from 1 to 1.5 pounds (450 to 680 grams). Females are usually larger than males. They can grow to be 10 inches (25 centimeters) long, with a tail that can add another 6 inches (15 centimeters) when they fully mature. They have an average lifespan of 10 to 15 years, although some have lived as long as 20 years in captivity.

▥ SPECIAL CONSIDERATIONS

Chinchillas should be handled calmly and gently to minimize stress. A protective reaction in chinchillas, known as **fur slip**, may occur if the animal is frightened, resulting in the release of a large patch of fur and revealing smooth, clean skin underneath. It may also occur with improper handling, fighting, or anything that causes overexcitement. The fur can take several months to regrow and may be a different shade. To prevent this, chinchillas should be handled gently with the least amount of stress by moving slowly and speaking softly. Tame, nonpregnant animals can be removed from a cage by grasping and lifting the base of the tail while using the opposite hand to support the body. Pregnant females should not be handled unless necessary.

Chinchillas are prone to **heat stroke** at temperatures greater than 80°F (27°C). While chinchillas can gradually adapt to outdoor temperatures less than 32°F (0°C), the chinchilla's preferred temperature range indoors is 50 to 60°F (10 to 16°C). The housing environment should be dry, free of drafts, moderately cool, and away from direct sun.

Taking your chinchilla with you when you travel is not recommended, as it can cause a great deal of stress to your pet. A better option is to locate a reliable pet sitter, or board your chinchilla in an appropriate facility. (Chinchillas should not be boarded in the same room with barking dogs.) If travel—such as a move—is unavoidable, planning ahead and taking certain precautions can minimize stress (*see* BOX).

■ SELECTING A CHINCHILLA

You can buy chinchillas at some pet stores or from chinchilla breeders. When selecting a pet chinchilla, it is important to determine that the animal is healthy and that it is used to being handled.

A chinchilla's eyes should be bright and shiny, but not watery. Discharges from the eyes, ears, or nose may indicate medical problems. Check the chinchilla's teeth. The upper and lower teeth should be fairly even when the jaw is closed, and there should be no signs of drooling. Check the body to be sure there are no obvious wounds. It might be better to choose your chinchilla later in the day so that you can observe whether it is active and alert. It is recommended that you take the chinchilla to a veterinarian to check its heart and test its droppings for protozoa and other parasites. Ask the breeder or supplier whether you can return the chinchilla if it is not healthy.

A chinchilla that cries and struggles to get away may not be used to human handling and may not make a good pet. A few weeks of regular contact and gradually increasing handling time may help. When first approaching a chinchilla, move slowly and quietly so as not to frighten it. Let it

When You Travel

Using a Pet Sitter or Boarding Facility

■ The best option may be locating a reliable pet sitter or boarding facility equipped to handle small mammals.

■ You should leave your pet sitter with detailed instructions on caring for your chinchilla, the phone number where you can be reached, and the address and phone number of your regular veterinarian, as well as a 24-hour emergency veterinary clinic.

■ It may be a good idea to have your pet sitter carry out the instructions once while you are there to be sure he or she fully understands the responsibilities involved.

Traveling in a Car

■ If you must take the chinchilla somewhere in a car, you must always be aware of the temperature inside the car. Excessive heat can be fatal to a chinchilla.

■ Put the chinchilla in a hard plastic, airline-type carrier that can be locked, and be sure the carrier is not in the sun.

Traveling on a Plane

■ Get an airline-approved carrier and call the airline well in advance of your trip to make a reservation for your chinchilla in the cabin so that you may place the carrier under your seat. Most airlines limit the number of pets allowed in the cabin on each flight.

■ If the airline will not allow the carrier in the cabin, be sure they have a climate controlled area of the cargo hold where they put pets.

Items to Take with You

■ Be sure to have plenty of fresh water, feed, hay, and bedding, and the chinchilla's toys and chew toys.

sniff at your fingers and then slowly and gently use both hands to lift the chinchilla.

■ PROVIDING A HOME FOR A CHINCHILLA

Many health problems of chinchillas can be avoided by providing a proper and consistent diet, appropriate housing, a clean source of water, nonabrasive bedding material, and frequent disinfection and sanitation of the cage and water bottle with soap and water.

Housing

Because chinchillas tend to be more active than some rodents, large, multi-level cages with ramps, perches, and platforms are recommended. Avoid plastic-coated wire. If wire mesh is used, the grid on the sides of the cage should be no wider than 1 by 2 inches (25 by 50 millimeters). The openings on the bottom of cages with a wire bottom should be no wider than ½ by ½ inches (15 by 15 millimeters). Wire-bottomed cages allow droppings to go through to the tray below. However, a solid area made from wood or hard plastic should be provided to allow a rest from standing on the wire. Without such relief, chinchillas can develop sore feet and a condition known as bumblefoot.

An appropriate bedding material, such as kiln-dried pine or recycled paper bedding, allows a place into which the chinchilla can snuggle. Chinchillas also seem

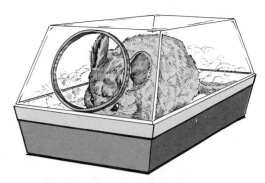

A regular dust bath helps keep the chinchilla's fur clean and groomed.

to prefer having a place to hide within their cage. This can be accommodated with materials such as small sections of PVC piping, which has the additional advantage of being easy to clean (just place in the dishwasher). Any wooden items used as part of the cage, as bedding materials, or as toys should be safe and nontoxic (*see* TABLE 3).

Dust Baths

Commercial dust baths, or mixtures of silver sand and Fuller's earth (9:1), 2 to 4 inches deep, should be offered to chinchillas daily for about 10 minutes. This satisfies the chinchilla's desire to keep itself clean and groomed and is necessary to maintain the animal's healthy skin and fur. Such mixtures should not remain in the cage for long periods of time because they will become soiled with chinchilla droppings and food debris.

Diet

In the wild, chinchillas eat a diet of high-fiber plants. Commercial pelleted diets formulated for chinchillas (available at most pet stores) provide adequate nutrition alone, but should be supplemented with high-quality hay to provide needed roughage in the diet. Hay should be stored in a well-ventilated, dry area and fed fresh daily. Chinchillas enjoy treats such as fresh or dried fruits (apples, grapes, or raisins), unsalted sunflower seeds, and dry

Table 3. Safe and Unsafe Wooden Items*	
Safe	**Unsafe**
Apple	Cedar
Ash	Cherry
Birch	Citrus wood (orange, lemon, grapefruit)
Elm	Fresh pine
Hazelnut	Oleander
Manzanite	Plum
Maple	Redwood
Pear	
Pine (without phenol oils)	

*Never use a wooden item that has been treated with chemicals or sprayed with pesticides, as these may be toxic to your chinchilla.

oatmeal; however, treats should be very limited to encourage your chinchillas to eat a complete diet of pellets. Hay and fruit not eaten within a day should be removed to avoid the growth of mold. If a proper diet is provided, there is usually no need for any nutritional supplements to be given.

Chinchillas' digestive systems are very sensitive. New ingredients in the diet should be introduced slowly to help prevent intestinal disorders. Gradually increase the amount of new food mixed in with the existing food over several weeks so your chinchilla has time to adjust to the new food. Chinchilla droppings are typically dry, and eating their own droppings is normal.

Fresh water should be available at all times. Providing water in a water bottle instead of a bowl decreases the chances of contamination. Watering systems should be washed thoroughly at least every other day to prevent contamination by opportunistic bacteria that can cause illness or death.

Exercise

Routine exercise is necessary for the health of your chinchilla. A roomy cage with toys is important. A 15-inch wheel provides running exercise, and chew toys and wooden parrot toys offer distractions to keep chinchillas from becoming bored. A 4-inch T- or Y-shaped PVC pipe gives your chinchilla a place to hide. Allowing chinchillas out of their cages for greater exercise and freedom of movement is acceptable; however, it is recommended that they be put in a "chinchilla-proof" room, wire pen, or plastic ball made for chinchillas. Otherwise, they require close supervision to prevent them from chewing furniture, electrical wires, walls, or other items.

Temperament

Chinchillas are easy-mannered and curious. If handled regularly when they are young, chinchillas can become quite tame and bond with their owners. Unless stressed, they rarely bite. Because chinchillas are nocturnal, they will sleep most of the day and be very active and playful in the evenings and at night. They should be kept in a fairly quiet area during the day.

■ ROUTINE HEALTH CARE

Pet chinchillas are typically seen by veterinarians for conditions related to age, trauma, or improper care. Infectious diseases are more common in colony animals raised for fur production than in pets. Viral diseases are uncommon. Tumors in chinchillas are very rare.

Signs of Illness

The chinchilla's overall appearance and behavior can provide clues to its well-

Routine Care of Your Chinchilla

When	To Do
Daily	Give fresh water
Daily	Give fresh food; remove any uneaten or partially eaten food from previous day
Daily	Give fresh hay
Daily	Let out of cage for about 2 hours of supervised exercise and play
Daily	Give 10-minute dust bath
Every other day	Clean food bowls or hoppers and water systems
Occasionally	Give a treat of fresh or dried fruit (less than 1 teaspoon/day)
Once a week	Clean and disinfect cage
When needed	Change bedding
When needed	Replace chew toys

being. It is a good idea to monitor your pet regularly for signs of illness. Sick chinchillas may show weight loss, hunched posture, scruffy hair coat, labored breathing, or difficulty walking normally. They may stop eating, have no energy, or not respond to stimulation. Respiratory conditions and digestive problems are the most common illnesses and may be signaled by discharges from the eyes and nose or diarrhea. Feet should be examined for sores or broken nails. Teeth may be discolored or overgrown. Ears should be examined for discharges or inflammation and eyes for discharges or conjunctivitis. The lower jaw and chin should be examined for swellings. Difficulty breathing and abnormal breath sounds should be noted.

Chinchillas produce 2 kinds of fecal pellets. One type is rich in nitrogen, and the chinchilla will normally eat these pellets. There is nothing wrong with your chinchilla if you observe this behavior.

Disease Treatment and Prevention

Sick chinchillas are easily stressed and should be handled very little. Although antibiotics are valuable medications against harmful bacteria, they are not well tolerated by chinchillas and can cause digestive problems. Oral medications or fluids can be given with a small syringe or eyedropper. If your pet is able to eat, medications can be mixed with food or water. Some medicines may have to be given intravenously, however. Dry animal droppings, dark urine, and skin tenting are signs of dehydration. Consult your veterinarian about how to replace the fluids in your dehydrated animal. Animals with a severe loss of appetite may require force feeding by syringe, which should be performed or supervised by a veterinarian.

Dental Care

A chinchilla's teeth are very important to its health. Tooth abnormalities are common in chinchillas. Drooling or a constant wet area under the chin (sometimes called **slobbers**) are signs of a dental problem. Uneven positioning of the upper and lower teeth when the jaw is closed is known as **malocclusion**. Malocclusion leads to poor use of food, rough hair coat, loss of appetite, and weight loss. Often, drooling results in loss of fur and swelling of the skin on the chin and neck. Lack of regular veterinary check-ups may lead to dental diseases.

Overgrown teeth or tooth roots can elongate and become impacted. In addition, the tooth surfaces may become sharp and can irritate the lining of the cheeks and the tongue. The appearance of mucus or pus or discharge from the eyes and nose may be signs of tooth overgrowth and malocclusion. Chewing becomes increasingly difficult, and severe malnutrition may lead to low blood sugar levels and ultimately seizures, paralysis, coma, and death. Premolar and molar teeth may be loose, broken, or sharply pointed. Sometimes feed or foreign bodies are wedged between the teeth and the gums.

During regular veterinary checkups, the chinchilla's mouth should be thoroughly

---

Health Care

Normal Readings

- Body temperature: 98.6 to 100.4°F (37 to 38°C)
- Heart rate: 100 to 150 beats per minute
- Number of teeth: 20 (16 molars and 4 incisors)

Signs of Illness

- Inactivity
- Loss of appetite or weight
- Discharge from the eyes, ears, or nose
- Hunched posture
- Abnormal walk
- Scruffy hair coat or hair loss
- Diarrhea
- Trouble breathing
- Drooling
- Seizures

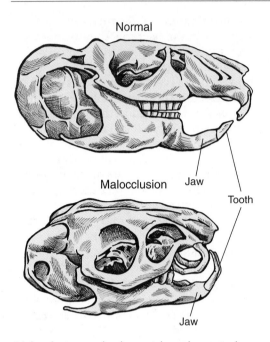

Normal

Malocclusion   Jaw

Tooth

Jaw

Malocclusion can lead to weight and appetite loss.

examined. X-rays can be used to check tooth position and look for overgrowth of the roots. Malocclusion is a condition requiring monthly care to guard against infection or disease. Treatment involves trimming and filing teeth, removing food or foreign bodies from the teeth, and cleaning any sores on the gums. Because chinchilla teeth grow constantly, appropriate materials (such as pumice stones or chew blocks) to gnaw are required. A commercial pelleted diet should provide adequate nutrition for preventing most dental diseases. However, the diet should also contain foods such as straw, hay, and gnawable items for optimal dental health. Teeth and body weight should be frequently monitored to avoid further problems. While individual chinchillas with malocclusion can be managed by careful observation and dental treatment, they should not be bred.

BREEDING AND REPRODUCTION

Pet owners are encouraged to maintain chinchillas in single-sex groups to provide companionship but avoid producing large numbers of offspring. Male chinchillas must be grouped before weaning or neutered to prevent fighting. When breeding, potential mates should be introduced before the female enters estrus, the time during which she is receptive to mating, to reduce fighting and increase compatibility. Males need a refuge box to escape potentially aggressive nonestrous females. Repeated aggression can teach the male to avoid females, making him an unsatisfactory breeder.

Pregnancies last for about 111 days. Pregnant females should be handled gently. As the female chinchilla approaches the time to give birth, she may become less active, lose her appetite, and become aggressive toward previously compatible cage mates. Chinchillas do not typically build nests as the time to give birth approaches, but a nesting box may help reduce the number of newborn deaths caused by drafts or cold stress. Kits with dangerously low body temperatures should be warmed and revived quickly to prevent death. Chinchillas have up to 4 kits per litter (2 is usual) and may have 1 to 3 litters per year. The kits are born with fur and open eyes and should be able to walk within an hour of birth. Weaning occurs at 6 to 8 weeks of age.

DISORDERS AND DISEASES

Furnishing adequate housing, a good diet, and considerate care will minimize disease in chinchillas, as with any other animal.

Heart and Blood Vessel Disorders

Heart murmurs that range from mild to moderate are sometimes seen in chinchillas, particularly young chinchillas. Usually these murmurs are not associated with any heart disease that needs treatment. However, if your chinchilla does have a heart murmur, you should be aware that the potential for the development of heart disease may exist.

Eye and Ear Disorders

Common eye and ear disorders in chinchillas include conjunctivitis and otitis media. Ear trauma is also common, due to the chinchilla's delicate ears.

Conjunctivitis

Conjunctivitis is an eye disease seen in some young chinchillas. It may be caused by a foreign body getting into the eye or a bacterial infection. Nursing kits may get conjunctivitis from direct contact with their mother if there is an infection in the birth canal. Chinchillas may also develop conjunctivitis if the dust from their baths gets into their eyes. Infected eyes may be blood-shot, swollen, and have a discharge. Infections usually are treated with topical antibiotic ointments or drops. Dust baths should be removed until the conjunctivitis is completely gone. As a preventive measure, dust baths should be avoided with pregnant females about to give birth in order to keep newborns from getting dust in their eyes or mouth.

Otitis Media

This ear disease may occur in young chinchillas after a respiratory infection or trauma. Scar tissue can enclose the healing ear canal and trap wax and debris inside. The eardrum may become thickened and swollen. The swelling may progress to the inner ear, which will result in the chinchilla becoming uncoordinated, being unbalanced, or circling and rolling. Surgery may be necessary to reopen a closed ear canal. Regular cleaning, in addition to antibiotics, can help ensure that the ear canal remains open until healing is complete. Ask your veterinarian to show you how to safely clean the ears.

Ear Trauma

The chinchilla's large, delicate ears are easily hurt, most often from bite wounds or, if exposed to extreme cold, frostbite. Treatment includes cleaning the wounded area with antiseptic solution and antibiotic ointment. Closing cuts with stitches in the ear is usually not effective and not recommended. If severe damage is present, the damaged part of the ear may need to be surgically removed. If wounds are left open, the proper antibiotics should be used to lower the chances of infection.

Digestive Disorders

Digestive disorders are among the most common disorders that occur in pet chinchillas. The cause may be infectious (such as a bacterial or viral disease), but noninfectious causes, such as changes in the diet or a diet that does not provide adequate nutrition or roughage, are also likely to cause digestive problems such as diarrhea, constipation, or bloat.

Diarrhea

Loose or watery stools occur in chinchillas with intestinal disorders caused by nutritional, bacterial, protozoal, parasitic, or stress-induced illnesses. Animals with these disorders may die quickly without signs or, in longterm cases, show a range of signs including lack of energy, loss of appetite, rough hair coat, staining near the anus, hunched posture, listlessness, dull eyes, dehydration, weight loss, stomach pain, excessive gas, fever or lower-than-normal body temperature, and diarrhea or constipation. The feces may look bloody or include mucus. Straining to have a bowel movement can lead to the lower part of the large intestine slipping out of place. Sudden changes in diet and the giving of inappropriate antibiotics can affect the bacteria that normally live in your chinchilla's digestive tract, causing digestive problems.

Treatment of diarrhea is similar for most causes. Dietary roughage (such as hay or straw) should be increased and grains and concentrates decreased. Although feeding *Lactobacillus* bacteria, in the form of yogurt with active cultures, is often recommended to help reestablish normal bacterial flora, the active cultures generally do not survive in the digestive tract. Instead, it may be beneficial to use probiotics with *Lactobacillus*. Several are readily available and can be added to the food or water of chinchillas. Giving the chinchilla fluids is very important. If your chinchilla will not drink water, then you need to get a veterinarian to provide fluids by injection.

There are many bacteria reported to cause gastroenteritis (inflammation of the stomach and intestines) and diarrhea in chinchillas. The most common sources of these bacteria are a contaminated environment and spoiled food. Protozoa such as *Giardia* are often present in apparently healthy normal chinchillas. These parasites may cause inflammation of the intestines and diarrhea. The disease signs occur under conditions of stress, poor sanitation, or at the same time that bacterial infection is causing inflammation of the intestines. A veterinarian can perform tests to find out if your chinchilla has any protozoa.

Gastroenteritis may also be caused by rapid changes in the chinchilla's normal diet. Diets low in fiber and high in carbohydrates, fats, and protein can cause medical problems. Feed or drinking water can also be contaminated by bacteria, molds, or chemicals. Vitamin A, B complex, or C deficiency may result in gastroenteritis. Young kits often develop diarrhea if their mothers cannot produce enough milk or after the use of milk replacers.

Constipation

More common than diarrhea, constipation most often occurs from a lack of dietary fiber and roughage. Dehydration, environmental stress, intestinal obstruction, obesity, lack of exercise, hairballs, and pregnancy may also cause constipation. Signs include straining to have a bowel movement and having fewer of them. Droppings are thin, short, and hard; have an unpleasant odor; and may be stained with blood. Longterm cases may lead to twisting, blockage, or displacement of the intestines. To provide relief, dietary fiber can be increased by providing alfalfa cubes, or mineral oil can be added to the feed. Persistent constipation may be due to several internal physical abnormalities. A veterinarian may be able to feel these or identify them on x-rays. Surgery may be required in such cases.

Bloat

Bloat can result from sudden dietary changes, especially overeating. It has been reported in nursing females 2 to 3 weeks after giving birth and may be related to hypocalcemia, a life-threatening imbalance of calcium metabolism. Gas production from the bacterial flora in unmoving bowels quickly builds up within 2 to 4 hours. Affected animals have no energy, difficulty breathing, and a painful, swollen stomach. They may roll or stretch while attempting to relieve their discomfort. Treatment by a veterinarian is usually required and may include passage of a stomach tube or insertion of a needle into the stomach to relieve gas build-up. Nursing females may respond favorably to calcium gluconate given intravenously.

Stomach Ulcers

Stomach ulcers are common in young chinchillas and are frequently caused by eating coarse, fibrous roughage or moldy feeds. Animals with stomach ulcers may not have an appetite or show no signs. You may not know that your chinchilla had an ulcer until after it has died and your veterinarian does an examination or necropsy (animal autopsy). Therefore, prevention is very important and includes providing appropriate types and amounts of dietary roughage and feeding commercial pellets formulated for chinchillas.

Lung and Airway Disorders

Infections of the respiratory tract can occur in chinchillas. The most common cause is a bacterial infection. Choking also poses a serious hazard in chinchillas because they lack the ability to vomit.

Upper Respiratory Tract Infections

Humid, crowded, and poorly ventilated housing conditions contribute to a greater chance of respiratory disease in chinchillas. Bacterial infections of the nasal sinuses and mucous membranes are seen more often in young or stressed chinchillas.

Signs include sneezing, a discharge from the nose, and conjunctivitis. In severe cases, animals can die suddenly. Untreated animals may progress to pneumonia (*see* below) or death. Diagnosis is based on signs and tests performed by a veterinarian. Treatment includes appropriate antibiotics and general supportive treatment, including gently soaking the nose and eyes with warm water compresses and removing any crusts. Prevention includes keeping young chinchillas in a warm and draft-free environment, maintaining good husbandry and sanitation, and separating affected or carrier animals from healthy ones.

Pneumonia

Pneumonia is usually associated with bacterial infection. Housing in cold, damp environments may lead to lowered resistance. Signs of respiratory distress include a thick, yellowish discharge from the nose, sneezing, and difficulty breathing. Pneumonia may be accompanied by eye infections, fever, weight loss, loss of energy, depression, or loss of appetite. Wheezing sounds from the lungs may be heard with a stethoscope. Sudden death from bacterial infection may spread quickly among animals. Diagnosis is based on signs, examination, and finding the bacteria in nasal or eye washes. Treatment usually does not work in severe cases, but your veterinarian may prescribe antibiotics or intravenous fluids in some cases. In addition, supportive treatment includes warm, dry housing and stress reduction.

Choke

Chinchillas do not have the ability to vomit and may choke when the airway is blocked by a large piece of food or bedding. Females may also choke when eating the placentas after delivering infants. Particles from these foreign bodies can irritate the lower respiratory tract and quickly lead to an accumulation of fluid in the lungs. This may be noticed as drooling, retching, coughing, and difficulty breathing as the chinchilla attempts to dislodge the foreign body. If untreated, choking may lead to asphyxiation and death.

Skin Disorders

Skin disorders in chinchillas may be caused by bacterial or fungal infection but can also result from behavioral issues such as fur chewing.

Ringworm (Dermatophytosis)

Ringworm, which is caused by fungi called dermatophytes, does not occur often in chinchillas. Small, patchy areas of baldness are seen mostly around the ears, nose, and feet, but can be found on any part of the body. Areas that are affected appear as irregular or circular-shaped, crusty, flaky skin with reddened edges. The disease is transferred by direct contact or by contact with items such as cage bedding, feeding equipment, or toys. Diagnosis is based on appearance, veterinary examination, or by finding the fungus in or on infected hairs. Some animals may be carriers and show no signs themselves. Effective treatment consists of 5 to 6 weeks of oral antifungal medicines. Isolated skin lesions may be treated effectively with topical antifungal creams applied daily for 7 to 10 days. Antifungal powders may be added to the chinchilla's regular dust bath. Prevention includes decreasing the potential for stress, isolating affected animals and quarantining any new additions, and adequate sanitation. Ringworm is contagious to humans and other animals.

Abscesses

Abscesses in chinchillas may occur after bite wounds or other trauma sites become infected. An abscess can be caused by several common bacteria. It may remain hidden under the animal's thick coat and only become evident after it ruptures. Ruptured abscesses should be completely drained and flushed with an antiseptic solution recommended by your veterinarian. Appropriate topical antibiotic creams may be applied as needed. Unruptured abscesses should be assessed by a veterinarian. They can be surgically removed and appropriate antibiotics given. Abscesses removed surgically often heal better than those that are lanced, drained, and flushed.

Fur Chewing

Currently thought to be an abnormal behavior, up to 30% of chinchillas may chew their own or each other's fur, resulting in a moth-eaten appearance. Fur chewing may be partly due to boredom, stress, malnutrition, warm or drafty environments, or increased hormonal activity. Mothers tend to pass this disorder to their offspring, and affected chinchillas usually have a nervous disposition. Hair loss is observed along the shoulders, flanks, sides, and paws. The affected areas appear darker due to the exposed underfur. A variety of approaches have been used to control the behavior. These include decreasing room humidity and temperature, changing the diet, and applying povidone-iodine ointment to the skin. Anything that causes the chinchilla stress should be removed or reduced. Papaya cubes or tablets may help prevent hairballs and potential intestinal blockage.

Chinchillas sometimes chew their own fur.

Ask your veterinarian about use of these products.

Disorders Affecting Multiple Body Systems

Some disorders affect more than one organ system. These are known as generalized or systemic disorders. Many are infections, but they can also be metabolic or hormonal problems.

Septicemia

Infections across multiple portions of your chinchilla's body may follow untreated bacterial gastroenteritis (*see* DIARRHEA, page 879), although other bacteria may also cause it. Animals may not show any signs and die suddenly or they may develop nonspecific signs such as loss of appetite and weight loss, inactivity, rough hair coat, and diarrhea. If these signs occur, a veterinary checkup is recommended. Diagnosis is based on finding certain bacteria in blood or affected organs. Treatment includes appropriate antibiotics and general supportive care.

Heat Stress

Chinchillas are very sensitive to sudden changes in their environment, especially temperatures above 80°F (27°C). Signs of heat stress include initial restlessness followed by rapid breathing, drooling, weakness, very high fever, congested lungs, coma, and death. To treat heat stress, the animal should be cooled down slowly and carefully with cool water baths and provided with general supportive care. Your veterinarian may provide intravenous fluids and corticosteroids for additional supportive care. To help prevent heat stress, make sure that your chinchilla's cage is placed away from direct sunlight.

Pseudomonas aeruginosa Infection

Found in unclean drinking water and the cage environment, *Pseudomonas aeruginosa* bacteria may cause infections in chinchillas with weakened or immature immune systems. The infection may be passed by direct contact or contaminated fecal droppings. Young kits may get it by nursing from an infected mother. Signs include loss of appetite and weight, depression, diarrhea or constipation, ulcers in the eyes or mouth, skin blisters containing pus, conjunctivitis, genital swellings, inflammation of the breasts, abortion, infertility, and acute death. A veterinarian should evaluate these signs and will also look for typical internal signs. Diagnosis is based on finding the bacteria; treatment includes appropriate antibiotics. To prevent infection, improved general animal husbandry and sanitation are required and disinfection practices should be intensified.

Listeria monocytogenes Infection

Listeria monocytogenes infection may occur when chinchillas live in environments with poor sanitation and contaminated food or water. It is seen most frequently in colony animals raised for fur, although it sometimes occurs in individual chinchillas. A chinchilla usually gets this infection by eating droppings with the bacteria in it. While *Listeria* can infect many species of animals and humans, chinchillas are particularly susceptible to it. The infection may occur in the intestines, bowels, and the brain. Signs, if present, include loss of appetite, depression, weight loss, constipation or diarrhea, and stomach pain. If the infection gets into the central nervous system, additional signs include droopy ears, twisted neck and head tilt, loss of coordination, circling, and convulsions leading to death. There are other internal signs a veterinarian would be able to find. Any organ may be affected. Diagnosis is based on finding the bacteria. There is no effective treatment for chinchillas showing signs of illness. Animals found to have the infection should be removed and attention given to cleaning the environment, water, and diet. Chinchillas not exhibiting signs can be vaccinated against it or treated with antibiotics that protect against the disease.

Yersinia Infection

Yersinia bacterial infections are uncommon in chinchillas kept as pets. Being exposed to wild rodents that are carriers of the disease is the most likely source of infection. Chinchillas can also get the disease by eating infected droppings or from their mothers either prior to birth or through milk while nursing. Infected pets may show no signs. Infection may spread quickly, causing chinchillas to have loss of energy, depression, loss of appetite, weight loss, constipation or diarrhea, or to die suddenly. There are other internal signs a veterinarian would be able to find. Diagnosis is based on finding the bacteria. Treatment of sick chinchillas does not work. Affected animals should be removed and attention given to cleaning the environment, water, and diet. Exposure to wild rodents should be eliminated.

Brain, Spinal Cord, and Nerve Disorders

Disorders that affect the central nervous system are not common in chinchillas. However, they may occur in animals as a result of infections by parasites, viruses, or other infectious organisms. Disorders of metabolism may also cause neurologic signs.

Roundworms

Chinchillas may be infected by a roundworm, *Baylisascaris procyonis*, normally found in raccoons. Chinchillas get it by eating feed contaminated with raccoon droppings. Infected chinchillas may show a variety of central nervous system signs, including loss of coordination, head tilt, tumbling, paralysis, lying down, coma, and death. There are tests a veterinarian can perform to diagnose this disease. There is no effective treatment. Prevention includes appropriate husbandry and adequate sanitation practices. The roundworm can be passed to humans and cause a fatal brain disease.

Protozoa

Certain protozoa (single-cell parasites) cause a disease called necrotic meningoencephalitis in chinchillas. Infections are rare. Signs may include poor coordination, inactivity, depression, loss of appetite, weight loss, difficulty breathing, a blue color to the skin, and a pus-like discharge of the nose. Your veterinarian will examine the chinchilla for additional internal signs. Active infections can be treated in some cases with antibiotics.

Herpesvirus 1 Infection

Human herpesvirus 1 infection has been reported in chinchillas. Signs include conjunctivitis and various neurologic signs, including seizures, disorientation, and inactivity, progressing to death. A veterinarian can determine other internal signs. Diagnosis is based on the signs and tests performed by a veterinarian. Treatment is not likely to be effective. Chinchillas may serve as a temporary reservoir for human herpesvirus infections.

Thiamine Deficiency

Thiamine (vitamin B_1) is required for normal carbohydrate metabolism and protein synthesis. Deficiency of this vitamin causes damage to peripheral motor nerves that is often reversible when thiamine is restored to the diet. Affected chinchillas may show neurologic signs such as trembling, circling, convulsions, or paralysis. Your veterinarian can treat this deficiency with injections of thiamine or B-complex vitamins. Sources of natural thiamine include leafy vegetables, high-quality hay, and wheat germ meal, or supplements can be added to the diet (1 milligram of thiamine per kilogram of feed) if needed.

Diseases that can be Spread from Chinchillas to People

Ringworm (Dermatophytosis)

Roundworm (*Baylisascaris procyonis*)

Toxoplasmosis

Herpesvirus 1

Bone and Muscle Disorders

The bones of chinchillas are thin and relatively fragile, so fractures are common. Other disorders include muscle spasms caused by dietary imbalance.

Fractures

Broken legs commonly happen when chinchillas accidentally catch their legs on wire caging or when the leg is grabbed. Healing begins quickly, within 7 to 10 days. See a veterinarian immediately for treatment. During the healing period, the chinchilla should be placed in a small cage or enclosure to limit its movement. To prevent potential limb injuries, caging should have solid floors or mesh openings no wider than ½ by ½ inches (15 by 15 millimeters).

Calcium:Phosphorus Imbalance

A dietary imbalance in the ratio of calcium to phosphorus or phosphorus deficiency may result in severe muscle spasms in young or pregnant chinchillas. Muscles of the hindlimbs, forelimbs, and face are affected. Treatment with calcium gluconate, given by a veterinarian, is recommended. Prevention is accomplished by feeding a well-balanced, nutritionally complete diet formulated for chinchillas.

Reproductive Disorders

If you intend to breed your chinchillas, you should seek the advice of your veterinarian or a qualified breeder on selecting the best chinchilla matches for breeding because some matches should be avoided. Breeding animals should have access to a fresh commercial pelleted diet and adequate roughage, and colonies should be screened carefully for any physical defects that may be inherited. (*See also* page 878.)

Infertility

Poor reproduction may be due to any of several possible causes, including malnutrition, abnormal sperm, hormonal imbalance, infectious disease, lack of experience, lethal genes from inappropriate crosses, or poor conditioning. Infectious and dietary factors are often the causes. Very fat females produce smaller litters. Matings between or among chinchillas with matched genes for White and Velvet coat color should be avoided.

Abortion or Resorption of Fetuses

The sudden ending of a pregnancy may be caused by improper handling, trauma, poor nutrition, bacterial infection, fever, or interruption of the blood supply to the uterus. Chinchillas may also resorb fetuses during early pregnancy if stressed. At term, suddenly startled females may abort. It is common for the female to eat the aborted kits. Abortion may take place unnoticed, but should be suspected if a female chinchilla suddenly loses weight. Often, a bloody vaginal discharge and staining near the anus are observed. A veterinarian should examine females after abortion and may provide treatment such as gently flushing the reproductive tract with an antiseptic solution and giving antibiotics.

Retained or Mummified Fetus

A fetus that dies late in pregnancy may be delivered along with the live young, remain in the uterus, or become mummified. If a dead fetus is not delivered, the pregnant female may neglect her live kits and become increasingly depressed as toxicity develops. A fetus that dies early in the pregnancy is normally resorbed without complication, but loss of fetal fluids may lead to mummification. A mummified fetus can remain within the uterus for a long time and prevent further pregnancies. Causes are thought to be similar to those for infertility (*see* page 884), with poor conditioning or infection being the most likely. All female chinchillas should be examined as soon as possible after giving birth to determine if any fetuses were not delivered. X-rays should be taken to provide a definitive diagnosis. A female not able to pass a retained fetus may require cesarean section, but chinchillas usually respond well to this procedure.

Difficulty Giving Birth (Dystocia)

Dystocia is an abnormal or difficult birth. This is very rare in chinchillas, but may be observed with an abnormally large or misplaced fetus or in young females bred too early. Poorly conditioned females may also develop a condition in which uterine contractions weaken or stop, or they may lack sufficient strength to deliver the kits. If labor continues for more than 4 hours, a veterinarian should administer a medicine that helps labor progress. If the chinchilla continues to experience difficulty giving birth, a cesarean section should be performed.

Metritis

A placenta or fetus that is not delivered may lead to bacterial contamination and inflammation of the uterus. Chinchillas with metritis may not walk normally and may have loss of appetite and weight, inadequate milk production, high fever, swollen and discolored genitals, and a vaginal discharge containing mucus and pus with an unpleasant odor. Kits are at risk of infection through contact with infected discharge. Early detection and treatment are essential because affected females can develop a severe, fatal bacterial infection with sudden deterioration and death. A veterinarian can give medicine that causes uterine contractions and forces out the infected debris. The veterinarian will then clean and disinfect the reproductive tract and the uterus. Antibiotics and general support are also provided.

Pyometra

Pyometra is a large accumulation of pus within the uterus. It may follow an episode of metritis or retained placenta, but is sometimes seen in unbred females. Signs include a rough hair coat and a vaginal discharge that may stain the genital area. Often, affected females are no longer capable of successful breeding and should be removed from the colony. There is no effective treatment for pyometra. An ovariohysterectomy, the removal of the ovaries and uterus, is recommended.

Lack of Milk

Advanced age, genetic factors, infection, or poor nutrition may cause inadequate milk production. Kits not receiving enough milk are vocal, restless, lose weight, and may die. Following pregnancy, the female's mammary glands should be examined for milk production. If females have not begun to produce adequate milk within 72 hours, oxytocin (a hormone that can help to stimulate milk flow) should be given by a veterinarian. Allowing kits to nurse from compatible nursing females or guinea pigs may be an option necessary in unresponsive cases or large litters. Otherwise hand feeding may be necessary.

Inflammation of the Mammary Glands (Mastitis)

The mammary glands of nursing females should be observed frequently for injuries caused by the sharp teeth of nursing kits. Minor wounds can be treated with topical antibiotics and warm compresses. More serious wounds can lead to infection. When this occurs, mammary glands are warm, firm, enlarged, and painful. Milk may be thick or bloody and clotted. Appropriate antibiotics are needed, and kits may need to be nursed by other nursing females or hand fed.

Hair Rings

In male chinchillas, a ring of hair may surround the penis within the foreskin and cause serious complications. Affected males may be observed grooming excessively, straining to urinate, and frequently cleaning their penis. Hair rings often develop following sexual intercourse. Treatment includes lubricating the penis or mild sedation to help with gentle removal of the hair ring. Your veterinarian can demonstrate the best technique for hair ring removal. You should routinely check male chinchillas for hair rings, especially any males that are used for breeding.

CHAPTER 64

Ferrets

■ INTRODUCTION

The domestic ferret is part of the Mustelidae animal family that includes weasels, badgers, and minks. However, unlike these wild species, they are fully domesticated and would likely starve if released outside. Ferrets have been in captivity for more than 2,000 years and are used as hunting animals in Europe, Australia, and New Zealand. They have become popular pets over the last decade in the United States.

■ DESCRIPTION AND PHYSICAL CHARACTERISTICS

Physically, ferrets are similar to cats. The male ferret, called a hob, can weigh up to 4 pounds (2 kilograms). The female, known as a jill, can weigh up to 2.5 pounds (1.2 kilograms). Ferrets come in a range of colors, but common variations include white with pink eyes, sable, cinnamon, and chocolate. White patches on the throat or toes are common. A ferret's coat will change color and density with the season; it will darken and thicken in winter, then lighten and shed in summer. Ferrets

Ferrets have become popular pets.

generally reach full size at 5 to 6 months of age and are considered adults at 1 year. The typical life span is 6 to 10 years, but many life spans are shortened due to accidents or illness (*see* TABLE 4).

Ferrets have less of the musky smell that is characteristic of this family of animals if the gonads are removed early in life. The anal scent glands are also usually removed at the same time. Many ferrets have these surgeries performed before you buy them. If not, it is important to have a female ferret spayed *before* she goes into heat for the first time in order to prevent life-threatening consequences such as the development of hyperadrenocorticism (*see* page 897).

Many adult ferrets have a large spleen due to increased production of red blood cells. Enlarged spleens are considered benign unless a ferret shows signs of illness, but have a veterinarian check to make sure the enlarged spleen is not a problem.

■ SPECIAL CONSIDERATIONS

Ferrets can quickly get into dangerous situations. They are intensely curious, nearly fearless, highly persistent, and have the ability to squeeze into very small openings. These traits may lead to serious injury or death. Ferrets also like to chew

Table 4. Ferrets at a Glance

Average weight	Male: 4 pounds (2 kilograms)
	Female: 2.5 pounds (1.2 kilograms)
Normal heart rate	200 to 250 beats per minute
Normal respiratory rate	30 to 40 breaths per minute
Average internal body temperature	100 to 103°F
Life expectancy	6 to 10 years
Recommended environmental temperature	65 to 75°F (never over 90°F)

on soft or plastic objects such as foam, pencil erasers, rubber bands, buttons and other objects commonly found around the home. These objects can pose a choking hazard or cause intestinal blockage. An intestinal blockage can be fatal and usually requires emergency surgery.

Before obtaining a ferret or ferrets, it is essential to "ferret-proof" your home (*see* TABLE 5). Seal all holes larger than 1 inch in walls, floors, or ductwork, and in appliances such as televisions, refrigerators, stoves, and washers. Use wire mesh rather

Table 5. Ensuring a Safe Environment

Area of Concern	Hazard	Prevention
Appliances—washers, dryers, stoves, dishwashers, and refrigerators	Exposure to electrical wires and moving parts, as well as entrapment inside a machine. Ferrets have been known to fall asleep in the laundry and end up in the washer or dryer. They also have crawled into refrigerators and stoves while the door was open and been trapped inside.	Seal all holes larger than 1 inch. Lower appliances to the floor and block access from all sides. Always check inside refrigerators, dishwashers, and stoves before closing the door or running the appliance. Examine clothing before placing it in the washer or dryer. If possible, restrict access to the laundry room at all times.
Air ducts	Entrapment, leading to starvation and dehydration.	Seal all holes larger than 1 inch where ductwork passes through a wall or floor.
Open railings	Falls.	Enclose railings or restrict access to the lower level of the home only.

(Continued on the following page)

Table 5. Ensuring a Safe Environment—*(Continued)*

Electrical wires	Electrocution.	Use a plastic wire protector. Apply bitter-tasting spray to discourage chewing behavior.
Open doors or doors with gaps.	Access to outdoors, where the ferret may become lost or injured.	Locate and possibly restrain ferrets before opening doors. Attach a door sweeper or weather stripping to bottom of a door with a gap.
Cabinets	Exposure to cleaning supplies, medications, and other toxic materials; entrapment.	Secure doors using sturdy, child-proof locks. Seal any openings between the cabinet and floor or baseboard.
Windows	Falls; access to outdoors.	Ensure screens are free of tears and fit securely. Because ferrets can tear holes in screens, it is best to keep windows closed.
Reclining furniture	Crushing injuries when position is changed; entrapment in wires or clamps.	Remove from home or modify to a stationary chair.
Couches, overstuffed chairs, rocking chairs	Suffocation or serious injury from being sat on; killed by rocking chair rails.	Supervise ferrets around couches, chairs, and similar furniture. Staple a carpet protector or sheet pulled tight to the underside of the couch, or consider replacing with a futon. Inspect cushions before sitting.
Houseplants	Possible poisoning hazard.	Remove from the home or place out of reach. (Remember that ferrets are excellent climbers.)
Box spring mattresses	Possible crush injury when someone lies on the bed.	Staple heavy fabric pulled tight or a plastic carpet protector to the bottom of the box spring.
Rugs	Crush injury while hiding or tunneling underneath.	Remove rugs or be careful when walking on them.
Any spongy, chewable household objects, including pencil erasers, balloons, Styrofoam, rubber bands, door stops, and tennis shoes	Intestinal blockage, choking.	Keep items out of reach of ferrets, either locked up or in areas that they cannot reach. Do not overlook waste in trash cans. Keep phone numbers for your local veterinarian and the National Animal Poison Control Center (888-426-4435) accessible.
Bathrooms—toilets, bathtubs, sinks	Drowning.	Keep toilet lids down, and possibly use a child lock. Do not leave tubs or sinks filled with water unattended.

than tape, which ferrets can remove. Put away anything small enough to be swallowed. Do not overlook toxic items, such as houseplants. Lock drawers, cabinets and doors; be aware that childproof locks may not stop a ferret. They are very good at manipulating objects with the front paws, and have been known to open zippers and untwist bottle caps. Get down to ferret eye level and look for small spaces behind furniture and around fixtures such as radiators and pipes, espe-

Biting

Biting is part of the natural behavior of ferrets. They may bite to get attention or as part of play. This is particularly true of young males 3 to 4 months of age that have spent most of their lives in a pet shop with other ferrets but little human interaction. Ferrets may play with humans in the same rough manner they play with other ferrets. If your ferret nips at you, return it to its cage for a brief "time-out" period. Done consistently, the animal will learn that biting is not appropriate behavior.

cially those that narrow and taper, where a ferret could become lost, stuck or suffocate. Recliners and sofa-sleepers also pose a hazard. When they cannot be adequately supervised, ferrets should be confined.

This "tunneling" instinct has also led to ferrets being stepped on while under rugs and sat on in couches. It may be helpful to provide ferrets with ready-made enclosures to satisfy the tunneling instinct. Consider flower pots, blankets, large piping, or rugs. Do not use items that might unravel or be chewed up.

Ferrets can be kept as pets in all states in the United States except California and Hawaii. However, some cities, such as New York City, prohibit owning ferrets. You should check with your local Fish and Game or Wildlife Department before purchasing a ferret.

Special consideration should be given to households with young children. Ferrets bite and scratch as a part of play, and out of protection if handled roughly (*see* Box). Rough handling may also injure the ferret.

▓ PROVIDING A HOME FOR A FERRET

Ferrets do not require much space, making them suitable for apartments and other small living spaces. However, appropriate housing must be provided for times when ferrets are alone or unsupervised. Ferrets

also require a high-quality diet, good hygiene, and appropriate levels of exercise and attention in order to remain healthy.

Housing

A wire cage at least 3 feet by 3 feet deep by 2 feet high is sufficient to supply a ferret with room for roaming while confined. Check the cage for sharp, jagged, or rough wire, and any openings large enough for the ferret to escape. Pad the bottom of the cage or buy one that has a solid bottom. Bare wire may harm the pads on a ferret's paws.

Most ferrets prefer to sleep in a relatively small, confined space. Ferrets often enjoy hammocks or fabric huts as sleeping quarters. For bedding, a clean towel or small blanket works well, but if fabric is used, check that it will not unravel and that the ferret does not eat it. Do not use newspaper or wood chips. These items can harbor bacteria or create dust that may irritate the respiratory tract. Cedar releases oil that may be toxic to ferrets.

The cage should contain feeding and watering areas. Ferrets often tip over water and food bowls, so use sturdy containers. Water bottles may be attached to the side of the cage as can several styles of food bowls.

Ferrets can be trained to use a litter box. They prefer to urinate and defecate in the same spot, away from sleeping and eating areas. Also, ferrets will drag the hindquarters across the floor after urinating or defecating to "wipe." This is not a sign of illness, but normal ferret behavior.

A cat litter box cut down to size and cat litter may be used. However, avoid using the clumping types of cat litter as these may cause respiratory problems in ferrets. Place the litter box in the cage, but do not place it too close to the ferret's sleeping or eating areas or it will not be used.

Place the cage away from drafts and dampness, and do not place it directly in front of windows. Ferrets are sensitive to heat and humidity because they do not have sweat glands. A temperature range of

65 to 75°F (18 to 23°C) is usually comfortable. Although they handle cold better than heat, food consumption may double when exposed to low temperatures.

Diet

Food and fresh water should be available at all times. Ferrets easily overheat and become dehydrated. They also have a high metabolism and short digestive tract, which require them to eat frequently.

Ferrets require high levels of fat and protein in the diet and should be fed commercial ferret food or high quality cat or kitten food. Because it is a carnivore, a ferret's diet should be meat-based. A diet high in plant proteins and ash (found in low quality foods) can cause bladder stones. Check the ingredients label before purchasing commercial food.

A diet of dry food (that is, kibble) is recommended. Prolonged feeding of soft, wet food leads to disease of the gums and teeth. Do not feed milk or other dairy products or foods rich in carbohydrates. All of these items are difficult for ferrets to digest. In addition, sugary foods may increase the risk of disease. Do not feed ferrets honey, raisins, fruit, or snacks containing sugar.

Keep treats to a minimum, no more than 5% of a ferret's daily caloric intake. Too many treats may lead to malnutrition. Good choices include meat, eggs, and freeze-dried muscle or organ meat, sold as cat or dog treats.

Ferrets do not react well to frequent diet changes. If changes must be made, introduce them gradually to avoid stressing the animal. For example, mix a new food in with the usual food for several days, slowly increasing the amount of the new food given. Vitamins and vitamin supplements are not necessary, except under special conditions or for older ferrets. Your veterinarian can advise you if these are needed.

Exercise

Ferrets are energetic, social animals that require a great deal of play and interaction. At a minimum, ferrets need 2 to 4 hours every day outside their cage to remain healthy. Leave the door of the cage open so that the ferret has access to food, water, and the litter box. Exercise also ensures your ferret will not mind being caged when necessary.

Temperament

Ferrets are often likened to kittens. They are playful, curious, highly active, and sociable, even as adults. They are quick learners and can be trained to do "tricks." They also are fearless and have short attention spans. Ferrets do not have a strong sense of territory or a homing instinct and will wander off if left outdoors. A young ferret may be frightened by sudden movement or a loud noise. It will hunch its back, puff out its fur, and screech. Older ferrets will only display this behavior if truly under attack by another animal. Talk quietly to the animal, but do not attempt to pick it up unless necessary for its safety. It will eventually calm down.

Feeding a Sick Ferret

Because healthy ferrets should mainly eat a diet of dry ferret food, they may be unaccustomed to eating moist or semi-moist foods. However, softer foods are often recommended for sick ferrets. Do not wait until your ferret is sick and cannot eat on its own to introduce it to softer foods. It is important for ferrets to take in nutrients when they are sick to avoid additional complications.

A popular choice is baby food. Remember that ferrets need a meat-based diet, and choose a baby food accordingly. Serve the food barely warm using fingers, a spoon, or syringe. If a syringe is used, push the plunger in slowly to avoid choking the animal. The ferret may not be interested the few first times you offer this new food. But eventually the ferret will start to eat the soft food and look forward to it as a treat.

As a general guideline, a sick ferret should be fed 15 to 20 milliliters of food every 2 to 4 hours, in addition to plenty of water. However, you should check with your veterinarian for specific instructions on feeding your sick pet.

When first let out of a cage, ferrets may run, jump, twist in the air, and violently collide with household objects. This is normal, healthy ferret behavior, and may be a sign of high spirits or simply good health.

Ferrets will sleep up to 18 hours a day. Young ferrets sleep especially deeply and may be difficult to wake, even when pinched or thumped on the chest. Many new owners worry the animal is dead or in a coma. A ferret that has a moist pink mouth, feels warm, and is breathing slowly but regularly is sleeping soundly. It is also normal for ferrets to shake and shiver when they wake up, and this should not be cause for alarm.

▓ ROUTINE HEALTH CARE

It may be difficult to find a veterinarian with experience in treating ferrets. Check with ferret clubs, local telephone directories, and online sources such as your state veterinary medical association for a recommendation. Do this before buying a ferret, or if you move, before an illness occurs. A yearly examination and vaccinations are recommended for pet ferrets; this is an excellent opportunity to establish a relationship with a veterinarian. Make sure the veterinarian is knowledgeable about ferrets and is located nearby. If possible, choose one who has after-hours emergency services, in case your ferret is injured or becomes ill late at night. Alternatively, know where he or she refers after-hours emergencies.

A plastic cat carrier is sufficient for transporting a ferret to the veterinarian's office.

Vaccination Schedule

Ferrets should be vaccinated annually for rabies and canine distemper. Reported cases of rabies in ferrets are rare, although like other mammals, ferrets are susceptible to the virus. Canine distemper is another viral disease that is fatal for ferrets.

For rabies, there is only 1 approved vaccine for use in the United States. The vaccine should first be given to ferrets when they are more than 16 weeks old and then repeated annually. For canine distemper, there are 2 approved vaccines. Be aware that vaccines made of mink or ferret tissue should not be used, as they may cause the disease. The vaccine is given at about 8, 10, and 12 weeks of age and then yearly.

Ferrets frequently have reactions to vaccines, which can include vomiting and diarrhea. In some ferrets, vaccines can cause shock and death. Owners of ferrets should remain in the veterinarian's office with their animal for 20 to 30 minutes after vaccination to watch for these signs. It is also recommended that ferrets not receive shots for both canine distemper and rabies on the same day to avoid possible reactions. Reactions can occur up to several hours after receiving a shot; however it is common for ferrets to be mildly lethargic for several days afterwards.

Dental Care

Ferrets explore their environment in large part through feel, especially using the mouth and teeth. Ferret teeth are unusually sharp, even when they are young. They will bite as part of play. You should have your ferret's teeth cleaned annually by a veterinarian to remove plaque and prevent gum disease and tooth loss. After administering general anesthesia, the veterinarian will use a steel scraper to remove buildup. He or she will also check for cracked or broken teeth. Teeth cleaning may be scheduled as part of a ferret's annual checkup. A diet of dry ferret food helps minimize plaque buildup.

Claw Trimming

Ferret claws are extremely sharp and should be trimmed every 1 to 2 weeks. Claws that are not regularly trimmed may become painfully long and more difficult to trim. There also is some risk that the ferret will injure itself or pull out the claw. Long claws may become more easily caught in carpet, towels, toys, and other items. A nail clipper made for humans

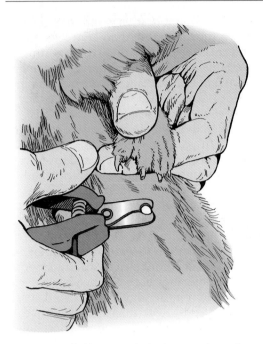

Proper care of ferrets includes keeping the nails trimmed.

may be used for trimming. The claws should be trimmed such that the end is parallel to the floor. Be careful not to cut the dark vein visible in each claw. You will hit the nerve as well as cause bleeding. Should you accidentally cut the vein, immediately apply styptic powder to stop the bleeding.

Ferrets should not be declawed. Claws are needed to walk and to grasp objects.

Ear Care

Ears should be cleaned once a month to remove the reddish wax buildup common in ferrets. Place drops of a commercial ear cleaning solution into the ear, then rub the ear to work it in. Ferrets will then shake or fling out the wax. Use a cotton swab to remove any remaining wax on the outer portion of the ear only. Work carefully and gently as the ear canal is very delicate.

Check for ear mites weekly. If wax is gray or granular, or the ear has an unpleasant odor, it is likely your ferret has mites.

Your veterinarian can confirm the presence of mites and prescribe medication to eliminate them (*see* PARASITES, page 895).

Hairballs

Ferrets are proficient self-groomers, requiring little human help. Because they shed each year in the spring and fall, hairballs may develop. Hairballs can cause vomiting, decreased appetite, or intestinal blockage. Use a soft brush to comb the fur. Loose hair can be controlled by changing bedding once a week. If your ferret is shedding a lot, you can treat it weekly with a malt-based cat or ferret laxative. However, many of these contain large amounts of sugar. Your veterinarian can recommend appropriate brands.

■ EMERGENCIES

Whenever a ferret appears to be lethargic or there is a sudden change in its behavior, a visit to the veterinarian is recommended (*see* TABLE 6). Ferrets may hide signs of illness or discomfort until the illness is advanced, so a sick ferret can rapidly become critically ill.

Ferrets with an intestinal blockage will stop eating and defecating and may cough, choke, or begin vomiting with advanced disease. Any ferret with signs of vomiting or diarrhea that lasts for more than 24 hours should be evaluated by a veterinarian because ferrets can quickly become dehydrated and weak. An occasional soft or irregular stool is not usually a problem. Bloody droppings can occur in both young and old ferrets for different reasons. Whatever the age of your ferret, if you notice bloody or dark, tarry droppings, you should seek veterinary care for your pet right away.

Poor eyesight and insatiable curiosity make ferrets susceptible to falls and other types of trauma, which may result in broken bones or internal injuries. Bent or disjointed limbs, limping, or difficulty coordinating the back legs may indicate a broken bone or other problems. There are many problems in ferrets that can lead to weakness of the back legs; any time this

Table 6. When to See a Veterinarian

See a veterinarian immediately if you notice:	See a veterinarian within 24 hours if you notice:
Weak pulse or low or quiet heart beat	Continuous sneezing or coughing
Bluish or white gums or tongue	Vomiting or diarrhea for more than 24 hours
Broken bones	Excessive water consumption
Puncture wounds to the abdomen or chest	Sudden change in behavior
Bite marks	Sleeping more than usual and unwilling to play
Heavy bleeding	Cloudy eyes, squinting, or inability to see
Burns, frostbite or a fever above 105°F (40.5°C)	A rash, excessive shedding, excessive head shaking, or persistent chewing or scratching of the body
Choking	A nose bleed for no apparent reason
Protruding rectum	Abnormal lumps that are not painful
Bloody, foul-smelling, or uncontrollable diarrhea	Lack of appetite, but no other signs of illness
Thick, black stools	Soft stools not accompanied by pain, blood, foul smells, or straining
Straining but failing to defecate or urinate	Sudden weight gain or loss
Extreme lethargy	Drooling
Seizures	Lameness for more than 24 hours
Staggering or other problems walking	Swollen joints
Sudden, severe lameness	Moderate itching
Severe or constant pain	Discharge from the eyes, ears, or other body openings
Failure to eat or drink for 24 hours	
Difficulty breathing, or shallow breathing	
Bloody urine, discomfort while urinating, or bleeding from the urinary or genital area	

problem is seen, a veterinarian should be consulted.

BREEDING AND REPRODUCTION

Ferrets reach sexual maturity between 4 and 8 months of age, occurring in the first spring after birth. The vast majority of ferrets are spayed or neutered before 6 weeks of age. This is primarily because females come into "heat" when they reach sexual maturity and will remain in heat unless bred. This condition can lead to a fatal infection or cause a drop in blood cell production, which also can be fatal.

Male ferrets that have not been neutered have a strong, musky smell when they come into season, which happens twice yearly. They also mark territory by urinating on it.

If your ferret is not spayed or neutered when you get it, you should talk to your veterinarian about performing the procedure. It is essential that all pet ferrets be spayed or neutered at an appropriate age.

■ INFECTIOUS DISEASES

Ferrets can be infected by a variety of microorganisms, including bacteria, viruses, fungi, and parasites. Some of these can also infect other types of pets and people.

Bacterial Diseases

Helicobacter mustelae is found in the stomach and in the small intestines of most, if not all, ferrets after weaning. It can cause chronic, persistent inflammation of the stomach (common in ferrets over 4 years of age) and cause ulcers similar to those found in humans. Gastric lymphoma, a stomach cancer, may occur in chronic cases. Signs include lack of appetite, vomiting, teeth clenching or grinding, diarrhea, stools stained black by blood, increased salivation, and abdominal pain. Lethargy, weight loss, and dehydration can also occur. An accurate diagnosis requires a biopsy and tests on the tissue collected, but often a suspected diagnosis can be made based on the history and the signs of the ferret. Treatment is with multiple antibiotics and usually lasts for 21 days.

Lawsonia intracellularis can cause a bowel disease characterized by excessive growth of intestinal tissue, especially in younger ferrets. Acute cases are often associated with stress. Signs include diarrhea, weight loss, and rectal prolapse, in which the rectum protrudes out of the anus and can be damaged or prevent defecation. Treatment is with antibiotics for 14 to 21 days.

Other bacterial infections seen in ferrets are similar to those seen in other mammals like dogs and cats and are treated similarly.

Viral Diseases

Ferrets are extremely susceptible to **canine distemper virus**. The disease affects multiple organs and damages the immune system. The virus can be transmitted by direct or indirect contact with an infected animal. It can be carried on the air, or on shoes, clothes, and skin.

Signs are seen 7 to 10 days after infection, starting with fever and a rash on the chin and groin area. This is followed by loss of appetite and thick discharge of mucus and pus from the eyes and nose. Brown crusts on the face and eyelids and thickening of the footpads also occur. Respiratory signs such as coughing, sneezing, and difficulty breathing can develop and progress rapidly. Canine distemper is fatal in ferrets. Death typically occurs 12 to 14 days after infection. There is no remedy or treatment. The best defense is yearly vaccination.

Human influenza virus causes fever, lethargy, lack of appetite, nasal discharge, and sneezing in ferrets. Treatment includes supportive care and antibiotics for secondary infections. Antiviral drugs are also available. Ferrets usually recover within 7 to 14 days.

Epizootic catarrhal enteritis is an inflammation of the intestines that is highly contagious. Ferrets usually contract the disease when a new, apparently healthy juvenile ferret is introduced into the home, or when exposed to contaminated objects such as food bowls, bedding, or clothing. The disease is most severe in older ferrets, which may take months to recover. Signs develop in 2 to 14 days and include lack of appetite; green, watery, or slimy diarrhea; stools stained black by blood; dehydration; lethargy; and weight loss. The virus damages the hair-like projections called villi that line the intestines, making it difficult for the affected animal to properly digest and absorb food.

It is not easy to accurately diagnose the virus; an intestinal biopsy is required. Treatment includes supportive care such as fluids, nutritional support (usually a bland, easily digestible diet), antibiotics, and substances that coat the intestines to protect their surface.

To avoid spreading the disease, wash hands and change clothes and shoes after handling any young or infected ferret before going near unaffected ferrets. Wash any new toy or bedding before giving it to your ferrets. Clean the litter box of the infected ferret at least daily. New ferrets brought into the home must be quarantined for at least 1 month.

Aleutian disease is a viral infection originally seen in mink, but at least 2 distinct ferret strains of the virus have been identified. The virus causes the ferret's antibodies to attack its own organs. The affected organs become inflamed and have difficulty functioning properly. The result is a variety of vague signs such as weight loss, weakness, clumsiness, an enlarged liver, and an enlarged spleen. Your veterinarian will make a diagnosis based on these signs and high levels of antibodies in the blood. No specific treatment exists. An infected ferret must be isolated to prevent the spread of the disease, and strict hygiene measures are recommended at all times.

Fungal Diseases

Ferrets are susceptible to **ringworm**, most commonly contracting 1 of 2 types, *Microsporum canis* or *Trichophyton mentagrophytes*. Transmission is by direct contact or contact with contaminated objects such as bedding or a grooming brush. It is often associated with overcrowding and exposure to cats. Infection is more common in infant and young ferrets. It is possible to transfer ringworm between people and ferrets. Wear gloves when handling an infected animal, and wash hands thoroughly afterward.

Other fungal diseases, such as fungal pneumonia (blastomycosis) and fungal infections of the central nervous system (cryptococcal meningitis), are very unusual in ferrets but have been reported.

Parasites

Ear mites are the most common parasite found in ferrets. The same organism is found in dogs and cats, and the disease can be passed between these species. Ferrets with dark, grayish ear wax and unpleasant smelling ears probably have ear mites. In many cases, there are no signs at all, and the mites are only discovered during a routine physical exam. A veterinarian will take a sample of the material in the ear and look at it under a microscope to diagnose ear mites. The drug ivermectin is commonly used for treatment.

Fleas are occasionally seen in ferrets, especially in households with multiple pets. They can be transmitted between ferrets, dogs, and cats. A large, untreated flea infestation can decrease red blood cells and cause weakness in ferrets. The most effective flea control products are available only through veterinarians. Many of the long-acting topical treatments last longer in ferrets because of the increased oily secretion in the coat. To rid an environment of fleas, thoroughly clean ferret cages and bedding, as well as the rugs, carpet, and furniture. Talk to your veterinarian about treating the entire environment (house or room) to get rid of fleas.

Mange (scabies) in ferrets is caused by a microscopic mite known as *Sarcoptes scabiei* and comes in 2 types. The first is a generalized inflammation of the skin that causes hair loss and severe itching. Red, raised areas filled with pus may develop. Ferrets scratch the affected area in an attempt to relieve the itch, quickly leading to damaged skin, secondary infection, and sores. The second form of the disease is limited to the feet, toes, and pads. The feet become red, swollen, and painful. It is also accompanied by intense itching.

The standard method of testing for mange is to take a skin scraping and identify the mites under a microscope. However, a negative scraping does not mean a ferret does not have mange. Diagnosis

Mange is caused by mites. It can cause hair loss and severe itching in ferrets.

may be based on history and the response to scabies medication. Mange can be treated by the drug ivermectin. Antibiotics may be needed to treat infections caused by scratching.

Ferrets that are housed outside may be infested with **bot fly larvae**. The larvae burrow into the skin, incubate for 30 days, then burrow back out and fall to the ground, leaving an open wound. In rare cases, the larvae burrow their way into the brain, nasal passages, or eyelids. Wounds are typically visible around the head, neck, and trunk, and may ooze pus. A veterinarian will open the pocket where the larvae have burrowed, pull out the larvae, and clean the wound.

Heartworm disease is a mosquito-transmitted illness seen primarily in dogs (*see* page 73). It can be found in ferrets, especially those given outdoor access in areas where heartworms are common. Once inside the ferret, the worm travels to the heart where it grows and eventually interferes with heart functions. Heartworms may also block the pulmonary arteries and cause respiratory problems. Because of a ferret's small size, even a single worm can cause disease and death. Signs include lethargy, coughing, difficulty breathing, and a buildup of fluid in the abdomen. Ferrets are at high risk of sudden death from heartworm disease. The disease may be difficult for your veterinarian to detect because of the relatively small number of worms present. Treatment is long-term and involves using drugs to prevent blood clots and kill the adult worms.

Heartworm disease is much easier to prevent than treat. In areas where heartworms occur, ferrets should be given an appropriate dose of a heartworm preventive medication, which can be obtained from your veterinarian. The drugs selamectin and ivermectin are commonly used to prevent heartworm disease. Keeping ferrets indoors will limit their exposure to mosquitoes that transmit heartworms.

Coccidiosis affects the lining of the intestines and can cause disease in young

Diseases that can be Spread from Ferrets to People
Influenza
Rabies
Ringworm

ferrets. Signs include diarrhea, lethargy, and rectal prolapse. Treatment is with antibiotics. If present, rectal prolapse usually resolves itself after the underlying disease is treated. Over-the-counter creams used to treat hemorrhoids may be helpful in treating rectal prolapse.

■ CANCERS AND TUMORS

Unfortunately, ferrets are very prone to a variety of cancers. In fact, the majority of pet ferrets will have some sort of tumor or cancer during their lifetime.

Mast Cell Tumor

Cutaneous mast cell tumors are probably the most common skin tumors in ferrets, often seen in animals over 3 years of age. These tumors can appear anywhere on the body, but typically affect the trunk and neck. The tumor appears as a raised, irregular, and often scabbed mass. Other signs are rare, but the tumors may bleed when scratched. Tumors are diagnosed by biopsy, and they should be surgically removed.

Lymphoma

Lymphoma is common in ferrets and can affect many organ systems, including the lymph nodes, spleen, liver, heart, thymus, and kidneys. Less commonly, lymphoma may affect the spine and central nervous system. Lymphoma can progress rapidly in young ferrets. In adults it is often a chronic disease. Clusters of lymphoma have been seen in ferrets that are related to one another and in ferrets that live together.

To diagnose lymphoma, a veterinarian will use a complete blood count, chemistry panel, x-rays, ultrasonography, and samples of any suspected tissues. Treatment for ferrets has not been standardized but may include removal of the abnormal tissue, chemotherapy, or radiation. Because chemotherapy suppresses the animal's normal immune response, careful monitoring by an experienced veterinarian is necessary.

Chordomas and Chondrosarcomas

Chordomas and chondrosarcomas have been reported in ferrets. Chordomas are tumors that typically appear as firm masses on the tail. They may form an ulcer from dragging on the ground, but otherwise they cause few problems. These tumors may also occur on the neck. Surgical removal is suggested when possible. Chondrosarcomas are tumors that can occur anywhere along the spine, ribs, or breast bone and tend to cause spinal cord compression and associated problems. They should be removed surgically, if possible.

Enlarged Spleen

An enlarged spleen is common in adult ferrets and is usually caused by an increased production of developing red blood cells. In most ferrets this is a benign condition. However, lymphoma and hemangiosarcoma, which are highly invasive, rapidly growing types of cancer, can occur in the spleen. Ultrasonography and needle aspiration of the spleen can be used to determine the cause of an enlarged spleen.

■ HORMONAL DISORDERS

Two hormonal (endocrine) disorders, insulinomas and hyperadrenocorticism, are common in ferrets. Both are described in this section.

Insulinomas

An insulinoma is a tumor found in the pancreas that overproduces insulin. These tumors are very common in ferrets older than 3 years of age. The elevated insulin levels result in low levels of blood sugar (hypoglycemia)—a condition that is the opposite of diabetes. Ferrets with insulinoma have signs such as weakness, lethargy, slight or partial paralysis of the rear

legs, increased salivation, and teeth clenching or grinding. In severe cases, seizures may occur. A veterinarian will make a diagnosis based on whether or not the ferret shows signs of hypoglycemia along with corresponding normal or elevated insulin levels. This is done using a "fasting" glucose test. You will be asked to withhold food from the ferret for about 4 hours before the appointment; a blood sample will then be drawn during the visit. Other blood work is usually normal. Ultrasonography only occasionally reveals these tumors.

Medical and surgical treatments are possible, but there is no cure. Surgical treatment involves either cutting out the mass or removing the part of the pancreas where the tumor is located. Because the cancer is found throughout the pancreas, it is unlikely that surgery will remove the entire tumor. A period of normal blood sugar levels occurs following surgery in some cases, but most ferrets require continued medical treatment. The benefits of surgery include reducing the severity of signs, easing management, and moderately increasing survival time. However, this does not reduce the tumor directly. Medical treatment is lifelong, and does not reduce the tumor directly. Glucose levels should be monitored 5 to 7 days after changing doses and at least every 3 months afterwards.

If a ferret goes into a seizure—signs include twitching, shaking, and unresponsiveness—it is possible to lay the animal on its side and rub honey or corn syrup on its gums using a cotton swab to return it to normal behavior. Check with your veterinarian once you have done this to see about adjusting your ferret's medications.

Hyperadrenocorticism

Hyperadrenocorticism in ferrets is caused by overproduction of the sex hormones (that is, progesterone, testosterone, and estrogen) by a portion of the adrenal gland. It can be seen in ferrets as young as 1.5 years old. Having your ferret spayed will help prevent this disease. The most common sign is hair loss beginning on the tail and rump and progressing up the body towards the head. In females, a swollen vulva and enlarged nipples may also be seen, while males may become aggressive and have difficulty urinating due to an enlarged prostate gland. Bone marrow suppression may follow severe elevation of estrogen levels in the blood. Ferrets with these signs should be taken to a veterinarian as soon as possible.

A veterinarian will make a preliminary diagnosis based on the history and physical examination of the ferret. The enlarged adrenal glands may be felt in front of the kidneys. Routine blood tests are usually normal. Ultrasonography may show enlarged gland(s), but your veterinarian needs to measure the sex hormones to make an accurate diagnosis.

Treatment for this condition includes medical and surgical options. Surgical removal of the adrenal gland(s) is more likely to cure the disease than medical management, but the disease will return in about half of all affected ferrets. If both sides are affected, a partial removal of the adrenal glands can be performed.

An examination of gland tissue may reveal that the disease has progressed to 1 of 3 levels: hyperplasia, adenoma, or adenocarcinoma. Functionally all 3 grades are similar, and the spread of cancer cells outside the glands is unlikely. Because the adrenal glands produce other hormones needed by the body, ferrets that have both adrenal glands completely or partially removed may develop other problems due to a lack of those hormones. This condition can be treated with supplements.

Signs can be reduced through medical management, but such treatment does not affect the adrenal gland, and the tumor may continue to enlarge. It is important to understand that this is a lifelong treatment to control the signs of the disease. Ferrets should be closely monitored if longterm medical treatment is used. Melatonin can be used to treat hair loss and may help with other signs as well. Other drugs used to control sex hormone levels in humans are beginning to be used in ferrets and show promise in controlling the signs.

OTHER NONINFECTIOUS DISEASES

Noninfectious diseases of ferrets include those that are not caused by viruses, bacteria, or other infectious agents. Some of the more commonly seen noninfectious diseases include gastric foreign bodies, dilated cardiomyopathy, and kidney disease.

Foreign Objects in the Stomach

Because of their inquisitive nature, ferrets often swallow foreign objects that can become lodged in the stomach or intestines. Foreign objects are usually soft rubber or plastic items, but can also be hairballs. Signs include loss of appetite, teeth clenching or grinding, overabundance of saliva, sharp abdominal pain, diarrhea, and stools stained black by blood. Vomiting is more common with gastritis (inflammation of the stomach lining) than with foreign objects. Veterinarians use x-rays to diagnose the problem. Surgery or endoscopy is usually required to remove the foreign object. Ferrets should be treated for inflammation of the stomach once the object has been removed.

Dilated Cardiomyopathy

Dilated cardiomyopathy (heart disease) occurs in ferrets that are more than 4 years old. The walls of the heart become thinner, reducing its ability to pump blood. Signs can be similar to those of insulinoma, a tumor that causes the body to overproduce insulin (see page 897). Your veterinarian should test for both problems. Signs include lethargy, weakness, and trouble breathing. Affected ferrets may also have an enlarged abdomen and decreased activity level. X-rays and echocardiography are used to diagnose the disease. Treatment is based on abnormalities revealed on the echocardiograph.

Kidney Disease

Kidney disease in ferrets is similar to that in other species. Kidney cysts are common in adult ferrets and usually do not cause a problem unless they are present in large numbers. Bladder stones can develop in ferrets fed diets high in plant proteins and are usually composed of crystals known as struvite.

CHAPTER **65**

Fish

▨ INTRODUCTION

Aquariums bring the beauty and wonder of the underwater world into your home. Although the average fish owner may not typically think of veterinary care for fish, aquatic medicine is becoming more mainstream, especially with the growth in popularity of the Japanese koi fish and Chinese fancy goldfish show industries. These show-quality fish can cost thousands of dollars, and veterinary care is common. Although a relatively small number of veterinarians throughout the United States work with fish, the numbers are increasing. To find a veterinarian who works with fish, contact the American Veterinary Medical Association or your local veterinarian for a recommendation.

Veterinary care for pet fish, exhibit animals, and valuable breeding stock includes radiology, ultrasonography, laboratory procedures including blood tests, and drug therapy. Advances in surgery have also improved diagnosis and treatment of diseases in fish.

The world of home aquariums is vast and varied. Aquariums and their inhabitants can be selected to be fiesty or serene, showy or subdued, social or solitary. They can also be low maintenance or require lighting schedules, intricate filtration systems, and precise environmental and nutritional management.

The 2 basic types of aquariums are freshwater and saltwater. A water environment in which saltwater and freshwater mix is known as brackish. In nature, this occurs in rivermouth deltas, marshes, and mangroves. In home aquariums, this is generally considered a freshwater environment.

Many different species of fish can be kept together in saltwater or freshwater worlds. For example, certain African river species can be kept with some Australian species; some types of Pacific reef fish can be kept with certain fish from Caribbean coastal flats. However, different species often have requirements that may differ greatly, and therefore they cannot be kept together. For example, water temperature and pH requirements can differ between species. Also, more aggressive species might attack or eat other fish in the tank. Therefore, you should learn as much as possible about the types of fish you are considering for your aquarium before purchase.

▨ DESCRIPTION AND PHYSICAL CHARACTERISTICS

Unlike mammals, fish are cold-blooded. This means that they do not maintain a constant internal body temperature; instead, their temperature is greatly influenced by their environment. True fish have a backbone and fins. Most also breathe with gills and have scales that cover their bodies. It is currently believed that fish began to evolve about 480 million years ago. There are about 22,000 known species of fish.

A fish's **fins** are used for balance and to help propel and steer through the water. Most fish have 2 types of fins: single fins that are found along the centerline (top and bottom) of the fish, and paired fins. The caudal fin, or tail fin, is the main fin used to move the fish forward in the water, while the dorsal and anal fins (on

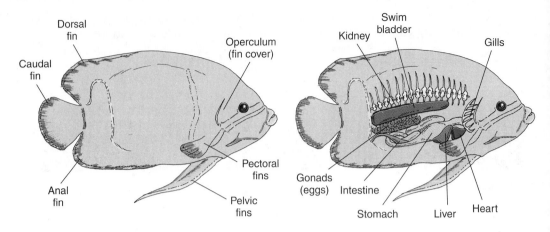

Anatomy of a fish

the top and bottom, respectively) help the fish balance and keep it from rolling over. The paired fins help with steering and hovering.

On the outside of the skin, most fish have **scales**. These overlap in rows and help protect the fish against injuries and infection. In some species (for example, puffer fish) the skin covers the scales—creating a living surface. Their edges are jagged and sharp in some fish, and smooth and rounded in others. Over the scales, fish secrete a mucous covering to further protect against infection. The mucus traps and immobilizes bacteria and viruses, keeping them from entering the fish's body. This covering also helps reduce friction, allowing the fish to move easily through the water.

In order to breathe underwater, fish have developed special organs called **gills**. The gills, found on the side of the fish just behind the head, contain thousands of capillaries, or tiny blood vessels. Water is constantly pumped over the gills, which filter the oxygen out of the water and directly into the fish's blood. A gill cover, called the operculum, is a flexible bony plate that helps protect the sensitive gills. Gills are also important for excretion of waste products, particularly ammonia, from the fish's bloodstream.

Fish have a unique internal organ known as the **swim bladder** or air bladder. It is usually found in the abdomen, and it helps fish move up or down in the water. By adjusting the amount of air in the bladder, fish can adjust the depth at which they float without continuously having to swim. In some fish, the swim bladder is also used to produce sounds. Members of the shark or ray family (elasmobranches) do not have a swim bladder.

Many fish have excellent vision and can see colors. They also have nostrils and are able to detect odors in water. Fish may or may not have teeth, depending on the species. Another organ of sense unique to fish is called the **lateral line**, located along the side of the fish. It contains small sensory hairs that help detect underwater vibrations and determine their source, enabling fish to navigate even in low light or murky water.

■ SPECIAL CONSIDERATIONS

A home aquarium must function as an ecosystem with specific conditions that are maintained at a constant level. Proper maintenance requires water quality monitoring, water changes, filtration, removal of waste materials, and aeration. The appropriate environmental conditions must be maintained regardless of the size of the aquatic environment, from a pond containing hundreds of gallons of water to the smallest goldfish bowl.

You will need to consider the various species of fish, which often have different behavioral characteristics, environmental and space needs, and dietary requirements. What species are aggressive or territorial? Is your tank large enough to house several species? Should the pH of the water be neutral or slightly alkaline? What temperature should the water be? Tropical fish need water kept near 77°F (25°C), while species from more temperate areas do better at lower temperatures. Will the same diet meet the nutritional needs of all species in the tank?

■ SELECTION

The best thing to do when considering a home aquarium is to learn as much as possible about the various types of aquariums and species of fish. Your veterinarian, books, hobby magazines, the Internet, and your local pet store can all be good sources of information. A reputable pet store can be a great resource, because experienced employees are often knowledgeable not only about setting up and maintaining home aquariums, but also about local conditions (such as the characteristics of the tap water in the area) and in-store products. They can help you determine whether freshwater or saltwater is right for you. A saltwater reef tank with live corals requires much more maintenance and upkeep than a goldfish in a bowl. They can also help you sort through the wide variety of species and select fish that can be kept in the same type of environment and that are likely to get along with each other.

Once you are ready to begin selecting individual fish for your aquarium, you should look for healthy specimens. Healthy fish generally have smooth, unblemished scales, fins, and skin surfaces. Skin and fins should be intact, not bloody or ragged. Eyes

should be bright, not cloudy. Fish should be swimming normally and steadily around the aquarium. Diseased fish often swim erratically (circling or drifting around the tank) or appear listless. The aquarium itself should be clean, and other fish in the environment should also appear healthy.

It is very important to make sure that your aquarium is properly set up and functioning for a while before you begin adding fish.

■ PROVIDING A HOME FOR FISH

Once you have chosen the type of fish you want to keep, you need to learn how to set up and maintain the best possible environment to keep them healthy. Important considerations include water quality, diet, cleaning, and prevention and treatment of disease.

Set Up

Creating and maintaining a healthy and balanced aquarium or pond begins with the set up. A good set up is also easier to clean. (For more information on routine cleaning and maintenance, *see* PREVENTIVE CARE, page 909.)

Placement

Your aquarium should be placed in a location that you can get to easily for feeding, cleaning, and general maintenance. The surface must be strong, level, and stable. This includes the floor and the tank stand or cabinet. Because 1 gallon (3.8 liters) of water weighs 8.3 pounds (3.8 kilograms), even a small aquarium can be extremely heavy relative to its size.

The tank should be located out of direct sunlight. This helps to limit the growth of algae in the tank. While a moderate amount of algae is not harmful, a buildup of algae on the glass or in the water is unsightly and makes it harder to spot any health problems with the fish or their environment. In addition, the tank requires more cleaning. Direct sunlight can also cause the water temperature in the tank to rise. The warmer the water becomes, the less oxygen it will hold. If the water gets too warm, the fish can suffocate and die.

The same principles apply to outdoor ponds, although direct sunlight may be unavoidable. If the pond contains aquatic plants, which can help oxygenate the water or supplement the fish's diet, some sunlight is necessary. Aquatic plants also help prevent the growth of algae by absorbing nutrients that would otherwise feed the algae. Plants, and floating plants in particular, can also minimize temperature changes by shading the water to keep it cool.

Another consideration in selecting a location is access to electrical outlets for the lights, filters, and pumps. Are there enough outlets close by or will you need extension cords and a power strip? Is the outlet grounded? Does it have a GFI (ground-fault interrupter)? In any case, you should consider a surge protector. The same is true for pumps, filters, and possibly lights operating for an outdoor pond. Outdoor plugs should be grounded and waterproof.

If you are installing an outdoor pond, either a preformed, rigid liner or a flexible EPMD sheet liner can be used. Make sure the hole is deep enough for your purposes, free of any debris that might puncture the liner, and ideally lined with sand, both to act as a cushion and to help prevent frost heave (the expansion and contraction of the ground during freeze-thaw cycles).

Filtration, Heaters, and Lights

Filtration is important to remove wastes and particulate matter. There are many kinds and types of filtration systems. The most common are under-gravel filters and hanging filters.

An under-gravel filtration system has a framework or grate that is placed underneath the gravel (or other substrate). Tubes are inserted into the framework through the gravel. Water is drawn up the tubes via either an external air pump or a submersible water pump (often called a power head). In an under-gravel system, the gravel acts as the filter media, which traps particulate matter and contains nitrifying bacteria that remove the primary fish waste, ammonia.

Hanging filters have an intake tube that reaches into the water. A small electric water pump draws water in through the intake. The water then passes through a replaceable filter cartridge that consists of filter floss, which collects particulate matter, and activated carbon, which removes certain chemicals and minerals. Many hanging filters also have some form of media to hold the nitrifying bacteria that remove fish waste.

A heater is necessary for tropical fish, both freshwater and saltwater. Do not plug in the heater until the tank is full of water. Most heaters are in a glass tube that may shatter if not surrounded by water, which regulates the temperature and prevents the tube from overheating.

Fish need a day/night cycle for optimal health. Leaving the lights on 24 hours a day, 7 days a week, stresses fish, leaving them more susceptible to disease.

Filters, pumps, heaters, and lights should not be turned on until after the tank is filled with water. Many electronics for aquariums and ponds, particularly submersible pumps, need the water to keep them cool and running safely. Certain fish, such as tangs that are in saltwater aquariums, are very sensitive to the extremely low charge that builds up in the water with the use of these electronics. This electrical charge can cause various health problems and stress. Use of a grounding probe is recommended to bleed off this charge.

In small aquariums, such as goldfish bowls and betta tanks, neither filtration nor a heater may be required. However, more frequent water changes are needed, with more water being changed out as well—perhaps as much as 50% per week. Goldfish and certain other temperate or cold water fish do fine in water that is room temperature.

Gravel and Decorative Objects

Usually, gravel is placed in a tank at the rate of 1 pound of gravel per 1 gallon of water. Before gravel is placed in the aquarium, it should be rinsed thoroughly to remove any accumulated dust. Dust can prematurely clog filters and damage water pumps. If using an under-gravel filter, pile the gravel higher at the back of the tank near the tubes so that it can act as the filtration medium. Creating a slope to the gravel can also make the tank appear to be deeper, front to back.

Larger decorative objects, such as large rocks, coral skeletons, or driftwood, are easier to place before the tank is filled with water because they can be moved much more easily. Decorative objects are not only aesthetically pleasing but also help "divide" the aquarium and allow fish to have their own territory. This can be very important for certain fish, such as freshwater cichlids and many saltwater reef fish.

Water

Poor water quality is the most common cause of environmentally-related diseases in fish. Water quality must be routinely monitored for levels of chlorine, pH (*see* Box), temperature, and salinity (level of salt). The water quality should always be tested before adding fish to the aquarium or pond to ensure that the water conditions are optimal. Your veterinarian or local pet store may offer this testing service, or you can purchase the testing equipment and do it yourself. Having your own testing kit also lets you include water quality testing as part of routine water changes and cleanings, including filter media changes.

An aquarium can be filled with tap water, filtered water, or reverse osmosis water. Obviously, tap water is the most convenient, the least expensive, and generally acceptable to use. Depending on its source (city or well), tap water will probably require treatment in one or several ways. Most city water is treated with chlorine or a combination of chlorine and ammonia (known as chloramine), both of which are toxic to fish and to the necessary bacteria that grow in your aquarium. Additives (dechlorinators) are available to remove both chlorine and chloramine

Explaining pH

pH is a measurement of the acidity or alkalinity of a substance. It is measured on a scale of 0 to 14, with 0 being the most acidic and 14 being the most alkaline. A pH of 7 means the substance is neutral. The pH scale is logarithmic, meaning the difference between any 2 whole numbers is a multiple of 10. It is important to recognize that small numerical changes represent significant changes in pH. The pH level of your aquarium should be monitored regularly because most fish have a narrow range of pH in which they will thrive.

Basic
- 14.0
- 9.0 (100 times more alkaline than pH of 7.0)
- 8.5
- 8.0 (10 times more alkaline than pH of 7.0)
- 7.5

7.0 (Neutral)

Acidic
- 6.5
- 6.0 (10 times more acidic than pH of 7.0)
- 5.5
- 5.0 (100 times more acidic than pH of 7.0)
- 0.0

from the water and should be used to treat any new water that goes in the aquarium. Dechlorinators are fast-acting, readily available, and inexpensive. Dissolved minerals can also lead to excess algae growth.

The pH level of tap water varies greatly from well to well or city to city. The level can easily be checked with one of many easy, inexpensive, and readily available home test kits. You can also take a sample of your water to your veterinarian or pet store for a more thorough analysis and determination of other water treatments that may be needed.

Filtered water has generally been passed through media to remove particulate matter, over activated carbon to remove chlorine and other chemicals and minerals, and possibly through or over another media that may remove other compounds. Reverse osmosis water is processed similarly, but the water is under pressure and forced through an extremely fine membrane and a similar activated carbon membrane to remove even more compounds from the water than are removed during normal filtration.

For a saltwater aquarium, the proper amount of commercial aquarium salt can be added to the tank before or after the water. Another option is to mix the salt with the water in a bucket before adding it to the tank. Regardless of method, you should follow the package directions and use the proper amount of salt to reach the desired salinity. For a saltwater environment, this is usually 30 to 33 parts per thousand. Commercial salts provide not only salinity but also necessary minerals and elements that are not found in tap, filtered, or distilled water. Commercial salts also raise the pH of the water and help buffer it to keep the pH stable.

Beneficial Bacteria

Beneficial bacteria feed on various wastes in the aquarium or pond. These can be solid wastes, such as uneaten food, decaying plant matter, and fish feces, or chemical wastes that the fish excrete—primarily ammonia. Prolonged ammonia exposure is highly toxic to fish. The ammonia is consumed by one type of bacteria that produces nitrites as its waste. These nitrites are also toxic to fish in high quantities. Another type of bacteria then consumes the nitrites to produce nitrates. Nitrates are much less toxic. They tend to accumulate more in saltwater tanks, however. Fortunately, nitrates can be used by plants and algae as food, or removed by water filtration.

These bacteria are common in the environment and will develop on their own in 4 to 6 weeks. Commercial products are sold that may speed up the process slightly, but these are not necessary for most home aquariums.

The bacterial colonies will generally grow to match the amount of available waste, but this takes time. Adding too many fish at once will overwhelm the available bacteria, and toxins will build up quickly. This is why it is best to add fish gradually, 1 or possibly 2 at a time, to

allow the bacterial colonies to grow to a level that can balance the amount of waste. The disadvantage of gradual addition of fish is that any time new fish are added to an established aquarium, there is a risk of introducing disease.

The maximum amount of fish that a system can safely handle can be a function of the available area, such as in many freshwater environments, or it can be a function of volume, as recommended in saltwater aquariums. A good freshwater guideline is 1 inch of fish for every 12 square inches of surface area, or 1 centimeter of fish for every 36 square centimeters of surface area. The ratio of fish to area should be reduced in a cold water environment, such as ponds and goldfish tanks, because the beneficial bacteria do not function as well at lower temperatures. A good saltwater guideline is 1 inch of fish for about every 5 gallons, or 1 centimeter per 8 liters. Home saltwater aquariums hold fewer fish than freshwater aquariums of the same size because saltwater carries less dissolved oxygen than freshwater. Also, saltwater fish tend to be more sensitive to crowding, which can cause undue stress and lead to illness. Ultimately, the carrying capacity of your aquarium is based on the filtration capacity (which can be determined by testing water quality) and the territory available for the fish.

Adding Fish

From a water quality perspective, it can be good to add fish slowly to a new aquarium, 1 or 2 at a time over a period of several weeks. The problem with this approach is that there is significant risk of accidentally introducing disease if the new fish have not been carefully quarantined (see page 907). An alternative strategy is to stock the new aquarium and monitor the water quality, especially ammonia and nitrite levels, on a daily basis. Rising levels of ammonia or nitrite can be controlled by frequent water changes. This approach is more work but can result in a stable and healthy group of fish.

When new fish are added to the aquarium, the current residents sometimes respond aggressively, chasing or attacking the new fish. Aggressiveness toward new fish is common among freshwater cichlids and other larger (more than 3 inches [7.6 centimeters]) freshwater species and, to a slightly lesser extent, among saltwater reef fish. This is particularly true when space and territory in the aquarium are at a premium. Aggressive behavior is stressful for all fish in the tank, so it is helpful to reduce aggression toward new fish by using the following techniques.

First, be sure to "float" the bag with the new fish in it to allow the temperature of the water in the bag to equalize with the temperature of the water in the tank or pond (about 20 to 30 minutes). Adding the fish directly, without a gradual equalization of temperature, can cause shock and stress. While the bag is floating, rearrange the decorative objects in the tank. This helps break up established territorial markers, which may reduce territorial aggression. This technique can also be helpful with aggression among established fish. When adding fish, never allow water from the transport bag to be introduced into the aquarium.

A second technique is to feed the fish in the tank at the same time the new fish are released. This is often enough to distract the aggressive fish from bothering the new fish.

A third technique is to release the new fish in the dark. When the tank light and the room lights are turned off, most fish will go into a "rest" mode within a few minutes. Float the bag with the new fish until the water temperature has acclimated and then release the new fish. After several minutes, turn the lights back on to feed or rearrange the decorative objects again if necessary.

If the aggression persists, the fish can be separated with a clear plastic tank divider. If this is not practical, and other options have failed, it may be necessary to remove either the aggressive fish or the new additions.

Aggression among pond fish such as koi and comet goldfish is fairly rare, but the same techniques can be used.

Diet

Like all other animals, fish benefit from a well-balanced diet, which is essential for good health. Quality foods and variety also improve coloration and behavior and reduce stress levels.

You need to know the type of diet your fish require, as well as where your fish naturally feed in the water column, such as at the surface, in the middle, or at the bottom. For instance, fish that prefer to feed at the bottom should not be fed flakes that float on the surface. A wide variety of processed and natural foods are available to meet the needs of nearly any fish. Commercial dried foods, such as pellets, flakes, or granules, are a good choice because they are usually formulated to contain the proper mix of nutrients for your fish when fed properly. Food should not be stored for excessive periods of time. It is better to buy smaller quantities of food frequently than a large container that is used for many months. In general, dried foods should be kept on hand for no more than 2 months.

Feeding methods and rates vary with species, age, system, and water temperature. In general, maintenance diets are fed at a rate of 1% to 2% of body weight per day, and growth diets at 3% to 5% of body weight per day. Overfeeding can lead to health problems as well as a dirty tank. A variety of foods should be fed, with one primary dietary source supplemented with other foods that provide necessary nutrients.

Live foods, while generally a good source of protein and fat, can lack sufficient amounts of other elements and may not provide a complete diet. Another consideration is that fish fed only live food from day one may refuse other foods. If the primary live food becomes unavailable, it may take some time to find another source. Finally, live foods can sometimes introduce parasites or diseases into the fish's environment.

Several kinds of pelleted food are formulated specifically for koi and goldfish in outdoor ponds. Natural foods such as shrimp pieces and plant material can be used as supplements. Insects that fall in the water are another source of live food in outdoor ponds. This amount should be reduced in colder weather, because the fish are not as active and do not need as much food.

Fresh vegetables are also a good addition to the diet of many fish. Zucchini can be diced, lightly cooked, and stored in the freezer. Feeding vegetables a few times a week as a supplement provides an excellent source of B and C vitamins.

> ### Common Signs of Illness in Fish
>
> - Lethargy
> - Not eating
> - Slow or rapid breathing
> - Loss of color
> - Discoloration or splotchiness
> - Spots
> - Scars
> - Ulcers (open sores)
> - Loss of scales
> - Scales sticking out or standing up
> - Swelling or bloating
> - Weight loss
> - Floating, drifting, or swimming erratically in unusual positions
> - Tumors and cystic growths
> - Puffy and/or fuzzy growths

ROUTINE HEALTH CARE

Preventing disease is always preferable to treating it. In most cases, a comprehensive fish health management program should focus on water quality, nutrition, sanitation (maintenance and cleaning), and quarantine.

Signs of Illness

Fish show signs of illness in a variety of ways. Some general signs of illness include changes in swimming behavior and noticeable changes in the color or condition of the body and fins (*see* BOX). The individual body systems sections of this chapter also list more specific signs as they relate to certain diseases.

Giving Medication

You will not be able to give your sick fish a pill or a spoonful of medicine. However, it is possible to give medications to fish to treat various disorders. Methods used to administer medication to pet fish include topical, injection, immersion, and in-food. Some of these need to be performed by your veterinarian (such as injections or surgery), while others can be

done at home. For example, many ulcerations and sores can be treated with a topical ointment. A number of scale, skin, and gill problems, particularly parasites, can be treated by placing the fish in a tank of medicated water for a period of time or by adding medication to the main tank or pond. Some freshwater fish can be treated by temporary immersion in mildly salty water, while saltwater fish can sometimes be treated by immersion in fresh or less-salty water. A few internal problems can also be treated by immersion methods. Simple internal problems can often be treated by feeding medicated food. More complicated diseases require veterinary treatment.

Certain drugs have been approved by the US Food and Drug Administration (FDA) for use in food fish, while others are listed as "low regulatory concern." These drugs and compounds can be used to treat pet fish. Because there are relatively few drugs approved for use in fish, drugs and compounds that have not been approved by the FDA are also sometimes used by veterinarians under controlled conditions. Federal and state regulations are of concern when treating outdoor ponds, because contamination of the general groundwater and other animals can be an issue.

Preventive Care

The best preventive care to keep fish and their environment healthy includes providing a good diet, monitoring the water quality, and maintaining a regular schedule of cleanings, water changes, and filter replacements (*see* BOX). Cleanings should include stirring up the gravel or other substrate to release solid wastes that have been trapped. The wastes can then be removed by the filtration units or by use of a net. A hydro-vac siphon can be used to remove solid waste from the gravel while water is being removed for a water change. Any new water should be dechlorinated before it is added to the aquarium or pond. If needed, salt and other supplements should be added to the new water.

Decorative objects should be cleaned every so often. Crevasses, cracks, and holes on rocks, wood, decorative corals, and other objects can capture waste that can pollute the water. Remove the decorations from the aquarium and run them under hot water. Rubbing or scrubbing with a towel or clean brush may be needed for more porous or obviously dirty pieces. Let the pieces drain completely, until they are no longer dripping. They can then be returned to the aquarium without much worry of harm from chlorine.

All filtration systems, regardless of type (including trickle filters, canister filters, sand filters, sump filters, ultraviolet sterilizers, and others) need regular maintenance. Replaceable cartridges should be changed once a month, or more often if needed, because the filter floss becomes clogged with wastes and the activated carbon loses effectiveness.

Quarantine

Quarantine means that new or sick animals are kept in a separate aquarium for a specific amount of time before joining others. The purpose of quarantine is to prevent the accidental introduction or

---

Essential Maintenance

Daily:
- Check fish, water temperature, and equipment
- Feed fish and remove any uneaten food
- Empty protein skimmer (saltwater tanks)

Weekly:
- Clean glass cover or condensation tray
- Add any water needed to compensate for evaporation
- Remove any algae from glass

Every 2 weeks:
- Change water—amount changed depends on stocking level
- Remove dead leaves from live plants and trim if needed
- Check pH, total alkalinity, ammonia levels, nitrate and nitrite levels, specific gravity (for saltwater and brackish tanks), and filter flow (clean if needed)
- Stir top of substrate and remove debris

Every 1 to 3 months:
- Replace carbon in filter
- Clean protein skimmer (marine saltwater tanks), filter pipework, and quartz sleeve of ultraviolet sterilizer (if applicable)
- Service power filters and air pump

Every 6 months:
- Check lighting
- Replace ultraviolet sterilizer tubes

---

spread of infectious disease to an established population of aquarium fish. Valuable pet fish should be quarantined for at least 30 to 60 days before being added to the general population. This can prevent the spread of disease from the new (or ill) fish to the entire population. A quarantine tank can be set up for new fish or for those showing signs of disease. Isolating the fish in question also allows easier observation and treatment. Quarantine systems should be completely broken down and disinfected between uses. Once quarantine is started, no new fish can be added or the quarantine period must be restarted.

Vaccination

In large-scale fish operations such as salmon hatcheries, vaccination is quite effective and commonly done. Vaccinations are still uncommon for pet fish, but it is likely that more vaccines will become available, such as the one that can prevent ulcer disease, a serious infection caused by *Aeromonas salmonicida, Aeromonas hydrophilia,* or other bacteria in koi and goldfish. The vaccine can be given either by injection or by immersion, with the size of the fish determining the method of administration. Routine vaccination of koi or goldfish is not recommended.

For all vaccines, water temperature affects the speed of the immune response, or how fast the body builds up antibodies for the disease. An experienced veterinarian or hobbyist can advise on how to properly administer vaccines to fish.

■ EMERGENCIES

Most home aquarium and pond emergencies are not truly medical in nature. They generally involve something going wrong with the aquatic environment such as a leak or an electrical problem with a heater or pump. In many cases, fast action can resolve the emergency. Make sure that all electrical items are grounded or have a circuit-breaking function along the power line. The possibility of leaks and spills, and their consequences, can also be lessened through planning and quick action.

Most emergencies can be avoided by planning and vigilant monitoring of the environment through water tests. Sudden releases of toxins (for example, chlorine, ammonia, or nitrite) from old activated carbon and certain water treatment chemicals may be identified ahead of time, or at least before they become fatal. Unfortunately, emergency medical treatment for pet fish is not as advanced or as readily available as it is for dogs and cats. If a veterinarian with fish experience is nearby, some instances of physical trauma to fish, such as an outdoor koi being attacked by a wild animal, can possibly be treated.

■ BREEDING AND REPRODUCTION

In an aquarium or pond, successful breeding largely depends on nutrition and environmental conditions that are sometimes very specific. In the wild, these conditions might be seasonal changes, water conditions, the amount of daylight, and the availability of specific food sources. The amount of daylight is generally less important in tropical species, because hours of sunlight in tropical regions nearer the equator stay fairly constant year round. Temperate or coldwater fish, such as goldfish and koi, may be more affected by shorter and longer days of the seasons further north or south. Certain conditions often trigger a particular species to breed. For instance, during the wet season in the tropics, rains may wash extra nutrients into the swollen rivers, leading to a greater abundance of available food and plants, which can be ideal breeding conditions for fish.

In aquarium and pond fish, healthy breeding stock must be of spawning age. You will need to research the nutritional and environmental needs of the particular species you want to breed. These conditions are almost as varied as the number of fish species (*see* TABLE 7). Proper substrate, cover, temperature, pH, live foods, lighting, and number of fish are all likely considerations.

Sexing Fish

Determining the sex of a fish can be difficult or easy, depending on whether physical differences are visible. Males of some species may be larger and showier than females. Information on how to sex a particular species may be obtained from your veterinarian, books, hobby magazines, the Internet, and other sources.

Live Bearers

Fish reproduce by bearing live young or by laying eggs. Livebearers give birth to fully formed and functional young, called fry. The eggs are fertilized and hatched within the female. Most livebearers have

Table 7. Types of Fish Reproduction

Types of Egg-Layers	Where Eggs are Laid	Fertilization Method	Common Species
Mouthbrooders	In water, then collected in mouth once fertilized and held there until birth; some hold fry in mouth for up to a week after birth	Fertilized by spawning before gathered in mouth	Fresh water cichlids, bettas, cardinal fish, gobies, blennies
Nest builders	A spot in substrate, a structure made of plant materials, bubble nest (foamy structure)	Spawning	Bass, bluegill, stickle-back, gourami, bettas
Egg scatterers	Sticky eggs are laid within a certain area under cover; non-sticky eggs set adrift in open water	Male swims by and sprays semen, or milt, around the area	Cardinal tetras, tiger barbs, zebra danios, goldfish, koi
Egg depositors	Sticky eggs are laid in one spot, usually substrate or glass	Male swims by and fertilizes eggs	Rainbow fish, killi-fish, dwarf cichlids, clownfish
Egg buriers	Buried in soft substrate	Male dives into substrate to fertilize eggs	Killifish, rare and endangered species in the wild

fewer and larger fry than egg layers, because the fry need to be more developed and large enough to fend for themselves after birth. Most species of livebearers kept in home aquariums are generally easy to breed. Identifying sexes is usually easy as well. Males are generally larger and have larger, longer, more ornate and colorful fins than females. For instance, only male swordtails have the "sword" on their tails, and male guppies have larger, more flowing tails that are brightly colored.

Fry should be separated from adults, because the adults (including the parents) tend to eat them. Small live or frozen food and crushed flakes are good for feeding fry. Species of freshwater livebearers include mollies, platys, swordtails, and guppies from the Americas, and the 20 or so half-beak species from Asia.

Egg Layers

Egg layers spawn by several means, including egg scattering, egg depositing, egg burying, nest building, and mouth-brooding. In all cases, eggs are laid and fertilized outside the body. Nest-builders and mouthbrooders are generally good parents, protecting the eggs and fry from aggressors. Many cichlid species, such as freshwater angelfish, are nest-builders.

Egg scatterers, egg depositors, and egg buriers may or may not defend the eggs and fry. Usually, the fry need to be separated from the adults to prevent the larger fish from eating them. Egg-scatterer females lay their sticky eggs in various places within a certain area (often in areas that provide some sort of cover), while others set nonsticky eggs adrift in open water. Egg depositors pick one general spot to lay sticky eggs, usually on the bottom substrate and sometimes on the aquarium glass. In saltwater, clownfish are depositors, guard their eggs and fry, and are the most likely species to be bred by hobbyists. Egg buriers either dive into soft substrate, or the male pushes the female into the soft substrate to lay. The male then dives in to fertilize the eggs. In a tank breeding environment, peat moss is often a good choice for the substrate.

Care for Newborns

Usually, fry should be separated from the adult fish and placed in a nursery environment. Mouthbrooders will eventually expel the fry, even though the fry are still quite vulnerable. Removing fry from outdoor ponds can be difficult. Ideally, a separate, smaller aquarium should be set up to receive them. Conditions should generally be kept much as they are in the main aquarium or pond. There should be some kind of cover for the fry, so they are safe, secure, and free from stress. The aquarium should be filtered, but the pump should not be so powerful that it sucks in the fry. Several commercial baby fish foods are available. Alternatively, finely crushed flake and tiny live or frozen foods can be fed.

Another option is to purchase a nursery. Nurseries are made of a box frame with a fine mesh netting for the walls and floor, or plastic grids for the same purpose. They are usually built to hang from the top lip of the aquarium into the water. The mesh or grid prevents the fry from escaping, while keeping them safe from the larger fish. The open tops allow access for feeding and other purposes.

■ DISORDERS AND DISEASES

Many of the disorders and diseases that are known to occur in fish are the result of stress, poor water quality, overcrowding, and failure to quarantine any new or sick fish to avoid spread of disease. These factors can all be minimized by appropriate care and good hygiene. Infections caused by bacteria, protozoa, viruses, fungi, or parasites may also occur.

Heart and Blood Vessel Disorders

Fish are cold-blooded, which means their body temperature is close to and fluctuates with the temperature of their environment. In addition, all their bodily processes are greatly influenced by the water temperature. Water that is very cold or that has been under pressure can become supersaturated with dissolved gases. If the temperature rises or the pressure drops suddenly, these gases may expand rapidly. If fish have already been exposed to this supersaturated water, the

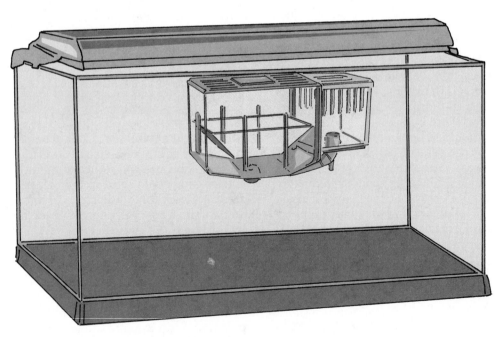

A nursery keeps fry separated from larger fish that may eat them.

gases they absorbed while breathing may also expand rapidly, releasing gas into the bloodstream. This is called **gas bubble disease**, and the small bubbles created can result in much tissue damage and death. Gas bubble disease in pond fish can be caused by owners filling an outdoor pond with well water using a hose. If the hose is submerged, gas in the incoming water will stay dissolved in the water and can cause problems. This is especially important if the water source is a deep well. To prevent this, the inflowing water can be sprayed as it hits the tank or pool.

Excess ammonia in a system is very harmful to fish. High levels of ammonia in an aquarium can be caused by several factors. Two syndromes that are characterized by very high levels of ammonia are well described. The first is called **new tank syndrome** and is a simple accumulation of ammonia that occurs when a new tank is stocked with fish before the biological filter is fully functional. In this case, the system will be recently set up, usually within the past 1 to 3 weeks. Ammonia accumulates because there are not enough bacteria in the biofilter to metabolize it. The situation can be managed by frequent (sometimes daily) water tests. When total ammonia levels are high (2 milligrams per liter or higher), at least 50% of the water in the aquarium should be changed. This intense management should only be necessary for 1 to 2 weeks, unless there are other unidentified problems with the system. Water quality monitoring will show a decline in ammonia, followed by an increase in nitrite as the bacterial colonies grow. The process is complete when nitrite levels also fall to normal.

The second type of ammonia problem is called **old tank syndrome**. While it is also characterized by high ammonia concentrations, it is completely different. This problem is caused by a sudden and drastic drop in pH, often below 6.0, which kills bacteria in the biofilter. The loss of bacteria results in the high concentrations of ammonia,

which are the hallmark of this problem. Simple water changes are not recommended, however, because an increase in pH may cause the ammonia present to become toxic, killing the fish.

Old tank syndrome is caused by a loss of buffering capacity, which allows the pH change to occur. The loss of buffering capacity is caused by improper water changes. Typically, this is caused by adding water to the aquarium to replace that lost by evaporation, but not actually removing old water from the tank during the water changing procedure. Removing old water from an aquarium is a very important part of the water change process. Failure to remove some of the old water at each water change allows organic acids to accumulate. These are produced by the fish and bacteria in the system and are normal. However, when the old water is not removed, the acids use up the buffering capacity of the water (measured by total alkalinity). When the total alkalinity falls to zero, the pH plummets, killing the biofilter and causing old tank syndrome.

Typically, a tank with old tank syndrome will have high ammonia levels (often higher than 10 milligrams per liter), little or no alkalinity, low pH (below 6.0), and high total hardness (several hundred milligrams per liter). In this situation fish should be moved to a separate holding tank, the aquarium should be totally broken down, everything should be thoroughly cleaned (including the biofilter), and then the entire system set up again as a new system. Because it is a new system without an established biofilter, you will need to monitor ammonia levels and do water changes as ammonia accumulates, until the new biofilter is established.

Anemia is a condition in which the number of red cells in the blood is low. The most obvious sign that fish are anemic is very pale gills. Observant fish owners may notice this. Although not a common finding, many things may cause anemia. These include various infections and folic acid deficiency, which has been reported in channel catfish. Longterm exposure to nitrite in the water may also lead to anemia. You should consult your veterinarian or other fish health professional if you suspect anemia is a problem in your fish.

Leeches are parasitic bloodsuckers that may carry various blood parasites. Because they consume blood themselves, a heavy infestation with leeches can cause anemia. This does not necessarily mean that blood parasites are present. Aquariums and ponds usually become infested with leeches by introduction of an infested fish or plant. There are some approved treatments, but avoiding leeches is best, and depopulating infested aquarium or pond fish and restarting the system is very effective.

Digestive Disorders

Parasites cause many digestive disorders in fish. Many parasites live harmoniously in, on, or around fish, but others cause problems such as weight loss and loss of appetite, and can lead to death in fry and other young fish. *Spironucleus* and *Hexamita* are protozoan parasites that attack the intestines of cichlids, bettas, gouramis, and other aquarium fish. The seriousness of the infection is directly related to the number of parasites present. Crowded conditions, shipping, handling, and other stressful situations can trigger outbreaks. Broodstock and ornamental cichlids should be watched especially carefully. Signs of infection may include lethargy, thinning, and white, stringy feces.

Another protozoan, *Cryptobia*, attacks the stomach of African cichlids. Affected fish stop eating and lose weight. There is no treatment for this parasite.

Both larval and adult **tapeworms** are sometimes found in fish. Aquarium fish and carp may be purchased with heavy infections, but they have limited exposure once in the aquarium unless they are fed infected intermediate hosts. Heavily infested fish may lose weight and appear lethargic. Treatment with an appropriate antiparasitic drug may be effective.

Eye Disorders

Eye disease in fish is common and can be caused by several disorders. Diseased eyes may appear swollen, enlarged (as in a pop-eyed appearance), bloody, ulcerated, or otherwise disfigured. A fish's eyes can be examined with a penlight or bright flashlight to determine if the abnormality is within the eye or in the surrounding tissue. Blood in the eye itself may be caused by injury or infection. Eye injuries commonly occur during transport and handling, especially when fish struggle in a net.

Parasites in the eye, such as **eye flukes**, may be found in wild-caught fish. Parasitized eyes may appear enlarged and possibly cloudy; sometimes tiny worms can be seen within the eye itself. Although this is unsightly, and may compromise the fish's vision, treatment is not necessary. There are no drugs that have been proven to be safe and effective for treating eye flukes in pet fish.

Tiny gas bubbles in the cornea (the thin, clear tissue covering the eye) may indicate **gas bubble disease**. Other signs of gas bubble disease include tiny bubbles in the fins or gills. A gill biopsy can be taken to confirm the diagnosis.

Cataracts (opacity of the lens of the eye) are also common in fish. These can be caused by eye flukes, nutritional deficiencies, or unknown factors.

Bone and Muscle Disorders

Bone and muscle disorders can be caused by nutritional imbalances, including deficiencies in ascorbic acid (vitamin C), vitamin E, and selenium. "**Broken back disease**," indicated by a bent backbone, is typical of vitamin C deficiency, though other problems could also cause deformation of the backbone.

Pleistophora hyphessobryconis is a parasite that attacks the skeletal muscle of neon tetra, angelfish, and other freshwater aquarium fish. Muscle damage leads to abnormal movement. Examination of diseased tissue with a microscope is necessary to confirm the infection. There is no treatment. All infected fish should be removed from the tank to prevent spread of the disease.

Brain, Spinal Cord, and Nerve Disorders

Neurologic disorders can be caused by nutritional imbalances, including deficiencies in thiamine, niacin, biotin, and pyridoxine.

Streptococcus **infection** can cause neurologic signs if it enters the brain. This infection is rare, but has been found in rainbow sharks, rosy barbs, danios, and some tetras and cichlids. All fish are considered susceptible. Sources of infection can be environmental or from infected live foods. The source must be identified and removed to prevent future outbreaks. Antibiotics are usually used to treat *Streptococcus* infections. Because *Streptococcus* is in a special group of bacteria, the gram-positive bacteria, specific antibiotics are necessary to treat these infections. Laboratory tests and assistance from your veterinarian or fish health professional are necessary to effectively treat a *Streptococcus* problem.

Neurologic disorders may also be caused by **ammonia toxicity**. This is common in fish with new tank syndrome (*see* page 911). Ammonia and pH should always be tested when neurologic disorders are observed.

Nutritional Disorders

One of the most common contributors to illness or death in aquarium and pond fish is improper nutrition. Nutritional disorders occur despite the fact that complete, nutritious food is commercially available in a variety of forms, such as pellets, flakes, and granules. One reason for this is the differing nutritional requirements for each type of fish. Some fish are herbivores (plant eaters), others are carnivores (meat eaters), and many are omnivores (plant and meat eaters). It is very important to learn what diet best matches the needs of your fish. You will probably need to feed more than one kind of food if you have several types of fish in your environment. Improper stor-

age of fish foods is a common cause of nutritional imbalance. Dry feeds should be kept in a cool, dry place and used or replaced every 2 months.

Many different types of nutritional deficiencies can occur, depending on the nutrient that is missing. Most of these are not diagnosed until the fish are very sick or dead. It is much easier to take the time to learn about and provide the correct diet for your fish than to correct the nutritional deficiency once it occurs.

Feeding live foods to your fish should be done carefully. Wild harvested live foods may harbor parasites or other harmful organisms that can cause disease in fish. You should purchase any live foods from a reputable source.

Feed intoxications can happen in aquarium settings. The most common of these is a result of feeding fish foods contaminated with the aflatoxin produced by *Aspergillus flavus*, a mold that grows on the feed. When this aflatoxin is eaten, it causes rapid growth of tumors and a high death rate. Moldy feeds should always be discarded.

Gill Disorders

The special organs called gills allow fish to breathe underwater. Gill disorders can be caused by environmental problems or infections.

Disorders Caused by Environmental Problems

Gas bubble disease can develop when water is supersaturated with dissolved gases. This is common in cold-water systems, when cold water introduced into the system is heated too rapidly, and the gas in the water builds up in the system. When the fish breathe through their gills, they take in this excess gas. Gas bubble disease has been linked to faulty pumps and, rarely, to ponds with heavy algal blooms that cause afternoon gas levels to be very high. Treatment involves vigorous aeration to blow the excess gas out of the water. Gas bubble disease is easily identified by a veterinarian by observing gas bubbles in gill capillaries when looking at a biopsy sample under a microscope. (*See also* HEART AND BLOOD VESSEL DISORDERS, page 910.)

Carbon dioxide can be toxic to fish when the concentration is greater than 20 milligrams per liter. Fish exposed to high levels of carbon dioxide appear lethargic and nonresponsive. When pH is tested, the water will be acidic. Treatment is vigorous aeration which blows the excess carbon dioxide out of the water and into the atmosphere. As the carbon dioxide concentration in the water decreases, the pH of the water increases.

Hydrogen sulfide (H_2S) is highly poisonous to fish. Excess hydrogen sulfide is usually found in water from a deep well or is the result of accumulated organic debris in the pond or holding tank. Hydrogen sulfide tests are available, but a strong sulfur odor is readily noticeable. Prevention involves thoroughly aerating any water introduced into the system and keeping the system sanitary to minimize buildup of organic wastes.

Disorders Caused by Infections

Dactylogyrus is a common parasite that infests the gills of fish and looks like a small worm under a microscope. It is commonly found on the gills of goldfish, koi, and discus but can also affect many other species of fish. Infested fish brush up against objects to try to remove the worms. Fish become pale, and their breathing becomes rapid and shallow. Gills are swollen and pale. A similar but larger parasite, *Neobenedinia*, infests salt water fish and can be devastating. These parasites lay eggs and this can cause reoccurring infection even after the adults have been killed. Formalin or praziquantel are most often used to treat these infestations. Quarantine can effectively prevent introducing these parasites into a healthy environment.

Many of the protozoan parasites mentioned under the section on skin disorders can also affect the gills of fish. Microscopic examination of infected tissue is necessary to identify all of these, but

treatment for these external gill and skin infections is very similar. Formalin is commonly used, and can be purchased at most pet stores. Other products may be used in some circumstances. Consultation with your veterinarian or fish health professional is recommended.

Bacterial gill disease is seen occasionally in aquarium fish. It usually begins in a system that is overcrowded and has poor water quality. Different types of bacteria are thought to cause this disease. Signs include swollen, mottled, and deformed gills. Because the gills cannot function properly, the fish have respiratory problems. Sanitation is critical to stop this disease and to prevent it in the future. Antibiotics can help treat bacterial infections, but if the underlying sanitation problem is not corrected, the infection is likely to reoccur.

Branchiomycosis is a fungal infection of the gills caused by *Branchiomyces* species. These organisms are commonly found in decaying organic material in the environment. Branchiomycosis causes respiratory problems and the death of gill tissue. It is typically found in warm ponds and can be prevented by avoiding overstocking and poor sanitation. This infection is extremely rare and has only been reported in the United States a few times.

A very serious **herpesvirus** has recently been described in koi. The death rate can be close to 100%. The main sign is destruction of the gills, which causes respiratory problems and death. Gills appear white and mottled and are obviously diseased. Laboratory tests to confirm the diagnosis are recommended. Your veterinarian may recommend destruction of diseased fish and any fish in contact with diseased fish. If this is done, the system should be thoroughly disinfected before restocking.

Skin Disorders

Skin disorders in fish are especially harmful. Any surface injury to the skin makes osmoregulation (fluid balance) more difficult and can lead to circulatory malfunction. The skin and mucus are extremely important protective barriers for fish. They seal the fish so fluid balance is more easily controlled. The mucus allows fish to slip through water more easily, so less energy is used while swimming. There are also several protective compounds in the mucus that protect the fish from bacteria and other organisms in the water. Various types of parasites, from tiny single-celled protozoa to larger lice and worms can cause skin disorders in fish, as can bacteria, viruses, and other organisms.

Sunburn can be a problem in fish that swim near the surface. Access to shade should be available to fish housed in outdoor ponds. Plants can be an excellent source of protection from direct sunlight.

Disorders Caused by Bacteria

Flavobacterium columnaris are bacteria that cause **columnaris disease** (sometimes called saddleback or cottonmouth disease). Signs may include skin lesions with slimy or cotton-like excretions. It is common in warmwater fish. Early treatment with potassium permanganate can help, but if not recognized until later, antibiotic treatment is generally needed.

Disorders Caused by Viruses

Carp pox is one of the oldest recognized fish diseases. It is caused by cyprinid herpesvirus-1. It is primarily a disease of koi. The skin abnormalities are smooth, raised, and have a milky appearance. They do not usually cause problems, but they can be a site of secondary bacterial infection. Carp pox is of particular interest to the koi enthusiast because the high value of these fish is based on appearance. Quarantine is essential, and any infected koi should be removed. Surgery to remove the pox lesions is not helpful.

Lymphocystis disease is a viral infection that can affect both saltwater and freshwater fish. In home aquariums, painted glass fish are especially susceptible. The main sign is cauliflower-like growths on the skin or fins. This does not usually cause a health problem, but it does affect the appearance of the fish. Micro-scopic examination of tissue is necessary to confirm that the problem is lymphocystis. Infections usually are not life-threatening and resolve without treatment.

Disorders Caused by Protozoa

A common protozoal infestation in home aquariums and ponds is called **ich** or **white spot disease**. This disease is caused by *Ichthyophthirius* in freshwater fish, and by *Cryptocaryon* in saltwater fish. The organisms attach to the fish and burrow into the skin and gills. The resulting cysts appear as visible white spots. Microscopic examination of diseased tissue is required to confirm the diagnosis. As the protozoa begin to reproduce, they leave a hole in the fish and sink to the bottom of the tank or pond to reproduce. One parasite can produce hundreds of new organisms. This rapid and massive reproduction is what makes this parasite so deadly. If there are large numbers of these parasites, the amount of damage can make the fish more susceptible to infection by other agents or cause a loss of bodily fluid. Treatment is with either copper sulfate or formalin, both of which can be obtained from your veterinarian or pet store. As with all medications, label instructions should be followed carefully. The treatment must be applied at specific intervals based on the water temperature, so advice from a fish health professional is recommended.

Another serious disease in aquarium fish is called **velvet** (also known as **rust** or **gold dust disease**). It is caused by protozoan parasites that attack the gills and skin, causing fine yellowish spots that are smaller and harder to see than the ones that occur with ich. Sometimes these appear as a thin, velvety film covering the skin. Other signs include loss of appetite, lethargy, and a tendency for affected fish to scratch against rocks or other hard objects. High death rates are common. Both freshwater and saltwater fish may be affected. In freshwater fish, the cause is *Piscinoodinium* (formerly known as

Oodinium, which may be the name used in older references). In saltwater fish, a related parasite called *Amyloodinium* is responsible. The parasites attach to the skin and gills. *Piscinoodinium* and *Amyloodinium* can be identified by your veterinarian following microscopic examination of gill,

Ich

Velvet

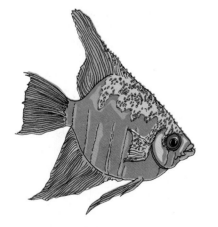

Skin slime due to protozoa

Protozoan parasites cause several common skin diseases in aquarium fish.

skin, or fin tissue. Chloroquine is an effective treatment and may be recommended to you. Instructions for giving it must be carefully followed. A recheck of the fish in 7 to 10 days may be needed.

Other protozoan parasites such as **Chilodonella**, **Brooklynella**, and the **trichodinids** may infest the gills or skin of aquarium fish. Infected fish may seem to have excessive amounts of slime or mucus. Microscopic examination of diseased tissue is required to confirm the diagnosis. Signs include dulled coloration, a light gray-white covering of mucus on the body of the fish, gill damage, and general weakness. Fish often rub against objects to relieve itching. Other observations may include rapid breathing, piping (swimming near the surface of the water, trying to gulp air), flashing (scratching), and loss of condition. Once the diagnosis is confirmed, fish can be treated. Formalin is often effective. The trichodinids in particular are often associated with overcrowding or poor sanitation, in which case cleaning the system is an important component of the treatment plan.

Tetrahymena corlissi and **Uronema species** are parasites that are usually found on the skin, gills, or fins, but they can also be found inside fish, including skeletal muscle and the fluids of the eye. These parasites are usually found in water that has a high level of organic matter. If the parasites are only on the surface of the fish, the infestation can be cleared with good sanitation and chemicals. If the parasites have moved inside the fish, the condition is not treatable.

Ambiphyra and **Apiosoma** are parasites that attack the skin and gills. These parasites are more common in pond fish than in aquarium fish, and usually do not affect saltwater species. Low numbers of these parasites are not a problem, but high numbers can damage the skin and gills, which compromises breathing and can leave the fish susceptible to other infections. Treating involves using formalin, copper sulfate, potassium permanganate, or salt. Excessive crowding and poor sanitation are predisposing factors and should be avoided.

Ichthyobodo **species** are common parasites of the skin and gills of aquarium, pond, and saltwater fish. They can be difficult to see but look like a flickering flame when infected tissue is examined with a microscope. Affected skin may appear to have a steel-gray discoloration, and mucus production called "blue slime" or "gray slime" may be seen. Behavioral signs include lethargy, poor appetite, piping (swimming near the surface, trying to gulp air), flashing (scratching), and overall weakness and loss of condition. Microscopic examination of infected tissue is required to confirm the diagnosis. Poor sanitation, crowding, or overfeeding can contribute to proliferation of the parasites and should be corrected. Salt, formalin, copper sulfate, or potassium permanganate baths can be effective treatments after underlying problems have been corrected.

Disorders Caused by Larger Parasites

The **anchor worm** (*Lernaea*) is an adult parasite that buries its head into the muscle tissue of a host fish. Despite the name, anchor worms are not worms, but crustaceans. They molt, and the larvae can damage gill tissue. Pond fish are the most common hosts. The fish may scratch against objects to try to knock the parasite off. The parasite can easily be seen, appearing as whitish-green threads hanging off the red, inflamed skin of the fish. The parasite can be removed, and the site of attachment can be treated with antibiotic ointments. Treatment is recommended to eliminate the parasite from the pond or aquarium.

Fish lice (*Argulus*) and **leeches** are parasites that attach themselves to a host fish, penetrate the skin, and feed on the blood. The fish scratch against objects to try to remove the lice. Lice look like small, clear disks that lie flat against the skin. Leeches are worm-like parasites that contract when touched. Treatment involves removing the parasites from the fish. The tank should be treated to kill any lice larvae that may be present. Leech infestations can be seasonal, but eggs may have been laid in the system, resulting in reinfection after the

adult parasites have been eliminated. Treatment is usually recommended if the system has no contact with surface water.

Gyrodactylus and *Dactylogyrus* are tiny flatworms that are skin and gill parasites of goldfish, koi, and other fish. The parasites are usually too small to be seen without a microscope. Fish become pale and can have skin sores with scattered hemorrhages and ulcerations. The death rate can be high when fish are heavily infested. Formalin or praziquantel are the treatments most often used for these infestations, and quarantine is a good practice to help prevent introduction of these parasites into a healthy environment.

As mentioned above, there are some **saltwater parasites** (*Neobenedinia* and related capsalid parasites) that have a similar effect as *Gyrodactylus* and *Dactylogyrus* do in freshwater fish. The marine organisms can be more virulent, however, because they are much larger and therefore can cause more damage to the fish. They also lay very sticky eggs that can be easily spread by nets or other objects to uninfected systems. Praziquantel is an effective treatment for the adults, but reinfection remains a threat if eggs have been released into the system.

Kidney and Urinary Tract Disorders

Sphaerospora auratus is a parasite that causes renal dropsy. It attacks the kidneys of pond-raised goldfish and can lead to severely enlarged, cystic kidneys and death. There is no practical treatment. Fortunately, infection is extremely rare.

Disorders Affecting Multiple Body Systems

Some disorders are widespread, affecting multiple organs and body systems. The most common types found in fish are discussed below.

Disorders Caused by Bacteria

Aeromonas **infection** is the most common bacterial infection of freshwater aquarium fish. Fish infected with *Aeromonas* or other closely related bacteria may show signs that include bloody spots or ulcers on the body, fluid accumulation in the abdomen ("dropsy" and "pinecone disease"), ragged fins, or enlarged eyes. Diagnosis of a bacterial infection requires laboratory testing. Many bacterial infections can be treated with antibiotics, but laboratory testing is necessary to determine which antibiotics will work against the particular bacteria causing the problem. Koi and goldfish are especially susceptible to a certain type of *Aeromonas* called *Aeromonas salmonicida*. This particular bacteria can cause deep ulcers and death in these fish. Antibiotic testing in a laboratory may be the only way to determine which drug should be used to control an outbreak of this disease.

Vibriosis is a common and potentially serious disease that affects many types of fish, although it is less common in freshwater species. *Vibrio* bacteria are responsible for causing bleeding and ulceration of the skin, fins, and tail. Internal organs can also bleed and break down. Preventive steps include minimizing stress and crowding. Antibiotics are useful but laboratory tests are needed to determine which ones will be effective. Bacterial populations change, and an antibiotic that worked in a previous outbreak may or may not be effective in a later outbreak. Rapidly changing antibiotics or "shotgunning" fish with many different drugs is a dangerous practice and can result in creation of resistant bacterial strains.

Edwardsiella tarda causes intestinal disease and skin ulcerations in many species of fish and can also infect reptiles and mammals (including people). Signs include gas-filled lesions that have a bad odor when they burst. Affected fish cannot swim normally because the gas-filled lesions affect their floating ability. The death rate from *Edwardsiella tarda* is usually low, often only 5 to 10% of the population. Antibiotics are effective, but as stated above, laboratory tests are needed to determine which drug will work best.

Mycobacteriosis is a bacterial infection that can affect aquarium fish, but it cannot be treated with antibiotics as most bacterial infections are. The mycobacterial organisms are protected from drugs because they have a way of hiding in the body of the fish where the antibiotics cannot reach them. These hiding places are often walled off by the body of the fish, forming nodules or "granulomas" in the tissues. Some fish may be infected early in their lives because their parents were infected or because they ate an infected fish. Other fish may develop the infection during periods of great stress. Others may pick up the disease because there are high numbers of *Mycobacterium* in their water. These organisms are common in our environment. Poor sanitation, low oxygen, and low pH create conditions that are favorable to these bacteria, increasing the threat to fish in such an aquarium. Diagnosis of *Mycobacterium* is difficult because signs resemble those of many other diseases. Signs could include weight loss, skin ulceration and bleeding, paleness, and skeletal deformity. Your veterinarian will diagnose *Mycobacterium* infection by examining different tissues with a microscope. Tissue may also be submitted for special laboratory tests to confirm the diagnosis. Infected fish are usually destroyed. The environment needs to be thoroughly cleaned with alcohol or phenolic compounds before starting over. *Mycobacterium* can infect people, but usually is restricted to a rash-like infection on the hands. People with immune system disorders should not be allowed contact with a *Mycobacterium*-positive aquarium. It is always wise to wash your hands after working in any aquarium, and people with compromised immune systems should probably not handle aquariums directly.

Disorders Caused by Fungi

Saprolegnia can affect fish and fish eggs. Signs include grayish-white, cotton-like growths on the skin, gills, eyes, or fins. This fungus can spread to the internal organs and deeper tissues of the body. Prevention consists of removing all potential sources of the fungus, such as correcting poor sanitation and removing any dead and decaying matter. If the environment is clean, and skin pathogens have been eliminated, a single treatment of potassium permanganate can often control external *Saprolegnia*.

Ichthyophonus hoferi is a fungus that causes internal infections, usually in older aquarium fish. It is usually identified through examination of fish that have died. Prevention includes removing infected fish and avoiding feeding raw fish products. This infection is very rare.

Cancer and Tumors

Like other animals, fish can develop cancer. The incidence can be higher in certain geographic areas and in certain species. Some tumors, such as the malignant melanoma of the gypsy-swordtail cross and fibromas or sarcomas of goldfish, are genetically linked and controlled. Tumors of the reproductive organs are common in koi. Affected fish have a swollen abdomen and lose condition. If the fish is not severely debilitated, some tumors can be removed surgically.

CHAPTER **66**

Gerbils

■ INTRODUCTION

Domesticated gerbils, *Meriones unguichlatus*, originated in the deserts of North Africa and central Asia and are sometimes referred to as Mongolian gerbils or Mongolian desert mice. Gerbils are relatives of mice and rats and have been bred as pets since the 1960s. Gerbils are known for their curious and mild temperament. Because they have almost no odor, require very little space, and are easy to care for, they make excellent pets. Gerbils are very social creatures, so they do best in the company of other gerbils.

Gerbils are known for their curious and mild temperament.

■ DESCRIPTION AND PHYSICAL CHARACTERISTICS

Adult gerbils weigh 2 to 3 ounces (50 to 90 grams). Males are slightly larger than females. The coats of gerbils in the wild are "agouti" colored, or a mix of gray, yellow, and black, with an off-white belly. Breeding has produced gerbils with many different coat colors, including black, buff, white, gray, and spotted. They are about the size of mice, with their bodies measuring about 4 inches (10 centimeters); their fur-covered tails can add an additional 3 inches (8 centimeters). Gerbils typically live for 2 to 3 years.

Both male and female gerbils have a **ventral marking gland** on their abdomen. The gland appears as an orange-tan hairless area that is usually oval in shape. It can sometimes be mistaken for a tumor. In male gerbils, the gland enlarges during puberty and produces an oily secretion. Male gerbils may use this as a way of "marking" territory, and they can

Both male and female gerbils have a ventral marking gland on the abdomen.

sometimes be seen rubbing their abdomen on objects.

■ SPECIAL CONSIDERATIONS

Never lift a gerbil up by its tail. Gerbils' tails are delicate and can be easily injured. The best way to remove a gerbil from its cage is to use both hands and scoop it up under its belly. Do not squeeze the gerbil. Until the gerbil is accustomed to being handled, hold it close to the ground so that if it falls, it will not fall far and hurt itself. It is recommended that you hold the gerbil over its cage or over your lap, so if it wriggles out of your hands, it cannot run away.

Because of their small size, gerbils cannot withstand rough handling and are not recommended as pets for very young children.

■ SELECTING A GERBIL

Gerbils are available at many pet stores, or they can often be obtained from a local breeder. When selecting a pet gerbil, you should look for one that has smooth glossy fur, clear eyes, and no obvious signs of trauma such as limping or hair loss on the body or tail. There should be no discharge from the eyes or nose, and no signs of diarrhea in the gerbil's environment. Healthy

gerbils are usually lively and curious. If any of the gerbils show signs of illness such as matted fur, a hunched posture, or dullness, you should look elsewhere for your new pet.

■ PROVIDING A HOME FOR A GERBIL

Gerbils are active and enjoy climbing and burrowing. Appropriate housing for these animals provides opportunities for both. Maintaining a clean environment and providing high-quality commercial diets formulated for gerbils help ensure that your pet remains healthy.

Housing

Gerbils must be kept in a cage with a solid (non-mesh) bottom, because they often stand up on their hind legs. An ordinary fish tank with a breathable (mesh) lid makes an excellent home for a gerbil. Solid plastic containers with connecting tunnels make an interesting environment. A rule of thumb is that each gerbil requires about 5 gallons of space; 1 gerbil needs at least a 5-gallon tank, 2 gerbils need a 10-gallon tank, and so on. Living quarters should be 60 to 70°F, and relatively dry (below 50% humidity). Whatever type of cage is chosen, it should be secure (to prevent escape) and easy to keep clean.

The cage should be about ⅓ filled with bedding materials to provide gerbils with a place to dig and hoard their food and a means to absorb their urine. Bedding made from aspen or corn cob shavings is a good choice and is commercially available. Recycled paper products marketed as bedding are safe and easy to clean. Cedar shavings contain oils that may be toxic to small animals, and their use remains controversial. Gerbil housing should be cleaned and disinfected often (once every 2 to 3 weeks) to prevent disease.

Nesting materials should be provided. Plain shredded facial tissue is suitable. Commercially-available nesting material is not recommended, as gerbils' small feet tend to get tangled in the strands. You may wish to provide a small wood, cardboard, or ceramic box in which the gerbil can build its nest. Gerbils may also benefit from regular sand or dust baths as described for chinchillas (*see* page 875); rolling in the sand is a way for these desert animals to help keep their fur clean.

Diet

The healthiest food choice is pellets formulated for gerbils. These pellets should contain 18 to 20% protein and are readily available in most pet stores. It is better to avoid the gerbil mixtures that contain pellets mixed with seeds, as the animals will often pick out the seeds and leave the pellets. To avoid obesity and diabetes, 5 grams of pellets per day is adequate. It is normal for gerbils to hoard their food, burying it in their bedding and around their cage. Homemade diets containing seeds or table scraps are usually not nutritionally balanced, although pumpkin or sunflower seeds can be offered as occasional treats. A consistent food source helps to prevent health problems.

Because gerbils are adapted to dry, desert-like conditions, they do not consume much water; 4 milliliters (less than 1 teaspoon) per day is average for an adult. However, plenty of fresh, clean water should be supplied daily. Water can be provided via a bottle with a metal spout or nipple, which can be hung from the lid of the tank, or via a small bowl. All water dispensers should be washed thoroughly when the water is refilled.

Exercise

In the wild, gerbils build elaborate burrows. Therefore many gerbil owners provide their pets with commercially-available plastic tubing and other environments that allow for climbing and burrowing. Other options are sturdy rocks, wooden planks, and ladders for climbing (when choosing toys, keep in mind that gerbils chew everything, so do not choose anything with pieces that may be harmful if swallowed).

Small cardboard boxes and toilet-paper tubes are quickly shredded but make excellent and readily available gerbil toys.

Some pet owners choose to provide their gerbils with an exercise wheel. However, the slats in a traditional hamster wheel can catch a gerbil's feet or delicate tail. When choosing an exercise wheel, either look for one with a solid surface, or cover the outside of a typical hamster wheel with tape to create a solid surface.

Rearranging the contents of the cage periodically will help keep your gerbil stimulated.

Temperament

Gerbils are highly social animals that live in family groups in the wild. Living alone may be stressful. Keeping gerbils in pairs, especially same-sex pairs from the same litter, is recommended.

Gerbils have a friendly temperament and are easy to socialize. However, they need time to adjust to their new surroundings and to your presence. Do not remove them from their cage immediately upon bringing them home. Begin by sitting quietly by their cage, talking softly to them, or offering them a treat from your open palm.

Gerbils may bite when they are stressed. In order to avoid stress when handling, do not startle a gerbil or pick it up while it is sleeping. While the gerbil is getting used to your presence, allow it to climb over your palm before lifting it out of its cage.

■ ROUTINE HEALTH CARE

Gerbils are relatively healthy animals. However, it is a good idea to monitor your gerbil's condition and behavior daily. There are early warning signs that may indicate illness. These include weight loss; decreases in activity; changes in the appearance of the fur; and a change in the color, consistency, smell, or amount of urine or feces. If any of these changes occur, it is best to bring your gerbil to a veterinarian.

Dental Care

Because gerbils' incisor teeth grow continuously, they need to constantly chew and gnaw to keep these teeth worn down. Overgrown teeth can cause lack of appetite and weight loss. Several varieties of chew toys are available; small rope and wood parrot toys are good choices for gerbils. Scrap lumber, as long as it is untreated, is another inexpensive option.

▊ BREEDING AND REPRODUCTION

Identifying male and female gerbils that are older than 7 weeks is relatively simple. Adult male gerbils have prominent testicles that can be seen under their tails. It is more difficult to determine the sex of gerbils that are less than 7 weeks old. Lifting the tail of a young gerbil reveals a small patch with no fur; this patch is farther away from the tail on males than on females. The easiest way to sex a gerbil under 7 weeks old is to compare it with another young gerbil whose sex is known. However, these methods are not always accurate.

Gerbils are generally monogamous, and paired gerbils will usually begin to mate at about 3 months of age. Mating can be identified by a ritual of chasing and mounting, with both gerbils checking their undersides after each round. Pregnancy lasts about 24 days, and a litter consists of 1 to 8 gerbil pups. Gerbils will begin mating again almost immediately after the female gives birth.

There are several causes of **infertility** in gerbils, including ovarian cysts, old age, sexual immaturity, exposure to pesticides or other toxins, nutritional deficiencies, and disease. Environmental causes of infertility in gerbils include overcrowding, incompatibility with a potential mate, environmental disturbances, and low temperatures. Ovarian cysts, which occur in 20% of older female gerbils, are the major cause of infertility and small litter sizes.

Care of Newborns

Gerbils instinctively take good care of their offspring, and no owner intervention is required. In fact, touching the pups or changing the layout of the cage can be harmful, so unless something is wrong, do not interfere during the pups' first few days of life. The male and female gerbil can both remain in the cage with the newborns.

Newborn gerbil pups can get lost or crushed under regular gerbil toys and exercise equipment. If you suspect that your female gerbil is pregnant, remove everything from the cage except food, water, nesting materials, and a reduced layer of bedding. Avoid cleaning the cage during the first few days of the pups' lives.

▊ DISORDERS AND DISEASES

Gerbils have few spontaneous illnesses. A proper and consistent diet, clean cage and bedding, and appropriate housing all contribute to maintaining good health.

Digestive Disorders

Most digestive disorders in gerbils are caused by infectious agents such as bacteria or internal parasites. Diarrhea is a common sign of many gastrointestinal diseases.

Malnutrition may also occur if gerbils are not fed a diet specifically formulated to meet their dietary needs.

Tyzzer's Disease

Tyzzer's disease, caused by *Clostridium piliforme* bacteria, is the most common infectious disease in gerbils. The bacteria are more likely to infect young or stressed gerbils. Signs of infection include depression, rough hair coat, hunched posture, loss of appetite, dehydration, and watery diarrhea. Because this disease is contagious, a sick gerbil should be separated from other gerbils. The bacteria are transmitted by contaminated feces, so the infected gerbil's cage must be thoroughly cleaned and disinfected. Sick gerbils should be handled after other gerbils, and you should always wash your hands thoroughly in between handling each gerbil.

Salmonellosis

Gerbils can be infected with several strains of *Salmonella* bacteria. Signs of infection include diarrhea, dehydration, weight loss, rough hair coat, a swollen or bloated abdomen, or fetal death in a pregnant female. Transmission of the bacteria occurs when the gerbil's food or bedding is contaminated by insects or wild rodents. Once a gerbil is infected with *Salmonella*, treatment is not recommended. The infected gerbil should be isolated and its environment should be thoroughly sanitized and disinfected. *Salmonella* infections can be transmitted to humans, even if the infected gerbil does not seem sick.

Pinworms

Gerbils can be infected with these intestinal parasites by exposure to another infected gerbil's feces. However, there may be no obvious signs. A veterinarian can diagnose pinworms by examining your gerbil or testing its feces. Several types of medication, which often must be mixed with the gerbil's feed or water, may be prescribed for treatment. The infected gerbil's cage should be thoroughly cleaned and disinfected because the worm's eggs may still be present.

Tapeworms

Gerbils can be infected with 2 kinds of tapeworms, *Rodentolepis nana* (dwarf tapeworm) and *Hymenolepis diminuta*. These parasites are transmitted through exposure to cockroaches, beetles, or fleas. The dwarf tapeworm can also infect humans. Gerbils usually do not have signs of tapeworms, but heavy infections can cause dehydration or diarrhea. A veterinarian can diagnose tapeworm infection with tests on your gerbil or its feces, and prescribe appropriate treatment. The cage of the infected gerbil should be thoroughly cleaned and sanitized, and whatever may have transmitted the infection (cockroaches, for example) should be eliminated.

Bone and Muscle Disorders

Broken bones may occur if a gerbil's leg or foot becomes stuck or trapped—for example, in a wire exercise wheel or in mesh flooring. The gerbil's delicate tail may also be injured in this way. Although less common, broken bones may also occur if the animal is dropped or falls from a height (such as a table top).

Skin Disorders

Disorders of the skin are relatively common in pet rodents, including hair loss and infestation with various parasites of the skin. There are several disorders that are specific to gerbils; however. These include porphyrin deposits around the nose and eyes, and a condition known as tail-slip.

Irritation of the Face and Nose

Environmental stressors, such as incompatible cage mates, high humidity, and overcrowding, can cause gerbils' tear glands to secrete an excess of **porphyrin**, a protein, around the nostrils and eyes. Accumulation of this reddish-brown porphyrin can cause skin irritation, which leads the gerbil to scratch and hurt itself. It can also lead to hair loss, skin redness, scabbing, and sores. These sores, in turn, can become infected, and the infection can spread. They are itchy, and if the gerbils scratch, the sores will bleed. Sometimes these sores heal by themselves, but more often the infection gets worse. Your veterinarian can diagnose these infections. Treatment includes careful cleaning of the affected area, and application of a prescribed antibiotic ointment. To prevent this condition, monitor the temperature (60 to 70°F) and humidity (below 50%) of your gerbil's environment, and separate any animals that are incompatible.

Hair Loss and Tail-slip

Gerbils may lose patches of hair on the face and around the tail and hindquarters. Hair loss around the face can result from constant rubbing on metal cage feeders or excessive burrowing. Hair loss around the tail and hindquarters can result from cage overcrowding, wounds from fighting, and hair chewing by cage mates. This can be prevented by fixing these environmental conditions and separating the animals that may be fighting.

Picking up a gerbil by the tail can result in fur loss or cause the skin on the tail to slip off. This is called tail-slip. The portions of the tail that are exposed by skin slippage often rot, and they must be treated by amputation. This problem can be prevented by never picking a gerbil up by the tail.

Rough Hair Coat

When humidity levels are too high, gerbils may develop rough and matted hair coats. This often occurs in gerbils that are kept in tanks without adequate ventilation. Be sure that the cage is adequately

Injury to a gerbil's tail can result in fur or skin loss called tail-slip.

ventilated and that the humidity level in the home is kept under 50%.

Mites

Gerbils can occasionally become infected with mites. Old age and infirmity can make a gerbil more susceptible to infection. Although mites are hard to see with the naked eye, gerbils may show other signs such as fur loss and dry, scaly, irritated skin on the back and rump. A veterinarian can prescribe medication for treatment. Bedding should be changed frequently and the cage sanitized and disinfected.

Tumors

In older gerbils, the ventral marking gland on the abdomen (*see* page 919) is at risk for developing tumors, some of which may be benign. The affected gland may develop open sores and become infected, but the tumors rarely spread. Other skin tumors may affect the ears or feet. Masses may be surgically removed. The outlook for a gerbil with a tumor varies with the size, stage, and timing of the removal. Prompt treatment by a veterinarian improves the chances of successful treatment.

Epilepsy (Seizures)

Gerbils may spontaneously develop seizures. These may be inherited, or they may be caused by sudden stress, improper handling, or introduction to a new environment. Seizures occur in about 20% of gerbils, but they are uncommon in many pet strains. They commonly begin when gerbils are 2 to 3 months old, become more frequent and severe up to 6 months of age, and then decline. Seizures last several minutes and can range from mildly trance-like behavior with twitching ears and whiskers to severe muscle convulsions and stiffness. Death from seizures is rare and there is no permanent damage. No medication is necessary. Seizures can be prevented or reduced in gerbils that are genetically predisposed if the gerbils are handled frequently during the first 3 weeks of life.

Kidney Disease

Gerbils that are more than 1 year old often develop an inflammation of the tiny blood vessels in the kidneys, a condition known as **glomerulonephritis**. Signs include excessive urination and thirst and weight loss. Supportive care with fluids may be required. Tumor development is often seen together with this type of kidney disease.

Masses in the Inner Ear

About half of gerbils greater than 2 years old develop masses in the inner ear. These masses—called **aural cholesteatomas**—push the eardrum far into the ear, causing permanent damage to the inner ear. Affected gerbils may tilt their head to one side.

Other Illnesses

Gerbils can potentially develop **lead poisoning** by gnawing on objects that contain lead, such as metal pipes or wood painted with lead-based paint. Gerbils

> ### Diseases that can be Spread from Gerbils to People
>
> Campylobacteriosis
> Salmonellosis
> Hantavirus infection
> Lymphocytic choriomeningitis
> Rabies
> Rat bite fever
> Tularemia

more than 10 months old can develop deposits of a certain kind of protein, called amyloid, in the spleen, liver, lymph nodes, pancreas, hormone glands, heart, and intestines. Signs of **amyloid deposits** include loss of appetite, dehydration, weight loss, and death.

Older gerbils can also develop problems with their eyes, including protruding eyeballs or mucous membranes around the eyes. Eye injuries may result when incompatible gerbils fight.

CHAPTER 67
Guinea Pigs

■ INTRODUCTION

Guinea pigs, also called cavies, are members of the Caviidae family, a group that includes several species of rodents from South America. All cavies are social animals that prefer to live in groups. They can be found in many habitats, including plains, marshes, and rocky areas. In the wild, cavies live in burrows and feed on vegetation including grass and leaves. They are popular pets and valuable research animals.

Cavies were domesticated in pre-Incan times (around 1400 AD). It is likely that the domesticated cavies originated in the highlands of Bolivia, Ecuador, and Peru.

In these areas, Native Americans used them for food and religious purposes. Europeans discovered these domesticated animals soon after their arrival in South America. Cavies were first imported into Europe in the early 1500s. Because Europeans believed they came from Guinea, cavies soon became known as guinea pigs.

There are 13 recognized breeds of guinea pigs.

Today, they are kept as pets around the world.

■ DESCRIPTION AND PHYSICAL CHARACTERISTICS

Guinea pigs, like other cavies, are stout and short-legged. They range from approximately 8 to 19 inches (20 to 50 centimeters) in length for a full grown adult. Adult guinea pigs are about 5 inches (13 centimeters) tall. The average adult weight is 30 to 35 ounces (850 to 1,000 grams). Their normal body temperature is 102 to 104°F (39 to 40°C). The life span of a guinea pig varies, but on average, they live 5 to 6 years (*see* TABLE 8).

There are currently at least 13 recognized breeds of guinea pigs. Some of the more common breeds include the American, which has short, smooth hair; the Abyssinian, with short hair that grows in whorls; and the Peruvian, which has longer, silky hair. Hairless breeds have also been developed. Guinea pigs come in several colors and color combinations, including black, tan, cream, brown, and white.

Guinea pig eyes are located on the sides of the head, allowing them to see both forward and backward, though they may have trouble seeing directly ahead. Their heads are blunt and have small ears. Guinea pigs have 4 digits (toes) on their front feet and 3 on each hind foot. Each toe

has a very sharp claw. Their hind legs are longer than their front legs. They have no external tail.

Guinea pigs have 20 teeth including upper and lower long incisors (for cutting and tearing), premolars, and molars. A guinea pig's teeth are "open rooted" and grow continuously throughout its life. They wear down their teeth by eating, chewing, and grinding food. Thus, it is important that your guinea pig's diet contain a sufficient amount of hays, grasses, and abrasive foods to maintain healthy teeth at the proper length. Fat pads, which are normal, on either side of the mouth can make examination of guinea pig teeth difficult.

■ SPECIAL CONSIDERATIONS

Guinea pigs are comfortable only in the narrow temperature range from 65 to 75°F (18 to 23°C). They also prefer a low relative humidity (below 50%). When exposed to temperatures above 85°F (29°C), they may develop heat stroke. Thus, special care needs to be exercised when transporting these animals during very cold or very hot days. They do not thrive in drafty locations and should not be constantly exposed to direct sunlight.

Because of their small size, guinea pigs often suffer injuries when outside their cages. They can be seriously injured when stepped on or if they fall off a table. Like

Table 8. Guinea Pigs at a Glance

Lifespan	5 to 6 years
Weight	30 to 35 ounces (0.8 to 1 kilogram)
Length	8 to 19 inches (20 to 50 centimeters)
Normal body temperature	102 to 104°F (39 to 40°C)
Heart rate	250 beats per minute
Estrus cycle	15 to 17 days
Duration of pregnancy	59 to 73 days
Litter size	1 to 7 (usually 3)
Weaning age	4 weeks
Environmental requirements	65 to 75°F

many other rodents, guinea pigs are attracted to anything that looks interesting to chew. Electrical cords are common hazards for these animals. Other pets, such as dogs, cats, and ferrets, may easily injure guinea pigs. In addition, many common houseplants are toxic for guinea pigs (*see* page 1175). Whenever your guinea pig is outside its cage, it should be very carefully monitored to keep it safe.

Unlike hamsters and rats, guinea pigs are mostly diurnal—that is, they are usually awake during the day and sleep at night. This makes them a good choice for a pet, because they will be active during the day when you can observe them and handle them without disturbing their rest.

Keeping more than one guinea pig provides companionship for your pet. Keeping only guinea pigs of the same sex prevents them from mating. If you plan to keep male guinea pigs together, they should either be neutered or be introduced to one another before they are finished weaning from their mothers. This will help prevent fighting. Guinea pigs may panic or become stressed if they come into contact with other pets, so keep them separate from dogs, cats, or other animals. This will also help prevent the spread of infectious diseases.

Guinea pigs have unusual sensitivities to many commonly used antibiotics when given orally, by injection, or rubbed on in creams. Many of the most widely used antibiotics can be toxic for your guinea pig. Do not use antibiotics or products containing antibiotics on your guinea pig without the guidance of a veterinarian (*see also* ANTIBIOTICS, page 931).

■ SELECTING A GUINEA PIG

When choosing a guinea pig for a pet, look for an animal that appears healthy, plump, and alert. The animal may initially be fearful or skittish but should, in a short time, respond positively to gentle stroking. Check over the animal carefully. The eyes should be bright and clean, not crusty or lusterless. The nose, eyes, ears, and anus

should be clear and free of any discharge or discoloration. The teeth should be clean and unstained and the long incisors in the upper jaw should overlap and just touch the bottom pair. Check the feet to be sure they are well-formed and move easily. The feet should be uninjured and without flakes, red spots, and scars.

Also, look at the housing for the guinea pigs you are considering. The cage or enclosure should be clean, with very little odor. The animals should not be too crowded, as this can lead to stress and may lessen resistance to disease. In many cases, guinea pigs will be kept in mixed (male and female) groups. Because female guinea pigs can become pregnant as young as 2 months of age, this often means that even a fairly young female guinea pig can be pregnant at the time of purchase.

Ask the seller about a prepurchase veterinary check. A responsible dealer will either allow a check by an outside veterinarian or will agree to accept back a diseased or pregnant animal that has been promptly examined by a veterinarian. If possible, have your new guinea pig examined by a veterinarian before you take it home or as soon as possible thereafter.

■ PROVIDING A HOME FOR A GUINEA PIG

Before you bring your guinea pig home, make sure you have already purchased and set up the cage and that you have appropriate food available. You should also have a supply of bedding for the cage and a suitable brush.

Housing

Commercial housing for guinea pigs is often undersized. Most cages sold for guinea pigs are designed for a single animal, not for 2 or more. It is recommended that 7 square feet of space be provided for a single guinea pig (for example, a cage 42 by 24 inches [106 by 61 centimeters]). An additional 2 to 4 square feet (0.6 to 1.2 square meters) of floor space should be provided for each additional guinea pig. A cage height of 18 inches (46 centimeters) is desirable. Cages of these sizes provide space for play and other activities that contribute to a healthy life for your guinea pig.

Cages can be constructed of glass, plastic, metal, or wire. Good ventilation is important to keep guinea pigs healthy, so if a cage with solid sides is selected, the top should be wire mesh that allows for plenty of air. Guinea pigs do not jump, so a lid is not required to control guinea pig activity; however, it may be recommended to protect the guinea pig from other pets in the household.

Because the small feet of guinea pigs are often injured by walking over wire mesh and other narrow objects, the cage bottom should be smooth and without rough ramps, mesh shelves, or floor grids. Using an exercise wheel with a wire mesh running surface may also injure guinea pig feet. Instead, select an exercise wheel with a solid running surface of sufficient size for your pet. Providing a small wood or cardboard box inside the cage will provide a sense of protection and a welcome place to sleep.

Place your guinea pig's home in an area out of direct sunlight and drafts where the temperature is between 65 to 75°F (18 to 23°C). This should be away from areas of heavy moisture (such as laundry rooms or damp basements). Guinea pigs should not be housed in the same cage or close to rabbits, as some infectious diseases can be transmitted between the species.

The bedding in your pet's home should not be allowed to get wet or accumulate moisture. Wood shavings (do not use cedar or raw pine) or shredded newspapers (printed with soy inks) should be provided and changed at least once a week. Sawdust and cat litter are poor choices because sawdust particles may be inhaled, causing damage to the lungs, and cat litter may be eaten. High quality soft grass is often used above the shavings or shredded newspapers, but good quality grass hay (timothy and orchard grass are popular) is often a better choice, as eating hay will provide

more of the abrasion your guinea pig needs for good dental health.

Diet

Guinea pigs are herbivores (plant eaters). A good quality guinea pig diet typically contains commercial pellets, hay, fruits, and vegetables. A small, smooth-surfaced heavy ceramic dish makes a good "dinner plate" because these dishes are hard to tip over and can be easily cleaned.

Most guinea pigs enjoy almost any type of vegetable but tend to be partial to green leafy vegetables such as carrot tops and lettuce. (Use romaine or green leaf lettuce rather than the less nutritious iceberg lettuce.) Small pieces of carrots and other vegetables and fruits are also welcome. Uneaten fresh food should be removed after a few hours. Good quality grass hay should be available at all times.

Guinea pig pellets, which are readily available in pet stores, should make up about two-thirds of your pet's diet. Before buying pellets, it is a good idea to scan the label. Good quality pellets should be free of animal byproducts and low in corn content. Many guinea pig pellets have a high alfalfa content. These pellets are suitable for young, growing, and pregnant guinea pigs; however, a timothy-based pellet, which provides less calcium, is a better choice for fully grown animals. Consult your veterinarian for advice on pellet content. Adult guinea pigs will eat about one-eighth of a cup of pellets a day assuming they have adequate access to hay and fresh vegetables and fruit. However, you should adjust the quantity of food based on your pet's consumption.

Guinea pigs, like people, lack the ability to synthesize vitamin C. They must get plenty of this vitamin in their diets to avoid scurvy. You should not substitute pellets formulated for other animals (such as rabbits) for guinea pig pellets, as these will not contain enough vitamin C. Commercially prepared guinea pig pellets should have sufficient vitamin C. However, much of the vitamin C may be lost if the pellets are stored for more than a few months. It is a good idea to supply adequate vitamin C in other ways, such as through fresh vegetables and fruits that contain high levels of this vitamin.

Fresh water should be available at all times to prevent dehydration. A drip bottle attached to the side of the cage at a height easily reached by your pet will keep contamination at a minimum. Clean the drip bottle and change the water daily. Do not add supplements to the water and avoid both distilled water and water with a high mineral content, especially water that has a high calcium content.

Guinea pigs can be picky eaters. They tend to develop preferences for foods at a very young age and they do not like to have their diet changed. It is a good idea, when purchasing or adopting a new guinea pig, to find out from the store or previous owner what foods it is accustomed to eating. If you are purchasing or raising a young guinea pig, you can try small amounts of different pellets, fruits, and vegetables to increase the range of foods the animal will accept.

Exercise

Routine exercise is necessary for the health of your guinea pig. Careful arrangement of your pet's cage will encourage activity. Placing the sleeping area (a small wooden or cardboard box) in one part of the cage, the water in a second location, and food in another encourages activity. Introducing a second level (accessed by a solid-floored ramp) or a small barrier can further encourage exercise. Placing a few pieces of PVC pipe (5 inches [13 centimeters] in diameter or larger) in the cage can provide a welcome runway for your pet and further encourage needed exercise.

Temperament

Guinea pigs are gentle, friendly, social, often highly vocal animals. They prefer to live in small groups (only 1 male in a mixed group, however). Guinea pigs can make a range of noises, from a "squeak" or "chirp" to a "tooth-chatter" noise that sounds like a purr.

Guinea pigs rarely bite, even when handled improperly. The correct way to pick up a guinea pig is to gently hold the animal near the shoulders in one hand while supporting the back with the other. Guinea pigs that are handled when they are young are often very affectionate and enjoy being held carefully.

ROUTINE HEALTH CARE

While guinea pigs do not require any vaccinations, it is recommended that you take your pet to a veterinarian familiar with guinea pigs at least once each year for a routine checkup.

Signs of Illness

Guinea pigs should be handled daily. This allows you a regular special time with your pet. It also provides you with the opportunity to check your pet for possible skin problems, injuries, sudden weight gain or loss, dental problems, and other health problems. Some signs to look for when a guinea pig is sick include loss of appetite, weight loss, hunched posture, an abnormal walk or a limp, a belly that is unusually skinny or abnormally large, a change in the consistency of the hair coat, or difficulty breathing. Sick guinea pigs may have decreased energy or not respond to noises or touch.

The most common health problems for these animals are problems with the lungs or the digestive system, so a sick guinea pig may also have discharge or oozing from the eyes or nose, or diarrhea. Dental problems are also common, so check your pet's mouth for drooling, overgrown teeth, or swelling. You should also check your pet's ears for oozing or irritation, and examine its feet for sores or broken nails.

If you notice any of these signs, it is best to take the guinea pig to the veterinarian promptly. These small pets can become sick quickly, and identifying and treating the problem right away can be critical.

Care Schedule for Your Guinea Pig

- Provide fresh, clean vegetables and grasses daily
- Provide fresh water daily
- Spot clean cage daily
- Clean cage every week
- Brush fur every week
- Trim nails every 8 to 12 weeks
- Bathe every 3 to 12 months

Grooming

Guinea pig nails require regular trims (whenever needed by your pet). Starting at a young age, trim the nails using a small animal nail clipper. Use care to note the "quick" and avoid cutting into the living part of the nail. A light shown from behind the nail will help you see the dark colored portion, which includes blood vessels. Cutting into the quick will be painful for your pet. If you accidentally cut into the quick, the bleeding that results can be controlled with a styptic pencil. To avoid injury, cut the nail cleanly about an eighth of an inch (0.3 centimeters) beyond the end of the quick. If you start nail clipping early and do it carefully, your pet will become accustomed to this needed care.

Guinea pigs seldom need baths. If they are required, use a shampoo specially formulated for small animals. Use of shampoos formulated for humans will dry the skin of a guinea pig. Bathe guinea pigs in a shallow bowl of warm water and avoid getting water or shampoo into their ears and eyes. Be sure to rinse thoroughly and dry your pet immediately to prevent chills. Guinea pigs with long hair need occasional brushing and grooming to keep hair clean and prevent matting.

■ BREEDING AND REPRODUCTION

In general, veterinarians do not recommend that individual pet owners attempt to breed guinea pigs. It is often difficult to find homes for young guinea pigs with caring and responsible pet owners. Breeding often reduces the lifespan of female guinea pigs and starting to breed after 8 months of age can be very dangerous for a female guinea pig. The cause of this is the normal stiffening of the symphysis (a joint of tough fibrous cartilage between the 2 pubic bones of the pelvis) when the female reaches adulthood. Sows who reach adulthood without a prior pregnancy may not be able to deliver their young normally. Cesarean sections are rarely successful in guinea pigs even when performed by a veterinarian who has experience with guinea pigs.

Spaying or neutering of pet guinea pigs can be done by a veterinarian experienced in dealing with small animals, but the surgery can be expensive and does carry risks. Neutering a male is generally easier than spaying a female. However, guinea pigs often do not react well to surgery, anesthesia, or being kept in unfamiliar surroundings. The safest, easiest, and least expensive way to prevent breeding is to house male and female guinea pigs separately.

If you do decide to have your guinea pig spayed or neutered, seek out a veterinarian who has successfully done a large number of these surgeries. After the surgery, keep your pet quiet and separated from other guinea pigs while recovering. A small, clean cage with towels for bedding works well. The towels should be changed at least twice a day. Check to see that the guinea pig is eating and drinking; extra vitamin C may also be helpful.

Male guinea pigs (boars) mature sexually and can mate as young as 3 months of age. Female guinea pigs (sows) mature sexually as young as 2 months of age (55 to 70 days). Females can have estrous or fertile periods at any time of the year, but they are most common in the spring. The estrous cycle length is 16 days. A female is fertile for about 6 to 11 hours, most often during night hours. They begin a new estrous cycle shortly after giving birth.

The guinea pig gestation period is 59 to 73 days. The litter size ranges from 1 to

8 pups, but a litter of 2 to 4 is more common. A female can give birth to up to 5 litters per year. When a guinea pig is about to give birth, any male guinea pigs near her will gather around and try to become the dominant male in order to both protect the female and mate with her. The female has a short postpartum estrus that will last for only about half a day and, without a dominant male, all of the males will try to mate with the new mother.

Care of Newborns

Newborn guinea pigs weigh about 3.5 ounces (100 grams). Even at such a small size, they have hair and are able to see and run. They will nurse from their mother, but are able to nibble at solid food (such as moistened pellets) within 2 days. The mother has a single pair of mammary glands from which the newborns will nurse until about 3 weeks of age. When they reach about 6 ounces (180 grams), the offspring will stop nursing and eat the same foods as their parents.

It is important to begin to carefully handle young guinea pigs when they are only 2 or 3 weeks old. This is the period when young guinea pigs will develop bonds with humans and learn to accept being held.

■ DISORDERS AND DISEASES

Health problems among guinea pigs that live alone are usually related to aging, dental disease, reproductive disorders, injury, or improper care. Infectious diseases such as certain viruses and bacteria usually occur only in guinea pigs that live with other guinea pigs. Intestinal parasites are not common. Tumors are rare in young guinea pigs, but are more common in guinea pigs that are more than 5 years old. Treatment of infectious diseases can be complicated by the fact that guinea pigs are more sensitive to antibiotics than other types of pets.

Prevention of health problems in guinea pigs is key. A proper diet that does not change from day to day, clean water, bedding materials that are gentle on your pet's skin, frequent cleaning and disinfecting of the cage, a low-stress environment, and sufficient exercise all help to prevent illness.

Sickness causes guinea pigs to be stressed; if your pet is sick, hold it as little as possible. Antibiotics can cause problems in guinea pigs' digestive tracts, so your pet may not tolerate these medications. Most disease treatments should include extra vitamin C. Diarrhea and other illnesses may cause your guinea pig to become dehydrated. Signs of dehydration include dry stools, dark urine, or skin "tenting" (if you pinch the skin it does not settle back to normal immediately but instead remains standing up for a few seconds). If your pet is dehydrated, your veterinarian may provide fluid treatment. Animals that will not eat may require a stomach tube.

Antibiotics

Guinea pigs are very sensitive to the effects of many antibiotics. These toxic effects may occur directly as a result of the medication (as in the case of the antibiotics streptomycin and dihydrostreptomycin). The antibiotics may also upset the balance of the bacteria that usually live in your pet's intestines. Many antibiotics, including penicillin, ampicillin, lincomycin, clindamycin, vancomycin, erythromycin, tylosin, tetracycline, and chlortetracycline, can cause this problem. If a guinea pig takes certain antibiotics, it may develop diarrhea, loss of appetite, dehydration, or a drop in body temperature. If treatment continues, it may die in less than a week. Inadequate nutrition and vitamin C deficiency can make your pet more likely to develop these problems. Even guinea pigs that do not show signs of problems with antibiotics may die suddenly. Your veterinarian can diagnose the toxic effects of antibiotics in your pet by examining the animal and testing its feces.

There is no effective treatment for this condition other than general support and stopping the antibiotics. In general, you should avoid giving your guinea pig any antibiotics unless specifically directed by a veterinarian familiar with these animals. If your guinea pig must take antibiotics, you will need to monitor its health carefully. If your pet develops diarrhea or stops eating during treatment, contact your veterinarian immediately. Antibiotic ointments used on the skin can be toxic if your pet licks or eats them.

Digestive Disorders

Digestive disorders in guinea pigs may be caused by infections or by an improper diet.

Diarrhea

Many types of bacteria, viruses, and parasites can upset a guinea pig's digestive system. Some signs that your pet's digestive system is upset are: diarrhea, weight loss, loss of energy, lack of appetite, and dehydration. Guinea pigs affected by these illnesses may die suddenly without seeming sick. Others may have a range of signs such as lack of energy, lack of appetite, rough fur coat, staining of the fur around the genital area with feces, loose stools, hunched posture, lack of energy, dull eyes, dehydration, weight loss, pain when the abdomen is touched or pressed, fever, or a low body temperature.

Treatment for diarrhea is usually the same, no matter what the cause. Roughage (fiber in the diet) should be increased and grains and sugars decreased. One way to do this is to provide hay in addition to commercial guinea pig feed. Feeding your guinea pig plain yogurt with active cultures, or a commercial supplement called a probiotic with live cultures, may help to restore the healthy balance of "good" bacteria in its digestive tract. Check with your veterinarian regarding the use of yogurt. It is important that your pet drink enough water. If your guinea pig will not voluntarily drink sufficient water, your veterinarian may provide additional fluids by injection. Antibiotics should only be used when absolutely necessary because their use can worsen the imbalance of bacteria in the digestive tract. Follow the treatment program prescribed by your veterinarian carefully. Keeping your

guinea pig's bedding, water bottle, and housing clean and sanitized and promptly removing uneaten food can help prevent infection by reducing the level of disease-causing organisms.

Dental Disease

Guinea pigs drool whenever there is a problem with chewing or swallowing. This condition is sometimes referred to as **slobbers**. The cause is usually a problem with the alignment of the teeth (called malocclusion). Malocclusion may occur due to heredity, lack of vitamin C, injury, or imbalances of certain minerals in the diet. The teeth of guinea pigs grow continuously throughout the animal's life. If the teeth or jaws do not meet properly, the teeth often become overgrown and chewing food becomes difficult. As a result, your pet may develop weight loss, bleeding from the mouth, or abscesses in the roots of its teeth that may spread infection to the animal's sinuses. These kinds of problems are very common in guinea pigs.

If your pet is slobbering or drooling, your veterinarian will evaluate this problem carefully. The molars in the back of the mouth are often the cause of this problem, even though teeth in the front of the mouth may seem normal. Some teeth may need to be clipped or filed to help your pet's jaw close properly. If the problem continues, monthly dental visits with your veterinarian may be necessary.

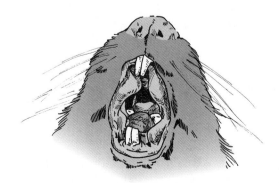

Normal teeth in an adult guinea pig

Eye and Ear Disorders

Signs of **conjunctivitis (pink eye)** include fluid oozing or dripping from the eye, inflammation of the lining of the eye, and redness around the edge of the eyelids. These infections are usually caused by bacteria, such as *Bordetella* or *Streptococcus* species, that cause general upper respiratory system disease (*see* page 935). Treatment may include antibiotic eye drops and antibiotics that affect your pet's whole body. An easy way to administer eye drops is to wrap the guinea pig securely in a towel first. As always with guinea pigs, watch your pet's reactions to the medication carefully.

Ear infections are rare in guinea pigs. When they do occur, they are usually the result of bacterial infection. They may occur at the same time as pneumonia or other respiratory disease. Signs of infection may include pus or discharge from the ears; however, sometimes there are no signs of infection. In severe cases, the animal may become deaf. If the infection spreads from the middle ear to the inner ear, your pet may show signs of problems with its nervous system, such as imbalance, tilting head, walking in circles, or rolling on the ground. The usual treatment is to help alleviate signs. Treatment for the ear infection itself does not usually work.

Nutritional Disorders

The most common nutritional disorder in guinea pigs is a lack of vitamin C. Loss of appetite also occurs and is usually a sign of another problem such as disease or problems with the teeth.

Vitamin C Deficiency (Scurvy)

Like people, apes, and monkeys, guinea pigs cannot produce their own vitamin C. If they do not get enough of this vitamin in their diet, their bodies' supply of vitamin C disappears quickly. This can cause problems with blood clotting and with the production of collagen, a protein necessary for healthy skin and joints. Reduced collagen can cause problems walking, swollen joints, and bleeding under the skin, in the

Some Fruits and Vegetables with High Vitamin C Content

- Turnip greens (260 milligrams per cup)
- Kale (192 milligrams per cup)
- Parsley (140 milligrams per cup)
- Green peppers (120 milligrams per cup)
- Strawberries (100 milligrams per cup)
- Broccoli florets (87 milligrams per cup; broccoli stems contain no vitamin C)
- Cabbage (50 milligrams per cup)
- Oranges (50 milligrams per cup)

muscles, in the membranes around the skull, in the brain, and in the intestines. Guinea pigs with a vitamin C deficiency may be weak, lack energy, and walk gingerly or with a limp. They may have a rough hair coat, lose their appetite, lose weight, have diarrhea, become ill, or die suddenly. Your veterinarian can diagnose vitamin C deficiency by finding out what your pet's diet is like, and by examining your pet, looking especially for bleeding or joint problems.

Some guinea pigs may develop a vitamin C deficiency even when they get enough vitamin C in their diets. This can happen if they have other illnesses or problems that prevent them from eating enough or prevent their bodies from absorbing vitamin C properly. Treatment includes giving your pet vitamin C daily, either by mouth (as directed by your veterinarian) or by injection at your veterinarian's office for 1 to 2 weeks. Multivitamins are not recommended because your pet may have problems with some of the other vitamins contained in them. To prevent vitamin C deficiency, guinea pig food should contain at least 10 milligrams of vitamin C daily (30 milligrams for pregnant females).

Appetite Loss

Loss of appetite can happen for many reasons, including disease, recovery from surgery, exposure to drafts, not having access to enough fresh water, not being able to chew properly because of an under-bite or overbite, and a condition called **ketosis**, in which your pet's body produces too much of one of the byproducts of digestion. Changes in the type of feed or water, or in the bowl or bottle that your pet eats or drinks from, may also trigger loss of appetite. If nothing is done for a guinea pig that is not eating, its condition may worsen very quickly, resulting in liver problems and death. Ketosis, which may be irreversible, can develop even in guinea pigs that begin to eat again. Your veterinarian will determine appropriate treatment, which may include giving your pet special foods such as a commercial hand-feeding formula or regular pelleted chow that has been ground up, vegetable baby foods, and vitamin C. Guinea pigs that refuse to eat may temporarily need to be force-fed by your veterinarian or by you if longer-term care is needed.

Metabolic Disorders

The most common metabolic disorders in guinea pigs involve abnormal metabolism of the mineral calcium.

Hardening of the Organs (Metastatic Calcification)

Guinea pigs that suffer from metastatic calcification (a hardening of the internal organs that spreads throughout the body) often die suddenly without any signs of illness. This condition usually occurs in male guinea pigs that are more than 1 year old. If your pet does have signs, they can include weight loss, muscle or joint stiffness, or increased urination (as part of kidney failure). The cause of this condition is uncertain, but is probably related to diets that have too much of the minerals calcium and phosphorus and not enough of the minerals magnesium and potassium. Most high-quality commercial guinea pig feed is formulated to contain the correct amounts of these vitamins and minerals. Check the nutrition information on the package label before buying pellets for your guinea pig, and do not give additional vitamin or mineral supplements.

Pregnancy Toxemia (Ketosis)

Ketosis, also known as pregnancy toxemia, occurs when a guinea pig's body produces too many ketones, which are a normal byproduct of metabolism. There are many causes of pregnancy toxemia in guinea pigs. These include obesity, large litter size, loss of appetite during the late stages of pregnancy, not eating enough, not exercising enough, environmental stress, and underdeveloped blood vessels in the uterus (an inherited condition). This problem usually happens in the last 2 to 3 weeks of pregnancy, or in the first week after a guinea pig gives birth. It most commonly affects guinea pigs that are pregnant with their first or second litters.

Although it occurs most often in pregnant female guinea pigs, ketosis can also happen in obese guinea pigs (male or female). A guinea pig may die suddenly of ketosis without ever demonstrating signs of illness. In other cases, a sick guinea pig has worsening signs that can include loss of energy, lack of appetite, lack of desire to drink, muscle spasms, lack of coordination or clumsiness, coma, and death within 5 days. Ketosis may cause fetal guinea pigs to die in the uterus.

Your veterinarian can diagnose ketosis by a blood test, and may also be able to identify a fatty liver and bleeding or cell death in the uterus or placenta. Treatment does not usually help, but options include giving your pet the medications propylene glycol, calcium glutamate, or steroids. However, once a guinea pig starts showing signs of this illness, the outcome is usually not good. To prevent ketosis, make sure your pet eats a high quality food throughout pregnancy, but limit the amount of food you give your pet in order to prevent obesity. Preventing exposure to stress in the last few weeks of pregnancy may also help.

Calcium Deficiency (Pregnant Females)

Because pregnancy and nursing require extra nutrients, pregnant guinea pigs may develop a sudden calcium deficiency. This happens most often in obese or stressed guinea pigs, or guinea pigs that have already been pregnant several times. The deficiency usually develops in the 1 to 2 weeks before, or shortly after, giving birth. In much the same way as in guinea pigs with pregnancy toxemia (*see* above), guinea pigs with this condition may die suddenly without signs, or may get sick slowly, with signs such as dehydration, depression, loss of appetite, muscle spasms, and convulsions. Your veterinarian will be able to identify similar problems as in a guinea pig with pregnancy toxemia, except they will likely be more severe. Guinea pigs with calcium deficiency should be treated with the mineral calcium gluconate. To prevent calcium deficiency, feed your pet only high-quality commercial guinea pig feed.

Lung and Airway Disorders

Respiratory diseases in guinea pigs can quickly become serious. If you notice that your guinea pig is having difficulty breathing, see your veterinarian as soon as possible.

Pneumonia

Pneumonia, or inflammation of the lungs, is the most frequent cause of death in guinea pigs. Pneumonia in guinea pigs is usually caused by bacterial infection (most often *Bordetella bronchiseptica*, but other bacteria such as *Streptococcus pneumoniae* or *Streptococcus zooepidemicus* may also be the cause). In rare cases, it may be caused by a type of virus known as adenovirus. All of these infectious agents can cause illness without leading to pneumonia (*see* below).

Signs of pneumonia include oozing or discharge from the nose, sneezing, and difficulty breathing. In addition, guinea pigs with pneumonia often suffer from inflammation of the eyes (commonly called pink eye), fever, weight loss, depression, or loss of appetite. Sudden death can occur when there are outbreaks among groups of guinea pigs. Your veterinarian can diagnose pneumonia from an examination or from special tests performed on the fluid that may be oozing from your pet's eyes or

nose. X-rays may also show pneumonia in the lungs.

In general, treatment for a guinea pig with pneumonia is really treatment for the signs of pneumonia instead of the pneumonia itself. This can include administering fluids (to ward off dehydration), forced feeding if necessary, oxygen therapy to help with breathing, and vitamin C. If the pneumonia is caused by bacterial infection, your veterinarian will likely prescribe longterm antibiotics. Although they can be toxic in guinea pigs (*see* page 931), certain antibiotics are safer than others, and your veterinarian may select one of these if needed. Commonly, the antibiotic is compounded into an oral suspension, which should then be given as directed. Watch any guinea pig receiving antibiotic treatment carefully. If the antibiotics cause diarrhea, the treatment should be stopped immediately and your veterinarian contacted. If you have more than 1 guinea pig, preventing and controlling outbreaks of pneumonia requires keeping your pets and their cages or tanks clean at all times, and removing guinea pigs that are sick from the company of the others.

Bordetella bronchisepta Infection

Guinea pigs without signs of illness may be infected with these bacteria in their nose or throat. Sometimes there can be an outbreak among groups of guinea pigs, during which all get sick and die quickly. Infection can be transmitted from one guinea pig to another when droplets are sprayed into the air by sneezing or coughing; in its genital form, infection can also be transmitted by sexual contact. Other animals, such as dogs, cats, rabbits, and mice, may be infected with these bacteria without showing any signs of illness, so pet owners should avoid letting their guinea pigs come into contact with other animals.

Streptococcosis

Guinea pigs may be infected with the *Streptococcus pneumoniae* bacteria without seeming sick. The bacteria can cause a sudden illness in previously healthy guinea pigs when they become stressed or stop eating; this can lead to death. One guinea pig can infect another by direct contact or by sneezing or coughing. Signs of streptococcosis include enlarged lymph nodes and difficulty breathing. Your veterinarian can spot other signs of infection with this bacteria, such as inflammation of the inner ear or eardrum (otitis media), inflammation of the joints (arthritis), and inflammation of the lining of the lungs, heart, abdomen, or uterus. He or she can diagnose streptococcosis based on these signs, other examination findings, and laboratory tests. Certain antibiotics can prevent one sick guinea pig from spreading the infection to other guinea pigs, but guinea pigs that do not seem sick may still be infected.

Adenovirus Infection

There is a type of adenovirus that is specific to guinea pigs. It may cause pneumonia (*see* page 935), but many guinea pigs have this virus without any signs of illness and are called carriers. Carriers can suddenly become sick as a result of stress or anesthesia. This occurs more often in guinea pigs that are young, old, or that have immune systems that are not working properly. Guinea pigs do not usually die from this virus, but those that do die often die suddenly without seeming sick. Signs of illness are similar to those seen in other viral or bacterial infections and include breathing difficulties, discharge from the nose, and weight loss.

Reproductive Disorders

Common reproductive problems in guinea pigs may involve the ovaries or breasts. There is also a metabolic disorder associated with improper calcium levels during pregnancy.

Ovarian cysts are very common in female guinea pigs between 18 months and 5 years of age. The cysts usually occur in both ovaries, but occasionally only the right ovary is affected. The cysts can often be felt in the abdomen. Other signs may include loss of appetite, energy, and sometimes hair loss on or around the abdomen.

To confirm the diagnosis, your veterinarian may use ultrasonography or x-rays. The only effective treatment is spaying (removing the ovaries and the uterus). If left untreated, the cysts may continue to grow and could potentially burst, placing the guinea pig's life in danger.

Mastitis is inflammation of the mammary glands. It is usually caused by a bacterial infection. This often occurs during the period when a female guinea pig's offspring are suckling. Injury—such as cuts or scrapes in the skin—can make it easier for bacteria in the environment to enter the body and cause infection. Mastitis is a painful and serious condition. The milk glands become painful and enlarged, warm, firm, and bluish in color. Without prompt treatment, the infection may spread to the guinea pig's bloodstream and cause fever, lack of appetite, depression, dehydration, a lack of milk production, neglect of offspring, and death. Milk may be thick or bloody and clotted. Your veterinarian may treat mastitis with appropriate antibiotics. To prevent this condition, make sure your pet is well taken care of, its living quarters are clean and sanitary, and its bedding does not cause irritation.

Bordetella **bacteria** can infect guinea pig genitals and can be spread by sexual contact. Infection can cause infertility, stillbirth, or sudden death of guinea pig fetuses in the uterus.

Because pregnancy and nursing require extra nutrients, pregnant guinea pigs may develop a sudden **calcium deficiency**. (For a more detailed discussion of CALCIUM DEFICIENCY, *see* page 934.)

Dystocia (difficulty giving birth) in female guinea pigs is caused by the normal stiffening of the tough fibrous cartilage which joins the 2 pubic bones. When the cartilage (the symphysis) stiffens, it limits the spread of the pubic bones. If the symphysis has not been stretched by a previous birth, the female will be unable to deliver her offspring normally. Cesarean sections are very risky for guinea pigs and the survival rate for the mother is poor. The safest option is to either breed the female between 4 and 5 months of age or prevent pregnancy altogether by housing male and female guinea pigs separately or by spaying and neutering.

Skin Disorders

Skin problems in guinea pigs are often first noticed as patches of hair loss. Several underlying problems can lead to hair loss, including infestations of fur mites or lice, ringworm, or fighting between incompatible animals. Another skin problem, pododermatitis, affects the feet.

Fur Mites

Severe infestation by fur mites may cause hair loss or itching along the rear end of a guinea pig's body. Some types of mites cause no signs, others cause hair loss but do not seem to affect the skin, and still others burrow into the skin and may cause intense itching, hair loss, and skin inflammation. This latter type of mite usually infects the inner thighs, shoulders, and neck. The skin underneath the affected fur may be dry or oily and thickened or crusty. In severely affected animals, the affected areas may become infected, which can cause the animals to lose weight, have low energy, or run around the cage. Left untreated, convulsions and death may result. Guinea pigs catch fur mites from other guinea pigs or from objects that are contaminated such as bedding. Your veterinarian can diagnose this condition either by examining your pet's fur or by looking at scrapings from your pet's skin under a microscope. To treat fur mites, your veterinarian will probably prescribe a powder or spray to be applied to your pet's skin or give your pet a series of injections. Infestations can be minimized or prevented by making sure that living quarters are clean and sanitary, and minimizing your pet's stress levels.

Lice

Guinea pigs that are infested with lice do not usually have signs, but in severe cases lice can cause itching, hair loss, and inflammation of the skin around the neck

Fur mites may cause hair loss or itching.

and ears. You can see the lice by looking at a piece of your pet's hair under a magnifying glass. To treat lice, your veterinarian will probably prescribe a powder or spray to be applied to your pet's skin. To prevent this condition, keep the guinea pig's cage clean and sanitary.

Ringworm

Skin infections in guinea pigs are most often caused by the fungus *Trichophyton mentagrophytes*, and less often by *Microsporum* species. The primary sign of ringworm is bald patches, usually starting at the head. The bald patches generally have crusty, flaky, red patches within them. When these patches appear on the face, it is usually around the eyes, nose, and ears. The disease may also spread to the back. A guinea pig can catch ringworm from another guinea pig or from contaminated objects such as bedding.

Your veterinarian can tell if your pet is infected with this condition by looking at the red patches on its skin, by shining a special ultraviolet light on its skin, or by a laboratory test. Ringworm usually goes away on its own if you take good care of your pet and keep its cage or tank clean and sanitary. The red, flaky patches can become infected, which causes them to become inflamed and pus-filled. Treatment is a 5- to 6-week course of an antifungal medicine called griseofulvin given by mouth. If there are only 1 or 2 bald patches or red, flaky areas that have not spread, they can be treated by applying an antifungal ointment recommended by your veterinarian every day for 7 to 10 days.

Ringworm is highly contagious to humans and other animals. If handling an infected guinea pig is necessary, you should wear disposable gloves or wash your hands thoroughly with soap and warm water after handling.

Barbering

Guinea pigs may chew or tear their own or each other's hair as a result of conflicts between adult males or between adults and juveniles. This is referred to as barbering. When this happens, the hair loss tends to be in patches, and there may be evidence of bite marks or skin inflammation underneath the fur. Barbering may be prevented by separating affected animals, minimizing stress, weaning baby guinea pigs from their mothers early, and feeding animals long-stemmed hay. Hair loss can also be caused by genetic problems or problems in metabolism, or the body's breakdown of food into energy; this is especially true in female guinea pigs that have been used for breeding. Young guinea pigs that are weaning from their mothers may have hair thinning as their coat changes to coarser adult fur, or if their diet does not have enough protein.

Pododermatitis (Bumblefoot)

Your pet's footpads can become inflamed, develop sores, or become overgrown over the course of many months. *Staphylococcus aureus* bacteria are often the cause and can enter your pet's feet through tiny cuts or scrapes. Factors that increase the risk of infection include obesity, wire floor caging, poor sanitation, and injury. When pododermatitis lasts for many months, it can lead to serious complications such as swelling of the lymph nodes, arthritis, inflammation of the tendons, and a buildup of a protein called amyloid in the kidney, liver, hormone glands, spleen, and pancreas. Your veterinarian can diagnose this condition by examining your guinea pig and by doing laboratory tests. If it is detected early, the condition may be treated simply by switching your pet's living quarters to ones with a smooth bottom, improving sanitation, and changing the bedding to softer material. Your veterinarian will likely clean any wounds, clip the hair around the affected areas, and trim any overgrown nails. Affected feet should be soaked in an antibiotic solution, and antibiotic ointment should be applied. In severe cases, animals may need antibiotics and pain medications. Guinea pigs that do not respond to therapy may require amputation of the affected area to avoid more serious complications.

Disorders Affecting Multiple Body Systems

Some guinea pig diseases affect more than one body system. These are also known as multisystemic or generalized diseases.

Enlarged Lymph Nodes ("Lumps" or Lymphadenitis)

Lymph nodes are glands that are located throughout the body that help fight infection. The lymph nodes around the neck often become enlarged or inflamed in guinea pigs. The usual cause of this problem is bacteria, most often *Streptococcus zooepidemicus*. The infected lymph nodes may become swollen and filled with pus (abscesses), sometimes only on one side. The infection can spread and cause an ear infection, inflammation of the eye, pneumonia, and toxins in the blood in younger animals. Other signs that you or your veterinarian might notice depend on which lymph nodes are affected, but may include tilting of the head, inflammation of the sinuses, inflammation of the eye, trouble breathing, skin that is pale or has a blue tint, blood or protein in the urine, fetal death or stillbirth in pregnant guinea pigs, arthritis, or inflammation of certain internal organs or tissues.

Guinea pigs catch this illness from other infected guinea pigs that are sneezing or coughing, by genital contact, or through cuts or scrapes in the skin or in the mouth. Your veterinarian can diagnose this condition by examination and laboratory tests. Antibiotics may or may not eliminate the infection. Abscesses might break open on their own, or they may be surgically opened and drained or removed. However, this may cause the bacteria to enter your pet's bloodstream. To help prevent infection of the lymph nodes, avoid any harsh or irritating bedding or food. Jaws that do not close properly or overgrown teeth should be fixed. Infections of the respiratory tract should be treated. Your pet's living quarters should be kept clean and sanitary, and sick animals should be housed away from other animals to prevent the spread of disease.

Salmonella Infection

Although occurrences are rare, *Salmonella* bacteria can infect guinea pigs. Some signs of infection include inflammation of the eye, fever, lack of energy, poor appetite, rough hair coat, enlarged spleen and liver, and swollen lymph nodes around the neck. The bacteria are spread by direct contact with infected guinea pigs or wild mice or rats or by sharing food, water, or bedding with infected animals. Fresh vegetables may also carry *Salmonella*. Because an animal that is treated may still continue to infect other animals even when it does not seem sick, treatment may not be recommended. Guinea pigs can spread *Salmonella* infection to humans by direct contact, so appropriate sanitation measures (such as wearing disposable gloves and washing hands thoroughly) should be taken when handling any sick guinea pig.

Yersinia Infection

Guinea pigs occasionally become infected with *Yersinia pseudotuberculosis* bacteria through contaminated food, bedding, or water. The bacteria can also enter a guinea pig's body through cuts or scrapes in the skin or through inhalation. If a guinea

---

Diseases that can be Spread from Guinea Pigs to People
Scabies
Ringworm
Salmonellosis
Campylobacteriosis
Yersiniosis

---

pig becomes infected, the illness may take several courses: 1) infection may spread to the bloodstream and cause sudden death; 2) infected guinea pigs may lose weight, develop diarrhea, and die over the course of 3 to 4 weeks; 3) swollen lymph nodes develop in the neck or shoulder; or 4) your pet may be infected without seeming sick. Veterinarians diagnose this infection by laboratory tests and examination of the sick guinea pig. All guinea pigs that are infected with these bacteria, or that have lived in close quarters with an infected guinea pig, must be euthanized (put to sleep), and the living quarters must be thoroughly sanitized and disinfected.

Cancers and Tumors

Younger guinea pigs may develop skin tumors or leukemia (a cancer of the blood), but most types of cancer are not common in guinea pigs until they are 4 to 5 years old. After that age, between one-sixth and one-third of guinea pigs will develop a tumor. Tumors are more common in strains of guinea pigs that have been inbred. Treatment, if recommended, will depend on the type and location of the tumor.

Benign skin tumors called **trichoepitheliomas** often occur in guinea pigs, commonly at the base of the tail. These can be easily removed with a simple surgical procedure.

Lymphosarcoma is the most common tumor in guinea pigs; it causes what is sometimes referred to as cavian leukemia. Signs may include a scruffy hair coat and occasionally masses in the chest area and/or an enlarged liver or spleen. The diagnosis is confirmed by a blood count and examination of fluids from the lymph nodes or chest cavity.

The outlook for survival is poor; most guinea pigs only live a few weeks after diagnosis.

CHAPTER 68

Hamsters

■ INTRODUCTION

Hamsters are rodents (members of the biological order Rodentia) and are distant relatives of mice and rats. Hamsters are small, almost tailless, relatively clean, affordable, easy to care for, and popular as pets.

The most common variety is the Syrian hamster, which is also known as the Golden hamster (*see* TABLE 9). This name comes from the coloring of the animal in its original wild home. Today, pet owners can find Syrian hamsters in many color and coat varieties. Other varieties kept as pets include the Russian dwarf hamster, Chinese hamster, and the European hamster (which is uncommon in the United States).

■ DESCRIPTION AND PHYSICAL CHARACTERISTICS

Adult Syrian hamsters are approximately 6 to 8 inches (15 to 20 centimeters) in length, and weigh 6 to 7 ounces (180

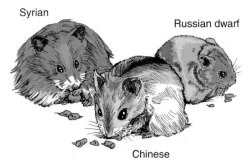

Syrian

Russian dwarf

Chinese

Different types of hamsters include the Syrian (golden), Chinese, and Russian dwarf.

to 210 grams). Most other varieties of hamsters are slightly smaller and weigh less. Hamsters kept as pets may live from 18 months to 3 years.

A unique feature of hamsters is the out-pouching of the checks on both sides of the mouth that extends along the sides of the head and neck all the way back to the shoulders. In the wild, these large pouches allow hamsters to gather food during foraging trips and then carry the food back to their nest for consumption later. Pet owners who suddenly see a fully distended pouch for the first time may fear their pet has some sort of fast-growing tumor or swelling.

Another unusual characteristic of hamsters is paired glands in the skin over the flanks. These glands appear as dark spots within the hair coat. They are much more obvious in males than in females. Hamsters use these glands to mark their territory. The glands also play a role in sexual behavior.

Most of the Syrian hamsters sold as pets originated in the Middle East or southeastern Europe. In their native environment, they live in dens beneath the ground where they store food and nest. They forage for food regularly, storing their finds in their pouches until they can carry it back to their dens. Most of the hamsters sold as pets today are the descendants of 3 littermates tamed in 1930.

■ SPECIAL CONSIDERATIONS

Hamsters are small animals with delicate bones that can be easily crushed if they are dropped or if they are handled

Table 9. Hamster Breeds Commonly Kept as Pets

Type	Color	Weight (grams)	Life Span (months)
Syrian	Golden originally, now bred in many colors	90 to 120	18 to 24
Chinese	Dark brown	40 to 60	30 to 36
Russian dwarf	Varied	35 to 50	18 to 24

roughly. In addition, they are nocturnal—meaning they are most active at night. Because of this, a hamster may not be the best pet to select for a young child.

While the popular Syrian or golden hamsters are normally classified as pets by regulatory agencies, some other types may be prohibited as foreign species. A check with your state's animal regulatory agency is advised before buying a hamster that is not a Syrian or golden hamster.

■ SELECTING A HAMSTER

When selecting a hamster as a possible pet, start by observing its environment. Does it appear and smell clean? Does the food appear fresh and are feeding containers clean? Are there sufficient water bottles for the number of animals in the cage? Are the water containers clean and without stains or deposits of foreign matter? Do the hamsters appear healthy? Do they have bright eyes? Are they alert and curious? Hamsters are most active at night, so you may want to consider selecting your new pet late in the afternoon or during evening hours.

Gently hold the animal you are considering. Most hamsters that have been held from a young age do not bite. Be cautious of any potential pet that does tend to bite. As you are holding the hamster, look carefully at its eyes; they should be clear and show an alert personality. Check the ears, feet, and fur. There should be no sign of injury, the toe nails should be unbroken and neatly trimmed, and the fur should be clean and without signs of mites, fleas, ringworm, or other diseases. Check the rump for any signs of problems. Avoid animals that show signs of diarrhea,

bloody discharge, irritation, or other problems. Check for any signs of excess drooling or slobbering, or any protruding teeth that could indicate a dental problem. Once you have looked at the general health of the animal, place the hamster in a confined area where it can move around. Does the animal move normally? Do not choose an animal that limps, appears lame, or is reluctant to move.

Before you make a commitment to purchase a pet, ask about having the animal checked by a veterinarian prior to purchase. If the seller will not permit a veterinarian check prior to purchase, ask about returns if the animal proves unhealthy after purchase. Responsible pet sellers will cooperate with veterinary checks.

If you do not have a cage for your hamster, consider asking the seller to hold your new pet for a day so that you can set up a proper home. Having the cage ready for your new pet will make the transition to your home less stressful for the hamster.

■ PROVIDING A HOME FOR A HAMSTER

Because of their small size, hamsters do not require large amounts of space compared to some other kinds of pets. In addition to a suitable cage, your hamster will need a balanced diet and regular time to play or exercise with you.

Housing

Your hamster will need a protected and safe environment within your home. Hamsters seem to prefer being housed in enclosures with solid floors, relatively deep bedding, and abundant nesting material.

This comes closest to the environments in which the animals lived in the wild. The enclosure should be secure; hamsters are outstanding escape artists and, once outside their cages, they are not only difficult to find, they are often reluctant to return to the cage.

Your hamster will need an enclosure with enough space to allow for some exercise, as well as areas for feeding and nesting. The enclosure should be at least 6 inches high, but enclosures 8 or more inches (20 centimeters or more) offer the advantage of allowing for deeper bedding. The floor should be solid and there should be no wood that can be gnawed and no sharp edges that might injure your pet. Smooth plastic or glass is preferred for cage walls, as wire can be chewed. Whatever cage or tank is selected, it should be easy to clean and sanitize, well ventilated, and easy to light. Ideally, a hamster's living environment should be kept at 64 to 79°F (17 to 26°C).

The hamster cage should be equipped with a water bottle with a sipping tip. The food container should be heavy (to resist tipping) and should have sides low enough for easy access to food but high enough to avoid accidental introduction of feces and urine. Ceramic dishes are good choices. All water and food containers should be easy to clean and sanitize.

Select bedding that is clean, nontoxic, absorbent, as dust-free as possible, and easy to change. Cedar chips and fresh pine materials should be avoided because of possible toxicity. Shredded paper (other than newspapers printed with conventional inks) and processed corn cobs make suitable bedding materials. For nesting materials, plain white facial tissues or unprinted paper towels cut into strips and placed on top of the bedding are well received by most hamsters. Cotton balls are potentially dangerous because the cotton can be caught in toe nails and feet and cause injury.

A nesting box made of sturdy cardboard or wood makes a suitable sleeping area.

A play area can be created using old packing tubes cut into short lengths; just be sure that the tube is large enough for your hamster to move through the space freely. For small hamsters, old toilet paper tubes make good running toys. In addition, boxes with holes cut into them make intriguing play areas for your hamster.

Hamsters are normally housed singly except during breeding periods. Sexually mature females are territorial and aggressive and frequently fight each other. Because of this, housing female hamsters in the same cage is not recommended. Breeding females are larger than mature males and the female hamster's aggressiveness often means that a male hamster will be injured by a female cage mate. Except while breeding, it is safest to house hamsters singly.

Diet

In the wild, hamsters eat both meat and vegetables. Commercially available food for mice and rats, which usually comes in pellet form, provides suitable nutrition as long as the food contains 15 to 20% protein. Extra vitamins are usually not necessary. Or you can feed commercially available pellets formulated for rabbits, which contain more fiber, or "roughage," than mice and rat food. If you are providing rabbit pellets for your hamster, you may choose to mix this in with mice and rat food occasionally. A few healthy treats—such as hay, fruits or vegetables, or chewy treats sold in pet stores—may be given but should be limited to not more than 10% of the total diet. Seeds should be given sparingly, because hamsters often prefer them over their pelleted food. Hamsters tend to hoard food, and will hide food pellets in their cheek pouches or around the floor of their cages. They usually eat their own feces.

Fresh, clean water should always be available. Your hamster's water bowl or bottle should be cleaned and sanitized regularly (usually daily) to prevent infection.

Exercise

Regular exercise is necessary for your hamster to stay happy and healthy. Often an exercise wheel is one part of providing the exercise your pet needs. Be sure to select a wheel with a solid running surface (to protect feet and bones). The wheel should also be large enough for your hamster to move freely inside and to easily enter and exit the wheel.

Pet stores often offer exercise balls that can confine the hamster while allowing it to move over a large area outside the cage. If buying an exercise ball for your hamster, be sure that the device is large enough for your pet, has sufficient ventilation, and is constructed securely. Even inside an exercise ball, hamsters can get into tight places and potentially hazardous situations. Keep a careful eye on your hamster if the animal is in an exercise ball and be sure to return your pet to its cage for food and, most critically, water after a reasonable exercise period.

Other encouragements to physical activity include providing a play area with tubes and boxes for play. Be sure all tubes and openings in boxes are large enough for your pet to easily enter and exit.

Temperament

Hamsters are active, curious, and fun to watch as they explore their environment. If they become accustomed to human handling early, they can be easily picked up and should not bite unless they are startled. Hamsters should not be housed in groups, as adults can become aggressive toward each other even if they are reared together.

Because they are nocturnal, hamsters are most active in the evening and at night and prefer to sleep during the day. Just as you do not like to be awakened or disturbed while you are sleeping, neither do hamsters. Plan your interaction with your hamster for the hours when the hamster is most likely to be awake and active. Evenings are usually good times for interactive play, cage cleaning, and other joint activity.

Hamsters are small animals; even the largest can sit comfortably on an adult human hand. Hamster bones and muscles are small and can be easily hurt. Handle these animals carefully and gently to avoid injuring them. One safe way to pick up a hamster is to put your hand under the entire animal and lift it gently. A second hand can then be placed gently over the animal to create a secure area.

ROUTINE HEALTH CARE

Locating a veterinarian for your hamster should not pose problems. Most small animal veterinarians will treat hamsters.

If you do not already have a good relationship with a veterinarian in your area, check with other pet owners for recommendations or consult your phone book's yellow pages. You can also go online and check the listings of your state's veterinary medical society. Call several practices. Select one that makes you feel comfortable, has experience in treating hamsters, and offers access to a 24-hour emergency care program. If you travel regularly, you may also want to ask about boarding for your hamster when you must be away from home.

Importance of Veterinary Care

There are many reasons for you to bring your hamster to a veterinarian for a health checkup as soon as possible, even before purchasing your pet. A prepurchase health checkup assures you that the hamster coming into your home is healthy. An early medical visit also establishes a basic medical record which your veterinarian can then use in keeping your pet healthy and in treating any medical conditions which may arise.

Signs of Illness

Pay attention to the way your pet routinely looks and acts, and how it interacts with you or with any cage mates. One good way to do this is to spend time with your hamster every day. This is not only a good way to develop a warm relationship with your pet, it gives you a regular opportunity to check for signs of illness. Problems that are noticed early are easier to solve (*see* BOX).

When a hamster is sick, it may also show signs of illness, such as weight loss, hunched posture, lack of energy, changes in the consistency of its fur or loss of fur, and difficulty breathing. Changes in behavior may also indicate illness; sick hamsters often stop exploring and playing in the cage as they usually do. Early signs of sickness include changes in the color, consistency, smell, and amount of urine and feces. The fur around a hamster's genitals should be checked for stains from feces, urine, or vaginal discharge. You should also keep an eye out for any fight wounds or other cuts and bruises that might become infected.

When you notice any changes in your hamster's appearance or behavior, you should take your hamster to your veterinarian for a checkup. The veterinarian may ask for a sample of your hamster's feces to check for worms or bacteria. He or she might check your hamster's mouth for overgrown teeth or cheek pouches that are blocked. Your hamster's ears and eyes will be examined to look for inflammation

How to Tell when Your Hamster is Sick
▨ Inactivity
▨ Loss of appetite or weight
▨ Discharge from the eyes, ears, or nose
▨ Hunched posture
▨ Abnormal walk
▨ Scruffy hair coat or hair loss
▨ Diarrhea ("wet tail")
▨ Trouble breathing

or oozing. Its feet should be examined for sores and overgrown or broken nails. Your veterinarian may push gently on your hamster's belly to feel for growths or lumps. As with humans, high temperature is a common sign of illness. So, your veterinarian will likely check your pet's temperature. A hamster's normal body temperature usually ranges from 98 to 101°F (36.7 to 38.3°C).

Hamsters are not normally aggressive, but they can become aggressive if they are startled or suddenly awakened, are sick, or are not handled gently. Therefore it may be easier to carefully scoop a sick hamster up in a small container than to pick it up with your hands.

Giving Medication

There are several ways to give medicine to hamsters. For pet owners, the most common method is by mouth. Often, you will be instructed to use a dropper to provide needed liquid medication. Take care to provide only the dosage prescribed by your veterinarian. Hamsters are very small and it is easy to overdose these small pets.

Veterinarians have additional options for providing necessary medications. For example, the veterinarian can place medicines directly into a hamster's stomach or give injections under the skin or into the abdomen.

Certain antibiotics can cause problems with hamsters' digestive tracts, so your pet may not tolerate these medications. Do not use antibiotic creams or other

Hunched posture or fluffed fur in a hamster may be signs of illness.

medications containing antibiotics on your hamster without specific directions from your veterinarian. Using antibiotics on your hamster could endanger your pet's life.

Diarrhea and other illnesses can cause hamsters to become dehydrated rapidly. If your pet becomes dehydrated, your veterinarian may need to provide fluid treatment.

Preventive Care

Prevention is the key to keeping your hamster healthy. To prevent illness, make sure your hamster has a proper diet, access to clean water and bedding, and a clean and sanitary cage.

The most important step you can take, after being sure your hamster's home is kept clean, is to be sure your hamster cannot get out of its cage. Many hamsters are seriously injured when they escape from their cages.

When taking your hamster out of its cage, handle it gently but carefully. Active hamsters can be dropped or can fall off tables or other furniture. These falls often result in broken bones, head injuries, or other serious problems. Whenever your hamster is outside its cage (for example, when you are cleaning the cage), place the hamster in a secure place, such as a second hamster cage, to prevent the hamster from wandering off into dangerous areas. Do not assume that your hamster will sit idly on a table while you clean the cage. Their instinct is to wander off in search of food as their ancestors did in the wild. So be sure that any hamster outside of its cage is carefully protected and secure.

Vaccinations

There are currently no vaccines that are required or recommended for hamsters.

Dental Care

Like other rodents, hamsters have incisor teeth that grow continuously throughout their lives. All hamsters need food and other items to chew that allow them to wear down their teeth naturally. Overgrown teeth can cause drooling, loss of appetite, and weight loss. If your ham-

ster's teeth are not worn down through normal gnawing and eating, your veterinarian will need to trim them occasionally. Hamster food that is ground into a powder can get trapped in a hamster's back teeth, causing cavities.

Hamsters tend to have fewer dental problems than some other rodents. However, it is a good idea to ask your veterinarian to check your pet's teeth for overgrowth and other problems.

Household Hazards

The average home holds many hazards for hamsters. They love to gnaw on such things as electrical cords, telephone wires, and other potentially dangerous objects. They will also chew on furniture and take advantage of any opening to get into areas under the kitchen cabinets, beneath the refrigerator or the oven, or inside dryer vents. Because they are so small, hamsters are easy to step on, and even a small child weighs enough to seriously injure or kill a hamster by crushing it underfoot. Hamsters should be kept safe from larger household pets such as dogs and cats.

▓ BREEDING AND REPRODUCTION

The best time for hamsters to have offspring is when they are between 10 weeks and 15 months old. Breeders use pairs with 1 male and 1 female, as well as groups of hamsters with 1 male and multiple females. Breeding of hamsters is best left to experienced breeders, as hamsters (particularly females) can become aggressive during mating. Also, there are a number of genetic defects associated with various types of hamsters, so breeding hamsters without having knowledge of their genetic heritage is not recommended.

Pregnancies usually last from 16 to 22 days, depending on the type of hamster. (Syrian or golden hamster pregnancies tend to last 16 to17 days.) You may notice a slight increase in girth or a larger abdomen in a pregnant female a few days before she gives birth. As pregnant hamsters approach the time to deliver the litter, they may become restless and active and may have

If Your Hamster is Pregnant

Do:

- Provide extra bedding.
- Take the hamster to the veterinarian for a prenatal checkup.
- Be sure the mother has a good diet and plenty of water throughout her pregnancy.
- Take the pups to the veterinarian for a check at about 1 month of age.

Do Not:

- Do not stress the mother.
- Do not disturb a new mother or her pups until a week after the birth.
- Do not give solid food until the pups are about 10 days old.

vaginal bleeding. When they are ready to give birth, provide them with nesting material. This helps them feel secure, and lowers the chance that new mothers will abandon or eat their offspring. Mothers and litters should not be disturbed for at least 7 days after the offspring are born, especially if the mother has never given birth before. Fostering abandoned offspring onto a different mother is rarely successful. Limit your activity around the cage to providing food and water as needed.

Normal litters contain 6 to 8 pups, and offspring are weaned after about 21 to 28 days. The pups are hairless and their eyes and ears are closed; however, pups have their front teeth (incisors) at birth. In most cases, it is safe to slowly begin handling the pups when they are about 7 days old. Solid food moistened with water can be offered to pups starting at about 10 days of age. Food and water should be located close to the floor within easy reach.

DISORDERS AND DISEASES

Furnishing adequate housing, a good diet, and routine preventive care will go a long way toward keeping your hamster safe, happy, and healthy.

Heart and Blood Vessel Disorders

Blood clots sometimes occur in hamsters inside one of the upper chambers of the heart. This condition is called **atrial thrombosis.** The blockages are often found in the left side of the heart.

Congestive heart failure, a condition in which the heart muscle weakens and can-

not pump blood efficiently throughout the body, also affects hamsters (*see* page 65). Both of these conditions happen more frequently in older female hamsters and are often connected with amyloidosis (*see* page 952). Signs include shortness of breath, an irregular heartbeat, and a blue tint to the skin. There is no effective treatment; however, your veterinarian may be able to suggest ways of managing this condition for a period of time.

Digestive Disorders

Diarrhea is one of the most common digestive system problems in hamsters and can be caused by several different disorders. Diarrhea in hamsters is also sometimes called "wet tail" because of how a hamster looks when it has diarrhea. Constipation is another common digestive problem in hamsters.

Diarrhea

Proliferative enteritis, an inflammation that spreads throughout the small intestine, causes diarrhea in hamsters. The culprit is the bacteria *Lawsonia intracellularis*, which is most likely to infect hamsters that are stressed due to being transported, living in an overcrowded cage, surgery or illness, or changes in diet. The condition is more common in young hamsters and occurs rapidly. Many hamsters with this infection get very sick and die quickly. Usually, the fur around the tail and belly is wet and matted. Common signs of this disease include low energy levels, loss of appetite, and weight loss.

Your veterinarian will likely make a diagnosis using the signs and history, and

A hamster with diarrhea will often have a wet tail. Diarrhea can be rapidly fatal and requires prompt veterinary care.

the animal's positive response to treatment. To treat a hamster with this condition, your veterinarian may give it fluids (either by mouth or by injection) in case it is dehydrated, and possibly antibiotics, which can be mixed into the hamster's drinking water. Sick hamsters should be kept separate from other hamsters to prevent spreading the illness, and the cages of both the sick and healthy animals should be thoroughly cleaned and sanitized.

Tyzzer's disease, a digestive illness caused by the bacteria *Clostridium piliforme*, can have many of the same signs as proliferative enteritis, above. These include loss of appetite, dehydration, watery diarrhea, and sudden death. Hamsters catch this illness by eating feces that contain the bacteria. This illness is more common in hamsters that are young or stressed. Your veterinarian can diagnose this illness by examination or by doing laboratory tests. Blood tests are only sometimes accurate. Your veterinarian may treat your hamster with fluids and antibiotics. Hamsters that have this illness or that have been in close contact with sick hamsters should be kept separate from other hamsters to prevent spreading the disease. The bacteria can form spores and spread through the environment, so the cage, food containers, and water sources used by both sick and healthy animals must be thoroughly cleaned and sanitized.

Inflammation of the small intestines may be related to **antibiotic use.** A certain group of antibiotics, known as gram-positive spectrum antibiotics (some examples are lincomycin, clindamycin, ampicillin, vancomycin, erythromycin, penicillin, and cephalosporins), can be fatal for hamsters. These medicines can cause inflammation of the small intestines, resulting in diarrhea and death within 2 to 10 days. They kill the bacteria that usually live in a hamster's digestive tract and allow the overgrowth of other bacteria. The pouch at the end of the small intestines (called the cecum) becomes swollen with fluid, and the hamster bleeds from inside its intestines. Your veterinarian can diagnose this problem by finding out what medications your pet has taken recently, and doing special laboratory tests. The bacterial overgrowth sometimes happens in hamsters that have not taken antibiotics. Once a hamster has this condition, the outlook is not good. One possible treatment your veterinarian may suggest is force-feeding the sick hamster feces from a hamster that is not sick; these "healthy" feces may help to re-establish the proper balance of bacteria in the sick hamster's intestines.

Salmonellosis, an inflammation of the intestines caused by *Salmonella* bacteria, is not common in hamsters. The signs and treatment approach for this disease are described in the gerbil chapter (*see* page 923).

The signs of illness when a hamster has an ***Escherichia coli* infection** are similar to other illnesses that cause diarrhea in hamsters. You veterinarian can identify this illness with a special laboratory test. Treatment and prevention are similar to that of proliferative enteritis (*see* page 946).

Protozoa are a special kind of single-cell animal, different from bacteria and viruses, that also cause illness. Healthy hamsters often carry protozoa in their digestive tracts without being sick, but hamsters that are young or stressed may develop intestinal infections and diarrhea as a result. Your veterinarian can identify this illness by doing a test on your hamster's feces. Treatment includes adding the medication metronidazole to your pet's drinking water.

Pinworms, a type of internal parasite, are a rare cause of disease of the digestive tract in hamsters. Diagnosis and treatment are as described for gerbils (*see* page 923).

Tapeworms are relatively common in hamsters compared to mice and rats. Infected hamsters typically have no signs. When a hamster has a serious case, the tapeworms can cause inflammation and blockage of the intestines and infection of the lymph nodes. Diagnosis and treatment are described in the chapter on gerbils (*see* page 923).

Constipation

Hamsters may become constipated if they have intestinal parasites such as tapeworms, if they eat their bedding and their intestines get blocked, or if a portion of the intestine folds inside itself, a condition called an **intussusception**.

Intussusception can be caused by inflammation of the intestines, pregnancy, poor diet, or not enough drinking water. It is sometimes seen as a tubular structure that protrudes from the anus. This is considered a medical emergency and requires immediate veterinary attention and surgery. Intussusception is fatal if not treated, and the chances for recovery are guarded even with prompt surgery.

Treatment of constipation requires identifying and treating the cause of the constipation. It may be necessary to surgically remove a portion of the intestines, or to create a bypass between 2 portions of the intestines that are not normally connected.

Actinomycosis

Actinomycosis is an infection caused by the fungus *Actinomyces bovis*. It is rare in hamsters. This illness can lead to rupture of the salivary glands, which may ooze pus. Your veterinarian can diagnose this illness with a laboratory test. Treatment includes lancing and draining the infected area and prescribing appropriate antibiotics.

Inflammation and Scarring of the Liver (Cholangiofibrosis)

Older hamsters, particularly females, sometimes suffer from longterm inflammation and degeneration of the liver (cirrhosis). Blood tests will show increases in enzymes produced by the liver. The cause of the disease is unknown, and there is no effective treatment.

Eye and Ear Disorders

Conjunctivitis (pink eye) is an inflammation of the eye or swelling of the face that may be the result of injury, overgrown or diseased teeth, or teeth that are not aligned properly. It may also be caused by a bacterial infection, irritation from dust in the bedding, or bite wounds. Warm water can be used to help gently remove crusted material from around the eyes and open eyelids. Your veterinarian may flush the affected eye with saline solution, and may prescribe an antibiotic ointment or other treatment.

Protrusion of the eyeball from the socket is common in hamsters. It can occur due to an infection of the eye or from trauma. The condition may also occur when the hamster is restrained too tightly by holding the skin at the back of the neck. This should be considered an emergency that requires veterinary attention. The sooner treatment is given, the more likely it is that the eye can be saved.

Bone, Joint, and Muscle Disorders

Lameness in hamsters is often caused by muscle or tendon strains. Broken bones most often occur when a hamster's leg becomes trapped in a wire exercise wheel or wire or mesh caging materials. For this reason, solid surface wheels and cage materials are recommended. Broken bones, including a broken back, may result if the hamster is dropped or falls from a height (such as a table top). Because hamsters are very small animals, broken limbs are difficult to treat. Any time your pet appears in pain or is reluctant to move, it is time to seek immediate professional help.

Nutritional Disorders

If a pregnant hamster does not get enough vitamin E, her fetuses can suffer degeneration of the nervous system. When this happens, the pregnant hamster usually delivers weak or stillborn offspring. She may also eat her offspring. Your veterinarian might notice bleeding or swelling in the skull or spine of the offspring. Adult hamsters with vitamin E deficiency can have muscle disorders or weakness, which can lead to paralysis. You can prevent this from happening by providing your pet with an appropriate, balanced diet. If you suspect your hamster is pregnant, check with your veterinarian regarding the amount of vitamin E in her diet.

Lung and Airway Disorders

Because of their small size, lung and other airway disorders in hamsters can quickly become serious. If you notice your hamster is wheezing or having difficulty breathing, see your veterinarian promptly.

Pneumonia

Pneumonia, or inflammation of the lungs, is not common in hamsters. When it does occur, it is usually the result of infection with one or more kinds of bacteria, either by themselves or together with viruses and other types of infectious agents. The bacteria that often cause pneumonia are normally present in the respiratory or digestive system in small numbers. These bacteria can multiply and lead to illness, however, when sudden changes in a hamster's environment, especially temperature, cause stress. Stress makes it harder for a hamster's body to fight off infection.

Signs that a hamster is sick with pneumonia include pus or mucus oozing from the nose or eyes, difficulty breathing, loss of appetite, and lack of activity. Your veterinarian can diagnose pneumonia by doing an examination or performing laboratory tests on the discharge. Treatment is usually not effective, but antibiotics can help in mild cases. Other things that can make a sick hamster more comfortable include giving it fluids by injection, keeping its cage warm and dry, and minimizing stress. If several hamsters live together, it is important to remove the sick hamster from the other hamsters, and to keep the living area clean and sanitary.

Sendai Virus (Parainfluenza 1) Infection

This virus is rare in hamsters, but it is highly contagious. The virus is spread from one hamster to another by sneezing or coughing. In newborn hamsters, this virus can cause dripping or oozing from the nose, trouble breathing, pneumonia, and death. Adult hamsters usually do not have signs. Bacterial infection can occur simultaneously with the viral infection. Your veterinarian can identify this illness by laboratory tests.

There is no treatment for the virus itself, but your veterinarian can treat the effects of the virus, with fluids under the skin for dehydrated animals, food supplements, and antibiotics if your hamster has a bacterial infection. To prevent infection with this virus, make sure your hamster does not come into contact with sick hamsters or other rodents and keep its cage clean.

Reproductive Disorders

Breeding female hamsters may have smaller litters or become infertile as a result of old age, malnutrition, a cold environment, not having enough nesting material, and not having a normal estrous cycle. Hamster reproduction is sensitive to the seasons and the cycle of light throughout the day and night. Also, a male and female pair may simply not be compatible. Hamster fetuses may die in the womb, and pregnant females may abandon or eat their offspring for a variety of reasons. These include eating a poor diet, having a large litter, being in a crowded or noisy environment, being handled too often, having a male in the cage after birth, not having enough nesting materials, not producing enough milk, having inflamed milk glands, or having sick or deformed offspring.

Milk (mammary) gland infection is usually caused by *Streptococcus* bacteria.

Infection usually becomes obvious 7 to 10 days after the female gives birth. Affected milk glands are swollen and may discharge pus or mucus. Mothers may eat their young as a result of this condition. Your veterinarian can identify the cause of the infection with a laboratory test, and may prescribe antibiotics for treatment.

Skin Disorders

Many skin disorders are caused by infections or parasites. You can help keep your hamster healthy by regularly checking its skin for signs of hair loss or other developing problems.

Skin Abscesses

Skin abscesses are infected pockets of pus under the skin. They are usually caused by bacterial infection of wounds received during fighting with cage mates or from injuries caused by sharp objects in the cage. Abscesses are often located around the head. If the lymph nodes around the neck are swollen, there may be an infection in the hamster's cheek pouches. In male hamsters, the glands over the hip called hypersecretory flank glands may be infected. Sometimes wood shavings from bedding can injure the feet or shoulders, which can lead to infection.

The particular type of bacteria causing the abscess is identified by a laboratory test. Treatment includes draining the abscess and antibiotics. For abscesses that have burst, your veterinarian will make sure all of the contents of the abscess have drained, and then flush the wound with an antibiotic liquid. Your hamster may also require antibiotic ointment. Abscesses that have not ruptured can be surgically removed and your veterinarian may inject antibiotics under the skin. If flank glands are infected, your veterinarian may shave the area around them, clean them, and apply ointment with antibiotics and steroids. Fighting hamsters should be separated from one another. Make sure your pet's cage has no sharp edges. Avoid bedding with wood shavings.

Hair loss can be a sign of several conditions and should be checked by your veterinarian.

Hair Loss (Alopecia)

Patchy hair loss can have many causes in hamsters. These include constant rubbing on parts of the cage, not enough protein in the diet, and hair chewing by cage mates (known as barbering). Hair loss may also be a sign of a type of T-cell lymphoma (a form of cancer) that involves the skin. This is relatively common in hamsters (*see* page 952). Infestation with mites, tumors in the adrenal glands, a thyroid gland imbalance, and problems with the kidneys are rarer conditions that can also cause hair loss.

Ringworm

Despite its name, ringworm is not caused by worms. Ringworm occurs when a hamster's skin becomes infected with a fungus. The most common ringworm-causing fungi are *Tricophyton mentagrophytes* and *Microsporum* species. Some hamsters have no signs. Other hamsters may have bald patches. These may be crusty, flaky, and red around the edges. Hamsters catch the disease from other animals or humans who are infected, or from infected objects such as bedding. Hamsters that spend time outside their cages may also be exposed to the fungi in your home. Your veterinarian can diagnose this condition by examining your pet, looking at the red spots under a special lamp, and by a laboratory test of hairs from the infected spots. To treat ringworm, your veterinarian may prescribe an antifungal ointment, a scrub made with iodine, a medicine to take by mouth called griseofulvin, and may shave the affected areas.

Ringworm is contagious to humans and other animals. If you suspect ringworm, be sure to wash your hands thoroughly following contact with your pet. Use disposable gloves when cleaning your pet's cage and its contents and wash your hands thoroughly following the cage cleaning.

Skin and Fur Mites

Infestation with mites is common in hamsters. The 2 species of mite that are most common are *Demodex criceti* and *Demodex aurati*. This condition is more common in males and older hamsters, because these groups are more prone to malnutrition and other diseases. When an animal is heavily infested with mites, its skin becomes inflamed, dry, and scaly, with hair loss over the back and rump area. Bald areas are dry and scaly, but not itchy. Treatment includes a prescription shampoo that contains selenium sulfide or an ointment that contains the medicine amitraz.

Other species of mites that are less common in hamsters include ear mites, nose mites, and tropical rat mites. Hamsters infested with ear mites can have inflammation of the skin around the ears, face, feet, and tail. Your veterinarian can identify this condition with a laboratory test on scrapings from the infected skin or hair. Treatment for these types of mites includes the medicine ivermectin. The bedding of the infested hamster should be changed often and the cage thoroughly cleaned and disinfected.

Kidney and Urinary Tract Disorders

Inflammation of the kidneys, which worsens over time, is more common in older and female hamsters. Hamsters with this condition lose weight, produce more urine than normal, and are unusually thirsty. The condition may be caused by viral infection, high blood pressure in the kidneys, or a disorder of the immune system. Sick hamsters may also have amyloidosis (*see* page 952).

Diseases Affecting Multiple Body Systems

Some diseases, including many infections, affect more than one body system. These are also known as generalized or systemic diseases.

Lymphocytic Choriomeningitis Virus (Arenavirus) Infection

This virus usually infects wild mice; hamsters become infected with it only occasionally. The virus is spread by contact with an infected rodent's urine or saliva, or by tiny droplets spread when sick rodents sneeze or cough. An infected pregnant hamster can pass it to her fetuses in the womb. The virus does not usually make hamsters sick, and it goes away on its own. However, sick hamsters can pass the virus to humans. Some hamsters that have this virus lose weight over time. Additional signs include convulsions, depression, and decreased reproduction in females. Your veterinarian might notice an enlarged liver, spleen, or kidneys, or swollen lymph nodes. The virus can be detected by laboratory tests. There is no effective treatment. Animals that are sick with arenavirus should be euthanized, and their living quarters must be thoroughly cleaned and sanitized. Any contact between your pet and wild rodents must be eliminated.

This virus is very contagious and very dangerous for humans. It can cause flu-like signs and inflammation of the brain, the membrane around the brain, and the spinal cord. To protect yourself and your family, wear disposable gloves when cleaning an infected hamster's cage. Be especially cautious about handling bedding and other materials that may contain urine. After you have finished cleaning the cage and all of its contents, dispose of potentially contaminated materials carefully (use gloves and place the materials in sealed plastic bags) then follow up with thorough handwashing including your arms. Immediately wash any clothing that may have come in contact with contaminated bedding or other items.

Amyloidosis

Amyloidosis is a condition in which the body produces sheets of dense protein called amyloid. The protein deposits build up in various organs, such as the liver and kidneys, and eventually interfere with the normal functions of those organs. This condition may affect hamsters that are more than 1 year old, or hamsters with longterm illnesses. It is more common in females. Hamsters with this condition usually do not appear sick until their kidneys stop working because of amyloid deposits. Kidney failure causes a buildup of chemicals in the blood, which can, in turn, lead to loss of appetite, a rough hair coat, hunched posture, accumulation of fluid in the body, depression, and death. Blood tests may show an increase in the proteins albumin and globulin, too much protein in the urine, and high cholesterol. There is no treatment for this illness except to make the hamster more comfortable (by giving it fluids, for example). Most hamsters with this illness live only a short time.

Polycystic Disease

This disease, which causes hamsters to develop fluid-filled sacs called cysts, is common in hamsters more than 1 year old. Usually, the hamster develops 1 or more cysts in its liver. The cysts are 3 centimeters or less in diameter. Other organs that can develop these cysts include accessory sex glands in males, the pancreas, the ovaries or the tissue lining the womb in females, and the adrenal glands.

Pseudotuberculosis

This illness is caused by the bacteria *Yersinia pseudotuberculosis*. Hamsters are exposed to the bacteria when the feces of wild birds or rodents get into their food or drinking water and can develop serious illness. Infection in hamsters usually leads to blood poisoning. Another sign is longterm extreme weight loss with occasional diarrhea. Your veterinarian might notice degeneration of the lymph nodes, spleen, liver, lungs, gallbladder, and the walls of the intestines. The bacteria can be detected with laboratory tests. There is no treatment.

Pseudotuberculosis is contagious to humans, so any hamsters with this disease, or any hamsters that have come into contact with them, must be euthanized. Contact with wild rodents or birds must be eliminated. The sick hamster's cage must be thoroughly cleaned and sanitized. Be sure to wear gloves when cleaning the cage and disposing of contaminated materials. Wash your hands and arms thoroughly when done.

Tularemia

This disease, caused by infection with the bacteria *Francisella tularensis*, is rare in hamsters. It can cause blood poisoning, with a high rate of severe illness and death. Hamsters catch this illness from infected ticks or mites. Sick hamsters may have a rough hair coat, and die within 48 hours of becoming ill. Your veterinarian might notice bleeding in the lungs, and enlarged liver, spleen, and lymph nodes. There is no treatment. This disease is contagious to humans, so any infected hamsters—or hamsters that have been exposed to infected hamsters—must be euthanized. The sick hamster's cage must be thoroughly cleaned and sanitized. Use gloves and dispose of bedding and other cage materials carefully. Minimize your pet's exposure to ticks and promptly treat any evidence of mite infestation (*see* page 951) to reduce any chance of developing tularemia.

Cancers and Tumors

Malignant, or cancerous, tumors occur in only about 4% of hamsters. Both genetic

Diseases that can be Spread from Hamsters to People
▓ Lymphocytic choriomeningitis virus (Arenavirus)
▓ Ringworm
▓ Salmonellosis
▓ Pseudotuberculosis
▓ Tularemia

and environmental factors may play a part in development of the disease. Most hamster tumors are not cancerous and occur in organs that produce hormones or digest food. The most common location of these benign tumors is in the adrenal gland, which is near the kidney.

Lymphoma may occur in older hamsters, with tumors in the lymph nodes, thymus, spleen, liver, and other sites. A type of T-cell lymphoma that affects the skin occurs in adult hamsters, with signs of low energy, weight loss, patchy hair loss, and skin inflammation.

Other tumors can develop in the womb, intestines, brain, skin, hair follicles, fat, or eyes. If you find an unexpected lump or bump on your hamster, have your pet checked by a veterinarian promptly. The sooner a tumor is discovered, the easier it is to treat.

CHAPTER **69**

Mice

▓ INTRODUCTION

House mice (scientific name *Mus musculus*) originated in the central and southern regions of Asia. Because they are very adaptable, they have spread all over the world. House mice were domesticated around 1800 by both Europeans and Asians who began to selectively breed them for their fur and coloring.

Mice have been used for many purposes over the centuries. Mice were used in religious rituals as early as 1100 BC by the Chinese, who referred to them as the "ancient ones." The Japanese believed that mice were messengers from the gods. The Greeks used them to predict the future and even worshipped them. Sailors and miners used them to test air quality in submarines and mines. Modern scientists use them to study genetics and diseases. They have even been sent into space.

▓ DESCRIPTION AND PHYSICAL CHARACTERISTICS

Adult mice typically weigh about 1 ounce (28 grams) and are approximately 2.5 to 3.5 inches (6 to 8 centimeters) long, not including the tail (*see* TABLE 10). Male mice are typically larger than females. Pet mice are available in many colors and coat patterns due to specialized breeding. Coats can be smooth, curly, longhaired or a combination. The most common color variations include brown, black, tan, gray, and albino, with lighter and darker shades of these as well. The usual life span of mice is 1.5 to 2.5 years.

▓ SPECIAL CONSIDERATIONS

Mice are easy to tame, handle, and look after, even by children. They are nocturnal by nature and usually spend most of the day sleeping; at night they are very active. Due to their small size, mice should be handled gently and may not be the best pet for very young children.

The best way to pick up a mouse is to gently grasp it by the middle or base of the tail and then place it in the palm of your hand. Avoid picking up a mouse by the tip of its tail. Owners should be careful not to drop their pet because even a short fall can

Table 10. Mice at a Glance

Lifespan	1.5 to 2.5 years
Weight	20 to 40 grams
Length (including tail)	6 to 7 inches (15 to 18 centimeters)
Normal body temperature	98 to 101°F (36°C)
Heart rate	450 to 600 beats per minute
Estrous cycle	4 to 5 days
Duration of pregnancy	19 to 21 days
Litter size	10 to 12 young
Weaning age	21 to 28 days

be harmful—or fatal—to the mouse. Mice may bite or try to escape if they become scared when they are handled or are in unfamiliar surroundings.

Because mice are social animals that need company, it is better to keep them in a group. However, they are also very prolific breeders, so males and females should be kept in different cages. Aggression is uncommon in mice that were raised together as littermates; however, when new groups of animals are housed together, they should be watched carefully for fighting, as this may cause injuries.

Mice have limited ability to regulate their body temperature, and they are very sensitive to heat and cold. They regulate their body temperature through dilation or constriction of the veins in their tails. They should be kept in a temperature range of 64 to 72°F (18 to 22°C), with a humidity level of 40 to 70%. Temperatures above 86°F (30°C) can cause heat stroke, especially if there is overcrowding in the cage. Although good lighting is important, mice should be kept away from direct sunlight.

■ SELECTING A MOUSE

Mice are widely available at pet stores, or they may be obtained from a local breeder. When selecting a pet mouse, you should look for one that has smooth glossy fur, clear eyes, and no obvious signs of trauma such as limping or hair loss on the body or tail. There should be no discharge from the eyes or nose, and no signs of diarrhea in the mouse's environment. Other signs of illness include matted fur, a hunched posture, and general dullness.

When awake, mice are usually lively and curious. Because mice are nocturnal, it may be best to visit a pet store and observe their mice in the evening rather than during the day.

■ PROVIDING A HOME FOR MICE

Your mice will be healthier and live longer if you provide them with appropriate, well ventilated housing, a nutritionally sound diet, and opportunity to exercise and explore their environment. Good sanitation is the key to preventing many types of disease.

Housing

A wide variety of cages are available for keeping mice. In general, a cage should have good ventilation, be easy to clean, and be escape proof. A plastic cage or glass aquarium or terrarium of sufficient size can make a good home for mice. Metal cages are not recommended because they can allow drafts (through mesh openings) and collect condensation. Cages made with wood are unacceptable for mice, as their urine will soak into the wood. This causes ammonia buildup, which can lead to respiratory disease. Mice may also chew through the wood, allowing them to escape.

Cages must have wire mesh on the top for good ventilation. The wire should be fine enough to prevent escape and strong enough to resist chewing from adult mice. A mesh with 1-centimeter squares is the recommended size. The minimum cage size for 2 to 3 mice is 18 inches (45 centimeters) long by 18 inches (45 centimeters) wide by 10 inches (25 centimeters) high. The bedding and floor covering should be absorbent. Wood shavings or prepared litter can provide soft bedding for mice. Cedar or pine shavings should be avoided as they may irritate the mouse's respiratory system. Hay or recycled paper may be added. Mice are nest builders and will make nests from their bedding for sleeping.

Fresh water should be available at all times to prevent dehydration. A water bottle with a hanger that allows mice to easily access the water is recommended. Holders with chew guards for the water bottle are available. These allow you to hang the bottle inside the cage. A water dish or bowl should be used only in emergencies, as mice often will spill the water or push shavings in it. If you use a food dish, it should be easy to clean and sturdy enough to prevent tipping.

Poor environmental quality, such as high ammonia levels and poor quality bedding materials, can increase the risk of bacterial or viral infections in mice. Cages should be cleaned with hot water at least once a week and the bedding should be changed at least twice weekly. Fresh water and food should be provided on a daily basis. All dishes and water bottles should be thoroughly cleaned before refilling.

Diet

Mice need a balanced diet that includes carbohydrates, fat, and protein. Commercial mouse diets are available and not only contain all the vitamins and minerals that mice need, but are also hard enough to wear down their constantly growing incisor teeth. Fresh vegetables, sunflower seeds, and fruit can be given in limited amounts as treats. On average, an adult mouse will eat 3 to 5 grams of food and drink 3 to 5 milliliters of water daily. Mice should be fed once a day (at night) and all uneaten food should be removed before fresh food is provided.

Exercise

Routine exercise is necessary for good health in all animals. Mice are extremely active and enjoy opportunities to exercise and play. Access to exercise wheels, tubes, ladders, and climbing blocks will fulfill this need. The cage should be large enough to accommodate some of these "cage toys" and allow comfortable movement around them.

Temperament

Mice are very social animals, and they appreciate being in a group. However mice owners should be careful when male mice are placed in the same cage, because they tend to fight unless they grew up together. Unrelated female mice can normally be placed in the same cage without any problems.

Usually, mice are good pets for children. However, they should be kept away from other pets in the house such as dogs, cats, birds, and other rodents. Remember, mice are the natural prey for several of these animals!

Because mice are nocturnal, they can be quite active at night. You may want to consider placing the cage in a location where sleeping family members will not be disturbed by their activity.

◼ ROUTINE HEALTH CARE

Mice are resilient animals and rarely get sick. Furnishing appropriate housing, a nutritious diet, good hygiene, and considerate care will minimize disease. Signs of illness in mice include a ruffled coat, depressed attitude, lethargy, closed or squinted eyes, reluctance to move even when handled, and a loss of appetite. Changes in the color, consistency, smell, or amount of urine or feces may also indicate that your mouse is sick. Any of these signs are a good indication that your mouse needs to see a veterinarian immediately.

Respiratory infections are common in mice, so they should be kept away from damp and drafts. Reducing dust from shavings and keeping the cage environment clean may help minimize the frequency of these infections.

Checking for Signs of Illness in Mice

▪ Look for general signs of illness, such as poor appetite, hunched posture, listlessness, and matted or puffed-up fur.

▪ Learn to spot signs of respiratory infections by listening for abnormal breathing or chattering and checking for any discharge from the eyes or nose. A mouse with a respiratory infection should be seen by a veterinarian.

▪ Check the teeth and gums for any misalignment or overgrowth of teeth, gum swelling, redness, pus, or foul odor. Oral infections can progress quickly and need early medical intervention to be resolved.

▪ Check the mouse's ears for discharge.

▪ Visually inspect your mouse's body for bleeding, wounds, or injuries.

▪ Look for signs of trauma such as limping, tilting, or circling when walking.

▪ Check for lumps, swelling, or areas of sensitivity that might indicate pain.

▪ Check the fur around the mouse's shoulders and neck for any scabs that might indicate parasites. Also watch your mouse's behavior to see if it is scratching excessively.

Dental Care

The incisor teeth of mice grow constantly and must be worn down by gnawing. Mice should be provided with appropriate materials, such as wooden gnawing blocks, to satisfy their need to gnaw. In addition, periodic trimming with nail clippers or a dental bur will prevent the teeth from growing too long. Overgrown incisors can lead to difficulty with eating, weight loss, dehydration, and oral trauma.

▪ BREEDING AND REPRODUCTION

Female mice reach sexual maturity at about 6 weeks of age; males take a week or two longer. From this age onward, females and males should be housed separately.

If you are planning to breed your mice, you should provide nesting material (tissue paper works well) in one corner of the cage. Females can have up to 15 litters a year and can become pregnant within 24 hours after giving birth. The average gestation time for mice is 19 to 21 days. Baby mice are called pups and are born deaf and blind. The average litter size is 10 to 12 pups. The cage should be kept in a quiet place and the litter should not be disturbed for at least 7 days after birth, especially if this is the female's first litter. Within 2 weeks, the baby mice will look like small adults.

Breeding and reproduction in mice can decrease due to various factors such as age, malnutrition, abnormal light cycles, cold environments, cysts on the ovaries, tumors, and inadequate nesting material. Pregnant females may abort, abandon, or eat their babies due to inadequate food or lack of water, overcrowded group housing, inadequate nesting materials, sick or deformed pups, or excessive noise.

▪ DISEASES AND DISORDERS

Diseases and disorders commonly seen in pet mice include infectious diseases, injuries due to trauma, and problems related to nutrition and aging. Although the treatment of disorders in rodents is becoming more sophisticated, prevention of disease (by providing an appropriate diet and practicing good management and hygiene) is usually more successful than treatment.

Digestive Disorders

A number of disorders can affect the digestive tract, including bacterial infections, viruses, and parasites. Signs of illness often include loss of appetite and weight and general signs such as rough or ruffled fur. Diarrhea may or may not be seen.

Often it is not possible to determine the exact cause of the disorder. If a bacterial infection is suspected, your veterinarian may recommend an antibiotic to eliminate the infection, along with supportive treatment. If parasites (such as pinworms) are the cause of illness, they can usually be eliminated with appropriate treatment. Good sanitation helps prevent many diseases.

Infections Caused by Bacteria

Bacterial infections of the digestive system are not common in mice kept as pets, although they occur frequently in breeding or research colonies. In most cases, young, stressed animals are more likely to be infected. Signs of illness may include loss of appetite, dehydration, watery diarrhea, ruffled fur, lethargy, and hunched posture. In most cases, the bacteria are transmitted by exposure to feces from infected animals. The infection is treated by giving appropriate antibiotics and administering supportive fluids or anti-diarrheal drugs if needed. Follow your veterinarian's advice regarding the isolation of infected animals and disinfection of cages and equipment.

Infections Caused by Viruses

Like bacterial infections, viral infections of the digestive system are seen more commonly in colonies of mice than in mice kept as pets. In addition, it can be difficult to distinguish whether an infection is viral, bacterial, or caused by other organisms. Young mice are more likely to be infected than adult mice. Signs of illness may include watery diarrhea and weight loss. There are only supportive treatments available.

Infections Caused by Protozoa

Various types of protozoa (microorganisms) are normally present in the digestive tract of mice and do not usually cause disease. However, in younger or stressed mice, these protozoa (most commonly *Spironucleus muris* and *Giardia muris*) can cause intestinal infections. Infection is transmitted by contaminated feces, and infected mice have diarrhea, weight loss, lethargy, and a rough hair coat. Young mice may show stunted growth. The protozoa can be controlled with appropriate drugs but cannot always be eliminated.

Pinworms

Pinworms are common intestinal parasites in mice. Mice normally carry pinworms with no sign of disease; however, a heavy infection can cause diarrhea due to intestinal inflammation. The disease is transmitted by eating materials contaminated with feces, and infected mice usually show few if any specific signs. The disease is diagnosed by identifying worms or their eggs in infected feces or on the area around the anus of the mouse. Several different medications available from a veterinarian can eliminate pinworm infection. Because pinworm eggs are light and may float in the air, it is important to sanitize and disinfect the cage as a part of the treatment program. Follow the advice of your veterinarian regarding medication and cage cleaning.

Tapeworms

The infection of mice with tapeworms is relatively uncommon and there are usually no clinical signs of infection. However, diarrhea, and weight loss may occur with a heavy infestation. The dwarf tapeworm can potentially infect humans if ingested. Care should be used when handling infected mice. Tapeworms are transmitted indirectly by cockroaches, beetles, or fleas. The infection is diagnosed by identifying tapeworm eggs in infected feces. Several medications are available for treatment. The cage should be sanitized and disinfected. Follow the advice of your veterinarian regarding medication and cage cleaning.

Lung and Airway Disorders

Disorders of the respiratory tract are common in pet mice. General signs of illness may include sniffling, difficulty breathing, discharge from the nose, or sneezing. Mice with respiratory disease also tend to make a noise called chattering. Infections may be caused by bacteria, viruses, or sometimes by several different microorganisms (known as a mixed infection).

Mycoplasmal Infection

This bacterial infection causes sudden and severe respiratory disease—as well as long-lasting respiratory and other problems—in mice. The infection is transmitted by direct contact, airborne bacteria, and sexual contact. It can also be passed on from a mother to her offspring during birth. The signs of the upper respiratory disease (in the nasal passages and middle ears) include sneezing, sniffling, rough hair coat, lethargy, labored breathing, weight loss, and reddish-brown staining around the eyes and nose. As the disease progresses, it will infect the lungs. The infection can become more severe in the presence of other bacterial and viral infections, often leading to pneumonia. Infection of the uterus and ovaries may occur in female mice infected with these bacteria, and genital infection may reduce fertility.

There is no cure or vaccine for mycoplasmal infection. However, infection and its signs can be suppressed with antibiotics. Keeping your mouse's home clean and ensuring early treatment of the infection are the only ways that you can fight this disease.

Other Respiratory Infections

Several other bacteria and viruses can cause respiratory infections in mice and all may have very similar signs of illness. Disease-causing organisms included in this group are cilia-associated respiratory *Bacillus, Streptococcus pneumoniae, Corynebacterium kutscheri, Pasteurella pneumotropica*, Sendai virus, pneumonia virus of mice, and *Pneumocystis carinii*. Of these, Sendai virus is the most likely to cause disease.

Signs common in these infections include sneezing, sniffling, labored breathing, rough hair coat, inactivity, weight loss, lack of appetite, and discharge from the eyes or nose. If you notice any of these signs, you should take your mouse to the veterinarian.

The diseases may be transmitted between mice by several routes, depending on the specific organism, including direct contact with infected animals, contaminated feces, or sneezing or coughing on one another. While most of these infections cannot be cured, your veterinarian may prescribe antibiotics to help reduce the severity of illness. Supportive care and keeping the mouse's environment clean

will also be helpful. Individuals showing signs of respiratory infection should be kept separate from other mice to reduce the spread of disease.

Skin Disorders

Some of the most common health problems in pet mice are disorders affecting the skin or fur. Skin inflammation and fur loss may be caused be infection, infestation with mites or other parasites, or barbering from incompatible cage mates.

Staphylococcus Infection

This infection is caused by bacteria that are commonly found on the skin of most animals, including mice. Infection occurs when the skin is damaged by scratching or bite wounds. Mice with weakened immune systems are more susceptible to the infection. Inflamed skin and sores may be observed on the head and neck, and the resulting abscesses may enlarge and spread under the skin to form lumps (tumors) around the face and head. The infection is treated with antibiotics or antibiotic/steroid ointments applied as directed. In order to prevent further damage caused by scratching, the toenails of the back feet should be clipped.

Scaly Skin Disease (*Corynebacterium bovis* Infection)

This bacterial infection causes no signs in most mice, but can cause scaly skin in hairless (nude) mice. Bacteria are present in the skin or in the mouth. This disease is transmitted by direct contact with infected mice or with contaminated objects such as bedding. Infected mice have yellow-white flakes on the skin and lose weight. Most mice recover. The infection is diagnosed using blood tests. Treatment with appropriate antibiotics decreases the signs.

Ringworm

Ringworm is caused not by worms but by fungi called dermatophytes that parasitize the skin. The infection is contagious and can infect humans and other animals. The fungal skin infections occur infrequently in mice. Usually, infected mice do not have any visible signs. However, some affected mice have areas of hair loss and reddened, irritated or flaky skin. The infection is transmitted by direct contact or by contaminated bedding, litter, or cage supplies. Treatment should be directed by your veterinarian and includes eliminating the fungal infection by using an appropriate fungicidal ointment, an antibiotic known to kill fungi, or both. This is important because even though the infection often clears on its own in several weeks, the animal can continue to harbor the infection only to have it reappear when conditions are again favorable for its growth.

To control the spread of infection, other household pets should be checked for ringworm and treated if needed. It is necessary to wash your hands and all materials that have come in contact with an infected animal. The use of disposable gloves is also helpful. If you notice signs of the fungal infection on yourself, you should check with your own physician regarding appropriate treatment. The infection is not dangerous and is often easily cured with over-the-counter antifungal creams.

Skin and Fur Mites

Several types of mites may infest the skin and fur of mice. Mites are external parasites. They are not bloodsuckers and often produce no visible signs. Heavily infested mice may have inflammation of the skin, and mites can be seen as white specks of dust on their hair follicles. In addition, they experience intense itching, leading to the scabs most frequently seen on the shoulders, neck, and face. The mouse fur mites do not infest humans or other animals. Infestation is diagnosed by identifying the mites or eggs from the hair and skin of the affected animal. Treatment usually involves applying a mite-killing drug to the skin, as either a powder (dust) or a solution. The solution is also sometimes given in the drinking water. Your veterinarian will advise you on the best treatment.

Under normal conditions mites are present in small numbers and do not bother their host; however, their numbers increase when the mouse is stressed, has decreased immunity due to other illnesses, or is unable to keep the numbers reduced by normal grooming. Therefore it is important that you provide proper regular care for your pet, including monitoring for illness. After treatment, the cage and all cage materials should be thoroughly cleaned and disinfected, because unhatched eggs may lead to reinfection.

Lice

Infestations of blood-sucking lice are common in wild mice, but are rarely seen in pet mice. Human beings will not be affected if their pet mice have these lice, because the lice do not cross over from one animal or species to another. Heavily infested mice show intense itching, restlessness, weakness, and anemia (lack of red blood cells). Infestation is diagnosed by identification of adult lice or eggs on the fur. Lice are treated similarly to mites (*see* above).

Fleas

Rodent fleas are uncommon in pet mice, but are sometimes seen if pets come into contact with wild rodents. The fleas are diagnosed by identifying them on the infested mice. Fleas are treated with medicated dusts or sprays. To prevent reinfestation, disinfect and clean the cage thoroughly. When holding or playing with mice other than your own, it is recommended that you wash and change clothes prior to handling your own mice.

Ringtail Syndrome

Low humidity, high temperatures, and drafts predispose young mice to develop a

---

Diseases that can be Spread from Mice to People

Lymphocytic choriomeningitis
Pneumocystis carinii infection
Ringworm
Salmonellosis

ring-like constriction of the tail called ringtail. This condition can also involve the feet or toes. Affected mice have swelling that leads to gangrene and death of cells in the portion of the tail below the constriction. Ringtail is diagnosed through medical history and signs; however, it is not common in mice kept as pets. Surgical removal of all or part of the tail is often necessary, and tail stumps usually heal without complication. Ringtail can be prevented by providing an environmental humidity of 40 to 70%, reducing drafts (use a cage with plastic or glass sides, rather than sides made of wire), and maintaining the cage temperature at 70 to 74°F (22 to 23°C).

Barbering (Fur Chewing)

This abnormal grooming behavior is occasionally seen in groups of male or female mice. Dominant members of the group chew the hair and whiskers of less dominant mice. Because the mouse chews the hair so close to the skin, it gives the appearance of being clean-shaven, hence the term barbering. Stress, boredom, and even heredity can lead to this behavior, and mice sometimes barber themselves. The most common places for barbering to be seen on the body are the stomach and front legs if caused by self-grooming, or on the muzzle, head, or shoulders of a cage mate. The skin is generally not affected, and its appearance will be normal without signs of inflammation, irritation, or cuts. Unless irritation develops, this condition does not require treatment. If barbering occurs because of the presence of a dominant mouse, the dominant animal should be removed for the well-being of the other cage mates.

Fight Wounds

Male mice often fight each other and cause injuries to the face, back, and genital areas. The skin will show patches of hair loss and scabs. The injury can become infected with bacteria and turn into an abscess. Tail biting can lead to

Barbering (fur chewing) may be due to boredom, stress, or a dominant mouse.

gangrene. Affected mice lose weight and sometimes die. Fight wounds are treated by cleaning them with a disinfectant solution, draining the abscesses, and applying appropriate antibiotic ointments as recommended or prescribed by your veterinarian. Mice that fight frequently should be separated.

Disorders Affecting Multiple Body Systems

Some disorders of mice can affect more than one body system. These conditions are also called generalized or systemic disorders.

Salmonellosis

This disease caused by *Salmonella* bacteria is uncommon in pet mice. However, pregnant females and infants are at higher risk of infection. The infection is transmitted by eating food contaminated by feces and is often associated with food, water, or bedding contaminated by wild rodents. Signs of infection include a distended abdomen (belly), diarrhea, dehydration, weight loss, rough hair coat, depression, and sudden death. There is no treatment. Infected mice should be isolated and the cage should be sanitized and disinfected to eliminate any potential source of contamination.

Salmonellosis can infect humans. Washing your hands before and after every contact with your mouse and its cage will help prevent the spread of this disease. Using disposable gloves when handling infected animals or cage contents provides additional protection.

Streptobacillus moniliformis Infection

This infection is caused by a bacteria normally found in the upper respiratory organs of rodents. Rats are the natural host for the bacteria, but infection can occur in mice. Infected mice may develop acute septicemia (presence of bacteria in the blood), which often is fatal. Mice that survive may have chronic arthritis and deformities in their legs and feet. Follow your veterinarian's advice regarding medication, supportive care for your pet, and cage cleaning needs.

Pseudomonas aeruginosa Infection

This infection of the nasal cavities and intestines is caused by drinking contaminated water. It does not cause signs in normal mice, but those with weakened immune systems may die suddenly with no sign of infection or develop rough hair coats, hunched posture, and weight loss. There is no treatment, and every effort should be made to prevent infection by supplying acidified or chlorinated drinking water and clean housing and supplies. Change your pet's water at least once a day; twice a day is better. Be sure that all water containers have been thoroughly cleaned before refilling them.

Mousepox

Mousepox infection is a highly contagious viral disease of mice that was only recently recognized in the United States. Mice are the only natural host of the virus. Pet mice are rarely infected unless they came from a colony where the members were infected. Thus it is important to get your pet from a reliable source. The acute (sudden onset) form of mousepox affects the entire body. Affected mice lack energy and may have a hunched posture, rough hair coat, diarrhea, inflammation of the eyes, and swelling of the face. Death often follows. Another form of the disease causes infected mice to develop a body-wide skin rash. The skin becomes swollen and

wounds appear on its surface. Because of the resulting pain, afflicted mice begin to chew on themselves, even to the point of amputating toes. The infection is transmitted through contact with contaminated feces or urine, or direct contact with wounds in the skin. Infection is diagnosed through blood tests. There is no specific treatment for this infection. Consult your veterinarian regarding supportive care for an infected mouse and control of the disease.

Parvovirus Infection

There are several parvoviruses that can infect mice, including **mouse parvovirus** and **minute virus of mice**. However, these infections are not likely to cause signs in healthy mice. All parvoviruses are highly contagious and transmission occurs through direct contact with infected urine or feces or by contamination of objects (such as bedding) in the environment. Disinfection of the cage is required to eliminate the virus. There is as yet no treatment.

Lymphocytic Choriomeningitis Virus Infection

This disease occurs primarily in wild mice. However, mice can carry the virus and transmit it without becoming ill. Mice can become infected at a pet store by contact with other infected rodents (rats and hamsters) or from contact with urine or feces from infected wild rodents. The virus is transmitted by coughing or sneezing or by direct contact with the urine or saliva of infected animals. Infection is diagnosed through blood tests. There is no effective treatment. Affected animals should be euthanized and the cage should be appropriately sanitized and disinfected.

Mice with this virus can infect humans, in whom it can cause serious illness. It may cause influenza-like signs or viral meningitis, an inflammation of the brain and spinal cord. Infection in pregnant women may result in miscarriage or birth defects.

Geriatric Diseases

Amyloidosis causes proteins to form dense deposits in the intestine, kidneys, lungs, thyroid, and lymph nodes of aged mice. Treatment is usually supplied to provide comfort, but there is no cure.

Atrial thrombosis is a heart disease that frequently occurs in older mice. The sick mice have an abnormally fast heart rate, bluish colored gums, and difficulty breathing. There is no effective treatment.

Osteoarthrosis is a type of arthritis that affects the joints in aged mice and can lead to difficulty of movement. Treatment is supportive and normally consists of supplying aspirin in the drinking water. Ask your veterinarian about dosage levels that are appropriate for your mouse.

Degeneration of the retina is often genetic (inherited). It may also be caused by exposure to high light levels. Retinal degeneration often causes blindness. Most mice compensate by using other senses such as smell and touch.

Cataracts may occur in older mice or after a decrease in tear production.

Cancers and Tumors

Tumor development in mice is dependent on various factors, including the breed of mouse, environment, age, and infection by viruses that cause cancer. Treatment usually requires surgery to

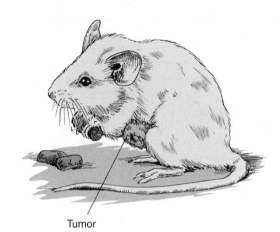

Tumor

Mammary tumors are common in mice.

remove the tumor because tumors may grow and spread to other locations in the body. Early removal allows for the best outcome with the least chance of complication and recurrence of the tumor.

Mammary tumors are commonly observed tumors in mice and can develop anywhere under the skin because mice have widely distributed mammary (breast) tissues. These tumors can be caused by infection with viruses that can be transmitted to baby mice through their mother's milk and placenta. Your veterinarian can remove the tumor during surgery, but the cancer often spreads to the lungs, and overall outcomes tend to be poor.

CHAPTER **70**

Prairie Dogs

■ INTRODUCTION

Black-tailed prairie dogs (*Cynomys ludovicianus*) are a type of ground squirrel kept by some people as pets, although not without some controversy. Although wild-caught prairie dogs can adapt to captive indoor environments and even bond with humans, especially if handled properly when young, they may also be stressed or injured when removed from their natural setting and social hierarchy. It should be noted that as of November 2003, it is now illegal in the United States to capture wild prairie dogs, especially with the intent of keeping them as pets. Prairie dogs will bite and may have diseases, such as monkeypox, that can be transmitted to people. Several prairie dog species are listed as threatened or endangered by the United States Fish and Wildlife Service.

■ DESCRIPTION AND PHYSICAL CHARACTERISTICS

Adult prairie dogs are 12 to 16 inches (30 to 40 centimeters) long and weigh 2 to 4 pounds (1 to 2 kilograms), with males slightly larger than females. Prairie dogs have short legs, sharp claws, a bark-like call and a need to chew. They have partially developed cheek pouches and tails covered with fur. The lifespan in captivity may reach 8 to 10 years.

In nature, prairie dogs live in large and complex social groups referred to as towns, which may cover many acres. Towns are subdivided into colonies or wards; these are further subdivided into distinct social family units called coteries. Coteries usually consist of an adult male, 1 to 4 adult females, and any offspring less than 2 years old. Prairie dogs are active during the day, particularly during the cooler hours of the day when they feed and socialize.

Female prairie dogs come into heat once a year and produce an average litter of 4 to 5 pups in the spring. Pregnancy lasts 34 to 36 days and pups are born blind and hairless. After weaning at 7 weeks of age, young males soon move away, while females typically spend their entire lives in their original coterie. Aggression from females directed at other females increases during pregnancy and the period of time in which they are nursing their young. Prairie dogs have a scent gland that can emit a strong musky odor.

■ SPECIAL CONSIDERATIONS

In June 2003, after pet prairie dogs were involved in an outbreak of monkeypox disease, the Centers for Disease Control and Prevention (CDC) and the Department of Health and Human Services issued a joint

Wild prairie dogs live in groups called coteries.

order that banned the transport, sale, or release of pet prairie dogs. On November 4, 2003, the CDC and the Food and Drug Administration issued a joint Interim Final Rule that makes this order permanent and includes some new restrictions. The new order specifically bans the capture of wild prairie dogs, as well as the trade of prairie dogs within states and between states. In short, it is illegal to transport, sell, capture, release, or relocate any prairie dog, even one that may be a healthy pet.

If you are moving to a new home and moving a pet prairie dog with you within the US, you must get permission from the Center for Veterinary Medicine at the Food and Drug Administration (*see* BOX, page 964). In most cases, this permission is given. However, it should be noted that some states do not allow prairie dogs as pets. The Center for Veterinary Medicine can provide you with the contact information of the state veterinarian for your state and that veterinarian will be able to tell you if prairie dogs are allowed.

The only time you can transport your prairie dog without permission is if it requires veterinary care due to illness or for a checkup, or if you are taking it to a shelter to be euthanized. If your prairie dog becomes ill, you should contact your veterinarian in advance to be sure they can provide care for your pet and to prepare for

FDA and CDC Contact Information

Food and Drug Administration
Center for Veterinary Medicine
Communications Staff, HFV-12
7519 Standish Place
Rockville, Maryland 20855
U.S.A.
(240) 276-9300
http://www.fda.gov/cvm/contactCVM.html

Centers for Disease Control and Prevention
1600 Clifton Rd.
Atlanta, GA 30333
U.S.A.
(404) 639-3311
Public Inquiries
English (800) CDC-INFO
Español (888) 246-2857
TTY (888) 232-6348
http://www.cdc.gov

its arrival. They will want to reduce any potential risk to themselves as well as waiting room patients. To transport your ill prairie dog, you should wear heavy gloves and long sleeves as protection against scratches, bites, or any body fluids. The animal should be contained securely in a portable cage or box during transport.

If your veterinarian determines that your prairie dog has monkeypox or any other disease that can be transmitted to humans, you should clean and disinfect anything that came into contact with the animal, including the area of the vehicle in which it was transported, the gloves and clothing worn when handling the animal, and its housing environment at your home. A suitable disinfectant can be created by adding ¼ cup of bleach to 1 gallon of water. If you want to discard the items, they should be disinfected and placed in a sealed plastic bag before being thrown away.

In general, prairie dogs should be handled with utmost care and housed and maintained separately from other wild rodent species. There is great potential for crossover of infectious diseases to this very susceptible host.

As with any animal that has the potential for transmitting diseases to humans, hands should be washed and disinfected before and after handling your pet and items in its environment.

▓ PROVIDING A HOME FOR A PRAIRIE DOG

Before bringing home a prairie dog, you should make sure you have a suitable, safe enclosure for your pet. You will also need to provide a complete diet and consider how you can meet your pet's exercise and socialization needs.

Housing

Housing for prairie dogs should be well-secured because their natural curiosity and chewing behavior will likely expose them to a number of household dangers such as toxic chemicals, poisonous household plants, or electrical cords. Animals kept as pets should be provided with a large enough space and materials for burrowing. Hay or wood shavings deep enough to allow your pet to burrow work well; however, cedar shavings should be avoided as they can irritate the respiratory tract. Nest boxes can be used to simulate the natural burrow environment. Large plastic rodent cages placed inside a larger container can help prevent bedding from spreading around when your pet digs or burrows. A large rock helps maintain a prairie dog's nails, and nonpoisonous dried tree branches or chew toys allow the gnawing action required to maintain appropriate tooth length. Prairie dogs do best in a cool, dry environment and should be kept at temperatures of 69 to 72°F (20 to 22°C) and relative humidity of 30 to 70%. Bedding materials should be replaced regularly, and enclosures cleaned and sanitized weekly to prevent disease. Prairie dogs can be trained to use a litter pan or box.

Diet

In the wild, prairie dogs mainly eat grasses, as well as some leaves and flower-

A proper enclosure for prairie dogs should be spacious and secure.

ing plants. Feeding your prairie dog a diet of good quality commercial rabbit or rodent pellets, alfalfa cubes, and timothy or grass hay will help keep it healthy. Pelleted diets and alfalfa should be decreased as animals mature to prevent obesity or gallbladder disease. Treats should be given sparingly, if at all, because obesity can shorten the life of your pet. Fruit can be given as an occasional treat. Prairie dogs have big appetites. During summer, they will normally store up fat reserves for hibernating in winter. Although prairie dogs are not true hibernators, they may enter an inactive state if they are kept at temperatures less than 55°F (13°C). Watering systems should be sanitized at least every other day to prevent bacterial contamination.

Exercise

Providing a housing enclosure that is large enough for the prairie dog to move around and play, as well as materials for burrowing, allows your pet the exercise required to help it stay healthy and fend off boredom. Adding chew toys and tubing (to simulate tunnels) can help keep your pet active and curious. Prairie dogs are not climbers, so shelving in the cage is not necessary.

Temperament

Prairie dogs can be very friendly and sociable with their owners; however, they can become stressed and may bite anyone to whom they have not bonded. Because prairie dogs are sociable animals, they require attention from and interaction with their owners. They can make a number of different sounds, and owners may come to recognize particular calls that indicate excitement, greeting, aggression, and others. If left alone, prairie dogs can become depressed and develop behavior problems. It is highly recommended that your pet be neutered; otherwise your prairie dog can become irritable and aggressive during breeding season.

■ ROUTINE HEALTH CARE

A proper enclosure and a suitable diet will help maintain your prairie dog's health. Routine visits to the veterinarian can also help assure that your pet is in good condition.

Signs of Illness

The prairie dog's overall appearance and behavior, particularly in relation to its cage mates, should be noted. Early signs of illness involve changes in the color, consistency, odor, and amount of urine and feces (firm pellets are normal). The hind end should be checked for stains that might indicate diarrhea, and females should be checked for vaginal discharges. The fur and skin should be examined for loss of hair, fight wounds or other trauma, fleas or mites, and elasticity for evidence of dehydration. If you gently pinch the skin, it should return to normal quickly; if not, your animal is dehydrated. Feet should be examined for sores and overgrown or broken nails. The body temperature of a healthy prairie dog is normally 96 to 102°F (35 to 39°C). If you notice any of these signs of illness, or if your prairie dog shows a lack of activity or responsiveness, you should contact your veterinarian.

A regular veterinary checkup will help keep your pet healthy. The veterinarian will check the mouth for overgrown teeth or impacted cheek pouches (food tightly wedged in the cheek pouches). Ears should be examined for discharges or inflammation and eyes for discharges or other evidence of illness. A sample of fecal pellets may be requested by your veterinarian in order to test for the presence of parasites or bacteria. Using a stethoscope designed for small animals, your veterinarian can listen to the heart and lungs. Spaying females and neutering males will help prevent related health problems.

Giving Medication

Medicines can be given to prairie dogs by mouth and by injection. Certain antibiotics can cause an imbalance in the prairie dog's naturally occurring intestinal bacteria, which can rapidly lead to blood poisoning and other serious problems as bacteria break down. Supplemental *Lactobacillus* in the diet may help offset the adverse effects of long-term use of antibiotics. Although feeding *Lactobacillus* in the form of yogurt with active cultures is often recommended to help reestablish normal bacterial flora, the active cultures generally do not survive in the digestive tract. Instead, it may be beneficial to use probiotics with *Lactobacillus*. Several are readily available and can be added to the food or water. Follow your veterinarian's advice as to what, if any, supplements to use in connection with antibiotic treatment. Medications or other fluids given by mouth can be given using an eyedropper. If necessary, a veterinarian can use a stomach tube to deliver medication directly into the stomach.

It may be necessary to give your pet anesthesia if intravenous injections or blood collection is necessary. Smaller amounts of blood can be collected by doing a toenail clip or puncturing a footpad or the outside of the ear.

Dehydration may occur with diarrhea or other illnesses. Your veterinarian will be able to determine the appropriate fluid treatment that should be used based on your pet's condition.

■ DISORDERS AND DISEASES

The most common diseases affecting prairie dogs include infections of the digestive system, injuries, and respiratory disorders. These and other diseases are discussed in this section.

Dental Disorders

A prairie dog's teeth grow continuously. Through the constant gnawing and grinding action of the opposing teeth, the prairie dog keeps this growth in check. However, uneven positioning of the upper and lower teeth when the jaw is closed, known as **malocclusion**, sometimes occurs. This may cause an overgrowth of the incisors (front teeth) or cheek teeth. If the condition interferes with eating, prairie dogs will eat less or not at all, and they may lose weight and condition. They may also drool. Excess moisture may accumulate on their muzzles and chest along with partially eaten food. As maloccluded teeth continue to grow, nearby tissues may be damaged. To treat this condition, your veterinarian will sedate or anesthetize your prairie dog, then trim the overgrown teeth back to normal length.

Teeth may be broken if prairie dogs chew on the wire mesh or bars of their cage. If teeth become fractured, your veterinarian should trim them to avoid further damage.

Odontoma is another dental condition seen in prairie dogs. This occurs when the root of the incisor enlarges to the point that the nasal passages become blocked, causing difficulty breathing. The cause is uncertain, but it may be related to vitamin or mineral imbalances, lack of sunlight, or inadequate wear or pressure on the incisor teeth. Treatment can be difficult because it includes addressing the underlying causes as well as surgery to correct the odontoma.

Diarrhea

Several conditions may cause diarrhea in prairie dogs, including overeating, rapid dietary changes, intestinal parasites, bacterial infections, such as those causing Tyzzer's disease (*see also* page 994), or antibiotic-induced changes in naturally occurring harmless bacteria in the intestines. Poor nutrition should be corrected; for example, providing more fiber in the form of good-quality hay can help prevent diarrhea. Supportive treatment includes injected fluids and bismuth subsalicylate (the active ingredient in antidiarrheal medications such as Pepto-Bismol® and Kaopectate®). Intestinal parasites may be treated with appropriate antibiotics. In cases of antibiotic-induced toxemia, your veterinarian may recommend giving *Lactobacillus* bacteria (such as that contained in probiotics) to help reestablish the natural balance of intestinal bacteria.

Fractures

Injuries due to fighting and accidents (such as being dropped when handled) can cause fractured leg bones. A lack of calcium in the diet can also lead to fractures. Unless the prairie dog is restrained from chewing off bandages, casts, or splints, affected limbs may require amputation. Fractures require at least 3 to 6 weeks to heal. Pelvic fractures (broken hips) are common in adult prairie dogs and may heal on their own if the animal is housed in a way that prevents climbing.

Hair Loss (Alopecia)

The most frequent causes of hair loss in prairie dogs include injury due to catching or rubbing the fur on wire cages, poor nutrition, skin parasites (such as fleas, lice, and ticks), and parasitic fungi that affect the skin, hair, or nails.

A prairie dog with a fungal skin infection such as **ringworm** may not show any signs or it may have small, patchy areas of hair loss. Other signs to look for include irregular or circular, crusty, flaky skin sores with reddened edges. Trans-

mission is by direct contact with infected animals and contaminated objects such as cage bedding. Diagnosis is based on physical signs and identification of the fungus in or on infected hairs by a laboratory test or by viewing the skin with an ultraviolet light called a Wood's lamp. Effective treatment may include fungicidal ointments, clipping hair from affected areas, povidone-iodine scrubs, or giving antifungal medication by mouth. Ringworm is contagious to humans and other animals.

Infestations of **fleas**, **lice**, or **ticks** can be treated with dips containing malathion or cat flea preventives and environmental control. Follow the treatment program, including careful attention to dosage levels, recommended by your veterinarian. Fleas on wild-caught prairie dogs pose a risk of carrying the organism that causes plague (*see* page 968).

Monkeypox Infection

In 2003, an outbreak of monkeypox virus in the United States resulted in a number of human and animal cases, including several in prairie dogs. The Centers for Disease Control and Prevention documented the transmission of the virus from infected Gambian rats to prairie dogs at an exotic pet distributor. Signs include large amounts of discharge from the nose, discharge from the eyes, difficulty breathing, enlargement of the lymph nodes, and sores on the skin and mucous membranes. Both animal-to-animal and animal-to-human transmission have been confirmed. Primary transmission is by direct contact with infected

---

Diseases that can be Spread from Prairie Dogs to People

Sylvatic plague
Ringworm
Tularemia
Monkeypox infection

animals or eating the undercooked meat of an infected animal. There is no effective treatment. Because monkeypox virus can be transmitted to humans, any infected animal (and all animals it may have been in contact with) should be euthanized. Potential sources of infection must be removed, and housing thoroughly sanitized and disinfected. Wild animal species of differing origins should be housed separately to prevent spread of the virus.

Plague

Plague is a disease that can occur in several species of animals, including rodents and humans. The form of the plague that occurs in rodents is known as sylvatic plague. Prairie dogs are highly susceptible to infection with the bacteria that cause sylvatic plague (*Yersinia pestis*). The same bacteria also cause plague in humans. This disease can be spread through flea bites, droplets in the air, and direct contact. Currently, sylvatic plague is widespread throughout the western United States. Rapid outbreaks of plague affect a high proportion of the animals exposed, and the high death rate in wild prairie dog populations within a colony may limit further spread.

Infected animals may have no energy or appetite and usually die rapidly. Plague is often diagnosed after death by examination of the animal's body, which may show signs such as abnormal enlargement of the spleen, bleeding and inflammation of the lymph nodes, and fluid in the lungs. Diagnosis is also based on the appearance of sudden, widespread illness and laboratory tests to detect the disease-causing bacteria.

Of all cases of human plague reported to the Centers for Disease Control and Prevention where a source of infection was identified, 13% were due to contact with wild prairie dogs. Infection may be transmitted from prairie dogs to humans by bites from infected fleas or by small droplets of fluid expelled in the air by coughing or sneezing. The risk of pet prairie dogs becoming infected and infecting their owners is very low; however, appropriate precautions should be taken with any newly wild-caught prairie dog. In addition, prairie dogs should not be kept in outside cages in areas where plague is known to be a problem.

Preventing the transmission of plague infections to humans requires adequate personal protective equipment (such as goggles, masks, respirators, gowns, and gloves), appropriate sanitation and disinfection, wild rodent control, flea removal from all animal species present, avoidance of sick or dead animals, and appropriate antibiotics (such as tetracyclines or trimethoprim-sulfa).

Pododermatitis

Literally meaning "inflammation of the skin of the foot," pododermatitis may occur in captive prairie dogs due to rough or wire cage floors, poor sanitation, or injuries of the feet. These conditions may lead to abrasions; pus-filled, slow-healing sores; and long-lasting infections. Diagnosis is based on signs and finding the agent causing infection in laboratory tests. If pododermatitis is detected early, animals should be switched to smooth-bottom flooring and sanitation should be improved, including more frequent changes of softer bedding material. Nails may require frequent trimming. Wounds should be cleaned and hair clipped around the sores. Affected feet should be soaked in a warm, disinfecting solution such as chlorhexidine or dimethyl sulfoxide combined with appropriate topical antibiotics. Your veterinarian can recommend the best treatment program. Severe cases may require injected antibiotics given by a veterinarian.

Preputial Blockage

Adult male prairie dogs that are not neutered and do not mate can develop a buildup of urine, discharges, and debris in the prepuce (the foreskin on the penis). If this material masses together and hardens, it may lead to discomfort, bacterial infection, and damage to the penis. This condition occurs most commonly during or following the annual reproductive season (October to January). A pus-filled discharge may be seen around the opening to the foreskin; you may also notice signs that the animal is unable to control urination. To treat this condition your veterinarian will need to sedate the animal, manually remove the debris under the foreskin, and thoroughly clean the area. If bacterial infection is suspected, the veterinarian will do laboratory tests to find which bacteria are present and recommend treatment.

Respiratory Disease

Respiratory disease in prairie dogs may be due to infectious causes (such as pneumonia caused by bacteria) or noninfectious causes (such as a dusty or humid environment). Noninfectious respiratory disease is more commonly seen in prairie dogs kept as pets. Diet and environmental conditions are suspected to be underlying causes. Obesity may also play a role in older prairie dogs. The airways may become blocked by inhalation of foreign bodies (such as dust or lint) or because of dental problems. Signs of respiratory disease in prairie dogs include open-mouth breathing, sneezing, and discharge from the nose. Noninfectious stuffy, runny nose or other allergic discharges often respond favorably to antihistamines and nasal decongestants given by mouth. Follow your veterinarian's dosage instructions and treatment program.

If infection is causing the respiratory problems, your veterinarian will likely advise treatment that includes general support and appropriate antibiotics. Early treatment will provide the best outcome.

Tularemia

This disease, caused by *Francisella tularensis* bacteria, is rare in prairie dogs. However, when infection does occur, it causes serious illness (such as pneumonia,

blood poisoning, and damage to the liver and spleen) with a high death rate. Transmission is either direct or indirect by bites from infected mosquitoes and ticks. Infected prairie dogs may show an inability to coordinate the movements of muscles, dehydration, severe diarrhea, and sudden death. There is no effective treatment for this infection. Because tularemia can be transmitted to humans, euthanasia is generally recommended when infection is suspected. In addition, potential sources of infection must be removed and housing thoroughly sanitized and disinfected.

Worms

Baylisascaris procyonis roundworm larvae have been found in some prairie dogs that come into contact with raccoons (the natural host of this roundworm). These larvae may migrate to the central nervous system and cause poor physical coordination, head tilt, and loss of the ability of affected prairie dogs to rise or right themselves. Major physical changes may not be apparent, but evidence of parasitic worms has been found in the brains of infected animals. There is no treatment.

Tapeworm larvae are common in wild prairie dogs, but they are rarely seen in animals kept as pets.

Cancers and Tumors

Tumors are uncommon in prairie dogs. Malignant tumors of the liver may occur, sometimes in association with chronic active hepatitis, a disease involving inflammation of the liver. Tumors in the sinus area of the upper jaw known as **odontomas** (*see* page 966) are significant causes of upper respiratory signs in prairie dogs and may be related to the constant chewing and grinding action of the upper incisor teeth. Other tumors found in prairie dogs include benign kidney tumors, malignant stomach tumors, benign fatty tissue tumors, and malignant tumors of the fibrous tissue of the cartilage at the base of the tongue.

CHAPTER 71

Potbellied Pigs

■ INTRODUCTION

Potbellied pigs are members of the Suidae family of animals. They are relatives of the pigs grown commercially for pork. The breed originated in Southeast Asia and was introduced to the United States in the mid-1980s; since then, they have become popular as pets.

■ DESCRIPTION AND PHYSICAL CHARACTERISTICS

Potbellied pigs have a short to medium wrinkled snout, small erect ears, large jowls in proportion to the head, a short neck, a pronounced potbelly, a swayed back, and a straight tail with a switch at the end. Most are black with occasional white on the snout, head, feet, or tail, but some are gray or completely white. Adult potbellied pigs should not exceed 18 inches at the shoulder (ideal height is about 14 inches at the shoulder). Newborns typically weigh from several ounces to a pound or more, and mature animals in trim condition weigh 50 to 95 pounds. Many adult potbellied pigs exceed this weight, and animals weighing over 150 pounds are common. Most potbellied pigs above 100 pounds are obese. They may live from 8 to 25 years, with a life span of 10 to 15 years common in healthy pigs. Obese or unusually small pigs may have shortened life spans.

■ SPECIAL CONSIDERATIONS

Potbellied pigs are very sensitive to extremes of heat and cold and should be provided a clean, dry, draft-free environment. Adults are usually comfortable in a temperature range of 65 to 75°F (18 to 24°C). Because pigs do not sweat, temperatures above 85°F (29.5°C) are stressful for adults. Extended exposure to high temperatures combined with high humidity may be fatal. Potbellied pigs are more susceptible to disease when kept in stressful environmental conditions. In general, the younger the pig, the more severe the impact of environmental stress.

Potbellied pigs are rooting animals and need an area suitable for this behavior. Owners should expect and tolerate rooting in lawns and gardens and/or the disturbance that results when potbellied pigs root in blankets, carpets, or other items inside the home. Using fencing to allow access only to certain areas will minimize damage. In addition, routine hoof maintenance and special dental care are required to keep these pigs healthy.

Most zoning ordinances classify potbellied pigs as livestock and not pets. They are, therefore, banned from residential properties in many urban and residential communities. To avoid zoning problems and litigation, individuals are advised to check local zoning regulations before acquiring a potbellied pig.

Potbellied pigs do not make suitable pets for apartment dwellers or residents of high-density condominium complexes.

■ SELECTING A POTBELLIED PIG

Before purchasing a potbellied pig, examine the location where the pig is being kept. Look for a clean, well-maintained environment and the presence of clean water and food along with a rooting area, "toilet" area, and shelter. If these conditions are not present, it is very likely the pig may have health problems caused by a poor environment.

Look for signs that the pig is healthy. It should be active and alert; free of any discharge from the nose, eyes, or ears; and free of sores and obvious distortions of the body (hidden tumors or lumps). Make sure the snout is of normal shape. Carefully observe the way the pig walks and moves. There should be no limping or difficulty in movement. Check that the teeth and hooves have been properly trimmed and cared for. There should be no cracks in the hooves and the teeth should not be too long. Observe the pig long enough to watch how it handles urination and defecation. Both processes should be easy and pain-free.

Observe the way the pig responds to you. It should be outgoing and interested. Avoid pigs that show signs of aggression or unfriendly behavior or pigs that are unduly shy or fearful.

Ask for a copy of any health records on the pig you are considering. A responsible seller will have vaccination records, birth records, and a history of the pig's health care. Ask to have the pig examined by a veterinarian of your choice before you buy it. If this is not possible, require a signed agreement stating that you may return the pig for a full refund if a prompt examination by a veterinarian shows the pig is not healthy. It is very risky to buy a pig if one of these conditions cannot be met.

■ PROVIDING A HOME FOR A POTBELLIED PIG

Housing

Housing for potbellied pigs may be provided outdoors, indoors, or both.

Outdoor Housing

A large pen equipped with a structure—such as a large dog house—to provide a sleeping, feeding, and watering area makes a suitable outdoor home. You should allow at least 50 square feet per pig. Pigs will instinctively eat and sleep in one area and defecate and urinate in another. Daily removal of feces and the addition of fresh dirt to cover and absorb urine are required for both the good health of the potbellied pig and the control of odor. Hay or straw may be added to partly satisfy the pig's need to root. Fresh dirt should be added weekly or more often if needed. Fencing should be well secured in the ground to prevent it from being "rooted up." Fencing

If kept outside, potbellied pigs need suitable shelter.

should also be removable, as the entire pen should be relocated periodically to prevent the buildup of wastes in the soil and to provide "new ground" for rooting. The old pen dirt should be smoothed out so that it is even with the surrounding soil surface and left unused for several months. If pens are maintained on solid surfaces (such as concrete pads), feces and urine should be removed daily, and fresh hay or straw provided 3 to 4 times per week. Water dispensers must be secured to prevent spilling or damage to the dispenser by chewing.

Indoor Housing

Potbellied pigs are territorial. If they are to be kept indoors, they need a defined space (such as a portion of a laundry room) with a sleeping and eating area in one corner and an elimination area in another. A large litter box with one side cut down to accommodate easy entry and exit often works well. Be sure the litter used is nontoxic; dry dirt or pine shavings are appropriate choices. Potbellied pigs are not only curious, they tend to chew on everything. Providing a blanket to burrow under or a box of dirt to satisfy the need to root will go a long way toward protecting your home furnishings.

Diet

Fresh water should be available at all times to prevent dehydration and salt toxicity. Balanced diets are essential to maintain health and prevent obesity. Starter, grower, and maintenance rations for potbellied pigs are available in many larger pet stores as crumbles or pellets. Provide the recommended amount per body weight and age divided into 2 or more meals per day. Meals should be presented at about the same time every day. Green leafy vegetables, alfalfa, and green grasses (but not weeds, because some are toxic) can be added to the ration to satisfy appetite. Fruits such as apples and grapes can be given in limited amounts. A regular source of citric acid, such as commercial products or oranges, is recommended to reduce the possibility of bladder infections and urolithiasis (the formation of kidney stones), which are common urinary problems in these animals. Many common house and garden plants are toxic to potbellied pigs, which like to root and are adventurous eaters (*see* POISONING, page 1145). To avoid potential danger, do not allow your pig to have access to such plants.

Potbellied pigs gain excess weight easily and have a very difficult time slimming down because, once obese, exercise options are limited. Overweight pigs are likely to become lame and develop health problems such as diabetes.

The best way to help keep your pig healthy is to provide a nutritionally sound diet that discourages obesity. Do not offer high calorie treats or table scraps to your pig. Instead, offer limited amounts of healthy treats such as apples, grapes, and other fruits. Do not forget to consider the impact of treats when planning your pig's overall diet.

Exercise

A daily routine that includes exercise and engaging activities is important for the mental and physical health of your potbellied pig. Regular exercise is necessary to maintain good health and prevent obesity.

A play time that does not include treats may help reduce boredom and discourage eating foreign objects, chewing on furniture, and other destructive or dangerous behaviors.

Potbellied pigs enjoy rooting in blankets or in a special towel box supplied just for play. A favorite toy can be hidden in blankets or towels as part of a rooting game. A dirt box can also supply needed play for your pig; the dirt should be changed regularly and the box thoroughly cleaned before new dirt is supplied.

These pigs may also be trained to walk on a leash. Daily walks and play are important in reducing boredom and avoiding undesirable behaviors. Like meals and other events, walks and exercise periods should occur at about the same time each day.

Temperament

Potbellied pigs are intelligent, curious animals, and they can be affectionate toward their owners. Boredom may result in destructive chewing or rooting or in aggression. The stimuli provided by regular exercise and access to an outside environment appear to have both health and temperament benefits.

These animals have a strong sense of place and rank in their herd or family. At approximately 2 years of age, many healthy potbellied pigs will develop a more aggressive personality and challenge other potbellied pigs and humans for the position of "top hog." Small children and even adults can be in danger from an aggressive 100-pound pig. It is at this stage that many potbellied pigs are either abandoned or placed in animal shelters.

Male potbellied pigs should not be kept as pets unless they are neutered. Neutering at an early age (2 to 3 months) is recommended to avoid development of an aggressive personality. A male pig that is rescued or adopted from a shelter should be neutered as soon as possible. Early spaying may also improve the temperament of female pigs. (*See also* BREEDING AND REPRODUCTION, page 974.)

ROUTINE HEALTH CARE

Locating a veterinarian with experience in caring for potbellied pigs may be difficult. Few small animal veterinarians have thorough training in this area. Similarly, livestock veterinarians may not be trained in potbellied pigs and may not be conveniently located. However, it is important to find professional medical care for your pig *before* an emergency occurs. Research the veterinarians listed in your phone directory or on the internet. A good source of information is the web site of your state veterinary medical association. Most state associations have an online referral service and information about specialized veterinary services.

Once you have compiled a list of possible veterinarians, call each one and ask if they have experience and training in the care of potbellied pigs. If a veterinarian does not feel comfortable caring for your pet, ask for a referral to another veterinarian who has the needed training and experience.

Importance of Veterinary Care

Ideally, a veterinary exam should be done before the potbellied pig is purchased to ensure that it is healthy. If this is not possible, be sure that you can return the animal to its previous owner if an initial medical examination shows that the animal has medical problems. Obtaining any medical records—such as records of any treatments or vaccinations—from the previous owner is very helpful. Bring these records to the first veterinary visit.

The first veterinary visit establishes a record of the animal in healthy condition. This information will be highly valuable should medical problems develop later. The veterinarian should provide any needed vaccinations, a fecal check for worms and deworming (if needed), skin scraping and treatment (or preventive treatment) for mange, and other common services.

Preventive Care

During your first veterinary appointment with your potbellied pig, you can set up a vaccination schedule and a program for hoof maintenance, parasite control, and dental care. These steps, in addition to preventing common injuries, will help your potbellied pig live a long, healthy life.

The hooves of potbellied pigs may become cracked or overgrown and cause lameness, discomfort, and, in extreme cases, infections and abscesses. Exercise on abrasive surfaces such as concrete helps wear down hoof ends and keep them at an appropriate length. For pigs living indoors or without access to exercise on abrasive surfaces, hoof trimming should be provided on an annual basis or more frequently if required. Your pig will likely be sedated or anesthetized for this procedure. The veterinarian may choose to combine hoof trimming with tooth trimming and routine dental care.

Vaccinations

Vaccination is important to protect against disease and also may be necessary for pet licensure in some areas. Follow the vaccination schedule recommended by your veterinarian (*see* Box).

Parasite Control

Many worms and other parasites can cause health problems for potbellied pigs. Further, some of these parasites can pose health problems for pig owners. Your pig's

---

Potbellied Pig Vaccinations

Generally, young potbellied pigs, or older potbellied pigs with no health care history (such as those that have been adopted from a rescue organization) are given their first vaccinations at or after 4 weeks of age. They are vaccinated a second time 3 to 4 weeks later. A booster vaccination may be given annually. Possible vaccination combinations include the following:

- Erysipelas
- Erysipelas and tetanus
- Erysipelas, tetanus, and leptospirosis
- Erysipelas, tetanus, leptospirosis, and *Actinobacillus pleuropneumoniae*

veterinarian should check routinely for the presence of worms (bring a fresh sample of your pig's droppings when you visit the veterinarian). If worms are found, a dewormer will be prescribed and should be used as directed.

Parasites, such as mange mites, can also live on the potbellied pig's skin. The most common disease caused by this type of parasite is sarcoptic mange (*see* page 981). Humans can easily develop this disease, so care should be taken to prevent mite infestations and to control mites as soon as they are found. Every young or newly acquired potbellied pig—particularly those obtained from sources such as a flea market or shelter—may harbor a few mange mites that are not yet causing itching, rubbing, or skin lesions. These pigs should receive routine preventive therapy to stop the development of mange disease and to prevent transmission to its owners. Your veterinarian can prescribe treatment for mites and other parasites as required.

Dental Care

Dental care is extremely important for potbellied pigs. Newborn pigs should have their 8 needle teeth trimmed to prevent injury to littermates and cuts on their mother's breasts and underside. At about 5 to 7 months of age, the permanent canine teeth will erupt. These canine teeth grow continuously throughout the pig's life. They should be first trimmed at about 1 year of age and then trimmed on an annual basis. Without trimming, the canine teeth will become elongated and cause discomfort and a misaligned bite. Pigs with elongated canine teeth may show persistent chewing motions and heavy salivation. Tooth trimming requires sedation or anesthesia and is often accompanied by a tetanus vaccination and removal of accumulated tartar and other debris from around other teeth to maintain good dental hygiene.

Elderly potbellied pigs may have abscessed and/or exposed tooth roots. An x-ray may be required to diagnose tooth root problems. Extraction of abscessed

teeth may be necessary. Most potbellied pigs respond well to extractions and recover rapidly with the help of antibiotics and tetanus shots.

Household Hazards

As with all pets, care should be exercised to protect potbellied pigs from injury. The most common injuries are intestinal problems caused by swallowing foreign objects and bone fractures from jumping onto or off furniture and other surfaces above the floor or ground. Keeping the area where your pig lives and plays free of easily swallowed objects can save your pig's life. Small toys and other foreign objects can easily block your pig's throat, stomach, or intestines and cause serious injury or death.

Fractures of leg and other bones often occur when pigs jump up on furniture or up to areas above the ground. To reduce the risk of broken bones and related injuries, gently but firmly discourage pigs from jumping on and off furniture and other above-ground surfaces. Play times should be arranged so that your pig remains on the floor or ground. Provide ramps rather than steps between levels, because steps are often difficult for pigs.

■ BREEDING AND REPRODUCTION

Although some basic information on breeding and reproduction is included here, breeding of potbellied pigs is not encouraged for the amateur owner. In addition, it is strongly recommended that male potbellied pigs be neutered early (at 2 to 3 months of age) to minimize the development of aggressive behavior. Males that have not been neutered do not make suitable pets.

Females

Female potbellied pigs are normally able to reproduce as early as 3 months of age. Lack of estrus in a female pig 3 months or older should be considered a possible sign of pregnancy, especially if the pig has been kept with male potbellied pigs. It is

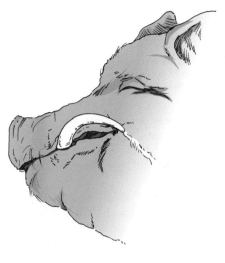

Overgrown tusk

Trimmed tusk

A potbellied pig's canine teeth (tusks) require regular trimming to prevent overgrowth.

recommended that female potbellied pigs kept as pets be completely spayed (the removal of both the uterus and ovaries, not just removal of the ovaries as is sometimes done) at 3 to 6 months of age. This will eliminate irritable behavior during estrus. Spaying also avoids the birth of unwanted pigs—a common problem—and reduces the chance that the pig may suffer from ovarian cysts, uterine tumors, or other problems.

The gestation period for potbellied pigs is 113 to 115 days. As the mother approaches delivery, she will develop a milk line along the teats. She may become restless or show nesting behavior. You will need to have a farrowing box ready. This is a box lightly padded with small blankets or similar soft bedding and large enough that your pig and her offspring can both move around and nestle together comfortably. The farrowing box should be placed out of drafts and away from any other pets. The number of piglets in a litter can range from 1 to 12. Ask your veterinarian for a list of items to have on hand for the delivery. A heat lamp or pad is often recommended because the piglets cannot maintain their own body temperature immediately after birth and require a

temperature of 80 to 90°F (26 to 32°C) for 10 to 12 days following birth. However, extreme caution is required when using heat lamps or pads. A heat lamp can easily overheat the mother, and it can burn the skin of the mother or piglets if it is too close. Also, exposed electrical cords of lamps or pads present a danger of electrocution if they are chewed by the piglets. At least a portion of the farrowing box should be kept cooler, as the mother can become overheated.

During birth, it is wise to keep an eye on the new piglets because they may be injured or killed if the mother pig lays on them. However, the new mother can be very protective of her offspring, and any disturbances or handling should be kept to a minimum. A small board placed between you and the mother may help your pig feel more secure during birthing. Once the afterbirth has arrived, be sure she has access to all her piglets.

Note that passage of the placenta (afterbirth) is the last event of farrowing. It almost always signifies that all pigs have been delivered. Retained afterbirth is rare in swine except when unborn pigs remain in the uterus, which quickly becomes a medical problem requiring professional assistance. Veterinarians use x-rays or ultrasonography to detect unborn pigs, and they may use medical or surgical treatment to attempt to remedy the problem.

Males

Potbellied pig boars (males) should be neutered (castrated) at 2 to 3 months of age. Males that are not neutered do not make suitable pets due to unpredictable behaviors around other animals and people and odor from their scent gland. Breeding boars should be kept in secure pens and not in homes. Neutered males can make good pets.

Care of Newborns

Newborn piglets need a warm farrowing box (between 80 to 90°F [26 to 32°C]) and easy access to their mother for nursing. Consumption of the first milk from the mother, known as colostrum, is very important for their health. Colostrum contains antibodies that provide protection against disease. Piglets need this protection during their first months of life.

Newborn piglets will instinctively find one teat and fight to use it. Mother pigs will grunt as they feed their offspring. When the milk is gone, it will take an hour or more for additional milk to be available. Small piglets, usually known as runts, need to nurse at least 4 minutes at a time. They may not fight for a teat and often do not get sufficient milk for growth and development. In such cases, you may have to either supplement their feed or hand feed the piglet entirely. Check with your veterinarian regarding appropriate milk for these piglets.

■ DISORDERS AND DISEASES

Furnishing adequate housing, a good diet, and routine preventive care will minimize disease in potbellied pigs, as with any other animal.

Digestive Disorders

Digestive disorders in potbellied pigs may be caused by organisms such as bacteria, or they may be due to problems caused by swallowing foreign objects or eating toxic substances.

Gastritis and Foreign Objects in the Digestive System

Potbellied pigs are omnivorous and, like small children, prone to swallowing anything they can get in their mouths. Plastic milk containers, toys, and even socks may be swallowed. This may be related to normal curiosity, boredom, or a seemingly insatiable appetite. The chances of your pig being hurt by swallowing an inedible object will be reduced by providing 2 or more small meals a day, including low- or no-calorie foods (lettuce, cabbage, celery, carrots, or green grasses) in the diet, providing an outlet for innate rooting needs, and providing stimulating activities on a daily basis.

If the object swallowed is small enough and pliable enough, it may pass through the body without incident, cause only mild stomach inflammation, or require treatment with antibiotics. Larger or sharp objects may lodge in the throat, stomach, or intestines and cause vomiting, colic, or infection, which may be mild or serious. Your veterinarian will use x-rays or other diagnostic tests to locate the foreign object and will check for infection and other signs of distress. Surgery is usually required to remove a large or sharp foreign object. In extreme cases, the damage to the body is so extensive that recovery is not possible. Following surgery, your potbellied pig will be given followup care, such as fluids, nutritional supplements, antibiotics, and a tetanus shot or booster, if needed.

Colibacillosis

Colibacillosis (*Escherichia coli* diarrhea) is common in young potbellied pigs. It is caused by *E. coli* bacteria, which are found in feces and wastewater contamination from humans, other animals, birds, and fish. Piglets who have not received colostrum by nursing from their mothers in the first hours of life are much more likely to die from this disease. Older pigs develop

Table 11. Emergencies

Sign	Response
Depressed, inactive, high temperature initially, followed by low body temperature; in direct sun or warm to hot environment	Likely caused by overheating. Use a fan to move air across the body. If in direct sun, provide shade. Wet head first with cool water for 10 to 15 minutes before wetting entire body surface for evaporative cooling. Do NOT apply cold water or ice as this can induce additional temperature shock. If possible, rest your pig on a cool (65 to 75°F) surface. Monitor carefully and get veterinary help if recovery does not occur promptly with cooling. Overheating can be fatal.
Lameness	Potbellied pigs are prone to weaknesses of the limbs and lower back and can easily break bones. Look for evidence of bites or other injuries. Minor scrapes or abrasions may be cleaned with soap and water, followed by the application of antiseptic or antibiotic cream. Check for evidence of more serious problems. If cracked hooves or evidence of animal bites are found, or if you do not find a minor problem, see your veterinarian for a prompt examination. Lameness accompanied by vocalization should be treated as a potential fracture and immediate veterinary care should be sought.
Extended straining to urinate or defecate	If your pig is having trouble urinating or defecating, this could be a sign of serious problems. Your pig may have swallowed a foreign object or have any of several serious medical problems. A prompt visit to the veterinarian is warranted. If a fresh fecal or urine sample is available, take that with you to the appointment.
Frequent urination, straining to urinate, and/or blood in the urine, especially with vocalization	A prompt veterinary examination can determine whether your pig has a serious urinary tract condition, such as a bladder inflammation (cystitis) or stones in the urinary tract (urolithiasis). Bring a fresh urine sample with your pig for the examination.

resistance to colibacillosis. The principal sign is diarrhea. The disease is diagnosed through a medical history and testing of a fecal sample. Good sanitation helps prevent the disease. Commercial swine vaccines to prevent colibacillosis are available, but they must be given to the female potbellied pig before she delivers. The vaccine stimulates immunity in the milk that bathes the gut of nursing piglets and prevents the attachment of the *E. coli* bacteria to the piglet's intestines. Colibacillosis can be effectively treated with appropriate antibiotics.

Salmonella Infections

Enterocolitis is an infection often caused by *Salmonella typhimurium* bacteria. Pigs can be infected at any age, but after weaning is most common. Sources of infection include waste food from over-turned garbage cans, exposure to other pigs with the infection, and wastes from other animals. The signs include mild to severe diarrhea with mucus and blood showing in the fecal matter. Fever, lethargy or weakness, and a bluish or purplish discoloration of the legs, ears, and jowls may also occur. Diagnosis is made by testing your pig's feces for the bacteria. At the same time, your veterinarian will test the bacteria to determine which medication can best treat your pet's infection. Untreated pigs may die from the infection, so prompt veterinary treatment is important.

Salmonella choleraesuis bacteria may also cause infection. The signs are similar to those of *S. typhimurium* infection, described above. Again, early veterinary intervention and treatment is important as this infection can cause death.

All *Salmonella* infections should be treated carefully because the bacteria can easily infect humans. Be sure to wash hands carefully and thoroughly with a strong soap, especially when disposing of waste materials. Children should not be exposed to pigs with any *Salmonella* infection as they can easily be infected.

Constipation

Constipation can be a problem for potbellied pigs and may result from ingestion of foreign objects, low water intake, or any of several diseases. The normal bowel movement of a potbellied pig consists of one main cylindrical formation made up of smaller, multiple fecal balls. This fecal construction is often confused with constipation. If you suspect that your pig is constipated, consult your veterinarian, who can examine your pet and make an evaluation. Take a fresh sample of feces to the appointment to make diagnosis easier.

Treatment for constipation varies based on the cause. In simple cases, an increase in water intake may solve the problem. Encourage additional water consumption by flavoring the liquid with fruit juice or liquid gelatin. In other cases, mineral oil, a mild laxative, or other stool softener may be prescribed. However, you should never force mineral oil or other drugs down the throat of a struggling, restrained potbellied pig. If the pig inhales the substance into its lungs, pneumonia can develop and can lead to death. Enemas may be more effective for some pigs. If the cause is a foreign object lodged in the intestines, surgery may be required. Follow your veterinarian's instructions for treatment carefully. Regular exercise is often helpful in preventing or treating constipation.

Rectal Prolapse

This is a painful condition in which one or more layers of the rectum protrude through the anus. The prolapse may involve only one rectal membrane (incomplete) or all the layers of the rectum (complete). The condition is most frequently associated with a prolonged but ineffectual effort to empty the rectum. It is most common in young animals with severe diarrhea and some other lower intestinal tract conditions. Eating foreign objects may trigger this condition. Straining to urinate can also be accompanied by rectal prolapse, so obtaining a correct diagnosis is important. Your veterinarian can treat this condition surgically, and recovery is considered routine. Once your pig has had a rectal prolapse, the chances of it happening again are greater.

Bone and Muscle Disorders

It is common for potbellied pigs to have lower back, hind limb, or forelimb weakness. Due to normal conformation, potbellied pigs are susceptible to muscle pulls and ligament damage as well as breaks in the bones of the back and legs.

Lameness

Lameness or favoring of a leg can be a sign that your pig has injured the affected leg or the back, especially if the lameness is accompanied by squealing or other vocalization. Pigs usually struggle against restraints and it is advised that these animals be sedated for extended exams, x-rays, hoof trimming, dental work, and other procedures to avoid self-injury. Thus, it is likely that your veterinarian will sedate your pig while determining the cause of the lameness. Minor injuries, including muscle sprains and strained ligaments, are usually treated with anti-inflammatory drugs. Other medications may be necessary if anti-inflammatory drugs do not control the signs.

Fractures

Breaks in leg bones and back bones are common in potbellied pigs and require surgery. Implanted pins, screws, plates, and other devices can help restore motion and strengthen the affected bone(s). Providing an environment that does not encourage your pig to jump on furniture or higher surfaces is the best way to reduce the chance of broken bones. Stairs

If your potbellied pig does not get enough exercise on rough surfaces, the hooves may overgrow.

are a challenge for pigs, and providing ramps between the levels in your home is a good way to solve this problem.

Arthritis

Arthritis can strike potbellied pigs at any age. Lameness is the most common sign. The affected joint(s) may or may not show swelling. Arthritis may be caused by several kinds of bacteria (infectious arthritis), or it may be caused by changes related to inflammation, joint stress, or aging (degenerative arthritis). Early treatment is needed to prevent distortion of the involved joints. Antibiotics may be effective if bacteria are the cause. In other cases, anti-inflammatory drugs can reduce the signs. Once the joints have been damaged, chronic lameness may occur, and pain management may be required. Arthritis in multiple joints may follow bacterial infection of the navel after birth. If degenerative arthritis and joint fusion from chronic inflammation are present, then euthanasia (putting the animal to sleep) may be advised.

Overgrown or Cracked Hooves

A potbellied pig's hooves continue to grow throughout its life. In the wild, hooves are worn down by exposure to rough surfaces. If your pig does not have access to rough surfaces such as concrete, then their hooves need routine annual trimming. Untrimmed hooves can cause damage to leg bones and encourage cracks. Cracks in hooves become infected easily and may require antiseptic cleaning and antibiotic medication to prevent more serious conditions.

Tetanus

Tetanus is an acute, often fatal, infectious disease caused by *Clostridium tetani* bacteria. Both humans and animals, including potbellied pigs, can be infected. The bacteria usually enter the body through a puncture wound, animal bite, open cut, or other injury. The first signs include muscle spasms, followed by uncontrollable, constant muscle contractions and inability to open the mouth (lockjaw). The best prevention is annual immunization; antitoxin and antibiotic medications following surgery or dental procedures may be used in unvaccinated animals.

Brain, Spinal Cord, and Nerve Disorders

Disorders of the nervous system in potbellied pigs may be caused by infection or by environmental problems such overheating or lack of water.

Bacterial Infection

Infections of the nervous system may be caused by several types of bacteria, including *Streptococcus suis* type 2, other *Streptococcus* species, *Salmonella choleraesuis*, *Haemophilus parasuis*, and *Escherichia coli*. These infections are most common during the first 6 months of life. Antibiotic treatment may be effective if started early, but death may occur before there are any signs of infection. Because *S. suis* type 2 can also be passed to humans, care should be taken to avoid exposure when handling a pot-bellied pig with suspected nervous system disease. Wearing disposable gloves and avoiding accidental hand contact with eyes or mouth while handling pigs showing neurologic signs will help prevent human infection. Also, use standard hand washing procedures with antiseptic soap immediately after handling these sick pigs, whether or not gloves are worn.

Signs of nervous system disease may include one or more of the following: fever, depression, lack of coordination, staggering, postural abnormality (such as dog-sitting position or holding a leg up like a bird dog on point), head tilt, circling, involuntary eye movement (nystagmus), and seizures.

Overheating

Because potbellied pigs do not sweat, they are easily overheated when exposed to temperatures above 85°F (29.5°C), especially if the humidity is also high. Overheated pigs may be depressed, inactive, and unresponsive. If an overheated pig has a subnormal rectal temperature (normal rectal temperature ranges from 99 to 102°F) before any attempt has been made to cool the animal, there is little chance for survival. Overheating is often fatal, although some pigs will respond to treatment for cooling.

Salt Poisoning

Salt poisoning or toxicity occurs after an extended lack of water (36 hours or more), followed by sudden water consumption. Less commonly, it may be caused by eating large amounts of high-salt foods. It may be difficult to carefully monitor water consumption when water is provided in open bowls or other containers. As a result, inactive pigs may not consume enough water to control salt concentrations in their bodies. Cool weather may also contribute to this problem for pigs housed outdoors. The signs of salt toxicity include seizures, walking aimlessly, blindness, or abnormal sitting or walking positions. If you notice any of these signs, you should seek immediate

veterinary assistance. Treatment for salt toxicity includes gradual rehydration and medications to reduce brain swelling. In severe cases, brain damage may result in permanent blindness and a vegetative state. In most such cases, euthanasia is recommended.

Seizures

Some potbellied pigs develop seizures of unknown cause. Pigs less than 1 year old are most likely to have such seizures. The frequency of these seizures varies greatly. A pig may have only 1 or 2 a month or as many as several each day. Pigs with only a few seizures may require no special medication. Animals with frequent seizures may be placed on medication to control the episodes. Some affected pigs may stop having seizures as they get older.

Lung and Airway Disorders

Young potbellied pigs are particularly susceptible to an infection of the upper respiratory system, atrophic rhinitis, that causes inflammation and discharge from the nose. Pneumonia can occur in potbellied pigs and should be considered a serious condition due to the small lung capacity of these animals.

Atrophic Rhinitis

This infectious disease of younger pigs initially causes sneezing, a runny or bloody nose, tearing, and distortion of the nose or snout. It is most often caused by *Bordetella bronchiseptica* and/or *Pasteurella multocida*, and less commonly by cytomegalovirus. It is usually transmitted from the mother to the piglet before weaning but can be transmitted from pig to pig after weaning. The more severe the rhinitis, the more likely it is that the pig's nose or snout will be permanently distorted. This distortion may become more pronounced as the pig grows.

Bleeding from the nose, with or without a crooked snout, is a common sign of the disease. Early treatment with antibiotics is recommended for acute cases. For pigs with chronic nose bleeds, cooling the area with cold water and keeping the pig calm are helpful. For pigs in dry climates, increasing the humidity of the air can offer some relief. Vaccines are available for atrophic rhinitis, but they must be used in pregnant mothers and unweaned pigs to be most effective. Watch newborn piglets for sneezing, nasal discharge, and tears. If these signs appear, your veterinarian should be consulted for prompt treatment.

Pneumonia

Like humans, potbellied pigs can develop pneumonia, an infection of the lungs with signs that include coughing, fever, lethargy, and difficulty breathing. Young pigs are exposed to pneumonia-causing microorganisms from their mothers or littermates or from contact with other infected pigs. Pneumonia is a serious disease for potbellied pigs because they have a relatively small lung capacity. The disease is often caused by *Mycoplasma hyopneumoniae*, which damages the immune capacity of the lungs. This is frequently followed by a more serious infection with the bacteria *Pasteurella multocida*. Antibiotic treatment can control the infection and is especially important when a litter of young pigs is involved. Vaccines are available for some types of pneumonia, but their use is probably not required unless your pet is routinely exposed to other pigs.

Pneumonia caused by *Actinobacillus pleuropneumoniae* is very dangerous for potbellied pigs. It is transmitted by mothers to their piglets or by exposure to other swine that have the disease. Pigs that are infected with the disease become carriers, and they can pass the infection to other pigs even though they might not have any signs. Common signs of infection include coughing, fever, and lethargy. Sudden death is possible. Prompt treatment with appropriate antibiotics is required. Even with prompt treatment,

recovered pigs usually have permanent tissue loss in the lungs and may have recurring respiratory problems. The best preventive step for this disease is vaccination. Commercial vaccines are readily available and should be included in your pig's vaccination schedule.

Skin Disorders

Skin disorders commonly seen in potbellied pigs can range from infectious diseases caused by bacteria or other organisms to skin tumors, dry skin, and sunburn.

Dry, Flaky Skin

Dry skin with itching that varies from mild to severe is seen in virtually all potbellied pigs. Bathing may worsen dry skin and can actually cause flaking if done too often. Instead, wipe the pig's skin with a wet towel each week to remove the flakes. Moisturizing lotions (such as those containing aloe vera) may be used as you might use a dry skin lotion. For some cases of dry, flaky skin, your veterinarian may recommend supplementing the diet with fatty acids, but these need to be used sparingly because the extra calories may lead to obesity.

Sarcoptic Mange

This skin disease is caused by mites, which are small parasites that live in the skin. The signs include intense itching, scratching, and skin sores. Affected pigs may attempt to lick the sores or rub them against a sharp or rough surface. Your veterinarian can test for the presence of mites and provide an injection of medication (usually an endectocide) to kill the mites. An additional injection is often required to completely rid your pig of mites. Because potbellied pigs can carry a small colony of mites without any signs, newly acquired pigs may be given a routine preventive injection of the medication during their first examination.

Skin Tumors

Skin tumors such as melanomas are commonly found in potbellied pigs and

Diseases that can be Spread from Potbellied Pigs to Humans

- Salmonellosis
- Erysipelas
- Streptococcal infections
- Leptospirosis
- Sarcoptic mange

other swine. These tumors may be malignant and spread to other parts of the body. Your veterinarian should remove any suspected tumor and have it evaluated by a pathologist. Occasionally, melanomas may regress on their own, resulting in a loss of hair and skin color of the entire body. In these cases, normal pigmentation usually returns, and affected pigs usually live normal life spans.

Sunburn

Sunburn can develop in potbellied pigs exposed to sudden high-intensity sunlight. The sunburn may or may not be obvious. Sunburned pigs may be "down in the back legs" and can show weakness or minor paralysis in the hind limbs accompanied by squeals or other vocalizations. Pigs will recover from sunburn; however, you may want to have your veterinarian suggest an appropriate skin lotion to provide pain relief for your pet. If the pig is kept in an outside pen, it is important to ensure that the animal always has some shade available to reduce the chance of sunburn or heat stress.

Erysipelas

This disease is a bacterial infection caused by *Erysipelothrix rhusiopathiae*. Infection can cause red spots on the skin and the death of skin cells. More serious complications are arthritis, heart problems, and even death. Routine monitoring of your pig's overall condition and alertness to changes in skin color and the presence of sores is recommended to catch this disease early. If you notice skin color changes or the presence of sores, you should have your veterinarian check your pig for erysipelas. Treatment with antibiotics such as penicillin is usually effective. Vaccination and annual booster shots are recommended to prevent this potentially fatal disease. People can be infected with this bacteria and care should be taken to isolate your pig to prevent spread of the disease to members of the family.

Kidney and Urinary Tract Disorders

Cystitis is inflammation of the bladder. **Urolithiasis** is the formation of stones, called calculi, in any portion of the urinary tract. Calculi are found in the bladder and urethra of potbellied pigs. In contrast, kidney stones that stay in the kidney area or pass painfully down the ureter to the bladder are the usual type in people. Stones or calculi can be painful, cause problems with urination, and cause blood in the urine. Both cystitis and urolithiasis are common in male and female potbellied pigs.

Signs of both conditions include frequent urination or straining to urinate, especially with vocalization. A prompt veterinary examination can determine if your pig has either condition. It speeds diagnosis if you can bring a fresh urine sample with your pig for the examination.

Antibiotics are the usual treatment for cystitis. Vaccination may help prevent possible kidney infection caused by *Leptospira* bacteria. *Leptospira* can be transmitted to humans, so care should be taken when handling the litter box or cleaning the area used by your pig for elimination (such as wearing disposable gloves), and thorough hand washing should follow any contact with your pig or its toys or food.

Treatment for urolithiasis can be an emergency situation if calculi are preventing urination. Immediate treatment usually involves sedating the pig and using x-rays or ultrasonography to determine whether the bladder is full; immediate relief of bladder pressure (if appropriate); then removing the calculi.

Routine urinalysis should be included in your pig's annual checkup. This can allow your veterinarian to catch these diseases early and prevent serious urinary tract disease.

Psychogenic Water Consumption

Pigs with this condition consume far more water than is required for normal body maintenance. Boredom may lead to psychogenic water consumption. Other causes of increased water consumption, such as cystitis or other urinary tract diseases should also be checked. To do this, your veterinarian can test your pig's urine both before and after a 12-hour water fast. Young pigs usually outgrow this condition. In some cases, water is restricted and offered only with meals. If this treatment is used, care must be taken to prevent salt poisoning (*see* page 980).

72
CHAPTER

Rabbits

■ INTRODUCTION

Rabbits are small mammals in the family Leporidae. The European or Old World rabbit (*Oryctolagus cuniculus*) is the only genus of domestic rabbits. Wild rabbits and hares include cottontail rabbits (*Sylvilagus*) and the "true" hares or jackrabbits (*Lepus*). In Western nations, rabbits have been kept as pets since the 1800s. As pets, they need a considerable amount of care and attention. Many different breeds of rabbits are available; common differences between breeds include size, color, and length of fur.

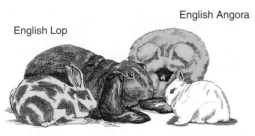

English Angora

English Lop

Beveren

Netherland Dwarf

There are many breeds of rabbits, including English Lop, English Angora, Netherland Dwarf, and Beveren.

A male rabbit is called a buck, a female is called a doe, and a baby is called a kit. Rabbits are born blind and hairless. In the wild, they are usually born and live in underground burrows.

■ DESCRIPTION AND PHYSICAL CHARACTERISTICS

Rabbits are small, furry, mammals with long ears, short fluffy tails, and strong, large hind legs. They have 2 pairs of sharp incisors (front teeth), one pair on top and one pair on the bottom. They also have 2 peg teeth behind the top incisors. Their teeth are specifically adapted for gnawing and grow continuously throughout their lives.

Using their powerful hind legs, rabbits move by hopping. They have 4 toes on their hind feet that are long and webbed to keep them from spreading apart as they jump. Their front paws have 5 toes each. Some species of rabbit can reach speeds of 35 to 45 miles per hour (55 to 70 kilometers per hour). Young rabbits seem to walk instead of hop.

Breeds of Rabbits

Small (2 to 6 pounds; 0.9 to 2.7 kilograms)

American Fuzzy Lop, Britannia Petite, Dutch, Dwarf Hotot, Florida White, Havana, Himalayan, Holland Lop, Jersey Wooly, Mini Lop, Mini Rex, Netherland Dwarf Polish, Silver, Tan

Medium (6 to 9 pounds; 2.7 to 4.1 kilograms)

American Sable, Belgian Hare, English Angora, English Spot, French Angora, Harlequin, Lilac, Rex, Rhinelander, Satin Angora, Silver Marten, Standard Chinchilla

Large (9 to 11 pounds; 4.1 to 5 kilograms)

American, American Chinchilla, Beveren, Californian, Champagne D'argent, Cinnamon, Crème D'argent, English Lop, Giant Angora, Hotot, New Zealand, Palomino, Satin, Silver Fox

Giant (more than 11 pounds; more than 5 kilograms)

Checkered Giant, Flemish Giant, French Lop, Giant Chinchilla

Rabbits vary in color and size, ranging in weight from 2 to 16 pounds (1 to 7 kilograms), depending on breed. Pet rabbits that have been well taken care of and spayed or neutered early in life have a life expectancy of 8 to 12 years.

■ SPECIAL CONSIDERATIONS

If a rabbit is not picked up or held properly, its back can possibly break; therefore, rabbits may be more suitable as pets for older teens and adults, rather than young children.

Rabbits may be housed inside or out; however, rabbits are sensitive to heat. Hot, humid weather, along with poorly ventilated hutches or transport in poorly ventilated vehicles, may lead to heat stress and death. Prolonged exposure to temperatures above 80°F (26°C) may cause your rabbit to become sick. Domesticated rabbits have difficulty with temperatures below 50°F (15°C). Rabbits kept outdoors in climates with temperature extremes must be provided with a fairly large shelter that is heated in winter and cooled in summer. If the rabbit is kept inside, a fairly large cage must be provided when the rabbit cannot be supervised. In addition, extra care must be taken to provide an area in which the rabbit cannot chew on electrical wires, carpeting, or other inappropriate items when allowed to roam free.

Rabbits have a physical and psychological need to chew. Providing your rabbit with a variety of items to chew on will not only allow them to keep wearing down their constantly growing teeth, but will also help to keep them from getting bored. Cardboard, paper, straw, untreated wicker baskets, nonpoisonous pieces of wood, and pine cones are all good choices for chewing.

Rabbits frequently groom themselves. Like cats, they swallow loose hair, which then passes through their digestive tracts and comes out in their droppings. Unfortunately, an excessive amount of hair can lead to the development of hairballs that may block digestion or cause other medical problems. Rabbit owners should regularly brush their pets with a soft brush to help prevent this from occurring. Rabbits with long fur require daily grooming, while rabbits with short fur should be brushed at least twice a week. In addition, rabbits shed every 3 months. One shedding may be light and the next one heavy. During these times, extra care must be taken to brush the rabbit and remove excess hair from its hutch or cage to reduce the possibility of hairballs. During these shedding periods, you may notice some bald spots. These should fill in again after the shedding period is over. Shedding can last anywhere from a day to a couple of weeks, depending on the type of rabbit.

Some people are allergic to rabbits, most commonly those that are also allergic to cats. There is another allergy consideration. Rabbits require hay at all times and if you are allergic to hay, a rabbit may not be the best pet for you.

Many states have legal statutes that forbid selling, offering for sale, bartering or giving away baby rabbits that are less than 2 months old. For complete and accurate statutes regarding rabbits, you should contact your state's Department of Conservation and Natural Resources or a local animal shelter. Also, those living within city limits may want to contact their county health department to inquire about possible restrictions concerning the keeping of rabbits prior to acquiring a rabbit as a pet.

SELECTING A RABBIT

There are several sources from which you can get a rabbit, including pet shops, humane societies, breeders, and rescue organizations. Questions you will want to consider before choosing a rabbit include who will the rabbit be a pet for; what size,

---

Buying Your First Rabbit

Questions to consider when buying a rabbit:

- Do you have a suitable location for a rabbit cage (indoors) or hutch (outdoors)?
- Whose pet will the rabbit be? A young child, an older child, or an adult?
- Do you want a small or large rabbit? Larger rabbits are more docile and robust; these are recommended for younger children with adult supervision. Smaller rabbits are more suited for older, more responsible children and adults; these require greater care when handling.
- Do you want a rabbit with long or short fur? Rabbits with short fur should be combed at least twice a week. Rabbits with long fur require more grooming. Combing rabbits helps prevent hairballs, which can block the intestines or cause other medical problems.
- What other characteristics are important to you (color, ear type, sex)?
- Do you plan to purchase more than 1 rabbit? Rabbits must be evaluated for compatibility; also keeping more rabbits means providing a larger cage or hutch.

---

color, and type of fur do you prefer; and where will you keep your rabbit. When selecting a rabbit, make sure the animal is healthy and that its environment is clean. Ask what type of diet the rabbit has been fed and how it was reared and handled. Rabbits are most active in the early morning and evening hours, so visiting at that time of day may give you a better picture of the rabbit's temperament.

A healthy rabbit should have well-groomed, shiny fur with no bare patches or obvious wounds. Fur that is wet or matted, especially around the chin or the vent, may be a sign of medical problems. There should be no discharge from the eyes or nose, and no discharge or crusting in the ears. Rabbits that are healthy are usually alert and curious when active. They should not be reluctant to move and should not show any lameness or stiffness.

PROVIDING A HOME FOR A RABBIT

Before you bring your rabbit home, you will need to prepare suitable housing, select a proper diet, and plan for your pet's exercise needs.

Housing

A rabbit hutch placed in the back yard, basement, or garage is a common way of housing rabbits. The hutch should be easy to access for proper care of the rabbit, as diseases of neglect are common in rabbits that are abandoned in a hutch at the back of the yard. There should be adequate ventilation and protection from dogs or other predators.

Rabbits can become a more integrated part of the household when they are kept indoors. They can be trained to use a litter box and accustomed to being kept in a cage part of the time. However, rabbits tend to chew on things and may gnaw furniture, curtains, carpeting, or electrical wiring. Chewing on electrical wiring is dangerous for the rabbit and creates a fire hazard. Rabbits should be confined to safe quarters when unsupervised.

Because rabbits gnaw, caging must be constructed of materials that will hold up. Cages should be easy to clean and sanitize. All-wire cages with a minimum of 12-gauge wire are preferred; 16-gauge wire is recommended for cage flooring to support the weight of the rabbit. Cages can be suspended from the ceiling with wire or set on metal frames. The size of the hutch depends on the size of the rabbit. Giant breeds, greater than 12 pounds (5.4 kilograms), require a minimum of 30 by 36 inches (75 by 90 centimeters) with a height of 16 to 18 inches (40 to 45 centimeters). Medium to large breeds, 7 to 12 pounds (3.2 to 5.4 kilograms), require 24 by 30 inches (60 by 76 centimeters). Smaller breeds can be accommodated by 18 by 24 inches (45 by 60 centimeters). Remember: these are minimum requirements and when more than 1 rabbit is housed, the cage should be larger.

The cage should be equipped with a feed hopper and a watering system. Feed hoppers are best constructed of sheet metal with holes or a screen in the bottom for removal of small broken feed particles. Rabbits drink more than other animals of similar size and they should be offered fresh water at all times. Rabbits often chew on the watering valve and eventually destroy it unless it is made of stainless steel or has a stainless centerpiece. Water bottles with sipper tubes work well. Crocks and cans are sometimes used for food and water; however, these containers are easily contaminated and should be washed and disinfected daily. A cage with nothing in it is inadequate; the cage environment should be enriched to give the rabbit something to do. Optimally, rabbits should be given run time outside of the cage on a daily basis.

If the rabbit is going to be bred, a nest box should be included in the cage. Nest boxes should be constructed so that they can be easily placed in the cage and later removed for cleaning and disinfecting between litters. Disinfecting the nest box after cleaning and again just before placing it in the cage helps reduce incidence of disease. The box should be large enough to prevent crowding but small enough to keep the kits warm. A standard size nest box for medium-sized rabbits is 16 by 10 by 8 inches (40 by 25 by 20 centimeters). Wooden, metal, or plastic nest boxes with nesting material such as straw, hardwood shavings, or shredded sugarcane work well in either warm or cold weather. Shredded paper, hay, leaves, and other materials have been used with less success. Rough edges, such as splintering wood, should be avoided as they contribute to mastitis (bacterial infection of the mammary glands) when does hop in and out of the nest box.

Pens should have a nonslip floor and may be bedded with straw or shredded paper covered with straw or hay to increase absorbency. Shavings or sawdust are not the best as the scent is too powerful. Pen sides should be at least 4 feet (1.2 meters) high to prevent rabbits from jumping out.

When setting up group housing, compatibility is a major factor. Personalities should be evaluated for docility and aggressiveness. Rabbits that have grown up together are best, although adult males may be so aggressive toward each other that serious fights occur. Neutering may improve compatibility. A general guide is "same sex and same size." Letting rabbits live in separate pens next to each other is a good idea prior to housing them together. Cages or pens should provide enough space for multiple rabbits. Floor space recommendations vary from 3.5 to 10 square feet (0.33 to 0.93 square meters) per rabbit to allow territory establishment. Others recommend 3.5 hop lengths per rabbit as a rule of thumb. Regardless, group-housed rabbits should be provided escape and hiding places and should be frequently monitored.

Cleaning frequency depends of the type of cage and number of rabbits. Rabbits typically choose a preferred elimination site, such as a corner of the cage or hutch. Poor sanitation leads to disease and deaths; therefore, cleaning and sanitizing must be regular. Nest boxes must be disinfected between uses. Cages, feeders, and watering equipment should be sanitized periodically with an effective and inexpensive sanitizing solution such as household chlorine bleach diluted to 1 ounce to 1 quart of water (30 milliliters to 1 liter of water) or other less corrosive disinfectants. Complete cleaning should be performed before housing new rabbits. Loose hair should be removed regularly to decrease the likelihood of hairballs. One of the most effective methods to remove hair from cages is washing. Pens or wire-floored cages should be brushed or hosed every 2 weeks. An acid wash may be required to descale rabbit urine from solid floor pans. Frequent manure removal is essential. Excess manure leads to unacceptable levels of ammonia in the air, which can cause respiratory disease.

Litter Box Training

Rabbits can be trained to use a litter box. Rabbits naturally prefer to use the same area (usually in a specific corner) when passing waste. Note where your rabbit likes to go and place an appropriately sized sturdy litter box in that spot. The rabbit should able to get in and out of it easily. Depending on available room within the cage, a medium-sized box works well for small breeds, while a large-sized box works best for rabbits that weigh 5 to 10 pounds. Larger breeds may require an extra-large box. Placing a few rabbit droppings in the box when it is first introduced into the cage will help the rabbit associate the smell with the new area to be used.

Many types of litter are available. Be sure the litter you use is safe for your rabbit. Your rabbit will spend a lot of time in the litter box and will often eat the litter. Litters made from alfalfa, oat, citrus, or paper are good choices for rabbits. You may also use a handful of hay as litter. The hay should be changed daily. Adding a few layers of newspaper under the hay is useful to absorb urine. Litters that are unsafe for rabbits include cedar or pine shavings, clumping litter, and clay litters.

It is important to clean the litter box often, not only to reduce the odor, but also for the health of your rabbit. The litter box should be completely emptied and disinfected at least once a week.

Diet

Rabbits are herbivores (plant eaters) with specialized feeding and digestive patterns. They are selective eaters and choose nutrient-rich leaves and new plant shoots over mature plant material that is higher in fiber. They have a high metabolic rate and only by selecting the most nutritious plant parts can they meet their requirements. A rabbit's droppings are small, hard pellets. However, they also expel "soft droppings" and eat them as they are expelling them. These soft droppings provide microbial protein, vitamins, and other nutrients essential in rabbit nutrition.

Rabbits digest fiber poorly. A generous amount of fiber in the diet (at least 15% crude fiber) is needed to allow for proper digestion and reduce the chances of intestinal disease. Fiber may also absorb poisons produced by bacteria and get rid of them through the hard animal droppings. Diets low in fiber increase the chances of intestinal problems, such as enterotoxemia, which can cause severe diarrhea and even death. However, diets too high in fiber (greater than 20% crude fiber) may result in an increased chance of constipation and a type of diarrhea called mucoid enteritis. A proper balance between fiber and other dietary components is critical for the health of your pet.

A dietary supply of vitamins A, D, and E is necessary. Bacteria in the gut produce a combination of B vitamins and vitamin K in adequate quantities; thus, dietary supplements of these vitamins are usually unnecessary. Diets containing alfalfa meal generally provide sufficient vitamin A. Lack of vitamin A in the diet may cause abortion, litters that are absorbed back into the body thereby ending the pregnancy, and water on the brain of unborn fetuses. Vitamin E deficiency has been

Table 12. Nutrient Requirements of Rabbits

	Protein (%) Total	Protein (%) Digestible	Fat (%)	Fiber (%)
Maintenance	12	9	1.5 to 2	14 to 20
Growth	16	12	2 to 4	14 to 16
Pregnancy	15	11	2 to 3	14 to 16
Lactation (7 to 8 kits)	17	13	2.5 to 3.5	12 to 14

associated with infertility, muscular dystrophy (a gradual wasting and weakening of muscles), and fetal and newborn deaths. Disease and stress may increase daily vitamin requirements. High-quality commercially available pelleted diets for rabbits should contain the proper nutrients and should be stored in airtight containers under cool, dry conditions to make sure that vitamins are not destroyed.

Although the basic components of your pet's diet (such as protein, fiber, fat, and energy) do not change, the amounts needed vary based on the life stage of the rabbit (such as growth, pregnancy, nursing, or maintenance), breed, condition, and lifestyle of the rabbit. Ratios should meet the nutrient requirements of the National Research Council (see TABLE 12).

Pelleted rabbit feeds provide good nutrition at reasonable cost. Fresh, clean water should always be available. Rabbits fed hay (alfalfa or clover) and grain (corn, oats, or barley) should be provided with a trace mineral salt block. Prolonged intake of typical commercial diets containing alfalfa meal may lead to kidney damage and calcium carbonate deposits in the urinary tract. Lowering the calcium level to 0.4 to 0.5% of the diet for non-nursing rabbits helps reduce these problems. This can be done by feeding pelleted diets that have a timothy hay base. Adult pet rabbits not intended for breeding should be fed a high-fiber pelleted diet, restricted to ¼ cup per 5 pounds of body weight (60 milliliters per 2.3 kilograms body weight) per day to prevent obesity and maintain a healthy digestive system. Having hay available at all times is necessary to avoid hair balls and to maintain a healthy digestive tract.

Rabbits are very efficient at converting poorly digestible materials into protein. Therefore, it is easy to overfeed or underfeed does and growing, adolescent rabbits. The amount to feed depends on the age of the adolescent rabbit or on the stage of pregnancy or lactation of the does. A general rule in feeding adolescents is to feed all that can be consumed in 20 hours, with the feed hopper empty about 4 hours per day. Does are usually allowed access to food at all times once they give birth to a litter. The general practice is to bring the doe from restricted to full feed slowly during the first week of nursing her young. Some plants are toxic to rabbits and should be avoided (see TABLE 13).

Exercise

Exercise is necessary for the health of your rabbit. A roomy cage that allows space to move around helps maintain both physical and emotional health. Allowing your rabbit some time each day to roam freely outside of its cage (under constant supervision) and providing it with a variety of toys and items on which to gnaw not only provides some exercise, but also helps to keep your pet from becoming bored.

Temperament

Rabbits are quiet, friendly, playful pets if treated correctly. They are social, but not all rabbits enjoy being handled. Before housing rabbits together, they should be carefully assessed for compatibility. Rabbits are most active at dawn and dusk.

Table 13. Plants and Foods that are Harmful to Rabbits

Restricted for Dietary Reasons	Toxic
Alfalfa hay	Aloe
Fruits	Azalea
Turnip greens	Calla lily
Broccoli leaves	Lily of the valley
Mustard greens	Philodendron
Kale	Apple seeds
Collard greens	Raw beans
Spinach	Cabbage
	Cauliflower
	Corn
	Rhubarb
	Potato or peels
	Chocolate
	Raw beans

In general, small rabbits do not really like to be handled and tend to struggle if picked up. Usually, medium to larger rabbits are calmer and easier to handle. When picking up or holding a rabbit, its hind end and legs should always be supported to prevent injury to the back. Proper handling and restraint of your rabbit is important. Rabbits have powerful hind limbs, which can kick out and lead to broken backs if they are not held securely. Rabbits should never be held by the ears. They should be picked up by grasping the loose skin over the shoulders with one hand while placing the other hand under the rump to support the weight. Toenails on the rear limbs may severely scratch unprotected arms when holding a rabbit.

■ ROUTINE HEALTH CARE

Rabbits should receive annual health checkups. Veterinarians may use techniques for physical examination of rabbits that are used for dogs and cats. A thorough examination of the mouth, including feeling the face and bottom of the jaw with the hands and fingers to distinguish between swellings that are solid and those that are filled with fluid, should be performed to evaluate dental health. An otoscope (an instrument with a light and magnifying glass usually used to examine ear canals) or a pediatric nasal speculum (an instrument with a mirror on it) can help in seeing the molars. Gender can be determined by depressing the external genitalia to reveal a slit-like vulva in females and a penis in males. The testicles descend at 10 to 12 weeks. Normal body temperature is 103 to 104°F (39.6 to 40°C). Body temperature less than 100.4°F (38°C) or greater than 105°F (40.6°C) is cause for concern.

Spaying or neutering helps prevent unwanted litters, spraying, aggressive behavior in males, and uterine cancer in females.

Nails should be trimmed every 1 to 2 months or as needed. Rabbits should never be declawed. They do not have the same type of nails as cats.

Routine vaccinations are not currently required for rabbits.

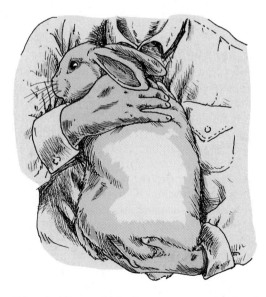

When holding a rabbit, always support its hind end to prevent injury.

Routine Care of Your Rabbit

When To Do

Daily	Give fresh water and food, including fresh hay
Daily	Let out of cage for supervised exercise and play
Daily	Brush and remove shed hair of rabbits with long fur
Daily	Clean out the litter box
Twice a week	Brush and remove shed hair of rabbits with short fur
Once a week	Clean and disinfect cage and food and water systems
Once a year	Veterinary checkup
When needed	Give fresh bedding
When needed	Give new chew toys

Signs of Illness

Signs of illness include discharge from the nose and eyes; fur loss and red, swollen skin; dark red urine; loss of energy, appetite, or weight; drooling; diarrhea or no droppings for more than 12 hours; not hopping or moving normally; and trouble breathing. A rabbit in pain may chatter or grind its teeth while sitting in a "hunched" position. If any of these signs occur, you should take the rabbit to your veterinarian immediately.

Giving Medication

Very few drugs are approved for use in rabbits. Occasionally, drugs approved for use in other species, such as cats or dogs, are used to treat rabbits. Caution is necessary when using antibiotics that suppress normal digestive system bacteria in rabbits. The use of inappropriate antibiotics may result in an imbalance in the normally occurring harmless intestinal bacteria, severe diarrhea, or even death. This has been called **antibiotic toxicity**. Antibiotics that should not be used in rabbits include clindamycin, lincomycin, erythromycin, ampicillin, amoxicillin/clavulanic acid, and cephalosporins. The flea treatment fipronil should not be used in rabbits, as it may be poisonous for some individuals.

Fasting before an operation is not required or recommended. Rabbits cannot vomit, and their stomachs are never empty, even after prolonged fasting. Your veterinarian may administer a pain-relieving medication prior to surgery to help reduce stress. It is critical to get rabbits eating after surgery, and treatment with pain medication for 1 to 2 days after surgery will help prevent loss of appetite. Hay and water should be offered as soon as possible following surgery. Alfalfa hay tends to entice rabbits with a poor appetite.

Signs of Illness in Rabbits

- Body temperature less than 100.4°F (38°C) or greater than 105°F (40.6°C)
- Discharge from the nose and eyes
- Fur loss and red, swollen skin
- Dark red urine
- Loss of energy
- Loss of appetite and weight
- Drooling
- Diarrhea, or no droppings for more than 12 hours
- Not hopping or moving normally
- Trouble breathing

If any of these signs occur, you should contact your veterinarian immediately.

Rabbits that will not eat after the surgery may require force feeding.

Rabbits will chew out skin sutures; therefore, veterinarians use an absorbable suture that is buried beneath the surface of the skin to close the incision. Rabbits also tolerate staples. Tissue glue has been used successfully as well.

Dental Care

Problems with the constantly-growing front teeth (incisors) are common in rabbits. Proper dental care will help prevent these sorts of problems.

Dental Malocclusion

All of a rabbit's teeth, the incisors, premolars, and molars, grow throughout the life of the rabbit. This growth is normally kept in check by the normal wearing action of chewing and grinding of opposing teeth. However, problems with overgrown teeth can occur when the teeth are positioned unevenly in the jaw. This is known as malocclusion. Malocclusion is probably the most common inherited disease in rabbits and leads to overgrowth of incisors (front teeth), resulting in difficulty eating and drinking.

The 2 types of malocclusion in rabbits are an underbite (where the lower teeth stick out in front of the upper teeth), and an overbite (where the upper teeth stick out in front of the lower teeth). A veterinarian can anesthetize a rabbit with malocclusion and trim the teeth to minimize problems. Malocclusion is generally inherited, but young rabbits can damage their incisor teeth by pulling on the cage wire, which results in misalignment and possible malocclusion as the teeth grow. This condition is difficult to differentiate from inherited malocclusion. Inherited malocclusion generally can be detected in rabbits as young as 3 to 8 weeks old.

Occasionally, the cheek teeth overgrow and cause severe tongue or cheek wounds.

Dental Abscesses

Infection of the tissue surrounding a tooth may lead to abscesses. These can be

Normal bite/dentition

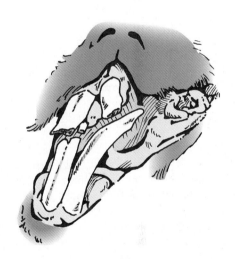

Malocclusion

Malocclusion of the teeth is usually inherited in rabbits but can be minimized with proper care.

caused by foreign objects (often plant material) that become embedded between the tooth and gum, exposure of the sensitive tissue at the center of a tooth (pulp) following tooth trimming, or other diseases or dietary problems. Several teeth are commonly affected. A thorough dental examination and x-rays are required to confirm the diagnosis. Pulling of the abscessed tooth may be necessary, along with procedures to prevent regrowth of the tooth. If multiple cheek teeth need to be pulled, the chance of recovery is small.

■ BREEDING AND REPRODUCTION

Rabbit breeds of medium to large size are sexually mature at 4 to 4.5 months, giant breeds at 6 to 9 months, and small breeds (such as the Polish Dwarf and Dutch) at 3.5 to 4 months of age. The release of eggs in female rabbits is triggered by sexual intercourse, not by a cycle of hormones as in humans. Contrary to popular belief, the rabbit has a cycle of mating receptivity; rabbits are receptive to mating about 14 of every 16 days. A doe is most receptive when the vagina is red and moist. Does that are not receptive have a whitish pink vaginal color with little or no moisture. Feeling the doe's abdomen for grape-sized embryos in the uterus is one technique for detecting pregnancy. The best time to do this is 12 days after breeding. False pregnancy, during which the rabbit shows signs of pregnancy but is not actually pregnant, is common in rabbits.

Pregnancy usually lasts about 31 to 33 days. Does with a small litter (usually 4 or less) seem to have longer pregnancies than those that produce larger litters. If a doe has not given birth by day 32 of her pregnancy, your veterinarian will likely induce labor; otherwise, a dead litter is almost always delivered sometime after day 34. Occasionally, pregnant does abort or resorb the fetuses due to nutritional deficiencies or disease.

Nest boxes should be added to the cage 28 to 29 days after breeding. If boxes are added too soon, they become fouled with urine and feces. A day or so before giving birth, the doe pulls fur from her body and builds a nest in the nest box.

Care of Newborns

Rabbit kits are born naked, blind, and deaf. They begin to show hair a few days after birth, and their eyes and ears are open by day 10. Newborn rabbits are unable to regulate their own body temperature until about day 7. Rebreeding can occur any time after giving birth. Most people raising rabbits for show or as pets rebreed 35 to 42 days after the birth of a litter.

Most medium- to large-sized female rabbits have 8 to 10 nipples, and many give birth to 12 or more young. If a doe is unable to nurse all the kits effectively, kits may be fostered by removing them from the nest box during the first 3 days and giving them to a doe of about the same age with a smaller litter. If the fostered kits are mixed with the doe's own kits and covered with hair of the doe, they are generally accepted. Moving the larger kits to the new litter instead of the smaller kits increases the chance of success. Does nurse only 1 to 2 times daily, and kits nurse for less than 3 minutes at a time. Kits are weaned around 4 to 5 weeks of age.

Kits can be reared by hand, but the death rate is high. They should be kept warm, dry, and quiet. Kitten milk replacer or a formula of ½ cup evaporated milk, ½ cup water, 1 egg yolk, and 1 tablespoon corn syrup can be used. Feedings vary from ½ teaspoon to 2 tablespoons, depending on the age of the kits. Kits start eating greens around day 15 to 18.

Young does may kill and eat their young for a number of reasons, including nervousness, neglect (failure to nurse), and severe cold. Dogs or predators entering a rabbitry often cause nervous does to kill and eat the young. Cannibalism of the dead young occurs as a natural, nest-cleaning instinct. If all management practices are proper and the doe kills 2 litters in a row, she should not be used for breeding.

■ DISORDERS AND DISEASES

Rabbits fed a suitable diet and kept in a healthy environment can live as long as 10 to 12 years. The most common diseases of rabbits include digestive system problems, respiratory infections, and skin disorders. These and other medical problems are discussed in this section. Some of these diseases can also be passed from rabbits to people (*see* Box).

Diseases that can be Spread from Rabbits to People

Disease	Organism
Dermatophytosis (ringworm)	*Trichophyton mentagrophytes* and *Microsporum canis*
Listeriosis	*Listeria monocytogenes*
Encephalitozoonosis	*Encephalitozoon cuniculi*
Mites	*Cheyletiella, Sarcoptes scabei,* and *Notoedres cati*
Tularemia	*Francisella tularensis*

Digestive Disorders

Digestive disorders in rabbits include both noninfectious (for example, hairballs) and infectious diseases. Intestinal infections are common problems and lead to diarrhea, which can quickly cause serious complications. If you notice that your rabbit has stopped eating or has other signs of a digestive problem, see your veterinarian promptly.

Hair Chewing and Hairballs

Rabbits groom themselves almost constantly, so their stomachs often contain hair. The hair is normally passed through the digestive tract and out through the animal's droppings. Hair chewing is usually caused by a low-fiber diet and can be corrected by increasing the fiber in the diet or feeding hay along with the pellets. Adding magnesium oxide to the diet at 0.25% also may be helpful. In some cases, hair chewing is a result of boredom. Providing toys and items on which to gnaw often stops this abnormal behavior.

The hair becomes a problem only if too much is consumed or if it builds up in the stomach and causes a blockage (commonly called a hairball). If this happens, the rabbit loses its appetite, loses weight, and dies within 3 to 4 weeks. Diagnosing the blockage before the rabbit dies can be difficult, because hairballs may be difficult to feel during a physical examination and they are rarely visible on x-rays. Providing adequate fiber in the diet is critical to maintaining good movement throughout the gastrointestinal tract and to preventing a slowdown or stop of the digestive process in the stomach. This is the most important hairball preventive treatment.

Once a blockage has occurred, the goals of treatment are to remove the obstruction, restore the digestive tract's delicate balance, get the digestive system working properly again, and relieve dehydration and loss of appetite. Treatment includes giving medications to stimulate the digestive system into working again, fluid treatment, pain medication, and anti-ulcer treatment. Reestablishing the natural balance of microorganisms in the animal's digestive system may be assisted by certain medications called probiotics or by having the rabbit eat the soft animal droppings that contain beneficial bacteria from healthy rabbits.

Several remedies have been proposed to assist in the break up or passage of a hairball. Pineapple juice contains the digestive enzyme bromelain and has been used to treat early cases of hairballs; an adult rabbit is given fresh or frozen juice directly into the stomach once or twice a day for 3 days. Both the fluid and the enzyme help to restore normal stomach function and to pass the hairball. Canned pineapple juice is not as effective because the canning process destroys the enzyme. Papaya contains the enzyme papain, also called papayazyme. Papain enzymes do not break down the hair itself, but may help break down the mucus that holds the hairball together. Human health food or nutrition stores carry bromelain and papayazyme supplements as aids to digestion. However, you should check with your veterinarian and always follow his or her recommendations for use of these supplements. Mineral oil, cat hairball treatments, and laxatives are not effective in removing the hair mass. Roughage (hay or straw) should be fed during the treatment to help carry the hair fibers through the digestive tract and out with the animal droppings. Surgical treatment is effective but may be risky.

Prevention is the best option. Providing a high fiber diet, avoiding stress and obesity, adding toys and items for chewing to the cage, and daily combing to remove loose hair effectively prevent this condition.

Intestinal Diseases

Intestinal disease is a major cause of death in young rabbits. Although most diarrheal diseases were once lumped together, specific diseases are now being described in more detail. Diet, antibiotic treatment, and other factors create disturbances of the naturally occurring bacteria and may make rabbits more susceptible to intestinal disease.

Diarrhea in your rabbit for any length of time is a cause for concern. If it occurs, you should promptly take your rabbit in for an examination.

Enterotoxemia causes rapidly developing, severe diarrhea, primarily in rabbits 4 to 8 weeks old. It occasionally affects adults and adolescent rabbits. Signs include lack of energy, rough coat, staining around the hind end, and death within 48 hours. Often a rabbit may look healthy in the evening and be dead the next morning. *Clostridium spiroforme* bacteria are the usual cause of enterotoxemia. Little is known about how the organism is spread; it is assumed to be an organism that is normally present in low numbers and causes no harm. Diet may be a factor in development of the disease. Enterotoxemia is seen less often when high-fiber diets are fed. When used in rabbits, certain antibiotics—including lincomycin, clindamycin, and erythromycin—seem to cause enterotoxemia and their use should be avoided. Diagnosis depends on history, signs, lesions, and detection of *Clostridium* bacteria.

Individual treatment for enterotoxemia should include supportive fluid treatment. There is little evidence that anti-

biotics are helpful. A drug used to treat high cholesterol in humans has been used with promising results, both as a preventive and a treatment. Reducing stress (such as crowding) in young rabbits and unlimited feeding of hay or straw are helpful in prevention. Adding copper sulfate to the diet of young rabbits may help prevent enterotoxemia. Check with your veterinarian regarding this medication.

Tyzzer's disease, caused by *Clostridium piliforme* bacteria, is characterized by large amounts of watery diarrhea. Other signs of illness are loss of appetite, dehydration, loss of energy, staining of the hindquarters, and death within 1 to 3 days in recently weaned rabbits. In severe outbreaks, more than 90% of affected rabbits may die. Some rabbits may develop long-lasting infections that appear as a wasting disease. The infection is spread when rabbits eat contaminated food or droppings and is associated with poor sanitation and stress. Internally, there is damage to the intestine, liver, and heart. A veterinarian can perform tests to confirm the diagnosis of Tyzzer's disease.

Most antibiotics used to treat this disease in other animals have not been effective in rabbits. However, the antibiotic oxytetracycline has helped in some cases. Following a disease outbreak, thorough disinfection and decontamination of the cage or hutch using either 1% peracetic acid or 3% bleach should be done to reduce the presence of bacteria.

Escherichia coli bacteria can cause rabbit diarrhea called **colibacillosis**. Their presence can be confusing, however, as these bacteria often multiply greatly in number when a rabbit develops diarrhea for any reason. Healthy rabbits do not have *E. coli* associated with their digestive tract.

Two types of colibacillosis are seen in rabbits, depending on their age. Rabbits 1 to 2 weeks old develop a severe yellowish diarrhea that is often fatal. It is common for entire litters to die of this disease. In weaned rabbits 4 to 6 weeks old, diarrhea very similar to that described for enterotoxemia (*see* page 994) is seen. Death often occurs in 5 to 14 days. Rabbits that survive are not healthy or strong and do not grow to their normal size. A veterinarian is able to make a diagnosis by doing a test to find *E. coli*. In severe cases, treatment is not successful; in mild cases, antibiotics may be helpful. Your rabbit's cage and other living areas should be thoroughly sanitized. High-fiber diets appear to help prevent the disease in weaned rabbits.

Proliferative enteropathy, caused by *Lawsonia intracellularis* bacteria, may cause diarrhea in recently weaned rabbits. Signs include diarrhea, depression, and dehydration, which go away within 1 to 2 weeks. This disease does not cause death unless it occurs together with infection by another organism that causes intestinal disease. Isolation of sick animals and treatment of signs is advised.

Mucoid enteritis is a diarrheal disease of rabbits that causes inflammation, an abnormally high level of secretions, and a buildup of mucus in the small and large intestines. While the cause is unknown, it may occur at the same time as other intestinal diseases. Factors that may contribute to the disease include recent dietary changes, too much or too little fiber in the diet, antibiotic treatment, environmental stress, and infection with other bacteria. Signs are gelatinous or mucus-covered droppings, loss of appetite, loss of energy, below normal temperature, dehydration, rough coat, and often a bloated abdomen due to excess water in the stomach. Your veterinarian may be able to feel an intestinal blockage. The hind end is often covered with mucus and signs of diarrhea. Diagnosis is based on signs and findings of gelatinous mucus in the colon after death. There is no effective treatment, but intense fluid therapy, an enema to remove the mucus, antibiotics, and pain relievers may be tried. Rabbits may live for about 1 week. Prevention is the same as for any rabbit intestinal disease.

Rotavirus causes diarrhea in rabbits. It is shed in the droppings of infected rabbits and, therefore, is probably transmitted by the droppings-mouth route. Young rabbits of weaning age are most susceptible. Rotavirus appears to be only mildly disease-causing on its own, but most rotavirus infections are complicated with disease-causing bacteria such as *Clostridium* or *Escherichia coli*. The mixed infection results in a much more deadly syndrome. There is no treatment, but the infection appears to be self-limiting if susceptible rabbits are not continually introduced into the population. Stopping breeding for 4 to 6 weeks seems to allow the disease to run its course, because infected does do not infect their offspring.

Rabbit calicivirus disease, also known as viral hemorrhagic disease, is highly infectious in European rabbits (*Oryctolagus*). Cottontail rabbits and jackrabbits are not susceptible. Humans and other mammals are also not affected. The calicivirus is highly contagious and can be transmitted by direct contact with infected rabbits or indirectly by inanimate objects. Infection results in a severe feverish disease causing liver damage, inflammation of the intestines, and damage to lymph nodes, followed by a condition in which the blood is unable to coagulate and massive ruptures of blood vessels in multiple organs. Rabbits show few signs and die within 24 hours of fever onset. The infection rate in an affected group is often close to 100% and the death rate is 60 to 90%.

Rabbit calicivirus disease was first reported in 1984 in the People's Republic of China. From there, it spread through the domestic and wild rabbit populations in continental Europe. The first report of the virus in the Western hemisphere was in Mexico City in 1988. Recent outbreaks of rabbit calicivirus disease occurred in Australia (1995), New Zealand (1997), and Cuba (1997). Rabbit calicivirus disease was confirmed in a group of 27 rabbits in Iowa in 2000, in the United States. The source of infection was not determined. The outbreak was contained, the virus eliminated, and the US remains disease free. This is a reportable disease, which means that any veterinarian who identifies it must notify the appropriate governmental authorities.

Coccidiosis is a common and worldwide disease in rabbits. It is caused by protozoa (single-celled organisms). There are 2 forms of the disease: hepatic, which affects the liver, and intestinal, which affects the intestines. Both types are caused by *Eimeria* protozoa. Transmission of both the forms is by ingestion, usually in contaminated feed or water. Rabbits that recover frequently become carriers.

Young rabbits are most susceptible to **hepatic coccidiosis**. Affected rabbits may have no appetite and have a rough coat. Disease is usually mild, but growing rabbits may fail to gain weight. Death occasionally occurs after a short period of illness.

Intestinal coccidiosis can occur in rabbits receiving the best of care, as well as in rabbits raised under unsanitary conditions. Typically, infections are mild and often no signs are seen. Good sanitation programs that can eliminate hepatic coccidiosis do not seem to eliminate intestinal coccidiosis.

Your veterinarian can perform laboratory tests to confirm the diagnosis of coccidiosis. Treatment is difficult, and is aimed at controlling rather than curing the disease. Antibacterial and/or anticoc-

cidial drugs may be prescribed. Rabbits that are treated successfully are immune to subsequent infections. Follow your veterinarian's treatment program carefully for the best results.

Treatment for coccidiosis will not be successful unless a sanitation program is started at the same time. Feed hoppers and water crocks must be cleaned and disinfected daily to prevent them from becoming contaminated with animal droppings. Hutches should be kept dry and the droppings removed often (twice a day is recommended). Wire cage bottoms should be brushed daily with a wire brush to help break the life cycle of the protozoa. Ammonia (10%) solution is the best choice to disinfect cages or other equipment exposed to the droppings.

Although adult **tapeworm** infections are rare in domestic rabbits, finding tapeworm larvae in rabbits is common. Rabbits serve as the intermediate hosts for 2 species of tapeworms found in dogs. Generally, there are no signs. Treatment is usually not attempted, but control is accomplished by restricting access of dogs (the final host of the tapeworm) to the area in which food and nesting material are stored. **Roundworms**, such as *Baylisascaris procyonis*, have been reported in rabbits. Signs may include ear infection or "wry neck." No effective treatment is available.

The rabbit **pinworm** usually does not cause disease but often is upsetting to owners. Transmission of the pinworm occurs by ingesting contaminated food or water. The adult worm lives in the large intestine. Diagnosis is made by finding the eggs during examination of the droppings. Single treatments are not very effective because the life cycle is direct and reinfection is common. Several drugs commonly used to treat worms in animals are effective in rabbits. Rabbit pinworms are not transmissible to humans.

Eye and Ear Disorders

Mature bucks and young rabbits are particularly susceptible to bacterial conjunctivitis (weepy eye), however, the incidence is low. Transmission is by direct contact with an infected rabbit or contaminated objects, such as bedding materials. Affected rabbits rub their eyes with their front feet. Eye ointments containing antibiotics, or antibiotics and a steroid, are usually recommended for treatment. Follow your veterinarian's treatment program carefully because many antibiotics are not suitable for use in rabbits. This infection commonly recurs. Flushing the tear duct with an antibiotic solution is often beneficial in chronically affected rabbits.

Bone and Muscle Disorders

Breaking or dislocating the lower back causing compression or severing of the spinal cord is common in rabbits. Common signs include hind end muscle weakness or paralysis and inability to control waste elimination. Initial signs of paralysis may go away within 3 to 5 days as swelling around the cord shrinks. Supportive treatment includes anti-inflammatory steroids to reduce damage from swelling. Paralysis and inability to control waste elimination after 1 to 2 weeks indicates that most likely the rabbit will not return to normal and requires putting the animal to sleep.

Splay leg is generally an inherited disorder, although it can occur after injury to the leg. The signs include abduction (distortion) of one or more legs as early as 3 to 4 weeks of age; an inability to walk or to support weight may also be seen. The right rear limb is most commonly affected. The condition may affect one or both sides of the body. There is no effective treatment.

Lung and Airway Disorders

Pasteurellosis, a bacterial infection caused by *Pasteurella multocida*, is common in domestic rabbits. It is highly contagious and is transmitted primarily by direct contact, although transmission by coughing or sneezing may also occur. In conventional colonies, 30 to 90% of apparently healthy rabbits may be carriers that show no signs of the disease. Signs of pasteurellosis include rhinitis (stuffy, runny nose), pneumonia (inflammation of one or both lungs), abscesses (pus-filled sores), reproductive tract infections, wry neck or head tilt (torticollis), and blood poisoning.

Rhinitis (snuffles or stuffy, runny nose) is inflammation of the mucous membranes of the air passages and lungs and can be short or long-lasting. *Pasteurella* bacteria are the usual culprits, but other bacteria may cause it as well. The initial sign is a thin, watery discharge from the nose and eyes. The discharge later becomes pus-filled. The fur on the inside of the front legs just above the paws may be matted and caked with dried discharge or this area may be clean with thinned fur as a result of pawing at the nose. Infected rabbits usually sneeze and cough. In general, rhinitis occurs when the resistance of the rabbit is low. Recovered rabbits are likely carriers.

Pneumonia is common in domestic rabbits. The cause is typically *Pasteurella* bacteria, but other bacteria may be involved. The infection causes inflammation of the lungs and of the membrane surrounding the lungs, accumulation of fluid in the lungs and chest, and ruptured blood vessels of the sac around the heart. Upper respiratory disease (rhinitis or snuffles, *see* above) often occurs before pneumonia. Inadequate ventilation, poor sanitation, and dirty nesting material are contributing causes. Affected rabbits lack appetite and energy, and may cough and have difficulty breathing or a fever. Rabbits usually die within 1 week after signs appear. Diagnosis depends on signs, physical changes, and laboratory test results. Antibiotic treatment often fails because the pneumonia is advanced before it is detected.

Reproductive Disorders

Reproductive disorders of rabbits include bacterial infections and metabolic disorders. (*See also* page 992.)

Pasteurella bacteria often cause **genital infections** (pasteurellosis), which may also be caused by several other organisms. The typical signs include inflammation of the reproductive tract and are usually seen in adults. Does are more often infected than bucks. If both horns of the uterus are affected, often the doe becomes sterile; if only one horn is involved, a normal litter may develop in the other. The only sign of an infection in the uterus may be a thick, yellowish-gray vaginal discharge. Bucks may discharge pus from the urethra or have an enlarged testicle. Longterm infection of the prostate and seminal vesicles is likely. Because the infection can be passed during breeding, infected animals should not be bred. Surgical removal of the infected reproductive organs along with antibiotic treatment is required for pet rabbits. The contaminated hutch and its equipment should be thoroughly disinfected. Diagnosis of pasteurellosis is based on signs and laboratory tests that detect the bacteria. Nasal swab tests can be performed to identify carriers. Treatment is difficult and may not completely get rid of the organism. Antibiotics seem to provide only temporary remission, and the next stress (such as giving birth to a litter) may cause relapse.

Ketosis (Pregnancy Toxemia)

Ketosis is a rare disorder that may result in death of does 1 to 2 days before giving birth. The disease is more common in first-litter does. Possible contributing factors include obesity and lack of exercise. Signs include loss of appetite, dullness of eyes, sluggishness, difficulty breathing, and lying down. The most significant physical change is fatty deposits in the liver and kidneys (noted after death has occurred). Injection of fluids that contain glucose may correct the disease. Breeding does early, before they become too fat, is also helpful. Hairballs in the stomach often predispose a rabbit to developing ketosis.

Treponematosis (Vent Disease, Rabbit Syphilis)

Treponematosis is a venereal disease of rabbits caused by *Treponema* bacteria. It occurs in both sexes and is transmitted through sexual intercourse and from the doe to her offspring. Although it is closely related to the organism that causes human syphilis, the bacteria is not transmissible to other domestic animals or humans. The incubation period is 3 to 6 weeks. Small blisters or slow-healing sores are formed, which then become covered with a heavy scab. These sores usually are confined to the genital region, but the lips and eyelids may also be involved. Infected rabbits should not be mated. Diagnosis is based on the signs and laboratory tests to identify the bacteria. Hutch burn (*see* page 999) is often confused with treponematosis because the diseases have very similar signs.

An injection of penicillin G is necessary to completely get rid of treponematosis. All rabbits in a group must be treated, even if no signs of disease are present. Sores usually heal within 10 to 14 days, and recovered rabbits can be bred without danger of transmitting the infection. A potential side effect of penicillin treatment is diarrhea and the possibility of an intestinal disease outbreak due to the increased levels of bacteria in the gut. Rabbits treated with penicillin should be switched to hay and treated with antidiarrheal medications immediately if needed (*see* INTESTINAL DISEASES, page 994). As with any antibiotic treatment for rabbits, your veterinarian's dosage instructions should be followed carefully and you should monitor the overall health of your pet for any signs of diarrhea or listlessness.

Mastitis (Blue Breasts)

Mastitis (inflammation of the breasts) affects nursing does and may progress to a blood infection that rapidly kills the doe. It is usually caused by staphylococcal bacteria, but other bacteria may be involved. Initially, the mammary glands become hot, reddened, and swollen. Later, they may become a bluish color, hence the common name, "blue bag" or "blue breasts." The doe will not eat but may crave water. Fever is often present.

If antibiotic treatment is started early (the first day the doe goes off feed), the rabbit may be saved and damage limited to 1 or 2 mammary glands. Because penicillin often causes diarrhea in rabbits, does treated with this antibiotic should be fed hay or some other high-fiber diet rather than a pelleted ration (*see* page 994). Kits should not be fostered to another doe because they will spread the infection. Handrearing of infected young may be attempted but is difficult.

The frequency of mastitis can be reduced if nest boxes are maintained without rough edges to the entrance, which can traumatize the teats when the doe jumps in and out of the nest box. Other preventive measures include sanitizing the nest box both before and after use.

Skin Disorders

Skin disorders in rabbits often lead to patches of hair loss (alopecia). Many of these problems are caused by parasites, such as mites, that will require medication from your veterinarian. Regular grooming will allow you to check your rabbit's skin and identify potential problems early.

Hutch Burn (Urine Burn)

Hutch burn is caused by wet and dirty hutch floors. It also occurs in rabbits that constantly dribble urine due to poor bladder control. The area surrounding the anus and genital region becomes inflamed and chapped. This is followed by infection with disease-causing bacteria. Brownish crusts cover the area and a bloody, pus-filled discharge may be present. Keeping hutch floors clean and dry and applying an antibiotic ointment to the sores speeds recovery.

Hutch burn is often confused with a bacterial disease called treponematosis (*see* page 998); only a veterinarian can determine the difference by finding the spirochete bacteria under a microscope.

Wet Dewlap (Moist Dermatitis)

Female rabbits have a heavy fold of skin on the front of the neck called a dewlap. As the rabbit drinks, this skin may become wet and soggy, which leads to inflammation. Possible causes include open water crocks and damp bedding. Dental malocclusion that causes excessive salivation can also be a cause. The hair may fall out, and the area may become infected or infested with fly larvae (maggots). The area often turns green if infected with *Pseudomonas* bacteria. If the area becomes infected, the hair should be clipped and antiseptic dusting powder applied. In severe cases, antibiotics injected by a veterinarian may be necessary.

Automatic watering systems with drinking valves generally prevent wet dewlaps. If open water receptacles are used, they should have small openings or be elevated.

Sore Hocks

This condition, sometimes called ulcerative pododermatitis, does not involve the hock (the ankle joint) but the sole of the hindfoot and, less commonly, the front paws. The cause is either pressure on the skin from bearing the body weight on wire-floored cages or trauma to the skin from stamping, with infection of the dead skin. Several factors, including a buildup of urine-soaked droppings, nervousness, hind-end paralysis after a spinal cord injury, and the type of wire used, may influence development of this disease. Genetics are also involved. Heavy-breed rabbits such as the Rex, Flemish Giant, and Checkered Giant are more susceptible. Rabbits with sore hocks sit in a peculiar position with their weight on their front feet; if all 4 feet are affected, they tiptoe when walking.

Various cleansing agents can be used to clean the sores, followed by topical and injected antibiotics. X-rays may be needed to check for inflammation of bone and bone marrow, which may be a complication. The rabbit must be removed from the cage or given a solid floor (board or mat) on which to sit or rest. Treatment is difficult and time consuming, and the condition often comes back. Because big feet and thick footpads are hereditary, selection of breeding stock for these traits has reduced the incidence of sore hocks.

Ringworm

Ringworm is a fungal infection that is common in rabbits. Affected animals develop raised, reddened, circular sores that are capped with white, bran-like, flaky material. The sores generally appear first on the head and then spread to other areas of the skin. Ringworm is generally associated with poor sanitation, poor nutrition, and other environmental stressors. The cause is most commonly the fungus *Trichophyton mentagrophytes* and occasionally *Microsporum canis*. Transmission is by direct contact. Objects such as hair brushes, which are often overlooked during disinfection, can play a significant role in spreading infection. Carriers without signs are very common. Your veterinarian can do tests to confirm the diagnosis.

Because infected rabbits can spread the disease to humans and other animals, they should be isolated and treated. Owners of infected rabbits should avoid close contact with their pets and use disposable gloves, followed by thorough hand and arm washing when handling infected rabbits, cleaning cages and equipment, or disposing of waste materials. Antifungal drugs are usually effective in treating ringworm. Antifungal creams applied to the skin also may be effective. You must carefully follow your veterinarian's treatment program to control this infection.

Myxomatosis

Myxomatosis is a deadly disease of all breeds of domesticated rabbits. It is caused by myxoma virus, a type of poxvirus. Myxomatosis is called "big head" and is characterized by skin sores or myxomas (benign tumors composed of mucus and a gelatinous material embedded in connective tissue). Wild rabbits are quite resistant and usually do not get myxomatosis. All other mammals are resistant to the virus. Myxomatosis has a worldwide distribution. In the US, myxomatosis is restricted largely to the coastal area of California and Oregon. These areas correspond to the geographic distribution of the California brush rabbit, the reservoir of the infection. Transmission is by bites from mosquitoes, fleas, biting flies, and by direct contact.

The first sign is conjunctivitis (inflammation of the eye) that rapidly becomes more noticeable and is accompanied by a milky discharge from the eye. The rabbit has no energy and no appetite, with a fever that may reach 108°F (42°C). In severe outbreaks, some rabbits die within 48 hours after signs appear. Those that survive become progressively weaker and develop a rough coat. The connective tissue of the eyelids, nose, lips, and ears fill with fluids, which gives a swollen appearance to the head. The ears may droop. In females, the vulva becomes inflamed and swollen with fluid; in males, the scrotum swells. Other signs include a pus-filled discharge from the nose, difficulty breathing, and coma leading to death, which usually occurs within 1 to 2 weeks after signs appear. Occasionally, a rabbit survives for several weeks; in these cases, thick lumps appear on the nose, ears, and forefeet.

The seasonal incidence of the disease, signs (especially the swollen genitalia), and high death rate all help veterinarians make the diagnosis.

A vaccine prepared from a myxomatosis virus has protected rabbits from infection, but it is not available in the US. Because there is no effective treatment, euthanasia is suggested. Preventive measures include protecting rabbits from exposure to insects and ticks that transmit diseases.

Shope Fibromas

Shope fibromas, a type of benign tumor, are found under natural conditions only in cottontails, although domestic rabbits can be infected by virus-containing material. Fibromas may be found in domestic rabbits in areas where these tumors occur in wild rabbits and where husbandry practices allow contact with insects and ticks that transmit diseases.

The fibromas are caused by a virus and usually occur on the legs, feet, and ears. The earliest physical sign is a slight thickening of the tissues just below the skin, followed by development of a soft swelling with distinct edges. These tumors may persist for several months before regressing, leaving the rabbit essentially normal.

Ear mites are common in rabbits and may require veterinary attention.

Papillomas

Two types of infectious benign tumors, known as papillomas, occur infrequently in domestic rabbits. Papillomas in the mouth, caused by the rabbit oral papillomavirus, consist of warts or small, grayish white, lumps attached by a narrow stalk on the bottom of the tongue or on the floor of the mouth. The second type, caused by the cottontail (Shope) papillomavirus, is characterized by horny warts on the neck, shoulders, ears, or abdomen and is primarily a natural disease of cottontail rabbits. Insects and ticks transmit the virus; therefore, insect control could be used as means of disease prevention. The oral papillomavirus is distinct from the Shope papillomavirus (which is also distinct from the Shope fibroma virus). Skin tumors caused by the Shope papillomavirus never occur in the mouth. Neither type of papillomatosis is treated, and the condition usually goes away on its own.

Mites and Fleas

Ear mites are a common parasite in rabbits. Mites irritate the lining of the ear and cause a watery fluid and thick brown crusts to build up, creating an "ear canker." Infested rabbits scratch at and shake their head and ears. They lose weight and may develop infections, which can damage the inner ear, reach the central nervous system, and result in torticollis or "wry

neck" (a twisting of the neck to one side, resulting in the head being tilted). Your veterinarian will remove the brown crumbly discharge and then treat the affected ear with one of the drugs that are approved for use in dogs and cats. Products containing a substance that breaks down the waxy secretions in the ear are particularly useful in removing the heavy, crusted material. The medication should be applied within the ear and down the side of the head and neck. Ear mite infestations are less likely to occur when rabbits are housed in wire cages than in solid cages. The mite is readily transmitted by direct contact.

Fur mites are also common on rabbits. Because these mites live on the surface of the skin and do not burrow into the skin, they do not cause the intense itching seen with sarcoptic mange. Fur mite infestations usually do not cause any signs unless the rabbit becomes weakened due to age, illness, or other stress. The mites may be noticed as "dandruff." Scraping the dandruff from the skin onto a dark paper or background will demonstrate this and has led to the nickname "walking dandruff" for this condition. Transmission is by direct contact. A diagnosis can be made by looking at skin scrapings under a microscope. Fur mites may cause a mild skin irritation or inflammation in humans. Weekly dusting of animals and bedding with permethrin powder can control these mites.

Rabbits are rarely infested with the **mange mites** that cause sarcoptic mange (canine scabies) or notoedric mange (feline scabies). These mites burrow into the skin and lay eggs. When infestation does occur, the rabbits are extremely itchy. It is difficult to get rid of these parasites on domestic rabbits. The condition is extremely contagious and can be transmitted to humans.

Fleas can affect rabbits and many other animals. Imidacloprid is a drug that kills adult fleas on contact; products containing this drug have been successfully used to treat rabbits infested with fleas. Products containing fipronil should never be used in rabbits. Ask your veterinarian for a treatment recommendation if your rabbit has fleas.

Kidney and Urinary Tract Disorders

The formation of mineral deposits in the urinary tract (sometimes known as kidney or bladder stones) is common in pet rabbits. The condition is generally suspected when blood is found in the urine. Several factors may contribute to the formation of kidney stones, including nutritional imbalance (especially the calcium:phosphorus ratio), heredity, infection, inadequate water intake, and metabolic disorders. Treatment involves surgically removing the stones, acidifying the urine, and reducing dietary calcium. Because alfalfa is high in calcium and is one of the main dietary components of rabbit pellets, switching the diet to grass or timothy hay and rolled oats may help prevent the condition from returning.

Disorders Affecting Multiple Body Systems

Several infectious diseases and other disorders can affect more than one body system in rabbits. The most common of these are described here.

Abscesses

Abscesses (pus-filled and inflamed sores) on the internal organs and below the skin, caused by *Pasteurella* bacteria, may not be apparent for long periods and then suddenly rupture. When bucks penned together fight, their wounds often develop abscesses. Your veterinarian will likely drain the abscess and prescribe an appropriate antibiotic. These signs frequently recur.

Heat Exhaustion

Rabbits are sensitive to heat. Hot, humid weather, along with poorly ventilated hutches or transport in poorly ventilated vehicles, may cause death, particularly in pregnant does. Affected rabbits stretch out and breathe rapidly. Outdoor hutches should be constructed so that they can be sprinkled in hot, humid weather. Unlimited access to cool water should be provided. When the environment can be controlled, optimal conditions include a temperature of 50 to 70°F (15 to 21°C) and a relative humidity of 40 to 60%, with good ventilation. Wire cages are preferable to solid hutches.

Treatment for heat exhaustion consists of immersing rabbits in cold water during the heat of the day, especially those that will give birth to a litter in the next day or two. Breeding bucks may lose a majority of viable sperm and might not breed successfully for several weeks while new sperm production replaces the sperm killed by heat stress.

Listeriosis

Listeriosis, a bacterial infection of the blood characterized by sudden death or abortion, is seen occasionally and is most common in does near the end of pregnancy. Poor husbandry and stress may be important in starting the disease. Signs may include loss of appetite, depression, and weight loss. The bacteria that cause listeriosis, *Listeria monocytogenes*, spreads by way of the blood to the liver, spleen, and uterus. It can infect many animals, including humans. Because diagnosis is rarely made before death, treatment is seldom attempted. If your pregnant doe becomes listless, loses weight, or seems depressed, you should contact your veterinarian promptly.

Tularemia

Tularemia (infection with *Francisella tularensis* bacteria) is rare in domestic rabbits, but wild rabbits and rodents are highly susceptible and have been involved in most outbreaks among domesticated rabbits. The bacteria also can infect people, and up to 90% of human cases are linked to wild rabbit exposure. The bacteria is found widely in the south central United States. It is highly infectious and can be passed through the skin, through the respiratory tract by way of aerosols, by ingestion, and by bloodsucking insects and ticks. Tularemia can cause a deadly blood infection. Diagnosis is based on findings made after death occurs, such as signs of bacterial blood infection, small bright white spots on the liver, and enlargement of the liver and spleen. There is no effective treatment for infected rabbits. Tularemia is a reportable disease and your veterinarian is required to tell public health authorities about any cases that occur.

Encephalitozoonosis

Encephalitozoonosis is a widespread protozoal infection of rabbits and occasionally of mice, guinea pigs, rats, and dogs. It causes pitting and sometimes inflammation of the kidneys; sometimes small masses occur in the brain and kidneys. Usually, no signs are seen. How it is transmitted is not definitely known, but the organism is shed in the urine. It seems to be mildly contagious in a rabbit colony. Your veterinarian can confirm a diagnosis using laboratory tests. Effective treatment has not been established. Prevention requires good sanitation.

Cancers and Tumors

By far, the most common tumor in rabbits is **uterine adenocarcinoma** (malignant tumor in the uterus). The likelihood of developing this cancer is related to breed. The disease may occur as multiple tumors that often spread to the liver, lungs, and other organs. This cancer is the primary reason for spaying (removing the ovaries and uterus) any nonbreeding female rabbits. Monitoring for the spread of the cancer should follow surgical removal of the uterine tumor. **Malignant lymphomas** (tumors in the lymph nodes) are relatively common and may occur in rabbits less than 2 years old. Typically, tumors in the lymph nodes cause enlargement of the kidneys, spleen, liver, and lymph nodes.

Papillomas and **Shope fibromas** are 2 types of benign skin tumors that occur in rabbits (*see* page 1000).

CHAPTER **73**

Rats

■ INTRODUCTION

Pet rats (scientific name *Rattus norvegicus*) originated from the Norway rat, found on the streets of cities and in the fields of rural areas. The Norway rat became domesticated in Victorian times and people began to selectively breed them for their fur and color. Rats have a long history in association with humans, although not always very pleasant. Some cultures regard rats benevolently; they are the first sign in the Chinese zodiac and are considered gods in some Indian religions. In Europe they were considered creatures of darkness, death, and disease because of the belief that they transmitted the plague. Today we know that it was not rats, but rather the fleas they harbored, that carried the infection.

▪ DESCRIPTION AND PHYSICAL CHARACTERISTICS

Adult female and male rats typically weigh 12 to 16 ounces (350 to 450 grams) and 16 to 23 ounces (450 to 650 grams), respectively (see TABLE 14). They are about 9 to 11 inches long without the tail. Male rats are usually larger than females. Pet rats are available in several colors and coat patterns due to specialized breeding. The common color variations include brown, black, tan, gray, and white with both lighter and darker shades as well. Some of the more exotic colors are Siamese, blue, silver black, silver fawn, lilac, cinnamon, black-eyed white, cinnamon pearl, lynx, silver agouti, silver lilac, and blaze. Rex rats have a curly coat. Tailless rats are born with no tails and hairless rats have no fur. The average life span of rats is about 2.5 to 3.5 years.

▪ SPECIAL CONSIDERATIONS

Domesticated rats are social, active, intelligent, and make good pets. They are nocturnal by nature and usually spend most of their time sleeping during the day; at night they are very active. In general, pet rats rarely bite.

Table 14. Rats at a Glance	
Lifespan	2.5 to 3.5 years
Length	Body: 9 to 11 inches (23 to 28 centimeters) Tail: 7 to 9 inches (18 to 23 centimeters)
Weight	12 to 23 ounces (350 to 650 grams)
Cage temperature range	64 to 78°F (18 to 26°C)
Relative humidity	40 to 70%
Breeding age	4 to 5 weeks
Estrous cycle	4 to 5 days
Gestation period	21 to 23 days
Litter size	6 to 12 young
Weaning age	21 days

The best way to pick up a rat is to grasp it gently over the shoulders and lift it up. They can also be steadied by grasping the base of the tail, but you should avoid picking up a rat by the tip of its tail. Move slowly to avoid startling the animal, and watch its behavior; a rat that rears up to face your approaching hand is more likely to bite.

Rats are social animals and need company; it is better to keep them in a group. However, they are also very prolific breeders, so keeping only rats of the same sex in the same cage is recommended. Aggression is uncommon in domesticated rats that are raised together as littermates. However, when new groups of animals are housed together, they should be watched carefully for fighting, as this may cause injuries.

Rats are very sensitive to heat and cold. They have a limited capacity to regulate their body temperature and do not sweat or pant. They regulate their body temperature through dilation or constriction of the veins in their tail. Rats should be kept in a temperature range of 64 to 78°F (18 to 26°C) with 40 to 70% humidity in the air. Temperatures above 86°F (30°C) can cause heat exhaustion, especially if the cage is overcrowded. Although good lighting is important, rats should be kept away from direct sunlight.

▪ SELECTING A RAT

When selecting a rat from a pet store or animal shelter, make sure that all the rats look healthy and alert, and that the animals are kept in clean and comfortable conditions. If any of the rats look sick, or if there is evidence of diarrhea or any bad smell in the cage, the rats may have been exposed to an infectious disease. Individual rats should have clean, shiny fur and the eyes and nose should be clear of any discharge.

Rats that have been handled should not be too skittish and are often naturally curious about humans. Because they are nocturnal, it is a good idea to view rats in the early evening when they are more likely to be fully awake and alert.

■ PROVIDING A HOME FOR A RAT

Your pet rat will need a suitable cage, a balanced diet, and the opportunity for exercise and socialization with you in order to remain in good health.

Housing

A wide variety of cages are available for pet rats. In general, a cage should have good ventilation, be easy to clean, and be escape-proof. It should have enough space to allow for some exercise, as well as areas for feeding and nesting. Extra space should be allowed if several rats are housed together. A plastic cage or glass aquarium or terrarium can make a good home for a pet rat; however the top should be mesh to allow plenty of ventilation. Metal or wire cages are less desirable because they can allow drafts (through mesh openings) and collect condensation. Metal cages are also harder to clean and disinfect and can corrode after long exposure to urine. Cages made with wood are unacceptable for housing rats, as their urine will soak into the wood. This causes ammonia buildup, which can lead to respiratory disease. Rats may also chew through the wood, allowing them to escape. The wood may also splinter, making it unsafe.

If wire shelves are used in the cage for the animals to climb on, they should be made of wire with openings no wider than ½ by ½ inch. Any wider opening might allow the rat's back foot to get caught in the opening, leading to injuries such as a broken leg. The new powder-coated wire rat cages with solid metal shelves and plastic cat pan bottoms are the easiest to clean, and rats seem to enjoy climbing on the various levels.

The bedding and floor covering should be absorbent. Wood shavings or prepared litter can provide soft bedding for rats. Hay may be added. Recycled paper products marketed as bedding are safe and easy to clean. Cedar shavings contain oils that may be toxic to small animals, and their use remains controversial.

A water bottle with a hanger that allows rats to easily drink water can be used. A water dish should be avoided as rats may spill the water or push shavings in it. Holders with chew guards for the water bottle are available. These allow you to hang the bottle inside the cage. If you use a feed dish, it should be easy to clean and sturdy enough to prevent tipping.

As with any pet, those living in a poor environment will develop health problems quickly. An unclean cage combined with poor quality bedding materials can increase the risk of bacterial and viral infection in rats. The cages should be cleaned with hot water at least once a week and the bedding should be changed at least twice weekly. Avoid allowing a buildup of ammonia (due to urine), which is produced when cage litter is not changed frequently enough.

Diet

In the wild, rats eat a varied diet. Domesticated rats need a balanced diet including carbohydrates, protein, and fat, as well as certain vitamins and minerals. Commercially prepared food is available at pet stores and not only contains all the vitamins and minerals that rats need but also provides pellets that are hard enough to wear down the constantly growing incisor teeth of the rat. Some mixtures contain pellets mixed with seeds; however, these should be avoided because rats will often pick out the seeds and leave the pellets. Rats may avoid new foods, so if you are changing from a seed mixture to pellets, it is best to introduce the new diet gradually. Fresh vegetables, sunflower seeds, and fruit can be given in limited amounts as treats. Fatty treats should be avoided, because older rats are prone to obesity.

Food should be available at all times; however, any uneaten food should be removed from the cage before fresh food is provided (at least once daily). Use solid containers for food that the rat cannot easily tip over. Fresh water should always be available from a water bottle mounted on or hung in the cage. All food and water containers should be cleaned thoroughly every day.

Exercise

Routine exercise is necessary for good health in all animals. Rats are extremely active and enjoy opportunities to exercise and play. Access to exercise wheels, tubes, ladders, and climbing blocks provides stimulation and is part of a balanced life. It may also help prevent obesity. If you get an exercise wheel for your rat, it should be at least 12 to 14 inches in diameter. The cage should be large enough to accommodate some of these "cage toys" and allow comfortable movement around them.

Temperament

Rats are very social creatures. They appreciate being in a group, and will often spend large amounts of time grooming themselves or fellow cage mates. Male rats tend to fight unless they grew up together. Females can be in the same cage without any problems.

Usually, rats are great with children but they should be kept away from other pets in the house such as dogs, cats, birds, and other rodents. Remember that rats are the natural predators or prey for several of these animals!

Because rats are nocturnal, they can be quite active at night. You may want to consider locating the cage in a place where sleeping family members will not be disturbed by their activity.

■ ROUTINE HEALTH CARE

Appropriate housing, a nutritious diet, good hygiene, and considerate care will minimize disease problems for your rat. Injuries can be prevented by keeping your pet in a cage free of hazards and always handling it carefully and gently. There are currently no vaccines for rats or other small rodents.

You should regularly examine your rat for any general signs that might indicate illness, trauma, or the presence of disease. These include loss of appetite or weight, hunched posture, discharge from the eyes or nose, hair loss, matted or fluffed fur, signs of trauma (bites, wounds, limping), or general dullness.

Signs of Illness

Loss of appetite or energy, dull coat, a puffy appearance of the coat, loud or raspy breathing, and labored breathing are all early signs of illness (*see* TABLE 15).

Table 15. Common Signs of Illness in Rats

Signs	Possible Cause
Wounds with patchy hair loss on the back, neck, and base of tail	This might be a sign of ringworm, barbering, or skin parasites such as mites or lice.
Reddish-brown discharge around the eyes	This might be a sign of a respiratory infection or infection by Sialodacryoadenitis virus. These infections are very serious and can lead to pneumonia.
Head tilt or circling	This might be a sign of ear infection, respiratory infection, or pituitary tumor.
Itching and scabs	This might be a sign of allergies, parasite infection (for example, mites, lice), high protein diet, or bacterial or fungal infection of the skin.
Lump	This might be an abscess, cyst, or tumor.
Paralysis	This might be due to brain or pituitary tumors (usually front leg paralysis), or stroke (usually one side and a rapid onset).
Sneezing, wheezing, or gasping	These might be a sign of allergies, heart failure, respiratory infection, or stroke.

Changes in the color, consistency, smell, or amount of urine or feces may also indicate that your rat is sick. Any of these signs is an indication that your rat needs to see a veterinarian promptly.

The Harderian gland, which lies behind the rat's eyeball, secretes a reddish-brown substance that lubricates the eye and eyelids. This secretion (sometimes referred to as **red tears**) gives the appearance of blood, but contains little or no blood. It is sometimes seen around the eyes and nose and may be a sign that your rat is ill or stressed.

Head tilt, often called "wry neck," is another sign of illness in rats. It is usually caused by an inner ear infection, but may also be caused by complications of respiratory infection, pituitary tumors, or even by a stroke. The rat should be seen by a veterinarian to determine the proper course of treatment.

Dental Care

Rats have incisor teeth that grow continuously throughout their lives. They have a need to wear down their growing teeth and should be provided with appropriate materials to gnaw. Wooden gnawing blocks hone down teeth and are a good solution. Rawhide chew sticks or hard dog biscuits can also be used. Cooked

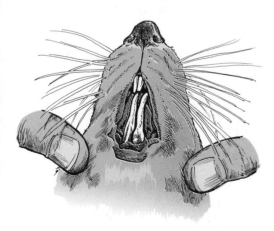

Rats have incisors that grow continuously. Overgrown incisors are a common problem in pet rats.

soup bones are a favorite of rats. When necessary, periodic trimming by your veterinarian will control the growing teeth. Overgrown incisors are a common problem in pet rats and can lead to difficulty in eating, weight loss, dehydration, and mouth trauma. If not kept trimmed, the teeth can grow into the nasal cavity.

■ BREEDING AND REPRODUCTION

Rats reach sexual maturity at about 4 to 5 weeks of age. From this age onward, females and males should be housed separately. The average gestation time is 21 to 23 days for rats, and pregnancy is sometimes detectable at about 2 weeks by feeling the abdomen or noticing weight gain or mammary (breast) development. Pregnant females will make a nest, and they should be provided with suitable materials. Tissue paper provides excellent material for nesting.

The usual litter size is 6 to 12 pups. When baby rats are born, they are deaf and blind. The cage should be kept in a quiet place and the litter should not be disturbed for at least 7 days after birth, especially if this is the female's first litter. Weaning occurs about 21 days after birth. Female rats can quickly become pregnant again after giving birth; however, it is not healthy for a female rat to be both pregnant and nursing a litter. It is recommended that the female be given a rest period of at least 2 months between pregnancies and litter rearing, to restore her body to full strength.

Breeding and reproduction in rats can decrease due to various factors such as age, malnutrition, abnormal light cycles, cold environment, cysts on the ovaries, tumors, and inadequate nesting material. Pregnant females may abort, abandon, or eat their babies due to inadequate food or lack of water, overcrowding in group housing, inadequate nesting materials, sick or deformed pups, or excessive noise. In healthy rats, however, reproductive problems are uncommon.

DISORDERS AND DISEASES

Infections, parasites, and cancer are some of the most common types of diseases and disorders in rats. Providing a balanced diet, proper housing, and routine veterinary care will help maintain your rat in the best condition possible.

Digestive Disorders

The most common digestive disorders of rats are caused by intestinal parasites or bacterial infection. These conditions are described in this section.

Intestinal Parasites

Pinworms are common intestinal parasites in rats. They only require one host (in this case, rats) and are transmitted through infected feces. Most infected rats have no signs, but a heavy infection of pinworms can cause diarrhea due to intestinal inflammation. The disease is diagnosed by identifying worms or their eggs in infected feces or on the area around the anus of the rat. Pinworm infections can be treated and controlled by using appropriate drugs prescribed by a veterinarian. Because pinworm eggs are light and may float in the air, it is important to sanitize and disinfect the cage on a regular basis.

The infection of rats with **tapeworms** is relatively uncommon, and there is usually no sign of infection. However, diarrhea and weight loss may occur with heavy infestation. The dwarf tapeworm can potentially infect humans if ingested. Tapeworms are transmitted indirectly through cockroaches, beetles, or fleas. The infection is diagnosed by identifying tapeworm eggs in infected feces. The worm infection is treated by using appropriate antiparasitic drugs. The cage should be sanitized and disinfected.

Rats are the intermediate host for the cat tapeworm, *Taenia taeniaformis*. Cat tapeworms can infect rats. Infection occurs when rats eat feed or come in contact with bedding contaminated with cat feces. Tapeworm cysts embed in the rat's liver, which becomes enlarged. It is important

for those who own both rodents and cats to eliminate potential sources of infection.

Protozoa

Various types of protozoa (microorganisms) are normally present in the digestive tract of rats and do not usually cause disease. However, in younger or stressed rats, these protozoa can cause intestinal infections. The infection is transmitted by contaminated feces, and infected rats have diarrhea, lethargy, rough hair coat, weight loss and, in severe cases, heavy bleeding that can lead to death. The protozoa can be controlled with appropriate drugs, but cannot always be eliminated.

Sialodacryoadenitis and Rat Coronavirus Infection

These related viruses infect the nasal cavities, lungs, Harderian gland (near the eyes), and salivary glands of rats. They are highly contagious and are transmitted by direct contact, airborne virus particles (such as from an infected rat's sneeze), or by exposure to contaminated bedding, feces, or other objects in the cage. To prevent the transmission of these diseases, it is important to wash your hands after handling animals in a pet shop or at a friend's house before handling your rat. Infection usually lasts 2 to 3 weeks.

Affected rats will sneeze and may seek to avoid direct or bright light. Enlarged salivary glands and lymph nodes can sometimes be felt. A rat may look as if it has mumps. Reddish brown pigments and discharge may be seen around the eyes, and eye involvement such as inflammation of the cornea or conjunctiva may occur; however, not all infected animals show these signs. There is no treatment, but infected animals usually recover and will develop resistance to future infections by these viruses.

Brain, Nerve, and Spinal Cord Disorders

Spinal cord degeneration can occur in rats older than 2 years. Affected rats' hind limbs are paralyzed.

Lung and Airway Disorders

Chronic respiratory disease (murine respiratory mycoplasmosis) is a bacterial infection. It causes both short- and long-term respiratory signs and other problems in rats. The infection is transmitted by direct contact, airborne bacteria, and sexual contact. It can also be passed on from a mother to her offspring during birth. The signs of infection vary but may include sneezing, sniffling, rough hair coat, lethargy, labored breathing, weight loss, head tilt, and reddish-brown staining around the eyes and nose. As the disease progresses, it will infect the lungs.

The infection can become more severe in the presence of other bacterial and viral infections. Infection of the uterus and ovaries may occur in female rats with chronic respiratory disease.

There is no cure for this condition. However, the signs of infection can be alleviated with antibiotics, and rats may live for 2 to 3 years with chronic respiratory disease. Keeping your rat's home clean—in particular by reducing ammonia levels in the cage—and early treatment of the infection are the best ways to fight this disease.

Several other bacteria and viruses can cause respiratory infections and pneumonia in rats. These all lead to similar signs, such as sneezing, sniffling, labored breathing, rough hair coat, inactivity, weight loss, lack of appetite, and discharge from the eyes or nose. If you notice any of these signs, you should take your rat to the veterinarian.

The diseases may be transmitted between rats by several routes, depending on the specific organism, including direct contact with infected animals, contaminated feces, or sneezing or coughing on one another. While most of these infections cannot be cured, your veterinarian may prescribe antibiotics to help reduce the severity of illness. Supportive care and keeping the rat's environment clean will also be helpful. Individuals showing signs of respiratory infection should be kept separate from other rats to reduce the spread of disease.

Skin Disorders

Skin disorders are common problems in rats. They can be caused by parasites, bacteria, or injury.

Barbering

This abnormal grooming behavior is occasionally seen in groups of male or female rats. Dominant members of the group chew the hair and whiskers of less dominant rats. Because the rat chews the hair so close to the skin, it gives the appearance of being clean-shaven, hence the term barbering. Stress, boredom, and even heredity can lead to this behavior, and rats sometimes barber themselves. The most common places barbering is seen on the body are the stomach and front legs if caused by self-grooming, or on the muzzle, head, or shoulders of a cage mate. The skin is generally not affected, and its appearance will be normal without signs of inflammation, irritation, or cuts. Unless irritation develops, this condition does not require treatment. If barbering occurs because of the presence of a dominant rat, the dominant rat should be removed for the well-being of the other cage mates.

Fight Wounds

Male rats often fight and cause injuries to the face, back, and genital areas. The skin will show patches of hair loss and scabs. Such injuries can become infected with bacteria, leading to the formation of abscesses. Tail biting can lead to gangrene. Affected rats lose weight and sometimes die. The fight wounds can be treated by cleaning them with a disinfectant solution, draining the abscesses, and applying appropriate antibiotic ointments, as recommended or prescribed by your veterinarian. Rats that fight frequently should be separated.

Fleas

Rodent fleas are uncommon in pet rats, but are sometimes seen if pets come into contact with wild rodents. The fleas are diagnosed by identifying them on the infested rats. Fleas are treated with medicated dusts or sprays. To prevent reinfestation, disinfect and clean the cage thoroughly. When holding or playing with rats other than your own, it is recommended that you wash and change clothes prior to handling your own rats.

Lice

Infestations of blood-sucking lice are common in wild rats, but are rarely seen in pet rats. Human beings will not be affected if their pet rat has these lice, because the lice do not cross over from one species to another. Heavily infested rats show intense itching, restlessness, weakness, and anemia (lack of red blood cells). Infestation is diagnosed by identification of adult lice or eggs on the rat fur. Lice are treated similarly to mites (*see* below).

Mites

Several types of mites may infest the skin and fur of rats. Mites are not bloodsuckers and often produce no visible signs. Heavily infested rats may have inflammation of the skin, and mites can be seen as white specks of dust on their hair follicles. In addition, they can cause intense itching, leading to the scabs most frequently seen on the shoulders, neck, and face. Rat fur mites do not infest humans or other animals. Infestation is diagnosed by identifying the mites or eggs from the hair and skin of the rat. Treatment usually involves applying a mite-killing drug to the skin, as either a powder (dust) or a solution. The solution may sometimes be given in the drinking water. Your veterinarian will advise you on the best treatment.

Under normal conditions mites are present in small numbers and do not bother their host, however their numbers increase when the rat is stressed, has decreased immunity due to other illnesses, and/or is unable to keep the numbers reduced by normal grooming. Therefore it

is important that you provide proper care for your pet, including monitoring for illness. After treatment, the rat's cage and all cage materials should be thoroughly cleaned and disinfected, because unhatched eggs may lead to reinfection.

Ringtail Syndrome

Low humidity, high temperatures, and drafts predispose young rats to develop a ring-like constriction of the tail called ringtail. This condition can also involve the feet or toes. Ringtail is most often seen in laboratory rats and is fairly rare in rats kept as pets. Affected rats have swelling that leads to gangrene and death of cells in the portion of the tail below the constriction. Surgical removal of all or part of the tail is often necessary, and tail stumps usually heal without complication. Ringtail can be prevented by providing an environmental humidity of 40 to 70%, reducing drafts (use a cage with plastic or glass sides, rather than sides made of wire), and maintaining cage temperature at 70 to 74°F (22 to 23°C).

Ringworm

Ringworm is caused by fungi called dermatophytes that parasitize the skin. The infection is spread by direct contact or by contaminated bedding, litter, or cage supplies, and it can infect humans and other animals. Ringworm occurs infrequently in rats. Infected rats may not have any visible signs. However, some affected rats have areas of hair loss and reddened, irritated, or flaky skin. Treatment should be directed by your veterinarian and includes eliminating the fungus by using an appropriate fungicidal ointment, an antibiotic known to kill fungi, or both. This is important because even though the infection often clears on its own in several weeks, the animal can continue to harbor the infection only to have it reappear when conditions are again favorable for its growth.

Staphylococcal Infection

This infection is caused by *Staphylococcus* bacteria that are commonly found

Diseases that can be Spread from Rats to People

Borreliosis

Leptospirosis

Melioidosis

Plague

Rat bite fever

Tularemia

Murine typhus

Hymenolepiasis (rat tapeworm)

Salmonellosis

humans. Diagnosis is based on blood tests or isolating the bacteria from the urine. Treatment is not recommended because of the risk of human infection.

Certain **roundworms** (nematodes) occasionally infect the rat's bladder, but these parasites are rarely reported. The treatment is similar to that for cases of intestinal pinworms (*see* page 1008).

Uroliths (stones) occur in the kidneys and bladders of older rats. Affected rats either show no signs or have blood in the urine, inflammation, and infection of the bladder. Surgery may be necessary to remove the stones. If the bladder is obstructed, death may occur due to kidney failure.

on the skin of most animals, including rats. Infection occurs when the skin is damaged by scratching or bite wounds. Rats with weakened immune systems are more likely to become infected. Inflamed skin and sores may be observed on the head and neck, and the resulting abscesses may enlarge and spread under the skin to form lumps (tumors) around the face and head. The infection is treated with antibiotics or antibiotic/steroid ointments applied as directed. In order to prevent further damage caused by scratching, the hind foot toenails should be clipped.

Kidney and Urinary Disorders

Chronic progressive nephrosis (glomerulonephrosis) is a common disease of older rats. It involves inflammation of the blood vessels in the kidney. The disease and its severity are influenced by the rat's gender and hereditary background and by dietary factors such as protein content and total calorie consumption. The disease occurs earlier and is more severe in male rats. Affected rats are lethargic and lose weight. They might also have kidney problems. Unfortunately, there is no treatment, and the condition is always fatal. Supportive treatment may be able to decrease the signs.

Leptospirosis is a bacterial infection of the urinary tract that is most often reported in wild rats and mice. It can potentially be transmitted to pet rats and

Disorders Affecting Multiple Body Systems

Some disorders of rats can affect more than one body system. These conditions are also called generalized or systemic disorders. The disorders that affect multiple body systems of rats are listed below.

Lymphocytic Choriomeningitis Virus Infection

Infection with this virus occurs occasionally in rats. Rats can become infected at pet stores by contact with other infected rodents (mice, guinea pigs, or hamsters), or from contact with the urine or feces of wild rodents, such as house mice. Infection is transmitted through aerosols or direct contact with urine or saliva of infected animals. Most infected rats do not show signs. However, some rats carry the virus and shed it in high quantities through urine. There is no effective treatment. Affected animals should be euthanized and the cage should be appropriately sanitized and disinfected.

It is possible that rats with this virus could pass the infection to humans, in whom it can cause serious illness. It may cause influenza-like signs, viral meningitis, and inflammation of the brain and spinal cord. However, human infections from pet rodents are rare.

Parvovirus Infection

This viral infection is uncommon in rats kept as pets. During the active stage of the infection, infected rats have small litters, stillborn pups, infertility, and runting. Infected male rats may develop a fatal hemorrhage (bleeding) and cell death in the brain and gonads. All parvoviruses are highly contagious and transmission occurs through direct contact with infected urine or feces or by contamination of objects (such as bedding) in the environment. Disinfection of the cage is required to eliminate the virus. There is as yet no treatment.

Polyarteritis Nodosa

Polyarteritis nodosa involves inflammation of the walls of the arteries and can affect many organs. The cause of disease is unknown. Heart attacks and aneurysms may occur in rats with polyarteritis nodosa.

Salmonellosis

This disease caused by *Salmonella* bacteria is uncommon in pet rats. However, pregnant females and infant rats are at higher risk of infection. The infection is transmitted by eating food contaminated by feces and is often associated with food, water, or bedding contaminated by wild rodents. Affected rats may have a distended abdomen (belly), diarrhea, dehydration, weight loss, rough hair coat, depression, and sudden death. Miscarriage may occur in pregnant rats. Infected rats can also transmit the disease to people. There is no treatment. Affected rats should be isolated and the cage sanitized and disinfected to eliminate any potential source of contamination.

Cancers and Tumors

Rats are very susceptible to the development of tumors. Your veterinarian will likely recommend surgical removal of the tumor because tumors may grow and spread to other locations in the body. Early removal allows for the best outcome with the least chance of complications and recurrence.

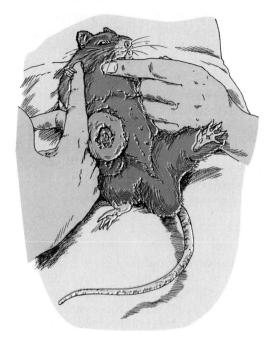

Mammary tumors may occur on the belly of female or male rats.

Keratocanthomas are benign tumors of the skin. They develop on the chest, back, or tail.

Mammary fibroadenomas are the most common tumors in rats. Because rats have widely distributed mammary (breast) tissue, tumors may be found under the skin anywhere on the belly side of the body, from chin to tail. Both female and male rats can develop tumors. Typically these tumors are soft, round, or somewhat flat growths that can be moved by firm pressure. Your veterinarian will perform surgery to remove the tumor, but recurrence in other parts of the body is common. These tumors normally do not become malignant (cancerous).

Tumors of the **pituitary gland**, a gland linked to the brain that controls hormonal secretion, are common in rats, especially females. The development of these tumors increases with the consumption of high-calorie diets. Affected rats have head tilt and depression and may die suddenly.

Most **testicular tumors** in rats are benign. The recommended treatment, when necessary, is the surgical removal of the testicle.

Tumors of the **Zymbal's gland** are infrequent in rats. They develop at the base of the ear in older rats. These tumors are not malignant.

CHAPTER 74
Reptiles

■ INTRODUCTION

Reptiles can be easily recognized by their horny or scaly skin. The class Reptilia has 4 orders: Rhynchocephalia, in which the sole species is the tuatara (a reptile that looks like an iguana but does not belong to the iguana family and is found only on islands off New Zealand); Crocodilia, which includes alligators, caimans, crocodiles, and gavials (a crocodile-like reptile native to India, Borneo, and Sumatra); Chelonia, which contains tortoises and turtles; and Squamata, which contains lizards and snakes.

■ DESCRIPTION AND PHYSICAL CHARACTERISTICS

There are many differences between reptiles and other vertebrates (animals with backbones). Most reptiles maintain their body temperature by absorbing heat from their environment and have a body temperature that changes according to the temperature of the local atmosphere, whereas most mammals and birds are able to maintain a constant body temperature despite changes in the temperature of their environment. With the exception of the crocodilians, reptiles do not have a heart with 4 chambers; yet the heart functions like a 4-chambered heart. Reptiles have both kidneys and a liver (see descriptions in the sections below). Fertilization of their eggs occurs internally, and the embryos develop within amnionic eggs; however, some reptiles lay eggs from

which their offspring hatch, while other reptiles give birth to live young.

Determining the sex of most reptiles (particularly snakes) can be tricky and in most cases is best left to a veterinarian or to an experienced breeder or dealer. The males and females of some species of lizards have distinguishing characteristics such as size, color, or scale pattern. However, Gila monsters, bearded lizards, and some skinks are hard to reliably identify as male or female. Male turtles have a longer tail than females, and the cloacal opening in males is more toward the tail tip. Among semiaquatic reptiles, males are smaller and have longer claws. They might also have a spur on the hindlegs. Terrestrial turtles and tortoises have distinct differences in the shape of their underbelly (plastron): it is concave (rounded) in males and flat in females. Some male tortoises also have a larger pair of scales on the head end of their underbelly (the gular scales).

Snakes

Snakes range in size from small (the size of a worm) to many feet in length. The skin of snakes is made up of scales that may be smooth or ridged. The scales on the belly (called scutes) are thicker than those on the sides and back of a snake to provide protection as it moves.

Snakes have some clear differences from other reptiles. They have no limbs, no moveable eyelids, and no ear openings. Most nonvenomous snakes have teeth

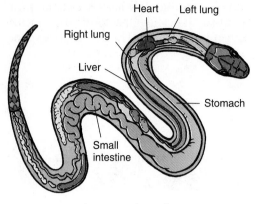

Anatomy of a snake

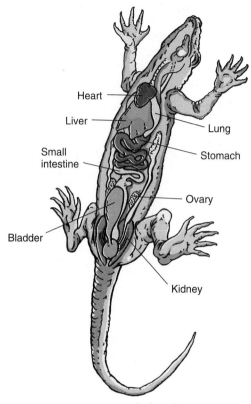

Anatomy of a lizard

that include 2 rows on top and 1 row on the bottom. The teeth are curved backwards to help keep struggling prey from escaping. Venomous snakes have grooved or hollow fangs that they use to inject venom into their prey. The bones in the lower jaw of snakes are long and flexible, which helps enable the snake to swallow large prey.

Internally, snakes have many sets of ribs to support their length. These ribs are also somewhat flexible to allow the prey to move through the snake's body. In addition, the organs inside a snake are long and narrow to allow them to fit inside the body cavity. There are several different ways in which snakes can move, including the familiar undulating crawl (slithering), sidewinding, and the accordion-like movement used to climb trees.

Snakes rely primarily on their senses of smell and touch. Their forked tongues assist in bringing small air particles into the mouth, where an organ on the roof of the mouth is used to identify smells. While snakes do not have external ears, they do have an ear bone that is used to detect vibrations of sound waves that move through the ground.

Lizards

There are more than 4,000 species of lizards, ranging in size from a few inches to the Komodo dragon, the largest lizard, which can reach up to 10 feet in length.

Lizards that are commonly kept as pets include geckos, anoles, iguanas, skinks, chameleons, and agamids (including bearded dragons).

Most lizards have dry skin made up of scales. The scales of lizards vary from the smoother scales of skinks to rough scales or even spikes. In many species, the tail is fragile and can break easily. It can regenerate; however, the new growth may look different.

Lizards are adapted to many different environments. Some are good swimmers, while others spend most of their time in trees. Many have clawed feet that help them climb and cling.

Like snakes, lizards use their tongues to help them smell. The tongue captures particles of air and brings them into the mouth, where a specialized organ can detect various smells. Lizards do have external ears and appear to be able to hear better than snakes. Most lizards have eyelids that clean and protect their eyes when they blink. A few, however, have fixed eyecaps like snakes.

Some lizards have developed special features to help them survive. Chameleons and some other species such as anoles can change the color of their scales to blend in with their surroundings. The males of some species have a loose flap of skin called the dewlap that can be extended to either intimidate a predator or to help attract a mate. And, as mentioned above, a lizard's tail can break off, which can help it escape from predators.

Turtles and Tortoises

Turtles and tortoises belong to a group of reptiles known as chelonians. They are easily distinguished by their hard protective shells that protect their upper and lower bodies. The upper covering is known as the carapace, while the bottom portion is called the plastron. The words "turtle" and "tortoise" are often used interchange-

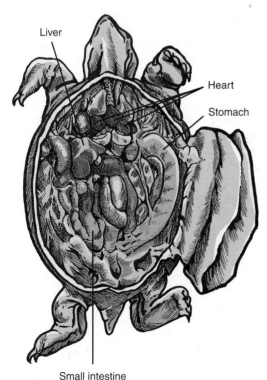

Liver

Heart

Stomach

Small intestine

Anatomy of a turtle

ably by people, and in different parts of the world they can mean different things. In general, however, a turtle spends most or a large portion of its time in water (including sea turtles and those found in ponds or rivers), whereas a tortoise generally lives on land.

Chelonians range in size from small (shells 3 to 4 inches in length) to very large (shell length of up to 8 feet). Many chelonians can be quite long-lived. Some species of tortoises have been known to survive in captivity for up to 150 years, and some aquatic turtles may live for 70 years.

The shells of turtles and tortoises are made up of a large number of bones that are covered by large scales called scutes. The shell is permanently attached at the spine and rib cage. Some turtles can tuck their head, legs, and tails inside their shells, but others cannot. The shell enlarges as the turtle grows, either by replacing old scutes (during shedding) with larger ones or by enlarging the diameter of existing scutes. In some cases, this can help determine the age of the animal.

Like snakes, turtles and tortoises hear by feeling vibrations in the ground or water. Many have good eyesight and a good sense of smell to help them locate food. They do not have teeth; rather, their mouths have a sharp edge that they use to bite or tear food. Many turtles and tortoises are omnivores, meaning they eat both plants and animals (such as insects or worms), although some eat only plants.

■ SPECIAL CONSIDERATIONS

Most reptiles cannot tolerate much handling and do best when provided with an environment as close to their natural habitat as possible and then left alone. In addition, reptiles require specialized diets often involving live prey, fresh vegetation, and vitamin and/or mineral supplements. Because of these requirements, reptiles are pets best suited to adults or older children who will enjoy observing their pet's behavior rather than playing with it.

Table 16. Diseases that can be Spread from Reptiles to People

Organism*	Found in	Disease it Causes	Human Symptoms
Salmonella	Turtles and tortoises, lizards, and snakes	Salmonellosis	Upset stomach, cramps, diarrhea, fever, nausea, and vomiting; can become life-threatening
Edwardsiella	Turtles and tortoises, snakes	Gastroenteritis; neonatal sepsis and meningitis	Same as salmonellosis plus more life-threatening illnesses
Spirometra	Snakes	Sparganosis	Painful and inflamed skin nodules, swelling and inflammation around the eye, could travel to the brain
Pentastomes (Tongue worms)	Snakes	Pentastomid infections	Inflammation of the prostate gland, eye infection, watery eyes, stomach pain, nose discharge, difficulty breathing and swallowing, vomiting, headaches, low tolerance of light, abnormal protrusion of the eyeball

*Note: This is not a comprehensive list of infections passed from reptiles to people, but it does include the ones that are most common. (For a more detailed discussion of diseases you can catch from animals, (*see* DISEASES SPREAD FROM ANIMALS TO PEOPLE (ZOONOSES), page 1088).

Reptiles can transfer some disease-causing organisms to humans. Children under the age of 10, pregnant women, the elderly, and people with a weakened immune system are susceptible. Even if your reptile is not sick, it can still pass a disease-causing organism on to you. *Salmonella* species, *Arizona* species, and *Edwardsiella* species bacteria, as well as various parasites, fungi, and protozoa, are just some of the potential disease-causing organisms transmitted from reptiles that can cause disease in humans (*see* TABLE 16).

Due to public health concerns, it is not recommended that you keep venomous snakes or reptiles as pets.

■ SELECTING A REPTILE

When choosing a pet reptile, it is important to have a clear understanding of both the care required for a particular species and the level of companionship you expect from a pet. Even though reptiles might seem like inactive "couch potatoes,"

keeping them as pets takes just as much of a commitment as caring for other, more assertively demanding companions such as birds or dogs. However, some species of reptiles require less effort and money to feed, house, and adequately care for over their life span than others.

Proper habitat is of the highest importance. If you are buying a tiny hatchling, make sure that you have enough space in your home to accommodate the cage of the fully grown reptile. Consider the type of food the animal will eat—feeding a frozen mouse to a pet snake is not usually for the squeamish, and the crickets that the leopard gecko has not yet eaten will be noisy. In general, reptiles are not social creatures or colony animals. Many prefer to live in solitary cages. A few species, such as green iguanas, bearded dragons, box turtles, king snakes, and boa constrictors, are more open to being handled, and they might even approach their human companions. Others, such as chameleons, are more likely to be stressed when touched or picked up. Finally, unlike

Preventing the Spread of Disease from Your Reptile to You

It is extremely important that you practice good sanitation every time you come into contact with your reptile or anything from its environment.

- Wash your hands with a disinfecting soap after handling the reptile and any of its environmental contents, especially after cleaning its cage and coming into contact with any animal droppings.
- Use disposable gloves.
- Disinfect the cage and its accessories often.
- Do not eat, drink, or smoke while handling your reptile or cleaning its environment.
- Do not kiss your pet reptile.
- Do not clean your reptile's cage or its contents in your kitchen or where any food preparation may take place.
- Disinfect the sink, tub, or counter you use to clean these items immediately after cleaning them to reduce the potential of disease-causing organisms being transmitted to you or anything you may use in the near future.
- Supervise children around the reptile.
- If your nonvenomous reptile bites or scratches you, wash the injured area immediately with a disinfecting soap and then apply a topical antibiotic ointment. If any signs of infection (such as redness, swelling, pus, or fever) develop, contact a doctor as soon as possible because whole system antibiotics may be needed.
- Do not keep venomous reptiles.
- Take your reptile to a veterinarian and have the reptile tested for potentially harmful organisms.

some other pets that live in enclosures (such as mice and hamsters), reptiles have rather long life spans. Consider the number of years that you will be willing to maintain and enlarge the reptile's habitat (*see* TABLE 17). Never release a pet reptile into the wild, even if the species is native to your area; instead, contact the local humane society or animal control agency.

It is important to know what is normal for a reptile before visiting the pet store or breeder. Look at a variety of pictures of your chosen reptile as a juvenile so that you can select one with a healthy size and appearance for its age. Choose a pet store or breeder whose reptile enclosures are clean and large enough to keep the inhabitants healthy and comfortable (*see* PROVIDING A HOME FOR A REPTILE, page 1018). Captive-bred animals make the best pets. They are less likely to bite than wild-caught animals, more likely to accept the food given to them, and less likely to harbor parasites.

Snakes

Healthy young snakes should have a rounded body, clear eyes, and a clean vent. Their spine should not stick out. Snakes should not wheeze or have mucus or bubbles near their nostrils. They should have no apparent skin cuts or parasite infestations. Choose a snake that flicks its tongue and is aware of and interested in its environment. When handled, the snake should seem to have strong muscles and lightly squeeze your hand or arm. Avoid nervous snakes that do not calm down after a bit of handling.

If you are a first-time snake owner, check with a reputable pet store regarding

Table 17. Average Life Span of Reptiles in Captivity	
Ball python	15 to 20 years
Boa constrictor	15 to 25 years
Bearded dragon	5 to 10 years
Corn snake	10 to 15 years
Eastern box turtle	25 to 50 years
Green anole	4 to 8 years
Green iguana	5 to 15 years
King snake	10 to 15 years
Leopard gecko	20+ years
Leopard tortoise	50+ years
Old World chameleons	3 to 8 years

recommended species for beginners. Also, it is wise to check any local laws regarding snake ownership; for example, keeping constricting snakes such as pythons is prohibited in many areas.

Lizards

Well-nourished, healthy lizards should not have projecting hip bones or visible tail bones. Their skin should not be scratched or bitten. The vent area should not be stained with urine or caked with feces. Eyes and nostrils should not be swollen, crusted, or show signs of discharge. However, it is normal for some species to have light salty deposits near their nostrils. Most species should have a pink interior mouth; yellow, white, or green spots in the mouth or on the tongue can indicate illness. Look for signs of mite infestation: tiny black, brown, reddish, or orange flecks that move on the head, neck, and belly. Even though this is fairly easy to treat, it can be a sign of unsanitary conditions. When handled, healthy lizards should seem strong. Most lizards will probably resist being caught or struggle. Tame lizards will be wide-eyed and alert when handled. Avoid lizards that are limp or unresponsive. Cool conditions can cause short-term sluggishness, but such habitats can lead to overall poor health.

If you are a first-time lizard owner, check with a reputable pet store regarding recommended species for beginners. Some lizards require more complex environments than others; also, some lizards can be handled frequently while others should be left alone for the most part.

Turtles and Tortoises

A healthy turtle or tortoise will have clear eyes and dry (not moist) skin without any wounds or evidence of parasites. The shell should not have any white or "weeping" areas or any evidence of erosion or previous damage. The animal should not wheeze or have mucus or bubbles near its nostrils. Any droppings in the enclosure should be firm and not liquid. Runny feces may be a sign of disease

caused by parasites. Captive-bred turtles or tortoises often tend to be healthier than those that are caught in the wild.

All turtles and tortoises with top shells less than 4 inches long are illegal to sell as pets in the US. This law was created in 1975 in the interest of public health: the popularity of keeping baby turtles as pets had led to more than 250,000 *Salmonella* infections in infants and children. (The reasoning behind the size restriction is that turtles larger than 4 inches are less likely to be kept and handled by children.) Nevertheless, baby turtles are still bought and sold as pets, especially in tourist areas. However, even baby turtles that are certified as free from *Salmonella* are illegal to sell in the US because of the risk of later infection.

Turtles and tortoises have complex housing and environmental needs. Although some species might be adorable as hatchlings, they grow quickly and are quite messy. They do not remain small if kept in a small container. Small fishbowl-type tanks are not adequate for housing turtles of any age or size.

■ PROVIDING A HOME FOR A REPTILE

Among the most important considerations for any pet are its housing and dietary requirements. Because reptiles cannot regulate their body temperature in the same way mammals can, they have stricter requirements for housing than many other pets, particularly regarding temperature and sanitation. Dietary needs vary widely by species.

Housing

Housing requirements for reptiles include an appropriate enclosure and sources of light, heat, and water. Be sure to have the habitat completely ready and secure before bringing your pet home.

Enclosure Design

Many reptiles appear nervous and insecure in captivity. This can be reduced by providing appropriate cage "furniture" and hiding spaces. Arboreal species (those that live in trees) should be provided with horizontal and vertical tree branches or other appropriate climbing material. Terrestrial species (those that live on the ground) usually require more horizontal space. Many terrestrial species, as well as those that like to dig or burrow, require hiding places such as boxes, tree trunks, rocks, or other objects. For some species, a solid black border painted on the glass wall 8 inches (20 centimeters) from the cage bottom provides added security.

Some species of reptiles are solitary and prefer to be housed alone. Housing animals of the same species together may sometimes be possible; however, groups should not include more than 1 male, as males of the same species may become aggressive toward each other. For experienced reptile owners, it may be possible to create an enclosure suitable for housing several compatible species together. Community housing of highly social species that are active during the day often requires placing several stations for basking, eating, and drinking that are all out of the view of dominant animals from the same species and any human observers. Overcrowding must be avoided to reduce stress and competition for food, water, basking sites, and mates. Aggressive species may have to be separated during feeding to prevent injury to cage mates. Fighting can be reduced significantly by housing only compatible species together.

The floor of the enclosure should be covered with a material that is disposable, inexpensive, nontoxic, and nonabrasive. The best ground coverings, or **substrates**, are those that provide the least amount of area for microbial growth and help make cage cleaning easy. Newspaper, sand, peat moss, potting soil, wood shavings, cypress mulch, corncob bedding, walnut bedding, gravel, alfalfa pellets, and artificial turf have all been used successfully for snakes. Cedar shavings should be avoided as the strong odors and vapors may cause breathing problems as well as potential neu-

rologic problems. Snakes less than 18 inches (45 centimeters) long should not be fed while on "loose" substrates such as shavings, corncob or walnut bedding, or small gravel because these substrates accumulate around the mouth (possibly causing inflammation of the mouth) and may be swallowed (possibly causing a blockage in the intestine). One solution is to remove the snake from its normal cage and feed it in a separate cage on newspaper. This results in conditioned behavior that is thought by some to decrease feeding frenzy activity in large snakes when approached in their normal, nonfeeding cage.

Ease of cleaning is a good reason to choose a less complicated substrate. In order to minimize parasites, bacteria, and other organisms that cause disease, it is essential to be able to clean thoroughly and frequently. Newspaper is the substrate of choice for sick reptiles because it is inexpensive, easy to clean, and allows regurgitated material or droppings to be easily observed.

The humidity level necessary for a particular reptile also determines substrate choice. Cypress mulch can hold moisture and is resistant to mold. In contrast, corncob bedding is readily available but is expensive and subject to severe molding if wet. Mixtures of sand, peat moss, and soil hold moisture and allow burrowing. Sand or soil can also be used for a drier substrate. Smaller environments within an enclosure can provide increased humidity without creating high humidity levels in the entire cage.

Sand, potting soil, and leaf litters are adequate substrates for many species of lizards, turtles, and tortoises. Alfalfa pellets (common rabbit pellets) are also useful bedding for turtles and tortoises. The pellets are inexpensive and easy to clean—and they are nutritious if eaten!

Aquatic turtles and crocodilians can be maintained on a combination of sand, gravel, and cement substrates if basking areas are provided. Gravel should be large enough so that it cannot be eaten.

Temperature

Most reptiles are **ectotherms** (often called "cold-blooded" animals), because they maintain their body temperatures by moving to different places in their environments. In their natural habitat, they are quite good at keeping their body temperature within a relatively narrow range compared with the outside temperature. To control daily changes in body temperature, many reptiles seek out cool or warm areas. For example, a reptile might bask on a rock that has been warmed by the sun to raise its body temperature.

The cage or enclosure used to house reptiles should provide a range of temperatures (within the preferred temperature range for each species) from one end of the enclosure to the other to keep the occupants healthy. A range of temperatures also helps with digestion, keeps their immune systems healthy, and increases the effectiveness of certain drugs. Tropical species generally prefer temperatures of 80 to 100°F (27 to 38°C) and temperate species, 68 to 95°F (20 to 35°C). Semi-aquatic turtles prefer a slightly lower range. The temperature in the enclosure must be carefully monitored; temperatures that exceed the upper limits by only 10°F (5°C) may prove deadly for some species of reptiles.

Most reptiles prefer basking sources of heat, perhaps because these are the most similar to their normal environment. Basking lights are preferred for turtles, tortoises, and lizards; this can be an incandescent bulb, infrared device, mercury vapor lamp, or a ceramic bulb heater. Heat lamps should be used with extreme caution, as overheating is common. These sources should all be protected from direct contact with reptiles and placed more than 18 inches (45 centimeters) from the ground covering. Smaller enclosures with limited ventilation should have a reptile thermostat with a probe attached to the heat source, and all cages should have a thermometer. It is a good idea to place thermometers in both the directly heated and unheated regions of the enclosure. Undertank heaters are also useful heat sources for lizards and snakes; when used with a basking light, they can provide heat at night as well as during the day. However, undertank heaters should cover no more than 30% of the available cage space and should be designed specifically for this use.

Two more recent products for heating reptile enclosures are mercury vapor bulbs and infrared heaters. Mercury vapor lamps are very good basking lights and also provide some ultraviolet (UV) light—the type of rays found in natural sunlight—that is necessary for reptile health (*see* LIGHTING REQUIREMENTS, below). Infrared panels are produced in many sizes and can easily be attached to the roof of the cage so as to radiate heat downward. Infrared heaters are unique because they heat objects in their path without overheating the enclosure. As with any basking light or heater, you should always check the temperature on top of the ground covering. If the heated surface is too warm for maintaining comfortable contact, it is too warm for the reptile as well. "Hot rocks" are not recommended because the heat they provide is not consistent and may cause burns.

Reptiles become inactive at lower temperatures. This is a normal seasonal event for many nontropical species, and it promotes the best conditions for reproduction and longterm physical well-being. However, hibernation should never be attempted with an ill reptile because its immune system is not as strong during seasonal changes and lower temperatures. Tropical species may decrease their level of activity due to minor temperature changes, but they should not be hibernated. Temperature extremes and fast changes of temperature should be avoided. You should ask your veterinarian or the person from whom you obtained the reptile about the proper temperature range and seasonal hibernation requirements for your pet.

Lighting Requirements

Feeding behavior, activity, and to a lesser extent, reproduction in reptiles are improved with full-spectrum light, which has qualities similar to natural sunlight and includes ultraviolet (UV) rays. Fluorescent bulbs that produce UVB wavelengths in the range of 290 to 320 nanometers are the most appropriate for reptile enclosures. Mercury vapor lamps are the only nonfluorescent bulbs available that can also provide ultraviolet light.

Providing the proper ultraviolet spectrum is essential in order to maintain healthy reptilian skin. While exposure to unfiltered sunlight is the best form of UV light available, sunlight filtered through most glass or plastic contains almost no ultraviolet rays. Ultraviolet-producing bulbs should be placed near resting or basking areas so that the reptile can obtain adequate ultraviolet exposure. Typical ultraviolet-producing lights should be within 18 inches of resting or basking areas, while mercury vapor lamps can be several feet away. The practice of using a black light in combination with full spectrum bulbs may promote reproductive activity in lizards, but does not significantly increase UVB exposure. Even the best full-spectrum bulbs available are a poor substitute for natural sunlight. A species-appropriate supplement that contains vitamin D_3 may be necessary (*see* NUTRIENT REQUIREMENTS, page 1023).

The daily cycle of light and darkness, called the **photoperiod**, affects the behavior and physical functions of all animals. Photoperiod requirements for reptiles are based on daily and yearly activity cycles. For reptiles that come from areas with seasonal temperature changes, the photoperiod provides cues to ensure that reproduction occurs within the best environmental conditions. For tropical species, variations in the photoperiod are less important. Changes in photoperiod from about 10 hours of daylight for winter months to about 14 hours of daylight for summer months are common for many

tropical and subtropical areas. Temperate areas experience changes in photoperiod ranging from about 8 hours of daylight during the winter to about 16 hours during the summer.

Water and Humidity

Semiaquatic reptiles, those that naturally live and grow near and in water, must be able to submerge themselves completely in water. Feeding, reproduction, and social interaction occur under water in many species. Filtering and aerating the water helps lower the level of toxic organic wastes and disease-causing organisms. For salt-water species, the salinity (level of salt) in the water should be carefully monitored. Water pH for some species of aquatic turtles may need to be adjusted to match their natural habitat.

Requirements for water intake are linked to the availability of water in the reptile's natural habitat. Aquatic and semiaquatic reptiles need more water, while species from drier environments tend to conserve water. It is very important that water be available at all times to avoid dehydration. Loss of water through the skin occurs in many species when deprived of soaking areas; likewise, absorbing water through the skin has also been documented. Many species drink readily from pools or bowls, but a number of small lizards (such as anoles and true chameleons) drink by lapping water droplets that accumulate through condensation. Misting the environment or creating a drip system provides options for water intake. Be sure to ask your veterinarian or local pet store the best way to ensure that your reptile is getting enough water.

The humidity should mimic that of the natural environment of the reptile. Excessively low humidity (less than 35%) can result in dry skin and abnormal skin shedding, especially in species that are not used to a dry environment. Excessively high humidity (greater than 70%) can result in skin infections. (*See* TABLE 18.)

Table 18. Reptile Housing Requirements

Temperature

Tropical species	80 to 100°F (27 to 38°C)
Temperate species	68 to 95°F (27 to 38°C)
Semiaquatic turtles	Slightly lower range

Humidity

All species	Varies by species; in general anything below 35% or above 70% may cause problems

Photoperiod

Subtropical and tropical species	10 hours (winter) to 14 hours (summer)
Temperate species	8 hours (winter) to 16 hours (summer)

Light

All species	UV and UVB: 290 to 320 nanometers
	Basking light: 50 to 75 watts at least 18 inches from basking area

Sanitation

Cleanliness is essential for successful longterm maintenance of reptiles. Cages should be kept free of any urine or animal droppings, and uneaten food should be removed and disposed of daily. Internal parasites are one of the most common health problems seen in reptiles in captivity; these parasites often need only one host—the reptile—and the offspring of the parasite can re-infect the same host. Therefore animal droppings should be removed in a timely manner. Tools used for scooping wastes should be disinfected before use in each cage to reduce the possibility of spreading the disease from cage to cage. Owners should check with their veterinarian regarding the most appropriate disinfectant or sanitizer to use for disinfecting their reptile's environment and

the frequency and concentration that is safest for their pet.

All substrates should be completely replaced at least every 3 months. Likewise, aquatic and terrestrial environments should be disassembled and disinfected at least every 3 months. Water dishes should be thoroughly cleaned at least once every 2 weeks. Although turtles appear to tolerate chlorine in treated water reasonably well, its effects are not known. While chlorine may result in temporary irritation of eyes in aquatic turtles not used to chlorine, it appears to be beneficial in controlling infection-causing bacteria and viruses in the water.

Diet

The nutritional requirements of reptiles are still being investigated. Most recommendations are based on experience and observation. The required levels of protein, carbohydrates, and fat in the diet are thought to be similar to those of mammals.

Feeding behavior and digestion are related to the environmental temperature. Because reptiles have a lower metabolism than mammals and other "warm-blooded" animals, they feed less frequently. Humidity, light, food type, and the presence of other animals also affect feeding behavior. In turtles and some plant-eating lizards, the color of the food contributes to food acceptance; red and yellow are often preferred colors. Some reptiles become accustomed to certain foods and are unwilling to accept alternatives. Providing a variety of foods at each feeding, especially to younger reptiles, may lessen this problem.

Quality is important when feeding whole-animal foods. Goldfish, mealworms, crickets, wax moth larvae, mice, or rats intended for use as reptile food should be fed a complete and balanced diet so that they provide adequate nutrients. Herbivores (animals that eat plants) and omnivores (animals that eat meat and plants) also require balanced rations. Vegetarian diets are often lacking in calories, protein, and calcium. Insects and grubs lack calcium, and supplementation is required.

The practice of **gut loading** is a common technique that involves providing insects with a nutritious mixture of cereals and vegetables immediately before being fed to the reptile—thus loading their gut with nutrients. Another common practice is the use of powdered vitamin/mineral supplements. Crickets brought home from a pet store and never fed have little nutritional value. Placing them in a bag with vitamin and mineral powders and shaking the bag will coat the insects with the powder. Although some of the powder will fall off, the newer microfine powders adhere remarkably well. Adding calcium and calcium-rich foods to the diet of crickets and wax moth larvae is another way to provide more calcium.

Nutrient Requirements

The **protein** content of a reptile diet has traditionally been recommended to be about 18 to 20% for meat-eaters and 11 to 12% for plant-eaters. Inadequate protein levels result in weight loss, muscle wasting, increased chances of infections, failure to reproduce, and slower healing after injury. An infection that will not go away after treatment can be the result of inadequate nutrition. Many newer commercial diets offer protein levels up to 28 to 32%, which may prompt rapid growth but can have severe longterm consequences such as hyperuricemia (*see* below). Consequently, lower protein levels are currently recommended, because reptiles excrete uric acid.

Excess protein levels occur in meat-eating lizards when excessive meat products are fed rather than whole animals. Feeding large amounts of high-protein cat foods has been shown to cause increased levels of protein and vitamin D_3. Many nutritionists recommend not feeding cat foods to reptiles. Dog food, especially low-fat varieties, can be used sparingly as part of a complete and balanced diet in both meat-eaters and plant-eaters. The overuse of high-protein diets prepared for meat-eaters has been shown to cause disease in tortoises and iguanas. Feeding excess protein can result in a condition called **hyperuricemia**, in which uric acid is deposited in internal organs. This may lead to gout of the affected organs, which can be fatal (*see* page 1031).

Most protein deficiencies are seen in plant-eating species on "salad-type" diets or in individual reptiles with no appetite. Diets for plant-eaters may be supplemented with alfalfa sprouts, bean sprouts, soybeans or meal, invertebrates (such as insects or worms), or soft-moist or low-fat dog food (used sparingly). Reptiles that refuse to eat may require force-feeding, a change in their environment, or enough variety in the diet to identify a preferred food item.

Fiber is required for the normal functioning of the digestive tract. In large land tortoises and other plant-eating species, adding roughage (such as hay) to the diet may eliminate chronic, smelly diarrhea.

Specific **fatty acid requirements** have not been determined for reptiles, but 0.2% linoleic acid (found in natural oils) in the diet is recommended. Atherosclerosis, a condition in which fatty material is deposited along the walls of arteries and then thickens, hardens, and eventually blocks the arteries, has been reported; restriction of cholesterol may be an important longterm dietary consideration in captive reptiles.

Mineral deficiencies are seen frequently in captive reptiles, especially turtles, tortoises, and lizards. Vitamin and mineral deficiencies are rare in snakes that are fed nutrient-rich whole prey. A vitamin/mineral supplement should be added to the diet of every captive reptile; many products designed for use in reptiles are available in pet stores. There is a delicate balance of calcium, phosphorus, and vitamin D_3 that is necessary to maintain good health in reptiles. If the balance is upset, hormonal disorders or bone diseases can occur.

Calcium imbalance is the most common mineral imbalance in reptile nutrition. Feeding a pure meat diet not only provides excessive protein but also is extremely poor in calcium and rich in phosphorus. Including whole prey or a low-fat, low-protein dog food in the diet can help reduce excess protein. Calcium should be supplemented with products developed for reptiles.

The exoskeleton of insects does not contain calcium. Therefore, reptiles that feed primarily on insects must obtain dietary calcium from insects "gut loaded" and powdered with calcium supplements. Plant-eating reptiles should be encouraged to eat items rich in calcium, including cabbage, kale, okra, sprouts, collard greens, and bok choy. These foods typically are also rich in vitamin A. A calcium supplement developed for reptiles should be routinely given to plant-eaters.

Vitamin D is also required for proper calcium metabolism and balance. Animals housed outside with access to natural, unfiltered sunlight usually have adequate levels of vitamin D_3. Access to ultraviolet light is strongly encouraged in reptiles that are not exposed to unfiltered sunlight (*see* Lighting Requirements, page 1021). Reptiles that are fed whole mammals (such as mice) as prey generally consume adequate levels of preformed vitamin D_3. The food items of reptiles that eat mostly insects should be fortified by gut loading and powdering. Plant-eating reptiles that have limited exposure to ultraviolet light should receive supplemental vitamin D_3. Most reptile supplements that contain calcium also contain adequate amounts of vitamin D_3. Care should be used when providing supplements, however, because excessive levels of vitamin D_3 in the diet can lead to excessive absorption and use of calcium.

Inappropriate levels of calcium, phosphorus, or vitamin D can result in an imbalance in the hormone that regulates calcium, phosphorus, and magnesium levels within the blood and bone. If these levels are not corrected, the bones may become weak and spongy and begin to bow outward as they are pulled upon by the muscles. This condition is most often seen in the jaw bones. Self-feeding becomes difficult and then impossible as the jaw bones become too soft. Force-feeding by tube is needed in extreme cases. Osteomalacia (softening of the bones), kidney stones, cloacal calculi (accumulated mineral deposits, similar to kidney stones), and rickets (which also leads to softening and weakening of the bones) are also possible results of a diet deficient in calcium or vitamin D_3. Broken bones, bone deformities, and soft or deformed shells in turtles may occur. Deadly signs may include seizures in which the muscles stay contracted.

Treatment consists of correcting the balance of these minerals and giving vitamin D_3, if necessary, either by exposure to an appropriate ultraviolet light source or by an injection given by a veterinarian. A dietary history of your reptile would be useful in helping the veterinarian evaluate any deficiencies and determine possible courses of treatment. If a calcium supplement is to be provided in the initial stages of treatment, it should not contain phosphorus. An excellent calcium source is calcium glubionate, given on the recommendation of a veterinarian. Other sources of dietary calcium include crushed cuttlebone, crushed oyster shells, crushed or pulverized calcium lactate, or commercially available products. In severe cases, a veterinarian can give a calcium injection before giving extra calcium by mouth.

Feeding of certain green foods that contain goiter-causing compounds, such as bok choy, broccoli, Brussels sprouts, cabbage, and soy, may cause an **iodine deficiency**. Signs of deficiency include a lack of normal energy and activity and an abnormal swelling (goiter) at the base of the neck where it meets the chest. The imbalance is corrected by supplementing with a balanced vitamin-mineral mixture containing iodine, or iodized salt (0.5% of the diet).

Vitamin A deficiency is common in captive, plant-eating turtles. Box turtles, particularly in the US, appear most at risk usually due to improper diets that do not contain enough vitamin A. Signs of vitamin A deficiency include swollen eyelids, chronic respiratory disease, and kidney disease. Sometimes a thickened, sticky discharge from the eyes, in addition to swollen eyelids, is seen. The eyes may eventually remain closed, impairing the ability of the turtle to find food. Treatment consists of short daily soaks to allow the turtle to drink and wash its eyes, application of an antibiotic ointment to the eyes, and vitamin A injections given by a veterinarian. For less severe cases, vitamin A can be supplied by adding a drop of cod liver oil to the reptile's food twice a week. Commercial vitamin products are also available for reptiles. Dietary levels of vitamin A should be increased for up to 6 weeks before hibernation in turtles and tortoises. However, caution should be used when supplementing, as too much vitamin A can cause severe thickening and irritation of the skin as well as incomplete and inadequate shedding of the skin.

Vitamin B$_1$ deficiency can result from diets containing fish with high thiaminase levels. Giving extra vitamin B$_1$ is required in such cases. Weight loss even though the reptile is eating enough food is a common sign, but neurologic problems (such as paralysis and lack of coordination or balance) can also occur. Goldfish have low thiaminase activity, while smelt have extremely high levels. Frozen fish have increased thiaminase levels. Deficiencies of the water-soluble vitamins often involve more than one vitamin and require treatment with a multivitamin preparation.

Deficiencies of other vitamins and minerals sometimes occur in reptiles and can be diagnosed and treated by your veterinarian.

Temperament

Aggression during mating and feeding is common in some semiaquatic turtles, some skinks and iguanas, and many other lizards and snakes. Injuries to cage mates can be severe and are best avoided by separating animals at feeding and reducing the number of animals allowed in a breeding group. When separated individuals are placed together for breeding, they should be carefully monitored. If reptiles are to be kept together, it is vital that the enclosure is large enough to accommodate a perch and/or hiding area for each reptile. Food and water is best placed in multiple locations to prevent dominant animals from intimidating the others.

■ ROUTINE HEALTH CARE

Good sanitation and nutrition and a properly designed environment play a major role in preventing many common health problems in reptiles. However, if medical attention is required, reptiles respond best to treatment from a veterinarian familiar with their special needs. When selecting a veterinarian for your reptile, ask about experience with reptiles and select the veterinarian with an appropriate level of experience and interest.

Importance of Veterinary Care

Even though no vaccinations are required for reptiles, an annual health check can help make sure that your pet is well nourished and free from diseases and parasites. Because not all reptiles are cared for as pets from the time they are hatched, a prompt visit to the veterinarian for an initial examination is also a good idea. The first veterinary visit establishes a record of the animal in healthy condition. This information will be highly valuable should medical problems develop later.

Chemical Restraint, Sedation, and Anesthesia

There are many circumstances where chemical restraint is needed to perform a complete and thorough physical examination. If the reptile is likely to injure veterinary personnel or itself during examination, chemical restraint should be used. Sedation and anesthesia will be needed during surgery. However, you should be sure that the veterinarian has knowledge of and experience with sedating a reptile, because several common anesthetic techniques are not appropriate for use in reptiles and other precautions particular to reptiles are required.

Signs of Illness

The sick reptile should be kept at a temperature near the upper limit preferred by the species to improve functioning of the immune system. Reptiles are unable to produce a true fever, but when infected with bacterial agents they move to warmer areas in their environment to create a "behavioral fever." Higher metabolic rates of reptiles with no appetite may require force-feeding or an increased rate of feeding. However, you should consult with your veterinarian regarding feeding, as it may raise uric acid levels and cause damage to the kidneys in conjunction with some commonly used antibiotics. Giving the reptile fluids should be considered as well.

Giving Medication

Antibiotics are usually given by injection in reptiles, although they are sometimes given by mouth in extremely small animals (such as the true chameleons and smaller geckos) that lack adequate muscle mass for injection. Intravenous injections are preferred in larger reptiles or when working around the head and mouth would be dangerous.

Shedding (Ecdysis)

Ecdysis is the process by which reptiles shed their outer skin in response to growth or wear. In snakes and some lizards, the process results in shedding the entire layer of skin as a single piece. Other lizards shed small sections of skin from time to time. Turtles shed coverings from individual scutes (plates) one at a time. Large, moderately abrasive rocks or other rough surfaces for reptiles to rub on during ecdysis help to ease a normal shed. Before shedding, snakes lose their appetite, and

their color becomes mildly translucent and dull. This is especially evident over the eyecaps, which become opaque. Increased irritability and aggressiveness are frequent. The shed begins around the mouth, and the old skin is turned inside out as it is shed.

Once a reptile becomes opaque, the humidity should be slightly increased to help the shedding progress and to decrease the risk of a retained shed (*see* DYSECDYSIS, page 1033). Lightly misting the cage at least once a day and providing a hidebox with moist sphagnum moss or a soaking container are all proven techniques.

■ EMERGENCIES

Even though pet reptiles live in carefully controlled environments, injuries and accidents are possible.

Burns

Burns may occur in reptiles due to the careless use of incandescent lights or other heat sources. They are treated by cleansing the site, applying antibiotic ointment, and placing the reptile in a clean, dry environment. In uninfected burns, sterile skin protectants can be applied to the area to act as a "second skin." These products allow the reptile to have access to the water and help keep contaminants out. In severe burn cases, fluids given through enemas or by injection may be needed to prevent dehydration, and whole system antibiotics may be required to prevent or treat bacterial infection. A veterinarian can advise you in providing supportive care, including pain management and assisted feeding techniques.

Crush Injuries

Crush injuries to turtles may result in fractures to the lower portion of the shell, the upper shell, or both. The turtle will need to be taken to a veterinarian who can remove the damaged or infected tissues and clean and bandage the injury. Whole system antibiotics will likely be prescribed.

Once the turtle is stable, the wounds should be cleaned again, and the fractures can be surgically realigned and repaired, using various types of epoxy, resin, or cement. Healing is slow and may require more than a year.

Fractures

Fractures due to trauma occur in all reptiles. Long bones may be repaired with splints or through surgery. A simple way of splinting the legs of lizards is to tape the injured leg to the body (front legs) or the tail (rear legs). These splints are tolerated well and protect the limb from further injury.

Injuries to the spinal column must be assessed individually, and x-rays are often needed to evaluate the extent of the injury. Spinal injuries of the tail may be tolerated, but injuries to the area between the skull and the tail often result in constipation and not being able to expel uric acid salts. Many green iguanas suffer spinal injuries just over the pelvis, leaving the lizard paralyzed in the rear. Changing the environment (such as providing low branches, a shallow water dish, and nonabrasive substrates) and learning how to empty the bowel content will allow the lizard to live a useful, comfortable life. Because these fractures often occur after metabolic bone disease, changes to the diet and vitamin/mineral supplements may be needed.

Rodent Bites

Rodent bites, which can be inflicted by uneaten prey, cause traumatic injuries. These injuries may then become infected and inflamed. When possible, rodents that have been freshly killed or frozen and thawed should be offered to prevent injury to the reptile (dead prey should be discarded after 24 hours if left uneaten). The feeding of live prey is illegal in many European countries. Fresh bite wounds may be treated by cleansing and treating with a mild disinfectant. An injection of antibiotics may be needed to treat certain types of infections. Untreated wounds that become infected are often seen as a soft or hard swelling. The pus-filled cavity should be removed surgically, and the wound closed with stitches. Infected tissue from open or draining sores should be surgically removed, disinfected, and injected antibiotics given. (*See also* ABSCESSES, page 1032.)

■ DISORDERS AND DISEASES

Furnishing adequate housing, a good diet, and routine parasite control will help to minimize disease in pet reptiles, as with any other animal.

Heart and Blood Vessel Disorders

Septicemia, a disease caused by bacteria in the blood, is a common cause of reptilian death. The disease affects the whole body and may occur after trauma, an isolated abscess (*see* ABSCESSES, page 1032), an infestation of parasites, or environmental stress. Death may be sudden or occur after longterm signs of illness. Common signs are trouble breathing, lack of energy, convulsions, and loss of muscle control. A tiny purplish red spot on the skin may be found on the lower part of the stomach, and turtles and tortoises develop a redness of the skin on the lower portion of the shell. Keeping a reptile's environment clean and well maintained can be important factors in reducing outbreaks of septicemia. Affected reptiles should be isolated, and antibiotic treatments started.

Digestive Disorders

Reptiles' digestive systems can be upset by viral infections, bacterial infections, protozoal infections, and infestation with parasites.

Adenoviruses

Adenoviruses may cause fatal liver or gastrointestinal diseases in certain snakes (gaboon vipers, ball pythons, boa constrictors, rosy boas, and rat snakes) and lizards (Jackson's chameleons, Savannah monitors, and bearded dragons). In bearded dragons, the adenovirus appears to be transmitted when contaminated animal droppings come in contact with the mouth. Signs of infection are more commonly noted in younger dragons but can affect adults, usually to a lesser extent. The signs are vague and include lack of energy, weakness, weight loss, diarrhea, and sudden death. The frequency of death is high in young bearded dragons, but good supportive care—such as giving fluids, force-feeding, and giving antibiotics for any secondary infections—can increase survival.

The signs of this disease in bearded dragons are similar to those caused by coccidia (see COCCIDIAL ORGANISMS, page 1035) and nutritional disorders, so it is important to have your veterinarian confirm the diagnosis, which can be done by a liver biopsy.

Recovered lizards should be quarantined for at least 3 months. The length of time required for a complete recovery (with no detectable virus) is unknown, so you should not plan to sell or trade a previously infected animal.

Infectious Stomatitis

An inflammation of the mucous tissue lining the mouth (infectious stomatitis) is seen in snakes, lizards, and turtles. Early signs include tiny purplish red spots in the mouth; firm, dry diseased tissue develops along the tooth row as the condition worsens. In severe cases, the infection can extend into the bony structures of the mouth. Bacteria that are commonly found in the mouth are the most frequent culprits. Respiratory or gastrointestinal infection may develop if the stomatitis is not treated promptly. Treatment requires the removal of any dead, damaged, or infected tissue from the wound in order to expose healthy tissue that will allow the wound to heal. The wound then needs to be cleansed with antiseptics or antibiotics. Finally, whole system antibiotics and supportive therapy should be given. Surgery may be needed in severe cases with slow-healing sores or inflamed growth. Vitamin supplementation, especially with vitamins A and C, may be helpful in some cases.

Intestinal Parasites

The stress of captivity coupled with a closed environment tends to cause a heavy burden of parasites that live inside reptiles. Many common internal parasites of reptiles have direct life cycles in which the offspring of the parasite can infect the same host it came from. For example, the adult parasite lives in the host's intestine, lays eggs that are passed in the animal droppings, and the eggs then infect the same host. These parasites can multiply to staggering numbers, and poor hygiene is often a factor. Every effort must be taken to rid reptiles of parasite burdens, and to rid the environment of intermediate hosts.

Treatment should be attempted when evidence of an infestation of parasites is found. Drugs called anthelmintics are usually needed to eliminate internal parasites. Many different anthelmintics—some of which are known as dewormers—are available. Your veterinarian can prescribe the one that is considered most effective for the particular parasite involved.

Roundworms of the stomach (**stomach worms**) are seen in lizards and, when infection is severe, can cause stomach ulcers. Numerous snakes are infected by a **hookworm** that lives in the upper gastrointestinal tract and causes wounds at sites of attachment. Large mineral deposits caused by this hookworm may cause intestinal obstruction.

Another group of roundworms, known as **ascarids**, also frequently infect reptiles. Severe wounds and death may be seen in infected snakes. Snakes infected with ascarids frequently regurgitate their partially digested food or adult worms and have no appetite. Infection may cause large masses of mineral deposits in the gastrointestinal tract; these wounds may become inflamed and filled with pus, and they may eventually make holes in the intestinal wall.

Many other species of roundworms may be found in reptiles on examination of the animal's droppings. The non-disease-causing parasites of prey items (such as the mouse pinworm) may be found when infected prey is consumed.

Protozoal Diseases

Protozoa are single-celled organisms, many of which can cause disease in animals. **Entamoeba invadens** is the most serious disease-causing protozoon of reptiles. Signs are loss of appetite and weight, vomiting, mucus-like or bloody diarrhea, and death. The disease may spread very quickly in large snake collections. Plant-eating reptiles appear to be less susceptible than meat-eating ones; however, a number of reptiles that seldom become affected or die can serve as carriers, including garter snakes, northern black racers, and box turtles. Other resistant groups include eastern king snakes, cobras (possibly as an adaptation that allows them to eat snakes), and most turtles. Most boas, colubrids (nonvenomous snakes such as king snakes, garter snakes, and water snakes), elapids (venomous snakes such as coral snakes and mambas), vipers, and crotalids (venomous pit vipers, rattlesnakes, and bushmasters) are highly susceptible. This protozoan is transmitted by direct contact with the cyst form. A veterinarian can do simple tests of the animal's droppings to look for the presence of *Entamoeba invadens*.

An antiprotozoal drug is usually prescribed for treatment. To help prevent transmission among reptiles, turtles and snakes should not be housed together. The potential for this disease to be passed on to humans should not be taken lightly, and strict sanitation and hygiene measures should be observed.

Cryptosporidiosis is an infectious condition caused by *Cryptosporidium* species of protozoa. It is often associated with regurgitating a meal, marked weight loss, and longterm reduction in strength and energy. In snakes, the organism affects the moist lining in the gastrointestinal tract, resulting in thickening of the natural ridges in the internal organs and loss of segmented movement. Often, but not always, a veterinarian can feel a mass in the stomach area. X-rays or an examination using a medical instrument called an endoscope may reveal ridge thickening. Many lizards, including Old World chameleons and Savannah monitors, are affected primarily in the intestines. A veterinarian can diagnose cryptosporidiosis by performing certain tests on the animal's droppings, on the regurgitated food, or through a medical procedure called an endoscopic gastric biopsy. While several treatments have been suggested, none have consistently worked. Intensive supportive care will often stabilize and help prolong the life of the affected reptile.

Cryptosporidiosis is a disease that can be transferred from animals to humans; however, it now appears that the strains commonly found in reptiles do not affect humans or other mammals.

Hormonal Disorders

Although hormonal (endocrine) disorders do not appear to be common in reptiles, **diabetes mellitus** (defects in insulin action) has been reported in turtles and tortoises. Signs of diabetes in these reptiles include sugar in the urine and abnormally high levels of sugar in the blood. A dramatically increased appetite might also be noticed.

Eye and Ear Disorders

Infections of the eyes are possible in all reptiles. Ear infections are most likely to occur in turtles.

Eye Abscesses and Conjunctivitis

Abscesses can occur below the clear covering over the eyes in snakes, and conjunctivitis occurs in other reptiles. The severity of this condition ranges from mild inflammation to inflammation involving all the tissues of the eyeball. It may occur as a result of the spreading of an infection of the mucous tissue lining the mouth (*see* INFECTIOUS STOMATITIS, page 1028). Topical antibiotic ointments are used in turtles and lizards without spectacles (the clear covering over the eyes). In snakes and lizards with spectacles, surgery is needed to drain the abscess and flush the space below it and the tear duct with an antibiotic solution. Some affected reptiles, especially turtles, may need supplemental vitamin A.

Ear Infections

Ear infections occur in turtles, most often in box turtles and aquatic turtles. Swelling may be seen at the eardrum, and firm, dry diseased tissue is present. Many bacteria have been found to cause ear infections. Drainage of the ear and whole system antibiotics are required. Surgery may be needed to scrape the inside surface of the area and to remove any abnormal growths or other tissue. The area should be flushed with diluted povidone-iodine or a similar product for a few days to prevent premature closure and to keep the area clean. Ear infections may occur after a vitamin A deficiency; injections and dietary supplementation of vitamin A may be beneficial.

Bone and Muscle Disorders

Abnormal beak growth, which interferes with feeding, occurs in turtles and tortoises; it is often associated with poor nutrition, a deficiency of calcium, or both. A calcium deficiency may cause the skull to become distorted as it develops. This interferes with normal positioning of the upper and lower beaks when the jaw is closed and can affect wear of the beaks. Feeding excessive amounts of dog food or monkey chow may contribute to this condition. Treatment consists of trimming or grinding the mouthparts into a more normal shape. The condition usually occurs again due to the original disorder of the upper and lower beaks growing in uneven positions, and longterm maintenance is required. "Chewable" foods that allow for some natural beak trimming and shaping should be provided to turtles and tortoises in captivity. Items that might be suitable include crunchy insects such as beetles, stink bugs, grasshoppers, and large mealworms. Fresh raw vegetables,

Abnormal beak growth in a turtle

such as bok choy and kale, are also good because they require tearing and more use of the mouth.

Brain, Spinal Cord, and Nerve Disorders

Star-gazing is a neurologic disorder with signs that include mental dullness, abnormal posture, and an inability to move forward normally. It is seen in, but not restricted to, snakes, and is characterized by a severely twisted neck, creating a "starward gaze." A retrovirus that causes a viral meningitis/encephalitis in certain snakes (boas and pythons) is the most commonly diagnosed star-gazing syndrome. This syndrome is referred to as **inclusion body disease** due to the presence of characteristic masses of virus particles inside cells, referred to as inclusion bodies (*see* INCLUSION BODY DISEASE OF BOID SNAKES, page 1036).

Other possible causes of star-gazing are heat damage, trauma, and infections caused by bacteria or other organisms. Bacterial meningitis or encephalitis usually results from an infection being spread through the blood or bacterial particles circulating in the blood from an abscess elsewhere in the body. The outcome of the disease varies, depending on the cause, but the outlook is generally guarded. Whole system antibiotics are usually necessary in bacterial cases. An injection of a corticosteroid may help to reduce the inflammation associated with these infections. Because sores may heal slowly, an early response to therapy is rarely seen, and good supportive care (including fluids and nutrient supplementation) is essential.

Nutritional Disorders

Nutritional disorders can be caused by an imbalance in various nutrients, including protein, vitamins, and minerals (*see also* page 1023), or by defects or other diseases that prevent proper utilization of nutrients.

Malnutrition and Dehydration

Reptiles that do not have an appetite may need to be force-fed to correct severe deficiencies. This is a process that is best directed by your veterinarian, because feeding a malnourished reptile with severe dehydration can lead to additional, serious health problems. Initial feedings should replace fluids and electrolytes. Dehydration is recognized by skin folds along the sides of the animal, saggy skin, and in severe cases, sunken eyes.

Fluids can be given by soaking the reptile in water, by letting the reptile drink the water, or by having a veterinarian give it by injection. The soaking of mildly dehydrated reptiles is an easy and practical means of rehydration. For reptiles that are alert enough, fluids given by mouth are preferred to other methods; however, if necessary, a veterinarian will know the best method and the correct amount of fluids to provide.

A malnourished or starving reptile is similar in appearance to one that is dehydrated. Loss of tissue below the skin, noticeable bones, and a gaunt, sunken appearance are noted. Initial force-feedings under the supervision of a veterinarian are best done with a prepared mixture rather than with whole animals. Once initial force-feedings have been done, small whole animals can be force-fed to snakes and meat-eating lizards. The prey should be coated with egg white and then gently advanced into the back of the mouth,

after which the reptile is allowed to swallow.

Environmental factors such as temperature, light, and humidity should be set to the best conditions for all reptiles showing a loss of appetite. Fluids and nutrients will not be used properly if conditions are not optimal.

Gout

Gout is not only a disease of humans; it is also seen in all orders of reptiles. It occurs when the amount of uric acid in the blood is too high. Two forms of gout have been reported. **Visceral gout** affects the organs, and **articular gout** affects the joints. X-rays often show mineralized salt deposits from uric acid in the affected organs and joints. Visceral gout can be due to too much protein in the diet (primary visceral gout) or to other causes such as dehydration or kidney damage (secondary visceral gout). Gout can be very painful, causing discomfort to the point that some reptiles refuse to move, eat, or drink.

Primary visceral gout is treated by correcting the diet. Secondary visceral gout is treated by trying to correct the underlying problem, be it dehydration or kidney failure. Drugs that have traditionally been used to treat gout in humans may be effective in reptiles if the diagnosis is made early. However, the outlook for recovery is poor in advanced cases. Medical treatment usually must be longterm, because signs of gout often occur again if treatment is discontinued. Euthanasia (putting the animal to sleep) should be considered in reptiles that appear to be in pain and have no appetite.

Lung and Airway Disorders

Respiratory infections, including pneumonia, are common in reptiles and can be affected by many things, such as parasites infesting the respiratory system or the whole body, unfavorable environmental temperatures, unsanitary conditions, another disease occurring at the same time, malnutrition, and vitamin A deficiency. Open-mouth breathing, discharge from the nose, and difficulty breathing are frequent signs. Septicemia (*see* page 1027) may develop in severe or prolonged cases. Treatment consists of improving environmental factors (such as cleanliness and temperature) and starting whole system antibiotics. A veterinarian will be able to advise you on the proper antibiotic treatment. Reptiles with respiratory infections should be kept at the mid to upper end of their preferred temperature range. Increased temperatures are important not only to stimulate the immune system but also to help increase the output of mucus in the respiratory tract. Turtles often have an underlying vitamin A deficiency, and an injection by a veterinarian may help. Many turtles treated for pneumonia fail to improve until after treatment for vitamin A deficiency.

Paramyxovirus

Paramyxovirus infections are more common in viper snakes, but have been reported in nonvenomous snakes as well. This highly contagious virus causes mostly breathing problems; it is not unusual to see discharge from the nose, open-mouth breathing, dried pus in the mouth, and labored breathing. It appears that the virus is passed from one animal to another through the moisture in their breath. Due to the severe inflammation caused by paramyxovirus, affected animals often develop additional bacterial infections. Neurologic symptoms, including tremors and abnormal posture (extreme stiffness with severe arching of the back and the head thrown backward), are sometimes seen.

A snake with a respiratory infection that does not respond to treatment with supportive care, antibiotics, and nebulization (a way of providing medication in the form of a fine mist or aerosol) may be infected with paramyxovirus. Tests can be performed by a veterinarian as screening tools to help eliminate infected animals and prevent carriers from entering noninfected collections. There is no specific treatment, but supportive care and antibiotics may be useful. Affected snakes should be isolated and strict hygiene used.

Skin Disorders

Reptiles are prone to a variety of skin diseases and disorders. Good sanitation practices—such as regular enclosure cleaning, providing fresh water, and removing uneaten food—can help prevent infection and parasite infestation.

Abscesses

Abscesses are pus-filled sores, often accompanied by inflammation, and usually caused by bacterial infection. They are seen in all orders of reptiles. Often, abscesses are triggered by traumatic injury, bite wounds, or poor environmental conditions. Infected sores under the skin are seen as small lumps or swellings. Other conditions that may appear similar include parasitic infections, tumors, and hematomas (semisolid masses of blood in the tissues, caused by injury, disease, or a clotting disorder). A number of organisms, often more than one kind at a time, have been recovered from abscesses in reptiles. Small, localized abscesses should be completely cut away to avoid a recurrence, which does happen often. Larger abscesses should be cut open, followed by thorough treatment of the wound. The lining of the abscess must be scraped to remove as much material as possible. Appropriate whole-system antibiotics may also be needed.

Dermatophytosis

Dermatophytosis, a fungal infection of the skin or nails, has been described in all reptiles. In most cases, an injury to the skin provides a point of entry for the fungus. Turtles and tortoises with fungal infections of the shell can be treated by removing the dead, damaged, or infected tissue and applying an antiseptic or disinfecting solution. For skin infections, an oral antifungal drug is usually needed, although antifungal creams have also been used with good effects. Exposure to ultraviolet light also may be beneficial. (*See also* DISEASES CAUSED BY FUNGI, page 1036.)

Dysecdysis

Dysecdysis refers to an incomplete or abnormal shedding of skin. Low humidity and other stresses, including decreased thyroid function, skin parasites, nutritional deficiencies, infectious diseases, and lack of suitable abrasive surfaces, may all contribute to an abnormal shed. Often, eyecaps or circular bands on the tail or digits are kept. Eyecaps are best treated by applying an ointment made especially for the eye area twice a day for several days until the remaining skin either falls off or can be grasped with a pair of fine forceps and removed. Be patient—eyecaps should never be forced off because of the possibility of damaging the spectacle (the transparent covering over the eyes).

Stubborn, retained skin is best treated by soaking the reptile in warm (77 to 82°F [25 to 28°C]) water for several hours and then pulling gently with a gauze sponge. A humidity chamber also works well. This can be as simple as a 10-gallon aquarium with an undertank heater in which wet bath towels are placed. The top can be covered with a light cloth to increase humidity levels, but excessive heat must be avoided and can be relieved by allowing more ventilation. It is easier to prevent than to treat an abnormal shed, so make sure that your reptile is free of disease and parasites, is kept at the correct humidity level, and has abrasive surfaces available to help slough its skin.

Skin Parasites

Parasites that live in the reptile's skin are often a problem with wild-caught and newly acquired reptiles. Infestations are best prevented by thorough examination and a period of quarantine for all new animals entering a collection.

Mites are distributed worldwide, and most species of reptiles are affected. Reduced energy and, in heavy infestations, anemia (a blood condition in which there are too few red blood cells) due to blood loss may occur. The skin of affected reptiles appears coarse, and incomplete and inadequate skin shedding may occur. The

Incomplete shedding (dysecdysis) in a snake may lead to retention of the eyecap.

mites are tiny—less than 1.5 millimeters long—and are often found near the eyes, folds around the face or neck area, or any other indentation on the reptile. Mites may also transmit disease-causing organisms from other infected animals.

Mites are visible to the naked eye but are hard to see in small numbers. If mites are suspected, placing the reptile on a piece of white paper and gently rubbing it to remove mites will allow the mites to be seen. Affected reptiles often spend a great deal of time soaking in water to drown the mites. If you examine the water dish, you might see the drowned remains of mites.

There are many methods of treatment. In all cases, cages should be cleaned thoroughly, and you should throw away substrate materials, branches, and disposable cage furniture. Newspaper bedding should be used until treatment is completed to help with frequent cleaning and to get rid of egg-laying sites. A veterinarian will be able to tell you the type of mites your reptile has and provide advice on eliminating them from your pet and its enclosure (such as recommending a safe insecticide).

Keep in mind that any enclosure in which insecticide is used should be well ventilated, and any water containers should be removed while spraying and replaced when spray has dried. Do not use any product without consulting your veterinarian, as some may be safe in certain species of reptiles, but deadly to others.

The larvae of **trombiculid mites (chiggers)** are seen occasionally but are not considered to cause disease.

Ticks are frequently found on reptiles, and have been associated with many diseases. Heavy infestations may result in anemia (a blood condition in which there are too few red blood cells) due to loss of blood. Certain ticks may cause paralysis, with muscle wasting at the site of the bite. Ticks can be removed manually. Whole system antibiotics are often needed due to infections associated with multiple skin bite wounds and, potentially, with transmission of disease-causing bacteria.

Leeches have been found on the legs, head, neck, and in the mouth of a variety of turtles and crocodilians.

Turtles frequently have **skin maggots**. Botflies create a skin wound in which to lay their eggs. These hatch into bots that live in their cyst-like structures until they are mature enough to leave the wound. The wounds often resemble a lump under the skin; on closer inspection, they have an opening that is often lined by a black, crusted material. Your veterinarian can remove the bot by slightly expanding the natural opening and using a forceps to extract it from the skin. The wound is then flushed with an antiseptic or disinfectant, and an antibiotic ointment is applied. Whole system antibiotics are needed in reptiles that have multiple wounds. Skin maggots may also occur in existing wounds, and the maggots must be manually removed and the underlying wound treated with topical and whole system antibiotics as needed. During heavy fly season, it is recommended that turtles be housed indoors or with screens over their enclosures to offer some protection.

Scale Rot

Scale rot (ulcerative or necrotic dermatitis) is seen in snakes and lizards. Humidity and unclean environments appear to be the main factors that cause this condition. Moist, unclean bedding allows bacteria and fungi to multiply. When coupled with exposure to animal droppings, this can cause small skin sores. Secondary infection with other bacteria may result in septicemia and death if untreated. Reddening of the skin, death of the skin tissue, slow-healing sores on the skin, and a skin discharge are common. Although sores are sometimes caused by skin injuries, they more often develop from within. This is the case with classic scale rot in the ball python, in which the disease can develop even when animals are kept under perfect conditions. The condition starts with bleeding into scales, followed by small, round, raised areas of inflamed skin filled with pus that eventually lead to open and slow-healing sores. Treatment with whole system antibiotics, topical antibiotic ointment, and excellent hygiene are essential.

Blister disease was originally considered to be a separate disease, but it is now recognized as simply an early stage of scale rot. The skin has small, round, raised areas of inflammation filled with pus or blisters. These may go away without development of slow-healing sores if treatment is started early. A low-grade heat injury may seem like blister disease due to the possible development of fluid-filled blisters.

Septicemic Cutaneous Ulcerative Disease (SCUD)

Septicemic cutaneous ulcerative disease (SCUD) in turtles is a bacterial disease in which the scales are pitted. The turtle may shed dead skin with an underlying pus-filled discharge. Loss of appetite, lack of energy, and bleeding red spots on the shell and skin are seen; liver damage is common. Whole system antibiotics are recommended. Good sanitation is critical in preventing septicemic cutaneous ulcerative disease.

Crustacean Bacteremia

Another shell disease of turtles is caused by *Beneckea chitinovora*, a bacteria commonly found in crustaceans. Reddening of the skin and pitting of the shell with slow-healing sores is seen. Septicemia

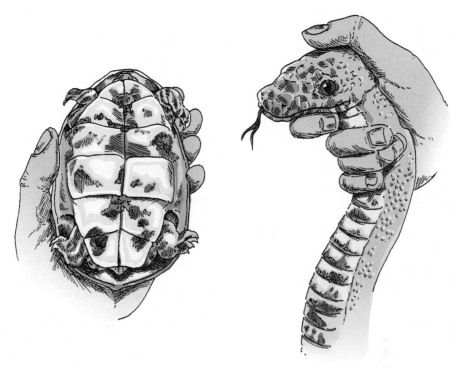

Bacteria often cause shell disease in turtles and scale rot in lizards and snakes.

(bacteria in the blood) is uncommon. Treatment with topical iodine is recommended. Feeding your turtle crayfish is often the cause of this condition and should be discouraged.

Disorders Affecting Multiple Body Systems

Some diseases affect more than one body system in a single animal, and other diseases have different effects in different species.

Bacterial Infections

Bacterial diseases are common in all reptiles. Most infections occur in reptiles whose immune systems are already weakened, most likely due to illness. Because of this, it is important not only to determine the type of bacteria that is causing the disease but also to correct environmental and nutritional deficiencies that contribute to ill health. Treatment with antibiotics for a specific type of bacteria will not be suc-

cessful without ensuring the proper heat, light, hydration, nutrition, and so on.

Coccidial Organisms

Several coccidial organisms have been reported to cause disease in reptiles. The severity of disease varies with the species of the coccidial organism and the type of reptile affected. These parasites can increase to tremendous numbers, especially in ill or diseased reptiles. The eggs of these parasites can survive for weeks in a dehydrated condition. Thorough daily cleaning is necessary to remove all animal droppings and contaminated food and water. Insects and other food items must be removed on a daily basis, as they are another source of contamination (for instance, crickets may eat the parasitic eggs while gathering fluid from the animal's droppings). Treatment should include an antimicrobial drug and may take 2 to 3 weeks. Even under the best conditions, treatment will get rid of these organisms in only 50% of cases. However, reducing the number of these organisms is still important, and a veterinarian should periodically check coccidial numbers.

Diseases Caused by Fungi

Excessively high humidity, low environmental temperature, already having another disease, malnutrition, and stress from poor husbandry may be factors in the development of diseases caused by fungi in reptiles. Little is known about the cause, development, and effects of fungal infections of the whole body, which can develop over a long period, but maintaining good sanitation and nutrition seems to reduce the number of these infections. Antifungal drugs may be used to treat whole-body infections, but reports of successful treatment in reptiles are few. For fungal infections that are limited to one area, surgical removal of the mass created by the fungus followed by local wound treatment may be helpful. *Basidiobolus* species, which can cause disease in mammals, are found in animal droppings of normal reptiles.

The most frequent sites of fungal infection in reptiles are the skin and respiratory tract. Slow-healing internal sores developing on gastrointestinal tissues have been associated with some fungal infections. Disease of the liver, kidneys, and spleen may also be caused by a fungal infection. Few signs other than weight loss—or in the case of respiratory infection, difficulty breathing—are seen before death. Animals may continue to eat until a few days before death.

Flagellates

Flagellates (a type of protozoal microorganism), especially *Hexamita* species, can cause urinary tract disease in turtles and tortoises and intestinal disease in snakes. A veterinarian with expertise can usually differentiate between the species and will be able to identify most of these organisms. An anthelmintic or antiprotozoal drug is usually prescribed for treatment.

Herpesviruses

Herpesviruses have been found in freshwater turtles, tortoises, and green sea turtles. In freshwater turtles, the virus may kill liver cells. In tortoises, the virus may cause death of mucous membrane cells in the mouth accompanied by loss of appetite, regurgitation, and discharge from the mouth and eyes. Herpesvirus infection can be diagnosed by a veterinarian.

Treatment in tortoises usually includes isolating the animal and providing supportive care, as well as giving an antiviral drug (either orally or in the form of an ointment applied directly to mouth sores).

Inclusion Body Disease of Boid Snakes

Boa constrictors and several species of pythons are most commonly affected by inclusion body disease, which is caused by a retrovirus. Boas are considered to be the normal host for this retrovirus because so many (up to 50% of those tested) are infected and they can harbor the virus for years without signs. In essence, inclusion body disease should be considered in every sick boa. Signs may appear suddenly due to any factor affecting the immune system and include a history of failure to absorb food, loss of appetite or weight, secondary bacterial infections, poor wound healing, skin ulcers, and regurgitation. Blood tests may show an increase in the number of white blood cells during the severe phase of the disease, but as the disease progresses, white cell counts tend to decline to levels that are below normal. As the disease becomes longterm (chronic) some boas will exhibit neurologic signs ranging from mild facial tics and abnormal tongue flicking to failure of the snake to right itself when laid on its back and severe seizures.

Pythons are thought to be an abnormal host of the retrovirus because the course of disease is more severe and neurologic signs are more extreme. Although the active disease can linger for months or more in boas, most pythons die within days or weeks of the appearance of signs.

Breeding, fight wounds, and contamination due to animal droppings coming in contact with the mouth are common ways of transferring the virus. Casual handling of an infected snake and then a normal snake does not appear to create enough exposure to cause infection. However, any reptile with a weakened immune system may be susceptible under the right circumstances. The snake mite is likely responsible for the spread of the virus in large, well-maintained collections.

Inclusion body disease is not curable, and many pet owners may choose to euthanize affected snakes. However, snakes can be isolated and treated with supportive measures to ease pain and symptoms. It is essential that you do not sell infected specimens or their offspring, as this has caused the disease to spread worldwide.

Infectious Cloacitis

Infection of the cloaca (the common passage for urine and feces in reptiles) is often caused by kidney stones or other hard accumulations of the lower intestine, urinary tract, or reproductive passages. It is characterized by swelling and bloody discharge from the cloaca. Accumulated mineral deposits, similar to kidney stones, may form when vitamin or mineral imbalances occur. These should be manually removed by a veterinarian and followed by dietary correction. When abscesses occur in the lower intestine, urinary tract, or reproductive passages, the infection can move within the body and inflame the brain and muscles throughout the animal. Upward-moving urinary or genital tract infections are common after infectious cloacitis. Aggressive treatment, including surgery to remove damaged or infected tissue from the wound, local wound treatment, and appropriate whole body antibiotics, is required. Your veterinarian may need to examine feces from your reptile to identify whether the infection is caused by parasites.

Internal Abscesses

Sores of internal organs may occur as a result of an infection in the blood. Abscesses of the female reproductive system are common and may lead to an infection of the abdomen. In this case, surgery is required, as whole system antibiotics alone are rarely successful.

Internal Parasites

Certain disease-causing **flatworms** (trematodes) infect the arteries and veins of turtles, and the mouth, respiratory system, kidneys, and the ducts that carry urine from the kidneys to the bladder of snakes.

Tapeworms are found in all orders of reptiles but are rare in crocodilians. The complex life cycle of tapeworms and the need for intermediate hosts limit the number of cases in captive reptiles. When present, segments of a tapeworm's body may be found in the lower intestine, urinary tract, or reproductive passages of the reptile, or typical tapeworm reproductive cells may be found in animal droppings. The infective larvae of some tapeworms may be found as soft swellings in the layer of connective tissue below the skin. These larval stages may be removed surgically.

Roundworms (nematodes) are found in all orders of reptiles. They are often microscopic, and include examples such as pinworms and hookworms. These parasites can inhabit the intestinal tract of reptiles; certain larvae are seen in the respiratory tract and respiratory cellular waste product, as well as in the mouth. They can sometimes be found in the animal's droppings. Infections often are mild but may lead to more serious diseases, such as pneumonia. In severe cases, death may result.

Some roundworm larvae may penetrate the skin, rather than entering the reptile through its mouth. This type of infection often goes unnoticed until the reptile is overwhelmed by parasites. Close attention to the immediate removal of animal droppings and urine-soaked areas of the substrate, as well as good sanitation practices, help to reduce parasite burdens in captive reptiles.

Skin sores caused by the **spirurid worm** (*Dracunculus* species) may be seen in reptiles. Numerous species of spirurids infect the stomach lining, body cavity, or blood vessels. These worms require an organism such as a mosquito or tick that transmits disease-causing microorganisms from infected animals to other animals, so they are less common in captive-bred reptiles or in reptiles that have been in longterm captivity. Treatment consists of increasing the environmental temperature to 95 to 98°F (35 to 37°C) for 24 to 48 hours. However, some "cool-adapted" reptiles may not tolerate this treatment.

Tongue worms (pentastomes) are found in a wide variety of reptiles, with variable abilities to cause disease. Infections are occasionally associated with signs of pneumonia, but these parasites can inhabit any tissue, and signs will vary with their migration path. Tongue worms were first noticed in tropical poisonous snakes; however, they have been seen in other reptiles as well. Treatment with the usual drugs (anthelmintics) often fails to eliminate these worms. In some cases, it may be possible for the veterinarian to use an endoscope to locate and mechanically remove all the adult worms. Recognition of these infestations is important because tongue worms are thought to present a risk of infection to humans. Euthanasia (putting the animal to sleep) is a valid consideration due to public health concerns.

Mycobacterial Infections

Mycobacterial infections are often associated with chronic wasting (a gradual loss of body condition caused by longterm infection). These infections generally affect the lungs of turtles and tortoises, whereas lizards, snakes, and crocodilians show small mass growths on their internal organs. The drugs required to fight these infections cause liver damage in reptiles, and their longterm use is unlikely to be safe.

Cancers and Tumors

Tumors are much more common in reptiles than previously thought. In addition to spontaneously developing cancerous (neoplastic) diseases, tumors have been associated with parasites and certain viruses. Tumors in reptiles are usually easily identified through various tests performed by a veterinarian. Once tumors are identified, treatment protocols similar to those used in other animals could be adapted. Your veterinarian will be able to recommend the appropriate treatment.

Retroviruses

Retroviruses found in Russell's vipers (viper virus), corn snakes (corn snake retrovirus), and California king snakes may sometimes be associated with malignant tumors.

Papillomas

European green lizards appear to pass viral particles from one lizard to another through bite wounds. The resulting papillomas (small growths) are approximately 1/16 to ¾ inches (2 to 20 millimeters) in diameter and may be single or multiple. While there are no signs in the initial phase, affected lizards may lose their energy and appetite and die. Diagnosis requires a veterinarian to test for signs of viral particles. Single masses can be surgically removed, but regrowth is common. Isolating any affected lizards may be the only way to prevent spread.

A papilloma-type virus also appears to affect Bolivian side-neck turtles and appears as white, oval skin sores distributed over the head. Slow-healing shell sores are also seen, primarily on the lower portion of the shell. Diagnosis requires a veterinarian to test for signs of viral particles. Treatment requires supportive care and treatment of signs; affected animals should be isolated from other turtles.

CHAPTER 75

Sugar Gliders

▒ INTRODUCTION

Sugar gliders (scientific name *Petaurus breviceps*) are small marsupials, mammals that nurse their offspring in pouches on their stomachs. Kangaroos, koalas, opossums, bandicoots and wombats are also marsupials. These exotic pets come originally from Australia and New Guinea and were first brought to the United States in 1994.

▒ DESCRIPTION AND PHYSICAL CHARACTERISTICS

Sugar gliders are generally 5 to 12 inches (120 to 320 millimeters) long with a tail that is 6 to 9 inches (150 to 230 millimeters) long. Their fur is bluish-gray with a pale belly and a dark stripe that runs down the back. Sugar gliders are similar to flying squirrels and have gliding membranes that allow efficient movement. These gliding membranes are called patagiums and stretch from the wrists to the ankles. Sugar gliders can glide up to 148 feet (45 meters) using their tails to steer and balance.

Female sugar gliders have stomach pouches in which the young develop. Mature males have a scent gland on the forehead that looks like a bald spot. They have a similar scent gland on the throat

A gliding membrane called the patagium allows these marsupials to glide up to 148 feet.

and near the base of the tail, which they use to mark each other and their territory. Males weigh 4 to 6 ounces (110 to 160 grams), and the slightly smaller females weigh 3 to 5 ounces (95 to 135 grams).

Sugar gliders are nocturnal, which means that they are most active at night and sleep throughout the day. They make noises such as chirping, barking, and chattering. They feed on insects and on the sap, gum, and nectar from various trees and plants. In the wild, they live in colonies that nest in tree hollows. Sugar gliders are generally strong and healthy when proper husbandry practices are followed. On average, they live 9 to 12 years in captivity. (*See* TABLE 19.)

▒ SPECIAL CONSIDERATIONS

Because sugar gliders are nocturnal, they should be kept in a fairly quiet area and allowed to sleep during the day. They can be easily stressed if awakened and

Sugar gliders originate from Australia and New Guinea.

Table 19. Sugar Gliders at a Glance	
Lifespan	9 to 12 years
Adult male body weight	110 to 160 grams (4 to 6 ounces)
Adult female body weight	95 to 135 grams (3 to 5 ounces)
Respiratory rate	16 to 40 breaths per minute
Heart rate	200 to 300 beats per minute
Body temperature	97.3°F (36.3°C)
Dentition (type of teeth)	Diprotodont (enlarged incisors or front teeth)
Puberty	7 to 10 months
Estrous cycle	29 days
Pregnancy duration	15 to 17 days
Litter size	2 (most common) or 1
Birth weight	0.2 gram (.007 ounce)
Pouch emergence	70 to 74 days
Weaning	110 to 120 days

taken out of their cages in daytime hours. This can increase the risk of illness. Sugar gliders are most active and playful in the evenings and at night. This is also when they are most vocal.

Sugar gliders should be provided with a large cage that is both sturdy and safe. Injury can result if the proper enclosure is not provided (*see* page 1041). A sugar glider should never be allowed to roam unsupervised outside of its cage as this may lead to injury. Bite wounds from other pets or other household hazards could be deadly.

The sharp claws of sugar gliders sometimes get caught in the fabric of clothing or other objects. Care must be taken when freeing them from the cloth or object; their toes, wrists, or ankles could easily be broken.

Sugar gliders are not domestic animals, and it is illegal to own them in certain states in the United States. Check with the United States Department of Agriculture's Animal Care Sector Office for your state to find out whether the laws in your area permit ownership of sugar gliders. If you own 4 or more breeding female sugar gliders, you may be subject to the Animal Welfare Act, which may require you to obtain a license and register your pets.

Behavioral disorders can occur in sugar gliders housed alone, with incompatible mates, or in inappropriate cages. It is very important to provide sugar gliders with a secure nest box or pouch. Anxiety may lead to overgrooming and fur loss, particularly at the base of the tail. Deliberately causing injury to themselves, over- or under-eating, abnormally excessive thirst, eating their own droppings, cannibalism, and pacing are also associated with stress. Priapism (persistant erection of the penis) has also been reported in adult male sugar gliders. This may result in trauma to the penis requiring surgical removal.

■ PROVIDING A HOME FOR A SUGAR GLIDER

Before bringing home a sugar glider, make sure you have made arrangements for suitable housing, diet, and exercise.

Temperament

Sugar gliders are very active, playful, intelligent, and inquisitive animals. They can develop strong bonds with their owners if given consistent and plentiful attention. Approximately 2 hours a day of interactive contact is recommended. Shorter or less frequent attention to a sugar glider that is a lone pet could result in the animal being depressed and could possibly lead to behavioral problems. Because they naturally live in colonies, sugar gliders are happy being raised in groups; however, they are also extremely territorial. Sugar gliders within a group are "marked" by the scent gland of the dominant male. Any sugar glider entering the group's territory without that scent can be violently attacked. It should be noted that the sugar glider will also "mark" you and anything in its surroundings with its scent.

Housing

A large cage, at least 20 by 20 by 36 inches (50 by 50 by 90 centimeters), with a secure lock is recommended for a single sugar glider. The enclosure should have enough room for exercise, as well as a place to put a food dish and a nest box or shelter in which your pet can sleep during the day. If the nest box is mounted high up in the cage, there must be enough room above the box to ensure that the sugar glider does not rub its elbows on the roof of the cage, which can cause their gliding membrane to tear. The mesh grid on wire cages should be no more than 1 by ½ inches (25 by 15 millimeters). Wire-bottomed cages allow droppings to go through to the tray below and can making cleaning easier.

Sugar gliders tolerate temperatures from 60 to 90°F (15 to 32°C); however, their preferred temperature range is 80 to 88°F (27 to 31°C). They should be kept in a warm room, away from heating or air conditioning vents and direct sunlight.

Appropriate bedding materials may include shredded newspaper or paper toweling, dry moss, cotton, leaves from a live branch, or wood shavings. Tree branches can be placed in the cage to allow climbing; however, certain woods are poisonous and should be avoided. Do not use almond, apricot, black walnut, cherry, or peach branches. Apple or citrus tree branches that have not been treated with pesticides are suitable. Some bird toys or other small animal toys, such as swings or chew toys, may also be appropriate.

Diet

In the wild, sugar gliders feed on tree sap, nectar, and insects. In captivity, they require a varied diet that includes fresh fruits and vegetables and protein from various sources (primarily insects). Fresh water must be available at all times.

Specially formulated mixtures for sugar gliders have been developed and are available in exotic pet stores or on the Internet. However, most of these are meant to be fed as part of a varied diet and should not be relied on as the only food source. The diet should also include appropriate vitamin and mineral supplements. Your veterinarian can recommend suitable supplements and provide directions on their usage.

Fat intake should be kept to a minimum. Nuts should be provided only as an occasional treat because they are high in fat and protein, and sugar gliders will often

Feeding Your Sugar Glider

Acceptable Food Items

- Commercial diets prepared for sugar gliders
- Artificial nectar mix (Leadbeater's mixture)
- Fruits (including apples, apricots, bananas, berries, cherries, grapes, melons, papaya, pears, plums, strawberries, dried fruits)
- Vegetables (carrots, corn, sweet potatoes, others not considered dangerous)
- Insects (mealworms, crickets)
- Other protein (meat such as cooked turkey or chicken, boiled eggs, feeder mice)
- Pure fruit juices (no sugar added)
- Occasional treats (such as nuts)

Potentially Dangerous Food Items

- Fruit with pits or seeds
- Certain vegetables, including avocado, broccoli, Brussels sprouts, cauliflower, leeks, lettuce, greens, garlic, onions, peas, and turnips
- Candy or chocolate
- Coffee, tea, soda
- Canned fruit
- Cat food (limited quantities can be fed if necessary)
- Nuts and seeds (can be fed as an occasional treat)
- Crickets raised on corn mash, outdoor insects
- Raw meats or eggs

eat them to the exclusion of healthier foods. Do not use canned fruit due to the preservatives and refined sugars in these products. Candy contains too much refined sugar and should not be given to your sugar glider. Chocolate must never be given to your sugar glider, as it is poisonous to them. Pits of fruits are also poisonous to sugar gliders. Small quantities of dry cat food can be fed as a source of protein if insects are unavailable. However, this should only be used until a supply of insects can be obtained, because feeding cat food to sugar gliders in large amounts or over an extended period may lead to medical problems.

It is important to thoroughly wash raw food items with fresh water before giving them to your pet to reduce the chances of exposure to various intestinal parasites that can cause diarrhea and vomiting.

Pet sugar gliders maintained on a mainly fruit diet are very susceptible to a nutritional condition in which there is a softening of the bones due to an imbalance of calcium and phosphorus intake (*see* page 1045). Diets should contain a daily protein source—a commercial extruded protein pellet, mealworms, crickets, or small amounts of cooked skinless chicken—as well as fruits and vegetables. Use of a balanced calcium/phosphorus supplement with vitamin D_3 and a multivitamin supplement can help prevent nutritional diseases.

Dental disease is more frequent in sugar gliders fed diets high in soft textured carbohydrates. Feeding insects with hard exoskeletons can help maintain dental health.

Exercise

Branches placed in the cage allow sugar gliders to climb. Small items from pet stores can be placed in the cage for the sugar gliders to climb, push, or carry. Taking your sugar glider out of its cage and interacting with it every day helps reduce boredom and behavioral problems. To reduce the possibility of injury, a sugar glider should never be left unattended outside of its cage.

◼ ROUTINE HEALTH CARE

Because sugar gliders are exotic animals, you should find a veterinarian who is familiar with these animals before your pet requires emergency care. A regular checkup in which the veterinarian performs a general physical examination and checks the animal's droppings for any parasites or harmful bacteria is recommended.

Signs of Illness

The sugar glider's overall appearance and behavior should be watched for signs of illness. Generally, sugar gliders should have bright eyes, a moist nose, pink nose and gums, the ability to grip with all 4 feet, a smooth fur coat, and good elasticity of their gliding membranes.

Wounds and signs of illness are similar to those seen in other animals, including depression, inactivity, and loss of appetite or weight. Other signs that your sugar glider is not well may include watery eyes, lack of energy, red and scaly skin, sores, abnormal droppings, excessive shedding or bald patches, labored breathing, and dragging the hind legs. If you notice any of these signs, you should bring your pet to a veterinarian immediately. Sugar gliders can very quickly pass the point of recovery if they do not receive prompt medical attention.

Sugar gliders can easily become dehydrated either from a lack of drinking water or due to a medical condition such as vomiting or diarrhea. This can be deadly if not addressed promptly. Signs of dehydration include sunken eyes, loose skin (the skin on the back will stay up after it is pinched), dry mouth and nose, lack of energy, abnormal breathing, and seizures. Immediately try to give the sugar glider water by mouth using a needle-less syringe and take the animal to a veterinarian. If needed, a veterinarian can inject fluids below the skin using a needle.

X-rays (radiographs) are useful tools in diagnosing medical problems in sugar gliders. It is particularly difficult to detect pneumonia in animals of this size without the use of radiography. Even extremely ill sugar gliders will generally tolerate short anesthesia to allow x-rays to be obtained.

Giving Medication

It is uncommon for owners to administer medication. If necessary, your veterinarian can advise you on the best way of giving medication to your sugar glider.

When needed, antibiotics are well tolerated by sugar gliders. Your veterinarian will be able to determine when antibiotics are necessary and will choose one based on your pet's particular illness. The drug will likely be administered by injection. To help in making clinical diagnoses, blood samples may be taken from the sugar glider after being given an anesthetic.

Preventive Care

Malnutrition is common in sugar gliders; therefore, a proper diet and supplementation (*see* DIET, page 1041) are very important. In addition to providing fresh water and a proper diet daily, regular cleaning of the enclosure, nest box, and the food and water dishes will help to keep your sugar glider healthy. Fresh fruit and vegetables should be promptly removed from the cage if not eaten within a few hours.

Sugar gliders can be infected by several common bacteria, including *Pasteurella*, staphylococci, streptococci, mycobacteria and clostridia. Several microorganisms that can be transmitted to and cause illness in humans also affect sugar gliders, including *Salmonella, Giardia, Cryptosporidium, Leptospira*, and *Toxoplasma* species. It is, therefore, very important to wash your hands thoroughly after cleaning your pet's enclosure and items within its cage, or after handling the sugar glider itself.

Diseases that can be Spread from Sugar Gliders to People

Cryptosporidiosis

Giardiasis

Leptospirosis

Salmonellosis

Toxoplasmosis

Dental Care

When sugar gliders are fed soft, carbohydrate-rich diets, gum disease and tartar are common problems that may require treatment by a veterinarian. Tartar buildup can be reduced if you include insects with hard exoskeletons, such as crickets and mealworms, in the sugar glider's diet.

Split or broken teeth or advanced tooth decay can lead to exposed root canals. The root canal is too small for filling and pulling the tooth could result in a break in the jawbone; therefore changing the diet is the best way to allow the sugar glider to cope with the exposed root. Follow your veterinarian's diet recommendations for the comfort and health of your pet.

■ BREEDING AND REPRODUCTION

Sugar gliders reach sexual maturity when they are 7 to 10 months old. They have an estrous cycle of about 29 days. As is common with marsupials, gestation (pregnancy) usually only lasts 15 to 17 days. After birth the babies, called joeys, crawl into their mother's pouch, where they remain until they are 70 to 74 days old. Young sugar gliders usually wean themselves at about 4 months of age. Sugar gliders have an average litter size of 2, each of which weighs about .007 ounces (0.2 grams) at birth. In the wild, female young leave the colony before reaching puberty. In captivity they may be attacked if not removed soon after weaning.

In the United States, many states require a breeding license for sugar gliders. Check with the United States Department of Agriculture office in your region to determine whether you need a license if you plan to breed these animals.

■ DISORDERS AND DISEASES

Many disorders and diseases that occur in sugar gliders are related to dietary imbalances, including malnutrition, obesity, and vitamin and mineral imbalances. Others are related to infection with bacteria, fungi, or parasites.

Aflatoxicosis

Aflatoxicosis is a liver disease caused by toxins produced by certain fungi in or on foods and feeds. Corn, peanuts, and cottonseed are the most likely to be contaminated with aflatoxins. Sugar gliders can get aflatoxicosis by eating contaminated peanuts or by eating crickets that have been fed contaminated corn. Therefore, it is important not to feed your sugar gliders peanuts and to know what kind of feed your insect supplier feeds its insects. Signs of aflatoxicosis are loss of appetite, anemia, jaundice, lack of energy, and diarrhea. Sudden death may occur. If diagnosed in time, aflatoxicosis is reversible. Take your sugar glider to a veterinarian immediately, and change its feed.

Constipation

Small, hard, dry animal droppings, or none at all, may be a sign of constipation. Possible causes of constipation are not enough liquids or fiber in the diet, poor overall diet, stress, lack of exercise, or digestive system problems. Some medications can also cause this problem. A medical examination by a veterinarian to determine the cause should be performed as soon as constipation is noticed.

Diarrhea and Vomiting

Several microscopic parasites, including *Cryptosporidium, Giardia*, and *Trichomonas* can cause diarrhea and occasional vomiting in sugar gliders, along with abdominal cramps, weight loss, and dehydration. Your veterinarian can perform tests to determine the cause of these signs and prescribe the appropriate medication. Because several of these parasites can also infect humans, it is important to use care when handling sick sugar gliders and to wash your hands thoroughly after cleaning the cage and before touching any food or any item that will be near your mouth. Until a followup test shows that the parasite has been eliminated, the sugar glider should be quarantined from other pets. The cage should also be thoroughly cleaned to reduce the possibility of reinfection.

Eye Disorders

Sugar gliders may be aggressive and can cause severe trauma to each other, particularly during mating and the introduction of new adults. These injuries often occur around the face and may include eye injuries and corneal scratches. Corneal scratches may develop slow-healing sores and conjunctivitis (inflammation of the tissue around the eye). Cataracts (white spots in the lens of the eye) also occur in sugar gliders. As in humans, this can lead to blindness.

Leptospirosis

Sugar gliders may become infected with this disease and pass it on to humans if they come into contact with water or food that has been contaminated with *Leptospira* bacteria. Signs include fever, kidney and liver problems. A veterinarian can test for the presence of these bacteria. Strict attention to thorough cage cleaning, food dish and water supply sanitation, and careful hand washing following contact with your pet or its environment are important to prevent both reinfection and transmission to you or other humans.

Lumpy Jaw (Actinomycosis)

Lumpy jaw is a condition in which the bacteria *Actinomyces israelii* infect the

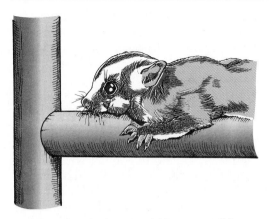

Lumpy jaw (actinomycosis) in a sugar glider

face and neck, creating a slowly enlarging, hard lump. The bacteria can also infect the lungs, intestinal tract, and other parts of the body. Discharge from the eyes and weight loss are other signs of infection. The facial tissues can become infected with the bacteria after surgery, trauma, or another infection. A common cause in sugar gliders is an abscess in the mouth. Lumpy jaw is deadly if left untreated; therefore, you should contact your veterinarian immediately if a hard lump appears on the face or neck of your pet or if you notice eye discharges or sudden weight loss. Treatment to get rid of the infection requires a prescribed medication. Because several disease-causing organisms may be involved, your veterinarian will perform tests to determine the most effective medication.

Mineral, Vitamin, and Protein Imbalances

Hypocalcemia is an abnormally low level of calcium in the blood and is due mainly to an imbalance of dietary calcium, phosphorus, and vitamin D. Not getting enough dietary protein causes **hypoproteinemia** and **anemia** (too few red blood cells in the blood). All of these conditions may be caused by longterm malnutrition and can lead to liver and kidney problems. Malnourished sugar gliders are weak and slow to respond, and usually thin and dehydrated. Anemic and hypoproteinemic sugar gliders may also have bruising, abnormal swelling, and pale mucous membranes. Weakened animals may develop additional infections. Treatment requires correcting the underlying dietary problems and providing general supportive care. Follow your veterinarian's advice regarding diet, supplements, water supplies, and environmental conditions.

Metabolic bone disease, also known as nutritional osteodystrophy, is a condition in which there is a softening of the bones due to an imbalance of the minerals calcium and phosphorus. The first signs are a weakening of the muscles in the sugar glider's hind end that progresses to paralysis of the hind legs. This can seem to happen very quickly. Pneumonia, heart problems, seizures, and broken bones can also occur as a result of this condition. X-rays reveal a loss of bone from the spinal column, pelvis, and long bones in particular. This disease, if treated quickly, can be reversible with proper diet and care. Treatment involves cage rest, giving calcium and vitamin D_3 supplements (which your veterinarian may give by injection), and correction of the diet.

To help prevent vitamin and mineral imbalances, insects in the diet can be gut-loaded with calcium or sprinkled with a calcium powder before being fed to sugar gliders. The practice of gut loading is a common technique that involves providing insects with a nutritious mixture of cereals and vegetables immediately before being fed to the sugar glider—thus loading their gut with nutrients. Another common practice is the use of powdered vitamin/mineral supplements. Crickets brought home from a pet store and never fed have little nutritional value. Placing them in a bag with vitamin and mineral powders and shaking the bag will coat the insects with the powder. Although some of the powder will fall off, the newer microfine powders adhere remarkably well.

Mites and Fleas

Wild sugar glider nests generally contain a range of host-specific mites and fleas, but these parasites that live on the outside of the body are uncommon in sugar gliders raised in captivity and indoors. Dusting with an insecticide recommended by your veterinarian is effective for controlling fleas and mites. Both the nesting box and the animal should be treated.

Obesity

Obesity can occur in captive sugar gliders that are fed a diet too high in calories. Lack of exercise also adds to the problem. Obesity can lead to heart and liver disease. Treatment of obesity requires a change in diet and an increase in exercise.

Pasteurellosis

Pasteurella multocida bacteria may spread from rabbits to sugar gliders. This infection is deadly for sugar gliders. Pus-filled, inflamed sores form on various organs, including the skin, causing sudden death.

Polioencephalomalacia

Polioencephalomalacia is a neurologic disease that causes deterioration in parts of the brain. Possible signs are loss of appetite, weight loss, lack of energy, weakness, dizziness, lack of coordination, disorientation, tremors, and gradual paralysis. It has been suggested that nutritional deficiencies may worsen this disease because some sugar gliders appear to have improved when given Vitamin B_1 (thiamine); however, the cause of this disease has not yet been determined. A severe case may prove deadly. A balanced and proper diet is most likely the best way to prevent this disease.

Toxoplasmosis

Toxoplasmosis is a disease often found in cats. Sugar gliders can get toxoplasmosis if they come into contact with cat litter or feces that have been contaminated with the parasite *Toxoplasma gondii* or if fed undercooked meats. Signs include lack of coordination, tremors, head tilt, diarrhea, loss of appetite and weight, loss of energy, below normal body temperatures, trouble breathing, and sudden death. This parasite can also be passed to humans; the signs include fever, sore throat and muscles, and loss of vision. The parasite is particularly dangerous for pregnant women; infection can cause miscarriage or birth defects. People with weakened immune systems are also very susceptible to becoming ill after contact with this parasite. To control this parasite, do not allow your sugar glider(s) to come in contact with a cat's litter box, provide only thoroughly cooked meats, and use gloves and thorough hand washing when handling cat litter.

Tumors

Tumors, particularly lymphoid neoplasia, are common in opossum and glider species. Tumors have been found in the spleen, liver, kidney, pouch, jaw, and lymph nodes of sugar gliders.

76 **Emergencies** **1050**
Introduction 1050
Emergency Care for Dogs and Cats 1051
Emergency Care for Horses 1059
Eye Emergencies 1063
Wound Management 1065
Lightning Strike and Electrocution 1068
Minor Injuries and Accidents 1069

77 **Diagnostic Tests and Imaging** **1070**
Introduction 1070
Types of Veterinary Medical Tests 1070
Tests Routinely Performed in Veterinary Medicine 1072
Diagnostic Imaging 1075
Radiation Therapy 1077

78 **Infections** **1078**
Introduction 1078
Defenses against Infection 1078
Development of Infection 1081
Infections in Animals with Impaired Defenses 1081
Preventing Infections 1082
Resident Flora 1082
Infections Caused by Bacteria 1082
Infections Caused by Rickettsiae 1085
Infections Caused by Parasites 1086
Infections Caused by Fungi 1086
Infections Caused by Viruses 1087

79 **Diseases Spread from Animals to People (Zoonoses)** **1088**
Introduction 1088
Preventing Zoonoses 1089
List of Zoonoses 1089

80 **Drugs and Vaccines** **1118**
Introduction 1118
How Drugs are Given in Animals 1119
Effect of Drug Treatment on the Fetus or Newborn Pet 1121
Guidelines for the Use of Antibiotic Drugs 1121
Drugs Used to Treat Heart and Blood Vessel Disorders 1122
Drugs Used to Treat Digestive Disorders 1124
Drugs Used to Treat Eye Disorders 1128
Drugs Used to Treat Bone and Muscle Disorders 1129
Drugs Used to Treat Brain, Spinal Cord, and Nerve Disorders 1130
Drugs Used to Treat Reproductive Disorders 1131
Drugs Used to Treat Lung and Airway Disorders 1132
Drugs Used to Treat Skin Disorders 1134
Drugs Used to Treat Kidney and Urinary Tract Disorders 1136
Antiviral Drugs 1138
Drugs Used to Treat Inflammation 1139

Drugs Used to Treat Cancers and Tumors 1140
Vaccines and Immunotherapy 1143

81 Poisoning.. 1145
Introduction 1145
Metabolism of Poisons 1145
Factors Affecting the Activity of Poisons 1145
Diagnosis 1146
General Treatment 1146
Algal Poisoning 1146
Arsenic Poisoning 1147
Bracken Fern Poisoning 1147
Cantharidin Poisoning (Blister Beetle Poisoning) 1148
Coal-tar Poisoning 1149
Copper Poisoning 1149
Cyanide Poisoning 1150
Ethylene Glycol (Antifreeze) Poisoning 1150
Fluoride Poisoning 1151
Food Hazards 1152
Fungal Poisoning 1154
Gossypol Poisoning 1159
Halogenated Aromatic Poisoning (PCB and Others) 1160
Herbicide Poisoning 1160
Household Hazards 1163
Insecticide Poisoning 1167
Lead Poisoning 1170
Mercury Poisoning 1171
Metaldehyde Poisoning 1171
Nitrate and Nitrite Poisoning 1172
Nonprotein Nitrogen Poisoning (Ammonia Poisoning) 1172
Pentachlorophenol Poisoning (Penta Poisoning) 1173
Petroleum Product Poisoning 1173
Plants Poisonous to Animals 1175
Poisoning from Human Over-the-counter Drugs 1181
Poisonings from Human Prescription Drugs 1194
Poisonings from Illicit and Abused Drugs 1198
Pyrrolizidine Alkaloidosis (*Senecio* Poisoning, Ragwort Poisoning) 1200
Quercus Poisoning (Oak Bud Poisoning, Acorn Poisoning) 1201
Rodenticide Poisoning 1201
Ryegrass Poisoning 1204
Salt Poisoning 1205
Selenium Poisoning 1205
Snakebite 1206
Sorghum Poisoning (Sudan Grass Poisoning) 1208
Spider Bites 1208
Strychnine Poisoning 1209
Sweet Clover Poisoning 1210
Toad Poisoning 1210
Zinc Poisoning 1211

82 Pain Management... 1211
Introduction 1211
Types of Pain 1211
Recognizing and Assessing Pain in Animals 1212
Pain Treatment 1213
Drugs Used to Relieve Pain 1213
Complementary and Alternative Therapies 1215
Treatment of Chronic Pain 1215

83 **Travel with Pets** **1216**

Introduction 1216
Travel with Service Animals 1216
Planning Your Trip 1217
Regulations Regarding Travel with Animals 1219
Vaccinations and Preventive Medications 1221
Returning to the United States 1221
Where to Stay 1223
Travel by Car 1223
Air Travel 1224
Travel by Ship 1226
Travel by Train 1226
Alternatives to Travel with Pets 1226

84 **Health and the Human-Animal Bond** **1228**

Introduction 1228
Health Benefits of Pet Ownership 1228
Animal-assisted Therapy and Activities 1229
Service and Other Working Dogs 1230
Animal Welfare 1231
Veterinary Family Practice or Bond-centered Practice 1231
Pet Loss and Grief 1232

85 **Cancer and Tumors** **1233**

Introduction 1233
What is Cancer? 1233
Development and Spread of Cancer 1235
Causes of Cancer 1235
Types of Cancer 1237
Reducing the Risk of Cancer 1238
Cancer Treatment 1240
Caring for a Pet with Cancer 1245
Quality of Life Issues 1248

CHAPTER 76

Emergencies

■ INTRODUCTION

Emergencies include serious injuries from accidents, burns, stings, bites, and possible poisoning. Sudden illness, or an ongoing illness that suddenly becomes worse, can also be an emergency. These conditions all require immediate veterinary attention.

You can reduce the likelihood of many of these situations, for example, by keeping harmful substances away from your pet. However, it is impossible to ensure that your pet will never have a medical emergency. By their very nature, emergencies are typically sudden and unexpected. Regardless, you can be prepared to respond if an emergency occurs.

Keep information about your pet's medical history and your veterinarian's phone number easily accessible. Make sure you know where the closest 24-hour veterinary hospital is located. It is also a good idea to keep a first aid kit on hand to treat minor emergencies.

Emergency patients present special challenges because underlying problems may not be evident for 24 to 48 hours. Many variables contribute to the overall success of emergency treatment, including the severity of the illness or injury, the amount of blood or fluid lost, age of the animal, previous health problems, and time delay in beginning therapy.

Emergencies resulting from poisonings are discussed in the chapter on poisoning (*see* page 1145) later in this section.

Know Your Pet

Knowing your pet's habits will help you recognize when something is wrong. Sudden changes in your pet's normal physical condition, gait, activity level, eating habits, elimination habits, or grooming habits can indicate a medical problem. Being able to recognize an emergency and get your pet to a veterinarian quickly is

Stocking a Pet First Aid Kit

You should keep a stocked first aid kit available and know how to use it. Check the expiration dates of all medications at least once a year, and replace them when necessary. Include the following items:

- Muzzle
- Bandaging materials (including gauze, sterile pads, stretch bandage, bandaging tape)
- Duct or packaging tape
- Small scissors
- Hydrogen peroxide
- Cotton balls or swabs
- Chlorhexidine wash (0.5%)
- Saline solution
- Antibiotic ointment
- Splinting materials
- Tweezers or forceps
- Bulb syringe
- Thermometer (for rectal use)
- Lubricating jelly
- Disposable gloves
- Kaolin-pectin (for mild diarrhea)*
- Activated charcoal (to deactivate poisons)*

*Always check with your veterinarian before using any over-the-counter medication.

one of the most important things you can do to ensure successful treatment.

First Aid Kit

You can purchase a ready-made pet first aid kit or make one yourself. A pet first aid kit generally includes basic items similar to those of a human first aid kit. The first aid kit should have a secure lid and be kept where you can find it quickly.

Be sure you know how to properly use the first aid kit. You may be able to enroll in animal first aid and CPR classes through your veterinarian's office, local community college, or groups such as the Red Cross.

Of course, a first aid kit is not a substitute for veterinary care. Take your pet to your veterinarian as soon as possible to determine the extent of the injury or illness and for followup care.

■ EMERGENCY CARE FOR DOGS AND CATS

Emergency care begins with your call to the veterinarian. Be prepared to describe the emergency situation. Your veterinarian may instruct you on how to administer first aid and how to safely transport your pet. You may be able to identify life-threatening airway, breathing, and circulation problems with the help of a veterinary professional on the telephone. Follow instructions regarding immediate treatment and transport. Calling ahead also gives the veterinary staff some time to prepare for your arrival.

What to Do at the Scene and Transport

You can provide basic medical care at the scene of the injury. Remember that *any animal that is injured or in pain may bite or scratch.* Injured animals must be approached carefully, and you should first take precautions for your own safety. Using a muzzle is often a prudent safety measure; one can be easily made from a piece of cloth or a ready-made muzzle can be included in the first aid kit. Never muzzle a dog with chest injuries or a dog with a short nose (brachycephalic breeds like Pugs), and never leave a muzzled dog alone. Placing a light towel or cloth over the animal's head can decrease the pet's awareness of nearby activity or noises that may cause fearful and aggressive reactions.

If your pet is not breathing, you may need to perform **mouth-to-nose resuscitation and chest compressions**. Request instructions from your veterinarian or pet emergency hotline. To perform mouth-to-nose resuscitation, close the animal's mouth, place your lips over the animal's

---

Emergencies Requiring Immediate Veterinary Care

- Severe trauma
- Heat exhaustion or stroke
- Frostbite or exposure to cold
- Electric shock
- Profuse bleeding from the nose, mouth, ears, or rectum
- Painful eyes with squinting, pupils that appear larger or smaller than usual, protruding eyeball
- Frequent vomiting and/or diarrhea, with or without blood
- Retching or unproductive vomiting, particularly if the stomach or abdomen looks bloated
- Difficulty breathing or other respiratory distress
- Collapse or coma
- Paralysis or severe neck or back pain (arching, twisted)
- Painful or bloated abdomen
- Clusters of seizures within a 24-hour period or a seizure that does not stop after several minutes
- Prolonged labor or difficulty giving birth
- Suspected poisonings, insect bite reactions, snake bites, scorpion bites, toad poisoning
- Extreme lethargy
- Prolapse of the rectum or uterus

(From *The Pill Book Guide to Medications for Your Dog and Cat* by Current Medical Directions Inc., copyright © 1998 by Bantam Books, a division of Random House Inc. Used by permission of Bantam Books, a division of Random House, Inc.)

---

nostrils, and initially give 3 to 4 strong breaths (*see* CARDIOPULMONARY-CEREBRAL RESUSCITATION, page 1057). If the animal does not start breathing on its own, breathe for the animal 10 to 12 times per minute. If you cannot detect a heartbeat, perform 5 chest compressions to 1 quick breath. Continue this pattern until the animal starts breathing on its own, or you get to veterinary assistance. Of course, in this situation, someone else will have to drive during transport.

| Step 1 | Step 2 | Step 3 |

A temporary muzzle can be created from a strip of cloth. Find a cloth bandage, rope, or other long strip of fabric. Tie a knot in the center of the bandage. Make another loose knot several inches above the first knot. Slip the loop over the dog's muzzle and gently pull the knot tight (Step 1). Cross the ends of the bandage under the dog's jaw (Step 2). Firmly tie the crossed ends behind the dog's neck (Step 3). Adapted, with permission, from *www.petfocused.com*, © morefocus group inc. 2007.

Bleeding requires immediate first aid. Press down firmly on the bleeding area with your fingers or the palm of your hand, and then apply a firm, but not tight, bandage. Any long pieces of fabric or gauze can be used. Often washcloths and hand towels are enough when applied with mild pressure. If the original bandage becomes soaked with blood, do not remove it; simply place additional material on top and continue to apply pressure. These bandages can be secured in place using duct or packaging tape.

Burns can be difficult to evaluate because the fur makes it hard to examine the injury. Large deep burns, chemical burns, and electrical burns need immediate attention, as do burns involving the airway or face. Use cold water on the affected area, and cover the burn with a nonstick dressing.

Dogs or cats that are **choking** may cough forcefully, drool, gag, or paw at their mouth. They may also hold their mouth open and show signs of agitation. If you think your pet is choking, do not stick your fingers in its mouth because you can easily be bitten or push the object further in. Instead, you can try to dislodge the object by thumping the animal between the shoulder blades or by applying several quick, squeezing compressions on both sides of the ribcage.

Do not remove **foreign objects** that have penetrated the skull, chest, or abdomen. Prevent the object from moving or penetrating further. If an arrow has penetrated the abdomen, do not let the shaft of the arrow move during transport. It may be necessary to stabilize the shaft of the arrow just outside the body and, holding it firmly, cut the shaft off.

Heat stroke is another emergency. Normal rectal temperature for cats and dogs is about 101.5°F to 102°F (38.6°C to 38.9°C). Signs of heat stroke include skin that is hot to the touch, vomiting, drooling, rapid panting, distress, loss of coordination, collapse, and unconsciousness. Remove the animal from the heat. Use cold water, ice packs, or wet towels to cool the head and body. Offer small amounts of water after the pet has begun to cool down. Do not immerse the animal in cold water.

Hypothermia (overexposure to cold) is rare in pets. It usually results when an animal has been lost or outside in very cold weather for a long time after another accident or injury, such as a car accident. Signs of hypothermia include slow pulse, shallow breathing, disorientation, collapse, and unconsciousness. Shivering is not a usual sign of hypothermia in pets. If the animal is wet, first dry it thoroughly, and then place wrapped warm (not hot) water bottles around the body. White, numb skin may be frozen or frostbitten. Thaw the area slowly; do not rub it or apply snow or warm water.

Dogs or cats that have neck or throat injuries caused by **strangulation**, such as hanging by their collar, should be taken to the veterinarian immediately. Remove the collar and use a makeshift harness from rope or an extra leash to control the animal.

Moving an Injured Animal

When moving or transporting an injured animal, minimize motion of its head, neck, and spine. A flat, firm surface of wood, cardboard, or thick fabric can be used to provide support. If the animal acts confused or disoriented after trauma, keep the head level or slightly elevated during transport. Avoid any jerking or thrashing motions, and prevent anything from pushing on the neck or jugular veins. Placing cats in boxes can minimize stress during transport. The box should have holes large enough so that you can see the cat.

Evaluation and Initial Treatment of Emergencies

In emergency medicine, the most life-threatening problems are treated first. When you arrive at the veterinary hospital, the veterinary staff will make a rapid assessment of your pet's physical condition and assign priority of care to each problem. They will ask about the current situation and probably for a brief medical history. Several observed problems or a history of problems may warrant immediate treatment regardless of physical findings. Trauma, shock, poisoning, severe burns, difficulty breathing, persistent seizures, abnormal heart rhythms, loss of consciousness, excessive bleeding, obstruction of the urethra, prolapsed organs, potential snake bite, heat stroke, open wounds exposing extensive soft tissue or bone, and difficult labor are usually treated immediately.

Common reasons for sudden death of an animal include airway blockage, breathing difficulty caused by buildup of air in the space around the lungs (called **tension pneumothorax**), fluid or blood in the lungs, severe narrowing of the airways (usually

---

Emergency Procedures to Discuss with your Veterinarian

Before you have to deal with an emergency, you should discuss the possibility with your veterinarian so that you can be prepared to take action quickly. You should know the answers to the following questions:

- What number should I call if my pet gets sick or injured after regular business hours?
- Where is the closest 24-hour emergency facility? (Visit their website, review any emergency tips, and download directions.)
- Are pet first aid classes available in my area?
- Do I have a complete pet first aid kit and do I know where it is located?
- What are some techniques for restraining my pet? Do I have a muzzle?
- What transport techniques are recommended?
- When and how should I perform the Heimlich maneuver in my pet if there is an obstruction of the airway due to a foreign object?

---

from an asthmatic or allergic reaction), cardiopulmonary arrest and loss of circulation, extremely slow or fast heart rate, or continued internal or external bleeding.

The veterinarian will evaluate your pet's airway, breathing, and circulation, as well as its level of consciousness. After your pet has been stabilized and initial emergency treatment begun, the veterinary staff will ask you additional questions about the animal's medical history and details of the current situation. Be prepared to provide information on your pet's past medical problems, medications, drug and food sensitivities, date of last vaccinations, and any other pertinent details.

The veterinarian will perform a complete physical examination of the animal, including listening to your pet's heart and lungs, checking the abdomen for pain, and examining the limbs and joints for pain or swelling. If abdominal pain is present, its source must be determined. Some signs, such as vomiting or diarrhea, can indicate which body systems may be involved. Samples of blood and urine may be collected for laboratory testing. All this information helps the veterinarian to identify specific problems and to determine a diagnosis, treatment, and monitoring plan.

Airway

Any obstruction of the airways can be life-threatening. If the large airways (the trachea, commonly called the windpipe, and its 2 main branches, called the bronchi) are completely obstructed, the animal is unable to breathe and will be unconscious. If the large airways are only partially obstructed, the animal's breathing will be noisy. The animal may be fearful, and its skin may appear to have a bluish tinge due to lack of oxygen. Possible causes of large airway problems include foreign objects, swelling (perhaps because of an allergic reaction), paralysis of the larynx, collapse of the trachea, and a longer soft palate than is usual. A potentially very serious situation called aspiration refers to breathing in stomach contents that have been vomited. This can lead to respiratory problems such as pneumonia and is one of the reasons why animals must be fasted before anesthesia and surgery.

Animals with severe small airway obstruction have difficulty breathing. They may wheeze and push out their diaphragm when exhaling. They may be fearful or anxious, and their skin, eyes, nailbeds, and other tissues may appear bluish. The animal may be sedated and given medication to expand the airways and make breathing easier. Common causes include allergic reactions; asthma (cats); and fluid, blood, mucus, or foreign material in the lungs.

If an animal is unconscious and not breathing, a tube will be placed through the larynx into the trachea to help it breathe. This is called **tracheal intubation**. If the upper airway is obstructed, oxygen can be given through a tube inserted below the obstruction to open the airway. The veterinarian will listen to ensure that the air is reaching the animal's lungs. Heart sounds and pulses are checked and when absent, cardiopulmonary-cerebral resuscitation is done.

If the large airways are only partially obstructed by a foreign object, the veterinarian will remove the object if possible. A tracheal tube may be placed to deliver oxygen. The animal may need to be sedated to relieve anxiety. When tracheal intubation is necessary, sedation, likely general anesthesia, will be needed.

Breathing

When animals have difficulty breathing, they breathe faster and breathing takes more effort. The breathing pattern often changes, followed by changes in posture. For example, dogs may stand with the elbows spread out and the back arched. Cats may crouch on all 4 limbs and raise their chest slightly, or sit high on the rear haunches and extend their head and neck. Obvious labored, open-mouth breathing and a blue tinge to the skin due to lack of oxygen develop last. These signs indicate significant loss of respiratory function.

The veterinarian will carefully observe the breathing pattern and listen to the animal's chest. X-rays or other tests may be necessary after the animal has been stabilized. Oxygen is administered by a tracheal tube, a mask, a hood, or other method. The animal may be sedated to relieve anxiety. After the animal has been stabilized, additional tests may be done.

One cause of breathing problems is **pleural space disease**. The pleural space is the area between the membrane covering the lungs and the membrane lining the chest cavity. In this condition, air, fluid, or abdominal contents are in the pleural space. The veterinarian will hear muffled lung sounds over the affected regions. Treatment of pleural space disease begins with the veterinarian using a needle or catheter to remove the air or fluid that is free in the chest cavity. This procedure relieves the tension within the chest, allowing the heart to beat and the lungs to expand. A chest tube is then placed to continue to relieve the pressure.

Circulation

Several indicators are used to determine how well the animal's circulatory system is functioning. These include heart rate, mucous membrane color, capillary refill time, and pulse intensity. Listening to the animal's heart and breath sounds will help the veterinarian determine what circulatory problems may exist.

Shock is the medical term for changes that develop when the body attempts to compensate for limited heart function, blood volume, or circulation. Shock can develop in many emergency situations, including head trauma, excessive blood or fluid loss, and severe infection. Signs of shock include a rapid heart rate, pale mucous membrane color, very low blood pressure, very little urinary output, and weak pulses. As shock progresses, delivery of oxygen and other nutrients to the tissues drops, eventually leading to organ failure and ultimately death.

Recognizing the type and stage of shock early is vital to treatment. Shock is typically classified into 3 categories: hypovolemic, cardiogenic, and distributive. **Hypovolemic shock** develops when blood volume is low, usually from loss of blood due to traumatic injury or loss of fluid through metabolic processes. **Cardiogenic shock** results when the heart fails, no longer pumping blood to the lungs or the rest of the body. **Distributive shock** is caused by blood flow being directed away from the central circulation because of a problem with peripheral blood vessels and is usually associated with serious widespread infections.

The goal of treatment for shock is to deliver blood to the tissues, bringing oxygen and other nutrients. Oxygen can be administered by a mask, bag, nasal or tracheal tube, or another method. Bleeding must be controlled. However, internal bleeding may not be evident until blood

pressure and circulation are restored. Fluids and blood products will be given intravenously as needed to replace what has been lost. Abdominal counterpressure may be used to reduce abdominal bleeding, when present.

Medication to relieve pain is usually provided quickly. Narcotics or local anesthetics can be used. Your veterinarian may use other medications as well.

Specific Diagnostics and Therapy

In an emergency, after your pet has been stabilized the veterinarian will ask you for a more complete history, conduct a more systematic physical examination, and begin specific diagnostic and treatment procedures.

Trauma

Accidents, falls, and fights with other animals may result in different types of trauma. In blunt trauma, the animal has been struck by an object (such as a car) but the skin was not penetrated. Blunt trauma is commonly associated with internal bleeding, organ rupture, fractures, and head injuries. In penetrating trauma, a sharp object, such as an arrow or bullet, pierces the skin, and injuries are related to the path of the penetrating object. Falling from a height can cause multiple bone fractures, as well as injuries to the chest and organs. A dog bitten by another larger dog can have deep penetrating bite wounds and will frequently have spinal injuries and tracheal rupture from the thrashing motions experienced during the attack.

For all types of trauma, airway, breathing, and circulation are evaluated and stabilized as described above. Control of bleeding, oxygen if needed, and pain relief are also given immediate attention. After stabilization, the nervous system, chest, abdomen, and bones are carefully evaluated. Blood tests, urine tests, and x-rays may be performed as needed. Trauma to the eye is also a common emergency (*see* EYE EMERGENCIES, page 1063).

Animals that have suffered a trauma often have multiple injuries, some of which may not be immediately obvious. Whenever the animal is moved or being examined, the neck and spine should be kept still in case there are spinal fractures or other problems that cannot be readily seen. Broken legs may be wrapped with bandages or splinted. Because many problems are not apparent for 12 to 24 hours after trauma occurs, your pet needs careful monitoring in the veterinary hospital.

Thoracic (Chest) Trauma

Some traumatic injuries to the chest are potentially life-threatening. Bruising of the lungs, air in the space around the lungs (called **pneumothorax**), heart rhythm problems, internal bleeding, and rib fractures are emergencies that may result from blunt trauma.

Tests to help determine the extent and severity of the problems include chest x-rays, blood tests, and an electrocardiogram (EKG). A procedure called centesis, in which a needle is inserted into the chest or abdomen of the animal to remove fluid or air, may also be performed. Laboratory examination of any fluid removed can help with diagnosis.

Severe bruising of the lungs causes labored breathing and lack of oxygen to the tissues. Oxygen treatment may require sedation and tracheal intubation, in which a tube is inserted into the trachea to help the animal breathe. When bruising is severe, ventilation (in which air is forced mechanically in and out of the lungs) may be required to provide the best chances for survival.

If air or fluid is trapped inside the animal's chest cavity, a tube may be inserted through an incision in the chest to drain the air or fluid. Surgery may be recommended either immediately or after several days if the animal does not improve.

A condition called **flail chest** may be caused by blunt trauma that breaks 3 or more ribs. The portions of ribs that have broken off, called flail segments, may be stabilized by using an external frame of metal rods or cast material that is formed to the shape of the chest. The animal must generally be anesthetized, and surgery is usually necessary.

Bite wounds over the chest must be cleaned and drained. The puncture holes seen on the skin from the bite are only a small portion of the significant damage that may have occurred to the muscles and tissues underneath the skin. Surgery may be required if the wound is penetrating or if there is significant bruising or swelling.

Heart rhythm abnormalities, particularly fast heart rhythms, are often seen after trauma. A sedative may be used to relieve anxiety and slow the animal's heart rate. The animal should be treated aggressively for shock, and an electrocardiogram should be done to look for primary heart rhythm problems.

Abdominal Trauma

The extent and severity of abdominal injuries are not always obvious immediately. If the abdominal wall is torn open, the injury is clearly serious. Bruising, road burns, cuts, scrapes, swelling, a change in the shape of the abdomen, or pain may indicate internal injuries. If your pet appears to have abdominal pain and is in shock, internal bleeding may be present. The spleen, liver, or kidneys may be injured. All abdominal organs have blood vessels that can be injured by blunt trauma.

It may take several hours for specific signs of an injury to an abdominal organ to appear. Your veterinarian will watch closely for sharp abdominal pain. Abdominal x-rays or ultrasonography may show the location of injury. If fluid is present in the abdomen, a needle may be inserted into various locations to remove it. The fluid is then examined for any evidence of infection, rupture of an organ, cancer, or other problems.

Sometimes, a catheter is placed through an incision in the animal's abdomen, and warm saline solution is flowed into the abdomen. The fluid is left in the abdomen for several minutes and then drained. This process is called **peritoneal lavage**. If the fluid is clear, significant internal abdominal bleeding is unlikely. Some blood in the fluid indicates mild bleeding. More blood in the fluid indicates significant abdominal bleeding that warrants careful monitoring and may require surgery. However, bleeding may be present even if the peritoneal lavage shows little or no blood in the fluid. Pelvic fractures in particular may cause complications, including bleeding, that often are not found by peritoneal lavage.

If internal bleeding or other serious internal problem is found, emergency surgery may be needed.

Cardiopulmonary-Cerebral Resuscitation

Cardiac arrest occurs when there is no heartbeat and breathing stops. The purpose of cardiopulmonary-cerebral resuscitation (CPCR) is to replace the work that the lungs and heart are not performing on their own. The success of CPCR efforts depends on the underlying cause of the cardiac arrest as well as on the speed and effectiveness of the treatment. The initial steps of CPCR are meant to get the needed oxygen and blood to the animal's tissues. CPCR progresses with advanced life support measures. Heart rhythms are monitored, drugs are administered, and the heart is defibrillated when necessary.

Mouth-to-nose resuscitation is the first step of cardiopulmonary-cerebral resuscitation.

Defibrillation is a process of shocking the heart in a specific way to restore a coordinated heart beat and a pulse. Often, immediate defibrillation offers the best chance of recovery after cardiac arrest. Defibrillation is considered the best treatment for one of the most common arrest arrhythmias, ventricular fibrillation. Other heart rhythm problems are generally thought not to be made any worse by the procedure.

Basic Life Support

Mouth-to-nose resuscitation is the first step of CPCR. This continues until the veterinary staff can insert a tube to deliver oxygen and help the animal breathe with mechanical ventilation. Chest compressions are used to promote circulation when no pulse is present. The animal is positioned on its back or its side (depending on size) and supported as needed while compressions are performed over the area of the heart. The goal is to improve the return of the blood to the heart between beats.

Constant monitoring is important during basic life support procedures. If circulation continues to fail, additional procedures or drugs may be necessary.

Advanced Life Support

In advanced life support, heart rhythms are monitored by electrocardiogram, and drugs or defibrillation may be used. The purpose is to reestablish the heartbeat.

Fluids are administered, usually intravenously (IV), to promote circulation. Sometimes, blood products are also given.

If basic life support has not been successful, meaning that the animal does not begin to breathe on its own or have a normal heartbeat after 5 to 10 minutes, open-chest cardiopulmonary resuscitation (CPR, *see* page 1058) may be started. Sometimes open-chest CPR is begun earlier. In severe trauma with blood loss, the chest may be opened to assess the injury as well as to perform CPR. In a large dog, external compressions may not generate enough blood flow. You should make your wishes known to the veterinary team as quickly as possible regarding your permission for open-chest CPR. This technique can be life-saving, but it carries additional expense and requires surgery to close the chest.

Open-chest Cardiopulmonary Resuscitation (Emergency Thoracotomy)

When chest compressions are not successful in restoring the heartbeat, the chest may need to be opened to allow access to the heart. The visual examination, along with the EKG, allows the type of heart arrhythmia to be determined. If blood has pooled around the heart in the tissue sac called the pericardium, the pressure from this fluid can be relieved by opening the sac. If the heart is not beating, the veterinarian grasps the heart with one or both hands and compresses it. The compression is then released to allow the heart chambers to refill with blood. If blood loss is severe or poor circulation has been prolonged, certain blood vessels may be clamped to direct blood flow to the brain. This is a temporary measure, usually up to 10 minutes.

If the heart begins to beat again, the open chest is rinsed with sterile, warm salt water, and a chest tube is placed before the chest is closed. Treatment continues while the underlying cause of the arrest is determined.

Fluid Therapy

Maintaining volume in the blood vessels and the tissues of the emergency patient is vital. Signs of dehydration (fluid loss in the tissues) include dry skin that does not "smooth" back into its normal position after being pinched, dry mucous membranes, and sunken eyes. When fluid is given, it is distributed evenly throughout the body. This rehydrates a dehydrated animal. However, excessive water volume can cause swelling, called edema. Specific types of fluids are given to injured animals to meet their specific bodily needs.

Monitoring the Critically Ill Animal

Critically ill animals must be monitored closely in the veterinary hospital for a period of time depending on the severity of the illness or injury. Close attention helps the veterinarian determine whether treatment is effective, or whether other treatments may be needed. Often, secondary problems become evident or develop during treatment.

Several parameters are generally evaluated daily or more often while the animal is hospitalized. These include the balance of fluids in the body, glucose (blood sugar) levels, electrolytes, oxygen levels, level of consciousness, blood pressure, heart rate and rhythm, coagulation of blood, red blood cell count and hemoglobin (a protein that carries oxygen) level, gastrointestinal function, kidney function, and effects of medications.

Nutrition

It is always preferable if an animal will eat on its own or at least take food orally. Small amounts of a liquid diet can generally be given orally. When the pet refuses oral feeding, a tube can be placed to provide nutrition through the gastrointestinal tract. In the rare event that nutrition cannot be given through the gastrointestinal tract, then nutrition is usually provided through specific intravenous fluids.

Pain Control

Signs of pain include fast heart rate and pale mucous membranes. These can mimic signs of shock. An animal in pain also has higher levels of stress hormones. However, animals may be in pain without showing obvious signs. In these cases, if the animal has a known painful condition, pain medication is generally administered. Pain medication makes the animal more comfortable but can also reduce signs of other conditions, possibly making diagnosis more difficult.

Nursing Care

Critically ill animals need skilled, knowledgeable, attentive nursing care.

Animals that are unable to walk should be turned from one side to the other, every 4 hours if possible, to prevent ulcers and other problems. Physical therapy to maintain range of motion, muscle tone, and blood flow may be a part of nursing care. Catheter sites should be inspected frequently for signs of infection or displacement. Bandages that become soiled or wet should be changed. If fluid collects in limbs, light compression wraps may be used. These should be changed every day. Any animal with a critical illness should have 24-hour nursing care.

After the Emergency

If your pet needs to stay in the veterinary hospital, ask about the visitation policy. Many veterinary hospitals encourage owner visits and have daily visiting hours. Talking to your pet and maintaining contact when possible can help reduce your pet's stress and anxiety (as well as your own).

When it is time to bring your pet home, make sure that you completely understand all care instructions. Often, you will be required to restrict an animal's activity for a certain period of time, particularly after surgery or if your pet has fractured a bone. Dogs can be crated or restrained in a small room; when taken outside, they should remain on a leash to prevent running or jumping. Cats can be kept in a small room where they will not be tempted to jump onto furniture or counters.

Medication should be given according to instructions, and all label directions followed closely. Tips on administering medications are given in the Dog Basics and Cat Basics chapters (*see* page 12 and page 338). Bandages should be changed as directed, and wounds or sutures (stitches) checked for any swelling, redness, or discharge that might indicate infection. You will probably be advised to avoid bathing your pet until any sutures are removed.

Your veterinarian will usually schedule a followup appointment to check on your pet's recovery. In the meantime, call if any problems arise or if you have any questions about care.

◼ EMERGENCY CARE FOR HORSES

Equine emergencies can be challenging for veterinarians and emotionally charged for owners. Preparation before an emergency occurs is key. Discuss the best facilities for treatment with your veterinarian ahead of time. Have phone numbers and other information on hand. Know how to get to the facility you have chosen, plan how you are going to transport the horse, and keep driving directions handy. Assemble and keep a first aid kit on hand to deal with immediate needs and transport in case your horse requires emergency treatment.

The most common types of equine emergencies are abdominal pain (colic), trauma and lacerations, and ill foals.

Common Emergency Procedures in Horses

Emergency procedures for horses follow the same general principles as those for small animals. However, there are special considerations for horses. Because horses cannot lie down for extended periods of time, some conditions that are considered less serious in other animals are emergencies in horses. Also, treatments often vary between smaller animals and horses.

Monitoring a horse in an emergency situation is crucial. In a horse that is in severe shock, pulse and breathing must be closely monitored.

Fluid Therapy

Preventing and treating dehydration is a primary concern. Horses require about 60 milliliters per kilogram of fluids per day normally. For an adult horse, this is about 1 liter (about 1 quart) per hour. Athletic horses often require more fluids. Heart rate, pulse, urine production, and other tests help determine whether a horse is dehydrated. Dehydration often develops along with other injuries and illnesses. Diarrhea is a major cause of dehydration, particularly in foals. If the horse is losing fluids, such as with diarrhea, very large quantities of fluids may be needed to correct the fluid loss. For example, a 1,000-pound horse that has become 5% dehydrated will need 25 liters (about 6¼ gallons) of fluids to correct that loss.

If a lot of blood has been lost, or the horse is exhausted or overheated, emergency fluid replacement is needed.

Nasogastric Intubation

Nasogastric intubation is an essential and possibly life-saving procedure commonly used in cases of equine colic. A tube is placed through the nostril down into the stomach to remove fluid that has accumulated in the stomach due to a blockage in the small intestine. Removing the fluid not only relieves the pain of the distended stomach, it may also prevent rupture of the stomach.

Abdominocentesis

In abdominocentesis, a needle or syringe is inserted through the abdominal wall to obtain a fluid sample. The fluid is used in the evaluation of abdominal diseases such as colic and weight loss. If the horse has suffered an intestinal rupture, this test will generally detect the problem. For the first 2 to 4 hours after a rupture of the intestine, the horse may not show any signs. Internal bleeding can also be detected by abdominocentesis.

Trocarization

Trocarization is a technique used to relieve the pressure in the abdomen when it becomes distended with gas due to an intestinal blockage. Such blockage can result in severe bloating (distention), pain, and rapid or uneven breathing. The veterinarian will identify the segment of intestine that is involved by rectal examination in adult horses. In foals or small horses, x-rays or ultrasonography can be used. If the problem is in the large intestine, trocarization may be used. After the pressure is relieved, the trocar is removed, and an antibiotic is infused. Because infection and other problems are possible after trocarization, the horse is usually monitored carefully for 24 hours for signs of any complications. Trocarization may not solve the blockage problem, and the horse may still need additional treatment or even abdominal surgery.

Tracheostomy

If the trachea is blocked due to swelling, a foreign object, or excessive bleeding, the airway needs to be opened. An emergency procedure for inserting a tube through the neck to allow breathing is called a tracheostomy. A local anesthetic may be given. The incision is made in the neck, and a tube is inserted into the trachea to help the horse breathe.

Once the horse can breathe without using the tube, it is removed. The incision site generally closes in 10 to 14 days and heals in 3 weeks. During that time, antibiotics may be used, and the site is cleaned and monitored.

Transporting an Injured Horse

In many equine emergencies, your veterinarian will travel to your location to assess and treat your horse. However, in some cases it may be necessary to transport your ill or injured horse for treatment.

Before loading an injured horse, be sure that the horse is stabilized and the injury immobilized as much as possible. A low ramp facilitates loading and unloading of an injured horse. While in the trailer, the horse may lean on the wall or partitions to help reduce the weight load on the injured leg. It will be easier for the horse to travel with partitions in place rather than loose in a makeshift stall. A sling can be placed under the abdomen to help the horse take weight off the injured limb. Many trailers have standing stalls at 45° angles (slant load trailers), which help horses balance during transport. If a regular straight-load trailer is used, the horse should face backward for a foreleg injury, and forward for a hindleg injury, to help cushion sudden stops. Providing hay helps relieve anxiety. Frequent stops should be made to check on the status of the horse and provide drinking water.

A horse with a severe injury may be loaded into a trailer using a blanket or tarp.

If the horse is severely injured and cannot stand, it can be pulled onto the trailer using a large tarp or blanket. The horse should be kept sedated during transport, to avoid injuries. A head protector or bandage can be used to protect the eyes and head from self-induced trauma. Bandages should also be applied to the lower legs to avoid trauma caused by paddling or thrashing.

Trauma and First Aid

Common traumatic injuries of horses include fractures, cuts, puncture wounds, infections, and a muscle weakness syndrome called exertional rhabdomyolysis. These conditions require immediate veterinary care. In cases of trauma, keeping the horse calm is a primary concern. This can help prevent further injury. Emergency first aid may also be required.

Eye Injuries

Eye injuries are usually caused by trauma. They include cuts, scratches, and penetrating injuries from foreign bodies. Direct blows to the eye can cause retinal detachment. The eyes should be protected from direct sunlight as much as possible (*see* EYE EMERGENCIES, page 1063).

Fractures and Dislocations

Bone fractures, particularly in the legs, are one of the more common musculoskeletal injuries in horses. Luxations, or dislocations, are also common. Initially, the goals are to relieve anxiety, prevent further injury, and allow safe transportation to the veterinary facility. Emergency splinting or other stabilization of injured legs should be performed.

Horses usually cannot bear weight on a leg with a traumatic fracture. Certain stress fractures and other skeletal and tendon injuries may take some weight. Generally, the first indication of a fracture is the sound of a loud crack (if you are present at the time of the injury) or sudden lameness. Other indications of a break are a misaligned or visibly unstable leg. A horse may lie down, or be unable to get up after a fall, if the injury is severe. If the horse is lying down, it should be examined before attempts are made to get it to stand. If the horse is standing, it should be examined before attempts are made to move it.

For examination, the horse should be restrained and sedated, if necessary, to relieve pain and anxiety. Fractures are often accompanied by significant skin and other tissue injuries. The veterinarian will begin by locating and assessing the injury. Bleeding must be controlled. Wounds are cleaned and debrided (foreign matter and dead tissue are removed), then bandaged. The fracture is then stabilized. A splint is usually used to stabilize the leg to prevent further injury during transport. Many splints are commercially available and are part of equine first aid kits. The splints should be well padded to avoid the development of sores.

Head Injuries

Head injuries can result in severe damage to the central nervous system. In many head injuries, swelling and bleeding continue after the initial injury, and quick veterinary care is needed to minimize the damage. Causes of head injury in horses include direct trauma from a fall, blows to the head, and falling over backward.

Horses with head injuries should be handled and moved with extreme caution. If the horse is down, it may need short-term general anesthesia.

Heat Stroke

Heat stroke is an emergency. A rectal temperature of more than 104.9°F (40.5°C) in a horse indicates overheating. Foals are especially susceptible to heat stroke. The first sign of heat stroke is that a horse stops sweating. Horses may also breathe heavily and begin to breathe through the mouth instead of the nose. Horses with heat stroke should be continuously hosed with cold water, stood in the shade and, if possible, placed in a cooling breeze. Seek veterinary attention immediately.

Wounds and Lacerations

Wounds and lacerations are common in horses. The steps involved in the management of these injuries are similar to those for small animals (see WOUND MANAGEMENT, page 1065). Control of bleeding is an immediate concern. In addition to wound management, a tetanus shot may be required.

Other Common Conditions Requiring Emergency Treatment

Two other common conditions that require emergency treatment in horses are esophageal obstruction (commonly called choke) and postcastration evisceration.

Esophageal Obstruction (Choke)

Esophageal obstruction, or choke, is common in horses (see also ESOPHAGEAL OBSTRUCTION, page 613). It is generally caused by feed blocking the esophagus. A horse is more likely to develop choke if it bolts its food or does not chew it completely, has been recently sedated, is dehydrated, or is fed poor-quality feed.

Coughing, drooling, and frequent attempts to swallow are obvious signs of choke. There may also be a discharge from the nose containing saliva and feed material. A veterinarian should be called immediately if choke is suspected.

If esophageal obstruction is confirmed, the horse is muzzled to prevent any further feed intake. The horse is then sedated to relax the muscles of the esophagus. This clears many obstructions without surgery. However, if the obstruction has not cleared after about 1 hour, a tube is usually inserted through the nose and into the esophagus. Water or saline solution is passed through the tube to flush the esophagus. Mineral oil should never be used because of the risks associated with aspiration. If repeated attempts to clear the obstruction are unsuccessful, further tests may be required to determine the cause of blockage (such as a foreign object).

Horses that have choked are at risk of recurrence for the next 2 to 4 weeks. In addition, the damaged esophagus may take 4 weeks or longer to heal. Feeding a slurried, pelleted diet or grass can help prevent recurrence. Permanent damage, resulting in a narrowed esophagus, sometimes develops as a result of choke.

Postcastration Evisceration

Evisceration, or internal tissue such as intestine protruding through the incision, is a risk after open castrations. The risk is increased in Standardbred and Belgian horses or after castration of an adult stallion.

Evisceration is first identified by a structure hanging out of the surgical incision. It is important to keep the horse quiet and to support the structure with a clean, moistened towel to avoid further stretching or damage. The horse is generally anesthetized for treatment, which often requires surgery.

Emergencies in Foals

Critically ill foals are common. Immediately after birth, the foal must begin breathing on its own and adapt to its new environment. These critical events are particularly difficult if the lungs are undeveloped, viral or bacterial infection is present, or the birth is abnormal.

The foal should begin breathing within 1 minute of birth. During the first hour of life, the breathing rate of a healthy foal can be high, but the rate should decrease to 30 to 40 breaths per minute within a few hours. It is not unusual for a newborn foal to appear slightly blue initially. This should resolve within minutes of birth.

The heart rate of a healthy newborn foal has a regular rhythm and should be at least 60 beats per minute. Heart murmurs are normal during the first few days. Murmurs that persist beyond the first week of life in an otherwise healthy foal should be investigated.

Slow or difficult labor or delivery (called dystocia) is associated with many emergency medical issues for both mares and foals. The goal in a normal birth of a healthy foal is to minimally disturb the bonding process. This also applies to high-risk births, although some disruption of normal bonding is inevitable.

A slow heart rate (less than 40 beats per minute) is expected during forceful contractions. The pulse rate should increase rapidly once the foal's chest clears the birth canal. If the heart rate does not increase, immediate intervention is required. Chest compressions may be used if no rib fractures are present in the foal.

Foals that are not spontaneously breathing are generally resuscitated using mouth-to-nose or artificial ventilation such as a squeeze bag attached to a face mask. The airway is checked to ensure that it is clear. The airway may be suctioned if necessary. If the foal does not breathe or move spontaneously within seconds of birth, it should be rubbed vigorously over its body. If vigorous rubbing does not result in spontaneous breathing, intubation is sometimes necessary to help the foal breathe.

Because approximately 5% of foals are born with fractured ribs, the ribs should be examined. Fractures are usually multiple and consecutive on one side of the chest. These fractures normally heal without intervention. However, chest compressions may not be possible on a foal with rib fractures.

■ EYE EMERGENCIES

Ophthalmic (eye) emergencies require fast diagnosis. Therapy must be appropriate and often aggressive to save the animal's vision.

Traumatic Proptosis

Traumatic proptosis is a bulging of the eye caused by injury. It may follow blunt trauma (such as being hit by a car or a fight with another animal), during which the eyeball is dislodged from the orbit. Eyelid spasms prevent the eyeball from returning to its proper position. Then, bleeding and swelling push the eye further from the orbit. The eye becomes dry, and vision may worsen or fail.

Treatment involves surgically replacing the eye into the socket. Stitches and stents placed during the surgery are removed when a brisk blink reflex returns (usually 7 to 21 days). Potential complications include corneal tears, optic nerve damage, vision loss, muscle injury, inflammation, and infection. About 40 to 60% of dogs, but very few cats, recover vision.

Bleeding in the Eye

If trauma damages the blood vessels in the eye, bleeding occurs. Proptosis may also be present. Parts of the eye may swell, or the animal may not be able to close the eye.

Therapy usually includes topical and systemic (whole body) antibiotics, corticosteroids, or other drugs. The upper and lower eyelids may need to be sewn together to protect the cornea until a brisk blink reflex returns. Glaucoma is a potential complication.

Foreign Objects in the Eye

Foreign objects in the eye are common in dogs, cats, and horses. These can be organic material, sand, metal fragments, glass shards, or other small objects. Redness, tearing, and swelling of the eye are common. The eyelids may spasm, and the animal may scratch at the affected eye. The animal may need to be sedated for examination and treatment. The foreign object can usually be removed by flushing the eye with saline solution or using small forceps that look like tweezers. Sutures may be used to close the wound. Topical and systemic (whole body) antibiotics, pain medication, and other drugs may be prescribed. Vision is usually restored after the foreign body is removed.

Penetrating Injuries

Injuries due to objects penetrating the eye are most common in dogs and cats. Lead pellets, bullets, splinters, and plant spines (such as cactus) can cause this type of injury. The eye should be examined for evidence of lens injury and other damage. Lens rupture is common with cat claw injuries. If the lens has been penetrated, it should be removed as soon as possible because perforation of the lens leads to rapid cataract formation. Bleeding, swelling, and glaucoma may develop also. Retinal detachments are common and often cause at least partial loss of vision.

Therapy aims to control swelling and maintain normal levels of pressure within the eye. A variety of drugs, including antibiotics and corticosteroids, may be used.

Corneal Injuries

Corneal ulcers may develop when the eye is not lubricated enough (for example, when there are not enough tears). They also may be caused by scratches or other injuries. Sometimes, the cornea erodes and weakens, resulting in a bulge. Iris prolapse is an abnormal shift of the iris. Dogs, cats, and horses are more likely to develop these problems, but they can be seen in other small animals as well. These conditions usually require immediate surgery, followed by appropriate medications. Potential complications include scarring or pigmentation of the cornea, cataract formation, and rarely, infection.

Corneal lacerations or tears are most common in dogs and horses and rare in cats. Bites, self-inflicted trauma, and other accidents can partially or totally penetrate the cornea. Partial-thickness corneal lacerations are usually very painful. The wound may need to be closed with sutures. To provide additional protection and support, the sutured laceration may be covered. This may include stitching the eyelids closed temporarily. Antibiotics and other medications may be prescribed. Potential complications include corneal scarring, cataracts, glaucoma, and other serious eye disease.

Glaucoma

Glaucoma is increased pressure in the eye. High intraocular pressure results in fluid buildup in the eye, bulging eyes, and signs of pain. Dog breeds most often affected with primary glaucoma include the American Cocker Spaniel, Basset Hound, Chow Chow, Akita, Chinese Shar-Pei, Norwegian Elkhound, and Samoyed. Glaucoma is diagnosed by measuring the pressure in the animal's eyes. This procedure is called tonometry. The goals of therapy are to lower pressure rapidly and to preserve as much vision as possible. Medication is usually tried first, but if the glaucoma does not improve, surgery may be needed. Referral to a veterinary ophthalmologist (eye specialist) may be required.

Dislocation of the Lens

The lens of the eye can become dislocated and push forward. Lens dislocation usually affects middle-aged dogs of the terrier breeds. It is most common in Smooth and Wire Fox Terriers and Jack Russell Terriers. The eye may bulge from excess fluid and high intraocular pressure and appear red. Spasm of the eyelid and tearing may be evident. Treatment consists of lowering the pressure within the eye to normal levels. The lens is removed as soon as possible. Topical and systemic (whole body) antibiotics and corticosteroids are usually prescribed.

Acute Vision Loss

Acute loss of vision may occur with many eye disorders, brain or nerve diseases, or generalized illnesses. Blindness may be sudden. Usually, vision is lost in both eyes at the same time, but loss of vision in one eye can occur. For acute vision loss, large amounts of the retina must be involved. The optic nerve may be damaged. Evaluation of vision requires a thorough examination. However, because visual field evaluation cannot be performed in animals, subjective tests of vision are necessary. The veterinarian may perform tests of your pet's response to flashing lights, moving objects, and other images. Referral to a veterinary ophthalmologist may be required.

Inflammation of the Optic Nerve

There are 2 main types of inflammation that affect the optic nerve. One, **papillitis**, is an inflamed optic nerve head that can be seen with an ophthalmoscope. In the other, **retrobulbar optic neuritis**, the animal's pupils are dilated, and blindness is common. Examination, blood tests, and other diagnostic procedures are done to confirm optic neuritis and to determine the type of problem. Because the inflammation is usually due to an underlying generalized disease, therapy is directed at the particular disease. Your veterinarian will watch for the pupils to return to normal size and respond to light. It may take several days for vision to be restored. Unfortunately, in some cases, optic neuritis can cause permanent blindness.

Degeneration or Detachment of the Retina

In **sudden acquired retinal degeneration**, vision is lost over several days. The pupils are generally much larger than normal and do not respond well to light. Middle-aged dogs are affected most often. Dogs with liver disease and certain hormone disorders may be more susceptible. There is no effective treatment.

Retinal detachment can cause vision loss in one or both eyes. Once retinal detachment is detected, immediate treatment can help restore vision. Some breeds, such as the Shih Tzu, are more prone to retinal detachment. Collie eye anomaly (*see* page 151) may also be related, but this form of retinal detachment is usually treatable. Trauma can cause retinal detachment. Certain diseases, including high blood pressure in cats and dogs, also contribute. Some retinal detachments involve holes and tears in the retina. Referral to a veterinary ophthalmologist may be required.

■ WOUND MANAGEMENT

Wounds are cuts, tears, burns, breaks, or other damage to living tissue. Wounds are often classified as clean, contaminated, or infected. Clean wounds are those created under sterile conditions, such as surgical incisions. The number of bacteria present determines the difference between contaminated and infected wounds.

Initial Wound Management

General wound care begins after the animal has been stabilized if it has undergone a trauma or is in shock. First aid, such as pressure to stop bleeding and basic bandaging, is generally done quickly.

Cleaning, or debridement, removes dead tissue and foreign material from the wound, reduces bacterial contamination, and helps prevent infection. If the wound is already infected, a tissue sample may be collected for culture. Irrigation of the wound, called lavage, washes away both visible and microscopic debris. This reduces the risk of infection. A syringe is used to spray a solution onto or into the wound to clean it. Antibiotics are used to treat bacterial infections. Medications for pain relief are also usually given.

After initial inspection, irrigation, and cleaning, the veterinarian will decide whether to close the wound or to manage it as an open wound. Each wound must be assessed individually. If there is too little skin to close the wound, or the risk of infection is high, the wound may not be closed.

Sutures, staples, or surgical glue can be used to close the wound. Sometimes, layers of closure are required. A wound may be closed after it has been treated for some time. This is common if an infection is present, but is successfully treated with antibiotics. Such wounds may be closed after 24 to 72 hours or longer.

Wounds that are left open are usually managed with repeated bandaging and debridement. Wet-to-dry dressings are often used. These dressings help clean the wound at every bandage change. In the early stages of healing, the bandage may need to be changed as often as twice daily. Dry, nonstick dressings are used after healing has progressed.

Drains

Drains are used to help remove fluid from a wound or body cavity. This prevents the body from "walling off" the fluid, which can lead to infection. Drains can be passive or active. In passive drainage techniques, gravity draws the fluid out. In active drainage techniques, some type of suction is required to pull fluid

from the wound. Laboratory tests may be run on the extracted fluid.

Bandages

Bandages help stop bleeding, keep the wound clean, protect the wound from further injury, and prevent the wound from excessive drying. Bandages have 3 layers.

The first layer of the bandage is directly on the wound and is sometimes called the dressing. It may be made of gauze or a mesh material that promotes early healing. This layer allows fluid to pass through to the secondary layer of the bandage, and also prevents tissue from drying out. Removing the bandages can cause some pain, but it helps debride and clean the tissue. Wet-to-dry bandages are made with moistened gauze that is placed directly on the wound. They can also be painful to remove but result in less tissue drying than dry bandages.

The second layer of a bandage absorbs fluid, pads the wound, and supports or immobilizes the limb. This layer is frequently cast padding or roll cotton.

The third layer provides some pressure on the wound, and holds the inner layers in place and protects them from the environment. This layer is usually adhesive tape or elastic wraps.

Before you bring your pet home, make sure you understand how to change your pet's bandages and clean the wound, if necessary.

Surgery

Sometimes, a wound requires surgical treatment. Different types of wounds need different surgical procedures. For example, flaps of skin may be stretched over the wound to close it. Muscle flaps are also used for deep wounds. Sometimes, skin (or muscle) from other areas, or grafts, are taken and surgically attached to cover a wound.

Wound Healing

Wounds heal in 4 stages (*see* BOX). Many factors affect how well and how quickly the wounds heal. Environment, the overall health of the animal, and drug treatments are among factors that influence healing. Temperature is one environmental factor that affects wound healing. The ideal temperature for wound healing is around 86°F (30°C). Cold weather may make wounds weaker, resulting in longer healing times. Wounds also need oxygen to heal. To maintain blood flow in the wound, bandages must not be excessively tight.

The overall health of the animal affects all aspects of care and healing. Some conditions, such as anemia, may interfere with wound healing by reducing oxygen levels. Malnutrition may alter the healing process. Although diabetes causes problems with wound healing in people, it has not been shown to cause problems in animals.

Many topical drugs are used to treat wounds. These may be intended to promote natural wound closure, prevent infection, or reduce pain. However, other topical drugs (used for other purposes) may slow wound healing. Your veterinarian will consider the risks and benefits when choosing the most appropriate treatment.

Management of Specific Wounds

Some specific types of wounds have special requirements or treatments.

Cuts and Tears (Lacerations)

Lacerations are cuts or tears in the skin. If they do not involve deep tissue or have other significant problems, they are called uncomplicated simple lacerations. Such cuts are usually managed by complete closure; however, this may not be possible if the wound is dirty or infected. Deep cuts can be treated similar to simple ones, depending on the extent of the injury. Damage to muscles, tendons, and other tissues must be treated before a wound can be closed.

Bite Wounds

Bite wounds are a major cause of injuries, especially in animals that spend a lot of time outdoors. Cat bites tend to be small puncture wounds that frequently become infected. Dog bites vary from simple puncture wounds to deep, wide gashes. Cultures are often taken of puncture wounds to determine the best antibiotic treatment. If tissue damage is extensive, as in the case of many dog bites, more involved treatment may be needed. Serious injuries may exist even if only small puncture marks or bruising are seen on the surface. For example, ribs may be broken or internal organs seriously damaged. For these reasons, any bite should be examined as soon as possible by

Stages of Wound Healing

Although there are many types of wounds, most undergo similar stages in healing. There are 4 major stages of wound healing after a full-thickness skin wound.

Inflammation is the first stage of wound healing. It can be divided into 2 phases. First, blood vessels constrict to control bleeding. Then, within minutes, blood vessels dilate. This causes swelling.

Debridement is the second stage of wound healing. This is removal of foreign material from the wound. It happens naturally on a cellular level. Certain white blood cells attack bacteria and other debris in the wound. The same term is used for the cleaning process used by doctors and veterinarians.

Repair is the third stage of wound healing. In a healthy wound, cells begin to grow and rebuild missing and damaged tissues. Small blood vessels develop to deliver a blood supply to the wound. Skin cells then migrate, and scabs form within hours of the initial wound. These skin, or epithelial, cells can cover a properly closed surgical incision within 48 hours. In an open wound, the creation of granulation tissue takes longer.

Maturation is the final stage of wound healing. During this period, the newly laid collagen fibers reorganize. This process allows wound strength to increase slowly over a long period (up to 2 years). Most wounds remain 15% to 20% weaker than the original tissue.

a veterinarian. After examination, the wound is generally cleaned thoroughly. Antibiotics and pain medication are commonly administered.

Degloving Injuries

In degloving injuries, the skin is sheared or torn off. Degloving injuries can occur on the limbs or torso as well as the paws. Loss of skin is often extensive, and deeper tissues are often involved. Animals hit by cars or caught underneath the hood often have degloving injuries. Sometimes the skin is not completely removed. It remains attached to surrounding skin but not to the tissues beneath the skin. The skin is loose, usually bruised, and fragile. It may die later because it lacks blood supply. Any dead skin or other tissue must be removed. Tissue that can heal is usually saved. Infection is a major complication, and preventing infection is a main goal of initial treatment.

Gunshot Injuries

In gunshot injuries, most of the damage is not visible. The wounds are typically very deep. Gunshot wounds are also contaminated because the bullet or pellet drags skin, hair, and dirt through the wound. If the bullet exits the body, the exit wound will be larger than the entrance wound. High-speed bullets create shock waves that affect surrounding tissue and organs. There may be blunt force trauma as a result.

Often, surgery is needed to determine the amount of damage done by a gunshot wound. Organ and deep tissue injuries can be life-threatening. Fractures are common and may require additional treatment or surgery.

Pressure Wounds

Pressure wounds, also called decubital ulcers, develop as a result of prolonged pressure on an area of skin. They are most common in paralyzed or immobile animals. When tissue does not get enough blood or oxygen, it begins to die. Pressure wounds can be extremely difficult to treat and are best prevented. Preventive mea-

sures include changing the position of the animal frequently, maintaining adequate nutrition and cleanliness, and providing a sufficiently padded bed. If pressure wounds are mild or caught early, cleaning and bandaging may be enough to prevent further damage. More severe wounds require surgery. Grafts may be needed.

■ LIGHTNING STRIKE AND ELECTROCUTION

Injury or death of a pet due to high-voltage electrical currents may be the result of lightning, fallen transmission wires, faulty electrical circuits, or chewing on an electrical cord. Lightning strike is seasonal and tends to be geographically restricted. Investigation of possible electrocution should always proceed with caution because the electrification resulting from broken transmission wires, for example, may still be present.

Certain types of trees, especially hardwoods such as oaks and those that are tall and have spreading root systems just beneath the ground surface, tend to be struck by lightning more often than others. Electrification of such roots charges a wide surface area, particularly when the ground is already damp; passage of charged roots beneath a shallow pool of water causes it to become electrified. Fallen or sagging transmission wires also may electrify a pool of water, fence, or building, and an animal may also directly contact such wires.

Varying degrees of electric shock may occur. In most instances of lightning strike, death is instantaneous and the animal falls without a struggle. Occasionally, the animal becomes unconscious but may recover in a few minutes to several hours; residual nervous signs (including depression, paraplegia, and increased skin sensitivity to normally painless stimulus) may persist for days or weeks or be permanent. Death from electric shock usually results from cardiac or respiratory arrest.

Lightning strike and electrocution should be considered true emergencies in which your veterinarian should be contacted right away. Even if the effect of electrocution appears mild (as in a pet chewing on an electrical cord), signs of shock or other complications may occur later. Animals that survive may require supportive and symptomatic therapy.

■ MINOR INJURIES AND ACCIDENTS

A number of minor injuries are generally not life-threatening but also demand immediate attention.

Broken Nails

Control any bleeding by applying pressure or using styptic power, cornstarch, or even white flour. Because broken nails can be very painful, you may need to place a muzzle on your dog (*see* FIGURE, page 1052). Try to gently remove the broken piece with clippers. Seek veterinary care if the broken nail cannot be removed easily.

Bumps, Bruises, Twists, and Sprains

Mild to moderate pain, tenderness, swelling, and limping can indicate a bruise, strain, or sprain. Keep your pet quiet and restrict exercise. Contact your veterinarian if signs continue for more than a few days.

Fish Hooks

Fish hooks often become lodged in the mouth, lips, nose, or paws. Do not try to remove a fish hook that is embedded in the eyes, mouth, or ears—this must be done under anesthesia by your veterinarian. If a hook embedded in the mouth is attached to a line, prevent your pet from swallowing the hook by tying the line to the animal's collar. Otherwise, cut the hook free from the line, but leave several inches of line attached so that the hook is easier to find (especially in thick fur). If the barb has entered the skin, push it through in the same direction so that you can snip off the barb with wire cutters or pliers. Then remove the hook by pulling it back out in the direction it entered the skin. Clean and

cover the wound, and take your pet to the veterinarian immediately.

Insect Bites and Stings

Bites and stings often occur on the face or elsewhere on the head. They are often so small that they cannot be seen through the fur. Apply a cold pack to the affected area to reduce swelling and itching. Look for a stinger. If you find one in the skin, you can use a credit card or other flat, rigid object to scrape it out. Do not squeeze a stinger with tweezers or other tool because this can release more venom into the wound. If your pet has an allergic reaction with a great deal of swelling in the head or neck area that may affect breathing, or if you find a stinger in the tongue or the roof of the mouth, take your pet to your veterinarian immediately.

Porcupine Quills

Porcupine quills have small barbs on their ends, which makes them very painful to remove. They should be removed by your veterinarian because of the need for anesthesia and the risk of more bleeding and tissue damage.

Skunking

Skunk spray is an oil that is best removed while still wet. If you can identify the specific area that was sprayed, clean it first before wetting the entire dog to avoid spreading the oil to other areas. There are numerous commercial products and recipes for homemade deskunking rinses. Be aware that many homemade concoctions are too harsh to use in the face and eye area, and many will bleach the hair coat. In addition to the objectionable odor, skunk spray can cause eye irritation and temporary blindness. Skunk bites can transmit rabies, but skunk spray has not been shown to transmit the virus.

Swallowed Objects

Dogs tend to swallow numerous inappropriate objects including toys, trash, or chicken bones. In many cases, swallowed objects can be treated with a wait-and-see approach; most of the time, the object will pass through without any trouble. However, swallowing sharp objects, such as needles or pieces of glass, or any type of long item, such as string, pantyhose, or fishing line, is very dangerous because a serious bowel condition can result. Although cats are more selective than dogs, they often swallow string, fishing line, or tinsel, or get the material wrapped and knotted around their tongue. In these situations, or if your pet has persistent vomiting, a tender abdomen, or is not having bowel movements, you should contact your veterinarian immediately.

CHAPTER 77

Diagnostic Tests and Imaging

■ INTRODUCTION

When you have a health problem, your doctor will order blood tests, x-rays, or other tests to help pinpoint the cause of the problem. When your pet has a health problem, your veterinarian will often order similar tests to determine the cause and seriousness of your pet's condition. Depending on the tests needed and the facilities available at your veterinarian's clinic, the tests may be performed in-house at the clinic or at a specialized laboratory or test facility in another location.

If the tests are to be carried out by the veterinarian or a technician within their clinic, then the staff has access to the medical history leading up to the problem. If the tests are to be performed elsewhere, it is important that a detailed history of the problem be included with the samples or be available when the pet arrives. The staff at the external laboratory will need this information to correctly perform the tests and interpret the results. Usually, the referring veterinary clinic will provide this information to the external laboratory. However, if you are asked to bring the information to the clinic with your pet, it is very important that you do so to help the laboratory do their work correctly.

■ TYPES OF VETERINARY MEDICAL TESTS

There are several categories of diagnostic tests that may be performed to help your veterinarian determine the cause of your pet's disorder.

Histology

Histology is the study of the structure, function, and chemical composition of cells within the body. Experts in histology (called pathologists) examine small tissue samples to determine if they are normal or diseased. These experts can often point to a cause for the abnormal cells.

Small tissue samples will often be sent to a pathologist if your veterinarian suspects conditions such as cancer or other diseases that cause tissue changes.

Microbiology

Microbiology is the study of small organisms such as bacteria, viruses, fungi, and other single-celled life forms. In a veterinary laboratory, specialists in microbiology can perform any of hundreds of tests looking for signs of infection. Common tests include growing and identifying bacteria, viruses, and fungi. Bacteria can also be tested to see which antibiotics should be effective for eliminating them from the body. Other tests use antibodies to detect the presence of microorganisms in a sample from an animal. Samples commonly used to culture microorganisms include blood, urine, feces, secretions from the nose or lungs, and swabs taken from a wound or abscess.

Toxicology

Toxicology is the branch of science that studies how poisons affect animals and how animals respond to poisons. If your veterinarian suspects that your pet has been poisoned, samples will be collected for toxicologic tests to identify the poison and the amount of damage it may have caused. For common poisons, the tests may be performed at the clinic to quickly identify the poison. Rapid identification of a poison can be critical for your pet's survival. In other cases, samples may be sent to an outside laboratory that can accurately test for a much wider range of poisons. If your pet has eaten something toxic, your veterinarian may ask you to bring a sample of it with you for testing.

Hematology

Hematology is the study of blood, its chemistry, and components. The most common blood test is a complete blood count (CBC). This test determines the number and type of white and red blood cells circulating in the bloodstream. It is most often used to check for signs of inflammation or infection (revealed by changes in the number and appearance of different kinds of white blood cells). Determining the number, size, and hemoglobin content of red blood cells helps identify disorders such as anemia. Platelets are also examined during a CBC; changes in platelets can help identify blood clotting disorders. (*See also* BLOOD SAMPLES, page 1073.)

Clinical Chemistry

Clinical chemistry is the study of the chemical composition of a sample. Usually, the sample is the liquid portion of blood (serum or plasma), although other body fluids may also be studied. Clinical chemistry tests are important for determining how well different organs are working. They can also help identify particular disorders, such as diabetes or pancreatitis.

Serology

Specialists in serology study the clear portions of body fluids. Most serologic tests determine the level of antibodies (called the titer) against a particular infectious microorganism. A high level of antibodies, or an increase in their level from one sample to another taken a few weeks later, shows that an animal has been exposed to the microorganism and its immune system has produced specific antibodies against the infectious agent. It used to be very cumbersome to test for specific antibodies in many different kinds of pets. Today, there are commercially available test kits for a wide range of serologic tests. The test kits are used on a regular basis by both in-house and outside laboratories to test for diseases such as heartworm disease, feline leukemia virus infection, Lyme disease, equine infectious anemia, and many others.

Cytology

The study of individual cells, their structure and origin, function(s), and death is known as cytology. Specialists in this field can provide a veterinarian with information about the cells in your pet's body. In particular, specialists in cytology are often called upon to identify cancerous cells or determine whether or not a tumor is benign or cancerous (malignant). Samples of tissue or fluid are collected, then slides are prepared and stained for microscopic examination to determine the type or types of cells present.

Fluid Analysis

Fluid analysis is the study of bodily fluids other than blood. Specialists in analyzing body fluids work closely with other specialists to help provide information about the health of an animal. Typically, fluid analysis includes checking the sample for cells and proteins.

■ TESTS ROUTINELY PERFORMED IN VETERINARY MEDICINE

Some of the most common basic tests performed by a veterinarian, veterinary technician, or laboratory personnel are discussed below. Tests may be performed at your veterinarian's office or clinic, samples may be sent out to a laboratory, or you may be asked to take your pet to a special test facility.

The Veterinarian

Just as your physician will check your vital signs, weight, and other conditions when you visit the doctor, your veterinarian will also want to check vital signs and obtain basic medical information about your pet. In addition to checking your pet's weight, looking at your pet's eyes, checking its ears, routine examination of the mouth and teeth, and observing the pet's movements, there are other simple tests that are often performed.

The veterinarian will use a stethoscope to listen for abnormal heart, lung, or digestive system sounds that may indicate problems with these organs.

The veterinarian may gently press on the pet's gums with a finger and then release the pressure to determine how long it takes for the capillaries in the gums to refill. A longer than normal capillary refill time may indicate that the pet is going into, or is already in, shock. Long refill times also occur in certain heart diseases. The color of the gums can also indicate problems such as jaundice (a sign of liver disease), shock, or anemia.

Veterinarians use their hands to check for the size and location of internal organs such as the liver, spleen, kidneys, and urinary bladder. This is called abdominal palpation. They will also check for enlargement of lymph nodes located throughout the body.

Specialized Tests

If your pet has a specific problem at the time of the examination, the veterinarian may perform additional tests that are not generally part of a routine physical examination. For example, examination of a dog with suspected vision problems might include tests that assess overall vision, examination with an ophthalmoscope (an instrument that allows the veterinarian to assess the interior portions of the eye) and various stains, and determination of the pressure within the eye (intraocular pressure). Similarly, examination of a lame horse might include a hands-on examination of the affected leg, blood and biochemical tests, muscle biopsy, and various types of imaging techniques.

The In-house Laboratory

Most veterinary clinics have at least basic laboratory facilities within their clinic. Several laboratory tests can be carried out in these facilities after the veterinarian collects the appropriate samples or after the pet owner collects the samples and brings them to the clinic. The complexity and types of tests done will vary from clinic to clinic. The following types of tests are frequently done at an in-house laboratory.

Stool Samples

Stool samples may be collected by the pet owner prior to a visit to the veterinary clinic or they may be collected by the veterinarian. A small amount of the stool sample is prepared and then examined under a microscope. In some cases, a small amount of the stool is placed in a liquid and then examined with a microscope. These steps are used to detect the presence of the cysts of various parasites such as *Giardia* and *Cryptosporidium*. The eggs of other parasites, such as roundworms, hookworms, and tapeworms, can be found in stool samples. Larval or adult worms or tapeworm segments may also be observed.

Urine Samples

Analysis of urine samples (urinalysis) is important for detecting various types of urinary tract diseases. Because significant changes occur in urine if it is left at room or higher temperature for any length of time, the sample should be analyzed immediately after collection, or refrigerated and transported to the laboratory as soon as possible after collection. Urine samples should not, however, be frozen because freezing will change several important characteristics of the urine. The tests usually carried out on urine samples include examining the appearance, chemistry, and sediment.

Normal urine is typically yellow or amber in color and is usually transparent or clear. The presence of diseases or infections may change the color or clarity. For most pet species, normal urine has a slight odor of ammonia; however, the urine of some pets (such as cats) normally has a pungent odor. A bacterial infection of the urinary tract may produce a strong ammonia odor in the urine.

Chemical analysis of urine may include determining its specific gravity (density) and pH level and measuring the amount of protein, glucose, or fragmented blood cells, all of which can indicate disease, injury, or defects. Microscopic examination of urine sediment (the solid part of urine) is part of a routine urinalysis. Large numbers of red blood cells in urine sediment usually indicate bleeding somewhere in the urinary tract, while large numbers of white blood cells usually indicate an infection. Other solid components of urine, known as casts, are long tubular structures formed by the congealing of protein in the kidneys. Large numbers of casts may indicate kidney disease. Crystals may be present but are generally not considered to be a problem. Bacteria may be present in small numbers in normally voided urine, but large numbers indicate infection. If your veterinarian suspects a bladder infection, a sample of urine to culture for bacteria may be collected directly from the bladder using a needle and syringe. This process is called cystocentesis.

Blood Samples

Analysis of the numbers and structure of blood cells is important in the diagnosis and monitoring of disease and infection. Blood samples are usually taken by the veterinarian or a veterinary technician for analysis.

There are 3 common tests carried out using **red blood cells**: packed cell volume, hemoglobin concentration, and red blood cell count. All 3 are interrelated and help your veterinarian diagnose diseases. The packed cell volume is the proportion of the whole volume of blood occupied by the red blood cells. When the proportion of red blood cells is high, the condition is called polycythemia. Polycythemia is common when a pet has dehydration or diarrhea. A low packed cell volume may suggest anemia or bleeding. The hemoglobin concentration in the blood sample indicates the oxygen-carrying capacity of the red blood cells. The red blood cell count is the number of red blood cells in a unit volume of blood. The results of the tests on red blood cells can tell your veterinarian a lot about the way your pet's body is functioning and suggest possible health problems.

There are 5 main types of **white blood cells** (*see* page 35). **Neutrophils** are the most common type of white blood cell. They engulf ("eat") infectious particles such as bacteria. They increase in number during inflammation, infection, and short-term stress. A related type of white blood cell is the **eosinophil**. The number of eosinophils goes up during allergic reactions and some tissue injuries. Their number also goes up in response to certain tumors and parasites. **Basophils** are the least common type of white blood cell. They are also related to neutrophils and eosinophils. An increase in the number of basophils is associated with inflammation. **Monocytes** are large cells that serve mainly as phagocytes and increase in number during chronic diseases. **Lymphocytes** are the white blood cells responsible for antibody production and cell-mediated immune responses (*see* page 164). Large increases in the number of lymphocytes often indicates leukemia, a type of cancer.

Platelets are cell-like particles in the blood (*see* page 36). Another name for platelets is thrombocytes. Platelets are much smaller than red or white blood cells. They perform a critical role in the clotting process to repair damaged blood vessels. Thus, injuries often prompt a large increase in number of platelets. Some autoimmune diseases, blood clotting disorders, and bone marrow problems cause a decrease in the number of platelets.

The Outside Laboratory or Test Center

Many of the tests the veterinarian uses to diagnose disease require highly specialized instruments or equipment. In other cases, specific training is required for the technicians performing the tests. For these reasons, many veterinarians will either send the samples to an outside laboratory or refer the patient to a special test facility. Some of the tests conducted are similar to those available in the clinic, but the availability of advanced testing equipment in a specialized facility may offer advantages in speed and accuracy. For example, the specialized laboratory may be able to more easily spot and identify abnormally shaped red or white blood cells, both of which can help confirm a disease diagnosis, during routine tests on a blood sample.

In addition, at an outside laboratory specialized tests may be performed, such as one to detect larval stages of parasites that are not easily found on standard tests. Because parasites also occur in samples other than stool samples, a direct smear of a pet's blood on a slide can be analyzed to detect the presence of blood parasites.

Most laboratories offer a basic group of tests, known as a basic test panel, which provides information regarding many general health problems (*see* TABLE 1). Having a laboratory perform these tests can help point to a diagnosis, particularly if the animal has signs and a history that could make it difficult to determine the problem. The basic group of blood tests for pets includes total protein, albumin, globulin (calculated as the difference between total protein and albumin), urea, creatinine, alanine amino transferase (ALT), and alkaline phosphatase (ALP). This group of tests may be modified as

Table 1. Tests Included in a Basic Test Panel

Test	What the Results may Mean
Total Protein	Increases due to dehydration or inflammation; may decrease due to bleeding, malnutrition, or congestive heart failure
Albumin	Increases due to dehydration; may decrease due to bleeding, congestive heart failure, or liver failure
Globulin	Calculated as the difference between total protein and albumin
Urea	Increases due to certain dietary excesses or deficiencies, congestive heart failure, kidney failure, or a ruptured bladder; decreases may be due to liver failure or low levels of dietary protein
Creatinine	Increases may be due to kidney disorders, muscle damage, or a ruptured bladder
Glucose	Increases may be caused by diabetes or short-term stress; decreases may be found in cases of neurologic disease or malnutrition
ALT and ALP	Increases in these enzymes may indicate liver damage, muscle damage, or increased thyroid gland activity

appropriate for other animals. Based on the results of this group of tests, other tests may be carried out as needed to reach a definite diagnosis.

It is important to identify the specific bacteria or other organisms causing an infection so that your veterinarian can carry out a proper treatment program. Although many microbiology tests can be performed at veterinary clinics, your veterinarian may prefer to have the samples tested at an outside laboratory that has specialized equipment and personnel with advanced training in microbiology. Your veterinarian will very carefully take a sample from a site on your pet that is typical of the disease or infection process. Samples are examined under a microscope, as well as cultured (grown on various substances) and then examined for the growth of colonies of the suspected organisms. Sometimes the bacteria have to be tested with different antibiotics to determine which one will be most effective. This takes a little longer but helps your veterinarian avoid treatment with an antibiotic that is not effective.

■ DIAGNOSTIC IMAGING

A number of imaging procedures have been developed to help diagnose diseases in humans, and many of these have been adapted for use in animals. Most imaging methods provide a large amount of information by noninvasive and economical means and, at the same time, do not change the disease process or cause unacceptable discomfort to the pet. However, because of the complexity and expense of the equipment and instruments, some of these procedures are carried out in facilities designed especially for their use.

X-ray Imaging

X-rays have been in use for many decades. Also known as radiography, this is the most commonly used imaging procedure in veterinary practices. The x-ray images are produced using the same processes used in human medicine except

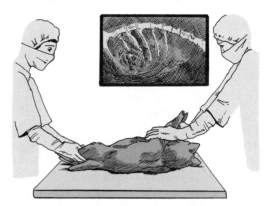

X-rays are often used to identify foreign objects that have been swallowed and are lodged in the gastrointestinal tract.

that the equipment is sized for use in a veterinary clinic. In most cases, this means equipment suitable for use with dogs, cats, and other small animals. However, portable equipment may be used in a large animal clinic that treats horses and other large animals. Although the procedure is painless, in some cases pets are sedated to reduce the anxiety and stress associated with the procedure and to help the animal stay still while the images are taken.

X-rays work well for imaging bones, foreign objects, and large body cavities. They are often used to help detect fractures, tumors, injuries, infections, and deformities. Although x-rays may not give enough information to determine the exact cause of your pet's problem, they can help your veterinarian determine which other tests may be needed to make a diagnosis.

The body's soft tissues do not absorb x-rays well and can be difficult to see using this technology alone. Specialized x-ray techniques, called contrast procedures, are used to help provide more detailed images of body organs. In these procedures the animal is given a dye that will block x-rays. This can be given intravenously to examine organs like the kidneys or heart, or by mouth to examine the digestive tract. A series of x-rays is taken after the dye is given, which will outline the organs where the dye collects. This makes it easier to spot any abnormalities.

The x-ray machine is positioned so that x-rays are beamed at the area to be examined. Exposure to x-rays lasts only a fraction of a second. However, the greater the exposure, the greater the risk that radiation may damage cells. For this reason, a very low dose is used, and lead shields may be used to protect areas that are not being x-rayed.

Traditional x-ray images are captured on film. However, recent advances in technology have made it possible for x-ray images to be stored on computers.

There are many advantages to storing x-ray images on computer. One of the most important is the ability to rapidly and economically transmit copies of the images to specialists or other clinics. Specialists or individuals at other clinics can study the images of your pet and help your veterinarian accurately diagnose and treat your pet's condition.

Ultrasonography

Ultrasonography (commonly called ultrasound) is the second most commonly used imaging procedure in veterinary practice. It uses ultrasonic sound waves to create images of body structures based on the pattern of echoes reflected from the tissues and organs. Ultrasound is much better than x-rays at showing the soft tissues within the body.

The technician usually performs an ultrasound scan by pressing a small probe against the animal's body, most frequently the abdominal wall. The sound waves are directed to various parts of the abdomen by moving the probe. Echoes occur as the sound beam changes velocity while passing through tissues of varying density. The echoes are converted into electrical impulses that are then converted into an image that represents the appearance of the tissues. In modern scanning systems, the sound beam is swept through the body many times per second, producing a dynamic, real-time image

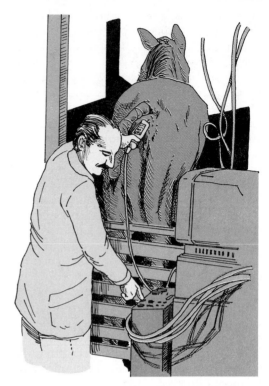

To check whether a mare is pregnant, a veterinarian can perform ultrasonography by inserting the wand into the horse's rectum.

that changes as the probe moves across the body.

An ultrasound scan can show the size and shape of many organs and can also show abnormalities within them. An ultrasound scan is both painless and noninvasive, and poses no risk of complications. This is the same diagnostic tool used in many medical facilities to check the condition of a human fetus in the womb.

Although ultrasound can be used to evaluate most soft tissues, the heart and abdominal organs are the most frequently scanned in veterinary clinics. Ultrasonic imaging of the heart is termed **echocardiography**. The structure and function of the heart and its valves can be evaluated by this procedure. There are limitations to ultrasonography. It cannot be used to scan gas-filled or bony tissues.

Computed Tomography

Computed tomography (CT) is a computer-enhanced x-ray procedure used to detect abnormalities in various body organs. Because of the expense and size of the equipment, and the need for specially trained technicians, this procedure is not often used for pets. However, it may be available in some locations (such as hospitals associated with veterinary schools or large specialty practices) and may occasionally be recommended.

In this procedure, the animal is placed on a motorized bed inside a CT scanner, which takes a series of x-rays from different angles. When one series, or scan, is completed, the bed is moved forward, and another scan is taken. CT scans differ from ordinary x-rays because they show different levels of tissue density and produce more detailed images. From these scans, a computer creates cross-sectional images of the body part under investigation and displays the images on a monitor. A dye that can be seen on x-rays may be injected intravenously to make it easier to see abnormalities in the images. By sequentially scanning a body area, an entire organ or other structure can be imaged without interference from neighboring or overlying structures. These scans can be used by the veterinarian to detect structural changes deep within the body, including tumors, abscesses, changes in blood vessels, and fractures.

Because of the need to remain still for a relatively long time while scanning is completed, animals undergoing a CT scan are anesthetized.

Magnetic Resonance Imaging

Magnetic resonance imaging (MRI) is the newest form of imaging in general use today. It is an alternative to computed tomography. With this procedure, a very powerful magnetic field generates detailed anatomic images. No x-rays are involved and it is extremely safe. However, because of the expense and size of the equipment and the need for specially

trained technicians, this procedure is not often used for pets. And, due to size constraints, it is not practical for use with horses or other large animals.

For the procedure, the animal is placed in a tubular electromagnetic chamber and pulsed with radio waves, causing tissues in the body to emit radio frequency waves that can be detected. Many repetitions of these pulses and subsequent emissions are required. The emitted waves are then converted into images that are displayed on a computer screen. The images can also be saved for additional study. Sequential examination of slices through the body is done in the same way as for computed tomography. Because the procedure is rather lengthy and the animal must not move throughout the procedure, general anesthesia is used in most cases.

Nuclear Medicine Imaging

Nuclear medicine imaging, also known as radionuclide imaging or scintigraphy, involves dosing the animal with an element that emits a type of radiation known as gamma rays. This element is then detected within the body by means of a special camera attached to a computer, which generates the image. The element is attached to a molecule that has an affinity for the organ or tissue of interest. If the molecule is metabolized by the organ or tissue or stays in the tissue for only a short time, consecutive camera images can be used to evaluate the function of the organ or tissue. Veterinarians most frequently use nuclear medicine imaging to analyze the lungs, kidneys, liver, thyroid, and heart, although other portions of a pet's body may also be studied with this technique.

■ RADIATION THERAPY

Although not a test or imaging procedure, radiation therapy is discussed here because, like several imaging techniques, it uses ionizing radiation. In veterinary practice, this treatment is very similar to the radiation therapy used in many human cancer patients.

Radiation therapy can help to control the growth of cancerous (malignant) tumor cells. With this treatment, a linear accelerator is used to produce powerful x-rays and electron beams that are carefully aimed at cancerous growths. The most frequent targets are deep-seated tumors and tumors of the skin and the tissues immediately below the skin.

Computerized treatment planning systems are used to ensure the greatest benefit from the radiation therapy. With these tools the dose to the tumor tissue is maximized and the damage to the surrounding normal tissue is kept as small as possible.

Whenever possible, removal of a tumor by surgery is preferred. However, it is often not possible to remove all of the tumor tissue. In these cases, radiation therapy is useful in treating the remaining cancerous tissue. This treatment is frequently combined with chemotherapy. Radiation therapy is often the treatment of choice for brain tumors, nasal tumors, and other cancers of the head and neck.

If your pet has radiation therapy, either with or without chemotherapy, there are a number of things you should know in order to provide the most supportive environment. It is common for pets undergoing radiation therapy to be more tired than normal and they may need a special diet. Ask your veterinarian for detailed instructions about what you need to do to support your pet during radiation therapy.

CHAPTER 78

Infections

▓ INTRODUCTION

Microorganisms are tiny living creatures, such as bacteria and viruses. Microorganisms are present everywhere. Despite their overwhelming abundance, relatively few of the thousands of species of microorganisms invade, multiply, and cause illness in animals and people.

Many microorganisms live on the skin and in the mouth, upper airways, and intestines without causing disease. Whether a microorganism lives harmlessly in or on a pet, or invades and causes disease depends on both the nature of the microorganism and the state of the pet's natural defenses.

This chapter provides a general introduction to the causes, signs, diagnosis, and treatment of various types of infections. Specific infections are discussed in the chapters covering the particular species and body system involved (for example, pneumonia is discussed in the chapter on lung and airway disorders).

▓ DEFENSES AGAINST INFECTION

Physical barriers and the immune system defend an animal's body against organisms that can cause disease. Physical barriers include outer coverings, such as skin, fur, feathers, and scales. Additional barriers include the mucous membranes, tears, ear wax, mucus, and stomach acid. The normal flow of urine is a mechanical barrier that can wash out microorganisms that have entered the urinary tract. The immune system uses white blood cells and antibodies to identify and eliminate organisms that manage to pass through the physical barriers.

Physical Barriers

Unless damaged—by injury, insect bite, or burn, for example—an animal's outer coverings usually prevent invasion by microorganisms. Other effective physical barriers are the mucous membranes, such as the linings of the mouth, nose, and eyelids. Typically, mucous membranes are coated with secretions that fight microorganisms. For example, the mucous membranes of the eyes are bathed in tears, which contain an enzyme that attacks bacteria and helps protect the eyes from infection.

The airways filter out particles that are present in the air that is breathed in. The walls of the nasal passages and airways are coated with mucus. Microorganisms in the air become stuck to the mucus, which is coughed up or blown out the nose. Mucus removal is aided by the coordinated beating of tiny hairlike projections, called cilia, that line the air passages. The cilia sweep the mucus up the airways, away from the lungs.

The digestive tract has a series of effective barriers, including stomach acid, pancreatic enzymes, bile, and intestinal secretions. The contractions of the intestine and the normal shedding of cells that line the intestine help remove harmful microorganisms.

The bladder is protected by the urethra, the tube through which urine passes as it leaves the body. In adult males, the long length of the urethra generally prevents bacteria from passing through it to reach the bladder. In females, the urethra is shorter, occasionally allowing bacteria outside the body to pass into the bladder. The flushing effect as the bladder empties is another defense mechanism in both sexes. The vagina is protected from harmful microorganisms by its normally acidic environment.

The Blood

Another way in which the body defends against infection is by increasing the number of certain types of white blood cells (neutrophils and monocytes) that surround and destroy invading microorganisms. The numbers can increase within several hours, largely because white blood cells can be released quickly from the bone marrow. The number of neutrophils increases first. If an infection persists, the number of monocytes increases. The number of eosinophils, another type of white blood cell, increases in allergic reactions and many parasitic infections but usually not in bacterial infections.

Inflammation

Any injury, including an invasion by microorganisms, results in a complex reaction in the affected area, called inflammation. Inflammation develops as a result of many different conditions. It begins through the release of different substances from the damaged tissue. It then directs the body's defenses to "wall off" the area, attack and kill any invading organisms, dispose of dead and damaged tissue, and begin the process of repair. However, inflammation may not be able to overcome large numbers of microorganisms.

During inflammation the blood supply also increases. This can be seen in an infected area near the surface of the body, which becomes red and warm. The walls of blood vessels become more porous, allowing fluid and white blood cells to pass into the affected tissue. The increase in fluid causes the inflamed tissue to swell. The white blood cells attack the invading microorganisms and release substances that continue the process of inflammation. Other substances trigger clotting in the tiny blood vessels in the inflamed area, which delays the spread of the microorganisms and their toxins. Many of the substances released during inflammation stimulate the nerves, causing pain, which can be hard to recognize in animals (*see* PAIN MANAGEMENT, page 1211). Reactions to the substances released during inflammation include the fever and muscle stiffness that commonly accompany infection.

Immune Response

When an infection develops, the immune system responds by producing several substances and agents that are designed to attack the specific invading microorganisms. For example, the immune system can create killer T cells (a type of white blood cell) that recognize and kill the invading microorganism. Also, the immune system produces antibodies that are specific to the invading microorganism. Antibodies attach to and immobilize microorganisms— killing them outright or helping the neutrophils target and kill them.

Fever

Body temperature increases as a protective response to infection and injury. The resulting fever enhances the body's defense mechanisms. Normal body temperature varies among species. Dogs and cats, for instance, have an average body temperature around 101.5° F, which is higher than that of people. Reptiles and amphibians are cold-blooded and do not maintain a set body temperature. Thus, they cannot develop a true fever as a response to infection. They sometimes seek out unusually warm locations, developing what is known as behavioral fever, to perform the same function (*see* REPTILES, page 1013).

The hypothalamus, which is a part of the brain, controls body temperature. When the thermostat of the hypothalamus is "reset," a fever results. The body increases its temperature by shunting blood from the skin surface to the interior of the body, thus reducing heat loss. Shivering (chills) may occur to increase heat production through muscle contraction. The body's efforts to conserve and produce heat continue until blood reaches the hypothalamus at the new, higher temperature, which is then maintained. Later, when the thermostat is reset to its normal level, the body eliminates excess heat through sweating and shunting blood to the skin.

Fever may follow a pattern: sometimes temperature peaks every day and then returns to normal. Alternatively, the tem-

Common Causes of Fever

- Infection
- Cancer
- Allergic reactions
- Autoimmune diseases
- Excessive exercise, especially in hot weather
- Certain drugs, including anesthetics
- Damage to the hypothalamus (the part of the brain that controls temperature), such as from a brain injury or tumor

perature may vary but does not return to normal. Some animals (such as the very old and the very young) may experience a drop in temperature as a response to severe infection.

Usually, fever is caused by an infection (for example, pneumonia or a urinary tract infection) that can often be diagnosed with a history, physical examination, and occasionally a few tests, such as a chest X-ray or a urinalysis. However, fever can also result from inflammation, cancer, or an allergic reaction. Sometimes, the cause cannot be easily determined. If fever continues for several days and has no obvious cause, a more detailed investigation is required. Potential causes of such a fever include infections, diseases caused by antibodies against the animal's own tissues (autoimmune diseases), and an undetected cancer (especially leukemia or lymphoma).

Your veterinarian will ask about your pet's present and previous signs and diseases, any medications your pet is currently receiving, exposure to infections (such as being boarded), and recent travel. The pattern of the fever usually does not help with the diagnosis. A history of exposure to certain materials or interaction with other animals is also important.

A thorough physical examination will be done to look for a source of infection or evidence of disease. Blood and other body fluids may be sent to a laboratory for culture, which is an attempt to grow the microorganism outside the body so that it can be specifically identified. Other blood tests may be done to detect antibodies against specific microorganisms. Increases in the white blood cell count usually indicate infection. The differential count (the proportion of different types of white blood cells) gives further clues. An increase in neutrophils, for example, suggests bacterial infection. An increase in eosinophils suggests the presence of parasites, such as roundworms or heartworms.

When an animal has a sustained fever for several weeks and extensive investigation does not reveal a cause, a veterinarian may refer to it as a **fever of unknown origin**. In such cases, the cause may be an unusual chronic infection or something other than infection, such as a connective tissue disease, cancer, or some other disease. Advanced diagnostic imaging techniques (for example, ultrasound, computed tomography [CT], or magnetic resonance imaging [MRI]) may help determine a diagnosis. A biopsy specimen from the liver, bone marrow, or another suspected site may be needed for examination.

■ DEVELOPMENT OF INFECTION

Infectious diseases are usually caused by microorganisms that invade the body and multiply. Invasion by most microorganisms begins when they adhere to cells in the body. Whether the microorganism remains near the invasion site or spreads to other sites depends on many factors, including whether it produces toxins, enzymes, or other substances. For example, *Clostridium tetani* in an infected wound produces a toxin that causes tetanus. Food poisoning is caused by toxins produced by staphylococcal organisms that are outside the body. Most toxins contain components that bind specifically with molecules on certain cells (target cells).

After invading the body, microorganisms start to multiply. One of 3 things can then happen: the microorganisms can continue to multiply and overwhelm the body's defenses, resulting in illness; a state of balance can be achieved, resulting in a chronic infection; or the body—with or without treatment—can destroy and eliminate the invading microorganism.

Many microorganisms that cause disease have properties that increase the severity of the disease and help them resist the body's defense mechanisms. For example, some bacteria produce enzymes that break down tissue, allowing the infection to spread faster. Other microorganisms have ways of blocking the body's defense mechanisms, such as by interfering with production of antibodies or T cells (a type of white blood cell). Others have outer coats (capsules) that resist being ingested by white blood cells. Some bacteria resist being destroyed by substances circulating in the bloodstream. Some even produce substances that counter the effects of antibiotics.

■ INFECTIONS IN ANIMALS WITH IMPAIRED DEFENSES

Many diseases, drugs, and other treatments can cause the body's natural defenses to break down. Such a breakdown can lead to infections, even by microorganisms that normally live harmlessly on or in the body. For example, the risk of infection is greatly increased in animals with extensive burns because damaged skin cannot prevent invasion by harmful microorganisms. Drugs such as the anticancer drugs used in chemotherapy can suppress the immune system. Radiation treatments can also suppress the immune system.

The ability to fight certain infections decreases dramatically in animals with immune disorders. Such animals are at particular risk of opportunistic infections (infections by microorganisms that generally do not cause infection in animals with a healthy immune system). They also become more severely ill from many common infections. Infections are more likely and usually more severe in older animals than in younger ones, probably because aging reduces the immune system's effectiveness.

■ PREVENTING INFECTIONS

Several steps help protect animals against infection. Sometimes, antibiotics are administered to prevent an infection from developing. This preventive measure is called prophylaxis. Many healthy animals that undergo certain types of surgery, such as intestinal surgery, are given prophylactic antibiotics.

Vaccination also can prevent infections. When a vaccination is given, it stimulates or enhances the body's ability to fight off certain disease-causing bacteria or viruses. In many animal species, vaccinations against certain diseases (such as rabies) are required. The vaccines available today are highly reliable and are usually well tolerated by most animals.

■ RESIDENT FLORA

A healthy animal lives in harmony with most microorganisms that establish themselves on or in the body. The microorganisms that usually live on or in a particular body site are called the resident flora. The resident flora at each site include several, or even several hundred, different types of microorganisms. Environmental factors such as diet or sanitary conditions influence what microorganisms make up an animal's resident flora. The resident flora are beneficial, often protecting the body against other organisms that can cause disease. Under nor-

mal conditions, if the resident flora are disturbed, they promptly reestablish themselves.

Under certain conditions, microorganisms that are part of an animal's resident flora may cause disease. Such conditions include the use of antibiotics or a weakened immune system. When antibiotics used to treat an infection kill a large proportion of the resident flora of the skin or intestine, other bacteria or fungi can multiply without being held in check.

■ INFECTIONS CAUSED BY BACTERIA

Bacteria are microscopic, single-celled organisms. Thousands of different kinds of bacteria live throughout the world. Some live in the environment, and others live on the skin, in the airways, in the mouth, and in the digestive and urinary tracts of animals and people. Only a few kinds of bacteria cause disease.

Bacteria commonly enter the bloodstream, but usually only a small number of bacteria do so at a time, and no signs develop. In addition, most bacteria that enter the bloodstream are rapidly removed by white blood cells. (For a more detailed discussion of this process, *see* page 35.) Sometimes, however, there are too many bacteria to be removed easily, and an infection develops. An infection that is widespread throughout the blood-

Types of Infectious Organisms

■ **Bacteria**: Bacteria are microscopic, single-celled organisms. Examples include *Escherichia coli*, *Salmonella* species, and *Staphylococcus* species.

■ **Viruses**: A virus is an infectious organism that is much smaller than a fungus, bacterium, or parasite. Viruses cannot reproduce on their own; a virus must invade a living cell and use that cell's own mechanisms to reproduce. Examples include canine parvovirus, equine influenza viruses, and feline enteric coronavirus.

■ **Fungi**: Fungi are actually a type of plant. Yeasts, molds, and mushrooms are all types of fungi. Examples include *Aspergillus, Candida albicans,* and dermatophytes (fungi that cause ringworm).

■ **Parasites**: A parasite is an organism, such as a worm or single-celled animal, that survives by living on or in another, usually much larger, organism (the host). Examples include *Dirofilaria immitis* (heartworm), *Ctenocephalides felis* (a common flea), *Sarcoptes* (sarcoptic mite), *Giardia,* and *Toxoplasma* (single-celled organisms called protozoa).

Cocci (sphere shaped)	Bacilli (rod shaped)	Spirochetes (spiral shaped)

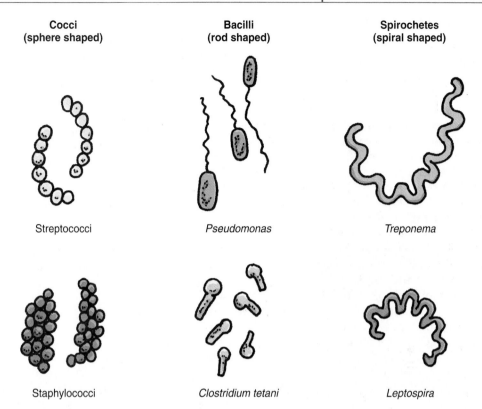

Streptococci | Pseudomonas | Treponema

Staphylococci | Clostridium tetani | Leptospira

Some common shapes of bacteria (modified with permission from *The Merck Manual of Medical Information*, Second Home Edition, 2003)

stream is called sepsis and causes severe signs.

Bacteremia and Sepsis

Bacteremia is the presence of bacteria in the bloodstream; sepsis, which is also called septicemia, is illness resulting from the persistence of microorganisms or their toxins in the bloodstream.

Temporary bacteremia may occur during dental procedures, because bacteria living on the gums around the teeth are freed and enter the bloodstream. Bacteria can also enter the bloodstream from the intestine, but they are rapidly removed when the blood passes through the liver. These conditions are usually not serious.

Sepsis is less common than bacteremia. Sepsis most often develops when there is another infection somewhere in the body, such as the lungs, abdomen, or urinary tract. Sepsis can also occur when surgery is performed on an infected area or on a part of the body where bacteria normally live, such as the intestine. The presence of a foreign object, such as an intravenous line or a drainage tube, may increase the risk of sepsis, and the chance of sepsis increases the longer the object is left in place. Sepsis is more likely to develop in animals with a suppressed immune system or other immune disorder. Rarely, nonbacterial infections can cause sepsis.

The circulating bacteria may settle in sites throughout the body if treatment is not started quickly. An infection can develop in the tissues surrounding the brain (meningitis), the sac around the heart (pericarditis), the bones (osteomyelitis), the joints (infectious arthritis), and other areas. Certain types of bacteria, such as staphylococci, can result in accumulations of pus that form abscesses in the organs they infect.

Signs and Diagnosis

Because the body is usually able to clear small numbers of bacteria quickly, temporary bacteremia rarely causes signs. When sepsis does develop, signs include shaking, fever, weakness, confusion, lack of interest in food, vomiting, and diarrhea. Other signs can also be present depending on the type and location of the initial infection.

A sudden high fever in an animal that has an infection may indicate sepsis. Bacteria in the bloodstream are usually difficult to find by simply examining the blood under a microscope. Several blood samples may be needed to make the diagnosis; the samples are sent to a laboratory for culture, a procedure to try to grow the bacteria for specific identification. Blood cultures can take several days. Unfortunately, bacteria may not always grow in a blood culture, particularly if the animal is taking antibiotics. Cultures of other fluids and substances (such as urine, cerebrospinal fluid, wound tissue, and material coughed up from the lungs) may also be analyzed for the presence of bacteria.

Treatment and Outlook

Bacteremia caused by surgery or dental procedures usually does not require treatment. However, animals at risk of developing serious infections (such as those with heart valve disease or a weakened immune system) generally are given antibiotics to prevent bacteria and sepsis before undergoing such procedures.

Sepsis is very serious and can lead to septic shock. Antibiotic treatment should begin immediately—even if test results confirming the diagnosis are not yet available. A delay in starting antibiotic treatment greatly decreases the animal's chances of survival. Initially, an antibiotic is selected based on the bacteria most likely to be present, which depends on where the infection started. Often, 2 or 3 antibiotics are given together to increase the chances of killing the bacteria, particularly when the source of the bacteria is unknown. Later, when the test results become available, the antibiotic may need to be changed to one that is most effective against the specific bacteria causing the infection. Surgery may sometimes be needed to eliminate the source of the infection.

Septic Shock

Septic shock is a life-threatening condition caused by an infection in the bloodstream (sepsis or blood poisoning) in which blood pressure falls dangerously low and many organs malfunction because of inadequate blood flow. Animals with low white blood cell counts or a chronic disease are at increased risk of developing septic shock.

Septic shock is caused by substances produced by the immune system to fight an infection (cytokines) and by toxins produced by some bacteria. These substances cause the blood vessels to widen, or dilate, which results in a drop in blood pressure. Blood flow to vital organs, particularly the kidneys and brain, is reduced even though the body tries to compensate by increasing both the heart rate and the volume of blood pumped. Eventually, the toxins and the increased work of pumping weaken the heart, which reduces blood flow even more. The walls of the blood vessels may leak, which allows fluid to escape from the bloodstream into tissues, causing swelling. In the lungs, this leakage and swelling causes difficulty breathing.

Signs and Diagnosis

Early signs of septic shock can include disorientation, a shaking chill, a rapid rise in temperature, warm skin, a rapid pulse, and rapid breathing or panting. Urinary output decreases. Tissues with poor blood flow release excess lactic acid into the bloodstream. When the blood becomes more acidic, many different organs malfunction. In later stages, body temperature often falls below normal.

As septic shock worsens, internal organs continue to fail. For example, the kidneys can greatly decrease or stop producing urine, allowing metabolic waste products (such as urea nitrogen) to accumulate in the blood. Problems in the lungs can lead to difficulty breathing and a reduced level of oxygen in the blood. The heart can fail, resulting in fluid retention and tissue swelling. Additionally, blood clots may form inside blood vessels.

Confirming a diagnosis of septic shock may require sophisticated analysis of several blood samples. Results of such analyses usually identify high or low levels of white blood cells, a decreased oxygen level, fewer platelets than normal, excess lactic acid, and increased levels of metabolic waste products. An electrocardiogram (EKG) may show irregularities in heart rhythm, indicating inadequate blood supply to the heart. Blood cultures are performed to identify the infecting organisms. Because there are causes of shock other than sepsis, additional tests may be needed.

Treatment and Outlook

As soon as signs of septic shock are apparent, large amounts of fluid are given intravenously to increase blood pressure. Drugs are given to increase blood flow to the brain, heart, and other organs. Oxygen is also administered.

After blood samples have been taken for laboratory cultures, high dosages of antibiotics are given intravenously. As in sepsis, 2 or 3 antibiotics may be given together to increase the chances of killing the bacteria. Once the specific bacteria causing the infection have been identified, the antibiotic may need to be changed.

Surgery may be needed to drain abscesses or to remove any dead tissue, such as gangrenous tissue of the intestine. Despite all efforts, many animals with septic shock do not survive.

■ INFECTIONS CAUSED BY RICKETTSIAE

Rickettsiae are an unusual type of bacteria that cause several diseases, including Rocky Mountain spotted fever. Rickettsiae differ from most other bacteria in that they can live and multiply only inside the cells of another organism (host) and cannot survive on their own in the environment.

Each of the rickettsiae has its own hosts and vectors (organisms that carry parasites to other organisms). Although some rickettsiae are found primarily in people, the usual host for most species is an animal. The population of animals that can serve as hosts is called the reservoir of infection. Animals in the reservoir may or may not be ill from the infection. People usually become infected through the bites of ticks, mites, fleas, and lice (vectors) that previously fed on an infected animal (*see* DISEASES SPREAD FROM ANIMALS TO PEOPLE (ZOONOSES), page 1088).

Signs and Diagnosis

The signs of a rickettsial infection vary among host species. In dogs, signs of infection may include fever, lack of appetite, depression, loss of stamina, lameness, and coughing. Such infections are usually seen during the warmer months and are not generally fatal. If the infection becomes chronic (longterm), severe problems can develop in the kidneys, lungs, brain, spleen, and bone marrow. Depression and weight loss are common, and death can result.

A history of exposure to ticks and fleas is a strong indicator in diagnosing rickettsial infections, but such contact may not always be apparent. Confirming the diagnosis is difficult, because rickettsiae cannot be identified using commonly available laboratory tests. Special cultures and blood tests for rickettsiae are not routinely available and take so long to process that treatment is usually needed before the test results are available.

Suspicion of rickettsial infection remains the most important factor in diagnosis.

Treatment

Rickettsial infections respond promptly to early treatment with antibiotics known to be effective against these bacteria. Improvement is usually noticeable in 1 to 2 days, and fever usually disappears in 2 to 3 days. Antibiotic treatment is needed for at least 1 week to clear the infection, or longer if the fever persists. Supportive care may be needed. When treatment begins late, improvement is slower and the fever lasts longer. Death can occur if the animal is not treated, or if treatment is begun too late.

■ INFECTIONS CAUSED BY PARASITES

A parasite is an organism that lives on or in another organism (usually referred to as the host), causing harm to the host. Parasites enter the body most often through the mouth or skin. Parasites that enter through the mouth are swallowed and can either remain in the intestine or burrow through the intestinal wall and invade other organs. Parasites that enter through the skin either bore directly through the skin or are introduced through the bites of infected insects. Some parasites enter through the skin or paws when an animal swims or bathes in water contaminated with the parasites.

Diagnosis of a parasitic infection usually requires samples of blood, feces, or urine for laboratory analysis. Repeated sample collections and examinations may be necessary to find the parasite. Less often, a tissue sample, or biopsy, is needed to find the parasite.

Some parasites, particularly those that are single-celled organisms, reproduce inside the host. Other parasites have complex life cycles, producing eggs or larvae that spend time in the environment or in an insect vector before becoming infective. If egg-laying parasites live in the digestive tract, their eggs may be found in the animal's feces when a sample is examined under a microscope.

■ INFECTIONS CAUSED BY FUNGI

Fungi are a type of organism, similar to plants, that can infect animals and people. Yeasts, molds, and mushrooms are all examples of fungi.

Some fungi reproduce by spreading microscopic spores. These spores are often present in the air, where they can be inhaled or come into contact with an animal's body surfaces. Consequently, fungal infections usually begin in the lungs or on the skin. Of the wide variety of spores that land on the skin or are inhaled into the lungs, most do not cause infection. Except for a few skin conditions, fungal infections are rarely passed from one animal to another. Because many fungal infections develop slowly, months or years may pass before a problem becomes noticeable.

Certain types of fungi are present on body surfaces or in the intestines. Although normally harmless, these fungi sometimes cause localized infections of the skin and claws, the sinuses, or the mouth. They seldom cause serious harm, except in animals with a weakened immune system. In this situation, fungal infections can be very aggressive, spreading quickly to other organs and often leading to death.

Sometimes, the normal balances that keep fungi in check are upset, and infections develop. For example, the bacteria normally present in the intestines limit the growth of certain fungi in the area. When antibiotics are given, those helpful bacteria can be killed—allowing the fungi to grow unchecked. The resulting overgrowth of fungi can cause signs, which are usually mild. As the bacteria grow back, the balance is restored, and the problem usually resolves.

Several drugs are effective against fungal infections, but the structure and chemical makeup of fungi make them

Identifying an Infectious Organism

Many different microorganisms can cause a given condition (for example, pneumonia can be caused by viruses, bacteria, or fungi). It is usually important to know what specific microorganism is causing an illness because the treatment is different for each organism.

There are many ways to identify microorganisms. Taking a sample from the site of infection and examining it under the microscope is often the most rapid method of identifying microorganisms. Sometimes, microorganisms can be recognized by characteristic shapes and colors. However, if the microorganisms are too few or too small to see under the microscope, they may not be found.

Another method of identifying an infectious organism is to grow it in the laboratory so that additional chemical tests can be done. The process of growing the organism is called a culture. Many microorganisms can be grown this way. Cultures can also be used to test the sensitivity of microorganisms to various antibiotics, which can help determine what drug to use to treat an infected animal. This strategy is particularly important because microorganisms are constantly developing resistance to antibiotics that were previously effective.

Some microorganisms are very difficult to culture. These infections can be identified by finding antibodies to the microorganisms in the infected animal's blood or other body fluids. Antibody-based tests are used to identify many infections, but they are not always reliable. Antibodies often stay in the body for many years after an infection has cleared. New tests, such as the polymerase chain reaction, can identify pieces of the genetic material (DNA) of the microorganism, which are present only when the organism is present. These tests are usually performed only when a particular disease is already suspected.

---

difficult to kill. Antifungal drugs can be applied directly to a fungal infection of the skin or other surface. In more severe infections, antifungal drugs are given by mouth or injected. Several months of treatment are often needed.

■ INFECTIONS CAUSED BY VIRUSES

Viruses are much smaller than fungi or bacteria, and they must invade a living cell to reproduce, or replicate. The virus attaches to a cell, enters it, and releases its DNA or RNA inside the cell. The DNA or RNA of the virus is its genetic information, which takes control of the cell and forces it to replicate the virus. The infected cell usually dies because the virus keeps it from performing its normal functions. Before it dies, however, the cell has already released new viruses, which go on to infect other cells.

Some viruses do not kill the cells they infect, but instead change the cells' functions. Sometimes, the infected cell loses control over normal cell division and cancer cells are produced. Some viruses that

do not kill the cells they infect leave their genetic material in the host cell, where it can remain inactive for a long time. This is called a latent infection. When the cell is disturbed, the virus may begin to replicate and cause disease.

Viruses are transmitted in a variety of ways, depending on the body system affected. For example, common viruses of the respiratory tract are usually inhaled, and viruses of the digestive tract are often swallowed. Other viral infections are transmitted by the bites of insects and other parasites (such as mosquitoes and ticks). Most viruses infect only one or a few species. For example, canine parainfluenza virus does not infect cats or people. Rabies is an exception and can affect any mammal.

The body has a number of defenses against viruses. Physical barriers, such as the skin, discourage easy entry. Infected cells also make substances (called interferons) that can help noninfected cells resist infection by many viruses.

When a virus enters the body, it triggers the body's immune defenses. These defenses begin with white blood cells, such as lymphocytes, which attack and destroy the virus or the cells it has infected. If the body survives the viral infection, the lymphocytes "remember" the invader and can respond more quickly and effectively to a later infection with the same virus. This is the basis of immunity. Immunity can also be produced by vaccination. Drugs that fight viral infections are called antiviral drugs. Antiviral drugs work by interfering with viral replication. Because viruses are tiny and replicate inside cells using the cells' own mechanisms, there are only a limited number of metabolic functions that antiviral drugs can target. In contrast, bacteria are larger organisms, commonly reproduce by themselves outside of cells, and have many metabolic functions against which antibiotics can be directed. Therefore, antiviral drugs are much more difficult to develop than antibiotics. In addition, viruses can develop resistance to antiviral drugs. The antiviral drugs themselves can also be toxic to animal and human cells.

Antibiotics are not effective against viral infections, but if a pet has a bacterial infection in addition to a viral infection, an antibiotic is generally needed.

ACKNOWLEDGMENT

Portions of this chapter have been modified, with permission, from *The Merck Manual of Medical Information*, Second Home Edition, 2003, pages 1086–1092.

CHAPTER **79**
Diseases Spread from Animals to People (Zoonoses)

▧ INTRODUCTION

Diseases that are passed from animals to people (called zoonotic diseases or zoonoses) present an ongoing public health concern. Many organisms (such as bacteria and viruses) that infect animals can also cause disease in people. These organisms can be passed on in a number of ways. Contact with the animal itself is one way that disease is spread, but other ways include contact with urine, feces, or respiratory secretions of an infected animal, or contact with other items in the animal's environment. Disease can also be spread through scratches or bites by a pet, or by insects (such as the Lyme-disease tick) that carry the infection from animals to humans.

Many known zoonotic diseases are passed from wild animals to people, or from wild animals to pets to people. Exposure to animals kept as pets is steadily increasing as the number of pets increases in the United States and other countries. The number of different types of animals kept as pets is also increasing. Exotic pets such as prairie dogs have become popular in many parts of the world. Such animals have brought diseases out of the wild and into human homes. For example, in 2003 an outbreak of monkeypox (a rare viral disease) occurred in people who were exposed to the virus by recently purchased prairie dogs. It was later determined that the prairie dogs likely were exposed to the virus when they came into contact with another exotic species, the Gambian rat, at a pet distributor.

In addition, exposure to wild animals is increasing as humans continue to clear land and build houses in areas that were formerly home to wildlife. Animals such as raccoons and opossums have adapted to urban conditions and are well known to spread infectious diseases such as rabies. People's desire to touch wild animals and livestock has resulted in the establishment of petting zoos. Public health officials in several countries, including the US, Canada, and United Kingdom, are trying to control the spread of disease at these zoos through inspections and rules, including handwashing with antibacterial soap.

People with weakened immune systems, such as those with AIDS (acquired immune deficiency syndrome) are much more likely to get diseases from animals, including tuberculosis and foodborne *Salmonella* infections. Some very rare diseases may emerge in individuals who have AIDS or other conditions that impair the body's ability to fight infections. Many of these organisms do not ordinarily cause disease.

▪ PREVENTING ZOONOSES

There are several things that can be done to minimize your exposure to the infectious organisms that cause disease. First, make sure your pet receives all of the recommended vaccinations for its species. This will keep your pet from becoming infected with certain dangerous diseases and spreading them to other pets or humans. Second, if you are thinking of acquiring a rare or exotic pet, make sure you check all local and regional regulations to ensure that it is legal to keep the animal as a pet in your area; also, check with your veterinarian about any possible health risks that might be associated with the animal. And always make sure that any new animal receives a checkup from your veterinarian to ensure that it is healthy and disease-free.

It is always a good idea to minimize contact between wild animals and your pet. If your pet is housed outdoors, it is more likely to come into contact with wild animals or insects that can spread disease. Take reasonable precautions—for example, if you and your dog go for a walk in an area known to be associated with Lyme disease, always check both yourself and your pet for ticks upon your return home. Use appropriate insect control products, such as flea and tick preventives. Avoid contact with droppings from other animals that could spread disease or parasites.

When your pet has an infectious disease, keep it separated from other pets and people in the household, if possible. Hands should always be thoroughly washed after any contact with the sick animal or its environment (bedding, toys, or food, for example). It may be necessary in some cases to thoroughly clean and sanitize the area, or even destroy some items such as bedding. Your veterinarian can provide appropriate guidelines, depending on the type of infection your pet has.

▪ LIST OF ZOONOSES

The following table lists the most important zoonoses that have been documented. Many of these are quite rare and only occur in certain areas of the world, or under certain conditions. The table is divided into categories, based on the type of organism that causes disease (for example, bacteria, viruses, parasites, and so on).

It is also important to note that, in the majority of zoonoses, infection is due to contact with a wild animal or an insect rather than a pet. For instance, where rodents are listed in the table, it is most commonly a wild rodent that is the source of disease, not one that has been bred and kept in captivity.

Many proven zoonoses, including some relatively rare viral infections carried by insects and infections caused by parasitic worms, have been omitted, as well as those diseases caused by fish and reptile toxins.

Table 2. Global Zoonoses*

Disease	Causative Organism	Principal Animals Involved
Bacterial Diseases		
Anthrax	*Bacillus anthracis*	Horses, livestock
Bordetellosis	*Bordetella bronchiseptica*	Dogs, rabbits, guinea pigs
Brucellosis	*Brucella abortus*	Cattle, bison, elk, caribou
	Brucella melitensis	Goats, sheep, camels
	Brucella suis	Wild and domestic pigs
	Brucella canis	Dogs
Campylobacter enteritis	*Campylobacter jejuni*	Dogs, cats
	Campylobacter coli, C. fetus, C. laridis	Domestic pigs
Capnocytophaga infection	*Capnocytophaga canimorsus, C. cynodegmi*	Dogs, cats
Cat scratch disease	*Bartonella henselae, B. quintana*	Cats
Clostridial diseases (*See also* Tetanus.)	*Clostridium perfringens*, type A	Domestic animals
	Clostridium septicum, C. novyi	Domestic animals
Erysipeloid	*Erysipelothrix rhusiopathiae*	Pigs, turkeys, pigeons, fish, marine mammals
Escherichia coli infections (Only some infections are considered zoonotic.)	Certain strains of *E. coli*, including O157:H7 and others	Cattle, humans
Glanders	*Burkholderia mallei*	Horses and related species
Leptospirosis	*Leptospira interrogans*	Common in rodents, dogs
Listeriosis	*Listeria monocytogenes*	Numerous mammals, birds
Lyme disease (Borreliosis)	*Borrelia* species	Deer, rodents

Known Distribution	Ways Spread to Humans	Signs in Humans
Worldwide; common in Africa, Asia, South America, eastern Europe	Work-related exposure; food-borne in Africa, Russia, and Asia; occasionally wounds or insect bites; rarely airborne	Skin rash, pneumonia, blood poisoning
Worldwide	Exposure to saliva or sputum	Pertussis-like pneumonia, usually in immunocompromised persons
Worldwide except North America	Work-related and recreational exposure	Fever lasting about a week, progressing to blood poisoning
Worldwide	Milk, cheese, contact	Fever lasting about a week with arthritis, progressing to blood poisoning
Northern hemisphere	Rarely airborne	Fever lasting about a week with arthritis, endocarditis; progressing to blood poisoning
Rare	Exposure to infectious material	Fever lasting about a week with arthritis, endocarditis; progressing to blood poisoning
Worldwide	Mainly foodborne, milk, water-borne, or work-related	Inflammation of the intestines, arthritis, blood poisoning
Less frequent		Inflammation of the intestines, arthritis
US	Bites or scratches	Fever to blood poisoning
Worldwide	Scratches, bites, "licks"	Enlargement of the lymph nodes to blood poisoning; skin rash in persons with AIDS
Worldwide	Foodborne; occasionally wound contaminant	Inflammation of the intestines, gas gangrene, blood poisoning
Worldwide	Wound infection	Inflammation of the intestines, gas gangrene, blood poisoning
Worldwide	Work-related, recreational exposure	Skin rash, blood poisoning
North and South America, Europe, South Africa, Japan, Australia	Eating undercooked ground beef or food or water contaminated with cattle feces	Inflammation of the intestines, diarrhea, abdominal pain, kidney failure
Rare except for some regions in Asia	Work-related exposure	Mucous membrane or skin rash, pneumonia, fever, blood poisoning
Worldwide	Work-related and recreational exposure; water- and foodborne	Fever, rash, pneumonia, inflammation of the covering of the brain, liver and kidney failure
Worldwide in cool environments	Raw contaminated milk, cheese, mud, water, and vegetables are infectious	Inflammation of the intestines and the covering of the brain, blood poisoning, fetal infection
Worldwide	Ticks	Fever, blood poisoning

(Continued on the following page)

Table 2. Global Zoonoses*—*(Continued)*

Disease	Causative Organism	Principal Animals Involved
Melioidosis (Pseudoglanders)	*Pseudomonas pseudomallei*	Rodents
Mycobacteriosis	*Mycobacterium avium-intracellulare* complex	Many species of mammals, some birds
Pasteurellosis	*Pasteurella multocida* and other species	Many species of animals, especially dogs and cats
Plague	*Yersinia pestis*	Rodents, cats, rabbits, related animals
Psittacosis and ornithosis	*Chlamydophila psittaci*	Parakeets, parrots, other domestic birds
Rat bite fever	*Streptobacillus moniliformis*	Rodents
	Spirillum minus	Rodents
Relapsing fever (Borreliosis)	*Borrelia recurrentis*	No animal reservoir for louseborne form; wild rodents (tickborne form)
Salmonellosis	*Salmonella enterica*	Horses, livestock, dogs, cats, reptiles, amphibians
Southern tick-associated rash illness	*Borrelia lonestari*	Uncertain
Streptococcal infections	*Streptococcus pyogenes*, other streptococci	Horses, livestock; occasionally other animals including dogs, cats
Tetanus	*Clostridium tetani*	Principally herbivores, but all animals may be intestinal carriers
Tuberculosis (*See also* Mycobacteriosis.)	*Mycobacterium bovis*	Livestock, monkeys
	Mycobacterium tuberculosis	Monkeys and other primates; dogs, cats, and other domestic animals, but only rarely
Tularemia	*Francisella tularensis*	Rabbits, rodents, cats

Known Distribution	Ways Spread to Humans	Signs in Humans
Asia, Africa, Australia, South America and US; rare	Wound infection and ingestion; organisms live in soil and surface water	Skin and lung lesions, hepatitis, organ abscesses
Worldwide	Primarily waterborne	Lung disease in elderly; spread throughout body in immunocompromised, especially persons with AIDS
Worldwide	Wounds, scratches, bites	Wound infections, inflammation of connective tissue, blood poisoning, inflammation of the covering of the brain
Areas of Western US, South America, Asia and Africa; rare	Fleas, airborne particles, handling infected animals	Skin rash, enlargement of lymph nodes, pneumonia, blood poisoning
Worldwide; common	Exposure to airborne particles	Pneumonia, blood poisoning
Worldwide; rare	Bites of rodents; can be water- or foodborne	Fever, skin rash, arthritis, blood poisoning
Asia	Bites of rodents; can be water- or foodborne	Fever, rash with plaques, wound reactivates, blood poisoning
Occasional epidemics	Crushing infected lice, tick bites	Relapsing fever (every 3 to 5 days, up to 10 episodes); blood poisoning
Worldwide; very common	Foodborne infection, especially in the elderly, infants, or immuno-compromised; work-related and recreational exposure	Inflammation of the intestines, blood poisoning
Southern US	Ticks	Bull's eye-shaped rash, arthritis, blood poisoning
Worldwide	Ingestion, especially of raw milk; direct contact	Inflammation of the throat and connective tissues, pneumonia, inflammation of the covering of the brain, arthritis, blood poisoning
Worldwide	Wound infection and injections	Muscle spasms and contractions (especially facial), seizures, high mortality
Worldwide; rare in US, Canada, Europe	Ingestion, inhalation, work-related exposure	Skin rash, inflammation of lymph nodes and the intestines
Worldwide	Exposure to animals infected with human tuberculosis	Lung disease, inflammation of lymph nodes and the covering of the brain, widespread organ abscesses
Polar regions of America, Europe, and Asia	Work-related and recreational exposure; insect bites; ingestion; inhalation	Skin ulcers; inflammation of the throat, lymph nodes, and intestines; pneumonia; blood poisoning

(Continued on the following page)

Table 2. Global Zoonoses*—(Continued)

Disease	Causative Organism	Principal Animals Involved
Vibriosis	*Vibrio parahaemolyticus; V. vulnificus* and other vibrios	Marine shellfish
	Vibrio cholerae	Crabs, shrimp, mussels
Yersiniosis	*Yersinia pseudotuberculosis*	Mammals, birds, puppies, kittens
	Yersinia enterocolitica	Domestic animals, especially pigs, dogs, cats
Rickettsial Diseases		
Boutonneuse fever, tick bite fever	*Rickettsia conorii*, related *Rickettsia*	Dogs, rodents, other animals
Ehrlichiosis	*Ehrlichia chaffeensis*	Deer, rodents, horses, dogs
	Anaplasma phagocytophilum	Deer, rodents, horses, dogs
	Ehrlichia sennetsu	Uncertain
	Ehrlichia ewingi	Uncertain
Eperythrozoonosis	*Mycoplasma (Eperythrozoon)* species	Livestock
Murine typhus	*Rickettsia typhi* and related species	Rats, cats, opossums, skunks, racoons
North Asian tickborne rickettsiosis	*Rickettsia siberica*	Wild rodents
Q fever (Query fever)	*Coxiella burnetii*	Livestock, cats, dogs, rodents, other mammals, birds
Queensland tick typhus	*Rickettsia australis*	Bandicoots, rodents
Rickettsial pox	*Rickettsia akari*	Mice
Rocky Mountain spotted fever	*Rickettsia rickettsii*	Rabbits, field mice, dogs
Spotted fever group	*Rickettsia parkeri*	Dogs and possibly cats
Scrub typhus	*Orientia tsutsugamushi* and related species	Rodents

Known Distribution	Ways Spread to Humans	Signs in Humans
Pacific basin, warm shores of Asia, Australia, North America; probably worldwide	Ingestion; wound infection	Inflammation of the intestines with diarrhea, abdominal pain, blisters and sores on skin; blood poisoning; more severe in immunocompromised individuals
Worldwide except Europe; epidemic in some developing countries	Ingestion; wound infection	Severe diarrhea, dehydration; deadly if untreated
Temperate zones	Ingestion; recreational exposure	Inflammation of the lymph nodes and intestines
Temperate zones	Ingestion; recreational exposure	Inflammation of the intestines with or without blood in stools, arthritis, blood poisoning
Europe, Asia, Africa	Bite of infected ticks	Skin burns or ulcerations, inflammation of the lymph nodes, rash, fever
US, Japan	Ticks	Fever, headache, fatigue, muscle aches
Worldwide	Ticks	Fever, headache, fatigue, muscle aches
Japan	Ticks	Fever, inflammation of the lymph nodes, blood poisoning, fever
Missouri	Dogs	Fever, headache, fatigue, muscle aches
Worldwide (animals); reports of human infection in China, Yugoslavia	Direct contact; through the placenta; insects	Low blood iron levels, hemolytic jaundice, fever, inflammation of the lymph nodes, hemoglobin in the urine; many patients show no signs
Worldwide	Infected rodent fleas, possibly cat fleas	Fever, skin rash, relatively mild
Siberia, Mongolia, China	Bite of infected ticks	Skin burns or ulcerations, inflammation of the lymph nodes, rash, fever
Worldwide; common	Mainly airborne; exposure to placenta, birth tissues, animal excreta; occasionally ticks and milk	Fever, pneumonia, inflammation of the liver and the lining of the heart
Australia	Bite of infected tick	Similar to Boutonneuse fever
Eastern US, Africa, Russia; rare	Bite of infected rodent mites	Scabbing, rash, fever; mild
Western hemisphere	Bite of infected ticks, also from crushing tick	Fever, rash, blood poisoning
Western hemisphere	Likely Gulf Coast tick and other related ticks	Fever, mild headache, widespread pain in the muscles and joints, rash
"Typhus islands" in Asia, Australia, East Indies	Bite of infected larval trombiculid mites	Scabbing, rash, fever, possibly pneumonia

(Continued on the following page)

Table 2. Global Zoonoses*—(Continued)

Disease	Causative Organism	Principal Animals Involved
Typhus	*Rickettsia prowazekii*	Flying squirrels
Fungal Diseases		
Actinomycosis	*Actinomyces israelii,* rarely other *Actinomyces* species	Mammals
Aspergillosis (Allergic broncho-pulmonary aspergillosis)	*Aspergillus* species	Birds and mammals; principally environmental in decaying vegetation or grains
Blastomycosis	*Blastomyces dermatitidis*	Dogs, cats, horses, sea mammals; principally environmental in moist soil
Candidiasis (Moniliasis)	*Candida* species	Birds and mammals
Coccidioidomycosis	*Coccidioides immitis*	Livestock, horses, dogs, desert rodents, other animals; principally environmental in specific dry areas
Cryptococcosis	*Cryptococcus neoformans*	Pigeons, cockatoos, cats, other mammals; principally environmental
Dermatophilosis	*Dermatophilus congolensis*	Livestock, horses, deer, other mammals
Histoplasmosis	*Histoplasma capsulatum*	Dogs; principally environmental in river valleys
Nocardiosis	*Nocardia* species	Dogs, other mammals; principally environmental in decomposing organic matter
Pneumocystis pneumonia	*Pneumocystis carinii* (human strain)	Rodents, dogs, cats, cattle
Rhinosporidiosis	*Rhinosporidium seeberi*	Horses, cattle, dogs, and birds; unidentified environmental sources
Ringworm (Dermatophytosis)	*Microsporum, Trichophyton,* and *Epidermophyton* species	Dogs, cats, cattle, rodents, other animals
Sporotrichosis	*Sporothrix schenckii*	Horses, other domestic and laboratory animals, birds; primarily environmental in vegetation (moss) and wood

Known Distribution	Ways Spread to Humans	Signs in Humans
Eastern US	Squirrel fleas or ticks suspected	Fever, rash, blood poisoning
Worldwide	Contact; rare	Fever, blood poisoning
Worldwide; sporadic	Environmental exposure	Pneumonia with system-wide spread in immunocompromised persons; chronic lung disease
Worldwide	Environmental exposure; also reported by animal exposure	Pneumonia, skin or bone lesions
Worldwide	Direct contact; often person to person	Skin and mucous membrane lesions; blood poisoning and spread to organs in immuno-compromised persons
Southwestern US, Mexico, Central and South America	Environmental exposure	Self-limited feverish illness; per-sistent inflammation of the cover-ing of the brain or infection of the bone in immunocompromised persons
Worldwide	Environmental exposure, espe-cially pigeon nests	Self-limiting masses in the lungs; inflammation of the covering of the brain and system-wide spread in immunocompromised persons
Worldwide	Contact; insects	Irritation of the skin with pus and peeling
Worldwide	Environmental exposure; grows abundantly in feces of chickens, blackbirds, bats	Flu-like, pneumonia, system-wide spread in immunocompromised persons
Worldwide	Environmental exposure	Pneumonia, system-wide spread in immunocompromised persons
Worldwide; common in persons with AIDS	Environmental exposure; person to person; source yet to be deter-mined, nor have animal strains been verified as human pathogens	Pneumonia, fever, dry cough
Worldwide, persistant in South Asia	Environmental exposure	Nasal and other mucous mem-brane masses and polyps; may cause obstruction
Worldwide	Direct contact with infected animals or material (bedding)	Skin and hair lesions; rarely, widespread skin involvement in immunocompromised persons
Worldwide	Work-related contact, including with animals	Skin ulcers may follow course of draining lymphatics of arms and legs; may spread throughout system in immunocompromised persons

(Continued on the following page)

Table 2. Global Zoonoses*—(Continued)

Disease	Causative Organism	Principal Animals Involved
Parasitic Diseases—Protozoans		
Babesiosis	*Babesia microti, B. bovis*	Wild rodents, cattle
	Babesia divergens	Mammals
Balantidiasis	*Balantidium coli*	Pigs, rats, primates
Chagas' disease (American trypanosomiasis)	*Trypanosoma cruzi*	Opossums, rodents, dogs, cats, other wild and domestic animals
Cryptosporidiosis	*Cryptosporidium parvum*	Cattle, other animals
Giardiasis	*Giardia lamblia*	Beavers, porcupines, dogs, other animals
Leishmaniasis (Kalaazar [visceral])	*Leishmania donovani* and other species	Dogs, wolves, other wild canids
Leishmaniasis (skin and mucosal)	*Leishmania tropica, L. braziliensis* complex	Dogs, wild canids, rodents, marsupials, sloths, other wild mammals
Malaria of nonhuman primates	Many species of *Plasmodium*	Monkeys, chimpanzees
Microsporidiosis	Microsporidia, *Enterocytozoon bieneusis, Encephalitozoon cuniculi, Encephalitozoon intestinalis, Encephalitozoon hellem*	Rodents, birds, other wild and domestic animals
Sarcocystosis (Sarcosporidiosis)	*Sarcocystis suihominis, S. hominis*	Pigs, cattle
Toxoplasmosis	*Toxoplasma gondii*	Mammals, especially cats, livestock, birds

Known Distribution	Ways Spread to Humans	Signs in Humans
Worldwide; rare	Bite of infected ticks	Fever and breakdown of red blood cells, low blood iron levels, especially severe in immunocompromised persons; repeated or longterm infections may develop
Europe	Bite of infected ticks	*See* above
Worldwide; low frequency	Ingestion, especially of water	Inflammation of the intestines; may involve the stomach
Southern US, Mexico, Central and South America	Feces of triatoma bug; contaminated bite wounds, abrasions, or mucous membranes; blood transfusion; through the placenta; tissue transplantation (infrequent)	Short-term—erratic fever, inflammation of the lymph nodes, enlargement of the spleen and liver, skin rash, inflammation of the heart or brain; worse in immunocompromised Longterm—enlargement of the heart, colon, and esophagus
Worldwide	Work-related contact and ingestion; waterborne	Inflammation of the intestine (cholera-like and persistent in immunocompromised persons); inflammation of the bladder
Worldwide; common	Water and less often food; person to person	Inflammation of the intestines; may be persistent
Southern Asia, South America, Africa	Bite of infected sand flies	Fever, enlargement of the spleen and liver, loss of red and white blood cells
Southern Asia, South America, Africa	Bite of infected sand flies	Raised bumps or ulcers on skin; may spread to oral mucous membranes and persist or recur
Tropical Americas, Asia, Africa	Mosquitoes	Fever; human infection is rare
Worldwide	Zoonotic transmission: contamination by feces; direct contact; waterborne possible; person to person common	Inflammation of the cornea of the eye (pain, redness, and visual blurring); short-term diarrhea (traveler's diarrhea); longterm diarrhea (immunocompromised persons)
Worldwide	Ingestion of raw pork or beef; ingestion of feces	Intestinal signs (from raw meat ingestion), muscular pain (from ingestion of feces)
Worldwide; common	Ingestion of feces of infected cats or found in meat or raw milk	Fever and inflammation of the lymph nodes; system-wide, multi-organ disease in immunocompromised persons, including brain abscess; infection of fetus may result in severe damage to central nervous system

(Continued on the following page)

Table 2. Global Zoonoses*—*(Continued)*

Disease	Causative Organism	Principal Animals Involved
Trypanosomiasis (African sleeping sickness)	*Trypanosoma brucei, T. brucei rhodesiense, T. brucei gambiense*	Wild and domestic dogs, other carnivores, ruminants

▓ Parasitic Diseases—Trematodes (Flukes)

Disease	Causative Organism	Principal Animals Involved
Clonorchiasis	*Clonorchis sinensis* (Chinese liver fluke)	Dogs, cats, pigs, rats, wild animals
Dicrocoeliasis	*Dicrocoelium dendriticum, D. hospes* (lancet fluke)	Cattle, sheep, goats
Echinostomiasis	*Echinostoma ilocanum* and other *Echinostoma* species	Cats, dogs, rodents, fish
Fascioliasis	*Fasciola hepatica, F. gigantica*	Cattle, sheep, other large ruminants
Fasciolopsiasis	*Fasciolopsis buski*	Pigs, dogs
Gastrodiscoidiasis	*Gastrodiscoides hominis*	Pigs, rats
Heterophyiasis	*Heterophyes* and other heterophids	Cats, dogs, foxes, fish-eating birds
Metagonimiasis	*Metagonimus yokogawai*	Cats, dogs, other fish-eating mammals, fish
Opisthorchiasis	*Opisthorchis felineus* (cat liver fluke)	Cats, dogs, foxes, pigs
	Opisthorchis viverrini (small liver fluke)	Dogs, cats, fish-eating mammals
	Amphimerus pseudofelineus	Dogs, cats, coyotes, opossums
Paragonimiasis (Lung fluke disease)	*Paragonimus westermani, P. africanus, P. mexicanus,* and other species	Dogs, cats, swine, wild carnivores

Known Distribution	Ways Spread to Humans	Signs in Humans
Africa; common south of the Sahara desert	Bite of infected tsetse fly	Painful sore at bite site, fever, headache, inflammation of lymph nodes, rash, drowsiness; gambiense disease may last years; rhodesiense disease may last weeks; both usually fatal without treatment
Asia	Ingestion of raw or partially cooked infected freshwater fish	Inflammation of the gallbladder; longterm infections associated with disease of the liver or cholangiocarcinoma (tumor of the bile duct)
Worldwide; Africa (*D. hospes*)	Ingestion of infected ants	Abdominal discomfort
Asia	Ingestion of uncooked fish, shellfish, or contaminated water	Abdominal discomfort, diarrhea
Worldwide; Africa and western Pacific (*F. gigantica*)	Ingestion of contaminated greens (such as watercress)	Colic, jaundice; migrating skin lesions seen with *F. gigantica*
Asian pig-raising regions	Ingestion of raw tubers and nuts of aquatic plants	Inflammation of the intestines with diarrhea, constipation, and vomiting; lack of appetite; facial, abdominal, and limb swelling may occur
Asia	Snails (larval flukes encyst on plants)	Mild diarrhea
Nile delta, Turkey, Asia	Ingestion of undercooked fish	Diarrhea with mucus; rarely heart or central nervous system involvement
Asia, Europe, Siberia	Ingestion of undercooked fish	Diarrhea with mucus
Eastern Europe, Asia, Siberia	Ingestion of uncooked fish containing encysted larvae	Fever; stomach pain associated with the bile system; enlarged liver due to inflammation of the bile ducts, abscess, or tumor of the bile duct
Thailand, Laos	Ingestion of undercooked fish containing encysted larva	*See* above
US, Central and South America	Undetermined	*See* above
China, India, Myanmar, Africa, tropical America	Ingestion of raw or partially cooked infected freshwater crustaceans	Lung disease resembling tuberculosis; less often inflammation of the brain and its covering and spreading skin nodules

(Continued on the following page)

Table 2. Global Zoonoses*—*(Continued)*

Disease	Causative Organism	Principal Animals Involved
Schistosomiasis (Bilharziasis)	*Schistosoma japonicum*	Cattle, pigs, dogs, cats, rodents
	Schistosoma mansoni	Baboons, rodents, cattle, dogs
	Schistosoma mattbeei	Cattle
	Schistosoma mekongi	Dogs, monkeys
	Schistosoma intercalatum	Cattle, sheep, goats, antelope
Swimmer's itch	Schistosome cercariae	Birds, mammals

■ Parasitic Diseases—Cestodes (Tapeworms)

Disease	Causative Organism	Principal Animals Involved
Asian taeniasis	*Taenia asiatica*	Domestic and wild pigs, cattle, monkeys
Bertielliasis	*Bertiella studeri, B. mucronata*	Primates, certain nonparasitic mites
Coenuriasis	*Taenia multiceps*	Dogs and wild canids, sheep, other herbivores
	Taenia serialis	Rabbits
	Taenia brauni	Wild rodents
Diphyllobothriasis (fish tapeworm infection)	*Diphyllobothrium latum, D. pacificum*	Humans, dogs, fish-eating animals, freshwater fish
Dipylidiasis (dog tapeworm infection)	*Dipylidium caninum*	Dogs, cats, fleas
Echinococcosis	*Echinococcus granulosus*	Dogs, livestock, rodents, deer, moose

Known Distribution	Ways Spread to Humans	Signs in Humans
Southeast Asia, China, Philippines	Penetration of unbroken skin by larvae from infected snails in water	Some cases have sudden onset (especially *S. japonicum, S. mansoni*) with fever, chills, cough, diarrhea, enlargement of the spleen and liver. In other chronic cases, bloody diarrhea, high blood pressure, vomiting of blood, and enlargement of spleen, liver, and other organs may occur. Central nervous system problems may be seen.
Africa, Arabia, tropical America	Penetration of unbroken skin by larvae from infected snails in water	*See above*
Southern Africa	Penetration of unbroken skin by larvae from infected snails in water	*See above*
Southeast Asia	Penetration of unbroken skin by larvae from infected snails in water	*See above*
Central Africa	Penetration of unbroken skin by larvae from infected snails in water	*See above*
Worldwide	Penetration of unbroken skin by larvae from infected snails in fresh- and saltwater	Hives
East and southeast Asia	Ingestion of undercooked meat	Vague abdominal complaints; spreading of worms
Asia, South America, Africa	Ingestion of infected insects	Abdominal pain, vomiting, diarrhea, constipation
Worldwide	Ingestion of tapeworm eggs in canine feces	Painless skin swelling; rarely neurologic involvement, including eye
Africa, Europe, US; rare	Ingestion of tapeworm eggs in canine feces	*See above*
Africa	Ingestion of tapeworm eggs in canine feces	*See above*
Worldwide	Ingestion of raw or partially cooked infected fish	Usually without signs; may cause mild abdominal distress; rarely anemia
Worldwide	Ingestion of dog or cat fleas	Usually in children, without signs or mild abdominal distress; pieces of worms in stool resemble cucumber seeds
Worldwide but mostly in Mediterranean region and southern South America	Ingestion of tapeworm eggs	Cause lesions of organs such as lung, liver, kidney; rarely affects central nervous system

(Continued on the following page)

Table 2. Global Zoonoses*—(Continued)

Disease	Causative Organism	Principal Animals Involved
Echinococcosis	*Echinococcus multilocularis*	Foxes, rodents, dogs and wild canids, cats, voles, lemmings, shrews
	Echinococcus vogeli	Dogs, some rodents
Hymenolepiasis (dwarf tapeworm infection)	*Hymenolepis nana*	Humans, rodents
Inermicapsifer infection	*Inermicapsifer madagascariensis*	Rodents
Mouse or rat tapeworm	*Hymenolepis nana, H. diminuta*	Rats, mice
Raillietina infection	*Raillietina* species	Birds, mammals
Sparganosis	*Spirometra* species	Cats, dogs, pigs, ferrets, rats, chickens, snakes, frogs, mice, monkeys
Taeniasis (beef tapeworm disease)	*Taenia saginata*	Cattle, water buffalo, reindeer, camels
Taeniasis (pork tapeworm disease); cysticercosis and neurocysticercosis	*Taenia solium*	Pigs, humans

Parasitic Diseases—Nematodes (Roundworms)

Disease	Causative Organism	Principal Animals Involved
Angiostrongyliasis	*Parastrongylus costaricensis*	Cotton rats, slugs
	Angiostrongylus cantonensis	Rats, snails, slugs, prawns, fish
Anisakiasis	Larvae of *Anisakis* and *Pseudoterranova* species	Fish, marine mammals and invertebrates
Capillariasis (intestinal)	*Capillaria philippinensis*	Aquatic birds, freshwater fish
Capillariasis (liver)	*Capillaria hepatica*	Rodents, other wild and domestic animals
Capillariasis (lung)	*Capillaria aerophila*	Dogs, cats, other carnivores

Known Distribution	Ways Spread to Humans	Signs in Humans
Alaska, Canada, Asia, Central Europe	Ingestion of tapeworm eggs	Usually large masses in liver, occasionally affects lungs or central nervous system
Central and South America	Ingestion of tapeworm eggs	Usually involves liver, may invade adjacent tissues
Worldwide	Accidental ingestion of tapeworm eggs or infected insects	Mild abdominal distress, may be accompanied by nausea or vomiting
Africa, southeast Asia, tropical America	Ingestion of infected insects	Mild abdominal signs, if any
Worldwide	Ingestion of infected insects (such as fleas or mealworms)	Mild abdominal signs of short duration
Tropical America, east Asia, Australia, Africa	Ingestion of infected insects	Vague discomfort
Worldwide; uncommon	Ingestion of infected crustacean (water flea) or raw infected animal flesh or application of animal flesh to human	Nodular, itchy skin rash that can spread; conjunctival and eyelid lesions; other organ involvement including central nervous system
Worldwide	Ingestion of undercooked meat containing larvae	Mild abdominal discomfort; tapeworm segments may appear in feces
Worldwide where pigs are raised (rare in US, Canada, United Kingdom, Scandinavia)	Ingestion of undercooked pork containing larvae	Usually no signs are seen for years until larvae result in central nervous system involvement (seizures) or involvement of the eye or heart; adult stage infection is mild or without signs
Central and South America, US	Accidental ingestion of slugs or plants contaminated by their secretions	May cause a syndrome resembling appendicitis, especially in children, called abdominal or intestinal angiostrongyliasis
Japan, east and southeast Asia to Australia, Pacific Islands, Africa	Accidental ingestion of slugs or plants contaminated by their secretions	Inflammation of the covering of the brain, eye involvement occurs with decreased vision, eye muscle paralysis
Japan, Holland, Scandinavia, western South America, western Europe, US	Ingestion of undercooked marine fish, squid, octopus	Inflammation of the lining of the stomach and intestines with pain may be accompanied by vomiting of blood; coughing
Northern Philippines, Thailand, east Asia, Egypt	Ingestion of infected fish	Intestinal disease, diarrhea, vomiting
Worldwide in scattered locations	Ingestion of embryonated eggs in soil	Inflammation of the liver
Worldwide	Accidental ingestion of infective eggs in soil or contaminated food	Fever, cough, bronchial spasm

(Continued on the following page)

Table 2. Global Zoonoses *—(Continued)

Disease	Causative Organism	Principal Animals Involved
Dioctophymosis (giant kidney worm infection)	*Dioctophyma renale*	Dogs, mink, other carnivores, frogs, fish
Dracunculiasis (Guinea worm infection)	*Dracunculus insignis*	Raccoons, mink, dogs
Dirofilariasis (heartworm infection)	*Dirofilaria immitis*	Dogs, cats, ferrets, raccoons, mosquitoes
Gnathostomiasis	*Gnathostoma spinigerum*	Dogs, cats, wild carnivores, freshwater fish
Gongylonemiasis	*Gongylonema pulchrum*	Ruminants, domestic and wild pigs, other mammals, beetles
Larva migrans, skin (*See also* Gnathostomiasis.)	*Ancylostoma braziliense, A. caninum, Uncinaria stenocephala*	Cats, dogs, wild carnivores
	Strongyloides stercoralis	Cats, dogs, sheep, pigs
Larva migrans, visceral (*See also* Angiostrongyliasis and Anisakiasis.)	*Toxocara canis, T. cati*	Dogs, cats
	Baylisascaris procyonis	Raccoons
Malayan filariasis	*Brugia malayi*	Cats, other carnivores, monkeys, mosquitoes
Strongyloidiasis	*Strongyloides stercoralis, S. fuelleborni*	Dogs, cats, foxes, primates
Thelaziasis	*Thelazia* species	Dogs, cats, other domestic and wild animals, flies

Known Distribution	Ways Spread to Humans	Signs in Humans
Europe, Asia, North and South America; rare	Ingestion of infected fish or frogs	Flank pain, kidney pain, blood in the urine, blockage of the ureter
North America	Ingestion of frogs and other hosts	Skin lesion that opens to reveal worm; allergic reaction and secondary infection may occur
Worldwide	Bite of infected mosquitoes	Fever, cough; longterm damage to blood vessels or damage in the lungs; often without signs; rarely involves eye
East Asia, India, Australia	Ingestion of infected fish or poultry	Shifting skin sores; may involve internal body parts or central nervous system
Worldwide; rare	Ingestion of infected insects	Intestinal discomfort
Worldwide in tropics and subtropics; common	Contact with infective larvae that penetrate skin	Itchy, slow-spreading, shifting skin lesions, usually of extremities; wheezing, cough, and hives may occur
Worldwide in tropics and subtropics; rare to common	Contact with infective larvae that penetrate skin	Itchy hives, usually on buttocks, groin, or trunk, along with intestinal signs; spreading with lung or central nervous system disease may occur in immunocompromised persons
Worldwide	Ingestion of eggs shed in feces of dogs and cats	Fever, wheezing cough; rash on trunk and extremities; may wax and wane for months; eye involvement (larvae may settle in retina and impair vision)
North America, Europe	Accidental ingestion of eggs in soil or material contaminated with feces	Can cause fatal inflammation of the brain and membrane surrounding the brain and spinal cord in infants; larvae may settle in retina and impair vision
Asia; common	Bite of infected mosquitoes	Skin rash, may include lymph node involvement
Worldwide	Contact with infective larvae that penetrate skin	Frequently without signs; features include abdominal pain, diarrhea, hive-like rash (waist, buttocks); abdominal pain and swelling, shock, lung and neurologic complications, blood poisoning, and death may occur in immunocompromised persons
East and south Asia; rare	Infected insects	Conjunctivitis

(Continued on the following page)

Table 2. Global Zoonoses *—(Continued)

Disease	Causative Organism	Principal Animals Involved
Trichinosis (Trichinellosis)	*Trichinella spiralis* and subspecies, *T. nativa, T. britovi, T. nelsoni, T. pseudospiralis*	Pigs, rodents, horses, wild carnivores, marine mammals
Tropical eosinophilia	*Brugia pahangi*	Cats, other carnivores, monkeys, mosquitoes
■ Parasitic Diseases—Others		
Hirudiniasis	*Limnatis nilotica* and other leeches	Livestock, horses, dogs
Macracanthorhynchosis	*Macracanthorhynchus hirudinaceus* and other species (thorny-headed worms)	Domestic and wild pigs, beetles, squirrels, muskrats, dogs, sea otters, fish, crustaceans
■ Diseases Spread by Insects, Ticks, or Mites		
Acariasis (Mange)	Mites of *Sarcoptes, Cheyletiella, Dermanyssus,* and *Ornithonyssus* species	Domestic animals
Myiasis	*Cochliomyia hominivorax* (screwworm)	Mammals
	Chrysomya bezziana (Old World screwworm)	Mammals
	Cordylobia anthropophaga (Tumbu fly)	Mammals
	Cuterebra species (rodent or rabbit bot fly)	Mammals
	Dermatobia hominis (human bot fly)	Mammals
	Gasterophilus species (equine bot fly)	Mammals
	Hypoderma lineatum	Mammals
	Hypoderma bovis (warbles)	Mammals
	Oestrus ovis, Rhinoestrus purpurensis	Cattle
	Wohlfahrtia species	Cattle
Nanophyetiasis	*Troglotrema salmincola*	Raccoons, skunks, snails
Pentastomid infections	*Linguatula serrata, Armillifer* species (tongue worms)	Dogs, snakes, other vertebrates

Known Distribution	Ways Spread to Humans	Signs in Humans
Worldwide, especially subarctic region	Ingestion of pork and flesh of wild animals containing cysts	Inflammation of the lining of the stomach and intestines followed by fever, severe pain in the joints, facial swelling; central nervous system or heart muscle involvement may follow
Asia; common	Bite of infected mosquitoes	Skin rash, may include lymph node involvement
Africa, Asia, Europe, Chile	Direct contact with leeches	Attaches to skin to suck blood; secondary infection may occur
Worldwide; uncommon	Ingestion of infected beetles	Inflammation of the intestines, may lead to gut perforation
Worldwide	Contact with infected individuals or animals; contaminated clothing	Itchy skin lesions
Tropical America	Eggs laid in fresh wounds or on skin	Skin wounds; nasal infestations; intestinal infestation; usually mild; some may be shifting and destructive causing burrows and boils
Asia, Africa	Eggs laid in fresh wounds or on skin	*See* above
Africa	Eggs laid in fresh wounds or on skin	*See* above
North America	Eggs laid in fresh wounds or on skin	*See* above
South America, Mexico	Can invade living tissue; eats dead tissue in wounds	*See* above
Worldwide	Can invade living tissue; eats dead tissue in wounds	*See* above
North America, Europe	Can invade living tissue; eats dead tissue in wounds	*See* above
Asia, North Africa	Can invade living tissue; eats dead tissue in wounds	*See* above
Worldwide	Eggs and their larvae	*See* above
North America, Europe, North Africa, Asia	Eggs and their larvae	*See* above
North America, Russia	Ingestion of fish or fish eggs (roe)	Mild gastrointestinal signs
Northern hemisphere, worldwide	Ingestion of infected animal tissues, water, or vegetation	Usually without signs; pressure from larvae may cause signs in lungs or other organs, including central nervous system and eye

(Continued on the following page)

Table 2. Global Zoonoses*—(Continued)

Disease	Causative Organism	Principal Animals Involved
Tick paralysis	Envenomization of ticks *Dermacentor andersoni, D. variabilis*, and sometimes *Ixodes, Haemaphysalis, Rhinocephalus*, and *Argas* species	Various animals
Tunga infections	*Tunga penetrans* (sand fleas, jiggers)	Dogs, humans, pigs, other mammals
Viral Diseases		
Argentinean, Bolivian, Brazilian, or Venezuela hemorrhagic fever	Various arenaviruses	Rodents
Central European tickborne encephalitis	Central European encephalitis virus	Rodents, birds, goats, sheep
Colorado tick fever	Colorado tick fever virus	Ground squirrels, chipmunks, porcupines, small rodents
Contagious ecthyma (Orf)	Orf virus (parapox)	Sheep, goats, wild hoofed mammals
Cowpox	Cowpox virus	Cattle, rodents, domestic and wild cats
Crimean-Congo hemorrhagic fever	Nairovirus	Cattle, rodents, sheep, goats, hares, birds
Eastern equine encephalomyelitis	Eastern equine encephalomyelitis virus	Wild and domestic birds, horses, mules, donkeys
Ebola hemorrhagic fever; Marburg hemorrhagic fever	Ebola and Marburg viruses	Primates and bats suspected
Encephalomyocarditis	Encephalomyocarditis virus	Rats, mice, squirrels, pigs, primates, elephants

Known Distribution	Ways Spread to Humans	Signs in Humans
North America, Australia, South Africa, Ethiopia	Direct contact (attachment) with tick	Inflammation of lining of stomach and intestines followed by nerve paralysis; burning or prickling sensation may be noted
Subtropical Africa, Americas, south Asia	Contact with contaminated soil	Penetration of skin and burrowing result in pain and itching; may be secondarily infected
Americas	Exposure to rodents or rodent excretions or secretions; person to person	Gradual onset of joint pain and fever; blood vessels may rupture, bleeding, central nervous system signs
Europe	Tick bites; may be milkborne	2-phase illness with inflammation of the brain occurring in second phase; paralysis or psychiatric signs may develop
Western US; common	Tick bites	2- to 3-phase illness with inflammation of the brain and its covering occurring in late phases; abdominal pain and vomiting may occur
Worldwide; common	Work-related exposure	Raised rash with sores, usually on hands
Worldwide; rare	Contact exposure	Blisters that may contain pus, usually on hands; regional inflammation of the lymph nodes
Africa, Middle East, central Asia, eastern Europe	Tick bites; work-related risk among animal workers	Fever, headache, inflammation of the throat, abdominal signs, rash, bleeding; very severe in pregnant women
Western hemisphere	Mosquito bites	Nonspecific fever, inflammation of the brain which may be severe and accompanied by seizures; neurologic signs occur in 30 to 50% of cases with inflammation of the brain
Central and southern Africa	Contact with infected animals or animal tissues	Abrupt onset of fever; joint and muscle pain; headache; gastrointestinal signs with vomiting; rash; hepatitis; widespread bleeding 3 to 4 days after onset; death rate 50 to 90% for Ebola, 20 to 30% for Marburg
Worldwide	Environmental contamination	Rare, sudden onset inflammation of the heart muscles

(Continued on the following page)

Table 2. Global Zoonoses*—(Continued)

Disease	Causative Organism	Principal Animals Involved
Far eastern tickborne encephalitis (Russian spring-summer encephalitis)	Far eastern (Russian spring-summer encephalitis) virus	Birds, small mammals, sheep
Foot-and-mouth disease	Foot-and-mouth disease virus	Cattle, pigs, other cloven-hoofed mammals
Hantaviral pulmonary syndrome	Sin Nombre virus, Black Creek Canal virus	Deer mice, cotton rats
Hemorrhagic fever with renal syndrome	Hantaan virus, Dobrava virus, Puumala virus, Seoul virus	Field mice, voles, rats
Hendra virus infection	Hendra virus	Horses, fruit bats
Hepatitis E	Hepatitis E virus	Pigs, deer, others
Herpes B virus disease	Cercopithecine herpesvirus 1 (Herpesvirus simiae, B virus)	Old World monkeys
Influenza type A (swine flu, avian flu, bird flu, Hong Kong flu)	Influenza virus (myxovirus)	Birds, pigs, other mammals; migratory waterfowl serve as reservoirs and carriers for highly pathogenic avian influenza
Japanese B encephalitis	Japanese encephalitis virus	Pigs, wild birds, horses
Kyasanur forest disease	Kyasanur forest virus	Rodents, monkeys
LaCrosse encephalitis	Bunyavirus species	Ground squirrels, other rodents
Lassa fever	Lassa virus	Wild rodents

Known Distribution	Ways Spread to Humans	Signs in Humans
Asia, Europe; rare	Tick bites	Similar to central European tick-borne inflammation of the brain; paralysis of shoulders and arms may be seen; fatality rate 20 to 25%; neurologic signs in 30 to 60% of survivors
Europe, Asia, Africa, South America	Contact exposure	Humans can become carriers but do not become ill
US, may be more widespread throughout Americas	Aerosols from rodent excretions and secretions	Fever, joint pain, respiratory failure, decrease in blood cell counts; death rate of 40 to 50%
China, Siberia, Korea, Manchuria, Japan, Balkan countries, Europe	Aerosols from rodent excretions and secretions	Abrupt onset of fever, back pain, rupture of blood vessels, bleeding, kidney failure; death rate 5 to 15%
Australia (Queensland)	Direct contact with infected animals or contaminated tissue	Respiratory infection, inflammation of the brain; can be fatal
Worldwide	Ingestion of contaminated fecal matter or raw or undercooked liver	Fever, gastrointestinal signs, jaundice; may be prolonged; worse in pregnancy
Worldwide; rare	Monkey bites and scratches; work-related exposure	Skin blisters followed by severe encephalitis with seizures, coma, paralysis; fatal in 70% of cases
Worldwide; common	Contact exposure; animals rarely a source	Upper and lower respiratory signs; may progress to influenza, pneumonia, or secondary bacterial pneumonia; seasonally endemic or epidemic
Asia, Pacific islands from Japan to the Philippines	Mosquito bites	Fever, intestinal signs to severe inflammation of the brain with seizures, paralysis; neurologic signs in up to 80% of survivors
India	Tick bites	Fever, rash, slowed heart rate; remission may be followed by inflammation of the brain and its covering
US, Canada	Mosquito bites	Fever, inflammation of the brain with seizures, paralysis, and other focal neurologic signs
Africa	Exposure to rodents or rodent excretions or secretions; person to person	Gradual onset of joint pain and fever; may develop severe swelling of head and neck; fluid in lungs or chest; bleeding less common

(Continued on the following page)

Table 2. Global Zoonoses*—(Continued)

Disease	Causative Organism	Principal Animals Involved
Louping ill	Louping ill virus	Sheep, goats, grouse, small rodents
Lymphocytic choriomeningitis	Lymphocytic choriomeningitis virus	House mice, dogs, guinea pigs, hamsters
Menangle virus infection	Menangle virus	Pigs, fruit bats
Milker's nodules (Pseudocowpox)	Pseudocowpox virus	Cattle
Monkeypox	Monkeypox virus	Prairie dogs, Gambian rats, other African rodents, other pet rodents in US, primates
Murray Valley encephalitis	Murray Valley encephalitis virus	Wild birds
Newcastle disease	Newcastle disease virus	Domestic fowl (poultry), wild birds
New World hemorrhagic fever	Arenavirus	Rodents
Nipah virus infection	Nipah virus	Pigs, dogs, fruit bats, other animals
Omsk hemorrhagic fever	Omsk hemorrhagic fever virus	Rodents, muskrats
Rabies and rabies-related infections	Lyssaviruses (Rabies virus, Duvenhage virus, Mokola virus, Ibadan shrew virus)	Wild and domestic dogs, ferrets, skunks, mink, civets, bats, other mammals
Rift Valley fever	Phlebovirus	Sheep, goats, cattle, camels

Known Distribution	Ways Spread to Humans	Signs in Humans
Great Britain, Northern Ireland; rare	Tick bites	2-phase illness with inflammation of the brain and its covering in second phase; relatively mild compared with central European tickborne encephalitis, which it resembles
Worldwide	Host excretions and secretions	Ranges from mild flu-like illness to severe inflammation of the covering of the brain in second phase; arthritis, swelling of the testes and/or salivary glands may occur; may cause abortion or birth defects
Australia	Respiratory secretions, feces	Fever
Worldwide; common	Work-related exposure to cattle	Painless, red nodules or bumps on skin, will resolve without treatment
West and central Africa; rare	Contact; aerosols	Usually mild, smallpox-like disease; even milder in those vaccinated for smallpox; swelling of the lymph nodes and other glands prominent
Australia, New Guinea; rare	Mosquito bites	No signs in most infections; when disease occurs it can be severe inflammation of the brain with neurologic signs
Worldwide; common	Work-related exposure	Conjunctivitis
Americas	Exposure to rodents or rodent excretions, secretions; person to person	Gradual onset of joint pain and fever; may develop rupture of the blood vessels, bleeding, central nervous system signs
Malaysia	Direct contact with infected animals or contaminated tissue	Fever, headache, vomiting, inflammation of the brain; 30% death rate
Omsk, Siberia; rare	Tick bites; direct contact with ticks	2-phase illness with inflammation of the brain occurring in second phase; deafness may follow infection
Worldwide except Australia, New Zealand, Great Britain, Ireland, Scandinavia, Japan, Taiwan; many smaller islands, including Hawaii, are free of infection	Bites of diseased animals; aerosols in closed environments	Tingling of the skin or pain at bite site, fever, joint pain, mood changes progress to excessively rapid breathing, general tingling of the skin, paralysis, seizures, fear of water; death rate more than 99%; other strains of virus very rare, but deadly
Africa; common to rare	Mosquitoes; contact during autopsy or handling of fresh meat	2-phase illness with slowed heart rate, rash or red spots on skin, bleeding

(Continued on the following page)

Table 2. Global Zoonoses*—(Continued)

Disease	Causative Organism	Principal Animals Involved
Ross River fever	Ross River virus	Undetermined
St. Louis encephalitis	St. Louis encephalitis virus	Wild birds, poultry
Severe acute respiratory syndrome (SARS)	Coronavirus	Civet cats most likely
Sindbis virus disease	Sindbis virus	Birds
Tahyna fever	Bunyavirus species	Hares, rodents, other mammals
Venezuelan equine encephalomyelitis	Venezuelan equine encephalitis virus	Rodents, horses and related species
Vesicular stomatitis	Vesicular stomatitis virus	Livestock, horses, bats, rodents, other wild mammals
Wesselsbron fever	Wesselsbron virus	Sheep
West Nile virus infection	West Nile virus	Wild birds, horses, other mammals
Western equine encephalomyelitis	Western equine encephalomyelitis virus	Wild birds, poultry, horses, mules, donkeys, bats, reptiles, amphibians
Yellow fever	Yellow fever virus	Monkeys, baboons
■ **Prion Diseases**		
Variant Creutzfeldt-Jakob disease	Prion protein (likely from bovine spongiform encephalopathy, also known as mad cow disease)	Cattle

*Many proven zoonoses, including some relatively rare viral infections carried by insects and infections caused by parasitic worms have been omitted, as well as those diseases caused by fish and reptile toxins.

Known Distribution	Ways Spread to Humans	Signs in Humans
Australia, South Pacific Islands	Mosquito bites	Fever, pain in the joints, rash, may persist for months; bruises on lower extremities
Western hemisphere	Mosquito bites	Inflammation of the brain, hepatitis, painful urination; more severe in elderly
China, southeast Asia	Direct contact suspected, person to person	Fever, joint pain, headache, diarrhea, pneumonia; fatality rate 10%
Eastern hemisphere; rare	Mosquito bites	Fever, arthritis, rash that may bleed, prominent joint pain
Europe, Africa	Mosquito bites	Fever, inflammation of the brain with seizures, paralysis, and other focal neurologic signs
Western hemisphere; common	Mosquito bites	Most have nonspecific fever and illness; fewer than 5% progress to inflammation of the brain with death rate of 20% of those patients
North and South America	Contact exposure and insect bites, including mosquitoes and biting flies	Fever, joint pain, inflammation of the throat, enlargement of the lymph nodes, blisters around mouth or rectum
Southern Africa, southeast Asia	Mosquito bites	Fever, muscle pain, increased sensitivity of skin, rash
Eastern and Western hemisphere; common	Mosquito bites; blood transfusion, tissue transplant rarely; may be milkborne	Fever, rash, worse in elderly; inflammation of the brain may be accompanied by paralysis and respiratory failure
Western and Central US, Canada, South America	Mosquito bites	Fever progresses to inflammation of the brain; worse in infants and children in whom neurologic signs are more likely
Tropical America, Africa	Mosquito bites	Fever, muscle pain, weakness; progressing to jaundice, slowed heart rate, liver and kidney failure in 20 to 50%; often fatal if bleeding occurs
Primarily in England, sporadic cases in France, Ireland, Italy, Canada, US, Japan	Ingestion of beef	Degeneration of nervous system; rapidly fatal

CHAPTER 80

Drugs and Vaccines

■ INTRODUCTION

If your pet has been diagnosed with a condition or disease that can be managed or cured, your veterinarian will most likely begin discussing treatment. He or she will recommend drugs that are necessary, safe, and effective for both the individual animal and the specific disorder. For many conditions, there are a variety of drugs that might be considered as an appropriate treatment. When selecting one to prescribe, veterinarians also consider the dose (amount), the method of action, how often to give the chosen drugs, the best way to give the drug, the particular form (for example, pills, liquid, or ointment) to be used, any public health or environmental effects, and local and state regulations.

This chapter provides some basic information on the types of formulations and application methods commonly used to treat diseases or disorders in animals, as well as a general discussion of the types of drugs used to treat disorders within certain body systems (such as the circulatory or digestive system). Specific drug therapies for individual conditions are not discussed here, however. For more detailed information on the treatment for a specific disease or disorder, you should refer to the chapter in this book where the condition is described.

Many chemicals and drugs can be used to combat disease-causing agents. Treatment with any drug involves a relationship between the host animal (your pet), the agent that causes disease, and the drug. The drug may be toxic only to the invading organism, but in many cases, it may also cause adverse effects in the host animal. Included in this category are drugs that are active against bacteria, viruses, fungi, parasites, and even tumors.

Your pet's natural defense mechanisms should be maximized when treating an infectious or parasitic disease in order to prevent an extended recovery time or a relapse. Minimizing stress, providing quality nutrition, and boosting the immune system are all approaches that may be used. An effective drug treatment program involves the veterinarian and the pet owner making informed decisions and carefully following all instructions.

As a pet owner, you should thoroughly discuss with your veterinarian any and all drugs—whether prescription, over-the-counter, or other medications (for example, herbal or other alternative preparations)—that you are thinking about giving to your pet. Inform yourself about how the drug works and any possible negative effects it may have. Even for drugs that seem easy to use or that you have given your pet before, it is important to carefully read the label and administer the correct dose as directed.

Extralabel Use of Drugs

Many of the drugs used in animals in the United States have not been formally approved by the Food and Drug Administration (FDA) for use in a particular species. However, veterinarians have the legal authority to prescribe drugs that have been approved for use in animals or humans for purposes beyond those for which they have been approved. This is referred to as extralabel (or off-label) use. The studies needed to gain FDA approval for a drug to treat a particular disease in a particular species usually require 7 or more years and millions of dollars. Because of these factors, the projected sales may not be large enough for a drug company to justify seeking approval in multiple species. Once a drug is approved for one use, however, it may also be prescribed by licensed professionals for other circumstances.

When deciding which drug to use to treat an animal, veterinarians rely on their training and experience, published reports in professional veterinary journals, and continuing education received at professional meetings. In order to prescribe a drug for your pet, your veterinarian must have what is called a valid veterinarian-client-patient relationship. This means that the veterinarian has agreed with you to serve your pet's medical needs, has recently examined your pet, and is available for followup care.

■ HOW DRUGS ARE GIVEN IN ANIMALS

A wide range of dosage formulations and delivery systems has been developed to provide for the care and welfare of animals. Using the correct dosage is very important in terms of effectiveness and safety. Drug treatment and delivery strategies can be complicated because of the variety of species and breeds treated, the wide range in body sizes, different animal rearing practices, seasonal variations, and the level of convenience, among other factors. Innovative solutions have been developed to meet many of these challenges—for example, the convenient dosing option offered by topical spot-on formulations for treating external and internal parasites on dogs and cats.

Drugs Given by Mouth

Oral dosage forms (given by mouth) include liquids (solutions, suspensions, and emulsions), semi-solids (pastes), and solids (tablets, capsules, powders, granules, premixes, and medicated blocks).

A **solution** is a mixture of 2 or more components that mix well and form a single phase that is consistent down to the molecular level (such as sugar water). Solutions are absorbed quickly and generally cause little irritation of the lining of the stomach and intestine. However, the taste of some drugs is more unpleasant when in solution. Oral solutions provide a convenient means of drug administration to newborn and young animals.

A **suspension** is a coarse dispersion of insoluble drug particles in a liquid (for example, flour mixed in water). Suspensions are useful for administering insoluble or poorly soluble drugs or in situations when the presence of a finely divided form of the material in the stomach and intestinal tract is required. The taste of most drugs is less noticeable in suspension than in solution because the drug is less soluble in suspension. Suspensions must typically be shaken vigorously just prior to administering.

An **emulsion** consists of 2 non-mixable liquids, one of which is dispersed throughout the other in the form of fine droplets (such as oil and vinegar salad dressing). Emulsions for oral administration are usually oil (the active ingredient) in water. They facilitate the administration of oily substances such as castor oil or liquid paraffin in a more palatable form.

A **paste** is a 2-component semi-solid in which a drug is dispersed as a powder in a liquid or fatty base. It is critical that pastes have a pleasant taste or are tasteless. Pastes are a popular dosage form for treating cats and horses, and can be easily and safely administered by owners.

A **tablet** consists of one or more active ingredients mixed with fillers. It may be a conventional tablet that is swallowed whole or a chewable tablet. Conventional and chewable tablets are the most common forms used to administer drugs to dogs and cats. Tablets can be more physically and chemically stable than liquid forms. The main disadvantages of tablets are the low absorption rate of poorly water-soluble drugs or simply poorly absorbed drugs, and the local irritation of the stomach or digestive tract lining that some drugs may cause.

A **capsule** is usually made from gelatin and filled with an active ingredient and fillers. Two common capsule types are available: hard gelatin capsules for solid-fill formulas, and soft gelatin capsules for liquid-fill or semi-solid-fill formulas. Capsules have no taste and are therefore good for drugs that are otherwise hard to give because of their bad flavor.

A **powder** is a formulation in which a drug powder is mixed with other powdered fillers to produce a final product. Most powders are added to food. Powders have better chemical stability than liquids and dissolve faster than tablets or capsules. Unpleasant tastes can be a factor with powders and are a particular concern when used in food because the animal may not eat all of it. In addition, sick animals often eat less and may not eat enough of the powdered drug for it to be effective.

A **granule** consists of powder particles that have been formed into larger pieces. Granulation is used when combining more than one form of medication. Granulation is especially effective for combining particles that are of different sizes because it helps prevent the separation or settling of the different particle sizes during storage or dose administration. Imagine granola clusters—if you just have granola mix, the smaller pieces fall to the bottom and are not eaten as often, but if you form it into clusters (large granules), you get every type of ingredient in each bite.

Drugs Given as Injections or Implants

A drug that is given parenterally—that is, by injection or as an implant—does not go through the gastrointestinal system. These drugs may be formulated in several different ways for use in animals, including solutions, suspensions, emulsions (*see* page 1119), and as a dry powder that is mixed with a liquid to become a solution or a suspension immediately prior to injection. Dry powders are used for those drugs that are unstable in liquid form.

The majority of **implants** used in veterinary medicine are compressed tablets or dispersed matrix systems in which the drug is uniformly dispersed within a non-degradable polymer. Implants are generally not used in dogs or cats but may be used in horses (for example, an ear implant for reproductive drugs used in mares).

Drugs Applied to the Skin or Mucous Membranes

The dosage forms applied to the skin or mucous membranes that are available for treating animals include solids (dusting powders), semi-solids (creams, ointments, and pastes), and liquids (solutions, suspension concentrates, and emulsifiable concentrates). These are known as topical drugs. Of special interest are transdermal delivery systems that work by carrying medications across the skin barrier to the bloodstream. Examples of these are transdermal gels and patches that are used in pets. There are also dosage forms that are unique to veterinary medicine, such as spot-on or pour-on formulations developed for the control of parasites.

A **dusting powder** is a fine-textured insoluble powder containing ingredients such as talc, zinc oxide, or starch in addition to the drug. Some feel gritty, and some have a smooth texture. Some dusting powders absorb moisture, which discourages bacterial growth. Others are used for their lubricant properties. The use of dusting powders is good for skin folds and not good for use on wet surfaces, as caking and clumping is likely to result.

A **cream** is a semi-solid emulsion formulated for application to the skin or mucous membranes. Cream emulsions are most commonly oil-in-water but may be water-in-oil. The oil-in-water creams easily rub into the skin (commonly called vanishing creams), and are easily removed by licking and washing. Water-in-oil emulsions are skin-softening and cleansing. Water-in-oil creams are also less greasy and spread more readily than ointments.

An **ointment** is a greasy, semi-solid preparation that contains dissolved or dispersed drugs. A range of ointment bases is used. Ointments are often effective at soothing because they block the skin from irritation. Ointments are useful for chronic, dry skin conditions and are not good for oozing or weeping areas of the skin.

A **paste** for skin use is a stiff preparation containing a high proportion of finely powdered solids such as starch, zinc oxide, calcium carbonate, and talc in addition to the drug(s). Pastes are less greasy than ointments. Pastes do not seal wounds.

Solutions are liquid formulations (*see* page 1119). Topical solutions include eye drops, ear drops, and lotions.

A **transdermal delivery gel** consists of a gel that delivers the active drug through the skin to the bloodstream. Not all drugs are suitable for this type of transdermal application, however. Transdermal gels are used to treat several diseases in dogs and cats, including undesirable behavior, cardiac disease, and hyperthyroidism. The dose is applied to the inner surface of the ear, making it easy to administer, especially in cats.

A **transdermal delivery patch** typically consists of a drug incorporated into a patch that is applied to the skin. The drug is absorbed across the skin over a long period of time. One type of pain reliever, which produces reactions like the body's own natural pain relievers, is delivered by transdermal patch in dogs, cats, and horses.

A **spot-on formulation** is a solution of active ingredient(s), which also typically contains a co-solvent and a spreading agent to ensure that the product is distributed to the entire body.

Insecticidal collars are plasticized polymer resins that contain an active ingredient. Collars for the control of ticks and fleas on dogs and cats release the active ingredient as a vapor, a dust, or a liquid, depending on the chemical. The animal's activity is an important factor in how well the insecticide moves from the collar to the animal.

■ EFFECT OF DRUG TREATMENT ON THE FETUS OR NEWBORN PET

An important aspect of medical treatment is the effect the treatment will have on the fetus or newborn when given to a pregnant or lactating animal. Many drugs are capable of crossing the placenta and affecting the fetus. Certain antibiotic drugs are toxic to a fetus, while others may affect developing cartilage, bones, and teeth. Some antifungal drugs and all cancer chemotherapeutic drugs are potentially harmful to a developing fetus. Glucocorticoids may cause cleft palate or other defects in puppies.

When medications are given to lactating animals, the excretion of the drug or its byproducts in milk and the possible effects on the suckling newborn must be taken into consideration.

■ GUIDELINES FOR THE USE OF ANTIBIOTIC DRUGS

Antibiotic drugs are commonly used in veterinary medicine to treat infectious diseases that are caused by bacteria and certain other microorganisms. There are many different classes of antibiotics available for use in animals, including penicillins, cephalosporins, cephamycins, aminoglycosides, quinolones, sulfonamides, tetracyclines, and macrolides. Some are effective against a wide range of organisms, while others are more closely targeted (for example, they may be effective against some bacteria but less effective against other bacteria). Thus, antibiotics are often referred to as broad-spectrum or narrow-spectrum drugs, respectively (*see* TABLE 3).

Successful antibiotic treatment is based on 4 principles: 1) identifying the disease-causing agent and selecting the appropriate drug for treatment; 2) attaining effective concentrations of the drug at the site of infection for a sufficient period of time; 3) choosing a dose rate, frequency, and method of administering the dose that maximizes the likelihood of a cure, prevents relapse, and minimizes the risk of developing resistance while causing no harm to the animal; and 4) using specific and appropriate supportive treatment to

Table 3. Common Antibiotics Used In Animals

Aminoglycosides	Amikacin, gentamicin, kanamycin, neomycin, netilmicin, streptomycin/dihydrostreptomycin
Cephalosporins	Cefadroxil, cefazolin, cephalexin, cephalothin, cephapirin
Imidazoles	Enilconazole, fluconazole, itraconazole, ketoconazole, thiabendazole
Penicillins	Amoxicillin, amoxicillin-clavulanic acid, ampicillin, benzathine penicillin G, cloxacillin, imepenem, penicillin V, potassium clavulanate/amoxicillin, potassium penicillin G, probenecid (prolongs blood levels of penicillins that have short plasma half-lives or that are costly), procaine penicillin G, sodium carbenicillin, sodium penicillin G, ticarcillin
Sulfonamides	Succinylsulfathiazole, sulfadiazine, sulfadimethoxine, sulfathiazole
Tetracyclines	Doxycycline, oxytetracycline, tetracycline
Quinolones	
Quinolone carboxylic acids	Enrofloxacin, norfloxacin, ciprofloxacin, orbifloxacin, pefloxacin, danofloxacin, difloxacin, marbofloxacin, rosoxacin, acrosoxacin, oxolinic acid
Naphthydridine carboxylic acids	Enoxacin, nalidixic acid
Cinnoline carboxylic acids	Cinoxacin
Pyridopyrimidine carboxylic acids	Pipemidic acid, piromidic acid
Quinolizine carboxylic acids	Ofloxacin, flumequine

improve the animal's ability to overcome the infection and associated disease conditions.

The emergence of bacteria that are resistant to currently available antibiotics within the animal or human population is of great concern. When resistance occurs, previously successful drugs can no longer be considered effective treatment, and new drugs must be developed. Resistance may develop in several different ways. However, when used properly (that is, the right antibiotic is used and it is given as prescribed for the appropriate amount of time), antibiotics are less likely to contribute to the selection of antibiotic-resistant organisms.

When given a prescription from your veterinarian for your pet, make sure that it is given exactly as instructed and that the entire prescription is given. Not following dosage schedules or not giving all of the prescription can cause a relapse, a reinfection, or development of antibiotic-resistant organisms.

■ DRUGS USED TO TREAT HEART AND BLOOD VESSEL DISORDERS

Many of the drugs used to treat heart disease in animals are the same medications used in people (*see* TABLE 4).

Positive Inotropes

Positive inotrope drugs increase the strength of the heart muscle by increasing the amount of calcium available for binding to muscle proteins. Increasing the amount of available calcium is done in different ways depending on the drug used. There are 3 classes of positive inotropes: cardiac glycosides, beta-adrenergic agonists, and phosphodiesterase inhibitors.

Angiotensin-converting Enzyme (ACE) Inhibitors

Angiotensin-converting enzyme (ACE) inhibitors are widely used to treat chronic congestive heart failure in dogs and cats. When angiotensin-converting enzyme

Table 4. Commonly Used Cardiovascular Drugs*

Drug	Animal(s)	Drug	Animal(s)
Amrinone	Dog, cat	Lidocaine¶	Dog
Amlodipine	Dog, cat	Mexiletine	Dog
Aspirin	Dog, cat	Nandrolone decanoate	Dog, cat, horse
Atenolol	Dog, cat	Nitroglycerin ointment	Dog, cat
Benazepril	Dog, cat	Nitroprusside	Dog
Boldenone undecylenate†	Horse	Oxymetholone	Dog, cat
Desmopressin	Dog	Phenytoin	Dog
Diltiazem	Dog, cat	Pimobendan	Dog
Digoxin‡	Dog, cat	Procainamide	Dog, cat, horse
Dobutamine	Dog, cat	Propranolol	Dog, cat
Dopamine	Dog	Quinidine sulfate	Dog, cat, horse
Enalapril§	Dog, cat	Quinidine gluconate	Horse
Epoetin alfa	Dog, cat	Stanozolol#	Dog, cat, horse
Folic acid	Dog, cat	Tocainide	Dog
Heparin, high dose	Dog, cat	tPA**	Cat
Heparin, low dose	Dog, cat, horse	Vitamin B₁₂††	Dog, cat
Hydralazine	Dog, cat	Warfarin	Dog, cat, horse
Iron (ferrous sulfate)	Dog, cat		

*Many of the drugs listed are not directly approved by the FDA for use in the species listed. Veterinarians decide what drug and dosage to use for an animal based on their experience, published reports, and continuing education.
†Approved by FDA as a supplemental treatment for debilitated horses.
‡Approved by FDA for treatment of heart failure and arrhythmias in dogs.
§Approved by FDA for treatment of mild, moderate, or severe heart failure in dogs due to mitral regurgitation and/or reduced ventricular contractility.
¶Several FDA-approved products are available; however, none are specifically approved for control of heart arrhythmias.
#Approved by FDA as a sterile suspension and oral tablets for use in dogs.
**Tissue plasminogen activator
††Several FDA-approved products are available.

formation is prevented, the narrowing of the blood vessels that is common in dogs with congestive heart failure is prevented. It also helps reduce the buildup of sodium and water in the body, which is another side effect of congestive heart failure. The use of these inhibitors helps increase the output of the heart and increases the animal's ability to exercise safely.

Vasoactive Drugs

Vasoactive drugs dilate or widen the blood vessels. There are 2 types of dilators.

Arterial dilators are drugs that dilate the arterioles, which makes it easier for the heart to pump blood away from itself. **Venous dilators** dilate the veins coming to the heart and increase the amount of blood that enters the heart.

Antiarrhythmics

Antiarrhythmics help the heart beat in its normal, rhythmic pattern. There are 4 classes of antiarrhythmics, grouped according to how they affect the heart cells. Class I drugs work to fix irregular heart rhythms and abnormal heart beats.

Class II antiarrhythmics work to prevent irregular heartbeats and block the effects of hormones (such as adrenaline) on the heart. Class III antiarrhythmics have no practical applications in veterinary medicine. Class IV drugs are referred to as calcium antagonists or calcium-channel blocking drugs. These work in the same way as Class II drugs.

Hematinics

Hematinics are drugs that increase the amount of hemoglobin (the portion of the red blood cell that carries oxygen throughout the body) and the number of red blood cells in the blood. These are used to treat anemia, a condition in which there are low numbers of red blood cells and too little hemoglobin.

Hemostatics

Hemostatics are used to help the blood clot. There are several types of drugs that function as hemostatics. **Lyophilized concentrates** are applied to the skin or to a particular area to help control capillary (small blood vessel) bleeding. These products are normally absorbed by the body. **Astringents** are used directly at the site of bleeding to control bleeding. They constrict the blood vessels and tissue to help slow and stop the blood flow. **Epinephrine** and **norepinephrine** are used to constrict the blood vessels and decrease blood flow to the tissues. They may be included in topical medications or applied up the nasal passage in tampons to help decrease and stop nosebleeds. **Systemic hemostatics** include fresh blood or blood components that are given to animals that cannot clot correctly.

Anticoagulants

Blood clots can be a serious problem. They can cause strokes or circulation problems and can block blood flow to vital organs. Anticoagulant drugs are used to stop or minimize the clotting process, usually by inactivating the body's natural clotting factors or increasing the rate at which the body dissolves clots.

Drugs Used for Prevention and Treatment of Heartworms

Several macrolide drugs (ivermectin, milbemycin oxime, moxidectin, and selamectin) can be given to prevent heartworm infection in dogs. Macrolides can also be used as preventives in cats. For dogs infected with heartworms, melarsomine dihydrochloride is the only available drug to kill the adult worms. Ivermectin can be used to kill microfilariae and immature heartworms, before giving melarsomine. Macrolides can also be prescribed to treat microfilariae in infected dogs, although they are not approved by the US Food and Drug Administration for this purpose.

■ DRUGS USED TO TREAT DIGESTIVE DISORDERS

A wide variety of drugs can be used to treat disorders of the digestive tract, including ones that affect the rate of movement of food through the intestines, antibiotics, drugs to suppress or induce vomiting, and drugs to treat ulcers or diarrhea.

Drugs that Affect Appetite

Appetite disorders, particularly a lack of appetite, are very common in sick animals. A veterinarian may suggest drug treatment to stimulate appetite for animals that cannot be coaxed to eat (*see* TABLE 5). There are several appetite-stimulating drugs; each drug works in a different way. Your veterinarian will prescribe the best drug for your pet based on how the drug can help stimulate your pet's appetite.

Drugs that Control or Stimulate Vomiting

Vomiting is caused by conditions that stimulate the emetic center of the brain. Sometimes vomiting can be beneficial (such as when a poison or toxin is eaten), but it can also be harmful in a sick or weakened animal that is likely to become dehydrated. Not all animals have

Table 5. Drugs Used to Stimulate Appetite*

Drug	Animal(s)
Boldenone undecylenate	Dog, cat, horse
Cyproheptadine	Cat
Diazepam	Cat
Megestrol acetate	Dog, cat
Oxazepam	Cat
Prednisone	Dog, cat, horse
Stanozolol	Dog, cat, horse

*Many of the drugs listed are not directly approved by the FDA for use in the species listed. Veterinarians decide what drug and dosage to use for an animal based on their experience, published reports, and continuing education.

Table 6. Drugs Used to Control or Stimulate Vomiting*

Drug	Animal(s)
Emetics (drugs that cause vomiting)	
Apomorphine	Dog, cat
Hydrogen peroxide	Dog, cat
Salt	Dog, cat
Syrup of ipecac	Dog, cat
Xylazine	Cat
Antiemetics (drugs that inhibit vomiting)	
Acepromazine	Dog, cat
Butorphanol	Dog
Chlorpromazine	Dog, cat
Cyclizine	Dog, cat
Dimenhydrinate	Dog, cat
Diphenhydramine	Dog, cat
Dolasetron	Dog, cat
Isopropamide	Dog, cat
Meclizine	Dog, cat
Metoclopramide	Dog, cat
Ondansetron	Dog, cat
Prochlorperazine	Dog, cat
Propantheline	Dog, cat

*Many of the drugs listed are not directly approved by the FDA for use in the species listed. Veterinarians decide what drug and dosage to use for an animal based on their experience, published reports, and continuing education.

the ability to vomit, so drugs that induce vomiting should not be given unless directed by a veterinarian or animal poison control specialist (*see* TABLE 6).

Emetic drugs are used to cause vomiting and are usually given in emergency situations after a pet has eaten a poison. They generally remove about 80% of the stomach contents. Syrup of ipecac is a well-known over-the-counter preparation that causes vomiting.

Antiemetic drugs are used to stop vomiting. Continual vomiting is physically exhausting and can cause dehydration, acid-base and electrolyte disturbances, and aspiration pneumonia. Antiemetic drugs are used to control excessive vomiting once a diagnosis has been made, to prevent motion sickness and psychologically-caused vomiting, and to control vomiting caused by radiation and chemotherapy.

Antacids

Stomach ulcers are a common problem in animals, in association with physiologic stress, dietary management, or as a side effect of drugs that can cause ulcers. The common antacids neutralize stomach acid to form water and a neutral salt.

Antacids frequently interfere with the gastrointestinal absorption of drugs that are administered at the same time. Because they are difficult to administer and require frequent dosing in dogs and cats, they are not as popular as newer therapies.

Histamine (H$_2$)-receptor Antagonists

H$_2$-receptor antagonists are used to treat ulcers of the gastrointestinal tract (*see* TABLE 7). They block stomach acid secretion by blocking H$_2$ receptors.

Table 7. Antiulcerative Drugs*

Drug	Animal(s)
Antacids	Dog, cat
Cimetidine	Dog, horse
Famotidine	Dog, horse
Misoprostol	Dog
Omeprazole	Dog, horse
Ranitidine	Dog, horse
Sucralfate	Dog, cat, horse

*Many of the drugs listed are not directly approved by the FDA for use in the species listed. Veterinarians decide what drug and dosage to use for an animal based on their experience, published reports, and continuing education.

Table 8. Antidiarrheal Drugs*

Activated charcoal

Aminopentamide

Bismuth subsalicylate

Diphenoxylate

Isopropamide

Kaolin-pectin

Loperamide

Paregoric

Propantheline

*Many of the drugs listed are not directly approved by the FDA for use in the species listed. Veterinarians decide what drug and dosage to use for an animal based on their experience, published reports, and continuing education.

Drugs Used to Treat Diarrhea

Treatment for diarrhea includes fluids, electrolyte (salt) replacement, maintenance of acid/base balance, and control of discomfort. Antiparasitic drugs or dietary treatment can also play an important role in the treatment of some types of diarrhea. Additional treatment may include intestinal protectants, motility modifiers, antibiotics, anti-inflammatory drugs, and antitoxins (*see* TABLE 8).

Mucosal Protectants and Adsorbents

Drugs such as kaolin-pectin formulas, activated charcoal, and bismuth subsalicylate are popular therapies for diarrhea. They work by protecting the lining of the intestines and/or absorbing the enterotoxins and endotoxins that cause some types of diarrhea.

These are all available as over-the-counter drugs, but they should not be given unless directed by your veterinarian. Some of these may change the color or consistency of feces.

Drugs that Modify Intestinal Action

Gastrointestinal motility is the rhythmic action of the intestines that moves food through the system. **Anticholinergic drugs** are common ingredients in antidiarrheal medications because they significantly

decrease intestinal motility and secretions. They relax spasms of smooth muscles in the intestine and decrease the urgency associated with some forms of diarrhea in cats and dogs, the amount of fluid secreted into the intestine, and abdominal cramping associated with an overactive intestine. Use of anticholinergic drugs is limited in veterinary medicine because few types of diarrhea in animals are classified as overactive.

Antibiotic Drugs

The effects of antibiotic drugs in the treatment of diarrhea are unknown or unproven in most situations. However, young animals are particularly susceptible to diarrhea and inflammation of the gastrointestinal system, and they can deteriorate rapidly from diarrhea. Antibiotics that are known to be effective against a broad spectrum of bacteria should be used in these cases.

Nonsteroidal Anti-inflammatory Drugs (NSAIDs)

Among their many effects, nonsteroidal anti-inflammatory drugs reduce the amount of prostaglandin produced in the body. (Prostaglandin is a hormone involved in the process of muscle contraction.) These drugs may be beneficial with some types of diarrhea. However, nonsteroidal anti-inflammatory drugs should be given cautiously because they can cause adverse gastrointestinal, liver, and kidney effects.

Gastrointestinal Prokinetic Drugs

Prokinetic drugs increase the movement of food through the gastrointestinal tract (*see* TABLE 9). They are useful in the treatment of motility disorders because they help coordinate motility patterns. Unfortunately, some prokinetic drugs can cause serious side effects, which complicates their use.

Cathartic and Laxative Drugs

Cathartics and laxatives increase the motility (movement) of the intestine or increase the bulk of feces (*see* TABLE 10). These drugs are administered to increase the passage of gastrointestinal contents associated with intestinal impaction, to cleanse the bowel before radiography or endoscopy, to eliminate toxins from the gastrointestinal tract, and to soften feces after intestinal or anal surgery. Some cathartics work by stimulating or irritating the nerves of the intestinal lining, while others draw fluid into the intestines

Table 9. Prokinetic Drugs*

Drug	Animal(s)
Cisapride	Dog, cat, horse
Domperidone	Dog, horse
Erythromycin	Dog
Metoclopramide	Dog, cat, horse
Nitazidine	Dog, rat
Neostigmine	Horse
Lidocaine	Horse
Ranitidine	Dog, rat

*Many of the drugs listed are not directly approved by the FDA for use in the species listed. Veterinarians decide what drug and dosage to use for an animal based on their experience, published reports, and continuing education.

Table 10. Cathartic and Laxative Drugs*

Drug	Animal(s)
Bisacodyl	Dog, cat
Castor oil	Dog
Docusate sodium, docusate calcium, docusate potassium	Dog, cat, horse
Lactulose	Dog, cat
Linseed oil	Horse
Magnesium hydroxide (milk of magnesia)	Dog, cat, horse
Magnesium sulfate (Epsom salts)	Dog, cat, horse

*Many of the drugs listed are not directly approved by the FDA for use in the species listed. Veterinarians decide what drug and dosage to use for an animal based on their experience, published reports, and continuing education.

and increase the bulk of feces. Laxatives and fecal softeners work by increasing the water content of feces or the amount of nondigestible material in the intestines.

Anthelmintics

Anthelmintics are drugs that combat parasitic worms, many of which infest the digestive tract. The most effective anthelmintics have a broad spectrum of activity against mature and immature parasites, are easy to give, inhibit reinfection for extended periods, have a wide margin of safety, and are compatible with other compounds.

There are several classes of anthelmintics: benzimidazoles and probenzimidazoles, salicylanilides and substituted phenols, imidazothiazoles, organophosphates, and macrocyclic lactones. Macrocyclic lactones are the drugs most widely used for the treatment and control of nematodes because of their broad spectrum, high efficiency, and persistent activity.

Benzimidazoles

Benzimidazoles treat roundworm and flatworm infections. In horses, benzimidazoles effectively remove almost all mature strongyle roundworms, although third and fourth stage larvae are more difficult to remove. Repeated dosages are thought to be effective because the lethal effect is a slow process. Benzimidazoles are now available and widely used as daily feed additives.

In dogs and cats, benzimidazoles are used for treatment of roundworms, hookworms, and tapeworms.

Tetrahydropyrimidines

These anthelmintics are effective against gastrointestinal roundworms. In horses, pyrantel is effective against adult ascarids, large and small strongyles, pinworms, and the ileocecal tapeworm *Anoplocephala perfoliata*. In dogs and cats, pyrantel pamoate is effective against the common gastrointestinal worms except for whipworms. Oxantel is sometimes added to preparations of pyrantel for dogs so that whipworms are affected.

Organophosphates

The use of organophosphates is declining. Dichlorvos is used as an anthelmintic in horses against small and large strongyles, ascarids, pinworms, and bots and in dogs and cats against roundworms, hookworms, and whipworms. Trichlorfon is used in horses against bots, ascarids, and pinworms and in dogs against roundworms, hookworms, and whipworms.

Macrocyclic Lactones

The macrocyclic lactones (avermectins and milbemycins) are products or chemical derivatives of soil microorganisms belonging to the genus *Streptomyces*.

Ivemectin and moxidectin are the only macrocyclic lactones available for use in horses. Both are effective against a broad range of adult and migrating larval stages of roundworm and insect parasites.

In dogs and cats, ivermectin, milbemycin oxime, moxidectin, and selamectin may be used for control of gastrointestinal roundworms (as well as prevention and control of heartworm infections).

Miscellaneous Anthelmintics

Piperazine is used against ascarid parasites in all species. Praziquantel is used against tapeworms in dogs, cats, and horses. Epsiprantel is used to treat the common tapeworm of dogs and cats. Bunamidine is used to treat tapeworms in dogs and cats. Nitroscanate is used in dogs and cats to treat roundworms, hookworms, and tapeworms.

■ DRUGS USED TO TREAT EYE DISORDERS

The 3 primary methods of administering medications to the eye are topical, local ocular (such as under the conjunctival tissue or into the vitreous portion of the eye), and systemic (given by mouth or injection). The most appropriate method of administration depends on the area of the eye to be medicated.

Drugs Used to Treat Glaucoma

Topical medications, such as gels or solutions containing **prostaglandins, miotics** (drugs that cause the pupil to contract), **beta-blocking adrenergics,** and **topical carbonic anhydrase inhibitors** (a type of diuretic), are the primary drugs for treatment of glaucoma, but these are often supplemented with drugs taken by mouth or injection.

Osmotic diuretics are used for the emergency treatment of sudden and severe glaucoma. Osmotic diuretics are used to reduce the pressure in the eye by reducing fluid buildup. **Oral carbonic anhydrase inhibitors** are also used in the treatment and management of short-term glaucoma. They reduce the amount of fluid within the eye.

Drugs Used to Treat Infectious Disease

Treatment of infectious diseases that affect the eyes will depend on the organism that causes the disease. Viral diseases (such as feline herpesvirus keratitis and conjunctivitis) can usually be treated with topical **antiviral drugs**. If topical treatment does not work, oral or injectable antiviral drugs may be required.

Antibacterial drugs may be given topically, orally, or by injection for most bacterial or protozoal infections. If inflammation is severe, topical corticosteroids or other anti-inflammatory drugs given by mouth or by injection may be helpful in reducing pain and inflammation.

Dogs and cats diagnosed with fungal infections affecting the eye require systemic treatment—that is, treatment with a drug that is distributed to all parts of the body. Along with systemic **antifungal drugs, topical and systemic anti-inflammatory drugs** and **topical mydriatics and cycloplegics** are needed to control pain in the eye.

Drugs Used to Treat Wounds or Trauma

All penetrating wounds of the eye should be considered infected and treated with systemic, broad-spectrum bactericidal **antibiotics**. Antibiotic treatment lasts for at least 14 to 21 days.

Penetrating eye trauma causes severe inflammation, so it is also treated with **nonsteroidal anti-inflammatory drugs**. These drugs are given intravenously or by mouth. Because treatment of eye injuries with these drugs may cause adverse effects on the digestive system, veterinarians often prescribe additional drugs to limit these effects, such as **H$_2$-blockers** or **proton pump inhibitors**.

Drugs Used to Treat Inflammation

Many infectious and noninfectious diseases cause inflammation within the eye (such as inflammation of the optic nerve or uvea). Irreversible damage and blindness may result if not caught early. Both topical and systemic **corticosteroids** and **nonsteroidal anti-inflammatory drugs**

are used to control inflammation, depending on the cause.

■ DRUGS USED TO TREAT BONE AND MUSCLE DISORDERS

Drugs that affect skeletal muscle function fall into several categories. Some, such as **neuromuscular blocking agents**, are used during surgery to produce paralysis. Others, such as **skeletal muscle relaxants**, reduce muscle rigidity and spasms associated with various neurologic and musculoskeletal conditions (*see* TABLE 11). In addition, there are several drugs that influence metabolic and other processes in skeletal muscle, including the nutrients that are required for normal muscle function and that are used to prevent or lessen degenerative muscular conditions. For example, selenium and vitamin E are used to prevent or treat muscular dystrophies such as white muscle disease in foals. The steroidal, nonsteroidal, and various other **anti-inflammatory drugs** are also commonly used to treat short- and longterm inflammatory conditions involving skeletal muscle. Anabolic steroids promote muscle growth and development and are administered in selected cases in which serious muscle deterioration has developed as a complication of another disease (*see* TABLE 12).

Table 11. Skeletal Muscle Relaxants*	
Drug	**Animal(s)**
Dantrolene	Horse
Diazepam	Cat
Guaifenesin	Dog, horse
Methocarbamol	Dog, cat, horse
Phenytoin	Horse

*Many of the drugs listed are not directly approved by the FDA for use in the species listed. Veterinarians decide what drug and dosage to use for an animal based on their experience, published reports, and continuing education.

Table 12. Anabolic Steroids*

Drug	Animal(s)
Boldenone undecylenate	Horse
Nandrolone decanoate	Dog, cat
Stanozolol	Dog, cat, horse

*Many of the drugs listed are not directly approved by the FDA for use in the species listed. Veterinarians decide what drug and dosage to use for an animal based on their experience, published reports, and continuing education.

■ DRUGS USED TO TREAT BRAIN, SPINAL CORD, AND NERVE DISORDERS

There are several categories of drugs used to treat disorders of the nervous system: anticonvulsants; tranquilizers, sedatives, and analgesics; and psychotropic agents.

Anticonvulsant Drugs

Anticonvulsant drugs are used to control seizures, including those caused by epilepsy (*see* TABLE 13). In epilepsy, treatment is essential to prevent overheating, brain damage, and disruption to the body's circulation. During a seizure, also called status epilepticus, anticonvulsants are given intravenously. However, they are usually given by mouth when used for longterm maintenance treatment. These drugs are usually started at a low dose, which is gradually adjusted until control of seizures occurs. To discontinue a drug, even when changing drugs, the dose should be tapered gradually to avoid triggering a seizure.

Tranquilizers, Sedatives, and Analgesics

Tranquilization reduces anxiety and gives a sense of calm without drowsiness. Drug-induced sedation has a more profound effect and produces drowsiness and hypnosis. Analgesia is the reduction of pain, which according to a drug's effect, may be more pronounced in either the

Table 13. Common Anticonvulsant Drugs*

Anticonvulsant Drug	Animal(s)
First-line anticonvulsant drugs	
Bromide (potassium salt)	Dog, cat, horse
Bromide (sodium salt)	
Diazepam	Dog, cat, horse
Phenobarbital	Dog, cat, horse
Second-line (add-on) anticonvulsant drugs	
Clonazepam	Dog
Clorazepate	Dog
Felbamate	Dog
Gabapentin	Dog
Levetiracetam	Dog
Topiramate	Dog
Valproic acid	Dog
Zonisamide	Dog

*Many of the drugs listed are not directly approved by the FDA for use in the species listed. Veterinarians decide what drug and dosage to use for an animal based on their experience, published reports, and continuing education.

body organs or the musculoskeletal system. A number of drugs may be used in animals for tranquilization, sedation, and analgesia (*see* TABLE 14 and TABLE 15). Many psychotropic drugs can function as either tranquilizers or sedatives according to the dose administered, and many sedatives are also analgesics. Also, drugs classified as tranquilizers, sedatives, or analgesics may have additional uses, such as behavior modification or control of nausea and vomiting.

Psychotropic Agents

Anxiolytics, antipsychotics, antidepressants, and mood stabilizers used to treat human behavior disorders are being used more commonly in veterinary medicine as aids to behavior modification treatment. Few veterinary clinical studies have been reported, so guidelines for vet-

Table 14. Tranquilizers and Sedatives without Analgesic Effects*

Drug	Animal(s)
Benzodiazepines	
Diazepam	Dog, cat, ferret, rabbit, horse
Midazolam	Rabbit
Butyrophenones	
Azaperone	Horse
Phenothiazines	
Acepromazine	Dog, cat, ferret, rabbit, horse
Chlorpromazine	Dog, cat, rabbit
Promazine	Dog, cat, horse
Triflupromazine	Dog, cat, horse

*Many of the drugs listed are not directly approved by the FDA for use in the species listed. Veterinarians decide what drug and dosage to use for an animal based on their experience, published reports, and continuing education.

Table 15. Analgesics*

Drug	Animal(s)
Opioid analgesics	
Buprenorphine	Dog, cat, ferret, rabbit
Butorphanol	Dog, cat, ferret, rabbit, horse
Meperidine	Dog, cat, ferret, rabbit, horse
Morphine	Dog, cat, ferret, rabbit, horse
Nalbuphine	Dog, cat, rabbit
Oxymorphone	Dog, cat, rabbit, horse
Pentazocine	Dog, cat, rabbit, horse
Nonopioid sedative analgesics	
Detomidine	Horse
Xylazine	Dog, cat, ferret, horse
Nonpsychotropic analgesics	
Acetaminophen	Dog
Aspirin	Dog, cat, ferret, rabbit, horse
Carprofen	Dog, cat, rabbit, horse
Dipyrone	Dog, cat, horse
Firocoxib	Dog, horse
Flunixin	Dog, cat, ferret, rabbit, horse
Ibuprofen	Dog, cat, rabbit
Indomethacin	Dog, rabbit
Ketoprofen	Dog, cat, rabbit, horse
Meclofenamic acid	Dog, cat, horse
Meloxicam	Dog, cat
Naproxen	Dog, horse
Phenylbutazone	Dog, cat, horse

*Many of the drugs listed are not directly approved by the FDA for use in the species listed. Veterinarians decide what drug and dosage to use for an animal based on their experience, published reports, and continuing education.

erinary use are based on their use in human medicine and on veterinarians' experience in treating pets with these drugs.

Anxiolytics have been used to treat generalized anxiety and panic disorder in humans and may help alleviate or diminish certain fear-related behaviors in animals (for example, thunderstorm anxiety in dogs and social anxiety in cats). **Antipsychotics** are used for nonselective tranquilization and diminishing behavioral arousal. **Mood-stabilizing drugs** are used in human medicine to treat bipolar disorder, impulsivity, emotional reactivity, and aggression. They may be used occasionally in animals (for example, to treat fear-related aggression). **Antidepressants** can be used to treat behavioral disorders, including compulsive behaviors, aggression, and inappropriate elimination. These drugs are classified as tricyclic compounds (tertiary amines, secondary amines), selective serotonin-reuptake inhibitors, and atypical antidepressants.

■ DRUGS USED TO TREAT REPRODUCTIVE DISORDERS

Drugs used to regulate and control the reproductive system are often naturally occurring **hormones** or chemical modifications of hormones. These are often used to induce or suppress estrus, the time during the reproductive cycle in animals when the female displays interest in mating, often called "heat." Some are also used to stimulate testicular function or sperm production. Some of the more commonly used hormones include gonadotropin-releasing hormone and related drugs, follicle-stimulating hormone, human chorionic gonadotropin, equine chorionic gonadotropin, estradiol compounds, progesterone and synthetic progestins, testosterone, and prostaglandins. Another hormone, oxytocin, is used to promote milk production and letdown and to cause contraction of the uterus to either induce labor or to enhance contraction of the uterus after the birth.

Dopaminergic agents may be used to treat false pregnancy in dogs. They can also be used with prostaglandin $F_{2\text{-alpha}}$ for terminating pregnancy (although this use is not approved in the US). **Dopamine antagonists** have shown promise for the manipulation of seasonal breeding species; their use speeds up the onset of estrous cycles in mares in the spring.

▓ DRUGS USED TO TREAT LUNG AND AIRWAY DISORDERS

Drugs used to treat respiratory conditions fall into several categories: cough suppressants, bronchodilators, expectorants, and decongestants. Antibiotics and anti-inflammatory drugs are also important in the treatment of many respiratory diseases.

Cough Suppressants

Cough suppressants stifle the coughing reflex (*see* TABLE 16). Most cough suppressants are narcotics that act directly on the part of the brain that prompts coughing, the medulla oblongata. **Morphine** is an effective cough suppressant at doses lower than those used to control pain or sedate. However, it is not commonly used because of its side effects and the poten-

Table 16. Cough Suppressants *

Drug	Animal(s)
Butorphanol	Dog
Codeine	Dog
Dextromethorphan	Dog, cat
Hydrocodone	Dog
Morphine	Dog

*Many of the drugs listed are not directly approved by the FDA for use in the species listed. Veterinarians decide what drug and dosage to use for an animal based on their experience, published reports, and continuing education.

tial for addiction. **Codeine** is found in many preparations, including tablets, liquids, and syrups. The potential for addiction is significantly lower than that for morphine. **Hydrocodone** is similar to codeine but is stronger. It is combined with an anticholinergic drug to discourage abuse by people. **Dextromethorphan** is not technically an opioid because it does not behave in the same way in the body and is not addictive or analgesic. **Butorphanol** is used as a painkiller and cough suppressant.

When prescribing a cough suppressant, your veterinarian will take into consideration the fact that some are not safe for use in cats. You should never give over-the-counter preparations intended for human use to your pet unless directed by a veterinarian.

Bronchodilators

In certain airway disorders, breathing becomes difficult because the muscles surrounding the airways constrict. Bronchodilators relieve this constriction by relaxing the muscles, which opens the airways and allows air to move more easily in and out of the lungs. Bronchodilators may also help relieve inflammation and clear mucus from the lungs. There are several categories of bronchodilators (*see* TABLE 17).

The **beta-adrenergic agonists** have beneficial effects in the treatment of broncho-

Table 17. Bronchodilator Drugs*

Drug	Animal(s)
Beta-adrenergic receptor agonists	
Albuterol	Dog, horse
Clenbuterol	Horse
Epinephrine	Dog, cat, horse
Isoproterenol	Dog, cat, horse
Terbutaline	Dog, cat, horse
Methylxanthine bronchodilators	
Aminophylline (injectable)	Dog, cat
Aminophylline (oral)	Dog, cat, horse
Theophylline (injectable)	Dog, horse
Theophylline (oral)	Dog, cat, horse
Theophylline (extended-release tablet)	Dog, cat, horse

*Many of the drugs listed are not directly approved by the FDA for use in the species listed. Veterinarians decide what drug and dosage to use for an animal based on their experience, published reports, and continuing education.

constrictive airway diseases. These have been shown to relax the bronchial smooth muscle, decrease the inflammatory response in the airways, and help the cilia clear mucus from the respiratory tract.

The **methylxanthines** are also used as bronchodilators. They cause relaxation of the bronchial smooth muscles, stimulation of the central nervous system, and mild heart stimulation. Methylxanthines also decrease the inflammatory response in the airways and help the cilia clear mucus from the respiratory system.

Anticholinergic drugs are effective bronchodilators that act by reducing the sensitivity of irritant receptors and inhibiting smooth muscles in the respiratory tract.

Anti-inflammatory Drugs

Glucocorticoids (a type of **corticosteroids**) help control inflammation of the airways by preventing the body's release of inflammatory chemicals. Because they suppress the immune system, glucocorticoids are gener-

ally not used in treating infectious respiratory diseases. In cases of severe attacks of allergic bronchitis, asthma, or recurrent airway inflammation, injection of glucocorticoids usually provides rapid relief. For longterm treatment in dogs and cats, oral treatment is usually used.

Antibiotics

Antibiotic treatment may or may not be necessary in the treatment of inflammatory airway diseases. Antibiotics may be prescribed when a true bacterial infection is present or when infection is making existing airway disease worse.

Inhalation Treatment

With inhalation treatment, high drug concentrations are delivered directly to the lungs by nebulizers or metered-dose inhalers. This helps to avoid or minimize certain adverse effects. Also, the drug's effects are seen more rapidly than with other delivery methods. Use of inhalation treatment in asthmatic cats, dogs with chronic bronchitis, and horses with recurrent airway inflammation is promising, but not scientifically based. Drugs available in metered-dose inhalers include several bronchodilators and anti-inflammatory drugs.

Expectorants and Mucus-producing Drugs

Expectorants and mucus-producing drugs make coughs more productive. They do this by increasing the amount of bronchial secretions, in addition to thinning the secretions. This clears the airways and eases breathing. They are usually given by mouth, although some can be nebulized and inhaled.

Decongestants

Decongestants, though commonly used in people to treat the sneezing and runny nose associated with allergies or hay fever, are rarely used for this purpose in animals. The alpha-adrenergic agonist drugs cause local constriction of the blood vessels, reducing swelling and edema.

They can be used topically as nasal decongestants in allergic or viral rhinitis. They can also be used systemically with antihistamines as respiratory tract decongestants. Antihistamines, when combined with alpha-adrenergic agonist drugs, are effective for treatment of allergic rhinitis in humans, but the effectiveness in animals has not been proven.

■ DRUGS USED TO TREAT SKIN DISORDERS

Drugs that may be used in or on the skin fall into several categories—antibiotics, antifungal drugs, antiparasitic drugs, nonsteroidal anti-inflammatory drugs, drugs that modulate the immune system, hormones, psychotropic agents, and vitamin and mineral supplements (*see* TABLE 18).

Several factors may contribute to the signs associated with skin disorders. Each factor should be identified and addressed if treatment is to succeed. Successful treatment of skin diseases may require longterm or lifelong treatment and is frequently a matter of successful control rather than cure.

Antibacterial Drugs

Certain bacteria commonly cause skin infections in animals. Until the particular bacteria can be identified, your veterinarian will probably treat your pet with an antibacterial drug from a class of drugs known to be effective against the most common bacteria. The duration of treatment varies with the type of infection present. In general, superficial infections should be treated for 7 days beyond surface healing; deep infections should be treated 7 to 21 days beyond apparent healing, which may require treatment durations of 8 to 12 weeks.

Antifungal Drugs

Several antifungal drugs are used to treat skin diseases in animals (*see* TABLE 18). Your veterinarian will make a determination, based on the fungus involved and your pet's species, which drug should be used for treatment. These drugs are usually given by mouth, although some may be given topically. The instructions should be followed carefully when these drugs are prescribed, as some may cause gastrointestinal upset or other adverse effects, and others may need to be taken with food or with another drug to increase the effectiveness of treatment.

Antiparasitic Drugs

Antiparasitic drugs are commonly used in all animals to combat infestation with parasites. This includes pests such as fleas and mites that can irritate the skin and cause disease, as well as parasites that live inside the animal's body.

One important class of drugs used to treat parasitic infestations is the **macrocyclic lactones**. Drugs from this class may be used to treat skin disorders caused by parasites, although their use is often off-label. ("Off-label" is a term that describes the use of an FDA-approved drug for a disorder other than that for which it was approved. It is a common practice in both human and veterinary medicine.) Depending on the drug, they may be given orally or topically.

Insect growth regulators halt or disrupt the development of the immature stages of some insects (larvae and/or eggs), leading to their death. These drugs are highly effective against insects such as fleas, flies, and mosquitoes that undergo complete metamorphosis, but they have little or no activity against ticks.

Chloronicotinyls (also known as **neonicotinoids**) kill fleas and lice, but have less activity against ticks. There are currently 2 drugs in this class, both of which have very different methods of action. One is administered topically and appears to paralyze fleas. The other is given orally and affects the nervous system of adult fleas, causing overstimulation and death.

Phenylpyrazoles have a broad spectrum of action and are effective against fleas, ticks, mites, and lice. Phenylpyrazoles are usually given topically.

Table 18. Drugs Commonly Used to Treat Skin Disorders

Class	Specific Drugs
Antistaphylococcal antibiotics	
Cephalosporins	Cefaclor, cephadroxil, cephalexin
Penicillins	Amoxicillin-clavulanate, oxacillin
Fluoroquinolones	Enrofloxacin, marbofloxacin, orbifloxacin
Sulfonamides	Trimethoprim-sulfadiazine, trimethoprim-sulfamethoxazole
Macrolides and lincosamides	Clindamycin, erythromycin, lincomycin
Antifungal medications	Amorolfine, amphotericin B, fluconazole, flucytosine, griseofulvin, itraconazole, ketoconazole, nystatin, potassium iodide, sodium iodide, terbenafine
Antihistamines	Clemastine, clorpheniramine, cyproheptadine, diphenhydramine, hydroxyzine, terfenadine, trimeprazine
Antiparasitics	Cythioate, ivermectin, lufenuron, milbemycin, moxidectin, nitenpyram, selamectin
Glucocorticoids	Betamethasone, dexamethasone, flumethasone, hydrocortisone (cortisol), methylprednisolone, prednisolone, prednisone, triamcinolone
Psychotropic drugs	Amitriptyline, clomipramine, diazepam, doxepin, fluoxetine

Formamidines are effective against ticks. The one drug approved for veterinary use in this category is used as a dip or impregnated in a collar marketed to control ticks in dogs.

Other, older drugs are occasionally used, but many have been replaced by the drugs discussed above, which are often more effective, safer, and better for the environment.

Antihistamines

Antihistamines work by blocking the receptors involved in the processes that cause itching and inflammation. Responses to antihistamines vary considerably, and several may need to be tried to find one that is effective for an animal (*see* TABLE 18). Antihistamines may enhance the effects of nonsteroidal anti-inflammatory drugs, corticosteroids, or fatty acid supplements and may allow dosages of these agents to be reduced in some cases. Some antihistamines can cause drowsiness and gastrointestinal signs. Overdoses can adversely affect the central nervous system and cause death.

Essential Fatty Acids

Fatty acids are important parts of cell membranes and play other important roles in the body, including maintaining healthy skin. They also have anti-inflammatory properties. Essential fatty acids cannot be made by the body and must be supplied in the diet. The essential fatty acids most important for balance in the skin of cats and dogs are linoleic acid and linolenic acid.

Essential fatty acids may be recommended to treat itching inflammatory diseases (such as allergies), conditions that cause crusting of the skin (such as discoid lupus erythematosus), and malformations of the nails or claws. Many commercial products are available. There are few side effects, but inflammation of the pancreas has been rarely reported. Large doses may also cause weight gain or diarrhea.

Hormonal Treatment

Hormonal treatment can be used to treat skin disorders. **Glucocorticoids** (a type of **corticosteroids**) may be used in either an anti-inflammatory or immunosuppressive capacity, depending on the dosage selected. Glucocorticoids are used for hypersensitivity skin conditions, contact dermatitis, immune-mediated diseases, and cancers. They are often prescribed to help curtail itching and inflammation.

Other hormones that may be prescribed to treat loss of hair or fur include thyroid hormone, progesterones, growth hormone, sex hormones, and melatonin.

Immunomodulators

Immunomodulators are drugs that help regulate the immune system's activity. Some drugs stimulate the immune system, while others suppress its actions. These drugs can be used to treat skin diseases and disorders. The most common use of immunostimulants in dogs is for chronic bacterial skin infections. Because the inflammatory process is directed by the immune system, immunosuppressants are often used to treat skin conditions involving inflammation and hypersensitivity (such as allergies), as well as various cancers and some types of arthritis.

Psychotropic Agents

Psychotropic drugs have been used off-label for treatment of feline psychogenic alopecia and canine acral lick dermatitis, syndromes that are characterized by excessive self-licking. Classes of drugs used include antidepressants, antipsychotics, opiate antagonists, anxiolytics, and mood stabilizers (*see* TABLE 18).

Vitamins and Minerals

Many vitamins and minerals play a role in maintaining skin health. Several can be used to treat skin diseases and disorders. **Retinoids**, which are naturally occurring and synthetic compounds with vitamin A activity, have been used for certain conditions involving the sebaceous (oil-producing) glands in the skin. The retinoids used most commonly are isotretinoin and acitretin.

Zinc is critical for the formation of keratin, the substance that forms the basis of skin, hair, and nails. Zinc supplementation can be given in cases of insufficient intestinal absorption, including deficiency syndrome I (Siberian Huskies, Alaskan Malamutes) and syndrome II (rapidly growing dogs on zinc-deficient diets). Diets high in phytates or minerals may inhibit zinc absorption. Supplementation is typically lifelong.

■ DRUGS USED TO TREAT KIDNEY AND URINARY TRACT DISORDERS

Drugs used to treat urinary disorders include antibiotics and antifungal medications for infections, diuretics for kidney failure, and a variety of other drugs for several other disorders.

Antibiotics

Antibiotic drugs are the basis of urinary tract infection treatment. Antibiotic treatment involves determining the type of bacteria present and choosing the appropriate drug. There are many types of antibiotics; your veterinarian will prescribe one that is excreted in an active form in the urine and is known to be effective against the particular bacteria present (*see* TABLE 19).

Many animals with recurrent urinary tract infections are treated with repeated courses of antibiotics. If the underlying cause of the infection is not found, the repeated courses of antibiotics can do more harm than good. Inappropriate treatment with the wrong antibiotic can cause bacteria to become resistant (*see* GUIDELINES FOR THE USE OF ANTIBIOTIC DRUGS, page 1121). Chronic urinary tract infections from highly resistant bacteria are very hard to treat.

If episodes occur more than once or twice yearly, and the causes of the urinary

Table 19. Antibiotic Drugs Commonly Used to Treat Urinary Tract Infections in Dogs and Cats*

Drug	Typical Antibacterial Activity
Amoxicillin	Staphylococci, streptococci, enterococci, *Proteus*
Ampicillin	Staphylococci, streptococci, enterococci, *Proteus*
Amoxicillin/clavulanic acid	Staphylococci, streptococci, enterococci, *Proteus*
Cephalexin/cefadroxil	Staphylococci, streptococci, *Proteus, Escherichia coli, Klebsiella*
Ceftiofur	*Escherichia coli, Proteus*
Enrofloxacin	Staphylococci, some streptococci, some enterococci, *Escherichia coli, Proteus, Klebsiella, Pseudomonas, Enterobacter*
Gentamicin	Staphylococci, some streptococci, some enterococci, *Escherichia coli, Proteus, Klebsiella, Pseudomonas, Enterobacter*
Nitrofurantoin	Staphylococci, some streptococci, some enterococci, *Escherichia coli, Klebsiella, Enterobacter*
Tetracycline	Streptococci, some activity against staphylococci and enterococci at high urine concentrations
Trimethoprim/sulfa	Streptococci, staphylococci, *Escherichia coli, Proteus*, some activity against enterococci and *Klebsiella*

*Many of the drugs listed are not directly approved by the FDA for treatment of the bacteria listed. Veterinarians decide what drug and dosage to use for an animal based on their experience, published reports, and continuing education.

tract infections cannot be found or corrected, longterm low-dose treatment with oral antibiotics may be necessary to prevent new episodes.

Antifungal Drugs

Although uncommon, fungal urinary tract infections occur in dogs and cats. Treatment involves removing any predisposing factors (excessive corticosteroids, urinary catheters) and giving antifungal drugs, with or without urinary alkalinization (*see* BOX).

Cystine-binding Agents

Cystinuria, with the formation of cystine kidney stones, is caused by an inherited disorder. Cystine kidney stones are dissolved with changes in the diet, urinary alkalinization or neutralization, and the use of cystine-binding agents. Once stones are dissolved, changes in the diet can help prevent them from coming back.

Diuretics

Diuretics are used to remove excess water from animals with swelling or volume overload, such as that which occurs with kidney failure. There are several classes of diuretics, grouped by the way they act in the body (*see* TABLE 20). **Loop diuretics** are named because of their effect on the ascending loop of Henle in the kidney. **Carbonic**

Controlling Urine pH

pH is the measure of how acidic or alkaline (basic) a substance is. Urine with abnormally high or low pH can contribute to the formation of certain types of kidney or bladder stones. In dogs, urine pH should be between 7 and 7.5. In cats, it should be between 6.3 and 6.6. **Potassium citrate** can be used to raise the pH, making it more alkaline (basic). **Ammonium chloride** or **DL-methionine** can be used to lower the pH, making it more acidic.

anyhdrase inhibitors work by decreasing the formation of carbonic acid, making more sodium bicarbonate, which takes water with it when it is excreted. Carbonic anhydrase inhibitors also enhance potassium excretion. **Thiazide diuretics** are infrequently used, but they may be given to animals that cannot tolerate the more potent loop diuretics. Thiazides can be combined with loop or potassium-sparing diuretics. They may also be used to treat diabetes insipidus, which affects the kidneys. **Potassium-sparing diuretics** do not cause the loss of potassium, which is beneficial in some conditions in which potassium levels may be low. These are usually used in combination with other diuretics, rather than alone. **Osmotic diuretics** keep water from being reabsorbed in the kidneys.

Other Drugs

Some angiotensin-converting enzyme (ACE) inhibitors (*see* page 1122), may be helpful in treating chronic kidney failure, and may reduce excess protein in the urine in some animals. Dimethyl sulfoxide (DMSO) has been used in dogs with amyloidosis with variable results.

Natural and synthetic hormones may help treat urinary incontinence (*see* Table 21). For example, a nonsteroidal estrogen derivative that closely resembles estradiol has been effective in treating urinary incontinence in female dogs.

Table 20. Diuretics*

Drug
Chlorothiazide
Dimethyl sulfoxide
Furosemide
Hydrochlorothiazide
Mannitol
Spironolactone

*Many of the drugs listed are not directly approved by the FDA for treatment in all species. Veterinarians decide what drug and dosage to use for an animal based on their experience, published reports, and continuing education.

Table 21. Drugs to Treat Urinary Incontinence*

Drug
Diethylstilbestrol
Ephedrine
Phenylpropanolamine
Pseudoephedrine
Testosterone cypionate
Testosterone propionate

*Many of the drugs listed are not directly approved by the FDA for treatment in all species. Veterinarians decide what drug and dosage to use for an animal based on their experience, published reports, and continuing education.

Alpha-adrenergic agents may also be helpful for this condition.

Muscle relaxants may help relieve urine retention due to tightening of the urethral muscles. Other drugs that may be tried include adrenergic antagonists or cholinergic agonists.

ANTIVIRAL DRUGS

The conventional approach to the control of viral diseases is to develop effective vaccines, but this is not always possible. The objective of antiviral activity is to eradicate the virus while minimally impacting the host and to prevent further viral invasion. However, because of their method of replication, viruses present a greater therapeutic challenge than do bacteria.

Viruses are made of a core of nucleic acid (DNA or RNA) surrounded by a protein shell or capsid. Some viruses are further surrounded by a lipoprotein membrane or envelope. Viruses cannot reproduce independently but depend on taking over the host cell's machinery to perform that task. Viral replication occurs in 5 steps: host cell penetration, disassembly, control of host protein and nucleic acid synthesis to produce new viral proteins, assembly of viral proteins, and release of the virus.

Drugs that target viral processes must penetrate host cells; in doing so, they are likely to disrupt normal cellular activities. Antiviral drugs are characterized by a narrow therapeutic margin, meaning that the difference between a dose that is effective and one that causes adverse effects is often small. Treatment is further complicated by viral latency, which is the ability of the virus to incorporate its genome into the host genome. The virus can remain inactive for a long time, then begin reproducing and cause illness again. In vitro susceptibility testing, which is used to tell what drugs a particular virus can be treated with, must depend on cell cultures, and these tests are expensive. More importantly, these laboratory tests do not necessarily predict which antiviral drugs will work in the animal.

Only a few agents have been found to be reasonably safe and effective against a limited number of viral diseases, and most of these have been developed in humans. Few have been studied in ani-

mals, and widespread clinical use of antiviral drugs is not common in veterinary medicine (*see* TABLE 22).

Most antiviral drugs interfere with viral nucleic acid synthesis or regulation. Such drugs generally are nucleic acid analogs that interfere with RNA and DNA production. Other mechanisms of action include interference with viral cell binding or interruption of virus uncoating. Some viruses contain unique metabolic pathways that serve as a target of drug treatment. Drugs that simply inhibit single steps in the viral replication cycle are called virustatic and only temporarily halt viral replication. Thus, optimal activity of some drugs depends on an adequate host immune response. Some antiviral drugs are designed to enhance the immune system of the host.

■ DRUGS USED TO TREAT INFLAMMATION

Inflammation is the response of the body to an injury or infection. It actually helps the body fight off foreign invaders, such as bacteria. Classic signs of inflammation include redness, heat, pain, and swelling; loss of function can also indicate inflammation.

However, inflammation can sometimes become so severe that it has negative effects on the body. In these cases, anti-inflammatory drugs may be prescribed to help reduce or limit inflammation. Several different types of anti-inflammatory drugs are used in veterinary medicine, depending on the cause and severity of the inflammation.

Antihistamines

Antihistamines selectively block specific histamine receptors in the body. One type, known as H_1 antagonists, help reduce the itching and swelling associated with inflammation in certain skin disorders, and are also useful in the treatment of immediate hypersensitivity reactions, a type of allergy.

Table 22. Antiviral Drugs*

Drug	Primary Use
Acyclovir	Feline herpesvirus, Pacheco's disease in birds
Amantadine	
Ganciclovir	
Idoxuridine	
Interferon alpha-2	Feline leukemia virus infection, feline infectious peritonitis, feline immunodeficiency virus infection
Ribavirin	Susceptible viral infections
Rimantadine	
Trifluridine	Herpesvirus infection of the eye
Vidarabine	Herpesvirus infection of the eye

*Many of the drugs listed are not directly approved by the FDA for treatment in all species. Veterinarians decide what drug and dosage to use for an animal based on their experience, published reports, and continuing education.

Corticosteroids

Corticosteroids are the most commonly used anti-inflammatory drugs. They can be highly effective in suppressing or preventing inflammation, but their effects also cause suppression of the immune response, which may increase the risk of infections.

Corticosteroids can be broken into 2 groups: mineralocorticoids and glucocorticoids. Mineralocorticoids are important in maintaining electrolyte (salt) balance. Glucocorticoids play significant roles in carbohydrate, protein, and lipid metabolism, the immune response, and the response to stress. Glucocorticoids can also affect fluid and electrolyte balance.

Glucocorticoids are commonly used to treat allergy and inflammation such as itching skin conditions and allergic lung and gastrointestinal diseases. In short-term allergic reactions or flea allergy dermatitis, these drugs can help relieve itching and limit self-trauma from scratching until the underlying cause is found. Glucocorticoids are also used in the management of chronic allergic bronchitis and feline asthma.

Nonsteroidal Anti-inflammatory Drugs

Nonsteroidal anti-inflammatory drugs (NSAIDs) have the potential to relieve pain and inflammation without the immunosuppressive and metabolic side effects that corticosteroids have. NSAIDs are often prescribed to treat musculoskeletal inflammation, osteoarthritis, pain following surgery, and laminitis and colic in horses.

There are many NSAIDs available for use in dogs, cats, and horses. Some, such as aspirin and acetaminophen are also used to treat pain in people. It is extremely important not to give these drugs to your pet unless directed by a veterinarian, however, as they can have serious adverse effects in certain species of animals. For example, cats have difficulty metabolizing aspirin and it stays in their system for much longer than in dogs, so it is rarely used in this species. Additionally, acetaminophen should never be used in cats.

Chondroprotective Agents

There are certain compounds that have been identified as having a protective effect against inflammation and the degeneration of cartilage that occurs in some types of arthritis or tissue inflammation. Two of these compounds that are familiar to many people are chondroitin sulfate and hyaluronic acid, because they are also used to treat these conditions in people. Research is still ongoing as to the effectiveness and mode of action of these compounds, but it appears that they have few adverse effects.

■ DRUGS USED TO TREAT CANCERS AND TUMORS

Antineoplastic (antitumor) chemotherapy is often used to treat dogs and cats, and it is routinely used for selected tumors in horses. Antineoplastic drugs can be grouped into general categories, based on their biochemical method of action: alkylating agents, antimetabolites, mitotic inhibitors, antineoplastic antibiotics, hormonal agents, and other miscellaneous drugs (*see* TABLE 23).

Chemotherapy drugs are usually given in various combinations of dosages and timing, which are referred to as regimens or protocols. This offers many advantages, because when drugs with different targets or mechanisms of actions are combined, the chances for success are greater.

Chemotherapy may be used in addition to surgery and radiation. Sometimes chemotherapy is started before surgery in an attempt to decrease tumor size or stage of malignancy, thus improving the chances of successful surgery.

The decision to use chemotherapy depends on the type of tumor to be treated, the stage of malignancy, the condition of the animal, and financial constraints. Responses to cancer chemotherapy can range from a decrease in day-to-day signs but no overall increased survival time to a complete remission. Some tumors respond better to chemotherapy than others. For example, canine

Table 23. Drugs Used to Treat Cancers and Tumors

Drug	Mechanism of Action	Main Tumor Types Treated
Alkylating agents		
Cyclophosphamide	Metabolized by the liver to an active form that affects duplication of DNA in actively dividing cells	Lymphoma, sarcomas, mammary adenocarcinoma, lymphocytic leukemia
Melphalan	Affects duplication of DNA in actively dividing cells	Multiple myeloma
Chlorambucil	Affects duplication of DNA in actively dividing cells; slowest-acting alkylating agent	Chronic lymphocytic leukemia, lymphoma
Carmustine	Affects duplication of DNA and RNA in actively dividing cells; not cross resistant with other alkylating agents	Central nervous system cancers (astrocytomas and gliomas), gastrointestinal carcinomas, multiple myeloma
Streptozocin*	Inhibits duplication of DNA; high affinity for pancreatic beta cells	Temporary remission of hypoglycemia resulting from functional pancreatic islet cell tumor
Dacarbazine	Metabolized by the liver to an active form that affects duplication of DNA and RNA in actively dividing cells	Lymphoma (for use in protocols after relapse)
Busulfan	Affects duplication of DNA in actively dividing cells	Chronic myelogenous leukemia, polycythemia vera
Antimetabolites		
Methotrexate	Inhibits metabolism of actively dividing cells	Lymphoma, Sertoli cell tumor, osteosarcoma, metastatic transmissible venereal tumor
5-Fluorouracil†	Interferes with duplication of DNA and may be incorporated into RNA to cause toxic effects	Gastrointestinal, lung, liver, and mammary carcinomas (by injection); skin carcinomas (topical)
Cytarabine	Interferes with duplication of DNA	Lymphoma (including central nervous system), leukemias
Dactinomycin (Actinomycin D)	Interferes with duplication of DNA; inhibits enzymes that affect DNA and RNA duplication; generates free radicals that break up DNA damage and cell membranes	Choriocarcinoma, testicular carcinoma, rhabdomyosarcoma, lymphoma
Antibiotic Antineoplastics		
Doxorubicin	Interferes with duplication of DNA; inhibits enzymes that affect DNA and RNA duplication; generates free radicals that break up DNA and damage cell membranes	Lymphoma, acute lymphocytic and granulocytic leukemia, sarcomas (osteosarcoma, hemangiosarcoma, rhabdomyosarcoma) and carcinomas (mammary, ovarian, small cell lung, thyroid, testicular, prostatic, transitional cell, squamous cell of the head and neck, cervical), plasma cell myeloma, hepatoma, neuroblastoma

(Continued on the following page)

Table 23. Drugs Used to Treat Cancers and Tumors—*(Continued)*

Drug	Mechanism of Action	Main Tumor Types Treated
Mitoxantrone	Degrades and breaks up DNA	Lymphoma, carcinomas (squamous cell, transitional cell, breast, thyroid, kidney), fibrosarcoma, hemangiopericytoma
Bleomycin	Generates oxygen radicals that break up DNA	Carcinomas (testicular, squamous cell of head and neck, cervical, penile) lymphoma, seminoma, malignant teratoma
Mitotic Inhibitors		
Vinblastine	Disrupts duplication of cells	Lymphoma and leukemias, mastocytoma
Vincristine	Disrupts duplication of cells	Transmissible venereal cell tumors, lymphoma and leukemias, central nervous system tumors, mast cell tumors, mammary adenocarcinoma, soft-tissue sarcomas, immune-mediated thrombocytopenia
Miscellaneous		
Cisplatin‡	Disrupts duplication of DNA	Osteosarcoma, carcinomas (transitional cell, testicular, squamous cell of head and neck, ovarian, cervical, bladder, and lung), mesothelioma
L-Asparaginase	Inhibits protein synthesis in tumor cells by binding the amino acid asparagine	Acute lymphocytic and lymphoblastic leukemia and lymphoma
Mitotane (o,p´DDD)	Destroys outer layers of the adrenal gland	Pituitary hyperadrenocorticism, relieves signs of adrenal cortical tumors
Hydroxyurea	Inhibits duplication of DNA by destroying an enzyme that is part of the process	Polycythemia vera, mastocytoma, granulocytic and basophilic leukemia, thrombocythemia
Etoposide	Breaks down DNA	Carcinomas (testicular, small cell lung)
Selegiline	Increases levels of the neurotransmitter dopamine in the pituitary gland	Pituitary hyperadrenocorticism, relieves signs caused by pituitary tumor
Hormones		
Prednisolone	Inhibits duplication of lymphocytes	Lymphoma, mast cell tumors, palliative treatment of brain tumors
Tamoxifen	Antiestrogenic; blocks the effects of estrogen on target tissues	Estrogen-receptor-positive breast carcinomas
Flutamide	Antiandrogenic; competes with testosterone for binding to androgen receptors	Testosterone-receptor-positive prostatic tumors; surgical castration preferred
Leuprolide	Mimics a brain hormone, which leads to reduced pituitary hormones and eventually to decreased concentration of testosterone (males) and estrogen (females)	Testosterone-receptor positive prostatic carcinomas or perianal tumors; surgical castration preferred

*Toxicities are so severe that use is very limited.
†Use on the skin in cats has resulted in fatal brain and liver toxicity.
‡May cause severe, potentially fatal buildup of fluid in the lungs in cats.

lymphoma is usually very responsive to chemotherapy. You should discuss the options and the risks and benefits of each with your veterinarian if you are considering chemotherapy to treat cancer in your pet.

VACCINES AND IMMUNOTHERAPY

The immune system protects the body against "foreign invaders" such as bacteria and other microorganisms that can cause disease. Certain proteins and other molecules of these invaders are known as antigens, and the immune-system defenses of the body respond to antigens by producing antibodies. (For a more detailed discussion of the immune system, *see* INFECTIONS, page 1078.)

Drugs can be used to affect the immune system in several ways. **Specific immunotherapy** is perhaps the most familiar type—it involves giving a specific antigen (such as a vaccine) to cause a specific, controlled immune system response. As a result, vaccines can provoke effective, and often very specific, longterm immunity. **Nonspecific immunotherapy** can cause the immune system to produce proteins and other compounds that strengthen immunity. It may also give the immune system an overall boost to help it resist infection. Nonspecific immunity includes **adjuvants**, which may be added to a vaccine to increase its effectiveness, and **immunostimulants**, which may be given to treat longterm disease in which the immune system may be suppressed.

Types of Vaccines

Several types of vaccines have been developed for use in animals. Traditionally, vaccines were grouped according to whether they contained living or killed organisms. Killed organisms are not as likely to provoke a strong immune response (providing immunity) as living ones. Because of this, vaccines that use killed organisms frequently also include additional compounds,

called adjuvants, intended to increase the overall effectiveness of the vaccine. A **killed vaccine** may contain the entire killed organism or just the portion of the organism that provokes the immune response. A Type 1 recombinant vaccine is also classified as killed.

Although vaccines that include live organisms tend to be more effective, there are some challenges involved in developing them, because the live organisms can also cause disease if not modified in some way. **Attenuated vaccines** are vaccines containing live organisms that have been altered so that they are less likely to cause disease. They can reproduce, which will cause the animal to mount a strong immune response. However, even if vaccines are attenuated, they can sometimes revert to virulence, causing the disease they were intended to prevent. To further ensure safety, Type 2 recombinant vaccines, or **gene-deleted vaccines**, were developed to safeguard against attenuated vaccines reverting to a form that can cause disease. The specific genes that cause disease in the host are found and deleted. The resulting vaccine includes live organisms that can reproduce and generate a strong immune response in the host, but can never cause disease.

Live vectored vaccines, or Type 3 recombinant vaccines, are an alternate method of inducing strong immunity with no risk of reversion to virulence. Using technology, the genes that code for a protective protein are removed from the disease-causing organisms and placed into a "vector" organism that does not cause disease. This vector reproduces in the host, producing high levels of the protective protein. The host develops a strong immune response to this protein, which then protects it from exposure to the original disease-causing organism. These vaccines are essentially free of adverse effects and are very stable.

DNA vaccines make it possible to immunize an animal by just injecting it with the DNA coding for a protein from the disease-causing organism. In addition to preventing diseases, DNA vaccine technology can also be used to treat diseases, including certain cancers.

In most countries, the production of vaccines is strictly controlled and regulated by government authorities. All vaccines are checked for safety and potency.

Giving Vaccines

The simplest and most common method used to give a vaccine is with an injection in the muscle or under the skin. This can be done with a needle or a new needle-free injector. Intranasal vaccines are also available for specific diseases, but they can be difficult to give, especially to large animals. Vaccines can also be given in feed or drinking water, a method that is most often used in the poultry industry. Fish can be vaccinated by immersion in a solution of antigen, which is absorbed through their gills. Transdermal (absorbed through the skin) vaccines are also being developed.

Vaccination Schedules

Vaccines stimulate an immune response, which lasts a varying amount of time depending on the specific vaccine and disease-causing organism. This means that a specific method and schedule of subsequent vaccine administration is needed to maintain immunity. In young animals there are challenges to mounting an immune response that must be considered, including the age of the animal and overcoming the immunity passed to the newborn by the mother. In mature animals some vaccinations must be given yearly, while vaccination every 2 to 3 years is sufficient to ensure immunity with others.

Pet owners should work with their veterinarian to determine the best vaccination schedule for their animal(s). Information on which vaccines are generally recommended for dogs, cats, and horses are found in the Basics chapters for these species. There are few vaccines available for other species of pets. Ferrets should be vaccinated against rabies and canine distemper. Psittacine birds (parrots and parakeets) should be vaccinated against avian polyomavirus.

Adverse Consequences

Modern, commercially produced, government-approved vaccines are generally very safe. The most common risks with vaccines include injection-site reactions (such as pain or swelling, which usually subside within a short time), allergic responses, incomplete inactivation, disease in animals with compromised immune systems, neurologic complications, and, rarely, contamination with other live agents. The stress of vaccination may be enough to activate an infection already present in the animal. Hypersensitivity reactions—which range from mild to anaphylactic shock—can also occur. All animals should be observed for a period of time following vaccination. Discuss with your veterinarian what signs you should watch for. In rare cases, certain vaccines have been linked to development of a type of skin cancer in cats at the site where the vaccine was given (*see* page 511).

Passive Immunity

In addition to vaccination, there are other ways of creating or increasing immunity against disease. **Passive immunity** involves one animal producing antibodies by active immunization, and then transferring those antibodies to a susceptible animal to confer immediate protection. The natural (and very important) form of passive immunization is the transfer of maternal antibodies to offspring across the placenta and in the colostrum (the first milk that is full of essential antibodies). Antisera may be produced in dogs against distemper and in cats against panleukopenia (also known as feline parvovirus enteritis). The effects of passive immunity are only temporary, however, as they only last for as long as the transferred antibody lasts, generally a few weeks.

In the same way, antibodies can be harvested from a portion of the blood to create immune globulin, which can then be given to another animal to provide immunity. For example, tetanus immune globulin (tetanus antitoxin) is given to animals and humans to confer immediate protection against tetanus.

CHAPTER 81

Poisoning

INTRODUCTION

Poisoning occurs when a toxic substance is swallowed, inhaled, or absorbed after coming in contact with the skin, eyes, or mucous membranes. Poisoning is also called toxicosis or intoxication. Because pets are unable to tell whether a substance is poisonous or not, they are often poisoned by eating something toxic, such as antifreeze or a poisonous plant. Pets can also be poisoned by a sting or bite from a venomous insect or snake, or even by a well-intentioned owner giving human drugs that are poisonous to animals.

An animal can be poisoned after a single exposure (with effects most pronounced during the first 24 hours) or after repeated or prolonged exposure to a poison. All toxic effects depend on the dose—the amount of poison present—and on the species. A small dose may be undetectable and have no harmful effects, while a large dose can be fatal.

METABOLISM OF POISONS

Poisons can be absorbed via the digestive tract, skin, lungs, eyes, mucous membranes (such as those of the nose or eye), mammary glands, and uterus, as well as from sites of injection. Toxic effects may be local, or the poison can be absorbed and spread by way of the bloodstream. Some poisons are excreted by the kidneys. Others are excreted in the bile and collect in fat deposits. Still others are excreted in milk. In most cases, the body attempts to detoxify the poison. The liver is most often the location of this metabolic process. Unfortunately, in some cases when the poison is metabolized, it is broken down into compounds that are more toxic than the original compound.

FACTORS AFFECTING THE ACTIVITY OF POISONS

The consequences of poisoning depend on many factors in addition to the actual toxicity of the poison itself. The dose is a primary concern, but the exact amount of poison an animal has been exposed to is seldom known. The length of time and the number of times the animal is exposed are important. The way in which the animal is exposed affects how much of the poison is absorbed, how it spreads through the body, and perhaps how it is metabolized. The time of intake of the poison can also be a factor. For example, if the stomach is empty when an animal eats a poisonous substance, vomiting may occur. If the stomach is partly filled, the poison may be retained and lead to toxic effects. Environmental factors, such as temperature and humidity, affect rates of consumption and even whether or not some toxic agents are present. For example, many plant poisons are associated with seasonal or climatic changes, such as winter cold and rainfall.

Different species can react differently to a particular poison because of variations in absorption, metabolism, or elimination. For example, species unable to vomit, such as horses or rabbits, can be poisoned with a lower dose. The age, size, nutritional status, stress level, and overall health of an animal are important factors. In young animals, metabolism is compromised by underdeveloped systems.

The chemical nature of a poison determines its ability to dissolve. Poisons that dissolve in water spread more easily than those that do not. Substances added to the active ingredient, such as binding agents, outer coatings, and sustained-release preparations, also influence absorption. Generally, as absorption is delayed, toxicity decreases.

Droplet size is an important consideration in sprays and dips, because the dose increases when the droplets are larger. This is one of many reasons to closely follow label instructions and recommended applications. Only formulations intended for animals should be used.

▨ DIAGNOSIS

Diagnosis of poisoning is based on history, signs, tissue changes, and laboratory examinations. Giving your veterinarian a complete history is important to help him or her make an accurate diagnosis and begin appropriate treatment. You should have the following information available: 1) sex, age, weight, and number of exposed or sick animals; 2) a list of signs of illness in the order they appeared; 3) any prior disease conditions; 4) any medications the animal is receiving; 5) possible related events, for example, change in diet or water source, other medications, feed additives, or pesticide applications; 6) description of the environment, including access to garbage, machinery, or vehicles; and 7) recent past locations and when moved (if applicable).

▨ GENERAL TREATMENT

Immediate, life-saving measures may be needed initially. Beyond this, treatment consists of preventing further absorption of the poison, providing supportive treatment, and administering specific antidotes, if available.

Thorough washing with soap and water can usually prevent further absorption of poisons on the skin. If the animal has a long or dense coat, the hair may need to be clipped. For some poisons that have been ingested, vomiting may be induced in dogs and cats. However, vomiting is *not* recommended if the suspected poison could damage the stomach or esophagus on its way up, if more than a few hours have passed, if the swallowing reflex is absent, if the animal is convulsing, or if there is a risk of aspiration pneumonia (vomited material being inhaled into the lungs). If the animal is unconscious, the stomach may be flushed with a stomach tube, or surgery on the stomach may be needed. Laxatives and medications used to empty the bowels may be recommended in some instances to help remove the poison from the gastrointestinal tract.

If the poison cannot be physically removed, sometimes activated charcoal can be administered by mouth to prevent further absorption from the gastrointestinal tract.

Supportive treatment is often necessary until the poison can be metabolized and eliminated. The type of support required depends on the animal's condition and may include controlling seizures, maintaining breathing, treating shock, controlling heart problems (for example, irregular heart beats), and treating pain.

In some cases, there is a known antidote for a specific poison.

▨ ALGAL POISONING

Algal poisoning is a severe and deadly condition caused by heavy growths of toxic blue-green algae in the drinking water. Deaths and severe illness of livestock, pets, wildlife, birds, and fish occur almost worldwide. Poisoning usually occurs during warm seasons when the algal waterblooms are larger and last longer. Most poisonings are seen among animals drinking algae-infested fresh water. Animal size and species sensitivity influence the degree of poisoning. Depending on bloom densities and toxin content, animals may need to ingest only a few ounces or up to several gallons of water to be poisoned.

More than 30 species of blue-green algae have been associated with toxic waterblooms. Some species produce toxins that damage nerve tissue. Others produce toxins that damage the liver, and others damage both nerve tissue and the liver. Death occurs within a few hours when the nervous system is affected because animals stop breathing. Liver failure causes death within a few days.

An affected animal may have muscle tremors, watery or bloody diarrhea, difficulty breathing, and go into a coma before death. A greenish algal stain may be seen on the mouth, nose, legs, and feet. When nerve tissue is affected, signs progress from muscle spasms to decreased movement, abdominal breathing, a bluish tinge to the skin and mucous membranes, convulsions, and death. Signs in birds are similar and also include spasm of the back muscles, which causes the head and legs to bend backward and the trunk to arch forward. In smaller animals, leaping movements often occur before death. In horses that survive sudden poisoning, the nose, ears, and back become sensitive to light, followed by hair loss and skin sloughing.

Affected animals should be moved to a protected area out of direct sunlight, away from the contaminated water supply. Ample quantities of water and good quality feed should be made available. Surviving animals have a good chance for recovery. Activated charcoal slurry may be beneficial if given shortly after toxin ingestion.

Keeping animals away from the affected water supply is essential. If no other water supply is available, animals should be allowed to drink only from shore areas kept free (by prevailing winds) of dense surface scums of algae. Cyanobacteria can be controlled by adding copper sulfate or other algicidal treatments to the water. Copper sulfate is best used to prevent bloom formation, and care should be taken to avoid water that contains dead algae cells, either from treatment with algaecide or natural aging of the bloom. This is because most toxin is freed in the water only after breakdown of the intact algae cells. Algaecide use should comply with local environmental and chemical registration regulations.

ARSENIC POISONING

Arsenic poisoning is caused by many different types of arsenic compounds. Poisoning is relatively infrequent due to the decreased use of arsenic compounds as pesticides, ant baits, and wood preservatives. Arsenites are used in some dips for tick control. Drinking water containing more than 0.25% arsenic is considered potentially toxic, especially for large animals. Cats may be more sensitive than other animals to arsenic poisoning.

Arsenic compounds that dissolve in water are well absorbed after ingestion by mouth. After absorption, most of the arsenic is bound to red blood cells and distributed to body tissues, with the highest levels found in the liver, kidneys, heart, and lungs. In longterm exposures, arsenic accumulates in skin, nails, hooves, sweat glands, and hair. Generally, the gastrointestinal tract, liver, kidneys, lungs, blood vessels, and skin are considered more vulnerable to arsenic damage.

Signs of poisoning are usually sudden and severe, typically developing within a few hours (or up to 24 hours). Arsenic poisoning has major effects on the gastrointestinal tract and cardiovascular system. Loss of blood and shock may occur. Large amounts of watery diarrhea, sometimes tinged with blood, are characteristic, as are severe colic, dehydration, weakness, depression, weak pulse, and collapse of circulation. The course may run from hours to several weeks depending on the quantity of arsenic ingested. In very severe poisoning, animals may simply be found dead.

In animals that have been recently exposed and are not yet showing signs, vomiting may be induced (in species that can vomit), followed by activated charcoal and a medication that causes emptying of the bowels. In dogs and cats, this may be followed 1 to 2 hours later by a medicine that prevents damage to the gastrointestinal tract, such as kaolin-pectin. Fluids are given as needed.

In animals already showing signs of poisoning, fluid treatment, blood transfusion (if needed), and dimercaprol (an antidote to arsenic) are recommended. Severely affected animals need supportive treatment, including intravenous fluids to restore blood volume and correct dehydration. Kidney and liver function should be monitored during treatment.

BRACKEN FERN POISONING

Bracken fern is widely distributed in upland and marginal areas throughout North and South America, Europe, Australia, and Asia. Ingestion of significant quantities results in signs of poisoning related to thiamine deficiency. The toxic effects appear to be cumulative and may require 1 to 3 months to develop, depending on the species of animal, quantity consumed, time of year, and other factors. Both leaves and rootstocks may be toxic. Most severe poisonings are seen after periods of drought when food is scarce. However, the plant is toxic even when present as a contaminant in hay, and cases have occurred in stabled animals. Horses seem to be particularly susceptible.

In horses, signs of bracken-induced thiamine deficiency (bracken staggers) include loss of appetite, weight loss, lack of coordination, and a crouching stance with the back and neck arched and the feet placed wide apart. When the horse is forced to move, its muscles may tremble. In severe cases, the heartbeat is very rapid and irregular. Death (usually 2 to 10 days after onset) is preceded by convulsions, muscle spasms, and spasms of the back muscles that cause the head and lower limbs to bend backward and the trunk to arch forward. The rectal temperature is usually normal but may reach 104°F (40°C).

Plants other than bracken fern, such as horsetail and turnip, can also cause thiamine deficiency. In horses, the condition must be distinguished from other nervous system disorders, including rabies or poisoning from *Crotalaria* species or ragwort. Blood tests can confirm the diagnosis.

Treatment is highly effective if thiamine deficiency is diagnosed early. Injection of a thiamine solution followed by oral supplementation is suggested. Animals similarly exposed but not yet showing signs should also be treated with thiamine, because signs can develop days or weeks after the source of bracken has been removed.

Bracken is usually grazed when more suitable food is not available, although individual animals may develop a taste for the plant, particularly the young tender shoots and leaves. The problem most often shows up in early spring (tender bracken shoots) or late summer (poor pasture conditions). The disease has been prevented in horses by improving pasture management and fertilization or by alternating bracken-contaminated and noncontaminated pasture at 3-week intervals.

Bracken fern growth can be hindered by close grazing or trampling in alternate grazing pasture systems. In time, bracken can be eliminated from a pasture using this approach or by regular cutting of the mature plant or, if the land is suitable, by deep plowing. Herbicide treatment using asulam or glyphosate can be an effective method of control, especially if combined with cutting before treatment.

■ CANTHARIDIN POISONING (BLISTER BEETLE POISONING)

Cantharidin is found in more than 200 species of beetles throughout the continental US. Beetles of the genus *Epicauta* are most often associated with toxicosis in horses. The striped blister beetles are particularly troublesome in the southwest.

Blister beetles usually feed on various weeds and occasionally move into alfalfa fields in large swarms. These insects live in groups and may be found in large numbers in hay when it is baled. One flake of alfalfa may contain several hundred beetles, but a flake from the other end of the same bale may have none. Animals are usually exposed by eating alfalfa hay or alfalfa products that contain blister beetles.

Cantharidin is odorless, colorless, and highly irritating. It causes blisters when in contact with skin or mucous membranes. As little as 0.1 to 0.2 ounces (4 to 6 grams) of dried beetles may be deadly to a horse. The toxicity of cantharidin does not decrease in stored hay, and cantharidin is also toxic to people, dogs, cats, rabbits, rats, cattle, sheep, and goats.

The severity of signs associated with cantharidin poisoning varies according to dose. Signs can range from mild depression or discomfort to severe pain, shock, and death. Common signs include abdominal pain, depression, loss of appetite, frequent attempts to drink small amounts of water or submerge the muzzle in water, and frequent attempts to urinate. Signs can last from hours to days. Affected horses always have dark, congested mucous membranes, even if other signs are barely noticeable. Horses that ingest a large amount of toxin may show signs of severe shock and die within hours.

Laboratory tests can detect cantharidin in stomach contents or urine. The amount of cantharidin in urine becomes too small to be detected in 3 to 4 days, so urine should be collected early in the course of disease for analysis. Microscopic evaluation of stomach contents of fatally poisoned horses may reveal fragments of blister beetles.

There is no specific antidote for cantharidin, and supportive treatment must be prompt to be successful. Administration of mineral oil helps flush the gastrointestinal tract, and repeated dosing may be recommended. Activated charcoal may be helpful if given early. Calcium and magnesium supplementation for prolonged periods is almost always recommended. Other supportive treatment includes administration of fluids, pain relievers, and medication that increases urine output. The outlook for affected horses improves daily if no complications occur.

Prevention is aimed at feeding beetle-free hay. The hay field must be scouted before it is cut and during baling, because the insects can be crushed during cutting, crimping, or baling of hay. Areas of the field that contain swarms of beetles must be avoided for a few days because most of the insects will leave. Once the beetles have left, these areas can be harvested.

First-cutting hay is almost always free of blister beetles, because the insects overwinter as subadults and usually do not emerge until late May or June in the southwest. Likewise, the last cutting of hay is often safe, because it is usually harvested after the adult insects are no longer active.

■ COAL-TAR POISONING

Coal-tar poisoning is often caused by chewing on or eating items that contain coal tar. Typical sources are clay pigeons, tar paper, creosote-treated wood, and bitumen-based flooring. Effects include liver damage with signs of jaundice, fluid build-up within the stomach, anemia, and death.

Coal tar contains 3 toxins: phenol, cresol, and pitch. Phenol is the most important toxin in coal-tar products. Cresols are used as disinfectants and are readily absorbed through the skin. Cats are especially sensitive to both phenol and cresol. Because cresol is toxic to wood-destroying fungi and insects, it is used as a wood preserver. Pitch is used as a binder in clay pigeons, road asphalt, insulation, tar paper, and roofing compounds. It is also used to cover iron pipes and to line wooden water tanks.

Diagnosis of coal-tar poisoning requires excluding poisoning by toxic plants and deficiency of vitamin E or selenium. Fragments of clay pigeons, tar paper, or other sources of coal tars found in the gastrointestinal tract, or chemical detection of coal-tar products in the liver, kidneys, blood, or urine can confirm the diagnosis.

There is no specific antidote for coal-tar poisoning. Supportive treatment is helpful, along with activated charcoal and medicines that cause the bowels to empty to reduce absorption. Antibiotics and high-quality protein diets may help recovery.

■ COPPER POISONING

Various breeds of dogs, especially Bedlington Terriers, have an inherited sensitivity to copper poisoning. Short-term poisoning is usually seen after accidental administration of excessive amounts of copper salts, which are sometimes part of medications for parasitic worms.

Low levels of molybdenum or sulfate in the diet can increase how much copper is absorbed and influence longterm copper poisoning. This can be caused by eating certain plants, such as subterranean clover.

Signs include abdominal pain, diarrhea, loss of appetite, dehydration, and shock. If the animal survives the gastrointestinal disturbances, destruction of red blood cells and blood in the urine may develop after 3 days. Diagnosis is confirmed by finding copper in the feces, kidneys, blood, or liver.

Often, treatment is not successful. Gastrointestinal sedatives and symptomatic treatment for shock may be useful. Medicines designed to remove toxic metals from the body may be useful if given early. Dietary supplementation with zinc acetate may reduce copper absorption.

■ CYANIDE POISONING

Cyanide kills tissues by lowering their ability to use oxygen. (*See also* SORGHUM POISONING [SUDAN GRASS POISONING], page 1208.) Cyanides are found in plants, fumigants (such as disinfectants), soil sterilizers, fertilizers, and rodent poisons (rodenticides). Poisoning can result from improper or malicious use, but another frequent cause is ingestion of plants that contain cyanogenic glycosides. This is most common in livestock. *Eucalyptus* species, kept as ornamental houseplants, have been implicated in deaths of dogs and cats.

Signs can begin within 15 to 20 minutes to a few hours after animals consume toxic plants. The animals become excited and breathe rapidly with a rapid heartbeat. Drooling, watery eyes, vomiting, and voiding of urine and feces may occur. Muscle spasms are common. Mucous membranes are bright red at first but then become a bluish color. Death usually occurs in 30 to 45 minutes during severe convulsions. Animals that live 2 hours or more after signs begin may recover, unless cyanide continues to be absorbed from the gastrointestinal tract.

The history, signs, and finding hydrocyanic acid in diagnostic specimens support a diagnosis of cyanide poisoning. The suspected source of poisoning (plant or otherwise), stomach contents, blood, liver, and muscle may all be tested for cyanide. If cyanide poisoning is suspected, it is important that specimens for testing are collected as soon as possible after death, preferably within 4 hours.

Immediate treatment is extremely important. Sodium nitrite and sodium thiosulfate are used as an antidote. Oxygen may also be helpful, especially in dogs and cats.

Pasture grasses (for example, Sudan grass and sorghum-Sudan grass hybrids) should not be grazed until they are 15 to 18 inches tall, and forage sorghums should be several feet tall. Animals should be fed before first turning out to pasture. Free-choice salt and mineral with added sulfur may help protect against toxicity. Grazing should be monitored closely during periods of environmental stress, for example, drought or frost. Abundant regrowth of sorghum can be dangerous. These shoots should be frozen and wilted before grazing. Although the process of curing sorghum hay and silage usually decreases the potential for cyanide toxicity, hazardous concentrations can still be present. Feeds should be analyzed before use if cyanide is suspected.

■ ETHYLENE GLYCOL (ANTIFREEZE) POISONING

Most ethylene glycol poisonings are associated with ingestion of radiator antifreeze. All animals are susceptible, with dogs and cats being affected most often. Ethylene glycol poisoning is common because antifreeze is widely used, it has a sweet taste and small lethal dose (only 3 to 4 teaspoons in dogs, 1 to 2 teaspoons in cats), and it is often stored and disposed of improperly. Sources of ethylene glycol other than antifreeze include some heat-exchange fluids used in solar collectors and ice-rink freezing equipment and some brake and transmission fluids. Absorption through the skin from topical products that contain ethylene glycol has caused toxicity in cats.

Ethylene glycol poisoning is most common in temperate and cold climates because antifreeze is used both to decrease the freezing point and to increase the boiling point of radiator fluid. In colder climates, ethylene glycol poisoning is often seasonal, with most cases occurring in the fall, winter, and early spring.

Signs begin almost immediately and resemble alcohol (ethanol) poisoning. Dogs and cats vomit due to gastrointestinal irritation, are excessively thirsty, and pass large amounts of urine. Neurologic signs

Antifreeze is a common cause of poisoning in dogs and cats due to its sweet taste.

develop, including depression, stupor, and lack of coordination. As the animal becomes more depressed, it drinks less and becomes dehydrated. Dogs may appear to briefly recover from these signs about 12 hours after ingestion. Severe kidney failure usually develops between 36 and 72 hours in dogs and between 12 and 24 hours in cats. Signs include a lack of energy, loss of appetite, dehydration, vomiting, diarrhea, mouth ulcers, drooling, rapid breathing, and possibly seizures or coma. The kidneys are often swollen and painful.

Diagnosis is often difficult because signs are similar to signs in other types of central nervous system disease or trauma, gastroenteritis, pancreatitis, diabetes, and severe kidney failure due to other causes. If ingestion of ethylene glycol is not witnessed, diagnosis is usually based on a combination of history, physical examination, and laboratory data.

The prognosis worsens as more time elapses between ingestion and treatment. Treatment involves reducing further absorption of ethylene glycol by inducing vomiting or flushing the stomach (or both), followed by administration of activated charcoal and sodium sulfate within 1 to 2 hours of ingestion. Once absorption has occurred, excess fluids are given to force the excretion of ethylene glycol through increased urine production and to correct dehydration. An antidote to ethylene glycol

is available for dogs, but is only effective if given before kidney failure develops. In cats, intravenous treatment with ethanol can be helpful if given early after ingestion of antifreeze. In dogs and cats with severe kidney failure, the outlook is poor.

Antifreeze should be stored securely, and old antifreeze should be discarded. Any antifreeze leaks should be cleaned up immediately. The area should then be covered with cat litter, sawdust, or another absorbent material to discourage pets from licking any small amount left on the ground.

Brands of antifreeze that contain propylene glycol instead of ethylene glycol are available. Although ingestion of propylene glycol is associated with a toxic syndrome similar to that of ethylene glycol poisoning, propylene glycol is less toxic that ethylene glycol and the outlook is usually better.

■ FLUORIDE POISONING

Fluorides are found throughout the environment and originate naturally from rocks and soil or from industrial processes. Toxic quantities of fluorides occur naturally. In certain areas, drinking water from deep wells may contain high levels of fluorides. Volcanic ash may be high in fluoride. Wastes from industrial processes, fertilizers, and mineral supplements are the most common causes of longterm fluoride poisoning. The fluoride-containing gases and dusts from manufacturing of fertilizers, mineral supplements, metal ores (steel and aluminum), and certain enamelling processes may contaminate forage crops. A 100-gram tube of fluoride toothpaste may contain 75 to 500 milligrams of sodium fluoride, depending on the brand.

Mouth or teeth-cleaning products present a danger to pets, especially dogs. Sodium fluoride at a dosage of 5 to 10 milligrams per kilogram can be fatal, and toxic effects can occur at less than 1 milligram per kilogram. Fluoride is absorbed quickly (most within 90 minutes). The stomach and intestines become inflamed, and the heart beats rapidly and irregularly. Nervous signs may also be seen, followed by collapse and death within a few hours of fluoride ingestion.

At high levels, fluorides bind calcium and replace the mineral part of bone. Longterm ingestion of fluoride at lower levels can cause changes in the enamel of developing teeth, leading to mottling, staining, and rapid wear. Signs develop in many animals when fluoride builds up in the bone. This results in abnormal bony growths and the hardening and thickening of tissue (sclerosis). Growing bones in the young and the ribs, jaws, and long bones are most affected.

A developing fluoride poisoning can be recognized by the following criteria (from most to least reliable): 1) chemical analyses to determine the amount of fluoride in the diet, urine, bones, and teeth; 2) tooth effects, in animals exposed at time of permanent teeth development; 3) lameness, as the result of fluoride buildup in bone; and 4) overall signs of loss of appetite and energy, weight loss, muscular wasting, and general mental and physical debilitation.

Severe fluoride poisoning can be treated with calcium gluconate given intravenously and magnesium hydroxide or milk given by mouth. This can help bind the fluoride before it is absorbed. In longterm exposure, control is difficult unless animals are removed from affected areas. Feeding calcium carbonate, aluminum oxide, aluminum sulfate, magnesium metasilicate, or boron can decrease absorption or increase excretion of fluoride, offering some control of longterm fluoride poisoning under some conditions. However, no treatment has been shown to cure the longterm effects of fluoride toxicity.

▓ FOOD HAZARDS

Many types of foods can cause illness in pets. Some of the most common examples are discussed below.

Avocado

All parts of the avocado—the fruit, leaves, stems, and seeds—can cause poisoning in animals. The leaves are the most toxic part. Horses, rabbits, guinea pigs, budgerigars, canaries, cockatiels, and fish are susceptible. Caged birds appear more sensitive to the effects of avocado. Budgerigars fed very small amounts of avocado fruit (0.04 ounces [1 gram]) can become agitated and begin feather pulling. An amount of 0.3 ounces (8.7 grams) of mashed avocado fruit can cause death within 48 hours.

In mammals and birds, heart muscle can be damaged within 24 to 48 hours of eating avocado. Horses may develop swelling of the head, tongue, and brisket. Birds develop a lack of energy, difficulty breathing, loss of appetite, swelling beneath the skin of neck and chest, and death. In nursing mammals, the mammary glands become inflamed within 24 hours of eating avocado. Affected mammary glands are firm and swollen, and milk production decreases by 75%.

Diagnosis of avocado poisoning relies on history of exposure and signs. There is no specific test to confirm the diagnosis. Treatment includes nonsteroidal anti-inflammatory drugs, pain relievers, and medications for congestive heart failure.

Bread Dough

Raw bread dough made with yeast poses hazards when eaten, including bloated stomach, metabolic abnormalities, and central nervous system depression. Although all species can be affected, dogs are most commonly involved because of their tendency to eat anything.

The warm, moist environment of the stomach serves as an efficient incubator for yeast to replicate, which expands the dough mass. The distended stomach reduces the flow of blood to the stomach wall and can result in breathing difficulties. The products of yeast fermentation include ethanol, which is absorbed into the bloodstream and results in poisoning and metabolic abnormalities.

Early signs can include unproductive attempts at vomiting, a distended stomach, and depression. As poisoning progresses, the animal becomes disoriented and uncoordinated. Eventually, severe depression, weakness, coma, dangerously low body temperature, or seizures may be seen. The expanding dough can also cause the digestive tract to twist abnormally in susceptible dog breeds.

A presumptive diagnosis is based on history of exposure, signs, and increased ethanol levels in the blood.

In animals that have eaten dough but are not yet showing any signs, inducing vomiting may be tried. However, the glutinous nature of the dough makes it difficult to vomit up. If vomiting is unsuccessful, the stomach may be flushed with cold water to slow the rate of yeast fermentation and help remove the dough. In some cases, the dough mass may need to be removed by surgery. Additional treatment includes medications to correct metabolic abnormalities and disturbances in heart rhythm, as well as to maintain normal body temperature. Fluids are administered to increase urine output and elimination of alcohol.

Chocolate

Ingestion of chocolate can result in potentially life-threatening heart rhythm abnormalities and central nervous system disturbances. Many species are susceptible, but chocolate poisoning is most common in dogs because of their tendency to eat any-

Chocolate poisoning is most common in dogs.

thing and the fact that chocolate is readily available. Deaths have also been reported in animals that have eaten mulch containing cocoa-bean hulls.

The toxic substances in chocolate are theobromine and caffeine. The following products are listed in order from highest to lowest of the amount of toxic substances they contain: dry cocoa powder, unsweetened (baker's) chocolate, cocoa bean hulls, semisweet chocolate and sweet dark chocolate, and milk chocolate. White chocolate contains insignificant amounts of theobromine and caffeine.

Theobromine and caffeine stimulate the central nervous system, increase urine output, and cause a rapid heartbeat. Severe signs and deaths vary depending on individual sensitivity to theobromine and caffeine. One ounce of milk chocolate per pound of body weight is a potentially fatal dosage in dogs.

Signs of poisoning usually begin within 6 to 12 hours of eating chocolate. The animal may become excessively thirsty, vomit, have diarrhea, and become restless. Signs may progress to hyperactivity, lack of coordination, tremors, and seizures. The animal may pass large amounts of urine. A very rapid and irregular heartbeat, rapid breathing, a bluish tinge to the skin and mucous membranes, high blood pressure, fever, and coma may develop.

Diagnosis is based on history of exposure and signs.

Animals showing signs of chocolate poisoning are stabilized with medications for tremors, seizures, and heart rhythm abnormalities. Fluids are given to increase urine output and excretion of theobromine and caffeine in the urine. In animals that are not yet showing signs, vomiting can be induced, followed by repeated doses of activated charcoal. Signs may persist up to 72 hours in severe cases.

Macadamia Nuts

Dogs are the only species in which illness after eating macadamia nuts has been reported. Within 12 hours of ingestion, dogs may vomit and become weak, depressed, and uncoordinated. Tremors and a fever may also be seen. Signs generally resolve within 12 to 48 hours. Diagnosis is based on history of exposure, signs, and excluding other possible conditions.

If the dog has eaten the nuts recently and is not yet showing signs, vomiting should be induced. Activated charcoal can also be helpful. Fortunately, most dogs recover without specific treatment. Severely affected dogs may need supportive treatment, including fluids, pain relievers, and medications to control the fever.

Raisins and Grapes

Ingestion of grapes or raisins has led to kidney failure in some dogs, and it has been reported in 1 cat. The amount of grapes associated with kidney injury in dogs is about 32 grams per kilogram. The amount of raisins associated with signs ranges from 11 to 30 grams per kilogram.

Dogs develop vomiting and/or diarrhea within 6 to 12 hours of eating grapes or raisins. Other signs include lack of energy, loss of appetite, abdominal pain, weakness, dehydration, excessive thirst, and tremors. Kidney failure develops within 1 to 3 days and usually results in death.

Diagnosis is based on history of exposure, signs, and excluding other causes of kidney failure.

If the animal has eaten the grapes or raisins within the last 15 to 20 minutes, vomiting can be induced, followed by administration of activated charcoal. If the animal has eaten a very large amount, or if vomiting or diarrhea has developed, fluids are given for 48 hours to increase urine output. If the dog is producing a small amount of urine, medications can be given to stimulate more urine production. If the dog is not producing any urine, survival is unlikely.

▓ FUNGAL POISONING

Important mycotoxic (fungal poisoning) diseases are seen in domestic animals worldwide (*see* TABLE 24). Mycotoxicoses are diseases caused by toxins of fungi. They can result from exposure to feed or bedding contaminated with toxins that can be produced when various fungi or molds grow on cereals, hay, straw, pastures, or any other fodder.

Sometimes 2 or more mycotoxins may be present in feedstuffs, making the signs more difficult to evaluate. Feed intake is often reduced, and animals may have reproductive difficulties. Some mycotoxins suppress the immune system, which can result in secondary disease caused by viruses, bacteria, or parasites. Other diagnoses must be excluded by evaluation of the history and signs and by diagnostic testing.

There are no specific antidotes for mycotoxins. Removing the source of the toxin (such as the moldy feedstuff) is necessary to prevent further exposure. If financial circumstances do not allow for disposal of the moldy feed, it can be blended with unspoiled feed just before feeding to reduce the toxin concentration, or fed to less susceptible species. When contaminated feed is blended with good feed, care must be taken to prevent further mold growth by thorough drying or by adding organic acids (for example, propionic acid) to the feed. Aluminosilicate can prevent the absorption of some mycotoxins (for example, aflatoxin).

Aflatoxicosis

Aflatoxins are produced by certain *Aspergillus* fungi on peanuts, soybeans, corn (maize), and other cereals either in the field or during storage when moisture content and temperatures are high enough for mold growth. Usually, this means day and night temperatures are consistently higher than 70°F (21°C). Signs in mammals vary depending on species, sex, age, nutritional status, amount of aflatoxins in the diet, and the length of time the diet has been fed. Aflatoxicosis is seen in many parts of the world. Dogs can be affected.

High doses of aflatoxins result in severe liver damage, while prolonged low dosages result in reduced growth rate and liver enlargement. In short-term outbreaks, deaths occur after a short period of a lack of appetite. Blood vessels rupture, causing internal bleeding, and jaundice often develops. Less severe outbreaks are more usual, and poor condition, weakness, loss of appetite, and sudden deaths can be seen. Breathing difficulties often develop, and response to treatment is usually poor.

History and examination of body tissues after death can point to the type of toxin. Feed should be analyzed for the presence and levels of aflatoxins. Aflatoxin can sometimes be detected in urine or the kidneys, or in milk of milk-producing animals if toxin intakes are high.

Batches of feed should be monitored for contamination with aflatoxin. Young, newly weaned, pregnant, and milk-producing animals require special protection from feeds suspected of being toxic. Contaminated feed can be diluted with noncontaminated feedstuff.

Fescue Poisoning (Summer Fescue Poisoning)

This warm season condition is characterized by reduced feed intake, weight gains, or milk production. Horses are affected during the summer when they are grazing or being fed tall fescue forage or seed contaminated with the fungus *Acremonium coenophialum*. The severity of the condition varies from field to field and year to year.

Signs may appear within 1 to 2 weeks after fescue feeding is started and include reduced performance, fever, rapid breathing, rough coat, lower prolactin levels (a hormone), and excessive drooling. The animals seek wet spots or shade. Decreased reproductive performance, including birth of weak foals and lack of milk production, can be seen in horses. The severity increases when environmental temperatures are higher than 75 to 80°F (24 to 27°C) and if high nitrogen fertilizer has been applied to the grass.

For control, toxic tall fescue pastures must be destroyed and reseeded with seed that does not contain the fungus, because the fungus transfers from plant to plant primarily through infected seed. Other measures to reduce severity of the disease include not using pastures during hot weather, diluting tall fescue pastures with interseeded legumes, clipping pastures to reduce seed formation, and offering other feedstuffs.

Fumonisin Poisoning

Equine leukoencephalomalacia is a mycotoxic disease of the central nervous system that affects horses, mules, and donkeys. It is seen in North and South America, South Africa, Europe, and China. It is associated with the feeding of moldy corn (maize), usually over a period of several weeks. Fumonisins are produced worldwide primarily by certain *Fusarium* fungi. Conditions favoring fumonisin production include a period of drought during the growing season, followed by cool, moist conditions during pollination and kernel formation.

Signs include mild depression, drowsiness, paralysis of the throat, blindness, circling, staggering, and a reluctance to stand. The signs may last several hours or several weeks, but are usually present 1 to 2 days. Brain damage is characteristic. Liver damage can be seen and lead to jaundice. Horses may develop leukoencephalomalacia from prolonged exposure to very small amounts of fumonisins in the diet.

No treatment is available. Avoiding moldy corn is the only prevention, although this is difficult because the corn may not look moldy or it may be part of a mixed feed. However, because most of the toxin is present in broken or small, poorly formed kernels, fumonisin concentration can be markedly reduced by cleaning grain to remove the screenings. Corn suspected of containing fumonisins should not be fed to horses.

Mycotoxic Lupinosis

Lupines cause 2 distinct forms of poisoning—lupine poisoning and lupinosis. Lupine poisoning is a nervous syndrome

Table 24. Fungal Poisoning in Domestic Animals

Disease	Fungi or Molds	Regions Where Reported
Aflatoxicosis	*Aspergillus flavus, A. parasiticus*	Widespread (warmer climatic zones)
Ergotism	*Claviceps purpurea*	Widespread
	Claviceps paspali, C. cinerea	Widespread
Fescue foot	*Acremonium coenophialum*	US, Australia, New Zealand, Italy
Leukoencephalomalacia	*Fusarium moniliforme*	Egypt, US, South Africa, Greece
Mycotoxic lupinosis (as distinct from alkaloid poisoning)	*Phomopsis leptostromiformis*	Widespread
Perennial ryegrass staggers	*Acremonium loliae*, an endophyte fungus confined to *Lolium perenne*	Australia, New Zealand, Europe, US
Sweet clover poisoning	*Penicillium, Mucor*, and *Aspergillus* species	North America
Tremorgen ataxia syndrome	*Penicillium crustosum, P. puberulum, P. verruculosum, P. roqueforti, Aspergillus flavus, A. fumigatus, A. clavatus,* and others	US, South Africa, probably worldwide
Trichothecene poisoning (fusariotoxicosis, vomiting and feed refusal in pigs)	*Fusarium sporotrichioides, F. culmorum, F. graminearum, F. nivale*; other fungal species	Widespread (except for deoxynivalenol, more likely in temperate to colder climates)
Stachybotryotoxicosis	*Stachybotrys atra (alternans)*	Former Soviet Union, southeast Europe
Myrotheciotoxicosis, Dendrodochiotoxicosis	*Myrothecium verrucaria, M. roridum*	Southeast Europe, former Soviet Union
	Myrothecium verrucaria	Brazil

Contaminated Toxic Foodstuff	Animal(s) Affected	Signs and Tissue Changes
Moldy peanuts, soybeans, cottonseeds, rice, sorghum, corn (maize), other cereals	Dogs	Major effects are slow growth and toxicity of the liver
Seedheads of many grasses, grains	Horses	Peripheral gangrene, late gestation suppression of lactation initiation
Seedheads of paspalum grasses	Horses	Acute tremors and incoordination (See PASPALUM STAGGERS, page 1158)
Tall fescue grass (*Festuca arundinacea*)	Horses	Lameness, weight loss, fever, dry gangrene of extremities, no milk production, thickened fetal membranes
Moldy corn (maize)	Horses, other equids	Depends on degree and specific site of brain lesion
Moldy seed, pods, stubble, and haulm of several *Lupinus* species affected by *Phomopsis* stem blight	Horses	Listlessness, no appetite, stupor, jaundice, marked liver injury; usually fatal
Endophyte-infected ryegrass pastures	Horses	Tremors, incoordination, collapse, convulsive spasms
Sweet clover (*Melilotus* species)	Horses	Stiffness, lameness, bleeding from the nose or into the gastrointestinal tract (See SWEET CLOVER POISONING, page 1210)
Moldy feed	All species	Tremors, rapid breathing, incoordination, collapse, convulsive spasms
Cereal crops, moldy roughage	Horses	Vomiting, feed refusal, loss of appetite and milk production, diarrhea, staggers, skin irritation, lowered immune function; recovery on removal of contaminated feed
Moldy roughage, other contaminated feed	Horses	Inflammation of the stomach, no appetite, low white blood cell counts, extensive bleeding in many organs, inflammation and tissue death in the gut, lowered immune function
Moldy rye stubble, straw	Horses	Acute—diarrhea, respiratory distress, inflammation of the stomach and intestine with bleeding, lowered immune function, death Chronic—formation of open sores in the stomach and intestine, unthriftiness, gradual recovery
Plants of *Baccharis* species that contain the toxins	Horses	Death of tissue lining the stomach and intestine

caused by bitter lupines. Lupinosis is a mycotoxic disease characterized by liver damage and jaundice, caused mainly by sweet lupines. Lupinosis is important in Australia and South Africa and also has been reported in New Zealand and Europe. Livestock and occasionally horses are affected.

The fungus that causes mycotoxic lupinosis is *Phomopsis leptostromiformis*. It produces sunken stem lesions that contain black masses, and it also affects the pods and seeds. The fungus also grows well on dead lupine material (haulm, pods, stubble) under favorable conditions, especially after rain. Complete loss of appetite and jaundice are the major signs. In severe outbreaks, deaths occur in 2 to 14 days. Feeding of moldy lupine material, together with signs and increased blood levels of liver enzymes, strongly indicate lupinosis.

Lupine fodder material should be monitored frequently for characteristic black spot fungal infestation, especially after rains.

Paspalum Staggers

This condition results from eating paspalum grasses infested by *Claviceps paspali*. The fungi mature in the seed heads in autumn. Ingestion causes nervous signs. Horses and guinea pigs are susceptible.

The time of onset of signs depends on the degree of the fungal infestation of the seed heads and the grazing habits of the animals. If large enough, a single dose can cause signs that last for several days. Large muscles tremble continuously, and movements are jerky and uncoordinated. Animals may be hostile and dangerous to approach or handle. If they try to run, the animals fall over in awkward positions. After prolonged exposure, complete paralysis can occur.

Recovery follows after animals are fed a diet free of fungus. Animals are less affected if left alone and provided readily available nutritious forages. Accidental access to ponds or rough terrain should be prevented to avoid the possibility of accidental trauma or drowning. Topping of the pasture to remove affected seed heads has been effective in control.

Slaframine Poisoning

Red clover (*Trifolium pratense*) can become infected with the fungus *Rhizoctonia leguminocola* (black patch disease), especially in wet, cool years. Rarely, other legumes (white clover, alsike, alfalfa) are infected. Slaframine is the toxic substance, and it is stable in dried hay and probably in silage. Horses are highly sensitive to slaframine.

Excessive drooling develops within hours after the contaminated hay is eaten. Signs also include tearing of the eyes, diarrhea, mild bloat, and frequent urination. After the contaminated hay is removed, animals recover within 24 to 48 hours.

Diagnosis is tentatively based on the signs and the presence of "black patch" on the forages. Analysis of the forages can detect slaframine. There is no specific antidote for slaframine toxicosis, although atropine may control some of the salivary and gastrointestinal signs. The contaminated hay must be removed from the diet. Preventing infection of clovers is difficult, although some varieties of clover may be relatively resistant to black patch disease. Using less red clover for forages or diluting the clover with other feeds is helpful.

Trichothecene Poisoning

The trichothecene mycotoxins are a group of closely related toxins of several families of fungi including species of *Fusarium, Trichothecium, Myrothecium, Cephalosporium, Stachybotrys, Trichodesma, Cylindrocarpon,* and *Verticimonosporium*. The term fusariotoxicosis is often used with trichothecene-related diseases, as well as bean hull poisoning of horses.

Animals typically refuse to eat the contaminated feedstuff, which limits intake of the toxin and development of other signs. If no other food is offered, animals may eat reluctantly. In some instances, excessive drooling and vomiting may occur. Irritation of the skin and mucous membranes, ulceration of the esophagus, and inflammation of the stomach and intestines are other typical signs. Blood vessels can rupture, and other serious blood disorders can develop. Weakness, seizures, and paralysis are seen in almost all species. Eventually, very low blood pressure may lead to death. Because trichothecenes suppress the immune system, secondary bacterial, viral, or parasitic infections may mask the primary illness.

In the former Soviet Union, Europe, and South Africa, a trichothecene-related disease known as **stachybotryotoxicosis** of horses has been diagnosed. Signs include tissue changes in skin and mucous membranes, disturbances of the nervous system, and abortions. Death may occur in 2 to 12 days. **Myrotheciotoxicosis** and **dendrodochiotoxicosis** have been seen in the former Soviet Union and New Zealand. The signs resemble those of stachybotryotoxicosis, but death may occur in 1 to 5 days.

Because the signs are nonspecific or masked by secondary infections, diagnosis is difficult. Analysis of feed is often costly and time consuming but ideally should be attempted. In the meantime, the feedstuff should be carefully examined for signs of mold growth or caking of feed particles. Changing the feed supply often results in immediate improvement and may provide another clue that the original feed was contaminated. Symptomatic treatment and feeding of uncontaminated feed are recommended.

■ GOSSYPOL POISONING

Gossypol poisoning is usually longterm, cumulative, and slowly and subtly harmful. It is caused by eating cottonseed or cottonseed products that contain excess free gossypol.

Gossypol is the major toxic ingredient in the cotton plant. Gossypol content of cottonseeds varies by plant species and variety and by environmental factors such as climate, soil type, and fertilization. Cottonseed is processed into edible oil, meal, linters (short fibers), and hulls. Cottonseed and cottonseed meal are widely used as protein supplements in animal feed. Cottonseed hulls are used as a source of additional fiber in animal feeds and usually contain much lower gossypol concentrations than whole cottonseeds.

All animals are susceptible. Domestic livestock are affected most often, but dogs fed diets that contain cottonseed meal have also developed gossypol poisoning. Guinea pigs and rabbits are most sensitive, followed by dogs and cats. Horses seem relatively unaffected. Toxic effects usually develop only after longterm exposure (weeks to months) to gossypol.

Signs reflect harmful effects on the heart, lungs, liver, kidneys, or reproductive system. Signs of prolonged excess gossypol exposure can include weight loss, weakness, loss of appetite, and increased susceptibility to stress. Prolonged exposure can cause sudden heart failure. Anemia can be another common result. In dogs, heart damage results in fluid buildup within the abdomen. Affected dogs may be very thirsty and have metabolic abnormalities and disturbances in heart rhythm.

Diagnosis is based on 1) a history of eating a diet containing cottonseed meal or cottonseed products over a relatively long period; 2) signs of heart, lung, and liver damage, with fluid buildup in various body cavities; and 3) no response to antibiotic treatment. However, samples of the diet may not be available to be analyzed for free gossypol levels if the feed has already been completely eaten.

Other causes of similar signs need to be excluded. These include antibiotics that can have toxic effects on the heart, nutritional or metabolic disorders (for example, selenium, vitamin E, or copper deficiency), infectious and noninfectious diseases, toxicoses caused by fungus-contaminated grain, and some plant poisonings.

There is no effective treatment for gossypol poisoning. All cottonseed products should be removed from the diet immediately if gossypol poisoning is suspected. However, severely affected animals may still die up to 2 weeks later. Recovery depends primarily on the extent of the toxic effects on the heart. Supportive treatment includes feeding a high-quality diet supplemented with lysine, methionine, and fat-soluble vitamins.

■ HALOGENATED AROMATIC POISONING (PCB AND OTHERS)

A class of organic chemical compounds called halogenated aromatics includes polychlorinated biphenyls (PCB), polybrominated biphenyls (PBB), naphthalenes, benzenes, and diphenyl ethers (PCDE, PBDE), as well as a number of pesticides such as DDT (*see* page 1167). Triclosan is a PCDE commonly used in antibacterial household products, and PBDE are used as flame retardants in plastics and electronic components. Most PCB use has been discontinued, but common PCB-containing products still in use include electrical transformers and capacitors and fluorescent light ballasts. These should be considered to contain PCB if manufactured before 1980 unless they are labeled otherwise. Other compounds resulting in persistent PCB contamination around farms and other facilities include hydraulic and heat transfer fluids, epoxy paints, and construction adhesives.

How long the poisoning lasts, how much toxin builds up in the body, and the types of toxic effects vary considerably among the many different halogenated aromatic compounds.

Livestock feed and pet food contamination as well as fish and fish meal were previously considered the major sources of exposure. Airborne and forage exposures are nearly universal, although at considerably lower levels.

Most toxic effects of halogenated aromatics are subtle and delayed but may be additive. Effects may include weight loss not necessarily accompanied by decreased food consumption, skin disorders, suppression of the immune system, enlarged liver, hormonal disruption, reproductive disorders, and cancer. Many effects may not become apparent until the animal is stressed or reaches adulthood. None of these signs are specific for poisoning by a halogenated aromatic compound and so cannot point to a specific diagnosis. Initial diagnosis is based on a complete history, inspection of the premises for potential exposures, and elimination of more common causes. Confirmation of poisoning relies on results of laboratory tests suggested by the medical history. Halogenated aromatic compounds are readily detected in blood as well as in body fat, milk fat, liver, feed, and other suspected sources.

Treatment is most likely to help when started as soon as possible after exposure. The source should be eliminated, and the animals bathed gently with detergent and cool water after skin exposure. Repeated large doses of activated charcoal given by mouth or flushing of the stomach may help prevent some absorption into the body after exposure by mouth. It is important to minimize stress. If the mother encounters persistent halogenated aromatics while pregnant, the offspring should not be allowed to nurse because the milk will be contaminated.

■ HERBICIDE POISONING

Herbicides are used routinely for weed control. Most herbicides are quite selective for specific plants and are not as poisonous for animals. Less selective compounds, such as arsenicals, chlorates, and dinitrophenols, are more toxic to animals. Most toxicity problems in animals result from exposure to excessive quantities of herbicides because of improper or careless use or disposal of containers. When herbicides are used properly, problems are rare.

Vegetation treated with herbicides at proper rates normally is not hazardous to animals, including people, and even less so after the herbicides have dried on the vegetation. Specific information on a particular herbicide is available on the label and from the manufacturer, cooperative extension services, or poison control centers.

Herbicide poisoning in animals is rare. With few exceptions, it is only when animals gain direct access to the product that severe poisoning occurs. The history is critical. Sickness after feeding, spraying of pastures or crops near pastures, a change in housing, or direct exposure may lead to a tentative diagnosis of herbicide poisoning. Severe gastrointestinal signs are frequent. Often the nature of exposure is hard to identify because of storage of herbicides in mislabeled or unlabeled containers. Other problems that can lead to exposure include unidentified spillage of liquid from containers or powder from broken bags near a feed source, or visual confusion with a dietary ingredient or supplement. Once a chemical source has been identified, an animal poison control center should be contacted for information on treatments, laboratory tests, and likely outcome.

Longterm disease caused by herbicides is even more difficult to diagnose. It may include a history of herbicide use close to the animal or the animal's feed or water source, or a gradual change in the animal's performance or behavior over several weeks, months, or even years. Occasionally, it involves manufacture or storage of herbicides nearby. Samples of possible sources (such as contaminated feed and water) for residue analysis, as well as tissues collected at necropsy, are essential. Months or even years may be required to successfully identify a problem of longterm exposure.

If poisoning is suspected, the first step in management is to stop further exposure. Any possible source should be removed from the animal's environment. Treatment includes stabilizing the animal and specific antidotal treatments when available. As with any potential poisoning, your veterinarian needs full disclosure of the circumstances (for example, unapproved use or improper storage of a chemical) to best make a diagnosis and begin treatment.

Inorganic Herbicides

The inorganic herbicides are older compounds that are less expensive and more toxic than newer compounds. They are no longer used much in developed countries.

The use of **inorganic arsenicals** (sodium arsenite and arsenic trioxide) as herbicides has been reduced greatly because of livestock losses, the long-lasting effects on the environment, and their association with causing cancer. Sodium arsenate and chromic copper arsenate are not currently registered with the Environmental Protection Agency. Arsenic derivatives continue to be available in other parts of the world in wood preservatives and insecticides. These compounds can be hazardous to animals when used as recommended.

The highly soluble **organic arsenicals** (methane arsonate, methyl arsonic acid) can concentrate in pools in toxic quantities after a rain has washed them from recently treated plants. (*See also* ARSENIC POISONING, page 1147.)

Ammonium sulfamate is not currently registered with the Environmental Protection Agency. It is used to kill brush and poison ivy.

Borax has been used as an herbicide and an insecticide. It is toxic to animals if consumed in moderate to large doses. Poisoning has not been reported when borax was used properly but has occurred when borax powder was scattered in the open for cockroach control. Signs of severe poisoning are diarrhea, rapid onset of weakness and an unwillingness to stand, and perhaps convulsions. An effective antidote is not known. Treatment consists of supportive care. Detergents containing borax should be stored away from where pets can get access to them.

Sodium chlorate is seldom used as an herbicide but remains registered. Treated plants and contaminated clothing are highly combustible and constitute fire hazards. Ingestion of treated plants and consumption of feed to which it is mistakenly added as salt can cause chlorate poisoning. Treatment with methylene blue must be repeated frequently. Blood transfusions, fluids, and mineral oil containing 1% sodium thiosulfate may be beneficial in treatment.

Organic Herbicides

Many organic herbicides can cause problems in pets.

Anilide or amide compounds (propanil, cypromid, clomiprop) are plant growth regulators, and some members of this group are more toxic than others. Exposure to these compounds can affect red blood cells and the immune system.

The **bipyridyl compounds or quaternary ammonium herbicides** include diquat and paraquat. These herbicides are used at low rates (2 ounces per acre [150 milliliters per hectare]), act quickly, are inactivated on soil contact, and quickly decompose in light. They produce toxic effects in the tissues of exposed animals. Skin irritation and clouding of the cornea can be seen after external exposure, and breathing in these chemicals is dangerous. Animals, including people, have died as a result of drinking from contaminated containers.

Diquat exerts most of its harmful effects in the gastrointestinal tract. Signs of kidney damage, central nervous system excitement, and convulsions occur in severely affected animals. Paraquat has 2 phases to its toxic action after ingestion. Immediate signs include excitement, convulsions, lack of coordination, inflammation of the gastrointestinal tract, loss of appetite, and possibly kidney involvement and breathing difficulty. Eye, nose, and skin irritation can be caused by direct contact, followed within days to 2 weeks by breathing problems.

Treatment includes administration of activated charcoal or other adsorbants in large quantities, medications that cause emptying of the bowels and that increase urine output, and supportive treatment.

Carbamate and thiocarbamate compounds (terbucarb, asulam, carboxazole, EPTC, pebulate, triallate, vernolate, butylate, thiobencarb) are moderately toxic. However, they are used at low concentrations, and normal use should not result in poisoning. Massive overdosage in accidental exposure causes lack of appetite, depression, breathing difficulty, diarrhea, weakness, and seizures.

Aromatic/benzoic acid compounds (chloramben, dicamba) have not caused poisoning after normal use. In overdosage, signs and tissue changes are similar to those described for poisoning by the phenoxyacetic compounds.

Phenoxyacetic and phenoxybutyric compounds (2,4-D [2-4-dichlorophenoxyacetic acid], 2,4,5-T [2,4,5-trichlorophenoxyacetic acid], 2,4-DB, MCPA) are commonly used for weed control. As a group, they are essentially nontoxic to animals when forage has been properly treated. When large doses are consumed, depression, loss of appetite, weight loss, tenseness, and muscular weakness (particularly of the hindquarters) are seen. In dogs, the muscles may remain contracted for longer than normal and have difficulty relaxing. Dogs also become uncoordinated and weak, and may have vomiting and diarrhea.

The use of 2,4,5-T was limited and its registration cancelled because extremely toxic contaminants, collectively called dioxins (TCDD and HCDD), were found.

Dinitrophenolic compounds include dinoseb, binapacryl, and DNOC. The old 2-4 dinitrophenol and dinitrocresol compounds were highly toxic to all animals. Poisoning can occur if animals are sprayed accidentally or have immediate access to forage that has been sprayed, because these compounds are readily absorbed through skin or lungs. Signs include fever, difficulty breathing, metabolic abnormalities, a rapid heartbeat, and convulsions, followed by coma and death. Cataracts can develop in animals with longterm dinitrophenol poisoning. Exposure to dinitro compounds may cause yellow staining of the skin, conjunctiva (of the eye), or hair. An effective antidote is not known. Affected animals should be cooled and sedated to help control fever. Atropine sulfate, aspirin, and fever reducers should not be used. Carbohydrate solutions given intravenously and vitamin A injections may be useful.

Organophospate compounds (for example glyphosate, bensulide) are widely used herbicides that have low toxicity. Exposure to toxic amounts is unlikely with recommended application and handling of containers.

Dogs and cats have shown eye, skin, and upper respiratory signs when exposed during or after an application to weeds or grass. Vomiting, staggering, and hindleg weakness have been seen in dogs and cats that were exposed to fresh chemicals on treated foliage. The signs usually disappear when exposure stops, and minimal symptomatic treatment is needed. Washing the chemical off the skin, emptying the stomach, and tranquilizing the animal are usually sufficient. (*See also* ORGANO-PHOSPHATES, page 1169.)

Other organic herbicides include phenyl or substituted urea compounds (diuron, fenuron, linuron, monolinuron), polycyclic alkanoic acids or aryloxyphenoxypropionic compounds (diclofop, fenoxaprop, fenthiaprop, fluazifop, haloxyfop), triazinylsulfonylurea or sulfonylurea compounds (chlorsulfuron, sulfometuron, ethametsulfuron, chloremuron), and triazine, methylthiotriazine, and triazinone compounds (atrazine, cyanazine, prometryn, metribuzin, simazine).

■ HOUSEHOLD HAZARDS

(*See also* RODENTICIDE POISONING, page 1201, POISONING FROM HUMAN OVER-THE-COUNTER DRUGS, page 1181, PLANTS POISONOUS TO ANIMALS, page 1175, and FOOD HAZARDS, page 1152.)

Hazardous chemicals—such as products containing alcohols, bleaches, or corrosives—often found in the home can be sources of poisoning in pets. It can be difficult to determine the specific toxicant(s) consumed and the amount ingested. Often a diagnosis must be based on the history of possible exposure and the development of relevant signs.

Alcohols

All species are susceptible to alcohol toxicosis. **Ethanol** is present in a variety of alcoholic beverages, some rubbing alcohols, drug elixirs, and fermenting bread dough (*see* page 1152). **Methanol** is most commonly found in windshield washer fluids. **Isopropanol** is found in rubbing alcohols and in alcohol-based flea sprays for pets. Overspraying pets with alcohol-based flea sprays is a common problem.

Alcohols can be absorbed through the gastrointestinal tract or the skin. They reach peak levels in the blood within 90 minutes to 2 hours. Signs generally begin within 30 to 60 minutes of ingestion and include vomiting, diarrhea, drooling, lack of coordination, depression, tremors, and difficulty breathing. Alcohols are very strong central nervous system depressants. Severe cases may progress to coma, dangerously low body temperature, low blood sugar, seizures, slow heart rate, and depressed breathing. Determination of blood alcohol levels may help to confirm the diagnosis of alcohol intoxication.

Severely affected animals must be stabilized and need supportive treatment, including regulation of body temperature and administration of fluids to increase urine output and elimination of alcohol. Medications are used to correct metabolic abnormalities, control seizures, and maintain or stimulate breathing. For animals that are not yet showing signs, vomiting may be induced in the first 20 to 40 minutes after ingestion. Activated charcoal is not often recommended. Bathing with mild shampoo is recommended for significant skin exposures.

Chlorine Bleaches

Exposure to undiluted chlorine bleaches may result in throat, skin, and eye irritation or ulceration as well as significant irritation of the respiratory tract. All species are susceptible. Caged birds are at increased risk of death from fumes of bleaches and other cleaning agents.

Chlorine bleaches are primarily used as household cleaners and pool sanitizers. Pets may be exposed by chewing on containers, drinking from buckets containing product, or swimming in recently treated pools. Products with low concentrations of bleach tend to be mild irritants. Products with higher concentrations of bleach may burn the skin. Diluting bleach with water according to the label directions often reduces its corrosive potential. Mixing household bleach and ammonia produces a highly toxic gas that can cause severe breathing distress within 12 to 24 hours of exposure.

Ingestion of dilute household bleach products rarely causes more than mild vomiting, excessive drooling, depression, loss of appetite, or diarrhea. Concentrated bleach products may cause significant corrosive injury to the gastrointestinal tract. Drinking or breathing significant amounts of chlorine bleach occasionally results in blood and metabolic abnormalities. Breathing a large amount can result in immediate coughing, gagging, sneezing, or retching. In addition, animals exposed to concentrated chlorine fumes may develop fluid in the lungs within 12 to 24 hours. In eye exposures, the eyes may water excessively, and the eyelids may swell and close tightly. Sores can develop on the cornea. Skin exposure can result in mild skin irritation and bleaching of the hair coat.

If the animal has ingested chlorine bleach, giving milk or water is advised. Because bleach is corrosive, vomiting should not be induced. Fluid treatment may help. Animals that have been exposed to fumes should be moved to an area with fresh air. Fluid in the lungs should be treated as needed. Bathing with mild shampoo and thorough rinsing is recommended for significant skin

exposures. Eye exposures should be treated immediately by flushing the eye with saline solution. Your veterinarian will stain the cornea to detect any corneal injuries.

Corrosives

Corrosives cause significant local tissue injury that can result in burns of the skin, cornea, and gastrointestinal tract. All species are susceptible. Heavy hair coats may provide some protection from skin exposure.

Corrosives are either acidic or alkaline. Common **acidic** corrosive products include anti-rust compounds, toilet bowl cleaners, gun-cleaning fluids, automotive batteries, swimming pool cleaning agents, and etching compounds. Common **alkaline** corrosive products include drain openers, automatic dishwasher detergents, toilet bowl cleaners, radiator cleaning agents, and swimming pool algaecides and "shock" agents.

Acids damage tissue immediately and are generally painful on contact. Alkaline agents also damage tissue immediately (causing it to liquefy), but they are not painful on contact, so prolonged exposure can result in deeper and more extensive burns. In addition, burns from alkaline agents may take up to 12 hours after contact to become apparent. Burns to the esophagus are more common with alkaline agents, and may be seen with or without significant mouth burns.

Signs after ingestion of corrosive agents include vocalization, lack of energy, excessive thirst, vomiting (with or without blood), abdominal pain, difficulty swallowing, swelling of the throat, difficulty breathing, and ulceration of the mouth, esophagus, or stomach. In severe cases, shock may develop quickly after exposure. The tissue may initially appear milky white to gray but gradually turns black as scabs form. Dead tissue may separate within days of exposure. After inhaling a corrosive agent, the animal may develop difficulty breathing, a bluish tinge to the skin and mucous membranes, and fluid in the lungs. Skin exposure may result in significant burns, with pain, redness, and separation of damaged tissue. Eye exposure may cause the eyes to water excessively, and the eyelids to swell and close tightly. Inflammation of the conjunctiva or sores on the cornea may develop.

Because corrosive agents act so quickly, much of the damage occurs before treatment can be started. Animals having difficulty breathing, in shock, or with severe, metabolic abnormalities must be stabilized. For recent mouth exposures, water or milk should be given immediately to dilute the corrosive agent. Vomiting should never be induced because of the risk of causing additional corrosive damage to the gastrointestinal tract. Likewise, the stomach should not be flushed because of the risk of tearing the weakened esophagus or stomach. Attempts to chemically neutralize an acid with a weak alkali (or an alkali with a weak acid) are also not recommended because the combining reaction produces heat that can result in heat burns. Activated charcoal is ineffective and can damage mucous membranes and delay wound healing.

Supportive care your veterinarian may provide includes monitoring for breathing difficulty and administering medications for pain and inflammation. In animals with significant burns to the mouth and esophagus, it may be necessary to place a tube through the body wall into the stomach to provide nutrition while affected tissues heal. Skin or eye exposures should be managed by flushing with large amounts of water or saline. Eyes should be flushed for at least 20 minutes, followed by special staining to determine the extent of damage to the cornea. Standard topical treatments for skin or eye burns are provided as needed.

Alkaline Batteries

Ingestion of alkaline batteries poses a risk of both corrosive injury to and obstruction of the digestive tract. Dogs are most commonly involved.

Alkaline batteries are found in many household electronic products, including remote controls, hearing aids, toys, watches, computers, and calculators. Nickel-cadmium and lithium batteries also often contain alkaline material. The alkaline gel in batteries causes tissue damage by liquefying the tissue on contact. The resulting burns can penetrate deeply into tissue. Lithium disc or "button" batteries can lodge in the esophagus and generate a current against the esophageal walls, resulting in circular ulcers that can lead to perforation. Some battery casings contain metals such as zinc or mercury, which pose hazards of foreign object obstruction and metal toxicosis if they remain in the stomach for a long time. Additionally, small batteries (especially disc batteries) can be inhaled and pose a choking hazard.

In foreign object obstruction, signs include vomiting, loss of appetite, abdominal discomfort, or urgent, painful, and unsuccessful attempts to defecate. The mucous membranes of the mouth, esophagus, or stomach may sustain burns. Perforation of the esophagus or stomach can lead to infection or severe blood loss.

For batteries that have been swallowed without being chewed, inducing vomiting may force the battery out. However, if there is any possibility that the battery casing has been punctured, vomiting should not be induced because of the risk of leakage of alkaline gel. When disc batteries have been ingested, giving small amounts of water (0.67 fluid ounces [20 milliliters]) every 15 minutes can decrease the severity and delay the development of current-induced ulcers in the esophagus. The decision on whether to remove a battery from the stomach depends on the size of the animal, the size of the battery, and evidence of battery puncture. X-rays can help to confirm the diagnosis as well as the location of the battery. Generally, batteries that have passed through the stomach usually continue to pass through the intestinal tract uneventfully. Adding bulk to the diet and carefully using medicines that cause emptying of the bowels may help ease passage. Usually, a series of x-rays is taken to monitor the progress of the battery through the gastrointestinal tract until the battery is expelled. Batteries that do not pass through the stomach within 48 hours of ingestion are unlikely to pass on their own. In these cases, the battery must be removed by surgery or endoscope. Batteries that have been punctured should be removed surgically. If ulceration of the mouth, esophagus, or stomach is suspected, it should be treated the same as other injuries caused by alkaline corrosives (*see* CORROSIVES, page 1164). Skin or eye exposures to alkaline gels should be managed by repeated rinsing with water (skin) or saline solution (eyes). The affected areas should be watched for development of ulcers and topical treatment given as needed.

Cationic Detergents

Exposure to cationic detergents can result in corrosive tissue injury and can affect the entire body. All species are susceptible. Cats are at increased risk of exposure by mouth due to grooming habits. Cationic detergents are found in a variety of algaecides, germicides, sanitizers, fabric softeners (including dryer softener sheets), and liquid potpourri. Cationic detergents are locally corrosive, causing skin, eye, and mucous membrane injury similar to that of alkaline corrosive agents. Whole-body effects range from central nervous system depression to fluid in the lungs.

Signs of oral exposure include inflammation and ulcers in the mouth, inflammation of the pharynx, excessive drooling, swollen tongue, depression, vomiting, abdominal discomfort, and increased breathing noises. A fever and a high white blood cell count are common. Other effects include metabolic abnormalities, central nervous system

depression, low blood pressure, coma, seizures, weakness, muscle spasms, collapse, and fluid in the lungs. Skin contact can cause skin irritation, redness, ulcers, and pain. Eye exposure can cause inflamed conjunctivae, swollen and tightly closed eyelids, tear production, and injuries to the cornea.

Your veterinarian can provide supportive treatment, including medications for any specific signs, such as seizures. Due to the potential for corrosive injury to mucous membranes, inducing vomiting and administration of activated charcoal are not recommended. For recent mouth exposures, milk or water can be given to dilute the agent. Mouth burns should be treated the same as other corrosive injuries (*see* CORROSIVES, page 1164). Skin and eye exposures should be managed by thorough flushing of the affected area with water or saline, followed by topical treatment. Pain relievers may be needed.

Detergents, Soaps, and Shampoos

Exposures to products containing anionic and nonionic detergents generally cause mild gastrointestinal irritation that responds well to symptomatic care. These products include human and pet shampoos, liquid hand dishwashing soaps, bar bath soaps (except homemade soaps, which may contain lye), many laundry detergents, and many household all-purpose cleaners. Some of these, such as electric dishwasher detergents, are also alkaline corrosives (*see* CORROSIVES, page 1164). All animals are susceptible.

These agents are not well absorbed by the body, and toxicity is limited to irritation of the eye, mouth, or gastrointestinal tract, which is usually mild and resolves on its own. Vomiting and diarrhea are the most common signs. Dehydration and metabolic abnormalities can develop in rare cases after prolonged vomiting or diarrhea.

Dilution with milk or water may reduce the risk of spontaneous vomiting. Vomiting usually resolves on its own after short periods of food and water restriction. In severe cases or in animals with sensitive stomachs, medications that prevent vomiting may be required. Rarely, fluid treatment is needed. Eyes should be flushed with water or saline for 5 minutes.

■ INSECTICIDE POISONING

All pesticide labels include directions for how to properly use the product. Because labels change to meet current government regulations, it is important that label directions are always followed. Labels must also carry warnings against use on unapproved species or under untested circumstances. Individuals have been prosecuted for failure to follow label directions or to heed label warnings.

Organic pesticides may have harmful effects on domestic species, fish, and wildlife. In no event should amounts greater than those specifically recommended be used, and maximal precautions should be taken to prevent drift or drainage to adjoining fields, pastures, ponds, streams, or other premises outside the treatment area.

Products stored under temperature extremes or held in partially full containers for long periods may deteriorate. Storing a chemical in anything but the original container is hazardous because its identification and label directions are then lost. Accidental contact with animals or people can then have disastrous consequences. Mixing compounds or using them in unapproved combinations can be very dangerous.

Poisoning by organic insecticides and acaricides (used to kill ticks and mites) may be caused by direct application, by eating feed or forage that has been treated to control plant parasites, or by accidental exposure.

Carbamate Insecticides

Carbamate insecticides include carbaryl, carbofuran, methomyl, and propoxur. Signs of toxicity include excessive drooling, abdominal cramping, vomiting, diarrhea, sweating, difficulty breathing, a bluish tinge to skin and mucous membranes, small pupils, muscle spasms, convulsions, buildup of fluid in the lungs, and death. Diagnosis usually depends on history of exposure to a particular carbamate and response to atropine treatment. When a history of exposure cannot be confirmed, but signs suggest carbamate or organophosphate poisoning, blood tests may help to confirm the diagnosis.

Treatment of carbamate poisoning is similar to that of organophosphate poisoning in that atropine injections are useful. (*See also* ORGANOPHOSPHATES, page 1169.)

Chlorinated Hydrocarbon Compounds

Use of these agents has been drastically reduced because of issues with tissue residues and longterm toxicity. Compounds that have been used in the past but are no longer registered in the US include adrin, DDT, dieldrin, chlordane, heptachlor, and toxaphene.

Benzene hexachloride was a useful insecticide for livestock and dogs but is highly toxic to cats in the concentrations necessary for parasite control. Only lindane is a useful insecticidal agent and it should be used in preference to other benzene hexachlorides (which are stored for excessively long periods in body tissues). Extremely thin or nursing animals are more susceptible to poisoning by lindane and should be treated with extreme caution.

Methoxychlor is one of the safest chlorinated hydrocarbon insecticides and one of the few registered for use in the US. Commercial products are available for garden, orchard, and field crops and for horses and ponies.

The chlorinated hydrocarbon insecticides are general central nervous system stimulants. The most obvious signs of poisoning are neuromuscular tremors, convulsions, and high fever. Affected animals initially become more alert or apprehensive. Muscle spasms begin in the face and gradually spread to involve the whole body. Convulsions may last from a few seconds to several hours and lead to coma. Animals may assume abnormal postures, such as resting the chest on the ground while remaining upright in the rear, keeping the head down between the forelegs, "head pressing" against a wall or fence, or continual chewing movements. Occasionally, an animal attacks other animals, people, or moving objects. Vocalization is common. Some animals are depressed, almost oblivious to their surroundings, and do not eat or drink. Usually, there is a large flow of thick saliva and an inability to control urination. Some animals have only a single convulsion and die, while others have numerous convulsions but then recover.

Chemical analysis of brain, liver, kidney, fat, and stomach contents is necessary to confirm the poisoning in dead animals. The suspected source, if it can be identified, should also be analyzed. Blood and urine from live animals may also be analyzed.

There are no known specific antidotes. When exposure is by spraying, dipping, or dusting, a thorough and gentle bath (no brushes), using detergents and large quantities of cool water is recommended. If the poison has been eaten, flushing the stomach is recommended. Giving digestible oils such as corn oil is not recommended, although heavy-grade mineral oil plus a medication that causes emptying of the bowels can speed removal of the chemical from the intestine. Activated charcoal can help prevent absorption from the gastrointestinal tract. If the animal is excited, a sedative or anticonvulsant is recommended. Any stress, such as noise or handling, should be stopped if possible. If the animal is depressed, dehydrated, and not eating, treatment should be directed toward rehydration and nourishment either intravenously or by stomach tube.

Insecticides Derived from Plants

Most insecticides derived from plants (such as derris [rotenone] and pyrethrum) are generally considered safe for use on animals. Nicotine in the form of nicotine sulfate is an exception. It must be used carefully, or poisoning may result. Affected animals show tremors, lack of coordination, difficulty breathing, coma, and death. Treatment consists of removing the material by flushing the stomach with tannic acid, administering activated charcoal, providing artificial respiration, and treating for cardiac arrest and shock. Mildly affected animals recover rapidly without treatment.

Pyrethrins and Pyrethroids

This group of naturally occurring compounds are the active insecticidal ingredients of pyrethrum. Pyrethrum is extracted from chrysanthemums and has been an effective insecticide for many years. Certain substances added to increase its stability and effectiveness, unfortunately, also increase its toxicity to mammals.

These are synthetic derivatives of natural pyrethrins and include allethrin, cypermethrin, decamethrin, fenvalerate, fluvalinate, permethrin, and tetramethrin. Generally, these compounds are more effective and less toxic to mammals than natural pyrethrins. Signs of toxicity usually begin within a few hours of exposure. Mildly affected animals often show excessive drooling, vomiting, diarrhea, mild tremors, and excitability or depression. More severely affected animals can have high fever, dangerously low body temperature, difficulty breathing, severe tremors, disorientation, and seizures. Death is caused by respiratory failure.

Generally, treatment is not required if a dilute pyrethrin or pyrethroid preparation has been consumed. Inducing vomiting is not usually recommended. Your veterinarian may use activated charcoal and a medication that causes emptying of the bowels. Because vegetable oils and fats promote the intestinal absorption of pyrethrum, they should be avoided. If skin exposure occurs, the animal should be bathed gently with a mild detergent and cool water. Further treatment consists of supportive care, including medications to control seizures.

d-Limonene

d-Limonene is used for flea control on cats and for other insect pests. At recommended dosages, the solution containing d-limonene appears to be safe. Increasing the concentration 5 to 10 times in sprays or dips increases the severity of toxic signs. These signs can include drooling, tremors, lack of coordination, and dangerously low body temperature. In dogs, ingestion of d-limonene by mouth causes vomiting.

Organophosphates

Organophosphates have replaced the banned organochlorine compounds and leave little tissue or environmental residue. Many organophosphates have been developed for plant and animal protection. However, organophosphates vary greatly in toxicity and are a major cause of animal poisoning.

Organophosphate insecticides include azinphos-methyl (or -ethyl), chlorpyrifos, coumaphos, diazinon, dichlorvos, dimethoate, disulfoton, fenthion, malathion, methyl parathion, naled, oxydemetonmethyl, parathion, phorate, phosmet, temephos, tetrachlorvinphos (low toxicity in dogs), and trichlorfon.

Flea collars containing dichlorvos may cause skin reactions in some pets. Malathion is one of the safest organophosphates. Parathion (diethyl parathion) is widely used for control of plant pests such as insects in orchards and on garden crops. Normally, because so little is used per acre, parathion presents no hazard. However, because of its potency, care should be taken to prevent accidental exposure.

Organophosphate insecticides not currently registered with the Environmental Protection Agency (as of 2002) include carbophenothion, chlorfenvinphos, crotoxyphos, demeton, dioxathion, EPN, famphur, mevinphos, ronnel (fenchlorphos), ruelene, terbufos, and tetraethyl pyrophosphate (TEPP).

Crotoxyphos is of rather low toxicity. EPN is related to parathion and is about one-half as toxic when applied externally; when ingested by mouth, it is about equally toxic. TEPP is one of the most severely toxic insecticides. It is not used on animals, but accidental exposure occurs occasionally, and deaths can occur within 40 minutes.

In organophosphate poisoning, certain nerve cells are overstimulated. Signs usually begin within hours after exposure but may be delayed for more than 2 days. Initial signs include excessive drooling, small pupils, frequent urination, diarrhea, vomiting, colic, and difficulty breathing, followed by muscle spasms and weakness, and finally nervousness, lack of coordination, apprehension, and seizures. Severity and course of poisoning is influenced mainly by the dosage and route of exposure. In sudden and severe poisoning, the primary signs may be breathing distress and collapse followed by death.

Blood tests can be an important diagnostic aid. Unfortunately, the results of the test do not necessarily correlate with the severity of the poisoning. Analyses performed after exposure may be negative because organophosphates do not remain long in tissues.

Specific treatment consists of atropine and the antidote pralidoxime (also called 2-PAM) to reverse signs of organophosphate poisoning. Removing the poison from the animal should also be attempted. If the organophosphate exposure was on the skin, the animal should be gently washed with detergent and water. Vomiting should be induced if the animal ingested the organophosphate less than 2 hours previously. Vomiting should not be induced if the animal is depressed. Mineral oil given by mouth decreases absorption from the gastrointestinal tract. Activated charcoal is also helpful. Artificial respiration or administration of oxygen may be required. Tranquilizers should not be given.

Pesticide Potentiating Agents

Piperonyl butoxide is used in many pesticide formulations including pyrethrins, pyrethroids, and d-limonene to make them more effective. It decreases breakdown of the chemical in the animal or insect's body. This makes the pesticide more toxic to the insect—but also to the host animal.

Solvents and Emulsifiers

Solvents and emulsifiers are required to make most liquid insecticides. Usually they have low toxicity, but they must be considered as possible causes of poisoning. Treatment is as for petroleum product poisoning (*see* page 1173).

The main signs of **acetone** poisoning are gastrointestinal irritation, unconsciousness, and kidney and liver damage. Treatment consists of flushing the stomach, providing supplemental oxygen, and feeding a low-fat diet. Additional supportive treatment can lessen signs.

Signs of poisoning by **isopropyl alcohol** include gastrointestinal pain, cramps, vomiting, diarrhea, dehydration, dizziness, stupor, coma, and death. The liver and kidneys are affected but may recover. Pneumonia may develop. Vomiting can be induced or the stomach flushed by your veterinarian, followed by providing respiratory support, and giving milk by mouth.

Methanol poisoning causes vomiting, abdominal pain, heightened reflexes, muscle spasms causing backward arching of the neck and spine, convulsions, fixed pupils, and inflammation of nerves. Large overdoses can lead to blindness. Treatment should include medications that cause vomiting followed by flushing of the stomach, saline laxatives, oxygen treatment, intravenous sodium bicarbonate, and pain relievers. Intensive and prolonged treatment is required, and the prognosis is poor.

Sulfur and lime-sulfur are 2 of the oldest insecticides. Elemental sulfur has practically no toxicity. Lime-sulfur may cause irritation, discomfort, or blistering. Death is rare. Treatment consists of removing residual material, applying bland protective ointments, and providing supportive measures.

■ LEAD POISONING

Lead poisoning is most common in dogs. In other species, lead poisoning is limited by reduced accessibility, more selective eating habits, or lower susceptibility. Lead poisoning is usually seen during renovation of old houses that have been painted with lead-based paint. Other sources of lead include linoleum, grease, lead weights, lead shot, improperly disposed of oil and batteries, and contaminated foliage growing near smelters or along roadsides.

Absorbed lead enters the blood and soft tissues, and eventually reaches the bone. The amount of lead absorbed is influenced by dietary factors such as calcium or iron levels. Lead causes bleeding and swelling of the brain, suppresses the immune system, and damages the kidneys and red blood cells.

In dogs, gastrointestinal signs, including loss of appetite, colic, vomiting, and diarrhea or constipation, may be seen. Anxiety, hysterical barking, jaw champing, drooling, blindness, lack of coordination, muscle spasms (with backward arching of the head, neck, and spine), and convulsions may develop. The central nervous system can be either depressed or stimulated.

In horses, lead poisoning usually results in a longterm syndrome characterized by weight loss, depression, weakness, colic, diarrhea, paralysis of the larynx and throat (roaring), and difficulty swallowing that often results in aspiration pneumonia.

In birds, loss of appetite, coordination, and condition; wing and leg weakness; and anemia are the main signs.

Specific concentrations of lead in the blood, liver, or kidneys can help to confirm the diagnosis in most species and to reflect the level or duration of exposure. They can also be used to determine a prognosis and monitor the success of treatment. Lead poisoning can be confused with other diseases that cause nervous or gastrointestinal abnormalities. In dogs, rabies, distemper, and hepatitis may appear similar to lead poisoning.

If tissue damage is extensive, particularly to the nervous system, treatment may not be successful. The vitamin thiamine lessens signs and reduces tissue deposition of lead. In dogs, thiamine is given along with calcium disodium edetate (Ca-EDTA). D-Penicillamine can also be administered, but side effects include vomiting and loss of appetite. Succimer is another agent that is useful in dogs as well as birds. Medications that cause emptying of the bowels may be useful to remove lead from the gastrointestinal tract. Medications to control seizures may also be needed.

■ MERCURY POISONING

Mercury exists in a variety of organic and inorganic forms. **Inorganic mercurials** include the volatile elemental form of mercury (used in thermometers) and the salted forms (mercuric chloride [sublimate] and mercurous chloride [calomel]). Ingested inorganic mercury is poorly absorbed and low in toxicity. However, large amounts are corrosive and can cause vomiting, diarrhea, colic, and kidney damage. In rare cases of longterm inorganic mercurial poisoning, the central nervous system effects resemble those of organic mercury poisoning. Mercury vapor from elemental mercury causes respiratory and neurologic signs. Inducing vomiting, followed by administration of dimercaprol, is recommended after ingestion by mouth.

Inorganic mercury is converted to the **organic forms**, methylmercury and ethylmercury, by microorganisms in the sediment of rivers, lakes, and seas. Marine life accumulates the most toxic form, methylmercury, and fish must be monitored for contamination. There are reports of commercial cat food causing severe neurologic disturbances in cats fed an exclusive tuna diet for 7 to 11 months.

The organic mercurials are absorbed through all routes and accumulate in the brain, kidneys, and muscle. Animals do not show signs until several weeks after being poisoned by organic mercury. Signs can include blindness, excitement, abnormal behavior and chewing, lack of coordination, and convulsions. Cats show hindleg rigidity, lack of coordination, and tremors. Neurologic signs may be irreversible.

Laboratory tests are used to detect concentrations of mercury associated with poisoning in tissue (especially whole blood, kidney, and brain) and feed.

Dimercaprol and penicillamine are sometimes used in treatment.

■ METALDEHYDE POISONING

Metaldehyde is the active ingredient in molluscicides, which are mostly used during the wet season for slug and snail control. In certain locations, metaldehyde is also used for rat control. (*See also* RODENTICIDE POISONING, page 1201.) Metaldehyde comes as a liquid or bait combined with bran, either as flakes or pellets, and is tasty to pets and farm animals. Some products also contain arsenic or an insecticide. All species are susceptible to metaldehyde poisoning, with dogs being the species most frequently poisoned (3 ounces of bait is enough to poison a 30-pound dog). Depending on stomach contents and the rate of stomach emptying, signs can vary greatly.

Signs of poisoning are similar in all mammals. Initial signs can include muscle tremors, lack of coordination, heightened senses, a rapid heartbeat, fever, and deep or fast breathing. The eyes may move rhythmically (most severe in cats), and muscle spasms can cause backward arching of the head, neck, and spine. All species develop vomiting, diarrhea, excessive drooling, metabolic abnormalities, and difficulty breathing. Horses also sweat a large amount.

Inducing vomiting in severe exposure may not be necessary because metaldehyde is a stomach irritant. However, the stomach is usually flushed with sodium bicarbonate. Fluid treatment is used to prevent possible liver damage. Medications are used to calm the animal and to reduce muscle activity and pain. Cold water rinses are recommended when fever is severe. Prognosis is good if fever and seizures can be controlled, but intensive treatment is usually needed for 4 or more days.

■ NITRATE AND NITRITE POISONING

Many species are susceptible to nitrate and nitrite poisoning, but cattle are affected most often. The effects of nitrite or nitrate toxicity are usually sudden but may be longterm.

Nitrates and nitrites are used in pickling and curing brines for preserving meats, certain machine oils and antirust tablets, gunpowder and explosives, and fertilizers. Poisonings occur most commonly from ingestion of plants that contain excess nitrate, especially by hungry animals that overeat and take in an enormous amount of nitrate. Nitrate poisoning can also result from accidental ingestion of fertilizer or other chemicals. Nitrate concentrations may be hazardous in ponds that receive extensive feedlot or fertilizer runoff; these types of nitrate sources may also contaminate shallow, poorly cased wells. Water transported in improperly cleaned liquid fertilizer tanks can also be extremely high in nitrate.

Crops that readily concentrate nitrate include cereal grasses (especially oats, millet, and rye), corn (maize), sunflower, and sorghums. Weeds that commonly have high nitrate concentrations are pigweed, lamb's quarter, thistle, Jimson weed, fireweed (*Kochia*), smartweed, dock, and Johnson grass. Anhydrous ammonia and nitrate fertilizers and soils naturally high in nitrogen tend to increase nitrate content in forage.

Signs of nitrite poisoning usually appear suddenly. Rapid, weak heartbeat with below normal body temperature and blood pressure, tremors, weakness, and lack of coordination are early signs of toxicosis.

Brown and bluish mucous membranes develop quickly. Difficulty breathing, rapid breathing, anxiety, drooling, and frequent urination are common. The abdomen may be painful, and the animal may have vomiting and diarrhea. Affected animals can also die suddenly without showing signs or have seizures. Under certain conditions, signs may not be apparent until animals have been eating nitrate-containing forages for days to weeks. Some animals develop emphysema and breathing distress, but most of these recover fully within 10 to 14 days. In longterm poisoning, signs include retarded growth, lowered milk production, vitamin A deficiency, reproductive problems, and increased susceptibility to infection.

Diagnosis relies on signs and blood tests to measure nitrate and nitrite levels in animals. Field tests for nitrate can also be performed.

Treatment includes slow intravenous injection of 1% methylene blue in various fluids. Trace mineral supplements and a balanced diet can help prevent nutritional or metabolic disorders associated with longterm excess dietary nitrate consumption. Feeding grain with high-nitrate forages may reduce nitrite production.

■ NONPROTEIN NITROGEN POISONING (AMMONIA POISONING)

Poisoning by ingestion of excess urea (a nitrogen compound) or other sources of nonprotein nitrogen is usually sudden, rapidly progressive, and highly deadly. After ingestion, nonprotein nitrogen undergoes a chemical reaction and releases excess ammonia into the gastrointestinal tract, which is absorbed and leads to excess ammonia in the blood.

The most common sources of nonprotein nitrogen in feeds are urea, urea phosphate, anhydrous ammonia, and salts such as monoammonium and diammonium phosphate. Because feed-grade urea is unstable, it is formulated (usually pelleted) to prevent degradation to ammonia. Horses are sometimes fed nonprotein nitrogen as a feed additive. Horses are more sensitive to urea than some other animals. Ammonium salts can be toxic and deadly to all species and ages of farm animals.

Diets low in energy and high in fiber are more commonly associated with nonprotein nitrogen toxicosis. Highly tasty supplements (such as liquid molasses) or improperly maintained lick tanks may lead to consumption of lethal amounts of nonprotein nitrogen. Early signs include muscle tremors (especially of face and ears), protrusion of eyeballs, abdominal pain, drooling, passing large amounts of urine, and grinding the teeth. Tremors progress to lack of coordination and weakness. Fluid in the lungs leads to difficulty breathing and gasping. Horses may exhibit head pressing. Eventually, there is a bluish tinge to the skin and mucous membranes, difficulty breathing, an absence of urine output, fever, and metabolic abnormalities. Death usually occurs within 3 to 12 hours in horses. Survivors recover in 12 to 24 hours with no lasting effects.

Ammonia or nitrogen poisoning is suggested by the history, signs, and dietary exposure. Blood and urine can be tested for ammonia nitrogen, and feed can be analyzed for nonprotein nitrogen. Definitive test results will probably not be possible in animals that have been dead more than a few hours in hot temperatures or 12 hours in moderate climates.

Examination and treatment may be difficult because of uncooperative behavior. Supportive treatment includes controlling fever, correcting dehydration with fluids, and calcium gluconate and magnesium solutions for muscle tremors.

PENTACHLOROPHENOL POISONING (PENTA POISONING)

Penta has been used as a fungicide, molluscicide, insecticide, and as a wood preservative, but its registrations for these purposes have gradually been cancelled over the years. It is currently registered only for industrial purposes; agricultural and domestic uses are prohibited.

Penta is intensely irritating to the skin and mucous membranes. Animals fed in troughs made of lumber treated with penta may salivate and have irritated mucous membranes of the mouth. Vaporization or leaching of penta in pens, enclosures, homes, and barns has caused illness and death. Signs of poisoning include nervousness, rapid pulse and breathing, weakness, muscle tremors, fever, convulsions, and death. Longterm poisoning results in fatty liver, kidney damage, and weight loss. Pentachlorophenol is considered to cause cancer and must be handled very carefully.

Blood tests for penta may aid in the diagnosis of poisoning, but diagnosis is usually made based on signs and treated lumber in the animal's environment.

There is no known antidote. Treatment includes removing the animal from the source of exposure, bathing animals that had skin exposure, administering activated charcoal by mouth, and providing supportive treatment, including cooling the animal and administering fluids, electrolytes (salts), and anticonvulsants. Bathing should be done gently with cold water and detergent.

PETROLEUM PRODUCT POISONING

Ingesting, inhaling, or direct skin contact with petroleum, petroleum condensate, gasoline, diesel fuel, kerosene, crude oil, or other hydrocarbon mixtures can cause illness and occasionally death in animals. Pipeline breaks, accidental release from storage tanks, and tank car accidents may contaminate land and water supplies. Animals may have access to open or leaky containers of fuel or other hydrocarbon materials.

Crude oil and gasoline contain varying amounts of aromatic hydrocarbons including benzene, toluene, ethyl-benzene, and xylene. These compounds, if ingested or inhaled in sufficient amounts, can have short- or longterm effects different from those caused by other hydrocarbons that make up most oil and gas products. Benzene, for example, is a known carcinogen at high levels of exposure and may damage red blood cells. Toluene can cause severe neurologic signs and damage. Gasoline, naphtha, and kerosene can damage lung tissue. Gasoline and naphtha may cause vomiting. Older formulations of lubricating oils and greases can be particularly dangerous because of toxic additives or contaminants (for example, lead).

Petroleum fractions have been used as pesticides for ticks and mites for many years. Small quantities applied to the skin cause few or no harmful effects, but large quantities and prolonged exposure can cause severe reactions. If their fur becomes contaminated, both dogs and cats can ingest petroleum products during grooming. Dogs can also ingest petroleum products directly when they are left in open containers. Animals confined to poorly ventilated areas where petroleum products have been used or stored can breathe in these compounds.

Petroleum hydrocarbon poisoning can involve the lungs, skin, gastrointestinal system, or the central nervous system. In most cases of ingestion, no signs are seen. Aspiration pneumonia (sometimes caused during vomiting) is usually the most serious conse-

quence of ingestion of these materials. Severe bloat is not consistently seen but can cause death very shortly after ingestion of gasoline or naphtha. Loss of appetite and mild depression begin in about a day and last 3 to 14 days depending on dose and content. Blood sugar can be low for several days after ingestion. These signs and weight loss may be the only signs in animals that do not bloat or draw the oil into their lungs. Some animals develop a longterm wasting condition.

The feces may become dry and formed several days after ingestion of kerosene or lighter hydrocarbon substances. In contrast, heavier hydrocarbon mixtures tend to cause emptying of the bowels. Oil may be found in feces up to 2 weeks after ingestion. Regurgitated or vomited oil may be seen on the muzzle and lips. Signs can include excitability or depression, shivering, head tremors, visual problems, and lack of coordination. Sudden, severe pneumonia with coughing, rapid and shallow breathing, reluctance to move, head held low, weakness, oily nose discharge, and dehydration are seen in some animals that breathe highly volatile mixtures into their lungs; death usually is seen within days. Respiratory signs may be limited to difficulty breathing shortly

Table 25. Poisonous Houseplants and Ornamentals

Common Name	Scientific Name (Family)
Autumn crocus, Crocus, Fall crocus, Meadow saffron, Wonder bulb	Colchicum autumnale (Liliaceae, Colchicaceae)
Avocado pear, Alligator pear	Persea americana (Lauraceae)

before death in animals that draw heavier hydrocarbons into their lungs.

Your veterinarian can confirm the diagnosis by the signs, along with analysis of gastrointestinal contents, lung, liver, kidney, and the suspected source.

If the animal has bloated, the pressure should be released by passing a stomach tube if necessary to save the animal's life. However, passing a stomach tube dramatically increases the risk of drawing the substance into the lungs. If the animal has not bloated, medications are given to cause emptying of the bowels, but there is no evidence that they improve prognosis. In dogs and cats, vomiting should not be induced, to avoid the risk of drawing the substance into the lungs. Activated charcoal can be used.

Animals with respiratory problems may need broad-spectrum antibiotic treatment. Treatment of aspiration pneumonia is rarely effective, and the prognosis is poor. In the case of skin exposure, the skin should be washed gently (no brushing or rubbing) with soap or mild detergents and large amounts of cool water. Further treatment is supportive, depending on the signs.

Petroleum hydrocarbon poisoning can be avoided only by preventing access. These substances must be stored properly, and fencing around high-risk petroleum facilities must be well maintained.

■ PLANTS POISONOUS TO ANIMALS

Many plants are poisonous to animals. The following are the more common plants that can be poisonous to pets.

Houseplants and Ornamentals

Pets often chew on or ingest household plants, which can result in poisoning (*see* TABLE 25). Houseplants vary in their degree of toxicity. Inquisitive puppies and kittens tend to mouth or chew almost everything. Many pets become bored or restless if left alone or confined for long periods, and chewing on objects for relief is common. Pets of all ages explore changes in their environment. For example, pets commonly chew the leaves or ripe berries of plants that are placed in the home during holidays.

Range Plants of Temperate North America

Poisonous range plants can affect animals in many ways, including longterm illness and debilitation, decreased weight gain, reproductive problems, and death

Toxic Parts and Effects	Treatment
Entire plant is toxic. Milk of lactating animals is a major excretory pathway. Observed signs are thirst, difficult swallowing, abdominal pain, profuse vomiting and diarrhea, weakness, and shock within hours of ingestion. Death from respiratory failure.	Prolonged course due to slow excretion of the toxin. Flush out stomach contents; supportive care for dehydration and electrolyte losses (fluid therapy); central nervous system, circulatory, and respiratory disturbances. Analgesics and atropine recommended for abdominal pain and diarrhea.
All above-ground parts (leaves in particular) reported toxic to cattle, horses, goats, rabbits, canaries, ostriches, and fish. Toxicity associated with loss of milk production (cattle, rabbits, goats), lung congestion, irregular heart beat, swelling of the jaw, sudden death (rabbits, caged birds, goats), respiratory distress, generalized congestion, subcutaneous swelling, and fluid around the heart (suggestive of cardiac failure, caged birds). In caged birds, signs may be seen within 24 hours (usually after 12 or more hours), with death 1 to 2 days after exposure.	Primarily symptomatic and supportive. (*See also* AVOCADO, page 1152.)

(Continued on the following page)

Table 25. Poisonous Houseplants and Ornamentals—*(Continued)*

Common Name	Scientific Name (Family)
Azalea, Rhododendron	*Rhododendron* species (Ericaceae)
Barbados aloe, Curacao aloe	*Aloe Barbadensis* (Liliaceae)
Caladium, Fancy leaf caladium, Angel wings	*Caladium* species (Araceae)
Century plant, American aloe	*Agave americana* (Agavaceae)
Cherry pepper, Chili pepper, Ornamental pepper, Capsicum	*Capsicum annuum* (Solanaceae)
Chinese evergreen, Painted drop tongue	*Aglaonema modestum* (Araceae)
Coontie, Florida arrowroot, Seminole bread, Cycad	*Zamia pumila* (Zamiaceae)
Cyclamen, Snowbread, Shooting star	*Cyclamen* species (Primulaceae)
Daffodils	*Narcissus* species (Amaryllidaceae)
Dragon tree	*Dracaena* species (Agavaceae)
Dumbcane	*Dieffenbachia* species (Araceae)
Easter lily, Trumpet lily	*Lilium longiflorum; L. tigrinum* (Liliaceae)
English holly, European holly	*Ilex aquifolium* (Aquifoliaceae)
Foxglove	*Digitalis purpurea* (Scrophulariacae)
Hyacinths	*Hyacinthus* species (Liliaceae)

Toxic Parts and Effects	Treatment
Entire plant, including pollen and nectar. Within hours of ingestion of toxic dose (1 gram/kilogram), drooling, tearing, vomiting, diarrhea, difficulty breathing, muscle weakness, convulsions, coma, and death. Signs may last several days, but toxin is not cumulative.	Supportive; flush out stomach contents, activated charcoal, saline cathartics, calcium injection, and antibiotics to control possible pneumonia suggested.
Latex of the leaves; higher concentrations in younger leaves. Upon eating, causes abrupt, severe diarrhea and/or low blood sugar, with vomiting in some cases.	Supportive—control diarrhea and fluid loss.
Entire plant is toxic. Ingestion causes immediate intense pain, irritation to mucous membranes, excess drooling, swollen tongue and pharynx, diarrhea, and difficulty breathing. Pets' access to plant associated with rhizomes brought indoors for winter storage.	Supportive
Leaves, seeds, and sap. Upon eating, causes skin and mouth irritation and swelling.	Supportive
Capsaicinoids (capsaicin) in the mature fruits, solanine and scopoletin in foliage; irritating to the stomach and intestinal tract, with vomiting and diarrhea. Not likely to be lethal.	Supportive; irritation relief—flush with cool water, topical or oral mineral or vegetable oil. Rarely topical anesthetics.
Entire plant. Upon eating, causes mouth irritation and swelling.	Supportive
Leaves, seeds, and stem. Ingestion associated with liver and stomach and intestinal disturbances and incoordination. Signs are persistent vomiting, diarrhea, abdominal pain, depression, and muscular paralysis.	No specific therapy; intravenous fluids and supportive care recommended.
Tuberous rhizomes cause stomach and intestine irritation, thereby increasing absorption and severe toxicity. Reduced appetite, diarrhea, convulsions, and paralysis can occur. Pets have greater access to these plants over winter months (both pets and plants are indoors).	Supportive
Same as for hyacinths (*see below*).	Same as for hyacinths (*see below*).
Leaves. Vomiting and severe diarrhea indicative of stomach and intestinal irritation expected. No cases have been reported.	Supportive, to correct fluid and electrolyte (salt) imbalance.
Entire plant, including sap. On ingestion, immediate intense pain, burning, and inflammation of mouth and throat, no appetite, vomiting, and possibly diarrhea, with tongue extended, head shaking, excessive drooling, and difficulty breathing. Immediate pain limits amount consumed. Death infrequent.	Supportive
Entire plant is toxic. Kidney system failure in cats 2 to 4 days post-ingestion. Not reported toxic to other species. Vomiting, depression, loss of appetite within 12 hours post-ingestion.	Emetics (induce vomiting), activated charcoal, saline cathartic, and nursing care—as for renal failure—within hours of ingestion. Delayed treatment is associated with poor prognosis.
Leaves, fruits, and seeds. Abdominal pain, vomiting, and diarrhea seen after ingestion of 2 or more berries. Death is rare.	Supportive (at best)
Entire plant is toxic. Generally, sudden abdominal pain, vomiting, bloody diarrhea, frequent urination, irregular slow pulse, tremors, convulsions, and rarely death.	Supportive
Bulbs. After ingestion of toxic dose (bulbs), vomiting, diarrhea, and rare deaths reported. Bulbs in storage may be accessible to pets.	Supportive

(Continued on the following page)

Table 25. Poisonous Houseplants and Ornamentals—*(Continued)*

Common Name	Scientific Name (Family)
Jerusalem cherry	*Solanum pseudocapsicum* (Solanaceae)
Kalanchoe, Air-plant, Cathedral-bells	*Kalanchoe* species (Crassulaceae)
Lily-of-the-valley, Conval lily, Mayflower	*Convallaria majalis* (Liliaceae)
Marijuana, Mary Jane, Grass, Pot, Hashish, Indian hemp, Reefer, Weed	*Cannabis sativa* (Cannabaceae)
Mistletoe	*Phoradendron flavescens* (Viscaceae)
Philodendron	*Philodendron* species (Araceae)
Poinsettia, Christmas flower, Christmas star	*Euphorbia pulcherrima* (Euphorbiaceae)
Sansevieria, Snake plant, Mother-in-law's tongue	*Sansevieria* species (Agavaceae)
Schefflera, Umbrella tree	*Schefflera* species (Araliaceae)
Spider plant, St. Bernard's lily, Airplane plant	*Chlorophytum* species (Liliaceae)
Yesterday-today-and-tomorrow, Lady-of-the-night	*Brunfelsia pauciflora floribunda* (Solanaceae)
Yew	*Taxus* species (Taxaceae)

Toxic Parts and Effects	Treatment
Leaves and fruits. Loss of appetite, abdominal pain, vomiting, diarrhea with blood, drooling, progressive weakness or paralysis, difficulty breathing, irregular heartbeat, circulatory collapse, dilated pupils, and convulsions reported.	Supportive; flush out stomach contents, activated charcoal, electrolytes and fluids, and anticonvulsants suggested.
Leaves. Within hours of ingesting toxic dose, depression, rapid breathing, teeth grinding, lack of coordination, paralysis, muscle spasms (rabbit), and death (rat).	Supportive; atropine has been effective in rabbits.
Leaves, flowers, rhizome, and water in which flowers have been kept. Variable period before signs arise depending on dose. Stomach and intestinal signs (vomiting, trembling, abdominal pain, diarrhea), progressive heart irregularities, and death. High blood pressure in sudden cases. Inflammation of the stomach and intestine, bleeding of small capillaries throughout.	Aimed at gut decontamination (flushing of stomach contents) and at correcting irregular heart beats and electrolyte (salt) imbalances. Monitoring of EKG and serum potassium necessary.
Leaves, stems, and flower buds of mature plants. Lethal dose for dogs is more than 3 grams/kilogram body weight. Pets' exposure usually from accidental access to this plant being used for in-home treatment of cancer patient or for illegal recreational uses by owner. Pets (dogs primarily) show incoordination, vomiting, dilated pupils, prolonged depression, excessive or irregular heartbeats, drooling, hyperexcitability, tremors, and fever. Death results when vital central nervous system regulatory centers are severely depressed.	Remove animal from source. Effectiveness of emetics limited by antiemetic effect of THC (the toxic compound in the plant). Oral tannic acid, activated charcoal followed by saline cathartics have been recommended. Stimulants (cardiac and respiratory) along with supportive therapy essential in severely depressed animals. Recovery slow at best. (*See also* MARIJUANA, page 1199.)
Entire plant is toxic. Vomiting, profuse diarrhea, dilated pupils, rapid labored breathing, shock, and death from cardiovascular collapse within hours of ingesting toxic dose.	Supportive.
Entire plant is toxic. On ingestion, immediate pain, local irritation to mucous membranes, excessive drooling, swollen tongue and pharynx, difficulty breathing, and kidney system failure. Excitability, nervous spasms, convulsions, and occasional brain swelling reported in cats.	Supportive.
Milky sap. Irritates mucous membranes and causes excessive drooling and vomiting but not death.	Supportive; flush out stomach contents, activated charcoal, and saline cathartics should be considered.
Leaves and flowers. Vomiting, drooling, diarrhea, and rupture of red blood cells related to stomach and intestinal activity of these compounds.	Supportive; fluids and electrolytes may be necessary.
Leaves. Mucous membrane irritation, drooling, loss of appetite, vomiting, and if severe enough, diarrhea.	Supportive.
Leaves and plantlets. Vomiting, drooling, retching, and varying degrees of loss of appetite seen in cats within hours of ingestion. Deaths and diarrhea not reported.	Supportive.
Flowers, leaves, bark, and roots. Upon eating, animals show abnormal heart rhythms, dry mouth, dilated pupils, difficulty breathing, tremors, depression, urinary retention, and sometimes coma (deep sedation). Not reported to cause death.	In severely depressed animals, stimulants (respiratory and cardiac), along with supportive therapy recommended.
Entire plant except the fleshy aril. Nervousness, trembling, incoordination, difficulty breathing, collapse; irregular heartbeats progressing to the heart stopping and death without struggle. Empty right side of heart; dark, tarry blood in left side of heart.	Supportive at best; usually futile once signs appear. Atropine may be helpful.

(*see* TABLE 26). Due to their diet and grazing habits, horses are much more likely to be poisoned by ingesting range plants than other companion animals. Usually, animals are poisoned by plants because hunger or other conditions cause them to graze plants that would not be eaten under normal circumstances. Overgrazing, trucking, trailing, corralling, or introducing animals onto a new range tend to induce hunger or change behavior, and poisoning may occur.

Poisonous plants do not always harm animals when eaten. For example, plants such as lupine and greasewood may be part of an animal's diet, and the animal is poisoned only when it consumes too much of the plant too fast.

Making a definitive diagnosis of plant poisoning is difficult. It is important to be familiar with the poisonous plants growing in the specific area and the conditions under which animals may be poisoned. A tentative diagnosis is possible if the following information is available: 1) local soil conditions, including deficiencies or excesses of various minerals, 2) the syndromes associated with each of the

Table 26. Poisonous Range Plants of Temperate North America

Common and Scientific Names	Habitat and Distribution	Affected Animal(s)
Dangerous Season: Spring and Fall		
Water hemlock; *Cicuta* species	Open, moist to wet environments; throughout North America	All
Dangerous Season: Spring		
African rue; *Peganum harmala*	Arid to semiarid ranges; southwest	Horses likely
Cocklebur; *Xanthium* species	Fields, waste places, exposed shores of ponds or rivers; throughout North America. Dangerous season spring and occasionally fall.	All animals
Death camas; *Zygadenus* species	Foothill grazing lands, occasionally boggy grasslands, low open woods; throughout North America	Horses
Oaks; *Quercus* species	Most deciduous woods; throughout North America	Horses
Pokeweed, Poke; *Phytolacca americana*	Disturbed rich soils such as recent clearings, pastures, waste areas; eastern North America	Horses, people

poisonous plants in the area, 3) the time of year when each plant is most likely to cause problems, 4) the history of the animal(s) over the last 6 to 8 months, and 5) any change of management or environmental condition that may have caused the animal to change its diet or grazing habits.

■ POISONING FROM HUMAN OVER-THE-COUNTER DRUGS

Safety of most over-the-counter human drugs or nutritional supplements has not been determined in animals; however, some are known to cause toxicity. Be sure to discuss the potential risks of using over-the-counter medications with your veterinarian before intentionally giving them to your pet. Store all medicines where your pet cannot reach them to avoid accidental ingestion.

Antihistamines

Antihistamines provide symptomatic relief of allergic signs (such as itchiness, hives, and difficulty breathing) caused by release of histamine in the body.

Toxic Parts and Effects	Comments and Treatment
Roots, stem base, young leaves. Toxicity retained when dry, except in hay. Rapid onset of signs, with death in 15 to 30 minutes. Drooling, muscular twitching, dilated pupils. Violent convulsions, coma, death. Poisoning in humans common.	Sedatives to control spasm and heart action. Outlook good if alive 2 hours after ingestion.
Seeds, leaves, stems; seeds more toxic. Loss of appetite, hindleg weakness, knuckling of fetlock, listlessness, excess drooling, subnormal temperature, frequent urination. Tissue changes include inflammation of the stomach and intestine, with bleeding on heart and under liver capsule.	Unpalatable. Eaten only under drought conditions.
Seeds and young seedlings. Loss of appetite, depression, nausea, vomiting, weakness, rapid weak pulse, difficulty breathing, muscle spasms, convulsions. Tissue changes include inflammation of the stomach, intestines, liver, and kidney.	Seedlings or grain contaminated with seeds. Oils and fats given by mouth may be beneficial; warmth, stimulants given in the muscle.
Entire plant. Drooling, vomiting, muscle weakness, incoordination or laying down, fast weak pulse, coma, death. No distinctive tissue changes.	Seeds most toxic. Leaves and stems lose toxicity as plant matures. Atropine and picrotoxin may be effective.
Young leaves and swollen or sprouting acorns. Loss of appetite, constipation, followed by dark tarry diarrhea, dry muzzle, frequent urination, rapid weak pulse, death. Tissue changes include swelling around the kidneys with inflammation, inflammation of the stomach and intestine.	Diet must consist of more than 50% oak buds and young leaves for a period of time. Kidney failure with diet history diagnostic. Treatment symptomatic. Oral ruminatorics helpful. (*See also* page 1201.)
Entire plant; roots most toxic. Vomiting, abdominal pain, bloody diarrhea, low blood cell counts. Terminal convulsions, death from respiratory failure. Tissue changes include open inflammation of the stomach and intestine, bleeding of the mucosa, dark liver.	Oils and protectants (stomach and intestinal tract). Dilute acetic acid orally, stimulants. Blood transfusion (hemolytic anemia).

(Continued on the following page)

Table 26. Poisonous Range Plants of Temperate North America—*(Continued)*

Common and Scientific Names	Habitat and Distribution	Affected Animal(s)
Dangerous Season: Spring and Summer		
Buckeye; *Aesculus* species	Woods and thickets; eastern US and California	Horses
Coffeepod, Sicklepod; *Cassia obtusifolia*	Found in cultivated (corn, soybean, or sorghum) and abandoned fields, along fences, roadsides; naturalized in eastern US	Horses
Coffee senna, Coffee weed, Styptic weed, Wild coffee; *Cassia occidentalis*	Common along roadsides, waste areas and pastures; naturalized in eastern US	Horses, rabbits
Fly poison, Staggergrass, Crow poison; *Amianthium muscaetoxicum*	Open woods, fields, and acid bogs; eastern North America	Horses
Larkspurs; *Delphinium* species	Either cultivated or wild, usually in open foothills or meadows and among aspen; mostly western. Dangerous season spring and summer, also seeds in fall.	Horses
Dangerous Season: Summer and Fall		
Black locust, False acacia, Locust tree; *Robinia pseudoacacia*	Open woods, roadsides, pinelands, on clay soils preferably; eastern US	Horses
Dogbanes; *Apocynum* species	Open woods, roadsides, fields; throughout North America	All
Flatweed, Cat's-ear, Gosmore; *Hypochaeris radicata*	Native to the Mediterranean and South America; widely distributed in the US, including Pacific, eastern and southeastern states	Horses
Nightshades, Jerusalem cherry, Potato, Horse nettle, Buffalo bur; *Solanum* species	Fence rows, waste areas, grain and hay fields; throughout North America	All

Toxic Parts and Effects	Comments and Treatment
Entire plant, especially seeds and leaves. Depression, incoordination, twitching, paralysis, inflammation of mucous membranes.	Young shoots and seeds especially poisonous. Stimulants and purgatives.
Toxic principles thought to be same as in *Cassia occidentalis*. Signs, although similar, less severe with *Cassia obtusifolia*.	Treatment ineffective in down animals.
Entire plant. Associated with stomach and intestinal dysfunction and degeneration of muscle. No fever, incoordination with diarrhea and coffee-colored urine. Affected animals are unable to stand but eat and are alert shortly before death. High blood pressure frequent. Tissue changes include heart and skeletal muscle degeneration. Congestion, fatty degeneration and tissue death in the liver and kidneys also reported. Death probably due to high blood pressure causing heart failure.	No specific treatment known. Symptomatic and supportive care essential. Although tissue changes are similar to those of vitamin E/selenium deficiency, this therapy is contraindicated. Remove animals from source.
Entire plant. Drooling, vomiting, rapid and irregular respiration, weakness, death from respiratory failure.	No practical treatment. Especially dangerous for animals new to pasture. Keep animals well fed.
Entire plant, fresh or dry. Straddled stance, arched back, repeated falling, forelegs first. Constipation, bloat, drooling, vomiting. Death (respiratory and heart failure). Most often no tissue changes.	Young plants and seeds more toxic. Toxicity decreases with maturity.
Entire plant, although flowers have been suggested as the toxic principles. Diarrhea, loss of appetite, weakness, hind end paralysis, depression, dilated pupils, cold extremities; frequently weak pulse. Death infrequent; recovery period extensive. Tissue changes after death restricted to stomach and intestinal tract.	Laxatives and stimulants suggested. Treatment supportive.
Leaves and stems of green or dry plants. Increased temperature and pulse, dilated pupils, loss of appetite, discolored mucous membranes, cold extremities, death.	Intravenous fluids and stomach protectants suggested.
Unknown; associated with but not proven cause of a neurologic condition called stringhalt, sudden onset of abnormal gait, knuckling of lower limb joints; paralysis of larynx; recovery possible, but condition could be permanent.	Tranquilizers, sedatives, mephenesin, and thiamine (questionable effectiveness); longterm phenytoin therapy seems helpful. Treatment with baclofen also reported helpful. Surgery reported helpful for gait problems.
Leaves, shoots, and unripe berries. Inflammation of the stomach and intestine with bleeding, weakness, excess drooling, difficulty breathing, trembling, progressive paralysis, laying down, death.	Pilocarpine, physostigmine, gastrointestinal protectants. Seeds may contaminate grain.

(Continued on the following page)

Table 26. Poisonous Range Plants of Temperate North America—*(Continued)*

Common and Scientific Names	Habitat and Distribution	Affected Animal(s)
Perilla mint, Beefsteak plant; *Perilla frutescens*	Ornamental originally from India, escaped to moist pastures, fields, roadsides, and waste places; eastern North America	Horses
Red maple; *Acer rubrum*	Moist land and swamps; eastern North America	Horses
Russian knapweed; *Centaurea repens*	Waste areas, roadsides, railroads, and overgrazed rangeland; not common in cultivated or irrigated pastures; mostly western and upper midwestern US	Horses
White snakeroot; *Eupatorium rugosum*	Woods, cleared areas, waste places, usually the moister and richer soils; eastern North America	Sheep, cattle, horses
Yellow star thistle, Yellow knapweed; *Centaurea solstitialis*	Waste areas, roadsides, pastures; mostly western North America	Horses
Dangerous Season: Fall and Winter		
Black walnut; *Juglans nigra*	Native to eastern US; now from eastern seacoast, west to Michigan and most of the Midwest, south to Georgia and Texas	Horses
Bladderpod, Rattlebox, Sesbane, Coffeebean; *Sesbania vesicaria*	Mostly open, low ground, abandoned cultivated fields; southeastern US coastal plain	All
Onions, (cultivated and wild); *Allium cepa, A. canadense*	Cultivated and grown on rich soils throughout US	Cattle, horses, dogs
Rattlebox, Purple serbane; *Daubentonia unica*	Cultivated and escaped, in waste places; southeastern US coastal plain	All
Rayless goldenrod, Burroweed; *Haplopappus heterophyllus*	Dry plains, grasslands, open woodlands, and along irrigation canals; southwest US	Horses

Toxic Parts and Effects	Comments and Treatment
Green or dry plant. Signs 2 to 10 days after exposure include difficulty breathing (especially on exhaling), open-mouth breathing, lowered head, reluctance to move, death on exertion. Tissue changes include fluid and swelling in the lungs.	Treatment ineffective once signs are severe. Injectable steroids, antihistamines, and antibiotics may help. Handle gently (prevents exertion and death).
Wilted leaves. Anemia, and destruction of blood cells; weakness, rapid breathing, rapid heart beat, depression, jaundice, poor oxygenation of blood, brownish discoloration of blood and urine.	Not common. Fluids, oxygen, and blood transfusion can be helpful. Methylene blue therapy not rewarding.
Fresh or dried plant. Chronic exposure, but sudden onset of signs. Inability to eat or drink, loss of facial tone, chewing, yawning, standing with head down, severe facial swelling, gait normal, head pressing, aimless walking or excitement most severe the first 2 days, become static thereafter. Death from starvation, dehydration, aspiration pneumonia.	More toxic than yellow star thistle (*C. solstitialis; see* below) but with similar pathology and prognosis. Some relief with massive doses of atropine but not an effective treatment. Euthanasia recommended.
Complex benzyl alcohol (tremetol in leaves and stems). Excreted via milk; cumulative. Weight loss, weakness, trembling (muzzle and legs) prominent after exercise, constipation, acetone odor, fatty degeneration of liver, partial paralysis of throat, death in 1 to 3 days.	"Milk sickness" or "trembles." Supportive treatment. Heart and respiratory stimulants and laxatives may be necessary. Remove animal from access to plant.
Entire plant. Involuntary chewing movements, twitching of lips, flicking of tongue. Mouth commonly held open. Unable to eat; death from dehydration, starvation, aspiration pneumonia.	Horses graze because of lack of other forage. Extended period of consumption essential for toxicity. Death of certain brain areas is diagnostic. No treatment. Euthanasia recommended.
Shavings with as little as 20% black walnut are toxic within 24 hours of exposure. Reluctance to move; depression; increased temperature, pulse, respiration rate, abdominal sounds, digital pulse, hoof temperature; distal limb swelling; lameness. Severe laminitis with continued exposure.	Nonfatal; laminitis and edema of lower limbs. Remove shavings promptly. Treat for limb edema and laminitis. Improvement in 1 to 2 days with no complications.
Green plant and seeds.	Green seeds are more toxic. Remove animal from source immediately. General supportive treatment—saline purgatives, intravenous fluids.
Entire parts. Livestock readily consume onions; low blood cell counts develop within days of exposure. Signs are hemoglobin in the urine, diarrhea, loss of appetite, jaundice, incoordination, collapse, and possible death if untreated. Hemolytic anemia reported in livestock ingesting wild onions. Swollen, pale, dying liver.	Signs similar to toxicity induced by S-methylcysteine sulfoxide (a rare toxic amino acid in *Brassica* species) in livestock. Susceptibility to onion poisoning varies across animal species: cattle more susceptible than horses and dogs, which are more susceptible than sheep and goats. Remove animals from source and prevent future access to cull onions. Symptomatic and supportive care essential.
Rapid pulse, weak respiration, diarrhea, death.	Seeds poisonous. Remove animal from source. Saline purgatives.
Primarily nursing young and nonlactating animals. Reluctance to move, trembling, weakness, vomiting, difficulty breathing, constipation, lying down, coma, death.	"Milk sickness." Separate foals from mares.

(Continued on the following page)

Table 26. Poisonous Range Plants of Temperate North America—*(Continued)*

Common and Scientific Names	Habitat and Distribution	Affected Animal(s)
Sweet clover, White sweet clover; *Melilotus officinalis* and *M. alba*	Commonly found on alkaline soils, fields, roadsides, and waste places; forage crop in southern and northern US	Horses
Dangerous Season: Fall, Winter, and Spring		
Chinaberry; *Melia azedarach*	Fence rows, brush, waste places; southeastern US	Horses
Dangerous Season: All Seasons		
Astragalus species (certain species only—selenium accumulators)	Areas high in selenium, mostly western and midwestern	Horses
Bracken fern; *Pteridium aquilinum*	Dry poor soil, open woods, sandy ridges	Horses
Castor bean; *Ricinus communis*	Cultivated in southern regions	All
Chokecherries, Wild cherries, Peaches; *Prunus* species	Waste areas, fence rows, woods, orchards, prairies, dry slopes	Horses
Corn cockle; *Agrostemma githago*	Weed, grainfields, and waste areas; throughout North America	All
Crotalaria, Rattlebox; *Crotalaria* species	Fields and roadsides; eastern and central US	All
Day-blooming jessamine and night-blooming jessamine, respectively; *Cestrum diurnum, C. nocturnum*	Open woods and fields; Gulf Coast states (Florida, Texas) and California	Horses, and dogs (ingesting cholecalciferol-based rodenticides)
Fraser's photinia, Chinese photinia, Red leaf photinia, Red tip photinia; *Photinia fraseri, P. serrulata, P. glabra*	Common ornamental (hedge or screen) in southern US	Horses
Groundsel, Senecio; *Senecio* species	Grassland areas; mostly western US	Horses, limited to US

Toxic Parts and Effects	Comments and Treatment
(*See* Sweet Clover Poisoning, page 1210.)	(*See* page 1210.)
Entire plant, fruit most toxic. Restlessness, vomiting, constipation, blue-tinged gums, rapid pulse, difficulty breathing, death within 24 hours.	Gastroenteritis usual. Recovery may be spontaneous. Laxatives and stomach and intestinal protectants suggested.
Selenium (chronic). Slow growth, reproductive failure, loss of hair, sore feet, acute death.	Avoid grazing seleniferous plants for extended periods. (*See* Selenium Poisoning, page 1205.)
(*See* Bracken Fern Poisoning, page 1147.)	(*See* page 1147.)
Entire plant, seeds especially toxic. Short to long course (death or recovery). Violent purgation, straining with bloody diarrhea, weakness, drooling, trembling, incoordination.	Diagnosis based on presence of seeds, red blood cell clumping, precipitin test. Specific antiserum, ideal antidote; sedatives, arecoline hydrobromide, followed by saline cathartics suggested.
Excitement leading to depression, difficulty breathing, incoordination, convulsions, prostration. Death may occur in 15 minutes.	Mucous membranes, bright pink color; blood, bright red color. (*See* Cyanide Poisoning, page 1150.)
Seeds. Short course. Profuse watery diarrhea, vomiting, dullness, general weakness, rapid breathing, hemoglobin in the urine, death.	Oils and stomach and intestinal protectants. Neutralize toxin. Blood transfusions may be necessary.
Entire plant, especially seeds. Chronic course. Horses—unthriftiness, incoordination, walking in circles, jaundice; Death may occur from a few weeks to months after ingestion.	Cumulative, fresh or dry. No treatment.
Entire plant, including fruit and sap. Inflammation of the stomach and intestine develops on ingestion of fruits. Vomiting, depression, loss of appetite, chronic weight loss with normal appetite, choppy stiff gait, increased pulse, persistent increases in blood calcemia and phosphate, calcium deposits in arteries, tendons, ligaments, and kidneys, destruction of the parathyroid glands, overgrowth of the thyroid gland, and increased bone density reported with chronic ingestion of leaves.	Prevent further access of animals to plants. In early stages, treatment might be effective. Correct fluid and electrolyte (salt) imbalances in cases with persistent vomiting or diarrhea. Reduce or prevent changes in blood calcium. Maintenance therapy of diuretics and steroids may be necessary.
Same as for Nandina (*see* page 1188).	Same as for Nandina (*see* page 1188).
Fresh or dry. Short-term poisoning not common. Dullness, aimless walking, increased pulse, rapid breathing, weakness, colic, delayed death (days to months). Nervous signs evident in later stages.	Liver biopsy diagnostic in early stages. No general treatment.

(Continued on the following page)

Table 26. Poisonous Range Plants of Temperate North America—*(Continued)*

Common and Scientific Names	Habitat and Distribution	Affected Animal(s)
Hound's tongue; *Cynoglossum officinale*	Common in waste places, roadsides, and pastured areas throughout US	Horses
Jimson weed, Thorn apple; *Datura stramonium*	Fields, barn lots, trampled pastures, and waste places on rich bottom soils; throughout North America	All
Johnson grass; *Sorghum halepense*	Weed of open fields and waste places; southern and scattered north to New York and Iowa	Horses
Laurel, Ivybush, Lambkill; *Kalmia* species	Rich moist woods, meadows, or acid bogs; eastern and north-western North America. Dangerous all seasons, especially winter and spring.	Horses
Laurel cherry, Cherry laurel; *Prunus caroliniana*	Woods, fence rows, and often escaped from cultivation; southern regions. Dangerous all seasons, especially winter and spring.	Horses
Locoweed; *Astragalus* species, *Oxytropis* species (certain species only)	Mostly western North America	All grazing animals
Lupines, Bluebonnet; *Lupinus* species	Dry to moist soils, roadsides, fields, and mountains; throughout, but poisoning mostly western North America	Horses
Milk vetch (and many other common names); *Astragalus* species (certain species only)	Nearly all	Horses
Milkweeds; *Asclepias* species	Dry areas, usually waste places, roadsides, streambeds	All
Mustards, Crucifers, Cress; *Brassica, Raphanus, Descurainia* species	Fields, roadsides; throughout North America	Horses
Nandina, Heavenly bamboo, Chinese sacred bamboo; *Nandina domestica*	Common ornamental in southern US	Horses
Oleander; *Nerium oleander*	Common ornamental in southern regions of the US	All

Toxic Parts and Effects	Comments and Treatment
Foliage. Unpleasant odor discourages consumption when fresh, becomes palatable in hay and is readily consumed. Signs are poor appetite, depression, rough hair coat, bleeding, bloody feces, incoordination, jaundice, death.	Know source and quality of hay. Treatment symptomatic and supportive at best. Affected animals seldom recover.
Entire plant, seeds in particular. Short course. Weak rapid pulse and heartbeat, dilated pupils, dry mouth, incoordination, convulsions, coma.	All parts, mainly in hay or silage. Urine from animal dilates pupils of laboratory animals (diagnostic). Treatment nonspecific; cardiac and respiratory stimulants.
Same as for *Sorghum vulgare* (*see* page 1190).	Same as for *Sorghum vulgare* (*see* page 1190).
Vegetative parts. Short course. Incoordination, excess drooling, vomiting, bloat, weakness, muscular spasms, coma, death.	Treatment includes laxatives, demulcents, nerve stimulants, atropine.
Wilted leaves, bark, and twigs. Short course. Difficult breathing, bloat, staggering, convulsions, followed by prostration and death. Mucous membranes and blood bright red.	(*See* CYANIDE POISONING, page 1150.)
Depression, emaciation, incoordination, dry lusterless hair. Abortions.	Avoid grazing of source. Both green and dry plants toxic.
Seeds (fresh and dry). Short course. No appetite, difficulty breathing, struggle, convulsions, death from respiratory paralysis.	Do not disturb sick animals; remove from source as they begin to recover. No effective treatment, but survivors recover completely. (*See also* MYCOTOXIC LUPINOSIS, page 1155.)
Hindlimb paralysis, goose-stepping, depression, rough coat, pulmonary emphysema, sudden death, spinal cord changes.	Avoid grazing of pre-flower stage.
Entire plant, green or dry. Staggering, tetanic convulsions, bloating, difficulty breathing, dilated pupils, rapid and weak pulse, coma, death.	Sedatives, laxatives, and intravenous fluids suggested.
Seeds and vegetative parts, fresh or dry. Sudden or long course. Loss of appetite, severe inflammation of the stomach and intestines, drooling, diarrhea, paralysis, sensitivity to light, hemoglobin in the urine.	Remove from source. Administer stomach and intestinal protectants (mineral oil).
Foliage and fruits. Hydrolyzed in stomach and intestinal tract to free cyanide, thereby affecting cellular respiration. Prognosis good if animal survives for 1 hour after signs begin. (*See* CYANIDE POISONING, page 1150.)	Acute outcome precludes effective treatment for most; Intravenous sodium nitrite/sodium thiosulfate treatment of choice. Picrate test indicates toxic potential of the plant. (*See* CYANIDE POISONING, page 1150.)
Entire plant, fresh or dry. Short course. Severe inflammation of the intestine and stomach, vomiting, diarrhea, increased pulse rate, weakness, death.	No specific treatment. Atropine in conjunction with propranolol reported helpful.

(Continued on the following page)

Table 26. Poisonous Range Plants of Temperate North America—*(Continued)*

Common and Scientific Names	Habitat and Distribution	Affected Animal(s)
Poison hemlock; *Conium maculatum*	Roadside ditches, damp waste areas; throughout North America	All
Privet, Ligustrum, Hedge plant; *Ligustrum* species	An ornamental; common as hedge; found at abandoned farm home sites, along fences, and in bottomlands.	Horses
Sorghum, Sudan grass, Kafir, Durra, Milo, Broom-corn, Schrock; *Sorghum vulgare*	Forage crops and escapes; throughout North America	All
St. John's-wort, Goatweed, Klamath weed; *Hypericum perforatum*	Dry soil, roadsides, pastures, ranges; throughout North America	Horses
Tall fescue; *Festuca arundinacea*	A coarse, hardy, drought-resistant grass; Pacific Northwest, Missouri, Oklahoma, and Kentucky; major pasture grass in southeastern US	Horses
Yellow jessamine, Evening trumpet flower, Carolina Jessamine; *Gelsemium sempervirens*	Open woods, thickets; southeast	All
Yew; *Taxus* species	Most of North America; Japanese and English yew common ornamentals	All

Antihistamines are often combined with other ingredients in many over-the-counter cold, sinus, and allergy medications. Commonly used antihistamines include chlorpheniramine, dimenhydrinate, diphenhydramine, promethazine, meclizine, and loratidine. Depending on the dose and the amount of time since ingestion, signs of antihistamine toxicity can include depression or hyperactivity, drooling, rapid breathing, rapid heartbeat, gastrointestinal upset, lack of coordination, tremors, fever, and seizures.

Treatment of antihistamine poisoning is primarily supportive. Vomiting should be considered only if the animal is not showing any signs. Fluids and other medications are used to support cardiovascular function and control seizures.

Decongestants

Several types of decongestants are available as over-the-counter drugs. The decongestants most toxic to pets are discussed below.

Imidazoline Decongestants

Oxymetazoline, xylometazoline, tetrahydrozoline, and **naphazoline** are derivatives of imidazoline that are found in over-the-counter decongestants. They are generally used in the nose and eyes for temporary relief of nasal congestion due to colds, allergies, or sinusitis.

Toxic Parts and Effects	Comments and Treatment
Vegetative parts. Short course. Dilated pupils; weakness; staggering gait; slow pulse, progressing to rapid and thready. Slow, irregular breathing; death from respiratory failure.	Toxin excreted via lungs and kidneys, mousy odor of breath and urine diagnostic. Administer saline cathartics; neutralize alkaloids with tannic acid, together with stimulants.
Leaves and fruit. Primarily intestine and stomach irritants. Diarrhea, abdominal pain, incoordination, muscle weakness, weak pulse, fever, convulsions, sometimes death.	Treatment symptomatic and supportive; correct dehydration.
Heavy in vegetative parts. Short course. Difficult breathing, bloat, staggering, convulsions, death. Blood bright red (cyanide) or chocolate brown (nitrate).	Hay safe for cyanide (volatile), not safe for nitrate (analyze). (*See* CYANIDE POISONING, page 1150, and NITRATE AND NITRITE POISONING, page 1172.)
Photodynamic pigment (hypericin). Short course. Sensitivity to light, pruritus and erythema, blindness, convulsions, diarrhea, hypersensitivity to cold water contact, death.	Remove animals from source and sunlight. Corticosteroids given by injection, topical antibiotics.
(*See* FESCUE POISONING [SUMMER FESCUE POISONING], page 1155.)	(*See* FESCUE POISONING [SUMMER FESCUE POISONING], page 1155.)
Entire plant. Short course. Weakness, incoordination, dilated pupils, convulsions, coma, death within 48 hours.	No specific treatment. Relaxants and sedatives suggested.
Bark, leaves, seeds. Gaseous distress, diarrhea, vomiting, tremors, difficulty breathing, dilated pupils, respiratory difficulty, weakness, fatigue, collapse, coma, convulsions, irregular heartbeat, circulatory failure, death. Death may be rapid.	Poisoning usually results when branches and trimmings fed to livestock.

In dogs, signs of poisoning may include vomiting, slow heart rate, abnormal heart rhythms, low or high blood pressure, panting, increased breathing sounds, depression, weakness, nervousness, hyperactivity, or shaking. Decongestants are absorbed rapidly, and these signs appear within 30 minutes to 4 hours after exposure. The gastrointestinal tract, heart, lungs, and nervous system can be affected.

Fluids are given to support heart function and to correct metabolic abnormalities, along with other medications to slow the heart rate and control apprehension and shaking. Yohimbine, a drug that cancels out the effect of the antihistamine on the body, can also be used.

Pseudoephedrine and Ephedrine

Ephedrine and pseudoephedrine are common over-the-counter medications used as nasal decongestants. Pseudoephedrine is found naturally in plants of the genus *Ephedra*. These drugs are not affected by the current Food and Drug Administration ban on products containing ephedra; in many areas, however, products containing pseudoephedrine are now kept behind the pharmacy counter due to their possible use in creating methamphetamine.

Pseudoephedrine and ephedrine overdose can result in enlarged pupils, rapid heartbeat, high blood pressure, abnormal heart rhythms, agitation, anxiety, hyperactivity, tremors, head bobbing, hiding, vomiting, and death. Treatment consists of removing any drug that has not been absorbed, controlling the central nervous system and cardiovascular effects, and supportive care. Vomiting should be induced or the stomach should be flushed, followed by administration of activated charcoal with a medicine that causes the emptying of the bowels. Hyperactivity, nervousness, seizures, and rapid heartbeat should be controlled through medication. Fluids should be given. Signs can last 1 to 4 days.

Nonsteroidal Anti-inflammatory Drugs (NSAIDs)

Nonsteroidal anti-inflammatory drugs are the most commonly used class of human medications in the world. Due to their widespread availability and use, human NSAIDs are often accidentally ingested by dogs and cats. Ibuprofen, aspirin, naproxen, and acetaminophen are some of the most common NSAIDs. These drugs should not be used in pets unless directed by your veterinarian.

Treatment of NSAID poisoning consists of removing any drug that has not been absorbed, protecting the gastrointestinal tract and kidneys, and providing supportive care. Vomiting should be induced in recent exposures, followed by administration of activated charcoal with a medication that empties the bowels. Fluids are given to increase urine output. The outlook for recovery depends on the amount ingested and the amount of time between ingestion and treatment.

Ibuprofen is used for its anti-inflammatory, fever-reducing, and pain-relieving properties in animals and people. It is rapidly absorbed after ingestion, but food in the stomach can slow this process. Ibuprofen can be used in dogs, but it has a narrow margin of safety. Prolonged use can cause stomach

ulcers and perforations, as well as kidney damage. In addition, central nervous system depression, low blood pressure, lack of coordination, heart effects, seizures, coma, and death can be seen. A single ingestion can lead to sudden and severe vomiting, diarrhea, abdominal pain, and loss of appetite.

Cats are more sensitive to ibuprofen than dogs, and toxicosis is seen at only half the dosage that causes problems in dogs. Ibuprofen toxicity is more severe in ferrets than in dogs that consume similar dosages.

Aspirin is rapidly absorbed from the gastrointestinal tract in animals. Aspirin poisoning is usually characterized by depression, fever, unusually deep or fast breathing, seizures, metabolic abnormalities, coma, stomach irritation or ulceration, liver damage, or increased bleeding time. Large dosages can be fatal in cats. Dogs tolerate aspirin better than cats, but prolonged use can result in stomach ulcers.

Naproxen is available as tablets, gelcaps, and as a suspension. Naproxen is similar to carprofen and ibuprofen. In people and dogs, naproxen is used for its anti-inflammatory, pain-relieving, and fever-reducing properties. It is rapidly absorbed after ingestion. Naproxen poisoning in dogs has caused bleeding into the bowels. Signs include black feces, frequent vomiting, abdominal pain, perforating ulcer of the small intestine, weakness, stumbling, pale mucous membranes, and anemia. Cats may be even more sensitive to naproxen toxicity than dogs.

Acetaminophen is commonly used in people to reduce fever and relieve pain. It has a lower risk of stomach ulceration than aspirin. Acetaminophen is rapidly absorbed, but absorption can be delayed with extended-release formulations. In dogs, signs of toxicity are usually not seen unless the dosage of acetaminophen is very high. Toxicity can be seen at lower dosages with repeated exposures. Cats are more sensitive to acetaminophen, and toxicity is seen at much lower dosages than in dogs.

Acetaminophen poisoning is characterized by changes in the hemoglobin in the blood and damage to the liver. Kidney damage is also possible. Cats primarily develop the changed hemoglobin in the blood within a few hours, resulting in a condition called Heinz body anemia. This results in mucous membranes becoming brown or muddy in color, and is usually accompanied by a rapid heartbeat, unusually deep or fast breathing, weakness, and lethargy. Other signs include depression, weakness, jaundice, vomiting, dangerously low body temperature, fluid buildup within the face or paws, a bluish tinge to the skin and mucous membranes, liver damage, and death.

Treatment of acetaminophen poisoning includes removing drug that has not been absorbed from the stomach, preventing or treating the blood changes and liver damage, and providing supportive care. Inducing vomiting is useful when performed early, followed by administration of activated charcoal with a medication that empties the bowels. Fluids and blood transfusions are given as needed.

Gastrointestinal Drugs

H$_2$-receptor antagonists, also called H$_2$ blockers, are commonly used to treat gastrointestinal ulcers, inflammation of the esophagus, and gastric reflux (a backward flow of stomach contents). Cimetidine, famotidine, and ranitidine are examples of this group. These drugs are rapidly absorbed, reaching peak blood concentrations within 1 to 3 hours.

H$_2$ blockers have a wide margin of safety. Overdoses typically result in minor effects such as vomiting, diarrhea, loss of appetite, and dry mouth. Treatment generally consists of monitoring and supportive care.

Antacids come in pill and liquid forms, and are frequently used to treat gastrointestinal upset. Common antacids include calcium carbonate, aluminum hydroxide, and magnesium hydroxide (milk of magnesia). These agents are poorly absorbed when ingested by mouth. Calcium- and aluminum-containing antacids generally cause constipation, while magnesium-containing antacids tend to cause diarrhea. Some products contain both aluminum and magnesium salts in an attempt to balance their constipating and laxative effects. Ingestion of calcium salts may cause a temporary excess of calcium in the blood, but significant whole-body effects are unlikely. Inducing vomiting within 2 to 3 hours of exposure may be helpful in preventing severe gastrointestinal upset.

Multivitamins and Iron

The common ingredients in multivitamins include ascorbic acid (vitamin C), cyanocobalamin (vitamin B$_{12}$), folic acid, thiamine (vitamin B$_1$), riboflavin (vitamin B$_2$), niacin (vitamin B$_3$), biotin, pantothenic acid, pyridoxine (vitamin B$_6$), calcium, phosphorus, iodine, iron, magnesium, copper, zinc, and vitamins A, D, and E. Among these ingredients, iron and vitamins A and D may cause significant problems if overdosed. Ingestion of large amounts of the other ingredients in pets can result in gastrointestinal upset (for example, vomiting, diarrhea, loss of appetite) that resolves on its own. However, toxicity is typically rare in pets.

Iron has direct corrosive or irritant effects on the lining of the gastrointestinal tract. It can also be a direct poison to liver cells. Signs of iron toxicosis usually develop within 6 hours. Initial vomiting and diarrhea, with or without blood, may be followed by shock, depression, fever, metabolic abnormalities, and liver failure 12 to 24 hours later, often with a period of apparent recovery in between. Shock may lead to kidney failure. An overdose of iron generally warrants inducing vomiting (or flushing the stomach), administering gastrointestinal protectants, and providing supportive treatment.

Vitamin A toxicity is not likely to occur after ingesting multivitamins. The amount of vitamin A needed to cause toxic effects is 10 to 1,000 times the dietary requirements for most species. Signs associated with vitamin A toxicity include general malaise, loss of appetite, peeling skin, weakness, tremors, convulsions, paralysis, and death.

Vitamin D is included in many calcium supplements to aid the absorption of the calcium. Most vitamins contain cholecalciferol (vitamin D_3). Vomiting, depression, passing large amounts of urine, excessive thirst, and high levels of phosphate in the blood may be seen within 12 hours, followed by high levels of calcium in the blood and sudden kidney failure 1 to 2 days after exposure. In addition to kidney failure, the heart and gastrointestinal tract may show signs of damage and mineralization. Initial treatment should include inducing vomiting (or flushing the stomach) and an analysis of the blood. Multiple doses of activated charcoal with a drug that empties the bowels should be given. If signs of toxicosis develop, treatment includes fluids and medications to increase urine output and to bind phosphate. Stabilization of blood calcium may require many days of treatment.

Nutritional Supplements

Guarana (*Paullinia cupana*), a natural source of caffeine, and **ma huang** (*Ephedra sinica*), a natural source of ephedrine, are contained in several herbal supplements that claim to help people lose weight and improve their energy level. In people, use of herbal supplements containing guarana and ma huang have been linked to inflammation of the liver (hepatitis), kidney stones, inflammation of the heart, and sudden death. In dogs, accidental ingestion of herbal supplements containing ma huang and guarana can lead to severe hyperactivity, tremors, seizures, vomiting, a rapid heartbeat, fever, and death within a few hours of exposure. The use of ephedra-containing supplements has been banned by the Food and Drug Administration (*see also* PSEUDOEPHEDRINE AND EPHEDRINE, page 1191).

5-Hydroxytryptophan or *Griffonia* seed extracts are contained in several over-the-counter herbal supplements that claim to treat depression, headaches, insom-

nia, and obesity. When taken by mouth, 5-hydroxytryptophan is rapidly absorbed. Signs can develop within 4 hours after ingestion and last up to 36 hours. Signs include seizures, depression, tremors, lack of coordination, vomiting, diarrhea, fever, temporary blindness, and death. Treatment consists of inducing vomiting (or flushing the stomach), administering fluids and medications to control central nervous system signs, and regulating body temperature (cool water bath, fans). Cyproheptadine, a drug that cancels out the effects of 5-hydroxytryptophan overdosage, may be used.

Topical Zinc Oxide

Zinc oxide ointments or creams are commonly used as topical skin protectants, astringents, and bactericidal agents. Most ointments contain 10 to 40% zinc oxide. Ingestion of these products usually results in vomiting, diarrhea, and liver and kidney damage. Signs are usually seen within 2 to 4 hours. Treatment is symptomatic and supportive.

■ POISONINGS FROM HUMAN PRESCRIPTION DRUGS

Pets commonly ingest prescription medications from countertops, pill minders, mail-order packages, or other sources. Safety data for human prescription drugs in certain animal species may not be available, because most are not approved for veterinary use.

Cardiovascular Medications

Cardiovascular medications (drugs used to treat heart disease) fall into several categories, including ACE inhibitors, calcium channel blockers, beta blockers, and diuretics. Some of these medications are used to treat heart diseases in animals, but all can be toxic if a pet accidentally eats a large number of pills.

Angiotensin-converting Enzyme (ACE) Inhibitors

Several ACE inhibitors (for example, enalapril, captopril, lisinopril) are used therapeutically in dogs and cats. The primary concern in cases of overdose is abnormally low blood pressure with secondary kidney damage. Onset occurs within a few hours of exposure, or longer for extended-release formulations. Other signs of overdose may include vomiting, pale mucous membranes, weakness, and a rapid or slow heartbeat. Activated charcoal can bind the drug from the gastrointestinal tract if given within 1 to 2 hours of ingestion. Blood pressure and kidney function should be monitored, and fluids given as needed.

Calcium Channel Blockers

Calcium channel blockers (for example, diltiazem, amlodipine, verapamil) affect the movement of calcium into the cells of the heart and blood vessels. As a result, they relax blood vessels and increase the supply of blood and oxygen to the heart. They are used in people for high blood pressure, chest pain (angina), and irregular heartbeats. The most common signs of overdose include low blood pressure, slow heart rate, gastrointestinal upset, and irregular heart rhythms. A very rapid heartbeat may develop in response to the drop in blood pressure.

Treatment of an overdose includes correcting the blood pressure and abnormal heart rhythm. In general, vomiting should not be induced unless this can be done within minutes of ingestion. Activated charcoal binds unabsorbed drug in the gastrointestinal tract and is most useful in the first hours after ingestion. If a sustained-release product was ingested, repeat doses of activated charcoal every 4 to 6 hours for a total of 2 to 4 doses can provide additional benefit. Specific medications should be started based on blood pressure, heart rate, electrocardiogram, and blood analysis. Fluids are recommended.

Beta Blockers

Beta blockers (for example, propanolol, atenolol, timolol) affect the response to some nerve impulses in certain parts of the body. As a result, they decrease the heart's need for blood and oxygen by reducing its workload. They also help the heart to beat more regularly. They are used in people most commonly to treat high blood pressure, relieve chest pain (angina), and correct abnormal heart rhythms. The most common signs of overdose in animals are slow heart rate and low blood pressure. Depressed breathing, coma, seizures, a high level of potassium in the blood, and low blood sugar level may develop. It is also possible to cause sudden congestive heart failure. Significant signs may be seen even at recommended dosages—however, no beta blockers are approved for veterinary use.

Because beta blockers are absorbed rapidly, vomiting should be induced only within minutes of ingestion. Administration of activated charcoal should be considered if either multiple tablets or capsules or sustained-release formulation tablets were ingested. Heart rate and the pet's condition should be monitored for at least 2 to 4 hours. Treatment includes fluids to increase blood pressure and medications to support heart function and decrease blood potassium levels.

Diuretics

Diuretics are used to increase urine output. Common diuretics include chlorothiazide, hydrochlorothiazide, furosemide, spironolactone, and triamterene. The most common signs of diuretic overdose include vomiting, depression, passing large amounts of urine, excessive thirst, and metabolic abnormalities (especially of potassium). Management should include monitoring fluids and electrolytes, with correction as needed.

Tranquilizers, Antidepressants, Sleep Aids, and Anticonvulsants

Tranquilizers, antidepressants, and related drugs are used in both pets and people, but can be very toxic if a pet consumes them by accident.

Benzodiazepines

Benzodiazepines are used to control seizures and to relieve anxiety. Commonly used benzodiazepines include diazepam, alprazolam, chlordiazepoxide, clonazepam, lorazepam, oxazepam, and triazolam. In general, all are rapidly and fairly completely absorbed. Cats may be more sensitive to adverse effects. The most common signs of toxicity in animals are central nervous system depression, depressed breathing, lack of coordination, weakness, disorientation, and vomiting. Some animals, especially at high doses, may initially show central nervous system excitation, followed by central nervous system depression. Other common signs are dangerously low body temperature, low blood pressure, a rapid heartbeat, and decreased muscle tone. Vomiting can be induced if the ingestion is recent and no signs are present. Flushing the stomach, followed by administration of activated charcoal can be performed if the ingested amount is very high. Close monitoring is needed. Additional treatment includes fluids, and medications to support respiratory function and to control central nervous system excitation.

Antidepressants

Antidepressants fall into several classes. One group, called the **selective serotonin reuptake inhibitors,** includes sertraline, fluoxetine, paroxetine, and fluvoxamine. The **tricyclic antidepressants**, another group, include amitriptyline, clomipramine, and nortriptyline. Signs of poisoning include agitation, confusion, fever, abnormal heart rhythms, high blood pressure, sudden muscular contractions, involuntary rhythmic movement of the eyes, seizures, metabolic abnormalities, an inability to urinate, dry mouth, enlarged pupils, and constipation. This may be followed by lethargy, lack of coordination, dangerously low body temperature, depressed breathing, a bluish tinge to skin and mucous membranes, low blood pressure, and coma.

Vomiting should be induced in cases of recent exposure if the animal is not showing any signs. This can be followed by activated charcoal (even several hours after ingestion) plus a medication that causes emptying of the bowels. Other medications are given to control seizures and heart rate and rhythm.

An overdose of almost any antidepressant can result in development of the **serotonin syndrome**. Signs of the serotonin syndrome include altered mental status, agitation, sudden muscular contractions, overactive reflexes, tremors, diarrhea, lack of coordination, and fever. This syndrome is often seen after overdose of substances that result in increased free levels of serotonin, such as antidepressants or profound stimulants (for example, amphetamines, cocaine, pseudoephedrine, and ephedra). Cyproheptadine is often used for treatment.

Barbiturates

Long-acting barbiturates, such as phenobarbital, mephobarbital, and primadone, are commonly used as anticonvulsants or sedatives. Short-acting barbiturates (butabarbital, pentobarbital, secobarbital) and ultra short-acting barbiturates (thiamylal and thiopental) are used mainly to induce anesthesia and to control seizures. The onset of signs after ingestion varies from 15 minutes to several hours, and effects can last up to several days for the long-acting class. The most common signs are sedation, lack of coordination, depressed breathing, coma, loss of reflexes, low blood pressure, and dangerously low body temperature.

Treatment begins with removing unabsorbed drug by inducing vomiting (if the exposure is very recent and no signs are seen) or by flushing the stomach. Additional treatment includes administration of activated charcoal and fluids, along with respiratory support and maintaining body temperature.

Sleep Aids

Zolpidem and zaleplon are sleep aids that act in a similar way as the benzodiazepines (*see* page 1195). Although sedation would be expected after ingestion, these drugs have been associated with the contradictory state of excitement. In addition to the obvious signs of sedation and lack of coordination, dogs have developed tremors, vocalizing, and pacing at low dosages.

Vomiting can be induced if the ingestion was recent and no signs are seen. For mild signs, keeping the pet quiet and in a safe place may be enough. If excitement develops, symptomatic treatment should be given and will vary with the signs and their intensity.

Tranquilizers

The most commonly used tranquilizers in veterinary medicine are acepromazine, chlorpromazine, and promazine. They are also used before general anesthesia, to prevent vomiting, and to treat central nervous system agitation after specific drug overdoses (amphetamines, cocaine). The most common signs of an overdose are sedation, weakness, lack of coordination, collapse, behavioral changes, dangerously low body temperature, low blood pressure, and either a rapid or slow heart rate. Treatment consists of symptomatic and supportive care. Because central nervous system signs begin rapidly, vomiting should be induced only if ingestion was recent, followed by administration of activated charcoal and a medication that causes emptying of the bowels. Body temperature, heart rate, and blood pressure should be monitored and treated symptomatically.

Muscle Relaxants

The most commonly used muscle relaxants include baclofen and cyclobenzaprine. Signs of poisoning may begin as soon as 30 minutes after ingestion. The most common signs are vocalization, drooling, vomiting, lack of coordination, weakness, tremors, shaking, coma, seizures, slow heart rate, dangerously low body temperature, and blood pressure abnormalities. Treatment consists of supportive care, including fluids and respiratory support. Vomiting should be induced if the exposure is recent and no signs are present, followed by administration of activated charcoal.

Topical Agents

Pets ingest many topical preparations, which most often results in only mild inflammation of the stomach and intestines. However, ingestion of certain topical agents, such as 5-fluorouracil and calcipotriene, can be fatal even at low doses.

5-Fluorouracil is available as an ointment or topical solution. It is used in people to treat skin cancers and precancerous skin growths caused by longterm sun exposure. Dogs and cats begin showing signs within a few hours of ingesting 5-fluorouracil. Initial signs include severe vomiting and diarrhea. Signs often progress to vomiting with blood, tremors, lack of coordination, and seizures. Generally, 5-fluorouracil affects the gastrointestinal tract, liver, kidneys, central nervous system, and bone marrow. The death rate in dogs is high.

Treatment consists primarily of supportive care. Vomiting should be induced after recent ingestion (within an hour) if the animal is not yet showing any signs, followed by activated charcoal and a medication that causes emptying of the bowels. If the animal is spontaneously vomiting or having seizures, medications are administered to protect the gastrointestinal tract and to control seizures and tremors. Fluids should be given and body temperature monitored. Blood and serum values are usually monitored for about 2 weeks. Surviving dogs may show evidence of bone marrow suppression later.

Calcipotriene, is used to treat psoriasis in people. It is available as an ointment and as a cream. Accidental ingestion in dogs is associated with life-threatening increases of calcium in the blood. Signs usually begin within 1 to 3 days of ingestion and include loss of appetite, vomiting, diarrhea, passing large amounts of urine, excessive thirst, depression, and weakness. Blood calcium is usually increased within 12 to 24 hours and may remain high for weeks. This is usually accompanied by an increase in blood phosphorus and soft-tissue mineralization. Kidney failure, coma, and death can occur in severe or untreated cases.

Treatment involves inducing vomiting and administering activated charcoal and a medication that empties the bowels. Fluids, corticosteroids, and diuretics are used to increase urine output and decrease blood calcium (*see* HYPERCALCEMIA, page 135). Blood levels of calcium and phosphorus, and kidney function usually must be monitored for several weeks.

Prescription Nonsteroidal Anti-inflammatory Drugs (NSAIDs)

There are many different prescription nonsteroidal anti-inflammatory drugs (NSAIDs) used to relieve pain and inflammation in both humans and animals. Some commonly prescribed NSAIDs in humans include diclofenac, naproxen, celecoxib, ketoprofen, meloxicam, etodolac, flurbuprofen, and ibuprofen. Accidental ingestion by animals of NSAIDs intended for human use is common. These drugs should never be given to pets unless prescribed by your veterinarian. Most NSAIDs have the potential to adversely affect the gastrointestinal tract, kidneys, and liver.

Signs of NSAID poisoning vary based on the particular drug and species of animal involved and the amount ingested. Signs may include vomiting, rapid breathing or heart rate, lack of coordination, and possibly seizures, coma, or death. If you suspect that your pet has ingested a prescription (or over-the-counter) NSAID, you should immediately contact your veterinarian or an animal poison control center.

Treatment of NSAID poisoning consists of removing any drug that has not been absorbed, protecting the gastrointestinal tract and kidneys, and providing supportive care. If the ingestion occurred recently, vomiting may be induced, followed by administration of activated charcoal with a medication that empties the bowels. Fluids may be given to increase urine output. The outlook for recovery depends on the amount ingested and the amount of time between ingestion and treatment.

▨ POISONINGS FROM ILLICIT AND ABUSED DRUGS

If your pet has been exposed to illicit or abused drugs, it is important that you provide an accurate and complete history to your veterinarian. This information is critical for your veterinarian to be able to make an accurate diagnosis and provide appropriate treatment. Illicit drugs are often adulterated with other pharmacologically active substances, which makes the diagnosis even more difficult. As with any potential poisoning, critical information includes the amount your pet has eaten, the amount of time between ingestion and appearance of signs, and a description of all signs that have developed.

Cocaine

Cocaine is obtained from the leaves of the coca plant. Common street names for cocaine include coke, gold dust, stardust, snow, "C", white girl, white lady, baseball, and speedball (cocaine and heroin). Free base cocaine is also called crack, rock, or flake. Cocaine is often "cut" or diluted with other substances, such as xanthine alkaloids, local anesthetics, and decongestants. Cocaine is primarily used illegally by people as a recreational drug, but it also has medical use as a topical anesthetic on the mucous membranes of the mouth, larynx, and nasal passages.

Cocaine poisoning is characterized by hyperactivity, shaking, lack of coordination, panting, agitation, nervousness, seizures, a rapid heartbeat, metabolic abnormalities, and fever. Central nervous system depression and coma may follow. Death may be due to very high fever or cardiac or respiratory arrest.

Diagnosis is based on a history of exposure and the characteristic signs. Identification of cocaine in blood, stomach contents, or urine can confirm exposure.

Animals with signs will need to be stabilized first before treatment can be attempted. Vomiting can be induced in a recent exposure if the animal is showing no signs. This should be followed by administration of activated charcoal with a medication that causes emptying of the bowels. If the animal's condition makes it inadvisable to induce vomiting (for example, presence of central nervous system signs or extremely rapid heartbeat) flushing the stomach should be performed.

Anticonvulsants and tranquilizers are used to control the central nervous system effects. Blood pressure, heart rate and rhythm, and body temperature will to be monitored often and treated as needed. Fluids should be administered and metabolic abnormalities monitored and corrected as needed. Treatment and monitoring should continue until all signs have resolved.

Amphetamines and Related Drugs

Amphetamines stimulate the central nervous system and the cardiovascular system. In people, amphetamines and their derivatives are commonly used for depression of appetite, narcolepsy, attention deficit disorder, Parkinson's disease, and some behavior disorders. Some common amphetamines or related drugs are benzphetamine, dextroamphetamine, pemoline, methylphenidate, phentermine, diethylpropion, phendimetrazine, methamphetamine, and phenmetrazine. Amphetamines sold on the street are often called speed, bennies, or uppers, and they are commonly "cut" or diluted with caffeine, ephedrine, or phenylpropanolamine.

Signs of amphetamine and cocaine poisoning are very similar. The only difference may be that the signs of amphetamine poisoning last longer. The most common signs are hyperactivity, aggression, fever, tremors, lack of coordination, a rapid heartbeat, high blood pressure, enlarged pupils, circling, and death.

Diagnosis and treatment are as for cocaine (see above), and the history given by the owner is extremely important. Most amphetamines and related drugs can be detected in stomach contents and urine.

Phenothiazine tranquilizers are used to control central nervous system signs in amphetamine poisoning. Anticonvulsants are used if needed. Heart rate and rhythm, body temperature, and electrolytes should be monitored and treated as needed.

Marijuana

Marijuana refers to a mixture of cut, dried, and ground flowers, leaves, and stems of the leafy green hemp plant *Cannabis sativa*. The plant grows in most tropical and temperate regions of the world. Street names for marijuana include pot, Mary Jane, hashish, weed, grass, THC, ganja, bhang, and charas. Marijuana or hashish sold on the streets may be contaminated with phencyclidine, LSD, or other drugs.

Marijuana is primarily used illegally by people as a recreational drug, but it has medical use to prevent vomiting in chemotherapy patients and to decrease pressure within the eye in glaucoma patients.

In dogs, the most common route of exposure is ingestion. Signs begin within 30 to 90 minutes and can last up to 3 days. The most common signs of poisoning are depression, lack of coordination, slow heart rate, dangerously low body temperature, vocalization, excessive drooling, vomiting, diarrhea, inability to control urination, seizures, and coma.

Diagnosis is based on a history of exposure and typical signs. Marijuana is difficult to detect in body fluids, however, urine testing in the early course of exposure may help confirm the diagnosis.

Treatment consists of supportive care, including medication to control seizures. Vomiting can be induced if the exposure is recent and the animal is not yet showing signs. Comatose animals should be given intravenous fluids and treated for dangerously low body temperature. Their position should be changed often to prevent fluid buildup and pressure sores. Treatment and monitoring should continue until all signs have resolved (up to 3 days in dogs).

Opiates

The term opioid refers to all drugs, natural or synthetic, that have morphine-like actions. Some of the common opioids are morphine, heroin, hydromorphone, oxymorphone, hydrocodone, codeine, oxycodone, butorphanol, methadone, propoxyphene, meperidine, diphenoxylate, fentanyl, loperamide, profadol, pentazocine, and buprenorphine. Tramadol is a synthetic opiate that is a derivative of codeine and is widely used in veterinary medicine as a pain reliever.

Opioids are used primarily as pain relievers, but also as cough suppressants and to treat diarrhea. Occasionally, opioids are also used for sedation before surgery and as a supplement to anesthesia. Toxicity of opioids in animals varies greatly among different species.

The primary effects of opioids are on the central nervous system, and on the respiratory, cardiovascular, and gastrointestinal systems. Common signs of poisoning include central nervous system depression, drowsiness, lack of coordination, vomiting, seizures, constricted pupils, coma, depressed breathing, low blood pressure, constipation, and death. Some animals—especially cats and horses—can show central nervous system excitation instead of central nervous system depression.

Diagnosis of opioid poisoning is based on a history of exposure and the signs. Urine can be analyzed to determine exposure to opioids.

Signs can be reversed with naloxone. Administration of naloxone should be repeated as needed because its duration of action may be shorter than the opioid being reversed. Animals should be closely monitored for depressed breathing and a ventilator provided if needed. Other signs should be treated symptomatically.

■ PYRROLIZIDINE ALKALOIDOSIS (*SENECIO* POISONING, RAGWORT POISONING)

Typically, pyrrolizidine alkaloidosis is a longterm poisoning that results in liver failure. It is caused by many toxic plants, most commonly of the genera *Senecio*, *Crotalaria*, *Heliotropium*, *Amsinckia*, *Echium*, *Cynoglossum*, and *Trichodesma*. These plants grow mainly in temperate climates, but some (for example, *Crotalaria* species) require tropical or subtropical climates. The plants most often implicated are ragwort (*Senecio jacobea*), woolly groundsel (*Senecio redellii*, *S. longilobus*), rattleweed (*Crotalaria retusa*), and seeds of yellow tarweed (*Amsinckia intermedia*).

Individual susceptibility varies greatly within species, with young, growing animals the most susceptible.

These plants, which under normal conditions are avoided by grazing animals, may be eaten during drought conditions. Some animals may eat these plants preferentially as roughage when they are available on extremely lush pasture. Animals are also poisoned by eating the plant material in hay, silage, or pellets. Seeds from *Crotalaria*, *Amsinckia*, and *Heliotropium* species, which have been harvested with grain, have caused pyrrolizidine alkaloidosis in horses.

Short-term poisoning is characterized by sudden death from liver damage and loss of blood from ruptured blood vessels. Animals rarely eat large amounts of these plants because of their poor taste. Long-term exposure is more typical, with the liver reflecting the cumulative and progressive effects of repeated ingestion of small amounts of toxin. Signs may not be seen for several weeks or months after initial exposure. The animal may have stopped eating the offending plant months earlier.

In horses, signs include loss of condition and appetite, dullness, and constipation or diarrhea. The animal may show straining and pain on defecation, and pass bloodstained feces. Fluid can build up within the abdomen, and jaundice may develop. Some animals become progressively weaker and reluctant to move. Liver damage can result in toxic substances accumulating in the blood, which affect brain function. In these animals, signs can also include head pressing, aimless wandering, lack of coordination, or frenzied and aggressive behavior. Animals may crave and eat nonfood substances (such as chalk, ashes, paint chips, clay, plaster, dirt or bones). Death may occur suddenly or after a prolonged coma caused by severe liver disease and high levels of ammonia in the blood.

Diagnosis is based on history, signs, and microscopic examination of liver and kidney tissue collected at necropsy.

Further intake of toxic plant material must be prevented. Animals showing signs rarely recover. Because high protein intake may prove harmful, rations high in carbohydrates are recommended. Veterinary treatment may include methionine in 10% dextrose solution, administered intravenously. Because the liver has a decreased ability to regenerate after pyrrolizidine alkaloid poisoning, the outlook is guarded.

■ *QUERCUS* POISONING (OAK BUD POISONING, ACORN POISONING)

Most animals are susceptible to *Quercus* poisoning, and most species of oak in Europe and North America are considered toxic. Signs occur several days after eating large quantities of young oak leaves in the spring or green acorns in the fall. The death rate is often high. Malformed foals and abortions have been reported in mares consuming acorns during the second trimester of pregnancy. The toxin causes gastrointestinal and kidney problems. Signs include loss of appetite, depression, weight loss, dehydration, urgent and painful defecation, smell of ammonia on the breath, clear discharge from the eyes or nose, excessive thirst, passing large amounts of urine, blood

in the urine, jaundice, and constipation followed by slimy or bloody diarrhea.

Feeding a pelleted ration supplement containing 10 to 15% calcium hydroxide plus providing access to more palatable feeds can be used as a preventive measure if exposure to acorns or oak leaves cannot be avoided. Calcium hydroxide and purgatives (such as mineral oil, sodium sulfate, or magnesium sulfate to aid in passing of feces) may be effective if given early in the course of disease. Fluid treatment may be beneficial. Recovery usually occurs within 60 days but is rare if kidney damage is severe.

■ RODENTICIDE POISONING

Pets often gain access to rodenticides by eating baits or the poisoned rodents. (*See also* STRYCHNINE POISONING, page 1209.) Many rodenticides are toxic to pets. Early veterinary intervention in cases of ingestion provides the best chance for successful treatment.

Anticoagulant Rodenticides (Warfarin and Related Compounds)

Anticoagulant rodenticides interfere with blood clotting. They are the most frequent cause of poisoning in pets. Pets may be poisoned directly from baits or indirectly by eating poisoned rodents. Different anticoagulants have different toxicity levels. Some require multiple feedings to result in toxicity, some require fewer feedings, and some are highly toxic after a single feeding.

Signs generally reflect blood loss from ruptured blood vessels, including anemia, semisolid masses of blood in the tissues, or bleeding into various areas of the body (the gastrointestinal tract, the eye, the nose, the lungs, or the urine). The animal can develop weakness, lack of coordination, colic, and panting or rapid breathing. Depression and loss of appetite are seen in all species even before bleeding occurs.

Anticoagulant rodenticide poisoning is usually diagnosed based on history of ingestion, blood tests, and a good response to vitamin K_1 treatment. Vitamin K_1 may need to continue for 2 to 4 weeks. Administration of oral vitamin K_1 with a fat-containing ration, such as canned dog food, increases its effectiveness 4 to 5 times as compared with vitamin K_1 given by mouth alone. Blood transfusions may be needed if bleeding is severe. Blood clotting should be monitored weekly until values remain normal for 5 to 6 days after treatment stops.

ANTU (Alpha-naphthylthiourea)

Use of ANTU has nearly been abandoned. However, dogs are occasionally poisoned. Animals with an empty stomach readily vomit after eating ANTU, but food in the stomach decreases the stimulation to vomit, and deadly quantities may be absorbed. Signs include vomiting, excessive drooling, coughing, and difficulty breathing. Animals prefer to sit. Fluid builds up in the lungs, and the skin and mucous membranes develop a bluish tinge. Other signs include weakness, lack of coordination, rapid weak pulse, and below normal temperature. Death can occur within 2 to 4 hours of ingestion, while animals that survive 12 hours may recover.

Medications that cause vomiting should be used only if the animal is not having trouble breathing. If respiratory distress is severe, the outlook is grave.

Bromethalin

Bromethalin is a nonanticoagulant rodenticide that can cause either a short- or longterm syndrome. In dogs, sudden, severe effects include hyperexcitability, muscle tremors, seizures, heightened reflexes of the hindlimbs, central nervous system depression, and death about 10 hours after ingestion. Longterm effects are seen with lower dosages and may appear 1 to 4 days after ingestion. This syndrome is characterized by vomiting, depression, lack of coordination, tremors, and a reluctance to stand. The effects may be reversible if exposure to bromethalin is discontinued. Bromethalin toxicosis should be considered when swelling of the brain or paralysis of the hind end is present.

Medical treatment is directed at blocking absorption from the gastrointestinal tract and reducing brain swelling. Using activated charcoal for several days may improve the recovery rate.

Cholecalciferol

Rodenticides containing cholecalciferol are a significant health threat to dogs and cats. Cholecalciferol produces excess calcium in the blood, which results in calcification (hardening) of soft tissue throughout the body. Signs generally develop within 18 to 36 hours of ingestion and can include depression, loss of appetite, passing large amounts of urine, and excessive thirst. As blood calcium concentrations increase, signs become more severe. Vomiting blood and bloody diarrhea may develop. As excess calcium in the blood continues, mineralization of the kidneys results in progressive kidney damage.

Diagnosis is based on history of ingestion, signs, and excess calcium in the blood (*see also* page 135).

Treatment usually includes removing the stomach contents, followed by administration of activated charcoal. Medications that increase urination are given for 2 to 4 weeks. Blood calcium levels should be monitored up to 2 weeks after stopping treatment. A low-calcium diet should be provided. Recently, pamidronate disodium has shown promise in treating dogs with cholecalciferol poisoning.

Metaldehyde

Metaldehyde is used as a snail or slug bait. (*See also* METALDEHYDE POISONING, page 1171.) Signs in dogs range from drooling and vomiting to anxiety and lack of coordination with muscle tremors, spasms, and heightened senses. Eventually, muscle spasms are continuous, leading to fever, physical weakness, and death. Diagnosis can be confirmed by finding metaldehyde bait or pellets in the vomited stomach contents.

Treatment is most effective if started early. Further absorption should be prevented by inducing vomiting, flushing the stomach, and giving activated charcoal. Tranquilizers, muscle relaxants, or even light anesthesia may be needed to control the muscle spasms. Fluid treatment promotes toxin excretion, and combats dehydration and metabolic abnormalities. Continuous supportive care is important. The outlook depends mostly on the amount of bait that was eaten.

Phosphorus

In its white (or yellow) form, phosphorus is hazardous to all domestic animals. It is infrequently used as a rodenticide today, but dogs occasionally become exposed by eating fireworks that contain white phosphorus. Phosphorus is locally corrosive and toxic to the liver when absorbed. Signs begin suddenly, with vomiting, severe diarrhea (often bloody), abdominal pain, and a garlic-like odor to the breath. Animals can appear to recover up to 4 days after ingestion, but additional signs of severe liver damage may develop, including blood loss from ruptured vessels, continued abdominal pain, and jaundice. Toxic substances may build up in the blood and affect the brain, leading to convulsions and death.

Prognosis is grave unless treatment is started early. Vomiting is induced and the stomach is flushed, followed by giving activated charcoal and medications that cause emptying of the bowels. Because fats favor additional absorption of phosphorus, a no-fat diet should be fed for at least 3 to 4 days. Mineral oil by mouth has been recommended because it dissolves phosphorus and prevents absorption.

Red Squill

This rodenticide is made from the plant *Urginea maritima*. It is rarely used. Red squill is more toxic to rats because they cannot vomit. Large quantities are required for poisoning in farm animals. Red squill is considered relatively safe, but dogs and cats have been poisoned.

Signs are vomiting, lack of coordination, and heightened senses, followed by paralysis, depression, convulsions, and heart abnormalities. The signs seldom last longer than 24 to 36 hours.

Treatment consists of supportive care, including emptying the gastrointestinal tract by flushing the stomach and using medications that cause emptying of the bowels. Medications to support heart function are also given.

Sodium Monofluoroacetate (1080)

1080 is a colorless, odorless, tasteless chemical, and its use is restricted to certain commercial applications. It is highly toxic to all animals, including people, because it overstimulates the central nervous system and causes numerous abnormalities of heart function. Central nervous system stimulation is the main effect in dogs, while the heart effects are more common in horses. Cats appear about equally affected by both.

Nervousness and restlessness begin 30 minutes or more after ingestion. Marked depression and weakness follow in all species except dogs. Animals rapidly become physically weak, and have a fast, weak pulse. Usually, dogs quickly develop muscle spasms, and many dogs show signs of severe pain. Dogs usually lose control of their bladder and bowels and can run in a frenzy. Animals die within hours after signs appear. Few animals that develop signs recover.

If signs are present, vomiting should not be induced. Flushing the stomach and giving activated charcoal and medications to control seizures are recommended. The outlook is grave if signs are severe.

The danger of secondary poisoning caused by eating rodents killed with 1080 is high. In the US, only certified, insured exterminators can purchase 1080, and a black dye must be mixed with it for identification.

Sodium Fluoroacetamide (1081)

1081 causes signs similar to those of 1080 (*see* above) and requires the same treatment.

Thallium Sulfate

Thallium sulfate can affect all species of animals. It has been banned for use as a rodenticide. Onset of signs may be delayed 1 to 3 days. All body systems are affected, with the gastrointestinal system, lungs, skin, and nervous system affected most commonly. Signs include inflammation of the gastrointestinal tract, abdominal pain, difficulty breathing, blindness, fever, conjunctivitis, inflammation of the gums, and tremors or seizures. After 4 to 5 days and an apparent recovery, or after repeated small doses, the skin can become inflamed, red, and thickened, and hair can be lost.

Treatment of thallium poisoning includes inducing vomiting, flushing the stomach, and administering sodium iodide. Diphenylthiocarbazone can be used as an antidote but is effective only if given within 24 hours of exposure. At the same time and for another 2 weeks, Prussian blue dissolved in water should be given. Symptomatic treatment of the diarrhea and convulsions is needed with particular attention to hydration, diet, prevention of secondary infection, and good nursing care.

Zinc Phosphide

Zinc phosphide has been used extensively around farms and barns as a rodent bait. Poisoning causes gastrointestinal tract irritation and cardiovascular collapse. Signs begin rapidly and include vomiting, abdominal pain, and aimless running and howling, followed by depression, difficulty breathing, and convulsions. Death is due to respiratory arrest. Diagnosis is based on history of exposure to zinc phosphide, signs, and detection of zinc phosphide in stomach contents. Zinc levels in the blood, liver, and kidneys may be increased. Treatment includes supportive care, fluids, calcium gluconate, and sodium bicarbonate to neutralize stomach acidity.

◼ RYEGRASS POISONING

Ryegrass is found in pastures throughout the world. Without careful management, it can be toxic to horses and other livestock.

Annual Ryegrass Staggers

This often deadly toxic disease affects the nervous system. It is seen in livestock of any age that graze pastures in which annual ryegrass (*Lolium rigidum*) is in the seedhead stage of growth (western and southern Australia and in South Africa from November to March). Hay of *Festuca rubra commutata* (Chewing's fescue) with *Rathayibacter toxicus*-infected seedhead galls has caused a similar disease in horses in Oregon.

In Australia, the responsible toxins are caused by a microscopic worm that carries a bacteria into seedhead galls of annual ryegrass. These bacteria-infected galls are present from early spring onward, but they are most toxic when the plants mature. Hence, animals show no signs until late spring and summer. Spread of worms to nearby healthy annual ryegrass pastures is slow.

Outbreaks occur 2 to 6 days after animals graze a pasture that contains infected annual ryegrass. Deaths can occur within hours, or up to 1 week after signs begin. Tissue changes include congestion, fluid buildup, ruptured blood vessels of the brain and lungs, and degeneration of the liver and kidneys.

Diagnosis is based on the characteristic nervous system signs of tremors, lack of coordination, rigidity, and collapse when stressed, with animals often becoming apparently normal again when left undisturbed. Nervous spasms can begin unexpectedly, and convulsions can be caused suddenly by either forced exercise or very hot weather. A thorough history and evaluation of the pastures will help differentiate staggers caused by other grasses.

Signs identical to those of annual ryegrass toxicity have recently been described in Australia in animals grazing annual blown grass (*Agrostis avenacea*), annual beard grass (*Polypogon monspeliensis*), or annual veldtgrass (*Ehrharta longiflora*) infected with worm galls.

These diseases have been called flood plain staggers, Stewart range syndrome, and veldtgrass staggers, respectively.

Perennial Ryegrass Staggers

This toxic condition affects the nervous system of grazing livestock and horses of all ages only in late spring, summer, and fall and only in pastures in which perennial ryegrass (*Lolium perenne*) or hybrid ryegrass are the major components. This includes parts of North and South America, Europe, and Australia.

The toxins are produced in perennial and hybrid ryegrasses infected with the fungus *Neotyphodium lolii*. The amounts in infected plants increase to toxic levels as the temperature rises in late spring and decrease again to safe levels in cooler weather.

The toxin affects the nervous system, causing lack of coordination. It also raises the temperature of animals in the warmer months of the year, causing heat stress. Signs develop gradually over a few days, beginning with fine tremors of the head and nodding movements. Noise, sudden exercise, or fright causes more severe head nodding with jerky movements and lack of coordination. Running movements are stiff and uncoordinated, often resulting in collapse with muscle spasms causing backward arching of the head, neck, and spine, involuntary rhythmic movement of the eyes, and flailing of stiffly extended limbs. In less severe cases, the attack soon subsides and within minutes the animal regains its feet. If the animal is again forced to run, the episode is repeated. The death rate is low (0 to 5%). Deaths are usually accidental, often by drowning when drinking from ponds or streams, or because the animals are unable to forage for food and water.

Because movement and handling of animals worsens signs, individual treatment is generally impractical. The condition resolves on its own in 1 to 2 weeks if animals are moved to nontoxic pastures or crops.

■ SALT POISONING

Salt (sodium chloride) toxicity can result when animals eat too much salt and do not have enough water to drink. Salt toxicity is directly related to water consumption and is unlikely if fresh drinking water is available. Mechanical failure of waterers, overcrowding, unpleasant tasting medicated water, new surroundings, or frozen water can all result in animals not drinking enough water. Signs generally involve the gastrointestinal tract and the central nervous system. Testing the blood and cerebrospinal fluid for sodium levels helps to confirm a diagnosis. Characteristic tissue changes in the brain and analyses of feed or water for sodium content are also useful for making a diagnosis.

There is no specific treatment. The offending feed or water must be removed immediately. Fresh water must be provided, initially in small amounts at frequent intervals. Drinking large amounts of water can worsen neurologic signs because fluid can build up in the brain. Severely affected animals should be given water via a stomach tube. The death rate may be more than 50% regardless of treatment. In dogs and cats, slow administration of fluids may be useful.

■ SELENIUM POISONING

Selenium is an essential element that is added to many feed supplements. Unfortunately, it has a narrow margin of safety. Too much selenium weakens the hooves, which tend to fracture when subjected to mechanical stress.

All animal species are susceptible to selenium poisoning. However, poisoning is more common in animals such as horses (and livestock) that may graze selenium-containing plants. Plants may accumulate selenium when the soil level is high—generally in alkaline soil with little rainfall. Different levels of selenium are absorbed from the soil depending on the type of plant.

Selenium toxicosis after ingestion of selenium-containing shampoos or selenium tablets is rare in pets. Severity of poisoning depends on how much was ingested and the length of exposure. Poisoning can be chronic or acute (*see* below). Diagnosis is based on signs, changes in tissues seen after death, and laboratory confirmation of high selenium levels in the diet (feed, forage, grains) or in blood or body tissues.

Chronic Selenium Poisoning (Alkali Disease)

Chronic selenium poisoning, also called alkali disease, usually develops when animals (livestock and horses) consume forages and grains containing selenium for many weeks or months. Affected animals are dull, very thin, and lack energy. The most distinctive signs involve the hair and the hooves. The hair coat becomes rough, and the long hairs of the tail or mane break off at the same level giving a "bob" tail and "roached" mane appearance. Abnormal growth and structure of hooves result in circular ridges and cracking of the hoof wall. Hooves may grow extremely long and turn upwards at the ends. Other effects include anemia, liver disease, fluid build-up within the abdomen, a weakened heart, and reduced reproductive performance. The animal's breath may have a garlicky odor.

Birds can also be affected with long-term selenium toxicosis. Eggs from birds in high selenium areas have a low hatching rate, and the embryos are usually deformed. Effects on development include underdeveloped feet and legs, malformed eyes, crooked beaks, and ropy feathers.

There is no specific treatment for selenium toxicosis. The source and exposure should be eliminated as soon as possible, and the animal given supportive care. Soil and forages should be tested regularly in high-selenium areas.

Acute Selenium Poisoning

Acute selenium poisoning is rare. Animals usually avoid these plants because of their offensive odor. However, when pasture is limited, these plants may be the only food available. Young animals are most susceptible. Signs are different from those of chronic toxicity and are characterized by abnormal behavior, breathing difficulty, gastrointestinal upset, and sudden death. Other signs include abnormal posture and depression, loss of appetite, unsteady gait, diarrhea, colic, increased pulse, rapid breathing, frothy discharge from the nose, and a bluish tinge to skin and mucous membranes. Death usually follows within a few hours of exposure. Multiple organs, including the lungs, liver, and kidneys, are damaged. Treatment consists of supportive care.

■ SNAKEBITE

Venomous snakes fall into 2 classes: 1) the elapines, which include the cobra, mamba, and coral snakes; and 2) the viperines, which include the true vipers (for example, puff adder, Russell's viper, and the common European adder) and the pit vipers (for example, rattlesnakes, cottonmouth moccasin, copperhead, and fer-de-lance). Pit vipers and coral snakes are found in North America.

Elapine snakes have short fangs and tend to hang on and "chew" venom into their victims. Elapine venom is toxic to the nervous system and paralyzes the breathing center. Animals that survive these bites generally recover completely. Viperine snakes have long, hinged, hollow fangs; they strike, inject venom, and withdraw. Viperine venom is typically toxic to the blood, killing cells and preventing normal clotting. The venom of some viperine species, for example, the Mojave rattlesnake, also affects the nervous system.

Deadly snakebites are more common in dogs than in any other domestic animal. Because many dogs are relatively small in size in proportion to the amount of venom injected, the bite of even a small snake can be fatal. Due to their large size, horses seldom die as a direct result of a snakebite, but bites on the muzzle, head, or

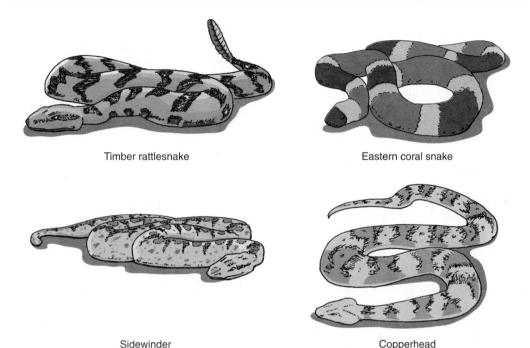

Timber rattlesnake   Eastern coral snake

Sidewinder   Copperhead

Some common North American poisonous snakes (colors not true to life; please consult a guide for proper identification of any snake)

neck that cause swelling and difficulty breathing can lead to death. Secondary damage can be serious; for example, a bite near the coronary band may cause a hoof to die and fall off.

A venomous snakebite is a true emergency. Rapid examination and appropriate treatment by a veterinarian are paramount. Owners should not spend time on first aid other than to keep the animal quiet and limit its activity.

In many instances, someone has witnessed the bite. Other conditions that are sometimes mistaken for snakebite include fractures, abscesses, spider bites, or allergic reactions to insect bites or stings. When possible, owners should bring the dead snake along with the bitten animal. The snake's head should not be damaged because identification often depends on the type of head.

Many bites do not result in venom being injected, or are made by nonpoisonous snakes. Typical pit viper bites are charac-

terized by severe local tissue damage that spreads from the bite site. The tissue becomes discolored within a few minutes, and dark, bloody fluid may ooze from the fang wounds if not prevented by swelling. Often the outer layer of the skin separates when the overlying hair is clipped or merely parted. Hair may hide the fang marks. Sometimes, only one fang mark or multiple punctures are present. In elapine snakebites, pain and swelling are usually minimal.

Intensive treatment should be started as soon as possible because irreversible effects of venom begin immediately after the bite. Animals bitten by an elapine snake can be treated with antivenin (which may be available through human hospital emergency rooms) and supportive care. An antivenin against North American pit vipers is available and should be used for all pit viper bites.

After injection of venom by a pit viper, signs are divided into 3 phases: the first

2 hours, the next 24 hours, and a variable period (usually about 10 days) afterward. In the first 2 hours, untreated animals usually die. If the animal is active and alert after 24 hours, death due to the direct effects of the venom is unlikely. The third phase is a recovery period, but infection can cause extensive cell damage, leading to tissue death that may involve an entire limb.

In dogs and cats, death rates are generally higher from bites to the chest or abdomen than from bites to the head or extremities. However, this may relate to the size and vulnerability of the victim, because smaller animals are more likely to be bitten on the body. Sensitivity to the venom of pit vipers varies among domestic animals, with horses being most sensitive, followed by dogs, rabbits, and cats.

Treatment for a pit viper bite includes treating for shock, neutralizing the venom, controlling blood clotting, and preventing secondary infection. Antivenin is highly beneficial because its action is the only direct and specific mechanism for neutralizing snake venom. Antivenin treatment is most effective if given within 24 hours of the bite. Antibiotic treatment should continue until all superficial tissue changes have healed. Tetanus antitoxin also should be given. In most cases, attempting to surgically remove the wound is impractical or unwarranted. There is also a vaccine available for dogs that may reduce the effects of a rattlesnake bite.

■ SORGHUM POISONING (SUDAN GRASS POISONING)

Sorghum poisoning is seen in horses, primarily in the southwestern US, after they have grazed hybrid Sudan pastures for weeks to months. The spinal cord softens and nerves degenerate in the spinal cord and brain. (*See also* CYANIDE POISONING, page 1150.)

Sorghum poisoning is characterized by lack of coordination of the hind end, inflammation and infection of the bladder, inability to urinate, and loss of hair

on the hindlegs due to urine scald. The lack of coordination may progress to limb paralysis. Reproductive problems, including deformed foals, can be seen. Affected horses often die from inflammation of the kidneys. Treatment with antibiotics may help, but a full recovery is rare.

■ SPIDER BITES

Poisonous spider bites are relatively uncommon and difficult to recognize. The bite of spiders of medical importance in the US is not particularly painful, so it is unusual for a spider bite to be suspected until signs appear. It is also unlikely that the offending spider will remain nearby the victim while signs develop, which may take 30 minutes to 6 hours. Poisonous spiders in the US belong to 2 groups—widow spiders and brown spiders.

Widow Spiders

Widow spiders usually bite only when accidentally touched. The most common species is the black widow, which is characterized by a red hourglass shape on the lower abdomen. Widow spider venom is very potent and causes severe, painful cramping of all large muscle groups.

Unless a widow spider bite has been witnessed, diagnosis must be based on signs, which include restlessness, anxiety, rapid and irregular breathing, shock, a rigid or tender abdomen, and painful muscles. The muscles may be rigid and will relax now and then.

Symptomatic treatment includes pain relievers and muscle relaxants. Tetanus antitoxin should also be given. Recovery may take some time, and weakness and partial paralysis may remain for several days.

Brown Spiders

There are at least 10 species of brown spiders in the US, but the brown recluse spider is the most common. Most of these spiders have a violin-shaped marking on the body, although it may be indistinct or even absent in some species. Brown recluse spider venom causes the blood vessels to narrow, which increases blood pressure and decreases blood flow. It also causes blood clots and destruction of red blood cells.

Unless a brown spider bite has been witnessed, a presumptive diagnosis may be based on the presence of a discrete, red, itchy spot on the skin that may bleed into surrounding tissue. Within 4 to 8 hours, a blister develops at the bite wound, and sometimes a pale area surrounds the redness of the lesion, so that it appears like a "bull's-eye." The central area sometimes appears pale or has a bluish tinge. The blister may turn into a slow-healing sore that may enlarge and extend to underlying tissues, including muscle. Sometimes, the blister may become raised, fill with pus, and then break down leaving a black scab. The affected area may take months to heal.

Additional signs may not appear for 3 to 4 days after the bite. They include destruction of red blood cells, effects on blood clotting, fever, vomiting, blood in the urine, kidney failure, and shock.

Early treatment can be successful, but unfortunately, many cases are not recognized until skin damage has become extensive. Treatment at that stage is less successful but can still help. Surgically removing the wound is of questionable value. In addition to cold packs and medication to prevent infection, tetanus vaccination may also be recommended by your veterinarian.

◼ STRYCHNINE POISONING

Strychnine is found in the seeds of the Indian tree *Strychnos nux-vomica*. It is mainly used as a pesticide to control rats, moles, gophers, and coyotes. Commercial baits are pelleted and often dyed red or green. Strychnine is highly toxic to most domestic animals. Strychnine poisoning in the US is sometimes seen in dogs and occasionally cats.

The highest concentrations of strychnine are found in the blood, liver, and kidneys. Depending on the amount ingested and the treatment administered, most of the toxic dose can be eliminated within 1 to 2 days. In strychnine poisoning, the muscles contract repeatedly for a long time. Signs begin rapidly, usually within 30 to 60 minutes. Food in the stomach can delay onset. Early signs, which may often be overlooked, consist of nervousness, tenseness, and stiffness. Vomiting usually does not occur. Severe, sustained muscle contractions may begin spontaneously or may be set off by a touch, sound, or sudden bright light. Extreme and overpowering muscle rigidity causes the legs to extend, giving the animal a "sawhorse" stance. Fever and seizures often develop in dogs. The muscle contractions may last from a few seconds to about a minute. Breathing may stop momentarily. Intermittent periods of relaxation seen during convulsions become less frequent as the disease progresses. The mucous membranes become a bluish color, and the pupils enlarge. Seizures become more frequent, and death eventually results from exhaustion and a lack of oxygen reaching body tissues. If untreated, the entire syndrome may last only 1 to 2 hours.

Tentative diagnosis of strychnine poisoning is usually based on history of exposure and signs. Diagnosis can be confirmed by finding strychnine on analysis of the stomach contents, vomit, liver, kidneys, or urine.

Strychnine poisoning is an emergency, and treatment should be started quickly. Treatment should be aimed at removing any strychnine that has not been absorbed, controlling seizures, and providing supportive care. Stomach contents can be removed by inducing vomiting or flushing the stomach, and by administering activated charcoal. However, because signs begin so rapidly, vomiting is often of limited value, and the stomach may need to be flushed. Fluids are given to increase urine output and maintain normal kidney function. Fever and metabolic abnormalities are treated. Artificial respiration may be needed.

■ SWEET CLOVER POISONING

Sweet clover poisoning is seen when animals eat spoiled sweet clover hay or silage. Any method of hay storage that allows sweet clover to mold increases the chance of a toxin forming in the hay. Weathered, large round bales, particularly the outer portions, usually contain the highest levels of toxin. When toxic hay or silage is eaten, blood clotting may be delayed and spontaneous bleeding may result (*see* BLOOD CLOTTING DISORDERS, page 50). Instances of poisoning have involved mainly cattle and some horses.

Signs are caused by faulty clotting of blood and loss of blood from ruptured blood vessels. The amount of time between eating toxic sweet clover and appearance of signs varies greatly. If the sweet clover has a low level of toxin, animals may eat it for months before disease appears.

The first signs may be stiffness and lameness, caused by bleeding into the muscles and joints. The animal may bleed from the nose or into the gastrointestinal tract. Death from massive bleeding after injury, surgery, or giving birth can occur suddenly without other signs.

Diagnosis is based on a history of eating sweet clover hay or silage over relatively long periods, signs, and a prolonged blood clotting time. Sweet clover poisoning is usually a problem in all animals in a herd. It is unlikely if bleeding or slow blood clotting are seen in a single animal from a group.

Blood transfusions are usually needed and can be repeated if necessary. Severely affected animals are also treated with vitamin K_1, which reverses the effects of the toxin. Several hours are needed for significant improvement, and more than 24 hours is needed for clotting to return to normal.

The only certain method of prevention is to avoid feeding sweet clover hay or silage. However, variations of sweet clover, low in the toxin and safe to feed (for example, Polara), have been developed.

A simple management technique is to alternate feeding (every 7 to 10 days) sweet clover hay suspected of containing the toxin with other roughage such as alfalfa or a grass-legume hay mixture. Pregnant animals should not receive sweet clover hay for at least 2 to 3 weeks, and preferably 4 weeks, before giving birth. Similarly, animals should not receive sweet clover hay for 3 to 4 weeks before castration or other surgery.

■ TOAD POISONING

Dogs and sometimes cats are poisoned by mouthing certain types of toads. All toads produce venom, but the potency of the venom varies with species and geographic locations. Toad venom is a thick, creamy white, highly irritating substance. It can affect the heart, the nervous system, and the blood vessels. The most toxic species in the US appears to be the giant or marine toad, *Bufo marinus*, an introduced species that is established in Florida, Hawaii, and Texas.

Encounters with toads are most common in warm or mild weather. Signs of poisoning vary and range from local effects in and around the mouth to convulsions and death. Local effects include frothy drooling, vigorous head shaking, pawing at the mouth, and retching. They are seen immediately, probably because the venom is extremely irritating. Vomiting is not unusual and may persist for several hours. Severe poisoning, as from *Bufo marinus* venom, causes life-threatening abnormal heart rhythms, difficulty breathing, a bluish tinge to skin and mucous membranes, and seizures.

There is no specific antidote. Treatment is directed at minimizing absorption of the venom, along with supportive treatment. The mouth should be immediately and thoroughly flushed with large amounts of water. Supportive treatment includes medications to reduce the amount of saliva and to correct the heart rhythm. Oxygen therapy may also be needed.

■ ZINC POISONING

Zinc is an essential trace metal that plays an important role in many biologic processes. Zinc toxicity has been seen in a wide range of animals. It is most common in pet dogs, possibly because of their indiscriminate eating habits and great availability of zinc-containing substances. Common sources of zinc include pennies, batteries, automotive parts, paints, zinc-oxide creams, herbal supplements, zippers, board-game pieces, screws and nuts on pet carriers, and the coating on galvanized metals such as pipes and cookware.

Zinc salts are formed in the stomach, absorbed from the small intestine, and quickly distributed to the liver, kidneys, prostate, muscles, bones, and pancreas. Zinc salts have direct irritant and corrosive effects on tissue and interfere with numerous metabolic processes, including the production and function of red blood cells. Diets containing high levels of zinc have caused longterm zinc toxicosis in livestock.

Signs vary based on the duration and degree of exposure. Signs progress from loss of appetite and vomiting to diarrhea, lethargy, jaundice, shock, destruction of red blood cells, blood in the urine, heart rhythm abnormalities, and seizures. Lameness has been reported in foals. The liver, kidney, and pancreas can be damaged. X-rays of the gastrointestinal tract can reveal zinc-containing foreign bodies. Zinc levels can be measured in blood or other tissues, and changes in the blood and urine reflect the effects on various organ systems.

After stabilizing the animal with fluids, oxygen, and blood products as necessary, removal of the source of zinc as early as possible is critical. This often requires surgery or the minimally invasive surgical procedure using an endoscope. Inducing vomiting is usually not recommended.

Administering fluids to increase urine output is recommended to promote kidney excretion of zinc and prevent kidney damage.

If diagnosed and treated early, the outlook for animals with zinc poisoning is generally good. Eliminating sources of zinc from the environment is essential to prevent recurrence.

CHAPTER 82

Pain Management

■ INTRODUCTION

Animals, just like people, feel pain when they are injured or sick. However, recognizing pain in animals can be difficult because animals do not act the same way that people do when they are in pain.

Pain management in veterinary medicine has become a routine part of the physical examination and treatment plan. Pain and the types of behaviors associated with it are good indicators of a physical problem. The type and extent of the pain can help the veterinarian diagnose the problem and select the appropriate treatment. Good pain management can help a sick or injured animal recover faster.

■ TYPES OF PAIN

Because pain is often a response to actual or potential tissue damage, it has a protective role. For example, if a muscle strain or pull causes pain in a limb, not putting weight on that limb can help prevent further injury.

Signs of Pain in Pets

You can play a central role in relieving your pet's pain by learning to recognize some common indicators of pain and discomfort.

Physical Signs

- Change in heart rate
- Heavy breathing
- Enlarged pupils
- Slowed reflexes

Behavioral Signs

- Reduced appetite
- Reluctance to lie down
- Unusual restlessness or anxiety
- Withdrawn behavior
- Mood or personality changes
- Licking, biting, or rubbing the site of pain
- Irritability

(Modified with permission from Colorado State University Animal Cancer Center web site, "How will I know if my pet is in pain?)

The most common types of pain can be categorized as acute, chronic, cancer, and neuropathic.

Acute pain is the normal, predictable, noticeable response to an undesirable stimulus (such as twisting, crushing, or burning) or tissue injury (such as bruises, wounds, and surgical incisions). People describe acute pain as sharp, throbbing, aching, or burning. Acute pain generally improves within the first 3 days after the event that caused it, but sometimes it can last for weeks or months.

Chronic pain persists for longer than the expected time frame for healing, or it can be associated with progressive noncancerous disease, such as osteoarthritis.

Cancer pain is the result of primary tumor growth, a spreading cancerous disease, or the toxic effects of chemotherapy or radiation.

Neuropathic pain results from damage to a nerve or some other part of the central nervous system. This type of pain is fre-

quently not diagnosed in veterinary medicine, mainly because animals cannot communicate a problem such as a tingling sensation.

◼ RECOGNIZING AND ASSESSING PAIN IN ANIMALS

Recognizing pain in animals is a challenge because animals cannot communicate the same way people do. However, there are some species-specific behaviors that can indicate pain and help us recognize it. For example, animals that are natural predators, such as dogs, behave differently when in pain than do prey animals, such as rabbits and horses. Prey animals tend to hide their pain, making recognition of pain even more difficult in these species.

In evaluating pain in animals, veterinarians consider vital signs, behavioral changes, pain scales, and the animal's history.

Vital Signs

Vital signs such as heart rate, respiratory rate, and blood pressure may be used to assess responses to an acute painful stimulus, particularly during surgery or after severe trauma. Measurement of vital signs can also be used to assess pain in some situations (such as horses with colic). However, measurements of vital signs do not differentiate between sources of pain, such as pain from surgery or another cause. In addition, vital signs may be normal in animals experiencing chronic pain. These indicators are not specific enough to distinguish pain from other stresses such as anxiety, fear, or physical responses to certain medical conditions (such as anemia). In other words, an animal can still be in pain even if its heart rate and breathing rate are normal.

Behavioral Changes

Recognizing pain-induced behaviors is difficult or impossible without knowing the normal behaviors of a particular species or breed. Behavioral changes associated with pain may be subtle and not easily recognized during routine checkups or examinations in animals. Many animals mask their pain with normal behaviors. For instance, dogs may wag their tails and greet people in spite of being in pain. In addition, behavioral changes in response to pain might be very different from the typical responses associated with people who are in pain. A cat sitting quietly in the back of the cage after surgery may be in pain; however, a caregiver might not recognize the pain if he or she expected to see more active signs of pain, such as pacing, agitation, or meowing.

In general, signs of chronic pain are less obvious and harder to recognize than signs of traumatic or surgical pain. Criteria that can be used to evaluate chronic pain (for example, lack of activity, decreased appetite, weight loss, and lack of grooming) are not specific signs of pain. Instead, these signs point only to an underlying problem that needs to be diagnosed. Your observations about changes in your pet's attitude or interaction with family members are essential to help your veterinarian evaluate chronic pain. Response to treatment, such as increased activity after administering a pain-relieving drug, may reveal a relationship between pain and the behavioral changes.

A pet with cancer pain may have some signs of acute pain (such as in response to tumor growth or after surgery, radiation, or chemotherapy) and some signs of chronic pain. If your pet has cancer, you should be alert for behavioral changes associated with both acute and chronic pain.

Pain Scales

A pain scale is one tool that veterinarians can use to rate an animal's pain. A pain scale is a questionnaire that includes the following characteristics: species, breed, age, gender, environment and rearing conditions, cause of pain (such as trauma or surgery), body region affected (such as the abdomen or muscle), and the duration and intensity of pain. Pain scales that consider species-specific behaviors

are likely to be more accurate than generic scales that rely heavily on subjective assessment and interpretation. Even if the severity of pain is correctly estimated, determining how well the individual animal is coping with the pain may be difficult. Current methods assess the effects of physical pain, but do not evaluate the mental or psychological effects of pain that an animal may experience.

▓ PAIN TREATMENT

Acute surgical, traumatic, and disease-related pain is generally treated with one or more **analgesic,** or pain-relieving, drugs. Selection of the most suitable drug or drug combination is based on the anticipated severity of pain, the pet's overall health, and the specific drugs helpful for the species. For more extensive injuries or disease-related tissue damage, analgesics from more than one drug class are often prescribed.

Reducing your pet's stress and providing all-around good care will maximize the benefit of the pain treatment regimen. Housing conditions, diet, and level of interaction with other animals and people should be tailored to the individual. For example, separating a pair of dogs that enjoy playing vigorously together might be stressful for the dogs under normal circumstances. But temporarily separating the dogs after one has had surgery (to allow the incision to start healing) is less stressful for the recovering dog if the human caregivers spend enough time interacting with it. Managing animals that are under stress and in pain requires a combination of good nursing care, non-drug methods (for example, bandaging, ice packs or heat, and physical therapy), and drug treatments.

▓ DRUGS USED TO RELIEVE PAIN

Types of drugs used to relieve pain include opioids, nonsteroidal anti-inflammatory drugs (NSAIDs), corticoster-

Principles of Pain Management

- Because signs of pain can be subtle and difficult to recognize, animals suspected of being in pain are usually treated and watched for improvement.

- Continuous (round-the-clock) administration of pain medication is often more effective at relieving pain than using an "as-needed" dosing schedule. For as-needed dosing to be an effective method of pain management, the animal must be one that shows pain behaviors and the caregiver must be able to recognize these behaviors.

- Many animals benefit from treatment with combinations of different types of analgesic drugs, rather than just one type.

- When analgesic drugs are prescribed in combination, a smaller-than-usual dose of each can usually provide adequate pain relief.

- Animals in pain can also have anxiety, so a veterinarian might prescribe an anti-anxiety drug for use after analgesic drugs have been given.

- Adequate pain relief after surgery or trauma allows the animal to rest. Dogs and cats often sleep more than usual for a few days after surgery, but a caregiver should be able to wake them up if the dosage of the analgesic drug is appropriate. If your pet cannot rest or cannot be awakened, call your veterinarian for reassessment.

- If pain-relief medication is given consistently for several days, the dose should be decreased gradually rather than stopped abruptly.

oids, and alpha$_2$ agonists. As with any other medication, it is always important to follow your veterinarian's instructions carefully regarding the correct dose to be given.

Opioids

Opioids (such as morphine) are used by licensed professionals primarily for their pain-relieving effects despite some well-known side effects. These drugs are the most effective analgesics available for the treatment of acute pain in many different animals, particularly cats and dogs.

Opioids relieve pain by acting on the central nervous system. Their side effects, such as sluggishness (sedation), change in mood (good or bad), and excitement, are related to other central nervous system processes. Different species—and even individual animals within a species—respond to opioids in different ways, so doses often require adjustment. For example, a horse might weigh 10 times as much as a large dog, yet the dose of morphine might be similar for both animals. The effect of an opioid depends on additional factors, including whether the animal is in pain, the overall health of the animal, the administration of other drugs at the same time, and individual sensitivity to opioid effects. For some opioids (such as butorphanol), a higher dose does not always bring more pain relief. This is called the ceiling effect.

Nonsteroidal Anti-inflammatory Drugs and Corticosteroids

For many animals, nonsteroidal anti-inflammatory drugs (NSAIDs) are useful as part of a pain management regimen after surgery or to relieve chronic pain, such as that caused by osteoarthritis. Carprofen, firocoxib, and meloxicam are some examples of drugs in this class. NSAIDs work by reducing inflammation, one cause of pain. They are readily available, relatively long-acting, and generally inexpensive. They can also be given at home after an animal has been released from the hospital. For these reasons, they have long been used for pain relief. Veterinarians may prescribe NSAIDs as one part of the total plan for pain relief, provided the animal does not have kidney, liver, blood clotting, or stomach problems.

NSAIDs intended for use in humans should never be given to your pet unless specifically prescribed by your veterinarian, as even small doses of drugs like aspirin or acetaminophen can cause severe adverse effects in some animals. For example, acetaminophen is toxic to cats and should never be used in this species.

Corticosteroids (such as prednisone and cortisol) also reduce inflammation and provide pain relief. They are used less frequently after surgery because they might weaken the immune system. Other possible side effects of corticosteroids include increased appetite and thirst, and increased need to urinate. Corticosteroids are not used at the same time as NSAIDs.

Alpha$_2$ Agonists

Alpha$_2$ agonists are used in large animals such as horses to provide both pain relief and sedative effects during procedures in which the animal remains standing. (Sedatives calm nervousness and reduce irritability and excitement.) Some evidence suggests that the sedative effect lasts longer than the pain relief. Alpha$_2$ agonists include xylazine, medetomidine, detomidine, and romifidine. Using both alpha$_2$ agonists and opioids results in pain relief and sedation that are greater than the effects of either drug alone.

Alpha$_2$ agonists are also used for anesthesia before and during surgery in a variety of animals. However, many veterinarians do not use these drugs to prolong pain relief after surgery or trauma because of the potential for adverse effects. In large animals, alpha$_2$ agonists can cause excessive sedation (such as sleepiness and reduced mental activity) and loss of muscle coordination. In small animals, pain-relieving doses of alpha$_2$ agonists also cause deep sedation. If alpha$_2$ agonists are prescribed after surgery, the dose will be much lower than that used before and during the procedure.

Local Pain Relief

Local anesthetics (such as lidocaine) numb just the area around a wound or surgical site. In large animals, local anesthetics are often used in surgeries—either alone or together with other types of anesthesia—to minimize the potential risks and complications of general anesthesia. In small animals, local anesthetics are usually used for minor procedures such as suturing of cuts. Using local anesthetics before surgery may allow veterinarians to reduce the amount of more powerful general anesthetics needed during longer and more complex surgical procedures. This, in turn, can minimize postoperative pain in animals and lead to a faster recovery.

■ COMPLEMENTARY AND ALTERNATIVE THERAPIES

Natural and holistic pain relief methods for pets, like those for people, have become a topic of much interest. Many different vitamins, herbal preparations, nutraceuticals, and natural remedies are available. Most of these therapies have not been tested in scientific trials, so they are not guaranteed as safe and effective. Some may prove neither helpful nor harmful, a few might be helpful, and others might actually be harmful. If you are interested in giving your pet a nutritional or herbal supplement, consult your veterinarian to make sure it will not interact with any other drugs your pet is taking.

Several scientific trials have been conducted using **acupuncture** as a pain relief technique for pets, with encouraging results. Soft tissue manipulation and massage may also provide relief from musculoskeletal pain, especially of the neck, back, and hips. Further research is needed to determine the optimal combination of pharmacological (drug) therapies and complementary or alternative techniques for various types of pain.

■ TREATMENT OF CHRONIC PAIN

As in acute pain, both drug and nondrug methods can be used to treat chronic pain. Some drugs that relieve acute pain are also used to treat chronic pain, such as opioids and nonsteroidal anti-inflammatory drugs. Depending on the situation, other drugs, such as an anti-anxiety or anticonvulsant drug, might be added to the treatment regimen.

Nondrug treatment of chronic pain depends on both the cause of the pain and the species of animal. For example, in a dog suffering from osteoarthritis pain, the goals of treatment are to increase the dog's ability to move around, to limit the progression of the disease, and even to help repair the tissue within the affected joints. Some or all of these goals might be achieved by weight control, moderate exercise, extra bedding or padding, and added warmth during cold or damp weather. Excessive exercise should be avoided because it causes further strain on the joints. Treatment with certain protec-

tive agents, such as chondroitin sulfate or glucosamine, may help heal the cartilage, prevent further breakdown of the cartilage, and stimulate cartilage regrowth. However, the effectiveness of these agents is still being reviewed and may vary based on the specific product used, how it is administered, and the animal's overall condition. Acupuncture and physical therapy have had some success in relieving osteoarthritis pain.

CHAPTER 83

Travel with Pets

■ INTRODUCTION

This chapter provides basic information on traveling with your pet, both within the United States and internationally. While the focus is on the United States as the "home country," many of the principles and suggestions are applicable to travel within or between other countries. Some of the issues facing owners who want or need to travel with their pets will also be addressed. Where complete discussion of a particular issue is not possible, places to obtain additional information are suggested. Alternatives to traveling with your pet are also discussed, because sometimes it is not possible or in your pet's best interest to bring it with you on your travels.

Cats and dogs are the most common pets to be taken along on trips. Most other pet animals are not routinely taken along on travels, so we have not included other specifics here. (For a more detailed discussion of ALTERNATIVES TO TRAVEL WITH PETS, *see* page 1226.)

■ TRAVEL WITH SERVICE ANIMALS

People who travel with service animals— for example, guide dogs for the visually impaired, or assistance dogs for those who

Daily Health Check

Regardless of the destination, you should perform a daily health check on your pet when away from home. In unfamiliar surroundings, the pet's appetite, energy level, and disposition may change. Signs of possible illness include any unusual discharges from the nose and eyes, excessive scratching or biting of any body part, abnormal urination or defecation, lack of appetite for longer than 24 hours, disorientation, or excessive water consumption. The pet should be checked by a local veterinarian if you become concerned about any physical or behavioral changes or if you note anything out of the ordinary.

are mobility impaired—do not have the choice of leaving their pet at home. In the United States, the Americans with Disabilities Act guarantees reasonable accommodations for the mobility of individuals using service dogs. Canada has similar laws in place that ensure the rights of its citizens with disabilities. However, even with service animals, advance planning for travel within the US is wise and sometimes essential. For example, travel to Hawaii with a service dog requires documentation of the animal's status and training, proof of current rabies vaccination, microchipping, testing for immunity to rabies, and other documentation. Although these requirements are less stringent than those for non-service animals (described later), they still require advance planning to ensure that the animal is not delayed upon arrival.

Individuals with disabilities should remember that beyond the borders of their home countries, accommodation needs should be approached creatively. If you anticipate foreign travel with a service animal, you should provide the destination country with as much advance notice as possible (at least 30 days) to avoid having to enter the country without these vital helpers. Sometimes it is necessary to be flexible about trying another nation's disability-related supports and services. When traveling internationally with an assistance dog, individuals with disabilities should contact organizations for the visually impaired and/or guide or service dog schools in the destination country to determine how practical international travel might be. It is important for disabled travelers to understand the laws and cultural norms of their destination.

▓ PLANNING YOUR TRIP

Travel with a pet can be as short as a car ride into town for a veterinary appointment or as lengthy as a permanent relocation to another country. Regardless of the type of travel, adequate planning and preparation will help avoid surprises and make the trip less stressful for both you and your pet.

Planning for US Travel

Even travel within the United States (especially between states) will be easier if you plan ahead. Remember to consider both the journey itself and the final destination when making plans. In all cases, your pet's vaccinations should be up-to-date; in particular, evidence of rabies vaccination may be needed for interstate travel.

Pet Travel Kit

- ▓ Brush or comb
- ▓ Favorite toy or pillow
- ▓ First-aid kit (commercially available or assembled on your own)
- ▓ Food
- ▓ Health certificate (issued within 10 days of trip)
- ▓ Leash
- ▓ Medications and prescription information
- ▓ Owner contact information
- ▓ Rabies vaccination certificate
- ▓ Veterinarian contact information
- ▓ Water (when possible, bringing a familiar source of water can help your pet avoid stomach upset)
- ▓ Any other records or forms required by the destination country

Check your pet carrier or crate to ensure that it is in good condition, large enough for your pet, and (if traveling by plane) approved for use on an airplane. Note that there are significant differences between carriers for use in the cabin, which are soft-sided, and those for use in the cargo hold, which are rigid. If possible, let your pet become accustomed to the carrier while you are still at home by feeding your animal in the carrier, having it take naps in the carrier, or leaving a favorite blanket or toy in it.

Make sure your pet's collar has identification tags including current contact information. If possible, attach a tag with your cell phone number, the phone number of where you will be staying, or the number of someone who can quickly locate you. Collars for cats should be of the breakaway type to avoid strangulation if the animal accidentally snags its collar.

Both libraries and online listings have phone numbers for veterinary clinics along travel routes or at destinations. The appropriate state veterinary association may also have listings. Knowing where to call for emergency veterinary care could save your pet's life.

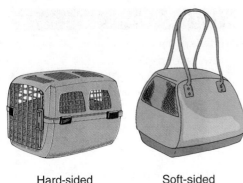

Hard-sided
(for cargo hold)

Soft-sided
(for passenger
compartment)

Pets traveling by plane must travel in an approved carrier.

If your travel is part of a relocation, your moving company may be able to provide helpful advice for transporting your pet and supplies (such as a fish tank), as well as how to help your pet adjust to its new home.

Planning for International Travel

The United States has become a nation of international travelers. In 1995 almost 19 million US citizens traveled to overseas sites. There are no records kept as to how many of these people traveled with pets; however, taking companion animals on overseas travel has certainly increased over the last several decades.

If you are considering taking your pet on a trip outside the US, you should first consult your veterinarian. The best advice that any veterinarian might give is simply to avoid, if possible, traveling abroad with your pet. Even with careful planning, traveling with a pet can be difficult. A pet traveling abroad can become separated from its owners or face a lengthy quarantine period. Even worse, the pet can acquire an unfamiliar disease or parasite. The danger of bringing these "uninvited guests" back into the US or other home country is a constant concern. For this reason, most countries have developed complex restrictions for the introduction (or reintroduction) of animals, animal products, and contaminated articles to prevent exotic infections from entering the country.

Some recent data show that during international trips, travelers from the US spent an average of 18 nights outside the country. For short trips such as these, the duration of overseas travel is far shorter than the length of the pet quarantine period often required by foreign countries. Thus, it makes sense that for short trips, pets should usually remain at home. The situation is far different for citizens temporarily residing outside of the country (for example, military personnel, consular personnel, missionaries, or expatriates). These citizens sometimes live outside of the US for months or years—and they often own dogs or cats that were either acquired in the US and transported to that foreign country or acquired in the foreign country.

If you decide to travel internationally with your pet, you should contact the embassy or consulate of the nation(s) to which you will be traveling to ensure that all necessary import requirements have been fulfilled and that the quarantine requirements (if any) are clearly understood. This should be done at least 9 months in advance of travel. Embassies are usually located in large metropolitan areas, such as New York City, Los Angeles, or Washington, DC. The US Department of State maintains a list of consulates and embassies on its web site.

As you are planning the details of your trip, be sure that the airports you intend to use will be able to provide the necessary customs and/or quarantine services you may require. If quarantine will be needed for your pet, find out whether a reservation is required and what the cost will be.

In addition to the regulations discussed below, you will want to know where to locate veterinary help if it is needed. If possible, research ahead of time (or ask a

Table 27. Government Agencies and Other Organizations with Information on Pet Travel

Organization	Scope	Web Site
American Veterinary Medical Association (AVMA)	Professional association for veterinarians	*www.avma.org*
Animal and Plant Health Inspection Service (APHIS)	Preservation of health of animals and agriculture in the US	*www.aphis.usda.gov/ac/ pettravel.html*
Centers for Disease Control and Prevention (CDC)	Prevention of human disease	*www.cdc.gov/ncidod/dq/ animal.htm*
Department for Environmental, Food, and Rural Affairs (DEFRA)	United Kingdom agency responsible for agricultural issues	*www.defra.gov.uk/animalh/ quarantine/index.htm*
International Airline Transport Association (IATA)	Standards for transportation of animals by air	*www.iata.org/whatwedo/cargo/ live_animals/index.htm*
US Department of State	Provides web sites of embassies and consulates	*http://usembassy.state.gov/*

friend or colleague in the destination country) to find contact information for local veterinarians or a veterinary association that can provide referrals. If you do not speak the language of the country you are traveling to, search for veterinarians that speak English or another language you understand. Phrase books often have sections for human medical emergencies and may be helpful if you need to explain your animal's condition to a veterinarian who speaks a different language.

■ REGULATIONS REGARDING TRAVEL WITH ANIMALS

The regulations for travel with animals are extensive and may seem burdensome (*see* TABLE 27). Remember, there are good reasons for such regulations: protecting your pet's health, protecting pets and other animals in the destination state or country, and protecting humans from diseases (such as rabies) that can be acquired from animals.

Travel within the United States

Each state has its own set of regulations for movement of animals across its borders. The Animal and Plant Health Inspection

Service (APHIS) web site provides links to the regulations for each state. In general, the pet owner should carry proof of current rabies vaccination and a current health certificate when traveling between states with dogs and cats.

A particular situation to take note of is travel to Hawaii, even from other US states. Because Hawaii is rabies free, its government has instituted a quarantine law to ensure that rabies is not introduced. This law covers all dogs and cats regardless of age or purpose. As an alternative to lengthy quarantine, a detailed process involving vaccination at specific times, microchipping, a blood test for rabies, and a 120-day waiting period may be followed. Successful completion of these requirements will allow the animal to be quarantined for 5 days or less; if not, the animal may be quarantined for up to 120 days. A similar requirement is in place even for animals originating in Hawaii and later returning, although the timing and waiting periods are different. The rabies requirement does not apply to horses, but the horse must originate in an area or county free of equine encephalomyelitis and be vaccinated prior to import. Please check the state of Hawaii's Agricultural Gateway web site for more details.

The island of Guam is also rabies free and has a quarantine period for import of dogs and cats. As with Hawaii, the quarantine time can be shortened significantly if specific microchipping, vaccination, and testing requirements are met prior to travel.

International Travel

If you plan to travel to other countries with your pet, you will need to research possible travel restrictions, vaccination requirements, quarantine, and other policies of the country or countries you will visit. The nearest consulate or embassy for that country and/or the country's government web site are places to begin your search for information. Your veterinarian may also be able to assist you by providing information on the federal and international agencies that should be contacted prior to foreign travel and/or possible re-entry with pets. Some countries require a health certificate and proof of rabies vaccination signed by a US government official.

If there are still questions or concerns about exporting animals to a foreign country, you should contact the US Department of Agriculture's Veterinary Services Area Office. Your veterinarian should be able to help you get in touch with the correct officials.

Required quarantine periods in some countries might be quite lengthy—as long as 6 months in some cases. Animals must be kenneled or stabled during the quarantine period, which also can be expensive, so owners might consider leaving the pet behind should the cost and effort (not to mention the stress of quarantine) outweigh the benefits of pet companionship. In particular, the United Kingdom's requirements for importation of pets are quite rigorous and can be found on their web site. It is important to remain up to date on requirements for importation, as they can change from one year to the next.

Various US federal agencies have rules for importing (or re-importing) pets, especially the Centers for Disease Control

and Prevention (CDC) and the Animal and Plant Health Inspection Service, a unit of the US Department of Agriculture (USDA). Both the Animal and Plant Health Inspection Service and the individual state veterinary services should be contacted regarding the importation of horses into the US and its territories. In addition, the US Customs Service also issues licensing and health requirements for both pets and wildlife. Neither the CDC nor the USDA requires a health certificate for routine pet importation; however, the CDC does require proof of current rabies vaccination for all imported dogs. The CDC also has rules dealing with other imported animals, including horses, cats, turtles, birds, snakes, fish, monkeys, civets, rodents, rabbits, and others. Furthermore, each state within the US has its own requirements for health and rabies vaccination certification.

Nearly every country has a different set of rules and regulations for the importation of pets, and these rules change periodically. For those reasons, it is difficult to summarize all the pertinent regulations here. However, some guidelines and examples of current regulations are provided below. In general, countries that are rabies free have the most stringent requirements for importation of dogs and cats.

Travel in Europe

European communities have become more open to international travelers. However, some countries in Europe, including the United Kingdom (UK), Sweden, and Norway, continue to require lengthy quarantines for animals from other countries. In these countries, most dogs and cats must be quarantined for 4 months (Sweden and Norway) or 6 months (United Kingdom), although the United Kingdom has recently implemented a program called the UK Pet Travel Scheme (PETS) that may eliminate the quarantine period for some qualified animals. However, like other "abbreviated quarantine" programs, it does require several months of preparation prior to travel. Dogs and cats may travel freely within other European countries if they are vaccinated against rabies and blood tests demonstrate adequate levels of antibodies. Dogs must also be vaccinated against canine distemper and leptospirosis.

The United Kingdom's Department for Environment, Food and Rural Affairs (DEFRA) is an important resource for people traveling to the UK or throughout Europe with pets. DEFRA also sponsors the Dog and Cat Travel and Risk Information (DACTARI) surveillance scheme. DACTARI provides for the reporting of exotic disease in dogs or cats whether they have been abroad or not. DEFRA encourages all pet owners to consider the potential risks of traveling in areas where exotic diseases occur and to seek veterinary advice before traveling overseas.

The European Union (EU) has recently instituted a "pet passport" program that makes it easier for pet owners to transport dogs, cats, and ferrets between member countries (and between the EU and certain other countries). This passport does not apply to animals first entering the EU from the United States; however, once an animal has met the requirements for entrance into an EU member country, its owner can contact a veterinarian in that country to apply for a passport.

A number of regulations cover import of horses into the UK and other parts of the EU. These depend in part on how long the horse will be in the destination country and the purpose of import. For example, the owners of horses present in the UK for longer than 30 days must obtain a "horse passport," a document that permanently identifies the animal and the medications it has received.

Travel to Asia and Africa

Regulations vary from country to country, although current health certificates and proof of rabies vaccination are near-universal requirements. Check with the appropriate embassy or consulate for specific information.

Travel to Australia

Australia is a rabies-free country and requires a 30-day quarantine of dogs and cats entering the country from the US. Horses must be quarantined in the US in an approved facility for 21 days, followed by quarantine in Australia for at least 14 days. These quarantine requirements are in addition to the various vaccinations and documentation required prior to import. Australia does not allow certain breeds of dog (such as American Pit Bull Terriers) into the country at all.

■ VACCINATIONS AND PREVENTIVE MEDICATIONS

Vaccination requirements vary from country to country. All dogs and cats should be vaccinated against rabies before they leave the United States. Rabies may be a nonexistent threat in some areas of the world, for example, in the United Kingdom, but may become an imposing problem in some remote areas of Africa or South America. The American Veterinary Medical Association recommends that pet owners travel with a rabies vaccination certificate if they cross international borders (including travel to Canada or Mexico).

While you are abroad with your pet, it is especially important that all vaccinations and preventive medications (such as those taken to prevent infection with heartworms or other parasites) be continued.

■ RETURNING TO THE UNITED STATES

There are a multitude of diseases and parasites that might be encountered in a foreign environment. The disease-causing organisms that animals may harbor have the potential to produce serious consequences. For example, in 2003 an outbreak of monkeypox in people in the United States was traced to Gambian giant rats, which carried the virus from Africa. The rats infected prairie dogs intended for the pet market, and the prairie dogs, in turn, infected people.

When citizens return to the United States, their pets—which may be infected with foreign diseases or parasites—are also presented for re-entry into the country. Dogs, cats, and certain other pets are subject to measures designed to prevent the introduction and spread of rabies and other zoonotic diseases (diseases that humans can acquire from infected animals). If an animal is found to have one of these diseases, the case must be reported to the appropriate state authorities, who in turn, will notify the proper federal agencies.

Before returning to the US, pets must undergo a complete physical examination, including blood tests to detect the presence of certain parasites. Pets should be dipped in a medicated solution to remove any fleas, ticks, or mites that may have infested the animal while overseas. A thorough examination of the feces is necessary to look for worms and other parasites. If the animal is found to be infected, suitable medications to kill the specific parasites will be administered.

Upon arrival in the US, owners must schedule another physical examination by a veterinarian. This examination should also include blood tests. Pets should again be dipped in a medicated solution to resolve any infestations that may have occurred while the animal was in transit. There may be additional restrictions if you enter the Unites States through Puerto Rico, Guam, or Hawaii. Before returning through these ports, travelers should contact animal health inspectors for additional information.

The general re-entry requirement is that all dogs and cats imported into the US be visually inspected by US Public Health Service personnel. Only those animals that are free of any evidence of infectious disease may be admitted. Animals showing signs of illness such as emaciation, skin sores, disturbances of the nervous system, jaundice, or diarrhea, must be examined, tested, or treated at the owner's expense by a licensed veterinarian designated by the agency.

Entry/Re-entry of Cats

Cats are subject only to the general requirements for entry as stated above. Rabies vaccination of cats is not a federal requirement; however, some states require vaccination prior to entry.

Entry/Re-entry of Dogs

Regardless of their age, dogs may be admitted to the US without restriction if they appear healthy and have been in a rabies-free area for at least the 6 months immediately preceding arrival in the US or since birth. The US Public Health Service provides a current list of rabies-free areas.

Dogs arriving from countries other than those listed as rabies-free may be admitted to the US if they are 3 months of age or older, free of any evidence of infectious disease, and accompanied by a valid certificate of rabies vaccination. All 3 requirements must be met. Vaccination certificates must identify the dog, be signed by a licensed veterinarian, and specify the expiration date, which must be after the date of arrival. If the expiration date is not indicated on the certificate, the certificate is considered to be valid for only 1 year from the date of issue. Vaccination certificates should also specify the date of vaccination, which must be at least 30 days before the arrival date.

For dogs that are at least 3 months old, are subject to the rabies vaccination requirement, and appear to be healthy but do not have a valid rabies certificate as outlined above, the Centers for Disease Control and Prevention (CDC) Form 75.37 must be completed (generally at the point of entry) and submitted to the appropriate Quarantine Station for distribution. The form may be signed by the owner or agent.

The US Public Health Service may release the dog if the owner agrees to place it in confinement for 30 days immediately upon arrival at the destination and to have it vaccinated against rabies within 4 days. Confinement is defined as restriction of an animal to a building or other enclosure, in isolation from other animals and people except for contact necessary for its care. If the dog is allowed out of the enclosure, the owner must muzzle the dog and use a leash.

The CDC Form 75.37 must also be prepared if the dog is older than 3 months of age and has a certificate showing a vaccination administered less than 30 days before arrival. The owner is required to confine the dog for the remainder of the 30 days.

Finally, Form 75.37 must be prepared for dogs younger than 3 months of age at the time of entry or re-entry. The owner is required to confine the dog until it is 3 months of age and then have it immunized against rabies. The dog must then be confined for an additional 30 days. A vaccination certificate presented for a puppy less than 3 months of age cannot be accepted.

The USDA should be contacted for requirements specific to dogs used for working livestock to prevent importation of *Echinococcus* species, which are tapeworms associated with the development of hydatid cysts in livestock and humans.

Entry/Re-entry of Horses

The CDC does not regulate importation of horses into the US unless the horse is known to carry a disease transmissible to humans. The USDA requires quarantine of horses for various time periods (3 to 60 days), depending on which country the horse is entering from. The owner or transporter should contact the port veterinarian at one of the USDA Animal Import Centers to reserve space at the quarantine facility.

■ WHERE TO STAY

If you will be staying in motels, hotels, or campgrounds along the way, check ahead of time to ensure that the establishment will accept pet visitors and what (if any) extra fees or restrictions there might be. Sources of information include the hotel's phone or web site, web sites dedicated to travelers with pets, or your travel agent. Travel associations such as the American Automobile Association (AAA) can provide information on accommodations for members wishing to travel with a pet.

If at all possible, do not leave your pet unattended in a hotel or motel room. Putting a "do not disturb" sign on the door will help to ensure that your pet is not accidentally released by housekeeping staff. Keeping the animal in its kennel will also help to ensure that it does not escape the room.

Even if you are planning to stay with friends or relatives, be sure to check whether they will be able to keep your pet in their home and, if so, whether it will need to be caged during its stay. Allergies, other pets in the home, and your pet's reaction to an unfamiliar environment should not be taken for granted.

If you are camping with your pet, do not allow it to wander unattended. Animals in unfamiliar surroundings can easily become lost or injured; wild animals such as skunks, raccoons, porcupines, and snakes can all be potential hazards for your pet. Remember to check for fleas and ticks during and after the trip. If you have any concerns, have your pet examined by a veterinarian upon return.

■ TRAVEL BY CAR

Before taking a long trip by car, it is helpful if you can take your pet for short rides in its carrier so that it becomes accustomed to being confined. Some pets have only been in their carriers during trips to the veterinarian, so they associate the carrier and car ride with an unpleasant experience. Enjoyable destinations such as a dog park can help your pet feel better about trips in the car.

Small animals should be kept within a travel carrier while riding in the car. This is the safest method not only for your pet, but also for other car passengers and even other drivers on the road. Within a carrier, your pet is more protected from sudden car movements. In addition, an excited animal can jump out of a car window or

Before traveling with a horse, practice entering and exiting the trailer.

distract (or even impede) the driver. Dogs that are too large to ride in a carrier should be kept in the back seat, ideally with an appropriate restraining harness. This minimizes their chances of interfering with the driver; in addition, it protects them from injury during an accident.

As much as they enjoy it, dogs should not be allowed to put their heads out of car windows. In addition to the risk of jumping out, they may suffer injury from flying debris or from their ears being flapped around. Similarly, a dog in the back of a pickup should be in a carrier.

A car can heat to dangerous levels in a very short time, even when the weather seems mild. Animals should not be left in a parked car if outside temperatures are above 72°F or below 55°F.

Animals (like their owners) should take frequent breaks while traveling by car. Stop about every 2 hours for a water and "potty" break. Be sure to keep your animal on a leash when leaving the car for such breaks. Feed your pet on its regular schedule if possible. Dry food is most convenient if the animal will take it; if moist food is needed, refrigerate or discard any leftovers.

Speak to your veterinarian if you know that your dog or cat does not travel well by car. For some animals, a small meal about 30 minutes before the trip will alleviate carsickness. If this does not work, your veterinarian may be able to recom-

mend an appropriate prescription or over-the-counter medication to help with nausea. Prescription tranquilizers are available as a last resort for animals that must travel by car but have difficulty doing so.

There are 2 general methods for transporting horses on the road. One is to tow the animal yourself; the other is to hire a horse transport company. Horse trailers can be rented; however, if you have not driven one before, you should practice with it before the trip. If your horse is not accustomed to trailering, you will need to spend time getting it used to entering and exiting the trailer. As with other pets, overnight accommodations should be thought out in advance. Some hotels and motels may allow a horse trailer to be parked overnight, or overnight boarding may be available along the route. Web sites dedicated to the traveler with horses are a good source for information about accommodations along the way.

■ AIR TRAVEL

The American Veterinary Medical Association provides thorough recommendations for air travel with pets; these apply to travel both inside and out of the US. Their recommendations include having a complete, physical examination before departure to determine whether your pet has any medical conditions that might make air travel dangerous, such as a heart condition that might not respond well to the changes in temperature or pressure that can occur on airplanes.

Pet owners should also contact their airline well in advance to check regulations and services. Most airlines that accept animals will have information on their web page about animal transportation, including travel tips. Many animal welfare organizations have similar information on their web sites.

US federal regulations require that pets be at least 8 weeks old and weaned for at least 5 days before flying. Federal Animal Welfare Act Regulations prohibit airlines from accepting dogs and cats for shipment if the airline cannot prevent exposure of the animal to temperatures less than 45°F (7°C) for more than 45 minutes while transferring the dog or cat between the terminal and the plane. This prohibition may be waived if a veterinarian provides an acclimation certificate stating that the dog or cat can be exposed to lower temperatures. However, a veterinarian cannot give a certificate allowing exposures to temperatures above 85°F (29°C) for more than 45 minutes. Some airlines will allow small dogs or cats to be transported in the passenger section if the carrier can fit under the seat and if the animal is able to sit quietly during the flight.

In order to minimize the chances of a pet getting lost or misdirected in transit, pet owners should try to book a direct flight or one with a minimal number of stops. Midweek flights tend to be less crowded and less stressful, providing favorable conditions for both owners and pets. The ages and size of pets; the time, length, and distance of the flight; and pet feeding routines must be considered. During warm months, the risk of overheating pets (in the cargo hold) can be reduced by selecting early morning or late evening flights. Some airlines will not ship animals when the temperatures are too hot or too cold to ensure safe travel in the cargo hold.

Travelers should arrive at the airport early, exercise the leashed pet lightly before the flight, and place the pet in a secure carrier or crate that is approved by the Federal Aviation Administration. The words "live animal" should appear on the crate in lettering at least 1 inch high, and the crate should be labeled with the owner's home and destination contact information. In general, tranquilizing pets is not recommended prior to flights. Consult your veterinarian regarding his or her specific recommendation for your pet.

Absorbent bedding or a comfortable pad should be placed in the carrier, and a favorite soft toy may be added. An item that has your scent (for example, an old shirt that you have worn overnight during sleep) can be placed in the carrier to help reassure your pet during travel. Pets should be familiarized with the crate well before the flight. This can be done by encouraging them to sleep, eat, and drink while in the crate.

Pets should be fed a light meal no less than 6 hours before departure. A handy way to provide your pet with water during the flight itself is to freeze water in its bowl prior to the trip and place the frozen bowl in its crate immediately prior to departure. This works best if the bowl can be affixed to the wire crate door. For trips lasting longer than 24 hours, provide some dry food in a durable plastic bag, contained in a cloth or mesh bag, attached to the outside of the crate. This can be fed by flight personnel should the need arise.

Pets should always be picked up promptly upon arrival at the destination. However, pets should not be let out of the carrier until you are in a quiet and secure area where there is no chance of escape.

When entering a country with a different language or dialect, it is wise to translate information (for example, the "live animal" notice and owner contact information) into the appropriate language so that local workers and baggage handlers will comprehend the importance of the contents of the pet carrier. A manila envelope containing copies of the pet's medical records should be taped to the outside of the carrier. Travelers should also carry a copy of these records with them at all times, together with contact information for the animal's veterinarian, color photographs of the pet, both with and without the owner (as a safeguard if pets are accidentally released or stolen during transit), and any pet medications.

Microchips implanted under the skin have recently become popular for identification of pets, and in some cases are required for travel. However, not all foreign countries have microchip scanning capabilities. Also, most of the microchips used in the United States operate on different frequencies that may not be picked up by scanners in other countries. Tattooing may still be beneficial in some foreign locales. Social security numbers should never be tattooed on animals as these numbers can be used to gain access to confidential personal information. Tattooing an email address is more suitable. In addition to a standard identification tag (which should be labeled with your name, home address, and phone number), the pet's collar should include a travel tag with information detailing where you are staying while away from home. Should your pet become lost, this will allow you to be contacted at your destination.

A number of companies specialize in air transport of horses and some have international experience. These companies may include door to door service and handling of much of the appropriate paperwork. Their fees will include the costs of the attendant required to travel with the horse.

▓ TRAVEL BY SHIP

Today, only one ocean liner provides regular voyages between the Unites States and England—Cunard's Queen Mary 2. For those individuals traveling by ocean liner, Cunard should be contacted for travel requirements and the amenities of their on-board kennels. Pet owners traveling on the Queen Mary 2 may take their dogs, cats, or birds with them in air-conditioned comfort. A valid health certificate from a veterinarian is required for the pet to be brought aboard. Dogs may be brought on board on a leash, but it is recommended that cats board in carriers or baskets. After embarkation, pets reside in kennels and are not permitted on any of the passenger decks, but owners may take their pets for walks on a designated area of the open deck. Interactions between owners and their pets are allowed daily. Owners should contact Cunard Lines for exact kennel dimensions; however, space limitations make it impossible to accommodate

dogs larger than a German Shepherd. There are no staff veterinarians aboard the ship.

Pets are not allowed on most other cruise lines, with the exception of service animals. If you are planning to cruise with a service animal, contact the cruise line as far in advance as possible in order to make sure that no problems arise. Most lines require you to provide food for your animal while on board the ship. In addition, some ports of call may have strict regulations and may not allow your animal to leave the ship.

▓ TRAVEL BY TRAIN

In the US, Amtrak does not allow animals aboard their trains, with the exception of service animals. In Europe, however, animals are often allowed to travel by train with their owners. You should check with the individual country to determine their regulations and restrictions. In some cases dogs are allowed to travel on leash, while in others they must travel by carrier. For other animals, appropriate carriers or cages are generally required.

As with air travel, it is important to make sure your pet has appropriate identification, and that you travel with copies of medical records (including vaccination history) and a health certificate, if required.

▓ ALTERNATIVES TO TRAVEL WITH PETS

If you decide that your pet should not travel with you, a number of alternative arrangements can be made. These vary in cost, quality, and convenience, so be sure to investigate the possibilities well before your trip to ensure that you are satisfied with the arrangement and that your desired facility or pet sitter will be available during the period of travel. Whether your pet stays in a boarding facility or in your home, be sure to provide accurate contact information, veterinarian information, medical records and proof of vaccinations if required, and any special care instructions to the caregiver.

Other than dogs and cats, most small pets are not routinely taken along on trips, so these travel alternatives may really be the only possibility for care during normal travel. If an unusual type of pet must be transported (for example, if the family is moving and intends to take the pet along), consult your veterinarian for advice. In the case of tropical fish, an aquarium supplier dealing in tropical fish may be able to help with properly "packing" the fish for a move.

Boarding Facilities (Kennels, Stables)

Your veterinarian is an excellent resource when looking for a boarding kennel, stable, or facility for your pet. Some veterinary clinics will board pets on site; this situation has the advantage that if your pet becomes ill, its normal veterinarian and records are close at hand. Check with friends who travel to see whether they can provide any recommendations.

Once you have located a boarding facility, be sure to visit it before boarding your pet to see whether the quarters appear to be comfortable, clean, and well-staffed. Facilities range from the bare-bones minimum cage or pen to elaborate "spa" or "day care" setups. Ask how often animals are fed and exercised. If you have particular concerns—such as a special diet or medicine for your pet that must be given daily—check to see whether the staff can accommodate your needs. For additional reassurance, some newer facilities even have cameras that allow owners to view their pets over the Internet. Facilities may also offer extra play time and special treats (usually at an additional cost).

The conditions under which horses are stabled and the treatment they receive is important and should be verified by the owner. At a minimum, the horse must be kept clean, suitably fed and exercised, and comfortably housed. The horse owner should pay close attention to the prospective stable environment and its overall construction. As with small animal boarding, it is important to seek recommendations from the veterinarian or other horse owners in the immediate area for suitable stabling facilities.

If you have a pet other than a dog, cat, or horse, your veterinarian may be able to suggest facilities that will be able to board the animal.

Your Home

Pets should never be left to fend for themselves while you are away. For a short trip, a neighbor or friend (especially one who knows your pet or is a pet owner) can provide care for your pet in the comfort of your home. Professional pet sitters are also available; the Internet can provide information on pet sitting associations and listings of their members, or you can ask pet-owning friends for recommendations. Ideally, have the potential sitter come to your home for a pre-trip interview to see how your pet reacts to him or her and to give you the opportunity to ask any questions you may have. Most reliable pet sitters will be able to provide references, so that you can check their reputation and past job experiences. Some pet sitters will also provide other services such as picking up the mail, and they can help provide a more "lived in" look to your home.

An ongoing relationship with a reliable pet sitter can be invaluable. In case of unexpected travel or absence (such as a family emergency), having a person who is already familiar with your pet and home can be a great relief.

As always, make sure the pet sitter knows how to contact you in case of illness or emergency, and be sure to provide a copy of your pet's veterinary records, as well as written instructions about any special care needs your pet might have.

CHAPTER 84

Health and the Human-Animal Bond

■ INTRODUCTION

The role of a pet has developed over the years from that of a simple outdoor guardian or mouse-catcher to one of a true companion and family member. Dogs, cats, and other pets have become an integral part of our everyday lives, and the relationship that exists between humans and animals has become known as the human-animal bond.

Not only has pet ownership become more common, but many pet owners also have more than one pet (*see* TABLE 28). As a result, there are now many specialty veterinarians, such as those serving only cat owners, owners of exotic pets, or those with more family-oriented practices. On average, pet owners in the US take their dogs to the veterinarian 1.9 times per year, and their cats to the veterinarian 1.0 times per year.

Many studies have shown that there are health benefits for owners who develop close bonds with a pet. Pet owners have fewer minor health problems, lower blood pressure and cholesterol levels, and better psychological well-being than people who do not have a pet. And pets appear to fill many of the same support functions as humans do for both adults and children. Animals are known to play a central, influential role in children's lives. Studies have reported that pet-owning preteens are more independent and have higher self-esteem.

Companion animals have also benefited from their closer association with people. In the past few decades, drugs and vaccines have been developed specifically for animals that have eliminated many of the infectious diseases that can shorten pets' lives. Recent surveys have shown that a pet's good health is a priority for many owners, and that they are willing to pay for both preventive care (such as vaccinations) and for advanced veterinary treatment for their companion animals.

With the greater esteem of companion animals in the household and in society, there has also come a greater emphasis on the animals' lifelong health. Albert Schweitzer's concept of "reverence for life" has become a standard for decision-making concerning animals for many people.

■ HEALTH BENEFITS OF PET OWNERSHIP

The company of a pet relaxes and entertains people, but the benefits of pet ownership go beyond simple joy. Studies have shown that keeping a pet improves the health and well-being of the people in the household. During stressful times, the comfort of a pet protects against depression and loneliness. People of all ages, both healthy and ill, benefit from living with a pet. In other studies, college-age women living with pets were less lonely than if they lived alone, and elderly women living with only a pet had better mental health than those who lived alone. Animal companions, both cats and dogs, help ward off depression and loneliness among people with AIDS and Alzheimer's disease. Stressful situations have less of an impact on elderly pet owners than on those who do not own pets—the pet owners visit the doctor less frequently during such times.

Pets allow their owners to feel needed as caregivers and nurturers, while also nurturing their owner. An owner's mood or physical capabilities do not change a pet's affection. An animal's unconditional affection often increases its owner's ability to cope with personal setbacks and depression. Pets reduce loneliness in a number of ways. Individuals who live "alone" with a pet are actually part of a family; they can look forward to being greeted and recognized when they walk in the door. The simple acts of feeding and caring for a pet can make its owner feel

Table 28. Pets in the United States (as of 2001)*

	Total Number of Pets (millions)	Number of Households with One or More as Pets (millions)
Dogs	61.6	37.9
Cats	70.8	33.2
Birds	10.1	4.8
Horses	5.1	1.8
Fish	49.3	6.4
Rabbits	4.8	1.8
Ferrets	1.0	0.5
Hamsters	0.9	0.7
Guinea pigs	0.6	0.5
Gerbils	0.3	0.2
Other rodents	0.8	0.3
Turtles	1.1	0.6
Snakes	0.7	0.3
Lizards	0.5	0.4

*Adapted from the 2002 *US Pet Ownership & Demographic Sourcebook*. Copyright, American Veterinary Medical Association.

needed and provide another reason for living and staying healthy.

Pets also motivate people to be more active and social. A pet is a powerful ally for starting conversations and making new acquaintances. Walking the dog provides not only physical exercise but also an opportunity to interact with humans, such as other dog owners and curious children. Many people are inspired by walking their dogs, using their pets as volunteers in nursing homes, or even just actively grooming, training, and pampering their pet. Without this bond, they would be less involved and engaged in living and more vulnerable to depression. Walking the dog and being outdoors where social contact is possible are healthful effects of living with a canine companion.

The daily comfort, social interaction, and motivation provided by pets improve cardiovascular health and lower blood pressure. Even relaxing with, talking to, or simply watching an animal can lower a person's blood pressure. One study of patients with high blood pressure showed that those who were given pets handled stressful tasks better than those who relied on blood pressure medication alone. Additionally, research shows people are more likely to survive the year after a heart attack if they have both a companion dog and a human social support network. Animal companionship is commonly linked to lower death rates and better longterm health.

■ ANIMAL-ASSISTED THERAPY AND ACTIVITIES

As the health benefits of pet ownership become more widely understood, there has been a greater effort to include pets in health research and practices. Involving animals as a type of therapy for the sick or elderly is becoming more popular.

Many pet owners volunteer their time and their companion pet in nursing or other rehabilitation centers. There is even a formal process (administered by the Delta Society) for screening animal companions and training their owners. After witnessing the positive effect such volunteer visits have on residents and patients, medical professionals (such as clinical psychologists, social workers, occupational therapists, physical therapists, and nurses) have begun to find ways to make interaction with animals a formal part of professional treatment. Some mental health facilities now provide animal-assisted therapy.

If short, occasional visits with animals are helpful for a person with special needs, then an animal's constant company might be even more beneficial for that individual. Service animals are now helping more than just people with physical disabilities. The use of psychiatric service dogs is growing. These dogs assist people with mental illnesses such as schizophrenia, bipolar disorder, fear of open places (agoraphobia), and anxiety. Psychiatric service dogs are specifically trained to meet their human companion's needs. For example, they might help distract a person with autism from a repetitive behavior or help their owner recover from a schizophrenic episode. Often, these dogs are specifically trained to create a protective, nurturing environment for their patients. It is also thought that the relationship between the animal and the owner is, in itself, therapeutic in many cases.

■ SERVICE AND OTHER WORKING DOGS

Just as dogs can be trained to provide therapy and companionship for the mentally disabled, they may also be trained to provide assistance to the physically disabled. These dogs are known as service dogs. Although initially service dogs were well known for providing guidance to the visually challenged, they can also be trained to assist people with hearing deficits, epi-

lepsy, limited mobility, and many other disabilities.

Dogs also provide a variety of other services for society. Working dogs have been trained to help law enforcement officers with tasks such as search and rescue and sniffing out everything from drugs to exotic pests to bombs. Many people remember the role that working dogs played in the days following the 9/11 terror attack on the World Trade Center in New York. However, they play equally important but less visible roles every day, such as helping police capture criminals or working at airports to assist with luggage screening.

Much time and money is needed for the specialized training these dogs and their handlers need. As the handlers build partnerships with their working dogs, they also form emotional bonds. Although service dogs might have several handlers in their early lives and training, when grown they typically spend all their waking hours with a single handler. Some working dogs might be kenneled in a separate facility during nonworking hours. However, many police dogs live with their handlers and their families.

Service dogs provide assistance and companionship.

Although service dogs are involved in a variety of work situations, all of these dogs are precious and valuable to their handlers. When a service dog needs medical attention, perhaps requiring it to be separated from its handler, the handler might need to make arrangements to accommodate the animal's absence. If a needed medical treatment, such as a drug that causes sleepiness, might alter a service dog's performance, handlers should be fully aware of all issues and potential side effects.

ANIMAL WELFARE

Most responsible pet owners and handlers have good intentions for their pets' welfare, and they work to reduce and prevent pain and promote well-being and pleasure in their companion animals. However, animal neglect and abuse still occur. People who intentionally and deliberately abuse animals are more likely to do the same to vulnerable human members of their household, such as children or the elderly. Reporting suspected animal abuse to local authorities might help save people from abuse, too.

Extreme cases of abuse are less common than cases of neglect and general poor care, some of which may not be done on purpose. This might include failing to feed the animal a proper, nutritious diet, not providing adequate space or housing, or simply not providing regular veterinary care or vaccinations.

Another serious problem occurs with animal hoarders, who may be mentally ill. Animal hoarders, perhaps without realizing it or intending to, acquire more animals than they can care for properly. Some communities address cases of animal hoarding by bringing in both animal control and mental health agencies.

A larger, society-wide animal welfare problem is the abandoning or killing of companion animals. Although the number of people who give up or abandon pets has dropped, the problem is still widespread. Pet owners who are not knowledgeable about animal care and training are more likely to relinquish their pets, especially if the pet has a behavior problem or if the owner had unrealistic expectations about life with a pet.

If you are considering becoming a pet owner for the first time, or keeping a new type of pet, it is highly recommended that you do research about the particular type of animal before you bring one home. This should include its diet and exercise needs, housing, amount of human interaction or daily care needed, and regular health care, including spaying or neutering. Having your pet spayed or neutered before it matures will not only prevent unwanted litters, it will also improve your pet's health and behavior. Breeders, veterinarians, pet stores, and animal shelters can help owners choose an appropriate pet and understand their responsibilities, reducing the likelihood that the owner will eventually give up the pet because it became a burden instead of a joy.

VETERINARY FAMILY PRACTICE OR BOND-CENTERED PRACTICE

Pet owners form deep attachments to their companions, and their expectations for veterinary care are becoming similar to their expectations for human medical care. Because pet owners today are willing to spend more time and money on proper pet care, the quality and style of veterinary medicine practices are growing increasingly important. New types of companion-animal practices have emerged. These are typically referred to as veterinary family practices or bond-centered practices.

Such practices build lifelong relationships with families and their animals. When a family gets a new pet, for example, a bond-centered veterinarian takes the opportunity to discuss the pet's life cycle with the family. The veterinarian might discuss building a positive relationship with the pet and explain how to minimize stressful, expensive behavior problems, such as destructive chewing.

A pet whose family understands its growth stages and needs is less likely to be banished to the back yard or given up for adoption. Veterinarians who practice in this way care for not only the medical needs and welfare of the animal, but also the social health of its family.

Pet owners with children should consider whether and how their veterinarian involves the whole family in the animal's care. Families may wish to select a pet care provider who communicates well with children, makes them comfortable, and accommodates them during the consultation—either by permitting them in the room or by providing a play area (*see* BOX).

It is also important, however, to choose a veterinarian that meets the needs of adult pet owners and the pet itself. If pet owners are comfortable at the veterinarian's office, the chances that the pet will be comfortable there increase as well. The medical staff may provide comfort by not only offering sound medical care and advice, but also emotional support. Good communication is crucial. A veterinarian should be willing to communicate with pet owners about the animal's needs, the treatment options available, and ways to keep pets happy and healthy. Pet owners can help build a positive relationship with their veterinarian by being neither neglectful nor over-involved, by listening to the doctor's advice, and by making sure their pet is under control, clean, and not a danger to others.

▨ PET LOSS AND GRIEF

As with all relationships, when an animal companion dies or is ill, its family will likely feel stress, sorrow, and grief. The effects may be felt by not only family members but also by neighbors, friends, and the veterinary care team.

Some communities, animal shelters, and veterinary colleges sponsor hotlines, support groups, and counseling for those who have just lost a companion animal. Veterinarians can also provide invaluable information and support to those who have lost a pet. The grieving process usually takes about a year as pet owners pass through significant family traditions and holidays before somewhat accepting the loss of a pet.

Even then, however, extra burdens may be experienced by the pet owner if they feel responsible for the death of the animal through euthanasia, commonly referred to as putting the pet to sleep. It is important for pet owners to understand all the options available to them and their pet before deciding that euthanasia is the best choice. Veterinarians can provide much of this information as well as support in decision making. The choice is not an easy one. Pet owners that are faced with the consideration of whether or not to euthanize their pet should be sure they are informed of all their options, choose the right veterinarian, and maintain a support network of friends and family to help cope with the loss of a companion.

Euthanasia

Euthanasia is defined as killing an animal in a humane manner, making death

---

Signs of a Client-centered Veterinary Practice

Veterinarians should provide their human and animal clients with more than just medical expertise. Look for the following signs that a veterinarian has taken into consideration not only the pet's needs but the family's needs as well:

▨ Areas for relaxation

▨ Softly lit public areas

▨ Comfortable seating in examination and waiting rooms

▨ Examination rooms without barriers from medical staff

▨ Spotlessly clean

▨ Excellent interpersonal skills: staff understand the emotional significance of medical care, and doctors take the time to ask and answer questions, build relationships, and even laugh with clients

▨ Regular followup communication

easy and painless for the animal. Euthanasia procedures are designed to prevent fear and distress. The exact method used might vary according to the situation, species, reason for euthanasia, and type of clinic.

Although there are many ways to end an animal's life that might seem quick, veterinarians are best equipped to make sure that an animal does not suffer in its last moments. Pet owners can choose to have a veterinarian euthanize a pet in order to relieve the pain and suffering of an untreatable illness or injury. The veterinarian aims for humane treatment before, during, and after the procedure. First, the veterinarian addresses the pain, anxiety, distress, and fear an animal might experience before it loses consciousness. Then, he or she makes sure the moment of death itself is pain-free.

In addition to the welfare of the pet, the veterinary team is also concerned with the safety and emotions of pet owners. If euthanasia is being considered by the owner, the veterinarian or another staff member will spend time explaining the process and any options or alternatives. They can usually offer suggestions of where to turn for additional support or help with making this difficult decision.

CHAPTER 85

Cancer and Tumors

▨ INTRODUCTION

The rate of cancer among dogs and cats is similar to the rate of cancer among humans. Cats seem to get cancer a little less frequently than humans while dogs seem to develop cancer slightly more frequently than humans. For most species, the chance that a pet will contract cancer goes up with age. For example, cancer is most common in pets that are 10 years old or older. Among dogs aged 10 or more, just under half of the deaths are due to cancer. However, even young animals can develop cancer; age is not the only factor involved in cancer development.

This chapter covers the general aspects of cancer in pets. Individual cancers and their treatments are covered in the chapters on specific body systems. For example, the description of melanoma and other skin cancers in dogs and cats can be found in the chapters on skin disorders for those species (*see* TABLE 29).

▨ WHAT IS CANCER?

Cancer is a group of abnormal cells often—though not always—consolidated into a mass called a tumor. The common characteristic of all cancer cells is the absence of normal growth control mechanisms. Normal, healthy cells grow and reproduce only to replace cells that have died or, in young animals, to support ordinary growth and development. Cancer cells have no such restraints; they keep growing and reproducing even when there is no need for new cells. They often invade and damage or destroy nearby healthy cells.

Any tissue in a body can develop cancer cells; no area of a body is immune to cancer. More than 100 types of cancer are known. Cancers are named based on the type of cell or organ in which the cancer develops. Thus, as an example, hepatocellular carcinoma is a specific type of cancer involving the liver.

Table 29. Common Cancers in Domestic Animals

Type of Cancer	Tissue Usually Affected	Page Reference
Dogs		
Bladder cancer	Urinary bladder	*See* page 297
Brain tumor	Brain	*See* page 197
Lipoma	Fat, subcutaneous tissue	*See* page 273
Lymphoma	Lymph nodes, spleen, bone marrow	*See* page 45
Malignant histiocytosis	Skin	*See* page 273
Mammary carcinoma	Breast (mammary gland)	*See* page 222
Mast cell tumor	Skin	*See* page 275
Melanoma	Skin	*See* page 276
Osteosarcoma	Bone	*See* page 193
Squamous cell carcinoma	Skin	*See* page 280
Cats		
Ceruminous gland adenocarcinoma	Ear canal	*See* page 437
Fibrosarcoma	Skin, subcutaneous tissue	*See* page 509
Infiltrative lipoma	Fat, subcutaneous tissue	*See* page 507
Lipoma	Fat, subcutaneous tissue	*See* page 507
Liposarcoma	Fat, subcutaneous tissue	*See* page 507
Mammary tumor	Breast (mammary gland)	*See* page 475
Mast cell tumor	Skin	*See* page 508
Osteosarcoma	Bone	*See* page 453
Sebaceous hyperplasia/adenoma	Skin	*See* page 509
Squamous cell carcinoma	Skin	*See* page 511
Synovial cell sarcoma	Joint	*See* page 450
Vaccine-associated sarcoma	Skin, subcutaneous tissue	*See* page 509
Horses		
Lymphoma	Lymph nodes, spleen	*See* page 590
Melanoma	Skin	*See* page 778
Sarcoid/fibrosarcoma of the skin, mouth, and salivary glands	Skin, mouth, salivary gland	*See* page 776
Squamous cell carcinoma	Skin	*See* page 779

While many types of cancer cause the development of tumors, not all tumors are malignant (cancerous). Tumors can be benign (noncancerous). Benign tumors, while they may need to be treated or removed, are not usually as dangerous as malignant tumors. Malignant tumors invade and destroy nearby cells and organs. They can be difficult to remove because of the involvement of nearby organs. Further, malignant tumors often spread (metastasize) to other parts of the body through the lymphatic system or the bloodstream.

■ DEVELOPMENT AND SPREAD OF CANCER

Transformation is the word used to describe the 2-step process by which a normal, healthy cell changes into a cancer cell. The first step in transformation is called initiation. During initiation, a cell's genetic material changes (mutates) and the growth inhibiting factor is reduced or lost. This change can occur spontaneously but it can also be caused by the presence of a substance (called a carcinogen) that encourages the mutation. Known carcinogens include chemicals, viruses, tobacco, radiation, and even sunlight. Not all cells are equally at risk when exposed to carcinogens. In some, a genetic flaw may make the cell more likely to mutate; in other cases, a cellular factor may make it more resistant to a specific carcinogen. Other factors may also contribute to initiation. Physical irritation over a long period can make a cell more vulnerable to carcinogens.

Promotion is the second step in the transformation of a healthy cell into a cancerous cell. Promotion is caused by agents known as promoters. The promoters stimulate the growth of the cell. With a damaged or lost growth inhibiting factor, the cell grows uncontrollably. Promotion cannot affect a cell that has not been initiated. That is why promoters do not, all by themselves, cause cancer. Substances found in the environment and certain drugs act as promoters.

Certain carcinogens are powerful enough to cause cancer on their own; they both initiate and promote cancer development. On the other side, not every carcinogen that an animal encounters will cause cancer. The DNA (genes) of animals, just like the DNA in humans, includes built-in repair mechanisms. An animal's DNA can protect the animal from the changes that cause cancer. Only when the protective mechanisms fail or are overwhelmed will an animal develop cancer.

Once a cell has turned cancerous, it starts growing and spreading. Because there is no control on the growth of these cells, the cancer will often take advantage of any available path to spread and find new places to grow. This process is called metastasizing. The 2 most common paths for cancerous cell spread are the lymphatic system and the bloodstream. The lymphatic system is made up of small vessels that collect the fluid surrounding cells and return that fluid to the bloodstream. Carcinomas are the malignant tumors formed of the epithelial cells lining the internal and external surfaces of the body. Carcinomas usually spread through the lymphatic system. Sarcomas are malignant tumors formed from bone, cartilage, fat, or other connective tissues. Sarcomas usually spread through the bloodstream.

■ CAUSES OF CANCER

Cancer is not a new disease. Physicians have been aware of cancer in humans for over 2,000 years. As a result, researchers have studied cancer in humans for generations. During the past hundred years, considerable progress has been made in understanding the spread and development of cancers in humans. Veterinarians know less about the specifics of cancer in animals because much less research has been done on malignancies in animals. However, new studies are being undertaken, often taking advantage of what has been learned about cancer in humans.

Many veterinarians and pet owners have observed that pets develop cancer more frequently during the late stages of their lives. Animal researchers do not yet understand the exact relationship between advancing age and cancer development. Some researchers, however, have speculated that age may weaken the immune system and make it easier for cells to mutate into precancerous (initiated) cells.

If this is true, age might play an important role in the observed higher rates of cancer in older animals.

Based on research in both humans and animals, we know that cancer is a complex process that can be triggered by hereditary, environmental, and nutritional factors. In both people and animals, cancer development is a complex process that proceeds gradually through the interaction of multiple factors.

Family History and Genetic Factors

Statistics on animal cancers support the idea that hereditary risk factors play a role in the occurrence of cancer among pets. For example, among dogs, Golden Retrievers, Boxers, and Bernese Mountain Dogs are generally more likely to develop cancer than other breeds. This suggests that there are genetic characteristics that contribute to the higher rates of cancer among these animals. The increased cancer risk these animals face may be caused by a combination of genes or by a single gene. More research is needed to gain a better understanding of which genetic factors are involved.

Environmental Factors

Research in humans shows that a large majority of human cancers are related to risk factors present either in the environment or in the diet. It is likely that these same risk factors play a major role in the development of cancers in pets. Because pets live in the same environment as their owners, pets are exposed to many of the same environmental hazards that have been identified as risk factors for humans.

Known carcinogens that may directly contribute to the development of cancer in pets include ultraviolet radiation (*see* VIRUSES, CARCINOGENS, AND OTHER KNOWN CAUSES OF CANCER, below) from long exposure to the sun; second-hand tobacco smoke; a variety of herbicides, insecticides, and pesticides commonly used in agriculture; and the air pollution and smog common in many urban areas. Nickel, uranium, benzidene, benzene,

radon, vinyl chloride, cadmium, and asbestos are all common substances that have been identified as carcinogens.

Just as humans differ in their response to carcinogens, so do animals. You pet is an individual and may have higher or lower sensitivity to risk factors. It is not possible to reliably establish whether a high rate of cancer in a particular family of animals is due to risk factors in the environment, hereditary factors, or to chance.

Age

Cancer occurs more frequently in older humans and animals. While we do not know the exact causes of cancer in either humans or animals, it is possible that the weakening of the immune system due to age plays a role in the body's ability to control mutated cells that could become malignant. Because healthy cells divide and reproduce continuously, veterinary cancer specialists speculate that as an animal ages it becomes more and more likely that a cell will divide incorrectly and produce a "mistake" that could lead to mutation. Such a mutation could, in turn, lead to cancer. Also, the longer a pet lives, the longer the animal is potentially exposed to environmental carcinogens and the higher the chance that a carcinogen could affect the genetic material (DNA and RNA) in a cell and cause cancer. Thus, there are multiple potential reasons for the observed relationship between advancing age and cancer.

Viruses, Carcinogens, and Other Known Causes of Cancer

The specific causes of some cancers have been identified by veterinary researchers. Almost all species of domestic animals develop squamous cell carcinoma. While researchers have not been able to pinpoint the exact cause of this common cancer, they have learned that prolonged exposure to the ultraviolet light that is present in sunlight is a significant risk factor. In addition, it has been shown that white cats, white dogs, and horses with white facial markings are more likely to develop squamous cell carcinoma.

Environmental carcinogens, such as those found in cigarette smoke, have been shown to contribute to the development of squamous cell carcinomas found in the mouths of cats. Mouth cancers in pets, including dogs and cats, are thought to be triggered by carcinogens in the air. The process may be very simple. The carcinogen lands on the coat of the animal and then transfers to the inside of the mouth as the animal licks itself while grooming.

Viruses are known causes of some cancers in pets. For example, feline leukemia virus is a common cause of death in cats. Up to 30% of cats persistently infected with this virus develop cancer. A type of cancerous wart (known as an oral papilloma) that develops in the mouth of dogs, especially younger dogs, is caused by a virus.

Some cancers are sexually transmitted. The genital cancer of dogs known as canine transmissible venereal tumor is transmitted during sexual intercourse. The cancerous cells are transferred during contact between a healthy animal and an affected animal.

While specific answers about the causes of many cancers are lacking, veterinarians and researchers do know that cancer cannot be caused by short-lived physical injuries such as bumps and bruises. However, the sites of serious traumatic injuries may develop cancer, occasionally years after the injury. For example, the location of bone fractures (especially if the fracture is recurring) or the sites of implants (such as pins or metal plates) have been shown to have a higher risk for sarcomas than other areas of the body. This information has caused speculation that chronic inflammation may contribute to cancer development.

Vaccinations are an important part of the care of your pet; they protect the health of your companion. However, in the early 1990s veterinarians began to notice that sarcomas were more likely than normal to occur at vaccination sites in some cats. In the years since, researchers have established a link between vaccination and sarcoma development in a small number of cases (*see* page 511). Researchers are now studying the problem to identify the exact cause and to look for ways to prevent this cancer.

Much research remains to be done about cancers of all kinds in both humans and animals. As we gain new information about the causes of cancer, the outlook for pets with cancer will be much more hopeful and our treatment of pets with cancer will improve. In the future, we hope to both prevent and cure cancer in our pets.

■ TYPES OF CANCER

As is the case with cancer in humans, some types of cancer are more common in pets than others. Breast (mammary) cancer, skin cancer, bone cancer, mouth (oral) cancer, connective tissue cancers (sarcomas), and lymphatic tissue cancers (lymphomas) are most frequently found in pets.

Cancers of the blood are known as **leukemias**. Cancers involving the blood-forming tissues are called **lymphomas**. Unlike cancers that form tumors, leukemias and lymphomas do not form a solid mass; they remain as separate cancerous cells. In the bone marrow and bloodstream, leukemia and lymphoma cells often crowd out and replace normal cells. Enlargement of multiple lymph nodes is often the first sign of lymphoma.

The cells that cover the surfaces of the body, produce hormones, and make up glands are known as epithelial cells. When epithelial cells mutate into cancer cells, the tumor is called a **carcinoma**. Cancers of the skin, lung, colon, stomach, breast, prostate, and thyroid gland all fall under the general category of carcinoma. Typically, younger animals develop carcinomas less frequently than older animals, although carcinomas can occur in animals of any age.

The cells that form muscles, connective tissues, and bones are collectively known as mesodermal cells. When these cells become cancerous, the tumor is called a

sarcoma. Bone cancer, also called osteosarcoma, is one well-known type of sarcoma.

■ REDUCING THE RISK OF CANCER

There are things that pet owners can do to reduce the risk of certain types of cancers in their pets. The most common cancer preventive step is spaying or neutering. Spaying young females does, to a large extent, prevent breast cancer. For example, female dogs that are spayed before their first heat (estrus) only rarely develop mammary cancer. Female dogs that have not been spayed have a risk for breast cancer that is 200 times greater than that for dogs that have been spayed before the first heat. Even dogs that were spayed after their first heat cycle are 10 times less likely to get breast cancer than unspayed females. The highest risk of breast cancer in female dogs is for those that are spayed after the fifth heat cycle or are never spayed. For male dogs, the risk of testicular cancer is eliminated with neutering.

While the degree of protection provided to female cats by spaying before the first heat cycle is less well documented than it is with dogs, most veterinarians believe that the risk of breast cancer in cats is also greatly reduced by spaying. The preventive key is doing this surgery before the first heat cycle or as soon after that as possible.

Unfortunately, similar proven steps for preventing other cancers are rare. And, there are some risk factors, such as genetic heritage, that are unavoidable. Even though we know very little about decreasing the risks of cancer, there are some steps pet owners can take to reduce the chance that their pets will develop cancer. Most of these steps involve lifestyle choices.

Good Nutrition and General Care

No diet has been proven to prevent cancer in animals. However, adequate nutrition and good general care not only provide what your pet needs to lead a healthy life, these things will also make it easier for your pet's body to fight cancer and other diseases. For many species of animals, nutritional guidelines have been established through research. Commercial producers of pet foods have used these guidelines to produce well-formulated foods; such products are readily available. Your pet's overall health and quality of life will be enhanced when you provide a diet that is nutritionally appropriate. Learn about your pet's nutritional needs and read pet food labels carefully to be sure the food you are providing meets those needs. This step may also contribute to reducing your pet's risk of cancer.

Reducing Known Risk Factors

Reducing known cancer risks in your pet's environment is a step toward cancer protection that you can take for the member of your family that is often the least able to avoid such risks. For example, by controlling your pet's exposure to sunlight and ultraviolet radiation, you can significantly reduce the risk of skin cancer. The areas on an animal's body that are most likely to develop skin cancer are those with little or no hair or those that do not have pigmentation (color). Therefore, the highest risk areas for skin cancer in cats include the eyelids, the tip of the nose, and the tips of the ears. For dogs, the abdomen is a vulnerable area. Animals with fair or white coloring are more likely to develop skin cancer than animals with dark hair. White or light skin or fur provide less protection from the ultraviolet rays in sunlight.

Owners of animals with white or light coats or skin should protect their pets from direct exposure to sunlight, especially during the hours when ultraviolet radiation is strongest. Ultraviolet rays are strongest during the summer months between the hours of noon and 4:00 P.M. Keeping pets indoors or in well-shaded areas as much as possible during these hours can significantly reduce the risk presented by ultraviolet radiation. Common sense is needed in applying this guideline. Short exposure to sunlight, such as during walks or normal "bathroom breaks," poses little risk; prolonged exposure, such as that of animals living outside, carries much more risk for skin cancer.

Among humans, smoking and other tobacco usage is a leading cause of cancer. Smoking is not only dangerous for the smoker; it also endangers the health of others exposed to tobacco smoke. This means that anyone living in a home where there is a smoker has an increased risk of health problems, including cancer. Pets that inhale secondhand smoke are more likely to develop cancer and other health problems than animals that live in a smoke-free environment. An owner's decision to stop smoking can, therefore, lower the chances that any pets living in the home will develop cancer.

Prevention and Early Detection

The earlier cancer is detected and diagnosed, the easier it is to treat and the better the outcome of the treatment is likely to be. Even if cancer cannot be avoided completely, early treatment offers the best chance for survival and a return to a normal, healthy life. Routine, thorough physical examination by a veterinarian is the best way for you to prevent fatal or debilitating cancer in your pet.

All animals, especially older animals, should be considered at risk for cancer and receive physical examinations by a veterinarian at least yearly. Exams should include blood and urine tests. These tests can lead to detection of cancer even though the animal may not look, feel, or act ill. Skin maps are used by some veterinarians to track skin masses on pets. These records allow the veterinarian to quickly identify any new masses or unexpected growth of existing masses and test them to determine whether or not such masses are cancerous. This is one method used to catch cancers early when treatment is easier and more likely to result in remission or a cure.

All pet owners should monitor their pet's health regularly. Some signs should alert you to possible cancer. Changes in your pet's body, appetite, and urinary or bowel habits are signs of possible illness. You should also note changes in personality, demeanor, or activity levels. Such changes can happen suddenly or gradually over time. These changes should alert you to have your pet examined by a veterinarian.

It is crucial to have your pet routinely screened for cancer by a veterinarian. In some cases, veterinarians may use advanced screening technologies such as x-rays, ultrasonography, magnetic resonance imaging (MRI), computed tomography (CT) scans, and examination of the colon (a colonscopy) to look for cancer. These tools can help your pet's veterinary team detect cancer at an early stage. Screening even when there is no sign of cancer is crucial because—just as with humans—the earlier cancer is detected, the better the treatment outcome is likely to be.

Possible Signs of Cancer

Various changes in a pet's behavior or appearance, such as those listed below, might indicate the development of cancer. These are not always signs of cancer; however, paying attention to such changes and bringing them to the attention of your veterinarian as soon as they occur can increase the chance that a cancer will be detected and treated at an early stage.

- A growing or changing lump
- Swollen lymph nodes
- Sudden abdominal swelling
- Unexplained bleeding from the mouth, nose, or genital area
- Difficulty when breathing, chewing, swallowing, urinating, or defecating
- Persistent sores or swelling
- Unexplained bad breath or other odor
- Dry cough
- Lowered stamina
- Recurrent vomiting or diarrhea
- Loss of weight or appetite
- Lack of interest in physical activities
- Indications of physical discomfort, such as lameness or stiffness

■ CANCER TREATMENT

Your veterinarian has several options for treating pets with cancer. There are 3 common treatment options for animal cancers: surgery, chemotherapy, and radiation therapy (also called radiotherapy). Each of these options can be used alone or in combination with other treatments. The specific treatment program your veterinarian will recommend will depend on the specifics of your pet's condition. In selecting the treatment, your veterinarian will consider the type of cancer, how quickly it grows and spreads (the stage or grade of the cancer), and the location of the cancer.

The goal of any cancer treatment program is to completely and permanently eradicate the cancer. Sadly, a complete cure is often not possible. For pets whose cancer cannot be cured, the veterinary team can provide treatment to minimize the animal's pain and discomfort and enhance its quality of life.

Oncology is the medical specialty that deals with all aspects of cancer in both humans and animals. Veterinary oncologists are veterinarians who study cancer in animals, including prevention, development, diagnosis, and treatment. A veterinary oncologist may be a part of the medical team treating your pet or the treatment may be conducted by your regular veterinarian and veterinary clinic staff.

Surgery

Surgery is considered the cornerstone for treating most cancers in animals. It is one of the oldest forms of cancer treatment and frequently the most effective one. Today, surgery may be combined with radiation therapy and/or chemotherapy, depending on the characteristics of the case.

When cancer surgery is performed, the main goal is usually to remove all the cancerous cells in the animal's body. Sometimes, if the cancer is detected early (before it grows too large or spreads to other parts of the body), surgery can completely cure

the animal. Other goals of cancer surgery can include removing an unsightly tumor to improve the animal's appearance or comfort or removal of a tumor that is interfering with the animal's normal body functions. These goals can improve the quality of life for the animal.

Surgery is most successful when the cancer involves a tumor that has not spread beyond its original location. Unfortunately, however, not all tumors can be surgically removed. Some are in inaccessible sites. And, there are times when the costs to the animal might outweigh the benefits. For example, removing a large tumor might require removing a vital organ or may cause a pet to lose a vital body function. If the cancer is in more than one location or has spread (metastasized), then surgery is not as likely to be an effective treatment.

A **biopsy** is a surgical procedure in which a piece of a tumor is removed for study and analysis by a pathologist. The pathologist's report to the veterinarian

---

Costs and Benefits of Cancer Surgery

Whenever cancer surgery is being considered, you should discuss its costs and benefits with your veterinarian.

Possible Benefits

■ Complete cure and a disease-free life

■ Reduced pain

■ Improved quality of life (even if complete cure is not possible)

■ Prolonged life (even if complete cure is not possible)

Possible Costs

■ Potential complications of surgery, including infections, bleeding, recurrence of the cancer, and undesirable changes in appearance

■ Short- or longterm pain and discomfort

■ Loss of normal function in affected limbs or organs (for example, as a result of amputation)

will provide important information such as the type of cancer and its characteristics. Combined with information about the size and location of the cancer, your veterinarian can develop the best treatment program for your pet.

Even if surgery cannot be used to completely remove a tumor, it can be used to remove part of a tumor, a process known as **debulking**. There are several possible benefits to debulking. First, partially removing a tumor can reduce the signs of cancer and make the animal more comfortable through improved mobility or reduced pain. Debulking can also be used to improve the effectiveness of radiation therapy or chemotherapy. These cancer treatments have the greatest chance for success when fewer cancer cells are present.

Surgery may also be prescribed by your veterinarian to manage or reduce the side effects of other treatments. During radiation therapy, for example, normal, healthy tissue may be damaged (*see* below). Removal of the damaged tissue will encourage more rapid healing. In other cases, the surgical placement of a feeding tube may be necessary when either the cancer or its treatment makes normal eating physically impossible or very painful.

Pain management is an important part of surgical treatment (*see* PAIN MANAGEMENT, page 1211). After the surgery, medication is usually provided to reduce pain and make the animal more comfortable.

Radiation Therapy

One of the most common treatments for cancer in both humans and animals is radiation therapy. This treatment is sometimes also called x-ray therapy, radioisotope irradiation, or cobalt therapy.

Cancer cells divide more frequently than normal cells. Cancer cells also have a weakness; they do not recover from radiation damage as quickly or completely as normal cells. Radiation works as a treatment for cancer because it kills cells that divide rapidly or, in other cases, because it damages the cancer cells so severely that they cannot

Radiation Therapy

Radiation therapy focuses a beam or field of intense energy on a certain area or organ of the body. The energy used in radiation therapy is similar to the energy used to create x-rays—except that either the radiation is many times stronger or the exposure time is much longer, so that the energy kills the cancer cells. Radiation can be applied to the cancer in 1 of 2 ways: from the outside using a machine, or from the inside using implants.

The more common method is external radiation therapy. In this technique, a linear accelerator beams rays to the site of the tumor. Normal tissue is shielded as much as possible from the destructive energy. To reduce exposure of normal tissue, multiple beam paths are often used. As a result, any negative side effects of the radiation are restricted to the area of treatment and do not affect the whole of the animal's body.

Internal radiation therapy is also a possible method of cancer treatment, but it is rarely used for animals. Doses of radiation are delivered in and around the tumor by an implanted radioactive substance (such as cobalt). This method is known as brachytherapy. It is seldom used to treat cancers in animals because the radioactive substance must be handled carefully and kept in place within the tumor to prevent exposing humans, other animals, or healthy body parts of the pet being treated. One exception to this is the use of radioactive iodine to treat thyroid adenomas in cats. Implantable radiation sources that are so small that they can be permanently implanted within the body are currently being researched and may increase the use of brachytherapy.

divide and grow (*see* BOX). Radiation therapists work to deliver just enough radiation to the cancer cells to destroy or injure them and prevent them from reproducing.

Radiation therapy is often used in addition to treatment with surgery or chemotherapy or both. The therapy or combination of therapies prescribed for a particular animal will be selected by your veterinarian based on which options offer the best chance of controlling or eradicating your pet's cancer. For brain tumors, nasal tumors, and other tumors in the head and neck, radiation therapy may be the treatment of choice. For cancers of the spine or pelvis, it may be the only practical treatment option.

Great strides have been made in recent years in radiation therapy. There has been a dramatic improvement in the sophistication of radiation therapy equipment and methods and a parallel rise in its success in eradicating cancer. Pet owners have also increased their requests for this treatment for their pets. However, radiation therapy is not a cure-all for cancer. Not all cancers are easily killed by radiation. Some cancers are highly resistant to radiation therapy and cancers of these types cannot be treated effectively with radiation. Thus, whether or not radiation therapy will be prescribed will depend, to a great extent, on the type of cancer to be treated.

Often, radiation therapy is used to either help make chemotherapy more effective or to decrease the size of a tumor in order to make surgical removal possible or more likely to succeed. Thus, radiation therapy is frequently used as a part of a combination treatment program.

Radiation therapy is not administered in a single "zap." It is delivered in a series of doses over an extended period. By administering the radiation in this way, the killing effect on the cancer cells is maximized while the toxic effects on healthy cells are minimized. This schedule allows healthy cells to repair themselves after radiation exposure. The exact dose and the schedule for delivery will be carefully set based on the type of cancer being treated, how advanced the cancer is, the animal's response to radiation therapy, and the goal of the treatment. For example, if the treatment goal is to reduce the size of a tumor prior to surgery, the treatment dose and schedule will be different than if the goal is to completely eradicate a tumor. Overall, a radiation therapy program will typically involve 5 doses per week for a period of 4 to 6 weeks.

A cancer cure is not the only possible goal for radiation therapy. In some cases, the radiation therapy goal is to provide some relief from the impact of a tumor or from the spread of cancer to other parts of the body. These steps may allow the animal to feel better even if its life is not lengthened by the treatment.

Great accuracy is required to target the radiation to destroy cancer cells while protecting healthy cells. However, even with great care and accuracy, radiation can damage normal cells close to the cancer. The cells most likely to be damaged are those that normally divide rapidly. These include the lining of the mouth, esophagus, and intestines; hair follicles; bone marrow; and the skin. Radiation can also damage the ovaries or testes.

There are some recognized adverse effects from radiation therapy. The extent and severity of these effects will depend on the size of the area being treated, the dose administered, and the location being radiated. When the radiation site is near sensitive tissues, the effects are likely to be more severe and prolonged. For example, treatment for tumors on the head or neck often causes damage to the overlying skin. Treatment of head tumors may cause inflammation or irritation of the lining of the mouth. For animals with this condition, a feeding tube may be recommended to reduce the discomfort of eating with a sore mouth. Dry eye is another side effect associated with radiation to the head. It is caused by a decrease in tear production due to the impact of radiation on the eyelids. This can sometimes be a permanent condition. Eye drops and other medications are available to help prevent sores from developing and relieve eye irritation. Radiation to any portion of the digestive tract may cause irritation resulting in nausea, lack of appetite, or diarrhea. For these animals, a change in diet may help control the signs.

Chemotherapy

Certain drugs destroy cancer cells. This type of treatment is called chemotherapy. It can be used to manage and treat several types of cancer. When it is used, the most common treatment goal is to shrink, stop the growth of, or destroy the cancer without longterm negative effects on the quality of life for the animal. Veterinarians will prescribe chemotherapy based on the type of cancer to be treated, the stage of the cancer, the overall condition of the animal to be treated, and any financial constraints that may be present.

In an ideal situation, a chemotherapy drug would kill cancer cells in an animal's body without harming normal healthy cells. Few such drugs have been found. Today, the drugs selected for chemotherapy have been designed to be more damaging to cancer cells than to normal cells. They specifically target cells that divide and grow rapidly. Normal cells will be affected to some extent by chemotherapy drugs; sometimes the drugs can have adverse effects. (*See* DRUGS USED TO TREAT CANCERS AND TUMORS, page 1140.)

Chemotherapy drugs are delivered either through the mouth or by injection. If injection is used, it can be into a vein (intravenous), muscle (intramuscular), or under the skin (subcutaneous). The delivery method will be selected with the comfort and quality of life for the pet in mind balanced against the goal of effective delivery of the drugs.

Some cancers do not respond to chemotherapy. How a cancer responds to a particular drug will depend on the type, size, rate of growth and spread, and location of the cancer. These factors are some of the most important ones in the selection of chemotherapy drugs, their combination, and their dosage. As is the case with other cancer treatments, chemotherapy is most effective when the tumor is small, is at an early stage in development, and has not spread to other parts of the body. When these conditions exist, most cancer cells divide quickly and the chemotherapy drugs are able to kill a larger number of the cancer cells.

Chemotherapy alone usually cannot cure cancer in pets. It is used most often to control cancer and its spread. Thus, chemotherapy is often used to treat cancers that affect the whole body, such as cancer of the lymphatic system (lymphoma). In other cases, chemotherapy is used to fight the remaining cancer cells when a tumor cannot be completely removed with surgery. Chemotherapy is also used to fight types of cancer that spread around the body early in their development.

Many of the chemotherapy drugs used to control cancer in people are used for the same purpose in pets. However, animals require dosages that are adjusted for their size and body type. In most cases, a combination of drugs will be used. Your veterinarian will evaluate the individual cancer and the particular needs of your pet when selecting the drug combination, dosage, and administration schedule. Quality of life issues, medical and nutritional support concerns, and pain control are other considerations that the prescribing veterinarian must evaluate when selecting a chemotherapy program. In all cases, your veterinarian must weigh the expected benefits of the drugs with possible adverse effects to select the most appropriate treatment for your pet. The veterinarian will carefully monitor your pet's physical and behavioral response to the treatment and adjust the dosage to maximize the effect on the cancer while reducing the side effects.

While improvements have been made in chemotherapy for humans—many of the well-known side effects such as nausea, vomiting, hair loss, and fatigue have been reduced in recent years—people still regard chemotherapy as a distinctly unpleasant experience. Animals, however, generally appear able to tolerate chemotherapy better than people. Animals can become nauseous from some chemotherapy drugs and this may lead to vomiting or a lack of interest in food. This side effect can be treated with anti-nausea medicine. Intravenous fluids can be used to control such side effects as vomiting, diarrhea, and dehydration. Some chemotherapy drugs may cause a reduction in the number of red blood cells (anemia), white blood cells (leukopenia), or the cells that clot blood (platelets). The loss of white blood cells is probably the most significant of these effects because white blood cell loss lowers your pet's ability to fight off infections. Your veterinarian will monitor your pet's condition by taking blood samples. If the white blood cell count becomes too low, antibiotics may be prescribed to prevent infections. For animals with a low platelet count, there is an increased risk of bleeding.

Hair loss is a common side effect of chemotherapy among people. This is less common in pets, though it varies among breeds. Dogs and cats receiving chemotherapy usually have good to excellent quality of life throughout the treatment program. Side effects, if any, are usually mild. The risk of life-threatening adverse effects is estimated at less than 5% for most types of chemotherapy. The most risky side effects can often be anticipated and either controlled or prevented entirely. If your pet will be undergoing chemotherapy, you should discuss the treatment program with your veterinarian in advance. You need to come to a mutual understanding about what can be expected for your pet and the level of risk that can be accepted.

Chemotherapy may be stopped before the end of the scheduled treatment program if the cancer being treated is not affected by the drugs or starts regrowing following a period of remission. A prescribed chemotherapy program may also be stopped when the animal has received the maximum acceptable total dose for a particular drug or if there are unacceptable adverse effects.

Combination Therapy

The term combination therapy refers to the use of 2 or more treatment options in the fight against cancer. Today, combination therapy is the most frequently used approach to treat cancer in pets. It offers the best opportunity to cure the cancer while maintaining the best possible quality of life for the animal.

Combination chemotherapy offers many advantages over single drug treatment programs. For example, when multiple chemotherapy drugs are used, and each one uses a different mechanism to kill cancer cells, it is less likely that the cancer will become drug resistant. This improves the chances that the treatment will be successful. Also, a combination of drugs can target different cancerous sites, increasing the likelihood of controlling any spread of the cancer. When using drugs with different side effects in combination, the probability is high that any side effects will be no worse than with a single drug given separately. These benefits combine to make a combination therapy program the best choice in many cases.

There is no single best treatment for all cancers. For some cancers, the best approach is one that combines surgery, radiation therapy, and chemotherapy. Tumors and other cancers that are confined to a localized area are often best treated with surgery or radiation therapy. Chemotherapy has the advantage of treating cancer cells that have spread from their original location. In other cases, radiation or chemotherapy is used to shrink a tumor to a size that makes surgical removal possible or more likely to succeed. Radiation or chemotherapy may be used following surgery to kill any cancer cells that may remain.

The stage of cancer development is a factor in selecting the treatment, whether a single treatment mode or a combination of treatment methods. For animals with advanced cancers that cannot be treated with surgery or radiation therapy, combination chemotherapy can be used to reduce the signs of the disease and prolong life.

Prospects for a Cure

During the past century, researchers have made enormous strides toward finding a cure for cancer. But we are not there yet. There is no single and complete cure for cancer in either humans or animals. However, much has been learned about managing and treating this ancient disease. Veterinarians have been successful in using surgery, chemotherapy, and radiation therapy to cure many animal cancers. Meanwhile, research is continuing and the prospects for better cancer treatments are strong. For example, a therapeutic vaccine for the treatment of melanoma in dogs recently received conditional approval from the United States Department of Agriculture. This represents the first approved vaccine for the treatment of cancer in either animals or humans.

■ CARING FOR A PET WITH CANCER

Caring for a pet with cancer is always a team effort. The owner of the animal is central to the treatment and management of the disease. The veterinarian and other members of the veterinary care team provide information and recommendations and perform tests and many of the treatments, but these steps come in response to the owner's decisions about the course of treatment. In addition, the owner, as primary care giver for the pet, will be directly and personally involved in the day-to-day care of the animal, including providing support, comfort, and delivery of medications. This is possible only when the owner works cooperatively with the veterinary care team and makes the effort to gain the knowledge and skills necessary to provide the needed decisions and care.

Supportive Care

All pets undergoing cancer treatment require supportive care. These tasks include giving prescribed medications, learning to recognize the signs of pain, and providing the nutrition your pet requires.

Giving Medication

Cancer treatment programs include medications for various reasons. If the animal is undergoing chemotherapy, there will be prescribed drugs to destroy the cancer cells. If surgery is included,

pain medications are usually prescribed to control postoperative pain. If the cancer itself causes pain, medications to control that pain will also be provided. Other possible medications include ones to reduce the adverse effects of chemotherapy or radiation therapy.

Some of the medications described above will be administered by your pet's medical team in a veterinary hospital or clinic. However, you may also have to give your pet medications at home. The timing of the medication is often critical to effective treatment. Thus, you play a vital role in making sure your pet receives the correct dose of medication at the prescribed times. As the primary care giver, you can also help your veterinarian by monitoring your pet's behavior and activity and reporting how well the medication seems to be working. If your pet does not respond as expected to the medication, or if your pet responds in an unusual or unexpected way, your veterinarian needs to be notified promptly so that dosages or medications can be adjusted.

You also should learn to recognize the signs of pain in your pet, so that pain-relieving medications can be prescribed as needed (*see* page 1246). Drugs that relieve pain are known as analgesics. Your veterinarian can prescribe any of several basic types of pain-relieving drugs. One type is known as **nonsteroidal anti-inflammatory drugs (NSAIDs)**. These drugs block the production of inflammatory molecules that contribute to pain and swelling. **Corticosteroids** (cortisone, for example) are a second type of pain reliever. Like the NSAIDs, corticosteroids are anti-inflammatory drugs that reduce pain and allow your pet to be more comfortable. However, caution is needed in giving steroids because they may have unwanted side effects when used for an extended period of time. **Opioids** are a third type of pain medication for cancer. Opioids include morphine and codeine. These are prescribed when advanced cancers cause prolonged, severe pain. Other types of pain medications that may be used include local anesthetics and alpha$_2$ agonists, although use of these medications is not as common as the use of other pain relievers.

Giving pain medication on a preset schedule is less difficult and more effective than providing pain medication "as needed." If your pet is in pain, it is likely to be stressed, nervous, and upset. This makes the administration of the medication more difficult for both you and your pet. Also, higher dosages of the medication may be required in these situations. The higher dosages increase the risk of adverse effects. The best plan is to set up a pain medication schedule in cooperation with your veterinarian before treatment and then follow that medication schedule as closely as possible.

Recognizing Cancer Pain

Pain in humans is a subjective experience and is difficult to measure accurately. Even if you have had your pet for a long time, recognizing and assessing pain during cancer treatment is challenging. Careful and close observation of your pet is needed.

Cancer pain is usually defined as the uncomfortable and disagreeable response of the body to the development and presence of cancer itself or the treatment for the disease. Some cancer-related pain may be acute. Acute cancer pain occurs when a tumor invades nearby tissues and expands. It may also occur in response to surgery, radiation therapy, or chemotherapy. Other cancer-related pain may be chronic. To assess your pet's pain level, you may have to look for behavioral changes that are associated with both acute and chronic pain. (*See also* TYPES OF PAIN, page 1211.)

For those who are not familiar with the normal behaviors of a particular species or an individual animal, assessing pain can be very difficult. The challenge is greater in some cases because many animals (such as birds) instinctively attempt to hide any behavior or sign that might show

they are weak or in pain. These difficulties are complicated by the fact that the amount of pain caused by various cancer treatments can vary greatly. Furthermore, pain is not simply physical; it can be emotional and psychological as well.

In the face of these challenges to pain assessment, owners are much more likely than veterinary care givers to notice the small variations in behavior that indicate pain. This is because owners are familiar with their pet's normal responses and movements, and their pet's reactions to a variety of situations. You are in the best position to take primary responsibility for judging your pet's tolerance for pain, for recognizing when your pet is in pain, and for taking the steps needed to reduce or eliminate it.

Nutritional Support

Every animal needs appropriate nutrition to live a healthy life. When cancer strikes, good nutrition takes on an even more important role in the life of the pet. While we do not yet fully understand the nutritional needs of animals with cancer, researchers have learned that animals undergoing cancer treatment may need different foods and different amounts of food than healthy animals.

Metabolism is the term that describes the physical and chemical processes used to build and maintain body tissues. Both cancer and cancer treatments can change your pet's metabolism. For example, your pet's usual diet may not provide sufficient nourishment while cancer is growing or while cancer treatments are being provided. Animals often lose their appetite during cancer treatment. If your pet does not eat enough to fuel its body, then tissues may be broken down to create the energy needed to survive. In these circumstances, your pet may "waste away" due to malnutrition. This occurs most frequently if the treatment continues for a long time. Another common risk is dehydration; pets with cancer may not drink enough water. Just as people can die more quickly from dehydration than starvation, so can animals. Drinking enough water is, therefore, as important as eating enough solid food.

Researchers are still studying the nutritional needs of animals with cancer. Thus far, some studies show that the high-carbohydrate and low-fat nutrition traditionally found in pet foods may not be the best for animals with cancer. Instead, these studies support the idea that animals with cancer need diets that are low in carbohydrates and high in fat; these may help reverse some of the negative changes found in the metabolism of pets with cancer.

If your pet is diagnosed with cancer, ask your veterinarian about any changes you may need to make in your pet's diet. During your conversation, also ask about any appetite stimulants and other medications to reduce side effects, such as pain, that can discourage healthy eating. Once the nutritional program has been developed, you may then need to adjust it to your pet's individual likes and dislikes. The goal is to supply your pet with the nutrition needed to fuel the normal functions of the animal's healthy organs and tissues.

Alternative ways of providing your pet with the needed nutrition may be required if the cancer or cancer treatment has caused metabolic changes that prevent your pet from consuming enough food and water. In some cases, special nutritional supplements may be needed or unusual feeding methods adopted. If, for example, part of the jaw has had to be removed due to mouth cancer, the pet will have to adapt to the new mouth shape. While recovering and adapting to the new shape, it may be necessary to feed your pet with a feeding tube. There are 3 common ways to provide a feeding tube. A tube may be run through the nasal passages to the stomach (nasogastric tube), through the neck into the esophagus (esophagostomy), or directly into the stomach (gastrostomy). These tubes are removed once the animal recovers sufficiently to eat on its own.

The metabolic changes caused by cancer or cancer treatment sometimes continue long after the cancer has been cured. In these cases, you need to provide the most appropriate diet after the cancer has been removed or destroyed. Follow your veterinarian's advice regarding the diet your pet needs following cancer.

Providing Comfort Care

Not all cancers can be cured and not all cancer treatments are fully successful. The cancer may be decreased or eliminated temporarily (in remission) and then return later. The treatment needed to control the cancer may cause considerable pain or cause significant adverse effects without any hope of curing the cancer. In such a case, you may need to decide at some point whether or not the continuation of treatment so degrades your pet's quality of life that it should be stopped. The issues become length of life in pain and misery versus a shorter life in less pain and discomfort.

When this point is reached, then the treatment focus shifts to one of providing as much comfort and nurturing care for the pet as possible in its final days or months. For situations where a cure is unlikely or not possible, where treatments have proved ineffective, or where the costs (especially any physical or emotional harm to the animal) outweigh the benefits, comfort care is the most appropriate answer.

The goal of comfort care, like the goal of hospice care for people, is to prevent pain and discomfort while providing emotional and physical support. This type of care allows you to focus on the quality of life for your pet rather than the quantity of life. A safe, stress-free environment in familiar surroundings helps your pet live out its life while you and your family emotionally adjust to your pet's terminal illness and prepare to say goodbye. (*See also* PET LOSS AND GRIEF, page 1232.)

In most cases, the best environment for comfort care is at home. This permits you and your family to spend more time with your ailing pet. It also permits you to be fully aware of its day-to-day needs and desires. This will allow you to react more quickly when the animal's needs and desires change. In addition, providing comfort care at home helps you prevent unnecessary pain, fear, and suffering as your pet approaches the end of its life.

Home-provided comfort care may not be for everyone. Caring for a terminally ill animal is an emotionally difficult and time-consuming responsibility. In most cases, the animal will lose some body functions, which will require you to provide an increased level of care. Owners who decide to provide comfort care at home should consult with a veterinarian who is knowledgeable about home comfort care and can provide information and support. In particular, a comfort care program should be developed, followed, and adjusted as the condition of the pet changes.

One primary goal of comfort care is the control of pain. Once that issue has been covered, other issues may also need to be addressed. For example, it may be necessary to relocate the pet's bed and change water and food containers to make sleeping, eating, and drinking easier and less painful. Family members may also rearrange their schedules to spend more time with the pet and provide more attention, well-loved treats, and affection. Because visits to the veterinarian are often stressful for a pet, you might elect to reduce the number of such visits. If so, you may need to learn how to perform medical tasks such as giving injections. These are all issues you will need to discuss with your veterinarian when you make the decision to provide home comfort care.

■ QUALITY OF LIFE ISSUES

At some point in a pet's life, the owner will be faced with this difficult question. The information below is provided as a guide to help you make the decisions you will need to make.

The quality of life for your pet should be the first priority during any treatment program. This is true for both pet owners and veterinary staff. When treating cancer, or any other disease, the goal should be to increase the pet's quality of life. Throughout the treatment program, the animal's quality of life needs to be assessed and adjustments made to support that goal as you move from diagnosis through treatment to the end of the pet's life.

Short-term problems—such as pain or temporary debility—can often be addressed with medications and changes to the living area to improve the pet's ability to move around a home. Eventually, however, there may come a time when it is impossible to control the effects of cancer and the animal may be in great pain, unable to control its bodily functions, or unable to eat or respond to others in its environment. Even comfort care may not control the animal's anguish and distress. In these cases, there are no positive aspects to the animal's life.

A humane and peaceful death is the best option in these situations. In making such decisions, having a set of guidelines or life quality standards is very helpful. Such criteria help a pet owner decide when prolonging an animal's life is worse than providing a peaceful end. Your veterinarian and other veterinary staff will provide information you need to understand euthanasia and a medical assessment of your pet's condition and recovery prospects. In many cases, as the time for such a decision arrives, you and your family have already realized that the time for euthanasia has arrived.

Euthanasia

When an animal's life becomes intolerably painful and distressing, the act of humanely ending that life is called euthanasia. The word comes from the Greek language and, literally, means "good death." Veterinarians are trained to provide an easy and painless death when that decision has been made. In many cases, deciding on euthanasia is an owner's final act of kindness and caring.

There are 3 goals when providing euthanasia. The first goal is to relieve pain and suffering. Second, there is a need to minimize any pain, anxiety, distress, and fear that the animal may have before consciousness is lost. The third goal is to provide a painless and distress-free death. The most common method of euthanasia is the injection of a high dose of anesthetic. This allows an animal to go to sleep, lose consciousness, and die peacefully.

During euthanasia, your veterinarian will monitor your pet, observing the animal's behavior and bodily responses to be sure the goals of euthanasia are being met. Just as humans have individual responses to events, so do animals. Monitoring euthanasia allows your veterinarian to provide the highest level of comfort for both you and your pet.

The process of euthanasia has been developed so that the loss of bodily functions does not cause your pet fear and distress. The first step is a rapid loss of consciousness, which eliminates fear and distress. Next, the ability to move is lost. Then, the animal's breathing and heart stop. Finally, permanent loss of brain function occurs. Throughout this process, the humane treatment of your pet is the primary concern.

Every pet has needs that should be recognized and respected. Pet owners often have feelings of guilt about making a euthanasia decision. These feelings can often be addressed through the use of a quality of life scale. Such a scale can also provide needed help in making the decisions about the care of animals with incurable diseases other than cancer. Some veterinarians have developed their own quality of life scales for use in pets (*see* BOX). Scales such as these provide a starting point for thought, discussion, and decision making. This is of course not the only way to make a quality of life decision.

No matter what decision is ultimately reached, every animal needs to be considered as an individual and receive kind and supportive care.

Saying Goodbye

Pets are a part of families. When they die, it is expected and natural for owners and family members to grieve and feel sorrow, anger, and stress. In some cases, the loss is felt not only in the animal's immediate family but also by neighbors and by the veterinary team that has provided care. And, given the relatively short lifetime of most pets, it means that owners can face the loss of several loved pets during a lifetime.

When a pet is to be euthanized, the decision can generate overwhelming feelings of guilt and the idea that there has to be one more step that could have been taken. Even with the support of family and your veterinarian, the guilt may not be reduced.

In some cases, owners decide to have the euthanasia take place at home, not only to create a private experience, but also because the pet will be in familiar and comfortable surroundings. Other individuals and families decide to have the euthanasia performed at a veterinary clinic, some of which offer a "comfort room" with surroundings that look more like a home than an examination room. Some people may find the euthanasia process so upsetting that they elect to say goodbye to their pet prior to the procedure, by spending time alone with the animal.

During the euthanasia procedure, some owners stay by their pet's side up to the moment of death. They may take a piece of the pet's hair as a keepsake, sing a song, or stroke the animal's body. It is perfectly natural for owners and family members to take time to say goodbye and stay by the animal for a period of time to achieve a closure. Veterinarians who treat cancer are familiar with these processes and have experience with owners who are going through the sorrow and grieving that accompany a pet's death.

In some communities and at some veterinary colleges, there are counseling

The HHHHHMM Scale

One quality of life scale, developed by a veterinarian, is known as the **HHHHHMM scale**. The letters stand for Hurt, Hunger, Hydration, Hygiene, Happiness, Mobility, and "More good days than bad days." Some of the issues raised in this scale are discussed in the text. They provide a starting point for thought, discussion, and decision making.

- **HURT:** Adequate pain control is the most important aspect of quality of life and it is first and foremost on the scale. This factor includes your pet's ability to breathe properly. Most pet owners do not realize that not being able to breathe is one of the most painful experiences for an animal, and is ranked at the top of the pain scale.

- **HUNGER:** Can your animal eat on its own? Has it lost interest in food? If your pet is not receiving adequate nutrition, by hand or force feeding, then a feeding tube should be considered, especially for cats. Malnutrition develops quickly in sick animals if the care giver is not knowledgeable about pet nutrition.

- **HYDRATION:** Is your animal hydrated? Fluids that are injected beneath the animal's skin are a very effective method to supplement the water intake of ailing pets. You can learn from your veterinarian how to perform this procedure on your own, which may take a few sessions.

- **HYGIENE:** Some questions to consider include: Can your pet be kept brushed and cleaned? Is the coat matted? Is your pet situated properly so that it will not have to lie in its own waste after elimination? Can your pet control its waste output?

- **HAPPINESS:** One important question to consider when contemplating euthanasia is: "Is your pet able to experience any joy or mental stimulation?" Pets often communicate their thoughts and emotions with their eyes. You should try to answer questions such as: Is your pet responsive and willing to interact with the family? If the animal is a cat, is it able to purr and enjoy being on the bed or in your lap? Is there a response to a bit of catnip or a favorite toy? Can your pet's bed be moved close to the family's activities and not left in an isolated or neglected area? Is your pet depressed, lonely, anxious, bored, or afraid?

- **MOBILITY:** You should determine whether your pet is able to move around on its own or with help in order to satisfy its desires. Does your pet feel like going out for a walk? Does your pet have central nervous system problems, such as seizures or stumbling? Can your pet be taken outdoors or helped into the litter box to eliminate with assistance? Will a harness, sling or cart be helpful? Is medication helping?

   The need for mobility seems dependent on the species and breed. You should bear in mind that cats and small lap dogs can and do enjoy life with much less mobility than large and giant-breed dogs.

- **MORE GOOD DAYS THAN BAD:** When there are too many bad days in a row or if your pet seems to be "turned off" to life, quality of life is compromised. Bad days are filled with undesirable experiences such as vomiting, nausea, diarrhea, frustration, and seizures. Bad days could be from profound weakness caused by anemia or from the discomfort caused by an obstruction or a large, inoperable tumor in the abdomen.

(Adapted from Villalobos, A.E., Quality of life scale helps make final call, *Veterinary Practice News*, September 2004.)

services and pet loss hotlines. Grieving owners can get support through these programs. Just as it takes time to recover from the loss of a human member of the family, so it takes time for people to recover from the loss of a pet. Some owners require a full year to achieve real closure and accept the loss of their pet. (*See also* page 1232.)

ACKNOWLEDGMENT

Portions of this chapter have been modified, with permission, from *The Merck Manual of Medical Information*, Second Home Edition, 2003, pages 1031–1047.

Glossary

A

abdomen The middle section of the body, between the chest and the pelvis.

abdominal cavity The body cavity between the chest and the pelvis.

abdominocentesis Surgical procedure in which a needle is inserted into the abdomen to withdraw fluid.

abortion The end of a pregnancy before the expelled fetus can survive independently, either by spontaneous abortion (miscarriage) or by a medical termination of pregnancy.

abscess A pocket of pus, usually caused by a bacterial infection.

acariasis Disease caused by a mite of the order Acarina.

acaricide A chemical agent used to kill mites.

ACE inhibitor Any of a class of drugs intended to lower blood pressure by widening blood vessels. ACE stands for angiotensin-converting enzyme.

acidic A liquid that has a pH lower than 7.

acquired Conditions that are not inborn and that develop during the animal's life.

acromegaly A disorder of excessive growth hormone secretion by the pituitary gland, resulting in excessive growth of bones in the legs.

actinobacillosis Disease caused by bacteria of the genus *Actinobacillus*.

actinomycosis A bacterial infection in humans, swine, and cattle that causes hard masses to form in the mouth and jaw.

acupuncture A procedure adapted from Chinese medical practice in which specific body areas are pierced with fine needles for therapeutic purposes.

acute A condition that has a brief or short course; signs often develop suddenly and may be severe.

acute pain The short-term sharp, throbbing, aching, or burning sensation in response to a stimulus (twisting, crushing, or burning) or tissue injury (bruises, wounds, and surgical incisions).

Addison's disease A deficiency of adrenal gland hormones.

adenocarcinoma A malignant tumor formed in the epithelium, or covering tissue, of an organ.

adenoma A benign tumor formed in glandular tissue.

adenovirus A virus of the family Adenoviridae.

adrenal gland A small, paired gland located near the kidneys that produces cortisol, epinephrine, and other hormones.

aerosol A suspension of particles dissolved in liquid and dispersed in a fine mist.

aflatoxicosis Poisoning caused by consumption of foods contaminated with a toxin produced by the fungus *Aspergillus flavus*.

African horse sickness An equine viral disease that is widespread in Africa. It is characterized by signs of lung and blood system impairment, and is most frequently transmitted by midges or mosquitoes.

agalactia Partial or complete lack of milk flow from the mammary gland.

agent Anything that produces an effect. For example, viruses and bacteria are agents that cause disease.

aggression Behavior that is related to conflict between individuals; includes both threats and attacks.

agonist A drug or other chemical that can bind to a receptor or cell to trigger a response typical of a naturally occurring substance.

agouti A mottled coat color in rodents, characterized by fur with bands of different colors.

airway Passage for air from the nose or mouth to the lungs.

algal poisoning A toxic and often deadly condition caused by heavy growths of blue-green algae in drinking water.

alkaline A substance with a pH higher than 7; also referred to as basic.

alkaloidosis Poisoning by alkaloids, plant toxins that damage the liver.

allergy An abnormally high sensitivity to certain substances, such as pollens, foods, or microorganisms.

alloimmune reaction A type of immune reaction that occurs when the body produces antibodies against the tissues of another animal. This may occur, for example, when one animal receives a blood transfusion from another animal of the same species but with a different blood type.

alopecia A partial or complete loss of hair in areas where it is usually found.

alternative therapy   Therapy used instead of conventional treatments (for example, homeopathic treatment).

alveoli   Plural form of the word alveolus.

alveolus   Tiny air-holding sac formed at the end of air passageways in the lungs, where the barrier between the air and the blood is a thin membrane.

amino acid   A chemical compound that forms the basic building block of proteins.

amoeba   A type of protozoa, or single-celled organism. Some are parasitic and can cause infection in animals.

amphetamine   A class of drugs that stimulates the central nervous system and the cardio-vascular system.

amphibian   A class of cold-blooded animals that spends at least part of their life cycle living in water.

amputation   The removal of a limb or other part of the body.

amyloid   A type of abnormally folded protein that may collect in various body tissues and interfere with their function.

amyloidosis   Disease characterized by accumulation of abnormal protein deposits.

anabolic   Pertaining to a metabolic process in which complex molecules are created from simpler ones.

analgesia   Treatment given to control pain; a deadening or absence of the sense of pain without loss of consciousness.

analgesic   A class of drugs that relieve pain.

anaphylactic shock   A rare, life-threatening, immediate allergic reaction to something that has entered the body, such as food, an injection, or an insect sting. Also called anaphylaxis.

anemia   An abnormally low red blood cell count caused by insufficient intake of iron in the diet, blood loss, or other medical conditions.

anesthesia   A lack of all sensation, particularly sensitivity to pain. It can be induced medically or result from trauma, and it can be limited to a small area (local anesthesia) or affect the entire body (general anesthesia).

anesthetic   An agent used to induce anesthesia, including injectable drugs and inhaled gases.

anestrus   An interval of sexual inactivity between 2 periods of estrus in female mammals that breed cyclically.

aneurysm   A dilation or bulging of a blood vessel caused by a weakening of its walls.

animal-assisted therapy   Using animals as therapy for the sick or elderly in nursing or other rehabilitation centers because of the positive effect such visits have on residents and patients.

animal welfare   Human efforts to reduce and prevent pain and suffering and promote well-being in animals.

anorexia   A lack or loss of appetite.

anoxia   Lack of oxygen in the blood or body tissues.

antacid   A medication that neutralizes acidity, especially in the stomach.

antagonist   A drug or substance that nullifies the effect of another substance.

anterior   Located toward the head or the front end of the body.

anterior uvea   Part of the front portion of the eye, including the iris and ciliary body.

anthelmintic   A class of drugs used to treat infection with parasitic worms.

anthrax   An often-fatal infectious disease caused by *Bacillus anthracis* bacteria that may infect all warm-blooded animals, including humans.

antibacterial   Destroying or inhibiting the growth of bacteria.

antibiotic   A class of drugs used to destroy bacteria while remaining safe for the human or animal being treated.

antibiotic resistance   Ability of a microorganism (such as bacteria) to resist the effects of an antibiotic drug.

antibody   A molecule produced by the immune system that attacks a particular foreign substance (antigen) in the body.

anticholinergic   A class of drugs that block acetylcholine receptors in nerves.

anticoagulant   A substance that stops blood from clotting.

anticonvulsant   A class of drugs used to prevent or relieve convulsions.

antidepressant   A class of drugs designed to relieve depression in humans; may also be used to help control behavior problems in pets.

antidote   A substance that counteracts the effect of a poison or toxin.

antiemetic   One of a group of drugs used to retard or stop vomiting.

antifungal   A class of drugs that destroy or prevent the growth of fungi.

antigen   Any substance that can stimulate an immune response.

antihistamine   A class of drugs used to relieve allergy signs by blocking the inflammatory action of histamines.

anti-inflammatory   Medication that prevents or reduces inflammation.

antimicrobial A large group of drugs used to fight infections caused by bacteria, fungi, and viruses.

antineoplastic A group of chemical agents or drugs used to combat cancer.

antioxidant A substance that inhibits oxidation of other compounds.

antiparasitic Any of a group of drugs used to combat infestation with parasites.

antiseptic solution A solution of a substance that kills or inhibits the growth of microbes.

antitoxin A compound that neutralizes a specific toxin.

antivenin An antidote to a particular venom; a serum that counteracts venom.

antiviral Compound that kills or inhibits the growth of viruses.

anus The opening at the end of the intestinal tract where solid wastes are pushed out of a body.

aorta The largest artery in the body. It carries blood away from the heart on its way to distribute oxygen to all body tissues except the lungs.

aortic arch The curved portion between the ascending and descending portions of the aorta.

aortic valve A heart valve comprising 3 flaps that controls the flow of blood from the left ventricle into the aorta.

aplasia Incomplete or incorrect development of a body part.

aquatic Describes organisms that live in water.

arboreal Describes species that spend most or all of their lives in trees.

arrhythmia An abnormal pattern of contraction of the heart, caused by a disturbance in conduction of the normal electrical impulses within the heart.

arsenical A substance (a drug or insecticide) containing arsenic.

arterial dilator A drug that dilates the small arteries, making it easier for the heart to pump blood away from itself.

artery Blood vessel that carries oxygen-rich blood away from the heart and toward the body's tissues.

arthritis Inflammation of a joint; often characterized by swelling, pain, and redness.

arthroscopy Examination of the interior of a joint, such as the knee, using a type of endoscope that is inserted into the joint through a small incision.

artificial insemination Introduction (with a syringe or other device) of semen into the uterus without sexual contact.

ascarid A class of roundworms whose larvae can cause disease.

ascites A condition in which fluid collects in the abdomen.

as-needed dosing Administering pain medication only when the animal shows recognizable signs of pain.

aspergillosis A fungal infection caused by several species of *Aspergillus* fungi.

asphyxiation A severe lack of oxygen resulting from inability to breathe.

aspiration The use of a suction device to withdraw fluid from the body.

aspiration pneumonia Inflammation caused by inhalation of food particles or fluids into the lungs.

asthma A respiratory condition marked by recurring episodes of labored breathing, wheezing, and coughing, triggered by oversensitivity to environmental conditions.

astringent A substance that causes tissues, such as mucous membranes, to shrink or dry out.

atherosclerosis A hardening of an artery caused by deposits made of cholesterol, other fatty substances, or cellular debris that accumulates inside the artery.

atopy Allergy characterized by itching and redness of the skin; may also include discharges from the eyes or nose.

atria Plural form of the word atrium.

atrial fibrillation Irregular contraction of the atria (upper heart chambers) caused by abnormal electrical activity in the heart.

atrial standstill A failure of the electrical impulses in the upper chambers of the heart, which results in a lack of contraction of those chambers.

atrial thrombosis A heart condition caused by a blood clot in the atrium of the heart.

atrioventricular valve The valve between the upper (atrial) and lower (ventricular) chambers of the heart.

atrium The upper chamber of the heart that receives blood from the veins and pushes it into the ventricle.

aural plaque In horses, a white growth caused by a virus that develops in and around the ears.

autoimmune An immune response that is developed against the animal's own tissues.

autonomic nervous system Specialized set of neurons controlling and regulating basic, unconscious bodily functions such as breathing and heart beat.

avian tuberculosis A slowly spreading, chronic infection of birds caused by the bacteria *Mycobacterium avium* and characterized by gradual weight loss.

awn A slender, bristle-like appendage found on the spikelets of many grasses.

axon Extensions of neurons that transmit electrical charges away from the cell body.

B

B cell A type of white blood cell that produces antibodies.

bacteremia The presence of bacteria in the bloodstream.

bacteria The plural form of the word bacterium.

bacterial disease Disease caused by invading bacteria or an overgrowth of usually harmless bacteria.

bacterium A microscopic, single-celled organism that may cause disease or may be a harmless, or even helpful, part of an animal's normal internal or external environment.

barbering Excessive chewing of hair or feathers that leads to bald patches of skin.

baroreceptors Nerve endings in blood vessels that are sensitive to blood pressure changes.

basal cells Cells at the base of the top layer of the skin.

basking The behavior of a cold-blooded animal lying in the sun to increase its body temperature.

basophil A type of white blood cell that releases histamine as part of the body's allergic response.

benign Something that is nonharmful or noncancerous.

besnoitiosis Infectious disease caused by protozoa of the genus *Besnoitia*, transmitted by certain biting flies and ticks, found in Africa, France, and Mexico.

beta cells Cells in the pancreas that produce insulin.

biceps brachii tendon Tendon of the biceps brachii, a major muscle of the upper front leg that acts to bend the elbow joint.

biopsy The removal of a small sample of tissue or fluid for examination. A sample is obtained in a way suited to the type of tissue and its location; it might be drawn out with a hollow needle and syringe, scraped with a curette, or cut away with a scalpel.

bladder A stretchable, membranous sac-like structure in the body that holds fluids; the term is used most often to refer to the urinary bladder.

blastoma A tumor composed of previously healthy young cells that never mature normally, but mutate into a cancer.

blastomycosis A disease caused by *Blastomyces* fungi that can affect several species of animals or humans; infection may occur in the skin, lungs, or other body organs.

blepharitis Inflammation of the eyelids.

blind spot The small circular area, insensitive to light, where the optic nerve enters the eye. *See also* optic disk.

blister A fluid-filled bump on the skin.

blood cell count The number of red blood cells, white blood cells, and platelets in a sample of blood. Also called a complete blood count (CBC).

blood cells Any of the cells contained in blood. *See also* erythrocyte, leukoctye, platelet.

blood clot A mass of blood cells, protein, and platelets, also known as a thrombus, that forms whenever there is a break or tear in a blood vessel.

blood poisoning A disorder, also known as septicemia, in which bacteria or their toxins circulate in the bloodstream.

blood pressure The force exerted by the blood against the walls of the blood vessels, especially the arteries.

blood transfusion A procedure in which another animal's blood is introduced into the body to counteract blood loss, anemia, or other conditions.

blood typing The identification of blood groups in order to match donor blood with the recipient's blood for a blood transfusion.

bloodborne Carried by or transmitted through blood.

bloodstream The flow of blood through the circulatory system of an organism.

body cavity An enclosed space in the body that contains organs, such as the cranial, spinal, thoracic, and abdominal cavities.

boid snakes Snakes related to boa constrictors. The group includes pythons.

bone marrow A soft tissue filling the spaces of the spongy tissue found at the ends of long bones. It produces red blood cells, most types of white blood cells, and platelets.

borreliosis Disease caused by bacteria of the genus *Borrelia*. *See* Lyme disease.

botulism Infection caused by ingesting food or dead flesh containing toxins produced by the bacterium *Clostridium botulinum*, or by absorbing toxins in the gastrointestinal tract. It results in rapid paralysis and death.

brachycephalic Short-headed or broad-headed.

brachygnathia Abnormal shortness or recession of the lower jaw.

brachytherapy A cancer treatment that involves internal radiation therapy.

brackish Water that is a mixture of fresh and salt water.

bradycardia A slower than normal heart rate.

brain The controlling center of the nervous system in vertebrates, connected to the spinal cord and enclosed in the cranium.

brain stem One of the 3 main sections of the brain; it controls many basic life functions.

brain stem auditory evoked response (BAER) Records electrical activity in the pathway from the sound receptors in the ear to the brain stem and cerebrum.

breed A group of animals or organisms having common ancestors and certain distinguishable characteristics.

breeding Sexual reproduction of animals, either spontaneously or planned and supervised by human beings.

broad-spectrum antibiotics Antibiotics that are effective against a wide range of bacteria.

bronchial Relating to the bronchi, the bronchial tubes, or the bronchioles, the body's airways.

bronchitis Inflammation of the bronchial airways.

bronchoscopy Interior examination of the airways with an endoscope.

buck The male of certain mammal species, such as rabbits, antelope, and deer.

budgerigar A small Australian parrot commonly kept as a pet; also called a budgie or parakeet.

bumblefoot A foot abscess in sheep, guinea pigs, or birds caused by a localized bacterial infection.

bursa A fluid-filled body sac located between a tendon and a bone or at points of friction.

C

calcification The abnormal hardening or stiffening of a body part caused by deposits of calcium.

calcinosis The abnormal depositing of calcium salts contributing to hardening of a part or tissue of the body.

calcinosis cutis A condition in which calcium deposits form in the skin; they can appear as small, thickened, "dots" on the abdomen.

calcitonin Hormone secreted by the parathyroid glands that regulates levels of calcium in the bloodstream.

calcium deficiency A lack of calcium in the body that can result from insufficient calcium or vitamin D in the diet and can cause bone deformities.

caloric Relating to heat or calories.

cancer A malignant tumor or growth that destroys healthy tissue.

cancer pain Pain resulting from primary tumor growth, a spreading cancerous disease, or the toxic effects of chemotherapy or radiation.

candidiasis A fungal disease caused by *Candida albicans* that affects the mucous membranes and the skin.

Canidae Scientific name for dogs, foxes, and wolves.

canine Relating to animals of the Canidae family, primarily dogs.

canine distemper (hardpad disease) A highly contagious, usually fatal viral disease of dogs, ferrets, mink, raccoons, and other mammals.

canine herpesviral infection A severe, often fatal, viral disease of puppies, sometimes referred to as fading or sudden-death syndrome. In adult dogs, it may be associated with upper respiratory infection or an inflammation of the vagina marked by pain and a pus-filled discharge (in females) or inflammation of the foreskin of the penis (in males).

canine thrombopathia A hereditary disorder of blood platelets that causes bleeding from the nose and gums, and tiny purple or red bruises as a result of bleeding under the skin.

canine tooth Long, pointed tooth used primarily for holding food in place in order to tear it.

cannibalism The act of eating a member of an animal's own species.

capillary The smallest type of blood vessel, which connects small blood vessels that branch off from arteries and veins.

capsule A medication consisting of an active ingredient and fillers, enclosed in a cylindrical coating usually made of gelatin; designed to be taken by mouth.

carcass The dead body of an animal.

carcinogen A cancer-causing substance or agent.

carcinoma An invasive, malignant tumor derived from epithelial tissues (tissues that make up the skin, glands, mucous membranes, and organ linings).

cardiac Of or relating to the heart.

cardiac output The amount of blood pumped from the heart during a specified period of time.

cardiac shunts   Abnormal openings between chambers of the left and right sides of the heart.

cardiac tamponade   A buildup of fluid in the sac around the heart, which increases pressure on the heart and gradually interferes with its ability to pump blood.

cardiomyopathy   A disease in which the heart muscle is weakened.

cardiopulmonary resuscitation (CPR)   An emergency procedure, often employed after cardiac arrest, in which massage of the heart, artificial respiration, and drugs are used to maintain the circulation of oxygenated blood to the body. Also called cardiopulmonary-cerebral resuscitation (CPCR).

cardiovascular system   The body system that consists of the heart and the blood vessels (veins and arteries).

carnivore   A flesh-eating animal.

carpal   Relating to bones in the wrist; a wrist bone.

carpal joint   Any of the joints between the carpal bones.

carrier   An animal that, without becoming ill, harbors or spreads disease-causing microorganisms.

cartilage   A somewhat elastic connective tissue that is found at the ends of bones and helps reduce friction as joints move.

castration   Most often refers to surgical removal of the testicles; less commonly may refer to removal of the ovaries.

cataract   Condition in which the lens of the eye progressively loses transparency, which often results in loss of vision.

cathartic   A drug given to increase the passage of gastrointestinal contents, to cleanse the bowel before radiography or endoscopy, to eliminate toxins from the gastrointestinal tract, and to soften feces after intestinal or anal surgery.

catheter   A thin flexible tube that is inserted into a body cavity, duct, or vessel to allow passage of fluids.

cationic   A substance or class of detergents that are locally corrosive, causing skin, eye, and mucous membrane injury similar to that of alkaline corrosive agents.

ceiling effect   Situation in which an increased dose of a pain-relieving drug provides incrementally smaller gains in pain relief.

cell   The smallest functioning unit in the structure of an organism.

cell body   The center portion of a neuron.

cellular infiltrates   Gas, fluid, or dissolved matter that enters cells or tissue.

centesis   Procedure in which a needle is inserted into a structure (for example, the chest or urinary bladder) of an animal to remove fluid or air.

central nervous system   The part of the nervous system that includes the brain and spinal cord.

cercariae   Parasitic larvae of trematode worms.

cerebellar hypoplasia   Lack of development of the cerebellum, the section of the brain that controls motor function.

cerebellum   The cauliflower-shaped brain structure located just behind the cerebrum and above the brain stem.

cerebrospinal fluid   The fluid surrounding the brain and spinal cord.

cerebrum   One of 3 main sections of the brain; area where sensory and motor nerve activity is coordinated.

cesarean section   A surgical procedure in which the abdomen and uterus are cut open and the young are delivered through the abdomen.

cestode   Intestinal parasitic worm of the class Cestoda, with a flat, segmented body; tapeworms.

chelonians   Tortoises and turtles.

chemotherapy   The use of chemical agents to treat diseases, especially cancer.

cherry eye   Swelling and inflammation of the third eyelid, especially in dogs.

chlamydiosis   Infection with a bacteria of the genus *Chlamydia*.

Chlamydophila   Bacteria that cause serious respiratory infections in birds.

cholesteatomas   Cysts on the eardrum that may extend into the middle ear.

chondrosarcoma   A malignant tumor of cartilage.

chordae tendineae   Strands of connective tissue in the heart that connect the valves to the papillary muscles of the heart's ventricles.

choroid   A membrane between the retina and sclera of the eye.

chromosome   Dense strands of material in the cell nucleus that carry the individual's genetic material (DNA).

chronic   A condition that persists over a long period of time, often months or longer.

chronic pain   Pain that persists for longer than the expected time frame for healing, or pain associated with progressive, noncancerous disease, such as osteoarthritis.

cilia   Tiny, hairlike projections that line the outer part of cells in some tissues, including the lower respiratory tract.

cilia-associated respiratory *Bacillus*   Bacteria that can cause chronic respiratory disease in rats and mice; transmitted by direct contact.

ciliary muscles The muscles in the eye that change the shape of the lens in order to keep vision in focus.

cleft palate A congenital abnormality that creates a gap along the center of the roof of the mouth.

cloaca In amphibians, fish, birds, and reptiles, an opening through which the digestive, urinary, and reproductive tracts exit the body.

cloacal prolapse A condition in which the cloaca protrudes outside the body.

cloacitis Inflammation of an animal's cloaca. *See* cloaca.

clostridia Bacteria that can cause severe intestinal disease or spread toxins through the bloodstream.

clot A collection of red blood cells, white cells, and platelets, bound together by protein fibers, that plugs holes in blood vessels.

coagulation The process by which liquid blood is transformed into a clot.

cobalt therapy A type of radiation therapy that uses radioactive cobalt to treat cancer.

Coccidia A group of protozoan parasites (small, single-celled organisms) that infect the intestinal tract of animals.

coccidioidomycosis A dustborne, noncontagious infection caused by inhalation of fungal spores.

coccidiosis A serious disease in cattle, sheep, goats, hogs, poultry, and rabbits, and less serious in dogs, cats, and horses. It is caused by protozoans (Coccidia) that invade and may destroy the lining of the intestines.

cochlea A snail-shaped cavity in the inner ear, containing the organs of hearing.

coelomitis Inflammation of the coelom, or abdomen, in retiles.

cognitive dysfunction Senility; similar to Alzheimer's disease in people.

cold-blooded Animals that do not maintain a constant internal body temperature; instead, their temperature is greatly influenced by their environment.

colibacillosis A form of diarrhea caused by *Escherichia coli* bacteria.

colic Severe abdominal pain caused by spasm, obstruction, or distention of the intestines; there are many possible causes.

colitis Inflammation of the colon.

collagen A fibrous protein that forms tendons, ligaments, and connective tissue; also found in skin, bone, and cartilage.

colon The large intestine.

colonoscopy Examination of the inside surface of the colon using a tube inserted through the rectum.

colony A group of organisms of one species that live and interact closely with each other in an organized fashion.

colostrum The watery fluid rich in antibodies and nutrients that is produced by a mother after giving birth and before producing true milk.

colt A young male horse.

colubrid A snake of the Colubridae family, including adders, vipers, cobras, rattlesnakes, and coral snakes.

combination chemotherapy Using a combination of drugs that target different sites or that employ different mechanisms to maximize destruction of cancer cells.

companion animal Any animal kept by humans for companionship or pleasure rather than for utility; a pet.

compensatory mechanism Any one of several specific responses the body uses in combating heart disease to maintain normal circulation.

complementary therapy Therapy used in addition to conventional treatments.

compulsive behavior Otherwise normal behaviors that occur out of context or so often that they interfere with normal activity.

computed tomography (CT) A computer-enhanced x-ray procedure used to detect abnormalities in various body organs.

conduction Passage of the electrical impulses that govern the pumping of the heart.

conformation The structure or outline of an item or entity, determined by the arrangement of its parts.

congenital defect An abnormality that is present at birth, as a result of either heredity or environmental influence such as a toxin or infection.

congestion An abnormal buildup of fluid in an organ or area of the body.

congestive heart failure A condition marked by weakness, shortness of breath, or an excessive buildup of fluid in the tissues or body cavities when the heart fails to maintain adequate blood circulation.

conjunctiva The mucous membrane lining the inside of the eyelids.

conjunctivitis Inflammation of the mucous membrane lining the inside of the eyelid. Also called pink eye.

constipation Difficulty in passing bowel movements; incomplete or infrequent passing of hard stools.

constricted toe syndrome A condition in newly hatched birds in which a tough ring of tissue forms around a toe joint, partially cutting off circulation.

contagious Describes a condition that can spread from one organism to another.

contaminated Unclean or polluted because of contact with harmful substances.

contraction Pumping action of the heart muscle or other muscles.

contrast procedure Specialized x-ray technique in which the animal is given a dye that shows up on the x-ray film to help provide more detailed images of body organs.

convulsion *See* seizure.

coprophagia Eating feces.

cornea The transparent outer part of the eye that covers the iris and pupil and admits light into the eyeball.

coronavirus A family of viruses that chiefly cause respiratory infections.

corticosteroid Any of the steroid hormones made by the adrenal gland or their synthetic equivalents; commonly used to reduce inflammation.

cortisol A steroid hormone produced by the adrenal gland that regulates carbohydrate metabolism and maintains blood pressure.

counterconditioning A method for reducing unwanted behavior by teaching a pet to replace it with a more favorable behavior.

counterirritant A substance that, when applied, irritates the skin and thereby reduces the inflammation of underlying tissue.

counterpressure Pressure applied to reduce bleeding.

cranial Relating to the skull, or cranium; toward the head end of the body.

cranium The portion of the skull enclosing the brain.

cream A semisolid mixture made for application to the skin or mucous membranes.

crop In many birds, a pouch in the gullet where food is stored and sometimes partially digested before passing to the stomach.

cross matching Blood typing test done to ensure that a blood donor and recipient have compatible blood types.

crotalids Snakes of the genus *Crotalidae*, including pit vipers (rattlesnakes, for example).

cryptococcosis A fungal disease that may affect the respiratory tract (especially the nasal cavity), central nervous system, eyes, and skin (particularly of the face and neck of cats).

cryptorchidism A developmental defect marked by the failure of one or both testes to descend into the scrotum.

cryptosporidiosis Intestinal infection with *Cryptosporidium* parasites, the primary sign of which is diarrhea.

Cryptosporidium A genus of single-celled protozoal parasites that causes intestinal infection in several species, including humans.

CT scan *See* computed tomography.

culture A method of encouraging a microorganism to grow in a laboratory in order to identify specific bacteria or viruses that may be present.

Cushing's disease A hormonal disease characterized by overproduction of cortisol from the adrenal gland; most often caused by a tumor of the pituitary gland in the brain.

cutaneous Of or relating to the skin.

cyst A closed, fluid-filled growth in otherwise normal tissue.

cystitis Inflammation of the bladder.

cystocentesis Extraction of a sample of urine directly from the bladder using a needle and syringe.

cytokine A protein secreted by cells of the immune system that helps regulate inflammatory responses.

cytology The study of the structure and function of individual cells.

cytotoxic Substance that is poisonous to cells.

D

debilitated Having greatly decreased energy and strength.

debulking A surgery done to remove part of a cancer or tumor.

decongestant A medication that reduces mucosal congestion.

defecate To expel feces from the intestinal tract.

defibrillation A process of shocking the heart in a specific way to restore a coordinated heart beat and a pulse.

deficiency A lack of something that is required for normal body function.

degeneration A condition that causes a gradual deterioration in the structure or function of a body part.

degenerative joint disease A form of arthritis characterized by gradual loss of cartilage of the joints. Also called osteoarthritis.

dehydration A lack of sufficient water within the body.

dendrite Extension of a neuron that receives signals from other neurons and transmits electrical charges to the cell body.

dental abscess An infected cavity in a tooth, soft tissue surrounding the teeth, or bone of the jaw.

dental malocclusion A misalignment of the teeth in which the upper and lower surfaces fail to come together properly.

depression In animals, this usually refers to lowered activity and lack of interest in surroundings.

dermatitis Inflammation of the skin.

dermatologist A specialist in the treatment of skin disorders.

dermatophytosis A fungal infection of the skin. Also known as ringworm.

dermis The middle layer of the 3 layers of the skin.

descending aorta The part of the aorta that passes through the chest and into the abdomen, supplying blood to the trunk and rear legs.

desensitization A way to gradually teach a pet to tolerate a situation by carefully exposing it to that situation in small steps.

detergent A cleansing substance, especially a liquid soap.

dewlap Loose skin on the underside of an animal's neck; this is normal in many species.

diabetes insipidus A metabolic disorder caused by a lack of antidiuretic hormone, which leads to production of large amounts of dilute urine and excessive thirst.

diabetes mellitus A metabolic disorder characterized by a deficiency in the hormone insulin and an accompanying inability to properly digest sugars; signs include excessive urination, too much sugar in the blood, thirst, hunger, and weight loss. *See also* insulin.

diagnosis The identification of a disease based on its signs, physical examination, and appropriate tests.

diaphragm A thin muscle that separates the abdominal and thoracic cavities and expands the chest during respiration.

diarrhea The abnormally frequent discharge of soft or liquid feces.

diastole The first half of a heartbeat, during which the upper chambers of the heart (atria) contract and send blood into the lower chambers (ventricles).

diestrus A short period of sexual inactivity between 2 estrus periods, during which the uterus is prepared for a fertilized egg.

dietary indiscretion Unhealthy eating, as of trash, large amounts of table scraps, or other inappropriate food.

digestion The process by which an animal processes food and absorbs nutrients.

digestive tract The system of organs responsible for digestion.

dilate To widen or enlarge.

dilated cardiomyopathy A heart disease in which the heart is enlarged and the heart muscle is weakened.

direct life cycle A pattern in which a parasite needs only 1 host in which to grow, breed, and reproduce itself.

discharge Any fluid that emerges from a sore or infection.

disinfectant A chemical used to kill germs.

dislocation Displacement of a body part, especially of a bone, from its usual fitting in a joint.

displacement activity The resolution of a behavior conflict by performing a seemingly unrelated activity such as grooming or sleeping.

disseminated intravascular coagulation A condition in which small blood clots develop throughout the bloodstream, blocking small blood vessels and destroying the platelets and clotting factors needed to control bleeding.

dissemination The spread of a disease-causing organism throughout the body, causing signs in multiple parts of the body.

distemper An airborne viral disease of dogs and some related animals such as raccoons; signs include fever, vomiting, diarrhea, loss of appetite, dehydration, tremors, weakness, and incoordination.

distended Swollen or expanded, as by pressure from within; dilated.

distillation The evaporation and subsequent collection of a liquid by condensation as a means of purification.

diuretic A medicine usually prescribed to reduce fluid overload; increases urine production.

DNA Deoxyribonucleic acid; the molecule that encodes genetic information in the nucleus of cells and is capable of self-replication.

doe A female of any of several species, including rabbits and deer.

dormant Existing in a temporarily inactive form or state, or biological rest.

duodenum The first and smallest portion of the small intestine, beginning at the stomach.

dustborne Carried by exterior or interior dusts, often used to describe bacteria transmitted in this way.

dysecdysis Improper or incomplete shedding of the skin in reptiles.

dysplasia Abnormal growth, development, or placement of body parts.

dystocia Abnormal or difficult birth.

dystrophy A degenerative condition caused by a nutritional defect or disorder.

E

ear canal The tube connecting the external ear with the eardrum.

ear mites Tiny organisms resembling ticks that can infect the ear canal of animals, especially dogs and cats.

eardrum The membrane at the end of the ear canal that transmits sound waves to the middle ear.

ecdysis The act of molting, or shedding, an outer skin layer.

echocardiography A type of ultrasonography used to examine the heart.

eclampsia A condition marked by a sudden drop in blood calcium levels, caused by the production of milk after giving birth; often leads to convulsions and coma.

ecosystem A community of interdependent living organisms and the environment they inhabit.

ectoparasite A parasite that lives on its host's skin, hair, or feathers, such as fleas and ticks.

ectotherm An animal that cannot regulate its own body temperature and is instead dependent on the temperature of its surroundings (for example, reptiles and amphibians); commonly referred to as cold-blooded.

ectropion A slack eyelid edge that is turned outward.

edema The abnormal accumulation of fluid in a tissue.

egg binding A condition in birds and reptiles in which the female is unable to lay a developed or partially developed egg.

ehrlichiosis A tickborne bacterial infection that affects white blood cells.

elapid A member of a family of venomous snakes with hollow fangs, such as cobras.

electrocardiogram (EKG) A recording of the heart's electrical activity made by attaching a set of electrodes to the skin.

electrocardiography Recording of the electrical activity of the heart.

electrolytes Ions, or salts, such as sodium and potassium, that are present in blood and other bodily fluids and help regulate various metabolic processes.

electromyography An electrical recording of muscle activity that aids in the diagnosis of diseases affecting muscles and peripheral nerves.

ELISA An abbreviation for enzyme-linked immunosorbent assay, a test used to detect a disease-causing agent such as a virus.

Elokomin fluke fever An infectious disease of dogs acquired by eating raw fish infected with flukes that carry the disease-causing bacteria.

emaciation A condition in which the animal is abnormally thin, generally as the result of malnutrition or disease.

embolism Obstruction of a blood vessel by a blood clot that breaks off from its point of origin and lodges elsewhere.

embolus Portion of a blood clot that breaks free and travels through the cardiovascular system.

embryo The earliest stage of development of an animal in the womb, before any of the major body organs have formed.

emphysema Abnormal accumulation of air in tissues; often affects the lungs and causes breathing difficulties.

emulsifier A chemical agent used to bind together substances that normally do not bind.

emulsion A suspension of one liquid in another with which the first will not mix (for example, oil and water).

encephalitis Inflammation of the brain; often caused by an infection.

encephalitozoonosis A protozoal infection of rabbits and occasionally of mice, guinea pigs, rats, and dogs that affects multiple organs; also called nosematosis.

encysted Enclosed in a cyst, sac, bladder, or vesicle (for example, an *encysted* tumor).

endocarditis Inflammation of the membranes lining the heart cavity.

endocrine Related to glands that deliver hormones into the bloodstream.

endoparasite A parasite that lives inside its host, such as a heartworm.

endoscope An instrument for examining visually the interior of a bodily canal or a hollow organ such as the colon, bladder, or stomach.

endoscopic gastric biopsy A sample of stomach tissue taken with an endoscope, a long, flexible tube equipped with a camera and other instruments that is inserted through the mouth into the stomach.

endoscopy A procedure in which a tube called an endoscope is inserted into a hollow organ. The tube generally has a camera for maneuvering and frequently has tools such as forceps or scissors attached.

endotoxin A substance found in the cell walls of some bacteria that causes toxic shock, fever, and inflammation in mammals.

endotracheal tube Tube inserted into the trachea to deliver oxygen or anesthetic gas.

engorge To fill with blood.

enterolith A hard mass composed of magnesium ammonium phosphate crystals that forms around a foreign object (such as a stone or nail) in the large intestine, most commonly in horses.

enterotoxemia The presence of bacterial toxins in the bloodstream.

entropion A turned-in edge of the eyelid, which leads to irritation of the eyeball from the eyelashes.

enzootic A disease that is continually present in a particular location.

enzyme A protein that speeds up a biological process such as digestion.

eosinopenia A decrease in the number of eosinophils (a type of white blood cell) in the bloodstream.

eosinophil A type of white blood cell that plays a role in the immune response by ingesting bacteria and other foreign cells, immobilizing and killing parasites, and participating in allergic reactions.

eosinophilia An increase in the number of eosinophils (a type of white blood cell) in the bloodstream.

epidemic An outbreak of a contagious disease that spreads rapidly and widely.

epidermis The outer layer of the 3 layers of the skin.

epidural anesthesia Injection of pain-relieving or numbing drugs into the space surrounding the spinal cord to decrease sensation in parts of the body below that portion of the spinal cord; often used to provide anesthesia for surgery.

epilepsy An inherited disease that causes seizures; generally requires treatment with anticonvulsants.

epithelial Having to do with the skin (epithelium).

epizootic lymphangitis A fungal disease that affects the skin, lymph vessels, and lymph nodes of the limbs and neck of horses.

equine Related to or having to do with horses.

equine granulocytic ehrlichiosis An infectious disease of horses caused by a bacterium found in the bloodstream and transmitted by ticks.

equine infectious anemia An incurable, viral bloodborne infection of horses transmitted by blood-sucking insects.

equine morbillivirus pneumonia A short-term, often fatal, viral respiratory infection of horses caused by the Hendra virus.

equine protozoal myeloencephalitis Protozoal infection of the nervous system of horses.

equine sarcoid See sarcoid.

equine viral arteritis A short-term, contagious, viral disease of the horse family that affects multiple body systems.

erosion A shallow or superficial ulcer or sore, typically on the skin.

erythrocyte A red blood cell.

erythropoiesis The formation and production of red blood cells.

erythropoietin A hormone secreted by the kidneys that triggers the production of red blood cells in bone marrow.

esophagus The muscular tube that connects the throat to the stomach.

estrous Of, relating to, or being in heat (estrus).

estrous cycle The recurring physiological and behavioral changes that take place from one period of estrus (heat) to another.

estrus A recurring period of increased sexual desire during which a female mammal will allow sexual activity and is capable of conceiving.

euthanasia The deliberate, painless killing of an incurably ill or injured animal; also called putting to sleep or putting down.

excretion The process for removing waste matter from the blood, tissues, or organs.

exertional rhabdomyolysis A metabolic disorder caused by intense exercise in which toxins from muscle injury can damage other tissues, especially the kidneys.

exoskeleton A skeletal structure outside the body, as in insects.

exotic pets Nontraditional pets; animals that are not domesticated.

expectorant A medicine that thins airway secretions, making them easier for the animal to cough up.

exposure Contact with or proximity to some environmental condition, toxin, or infectious agent.

eyelid atresia A congenital condition in which the eye opening is reduced or closed entirely over otherwise normal eyes.

F

failing heart Any heart with a reduced ability to contract.

farcy A contagious, incurable bacterial infection of horses that may affect the skin or lungs. Also called glanders.

farrier A person who makes and fits horseshoes.

fasting Withholding food from an animal for a certain length of time.

fatal Causing or capable of causing death.

fatty acid One of the major components of fat, used by the body to supply energy and build tissues.

fecal Relating to or consisting of feces.

feces The solid waste from an animal.

feed hopper A simple device that uses gravity to keep a trough or bowl filled with food as animals eat.

feline Of or having to do with cats.

feline distemper *See* feline panleukopenia.

feline infectious enteritis *See* feline panleukopenia.

feline infectious peritonitis A progressive viral infection of cats that affects multiple body systems and causes a variety of signs.

feline leukemia virus A cancer-causing virus of cats that infects cells of the immune system and frequently results in death.

feline lymphoma A tumor of the immune system that is the most frequently diagnosed cancer of cats.

feline panleukopenia A viral infection of cats that affects multiple body systems; most infections cause no signs, but if signs are present the infection is serious and usually fatal.

femur The large bone of the upper hind limb; also known as the thigh bone.

fertility The ability to produce offspring.

fertilization The combination of a sperm cell and an egg cell into a developing organism.

fetal Having to do with a fetus or its development.

fetal membranes The thin layers of tissue that surround the embryo during its development. Also called amniotic sac.

fetus A developing animal from the stage at which the major organs form until birth. *See also* embryo.

fever Abnormally high body temperature.

fibrocartilage A type of strong, relatively inelastic connective tissue.

fibroma A benign tumor formed in fibrous or connective tissue.

fibromatosis A thickening and invasive growth in tendon sheaths.

fibropapillomatosis A condition characterized by the presence of abnormal growths of tissue (fibrous papillomas) in both the epidermal and dermal skin layers.

fibrosarcoma A malignant tumor that arises from cells that produce connective tissue, predominantly found in the area around bones or in soft tissue.

fibrosis The formation of excessive, dense, tough connective tissue.

fibrous osteodystrophy Generalized loss of mineral salts throughout the skeleton due to an increased rate of bone destruction resulting from hyperparathyroidism (excess parathyroid hormone secretion). Also known as osteitis fibrosa cystica.

fibrous tissue Tissue consisting primarily of high-strength fibers, such as ligaments and tendons.

filly A young female horse.

filtration The process of removing waste and particulate matter from water.

first aid Emergency medical treatment given until more thorough, professional veterinary treatment can be obtained.

fistulous withers A condition in which connective tissue in a horse's withers region becomes infected and inflamed.

flagellate A single-celled organism with one or more flagella, whip-like appendages used for locomotion.

flashing Scratching (as pertains to fish).

flea A small, wingless insect that lives on the skin of mammals or birds and feeds on their blood.

flexor tendons Any of several tendons that act to bend a joint.

flora Bacteria that normally live in a part of the body, such as the intestines.

fluke Any of almost 6,000 species of parasitic flatworms.

fluorescein staining A test that uses orange dye (fluorescein) and a specialized light to detect foreign bodies or scratches in the eye.

fly strike A condition in which flies lay their eggs on wounds, dead skin, or skin covered with feces. The maggots that hatch can destroy large areas of skin. Also called cutaneous myiasis.

foal The offspring of a horse or other equid, up to the age of 1 year.

forceps A surgical instrument used to grasp and hold tissue.

forebrain The front segment of the brain that includes the cerebrum, thalamus, and hypothalamus.

foreskin The loose fold of skin that covers the glans of the penis. Also called prepuce.

fossorial species An animal that is specially adapted for digging.

fracture The partial or complete break of a bone.

frostbite Tissue damage caused by freezing temperatures, which can result in tissue death if exposure is extensive.

fry Newly hatched fish.

fungal Caused by, or related to, a fungus.

fungus A classification of living things that are immobile but cannot gain energy from sunlight, as plants can; some cause infections in animals and people.

fur mite External parasites that live on the skin and fur and cause itching.

fur slip A condition in chinchillas in which patches of fur are lost due to rough handling or fighting.

G

gait The manner of walking or moving.

gastrin A hormone that prompts the release of gastric acid in the stomach, usually secreted by the stomach and small intestine.

gastrinoma A tumor of the pancreatic islet cells.

gastroenteritis Inflammation of the stomach and intestine, often resulting in diarrhea, vomiting, and cramps.

gastrointestinal Having to do with the stomach and intestines.

gastrointestinal system The internal organs responsible for digestion, including the stomach and the intestines.

gastrostomy Insertion of a tube directly into the stomach for the purpose of providing nutrition.

genetic Having to do with genes or heredity.

genitalia External sex organs.

geotrichosis A rare fungal infection caused by *Geotrichum candidum*, a fungus found in soil, decaying organic matter, and contaminated food.

gestation The period of development of an animal inside its mother's womb.

Giardia A water-dwelling, single-celled microorganism that causes diarrhea in many species, including humans.

giardiasis A gastrointestinal disorder caused by infection with *Giardia* microorganisms, characterized by diarrhea, stomach cramps, nausea, and vomiting.

gingivitis Inflammation of the gums.

glanders A contagious, incurable, slowly progressive bacterial infection of horses that may affect the skin or lungs. Also called farcy.

glaucoma An eye disorder marked by increased pressure within the eye, which can damage the interior of the eye and lead to blindness.

gliding membrane A flap of skin which allows an animal to glide but not fly, as is found in sugar gliders and flying squirrels. Also called a patagium.

globin A globular protein that combines with heme to form hemoglobin. *See* hemoglobin.

glomerulonephritis Inflammation of the glomeruli of the kidney.

glomerulonephrosis A common disease of older rats involving inflammation of the blood vessels in the kidney.

glomerulus Structure in the kidney made up of special blood vessels that help filter blood; each kidney contains thousands of these.

glossitis Inflammation of the tongue.

glucagon A hormone that helps convert stored carbohydrates into glucose (sugar) so they can be used as energy.

glucocorticoid A type of corticosteroid (*see* corticosteroid) that is involved with metabolism of carbohydrates, protein, and fat. They are frequently used in medicine for their anti-inflammatory and immunosuppressive properties.

glucose A simple sugar that is one of the body's main sources of energy.

glucosuria The presence of glucose, a sugar, in the urine.

gnat A small, 2-winged biting fly.

goiter An enlarged thyroid, often caused by iodine deficiency.

goitrogen A goiter-producing substance.

gonads The sex organs that produce reproductive cells (sperm and eggs). In the male, these are the testes; in the female, the ovaries.

gout A painful inflammation of joints, often in the foot, that is most often caused by a buildup of uric acid and salts.

granule A small grain or particle; or a compound of powder particles that have been formed into larger pieces.

granulocyte A specialized type of white blood cell, produced in the bone marrow, that plays a role in immune responses to invading microorganisms.

gray patch disease A herpesviral infection of the skin that affects turtles, characterized by sores that spread across the turtle's body.

growth plate Zone of cartilage near the ends of long bones where new bone is formed.

gut loading The process of feeding prey animals highly nutritious food in order to pass the nutrients on to animals that eat them.

guttural pouch Areas of the eustachian tubes that form a bag or pouch, located under the base of the skull in horses.

H

habituation A simple form of learning that involves the ending of, or decrease in, a reaction to a situation as a result of repeated or prolonged exposure to that situation.

halogenated Combined or treated with a halogen (fluorine, chlorine, bromine, iodine).

hardpad disease *See* canine distemper.

head tilt A condition in which the head is kept tipped to one side; can be caused by many different diseases, including inner ear infection and neurological problems.

heart disease Any structural or functional abnormality of the heart that impairs its normal functioning.

heart failure Any heart abnormality that results in failure of the heart to pump enough blood to meet the body's needs.

heat *See* estrus.

heat exhaustion A condition caused by overexertion in high temperatures or overexposure to the sun.

heat stroke A collapse brought on by prolonged periods of heat stress or heat exhaustion. Signs include cessation of sweating or panting, extremely high body temperature, and unconsciousness.

helminth A general term for a group of parasitic worms.

hemangiosarcoma A rare, rapidly growing, highly invasive cancer that originates from cells that line blood vessels (endothelial cells).

hematology The study of blood, its chemistry and components.

hematoma A mass of blood, generally clotted, that forms in an organ or body cavity due to a ruptured blood vessel.

hematopoiesis The formation and development of the various blood cells.

heme A complex molecule containing iron that combines with globin to form hemoglobin.

hemoglobin The iron-rich compound in blood that carries oxygen throughout the body.

hemolysis A condition in which red blood cells are ruptured.

hemorrhage Bleeding; escape of blood from a broken blood vessel.

hemostasis A process that stops blood flow, particularly clot formation.

hemostatic A compound that inhibits bleeding.

hepatic Related to or affecting the liver.

hepatic encephalopathy A syndrome that occurs as a result of liver disease; signs include circling, head pressing, aimless wandering, weakness, poor coordination, blindness, excessive drooling, aggression, dementia, seizures, and coma.

hepatitis Inflammation of the liver.

hepatopathy General scientific term for liver disease.

herbicide One of a group of chemicals used to destroy weeds.

herbivores Animals, such as rabbits or horses, that eat only plants.

hereditary Transmitted genetically from parent to offspring.

hernia The protrusion of a body part through the lining that normally encloses it.

herpesvirus Any of a group of viruses that cause disease in humans and animals. Herpesviruses often cause sores or rashes and generally remain in the body even when not causing signs.

hibernation A state of inactivity and unconsciousness, generally during the winter months.

histiocytoma A soft tissue giant cell tumor.

histology The anatomical study of the microscopic structure of tissue.

histoplasmosis A noncontagious infection caused by a soil fungus, occurring when airborne spores are inhaled.

hives The least severe type of anaphylactic (allergic) reaction. Small bumps occur on the skin. The hair may stand up over these swellings and sometimes they itch.

hock The ankle joint of rabbits, horses, and other 4-legged animals that walk on the same bones that form the toes in humans.

hormone A compound produced by a gland in the body that stimulates other parts of the body and controls their activity.

host A living animal or plant on or in which a parasite lives. *See* parasite.

hot packing A supportive treatment that involves application of moist heat to reduce inflammation.

human-animal bond The emotional relationship existing between humans and companion animals.

husbandry The care provided to maintain domestic animals.

hutch A pen or coop for a small animal, such as a rabbit.

hutch burn A disease caused by wet and dirty hutch floors in which the area surrounding the anus and genital region becomes inflamed and chapped, and then infected with disease-causing bacteria.

hydration The process of providing an adequate amount of fluids to body tissues.

hydrocephalus A condition in which excess fluid accumulates within the skull because of a blockage in the normal channels that allow it to flow out of the skull.

hygiene Actions taken to maintain cleanliness and health.

hygroma A cyst or sac filled with fluid.

hyper- Prefix meaning over, above, too much, too high, excessive.

hyperadrenocorticism A disease caused by production of too much cortisol. Also called Cushing's disease.

hypercalcemia Abnormally high levels of calcium in the blood, characterized by weakness, nausea, confusion, and lethargy.

hyperextension Extension of a joint beyond its normal range of motion.

hyperlipemia Excessive levels of fat in the blood.

hyperparathyroidism An excess of parathyroid hormone in the blood.

hyperplasia An abnormal increase in the number of cells in an organ or tissue with consequent enlargement.

hypertension An increase in the body's blood pressure.

hyperthermia Abnormally high body temperature.

hyperthyroidism A disorder caused by an excess of the thyroid hormones.

hypertrichosis A common endocrine disorder resulting from chronic excess of the hormone cortisol (Cushing's disease). Signs include development of an abnormally long or heavy hair coat, excessive thirst and urination, increased appetite and weight, an enlarged abdomen, and bulging eyes.

hypertrophy Enlargement of an organ or tissue.

hyperuricemia Abnormally high levels of uric acid in the blood, caused by excessive production or insufficient excretion of the compound.

hypo- Prefix meaning below, less than normal, deficient, too little, too low.

hypoadrenocorticism A deficiency of adrenal gland hormones. Also called Addison's disease.

hypocalcemia Abnormally low levels of calcium in the blood.

hypoglycemia Abnormally low levels of glucose in the blood, often caused by a deficiency of insulin, characterized by trembling, weakness, hunger, confusion, unconsciousness, and in severe cases, death.

hypoparathyroidism Disorder characterized by low calcium levels, high phosphate levels, and either temporary or permanent insufficiency of parathyroid hormone.

hypoplasia A condition of abnormal development in which a body part remains small, immature, or underdeveloped.

hypoproteinemia Abnormally low levels of protein in the blood.

hypothalamus The part of the brain below the thalamus that functions to regulate bodily temperature and certain metabolic processes.

hypothermia Abnormally low body temperature.

hypothyroidism A deficiency of thyroid hormone, which can cause weight gain, constipation, and cold sensitivity.

hypoxia Condition in which the level of oxygen in the blood is too low; anoxia.

I

idiopathic Used to describe a disorder or disease that has no apparent cause.

immersion A method of administering medication to or treating fish by placing them in a tank containing the medication.

immune Resistant to infection or disease.

immune response The body's reaction to an infectious agent or other foreign "invader." This includes recognition of the invader and development of a protective defense.

immune system The system within an animal that recognizes an infectious agent or other foreign "invader" and mounts an immune response. The immune system includes various organs, such as the thymus gland, spleen, and lymph nodes, as well as specialized cells found throughout the body.

immune-mediated Describes a process initiated or controlled by the immune system.

immunization The process of making an individual immune to a given disease, generally through vaccination.

immunized Rendered resistant to toxins or infectious agents, especially by injection or vaccination.

immunodeficiency An inability of the immune system to produce a normal immune response.

immunoglobulin Protein antibodies produced by the body to fight a disease.

immunomodulator A drug that helps regulate the immune system's activity.

immunostimulant A drug or agent that increases an immune response.

immunosuppressed A state in which the immune system is inhibited by medications during the treatment of other disorders, or by stress or infection.

immunosuppression Interference with the normal function of the immune system.

immunotherapy Any of several treatments of disease that involve inducing, enhancing, or suppressing an immune response.

impedance Obstruction of normal flow or passage, such as an obstruction of blood flow.

implant A drug, such as a long-lasting tablet, inserted under the skin.

incisor Front teeth that are used to grasp or cut food.

inclusion body disease Any disease characterized by inclusion bodies, small foreign bodies within cells.

incontinence The inability to control urination or defecation.

incubation period The time after an infection has been contracted but before any signs are apparent.

infection A disorder that occurs when microorganisms invade the body and multiply. Infectious microorganisms include bacteria, viruses, fungi, and parasites.

infectious A condition that is passed from animal to animal by a virus, bacterium, or other agent.

infectious canine hepatitis A contagious viral disease of dogs with signs that vary from a slight fever and congestion of the mucous membranes to severe depression, severe reduction in white blood cells, and deficiency of blood clotting.

infertility The inability to produce offspring.

infest To live as a parasite in or on.

infestation The act of infesting or state of being infested.

infiltrate Material deposited within the space between cells in a tissue.

inflammation A localized protective response to injury or other tissue damage. The response includes increased blood flow in the surrounding capillaries (causing redness), swelling, increased temperature in the area, and pain.

inflammatory Characterized or caused by inflammation.

influenza A respiratory infection caused by an influenza (flu) virus.

ingest To take food or liquid into the body by swallowing or absorption; eat.

inhalation The act of breathing in.

inherited Passed genetically from parents to offspring.

inhibitor A substance that restrains or retards physiological, chemical, or enzyme action.

initiation The first step in the transformation of healthy cells into cancerous cells.

inoculation Introduction of a substance into the tissues or fluids of the body; this is often done for the purpose of preventing or curing certain diseases.

inorganic Composed of minerals rather than living material; without carbon.

insect growth regulator A class of drugs that helps control pests such as fleas by disrupting their development and maturation.

insecticidal Of or related to a chemical substance used to kill insects.

insulin A hormone secreted by the pancreas that is essential for digestion, especially that of carbohydrates. *See also* diabetes mellitus.

insulinoma A common pancreatic islet tumor that affects the insulin-secreting beta cells.

interdigital furunculosis Abscesses on the webbing between the toes.

interferon Protein produced by immune cells that helps fight viral infection. *See also* cytokines.

intermediate host An animal in which juvenile parasites reside before passing to the final host animal to develop into adults and breed.

intestinal protozoan Any of a number of single-celled microorganisms that infect or dwell within the intestines. Many cause disease, but others are harmless or even beneficial.

intestine The part of the digestive tract between the stomach and the anus, divided into the small intestine and the large intestine.

intoxication Another term for poisoning or toxicosis.

intramuscular Directly in or into the muscle.

intraocular Having to do with, entering, or residing within the interior of the eye.

intravascular Inside the blood vessels.

intravenous A method of administering fluids or medications directly into a vein. Also known by the abbreviation IV.

intubation Insertion of a breathing tube into the trachea.

intussusception The doubling up of a section of intestine on itself in accordion-like folds, causing obstruction.

invasive A tumor that tends to spread locally into adjacent tissues.

invertebrate An animal without a backbone, such as an insect or spider.

involuntary Spontaneous or automatic; not controllable by the conscious mind.

iodine deficiency Insufficient iodine in the diet that can lead to goiter.

iodine toxicity Harmful effects, which may include goiter, of an excess of iodine in the diet.

iris The muscular diaphragm in the eye that controls the size of (and therefore the amount of light passing through) the pupil.

irradiation Bombardment with radiation, generally as a treatment for tumors.

islet cell tumor A cancer of the islet cells of the pancreas.

islet of Langerhans Cluster of 3 kinds of endocrine cells scattered throughout the pancreas that secrete several hormones, including insulin.

isolation The process of keeping diseased or potentially diseased animals separate from other susceptible animals.

J

jaundice A condition characterized by yellowing of the skin, eyes, and mucous membranes caused by an excess of bile products in the blood.

joint The site where 2 or more bones meet. Joints may be movable or immovable.

joint mice Fragments of cartilage in joints.

jugular Of, relating to, or located in the region of the neck or throat.

K

keratin The hard protein that makes up hair, fingernails, claws, horns, scales, and the shafts of feathers.

keratinization Creation of new skin cells near the base of the epidermis that migrate upwards, producing a compact layer of dead cells on the skin surface.

keratoacanthoma A benign skin tumor of dogs that includes a cyst filled with keratin.

ketosis A condition resulting from excess buildup of ketones, a waste product, in the blood.

kidney Either of a pair of abdominal organs that filter waste from the blood and help maintain proper water and salt balance.

kidney failure Loss of normal function of the kidneys, which can be either a short- or longterm condition.

kit The young of any of a number of mammals, such as foxes and rabbits.

L

laceration A cut or tear in the skin.

lacrimal gland The gland near the eye that produces tears.

lactation The production of milk by a female mammal.

***Lactobacillus* species** A group of bacteria that create lactic acid and play a normal, often beneficial, role in many animals' bodies.

lagenidiosis A fungal infection of dogs that affects the skin and blood vessels.

lagophthalmos An inability to completely close the eyelids due to malformation.

lameness An inability to walk or move normally, often, but not always, caused by pain in the limb.

larva An immature form or life stage of an insect or parasite.

larvae Plural form of the word larva.

larval Of or pertaining to larvae.

larynx The part of the throat often called the "voice box" in humans.

latent In an inactive or hidden stage.

laxative A drug used to promote bowel movements.

leg banding The process of putting coded bands onto the legs of captive birds, generally while they are young, for purposes of identification.

Legg-Calvé-Perthes disease Deterioration of the top of the femur (the femoral head) seen in young miniature and small breeds of dogs, characterized by a lack of blood supply and destruction of blood vessels of the bone.

lens The transparent, oval-shaped part of the eye that focuses light on the retina.

leptospirosis An infection characterized by fever and jaundice caused by bacteria of the genus *Leptospira*.

lesion Any abnormal change in the structure or function of a part of the body.

lethargy Lack of energy; apathy.

leukemia A cancer of the blood and bone marrow, characterized by increased numbers of white blood cells.

leukocyte Blood cell type involved in immune responses; commonly called white blood cells.

leukocytic Having to do with leukocytes.

leukocytosis An increase in the number of white blood cells in the bloodstream.

leukogram A diagnostic blood test that counts the number of different white blood cells circulating in the bloodstream.

leukopenia A decrease in the number of white blood cells in the bloodstream.

libido Sexual drive; desire to mate.

lice A group of small, wingless insects that live on the skin of birds and mammals and suck their blood.

life cycle A description of all the stages in the life of an organism.

ligament A band of tough, fibrous tissue connecting bones or cartilage at a joint, or supporting an organ.

liposarcoma A benign tumor of fatty tissue.

listeriosis An infection by the bacteria *Listeria monocytogenes* which can affect the nervous system, or lead to abortion or blood poisoning.

liver A large abdominal organ with many functions, such as filtering and removing toxins from the blood, storing glycogen, and producing and secreting bile.

localized Restricted or limited to a specific body part or region.

lockjaw A spasm of the jaw muscles that keeps them tightly closed, most frequently caused by tetanus. *See also* tetanus.

long bones Any of several elongated bones of the legs (for example, the femur and humerus) that have a roughly cylindrical shaft.

lordosis An abnormal inward curving of the spine in the lower area of the back.

lumpectomy Surgical excision of a tumor with minimal removal of surrounding tissue.

lumpy jaw The most common and least severe form of actinomycosis, a bacterial infection that causes hard masses to form in the mouth and jaw.

lung Either of 2 spongy, saclike respiratory organs that occupy the chest cavity and provide the blood with oxygen while removing carbon dioxide during respiration.

luxation Dislocation.

Lyme disease Tickborne infection of animals and humans caused by *Borrelia burgdorferi* bacteria that can cause rash and arthritis. Also known as Lyme borreliosis.

lymph node Small organ of the immune system that contains cells that fight infections, neutralize toxins, and produce antibodies.

lymph A clear, watery fluid derived from body tissues that collects through the lymphatic system and is then returned to the bloodstream.

lymphadenitis Inflammation of the lymph nodes.

lymphangitis Inflammation of lymphatic vessels.

lymphatic system The network of small vessels that collects the fluid surrounding the cells and returns it to the bloodstream.

lymphocyte White blood cells that produce antibodies, neutralize toxins, and fight infections and cancer.

lymphocytic choriomeningitis A viral infection of mice characterized by fever, vomiting, neck stiffness, and slow pulse.

lymphocytosis An increase in the number of lymphocytes in the bloodstream.

lymphoid Of or relating to the lymph or lymphatic tissue.

lymphoma A cancer of certain white blood cells that begins in a lymph node or other lymphoid tissue.

lymphopenia A decrease in the number of lymphocytes in the bloodstream.

M

macrophage A type of white blood cell, larger than most, that consumes infectious agents and other foreign cells and destroys them.

maggot The legless, soft-bodied, wormlike larva of any of various flies, often found in decaying matter.

magnetic resonance imaging (MRI) An advanced, noninvasive diagnostic imaging technique that uses powerful magnets to examine tissues and organs.

malabsorption Faulty or abnormal absorption of nutrients from the digestive tract.

malaise A feeling of illness or depression.

maldigestion Abnormal breakdown and absorption of foods from the digestive tract.

malignant Cancerous; a tumor that invades other nearby tissues or spreads throughout the body.

malnourished Affected by an improper or insufficient diet; undernourished.

malocclusion *See* dental malocclusion.

mammals Animals that produce milk to feed their young and have 4 limbs and at least some hair.

mammary Of or relating to the mammary glands of a female mammal.

mammary glands The organs that produce milk.

mange Any of several skin disorders caused by an infestation of mange mites.

marking Depositing urine or feces to send a social signal, such as claiming territory.

marsupials Mammals, chiefly but not exclusively from Australia, that carry their young in an external pouch.

masking behavior Behavior to hide injury or weakness, especially by prey animals.

mass Another word for a tumor or growth.

mast cell A cell that secretes histamine found in connective tissue.

mastitis Inflammation of the mammary glands, often caused by bacterial infection.

maternal immunity The resistance to disease provided by antibodies passed through the mother's first milk (colostrum) to newborn mammals, usually lasting for several weeks.

mechanism A process by which something is accomplished.

megakaryocyte A large cell found in bone marrow that produces platelets.

melanoma A type of skin tumor, often malignant, that contains dark pigment.

melioidosis An uncommon bacterial infection, usually of rodents, that can be passed to humans.

membrane A thin layer of tissue that lines an organ or body cavity.

meninges Thin layers of tissue that line the brain and spinal cord.

meningitis Inflammation of the meninges.

meningoencephalitis Inflammation of the brain and of the membrane lining the brain and spinal cord.

metabolic activity The chemical processes occurring within a living cell or organism that are essential to maintenance of life.

metabolic bone disease Any of several diseases of the bones caused by an imbalance of calcium and other minerals in response to abnormal metabolism.

metabolic disorder Any disorder in which normal body processes are disturbed, leading to an increase or decrease in the end products of those processes.

metabolic rate Metabolism over time; the speed at which metabolism occurs.

metabolism The physical and chemical processes that take place in the body to maintain life.

metacarpal bones Bones in a vertebrate animal's forefoot similar to the bones in the human hand between the wrist and the fingers.

metastasis The spread of a malignant tumor to distant parts of the body.

metastatic calcification Abnormal, hardened deposits of calcium in soft tissues.

metastatic tumor A tumor formed from cells that have traveled from the original tumor to another site in the body.

metatarsal bones Bones in a vertebrate animal's hind foot similar to bones in the human foot between the toes and the ankle.

metritis Inflammation of the uterus.

microbiology The study of small organisms such as bacteria, viruses, fungi, and other single-celled life forms.

microchipping A method of identifying pets that involves the insertion of a small glass-encased electronic chip under the skin.

microfilaria Immature life stage of heartworms that is found in the bloodstream.

microhabitat The small, specialized environment in which an organism lives.

microorganism A bacterium, virus, or other organism that is too small to see without a microscope.

midges Gnatlike flies that are often found near water; some species bite and feed on blood.

miliary dermatitis Skin irritation with small, solid, bumps typically spread over the back, neck, and face.

mineralocorticoids Hormones produced by the adrenal cortex that help control the body's balance of sodium and potassium salts.

mineral A solid crystalline substance arising from inorganic processes. Many minerals are nutrients that are needed for normal body functions.

mite Any of a number of very small arachnids, related to spiders and scorpions, many of which live as parasites on various species of animals.

mitral valve The valve between the left chambers of the heart, through which the blood flows from the atrium to the ventricle.

molar A large grinding tooth in the back of the mouth.

mold Any of various fungi that often cause disintegration of organic matter.

molt In birds, the normal loss of feathers in preparation for the growth of new feathers. In reptiles, the normal shedding of skin; also called ecdysis.

Mongolian desert mice Another term for gerbils, related to their origin.

monkeypox A viral disease, similar to but milder than smallpox, originally detected in monkeys.

monocyte A type of white blood cell that plays a role in immune defense by moving from the bloodstream into the tissues, enlarging, and becoming a macrophage. *See also* macrophage.

monocytopenia A decrease in the number of monocytes in the bloodstream.

monocytosis An increase in the number of monocytes in the bloodstream.

mortality The rate of death in a population.

mosquito A winged insect that feeds on blood and can transmit disease.

motor Relating to motion, or body movement.

motor function The ability to produce body movement by complex interaction of the brain, nerves, and muscles.

motor neurons Nerve cells that carry signals from the brain that control muscle activity.

MRI *See* magnetic resonance imaging.

mucosa *See* mucous membrane.

mucous membrane The layer of cells that lines the tubular organs of the body, such as the digestive and respiratory tracts.

mucus A slippery secretion produced by glands of the mucous membranes.

multifocal Relating to or arising from many locations.

murmur A vibration heard coming from the heart or major blood vessels.

muscle A tissue composed of fibers capable of contracting (and thus producing motion).

muscular wasting The steady loss of muscle mass and strength.

musculoskeletal Having to do with the muscles, bones, and joints.

Mustelidae Latin term for the scientific family that includes ferrets, mink, and skunks.

mutation A spontaneous, permanent change in genetic material that is passed to the organism's offspring.

muzzle An animal's nose and jaws.

mycetoma Infection of the skin and underlying tissues that has the appearance of a nodule or tumor.

mycobacterial infections *See* mycobacteriosis.

mycobacteriosis Infection by mycobacteria, a group that includes the bacteria responsible for leprosy and tuberculosis.

mycoplasma The smallest known type of bacteria, which lack cell walls.

mycosis Fungal infection.

mycotoxicosis Disease caused by toxins produced by fungi.

myelography A specialized x-ray procedure in which a dye is injected into the cerebrospinal canal to outline the spinal cord.

myiasis Maggot infestation. Also known as strike.

myocardial disease A disorder of the heart muscle.

myocarditis A local or widespread inflammation of the heart muscle with degeneration or death of the heart muscle cells.

myocardium The muscular tissue of the heart.

myopathy General term referring to any skeletal muscle disease.

myositides Diseases that produce a mainly inflammatory reaction in muscle.

myositis Inflammation of a muscle, characterized by pain, tenderness, and sometimes spasm in the affected area.

myxomatosis A severe viral disease in rabbits, characterized by the formation of myxoma, or soft, gelatinous tumors, and subsequent swelling around the head, face, and genitals.

N

nagana An often fatal disease of vertebrates transmitted by the bite of the tsetse fly; may affect multiple body systems and often causes anemia.

nares The openings of the nose.

nasal Having to do with the nose, often its interior.

nasal cavity The air-filled space above and behind the nose, on either side of the septum.

nasal discharge Material, typically mucus, emerging from the nose.

nasogastric tube A feeding tube that is inserted through the nose into the stomach.

nasolacrimal duct A duct that moves tears from the eye to the nose.

nebulization Conversion of a substance, such as a medication, from a liquid or solid state into a fine mist or vapor.

necropsy An animal autopsy.

necrotic dermatitis Inflammation of the skin characterized by localized death of tissue.

necrotic meningoencephalitis A disease caused by infection of the brain with microorganisms, with signs that may include depression, lethargy, labored breathing, loss of appetite, bluish skin, and a pus-like discharge from the nose.

nematode A parasitic worm; also called a roundworm.

neonatal Having to do with newborn offspring.

neoplasia The formation of a tumor.

neoplasm A tumor.

neosporosis An infectious disease of dogs and other animals caused by the protozoan parasite *Neospora caninum*.

nephritis Inflammation of the kidney.

nephrotic Of or relating to the kidneys.

nephrotic syndrome Signs of disease in the kidney that may include protein in the urine, low levels of protein in the blood, a buildup of fluid in the abdomen, shortness of breath, and swelling in the legs.

nerve Specialized tissues that transmit electrical impulses serving to relay sensory or motor information between the nervous system and body organs.

nest box A man-made box provided for animals to nest in.

neuroendocrine tissue tumors Tumors that can develop from neuroendocrine cells (found in tissues that have both nervous system and hormone-producing functions) in the adrenal or thyroid glands.

neurologic Of or pertaining to the nervous system.

neurologic signs Impairments of perception or behavior caused by damage to the central nervous system.

neuromuscular Having to do with the terminations of nerves in muscle tissue.

neuron The specialized cells of the nervous system responsible for transmitting electrical signals.

neuropathic pain Pain resulting from damage to a nerve or some other part of the central nervous system.

neurotransmitter A chemical released by a nerve cell that passes signals to other nerve cells, or to muscles or glands.

neuter To remove the internal reproductive organs (that is, the ovaries and uterus or testes) of an animal in order to prevent reproduction.

neutropenia A decrease in the number of neutrophils in the bloodstream.

neutrophil A common type of white blood cell that engulfs and destroys bacteria and other foreign cells.

neutrophilia An increase in the number of neutrophils in the bloodstream.

nevus A congenital pigmented area on the skin; sometimes called a birthmark.

Newcastle disease A contagious viral disease in birds, whose signs include coughing, sneezing, diarrhea, tremors, and twitching.

nictitating membrane A thin membrane in many animals that can extend across the eye to protect it; also called the third eyelid.

nit The small egg of a louse, typically found glued to hair.

nitrates Chemical compounds that can be used by plants and algae as food, or removed by water filtration.

nocardiosis A chronic, noncontagious disease caused by *Nocardia* bacteria found in soil, decaying vegetation, and other environmental sources.

nocturnal An animal that is active only or primarily at night.

nodule A small, irregular, rounded mass.

noncontagious Not contagious; not communicable by contact.

nonregenerative anemia A decrease in the number of red blood cells, which the bone marrow is not able to fully compensate for by creating new red blood cells.

nonsteroidal anti-inflammatory drug (NSAID) A group of medications other than corticosteroids that relieve pain, fever, and inflammation.

nonviremic Animals that, despite being infected by a virus, show no evidence of it in the bloodstream.

nuclear scintigraphy A diagnostic procedure involving dosing the animal with a radioactive element. This element is then detected within the body by means of a special camera attached to a computer, which generates the image.

nutrient A substance that nourishes a living thing.

nutrition A source of nourishment; food.

nutritional deficiency A lack in the type or amount of nutrients an organism receives.

nutritional osteodystrophy Defective bone formation, as in rickets, caused by an imbalance of calcium and phosphorus in the diet.

nymph The larval form of certain insects.

nymphomania Prolonged estrus or sexually receptive behavior in a female animal.

nystagmus Abnormal, involuntary, usually rapid movement of the eyeballs as a result of dizziness, head injury, or disease.

O

obstruction Blockage of a passage in the body, as of the intestines.

ocular Of or relating to the eye.

ocular fundus The back layer of the eye opposite the pupil where light is detected by specialized nerve cells.

ointment A healing salve intended for external application.

oncologist A cancer specialist.

oncology The field of medicine dedicated to the study, diagnosis, and treatment of cancer.

oocyst A fertilized egg in the process of development; a zygote.

oomycosis Infection with Oomycetes fungi, most common among fish.

opaque Something through which light cannot pass.

ophthalmoscope An instrument for viewing the interior of the eye.

opiate A class of narcotic drugs derived from opium that can reduce pain, induce sleep, and suppress coughing.

opioid Any of a class of synthetic drugs that are not derived from opium but have similar properties. *See* opiate.

opportunistic agent An infectious substance or microorganism, not normally dangerous, that can cause disease when the body's immune system is impaired or weakened.

opportunistic infection An infection by a microorganism that normally does not cause disease but becomes capable of doing so when the body's immune system is impaired or weakened.

optic disk The point on the retina where the optic nerve enters the eye. Also called the blind spot.

optic nerve The nerve that connects the eye to the brain and transmits visual information; also called the second cranial nerve.

optimal temperature zone The preferred temperature range for a species.

oral Having to do with the mouth.

oral cavity The interior of the mouth.

orbit The part of the skull that encloses and protects the eye and related structures.

organ A structure composed of various types of tissues that has a specific function; most organs function as part of an organ system.

organic Relating to a substance derived from a living organism; containing carbon.

organism An individual form of life, such as a plant, an animal, a bacterium, or a fungus.

osmoregulation Maintenance of an optimal balance in the concentration of salts in the body's fluids.

osteoarthritis *See* degenerative joint disease.

osteochondritis dissecans A condition usually seen in young animals in which the immature joint cartilage separates from the underlying bone.

osteochondrosis A condition in which immature joint cartilage separates from the bone and floats loosely in the joint cavity, where it can cause inflammation and interfere with proper bone formation.

osteomalacia A condition in adult animals in which the bones soften because of an imbalance in calcium and phosphorus metabolism.

osteomyelitis Inflammation of the bones caused by a bacterial infection.

osteoporosis A condition marked by loss of bone mass due to poor nutrition, age, or nursing.

osteosarcoma A malignant bone tumor.

otitis Inflammation of the ear.

otitis externa Inflammation of the external ear canal.

otitis interna Inflammation of the inner ear.

otitis media Inflammation of the middle ear.

otoscope An instrument with a light and a magnifying lens to aid visual examination of the ear canal.

outbreak A sudden occurrence or appearance, as of a disease.

ovary The female reproductive organ that produces eggs, as well as the hormones estrogen and progesterone.

ovariohysterectomy The surgical removal of the ovaries and uterus.

over-the-counter Sold directly to the public without a doctor's prescription.

ovulation The release of an egg (ovum) from the ovary for possible fertilization.

oxygenate To treat, combine, or infuse with oxygen.

oxytocin A hormone that stimulates milk flow, causes the uterus to contract during and after birth, and increases maternal behavior.

P

paecilomycosis An infection caused by fungi of the genus *Paecilomyces* that affects the lungs and other organs.

palliative A drug or medicine used to relieve or soothe the signs of disease.

palpation Examination by finger pressure to detect growths, changes in underlying organs, and unusual tissue reactions to pressure.

pancreas A large gland that secretes digestive enzymes and hormones, such as insulin, that regulate blood sugar levels.

panhypopituitarism A disorder in which the pituitary gland and nearby tissues, including the hypothalamus, are compressed or damaged, leading to a lack of several different hormones.

papilloma A wart or other benign growth on the skin or other vascular tissues.

papillomatosis Any condition marked by the presence of many papillomas. *See* papilloma.

papule A small, hard, round bump or protuberance on the skin.

paralysis Partial or total loss of motor function or sensation in part of the body.

paramyxovirus Any of a group of viruses including those that cause measles, mumps, rubella, and Newcastle disease.

paranasal Adjacent to the nasal cavity.

parasite Any living organism that lives inside, with, or close to another living creature (called a host) and uses the host as a source of food, shelter, or other requirements.

parasitic Of, related to, or caused by a parasite.

parasitism A close relationship in which one species, the parasite, benefits at the expense of the other, the host.

parathyroid glands Glands that secrete parathyroid hormone and calcitonin.

parathyroid hormone A hormone that acts with vitamin D and another hormone, calcitonin, to regulate the levels of calcium in the body.

parvovirus A family of viruses including a type that causes a highly contagious intestinal disease of dogs.

passerine Describes the group of perching birds and songbirds such as jays, blackbirds, finches, warblers, and sparrows.

paste A semisolid drug dosage form for treating animals.

pasteurellosis Infection with *Pasteurella* bacteria, which most frequently infect the respiratory tract.

patagium *See* gliding membrane.

patella Kneecap; a flat triangular bone located at the front of the knee joint.

patellar luxation Displacement of the kneecap.

patent ductus arteriosus A heart defect in which the ductus arteriosus (the temporary fetal blood vessel connecting the aorta and the pulmonary artery) does not close at birth.

pathogenic Producing disease, or having the capability to cause disease.

pathologic Relating to or caused by disease.

pathologist A veterinarian or physician who specializes in examining tissue samples to identify the cause of disease or death.

pectoral muscle Any of the muscles that connect to the chest at one end and to the bones of the front limbs at the other end.

pelvic canal The passage from the abdomen through the bones of the pelvis to the outside of the body.

penicillosis Infection by mold of the genus *Penicillium*, which usually affects the nose and sinuses.

penis The external male organ of copulation, used to transfer semen to the female and to expel urine.

pentastomes Worms that infest the respiratory system of birds, reptiles, and mammals. Also called tongue worms due to their appearance.

perianal Situated or occurring around the anus.

pericardial disease Disease of the pericardium, the sac surrounding the heart.

pericardiocentesis Insertion of a needle through the pericardium (the sac surrounding the heart) to withdraw fluid.

pericarditis Inflammation of the sac or lining around the heart.

pericardium The sac-like membrane surrounding the heart.

periodontal Of or relating to the gums.

perioperative The period immediately before and after a surgical procedure.

peripheral nervous system The parts of the nervous system outside of the brain and spinal cord.

peritoneal cavity The space between the membranes lining the abdominal cavity and the abdominal organs.

peritoneal lavage Rinsing of the peritoneal cavity with saline or other fluids as a part of a diagnostic test to look for signs of infection or inflammation.

peritoneum The membrane lining the abdominal cavity and the organs found within it.

peritonitis Inflammation of the peritoneum, often caused by infection or injury to the gastrointestinal tract.

permeability The rate at which a liquid or gas passes through a membrane or other porous material.

persistent Tenaciously or obstinately continuing, often for a long time.

pesticide A chemical that kill pests, especially insects.

pH A measure of the acidity or alkalinity of a fluid or damp substance.

phaeohyphomycosis A fungal infection that usually occurs because of contamination of tissue at the site of an injury.

phagocyte A cell that ingests and kills other substances, especially microorganisms.

phagocytosis The process by which cells engulf and digest microorganisms and cellular debris; an important defense against infection.

phalanx Any of the bones that form the digits, corresponding to fingers and toes in humans.

pharmacology The science that deals with the chemistry, development, uses, and metabolism of drugs.

pharynx The throat.

pheochromocytoma A tumor of the adrenal gland that is able to secrete adrenaline (epinephrine) and other hormones.

pheromone A chemical secreted by an animal that influences the behavior or development of others of the same species; often serving to attract the opposite sex.

phobia An intense and excessive fear of something.

photoperiod The amount of time per day that an organism is exposed to sunlight or artificial light.

photoreceptor Any structure that senses the presence of light.

photosensitization A condition in which skin is overly sensitive to sunlight; distinct from sunburn.

pica The eating of non-food items, such as gravel or dirt.

pigmentation The deposition of coloring matter (pigment) in a cell or tissue.

pink eye *See* conjunctivitis.

pinna The large visible portion of the external ear.

pinworm Any of a group of small, parasitic nematodes that live in the intestines of vertebrates.

piping Refers to the activity of fish swimming near the surface of the water trying to gulp air.

pituitary Related to the pituitary gland of the brain that produces hormones critical for control of many bodily functions.

pituitary dwarfism Disorder of the pituitary gland in which a shortage of growth hormone leads to smaller than normal size.

pituitary gland A small, oval, endocrine gland attached to the base of the brain which secretes hormones that control many other endocrine glands.

placenta The organ that connects the fetus to the mother in most mammals and regulates the exchange of nutrients between them.

placental Of or relating to the placenta.

plague An acute and sometimes fatal bacterial disease, transmitted primarily by the fleas of rats and other rodents.

plasma The clear, yellowish fluid portion of blood or lymph in which cells are suspended.

plasmodial organisms Single-celled protozoal parasites that live within the bloodstream and cause malaria.

platelet A type of small blood cell responsible for clotting. Also called a thrombocyte.

pleura The membranes lining the outside of the lungs and the chest cavity.

pleural cavity The space between the membranes lining the chest wall and the lungs.

pleurisy Inflammation of the lining around the lungs (the pleura), causing pain, cough, chest tenderness, and shortness of breath.

pneumonia Inflammation of the lung tissue, often accompanied by inflammation of the trachea and other large airways; also known as pneumonitis.

pneumonitis *See* pneumonia.

pneumothorax Air in the space between the lungs and the chest wall.

pododermatitis Inflammation of the skin near the foot or hoof.

poison A substance that causes illness, injury, or death if ingested.

polioencephalomalacia A neurologic disease that leads to softening and degeneration in the outer layer of the brain.

poll evil Bacterial infection and inflammation of a sac surrounding a tendon near the base of the skull in horses.

polyarteritis nodosa Inflammation of the walls of arteries that affects multiple organs.

polycythemia An increase in the number of red blood cells circulating in the bloodstream.

polydactyly The presence of extra toes, which is a common inherited condition in cats.

polyp A growth or mass projecting from the tissue of a membrane, sometimes tumorous.

polyphagia Excessive appetite or overeating.

polysaccharide A complex carbohydrate such as starch or cellulose, made up of sugar molecules in a chain structure.

porphyrin A protein molecule that is one of the building blocks of hemoglobin, the molecule that carries oxygen in the bloodstream.

portosystemic shunt A congenital defect in the blood vessels of the liver that reduces the ability of the liver to process waste products.

positive inotrope Any of a class of drugs used to help the heart muscle contract.

postpartum hypocalcemia *See* puerperal hypocalcemia.

powder A formulation in which a drug powder is mixed with other powdered fillers to produce a final product.

predation The hunting and eating of other animals.

predilection A particular liking or preference.

predisposing factor A condition or situation that increases the susceptibility to a particular disease or injury.

pregnancy toxemia An often-fatal metabolic condition of pregnant guinea pigs, cows, and sheep, more common in those that are overweight, in which a buildup of toxins occurs in the bloodstream.

prenatal Of or relating to the period before birth.

prepuce A retractable fold of skin covering the penis in many mammals.

prevalent Widely or commonly occurring.

priapism An abnormal, persistent erection of the penis, often caused by spinal cord injury or injury to the penis.

primary factor The main cause, or one of the main causes, of a disease or injury.

prognathia Abnormal protrusion of the jaw, commonly the lower jaw.

prognosis The prospect of survival or recovery following a disease or injury.

progressive Tending to become more severe or wider in scope.

prokinetic A drug that increases the movement of food through the gastrointestinal tract.

prolapse The displacement of a body part from its usual position.

proliferative enteropathy A disease of the intestinal tract in young pigs characterized by severe diarrhea and anemia; possibly caused by bacteria.

promoter An agent that facilitates the development of cancer in cells.

promotion The second step in the development of cancer.

prophylaxis Administering antibiotics as a preventive measure to keep an infection from developing.

prostate gland An organ of the male reproductive system that creates part of the fluid portion of semen.

prostration Total exhaustion or weakness; collapse.

protein Complex molecules made of amino acids that include many substances (such as enzymes, hormones, and antibodies) necessary for the proper functioning of an organism.

protocol A method or regimen of treatment.

protozoa Plural of protozoan.

protozoal Of, related to, or caused by protozoa.

protozoan Any of a large group of single-celled, usually microscopic organisms, that may be parasites.

protrusion Something that sticks out.

pruritus Severe itching; usually signalled by scratching.

pseudomyiasis False strike (maggot infestation); the presence of fly maggots in the gastrointestinal tract (from ingestion) but without tissue infestation.

psittacine Of or belonging to the family Psittacidae, which includes parrots, macaws, and parakeets.

psychotropic drug Any of a group of drugs that are used to modify an animal's behavior, including antidepressants, anti-anxiety drugs, and sedatives.

puberty The phase during which an animal becomes sexually mature.

puerperal hypocalcemia A life-threatening decrease in calcium usually seen in dogs 2 to 3 weeks after giving birth, caused by the loss of calcium from producing milk.

puerperal tetany See puerperal hypocalcemia.

pulmonary Of, relating to, or affecting the lungs.

pulmonary artery The artery that carries venous blood from the right ventricle of the heart to the lungs.

pulmonary edema Fluid in the lungs.

pulmonary hypertension High blood pressure in the blood vessels of the lungs.

pulmonary valve The valve that releases blood out of the right ventricle of the heart into the pulmonary artery.

pulse The rhythmic throbbing of arteries produced by the regular contractions of the heart.

pupa The nonfeeding, transformative stage between the larva and adult in insects.

pupil The black circle in the center of the iris in the eye; the hole through which light enters the eye.

pus A thick, yellowish-white fluid seen in wounds and sores and containing white blood cells, microorganisms, and tissue debris.

pustules Small, inflamed, elevations of the skin filled with pus.

pyloric stenosis A muscular constriction between the stomach and intestines.

pyoderma Any skin disorder that includes formation of pustules or pimples.

pyometra A disorder characterized by the accumulation of a large amount of pus in the uterus.

pythiosis A disease caused by *Pythium insid-iosum*, an organism similar to a fungus, which can affect the skin or gastrointestinal tract in dogs or cause skin disorders in horses or cats.

Q

Q fever A bacterial infection that mainly affects the respiratory or reproductive tracts of ruminants such as cattle and sheep, although other domestic animals, including dogs and cats may be infected. Also known as query fever.

quadriceps Large muscle at the front of the thigh that acts to extend the knee.

qualitative Of or related to a categorical observation of an object, for example breed or sex.

quantitative Of or related to a numerical observation of an object, such as 5 pounds or 3 meters.

quarantine To keep an animal separate from other animals to avoid spreading a disease or infection.

queen A mature female cat, especially one kept for breeding purposes.

R

rabbit calicivirus disease A highly infectious, contagious, and mostly fatal disease of domestic rabbits that affects the digestive system and causes internal bleeding. Also called viral hemorrhagic disease.

rabbitpox An often fatal, generalized, viral disease of rabbits that causes pox marks on the skin as well as discharges from the nose and eyes.

rabbitry A place where rabbits are kept or bred.

radiation High-intensity energy waves emitted by radioactive elements, for example, x-rays.

radiation therapy The use of radiation or radioactive substances to treat disease.

radiography An imaging technique that produces an image on film or other sensitive surface by radiation, such as x-rays passing through an object.

radioisotope irradiation A type of radiation therapy. *See* radiation therapy.

radiotherapy *See* radiation therapy.

radius The shorter and thicker bone in the lower forelimb of animals.

radon A colorless, radioactive gaseous element used in radiotherapy.

range (as in range plants) Extensive open land area where livestock wander and graze.

rash A temporary outbreak on the skin's surface that is often reddish and itchy.

receptor A sensory nerve ending that responds to one of several stimuli, such as touch, temperature, light, taste, or pain.

recurrence A repeated occurrence; reappearance or repetition.

recurrent Happening again and again.

reflex An unconscious, automatic movement that occurs in response to sensory stimulation, for example the extension of the knee when the tendon below the knee is tapped.

regenerative anemia A form of anemia in which the bone marrow responds to the decreased number of red blood cells by increasing red blood cell production.

regurgitate To flow in the opposite direction than normal, as in backward flow of blood within the heart; to bring undigested food up from the esophagus (rather than the stomach) to the mouth.

reinfestation A reoccurrence of an infestation, as by fleas.

reinforcement Reward; any event that increases the chances that a certain behavior will be repeated.

relapse The return of an illness, especially after a period of apparent health or improvement.

remission A decrease in or a temporary disappearance of the signs of disease.

renal Of, relating to, or in the region of the kidneys.

replicate Reproduce.

reproduction The process that gives rise to offspring.

reproductive system The organs involved in reproduction.

reptile Any of a class of air-breathing, usually ectothermic (cold-blooded), vertebrate animals, generally covered in scales or plates; examples include lizards, snakes, and turtles.

resistance An organism's ability to keep from being affected by an infection; ability of a microorganism to withstand the effects of a previously effective drug or dosage.

resistant Having the capacity to withstand; relating to or conferring immunity.

resorption The process of reclaiming an established organ or structure in order to use its nutrients.

respiratory Of, relating to, used in, or affecting respiration (breathing).

respiratory failure Inadequate gas exchange or airflow in the respiratory system.

respiratory sinus arrhythmia The small variations in heart rate in healthy, quiet animals that are caused by pressure changes in the chest associated with breathing.

respiratory system The organs responsible for breathing, including the lungs, trachea, mouth, nose, and throat.

respiratory tract The passages through which air enters and leaves the body.

reticulocyte An immature red blood cell.

retina The rear inner surface of the eye, responsible for picking up light and transmitting it to the brain as visual signals via the optic nerve.

retrovirus Any of a family of viruses that store their genetic material as single-stranded RNA rather than 2-stranded DNA.

reverse osmosis Purification process by which water is forced through an extremely fine membrane and a carbon filter to remove even more compounds than are removed during normal filtration.

rhabdomyolysis (sporadic exertional) Severe cramping and stiffness of muscles following heavy exercise, leading to disintegration of muscle fibers; also called tying up.

rhinitis Inflammation of the nose.

rhinosporidiosis A chronic, nonfatal, fungal infection, primarily of the lining of the nasal passages and, occasionally, of the skin.

rickets A nutritional disorder of young animals caused by a lack of phosphorus or vitamin D, leading to malformation of bones and lameness.

rickettsiae A group of small bacteria that can live only within cells and that cause several diseases, including Rocky Mountain spotted fever, in animals and people.

ringtail A ring-like constriction of the tail, affecting mice, rats, or hamsters, caused by low humidity and high temperatures, and eventually causing gangrene and loss or partial loss of the tail.

ringworm A fungal skin infection affecting many animals and humans; dermatophytosis.

RNA Ribonucleic acid; a nucleic acid found in all living cells essential for the manufacture of proteins and carrying genetic information.

Rocky Mountain spotted fever An infection of humans, dogs, and other animals that is caused by *Rickettsia rickettsii* bacteria, transmitted by ticks.

rodenticide A compound used to poison rodents.

root canal The central cavity of a tooth that extends down into the roots of the tooth.

Rotavirus A genus of viruses that cause intestinal infection in young animals of several species, including birds and pigs.

roughage Another term for fiber, which aids digestion.

roundworm *See* nematode.

ruminant Any of various hoofed, even-toed, mammals such as cattle, sheep, goats, and deer, characteristically having a 4-compartment stomach and chewing a cud consisting of partially digested food.

S

saline A solution of salt (sodium chloride) and purified water that has the same concentration of salts as the bloodstream.

saliva The clear liquid containing digestive enzymes and immune cells that is secreted into the mouth by the salivary glands.

salmon poisoning disease An infectious disease in which the infective agent is transmitted through the various life cycle stages of a flatworm known as a fluke. *See* Elokomin fluke fever.

salmonellosis Infection with *Salmonella* bacteria, most often characterized by gastrointestinal signs such as diarrhea.

sanitation Measures and actions to maintain health through good hygiene.

sarcocystosis Disease in which the muscles and other soft tissues are invaded by intermediate life stages of single-celled organisms of the genus *Sarcocystis.*

sarcoid (equine) Fibrous tumor masses that resemble large warts. They commonly occur on the lower legs of horses.

sarcoma A malignant tumor formed in connective tissue, bone, cartilage, or certain types of muscle.

scabies Infestation by mites of the genus *Sarcoptes*, which affect dogs, cats, horses, pigs, and other species; sarcoptic mange.

scar tissue The pale, inflexible connective tissue that forms at the site of an injury.

scintigraphy *See* nuclear scintigraphy.

sclera The white outer coating that covers the eyeball, except for the central round area covered by the transparent cornea.

scoliosis A congenital sideways curvature or deformation of the spine.

scraping Cellular material obtained for examination by scratching a specific tissue with a clinical instrument.

screwworm The larval stage of certain disease-spreading flies.

scrotum The external pouch of skin and muscle containing the testes in male mammals.

scurvy A nutritional disorder caused by a lack of vitamin C and characterized by bleeding of the skin and mucous membranes, tooth loss, weakness, and spongy gums.

scute An external bony or horny plate or scale covering the skin of some reptiles, such as the shell of a turtle.

sebaceous gland A skin gland that secretes the oil known as sebum into the hair follicles and onto the skin.

seborrhea A disease of the sebaceous glands characterized by excessive secretion of sebum or an alteration in its quality, resulting in an oily coating, crusts, or scales on the skin.

sebum Oily secretion from the sebaceous gland that helps lubricate the skin.

secondary hyperparathyroidism The excessive secretion of parathyroid hormone by the parathyroid glands in response to hypocalcemia (low blood calcium levels).

secretion The process of secreting (generating) a substance from cells, or bodily fluids such as saliva, mucus, or tears.

sedate To administer sedatives, bringing about a relaxed state.

sedative A drug or other agent that induces sedation, a state of calm, restfulness, or drowsiness.

sedentary An adjective used to describe an animal or human that exercises little.

seizure Any of several types of interruption in normal bodily control or thought processes, often characterized by uncontrollable stiffness or jerking of the body, face, or limbs.

semen The viscous, whitish fluid containing sperm and seminal fluid that a male ejaculates during breeding.

semiaquatic An animal that frequents water but does not completely live in it.

semilunar valves Valves between the heart and the aorta, and between the heart and the pulmonary artery.

sensory Of or relating to sensations of pain, position, touch, temperature, taste, hearing, vision, and smell.

sepsis Illness resulting from the persistent presence of microorganisms or their toxins in the bloodstream. Also called septicemia or blood poisoning.

septal defect A hole in the membrane, or muscle wall, dividing the chambers of the heart.

septic shock A life-threatening condition caused by an infection in the bloodstream in which blood pressure falls dangerously low and many organs malfunction because of inadequate blood flow. *See* sepsis.

septicemia *See* sepsis.

septicemic cutaneous ulcerative disease (SCUD) A bacterial disease in turtles in which the scales are pitted.

serotype A group of related microorganisms that are neutralized by the same antibodies.

service animal Companion animal that is trained to help a person with disabilities, aid law enforcement personnel, help search for lost people, or other tasks.

sheath An enveloping tubular structure, such as the tissue that encloses a muscle or nerve fiber.

shock A condition of sudden failure of the circulatory system, brought on by excessive blood loss, severe infection, or nervous system dysfunction, among other causes.

sign Indication or evidence of disease, for example weakness, coughing, or diarrhea.

silage Animal feed made by storing green plant material, as in a silo.

sinoatrial node The heart's natural pacemaker, which generates rhythmic impulses that cause contractions of the muscle fibers of the heart.

sinus (cardiology) A dilated channel or receptacle containing chiefly venous blood.

sinus (respiratory system) Any of several bony cavities in the head connected to the nasal cavity.

sinus arrest A pause or cessation of cardiac sinus pacemaker activity.

sinusitis Inflammation of the lining of the sinuses in the head.

skeletal disorder Disease affecting the development or structure of the bones.

skin appendage A small or secondary attachment to the skin, such as hair follicles, oil and sweat glands, and claws.

skin tenting Condition that occurs when a small section of skin is pinched away from the body does not snap back to its original position. It can be used to indicate the degree of dehydration of an animal.

small intestine The long, narrow part of the digestive tract that lies between the stomach and the colon.

smear A medical screening or diagnostic procedure in which a sample of cells (blood, for example) is collected and spread on a microscope slide for examination.

soft tissue Any of the body tissues other than bone and cartilage.

solution A drug dosage form that is dissolved in liquid, usually water.

solvent A substance in which other substances are dissolved to create a solution.

somatostatin A hormone produced chiefly by the hypothalamus that inhibits the secretion of growth hormone and various other hormones.

soundness Freedom from injury, disease, or illness; without damage.

spasm A sudden, involuntary contraction of a muscle or group of muscles.

spawning The process by which some animals, such as certain fish, reproduce.

spay To remove the internal reproductive organs (ovaries, uterus) of a female animal in order to prevent reproduction.

species A subdivision of a basic biological group, the genus, containing individuals that resemble one another and that may interbreed.

spina bifida A congenital defect in which the spinal column is imperfectly closed.

spinal Of, relating to, or situated near the spine or spinal cord.

spinal cord The long bundle of nerve tissue that runs from the brain to the end of the spinal column and connects to the majority of the peripheral nerves.

spine The backbone of a vertebrate.

spirurid A worm, transmitted by mosquitoes or ticks, that may cause skin sores or infect the stomach lining, body cavity, or blood vessels.

splay leg A leg or pelvic socket deformity causing the legs to spread out (splay).

spleen A glandlike, lymphoid organ that is part of the immune system and that stores blood cells and produces some types of white blood cells.

splint A rigid device used to prevent motion of a joint or of the ends of a fractured bone.

sporadic Happening or appearing at irregular intervals.

spore A reproductive cell, produced by bacteria or fungi, capable of developing into a new individual without fusing with another reproductive cell.

sporocyst The first sac-like reproductive stage in many parasitic flatworms that buds off cells.

sporotrichosis An infectious disease caused by a yeast-like organism that affects many species, including humans, and that often takes the form of localized, ulcerated skin sores.

spot-on A solution of active ingredients for application to the skin which typically contains a cosolvent and a spreading agent to ensure that the product is distributed to the entire body.

squamous Referring to the portion of the epithelium (skin) composed of flat, plate-like cells.

squamous cell carcinoma A form of skin cancer that usually originates in sun-damaged areas.

stamina Endurance.

star-gazing A sign of neurologic disease in which the neck is twisted backward and the animal appears to be looking up into the sky.

stenosis A constriction or narrowing of a duct or passage; an obstruction.

stereotypic behavior Repetitious, relatively unvaried actions that have no obvious purpose or function.

stethoscope An instrument used to magnify sounds produced within the body in order to determine health or diagnose disease.

stifle joint Knee joint; the tendons, ligaments, and other tissues that connect the upper and lower long bones of the rear leg.

stillbirth Unintentional death of the fetus in the uterus.

stimulant A drug or other agent that produces an increase in function of an organ or body part.

stimulation To cause physical reaction in something such as a nerve or organ.

stimulus An agent or condition that elicits a reaction or response from an organism.

stomatitis Inflammation of the mouth.

strain A group of organisms of the same species, having distinctive characteristics but not usually considered a separate breed or variety.

strike Maggot infestation, or myiasis.

stunting A reduction in overall growth or progress.

stye An infection of one or more of the glands at the edge of the eyelid or under it.

subcutaneous Located just beneath the skin.

subcutis The innermost of the 3 layers of the skin.

subspectacle abscessation A common bacterial eye infection in snakes.

substrate Ground covering such as newsprint, sand, peat moss, potting soil, wood shavings, or cypress mulch that are used to cover the bottom of cages for animals such as rodents or reptiles.

subvalvular Located below one of the heart valves.

superficial Located at the surface, or only affecting the surface.

superficial flexor tendon A tendon that flexes the joints of the lower leg.

supplement Something added to complete a thing, make up for a deficiency, or extend or strengthen the whole.

supportive care A wide range of nonspecific treatments for sick or injured animals designed to relieve the signs of illness and that may include injectable fluids, supplemental feeding, heat, or removal of stress.

suppression The reduction or stoppage of a normal bodily function.

supravalvular Located above one of the heart valves.

surgery Medical procedure to treat injury or disease involving an operation, such as removal or replacement of a diseased organ or tissue.

susceptibility The likelihood of being affected or infected; vulnerability.

suspension A dispersion of insoluble or poorly soluble drug particles in a liquid.

suspensory ligament A ligament that provides support for the fetlock joint in horses.

suture Any of the fine threads of specialized material used surgically to close a wound or join tissues; also the act of surgically closing a wound or joining tissues using a stitch or stitches.

syndrome A group of signs that occur together and signal a particular abnormal condition.

synostosis An abnormality in which 2 adjacent bones, such as vertebrae, fuse together.

synovial fluid Fluid contained within a joint cavity that helps lubricate the joint.

synovial membrane Membrane surrounding a joint between bones.

systemic A disease or condition that affects or spreads throughout the entire body rather than being confined to a single location. Also called generalized.

systole The second half of the heartbeat, characterized by the sound of the aortic and pulmonary valves closing, when the ventricles contract.

T

T cell A type of white blood cell that participates in immune responses to infections and other diseases.

T$_3$, T$_4$ Two iodine-containing hormones produced by the thyroid gland that act on many cellular processes to regulate metabolic rate.

tablet A solid pellet made up of one or more compressed powdered drugs and perhaps fillers to be taken by mouth.

tachycardia A rapid heartbeat.

tarsal joint The hock, or ankle joint of the lower rear leg.

tarsal Of, relating to, or situated near the bones of the ankle.

tartar A hard deposit of organic material that forms on teeth.

temperate Mild or restrained in behavior or attitude. As refers to climate, neither very hot nor very cold.

tendinitis Inflammation of a tendon.

tendon An inelastic band of tough fibrous connective tissue attaching a muscle to a bone or other part.

tension pneumothorax A buildup of air in the space between the lungs and the chest wall; can lead to collapse of a lung.

tentative diagnosis Early, most likely diagnosis based on the history, physical examination, and signs of a disorder.

teratogen Agents or factors that cause or increase the incidence of a congenital defect.

terrestrial Living on the ground or underneath its surface.

testes The reproductive organs in a male vertebrate, which produce sperm and the hormone testosterone.

tetanus An often-fatal disease characterized by spastic contraction of muscles and caused by a toxin produced by *Clostridium tetani* bacteria. Also called lockjaw.

tetany Continuous, spastic contraction of muscles, causing rigidity of limbs.

tetralogy of Fallot A complex congenital heart defect that produces a bluish tinge to skin and membranes caused by insufficient oxygen in the blood.

therapy Treatment for an illness.

thermography An imaging technique that records the heat emitted by bodies as infrared radiation; used to diagnose musculoskeletal disorders.

third eyelid *See* nictitating membrane.

third phalanx The outermost bone of a finger or toe.

thoracentesis Procedure in which a needle is inserted into the chest cavity to withdraw excess fluid.

thoracic Of, relating to, or situated in or near the chest (thorax).

thorax The chest cavity, encased by the ribs and containing the heart, lungs, and other organs.

thrombocyte *See* platelet.

thrombopoietin A hormone that regulates the production of blood platelets.

thrombosis Obstruction of an artery by a blood clot.

thrombus A blood clot formed in an artery or vein, frequently causing blockage of the blood vessel.

thymus A gland in the upper chest or the base of the neck that is the site of maturation of some types of lymphocytes, a class of white blood cell.

thyroid gland An endocrine organ in the base of the neck that regulates metabolism.

thyroid hyperplasia Enlargement of the thyroid gland. Also known as goiter.

tick Parasitic invertebrates with 8 legs that suck blood and can transmit several diseases.

tick fever *See* Rocky Mountain spotted fever.

tissue Interconnected cells that perform a similar function within an organism.

tonometer A device for measuring pressure, particularly pressure inside the eye.

tonsillitis Inflammation of the tonsils.

tonsil A small mass of lymphoid tissue in the throat.

topical Involving local application to a part of the body, especially on the skin; for instance, a topical ointment.

torpor A state of deep unconsciousness, usually brought on as a result of environmental conditions such as low temperature.

torticollis A twisting of the neck to one side, resulting in the head being tilted; can be caused by an ear infection or neurologic disease. Also called wry neck.

toxemia A condition brought on by toxins in the blood, especially those produced by bacteria or a metabolic disturbance.

toxic Containing or being a toxin; poisonous.

toxicant A toxic substance.

toxicity The degree to which something is poisonous.

toxicology The branch of science that studies how poisons affect animals and people and how they respond to poisons.

toxicosis Disease or condition resulting from poisoning.

toxin A poisonous material; most often used to describe poisons produced by plants, animals (such as venomous snakes), and some bacteria.

toxoid A substance that has been treated to destroy its toxic properties but retains the capacity to stimulate production of antibodies that can neutralize the original toxin.

toxoplasmosis Infection by *Toxoplasma* microorganisms, which can cause serious damage to the central nervous system, especially in young animals.

trachea The thin-walled, cartilaginous tube that connects the throat to the lungs. Also called the windpipe.

tracheal intubation Insertion of a tube into the trachea to help an animal breathe or to administer anesthesia.

tracheobronchitis Inflammation of the trachea and large airways (bronchi).

tracheostomy An emergency procedure for inserting a tube through the neck into the trachea to allow breathing.

tranquilizer Any of a class of drugs used to produce a calming or soothing effect.

transdermal Describes a medication delivery form that is absorbed through the skin into the bloodstream, such as a patch or an ointment.

transformation The 2-step process of development of cancerous cells from healthy cells, consisting of initiation and promotion.

transfusion The transfer of whole blood or blood products, such as packed red blood cells, from one individual to another.

transmission The passing of an infection from one individual to another.

trauma Damage to living tissue caused by an outside source; a wound.

trematodes Parasitic flatworms.

treponematosis Infection by bacteria of the genus *Treponema*, which includes syphilis.

trichinellosis A parasitic disease caused by a type of roundworm, transmittable to humans and often associated with eating undercooked pork. Also called trichinosis.

tricuspid valve The valve between the right chambers of the heart, through which blood flows from the right atrium to the right ventricle.

trocarization A technique used to relieve the pressure in the abdomen when it becomes distended with gas due to an intestinal blockage.

tube feeding Delivery of nutrients, either a special liquid formula or pureed food, through a tube advanced through the nose or mouth into the stomach.

tuberculosis Disease of many animal species and humans caused by infection with bacteria of the genus *Mycobacterium*, which typically affects the respiratory system.

tularemia A highly contagious bacterial infection found especially in wild rabbits and rodents that may also affect humans, and which may be transmitted by ticks or direct contact with an infected animal.

tumor An abnormal, usually well defined, mass of tissue within an animal; can be either malignant (cancerous) or benign.

tympanic bullae The round bones behind the ears.

Tyzzer's disease A common infection of rabbits and rodents, caused by *Clostridium piliforme* bacteria, that typically affects the digestive system. Other species are occasionally affected.

U

ubiquitous Existing everywhere.

udder Another term for the mammary glands of farm animals, including cows, pigs, and horses.

ulcer A sore of the skin or of a mucous membrane (for instance, the mouth or stomach lining) characterized by erosion and loss of surface tissue.

ulcerate To develop an ulcer.

ulcerative dermatitis A skin disorder characterized by formation of ulcers in multiple locations; can be a result of itching and scratching caused by another condition.

ulna One of the 2 long bones of the lower part of the front leg.

ultrasonography A diagnostic test that uses a machine which emits ultrasonic sound waves, or sounds above the range that humans can hear, to produce a 2-dimensional image of the inside of a body cavity.

ultraviolet (UV) radiation Light energy radiating from the sun that is not visible to the human eye and that can cause sunburn and increase the risk of skin cancer.

umbilical Related to or situated in the umbilical cord, the navel, or the area surrounding the navel.

umbilical cord The flexible tube connecting the fetus to the placenta, through which nutrients are delivered and waste is expelled.

unconscious Lacking awareness and the capacity for sensory perception; not conscious.

unthriftiness Failure of a young animal to grow or gain weight at a normal rate in spite of an adequate diet and absence of obvious illness.

upper airways The portion of the respiratory tract that extends from the nostrils or mouth through the throat (pharynx).

urate A salt formed from uric acid. *See* uric acid.

uremia A buildup of toxic chemicals in the blood that occurs when the kidneys are not functioning properly.

ureter The narrow tube that connects the kidney to the bladder.

urethra The tube from the urinary bladder through which urine exits the body.

uric acid A weak acid present in the urine, which can lead to gout or other disorders in birds if it builds up to high levels.

urinalysis Laboratory analysis of urine, used to aid in the diagnosis of disease.

urinate To expel liquid waste from the body by contracting the urinary bladder.

urine scalding Skin inflammation caused by prolonged contact with urine.

urogenital tract Relating to or involving the organs of the urinary tract and the reproductive system.

urolith A buildup of mineral salts in any part of the urinary tract; also called a urinary calculus or stone.

urolithiasis A condition brought on by the formation of stones (calculi) in the urinary system of an animal.

urticaria *See* hives.

uterus The organ of the female reproductive system in which the fetus develops.

uvea The middle layer of the eye, which includes the iris and the muscles that control it.

uveitis Inflammation of the uvea.

V

vaccination The administration of a substance to produce immunity against a specific disease; immunization.

vaccine A product, including dead or weakened forms of an infectious agent or molecules that are part of the agent, that prompts the immune system to develop defenses against that specific organism.

vagina The lubricated muscular tube of female mammals that connects the cervix to the vulva, forming the external opening of the genitals.

valve A membranous structure that closes to prevent the backward flow of material through a canal or passage.

valvular disease Disease resulting in failure of the heart valves to open or close properly.

vascular Of, characterized by, or containing vessels that carry fluids, such as blood or lymph, through the body of an animal.

vascular network The collection of vessels that carry or circulate bodily fluids.

vasculitis Inflammation of the blood vessels.

vasodilator Any of a class of drugs intended to lower blood pressure by widening blood vessels, thus increasing blood flow.

vector An organism, such as a tick or mosquito, that carries an infectious agent between susceptible animals. A vector may also be mechanical (nonliving), such as clothing or equipment.

vein Any of the system of blood vessels that carry blood toward the heart.

venae cavae The 2 largest veins, which return blood from the body to the right atrium.

venereal disease A contagious disease typically spread through sexual activity.

venom A poisonous fluid injected by the bite or sting of an animal.

venous dilator A drug that dilates the veins coming to the heart and increases the amount of blood that enters the heart.

ventricle Either of the 2 lower chambers of the heart.

ventricular fibrillation A common arrhythmia of the heart characterized by chaotic, ineffective contraction of the heart muscle.

vertebra Any of the bones forming the spinal column.

vertebrate An animal with a backbone, such as fish, reptiles, mammals, and birds.

vesicle A small, raised area of skin, containing fluid; blister.

vesicular stomatitis An acute viral disease of horses and pigs, transmitted by mosquitoes and other insects and signaled by excessive drooling, loss of appetite due to mouth blisters, and lameness due to foot ulcers.

vestibular system The organs in the inner ear that control balance.

veterinarian An individual trained and licensed to treat the medical conditions of animals; a doctor of veterinary medicine.

veterinary dermatologist A veterinarian specializing in the treatment of skin disorders.

veterinary family practice Also known as "bond-centered practice," in which the veterinarian establishes a lifelong relationship with families and their animals and cares not only for the medical welfare of the animal, but also for the social health of its family.

vipers A group of highly poisonous snakes whose long fangs fold back when not in use.

viral Of, relating to, or caused by a virus.

virus A tiny infectious agent consisting of a genetic material (RNA or DNA) in a protein coat, which relies on host cells to reproduce.

visceral Relating to or affecting one or more of the soft internal organs of the body, especially those within the abdominal cavity.

visceral gout An inflammatory buildup of uric acid metabolites in the internal organs of reptiles or birds, leading to pain and discomfort.

visceral leishmaniasis A chronic, severe disease of humans, dogs, and certain rodents caused by protozoa, characterized by skin lesions, lymph node enlargement, weight loss, anemia, lameness, and kidney failure.

vitamin Any of a group of compounds that are essential for proper body function and growth.

vitamin D A fat-soluble vitamin required for normal metabolism of calcium and phosphorus.

volume overload A form of heart failure that results in an increase in the size of the one or both ventricles, the lower chambers of the heart.

vomit To expel the contents of the stomach; to throw up.

vulva The external female reproductive organs.

W

warm-blooded An animal that maintains a relatively constant and warm body temperature independent of environmental temperature. Also called homeothermic.

wart A hard, rough lump growing on the skin.

water mold An aquatic fungus living chiefly in fresh water or moist soil.

water salinity A measure of the amount of salt in water.

weaning The process of getting an infant mammal adjusted to eating food rather than drinking its mother's milk.

wheal A localized area of fluid buildup in the skin that may be pale or reddened and may itch; a hive.

white blood cell Any of a group of infection-fighting blood cells. *See* leukocyte.

withers The ridge between the shoulder blades of a horse.

womb Another word for uterus. *See* uterus.

worms Soft-bodied organisms, many of which are parasitic and infect animals and/or humans.

X

x-ray A high-energy form of electromagnetic radiation that can be used to produce images that allow a veterinarian to see inside the body; also used to describe the pictures produced by the rays, which are also called radiographs.

x-ray therapy *See* radiation therapy.

Y

yeast A small, single-celled fungus that ferments carbohydrates; some types can infect humans and animals.

yellow fat disease A condition in cats involving inflammation of the fatty tissue, thought to be due to an excess of unsaturated fatty acids in food combined with a deficiency of vitamin E.

Z

zinc toxicity A typically chronic form of poisoning caused by consumption of items containing the metal zinc and characterized by lameness and stiffness.

zoonosis A disease that can be passed from animals to people.

zoonotic risk The likelihood that a disease will be passed from an animal to people.

zygomycosis A fungal infection of the lining of the mouth, nasal passages, and tissue beneath the skin, or the sides of the head, neck, and body.

Index

Note: Page numbers in *italics* refer to illustrations, tables, or sidebars. Entries are indexed by disorder and by animal species. To locate a specific disorder, for example heartworm in dogs, it will be easiest to look first under heartworm and then find the subentry for dogs. In most cases both common names and proper names for disorders are indexed.

A

Abdomen
  traumatic injuries to 1056
Abdominocentesis
  as emergency treatment in
    horses 1060
  for treatment of heart failure
    68
Abortion
  associated with equine viral
    arteritis 800
  associated with feline leuke-
    mia virus 535
  in mares 732
Abscesses
  between toes
    in dogs 247
  in chinchillas 881
  in hamsters 950
  pancreatic
    in cats 409
    in dogs 119
  in rabbits 1002
  in reptiles 1027, 1029, 1032,
    1037
Acariasis (*see* Mange)
ACE inhibitors (*see*
    Angiotensin-converting
    enzyme (ACE) inhibitors)
Acetaminophen 1140
  poisoning from 1192
Acetone poisoning 1170
Achilles tendon disruption
    (dropped hock)
  in dogs 190
Acorn poisoning 1201, *1180*
Acquired immunedeficiency
    syndrome (AIDS)
  and susceptibility to
    zoonoses 1089
Acquired laryngeal paralysis
  in dogs 202
Acromegaly
  in cats 421

Actinobacillosis
  in dogs 306
  in horses 794
Actinomycosis (Lumpy jaw)
    1096
  in dogs 307
  in hamsters 948
  in horses 795
  in sugar gliders 1044
Activated charcoal 1126
Acupuncture
  in pain management 1215
Acute bronchointerstitial
    pneumonia
  in foals 748
Acute idiopathic polyradiculo-
    neuritis
  in cats 460
  in dogs 202
Acute pain 1212 (*see also* Pain)
Addison's disease
  in cats 417
  in horses 644
  in dogs 132
Adenocarcinomas
  of apocrine gland
    in dogs 281
    in horses 780
  of perianal gland
    in dogs 277
  of sebaceous glands
    in cats 509
    in dogs 278
Adenomas
  of apocrine gland
    in dogs 281
    in horses 780
  of sebaceous glands
    in dogs 278
    in horses 779
Adenovirus infection
  in guinea pigs 936
  in reptiles 1027
Adhesions
  in horses 619

Adjuvants 1143
Adrenal crisis
  in dogs 132
Adrenal gland disorders
  in cats 417
  in dogs 131
Adrenal glands
  of cats 417
  of dogs 131
  of horses 641
Adult-onset panhypopituitar-
    ism
  in cats 421
  in dogs 137
Aerosol poisoning
  in birds 857
Aflatoxicosis 1154, *1156*
  in sugar gliders 1044
Aflatoxins 1154
Africa
  travel with pets to 1221
African horse sickness 795
African Grey parrots *818*
  calcium deficiency in 845
African sleeping sickness (*see*
    Trypanosomiasis)
Agalactia
  in cats 472
  in dogs 217
Age determination
  in horses 609
Aggression (*see also* Behavior
    problems)
  in breeding stallions 576
  in cats 346, 352
  in dogs 18, 25
  in horses 572, *573*, 574
  types of
    in cats 352
    in dogs 25
    in horses 572
Aging
  and cancer 1236
Air travel with pets 1224
Airsacculitis 846

Air sac mites 848
Airway blockage
  emergency care of dogs and
    cats with 1054
Airway disorders (*see* Lung
    and airway disorders)
Albinism
  in cats 491
  in dogs 244
  in horses 758
Alcohol poisoning 1163
Aldosterone *130*
Aleutian disease
  in ferrets 895
Algaecide poisoning 1166
Algal poisoning 1146
Alkali disease (*see* Selenium
    poisoning)
Alkaline batteries
  ingestion of 1165
Allergic asthma
  in cats 440
Allergic bronchiolitis
  in cats 440
Allergic bronchitis
  in cats 487
  in dogs 168
Allergic bronchopulmonary
    aspergillosis *1089*
Allergic pneumonitis
  in cats 479
  in dogs 227
Allergic reactions (*see* Ana-
    phylactic reactions)
Allergic rhinitis
  in dogs 168
Allergies (*see also* Anaphy-
    lactic reactions)
  in cats 441, 492
  in dogs 245
    food allergies 168
    immunotherapy for 246
    nasal 168
  from food (*see* Food allergies)
  in horses 759
  to rabbits 984
Alloimmune hemolysis
  in dogs 39
Aloe poisoning *1176*
Alopecia (*see also* Hair loss)
  in cats 491, 498
  color dilution
    in dogs 242
  in dogs 242, 255
  in horses 766
Alpha$_2$ agonists
  in pain management
    1215

Alprazolam poisoning
    1196
Alternative therapies
  for pain management 1215
Aluminum phosphide poison-
    ing 1204
Amebiasis
  in cats 405
  in dogs 115
American canine hepato-
    zoonosis 43
American Board of Veterinary
    Practitioners 832
American trypanosomiasis
    1098 (*see also* Chagas'
    disease)
American Veterinary Medical
    Association
  board certification *19, 352, 567*
Ammonia poisoning 1172
Amphetamines
  poisoning from 1199
Amphibians 864
  bacterial diseases in 868
  characteristics of 864
  diet of 867
  diseases caused by parasites
    870
  frogs *864*
  fungal diseases in 869
  handling of 864
  housing for 865
  metabolic disease 872
  musculoskeletal disease 872
  newts *865*
  nutritional deficiencies 872
  nutritional requirements 867
  obesity 872
  salamanders *865*
  temperature requirements 865
  thiamine deficiency in 872
  toads *864*
  tumors in 872
  viral diseases in 871
  water requirements 866
Amputation neuromas
  in dogs 278
Amyloidosis
  in cats 530
  in dogs 307
  in gerbils 925
  in hamsters 952
  in horses 796
  of the kidneys
    in dogs 294
  of the liver
    in cats 413
    in dogs 124

  in horses 639
  in mice 962
Anabolic steroids 1129, *1130*
Anal disorders
  in cats 414
  in dogs 125
  in horses 640
Analgesic drugs 1130, *1131*
  in pain management 1213
Anal sac disease
  in cats 414
  in dogs 125
Anal sacs (Anal glands)
  of cats 414
  of dogs 7, 125
Anaphylactic reactions
  anaphylactic shock (*see* Ana-
    phylactic shock)
  atopy 169
    in cats 439
    in dogs 167
  food allergies
    in cats 440
    in dogs 168
  hives
    in cats 439
    in dogs 168
    in horses 660
  in horses 660
  PIE (Pulmonary infiltration
    with eosinophilia)
    syndrome 168, 440
  skin allergies 441, 660
  sweet itch 660
Anaphylactic shock
  in cats 439
  in dogs 167
  in horses 660
Anaphylaxis 166
Anaplasmosis
  in horses 796
Anchor worms 917
Anemia
  in cats 362
  of chronic disease
    in cats 363
    in dogs 41
  cold agglutinin (hemolytic)
    disease 661
  diagnosis of 1073
  in dogs 37, 169
  equine infectious 716, 799
  in horses 584
  immune-mediated hemolytic
    169, 441, 661
  and nutritional deficiencies
    in dogs 40
  in sugar gliders 1045

Anesthesia
  local 1215
  and malignant hyperthermia
    in dogs 304
  of reptiles 1025
Aneurysms
  in cats 382
  in dogs 76
  in horses 601
Angiosarcomas
  in cats 507
  in dogs 272
  in horses 780
Angiostrongyliasis *1104*
Angiotensin-converting
    enzyme (ACE) inhibitors
    58, 1122
  poisoning from 1194
Angular limb deformities
  in dogs 190
  in horses 670
Animal hoarders 1231
Animal welfare 1231
Animal and Plant Health
    Inspection Service
    (APHIS)
  pet travel regulations of 1220
Animal-assisted therapy 1229
  (*see also* Service ani-
    mals)
Anisakiasis *1104*
Ankle injuries
  in dogs 187
Ankyloglossia
  in dogs 82
Annual ryegrass staggers 1204
Anoles (*see* Lizards)
Anorectal strictures
  in cats 414
  in dogs 127
  in horses 640
Antacids 1125
  poisoning from 1193
Anterior uvea
  disorders of
    in cats 428
    in dogs 148
    in horses 650
Anterior uveitis
  in cats 429, 443
  in dogs 148, 171
  in horses 662
Anthelmintics 1127
Anthrax *1090*
  in cats 531
  in dogs 308
  in horses 797
Antiarrhythmic drugs 1123

Antibacterial drugs
  for skin infections 1134
Antibiotics
  common types of *1122*
  and diarrhea 1126
  for disease prevention 1082
  for ear disorders
    in dogs 162
  guidelines for use of 1121
  for rabbits 990, 994
  resistance to 1122
  for respiratory diseases
    1133
  for rickettsial infections
    1086
  sensitivity to
    in guinea pigs 931
    in hamsters 947
    in rabbits 990
  for sepsis 1084
  for urinary tract infections
    1136, *1137*
  use in veterinary medicine
    1121
Antibodies *165*
Anticholinergic drugs 1126,
    1133
Anticoagulant drugs 1124
Anticonvulsant drugs 1130,
    1130
Antidepressant drugs 1131
Antidepressants
  poisoning from 1196
  tricyclic *23, 350* (*see* Tri-
    cyclic antidepressants)
Antidiarrheal drugs *1126*
Antidiuretic hormone *130*
Antiemetic drugs 1125, *1125*
Antifreeze poisoning 1150
Antifungal drugs 1086,
    1134, 1137
Antigen detection test
  for diagnosis of heartworm
    infection 75
Antigen presenting cells *165*,
    166
Antigens 164, *165*
Antihistamines 1134, 1135,
    1139
  poisoning from 1181
Anti-inflammatory drugs
  corticosteroids 1133 (*see also*
    Corticosteroids)
  nonsteroidal 1134, 1214 (*see
    also* Nonsteroidal anti-
    inflammatory drugs
Antineoplastic chemotherapy
    1140

Antiparasitic drugs 1134
Antipsychotic drugs 1131
Antiulcerative drugs *1126*
Antiviral drugs 1088, 1138,
    1139
ANTU poisoning 1202
Anxiety (*see also* Separation
    anxiety)
  in cats 346
  in dogs 18
  in horses 567, 574
  treatment of 1131
Anxiolytic drugs 1131
Aortic stenosis
  in cats 374
  in dogs 60
APHIS (*see* Animal and Plant
    Health Inspection
    Service)
Aplasia cutis
  in cats 491
  in dogs 242
  in horses 758
Aplastic anemia
  in cats 363
  in dogs 41
  in horses 585
Apocrine gland
  adenocarcinomas of
    in dogs 281
    in horses 780
  adenomas of
    in dogs 281
    in horses 780
  cysts of
    in dogs 280
  tumors of
    in cats 512
    in dogs 270
Appetite disorders
  drugs for 1124, *1125*
Appetite loss
  in horses 572
Aquariums 899
  adding fish to 904, 905
  bacteria in 904
  betta tanks 902
  carbon dioxide in 914
  cleaning 907, *907*
  emergencies in 908
  excess ammonia in 911, 913
  feed intoxications in 913
  filtration of 902, 907
  freshwater 903, 904
  freshwater vs saltwater 901
  goldfish bowls 902
  gravel in 902
  heaters for 902

Aquariums (*continued*)
  hydrogen sulfide in 914
  maintenance of 900, 901,
      907, *907*
  new tank syndrome 911
  nursery environment in 909
  old tank syndrome 911
  pH of *903*
  quarantine tanks 907
  saltwater 904
  selecting fish for 901
  set up of 901
  toxins in 904
  water quality in 903
  water temperature of 902
  water treatment for 903
Aquatic medicine (*see* Fish)
Aquatic plants 902
Arenavirus
  in hamsters 951
Argentinean hemorrhagic
      fever *1110*
Arrhythmias
  description of 55
  in horses 594
Arrhythmogenic right ventric-
      ular cardiomyopathy
  in dogs 71
Arsenic poisoning 1147, 1161
Arterial dilators 1123
Arteritis
  equine viral 746, 800
Arthritis
  cancerous
    in cats 450
    in dogs 186
  canine rheumatoid 172
  in cats 449
  in dogs 172, 185
  in horses 675
  immune-mediated
    in cats 450
    in dogs 172
  of lumbar vertebrae
    in horses 702
  plasmacytic-lymphocytic
      synovitis 172
  in potbellied pigs 979
  septic
    in cats 449
    in dogs 185
    in horses 676, 692
  of shoulder joint
    in horses 694
  traumatic
    in horses 675
Arthrogryposis
  in foals 669

Arthroscopy
  in dogs 178
  in horses 668
Arytenoid chondritis
  in horses 741
Ascarids (*see also* Round-
      worms)
  in horses 629
  in reptiles 1028
Ascites
  in cats 390, 409
  in dogs 121
  in horses 608
Asia
  travel with pets to 1221
Asian taeniasis *1102*
Aspergillosis *1096*
  in birds 846
  in cats 537
  in dogs 312
  in horses 801
Aspiration pneumonia
  in cats 485
  in dogs 234
  in horses 740
Aspirin 1140
Aspirin poisoning 1192
Asthma
  in cats 440, 487
  in macaws 847
Atlantoaxial subluxation
  in dogs 201
Atopy (*see also* Skin
      allergies)
  in cats 493
  in dogs 169, 246
  in horses 759
Atresia
  tricuspid
    in horses 598
  of intestinal tract
    in horses 608
Atrial fibrillation
  in horses 594
Atrial septal defects
  in cats 375
  in dogs 62
Atrial standstill
  in cats 379
  in dogs 71
Atrial thrombosis
  in hamsters 946
  in mice 962
Atrophic rhinitis
  in potbellied pigs 980
Atrophy
  of right liver lobe
    in horses 639

Attention seeking behavior
  in dogs 27
Attenuated vaccines 1143
Aural plaques 658
Aural cholesteatoma
  in gerbils 925
Aurotrichia
  in dogs 244
Australia
  travel with pets to 1221
Australian stringhalt 714
Autoimmune adrenalitis 173
Autoimmune skin disorders
  in dogs 170
Autoimmune thyroiditis 173
Automobile travel with pets
      1223
Avian gastric yeast 840
Avian influenza 847, *1112* (*see
      also* Influenza type A)
Avian tuberculosis 855
Avocado poisoning *1152*, *1174*
Azalea poisoning *1176*
Azinphos poisoning 1169
Azotemia 292

B

Babesiosis *1098*
  in cats 364
  in dogs 42
  in horses 586
Back disorders
  in horses 701
Bacteremia 1083
Bacteria
  in bloodstream 1083
  infections caused by 1082
  and purpura hemorrhagica 662
  resistance to antibiotics 1121
  rickettsiae 1085
  sepsis 1083
Bacterial cystitis
  in cats 517
  in dogs 288
  in horses 784
Bacterial infections
  in birds 855
  in ferrets 894
  in reptiles 1035
Balanoposthitis
  in dogs 218
Balantidiasis *1098*
Bandage types 1066
Barbering
  in guinea pigs 938
  in mice 960
  in rats 1009

Barbiturates
  poisoning from 1196
Basal cell carcinoma
  in cats 506
  in dogs 271
  in horses 776
Basal cell tumors
  in cats 506
  in dogs 270
  in horses 776
Basic test panel *1074*
Basidiobolomycosis
  in horses 805
Basking lights 1020
Basophilia
  in dogs 51
Baylisascaris procyonis
    infection
  in chinchillas 883
B cells 35, *165*
Beaks
  of birds
    trimming of 835
    types of 824
  of turtles and tortoises 1030
Bedding material
  for chinchillas 875
  for gerbils 920
  for guinea pigs 928
  for rats 1005
Behavior
  of cats 345
    social behavior 351
  of dogs 17
    social behavior 24
  of horses 566
    social behavior 570
  modification techniques
    for cats 347
    for dogs 19
    for horses 568
  pain-induced changes in
    1212
Behavioral fever 1080
Behavior problems
  in cats 345, 352
  in dogs 17, 25
  in horses 566, 571, 572, *573*
Beneckea chitinovora
    infection
  in turtles 1034
Benzene hexachloride poison-
    ing 1167
Benzene poisoning 1160
Benzimidazoles 1127
Benzodiazepines
  poisoning from 1195
Bertilliasis *1102*

Besnoitiosis
  in horses 798
Beta-adrenergic agonists 1132
Beta blockers
  poisoning from 1195
Biceps brachii tendon
    inflammation
  in dogs 189
Bicipital bursitis
  in horses 695
Bile duct disorders
  in cats 413
  in dogs 125
Bile duct obstruction
  in cats 413
  in dogs 125
Bilharziasis *1102*
Biopsy 1240
Bird flu (*see* Avian influenza)
Birds 816
  air sac mites 848
  aspergillosis 846
  avian gastric yeast 840
  avian influenza 847
  avian tuberculosis in 855
  bacterial diseases in 855
  beak and feather disease 852
  beaks of 824
  beak trimming 835
  birth defects in 838
  bone fractures in 843
  breeding of 836
  and cage mate trauma 831
  cages for 829, 857
  cancer in 858
  candidiasis in 840
  cardiovascular disorders in
    839
  care during illness or injury
    840
  cataracts in 843
  chronic heart disease in 839
  clostridial diseases in 856
  cockatiels 817
  communication by 823
  conjunctivitis in 843
  constricted toe syndrome 839
  crop burns 838
  crop of 824
  developmental problems in
    838
  diabetes mellitus in 843
  diet of 830, 844, 850
  digestive disorders in 840
  digestive system 826
  ears of 822
  egg binding in 849
  exercising 831

eye disorders in 843
eyelid atresia in 839
fatty liver disease 838
feather disorders 850
feather loss *853*
feather plucking 850, *851*
feathers 821, 825
  ear coverts 822
  mites of 852
feet of 824
first aid kit for *859*
flight of 824
gapeworms 848
gastrointestinal parasites
    in 842
giardiasis in 842
giving medication to 833, *834*
gizzard of 826
goiters in 845
gout in 844, 852
grooming 834
health care for 832
hearing of 822
herpesvirus infections in 855
hormonal disorders in 843
household hazards 835,
    836, 857
identifying gender of 837
inflammation of the eye 843
injuries of 859
kidney disorders in 852
lead poisoning in 857, 1170
leg banding 835
life span of 826
lockjaw in 839
metabolism of 821
microchipping 835
mites of 852
molting of 825, *853*
mycobacteriosis in 855
nail trimming 835
newborn care 837
Newcastle disease 848
nutritional disorders in 844
nutritional requirements 830
ownership considerations
    817, 826
Pacheco's disease in 854
papillomas in 855
papillomatosis in 841
physical characteristics of
    816, *817*
poisoning in *836*, 857, 1145
polyomavirus in 854
popular types *817*
poxvirus infections in 855
proventricular dilatation
    disease in 841

Birds (*continued*)
  psittacine beak and feather
    disease 852
  psittacosis in 855
  reproduction of 836
  reproductive disorders in 848
  respiratory disorders in 846
  respiratory parasites 848
  ringworm 851
  roundworms in 842
  sarcocystosis in 848
  selection of 828
  senses of 820
  signs of illness 821, 832
  skin infections of 851
  skin of 823, 825
  sleeping patterns of 831
  sources for 828
  splay leg 838
  swallowing foreign objects
    837
  tapeworms in 842
  temperament of 831
  temperature regulation in
    821
  transmission of disease to
    humans 856
  tumors of 858
  urinary tract disorders in
    852
  vaccination of 835
  veterinarians for 832
  vision 822
  vitamin and mineral defi-
    ciencies 844, 845
  Vitamin D toxicosis in 845
  water requirements 830
  wing trimming 834
  zinc poisoning 857
Birkeland fractures 687
Birth defects (*see* Congenital
    disorders)
Bismuth subsalicylate *1126*
Bite wounds
  emergency care of dogs and
    cats 1056
  management of 1067
  in mice 960
Biting
  by ferrets *889*
Black disease (*see* Infectious
    necrotic hepatitis)
Black flies
  in dogs 252
  in horses 762
Black hair follicle dysplasia
  in dogs 243
Black walnut poisoning *1184*

Bladder
  congenital disorders of
    in cats 516
    in dogs 286
    in horses 784
  infections of
    in cats 517
    in dogs 288
    in horses 784
Bladder stones (*see also*
    Uroliths)
  in ferrets 899
  in rabbits 1002
Blastomycosis *1096*
  North American
    in cats 539
    in dogs 315
Bleach poisoning 1163
Bleeding (*see also* Hemorrhage)
  into the eye 1064
    in cats 427
    in dogs 146
  first aid for, in dogs and
    cats 1052
  from thrombocytopenia 170
Bleeding disorders
  in cats 366
  in dogs 46
  in horses 587
Blepharitis
  in cats 425
  in dogs 144
  in horses 648
Blindness 1065 (*see also*
    Vision)
Blister beetle poisoning 1148
Blister diseases
  in reptiles 1034
Bloat
  in chinchillas 880
  in dogs 103
Blood samples 1073
Blood cell counts *39*
Blood cells
  types of 33, *36, 360*
Blood clots
  in cats 382
  in dogs 76
  in hamsters 946
  in horses 600
Blood clotting
  and thrombocytopenia 441
Blood clotting disorders
  in cats 366, 368
  in dogs 46, 50
  in horses 587, 589
Blood disorders
  in cats 359

anemia 362
hemophilia 367
leukemia 363
neonatal isoerythrolysis
  362
in dogs 33
  anemia 37
  hemophilia 47
  leukemia 41, 52
  lymphoma 52
in horses 581
  anemia 584
  aplastic anemia 585
  babesiosis 586
  hemophilia 588
  leukemia 585, 590
  lymphangitis 591
  lymphoma 590
  neonatal isoerythrolysis
    585
  pigeon fever 591
  platelet disorders 588
  Surra 586
  thrombocytopenia 588
  trypanosomiasis 586
  tsetse fly disease 586
Blood infection (*see*
    Septicemia)
Blood loss anemia
  in dogs 38
Blood pressure
  and heart rate 54
Blood tests (*see also* Diagnos-
    tic tests)
  hematology 1071
Blood transfusions
  in cats 361
  in dogs 37
  in horses 584
Blood types
  of cats 361
  of dogs 37, 361
  of horses 581, 584
Blood vessel disorders
  in cats 368, 370
    aneurysms 382
    aortic stenosis 374
    blood clots 382
    heartworm disease 380
    hypertension 380
    patent ductus arteriosus 374
  in dogs 50, 53
    aneurysms 76
    blood clots 76
    heartworm disease 73
    hypertension 73
    patent ductus arteriosus 59
    vasculitis 171

in horses 589, 592
  aneurysms 600
  blood clots 600
  hypertension 600
  patent ductus arteriosus 597
  vasculitis 662
Blow flies
  in horses 763
Blue breasts (see Mastitis)
"Blue eye"
  in dogs 318
Blue-green algae poisoning 1146
Blunt trauma
  1056 (see also Trauma)
Boarding facilities 1227
Body temperature regulation
  in dogs 303
Bog spavin 696
Bolivian hemorrhagic fever 1089
Boluses 561
Bone disorders (see Musculoskeletal disorders)
Bone fractures (see Fractures)
Bone marrow disease
  in cats 363
  in dogs 41
Bone spavin
  in horses 696
Bone tumors
  in cats 453
  in dogs 193
Borax poisoning 1161
Bordetella
  vaccination in dogs 13
Bordetella bronchisepta
  infection
    in guinea pigs 935
Bordetellosis 1090
Borreliosis (see Lyme disease)
Bot fly larvae infestation
  in cats 496
  in dogs 252
  in ferrets 896
Bots
  in horses 563, 629
Bottle flies
  and skin disorders
    in horses 763
Botulism
  in dogs 309
  in horses 714, 798
Boutonneuse fever 1094
Bowen's disease
  feline 512

Brachial plexus avulsion
  in cats 461
  in dogs 204
Brachygnathia
  in cats 387
  in dogs 82
  in horses 606
Brachytherapy 1241
Bracken fern poisoning 1147, 1186
Bracken staggers 1148
Brain stem auditory evoked response (BAER) 199
Brain injuries
  in cats 456
  in dogs 196
  in horses 710
Brain tumors
  in dogs 197
Branchiomycosis 914
Bran disease 674 (see also Osteomalacia)
Brazilian hemorrhagic fever 1110
Bread dough poisoning 1152
Breathing difficulties
  emergency care for 1054
Breeding
  of cats 343
  of chinchillas 878, 884
  of dogs 15
  of ferrets 893
  of fish 908
  of gerbils 922
  of guinea pigs 930
  of hamsters 945, 949
  of horses 565
  of mice 956
  of pet birds 836
  of potbellied pigs 974
  of rabbits 986, 992
  of rats 1007
  of sugar gliders 1043
Breeding management
  of cats 471
  of dogs 215
  of horses 727
Broken back disease 912
Broken bones (see Fractures)
Bromethalin poisoning 1202
Bronchial asthma
  in cats 487
Bronchitis (see also Tracheobronchitis)
  in cats 479
  in dogs 168, 228, 237
Bronchodilator drugs 1132, 1133

Broodmares
  vaccination of 729
Brown spider bites 1208
Brucellosis 1090
  in dogs 223
  in horses 733
Bruised sole
  in horses 679
Bubonic plague (see Plague)
Bucked shins
  in horses 689
Budgerigars 817 (see also Birds)
  goiters in 845
  gout in 853
  mites of 852
Buffalo flies
  and skin disorders
    in horses 762
Bullous pemphigoid 170
Bumblefoot (see Pododermatitis)
Bunamidine 1128
Burns
  chemical 1164
  first aid for, in dogs and cats 1052
  management of 1065
  of the mouth
    in cats 394
    in dogs 93
  in reptiles 1026
Bursitis
  bicipital
    in horses 695
  in horses 677
  trochanteric
    in horses 701
Butorphanol 1132
Buttress foot
  in horses 685

C

Caffeine toxicity 1153
Cage mate trauma
  in birds 831
Cages
  for birds 829
  for chinchillas 875
  for ferrets 889
  for gerbils 920
  for guinea pigs 927
  for hamsters 941
  for mice 954
  for prairie dogs 964
  for rabbits 985
  for rats 1005

Cages (*continued*)
  for reptiles 1018
  for sugar gliders 1040
Caiques *817*
Calcinosis
  enzootic
    in horses 674
Calcipotriene poisoning
  1197
Calcitonin *130*, 135
Calcium
  imbalances
    in cats 453
    in dogs 180
    in horses 673
    in reptiles 1024
  low blood levels of (*see*
    Hypocalcemia)
  metabolism disorders
    in cats 419, 525
    in dogs 134, 302
    in horses 790
  needs of guinea pigs 934
Calcium deficiency
  in African Grey parrots 845
Calcium channel blockers
  poisoning from 1195
Calculi
  in cats 524, *525*
  in dogs 299
  in horses 787
Camping
  with pets 1223
Campylobacter enteritis *1090*
Campylobacteriosis
  in cats 402
  in dogs 109
Canaries 816, *817* (*see also*
    Birds)
  beaks of 824
  feather cysts 850
Cancer 1233 (*see also* individ-
    ual tumor types)
  and age 1236
  in birds 858
  carcinomas 1237
  caring for pets with 1245
  causes of 1235
  chemotherapy for 1242
  combination therapy for
    1244
  common types in pets *1234*,
    1237
  cure for 1244
  development of 1235
  diagnosis of 1239
  drugs for *1141* (*see also*
    Chemotherapy)

environmental factors for
    1236
  and euthanasia 1248
  of the eye
    in cats 432
    in dogs 154
    in horses 654
  in ferrets 896
  in fish 919
  in hamsters 952
  of immune system 175, 444
  incidence of 1233
  leukemias 1237
  of the liver
    in cats 412
    in dogs 124
  lymphomas 175, 1237
  in mice 962
  and nutrition 1238
  nutritional needs of pets
    with 1246
  pain from 1212 (*see also*
    Pain)
  pain management 1245, 1248
  pancreatic
    in cats 409
    in dogs 119
  in prairie dogs 969
  prevention of 1239
  and quality of life for pets
    1247, 1248
  in rabbits 1003
  radiation therapy for 1077,
    1241
  in rats 1012
  reducing risk of 1238
  in reptiles 1038
  of respiratory system
    in cats 479
    in dogs 228
  sarcomas 1238
  sexual transmission of 1237
  signs of 1239, *1239*
  of skin (*see* Skin cancer)
  spread of 1235
  squamous cell carcinoma
    1236
  surgery for 1240, *1240*
  testing for 1071
  treatment of 1240 (*see also*
    Chemotherapy; Radia-
    tion therapy)
  and viruses 1237
Cancer pain
  signs of 1213
Candida albicans infection
  (*see* Candidiasis)
Candidiasis *1096*

in birds 840
  in cats 537
  in dogs 313
  in horses 802
Canine demodicosis 262
Canine distemper 309
  in ferrets 894
Canine distemper encephalo-
    myelitis 206
Canine extramedullary plas-
    macytomas 274
Canine heartworm pneumoni-
    tis 228
Canine herpesvirus 50, 310
Canine ichthyosiform derma-
    toses 243
Canine juvenile cellulitis 158
Canine malignant lymphoma
    45
Canine mucous membrane
    papillomatosis 282
Canine nasal mites 230
Canine scabies 260
Canine thrombopathia 49
Canine warty dyskeratomas
    271
Canker (*see also* Trichomon-
    iasis)
  in horses 680
Cannibalism of young
  by rabbits 992
Cannon bone fractures
  in horses 691
Cantharidin poisoning (blister
    beetle poisoning) 1148
Capillaria worm infection
    1104
  in cats 518
  in dogs 289
Capnocytophaga infection
    1090
Capped elbow
  in horses 677
Capped hock
  in horses 677
Capsules 1119
Car travel with pets 1223
Carbamate poisoning 1167
Carbonic anhydrase inhibitors
    1128
Carcinogens 1235
  environmental 1237
  tobacco 1239
  ultraviolet (UV) radiation
    1236
Carcinomas 1237
  basal cell
    in cats 506

in dogs 271
in horses 776
renal cell
in horses 787
of the renal tubules
in dogs 296
spread of 1235
squamous cell
in cats 511
in dogs 280
in horses 779
transitional cell
in dogs 297, 298
in horses 787
Cardiac catheterization *57*
Cardiac tamponade
in cats 380
in dogs 72
in horses 600
Cardiogenic shock 1055
Cardiomyopathy
and blood clotting in cats 368
in cats 378
in dogs 69
Cardiopulmonary-cerebral
resuscitation (CPCR)
defibrillation 1057
of dogs and cats 1051, 1057
Cardiopulmonary resuscitation (CPR)
in dogs and cats 1058
Cardiovascular disease (*see*
Heart and blood vessel
disorders)
Cardiovascular system
of cats 370
of dogs 53, 55
of horses 592
Carpal bones
fractures of
in horses 690
Carp pox 915
Carprofen
poisoning from 1198
Carpus
deformities of
in horses 670
disorders of
in horses 689
Carriers (*see* Pet carriers)
Castor bean poisoning *1186*
Castration
postcastration evisceration
of horses 1063
Cataracts
in birds 843
in cats 429
in dogs 149, *151*

in horses 652
in mice 962
Cathartic drugs 1127, *1127*
Cats
acromegaly in 421
Addison's disease in 417
aggression in 346, 352
allergic asthma in 440
allergic bronchiolitis in 440
allergic reactions in 439
allergies in 492
amyloidosis in 530
anaphylactic reactions in
439
anemia in 362
anterior uveitis in 443
aspergillosis in 537
asthma in 440
babesiosis in 364
behavior modification techniques 347
behavior of 335, 345, 351
behavior problems of 345,
352
medications for 349, *350*
bile duct disorders in 413
bleeding disorders in 366
blood clotting disorders in
368
blood disorders 359
blood types of 361
blood vessel disorders in
370, 382
boarding facilities for 1227
bone disorders in 452
breeders of 335
breeding of 343
breeds of 330, 335
candidiasis in 537
cardiomyopathy in 378
cardiovascular disease in
370, 378
cell-mediated immune reactions in 443
Chagas' disease in 366
chemotherapy for 445
Chlamydial conjunctivitis
432
claws of 332
trimming 332
coccidioidomycosis in 538
congenital disorders in 529
congenital erythropoietic
porphyria in 526
congenital heart defects in
373
congenital skin disorders
in 491

conjunctival disorders in
427
conjunctivitis in 427
constipation in 399
cryptococcosis in 538
Cushing's disease in 420
cytauxzoonosis in 364
cytotoxic disorders in 441
deafness of 435
declawing 332
dental care for 342
dental development in 390
dental disorders in 390
dermatitis in 489
diabetes mellitus in 418
diet of 337
digestive disorders in 383
digestive system infections
in *385*
digestive system of 333, 383
diseases affecting multiple
systems 528
dry eye in 427
ear cleaning 342
ear disorders of 433
ehrlichiosis in 532
emergency care of 1051
esophageal disorders in
397
exercise for 337
eye disorders of 423
eyelash abnormalities 425
eyelid disorders of 425
eye structure and function
in 423
feline immunodeficiency
virus in 444
feline infectious anemia in
365
feline infectious peritonitis
532
feline leukemia virus in
444, 533
feline panleukopenia (distemper) in 536
flea control 342
flea infestations 494
food allergies in 440
fungal infections in 537
fur of *333, 333*
gall bladder disorders in
409, 413
gammopathies in 445
gastrointestinal disorders 398
gastrointestinal parasites in
341, 403
genetic storage diseases in
526, *526*

Cats (*continued*)
giving medication to 338
glanders (farcy) in 540
glomerulonephritis in 442
granulomatous reactions
in 443
grooming 342
hairballs in *398*
hair loss (alopecia) of 491,
498
hair types *333*
health of *336*
hearing of 331
heart disorders in 370
heartworm disease in 380
heat stroke in 1052
hemophilia in 367
hepatozoonosis in 365
hernias in 388
histoplasmosis in 538
hives and skin rashes 439, 499
hormonal disorders of 415
household hazards for 343
housetraining of 353
hypercalcemia in *420*
hyperesthesia in 353
hypertension in 380
hyperthyroidism in 422
hypothermia in 1052
immune disorders in 439
immune system tumors in
444
indoor versus outdoor 336
itching in 499
joint disorders in 449
kidney disorders in 514
kitten care 343
lameness in 446
lens disorders in 429
leukemia in 363, 444, 534
lice infestations 500
life expectancy of 330
litter boxes for 337
liver disorders in 409
lupus in 442
Lyme disease in 541
lymphoma in 444, 534
malignant hyperthermia in
528
mange in 436
mange mites of 342
marking behavior of 335,
352, 353
melioidosis in 541
metabolism of 330
motion sickness in 467
musculoskeletal disorders
in 445

myasthenia gravis in 442
mycetomas in 539
nasal cavity disorders in
426
nervous system disorders
of 455
nocardiosis in 542
North American blasto-
mycosis in 539
nutritional requirements
337
obesity in 337
oral tumors in 395
pancreatic disorders in 407,
417
parasite control 340
parasites of *341*
parvovirus in 444
pemphigus in 425, 442
peritonitis in 542
phaeohyphomycosis in 540
phagocytosis deficiencies
in 443
pharyngeal disorders in 396
phobias in 346
physiologic values of *330*
PIE (pulmonary infiltration
with eosinophilia)
syndrome in 440
plague in 543
platelet disorders in 368
poisoning in 1145
polycythemia in 370
pregnancy of 343
pruritus (itching) in 490, 499
Q fever in 544
rabies in 467
rectal and anal disorders in
414
reproduction of 343, 471
reproductive disorders of
469
respiratory disorders in 475
retinal disorders in 430
rhinosporidiosis in 540
salivary disorders in 395
selecting 334, *336*
senses of 331
signs of illness in 338
signs of pain in 1213
skin allergies in 441
skin disorders in 488
skin of 332
skin tumors in 505
spaying/neutering of 343
sporotrichosis in 540
Surra 366
tear duct disorders in 426

teeth of 333, *333*
temperament of 334
temperature regulation 330
tetanus in 464, 544
thrombocytopenia in 368
tick infestations of 505
toxoplasmosis in 545
travel with 1216
trichinellosis (trichinosis)
in 546
trypanosomiasis in 365
tuberculosis in 546
tularemia in 547
urinary system of 334
urinary tract disorders in 514
treatment *1137*
urination problems in
523
uveitis in 428
vaccination of 339, *339*
vaccine-associated tumors
in 511
veterinary care of 338
vision of 331, 424
vomiting 397
whiskers of *333*, 333
worms in 340
Cat scratch disease *1090*
Caudal cervical spondylo-
myelopathy
in dogs 201
Cavies (*see* Guinea pigs)
Cavities 90
CDC (*see* Centers for Disease
Control and Prevention)
Cell-mediated immune reactions
in cats 443
in dogs 172, 173
in horses 663
Center for Veterinary Medicine 963, *964*
Centers for Disease Control
and Prevention (CDC)
963, *964*, 967
pet travel regulations of
1220
Central European tickborne
encephalitis *1110*
Central nervous system (*see*
Nervous system)
Cerebellar abiotrophies
in dogs 201
in horses 713
Cerebellar hypoplasia
in cats 460
in dogs 201
in horses 713

Cerebrospinal fluid
analysis of 199
Cervical line lesions
in cats 392
Cervical stenotic myelopathy
in horses 713
Cestodes (*see* Tapeworms)
Chagas' disease *1098*
in cats 366
in dogs 44
Chameleons 1014 (*see also*
Lizards)
Chédiak-Higashi syndrome
in cats 368, 369
Chemical burns
from corrosive agents 1164
Chemistry 1071
Chemosis
in cats 427
in dogs 146
Chemotherapy 1140, 1242
administration of 1243
adverse effects of 1243
efficacy of 1243
and infection 1081
poisoning from 1197
protocols 1140
resistance to 1243
Cherry eye
in dogs 144
Chest
traumatic injuries to 1056
Chewable tablets 1119
Cheyletiellosis
in cats 501
in dogs 261
Chiggers
on horses 770
Chinchillas 873
abortion in 885
abscesses in 881
bite wounds in 881
bloat in 880
breeding of 878, 884
caring for 873, 876
choking 881
conjunctivitis in 879
constipation in 880
dental care for 877
diarrhea in 879
diet of 875, 878, 880, 884
digestive disorders in 879
dust baths for 875
dystocia 885
ear disorders in 879
ear trauma in 879
exercise for 876
eye disorders in 879

fractured bones in 884
fur chewing by 882
fur of 873, 882
fur slip in 873
gastroenteritis in 880
hair rings 886
heart murmurs in 878
heat stress in 874, 882
herpesvirus 1 in 884
household hazards *875*
housing for 875, *875*, 876
infertility 884
Listeria monocytogenes in
883
mastitis 886
metritis 885
nutritional requirements of
875, 884
otitis media in 879
pneumonia in 881
pregnancy of 878
protozoal infections in 884
Pseudomonas aeruginosa
infection in 882
pyometra 885
reproduction of 878, 884
resorption of fetuses 885
respiratory tract infections
in 880
retained fetus 885
ringworm in 881
roundworms in 883
routine health care 876
selecting 874
septicemia in 882
signs of illness in 876, 877,
877
skin disorders in 881
stomach ulcers in 880
teeth of 877
temperament of 876
thiamine deficiencies in 884
traveling with *874*
treating disease in 877
Yersinia infections in 883
zoonoses in *884*
Chlamydial conjunctivitis
in cats 432
Chlamydial pneumonia
in cats 486
Chlamydiosis
in amphibians 868
in birds 855
Chlorinated hydrocarbon
compounds
poisoning from 1167
Chlorine bleach poisoning 1163
Chloronicotinyls 1134

Chlorpyrifos poisoning
1169
Choanal atresia
in horses 740
Chocolate poisoning 1153
Choke (*see* Esophageal
obstruction)
in horses 613
Choking
first aid for, in dogs and
cats 1052
Cholangiofibrosis
in hamsters 948
Cholangiohepatitis
in cats 410
in horses 635
Cholecalciferol poisoning
1202
Cholecystitis
in cats 413
in dogs 125
Chondroitin sulfate 1140
Chondroprotective agents
1140
Chorioptic mange (*see also*
Mange)
in horses 769
Chorioretinitis
in cats 430
in dogs 152
in horses 653
Chromomycosis
in amphibians 869
Chronic allergic bronchitis
in dogs 168
Chronic pain 1212
Chronic hepatitis
in dogs 123
Chronic inflammatory demyelinating polyneuropathy
in cats 460
Chronic kidney disease
in cats 518
signs of *519*
in dogs 290
signs of *291*
in horses 785
Chronic kidney failure
and hypocalcemia
in cats 419
in dogs 135
Chronic pain (*see also* Pain)
signs of 1213, 1246
treatment of 1215
Chronic respiratory disease
in rats 1009
Chronic ulcerative stomatitis
in dogs 91

Chylothorax
  in cats 478
  in dogs 227
  in horses 739
Chytridiomycosis
  in amphibians 870
Cimetidine poisoning 1193
Cirrhosis
  in dogs 122
  in hamsters 948
Claws
  of cats 332
Claw trimming (*see* Nail
    trimming)
Cleaning products
  poisoning from 1166
Cleft lip
  in cats 387
  in dogs 82
  in horses 606
Cleft palate
  in cats 387
  in dogs 82
  in horses 606
Clicker training 21, 348
Clinical chemistry tests
    1071
Cloacal prolapse
  in birds 849
Clomiprop poisoning 1162
Clonazepam poisoning 1195
Clonorchiasis *1100*
Clostridia-associated intestinal
    inflammation
  in horses 624, 806
Clostridial disease *1090* (*see
    also* Tetanus)
  in birds 856
Clotting protein disorders
  in cats 367
  in dogs 47
  in horses 587
Coal-tar poisoning 1149
Cocaine poisoning 1198
Coccidioidomycosis *1096*
  in cats 411, 538
  in dogs 123, 313
  in horses 802
Coccidiosis
  in cats 406
  in dogs 116
  in ferrets 896
  in rabbits 996
  in reptiles 1035
Cockatiels *817, 838* (*see also*
    Birds)
  eyelid atresia in 839
  gout in 853

one week post-purchase
    syndrome 838
  splay leg 838
Cockatoos *818* (*see also* Birds)
  cloacal prolapse in 849
  psittacine beak and feather
    disease 852
  sarcocystosis in 848
  tapeworms in 842
Codeine 1132
  poisoning from 1200
Coenuriasis *1102*
Coenurosis
  in dogs 208
  in horses 720
Coffee weed poisoning
    1182
Coggins test *558*
Cognitive dysfunction 27
Colibacillosis
  in potbellied pigs 976
  in rabbits 994
Colic
  emergency treatment of
    1060
  in horses 603, 616, *617*
  signs of *555, 556*
Colitis-X
  in horses 624
Collagenous nevi
  in cats 506
  in dogs 271
  in horses 776
Collar galls 773
Collars
  insecticidal 1121
Collie eye anomaly 151
Collie nose 263
Coloboma
  in kittens 425
Colon
  inflammation of
    in cats 398
    in dogs 102
Colorado tick fever *1110*
Color dilution alopecia
  in dogs 242
Columnaris disease 915
Combination therapy
  as cancer treatment 1244
Comfort index 559, *560*
Common digital extensor
    tendon
  rupture of
    in horses 691
Companion animals
  and humans 1228
Complete blood count 1071

Compulsive behavior
  in cats 353
  in dogs 27
Computed tomography (CT)
    1077
Conditioning
  of cats 347
  of dogs 21
  of horses 569
Congenital deafness (*see*
    Deafness)
Congenital disorders
  affecting multiple body
    systems
    in cats 529
    in dogs 305
    in horses 794
  causes of
    in cats 529
    in dogs 306
    in horses 794
  of musculoskeletal system
    in cats 447
    in dogs 179
    in horses 669
  of nervous system
    in cats 457, 459
    in dogs 200
    in horses 710, 712
Congenital erythropoietic
    porphyria
  in cats 526
Congenital heart defects
  in cats 373
    aortic stenosis 374
    atrial septal defects 375
    cor triatriatum sinister 376
    endocardial fibroelastosis
      376
    mitral valve dysplasia 375
    patent ductus arteriosus
      374
    pulmonic stenosis 375
    tetralogy of Fallot 375
    tricuspid valve dysplasia
      375
  in dogs 58
    aortic stenosis 60
    atrial septal defects 62
    cor triatriatum dexter 64
    mitral stenosis 63
    mitral valve dysplasia 63
    patent ductus arteriosus 59
    peritoneopericardial dia-
      phragmatic hernia 64
    persistent right aortic
      arch 61
    pulmonic stenosis 60

tetralogy of Fallot 62
tricuspid dysplasia 64
ventricular septal defects 61
in horses 596
patent ductus arteriosus 597
tetralogy of Fallot 597
tricuspid dysplasia 598
ventricular septal defects 596
Congenital megaesophagus
in cats 460
Congenital papillomas
of foals 781
Congestive heart failure
in dogs 56
in hamsters 946
treatment of 1122
Conidiobolomycosis
in horses 805
Conjunctiva
in cats 427
in dogs 145
in horses 649
Conjunctivitis
in birds 843
in cats 427
in chinchillas 879
in dogs 146
in guinea pigs 933
in hamsters 948
in horses 649
in rabbits 997
in reptiles 1029
Constipation
in cats 399
in chinchillas 879
in dogs 102
in hamsters 948
in potbellied pigs 978
in sugar gliders 1044
Constricted toe syndrome 839
Contagious equine metritis 733
Contagious ecthyma
in dogs 248, 1110
Contracted flexor tendons
of foals 669
of horses 672
Contracted heel
in horses 680
Conures 818
Coonhound paralysis 202
Copper poisoning 1149
Copper-associated hepatopathy
in cats 390
in dogs 86
Coprophagia
in horses 572

Cornea
deterioration of
in cats 428
in dogs 148
ulcers of
in cats 428
in dogs 147
in horses 650
Corneal inflammation
in dogs 146
Corneal sequestration
in cats 428
Cornifying epitheliomas
in dogs 272
Corns
in horses 679
Coronavirus
infection in rats 1008
vaccination in dogs 13
Corrosive agents
poisoning from 1164
Corticosteroids 1133, 1136, 1140
for allergic asthma 440
for eye inflammation 1129
in pain management 1215
Corticotropin 130
Cortisol 130
Cor triatriatum dexter
in dogs 64
Cor triatriatum sinister
in cats 376
Cottonseed poisoning 1159
Coughs
in dogs 238
Cough suppressants 1132, 1132
Coumaphos poisoning 1169
Counterconditioning (see also
Conditioning
of cats 349
of dogs 22
of horses 570
Cowpox 1110
Coxitis
in horses 700
CPCR 1057 (see Cardio-
pulmonary-cerebral
resuscitation)
Cranial cruciate ligament tear
in cats 450
in dogs 186
Cranial nerves
of cats 457
of dogs 198
of horses 711
Craniomandibular osteopathy
in dogs 191

Crates
for travel (see Pet carriers)
Creams 1120
Cresol poisoning 1149
Creutzfeldt-Jakob disease 1116
Cribbing behavior
in horses 575
Cricopharyngeal achalasia
in dogs 84, 97
Crimean-Congo hemorrhagic
fever 1110
Crocodilians 1013 (see also
Reptiles)
Crop
burns of 838
candidiasis of 841
Crotalaria poisoning 1186
Crustacean bacteremia
in reptiles 1034
Cryptococcosis 1096
in cats 538
in dogs 314
in horses 802
Cryptorchidism
in cats 473
in dogs 218
in horses 731, 794
Cryptosporidiosis 1098
in horses 632
in reptiles 1029
CT scans (see Computed
tomography)
Culicoid hypersensitivity
in horses 762
Culture of infectious organisms 1087
Curb
in horses 697
Currying 564
Cushing's disease
in cats 420
in dogs 132, 136
in horses 643
Cutaneous asthenia (see
Ehlers-Danlos syndrome)
Cutaneous habronemiasis
in horses 770
Cutaneous lymphosarcoma
in dogs 275
in horses 778
Cutaneous mucinosis
in dogs 244
Cuterebriasis
in cats 496
in dogs 252
Cuts
management of 1065
Cyanide poisoning 1150

Cyclamen poisoning *1176*
Cyclic hematopoiesis
  of Gray Collies 52
Cysticercosis *1104*
Cystine-binding agents 1137
Cystitis
  bacterial
    in cats 517
    in dogs 288
    in horses 784
  feline idiopathic 521
  feline interstitial 521
  in potbellied pigs 982
Cystoadenocarcinomas
  in dogs 296
Cystocentesis 1073
Cysts
  of apocrine gland
    in dogs 280
  dentigerous
    in horses 607, 758
  dermoid
    in dogs 242, 273
    in horses 758, 777
  follicular
    in horses 758
  of the head and neck
    in dogs 84
    in horses 607
  of kidneys
    in cats 515
    in dogs 286
    in horses 783
  of the liver
    in cats 390, 412
    in dogs 86, 123
    in horses 608
  of the ovaries (follicular)
    in cats 474
    in dogs 220
  in pedal bones
    of horses 679
  periauricular
    in horses 758
  of prostate gland
    in dogs 220
  of the sinuses
    in horses 743
  of the skin
    in cats 507
    in dogs 273
    in horses 777
  of the stifle
    in horses 700
  subchondral
    in horses 676, 692
  subepiglottic
    in horses 754

urachal
  in cats 516
  in dogs 287
  in horses 783
Cytauxzoonosis
  in cats 364
Cytokines *165*
Cytologic tests 1071
Cytotoxic disorders
  in cats 441
  in dogs 169
  in horses 661

D

Dacryocystitis
  in cats 426
  in dogs 145
  in horses 649
Dactylogyrus infection
  in fish 914, 917
Daffodil poisoning *1176*
Dancing Doberman disease
  202
Deafness
  in cats 435
  in dogs 157
    congenital 202
  in horses 657
Dechlorinators 903
Declaw surgery 332
Decongestants 1133
  poisoning from 1190
Decubital ulcers 1068
Deer flies
  and skin disorders
    in cats 496
    in dogs 253
Defibrillation 1057
Degenerative joint disease (*see*
  Osteoarthritis)
Degenerative lumbosacral
  stenosis
  in cats 462
  in dogs 204
Degenerative valve disease
  in cats 378
  in dogs 68
  in horses 599
Degloving injuries
  management of 1068
Dehydration
  in potbellied pigs 980
  in reptiles 1031
  treatment of 1059 (*see also*
    Fluid therapy)
Demodectic mange
  in horses 770

Demodicosis
  in cats 501
  in dogs 262
Dendrodochiotoxicosis *1156,
  1159*
Dental abnormalities
  in cats 387
  in dogs 83
  in horses 607
Dental care
  for cats 342
  for chinchillas 877
  for dogs 14
  for ferrets 891
  for gerbils 922
  for hamsters 945
  for mice 956
  for potbellied pigs 974
  for rabbits 991
  for rats 1007
Dental development
  in cats 390
  in dogs 86
  in horses 609
Dental disorders
  in cats 390
  in dogs 87
  in guinea pigs 932
  in horses 610
Dentigerous cysts
  in horses 607, 758
Dentition
  of cats 333, *333*
  of dogs 6, *6*
  of horses 554, *555*, 564, *564*
Dermatitis
  in cats 489
  in dogs 240
  flea allergy
    in cats 495
    in dogs 250
    in horses 756
  nasal solar
    in dogs 263
  summer
    in horses 762
Dermatomyositis
  familial
    in dogs 245
Dermatophilosis *1096*
  in dogs 248
  in horses 760
Dermatophytosis (*see* Ringworm)
Dermatosis
  in dogs 159
  psoriasiform-lichenoid
    in dogs 243

Dermatosparaxis
  in cats 491
  in dogs 244
Dermographism
  in horses 767
Dermoid cysts
  in dogs 242, 273
  in horses 758, 777
Dermoid sinuses 758
Desensitization
  of dogs 22
  of horses 570
  of cats 349
Deskunking 1069
Desmitis
  in horses 690
Detergents
  poisoning from 1166
Dew claws 5
Deworming
  drugs for 1127
  in horses 563
  in kittens 344
  in puppies 16
Dextromethorphan 1132
Diabetes insipidus
  in cats 421
  in dogs 138
Diabetes mellitus
  in birds 843
  in cats 418
  in dogs 133
  in horses 644
  and liver disease
    in cats 412
    in dogs 123
  in reptiles 1029
Diabetic neuropathy
  in cats 460
Diagnostic imaging 1075
  for cancer 1239
  computed tomography
    (CT) 1077
  echocardiography 1076
  magnetic resonance imaging
    (MRI) 1077
  nuclear medicine imaging
    1077
  ultrasonography 1076
  x-rays 1075
Diagnostic tests 1070
  basic test panel 1074, *1074*
  blood samples 1073
  for cancer 1239
  clinical chemistry 1071
  cytology 1071
  fluid analysis 1071
  hematology 1071

histology 1070
  for infections 1080
  microbiology 1070
  serology 1071
  at specialized laboratories
    1074
  stool samples 1072
  toxicology 1071
  urinalysis 1073
  in veterinary medicine 1072
Diaphragmatic hernias
  in cats 480
  in dogs 64, 230
  in horses 740
Diarrhea
  and antibiotics 1126
  in cats 384
  in chinchillas 879
  in dogs 7, 78
  drugs for *1126*
  in foals 625
  in guinea pigs 932
  in hamsters 946
  in horses 602, 621, *621*
  in mice 957
  in potbellied pigs 976, 977
  in prairie dogs 967
  in rabbits 994
  treatment of 1126
Diazepam poisoning 1195
Diazinon poisoning 1169
DIC (*see* Disseminated
    intravascular coagula-
    tion)
Dichlorvos poisoning 1169
Dicrocoeliasis *1100*
Diet
  of amphibians 867
  of birds 830
  of cats 337
  of chinchillas 875
  of dogs 10, *16*
  of ferrets 890
  of fish 905
  of gerbils 921
  of guinea pigs 928
  of hamsters 942
  of horses 559
  of mice 955
  of potbellied pigs 972
  of puppies 16
  of rabbits 987
  of rats 1005
  of reptiles 1022
  of sugar gliders 1041, *1041*
Digestive disorders
  in cats 383
    amebiasis 405

campylobacteriosis 402
    coccidiosis 406
    constipation 399
    feline enteric coronavirus
      399
    gastritis 400
    giardiasis 407
    inflammation of the large
      intestine 398
    inflammatory bowel dis-
      ease 401
    malabsorption 402
    obstruction 400
    Salmonella infection 403
    Tyzzer's disease 403
    ulcers 401
  in chinchillas 879
  in dogs 77
    amebiasis 115
    bloat 103
    campylobacteriosis 109
    coccidiosis 116
    constipation 102
    diarrhea 78
    gastritis 104
    gastrointestinal parasites
      110, *111*
    giardiasis 116
    Helicobacter infection
      109
    hemorrhagic gastroenteri-
      tis 106
    inflammation of the large
      intestine 102
    inflammatory bowel dis-
      ease 107
    obstruction 104
    parvovirus 101
    Salmonella infection 109
    tumors 104
    Tyzzer's disease 110
    ulcers 106
    vomiting 100
  drugs for 1124
  in hamsters 946
  in horses 602
    colic 616
    cryptosporidiosis 632
    giardiasis 632
    obstructions 615
    tumors 626
  in mice 956
  in rabbits 993
Digestive system
  of cats 333
  of dogs 6, 77
  of horses 555, 602
Dilated pores of Winer 507

Dilated cardiomyopathy
  in cats 378
  in dogs 69
  in ferrets 898
Dinitrocresol poisoning 1162
Dinitrophenol poisoning 1162
Dioctophymosis (giant kidney
    worm infection) *1106*
  in dogs 289
Dioxin poisoning 1160, 1162
Diphyllobothriasis (fish tape-
    worm infection) *1102*
Dipylidiasis (dog tapeworm
    infection) *1102*
Diquat poisoning 1162
Dirofilariasis (*see* Heartworm
    infection)
Dishwasher detergents
  poisoning from 1164
Diskospondylitis
  in cats 462
  in dogs 205
Dislocations
  in horses 701
    emergency care 1061
Disseminated intravascular
    coagulation (DIC)
  in cats 367
  in dogs 48
  in horses 588
Distemper
  in cats (*see* Feline panleuko-
    penia)
  in dogs 309
  in ferrets 894
  in horses 753
  vaccination
    in cats *339*
    in dogs *13*
Distributive shock 1055
Diuretics 1137, *1138*
  poisoning from 1195
Diverticula
  esophageal
    in cats 397
    in dogs 84, 99
d-Limonene
  poisoning from 1169
DNA vaccines 1143
Dogs 2
  actinobacillosis in 306
  actinomycosis in 307
  activity levels of 7
  Addison's disease in 132
  aggression in 18, 25
  allergic rhinitis in 168
  allergies in 245
  amyloidosis in 307

anal glands of 7
anaphylactic reactions in
    167
anemia in 37, 169
anterior uveitis in 171
arthritis in 172
aspergillosis in 174, 312
atopy in 169
autoimmune adrenalitis in
    173
autoimmune thyroiditis in
    173
babesiosis in 42
behavior modification tech-
    niques 19
behavior of 17, 24
behavior problems 17, 25, 27
    medications for 23, *23*
bleeding disorders in 46
blood clotting disorders in
    50
blood disorders in 33
blood types of 37
blood vessel disorders in 53,
    76
boarding facilities for 1227
body temperature regulation
    303
bone disorders in 190
bone marrow disease in 41
botulism in 309
breeding of 15
bronchitis in 168, 237
bullous pemphigoid in 170
candidiasis in 313
canine herpesvirus in 50
canine juvenile cellulitis in
    158
canine rheumatoid arthritis
    in 172
cardiovascular disease in
    53
cell-mediated immune reac-
    tions in 172
Chagas' disease in 44
coccidioidomycosis (Valley
    fever) in 313
combined immunodeficiency
    disease 174
compulsive disorders in 27
congenital heart defects in
    58
congenital skin disorders in
    242
congestive heart failure in
    56
conjunctivitis in 146
constipation in 102

contact hypersensitivity in 173
cryptococcosis in 314
Cushing's disease in 132, 136
cytotoxic disorders in 169
deafness of 157
dental care for 14
dental development in 86
dermatitis in 240
dermatophilosis 248
dermatosis in 159
diabetes mellitus in 133
diet of 10, *16*, 168
digestive disorders in 77, *80*
digestive system of 6, 77
diseases affecting multiple
    systems 305
dry eye in 145
ear disorders of 155
Ehlers-Danlos syndrome in
    50
ehrlichiosis in 310
Elokomin fluke fever in 325
emergency care of 1051
encephalitis in 173
endocrine diseases
  of the liver 123
enterotoxemia in 311
esophageal disorders in 97
estrous cycle in *15*
exercise for 11
eye disorders of 140
eyelash abnormalities 144
eyelid disorders of 143
false pregnancy in 27
fearful behavior in 27
flea infestations 249
food allergies in 168
frostbite 159
fungal infections in 312
gall bladder disorders in
    120, 125
gammopathies in 175
gastrointestinal disorders
    100
gastrointestinal parasites
    in 110
genetic storage diseases in
    300, *301*
giving medication to 12
glanders (farcy) in 317
glaucoma in 149, 1064
glomerulonephritis in 171
granulomatous reactions
    in 173
grooming of 5, 14
hair loss (alopecia) of 242,
    255
hair of 5

hearing of 4
heart disorders in 53
heart failure in 65
heartworm disease in 73
heat stroke in 3, 1052
hemophilia in 47
hepatozoonosis in 43
hernias in 84, 85
herpesvirus infection in 310
histoplasmosis in 314
hives and skin rashes 168,
    256
hormonal disorders of 128
household hazards for 15
housetraining of 16, 16, 26
housing for 10
hyperactivity in 27
hyperadrenocorticism in
    132, 136
hypercalcemia in135, 136
hypertension in 73
hypoadrenocorticism in 132
hypocalcemia in 137
hypothermia in 1052
hypothyroidism in 139
immune disorders in 164
immune-mediated arthritis
    in 172
immune-mediated diseases
    in 159
immune system tumors in
    175
immunoglobulin deficiency
    in 174
importing of 1220
infectious hepatitis in 318
itching in 258
jaundice in 125
joint disorders in 183
keratoconjunctivitis sicca in
    145, 173
kidney disorders in 285
lagenidiosis in 316
lameness in 178
lead poisoning in 1170
leishmaniasis in 318
leptospirosis in 319
leukemia in 41, 52
lice infestations 259
liver disorders in 120
lupus in 171
Lyme disease in 320
lymphoma in 45, 52
malignant hyperthermia in
    304
marking behavior of 26
megaesophagus in 98
melioidosis in 321

meningitis in 172
metabolic disorders in
    300
motion sickness in 211
muscular fatigue in 303
musculoskeletal disorders
    in 176
myasthenia gravis in 170
mycetomas in 315
nails of 4
nasal allergies in 168
nasal cavity disorders in 144
neosporosis in 322
nervous system disorders
    of 194
nocardiosis in 322
North American blastomy-
    cosis in 315
nutritional requirements
    10
obesity in 11
oral tumors in 94
outdoor dogs 10, 10
pancreatic disorders in 117
panting in 3
parasite control 13
parvovirus in 101
pemphigus foliaceus in 170
pemphigus in 144
pemphigus vulgaris in 170
pericardial disease in 72
peritonitis in 323
phaeohyphomycosis in 316
pharyngeal disorders in 97
phobias in 19, 27
PIE (pulmonary infiltration
    with eosinophilia)
    syndrome in 168
plague in 323
plasmacytic-lymphocytic
    synovitis in 172
platelet disorders in 48
poisoning in 1145
polycythemia in 52
puppy care 15
pythiosis in 316
rabies in 211, 1222
rectal and anal disorders in
    125
reproduction of 15, 215
reproductive disorders of
    214
respiratory disorders in
    224
rhinosporidiosis in 317
Rocky Mountain spotted
    fever in 50, 324
salivary disorders in 95

salmon poisoning disease
    in 325
seborrhea in 159
selecting 7, 9
senility in 27
senses of 3
separation anxiety in 27
signs of illness in 12, 167,
    168, 175
signs of pain in 1213
skin allergies in 169
skin disorders in 170, 238
skin of 5
skin tumors in 269
spaying/neutering of 15
sporotrichosis in 317
Surra in 44
tear duct disorders in 144,
    145
teeth of 6, 6
temperament of 7, 9, 11
tetanus in 207, 326
thrombocytopenia in 48
tick infestations of 268
toxoplasmosis in 326
training of 16, 20
travel with 1216
trichinellosis (trichinosis)
    in 327
trypanosomiasis in 44
tuberculosis in 327
tularemia in 328
urinary tract disorders in
    283
urinary tract infections 1137
urination problems in 298
vaccination of 12, 13
vasculitis in 171
veterinary care of 9, 11
vision in 3, 141
vomiting in 100
working dogs 1230
Dog tapeworm infection 1102
Dog trainers
    selecting 20
Dominance aggression
    in dogs 25
Dominance behavior
    in dogs 18
    in horses 567
Dopamine antagonists 1132
Dopaminergic agents 1132
Dorsal displacement of soft
    palate
    in horses 743
Dourine
    in horses 587, 736
Doves 818

Dracunculus infection *1106*
  in cats 502
  in dogs 263
Dropped hock (*See* Achilles
    tendon disruption)
Drugs 1118
  administering in animals
    1119
  analgesics 1130, *1131*
  angiotensin-converting
    enzyme (ACE) inhibitors
    1122
  antacids 1125
  anthelmintics 1127
  antiarrhythmics 1123
  anticholinergic 1126, 1133
  anticoagulants 1124
  anticonvulsant 1130, *1130*
  antidepressants 1131
  antidiarrheal *1126*
  antiemetic 1125, *1125*
  antifungal 1134, 1137
  antihistamines 1134,
    1135, 1139
  anti-inflammatory 1133 (*see
    also* Nonsteroidal anti-
    inflammatory drugs)
  antineoplastic chemother-
    apy 1140
  antiparasitic 1134
  antipsychotics 1131
  antiulcerative *1126*
  antiviral 1088, 1138, *1139*
  anxiolytics 1131
  and appetite 1124, *1124*
  applied to skin 1120
  arterial dilators 1123
  benzimadazoles 1127
  bronchodilators 1132, *1133*
  for cancer treatment
    1140, *1141*
  for cardiovascular disease
    1122, *1123*
  cathartics 1127, *1127*
  chondroprotective agents
    1140
  corticosteroids 1133, 1140
  cough suppressants 1132,
    1132
  decongestants 1133
  for diarrhea 1126
  for digestive disorders 1124
  diuretics 1137, *1138*
  emetic 1125, *1125*
  essential fatty acids 1135
  expectorants 1133
  extralabel use of 1118
  for eye disorders 1128

  for fish 906
  for glaucoma 1128
  for hamsters 944
  for heartworms 1124
  hematinics 1124
  hemostatics 1124
  histamine (H$_2$)-receptor
    antagonists 1125
  hormonal treatment 1136
  immune system modulators
    1136
  immunotherapy 1143
  implants 1120
  for inflammation 1139
  injectable types of 1120
  insecticidal collars 1121
  for kidney disease or failure
    1136
  laxatives 1127, *1127*
  macrocyclic lactones
    1128, 1134
  mood-stabilizing 1131
  mucus-producing 1133
  muscle relaxants *1129*
  for musculoskeletal disor-
    ders 1129
  for nervous system disorders
    712, 1130
  nonsteroidal anti-inflamma-
    tory drugs (NSAIDs)
    1126, 1140
  organophosphates 1128
  for pain management in
    cancer 1245
  patches 1121
  positive inotropes 1122
  prescription of 1119
  prokinetic 1127, *1127*
  psychotropic agents 1130,
    1136
  regulation of 1118
  for reproductive disorders
    1131
  for reptiles 1026
  for respiratory disorders
    1132
  sedatives 1130, *1131*
  for skin disorders 1134, *1135*
  spot-on formulations 1121
  steroids *1130* (*see also*
    Corticosteroids)
  tetrahydropyrimidines 1128
  topical types of 1120
  tranquilizers 1130, *1131*
  transdermal delivery gels
    1121
  for treatment of parasites
    1127

  for urinary disorders 1136,
    1138
  vasoactive 1123
  venous dilators 1123
  for vomiting 1124, *1125*
Dry eye
  in cats 427
  in dogs 145
  in horses 649
Dry mouth (*see* Xerostomia)
Dummy foal syndrome 721
Dust baths
  for chinchillas 875
  for gerbils 921
Dusting powders 1120
Dysautonomia
  in cats 464
  in dogs 207
  in horses 718
Dyschondroplasia
  in dogs 179
Dysecdysis (*see also* Ecdysis)
  in reptiles 1033
Dysfibrinogenemia 47
Dyskeratomas
  warty
    in dogs 271
Dysplasia
  black hair follicle
    in dogs 243
  of the elbow
    in dogs 184
  of the hip
    in cats 449
    in dogs 184
Dystocia (abnormal labor and
    delivery)
  in cats 471, 474
  in dogs 216, 220
  in guinea pigs 936
  in horses 1063

E

Ear disorders
  of cats 433
    hematomas 435
    otitis externa 437
    otitis interna 437
    otitis media 437
    pinna (outer ear) 435
    polyps 438
    solar dermatitis 436
  of chinchillas 879
  deafness (*see* Deafness)
  of dogs 155
    canine juvenile cellulitis 158
    caused by insects 158

dermatosis 159
fly strike (fly bites) 158
hematomas 158
otitis externa 160
otitis interna 161
otitis media 161
pinna (outer ear) 158
ruptured ear drum 162
seborrhea 159
tumors 163, 437
of horses 655
aural plaques 658
caused by insects 657
fly strike (fly bites) 658
otitis externa 659
otitis interna 659
otitis media 659
pinna (outer ear) 657
Eardrum
ruptured
in dogs 162
Ear hematomas
in cats 435
in dogs 158
Ear infections
in cats 434
in dogs 156
in guinea pigs 933
Ear mites (*see also* Mites)
of cats 501
of dogs 261
of ferrets 895
of rabbits 1001
Ears
cleaning of
in dogs 161, *162*
disorders of (*see* Ear disorders)
examination of
in cats 434
in dogs 156, 160, 161
in horses 657
parasites of
in cats 435
in dogs 158
in horses 657
structure of
in cats 433
in dogs 155
in horses 655
tumors of
in cats 437
in dogs 163
Ear ticks
of cats 437
of dogs 159
of horses 659
Earwax gland tumors
of cats 438

of dogs 163
Easter lily poisoning *1176*
Eastern equine encephalomyelitis *1110*
Ebola hemorrhagic fever *1110*
Eccrine gland
tumors of
in dogs 281
Ecdysis 1026
Echinococcosis *1102*
in dogs 209
Echinostomiasis *1100*
Echocardiography *57*, 1076
Eclampsia (*see* Puerperal
hypocalcemia)
Eclectus parrots *818*
Ectopic ureter
in cats 516
in dogs 286
in horses 783
Ectropion
in cats 425
in dogs 143
Edema
malignant
in horses 808
Egg binding 849
Ehlers-Danlos syndrome
in cats 368, 492
in dogs 50, 244
in horses 589
Ehrlichiosis *1094*
in cats 532
in dogs 310
equine granulocytic (*see*
Anaplasmosis)
and spinal cord dysfunction
in dogs 205
Elbow
bursitis of
in horses 677
dislocation of
in dogs 187
disorders of
in horses 694
dysplasia
in dogs 184
fractures of
in horses 695
Electrocardiography *57*
Electrocution 1068
Electroencephalogram 199
Electromyogram 199
Elokomin fluke fever
in dogs 325
Embolism
in horses 601
Embolus 76

Emergencies 1050 (*see also*
Emergency care)
electrocution 1068
lightning strikes 1068
preparing for 1050, *1053*
Emergency care
of dogs and cats 1051
airway blockage 1054
breathing difficulties 1054
cardiopulmonary-cerebral
resuscitation (CPCR)
1051, 1057
fluid therapy 1058
nursing care 1058
nutrition 1058
pain control 1058
at scene of injury 1051
shock 1055
transport 1053
with trauma 1055
evaluating need for *1051*
eye emergencies 1063
first aid kits for 1050, *1050*
of horses 1059
esophageal obstruction 1062
foal emergencies 1063
fractures 1061
head injuries 1062
postcastration eviscera-
tion 1063
transport 1060
traumatic injuries 1061
of insect bites or stings 1069
of minor injuries 1069
veterinary evaluation of
injuries 1053
Emetic drugs 1125, *1125*
Emphysema
in cats 481
in dogs 231
Emulsifiers
poisoning from 1170
Emulsions 1119, 1120
Enamel defects of the teeth
in cats 393
in dogs 90
Enamel points
in horses 611
Encephalitis
in cats 466
Central European tickborne
1110
in dogs 173, 210
Far eastern tickborne (Russian spring-summer
encephalitis) *1112*
in horses 718, 722
Japanese B *1112*

Encephalitis (*continued*)
LaCrosse *1112*
Murray Valley *1114*
St. Louis *1116*
Encephalitozoonosis
in rabbits 1003
Encephalomyelitis
Eastern equine *1110*
in horses 724
vaccination in horses *562*
Venezuelan equine *1116*
Western equine *1116*
Encephalomyocarditis *1110*
Encephalopathy
neonatal
in horses 721
Endocardial fibroelastosis
in cats 376, 379
in dogs 71
Endocarditis
in dogs 71
in horses 600
Endocrine disorders (*see*
Hormonal disorders)
Endocrine system
of cats 415
of dogs 128
of horses 641
Endodontic disease
in cats 391
in dogs 89
Endurance events
and fatigue
in horses 791
Entamoeba invadens infections
in reptiles 1029
Enteric coronavirus
in cats 399
Enterocolitis
clostridia-associated
in horses 806
Enteroliths
in horses 620
Enterotoxemia
in dogs 311
in foals 807
in rabbits 994
Entropion
in cats 425
in dogs 143
in horses 648
Enzootic calcinosis
in horses 674
Eosinopenia
in cats 369
in dogs 51
Eosinophil *165*

Eosinophilia (*see also* Tropical
eosinophilia)
in cats 369
in dogs 51
in horses 590
Eosinophilic granuloma complex
in cats 493
in dogs 248
in horses 760
Eosinophilic plaques
in cats 493
Eosinophilic ulcers
in cats 493
Eosinophils 35
Eperythrozoonosis *1094*
Ephedrine poisoning 1191
Epidermal hamartomas
in dogs 271
Epidermolysis bullosa syndromes
in cats 492
in dogs 244
in horses 759
Epididymis
inflammation of
in cats 473
in dogs 218
Epiglottis
entrapment of
in horses 744
Epilepsy
in dogs 200
drugs for 1130
in gerbils 924
in horses 713
Epinephrine *130*, 1124
Epiphora
in cats 426
Epitheliogenesis imperfecta
in cats 491
in dogs 242
in horses 758
Epitheliomas
cornifying
in dogs 272
Epizootic catarrhal enteritis
in ferrets 894
Epizootic lymphangitis
in horses 802
Epsiprantel 1128
Epulides
in cats 395
in dogs 94
Equine aural plaques 658
Equine coital exanthema 734
Equine degenerative myeloencephalopathy 713, 716

Equine dysautonomia 718
Equine granulocytic ehrlichiosis 796
Equine herpesvirus infection
744
Equine herpesvirus-1 myeloencephalopathy 717
Equine infectious anemia
716, 799
Equine influenza 745
Equine leukoencephalomalacia 1155
Equine morbillivirus pneumonia 746, 799
Equine motor neuron disease
716
Equine protozoal myeloen-
cephalitis 717, 719
Equine recurrent uveitis
(periodic ophthalmia,
moon blindness) 651,
662, 807
Equine rhinopneumonitis
as cause of abortion in
mares 732
Equine sarcoids 655, 776
Equine ulcerative keratomycosis
in horses 650
Equine venereal balanitis 734
Equine viral arteritis 746, 800
as cause of abortion in
mares 733
Equine viral encephalomyelitis 718
Equine viral rhinopneumonitis 744
vaccination in horses *562*
Ergotism *1156*
Erysipelas
in potbellied pigs 982
Erysipeloid *1090*
Erythrocytes 33
Erythropoietin 34
Escherichia coli infection *1090*
in hamsters 947
in rabbits 994
Esophageal disorders
in cats 397
in dogs 97
in horses 613
Esophageal diverticula
in cats 388, 397
in dogs 84, 99
Esophageal obstruction
in horses 613, 1062
Esophageal strictures
in cats 397

in dogs 98
in horses 614
Esophageal worms
in dogs *111*
Esophagitis
in cats 397
in dogs 99
Esophagus
inflammation of (*see*
Esophagitis)
Essential fatty acids 1135
Estrogen *131*
Estrous (heat) cycle
of cats 470
of dogs *15*, 215
of horses 565, 727
Ethanol poisoning 1163
Ethmoid hematoma
in horses 743
Ethylene glycol poisoning
1150
Eumycotic mycetomas
in cats 539
in dogs 315
Europe
travel with pets to 1220
European Union pet passport
program 1221
Euthanasia 1232
for animals with cancer 1248
Exercise
for birds 831
for cats 337
for dogs 11
for ferrets 890
for gerbils 921
for guinea pigs 929
for hamsters 943
for horses 560
for potbellied pigs 972
for sugar gliders 1042
Exercise-induced pulmonary
hemorrhage
in horses 747
Exertional myopathy (rhabdomyolysis)
in dogs 189
in horses 704, 789
Exocrine pancreatic insufficiency
in cats 408
in dogs 118
Expectorants 1133
Eye disorders
of birds 843
of cats 423
of anterior uvea 428
cancer and tumors 432

cataracts 429
chorioretinitis 430
conjunctivitis 427
corneal ulcers 428
dry eye 427
eyeworm disease 432
glaucoma 429
interstitial keratitis 428
lens displacement 430
optic atrophy 431
optic nerve hypoplasia 431
progressive retinal atrophy
430
prolapse of the eye 431
ruptured blood vessels 427
tear sac inflammation
(dacrocystitis) 426
of dogs 140
of anterior uvea 148
cancer and tumors 154
cataracts 149, *150*
cherry eye 144
chorioretinitis 152
Collie eye anomaly 151
conjunctivitis 146
corneal inflammation 146
corneal ulcers 147
dry eye 145
eyeworm disease 154
glaucoma 149
interstitial keratitis 147
of the iris 148
lens displacement 150
optic atrophy 153
optic nerve hypoplasia 152
orbital cellulitis 153
papilledema 153
progressive retinal atrophy
151
prolapse of the eye 153
retinal degeneration 152
retinal detachments 152
ruptured blood vessels 146
tear sac inflammation
(dacrocystitis) 145
drugs for 1128
of horses 646
of anterior uvea 650
cancer and tumors 654
cataracts 652
conjunctivitis 649
corneal ulcers 650
dry eye 649
eyeworm disease 654
from flies 763
glaucoma 652
lens displacement 652
optic nerve hypoplasia 653

prolapse of the eye 653
retinal detachments 653
tear sac inflammation
(dacrocystitis) 649
of rabbits 996
of reptiles 1029
Eye emergencies 1063
bleeding in the eye 1064
foreign objects in the eye
1064
glaucoma 1064
injuries to the cornea 1064
lacerations 1064
lens dislocation 1065
penetrating injuries 1064
retinal degeneration or
detachment 1065
traumatic proptosis 1063
vision loss 1065
Eye flukes
in fish 912
Eye gnats
in dogs 252
in horses 763
Eye infections
drugs for 1128
Eye injuries 1063 (*see also* Eye
emergencies)
of horses 1061
Eyelash abnormalities
in cats 425
in dogs 144
Eyelids
disorders of
in cats 425
in dogs 143
in horses 648
structure
in cats 424
in dogs 142
in horses 647
tumors of
in cats 432
in dogs 154
Eyes
cancer of
in cats 432
in dogs 154
in horses 654
of cats 423
disorders of (*see* Eye disorders)
of dogs 140
of horses 646
prolapse of
in cats 431
in dogs 153
in horses 653

Eye trauma
  treatment of 1129
Eyeworms
  in cats 432
  in dogs 154
  in horses 654

F

Fabric softeners
  poisoning from 1166
Face flies
  in horses 763
Facial nerve injuries (*see also*
    Facial paralysis)
  in horses 715
Facial paralysis
  in cats 464
  in dogs 208
  in horses 720
Fading syndrome
  in puppies 310
False pregnancy (pseudo-
    pregnancy)
  in cats 474
  in dogs 27, 220
False strangles 591
Familial dermatomyositis
  in dogs 245
Familial footpad hyperkerato-
    sis
  in dogs 243
Familial vasculopathy
  in dogs 245
Famotidine poisoning 1193
Fanconi syndrome
  in dogs 295
Farcy (*see* Glanders)
Far eastern tickborne encepha-
    litis *1112*
Farrowing box 975
Fascioliasis *1100*
Fasciolopsiasis *1100*
Fatigue
  in dogs 303
  in horses 790
Fatty acids 1135
Fatty liver disease
  in birds 838
Fear
  behavior problems in dogs
    27
Feather cysts 850
Feather mites 852 (*see also*
    Mites)
Feathers
  damage to *853*
  disorders of 850

ear coverts 822
  loss of *853*
  maintenance of 825
  molting of 825
  plucking of 850, *851*
  types of 825
Federal agencies
  pet travel regulation by *1219*,
    1220, 1224
Feed hoppers 986
Feed intoxications
  of fish 913
Feline acromegaly 421
Feline atopy 493
Feline Bowen's disease 512
Feline calicivirus 481
  vaccination *339*
Feline chlamydiosis 486
  vaccination *339*
Feline demodicosis 501
Feline distemper 536
Feline enteric coronavirus 399
Feline gingivitis/stomatitis
    syndrome 391
Feline herpesviral rhinotra-
    cheitis 481
Feline herpesvirus type 1
  vaccination *339*
Feline idiopathic cystitis 521
Feline immunodeficiency
    virus 444
  vaccination *339*
Feline infectious anemia 365
Feline infectious enteritis 536
Feline infectious peritonitis
    411, 462, 532
  vaccination *340*
Feline interstitial cystitis 521
Feline leukemia 369
Feline leukemia virus 444, 533
  myelopathy associated
    with 462
  vaccination *340*
Feline lower urinary tract
    disease (FLUTD) *517*
Feline lymphosarcoma-
    leukemia complex 433
Feline miliary dermatitis 495
Feline odontoclastic resorp-
    tive lesions (FORL) 392
Feline panleukopenia 536
Feline progressive polyarthri-
    tis 450
Feline respiratory disease
    complex 481, *482*
Feline scabies 500
Feline solar dermatitis 436
Feline stomatitis 393

Feline viral rhinotracheitis
  vaccination *339*
FeLV (*see* Feline leukemia
    virus)
Femoral nerve injuries
  in horses 715
Fentanyl poisoning 1200
Ferrets 886
  Aleutian disease in 895
  bacterial disease in 894
  biting by *889*
  bot fly larvae in 896
  breeding of 893
  broken bones in 892
  cancer in 896
  canine distemper in 894
  claw trimming 891
  coccidiosis in 896
  dental care for 891
  diet of 890, *890*
  dilated cardiomyopathy in
    898
  ear care for 892
  ear mites in 895
  emergency care for 892, *893*
  enlarged spleen in 897
  epizootic catarrhal enteritis
    in 894
  exercise for 890
  flea infestations of 895
  fungal disease in 895
  grooming 892
  hairballs 892
  health care for 891
  heartworm disease in 896
  hormonal disorders in 897
  household hazards 887, *887*
  housing for *887*, 889
  hyperadrenocorticism in 897
  infectious diseases of 894
  influenza in 894
  insulinomas in 897
  intestinal blockage in 892
  kidney disease in 898
  life span of 887, *887*
  mange in 895
  nutritional requirements
    of 890
  ownership restrictions 889
  reproduction of 893
  ringworm in 895
  signs of illness in 892, *893*
  sleeping habits of 891
  spaying or neutering 893
  swallowed objects in 898
  teeth of 891
  temperament of 890
  transporting 891

tumors of 896
vaccination of 891
veterinary care for 891,
    892, *893*
viral diseases in 894
Fescue foot *1156*
Fescue grass poisoning
  as cause of abortion in
    mares 732
Fescue poisoning 1155, *1190*
Fetlock disorders
  in horses 687
Fever
  causes of *1080*, 1080
  purpose of 1080
  in reptiles and amphibians
    1080
Fever of unknown origin 1081
  in cats 527
  in dogs 303
  in horses 792
Fibroblastic tumors
  in cats 506
  in dogs 271
Fibroma
  in cats 506
  in dogs 271
  gingival
    in cats 395
    in dogs 94
Fibromatosis
  in cats 510
  in dogs 279
  in horses 777
Fibrosarcoma
  in cats 510
  in dogs 279
  vaccine-associated
    in cats 339, 511, 1144
Fibrosis of the liver
  in dogs 122, 124
Fibrotic myopathy
  in dogs 188
Fibrous histiocytomas
  in cats 509
  in dogs 278
  in horses 779
Fibrous osteodystrophy
  in dogs 181
Filters
  for aquariums 902
    maintenance of 907
Finches *818* (*see also* Birds)
  tapeworms in 842
Fins
  of fish 899
First aid
  for minor injuries 1069

First aid kits 1050, *1050*
Fish 899
  and ammonia 911, 913
  anchor worms in 917
  anemia in 911
  aquariums for 900
  bacterial infections of 917
  bone and muscle disorders
    in 912
  branchiomycosis in 914
  breeding of 908
  cancer in 919
  and carbon dioxide 914
  care of young 909
  carp pox in 915
  circulatory disorders of 910
  columnaris disease in 915
  determining sex of 908
  diet of 905, 913
  digestive disorders of 912
  emergency treatment for 908
  eye disorders of 912
  feeding 905, 913
  fry 908, 909
  fungal diseases of 918
  gas bubble disease in 911,
    913
  gill disorders in 913
  herpesvirus in 914
  hydrogen sulfide in 914
  ich (white spot disease) in
    915
  importing of 1220
  intestinal parasites of 912
  kidney disease 917
  and leeches 912, 917
  lice on 917
  lymphocystis disease in
    915
  medication for 906
  mycobacteriosis in 918
  neurologic disorders in 913
  new tank syndrome in 911
  nurseries for 909
  nutritional deficiencies in
    912, 913
  nutritional requirements
    of 905
  old tank syndrome in 911
  parasites of 912, 916
  ponds 900
  preventing disease in 906, 907
  reproduction of 908
  selecting 901
  senses of 900
  separating 909
  signs of illness in 901, 906,
    906

skin and gill parasites of 914,
    915, 917
skin disorders of 914
skin slime in 916
sunburn of 915
tapeworms in 912
tropical (*see* Tropical fish)
vaccination of 908, 1144
velvet disease in 915
veterinary care for 899
vibriosis in 918
Fish hook injuries 1069
Fish lice 917
Fish tanks (*see* Aquariums)
Fistulous withers
  in horses 677
Flail chest 1056
Flatworms
  in reptiles 1037
  treatment of 1127
Flea allergy dermatitis
  in cats 495
  in dogs 250
Flea collars
  insecticidal 1121
  skin irritation from 1169
Fleas
  in cats *341*, 494
  in dogs 249
  in ferrets 895
  life cycle of 249
  in mice 959
  in rabbits 1002
  in rats 1009
  in sugar gliders 1046
  treatment of 1134
Flesh flies
  in horses 763
Flexor tendon deformities
  of foals 669
  of horses 672
Flies
  as a cause of ear irritation
    in dogs 158
    in horses 658
  and disease transmission
    in cats 496
    in dogs 251
    in horses 761
  and skin disorders
    in cats 496
    in dogs 251
    in horses 761
Floating
  of the teeth
    in horses 610
Flu (*see* Influenza)
Fluid analysis 1071

Fluid therapy
  for dogs and cats 1058
  for horses 1059
Flukes
  in cats *341*, 341, *405*, *406*
  in dogs 114, *115*
  lung
    in cats 483
    in dogs 232
  and nervous system
      disorders
    in cats 465
    in dogs 209
Fluoride poisoning 1151
Fluoxetine poisoning 1196
FLUTD (*see* Feline lower uri-
    nary tract disease)
Fluvoxamine poisoning
    1196
Fly bites
  in horses *657*
Fly control
  for horses 563
Fly strike
  in cats 496
  in dogs 158, 253
  in horses 658, 764
Foal heat diarrhea 625
Foal pneumonia 747
Foaling
  preparations for 729
Foal rejection 575
Foals (*see also* Horses)
  care of 565
  emergency care 1063
  hypothyroidism in 645
  socialization of 566
  vaccinations for 566
Follicle-stimulating hormone
    130
Follicular cysts
  in cats 474
  in dogs 220
  in horses 758
Food allergies
  in cats 440, 493
  in dogs 168, 246
  in horses 759
Food and Drug Administration
    (FDA) *963*, 1118
Foot-and-mouth disease
    1112
Foot injuries
  in horses 684
Footpad hyperkeratosis
  in dogs 243
Forage
  for horses 559

Foreign objects
  in esophagus
    in cats 397
    in dogs 99
  in the eye 1064
  first aid for, in dogs and
      cats 1052
  swallowing of 1069
Formamidines 1135
Founder (*see* Laminitis)
Fourth branchial arch
    defect
  in horses 742
Fractures
  in birds 843
  of the bone
    in cats 453
    in dogs 193
    in hamsters 948
  of cannon bones
    in horses 691
  of the carpal bones
    in horses 690
  in chinchillas 884
  of the elbow bones
    in horses 695
  emergency care
    in horses 1061
  of fetlock
    in horses 687
  of the hock
    in horses 697
  of the joint
    in dogs 187
  of long pastern bone
    in horses 687
  of navicular bone
    in horses 681
  of the pelvis
    in horses 701
  in potbellied pigs 978
  in reptiles 1027
  of short pastern bone
    in horses 687
  of shoulder bones
    in horses 695
  of the splint bones
    in horses 691
  of stifle
    in horses 699
  of the tarsus
    in horses 697
  of the vertebrae
    in horses 701
Fragile skin syndrome
  in cats 513
Frogs 864 (*see also* Amphibi-
    ans)

Frostbite
  in dogs 159
  in horses 658
Frounce 842
Fumes
  dangers to birds from 857
Fumonisin poisoning 1155
Fungal infections 1086
  in cats 537
  in dogs 312
  drugs for 1134
  in ferrets 895
  in fish 918
  in horses 801
  transmitted to people *1096*
Fungal pneumonia
  in cats 486
  in dogs 234, *235*
Fungal poisoning 1154, *1156*
Fungal stomatitis
  in cats 394
  in dogs 92
Fur
  of cats *333*, 333
Fur chewing (*see also* Barber-
    ing)
  in chinchillas 882
  in rabbits 993
Fur mites 951, 1001 (*see also*
    Mites)
Fur slip 873
Furuncles 247
Fusariotoxicosis 1158

G

Gait
  of horses 552
  evaluation of 711
Gallbladder disorders
  in cats 409
    cholecystitis 413
    gallstones 413
    rupture 414
  in dogs 120
    cholecystitis 125
    gallstones 125
    rupture 125
Gallstones
  in cats 413
  in dogs 125
  in horses 636
Gammopathies
  in cats 445
  in dogs 175
Gapeworms 848
Gas bubble disease 910, 912,
    913

Gasoline poisoning 1173
Gastric ulcers (*see also* Gastrointestinal ulcers)
 in horses 614
Gastrinomas
 in dogs 134
Gastritis
 in cats 400
 in dogs 104
Gastrocnemius rupture
 in horses 698
Gastrodiscoidiasis *1100*
Gastroenteritis
 in chinchillas 880
 hemorrhagic
  in dogs 106
Gastroesophageal reflux
 in horses 615
Gastrointestinal disorders (*see* Digestive disorders)
Gastrointestinal drugs 1124
 poisoning from 1193
Gastrointestinal obstruction
 in cats 400
 in dogs 104
 in horses 615
Gastrointestinal parasites
 in cats 403
  flukes 405
  hookworms 405
  roundworms 403
  tapeworms 405
 in dogs 110
  flukes 114
  hookworms 112
  roundworms 110
  tapeworms 114
  whipworms 114
 in horses 629
  ascarids 629
  bots 629
  large strongyles 631
  small strongyles 631
  tapeworms 632
 in reptiles 1028
Gastrointestinal tract (*see* Digestive system)
Gastrointestinal ulcers (*see also* Gastric ulcers)
 in cats 401
 in dogs 106, *106*
Geckos 1014 (*see also* Lizards)
Gene-deleted vaccines 1143
Generalized disease
 in cats 528
 in dogs 305
 in horses 793

Genetics
 and cancer 1236
 and metabolic disorders
  of cats 526
  of dogs 301
Genetic storage diseases
 in cats 526, *526*
 in dogs 301, *301*
Genital horsepox (*see* Equine coital exanthema)
Geotrichosis
 in dogs 314
Gerbils 919
 amyloid deposits 925
 aural cholesteatoma 925
 breeding 922
 broken bones of 923
 cages for 920
 dental care 922
 diet of 921
 digestive disorders 922
 diseases transmitted to people from *925*
 exercise for 921
 hair loss in 924
 handling of 920
 infertility in 922
 kidney disease 925
 lead poisoning in 925
 mite infestations in 924
 newborns 922
 nutritional requirements 921
 pinworms in 923
 porphyrin deposits 923
 reproduction 922
 salmonellosis in 923
 seizures in 924
 selecting 920
 sex determination 922
 signs of illness 921
 skin disorders of 923
 tail injuries of 923
 tapeworms in 923
 temperament of 921
 tumors of 924
 Tyzzer's disease in 923
 ventral marking gland 919
  tumors 924
 water requirements of 921
Giant cell tumors
 of soft tissue
  in cats 509
  in dogs 278
  in horses 779
Giant kidney worm infection *1106*
 in dogs 289

Giardiasis *1098*
 in birds 842
 in cats 407
 in dogs 116
 in horses 632
 vaccination
  in cats *340*
  in dogs 12, *13*
Gid
 in dogs 208
 in horses 720
Gills
 of fish 900
 disorders of 913, 914, 915
Gingival fibroma
 in cats 395
 in dogs 94
Gingivitis
 in cats 390
 in dogs 88
Gizzard 824, 826
Glanders (farcy) *1090*
 in cats 540
 in dogs 317
 in horses 805
Glaucoma 1064
 in cats 429
 in dogs 149
 drugs for 1128
 in horses 652
Glomerular disease
 in cats 520
 in dogs 293
 in horses 786
Glomerulonephritis
 in cats 442, 520
 in dogs 171, 293
 in gerbils 925
Glossitis
 in cats 394
 in dogs 93
Glucagon *130*
Glucocorticoids 1133, 1136 (*see also* Corticosteroids)
Glycogen branching enzyme deficiency
 in horses 671
Glycogen storage disease (glycogenosis)
 in cats 447
 in dogs 124, 179
 in horses 669
Gnathostomiasis *1106*
Gnats
 and skin disorders
  in dogs 252
  in horses 761, 763

Goiters
  in horses 645
  in pet birds 845
Gold dust disease 915
Golden hamsters 940 (*see*
    Hamsters)
Goldfish (*see also* Fish)
  parasites of 917
  water temperature for 902
Gongylonemiasis *1106*
Gonitis
  in horses 699
Gossypol poisoning 1159
Gout
  in birds 844, 852
  in reptiles 1031
Granules 1120
Granulocytes 35
Granulomas
  eosinophilic
    in cats 493
Granulomatous reactions
  in cats 443
  in dogs 173
  in horses 663
Granulomatous meningo-
    encephalomyelitis
  in dogs 206
Granulomatous sebaceous
    adenitis
  in dogs 243
Grapes
  poisoning from 1154
Grass parakeets *818*
Grass sickness
  in horses 718
Gray Collie syndrome 52
Greasy heel
  in horses 686
Greyhound polyarthritis 185
Grief
  and loss of pet 1232, 1249
Grit
  for birds 830
Grooming
  of cats 342
  of dogs 14
  excessive, in cats 353
  of horses 559, 564
Groundsel poisoning *1186*
Growth hormone *130*
Grubs
  and skin disorders
    in cats 496
    in dogs 252
Guarana poisoning 1194
Guide dogs (*see* Service ani-
    mals)

Guinea pigs, 925
  antibiotic sensitivity 927, 931
  appetite loss in 933
  bacterial infections of 935, 939
  barbering 938
  breeding of 930
  breeds 926
  calcium deficiency in 934
  cancers of 939
  conjunctivitis in 933
  dehydration in 931
  dental disease in 932
  diarrhea in 932
  diet of 928
  digestive disorders of 932
  disease prevention 931
  ear infections in 933
  enlarged lymph nodes in
    938
  exercise 929
  grooming 930
  hair loss in 937
  handling of 929
  housing for 927
  ketosis (pregnancy toxemia)
    934
  lice in 937
  mastitis in 936
  metastatic calcification in
    934
  mite infestations in 937
  neutering of 930
  newborn care 931
  nutritional requirements of
    928
  ovarian cysts in 936
  pneumonia in 935
  pododermatitis 938
  reproduction 930
  reproductive disorders of 936
  ringworm in 937
  routine health care 929, *930*
  Salmonella infection 939
  selecting 927
  signs of illness 929
  skin disorders of 937, 939
  sleeping habits of 927
  slobbers 932
  spaying 930
  teeth 926
  temperament of 929
  temperature requirements of
    926
  tumors in 939
  viral infections in 936
  vitamin C needs 928, 933
  water requirements of 929
  Yersinia infection 939

Guinea worm infection *1106*
Gum disease
  in cats 390
    gingivitis 390
    periodontitis 391
    prevention of 391
  in dogs 87
    gingivitis 88
    periodontitis 88
    prevention of 89
  in horses 611
Gunshot injuries
  management of 1068
Gut loading 1023, 1024, 1045
Guttural pouch empyema749
Guttural pouch infection749
Guttural pouch mycosis 749,
    801
Guttural pouch tympany 750
Gyrodactylus infection
  in fish 917

H

H_1 antagonists 1139
H_2 blockers
  poisoning from 1193
Habituation
  in cats 347
  in dogs 20
  in horses 568
Habronemiasis
  in horses 770
Hair (*see also* Fur)
  of dogs 5
  of horses 756
Hairballs
  in cats *398*
  in ferrets 892
  in rabbits 988, 993
Hair follicles
  of cats 489
  of dogs 239
  tumors of
    in cats 512
    in dogs 272
Hair growth abnormalities
  in cats 491
Hairlessness
  in cats 491
Hair loss
  in cats 491, 498
  in dogs 159, 242, 255
  in gerbils 924
  in guinea pigs 937
  in hamsters 950
  in horses 766
  in prairie dogs 967

Hairworms
  in horses *630*
Halogenated aromatic poison-
    ing 1160
Hamartomas
  epidermal
    in dogs 271
  of sebaceous glands
    in dogs 278
Hamsters 940
  abscesses in 950
  actinomycosis in 948
  aggressiveness in 944, 945
  amyloidosis in 952
  bacterial infections in 947
  barbering by 950
  blood clots in 946
  breeding of 945, 949
  breeds of *941*
  broken bones of 948
  cages for 941, 945
  cancer in 952
  cardiovascular disease in946
  caring for 940, 943
  cirrhosis of 948
  congestive heart failure in
      946
  conjunctivitis in 948
  constipation of 948
  dental care for 945
  diarrhea 946
  diet 942, 949
  digestive disorders in 946
  disease prevention 945
  exercise for 943
  eye trauma in 948
  giving medication to 944
  glands of 940
  hair loss 950
  handling of 943, 945
  health care for 943
  household hazards 945
  intussusception in 948
  kidney disease in 951, 952
  lameness in 948
  lifespan of 940
  liver disorders of 948
  lymphocytic choriomeningi-
      tis virus 951
  lymphoma in 953
  mammary gland infection
      in 949
  mite infestations 951
  newborn care 946
  nutritional disorders in 949
  nutritional requirements 942
  ownership regulations 941
  pinworms in 948

  pneumonia in 949
  polycystic disease in 952
  pregnancy of 945, *946*, 949
  proliferative enteritis 946
  protozoal infections in 947
  pseudotuberculosis in 952
  reproduction of 945
  reproductive disorders in 949
  respiratory disorders in 949
  ringworm in 950
  salmonellosis 947
  selecting 941
  Sendai virus in 949
  signs of illness in 943, *944*
  skin disorders of 950
  tapeworms in 948
  teeth of 945
  temperament 943
  tularemia in 952
  tumors in 952
  Tyzzer's disease in 947
  veterinary examination of
      941, 943
  vitamin deficiencies in 949
  water requirements 942
Hantavirus *1112*
Harderian gland
  in rats 1007
Hardpad disease 309
Harelip (*see* Cleft lip)
Harvest mites
  on horses 770
Hawaii
  quarantine law 1219
Head injuries
  of horses 1062
Head tilt
  in rats 1007
Health
  benefits of pet ownership
      1228
  and human-animal bond 1228
Hearing
  of birds 822
  of cats 331
  of dogs 4
  of horses 552
Heart and blood vessel
    disorders
  in cats 370
    atrial septal defects 375
    atrial standstill 379
    blood clots 382
    blood vessel disorders 382
    cardiomyopathy 378
    congenital abnormalities
        373
    cor triatriatum sinister 376

    degenerative valve disease
        378
    endocardial fibroelastosis
        376
    heart failure 376
    heartworm disease 380
    infective endocarditis 379
    mitral valve dysplasia 375
    pericardial disease 380
    pulmonic stenosis 375
    tetralogy of Fallot 375
    tricuspid valve dysplasia
        375
    ventricular septal defects
        375
  in chinchillas 878
  in dogs 53
    aneurysm 76
    aortic stenosis 60
    atrial septal defects 62
    atrial standstill 71
    cardiac tamponade 72
    congenital abnormalities 58
    cor triatriatum dexter 64
    degenerative valve disease
        68
    dilated cardiomyopathy 69
    endocardial fibroelastosis 71
    heart failure 65
    heartworm disease 73
    infective endocarditis 71
    mitral stenosis 63
    mitral valve dysplasia 63
    myocarditis 70
    pericardial disease 72
    persistent right aortic arch
        61
    pulmonic stenosis 60
    signs of 56
    tetralogy of Fallot 62
    tricuspid dysplasia 64
    ventricular septal defects
        61
  drugs for 1122, *1122*
  in horses 592
    aneurysm 601
    blood clots 600
    congenital abnormalities
        596
    degenerative valve disease
        599
    heart failure 598
    infective endocarditis600
    myocarditis 599
    pericardial disease 600
    pericarditis 600
    signs of 595
    tetralogy of Fallot 597

Heart and blood vessel disorders
in horses (*continued*)
tricuspid dysplasia 598
ventricular septal defects
596
incidence of 55
Heart failure
in cats 376
in dogs 65
drugs for 58
in horses 598
types of 65
Heart murmurs
in cats 371, 593
in chinchillas 878
in dogs 54
Heart rate
and blood pressure 54
in cats 371
in dogs 54
in horses 593
Heartworms *1106*
in cats *341, 342*, 380
in dogs 14, 73
drugs for prevention of 1124
drugs for treatment of 1124
in ferrets 896
pneumonitis from
in cats 479
in dogs 227
Heat sources
for reptiles 1020
Heat stress
in chinchillas 882
in horses 559, *560*
in potbellied pigs 980
in rabbits 984, 1002
Heat stroke
in chinchillas 874
in dogs 3
emergencies 1052
in horses 1062
Heaves 752
Heel
contracted
in horses 680
sheared
in horses 686
Heel crack
in horses 685
Helicobacter infection
in dogs 109
Helicobacter mustelae infection
in ferrets 894
Hemangiomas
in cats 507
in dogs 271
in horses 780

Hemangiopericytomas
in dogs 272
Hematinic drugs 1124
Hematologic tests 1071
Hematoma
of the ear
in cats 435
in dogs 158
ethmoid
in horses 743
Hemobartonellosis
in cats 365
Hemochromatosis
in horses 639
Hemoglobin 1124
Hemolysis
alloimmune
in dogs 39
microangiopathic
in dogs 40
Hemolytic anemia
in cats 362
in dogs 39
Hemophilia
in cats 367
in dogs 47
in horses 588
Hemorrhage 1064 (*see also*
Bleeding)
Hemorrhagic fever *1110*
Hemorrhagic gastroenteritis
in dogs 106
Hemostatic drugs 1124
Hemothorax
in cats 478
in dogs 227
in horses 739
Hendra virus infection *1112*
in horses 746, 799
Hepatic amyloidosis
in cats 413
in dogs 124
Hepatic coccidiosis
in rabbits 996
Hepatic cysts
in cats 390
in dogs 86
in horses 608
Hepatic encephalopathy
in cats 409
in dogs 121, 201
in horses 633
Hepatic lipidosis
in cats 410
in horses 638
Hepatitis
in cats
lymphocytic portal 411

in dogs
chronic 123
infectious 318
vaccination *13*
in horses
acute 635
chronic active 638
infectious necrotic 805
Hepatitis E *1112*
Hepatocutaneous syndrome
in cats 412
Hepatoid tumors
in dogs 277
Hepatozoonosis
in cats 365
in dogs 43
Herbal supplements
in pain management
1215
poisoning from 1194
Herbicide poisoning 1160
Hereditary equine regional
dermal asthenia (HERD)
758
Hereditary deafness (*see* Deafness)
Heredity
and cancer 1236
Hernia
in cats 388, 480
in dogs 84, *85*, 127, 230
in horses 607, 740
Herpes B virus disease
1112
Herpesvirus
in dogs 310
in horses 744
in koi 914
in reptiles 1036
Herpesvirus 1 infection
in chinchillas 884
Herpesvirus 1 myeloencephalopathy
in horses 717
Heterophyiasis *1100*
Hiatal hernias
in cats 388
in dogs 84, *85*
Hibernation
of reptiles 1020
High blood pressure (*see*
Hypertension)
Hip dislocation
in cats 451
in dogs 187
in horses 701
Hip disorders
in horses 700

Hip dysplasia
  in cats 449
  in dogs 180, 184
Hirudiniasis *1108*
Histamine (H₂) antagonists 1125
Histiocytomas
  in dogs 273
  fibrous
    in cats 509
    in dogs 278
    in horses 779
Histologic tests 1070
Histoplasmosis *1096*
  in cats 411, 538
  in dogs 123, 314
Hives
  in cats 439, 499
  in dogs 168, 256
  in horses 660, 767
Hoarding of pets 1231
Hock
  bursitis of
    in horses 677
  dropped
    in dogs 190
  fractures of
    in horses 697
Hollow wall
  in horses 686
Holly berries
  poisoning from *1176*
Home care
  of injured dogs and cats 1059
Hong Kong flu (*see* Influenza type A)
Hoof care
  in horses 564
  in potbellied pigs 973
Hookworms
  in cats *341*, *404*, 405
  in dogs *111*, 112
  in reptiles 1037
  treatment of 1127
Hooves
  of horses
    anatomy of 553
    applying medication to 561
    routine care of 564
    trimming 565
  of potbellied pigs 973
Hormonal disorders
  of cats 415
    Addison's disease 417
    adrenal gland disorders 417
    adult-onset panhypo-pituitarism 421

calcium metabolism disorders 419
    Cushing's disease 420
    diabetes insipidus 421
    diabetes mellitus 418
    hyperadrenocorticism 420
    hypercalcemia 420, *420*
    hyperthyroidism 422
    hypoadrenocorticism 417
    hypocalcemia 419
    hypoparathyroidism 419
    hypothyroidism 422
    insulinomas 418
    pancreatic disorders 417
    parathyroid gland disorders 419
    pituitary gland disorders 420
    thyroid gland disorders 422
  of dogs 128
    Addison's disease 132
    adrenal gland disorders 131
    adult-onset panhypopitu-itarism 137
    calcium metabolism disorders 134
    Cushing's disease 132, 136
    diabetes insipidus 138
    diabetes mellitus 133
    gastrinomas 134
    hyperadrenocorticism 132, 136
    hypercalcemia 135, *136*
    hyperthyroidism 140
    hypoadrenocorticism 132
    hypocalcemia 135, *136*
    hypoparathyroidism 135
    hypothyroidism 139
    insulinomas 134
    juvenile-onset panhypopi-tuitarism 138
    neuroendocrine tissue tumors 140
    pancreatic disorders 132
    parathyroid gland disorders 134
    pheochromocytomas 132
    pituitary gland disorders 136
    thyroid gland disorders 139
  of ferrets 897
  of horses 641
    Addison's disease 644
    Cushing's disease 643
    diabetes mellitus 644
    goiters 645

hyperadrenocorticism 643
    hypoadrenocorticism 644
    hypothyroidism 645
Hormonal treatment
  for reproductive disorders 1131
  of skin disorders 1136
  for urinary incontinence 1138
Hormone replacement therapy
  in dogs 140
  in horses 643
  monitoring 131
Hormones *130* (*see also* Endocrine system)
  for behavior problems
    in cats *349*
    in dogs *23*
  calcium-regulating 134
  deficiency of (*see* Hormonal disorders)
  functions of 128
Horn flies
  in horses 764
Horse bots 629, *630*
Horse flies
  in cats 496
  in dogs 253
  in horses 764
Horse pills 561
Horses (*see also* Foals)
  actinobacillosis in 794
  actinomycosis in 795
  Addison's disease in 644
  African horse sickness in 795
  age of 609
  aggression in 572, *573*, 574, 576
  allergies in 759
  amyloidosis in 796
  anaphylactic reactions in 660
  anemia in 584, 661
  anterior uveitis in 662
  anthrax in 797
  appetite loss 572
  aspergillosis in 801
  babesiosis in 586
  back disorders in 701
  behavior modification techniques 568
  behavior problems 566, 571, 572, *573*
    medications for 570
  besnoitiosis in 798
  blood clotting disorders in 589

Horses (*continued*)
  blood disorders in 581
  blood types of 581, 584
  blood vessel disorders in
    592
  boarding facilities for 1227
  bone fractures 1061
  botulism in 798
  bracken staggers in 1148
  breeding of 565
  breeds of 557
  candidiasis in 802
  cardiovascular disease in
    592
  cell-mediated immune
    reactions in 663
  coccidioidomycosis (Valley
    fever) in 802
  cold agglutinin (hemolytic)
    disease in 661
  colic in *556*, 603, 616
  combined immunodeficiency
    disease in 664
  congenital disorders in
    794
  conjunctivitis in 649
  contact hypersensitivity in
    663
  coprophagia in 572
  cryptococcosis in 802
  Cushing's disease in 643
  cytotoxic disorders in 661
  deafness in 657
  dental care for 564, *564*
  dental development in
    609
  dental disorders in 610
  dermatitis in 756
  dermatophilosis in 760
  deworming programs for
    563
  diabetes mellitus in 644
  diet of 559
  digestive disorders in 602
  digestive system infections
    in *604*
  digestive system of 555, 602
  dourine in 587
  dystocia in 1063
  ear disorders of 655
  elbow disorders in 694
  emergency care of 1059
  enterocolitis in 806
  enterotoxemia in 807
  epizootic lymphangitis in
    802
  equine infectious anemia
    in 799

  equine morbillivirus pneu-
    monia in 799
  equine viral arteritis in
    800
  esophageal disorders in
    613
  estimation of age in 554, *555*
  exercise for *560*, 560
  exertional rhabdomyolysis
    in 789
  eye disorders of 646
  eyelid disorders of 648
  eyes of 551
  fetlock disorders in 687
  foal rejection 575
  foals 565, 569
  food allergies in 759
  frostbite in 658
  fungal infections in 801
  gaits of 552
  gastric ulcers in 614
  gastrointestinal parasites
    in 629
  giving medication to
    561
  glanders (farcy) in 805
  goiters in 645
  granulomatous reactions
    663
  grooming of 559, 564
  hair of 553, 756
  hearing of 552
  heart disorders in 592
  heat stress in 559, *560*,
    1062
  hemophilia in 588
  hernias in 607
  hip disorders in 700
  hives in 660, 767
  hooves of 553
  hormonal disorders of
    641
  housing for 559
  hypertrichosis in 643
  immune disorders in 659
  importing of 1220
  infectious necrotic hepatitis
    in 805
  infertility in 731
  insect bites *657*, 658
  intestinal disorders in 621
  itching in 757, 768
  joint disorders in 675
  kidney disorders in *556*,
    781
  kidney injuries in 556
  lameness in 666
  laminitis in 682

  leptospirosis in 807
  leukemia in 585
  leukoencephalomalacia
    1155
  lice infestations 768
  life expectancy of 550
  liver disorders in 633
  Lyme disease in 808
  malignant edema in
    808
  mange 659
  melioidosis in 808
  metabolism of 550
  milk allergies in 660
  "Monday morning" sickness
    in 560
  moon blindness in 662,
    807
  muscular fatigue in 790
  musculoskeletal disorders
    in 664
  nasal cavity disorders in
    648
  nervous system disorders
    of 708
  nocardiosis in 809
  nuchal ligament of 550
  nutritional requirements
    559
  pain management in
    1215
  parasites of 563, *563*
  pastern disorders in 687
  peritonitis in 809
  phaeohyphomycosis in
    804
  phobias in 568
  photosensitization in 772
  platelet disorders in 588
  pneumonia in 799
  poisoning in 1145
  prepurchase examination of
    558, *558*
  purpura hemorrhagica in
    662
  pythiosis in 803
  quarantine of 662
  rabies in 723
  rectal and anal disorders in
    640
  recurrent uveitis in 807
  reproduction of 565, 727
  reproductive disorders of
    726
  respiratory disorders in
    736
  rhinosporidiosis in 804
  selecting 557

senses of 551, *551*
septicemia in 810
septic shock in 811
sexual behaviors of 575
shoes of 564, 565
shoulder disorders in 694
signs of illness in 561
skin allergies in 660
skin disorders in *554*, 554, 755
skin of 553, *554*
skin tumors in 775
sporotrichosis in 804
stall behavior *574*, 574
stay apparatus 553
stifle joint disorders of
    699
Surra in 586
sweet itch in 660
tarsus disorders in 696
teeth of 554, *555*, 564, *564*
temperament of 557, *573*
temperature regulation 550
tetanus (lockjaw) in 718, 811
thrombocytopenia in 588
tick infestations of 774
trailering problems 576
transportation of 576,
    1224
    by air 1224
trichinellosis (trichinosis)
    in 813
trypanosomiasis in 586
Tsetse fly disease in 586
tuberculosis in 813
tularemia in 813
urinary tract disorders in
    781
uterine prolapse in 735
vaccination of 561, *562*
vasculitis in 662
vesicular stomatitis in
    813
veterinary care of 560
vision in 551, *551*, 646
wood chewing in 572
zygomycosis in 805
Horse shoes
    routine care of 564
    types of 565
House flies
    and skin disorders
        in horses 763
Household hazards 1163
    for birds 835
    for cats 343
    for chinchillas *875*
    for dogs 15
    for ferrets 887

Houseplants poisonous to
    animals *1174*, 1175
Housetraining
    of cats 353
    of dogs 16, *16*, 26
Housing
    for amphibians 865
    for birds 829
    for chinchillas 875
    for dogs 10
    for ferrets 889
    for gerbils 920
    for guinea pigs 927
    for hamsters 941
    for horses 559
    for mice 954
    for potbellied pigs 971
    for prairie dogs 964
    for rabbits 985
    for rats 1005
    for sugar gliders 1040
Human-animal bond 1228
    health benefits of
        1228
Hutch burn
    in rabbits 999
Hutches
    for rabbits 985
Hyacinth bulbs
    poisoning from *1176*
Hyaluronic acid 1140
Hydranencephaly
    in cats 460
Hydrocephalus
    in dogs 200
    in horses 794
Hydrocodone 1132
Hydrothorax
    in cats 478
    in dogs 227
    in horses 739
Hygroma
    in dogs 257
    in horses 691
Hymenolepiasis (dwarf tape-
    worm infection) *1104*
Hyperactivity
    in dogs 27
Hyperadrenocorticism
    in cats 420
    in dogs 132, 136
    in ferrets 897
    in horses 643
    and liver disease
        in dogs 123
    and skin disorders
        in cats 513
Hyperammonemia

in horses 639
Hypercalcemia
    in cats 419, *420*
    in dogs 135, *136*
Hypereosinophilic syndrome
    in cats 369
Hyperesthesia
    in cats 353
Hyperkalemic periodic
        paralysis
    in horses 671, 706, 714
Hyperlipemia
    in horses 638
Hypermagnesemia
    in cats 527
    in dogs 303
    in horses 790
Hyperparathyroidism
    in dogs 181
    nutritional secondary
        in cats 453
    and rubber jaw syndrome
        in cats 448
    in dogs 181
Hyperpigmentation
    in dogs 257
Hyperplastic syndromes
    in dogs 243
Hypersensitivity pneumonitis
    in horses 662
Hypersensitivity reactions
    after vaccination 1144
Hypertension
    in cats 380
    in dogs 73
    in horses 600
Hyperthermia (*see* Malignant
        hyperthermia)
Hyperthyroidism
    in cats 412, 422
    in dogs 140
Hypertrichosis 643 (*see also*
        Cushing's disease)
Hypertrophic cardiomyopathy
    in cats 379
    in dogs 70
Hypertrophic osteodystrophy
    in dogs 191
Hypertrophic osteopathy
    in dogs 192
Hyperuricemia
    in reptiles 1023
Hypervitaminosis A
    in cats 453, 463
Hypoadrenocorticism
    in cats 417
    in dogs 132
    in horses 644

Hypocalcemia
  in cats 420, 526
  in dogs 135, *137*, 301
  in sugar gliders 1045
Hypocalcemic tetany
  in horses 790
Hypofibrinogenemia 47
Hypoglycemia
  in cats 526
  in dogs 301
Hypokalemic polymyopathy
  in cats 452
Hypoparathyroidism
  in cats 419
  in dogs 135, 182
Hypophosphatemia
  in cats 363
Hypoproteinemia
  in sugar gliders 1045
Hypospadias
  in dogs 287
Hypothermia
  first aid for 1052
Hypothyroidism
  in cats 422, 513
  in dogs 139, 283
  in horses 645
Hypothyroid neuropathy
  in dogs 203
Hypovolemic shock 1055
Hystiocytosis
  in dogs 273

I

Ibuprofen poisoning 1192
Ich (white spot disease)
  in fish 915
Ichthyosiform dermatoses
  in dogs 243
Identification tags
  for travel 1217, 1225
Iguanas 1014 (*see also* Lizards)
Imaging techniques 1075 (*see also* Diagnostic imaging)
  for diagnosis of heart disease
    57
  in diagnosis of lameness
    in horses *668*
Immune response 164
Immune complex disorders
  in cats 442
  in dogs 171
  in horses 662
Immune deficiency diseases
  in cats 443
  in dogs 173
  in horses 663

Immune disorders
  in cats 439
    allergic asthma 440
    allergic bronchiolitis 440
    anaphylactic reactions
      439
    anterior uveitis 443
    feline immunodeficiency
      virus 444
    feline leukemia virus 444
    food allergies 440
    gammopathies 445
    glomerulonephritis 442
    granulomatous reactions
      443
    hives 439
    immune deficiency dis-
      eases 443
    immune-mediated
      hemolytic anemia 441
    immune-mediated
      thrombocytopenia 441
    immune system tumors
      444
    lymphoma 444
    myasthenia gravis 442
    parvovirus 444
    pemphigus 442
    phagocytosis deficiencies
      443
    PIE (pulmonary infiltration
      with eosinophilia) syn-
      drome 440
    skin allergies 441
    systemic lupus erythema-
      tosus 442
    from viruses 444
  in dogs 164
    allergic bronchitis 168
    allergic rhinitis 168
    anaphylactic reactions
      167
    anemia 169
    anterior uveitis 171
    atopy 169
    autoimmune adrenalitis
      173
    autoimmune skin disor-
      ders 170
    autoimmune thyroiditis
      173
    combined immuno-
      deficiency disease
      174
    contact hypersensitivity
      173
    encephalitis 173
    food allergies 168

    gammopathies 175
    glomerulonephritis 171
    granulomatous reactions
      173
    hives 168
    immune-deficiency dis-
      eases 173
    immune-mediated arthritis
      172
    immune-mediated
      hemolytic anemia 169
    immune-mediated
      thrombocytopenia 170
    immunoglobulin defi-
      ciency 174
    keratoconjunctivitis sicca
      173
    lupus 171
    meningitis 172
    myasthenia gravis 170
    old dog encephalitis 173
    PIE (Pulmonary infiltration
      with eosinophilia) syn-
      drome 168
    selective immunodeficien-
      cies 174
    skin allergies 169
    from tumors 175
    uveitis 171
    vasculitis 171
    from viruses 174
  in horses 659
    anaphylactic reactions
      660
    anterior uveitis 662
    cell-mediated immune
      reactions 663
    cold agglutinin (hemolytic
      disease) 661
    combined immunodefi-
      ciency disease 664
    contact hypersensitivity
      663
    granulomatous reactions
      663
    hives 660
    hypersensitivity pneu-
      monitis 662
    immune-deficiency dis-
      eases 663
    immune-mediated
      hemolytic anemia
      661
    immune-mediated
      thrombocytopenia
      661
    immunoglobulin defi-
      ciency 663

moon blindness 662
purpura hemorrhagica
662
skin allergies 660
sweet itch 660
vasculitis 662
and infection 1081
Immune-mediated arthritis
in cats 450
in dogs 172
Immune-mediated diseases
in cats 439
in dogs 164
in horses 659
Immune-mediated hemolytic
anemia
in cats 441
in dogs 169
in horses 661
Immune-mediated myositis
in horses 707
Immune-mediated thrombo-
cytopenia
in cats 441
in dogs 170
in horses 661
Immune system
antibodies in *165*
cells of *165*
functions of 1078
and infections 1080
nonspecific immunity
165
physical barriers of 164
response of 165
specific immunity 165
tumors in 175
Immunization (*see also*
Vaccination)
passive 1144
Immunodeficiencies (*see*
Immune deficiency
diseases)
Immunodepressant drugs
1136
Immunoglobulins *165*
Immunomodulators 1136
Immunostimulant drugs
1136
Immunotherapy 1143
Implants 1120
Inclusion body disease of boid
snakes 1030, 1036
Incontinence
treatment of 1138, *1138*
urinary
in cats 523
in dogs 298

Inermicapsifer infection *1104*
Infections 1078
bacterial 1082
of birds 851
and blood cells 1079
caused by fungi 1086
caused by parasites 1086
caused by rickettsiae
1085
caused by viruses 1087
defense against 1078
development of 1081
diagnosis of 1080, *1087*
and fever 1080
immune response to
1080
and inflammation 1079
microorganisms that cause
1082
natural barriers to 1078
prevention of 1082
and sepsis 1083
spread of 1081
susceptibility of animals to
1081
Infectious canine hepatitis
122, 318
Infectious cloacitis
in reptiles 1037
Infectious necrotic hepatitis
in horses 805
Infective arthritis (*see* Septic
arthritis)
Infective endocarditis
in cats 379
in dogs 71
in horses 600
Infertility (*see also* Breeding,
Reproductive disorders)
in cats 472, 535
in dogs 217
in horses 731
Inflammation
antihistamines for 1139
chondroprotective agents
for 1140
corticosteroids for 1140
drugs for 1139
negative effects of 1139
nonsteroidal anti-inflammatory drugs (NSAIDs) for
1140
role of 1079
of skin (*see* Dermatitis)
Inflammatory process
1079
Inflammatory airway disease
in horses 750

Inflammatory bowel disease
in cats 401
in dogs 107
in horses 627
Influenza
avian 847
in ferrets 894
in horses 745
vaccination *562*
Influenza type A *1112*
Infrared panels 1020
Inguinal hernias
in dogs *85*
in horses 607, 620
Inhalation treatment 1133
Injections 1120
Injuries (*see also* Emergencies,
Trauma)
of birds 859
emergency care of, in horses
1061
to the eye (*see* Eye emergencies)
of ferrets 892
minor 1069
of rats 1009
veterinary evaluation of
1053, 1056
Insect growth regulators
1134
Insecticide poisoning 1167
Insects
bites or stings 1069
and skin disorders
in cats 494, 496
in dogs 249, 251
in horses 761
as a source of ear irritation
in horses *657*
Insulin *130*
Insulinomas
in cats 418
in dogs 134
in ferrets 897
Insulin production
in cats 418
in dogs 133
in horses 641
Interdigital furunculosis 247
Interstitial cystitis
in cats 521
Interstitial keratitis
in cats 428
in dogs 147
Interstitial nephritis
in cats 518
in dogs 289
in horses 785

Intervertebral disk disease
  in cats 462
  in dogs 204
Intestinal blockages (*see*
    Gastrointestinal
    obstruction)
Intestinal capillariasis
  1089
Intestinal clostridiosis
  in horses 806
Intestinal coccidiosis
  in rabbits 996
Intestinal disorders (*see* Diges-
    tive disorders)
Intestinal flukes
  in dogs *115*
Intestinal parasites (*see* Gas-
    trointestinal parasites)
Intoxication (*see* Poisoning)
Intubation 1054, 1060
Intussusception
  in dogs 105
  in hamsters 948
Iodine deficiency
  in horses 645
  in reptiles 1024
Iodine toxicity
  in horses 646
Ionophore toxicity
  in horses 707, 715
Ipecac 1125
Iridoviruses
  in amphibians 872
Iron poisoning 1193
Iron storage disease
  in birds 846
Ischemic neuromyopathy
  in cats 461
Islet cell tumors
  functional
    in cats 418
    in dogs 134
  gastrin secreting
    in dogs 134
Isopropanol poisoning 1163
Isopropyl alcohol poisoning
    1170
Itching
  in cats 490, 499
  in dogs 240, 258
  in horses 757, 768

J

Japanese B encephalitis *1112*
Jaundice
  in dogs 125
Jimson weed poisoning *1188*

Johnson grass poisoning
  1188
Joint capsule
  inflammation of
    in horses 694
Joint disorders (*see also*
    Musculoskeletal disor-
    ders)
  in cats 449
  in dogs 183
  in horses 675
Joint rigidity (*see* Arthrogrypo-
    sis)
Jugular vein thrombosis
  in horses 601
Juvenile epilepsy
  in horses 713
Juvenile-onset panhypo-
    pituitarism
  in dogs 138

K

Kaolin-pectin 1126
Kasen
  in horses 762
Kennel cough
  in dogs 238
    vaccination *13*
Kennels
  as boarding facilities 1227
Keratinized skin cysts
  in cats 507
  in dogs 273
  in horses 777
Keratoacanthomas
  in rats 1012
Keratoconjunctivitis sicca (*see*
    Dry eye)
Keratoma
  in horses 682, 777
Kerosene poisoning 1173
Ketosis
  in guinea pigs 934
  in rabbits 998
Kicking behavior
  in horses 574
Kidney disorders (*see also*
    Urinary tract disorders)
  in cats 514
    acute kidney disease 520
    chronic kidney disease 518
    cysts 515
    dysplasia 515
    glomerular disease 520
    hypoplasia 515
    infection (pyelonephritis)
      517

  kidney failure 518
  renal tubular acidosis 522
  tumors 522
in dogs 283
  acute kidney disease 292
  chronic kidney disease 290
  cysts 286
  dysplasia 285
  Fanconi syndrome 295
  giant kidney worm infec-
    tion 289
  glomerular disease 293
  hypoplasia 285
  infection (pyelonephritis)
    288
  kidney failure 290
  renal tubular acidosis
    294
  tumors 296
drugs for 1136
in ferrets 898
in gerbils 925
in hamsters 951
in horses 781
  acute kidney disease
    786
  chronic kidney disease
    785
  cysts 783
  dysplasia 783
  glomerular disease 786
  hypoplasia 783
  infection (pyelonephritis)
    784
  kidney failure 785
  renal tubular acidosis 787
  tumors 787
Kidney failure
  in cats 518
  in dogs 290
  in horses 785
Kidneys
  congenital disorders of
    in cats 515
    in dogs 285
    in horses 783
  polycystic
    in cats 515
    in dogs 285
    in horses 783
Kidney stones (*see also* Uro-
    liths, Urinary stones)
  in rabbits 1002
  in reptiles 1024
  treatment of 1137
Killed vaccines 1143
Kissing spine syndrome
  in horses 702

Kittens (*see also* Cats)
  care of 343
  nutritional requirements
    of 344
  socialization of 344
  vaccination of 344
  worms in 344
Kneecap displacement
  in cats 449
  in dogs 183
  in horses 700
Koi (*see also* Fish)
  carp pox in 915
  herpesvirus in 914
  parasites of 917
  tumors of 919
Kunkers 803
Kyasanur forest disease *1112*
Kyphosis
  in horses 671

L

Labor and delivery
  in cats 471
  in dogs 216
  in horses 729
Lacerations
  emergency care of, in horses
    1062
  of the eye 1064
  of the lip
    in horses 612
  management of 1067
Lacrimal (tear) glands
  of cats 424
  of dogs 142
  of horses 647
LaCrosse encephalitis *1112*
Lactase deficiency
  in foals 628
Lactation tetany
  in horses 790
Lactobacillus
  (*see* Probiotics)
Lactose intolerance
  in foals 628
Lagenidiosis
  in dogs 316
Lagophthalmos
  in cats 425
  in dogs 143
Lameness
  in cats 446
  in dogs 178
  in hamsters 948
  in horses 666, *668*
  in potbellied pigs 978

Laminitis (founder)
  and blood clots 589
  in horses 682
Large intestine
  inflammation of
    in cats 398
    in dogs 102
Large strongyles
  in horses 631
Larkspur poisoning *1182*
Larval cyathostomiasis
  in horses 631
Larva migrans *1106*
Laryngeal chondropathy
  in horses 741
Laryngeal hemiplegia
  in horses 741
Laryngitis
  in cats 483
  in dogs 231
Larynx
  disorders of
    in horses 741
  inflammation of (*see*
    Laryngitis)
  paralysis of
    in cats 484
    in dogs 233
    in horses 741
Lassa fever *1112*
Lateral line 900
Lavage
  peritoneal 1056
Lawsonia intracellularis
  infection
    in ferrets 894
Laxatives 1127, *1127*
Lead poisoning 1170
  in birds 857
  in gerbils 925
Leeches
  and fish 912, 917
  found on reptiles 1034
Left-sided congestive heart
  failure 67
Leg banding
  in birds 835
Legg-Calvé-Perthes disease
  in dogs 183
Leg mange
  in horses 769
Leg paralysis
  in cats 466
  in dogs 209
  in horses 721
Leishmaniasis *1098*
  in cats 541
  in dogs 318

Lens displacement
  in cats 430
  in dogs 150
  in horses 652
Lens disorders
  in cats 429
  in horses 652
Lentigo
  in cats 491
Leptospirosis *1090*
  as cause of abortion in mares
    733
  in dogs *13*, 122, 319, *320*
  in horses 807
  and kidney failure
    in horses 785
  in rats 1011
  in sugar gliders 1044
Leukemia 1237
  in cats 363, 369, 444, 534
  in dogs 41, 52
  in guinea pigs 939
  in horses 585, 590
Leukocytosis 51
  in horses 590
Leukoencephalomalacia *1156*
Leukopenia 51
Libido
  equine problems 575
Lice
  in dogs 259
  drugs for 1134
  in guinea pigs 937
  in horses 768
  in mice 959
  in rats 1010
  and skin disorders
    in cats 500
    in dogs 259
    in horses 768
Life support 1057
Ligament strain
  in horses 702
Lightning strikes 1068
Limb deformities
  in horses 670
Lime-sulfur poisoning 1170
Lip disorders
  in dogs 91
Lip fold dermatitis
  in dogs 91
Lip lacerations
  in horses 612
Lipomas
  in birds 858
  in cats 507
  in dogs 273
  in horses 777

Liposarcomas
  in cats 507
  in dogs 273
  in horses 777
Listeria monocytogenes
    infection
  in chinchillas 883
Listeriosis *1090*
  in rabbits 1002
Litter boxes
  avoidance of, in cats 353
  for cats 337
  for ferrets 889
  for rabbits 987
Live vectored vaccines 1143
Liver
  functions of 120, *120*
Liver capillariasis *1089*
Liver disorders
  in cats 409
    ascites 409
    cancer 412
    cholangiohepatitis 410
    endocrine diseases 412
    hepatic amyloidosis 413
    hepatic encephalopathy
      409
    hepatic lipidosis 410
    hepatocutaneous syn-
      drome 412
    infectious diseases 411
    liver cysts 412
    lymphocytic portal hepati-
      tis 411
    poisons 411
    portosystemic shunts 411
    tumors 412
  in dogs 120
    ascites 121
    cancer 124
    chronic hepatitis 123
    cirrhosis 122
    endocrine diseases 123
    fibrosis 122, 124
    glycogen storage disease
      (glycogenosis) 124
    hepatic amyloidosis 124
    hepatic encephalopathy
      121
    infectious diseases 122
    liver cysts 123
    nodular hyperplasia 123
    poisons 122
    portosystemic shunts 122
    tumors 124
  in horses 633
    acute hepatitis 635
    amyloidosis 639

cholangiohepatitis 635
chronic active hepatitis
  638
gallstones 636
hemochromatosis 639
hepatic encephalopathy
  633
hepatic lipidosis 638
hyperlipemia 638
lobe torsion 639
poisons 636, *637*
portosystemic shunts 640
primary hyperammonemia
  639
right lobe atrophy 639
serum sickness 635
Theiler's disease 635
Tyzzer's disease 635
Liver flukes
  in cats 413
  in dogs *115*, 115
Lizards 1014 (*see also* Rep-
    tiles)
  adenovirus infections 1027
  cryptosporidiosis in 1029
  papillomas in 1038
  scale rot in 1034
  selecting 1018
  sex determination 1013
  signs of illness 1018
  stomach worms in 1028
  stomatitis in 1028
Local anesthetics 1215
Lockjaw (*see* Tetanus)
Locoweed poisoning *1188*
Lodging
  during travel with pets 1223
Lorazepam poisoning *1195*
Lordige (*see* West Nile
    encephalomyelitis)
Lordosis
  in horses 671
Lories *819* (*see also* Birds)
  diet of 830
Lorikeets *819* (*see also* Birds)
  diet of 830
Loss of appetite
  in animals with cancer 1246
Louping ill *1114*
Lovebirds *819* (*see also* Birds)
Lucké tumors
  in amphibians 872
Lumps (*see* Lymphadenitis)
Lumpy jaw (*see* Actinomyco-
    sis)
Lung cancer
  in cats 480
  in dogs 229

Lung capillariasis *1089*
Lung hemorrhage
  in horses 747
Lung and airway disorders 227
  in birds 846
  in cats 475
    allergic pneumonitis (PIE
      syndrome) 479
    aspiration pneumonia 485
    cancer and tumors 479
    chlamydial pneumonia 486
    chylothorax 478
    diaphragmatic hernias 480
    emphysema 481
    feline respiratory disease
      complex 481, *482*
    fungal pneumonia 486
    heartworm pneumonitis
      479
    hemothorax 478
    hydrothorax 478
    laryngeal paralysis 484
    laryngitis 483
    lung flukes 483
    lungworms 484
    nasopharyngeal polyps 484
    pharyngitis 484
    pneumonia 485
    pneumothorax 479
    pulmonary edema 486
    respiratory distress 476
    rhinitis 486
    sinusitis 486
    tonsillitis 487
    tracheobronchitis 487
  in chinchillas 880
  in dogs 224
    allergic pneumonitis (PIE
      syndrome) 229
    aspiration pneumonia 234
    cancer and tumors 228
    chylothorax 227
    diaphragmatic hernias 230
    emphysema 231
    fungal pneumonia 234
    heartworm pneumonitis
      227
    hemothorax 228
    hydrothorax 228
    kennel cough 238
    laryngeal paralysis 233
    laryngitis 231
    lung flukes 232
    lungworms 232
    nasal mites 230
    pharyngitis 233
    pneumonia 233
    pneumothorax 227

pulmonary edema 235
rhinitis 235
sinusitis 235
tonsillitis 236
tracheal collapse 237
tracheobronchitis 237
drugs for 1132, *1133*
in hamsters 949
in horses 736
  acute bronchointerstitial
    pneumonia 748
  arytenoid chondritis 741
  aspiration pneumonia 740
  choanal atresia 740
  chylothorax 739
  diaphragmatic hernias 740
  distemper 753
  dorsal displacement of soft
    palate 743
  epiglottic entrapment 744
  equine herpesvirus infec-
    tion 744
  equine morbillivirus pneu-
    monia 746
  equine viral arteritis 746
  ethmoid hematoma 743
  exercise-induced pulmo-
    nary hemorrhage 747
  foal pneumonia 747
  fourth branchial arch
    defect 742
  guttural pouch empyema
    749
  guttural pouch mycosis 749
  guttural pouch tympany
    750
  hemothorax 739
  hydrothorax 739
  inflammatory airway
    disease 750
  influenza 745
  laryngeal disorders 741
  laryngeal hemiplegia 741
  lungworms 750
  nasal polyps 751
  nasal septum disorders742
  of paranasal sinuses 742
  pharyngeal lymphoid
    hyperplasia 751
  pleuropneumonia 752
  pneumothorax 740
  recurrent airway obstruc-
    tion (heaves) 752
  respiratory distress 737
  sinus cysts 743
  sinusitis 743
  strangles 753
  subepiglottic cysts 754

in mice 957
in prairie dogs 969
Lung flukes
  in cats 483
  in dogs 232
Lungs
  inflammation of (*see*
    Pneumonia)
Lungworms
  in amphibians 871
  in cats 484
  in dogs 232
  in horses 750
Lupine poisoning 1155,
    1188
Lupinosis 1155
Lupoid dermatosis
  hereditary
    in dogs 245
Lupus (*see* Systemic lupus
    erythematosus)
Luteinizing hormone *130*
Luxations (*see* Dislocations)
Lyme disease (borreliosis)
    1090
  in cats 541
  in dogs 13, 320, *321*
  in horses 808
Lymphadenitis
  in guinea pigs 938
Lymphangitis
  in horses 591
    epizootic 802
Lymphocystis disease
    915
Lymphocytes *165*
  functions of 35
Lymphocytic choriomeningi-
    tis virus infection
    1114
  in hamsters 951
  in mice 961
  in rats 1011
Lymphocytic portal hepatitis
  in cats 411
Lymphocytosis
  in dogs 51
  in horses 590
Lymphoma 1237
  in birds 858
  in cats 369, 444, 463, 508,
    534
  in dogs 45, 52, 175
  in hamsters 953
  in horses 590
Lymphopenia
  in dogs 51
  in horses 590

Lymphosarcoma
  in cats 508
  in dogs 275
  in guinea pigs 939
  in horses 778

M

Ma huang poisoning 1194
Macadamia nut poisoning
    1153
Macaw respiratory hyper-
    sensitivity 847
Macaws *819* (*see also* Birds)
  asthma in 847
  feather cysts 850
  papillomatosis in 841
  wasting disease in 841
Macracanthorhynchosis
    1108
Macrocyclic lactones 1128,
    1134
Maggots
  in cats 496
  in dogs 253
  in horses 764
Magnesium metabolism
    disorders
  in cats 527
  in dogs 303
  in horses 790
Magnetic resonance imaging
    (MRI) 1077
Malabsorption
  in cats 389, 402
  in dogs 85
  in horses 608, 627
Malaria *1098*
Malathion poisoning 1169
Malayan filariasis *1106*
Maldigestion
  in dogs 85
  in horses 608, 627
Malignant edema
  in horses 808
Malignant hyperthermia
  in cats 528
  in dogs 189, 304
  in horses 793
Malnutrition (*see also* Diet,
    Nutritional requirements)
  and cancer 1246
  in reptiles 1031
Malocclusion
  in guinea pigs 932
  in chinchillas 877
  in prairie dogs 966
  in rabbits 991

Mammary glands
  infection of
    in hamsters 949
Mammary tissue
  overgrowth of (hypertrophy)
    in cats 474
Mammary tumors
  in cats 475
  in dogs 222
  in mice 962
  in rats 1012
Mane mange 769
Mange
  in cats 436, 500
  in dogs 159, 260
  in ferrets 895
  in horses 659, 769
  in potbellied pigs 974, 981
  transmission to people 1108
Mange mites (see also Mites)
  in cats 342
  in potbellied pigs 974
Marburg hemorrhagic fever
    1110
Mare reproductive loss syn-
    drome 732
Marijuana poisoning 1178,
    1199
Marking behavior
  of cats 353, 335, 351
  of dogs 26
Marsupials
  sugar gliders (see Sugar
    gliders)
Massage
  in pain management 1215
Mast cells 165
Mast cell tumors
  in cats 508
  in dogs 275
  in horses 778
Masticatory myositis
  in dogs 188
Mastitis
  in cats 474
  in dogs 221
  in guinea pigs 936
  in horses 734
  in rabbits 998
Medicated shampoos
  for dogs 242, 268
  for horses 757
Medication (see Drugs)
Megacolon
  in cats 399
Megaesophagus
  in cats 388, 460
  in dogs 84, 98

Melanoma
  in cats 433, 509
  in dogs 276
  in horses 778
  in potbellied pigs 981
Melioidosis 1092
  in cats 541
  in dogs 321
  in horses 808
Menangle virus infection
    1114
Meningitis
  in cats 466
  in dogs 172, 210
  in horses 722
Meningoencephalitis
  in cats 466
  in dogs 210
  in horses 722
Meningoencephalomyelitis
  in cats 463
  in dogs 206
Mercury poisoning 1171
Mercury vapor lamps 1020,
    1021
Metabolic disorders
  of cats
    acquired 526
    genetic 526
    malignant hyperthermia
      528
    production-related 526
    puerperal hypocalcemia
      527
  of dogs 300
    acquired 301
    genetic 301
    malignant hyperthermia
      304
    production-related 301
    puerperal hypocalcemia
      302
    and fever 303
  of horses
    acquired 789
    malignant hyperthermia
      793
    production-related
      789
Metabolic osteodystrophies
  in cats 448
Metabolic storage disorders
  in cats 526
  in dogs 300
  in horses 788
Metabolism
  disorders of (see Metabolic
    disorders)

Metacarpus
  of horses
    disorders of 689
Metagonimiasis 1100
Metaldehyde poisoning 1171,
    1202
Metastatic calcification
  in guinea pigs 934
Methadone poisoning 1200
Methanol poisoning 1163, 1170
Methoxychlor poisoning 1167
Methylxanthines 1133
Metritis
  in cats 474
  in dogs 221
  in horses 735
    contagious equine 733
Mice 953, 953
  amyloidosis in 962
  atrial thrombosis in 962
  bacterial diseases 958
  barbering 960
  breeding of 956
  cancer in 962
  dental care 956
  diarrhea in 957
  diet of 955
  digestive disorders in 956
  exercise for 955
  eye disorders 962
  fleas in 959
  geriatric diseases 962
  handling of 953
  housing for 954, 955
  lice in 959
  mites in 959
  mousepox in 961
  mycoplasmal infection 957
  nutritional requirements
    of 955
  osteoarthrosis in 962
  parvovirus infections in 961
  pinworms in 957
  protozoal infections 957
  reproduction of 956
  respiratory disorders in 957
  ringtail syndrome in 959
  ringworm in 958
  salmonellosis in 960
  scaly skin disease in 958
  signs of illness 955, 956
  skin disorders in 958
  tapeworms in 957
  teeth of 956
  temperament of 955
  temperature requirements
    954
  tumors in 962

viral diseases 958
water requirements of 955
wounds in 960
Microbiologic tests 1070
Microchipping
  of birds 835
  for identification of lost
    pets 1225
Microglossia
  in dogs 82
Microorganisms
  and disease 1078
  resident flora 1082
Microsporidiosis *1098*
Midges
  skin allergies from
    in horses 660
  and skin disorders
    in dogs 252
    in horses 761
Miliary dermatitis
  in cats 436, 495
Milk allergy
  in horses 660
Milker's nodules (pseudocow-
    pox) *1114*
Milk glands (*see* Mammary
    glands)
Milk vetch
  poisoning from *1188*
Milkweed poisoning *1188*
Mineral deficiencies (*see also*
    Nutritional deficiencies)
  of reptiles 1023
Minute virus of mice 961
Miotics 1128
Mistletoe poisoning *1178*
Mites (*see also* Mange mites)
  air sac mites 848
  canine nasal 230
  ear mites
    of cats 501
    of dogs 261
    of horses 659
  feather mites 852
  in gerbils 924
  in guinea pigs 937
  in hamsters 951
  in horses 659, 770
  leg mites 852
  mange mites
    in cats 500
    in dogs 260
    in horses 769
  in mice 959
  in rabbits 1001
  in rats 1010
  in reptiles 1033

scaly face mites 852
  and skin disorders
    in cats 500
    in dogs 260
  in sugar gliders 1046
  treatment of 1134
Mitral stenosis
  in dogs 63
Mitral valve dysplasia
  in cats 375
  in dogs 63
Molting 825, *853*
"Monday Morning" sickness
    560
Mongolian gerbils (*see* Gerbils)
Moniliasis *1096* (*see* Candidia-
    sis)
Monkeypox 963, 964, 967,
    1114
Monocytes 35 (*see also* White
    blood cells)
Monocytosis
  in dogs 52
Mood-stabilizing drugs 1131
Moon blindness (*see* Equine
    recurrent uveitis)
Mosquitoes
  and disease transmission
    in cats 497
    in dogs 254
    in horses 765
  and skin disorders
    in cats 436, 497
    in dogs 254
    in horses 765
Motility disorders
  drugs for 1127
Motion sickness
  in cats 467
  in dogs 211
Motor neuron disease
  in horses 716
Mouse (*see* Mice)
Mouse parvovirus 961
Mousepox 961
Mouse tapeworm *1104*
Mouth disorders
  in cats
    burns 394
    inflammation 393
  in dogs
    burns 93
    inflammation 91
    ulcers 91
  in horses
    lip lacerations 612
    paralysis of the tongue 612
    stomatitis 612

Mouth-to-nose resuscitation
    1051 (*see also* Cardio-
    pulmonary-cerebral
    resuscitation)
MRI (*see* Magnetic resonance
    imaging)
Mucocele
  salivary
    in cats 395
    in dogs 95
Mucoid enteritis
  in rabbits 995
Mucus-producing drugs
    1133
Murine respiratory mycoplas-
    mosis
  in rats 1009
Murine typhus *1094*
Murray Valley encephalitis
    1114
Muscle disorders (*see* Musculo-
    skeletal disorders)
Muscle relaxants *1129*
  poisoning from 1197
Muscle strain
  in horses 702
Muscle tumors
  in cats 452
  in dogs 190
Muscular dystrophy
  in cats 447
  in dogs 179
Muscular fatigue
  in dogs 303
  in horses 790
Musculoskeletal disorders
  in cats 445
    arthritis 449
    bone disorders 452
    congenital disorders 447
    hip dysplasia 449
    joint disorders 449
    joint trauma 450
    muscle disorders 451
    nutritional osteopathies
      453
    osteodystrophy 447
    osteogenesis imperfecta 447
    osteomalacia (adult rick-
      ets) 448
    osteomyelitis 452
    rickets 447
    rubber jaw syndrome 448
  in dogs 176
    arthritis 185
    bone disorders 190
    bone fractures 193
    congenital disorders 179

Musculoskeletal disorders
  in dogs (*continued*)
    elbow dysplasia 184
    hip dysplasia 180, 184
    hypertrophic osteodystro-
      phy 191
    hypertrophic osteopathy
      192
    joint disorders 183
    joint fractures 187
    joint trauma 186
    muscle disorders 188
    muscle or tendon trauma
      189
    nutritional osteopathies
      192
    osteochondrosis 180, 184
    osteodystrophy 181
    osteogenesis imperfecta
      180
    osteomalacia (adult rick-
      ets) 181
    osteomyelitis 192
    panosteitis 191
    polymyositis 188
    rickets 180
    rubber jaw syndrome 181
  drugs for 1129
  in horses 664
    arthritis 675
    back disorders 701
    bog spavin 696
    bone fractures of foot 681
    bone spavin 696
    bursitis 677, 695
    cannon bone fractures 691
    carpal bone fractures 690
    carpal disorders 689
    congenital disorders 669
    contracted flexor tendons
      669, 672
    elbow disorders 694
    exertional myopathies 704
    fetlock disorders 687
    foot injuries 684
    hip disorders 700
    joint disorders 675
    lameness 666
    laminitis 682
    metacarpal disorders 689
    muscle disorders 704
    nutritional myopathies 704
    osteochondritis dissecans
      669, 671, 675
    pastern disorders 687
    physitis 672
    shoulder disorders 694
    spine deformities 670

    splint bone fractures 691
    splints 692
    of stifle joint 699
    stringhalt 698
    tarsus disorders 696
    tendinitis 678
    tenosynovitis 678
Myasthenia gravis
  in cats 442, 460
  in dogs 170, 202
Mycetomas
  in cats 539
  in dogs 315
Mycobacteriosis *1092*
  in amphibians 868
  in birds 855
  in fish 918
  in reptiles 1038
Mycoplasmal infection
  in mice 957
Mycosis
  of guttural pouch 749
Mycotic pneumonia (*see* Fungal pneumonia)
Mycotoxic lupinosis
  1156
Mycotoxins (*see* Fungal poisoning)
Myelodysplasia
  in cats 363
  in dogs 42
Myeloencephalitis
  in horses 717
Myelofibrosis
  in cats 364
  in dogs 42
Myelography 199
Myelopathy
  in cats with feline leukemia
    virus 462
Myiasis *1108*
  in cats 466, 496
  in dogs 209, 253
  in horses 721, 764
Mynas (Mynahs) *819* (*see also*
  Birds)
Myocarditis
  in dogs 70
  in horses 599
Myopathies (*see also* Musculoskeletal disorders)
  dystrophy-like
    in cats 447
    in dogs 179
  fibrotic
    in dogs 188
  fibrotic and ossifying
    in horses 707

  nutritional
    in horses 704
  related to toxic plant inges-
    tion
    in horses 707
Myositis
  immune-mediated
    in horses 707
Myositis ossificans
  in dogs 188
Myotonia congenita
  in horses 714
Myrotheciotoxicosis *1156*, 1159
Myxomatosis 1000

N

Nagana
  in horses 766
Nail bind 684
Nail prick 684
Nails
  minor injuries to 1069
Nail trimming
  in birds 835
  in cats 332
  in ferrets 891
  in guinea pigs 930
  in rabbits 989
Nanophyetiasis *1108*
Naphthalene poisoning
  1160
Naproxen poisoning 1192
Narcolepsy
  in horses 713
Nasal allergies
  in dogs 168
Nasal aspergillosis
  in dogs *312*
Nasal cavity
  disorders of
    in cats 426
    in dogs 144
    in horses 648
Nasal dermatoses
  of dogs 263
Nasal mites
  in dogs 230
Nasal polyps
  in horses 751
Nasal septum disorders
  in horses 742
Nasal solar dermatitis
  in dogs 263
Nasogastric intubation
  of horses 1060
Nasopharyngeal polyps
  in cats 484

Natural remedies
  for pain management 1215
Navel ill
  in horses 676
Navicular bone fractures
  in horses 681
Navicular disease
  in horses 683
Near eastern equine encephali-
    tis (see West Nile
    encephalomyelitis)
Negative reinforcement
    (see Reinforcement of
    behavior)
Neobenedinia infection
  in fish 914, 917
Neonatal encephalopathy
  in horses 721
Neonatal isoerythrolysis
  in cats 362
  in dogs 40
  in horses 585
Neonatal maladjustment
    syndrome (see Neonatal
    encephalopathy)
Neosporosis
  in dogs 206, 322
Nephritis
  interstitial
    in cats 518
    in dogs 289
    in horses 785
Nephroblastoma
  in dogs 207, 296
  in horses 783
Nerve sheath tumors
  in dogs 203, 210, 278
Nervous system
  of cats 455
  of dogs 194
  of horses 708
Nervous system disorders
  of cats 455
    brain injuries 457
    caused by parasites 465
    congenital disorders 457,
      459
    diabetic neuropathy 460
    diskospondylitis 462
    dysautonomia 464
    encephalitis 466
    facial paralysis 464
    feline infectious peritonitis
      462
    fungal diseases 462
    infections 457
    leg paralysis 466
    meningitis 466

meningoencephalitis 466
myasthenia gravis 460
peripheral nerves 460
poisoning 460, 464
rabies 467
spinal column and cord
  456, 462
tetanus 464
tick paralysis 461, 469
of dogs 196
  acquired laryngeal paraly-
    sis 202
  autoimmune disorders
    197
  brain injuries 198
  caused by parasites 208
  congenital disorders 197, 200
  deafness 202
  degenerative lumbosacral
    stenosis 204
  diskospondylitis 205
  drugs for 200
  dysautonomia 207
  encephalitis 211
  epilepsy 200
  facial paralysis 208
  fungal diseases 206
  hypothyroid neuropathy
    203
  infections 196
  intervertebral disk disease
    204
  leg paralysis 209
  meningitis 210
  meningoencephalitis
    210
  metabolic disorders 197
  myasthenia gravis 202
  peripheral nerves 201
  poisoning 203, 207
  rabies 211
  rickettsial diseases 205
  spinal column and cord
    196, 204
  tetanus 207
  tick paralysis 203, 213
  trigeminal neuritis 202
  tumors 197
  drugs for 1130
  of horses 708
    botulism 714
    caused by parasites 720
    congenital disorders 710,
      712
    drugs for 712
    dysautonomia 718
    encephalitis 722
    epilepsy 713

equine degenerative
  myeloencephalopathy
  716
equine protozoal myelo-
  encephalitis 717, 719
facial paralysis 720
fungal diseases 717
herpesvirus-1 myelo-
  encephalopathy 717
infections 710
ionophore toxicity 715
leg paralysis 721
meningitis 722
meningoencephalitis 722
motor neuron disease 716
narcolepsy 713
neonatal encephalopathy
  721
peripheral nerves 714
poisoning 717
polyneuritis equi 714
rabies 723
spinal column and cord 716
stringhalt 714
tetanus 718
treatment of 712
viral encephalomyelitis
  718
West Nile encephalomyeli-
  tis 724
Nest boxes
  for rabbits 986, 992, 999
Neuraxonal dystrophy
  in horses 713
Neuroendocrine tissue tumors
  in dogs 140
Neurofibromas
  in cats 509
  in dogs 278
  in horses 778
Neurofibrosarcomas
  in cats 509
  in dogs 278
  in horses 778
Neurologic disorders (see Nervous system disorders)
Neuromas
  associated with amputation
    in dogs 278
Neurons 196
Neuropathic pain 1212 (see
  also Pain)
Neutering
  and cancer 1238
  of cats 343
  of dogs 15
  of guinea pigs 930
  of potbellied pigs 974

Neutropenia
  in cats 369
  in dogs 51
  in horses 590
Neutrophilia
  in cats 369
  in dogs 51
  in horses 590
Neutrophils 35, *165 (see also*
    White blood cells)
Nevus
  collagenous
    in cats 506
    in dogs 271
    in horses 776
  in dogs 242
  in horses 758
Newcastle disease 848, *1114*
New tank syndrome 911
Newts 865 (*see also*
    Amphibians)
New World hemorrhagic fever
    1114
Nicotine sulfate poisoning
    1168
Nictitating membrane
  of cats 331, 424
  of dogs 4, 142
  of horses 647
Nightshades
  poisoning from *1182*
Nipah virus infection *1114*
Nitrate poisoning 1172
Nitrite poisoning 1172
Nitroscanate 1128
Nocardiosis *1096*
  in cats 542
  in dogs 322
  in horses 809
Nodular hyperplasia
  in dogs 123
Nonprotein nitrogen poison-
    ing 1172
Nonspecific immunity 165
Nonsteroidal anti-inflamma-
    tory drugs (NSAIDs) 1126,
    1140
  in pain management 1214
  poisoning from 1192
  prescription (human),
    poisoning from 1198
  toxicity in horses 627
Norepinephrine *130*, 1124
North American blastomycosis
  in cats 539
  in dogs 315
North Asian tickborne rickett-
    siosis *1094*

Notoedric mange
  in cats 436, 500
NSAIDs (*see* Nonsteroidal
    anti-inflammatory
    drugs)
Nuchal ligament 550
Nuclear medicine imaging
    1077
Nursing care
  for critically ill animals 1058
Nutraceuticals
  in pain management 1215
Nutrition
  importance of 1238
  for injured dogs and cats
    1058
Nutritional deficiencies
  of birds 850
  and skin disorders
    in dogs 282
Nutritional deficiency ane-
    mias
  in dogs 40
Nutritional myopathies
  in horses 704
Nutritional osteodystrophy
  in sugar gliders 1045
Nutritional osteopathies
  in cats 453
  in dogs 192
Nutritional requirements
  of birds 830, 844
  of cats 337
  of chinchillas 875, 884
  of dogs 10
  of ferrets 890
  of hamsters 942
  of horses 559
  of mice 955
  for pets with cancer 1246
  of rabbits 987
  of rats 1005
Nutritional secondary hyper-
    parathyroidism
  in cats 453
Nutritional supplements
  for animals with cancer 1247
  poisoning from 1194
Nymphomania
  in mares 576

O

Oak bud poisoning 1201, *1180*
Obesity
  in amphibians 872
  in dogs 11
  in horses 574

  in cats 337
  in potbellied pigs 972
  in sugar gliders 1046
Obstruction
  of bile duct
    in cats 413
    in dogs 125
  gastrointestinal
    in cats 400
    in dogs 104
    in horses 615
Occipitoatlantoaxial malfor-
    mation
  in horses 713
Ocular fundus
  of cats 430
  of dogs 151
  of horses 652
Odontoma
  in prairie dogs 966
"Off-label" use of drugs 1118
Oil glands
  of cats 489
  of dogs 240
  of horses 756
Ointments 1120
Old dog encephalitis 173
Old tank syndrome 911
Omsk hemorrhagic fever
    1114
Onchocerciasis
  in horses 771
Onions
  poisoning from *1184*
Open-chest cardiopulmonary
    resuscitation (*see*
    Cardiopulmonary
    resuscitation)
Ophthalmic emergencies (*see*
    Eye emergencies)
Opioids
  in pain management 1214
  poisoning from 1200
Opisthorchiasis *1100*
Optic atrophy
  in cats 431
  in dogs 153
Optic nerve hypoplasia
  in cats 431
  in dogs 152
  in horses 653
Orbital cellulitis
  in dogs 153
Organophosphates 1128
  poisoning from 1169
    in cats 460, 464
    in dogs 203, 207
    in horses 715, 717

Ornithosis *1092*
Osmotic diuretics 1128
Osselets
  in horses 688
Osteitis
  pedal
    in horses 684
Osteoarthritis (degenerative
      joint disease)
  in cats 449
  in dogs 185
  in horses 676, 691
  treatment of pain 1215
Osteoarthrosis
  in mice 962
Osteochondritis dissecans
  in horses 669, 671, 675
Osteochondroma
  in horses 691
Osteochondromatosis
  in cats 452
  in dogs 191
Osteochondrosis
  in dogs 180, 184
Osteodystrophy
  in cats 447, 452
  in dogs 180, 191
  in horses 673
Osteogenesis imperfecta
  in cats 447
  in dogs 180
Osteomalacia (adult rickets)
  in cats 448
  in dogs 181
  in horses 674
  in reptiles 1024
Osteomyelitis
  in birds 843
  in cats 452
  in dogs 192
Osteopathy
  craniomandibular
    in dogs 191
  hypertrophic
    in dogs 192
  nutritional
    in cats 453
    in dogs 192
Osteopetrosis
  in dogs 180
Otitis externa
  in cats 437
  in dogs 160
  in horses 659
Otitis interna
  in cats 437
  in dogs 161
  in horses 659

Otitis media
  in cats 437
  in chinchillas 879
  in dogs 161
  in horses 659
Otodectic mange
  in cats 436, 501
  in dogs 261
Ovarian cysts
  in guinea pigs 936
Ovarian remnant syndrome
  in cats 475
  in dogs 221
Ovaries
  underdevelopment of
    in mares 732
Overheating (*see* Heat stress)
Over-the-counter drugs
  poisoning from 1181
Over-training
  of horses 791
Oxycodone poisoning
    1200
Oxytocin *130*

P

Pacheco's disease 854
Pain
  assessment methods 1212
  behaviors in animals 1212
  signs of *1212*, 1212, 1213, 1246
  treatment of 1213
  types of 1211
Pain scales 1213
Pain management 1211
  in cancer 1245, 1248
    drugs used for 1245
  complementary and alter-
      native therapies 1215
  corticosteroids for 1215
  in emergency care 1058
  local anesthetics in 1215
  nonsteroidal anti-
      inflammatory drugs for
      1214
  opioids for 1214
  and quality of life *1250*
Palmar carpal ligament break-
      down
  in cats 451
  in dogs 188
Palmar intercarpal ligament
      tear
  in horses 693
Pancreatic abscesses
  in cats 409
  in dogs 119

Pancreatic cancer
  in cats 409
  in dogs 119
Pancreatic disorders
  in cats 407, 417
    abscesses 409
    exocrine pancreatic insuffi-
        ciency 408
    pancreatic cancer 409
    pancreatitis 408
    pseudocysts 409
  in dogs 117, 132
    abscesses 119
    exocrine pancreatic insuffi-
        ciency 118
    pancreatic cancer 119
    pancreatitis 117
    pseudocysts 119
Panhypopituitarism
  adult-onset
    in cats 421
    in dogs 137
  juvenile onset
    in dogs 138
Panleukopenia
  vaccination in cats *339*
Pannus
  in dogs 147
Panosteitis
  in dogs 191
Papillar stomatitis
  in horses 613
Papilledema
  in dogs 153
Papillitis 1065
Papillomas
  of birds 855
  of cats 513
  of dogs 94, 282
  of foals 781
  of horses 781
  of rabbits 1001
  of reptiles 1038
Papillomatosis
  in birds 841
Parafilaria multipapillosa
    infestation
  in horses 771
Paragonimiasis (lung fluke
    disease) *1100*
Parakeets *817* (*see also* Birds)
Paralysis
  caused by tumors
    in dogs 210
  facial
    in cats 464
    in dogs 208
    in horses 720

Paralysis (*continued*)
  hyperkalemic periodic
    in horses 714
  of the leg
    in cats 466
    in dogs 209
    in horses 721
  from ticks
    in cats 469
    in dogs 213
Paramyxovirus infections
  in snakes 1032
Paranasal sinus disorders
  in horses 742
Paraneoplastic neuropathy
  in dogs 203
Paraphimosis
  in cats 473
  in dogs 219
Paraquat poisoning 1162
Parasites
  bloodborne
    of cats 364
    of dogs 42
    of horses 586
  in cats 340, *341*
  in dogs 13
  drugs for 1134
  of the ear
    in cats 435
    in dogs 158
    in horses 657
  external
    in horses 563
  eyeworms
    of cats 432
    of dogs 154
    of horses 654
  in fish 912, 914
  gastrointestinal
    in cats 403
    in dogs 110
    in horses *563, 564,* 629
  infections caused by
    1086
  mites (*see* Mites)
  in potbellied pigs 973
  of saltwater fish 917
  strongyles 563
  testing for 1072
  treatment of 1127
Parathion poisoning 1169
Parathyroid gland disorders
  in cats 419
  in dogs 134
Parathyroid hormone *130, 134*
Paroxetine poisoning
  1196

Parrot fever 855
Parrotlets *819*
Parrot mouth
  in horses 611
Parrots *817* (*see also* Birds)
  beaks of 824
  communication by 823
  gout in 853
  life span of 826
  Pacheco's disease in 854
  papillomatosis in 841
  psittacine beak and feather
    disease 852
  sarcocystosis in 844, 848
  skin infections of 851
  tapeworms in 842
  temperament of 831
Parvovirus
  in cats 444
  in dogs *13,* 101, 175
  in mice 961
  in rats 1012
Paspalum staggers 1158
Passive immunity 1144
Pastern disorders
  in horses 687
Pastes 1119, 1120
Pasteurellosis *1092*
  in rabbits 997, 998
  in sugar gliders 1046
Patagium 1039
Patent ductus arteriosus
  in cats 374
  in dogs 59
  in horses 597
Patent urachus
  in horses 784
Pawing behavior
  in horses 574
Paws
  of cats 332
  of dogs 4
PBB (*see* Polybrominated
  biphenyl poisoning)
PCB (*see* Polychlorinated
  biphenyl poisoning)
Pedal bone
  cysts
    in horses 679
  fractures of
    in horses 681
  inflammation of
    in horses 684
Pedal osteitis
  in horses 684
Pelger-Huët anomaly
  in cats 369
  in dogs 52

Pelodera dermatitis
  in dogs 264
  in horses 771
Pelvis fractures
  in horses 701
Pemphigus
  in cats 425, 442
  in dogs 144
Pemphigus foliaceus 170
Pemphigus vulgaris 170
Pentachlorophenol poisoning
  (Penta poisoning)
  1173
Pentastomid infections
  1108
Perennial ryegrass staggers
  1205
Perianal fistula
  in dogs 126
Perianal gland tumors
  in dogs 277
Periauricular cysts
  in horses 758
Pericardial disease
  in cats 380
  in dogs 72
  in horses 600
Perineal hernia
  in dogs 127
Periodic ophthalmia (*see*
  Equine recurrent uveitis)
Periodontal disease (*see* Gum
  disease)
Periodontitis
  in cats 391
  in dogs 88
Peripheral nerve disorders
  of cats 460
  of dogs 201
  of horses 715
Peripheral nerve sheath
  tumors
  in dogs 278
Peripheral nervous system (*see*
  Nervous system)
Peritoneal lavage 1056
Peritoneopericardial diaphragmatic hernia
  in dogs 64, *85*
Peritonitis
  in cats 542
    feline infectious 532
  in dogs 323
  in horses 809
Persistent right aortic arch
  in dogs 61
Pesticide poisoning 1167
Pet sitters 1227

Pet carriers 1217
  for air travel 1225
  for car travel 1223
Petroleum product poisoning
    1173
Pets
  abuse of 1231
  in animal-assisted therapy
      1229
  euthanasia for 1232
  health benefits for owners
      1228
  loss of 1232
  ownership considerations
      1231
  populations in the U.S. *1229*
  travel with 1216
  welfare of 1231
pH
  scale *903*
  of urine *1137*
Phaeohyphomycosis
  in cats 540
  in dogs 316
  in horses 804
Phagocytes 35
Pharyngeal disorders
  in cats 396
  in dogs 97
  in horses 751
Pharyngeal lymphoid hyper-
      plasia
  in horses 751
Pharyngeal paralysis
  in cats 396
  in dogs 97
  in horses 613
Pharyngitis
  in cats 484
  in dogs 233
  in horses 751
Pharynx
  disorders of (*see* Pharyngeal
      disorders)
  inflammation of (*see*
      Pharyngitis)
Phenol poisoning 1149
Phenylpyrazoles 1134
Pheochromocytomas
  in dogs 132
Phimosis
  in cats 473
  in dogs 219
Phobias (*see also* Behavior
      problems)
  in cats 346
  in dogs 19, 27
  in horses 568

Phosphorus
  imbalances
    in cats 447
    in dogs 180
    in horses 673
  poisoning from 1203
Photoperiod *1022*
Photosensitization
  in cats 502
  in dogs 264
  in horses 633, 772
Physitis
  in horses 672
Pica
  in horses 572
PIE (Pulmonary infiltration
      with eosinophilia)
      syndrome
  in cats 440
  in dogs 168
Pigeon fever
  in horses 591
Pigeons *819*
Pigmentary abnormalities
  in cats 491
  in dogs 244, 257
  in horses 758
Pigs
  potbellied (*see* Potbellied pigs)
Pink eye (*see* Conjunctivitis)
Pinna
  disorders of
    in cats 435
    in dogs 158
    in horses 657
Pinworms
  in gerbils 923
  in hamsters 948
  in horses *563*, *630*
  in mice 957
  in rabbits 996
  in rats 1008
  in reptiles 1037
Pionus parrots *819*
Piperazine 1128
Piperonyl butoxide 1169
Pitch poisoning 1149
Pituitary adenomas
  in birds 859
Pituitary dwarfism
  in dogs 138
Pituitary gland disorders
  in cats 420
  in dogs 136
Pituitary gland tumors
  in dogs 132
  in rats 1012
Placenta

retained
    in horses 735
Placental subinvolution
  in dogs 222
Plague *1092*
  in cats 543
  in dogs 323
  in prairie dogs 968
Plants (*see also* Houseplants,
      Range plants)
  aquatic (*see* Aquatic plants)
  poisonous to animals 1175
Plasmacytomas
  extramedullary
    in dogs 274
Platelets 1074
  disorders of
    in cats 368
    in dogs 48
    in horses 588
  functions of 36
Pleural space disease
  in dogs and cats 1054
Pleuroperitoneal hernias
  in dogs *85*
Pleuropneumonia
  in horses 752
Pneumocystis pneumonia *1096*
Pneumonia
  aspiration
    in cats 485
    in dogs 234
    in horses 740
  in cats 485
  in chinchillas 881
  in dogs 233
  equine morbillivirus 746
  in foals 747, 748
  fungal
    in cats 486
    in dogs 234
  in guinea pigs 935
  in hamsters 949
  in horses 752, 799
  in potbellied pigs 981
  in rabbits 997
Pneumonitis
  allergic
    in cats 479
    in dogs 227
  in cats 486
Pneumothorax 1053, 1056
  in cats 479
  in dogs 227
  in horses 740
Pododermatitis
  in guinea pigs 938
  in prairie dogs 968

Poicephalus parrots *819*
Poinsettia poisoning *1178*
Poison hemlock *1190*
Poisoning 1145 (*see also* Poisons)
Poisons
  1080 poisoning 1203
  1081 poisoning 1203
  5-Fluorouracil 1197
  affecting the liver
    in cats 411
    in dogs 122
    in horses 636, *637*
  aflatoxins 1154
  algae 1146
  algaecide 1147
  ammonia 1172
  amphetamines 1199
  antifreeze 1150
  arsenic 1147, 1161
  avocado 1152
  in birds *836*, 857
  bleaches 1163
  bracken fern 1147
  bread dough 1152
  cantharidin 1148
  chocolate 1153
  cleaning products 1166
  coal tar 1149
  cocaine 1198
  copper 1149
  cottonseeds 1159
  cyanide 1150
  dinitro compounds 1162
  emulsifiers 1170
  ethylene glycol (antifreeze) 1150
  fescue 1155
  fluorides 1151
  fungi 1154, *1156*
  gossypol 1159
  grapes 1154
  halogenated aromatics 1160
  herbicides 1160
  household chemicals 1163
  houseplants *1174*, 1175
  human over-the-counter drugs 1181
  human prescription drugs 1194
  insecticides 1167
  iron 1193
  lead 1170
  lupines 1155
  macadamia nut 1153
  marijuana 1199
  mercury 1171
  metaldehyde 1171, 1202

  nitrates 1172
  nitrites 1172
  nonprotein nitrogen poisoning 1172
  opiates 1200
  organophosphates 1169
  paspalum grasses 1158
  pentachlorophenol 1173
  petroleum products 1173
  pyrethrins 1168
  raisins 1154
  range plants 1175, *1180*
  rodenticides 1201
  ryegrass *1156*, 1204
  salt (sodium chloride) 1205
  sanitizers 1166
  selenium 1205
  snakebites 1206
  solvents 1170
  sorghum 1150
  spiderbites 1208
  strychnine 1209
  sweet clover *1156*, 1210
  toad venom 1210
  urea 1172
  vitamin overdose 1193
  zinc 1211
Pokeweed poisoning *1180*
Polioencephalomalacia
  in sugar gliders 1046
Polioencephalomyelitis
  in cats 463
Poll evil
  in horses 677
Polyarteritis nodosa
  in rats 1012
Polybrominated biphenyls
  poisoning from 1160
Polyclonal gammopathies
  in cats 445
  in dogs 175
Polycystic disease
  in dogs 123
  in hamsters 952
Polycystic kidneys
  in cats 515
  in dogs 285
  in horses 783
Polycythemia
  in cats 370
  diagnosis of 1073
  in dogs 52
Polydactyly
  in horses 670
Polymyopathy
  hypokalemic
    in cats 452

Polymyositis
  in dogs 188
Polyneuritis equi 714
Polyomavirus 854
Polyps
  nasal
    in horses 751
  nasopharyngeal 438
    in cats 484
  rectal
    in cats 414
    in dogs 127
Polyradiculoneuritis
  in dogs 202
Polysaccharide storage myopathy
  in horses 705
Ponds
  set up for fish 902
Porcupine quills
  injuries from 1069
Pork tapeworm disease *1104*
Porphyria
  in cats 492
Porphyrin deposits
  in gerbils 923
Portosystemic shunt
  in cats 389, 411
  in dogs 86, 122
  in horses 608, 640
Positive inotropes 1122
Postcastration evisceration
  of horses 1063
Postpartum hypocalcemia (*see* Puerperal hypocalcemia)
Post-traumatic sarcoma
  in cats 433
Potbellied pigs 970
  aggression in 972
  arthritis 979
  atrophic rhinitis 980
  bacterial infections 979
  breeding 974
  calculi (stones) 982
  colibacillosis 976
  constipation 978
  cystitis 982
  dehydration 980
  dental care 974
  diarrhea 976, 977
  diet 972
  digestive disorders 976
  dry skin in 981
  enterocolitis 977
  erysipelas 982
  exercising 972
  fractures 978

hoof problems 973, 979
household hazards 974
housing 971
lameness 978
nervous system disorders 979
neutering/spaying 972, 975, 976
newborn care 976
nutritional requirements of 972
obesity in 972
overheating 980
ownership restrictions 970
parasite control 973
pneumonia 981
pregnancy 975
rectal prolapse 978
reproduction 974
rooting 970
routine health care 973
Salmonella infections 977
salt poisoning 980
sarcoptic mange 974, 981
seizures 980
selecting 970
skin disorders 981
sunburn 982
swallowed objects 976
teeth 974
   trimming of 974
temperament 972
temperature requirements of 970, 980
tetanus 979
tumors 981
urolithiasis 982
vaccination of 973, *973*
veterinary care for 973
water requirements of 972, 983
Potomac horse fever 623
as cause of abortion in mares 733
vaccination in horses 562
Powdered vitamin/mineral supplements
for reptiles 1023
Powders 1120
dusting 1120
Poxvirus infections
in birds 855
in cats 503
Prairie dogs 962
aggression in 963, 965
lifespan of 963
antibiotic use in 966

cancer in 969
dehydration in 966
dental disorders 966
diarrhea in 967
diet of 964
diseases transmitted to humans from 964, *967*
exercising 965
fleas and ticks in 967
fractured bones in 967
hair loss in 967
housing for 964
malocclusion in 966
and monkeypox 963, 964, 967
odontoma in 966
ownership restrictions 962, 963
plague in 968
pododermatitis in 968
preputial blockage in 968
reproduction 963
respiratory disease in 969
ringworm in 967
roundworms in 969
signs of illness in 965
spaying and neutering of 966
teeth of 966
temperament 965
tularemia in 969
tumors in 969
veterinary care for 965
water requirements 965
Praziquantel 1128
Preen gland 825
Pregnancy (*see also* False pregnancy, Reproduction)
in cats 471
in dogs 216
and drugs 1121
in hamsters 945
in horses 728
Pregnancy toxemia (*see* Ketosis)
Prepuce
inflammation of
in dogs 218
Prepurchase examination
of horses 558, *558*
Prescription drugs (human)
poisoning from 1194
Pressure wounds
management of 1068
Primary hyperammonemia
in horses 639
Primary hyperparathyroidism
in dogs 181

Probiotics
for prairie dogs 966
for rabbits 993
Production-related metabolic disorders
of cats 526
of dogs 301
of horses 789
Progesterone *131*
Prognathia
in cats 387
in dogs 82
in horses 607
Progressive retinal atrophy
in cats 430
in dogs 151
Prokinetic drugs 1127, *1127*
Prolactin *130*
Prolapse
rectal
in cats 415
in dogs 128
in horses 640
Proliferative enteritis
in hamsters 946
Proliferative enteropathy
in rabbits 995
Propanil poisoning 1162
Prophylaxis 1082
Prostaglandin 1126
Prostate
cancer of
in dogs 220
disorders of
in cats 473
in dogs 219
Proventricular dilatation disease 841
Proventriculus 826
Pruritus
in cats 490, 499
in dogs 242, 259
in horses 768
Pseudocowpox *1114*
Pseudoephedrine poisoning 1191
Pseudoglanders *1092*
Pseudomonas aeruginosa infection
in chinchillas 882
in mice 961
Pseudotuberculosis
in hamsters 952
Psittacine beak and feather disease 852
Psittacosis 855, *1092*
Psitticula parakeets *820*

Psoriasiform-lichenoid
    dermatosis
  in dogs 245
Psoroptic mange
  in horses 659, 769
Psychotropic agents 1130, 1136
Ptyalism (*see* Salivation)
Puerperal hypocalcemia
  in cats 527
  in dogs 302
Pulmonary edema
  in cats 486
  in dogs 235
Pulmonary hemorrhage
  exercise-induced
  in horses 747
Pulmonary infiltrates with
    eosinophilia (PIE) syn-
    drome (*see* Allergic
    pneumonitis)
Pulmonic stenosis
  in cats 375
  in dogs 60
Punishment
  of cats 349
  of dogs 22
  of horses 570
Puppies (*see also* Dogs)
  care of 15
  nutritional requirements of 16
  vaccination of 15
  worms in 16
Puppy hypoglycemia 201
Pure red cell aplasia
  in cats 363
  in dogs 41
  in horses 585
Purpura hemorrhagica
  in horses 662
Pyelonephritis
  in cats 517
  in dogs 288
  in horses 784
Pyloric stenosis
  in cats 389
  in dogs 85
  in horses 608
Pyoderma
  in cats 504
  in dogs 265
Pyometra
  in cats 475
  in dogs 221
  in horses 735
Pyramidal disease
  in horses 685
Pyrethrins
  poisoning from 1168

Pyrethroids
  poisoning from 1168
Pyrrolizidine alkaloidosis
    1200
Pythiosis
  in dogs 316
  in horses 803

Q

Q fever (Query fever) *1094*
  in cats 544
Quadriceps contracture (stiff
    stifle disease)
  in dogs 190
Quaker (Monk) parakeets *820*
Quality of life
  for animals with cancer
    1247, 1248
  scale 1249, *1250*
Quarantine laws
  for domestic travel 1219
  for international travel 1220
Quarantine tanks
  for fish 907
Quarter crack
  in horses 685
Queensland itch
  in horses 762
Queensland tick typhus *1094*
Quercus poisoning (oak bud
    poisoning, acorn poison-
    ing) 1201, *1180*
Query fever (*see* Q fever)
Quidding *564*
Quittor
  in horses 685

R

Rabbit calicivirus disease
    995
Rabbits 983
  abscesses in 1002
  allergies to 984
  and antibiotics 990, 994
  bacterial infections of 994
  bladder stones of 1002
  breeding 986, 992
  breeds of 983, *984*
  broken bones in 997
  calicivirus disease in 995
  cancer in 1003
  cannibalism of young 992
  caring for 984, *985*, 986, 990
  coccidiosis 996
    hepatic 996
    intestinal 996

  compatibility of 988
  conjunctivitis in 996, 1000
  dental abscesses 991
  dental care 991
  diarrhea in 994
  diet of 987, *989*
  digestive disorders 993
  disease prevention in 986
  diseases transmitted to
    humans from *993*
  encephalitozoonosis in
    1003
  enterotoxemia in 994
  exercise needs of 986, 988
  flea infestations in 1002
  food hazards *989*
  genital infections in 998
  grooming of 984
  hairballs 984, 988, 993
  hair chewing 993
  handling of 989
  hay for 988
  heat stress in 984, 1002
  housing for 985, 988, 1002
  hutch burn in 999
  intestinal disease in 987, 994
  ketosis in 998
  kidney stones of 1002
  life span of 984
  listeriosis in 1002
  litter box training for 987
  malocclusion in 991
  mastitis in 998
  mites of 1001
  moist dermatitis of 999
  myxomatosis in 1000
  nest boxes for 992, 999
  newborn care 992
  nutritional requirements of
    987, 988
  papillomas in 1001
  pasteurellosis in 997, 998
  pinworms in 996
  pneumonia in 997
  reproduction 992
  reproductive disorders in
    998
  respiratory disorders in
    997
  rhinitis in 997
  ringworm 1000
  rotaviral infection in 995
  roundworms in 996
  selecting 985, *985*
  shedding by 984
  shope fibromas in 1000
  signs of illness in 990, *990*
  skin disorders in 999

sore hocks in 999
spaying/neutering 989
splay leg in 997
tapeworms in 996
teeth of 983, 991
temperament of 988
torticollis in 1001
treponematosis in 998
tularemia in 1003
tumors in 1003
Tyzzer's disease in 994
ulcerative pododermatitis
  in 999
vaccination of 989
venereal disease in 998
veterinary care for 989
wet dewlap in 999
Rabbit syphilis 998
Rabies *1114*
  in cats 467
  in dogs 211
  in horses 723
  quarantine laws 1219
  vaccination programs
    in cats *339*
    in dogs *13*, 212
    in ferrets 891
    in horses *562*
    for travel purposes 1221,
      1222
Radiation therapy 1077,
  1241, *1241*
  brachytherapy *1241*
  and infection 1081
Radiography 1075
Radionuclide imaging 1077
Ragwort poisoning 1200
Raillietina infection *1104*
Raisins
  poisoning from 1154
Range plants poisonous to
  animals 1175, *1180*
Ranitidine poisoning 1193
Rashes
  in cats 499
Rat bite fever *1092*
Rat coronavirus infection
  1008
Rat poison 1201 (*see* Rodenticide poisoning)
Rats 1003
  barbering 1009
  breeding 1007
  cages for 1004, 1005
  cancer in 1012
  chronic respiratory disease
    1009
  compatibility 1004

dental care 1007
diet 1005
digestive disorders 1008
exercising 1006
eye disorders 1007
fight wounds 1009
flea infestations of 1009
handling 1004
head-tilt in 1007
kidney and urinary disorders
  1011
lice of 1010
lymphocytic choriomeningitis virus infection in
  1011
mammary tumors 1012
mite infestations in 1010
nutritional requirements
  1005
parvovirus infection in
  1012
pinworms in 1008
polyarteritis nodosa 1012
protozoal infections 1008
reproduction 1007
respiratory disorders 1009
ringtail syndrome 1010
ringworm in 1010
roundworms in 1011
salivary gland
    inflammation 1008
salmonellosis 1012
selecting 1004
sialodacryoadenitis 1008
signs of illness 1006, *1006*
skin disorders of 1009
spinal cord degeneration
  in 1008
tapeworms in 1008
teeth 1007
temperament 1006
tumors in 1012
water requirements
  1005
Rat tapeworm *1104*
Recluse spider bites 1208
Rectal disorders
  in cats 414
  in dogs 125
  in horses 640
Rectal polyps
  in cats 414
  in dogs 127
Rectal prolapse
  in cats 415
  in dogs 128
  in horses 640
  in potbellied pigs 978

Rectal strictures
  in cats 414
  in dogs 127
  in horses 640
Rectal tears
  in cats 415
  in dogs 128
  in horses 640
Rectal tumors
  in cats 414
  in dogs 127
Recurrent airway obstruction
  in horses 752
Recurrent uveitis
  in horses 807
Red squill poisoning 1203
Red blood cells 33
Red-leg syndrome
  in amphibians 868
Red tears 1007
Reflexes
  of cats 455
  of dogs 194
Reinforcement of behavior
  in cats 348
  in dogs 21
  in horses 569
Relapsing fever (borreliosis)
  1092
Renal adenocarcinomas
  (Lucké tumors)
  in amphibians 872
Renal cell carcinoma
  in horses 787
Renal disorders (*see* Kidney
  disorders)
Renal dropsy
  in fish 917
Renal tubular acidosis
  in cats 522
  in dogs 294
  in horses 787
Reproduction
  of birds 836
  of cats 343
  of chinchillas 878, 884
  of dogs *15*, 15
  of ferrets 893
  of fish 908
  of gerbils 922
  of guinea pigs 930
  of hamsters 945
  of horses 565
  of mice 956
  of potbellied pigs 974
  of rabbits 992
  of rats 1007
  of sugar gliders 1043

Reproduction management
    of cats 471
    of dogs 215
    of horses 727
Reproductive cycle
    of cats 470
    of dogs 215
    of horses 727
Reproductive disorders
    of birds 848
    of cats 469
        cryptorchidism 473
        dystocia (abnormal labor
            and delivery) 471, 474
        false pregnancy 474
        follicular cysts 474
        infertility 472
        mammary hypertrophy
            (overgrowth) 474
        mammary tumors 475
        mastitis 474
        metritis 474
        paraphimosis 473
        phimosis 473
        prostate disorders 473
        pyometra 475
    of dogs 214
        balanoposthitis 218
        brucellosis 223
        cryptorchidism 218
        dystocia (abnormal labor
            and delivery) 216, 220
        false pregnancy 220
        follicular cysts 220
        infertility 217
        mammary tumors 222
        mastitis 221
        metritis 221
        paraphimosis 219
        phimosis 219
        prostate disorders 219
        pyometra 221
        transmissible venereal
            tumors 223
        vaginitis 222
    drugs for 1131
    of horses 726
        abortion 732
        brucellosis 733
        contagious equine metritis
            733
        cryptorchidism 731
        dourine 736
        equine coital exanthema
            734
        mare reproductive loss
            syndrome 732
        mastitis 734

    metritis 735
    pyometra 735
    retained placenta 735
    vaginitis 736
    vulvitis 736
Reproductive system
    of cats 469
    of dogs 214
    of horses 726
Reptiles 1013
    abscesses in 1037
    aggression in 1019
    bacterial infections in 1035
    bite injuries 1027
    bone and muscle disorders
        1030
    burn injuries 1026
    cancer of 1038
    crush injuries 1026
    diabetes mellitus in 1029
    diet of 1022
    digestive disorders 1027
    diseases transmitted to
        humans from 1016, 1016
    ear disorders 1029
    emergency care 1026
    enclosures for 1018
    eye disorders 1029
    fractures 1027
    fungal infections in 1032,
        1036
    gout in 1031
    hibernation 1020
    housing requirements 1022
    humidity requirements
        1021, 1022
    hyperuricemia in 1023
    intestinal parasites in
        1028
    lighting requirements
        1021, 1022
    medications for 1026
    nervous system disorders
        1030
    nutritional disorders 1031
    nutritional requirements
        1022, 1023
    parasites of 1037
    protozoal diseases 1029
    respiratory disorders 1031
    selecting 1016
    septicemia in 1027
    skin disorders 1032
    skin parasites of 1033
    temperament 1025
    temperature requirements
        1020, 1022, 1026
    tumors of 1038

    vitamin and mineral require-
        ments of 1023
    water requirements 1021,
        1022
Resident flora 1082
Respiratory disorders (see
        Lung and airway disor-
        ders)
Respiratory distress
    in cats 476
    in dogs 224
    in horses 737
Respiratory system
    of cats 475
    of dogs 224
    of horses 556, 736
Restrictive cardiomyopathy
    in cats 379
Retained placenta
    in horses 735
Retained ulnar cartilage cores
    in dogs 192
Retinal degeneration 1065
    in dogs 152
    in mice 962
Retinal detachments 1065
    in cats 431
    in dogs 152
    in horses 653
Retinal dysplasia
    in cats 430
    in dogs 151
Retinal inflammation
    in cats 430
    in dogs 152
Retinoids 1136
Retrobulbar hemorrhage
    1064
Retrobulbar optic neuritis
    1065
Rhabdiasis
    in amphibians 871
Rhabdomyolysis (see Exer-
        tional myopathy)
Rheumatoid arthritis
    in dogs 172, 185
Rhinitis
    in cats 486
    in dogs 235
    in rabbits 997
Rhinopneumonitis
    equine viral 744
Rhinosinusitis
    in cats 486
Rhinosporidiosis 1096
    in cats 540
    in dogs 317
    in horses 804

Rhodococcus equi pneumonia
in foals 747
Rhododendron poisoning *1176*
Rickets
in cats 447, 448
in dogs 180, 181
in horses 674
in reptiles 1024
Rickettsial diseases 1085
(*see also individual
diseases*)
in dogs 312
feline infectious anemia 365
Rocky Mountain spotted fever
1094
in dogs 50
transmitted to people *1094*
Rickettsial pox *1094*
Rift Valley fever *1114*
Right liver lobe atrophy
in horses 639
Right-sided congestive heart
failure 67
Ringbone
in horses 688
Ringtail syndrome
in mice 959
in rats 1010
Ringworm *1096*
in birds 851
in cats 504
in chinchillas 881
in dogs 266
in ferrets 895
in guinea pigs 937
in hamsters 950
in horses 773
in mice 958
in prairie dogs 967
in rabbits 1000
in rats 1010
in reptiles 1032
Roaring
in horses 741
Rocky Mountain spotted fever
1094
in dogs 50, 324
Rodenticide poisoning 1201
Rodents (*see individual
species*)
importing of 1220
Rosellas *820*
Ross River fever *1116*
Rotavirus
vaccination in horses *562*
Rotavirus infection
in foals 626
in rabbits 995

Roundworms
in amphibians 871
in birds 842
in cats 340, *341*, 403, *404*,
465
in chinchillas 883
in dogs 110, *111*, 210
in horses *563*, 721
in prairie dogs 969
in rabbits 996
in rats 1011
in reptiles 1028, 1037
treatment of 1127
Rubber jaw syndrome
in cats 448
in dogs 181
Rubber puppy disease (*see
Ehlers-Danlos syndrome*)
Rupture
of bile duct
in cats 414
in dogs 125
of common digital extensor
tendon
in horses 691
of gallbladder
in cats 414
in dogs 125
Russian spring-summer
encephalitis *1112*
Rust 915
Ryegrass poisoning 1204, *1156*
Ryegrass staggers
annual 1204
perennial 1205

S

Sacroiliac injury
in horses 703
Saddle sores 773
Salamanders *865* (*see also
Amphibians*)
Salivary disorders
in cats 395
excessive salivation 395
salivary gland tumors
396
salivary mucocele 395
xerostomia 396
in dogs 95
excessive salivation 95
inflammation of salivary
gland 96
salivary fistula 96
salivary gland tumors 96
salivary mucocele 95
xerostomia 96

Salivation
excessive
in cats 395
in dogs 95, *95*
Salmonella infection *1092*
in cats 403
in dogs 109
in gerbils 923
in guinea pigs 939
in hamsters 947
in horses 621
in mice 960
in rats 1012
Salmon poisoning disease
in dogs 325
Salt (sodium chloride) poisoning 1205
in potbellied pigs 980
Sandcrack (Toe crack, Quarter
crack, Heel crack)
in horses 685
Sand flies
in cats 497
in dogs 254
Saprolegnia infection
in amphibians 870
in fish 918
Sarcocystosis *1098*
in birds 844, 848
in cats 454
in dogs 194
in horses 708
Sarcoids
in horses 776
Sarcomas 1238
anaplastic
in cats 513
in dogs 281
soft tissue
in cats 509
in dogs 279
spread of 1235
undifferentiated
in cats 513
in dogs 281
Sarcoptic mange
in cats 436
in dogs 159, 260
in horses 769
in potbellied pigs 974, 981
SARS (*see Severe acute respiratory syndrome*)
Saucer fractures
in horses 689
Scabies (*see also* Mange)
in cats 500
in dogs 260
in horses 769

Scale rot
  in reptiles 1034
Scales
  of fish 900
Scaly skin disease
  in mice 958
Schistosomiasis (bilharziasis)
  1102
Sciatic nerve injuries
  in cats 461
  in dogs 204
  in horses 715
Scintigraphy 1077
Scoliosis
  in horses 670
Scottish fold osteodystrophy
  452
Scratches (greasy heel)
  in horses 686
Screening for cancer
  1239
Screwworms
  and skin disorders
    in dogs 254
    in horses 764
Scrotal hernias
  in dogs 85
Scrub typhus *1094*
SCUD (*see* Septicemic cutaneous ulcerative disease)
Scurvy (*see* Vitamin C
  deficiency)
Sea travel with pets 1226
Sebaceous glands
  of cats 489
  of dogs 240
  of horses 756
  tumors of
    in cats 509
    in dogs 278
    in horses 779
Seborrhea
  in dogs 159, 266
Seborrheic syndromes
  in dogs 243
Second-hand smoke and pets
  1239
Sedatives 1130, *1131*
Seedy toe (hollow wall)
  in horses 686
Segmental aplasia
  in horses 608
Seizures
  drugs for 1130, *1130*
  epileptic
    in dogs 200
  in gerbils 924
  in potbellied pigs 980

Selective immunodeficien-
  cies 174
Selective serotonin reuptake
  inhibitors (SSRI)
  poisoning from 1196
Selenium
  deficiency
    in horses 704
  poisoning from 1205
Self-mutilation
  in horses 575
Sendai virus
  in hamsters 949
  in mice 958
Senecio poisoning 1200,*1186*
Senility
  in dogs 27
Senna poisoning *1182*
Sense of smell
  in cats 331
  in dogs 4
  in horses 552
Sensitivity to sunlight (*see*
  Photosensitization)
Separation anxiety
  in dogs 27
Sepsis 1083 (*see also* Septicemia)
Septic arthritis
  in cats 449
  in dogs 185
  in horses 676, 692
Septicemia
  in chinchillas 882
  in foals 810
  in reptiles 1027
Septicemic cutaneous ulcerative disease (SCUD)
  in reptiles 1034
Septic shock 1084
  in horses 811
Serologic tests 1071
Serotonin syndrome
  1196
Sertraline poisoning
  1196
Serum sickness
  in horses 635
Service animals 1230
  for psychiatric disorders
    1230
  travel with 1216, 1226
Sesamoiditis
  in horses 689
Severe acute respiratory syndrome (SARS) *1116*
Shaker foal syndrome 714,
  798

Shampoos
  for dogs 5
  poisoning from 1166
Shampoo therapy
  for dogs *242*
  for horses *757*
Sheared heels
  in horses 686
Shedding
  in cats 489, *499*
  in dogs 240, *256*
  of skin, in reptiles 1026
Shins
  disorders of
    in horses 689
Shock
  emergency care of animals
    with 1055
  types of 1055
Shope fibromas
  in rabbits 1000
Shoulder disorders
  in dogs 189
  in horses 694
Shoulder fractures
  in horses 695
Sialodacryoadenitis
  in rats 1008
Sialosis (*see* Salivation)
Sidebone
  in horses 687
Sight
  of birds 822
  of cats 331, 424
  of dogs 3, 141
  of horses 551, 552, 646
Sindbis virus disease *1116*
Sinoatrial node 54
Sinus cysts
  in horses 743
Sinus disorders
  in horses 742
Sinusitis
  in cats 486
  in dogs 235
  in horses 743
Skin
  of amphibians 864
  of cats 332, 488
  of dogs 5, 240
  of horses 755
Skin allergies
  in cats 441, 492
  in dogs 169, 247
  in horses 660, 759
Skin cancer
  in cats 505
  in dogs 271

in horses 775
reducing risk of 1238
Skin color abnormalities
in cats 491
in dogs 245
in horses 758
Skin cysts
in dogs 275
in horses 777
Skin disorders
in cats 488
allergy-related 492
associated with disorders of
internal organs 513
associated with hypera-
drenocorticism 513
associated with hypothy-
roidism 513
atopy 493
bot fly larvae infestation
496
cancer 505
congenital disorders 491
cysts 507
demodicosis 501
dermatitis 489
diagnosis of 490, 490
eosinophilic granuloma
complex 493
fibromatosis 510
flea allergy dermatitis 495
fleas 494
from flies 496, 497
fragile skin syndrome 513
hair loss (alopecia) 491, 498
hives and rashes 499
itching 490, 499
lice 500
from maggots (myiasis)
496
mange (scabies) 500
mite infestation 500
from mosquitoes 497
from parasitic worms 502
photosensitization 502
pox virus infections 503
pyoderma 504
ringworm 504
solar keratosis 511
tick infestation 505
treatment of 490
trombiculosis 502
tumors 505
vaccine-associated tumors
511
walking dandruff (cheyle-
tiellosis) 501
warts (papillomas) 513

in chinchillas 881
in dogs 170, 240
abnormal skin growth 243
abscesses between toes 247
allergy-related 245
associated with disorders of
internal organs 283
associated with hypothy-
roidism 283
associated with nutritional
deficiencies 282
atopy 246
autoimmune 170
bot fly larvae infestation
252
bullous pemphigoid 170
cancer 269
congenital disorders 242,
267
cysts 273
demodicosis 262
dermatitis 240
dermatophilosis 248
diagnosis of 241, 240
Dracunculus infection 263
eosinophilic granuloma
complex 248
fibromatosis 279
flea allergy dermatitis 250
fleas 249
from flies 251, 252, 253,
254
from gnats 252
hair loss (alopecia) 242, 255
hives and rashes 256
hygromas 257
hyperpigmentation 257
ichthyosiform dermatoses
243
itching 240, 258
lice 259
from maggots (myiasis) 253
mange (scabies) 260
from midges 252
mite infestation 260
from mosquitoes 254
nasal dermatoses 263
from parasitic worms 263
Pelodera dermatitis 264
pemphigus foliaceus 170
pemphigus vulgaris 170
photosensitization 264
pyoderma 265
ringworm 266
seborrhea 266
solar keratosis 280
tick infestation 268
treatment of 241

trombiculosis 262
tumors 269
walking dandruff (cheyle-
tiellosis) 261
warts (papillomas) 282
drugs for 1134, 1135
in hamsters 950
hormonal treatment for
1136
in horses 755
allergy-related 759
atopy 759
cancer 775
from chiggers 770
congenital disorders 758
cutaneous habronemiasis
(summer sores) 770
cysts 758, 777
dermatitis 756
dermatophilosis 760
diagnosis of 757
eosinophilic granuloma
complex 760
fibromatosis 777
from flies 761
from gnats 761, 763
hair loss (alopecia) 766
hives (urticaria) 767
itching 757, 768
lice 768
from maggots (myiasis) 764
mange (mite infestation)
769
from midges 761, 771
from mites 770
from mosquitoes 765
onchocerciasis 771
from parasitic worms
770, 771
photosensitization 772
pigmentary abnormalities
758
ringworm 773
saddle sores 773
from ticks 774
treatment 757
tumors 775
warts (papillomas) 781
in mice 958
in potbellied pigs 981
in rabbits 999
in reptiles 1033
vitamins and minerals for
1136
Skin inverted papillomas
of dogs 282
Skinks 1014 (see also Lizards)
Skin mites (see Mites)

Skin tags
  in dogs 271
Skin warts
  of dogs 282
Skunking 1069
Slaframine poisoning 1158
  in horses 612
Sleep aids
  poisoning from 1196
Slobbers
  in guinea pigs 932
Small strongyles
  in horses 631
Smooth muscle tumors
  in dogs 278
Snail and slug control
    products
  poisoning from 1171
Snakebites 1206
Snakes 1013 (see also Reptiles)
  adenovirus infections
    1027
  ascarids in 1028
  inclusion body disease
    1036
  cryptosporidiosis in 1029
  importing of 1220
  paramyxovirus infections
    in 1032
  scale rot in 1034
  selecting 1017
  signs of illness 1017
  star-gazing in 1030
  stomatitis in 1028
Snuffles 997 (see also Rhinitis)
Soaps
  poisoning from 1166
Sodium chlorate poisoning
    1161
Sodium fluoroacetamide
    poisoning 1203
Sodium monofluoroacetate
    poisoning 1203
Soft palate displacement
  in horses 743
Soft tissue giant cell tumors
  in cats 509
  in dogs 278
  in horses 779
Solar dermatitis 436
Solar keratosis
  in cats 511
  in dogs 280
Solutions 1119, 1121
Solvents
  poisoning from 1170
Sore hocks
  in rabbits 999

Sorghum poisoning 1150,
    1208, 1190
  in horses 718
Southern tick-associated rash
    illness 1092
Sparganosis 1104
Spaying
  and cancer 1238
  of cats 343
  of dogs 15
  of guinea pigs 930
Specific immunity 165
Spider bites 1208
Spina bifida
  in horses 714
Spina bifida occulta
  in Manx cats 460
Spinal column and cord
    disorders
  in cats 462
  in dogs 204
  in horses 670
Spinal cord injuries
  in cats 456
  in dogs 196
  in horses 710
Spindle-cell sarcomas (see Sar-
    comas)
Spinous ear ticks
  in horses 774
Spirurid worms
  in reptiles 1038
Splay leg
  in birds 838
  in rabbits 997
Spleen
  enlarged, in ferrets 897
Splint bone fractures
  in horses 691
Splints
  in horses 692
Spores 1086
Sporotrichosis 1096
  in cats 540
  in dogs 317
  in horses 804
Spotted fever group 1094
Spraying (see Marking
    behavior)
Springhalt (see Stringhalt)
Squamous cell carcinoma
  in birds 858
  in cats 395, 511
  in dogs 280
  in horses 655, 779
  risk factors for 1236
SSRI (see Selective serotonin
    reuptake inhibitors)

St. Louis encephalitis 1116
Stable flies
  in cats 498
  in dogs 255
  in horses 765
Stables
  as boarding facilities 1227
Stachybotryotoxicosis 1156,
    1159
Staggering disease
  in cats 463
Staggers
  in dogs 208
  in horses 720
  paspalum 1158
  ryegrass, annual 1204
  ryegrass, perennial 1156,
    1205
Stall walking or circling 574
Staphylococcus infection
  in mice 958
  in rats 1010
Star-gazing
  in reptiles 1030
Stay apparatus 553
Steatitis (see Yellow fat disease)
Stenosis
  degenerative lumbosacral
    in cats 462
    in dogs 204
Step mouth
  in horses 611
Stereotypic behaviors
  in cats 347
  in dogs 19
  in horses 568
Steroids 1129 (see also Corti-
    costeroids)
  anabolic 1130
Stiff stifle disease
  in dogs 190
Stifle
  fractures of
    in horses 699
  joint disorders
    in horses 699
Stomach
  inflammation of
    in cats 400
    in dogs 104
  ulcers (see Ulcers)
Stomach disorders (see Diges-
    tive disorders)
Stomach worms
  in cats 404
  in dogs 111
  in horses 630
  in reptiles 1028

Stomatitis
  in cats 393
  fungal
    in cats 394
    in dogs 92
  infectious
    in reptiles 1028
  in horses 612
  ulcerative
    in dogs 91
  vesicular
    in horses 813
Stool samples
  testing of 1072
Strangles
  in horses 753
    vaccination *562*
Strangulation 1053
Strawberry footrot (*see* Dermatophilosis)
Straw itch mites
  in horses 770
Streptobacillus moniliformis
  in mice 961
Streptococcal infections
    1092
  in fish 913
  in guinea pigs 935
Stress management
  in pain treatment regimens
    1213
Strike (*see* Fly strike)
Stringhalt (springhalt)
  in horses 698, 714
Strongyles *563*, 563
  in horses 630, 631
Strongyloidiasis *1106*
Strychnine poisoning
    1209
Subchondral cysts
  in horses 676, 692
Subepiglottic cysts
  in horses 754
Sudan grass poisoning 1208,
    1190
Sudden death syndrome
  in puppies 310
Sugar gliders 1039
  aflatoxicosis in 1044
  aggression in 1040
  antibiotic use in 1043
  breeding 1044
  constipation in 1044
  dehydration in 1042
  dental care 1042, 1043
  diet 1041, 1045
  digestive disorders in
    1044

diseases transmitted to
    humans 1043, *1043*, 1044
exercise for 1042
eye disorders 1044
fleas 1046
food hazards *1041*
housing requirements 1040,
    1041
leptospirosis in 1044
lumpy jaw (actinomycosis)
    in 1044
mites 1046
nutritional requirements
    1041, *1041*, 1045
obesity 1046
ownership restrictions 1040
pasteurellosis in 1046
polioencephalomalacia
    1046
reproduction 1043
signs of illness 1042
temperament 1040
temperature requirements
    1041
toxoplasmosis 1046
tumors in 1046
Sulfur poisoning 1170
Summer fescue poisoning 1155
Summer bleeding
  in horses 771
Summer dermatitis
  in horses 762
Summer sores
  in horses 770
Superficial flexor tendon
  displacement of
    in horses 697
Suprascapular nerve injuries
  in horses 715
Surgery
  as cancer treatment
    1240, *1240*
  for wound repair 1066
Surra (*Trypanosoma evansi*
    infection)
  in cats 366
  in dogs 44
  in horses 586
Suspensions 1119
Suspensory desmitis
  in horses 692
Suspensory ligament
  inflammation of
    in horses 692
Swallowed items
  in cats 397
  in dogs 99
  treatment for 1069

Swallowing disorders (*see*
    Esophageal disorders)
Sweat glands
  of horses 756
Sweat gland tumors
  in cats 512
  in dogs 280
  in horses 780
Sweeney
  in horses 695
Sweet clover poisoning 1210,
    1156, *1186*
Sweet itch
  in horses 660, 762
Swim bladder 900
Swimmer's itch *1102*
Swine flu *1112*
Sylvatic plague (*see* Plague)
Synchronous diaphragmatic
    flutter
  in horses 791
Synostosis
  in horses 670
Synovial cell sarcoma
  in cats 450
  in dogs 186
Synovial hernia
  in horses 693
Synovial joint membrane
  inflammation of
    in horses 694
Synovitis
  plasmacytic-lymphocytic
    in dogs 172
  villonodular
    in horses 689
Syrian hamster 940 (*see*
    Hamsters)
Systemic diseases
  in cats 528
  in dogs 305
  in horses 793
Systemic lupus erythematosus
  in cats 442, 450
  in dogs 171, 185
Systole 54

T

T$_3$ *130*
T$_4$ *130*
Tablets 1119
Taeniasis, Asian *1104*
Taeniasis (beef tapeworm
    disease) *1104*
Taeniasis (pork tapeworm
    disease) *1104*
Tahyna fever *1116*

Tail-slip
  in gerbils 924
Talons 824
Tapeworms
  in birds 842
  in cats *341, 404*, 405
  in dogs *111*, 114
  in fish 912
  in gerbils 923
  in hamsters 948
  in horses *563, 563, 630*, 632,
    720
  in mice 957
  in rabbits 996
  in rats 1008
  in reptiles 1037
  treatment of 1127
Tarsus
  deformities of
    in horses 670
  disorders of
    in horses 696
  fractures of
    in horses 697
Tattooing
  for identification of lost pets
    1226
T cells 35, *165* (*see also* White
    blood cells)
  in the immune response
    1080
Tear ducts
  disorders of
    in cats 426
    in dogs 144, 145
    in horses 648
Teeth
  of cats 333
  of chinchillas 877
  of dogs 6
  enamel defects
    in cats 393
    in dogs 90
  of ferrets 891
  of gerbils 922
  of guinea pigs 926
  of hamsters 945
  of horses 554, *555*, 564,
    564
    estimating age 554,
      555
  of mice 956
  of potbellied pigs 974
  of rabbits 983, 991
  of rats 1007
  of sugar gliders 1043
Tendinitis
  in horses 678

Tendon ruptures
  hindlimb
    in horses 698
Tendon sheath inflammation
  in horses 693
Tenosynovitis
  in horses 678
Testes
  inflammation of
    in cats 473
    in dogs 218
Testicular tumors
  of rats 1013
Testosterone *130*
Tetanus *1092*
  in birds 839
  in cats 464, 544
  in dogs 207, 326
  in horses *562*, 718, 811
  in potbellied pigs 979
Tetany
  hypocalcemic
    in horses 790
  lactation
    in horses 790
  transport
    in horses 790
Tetrahydropyrimidines
    1128
Tetralogy of Fallot
  in cats 375
  in dogs 62
  in horses 597
Thallium sulfate poisoning
    1204
Theiler's disease
  in horses 635
Thelaziasis *1106*
  of cats 432
  of dogs 154
  of horses 654
Theobromine toxicity
    1153
Thiamine deficiency
  in amphibians 872
  bracken-induced 1147
Third eyelid (*see* Nictitating
    membrane)
Thoracentesis
  for treatment of heart failure
    68
Thoroughpin
  in horses 699
Threadworms
  in cats *404*
  in dogs *111*
Thrombocytes 1074 (*see also*
    Platelets)

Thrombocytopenia
  in cats 368
  in dogs 48
  in horses 588
  immune-mediated 441, 661
Thrombopathia
  in dogs 49
Thrombosis (*see also* Atrial
    thrombosis, Blood clots)
  in horses 600
Thrombus 76
Thrush (*see* Candidiasis)
Thyroid gland
  of horses 642
Thyroid gland disorders
  in cats 422
  in dogs 139, 173
Thyroid hormones *130*
Tick bite fever *1094*
Tickborne encephalitis
    1112
Tick fever (*see also* Rocky
    Mountain spotted fever)
  Colorado tick fever *1110*
Tick paralysis *1110*
  in cats 461, 469
  in dogs 203, 213
Ticks
  and disease transmission
    in cats 505
    in dogs 268
    in horses 774
  of the ear (*see* Ear ticks)
  ehrlichiosis from *1094*
  removal of
    in cats 505
    in dogs 269
  of reptiles 1034
  and skin disorders
    in cats 505
    in dogs 268
    in horses 774
  Southern tick-associated
    rash illness *1092*
  species of 268
  treatment of 1134
Tight-lip syndrome
  in Shar-Peis 83
Toad poisoning 1210
Toads *864* (*see also* Amphibi-
    ans)
Toe crack
  in horses 685
Toilet bowl cleaners
  poisoning from 1164
Tongue
  paralysis of
    in horses 612

Tongue inflammation
  in cats 394
  in dogs 93
Tongue worms (see also Pentastomid infections)
  in reptiles 1038
Tonsillitis
  in cats 487
  in dogs 236
Tooth decay
  in dogs 90
Tooth infection
  in horses 611
Topical drugs 1120
Torticollis
  in rabbits 1001
Tortoises 1015 (see also Reptiles)
  abnormal beak growth in 1030
  fungal infections in 1032
  herpesviruses in 1036
  selecting 1018
  sex determination 1013
  signs of illness in 1018
Toucans 820 (see also Birds)
Toxic waterblooms 1146
Toxicologic tests 1071
Toxicosis (see Poisoning)
Toxoplasmosis 341, 1098
  in cats 412, 463, 545
  in dogs 123, 326
  in sugar gliders 1046
  transmission to people 545
Tracheal collapse
  in dogs 237
Tracheal intubation
  in emergency care 1054
Tracheobronchitis
  in cats 487
  in dogs 13, 237
  infectious 238
Tracheostomy
  of horses 1060
Trailering
  of horses 576, 1224
Train travel with pets 1226
Tranquilizers 1130, 1131
  poisoning from 1197
Transdermal delivery of drugs 1120
  gels 1121
  patches 1121
Transitional cell carcinomas
  of the urinary tract
  in dogs 296, 297

Transmissible venereal tumors
  in dogs 223
Transportation
  of horses 576, 1224
Transport tetany
  in horses 790
Trauma
  abdominal 1056
  emergency care of dogs and cats 1055
  emergency care of horses 1061
  eye emergencies 1063
  thoracic (chest) 1056
Traumatic arthritis
  in horses 675
Traumatic proptosis 1063
Travel kit
  for pets 1217
Travel with pets 1216
  to Africa 1221
  by airplane 1224
  alternatives to 1226
  to Asia 1221
  to Australia 1221
  camping 1223
  by car 1223
  carriers for 1217
  to Europe 1220
  identification tags for 1225
  international travel 1218, 1225
    regulations 1220
  lodging 1223
  quarantine laws 1219, 1220
  regulations regarding 1219
    by US federal agencies 1220
  service animals 1216, 1226
  by ship 1226
  signs of illness during 1216
  by train 1226
  travel kit for 1217
  within the United States 1217
  vaccination requirements 1221
Trematodes (see Flukes)
Tremorgen ataxia syndrome 1156
Trenchmouth
  in dogs 92

Treponematosis
  in rabbits 998
Trichinellosis (trichinosis) 1108
  in cats 546
  in dogs 327
  in horses 813
Trichinosis (see Trichinellosis)
Trichlorfon poisoning 1169
Trichoepitheliomas
  in cats 512
  in dogs 273
  in guinea pigs 939
Tricholemmomas
  in dogs 272
Trichomoniasis
  in birds 842
Trichothecene poisoning 1156, 1158
Tricuspid dysplasia
  in cats 375
  in dogs 64
  in horses 598
Tricyclic antidepressants
  poisoning from 1196
Trigeminal neuritis
  in cats 460
  in dogs 202
Trocarization
  of horses 1060
Trochanteric bursitis
  in horses 701
Trombiculosis
  in cats 502
  in dogs 262
Tropical eosinophilia 1108
Tropical fish (see also Fish)
  water temperature for 902
Trypanosoma cruzi infection (see Chagas' disease)
Trypanosoma evansi infection (see Surra)
Trypanosomiasis
  American (see Chagas' disease)
  African sleeping sickness 1100
  in cats 365
  in dogs 44
  in horses 586
Tsetse flies
  and disease transmission
    in dogs 255
    in horses 766

Tsetse fly disease (*see* Trypanosomiasis)
Tuberculosis *1092* (*see also* Mycobacteriosis)
  in cats 546
  in dogs 327
  in horses 813
Tularemia *1092*
  in cats 547
  in dogs 328
  in hamsters 952
  in horses 813
  in prairie dogs 969
  in rabbits 1003
  transmission to people *1092*
Tumors 1233
  associated with feline leukemia virus 534
  basal cell
    in horses 776
  biopsy of 1240
  in birds 858
  of the bladder
    in horses 787
  of bones
    in cats 453
    in dogs 193
  chemotherapy for 1242
  development of 1235
  drugs for *1141* (*see also* Chemotherapy)
  of endocrine glands
    in cats 416
    in dogs 129
  of the eye
    in cats 432
    in dogs 154
    in horses 654
  in ferrets 896
  fibroblastic
    in cats 506
    in dogs 271
  in fish 919
  gastrointestinal
    in dogs 104
    in horses 626
  in gerbils 924
  of hair follicles
    in cats 512
  in hamsters 952
  of immune system 175,444
  of the kidneys
    in cats 522
    in dogs 296
    in horses 787
  of larynx and trachea
    in cats 480
    in dogs 229

  of the liver
    in cats 412
    in dogs 124
  lung
    in cats 480
    in dogs 229
  lymphoma 175
  mammary
    in cats 475
    in dogs 222
  mast cell
    in cats 508
    in dogs 275
    in horses 778
  in mice 962
  of muscles
    in cats 452
    in dogs 190
  nerve sheath
    in dogs 203
  of nervous system
    in cats 457
    in dogs 197
  of neuroendocrine tissue
    in dogs 140
  of nose and sinuses
    in cats 479
    in dogs 228
  oral
    in cats 395
    in dogs 94
    in horses 612
  in prairie dogs 969
  in rabbits 1000, 1001, 1003
  radiation therapy for 1078, 1241
  in rats 1012
  rectal
    in cats 414
    in dogs 127
  in reptiles 1038
  of the salivary gland
    in cats 396
    in dogs 96
  of sebaceous glands
    in cats 509
    in dogs 278
    in horses 779
  of the skin
    in cats 492, 505
    in dogs 269
    in horses 775
  of spinal column or cord
    in cats 463
    in dogs 207
  in sugar gliders 1046
  surgical removal of 1240

  of sweat glands
    in cats 512
    in dogs 280
    in horses 780
  transmissible venereal
    in dogs 223
  of the urinary tract
    in cats 522
    in dogs 297
    in horses 787
  vaccine-associated
    in cats 511
  wart-like
    in cats 507
    in dogs 271
Tunga infections *1110*
Turtles 1015 (*see also* Reptiles)
  abnormal beak growth in 1030
  crush injuries 1026
  crustean-borne bacteremia in 1034
  ear infections in 1030
  fungal infections in 1032
  herpesviruses in 1036
  importing of 1220
  ownership restrictions 1018
  papillomas in 1038
  selecting 1018
  septicemic cutaneous ulcerative disease (SCUD) in 1034
  sex determination 1013
  signs of illness in 1018
  skin maggots in 1034
  stomatitis in 1028
Type I reactions
  chronic allergic bronchitis
    in dogs 168
  PIE (Pulmonary infiltration with eosinophilia) syndrome
    in cats 440
    in dogs 168
Type II muscle fiber deficiency
  in dogs 188
Type II reactions
  pemphigus vulgaris
    in dogs 170
Type III reactions
  anterior uveitis
    in dogs 171
    in horses 662
Type IV reactions
  old dog encephalitis 173

Typhus *1096* (*see also* Murine typhus, Queensland tick typhus, Scrub typhus)
Tyzzer's disease
  in cats 403
  in dogs 110
  in gerbils 923
  in hamsters 947
  in horses 635
  in rabbits 994

U

Uberreiter's disease
  in dogs 147
Ulcerative keratitis
  in cats 428
  in dogs 147
Ulcerative pododermatitis
  in rabbits 999
Ulcerative stomatitis
  in dogs 91
Ulcers
  decubital (*see* Pressure wounds)
  drugs for *1126*
  eosinophilic
    in cats 493
  gastrointestinal
    in cats 401
    in chinchillas 880
    in dogs 106, *106*
    in horses 614
Ulna
  deformities of
    in dogs 190, 192
  fractures of
    in horses 695
Ultrasonography 1076
Ultrasound (*see* Ultrasonography)
Umbilical hernias
  in cats 389
  in dogs 85
United Kingdom
  travel with pets to 1220
Urachal diverticula
  in cats 516
  in dogs 286
  in horses 784
Urachal remnants
  in cats 516
  in dogs 286
  in horses 783
Urea poisoning 1172
Ureterocele
  in horses 783

Ureters
  congenital disorders of
    in cats 516
    in dogs 286
    in horses 783
Urethra
  congenital disorders of
    in cats 516
    in dogs 287
    in horses 784
Urethrorectal fistulas
  in dogs 287
Urinalysis 1073
Urinary incontinence (*see also* Incontinence)
  drugs for *1138*
Urinary stones
  in cats 524, *525*
  in dogs 299
  in horses 787
Urinary system
  of cats 334
  of dogs 6
  of horses 556
Urinary tract disorders
  in cats 334, 514
    blockage 522
    Capillaria worm infection 518
    congenital disorders 515
    infections 516
    tumors 522
    urachal remnants 516
    urinary stones (calculi, uroliths) 524
    urination problems 523
  in dogs 283
    blockage 295
    Capillaria worm infection 289
    congenital disorders285
    infections 287
    tumors 296
    urachal remnants 286
    urinary stones (calculi, uroliths) 299
    urination problems 299
  drugs for 1136, *1137*
  in horses 781
    congenital disorders 783
    infections 784
    tumors 787
    urachal remnants 783
    urinary stones (calculi, uroliths) 787
    uroperitoneum 788
  in turtles 1036

Urination problems
  in cats 523
  in dogs 299
  in horses 788
Urine pH *1137*
Urine burn (*see* Hutch burn)
Urine leakage
  in cats 523
  in dogs 298
  in horses 788
Urine marking (*see* Marking behavior)
Urine tests (*see* Urinalysis)
Uroliths
  in cats 524, *525*
  in dogs 299
  in horses 787
  in potbellied pigs 982
  in rats 1011
Uroperitoneum
  in horses 788
Urticaria (*see* Hives)
Uterine adenocarcinoma
  in rabbits 1003
Uterine prolapse
  in horses 735
Uvea
  disorders in cats 428
Uveitis
  in birds 843
  in cats 443
  in dogs 171
  in horses 662

V

Vaccination (*see also* Immunization)
  of birds 835, 854
  of broodmares *729*
  of cats 339, *339*
  of dogs 12, *13*
  of ferrets 891
  of fish 908
  of foals 566
  of horses 561, *562*
  of kittens 344
  of potbellied pigs 973, *973*
  to prevent spread of zoonoses 1089
  of puppies 15
  required for travel 1221
  role in preventing infections 1082
  schedules for 1144
Vaccine-associated tumors
  in cats 511

Vaccines 1143
administering 1144
adverse effects of
1144
attenuated 1143
DNA 1143
gene-deleted 1143
killed 1143
live vectored 1143
types of 1143
Vaginal hypertrophy (overgrowth)
in dogs 222
Vaginal prolapse
in dogs 222
Vaginitis
in dogs 222
in horses 736
Valley fever
in dogs 313
in horses 802
Variant Creutzfeldt-Jakob
disease *1116*
Vascular ring entrapment
in cats *388*
in dogs *84*
Vasculitis
in dogs 171
in horses 662
Vasculopathy
familial
in dogs 245
Vasoactive drugs 1123
Vasopressin *130*
Velvet disease
in fish 915
Venezuelan equine
encephalomyelitis
1116
Venezuelan hemorrhagic fever
1110
Venous dilators 1123
Vent disease (*see* Treponematosis)
Vent prolapse
in birds 849
Ventral marking gland
of gerbils 919
Ventricular septal defects
in cats 375
in dogs 61
in horses 596
Verminous myelitis
in cats 463
in dogs 206
Verminous myelitis and
encephalitis
in horses 717

Vertebrae
degenerative disease of
in horses 702
fractures of
in horses 701
malformations of
in dogs 201
Vesicular stomatitis *1116*
in horses 813
Veterinary behaviorists *19,*
352, 567
Veterinary oncologists
1240
Veterinary care
of cats 338
of dogs 9, 11
during domestic travel
1217
during international travel
1218
family practice 1231,
1232
of ferrets 891, 892, *892*
of hamsters 943
of horses 560
of pet birds 832
of puppies 15
of reptiles 1025
routine examinations 1072
Veterinary tests (*see*
Diagnostic tests)
Vibriosis 918, *1089*
Vietnamese potbellied pigs
(*see* Potbellied pigs)
Villonodular synovitis
in horses 689
Viral hemorrhagic disease
in rabbits 995
Viral papillomas
in horses 613
Viruses 1087
and cancer 1237
immune defense against
1087
infections caused by
1087
latent infection from
1087
transmission of 1087
treatment of 1088
Visceral leishmaniasis
in dogs 318
Vision
of birds 822
of cats 331, 423
of dogs 3, 140
of horses 551, *552*, 646
sudden loss of 1065

Vital signs
in pain assessment
1212
Vitamin overdose 1193
Vitamin A
imbalances
in cats 453
Vitamin C
natural sources *933*
deficiency
of guinea pigs 928, 933
Vitamin D
imbalances
in cats 447
in dogs 180
in horses 673
for reptiles 1024
Vitamin deficiencies
in chinchillas 884
in reptiles 1025
Vitamin D toxicosis
in birds 845
Vitamin E
deficiency of
in horses 704
requirements of hamsters
949
Vitiligo
in cats 492
in dogs 244
in horses 758
Volvulus
in horses 620
Vomiting
in cats 397
control of 1124, *1125*
in dogs 100
Von Willebrand's disease
in cats 368
in dogs 49
Vulvitis
in horses 736

W

Walking dandruff
in cats 501
in dogs 261
Warts (*see also* Viral papillomas)
of cats 513
of dogs 282
of horses 781
viral
of dogs 94
Water mold
of amphibians (*see* Saprolegniasis)

Water quality requirements
  for amphibians 866
  for fish 903
Wave mouth
  in horses 611
Weaving behavior
  in horses 574
Weed killer poisoning (*see* Herbicide poisoning)
Wesselsbron fever *1116*
Western equine encephalomyelitis *1116*
West Nile virus infection *1116*
  in horses 718, 724
  transmission to people 725, *1116*
  vaccination in horses *562*
Wet dewlap
  in rabbits 999
Whipworms
  in dogs *111*, 114
Whiskers
  of cats *333, 333*
White blood cells (*see also* Phagocytes, Lymphocytes)
  functions of 35
  in the immune response 1080
  role in preventing infections 1079
  types of 35, 1073
  and viruses 1087
White spot disease
  in fish 915
Widow spider bites 1208
Wild animals
  diseases from (*see* Zoonoses)
Windgalls (windpuffs)
  in horses 689
Windsucking behavior (*see* Cribbing behavior)

Wings
  shape of 824
  trimming of 834
Wobbler syndrome
  in dogs 201
  in horses 713
Wood-chewing
  in horses 572
Wooden tongue
  in horses 795
Worms (*see also* Gastrointestinal parasites, Heartworms)
  in cats 340
  in kittens 344
  and skin disorders
    in cats 502
    in dogs 263
    in horses 770
  treatment of 1127
Wounds
  of the eye 1063
  management of 1065
  in mice 960
  stages of healing 1066, *1067*
  surgical treatment of 1066
Wry neck
  in rats 1007

X

Xanthomas
  in birds 858
Xerostomia
  in cats 396
  in dogs 96
X-ray imaging 1075

Y

Yellow fat disease (steatitis)
  in cats 451
  in horses 704
Yellow fever *1116*
Yersinia infection *1094*
  in chinchillas 883
  in guinea pigs 939
Yew poisoning *1190*

Z

Zinc 1136
  for treating skin disorders 1136
Zinc oxide poisoning 1194
Zinc phosphide poisoning 1204
Zinc deficiency syndromes
  in dogs 245
Zinc poisoning 1211
  in birds 857
Zoonoses 1088, *1090*
  from chinchillas *884*
  from gerbils *925*
  prevention of 1089
  from rabbits *993*
  from reptiles 1016, *1016, 1017*
  from sugar gliders 1043, *1043*, 1044
  transmission of 1088
Zygomycosis
  in horses 805
Zymbal's gland
  tumors of
    in rats 1013